Pocket Italian Dictionary

Fourth Edition

Italian ·····> English
English ·····> Italian

Editors
Pat Bulhosen
Francesca Logi
Loredana Riu

OXFORD
UNIVERSITY PRESS

OXFORD

UNIVERSITY PRESS

Great Clarendon Street, Oxford OX2 6DP

Oxford University Press is a department of the University of Oxford.
It furthers the University's objective of excellence in research, scholarship,
and education by publishing worldwide in

Oxford New York

Auckland Cape Town Dar es Salaam Hong Kong Karachi
Kuala Lumpur Madrid Melbourne Mexico City Nairobi
New Delhi Shanghai Taipei Toronto

With offices in

Argentina Austria Brazil Chile Czech Republic France Greece
Guatemala Hungary Italy Japan Poland Portugal Singapore
South Korea Switzerland Thailand Turkey Ukraine Vietnam

Oxford is a registered trade mark of Oxford University Press
in the UK and in certain other countries

Published in the United States
by Oxford University Press Inc., New York

© Oxford University Press 1997, 2000, 2004, 2006, 2010

The moral rights of the author have been asserted

Database right Oxford University Press (maker)

First edition 1997
Reissued with new cover 2000
Second edition 2004
Third edition 2006
Fourth edition 2010

British Library Cataloguing in Publication Data

Data available

Library of Congress Cataloging in Publication Data

Data available

Typeset in Nimrod, Arial and Meta by Datagrafix, Inc
Printed in Great Britain by Clays Ltd, St Ives plc

ISBN 978-0-19-957616-6
ISBN 978-0-19-964005-8 (Special edition)

10 9 8 7 6 5 4 3 2

1352733675456227

Preface / Prefazione

This dictionary has been designed to meet the needs of students, tourists, and all those who require quick and reliable answers to their translation questions. It provides clear guidance on selecting the most appropriate translation, illustrative examples to help with construction and usage, and precise information on grammar and style.

Focusing on everyday, idiomatic Italian and English, both spoken and written, this easy-to-use dictionary offers up-to-the-minute coverage of a wide range of vocabulary. New words and senses have been drawn from an exciting initiative, the Oxford Languages Tracker, which enables us to track the latest developments in Italian and other modern languages. Additionally, for the first time in a dictionary of this size, 2000 of the most frequently used words in Italian and English have been marked.

This new edition also offers a wide range of supplementary materials such as a revised and updated A–Z of Italian life and culture, a calendar of festive days in Italy, a correspondence section containing model letters to help with personal and business letter-writing in Italian, a guide to text messaging, a new section on navigating online services in Italian, and a grammar summary.

Questo dizionario è stato creato per soddisfare le esigenze degli studenti, dei turisti e di tutti coloro che hanno bisogno di risposte rapide e sicure ai problemi di traduzione. Il lettore è guidato con chiarezza nella scelta del termine più appropriato, con esempi di uso della lingua e con indicazioni precise di grammatica e di stile.

Basandosi sull'uso contemporaneo dell'inglese e dell'italiano, scritto e parlato, questo dizionario di facile consultazione offre una trattazione aggiornata di un'ampia gamma di vocaboli. Neologismi e nuove accezioni sono stati individuati grazie ad un nuovo strumento, l'Oxford Languages Tracker, che permette di monitorare gli sviluppi più recenti dell'inglese e di altre lingue moderne. Inoltre, per la prima volta in un dizionario di queste dimensioni, vengono segnalate 2000 delle parole d'uso più frequente in italiano e in inglese.

Questa quarta edizione contiene anche un vasto repertorio di materiali supplementari: una sezione aggiornata su aspetti della civiltà britannica e statunitense, le principali festività nel Regno Unito e negli Stati Uniti, una sezione di corrispondenza che propone modelli di lettere in inglese, una guida agli sms, una nuova sezione sulla navigazione di servizi online in lingua inglese e note di grammatica.

List of contributors / Hanno collaborato

First edition/Prima edizione

Editors/Redazione
Debora Mazza
Jane Goldie
Donatella Boi
Francesca Logi
Peter Terrell
Sonia Tinagli-Baxter
Carla Zipoli

Allan Cameron
Michela Masci
Ilaria Panuccio

Copy editors/Segreteria di redazione
Alice Grandison
Mary Rigby
Daphne Trotter

Project management by/A cura di
LEXUS

Second edition/Seconda edizione

Pat Bulhosen
Francesca Logi
Loredana Riu

Third edition/Terza edizione

Joanna Brough
Stephen Curtis
Penelope Isaac
Francesca Logi

Fourth edition/Quarta edizione

Joanna Rubery
Loredana Riu

Contents / Indice

Introduction / Introduzione

Here is some basic information on the way the entries in this dictionary are organized.

A swung dash ∼ is used to replace the headword within the entry.

Compounds are listed in alphabetical order. Remember this when looking for a word. The entry 'password', for example, is entered alphabetically – at some distance from the entry 'pass'. Likewise 'paintbrush' and 'paintpot' will have 'painter', 'pain threshold' and 'painting' entered in between.

Indicators are provided to guide the user to the best translation for a specific sense of a word. Types of indicator are:

field labels (see the list on p x), which indicate a general area of usage (commercial, computing, photography etc);

sense indicators, eg: **bore** n (of gun) calibro m; (person) seccatore, -trice mf;

typical subjects of verbs, eg: **bond** vt ‹glue› attaccare;

typical objects of verbs, placed after the translation of the verb, eg: **boost** vt stimolare ‹sales›; sollevare ‹morale›;

nouns that typically go together with certain adjectives, eg: **rich** a ricco; ‹food› pesante.

❶, ❷, etc mean that the same word is being translated as a different part of speech, eg. **partition** ❶ n ... ❷ vt ...

A solid black square is used to

Ecco le informazioni essenziali su come sono organizzate le voci nel dizionario.

Un trattino ondulato ∼ è utilizzato al posto del lemma all'interno della voce.

I vocaboli composti sono in ordine alfabetico. È importante ricordarlo quando si cerca la parola che interessa. La voce 'password', ad esempio, essendo in ordine alfabetico, compare a una certa distanza dopo la voce 'pass'. Per la stessa ragione fra 'paintbrush' and 'paintpot' compaiono 'painter', 'pain threshold' e 'painting'.

Degli indicatori vengono forniti per indirizzare l'utente verso la traduzione corrispondente al senso voluto di una parola. I tipi di indicatori sono:

etichette semantiche (vedi la lista a p x), indicanti l'ambito specifico in cui la parola viene generalmente usata in quel senso (commercio, informatica, fotografia ecc);

indicatori di significato, es.: **redazione** nf (ufficio) editorial office; (di testi) editing;

soggetti tipici di verbi, es.: **trovarsi** vr ‹luogo› be;

complementi oggetti tipici di verbi, collocati dopo la traduzione dello stesso verbo, es: **superare** vt overtake ‹veicolo›; pass ‹esame›;

sostantivi che ricorrono tipicamente con certi aggettivi, es.: **solare** a ‹energia, raggi› solar; ‹crema› sun.

❶, ❷, ecc indicano che la stessa

identify phrasal verbs, eg ■ **strip down** *vt* ... Phrasal verbs are listed in alphabetical order directly after the main verb. So 'strip down' comes after 'strip' and before 'strip cartoon'.

English pronunciation is given for the Italian user in the International Phonetic Alphabet (see p ix).

Italian stress is shown by a ' placed in front of the stressed syllable in a word.

Square brackets are used around parts of an expression which can be omitted without altering the sense.

The ✓ symbol marks a word identified as being among the most frequently-used words in English or Italian.

parola viene tradotta come una diversa parte del discorso, es. **calcolatore** ① *a* ... ② *nm* ...

Un quadratino nero viene utilizzato per indicare i phrasal verbs, ad esempio: ■ **strip down** *vt* ... I phrasal verbs si trovano in ordine alfabetico immediatamente dopo il verbo principale. Così 'strip down' viene subito dopo 'strip' e subito prima di 'strip cartoon'.

La pronuncia inglese è data usando l'Alfabetico Fonetico Internazionale (vedi p ix).

L'accento tonico nelle parole italiane è indicato dal segno ' collocato davanti alla sillaba accentata.

Delle parentesi quadre racchiudono parti di espressioni che possono essere omesse senza alterazioni di senso.

Il simbolo ✓ contrassegna una parola identificata come una delle parole d'uso più frequente in inglese o in italiano.

Proprietary terms / Marche depositate

This dictionary includes some words which are, or are asserted to be, proprietary names or trademarks. Their inclusion does not imply that they have acquired for legal purposes a non-proprietary or general significance, nor is any other judgment implied concerning their legal status. In cases where the editor has some evidence that a word is used as a proprietary name or trademark this is indicated by the symbol ®, but no judgment concerning the legal status of such words is made or implied thereby.

Questo dizionario include alcune parole che sono o vengono considerate nomi di marche depositate. La loro presenza non implica che abbiano acquisito legalmente un significato generale, né si suggerisce alcun altro giudizio riguardo il loro stato giuridico. Qualora il redattore abbia trovato testimonianza dell'uso di una parola come marca depositata, questa è stata contrassegnata dal simbolo ®, ma nessun giudizio riguardo lo stato giuridico di tale parola viene espresso o suggerito in tal modo.

······································

Pronunciation of Italian
······································

Vowels

a	is broad like *a* in *father*: **casa**.
e	has two sounds: closed like *ey* in *they*: **sera**; open like *e* in *egg*: **sette**.
i	is like *ee* in *feet*: **venire**.
o	has two sounds: closed like *o* in *show*: **croma**; open like *o* in *dog*: **bocca**.
u	is like *oo* in *moon*: **luna**.

When two or more vowels come together each vowel is pronounced separately: **buono**; **baia**.

······································
Consonants

b, **d**, **f**, **l**, **m**, **n**, **p**, **t**, **v** are pronounced as in English. When these are double they are sounded distinctly: **bello**.

c	before **a**, **o**, or **u** and before consonants is like *k* in *king*: **cane**. before **e** or **i** is like *ch* in *church*: **cena**.
ch	is also like *k* in *king*: **chiesa**.
g	before **a**, **o**, or **u** is hard like *g* in *got*: **gufo**. before **e** or **i** is like *j* in *jelly*: **gentile**.
gh	is like *g* in *gun*: **ghiaccio**.
gl	when followed by **a**, **e**, **o**, or **u** is like *gl* in *glass*: **gloria**.
gli	is like *lli* in *million*: **figlio**.
gn	is like *ni* in *onion*: **bagno**.
h	is silent.
ng	is like *ng* in *finger* (not *singer*): **ringraziare**.
r	is pronounced distinctly.
s	between two vowels is like *s* in *rose*: **riso**. at the beginning of a word it is like *s* in *soap*: **sapone**.
sc	before *e* or *i* is like *sh* in *shell*: **scienza**.
z	sounds like *ts* within a word: **fazione**; like *dz* at the beginning: **zoo**.

The stress is shown by the sign ' printed before the stressed syllable.

Pronuncia inglese

Simboli fonetici

Vocali e dittonghi

æ	bad	ʊ	put	aʊ	now
ɑ:	ah	u:	too	aʊə	flour
e	wet	ə	ago	ɔɪ	coin
ɪ	sit	ɜ:	work	ɪə	here
i:	see	eɪ	made	eə	hair
ɒ	got	əʊ	home	ʊə	poor
ɔ:	door	aɪ	five		
ʌ	cup	aɪə	fire		

Consonanti

b	boy	l	leg	t	ten
d	day	m	man	tʃ	chip
dʒ	page	n	new	θ	three
f	foot	ŋ	sing	ð	this
g	go	p	pen	v	verb
h	he	r	run	w	wet
j	yes	s	speak	z	his
k	coat	ʃ	ship	ʒ	pleasure

Note:
ˈ precede la sillaba accentata.
La vocale nasale in parole quali *nuance* è indicata nella trascrizione fonetica come ñ: njuːɒs.

Abbreviations / Abbreviazioni

adjective	adj	aggettivo	masculine or feminine	mf	maschile o femminile
abbreviation	abbr	abbreviazione	military	Mil	militare
administration	Admin	amministrazione	music	Mus	musica
adverb	adv	avverbio	noun	n	sostantivo
aeronautics	Aeron	aeronautica	nautical	Naut	nautica
American	Am	americano	old use	old	antiquato
anatomy	Anat	anatomia	pejorative	pej	peggiorativo
archaeology	Archaeol	archeologia	personal	pers	personale
architecture	Archit	architettura	photography	Phot	fotografia
astrology, astronomy	Astr	astrologia, astronomia	physics	Phys	fisica
attributive	attrib	attributo	plural	pl	plurale
automobiles	Auto	automobile	politics	Pol	politica
auxiliary	aux	ausiliario	possessive	poss	possessivo
biology	Biol	biologia	past participle	pp	participio passato
botany	Bot	botanica	prefix	pref	prefisso
British English	Br	inglese britannico	preposition	prep	preposizione
Chemistry	Chem	chimica	present tense	pres	presente
commerce	Comm	commercio	pronoun	pron	pronome
computers	Comput	informatica	psychology	Psych	psicologia
conjunction	conj	congiunzione	past tense	pt	tempo passato
cooking	Culin	cucina		qcno	qualcuno
definite article	def art	articolo determinativo		qcsa	qualcosa
	ecc	eccetera	proprietary term	®	marca depositata
economics	Econ	economia	rail	Rail	ferrovia
electricity	Electr	elettricità	reflexive	refl	riflessivo
et cetera	etc	et cetera	religion	Relig	religione
feminine	f	femminile	relative pronoun	rel pron	pronome relativo
familiar	fam	familiare	somebody	sb	
figurative	fig	figurato	school	Sch	scuola
finance	Fin	finanza	singular	sg	singolare
formal	fml	formale	slang	sl	gergo
geography	Geog	geografia	something	sth	
geology	Geol	geologia	suffix	suff	suffisso
grammar	Gram	grammatica	technical	Techn	tecnico
humorous	hum	umoristico	telephone	Teleph	telefono
indefinite article	indef art	articolo indeterminativo	theatrical	Theat	teatrale
interjection	int	interiezione	television	TV	televisione
interrogative	inter	interrogativo	typography	Typ	tipografia
invariable (no plural form)	inv	invariabile	university	Univ	università
journalism	Journ	giornalismo	auxiliary verb	v aux	verbo ausiliare
law	Jur	legge/giuridico	intransitive verb	vi	verbo intransitivo
literary	liter	letterario	reflexive verb	vr	verbo riflessivo
masculine	m	maschile	transitive verb	vt	verbo transitivo
mathematics	Math	matematica	transitive and intransitive	vt/i	verbo transitivo e intransitivo
mechanics	Mech	meccanica	vulgar	vulg	volgare
medicine	Med	medicina			
meteorology	Metereol	meteorologia	cultural equivalent	≈	equivalenza culturale

Aa

a (**ad** *before vowel*) *prep* to; (stato in luogo, tempo, età) at; (con mese, città) in; (mezzo, modo) by; **dire qualcosa a qualcuno** tell somebody something; **alle tre** at three o'clock; **a vent'anni** at the age of twenty; **a Natale** at Christmas; **a dicembre** in December; **ero al cinema** I was at the cinema; **vivo a Londra** I live in London; **a due a due** two by two; **a piedi** on *or* by foot; **maglia a maniche lunghe** long-sleeved sweater; **casa a tre piani** house with three floors; **giocare a tennis** play tennis; **50 km all'ora** 50 km an hour; **2 euro al chilo** 2 euros a kilo; **al mattino/alla sera** in the morning/evening; **a venti chilometri/due ore da qui** twenty kilometres/two hours away

'abaco *nm* abacus

a'bate *nm* abbot

abbacchia'mento *nm* fam dejection

abbacchi'ato *adj* fam dejected, downhearted

ab'bacchio *nm* [young] lamb
- **abbacchio alla romana** spring lamb

abbaci'nare *vt* dazzle, blind; fig deceive

abbagli'ante ① *adj* dazzling
② *nm* headlight, high-beam Am; **mettere gli abbaglianti** put the headlights on full beam

abbagli'are *vt* dazzle

ab'baglio *nm* blunder; **prendere un ~** make a blunder

abbaia'mento *nm* barking

abbai'are *vi* bark

abba'ino *nm* dormer window; (mansarda) loft

abbando'nare *vt* abandon; leave ‹luogo›; give up ‹piani ecc›; **~ il campo** Mil desert in the face of the enemy

abbando'narsi *vr* let oneself go; **~ a** give oneself up to ‹ricordi ecc›

abbando'nato *adj* abandoned

abban'dono *nm* abandoning; fig abandon; (stato) neglect

abbarbi'carsi *vr* **~ a** cling to

abbassa'mento *nm* (di temperatura, acqua, prezzi) drop

abbas'sare *vt* lower; turn down ‹radio, TV›; **~ i fari** dip the headlights

abbas'sarsi *vr* stoop; ‹sole ecc› sink; fig demean oneself

ab'basso ① *adv* below
② *int* down with

abba'stanza *adv* enough; (alquanto) quite; **~ nuovo** newish; **ne ho ~!** I've had enough!, I'm fed up!

ab'battere *vt* demolish; shoot down ‹aereo›; put down ‹animale›; topple ‹regime›; fig (demoralizzare) dishearten

ab'battersi *vr* (cadere) fall; fig be discouraged; **~ a terra/al suolo** fall down

abbatti'mento *nm* (morale) despondency

abbat'tuto *adj* despondent, down-in-the-mouth

abba'zia *nf* abbey

abbelli'mento *nm* embellishment

abbel'lire *vt* embellish

abbel'lirsi *vr* adorn oneself

abbeve'rare *vt* water

abbevera'toio *nm* drinking trough

abbicci *nm inv* fig rudiments *pl*; **l'~ di the** ADC of

abbi'ente *adj* well-to-do

abbi'etto *adj* despicable, abject

abbiglia'mento *nm* clothes *pl*; (industria) clothing industry, rag trade fam
- **abbigliamento da bambino** children's wear; **abbigliamento da donna** ladies' wear; **abbigliamento per uomo** menswear; **abbigliamento sportivo** sportswear

abbigli'are *vt* dress

abbigli'arsi *vr* dress up

abbina'mento *nm* combining

abbi'nare *vt* combine; match ‹colori›

abbindo'lare *vt* cheat

abbocca'mento *nm* interview; (conversazione) talk

abboc'care *vi* bite; ‹tubi› join; fig swallow the bait

abboc'cato *adj* ‹vino› fairly sweet

abbof'farsi = ABBUFFARSI

abbona'mento *nm* subscription; (ferroviario ecc) season-ticket; **fare l'~** take out a subscription
- **abbonamento all'autobus** bus pass; **abbonamento mensile** monthly ticket; **abbonamento alla televisione** television licence

abbo'nare *vt* make a subscriber

abbo'narsi *vr* subscribe (**a** to); take out a season-ticket (**a** for) ‹teatro, stadio›

abbo'nato, -a *nmf* subscriber

abbon'dante *adj* abundant; ‹quantità› copious; ‹nevicata› heavy; ‹vestiario› roomy; **~ di** abounding in

abbondante'mente *adv* ‹mangiare› copiously

abbon'danza *nf* abundance

abbon'dare *vi* abound

abbor'dabile *adj* ⟨persona⟩ approachable; ⟨prezzo⟩ reasonable

abbor'daggio *nm* Mil boarding

abbor'dare *vt* board ⟨nave⟩; approach ⟨persona⟩; fam (attaccar bottone a) chat up; tackle ⟨compito ecc⟩

abbotto'nare *vt* button up

abbotto'nato *adj* fig tight-lipped

abbottona'tura *nf* [row of] buttons; **con ∼ da donna/uomo** ⟨giacca⟩ that buttons on the left/right

abboz'zare ① *vt* sketch [out] ⟨disegno⟩; draft ⟨documento⟩; **∼ un sorriso** give a little smile
② *vi* fam (rassegnarsi) resign oneself

ab'bozzo *nm* (di disegno) sketch; (di documento) draft

♪ **abbracci'are** *vt* embrace ⟨causa⟩; hug, embrace ⟨persona⟩; take up ⟨professione⟩; fig include

ab'braccio *nm* hug

abbrevi'are *vt* shorten; (ridurre) curtail; abbreviate ⟨parola⟩

abbreviazi'one *nf* abbreviation

abbron'zante *nm* suntan lotion

abbron'zare *vt* bronze; tan ⟨pelle⟩

abbron'zarsi *vr* get a tan

abbron'zato *adj* tanned

abbronza'tura *nf* [sun]tan

abbrusto'lire *vt* toast; roast ⟨caffè ecc⟩

abbruti'mento *nm* brutalization

abbru'tire *vt* brutalize; ⟨lavoro⟩ stultify

abbru'tirsi *vr* become brutalized

abbuf'farsi *vr* fam stuff oneself

abbuf'fata *nf* fam blowout

abbuo'nare *vt* reduce; fig overlook ⟨mancanza, errore⟩

abbu'ono *nm* allowance; Sport handicap

abdi'care *vi* abdicate

abdicazi'one *nf* abdication

aber'rante *adj* aberrant

aberrazi'one *nf* aberration

abe'taia *nf* wood of fir trees

a'bete *nm* fir

abi'etto *adj* despicable

abiezi'one *nf* degradation

abige'ato *nm* Jur cattle-stealing, rustling

'abile *adj* able; (idoneo) fit; (astuto) clever

abilità *nf inv* ability; (idoneità) fitness; (astuzia) cleverness

abili'tante *adj* **corso ∼** [officially recognized] training course

abili'tare *vt* qualify

abili'tato *adj* qualified

abilitazi'one *nf* qualification; (titolo) diploma

abil'mente *adv* ably; (con astuzia) cleverly

abis'sale *adj* abysmal

a'bisso *nm* abyss

abi'tabile *adj* inhabitable

abitabilità *nf* fitness for human habitation; **licenza di ∼** document certifying that a building is fit for human habitation

abi'tacolo *nm* Auto passenger compartment

abi'tante *nmf* inhabitant

♪ **abi'tare** *vi* live

abi'tato ① *adj* inhabited
② *nm* built-up area

abitazi'one *nf* house; **crisi delle abitazioni** housing problem

abi'tino *nm* Relig scapular

♪ **'abito** *nm* (da donna) dress; (da uomo) suit; **abiti** *pl* clothes
■ **abito da ballo** ball dress; **abito da cerimonia** formal dress; **abito da cocktail** cocktail dress; **abito mentale** mentality; **'abito scuro'** (su inviti) 'black tie'; **abito da sera** evening dress; **abito talare** cassock; **abito da uomo** suit

abitu'ale *adj* usual, habitual

abitual'mente *adv* usually

♪ **abitu'are** *vt* accustom

abitu'arsi *vr* **∼ a** get used to

abitu'ato *adj* **∼ a** used to

abitudi'nario, -a ① *adj* of fixed habits
② *nmf* person of fixed habits

♪ **abi'tudine** *nf* habit; **d'∼** usually; **per ∼** out of habit; **avere l'∼ di fare qualcosa** be in the habit of doing something; **abitudini** *pl* customs

abiu'rare *vt* renounce

abla'tivo *nm* ablative

abluzi'oni *nfpl* **fare le ∼** wash

abnegazi'one *nf* self-sacrifice

ab'norme *adj* abnormal

abo'lire *vt* abolish; repeal ⟨legge⟩

abolizi'one *nf* abolition; (di legge) repeal

abolizio'nismo *nm* abolitionism

abolizio'nista *adj & nmf* abolitionist

abomi'nevole *adj* abominable

abo'rigeno, -a *adj & nmf* aboriginal

abor'rire *vt* abhor

abor'tire *vi* miscarry; (volontariamente) have an abortion; fig fail

abor'tista *adj* pro-choice

abor'tivo *adj* abortive

a'borto *nm* miscarriage; (volontario) abortion

abrasi'one *nf* abrasion

abra'sivo *adj & nm* abrasive

abro'gare *vt* repeal

abroga'tivo *adj* **referendum ∼** referendum to repeal a law

abrogazi'one *nf* repeal

abruz'zese ① *adj* Abruzzi *attrib*

♪ indicates a very frequent word

2 *nmf* person from the Abruzzi
3 *nm* Abruzzi dialect

'abside *nf* apse

abu'lia *nf* apathy

a'bulico *adj* apathetic

abu'sare *vi* ∼ **di** abuse; over-indulge in ‹alcol›; (approfittare di) take advantage of; (violentare) rape

abusi'vismo *nm* large-scale abuse
■ **abusivismo edilizio** building without planning permission

abu'sivo *adj* illegal

a'buso *nm* abuse; **'ogni** ∼ **sarà punito'** 'penalty for misuse'
■ **abuso di confidenza** breach of confidence; **abusi** *pl* **sessuali** sexual abuse

a.C. *abbr* (**avanti Cristo**) BC

a'cacia *nf* acacia

'acaro *nm* Zool mite

'acca *nf* fam **non ho capito un'** ∼ I understood damn all

acca'demia *nf* academy
■ **Accademia di Belle Arti** Academy of Fine Arts; **accademia militare** military academy

acca'demico, -a **1** *adj* academic
2 *nmf* academician

⚹ **acca'dere** *vi* happen; **accada quel che accada** come what may

acca'duto *nm* event

accalappia'cani *nm inv* dog-catcher

accalappi'are *vt* catch; fig allure

accal'care *vt* cram together

accal'carsi *vr* crowd

accal'darsi *vr* get overheated; (per fatica) got hot; fig get excited

accal'dato *adj* overheated; (per fatica) hot; fig excited

accalo'rarsi *vr* get excited

accampa'mento *nm* camp

accam'pare *vt* fig put forth

accam'parsi *vr* camp

accani'mento *nm* tenacity; (odio) rage

acca'nirsi *vr* persist; (infierire) rage

accanita'mente *adv* ‹odiare› fiercely; ‹insistere› persistently; ‹lavorare› assiduously

acca'nito *adj* persistent; ‹odio› fierce; ‹fumatore› inveterate; ‹lavoratore› assiduous

⚹ **ac'canto** *adv* near; ∼ **a** *prep* next to; **la ragazza della porta** ∼ the girl next door

accanto'nare *vt* set aside; Mil billet

accaparra'mento *nm* hoarding; Comm cornering

accapar'rare *vt* hoard

accapar'rarsi *vr* grab; corner ‹mercato›

accaparra|'tore, -trice *nmf* hoarder

accapigli'arsi *vr* scuffle; (litigare) squabble

accappa'toio *nm* bathrobe; (per spiaggia) beachrobe

accappo'nare *vt* **fare** ∼ **la pelle a qualcuno** make somebody's flesh creep

accarez'zare *vt* caress, stroke; fig cherish

accartocci'are *vt* scrunch up

accartocci'arsi *vr* curl up

acca'sarsi *vr* get married

accasci'arsi *vr* flop down; fig lose heart

accata'stare *vt* pile up

accatti'vante *adj* beguiling

accatti'varsi *vr* ∼ **le simpatie/la stima/l'affetto di qualcuno** gain somebody's sympathy/respect/affection

accatto'naggio *nm* begging

accat'tone, -a *nmf* beggar

accaval'lare *vt* cross ‹gambe›

accaval'larsi *vr* pile up; fig overlap

acce'cante *adj* ‹luce› blinding

acce'care **1** *vt* blind
2 *vi* go blind

ac'cedere *vi* access; ∼ **a** enter; (acconsentire) comply with; Comput access

accele'rare **1** *vi* accelerate
2 *vt* speed up, accelerate; ∼ **il passo** quicken one's pace

accele'rata *nf* sudden acceleration

accele'rato *adj* rapid

accelera'tore *nm* accelerator
■ **acceleratore grafico** Comput graphics accelerator

accelerazi'one *nf* acceleration

⚹ **ac'cendere** *vt* light; turn on, switch on ‹luce, TV ecc›; fig inflame; **ha da** ∼**?** have you got a light?

ac'cendersi *vr* catch fire; (illuminarsi) light up; fig become inflamed; ‹TV, computer› turn on, switch on

accendi'gas *nm inv* gas lighter; (su cucina) automatic ignition

accen'dino *nm* lighter

accendi'sigari *nm inv* cigar-lighter

accen'nare **1** *vt* indicate; hum ‹melodia›; give a hint of ‹sorriso›
2 *vi* ∼ **a** beckon to; fig hint at; (far l'atto di) make as if to; **accenna a piovere** it looks like rain

ac'cenno *nm* gesture; (con il capo) nod; fig hint

accensi'one *nf* lighting; (di motore) ignition

accen'tare *vt* accent; (con accento tonico) stress

accentazi'one *nf* accentuation

ac'cento *nm* accent; (tonico) stress
■ **accento acuto** acute [accent]; **accento circonflesso** circumflex [accent]; **accento grave** grave [accent]

accentra'mento *nm* centralizing

accen'trare *vt* centralize

accentra'tore *adj* ⟨*persona*⟩ who refuses to delegate; ⟨*politica*⟩ of centralization

accentu'are *vt* accentuate

accentu'arsi *vr* become more noticeable

accentu'ato *adj* marked

accerchia'mento *nm* surrounding

accerchi'are *vt* surround

accerchi'ato *adj* surrounded

accer'tabile *adj* ascertainable

accerta'mento *nm* check; **accertamenti** *pl* [medici] tests

accer'tare *vt* ascertain; (controllare) check; assess ⟨*reddito*⟩

ac'ceso *adj* lighted; ⟨*radio, TV ecc*⟩ on; ⟨*colore*⟩ bright

acces'sibile *adj* accessible; ⟨*persona*⟩ approachable; ⟨*spesa*⟩ reasonable

ac'cesso *nm* access; Med (di rabbia) fit; 'vietato l'∼' 'no entry'; '∼ riservato a ...' 'access restricted to ...'

■ **accesso diretto** Comput direct access; **accesso disabili** wheelchair access; **accesso a Internet** Comput Internet access; **accesso multiplo** Comput multi-access; **accesso remoto** Comput remote access

accessori'ato *adj* accessorized

acces'sorio ⟨1⟩ *adj* accessory; (secondario) of secondary importance

⟨2⟩ *nm* accessory; **accessori** *pl* (rifiniture) fittings

■ **accessori** *pl* **per il bagno** bathroom fittings; **accessori** *pl* **moda** fashion accessories

ac'cetta *nf* hatchet

accet'tabile *adj* acceptable

✶ **accet'tare** *vt* accept; (aderire a) agree to

accettazi'one *nf* acceptance; (luogo) reception; [banco] **accettazione** check-in [desk]; **accettazione** [bagagli] check-in

ac'cetto *adj* agreeable; **essere bene** ∼ be very welcome

accezi'one *nf* meaning

acchiap'pare *vt* catch

+acchiotto *suff* **lupacchiotto** *nm* wolf cub; (affettuoso) baby wolf; **orsacchiotto** *nm* teddy bear; **fessacchiotto** *nm* nitwit

ac'chito *nm* **di primo** ∼ at first

acciac'care *vt* crush; fig prostrate

acciac'cato, -a *adj* **essere** ∼ ache all over

acci'acco *nm* infirmity; *pl* **acciacchi** (afflizioni) aches and pains

acciaie'ria *nf* steelworks

acci'aio *nm* steel

■ **acciaio inossidabile** stainless steel

acciambel'larsi *vr* curl up

acciden'tale *adj* accidental

accidental'mente *adv* accidentally

acciden'tato *adj* ⟨*terreno*⟩ uneven

✶ **acci'dente** *nm* accident; Med stroke; **non capisce/non vede un** ∼ fam he doesn't understand/can't see a damn thing; **mandare un** ∼ **a qualcuno** fam tell somebody to go to hell

acci'denti *int* fam damn!; ∼ **a te!** damn you!, blast you!

ac'cidia *nf* sloth

accigli'arsi *vr* frown

accigli'ato *adj* frowning

ac'cingersi *vr* ∼ **a** be about to

+accio *suff* **erbaccia** *nf* weed; **donnaccia** *nf* tart; **faticaccia** *nf* hard slog; **lavoraccio** *nm* (lavoro faticoso) helluva job fam; (lavoro malfatto) botched job; **fattaccio** *nm* (hum) foul deed; **parolaccia** *nf* swear word; **avaraccio** *nm* skinflint

acciotto'lato *nm* cobbled paving, cobblestones *pl*

acci'picchia *int* good Lord!

acciuf'fare *vt* catch

acci'uga *nf* anchovy

accla'mare *vt* applaud; (eleggere) acclaim

acclamazi'one *nf* applause

acclima'tare *vt* acclimatize

acclima'tarsi *vr* get acclimatized

acclimatazi'one *nf* acclimatization

ac'cludere *vt* enclose

ac'cluso *adj* enclosed

accocco'larsi *vr* squat

acco'darsi *vr* tag along

accogli'ente *adj* welcoming; (confortevole) cosy

accogli'enza *nf* welcome

✶ **ac'cogliere** *vt* receive; (con piacere) welcome; (contenere) hold

accol'lare *vt* ∼ **qualcosa a qualcuno** fig saddle somebody with something

accol'larsi *vr* take on ⟨*responsabilità, debiti, doveri*⟩

accol'lato *adj* ⟨*maglia*⟩ high-necked

accoltel'lare *vt* knife

accoman'dante *nmf* Jur sleeping partner

accomanda'tario, -a *nmf* Jur general partner

accoman'dita *nf* Jur limited partnership

■ **accomandita per azioni** limited partnership based on shares

accomia'tare *vt* dismiss

accomia'tarsi *vr* take one's leave (**da** of)

accomoda'mento *nm* arrangement

accomo'dante *adj* accommodating

✶ **accomo'dare** *vt* (riparare) mend; (disporre) arrange

accomo'darsi *vr* make oneself at home; **si accomodi!** come in!; (si sieda) take a seat!

accompagna'mento *nm* accompaniment; (seguito) retinue

✶ indicates a very frequent word

accompa'gnare *vt* accompany; ~ qualcuno a casa see somebody home; ~ qualcuno alla porta show somebody to the door; ~ qualcuno con lo sguardo follow somebody with one's eyes

accompa'gnarsi *vr* ‹cibi, colori ecc› go [well] together; ~ con o a qualcuno accompany somebody

accompagna|'tore, -trice *nmf* companion; (di comitiva) escort; Mus accompanist

■ ~ turistico tour guide

accomu'nare *vt* pool

acconci'are *vt* arrange

acconci'arsi *vr* do one's hair

acconcia'tura *nf* hairstyle; (ornamento) headdress; **'acconciature** 'ladies' hairdresser'

accondiscen'dente *adj* too obliging

accondiscen'denza *nf* excessive desire to please

accondi'scendere *vi* ~ a condescend; comply with ‹desiderio›; (acconsentire) consent to

acconsen'tire *vi* consent

acconten'tare *vt* satisfy

acconten'tarsi *vr* be content (di with)

ac'conto *nm* deposit; in ~ on account; lasciare un ~ leave a deposit

■ acconto di dividendo interim dividend

accop'pare *vt* fam bump off

accoppia'mento *nm* coupling; (di animali) mating

accoppi'are *vt* couple; mate ‹animali›

accoppi'arsi *vr* pair off; ‹animali› mate

accoppi'ata *nf* (scommessa) *bet placed on two horses for first and second place*; sono una strana ~ they make strange bedfellows; **accoppiata vincente** fig winning combination

accoppia'tore *nm*

■ accoppiatore acustico Comput acoustic coupler

acco'rato *adj* sorrowful

accorci'are *vt* shorten

accorci'arsi *vr* get shorter

accor'dare *vt* concede; match ‹colori ecc›; Mus tune

accor'darsi *vr* agree

accorda|'tore, -trice *nmf* Mus tuner

ac'cordo *nm* agreement; Mus chord; (armonia) harmony; andare d'~ get on well; d'~! agreed!; essere d'~ agree; in ~ con in collusion with; prendere accordi con qualcuno make arrangements with somebody

■ accordo collettivo joint agreement

ac'corgersi *vr* ~ di notice; (capire) realize

accorgi'mento *nm* shrewdness; (espediente) device

accorpa'mento *nm* amalgamation

accor'pare *vt* amalgamate

ac'correre *vi* hasten

accorta'mente *adv* astutely

accor'tezza *nf* (previdenza) forethought

ac'corto *adj* shrewd; mal ~ incautious

accosta'mento *nm* (di colori) combination

acco'stare *vt* draw close to; approach ‹persona›; put ajar ‹porta ecc›

acco'starsi *vr* ~ a come near to

accovacci'arsi *vr* crouch, squat down

accovacci'ato *adj* squatting

accoz'zaglia *nf* jumble; (di persone) mob

accoz'zare *vt* ~ colori mix colours that clash

accredi'tabile *adj* reliable

accredita'mento *nm* credit

■ accreditamento tramite bancogiro Bank Giro Credit

accredi'tare *vt* confirm ‹notizia›; Comm credit

accredi'tato *adj* accredited; ‹notizia› reliable

ac'crescere *vt* increase

ac'crescersi *vr* grow larger

accresci'mento *nm* increase

accresci'tivo *adj* augmentative

accucci'arsi *vr* ‹cane› lie down; ‹persona› crouch

accu'dire *vi* ~ a attend to

accumu'lare *vt* accumulate

accumu'larsi *vr* pile up, accumulate

accumula'tore *nm* accumulator; Auto, Comput battery

accumulazi'one *nf* accumulation

ac'cumulo *nm* (di merce) build-up

accurata'mente *adv* carefully

accura'tezza *nf* care

accu'rato *adj* careful

ac'cusa *nf* accusation; Jur charge; essere in stato di ~ Jur have been charged; mettere qualcuno sotto ~ Jur charge somebody; la Pubblica Accusa Jur the public prosecutor

accu'sare *vt* accuse; Jur charge; complain of ‹dolore›; ~ ricevuta di Comm acknowledge receipt of

accusa'tivo *nm* Gram accusative

accu'sato, -a *nmf* accused

accusa'tore ① *adj* accusing ② *nm* Jur prosecutor

a'cerbo *adj* sharp; (non maturo) unripe

'acero *nm* maple

a'cerrimo *adj* implacable

ace'tato *nm* acetate

a'ceto *nm* vinegar

■ aceto di vino wine vinegar

ace'tone *nm* nail polish remover

ace'tosa *nf* Culin [edible] sorrel

aceto'sella *nf* Bot sorrel

A.C.I. *nf abbr* (**Automobile Club d'Italia**) Italian Automobile Association, ≈ AAA Am, ≈ RAC Br

acidità *nf* acidity
■ acidità di stomaco acid stomach

'acido ① *adj* acid; ⟨persona⟩ sour ② *nm* acid
■ ~ cloridrico hydrochloric acid

a'cidulo *adj* slightly sour

'acino *nm* berry; (chicco) grape

'acme *nf* acme

'acne *nf* acne

✐ **'acqua** *nf* water; fare ~ Naut leak; ~ in bocca! fig mum's the word!; avere l'~ alla gola, essere con l'~ alla gola fig be pushed for time; ho fatto un buco nell'~ fig I had no luck whatsoever; in cattive acque in deep water; navigare in cattive acque be in financial difficulties
■ acqua calda hot water; acqua di Colonia eau de Cologne; acqua corrente running water; acqua dolce fresh water; acqua minerale mineral water; acqua minerale gassata fizzy mineral water; acqua naturale still mineral water; acqua potabile drinking water; acqua del rubinetto tap water; acqua salata salt water; acqua saponata suds; acqua tonica tonic water

acqua'forte *nf* etching

acqua'gym *nf* aquarobics *sg*

ac'quaio *nm* sink

acquama'rina *adj* aquamarine

acquapark *nm inv* waterpark

acqua'plano *nm* hydroplane

acqua'ragia *nf* white spirit

acqua'rello *nm* watercolour

a'cquario *nm* aquarium, fish tank; Astr Aquarius

acquartie'rare *vt* Mil billet

acqua'santa *nf* holy water

acquasanti'era *nf* font

acqua'scivolo *nm* water slide

acqua'scooter *nm inv* water-scooter

a'cquata *nf* fam downpour

a'cquatico *adj* aquatic; sport acquatico water sport

acquat'tarsi *vr* crouch

acqua'vite *nf* brandy

acquaz'zone *nm* downpour

acque'dotto *nm* aqueduct

'acqueo *adj* vapore ~ steam, water vapour

acque'rello *nm* watercolour

acquicol'tura *nf* aquaculture

acquie'scente *adj* acquiescent

acquie'tare *vt* appease; calm ⟨dolore⟩

acquie'tarsi *vr* calm down

acqui'rente *nmf* purchaser

acqui'sire *vt* acquire

acqui'sito *adj* acquired

acquisizi'one *nf* attainment

✐ **acqui'stare** *vt* purchase; (ottenere) acquire; ~ in ⟨prestigio, bellezza⟩ gain in

a'cquisto *nm* purchase; uscire per acquisti go shopping; fare acquisti shop; ufficio acquisti purchasing department
■ acquisto rateale hire purchase, HP, install-ment plan Am; acquisto d'impulso impulse buy; acquisto a termine Fin forward buying

acqui'trino *nm* marsh

acquo'lina *nf* far venire l'~ in bocca a qualcuno make somebody's mouth water; ho l'~ in bocca my mouth is watering

a'cquoso *adj* watery

'acre *adj* acrid; (al gusto) sour; fig harsh

a'credine *nf* acridness; (al gusto) sourness; fig harshness

acre'mente *adv* acridly

a'crilico *nm* acrylic

a'critico *adj* acritical

a'crobata *nmf* acrobat

acro'batico *adj* acrobatic

acroba'zia *nf* acrobatics *pl*

acroba'zie *nfpl* acrobatics; fare ~ fig do acrobatics

a'cronimo *nm* acronym

a'cropoli *nf* acropolis

acu'ire *vt* sharpen

acu'irsi *vr* become more intense

a'culeo *nm* sting; Bot prickle

a'cume *nm* acumen

acumi'nato *adj* pointed

a'custica *nf* acoustics *pl*

acustica'mente *adv* acoustically

a'custico *adj* acoustic

acuta'mente *adv* shrewdly

acu'tezza *nf* acuteness; fig shrewdness; (di suoni) shrillness

acutiz'zare *vt* aggravate ⟨dolore⟩

acutiz'zarsi *vr* become worse

a'cuto ① *adj* sharp; ⟨suono⟩ shrill; ⟨freddo, odore⟩ intense; Gram, Math, Med acute ② *nm* Mus high note

ad ① *prep* (before vowel) = A ② *nm* (abbr **amministratore delegato**) managing director

A.D. *abbr* Pol ⟨**Alleanza Democratica**⟩ Democratic Alliance

adagi'are *vt* lay down

adagi'arsi *vr* lie down

a'dagio ① *adv* slowly ② *nm* Mus adagio; (proverbio) adage

ada'mitico *adj* in costume ~ in one's birthday suit, stark naked

adat'tabile *adj* adaptable

adattabilità *nf* adaptability

✐ indicates a very frequent word

adatta'mento *nm* adaptation; **avere spirito di** ∼ be adaptable
■ **adattamento cinematografico** film adaptation, adaptation for the cinema
adat'tare *vt* adapt; (aggiustare) fit
adat'tarsi *vr* adapt
adatta'tore *nm* adaptor
◆ **a'datto** *adj* suitable (**a** for) (giusto) right
addebita'mento *nm* debit
■ **addebitamento diretto** direct debit
addebi'tare *vt* debit; fig ascribe ‹*colpa*›
ad'debito *nm* charge
addensa'mento *nm* thickening; (di persone) gathering
adden'sare *vt* thicken
adden'sarsi *vr* thicken; (affollarsi) gather
adden'tare *vt* bite
adden'trarsi *vr* penetrate
ad'dentro *adv* deeply; **essere** ∼ **in** be in on
addestra'mento *nm* training
■ **addestramento iniziale** basic training
adde'strare *vt* train
adde'strarsi *vr* train
addestra|'tore, -trice *nmf* trainer
ad'detto, -a ① *adj* assigned ② *nmf* employee; (diplomatico) attaché
■ **adetti** *pl* **ai lavori** persons involved in the work; **'vietato l'ingresso ai non addetti ai lavori'** 'staff only'; **addetto commerciale** salesman; **addetto culturale** cultural attaché; **addetto stampa** information officer, press officer; **addetto ai traslochi** removal man
addì *adv* ∼ **15 settembre 2010** on 15th September 2010
addi'accio *nm* **dormire all'**∼ sleep in the open
addi'etro *adv* (indietro) back; (nel passato) before
◆ **ad'dio** *nm & int* goodbye
■ **addio al celibato** stag night, stag party; **addio al nubilato** hen night; **cena d'addio** farewell dinner
◆ **addirit'tura** *adv* (perfino) even; (assolutamente) absolutely; ∼**!** really!
ad'dirsi *vr* ∼ **a** suit
addi'tare *vt* point at; (per identificare) point out; fig point to
addi'tivo *adj & nm* additive
addizio'nale ① *adj* additional ② *nf* (imposta) surtax
addizional'mente *adv* additionally
addizio'nare *vt* add [up]
addiziona'trice *nf* adding machine
addizi'one *nf* addition
addob'bare *vt* decorate
ad'dobbo *nm* decoration
addol'cire *vt* sweeten; tone down ‹*colore*›; fig soften
addol'cirsi *vr* fig mellow

addolo'rare *vt* grieve
addolo'rarsi *vr* be upset (**per** by)
addolo'rato *adj* pained, distressed
ad'dome *nm* abdomen
addomesti'care *vt* tame
addomestica'tore, -trice *nmf* tamer
addomi'nale ① *adj* abdominal ② *nmpl* **addominali** abdominals
◆ **addormen'tare** *vt* put to sleep
addormen'tarsi *vr* go to sleep
addormen'tato *adj* asleep; fig slow
addos'sare *vt* ∼ **a** (appoggiare) lean against; (attribuire) lay on
addos'sarsi *vr* (ammassarsi) crowd; shoulder ‹*responsabilità ecc*›
◆ **ad'dosso** *adv* on; ∼ **a** *prep* on; (molto vicino) right next to; **andare/venire** ∼ **qualcuno** run into somebody; **mettere gli occhi** ∼ **a qualcuno/qualcosa** hanker after somebody/something; **non mettermi le mani** ∼**!** keep your hands off me!; **stare** ∼ **a qualcuno** fig be on somebody's back; **farsela** ∼ fam (bisogni corporali) dirty oneself; (pipì) wet oneself
ad'durre *vt* produce ‹*prova, documento*›; give ‹*pretesto, esempio*›
adegua'mento *nm* adjustment
adegu'are *vt* adjust
adegu'arsi *vr* conform
adeguata'mente *adv* suitably
adegua'tezza *nf* suitability
adegu'ato *adj* suitable; ∼ **a** suited to, suitable for
a'dempiere *vt* fulfil
adempi'mento *nm* fulfilment
adem'pire *vt* fulfil
ade'noidi *nfpl* adenoids
a'depto, -a *nmf* adherent
ade'rente ① *adj* adhesive; ‹*vestito*› tight ② *nmf* follower
ade'renza *nf* adhesion; **aderenze** *pl* connections
ade'rire *vi* ∼ **a** stick to, adhere to; support ‹*sciopero, petizione*›; agree to ‹*richiesta*›
adesca'mento *nm* Jur soliciting
ade'scare *vt* bait; fig entice
adesca'trice *nf* fille de joie
adesi'one *nf* adhesion; fig agreement
ade'sivo ① *adj* adhesive ② *nm* sticker; Auto bumper sticker
◆ **a'desso** *adv* now; (poco fa) just now; (tra poco) any moment now; **da** ∼ **in poi** from now on; **per** ∼ for the moment; **fino** ∼ up till now
adia'cente *adj* adjacent; ∼ **a** next to
adia'cenze *nfpl* adjacent areas
adi'bire *vt* ∼ **a** put to use as
'adipe *nm* adipose tissue
adi'poso *adj* adipose
adi'rarsi *vr* get irate

adi'rato *adj* irate
a'dire *vt* resort to; ~ **le vie legali** take legal proceedings; ~ **la successione** Jur take possession of an inheritance
'adito *nm* dare ~ **a** give rise to
ADM *nfpl abbr* (**Armi di Distruzione di Massa**) WMD
adocchi'are *vt* eye; (con desiderio) covet
adole'scente *adj & nmf* adolescent *attrib*
adole'scenza *nf* adolescence
adolescenzi'ale *adj* adolescent
adombra'mento *nm* darkening
adom'brare *vt* darken; fig veil
adom'brarsi *vr* (offendersi) take offence
◦′ **adope'rare** *vt* use
adope'rarsi *vr* take trouble
ado'rabile *adj* adorable
◦′ **ado'rare** *vt* adore
adorazi'one *nf* adoration; **in** ~ adoring
ador'nare *vt* adorn
a'dorno *adj* adorned (**di** with)
adot'tare *vt* adopt
adot'tivo *adj* adoptive
adozi'one *nf* adoption
adrena'lina *nf* adrenalin
adri'atico ☐1☐ *adj* Adriatic
☐2☐ *nm* **l'Adriatico** the Adriatic
adu'lare *vt* flatter
adula|'tore, -trice *nmf* flatterer
adula'torio *adj* sycophantic
adulazi'one *nf* flattery
a'dultera *nf* adulteress
adulte'rare *vt* adulterate
adulte'rato *adj* adulterated
adulte'rino *adj* adulterous
adul'terio *nm* adultery
a'dultero ☐1☐ *adj* adulterous
☐2☐ *nm* adulterer
◦′ **a'dulto, -a** *adj & nmf* adult; (maturo) mature
adu'nanza *nf* assembly
adu'nare *vt* gather
adu'nata *nf* Mil parade
a'dunco *adj* hooked
adunghi'are *vt* claw
ae'rare *vt* air ‹stanza›
aera'tore *nm* ventilator
aerazi'one *nf* ventilation
a'ereo ☐1☐ *adj* aerial; (dell'aviazione) air *attrib*
☐2☐ *nm* aeroplane, plane; **andare in** ~ fly
■ **aereo da carico** cargo plane; **aereo da guerra** warplane; **aereo di linea** airliner; **aereo navetta** shuttle; **aereo a reazione** jet [plane]
ae'robica *nf* aerobics *sg*
ae'robico *adj* aerobic
aerodi'namica *nf* aerodynamics *sg*

aerodi'namico *adj* aerodynamic
aero'grafo *nm* airbrush
aero'gramma *nm* aerogram[me]
aero'linea *nf* airline
aero'mobile *nm* aircraft
aeromo'dello *nm* model aircraft
aero'nautica *nf* aeronautics *sg*; Mil Air Force
aero'nautico *adj* aeronautical
aerona'vale *adj* air and sea *attrib*
◦′ **aero'plano** *nm* aeroplane
aero'porto *nm* airport
aeroportu'ale *adj* airport *attrib*
aero'scalo *nm* cargo and servicing area
aero'sol *nm inv* aerosol
■ **apparecchio per aerosol** vaporizer
aerospazi'ale *adj* aerospace *attrib*
aero'statico *adj*
■ **pallone aerostatico** aerostat
ae'rostato *nm* aerostat
aerostazi'one *nf* air terminal
aerosti'ere *nm* balloonist
aero'via *nf* air corridor
A.F. *abbr* (**alta frequenza**) HF
'afa *nf* sultriness
af'fabile *adj* affable
affabilità *nf* affability
affaccen'darsi *vr* busy oneself (**a** with)
◦′ **affacci'arsi** *vr* show oneself; ~ **alla finestra** appear at the window
affacen'dato *adj* busy
affa'mare *vt* starve [out]
affa'mato *adj* starving
affan'nare *vt* leave breathless
affan'narsi *vr* busy oneself; (agitarsi) get worked up
affan'nato *adj* breathless; **dal respiro** ~ wheezy
af'fanno *nm* breathlessness; fig worry; **essere in** ~ **per** be anxious about
affannosa'mente *adv* breathlessly
affan'noso *adj* exhausting; **respiro** ~ heavy breathing
◦′ **af'fare** *nm* matter; (occasione) bargain; Comm transaction, deal; **pensa agli affari tuoi** mind your own business; **non sono affari tuoi** fam it's none of your business; **fare affari d'oro** have a field day; **affari** *pl* business; **d'affari** ‹uomo, cena, viaggio› business; **affari** *pl* **esteri** foreign affairs; **ministro degli affari esteri** Foreign Secretary Br, Secretary of State Am
affa'rismo *nm* pej wheeling and dealing
affa'rista *nmf* wheeler-dealer
affasci'nante *adj* fascinating; ‹persona, sorriso› bewitching
affasci'nare *vt* bewitch; fig charm
affastel'lare *vt* tie up in bundles

◦′ indicates a very frequent word

affatica'mento *nm* fatigue

affati'care *vt* tire; (sfinire) exhaust

affati'carsi *vr* tire oneself out; (affannarsi) strive

affati'cato *adj* fatigued, suffering from fatigue; ∼ **dal troppo lavoro** overworked

∮ **af'fatto** *adv* completely; **non ... ∼** not ... at all; **niente ∼!** not at all!

∮ **affer'mare** *vt* affirm; (sostenere) assert

affer'marsi *vr* establish oneself

affermativa'mente *adv* in the affirmative

afferma'tivo *adj* affirmative

affer'mato *adj* established

affermazi'one *nf* assertion; (successo) achievement

affer'rare *vt* seize; catch ‹oggetto›; (capire) grasp; ∼ **al volo** fig be quick on the uptake

affer'rarsi *vr* ∼ **a** grasp at, clutch at

affet'tare *vt* slice; (ostentare) affect

affet'tato ① *adj* sliced; ‹sorriso, maniere› affected ② *nm* cold meat, sliced meat

affetta'trice *nf* bacon-slicer

affettazl'one *nf* affectation

affet'tivo *adj* affective; **rapporto affettivo** emotional tie

af'fetto¹ *nm* affection; **con ∼** affectionately; **gli affetti familiari** family ties

af'fetto² *adj* ∼ **da** suffering from

affettuosa'mente *adv* affectionately

affettuosità *nf inv* (gesto) affectionate gesture

∮ **affettu'oso** *adj* affectionate

affezio'narsi *vr* ∼ **a** grow fond of

affezio'nato *adj* devoted, attached (**a** to)

affezi'one *nf* affection; Med ailment

affian'care *vt* put side by side; Mil flank; fig support

affian'carsi *vr* come side by side, fig stand together, stand shoulder to shoulder; ∼ **a qualcuno** fig help somebody out

affiata'mento *nm* harmony

affia'tarsi *vr* get on well together

affia'tato *adj* close-knit; **una coppia affiatata** a very close couple

affibbi'are *vt* ∼ **qualcosa a qualcuno** saddle somebody with something; ∼ **un pugno a qualcuno** let fly at somebody

affi'dabile *adj* reliable, dependable

affidabilità *nf* reliability, dependability

affida'mento *nm* Jur (dei minori) custody; **fare ∼ su qualcuno** rely on somebody; **non dare ∼ (a qualcuno)** not inspire confidence (in somebody)

∮ **affi'dare** *vt* entrust

affi'darsi *vr* ∼ **a** rely on

affida'tario *adj* (famiglia) foster

af'fido *nm* **un bambino in ∼** a foster child

affievoli'mento *nm* weakening

affievo'lirsi *vr* grow weak

af'figgere *vt* affix

affilacol'telli *nm inv* knife sharpener

affi'lare *vt* sharpen

affili'are *vt* affiliate

affili'arsi *vt* become affiliated

affiliazi'one *nf* affiliation

affi'nare *vt* sharpen; (perfezionare) refine

affinché *conj* so that, in order that

af'fine *adj* similar

affinità *nf inv* affinity

affiora'mento *nm* emergence; Naut surfacing

affio'rare *vi* emerge; fig come to light

affissi'one *nf* bill-posting; **'divieto di ∼'** 'stick no bills'

af'fisso *nm* bill; Gram affix

affitta'camere ① *nm inv* landlord ② *nf inv* landlady

affit'tare *vt* (dare in affitto) let; (prendere in affitto) rent

■ **af'fittasi** to let, for rent

af'fitto *nm* rent; **contratto d'∼** lease; **dare in ∼** let; **prendere in ∼** rent

affittu'ario, -a *nmf* Jur lessee

af'fliggere *vt* torment

af'fliggersi *vr* distress oneself

af'flitto *adj* distressed

afflizi'one *nf* distress; fig affliction

afflosci'are *vt* **la pioggia ha afflosciato le foglie** the rain has made the leaves go all limp

afflosci'arsi *vr* become floppy; (accasciarsi) flop down

afflu'ente *adj* & *nm* tributary

afflu'enza *nf* flow; (di gente) crowd

afflu'ire *vi* flow; fig pour in

af'flusso *nm* influx

affoga'mento *nm* drowning

affo'gare *vt/i* drown; Culin poach; ∼ **in** fig be swamped with

affo'garsi *vr* (suicidarsi) drown oneself

affo'gato *adj* ‹persona› drowned; ‹uova› poached

■ **affogato al caffè** *ice cream with hot espresso poured over it*

affolla'mento *nm* crowd

affol'lare *vt* crowd

affol'larsi *vr* crowd

affol'lato *adj* crowded

affonda'mento *nm* sinking

affon'dare *vt/i* sink

affon'darsi *vr* sink

affossa'mento *nm* (avvallamento) pothole; fig burial

affran'care *vt* redeem ‹bene›; stamp ‹lettera›; free ‹schiavo›

affran'carsi *vr* free oneself

affran'cato *adj* ⟨lettera⟩ stamped; ⟨schiavo⟩ freed; **già ~** ⟨busta⟩ prepaid

affranca'trice *nf* franking machine, franker

affranca'tura *nf* stamping; (di spedizione) postage
- **affrancatura a carico del destinatario** freepost; **affrancatura per l'estero** postage abroad

af'franto *adj* prostrate with grief, grief-stricken; (esausto) worn out

affre'scare *vt* paint a fresco on

af'fresco *nm* fresco

affret'tare *vt* speed up

affret'tarsi *vr* hurry

affrettata'mente *adv* hastily

affret'tato *adj* ⟨passo⟩ fast; ⟨decisione⟩ hasty; ⟨lavoro⟩ rushed

⚬ **affron'tare** *vt* face; confront ⟨nemico⟩; meet ⟨spese⟩

affron'tarsi *vr* clash

af'fronto *nm* affront, insult; **fare un ~ a qualcuno** insult somebody

affumi'care *vt* fill with smoke; Culin smoke

affumi'cato *adj* ⟨prosciutto, formaggio⟩ smoked; ⟨lenti, vetro⟩ tinted

affuso'lare *vt* taper [off]

affuso'lato *adj* tapering

Af'ganistan *nm* Afghanistan

af'gano *adj & nmf* Afghani, Afghan

AFI *nm abbr* (**Alfabeto Fonetico Internazionale**) IPA

aficio'nado, -a *nmf* aficionado

'afide *nm* aphid

'afono *adj* (rauco) hoarse

afo'risma *nm* aphorism

a'foso *adj* sultry

'Africa *nf* Africa
- **Africa orientale** East Africa; **Africa nera** Black Africa; **Africa del Nord** North Africa

afri'cano, -a *adj & nmf* African

afri'kaans *nm* Afrikaans

afroameri'cano, -a *adj & nmf* Afro-American

afroasi'atico *adj* Afro-Asian

afroca'ribico *adj* Afro-Caribbean

afrocu'bano *adj* Afro-Cuban

afrodi'siaco *adj & nm* aphrodisiac

a'genda *nf* diary
- **agenda elettronica** personal organizer, electronic organizer; **agenda da tavolo** desk diary

agen'dina *nf* pocket-diary

⚬ **a'gente** *nm* agent; **agenti** *pl* **atmosferici** atmospheric agents
- **agente di cambio** stockbroker; **agente di custodia** prison warder; **agente del fisco**

assessor; **agente immobiliare** estate agent, realtor Am; **agente marittimo** shipping agent; **agente di polizia** police officer; **agente segreto** secret agent; **agente teatrale** theatrical agent; (di compagnia) impresario; **agente di viaggio** travel agent

agen'zia *nf* agency; (filiale) branch office; (di banca) branch
- **agenzia di collocamento** employment exchange; **agenzia immobiliare** estate agency, realtor Am; **agenzia matrimoniale** dating agency; **agenzia pubblicitaria** advertising agency; **agenzia di recupero crediti** debt collection agency; **agenzia di stampa** news agency, press agency; **agenzia di viaggi** travel agency

agevo'lare *vt* facilitate

agevolazi'one *nf* facilitation
- **agevolazioni** *pl* **fiscali** tax breaks

a'gevole *adj* easy; ⟨strada⟩ smooth

agevol'mente *adv* easily

agganci'are *vt* hook up; Rail couple

agganci'arsi *vr* ⟨vestito⟩ hook up; **~ a** ⟨maglia⟩ catch on; ⟨rimorchio⟩ hook onto

ag'gancio *nm* Aeron docking

ag'geggio *nm* gadget

agget'tivo *nm* adjective

agghiacci'ante *adj* terrifying

agghiacci'are *vt* fig **~ qualcuno** make somebody's blood run cold

agghiacci'arsi *vr* freeze

agghin'dare *vt* fam dress up

agghin'darsi *vr* fam doll oneself up

agghin'dato *adj* dressed up; ⟨sala⟩ decorated; fig ⟨stile⟩ stilted

aggiornabilità *nf* Comput upgradability

aggiorna'mento *nm* update; (azione) updating; **corso di ~** refresher course

aggior'nare *vt* (rinviare) postpone; (mettere a giorno) bring up to date, update

aggior'narsi *vr* get up to date

aggior'nato *adj* up-to-date; ⟨versione⟩ updated

aggio'taggio *nm* Jur manipulation of the market

aggira'mento *nm* Mil outflanking

aggi'rare *vt* surround; fig (ingannare) trick

aggi'rarsi *vr* hang about; **~ su** ⟨discorso ecc⟩ be about; ⟨somma⟩ be around

aggiudi'care *vt* award; (all'asta) knock down

aggiudi'carsi *vr* win

⚬ **aggi'ungere** *vt* add

aggi'unta *nf* addition; **in ~** in addition

aggiun'tare *vt* splice

aggiun'tivo *adj* supplementary

aggi'unto ① *adj* added
② *adj & nm* (assistente) assistant

⚬ **aggiu'stare** *vt* mend; (sistemare) settle; fam (mettere a posto) fix; **ora l'aggiusto io** fig I'll sort him out

aggiu'starsi vr adapt; (mettersi in ordine) tidy oneself up; (decidere) sort things out; ‹tempo› clear up

aggiusta'tina nf dare un'∼ a neaten

agglomera'mento nm conglomeration

agglome'rante nm binder

agglome'rato nm built-up area

aggrap'pare vt grasp

aggrap'parsi vr ∼ a cling to

aggrava'mento nm worsening; (di pena) increase

aggra'vante Jur 1 nf aggravation 2 adj aggravating; **circostanza aggravante** aggravation

aggra'vare vt (peggiorare) make worse; increase ‹pena›; (appesantire) weigh down

aggra'varsi vr worsen

ag'gravio nm
■ aggravio fiscale tax burden

aggrazi'ato adj graceful

aggre'dire vt attack

aggre'gare vt add; (associare a un gruppo ecc) admit

aggre'garsi vr ∼ a join

aggre'gato 1 adj associated 2 nm aggregate; (di case) block

aggregazi'one nf (di persone) gathering

aggressi'one nf aggression; (atto) attack
■ aggressione a mano armata armed assault

aggressività nf aggressiveness

aggres'sivo adj aggressive

aggres'sore nm aggressor

aggrin'zare, aggrinzire vt wrinkle

aggrin'zirsi vr wrinkle

aggrot'tare vt ∼ le ciglia/la fronte frown

aggrovigli'are vt tangle

aggrovigli'arsi vr get entangled; fig get complicated

aggrovigli'ato adj entangled; fig confused

agguan'tare vt catch

agguan'tarsi vr ∼ a grasp

aggu'ato nm ambush; (tranello) trap; **stare in** ∼ lie in wait; **tendere un** ∼ **a qualcuno** set an ambush for somebody

agguer'rito adj fierce

agiata'mente adv comfortably

agia'tezza nf comfort

agi'ato adj ‹persona› well off; ‹vita› comfortable

a'gibile adj ‹palazzo› fit for human habitation

agibilità nf fitness for human habitation

'agile adj agile

agilità nf agility

agil'mente adv agilely

'aglo nm ease; **mettersi a proprio** ∼ make oneself at home

a'gire vi act; ‹comportarsi› behave; (funzionare) work; ∼ **su** affect

agi'tare vt shake; wave ‹mano›; fig (turbare) trouble; '∼ **prima dell'uso'** 'shake before using'

agi'tarsi vr toss about; (essere inquieto) be restless; ‹mare› get rough

agi'tato adj restless; ‹mare› rough

agita|'tore, -trice nmf (persona) agitator

agitazi'one nf agitation; **mettere in** ∼ **qualcuno** send somebody into a flat spin

'agli = A + GLI

'aglio nm garlic

a'gnello nm lamb

agno'lotti nmpl ravioli sg

a'gnostico, -a adj & nmf agnostic

'ago nm needle; **a 9 aghi** ‹stampante› 9-pin
■ ago di pino pine-needle

ago'gnare vt (liter) yearn for, thirst for

ago'nia nf agony

ago'nismo nm competitiveness

ago'nistica nf competition

ago'nistico adj competitive

agoniz'zante adj in one's death throes

agoniz'zare vi be on one's deathbed

agopun|'tore, -trice nmf acupuncturist

agopun'tura nf acupuncture

agorafo'bia nf agoraphobia

ago'rafobo, -a nmf agoraphobic

agostini'ano, -a adj & nmf Augustinian

a'gosto nm August

a'graria nf agriculture

a'grario 1 adj agricultural 2 nm landowner

a'greste adj rustic

a'gricolo adj agricultural

agricol'tore nm farmer

agricol'tura nf agriculture
■ agricoltura biologica organic farming

agri'foglio nm holly

agrimen'sore nm land-surveyor

agritu'rismo nm farm holidays, agrotourism

'agro¹ adj sour; **all'**∼ Culin pickled

'agro² nm countryside around a town

agroalimen'tare adj food attrib

agro'dolce adj bitter-sweet; Culin sweet-and-sour; **in** ∼ sweet and sour

agrono'mia nf agronomy

a'gronomo, -a nmf agriculturalist

agropasto'rale adj based on farming

a'grume nm citrus fruit; (pianta) citrus tree

agru'meto nm citrus plantation

aguz'zare vt sharpen; ∼ **le orecchie** prick up one's ears; ∼ **la vista** look hard

aguz'zino nm slave-driver; (carceriere) jailer

a'guzzo adj pointed

a

ꞔ **ah** *int* ah!; ah, davvero? oh really?

ahi *int* ow!

ahimè *int* alas!

'ai = A + I

'aia *nf* threshing-floor

'Aia *nf* L'∼ The Hague

Aids *nm* Aids

AIE *abbr* (**Associazione Italiana degli Editori**) *association of Italian publishers*

air bag *nm inv* Auto air bag

ai'rone *nm* heron

air terminal *nm inv* air terminal

ai'tante *adj* sturdy

aiu'ola *nf* flowerbed

aiu'tante ① *nmf* assistant
② *nm* Mil adjutant
■ aiutante di campo aide-de-camp

ꞔ **aiu'tare** *vt* help

ꞔ **ai'uto** *nm* help, aid; (assistente) assistant; dare un ∼ lend a hand; venire in ∼ a qualcuno come to somebody's rescue; ∼! help!; aiuti *pl* alimentari food aid
■ aiuti *pl* umanitari relief supplies; aiuto chirurgo assistant surgeon; aiuto domestico mother's help; aiuto infermiere nursing auxiliary; aiuto in linea Comput on-line help

aiz'zare *vt* incite; ∼ contro set on

al = A + IL

ꞔ **'ala** *nf* wing; fare ∼ make way; avere le ali ai piedi fig run like the wind; tarpare le ali a qualcuno fig clip somebody's wings
■ ala destra/sinistra (in calcio) right/left wing

ala'bastro *nm* alabaster

'alacre *adj* brisk

alam'bicco *nm* alembic

a'lano *nm* Great Dane

a'lare *nm* firedog; apertura alare wingspan

A'laska *nf* Alaska

ꞔ **'alba** *nf* dawn

alba'nese *adj & nmf* Albanian

Alba'nia *nf* Albania

'albatro *nm* albatross

albeggi'are *vi* dawn

albe'rare *vi* line with trees ‹strada›

albe'rato *adj* wooded; ‹viale› tree-lined

albera'tura *nf* Naut masts *pl*

albe'rello *nm* sapling

alber'gare ① *vt* ‹edificio› accommodate
② *vi* (liter) lodge

alberga|'tore, -trice *nmf* hotel-keeper

alberghi'ero *adj* hotel *attrib*

ꞔ **al'bergo** *nm* hotel
■ albergo diurno *hotel where rooms are rented during the daytime*; albergo a 3 stelle 3-star hotel

ꞔ **'albero** *nm* tree; Naut mast; Mech shaft

ꞔ indicates a very frequent word

■ albero a camme camshaft; albero a foglie caduche deciduous tree; albero da frutto fruit tree; albero genealogico family tree; albero a gomiti crankshaft; albero della gomma rubber tree; albero maestro Naut mainmast; albero di Natale Christmas tree; albero di trasmissione Mech transmission shaft, prop shaft

albi'cocca *nf* apricot

albi'cocco *nm* apricot (tree)

al'bino *nm* albino

'albo *nm* register; (libro ecc) album; (per avvisi) notice board

album *nm inv* album
■ album da colorare colouring book; album da disegno sketch-book

al'bume *nm* albumen

albu'mina *nf* albumin

alca'lino *adj* alkaline

'alce *nm* elk

alchi'mia *nf* alchemy

alchi'mista *nm* alchemist

'alcol *nm* alcohol; Med spirit; (liquori forti) spirits *pl*; darsi all'∼ take to drink
■ alcol denaturato meths, surgical spirit; alcol etilico ethyl alcohol

alcolicità *nf* alcohol content

al'colico ① *adj* alcoholic
② *nm* alcoholic drink

alco'lismo *nm* alcoholism

alco'lista *nmf* alcoholic

alcoliz'zato, -a *adj & nmf* alcoholic

alcol'test® *nm inv* (prova) breath test(ing); (apparecchio) Breathalyzer®

al'cova *nf* alcove

ꞔ **al'cun, alcuno** *adj & pron* any; non ha ∼ amico he hasn't any friends, he has no friends; alcuni *pl* some, a few; alcuni suoi amici some of his friends

aldilà *nm* next world, hereafter

alea'torio *adj* unpredictable; Jur aleatory

aleggi'are *vi* ‹brezza› blow gently; ‹profumo› waft

a'letta *nf* Mech fin

alet'tone *nm* Aeron aileron; Auto stabilizer

'alfa *nf inv* alpha

alfa'betico *adj* alphabetical

alfabetizzazi'one *nf*
■ alfabetizzazione della popolazione teaching people to read and write; tasso di alfabetizzazione literacy rate

alfa'beto *nm* alphabet
■ Alfabeto Fonetico Internazionale International Phonetic Alphabet; alfabeto Morse Morse code

alfanu'merico *adj* alphanumeric

alfi'ere *nm* (negli scacchi) bishop

al'fine *adv* eventually, in the end

'alga *nf* weed; alghe *pl* marine seaweed

'algebra nf algebra
Al'geri nf Algiers
Alge'ria nf Algeria
alge'rino, -a adj & nmf Algerian
algocol'tura nf seaweed farming
algo'ritmo nm algorithm
ali'ante nm glider
'alibi nm inv alibi
a'lice nf anchovy
alie'nabile adj Jur alienable
alie'nare vt alienate
alie'narsi vr become estranged; ∼ le simpatie di qualcuno lose somebody's good will
ali'enato, -a ① adj alienated ② nmf lunatic
alienazi'one nf alienation
a'lieno, -a ① nmf alien ② adj è ∼ da invidia envy is foreign or alien to him
alimen'tare ① vt feed; fig foment ② adj food attrib; ‹abitudine› dietary ③ nm alimentari pl foodstuffs
alimenta'tore nm power unit
■ alimentatore automatico di documenti automatic paper feed
alimentazi'one nf feeding; (cibo) food; (elettrica, a gas ecc) supply
ali'mento nm food; alimenti pl food; Jur alimony
a'liquota nf share; (di imposta) rate
■ aliquota minima basic rate; ad ∼ zero zero-rated
ali'scafo nm hydrofoil
'alito nm breath; alito cattivo bad breath
ali'tosi nf inv halitosis
all. abbr (allegato) encl
'alla = A + LA
allaccia'mento nm connection
allacci'are vt fasten ‹cintura›; lace up ‹scarpe›; do up ‹vestito›; (collegare) connect; form ‹amicizia›
allacci'arsi vr do up, fasten ‹vestito, cintura›
allaga'mento nm flooding
alla'gare vt flood
alla'garsi vr to become flooded
allampa'nato adj lanky
allarga'mento nm (di strada, ricerche) widening
⚹ **allar'gare** vt widen; open ‹braccia, gambe›; let out ‹vestito ecc›; fig extend
allar'garsi vr to widen
allar'mante adj alarming
allar'mare vt alarm
allar'mato adj panicky, alarmed
al'larme nm alarm; dare l'∼ raise the alarm; mettere in ∼ qualcuno alarm somebody; far scattare il campanello d'∼ set

the alarm bells ringing
■ falso allarme fig false alarm; allarme aereo air-raid siren; (suono) air-raid warning; allarme antifumo smoke alarm; allarme antincendio fire alarm; allarme rosso red alert
allar'mismo nm alarmism
allar'mista nmf alarmist
allatta'mento nm (di animale) suckling; (di neonato) feeding
allat'tare vt suckle ‹animale›; feed ‹neonato›; ∼ artificialmente bottle feed
'alle = A + LE
alle'anza nf alliance
■ Alleanza Democratica Pol Democratic Alliance; Alleanza Nazionale Pol National Alliance
alle'are vt unite
alle'arsi vr form an alliance
⚹ **alle'ato, -a** ① adj allied ② nmf ally
alle'gare¹ vt Jur allege
alle'gare² vt (accludere) enclose; set on edge ‹denti›
alle'gato ① adj enclosed; Comput attached ② nm enclosure; Comput attachment; in ∼ attached, appended
allegazi'one nf Jur allegation
alleggeri'mento nm alleviation
allegge'rire vt lighten; fig alleviate
allegge'rirsi vr become lighter; (vestirsi leggero) put on lighter clothes
allego'ria nf allegory
alle'gorico adj allegorical
allegra'mente adv breezily
alle'gria nf gaiety
⚹ **al'legro** ① adj cheerful; ‹colore› bright; (brillo) tipsy ② nm Mus allegro
alle'luia int hallelujah
allena'mento nm training
alle'nare vt train
alle'narsi vr train
allena|'tore, -trice nmf trainer, coach
allen'tare vt loosen; fig relax
allen'tarsi vr become loose; Mech work loose
aller'gia nf allergy
al'lergico adj allergic
aller'gologo, -a nmf allergist
al'lerta nf stare ∼ be alert, be on the alert; essere in stato di ∼ Mil be in a state of alert; mettere in stato di ∼ put on the alert
allesti'mento nm preparation; in ∼ in preparation
■ allestimento scenico Theat set
alle'stire vt prepare; stage ‹spettacolo›; Naut fit out
allet'tante adj alluring; poco ∼ unattractive

allet'tare vt entice

allet'tato adj bed-bound, laid up

⚲ **alleva'mento** nm breeding; (processo) bringing up; (luogo) farm; (per piante) nursery; **pollo di allevamento** battery chicken
- **allevamento in batteria** battery farming; **allevamento a terra** free-range farming; **pollo/uova di allevamento a terra** free-range chicken/eggs

⚲ **alle'vare** vt bring up ‹bambini›; breed ‹animali›; grow ‹piante›

alleva|'tore, -trice nmf breeder

allevia'mento nm alleviation

allevi'are vt alleviate; fig lighten

alli'bito adj astounded; **rimanere** ∼ be astounded

allibra'tore nm bookmaker

allie'tare vt gladden

allie'tarsi vr rejoice

⚲ **alli'evo, -a** ① nmf pupil ② nm Mil cadet

alliga'tore nm alligator

allinea'mento nm alignment

alline'are vt line up; Typ align; Fin adjust

alline'arsi vr line up; fig fall into line; ∼ **con qualcuno** fig align oneself with somebody

alline'ato adj lined up; **i paesi non allineati** the non-aligned states

'allo = A + LO

allo'care vt allocate

al'locco¹ nm tawny owl

al'locco², -a nmf fig idiot

allocuzi'one nf speech

al'lodola nf [sky]lark

alloggi'are ① vt ‹persona› put up; ‹casa› provide accommodation for; Mil billet ② vi put up, stay; Mil be billeted

al'loggio nm (appartamento) flat, apartment Am; Mil billet
- **alloggio popolare** council flat

allontana'mento nm removal

⚲ **allonta'nare** vt move away; (licenziare) dismiss; avert ‹pericolo›

allonta'narsi vr go away

allopa'tia nf allopathy

⚲ **al'lora** adv then; (in quel tempo) at that time; (in tal caso) in that case; ∼ ∼ just then; **d'**∼ **in poi** from then on; **e** ∼**?** what now?; (e con ciò?) so what?; **fino** ∼ until then

allorché conj when, as soon as

al'loro nm laurel; Culin bay; **dormire sugli allori** rest on one's laurels

'alluce nm big toe

alluci'nante adj fam incredible; **sostanza allucinante** hallucinogen

---

⚲ indicates a very frequent word

alluci'nato, -a nmf person who suffers from hallucinations; fam space cadet

allucina'torio adj hallucinatory

allucinazi'one nf hallucination

allucino'geno adj ‹sostanza› hallucinatory

al'ludere vi ∼ **a** allude to

allu'minio nm aluminium

allu'naggio nm moon-landing

allu'nare vi land on the moon

⚲ **allun'gare** vt lengthen; stretch out ‹mano›; stretch ‹gamba›; extend ‹tavolo›; (diluire) dilute; ∼ **il collo** crane one's neck; ∼ **il muso** pull a long face; ∼ **il passo** quicken one's step; ∼ **le mani su qualcuno** touch somebody up; (picchiare) start fighting with somebody; ∼ **uno schiaffo a qualcuno** slap somebody

allun'garsi vr grow longer; (crescere) grow taller; (sdraiarsi) lie down, stretch out

allun'gato adj ‹forma› elongated

al'lungo nm (nel calcio) pass; (nella corsa) spurt; (nel pugilato) lunge

allusi'one nf allusion

allu'sivo adj allusive

alluvio'nale adj alluvial

alluvio'nato adj ‹popolazione› flooded out; ‹territorio› flooded

alluvi'one nf flood

alma'nacco nm almanac
- **almanacco nobiliare** peerage

⚲ **al'meno** adv at least; [se] ∼ **venisse il sole!** if only the sun would come out!

a'logena nf halogen lamp

a'logeno ① nm halogen ② adj **lampada alogena** halogen lamp

a'lone nm halo

alo'pecia nf Med alopecia

al'paca nm inv alpaca

al'pestre adj Alpine

'Alpi nfpl **le** ∼ the Alps

alpi'nismo nm mountaineering

alpi'nista nmf mountaineer

alpi'nistico adj mountaineering attrib

al'pino ① adj Alpine ② nm Mil **gli Alpini** the Alpine troops

al'quanto ① adj a certain amount of ② adv rather

Al'sazia nf Alsace

alt int stop; **intimare l'**∼ give the order to halt

alta'lena nf swing; (tavola in bilico) see-saw

altale'nare vi fig vacillate

alta'mente adv highly

al'tare nm altar

alta'rino nm **scoprire gli altarini di qualcuno** reveal somebody's guilty secrets

alte'rabile *adj* which can be changed, alterable

alte'rare *vt* alter; adulterate ‹*vino*›; (falsificare) falsify

alte'rarsi *vr* be altered; ‹*cibo*› go bad; ‹*merci*› deteriorate; (arrabbiarsi) get angry

alte'rato *adj* ‹*suono*› distorted; ‹*viso*› careworn; ‹*cibo*› spoilt; ‹*vino*› adulterated; (arrabbiato) angry

alterazi'one *nf* alteration; (di vino) adulteration

al'terco *nm* altercation

alte'rigia *nf* haughtiness

alter'nanza *nf* alternation; (in agricoltura) rotation; Pol regular change in government

alter'nare *vt* alternate

alter'narsi *vr* alternate

alterna'tiva *nf* alternative

alterna'tivo *adj* alternate; **medicina alternativa** alternative medicine

alter'nato *adj* alternating

alterna'tore *nm* Electr alternator

al'terno *adj* alternate; **a giorni alterni** every other day

al'tero *adj* haughty

⚬ᶠ **al'tezza** *nf* height; (profondità) depth; (suono) pitch; (di tessuto) width; (titolo) Highness; **essere all'~ di** be on a level with; fig be up to ∎ **altezza libera di passaggio** headroom

altezzosa'mente *adv* haughtily

altezzosità *nf* haughtiness

altez'zoso *adj* haughty

al'ticcio *adj* tipsy, merry

al'timetro *nm* altimeter

altipi'ano *nm* plateau

altiso'nante *adj* high-sounding

alti'tudine *nf* altitude

⚬ᶠ **'alto** ① *adj* high; (di statura) tall; (profondo) deep; ‹*suono*› high-pitched; ‹*tessuto*› wide; Geog northern; **a notte alta** in the middle of the night; **avere degli alti e bassi** have some ups and downs; **di ~ bordo** high-class; **di ~ rango** high-ranking; **ad alta definizione** high-definition; **ad alta fedeltà** high-fidelity; **ad ~ livello** high-level; **a voce alta, ad alta voce** in a loud voice; ‹*leggere*› aloud; **essere in ~ mare** be on the high seas; fig be all at sea ∎ **alta borghesia** *nf* gentry; **alta finanza** *nf* high finance; **alta frequenza** *nf* high frequency; **alta moda** *nf* high fashion; **alta pressione** *nf* (meteorologica) high pressure; **alta società** *nf* high society; **alta tensione** *nf* high voltage; **alto commissariato** *nm* High Commission; **alto medioevo** *nm* Dark Ages; **alto tradimento** *nm* high treason
② *adv* high; **in ~** ‹*essere*› at the top; ‹*guardare*› up; **mani in ~!** hands up!; **dall'~** from above; **guardare qualcuno dall'~ in basso** look down on somebody

altoate'sino *adj* South Tyrolean

alto'forno *nm* blast furnace

altolà *int* halt there!

altolo'cato *adj* highly placed

altopar'lante *nm* loudspeaker

altopi'ano *nm* plateau

⚬ᶠ **altret'tanto** ① *adj & pron* as much; (*pl*) as many
② *adv* likewise; **buona fortuna! - grazie, ~** good luck! - thank you, the same to you

⚬ᶠ **altri'menti** *adv* otherwise

⚬ᶠ **'altro** ① *adj* other; **un ~, un'altra** another; **l'altr'anno** last year; **l'~ ieri** the day before yesterday; **doman l'~** the day after tomorrow; **l'ho visto l'~ giorno** I saw him the other day
② *pron* other [one]; **un ~, un'altra** another [one]; **ne vuoi dell'~?** would you like some more?; **l'un l'~** one another; **nessun ~** nobody else; **gli altri** (la gente) other people
③ *nm* something else; **non fa ~ che lavorare** he does nothing but work; **desidera ~?** (in negozio) anything else?; **più che ~,** sono stanco I'm tired more than anything; **se non ~** at least; **senz'~** certainly; **tra l'~** what's more; **~ che!** absolutely!

⚬ᶠ **altroché** *adv* absolutely!

altroi'eri *nm* **l'~** the day before yesterday

al'tronde: **d'~** *adv* on the other hand

⚬ᶠ **al'trove** *adv* elsewhere

al'trui ① *adj* other people's
② *nm* other people's belongings *pl*

altru'ismo *nm* altruism

altruista *nmf* altruist

al'tura *nf* high ground; Naut deep sea

a'lunno, -a *nmf* pupil

alve'are *nm* hive

'alveo *nm* bed

alzaband'iera *nm* inv flag-raising

alzacri'stallo *nm* Auto window winder

⚬ᶠ **al'zare** *vt* lift, raise; (costruire) build; Naut hoist; **~ le spalle** shrug one's shoulders; **~ i tacchi** fig take to one's heels; **~ la voce** raise one's voice; **~ il volume** turn up the volume

al'zarsi *vr* (in piedi) stand up; (da letto) get up; ‹*vento, temperatura*› rise

al'zata *nf* lifting; (aumento) rise; (da letto) getting up; Archit elevation ∎ **alzata di spalle** shrug of the shoulders

alza'taccia *nf* fam **fare un'~** get up at the crack of dawn

al'zato *adj* up

A.M. *abbr* (**aeronautica militare**) Air Force

a'mabile *adj* lovable; ‹*vino*› sweet

amabilità *nf* kindness

amabil'mente *adv* kindly

a'maca *nf* hammock

a'malgama *nm* amalgam

amalga'mare *vt* amalgamate

amalga'marsi vr amalgamate

ama'nita nf Bot amanita

✓ **a'mante** ☐1 adj ~ **di** fond of
☐2 nmf fig lover
■ **amante degli animali** animal lover; **amante della lettura** book lover
☐3 nm lover
☐4 nf mistress

amara'mente adv bitterly

ama'ranto ☐1 nm Bot amarant[h]us; (colore) rich purple
☐2 adj rich purple

✓ **a'mare** vt love; be fond of ‹musica, sport ecc›

amareggia'mento nm bitterness

amareggi'are vt embitter

amareggi'arsi vr become embittered

amareggi'ato adj embittered

ama'rena nf sour black cherry

ama'retto nm macaroon

ama'rezza nf bitterness; (dolore) sorrow

a'maro ☐1 adj bitter
☐2 nm bitterness; (liquore) bitters pl

ama'rognolo adj rather bitter

a'mato, -a ☐1 adj loved
☐2 nmf beloved

ama|'tore, -trice nmf lover

a'mazzone nf (in mitologia) Amazon; **all'~** side saddle

Amaz'zonia nf Amazonia

amaz'zonico adj Amazonian

ambasce'ria nf diplomatic mission

ambasci'ata nf embassy; (messaggio) message

ambascia|'tore, -trice ☐1 nm ambassador
☐2 nf ambassadress

ambe'due adj & pron both

ambi'destro adj ambidextrous

ambien'tale adj environmental

ambienta'lismo nm environmentalism

ambienta'lista adj & nmf environmentalist

ambienta'mento nm acclimatization

ambien'tare vt acclimatize; set ‹storia, film ecc›

ambien'tarsi vr get acclimatized

✓ **ambi'ente** nm environment; (stanza) room

ambiguità nf inv ambiguity; (di persona) shadiness

am'biguo adj ambiguous; ‹persona› shady

am'bire vi ~ **a** aspire to

am'bito¹ adj ‹lavoro, incarico› much sought-after

'ambito² nm sphere

ambiva'lente adj ambivalent

ambiva'lenza nf ambivalence

ambizi'one nf ambition

✓ indicates a very frequent word

---

ambizi'oso adj ambitious

amblio'pia nf lazy eye

'ambo ☐1 adj inv both
☐2 nm (in tombola, lotto) double

'ambra nf amber

am'brato adj amber

ambu'lante adj wandering; **venditore ambulante** hawker

ambu'lanza nf ambulance

ambulatori'ale adj **essere trattato con intervento ~** have day surgery

ambula'torio nm (di medico) surgery; (di ospedale) out-patients' [department]
■ **ambulatorio dentistico** dental clinic

Am'burgo nf Hamburg

a'meba nf amoeba

a'mebico adj amoebic

'amen int amen; **e allora ~!** well, so be it!

amenità nf inv (facezia) pleasantry

a'meno adj pleasant

amenor'rea nf Med amenorrhoea

A'merica nf America
■ **America centrale** Central America; **America Latina** Latin America; **America del Nord/Sud** North/South America

america'nata nf pej (film) American rubbish

america'nismo nm Americanism; (patriottismo) flag-waving

americaniz'zarsi vr become Americanized

✓ **ameri'cano, -a** adj & nmf American

ame'rindio adj Native American

ame'tista nf amethyst

ami'anto nm asbestos

ami'chevole adj friendly

✓ **ami'cizia** nf friendship; **fare ~ con qualcuno** make friends with somebody; **amicizie** pl (amici) friends

✓ **a'mico, -a** ☐1 adj ‹parola, persona› friendly
☐2 nmf friend
■ **amico del cuore** bosom friend; **amico d'infanzia** childhood friend; **amico intimo** close friend; **amico di penna** penfriend, penpal

'amido nm starch

ammac'care vt dent ‹metallo›; bruise ‹frutto›

ammac'carsi vr ‹metallo› get dented; ‹frutto› bruise

ammac'cato adj ‹metallo› dented; ‹frutto› bruised

ammacca'tura nf dent; (livido) bruise

ammaestra'mento nm training

ammae'strare vt (istruire) teach; train ‹animale›

ammae'strato adj trained

ammaestra|'tore, -trice nmf trainer

ammainabandi'era nm inv flag-lowering

ammai'nare vt lower ‹bandiera›; furl ‹vele›

🔑 **amma'larsi** vr fall ill

amma'lato, -a ① adj ill
② nmf sick person; (paziente) patient

ammali'are vt bewitch

ammali'ato adj bewitched

ammalia|'tore, -trice ① adj bewitching
② nm enchanter
③ nf enchantress

am'manco nm deficit

ammanet'tare vt handcuff

ammani'carsi vr fig acquire connections

ammani'cato adj essere ∼ have connections

ammanigli'arsi vr fig = AMMANICARSI

ammanigli'ato adj fig = AMMANICATO

amman'sire vt tame, domesticate ‹animali›; fig pacify, placate

amman'sirsi vr ‹animali› become tame; fig calm down

amman'tarsi vr ‹persona› wrap oneself up in a cloak; ∼ **di** fig feign ‹virtù›

amma'raggio nm splashdown

amma'rare vi put down on the sea; ‹navicella spaziale› splash down

ammassa'mento nm Mil build-up

ammas'sare vt amass

ammas'sarsi vr crowd together

am'masso nm mass; (mucchio) pile

ammat'tire vi go mad

ammazzacaffè nm inv liqueur

ammazza'fame nm inv stodge

🔑 **ammaz'zare** vt kill

ammaz'zarsi vr fig (suicidarsi) kill oneself; (rimanere ucciso) be killed

am'menda nf amends pl; (multa) fine; **fare** ∼ **di qualcosa** make amends for something

am'messo ① pp di AMMETTERE
② conj ∼ **che** supposing that

🔑 **am'mettere** vt admit; (riconoscere) acknowledge; (supporre) suppose; **ammettiamo che … let's suppose [that]…**

ammez'zato nm (piano ammezzato) mezzanine

ammic'care vi wink

ammini'strare vt administer; (gestire) run

ammini'strarsi vr fig manage one's finances

amministra'tivo adj administrative

amministra|'tore, -trice nmf administrator; (di azienda) manager; (di società) director
■ **amministratore aggiunto** associate director; **amministratore del condominio** property manager; **amministratore delegato** managing

director; **amministratore unico** sole director

🔑 **amministrazi'one** nf administration; **fatti di ordinaria** ∼ fig routine matters
■ **amministrazione aziendale** (studi) business studies; **amministrazione comunale** local council; **amministrazione controllata** receivership; **amministrazione pubblica** civil service; **amministrazione regionale** regional council

ammino'acido nm amino acid

ammi'rabile adj admirable

ammi'raglia nf flag-ship

ammiragli'ato nm admiralty

ammi'raglio nm admiral

ammi'rare vt admire

ammi'rato adj restare/essere ∼ be full of admiration

ammira|'tore, -trice nmf admirer

ammirazi'one nf admiration

ammis'sibile adj admissible

ammissibilità nf acceptability

ammissi'one nf admission; (approvazione) acknowledgement

ammobili'are vt furnish

ammobili'ato adj furnished; **stanza ammobiliata** furnished room

ammoderna'mento nm modernization

ammoder'nare vt modernize

ammoder'narsi vr move with the times

am'modo ① adj proper
② adv properly

ammogli'are vt marry off

ammogli'arsi vr get married

ammogli'ato ① adj married
② nm married man

am'mollo nm in ∼ soaking; **mettere in** ∼ pre-soak

ammo'niaca nf ammonia

ammoni'mento nm warning; (di rimprovero) admonishment

ammo'nire vt warn; (rimproverare) admonish

ammoni'tore adj admonishing

ammonizi'one nf Sport warning; (rimprovero) admonishment

ammon'tare ① vi ∼ **a** amount to
② nm amount

ammonticchi'are vt heap up, pile up

ammonticchi'arsi vr pile up

ammor'bare vt (con odore) pollute; (con malattie) infect

ammorbi'dente nm (per panni) softener

ammorbi'dire vt soften

ammorbi'dirsi vr soften

ammorta'mento nm Comm amortization

ammor'tare vt pay off ‹spesa›; Comm amortize ‹debito›

ammortiz'zare vt ① Comm = AMMORTARE
② Mech damp

a

ammortizza'tore nm shock-absorber
ammosci'are vt make flabby
ammosci'arsi vi get flabby
ammucchi'are vt pile up
ammucchi'arsi vr pile up
ammucchi'ata nf sl (orgia) orgy; **un'~ di** fam (ammasso) loads of
ammuf'fire vi go mouldy
ammuf'firsi vr go mouldy
ammuf'fito adj mouldy; fig stuffy
ammutina'mento nm mutiny
ammuti'narsi vr mutiny
ammuti'nato ⨯1⨯ adj mutinous
    ⨯2⨯ nm mutineer
ammuto'lire vi be struck dumb
ammuto'lirsi vr fall silent
amne'sia nf amnesia
amni'stia nf amnesty
amnisti'are vt amnesty
'amo nm hook; fig bait
amo'rale adj amoral
amoralità nf amorality
⚥ **a'more** nm love; **d'~** ‹canzone, film› love; **fare l'~** make love; **per l'amor di Dio/del cielo!** for heaven's sake!; **andare d'~ e d'accordo** get on like a house on fire; **amor proprio** self-respect; **amor cortese** courtly love; **è un ~** ‹persona› he's/she's a darling; **per ~ di** for the sake of; **amori** pl love affairs
amoreggi'are vi flirt
amo'revole adj loving
amorevol'mente adv lovingly
a'morfo adj shapeless; ‹persona› colourless, grey
amo'rino nm cherub
amorosa'mente adv lovingly
amo'roso adj loving; ‹sguardo ecc› amorous; ‹lettera, relazione› love attrib
am'pere nm inv ampere; **da 15 ~** 15-amp
ampe'rometro nm ammeter
ampia'mente adv widely
ampi'ezza nf (di esperienza) breadth; (di stanza) spaciousness; (di gonna) fullness; (importanza) scale
■ **ampiezza di vedute** broadmindedness
⚥ **'ampio** adj ample; ‹esperienza› wide; ‹stanza› spacious; ‹vestito› loose; ‹gonna, descrizione› full; ‹pantaloni› baggy; **di ampie vedute** broadminded
am'plesso nm embrace
amplia'mento nm (di cosa, porto) enlargement; (di strada, conoscenze) broadening
ampli'are vt broaden, widen ‹strada, conoscenze›; enlarge ‹casa›
ampli'arsi vr broaden, grow wider
amplifi'care vt amplify; fig magnify

⚥ indicates a very frequent word

amplifica'tore nm amplifier
amplificazi'one nf amplification
am'polla nf cruet
ampol'loso adj pompous
ampu'tare vt amputate
amputazi'one nf amputation
amu'leto nm amulet
A.N. abbr Pol (**Alleanza Nazionale**) National Alliance (right-wing party)
anabbagli'ante ⨯1⨯ adj Auto dipped
    ⨯2⨯ nm **anabbaglianti** pl dipped headlights
anaboliz'zante nm anabolic steroid
ana'cardi nmpl cashew nuts
ana'cardio nm cashew
ana'conda nf Zool anaconda
anacro'nismo nm anachronism
anacro'nistico adj anachronistic; **essere ~** be an anachronism
anae'robico adj anaerobic
anafi'lassi nf anaphylaxis
anafi'lattico adj shock **~** Med anaphylactic shock
a'nagrafe nf (ufficio) registry office; (registro) register of births, marriages and deaths
ana'grafico adj dati pl anagrafici personal data
ana'gramma nm anagram
anal'colico ⨯1⨯ adj non-alcoholic
    ⨯2⨯ nm soft drink, non-alcoholic drink
a'nale adj anal
analfa'beta adj & nmf illiterate
analfabe'tismo nm illiteracy
anal'gesico nm painkiller
a'nalisi nf inv analysis; Med test; **in ultima ~** in the final analysis
■ **analisi grammaticale/del periodo/logica** parsing; **analisi di mercato** market research; **analisi del percorso critico** critical path analysis; **analisi del sangue** blood test
ana'lista nmf analyst
■ **analista economico** economic analyst; **analista finanziario** business analyst
ana'litico adj analytical
analiz'zabile adj analysable
analiz'zare vt analyse; Med test, analyse
anal'lergico adj hypoallergenic
analoga'mente adv analogously
analo'gia nf analogy
ana'logico adj analogue
analo'gismo nm reasoning by analogy
a'nalogo adj analogous
anam'nesi nf inv medical history
'ananas nm inv pineapple
anar'chia nf anarchy
a'narchico, -a ⨯1⨯ adj anarchic
    ⨯2⨯ nmf anarchist
anar'chismo nm anarchism

A.N.A.S. *nf abbr* (**Azienda Nazionale Autonoma delle Strade**) *national road maintenance authority*

ana'tema *nm* anathema

anato'mia *nf* anatomy

ana'tomico *adj* anatomical; ‹sedia› contoured, ergonomic

'anatra *nf* duck

■ anatra selvatica mallard

ana'troccolo *nm* duckling

'anca *nf* hip; (di animale) flank

ance'strale *adj* ancestral

⚹ **'anche** *conj* also, too, as well; (persino) even; parla ∼ francese he also speaks French, he speaks French too, he speaks French as well; ∼ se even if

ancheggi'are *vi* wiggle one's hips

anchilo'sarsi *vr* fig stiffen up

anchilo'sato *adj* fig stiff

⚹ **an'cora**[1] *adv* still; (con negazione) yet; (di nuovo) again; (di più) some more; ∼ una volta once more; non ∼ not yet; ∼ esistente extant; ∼ più bello even more beautiful; ∼ una birra another beer, one more beer

'ancora[2] *nf* anchor; gettare l'∼ drop anchor

■ ancora di salvezza fig last hope

anco'raggio *nm* anchorage

anco'rare *vt* anchor

anco'rarsi *vr* anchor; drop anchor; ∼ a fig cling to

Andalu'sia *nf* Andalusia

anda'luso, -a *adj & nmf* Andalusian

anda'mento *nm* (del mercato, degli affari) trend

an'dante [1] *adj* (corrente) current; (di poco valore) cheap
[2] *nm* Mus andante

⚹ **an'dare** [1] *vi* go; (funzionare) work; (essere di moda) be in; ∼ via (partire) leave; ‹macchia› come out; ∼ a piedi walk; ∼ a sciare go skiing; ∼ [bene] (confarsi) suit; ‹taglia› fit; ti va bene alle tre? does three o'clock suit you?; non mi va di mangiare I don't feel like eating; ∼ di fretta be in a hurry; ∼ fiero di be proud of; ∼ di moda be in fashion; va per i 40 anni he's nearly 40; ma va' [là]! come on!; come va? how are things?; ∼ a male go off; ∼ a fuoco go up in flames; ∼ perduto be lost; va spedito [entro] stamattina it must be sent this morning; ne va del mio lavoro my job is at stake; come è andata a finire? how did it turn out?; cosa vai dicendo? what are you talking about?; andarsene go away; (morire) pass away
[2] *nm* going; ∼ e venire (andirivieni) comings and goings *pl*; a lungo ∼ eventually; a tutto ∼ at full speed; con l'∼ del tempo with the passing of time

an'data *nf* going; (viaggio) outward journey; biglietto di sola andata/di andata e ritorno single/return [ticket]

anda'tura *nf* walk; (portamento) bearing; Naut tack; Sport pace

an'dazzo *nm* fam turn of events; prendere un brutto ∼ turn nasty

'Ande *nfpl* le ∼ the Andes

an'dino *adj* Andean

andirivi'eni *nm inv* comings and goings *pl*

'andito *nm* passage

An'dorra *nf* Andorra

an'drone *nm* entrance

andro'pausa *nf* male menopause

a'neddoto *nm* anecdote

ane'lare *vt* ∼ a long for

a'nelito *nm* longing

⚹ **a'nello** *nm* ring; (di catena) link

■ anello di fidanzamento engagement ring; anello d'oro gold ring

ane'mia *nf* anaemia

a'nemico *adj* anaemic

a'nemone *nm* anemone

aneste'sia *nf* anaesthesia; (sostanza) anaesthetic

■ anestesia peridurale epidural

aneste'sista *nmf* anaesthetist

ane'stetico *adj & nm* anaesthetic

anestetiz'zare *vt* anaesthetize

a'neto *nm* dill

anfeta'mina *nf* amphetamine

an'fibi *nmpl* (scarponi) army boots

an'fibio [1] *nm* amphibian
[2] *adj* amphibious

anfite'atro *nm* amphitheatre

'anfora *nf* amphora

an'fratto *nm* ravine

an'gelico *adj* angelic

⚹ **'angelo** *nm* angel

■ angelo custode guardian angel

anghe'ria *nf* harassment

an'gina *nf inv*

■ angina [pectoris] angina [pectoris]

angi'ologo, -a *nmf* Med angiologist

anglica'nesimo *nm* Relig Anglicanism

angli'cano, -a *adj & nmf* Relig Anglican

angli'cismo *nm* Anglicism

angliciz'zare *vt* anglicize

anglo+ *pref* Anglo+

angloameri'cano, -a *nmf* Anglo-American

an'glofilo, -a *adj & nmf* Anglophile

an'glofono, -a *nmf* English-speaker

anglofran'cese *adj* Anglo-French

anglo'sassone *adj & nmf* Anglo-Saxon

An'gola *nf* Angola

ango'lano, -a *adj & nmf* Angolan

ango'lare *adj* angular

angolazi'one *nf* angle shot; fig point of view

angoli'era *nf* (mobile) corner cupboard

◆ **'angolo** *nm* corner; Math angle; **dietro l'**∼ round the corner; **fare** ∼ **con** ‹*negozio, casa*› be on the corner of

■ **angolo acuto** acute angle; **angolo [di] cottura** kitchenette; **angolo retto** right angle

ango'loso *adj* angular; ‹*carattere*› difficult to get on with

'angora *nf*

■ **[lana d']angora** angora

an'goscia *nf* anguish

angosci'are *vt* torment

angosci'arsi *vr* (preoccuparsi) worry oneself sick, torment oneself

angosci'ato *adj* agonized

angosci'oso *adj* (disperato) anguished; (che dà angoscia) distressing

angu'illa *nf* eel

an'guria *nf* water-melon

an'gustia *nf* (ansia) anxiety; (penuria) poverty

angusti'are *vt* distress

angusti'arsi *vr* be distressed (**per** about)

angusti'ato *adj* distressed

an'gusto *adj* narrow

'anice *nm* anise; Culin aniseed; (liquore) anisette

ani'cino *nm* (biscotto) aniseed biscuit

ani'dride *nf*

■ **anidride carbonica** carbon dioxide; **anidride solforosa** sulphur dioxide

◆ **'anima** *nf* soul; **non c'era** ∼ **viva** there was not a soul about; **all'**∼ **!** good grief!; **mi fa dannare l'**∼ **!** he'll be the death of me!; **l'** ∼ **della festa** the life and soul of the party; **un'**∼ **in pena** a soul in torment; **volere un bene all'**∼ **a qualcuno** love somebody to death; **la buon'**∼ **della zia** my late aunt, God rest her soul

■ **anima gemella** soul mate

◆ **ani'male** *adj* & *nm* animal

■ **animali** *pl* **domestici** pets; **animali** *pl* **selvatici** wild animals

anima'lesco *adj* animal

anima'lista *nmf* animal rights activist

ani'mare *vt* give life to; (ravvivare) enliven; (incoraggiare) encourage

ani'marsi *vr* come to life; (accalorarsi) become animated

ani'mato *adj* animate; ‹*discussione*› animated; ‹*strada, paese*› lively

anima|'tore, -trice *nmf* leading spirit; Cinema animator

animazi'one *nf* animation; **con** ∼ animatedly

■ **animazione elettronica** animatronics *sg*

ani'melle *nfpl* (di agnello, vitello) sweet-bread

◆ **'animo** *nm* (mente) mind; (indole) disposition; (cuore) heart; **perdersi d'**∼ lose heart; **farsi** ∼ take heart

animosa'mente *adv* with animosity

animosità *nf* animosity

ani'moso *adj* brave; (ostile) hostile

ani'setta *nf* anisette

'anitra *nf* duck

annacqua'mento *nm* fig watering down, dilution

annac'quare *vt* anche fig water down

annac'quato *adj* watered down; ‹*colore, resoconto*› insipid

annaffi'are *vt* water

annaffia'toio *nm* watering-can

an'nali *nmpl* annals; **restare negli** ∼ go down in history

anna'spare *vi* flounder

an'nata *nf* year; (importo annuale) annual amount; ‹*di vino*› vintage

■ **vino d'annata** vintage wine

annebbia'mento *nm* fog build-up; fig clouding

annebbi'are *vt* cloud ‹*vista, mente*›

annebbi'arsi *vr* get misty; (in città, su autostrada) get foggy; ‹*vista, mente*› grow dim

annega'mento *nm* drowning

anne'gare *vt/i* drown

anne'rire *vt/i* blacken

anne'rirsi *vr* become black

an'nessi *nmpl* (costruzioni) outbuildings; **tutti gli** ∼ **e i connessi** all the appurtenances

annessi'one *nf* (di nazione) annexation

an'nesso [1] pp di ANNETTERE
[2] *adj* attached; ‹*stato*› annexed

an'nettere *vt* add; (accludere) enclose; annex ‹*stato*›

annichi'lire *vt* annihilate

anni'darsi *vr* nest

annienta'mento *nm* annihilation

annien'tare *vt* annihilate

annien'tarsi *vr* abase oneself

anniver'sario *adj* & *nm* anniversary

■ **anniversario di matrimonio** *o* **di nozze** wedding anniversary

◆ **'anno** *nm* year; **Buon Anno!** Happy New Year!; **quanti anni ha?** how old are you?; **Tommaso ha dieci anni** Thomas is ten [years old]; **gli anni '30** the '30s

■ **anno accademico** academic year; **anno bisestile** leap year; **anno civile** calendar year; **anno giudiziario** law year; **anno luce** light year; **anno nuovo** New Year; **anno sabbatico** Univ sabbatical; **anni verdi** *pl* salad days

anno'dare *vt* knot; do up ‹*cintura*›; fig form

anno'darsi *vr* become knotted

◆ **annoi'are** *vt* bore; (recare fastidio) annoy

annoi'arsi *vr* get bored; (condizione) be bored

◆ indicates a very frequent word

annoi'ato *adj* bored
an'noso *adj* ‹questione› age-old
anno'tare *vt* note down; annotate ‹testo›
annotazi'one *nf* note
annove'rare *vt* number
annu'ale *adj* annual, yearly
annual'mente *adv* annually
annu'ario *nm* year-book
annu'ire *vi* nod; (acconsentire) agree
annulla'mento *nm* annulment; (di appuntamento) cancellation
annul'lare *vt* annul; cancel ‹appuntamento›; (togliere efficacia a) undo; disallow ‹gol›; (distruggere) destroy
annul'larsi *vr* cancel each other out
an'nullo *nm* (timbro) franking
✇ **annunci'are** *vt* announce; (preannunciare) foretell
annuncia|'tore, -trice *nmf* announcer
annunciazi'one *nf* Annunciation
an'nuncio *nm* announcement; (pubblicitario) advertisement, ad; (notizia) news
■ **annunci** *pl* **economici** classified advertisements; **annunci** *pl* **mortuari** obituaries, death notices; **annuncio personale** personal ad; **annuncio pubblicitario** advertisement
'annuo *adj* annual, yearly
annu'sare *vt* sniff
annu'sata *nf* **dare un'∼ a** have a sniff at
annuvola'mento *nm* clouding over
annuvo'lare *vt* cloud
annuvo'larsi *vr* cloud over
'ano *nm* anus
a'nodino *adj* anodyne
'anodo *nm* anode
anoma'lia *nf* anomaly
a'nomalo *adj* anomalous
a'nonima *nf*
■ **Anonima Alcolisti** Alcoholics Anonymous; **anonima sequestri** *Italian criminal organization specializing in kidnapping*
anoni'mato *nm* **mantenere l'∼** remain anonymous
anonimità *nf* anonymity
a'nonimo, -a [1] *adj* anonymous
[2] *nmf* unknown person; (pittore, scrittore) anonymous painter/writer
anores'sia *nf* Med anorexia
ano'ressico, -a *nmf* anorexic
anor'male [1] *adj* abnormal
[2] *nmf* deviant, abnormal person
anormalità *nf inv* abnormality
'ansa *nf* handle; (di fiume) bend
ANSA *nf abbr* (**Agenzia Nazionale Stampa Associata**) *Italian press agency*
an'sante *adj* panting
an'sare *vi* pant
✇ **'ansia, ansietà** *nf* anxiety; **stare/essere in ∼ per** be anxious about

ansi'mante *adj* breathless
ansi'mare *vi* gasp for breath
ansio'litico *nm* tranquillizer
ansi'oso *adj* anxious
'anta *nf* (di finestra) shutter; (di armadio) door
antago'nismo *nm* antagonism
antago'nista *nmf* antagonist
antago'nistico *adj* antagonistic
an'tartico *adj & nm* Antarctic
An'tartide *nf* Antarctica
ante'bellico *adj* pre-war
antece'dente [1] *adj* preceding
[2] *nm* precedent
ante'fatto *nm* prior event
ante'guerra [1] *adj* pre-war
[2] *nm* pre-war period
ante'nato, -a *nmf* ancestor
an'tenna *nf* Radio, TV aerial; (di animale) antenna; Naut yard; **rizzare le antenne** fig prick up one's ears
■ **antenna parabolica** satellite dish; **antenna radar** radar scanner
ante'porre *vt* put before
ante'prima *nf* preview; **vedere qualcosa in ∼** have a sneak preview of something
■ **anteprima di stampa** Comput print preview
anteri'ore *adj* front *attrib*; (nel tempo) previous
anterior'mente *adv* (nel tempo) previously; (nello spazio) in front
antesi'gnano, -a *nmf* fig forerunner
anti+ *pref* anti+
antiabor'tista [1] *nmf* antiabortionist
[2] *adj* antiabortion *attrib*
anti'acido *nm* antacid
antiade'rente *adj* ‹padella› nonstick
antia'ereo *adj* anti-aircraft *attrib*
antial'lergico *adj* hypoallergenic
antia'partheid *adj inv* antiapartheid
antia'tomico *adj* anti-nuclear; **rifugio antiatomico** fallout shelter
antibat'terico *adj* antibacterial
antibi'otico *adj & nm* antibiotic
antibloc'caggio *adj inv* antilock *attrib*
anti'caglia *nf* (oggetto) piece of old junk
antical'care *nm* softener
antica'mente *adv* in ancient times, long ago
anti'camera *nf* ante-room; **fare ∼** be kept waiting
antichità *nf inv* antiquity; (oggetto) antique
antici'clone *nm* anticyclone
antici'clonico *adj* ‹area› anti-cyclonic
antici'pare [1] *vt* advance; Comm pay in advance; (prevedere) anticipate; (prevenire) forestall
[2] *vi* be early
anticipata'mente *adv* in advance

a

antici'pato *adj* upfront; **pagamento anticipato** advance payment

anticipazi'one *nf* anticipation; (notizia) advance news

an'ticipo *nm* advance; (caparra) deposit; **in ~** early; (nel lavoro) ahead of schedule; **giocare d'~** Sport fig anticipate the next move

⚘ **an'tico** ① *adj* ancient; ‹mobile ecc› antique; (vecchio) old; **all'antica** old-fashioned ② *nm* **gli antichi** the ancients

anticomu'nista *adj & nmf* anti-communist

anticoncezio'nale *adj & nm* contraceptive

anticonfor'mismo *nm* unconventionality

anticonfor'mista *nmf* nonconformist

anticonfor'mistico *adj* unconventional, nonconformist

anticonge'lante *adj & nm* anti-freeze

anticonsu'mismo *nm* anti-consumerism

anti'corpo *nm* antibody

anticostituzio'nale *adj* unconstitutional

anti'crimine *adj inv* ‹squadra› crime *attrib*

antidemo'cratico *adj* undemocratic

antidepres'sivo *nm* antidepressant

antidiluvi'ano *adj* fig antediluvian

antidolo'rifico *nm* painkiller

anti'doping *nm inv* Sport dope test

an'tidoto *nm* antidote

anti'droga *adj inv* ‹compagna› anti-drugs; ‹squadra› drug *attrib*

antie'stetico *adj* ugly

antie'tà *adj inv* anti-ageing

antifa'scismo *nm* anti-fascism

antifa'scista *adj & nmf* anti-fascist

an'tifona *nf* fig dull and repetitive speech; **capire l'~** take the hint; **sempre la stessa ~** always the same old story

anti'forfora *adj inv* dandruff *attrib*

anti'fumo *adj inv* anti-smoking

anti'furto ① *nm* anti-theft device; (allarme) alarm
  ■ **antifurto della macchina** car alarm
  ② *adj inv* ‹sistema› anti-theft

anti'gelo ① *adj inv* anti-freeze ② *nm* antifreeze; (parabrezza) defroster

anti'gene *nm* antigen

antigi'enico *adj* unhygienic

anti'graffio *adj* scratch-resistant

anti-inflazi'one *adj inv* anti-inflation

An'tille *nfpl* **le ~** the West Indies

an'tilope *nf* antelope

⚘ indicates a very frequent word

anti'mafia *adj inv* anti-Mafia

antimilita'rista ① *adj inv* anti-militaristic, anti-war ② *nmf* anti-militarist

antin'cendio *adj inv* **allarme ~** fire alarm; **porta ~** fire door

anti'nebbia *adj inv* [faro] ~ Auto foglamp, foglight

antine'vralgico ① *adj* pain-killing ② *nm* pain-killer

antinfiamma'torio *adj & nm* anti-inflammatory

antinflazio'nistico *adj* anti-inflationary

antinquina'mento *adj inv* anti-pollution

antinucle'are *adj* anti-nuclear

antio'rario *adj* anti-clockwise, counter-clockwise Am

antiparassi'tario *nm* insecticide

antiparlamen'tare *adj* unparliamentary

antipasti'era *nf* hors d'oeuvre dish

anti'pasto *nm* hors d'oeuvre, starter
  ■ **antipasti** *pl* **caldi** hot starters; **antipasti** *pl* **freddi** cold starters; **antipasti** *pl* **misti** variety of starters

antipa'tia *nf* antipathy

anti'patico *adj* unpleasant

an'tipodi *nmpl* Antipodes; **essere agli ~** fig be poles apart

anti'polio ① *nf inv* (vaccino) polio vaccine; **fare l'~** have a polio injection ② *adj* ‹siero, vaccino› polio *attrib*

antipopo'lare *adj* anti-working-class

antiprobizio'nismo *nm* anti-prohibitionism

antiproibizio'nista *adj & nmf* anti-prohibitionist

antiproi'ettile *adj inv* bullet-proof

antiquari'ato *nm* antique trade; **pezzo d'antiquariato** antique

anti'quario, -a *nmf* antique dealer

anti'quato *adj* antiquated

antiraz'zismo *nm* antiracism

antiraz'zista *adj* anti-racist

antiretrovi'rale *adj* antiretroviral

antireu'matico *adj & nm* anti-rheumatic

antiri'flesso *adj inv* antiglare

anti'ruggine ① *nm inv* rust-inhibitor ② *adj* anti-rust

anti'rughe *adj inv* anti-wrinkle *attrib*

anti'scasso *adj inv* ‹porta› burglar-proof

antisci'opero *adj inv* anti-strike

anti'scippo *adj inv* theft-proof

anti'scivolo *adj inv* nonskid

antise'mita *adj* anti-Semitic

antisemi'tismo *nm* anti-Semitism

anti'settico *adj & nm* antiseptic

antisinda'cale *adj* ‹comportamento› anti-trade-union

anti'sismico *adj* earthquake-proof

antisoci'ale *adj* anti-social

antiso'lare *adj & nm* suntan

antisommer'gibile 1 *adj inv* anti-submarine

2 *nm* submarine hunter

antista'minico *nm* antihistamine

anti'stante *prep* ~ **a** in front of

anti'tarlo *nm inv* woodworm treatment

anti'tarmico *adj* mothproof

antiterro'rismo *nm* counter-terrorism

antiterro'rista *adj* antiterrorist

antiterro'ristico *adj* antiterrorist

an'titesi *nf inv* antithesis

antite'tanica *nf* tetanus injection

antite'tanico *adj* tetanus *attrib*

anti'tetico *adj* antithetical

anti'trust *adj* antitrust

antitumo'rale *adj* which stops the growth of tumours

anti'urto *adj* shockproof

antivaio'losa *nf* smallpox injection

anti'vipera *adj* siero ~ snakebite antidote

antivi'rale *adj* anti-viral

anti'virus *nm inv* Comput antivirus software

antolo'gia *nf* anthology

an'tonimo *nm* antonym

antono'masia per ~ *adj* ‹poeta› quintessential

antra'cite *nf* anthracite; (colore) charcoal [grey]

'antro *nm* cavern

antro'pofago *adj* man-eating, cannibalistic

antropolo'gia *nf* anthropology

antropo'logico *adj* anthropological

antro'pologo, -a *nmf* anthropologist

anu'lare *nm* ring-finger

An'versa *nf* Antwerp

✧ **'anzi** *conj* in fact; (o meglio) or better still; (al contrario) on the contrary

anzianità *nf* old age; (di servizio) seniority

anzi'ano, -a 1 *adj* old, elderly; (di grado ecc) senior

2 *nmf* elderly person

anziché *conj* rather than

anzi'tempo *adv* prematurely

anzi'tutto *adv* first of all

a'orta *nf* aorta

A'pache *mf inv* Apache

apar'theid *nf* apartheid

apar'titico *adj* unaligned

apa'tia *nf* apathy

a'patico *adj* apathetic

'ape *nf* bee

■ **ape regina** queen bee

aperi'tivo *nm* aperitif

aperta'mente *adv* openly

✧ **a'perto** *adj* open; **all'aria aperta** in the open air; **all'~** ‹teatro› open-air; ‹piscina› outdoor; ~ **a tutti** open to all comers; **rimanere a bocca aperta** be dumbfounded

aper'tura *nf* opening; (inizio) beginning; (ampiezza) spread; (di arco) span; Pol overtures *pl*; Phot aperture

■ **apertura alare** wing span; **apertura di credito** loan agreement; **apertura di credito presso un negozio** charge account; **apertura domenicale [dei negozi]** Sunday trading; **apertura mentale** openness

api'ario *nm* apiary

'apice *nm* apex; **l'~ di** the acme of

apicol|'tore, -trice *nmf* beekeeper

apicol'tura *nf* beekeeping

a'plomb *nm inv* (di un abito) hang; fig aplomb, self-assurance

ap'nea *nf*

■ **immersione in apnea** free diving

Apoca'lisse *nf* **l'~** the Apocalypse

apoca'littico *adj* apocalyptic

a'pocrifo *adj* apocryphal

apo'geo *nm* apogee

a'polide 1 *adj* stateless

2 *nmf* stateless person

apo'litico *adj* apolitical

A'pollo *nm* Apollo

apolo'geta *nmf* apologist (di for)

apolo'gia *nf* apologia; (celebrazione) eulogy

■ **apologia di reato** condoning of a criminal act

apoples'sia *nf* apoplexy

apo'plettico *adj* apoplectic

a'postolo *nm* apostle

apostro'fare *vt* (mettere un apostrofo a) write with an apostrophe; reprimand ‹persona›

a'postrofo *nm* apostrophe

apote'osi *nf* apotheosis

appaga'mento *nm* fulfilment

appa'gare *vt* satisfy

appa'garsi *vr* ~ **di** be satisfied with

appa'gato *adj* sated

appai'are *vt* pair; mate ‹animali›

appallotto'lare *vt* roll into a ball

appallotto'larsi *vr* ‹gatto› curl up in a ball; ‹farina› become lumpy

appal'tare *vt* contract out; ~ **a imprese esterne** outsource

appalta'tore *nm* contractor

ap'palto *nm* contract; **dare in** ~ contract out; **appalto a imprese esterne** outsourcing; **gara di appalto** call for tenders

appan'naggio *nm* (in denaro) annuity; fig prerogative

appan'nare *vt* mist ‹vetro›; dim ‹vista›

appan'narsi *vr* mist over; ‹vista› grow dim

appa'rato *nm* apparatus; (apparecchiamento) array; (pompa) display
■ **apparato digerente** digestive system; **apparato scenico** set

apparecchi'are [1] *vt* prepare [2] *vi* lay the table Br, set the table

apparecchia'tura *nf* (impianti) equipment

✦ **appa'recchio** *nm* apparatus; (congegno) device; (radio, TV ecc) set; (aeroplano) aircraft; (telefono) phone
■ **apparecchio acustico** hearing aid

appa'rente *adj* apparent

apparente'mente *adv* apparently

appa'renza *nf* appearance; **in ~** apparently

✦ **appa'rire** *vi* appear; (sembrare) look

appari'scente *adj* striking; pej gaudy

apparizi'one *nf* apparition

✦ **apparta'mento** *nm* flat, apartment Am
■ **appartamento ammobiliato** furnished flat; **appartamento in multiproprietà** timeshare

appar'tarsi *vr* withdraw

appar'tato *adj* secluded

apparte'nente *adj* **~ a** belonging to

apparte'nenza *nf* membership

✦ **apparte'nere** *vi* belong

appassio'nante *adj* (storia, argomento) exciting

appassio'nare *vt* excite; (commuovere) move

appassio'narsi *vr* **~ a** become excited by

appassio'nato *adj* passionate; **~ di** (entusiastico) fond of

appas'sire *vi* wither

appas'sirsi *vr* fade

appas'sito *adj* faded

appel'larsi *vr* **~ a** appeal to

ap'pello *nm* appeal; (chiamata per nome) rollcall; (esami) exam session; **fare l'~** call the roll

✦ **ap'pena** [1] *adv* just; (a fatica) hardly [2] *conj* [non] **~** as soon as, no sooner ... than; **~ prima di** just before

ap'pendere *vt* hang [up]

appendi'abiti *nm inv* hat-stand, hallstand

appen'dice *nf* appendix; **romanzo d'appendice** novel serialized in a magazine or newspaper

appendi'cite *nf* appendicitis

Appen'nini *nmpl* **gli ~** the Apennines

appen'ninico *adj* Apennine

appesan'tire *vt* weigh down

appesan'tirsi *vr* become heavy

ap'peso [1] pp di APPENDERE

[2] *adj* hanging; (impiccato) hanged

✦ **appe'tito** *nm* appetite; **aver ~** be hungry; **buon ~!** enjoy your meal!

appeti'toso *adj* appetizing; fig tempting

appezza'mento *nm* plot of land

appia'nare *vt* level; fig smooth over

appia'narsi *vr* improve

appiat'tire *vt* flatten

appiat'tirsi *vr* flatten oneself; fig level out

appic'care *vt* **~ il fuoco a** set fire to

appicci'care [1] *vt* stick; **~ a** fig (appioppare) palm off on [2] *vi* be sticky

appicci'carsi *vr* stick; ‹cose› stick together; **~ a qualcuno** fig stick to somebody like glue

appiccica'ticcio *adj* sticky; fig clingy

appicci'cato *adj* **stare ~ a qualcuno** be all over somebody

appicci'coso *adj* sticky; fig clingy

appie'dato *adj* **sono ~** I don't have the car; **sono rimasto ~** I was stranded

appi'eno *adv* fully

appigli'arsi *vr* **~ a** get hold of; fig stick to

ap'piglio *nm* fingerhold; (per piedi) foothold; fig pretext

appiop'pare *vt* **~ a** palm off on; fam (dare) give; **~ un ceffone a qualcuno** slap somebody

appiso'larsi *vr* doze off

applau'dire *vt/i* applaud

ap'plauso *nm* applause

appli'cabile *adj* applicable

✦ **appli'care** *vt* apply; enforce ‹legge ecc›

appli'carsi *vr* apply oneself

appli'cato [1] *nmf* (impiegato) senior clerk [2] *adj* (nel ricamo) appliqué; **matematica applicata** applied mathematics *sg*

applica'tore *nm* applicator

applicazi'one *nf* application; (di legge) enforcement
■ **applicazioni** *pl* **tecniche** handicrafts

✦ **appoggi'are** *vt* lean (a against); (mettere) put; (sostenere) back

appoggi'arsi *vr* **~ a** lean against; fig rely on

appoggi'ato *adj* leaning (**su** on; **contro, a** against)

ap'poggio *nm* support; **appoggi** *pl* fig influential contacts

appollai'arsi *vr* fig perch

ap'porre *vt* affix

appor'tare *vt* bring; (causare) cause; **~ delle modifiche a qualcosa** modify something

ap'porto *nm* contribution

apposita'mente *adv* (specialmente) especially; **fatto ~** purpose-made

ap'posito *adj* proper

✦ indicates a very frequent word

apposizi'one *nf* apposition

✧ ap'posta *adv* on purpose; (espressamente) specially; **neanche a farlo ∼!** what a coincidence!

apposta'mento *nm* ambush; (caccia) lying in wait

appo'stare *vt* post ‹*soldati*›

appo'starsi *vr* lie in wait

ap'prendere *vt* understand; (imparare) learn

apprendi'mento *nm* learning
■ apprendimento assistito dal computer computer-aided learning

appren'dista *nmf* apprentice

apprendi'stato *nm* apprenticeship

apprensi'one *nf* apprehension; **essere in ∼ per** be anxious about

appren'sivo *adj* apprehensive

ap'presso *adv & prep* (vicino) near; (dietro) behind; **come ∼** as follows

appre'stare *vt* prepare

appre'starsi *vr* get ready

apprez'zabile *adj* appreciable

apprezza'mento *nm* appreciation; (giudizio) opinion

apprez'zare *vt* appreciate

apprez'zato *adj* appreciated

ap'proccio *nm* approach

appro'dare *vi* land; **∼ a** fig come to; **non ∼ a nulla** come to nothing

ap'prodo *nm* landing; (luogo) landing-stage

✧ approfit'tare *vi* take advantage (**di** of), profit (**di** by)

approfitta|'tore, -trice *nmf* chancer

approfondi'mento *nm* deepening; **di ∼** ‹*corso*› advanced

approfon'dire *vt* broaden, widen ‹*indagine, conoscenze*›

approfon'dirsi *vr* ‹*divario*› widen

approfon'dito *adj* ‹*studio, ricerca*› in-depth

appron'tare *vt* get ready, prepare

appropri'arsi *vr* **∼ a** (essere adatto a) suit; **∼ di** take possession of; **∼ indebitamente di** embezzle, misappropriate

appropri'ato *adj* appropriate

appropriazi'one *nf* Jur appropriation
■ appropriazione indebita Jur embezzlement

approssi'mare *vt* **∼ per eccesso/difetto** round up/down

approssi'marsi *vr* draw near

approssimativa'mente *adv* approximately

approssima'tivo *adj* approximate

approssimazi'one *nf* approximation

✧ appro'vare *vt* approve of; approve ‹*legge*›

approvazi'one *nf* approval

approvvigiona'mento *nm* supplying; approvvigionamenti *pl* provisions

approvvigio'nare *vt* supply

approvvigio'narsi *vr* stock up

✧ appunta'mento *nm* appointment; fam date; **fissare un ∼, prendere un ∼** make an appointment; **darsi ∼** decide to meet

appun'tare *vt* (annotare) take notes; (fissare) fix; (con spillo) pin; (appuntire) sharpen

appun'tarsi *vr* **∼ su** ‹*teoria*› be based on

appun'tato *nm* (carabiniere) *lowest rank in the Carabinieri*

appuntel'larsi *vr* (sostenersi) support oneself

appun'tino *adv* meticulously

appun'tire *vt* sharpen

appun'tito *adj* ‹*matita*› sharp; ‹*mento*› pointed

ap'punto[1] *nm* note; (piccola critica) niggle

✧ ap'punto[2] *adv* exactly; **per l'∼!** exactly!; **stavo ∼ dicendo ...** I was just saying ...

appura'mento *nm* verification

appu'rare *vt* verify

a'pribile *adj* that can be opened; **tettuccio apribile** Auto sun roof

apribot'tiglie *nm inv* bottle-opener

✧ a'prile *nm* April
■ primo d'aprile April Fool's Day

aprio'ristico *adj* a priori

✧ a'prire *vt* open; turn on ‹*luce, acqua ecc*›; (con chiave) unlock; open up ‹*ferita ecc*›; **∼ le ostilità** Mil commence hostilities; **apriti cielo!** heavens above!

a'prirsi *vr* open; (spaccarsi) split; (confidarsi) confide (**con** in)

apri'scatole *nf inv* tin opener Br, can opener

APT *abbr* (**Azienda di Promozione Turistica**) Tourist Board

aqua'planing *nm* **andare in ∼** aquaplane

'aquila *nf* eagle; **non è un'∼!** fig he's no genius!

aqui'lino *adj* aquiline

aqui'lone *nm* (giocattolo) kite

aqui'lotto *nm* (piccolo dell'aquila) eaglet

AR (a) *abbr* (**andata e ritorno**) return [ticket]
(b) *abbr* (**avviso di ricevimento**) return receipt for registered letters

ara'besco *nm* arabesque; (hum) scribble

A'rabia *nf* Arabia
■ l'Arabia Saudita Saudi Arabia

✧ 'arabo, -a [1] *adj* Arab; ‹*lingua*› Arabic
[2] *nmf* Arab
[3] *nm* (lingua) Arabic

arabo-israeli'ano *adj* Arab-Israeli

a'rachide *nf* peanut

arago'nese *adj* Aragonese

ara'gosta *nf* lobster

a'raldica *nf* heraldry

a'raldico *adj* heraldic

····✧

a

aran'ceto nm orange grove

ᕁ **a'rancia** nf orange; **succo d'arancia** orange juice

aranci'ata nf orangeade

a'rancio nm orange (tree); (colore) orange

aranci'one adj & nm orange

a'rare vt plough

ara'tore nm ploughman

a'ratro nm plough

ara'tura nf ploughing

a'razzo nm tapestry

arbi'traggio nm Comm arbitrage; Sport refereeing; Jur arbitration

arbi'trare vt arbitrate in; Sport referee

arbitrarietà nf arbitrariness

arbi'trario adj arbitrary

arbi'trato nm arbitration

ar'bitrio nm will; **è un** ~ it's very high-handed

'arbitro nm arbiter; Sport (nel calcio, boxe) referee, ref fam; (nel baseball, tennis, cricket) umpire

arboricol'tura nf arboriculture

ar'busto nm shrub

'arca nf ark; (cassa) chest
■ **l'~ di Noè** Noah's Ark

ar'caico adj archaic

arca'ismo nm archaism

ar'cangelo nm archangel

ar'cano [1] adj mysterious
[2] nm mystery

ar'cata nf arch; (serie di archi) arcade

archeolo'gia nf archaeology

archeo'logico adj archaeological

arche'ologo, -a nmf archaeologist

ar'chetipo nm archetype

ar'chetto nm Mus bow

architet'tare vt fig devise; **cosa state architettando?** fig what are you plotting?

ᕁ **archi'tetto** nm architect
■ **architetto d'interni** interior designer

architet'tonico adj architectural

architet'tura nf anche Comput architecture

archi'trave nm lintel

archivi'abile adj that can be filed

archivi'are vt file, archive; Jur close

archiviazi'one nf filing; Jur (di caso) closing
■ **archiviazione dati** data storage

ar'chivio nm archives pl; Comput file

archi'vista nmf filing clerk

archi'vistica nf rules governing the keeping of archives and records

ARCI nf abbr (**Associazione Ricreativa Culturale Italiana**) Italian cultural and leisure association

arci'duca nm archduke

arcidu'chessa nf archduchess

arci'ere nm archer

ar'cigno adj grim

arci'one nm saddle

arci'pelago nm archipelago

arci'vescovo nm archbishop

ᕁ **'arco** nm arch; Math arc; (arma, Mus) bow; **nell'~ di una giornata/due mesi** in the space of a day/two months
■ **arco rampante** flying buttress; **arco temporale** time-frame

arcoba'leno nm rainbow

arcu'are vt bend; ~ **la schiena** ‹gatto› arch its back

arcu'arsi vr bend

arcu'ato adj bent; ‹schiena di gatto› arched

ar'dente adj burning; fig ardent
■ **camera ardente** chapel of rest

ardente'mente adv ardently

'ardere vt/i burn
■ **legna da ardere** firewood

ar'desia nf slate

ardi'mento nm boldness

ar'dire [1] vi dare
[2] nm (coraggio) daring, boldness; (sfrontatezza) impudence

ar'dito adj daring; (coraggioso) bold; (sfacciato) impudent

ar'dore nm (calore) heat; fig ardour

'arduo adj arduous; (ripido) steep

'area nf area; (superficie) surface
■ **area fabbricabile** building land; **area di rigore** (in calcio) penalty area, penalty box; **area di servizio** service area; **area soggetta a vincoli ambientali** conservation area; **area [di sosta] per roulotte** trailer park Am, caravan site; **area di sviluppo** growth area

a'rena nf arena

are'naria nf sandstone

are'narsi vr run aground; fig ‹trattative› reach deadlock; **mi sono arenato** I'm stuck

are'nile nm stretch of sand

areo'plano nm aeroplane

'argano nm winch

argen'tato adj silver-plated

ar'genteo adj silvery

argente'ria nf silver[ware]

argenti'ere nm silversmith

argen'tina nf (maglia) round-necked pullover

Argen'tina nf Argentina

argen'tino¹ adj silvery

argen'tino², -a adj & nmf Argentinian

ar'gento nm silver; **d'**~ silver
■ **argento vivo** Chem quicksilver

ar'gilla nf clay

ᕁ indicates a very frequent word

argil'loso *adj* ‹terreno› clayey; (simile all'argilla) clay-like

argi'nare *vt* embank; fig hold in check, contain

'argine *nm* embankment; (diga) dike; **fare ~ a** fig hold in check, contain

argomen'tare *vi* argue

⚹ **argo'mento** *nm* argument; (motivo) reason; (soggetto) subject

argu'ire *vt* deduce

arguta'mente *adv* (con astuzia) shrewdly; (con facezia) wittily

ar'guto *adj* witty; (astuto) shrewd

ar'guzia *nf* wit; (battuta) witticism; (astuzia) shrewdness

⚹ **'aria** *nf* air; (aspetto) appearance; Mus tune; Auto choke; **avere l'~… look …**; **mandare all'~ qualcosa** fig ruin something; **andare all'~** fig fall through; **a tenuta d'~** draughtproof; **avere la testa per ~** fig be absent-minded, have one's head in the clouds; **che ~ tirava?** fig what was the atmosphere like?; **cambiare ~** fig have a change of scene; **cambia ~ !** (hum) get out of here!

■ **corrente d'aria** draught; **aria-aria** *adj inv* Mil air-to-air; **aria condizionata** air-conditioning; **aria-terra** *adj inv* air-to-ground

ari'ano *adj* Aryan

arida'mente *adv* without emotion

aridità *nf* aridity

'arido *adj* arid

arleggi'are *vt* air; **~ una stanza** give a room an airing

arieggi'ato *adj* airy

ari'ete *nm* ram, (strumento) battering-ram; Ariete Astr Aries

ari'etta *nf* (brezza) breeze

a'ringa *nf* herring

ari'oso *adj* ‹locale› light and airy

'arista *nf* chine of pork

aristo'cratico, -a ① *adj* aristocratic ② *nmf* aristocrat

aristocra'zia *nf* aristocracy

arit'metica *nf* arithmetic

arit'metico *adj* arithmetical

arlec'chino *nm* Harlequin; fig buffoon

⚹ **'arma** *nf* weapon; (forze armate) [armed] forces; **armi** *pl* arms; **chiamare alle armi** call up; **sotto le armi** in the army; **alle prime armi** fig inexperienced, fledg[e]ling; **prendere/deporre le armi** take up arms/put down one's arms; **passare qualcuno per le armi** execute somebody; **confrontarsi ad armi pari** compete on an equal footing

■ **arma bianca** knife; **arma a doppio taglio** fig double-edged sword; **arma a fuoco** firearm; **arma di distruzione di massa** weapon of mass destruction; **arma impropria** makeshift weapon; **arma segreta** fig secret weapon; **armi**

pl **nucleari** nuclear weapons

armadi'etto *nm* locker, cupboard; (in aereo) overhead locker

■ **armadietto del bagno** bathroom cabinet; **armadietto dei medicinali** medicine cabinet

arma'dillo *nm* armadillo

ar'madio *nm* cupboard; (guardaroba) wardrobe

■ **armadio a muro** fitted cupboard

armamen'tario *nm* tools *pl*; fig paraphernalia

arma'mento *nm* armament, weaponry; Naut fitting out

⚹ **ar'mare** *vt* arm; (equipaggiare) fit out; Archit reinforce

ar'marsi *vr* arm oneself (**di** with)

ar'mata *nf* army; (flotta) fleet

ar'mato *adj* armed; **rapina a mano armata** armed robbery

arma'tore *nm* shipowner

arma'tura *nf* framework; (impalcatura) scaffolding; (di guerriero) armour

armeggi'are *vi* fig manoeuvre

Ar'menia *nf* Armenia

ar'meno, -a *adj & nmf* Armenian

arme'ria *nf* Mil armoury

armi'stizio *nm* armistice

armo'nia *nf* harmony

ar'monica *nf*

■ **armonica [a bocca]** mouth-organ

ar'monico *adj* harmonic

armoniosa'mente *adv* harmoniously

armoni'oso *adj* harmonious

armoniz'zare ① *vt* harmonize ② *vi* match

armoniz'zarsi *vr* ‹colori› go together, match

ar'nese *nm* tool; (oggetto) thing; (congegno) gadget; **male in ~** in bad condition

'arnia *nf* beehive

a'roma *nm* aroma; **aromi** *pl* herbs; **aromi** *pl* **naturali/artificiali** natural/artificial flavourings

aromatera'pia *nf* aromatherapy

aro'matico *adj* aromatic

aromatiz'zare *vt* flavour

'arpa *nf* harp

ar'peggio *nm* arpeggio

ar'pia *nf* harpy

arpi'one *nm* hook; (pesca) harpoon

ar'pista *nmf* harpist

arrabat'tarsi *vr* do all one can

⚹ **arrabbi'arsi** *vr* get angry

arrabbi'ato *adj* angry

arrabbia'tura *nf* rage; **prendersi un'~** fly into a rage

arraf'fare *vt* grab

arraf'fone *nmf* fam thief

a

arrampi'carsi *vr* climb [up]; ~ **sugli specchi** fig clutch at straws

arrampi'cata *nf* climb

arrampica|'tore, -trice *nmf* climber
■ **arrampicatore sociale** social climber

arran'care *vi* limp, hobble; fig struggle, limp along

arrangia'mento *nm* arrangement

arrangi'are *vt* arrange

arrangi'arsi *vr* manage; ~ **alla meglio** get by; **ar'rangiati!** get on with it!

arrangia|'tore, -trice *nmf* Mus arranger

arra'parsi *vr* vulg get randy

arre'care *vt* bring; (causare) cause

arreda'mento *nm* interior decoration; (l'arredare) furnishing; (mobili ecc) furnishings *pl*

arre'dare *vt* furnish

arreda|'tore, -trice *nmf* interior designer

ar'redo *nm* furnishings *pl*

arrem'baggio *nm* **lanciarsi all'**~ fig stampede

ar'rendersi *vr* surrender; ~ **all'evidenza dei fatti** face facts

arren'devole *adj* ‹persona› yielding

arrendevo'lezza *nf* softness

ℱ **arre'stare** *vt* arrest; (fermare) stop

arre'starsi *vr* halt

ar'resto *nm* stop; Jur arrest; **la dichiaro in [stato d']** ~ you are under arrest
■ **mandato di arresto** warrant; **arresto cardiaco** heart failure, cardiac arrest; **arresti** *pl* **domiciliari** Jur house arrest

arretra'mento *nm* withdrawal

arre'trare ① *vt* withdraw; pull back ‹giocatore›
② *vi* withdraw

arre'trato ① *adj* (paese ecc) backward; Mil (posizione) rear; **numero arretrato (di rivista)** back number; **del lavoro** ~ a backlog of work
② *nm* (di stipendio) back pay; **essere in** ~ be behind schedule; **arretrati** *pl* arrears
■ **arretrati** *pl* **di paga** back pay

arricchi'mento *nm* enrichment

arric'chire *vt* enrich

arric'chirsi *vr* get rich

arric'chito, -a *nmf* nouveau riche

arricciaca'pelli *nm inv* tongs

arricci'are *vt* curl; ~ **il naso** turn up one's nose

ar'ridere *vi* ~ **a qualcuno** ‹sorte› smile on somebody

ar'ringa *nf* Jur closing address

arrin'gare *vt* harangue

arrischi'arsi *vr* dare

arrischi'ato *adj* risky; (imprudente) rash

ℱ **arri'vare** *vi* arrive; ~ **a** (raggiungere) reach; (ridursi) be reduced to

arri'vato, -a ① *adj* successful; **ben** ~**!** welcome!
② *nmf* successful person; **il primo/secondo** ~ (in gare) the first/second to finish

arrive'derci *int* goodbye; ~ **a domani** see you tomorrow

arri'vismo *nm* social climbing; (nel lavoro) careerism

arri'vista *nmf* social climber; (nel lavoro) careerist

ℱ **ar'rivo** *nm* arrival; Sport finish; ~ **previsto per le ore ...** expected time of arrival ...

arro'gante *adj* arrogant

arro'ganza *nf* arrogance

arro'garsi *vr* ~ **il diritto di fare qualcosa** take it upon oneself to do something; ~ **il merito** take the credit

arrossa'mento *nm* reddening

arros'sare *vt* make red, redden ‹occhi›

arros'sarsi *vr* go red

arros'sire *vi* blush, go red

arro'stire *vt* roast; toast ‹pane›; (ai ferri) grill

arro'stirsi *vr* fig broil

ar'rosto *adj* & *nm* roast; **molto fumo e niente** ~ fig all show and no substance
■ **arrosto d'agnello** roast lamb

arro'tare *vt* sharpen; fam (investire) run over

arro'tino *nm* knife-sharpener

arroto'lare *vt* roll up

arroton'dare *vt* round; Math ecc round off; ~ **lo stipendio** supplement one's income

arroton'darsi *vr* become round; ‹persona› get plump

arrovel'larsi *vr* ~ **il cervello** rack one's brains

arroven'tare *vt* make red-hot

arroven'tarsi *vr* become red-hot

arroven'tato *adj* red-hot; fig ‹discorso› fiery

aruf'fare *vt* ruffle; fig confuse

arruf'farsi *vr* become ruffled

arruf'fato *adj* ‹capelli› dishevelled, tousled

arruffia'narsi *vr* ~ **[con] qualcuno** fig butter somebody up

arruggi'nire *vt* rust

arruggi'nirsi *vr* go rusty; fig (fisicamente) stiffen up; ‹conoscenze› go rusty

arruggi'nito *adj* rusty

arruola'mento *nm* enlistment

arruo'lare *vt/i* enlist

arruo'larsi *vr* enlist

arse'nale *nm* arsenal; (cantiere) [naval] dockyard

ar'senico *nm* arsenic

'arso ① *pp di* ARDERE

ℱ indicates a very frequent word

2 *adj* burnt; (arido) dry

ar'sura *nf* burning heat; (sete) parching thirst

art déco *nf* art deco

⚔ **'arte** *nf* art; (abilità) craftsmanship; **senza ∼ né parte** incapable; **nome d'arte** professional name
- **arte drammatica** dramatics; **le belle arti** *pl* the fine arts; **arti** *pl* **figurative** figurative arts; **arti** *pl* **dello spettacolo** performing arts

arte'fare *vt* adulterate ⟨vino⟩; disguise ⟨voce⟩

arte'fatto *adj* fake; ⟨vino⟩ adulterated

ar'tefice **1** *nm* craftsman; fig author
2 *nf* craftswoman

ar'teria *nf* artery
- **arteria [stradale]** arterial road

arterio'sclerosi *nf* arteriosclerosis, hardening of the arteries

arterioscle'rotico *adj* senile

arteri'oso *adj* Anat arterial

'artico *adj* Arctic

'Artico *nm* **l'∼** the Arctic

artico'lare **1** *adj* articular
2 *vt* articulate; (suddividere) divide

artico'larsi *vr* fig **∼ in** consist of

artico'lato *adj* Auto articulated; fig well-constructed

articolazi'one *nf* Anat articulation

⚔ **ar'ticolo** *nm* article; **articoli** *pl* **per la casa** household goods; **articoli** *pl* **per la cucina** kitchenware; **articoli** *pl* **di marca** brand name goods; **articoli** *pl* **da regalo** gifts; **articoli** *pl* **da spiaggia** beach gear; **articoli** *pl* **sportivi** sports gear, negozio di articoli sportivi sports shop; **articoli** *pl* **vari** sundries
- **articolo civetta** Comm loss leader; **articolo determinativo** Gram definite article; **articolo di fondo** leader, leading article; **articolo indeterminativo** Gram indefinite article; **articolo di prima pagina** Journ cover story; **articolo principale** Journ lead story

'Artide *nf* **l'∼** the Arctic [region]

artifici'ale *adj* artificial

artifici'ere *nm* Mil explosives expert, bomb disposal expert

arti'ficio *nm* artifice; (affettazione) affectation

artificiosità *nf* artificiality

artifici'oso *adj* artful; (affettato) affected

artigi'ana *nf* craftswoman

artigia'nale *adj* made by hand; (hum) amateurish

artigianal'mente *adv* with craftsmanship; (hum) amateurishly

artigia'nato *nm* craftsmanship; (ceto) craftsmen *pl*

artigi'ano *nm* craftsman

artigli'ato *adj* with claws

artigli'ere *nm* artilleryman

artiglie'ria *nf* artillery
- **artiglieria antiaerea** flak

ar'tiglio *nm* claw; fig clutch; **sfoderare gli artigli** fig show one's claws

⚔ **ar'tista** *nmf* artist

artistica'mente *adv* artistically

ar'tistico *adj* artistic

arti'stoide *adj* arty

art nouveau *nf* art nouveau

'arto *nm* limb

ar'trite *nf* arthritis

ar'tritico, -a *nmf* arthritic

ar'trosi *nf* rheumatism

arzigogo'lato *adj* fantastic, bizarre

ar'zillo *adj* sprightly

a'scella *nf* armpit

ascen'dente **1** *adj* ascending
2 *nm* (antenato) ancestor; (influenza) ascendancy; Astr ascendant

ascen'denza *nf* ancestry

a'scendere *vi* ascend

ascensi'one *nf* ascent; **l'Ascensione** the Ascension

ascen'sore *nm* (in una costruzione) lift, elevator Am; Comput scroll box

a'scesa *nf* ascent; (al trono) accession; (al potere) rise

a'scesi *nf* asceticism

a'scesso *nm* abscess

a'sceta *nmf* ascetic

a'scetico *adj* ascetic

'ascia *nf* axe

asciugabianche'ria *nm inv* (stenditoio) clothes horse; (macchina) tumble-drier

asciugaca'pelli *nm inv* hair dryer, hairdrier

asciuga'mano *nm* towel
- **asciugamano di carta** paper towel

⚔ **asciu'gare** *vt* dry; **∼ le stoviglie** do the drying-up

asciu'garsi *vr* dry oneself; (diventare asciutto) dry up; **∼ le mani** dry one's hands

asciuga'trice *nf* tumble dryer

asci'utto *adj* dry; (magro) wiry; ⟨risposta⟩ curt; **essere all'∼** fig be hard up

⚔ **ascol'tare** **1** *vt* listen to
2 *vi* listen

ascolta|'tore, -trice *nmf* listener

a'scolto *nm* listening; **dare ∼ a** listen to; **essere in ∼** Radio be listening; **mettersi in ∼** Radio tune in; **prestare ∼** listen

a'scrivere *vt* (attribuire) ascribe; **∼ a** (annoverare) number among

asessu'ato *adj* asexual

a'settico *adj* aseptic

asfal'tare *vt* asphalt

asfal'tato *adj* tarmac

a'sfalto *nm* asphalt

asfis'sia *nf* asphyxia

asfissi'ante *adj* ‹caldo› oppressive; fig ‹persona› annoying

asfissi'are *vt* asphyxiate; fig annoy

'Asia *nf* Asia
- ■ Asia Minore Asia Minor

asi'ago *nm full-fat white cheese*

asi'atico, -a *adj & nmf* Asian

a'silo *nm* shelter; (d'infanzia) nursery school
- ■ asilo infantile day nursery; asilo nido day nursery; asilo politico political asylum

asim'metrico *adj* asymmetric[al]

a'sincrono *adj* asynchronous

'asino *nm* donkey; fig (persona stupida) ass; Sch dunce; **qui casca l'~!** fig that's where it falls down!

'asma *nf* asthma

a'smatico *adj* asthmatic

asoci'ale *adj* asocial

'asola *nf* buttonhole

a'sparagi *nmpl* asparagus *sg*

aspara'gina *nf* Bot asparagus fern

a'sparago *nm* asparagus

a'spergere *vt* ~ **con/di** sprinkle with

asperità *nf inv* harshness; (di terreno) roughness

asper'sorio *nm* aspergillum, holy-water sprinkler

🔹 **aspet'tare** ⬚1 *vt* wait for; (prevedere) expect; **~ un bambino** be expecting [a baby]; **fare ~ qualcuno** keep somebody waiting ⬚2 *vi* wait

aspet'tarsi *vr* expect

aspetta'tiva *nf* expectation; (nel lavoro) leave of absence; **all'altezza delle aspettative** up to expectations; **inferiore alle aspettative** not up to expectations
- ■ aspettativa per malattia sick leave; aspettativa per maternità maternity leave

a'spetto¹ *nm* look; (di problema) aspect; **di bell'~** good-looking

🔹 **a'spetto²** *nm*
- ■ sala d'aspetto waiting room

'aspic *nm* aspic

aspi'rante ⬚1 *adj* aspiring; ‹pompa› suction *attrib* ⬚2 *nmf* (a un posto) applicant; (al trono) aspirant; **gli aspiranti al titolo** the contenders for the title

aspira'polvere *nm inv* vacuum cleaner; **passare l'~** vacuum, hoover

aspi'rare ⬚1 *vt* inhale; Mech suck in; (con elettrodomestici) vacuum, hoover ⬚2 *vi* ~ **a** aspire to

aspi'rato *adj* aspirate

aspira'tore *nm* extractor fan

aspirazi'one *nf* inhalation; Mech suction; (ambizione) ambition

---
🔹 indicates a very frequent word

aspi'rina® *nf* aspirin

aspor'tare *vt* take away

a'sporto *nm* da ~ take-away

aspra'mente *adv* (duramente) severely

a'sprezza *nf* (al gusto) sourness; (di clima) severity; (di carattere, parole, suono) harshness; (di odore) pungency; (di litigio) bitterness

a'sprigno *adj* slightly sour

'aspro *adj* ‹al gusto› sour; ‹clima› severe; ‹suono, parole› harsh; ‹odore› pungent; ‹litigio› bitter

assaggi'are *vt* taste

assaggia|'tore, -trice *nmf* taster

assag'gini *nmpl* Culin samples

as'saggio *nm* tasting; (piccola quantità) taste; fig (campione) sample

🔹 **as'sai** *adv* very; (moltissimo) very much; (abbastanza) enough

assa'lire *vt* attack

assali|'tore, -trice *nmf* assailant

assal'tare *vt* Mil attack, charge; hold up ‹banca, treno›

assalta'tore *nm* hold-up man

as'salto *nm* attack; **d'~** ‹giornalismo› aggressive; **prendere d'~** storm ‹città›; fig mob ‹persona›; hold up ‹banca›

assapo'rare *vt* savour

assas'sina *nf* murderess

assassi'nare *vt* murder, assassinate; fig murder

assas'sinio *nm* murder, assassination

🔹 **assas'sino** ⬚1 *adj* murderous ⬚2 *nm* murderer

'asse ⬚1 *nf* board ⬚2 *nm* Techn axle; Math axis
- ■ asse da stiro ironing board

assecon'dare *vt* satisfy; (favorire) support; **~ i capricci di qualcuno** indulge somebody's every whim; **~ i desideri di qualcuno** comply with somebody's wishes

assedi'are *vt* besiege

assedi'ato *adj* besieged

as'sedio *nm* siege

assegna'mento *nm* allotment; **fare ~ su** rely on

asse'gnare *vt* allot; award ‹premio›

assegna'tario, -a *nmf* recipient

assegnazi'one *nf* (di alloggio, denaro, borsa di studio) allocation; (di premio) award

as'segno *nm* allowance; (bancario) cheque; **contro ~** cash on delivery; **pagare con un ~** pay by cheque
- ■ assegno circolare bank draft; assegni familiari *pl* family allowance; assegno post-datato post-dated cheque; assegno sbarrato crossed cheque; assegno non trasferibile cheque made out to "account payee only"; assegno turistico traveller's cheque; assegno a vuoto bad cheque, dud cheque

assem'blaggio *nm* assemblage

assem'blare *vt* assemble

assem'blea *nf* assembly; (adunanza) gathering
- **assemblea generale annuale** Annual General Meeting, AGM

assembra'mento *nm* gathering

assem'brare *vt* gather

assen'nato *adj* sensible

as'senso *nm* assent

assen'tarsi *vr* go away; (da stanza) leave the room

as'sente [1] *adj* absent; (distratto) absent-minded
[2] *nmf* absentee

assente'ismo *nm* absenteeism

assente'ista *nmf* frequent absentee

assen'tire *vi* acquiesce (**a** in)

as'senza *nf* absence; (mancanza) lack
- **assenza di gravità** zero gravity; **assenze** *pl* **ingiustificate** (a scuola) truancy

asse'rire *vi* assert

asserragli'arsi *vr* barricade oneself

asser'tivo *adj* assertive

asser|'tore, -trice *nmf* supporter

asservi'mento *nm* subservience

asser'vire *vt* fig enslave

asser'virsi *vr* fig be subservient

asserzi'one *nf* assertion

assesso'rato *nm* [council] department

asses'sore *nm* councillor

assesta'mento *nm* settlement

asse'stare *vt* arrange; ∼ **un colpo** deal a blow

asse'starsi *vr* settle oneself

asse'stato *adj* ben ∼ well-judged

asse'tato *adj* parched

as'setto *nm* order; Naut, Aeron trim; **in** ∼ **di guerra** on a war footing; **cambiare l'**∼ **territoriale dell'Europa** change the map of Europe

assi'cella *nf* lath

assicu'rabile *adj* insurable

assicu'rare *vt* assure; Comm insure; register ‹posta›; (fissare) secure; (accertare) ensure

assicu'rarsi *vr* (con contratto) insure oneself; (legarsi) fasten oneself; ∼ **che** make sure that

assicu'rata *nf* registered letter

assicura'tivo *adj* insurance *attrib*

assicu'rato *adj* insured; **lettera assicurata** registered letter

assicura|'tore, -trice [1] *nmf* insurance agent
[2] *adj* insurance; **società assicuratrice** insurance company

assicurazi'one *nf* assurance; (contratto) insurance; **fare un'**∼ take out insurance
- **assicurazione multirischi** blanket cover;

assicurazione sanitaria medical insurance; **assicurazione di viaggio** travel insurance

assidera'mento *nm* exposure

asside'rarsi *vr* fam be frozen; Med be suffering from exposure

asside'rato *adj* Med suffering from exposure; fam frozen

assidua'mente *adv* assiduously

assiduità *nf* assiduity

as'siduo *adj* assiduous; ‹cliente› regular

assi'eme *adj* [together] with

assil'lante *adj* ‹persona, pensiero› nagging

assil'lare *vt* pester

assil'larsi *vr* torment oneself

as'sillo *nm* worry

assimi'lare *vt* assimilate

assimilazi'one *nf* assimilation

assi'oma *nm* axiom

assio'matico *adj* axiomatic

As'siria *nf* Assyria

as'sise *nfpl* assizes; **Corte d'Assise** Court of Assize[s]

assi'stente *nmf* assistant
- **assistente sociale** social worker; **assistente sociosanitario** care worker; **assistente universitario** assistant lecturer; **assistente di volo** flight attendant

assi'stenza *nf* assistance; (presenza) presence
- **assistenza alla clientela** customer care; **assistenza medica** medical care; **assistenza ospedaliera** hospital treatment; **assistenza sanitaria** health care; **assistenza sociale** social work

assistenzi'ale *adj* welfare

assistenzia'lismo *nm* abuse of the welfare state

as'sistere [1] *vt* assist; (curare) nurse
[2] *vi* ∼ **a** (essere presente) be present at; watch ‹spettacolo ecc›

assi'stito *adj* ∼ **da computer** computer-aided

'asso *nm* ace; **piantare in** ∼ leave in the lurch
- **asso nella manica** trump card

associ'are *vt* join; (collegare) associate

associ'arsi *vr* join forces; Comm enter into partnership; ∼ **a** join; subscribe to ‹giornale ecc›

associ'ato, -a [1] *adj* associate
[2] *nmf* partner

associazi'one *nf* association
- **associazione di categoria** trade-union; **associazione per delinquere** criminal organization; **Associazione Europea di Libero Scambio** European Free Trade Association; **associazione in partecipazione** Comm joint venture

associazio'nismo *nm* Pol excessive tendency to form associations; Psych ⋯▸

associationism
asso'dare *vt* ascertain ‹verità›
assogget'tare *vt* subject
assogget'tarsi *vr* submit
asso'lato *adj* sunny
assol'dare *vt* recruit
as'solo *nm* Mus solo
as'solto *pp* di ASSOLVERE
assoluta'mente *adv* absolutely
assolu'tismo *nm* absolutism
assolu'tista *nmf* absolutist
assolu'tistico *adj* absolutist
✓ **asso'luto** *adj* absolute
assolu'torio *adj* formula assolutoria acquittal
assoluzi'one *nf* acquittal; Relig absolution
as'solvere *vt* perform ‹compito›; Jur acquit; Relig absolve
assolvi'mento *nm* performance
✓ **assomigli'are** *vi* ~ a be like, resemble
assomigli'arsi *vr* resemble each other
assom'marsi *vr* combine; ~ a qualcosa add to something
asso'nanza *nf* assonance
asson'nato *adj* drowsy
asso'pirsi *vr* doze off
assor'bente *adj* & *nm* absorbent
■ assorbente igienico sanitary towel
assor'bire *vt* absorb
assor'dante *adj* deafening
assor'dare *vt* deafen
assorti'mento *nm* assortment
assor'tire *vt* match ‹colori›
assor'tito *adj* assorted; ‹colori, persone› matched
as'sorto *adj* engrossed
assottiglia'mento *nm* thinning; (aguzzamento) sharpening
assottigli'are *vt* make thin; (aguzzare) sharpen; (ridurre) reduce
assottigli'arsi *vr* grow thin; ‹finanze› be whittled away
assue'fare *vt* accustom
assue'farsi *vr* ~ a get used to
assue'fatto *adj* (a caffe, aspirina) immune to the effects; (a droga) addicted
assuefazi'one *nf* (a caffè, aspirina) immunity to the effects; (a droga) addiction
✓ **as'sumere** *vt* assume; take on ‹impiegato›; ~ informazioni make inquiries
as'sunto ⓵ *pp* di ASSUMERE ⓶ *nm* task
assunzi'one *nf* (di impiegato) employment; Relig l'Assunzione Assumption
assurdità *nf inv* absurdity; dire delie ~ talk nonsense
✓ **as'surdo** *adj* absurd

✓ indicates a very frequent word

'**asta** *nf* pole; Mech bar; Comm auction; a mezz'~ at half-mast
■ asta di livello [dell'olio] Auto dip-stick
a'stemio *adj* abstemious
aste'nersi *vr* abstain (da from)
astensi'one *nf* abstention
astensio'nismo *nm* persistent abstention
astensio'nista *nmf* persistent abstainer
astensio'nistico *adj* tendenza astensionistica tendency to abstain
aste'nuto, -a *nmf* abstainer
aste'risco *nm* (simbolo) asterisk; (tasto) star key, asterisk key
aste'roide *nm* asteroid
'**astice** *nm* crayfish
asti'cella *nf* stick; (in salto in alto) bar
astig'matico *adj* astigmatic
astigma'tismo *nm* astigmatism
asti'nenza *nf* abstinence; crisi di astinenza withdrawal symptoms
'**astio** *nm* rancour; avere ~ contro qualcuno bear somebody a grudge
asti'oso *adj* resentful
a'stragalo *nm* anklebone
'**astrakan** *nm* astrakhan
astrat'tezza *nf* abstractness
astrat'tismo *nm* abstractionism
a'stratto *adj* abstract
astrin'gente *adj* & *nm* astringent
+**astro** *suff* giovinastro *nm* lout; giallastro *adj* yellowish; dolciastro *adj* sweetish
'**astro** *nm* star
astro'fisica *nf* astrophysics *sg*
astro'fisico, -a ⓵ *adj* astrophysical ⓶ *nmf* astrophysicist
astrolo'gia *nf* astrology
astro'logico *adj* astrological
a'strologo, -a *nmf* astrologer
astro'nauta *nmf* astronaut
astro'nautica *nf* astronautics *sg*
astro'nave *nf* spaceship
astro'mia *nf* astronomy
astro'nomico *adj* anche fig astronomic, astronomical
a'stronomo *nm* astronomer
astrusità *nf* abstruseness
a'struso *adj* abstruse
a'stuccio *nm* case
a'stuto *adj* shrewd; (furbo) cunning
a'stuzia *nf* shrewdness; (azione) trick
a'tavico *adj* atavistic
ate'ismo *nm* atheism
ate'lier *nm inv* (di alta moda) atelier; (di artista) [artist's] studio
A'tene *nf* Athens
ate'neo *nm* university
ateni'ese *adj* & *nmf* Athenian

'ateo, -a *adj & nmf* atheist

a'tipico *adj* atypical

at'lante *nm* atlas; **i monti dell'Atlante** the Atlas Mountains

at'lantico *adj* Atlantic; **l'[Oceano] Atlantico** the Atlantic [Ocean]

at'leta *nmf* athlete

a'tletica *nf* athletics *sg*
- **atletica leggera** track and field events; **atletica pesante** *weight-lifting, boxing, wrestling, etc*

a'tletico *adj* athletic

atle'tismo *nm* athleticism

⚡ **atmo'sfera** *nf* atmosphere

atmo'sferico *adj* atmospheric

a'tollo *nm* atoll

a'tomica *nf* atom bomb

a'tomico *adj* atomic

atomiz'zare *vt* atomize

atomizza'tore *nm* atomizer

'atomo *nm* atom

'atono *adj* unstressed

'atrio *nm* entrance hall, lobby

a'troce *adj* atrocious; ‹*terrible*› dreadful

atroce'mente *adv* atrociously

atrocità *nf inv* atrocity

atro'fia *nf* atrophy

atrofiz'zare *vt* atrophy

atrofiz'zarsi *vr* Med fig atrophy

attac'cabile *adj* attachable

attaccabot'toni *nmf inv* [crashing] bore

attacca'brighe *nmf inv* troublemaker

attacca'mento *nm* attachment

attac'cante ① *adj* attacking
② *nm* Sport forward

attacca'panni *nm inv* [coat-]hanger; (a muro) [clothes-]hook

⚡ **attac'care** ① *vt* attach; (legare) tie; (appendere) hang; (cucire) sew on; (contagiare) pass on; (assalire) attack; (iniziare) start
② *vi* stick; (diffondersi) catch on

attac'carsi *vr* cling; (affezionarsi) become attached; (litigare) quarrel

attacca'ticcio *adj* sticky; fig clinging and tiresome

attac'cato *adj* stuck

attacca'tura *nf* junction
- **attaccatura dei capelli** hairline

attac'chino *nm* billposter

at'tacco *nm* attack; (punto d'unione) junction; (accesso) fit
- **attacco aereo** air attack; **attacco cardiaco** heart attack; **attacco epilettico** epileptic fit

attanagli'are *vt* fig (tormentare) haunt

attar'darsi *vr* stay late; (indugiare) linger

attec'chire *vi* take; (moda ecc) catch on

⚡ **atteggia'mento** *nm* attitude

atteggi'are *vt* assume

atteggi'arsi *vr* ~ **a** pose as

attem'pato *adj* elderly

atten'darsi *vr* camp, pitch camp

atten'dente *nm* Mil batman

⚡ **at'tendere** ① *vt* wait for
② *vi* ~ **a** attend to

at'tendersi *vr* expect

atten'dibile *adj* reliable

attendibilità *nf* reliability

atte'nersi *vr* ~ **a** stick to

attenta'mente *adv* attentively

atten'tare *vi* ~ **a** make an attempt on

atten'tato *nm* act of violence; (contro politico ecc) assassination attempt; ~ **alla vita di** attempted murder of
- **attentato dinamitardo** bombing; **attentato suicida** suicide attack

attenta'tore, -trice *nmf* attacker; (a scopo politico) terrorist

⚡ **at'tento** *adj* attentive; (accurato) careful; **~!** look out!; **stare ~** pay attention; **'attenti al cane'** 'beware of the dog'

attenu'ante *nf* extenuating circumstance

attenu'are *vt* attenuate; (minimizzare) minimize; subdue ‹*colori ecc*›; calm ‹*dolore*›; soften ‹*colpo*›

attenu'arsi *vr* diminish

attenuazi'one *nf* lessening

⚡ **attenzi'one** *nf* attention; (cura) care; **fare ~** be careful; **~!** watch out!; **~, prego** your attention, please; **coprire di attenzioni** lavish attention on

atter'raggio *nm* landing
- **atterraggio di fortuna** emergency landing

atter'rare ① *vt* knock down
② *vi* land

atter'rire *vt* terrorize

atter'rirsi *vr* be terrified

⚡ **at'tesa** *nf* waiting; (aspettativa) expectation; **in ~ di** waiting for

at'teso pp di ATTENDERE

atte'stabile *adj* certifiable

atte'stare *vt* state; (certificare) certify

atte'stato *nm* certificate

attestazi'one *nf* certificate; (dichiarazione) declaration

'Attica *nf* Attica

'attico¹ *nm* (lingua) Attic

'attico² *nm* (appartamento) penthouse

at'tiguo *adj* adjacent

attil'lato *adj* ‹*vestito*› close-fitting

⚡ **'attimo** *nm* second; **un ~!** just a sec!; **in un ~** in double-quick time; **non ho avuto un ~ di respiro** I haven't had time to draw breath

atti'nente *adj* ~ **a** pertaining to

at'tingere *vt* draw; fig obtain

atti'rare *vt* attract

atti'rarsi *vr* draw ‹*attenzione*›; incur ‹*odio*›

a

attitudi'nale *nm*
■ test attitudinale aptitude test

atti'tudine *nf* (disposizione) aptitude; (atteggiamento) attitude

atti'vare *vt* activate

attivazi'one *nf* setting in motion, turning on; Phys, Chem activation

atti'vismo *nm* activism

atti'vista *nmf* activist

✧ **attività** *nf inv* activity; Comm assets *pl*
■ attività fisse *pl* fixed assets; **attività liquide** *pl* Comm liquid assets

✧ **at'tivo** 1 *adj* active; Comm productive
2 *nm* assets *pl*

attiz'zare *vt* poke; fig stir up

attizza'toio *nm* poker

✧ **'atto** *nm* act; (azione) action; Comm, Jur deed; (certificato) certificate; **fare ∼ di presenza** put in an appearance; **mettere in ∼** put into action; **atti** *pl* (di società ecc) proceedings; **atti** *pl* **di libidine violenta** indecent assault; **atti** *pl* **osceni** gross indecency
■ atto di vendita bill of sale

+attolo *suff* vermiciattolo *nm* slimy individual

at'tonito *adj* astonished

attorcigli'are *vt* twist

attorcigli'arsi *vr* get twisted

✧ **at'tore** *nm* actor

attorni'are *vt* surround

attorni'arsi *vr* ∼ **di** surround oneself with

✧ **at'torno** 1 *adv* around, about
2 *prep* ∼ **a** around, about

attrac'care *vt/i* dock

attra'ente *adj* attractive

at'trarre *vt* attract

at'trarsi *vr* be attracted to each other

attrat'tiva *nf* charm, attraction

attraversa'mento *nm* (di strada) crossing
■ attraversamento pedonale pedestrian crossing, crosswalk Am

✧ **attraver'sare** *vt* cross; (passare) go through

✧ **attra'verso** *prep* through; (obliquamente) across

attrazi'one *nf* attraction; **attrazioni** *pl* **turistiche** tourist attractions

attrez'zare *vt* equip; Naut rig

attrez'zarsi *vr* kit oneself out

attrezza'tura *nf* equipment; Naut rigging
■ attrezzatura da campeggio camping equipment

at'trezzo *nm* tool; **at'trezzi** *pl* equipment; Sport appliances *pl*

attribu'ibile *adj* attributable

✧ **attribu'ire** *vt* attribute

attribu'irsi *vr* ascribe to oneself; ∼ **il merito di** claim credit for

attri'buto *nm* attribute

attribuzi'one *nf* attribution

at'trice *nf* actress

at'trito *nm* friction

attrup'pare *vt* assemble

attrup'parsi *vr* gather

attu'abile *adj* feasible

attuabilità *nf* viability

attu'ale *adj* present; (di attualità) topical; (effettivo) actual

attualità *nf inv* topicality; (avvenimento) news; **programma di attualità** current affairs programme

attualiz'zare *vt* update

attual'mente *adv* at present

attu'are *vt* carry out

attu'ario, -a *nmf* actuary

attu'arsi *vr* be realized

attua'tore *nm* Techn actuator

attuazi'one *nf* carrying out

attuti'mento *nm* (di colpo) softening; (di suoni) muffling

attu'tire *vt* deaden; ∼ **il colpo** soften the blow

au'dace *adj* daring, bold; (insolente) audacious

au'dacia *nf* daring, boldness; (insolenza) audacity

audiapprendi'mento *nm* audio-based learning

'audience *nf inv* (telespettatori) audience

'audio *nm* audio

audiocas'setta *nf* audio cassette

audio'leso *adj* hearing-impaired

audio'libro *nm* audiobook, talking book

audio'metrico *adj* Med aural

audiovi'sivo *adj* audiovisual

'auditing *nm* auditing

audi'torio *nm* auditorium

audizi'one *nf* audition; Jur hearing

'auge *nm* height; **essere in ∼** be popular

augu'rare *vt* wish

augu'rarsi *vr* hope

au'gurio *nm* wish; (presagio) omen; **auguri!** all the best!; (a Natale) Happy Christmas!; **tanti auguri** best wishes

au'gusto *adj* august

'aula *nf* classroom; Univ lecture-hall; (sala) hall; **silenzio in ∼!** silence in court!
■ aula bunker (in tribunale) secure courtroom; **aula magna** Univ great hall; **aula del tribunale** courtroom

✧ **aumen'tare** *vt/i* increase; ∼ **di peso** gain weight

au'mento *nm* increase; (di stipendio) [pay] rise
■ aumento di prezzo price increase

'aureo *adj* golden

✧ indicates a very frequent word

au'reola nf halo
au'rora nf dawn
■ **aurora boreale** aurora borealis, Northern Lights
auscul'tare vt Med auscultate
ausili'are adj & nmf auxiliary
auspi'cabile adj è ~ **che …** it is to be hoped that …
auspi'care vt hope for
au'spicio nm omen; **auspici** pl (protezione) auspices; **è di buon** ~ it is a good omen
austerità nf austerity
au'stero adj austere
Austra'lasia nf Australasia
au'strale adj southern
Au'stralia nf Australia
australi'ano, -a adj & nmf Australian
'Austria nf Austria
au'striaco, -a adj & nmf Austrian
austroun'garico adj Austro-Hungarian
autar'chia nf autarchy
au'tarchico adj autarchic
aut aut nm inv either-or [choice]
autenti'care vt authenticate
autenti'cato adj certified
autenticità nf authenticity
au'tentico adj authentic; (vero) true
au'tismo nm autism
au'tista nm driver
au'tistico adj autistic
'auto nf inv car; **viaggiare in** ~ travel by car
■ **auto blindata** armour-plated car; **auto a quattro ruote motrici** four-wheel drive car; **auto sportiva** sports car; **auto a trazione anteriore** front-wheel drive car; **auto usata** second-hand car
auto+ pref self+
autoabbron'zante [1] nm self-tan
  [2] adj self tanning
autoaccesso'rista nmf car accessory supplier
autoade'sivo [1] adj self-adhesive
  [2] nm sticker
autoaffermazi'one nf self-assertion
autoambu'lanza nf ambulance
autoa'nalisi nf self-analysis
autoartico'lato nm articulated lorry
autobiogra'fia nf autobiography
autobio'grafico adj autobiographical
auto'blinda nf armoured car
auto'bomba nf car-bomb
auto'botte nf tanker
'autobus nm inv bus
auto'carro nm lorry
autocertificazi'one nf self-certification
autoci'sterna nf tanker
auto'clave nf (contenitore ad alta pressione) autoclave; (idraulica) surge tank

autocombusti'one nf spontaneous combustion
autocommiserazi'one nf self-pity
autocompiaci'mento nm smugness, self-satisfaction
autocompiaci'uto adj smug, self-satisfied
autoconcessio'nario nm car dealer
autocon'trollo nm self-control
au'tocrate nm autocrat
auto'cratico adj autocratic
auto'critica nf self-criticism
au'toctono adj native, aboriginal
autode'nuncia nf spontaneous confession
autodeterminazi'one nf self-determination
autodi'datta [1] adj self-taught
  [2] nmf self-educated person, autodidact
autodi'fesa nf self-defence
autodisci'plina nf self-discipline
autodi'struggersi vr self destruct, auto-distruct
autodistrut'tivo adj self-destructive
autodistruzi'one nf self-destruction
autoferrotranvi'ario adj public transport attrib
autoferrotranvi'eri nmpl public transport workers
autoffi'cina nf garage
autofinanzia'mento nm self-financing
autofinanzi'arsi vr be self-financing; ‹persona› use one's own finance
autogesti'one nf self-management
autoge'stirsi vr ‹operai, studenti› be self-managing
autoge'stito adj self-managed
auto'gol nm inv Sport own goal
autogo'verno nm home rule, self-rule
au'tografo adj & nm autograph
auto'grill nm inv motorway café
autogrù nf inv breakdown truck, recovery vehicle
autogui'dato adj homing attrib
autoim'mune adj autoimmune
autoiro'nia nf self-mockery
autola'vaggio nm car wash
autolesi'one nf self-inflicted wound
autolesio'nismo nm self-harm; fig self-destruction
autolesio'nistico adj self-destructive
auto'linea nf bus line
au'toma nm robot
automatica'mente adv automatically
auto'matico [1] adj automatic; **auto con cambio** ~ automatic
  [2] nm (bottone) press-stud; (fucile) automatic
automatiz'zare vt automate

a

automatizzazi'one *nf* automation

automazi'one *nf* automation

auto'mezzo *nm* motor vehicle; **uscita automezzi** motor vehicles exit

⚡ **auto'mobile** *nf* [motor] car
■ **automobile da corsa** racing car

automobi'lina *nf* toy car

automobi'lismo *nm* motoring

automobi'lista *nmf* motorist

automobi'listico *adj* ⟨industria⟩ automobile *attrib*

automodel'lismo *nm* model car making; (collezione) model car collecting

autono'leggio *nm* car rental

autonoma'mente *adv* autonomously

autono'mia *nf* autonomy; Auto range; (di laptop, cellulare) battery life

⚡ **au'tonomo** *adj* autonomous

auto'parco *nm* (insieme di auto) fleet of cars

autopat'tuglia *nf* patrol car

auto'pista *nf* [fairground] race track

auto'pompa *nf* fire engine

auto'psia *nf* autopsy

autopunizi'one *nf* self-punishment

auto'radio *nf inv* car radio; (veicolo) radio car

au|'tore, -trice *nmf* author; (di pitture) painter; (di furto ecc) perpetrator; **quadro d'**∼ genuine master

autoreg'gente *nf* (calza) hold-up, stay-up

autoregolamentazi'one *nf* self-regulation

autore'parto *nm* Mil mechanized unit

auto'revole *adj* authoritative; (che ha influenza) influential

autorevo'lezza *nf* authority

autoriduzi'one *nf protest which takes the form of paying less than the requisite amount*

autori'messa *nf* garage

autoriparazi'oni *nfpl* '∼' 'car repairs', 'auto repairs'

⚡ **autorità** *nf inv* authority

autori'tario *adj* autocratic

autorita'rismo *nm* authoritarianism

autori'tratto *nm* self-portrait

autoriz'zare *vt* authorize

autorizzazi'one *nf* authorization

auto'scatto *nm* Phot automatic shutter release

auto'scontro *nm inv* bumper car

autoscu'ola *nf* driving school

autosno'dato *nm* articulated bus

autosoc'corso *nm* breakdown service; (veicolo) breakdown van, breakdown truck

auto'starter *nm inv* Auto self-starter

auto'stop *nm* hitch-hiking, hitching; **fare l'**∼ hitch-hike, hitch

autostop'pista *nmf* hitch-hiker

auto'strada *nf* motorway, highway Am
■ **autostrada dell'informazione** information superhighway; **autostrada a pedaggio** toll motorway; **Autostrada del Sole** Highway of the Sun (*connecting Milan and Reggio Calabria*)

autostra'dale *adj* motorway *attrib*, highway *attrib* Am

autosuffici'ente *adj* self-sufficient

autosuffici'enza *nf* self-sufficiency

autosuggesti'one *nf* autosuggestion

autotrasporta|'tore, -trice *nmf* haulier, carrier

autotra'sporto *nm* road haulage

auto'treno *nm* articulated lorry, roadtrain

autove'icolo *nm* motor vehicle

auto'velox *nm inv* speed camera

autovet'tura *nf* motor vehicle

autun'nale *adj* autumnal; (giornata, vestiti) autumn *attrib*

au'tunno *nm* autumn

aval'lare *vt* endorse, back ⟨cambiale⟩; fig endorse

a'vallo *nm* endorsement

avam'braccio *nm* forearm

avam'posto *nm* Mil forward position

a'vana [1] *nm inv* (sigaro) Havana [cigar]; (colore) tobacco, dark brown
[2] *adj inv* (colore) tobacco-coloured, dark brown

A'vana *nf* Havana

avangu'ardia *nf* vanguard; fig avant-garde; **essere all'**∼ be in the forefront; Techn be at the leading edge; **d'**∼ avant-garde

avansco'perta *nf* reconnaissance; **andare in** ∼ reconnoitre

avanspet'tacolo *nm* **da** ∼ in poor taste

⚡ **a'vanti** [1] *adv* (in avanti) forward; (davanti) in front; (prima) before; ∼! (entrate) come in!; (suvvia) come on!; '∼' (su semaforo) 'cross now', 'walk' Am; ∼ **diritto** straight ahead; **più** ∼ further on; **va'** ∼! go ahead!; **andare** ∼ (precedere) go ahead; ⟨orologio⟩ be fast; ∼ **e indietro** backwards and forwards
[2] *adj* (precedente) before
[3] *prep* ∼ **a** before; (in presenza di) in the presence of

avanti'eri *adv* the day before yesterday

avan'treno *nm* front axle assembly

avanza'mento *nm* progress; (promozione) promotion

⚡ **avan'zare** [1] *vi* advance; (progredire) progress; (essere d'avanzo) be left [over]
[2] *vt* advance; (superare) surpass; (promuovere) promote

avan'zarsi *vr* advance; (avvicinarsi) approach

avan'zata *nf* advance

⚡ indicates a very frequent word

avan'zato *adj* advanced; (nella notte) late; **in età avanzata** elderly

a'vanzo *nm* remainder; Comm surplus; **avanzi** *pl* (rovine) remains; (di cibo) left-overs ■ **avanzo di galera** jailbird

ava'raccio *nm* Scrooge

ava'ria *nf* (di motore) engine failure

avari'arsi *vr* spoil

avari'ato *adj* ‹frutta, verdura› rotten; ‹carne› tainted

ava'rizia *nf* avarice

a'varo, -a [1] *adj* stingy
[2] *nmf* miser

a'vena *nf* oats *pl*

✧ **a'vere** [1] *vt* have; (ottenere) get; (indossare) wear; (provare) feel; **ho trent'anni** I'm thirty; **ha avuto il posto** he got the job; **~ fame/freddo** be hungry/cold; **ho mal di denti** I've got toothache; **cos'ha a che fare con lui?** what has it got to do with him?; **~ da fare** be busy; **~ luogo** take place; **che hai?** what's the matter with you?; **nei hai per molto?** will you be long?; **quanti ne abbiamo oggi?** what date is it today?; **avercela con qualcuno** have it in for somebody
[2] *v aux* have; **non l'ho visto** I haven't seen him; **lo hai visto?** have you seen him?; **l'ho visto ieri** I saw him yesterday
[3] *nm* **averi** *pl* wealth *sg*

avia|'tore, -trice *nmf* aviator

aviazi'one *nf* aviation; Mil Air Force

avicol'tura *nm* poultry farming

avida'mente *adv* avidly

avidità *nf* avidness

'avido *adj* avid

avi'ere *nm* aircraft[s]man

avio'getto *nm* jet [plane]

avio'linea *nf* airline

aviotraspor'tato *adj* airborne

avitami'nosi *nf* vitamin deficiency

a'vito *adj* ancestral

'avo, -a *nmf* ancestor

avo'cado *nm inv* avocado

a'vorio *nm* ivory

a'vulso *adj* **~ dal contesto** fig taken out of context

Avv. *abbr* (**avvocato**) lawyer

avva'lersi *vr* avail oneself (**di** of)

avvalla'mento *nm* depression

avvalo'rare *vt* bear out ‹tesi›; endorse ‹documento›; (accrescere) enhance

avvam'pare *vi* flare up; (arrossire) blush

avvantaggi'are *vt* favour

avvantaggi'arsi *vr* **~ di** benefit from; (approfittare) take advantage of

avve'dersi *vr* (accorgersi) notice; (capire) realize

avve'duto *adj* shrewd

avvelena'mento *nm* poisoning

avvele'nare *vt* poison

avvele'narsi *vr* poison oneself

avvele'nato *adj* poisoned

avve'nente *adj* attractive

avve'nenza *nf* attraction, charm

✧ **avveni'mento** *nm* event

✧ **avve'nire** [1] *vi* happen; (aver luogo) take place
[2] *nm* future

avveni'rismo *nm* excessive confidence in the future

avveni'ristico *adj* futuristic

avven'tarsi *vr* fling oneself

avventata'mente *adv* recklessly

avven'tato *adj* ‹decisione› rash

avven'tizio *adj* (personale) temporary; (guadagno) casual

av'vento *nm* advent; Relig Advent

avven'tore *nm* regular customer

✧ **avven'tura** *nf* adventure; (amorosa) affair; **d'~** ‹film› adventure *attrib*

avventu'rarsi *vr* venture

avventuri'ero, -a [1] *nm* adventurer
[2] *nf* adventuress

avventu'rismo *nm* adventurism

avventu'ristico *adj* adventurist

avventu'roso *adj* adventurous

avve'rabile *adj* ‹previsione› that may come true

avve'rarsi *vr* come true

av'verbio *nm* adverb

avver'sare *vt* oppose

✧ **avver'sario, -a** [1] *adj* opposing
[2] *nmf* opponent

avversi'one *nf* aversion

avversità *nf inv* adversity

av'verso *adj* (sfavorevole) adverse; (contrario) averse

avver'tenza *nf* (cura) care, (avvertimento) warning; (avviso) notice; (premessa) foreword; **avvertenze** *pl* (istruzioni) instructions

avver'tibile *adj* (disagio) perceptible

avverti'mento *nm* warning

✧ **avver'tire** *vt* warn; (informare) inform; (sentire) feel

avvertita'mente *adv* deliberately

avvez'zare *vt* accustom

avvez'zarsi *vr* accustom oneself

av'vezzo *adj* **~ a** used to

avvia'mento *nm* starting; Comm goodwill

✧ **avvi'are** *vt* start

avvi'arsi *vr* set out

avvi'ato *adj* under way; **bene ~** thriving

avvicenda'mento *nm* (in agricoltura) rotation; (nel lavoro) replacement; (delle stagioni) change

avvicen'dare *vt* rotate

avvicen'darsi *vr* take turns, alternate

avvicina'mento *nm* approach

◆ **avvici'nare** *vt* bring near; approach ‹persona›

avvici'narsi *vr* come nearer, approach; avvicinarsi a come nearer to, approach

avvi'lente *adj* demoralizing; (umiliante) humiliating

avvili'mento *nm* despondency; (degradazione) degradation

avvi'lire *vt* dishearten; (degradare) degrade

avvi'lirsi *vr* lose heart; (degradarsi) degrade oneself

avvi'lito *adj* disheartened; (degradato) degraded

avvilup'pare *vt* envelop

avvilup'parsi *vr* wrap oneself up; (aggrovigliarsi) get entangled

avvinaz'zato *adj* drunk

avvin'cente *adj* ‹libro ecc› enthralling

av'vincere *vt* enthral

avvinghi'are *vt* clutch

avvinghi'arsi *vr* cling

av'vio *nm* start-up; **dare l'~ a qualcosa** get something under way; **prendere l'~** get under way

avvi'saglia *nf* (di malattia) first sign

avvi'sare *vt* inform; (mettere in guardia) warn

av'viso *nm* notice; (annuncio) announcement; (avvertimento) warning; (pubblicitario) advertisement; **a mio ~** in my opinion

■ **avviso di accreditamento** advice slip; **avviso a cura del ministero della salute** government health warning; **avviso di chiamata in linea** call waiting; **avviso di garanzia** Jur *notification that one is to be the subject of a legal enquiry*

avvista'mento *nm* sighting

avvi'stare *vt* catch sight of; **~ terra** make landfall

avvi'tare *vt* screw in; screw down ‹coperchio›

avvi'tarsi *vr* ‹aereo› go into a spin

avvi'tata *nf* (di aereo) spin

avviz'zire *vi* wither

avviz'zito *adj* withered

◆ **avvo'cato** *nm* lawyer; fig advocate

■ **avvocato del diavolo** devil's advocate

avvoca'tura *nf* legal profession; (insieme di avvocati) lawyers

av'volgere *vt* wrap [up]

av'volgersi *vr* wrap oneself up

avvol'gibile *nm* roller blind

avvolgi'mento *nm* winding

av'volto *adj* **~ in** wrapped in

avvol'toio *nm* vulture

aza'lea *nf* azalea

Azerbaigi'an *nm* Azerbaijan

azerbaigi'ano, -a *adj & nmf* Azerbaijani

azi'enda *nf* business, firm

■ **azienda agricola** farm; **azienda elettrica** electricity board; **azienda a partecipazioni statali** *enterprise in which the government has a shareholding*; **azienda di soggiorno** tourist bureau

azien'dale *adj* ‹politica, dirigente› company *attrib*; ‹giornale› in-house

azienda'listico *adj* company *attrib*

azio'nabile *adj* which can be operated

aziona'mento *nm* operation

azio'nare *vt* operate

azio'nario *adj* share *attrib*; **mercato azionario** share market

◆ **azi'one** *nf* action; Fin share; **d'~** ‹romanzo, film› action[-packed]; **ad ~ ritardata** delayed action

■ **azione sindacale** industrial action

azio'nista *nmf* shareholder

a'zoto *nm* nitrogen

az'teco, -a *adj & nmf* Aztec

azzan'nare *vt* seize with its teeth; sink its teeth into ‹gamba›

azzar'dare *vt* risk

azzar'darsi *vr* dare

azzar'dato *adj* risky; (precipitoso) rash

az'zardo *nm* hazard

■ **gioco d'azzardo** game of chance

azzec'care *vt* hit; fig (indovinare) guess

azzera'mento *nm* setting to zero; fig

■ **corso di azzeramento** remedial classes *pl*

azze'rare *vt* reset

azzi'mato *adj* dapper

'azzimo *adj* unleavened

azzit'tire *vt* silence, hush

azzit'tirsi *vr* go quiet, fall silent

azzop'pare *vt* lame

Az'zorre *nfpl* **le ~** the Azores

azzuf'farsi *vr* come to blows

azzur'rato *adj* ‹lenti› blue-tinted

◆ **az'zurro** *adj & nm* blue; **principe azzurro** Prince Charming; **gli azzurri** *the Italian national team*

azzur'rognolo *adj* bluish

Bb

babà *nm inv* ~ **al rum** rum baba

bab'beo 1 *adj* foolish
2 *nm* idiot

'babbo *nm* fam dad, daddy
■ **Babbo Natale** Father Christmas

bab'buccia *nf* slipper

babbu'ino *nm* baboon

ba'bordo *nm* Naut port side

baby boom *nm* baby boom

baby'sitter *nmf inv* baby-sitter; **fare il/ la** ~ babysit, do baby-sitting

ba'cato *adj* worm-eaten; **avere il cervello** ~ have a slate loose

'bacca *nf* berry

baccalà *nm inv* dried salted cod

bac'cano *nm* din

bac'cello *nm* pod

bac'chetta *nf* rod; (magica) wand; (di direttore d'orchestra) baton; (di tamburo) drumstick

ba'checa *nf* showcase; (in ufficio) notice board
■ **bacheca elettronica** Comput bulletin board

bacia'mano *nm* kiss on the hand; **fare il** ~ **a qualcuno** kiss somebody's hand

baci'are *vt* kiss

baci'arsi *vr* kiss [each other]

ba'cillo *nm* bacillus

baci'nella *nf* basin; (contenuto) basinful

ba'cino *nm* basin; Anat pelvis; (di porto) dock; (di minerali) field
■ **bacino carbonifero** coalfield; **bacino d'utenza** catchment area

'bacio *nm* kiss; **bacio sulla bocca** kiss on the lips

backgammon *nm* backgammon

'baco *nm* worm
■ **baco da seta** silkworm

'bacon *nm* bacon

ba'cucco *adj* **un vecchio** ~ a senile old man

'bada *nf* **tenere qualcuno a** ~ keep somebody at bay

ba'dare *vi* take care (**a** of); (fare attenzione) look out; **bada ai fatti tuoi!** mind your own business!

ba'dia *nf* abbey

ba'dile *nm* shovel

'badminton *nm* badminton

'baffi *nmpl* moustache *sg*; (di animale) whiskers; **mi fa un baffo** I don't give a damn; **ridere sotto i** ~ laugh up one's sleeve

baf'futo *adj* moustached

ba'gagli *nmpl* luggage, baggage; **ritiro bagagli** baggage claim

bagagli'aio *nm* Rail luggage van, baggage car Am; Auto boot

ba'gaglio *nm* luggage, baggage; Mil kit; **un** ~ a piece of luggage
■ **bagaglio a mano** hand-luggage, hand-baggage; **bagaglio in eccesso, bagaglio eccedente** excess baggage

baga'rino *nm* ticket tout

baga'tella *nf* trifle; Mus bagatelle

baggia'nata *nf* piece of nonsense; **non dire baggianate** don't talk nonsense

Bagh'dad *nf* Baghdad

bagli'ore *nm* glare; (improvviso) flash; fig (di speranza) glimmer

bagna'cauda *nf* vegetables (*especially raw*) *in an oil, garlic and anchovy sauce typical of Piedmont*

ba'gnante *nmf* bather

ba'gnare *vt* wet; (inzuppare) soak; (immergere) dip; (innaffiare) water; ‹mare, lago› wash; ‹fiume› flow through

ba'gnarsi *vr* get wet; (al mare ecc) swim, bathe; **'vietato** ~**'** 'no bathing'

bagnasci'uga *nm inv* edge of the water, waterline

ba'gnato *adj* wet; **bagnato fradicio** soaked

ba'gnino, -a *nmf* life guard

'bagno *nm* bath; (stanza) bathroom; (gabinetto) toilet; (al mare) swim, bathe; **bagni** *pl* (stabilimento) lido; **fare il** ~ have a bath; (nel mare ecc) [have a] swim, bathe; **andare in** ~ go to the bathroom, go to the toilet; **mettere a** ~ soak; **con** ~ ‹camera› en suite
■ **bagno oculare** eyebath; **bagno rivelatore** Phot developing bath; **bagno di sangue** bloodbath; **bagno di sviluppo** Phot developing bath; **bagno turco** Turkish bath

bagnoma'ria *nm* **cuocere a** ~ cook in a double saucepan

bagnoschi'uma *nm inv* bubble bath, foam bath

ba'guette *nf inv* French loaf, baguette

Ba'hamas *nfpl* **le** ~ the Bahamas

Bah'rain *nm* Bahrain, Bahrein

'baia *nf* bay

baio'netta *nf* bayonet

'baita *nf* mountain chalet

bala'ustra, balaustrata *nf* balustrade

balbet'tare *vt/i* stammer; ‹bambino› babble

balbet'tio *nm* stammering; (di bambino) babble

bal'buzie *nf* stutter

balbuzi'ente [1] *adj* stuttering [2] *nmf* stutterer

Bal'cani *nmpl* Balkans

bal'canico *adj* Balkan

balco'nata *nf* Theat balcony, dress circle

balcon'cino *nm*
■ reggiseno a balconcino underwired bra

✧ **bal'cone** *nm* balcony

baldac'chino *nm* canopy; **letto a baldacchino** four-poster bed

bal'danza *nf* boldness

baldan'zoso *adj* bold

bal'doria *nf* revelry; **far ∼ have a riotous time**

Bale'ari *nfpl* **le [isole] ∼** the Balearics, the Balearic Islands

ba'lena *nf* whale

bale'nare *vi* lighten; fig flash; **mi è balenata un'idea** I've just had an idea

bale'niera *nf* whaler

ba'leno *nm* **in un ∼** in a flash

balenot'tera *nf*
■ balenottera azzurra blue whale

ba'lera *nf* dance hall

ba'lestra *nf* crossbow

ba'lia[1] *nf* **in ∼ di** at the mercy of

'balia[2] *nf* wetnurse

ba'listico *adj* ballistic; **perito balistico** ballistics expert

'balla *nf* bale; fam (frottola) tall story

bal'labile *adj* **essere ∼** be good for dancing to

✧ **bal'lare** *vi* dance; **andare a ∼** go dancing

bal'lata *nf* ballad

balla'toio *nm* (nelle scale) landing

balle'rino, -a [1] *nmf* dancer; (classico) ballet dancer [2] *nf* (classica) ballet dancer, ballerina

bal'letto *nm* ballet

bal'lista *nmf* fam bullshitter

✧ **'ballo** *nm* dance; (il ballare) dancing; **sala da ballo** ballroom; **essere in ∼** ‹lavoro, vita› be at stake; ‹persona› be committed; **tirare qualcuno in ∼** involve somebody
■ ballo liscio ballroom dancing; **ballo in maschera** masked ball

ballonzo'lare *vi* skip about

ballot'taggio *nm* second count [of votes]

balne'are *adj* bathing *attrib*; **stagione balneare** swimming season; **stazione balneare** seaside resort

balneazi'one *nf*
■ ‘divieto di balneazione’ ‘no bathing’

✧ indicates a very frequent word

ba'lordo *adj* foolish; (stordito) stunned; **tempo ∼** nasty weather

bal'samico *adj* ‹aria› balmy

'balsamo *nm* balsam; (per capelli) conditioner; (lenimento) remedy

'baltico *adj* Baltic; **il [mar] Baltico** the Baltic [Sea]

balu'ardo *nm* bulwark

'balza *nf* crag; (di abito) flounce

bal'zano *adj* (idea) weird

bal'zare *vi* bounce; (saltare) jump; **∼ in piedi** leap to one's feet

'balzo *nm* bounce; (salto) jump; **prendere la palla al ∼** fig seize an opportunity

bam'bagia *nf* cotton wool; **vivere nella ∼** fig be in clover

✧ **bam'bina** *nf* little girl; (piccola) baby; **ha avuto una ∼** she had a [baby] girl

bambi'naia *nf* nursemaid, nanny

bambi'nata *nf* childish thing to do/say

✧ **bam'bino** *nm* child; (appena nato) baby; **avere un ∼** have a baby; (maschio) have a [baby] boy; **bambini** *pl* children, kids; (piccoli) babies
■ bambino prodigio child prodigy

bambi'none, -a *nmf* pej big *or* overgrown child

bam'boccio *nm* chubby child; (sciocco) simpleton; (fantoccio) rag doll

'bambola *nf* doll

bambo'lotto *nm* male doll

bambù *nm* bamboo

ba'nale *adj* banal

banalità *nf inv* banality

banaliz'zare *vt* trivialize

ba'nana *nf* banana

ba'nano *nm* banana (tree)

✧ **'banca** *nf* bank
■ banca d'affari merchant bank, investment bank; **banca [di] dati** databank; **banca etica** ethical bank; **Banca Europea per la Ricostruzione e lo Sviluppo** European Bank for Reconstruction and Development; **banca degli occhi** eye bank; **banca del sangue** blood bank; **banca dello sperma** sperm bank

banca'rella *nf* stall

bancarel'lista *nmf* stallholder

ban'cario, -a [1] *adj* banking *attrib*; **trasferimento bancario** bank transfer [2] *nmf* bank employee

banca'rotta *nf* bankruptcy; **fare ∼** go bankrupt

banchet'tare *vi* banquet

ban'chetto *nm* banquet

banchi'ere *nm* banker

ban'china *nf* Naut quay; (in stazione) platform; (di strada) path
■ banchina spartitraffico central reservation, median strip Am; **banchina non transitabile** soft verge

ban'chisa nf floe

ᕦ **'banco** nm (di scuola) desk; (di negozio) counter; (di officina) bench; (di gioco, banca) bank; (di mercato) stall; (degli imputati) dock; **sotto ~ under the counter; medicinale da banco** over the counter medicines
■ **banco dei formaggi** (in supermercato) cheese counter; (in mercato) cheese stall; **banco di ghiaccio** ice floe; **banco informazioni** information desk; **banco di nebbia** fog bank; **banco di sabbia** sandbank

'bancomat® nm inv (sportello) cash dispenser, cash machine, cashpoint; (carta) bank card, cash card

ban'cone nm counter; (in bar) bar

banco'nota nf banknote, bill Am; **banco'note** pl paper currency

'banda nf band; (di delinquenti) gang
■ **banda d'atterraggio** Aeron landing strip; **banda larga** Comput broadband; **banda passante** bandwidth; **banda rumorosa** rumble strip

ban'dana nf bandanna

banderu'ola nf weathercock; Naut pennant

ᕦ **bandi'era** nf flag; **cambiare ~ change sides, switch allegiances**

bandie'rina nf (nel calcio) corner flag

bandie'rine nfpl bunting

ban'dire vt banish; (pubblicare) publish; fig dispense with ‹formalità, complimenti›

ban'dista nmf bandsman

bandi'tismo nm banditry

ban'dito nm bandit

bandi'tore nm (di aste) auctioneer

'bando nm proclamation
■ **bando di concorso** job advertisement (published in an official gazette for a job for which a competitive examination has to be sat)

bang nm inv wham
■ **bang sonico** sonic boom

Bangla'desh nm Bangladesh

ᕦ **bar** nm inv bar

'bara nf coffin

ba'racca nf hut; (catapecchia) hovel; **mandare avanti la ~ keep the ship afloat**

barac'cato, -a [1] adj living in a shanty town
[2] nmf shanty town dweller

barac'chino nm (di gelati, giornali) kiosk; Radio CB radio

barac'cone nm (roulotte) circus caravan; (in luna park) booth; fig (organizzazione) lumbering great dinosaur of an organization

barac'copoli nf inv shanty town

bara'onda nf chaos; **non fare ~ don't make a mess**

ba'rare vi cheat

'baratro nm chasm

barat'tare vt barter

ba'ratto nm barter

ba'rattolo nm jar; (di latta) tin

ᕦ **'barba** nf beard; fam (noia) bore; **farsi la ~ shave; in ~ a in spite of; è una ~ (noia) it's boring**

barbabi'etola nf beetroot; **barbabietole** pl beetroot
■ **barbabietola da zucchero** sugar beet

Bar'bados nfpl le ~ Barbados

barbagi'anni nm inv barn owl

bar'barico adj barbaric

bar'barie nf inv barbarity

barba'rismo nm barbarism

'barbaro [1] adj barbarous
[2] nm barbarian

'barbecue nm inv barbecue, BBQ

bar'betta nf Naut painter

barbi'ere nm barber; (negozio) barber's

bar'biglio nm barb

barbi'turico nm barbiturate

bar'bone, -a [1] nm (vagabondo) vagrant; (cane) poodle
[2] nf bag lady

bar'boso adj fam boring

barbu'gliare vi mumble

bar'buto adj bearded

'barca nf boat; **una ~ di fig a lot of**
■ **barca a motore** motorboat; **barca da pesca** fishing boat; **barca a remi** rowing boat, rowboat Am; **barca di salvataggio** lifeboat; **barca a vela** sailing boat, sailboat Am

barcai'olo nm boatman

barcame'narsi vr manage

barca'rola nf Mus barcarole

Barcel'lona nf Barcelona

barcol'lare vi stagger

barcol'loni adv camminare ~ stagger

bar'cone nm barge; (di ponte) pontoon

bar'dare vt harness

bar'darsi vr (hum) dress up

barda'tura nf (per cavallo) harness

ba'rella nf stretcher

barelli'ere nm stretcher-bearer

'Barents nm
■ **mare di Barents** Barents Sea

ba'rese adj from Bari

bari'centro nm centre of gravity

ba'rile nm barrel

bari'lotto nm fig tub of lard

ba'rista [1] nm barman
[2] nf barmaid

ba'ritono nm baritone

bar'lume nm glimmer; **un ~ di speranza** a glimmer of hope

'barman nm inv barman

b

'**baro** *nm* cardsharp
ba'rocco *adj & nm* baroque
ba'rometro *nm* barometer
baro'nale *adj* baronial
ba'rone *nm* baron; **i baroni** fig the top brass
baro'nessa *nf* baroness
'**barra** *nf* bar; (lineetta) oblique; Naut tiller
  ■ **barra delle applicazioni** Comput task bar; **barre** *pl* **laterali antintrusione** Auto side impact bars; **barra dei menu** Comput menu bar; **barra di navigazione** navigation bar; **barra retroversa** backslash; **barra di rimorchio** tow bar; **barra di scorrimento** Comput scroll bar; **barra spaziatrice** space bar; **barra di stato** Comput status bar; **barra degli strumenti** Comput tool bar; **barra di titolo** Comput title bar
bar'rage *nm inv* Sport jump-off
bar'rare *vt* block off ‹strada›
barri'care *vt* barricade
barri'cata *nf* barricade
barri'era *nf* barrier; (stradale) road-block; Geol reef
  ■ **barriera corallina** coral reef; **barriera linguistica** language barrier; **barriera razziale** colour bar; **barriera del suono** sound barrier
bar'rire *vi* trumpet
bar'rito *nm* trumpeting
ba'ruffa *nf* scuffle; **far ~** quarrel
barzel'letta *nf* joke; **~ sporca** *o* **spinta** dirty joke
basa'mento *nm* base; Geol bedrock
ba'sare *vt* base
ba'sarsi *vr* **~ su** be based on; **mi baso su ciò che ho visto** I'm going on [the basis of] what I saw
'**basco, -a** ① *adj & nmf* Basque ② *nm* (copricapo) beret
⚔ '**base** *nf* basis; (fondamento) foundation; Mil base; Pol rank and file; **a ~ di** containing; **in ~ a** on the basis of
  ■ **base di controllo** ground control; **base [di] dati** database; **base d'intesa** common ground; **base logica** logical basis; **base navale** naval base
'**baseball** *nm* baseball
ba'setta *nf* sideburn
basi'lare *adj* basic
ba'silica *nf* basilica
Basili'cata *nf* Basilicata
ba'silico *nm* basil
ba'sista *nm* grass roots politician; (di un crimine) mastermind
'**basket** *nm* basketball
bas'sezza *nf* lowness; (di statura) shortness; (viltà) vileness
bas'sista *nmf* bassist
⚔ '**basso** ① *adj* low; (di statura) short; ‹acqua› shallow; ‹televisione› quiet; (vile) despicable;

parlare a bassa voce speak quietly, speak in a low voice; **la bassa Italia** southern Italy ② *nm* lower part; Mus bass [guitar]; **guardare in ~** look down
basso'fondo *nm* (*pl* **bassifondi**) shallows; **bassifondi** *pl* (quartieri poveri) slums
bassorili'evo *nm* bas-relief
bas'sotto *nm* dachshund
ba'stardo, -a ① *adj* bastard; (di animale) mongrel ② *nmf* bastard; (animale) mongrel
⚔ **ba'stare** *vi* be enough; (durare) last; **basta!** that's enough!, that'll do!; **basta che** (purché) provided that; **basta così** that's enough; **basta così?** is that enough?, will that do?; (in negozio) will there be anything else?; **basta andare alla posta** you only have to go to the post office; **basta che tu lo faccia bene** make sure you do it well
Basti'an con'trario *nm* contrary old so-and-so
basti'mento *nm* ship; (carico) cargo
basti'one *nm* bastion
basto'nare *vt* beat
basto'nata *nf* **dare una ~** a beat with a stick
baston'cino *nm* (da sci) ski pole
  ■ **bastoncino di pesce** fish finger, fish stick Am
ba'stone *nm* stick; (da golf) club; (da passeggio) walking stick
  ■ **bastone da hockey** hockey stick
ba'tosta *nf* blow
bat'tage *nm inv*
  ■ **battage pubblicitario** media hype
⚔ **bat'taglia** *nf* battle; (lotta) fight
battagli'are *vi* battle; fig fight
bat'taglio *nm* (di campana) clapper; (di porta) knocker
battagli'one *nm* battalion
bat'tello *nm* boat; (motonave) steamer
bat'tente *nm* (di porta) wing; (di finestra) shutter; (battaglio) knocker
⚔ '**battere** ① *vt* beat; hit, knock ‹testa, spalla›; (percorrere) scour; thresh ‹grano›; break ‹record› ② *vi* (bussare, urtare) knock; ‹cuore› beat; ‹ali ecc› flap; Tennis serve; **~ a macchina** type; **~ gli occhi** blink; **~ il piede** tap one's foot; **~ le mani** clap [one's hands]; **~ le ore** strike the hours
bat'teri *nmpl* bacteria
batte'ria *nf* battery; Mus drums *pl*; Sport (eliminatoria) heat
  ■ **batteria a bottone** button battery
bat'terico *adj* bacterial
bat'terio *nm* bacterium
batteriolo'gia *nf* bacteriology
batterio'logico *adj* bacteriological
batte'rista *nmf* drummer
'**battersi** *vr* fight

⚔ indicates a very frequent word

bat'tesimo *nm* baptism, christening

battez'zare *vt* baptize, christen

battiba'leno *nm* in un ∼ in a flash

batti'becco *nm* squabble

batticu'ore *nm* palpitation; **mi venne il** ∼ I was scared

bat'tigia *nf* water's edge

batti'mano *nm* applause

batti'panni *nm inv* carpetbeater

batti'scopa *nm inv* skirting board

batti'stero *nm* baptistery

batti'strada *nm inv* outrider; (di pneumatico) tread; Sport pacesetter

battitap'peto *nm inv* carpet sweeper

'battito *nm* (alle tempie) throbbing; (di orologio) ticking; (della pioggia) beating
- **battito cardiaco** heartbeat

batti|'tore, -trice *nmf* Sport batsman

bat'tuta *nf* beat; (colpo) knock; (spiritosaggine) wisecrack; (osservazione) remark; Mus bar; Tennis service; Theat cue; (dattilografia) stroke
- **battuta d'arresto** setback

ba'tuffolo *nm* flock

ba'ule *nm* trunk

bau'xite *nf* bauxite

'bava *nf* dribble; (di cane ecc) slobber; **aver la** ∼ **alla bocca** foam at the mouth

bava'glino *nm* bib

ba'vaglio *nm* gag

bava'rese *nf* ice-cream cake with milk, eggs and cream

'bavero *nm* collar

ba'zar *nm inv* bazaar

ba'zooka *nm inv* bazooka

baz'zecola *nf* trifle

bazzi'care *vt/i* haunt

baz'zotto *adj* soft-boiled

be'arsi *vr* delight (**di** in)

beata'mente *adv* blissfully

beatifi'care *vt* beatify

beati'tudine *nf* bliss

✧ **be'ato** *adj* blissful; Relig blessed; ∼ **te!** lucky you!

beauty-'case *nm inv* toilet bag

bebè *nm inv* baby

bec'caccia *nf* woodcock

bec'care *vt* peck; fig catch

bec'carsi *vr* (litigare) quarrel

bec'cata *nf* beakful; (colpo) peck

beccheggi'are *vi* pitch

bec'chime *nm* birdseed

bec'chino *nm* gravedigger

'becco *nm* beak; (di caffettiera ecc) spout; **chiudi il** ∼ fam shut your trap; **non ha il** ∼ **di un quattrino** fam he's skint; **restare a** ∼ **asciutto** fam end up with nothing
- **becco Bunsen** Bunsen [burner]; **becco a gas** gas burner

bec'cuccio *nm* spout

'beeper *nm inv* beeper

be'fana *nf* legendary old woman who brings presents to children on Twelfth Night; (giorno) Twelfth Night; (donna brutta) old witch

'beffa *nf* hoax; **farsi beffe di qualcuno** mock somebody

bef'fardo *adj* derisory; ‹persona› mocking

bef'fare *vt* mock

bef'farsi *vr* ∼ **di** make fun of

beffeggi'are *vt* taunt

'bega *nf* quarrel; **è una bella** ∼ it's really annoying

be'gonia *nf* begonia

beh *int* well

'beige *adj inv & nm* beige

Bei'rut *nf* Beirut

be'lare *vi* bleat

be'lato *nm* bleating

'belga *adj & nmf* Belgian

'Belgio *nm* Belgium

Bel'grado *nf* Belgrade

Be'lize *nm* Belize

'bella *nf* (in carte, Sport) decider; (innamorata) sweetheart
- **bella di giorno** Bot morning glory; **bella di notte** fig lady of the night

✧ **bel'lezza** *nf* beauty; **che** ∼! how lovely!; **per** ∼ (per decorazione) for decoration; **chiudere/finire in** ∼ end on a high note; **la** ∼ **di tre mesi/500 euro** all of three months/500 euros

belli'cismo *nm* warmongering

belli'cistico *adj* warmongering

'bellico *adj* war *attrib*; **periodo bellico** wartime

bellicosità *nf* belligerence

belli'coso *adj* warlike

bellige'rante *adj & nmf* belligerent

bellige'ranza *nf* belligerence

bellim'busto *nm* dandy

✧ **'bello** [1] *adj* nice; (di aspetto) beautiful; ‹uomo› handsome; (moralmente) good; **cosa fai di** ∼ **stasera?** what are you up to tonight?; **oggi fa** ∼ it's a nice day today; **una bella cifra** a lot; **un bel piatto di pasta** a big plate of pasta; **nel bel mezzo** right in the middle; **un bel niente** absolutely nothing; **bell'e fatto** over and done with; **bell'amico sei!** fine friend you are!; **questa è bella!** that's a good one!; **bel voto** good mark; **il bel mondo** the beautiful people; **le belle arti** the fine arts [2] *nm* (bellezza) beauty; (innamorato) sweetheart; **sul più** ∼ at the crucial moment; **il** ∼ **è che** … the funny thing is that …

beltà *nf* (liter) beauty

'belva *nf* wild beast

be'molle *nm* Mus flat

b

ben ▶ BENE

benché *conj* though, although

'benda *nf* bandage; (per occhi) blindfold

ben'dare *vt* bandage; blindfold ‹occhi›

bendi'sposto *adj* essere ~ **verso** be well-disposed towards

☞ **'bene** [1] *adv* well; **ben** ~ thoroughly; ~**!** good!; **star** ~ (di salute) be well; ‹vestito, stile› suit; (finanziariamente) be well off; **non sta** ~ (non è educato) it's not nice; **sta/va** ~**!** all right!; **ti sta** ~**!** [it] serves you right!; **ti auguro** ~ I wish you well; **voler** ~ **a** love; **di** ~ **in meglio** better and better; **fare** ~ (aver ragione) do the right thing; **fare** ~ **a** ‹cibo› be good for; **una persona per** ~ a good person; **per** ~ (fare) properly; **è ben difficile** it's very difficult; **ben cotto** well done; **come tu ben sai** as you well know; **lo credo** ~**!** I can well believe it!

[2] *nm* good; **per il tuo** ~ for your own good; **beni** *pl* (averi) property *sg*; **un** ~ **di famiglia** a family heirloom; Fin assets

■ **beni ambientali** *pl* environment; **beni di consumo** *pl* consumer products, consumer goods; **beni culturali** *pl* cultural heritage; **beni immobili** *pl* real estate, realty Am; **beni mobili** *pl* movables

benedet'tino *adj & nm* Benedictine

bene'detto *adj* blessed

☞ **bene'dire** *vt* bless; **mandare qualcuno a farsi** ~ fam tell somebody to get lost

benedizi'one *nf* blessing

benedu'cato *adj* well-mannered

benefat|'tore, -'trice *nmf* benefactor; benefactress

benefi'care *vt* help

benefi'cenza *nf* charity

benefici'are *vi* ~ **di** profit by

benefici'ario, -a *adj & nmf* beneficiary

bene'ficio *nm* benefit; **con** ~ **di inventario** with reservations

■ **beneficio accessorio** perquisite

be'nefico *adj* beneficial; (di beneficenza) charitable

'Benelux *nm* Benelux

beneme'renza *nf* benevolence

bene'merito *adj* worthy

bene'placito *nm* consent, approval

be'nessere *nm* well-being

bene'stante [1] *adj* well off [2] *nmf* well-off person

bene'stare *nm* consent

benevo'lenza *nf* benevolence

be'nevolo *adj* benevolent

ben'fatto *adj* well-made

Ben'gala *nm* Bengal

ben'godi *nm* **il paese di** ~ a land of plenty

benia'mino *nm* favourite

be'nigno *adj* kindly; Med benign

Be'nin *nm* Benin

beninfor'mato [1] *adj* well-informed [2] *npl* **i beninformati** those in the know

benintenzio'nato, -a [1] *adj* well-meaning [2] *nmf* well-meaning person

benin'teso *adv* needless to say, of course; ~ **che** ... of course, ...

be'nissimo *int* fine

benpen'sante *adj & nmf* self-righteous

benser'vito *nm* **dare il** ~ **a qualcuno** give somebody the sack

bensì *conj* but rather

benve'nuto *adj & nm* welcome; **benvenuta!** welcome!

ben'visto *adj* essere ~ (da qualcuno) go down well (with somebody)

benvo'lere *vt* **farsi** ~ **da qualcuno** win somebody's affection; **prendere a** ~ **qualcuno** take a liking to somebody; **essere benvoluto da tutti** be well-liked by everyone

benvo'luto *adj* well-liked

ben'zene *nm* benzene

ben'zina *nf* petrol, gas Am; **far** ~ get petrol

■ **benzina avio** aviation fuel; **benzina con piombo** leaded petrol; **benzina senza piombo** *o* **verde** leadfree petrol, unleaded petrol; **benzina super** four-star petrol, premium gas Am

benzi'naio, -a *nmf* petrol station attendant, gas station attendant Am

be'one, -a *nmf* fam boozer

'berbero, -a *adj & nmf* Berber

☞ **'bere** [1] *vt* drink; (assorbire) absorb; fig swallow; ~ **una tazza di tè** have a cup of tea [2] *nm* drinking; **da** ~ **e da mangiare** food and drink

berga'motto *nm* bergamot

'Bering *nm* **il mare di** ~ the Bering Sea; **lo stretto di** ~ the Bering Straits

ber'lina *nf* Auto saloon; **mettere alla** ~ **qualcuno** ridicule somebody

berli'nese [1] *nmf* Berliner [2] *adj* Berlin *attrib*

Ber'lino *nm* Berlin

■ **Berlino Est** East Berlin

ber'muda *nfpl* (pantaloni) Bermuda shorts

Ber'muda *nfpl* **le** ~ the Bermudas

'Berna *nf* Berne

ber'noccolo *nm* bump; (disposizione) flair

ber'retto *nm* beret, cap

■ **berretto a pompon** bobble hat

bersagli'are *vt* fig bombard

ber'saglio *nm* target

bescia'mella *nf* béchamel, white sauce

☞ indicates a very frequent word

be'stemmia nf swearword; (maledizione) oath; (sproposito) blasphemy

bestemmi'are vi swear

✧ **'bestia** nf animal; (persona brutale) beast; (persona sciocca) fool; **andare in** ∼ fam blow one's top; **lavorare come una** ∼ slave away
■ bestia nera fig pet hate

besti'ale adj bestial; ⟨espressione, violenza⟩ brutal; fam ⟨freddo, fame⟩ terrible; **fa un caldo/freddo** ∼ it's dreadfully hot/cold

bestialità nf inv bestiality; fig nonsense

besti'ame nm livestock

betabloc'cante nm betablocker

Be'tlemme nf Bethlehem

betoni'era nf concrete mixer

'bettola nf fig dive

be'tulla nf birch
■ betulla bianca silver birch

be'vanda nf drink
■ bevanda alcolica alcoholic drink

bevi|'tore, -trice nmf drinker

be'vuta nf drink

be'vuto pp di BERE

Bhu'tan nm Bhutan

bi+ pref bi+

bi'ada nf fodder

✧ **bianche'ria** nf linen
■ biancheria per la casa household linen; biancheria intima underwear; (da donna) lingerie; biancheria da letto bed linen

bian'chetto nm whitener

✧ **bi'anco, -a** ① adj white; ⟨foglio⟩ blank; **voce bianca** treble voice
② nmf white
③ nm white; **mangiare in** ∼ eat bland food; **andare in** ∼ fam not score; **in** ∼ **e nero** (film, fotografia) black and white, monochrome; **passare una notte in** ∼ have a sleepless night
■ bianco sporco off white; bianco d'uovo egg white

biancomangi'are nm blancmange

bian'core nm (bianchezza) whiteness

bianco'segno nm Jur blank document bearing a signature

bianco'spino nm hawthorn

biasci'care vt (mangiare) eat noisily; (parlare) mumble

biasi'mare vt blame

biasi'mevole adj blameworthy

bi'asimo nm blame

'Bibbia nf Bible

bibe'ron nm inv [baby's] bottle

'bibita nf [soft] drink
■ bibita alcolica alcopop; bibita gasata fizzy drink

'biblico adj biblical

bibliogra'fia nf bibliography

biblio'grafico adj bibliographical

biblio'teca nf library; (mobile) bookcase

bibliote'cario, -a nmf librarian

bicame'rale adj two-chamber attrib, bicameral

bicarbo'nato nm bicarbonate
■ bicarbonato di sodio bicarbonate of soda

bicchie'rata nf glassful

✧ **bicchi'ere** nm glass

bicchie'rino nm fam tipple

bicente'nario nm bicentenary

'bici nf fam bike

✧ **bici'cletta** nf bicycle, bike; **andare in** ∼ cycle, go by bike; (saper portare la bicicletta) ride a bicycle
■ bicicletta da corsa racer

bi'cipite nm biceps

bi'cocca nf hovel

bico'lore adj two-coloured

bidè nm inv bidet

bi'dello, -a nmf janitor, [school] caretaker

bidirezio'nale adj bidirectional

bido'nare vt con, swindle; **farsi** ∼ be conned

bido'nata nf fam swindle

bi'done nm bin; fam (truffa) swindle; **fare un** ∼ **a qualcuno** fam stand somebody up
■ bidone dell'immondizia, bidone della spazzatura rubbish bin, trash can Am

bidon'ville nf inv shantytown

bi'eco adj callous

bi'ella nf connecting rod

Bielo'russia nf Belarus

bielo'russo, -a adj & nmf Belorussian

bien'nale adj biennial

bi'ennio nm two-year period

bi'erre nf/pl (Brigate Rosse) Red Brigades

bi'etola nf beet

bifo'cale adj bifocal

bi'folco, -a nmf fig boor

bifor'carsi vr fork

biforcazi'one nf fork

bifor'cuto adj forked

biga'mia nf bigamy

'bigamo, -a ① adj bigamous
② nmf bigamist

big bang nm big bang

bighello'nare vi loaf around

bighel'lone nm loafer

bigiotte'ria nf costume jewellery; (negozio) jeweller's

bigliet'taio nm booking clerk; (sui treni) ticket-collector

bigliette'ria nf ticket-office; Theat box-office
■ biglietteria automatica ticket vending machine

⚘ **bigli'etto** *nm* ticket; (lettera breve) note; (cartoncino) card; (di banca) banknote
- biglietto di sola andata single [ticket]; biglietto di andata e ritorno return [ticket]; biglietto di auguri card; biglietto chilometrico *ticket allowing travel up to a maximum specified distance*; biglietto collettivo group ticket; biglietto elettronico e-ticket; biglietto giornaliero day pass; biglietto d'ingresso entrance ticket; biglietto d'invito invitation card; biglietto della lotteria lottery ticket; biglietto da visita business card

bigliet'tone *nm* fam (soldi) big one

bignè *nm inv* puff
- bignè alla crema cream puff

bigo'dino *nm* roller

bi'gotto *nm* bigot

bi'kini *nm inv* bikini

bi'lancia *nf* scales *pl*; (di orologio, Comm) balance; Bilancia Astr Libra
- bilancia commerciale balance of trade; bilancia da cucina kitchen scales; bilancia dei pagamenti balance of payments; bilancia pesapersone scales

bilanci'are *vt* balance; fig weigh

bilancia'tura *nf*
- bilanciatura gomme wheel-balancing

bilanci'ere *nm* (in sollevamento pesi) bar-bell; (di orologio) balance wheel

bi'lancio *nm* budget; Comm balance [sheet]; fare il ~ balance the books; fig take stock; chiudere il ~ in attivo/passivo to end the financial year in profit/with a loss
- bilancio patrimoniale balance sheet; bilancio preventivo budget

bilate'rale *adj* bilateral

'bile *nf* bile; fig rage

bili'ardo *nm* billiards *sg*

'bilico *nm* equilibrium; in ~ in the balance

bi'lingue *adj* bilingual

bilingu'ismo *nm* bilingualism

bili'one *nm* billion

bili'oso *adj* bilious

bilo'cale 1 *adj* two-room
2 *nm* two-room flat

'bimbo, -a *nmf* child
- ~ in fasce babe in arms

bimen'sile *adj* fortnightly Br, twice-monthly

bime'strale *adj* bimonthly

bi'mestre *nm* two months

bi'nario *nm* track; (piattaforma) platform

bi'nocolo *nm* binoculars *pl*

bi'nomio *nm* binomial

bio+ *pref* bio+

bioagricol'tore *nm* organic farmer

bioagricol'tura *nf* organic farming

bio'chimica *nf* biochemistry

bio'chimico, -a 1 *nmf* biochemist
2 *adj* biochemical

biocompa'tibile *adj* biocompatible

biodegra'dabile *adj* biodegradable

biodiversità *nf* biodiversity

bio'etica *nf* bioethics *sg*

bio'fisica *nf* biophysics *sg*

bio'gas *nm* biogas

biogra'fia *nf* biography

bio'grafico *adj* biographical

bi'ografo, -a *nmf* biographer

bioingegne'ria *nf* bioengineering

biolo'gia *nf* biology

biologica'mente *adv* biologically

bio'logico *adj* biological; ‹agricoltura› organic

bi'ologo, -a *nmf* biologist

bi'onda *nf* blonde
- bionda ossigenata peroxide blonde; bionda platinata platinum blonde

⚘ **bi'ondo** 1 *adj* blond
2 *nm* fair colour; (uomo) fair-haired man
- biondo cenere ash blond; biondo platino platinum blonde

bi'onico *adj* bionic

bio'psia *nf* biopsy

bio'ritmo *nm* biorhythm

bio'sfera *nf* biosphere

bi'ossido *nm* dioxide
- biossido di carbonio carbon dioxide

biotecnolo'gia *nf* biotechnology

bioterro'rismo *nm* bioterrorism

bip *nm inv* blip

bipar'titico *adj* bipartisan

biparti'tismo *nm* two-party system

bipar'tito 1 *adj* bipartite, two-party *attrib*
2 *nm* two-party coalition

bipartizi'one *nf* division into two parts

bipo'lare *adj* Electr bipolar; Pol dominated by two large parties

bipola'rismo *nm* Pol *system in which the numerous parties line up behind two main parties*

bipolarizazzi'one *nf* Pol *tendency towards 'bipolarismo'*

bi'posto *adj inv & nm inv* two-seater

'birba *nf*, **birbante** *nm* rascal, rogue

birbo'nata *nf* trick

bir'bone *adj* wicked

birdie *nm inv* (golf) birdie

biri'chino, -a 1 *adj* naughty
2 *nmf* little devil

bi'rillo *nm* skittle; (di segnaletica stradale) traffic cone

Bir'mania *nf* Burma

bir'mano, -a *adj & nmf* Burmese

'birra *nf* beer; a tutta ~ fig flat out

■ **birra chiara** lager; **birra grande** ≈ pint; **birra piccola** ≈ half-pint; **birra scura** dark beer, brown ale Br

birre'ria *nf* beer-house; (fabbrica) brewery

bis *nm inv* encore

bi'saccia *nf* haversack

bi'sbetica *nf* shrew

bi'sbetico *adj* bad-tempered

bisbigli'are *vt/i* whisper

bi'sboccia *nf* **fare** ~ make merry

'bisca *nf* gambling-house

Bi'scaglia *nf* **il golfo di** ~ the Bay of Biscay

'biscia *nf* snake

biscotti'era *nf* biscuit barrel, biscuit tin

bi'scotto *nm* biscuit

■ **biscotto per cani** dog-biscuit

bisessu'ale *adj & nmf* bisexual

bise'stile *adj* **anno** ~ leap year

bisettima'nale *adj* twice-weekly

biset'trice *nf* bisector

bisezi'one *nf* bisection

bisil'labico *adj* two-syllable *attrib*, bisyllabic

bi'slacco *adj* peculiar

bi'slungo *adj* oblong

bi'snonno, -a [1] *nm* great-grandfather [2] *nf* great-grandmother

🗲 **biso'gnare** *vi* **bisogna agire subito** we must act at once; **bisogna farlo** it is necessary to do it; **non bisogna scongelarlo** you don't need to defrost it

🗲 **bi'sogno** *nm* need; (povertà) poverty; **aver** ~ **di** need

biso'gnoso *adj* needy, (povero) poor; ~ **di** in need of

bi'sonte *nm* bison

bi'stecca *nf* steak

■ **bistecca di cavallo** horsemeat steak; **bistecca ai ferri** grilled steak; **bistecca alla fiorentina** large grilled beef steak

bi'sticci *nmpl* bickering

bisticci'are *vi* quarrel

bi'sticcio *nm* quarrel; (gioco di parole) pun

bistrat'tare *vt* mistreat

bistrò *nm inv* bistro

'bisturi *nm inv* scalpel

bi'sunto *adj* very greasy

bit *nm inv* bit

bito'nale *adj* two-tone

bi'torzolo *nm* lump

'bitter *nm inv* bitter aperitif

bi'tume *nm* bitumen

bivac'care *vi* bivouac

bi'vacco *nm* bivouac

'bivio *nm* crossroads; (di strada) fork

bizan'tino *adj* Byzantine

'bizza *nf* tantrum; **fare le bizze** ‹bambini› play up

bizzar'ria *nf* eccentricity

biz'zarro *adj* bizarre

biz'zeffe *adv* **a** ~ galore

'blackjack *nm* blackjack

blan'dire *vt* soothe; (allettare) flatter

'blando *adj* mild

bla'sfemo *adj* blasphemous

bla'sone *nm* coat of arms

blate'rare *vi* blather; ~ **di qualcosa** burble on about something

'blatta *nf* cockroach

'bleso *adj* lisping

blin'dare *vt* armour-plate

blin'dato *adj* armoured

'blinker *nm inv* blinker

'blister *nm inv* blister pack

blitz *nm inv* blitz

🗲 **bloc'care** *vt* block; (isolare) cut off; Mil blockade; Comm freeze; stop ‹assegno›; ~ **l'accesso a** seal off

bloc'carsi *vr* Mech jam

blocca'sterzo *nm* steering lock

bloc'cato *adj* blocked

bloc'chetto *nm*

■ **blocchetto per appunti** memo pad; **blocchetto di biglietti** book of tickets

'blocco *nm* block; Mil blockade; (dei fitti) restriction; (di carta) pad; (unione) coalition; **in** ~ Comm in bulk

■ **blocco chiamate** Teleph call barring; **blocco per appunti** notepad; **blocco psicologico** mental block; **blocco stradale** road-block

block-notes *nm inv* memo pad

blog'gare *vi* blog

blogos'fera *nf* blogosphere

🗲 **blu** *adj & nm* blue

blu'astro *adj* bluish

blue chip *nf inv* Fin blue chip

blue-'jeans *nmpl* jeans

bluff *nm inv* (carte, fig) bluff

bluf'fare *vi* (carte, fig) bluff

'blusa *nf* blouse

'boa [1] *nm* boa [constrictor]; (sciarpa) [feather] boa [2] *nf* Naut buoy

bo'ato *nm* rumbling

bo'bina *nf* spool; (di film) reel; Electr coil

bobi'nare *vt* spool

🗲 **'bocca** *nf* mouth; **a** ~ **aperta** fig dumbfounded; **in** ~ **al lupo!** fam break a leg!; **fare la respirazione** ~ **a** ~ **a qualcuno** give somebody mouth to mouth resuscitation, give somebody the kiss of life; **essere di** ~ **buona** eat anything; fig be easily satisfied; **essere sulla** ~ **di tutti** be the talk of the town

■ **bocca del camino** chimneybreast; **bocca di leone** snapdragon

boccac'cesco *adj* licentious

boc'caccia *nf* grimace; **far boccacce** make faces

boc'caglio *nm* nozzle

boc'cale *nm* jug; (da birra) mug

bocca'porto *nm* Naut hatch

bocca'scena *nm inv* proscenium

boc'cata *nf* (di fumo) puff; **prendere una ~ d'aria** get a breath of fresh air

boc'cetta *nf* small bottle

boccheggi'are *vi* gasp

boc'chino *nm* cigarette holder; (di pipa, Mus) mouthpiece

'boccia *nf* (palla) bowl; **bocce** *pl* (gioco) bowls *sg*; **giocare a bocce** play bowls

bocci'are *vt* (agli esami) fail; (respingere) reject; (alle bocce) hit; **essere bocciato** fail; (ripetere) repeat a year

boccia'tura *nf* failure

bocci'olo *nm* bud

'boccolo *nm* ringlet

boccon'cino *nm* morsel

boc'cone *nm* mouthful; (piccolo pasto) snack

boc'coni *adv* face down[wards]

Bo'emia *nf* Bohemia

bo'emo, -a *adj & nmf* Bohemian

bo'ero, -a *nmf* Afrikaner

bofonchi'are *vi* grumble

boh *int* dunno

'boia *nm* executioner; **fa un freddo ~ fam** it's brass-monkey weather; **ho un sonno ~ fam** I can't keep my eyes open

boi'ata *nf* fam rubbish

boicot'taggio *nm* boycotting

boicot'tare *vt* boycott

bo'lero *nm* bolero

'bolgia *nf* (caos) bedlam

'bolide *nm* meteor; **passare come un ~** shoot past [like a rocket]

Bo'livia *nf* Bolivia

bolivi'ano, -a *adj & nmf* Bolivian

'bolla *nf* bubble; (vescica, in tappezzeria) blister; **finire in una ~ di sapone** go up in smoke

■ **bolla di accompagnamento** packing list; **bolla d'aria** (in acqua) air bubble; **bolla di consegna** packing list; **bolla speculativa** speculative bubble

bol'lare *vt* stamp; fig brand

bol'lato *adj* fig branded; **carta bollata** *paper with stamp showing payment of duty*

bol'lente *adj* boiling [hot]

bol'letta *nf* bill; **essere in ~** be hard up

bollet'tino *nm* bulletin; Comm list

■ **bollettino d'informazione** fact sheet; **bollettino meteorologico** weather report;

bollettino ufficiale gazette

bolli'latte *nm* milk pan

bol'lino *nm* coupon

bol'lire *vt/i* boil

bol'lito *nm* boiled meat

bolli'tore *nm* boiler; (per l'acqua) kettle

bolli'tura *nf* boiling

'bollo *nm* stamp; Auto tax disc

bol'lore *nm* boil; (caldo) intense heat; fig ardour

Bo'logna *nf* Bologna

bolo'gnese *nmf* person from Bologna; **spaghetti alla bolognese** spaghetti bolognese

✧ **'bomba** *nf* bomb; **a prova di ~** bomb-proof; **tornare a ~** get back to the point

■ **bomba atomica** nuclear bomb; **bomba intelligente** smart bomb; **bomba a mano** hand grenade; **bomba molotov** petrol bomb; **bomba ad orologeria** time bomb; **bomba sporca** dirty bomb

✧ **bombarda'mento** *nm* shelling; (con aerei) bombing; fig bombardment

■ **bombardamento aereo** air raid

bombar'dare *vt* shell; (con aerei) bomb; fig bombard; **~ a tappeto** carpet-bomb

bombardi'ere *nm* bomber

bom'bato *adj* domed

'bomber *nm inv* bomber jacket

bom'betta *nf* bowler [hat]

'bombo *nm* bumblebee

'bombola *nf* cylinder

■ **bombola di gas** gas bottle, gas cylinder

bombo'letta *nf* spray can

bombo'lone *nm* doughnut

bomboni'era *nf* wedding keep-sake

bo'naccia *nf* Naut calm

bonacci'one, -a [1] *nmf* good-natured person

[2] *adj* good-natured

bo'nario *adj* kindly

bo'nifica *nf* land reclamation

bonifi'care *vt* reclaim

bo'nifico *nm* Comm discount

■ **bonifico [bancario]** [credit] transfer

✧ **bontà** *nf* goodness; (gentilezza) kindness

'bonus-'malus *nm inv* Auto *car insurance policy with no claims bonus clause*

'boogie *nm* boogie

'bookmaker *nm inv* bookmaker

'boomerang *nm inv* boomerang

boot *nm* Comput boot-up; **eseguire il ~** boot up

'bora *nf cold north-east wind in the upper Adriatic*

borbot'tare *vi* mumble; (stomaco) rumble

borbot'tio *nm* mumbling; (di stomaco) rumbling

'borchia *nf* stud

borchi'ato *adj* studded

bor'dare *vt* border

bor'data *nf* Naut broadside

borda'tura *nf* border

bor'deaux ① *nm inv* (vino) claret, Bordeaux
② *adj inv* (colore) claret

bor'dello *nm* brothel; fig bedlam; (disordine) mess

bor'dino *nm* narrow border

⚡ **'bordo** *nm* border; (estremità) edge; **a ~** Aeron, Naut on board; **d'alto ~** ‹prostituta› high-class
■ **bordo d'attacco** Aeron leading edge

bor'dura *nf* border

bor'gata *nf* hamlet

⚡ **bor'ghese** *adj* bourgeois; ‹abito› civilian; **in ~** in civilian dress; ‹poliziotto› in plain clothes

borghe'sia *nf* middle classes *pl*

'borgo *nm* village; (quartiere) district

'boria *nf* conceit

bori'oso *adj* conceited

bor'lotto *nm*
■ [fagiolo] borlotto pinto bean

'Borneo *nm* Borneo

boro'talco *nm* talcum powder

bor'raccia *nf* flask

⚡ **'borsa** *nf* bag; (borsetta) handbag
■ borsa dell'acqua calda hot-water bottle; borsa frigo cool-box; borsa della spesa shopping bag; borsa di studio scholarship; borsa termica cool bag; borsa da viaggio travel bag

'Borsa *nf*
■ Borsa [valori] Stock Exchange

borsai'olo *nm* pickpocket

bor'seggio *nm* pickpocketing

borsel'lino *nm* purse

bor'sello *nm* (portamonete) purse; (borsetto) man's handbag

bor'setta *nf* handbag

bor'setto *nm* man's handbag

bor'sino *nm* Fin dealing room

bor'sista *nmf* Fin speculator; Sch scholarship holder

bor'sone *nm* carryall

bo'scaglia *nf* woodlands *pl*

boscai'olo *nm* woodman; (guardaboschi) forester

bo'schetto *nm* grove

⚡ **'bosco** *nm* wood

bo'scoso *adj* wooded

'Bosnia *nf* Bosnia

bos'niaco, -a *adj & nmf* Bosnian

Bosnia-Erzego'vina *nf* Bosnia-Herzegovina

boss *nm inv*
■ boss mafioso Mafia boss

'bosso *nm* boxwood

'bossolo *nm* cartridge case

Bot *nm abbr* (**Buoni Ordinari Del Tesoro**) T-bills

bo'tanica *nf* botany

bo'tanico ① *adj* botanical
② *nm* botanist

'botola *nf* trapdoor

Bot'swana *nm* Botswana

'botta *nf* blow; (rumore) bang; **fare a botte** come to blows
■ botta e risposta fig thrust and counter-thrust

botta'trice *nf* monkfish

'botte *nf* barrel

bot'tega *nf* shop; (di artigiano) workshop

botte'gaio, -a *nmf* shopkeeper

botte'ghino *nm* Theatr box-office; (del lotto) lottery-shop

⚡ **bot'tiglia** *nf* bottle; **in ~** bottled

bottiglie'ria *nf* wine shop

bot'tino *nm* loot; Mil booty

'botto *nm* bang; **di ~** all of a sudden

bot'tone *nm* button; Bot bud
■ bottone di carica winder

botu'lismo *nm* botulism

'bourbon *nm inv* bourbon

bo'vini *nmpl* cattle

bo'vino *adj* bovine
■ carne bovina beef

'bowling *nm* bowling, tenpin bowling Br

box *nm inv* (per cavalli) loosebox; (recinto per bambini) play-pen

'boxe *nf* boxing

'boxer *nmpl* jockey shorts

'bozza *nf* draft; Typ proof; (bernoccolo) bump
■ bozza in colonna galley [proof]; bozza definitiva page proof; bozza impaginata page proof; bozza di stampa page proof

boz'zetto *nm* sketch

'bozzolo *nm* cocoon

BR *nfpl abbr* (**Brigate Rosse**) Red Brigades

brac'care *vt* hunt

brac'cetto *nm* **a ~** arm in arm

bracci'ale *nm* bracelet; (fascia) armband

braccia'letto *nm* bracelet; (di orologio) watch-strap
■ braccialetto identificativo identity bracelet

bracci'ante *nm* day labourer

bracci'ata *nf* (nel nuoto) stroke

⚡ **'braccio** *nm* (*pl nf* **braccia**) arm (di fiume, *pl* **bracci**) arm
■ braccio di ferro arm wrestling

bracci'olo *nm* (di sedia) arm[rest]; (da nuoto) armband

'bracco *nm* hound

bracconi'ere *nm* poacher

'brace *nf* embers *pl*; **alla ~** char-grilled

'**brache** *nfpl* fam (pantaloni) britches; **calare le ~** fig chicken out

braci'ere *nm* brazier

braci'ola *nf* chop
■ braciola di maiale pork chop

'**brado** *adj* **allo stato ~** in the wild

braille *nm* Braille

brain-'storming *nm inv* brainstorming

'**brama** *nf* longing

bra'mare *vt* long for

bra'mino *nm* Brahmin

bramo'sia *nf* yearning

'**branca** *nf* branch

'**branchia** *nf* gill

'**branco** *nm* (di cani) pack; pej (di persone) gang

branco'lare *vi* grope

'**branda** *nf* camp-bed

bran'dello *nm* scrap; **a brandelli** in tatters

bran'dina *nf* cot

bran'dire *vt* brandish

'**brandy** *nm inv* brandy

'**brano** *nm* piece; (di libro) passage

bran'zino *nm* sea bass

bra'sare *vt* braise

bra'sato *nm* braised beef with herbs

Bra'sile *nm* Brazil

brasili'ano, -a *adj & nmf* Brazilian

bra'vata *nf* bragging

◆ '**bravo** *adj* good; (abile) clever; (coraggioso) brave; **~!** well done!

bra'vura *nf* skill

'**breccia** *nf* breach; **sulla ~** fig very successful, at the top

brecci'ame *nm* loose chipping *pl*

bre'saola *nf* dried, salted beef sliced thinly and eaten cold

Bre'tagna *nf* Brittany

bre'tella *nf* shoulder-strap; (strada) link road; Mech brace; **bretelle** *pl* (di calzoni) braces, suspenders Am

bretone *adj & nmf* Breton

◆ '**breve** *adj* brief, short; **in ~** briefly; **tra ~** shortly

brevet'tare *vt* patent

bre'vetto *nm* patent; (attestato) licence

brevità *nf* shortness

'**brezza** *nf* breeze

bricco'nata *nf* dirty trick

bric'cone *nm* blackguard; (hum) rascal

'**briciola** *nf* crumb; fig grain

'**briciolo** *nm* fragment; **non hai un ~ di cervello!** you don't have an ounce of common sense!

bridge *nm inv* (carte) bridge

◆ indicates a very frequent word

'**briga** *nf* (fastidio) trouble; (lite) quarrel; **attaccar ~** pick a quarrel; **prendersi la ~ di fare qualcosa** go to the trouble of doing something

◆ **brigadi'ere** *nm* (dei carabinieri) sergeant

brigan'taggio *nm* highway robbery

bri'gante *nm* bandit; (hum) rogue

bri'gare *vi* to intrigue

bri'gata *nf* brigade; (gruppo) group

briga'tista *nmf* Pol member of the Red Brigades

'**briglia** *nf* rein; **a ~ sciolta** at full gallop; fig at breakneck speed

bril'lante ① *adj* brilliant; (scintillante) sparkling
② *nm* diamond

brillan'tina *nf* brilliantine

◆ **bril'lare** *vi* shine; ‹metallo› glitter; (scintillare) sparkle

'**brillo** *adj* tipsy

'**brina** *nf* hoar-frost

brin'dare *vi* toast; **~ a qualcuno** drink a toast to somebody

'**brindisi** *nm inv* toast

'**brio** *nm* vivacity

bri'oche *nf inv* croissant

bri'oso *adj* vivacious

'**briscola** *nf* (seme) trumps

bri'tannico *adj* British

'**brivido** *nm* shiver; (di paura ecc) shudder; (di emozione) thrill; **avere i brividi** have the shivers; **dare i brividi a qualcuno** give somebody the shivers

brizzo'lato *adj* ‹capelli, barba› greying

'**brocca** *nf* jug

broc'cato *nm* brocade

'**broccoli** *nmpl* broccoli *sg*

bro'daglia *nf* pej dishwater

'**brodo** *nm* broth; (per cucinare) stock
■ brodo di manzo beef tea; brodo di pollo chicken broth; (per cucinare) chicken stock; brodo ristretto consommé; brodo vegetale clear broth; (per cucinare) vegetable stock

'**broglio** *nm*
■ broglio elettorale gerrymandering

'**broker** *nmf inv* broker
■ broker d'assicurazioni insurance broker

'**bromo** *nm* Chem bromine

bro'muro *nm* bromide

bronchi'ale *adj* bronchial

bron'chite *nf* bronchitis

bron'chitico *adj* chesty

'**broncio** *nm* sulk; **fare il ~** sulk

bronto'lare *vi* grumble; ‹tuono ecc› rumble; **~ contro qualcuno/qualcosa** grumble or grouch about somebody/something

bronto'lio *nm* grumbling; (di tuono, stomaco) rumbling

bronto'lone, **-a** *nmf* grumbler
'bronzo *nm* bronze; **una faccia di ~** fam a brass neck
bros'sura *nf*
■ edizione in **brossura** paperback
browser *nm* Comput browser
bru'care *vt* ‹pecora› graze
bruciacchi'are *vt* scorch
bruci'ante *adj* burning
brucia'pelo *adv* **a ~** point-blank
✧ **bruci'are** 1 *vt* burn; (scottare) scald; (incendiare) set fire to
2 *vi* burn; (scottare) scald
bruci'arsi *vr* burn oneself
bruci'ato *adj* burnt; fig burnt-out
brucia'tore *nm* burner
brucia'tura *nf* burn
bruci'ore *nm* burning sensation
'bruco *nm* grub
'brufolo *nm* spot, pimple
brufo'loso *adj* spotty, pimply
brughi'era *nf* heath
bruli'care *vi* swarm
bruli'chio *nm* swarming
'brullo *adj* bare
'bruma *nf* mist
Bru'nei *nm* Brunei
✧ **'bruno** *adj* brown; ‹occhi, capelli› dark
brusca'mente *adv* (di colpo) suddenly; (in tono brusco) sharply
bru'schetta *nf* toasted bread rubbed with garlic and sprinkled with olive oil
'brusco *adj* sharp; (persona) brusque, abrupt; (improvviso) sudden
bru'sio *nm* buzzing
bru'tale *adj* brutal
brutalità *nf* brutality
brutaliz'zare *vt* brutalize
'bruto *adj* & *nm* brute
brut'tezza *nf* ugliness
✧ **'brutto** *adj* ugly; ‹tempo, tipo, situazione, affare› nasty; (cattivo) bad
■ **brutta copia** *nf* rough copy; **~ tiro** *nm* dirty trick
brut'tura *nf* ugly thing
bub'bone *nm* Med swelling
'buca *nf* hole; (avvallamento) hollow
■ **buca delle lettere** letter-box
buca'neve *nm inv* snowdrop
bucani'ere *nm* buccaneer
bu'care 1 *vt* make a hole in; (pungere) prick; punch ‹biglietti›
2 *vi* have a puncture
'Bucarest *nf* Bucharest
bu'carsi *vr* prick oneself; (con droga) shoot up
buca'tini *nmpl* pasta similar to spaghetti but thicker and hollow

bu'cato *nm* washing; **fare il ~** do the washing
'buccia *nf* peel, skin; **bucce** *pl* (di frutta) parings
■ **buccia di banana** banana skin
bucherel'lare *vt* riddle
bucherel'lato *adj* pitted
✧ **'buco** *nm* hole
■ **buco della serratura** keyhole
bu'colica *nf* bucolic
bu'colico *nm* bucolic
'Budda *nm* Buddha
bud'dista *nmf* Buddhist
bu'dello *nm* (*pl nf* **budella**) bowel
'budget *nm inv* budget
■ **budget provvisorio** minibudget
budge'tario *adj* budgetary
bu'dino *nm* pudding
✧ **'bue** *nm* (*pl* **buoi**) ox
'bufalo *nm* buffalo
bu'fera *nf* storm; (di neve) blizzard
bufferiz'zato *adj* Comput buffered
buf'fet *nm inv* snack bar; (mobile) sideboard; (pasto) buffet
buf'fetto *nm* cuff
'buffo 1 *adj* funny; Theat comic
2 *nm* funny thing
buffo'nata *nf* (scherzo) joke
buf'fone *nm* buffoon; **fare il ~** play the fool
✧ **bu'gia** *nf* lie; **~ pietosa** white lie
bugi'ardo, **-a** 1 *adj* lying
2 *nmf* liar
bugi'gattolo *nm* cubby-hole
✧ **'buio** 1 *adj* dark
2 *nm* darkness; **al ~** in the dark; **~ pesto** pitch dark
'bulbo *nm* bulb; (dell'occhio) eyeball
Bulga'ria *nf* Bulgaria
'bulgaro, **-a** *adj* & *nmf* Bulgarian
buli'mia *nf* bulimia
bu'limico *nmf* bulimic
'bullo *nm* bully
bul'lone *nm* bolt
'bunker *nm inv* bunker
buona'fede *nf* good faith
buo'nanima *nf* **la ~ di mio zio** my late uncle, God rest his soul
buona'notte *int* good night
buona'sera *int* good evening
buonco'stume *nf* Vice Squad
buondì *int* good day!
✧ **buon'giorno** *int* good morning; (di pomeriggio) good afternoon
buon'grado *nm* **di ~** willingly
buongu'staio, **-a** *nmf* gourmet, foodie fam
buon'gusto *nm* good taste
✧ **bu'ono** 1 *adj* good; (momento) right; **dar ~** (convalidare) accept; **alla buona** easy-going; ···⁝·

‹cena› informal; **buona fortuna!** good luck!; **buona notte/sera** good night/evening; **buon compleanno/Natale!** happy birthday/merry Christmas!; **buon viaggio!** have a good trip!; **buon appetito!** enjoy your meal!; ∼ **senso** common sense; **di buon'ora** early; **a buon mercato** cheap; **una buona volta** once and for all; **buona parte di** the best part of; **tre ore buone** three good hours
2 *nm* good; (in film) goody; (tagliando) voucher; (titolo) bond; **con le buone** gently
■ **buono acquisto** gift token; **buono sconto** money-off-coupon
3 *nmf* **buono, -a a nulla** dead loss
buontem'pone, -a *nmf* happy-go-lucky person
buonu'more *nm* good temper
buonu'scita *nf* retirement bonus; (di dirigente) golden handshake
buratti'naio *nm* puppeteer
burat'tino *nm* puppet
'burbero *adj* surly; (nei modi) rough
bu'rino, -a *nmf* hick
Bur'kina 'Faso *nm* Burkina (Faso)
'burla *nf* joke; **fare una** ∼ **a** play a trick on; **per** ∼ for fun
bur'lare *vt* make a fool of
bur'larsi *vr* ∼ **di** make fun of
bu'rocrate *nm* bureaucrat
burocra'tese *nm* gobbledygook
buro'cratico *adj* bureaucratic
burocra'zia *nf* bureaucracy
bu'rotica *nf* office automation
bur'rasca *nf* storm

burra'scoso *adj* stormy
'burro *nm* butter
■ **burro di arachidi** peanut butter
bur'rone *nm* ravine
Bu'rundi *nm* Burundi
bus *nm inv* Comput bus
■ **bus locale** local bus
bu'scare *vt* catch; **buscarle** fam get a hiding
bu'scarsi *vr* catch
bus'sare *vt* knock
'bussola *nf* compass; **perdere la** ∼ lose one's bearings
'busta *nf* envelope; (astuccio) case
■ **busta affrancata** business reply envelope; **busta a finestra** window envelope; **busta imbottita** Jiffy bag®, padded envelope; **busta paga** pay-packet
busta'rella *nf* bribe
bu'stina *nf* (di tè) tea bag; (per medicine) sachet
'busto *nm* bust; (indumento) girdle; **a mezzo** ∼ half-length
bu'tano *nm* Calor gas®
buttafu'ori *nm inv* bouncer
⚡ **but'tare** *vt* throw; ∼ **giù** (demolire) knock down; (inghiottire) gulp down; scribble down ‹scritto›; fam put on ‹pasta›; (scoraggiare) dishearten; ∼ **via** throw away
but'tarsi *vr* throw oneself; (saltare) jump
butte'rato *adj* pitted
buz'zurro *nm* fam yokel
byte *nm inv* Comput byte

Cc

c.a. *abbr* (**cortese attenzione**). attn.
caba'ret *nm inv* cabaret
cabaret'tistico *adj* cabaret *attrib*
ca'bina *nf* Naut Aeron cabin; (al mare) beach hut; (di funivia) [cable] car
■ **cabina elettorale** polling booth; **cabina di pilotaggio** cockpit; (di aereo di linea) flight deck; **cabina di prova** fitting room; **cabina telefonica** telephone box Br, phone booth
cabi'nato *nm* cabin cruiser
ca'blaggio *nm* Electr wiring
ca'blato *adj* ‹messaggio› cable *attrib*
cablo'gramma *nm* cablegram
cabo'taggio *nm* Naut coastal navigation
cabrio'let *nm inv* Auto convertible

ca'cao *nm* cocoa
ca'care *vi* vulg have a crap
caca'toa *nm inv* cockatoo
'cacca *nf* fam poo, number two
'cacchio *nm* fam hell; **ma che** ∼ **fai/dici?** fam what the hell are you doing/saying?
⚡ **'caccia** **1** *nf* hunt; (con fucile) shooting; (inseguimento) chase; (selvaggina) game
2 *nm inv* Aeron fighter; Naut destroyer; **andare a** ∼ go hunting
■ **caccia alla balena** whaling; **caccia grossa** big game; **caccia all'uomo** man-hunt; **caccia alla volpe** fox hunting
cacciabombardi'ere *nm* Aeron fighter-bomber
cacciagi'one *nf* game

⚡ indicates a very frequent word

cacci'are [1] *vt* hunt; (mandar via) chase away; (scacciare) drive out; (ficcare) shove; **caccia [fuori] i soldi!** fam out with the money!; **~ un urlo** fam let out a yell [2] *vi* go hunting

cacci'arsi *vr* (nascondersi) hide; (andare a finire) get to; **~ nei guai** get into trouble

caccia'tora *nf* **alla ~** Culin chasseur

caccia|'tore, -trice *nmf* hunter
■ **cacciatore di dote** gold digger; **cacciatore di frodo** poacher; **cacciatore di taglie** bounty hunter; **cacciatore di teste** Comm head-hunter

cacciatorpedini'ere *nm inv* destroyer

caccia'vite *nm inv* screwdriver

cacci'ucco *nm*
■ **cacciucco alla livornese** *soup of seafood, tomato and wine served with bread*

cache-'sexe *nm inv* thong

ca'chet *nm inv* Med capsule; (colorante) colour rinse; (stile) cachet

'cachi [1] *nm inv* persimmon [2] *adj inv* (colore) khaki

'cacio *nm* (formaggio) cheese

caci'otta *nf* creamy, fairly soft cheese

'caco *nm* fam persimmon

cacofo'nia *nf* cacophony

'cactus *nm inv* cactus

cada'uno *adj* each

ca'davere *nm* corpse

cada'verico *adj* fig deathly pale

ca'dente *adj* falling; (casa) crumbling

ca'denza *nf* cadence; (ritmo) rhythm; Mus cadenza

caden'zare *vt* give rhythm to

caden'zato *adj* measured

ca'dere *vi* fall; (capelli ecc) fall out; (capitombolare) tumble; (vestito ecc) hang; **far ~** (di mano) drop; **~ dal pero** fam be flabbergasted; **~ dal sonno** feel very sleepy; **lasciar ~** drop; **~ dalle nuvole** fig be taken aback; **~ dalla finestra** fall out of the window

ca'detto *nm* cadet

ca'duta *nf* fall; fig downfall
■ **caduta dei capelli** hair loss; **caduta libera** freefall; **caduta massi** rockfall; (avviso) falling rocks

ca'duto *nm* **i caduti** the dead; **monumento ai caduti** war memorial

caffè *nm inv* coffee; (locale) café
■ **caffè corretto** espresso with a dash of liqueur; **caffè Internet** cybercafé, Internet café; **caffè lungo** weak black coffee; **caffè macchiato** coffee with a dash of milk; **caffè ristretto** extra-strong espresso coffee; **caffè solubile** instant coffee

caffe'ina *nf* caffeine

caffel'latte *nm inv* white coffee

caffette'ria *nf* coffee bar

caffetti'era *nf* coffee-pot

■ **caffettiera a stantuffo** cafetière

cafo'naggine *nf* boorishness

cafo'nata *nf* boorishness

ca'fone, -a *nmf* boor

cafone'ria *nf* (comportamento) boorishness; **è stata una ~** it was boorish

ca'gare *vi* vulg crap; **va' a ~!** go and get stuffed!

cagio'nare *vt* cause

cagio'nevole *adj* delicate

cagli'are *vi* curdle

cagli'arsi *vr* curdle

cagli'ata *nf* curd cheese

caglia'tura *nf* curdling

'cagna *nf* bitch

ca'gnara *nf* fam din

ca'gnesco *adj* **guardare qualcuno in ~** scowl at somebody

ca'gnetto *nm* lapdog

C.A.I. *nm abbr* (**Club Alpino Italiano**) *Italian mountain sports association*

cai'mano *nm* cayman

'caio *nm* so-and-so

'Cairo *nm* **il ~** Cairo

'cala *nf* creek

cala'brese *adj & nmf* Calabrian

Ca'labria *nf* Calabria

cala'brone *nm* hornet

cala'maio *nm* inkpot

calama'retto *nm* small squid

cala'mari *nmpl* squid *sg*

cala'maro *nm* squid

cala'mita *nf* magnet

calamità *nf inv* calamity; **~ pl naturali** natural disasters

calami'tare *vt* draw (attenzione)

ca'lante *adj* waning

ca'lare [1] *vi* come down; (vento) drop; (diminuire) fall; (tramontare) set; **~ di peso** lose weight; **~ di tono** fig drag [2] *vt* (abbassare) lower; (nei lavori a maglia) decrease [3] *nm* (di luna) waning

ca'larsi *vr* lower oneself

ca'lata *nf* (invasione) invasion

'calca *nf* throng

cal'cagno *nm* (*pl f* **calcagna**) heel; **stare alle calcagna di qualcuno** fig follow somebody around

cal'care[1] *nm* limestone

cal'care[2] *vt* tread; (premere) press [down]; **~ la mano** fig exaggerate; **~ le orme di qualcuno** fig follow in somebody's footsteps; **~ le scene** fig tread the boards

'calce[1] *nf* lime
■ **calce viva** quicklime

'calce[2] *nm* **in ~** at the foot of the page

calce'struzzo *nm* concrete

cal'cetto *nm* Sport five-a-side [football]; (da tavolo) table football

calci'are *vt* kick

calcia'tore *nm* footballer

calcifi'carsi *vr* calcify

calcificazi'one *nf* calcification

cal'cina *nf* mortar

calci'naccio *nm* (pezzo di intonaco) flake of plaster; (pezzo di muro) piece of rubble

🔹 **'calcio¹** *nm* kick; Sport football; (di arma da fuoco) butt; **dare un ~ a** kick; **giocare a ~** play football
 ▪ **calcio d'angolo** corner [kick]; **calcio di punizione** free kick; **calcio di rigore** penalty [kick]

'calcio² *nm* Chem calcium

calcio-mer'cato *nm inv* transfer market

'calco *nm* (con carta) tracing; (arte) cast

calco'lare *vt* calculate; (considerare) consider

calco'lato *adj* calculated

calcola'tore 1 *adj* calculating
 2 *nm* calculator; (macchina elettronica) computer
 ▪ **calcolatore digitale** (calcolatrice) calculator

calcola'trice *nf* calculating machine

'calcolo *nm* calculation; Med stone; **per ~** fig out of self-interest; **mi sono fatto i calcoli** fig I've weighed up the pros and cons
 ▪ **calcolo approssimativo** guesstimate; **calcolo biliare** gallstone; **calcolo renale** kidney stone

cal'daia *nf* boiler
 ▪ **caldaia ad accumulo** storage heater

caldar'rosta *nf* roast chestnut

caldeggi'are *vt* support

🔹 **'caldo** 1 *adj* warm; (molto caldo) hot; ‹situazione, zona› dangerous; ‹notizie› latest; **non gli fa né ~ né freddo** fig he doesn't give a damn; **ondata di caldo** heatwave; **tavola calda** snack bar
 2 *nm* heat; **avere ~** be warm, be hot; **fa ~** it's warm, it's hot

caleido'scopio *nm* kaleidoscope

calen'dario *nm* calendar
 ▪ **calendario sportivo** sporting calendar

ca'lesse *nm* gig

cali'brare *vt* calibrate

cali'brato *adj* calibrated; fig balanced; **taglie** *pl* calibrate clothes for non-standard sizes

'calibro *nm* calibre; (strumento) callipers *pl*; **di grosso ~** ‹persona› top *attrib*

'calice *nm* goblet; Relig chalice

californi'ano, -a *adj & nmf* Californian

ca'ligine *nm* fog; (industriale) smog

call-girl *nf inv* call girl

calligra'fia *nf* handwriting; (cinese) calligraphy

calli'grafico *adj* **perizia calligrafica** handwriting analysis

cal'ligrafo, -a *nmf* calligrapher

cal'lista *nmf* chiropodist

'callo *nm* corn; **fare il ~ a** become hardened to

cal'loso *adj* callous

🔹 **'calma** *nf* calm; **mantenere la ~** keep calm; **prendersela con ~** fig take it easy; **fare qualcosa con ~** take one's time doing something

cal'mante 1 *adj* calming
 2 *nm* sedative

🔹 **cal'mare** *vt* calm [down]; (lenire) soothe

cal'marsi *vr* calm down; ‹vento› drop; ‹dolore› die down

calmie'rare *vt* control the prices of

calmi'ere *nm* price control

🔹 **'calmo** *adj* calm

'calo *nm* Comm fall; (di volume) shrinkage; (di peso) loss; **in ~** dwindling

ca'lore *nm* heat; (moderato) warmth; **in ~** (di animale) on heat

calo'ria *nf* calorie

ca'lorico *adj* calorific

calo'rifero *nm* radiator

calorosa'mente *adv* warmly

calorosità *nf* fig warmth

calo'roso *adj* warm

ca'lotta *nf*
 ▪ **calotta cranica** skullcap; **calotta glaciale** icecap; **calotta polare** polar icecap

calpe'stare *vt* trample [down]; fig trample on ‹diritti, sentimenti›; **'vietato ~ l'erba'** 'keep off the grass'

calpe'stio *nm* (passi) footsteps *pl*; (rumore) stamping

ca'lunnia *nf* slander

calunni'are *vt* slander

calunni'oso *adj* slanderous

ca'lura *nf* heat

cal'vario *nm* Calvary; fig trial

calvi'nismo *nm* Calvinism

calvi'nista *nmf* Calvinist

cal'vizie *nf* baldness

'calvo *adj* bald

🔹 **'calza** *nf* (da reggicalze) stocking; (da uomo) sock
 ▪ **calza della befana** ≈ Christmas stocking

calza'maglia *nf* tights *pl*; (per danza) leotard

cal'zante *adj* fig fitting

cal'zare 1 *vt* (indossare) wear; (mettersi) put on
 2 *vi* fit; **~ a pennello** ‹indumenti› fit like a glove

calza'scarpe *nm inv* shoehorn

calza'tura *nf* footwear; **calzature** *pl* footwear *sg*

calzaturi'ficio *nm* shoe factory

cal'zetta *nf* ankle sock; **è una mezza ~** *fig* he's no use

calzet'tone *nm* knee-length woollen sock

cal'zino *nm* sock

calzo'laio *nm* shoe mender

calzole'ria *nf* (negozio) shoe shop

calzon'cini *nmpl* shorts
- **calzoncini da bagno** swimming trunks

cal'zone *nm* Culin *folded pizza with tomato, mozzarella etc inside*

cal'zoni *nmpl* trousers, pants Am
- **calzoni alla cavallerizza** jodhpurs

camale'onte *nm* chameleon

cambi'ale *nf* Comm bill of exchange

cambia'mento *nm* change
- **cambiamento climatico** climate change

✰ **cambi'are** ① *vt* change; move ‹casa›; (fare cambio di) exchange; **~ canale** TV switch over; **~ rotta** Naut alter course; **~ l'aria in una stanza** air a room; **~ sesso** have a sex change
② *vi* change; (fare cambio) exchange

cambi'arsi *vr* change

cambiava'lute *nm* bureau de change

✰ **'cambio** *nm* change; Comm (scambio) exchange; Mech gear; **dare il ~ a qualcuno** relieve somebody; **in ~ di** in exchange for
- **cambio della guardia** changeover; **cambio dell'olio** oil change

Cam'bogia *nf* Cambodia

cambogi'ano *adj* & *nmf* Cambodian

cam'busa *nf* pantry

ca'melia *nf* camellia

✰ **'camera** *nf* room; (mobili) [bedroom] suite; Camera Pol, Comm Chamber
- **camera ammobiliata** bedsit; **camera ardente** chapel of rest; **camera d'aria** inner tube; **camera blindata** strong room; **Camera di Commercio** Chamber of Commerce; **Camera dei Comuni** House of Commons; **Camera dei Deputati** ≈ House of Commons; **Camera dei Lord** House of Lords; **Camera dei Rappresentanti** House of Representatives; **camera doppia** double room; **camera a gas** gas chamber; **camera da letto** bedroom; **camera a due letti** twin room; **camera matrimoniale** double room; **camera oscura** darkroom; **camera degli ospiti** guest room; **camera singola** single room

came'rata¹ *nf* (dormitorio) dormitory; Mil barrack room

came'rata² *nmf* mate

camera'tesco *adj* comradely

camera'tismo *nm* comradeship

cameri'era *nf* maid; (di ristorante) waitress; (in albergo) chamber-maid

✰ **cameri'ere** *nm* manservant; (di ristorante) waiter

came'rino *nm* dressing-room

came'ristico *adj* Mus chamber

'Camerun *nm* il **~** Cameroon

'camice *nm* overall

camice'ria *nf* shirt shop

cami'cetta *nf* blouse

✰ **ca'micia** *nf* shirt; **essere nato con la ~** *fig* be born lucky
- **uovo in camicia** poached egg; **camicia di forza** strait-jacket; **camicia nera** Blackshirt; **camicia da notte** nightdress; (da uomo) nightshirt

camici'aio *nm* (venditore) shirtseller; (sarto) shirtmaker

camici'ola *nf* vest

cami'netto *nm* fireplace
- **caminetto alimentato a carbone** coalfire

ca'mino *nm* chimney; (focolare) fireplace, hearth

'camion *nm inv* lorry Br, truck
- **camion della nettezza urbana** dust-cart Br, garbage truck Am

camion'cino *nm* van

camio'netta *nf* jeep

camio'nista *nmf* lorry driver Br, truck driver

'camma *nf* cam; **albero a camme** Auto camshaft

cam'mello ① *nm* camel; (tessuto) camel-hair
② *adj inv* (colore) camel

cam'meo *nm* cameo

✰ **cammi'nare** *vi* walk; ‹auto, orologio› go; **~ avanti e indietro** pace up and down

cammi'nata *nf* walk; **fare una ~** go for a walk

✰ **cam'mino** *nm* way; **essere in ~** be on the way; **mettersi in ~** set out; **cammin facendo** on the way

camo'milla *nf* camomile; (bevanda) camomile tea

camo'millarsi *vr sl* **camomillati!** don't get your knickers in a twist!, cool it!

Ca'morra *nf* local mafia

camor'rista *nmf* member of the 'Camorra'

ca'moscio *nm* chamois; (pelle) suede

✰ **cam'pagna** *nf* country; (paesaggio) countryside; Comm, Mil campaign; **in ~** in the country
- **campagna elettorale** election campaign; **campagna promozionale** promotional campaign, marketing campaign; **campagna pubblicitaria** publicity campaign

campa'gnola *nf* Auto cross-country vehicle

campa'gnolo, -a ① *adj* rustic
② *nm* countryman
③ *nf* countrywoman

cam'pale *adj* field *attrib*; **giornata campale** fig strenuous day

cam'pana *nf* bell; (di vetro) belljar; **a ∼** bellshaped; **essere sordo come una ∼** be as deaf as a doorpost; **sentire anche l'altra ∼** fig hear the other side of the story; **vivere sotto una ∼ di vetro** fig be mollycoddled; **campane** *pl* **eoliche** wind chimes; **campane** *pl* **a morto** death knell

campa'naccio *nm* cowbell

campa'naro *nm* bell-ringer

campa'nella *nf* (di tenda) curtain ring

campa'nello *nm* door-bell; (cicalino) buzzer

Cam'pania *nf* Campania

campa'nile *nm* bell tower

campani'lismo *nm* parochialism

campani'lista *nmf* person with a parochial outlook

campani'listico *adj* parochial

cam'panula *nf* Bot campanula

cam'pare *vi* live; (a stento) get by; **tirare a ∼** fig live from day to day

cam'pato *adj* **∼ in aria** unfounded

campeggi'are *vi* camp; (spiccare) stand out; **'vietato ∼'** 'no camping'

campeggia|'tore, -trice *nmf* camper

cam'peggio *nm* camping; (terreno) campsite; **andare in ∼** go camping; **fare ∼ libero** camp in the wild

■ **campeggio per roulotte** caravan site

'camper *nm inv* camper (van)

cam'pestre *adj* rural

Campi'doglio *nm* Capitol

'camping *nm inv* campsite

campiona'mento *nm* sampling

campio'nario ① *nm* [set of] samples ② *adj* **fiera campionaria** trade fair

campio'nato *nm* championship

■ **Campionato Mondiale di Calcio** World Cup

campiona'tura *nf* (di merce) range of samples; (in statistica) sampling

■ **campionatura casuale** random sample

⚘ **campi'one** *nm* champion; Comm sample; (esemplare) specimen; **indagine campione** (in statistica) sample

■ **campione gratuito** free sample; **'∼ senza valore'** 'sample, no commercial value'

campio'nessa *nf* ladies' champion

⚘ **'campo** *nm* field; (accampamento) camp; Mil encampment; **abbandonare il ∼** Mil desert in the face of the enemy; fig throw in the towel; **a tutto ∼** fig wide-ranging; **avere ∼ libero** fig have a free hand; **non avere ∼** ‹cellulare› to be out of range; **giocare a tutto ∼** Sport cover the entire pitch

■ **campo d'aviazione** airfield; **campo base** base camp; **campo di battaglia** battlefield; **campo da calcio** football pitch; **campo di**

concentramento concentration camp; **campo in erba** grass court; **campo da golf** golf course; **campo di grano** cornfield; **campo da hockey** hockey field; **campo di mais** cornfield; **campo di prigionia** prison camp; **campo profughi** refugee camp; **campo sportivo** sports ground; **campo di sterminio** death camp; **campo in superficie dura** hard court; **campo da tennis** tennis court

campo'santo *nm* cemetery

'campus *nm inv* (di università) campus

camuf'fare *vt* disguise

camuf'farsi *vr* disguise oneself

ca'muso *adj* **naso ∼** snub nose

'Canada *nm* Canada

cana'dese *adj & nmf* Canadian

ca'naglia *nf* scoundrel; (plebaglia) rabble

⚘ **ca'nale** *nm* channel; (artificiale) canal

■ **Canal Grande** Gran Canal; **canale della Manica** English Channel; **canale di scolo** dyke

canaliz'zare *vt* channel ‹acque, energie›

canalizzazi'one *nf* channelling; (rete) pipes *pl*

'canapa *nf* hemp

■ **canapa indiana** (droga) cannabis

Ca'narie *nfpl* **le ∼** the Canaries

cana'rino *nm* canary

ca'nasta *nf* (gioco) canasta

cancel'labile *adj* erasable; ‹impegno, incontro› which can be cancelled

⚘ **cancel'lare** *vt* cross out; (con la gomma) rub out; fig wipe out; (annullare) cancel; Comput delete, erase

cancel'larsi *vr* be erased, be wiped out

cancel'lata *nf* railings *pl*

cancel'lato *adj* cancelled

cancella'tura *nf* erasure

cancellazi'one *nf* cancellation; Comput deletion; **∼ del debito** (ai paesi poveri) debt relief

cancelle'ria *nf* chancellery; (articoli per scrivere) stationery

cancel'letto *nm* hash sign

cancelli'ere *nm* chancellor; (di tribunale) clerk

cancel'lino *nm* duster

can'cello *nm* gate

cance'rogeno ① *nm* carcinogen ② *adj* carcinogenic

cance'roso *adj* cancerous

can'crena *nf* gangrene; **andare in ∼** become gangrenous

cancre'noso *adj* gangrenous

'cancro *nm* cancer; **Cancro** Astr Cancer; **tropico del Cancro** Tropic of Cancer

candeggi'are *vt* bleach

candeg'gina *nf* bleach

can'deggio *nm* bleaching

can'dela *nf* candle; Auto spark plug; **a lume di** ~ by candle-light; ‹*cena*› candlelit; **tenere la** ~ fig play gooseberry; **il gioco non vale la** ~ the game is not worth the candle
■ **candela magica** sparkler

cande'labro *nm* candelabra

cande'letta *nf* Med pessary

candeli'ere *nm* candlestick

cande'line *nfpl* candles

cande'lotto *nm* (di dinamite) stick
■ **candelotto lacrimogeno** tear gas grenade

candida'mente *adv* innocently

candi'dare *vt* put forward as a candidate

candi'darsi *vr* stand as a candidate

candi'dato, -a *nmf* candidate

candida'tura *nf* Pol candidacy; (per lavoro) application

'candido *adj* snow-white; (sincero) candid; (puro) pure

can'dito 1 *adj* candied 2 *nm* piece of candied fruit

can'dore *nm* whiteness; fig innocence

⚥ **'cane** *nm* dog; (di arma da fuoco) cock; **un tempo da cani** foul weather; **fa un freddo** ~ it's bitterly cold; **non c'era un** ~ fig there wasn't a soul about; **solo come un** ~ fig all on one's own; **essere come** ~ **e gatto** fig fight like cat and dog; **essere un** ~ ‹*attore, cantante*› be appalling, be a dog sl; **fatto da cani** fig ‹*lavoro*› botched; **mangiare da cani** fig eat very badly; **figlio di un** ~ fam son of a bitch
■ **cane da caccia** hunting dog; **cane per ciechi** guide-dog; **cane da corsa** greyhound; **cane da guardia** guard-dog; **cane lupo** alsatian; **cane poliziotto** police dog; **cane da salotto** lapdog; **cane sciolto** fig maverick

ca'nestro *nm* basket; **fare** ~ score a basket

'canfora *nf* camphor

cangi'ante *adj* iridescent; **seta cangiante** shot silk

can'guro *nm* kangaroo

ca'nicola *nf* scorching heat

ca'nile *nm* kennel; (di allevamento) kennels *pl*
■ **canile municipale** dog pound

ca'nino *adj & nm* canine

ca'nizie *nm* white hair

'canna *nf* reed; (da zucchero) cane; (di fucile) barrel; (bastone) stick; (di bicicletta) crossbar; (asta) rod; fam (hashish) joint; **povero in** ~ destitute
■ **canna fumaria** flue; **canna da pesca** fishing-rod; **canna da zucchero** sugar cane

cannabis *nf* cannabis

can'nella *nf* cinnamon

cannel'loni *nmpl*
■ **cannelloni al forno** rolls of pasta stuffed with meat and baked in the oven

can'neto *nm* bed of reeds

can'nibale *nm* cannibal

canniba'lismo *nm* cannibalism

cannocchi'ale *nm* telescope

can'noli *nmpl*
■ **cannoli alla siciliana** *cylindrical pastries filled with ricotta and candied fruit*

canno'nata *nf* cannon shot; **è una** ~ fig it's brilliant

cannon'cino *nm* (dolce) cream horn

can'none *nm* cannon; fig ace

cannoneggia'mento *nm* cannonade

cannoni'era *nf* gunboat

cannoni'ere *nm* (soldato) gunner; (calciatore) top goal scorer

can'nuccia *nf* [drinking] straw; (di pipa) stem

ca'noa *nf* canoe

cano'ismo *nm* canoeing

'canone *nm* canon; (del telefono) standing charge; (affitto) rent; **equo canone** rent set by law

ca'nonica *nf* manse

ca'nonico *nm* canon

canoniz'zare *vt* canonize

canonizzazi'one *nf* canonization

ca'noro *adj* melodious

ca'notta *nf* (estiva) vest top, singlet

canot'taggio *nm* canoeing; (voga) rowing

canotti'era *nf* vest, singlet

canotti'ere *nm* oarsman

ca'notto *nm* [rubber] dinghy

cano'vaccio *nm* (trama) plot; (straccio) duster; (per ricamo) canvas

can'tante *nmf* singer
■ **cantante lirico** opera-singer

⚥ **can'tare** *vt/i* sing; ~ **vittoria** fig crow; **fare** ~ **qualcuno** sl make somebody talk; **me le ha cantate** fam he told me off

canta'storie *nmf inv* story-teller

can'tata *nf* Mus cantata

can'tato *adj* sung

cantau|'tore, -trice *nmf* singer-song-writer

canticchi'are *vt* sing softly; (a bocca chiusa) hum

'cantico *nm* hymn

canti'ere *nm* yard; Naut shipyard; (di edificio) construction site
■ **cantiere navale** naval dockyard; (per piccole imbarcazioni) boatyard

cantie'ristica *nf* construction

canti'lena *nf* singsong; (ninna-nanna) lullaby

can'tina *nf* cellar; (per vini) wine cellar; (osteria) wine shop

⚥ **'canto¹** *nm* singing; (canzone) song; Relig chant; (poesia) poem
■ **canto di Natale** *o* **natalizio** Christmas carol; **canto degli uccelli** birdsong

'**canto²** *nm* (angolo) corner; (lato) side; **dal** ∼ **mio** for my part; **d'altro** ∼ on the other hand

canto'nale *adj* cantonal

canto'nata *nf* **prendere una** ∼ fig drop a clanger

can'tone *nm* canton; (angolo) corner

can'tore *nm* chorister

can'tuccio *nm* nook; **stare in un** ∼ fig hold oneself aloof

ca'nuto *adj* liter whitehaired

canzo'nare *vt* tease

canzona'torio *adj* teasing

canzona'tura *nf* teasing

⚜ **can'zone** *nf* song
■ **canzone d'amore** love song

canzo'netta *nf* fam pop song

canzoni'ere *nm* songbook

'**caos** *nm* chaos

ca'otico *adj* chaotic

cap. *abbr* (**capitolo**) chap., chapter

C.A.P. *nm abbr* (**Codice di Avviamento Postale**) post code, zip code Am

⚜ **ca'pace** *adj* able; (esperto) skilled; ⟨*stadio, contenitore*⟩ big; ∼ **di** (disposto a) capable of; **è** ∼ **a cantare?** can he sing?

capacità *nf inv* ability; (attitudine) skill; (capienza) capacity
■ **capacità d'assorbimento** absorbency; **capacità di credito** creditworthiness; **capacità di memorizzazione** retentiveness; **capacità produttiva** production capacity; **capacità di resistenza** staying power

capaci'tarsi *vr* ∼ **di** (rendersi canto) understand; (accorgersi) realize

ca'panna *nf* hut

capan'nello *nm* knot of people; **fare** ∼ **intorno a qualcuno/qualcosa** gather round somebody/something

ca'panno *nm*
■ **capanno degli attrezzi** garden shed; **capanno da spiaggia** beach hut, cabana

capan'none *nm* shed; Aeron hangar

caparbietà *nf* obstinacy

ca'parbio *adj* obstinate

ca'parra *nf* deposit

capa'tina *nf* short visit; **fare una** ∼ **in città/da qualcuno** pop into town/in on somebody

⚜ **ca'pello** *nm* hair; **non torcere un** ∼ **a qualcuno** fig not lay a finger on somebody; **capelli** *pl* (capigliatura) hair *sg*; **avere i capelli a spazzola** have a crew-cut; **spaccare il** ∼ **in quattro** split hairs; **averne fin sopra i capelli** fig be fed up to the back teeth; **mettersi le mani nei capelli** fig tear one's hair out; **capelli** *pl* **d'angelo** vermicelli

capel'lone *nm* long-haired type, hippie

capel'luto *adj* hairy; **cuoio capelluto** scalp

ca'pestro *nm* noose; **contratto capestro** strait-jacket of a contract

capez'zale *nm* bolster; fig bedside

ca'pezzolo *nm* nipple

capi'ente *adj* capacious

capi'enza *nf* capacity

capiglia'tura *nf* hair

capil'lare *adj* capillary

⚜ **ca'pire** *vt* understand; **non capisco** I don't understand; ∼ **male** misunderstand; **si capisce!** naturally!; **sì, ho capito** yes, I see

⚜ **capi'tale** ① *adj* Jur capital; (principale) main
② *nf* (città) capital
③ *nm* Comm capital
■ **capitale di avviamento** start-up capital; **capitale azionario** Fin equity capital, share capital; **capitale di investimento** investment capital; **capitale di rischio** venture capital; **capitale sociale** Fin share capital

capita'lismo *nm* capitalism

capita'lista *nmf* capitalist

capita'listico *adj* capitalist

capitaliz'zare *vt* capitalize

capitalizzazi'one *nf* capitalization

capita'nare *vt* lead ⟨*rivolta*⟩; Sport captain

capitane'ria *nf*
■ **capitaneria di porto** port authorities *pl*

⚜ **capi'tano** *nm* captain
■ **capitano di lungo corso** Naut captain

⚜ **capi'tare** *vi* (giungere per caso) come; (accadere) happen

'**capite**: **pro** ∼ *adv* per capita

capi'tello *nm* Archit capital

capito'lare *vi* capitulate

capitolazi'one *nf* capitulation

ca'pitolo *nm* chapter

capi'tombolo *nm* headlong fall; **fare un** ∼ tumble down

⚜ '**capo** *nm* head; (chi comanda) boss fam; (di vestiario) item; Geog cape; (in tribù) chief; (parte estrema) top; **a** ∼ (in dettato) new paragraph; **da** ∼ over again; **giramento di** ∼ dizziness; **mal di** ∼ headache; **in** ∼ **a un mese** within a month; **non ha né** ∼ **né coda** ⟨*discorso, ragionamento*⟩ I can't make head nor tail of it
■ **capo d'abbigliamento** item of clothing; **capo d'accusa** Jur charge, count; **capo di bestiame** head of cattle; **Capo di Buona Speranza** Cape of Good Hope; **capo reparto** head of department; **il Capo Verde** Cape Verde

capo'banda *nm* Mus band-master; (di delinquenti) ringleader

capocameri'ere, -a ① *nm* head waiter
② *nf* head waitress

⚜ indicates a very frequent word

ca'pocchia *nf*
■ capocchia di spillo pinhead

ca'poccia *nm* fam (testa) nut

capocci'one, **-a** *nmf* fam brainbox

capo'classe *nmf* ≈ form captain

capocor'data *nmf* (alpinista) leader

capocu'oco, **-a** *nmf* head cook

capo'danno *nm* New Year's Day

capofa'miglia *nm* head of the family

capoffi'cina *nm* head mechanic

capo'fitto *nm* a ~ headlong

capo'giro *nm* giddiness

capo'gruppo *nm* group leader

capola'voro *nm* masterpiece

capo'linea *nm* terminus

capo'lino *nm* fare ~ peep in

capo'lista *nmf* Sport league leaders *pl*; Pol *candidate whose name appears first on the list*

capolu'ogo *nm* main town

capo'mafia *nm* Mafia boss

capo'mastro *nm* master builder

⚔ **capo'rale** *nm* lance-corporal

capore'parto *nmf* department head, head of department

capo'sala *nf inv* Med ward sister

capo'saldo *nm* stronghold

capo'scalo *nm* airline manager

capo'squadra *nm inv* foreman; Sport team captain

capostazi'one *nm inv* stationmaster

capo'stipite *nmf* (di famiglia) progenitor; (di esemplare) archetype

capo'tavola *nmf* (persona) head of the table; sedere a ~ sit at the head of the table

capo'treno *nm* guard

ca'potta *nf* top

capot'tare *vi* somersault

capouf'ficio *nmf* department head

capo'verso *nm* first line; Jur paragraph

capo'volgere *vt* overturn; fig reverse

capo'volgersi *vr* overturn; ‹barca› capsize; fig be reversed

capovolgi'mento *nm* turnaround

capo'volto ① pp di CAPOVOLGERE ② *adj* upside down

'cappa *nf* cloak; (di camino) cowl; (di cucina) hood

cappa'santa *nf* Culin scallop

cap'pella *nf* chapel
■ la Cappella Sistina the Sistine Chapel

cappel'lano *nm* chaplain

cappel'letti *nmpl* small filled pasta parcels

cappelli'era *nf* (per cappelli) hatbox; (in aereo) overhead locker

cappel'lino *nm*
■ cappellino di carta party hat

⚔ **cap'pello** *nm* hat; **tanto di ~! I take my hat off to you!**
■ cappello a cilindro top hat; cappello da cowboy stetson, cowboy hat; cappello di feltro homburg; cappello di paglia straw hat; cappello da sole sun hat

'cappero *nm* caper; capperi! fam gosh!

'cappio *nm* noose; avere il ~ al collo fig have a millstone round one's neck; ‹marito› be henpecked

cap'pone *nm* capon

cap'potto *nm* [over] coat

cappuc'cino *nm* (frate) Capuchin [friar]; (bevanda) white coffee

cap'puccio *nm* hood; (di penna stilografica) cap

'capra *nf* goat; salvare ~ e cavoli fig run with the hare and hunt with the hounds

ca'pretto *nm* kid

ca'priccio *nm* whim; (bizzarria) freak; **fare i capricci** have tantrums

capricci'oso *adj* capricious; ‹bambino› naughty

Capri'corno *nm* Astr Capricorn

capri'foglio *nm* honeysuckle

ca'prino *nm* goat's cheese

capri'ola *nf* somersault

capri'olo *nm* roe (deer)

'capro *nm* [billy-]goat
■ capro espiatorio scapegoat

ca'prone *nm* [billy-] goat

'capsula *nf* capsule; (di proiettile) cap; (di dente) crown

cap'tare *vt* Radio, TV pick up; catch ‹attenzione›

C.A.R. *nm abbr* (**Centro Addestramento Reclute**) basic training camp

cara'bina *nf* carbine

⚔ **carabini'ere** *nm* carabiniere; carabini'eri *pl Italian police force (which is a branch of the army)*

ca'raffa *nf* carafe

Ca'raibi *nmpl* (zona) Caribbean *sg*; (isole) Caribbean Islands; il mar dei ~ the Caribbean [Sea]

Cara'ibico *adj* Caribbean

cara'mella *nf* sweet
■ caramella alla menta mint

cara'mello *nm* caramel

ca'rato *nm* carat

⚔ **ca'rattere** *nm* character; (caratteristica) characteristic; di buon ~ good-natured; in ~ con (intonato) in keeping with; è una persona di ~ (deciso) he's got character
■ carattere jolly Comput wild card; carattere tipografico typeface

caratte'rino *nm* difficult nature

caratte'rista ① *nm* character actor ② *nf* character actress

c

⚘ **caratte'ristico, -a** ❶ adj characteristic; (pittoresco) quaint
❷ nf characteristic

caratteriz'zare vt characterize

caratterizzazi'one nf characterization

cara'tura nf carats; Comm part-ownership

'caravan nm inv caravan

carboi'drato nm carbohydrate

car'bonchio nm anthrax

carbon'cino nm (per disegno) charcoal

⚘ **car'bone** nm coal; **stare sui carboni ardenti** fig be on tenterhooks
■ **carbone fossile** anthracite

carbo'nifero adj carboniferous

car'bonio nm carbon
■ **carbonio 14** carbon-14

carboniz'zare vt burn to a cinder, burn to a crisp; **é morto carbonizzato** he was burned to death

carboniz'zato adj charred

carbu'rante nm fuel

carbu'rare ❶ vt carburize
❷ vi fig be firing on all four cylinders; **il motore carbura male** the mixture is wrong

carbura'tore nm carburettor

carburazi'one nf carburation

car'cassa nf carcass; fig old wreck

carce'rario adj prison attrib

carce'rato, -a nmf prisoner

carcerazione nf imprisonment

⚘ **'carcere** nm prison; (punizione) imprisonment
■ **carcere di massima sicurezza** maximum security prison

carceri'ere, -a nmf gaoler

carci'noma nm carcinoma

carcio'fino nm baby artichoke

carci'ofo nm artichoke

cardel'lino nm goldfinch

car'diaco adj cardiac; **disturbo cardiaco** heart disease

'cardigan nm inv cardigan

cardi'nale adj & nm cardinal

'cardine nm hinge

cardiochi'rurgo nm heart surgeon

cardiolo'gia nf cardiology

cardi'ologo nm heart specialist

cardio'patico nmf person suffering from a heart complaint

cardio'tonico nm heart stimulant

cardiovasco'lare adj cardiovascular

'cardo nm thistle

ca'rena nf Naut bottom

care'naggio nm
■ **bacino di carenaggio** dry dock

ca'rente adj ∼ **di** lacking in

ca'renza nf lack; (scarsità) scarcity

⚘ indicates a very frequent word

care'stia nf famine; (mancanza) dearth

ca'rezza nf stroke; (di madre, amante) caress; **fare una** ∼ **a** stroke; (madre, amante) caress

carez'zare vt stroke; ‹madre, amante› caress

carez'zevole adj fig sweet

'cargo nm inv (nave) cargo boat, freighter; (aereo) cargo plane, freight plane

cari'are vt decay

cari'arsi vi decay

cari'ato adj decayed

⚘ **'carica** nf office; Mil, Electr charge; fig drive; **dotato di una forte** ∼ **di simpatia** really likeable
■ **carica esplosiva** payload

caricabatte'ria nm inv battery charger

⚘ **cari'care** vt load ‹camion, software›; Mil, Electr charge; wind up ‹orologio›; Comput upload ‹programma›

cari'carsi vr Electr charge [up]; ∼ **di lavoro** take on too much work

cari'cato adj fig affected

carica'tore nm (per proiettile) magazine; (per diapositive) carousel

carica'tura nf caricature

caricatu'rale adj grotesque

caricatu'rista nmf caricaturist

⚘ **'carico** ❶ adj loaded (**di** with); ‹colore› strong; ‹orologio› wound [up]; ‹batteria› charged
❷ nm load; (di nave) cargo; (il caricare) loading; **avere un** ∼ **di lavoro** have a heavy workload; **testimone a** ∼ Jur witness for the prosecution; **a** ∼ **di** Comm to be charged to; ‹persona› dependent on
■ **carico utile** payload

'carie nf [tooth] decay

caril'lon nm inv musical box

carino adj pretty, nice-looking; (piacevole) agreeable

ca'risma nm charisma

cari'smatico adj charismatic

⚘ **carità** nf charity; **per** ∼! (come rifiuto) God forbid!

carita'tevole adj charitable

car'linga nf fuselage

car'lino nm pug

carnagi'one nf complexion

car'naio nm fig shambles

car'nale adj carnal; **cugino carnale** first cousin

⚘ **'carne** nf flesh; (alimento) meat; **di** ∼ meaty
■ **carne macinata** mince, ground beef Am; **carne di maiale** pork; **carne di manzo** beef; **carne di vitella** veal

car'nefice nm executioner

carnefi'cina nf slaughter

carne'vale nm carnival

carneva'lesco *adj* carnival

car'nivoro ⟦1⟧ *nm* carnivore
⟦2⟧ *adj* carnivorous

car'noso *adj* fleshy

⚥ **'caro, -a** ⟦1⟧ *adj* dear; **cari saluti** kind regards
⟦2⟧ *nmf* fam darling, dear; **i miei cari** my nearest and dearest

⚥ **ca'rogna** *nf* carcass; fig bastard

caro'sello *nm* merry-go-round

ca'rota *nf* carrot

caro'vana *nf* caravan; (di veicoli) convoy

caro'vita *nm* high cost of living

'carpa *nf* carp

car'paccio *nm finely sliced raw beef with oil, lemon and slivers of Parmesan*

Car'pazi *nmpl* **i ∼** the Carpathians

carpenti'ere *nm* carpenter

car'pire *vt* seize; (con difficoltà) extort

car'pone, carponi *adv* on all fours; **camminare ∼** crawl

car'rabile *adj* suitable for vehicles; **passo ∼ = PASSO CARRAIO**

car'raio *adj* **passo ∼** *entrance to driveway, garage etc where parking is forbidden*

carreggi'ata *nf* roadway; **doppia carreggiata** dual carriageway, divided highway Am; **rimettersi in ∼** fig straighten oneself out

carrel'lata *nf* TV pan; fig (di notizie) round-up

car'rello *nm* trolley; (di macchina da scrivere) carriage; Aeron undercarriage; Cinema, TV dolly
■ **carrello d'atterraggio** Aeron landing gear; **carrello dei dolci** dessert trolley; **carrello portabagagli** luggage trolley, baggage cart Am; **carrello della spesa** shopping trolley

car'retta *nf* (veicolo vecchio) old banger; **tirare la ∼** fig plod along

car'retto *nm* cart

⚥ **carri'era** *nf* career; **di gran ∼** at full speed; **fare ∼** get on

carrie'rismo *nm* careerism

carrie'rista *nmf* **è un ∼** his career is all that matters

carri'ola *nf* wheelbarrow

'carro *nm* cart
■ **carro armato** tank; **carro attrezzi** breakdown vehicle, tow truck, wrecker Am; **carro funebre** hearse; **carro merci** truck

⚥ **car'rozza** *nf* carriage; Rail coach, car
■ **carrozza bagagliaio** Rail guard's van; **carrozza belvedere** Rail observation car; **carrozza cuccette** sleeping car; **carrozza fumatori** Rail smoker; **carrozza letti** Rail sleeping car; **carrozza ristorante** Rail restaurant car, buffet car

carroz'zella *nf* (per bambini) pram; (per invalidi) wheelchair

carrozze'ria *nf* bodywork; (officina) bodyshop

carrozzi'ere *nm* panel beater

carroz'zina *nf* pram; (pieghevole) push-chair, stroller Am

carroz'zone *nm* (di circo) caravan; fig (organizzazione) slow-moving great monster of an organization

car'ruba *nf* carob

car'rubo *nm* carob

car'rucola *nf* pulley

⚥ **carta** *nf* paper; (da gioco) card; (statuto) charter; Geog map
■ **carta di addebito** charge card; **carta d'argento** senior citizens' railcard; **carta assegni** cheque card; **carta assorbente** blotting-paper; **carta carbone** carbon paper; **carta di credito** credit card; **carta crespata** crepe paper; **carta di debito** debit card; **carta fedeltà** loyalty card; **carta geografica** map; **carta d'identità** identity card; **carta igienica** toilet-paper; **carta d'imbarco** boarding pass, boarding card; **carta intelligente** smart card; **carta da lettere** writing-paper; **carta millimetrata** graph paper; **carta da pacchi** wrapping paper; **carta da parati** wallpaper; **carta da regali** giftwrap; **carta di riso** rice paper; **carta SIM** SIM card; **carta smerigliata** emery paper; **carta stagnola** silver paper, silver foil; Culin aluminium foil; **carta straccia** waste paper; **carta stradale** road map; **carta termica** thermal paper; **carta topografica** ≈ Ordnance Survey Map; **carta velina** tissue-paper; **carta verde** Auto green card; **carta vetrata** sandpaper; **carta dei vini** wine-list

car'taccia *nf* waste paper

car'taceo *adj* paper

carta'modello *nm* pattern

cartamo'neta *nf* paper money

carta'pecora *nf* vellum

carta'pesta *nf* papier mâché

cartave'trare *vt* sand [down]

car'teggio *nm* correspondence

car'tella *nf* (per documenti ecc) briefcase; (di cartoncino) folder; (di scolaro) satchel, schoolbag
■ **cartella clinica** medical record

cartel'lina *nf* document wallet, folder

cartel'lino *nm* (etichetta) label; (dei prezzi) price-tag; (di presenza) time-card; **timbrare il ∼** clock in; (all'uscita) clock out

car'tello *nm* sign; (pubblicitario) poster; (stradale) road sign; (di protesta) placard; Comm (di droga) cartel

cartel'lone *nm* poster; Theat bill
■ **cartellone pubblicitario** billboard

cartello'nista *nmf* poster designer

cartello'nistica *nf* poster designing

carti'era *nf* paper-mill

carti'lagine nf cartilage

cartina nf (geografica) map; (per sigarette) cigarette paper
■ cartina di tornasole litmus paper

car'toccio nm paper bag; **al ~** Culin baked in foil

cartogra'fia nf cartography

car'tografo nm cartographer

carto'laio, -a nmf stationer

cartole'ria nf stationer's [shop]

cartolibre'ria nf stationer's and book shop

❖ **carto'lina** nf postcard
■ cartolina postale postcard; cartolina [precetto] call-up papers

carto'mante nmf fortune-teller

carton'cino nm (materiale) card; (biglietto) card

car'tone nm cardboard; (arte) cartoon
■ cartone animato [animated] cartoon; cartone ondulato corrugated cardboard; cartone di uova egg box

car'tuccia nf cartridge; **mezza ~** fig weakling
■ cartuccia d'inchiostro ink cartridge

❖ **'casa** nf house; (abitazione propria) home; (ditta) firm; **amico di ~** family friend; **andare a ~** go home; **uscire di ~** leave the house; **essere di ~** be like one of the family; **fatto in ~** home-made; **~ per ~** house-to-house
■ casa d'aste auction house; casa di correzione ≈ reform school; casa di cura nursing home; casa del custode gatehouse; casa famiglia care home; casa madre Comm parent company; casa di mode fashion house; casa in multiproprietà timeshare; casa popolare council house; casa rifugio women's refuge; casa di riposo old people's home, retirement home; casa dello studente hall of residence; casa per le vacanze holiday home

ca'sacca nf military coat; (giacca) jacket

ca'saccio adv **a ~** at random; **sparare a ~ su qualcuno/qualcosa** take a potshot at somebody/something

ca'sale nm (gruppo di case) hamlet; (casolare) farmhouse

casa'linga nf housewife

casa'lingo ① adj domestic; (fatto in casa) home-made; (amante della casa) home-loving; (semplice) homely
② nm **casalinghi** pl household goods

casa'nova nm inv (donnaiolo) Casanova

ca'sata nf family

ca'sato nm family name

ca'scante adj falling; (floscio) flabby

❖ **ca'scare** vi fall [down]

ca'scata nf (di acqua) waterfall

casca'tore, -trice ① nm stuntman
② nf stuntwoman

cas'chetto nm
■ [capelli a] caschetto bob

ca'scina nf farm building

casci'nale nm farmhouse

'casco nm crash-helmet; (asciugacapelli) [hair-]drier
■ casco di banane bunch of bananas; Caschi blu pl Mil Blue Helmets, Blue Berets

caseggi'ato nm block of flats Br, apartment block

casei'ficio nm dairy

ca'sella nf pigeon-hole
■ casella postale post office box, PO box; (elettronica) mailbox

casel'lante nmf (per treni) signalman; (in autostrada) toll collector

casel'lario nm (mobile) filing cabinet; (di documenti) file
■ casellario giudiziario record of convictions; avere il ~ giudiziario vuoto have no criminal record

ca'sello nm (di autostrada) [motorway] toll booth

case'reccio adj home-made

ca'serma nf barracks pl; **da ~** ‹linguaggio› barrack room attrib
■ caserma dei carabinieri military police station; caserma dei pompieri, caserma dei vigili del fuoco fire station

caser'mone nm pej barracks pl

cash and carry nm inv cash-and-carry

casi'nista nmf fam muddler

ca'sino nm fam (bordello) brothel; fig sl (confusione) racket; (disordine) mess; **un ~ di** loads of; **è un ~** (complicato) it's too complicated

casinò nm inv casino

ca'sistica nf (classificazione) record of occurrences

❖ **'caso** nm chance; (fatto, circostanza, Med, Gram), case; **a ~** at random; **~ mai** if need be; **far ~ a** pay attention to; **non far ~ a** take no account of; **per ~** by chance
■ caso [giudiziario] [legal] case, court case; caso urgente Med emergency case

caso'lare nm farmhouse

'caspita int good gracious

❖ **'cassa** nf till; (di legno) crate; Comm cash; (luogo di pagamento) cash desk; (mobile) chest; (istituto bancario) bank
■ cassa automatica prelievi cash dispenser, automatic teller; cassa comune kitty; cassa continua cash machine; cassa da morto coffin; cassa di risparmio savings bank; cassa toracica ribcage

cassa'forte nf safe

cassa'panca nf linen chest

cas'sata nf ice-cream cake

cas'sero nm Naut quarterdeck

casseru'ola *nf* saucepan

cas'setta *nf* case; (per registratore) cassette; **far buona** ∼ Theatr be good box-office
■ **cassetta degli attrezzi** toolbox; **cassetta delle lettere** postbox, letterbox; **cassetta delle offerte** charity box; **cassetta portapane** breadbin; **cassetta portavalori** cash box; **cassetta del pronto soccorso** first-aid kit; **cassetta di sicurezza** strong-box, safe-deposit box

cas'setto *nm* drawer; (di fotocopiatrice ecc) tray
■ **cassetto di inserimento [dei] fogli** paper feed tray

casset'tone *nm* chest of drawers

cassi'ere, -a *nmf* cashier; (di supermercato) checkout assistant, checkout operator; (di banca) teller

cassinte'grato, -a *nmf* person who has been laid off

cas'sone *nm* (cassa) chest; (per acqua) cofferdam

casso'netto *nm* rubbish bin, wheelie bin, trash can Am

'casta *nf* caste

ca'stagna *nf* chestnut; **prendere qualcuno in** ∼ fig catch somebody in the act
■ **castagna d'India** horse chestnut

casta'gnaccio *nm* tart from Tuscany made with chestnut flour

casta'gneto *nm* chestnut grove

ca'stagno *nm* chestnut[-tree]

casta'gnola *nf* (petardo) firecracker

ca'stano *adj* chestnut; ‹occhi, capelli› brown

ca'stello *nm* castle; (impalcatura) scaffold
■ **castello incantato** enchanted castle; **castello di sabbia** sandcastle

casti'gare *vt* punish

casti'gato *adj* (casto) chaste; ‹abito, atteggiamento› prim and proper

ca'stigo *nm* punishment

castità *nf* chastity

'casto *adj* chaste

ca'storo *nm* beaver

ca'strante *adj* fig frustrating

ca'strare *vt* castrate

ca'strato *adj* castrated; (inibito) inhibited; (cantante) castrato

castrazi'one *nf* gelding

ca'strone *nm* gelding

castrone'ria *nf* fam rubbish

'casual *nm inv* casual wear

casu'ale *adj* chance *attrib*

casual'mente *adv* by chance

ca'supola *nf* little house

cata'clisma *nm* fig upheaval

cata'comba *nf* catacomb

cata'falco *nm* catafalque

cata'fascio *nm* **andare a** ∼ go to rack and ruin

cata'litico *adj* **marmitta catalitica** Auto catalytic converter

cataliz'zare *vt* fig heighten

cataliz'zato *adj* Auto fitted with a catalytic converter

catalizza'tore ① *adj* Phys catalysing; **centro** ∼ fig catalyst
② *nm* Auto catalytic converter; fig catalyst

catalo'gabile *adj* which can be listed

catalo'gare *vt* catalogue

catalogazi'one *nf* cataloguing

cata'logna *nf* type of chicory with large leaves

ca'talogo *nm* catalogue

catama'rano *nm* (da diporto) catamaran

cata'pecchia *nf* hovel; fam dump

cata'pulta *nf* catapult

catapul'tare *vt* (scaraventare fuori) eject

catapul'tarsi *vr* (precipitarsi) dive

catarifran'gente *nm* reflector

ca'tarro *nm* catarrh

catar'roso *adj* ‹voce› catarrhal

ca'tarsi *nf inv* catharsis

ca'tartico *adj* cathartic

ca'tasta *nf* pile

cata'stale *adj* **registro** ≈ land registry; **rendita** ≈ revenue from landed property

ca'tasto *nm* land register

ca'tastrofe *nf* catastrophe

cata'strofico *adj* catastrophic

catastro'fismo *nm* catastrophe theory

catch *nm* all-in wrestling

cate'chismo *nm* catechism

catego'ria *nf* category

cate'gorico *adj* categorical

categoriz'zare *vt* categorize

ca'tena *nf* chain
■ **catena montuosa** mountain range; **catene da neve** *pl* [snow] chains

cate'naccio *nm* bolt

cate'nella *nf* (collana) chain; (di orologio) watch chain; **tirare la** ∼ (del gabinetto) flush, pull the plug

cate'nina *nf* chain

cate'ratta *nf* cataract

ca'terva *nf* **una** ∼ **di** heaps of, loads of

ca'tetere *nm* catheter

'catgut *nm inv* catgut

cati'nella *nf* basin; **piovere a catinelle** bucket down

ca'tino *nm* basin

ca'todico *adj* cathode; **raggi catodici** cathode rays

ca'torcio *nm* fam old wreck

catra'mare *vt* tar

ca'trame *nm* tar

'cattedra *nf* (tavolo di insegnante) desk; (di università) chair

catte'drale *nf* cathedral

catte'dratico, -a ① *nmf* professor ② *adj* ‹pedante› pedantic; ‹insegnamento› university *attrib*

catti'veria *nf* wickedness; (azione) wicked action; **fare una ∼ a qualcuno** be nasty to somebody

cattività *nf* captivity

✧ **cat'tivo** *adj* bad; ‹bambino› naughty

cattocomu'nista *nmf* Catholic-communist

cattoli'cesimo *nm* Catholicism

✧ **cat'tolico, -a** *adj & nmf* [Roman] Catholic

cat'tura *nf* capture

cattu'rare *vt* capture

cau'casico, -a *nmf* Caucasian

'Caucaso *nm* **il ∼** the Caucasus

cauc'ciù *nm* rubber

✧ **'causa** *nf* cause; Jur lawsuit; **far ∼ a qualcuno** sue somebody
■ **causa di forza maggiore** circumstances beyond one's control; (in assicurazione) act of God

cau'sale *adj* causal

cau'sare *vt* cause

'caustico *adj* caustic

cauta'mente *adv* cautiously

cau'tela *nf* caution

caute'lare *vt* protect

caute'larsi *vr* take precautions

cauteriz'zare *vt* cauterize

cauterizzazi'one *nf* cauterization

'cauto *adj* cautious

cauzi'one *nf* security; (per libertà provvisoria) bail; (deposito) deposit

cav. *abbr* (**cavaliere**) Kt, Knight

'cava *nf* quarry; fig mine

caval'care *vt* ride; (stare a cavalcioni) sit astride

caval'cata *nf* ride; (corteo) cavalcade

cavalca'via *nm* flyover

cavalci'oni: a ∼ *adv* astride

✧ **cavali'ere** *nm* rider; (titolo) knight; (accompagnatore) escort; (al ballo) partner

cavalle'resco *adj* chivalrous

cavalle'ria *nf* chivalry; Mil cavalry

cavalle'rizzo, -a ① *nm* horseman ② *nf* horsewoman

caval'letta *nf* grasshopper

caval'letto *nm* trestle; (di macchina fotografica) tripod; (di pittore) easel

caval'lina *nf* (ginnastica) horse; (gioco) leapfrog; **correre la ∼** fig pursue a life of pleasure

caval'lino *adj* equine

✧ indicates a very frequent word

✧ **ca'vallo** *nm* horse; (misura di potenza) horsepower; (scacchi) knight; (dei pantaloni) crotch; **a ∼** on horseback; **andare a ∼** go horse-riding
■ **cavallo di battaglia** war horse; **cavallo a dondolo** rocking-horse; **cavallo da tiro** carthorse; **cavallo di Troia** Trojan horse

caval'lona *nf* pej ungainly female

caval'lone *nm* (ondata) roller

caval'luccio *nm*
■ **cavalluccio marino** sea horse

✧ **ca'vare** *vt* take out; (di dosso) take off; **cavarsela** get away with it; **se la cava bene** he's/she's doing all right

cavasti'vali *nm inv* bootjack

cava'tappi *nm inv* corkscrew

ca'veau *nm inv* (di banca) vault

ca'verna *nf* cave

caver'nicolo, -a *nmf* cave dweller

caver'noso *adj* ‹voce› deep

ca'vetto *nm* Electr lead

ca'vezza *nf* halter; **mettere la ∼ al collo a qualcuno** put somebody on a tight rein

'cavia *nf* guinea-pig

cavi'ale *nm* caviar

ca'viglia *nf* ankle

cavil'lare *vi* quibble

ca'villo *nm* quibble

cavil'loso *adj* pettifogging

cavità *nf inv* cavity

'cavo ① *adj* hollow ② *nm* cavity; (di metallo) cable; Naut rope
■ **televisione via cavo** cable TV; **cavo di collegamento** [connecting] cable; **cavo seriale** serial cable; **cavo di spiegamento** ripcord

cavo'lata *nf* fam rubbish; **non dire cavolate** fam don't talk rubbish; **non fare cavolate** fam don't act like an idiot

cavo'letto *nm*
■ **cavoletto di Bruxelles** Brussels sprout

cavolfi'ore *nm* cauliflower

'cavolo *nm* cabbage; **∼!** fam sugar!; **non ho capito un ∼** fam I understood bugger-all; **che ∼ succede?** what the heck is going on?
■ **cavolo cappuccio** spring cabbage

caz'zata *nf* vulg shit; **non dire cazzate** don't talk shit; **non fare cazzate** don't fuck things up

'cazzo ① *vulg nm* prick ② *int* fuck!; **non capisce un ∼** he doesn't understand a fucking thing; **non me ne importa un ∼!** I don't give a fuck!; **sono cazzi miei!** it's my fucking business!

caz'zotto *nm* punch; **prendere qualcuno a cazzotti** beat somebody up

cazzu'ola *nf* trowel

CB *nf abbr* (**banda cittadina**) CB

cc *abbr* (**centimetri cubi**) cc

c/c *abbr* (**conto corrente**) c/a

ccn *nf abbr* (**copia carbone nascosta**) bcc

CCT *nm abbr* (**Certificato di Credito del Tesoro**) T-bill

CD *nm inv* CD

CD-ROM *nm inv* CD-Rom

⚥ **ce** ⓵ *pers pron* (a noi) us; **ce lo ha dato** he gave it to us
⓶ *adv* there; **ce ne sono molti** there are many; **ce ne vuole!** it takes some doing!

cec'chino *nm* sniper; Pol *MP who votes against his own party*

'cece *nm* chickpea

Ce'cenia *nf* Chechnya

cecità *nf* blindness

'ceco, -a *adj & nmf* Czech; **la Repubblica Ceca** the Czech Republic

Cecoslo'vacchia *nf* Hist Czechoslovakia

⚥ **'cedere** ⓵ *vi* (arrendersi) surrender; (concedere) yield; (sprofondare) subside
⓶ *vt* give up; make over ‹proprietà ecc›

ce'devole *adj* ‹terreno ecc› soft; fig yielding

ce'diglia *nf* cedilla

cedi'mento *nm* (di terreno) subsidence

'cedola *nf* coupon

cedo'lino *nm* (dello stipendio) wage slip

'cedro *nm* (albero) cedar; (frutto) citron

C.E.E. *nf abbr* (**Comunità Economica Europea**) E[E]C

cefa'lea *nf* headache

ce'falo *nm* mullet

'ceffo *nm* (muso) snout; pej (persona) mug

cef'fone *nm* slap

ce'lare *vt* conceal

ce'larsi *vr* conceal oneself

ce'lato *adj* concealed

cele'brare *vt* celebrate, observe ‹festività›

celebra'tivo *adj* celebratory

celebrazi'one *nf* celebration

⚥ **'celebre** *adj* famous

celebrità *nf inv* celebrity

'celere ⓵ *adj* swift; **corso celere** crash course
⓶ *nf* (polizia) flying squad

celerità *nf* speed; **con ∼** speedily

ce'leste ⓵ *adj* (divino) heavenly
⓶ *adj & nm* (colore) pale blue

celesti'ale *adj* celestial

celi'bato *nm* celibacy

'celibe ⓵ *adj* single
⓶ *nm* bachelor

'cella *nf* cell
■ **cella frigorifera** cold store; **cella di isolamento** solitary confinement

+cello *suff* **monticello** *nm* mound; **praticello** *nm* small meadow

'cellofan *nm inv* cellophane; Culin cling film

cellofa'nare *vt* wrap in cling film

⚥ **'cellula** *nf* cell
■ **cellula fotoelettrica** electronic eye

cellu'lare *nm* (telefono) mobile (phone), cell phone; **furgone ∼** police van; **telefono ∼** mobile (phone)

cellu'lite *nf* cellulite

cellu'litico *adj* full of cellulite

cellu'loide *adj* celluloid; **il mondo della ∼** fig the celluloid world

cellu'losa *nf* cellulose

'Celsius *adj inv* Celsius

'celta *nm* Celt

'celtico *adj* Celtic

'cembalo *nm* Mus cembalo, harpsichord

cemen'tare *vt* cement

cementifi'care *vt* turn into a cement jungle

cementificazi'one *nf* turning into a cement jungle

cementi'ficio *nm* cement factory

cemen'to *nm* cement
■ **cemento armato** reinforced concrete

⚥ **'cena** *nf* dinner; (leggera) supper; (festa) dinner party

ce'nacolo *nm* circle

ce'nare *vi* have dinner; **∼ fuori** eat out

'cencio *nm* rag; (per spolverare) duster; **bianco come un ∼** white as a sheet

cenci'oso *adj* in rags

'cenere *nf* ash; (di carbone ecc) cinders *pl*; **le Ceneri** *pl* Ash Wednesday

Cene'rentola *nf* Cinderella

ce'netta *nf* (cena semplice) informal dinner; (cena intima) romantic dinner

'cenno *nm* sign; (col capo) nod; (con la mano) wave; (allusione) hint; (breve resoconto) mention; **far ∼ di sì** nod

ce'none *nm* **il ∼ di Capodanno/Natale** *special New Year's Eve/Christmas Eve dinner*

ceno'tafio *nm* cenotaph

censi'mento *nm* census

cen'sire *vt* take a census of

CENSIS *nm abbr* (**Centro Studi Investimenti Sociali**) *national opinion research institute*

cen'sore *nm* censor

cen'sura *nf* censorship

censu'rare *vt* censor

centelli'nare *vt* sip; fig measure out carefully

cente'nario, -a ⓵ *adj & nmf* centenarian
⓶ *nm* (commemorazione) centenary

centen'nale *adj* centennial

cen'tesimo ⓵ *adj* hundredth ⋯⟶

2 *nm* hundredth; (di dollaro, euro) cent; **non avere un** ~ be penniless

cen'tigrado *adj* centigrade

cen'tilitro *nm* centilitre

cen'timetro *nm* centimetre

centi'naia *nfpl* hundreds

◆ **centi'naio** *nm* hundred

◆ **'cento** *adj & nm* a *or* one hundred; **per** ~ percent

centodi'eci *nm* a *or* one hundred and ten; ~ **e lode** Univ ≈ first class honours

centome'trista *nmf* Sport one hundred metres runner

cento'mila *nm* a *or* one hundred thousand

◆ **cen'trale** **1** *adj* central
2 *nf* (di azienda ecc) head office
■ **centrale atomica** atomic power station; **centrale elettrica** power station, power plant; **centrale idroelettrica** hydroelectric power station; **centrale nucleare** nuclear power station; **centrale operativa** (di polizia) operations room; **centrale telefonica** [telephone] exchange

centra'lina *nf* Teleph switchboard; (apparecchiatura) junction box

centralinista *nmf* (switchboard/telephone) operator

centra'lino *nm* Teleph exchange; (di albergo ecc) switchboard

centra'lismo *nm* centralism

centraliz'zare *vt* centralize

cen'trare *vt* ~ **qualcosa** hit something in the centre; (fissare nel centro) centre; fig hit on the head ⟨idea⟩

cen'trato *adj* ⟨tiro, colpo⟩ well-aimed; fig ⟨osservazione⟩ right on target

centrat'tacco *nm* Sport centre forward

cen'trifuga *nf* spin-drier
■ **centrifuga [asciugaverdure]** shaker; **centrifuga elettrica** juice extractor

centrifu'gare *vt* Techn centrifuge; ⟨lavatrice⟩ spin

cen'trino *nm* doily

cen'trismo *nm* Pol centrism

cen'trista *adj* Pol centrist

◆ **'centro** *nm* centre; **in** ~ ⟨essere⟩ in town; ⟨andare⟩ into town
■ **centro di accoglienza** detention centre; **centro di attrazione** focal point; **centro benessere** wellness centre; **centro città** city centre, midtown Am; **centro commerciale** shopping centre, mall; **centro di costi** Comm cost centre; **centro culturale** arts centre; **centro di gravità** centre of gravity; **centro di identificazione ed espulsione** immigration removal centre; **centro di informazioni turistiche** tourist information office; **centro operativo** Mil operations room; **centro polisportivo** sports centre; **centro di**

◆ indicates a very frequent word

riabilitazione halfway house; **centro sociale** community centre; **centro sportivo** leisure centre; **centro storico** old town

centrocam'pista *nm* Sport midfield player, midfielder

centro'campo *nm* midfield

centro'destra *nm inv* Pol centre right

centromedi'ano *nm* Sport centre half

centrosi'nistra *nm inv* Pol centre left

centro'tavola *nm inv* centre-piece

centupli'care *vt* fig multiply

'ceppo *nm* (di albero) stump; (da ardere) log; fig (gruppo) stock

'cera *nf* wax; (aspetto) look
■ **cera d'api** beeswax; **cera per auto** car wax; **cera per il pavimento** floor-polish

cera'lacca *nf* sealing-wax

ce'ramica *nf* (arte) ceramics *sg*; (materia) pottery; (oggetto) piece of pottery

cera'mista *nmf* ceramicist

ce'rata *nf* (giacca) waxed jacket

ce'rato *adj* ⟨tela⟩ waxed

cerbi'atto *nm* fawn

cerbot'tana *nf* blowpipe

'cerca *nf* andare in ~ **di** look for

cercaper'sone *nm inv* beeper; **chiamare con il** ~ beep

◆ **cer'care** **1** *vt* look for
2 *vi* ~ **di** try to

cerca|'tore, -trice *nmf*
■ **cercatore d'oro** gold seeker

'cerchia *nf* circle
■ **cerchia familiare** family circle

cerchi'are *vt* circle, draw a circle around ⟨parola⟩

cerchi'ato *adj* ⟨occhi⟩ black-ringed

cerchi'etto *nm* (per capelli) hairband

'cerchio *nm* circle; (giocattolo) hoop

cerchi'one *nm* alloy wheel

cere'ale *nm* cereal

cerea'licolo *adj* grain *attrib*, cereal *attrib*

cere'brale *adj* cerebral

'cereo *adj* waxen

ce'retta *nf* depilatory wax; **fare la** ~ wax

cer'foglio *nm* chervil

◆ **ceri'monia** *nf* ceremony
■ **cerimonia inaugurale** induction ceremony; **cerimonia nuziale** marriage ceremony; **cerimonia di premiazione** awards ceremony

cerimoni'ale *nm* ceremonial

cerimoni'ere *nm* master of ceremonies

cerimoni'oso *adj* ceremonious

ce'rino *nm* [wax] match

cerni'era *nf* hinge; (di borsa) clasp
■ **cerniera lampo** zip[-fastener], zipper Am

'cernita *nf* selection

'cero *nm* candle

ce'rone *nm* greasepaint

ce'rotto *nm* [sticking] plaster

■ cerotto callifugo corn plaster; cerotto [transdermico] alla nicotina nicotine patch

certa'mente *adv* certainly

cer'tezza *nf* certainty

certifi'care *vt* certify

certifi'cato *nm* certificate

■ certificato medico doctor's note, sick note; certificato di morte death certificate

certificazi'one *nf* certification

■ certificazione di bilancio Fin auditors' report

⚹ **'certo** ⃞1 *adj* certain; ‹notizia› definite; (indeterminativo) some; **sono ~ di riuscire** I am certain to succeed; **a una certa età** at a certain age; **certi giorni** some days; **un ~ signor Giardini** a Mr Giardini; **una certa Anna** somebody called Anna; **certa gente** *pej* some people; **ho certi dolori!** I'm in such pain!; **certi** *pron pl* some; (alcune persone) some people

⃞2 *adv* of course; **sapere per ~** know for certain, know for sure; **di ~** surely; **~ che … surely …**

cer'tosa *nf* Carthusian monastery

certo'sino *nm* Carthusian [monk]; **pazienza certosina** exceptional patience

cer'tuni *pron* some

ce'rume *nm* earwax

⚹ **cer'vello** *nm* brain; **avere un ~ da gallina** be a bird-brain

cervel'lone, -a *nmf* hum brainbox

cervel'lotico *adj* (macchinoso) over-elaborate

cervi'cale *adj* cervical

'cervice *nf* cervix

'cervo *nm* deer

ce'sareo *adj* Med Caesarean; **parto cesareo** Caesarean

cesel'lare *vt* chisel

cesel'lato *adj* chiselled

cesella'tura *nf* chiselling

ce'sello *nm* chisel

ce'soie *nfpl* shears

'cespite *nm* source of income

ce'spuglio *nm* bush

cespugli'oso *adj* ‹terreno› bushy

⚹ **ces'sare** ⃞1 *vi* stop, cease

⃞2 *vt* stop

ces'sate *nm*

■ cessate il fuoco ceasefire

ces'sato *adj* **~ allarme/pericolo** all clear

cessazi'one *nf* cessation

■ cessazione d'esercizio closing down

cessi'one *nf* handover

'cesso *nm sl* (gabinetto) bog, john Am; fig (locale, luogo) dump

'cesta *nf* [large] basket

ce'stello *nm* (di lavatrice) drum

cesti'nare *vt* throw away; bin ‹lettera›; turn down ‹proposta›

ce'stino *nm* [small] basket; (per la carta straccia) waste-paper basket; Comput recycle bin, trashcan Am

'cesto *nm* basket

■ cesto della biancheria linen basket

ce'sura *nf* caesura

ce'taceo *nm* cetacean

'ceto *nm* [social] class

'cetra *nf* lyre

cetrio'lino *nm* gherkin

cetri'olo *nm* cucumber

cfr *abbr* (**confronta**) cf

C.G.I.L. *nf abbr* (**Confederazione Generale Italiana del Lavoro**) *trades union organization*

'Chad *nm* Chad

cha'let *nm inv* chalet

cham'pagne *nm inv* champagne

'chance *nf inv* chance

chape'ron *nm inv* chaperone

char'lotte *nf inv* ice-cream cake with fresh cream, biscuits and fruit

'charter *nm inv* charter plane; **volo charter** charter flight

chat'tare *vi* chat

⚹ **che** ⃞1 *rel pron* (persona: soggetto) who; (persona: oggetto) whom; (cosa, animale) which; **questa è la casa ~ ho comprato** this is the house [that] I've bought; **il ~ mi sorprende** which surprises me; **dal ~ deduco che …** from which I gather that …; **avere di ~ vivere** have enough to live on; **grazie! - non c'è di che!** thank you - don't mention it; **il giorno ~ ti ho visto** fam the day I saw you

⃞2 *inter adj* what; (esclamativo: con aggettivo) how; (con nome) what a; **~ macchina prendiamo, la tua o la mia?** which car are we taking, yours or mine?; **~ bello!** how nice!; **~ idea!** what an idea!; **~ bella giornata!** what a lovely day!

⃞3 *inter pron* what; **a ~ pensi?** what are you thinking about?

⃞4 *conj* that; (comparazioni) than; **credo ~ abbia ragione** I think [that] he is right; **era così commosso ~ non riusciva a parlare** he was so moved, [that] he couldn't speak; **aspetto ~ telefoni** I'm waiting for him to phone; **è da un po' ~ non lo vedo** it's been a while since I saw him; **mi piace più Roma ~ Milano** I like Rome better than Milan; **~ ti piaccia o no** whether you like it or not; **~ io sappia** as far as I know

'checca *nf* fam queen

checché *pron* whatever

check-'in *nm inv* check-in; **fare il ~ check in**

check-'up *nm inv* Med check-up; **fare un ~** have a check-up

cheese'burger *nm inv* cheeseburger

'chef nm inv chef
'chela nf nipper
chemiotera'pia nf chemotherapy, chemo fam
chemisi'er nm inv chemise
chero'sene nm paraffin
cheru'bino nm cherub
che'tare vt quieten
che'tarsi vr quieten down
cheti'chella: alla ∼ adv silently
'cheto adj quiet
⚜ **chi** ① rel pron whoever; (coloro che) people who; **ho trovato ∼ ti può aiutare** I found somebody who can help you; **c'è ∼ dice che …** some people say that …; **senti ∼ parla!** look who's talking!
② inter pron (soggetto) who; (oggetto, con preposizione) whom; (possessivo) **di ∼** whose; **∼ sei?** who are you?; **∼ hai incontrato?** who did you meet?, whom did you meet? fml; **di ∼ sono questi libri?** whose books are these?; **con ∼ parli?** who are you talking to?, to whom are you talking? fml; **a ∼ lo dici!** tell me about it!
chi'acchiera nf chat; (pettegolezzo) gossip; **chiacchiere** pl chitchat; **far quattro chiacchiere** have a chat
chiacchie'rare vi chat; (far pettegolezzi) gossip
chiacchie'rato adj essere ∼ ⟨persona⟩ be the subject of gossip
chi'acchiere nfpl (dolci) sweet pastries fried and sprinkled with icing sugar
chiacchie'rone, -a ① adj talkative ② nmf chatterbox
⚜ **chia'mare** vt call; (far venire) send for; **come ti chiami?** what's your name?; **mi chiamo Roberto** my name is Robert; **∼ alle armi** call up; **mandare a ∼** send for; **∼ a rapporto** debrief
chia'marsi vr be called
chia'mata nf call; Mil call-up
■ **chiamata a carico del destinatario** reverse charge call, transferred charge call; **chiamata interurbana** long-distance call; **chiamata in teleselezione** direct dialling, toll call Am; **chiamata urbana** local call
chi'appa nf fam cheek
chiara'mente adv clearly
chia'rezza nf clarity; (limpidezza) clearness
chiarifi'care vt clarify
chiarifica'tore adj clarificatory
chiarificazi'one nf clarification
chiari'mento nm clarification
chia'rire vt make clear; (spiegare) clear up
chia'rirsi vr become clear
⚜ **chi'aro** adj clear; (luminoso) bright; ⟨colore⟩ light; ⟨capelli⟩ fair

⚜ indicates a very frequent word

chia'rore nm glimmer
chiaro'scuro nm (tecnica) chiaroscuro
chiaroveg'gente ① adj clear-sighted ② nmf clairvoyant
chi'asso nm din
chiassosa'mente adv (rumorosamente) rowdily; (vistosamente) gaudily
chias'soso adj (rumoroso) rowdy; (vistoso) gaudy
chi'atta nf canal boat, canal barge
⚜ **chi'ave** nf key; **chiudere a ∼** lock
■ **chiave dell'accensione** ignition key; **chiave di basso** Mus bass clef; **chiave inglese** monkey-wrench; **chiave [inglese] a rullino** adjustable spanner; **chiave USB** ▶ CHIAVETTA USB
chia'vetta nf (in tubi) key
■ **chiavetta USB** USB key
chiavi'stello nm latch
chi'azza nf stain
■ **chiazza di petrolio** oil-slick
chiaz'zare vt stain
chiaz'zato adj dappled
chic adj inv chic
chicches'sia pron anybody
chicchirichì nm inv cock-a-doodle-doo
'chicco nm grain; (di caffe) bean; (d'uva) grape
■ **chicco di caffè** coffee bean; **chicco di grandine** hailstone; **chicco d'orzo** barleycorn
⚜ **chi'edere** vt ask; (per avere) ask for; (esigere) demand; **∼ notizie di** ask after
chi'edersi vr wonder
chieri'chetto nm altar boy
chi'erico nm cleric
⚜ **chi'esa** nf church
■ **Chiesa anglicana** Church of England
chi'esto pp di CHIEDERE
chif'fon nm chiffon
'chiglia nf keel
chi'gnon nm inv bun
'chilo nm kilo
⚜ **chilo'grammo** nm kilogram[me]
chilo'hertz nm inv kilohertz
chilome'traggio nm Auto ≈ mileage
chilo'metrico adj in kilometres; fig endless
⚜ **chi'lometro** nm kilometre
'chilowatt nm inv kilowatt
chilowat'tora nm inv kilowatt hour
chi'mera nf fig illusion
'chimica nf chemistry
■ **chimica organica** organic chemistry
'chimico, -a ① adj chemical ② nmf chemist
chi'mono nm kimono
'china nf (declivio) slope; **inchiostro di china** Indian ink
chi'nare vt lower

chi'narsi *vr* stoop

chincaglie'rie *nfpl* knick-knacks

chinesitera'pia *nf* physiotherapy

chi'nino *nm* quinine

'chino *adj* bent

chi'notto *nm sparkling soft drink*

chintz *nm* chintz

chi'occia *nf* sitting hen

chi'occiola *nf* snail; Comput at sign, @
■ **scala a chiocciola** spiral staircase

chio'dato *adj* pneumatici chiodati snow
tyres; **scarpe chiodate** shoes with crampons

chi'odo *nm* nail; (idea fissa) obsession
■ **chiodo di garofano** clove

chi'oma *nf* [head of] hair; (fogliame) foliage

chi'osco *nm* kiosk; (per giornali) news-stand

chi'ostro *nm* cloister

chip *nm inv*
■ **chip** [di silicio] chip

'chipset *nm inv* chipset

chiro'mante *nmf* fortune teller, palmist

chiroman'zia *nf* palmistry

chiro'pratico, -a *nmf* chiropractor

chirur'gia *nf* surgery
■ **chirurgia endoscopica** keyhole surgery;
chirurgia estetica cosmetic surgery

chirurgica'mente *adv* surgically

chi'rurgico *adj* surgical

chi'rurgo *nm* surgeon

ᵍ **chissà** *adv* who knows; ~ **quando arriverà**
I wonder when he will arrive

chi'tarra *nf* guitar
■ **chitarra acustica** acoustic guitar; **chitarra
basso** bass guitar

chitar'rista *nmf* guitarist

ᵍ **chi'udere** ① *vt* shut, close; (con chiave)
lock; turn off, switch off ‹luce ecc›; turn off
‹acqua›; (per sempre) close down ‹negozio,
fabbrica ecc›; (recingere) enclose; **chiudi il
becco!** shut up!
② *vi* shut, close; (con chiave) lock up

chi'udersi *vr* shut; ‹tempo› cloud over;
‹ferita› heal over; fig withdraw into oneself

ᵍ **chi'unque** ① *pron* anyone, anybody
② *rel pron* whoever

chi'usa *nf* enclosure; (di canale) lock;
(conclusione) close

chi'uso ① *pp di* CHIUDERE
② *adj* closed, shut; ‹cielo› overcast;
‹persona› reserved; '~ **per turno**' 'closing
day'

chiu'sura *nf* closing; (sistema) lock;
(allacciatura) fastener; '~ **settimanale il lunedi**'
'closed on Mondays'
■ **chiusura centralizzata** Auto central locking;
chiusura lampo zip, zipper Am

ᵍ **ci** ① *pron* (personale) us; (riflessivo) ourselves;
(reciproco) each other; (a ciò, di ciò ecc) about
it; **non ci disturbare** don't disturb us;
aspettateci wait for us; **ci ha detto tutto** he

told us everything; **ci consideriamo ... we**
consider ourselves ...; **ci laviamo le mani**
we wash our hands; **ci odiamo** we hate each
other; **non ci penso mai** I never think about
it; **pensaci!** think about it!
② *adv* (qui) here; (lì) there; (moto per luogo)
through it; **ci siamo** here we are; **ci siete?**
are you there?; **ci siamo passati tutti** we
all went through it; **c'è** there is; **ci vuole
pazienza** it takes patience; **non ci vedo/
sento** I can't see/hear

C.ia *abbr* (**compagnia**) Co.

cia'batta *nf* slipper

ciabat'tare *vi* shuffle

ciabat'tino *nm* cobbler

ci'ac *nm inv* Cinema ~ **sigira!** action!

ci'alda *nf* wafer

cial'trone *nm* (mascalzone) scoundrel;
(fannullone) wastrel

ciam'bella *nf* Culin ring-shaped cake;
(salvagente) lifebelt; (gonfiabile) rubber ring

ci'ance *nfpl* yapping

cianci'are *vi* gossip

cianfru'saglie *nfpl* knick-knacks

cia'notico *adj* ‹viso› puce

cia'nuro *nm* cyanide

ᵍ **ci'ao** *int* fam (all'arrivo) hello!, hi!; (alla partenza)
bye-bye!, cheerio!

ciar'lare *vi* chat

ciarla'tano *nm* charlatan

ciarli'ero *adj* (loquace) talkative

ᵍ **cia'scuno** ① *adj* each
② *pron* everyone, everybody; (distributivo)
each [one]; **per** ~ each

ci'bare *vt* feed

ci'barie *nfpl* provisions

ci'barsi *vr* eat; ~ **di** live on

ciber'netica *nf* cybernetics *sg*

ciber'netico *adj* cybernetic

ciber'spazio *nm* cyberspace

ᵍ **'cibo** *nm* food; **non toccare** ~ leave one's
food untouched; **non ha toccato** ~ **da ieri** he
hasn't had a bite to eat since yesterday
■ **cibo per animali** pet food; **cibi** *pl* **precotti**
ready meals

ci'cala *nf* cicada

cica'lino *nm* buzzer

cica'trice *nf* scar

cicatriz'zante *nm* ointment

cicatriz'zare *vi* heal [up]

cicatriz'zarsi *vr* heal [up]

cicatrizzazi'one *nf* healing

'cicca *nf* cigarette end; fam (sigaretta) fag; fam
(gomma) [chewing] gum

cic'chetto *nm* fam (bicchierino) nip;
(rimprovero) telling-off

'ciccia *nf* fam fat, flab

cicci'one, -a *nmf* fam fatty, fatso

cice'rone *nm* guide

cicla'mino *nm* cyclamen
ciclica'mente *adv* cyclically
'ciclico *adj* cyclical
ci'clismo *nm* cycling
ci'clista *nmf* cyclist
'ciclo *nm* cycle; (di malattia) course
■ **ciclo economico** business cycle
ciclo'cross *nm inv* cyclo-cross
ciclomo'tore *nm* moped
ci'clone *nm* cyclone
ci'clonico *adj* cyclonic
ciclosti'lare *vt* duplicate
ciclosti'lato ① *nm* duplicate [copy]
② *adj* duplicate
ci'cogna *nf* stork
ci'coria *nf* chicory
ci'cuta *nf* hemlock
C.I.E. *nm abbr* (**centro di identificazione ed espulsione**) immigration removal centre
⚡ **ci'eco, -a** ① *adj* blind
② *nmf* blind man; blind woman; **i parzialmente ciechi** the partially sighted
ciel'lino *nmf* Pol *member of the Comunione e Liberazione movement*
⚡ **ci'elo** *nm* sky; Relig heaven; **al settimo ~** in seventh heaven; **santo ~!** good heavens!
⚡ **'cifra** *nf* figure; (somma) sum; (monogramma) monogram; (codice) code; **una ~ sl** like crazy
ci'frare *vt* embroider with a monogram; (codificare) code
ci'frato *adj* monogrammed; (codificato) coded
'ciglio *nm* (bordo) edge; (degli occhi) eyelash; **ciglia** *pl* eyelashes
'cigno *nm* swan
cigo'lante *adj* squeaky
cigo'lare *vt* squeak
cigo'lio *nm* squeak
'Cile *nm* Chile
ci'lecca *nf* **far ~** miss
ci'leno, -a *adj & nmf* Chilean
cili'egia *nf* cherry
cili'egio *nm* cherry[-tree]
cilin'drata *nf* cubic capacity, c.c.; **macchina di grossa ~** highpowered car
ci'lindro *nm* cylinder; (cappello) top hat, topper
⚡ **'cima** *nf* top; fig (persona) genius; **in ~ a** at the top of; **da ~ a fondo** from top to bottom
■ **cima alla genovese** *baked veal stuffed with chicken and chopped vegetables, served cold*; **cime di rapa** *pl* turnip greens
ci'melio *nm* relic; **cimeli** *pl* memorabilia
cimen'tare *vt* put to the test
cimen'tarsi *vr* (provare) try one's hand; **~ in** (arrischiarsi) venture into

'cimice *nf* bug; (puntina) drawing pin, thumbtack Am
cimini'era *nf* chimney; Naut funnel
⚡ **cimi'tero** *nm* cemetery
■ **cimitero delle macchine** breaker's yard
ci'mosa *nf* selvage, selvedge
ci'murro *nm* distemper
'Cina *nf* China
cincial'legra *nf* great tit
cincia'rella *nf* blue tit
cincillà *nm inv* chinchilla
cin cin *int* cheers!
cincischi'are *vi* fiddle
cincischi'arsi *vr* mess around
'cine *nm* fam cinema
cine'asta *nmf* film maker
Cinecittà *nf* (stabilimento) *film complex in the suburbs of Rome*
cine'club *nm inv* film club
ci'nefilo, -a *nmf* cinemagoer, film buff
cinegior'nale *nm* newsreel
⚡ **cinema** *nm inv* cinema, movie theater Am
■ **cinema d'essai** arts cinema
cine'matica *nf* kinematics *sg*
cinematogra'fare *vt* film
cinematogra'fia *nf* cinematography
cinemato'grafico *adj* film *attrib*
cinema'tografo *nm* cinema
cine'presa *nf* cine-camera
ci'nereo *adj* ashen
ci'nese *adj & nmf* Chinese
cinese'rie *nfpl* chinoiserie
cine'teca *nf* (raccolta) film collection
ci'netica *nf* kinetics *sg*
ci'netico *adj* kinetic
'cingere *vt* (circondare) surround
'cinghia *nf* strap; (cintura) belt
■ **cinghia del ventilatore** fanbelt; **cinghia della ventola** fanbelt
cinghi'ale *nm* wild boar; **pelle di cinghiale** pigskin
cinghi'ata *nf* lash
cingo'lato ① *adj* (mezzi) caterpillar *attrib*
② *nm* caterpillar
'cingolo *nm* Mech belt
cinguet'tare *vi* twitter
cinguet'tio *nm* twittering
cinica'mente *adv* cynically
'cinico *adj* cynical
ci'niglia *nf* (tessuto) chenille
ci'nismo *nm* cynicism
ci'nofilo *adj* ⟨unità⟩ dog-loving
⚡ **cin'quanta** *adj & nm* fifty
cinquanten'nale *nm* fiftieth anniversary
cinquan'tenne *adj & nmf* fifty-year-old
cinquan'tesimo *adj & nm* fiftieth

cinquan'tina *nf* una ∼ di about fifty
⚔ **'cinque** *adj & nm* five
cinquecen'tesco *adj* sixteenth-century
cinque'cento [1] *adj* five hundred
[2] *nm* il Cinquecento the sixteenth century
cinque'mila *adj & nm* five thousand
cin'quina *nf* (in tombola) five in a row
'cinta *nf* (di pantaloni) belt; muro di cinta [boundary] wall
cin'tare *vt* enclose
'cintola *nf* (di pantaloni) belt
cin'tura *nf* belt
■ cintura nera black belt; cintura di salvataggio lifebelt; cintura di sicurezza Aeron, Auto seat belt
cintu'rato *nm* Auto radial tyre
cintu'rino *nm*
■ cinturino [dell'orologio] watch-strap; (di metallo) bracelet
⚔ **ciò** *pron* this; that; ∼ che what; ∼ nondimeno nevertheless
ci'occa *nf* lock
ciocco'lata *nf* chocolate; (bevanda) [hot] chocolate
■ cioccolata in polvere drinking chocolate
cioccola'tino *nm* chocolate
ciocco'lato *nm* chocolate
■ cioccolato fondente plain chocolate, dark chocolate; cioccolato al latte milk chocolate; cioccolato da pasticceria cooking chocolate
⚔ **cioè** *adv* that is
ciondo'lare *vi* dangle
ciondo'lio *nm* dangling
ci'ondolo *nm* pendant
ciondo'loni *adv* fig hanging about
cionono'stante *adv* nonetheless
ci'otola *nf* bowl
ci'ottolo *nm* pebble; ciottoli *pl* (in spiaggia) shingle
ci'piglio *nm* frown; con ∼ with a frown
ci'polla *nf* onion; (bulbo) bulb
cipol'lotto *nm* green onion
ci'presso *nm* cypress
'cipria *nf* [face] powder
cipri'ota *adj & nmf* Cypriot
'Cipro *nm* Cyprus
⚔ **'circa** *adv & prep* about
cir'cense *adj* circus *attrib*
'circo *nm* circus
circo'lare [1] *adj* circular
[2] *nf* circular; (di metropolitana) circle line
[3] *vi* circulate
circola'torio *adj* Med circulatory
circolazi'one *nf* circulation; (traffico) traffic
'circolo *nm* circle; (società) club
■ circolo del golf golf-club; Circolo polare antartico Antarctic Circle; Circolo polare artico Arctic Circle; circolo sociale social club

circon'cidere *vt* circumcise
circoncisi'one *nf* circumcision
⚔ **circon'dare** *vt* surround
circon'dario *nm* (amministrativo) administrative district; (vicinato) neighbourhood
circon'darsi *vr* ∼ di surround oneself with
circonfe'renza *nf* circumference
■ circonferenza del collo collar size; circonferenza dei fianchi hip measurement; circonferenza [della] vita waist measurement
circon'flesso *adj* e con l'accento ∼ circumflex e
circonvallazi'one *nf* ring road
circo'scritto [1] pp di CIRCOSCRIVERE
[2] *adj* limited
circo'scrivere *vt* circumscribe
circoscrizio'nale *adj* area
circoscrizi'one *nf* area
■ circoscrizione elettorale constituency
circo'spetto *adj* wary
circospezi'one *nf* con ∼ warily
circo'stante *adj* surrounding
⚔ **circo'stanza** *nf* circumstance; (occasione) occasion
circostanzi'ato *adj* circumstantial
circu'ire *vt* (ingannare) trick
circuite'ria *nf* circuitry
cir'cuito *nm* circuit
circumnavi'gare *vt* circumnavigate
circumnavigazi'one *nf* circumnavigation
ci'rillico *adj* Cyrillic
cir'ripede *nm* barnacle
cir'rosi *nf* cirrhosis
Cisgior'dania *nf* West Bank
C.I.S.L. *nf abbr* (Confederazione Italiana Sindacati Lavoratori) *trades union organization*
C.I.S.N.A.L. *nf abbr* (Confederazione Italiana Sindacati Nazionali dei Lavoratori) *trades union organization*
'cispa *nf* (nell'occhio) sleep
ci'sposo *adj* bleary-eyed
'ciste *nf inv* cyst
ci'sterna *nf* cistern; (serbatoio) tank
'cisti *nf inv* cyst
cisti'fellea *nf* gall bladder
ci'stite *nf* cystitis
C.I.T. *nm abbr* (Compagnia Italiana Turismo) *Italian tourist organization*
ci'tare *vt* (riportare brani ecc) quote; (come esempio) cite; Jur summons
citazi'one *nf* quotation; Jur summons *sg*
citofo'nare *vt* buzz
ci'tofono *nm* entry phone; (in ufficio, su aereo ecc) intercom
cito'logico *adj* cytological

'citrico *adj* citric
ci'trullo *nmf* fam dimwit
✓ **città** *nf inv* town; (grande) city
  ■ **Città del Capo** Cape Town; **città dormitorio** dormitory town; **città fantasma** ghost town; **città giardino** garden city; **città stato** city state; **Città del Vaticano** Vatican City
citta'della *nf* citadel
citta'dina *nf* town
cittadi'nanza *nf* citizenship; (popolazione) citizens *pl*
✓ **citta'dino, -a** *nmf* citizen; (abitante di città) city dweller
ciucci'are *vt* fam suck
ci'uccio *nm* fam dummy
ci'uco *nm* ass
ci'uffo *nm* tuft
ci'urma *nf* Naut crew
ciur'maglia *nf* (gentaglia) rabble
ci'vetta *nf* owl; fig (donna) flirt; [auto] civetta unmarked police car
civet'tare *vi* flirt
civette'ria *nf* flirtatiousness, coquettishness
civettu'olo *adj* flirtatious, coquettish
'civico *adj* civic
✓ **ci'vile** ① *adj* civil ② *nm* civilian
civi'lista *nmf* (avvocato) specialist in civil law
civiliz'zare *vt* civilize
civiliz'zarsi *vr* become civilized
civiliz'zato *adj* ‹paese› civilized
civilizzazi'one *nf* civilization
civil'mente *adv* civilly
✓ **civiltà** *nf inv* civilization; (cortesia) civility
ci'vismo *nm* public spirit
cl *abbr* (**centilitro**) centilitre(s)
CL *nf abbr* (**Comunione e Liberazione**) young Catholics association
'clacson *nm inv* horn
clacso'nare *vi* beep the horn, hoot
cla'more *nm* clamour; **fare ∼** cause a sensation
clamorosa'mente *adv* ‹sbagliare› sensationally
clamo'roso *adj* noisy; ‹sbaglio› sensational
clan *nm inv* clan; fig clique
clandestina'mente *adv* secretly
clandestinità *nf* secrecy; **vivere nella ∼** live underground
clande'stino *adj* clandestine; **movimento ∼** underground movement; **passeggero ∼** stowaway
claque *nf inv* claque
clarinet'tista *nmf* clarinettist
clari'netto *nm* clarinet

✓ indicates a very frequent word

✓ **'classe** *nf* class; (aula) classroom; **di prima ∼** first-class
  ■ **classe economica** economy class; **classe operaia** working class; **classe turistica** tourist class
classicheggi'ante *adj* classical
classi'cismo *nm* classicism
classi'cista *nmf* classicist
'classico ① *adj* classical; (tipico) classic ② *nm* classic
classifica *nf* classification; Sport league
  ■ **classifica dei singoli** singles charts
classifi'cabile *adj* classifiable
classifi'care *vt* classify
classifi'carsi *vr* be placed
classifica'tore *nm* (cartella) folder; (mobile) filing cabinet
classificazi'one *nf* classification
clas'sista ① *adj* class-conscious ② *nmf* class-conscious person
claudi'cante *adj* lame
'clausola *nf* clause
  ■ **clausola penale** Jur, Comm penalty clause; **clausola di recesso** Jur, Comm escape clause
claustrofo'bia *nf* claustrophobia
claustro'fobico *adj* claustrophobic
clau'sura *nf* Relig cloistered life; **di ∼** ‹suora› cloistered; **essere in ∼** fig shut oneself up; **vivere in ∼** fig live like a hermit
'clava *nf* club
clavicemba'lista *nmf* harpsichord player
clavi'cembalo *nm* harpsichord
cla'vicola *nf* collar-bone
clavi'cordo *nm* clavichord
cle'mente *adj* merciful; ‹tempo› mild
cle'menza *nf* mercy, clemency
clep'tomane *nmf* kleptomaniac
cleptoma'nia *nf* kleptomania
cleri'cale *adj* clerical
'clero *nm* clergy
cles'sidra *nf* hourglass
clic *nm inv* Comput click; **fare ∼ su** click on; **fare doppio ∼** double-click
clic'care *vi* Comput click; **∼ su** click on
cliché *nm inv* cliché
click ▶ CLIC
✓ **cli'ente** *nmf* client; (di negozio) customer
✓ **clien'tela** *nf* customers *pl*, clientele; (di avvocato) clientele
cliente'lare *adj* Pol nepotistic
cliente'lismo *nm* nepotism
'clima *nm* climate
clima'terio *nm* climacteric
climatica'mente *adv* climatically
cli'matico *adj* climatic; **stazione climatica** health resort
climatizza'tore *nm* air conditioner

climatizzazi'one *nf* air conditioning

'**clinica** *nf* clinic
■ **clinica di allergologia** allergy clinic; **clinica odontoiatrica** dental clinic; **clinica ostetrica** maternity hospital; **clinica psichiatrica** mental hospital

'**clinico** [1] *adj* clinical
[2] *nm* clinician

clip *nf inv* paper-clip; (di orecchino) clip

cli'stere *nm* Med enema

clo'aca *nf* sewer

cloche *nf inv* cloche hat

clo'nare *vt* clone

clonazi'one *nf* cloning

'**clone** *nm* clone

clo'rato *adj* chlorate

'**cloro** *nm* chlorine

cloro'filla *nf* chlorophyll

clorofluorocar'buro *nm* chlorofluorocarbon, CFC

cloro'formio *nm* chloroform

clou *adj inv* momenti ~ highlights

club *nm inv* club
■ **club per i giovani** youth club; **club sportivo** sports club

club-'sandwich *nm inv* club sandwich

cm *abbr* (**centimetro**) cm

CNR *nm abbr* (**Consiglio Nazionale delle Ricerche**) national research council

Co. *abbr* (**compagnia**) Co

coabi'tare *vi* live together

coabitazi'one *nf* (di razze) coexistence

coadiu|'tore, -trice *nmf* (in ufficio) assistant

coadiu'vare *vt* cooperate with

coagu'lante *nm* coagulant

coagu'lare *vt* coagulate

coagu'larsi *vr* coagulate

coagulazi'one *nf* coagulation

coalizi'one *nf* coalition

coaliz'zare *vt* fig unite

coaliz'zarsi *vr* unite

co'atto *adj* Jur compulsory

co'balto *nm* cobalt, (colore) cobalt blue

COBAS *nmpl abbr* (**Comitati di Base**) *independent trade unions*

'**cobra** *nm inv* cobra

'**Coca**® *nf* Coke®

Coca 'cola® *nf* Coca Cola

coca'ina *nf* cocaine

cocai'nomane *nmf* cocaine addict

coc'carda *nf* rosette

cocchi'ere *nm* coachman

coc'chio *nm* coach

'**coccige** *nm* coccyx

cocci'nella *nf* ladybird

'**coccio** *nm* earthenware; (frammento) fragment

cocciu'taggine *nf* stubbornness

cocciuta'mente *adv* stubbornly

cocci'uto *adj* stubborn

'**cocco** *nm* coconut palm; fam love; **noce di cocco** coconut

coccodè *nm inv* cluck

cocco'drillo *nm* crocodile

cocco'lare *vt* cuddle

co'cente *adj* ‹sole› burning; ‹lacrime, delusione› bitter

'**cocker** *nm inv*
■ **cocker [spaniel]** cocker spaniel

'**cocktail** *nm inv* (ricevimento) cocktail party

co'comero *nm* watermelon

co.co.pro. *nf abbr* (**collaborazione coordinata a progetto**) *type of freelance work for a planned activity and a fixed period on a client's behalf*

co'cuzzolo *nm* top; (di testa, cappello) crown

'**coda** *nf* tail; (di abito) train; (fila) queue; (di traffico) tailback; **fare la** ~ queue [up], stand in line Am
■ **coda di cavallo** (acconciatura) pony tail; **coda dell'occhio** corner of one's eye; **coda di paglia** guilty conscience

co'dardo, -a [1] *adj* cowardly
[2] *nmf* coward

co'dazzo *nm* train

code'ina *nf* codeine

co'desto *adj* that

'**codice** *nm* code; in ~ ‹messaggio› coded, in code; **mettere in** ~ encode
■ **codice di avviamento postale** postal code, zip code Am; **codice a barre** bar-code; **codice civile** civil code; **codice fiscale** National Insurance number Br, tax code; **codice penale** penal code; **codice PIN** PIN; **codice della strada** highway code

codi'cillo *nm* codicil

co'difica *nf* coding

codifi'care *vt* encode; codify ‹legge›

codifica|'tore, -trice *nmf* Comput encoder

codificazi'one *nf* encoding; (di legge) codification

co'dini *nmpl* bunches

coeffici'ente *nm* coefficient

coercizi'one *nf* coercion

coe'rente *adj* consistent

coe'renza *nf* consistency

coesi'one *nf* cohesion

coe'sistere *vi* coexist

coe'sivo *adj* cohesive

coe'taneo, -a *adj & nmf* contemporary

cofa'netto *nm* casket

'**cofano** *nm* (forziere) chest; Auto bonnet, hood Am

cofirma'tario, -a *nmf* cosignatory

coge'stire *vt* co-manage

cogi'tare *vi* ponder

🌢 **'cogliere** *vt* pick; (sorprendere) catch; (afferrare) seize; (colpire) hit; ~ **la palla al balzo** seize the opportunity; ~ **di sorpresa** take by surprise

co'glione *nm* vulg ball; (sciocco) dickhead; **rompere i coglioni a qualcuno** get on somebody's tits

'Cognac *nm* cognac

co'gnato, -a [1] *nm* brother-in-law [2] *nf* sister-in-law

cognizi'one *nf* knowledge; **con ~ di causa** on an informed basis

🌢 **cognome** *nm* surname, second name ■ **cognome da ragazza/da nubile** maiden name

cogu'aro *nm* cougar

'coi = CON + I

coi'bente *adj* insulating

coinci'denza *nf* coincidence; (di treno ecc) connection

coin'cidere *vi* coincide

coinqui'lino *nm* flatmate

cointesta'tario *nm* Fin joint account-holder

coin'volgere *vt* involve

coinvolgi'mento *nm* involvement

coin'volto *adj* involved

'coito *nm* coitus

col = CON + IL

colà *adv* there

cola'brodo *nm inv* strainer; **ridotto a un ~** fam full of holes

cola'pasta *nm inv* colander

co'lare [1] *vt* strain; (versare lentamente) drip [2] *vi* (gocciolare) drip; (perdere) leak; ~ **a picco** Naut sink

co'lata *nf* (di metallo) casting; (di lava) flow

🌢 **colazi'one** *nf* (del mattino) breakfast; (di mezzogiorno) lunch; **far ~** have breakfast/lunch
■ **prima colazione** breakfast; **colazione di lavoro** working lunch; **colazione al sacco** packed lunch

col'bacco *nm* fur hat

co'lei *pron f* the one

co'lera *nm* cholera

coleste'rolo *nm* cholesterol

colf *nf inv abbr* (**collaboratrice familiare**) home help

colibrì *nm inv* humming-bird

'colica *nf* colic

co'lino *nm* [tea] strainer

'colla *nf* glue; (di farina) paste
■ **colla di pesce** gelatine

collabo'rare *vi* collaborate; ~ **con** ‹polizia› co-operate with; ~ **a** ‹rivista› contribute to

collabora|'tore, -trice *nmf* collaborator; (di rivista) contributor
■ **collaboratrice familiare** domestic help

collaborazi'one *nf* collaboration; (con polizia) co-operation

collaborazio'nista *nmf* collaborator

col'lage *nm inv* collage

col'lana *nf* necklace; (serie) series
■ **collana di perle** pearl necklace

col'lant *nmpl* tights
■ **collant velati** sheer tights

col'lante *adj* adhesive

col'lare *nm* collar

colla'rino *nm* dog collar

col'lasso *nm* collapse
■ **collasso cardiaco** syncope; **collasso renale** kidney failure

collate'rale *adj* collateral

collau'dare *vt* test

collauda|'tore, -trice *nmf* tester

col'laudo *nm* test

collazio'nare *vt* collate

'colle *nm* hill; (passo) pass

🌢 **col'lega** *nmf* colleague

colle'gabile *adj* compatible (**a** with)

collega'mento *nm* connection; Mil liaison; Radio ecc link
■ **collegamento dati** data link; **collegamento ipertestuale** hyperlink; **collegamento in rete** networking

colle'gare *vt* connect

colle'garsi *vr* TV, Radio link up (**a** with); Comput (a una rete ecc) go on line (**a** to)

collegi'ale [1] *nmf* boarder [2] *adj* ‹responsabilità, decisione› collective

col'legio *nm* (convitto) boarding-school
■ **collegio elettorale** constituency

'collera *nf* anger; **andare in ~** get angry

col'lerico *adj* irascible

col'letta *nf* collection

collettività *nf inv* community

collet'tivo [1] *adj* collective; ‹interesse› general; **biglietto collettivo** group ticket [2] *nm* (studentesco, femminista) collective

col'letto *nm* collar

collet'tore *nm* (di fognatura) main sewer

collezio'nare *vt* collect

collezi'one *nf* collection
■ **collezione invernale** winter collection

collezio'nismo *nm* collecting

collezio'nista *nmf* collector
■ **collezionista di francobolli** stamp collector

colli'mare *vi* coincide

🌢 **col'lina** *nf* hill

colli'nare *adj* hill *attrib*

colli'netta *nf* knoll

🌢 indicates a very frequent word

colli'noso *adj* ‹terreno› hilly

col'lirio *nm* eyewash

collisi'one *nf* collision

◈ **'collo** *nm* neck; (pacco) package; **a ~ alto** high-necked; **a rotta di ~** breakneck
■ **collo del piede** instep

colloca'mento *nm* placing; (impiego) employment

collo'care *vt* place

collo'carsi *vr* take one's place

collocazi'one *nf* placing

colloqui'ale *adj* ‹termine› colloquial; ‹tono› informal

col'loquio *nm* conversation; (udienza ecc) interview; (esame) oral [exam]

col'loso *adj* glutinous

col'lottola *nf* nape

collusi'one *nf* collusion

colluttazi'one *nf* scuffle

col'mare *vt* fill; bridge ‹divario›; **~ qualcuno di gentilezze** overwhelm somebody with kindness

'colmo [1] *adj* full; **un cucchiaio ~ a** heaped spoonful
[2] *nm* top; fig height; **al ~ della disperazione** in the depths of despair; **questo è il ~!** (con indignazione) this is the last straw!; (con stupore) I don't believe it!; **per ~ di sfortuna** to crown it all

+colo *suff* **poetucolo** second rate poet

co'lomba *nf* dove
■ **colomba pasquale** *dove shaped cake with candied fruit eaten at Easter*

colom'baccio *nm* wood pigeon

colom'baia *nf* dovecote

Co'lombia *nf* Colombia

colombi'ano *adj & nmf* Colombian

co'lombo *nm* pigeon; **colombi** *pl* (innamorati) lovebirds

colonia *nf* colony; (per bambini) holiday camp, summer camp

Co'lonia *nf* Cologne; **[acqua di] colonia** [eau de] Cologne

coloni'ale *adj* colonial

colonia'lista *nmf* colonialist

co'lonico *adj* ‹terreno, casa› farm *attrib*

coloniz'zare *vt* colonize

colonizza|'tore, -trice *nmf* colonizer

colonizzazi'one *nf* colonization

co'lonna *nf* column; (di auto) tailback
■ **colonna sonora** sound-track; **colonna vertebrale** spine

colon'nato *nm* colonnade

colon'nello *nm* colonel

colon'nina *nf* (distributore) petrol pump, gas pump Am

co'lono *nm* tenant farmer

colo'rante *nm* colouring
■ **colorante alimentare** food colouring

colo'rare *vt* colour; colour in ‹disegno›

◈ **co'lore** *nm* colour; (carte) suit; **a colori** in colour; **di ~** coloured; **farne di tutti i colori** get up to all sorts of mischief; **passarne di tutti i colori** go through hell; **diventare di tutti i colori** fig turn scarlet
■ **colore a olio** oil paint; **colore primario** primary colour

colori'ficio *nm* paint and dyes shop

colo'rito [1] *adj* coloured; ‹viso› rosy; ‹racconto, linguaggio› colourful
[2] *nm* complexion

co'loro *pron pl* the ones

colos'sale *adj* colossal

Colos'seo *nm* Coliseum

co'losso *nm* colossus

◈ **'colpa** *nf* fault; (biasimo) blame; (colpevolezza) guilt; (peccato) sin; **dare la ~ a** blame; **essere in ~** be at fault; **per ~ di** because of; **è ~ mia** it's my fault

col'pevole [1] *adj* guilty
[2] *nmf* culprit

◈ **col'pire** *vt* hit, strike; fig strike; **~ nel segno** hit the nail on the head

◈ **'colpo** *nm* blow; (di arma da fuoco) shot; (urto) knock; (emozione) shock; Med, Sport stroke; (furto) robbery; **di ~** suddenly; **far ~** make a strong impression; **far venire un ~ a qualcuno** fig give somebody a fright; **perdere colpi** ‹motore› keep missing; **a ~ d'occhio** at a glance; **a ~ sicuro** for certain
■ **colpo d'aria** chill; **colpo basso** blow below the belt; **colpo di frusta** Med whiplash injury; **colpo di grazia** kiss of death; **colpo da maestro** masterstroke; **colpo di scena** sensational development; **colpo di sole** sunstroke; **colpi di sole** *pl* (su capelli) highlights; **colpo di Stato** coup [d'état]; **colpo di telefono** ring, call; **dare un ~ di telefono a qualcuno** give somebody a ring *or* call; **colpo di testa** [sudden] impulse; **colpo di vento** gust of wind

col'poso *adj* **omicidio ~** manslaughter

coltel'lata *nf* stab

coltelle'ria *nf* cutlery shop

◈ **col'tello** *nm* knife; **avere il ~ dalla parte del manico** have the upper hand
■ **coltello per il pane** breadknife; **coltello a serramanico** jackknife

◈ **colti'vare** *vt* cultivate

coltiva|'tore, -trice *nmf* farmer

coltivazi'one *nf* farming; (di piante) growing
■ **coltivazione intensiva** intensive farming

'colto [1] *pp di* COGLIERE
[2] *adj* cultured

'coltre *nf* blanket

col'tura *nf* cultivation
■ **coltura alternata** crop rotation

◈ **co'lui** *pron m* the one

'colza *nf* Bot (oilseed) rape

'coma *nm inv* coma; in ~ in a coma; in ~ irreversibile brain dead

comanda'mento *nm* commandment

coman'dante *nm* commander; Naut, Aeron captain

⚘ **coman'dare** [1] *vt* command; Mech control; ~ a qualcuno di fare qualcosa order somebody to do something
[2] *vi* be in charge

⚘ **co'mando** *nm* command; (di macchina) control

co'mare *nf* (pettegola) gossip

coma'toso *adj* Med comatose

combaci'are *vi* fit together; ‹testimonianze› concur

combattente [1] *adj* fighting
[2] *nm* combatant
■ ex combattente ex-serviceman; combattente per la libertà freedom fighter

⚘ **com'battere** *vt/i* fight

combatti'mento *nm* fight; Mil battle; fuori ~ ‹pugilato› knocked out

combat'tuto *adj* ‹gara› hard fought; (tormentato) torn; ‹discussione› heated

⚘ **combi'nare** *vt/i* arrange; (mettere insieme) combine; fam (fare) do; cosa stai combinando? what are you doing?

combi'narsi *vr* combine; (mettersi d'accordo) come to an agreement

combinazi'one *nf* combination; (caso) coincidence; per ~ by chance

com'briccola *nf* gang

combu'stibile [1] *adj* combustible
[2] *nm* fuel

combusti'one *nf* combustion

com'butta *nf* gang; in ~ in league

⚘ **'come** [1] *adv* like; (in qualità di) as; (interrogativo, esclamativo) how; questo vestito è ~ il tuo this dress is like yours; ~? pardon?; ~ stai? how are you?; ~ va? how are things?; ~ mai? how come?; ~? what?; non sa ~ fare he doesn't know what to do; ~ sta bene! how well he looks!; ~ no! that will be right!; ~ tu sai as you know; fa' ~ vuoi do as you like; ~ se as if
[2] *conj* (non appena) as soon as

come'done *nm* blackhead

co'meta *nf* comet

'comfort *nm inv* comfort; con tutti i ~ with all mod cons

'comico [1] *adj* comical; ‹teatro, attore› comic
[2] *nm* funny side; (attore) comic actor, comedian
[3] *nf* comedienne; (attrice) comic actress, comedienne; (a torte in faccia) slapstick sketch

co'mignolo *nm* chimney-pot

⚘ **cominci'are** *vt/i* begin, start; a ~ da oggi from today; per ~ to begin with;

cominciamo bene! we're off to a fine start!

comi'tato *nm* committee
■ comitato consultivo advisory committee; comitato direttivo steering committee; comitato esecutivo executive committee; comitato di gestione management committee

comi'tiva *nf* party, group

co'mizio *nm* meeting
■ comizio elettorale election rally

'comma *nm* (capoverso) paragraph

com'mando *nm inv* commando

com'media *nf* comedy; (opera teatrale) play; fig sham
■ commedia musicale musical

commedi'ante [1] *nm* comic actor; fig pej phoney
[2] *nf* comic actress; fig pej phoney

commedi'ografo, -a *nmf* playwright

commemo'rare *vt* commemorate

commemorazi'one *nf* commemoration
■ commemorazione dei defunti (2 novembre) All Soul's Day

commenda'tore *nm* commander

commen'sale *nmf* fellow diner

commen'tare *vt* comment on; (annotare) annotate

commen'tario *nm* commentary

commenta|'tore, -trice *nmf* commentator

com'mento *nm* comment; TV, Radio commentary
■ commento musicale music

⚘ **commerci'ale** *adj* commercial; ‹relazioni, trattative› trade; ‹attività›; business; centro commerciale shopping centre

commerci'alista *nmf* business consultant; (contabile) accountant, certified public accountant Am

commercializ'zare *vt* market; pej commercialize

commercializzazi'one *nf* marketing; pej commercialization
■ commercializzazione di massa mass-marketing

commerci'ante *nmf* trader, merchant; (negoziante) shopkeeper
■ commerciante all'ingrosso wholesaler; commerciante di oggetti d'arte art dealer

commerci'are *vi* ~ in deal in

⚘ **com'mercio** *nm* commerce; (internazionale) trade; (affari) business; in ~ (prodotto) on sale
■ commercio al dettaglio o al minuto retail trade; commercio all'ingrosso wholesale trade

com'messo, -a [1] *pp di* COMMETTERE
[2] *nmf* shop assistant; commessi *pl* counter staff
■ commesso viaggiatore commercial traveller
[3] *nf* (ordine) order

comme'stibile [1] *adj* edible
[2] *nm* commestibili *pl* groceries

⚘ indicates a very frequent word

♂ **com'mettere** *vt* commit; make ‹sbaglio›; ∼ **un reato** commit an offence

commi'ato *nm* leave; **prendere** ∼ **da** take leave of

commise'rare *vt* commiserate

commise'rarsi *vr* feel sorry for oneself

commissari'ato *nm* (di polizia) police station

commis'sario *nm* ≈ [police] superintendent; (membro di commissione) commissioner; Sport steward; Comm commission agent
■ **commissario di bordo** purser; **commissario capo** chief superintendent; **commissario d'esame** examiner; **commissario di gara** race official, steward; **commissario tecnico** (della nazionale) national team manager

commissi'one *nf* (incarico) errand; (comitato, percentuale) commission; Comm (di merce) order; **commissioni** *pl* (acquisti) **fare commissioni** go shopping
■ **commissione d'esame** board of examiners; **Commissione Europea** European Commission; **commissione d'inchiesta** court of inquiry

commit'tente *nmf* purchaser

com'mosso ① pp di COMMUOVERE ② *adj* moved

commo'vente *adj* moving

commozi'one *nf* emotion
■ **commozione cerebrale** concussion

♂ **commu'overe** *vt* touch, move

commu'oversi *vr* be touched

commu'tare *vt* change; Jur commute

commuta'tore *nm* Electr commutator

commutazi'one *nf* (di pena) commutation

comò *nm inv* chest of drawers

comoda'mente *adv* comfortably

como'dino *nm* bedside table

♂ **comodità** *nf inv* comfort; (convenienza) convenience

♂ **'comodo** ① *adj* comfortable; (conveniente) convenient; (spazioso) roomy; (facile) easy; **stia comodo!** don't get up!; **far** ∼ be useful ② *nm* comfort; **fare il proprio** ∼ do as one pleases; **prendila con** ∼! take it easy!

Co'more *nfpl* **le (isole)** ∼ Comoros

'compact disc *nm inv* compact disc

compae'sano, -a ① *nm* fellow countryman ② *nf* fellow countrywoman

com'pagine *nf* (squadra) team

♂ **compa'gnia** *nf* company; (gruppo) party; **fare** ∼ **a qualcuno** keep somebody company; **essere di** ∼ be sociable
■ **compagnia aerea** airline; **compagnia di bandiera** (aerea) national airline; **compagnia low cost** budget airline, no frills airline

♂ **com'pagno, -a** *nmf* companion; (Comm, Sport, in coppia) partner; Pol comrade

■ **compagno di classe** classmate; **compagno di scuola** schoolmate, schoolfriend; **compagno di squadra** team-mate; **compagno di viaggio** fellow traveller

compa'rabile *adj* comparable

compa'rare *vt* compare

compara'tivo *adj* & *nm* comparative

comparazi'one *nf* comparison

com'pare *nm* sidekick

♂ **compa'rire** *vi* appear; (spiccare) stand out; ∼ **in giudizio** appear in court

com'parso, -a ① pp di COMPARIRE ② *nf* appearance; Cinema extra; Theat walk-on

compartecipazi'one *nf* sharing; (quota) share

comparti'mento *nm* compartment; (amministrativo) department

compas'sato *adj* calm and collected

compassi'one *nf* compassion; **aver** ∼ **per** feel pity for; **far** ∼ arouse pity

compassio'nevole *adj* compassionate

com'passo *nm* [pair of] compasses *pl*

compa'tibile *adj* (conciliabile) compatible; (scusabile) excusable

compatibilità *nf* compatibility

compatibil'mente *adv* ∼ **con i miei impegni** if my commitments allow

compati'mento *nm* **un'aria di** ∼ air of condescension

compa'tire *vt* pity; (scusare) make allowances for

compatri'ota *nmf* compatriot

compat'tezza *nf* (di materia) compactness; fig (di partito) solidarity

com'patto *adj* compact; (denso) dense; (solido) solid; fig united

compendi'are *vt* (fare un sunto) summarize

com'pendio *nm* outline; (sunto) synopsis; (libro) compendium

compene'trare *vt* pervade

compen'sare *vt* compensate; (supplire) make up for

compen'sarsi *vr* balance each other out

compen'sato *nm* (legno) plywood

compensazi'one *nf* compensation

♂ **com'penso** *nm* compensation; (retribuzione) remuneration; **in compenso** (in cambio) in return; (d'altra parte) on the other hand; (invece) instead

'compera *nf* purchase; **far compere** do some shopping

compe'rare *vt* buy

compe'tente *adj* competent; ‹ufficio› appropriate

compe'tenza *nf* competence; (responsabilità) responsibility; **competenze** *pl* (onorari) fees

com'petere *vi* compete; ~ **a** *‹compito›* be the responsibility of

competitività *nf* competitiveness

competi'tivo *adj* *‹prezzo, carattere›* competitive

competi|'tore, -trice *nmf* competitor

competizi'one *nf* competition

compia'cente *adj* obliging

compia'cenza *nf* obligingness; **avere la** ~ **di …** be so obliging as to …

compia'cere *vt/i* please

compia'cersi *vr* (congratularsi) congratulate; ~ **di** (degnarsi) condescend to

compiaci'mento *nm* satisfaction; pej smugness

compiaci'uto *adj* satisfied; *‹aria, sorriso›* smug

compi'angere *vt* pity; (per lutto ecc) sympathize with

⌁ **'compiere** *vt* (concludere) complete; commit *‹delitto›*; ~ **gli anni** have one's birthday

'compiersi *vr* end; (avverarsi) come true

compi'lare *vt* compile; fill in *‹modulo›*

compila|'tore, -trice *nmf* compiler

compilazi'one *nf* compilation

compi'mento *nm* completion; **portare a** ~ **qualcosa** conclude something

com'pire *vt* = COMPIERE

compi'tare *vt* spell

⌁ **'compito¹** *nm* task; (dovere) duty; Sch homework; **fare i compiti** do one's homework

com'pito² *adj* polite

compiu'tezza *nf* completeness

compi'uto *adj* **avere 30 anni compiuti** be over 30

comple'anno *nm* birthday

complemen'tare *adj* complementary; (secondario) subsidiary

comple'mento *nm* complement; Mil draft
■ **complemento oggetto** Gram direct object

comples'sato *adj* hung-up

complessità *nf* complexity

complessiva'mente *adv* on the whole; (in totale) altogether

comples'sivo *adj* comprehensive; (totale) total

⌁ **com'plesso** ⓵ *adj* complex; (difficile) complicated
⓶ *nm* complex, hang up fam; Psych complex; (di cantanti ecc) group; (di circostanze, fattori) combination; **in** ~ on the whole; (in totale) altogether
■ **complesso di inferiorità** inferiority complex

completa'mente *adv* completely

completa'mento *nm* completion

⌁ **comple'tare** *vt* complete

⌁ indicates a very frequent word

comple'tezza *nf* completeness

⌁ **com'pleto** ⓵ *adj* complete; (pieno) full [up]; **al** ~ *‹teatro›* sold out; *‹albergo›* full; '~ ' 'no vacancies'; **la famiglia al** ~ the whole family
⓶ *nm* (vestito) suit; (insieme di cose) set

⌁ **compli'care** *vt* complicate

compli'carsi *vr* become complicated

compli'cato *adj* complicated

complicazi'one *nf* complication; **salvo complicazioni** all being well

'complice ⓵ *nmf* accomplice
⓶ *adj* *‹sguardo›* knowing

complicità *nf* complicity

complimen'tare *vt* compliment

complimen'tarsi *vr* ~ **con** congratulate

⌁ **compli'mento** *nm* compliment; **complimenti** *pl* (ossequi) regards; (congratulazioni) congratulations; **fare complimenti** stand on ceremony

complot'tare *vi* plot

com'plotto *nm* plot

compo'nente ⓵ *adj & nm* component
⓶ *nmf* member

componen'tistica *nf* (per auto, elettronica) accessories *pl*

compo'nibile *adj* *‹cucina›* fitted; *‹mobili›* modular

componi'mento *nm* composition; (letterario) work

⌁ **com'porre** *vt* compose; (sistemare) put in order; Typ set; lay out *‹salma›*; settle *‹lite›*

com'porsi *vr* ~ **di** be made up of

comportamen'tale *adj* behavioural

comporta'mento *nm* behaviour

⌁ **compor'tare** *vt* (implicare) involve

compor'tarsi *vr* behave

com'posito *adj* Chem, Phot composite

composi|'tore, -trice *nmf* composer; Typ compositor

composizi'one *nf* composition
■ **composizione floreale** flower arrangement

com'posta *nf* stewed fruit; (concime) compost

compos'taggio *nm* composting

compo'stezza *nf* composure

com'posto ⓵ *pp di* COMPORRE
⓶ *adj* *‹parola›* compound; **essere** ~ **da** consist of, comprise; **stai** ~! sit properly!
⓷ *nm* Chem compound; Culin mixture

⌁ **com'prare** *vt* buy; fig (corrompere) buy off, bribe

compra|'tore, -trice *nmf* buyer

compra'vendita *nf* buying and selling; **atto di compravendita** deed of sale

⌁ **com'prendere** *vt* understand; (includere) comprise

compren'donio *nm* essere duro di ∼ be slow on the uptake

compren'sibile *adj* understandable

comprensibil'mente *adv* understandably

comprensi'one *nf* understanding

compren'sivo *adj* understanding; (che include) inclusive

com'preso [1] pp di COMPRENDERE [2] *adj* included; **tutto compreso** ⟨*prezzo*⟩ all-in; **da lunedì a venerdì** ∼ Monday to Friday inclusive

com'pressa *nf* compress; (pastiglia) tablet

compressi'one *nf* compression
■ **compressione dati** Comput data compression

com'presso [1] pp di COMPRIMERE [2] *adj* compressed

compres'sore *nm* (rullo) steamroller

compri'mario, -a [1] *nm* Theat supporting actor [2] *nf* supporting actress

com'primere *vt* press; (reprimere) repress; Comput compress

compro'messo [1] pp di COMPROMETTERE [2] *nm* compromise; (contratto) *preliminary but binding agreement*

compromet'tente *adj* compromising

compro'mettere *vt* compromise

comproprietà *nf* multiple ownership

comproprie'tario, -a *nmf* joint owner

compro'vare *vt* prove

com'punto *adj* contrite

compunzi'one *nf* compunction

compu'tare *vt* calculate; (addebitare) estimate

com'puter *nm inv* computer
■ **computer da casa** home computer

computeriz'zare *vt* computerize

computeriz'zato *adj* computerized

computerizzazi'one *nf* computerization

computiste'ria *nf* book-keeping

'computo *nm* calculation

comu'nale *adj* municipal

◆ **co'mune** [1] *adj* common; ⟨*parti*⟩ communal, common; ⟨*amico*⟩ mutual; (ordinario) ordinary [2] *nm* municipality; **in** ∼ shared; **fuori del** ∼ out of the ordinary; **avere qualcosa in** ∼ have something in common [3] *nf* collective farm; commune

comu'nella *nf* fare ∼ form a clique

comune'mente *adv* commonly

comuni'cante *adj* interconnecting

◆ **comuni'care** *vt* communicate; pass on ⟨*malattia*⟩; Relig administer Communion to

comuni'carsi *vr* receive Communion

comunica'tiva *nf* communicativeness

comunica'tivo *adj* communicative

comuni'cato *nm* communiqué
■ **comunicato commerciale** Radio commercial; **comunicato stampa** press release

◆ **comunicazi'one** *nf* communication; Teleph [phone] call; **avere la** ∼ get through; **dare la** ∼ **a qualcuno** put somebody through
■ **comunicazione dati** Comput data communications

comuni'one *nf* communion; Relig [Holy] Communion

comu'nismo *nm* communism

◆ **comu'nista** *adj & nmf* communist

comunità *nf inv* community
■ **Comunità [Economica] Europea** European [Economic] Community; **Comunità degli Stati Indipendenti** Commonwealth of Independent States; **comunità terapeutica** rehabilitation centre

◆ **co'munque** [1] *conj* however [2] *adv* anyhow

◆ **con** *prep* with; (mezzo) by; ∼ **facilità** easily; ∼ **mia grande gioia** to my great delight; **è gentile** ∼ **tutti** he is kind to everyone; **col treno** by train; ∼ **questo tempo** in this weather

co'nato *nm*
■ **conato di vomito** retching

'conca *nf* basin; (valle) dell

concate'nare *vt* link together

concate'narsi *vr* ⟨*idee*⟩ be connected

concatenazi'one *nf* connection

'concavo *adj* concave

◆ **con'cedere** *vt* grant; award ⟨*premio*⟩; (ammettere) admit

con'cedersi *vr* allow oneself ⟨*pausa*⟩; treat oneself to ⟨*lusso, vacanza*⟩

concentra'mento *nm* concentration

concen'trare *vt* concentrate

concen'trarsi *vr* concentrate

concen'trato [1] *adj* concentrated [2] *nm* concentrate
■ **concentrato di pomodoro** tomato purée

concentrazi'one *nf* concentration

con'centrico *adj* concentric

concepi'mento *nm* conception

conce'pire *vt* conceive ⟨*bambino*⟩; (capire) understand; (figurarsi) conceive of; devise ⟨*piano ecc*⟩

con'cernere *vt* concern

concer'tare *vt* Mus harmonize; (organizzare) arrange

concer'tarsi *vr* agree

concer'tista *nmf* concert performer

con'certo *nm* concert; (composizione) concerto
■ **concerto rock** rock concert

concessio'nario *nm* agent

concessi'one *nf* concession

con'cesso pp di CONCEDERE

con'cetto *nm* concept; (opinione) opinion

concet'toso *adj* cerebral

concezi'one *nf* conception; (idea) concept

con'chiglia *nf* [sea] shell

■ **conchiglia del pellegrino** scallop shell; **conchiglia di san Giacomo** scallop shell

'**concia** *nf* tanning; (di tabacco) curing

conci'are *vt* tan; cure ‹*tabacco*›; ∼ **qualcuno per le feste** give somebody a good hiding

conci'arsi *vr* (sporcarsi) get dirty; (vestirsi male) dress badly

conci'ato *adj* ‹*pelle, cuoio*› tanned; **essere** ∼ **come un barbone** look like something the cat dragged in

concili'abile *adj* compatible

concili'abolo *nm* private meeting

concili'ante *adj* conciliatory

concili'are *vt* reconcile; pay ‹*contravvenzione*›; (favorire) induce

concili'arsi *vr* go together; (mettersi d'accordo) become reconciled

conciliazi'one *nf* reconciliation; Jur settlement

con'cilio *nm* Relig council; (riunione) assembly

conci'maia *nf* dunghill

conci'mare *vt* feed ‹*pianta*›

con'cime *nm* manure; (chimico) fertilizer

concisi'one *nf* conciseness

con'ciso *adj* concise

conci'tato *adj* excited

concitta'dino, **-a** *nmf* fellow citizen

concla'mato *adj* Med full blown

con'clave *nm* conclave

✧ **con'cludere** *vt* conclude; (finire con successo) successfully complete

con'cludersi *vr* come to an end

conclusi'one *nf* conclusion; **in** ∼ (insomma) in short

conclu'sivo *adj* conclusive

con'cluso pp di CONCLUDERE

concomi'tante *adj* contributory

concomi'tanza *nf* (di circostanze, fatti) combination; **in** ∼ **con** combined with, in conjunction with

concor'danza *nf* agreement

concor'dare ① *vt* agree [on]; Gram make agree ② *vi* (sul prezzo) agree

concor'dato *nm* agreement; Jur, Comm composition

con'corde *adj* in agreement; (unanime) unanimous

con'cordia *nf* concord

concor'rente ① *adj* concurrent; (rivale) competing

② *nmf* Comm, Sport competitor; (candidato) candidate; (a quiz, concorso di bellezza) contestant

concor'renza *nf* competition

■ **concorrenza sleale** unfair competition

concorrenzi'ale *adj* competitive

con'correre *vi* (contribuire) combine; (andare insieme) go together; (competere) compete

con'corso ① pp di CONCORRERE

② *nm* competition; **fuori** ∼ not in the official competition

■ **concorso di bellezza** beauty contest; **concorso di circostanze** combination of circumstances; **concorso di colpa** contributory negligence; **concorso ippico** showjumping event; **concorso a premi** prize-winning competition; **concorso in reato** Jur complicity; **concorso per titoli** *competition in which exam results are not the sole criterion*

concreta'mente *adv* concretely

concre'tare, **concretizzare** *vt* put into concrete form

con'creto *adj* concrete; **in** ∼ in concrete terms

concu'bina *nf* concubine

concussi'one *nf* acceptance of a bribe

con'danna *nf* sentence; **pronunziare una** ∼ hand down a sentence

■ **condanna a morte** death sentence; **condanna penale** prison sentence

✧ **condan'nare** *vt* (disapprovare) condemn; Jur sentence

condan'nato, **-a** ① *adj* (destinato) forced ② *nmf* prisoner

con'densa *nf* condensation

conden'sare *vt* condense

conden'sarsi *vr* condense

condensa'tore *nm* Electr condenser

condensazi'one *nf* condensation

condi'mento *nm* seasoning; (salsa) dressing

■ **condimento per insalata** salad dressing

con'dire *vt* flavour; dress ‹*insalata*›

condiscen'dente *adj* indulgent; pej condescending; (arrendevole) compliant

condiscen'denza *nf* indulgence; pej condescension; (arrendevolezza) compliance

con'dito *adj* Culin seasoned

condi'videre *vt* share

condizio'nale ① *adj* & *nm* conditional ② *nf* Jur suspended sentence

condiziona'mento *nm* Psych conditioning

condizio'nare *vt* condition

condizionata'mente *adv* conditionally

condizio'nato *adj* conditional (da on); **aria condizionata** air-conditioning

condiziona'tore *nm* air conditioner

✧ **condizi'one** *nf* condition; **a** ∼ **che** on condition that; **condizioni** *pl* **di credito** credit terms

---

✧ indicates a very frequent word

■ condizione imprescindibile precondition

condogli'anze *nfpl* condolences; **fare le ~ a** offer one's condolences to

'condom *nm inv* condom

condomini'ale *adj* ‹spese› common; ‹riunione› tenants' *attrib*

condo'minio *nm* joint ownership; (edificio) condominium

condo'mino, -a *nmf* joint owner

condo'nare *vt* remit

con'dono *nm* remission

con'dotta *nf* conduct; (circoscrizione di medico) country practice; (di gara ecc) management; (tubazione) pipe

con'dotto [1] pp di CONDURRE
■ medico condotto country doctor
[2] *nm* pipe; Anat duct
■ condotto dell'aria air duct; **condotto sotterraneo** culvert

condu'cente *nm* driver
■ conducente di autobus bus driver

⚘ **con'durre** *vt* lead; drive ‹veicoli›; (accompagnare) take; conduct ‹gas, elettricità ecc›; (gestire) run; **~ a termine** complete; **~ delle indagini** carry out an investigation

con'dursi *vr* behave

condut|'tore, -trice [1] *nmf* TV presenter; (di veicolo) driver
[2] *nm* Electr conductor

condut'tore *adj*
■ filo conduttore leitmotif

condut'tura *nf* duct
■ conduttura del gas gas main

conduzi'one *nf* conduction

confabu'lare *vi* have a confab

confa'cente *adj* suitable

con'farsi *vr* confarsi a suit

confederazi'one *nf* confederation
■ Confederazione elvetica Swiss Confederation

confe'renza *nf* (discorso) lecture; (congresso) conference
■ conferenza stampa press conference, news conference

conferenzi'ere, -a *nmf* lecturer, speaker

confe'rire [1] *vt* (donare) confer
[2] *vi* (consultarsi) confer

con'ferma *nf* confirmation; **dare ~** confirm

⚘ **confer'mare** *vt* confirm

⚘ **confes'sare** *vt* confess

confes'sarsi *vr* confess

confessio'nale [1] *adj* ‹segreto› of the confession
[2] *nm* confessional

⚘ **confessi'one** *nf* confession

confes'sore *nm* confessor

con'fetto *nm* (di mandorla) sugared almond

confet'tura *nf* jam

confezio'nare *vt* tailor ‹vestito›; package ‹prodotto›; **~ sottovuoto** vacuum-pack

confezio'nato *adj* ‹vestiti› off-the-peg; ‹gelato› wrapped

confezi'one *nf* manufacture; (di abiti) making; (di pacchi) packaging; **di ~** ‹abiti› off-the-peg; **confezioni** *pl* clothes
■ confezione economica economy pack, economy size; **confezione famiglia** family size; **confezione multipla** multipack; **confezione regalo** gift set; **confezione da sei** (di bottiglie, lattine) six-pack

confic'care *vt* thrust

confic'carsi *vr* lodge

confic'cato *adj* **~ in** lodged in, embedded in

confi'dare [1] *vt* confide
[2] *vi* **~ in** trust

confi'darsi *vr* **~ con** confide in

confi'dente [1] *adj* confident
[2] *nmf* confidant; (informatore) informer

confi'denza *nf* confidence; (familiarità) familiarity; **prendersi delle confidenze** take liberties

confidenzi'ale *adj* confidential; ‹tono› familiar; **in via ~** confidentially

configu'rare *vt* Comput configure

configurazi'one *nf* configuration

confi'nante *adj* neighbouring

confi'nare [1] *vt* (relegare) confine
[2] *vi* **~ con** border on

confi'narsi *vr* (ritirarsi) withdraw

confi'nato [1] *adj* confined
[2] *nm* prisoner

CONFIN'DUSTRIA *nf abbr* **(Confederazione generale dell'Industria italiana)** ≈ CBI

⚘ **con'fine** *nm* border; (tra terreni) boundary

con'fino *nm* political exile

con'fisca *nf* (di proprietà) confiscation

confi'scare *vt* confiscate

conflagrazi'one *nf* conflagration

con'flitto *nm* conflict
■ conflitto aereo air war

conflittu'ale *adj* adversarial

conflittualità *nf* adversarial nature

conflu'enza *nf* confluence; (di strade) junction

conflu'ire *vi* ‹fiumi› flow together; ‹strade› meet

⚘ **con'fondere** *vt* confuse; (imbarazzare) embarrass

con'fondersi *vr* (mescolarsi) mingle; (sbagliarsi) be mistaken

confor'mare *vt* standardize (**a** in line with)

confor'marsi *vr* conform

conformazi'one *nf* conformity (**a** with); (del terreno) nature

con'forme *adj* standard
conforme'mente *adv* accordingly
confor'mismo *nm* conformity
confor'mista *nmf* conformist
conformità *nf* (a norma) conformity (a with); **in ~ a** in accordance with, in conformity with
confor'tante *adj* comforting
confor'tare *vt* comfort
confor'tevole *adj* (comodo) comfortable
con'forto *nm* comfort; **a ~ di** ‹una tesi› in support of; **conforti** *pl* **religiosi** last rites
confra'telli *nmpl* brethren
confra'ternita *nf* brotherhood
confron'tare *vt* compare
⚘ **con'fronto** *nm* comparison; **in ~ a** by comparison with; **nei tuoi confronti** towards you; **senza ~** far and away, by far
   ■ **confronto diretto** head to head
confusio'nario *adj* ‹persona› muddle-headed
confusi'one *nf* confusion; (baccano) racket; (disordine) mess; (imbarazzo) embarrassment
con'fuso [1] *pp di* CONFONDERE
   [2] *adj* confused; (indistinto) indistinct; (imbarazzato) embarrassed
confu'tare *vt* confute
conge'dare *vt* dismiss; Mil discharge
conge'darsi *vr* take one's leave
con'gedo *nm* leave; **essere in ~** be on leave
   ■ **congedo malattia** sick leave; **congedo [di] maternità** maternity leave; **congedo [di] paternità** paternity leave
conge'gnare *vt* devise; (mettere insieme) assemble
con'gegno *nm* device
congelamento *nm* freezing; Med frostbite
   ■ **congelamento dei prezzi** price freeze
conge'lare *vt* freeze
conge'lato *adj* ‹cibo› deep-frozen
congela'tore *nm* freezer
congeni'ale *adj* congenial
con'genito *adj* congenital
congestio'nare *vt* congest
congestio'nato *adj* ‹traffico› congested; ‹viso› flushed
congesti'one *nf* congestion
conget'tura *nf* conjecture
congi'ungere *vt* join ‹mani›; combine ‹sforzi›
congi'ungersi *vr* join, connect
congiunti'vite *nf* conjunctivitis
congiun'tivo *nm* subjunctive
congi'unto [1] *pp di* CONGIUNGERE

⚘ *indicates a very frequent word*

   [2] *adj* joined; ‹azione› joint; ‹forze, sforzo› combined
   [3] *nm* relative
congiun'tura *nf* junction; (situazione) situation
congiuntu'rale *adj* economic
congiunzi'one *nf* Gram conjunction
congi'ura *nf* conspiracy
congiu'rare *vi* conspire
conglome'rato *nm* conglomerate; fig conglomeration; (da costruzione) concrete
'Congo *nm* Congo
congo'lese *adj & nmf* Congolese
congratu'larsi *vr* **~ con qualcuno per** congratulate somebody on
congratulazi'oni *nfpl* congratulations
con'grega *nf* band
congre'gare *vt* gather
congre'garsi *vr* congregate
congregazi'one *nf* congregation
congres'sista *nmf* convention participant
con'gresso *nm* congress, convention; (americano) Congress
   ■ **Congresso Nazionale Africano** African National Congress
'congrua *nf* stipend
'congruo *adj* proper; (giusto) fair
conguagli'are *vt* balance
congu'aglio *nm* balance
coni'are *vt* coin
conia'tura *nf* coinage
coniazi'one *nf* coinage
'conico *adj* conical
co'nifera *nf* conifer
co'niglia *nf* female rabbit, doe
conigli'era *nf* rabbit hutch
conigli'etta *nf* bunny girl
conigli'etto *nm* bunny
co'niglio *nm* rabbit
coniu'gale *adj* marital; ‹vita› married
coniu'gare *vt* conjugate
coniu'garsi *vr* get married; Gram conjugate
coniu'gato *adj* (sposato) married
coniugazi'one *nf* conjugation
'coniuge *nmf* spouse
connazio'nale *nmf* compatriot
connessi'one *nf* connection
   ■ **connessione a banda larga** broadband connection
con'nesso *pp di* CONNETTERE
con'nettere [1] *vt* connect
   [2] *vi* think rationally
con'nettersi *vr* Comput (a Internet) log on (a to)
connet'tore *nm* connector
conni'vente *adj* conniving

conno'tare *vt* connote

conno'tato *nm* distinguishing feature; **connotati** *pl* description; **rispondere ai connotati** fit the description; **cambiare i connotati a qualcuno** (hum) re-arrange somebody's face

con'nubio *nm* fig union

'cono *nm* cone

cono'scente *nmf* acquaintance

✦ **cono'scenza** *nf* knowledge; (persona) acquaintance; (sensi) consciousness; **perdere ~** lose consciousness; **riprendere ~** regain consciousness, come to
■ **conoscenza di lavoro** business contact

✦ **co'noscere** *vt* know; (essere a conoscenza di) be acquainted with; (fare la conoscenza di) meet; **~ qualcosa a fondo** know something inside out

conosci'|tore, -trice *nmf* connoisseur

conosci'uto [1] pp di CONOSCERE [2] *adj* well-known

con'quista *nf* conquest

✦ **conqui'stare** *vt* conquer; fig win

conquista'tore *nm* conqueror; fig ladykiller

consa'crare *vt* consecrate; ordain ‹sacerdote›; (dedicare) dedicate

consa'crarsi *vr* devote oneself

consa'crato *adj* ‹suolo› hallowed

consacrazi'one *nf* consecration

consangu'ineo, -a *nmf* blood relation

consa'pevole *adj* conscious

consapevo'lezza *nf* consciousness

consapevol'mente *adv* consciously

conscia'mente *adv* consciously

'conscio *adj* conscious

consecu'tivo *adj* consecutive; (seguente) next

con'segna *nf* delivery; (merce) consignment; (custodia) care; (di prigioniero) handover; Mil (ordine) orders *pl*; Mil (punizione) confinement to barracks; **pagamento alla consegna** cash on delivery
■ **consegna della posta** mail delivery

✦ **conse'gnare** *vt* deliver; Mil confine to barracks; hand over ‹prigioniero, chiavi›

consegna'tario *nm* consignee

consegu'ente *adj* consequent

✦ **consegu'enza** *nf* consequence; **di ~** (perciò) consequently; ‹agire, comportarsi› accordingly

consegui'mento *nm* achievement

consegu'ire [1] *vt* achieve [2] *vi* follow

✦ **con'senso** *nm* consent; (della popolazione) consensus

consensu'ale *adj* consensus-based

✦ **consen'tire** [1] *vi* consent [2] *vt* allow

consenzi'ente *adj* consenting

con'serto *adj* **a braccia conserte** with one's arms folded

con'serva *nf* preserve; (di frutta) jam; (di agrumi) marmalade
■ **conserva di pomodoro** tomato sauce

✦ **conser'vare** *vt* preserve; (mantenere) keep; **~ in frigo** keep refrigerated; **~ in luogo asciutto** keep dry

conser'varsi *vr* keep; **~ in salute** keep well

conserva'|tore, -trice *adj & nmf* Pol conservative; **partito conservatore** Conservative Party, Tory Party Br

conserva'torio *nm* conservatory, school of music

conservato'rismo *nm* conservatism

conservazi'one *nf* preservation; **a lunga ~** long-life

con'sesso *nm* assembly

✦ **conside'rare** *vt* consider; (stimare) regard

conside'rato *adj* (stimato) esteemed

considerazi'one *nf* consideration; (osservazione, riflessione) remark; (stima) respect

conside'revole *adj* considerable

consigli'abile *adj* advisable

✦ **consigli'are** *vt* advise; (raccomandare) recommend

consigli'arsi *vr* **~ con qualcuno** ask somebody's advice

consigli'ere, -a *nmf* adviser; (membro di un consiglio) councillor
■ **consigliere d'amministrazione** board member; **consigliere delegato** managing director

✦ **con'siglio** *nm* advice; (ente) council; **un ~** a piece of advice
■ **consiglio d'amministrazione** board of directors; **consiglio di guerra** war cabinet; **consiglio d'istituto** parent-teacher association; **consiglio dei ministri** Cabinet; **consiglio scolastico** education committee; **Consiglio di Sicurezza** (dell'ONU) Security Council; **Consiglio Superiore della Magistratura** *body responsible for ensuring the independence of the judiciary*

con'simile *adj* similar

consi'stente *adj* substantial; (spesso) thick; fig ‹argomento› solid

consi'stenza *nf* consistency; (spessore) thickness; fig (di argomento) solidity

✦ **con'sistere** *vi* **~ in** consist of

consoci'arsi *vr* go into partnership

consoci'ata *nf* (azienda) subsidiary

consociati'vismo *nm* excessive tendency to form associations

consoci'ato *nm* associate

con'socio, -a *nmf* fellow-member

conso'lante *adj* consoling

conso'lare¹ *adj* consular

ꟈ **conso'lare**[2] *vt* console
conso'larsi *vr* console oneself
conso'lato *nm* consulate
consolazi'one *nf* consolation
'console[1] *nm* consul
con'sole[2] *nf inv* (tastiera) console
■ **console per videogiochi** games console
consolida'mento *nm* consolidation
consoli'dare *vt* consolidate
consoli'darsi *vr* consolidate
consommé *nm inv* consommé
conso'nante *nf* consonant
conso'nanza *nf* consonance
'consono *adj* appropriate (**a** to), suitable (**a** for)
con'sorte *nmf* consort
con'sorzio *nm* consortium
con'stare *vi* ~ **di** consist of; (risultare) appear; **a quanto mi consta** as far as I know; **mi consta che** … seemingly …
consta'tare *vt* ascertain
constatazi'one *nf* statement of fact
consu'eto[1] *adj* usual
[2] *nm* **più del** ~ more than usual
consuetudi'nario *adj* ‹diritto› common; ‹persona› set in one's ways
consue'tudine *nf* habit; (usanza) custom
consu'lente *nmf* consultant
■ **consulente aziendale** management consultant; (azienda) management consultancy; **consulente matrimoniale** marriage guidance counsellor
consu'lenza *nf* consultancy
consul'tare *vt* consult
consul'tarsi *vr* ~ **con** consult with
consultazi'one *nf* consultation
consul'tivo *adj* consultative
con'sulto *nm* consultation
consul'torio *nm* free clinic providing treatment for sexual problems and advice
ꟈ **consu'mare** *vt* (usare) consume; wear out ‹abito, scarpe›; consummate ‹matrimonio›; commit ‹delitto›
consu'marsi *vr* consume; ‹abito, scarpe› wear out; (struggersi) pine; '**da** ~ **preferibilmente entro il** …' best before …
consu'mato *adj* ‹politico› consummate; ‹scarpe, tappeto› worn [out]
consuma'|tore, -trice *nmf* consumer
consumazi'one *nf* consumption; (bibita) drink; (spuntino) snack; (di matrimonio) consummation; (di delitto) commission
consu'mismo *nm* consumerism
consu'mista *nmf* consumerist
con'sumo *nm* consumption; (uso) use; **generi di consumo** consumer goods
■ **consumo [di carburante]** [fuel] consumption

ꟈ indicates a very frequent word

consun'tivo *nm* **fare il** ~ **di** fig take stock of
■ **bilancio consuntivo** balance sheet
con'sunto *adj* well-worn
conta'balle *nmf* fam storyteller
con'tabile[1] *adj* book-keeping
[2] *nmf* accountant
contabilità *nf inv* accounting; (ufficio) accounts department; **tenere la** ~ keep the accounts
■ **contabilità di gestione** management accounts; **contabilità in partita doppia** double entry book-keeping
contachi'lometri *nm inv* mileometer, odometer Am
ꟈ **conta'dino, -a** *nmf* farm-worker, agricultural labourer; (proprietario) farmer; (medievale) peasant
contagi'are *vt* infect; **la sua allegria contagia tutti** his cheerfulness is very contagious
contagi'ato *adj* infected
con'tagio *nm* contagion
contagi'oso *adj* contagious
conta'giri *nm inv* rev counter
conta'gocce *nm inv* dropper; **dare qualcosa col** ~ fig dole something out in dribs and drabs
contami'nare *vt* contaminate
contaminazi'one *nf* contamination
■ **contaminazione incrociata** cross-contamination
contami'nuti *nm inv* timer
con'tante *nm* cash; **pagare in contanti** pay cash
ꟈ **con'tare**[1] *vt* count; (tenere conto di) take into account; **devi** ~ **un'ora per il viaggio** you have to allow an hour for the journey
[2] *vi* count; ~ **di fare qualcosa** plan to do something
conta'scatti *nm inv* Teleph time-unit counter
con'tato *adj* ‹giorni, ore› numbered
conta'tore *nm* meter
■ **contatore del gas** gas meter
contat'tare *vt* contact
ꟈ **con'tatto** *nm* contact; **essere in** ~ **con** be in touch or contact with; **mettersi in** ~ **con** contact, get in touch with
ꟈ **'conte** *nm* count, earl Br
con'tea *nf* county
conteggi'are[1] *vt* include
[2] *vi* calculate
con'teggio *nm* calculation
■ **conteggio alla rovescia** countdown
con'tegno *nm* behaviour; (atteggiamento) attitude; **darsi un** ~ pull oneself together
conte'gnoso *adj* dignified
contem'plare *vt* contemplate; (fissare) gaze at

contempla'tivo *adj* contemplative

contemplazi'one *nf* contemplation

con'tempo *nm* nel ∼ in the meantime

contemporanea'mente *adv* at the same time

contempo'raneo, -a *adj & nmf* contemporary

conten'dente *nmf* competitor

con'tendere ① *vi* compete; (litigare) quarrel ② *vt* dispute

con'tendersi *vr* ∼ qualcosa compete for something

⚬ **conte'nere** *vt* contain; (reprimere) repress

conte'nersi *vr* contain oneself

conteni'tore *nm* container

conten'tabile *adj* facilmente ∼ easy to please

conten'tare *vt* please

conten'tarsi *vr* ∼ di be content with

conten'tezza *nf* happiness

conten'tino *nm* placebo

⚬ **con'tento** *adj* glad; (soddisfatto) happy

conte'nuto *nm* contents *pl*; (di libro, testo) content

contenzi'oso ① *adj* contentious ② *nm* dispute; (ufficio) legal department

con'tesa *nf* disagreement; Sport contest

con'teso ① *pp di* CONTENDERE ② *adj* contested

con'tessa *nf* countess

conte'stare *vt* contest; Jur give notification of ‹contravvenzione›; ∼ un reato a qualcuno charge somebody with an offence

contesta|'tore, -trice ① *nmf* person who is anti-authority ② *adj* anti-authority

contestazi'one *nf* (disputa) dispute; (protesta) protest; (di contravvenzione) notification

con'testo *nm* context

con'tiguo *adj* adjacent

continen'tale *adj* continental

⚬ **conti'nente** *nm* continent

conti'nenza *nf* continence

contin'gente *nm* contingent; (quota) quota

contin'genza *nf* contingency

continua'mente *adv* (senza interruzione) continuously; (frequentemente) continually

⚬ **continu'are** *vt/i* continue; (riprendere) resume; ∼ gli studi stay on at school

continua'tivo *adj* on-going, continuous

continuazi'one *nf* continuation

continuità *nf* continuity

⚬ **con'tinuo** *adj* continuous; (molto frequente) continual; di ∼ continuously; (frequentemente) continually; **corrente continua** direct current

con'tinuum *nm inv* continuum

⚬ **'conto** *nm* calculation; (in banca, negozio) account; (di ristorante ecc) bill, check Am; (stima) consideration; **a conti fatti** all things considered; **ad ogni buon** ∼ in any case; **di poco/nessun** ∼ of little/no importance; **in fin dei conti** when all's said and done; **per** ∼ **di** on behalf of; **per** ∼ **mio** (a mio parere) in my opinion; (da solo) on my own; **per** ∼ **terzi** for a third party; **sul** ∼ **di qualcuno** ‹voci, informazioni› about somebody; **far** ∼ **di** (supporre) suppose; (proporsi) intend; **far** ∼ **su** rely on; **fare i propri conti** do one's accounts; **fare i conti con qualcuno** fig sort somebody out; **fare i conti in tasca a qualcuno** estimate how much somebody is worth; **fare i conti senza l'oste** forget the most important thing; **render** ∼ **a qualcuno di qualcosa** be accountable to somebody for something; **rendersi** ∼ **di qualcosa** realize something; **starsene per** ∼ **proprio** be on one's own; **tener** ∼ **di qualcosa** take something into account; **tenere da** ∼ **qualcosa** look after something

■ **conto in banca** bank account; **conto congiunto** joint account; **conto corrente** current account, checking account Am; **conto [corrente] comune** joint account; **conto corrente postale** Giro account; **conto profitti e perdite** profit and loss account; **conto alla rovescia** countdown; **conto spese** expense account

con'torcere *vt* twist

con'torcersi *vr* twist about

contor'nare *vt* surround

con'torno *nm* contour; Culin vegetables *pl*

contorsi'one *nf* contortion

contorsio'nista *nmf* contortionist

con'torto ① *pp di* CONTORCERE ② *adj* twisted

contrabban'dare *vt* smuggle

contrabbandi'ere, -a *nmf* smuggler

contrab'bando *nm* contraband

contrabbas'sista *nmf* double bass player

contrab'basso *nm* double bass

contraccambi'are *vt* return

contrac'cambio *nm* return

contraccet'tivo *nm* contraceptive

contraccezi'one *nf* contraception

contrac'colpo *nm* rebound; (di arma da fuoco) recoil; fig repercussion

con'trada *nf* (rione) district

contrad'detto *pp di* CONTRADDIRE

contrad'dire *vt* contradict

contraddi'stinguere *vt* differentiate, distinguish

contraddi'stinto ① *pp di* CONTRADDISTINGUERE ② *adj* ∼ da distinguished by

contraddit'torio *adj* contradictory

contraddizi'one *nf* contradiction
contra'ente *nmf* contracting party
contra'ereo *adj* anti-aircraft
contraf'fare *vt* disguise
contraf'fatto ① pp di CONTRAFFARE
  ② *adj* disguised
contraffazi'one *nf* disguising
contraf'forte *nm* buttress
con'tralto ① *nm* counter-tenor
  ② *nf* contralto
contrap'peso *nm* counterbalance
contrap'porre *vt* (confrontare) compare;
  ∼ A a B counter B with A
contrap'porsi *vr* be in opposition; ∼ a
  contrast with; (opporsi a) be opposed to
contrap'punto *nm* Mus counterpoint
contraria'mente *adv* ∼ a contrary to;
  ∼ a me unlike me
contrari'are *vt* oppose; (infastidire) annoy
contrari'arsi *vr* get annoyed
contrarietà *nf inv* adversity; (ostacolo)
  set-back
♂ **con'trario** ① *adj* contrary, opposite;
  ‹direzione› opposite; ‹esito, vento›
  unfavourable
  ② *nm* contrary, opposite; **al** ∼ on the
  contrary
con'trarre *vt* contract
contrasse'gnare *vt* mark
contras'segno *nm* mark; **[in]** ∼
  ‹spedizione› cash on delivery, COD
  ■ contrassegno IVA VAT receipt
contra'stante *adj* contrasting
contra'stare ① *vt* oppose; (contestare)
  contest
  ② *vi* contrast; ‹colori› clash
con'trasto *nm* contrast; (di colori) clash;
  (litigio) dispute
contrattac'care *vt* counter-attack
contrat'tacco *nm* counter-attack
contrat'tare *vt/i* negotiate; (mercanteggiare)
  bargain
contrattazi'one *nf* contravention;
  (salariale) bargaining
  ■ contrattazione di azioni share dealing
contrat'tempo *nm* hitch
♂ **con'tratto** ① pp di CONTRARRE
  ② *nm* contract
  ■ contratto di lavoro employment contract;
  contratto a termine fixed-term contract;
  contratti a termine *pl* Fin futures
contrattu'ale *adj* contractual
contravve'nire *vi* contravene a law
contrazi'one *nf* contraction; (di prezzi)
  reduction
contribu'ente *nmf* contributor; (del fisco)
  taxpayer
contribu'ire *vi* contribute

contribu'tivo *adj* contributory
contri'buto *nm* contribution; **contributi** *pl*
  pensionistici pension contributions
con'trito *adj* contrite
♂ **'contro** ① *prep* against; ∼ **di me** against
  me
  ② *nm* **il pro e il** ∼ the pros and cons *pl*
contro'battere *vt* counter
controbilanci'are *vt* counterbalance
controcor'rente ① *adj* ‹idee, persona›
  nonconformist
  ② *adv* upriver; fig upstream; **andare** ∼ fig
  swim against the tide
controcul'tura *nf* counterculture
contro'curva *nf* second bend
contro'esodo *nm* massive return from
  holiday
controfa'gotto *nm* double bassoon
controffen'siva *nf* counter-offensive
controfi'gura *nf* stand-in
controfi'letto *nm* sirloin
contro'firma *nf* countersignature
controfir'mare *vt* countersign
controindicazi'one *nf* Med
  contraindication
controinterroga'torio *nm* cross-
  examination
control'labile *adj* ‹emozione›
  controllable; Tech which can be monitored
♂ **control'lare** *vt* control; (verificare) check
control'larsi *vr* control oneself
control'lato *adj* controlled
con'troller *nm inv* Fin controller
con'trollo *nm* control; (verifica) check; Med
  check-up; **perdere il** ∼ **di** lose control of
  ■ controllo degli armamenti arms control;
  controllo automatico della velocità automatic
  speed check; **controllo bagagli** baggage
  control; **controllo biglietti** ticket inspection;
  controllo dei cambi exchange control;
  controllo del credito credit control; **controllo**
  medico check-up; **controllo delle nascite**
  birth control; **controllo ortografico** Comput
  spellchecker; **fare il** ∼ **ortografico** spellcheck;
  controllo passaporti passport control;
  controllo [di] qualità quality control
control'lore *nm* controller; (sui treni ecc)
  [ticket] inspector
  ■ controllore di volo air-traffic controller
contro'luce *nf* in ∼ against the light
contro'mano *adv* in the wrong direction
contromi'sura *nf* countermeasure
contropar'tita *nf* compensation; **in** ∼
  in return
contropi'ede *nm* Sport breakaway;
  prendere in ∼ fig catch off guard
controprodu'cente *adj* counter-
  productive

♂ indicates a very frequent word

contro'prova *nf* cross-check; **fare la ~ di qualcosa** cross-check something

con'trordine *nm* counter order; **salvo contrordini** unless I/you hear to the contrary

contro'senso *nm* contradiction in terms

controspio'naggio *nm* counterespionage

controten'denza *nf* countertrend

controva'lore *nm* equivalent

contro'vento *adv* against the wind

contro'versia *nf* controversy; Jur dispute

contro'verso *adj* controversial

controvo'glia *adv* unwillingly

contu'mace *adj* Jur in default, absent

contu'macia *nf* default; **in ~** in one's absence

contun'dente *adj* ‹corpo, arma› blunt

contur'bante *adj* perturbing

contur'bare *vt* perturb

contusi'one *nf* bruise

con'tuso *nm* person suffering from cuts and bruises

convale'scente *adj & nmf* convalescent

convale'scenza *nf* convalescence; **essere in ~** be convalescing

con'valida *nf* ratification; (di nomina) confirmation; (di biglietto) validation

convali'dare *vt* ratify; confirm ‹nomina›; validate ‹atto, biglietto›

con'vegno *nm* meeting; (congresso) convention, congress

conve'nevole *adj* suitable

conve'nevoli *nmpl* pleasantries

conveni'ente *adj* convenient; (vantaggioso) advantageous; ‹prezzo› attractive

conveni'enza *nf* convenience; (interesse) advantage; (di prezzo) attractiveness

✒ **conve'nire** ① *vi* agree; (riunirsi) gather; (essere opportuno) be convenient; **ci conviene andare** It's better to go, **non mi conviene stancarmi** I'd better not tire myself out
② *vt* agree [on]

conven'ticola *nf* clique

✒ **con'vento** *nm* (di suore) convent; (di frati) monastery

conve'nuto *adj* agreed

convenzio'nale *adj* conventional

convenzio'nato *adj* ‹prezzo› controlled

convenzi'one *nf* convention

conver'gente *adj* converging

conver'genza *nf* convergence

con'vergere *vi* converge

con'versa *nf* lay sister

conver'sare *vi* converse

conversa|'tore, -trice *nmf* conversationalist

conversazi'one *nf* conversation

conversi'one *nf* conversion

con'verso *pp di* CONVERGERE

conver'tibile *nf* Auto convertible

conver'tire *vt* convert

conver'tirsi *vr* convert

conver'tito, -a ① *adj* converted
② *nmf* convert

converti'tore *nm* converter

con'vesso *adj* convex

convezi'one *nf* convection

convin'cente *adj* convincing

✒ **con'vincere** *vt* convince

con'vinto *adj* convinced

convinzi'one *nf* conviction

convi'tato *nm* guest

con'vitto *nm* boarding school

convi'vente ① *nm* common-law husband
② *nf* common-law wife

convi'venza *nf* cohabitation

con'vivere *vi* live together

convivi'ale *adj* convivial

convo'care *vt* summon; Jur summons; convene ‹riunione›

convocazi'one *nf* summoning; Jur summoning; (atto) summons; (riunione) meeting

convogli'are *vt* convey; ‹navi› convoy

con'voglio *nm* convoy; (ferroviario) train

convolare *vi* **~ a giuste nozze** (hum) tie the knot

convulsa'mente *adv* convulsively

convulsi'one *nf* convulsion; fig fit

convul'sivo *adj* Med convulsive; ‹riso› hysterical

coope'rante *nmf* aid worker

coope'rare *vi* co-operate

coopera'tiva *nf* co-operative

cooperazi'one *nf* co-operation

coordina'mento *nm* co-ordination

coordi'nare *vt* co-ordinate

coordi'nata *nf* Math co-ordinate; **coordinate** *pl* (su mappa) grid reference; **coordinate** *pl* **bancarie** bank details

coordi'nato ① *adj* co-ordinated
② *nm* (intimo) lingerie set

coordina|'tore, -trice *nmf* co-ordinator

coordinazi'one *nf* co-ordination

■ **coordinazione occhio-mano** hand-eye coordination

co'perchio *nm* lid; (copertura) cover

co'perta *nf* blanket; (copertura) cover; Naut deck

■ **coperta elettrica** electric blanket

coper'tina *nf* cover; (di libro) dust-jacket

co'perto ① *pp di* COPRIRE
② *adj* covered; (vestito) wrapped up; ‹cielo› overcast; ‹piscina› indoor
③ *nm* (a tavola) place; (prezzo del coperto) cover charge; **al ~** under cover

coper'tone *nm* tarpaulin; (gomma) tyre

coper'tura *nf* cover; (azione) covering; (di strada) surfacing; (di malefatta) cover-up
- **copertura globale** blanket coverage

'copia *nf* copy; **bella/brutta ∼** fair/rough copy; **essere la ∼ spiccicata di qualcuno** be the spitting image of somebody
- **copia su carta** hard copy; **copia pirata** pirate copy; **copia di riserva** Comput backup copy

'copia e in'colla *nm inv* Comput copy and paste; **fare un ∼** copy and paste

copi'are *vt* copy

copia'trice *nf* copier

copi'lota *nmf* co-pilot; (di auto) co-driver

copi'one *nm* Cinema, TV script

copi'oso *adj* copious

'coppa *nf* (calice) goblet; (bicchiere) glass; (per gelato ecc) dish; Sport cup
- **coppa [di] gelato** ice-cream (*served in a dish*); **coppa del mondo** World Cup

cop'petta *nf* (di ceramica, vetro) bowl; (di gelato) small tub

'coppia *nf* couple; **∼ di fatto** de facto couple; (in carte, voga) pair

co'prente *adj* (cipria, vernice) thick; ‹collant› opaque

copri'capo *nm* head covering

coprifu'oco *nm* curfew

copri'letto *nm* bedspread

copri'mozzo *nm* hub-cap

copriobiet'tivo *nm* lens cap

copripiu'mino *nm* duvet cover

⚡ **co'prire** *vt* cover; drown [out] ‹suono›; hold ‹carica›

co'prirsi *vr* (vestirsi) cover oneself up; (vestirsi pesante) dress warmly; fig cover up; (proteggersi) cover oneself; ‹cielo› become overcast

copritei'era *nm* tea cosy

co-protago'nista *nmf* Cinema co-star

'coque: alla ∼ *adj* ‹uovo› soft-boiled

⚡ **co'raggio** *nm* bravery, courage; (sfacciataggine) nerve; **∼!** chin up!

coraggiosa'mente *adv* bravely, courageously

coraggi'oso *adj* brave, courageous

co'rale *adj* choral

co'rallo *nm* coral

co'rano *nm* Koran

co'razza *nf* armour; (di animali) shell

coraz'zata *nf* battleship

coraz'zato *adj* ‹nave› armour-plated

corazza'tura *nf* armour plating

corazzi'ere *nm* cuirassier

corbelle'ria *of* piece of nonsense; **dire corbellerie** talk nonsense

⚡ **'corda** *nf* cord; (spago, Mus) string; (fune) rope; (cavo) cable; **essere giù di ∼** be down; **dare ∼ a qualcuno** encourage somebody; **tagliare la ∼** cut and run; **tenere qualcuno sulla ∼** keep somebody on tenterhooks; **corde** *pl* **vocali** vocal cords
- **corda per il bucato** washing line

cor'data *nf* roped party

cordi'ale ① *adj* cordial; **cordiali saluti** best wishes ② *nm* (bevanda) cordial

cordialità *nf inv* cordiality; **∼** *pl* (saluti) best wishes

'cordless *nm inv* Teleph cordless (phone)

cor'doglio *nm* grief; (lutto) mourning

cor'done *nm* cord; (schieramento) cordon
- **cordone ombelicale** umbilical cord; **cordone sanitario** cordon sanitaire

Corea *nf* Korea
- **Corea del Nord** North Korea; **Corea del Sud** South Korea

core'ano, -a *adj* & *nmf* Korean

coreogra'fare *vt* choreograph

coreogra'fia *nf* choreography; **fare la ∼ di** choreograph

core'ografo, -a *nmf* choreographer

Corfù *nf* Corfu

cori'aceo *adj* tough

cori'andoli *nmpl* (di carta) confetti *sg*

cori'andolo *nm* (spezia) coriander

cori'care *vt* put to bed

cori'carsi *vr* go to bed

Co'rinto *nf* Corinth

co'rista *nmf* choir member

'corna ▶ CORNO

cor'nacchia *nf* crow

corna'musa *nf* bagpipes *pl*

'cornea *nf* cornea

'corner *nm inv* corner; **salvarsi in ∼** fig have a lucky escape

cor'netta *nf* Mus cornet; (del telefono) receiver

cor'netto *nm* (brioche) croissant
- **cornetto acustico** ear trumpet

cor'nice *nf* frame
- **cornice a giorno** clip frame; **cornice digitale** digital frame

cornici'one *nm* cornice

cornifi'care *vt* fam cheat on

⚡ **'corno** *nm* (*pl f* **corna**) horn; **fare le corna a qualcuno** fam cheat on somebody; **fare le corna (per scongiuro)** ≈ touch wood; **un ∼!** you must be joking!; (per niente) nonsense!
- **corno da caccia** French horn

Corno'vaglia *nf* Cornwall

cornu'copia *nf* cornucopia

cor'nuto ① *adj* horned ② *nm* fam (marito tradito) cuckold; (insulto) bastard

---

'coro *nm* chorus; Relig choir

co'rolla *nf* corolla

corol'lario *nm* corollary

co'rona *nf* crown; (di fiori) wreath; (rosario) rosary

corona'mento *nm* (di sogno) fulfilment; (di carriera) crowning achievement

coro'nare *vt* fulfil ‹sogno›

coro'nario *adj* ‹arteria› coronary

cor'petto *nm* bodice

✧ **'corpo** *nm* body; Mil (diplomatico) corps *inv*; [a] ~ a ~ Mil hand to hand; **lottare** [a] ~ a ~ have a punch-up, slug it out; **dare** ~ **a qualcosa** give substance to something; **buttarsi a** ~ **morto in qualcosa** throw oneself desperately into something; **andare di** ~ move one's bowels

■ **corpo di ballo** corps de ballet; **corpo estraneo** foreign body; **corpo insegnante** teaching staff; **corpo del reato** murder weapon

corpo'rale *adj* corporal

corporati'vismo *nm* corporatism

corpora'tura *nf* build

corporazi'one *nf* corporation

cor'poreo *adj* bodily

cor'poso *adj* full-bodied

corpu'lento *adj* stout

'corpus *nm inv* corpus

cor'puscolo *nm* corpuscle

corre'dare *vt* (di note) supply (**di** with); **corredato di curriculum** accompanied by a CV

corre'dino *nm* (per neonato) layette

cor'redo *nm* (nuziale) trousseau; (di informazioni ecc) set

correggere *vt* correct; lace ‹bevanda›; ~ **le bozze** proof-read

corre'lare *vt* correlate

✧ **cor'rente** **[1]** *adj* running; (in vigore) current; (frequente) everyday; ‹inglese ecc› fluent

[2] *nf* current; (d'aria) draught; **essere al** ~ **di qualcosa** be aware of something; **tenersi al** ~ keep up to date (**di** with)

■ **corrente continua** direct current; **corrente trasversale** cross current

corrente'mente *adv* ‹parlare› fluently; (comunemente) commonly

✧ **'correre** **[1]** *vi* run; (affrettarsi) hurry; Sport race; ‹notizie› circulate; **lascia** ~**!** let it go!; ~ **dietro a** run after; **tra loro non corre buon sangue** there is bad blood between them **[2]** *vt* run; ~ **un pericolo** run a risk; **corre voce che …** there's a rumour that …

correspon'sabile *nmf* person jointly responsible

corresponsi'one *nf* payment

corretta'mente *adv* correctly; ‹sedersi, mangiare› properly; ‹trattare, fare qualcosa› right

corret'tivo *nm* corrective

cor'retto **[1]** *pp di* CORREGGERE **[2]** *adj* correct; ‹caffè› with a drop of alcohol

corret'|tore, -trice **[1]** *nmf* ■ **correttore di bozze** proof-reader **[2]** *nm* ■ **correttore grammaticale** Comput grammar checker; **correttore ortografico** Comput spellchecker

correzi'one *nf* correction ■ **correzione di bozze** proof-reading; **correzione errori** Comput error correction

cor'rida *nf* bullfight

corri'doio *nm* corridor; Aeron aisle

corri'|dore, -trice *nmf* (automobilistico) driver; (ciclista) cyclist; (a piedi) runner

corri'era *nf* coach, bus

corri'ere *nm* courier; (posta) mail; (spedizioniere) carrier ■ **corriere della droga** drug mule

corri'mano *nm* hand rail

corrispet'tivo *nm* amount due

corrispon'dente **[1]** *adj* corresponding **[2]** *nmf* correspondent ■ **corrispondente estero** foreign correspondent

corrispon'denza *nf* correspondence; **tenersi in** ~ **con** correspond with; **per** ~ ‹fare un corso› by correspondence; **corso per corrispondenza** correspondence course; **vendite per corrispondenza** mail-order [shopping]

corri'spondere *vi* correspond; ‹stanza›; communicate; ~ **a** (contraccambiare) return

corri'sposto *adj* ‹amore› reciprocated

corrobo'rare *vt* strengthen; fig corroborate

cor'rodere *vt* corrode

cor'rodersi *vr* corrode

cor'rompere *vt* corrupt; (con denaro) bribe

corrosi'one *nf* corrosion

corro'sivo *adj* corrosive

cor'roso *pp di* CORRODERE

cor'rotto **[1]** *pp di* CORROMPERE **[2]** *adj* corrupt

corrucci'arsi *vr* be vexed

corrucci'ato *adj* vexed

corru'gare *vt* wrinkle; ~ **la fronte** knit one's brows

corrut'tela *nf* depravity

corruzi'one *nf* corruption; (con denaro) bribery

✧ **'corsa** *nf* running; (rapida) dash; Sport race; (di treno ecc) journey; **di** ~ at a run; **di gran** ~ in a great hurry; **fare una** ~ (sbrigarsi) run, hurry

■ **corsa agli armamenti** arms race; **corsa ciclistica** cycle race; **corsa ippica** horse race; **corsa all'oro** gold rush; **corsa a ostacoli** obstacle race; **corsa piana** flat racing; **corsa semplice** one way [ticket]

cor'sia nf gangway; (di ospedale) ward; Aut lane; (di supermercato) aisle
■ **corsia autobus** bus lane; **corsia d'emergenza** Aut hard shoulder; **corsia a scorrimento veloce** express lane; **corsia di sorpasso** fast lane, outside lane

'Corsica nf Corsica

cor'sivo nm italics pl; **in ~** in italics

⚘ **'corso** [1] pp di CORRERE
[2] nm course; (strada) main street; Comm circulation; (in borsa) price, quotation; **essere in ~** be underway; **lavori in ~** work in progress; **nel ~ di** during; **avere ~ legale** be legal tender
■ **corso d'acqua** waterway; **corso per corrispondenza** correspondence course; **corso di formazione** training course; **corso di formazione professionale** vocational course; **corso full immersion** immersion course; **corso del giorno** current daily price; **corso di laurea** degree course; **corso serale** evening class; **corsi** pl **di studio a distanza** distance learning

⚘ **'corte** nf [court] yard; Jur (regale) court; **fare la ~ a qualcuno** court somebody
■ **corte d'appello** court of appeal; **corte d'assise** crown court; **Corte di cassazione** supreme court of appeal; **Corte dei conti** National Audit Office; **Corte europea per i diritti dell'uomo** European Court of Human Rights; **Corte europea di giustizia** European Court of Justice; **corte di giustizia** court of law

cor'teccia nf bark

corteggia'mento nm courtship

corteggi'are vt court

corteggia'tore nm admirer

cor'teo nm procession
■ **corteo di auto** motorcade; **corteo funebre** funeral cortège; **corteo nuziale** bridal party

cor'tese adj courteous

corte'sia nf courtesy; **per ~** please

cortigi'ano, -a [1] nmf courtier
[2] nf courtesan

⚘ **cor'tile** nm courtyard

cor'tina nf curtain; (schermo) screen

⚘ **'corto** adj short; **per farla corta** to cut a long story short; **a ~ di** short of, hard up for
■ **corto circuito** nm short [circuit]

cortome'traggio nm Cinema short

cor'vino adj jet-black

'corvo nm raven

⚘ **'cosa** nf [1] thing; (faccenda) matter
[2] inter, rel pron what; **[che] ~** what; **nessuna ~** nothing; **ogni ~** everything; **per prima ~** first of all; **tante cose** [so] many things; (augurio) all the best; **~?** what?; **~ hai detto?** what did you say?; **le cose le vanno bene** she's doing all right

'cosca nf clan

'coscia nf thigh; Culin leg; **cosce** pl **di rana** frogs' legs

cosci'ente adj conscious

⚘ **cosci'enza** nf conscience; (consapevolezza) consciousness; **mettersi la ~ a posto** salve one's conscience

coscienziosa'mente adv conscientiously

coscienzi'oso adj conscientious

cosci'otto nm leg

co'scritto nm conscript

coscrizi'one nf conscription

⚘ **così** [1] adv so; (in questo modo) like this, like that; (perciò) therefore; **le cose stanno ~** that's how things stand; **fermo ~!** hold it!; **proprio ~!** exactly!; **basta ~!** that will do!; **ah, è ~?** it's like that, is it?; **~ ~** so-so; **e ~ via** and so on; **per ~ dire** so to speak; **più di ~** any more; **una ~ cara ragazza!** such a nice girl!; **è stato ~ generoso da aiutarti** he was kind enough to help you
[2] conj (allora) so
[3] adj inv (tale) like that, such; **una ragazza ~** a girl like that, such a girl

cosicché conj and so

cosid'detto adj so-called

co'smesi nf beauty treatment

co'smetico [1] adj cosmetic
[2] nm **cosmetici** pl cosmetics; (trucchi) make-up

'cosmico adj cosmic

'cosmo nm cosmos

cosmo'nauta nmf cosmonaut

cosmopo'lita adj cosmopolitan

co'spargere vt sprinkle; (disseminare) scatter; **~ il pavimento di cera** spread wax on the floor

co'spetto nm **al ~ di** in the presence of

co'spicuo adj conspicuous; ‹somma ecc› considerable

cospi'rare vi conspire, plot

cospira|'tore, -'trice nmf conspirator, plotter

cospirazi'one nf conspiracy, plot

⚘ **'costa** nf coast, coastline; Anat rib; **sotto ~** inshore
■ **Costa d'Avorio** Ivory Coast; **Costa Azzurra** Côte d'Azur; **Costa Smeralda** Emerald coast (in Sardinia)

costà adv there

co'stante adj & nf constant

co'stanza nf constancy

⚘ **co'stare** vi cost; **quanto costa?** how much is it?; **costi quel che costi** whatever the cost

'Costa 'Rica nm Costa Rica

co'stata nf chop
■ **costata [di manzo]** rib steak

co'stato nm ribs pl

⚘ indicates a very frequent word

costeggi'are *vt* (per mare) coast; (per terra) skirt

co'stei *pers pron* (soggetto) she; (complemento) her

costellazi'one *nf* constellation

coster'nato *adj* dismayed

costernazi'one *nf* consternation

costi'era *nf* stretch of coast

costi'ero *adj* coastal

co'stine *nfpl* (di maiale) spare ribs

'**costing** *nm inv* costing

costi'pato *adj* constipated; **essere ~** (raffreddato) have a bad cold

costipazi'one *nf* constipation; (raffreddore) bad cold

⚡ **costitu'ire** *vt* constitute; (essere) be; (formare) form; (nominare) appoint

costitu'irsi *vr* ‹criminale› give oneself up

costituzio'nale *adj* constitutional

costituzional'mente *adv* Pol constitutionally

costituzi'one *nf* constitution; (formazione) formation

⚡ '**costo** *nm* cost; **a nessun ~** on no account; **a ~ di perdere la salute** at the cost of one's health; **sotto ~** at less than cost price; **costi** *pl* **di gestione** administration costs; **costi** *pl* **spedizione** freight charges
- **costo del denaro** Fin cost of money; **costo unitario** unit cost; **costo della vita** cost of living

'**costola** *nf* rib; (di libro) spine; **stare alle costole di qualcuno** follow somebody around

costo'letta *nf* cutlet

co'storo *pron* (soggetto) they; (complemento) them

co'stoso *adj* costly

co'stretto pp di COSTRINGERE

⚡ **co'stringere** *vt* force, compel

costrit'tivo *adj* coercive

costrizi'one *nf* compulsion

⚡ **costru'ire** *vt* build, construct

costrut'tivo *adj* constructive

⚡ **costruzi'one** *nf* building, construction; (edificio) building

⚡ **co'stui** *pers pron* (soggetto) he; (complemento) him

co'stume *nm* (usanza) custom; (indumento) costume; **costumi** *pl* (morale) morals
- **costume da bagno** swim-suit; (da uomo) swimming trunks; **costume intero** one-piece; **costume tradizionale** traditional costume

costu'mista *nmf* wardrobe assistant

cote'chino *nm* spiced pork sausage

co'tenna *nf* pigskin; (della pancetta) rind
- **cotenna arrostita** crackling

co'togna *nf* quince

coto'letta *nf* cutlet

- **cotoletta alla milanese** veal cutlet in breadcrumbs

coto'nato *adj* ‹capelli› back-combed

co'tone *nm* cotton
- **cotone idrofilo** cotton wool, absorbent cotton Am

cotoni'ficio *nm* cotton mill

'**cotta** *nf* Relig surplice; fam (innamoramento) crush; **prendere una ~ per qualcuno** fam have a crush on somebody

'**cottimo** *nm* piece-work

'**cotto** ① pp di CUOCERE
② *adj* done; fam (innamorato) in love; (sbronzo) drunk; **ben ~** well cooked; ‹carne› underdone; **troppo ~** overcooked; ‹carne› overdone

cotton fi'oc® *nm inv* cotton bud

cot'tura *nf* cooking

'**country** *nm inv* country and western

cou'pon *nm inv* coupon

cou'scous *nm inv* couscous

co'vare *vt* hatch; sicken for ‹malattia›; harbour ‹rancore›

co'vata *nf* brood

'**covo** *nm* den

co'vone *nm* sheaf

cow-'boy *nm inv* cowboy

'**cozza** *nf* mussel
- **cozze alla marinara** *pl* moules marinière

coz'zare *vi* **~ contro** bump into

'**cozzo** *nm* fig clash

C.P. *abbr* (**Casella Postale**) PO Box

crac *nm inv* crack; (di tessuto) rip

crack *nm* (droga) crack

Cra'covia *nf* Cracow

'**crafen** *nm inv* cream doughnut

'**crampo** *nm* cramp

'**cranio** *nm* skull

cra'tere *nm* crater

cra'vatta *nf* tie; (a farfalla) bow-tie

cre'anza *vt* manners *pl*; **mala ~** bad manners

⚡ **cre'are** *vt* create; **~ assuefazione** be habit-forming

creatività *nf* creativity

crea'tivo *adj* creative

cre'ato *nm* creation

crea|'tore, -trice *nmf* creator; **andare al ~** go to meet one's maker

⚡ **crea'tura** *nf* creature; (bambino) baby; **povera ~!** poor thing!

creazi'one *nf* creation

cre'dente *nmf* believer

cre'denza *nf* belief; Comm credit; (mobile) sideboard

credenzi'ali *nfpl* credentials

⚡ '**credere** ① *vt* believe; (pensare) think
② *vi* **~ in** believe in; **credo di sì** I think so; **non ti credo** I don't believe you; **non posso crederci!** I can't believe it!

'credersi *vr* think oneself to be; **si crede uno scrittore** he flatters himself he is a writer

cre'dibile *adj* credible, believable

credibilità *nf* credibility

credi'tizio *adj* credit *attrib*

'credito *nm* credit; (stima) esteem; **comprare a ~** buy on credit; **dare ~ a qualcosa** give credence to something; **fare ~** give credit
■ **credito all'esportazione** export credit; **credito inesigibile** bad debt

credi|'tore, -trice *nmf* creditor

'credo *nm inv* credo

credulità *nf* credulity

'credulo *adj* credulous

credu'lone, -a *nmf* simpleton

'crema *nf* cream; (di uova e latte) custard
■ **crema base per il trucco** vanishing cream; **crema depilatoria** depilatory [cream]; **crema detergente** cleansing cream; **crema idratante** moisturizer; **crema per le mani** hand cream; **crema pasticciera** confectioner's custard; **crema per la pelle** skin cream; **crema protettiva** barrier cream; **crema solare** suntan lotion; **crema per il viso** face cream

cremagli'era *nf* ratchet

cre'mare *vt* cremate

crema'torio *nm* crematorium

cremazi'one *nf* cremation

crème cara'mel *nf* crème caramel

creme'ria *nf* dairy (*also selling ice cream and cakes*)

Crem'lino *nm* Kremlin

cre'moso *adj* creamy

cren *nm* horseradish

'crepa *nf* crack

cre'paccio *nm* cleft; (di ghiacciaio) crevasse

crepacu'ore *nm* heart-break

crepa'pelle: a ~ *adv* fit to burst

cre'pare *vi* crack; fam (morire) kick the bucket; **~ dal ridere** laugh fit to burst

crepa'tura *nf* crevice

crêpe *nf inv* pancake

crepi'tare *vi* crackle

crepi'tio *nm* crackling

cre'puscolo *nm* twilight

cre'scendo *nm* crescendo

cre'scenza *nf creamy white cheese*

⚔ **'crescere** ① *vi* grow; (aumentare) increase, grow
② *vt* (allevare) bring up; (aumentare) increase

cresci'one *nm* watercress

'crescita *nf* growth; (aumento) increase, growth

cresci'uto *pp di* CRESCERE

'cresima *nf* confirmation

cresi'mare *vt* confirm

cre'spato *adj* crinkly

cre'spella *nf* pancake

'crespo ① *adj* ‹capelli› frizzy
② *nm* crêpe

'cresta *nf* crest; (cima) peak; **abbassare la ~** become less cocky; **alzare la ~** become cocky; **sulla ~ dell'onda** on the crest of a wave

'creta *nf* clay

'Creta *nf* Crete

cre'tese *adj & nmf* Cretan

creti'nata *nf* something stupid; **dire cretinate** talk nonsense

⚔ **cre'tino, -a** ① *adj* stupid
② *nmf* idiot

C.R.I. *abbr* (**Croce Rossa Italiana**) Italian Red Cross

'cribbio *int* gosh!, golly!

cric *nm inv* jack

'cricca *nf* gang

'cricco *nm* jack

cri'ceto *nm* hamster

'cricket *nm* cricket

crimi'nale *adj & nmf* criminal

criminalità *nf* crime
■ **criminalità organizzata** organized crime

'crimine *nm* crime

criminolo'gia *nf* criminology

crimi'nologo, -a *nmf* criminologist

crimi'noso *adj* criminal

'crine *nm* horsehair

crini'era *nf* mane

crino'lina *nf* crinoline

crioge'nia *nf* cryogenics *sg*

'cripta *nf* crypt

crip'tare *vt* encrypt

crisan'temo *nm* chrysanthemum

⚔ **'crisi** *nf inv* crisis; Med fit; **essere in ~ di astinenza** be having withdrawal symptoms, be cold turkey fam
■ **crisi di nervi** hysterics; **crisi del settimo anno** seven-year itch

cristal'lino ① *adj* crystal clear
② *nm* crystalline lens

cristalliz'zare *vt* crystallize

cristalliz'zarsi *vr* crystallize; fig ‹parola, espressione› become part of the language

cri'stallo *nm* crystal

cristia'nesimo *nm* Christianity

cristianità *nf* Christendom

⚔ **cristi'ano, -a** *adj & nmf* Christian

⚔ **'Cristo** *nm* Christ; **avanti ~** BC; **dopo ~** AD; **un povero c~** a poor beggar

cri'terio *nm* criterion; (buon senso) [common] sense

'critica *nf* criticism; (recensione) review; **fare la ~ di** review ‹film, libro›
■ **critica letteraria** literary criticism

criti'care *vt* criticize

'critico ① *adj* critical
② *nm* critic
■ **critico letterario** literary critic

criti'cone, -a *nmf* fault finder

crittazi'one *nf*
■ **crittazione [dei] dati** Comput data encryption

crivel'lare *vt* riddle (**di** with)

cri'vello *nm* sieve

cro'ato, -a *adj & nmf* Croatian, Croat

Cro'azia *nf* Croatia

croc'cante ① *adj* crisp
② *nm* type of crunchy nut biscuit

croc'chetta *nf* croquette

'crocchia *nf* bun

'crocchio *nm* cluster

'croce *nf* cross; **a occhio e** ∼ roughly; **fare testa e** ∼ toss a coin; **fare** *o* **mettere una** ∼ **sopra qualcosa** fig forget about something; **mettere in** ∼ (criticare) crucify; (tormentare) nag nonstop
■ **Croce Rossa** Red Cross

croceros'sina *nf* Red Cross nurse

croce'via *nm inv* crossroads *sg*

croci'ata *nf* crusade

croci'ato ① *adj* cruciform
② *nm* crusader

cro'cicchio *nm* crossroads *sg*

croci'era *nf* cruise; **velocità di crociera** cruising speed

croci'figgere *vt* crucify

crocifissi'one *nf* crucifixion

croci'fisso ① *pp di* CROCIFIGGERE
② *adj* crucified
③ *nm* crucifix

crogio'larsi *vr* bask

crogi'olo *nm* crucible; fig melting pot

croglu'olo = CROGIOLO

crois'sant *nm inv* croissant

crol'lare *vi* collapse; ‹prezzi› slump

'crollo *nm* collapse; (dei prezzi) slump

'croma *nf* quaver

cro'mato *adj* chromium-plated

'cromo *nm* chrome

cromo'soma *nm* chromosome

'cronaca *nf* chronicle; (di giornale) news; TV, Radio commentary; **fatto di** ∼ news item
■ **cronaca mondana** gossip column; **cronaca nera** crime news

'cronico *adj* chronic

cro'nista *nmf* reporter; (di partita) commentator

croni'storia *nf* chronicle

cro'nografo *nm* chronograph

cronolo'gia *nf* chronology

cronologica'mente *adv* chronologically

crono'logico *adj* chronological

cronome'traggio *nm* timing

cronome'trare *vt* time

cronome'trista *nmf* Sport timekeeper

cro'nometro *nm* chronometer; Sport stopwatch

cross *nm* (corsa campestre) cross-country; (motocross) motocross

cros'sista *nmf* scrambler; (a piedi) cross-country runner

'crosta *nf* crust; (di formaggio) rind; (di ferita) scab; (quadro) daub

cro'staceo *nm* shellfish

cro'stata *nf* tart
■ **crostata di frutta** fruit tart; **crostata di mele** apple pie

cro'stino *nm* croûton; **crostini** *pl* pieces of toasted bread served as a starter

croupi'er *nmf inv* croupier

crucci'are *vt* torment

crucci'arsi *vr* torment oneself

'cruccio *nm* torment

cruci'ale *adj* crucial

cruci'verba *nm inv* crossword [puzzle]

cru'dele *adj* cruel

crudel'mente *adv* cruelly

crudeltà *nf inv* cruelty

'crudo *adj* raw; ‹linguaggio› crude

cru'ento *adj* bloody

crumi'raggio *nm* strike-breaking

cru'miro *nm* blackleg, scab

'crusca *nf* bran

cru'scotto *nm* dashboard

C.S.I. *nf abbr* (**Comunità degli Stati Indipendenti**) CIS

'Cuba *nf* Cuba

cu'bano, -a *adj & nmf* Cuban

cu'betto *nm*
■ **cubetto di ghiaccio** ice cube

'cubico *adj* cubic

cu'bismo *nm* cubism

cu'bista *adj & nmf* cubist

cubi'tale *adj* **a caratteri cubitali** in enormous letters

'cubo *nm* cube

cuc'cagna *nf* abundance; (baldoria) merry-making; **paese della** ∼ land of plenty

cuc'cetta *nf* (su un treno) couchette; Naut berth

cucchiai'ata *nf* spoonful

cucchia'ino *nm* teaspoon; (contenuto) teaspoon[ful]

cucchi'aio *nm* spoon; **un** ∼ a spoon[ful] (**di** of); **al** ∼ ‹dolce› creamy
■ **cucchiaio di legno** wooden spoon; **cucchiaio da minestra** soup-spoon; **cucchiaio da tavola** tablespoon; (contenuto) tablespoon[ful]

cucchiai'one *nm* serving spoon

'cuccia *nf* basket; (in giardino) kennel; **[fa' la]** ∼**!** down!

cuccio'lata *nf* litter

'cucciolo nm puppy

ᛉ **cu'cina** nf kitchen; (il cucinare) cooking; (cibo) food; (apparecchio) cooker; **far da ∼** cook; **libro di cucina** cook[ery] book

■ **cucina casalinga** home cooking; **cucina componibile** fitted kitchen; **cucina a gas** gas cooker

cuci'nare vt cook

cuci'nino nm kitchenette

cu'cire vt sew; **macchina da cucire** sewing-machine; **cucilo a macchina** do it on the machine

cu'cito nm sewing

cuci'tura nf seam

cucù nm inv cuckoo; ∼! peekaboo!

'cuculo nm cuckoo

cuffia nf bonnet; (ricevitore) headphones pl

■ **cuffia da bagno** bathing cap; **cuffia con microfono** (per telefonino) headset

cu'gino, -a nmf cousin

ᛉ **'cui** pron rel (persona: con prep) who[m]; (cose, animali: con prep) which; (tra articolo e nome) whose; **la persona con ∼ ho parlato** the person I spoke to, the person to whom I spoke fml; **la ditta per ∼ lavoro** the company I work for, the company for which I work; **l'amico il ∼ libro è stato pubblicato** the friend whose book was published; **in ∼** (dove) where; (quando) that; **per ∼** (perciò) so; **la città in ∼ vivo** the city I live in, the city where I live; **il giorno in ∼ l'ho visto** the day [that] I saw him

cu'latta nf breech

culi'naria nf cookery

culi'nario adj culinary

'culla nf cradle

cul'lare vt rock; fig cherish ‹sogno, speranza›

cul'larsi vr ∼ **nella speranza di** (liter) cherish the fond hope that

culmi'nante adj culminating

culmi'nare vi culminate

'culmine nm peak

'culo nm vulg arse; (fortuna) luck; **prendere qualcuno per il ∼** take the piss out of somebody

'culto nm cult; Relig religion; (adorazione) worship

ᛉ **cul'tura** nf culture

■ **cultura generale** general knowledge; **cultura di massa** mass culture

cultu'rale adj cultural

cultu'rismo nm body-building

cultu'rista nmf body-builder

cu'mino nm

■ **cumino nero** cumin

cumula'tivo adj cumulative; ‹prezzo› all-in, all-inclusive; **biglietto cumulativo** group ticket

'cumulo nm pile; (mucchio) heap; (nuvola) cumulus

'cuneo nm wedge

cu'netta nf gutter

cu'nicolo nm tunnel

ᛉ **cu'ocere** 1 vt cook; fire ‹ceramica›
  2 vi cook; ‹ceramica› fire

cu'oco, -a nmf cook

cu'oia nfpl **tirare le ∼** fam kick the bucket

cu'oio nm leather

■ **cuoio capelluto** scalp

ᛉ **cu'ore** nm heart; **cuori** pl (carte) hearts; **di [buon] ∼** ‹persona› kind-hearted; **di tutto ∼** wholeheartedly; **ti ringrazio di tutto ∼** many thanks; **nel profondo del ∼** in one's heart of hearts; **nel ∼ della notte** in the middle of the night; **senza ∼** heartless; **mettersi il ∼ in pace** come to terms with it; **parlare a ∼ aperto** have a heart-to-heart (con with); **stare a ∼ a qualcuno** be very important to somebody

■ **cuore tenero** (persona) softy

cupa'mente adv darkly

cupi'digia nf greed

Cu'pido nm Cupid

'cupo adj gloomy; ‹voce› deep

'cupola nf dome; **a ∼** domed

ᛉ **'cura** nf care; (amministrazione) management; Med treatment; **aver ∼ di** look after; **a ∼ di** ‹libro› edited by; **in ∼** under treatment; **fare delle cure termali** take the waters

■ **cura dimagrante** diet; **cura della fertilità** fertility treatment

cu'rabile adj curable

cu'rante adj **medico ∼** GP, doctor

ᛉ **cu'rare** vt take care of, look after; Med treat; (guarire) cure; edit ‹testo›

cu'rarsi vr take care of oneself, look after oneself; ∼ **dei fatti propri** mind one's own business

cu'rato nm parish priest

cura|'tore, -trice nmf trustee; (di testo) editor

■ **curatore fallimentare** official receiver

'curcuma nf turmeric

curcu'mina nf turmeric

'curdo, -a 1 nmf Kurd
  2 adj Kurdish

'curia nf curia

curio'saggine nf nosiness

curio'sare vi be curious; (mettere il naso) pry (in into); (nei negozi) look around

ᛉ **curiosità** nf inv curiosity

ᛉ **curi'oso** 1 adj curious; (strano) odd, curious
  2 nm busybody

'curling nm inv Sport curling

cur'ricolo nm curriculum

cur'riculum nm inv curriculum

ᛉ indicates a very frequent word

'curry *nm inv* curry
- curry in polvere curry powder

cur'sore *nm* Comput cursor

'curva *nf* curve; (stradale) bend
- curva a gomito dogleg; **curva di apprendimento** learning curve

cur'vare *vt/i* bend, curve

cur'varsi *vr* bend, curve

'curvo *adj* curved; (piegato) bent

cusci'netto *nm* pad; Mech bearing
- cuscinetto puntaspilli pincushion; **cuscinetto a sfere** ball bearing

cu'scino *nm* cushion; (guanciale) pillow
- cuscino gonfiabile air cushion

cu'scus *nm inv* couscous

'cuspide *nf* spire

cu'stode *nm* caretaker; (di abitazione) concierge; (di fabbrica) guard; (di museo) custodian
- ~ giudiziario official receiver

cu'stodia *nf* care; Jur custody; (astuccio) case; **ottenere la ~ di** get custody of
- custodia cautelare remand

custo'dire *vt* keep; (badare) look after

cu'taneo *adj* skin *attrib*

'cute *nf* skin

cu'ticola *nf* cuticle

'cutter *nm inv* cutter

CV *abbr* (**cavallo vapore**) hp

cyber'spazio *nm* cyberspace

cyberterro'rismo *nm* cyberterrorism

cy'clette® *nf inv* exercise bicycle

· ·

D d

· ·

da *prep* from; (con verbo passivo) by; (moto a luogo) to; (moto per luogo) through; (stato in luogo) at; (temporale) since; (continuativo) for; (causale) with; (in qualità di) as; (con caratteristica) with; (come) like; **da Roma a Milano** from Rome to Milan; **staccare un quadro dalla parete** take a picture off the wall; **i bambini dai 5 ai 10 anni** children between 5 and 10; **vedere qualcosa da vicino/lontano** see something from up close/from a distance; **amato da tutti** loved by everybody; **scritto da** written by; **andare dal panettiere** go to the baker's; **passo da te più tardi** I'll come over to your place later; **passiamo da qui** let's go this way; **un appuntamento dal dentista** an appointment at the dentist's; **il treno passa da Venezia** the train goes through Venice; **dall'anno scorso** since last year; **vivo qui da due anni** I've been living here for two years; **da domani** from tomorrow; **piangere dal dolore** cry with pain; **ho molto da fare** I have a lot to do; **occhiali da sole** sunglasses; **qualcosa da mangiare** something to eat; **un uomo dai capelli scuri** a man with dark hair; **è un oggetto da poco** it's not worth much; **da solo** alone; **l'ho fatto da solo** I did it by myself; **si è fatto da sé** he is a self-made man; **vive da re** he lives like a king; **non è da lui** it's not like him

dab'bene *adj* honest

dac'capo *adv* again; (dall'inizio) from the beginning

dacché *conj* since

dada'ismo *nm* (arte) Dadaism

dada'ista *adj & nmf* Dadaist

'dado *nm* dice; Culin stock cube; Techn nut

- dado ad alette wing nut

daf'fare *nm* work

'dagli = DA + GLI

dai¹ =DA + I

dai² *int* come on!; ~, **non fare così!** come on, don't be like that!; ~, **sbrigati!** come on, get a move on!

'daino *nm* deer; (pelle) buckskin

dal = DA + IL

'dalia *nf* dahlia

'dalla = DA + LA

'dalle – DA + LE

'dallo = DA + LO

'dalmata *nm* (cane) Dalmatian

Dal'mazia *nf* Dalmatia

dal'tonico *adj* colour-blind

'dama *nf* lady; (nei balli) partner; (gioco) draughts
- dama di compagnia lady's companion; **dama di corte** lady-in-waiting

dama'scato *adj* damask

da'masco *nm* (tessuto) damask

dame'rino *nm* (bellimbusto) dandy

dami'gella *nf* (di sposa) bridesmaid

damigi'ana *nf* demijohn

dam'meno *adv* non essere ~ be no less good (di than)

DAMS *nm abbr* (**Discipline delle Arti, della Musica e dello Spettacolo**) (corso di laurea) *degree in fine art, music and drama*

da'naro = DENARO

dana'roso *adj* fam (ricco) loaded

da'nese [1] *adj* Danish ···>

d

2 *nmf* Dane

3 *nm* (lingua) Danish

Dani'marca *nf* Denmark

dan'nare *vt* damn; **far ~ qualcuno** drive somebody mad

dan'narsi *vr* fig wear oneself out; **~ l'anima (a fare qualcosa)** wear oneself out (doing something)

dan'nato, -a 1 *adj* damned, damn fam

2 *nmf* damned person; **lavorare/studiare come un ~** fig work/study like mad

dannazi'one *nf* damnation

danneggia'mento *nm* damage

danneggi'are *vt* damage; (nuocere) harm

danneggi'ato *adj* Jur injured

♂ **'danno** *nm* damage; (a persona) harm; **danni** *pl* damage; **danni collaterali** collateral damage; **danni** *pl* **alla struttura portante** structural damage

dan'noso *adj* harmful

dan'tesco *adj* Dantean, Dantesque

danubi'ano *adj* Danubian

Da'nubio *nm* Danube

'danza *nf* dance; (il danzare) dancing
■ **~ folcloristica** country dancing

dan'zante *adj* **serata ~** dance

dan'zare *vi* dance

danza|'tore, -trice *nmf* dancer
■ **danzatrice del ventre** belly dancer

♂ **dapper'tutto** *adv* everywhere

dap'poco *adj* worthless

♂ **dap'prima** *adv* at first

Darda'nelli *nmpl* **i ~** the Dardanelles

'dardo *nm* dart

♂ **'dare** 1 *vt* give; sit ‹esame›; have ‹festa›; **~ qualcosa a qualcuno** give somebody something; **~ da mangiare a qualcuno** give somebody something to eat; **~ fuoco a qualcosa** set fire to something; **~ il benvenuto a qualcuno** welcome somebody; **~ la buonanotte a qualcuno** say good night to somebody; **~ del tu/del lei a qualcuno** address somebody as "tu/lei"; **~ del cretino a qualcuno** call somebody an idiot; **~ qualcosa per scontato** take something for granted; **~ fastidio a** annoy; **~ cosa danno alla TV stasera?** what's on TV tonight?; **darle a qualcuno** (picchiare) give somebody a walloping

2 *vi* **~ nell'occhio** be conspicuous; **~ alla testa** go to one's head; **~ su** ‹finestra, casa› look on to; **~ sui o ai nervi a qualcuno** get on somebody's nerves

3 *nm* Comm debit

'darsena *nf* dock

'darsi *vr* (scambiarsi) give each other; **~ da fare** get down to it; **si è dato tanto da fare!** he went to so much trouble!; **~ a** (cominciare)

take up; **~ al bere** take to drink; **~ per** ‹malato› pretend to be; **~ per vinto** give up; **può ~** maybe

darvini'ano *adj* Darwinian

darvi'nista *nmf* Darwinist

♂ **'data** *nf* date; **di lunga ~** old established
■ **data di emissione** date of issue; **data di nascita** date of birth; **data di scadenza** expiry date; (su alimenti) best before date

data'base *nm inv* database
■ **database relazionale** relational database

da'tabile *adj* datable

da'tare *vt* date; **a ~ da** as from

da'tario *nm* (su orologio) calendar

da'tato *adj* dated

da'tivo *nm* dative

'dato 1 *adj* given; (dedito) addicted; **~ che** seeing that, given that

2 *nm* datum; **dati** *pl* data
■ **dato di fatto** well established fact; **dati sensibili** sensitive data

da'tore *nm* giver
■ **datore di lavoro** employer

'dattero *nm* date

dattilogra'fare *vt/i* type; **~ a tastiera cieca** touch-type

dattilogra'fia *nf* typing
■ **dattilografia a tastiera cieca** touch-typing

datti'lografo, -a *nmf* typist

dattilo'scritto *adj* ‹copia› typewritten, typed

dat'torno *adv* **togliersi ~** clear off

♂ **da'vanti** 1 *adv* before; (dirimpetto) opposite; (di fronte) in front

2 *adj inv* front

3 *nm* front; **~ di dietro** ‹maglia› back-to-front; **~ a** *prep* before, in front of; **passare ~ a** pass, go past

davan'zale *nm* window sill

da'vanzo *adv* **ce n'è ~** there is more than enough

♂ **dav'vero** *adv* really; **per ~** in earnest; **dici ~?** honestly?

dazi'ario *adj* excise

'dazio *nm* duty; (ufficio) customs *pl*
■ **dazi doganali** *pl* customs duties; **dazio d'importazione** import duty

d.C. *abbr* (**dopo Cristo**) AD

D.C. *nf abbr* (**Democrazia Cristiana**) Christian Democratic Party

D.D.T. *nm* (insetticida) DDT

'dea *nf* goddess

deambula'torio *adj* ambulatory

debel'lare *vt* defeat

debili'tante *adj* weakening

debili'tare *vt* weaken

debili'tarsi *vr* become debilitated

debilitazi'one *nf* debilitation

debita'mente *adv* duly

♂ indicates a very frequent word

'debito [1] adj due; **a tempo ~** in due course
[2] nm debt
■ **debito pubblico** national debt
debi|'tore, -trice nmf debtor
'debole [1] adj weak; ‹luce› dim; ‹suono› faint
[2] nm weak point; **avere un ~ per qualcuno** have a soft spot for somebody; **avere un ~ per qualcosa** have a weakness for something
debo'lezza nf weakness
debor'dare vi overflow
debosci'ato adj debauched
debrai'ata nf Auto declutching
debut'tante [1] adj beginner
[2] nmf beginner; (attore) actor/actress making his/her début
debut'tare vi make one's début
de'butto nm début
'decade nf period of ten days
deca'dente adj decadent
decaden'tismo nm decadence
deca'denza nf decline; Jur loss
deca'dere vi lapse
decadi'mento nm (delle arti) decline
deca'duto adj ‹persona› impoverished; ‹decreto, norma› no longer in force
decaffei'nato [1] adj decaffeinated
[2] nm decaffeinated coffee, decaf fam
deca'grammo nm decagram
decal'care vt trace
decalcifi'carsi vr become brittle
decalcificazi'one nf (condizione) brittle bones
decalcoma'nia nf transfer
de'calitro nm decalitre
de'calogo nm fig rule book
de'cametro nm decametre
de'cano nm dean
decan'tare vt (lodare) praise
decapi'tare vt decapitate; behead ‹condannato›
decapitazi'one nf decapitation; beheading
decappot'tabile adj convertible
decappot'tare vt take down the hood of
'decathlon nm inv decathlon
de'cedere vi (morire) die
dece'duto adj deceased
decele'rare vt/i slow down, decelerate
decelerazi'one nf deceleration
decen'nale [1] adj ten-yearly
[2] nm (anniversario) tenth anniversary
de'cenne adj ‹bambino› ten-year-old
de'cennio nm decade
de'cente adj decent
decente'mente adv decently

decentraliz'zare vt decentralize
decentra'mento nm decentralization
decen'trare vt decentralize
de'cenza nf decency
de'cesso nm death, decease fml; **atto di decesso** death certificate
'decibel nm inv decibel
de'cidere vt decide; settle ‹questione›
de'cidersi vr make up one's mind
deci'frabile adj decipherable
deci'frare vt decipher; (documenti cifrati) decode
decifrazi'one nf deciphering
de'cigrado nm tenth of a degree
deci'grammo nm decigram
de'cilitro nm decilitre
deci'male adj decimal
deci'mare vt decimate
de'cimetro nm decimetre
'decimo adj & nm tenth
de'cina nf Math ten; **una ~ di** (circa dieci) about ten
decisa'mente adv definitely, decidedly
decisio'nale adj decision-making
decisi'one nf decision; **prendere una ~** make or take a decision; **con ~** decisively
decisio'nismo nm tendency to make decisions without consulting others
decisio'nista nmf person who does not consult others before making decisions
deci'sivo adj decisive
de'ciso [1] pp di DECIDERE
[2] adj decided
decla'mare vt/i declaim
declama'torio adj ‹stile› declamatory
declas'sare vt downgrade
decli'nabile adj Gram declinable; ‹offerta› that can be refused
decli'nare [1] vt decline; turn down, refuse ‹invito›; **~ ogni responsabilità** disclaim all responsibility
[2] vi go down; (tramontare) set
declinazi'one nf Gram declension
de'clino nm decline; **in ~** ‹popolarità› on the decline
de'clivio nm downward slope
dé'co adj inv Art Deco
de'coder nm inv TV set-top box
deco'difica nf decoding
decodifi'care vt decode
decodifica'tore nm TV descrambler
decodificazi'one nf decoding
decol'lare vi take off
décolle'té [1] adj inv low cut
[2] nm inv low neckline
de'collo nm take-off
decolonizzazi'one nf decolonization
decolo'rante nm bleach

decolo'rare *vt* bleach
decolorazi'one *nf* bleaching
decom'porre *vt* decompose
decom'porsi *vr* decompose
decomposizi'one *nf* decomposition
decompressi'one *nf* decompression
decom'primere *vt* decompress
deconcen'trarsi *vr* become distracted
deconge'lare *vt* defrost
decongestio'nare *vt* Med fig relieve
congestion in
decontami'nare *vt* Techn decontaminate
decontaminazi'one *nf*
decontamination
decontrazi'one *nf* relaxation
deco'rare *vt* decorate
decora'tivo *adj* decorative
deco'rato *adj* (ornato) decorated
decora|'tore, -trice *nmf* decorator
decorazi'one *nf* decoration
■ decorazione floreale flower arranging
de'coro *nm* decorum
decorosa'mente *adv* decorously
deco'roso *adj* dignified
decor'renza *nf* ~ dal ... with effect
from ..., effective ...
de'correre *vi* pass; a ~ da with effect
from
de'corso [1] pp di DECORRERE
[2] *nm* passing; Med course
decre'mento *nm* decrease
de'crepito *adj* decrepit
decre'scente *adj* decreasing
de'crescere *vi* decrease; ‹prezzi› go
down; ‹acque› subside
decre'tare *vt* decree; ~ lo stato
d'emergenza declare a state of emergency
de'creto *nm* decree
■ decreto ingiuntivo decree; decreto legge
decree which has the force of law; decreto
legislativo decree requiring the approval of
Parliament
decre'tone *nm* Pol portmanteau bill
de'cubito *nm*
■ piaghe da decubito bedsores
decur'tare *vt* reduce
decurtazi'one *nf* reduction
'dedalo *nm* maze
'dedica *nf* dedication
⚹ **dedi'care** *vt* dedicate
dedi'carsi *vr* dedicate oneself
'dedito *adj* ~ a given to; (assorto) engrossed
in; addicted to ‹vizi›
dedizi'one *nf* dedication
de'dotto [1] pp di DEDURRE
[2] *adj* deduced
dedu'cibile *adj* ‹tassa› allowable

de'durre *vt* deduce; (sottrarre) deduct
dedut'tivo *adj* deductive
deduzi'one *nf* deduction
défail'lance *nf inv* (cedimento) collapse
defal'care *vt* deduct
defalcazi'one *nf* deduction
defe'care *vi* defecate
defecazi'one *nf* defecation
defene'strare *vt* fig remove from office
defe'rente *adj* deferential
defe'renza *nf* deference
deferi'mento *nm* referral
defe'rire *vt* Jur remit
defezio'nare *vi* (abbandonare) defect
defezi'one *nf* defection
defezio'nista *nmf* defector
defici'ente [1] *adj* (mancante) deficient;
Med mentally deficient
[2] *nmf* mental defective; pej half-wit
defici'enza *nf* deficiency; (lacuna) gap; Med
mental deficiency
'deficit *nm inv* deficit, shortfall; essere
in ~ be in deficit
defici'tario *adj* ‹bilancio› deficit *attrib*;
‹sviluppo› insufficient
defi'larsi *vr* (scomparire) slip away; ~ da
qualcosa sneak away from something
défi'lé *nm inv* fashion show
defi'nibile *adj* definable; ~ dall'utente
Comput user-definable
defi'nire *vt* define; (risolvere) settle
definitiva'mente *adv* for good
defini'tivo *adj* definitive
defi'nito *adj* definite
definizi'one *nf* definition; (soluzione)
settlement
defiscaliz'zare *vt* abolish the tax on
defiscalizzazi'one *nf* abolition of tax
defla'grare *vt* (esplodere) explode
deflagrazi'one *nf* (esplosione) explosion
deflazio'nare *vt* deflate
deflazi'one *nf* deflation
deflazio'nistico *adj* deflationary
deflet'tore *nm* Auto quarterlight
deflu'ire *vi* ‹liquidi› flow away; ‹persone›
stream out
de'flusso *nm* (di marea) ebb
defogli'ante [1] *adj* defoliating
[2] *nm* defoliant
deforestazi'one *nf* deforestation
defor'mante *adj* artrite ~ acute arthritis
defor'mare *vt* deform ‹arto›; fig distort
defor'marsi *vr* lose its shape
defor'mato *adj* warped
deformazi'one *nf* (di fatti) distortion; è
una ~ professionale put it down to the job
de'forme *adj* deformed
deformità *nf inv* deformity

deframmen'tare *vt* defragment fam; defrag

defrau'dare *vt* defraud

de'funto, -a *adj & nmf* deceased

degene'rare *vi* degenerate

degenera'tivo *adj* ‹processo› degenerative

degene'rato *adj* degenerate

degenerazi'one *nf* degeneration

de'genere *adj* degenerate

de'gente ① *adj* bedridden ② *nmf* patient

de'genza *nf* confinement
■ degenza ospedaliera stay in hospital

'degli = DI + GLI

deglu'tire *vt* swallow

deglutizi'one *nf* swallowing

de'gnare *vt* ~ qualcuno/qualcosa di uno sguardo deign *or* condescend to look at somebody/something

de'gnarsi *vr* deign, condescend

⚘ **'degno** *adj* worthy; (meritevole) deserving
■ degno di lode praiseworthy, degno di nota noteworthy

degrada'mento *nm* degradation

degra'dante *adj* demeaning

degra'dare *vt* degrade

degra'darsi *vr* lower oneself; ‹città› fall into a state of disrepair

degradazi'one *nf* degradation

de'grado *nm* deterioration
■ degrado ambientale environmental damage; degrado urbano urban blight, urban decay

degu'stare *vt* taste

degustazi'one *nf* tasting
■ degustazione di vini wine tasting

'dei = DI + I

deindiciz'zare *vt* deindex

déjà vu *nm inv* déjà vu

del = DI + IL

dela|'tore, -trice *nmf* [police] informer

delazi'one *nf* informing

'delega *nf* proxy; legge ~ *law that does not require Parliamentary approval*

dele'gante *nmf* Jur representative

dele'gare *vt* delegate

dele'gato *nm* delegate

delegazi'one *nf* delegation

delegitti'mare *vt* delegitimize

dele'terio *adj* harmful

del'fino *nm* dolphin; (stile di nuoto) butterfly [stroke]; nuotare a ~ do the butterfly

de'libera *nf* bylaw

delibe'rante *adj* ‹organo› decision making

delibe'rare *vt/i* deliberate; ~ su/in rule on/in

deliberata'mente *adv* deliberately

delibe'rato *adj* (intenzionale) deliberate

delicata'mente *adv* delicately

delica'tezza *nf* delicacy; (fragilità) frailty; (tatto) tact

deli'cato *adj* delicate; ‹salute› frail; ‹suono, colore› soft

delimi'tare *vt* define

delimita'tivo *adj* defining

delimitazi'one *nf* definition

deline'are *vt* outline

deline'arsi *vr* be outlined; fig take shape

deline'ato *adj* outlined

delineazi'one *nf* outline

⚘ **delinqu'ente** *nmf* delinquent
■ delinquente minorile young offender; delinquente recidivo habitual offender

delinqu'enza *nf* delinquency
■ delinquenza minorile juvenile crime

delinquenzi'ale *adj* criminal

de'linquere *vi* commit a criminal act; associazione per delinquere conspiracy [to commit a crime]; istigazione a delinquere incitement to crime

de'liquio *nm* cadere in ~ swoon

deli'rante *adj* Med delirious; (assurdo) insane; (sfrenato) frenzied

deli'rare *vi* be delirious

de'lirio *nm* delirium; fig frenzy; mandare/ andare in ~ fig send/go into a frenzy

⚘ **de'litto** *nm* crime
■ delitto passionale crime of passion

delittu'oso *adj* criminal

de'lizia *nf* delight

delizi'are *vt* delight

delizi'arsi *vr* ~ di delight in

delizi'oso *adj* delightful; (cibo) delicious

'della = DI + LA

'delle = DI + LE

'dello = DI + LO

'delta *nm inv* delta

delta'plano *nm* hang-glider; fare ~ go hang-gliding

deluci'dare *vt* fig clarify

delucidazi'one *nf* clarification

delu'dente *adj* disappointing

⚘ **de'ludere** *vt* disappoint

delusi'one *nf* disappointment

de'luso *adj* disappointed; essere ~ di qualcosa/qualcuno be disillusioned with something/somebody

dema'gogico *adj* popularity-seeking, demagogic

dema'gogo *nm* demagogue

deman'dare *vt* entrust

demani'ale *adj* ‹proprietà› government attrib

de'manio *nm* government property

demar'care *vt* demarcate

demarcazi'one *nf* demarcation; linea di demarcazione demarcation line

de'mente *adj* demented

de'menza *nf* dementia
■ demenza senile senile dementia

demenzi'ale *adj* (assurdo) zany

de'merito *nm* nota di ∼ demerit mark

demilitariz'zare *vt* demilitarize

demilitarizzazi'one *nf* demilitarization

demistifi'care *vt* debunk

demistifica|'tore, -trice *nmf* debunker

demistifica'torio *adj* debunking

demistificazi'one *nf* debunking

demitiz'zare *vt* demythologize

demitizzazi'one *nf* demythologization

democratica'mente *adv* democratically

demo'cratico *adj* democratic

democratiz'zare *vt* democratize

democra'zia *nf* democracy

democristi'ano, -a *adj & nmf* Christian Democrat

'demodisk *nm inv* Comput demo disk

demogra'fia *nf* demography

demo'grafico *adj* demographic; incremento demografico increase in population

demo'lire *vt* demolish

demo'lito *adj* demolished

demolizi'one *nf* demolition

'demone *nm* demon

demo'niaco *adj* demonic

de'monio *nm* demon

demoniz'zare *vt* demonize

demonizzazi'one *nf* demonization

demoraliz'zante *adj* demoralizing

demoraliz'zare *vt* demoralize

demoraliz'zarsi *vr* become demoralized

demoraliz'zato *adj* demoralized

de'mordere *vi* give up

demoti'vare *vt* demotivate

demoti'varsi *vr* become demotivated

demoti'vato *adj* demotivated

demotivazi'one *nf* demotivation

de'nari *nmpl* (nelle carte) diamonds

⚘ **de'naro** *nm* money
■ denaro virtuale e-cash

denatu'rato *adj* alcol ∼ methylated spirits

denazionaliz'zare *vt* denationalize

deni'grare *vt* denigrate

denigra|'tore, -trice 1 *adj* denigrating 2 *nmf* denigrator

denigra'torio *adj* denigratory

denigrazi'one *nf* denigration

denomi'nare *vt* name

denomi'narsi *vr* be named

denomina'tivo *adj* denominative

denomina'tore *nm* denominator

denominazi'one *nf* denomination
■ denominazione di origine controllata *mark guaranteeing the quality of a wine*

deno'tare *vt* denote

denotazi'one *nf* denotation

densa'mente *adv* densely

densità *nf* density
■ ad alta/bassa densità di popolazione densely/sparsely populated

'denso *adj* thick, dense

den'tale *adj* dental

den'tario *adj* dental

den'tata *nf* bite

den'tato *adj* ‹lama› serrated

denta'tura *nf* teeth *pl*; Techn serration

⚘ **'dente** *nm* tooth; (di forchetta) prong; (di montagna) jagged peak; al ∼ Culin just slightly firm; lavarsi i denti brush one's teeth
■ dente del giudizio wisdom tooth; dente di latte milk tooth; dente di leone Bot dandelion

'dentice *nm* dentex (*type of sea bream*)

denti'era *nf* dentures *pl*, false teeth *pl*; mettersi la ∼ put one's false teeth in

denti'fricio *nm* toothpaste

den'tista *nmf* dentist

⚘ **'dentro** 1 *adv* in, inside; (in casa) indoors; da ∼ from within; qui ∼ in here; metter ∼ fam (in prigione) lock up, put inside 2 *prep* in, inside; (di tempo) within, by 3 *nm* inside

denucleariz'zare *vt* denuclearize

denucleariz'zato *adj* nuclear-free, denuclearized

denuclearizzazi'one *nf* denuclearization

denu'dare *vt* bare

denu'darsi *vr* strip

de'nuncia *nf* denunciation; (alla polizia) reporting; fare una ∼ draw up a report
■ denuncia dei redditi income tax return

⚘ **denunci'are** *vt* denounce; (accusare) report

de'nunzia = DENUNCIA

denu'trito *adj* underfed

denutrizi'one *nf* malnutrition

deodo'rante *adj & nm* deodorant
■ deodorante antitraspirante antiperspirant; deodorante per ambienti air-freshener; deodorante a sfera roll-on

deodo'rare *vt* deodorize

deontolo'gia *nf* (etica professionale) code of conduct

depenaliz'zare *vt* decriminalize

depenalizzazi'one *nf* decriminalization

dépen'dance *nf inv* outbuilding

depe'ribile *adj* perishable

⚘ indicates a very frequent word

deperi'mento *nm* wasting away; (di merci) deterioration

depe'rire *vi* waste away

depe'rito *adj* wasted

depi'lare *vt* depilate

depi'larsi *vr* shave ‹gambe›; pluck ‹sopracciglia›

depila'tore ① *adj* depilatory ② *nm* (apparecchio) hair remover

depila'torio *nm* depilatory

depilazi'one *nf* hair removal
∎ **depilazione diatermica** electrolysis

depi'staggio *nm* fig diversionary manoeuvre

depi'stare *vt* fig throw off the track

dépli'ant *nm inv* brochure, leaflet

deplo'rabile *adj* deplorable

deplo'rare *vt* deplore; (dolersi di) grieve over

deplo'revole *adj* deplorable

depoliticiz'zare *vt* depoliticize

de'porre *vt* put down; lay down ‹armi›; lay ‹uova›; (togliere da una carica) depose; (testimoniare) testify

depor'tare *vt* deport

depor'tato, -a *nmf* deportee

deportazi'one *nf* deportation

deposi'tante *nmf* Fin depositor

deposi'tare *vt* Fin deposit; (lasciare in custodia) leave; (in magazzino) store

deposi'tario, -a *nmf* (di segreto) repository

deposi'tarsi *vr* settle

de'posito *nm* deposit; (luogo) warehouse; Mil depot
∎ **deposito d'armi** arms dump; **deposito bagagli** left-luggage office, baggage checkroom Am; **deposito bagagli automatico** left-luggage lockers; **deposito bancario** deposit account; **deposito bancario vincolato** fixed term deposit account

deposizi'one *nf* deposition; (da una carica) removal

de'posto *adj* deposed

depotenzi'are *vt* weaken

depra'vare *vt* deprave

depra'vato *adj* depraved

depravazi'one *nf* depravity

depre'cabile *adj* appalling

depre'care *vt* deprecate

depre'dare *vt* plunder

depressio'nario *adj* **area depressionaria** Metereol area of low pressure

depressi'one *nf* depression; **area di depressione** Metereol area of low pressure; Econ depressed area

depres'sivo *adj* depressive

de'presso ① *pp di* DEPRIMERE ② *adj* depressed

depressuriz'zare *vt* depressurize

depressurizzazi'one *nf* depressurization

deprezza'mento *nm* depreciation

deprez'zare *vt* depreciate

deprez'zarsi *vr* depreciate

depri'mente *adj* depressing

de'primere *vt* depress

de'primersi *vr* get depressed

deprivazi'one *nf* deprivation

depu'rare *vt* purify

depu'rarsi *vr* be purified

depura'tore *nm* purifier

depurazi'one *nf* purification; (di detriti) effluent

depu'tare *vt* delegate

depu'tato, -a *nmf* ≈ Member of Parliament, MP

deputazi'one *nf* deputation

dequalifi'care *vt* disqualify

dequalifi'carsi *vr* disqualify oneself

dequalificazi'one *nf* disqualification

deraglia'mento *nm* derailment

deragli'are *vi* go off the lines; **far ~** derail

deraglia'tore *nm* derailleur gears *pl*

dera'pare *vi* Auto skid; ‹sciatore› sideslip

derattiz'zare *vt* clear of rats

derattizzazi'one *nf* rodent control

'derby *nm inv* Sport local derby

deregolamen'tare *vt* Comm deregulate

deregolamentazi'one *nf* deregulation

dere'litto *adj* derelict

deresponsabiliz'zare *vt* deprive of responsibility

deresponsabiliz'zarsi *vr* abdicate responsibility

deresponsabilizzazi'one *nf* depriving of responsibility

dere'tano *nm* backside, bottom

de'ridere *vt* deride

derisi'one *nf* derision

deri'sorio *adj* derisory

de'riva *nf* drift; **andare alla ~** drift

deri'vabile *adj* derivable

deri'vare ① *vi* **~ da** (provenire) derive from ② *vt* derive; (sviare) divert

deri'vata *nf* Math derivative

deri'vato ① *adj* derived ② *nm* by-product

derivazi'one *nf* derivation; (di fiume) diversion

derma'tite *nf* dermatitis

dermatolo'gia *nf* dermatology

dermato'logico *adj* dermatological

derma'tologo, -a *nmf* dermatologist

derma'tosi *nf* dermatosis

dermoprotet'tivo *adj* ‹crema› skin attrib; ‹azione› protective

'deroga *nf* dispensation

dero'gare *vi* ~ **a** depart from
deroga'torio *adj* derogatory
der'rata *nf* merchandise
■ **derrate alimentari** *pl* foodstuffs
deru'bare *vt* rob
deru'bato *adj* robbed
desaliniz'zare *vt* desalinate
desalinizzazi'one *nf* desalination
desapare'cido *nmf* (*pl* ~**s**) disappeared man/woman, desaparecido
descolarizzazi'one *nf* deschooling
descrit'tivo *adj* descriptive
de'scritto *pp di* DESCRIVERE
♂ **de'scrivere** *vt* describe
descri'vibile *adj* describable
descrizi'one *nf* description
desensibiliz'zare *vt* desensitize
desensibilizzazi'one *nf* desensitization
de'sertico *adj* desert
♂ **de'serto** ① *adj* uninhabited
② *nm* desert
deside'rabile *adj* desirable
♂ **deside'rare** *vt* wish; (volere) want; (intensamente) long for; (bramare) desire; **desidera?** what would you like?, can I help you?; **lasciare a** ~ leave a lot to be desired
deside'rato *adj* intended
♂ **desi'derio** *nm* wish; (brama) desire; (intenso) longing
deside'roso *adj* desirous; (bramoso) longing
desi'gnare *vt* appoint, designate; (fissare) fix
desi'gnato *adj* designate *attrib*
designazi'one *nf* appointment
de'signer *nmf inv* designer
desi'nare ① *vi* dine
② *nm* dinner
desi'nenza *nf* ending
de'sistere *vi* ~ **da** desist from
'desktop 'publishing *nm inv* desktop publishing, DTP
deso'lante *adj* distressing
deso'lare *vt* distress
deso'lato *adj* desolate; (spiacente) sorry; **siamo desolati di dovervi comunicare che …** (in lettere) we are sorry to have to inform you that …
desolazi'one *nf* desolation
'despota *nm* despot
desqua'marsi *vr* flake off
desquamazi'one *nf* flaking off
destabiliz'zante *adj* destabilizing
destabiliz'zare *vt* destabilize
destabilizzazi'one *nf* destabilization
de'stare *vt* waken; fig awaken

de'starsi *vr* waken; fig awaken
♂ **desti'nare** *vt* destine; (nominare) appoint; (assegnare) assign; (indirizzare) address
destina'tario *nm* (di lettera, pacco) addressee
desti'nato *adj* **essere** ~ **a fare qualcosa** be destined *or* fated to do something
destinazi'one *nf* destination; fig purpose; **con** ~ **Parigi** (aereo, treno) destined for Paris
♂ **de'stino** *nm* destiny; (fato) fate
destitu'ire *vt* dismiss
destitu'ito *adj* ~ **di** devoid of
destituzi'one *nf* dismissal
'desto *adj* (liter) awake
♂ **'destra** *nf* (parte) right; (mano) right hand; **prendere a** ~ turn right; **a** ~ (essere) on the right; (andare) to the right; **la prima a** ~ the first on the right; **sulla** ~ on the right-hand side; **di** ~ Pol right wing; **la** ~ Pol the Right
destreggi'are *vi* manoeuvre
destreggi'arsi *vr* manoeuvre
de'strezza *nf* dexterity; (abilità) skill
'destro *adj* right; (abile) skilful
de'stroide *adj* Pol right-wing
destruttu'rato *adj* (incoerente) unstructured
desu'eto *adj* obsolete
de'sumere *vt* (congetturare) infer; (ricavare) obtain
desu'mibile *adj* inferable
detas'sare *vt* abolish the tax on
detassazi'one *nf* abolition of tax
detei'nato *adj* tannin free
dete'nere *vt* hold; (polizia) detain
deten'tivo *adj* **pena detentiva** custodial sentence
deten'|tore, -trice *nmf* holder
■ **detentore del titolo** titleholder
dete'nuto, -a *nmf* prisoner
detenzi'one *nf* detention
deter'gente ① *adj* cleaning; (latte, crema) cleansing
② *nm* detergent; (per la pelle) cleanser
deteriora'mento *nm* deterioration
deterio'rare *vt* cause to deteriorate (cibo, relazione)
deterio'rarsi *vr* deteriorate
determi'nabile *adj* determinable
determinabilità *nf* determinability
determi'nante *adj* decisive
determi'nare *vt* determine
determi'narsi *vr* ~ **a** resolve to
determina'tezza *nf* determination
determina'tivo *adj* (articolo) definite; **pronome** ~ determiner
determi'nato *adj* (risoluto) determined; (particolare) specific; (stabilito) certain
determinazi'one *nf* determination; (decisione) decision

♂ indicates a very frequent word

determi'nismo *nm* determinism

deter'rente *adj* & *nm* deterrent

deter'sivo *nm* detergent
- detersivo biologico biological powder; detersivo per bucato washing powder; detersivo per i piatti washing-up liquid, dishwashing liquid Am

dete'stare *vt* detest, hate

dete'starsi *vr* hate oneself

deto'nare *vi* detonate

detona'tore *nm* detonator

detonazi'one *nf* detonation

detra'ibile *adj* deductible

de'trarre *vt* deduct (da from)

de'tratto ① pp di DETRARRE ② *adj* deducted

detrat|'tore, -trice *nmf* detractor

detrazi'one *nf* deduction; (da tasse) tax allowance

detri'mento *nm* detriment; **a ~ di** to the detriment of

de'trito *nm* debris; **detriti** *pl* (di fiume) detritus
- detrito di falda scree

detroniz'zare *vt* dethrone

'detta *nf* **a ~ di** according to

dettagli'ante *nmf* Comm retailer

dettagli'are *vt* detail

dettagliata'mente *adv* in detail

det'taglio *nm* detail; **al ~** Comm retail

det'tame *nm* dictate; **i dettami della moda** the dictates of fashion

det'tare *vt* dictate; **~ legge** fig lay down the law

det'tato *nm* Sch dictation

detta'tura *nf* dictation

'detto ① *adj* said; (chiamato) called; (soprannominato) nicknamed; **~ fatto** no sooner said than done ② *nm* **~** [popolare] saying

detur'pare *vt* disfigure

deturpazi'one *nf* disfigurement

deumidifi'care *vt* dehumidify

deumidifica'tore *nm* dehumidifier

deumidificazi'one *nf* dehumidification

devalutazi'one *nf* devaluation

deva'stante *adj* devastating

deva'stare *vt* devastate

deva'stato *adj* devastated

devasta|'tore, -trice ① *adj* destructive; fig devastating ② *nmf* destroyer

devastazi'one *nf* devastation; fig ravages *pl*

devi'ante *adj* deviant

devi'anza *nf* deviance

devi'are ① *vi* deviate ② *vt* divert

devi'ato *adj* ‹mente› warped

deviazi'one *nf* deviation; (stradale) diversion; **fare una ~** Auto make a detour

devitaliz'zare *vt* kill the nerve of, devitalize fml

devitalizzazi'one *nf* killing of the nerve, devitalization fml

devo'luto ① pp di DEVOLVERE ② *adj* devolved

devoluzi'one *nf* devolution

de'volvere *vt* devolve; **~ qualcosa in beneficenza** give something to charity

devota'mente *adv* devoutly

de'voto *adj* devout; (affezionato) devoted

devozi'one *nf* devotion

dg *abbr* (**decigrammi**) decigrams

di *prep* of; (partitivo) some; (scritto da) by; ‹parlare, pensare ecc› about; (con causa, mezzo) with; (con provenienza) from; (in comparazioni) than; (con infinito) to; **la casa di mio padre/dei miei genitori** my father's house/my parents' house; **compra del pane** buy some bread; **hai del pane?** do you have any bread?; **un film di guerra** a war film; **piangere di dolore** cry with pain; **coperto di neve** covered with snow; **sono di Genova** I'm from Genoa; **uscire di casa** leave one's house; **mi è uscito di mente** it slipped my mind; **più alto di te** taller than you; **è ora di partire** it's time to go; **crede di aver ragione** he thinks he's right; **dire di sì** say yes; **di domenica** on Sundays; **di sera** in the evening; **una pausa di un'ora** an hour's break; **un corso di due mesi** a two-month course

dia'bete *nm* diabetes

dia'betico, -a *adj* & *nmf* diabetic

diabolica'mente *adv* devilishly

dia'bolico *adj* diabolic[al]

di'acono *nm* deacon

dia'critico *adj* diacritic

dia'dema *nm* diadem; (di donna) tiara

di'afano *adj* diaphanous

dia'framma *nm* diaphragm; (divisione) screen

di'agnosi *nf inv* diagnosis
- diagnosi precoce early detection, early diagnosis

dia'gnostica *nf* Med diagnostics *sg*

diagnosti'care *vt* diagnose

dia'gnostici *nmpl* Comput diagnostics *sg*

dia'gnostico *adj* diagnostic

diago'nale *adj* & *nf* diagonal

diagonal'mente *adv* diagonally

dia'gramma *nm* diagram
- diagramma a barre bar chart; diagramma di flusso flowchart

dialet'tale *adj* dialect *attrib*; **poesia dialettale** poetry in dialect

dialettaleggi'ante *adj* dialect *attrib*

dia'lettica *nf* dialectics *sg*

dia'lettico *adj* dialectic

dia'letto *nm* dialect

di'alisi *nf* dialysis

dialo'gante *adj* unità ∼ Comput interactive terminal

dialo'gare ① *vt* write the dialogue for ‹scena›
② *vi* ∼ **con** converse with

dialo'gato *adj* in dialogue

dialo'ghista *nmf* (scrittore) dialogue writer

di'alogo *nm* dialogue

dia'mante *nm* diamond

diaman'tifero *adj* diamond bearing

diametral'mente *adv* diametrically

di'ametro *nm* diameter

di'amine *int* che ∼... what on earth ...

di'apason *nm inv* (per accordatura) tuning fork

diaposi'tiva *nf* slide

di'aria *nf* daily allowance

di'ario *nm* diary
■ **diario di bordo** logbook; **diario di classe** class register

dia'rista *nmf* (scrittore) diarist

diar'rea *nf* diarrhoea

di'aspora *nf* Diaspora

dia'triba *nf* diatribe

diavole'ria *nf* (azione) devilment; (marchingegno) weird contraption

diavo'letto *nm* imp; hum (bambino) little devil

✦ **di'avolo** *nm* devil; **va' al ∼!** fam go to hell!; **che ∼ fai?** fam what the hell are you doing?

di'battere *vt* debate

di'battersi *vr* struggle

dibattimen'tale *adj* Jur of the hearing

dibatti'mento *nm* (discussione) debate; Jur hearing

di'battito *nm* debate; (meno formale) discussion

dica'stero *nm* office

di'cembre *nm* December

dice'ria *nf* rumour

✦ **dichia'rare** *vt* state; (ufficialmente) declare; ∼ **colpevole** Jur convict; **niente da ∼?** anything to declare?

dichia'rarsi *vr* (in amore) declare one's love; ∼ **soddisfatto** declare oneself satisfied; **si dichiara innocente** he says he's innocent; ∼ **a favore di qualcosa** declare oneself in favour of something; **si dichiara che ...** (in documenti) it is hereby declared that ...; ∼ **vinto** acknowledge defeat

dichia'rato *adj* avowed

dichiarazi'one *nf* statement; (documento, di guerra, d'amore) declaration; **fare una ∼** (ufficialmente) make a statement
■ **dichiarazione dei diritti** Pol bill of rights;

dichiarazione doganale customs declaration; **dichiarazione dei redditi** [income] tax return

dician'nove *adj & nm* nineteen

dicianno'venne *adj & nmf* nineteen-year-old

dicianno'vesimo *adj & nm* nineteenth

dicias'sette *adj & nm* seventeen

diciasset'tenne *adj & nmf* seventeen-year-old

diciasset'tesimo *adj & nm* seventeenth

diciot'tenne *adj & nmf* eighteen-year-old

diciot'tesimo *adj & nm* eighteenth

dici'otto *adj & nm* eighteen; Univ pass mark

dici'tura *nf* wording

dicoto'mia *nf* dichotomy

didasca'lia *nf* (di film) subtitle; (di illustrazione) caption; Theat stage direction

dida'scalico *adj* ‹letteratura› didactic

di'dattica *nf* didactics *sg*

didattica'mente *adv* didactically

di'dattico *adj* didactic; ‹televisione› educational

di'dentro *adv* inside

didi'etro ① *adv* behind
② *nm* (hum) hindquarters *pl*

✦ **di'eci** *adj & nm* ten

dieci'mila *adj & nm* ten thousand

die'cina = DECINA

di'eresi *nf* diaeresis

'diesel *adj & nm inv* diesel

di'esis *nm inv* sharp

di'eta *nf* diet; **a ∼** on a diet
■ **dieta mediterranea** Mediterranean diet

die'tetica *nf* dietetics *sg*

die'tetico *adj* diet

die'tista *nmf* dietician

die'tologo *nmf* dietician

✦ **di'etro** ① *adv* behind
② *prep* behind; (dopo) after
③ *adj* back; ‹zampe› hind
④ *nm* back; **le stanze di ∼** the back rooms; **le zampe di ∼** the hind legs

dietro'front *nm inv* about-turn; fig U-turn; ∼**!** about turn!

dietrolo'gia *nf* obsessive search for supposedly hidden motives behind events or behind people's actions and words

di'fatti *adv* in fact

✦ **di'fendere** *vt* defend

di'fendersi *vr* defend oneself; fam (cavarsela) get by

difen'dibile *adj* defendable, defensible

difen'siva *nf* **stare sulla ∼** be on the defensive

difen'sivo *adj* defensive

difen'sore ① *adj* **avvocato ∼** defence counsel
② *nm* defender

■ **difensore civico** ombudsman

◆ **di'fesa** *nf* defence; **prendere le difese di qualcuno** come to somebody's defence

■ **difesa civile** Civil Defence

di'feso ① pp di DIFENDERE
② *adj* defended; (luogo) sheltered

difet'tare *vi* be defective; ~ **di** lack

difet'tivo *adj* defective

◆ **di'fetto** *nm* defect; (morale) fault, flaw; (mancanza) lack; (in tessuto, abito) flaw; **essere in** ~ be at fault; **far** ~ be lacking

■ **difetto di pronuncia** speech impediment

difet'toso *adj* defective; (abito) flawed

diffa'mare *vt* (con parole) slander; (per iscritto) libel

diffama|'tore, -trice *nmf* slanderer; (per iscritto) libeller

diffama'torio *adj* slanderous; (per iscritto) libellous

diffamazi'one *nf* slander; (scritta) libel

diffe'rente *adj* different

differente'mente *adv* differently

◆ **diffe'renza** *nf* difference, **a** ~ **di** unlike; **non fare** ~ make no distinction (**fra** between)

■ **differenza di fuso orario** time difference

differenzi'abile *adj* differentiable

differenzi'ale *adj & nm* differential

differenzi'are *vt* differentiate

differenzi'arsi *vr* ~ **da** differ from

differenzi'ato *adj* differentiated

differenziazi'one *nf* differentiation

diffe'ribile *adj* postponable

diffe'rire ① *vt* postpone
② *vi* be different

diffe'rita *nf* **in** ~ TV prerecorded

◆ **dif'ficile** ① *adj* difficult; (duro) hard; (improbabile) unlikely
② *nm* difficulty

difficil'mente *adv* with difficulty

◆ **difficoltà** *nf inv* difficulty; **trovarsi in** ~ be in trouble; **mettere qualcuno in** ~ put somebody on the spot

■ **difficoltà d'apprendimento** special needs; **bambini con** ~ **d'apprendimento** children with special needs

dif'fida *nf* warning

diffi'dare ① *vi* ~ **di** distrust
② *vt* warn

diffi'dente *adj* mistrustful

diffi'denza *nf* mistrust

◆ **dif'fondere** *vt* spread; diffuse (calore, luce ecc)

dif'fondersi *vr* spread

difformità *nf inv* deformation; (di opinioni) difference of opinion

diffusa'mente *adv* at length

diffusi'one *nf* diffusion; (di giornale) circulation

dif'fuso ① pp di DIFFONDERE
② *adj* common; (malattia) widespread; (luce) diffuse

diffu'sore *nm* (per asciugacapelli) diffuser

difi'lato *adv* straight; (subito) straightaway

di'fronte *adj inv & adv* opposite;
~ **all'ingresso** in front of the entrance;
(dall'altro lato della strada) opposite the entrance

difte'rite *nf* diphtheria

'diga *nf* dam; (argine) dike

dige'rente *adj* alimentary

dige'ribile *adj* digestible

digeribilità *nf* digestibility

dige'rire *vt* digest; fam stomach

digesti'one *nf* digestion

dige'stivo ① *adj* digestive
② *nm* digestive; (dopo cena) liqueur

Digi'one *nf* Dijon

digi'tale ① *adj* digital; (delle dita) finger *attrib*
② *nf* (fiore) foxglove

digitaliz'zare *vt* digitalize

digitalizzazi'one *nf* digitalizing

digi'tare *vt* key in (dati)

digiu'nare *vi* fast

digi'uno ① *adj* **essere** ~ have an empty stomach
② *nm* fast; **a** ~ (bere ecc) on an empty stomach

dignità *nf* dignity

digni'tario *nm* dignitary

dignitosa'mente *adv* with dignity

digni'toso *adj* dignified

DIGOS *nf abbr* (**Divisione Investigazioni Generali e Operazioni Speciali**) ≈ riot police

digressi'one *nf* digression

digri'gnare *vi* ~ **i denti** grind one's teeth

digros'sare *vt* fig impart basic concepts to

dik'tat *nm inv* (trattato) diktat

dila'gare *vi* flood; fig spread

dilani'are *vt* tear to pieces

dilapi'dare *vt* squander

dilapidazi'one *nf* squandering

dila'tare *vt* dilate

dila'tarsi *vr* dilate; (legno) swell; (metallo, gas) expand

dila'tato *adj* dilated; (legno) swollen; (metallo, gas) expanded

dilatazi'one *nf* dilation; (di legno) swelling; (di metallo, gas) expansion

dilazio'nabile *adj* postponable

dilazio'nare *vt* delay

dilazi'one *nf* delay

dileggi'are *vt* mock

dilegu'are *vt* disperse

dilegu'arsi *vr* disappear

di'lemma *nm* dilemma

dilet'tante *nmf* amateur
dilettan'tesco *adj* amateurish
dilettan'tismo *nm* amateurism
dilettan'tistico *adj* amateurish
dilet'tare *vt* delight
dilet'tarsi *vr* ~ di delight in
dilet'tevole *adj* delightful
di'letto, -a [1] *adj* beloved
  [2] *nm* (piacere) delight
  [3] *nmf* (persona) beloved
dili'gente *adj* diligent; ‹lavoro› accurate
dili'genza *nf* diligence
dilu'ente *nm* Techn diluent; (per vernici) thinner
diluire *vt* dilute
diluizione *nf* dilution
dilun'gare *vt* prolong
dilun'garsi *vr* ~ su dwell on ‹argomento›
diluvi'are *vi* pour [down]
di'luvio *nm* downpour; fig flood
  ■ il ~ universale the Flood
dima'grante *adj* slimming, diet
dimagri'mento *nm* loss of weight
dima'grire *vi* lose weight
dima'grirsi *vr* lose weight
dime'nare *vt* wave; wag ‹coda›
dime'narsi *vr* be agitated
dimensio'nare *vt* fig get into proportion
◆ **dimensi'one** *nf* dimension; (misura) size
dimenti'canza *nf* forgetfulness; (svista) oversight; per ~ accidentally
◆ **dimenti'care** *vt* forget; l'ho dimenticato a casa I left it at home
dimenti'carsi *vr* ~[di] forget
dimentica'toio *nm* andare/finire nel ~ hum fall into oblivion
di'mentico *adj* ~ di (che non ricorda) forgetful of; (non curante) oblivious of
dimessa'mente *adv* modestly
di'messo [1] *pp di* DIMETTERE
  [2] *adj* humble; (trasandato) shabby; ‹voce› low
dimesti'chezza *nf* familiarity
di'mettere *vt* dismiss; (da ospedale ecc) discharge
di'mettersi *vr* resign
dimez'zare *vt* halve
diminu'ire *vt/i* diminish; (in maglia) decrease
diminu'ito *adj* Mus diminished
diminu'tivo *adj* & *nm* diminutive
diminuzi'one *nf* decrease; (riduzione) reduction; in ~ dwindling
dimissio'nario [1] *adj* outgoing
  [2] *nmf* outgoing chairman/president etc
dimissi'oni *nfpl* resignation *sg*; dare le ~ resign

◆ *indicates a very frequent word*

di'mora *nf* residence
dimo'rare *vi* reside
dimo'strabile *adj* demonstrable
dimostrabilità *nf* demonstrability
dimo'strante *nmf* demonstrator
◆ **dimo'strare** *vt* demonstrate; (provare) prove; (mostrare) show
dimo'strarsi *vr* prove [to be]
dimostra'tivo *adj* demonstrative
dimostrazi'one *nf* demonstration; Math proof
di'namica *nf* dynamics *sg*; ~ dei fatti sequence of events
di'namico *adj* dynamic
dina'mismo *nm* dynamism
dinami'tardo [1] *adj* attentato ~ bomb attack
  [2] *nmf* bomber
dina'mite *nf* dynamite
'dinamo *nf inv* dynamo
◆ **di'nanzi** [1] *adv* in front
  [2] *prep* ~ a in front of
'dinaro *nm* (moneta) dinar
dina'stia *nf* dynasty
di'nastico *adj* dynastic
din'don *nm inv* dingdong
'dingo *nm* (cane) dingo
dini'ego *nm* denial
dinocco'lato *adj* lanky
dino'sauro *nm* dinosaur
din'torni *nmpl* outskirts; nei ~ di in the vicinity of
din'torno *adv* around
◆ **'dio** *nm* (*pl* dei) god; Dio God; Dio mio! my God!
dioce'sano *adj* diocesan
di'ocesi *nf inv* diocese
dioni'siaco *adj* Dionysian
dios'sina *nf* dioxin
diot'tria *nf* dioptre
dipa'nare *vt* wind into a ball; fig unravel
diparti'mento *nm* department
dipen'dente [1] *adj* depending
  [2] *nmf* employee
dipen'denza *nf* dependence; (edificio) annexe
◆ **di'pendere** *vi* ~ da depend on; (provenire) derive from; dipende it depends
◆ **di'pingere** *vt* paint; (descrivere) describe
di'pinto [1] *pp di* DIPINGERE
  [2] *adj* painted
  [3] *nm* painting
di'ploma *nm* diploma
diplo'mare *vt* graduate
diplo'marsi *vr* graduate
diplomatica'mente *adv* diplomatically
diplo'matico [1] *adj* diplomatic
  [2] *nm* diplomat; (pasticcino) millefeuille (*with alcohol*)

diplo'mato [1] *nmf person with school qualification*
[2] *adj* qualified

diploma'zia *nf* diplomacy

di'porto *nm* imbarcazione da ∼ pleasure craft

dirada'mento *nf* thinning out

dira'dare *vt* thin out; make less frequent ⟨visite⟩

dira'darsi *vr* thin out; ⟨nebbia⟩ clear

dira'mare *vt* issue

dira'marsi *vr* branch out

diramazi'one *nf* (di strada, fiume) fork; (di albero, impresa) branch; (di ordine) issuing

⚘ **'dire** [1] *vt* say; (raccontare, riferire) tell; ∼ quello che si pensa speak one's mind; voler ∼ mean; volevo ben ∼! I wondered!; ∼ di sì/no say yes/no; si dice che … rumour has it that …; come si dice "casa" in inglese? what's the English for "casa"?; questo nome mi dice qualcosa the name rings a bell; che ne dici di…? how about…?; non c'è che ∼ there's no disputing that; e ∼ che … to think that …; a dir poco/tanto at least/most
[2] *vi* ∼ bene/male di speak highly/ill of somebody; dica pure (in negozio) how can I help you?; dici sul serio? are you serious?; per modo di ∼ as it were

di'retta *nf* TV live broadcast; in ∼ live

diretta'mente *adv* directly

diret'tissima *nf* (strada) main route; per ∼ Jur ⟨processare⟩ without going through the normal procedures

diret'tissimo *nm* fast train

diret'tiva *nf* directive; direttive *pl* (indicazioni) guidelines

diret'tivo [1] *adj* (dirigente) management *attrib*, managerial
[2] *nm* Pol executive

di'retto [1] *pp di* DIRIGERE
[2] *adj* direct; il mio ∼ superiore my immediate superior; ∼ a (inteso) meant for; essere ∼ a be heading for; in diretta ⟨trasmissione⟩ live
[3] *nm* (treno) through train

⚘ **diret'tore** *nm* manager; (più in alto nella gerarchia) director; (di scuola) headmaster
■ direttore amministrativo company secretary; direttore artistico artistic director; direttore del carcere prison governor; direttore di filiale branch manager; direttore di gara referee; direttore generale managing director, chief executive officer; direttore di giornale newspaper editor; direttore d'istituto Univ department head; direttore d'orchestra conductor; direttore del personale personnel manager/director; direttore di produzione production manager/director; direttore spirituale spiritual advisor; direttore sportivo team manager; direttore tecnico Sport manager; direttore di zona area manager, regional director

diret'trice *nf* manageress; (di scuola) headmistress; (indirizzo) guiding principle

direzio'nale *adj* directional

direzio'nare *vt* direct

⚘ **direzi'one** *nf* direction; (di società) management; Sch headmaster's/ headmistress's office (*primary school*); in ∼ nord (traffico) northbound; 'tutte le direzioni' Auto 'all routes'

diri'gente [1] *adj* ruling
[2] *nmf* executive
■ dirigente d'azienda company director; dirigente di partito Pol party leader

diri'genza *nf* (gestione) management; (i dirigenti) top management; Pol leadership
■ dirigenza aziendale business management

dirigenzi'ale *adj* management *attrib*, managerial

⚘ **di'rigere** *vt* direct; conduct ⟨orchestra⟩; run ⟨impresa⟩

di'rigersi *vr* ∼ verso head for

diri'gibile *nm* airship

dirim'petto [1] *adv* opposite
[2] *prep* ∼ a facing

⚘ **di'ritto**[1] [1] *adj* straight; (destro) right
[2] *adv* straight; andare ∼ go straight on; sempre ∼ straight ahead, straight on
[3] *nm* right side; Tennis forehand; fare un ∼ (a maglia) knit one

⚘ **di'ritto**[2] *nm* right; Jur law
■ diritti degli animali *pl* animal rights; diritti d'autore *pl* royalties; diritti civili *pl* civil rights; diritti di prelievo *pl* Fin drawing rights; diritti umani *pl* human rights; diritto civile civil law; diritto commerciale commercial law; diritto penale criminal law; diritto di voto right to vote, suffrage

dirit'tura *nf* straight line; fig honesty
■ ∼ d'arrivo Sport fig home straight

diroc'cato *adj* tumbledown

dirom'pente *adj* anche fig explosive

dirotta'mento *nm* hijacking

dirot'tare [1] *vt* reroute ⟨treno, aereo⟩; (illegalmente) hijack; divert ⟨traffico⟩
[2] *vi* alter course

dirotta|'tore, -trice *nmf* hijacker; (solo di aereo) skyjacker

di'rotto *adj* ⟨pioggia⟩ pouring; ⟨pianto⟩ uncontrollable; piovere a ∼ rain heavily

di'rupo *nm* precipice

di'sabile [1] *adj* disabled
[2] *nmf* disabled person

disabili'tare *vt* disable

disabi'tato *adj* uninhabited

disabitu'arsi *vr* ∼ a get out of the habit of

disac'cordo *nm* disagreement

disadatta'mento *nm* maladjustment

disadat'tato, -a [1] *adj* maladjusted
[2] *nmf* misfit

disa'dorno *adj* unadorned

d

disaffezi'one *nf* disaffection

disa'gevole *adj* (scomodo) uncomfortable; (difficile) inconvenient

disagi'ato *adj* poor; ‹vita› hard; (scomodo) uncomfortable

di'sagio *nm* discomfort; (difficoltà) inconvenience; (imbarazzo) embarrassment, uneasiness; **sentirsi a ~** feel uncomfortable; **disagi** *pl* (privazioni) hardships
■ **disagio sociale** social distress

di'samina *nf* close examination

disamora'mento *nm* estrangement

disanco'rare *vt* Fin de-link

disappro'vare *vt* disapprove of

disapprovazi'one *nf* disapproval

disap'punto *nm* disappointment; **con suo grande ~** [much] to his chagrin

disarcio'nare *vt* unseat

disar'mante *adj* fig disarming

disar'mare *vt/i* disarm

disar'mato *adj* disarmed; fig defenceless

di'sarmo *nm* disarmament

disartico'lato *adj* fig disjointed

disa'strato, -a ① *adj* devastated
② *nmf* victim (*of flood, earthquake ecc*)

di'sastro *nm* disaster; fam (grande confusione) mess; fam (persona) disaster area
■ **disastro aereo** air crash

disastrosa'mente *adv* disastrously

disa'stroso *adj* disastrous

disat'tento *adj* inattentive

disattenzi'one *nf* inattention; (svista) oversight

disatti'vare *vt* de-activate

disa'vanzo *nm* deficit

disavve'duto *adj* thoughtless

disavven'tura *nf* misadventure

disavver'tenza *nf* inadvertence

di'sbrigo *nm* dispatch

di'scapito *nm* **a ~ di** to the detriment of

di'scarica *nf* scrap-yard

di'scarico *nm* (di merce) unloading; **prova a discarico** evidence for the defence; **testimone a discarico** witness for the defence

discen'dente ① *adj* descending
② *nmf* descendant

discen'denza *nf* descent; (discendenti) descendants *pl*

ꟷ **di'scendere** ① *vi* (dal treno) get off; (da cavallo) dismount; (sbarcare) land; **~ da** (trarre origine da) be a descendant of
② *vt* descend

discen'sore *nm* (attrezzo) karabiner

di'scepolo, -a *nmf* disciple

di'scernere *vt* discern

discerni'mento *nm* discernment

ꟷ indicates a very frequent word

di'scesa *nf* descent; (pendio) slope; **~ in picchiata** (di aereo) nosedive; **essere in ~** ‹strada› go downhill
■ **discesa libera** (in sci) downhill race

disce'sista *nmf* (sciatore) downhill skier

di'sceso pp di DISCENDERE

di'schetto *nm* Comput diskette

dischi'udere *vt* open; (svelare) disclose

dischi'udersi *vr* open up

di'scinto *adj* scantily dressed

disci'ogliere *vt* ‹acido› dissolve; ‹neve› thaw; (fondersi) melt

disci'olto pp di DISCIOGLIERE

disci'plina *nf* discipline

discipli'nare ① *adj* disciplinary
② *vt* discipline

discipli'nato *adj* disciplined

disc-'jockey *nm inv* disc jockey, DJ

ꟷ **'disco** *nm* disc; Sport discus; Mus record; **ernia del disco** slipped disc
■ **disco a 33 giri** LP; **disco a 45 giri** single; **disco fisso** Comput fixed disk, hard disk; **disco dei freni** brake disc; **disco master** Comput master disk; **disco rigido** Comput hard disk; **disco volante** flying saucer

discogra'fia *nf* (insieme di incisioni) discography; (industria) record industry

disco'grafico ① *adj* ‹industria› record attrib, recording; ‹mercato, raccolta› record attrib; **casa discografica** record company, recording company
② *nmf* record producer

'discolo ① *nmf* rascal
② *adj* unruly

di'scolpa *nf* clearing; **a sua ~ si deve dire che …** in his defence it must be said that …

discol'pare *vt* clear

discol'parsi *vr* clear oneself

discon'nettere *vt* disconnect

disco'noscere *vt* deny; disown ‹figlio›

discontinuità *nf inv* (nel lavoro) irregularity; (di stile) unevenness

discon'tinuo *adj* intermittent; fig ‹impegno, rendimento› uneven

discopa'tia *nf* disc problems *pl*

discor'dante *adj* discordant

discor'danza *nf* discordance; **essere in ~** clash

discor'dare *vi* ‹opinioni› conflict

di'scorde *adj* clashing

di'scordia *nf* discord; (dissenso) dissension

discor'rere *vi* talk (**di** about)

discor'sivo *adj* colloquial

ꟷ **di'scorso** ① pp di DISCORRERE
② *nm* speech; (conversazione) talk
■ **discorso indiretto** indirect speech; **discorso di ringraziamento** vote of thanks

di'scosto ① *adj* distant
② *adv* far away; **stare ~** stand apart

disco'teca *nf* disco; (raccolta) record library

discote'caro *nmf* pej disco freak

di'scount *nm inv* discount store

discredi'tare *vt* discredit

di'scredito *nm* discredit

discre'pante *adj* contradictory

discre'panza *nf* discrepancy

✔ **di'screto** *adj* discreet; (moderato) moderate; (abbastanza buono) fairly good

discrezionalità *nf* discretion

discrezi'one *nf* discretion; (giudizio) judgement; **a ∼ di** at the discretion of

discrimi'nante 1 *adj* extenuating 2 *nf* Jur extenuating circumstances *pl*

discrimi'nare *vt* discriminate

discrimina'tivo *adj* ‹provvedimento› discriminatory

discrimina'torio *adj* ‹atteggiamento› discriminatory

discriminazi'one *nf* discrimination ■ **discriminazione in base all'età** age discrimination; **discriminazione sessuale** sexual discrimination

discussi'one *nf* discussion; (alterco) argument; **messa in ∼** questioning

di'scusso 1 *pp di* DISCUTERE 2 *adj* controversial

✔ **di'scutere** 1 *vt* discuss; (formale) debate; (litigare) argue 2 *vi* ∼ **su qualcosa** discuss something

discu'tibile *adj* debatable; ‹gusto› questionable

disde'gnare *vt* disdain

di'sdegno *nm* disdain

disde'gnoso *adj* disdainful

di'sdetta *nf* retraction; (sfortuna) bad luck; Comm cancellation

di'sdetto *pp di* DISDIRE

disdi'cevole *adj* unbecoming

di'sdire *vt* retract; (annullare) cancel

disedu'care *vt* have a bad effect on

diseduca'tivo *adj* bad for children

dise'gnare *vt* draw; (progettare) design

disegna|'tore, -trice *nmf* designer ■ **disegnatore di moda** fashion designer

✔ **di'segno** *nm* drawing; (progetto, linea) design ■ **disegno di legge** bill; **disegno in scala** scale drawing; **disegno tecnico** technical drawing; **disegno dal vero** life drawing

diser'bante 1 *nm* herbicide, weed-killer 2 *adj* herbicidal, weed-killing

diser'bare *vt* weed

disere'dare *vt* disinherit

disere'dato 1 *adj* dispossessed 2 *nmf* **i diseredati** the dispossessed

diser'tare *vt/i* desert; ∼ **la scuola** stay away from school

diser'tore *nm* deserter

diserzi'one *nf* desertion

disfaci'mento *nm* decay; fig decline; **in ∼** decaying; fig in decline

di'sfare *vt* undo; strip ‹letto›; (smantellare) take down; (annientare) defeat; ∼ **le valigie** unpack [one's bags]

di'sfarsi *vr* fall to pieces; (sciogliersi) melt; ∼ **di** (liberarsi di) get rid of; ∼ **in lacrime** dissolve into tears

di'sfatta *nf* defeat

disfat'tismo *nm* defeatism

disfat'tista *adj & nmf* defeatist

di'sfatto *adj* fig worn out

disfunzio'nale *adj* dysfunctional

disfunzi'one *nf* disorder

disge'lare *vt/i* thaw

disge'larsi *vr* thaw

di'sgelo *nm* thaw

disgi'ungere *vt* disconnect

disgi'unto *adj* ‹firme› separate

✔ **di'sgrazia** *nf* misfortune; (incidente) accident; (sfavore) disgrace

disgraziata'mente *adv* unfortunately

✔ **disgrazi'ato, -a** 1 *adj* unfortunate 2 *nmf* wretch

disgrega'mento *nm* disintegration

disgre'gare *vt* break up

disgre'garsi *vr* disintegrate

disgrega'tivo *adj* disintegrating

disgrega'tore *adj* disintegrating

disgregazi'one *nf* (di società) break-up

disgu'ido *nm* ■ **disguido postale** mistake in delivery

disgu'stare *vt* disgust

disgu'starsi *vr* ∼ **di** be disgusted by

di'sgusto *nm* disgust

disgustosa'mente *adv* disgustingly; ∼ **dolce** nauseatingly sweet

disgu'stoso *adj* disgusting

disidra'tante *adj* dehydrating

disidra'tare *vt* dehydrate

disidra'tarsi *vr* become dehydrated

disidra'tato *adj* dehydrated

disidratazi'one *nf* dehydration

disil'ludere *vt* disenchant, disillusion

disil'ludersi *vr* become disenchanted, become disillusioned

disillusi'one *nf* disenchantment, disillusionment

disil'luso *adj* disenchanted, disillusioned

disimbal'laggio *nm* unpacking

disimbal'lare *vt* unpack

disimpa'rare *vt* forget

disimpe'gnare *vt* release; (compiere) fulfil; redeem ‹oggetto dato in pegno›

disimpe'gnarsi *vr* disengage oneself; (cavarsela) manage

d

disim'pegno nm (locale) vestibule; (disinteresse) lack of interest

disimpi'ego nm re-allocation; (di truppe) reassignment

disincagli'are vt Naut refloat

disincagli'arsi vr Naut float off

disincan'tato adj (disilluso) disillusioned, disenchanted

disincar'nato adj disembodied

disincenti'vante adj demotivating

disincenti'vare vt demotivate

disincen'tivo nm disincentive

disincroci'are vt uncross

disinfe'stare vt disinfest

disinfestazi'one nf disinfestation

disinfet'tante adj & nm disinfectant

disinfet'tare vt disinfect

disinfezi'one nf disinfection

disinfiam'marsi vr become less inflamed

disinflazio'nare vt disinflate

disinflazi'one nf disinflation

disinflazio'nistico adj disinflationary

disinfor'mato adj uninformed

disinformazi'one nf lack of information; (informazione erronea) misinformation

disingan'nare vt disabuse

disin'ganno nm disillusion

disini'birsi vr lose one's inhibitions

disini'bito adj uninhibited

disinne'scare vt defuse

disin'nesco nm (di bomba) bomb disposal

disinne'stare vt disengage

disinne'starsi vr disengage

disin'nesto nm disengagement

disinquina'mento nm cleaning up

disinqui'nare vt clean up

disinse'rire vt disconnect

disinse'rito adj disconnected

disinte'grare vt disintegrate

disinte'grarsi vr disintegrate

disintegrazi'one nf disintegration

disinteressa'mento nm lack of interest

disinteres'sarsi vr ~ di take no interest in

disinteressata'mente adv without interest; (senza secondo fine) disinterestedly

disinteres'sato adj uninterested; (senza secondo fine) disinterested

disinte'resse nm indifference; (oggettività) disinterestedness

disintossi'care vt detoxify

disintossi'carsi vr come off drugs; ‹alcolizzato› dry out, detox

disintossicazi'one nf giving up alcohol/drugs, detox; **programma di ~** detox programme

disinvolta'mente adv in a relaxed way

disin'volto adj relaxed

disinvol'tura nf confidence

disi'stima nf lack of respect

disles'sia nf dyslexia

di'slessico adj dyslexic

disli'vello nm difference in height; fig inequality

disloca'mento nm Mil posting

dislo'care vt Mil post

dismenor'rea nf dysmenorrhoea

dismi'sura nf excess; **a ~** excessively

disobbedi'ente adj disobedient

disobbe'dire vt disobey

disoccu'pato, -a [1] adj unemployed [2] nmf unemployed person

disoccupazi'one nf unemployment

disonestà nf dishonesty

diso'nesto adj dishonest

disono'rare vt dishonour

disono'rato adj dishonoured

diso'nore nm dishonour

di'sopra [1] adv above [2] adj upper [3] nm top

disordi'nare vt disarrange

disordinata'mente adv untidily

disordi'nato adj untidy; (sregolato) immoderate

✧ **di'sordine** nm disorder, untidiness; (sregolatezza) debauchery

disores'sia nf eating disorder

disor'ganico adj inconsistent

disorganiz'zare vt disorganize

disorganiz'zato adj disorganized

disorganizzazi'one nf disorganization

disorienta'mento nm disorientation

disorien'tare vt disorientate

disorien'tarsi vr lose one's bearings

disorien'tato adj fig bewildered

disos'sare vt bone

disos'sato adj boned

di'sotto [1] adv below [2] adj lower [3] nm bottom

di'spaccio nm dispatch

dispa'rato adj disparate

'dispari adj odd, uneven

dispa'rire vi disappear

disparità nf inv disparity

di'sparte adv **in ~** apart; **stare in ~** stand aside

di'spendio nm expenditure; pej waste

dispendiosa'mente adv extravagantly

dispendi'oso adj expensive

di'spensa nf pantry; (distribuzione) distribution; (mobile) cupboard; Jur

✧ indicates a very frequent word

exemption; Relig dispensation; (pubblicazione periodica) number

dispen'sare *vt* distribute; (esentare) exonerate

dispen'sario *nm* dispensary

di'spenser *nm inv* display rack; (confezione) dispenser

◈ **dispe'rare** *vi* despair (**di** of)

dispe'rarsi *vr* despair

disperata'mente *adv* ‹piangere› desperately; ‹studiare› like mad

dispe'rato *adj* desperate; ‹tentativo› last-ditch

◈ **disperazi'one** *nf* despair

di'sperdere *vt* scatter; disperse

di'sperdersi *vr* scatter; disperse

dispersi'one *nf* dispersion; (di truppe) dispersal

disper'sivo *adj* disorganized

di'sperso ① pp di DISPERDERE
② *adj* scattered; (smarrito) lost
③ *nm* missing soldier

di'spetto *nm* spite; **a ~ di** in spite of; **fare un ~ a qualcuno** spite somebody

dispet'toso *adj* spiteful

◈ **dispia'cere** ① *nm* upset; (rammarico) regret; (dolore) sorrow; (preoccupazione) worry
② *vi* **mi dispiace** I'm sorry; **non mi dispiace** I don't dislike it; **se non ti dispiace** if you don't mind

dispiaci'uto *adj* sorry

dispie'gare *vt* unfold

dispie'garsi *vr* unfurl

dispo'nibile *adj* available; (gentile) helpful

disponibilità *nf* availability; (gentilezza) helpfulness

■ **disponibilità correnti** *pl* Fin current assets

◈ **di'sporre** ① *vt* arrange
② *vi* dispose; (stabilire) order; **~ di** have at one's disposal

di'sporsi *vr* (in fila) line up

disposi'tivo *nm* device

■ **dispositivo di emergenza** emergency button/handle; **dispositivo di puntamento** Comput pointing device

◈ **disposizi'one** *nf* disposition; (ordine) order; (libera disponibilità) disposal

di'sposto ① pp di DISPORRE
② *adj* ready; (incline) disposed; **essere ben disposto verso** be favourably disposed towards

dispotica'mente *adv* despotically

di'spotico *adj* despotic

dispo'tismo *nm* despotism

dispregia'tivo *adj* disparaging

disprez'zabile *adj* despicable

disprez'zare *vt* despise

di'sprezzo *nm* contempt

'disputa *nf* dispute

dispu'tare *vi* dispute; (gareggiare) compete

dispu'tarsi *vr* **~ qualcosa** contend for something

disqui'sire *vi* discourse

disquisizi'one *nf* disquisition

dissa'crante *adj* debunking

dissa'crare *vt* debunk

dissacra|'tore, -trice *nmf* debunker

dissacra'torio *adj* debunking

dissacrazi'one *nf* debunking

dissangua'mento *nm* loss of blood; fig impoverishment

dissangu'are *vt* bleed; fig bleed dry

dissangu'arsi *vr* bleed; fig become impoverished

dissangu'ato *adj* bloodless; fig impoverished

dissa'pore *nm* disagreement

dissec'care *vt* dry up

dissec'carsi *vr* dry up

dissemi'nare *vt* disseminate; (notizie) spread

dissen'nato *adj* ‹politica› senseless

dis'senso *nm* dissent; (disaccordo) disagreement

dissente'ria *nf* dysentery

dissen'tire *vi* disagree (**da** with)

dissepelli'mento *nm* exhumation

dissepel'lire *vt* exhume ‹cadavere›; disinter ‹rovine›; fig unearth

dissertazi'one *nf* dissertation

disser'vizio *nm* poor service

disse'stare *vt* upset; Comm damage

disse'stato *adj* ‹strada› uneven; ‹azienda› shaky

dis'sesto *nm* ruin

disse'tante *adj* thirst-quenching

disse'tare *vt* **~ qualcuno** quench somebody's thirst

disse'tarsi *vr* quench one's thirst

dissezio'nare *vr* dissect

dissezi'one *nf* dissection

dissi'dente *adj* & *nmf* dissident

dissi'denza *nf* dissidence

dis'sidio *nm* disagreement

dis'simile *adj* unlike, dissimilar

dissimu'lare *vt* conceal

dissimu'lato *adj* concealed

dissimula|'tore, -trice *nmf* dissembler

dissimulazi'one *nf* concealment

dissi'pare *vt* dissipate; (sperperare) squander

dissi'parsi *vr* ‹nebbia› clear; ‹dubbio› disappear

dissipa'tezza *nf* dissipation

dissi'pato *adj* dissipated

dissipa'tore *nm*

■ **dissipatore termico** heat sink

d

dissipazi'one *nf* squandering
dissoci'abile *adj* separable
dissoci'are *vt* dissociate
dissoci'arsi *vr* dissociate oneself
dissoci'ato, -a ① *adj* Pol dissenting
  ② *nmf* Pol dissenter
dissociazi'one *nf* Pol dissociation
dissoda'mento *nm* tillage
disso'dare *vt* till
dis'solto *pp di* DISSOLVERE
disso'lubile *adj* dissoluble
dissolu'tezza *nf* dissoluteness
dissolu'tivo *adj* divisive
disso'luto *adj* dissolute
dissol'venza *nf* (di immagine) fade-out,
  dissolve
dis'solvere *vt* dissolve; (disperdere) dispel
dis'solversi *vr* dissolve; (disperdersi) clear
disso'nante *adj* dissonant
disso'nanza *nf* dissonance
dissotterra'mento *nm* disinterment
dissotter'rare *vt* disinter ‹bara›; fig
  resurrect ‹rancore›
dissua'dere *vt* dissuade
dissuasi'one *nf* dissuasion
dissua'sivo *adj* dissuasive
distacca'mento *nm* Mil detachment
distac'care *vt* detach; Sport leave behind
distac'carsi *vr* be detached
distac'cato *adj* ‹tono, voce› expressionless
di'stacco *nm* detachment; (separazione)
  separation; Sport lead
di'stante ① *adj* far away; fig ‹person›
  detached
  ② *adv* far away
✧ **di'stanza** *nf* distance
distanzia'mento *nm* spacing [out]; Sport
  outdistancing
distanzi'are *vt* space out; Sport
  outdistance
di'stare *vi* be distant; **quanto dista?** how
  far is it?; **Roma dista 20 chilometri da qui**
  Rome is 20 kilometres away, Rome is
  20 kilometres from here
di'stendere *vt* stretch out ‹parte del
  corpo›; (spiegare) spread; (deporre) lay
di'stendersi *vr* stretch; (sdraiarsi) lie down;
  (rilassarsi) relax
distensi'one *nf* stretching; (rilassamento)
  relaxation; Pol détente
disten'sivo *adj* relaxing
di'stesa *nf* expanse
di'steso *pp di* DISTENDERE
distil'lare *vt/i* distil
distil'lato ① *adj* distilled
  ② *nm* distillate
distillazi'one *nf* distillation

distille'ria *nf* distillery
di'stinguersi *vr* (per bravura ecc)
  distinguish oneself; **si distingue dagli altri**
  per ... it is distinguished from the others
  by ...
distin'guibile *adj* distinguishable
di'stinguo *nm inv* distinction
di'stinta *nf*
  ■ **distinta di pagamento** receipt; **distinta di**
  versamento paying-in slip
distinta'mente *adv* (separatamente)
  individually, separately; (chiaramente)
  clearly; (in modo elegante) in a distinguished
  way; **vi saluto ～** Yours truly
distin'tivo ① *adj* distinctive
  ② *nm* badge
di'stinto ① *pp di* DISTINGUERSI
  ② *adj* distinct; (signorile) distinguished;
  distinti saluti Yours faithfully
distinzi'one *nf* distinction
di'stogliere *vt* ～ **da** (allontanare) remove
  from; (dissuadere) dissuade from
di'stolto *pp di* DISTOGLIERE
di'storcere *vt* twist; distort ‹suono›
di'storcersi *vr* sprain ‹caviglia›
distorsi'one *nf* Med sprain; (alterazione)
  distortion
di'storto *adj* warped; ‹suono› distorted
✧ **di'strarre** *vt* distract; (divertire) amuse
di'strarsi *vr* (deconcentrarsi) be distracted;
  (svagarsi) amuse oneself; **non ti distrarre!** pay
  attention!
distratta'mente *adv* absently
di'stratto ① *pp di* DISTRARRE
  ② *adj* absentminded; (disattento) inattentive
distrazi'one *nf* absent-mindedness;
  (errore) inattention; (svago) amusement;
  errore di distrazione absent-minded mistake
di'stretto *nm* district
distrettu'ale *adj* district *attrib*
✧ **distribu'ire** *vt* distribute; (disporre)
  arrange; deal ‹carte›
distribu'tore *nm* distributor; (di benzina)
  petrol pump, gas pump Am; (automatico) slot
  machine
  ■ **distributore automatico di biglietti** ticket
  machine; **distributore di bevande** drinks
  dispenser; **distributore di monete** change
  machine
distribuzi'one *nf* distribution
distri'care *vt* disentangle
distri'carsi *vr* fig get out of it
distro'fia *nf*
  ■ **distrofia muscolare** muscular dystrophy
di'strofico *adj* dystrophic
✧ **di'struggere** *vt* destroy
di'struggersi *vr* **si distrugge col bere**
  he is destroying himself with drink; **la**
  macchina si è distrutta the car has been
  written off

✧ indicates a very frequent word

distruttività *nf* destructiveness

distrut'tivo *adj* destructive; ‹critica› negative

di'strutto ① *pp di* DISTRUGGERE
  ② *adj* destroyed; **un uomo ∼** a broken man

distrut'tore *nm*
■ distruttore di documenti paper shredder

distruzi'one *nf* destruction

⚜ **distur'bare** *vt* disturb; (sconvolgere) upset

distur'barsi *vr* trouble oneself; **non si disturbi** please don't trouble yourself

distur'bato *adj* Med ‹mente› disordered; ‹intestino› upset

⚜ **di'sturbo** *nm* bother; (indisposizione) trouble; Med problem; Radio, TV interference; **disturbi** *pl* Radio, TV static
■ disturbo da deficit dell'attenzione attention deficit disorder; **disturbi di stomaco** *pl* stomach trouble

disubbidi'ente *adj* disobedient

disubbidi'enza *nf* disobedience

disubbi'dire *vi* ∼ **a** disobey

disuguagli'anza *nf* disparity; (eterogeneità) irregularity

disugu'ale *adj* unequal; (eterogeneo) irregular

disumanità *nf* inhumanity

disu'mano *adj* inhuman

disuni'one *nf* disunity

disu'nire *vt* divide

di'suso *nm* **cadere in ∼** fall into disuse

di'tale *nm* thimble

di'tata *nf* poke; (impronta) finger-mark

⚜ **'dito** *nm* (*pl nf* **dita**) finger; (di vino, acqua) finger
■ dito del piede toe

'ditta *nf* firm
■ ditta di vendita per corrispondenza mail order firm

dit'tafono *nm* dictaphone

ditta'tore *nm* dictator

dittatori'ale *adj* dictatorial

ditta'tura *nf* dictatorship

dit'tongo *nm* diphthong

diu'retico *adj* diuretic

di'urno *adj* daytime; **spettacolo diurno** matinée

'diva *nf* diva

diva'gare *vi* digress

divagazi'one *nf* digression
■ divagazione sul tema digression

divam'pare *vi* burst into flames; fig spread like wildfire

di'vano *nm* settee, sofa
■ divano letto sofa bed

divari'care *vt* open

divari'carsi *vr* splay

divari'cata *nf* splits *pl*

divari'cato *adj* ‹gambe, braccia› splayed

di'vario *nm* discrepancy; **un ∼ di opinioni** a difference of opinion

di'vellere *vt* (sradicare) uproot

di'velto *pp di* DIVELLERE

⚜ **dive'nire** *vi* = DIVENTARE

⚜ **diven'tare** *vi* become; (lentamente) grow; (rapidamente) turn

dive'nuto *pp di* DIVENIRE

di'verbio *nm* squabble

diver'gente *adj* divergent

diver'genza *nf* divergence
■ divergenza di opinioni difference of opinion

di'vergere *vi* diverge

diversa'mente *adv* (altrimenti) otherwise; (in modo diverso) differently
■ diversamente abile differently abled

di'versi *adj & pron* (parecchi) several

diversifi'care *vt* diversify

diversifi'carsi *vr* differ; be different

diversifi'cato *adj* broad-based

diversificazi'one *nf* diversification

diversi'one *nf* diversion

diversità *nf inv* diversity; **ci sono molte ∼** there are many differences

diver'sivo ① *adj* diversionary
  ② *nm* diversion

⚜ **di'verso** *adj* different

diver'tente *adj* amusing

diver'ticolo *nm* digression

diverti'mento *nm* fun, amusement; **buon ∼!** enjoy yourself!, have fun!

⚜ **diver'tire** *vt* amuse

diver'tirsi *vr* enjoy oneself, have fun

diver'tito *adj* amused

divi'dendo *nm* dividend

⚜ **di'videre** *vt* divide; (condividere) share

di'vidersi *vr* (separarsi) separate

divi'eto *nm* prohibition; '∼ **di pesca**' 'fishing prohibited'; '∼ **di sosta**' 'no parking'

divina'mente *adv* divinely

divinco'larsi *vr* wriggle

divinità *nf inv* divinity

di'vino *adj* divine

di'visa *nf* uniform; Fin currency

divi'sibile *adj* divisible

⚜ **divisi'one** *nf* division

divisio'nismo *nm* (in arte) pointillism

di'vismo *nm* worship; (atteggiamento) superstar mentality

di'viso ① *pp di* DIVIDERE
  ② *adj* divided

divi'sore *nm* divisor

divi'sorio *adj* dividing; **muro divisorio** partition wall

'divo, -a *nmf* star

divo'rare *vt* devour

divo'rarsi *vr* ~ **da** be consumed with

divorzi'are *vi* divorce

divorzi'ato, -a *nmf* divorcee

di'vorzio *nm* divorce

divul'gare *vt* divulge; (rendere popolare) popularize

divul'garsi *vr* spread

divulga'tivo *adj* popular

divulgazi'one *nf* spread; (di cultura, scienza) popularization

dizio'nario *nm* dictionary

■ dizionario dei sinonimi thesaurus

dizi'one *nf* diction

DJ *nm inv* DJ

DNA *nm inv* DNA

do *nm* Mus (chiave, nota) C

D.O.C. *abbr* (**Denominazione di Origine Controllata**) *mark guaranteeing the quality of a wine*

'doccia *nf* shower; (grondaia) gutter; **fare la** ~ have a shower, shower

doccia'tura *nf* Med douche

do'cente 1 *adj* teaching

2 *nmf* teacher; (di università) lecturer

do'cenza *nf* university teacher's qualification

D.O.C.G. *abbr* (**Denominazione di Origine Controllata e Garantita**) *mark guaranteeing the high quality of a wine*

'docile *adj* docile

docilità *nf* docility

documen'tare *vt* document

documen'tario *adj & nm* documentary

documen'tarsi *vr* gather information (su about)

documen'tato *adj* well-documented; ‹persona› well-informed

documentazi'one *nf* documentation

✍ **docu'mento** *nm* document; **documenti** *pl* papers

■ documento d'identità ID

dodeca'fonico *adj* Mus dodecaphonic

Dodecan'neso *nm* il ~ the Dodecanese

dodi'cenne *adj & nmf* twelve-year-old

dodi'cesimo *adj & nm* twelfth

✍ **'dodici** *adj & nm* twelve

do'gana *nf* customs *pl*; (dazio) duty

■ dogana merci customs for freight; dogana passeggeri passenger customs

doga'nale *adj* customs *attrib*

dogani'ere *nm* customs officer

'doglie *nfpl* labour pains

'dogma *nm* dogma

dog'matico *adj* dogmatic

dogma'tismo *nm* dogmatism

✍ **'dolce** 1 *adj* sweet; ‹clima› mild; ‹voce, consonante› soft; ‹acqua› fresh

2 *nm* (portata) dessert; (torta) cake; **non mangio dolci** I don't eat sweet things; **dolci** *pl* **della casa** (in menu) home-made cakes

dolce'mente *adv* sweetly

dolce'vita *adj inv* (maglione) rollneck

dol'cezza *nf* sweetness; (di clima) mildness

dolci'ario *adj* confectionery

dolci'astro *adj* sweetish

dolcifi'cante 1 *nm* sweetener

2 *adj* sweetening

dolcifica'tore *nm* (per acqua) softener

dolci'umi *nmpl* sweets

do'lente *adj* painful; (spiacente) sorry; **punto** ~ sore point

do'lere *vi* ache, hurt; (dispiacere) regret

do'lersi *vr* regret; (protestare) complain; ~ **di** be sorry for

'dollaro *nm* dollar

'dolly *nm inv* Cinema, TV dolly

'dolmen *nm inv* dolmen

'dolo *nm* Jur malice; (truffa) fraud

Dolo'miti *nfpl* le ~ the Dolomites

dolo'mitico *adj* Dolomite, of the Dolomites

dolo'rante *adj* aching

✍ **do'lore** *nm* pain; (morale) sorrow; **avere dei dolori** be in pain

■ dolori post-partum *pl* after-pains

dolorosa'mente *adv* painfully

dolo'roso *adj* painful

do'loso *adj* malicious

✍ **do'manda** *nf* question; (richiesta) request; (scritta) application; Comm demand; ~ **e offerta** supply and demand; **fare una** ~ **(a qualcuno)** ask (somebody) a question

■ domanda di impiego job application; domanda riconvenzionale counterclaim; domanda trabocchetto trick question

✍ **doman'dare** *vt* ask; (esigere) demand; ~ **qualcosa a qualcuno** ask somebody for something

doman'darsi *vr* wonder

✍ **do'mani** 1 *adv* tomorrow; ~ **sera** tomorrow evening; **a** ~ see you tomorrow

2 *nm* il ~ the future

do'mare *vt* tame; fig control ‹emozioni›

doma|'tore, -trice *nmf* tamer

■ domatore di cavalli horsebreaker

✍ **domat'tina** *adv* tomorrow morning

doma'tura *nf* (di cavallo) breaking

✍ **do'menica** *nf* Sunday; **di** ~ on Sundays

■ Domenica delle Palme Palm Sunday

domeni'cale *adj* Sunday *attrib*

domeni'cano *adj* Dominican

do'mestico, -a 1 *adj* domestic; **le pareti domestiche** one's own four walls

2 *nm* servant

3 *nf* maid

✍ indicates a very frequent word

domicili'are *adj* arresti domiciliari Jur house arrest; **perquisizione domiciliare** Jur house search

domicili'arsi *vr* settle

domi'cilio *nm* domicile; (abitazione) home; **recapitiamo a** ∼ we do home deliveries

domi'nante *adj* ‹nazione, colore› dominant; ‹carattere› chief; ‹opinione› prevailing; ‹motivo› main

domi'nanza *nf* Biol, Zool dominance

domi'nare ① *vt* dominate; (controllare) control
② *vi* rule over; (prevalere) be dominant

domi'narsi *vr* control oneself

domina|'tore, -trice ① *adj* domineering
② *nmf* ruler

dominazi'one *nf* domination

Domi'nica *nf* Dominica

domini'cano *adj* la Repubblica Dominicana the Dominican Republic

do'minio *nm* control; Pol dominion; (ambito) field; **di** ∼ **pubblico** common knowledge

'domino *nm* (gioco) dominoes

⚜ **don** *nm inv* (ecclesiastico) Father

do'nare ① *vt* give; donate ‹sangue, organo›
② *vi* ∼ **a** (giovare esteticamente) suit

do'narsi *vr* dedicate oneself

dona|'tore, -trice *nmf* donor
■ **donatore di organi** organ donor; **donatore del seme** sperm donor

donazi'one *nf* donation

dondo'lare ① *vt* swing; (cullare) rock
② *vi* sway

dondo'larsi *vr* swing

dondo'lio *nm* rocking

'dondolo *nm* swing; **cavallo/sedia a** ∼ rocking-horse/chair

dongio'vanni *nm inv* Romeo, Don Juan

⚜ **'donna** *nf* woman; **fare la prima** ∼ act like a prima donna; **'donne'** 'ladies'
■ **donna d'affari** businesswoman; **donna delle pulizie** cleaner; **donna di servizio** domestic help; **donna di vita** (prostituta) lady of the night

don'naccia *nf* pej hussy

donnai'olo *nm* womanizer

donnicci'ola *nf* fig old woman

'donnola *nf* weasel

'dono *nm* gift

'doping *nm inv* Sport drug-taking; **fa uso di** ∼ he takes drugs

⚜ **'dopo** ① *prep* after; (a partire da) since
② *adv* after; afterwards; (più tardi) later; (in seguito) later on; ∼ **di me** after me

dopo'barba *nm inv* aftershave

dopo'cena *nm inv* evening

dopodiché *adv* after which

dopodo'mani *adv* the day after tomorrow

dopogu'erra *nm inv* post-war period

dopola'voro *nm inv* working man's club

dopo'pranzo *nm inv* afternoon

dopo'sci *adj & nm inv* après-ski

doposcu'ola *nm inv* after-school activities *pl*

dopo-'shampoo ① *nm inv* conditioner
② *adj inv* conditioning

dopo'sole ① *nm inv* aftersun cream
② *adj inv* aftersun

⚜ **dopo'tutto** *adv* after all

doppi'aggio *nm* dubbing

doppia'mente *adv* (in misura doppia) doubly

doppi'are *vt* Naut double; Sport lap; Cinema dub

doppia|'tore, -trice *nmf* dubber

doppi'etta *nf* (fucile) double-barrelled shotgun; Auto double-declutch; (in calcio) two goals, (in pugilato) one-two

doppi'ezza *nf* duplicity

⚜ **'doppio** ① *adj & adv* double
■ **doppia nazionalità** dual nationality; **doppi vetri** double glazing; **doppio clic** Comput double click; **fare un** ∼ **su** double-click on; **doppio fallo** Tennis double fault; **doppio gioco** double-dealing; **doppio mento** double chin; **doppio senso** double entendre
② *nm* double, twice the quantity; Tennis doubles *pl*
■ **doppio misto** Tennis mixed doubles

doppio'fondo *nm* Naut double hull; (in valigia) false bottom

doppiogio'chista *nmf* double-dealer

doppi'one *nm* duplicate

doppio'petto *adj* double-breasted

dop'pista *nmf* Tennis doubles player

do'rare *vt* gild; Culin brown

do'rato *adj* gilt; (color oro) golden

dora'tura *nf* gilding

'dorico *adj* Archit Doric

do'rifora *nf* Colorado beetle

dormicchi'are *vi* doze

dormigli'one, -a *nmf* sleepyhead; fig lazybones

⚜ **dor'mire** *vi* sleep; (essere addormentato) be asleep; fig be asleep; **andare a** ∼ go to bed; ∼ **come un ghiro** sleep like a log; ∼ **in piedi** fig be half asleep; (essere stanco) be dead tired; **dormirci sopra** sleep on it

dor'mita *nf* good sleep; **fare una bella** ∼ have a good sleep

dormi'tina *nf* nap

dormi'torio *nm* dormitory
■ **dormitorio pubblico** night shelter

dormi'veglia *nm* **essere nel** ∼ be half asleep

dor'sale ① *adj* dorsal
② *nf* (di monte) ridge

dor'sista *nmf* backstroke swimmer

'dorso *nm* back; (di libro) spine; (di monte) crest; (nel nuoto) backstroke; **a ~ di cavallo** on horseback

do'saggio *nm* dosage; *fig* weighing; **sbagliare il ~** get the amount wrong

do'sare *vt* dose; *fig* measure; **~ le parole** weigh one's words

do'sato *adj* measured

dosa'tore *nm* measuring jug

'dose *nf* dose; **~ eccessiva** overdose; **in buona ~** *fig* in good measure

dos'sier *nm inv* (raccolta di dati, fascicolo) file

'dosso *nm* (dorso) back; (su strada) bump; **levarsidi ~ gli abiti** take off one's clothes
■ **dosso di rallentamento** road hump, speed hump

do'tare *vt* endow; (di accessori) equip

do'tato *adj* ‹persona› gifted; (fornito) equipped

dotazi'one *nf* (attrezzatura) equipment; (mezzi finanziari) endowment; **avere qualcosa in ~** be equipped with something

⚘ **'dote** *nf* dowry; (qualità) gift

dott. *abbr* (**dottore**) Dr

'dotto [1] *adj* learned
[2] *nm* scholar; *Anat* duct

dotto'rale *adj* doctoral; *pej* pedantic

dotto'rando, -a *nmf* postgraduate student

dotto'rato *nm* doctorate

⚘ **dot'tor|e, dottor'essa** *nmf* doctor

dot'trina *nf* doctrine

dott.ssa *abbr* (**dottoressa**) Dr

double-'face *adj inv* reversible

⚘ **'dove** *adv* where; **di ~ sei?** where do you come from; **fin ~?** how far?; **per ~?** which way?

⚘ **do'vere** [1] *vi* (obbligo) have to, must; **devo andare** I have to go, I must go; **devo venire anch'io?** do I have to come too?; **avresti dovuto dirmelo** you should have told me, you ought to have told me; **devo sedermi un attimo** I must sit down for a minute, I need to sit down for a minute; **dev'essere successo qualcosa** something must have happened; **come si deve** properly
[2] *vt* (essere debitore di, derivare) owe; **essere dovuto a** be due to
[3] *nm* duty; **per ~** out of duty; **rivolgersi a chi di ~** apply to the appropriate authorities

dove'roso *adj* right and proper

do'vizia *nf* **con ~ di particolari** in great detail

do'vunque [1] *adv* (dappertutto) everywhere; (in qualsiasi luogo) anywhere
[2] *conj* wherever

dovuta'mente *adv* duly

do'vuto *adj* due; (debito) proper; **essere ~ a** be attributable to; **ha fatto più del ~** he did more than he had to

⚘ indicates a very frequent word

Down: **sindrome di ~** *nf* *Med* Down's syndrome

doz'zina *nf* **una ~ di uova** a dozen eggs; **mezza ~ di uova** half a dozen eggs

dozzi'nale *adj* cheap

'draga *nf* (scavatrice) dredger

draga'mine *nf* minesweeper

dra'gare *vt* dredge

'drago *nm* dragon

'dramma *nm* drama; **fare un ~ di qualcosa** *fig* make a drama out of something

drammatica'mente *adv* dramatically

drammaticità *nf* dramatic force

dram'matico *adj* dramatic

drammatiz'zare *vt* dramatize

drammatizzazi'one *nf* dramatization

drammatur'gia *nf* (genere) drama

dramma'turgo *nm* playwright

dram'mone *nm* (film) tear-jerker, weepy

drappeggi'are *vt* drape

drap'peggio *nm* drapery

drap'pello *nm* *Mil* squad; (gruppo) band

'drappo *nm* (tessuto) cloth

drastica'mente *adv* drastically

'drastico *adj* drastic

dre'naggio *nm* drainage
■ **drenaggio di capitali** transfer of capital; **drenaggio fiscale** fiscal drag

dre'nare *vt* drain

'Dresda *nf* Dresden

dres'sage *nm inv* (gara) dressage

drib'blare *vt* (in calcio) dribble; *fig* dodge

'dribbling *nm inv* (in calcio) dribble

'dritta *nf* (mano destra) right hand; *Naut* starboard; (informazione) pointer; tip; **a ~ e a manca** (dappertutto) left, right and centre

dritta'mente *adv* (furbescamente) craftily

'dritto, -a [1] *adj* = DIRITTO[1]
[2] *nmf* *fam* crafty so-and-so

drive *nm inv* *Comput* drive

drive-'in *nm inv* drive-in

driz'zare *vt* straighten; (rizzare) prick up

driz'zarsi *vr* straighten [up]; (alzarsi) raise; **mi sono drizzati i capelli** *fig* my hair stood on end

'droga *nf* drug
■ **droga leggera** soft drug; **droga di passaggio** gateway drug; **droga pesante** hard drug

dro'gare *vt* drug

dro'garsi *vr* take drugs

drogato, -a [1] *adj* drugged
[2] *nmf* drug addict

droghe'ria *nf* grocery

droghi'ere, -a *nmf* grocer

drome'dario *nm* dromedary

'druso *nmf* Druse

dua'lismo *nm* dualism; (contrasto) conflict

⚘ **'dubbio** [1] *adj* doubtful; (ambiguo) dubious

2 *nm* doubt; (sospetto) suspicion; **mettere in** ∼ doubt; **essere fuori** ∼ be beyond doubt; **essere in** ∼ be doubtful

dubbiosa'mente *adv* doubtfully

dubbi'oso, dubitante *adj* doubtful

dubi'tare *vi* doubt; ∼ **di** doubt; (diffidare) mistrust; **dubito che venga** I doubt whether he'll come

dubita'tivo *adj* (ambiguo) ambiguous

Du'blino *nf* Dublin

'duca *nm* duke

du'cale *adj* ducal

'duce *nm* (nel fascismo) Duce

du'chessa *nf* duchess

✦ **'due** *adj & nm* two

duecen'tesco *adj* thirteenth-century

duecen'tesimo *nm* two hundredth

duecento *adj & nm* two hundred

duel'lante *nmf* dueller

duel'lare *vi* duel

du'ello *nm* duel

due'mila *adj & nm* two thousand

due'pezzi *nm inv* (bikini) bikini; (vestito) two-piece suit

du'etto *nm* duo; Mus duet

'dumping *nm inv* Fin dumping

'duna *nf* dune

dune 'buggy *nm inv* beach buggy

✦ **'dunque** *conj* therefore; (allora) well [then]; **arrivare al** ∼ get down to the nitty-gritty

'duo *nm inv* duo; Mus duet

duodeci'male *adj* duodecimal

duode'nale *adj* ulcera ∼ duodenal ulcer

duo'deno *nm* duodenum

du'omo *nm* cathedral

'duplex *nm* Teleph party line

dupli'care *vt* duplicate

dupli'cato *nm* duplicate

duplicazi'one *nf* duplication

'duplice *adj* double; **in** ∼ in duplicate

duplicità *nf* duplicity

dura'mente *adv* ‹lavorare› hard; ‹rimproverare› harshly

✦ **du'rante** *prep* during

✦ **du'rare** **1** *vi* last; ‹cibo› keep; (resistere) hold out; **così non può** ∼ this can't go on any longer; ∼ **in carica** remain in office; **finché dura** as long as it lasts
2 *vt* ∼ **fatica** sweat blood

du'rata *nf* duration
■ **durata del collegamento** on-line time; **durata di conservazione** shelf-life; **durata della vita** life span

dura'turo *adj* lasting

du'revole *adj* ‹pace› lasting, enduring

du'rezza *nf* hardness; (di carne) toughness; (di voce, padre) harshness

✦ **'duro, -a** **1** *adj* hard; ‹persona, carne› tough; ‹voce› harsh; ‹pane› stale; **tieni** ∼**!** (resistere) hang in there!; ∼ **d'orecchio** hard of hearing
2 *nmf* (persona) tough person, toughie fam

du'rone *nm* hardened skin

'duttile *adj* ‹materiale› ductile; ‹carattere, persona› malleable

duttilità *nf* (di materiale) ductility; (di individuo) malleability

'duty free *nm inv* duty-free shop

DVD **1** *nm inv* (disco) DVD
2 *nm inv* (lettore) DVD player

Ee

✦ **e** *conj* and

eba'nista *nmf* cabinet-maker

'ebano *nm* ebony

✦ **eb'bene** *conj* well [then]

eb'brezza *nf* inebriation; (euforia) elation; **guida in stato di** ∼ drink-driving; **l'**∼ **della velocità** the thrill of speed

'ebbro *adj* inebriated; ∼ **di gioia** delirious with joy

'ebete *adj* stupid

ebollizi'one *nf* boiling

e'braico *adj & nm* Hebrew

ebra'ismo *nm* Judaism

e'breo, -a **1** *adj* Jewish

2 *nm* Jew
3 *nf* Jewess

'Ebridi *nfpl* **le** ∼ the Hebrides

eca'tombe *nf* **fare un'**∼ wreak havoc

ecc *abbr* (**eccetera**) etc

ecce'dente *adj* ‹peso, bagaglio› excess

ecce'denza *nf* excess; (d'avanzo) surplus; **avere qualcosa in** ∼ have an excess of something; **bagagli in** ∼ excess baggage
■ **eccedenza di cassa** surplus; **eccedenza di peso** excess weight

ec'cedere **1** *vt* exceed
2 *vi* go too far; ∼ **nel bere** drink to excess; ∼ **nel mangiare** overeat

eccel'lente *adj* excellent

ꙮ **eccel'lenza** nf excellence; (titolo) Excellency; **per ~ par** excellence

ec'cellere vi excel (**in** at)

eccentricità nf inv eccentricity

ec'centrico, -a adj & nmf eccentric

ecce'pire vt object to

eccessiva'mente adv excessively

ecces'sivo adj excessive

ec'cesso nm excess; **andare agli eccessi** go to extremes; **dare in eccessi** fly into a temper; **all'~** to excess

■ **eccesso di personale** over-manning; **eccesso di peso** excess weight; **eccesso di velocità** speeding

ꙮ **ec'cetera** adv et cetera

ec'cetto prep except; **~ che** (a meno che) unless

eccettu'are vt except

ꙮ **eccezio'nale** adj exceptional; **in via [del tutto] ~** as an exception

eccezional'mente adv exceptionally; (contrariamente alla regola) as an exception

eccezi'one nf exception; Jur objection; **a ~ di** with the exception of; **d'~** exceptional

ec'chimosi nf inv bruising

eccì int atishoo

ec'cidio nm massacre

ecci'tabile adj ⟨persona, carattere⟩ excitable

eccita'mento nm excitement

ecci'tante ① adj exciting; ⟨sostanza⟩ stimulant ② nm stimulant

ecci'tare vt excite; (sessualmente) excite, arouse

ecci'tarsi vr get excited; (sessualmente) become aroused or excited

ecci'tato adj excited; (sessualmente) excited, aroused; **~ da** flushed with

eccitazi'one nf excitement; (sessuale) arousal, excitement

ecclesi'astico ① adj ecclesiastical ② nm priest

ꙮ **'ecco** adv (qui) here; (là) there; **~!** (con approvazione) that's right!; **~ qua!** (dando qualcosa) here you are!; **~ la tua borsa** here is your bag; **~ mio figlio** there is my son; **eccomi** here I am; **~ fatto** there we are; **~ perché** this is why; **~ tutto** that is all

ec'come adv & int and how!

ECG abbr (**elettrocardiogramma**) ECG

echeggi'are vi echo

e'clettico adj eclectic

eclet'tismo nm eclecticism

eclis'sare vt fig eclipse

eclis'sarsi vr (sparire) disappear

e'clissi nf inv eclipse

■ **eclissi di sole** solar eclipse

─────────────────────

ꙮ indicates a very frequent word

'eco nmf (pl m **echi**) echo; **ha suscitato una vasta ~** it caused a great stir

eco+ pref eco+; **eco-guerrigliero** eco-warrior

ecogra'fia nf scan

ecolo'gia nf ecology

eco'logico adj ecological; ⟨prodotto⟩ environmentally friendly, eco-friendly

e'cologo, -a nmf ecologist

e commerci'ale nf ampersand

econo'mia nf economy; (scienza) economics sg; **fare ~** economize (**di** on); **[fatto] in ~** [done] on the cheap; **senza ~** unstintingly; **fare qualcosa senza ~** spare no expense doing something

■ **economia aziendale** business administration; **economia domestica** Sch home economics; **economia di mercato** market economy; **economia di libero mercato** free market; **economia mista** mixed economy; **economia sommersa** black economy

economicità nf economy

ꙮ **eco'nomico** adj economic; (a buon prezzo) cheap; (con pochi costi) economical; **difficoltà economiche** financial difficulties; **classe economica** economy class; **edizione economica** paperback

econo'mie nfpl (risparmi) savings

econo'mista nmf economist

economiz'zare ① vt save ⟨tempo, denaro⟩ ② vi economize (**su** on)

economizza'tore nm Auto fuel economizer

e'conomo, -a ① adj thrifty ② nmf (di collegio) bursar

ecosi'stema nm ecosystem

eco'tassa nf carbon tax

ecoterro'rismo nm ecoterrorism

é'cru adj inv fawn

Ecua'dor nm Ecuador

ecuadori'ano, -a adj & nmf Ecuadorian

ecu'menico adj ecumenical

ec'zema nm eczema

ed ▸ conj E

e'dema nm oedema

'Eden nm Eden

'edera nf ivy

e'dicola nf [newspaper] kiosk

edifi'cabile adj ⟨area, terreno⟩ classified as suitable for development

edifi'cante adj edifying

edifi'care vt build; (indurre al bene) edify

edi'ficio nm building; fig structure

e'dile ① adj building attrib ② nm **edili** pl construction workers

edi'lizia nf building trade

edi'lizio adj building attrib

Edim'burgo nf Edinburgh

E'dipo *nm* Oedipus; **complesso di Edipo** Oedipus complex

edi'tare *vt* edit

'editing *nm* editing

'edito *adj* published

edi|'tore, -trice [1] *adj* publishing [2] *nmf* publisher; (curatore) editor

edito'ria *nf* publishing
■ **editoria elettronica** desktop publishing, electronic publishing; **editoria telematica** online publishing

editori'ale [1] *adj* publishing [2] *nm* (articolo) editorial, leader

e'ditto *nm* edict

edizi'one *nf* edition; (di manifestazione) performance; **in ~ italiana** ⟨film⟩ dubbed into Italian
■ **edizione ridotta** abridgement, abridged version; **edizione della sera** (di telegiornale) evening news

edo'nismo *nm* hedonism

edo'nistico *adj* hedonistic

educaЙ'oco *nm* edutainment

edu'canda *nf* [convent school] boarder; fig prim and proper girl

⚘ **edu'care** *vt* educate; (allevare) bring up

educa'tivo *adj* educational

edu'cato *adj* polite

educa|'tore, -trice *nmf* educator

⚘ **educazione** *nf* education; (di bambini) upbringing; (buone maniere) [good] manners *pl*; **bella ~!** what manners!
■ **educazione alla cittadinanza** education for citizenship; **educazione fisica** physical education; **educazione sessuale** sex education

edulco'rare *vt* **~ la pillola** sweeten the pill

EED *abbr* (**elaborazione elettronica [dei] dati**) EDP

e'felide *nf* freckle

effemi'nato *adj* effeminate

effe'rato *adj* brutal

efferve'scente *adj* effervescent; (frizzante) fizzy; ⟨aspirina®⟩ soluble

effettiva'mente *adv* **è troppo tardi - ~** it's too late - so it is

effet'tivo [1] *adj* actual; (efficace) effective; ⟨personale⟩ permanent; Mil regular [2] *nm* (somma totale) sum total

⚘ **ef'fetto** *nm* effect; (impressione) impression; (cambiale) bill; **fare ~** ⟨medicina⟩ take effect; **fare ~ su** have an effect on, affect; **in effetti** in fact; (a tutti gli effetti) to all intents and purposes; **ad effetto** ⟨frase⟩ catchy; **la vista del sangue mi fa ~** I can't stand the sight of blood; **tiro con ~** spin
■ **effetto boomerang** boomerang effect; **effetto domino** domino effect; **effetto di luce** trick of the light; **effetti personali** *pl*

personal belongings, personal effects fml; **effetto ritardato** delayed effect; **effetto serra** greenhouse effect; **effetto sonoro** sound effect; **effetto speciale** Cinema, TV special effect

effettu'are *vt* effect; carry out ⟨controllo, sondaggio⟩

effettu'arsi *vr* take place; **'si effettua dal ... al ...'** this service is available from ... till ...

effi'cace *adj* effective

effi'cacia *nf* effectiveness

effici'ente *adj* efficient

effici'enza *nf* efficiency; **in piena ~** in full swing

ef'figie *nf* effigy

ef'fimero *adj* ephemeral

ef'flusso *nm* outflow

ef'fluvio *nm* stink

ef'fondersi *vr* **~ in ringraziamenti** be profuse in one's thanks

effrazi'one *nf*
■ **effrazione con scasso** Jur breaking and entering

effusi'one *nf* effusion

'Egadi *nfpl* **le [isole] ~** the Egadi Islands

egemo'nia *nf* hegemony

E'geo *nm* **l'~** the Aegean [Sea]

e'gida *nf* **sotto l'~ di** under the aegis of

E'gitto *nm* Egypt

egizi'ano, -a *adj & nmf* Egyptian

e'gizio, -a *adj & nmf* Ancient Egyptian

⚘ **'egli** *pers pron* he; **~ stesso** he himself

ego'centrico, -a [1] *adj* egocentric [2] *nmf* egocentric person

egocen'trismo *nm* egocentricity

ego'ismo *nm* selfishness

ego'ista [1] *adj* selfish [2] *nmf* selfish person

egoistica'mente *adv* selfishly

ego'istico *adj* selfish

Egr. *abbr* (**egregio**) **~ Sig.** (su busta) Mr

e'gregio *adj* distinguished; **Egregio Signore** Dear Sir

eguali'tario *adj & nm* egalitarian

⚘ **eh** *int* huh!

⚘ **'ehi** *int* hey!

ehilà *int* hi!

ehm *int* um

eiacu'lare *vi* ejaculate

eiaculazi'one *nf* ejaculation

eiet'tabile *adj* ⟨sedile⟩ ejector

eiezi'one *nf* Aeron ejection

'Eire *nf* Eire

elabo'rare *vt* elaborate; process ⟨dati⟩

elabo'rato [1] *adj* elaborate [2] *nm* (tabulato) preprinted form

elabora'tore *nm*
■ **elaboratore [di testi]** word processor

e

elaborazione *nf* elaboration; (di dati) processing
- **elaborazione [dei] dati** data processing; **elaborazione elettronica [dei] dati** electronic data processing; **elaborazione sequenziale** Comput batch processing; **elaborazione [di] testi** word processing

elar'gire *vt* lavish

elasticità *nf* elasticity
- **elasticità mentale** mental agility; **elasticità di movimento** litheness

elasticiz'zato *adj* ‹stoffa› elasticated

e'lastico [1] *adj* elastic; ‹tessuto› stretch; ‹passo› springy; ‹orario, mente› flexible; ‹persona› easy-going; ‹morale› lax; **collant** *pl* **elastici** support tights
[2] *nm* elastic; (fascia) rubber band

'Elba *nf* Elba

eldo'rado *nm* eldorado

ele'fante *nm* elephant; **avere una memoria da ~** have a memory like an elephant; **fare passi da ~** thump about
- **~ marino** sea-elephant

elefan'tesco *adj* elephantine

elefan'tessa *nf* cow-[elephant]

elefan'tiaco *adj* (enorme) elephantine

♂ **ele'gante** *adj* elegant

elegante'mente *adv* elegantly

ele'ganza *nf* elegance

♂ **e'leggere** *vt* elect

eleg'gibile *adj* eligible

ele'gia *nf* elegy

elemen'tare *adj* elementary; **scuola elementare** primary school

♂ **ele'mento** *nm* element; (componente) part; **trovarsi nel proprio ~** be in one's element; **elementi** *pl* (fatti) data; (rudimenti) elements

ele'mosina *nf* charity; **chiedere l'~** beg; **vivere d'~** live on charity; **fare l'~** give money to beggars

elemosi'nare *vt/i* beg

elen'care *vt* list

e'lenco *nm* list
- **elenco [degli] abbonati** Teleph telephone directory; **elenco telefonico** telephone directory

elet'tivo *adj* ‹carica› elective

e'letto, -a [1] *pp di* ELEGGERE
[2] *adj* chosen
[3] *nmf* (nominato) elected member; **per pochi eletti** fig for the chosen few

eletto'rale *adj* electoral

elettora'lismo *nm* electioneering

eletto'rato *nm* electorate

elet|'tore, -trice *nmf* voter

elet'trauto *nm* electrics garage

elettri'cista *nm* electrician

elettricità *nf* electricity; **togliere l'~** cut the electricity off; **è mancata l'~** there was a power cut

♂ **e'lettrico** *adj* electric

elettriz'zante *adj* ‹notizia, gara› electrifying

elettriz'zare *vt* fig electrify

elettriz'zato *adj* fig electrified

elettro+ *pref* electro+

elettrocardio'gramma *nm* electrocardiogram, ECG

elettrocuzi'one *nf* electrocution

e'lettrodo *nm* electrode

elettrodo'mestico *nm* [electrical] household appliance

elettroencefalo'gramma *nm* electroencephalogram

elettroesecuzi'one *nf* electrocution

elet'trogeno *adj* **gruppo ~** generator

elet'trolisi *nf* electrolysis

elettromo'tore *nm* electric motor

elettromo'trice *nf* electric train

elet'trone *nm* electron

elet'tronico, -a [1] *adj* electronic
[2] *nf* electronics *sg*

elettroshocktera'pia *nf* electroshock therapy, electroshock treatment, EST

elettro'tecnica *nf* electrical engineering

elettro'tecnico *nm* electrical engineer

elettro'treno *nm* electric train

♂ **ele'vare** *vt* raise; (promuovere) promote; (erigere) erect; fig (migliorare) better; **~ al quadrato/cubo** square/cube

ele'varsi *vr* rise; ‹edificio› stand

ele'vato *adj* high; fig (sentimento) lofty; **~ al cubo/al quadrato** cubed/squared; **~ a dieci** raised to the power of ten

eleva'tore *nm* fork-lift truck

elevazi'one *nf* elevation

elezi'one *nf* election; **elezioni** *pl* **amministrative** local council elections; **elezioni** *pl* **politiche** general election

eliambu'lanza *nf* air ambulance

'elica *nf* Naut screw, propeller; Aeron propeller; (del ventilatore) blade

eli'cottero *nm* helicopter

elimi'nabile *adj* which can be eliminated

elimi'nare *vt* eliminate

elimina'toria *nf* Sport [preliminary] heat

eliminazi'one *nf* elimination

'elio *nm* (gas) helium

eli'porto *nm* heliport

elisabetti'ano *adj* & *nmf* Elizabethan

é'lite *nf inv* élite

eli'tista *adj* élitist

'ella *pers pron* (liter) she; **~ stessa** she herself

el'lenico *adj* Hellenic

elle'nistico *adj* Hellenistic

ellepì *nm inv* LP

+ellino *suff* **campanellino** *nm* [small] bell; **fiorellino** *nm* [little] flower; **gonnellina** *nf* short skirt

el'lisse *nf* ellipse

el'lissi *nf inv* ellipsis

el'littico *adj* elliptical

+ello *suff* **finestrella** *nf* little window; **pecorella** *nf* woolly sheep; **saltello** *nm* skip

el'metto *nm* helmet

elogi'are *vt* praise

elogia'tivo *adj* laudatory

e'logio *nm* praise; (discorso, scritto) eulogy; **degno di ∼** laudable, praiseworthy; **ti faccio i miei elogi per** congratulations on ■ **∼ funebre** funeral oration

elo'quente *adj* eloquent; fig tell-tale

elo'quenza *nf* eloquence

El Salva'dor *nm* El Salvador; **nel Salvador** in El Salvador

e'ludere *vt* elude; evade ‹sorveglianza, controllo›

elusi'one *nf* ■ **elusione fiscale** tax avoidance

elu'sivo *adj* elusive

el'vetico *adj* Swiss; **Confederazione Elvetica** Swiss Confederation

emaci'ato *adj* emaciated

e-mail *nf inv* e-mail; **mandare per ∼** e-mail, send by e-mail; **indirizzo ∼** e-mail address

ema'nare 1 *vt* give off; pass ‹legge› 2 *vi* emanate

emanazi'one *nf* giving off; (di legge) enactment

emanci'pare *vt* emancipate

emanci'parsi *vr* become emancipated

emanci'pato *adj* emancipated

emancipazi'one *nf* emancipation

emargi'nato *nm* marginalized person

emarginazi'one *nf* marginalization

ema'toma *nm* haematoma

em'bargo *nm* embargo ■ **embargo sulle armi** arms embargo

em'blema *nm* emblem

emble'matico *adj* emblematic

embo'lia *nf* embolism

'embolo *nm* embolus

embrio'nale *adj* Biol fig embryonic; **allo stato ∼** ‹progetto, idea› embryonic

embri'one *nm* embryo

emenda'mento *nm* amendment

emen'dare *vt* amend

emen'darsi *vr* reform

emer'gente *adj* emergent

emer'genza *nf* emergency; **in caso di ∼** in an emergency; **di ∼** (di riserva) stand-by;

uscita d'emergenza emergency exit ■ **emergenza sanitaria** ambulance

e'mergere *vi* emerge; ‹sottomarino› surface; (distinguersi) stand out

e'merito *adj* ‹professore› emeritus; **un ∼ imbecille** a prize idiot

e'merso pp di EMERGERE

e'messo pp di EMETTERE

e'metico *adj* emetic

e'mettere *vt* emit; give out ‹luce, suono›; let out ‹grido›; (mettere in circolazione) issue

emi'crania *nf* migraine

emi'grare *vi* emigrate

emi'grato, -a *nmf* immigrant

emigrazi'one *nf* emigration

emi'nente *adj* eminent

emi'nenza *nf* eminence; **Sua Eminenza** His/Your Eminence ■ **eminenza grigia** éminence grise

emi'rato *nm* emirate; **Emirati** *pl* **Arabi Uniti** United Arab Emirates

e'miro *nm* emir

emi'sfero *nm* hemisphere

emis'sario *nm* emissary; (fiume) effluent

emissi'one *nf* emission; (di denaro, francobolli) issue; (trasmissione) broadcast; '**∼ del biglietto**' 'take your ticket here'; **a emissioni zero** carbon neutral; **a basse emissioni** low-carbon; **emissioni di CO_2** carbon emissions

emit'tente 1 *adj* issuing; (trasmittente) broadcasting 2 *nf* Radio transmitter

'emmental *nm* Emmenthal

emofi'lia *nf* haemophilia

emofi'liaco, -a *nmf* haemophiliac

emoglo'bina *nf* haemoglobin

emorra'gia *nf* haemorrhage; **avere un'∼** haemorrhage

emor'roidi *nfpl* haemorrhoids, piles

emo'statico *adj* haemostatic

emotiva'mente *adv* emotionally

emotività *nf* emotional make-up

emotivo *adj* emotional; **con turbe emotive** emotionally disturbed

emozio'nante *adj* exciting; (commovente) moving

emozio'nare *vt* excite; (commuovere) move

emozio'narsi *vr* become excited; (commuoversi) be moved

emozio'nato *adj* excited; (commosso) moved

emozi'one *nf* emotion; (agitazione) excitement

empietà *nf* impiety

'empio *adj* impious; (spietato) pitiless; (malvagio) wicked

em'pirico *adj* empirical

empi'rismo *nm* empiricism

empi'rista *nmf* empiricist

em'porio *nm* emporium; (negozio) general store

emù *nm inv* emu

emu'lare *vt* emulate

emulazi'one *nf* emulation

■ emulazione di terminale terminal emulation

emulsio'nare *vt* emulsify

emulsio'narsi *vr* emulsify

emulsi'one *nf* emulsion

ena'lotto *nm* weekly lottery

encefa'lite *nf*

■ encefalite spongiforme bovina Bovine Spongiform Encephalopathy, BSE

encefalo'gramma *nm* encephalogram

en'ciclica *nf* encyclical

enciclope'dia *nf* encyclopaedia

enciclo'pedico *adj* ‹mente, cultura, dizionario› encyclopaedic

encomi'are *vt* commend

en'comio *nm* commendation

ende'mia *nf* (situazione) endemic

en'demico *adj* endemic

endocrinolo'gia *nf* endocrinology

endo'vena ⊡ *nf* intravenous injection ⊡ *adv* intravenously

endove'noso *adj* intravenous; per via endovenosa intravenously

ener'getico *adj* ‹risorse, crisi› energy *attrib*; ‹alimento› energy-giving

✧ **ener'gia** *nf* energy; pieno di ∼ full of energy

■ energia alternativa alternative energy; energia atomica atomic energy; energia elettrica electricity; energia eolica windpower; energia idroelettrica hydroelectricity; energia nucleare nuclear energy, nuclear power; energia solare solar energy, solar power

energica'mente *adv* energetically

e'nergico *adj* energetic; (efficace) strong

ener'gumeno *nm* Neanderthal

'enfasi *nf* emphasis

en'fatico *adj* emphatic

enfatiz'zare *vt* emphasize

enfi'sema *nm* emphysema

e'nigma *nm* enigma

enig'matico *adj* enigmatic

enig'mistica *nf* puzzles *pl*

E.N.I.T. *nm abbr* (Ente Nazionale Italiano per il Turismo) Italian State Tourist Office

en'nesimo *adj* Math nth; fam umpteenth; all'ennesima potenza Math fig to the nth power/degree

eno'logico *adj* wine *attrib*

✧ indicates a very frequent word

✧ **enorme** *adj* enormous, great big fam; è un'ingiustizia ∼ it's enormously unfair

enorme'mente *adv* massively

enormità *nf inv* enormity; (assurdità) absurdity

eno'teca *nf* wine-tasting shop

eno'tera *nf* evening primrose

en pas'sant *adv* in passing

'ente *nm* board; (società) company; (in filosofia) being

ente'rite *nf* enteritis

entero'clisma *nm* Med enema

entità *nf inv* (filosofia) entity; (gravità) seriousness; (dimensione) extent

entomolo'gia *nf* entomology

entou'rage *nm inv* entourage

✧ **en'trambi** *adj & pron* both

✧ **en'trare** *vi* go in, enter; ∼ in go into; (stare in, trovar posto in) fit into; (arruolarsi) join; entrarci (avere a che fare) have to do with; tu che c'entri? what has it got to do with you?; da che parte si entra? how do you get in?; fallo ∼ (in ufficio, dal medico ecc) show him in; 'vietato ∼' 'no entry'

✧ **en'trata** *nf* (a) entry, entrance (b) (*pl* entrate) Comm takings; (reddito) income *sg*

■ entrata libera admission free; entrata di servizio tradesman's entrance

entre'côte *nf inv* beef entrecôte

✧ **'entro** *prep* (tempo) within; ∼ oggi by the end of today

entro'bordo *nm* (motore) inboard motor; (motoscafo) speedboat

entro'terra *nm inv* hinterland

entusia'smante *adj* fascinating, exciting

entusia'smare *vt* arouse enthusiasm in

entusia'smarsi *vr* be enthusiastic (per about)

✧ **entusi'asmo** *nm* enthusiasm

entusi'asta ⊡ *adj* enthusiastic ⊡ *nmf* enthusiast

entusi'astico *adj* enthusiastic

enucle'are *vt* define

enume'rare *vt* enumerate

enumerazi'one *nf* enumeration

enunci'are *vt* enunciate

enunciazi'one *nf* enunciation

E'olie *nfpl* le ∼ the Aeolian Islands

epa'tite *nf* hepatitis

ep'eira *nf* garden spider

epi'centro *nm* epicentre

'epico *adj* epic

epide'mia *nf* epidemic

epi'dermide *nf* epidermis

epidu'rale *adj* Med (anestesia) epidural

Epifa'nia *nf* Epiphany

epi'gramma *nm* epigram

epiles'sia *nf* epilepsy
epi'lettico, -a *adj & nmf* epileptic
e'pilogo *nm* epilogue
episco'pato *nm* episcopacy
epi'sodico *adj* episodic; **caso ∼** one-off case
⚔ **epi'sodio** *nm* episode
e'pistola *nf* epistle
episto'lare *adj* epistolary
episto'lario *nm* correspondence, letters *pl*
epi'taffio *nm* epitaph
e'piteto *nm* epithet
⚔ **'epoca** *nf* age; (periodo) period; **a quell'∼** in those days; **un avvenimento che ha fatto ∼** an epoch-making event; **auto d'epoca** vintage car; **mobile d'epoca** period furniture
e'ponimo *adj* eponymous
epo'pea *nf* epic
⚔ **ep'pure** *conj* [and] yet
E.P.T. *abbr* (**Ente Provinciale per il Turismo**) *Italian local tourist board*
epu'rare *vt* purge; purify ‹acqua›
epura'tore *nm* water purifier
epurazi'one *nf* purging; (di acqua) purification
■ **epurazione etnica** ethnic cleansing
equalizza'tore *nm* equalizer
e'quanime *adj* level-headed; (imparziale) impartial
equa'tore *nm* equator
equatori'ale *adj* equatorial
equazi'one *nf* equation
e'questre *adj* equestrian; **circo equestre** circus
equidi'stante *adj* equidistant
equi'latero *adj* equilateral
equili'brare *vt* balance
equili'brato *adj* (persona) well-balanced
equi'librio *nm* balance; (buon senso) common sense; (di bilancia) equilibrium
equili'brismo *nm* **fare ∼** do a balancing act
equili'brista *nmf* tightrope walker
e'quino *adj* horse *attrib*
equi'nozio *nm* equinox
equipaggia'mento *nm* equipment
equipaggi'are *vt* equip; (di persone) man
equi'paggio *nm* crew; Aeron cabin crew
■ **equipaggio di volo** aircrew
equipa'rare *vt* make equal
equipa'rato *adj* equal
é'quipe *nf inv* team
equità *nf* equity
equitazione *nf* riding, horseriding, horseback riding Am
equiva'lente *adj & nm* equivalent
equiva'lenza *nf* equivalence

equiva'lere *vi* **∼ a** be equivalent to
equivo'care *vi* misunderstand
e'quivoco ☐ *adj* equivocal; (sospetto) suspicious; **un tipo ∼** a shady character
☐ *nm* misunderstanding; **a scanso di equivoci** to avoid any misunderstandings; **giocare sull'∼** equivocate
'equo *adj* fair, just
equosoli'dale *adj* fair trade
'era *nf* era
■ **era glaciale** Ice Age
⚔ **'erba** *nf* grass; (medicinale) herb; **in ∼** ‹atleta, attore› budding
■ **erba cipollina** chives
er'baccia *nf* weed
er'baceo *adj* herbaceous
erbi'cida *nm* weedkiller
erbi'voro ☐ *adj* herbivorous
☐ *nm* herbivore
erbo'rista *nmf* herbalist
erboriste'ria *nf* herbalist's shop
er'boso *adj* grassy
Erco'lano *nf* Herculaneum
'Ercole *nm* Hercules
er'culeo *adj* ‹forza› herculean
e'rede ☐ *nm* heir
☐ *nf* heiress
eredità *nf inv* inheritance; Biol heredity
eredi'tare *vt* inherit
ereditarietà *nf* heredity
eredi'tario *adj* hereditary
erediti'era *nf* heiress
+erello *suff* furterello *nm* petty theft; pioggerella *nf* drizzle
ere'mita *nm* hermit
'eremo *nm* isolated place; fig retreat
ere'sia *nf* heresy
e'retico, -a ☐ *adj* heretical
☐ *nmf* heretic
e'retto ☐ *pp di* ERIGERE
☐ *adj* erect
erezi'one *nf* erection; (costruzione) building
ergasto'lano, -a *nmf* prisoner serving a life sentence, lifer fam
er'gastolo *nm* life sentence; (luogo) prison
ergono'mia *nf* ergonomics *sg*
ergo'nomico *adj* ergonomic
ergotera'pia *nf* occupational therapy
ergotera'pista *nmf* occupational therapist
'erica *nf* heather
e'rigere *vt* erect; fig (fondare) found
eri'tema *nm* (cutaneo) inflammation; (solare) sunburn
■ **eritema da pannolini** nappy rash
Eri'trea *nf* Eritrea
eri'treo, -a *adj & nmf* Eritrean
ermafro'dito *adj & nm* hermaphrodite

e

ermel'lino *nm* ermine

ermetica'mente *adv* hermetically

er'metico *adj* hermetic; (a tenuta d'aria) airtight

'ernia *nf* hernia

e'rodere *vi* erode

⚔ **e'roe** *nm* hero

ero'gare *vt* distribute; (fornire) supply

erogazi'one *nf* supply

e'rogeno *adj* erogenous

eroica'mente *adv* heroically

e'roico *adj* heroic

ero'ina *nf* heroine; (droga) heroin

eroi'nomane *nmf* heroin addict

ero'ismo *nm* heroism

'eros *nm* Eros

erosi'one *nf* erosion

e'rotico *adj* erotic

ero'tismo *nm* eroticism

'erpice *nm* harrow

er'rante *adj* wandering

er'rare *vi* (vagare) wander; (sbagliare) be mistaken

er'rato *adj* (sbagliato) mistaken; **se non vado ~** if I'm not mistaken

'erre *nf*
∎ **erre moscia** burr

erronea'mente *adv* mistakenly

⚔ **er'rore** *nm* error, mistake; (di stampa) misprint; **essere in ~** be wrong
∎ **errore giudiziario** miscarriage of justice; **errore di stampa** printing error, typo

'erta *nf* **stare all'~** be on the alert

eru'dirsi *vr* get educated

eru'dito *adj* learned

erut'tare **[1]** *vt* ‹vulcano› erupt **[2]** *vi* (ruttare) belch

eruzi'one *nf* eruption; Med rash

Es *nm* Psych l'~ the id

es. *abbr* (**esempio**) eg

esacer'bare *vt* exacerbate

⚔ **esage'rare** **[1]** *vt* exaggerate; **~ le cose** exaggerate things, go over the top **[2]** *vi* exaggerate; (nel comportamento) go over the top; **~ nel mangiare** eat too much

esagerata'mente *adv* excessively

esage'rato **[1]** *adj* exaggerated; ‹prezzo› exorbitant **[2]** *nm* **è un ~** he exaggerates

esagerazi'one *nf* exaggeration; **è costato un'~** it cost the earth; **senza ~** with no exaggeration

esago'nale *adj* hexagonal

e'sagono *nm* hexagon

esa'lare **[1]** *vt* give off; **~ l'ultimo respiro** breathe one's last **[2]** *vi* emanate

esalazi'one *nf* emission; **esalazioni** *pl* fumes

esal'tare *vt* exalt; (entusiasmare) elate

esal'tarsi *vr* (entusiasmarsi) get excited (**per** about)

esal'tato **[1]** *adj* (fanatico) fanatical **[2]** *nm* fanatic

esaltazi'one *nf* exaltation; (in discorso) fervour

⚔ **e'same** *nm* examination, exam; **dare un ~** take *or* sit an exam; **prendere in ~** examine
∎ **esame di ammissione** Sch entrance examination; **esame di coscienza** soul-searching; **esame di guida** driving test; **esami di maturità** ≈ A-levels; **esame orale** Sch, Univ viva; **esame del sangue** blood test; **esame della vista** eye test

esami'nando, -a *nmf* examinee

esami'nare *vt* examine

esamina|'tore, -'trice *nmf* examiner

e'sangue *adj* bloodless

e'sanime *adj* lifeless

esaspe'rante *adj* exasperating

esaspe'rare *vt* exasperate

esaspe'rarsi *vr* get exasperated

esasperazi'one *nf* exasperation

esatta'mente *adv* exactly

esat'tezza *nf* exactness; (precisione) precision; (di risposta, risultato) accuracy

⚔ **e'satto** *adj* exact; (risposta, risultato) correct; ‹orologio› right; **hai l'ora esatta?** do you have the right time?; **sono le due esatte** it's two o'clock exactly

esat'tore *nm* collector
∎ **esattore dei crediti** Fin debt collector; **esattore delle imposte** tax collector, tax man

esau'dire *vt* grant; fulfil ‹speranze›

esauri'ente *adj* exhaustive

esauri'mento *nm* exhaustion; **'fino ad ~ delle scorte'** 'subject to availability'
∎ **esaurimento nervoso** nervous breakdown

esau'rire *vt* exhaust

esau'rirsi *vr* exhaust oneself; ‹merci ecc› run out

esau'rito *adj* exhausted; ‹merci› sold out; ‹libro› out of print; **fare il tutto ~** ‹spettacolo› play to a full house; **'tutto ~'** 'sold out'

esazi'one *nf* collection
∎ **esazione crediti** debt collection

'esca *nf* bait

escande'scenza *nf* outburst; **dare in escandescenze** lose one's temper

escava'tore *nm* excavator

escava'trice *nf* excavator

escla'mare *vi* exclaim

esclama'tivo *adj* exclamatory

esclamazi'one *nf* exclamation

⚔ **e'scludere** *vt* exclude; rule out ‹possibilità, ipotesi›

⚔ indicates a very frequent word

esclusi'one *nf* exclusion; **senza ~ di colpi** *‹attacco›* all-out

esclu'siva *nf* exclusive right, sole right; **in ~** exclusive

esclusiva'mente *adv* exclusively

esclusi'vista *nmf* exclusive agent

esclu'sivo *adj* exclusive

e'scluso ① *pp di* ESCLUDERE
② *adj* **non è ~ che ci sia** it's not out of the question that he'll be there; **esclusi i presenti** with the exception of those present; **esclusi sabati e festivi** except Saturdays and Sundays/holidays
③ *nm* outcast

escogi'tare *vt* contrive

escoriazi'one *nf* graze

escre'mento *nm* excrement; **escrementi** *pl* excrement

escursi'one *nf* (gita) excursion; (camminata) hike; (scorreria) raid
■ **escursione termica** *difference between the lowest and the highest temperature in a 24 hours period*

escursio'nismo *nm* hiking

ese'crabile *adj* abominable

ese'crare *vt* abhor

esecu'tivo *adj & nm* executive

esecu'|tore, -trice *nmf* executor; Mus performer

esecuzi'one *nf* execution; Mis performance
■ **esecuzione capitale** capital punishment

esegu'ibile *nm* Comput executable file

✓ **esegu'ire** *vt* carry out; Jur execute; Mus perform

✓ **e'sempio** *nm* example; **ad o per ~** for example; **dare l'~ a qualcuno** set somebody an example; **fare un ~** give an example

esem'plare ① *adj* examplary
② *nm* specimen; (di libro) copy

esemplifi'care *vt* exemplify

esen'tare *vt* exempt

esen'tarsi *vr* free oneself

esen'tasse *adj* tax-free

e'sente *adj* exempt
■ **esente da imposta** duty-free; **esente da IVA** VAT exempt

e'sequie *nfpl* funeral rites

eser'cente *nmf* shopkeeper

✓ **eserci'tare** *vt* exercise; (addestrare) train; (fare uso di) exert; (professione) practise

eserci'tarsi *vr* practise; **~ nella danza** practise dancing

eserci'tato *adj ‹occhio›* practised; **tenere la memoria esercitata** give one's memory some exercise

esercitazi'one *nf* exercise; Mil drill; (di musica, chimica) practical class

✓ **e'sercito** *nm* army
■ **Esercito della Salvezza** Salvation Army

eser'cizio *nm* exercise; (pratica) practice; Comm financial year; (azienda) business; **essere fuori ~** be out of practice; **nell'~ delle proprie funzioni** in the line of duty
■ **esercizio finanziario** financial year; **esercizio fiscale** fiscal year, tax year; **esercizi a terra** *pl* floor exercises; **esercizio tributario** fiscal year, tax year

esi'bire *vt* show off; produce *‹documenti›*

esi'birsi *vr* Theat perform; fig show off

esibizi'one *nf* Theat performance; (di documenti) production
■ **esibizione in volo** Aeron air display

esibizio'nismo *nm* showing off

esibizio'nista *nmf* exhibitionist

esi'gente *adj* exacting; (pignolo) fastidious

esi'genza *nf* demand; (bisogno) need

e'sigere *vt* demand; (riscuotere) collect

e'siguo *adj* meagre

esila'rante *adj* exhilarating

esila'rare *vt* exhilarate

'esile *adj* slender; *‹voce›* thin

esili'are *vt* exile

esili'arsi *vr* go into exile

esili'ato, -a ① *adj* exiled
② *nmf* exile

✓ **e'silio** *nm* exile

e'simere *vt* release

e'simersi *vr* **~ da** get out of

e'simio *adj* distinguished

esi'stente *adj* existing

✓ **esi'stenza** *nf* existence

esistenzi'ale *adj* existential

esistenzia'lismo *nm* existentialism

✓ **e'sistere** *vi* exist

esi'tante *adj* hesitating; *‹voce›* faltering

✓ **esi'tare** *vi* hesitate

esitazi'one *nf* hesitation

'esito *nm* result; **avere buon ~** be a success

'esodo *nm* exodus; **l'~ estivo, il grande ~** (per le vacanze) the summer *or* holiday exodus

e'sofago *nm* oesophagus

esone'rare *vt* exempt

e'sonero *nm* exemption

esorbi'tante *adj* exorbitant

esorbi'tare *vi* **~ da** exceed

esor'cismo *nm* exorcism

esor'cista *nmf* exorcist

esorciz'zare *vt* exorcize

esordi'ente *nmf* person making his/her début

e'sordio *nm* opening; (di attore) début

esor'dire *vi* début

esor'tare *vt* (pregare) beg; (incitare) urge

eso'terico *adj* esoteric

e'sotico *adj* exotic

espa'drillas *nfpl* espadrilles

e'spandere *vt* expand

e'spandersi *vr* expand; (diffondersi) extend

espan'dibile *adj* Comput upgradeable

espandibilità *nf inv* Comput upgradeability

espansi'one *nf* expansion; **in ~** expanding

espansio'nista *nmf* expansionist

espansio'nistico *adj* expansionist

espan'sivo *adj* expansive; ‹persona› friendly

espatri'are *vi* leave one's country

espatri'ato, -a *nmf* expatriate, expat fam

e'spatrio *nm* expatriation

espedi'ente *nm* expedient; **vivere di espedienti** live by one's wits

e'spellere *vt* expel; send off ‹calciatore›

ᕱ **esperi'enza** *nf* experience; **per ~** ‹sapere, parlare› from experience; **non ha ~** he doesn't have any experience

esperi'mento *nm* experiment

e'sperto, -a *adj & nmf* expert
■ **esperto di computer** computer expert

espi'are *vt* atone for

espia'torio *adj* expiatory

espi'rare *vt/i* breathe out

espirazi'one *nf* exhalation; (scadenza) expiry

espli'care *vt* carry on

esplicita'mente *adv* explicitly

e'splicito *adj* explicit

e'splodere ① *vi* explode
② *vt* ‹arma› fire

esplo'rare *vt* explore

esplora|'tore, -trice *nmf* explorer; **giovane esploratore** boy scout; **giovane esploratrice** girl guide

esplorazi'one *nf* exploration

esplosi'one *nf* explosion

esplo'sivo *adj & nm* explosive

espo'nente *nm* exponent; **2 all'~** superscript 2

esponenzi'ale *adj* exponential

ᕱ **e'sporre** *vt* expose; display ‹merci›; (spiegare) expound; exhibit ‹quadri ecc›

e'sporsi *vr* (compromettersi) compromise oneself; (al sole) expose oneself; (alle critiche) lay oneself open

espor'tare *vt* Comm, Comput export

esporta|'tore, -trice *nmf* exporter

esportazi'one *nf* export

espo'simetro *nm* light meter

esposi|'tore, -trice ① *nmf* exhibitor
② *nm* display rack

ᕱ **esposizi'one** *nf* (mostra) exhibition; (in vetrina) display; (spiegazione ecc) exposition; (posizione, fotografia) exposure; **con ~ a nord/sud** north-/south-facing

■ **esposizione a radiazioni** radiation exposure

e'sposto ① *pp di* ESPORRE
② *adj* exposed; ‹merce› on show; ‹spiegato› set out; **~ a nord/sud** north-/south-facing
③ *nm* submission

espressa'mente *adv* expressly; **non l'ha detto ~** he didn't put it in so many words

ᕱ **espressi'one** *nf* expression

espressio'nismo *nm* expressionism

espressio'nista *adj & nmf* expressionist

espressio'nistico *adj* expressionistic

espres'sivo *adj* expressive

e'spresso ① *pp di* ESPRIMERE
② *adj* express
③ *nm* (lettera) special delivery; (treno) express train; (caffè) espresso; **per ~** ‹spedire› [by] express [post]; **piatto ~** meal made to order

ᕱ **e'sprimere** *vt* express

e'sprimersi *vr* express oneself

espropri'are *vt* dispossess

espropriazi'one *nf* Jur expropriation

e'sproprio *nm* expropriation

espulsi'one *nf* expulsion

e'spulso *pp di* ESPELLERE

esqui'mese *adj & nmf* Eskimo

es'senza *nf* essence

essenzi'ale ① *adj* essential
② *nm* important thing; **l'~** (di teoria ecc) the bare bones; **l'~ è …** (la cosa più importante) the main thing is …

essenzial'mente *adj* essentially

ᕱ **'essere** ① *vi* be; **c'è** there is; **ci sono** there are; **ci sono!** (ho capito) I've got it!; **ci siamo!** (siamo arrivati) here we are at last!; **non ce n'è più** there's none left; **c'è di che essere contenti** there's a lot to be happy about; **che ora è? - sono le dieci** what time is it? - it's ten o'clock; **chi è? - sono io** who is it? - it's me; **è stato detto che** it has been said that; **siamo in due** there are two of us; **questa camicia è da lavare** this shirt is to be washed; **non è da te** it's not like you; **~ di** belong to; (provenire da) be from; **~ per** (favorevole) be in favour of; **se fossi in te, …** if I were you, …; **sarà!** if you say so!; **come sarebbe a dire?** what are you getting at?
② *v aux* have; (in passivi) be; **siamo arrivati** we have arrived; **ci sono stato ieri** I was there yesterday; **sono nato a Torino** I was born in Turin; **è riconosciuto come…** he is recognized as …
③ *nm* being; **~ umano** human being; **~ vivente** living creature

essic'care *vt* dry

essic'cato *adj* dried; ‹noce di cocco› desiccated

ᕱ **'esso, -a** *pers pron* he, she; (cosa, animale) it

est *nm* east; **l'Est europeo** Eastern Europe

'estasi *nf* ecstasy; **andare in ~ per** go into raptures over

estasi'are *vt* enrapture

estasi'arsi *vr* go into raptures

♂ **e'state** *nf* summer

e'statico *adj* ecstatic

estempo'raneo *adj* impromptu

♂ **e'stendere** *vt* extend

e'stendersi *vr* spread; (allungarsi) stretch

estensione *nf* extension; (ampiezza) expanse; Mus range

■ **estensione del file** Comput file extension

esten'sivo *adj* extensive

estenu'ante *adj* exhausting

estenu'are *vt* exhaust

estenu'arsi *vr* exhaust oneself

'estere *nm* ester

esteri'ore *adj & nm* exterior

esteriorità *nf inv* outward appearance; badare all'~ judge by appearances

esterioriz'zare *vt* externalize

esterior'mente *adv* externally; (di persone) outwardly

esterna'mente *adv* on the outside

ester'nare *vt* express, show

♂ **e'sterno, -a** **1** *adj* external; (scala) outside; **per uso** ~ for external use only **2** *nm* Archit exterior; (in film) location shot **3** *nmf* day-pupil

♂ **'estero** **1** *adj* foreign **2** *nm* foreign countries *pl*; **all'**~ abroad; **ministero degli esteri** ≈ Foreign Office Br, State Department Am

esterofi'lia *nf* xenophilia

este'rofilo *adj* xenophile

esterre'fatto *adj* horrified

e'steso **1** pp di ESTENDERE **2** *adj* extensive; (diffuso) widespread; **per** ~ ‹scrivere› in full

e'steta *nmf* aesthete

e'stetica *nf* aesthetics *sg*

estetica'mente *adv* aesthetically

esteticità *nf* aestheticism

e'stetico *adj* aesthetic; ‹chirurgia, chirurgo› plastic

este'tismo *nm* (dottrina, carattere) aestheticism

este'tista *nmf* beautician

estima'tore, -trice *nmf* fan

'estimo *nm* estimate

e'stinguere *vt* extinguish; close ‹conto›

e'stinguersi *vr* die out

e'stinto, -a **1** pp di ESTINGUERE **2** *nmf* deceased

estin'tore *nm* [fire] extinguisher

estinzi'one *nf* extinction; (di incendio) putting out

estir'pare *vt* uproot; extract ‹dente›; fig eradicate ‹crimine, malattia›

estirpazi'one *nf* eradication; (di dente) extraction

e'stivo *adj* summer *attrib*

'estone *adj & nm* Estonian

E'stonia *nf* Estonia

e'storcere *vt* extort

estorsi'one *nf* extortion

e'storto pp di ESTORCERE

estradizi'one *nf* extradition

estra'gone *nm* tarragon

estra'ibile *adj* removable

♂ **e'straneo, -a** **1** *adj* extraneous; (straniero) foreign **2** *nmf* stranger

estrani'are *vt* estrange

estrani'arsi *vr* become estranged

estrapo'lare *vt* extrapolate

e'strarre *vt* extract; (sorteggiare) draw

e'stratto **1** pp di ESTRARRE **2** *nm* extract; (brano) excerpt; (documento) abstract

■ **estratto conto** statement [of account], bank statement

estrazi'one *nf* extraction; (a sorte) draw

■ **estrazione a premi** prize draw

estrema'mente *adv* extremely

estre'mismo *nm* extremism

estre'mista *nmf* extremist

estremità **1** *nf inv* extremity; (di una corda) end **2** *pl* Anat extremities

♂ **e'stremo** **1** *adj* extreme; (ultimo) last; **misure estreme** drastic measures; **fare un** ~ **tentativo** make one last try; **l'Estremo Oriente** the Far East; ~ **saluto** Mil military funeral; **l'estrema unzione** last rites **2** *nm* (limite) extreme; **all'**~ in the extreme; **passare da un** ~ **all'altro** go from one extreme to the other; **estremi** *pl* (di documento) main points; (di reato) essential elements; **essere agli estremi** be at the end of one's tether; **andare agli estremi** go to extremes; **essere all'**~ **delle forze** have no strength left

'estro *nm* (disposizione artistica) talent; (ispirazione) inspiration; (capriccio) whim

e'strogeno *nm* oestrogen

estro'mettere *vt* expel

estromissi'one *nf* ejection

e'stroso *adj* talented; (capriccioso) unpredictable

estro'verso **1** *adj* extroverted **2** *nm* extrovert

estu'ario *nm* estuary

esube'rante *adj* exuberant

esube'ranza *nf* exuberance

e'subero *nm*

■ **esubero cassa integrazione** voluntary redundancy

esu'lare *vt* ~ **da** be beyond the scope of

'esule *nmf* exile

esul'tante *adj* exultant

esul'tanza *nf* exultation

esul'tare *vi* rejoice

esu'mare *vt* exhume

ᵍ **età** *nf* age; **raggiungere la maggiore ~** come of age; **un uomo di mezz'~** a middle-aged man; **avere la stessa ~** be the same age; **che ~ gli daresti?** how old would you say he was?; **fin dalla più tenera ~** from his/her etc earliest years; **in ~ avanzata** of advanced years; **è senza ~** it's hard to tell his age
■ **età del bronzo** Bronze Age; **età della pensione** retirement age

e'tano *nm* ethane

eta'nolo *nm* ethanol

'etere *nm* ether
■ **etere etilico** ether

e'tereo *adj* ethereal

eterna'mente *adv* eternally

eternità *nf* eternity; **è un'~ che non la vedo** I haven't seen her for ages

ᵍ **e'terno** *adj* eternal; ‹*questione, problema*› age-old; *fig* ‹*dicorso, conferenza*› never-ending; **in ~** *fam* for ever; **giurare amore ~** swear undying love; **un ~ bambino** a child

etero'geneo *adj* diverse, heterogeneous

eterosessu'ale *adj & nmf* heterosexual

eterosessualità *nf* heterosexuality

'etica *nf* ethics *sg*

eti'chetta¹ *nf* label; (con il prezzo) price-tag

eti'chetta² *nf* (cerimoniale) etiquette

etichet'tare *vt* label

etichetta'trice *nf* labelling machine

etichetta'tura *nf* (operazione) labelling

'etico *adj* ethical

eti'lometro *nm* Breathalyzer®

etimolo'gia *nf* etymology

e'tiope *adj & nmf* Ethiopian

Eti'opia *nf* Ethiopia

eti'opico *adj* Ethiopian

'Etna *nm* Etna

et'nia *nf* ethnic group

'etnico *adj* ethnic

etnolo'gia *nf* ethnology

e'trusco *adj & nmf* Etruscan

'ettaro *nm* hectare

+ettino *suff* **cosettina** *nf* small thing; **è una cosettina da niente** it's nothing

+etto *suff* **cameretta** *nf* little bedroom; **scherzetto** *nf* prank; **piccoletto** *nm pej* shorty

'etto, ettogrammo *nm* hundred grams, quarter pound

et'tolitro *nm* hectolitre

euca'lipto *nm* eucalyptus

eucari'stia *nf* Eucharist

eufe'mismo *nm* euphemism

eufe'mistico *adj* euphemistic

eufo'ria *nf* elation; *Med* euphoria

eu'forico *adj* elated; *Med* euphoric

euge'netica *nf* eugenics *sg*

eu'nuco *nm* eunuch

Eur'asia *nf* Eurasia

eurasi'atico *adj* Eurasian

'EURATOM *nf abbr* (**Comunità Europea dell'Energia Atomica**) EURATOM

ᵍ **'euro** *nm inv* *Fin* euro

euro+ *pref* Euro+

eurobbligazi'one *nf* Eurobond

euro'cheque *nm inv* Eurocheque

Euro'city *nm inv* *Rail* international intercity

eurodepu'tato *nm* Euro MP, MEP

eurodi'visa *nf* Eurocurrency

euro'dollaro *nm* Eurodollar

Eu'ropa *nf* Europe

europe'ismo *nm* Europeanism

ᵍ **euro'peo, -a** *adj & nmf* European

euro'scettico *nm* Euro-sceptic

Euro'zona *nf* Eurozone

eutana'sia *nf* euthanasia

evacu'are *vt* evacuate

evacuazi'one *nf* evacuation

e'vadere **1** *vt* evade; (sbrigare) deal with **2** *vi* **~ da** escape from

evane'scente *adj* vanishing

evan'gelico *adj* evangelical

evange'lista *nm* evangelist

evan'gelo = VANGELO

evapo'rare *vi* evaporate

evaporazi'one *nf* evaporation

evasi'one *nf* escape; (fiscale) evasion; *fig* escapism

evasiva'mente *adv* evasively

eva'sivo *adj* evasive

e'vaso, -a **1** pp di EVADERE **2** *nmf* fugitive

eva'sore *nm*
■ **evasore fiscale** tax evader

eveni'enza *nf* eventuality; **in ogni ~** if need be

e'vento *nm* event

eventu'ale *adj* possible

eventualità *nf inv* eventuality; **in ogni ~** at all events; **nell'~ che** in the event that

eventual'mente *adv* if necessary

ever'sivo *adj* subversive

evi'dente *adj* evident

evidente'mente *adv* evidently

evi'denza *nf* evidence; **mettere in ~** emphasize; **mettersi in ~** make oneself conspicuous; **arrendersi all'~** face the facts

evidenzi'are *vt* highlight

evidenzia'tore *nm* (penna) highlighter

evi'rare *vt* emasculate

ᵍ indicates a very frequent word

evi'tare *vt* avoid; (risparmiare) spare

'evo *nm* age

evo'care *vt* evoke

evolu'tivo *adj* evolutionary

evo'luto [1] *pp di* EVOLVERE
[2] *adj* evolved; (progredito) progressive; ‹civiltà, nazione› advanced; **una donna evoluta** a modern woman

evoluzi'one *nf* evolution; (di ginnasta, aereo) circle

e'volvere *vt* develop

e'volversi *vr* evolve

ev'viva *int* hurray; ∼ **il Papa!** long live the Pope!; **gridare** ∼ cheer; ∼ **la modestia!** what modesty!

ex *prep* ex, former; **ex moglie** ex-wife

ex 'aequo *adv* arrivare ∼ come in joint first

ex-Jugo'slavia *nf* ex-Yugoslavia

ex-jugo'slavo *adj & nmf* ex-Yugoslav

ex 'libris *nm inv* bookplate

ex'ploit *nm inv* feat, exploit

'extra [1] *adj inv* extra; ‹qualità› first-class
[2] *nm inv* extra

extracomuni'tario, -a [1] *adj* non-EC, non-EU
[2] *nmf immigrant from outside the EU*

extraconiu'gale *adj* extramarital

extraeuro'peo *adj* non-European

extraparlamen'tare *adj* extraparliamentary

extrasco'lastico *adj* extra-curricular

extrasensori'ale *adj* extrasensory

extrater'restre *nmf* extra-terrestrial

extrauniversi'tario *adj* extramural

ex 'voto *nm inv* ex voto

Ff

fa¹ *nm inv* Mus (chiave, nota) F

fa² *adv* ago; **due mesi** ∼ two months ago

fabbi'sogno *nm* requirements *pl*, needs *pl*
■ **fabbisogno dello Stato** government spending estimates

'fabbrica *nf* factory

fabbri'cabile *adj* ‹area, terreno› that can be built on

fabbri'cante *nm* manufacturer
■ **fabbricante d'armi** arms manufacturer

fabbri'care *vt* build; (produrre) manufacture; fig (inventare) fabricate

fabbri'cato *nm* building

fabbricazi'one *nf* manufacturing; (costruzione) building

'fabbro *nm* blacksmith

fac'cenda *nf* matter; **faccende** *pl* domestiche housework *sg*

faccendi'ere *nm* wheeler-dealer

fac'chino *nm* porter

'faccia *nf* face; (di foglio) side; ∼ **a** ∼ face to face; ∼ **tosta** cheek; **voltar** ∼ change sides; **di** ∼ (palazzo) opposite; **alla** ∼ **di** fam (a dispetto di) in spite of; **alla** ∼**!** (stupore) bloody hell!

facci'ata *nf* façade; (di foglio) side; fig (esteriorità) outward appearance

fa'cente *nmf*
■ **facente funzioni** deputy

fa'ceto *adj* facetious; **tra il serio e il** ∼ half joking

fa'cezia *nf* (battuta) witticism

fa'chiro *nm* fakir

'facile *adj* easy; (affabile) easy-going; **essere** ∼ **alle critiche** be quick to criticize; **essere** ∼ **al riso** laugh a lot; ∼ **a farsi** easy to do; **è** ∼ **che piova** it's likely to rain

facilità *nf inv* ease; (disposizione) aptitude; **avere** ∼ **di parola** express oneself well
■ **facilità d'uso** ease of use, user-friendliness

facili'tare *vt* facilitate

facilitazi'one *nf* facility; **facilitazioni** *pl* Fin special terms; **facilitazioni** *pl* **di pagamento** easy terms; **facilitazioni** *pl* **creditizie** credit facilities

facil'mente *adv* (con facilità) easily; (probabilmente) probably

faci'lone *adj* slapdash

facilone'ria *nf* slapdash attitude

facino'roso *adj* violent

facoltà *nf inv* faculty; (potere) power; **essere nel pieno possesso delle proprie** ∼ be compos mentis

facolta'tivo *adj* optional; **fermata facoltativa** request stop

facol'toso *adj* wealthy

fac'simile *nm* facsimile

fac'totum [1] *nm inv* man Friday
[2] *nf inv* girl Friday

'faggio *nm* beech

fagi'ano *nm* pheasant

fagio'lino *nm* French bean

fagi'olo *nm* bean; **a** ∼ ‹arrivare, capitare› at the right time
■ **fagiolo borlotto** borlotti bean; **fagiolo bianco di Spagna** runner bean, haricot bean

fagoci'tare *vt* gobble up ‹società›

fa'gotto *nm* bundle; Mus bassoon

Fahren'heit *adj* Fahrenheit

'faida *nf* feud

fai da te *nm* do-it-yourself, DIY

fa'ina *nf* weasel

fa'lange *nf* (dito, Mil) phalanx

fal'cata *nf* stride

'falce *nf* scythe
■ **falce e martello** (simbolo) the hammer and sickle

fal'cetto *nm* sickle

falci'are *vt* cut; fig mow down

falci'ata *nf* (quantità d'erba) swathe

falcia'trice *nf* [lawn]mower

'falco *nm* hawk

fal'cone *nm* falcon

'falda *nf* stratum; (di neve) flake; (di cappello) brim; (di cappotto, frac) coat-tails; (pendio) slope
■ **falda freatica** water table

fale'gname *nm* carpenter

falegname'ria *nf* carpentry

fa'lena *nf* moth

'Falkland *nfpl* **le [isole]** ~ the Falklands

'falla *nf* leak

fal'lace *adj* deceptive

'fallico *adj* phallic

fallimen'tare *adj* disastrous; Jur bankruptcy

falli'mento *nm* Comm bankruptcy; fig failure

fal'lire ① *vi* Comm go bankrupt; fig fail ② *vt* miss ‹colpo›

fal'lito ① *adj* unsuccessful ② *adj & nm* bankrupt

'fallo *nm* fault; (errore) mistake; Sport foul; (imperfezione) flaw; **senza** ~ without fail; **cogliere in** ~ catch red-handed; **mettere un piede in** ~ slip
■ **fallo di mano** (in calcio) handball

falò *nm inv* bonfire

fal'sare *vt* alter; (falsificare) falsify

falsa'riga *nf* **sulla** ~ **di** along the same lines as

fal'sario, -a *nmf* forger; (di documenti) counterfeiter

fal'setto *nm* falsetto

falsifi'care *vt* fake; (contraffare) forge

falsificazi'one *nf* (di documenti) falsification

falsità *nf* falseness

✐ **'falso** ① *adj* false; (sbagliato) wrong; ‹opera d'arte ecc› fake; ‹gioielli, oro› imitation; **essere un** ~ **magro** be fatter than one looks ② *nm* forgery; **giurare il** ~ commit perjury
■ **falso in atto pubblico** forgery of a legal document

'fama *nf* fame; (reputazione) reputation

✐ **'fame** *nf* hunger; **aver** ~ be hungry; **fare la** ~ barely scrape a living; **da** ~ ‹stipendio› miserly; **avere una** ~ **da lupo** be ravenous

fa'melico *adj* ravenous

famige'rato *adj* infamous

✐ **fa'miglia** *nf* family
■ **famiglia affidataria** foster family, foster home

famili'are ① *adj* family *attrib*; (ben noto) familiar; (senza cerimonie) informal ② *nmf* relative, relation

familiarità *nf* familiarity; (informalità) informality

familiariz'zarsi *vr* familiarize oneself

✐ **fa'moso** *adj* famous

fa'nale *nm* lamp; Auto ecc light
■ **fanali posteriori** *pl* Auto rear lights

fana'lino *nm*
■ **fanalino di coda** Auto tail light; **essere il** ~ **di coda** fig bring up the rear, be the back marker

fa'natico, -a ① *adj* fanatical; **essere** ~ **di calcio/cinema** be a football/cinema fanatic ② *nmf* fanatic

fana'tismo *nm* fanaticism

fanciul'lezza *nf* childhood

fanci'ullo, -a *nmf* liter young boy; young girl

fan'donia *nf* lie; **fandonie!** nonsense!

fan'fara *nf* fanfare; (complesso) brass band

fanfaro'nata *nf* brag; **fanfaronate** *pl* bragging

fanfa'rone, -a *nmf* braggart

fan'ghiglia *nf* mud

'fango *nm* mud

fan'goso *adj* muddy

fannul'lone, -a *nmf* idler

fantasci'enza *nf* science fiction

✐ **fanta'sia** *nf* fantasy; (immaginazione) imagination; (capriccio) fancy; (di tessuto) pattern; **fantasie** *pl* (sciocchezze) moonshine

fantasi'oso *adj* ‹stilista, ragazzo› imaginative; ‹resoconto› improbable, fanciful

fan'tasma *nm* ghost; **essere il** ~ **di se stesso** be a shadow of one's former self; **città fantasma** ghost town; **governo fantasma** shadow cabinet

fantasti'care *vi* day-dream, fantasize

fantastiche'ria *nf* day-dream, fantasy

fan'tastico *adj* fantastic; ‹racconto› fantasy *attrib*

'fante *nm* infantryman; (nelle carte) jack

fante'ria *nm* infantry

fan'tino *nm* jockey

fan'toccio *nm* puppet

fanto'matico *adj* (inafferrabile) phantom *attrib*; (immaginario) mythical

fara'butto *nm* trickster

fara'ona *nf* (uccello) guinea-fowl

'farcia *nf* stuffing; (di torta) filling

farcire ⋯⋮⟩ fatato ⋯⋯

far'cire *vt* stuff; fill ‹*torta*›

far'cito *adj* stuffed; ‹*dolce*› filled

fard *nm inv* blusher

far'dello *nm* bundle; fig burden

🖉'fare **1** *vt* do; make ‹*dolce, letto, ecc*›; (recitare la parte di) play; (trascorrere) spend; **~ una pausa/un sogno** have a break/a dream; **~ colpo su** impress; **~ paura a** frighten; **~ piacere a** please; **farla finita** put an end to it; **~ l'insegnante** be a teacher; **~ lo scemo** play the idiot; **~ una settimana al mare** spend a week at the seaside; **3 più 3 fa 6** 3 and 3 makes 6; **quanto fa? - fanno 50 euro** how much is it? - it's 50 euros; **far ~ qualcosa a qualcuno** get somebody to do something; (costringere) make somebody do something; **~ vedere** show; **fammi parlare** let me speak; **niente a che ~ con** nothing to do with; **non c'è niente da ~** (per problema) there is nothing we/you etc can do; **fa caldo/ buio** it's warm/dark; **non fa niente** it doesn't matter; **strada facendo** on the way; **farcela** (riuscire) manage

2 *vi* **fai in modo di venire** try and come; **~ da** act as; **~ per** make as if to; **~ presto** be quick; **non fa per me** it's not for me

3 *nm* (comportamento) manner; **sul far del giorno** at daybreak

fa'retto *nm* spot[light]

far'falla *nf* butterfly

farfal'lino *nm* (cravatta) bow tie

farfugli'are *vt* mutter

fa'rina *nf* flour

■ **farina di ceci** chickpea flour, gram flour; **farina gialla** maize flour; **farina integrale** wholemeal flour; **farina lattea** powdered milk for babies; **farina d'ossa** bonemeal

fari'nacei *nmpl* starchy food *sg*

fa'ringe *nf* pharynx

farin'gite *nf* pharyngitis

fari'noso *adj* ‹*neve*› powdery; ‹*mela*› soft; ‹*patata*› floury

farma'ceutico *adj* pharmaceutical; **industria farmaceutica** pharmaceuticals industry

farma'cia *nf* pharmacy; (negozio) chemist's [shop]

■ **farmacia di turno** duty pharmacy

farma'cista *nmf* chemist, pharmacist

'farmaco *nm* drug; **essere sotto farmaci** be on medication

'faro *nm* Auto headlight; Aeron beacon; (costruzione) lighthouse; **abbassare i fari** dip one's headlights; **accendere i fari** switch on one's lights

■ **fari antinebbia** *pl* fog lamps; **fari posteriori** *pl* rear lights

farragi'noso *adj* confused

'farsa *nf* farce

far'sesco *adj* farcical

'farsi *vr* (diventare) get; sl (drogarsi) shoot up; **~ avanti** come forward; **~ i fatti propri** mind one's own business; **~ la barba** shave; **~ la villa** fam buy a villa; **~ il ragazzo** fam find a boyfriend; **~ due risate** have a laugh; **~ male** hurt oneself; **~ un nome** make a name for oneself; **farsela sotto** fam wet oneself

Far 'west *nm* Wild West

fa'scetta *nf* strip; (per capelli) hair band; (di giornale) wrapper

'fascia *nf* band; (zona) area; (ufficiale) sash; (benda) bandage; (di smoking) cummerbund; (in statistica) bracket; **le fasce deboli** the underprivileged

■ **fascia per capelli** hair band; **fascia elastica** crepe bandage; (ventriera) girdle; **fascia d'età** age bracket, age group; **fascia d'ozono** ozone layer; **fascia di reddito** income bracket

fasci'are *vt* bandage; cling to ‹*fianchi*›

fasci'arsi *vr* bandage; **~ la testa prima di rompersela** worry about something that might never happen

fascia'tura *nf* dressing; (azione) bandaging

fascicola'tore, -trice *nmf* sorter

fa'scicolo *nm* file; (di rivista) issue; (libretto) booklet

fa'scina *nf* faggot

'fascino *nm* fascination

fasci'noso *adj* charming

'fascio *nm* bundle; (di fiori) bunch

■ **fascio di luce** beam of light

fa'scismo *nm* fascism

🖉 fa'scista *adj & nmf* fascist

'fase *nf* phase; **il motore è fuori ~** the timing is wrong; **sono fuori ~** I'm not firing on all four cylinders; **essere in ~ di miglioramento** be on the mend, be recovering; **essere in ~ di espansione** be expanding

fast 'food *nm inv* fast food; (ristorante) fast food restaurant

🖉 fa'stidio *nm* nuisance; (scomodo) inconvenience; **fastidi** *pl* (preoccupazioni) worries; (disturbi) troubles; **dar ~ a qualcuno** bother somebody

fastidi'oso *adj* tiresome

'fasto *nm* pomp

fa'stoso *adj* sumptuous

fa'sullo *adj* bogus

'fata *nf* fairy

fa'tale *adj* fatal; (inevitabile) fated; **donna fatale** femme fatale

fata'lismo *nm* fatalism

fata'lista **1** *nmf* fatalist

2 *adj* fatalistic

fatalità *nf inv* fate; (caso sfortunato) misfortune

fatal'mente *adv* inevitably

fa'tato *adj* ‹*anello, bacchetta*› magic

f

⚬ **fa'tica** *nf* effort; (lavoro faticoso) hard work; (stanchezza, di metalli) fatigue; **a ∼** with great difficulty; **è ∼ sprecata** it's a waste of time; **fare ∼ a fare qualcosa** find it difficult to do something; **senza [nessuna] ∼** without [any] effort; **fare ∼ a finire qualcosa** struggle to finish something; **uomo di fatica** odd-job man

fati'caccia *nf* pain

fati'care *vi* toil; **∼ a** (stentare) find it difficult to

fati'cata *nf* effort; (sfacchinata) grind

fati'coso *adj* tiring; (difficile) difficult

fati'scente *adj* crumbling

'fato *nm* fate

fat'taccio *nm hum* foul deed

fat'tezze *nfpl* features

fat'tibile *adj* feasible

fatti'specie *nf* **nella ∼** in this case

⚬ **'fatto** ⨯1⨯ (pp di FARE); **ormai è fatta!** what's done is done
⨯2⨯ *adj* made; **∼ a mano/in casa** handmade/home-made; **essere ben ∼** ‹persona› have a nice figure; **un uomo ∼** a grown man
⨯3⨯ *nm* fact; (azione) action; (avvenimento) event; (faccenda) business, matter; **sa il ∼ suo** he knows his business; **le ho detto il ∼ suo** I told her what I thought of her; **di ∼** in fact; **in ∼ di** as regards; **∼ sta che** the fact remains that; **mettere di fronte al ∼ compiuto** present with a fait accompli

fat'tore *nm* (causa, Math) factor; (di fattoria) farm manager
■ **fattore di protezione solare** protection factor

fatto'ria *nf* farm; (casa) farmhouse

fatto'rino *nm* messenger [boy]
■ **fattorino d'albergo** bellboy

fattucchi'era *nf* witch

fat'tura *nf* (stile) cut; (lavorazione) workmanship; Comm invoice
■ **fattura di acqusto** purchase invoice; **fattura pro-forma** pro forma [invoice]; **fattura di vendita** sales invoice

fattu'rare *vt* invoice; (adulterare) adulterate

fattu'rato *nm* turnover, sales *pl*

fatturazi'one *nf* invoicing, billing

'fatuo *adj* fatuous

'fauci *nfpl* (di leone) maw *sg*, jaws *pl*

'fauna *nf* fauna

'fausto *adj* propitious

fau'tore *nm* supporter

'fava *nf* broad bean

fa'vella *nf* speech

fa'villa *nf* spark

'favo *nm* honeycomb

'favola *nf* fable; (fiaba) story; (oggetto di pettegolezzi) laughing-stock; **è una ∼!** (meraviglia) it's divine!

favo'loso *adj* fabulous

⚬ **fa'vore** *nm* favour; **essere a ∼ di** be in favour of; **per ∼** please; **di ∼** ‹condizioni, trattamento› preferential; **col ∼ delle tenebre** under cover of darkness

favoreggia'mento *nm* Jur aiding and abetting

favo'revole *adj* favourable

favorevol'mente *adv* favourably

⚬ **favo'rire** *vt* favour; (promuovere) promote; **vuol ∼?** (a cena, pranzo) will you have some?; (entrare) will you come in?; **favorisca alla cassa** please pay at the cash-desk; **favorisca i documenti** your papers please

favo'rito, -a *adj & nmf* favourite

fax *nm inv* fax; **inviare via ∼** fax, send by fax
■ **fax a carta comune** plain paper fax

fa'xare *vt* fax

fazi'one *nf* faction

faziosità *nf* bias

fazi'oso *nm* sectarian

fazzolet'tino *nm*
■ **fazzolettino [di carta]** [paper] tissue

fazzo'letto *nm* handkerchief, hanky; (da testa) headscarf

feb'braio *nm* February

'febbre *nf* fever; **avere la ∼** have o run a temperature
■ **febbre da fieno** hay fever

febbrici'tante *adj* fevered

feb'brile *adj* feverish

febbril'mente *adv* feverishly

'feccia *nf* dregs *pl*

'fecola *nf* potato flour

fecon'dare *vt* fertilize

feconda'tore *nm* fertilizer

fecondazi'one *nf* fertilization
■ **fecondazione artificiale** artificial insemination; **fecondazione in vitro** in vitro fertilization, IVF

fe'condo *adj* fertile

⚬ **'fede** *nf* faith; (fiducia) trust; (anello) wedding ring; **in buona/mala ∼** in good/bad faith; **prestar ∼ a** believe; **tener ∼ alla parola** keep one's word; **aver ∼ in qualcuno** have faith in somebody, believe in somebody; **degno di ∼** reliable; **in ∼** Yours faithfully

⚬ **fe'dele** ⨯1⨯ *adj* faithful
⨯2⨯ *nmf* believer, worshipper; (seguace) follower; **i fedeli** the faithful

fedel'mente *adv* faithfully

fedeltà *nf* faithfulness; **alta fedeltà** high fidelity

'federa *nf* pillowcase

fede'rale *adj* federal

federa'lismo *nm* federalism

federa'lista *adj* federalist

fede'rato *adj* federate

federazi'one *nf* federation

⚬ indicates a very frequent word

fe'difrago, -a ① adj faithless; hum two-timing
② nm faithless wretch; hum two-timer
fe'dina nf avere la ∼ **penale sporca/pulita** have a/no criminal record
fega'telli nmpl (di maiale) pork liver
fega'tino nm fegatini pl di pollo chicken livers
'fegato nm liver; fig guts pl; **mangiarsi il ∼, rodersi il ∼** be consumed with rage
'felce nf fern
⚘ **fe'lice** adj happy; (fortunato) lucky; ∼ **come una Pasqua** blissfully happy
felice'mente adv happily; (con successo) successfully
⚘ **felicità** nf happiness
felici'tarsi vr ∼ **con** congratulate
felicitazi'oni nfpl congratulations
fe'lino adj feline
'felpa nf (indumento) sweatshirt; (stoffa) felt
fel'pato adj brushed; ⟨passo⟩ stealthy
'feltro nm felt; (cappello) felt hat
⚘ **'femmina** nf female
femmi'nile ① adj feminine; ⟨rivista, abbigliamento⟩ women's; ⟨sesso⟩ female
② nm feminine
femminilità nf femininity
femmi'nismo nm feminism
'femore nm femur
'fendere vt split
fendi'nebbia nm inv fog lamp
fendi'tura nf split; (in roccia) crack
fe'nice nf phoenix
feni'cottero nm flamingo
fenome'nale adj phenomenal
⚘ **fe'nomeno** nm phenomenon
'feretro nm coffin
feri'ale adj weekday; **giorno feriale** weekday
'ferie nfpl holidays; (di università, tribunale ecc) vacation sg; **andare in ∼** go on holiday; **prendere le ∼** go on holiday; **prendere delle ∼** take time off; **prendere un giorno di ∼** take a day off
feri'mento nm wounding
⚘ **fe'rire** vt wound; (in incidente) injure; fig hurt
fe'rirsi vr injure oneself
⚘ **fe'rita** nf wound
■ **ferita d'arma da fuoco** gunshot wound
fe'rito ① adj wounded
② nm wounded person; Mil casualty; ∼ **grave** seriously injured person; **i feriti** the injured
feri'toia nf loophole; feritoie pl **per le schede di espansione** Comput expansion slots
'ferma nf Mil period of service
fermacal'zoni nm inv cycle clip
fermaca'pelli nm inv hair slide

ferma'carte nm inv paperweight
ferma'coda nm inv (di stoffa) scrunchie
fermacra'vatta nm inv tiepin
ferma'fogli nm inv bulldog clip
fer'maglio nm clasp; (spilla) brooch; (per capelli) hair slide
ferma'mente adv firmly
ferma'porta nm inv doorstop
⚘ **fer'mare** ① vt stop; (fissare) fix; Jur detain
② vi stop
fer'marsi vr stop
fer'mata nf stop; '∼ **prenotata**' 'bus stopping'; **senza fermate** ⟨tragitto⟩ non-stop
■ **fermata dell'autobus** bus stop; **fermata obbligatoria** compulsory stop; **fermata a richiesta** request stop
fermen'tare vi ferment
fermentazi'one nf fermentation
fer'mento nm ferment; (lievito) yeast; **essere in ∼** be in/get into a tizzy
fer'mezza nf firmness
⚘ **'fermo** ① adj still; ⟨veicolo⟩ stationary; (stabile) steady; ⟨orologio⟩ not working; ∼**!** don't move!; ∼ **restando che ...** it being understood that ...; '∼ **per manutenzione**' 'closed for repairs'
② nm Jur detention; Mech catch; **in stato di fermo** in custody
■ **fermo immagine** TV freeze frame; **fermo posta** poste restante, general delivery Am
fer'net® nm inv bitter digestive liqueur
fe'roce adj fierce, ferocious; ⟨bestia⟩ wild; ⟨freddo, dolore⟩ unbearable
feroce'mente adv fiercely, ferociously
fe'rocia nf ferocity
fer'raglia nf scrap iron
ferra'gosto nm 15 August (bank holiday in Italy); (periodo) August holidays pl
ferra'menta nfpl ironmongery sg; **negozio di ferramenta** ironmonger's
fer'rare vt shoe ⟨cavallo⟩
fer'rato adj ∼ **in** (preparato in) well up in
'ferreo adj iron
⚘ **'ferro** nm iron; (attrezzo) tool; (di chirurgo) instrument; **di ∼** ⟨memoria⟩ excellent; ⟨alibi⟩ cast-iron; **salute di ∼** iron constitution; **ai ferri** ⟨bistecca⟩ grilled; **essere ai ferri corti** be at daggers drawn; **mettere il paese a ∼ e fuoco** put a country to the sword; **i ferri del mestiere** the tools of the trade
■ **ferro battuto** wrought iron; **ferro da calza** knitting needle; **ferro di cavallo** horseshoe; **ferro da stiro** iron; **ferro a vapore** steam iron
fer'roso adj ferrous
ferro'vecchio nm scrap merchant
ferro'via nf railway, railroad Am; **Ferrovie** pl **dello Stato** Italian State Railways
ferrovi'ario adj railway attrib, railroad Am attrib

ferrovi'ere *nm* railwayman, railroad worker Am

'fertile *adj* fertile

fertilità *nf* fertility

fertiliz'zante *nm* fertilizer

fertilizzazi'one *nf* fertilization

fer'vente *adj* blazing; fig fervent

fervente'mente *adv* fervently

'fervere *vi* ‹preparativi›; be well under way

fervida'mente *adv* fervently

'fervido *adj* fervent; **fervidi auguri** best wishes

fer'vore *nm* fervour; (di discussione) heat

'fesa *nf* (carne) rump

fesse'ria *nf* dire/fare una ∼ fam say/do something stupid

'fesso 1 pp DI FENDERE
2 *adj* cracked; fam (sciocco) foolish
3 *nm* fam (idiota) fool; **far ∼ qualcuno** fam con somebody

fes'sura *nf* crack; (per gettone ecc) slot
■ **fessura [per la scheda] di espansione** Comput expansion slot

⚬ **'festa** *nf* feast; (giorno festivo) holiday; (compleanno) birthday; (ricevimento) party; fig joy; **fare ∼ a qualcuno** welcome somebody; **essere in ∼** be on holiday; **far ∼** celebrate; **della ∼** ‹vestito, tovaglia› best; **conciare qualcuno per le feste** give somebody a sound thrashing; **le feste** (Natale, Capodanno ecc) the holidays
■ **festa di addio al celibato** stag night, stag party; **festa di addio al nubilato** hen party; **festa di compleanno** birthday party; **festa della mamma** Mother's Day, Mothering Sunday; **festa mascherata** fancy dress party; **festa nazionale** public holiday, legal holiday Am; **festa del papà** Father's Day

festai'olo, -a 1 *adj* festive
2 *nmf* party animal

festeggia'mento *nm* celebration; (manifestazione) festivity; **festeggiamenti** *pl* celebrations

festeggi'are *vt* celebrate; (accogliere festosamente) give a hearty welcome to

fe'stino *nm* party

'festival *nm inv* festival
■ **festival cinematografico** film festival

festività *nfpl* festivities

fe'stivo *adj* holiday; (lieto) festive; **festivi** *pl* public holidays

fe'stone *nm* (nel cucito) scallop, scollop; (di carta) paper chain

fe'stoso *adj* merry

fe'tente 1 *adj* evil smelling; fig revolting
2 *nmf* fam bastard

fe'ticcio *nm* fetish

'feto *nm* foetus

fe'tore *nm* stench

'fetta *nf* slice; **a fette** sliced
■ **fetta biscottata** *slices of crispy toast-like bread*

fet'tina *nf* thin slice

fet'tuccia *nf* tape; (con nome) name tape

fettuc'cine *nfpl* ribbon-shaped pasta

feu'dale *adj* feudal

'feudo *nm* feud

fez *nm inv* fez

FFSS *abbr* (**Ferrovie dello Stato**) Italian State Railways

fi'aba *nf* fairy-tale

fia'besco *adj* fairy-tale *attrib*

fi'acca *nf* weariness; (indolenza) laziness; **battere la ∼** be sluggish

fiac'care *vt* weaken

fi'acco *adj* weak; (indolente) slack; (stanco) weary; ‹partita› dull

fi'accola *nf* torch

fiacco'lata *nf* torchlight procession

fi'ala *nf* phial

fia'letta *nf* phial
■ **fialetta puzzolente** stink bomb

fi'amma *nf* flame; Naut pennant; **in fiamme** in flames; **andare in fiamme** go up in flames; **dare alle fiamme** commit to the flames; **alla ∼** Culin flambé; **le Fiamme Gialle** body responsible for border control and investigating fraud
■ **fiamma ossidrica** blowtorch

fiam'mante *adj* flaming; **nuovo ∼** brand new

fiam'mata *nf* blaze

fiammeggi'are 1 *vi* blaze
2 *vt* singe ‹pollo›

fiam'mifero *nm* match

fiam'mingo, -a 1 *adj & nm* Flemish
2 *nmf* Fleming

fian'cata *nf* wing

fiancheggi'are *vt* border; fig support

⚬ **fi'anco** *nm* side; (di persona) hip; (di animale) flank; Mil wing; **al mio ∼** by my side; **∼ a ∼** ‹lavorare› side by side

Fi'andre *nfpl* le ∼ Flanders

fia'schetta *nf* hip flask

fiaschette'ria *nf* wine shop

fi'asco *nm* flask; fig fiasco; **fare ∼** be a fiasco

fia'tare *vi* breathe; (parlare) breathe a word

⚬ **fi'ato** *nm* breath; (vigore) stamina; **strumenti a ∼** wind instruments; **avere il ∼ corto** be short of breath; **senza ∼** breathlessly; **tutto d'un ∼** ‹bere, leggere› all in one go

'fibbia *nf* buckle

'fibra *nf* fibre; **fibre** *pl* (alimentari) roughage
■ **fibre artificiali** *pl* man-made fibres; **fibra ottica** optical fibre; **a fibre ottiche** ‹cavo› fibre optic; **fibra sintetica** man-made fibre, synthetic; **fibra di vetro** fibreglass

---

⚬ indicates a very frequent word

fi'broma *nm* fibroid
fi'broso *adj* fibrous
ficca'naso *nmf inv* nosey parker
fic'care *vt* thrust; drive ‹*chiodo ecc*›; fam (mettere) shove
fic'carsi *vr* thrust oneself; (nascondersi) hide; ∼ **nei guai** get oneself into trouble
'fiche *nf inv* (gettone) chip
'fico¹ *nm* (albero) fig-tree; (frutto) fig; **non me ne importa un** ∼ **[secco]** fam I don't give a damn; **non capisce un** ∼ **[secco]** fam he doesn't understand a bloody thing; **non vale un** ∼ **[secco]** fam it's totally worthless
  ■ **fico d'India** prickly pear
'fico², -a ⦗1⦘ *nmf* fam cool sort
  ⦗2⦘ *adj* cool
fidanza'mento *nm* engagement; **rompere il** ∼ break off one's engagement, break it off
fidan'zarsi *vr* get engaged
fidan'zata *nf* (ufficiale) fiancée; (innamorata) girlfriend
fidan'zato *nm* (ufficiale) fiancé; (innamorato) boyfriend
fi'darsi *vr* ∼ **di** trust
fi'dato *adj* trustworthy
'fido ⦗1⦘ *adj* ‹*compagno*› loyal
  ⦗2⦘ *nm* devoted follower; Comm credit
fi'ducia *nf* confidence; **degno di** ∼ trustworthy; **persona di** ∼ reliable person; **di** ∼ ‹*fornitore, banca*› regular, usual; **avere** ∼ **in se stessi** believe in oneself; **incarico di** ∼ important job
fiduci'ario, -a ⦗1⦘ *adj* ‹*rapporto, transazione*› based on trust
  ⦗2⦘ *nmf* trustee
fiduci'oso *adj* hopeful
fi'ele *nm* bile; fig bitterness; **amaro come il** ∼ bitter
fienagi'one *nf* haymaking
fie'nile *nm* barn
fi'eno *nm* hay
fi'era *nf* fair
  ■ **fiera commerciale** trade fair; **fiera del libro** book fair
fie'rezza *nf* (dignità) pride
fi'ero *adj* proud
fi'evole *adj* faint; ‹*luce*› dim
'fifa *nf* fam jitters; **aver** ∼ have the jitters
fi'fone, -a *nmf* fam chicken, yellowbelly
FIGC *nf abbr* (**Federazione Italiana Gioco Calcio**) Italian Football Association
Figi *nfpl* **le isole** ∼ Fiji
'figli *nmpl* children
'figlia *nf* daughter
  ■ **figlia unica** only child
figli'are *vi* ‹*animale*› calve
figli'astra *nf* stepdaughter
figli'astro *nm* stepson

'figlio *nm* son; (generico) child; **è** ∼ **d'arte** he was born in a trunk
  ■ **figlio adottivo** adopted child; **figlio di papà** spoilt brat; **figlio di puttana** vulg son of a bitch; **figlio unico** only child
figli'occia *nf* goddaughter
figli'occio *nm* godson
figli'ola *nf* girl
figlio'lanza *nf* offspring
figli'olo *nm* boy; **figlioli** *pl* children
'figo, -a *adj* ▶ FICO²
fi'gura *nf* figure; (aspetto esteriore) shape; (illustrazione) illustration; (in carte da gioco) picture [card]; **far bella/brutta** ∼ make a good/bad impression; **mi hai fatto fare una brutta** ∼ you made me look a fool; **che** ∼**!** how embarrassing!
  ■ **figura paterna** father figure; **figura retorica** figure of speech
figu'raccia *nf* bad impression
figu'rare ⦗1⦘ *vt* represent; (simboleggiare) symbolize; (immaginare) imagine
  ⦗2⦘ *vi* (far figura) cut a fine figure; (in lista) appear, figure; ∼ **in testa al cartellone** Theat get top billing
figu'rarsi *vr* (immaginarsi) imagine; **figurati!** imagine that!; **posso? - [ma] figurati!** may I? - of course!
figura'tivo *adj* figurative
figu'rina *nf* (da raccolta) cigarette card; (statuetta) figurine
figuri'nista *nmf* dress designer
figu'rino *nm* fashion sketch
fi'guro *nm* **un losco** ∼ a shady character
figu'rone *nm* **fare un** ∼ make an excellent impression
fil *nm*
  ■ **fil di ferro** wire
'fila *nf* line; (di soldati ecc) file; (di oggetti) row; (coda) queue; **di** ∼ in succession; **fare la** ∼ queue [up], stand in line Am; **in** ∼ **indiana** single file
fila'mento *nm* filament
fi'lanca® *nf* type of synthetic stretch fabric
fi'lante *adj* ‹*formaggio*› stringy; **stella filante** (di carta) streamer
filantro'pia *nf* philanthropy
filan'tropico *adj* philanthropic
fi'lantropo, -a *nmf* philanthropist
fi'lare ⦗1⦘ *vt* spin; Naut pay out
  ⦗2⦘ *vi* (andarsene) run away; ‹*liquido*› trickle; ‹*ragionamento*› hang together; **fila!** fam scram!; ∼ **con** fam (amoreggiare) go out with; ∼ **dritto** toe the line
  ⦗3⦘ *nm* (di viti, alberi) row
filar'monica *nf* (orchestra) orchestra
filar'monico *adj* philharmonic
fila'strocca *nf* rigmarole; (per bambini) nursery rhyme
filate'lia *nf* philately, stamp collecting

fila'telico, -a nmf philatelist

fi'lato [1] adj spun; (ininterrotto) running; (continuato) uninterrupted; di ~ (subito) immediately; andare dritto ~ a go straight to
[2] nm yarn

fila|'tore, -trice nmf spinner

fila'tura nf spinning; (filanda) spinning mill

file nm inv Comput file

filetta'tura nf (di vite) thread

fi'letto nm (bordo) border; ‹di vite› thread; Culin fillet
■ filetto ai ferri grilled fillet of beef

fili'ale [1] adj filial
[2] nf Comm branch

filibusti'ere nm rascal

fili'forme adj stringy

fili'grana nf filigree; (su carta) watermark

fi'lippica nf invective

filip'pino, -a adj & nmf Filipino

✧ film nm inv film
■ film catastrofico disaster movie; film comico comedy; film drammatico drama; film di fantascienza science fiction film; film giallo thriller; film a lungometraggio feature film; film dell'orrore horror film; film poliziesco detective film; film verità docudrama

fil'mare vt film

fil'mato [1] adj filmed
[2] nm short film

fil'mina nf film strip

fil'mino nm cine film

✧ 'filo nm thread; (tessile) yarn; (metallico) wire; (di lama) edge; (venatura) grain; (di perle) string; (d'erba) blade; (di luce) ray; un ~ di (poco) a drop of; con un ~ di voce in a whisper; per ~ e per segno in detail; fare il ~ a qualcuno fancy somebody; perdere il ~ lose the thread; essere appeso a un ~ be hanging by a thread; essere sul ~ del rasoio be on a knife-edge; un ~ d'aria a breath of air; un ~ di speranza a glimmer of hope
■ filo interdentale dental floss; filo a piombo plumb-line; filo spinato barbed wire

filo+ pref philo+

filoameri'cano adj pro-American

'filobus nm inv trolleybus

filocomu'nista adj pro-communist

filodiffusi'one nf rediffusion

filodram'matica nf amateur dramatic society

filolo'gia nf philology

filo'logico adj philological

fi'lologo, -a nmf philologist

filon'cino nm ≈ French stick

fi'lone nm vein; (di pane) long loaf, Vienna loaf

fi'loso adj stringy

─────────────────
✧ indicates a very frequent word

filoso'fia nf philosophy

fi'losofo, -a nmf philosopher

fil'traggio nm filtering

fil'trare vt filter

'filtro nm filter
■ filtro chiamate Teleph call screening; filtro dell'olio oil filter

'filza nf string

fin ▶ FINO[1]

fi'nale [1] adj final
[2] nm end; ~ a sorpresa surprise ending
[3] nf Sport final

fina'lista nmf finalist

finalità nf inv finality; (scopo) aim

final'mente adv at last; (in ultimo) finally

fi'nanza nf finance; Guardia di ~ body of police officers responsible for border control and for investigating fraud; intendenza di ~ inland revenue office

finanzia'mento nm funding

finanzi'are vt fund, finance

finanzi'aria nf investment company; (holding) holding company; Jur finance bill

finanzi'ario adj financial

finanzia|'tore, -trice nmf backer

finanzi'ere nm financier; (guardia di finanza) customs officer

✧ finché conj until; (per tutto il tempo che) as long as

✧ 'fine [1] adj fine; (sottile) thin; ‹udito, vista› keen; (raffinato) refined
[2] nf end; alla ~ in the end; alla fin ~ after all; in fin dei conti when all's said and done; andare a buon ~ be successful; te lo dico a fin di bene I'm telling you for your own good; che ~ ha fatto Anna? what became of Anna?; che ~ hanno fatto le chiavi? where have the keys got to?; senza ~ endless
[3] nm aim
■ fine settimana weekend

✧ fi'nestra nf window
■ finestra a battenti casement window

fine'strella nf Comput box
■ finestrella di aiuto help window; finestrella di dialogo dialog box, dialogue box Br; finestrella di messaggio message box

fine'strino nm Rail, Auto window

fi'nezza nf fineness; (sottigliezza) thinness; (raffinatezza) refinement

'fingere vt pretend; feign ‹affetto ecc›

'fingersi vr pretend to be

fini'menti nmpl finishing touches; (per cavallo) harness sg

fini'mondo nm end of the world; fig pandemonium

✧ fi'nire vt finish, end; (smettere) stop; (diventare, andare a finire) end up; finiscila! stop it!

fi'nito adj finished; (abile) accomplished

fini'tura nf finish

finlan'dese [1] adj Finnish

2 *nmf* Finn
3 *nm* (lingua) Finnish
Fin'landia *nf* Finland

🗸 **'fino¹** *prep* ∼ a till, until; (spazio) as far
as; ∼ **all'ultimo** to the last; ∼ **alla nausea**
‹ripetere, leggere› ad nauseam; **fin da** (tempo)
since; (spazio) from; **fin dall'inizio** from the
beginning; **fin qui** as far as here; **fin troppo**
too much; ∼ **a che punto** how far

'fino² *adj* fine; (acuto) subtle; (puro) pure

fi'nocchio *nm* fennel; fam (omosessuale)
poof

🗸 **fi'nora** *adv* so far, up till now

'finta *nf* pretence, sham; Sport feint; **far** ∼ **di**
pretend to; **far** ∼ **di niente** act as if nothing
had happened; **per** ∼ (per scherzo) for a laugh

'finto, -a 1 pp di FINGERE
2 *adj* false; (artificiale) artificial; **finta pelle**
fake leather; **fare il** ∼ **tonto** act dumb

finzi'one *nf* pretence

fi'occo *nm* bow; (di neve) flake; (nappa)
tassel; Naut jib; **coi fiocchi** fig excellent;
fiocchi *pl* **di avena** oatmeal; (cotti) porridge;
fiocchi *pl* **di granoturco** cornflakes; **fiocchi**
pl **di latte** cottage cheese
■ **fiocco di neve** snowflake

fi'ocina *nf* harpoon

fi'oco *adj* weak; ‹luce› dim

fi'onda *nf* catapult

fio'raio, -a *nmf* florist

fiorda'liso *nm* cornflower

fi'ordo *nm* fiord

🗸 **fi'ore** *nm* flower; **a fior d'acqua** on the
surface of the water; **a fiori** flowery; **in** ∼
flowering; **fior di** (abbondanza) a lot of; **il fior**
∼ **di** the cream of; **ha i nervi a fior di pelle**
his nerves are on edge; **nel** ∼ **degli anni** in
one's prime; **è il suo** ∼ **all'occhiello** that's
a feather in his cap; **suo figlio è il suo** ∼
all'occhiello his son is his pride and joy
■ **fiori d'arancio** *pl* orange blossom; **fiore di
campo** wild flower; **fior di latte** (formaggio) soft
cheese; **fiore selvatico** wild flower; **fiori di
zucca fritti** *pl* fried pumpkin flowers

fio'rente *adj* ‹industria› booming

fioren'tina *nf* (bistecca) T-bone steak

fioren'tino *adj* Florentine

fio'retto *nm* (scherma) foil; Relig act of
mortification

fi'ori *nmpl* (nelle carte) clubs

fiori'era *nf* container

fio'rino *nm*
■ **fiorino olandese** guilder

fio'rire *vi* flower; ‹albero› blossom; fig
flourish

fio'rista *nmf* florist; (negozio) florist's

fiori'tura *nf* flowering; (di albero)
blossoming; (insieme di fiori) flowers *pl*

fio'rone *nm* (fico) early fig

fi'otto *nm* (di sangue) spurt; **scorrere a flotti**
pour out; **piove a fiotti** the rain is pouring
down

Fi'renze *nf* Florence

🗸 **'firma** *nf* signature; (nome) name

firma'mento *nm* firmament

🗸 **fir'mare** *vt* sign

firma'tario, -a *nmf* signatory

fir'mato *adj* ‹quadro, lettera› signed; ‹abito,
borsa› designer *attrib*

fisar'monica *nf* accordion

fi'scale *adj* fiscal

fisca'lista *nmf* tax consultant

fiscaliz'zare *vt* finance with government
funds

fischi'are 1 *vi* whistle; **mi fischiano le
orecchie** I've got a ringing noise in my ears;
fig my ears are burning
2 *vt* whistle; (in segno di disapprovazione) boo

fischi'ata *nf* whistle

fischiet'tare *vt* whistle

fischiet'tio *nm* whistling

fischi'etto *nm* whistle

'fischio *nm* whistle; **fischi** *pl* Theat booing;
prendere fischi per fiaschi get hold of the
wrong end of the stick

'fisco *nm* Inland Revenue Br, IRS Am; (tasse)
taxation; **il** ∼ the taxman

'fisica *nf* physics *sg*
■ **fisica atomica** atomic physics; **fisica
nucleare** nuclear physics

fisica'mente *adv* physically

🗸 **'fisico, -a** 1 *adj* physical
2 *nmf* physicist
■ **fisico nucleare** atomic scientist
3 *nm* physique

'fisima *nf* whim

fisiolo'gia *nf* physiology

fisio'logico *adj* physiological

fisi'ologo, -a *nmf* physiologist

fisiono'mia *nf* features *pl*, face; (di
paesaggio) appearance

fisiotera'pia *nf* physiotherapy

fisiotera'pista *nmf* physiotherapist,
physio fam

fissa'mente *adv* fixedly; (permanentemente)
steadily

🗸 **fis'sare** *vt* fix, fasten; (guardare fissamente)
stare at; arrange ‹appuntamento, ora›

fis'sarsi *vr* (stabilirsi) settle; (fissare lo sguardo)
stare; ∼ **su** (ostinarsi) set one's mind on; ∼ **di
fare qualcosa** become obsessed with doing
something

fissa'tivo *nm* Phot fixative

fis'sato, -a 1 *adj* (al muro) fixed; (prezzo)
agreed
2 *nm* (persona) person with an obsession

fissa'tore *nm* hair spray

fissazi'one *nf* fixation; (ossessione) obsession

⚡ **'fisso** ① *adj* fixed; **un lavoro** ∼ a regular job; **senza fissa dimora** of no fixed abode; **avere una ragazza fissa** have a steady girlfriend
② *adv* fixedly; **guardare** ∼ **negli occhi qualcuno** stare at somebody; ⟨*innamorato*⟩ gaze into somebody's eyes

fitotera'pia *nf* herbalism; (per piante) plant health

'fitta *nf* sharp pain

fit'tavolo *nm* tenant

fit'tizio *adj* fictitious

'fitto¹ ① *adj* thick; ∼ **di** full of
② *nm* depth

'fitto² *nm* (affitto) rent; **dare a** ∼ let; **prendere a** ∼ rent; (noleggiare) hire

fiu'mana *nf* swollen river; fig stream

⚡ **fi'ume** ① *nm* river; fig stream
② *adj inv* ⟨*discussione*⟩ endless, never-ending; **romanzo fiume** roman-fleuve

fiu'tare *vt* smell; ⟨*animale*⟩ scent; snort ⟨*cocaina*⟩

fi'uto *nm* [sense of] smell; fig nose

'flaccido *adj* flabby

fla'cone *nm* bottle

flagel'lare *vt* flog

flagellazi'one *nf* flagellation

fla'gello *nm* scourge

fla'grante *adj* flagrant; **in** ∼ in the act

fla'menco *nm* flamenco

flan *nm inv* baked custard

fla'nella *nf* flannel

'flangia *nf* (su ruota) flange

flash *nm inv* Journ newsflash

flau'tista *nmf* flautist

'flauto *nm* flute
■ **flauto diritto** recorder; **flauto traverso** flute

'flebile *adj* feeble

fle'bite *nf* phlebitis

flebo'clisi *nf* drip

'flemma *nf* calm; Med phlegm

flem'matico *adj* phlegmatic

fles'sibile *adj* flexible

flessibilità *nf* flexibility

flessi'one *nf* (del busto in avanti) forward bend; (a terra) sit-up; (delle ginocchia) kneebend; (di vendite, produzione) drop, fall

fles'sivo *adj* Gram inflected

'flesso ① pp di FLETTERE
② *adj* Gram inflected

flessu'oso *adj* supple

'flettere *vt* bend

flip-'flop *nm inv* flip flop

flir'tare *vi* flirt

F.lli *abbr* (**fratelli**) Bros.

'floppy disk *nm inv* floppy disk

'flora *nf* flora

'florido *adj* flourishing

florovivа'istica *nf* ⟨*attività*⟩ growing under glass

'floscio *adj* limp; (flaccido) flabby

'flotta *nf* fleet

flot'tiglia *nf* flotilla

flu'ente *adj* fluent

fluidità *nf* fluidity; (nel parlare) fluency

flu'ido *nm* fluid

flu'ire *vi* flow

fluore'scente *adj* fluorescent

fluore'scenza *nf* fluorescence

flu'oro *nm* fluorine

fluo'ruro *nm* fluoride

'flusso *nm* flow; Med flux; (del mare) flood-tide
■ **flusso e riflusso** ebb and flow; **flusso di cassa** cash flow

'flutti *nmpl* billows

fluttu'ante *adj* fluctuating

fluttu'are *vi* ⟨*prezzi*⟩ fluctuate; ⟨*moneta*⟩ float

fluttuazi'one *nf* fluctuation; (di moneta) floating

fluvi'ale *adj* river

fo'bia *nf* phobia

'fobico *adj* phobic

'foca *nf* seal

fo'caccia *nf* (pane) flat bread; (dolce) ≈ raisin bread

fo'cale *adj* ⟨*distanza, punto*⟩ focal

focaliz'zare *vt* get into focus ⟨*fotografia*⟩; focus ⟨*attenzione*⟩; define ⟨*problema*⟩

'foce *nf* mouth

fo'chista *nm* stoker

foco'laio *nm* Med focus; fig centre

foco'lare *nm* hearth; (caminetto) fireplace; Techn furnace

fo'coso *adj* fiery

'fodera *nf* lining; (di libro) dust-jacket; (di poltrona ecc) loose cover

fode'rare *vt* line; cover ⟨*libro*⟩

fode'rato *adj* lined; ⟨*libro*⟩ covered

'foga *nf* impetuosity

'foggia *nf* fashion; ⟨*maniera*⟩ manner; (forma) shape

foggi'are *vt* mould

⚡ **'foglia** *nf* leaf; (di metallo) foil; **mangiare la** ∼ catch on
■ **foglia di alloro** bay leaf

fogli'ame *nm* foliage

fogliet'tino *nm*
■ **fogliettino igienico** (per pannolini) nappy liner

fogli'etto *nm* (pezzetto di carta) piece of paper

⚡ indicates a very frequent word

'foglio *nm* sheet; (pagina) leaf; (di domanda, iscrizione) form
■ **foglio di carta** sheet of paper; **foglio elettronico** Comput spreadsheet; **foglio illustrativo** instruction leaflet; **foglio protocollo** foolscap; **foglio rosa** provisional driving licence; **foglio di via** expulsion order

'fogna *nf* sewer

fogna'tura *nf* sewerage

fohn *nm inv* hair dryer

fo'lata *nf* gust

fol'clore *nm* folklore

folclo'ristico *adj* folk; (bizzarro) weird

folgo'rante *adj* ‹idea› brilliant

folgo'rare ① *vi* (splendere) shine
② *vt* (con un fulmine) strike

folgo'rato *adj* fig thunderstruck

folgorazi'one *nf* (da fulmine, elettrica) electrocution; fig (idea) brainwave

'folgore *nf* thunderbolt

'folio: in ~ *adj* folio

'folla *nf* crowd

'folle *adj* mad; ‹velocità› breakneck; **in** ~ Auto in neutral; **andare in** ~ Auto coast

folleggi'are *vi* paint the town red

folle'mente *adv* madly

fol'letto *nm* elf

fol'lia *nf* madness; **alla** ~ ‹amare› to distraction; **costare una** ~ cost the earth; **fare una** ~ go mad; **farei follie per lei** I'd do anything for her

'folto *adj* thick

fomen'tare *vt* stir up

fond'ale *nm* Theat backcloth
■ **fondale marino** sea bed

fonda'menta *nfpl* foundations

fondamen'tale *adj* fundamental

fondamenta'lismo *nm* fundamentalism

fondamenta'lista *nmf* fundamentalist

fonda'mento *nm* (di principio, teoria) foundation; **privo di** ~ groundless, without foundation

fon'dant *nm inv* fondant

fon'dare *vt* establish; base ‹ragionamento, accusa›

fon'darsi *vr* be based (**su** on)

fon'dato *adj* ‹ragionamento› well-founded; ~ **su** based on

fondazi'one *nf* establishment; **fondazioni** *pl* (di edificio) foundations

fon'delli *nmpl* **prendere qualcuno per i** ~ fam pull somebody's leg

fon'dente *adj* ‹cioccolato› dark

'fondere ① *vt* melt; fuse ‹metallo›
② *vi* melt; ‹metallo› fuse; ‹colori› blend

fonde'ria *nf* foundry

'fondersi *vr* melt; Comm merge

'fondo ① *adj* deep; **è notte fonda** it's the middle of the night

② *nm* bottom; (fine) end; (sfondo) background; (indole) nature; (somma di denaro) fund; (feccia) dregs *pl*; (terreno) land; **[sci di]** ~ cross-country skiing; **andare a** ~ ‹nave› sink; **in** ~ after all; **in** ~ **a** at the end/ bottom of; **in** ~ **in** ~ deep down; **fino in** ~ right to the end; ‹capire› thoroughly; **andare fino in** ~ **a qualcosa** get to the bottom of something; **dar** ~ **a** use up; **a doppio** ~ false bottomed; **toccare il** ~ touch bottom; fig hit rock bottom; **senza** ~ bottomless; **fondi** *pl* (denaro) funds; (di caffè) grounds; **fondi** *pl* **di magazzino** old stock; **fondi** *pl* **neri** slush fund; **fondi** *pl* **sovrani** sovereign wealth funds
■ **articolo di fondo** (in giornale) editorial; **fondo fiduciario** trust fund; **fondo [comune] di investimento** investment trust; **Fondo Monetario Internazionale** International Monetary Fund; **fondo pensione** pension fund; **fondo per la ricostruzione** disaster fund; **fondo sopravvenienze passive** contingency fund; **fondo stradale** road surface

fondo'tinta *nm inv* foundation [cream]

fon'due *nf* (di formaggio) fondue

fon'duta *nf* fondue

fo'nema *nm* phoneme

fo'netica *nf* phonetics *sg*

fo'netico *adj* phonetic

fonolo'gia *nf* phonology

fon'tana *nf* fountain; (di farina) well

fonta'nella *nf* drinking fountain; Anat fontanelle

'fonte ① *nf* spring; fig source
② *nm* font

fon'tina *nf* soft mature cheese often used in cooking

'football *nm*
■ **football americano** American football

foraggi'are *vt* fodder

fo'raggio *nm* forage

fo'rare ① *vt* pierce: punch ‹biglietto›
② *vi* puncture

fo'rarsi *vr* ‹gomma, pallone› go soft

fora'tura *nf* puncture

'forbici *nfpl* scissors; **un paio di** ~ a pair of scissors
■ **forbici da siepe** garden shears; **forbici a zigzag** pinking shears, pinking scissors

forbi'cina *nf* earwig; **forbicine** *pl* (per le unghie) nail scissors

for'bito *adj* erudite

'forca *nf* fork; (patibolo) gallows *pl*

for'cella *nf* fork; (per capelli) hairpin

for'chetta *nf* fork; **essere una buona** ~ enjoy one's food

forchet'tata *nf* (quantità) forkful

forchet'tone *nm* carving fork

for'cina *nf* hairpin

'forcipe *nm* forceps *pl*

for'cone *nm* pitchfork

for'ense *adj* forensic

✛ **fo'resta** *nf* forest
  ■ **foresta equatoriale** rain forest; **Foresta Nera** Black Forest

fore'stale *adj* forest *attrib*; **la Forestale** branch of the police with responsibility for national forests

foreste'ria *nf* guest rooms *pl*

foresti'ero, -a 1 *adj* foreign 2 *nmf* foreigner

for'fait *nm inv* fixed price; **dare** ∼ (abbandonare) give up; **prezzo [a] forfait** all-in price; **contratto [a] forfait** lump-sum contract

forfe'tario *adj* flat rate

'forfora *nf* dandruff

'forgia *nf* forge

forgi'are *vt* forge

✛ **'forma** *nf* form; (sagoma) shape; Culin mould; (per scarpe) shoe tree; (di calzolaio) last; **essere in** ∼ be in good form; **in (gran)** ∼ (very) fit, on (top) form; **a** ∼ **di** in the shape of; **sotto** ∼ **di** in the form of; **forme** *pl* (del corpo) curves; (convenzioni) appearances

formag'gera *nf* [covered] cheese board

formag'gino *nm* processed cheese

✛ **for'maggio** *nm* cheese
  ■ **formaggio erborinato** blue cheese

for'male *adj* formal

forma'lina *nf* formalin

forma'lismo *nm* formalism

forma'lista *nmf* formalist

formalità *nf inv* formality

formaliz'zare *vt* formalize

formaliz'zarsi *vr* stand on ceremony, be formal

formal'mente *adv* formally

'forma 'mentis *nf inv* way of thinking, mindset

✛ **for'mare** *vt* form; dial (numero di telefono)

for'marsi *vr* form; (svilupparsi) develop

for'mato *nm* size; (di libro, dischetto) format
  ■ **formato famiglia** economy pack, economy size; **formato tessera** (fotografia) passport-size

format'tare *vt* format

formattazi'one *nf* formatting

formazione *nf* formation; Sport line-up; **in** ∼ in the process of being formed
  ■ **formazione professionale** vocational training; **formazione professionale postlaurea** graduate training scheme

for'mella *nf* tile

for'mica[1] *nf* ant

'formica®[2] *nf* Formica

formi'caio *nm* anthill

formichi'ere *nm* anteater

formico'lare *vi* (braccio ecc) tingle; ∼ **di** be swarming with; **mi formicola la mano** I have pins and needles in my hand

formico'lio *nm* swarming; (di braccio ecc) pins and needles *pl*

formi'dabile *adj* (tremendo) formidable; (eccezionale) tremendous

for'mina *nf* mould

for'moso *adj* curvy

✛ **'formula** *nf* formula; **assolvere con** ∼ **piena** acquit
  ■ **formula di cortesia** polite form of address

formu'lare *vt* formulate; (esprimere) express

formulazi'one *nf* formulation

for'nace *nf* furnace; (per laterizi) kiln

for'naio, -a *nmf* baker; (negozio) bakery

fornel'letto *nm*
  ■ **fornelletto da campeggio** camping stove; **fornelletto a gas** gas stove

for'nello *nm* stove; (di pipa) bowl
  ■ **fornello da campeggio** camping stove

fornicazi'one *nf* fornication

✛ **for'nire** *vt* supply (di with); ∼ **qualcosa a qualcuno** supply somebody with something

for'nirsi *vr* ∼ **di** provide oneself with

forni'tore *nm* supplier
  ■ **fornitore di servizi [Internet]** [Internet] service provider

forni'tura *nf* supply; **forniture** *pl* **per ufficio** office supplies

'forno *nm* oven; (panetteria) bakery; **al** ∼ roast; **da** ∼ (stoviglie) ovenproof
  ■ **forno autopulente** self-cleaning oven; **forno crematorio** cremator; **forno elettrico** electric oven; **forno a gas** gas oven; **forno a microonde** microwave [oven]

'foro *nm* hole; (romano) forum; (tribunale) [law] court

✛ **'forse** *adv* perhaps, maybe; **essere in** ∼ be in doubt

forsen'nato, -a 1 *adj* mad 2 *nmf* madman; madwoman

✛ **'forte** 1 *adj* strong; (colore) bright; (suono) loud; (resistente) tough; (spesa) considerable; (dolore) severe; (pioggia) heavy; fam (simpatico) great; (taglia) large; **essere** ∼ **in qualcosa** be good at something 2 *adv* strongly; (parlare) loudly; (velocemente) fast; (piovere) heavily 3 *nm* (fortezza) fort; (specialità) strong point

for'tezza *nf* fortress; (forza morale) fortitude

fortifi'care *vt* fortify

fortifi'cato *adj* (città) walled

for'tino *nm* Mil blockhouse

for'tissimo *adj* (caffè, liquore) extra-strong

for'tuito *adj* fortuitous; **incontro fortuito** chance encounter

---

✛ indicates a very frequent word

for'tuna *nf* fortune; (successo) success; (buona sorte) luck; **atterraggio di** ~ forced landing; **aver** ~ be lucky; **buona** ~! good luck!; **di** ~ makeshift; **per** ~ luckily; **hai una** ~ **sfacciata!** fam you lucky blighter!

fortu'nale *nm* storm

fortunata'mente *adv* fortunately

fortu'nato *adj* lucky, fortunate; ⟨impresa⟩ successful

fortu'noso *adj* ⟨giornata⟩ eventful

fo'runcolo *nm* pimple; (grosso) boil

forunco'loso *adj* spotty

'forza *nf* strength; (potenza) power; (fisica) force; **di** ~ by force; **a** ~ **di** by dint of; **con** ~ hard; ~! come on!; **in** ~ **di** under, in accordance with; ~ **maggiore** circumstances beyond one's control; **la** ~ **pubblica** the police; **le forze armate** the armed forces; **per** ~ against one's will; (naturalmente) of course; **farsi** ~ bear up; **mare** ~ **8** force 8 gale; **bella** ~! fam big deal!; **che** ~! (che simpatico, divertente) cool eh?

■ **forza di gravità** [force of] gravity; **forza lavoro** workforce; **forze** *pl* **di mercato** market forces; **forza di volontà** will-power

for'zare *vt* force; (scassare) break open; (sforzare) strain

for'zato ① *adj* forced; ⟨sorriso⟩ strained ② *nm* convict

forza'tura *nf* (di cassaforte) forcing; **sostenere che ... è una** ~ to maintain that ... is forcing things

forzi'ere *nm* coffer

for'zuto *adj* strong

fo'schia *nf* haze, mist

'fosco *adj* dark

fo'sfato *nm* phosphate

'fosforo *nm* phosphorus

'fossa *nf* pit; (tomba) grave

■ **fossa biologica** cesspool; **fossa comune** mass grave; **fossa dell'orchestra** orchestra pit

fos'sato *nm* (di fortificazione) moat

fos'setta *nf* (di guancia) dimple

'fossile *nm* fossil

'fosso *nm* ditch; Mil trench

'foto *nf inv* fam photo; **fare delle** ~ take some photos

foto'camera *nf* camera

■ **fotocamera digitale** digital camera, fam digicam

foto'cellula *nf* photocell

fotocomposi'tore, -trice *nmf* filmsetter

fotocomposizi'one *nf* filmsetting, photo-composition

foto'copia *nf* photocopy

fotocopi'are *vt* photocopy

fotocopia'trice *nf* photocopier

foto'finish *nm inv* photo finish

foto'genico *adj* photogenic

fotogiorna'lista *nmf* photojournalist

fotogra'fare *vt* photograph

fotogra'fia *nf* (arte) photography; (immagine) photograph; **fare fotografie** take photographs

■ **fotografia aerea** aerial photography

foto'grafico *adj* photographic; **macchina fotografica** camera

fo'tografo, -a *nmf* photographer; (negozio) photographer's

foto'gramma *nm* frame

fotoincisi'one *nf* photoengraving

fotomo'dello, -a *nmf* [photographer's] model

fotomon'taggio *nm* photomontage

foto'ottica *nf* camera shop and optician's

fotorepor'tage *nm inv* photo essay

fotore'porter *nmf inv* newspaper photographer; (di rivista) magazine photographer

fotori'tocco *nm* retouching, image manipulation

fotoro'manzo *nm* photo story

foto'sintesi *nf* photosynthesis

'fottere *vt* sl (rubare) nick; sl (imbrogliare) screw; vulg fuck, screw

'fottersene *vr* vulg not give a fuck; **va' a farti** ~! vulg fuck off!

fot'tuto *adj* sl (maledetto) bloody

fou'lard *nm inv* scarf

'foxhound *nm inv* foxhound

fox-'terrier *nm inv* fox terrier

fo'yer *nm inv* foyer

fra *prep* (in mezzo a due) between; (in un insieme) among; (tempo, distanza) in; **detto** ~ **noi** between you and me; ~ **sé e sé** to oneself; ~ **l'altro** what's more; ~ **breve** soon; ~ **quindici giorni** in two weeks' time; ~ **tutti, siamo in venti** there are twenty of us altogether

fracas'sare *vt* smash

fracas'sarsi *vr* shatter

fracas'sato *adj* smashed

fra'casso *nm* din; (di cose che cadono) crash

fracas'sone, -a *nmf* clumsy person

'fradicio *adj* (bagnato) soaked; **ubriaco** ~ blind drunk

'fragile *adj* fragile; fig frail

fragilità *nf* fragility; fig frailty

'fragola *nf* strawberry

fra'gore *nm* uproar; (di cose rotte) clatter; (di tuono) rumble

frago'roso *adj* uproarious; ⟨tuono⟩ rumbling; ⟨suono⟩ clanging

fra'grante *adj* fragrant

fra'granza *nf* fragrance

frain'tendere *vt* misunderstand

frain'tendersi *vr* be at cross-purposes

frain'teso pp di FRAINTENDERE

frammen'tario *adj* fragmentary

fram'mento *nm* fragment

fram'misto *adj* ∼ **di** interspersed with

'frana *nf* landslide; fam (persona) walking disaster area

fra'nare *vi* slide down

franca'mente *adv* frankly

france'scano *adj & nm* Franciscan

❤ **fran'cese** ⚊**1**⚊ *adj* French
⚊**2**⚊ *nm* Frenchman; (lingua) French
⚊**3**⚊ *nf* Frenchwoman

france'sina *nf* (scarpa) brogue

fran'chezza *nf* frankness; **in tutta** ∼ in all honesty

fran'chigia *nf*
■ **franchigia bagaglio** (per aereo) baggage allowance

'Francia *nf* France

'franco¹ *adj* frank; Comm free; **farla franca** get away with something; **parlare** ∼ speak frankly
■ **franco a bordo** free on board; **franco domicilio** delivered free of charge; **franco fabbrica** ex-works; **franco di porto** carriage free, carriage paid

'franco² *nm* (moneta) franc

franco'bollo *nm* stamp

franco-cana'dese *adj & nmf* French Canadian

fran'cofono *adj* Francophone, French-speaking

Franco'forte *nf* Frankfurt

fran'gente *nm* (onda) breaker; (scoglio) reef; fig (momento difficile) crisis; **in quel** ∼ in the circumstances

fran'getta *nf* fringe

'frangia *nf* fringe

frangi'flutti *nm inv* bulwark

frangi'vento *nm* windbreak

fra'noso *adj* subject to landslides

fran'toio *nm* olive-press

frantu'mare *vt* shatter

frantu'marsi *vr* shatter

fran'tumi *nmpl* splinters; **in** ∼ smashed; **andare in** ∼ be smashed to smithereens

frappé *nm inv* milkshake

frap'porre *vt* interpose

frap'porsi *vr* intervene

fra'sario *nm* vocabulary; (libro) phrase book

'frasca *nf* [leafy] branch; **saltare di palo in** ∼ jump from subject to subject

❤ **'frase** *nf* sentence; (espressione) phrase
■ **frase fatta** cliché

fraseolo'gia *nf* phrases *pl*

'frassino *nm* ash [tree]

frastagli'are *vt* make jagged

frastagl'iato *adj* jagged

frastor'nare *vt* daze

frastor'nato *adj* dazed

frastu'ono *nm* racket

'frate *nm* friar; (monaco) monk

fratel'lanza *nf* brotherhood

fratel'lastro *nm* step brother, half-brother

fratel'lino *nm* little brother

❤ **fra'tello** *nm* brother; **fratelli** *pl* (fratello e sorella) brother and sister; Relig brethren
■ **fratello gemello** twin brother; **fratello di sangue** blood brother

fraternità *nf* brotherhood

fraterniz'zare *vi* fraternize

fra'terno *adj* brotherly

fratri'cida ⚊**1**⚊ *adj* fratricidal
⚊**2**⚊ *nm* fratricide

frat'taglie *nfpl* (di pollo ecc) giblets

frat'tanto *adv* in the meantime

frat'tura *nf* fracture

frattu'rare *vt* break

frattu'rarsi *vr* break

fraudo'lento *adj* fraudulent

frazi'one *nf* fraction; (borgata) hamlet; (paese) *administrative division of a municipality*

'freccia *nf* arrow; Auto indicator

frecci'ata *nf* (osservazione pungente) cutting remark

fredda'mente *adv* coldly

fred'dare *vt* cool; fig (con sguardo, battuta) cut down; (uccidere) kill

fred'dezza *nf* coldness

❤ **'freddo** *adj & nm* cold; **aver** ∼ be cold; **fa** ∼ it's cold; **a** ∼ ‹*sparare*› in cold blood; ‹*lavare*› in cold water

freddo'loso *adj* sensitive to cold, chilly

fred'dura *nf* pun

❤ **fre'gare** *vt* rub; fam (truffare) cheat; fam (rubare) swipe; **fregarsene** fam not give a damn; **me ne frego!** I don't give a damn!; **chi se ne frega!** what the heck!

fre'garsi *vr* rub ‹*occhi, mani*›

fre'gata *nf* rub; (nave) frigate

frega'tura *nf* fam (truffa) swindle; (delusione) letdown

'fregio *nm* Archit frieze; (ornamento) decoration

'fregola *nf* rutting; **avere la** ∼ **di fare qualcosa** fam have a craze for doing something

fre'mente *adj* quivering

'fremere *vi* quiver

'fremito *nm* quiver

fre'nare ⚊**1**⚊ *vt* brake; fig restrain; hold back ‹*lacrime, impazienza*›
⚊**2**⚊ *vi* brake

fre'narsi *vr* check oneself

❤ indicates a very frequent word

fre'nata *nf* fare una ∼ **brusca** hit the brakes

frene'sia *nf* frenzy; (desiderio smodato) craze

frenetica'mente *adv* frantically

fre'netico *adj* frantic

'freno *nm* brake; fig check; **togliere il** ∼ release the brake; **usare il** ∼ apply the brake; **tenere a** ∼ restrain; **tenere a** ∼ **la lingua** hold one's tongue; **porre un** ∼ **a** fig rein in; **freni** *pl* **a disco** disc brakes
■ **freno a mano** handbrake; **freno a pedale** footbrake

✧ **frequen'tare** *vt* frequent; attend ‹scuola ecc›; mix with ‹persone›; **non ci frequentiamo più** we don't see each other any more

fre'quente *adj* frequent; **di** ∼ frequently

fre'quenza *nf* frequency; (assiduità) attendance

'fresa *nf* mill

fre'sare *vt* mill

fre'schezza *nf* freshness; (di temperatura) coolness

✧ **'fresco** ① *adj* fresh; ‹temperatura› cool; ∼ **di studi** fresh out of school; **stai** ∼! fam you're for it!; **se ti vede stai** ∼ fam you're done for if he sees you
② *nm* coolness; **far** ∼ be cool; **mettere/tenere in** ∼ put/keep in a cool place; **al** ∼ fam (in prigione) inside

fre'scura *nf* cool

'fresia *nf* freesia

✧ **'fretta** *nf* hurry, haste; **aver** ∼ be in a hurry; **far** ∼ **a qualcuno** hurry somebody; **in** ∼ **e furia** in a great hurry; **andarsene in** ∼ rush away; **senza [nessuna]** ∼ at your/his etc leisure

frettolosa'mente *adv* hurriedly

fretto'loso *adj* ‹persona› hasty; ‹lavoro› rushed, hurried

fri'abile *adj* crumbly

fricas'sea *nf* stewed meat served with an egg and lemon sauce

'friggere ① *vt* fry; **vai a farti** ∼! get lost!
② *vi* sizzle; ∼ **di impazienza** be on tenterhooks

friggi'trice *nf* electric chip pan

frigidità *nf* frigidity

'frigido *adj* frigid

fri'gnare *vi* whine

fri'gnone, -a *nmf* whiner

'frigo *nm inv* fridge

frigo'bar *nm inv* minibar

frigocongela'tore *nm* fridge-freezer

frigo'rifero ① *adj* refrigerating; ‹camion› refrigerated
② *nm* refrigerator

fringu'ello *nm* chaffinch

'frisbee® *nm inv* frisbee

frit'tata *nf* omelette

frit'tella *nf* fritter; fam (macchia d'unto) grease stain

'fritto ① pp di FRIGGERE
② *adj* fried; **essere** ∼ be done for
③ *nm* fried food
■ **fritto misto** mixed fried fish/vegetables

frit'tura *nf* (pietanza) fried dish
■ **frittura di pesce** variety of fried fish

frivo'lezza *nf* frivolity

'frivolo *adj* frivolous

frizio'nare *vt* rub

frizi'one *nf* friction; Mech clutch; (di pelle) rub

friz'zante *adj* fizzy; ‹vino› sparkling; ‹aria› bracing

'frizzo *nm* gibe

fro'dare *vt* defraud

'frode *nf* fraud; **con la** ∼ Jur under false pretences
■ **frode fiscale** tax evasion

frol'lino *nm* (biscotto) ≈ shortbread biscuit

'frollo *adj* tender; ‹selvaggina› high; ‹persona› spineless, **pasta frolla** short[crust] pastry

'fronda *nf* [leafy] branch; fig rebellion

fron'doso *adj* leafy

fron'tale *adj* frontal; ‹scontro› head-on

✧ **'fronte** ① *nf* forehead; (di edificio) front; **di** ∼ opposite; **di** ∼ **a** opposite, facing; (a paragone) compared with
② *nm* Mil, Pol front; **far** ∼ **a** face

fronteggi'are *vt* face

fronte'spizio *nm* title page

fronti'era *nf* frontier, border

fron'tone *nm* pediment

'fronzolo *nm* frill

'frotta *nf* swarm; (di animali) flock

'frottola *nf* fib; **frottole** *pl* nonsense *sg*

fru'gale *adj* frugal

fru'gare ① *vi* rummage
② *vt* search

fru'ire *vi* ∼ **di** make use of, take advantage of

frul'lare ① *vt* Culin whisk
② *vi* ‹ali› whirr

frul'lato *nm*
■ **frullato di frutta** fruit drink with milk and crushed ice

frulla'tore *nm* [electric] mixer

frul'lino *nm* whisk

fru'mento *nm* wheat

frusci'are *vi* rustle

fru'scio *nm* rustle; (radio, giradischi) ground noise; (di acque) murmur

'frusta *nf* whip; (frullino) whisk

fru'stare *vt* whip

fru'stata *nf* lash

fru'stino *nm* riding crop

fru'strare *vt* frustrate

fru'strato *adj* frustrated

frustrazi'one *nf* frustration

⚜ **'frutta** *nf* fruit; **negozio di ∼ e verdura** greengrocer's
  ■ **frutta esotica** exotic fruit, tropical fruit; **frutta fresca di stagione** seasonal fruit; **frutta secca** nuts *pl*

frut'tare ⑴ *vi* bear fruit; Comm give a return
  ⑵ *vt* yield

frut'teto *nm* orchard

frutticol'tore *nm* fruit farmer

frutticol'tura *nf* fruit farming, fruit growing

frutti'era *nf* fruit bowl

frut'tifero *adj* ‹albero› fruit-bearing; Fin ‹deposito› interest-bearing

frutti'vendolo, -a *nmf* greengrocer

⚜ **'frutto** *nm* anche fig fruit; Fin yield; **frutti di bosco** *pl* fruits of the forest; **frutti di mare** *pl* seafood *sg*
  ■ **frutto della passione** passion fruit

fruttu'oso *adj* profitable

FS *abbr* (**Ferrovie dello Stato**) Italian State Railways

f.to *abbr* (**firmato**) signed

fu *adj* (defunto) late; **il fu signor Rossi** the late Mr Rossi

fuci'lare *vt* shoot, execute by firing squad

fucilazi'one *nf* execution [by firing squad]

fu'cile *nm* rifle
  ■ **fucile ad aria compressa** air rifle; **fucile a canne mozze** sawn-off shotgun

fucil'lata *nf* shot

fu'cina *nf* forge

'fuco *nm* kelp

'fucsia *nf* fuchsia

⚜ **'fuga** *nf* escape; (perdita) leak; (di ciclisti) breakaway; Mus fugue; **darsi alla ∼** take to flight; **mettere qualcuno in ∼** put somebody to flight
  ■ **fuga di cervelli** brain drain; **fuga di gradini** flight of steps; **fuga di notizie** leak; **fuga romantica** elopement

fu'gace *adj* fleeting

fug'gevole *adj* short-lived

fuggi'asco, -a *nmf* fugitive

fuggi'fuggi *nm* stampede

⚜ **fug'gire** *vi* flee; ‹innamorati› elope; fig fly

fuggi'tivo, -a *nmf* fugitive

'fulcro *nm* fulcrum

ful'gore *nm* splendour

fu'liggine *nf* soot

fuliggi'noso *adj* sooty

full *nm inv* (nel poker) full house

fulmi'nante *adj* (sguardo) withering; **è morto di leucemia ∼** he died very soon after

contracting leukaemia

fulmi'nare *vt* strike by lightning; (con sguardo) look daggers at; (con scarica elettrica) electrocute

fulmi'narsi *vr* burn out

fulmi'nato *adj* rimanere ∼ electrocute oneself

'fulmine *nm* lightning; **colpo di fulmine** fig love at first sight; **un ∼ a ciel sereno** a bolt from the blue

ful'mineo *adj* rapid; ‹sguardo› withering

'fulvo *adj* tawny

fumai'olo *nm* funnel; (di casa) chimney

fu'mante *adj* ‹minestra, tazza› steaming

⚜ **fu'mare** *vt/i* smoke; (in ebollizione) steam; 'vietato ∼' 'no smoking'

fu'mario *adj* (canna) flue

fu'mata *nf* (segnale) smoke signal

fuma|'tore, -trice *nmf* smoker; **non fumatori** ‹scompartimento› non-smoker, non-smoking

fu'metto *nm* comic strip; **fumetti** *pl* comics

⚜ **'fumo** *nm* smoke; (vapore) steam; fig hot air; **andare in ∼** vanish; **vendere ∼** put on an act; **cercava di vendere ∼** it was all hot air; **fumi** *pl* (industriali) fumes; **sotto i fumi dell'alcol** under the influence of alcohol
  ■ **fumo passivo** passive smoking

fu'mogeno *adj* **cortina fumogena** smoke screen

fu'moso *adj* ‹ambiente› smoky; ‹discorso› vague

funambo'lesco *adj* acrobatic

fu'nambolo, -a *nmf* tightrope walker

'fune *nf* rope; (cavo) cable

'funebre *adj* funeral; (cupo) gloomy

⚜ **fune'rale** *nm* funeral

fu'nereo *adj* ‹aria› funereal

fu'nesto *adj* sad

'fungere *vi* ∼ **da** act as

'fungo *nm* mushroom; Bot, Med fungus; **funghi** *pl* Bot fungi
  ■ **fungo atomico** mushroom cloud; **fungo commestibile** edible mushroom

funico'lare *nf* funicular [railway]

funi'via *nf* cableway

funzio'nale *adj* functional

funzionalità *nf* functionality

funziona'mento *nm* functioning

⚜ **funzio'nare** *vi* work, function; ∼ **da** (fungere da) act as

funzio'nario *nm* official
  ■ **funzionario statale** civil servant

⚜ **funzi'one** *nf* function; (carica) office; Relig service; **entrare in ∼** take up office; **mettere in ∼** ‹motore› start up; **vivere in ∼ di** live for

⚜ **fu'oco** *nm* fire; (fisica, fotografia) focus; **far ∼** fire; **dar ∼ a** set fire to; **andare a ∼** go up in flames; **prendere ∼** catch fire; **a ∼ vivo**

‹*cuocere*› on a high heat; **a ~ lento** ‹*cuocere*› on a low heat; **'vietato accendere fuochi'** 'no campfires'; **fuochi** *pl* **d'artificio** fireworks
■ **fuoco amico** friendly fire; **fuoco di paglia** nine-days' wonder; **fuochi** *pl* **pirotecnici** pyrotechnics

fuorché *prep* except

⚹ **fu'ori** **1** *adv* out; (all'esterno) outside; (all'aperto) outdoors; **~!** fam get out!; **~ i soldi!** fork up!; **andare di ~** (traboccare) spill over; **essere ~ di sé** be beside oneself; **essere in ~** (sporgere) stick out; **far ~** fam get rid of; **fuori commercio** not for sale; **~ luogo** (inopportuno) out of place; **~ mano** out of the way; **~ moda** old-fashioned; **~ pasto** between meals; **~ pericolo** out of danger; **~ programma** unscheduled; **~ questione** out of the question; **fuori uso** out of use **2** *nm* outside

fuori'bordo *nm* speedboat (*with outboard motor*), powerboat

fuori'campo *adj inv* Cinema ‹*voce*› off-screen

fuori'classe *nmf inv* champion

fuoricombatti'mento *nm* knockout

fuorigi'oco *nm* & *adv* offside

fuori'legge *nmf* outlaw

fuori'pista *nm inv* (sci) off-piste skiing

fuori'serie **1** *adj* custom-made **2** *nf* Auto custom-built model

fuori'strada *nm inv* off-road vehicle, off-roader

fuoriu'scita *nf* (perdita) leak

fuoriu'scito, -a *nmf* exile

fuorvi'are **1** *vt* lead astray **2** *vi* go astray

furbacchi'one *nm* crafty old devil

fur'bastro, -a *nmf* crafty devil

furbe'ria *nf* cunning

fur'besco *adj* sly, cunning

fur'bizia *nf* cunning

'furbo *adj* sly, cunning; (intelligente) clever; (astuto) shrewd; **bravo ~!** nice one!; **fare il ~** try to be clever

fu'rente *adj* furious

fu'retto *nm* ferret

fur'fante *nm* scoundrel

furgon'oino *nm* delivery van

fur'gone *nm* van
■ **furgone postale** mail van

'furia *nf* fury; (fretta) haste; **a ~ di** by dint of; **andare su tutte le furie** fly into a rage

furi'bondo *adj* furious

furi'ere *nm* Mil quartermaster

furiosa'mente *adv* furiously

furi'oso *adj* furious; ‹*litigio*› violent

fu'rore *nm* fury; (veemenza) frenzy; **far ~** be all the rage

furoreggi'are *vi* be a great success

furtiva'mente *adv* covertly, stealthily

fur'tivo *adj* furtive, stealthy

⚹ **'furto** *nm* theft; **commettere un ~** steal; **è un ~!** fig it's daylight robbery!
■ **furto d'auto** car theft; **furto di minore entità** petty theft; **furto con scasso** burglary

'fusa *nfpl* **fare le ~** purr

fu'scello *nm* (di legno) twig; (di paglia) straw; **sei un ~** you're as light as a feather

fu'seaux *nmpl* leggings

fu'sibile *nm* fuse

fu'silli *nmpl* pasta twirls

fusi'one *nf* fusion; Comm merger
■ **fusione fredda** Phys cold fusion

'fuso **1** pp di FONDERE **2** *adj* melted **3** *nm* spindle; **a ~** spindle-shaped
■ **fuso orario** time zone

fusoli'era *nf* fuselage

fu'stagno *nm* corduroy

fu'stella *nf* (talloncino) *part of packaging on prescribed medicine returned by the pharmacist to claim a refund*

fustl'gare *vt* flog; fig castigate

fu'stino *nm* (di detersivo) box

'fusto *nm* stem; (tronco) trunk; (recipiente di metallo) drum; (di legno) barrel
■ **fusto del letto** bedstead

'futile *adj* futile

futilità *nf* futility

futu'rismo *nm* futurism

futu'rista *nmf* futurist

⚹ **fu'turo** *adj* & *nm* future; **predire il ~** tell fortunes, foretell
■ **futuro anteriore** Gram future perfect

f

Gg

gabardine *nf* (tessuto) gabardine
gab'bare *vt* cheat
gab'barsi *vr* ~ **di** make fun of
'gabbia *nf* cage; (da imballaggio) crate
■ **gabbia dell'ascensore** lift cage; **gabbia degli imputati** dock; **gabbia toracica** rib cage
gabbi'ano *nm* [sea]gull
■ **gabbiano comune** common gull
gabi'netto *nm* (di medico) consulting room; Pol cabinet; (toilette) toilet; (laboratorio) laboratory; **andare al** ~ go to the toilet; **gabinetti** *pl* **pubblici** public convenience
'Gabon *nm* Gabon
ga'elico *nm* Gaelic
'gaffa *nf* boathook
'gaffe *nf inv* blunder
gagli'ardo *adj* vigorous
gai'ezza *nf* gaiety
'gaio *adj* cheerful
'gala *nf* gala
ga'lante *adj* gallant
galante'ria *nf* gallantry
galantu'omo *nm* (*pl* **galantuomini**) gentleman
ga'lassia *nf* galaxy
gala'teo *nm* [good] manners *pl*; (trattato) book of etiquette
gale'otto *nm* (rematore) galley-slave; (condannato) convict
ga'lera *nf* (nave) galley; fam slammer
'galla *nf* Bot gall; **a** ~ afloat; **venire a** ~ surface
galleggi'ante ① *adj* floating ② *nm* craft; (boa) float
galleggi'are *vi* float
galle'ria *nf* (traforo) tunnel; (d'arte) gallery; Theat circle; (arcata) arcade; **prima galleria** dress circle
■ **galleria aerodinamica** wind tunnel; **galleria d'arte** art gallery
'Galles *nm* Wales
gal'lese ① *adj* Welsh ② *nm* Welshman; (lingua) Welsh ③ *nf* Welshwoman
gal'letta *nf* cracker
gal'letto *nm* cockerel; **fare il** ~ show off, impress the girls
'gallico *adj* Gallic
gal'lina *nf* hen
galli'nella *nf*
■ **gallinella d'acqua** moorhen

gal'lismo *nm* machismo
'gallo *nm* cock
■ **gallo cedrone** capercaillie
gal'lone *nm* stripe; (misura) gallon
galop'pante *adj* galloping
galop'pare *vi* gallop
galop'pino *nm* **fare da** ~ **a qualcuno** fam be somebody's gopher
ga'loppo *nm* gallop; **al** ~ at a gallop
galvaniz'zare *vt* galvanize
♂ **'gamba** *nf* leg; (di lettera) stem; **darsela a gambe** take to one's heels; **essere in** ~ (essere forte) be strong; (capace) be smart
gam'bale *nm* (di stivale) bootleg
gamba'letto *nm* pop sock
gambe'retti *nmpl* shrimps
■ **gamberetti in salsa rosa** prawn cocktail
'gambero *nm* prawn; (di fiume) crayfish
gambe'roni *nmpl* king prawns
'Gambia *nf* the Gambia
gambiz'zare *vt* kneecap
'gambo *nm* stem; (di pianta) stalk
ga'mella *nf* billy
game 'point *nm inv* game point
ga'mete *nm* gamete
'gamma *nf* Mus scale; fig range
■ **gamma d'onda** waveband; **gamma di prezzi** price range; **gamma di prodotti** product range
ga'nascia *nf* jaw; **ganasce** *pl* **del freno** brake shoes
'gancio *nm* hook
'Gange *nm* Ganges
'ganghero *nm* **uscire dai gangheri** fig get into a temper
'gangster *nm inv* gangster
♂ **'gara** *nf* competition; (di velocità) race; **fare a** ~ compete
■ **gara d'appalto** call for tenders; **gara a cronometro** time trial
ga'rage *nm inv* garage
gara'gista *nmf* garage owner
ga'rante *nmf* guarantor
♂ **garan'tire** *vt* guarantee; (rendersi garante) vouch for; (assicurare) assure
garan'tirsi *vr* ~ **contro**, ~ **da** guard against, insure against
garan'tismo *nm* protection of civil liberties
garan'tito *adj* guaranteed
garan'zia *nf* guarantee; **in** ~ under guarantee

♂ indicates a very frequent word

■ **garanzia collaterale** collateral; **garanzia di rimborso** money-back guarantee; **garanzia a vita** lifetime guarantee

gar'bare *vi* like; **non mi garba** I don't like it

gar'bato *adj* courteous

'garbo *nm* courtesy; (grazia) grace; **con ~** graciously

gar'buglio *nm* muddle

gar'denia *nf* gardenia

gareggi'are *vi* compete

garga'nella *nf* **a ~** from the bottle

garga'rismo *nm* gargle; **fare i gargarismi** gargle

ga'ritta *nf* sentry box

ga'rofano *nm* carnation; **chiodo di garofano** clove

gar'retto *nm* shank

gar'rire *vi* chirp

gar'rotta *nf* garrotte

'garrulo *adj* garrulous

'garza *nf* gauze

gar'zone *nm* boy

■ **garzone di stalla** stable-boy

✱ **gas** *nm inv* gas; **dare ~** Auto accelerate; **a ~** gas-fired; **a tutto ~** flat out

■ **gas asfissiante** poisonous gas; **gas esilarante** laughing gas; **gas lacrimogeno** tear gas; **gas nobile** inert gas; **gas propellente** propellant; **gas di scarico** *pl* exhaust fumes

gas'dotto *nm* natural gas pipeline

ga'solio *nm* diesel oil

■ **gasolio invernale** diesel containing anti-freeze

ga'sometro *nm* gasometer

gas'sare *vt* aerate; (uccidere col gas) gas

gas'sato *adj* gassy

gas'soso, -a *adj* gaseous

'gastrico *adj* gastric

ga'strite *nf* gastritis

gastroente'rite *nf* gastro-enteritis

gastrono'mia *nf* gastronomy

gastro'nomico *adj* gastronomic[al]

ga'stronomo, -a *nmf* gourmet

'gatta *nf* **una ~ da pelare** a headache

gatta'buia *nf hum* clink

gatta'iola *nf* catflap

gat'tile *nm* cattery

gat'tino, -a *nmf* kitten

✱ **'gatto, -a** *nmf* cat; **c'erano solo quattro gatti** there were only a few people

■ **gatto delle nevi** snowmobile; **gatto a nove code** cat-o'-nine-tails; **gatto selvatico** wildcat

gat'toni *adv* on all fours

gat'tuccio *nm* dogfish

gau'dente *adj* pleasure-loving

'gaudio *nm* joy

ga'vetta *nf* mess tin; **fare la ~** rise through the ranks

gay *adj inv* gay

Gaza *nf* **la striscia di ~** Gaza strip

ga'zebo *nm inv* gazebo

'gazza *nf* magpie

gaz'zarra *nf* racket; **fare ~** make a racket

gaz'zella *nf* gazelle; Auto police car

gaz'zetta *nf* gazette

■ **Gazzetta Ufficiale** official journal

gazzet'tino *nm* (titolo) title page; (rubrica) page

gaz'zosa *nf* clear lemonade

GB *abbr* (**Gran Bretagna**) GB

'geco *nm* gecko

ge'lare *vt/i* freeze; **far ~ il sangue** make somebody's blood run cold

ge'lata *nf* frost

gela'taio, -a ① *nmf* ice-cream seller ② *nm* (negozio) ice-cream shop

gelate'ria *nf* ice-cream parlour

gelati'era *nf* ice-cream maker

gela'tina *nf* gelatine; (dolce) jelly

■ **gelatina di frutta** fruit jelly

gelati'noso *adj* gelatinous

ge'lato ① *adj* frozen ② *nm* ice-cream

■ **gelato alla vaniglia** vanilla ice-cream

'gelido *adj* freezing

'gelo *nm* (freddo intenso) freezing cold; (brina) frost; fig chill

ge'lone *nm* chilblain

gelosa'mente *adv* jealously

gelo'sia *nf* jealousy

✱ **ge'loso** *adj* jealous

'gelso *nm* mulberry[-tree]

gelso'mino *nm* jasmine

gemel'laggio *nm* twinning

gemel'lare ① *vt* twin ② *adj* twin

ge'mello, -a *adj & nmf* twin; **gemelli** *pl* (di polsino) cuff-link; **Gemelli** *pl* Astr Gemini *sg*

■ **gemelli** *pl* **monozigoti** identical twins

'gemere *vi* groan

'gemito *nm* groan

'gemma *nf* gem; Bot bud

gemmolo'gia *nf* gemmology

gen'darme *nm* gendarme

'gene *nm* gene

genealo'gia *nf* genealogy

genea'logico *adj* genealogical

✱ **gene'rale¹** *adj* general; **in ~** (tutto sommato) in general, on the whole; **parlando in ~** generally speaking

✱ **gene'rale²** *nm* Mil general

■ **generale di divisione** major-general

generalità *nf inv* (qualità) generality, general nature; (maggior parte) majority; **~** *pl* (dati) particulars *pl*

generaliz'zare *vt* generalize

g

generalizzazi'one *nf* generalization

general'mente *adv* generally

gene'rare *vt* give birth to; (causare) breed; Techn generate

genera'tore *nm* Techn generator

generazio'nale *adj* generation *attrib*

ꞏ⸰ **generazi'one** *nf* generation; **di ~ in ~** from generation to generation

ꞏ⸰ **'genere** *nm* kind; Biol genus; Gram gender; (letterario, artistico) genre; (prodotto) product; **cose del ~** such things; **il ~ umano** mankind; **in ~** generally; **generi** *pl* **alimentari** provisions; **generi** *pl* **di prima necessità** essentials

generica'mente *adv* generically

ge'nerico *adj* generic; **medico generico** general practitioner

'genero *nm* son-in-law

generosa'mente *adv* generously

generosità *nf* generosity

ꞏ⸰ **gene'roso** *adj* generous

'genesi *nf* genesis

genetica'mente *adv* genetically; **~ modificato** genetically modified

ge'netico, -a ⓵ *adj* genetic ⓶ *nf* genetics *sg*

gene'tista *nmf* geneticist

gen'giva *nf* gum

geni'ale *adj* ingenious; (congeniale) congenial

geni'ere *nm* Mil sapper

'genio *nm* genius; **andare a ~** be to one's taste
■ **genio civile** civil engineering; **genio incompreso** misunderstood genius; **genio [militare]** Engineers

geni'tale ⓵ *adj* genital ⓶ *nm* **genitali** *pl* genitals

ꞏ⸰ **geni'tore** *nm* parent

gen'naio *nm* January

geno'cidio *nm* genocide

ge'noma *nm* genome

geno'teca *nf* gene library

'Genova *nf* Genoa

geno'vese *adj* Genoese

gen'taglia *nf* rabble

ꞏ⸰ **'gente** *nf* people *pl*

ꞏ⸰ **gen'tile** *adj* kind; **Gentile Signore** (in lettere) Dear Sir

genti'lezza *nf* kindness; **per ~** (per favore) please

gentil'mente *adv* kindly

gentilu'omo (*pl* **gentiluomini**) *nm* gentleman

genu'flettersi *vr* kneel down

genuina'mente *adv* genuinely

genu'ino *adj* genuine; «*cibo, prodotto*» natural

genzi'ana *nf* gentian

geo'fisica *nf* geophysics *sg*

geo'fisico, -a *nmf* geophysician

geogra'fia *nf* geography

geo'grafico *adj* geographical

ge'ografo, -a *nmf* geographer

geolo'gia *nf* geology

geo'logico *adj* geological

ge'ologo, -a *nmf* geologist

ge'ometra *nmf* surveyor

geome'tria *nf* geometry

geometrica'mente *adv* geometrically

geo'metrico *adj* geometric[al]

geopo'litico *adj* geopolitical

Ge'orgia *nf* Georgia

geo'termico *adj* geothermal, geothermic

ge'ranio *nm* geranium

gerar'chia *nf* hierarchy

gerarchica'mente *adv* hierarchically

ge'rarchico *adj* hierarchic[al]

ger'billo *nm* gerbil

ge'rente ⓵ *nm* manager ⓶ *nf* manageress

'gergo *nm* jargon; (dei giovani) slang
■ **gergo burocratico** bureaucratic jargon

geri'atra¹ *nmf* geriatrician

geria'tria² *nf* geriatrics *sg*

geri'atrico *adj* geriatric

'gerla *nf* wicker basket

Ger'mania *nf* Germany
■ **Germania [dell']Est** East Germany; **Germania [dell']Ovest** West Germany

ger'manico *adj* Germanic

'germe *nm* germ; fig (principio) seed
■ **germe di grano** wheat germ

germogli'are *vi* sprout

ger'moglio *nm* sprout; **in ~** Bot sprouting; **germogli** *pl* **di soia** beansprouts

gero'glifico *nm* hieroglyph; **geroglifici** *pl* hieroglyphics

geron'tologo, -a *nmf* gerontologist

ge'rundio *nm* gerund

Gerusa'lemme *nf* Jerusalem

ges'setto *nm* chalk

'gesso *nm* chalk; Med (scultura) plaster

ge'staccio *nm* ≈V-sign

gestazi'one *nf* gestation

gestico'lare *vi* gesticulate

gestio'nale *adj* management *attrib*

gesti'one *nf* management
■ **gestione aziendale** business management; **gestione dei dati** Comput data management; **gestione disco** Comput disk management; **gestione dell'energia** energy resource management; **gestione del flusso di cassa**

ꞏ⸰ indicates a very frequent word

cashflow management; **gestione patrimoniale** financial management

ge'stire *vi* manage; ∼ **male** mishandle

ge'stirsi *vr* budget one's time and money

✧ **'gesto** *nm* gesture (*pl f* **gesta**) (*azione*) deed

ge'store *nm* manager

Gesù *nm* Jesus
■ **Gesù bambino** baby Jesus

gesu'ita *nm* Jesuit

gesu'itico *adj* Jesuit *attrib*

✧ **get'tare** *vt* throw; (*scagliare*) fling; (*emettere*) spout; Techn fig cast; ∼ **via** throw away

get'tarsi *vr* throw oneself; ∼ **in** ‹fiume› flow into

get'tata *nf* throw; Techn casting

'gettito *nm*
■ **gettito fiscale** tax revenue

'getto *nm* throw; (*di liquidi, gas*) jet; **a** ∼ **continuo** in a continuous stream; **di** ∼ straight off

getto'nato *adj* ‹canzone› popular

get'tone *nm* token; (*per giochi*) counter; **a** ∼ coin operated

gettoni'era *nf* coin box

'geyser *nm inv* geyser

'Ghana *nm* Ghana

ghe'pardo *nm* cheetah

'gheppio *nm* kestrel

gher'mire *vt* grasp

'ghette *nfpl* (*per neonato*) leggings

ghettiz'zare *vt* ghettoize

'ghetto *nm* ghetto

ghiacci'aia *nf* glacier

ghiacci'aio *nm* glacier

ghiacci'are *vt/i* freeze

ghiacci'ato *adj* frozen; (*freddissimo*) ice-cold

✧ **ghi'accio** *nm* ice; Auto black ice
■ **ghiaccio secco** dry ice

ghiacci'olo *nm* icicle; (*gelato*) ice lolly

ghi'aia *nf* gravel

ghiai'oso *adj* gritty

ghi'anda *nf* acorn

ghian'daia *nf* jay

ghi'andola *nf* gland
■ **ghiandola pituitaria** pituitary gland; **ghiandola sudoripara** sweat gland; **ghiandola surrenale** adrenal gland

ghigliot'tina *nf* guillotine

ghi'gnare *vi* sneer

'ghigno *nm* sneer

ghi'otto *adj* greedy, gluttonous; (*appetitoso*) appetizing

ghiot'tone, -a *nmf* glutton

ghiottone'ria *nf* (*caratteristica*) gluttony; (*cibo*) tasty morsel

ghiri'goro *nm* flourish

ghir'landa *nf* (*corona*) wreath; (*di fiori*) garland

'ghiro *nm* dormouse; **dormire come un** ∼ sleep like a log

'ghisa *nf* cast iron

✧ **già** *adv* already; (*un tempo*) formerly; ∼**!** indeed!; ∼ **da ieri** since yesterday

✧ **gi'acca** *nf* jacket
■ **giacca a vento** windcheater

giacché *conj* since

giac'cone *nm* jacket

gia'cenza *nf* **giacenze** *pl* **di magazzino** unsold stock

gia'cere *vi* lie

giaci'mento *nm* deposit
■ **giacimento di petrolio** oil deposit

gia'cinto *nm* hyacinth

gi'ada *nf* jade

giaggi'olo *nm* iris

giagu'aro *nm* jaguar

gial'lastro *adj* yellowish

✧ **gi'allo** *adj* & *nm* yellow; [libro] **giallo** crime novel; [film] **giallo** thriller
■ **giallo dell'uovo** egg yolk

Gia'maica *nf* Jamaica

giamai'cano, -a *adj* & *nmf* Jamaican

gian'duia *nm inv* soft hazelnut chocolate typical of Piedmont

Giap'pone *nm* Japan

giappo'nese *adj* & *nmf* Japanese

gi'ara *nf* jar

giardi'naggio *nm* gardening

giardini'ere, -a ① *nmf* gardener ② *nf* Auto estate car
■ **giardiniera di verdure** *diced, mixed vegetables, cooked and pickled*

✧ **giar'dino** *nm* garden
■ **giardino d'infanzia** kindergarten; **giardino pensile** roof-garden; **giardini** *pl* **pubblici** park; **giardino zoologico** zoo

giarretti'era *nf* garter

Gi'ava *nf* Java

giavel'lotto *nm* javelin

Gi'buti *nf* Djibouti

gi'gante *nm* giant

gigan'tesco *adj* gigantic

gigantogra'fia *nf* blow-up

'giglio *nm* lily

gilè *nm inv* waistcoat

gin *nm inv* gin

gin'cana *nf* gymkhana

ginecolo'gia *nf* gynaecology

gineco'logico *adj* gynaecological

gine'cologo, -a *nmf* gynaecologist

gi'nepro *nm* juniper

gi'nestra *nf* broom

Gi'nevra *nf* Geneva

gingil'larsi *vr* fiddle; (perder tempo) potter

gin'gillo *nm* plaything; (ninnolo) knick-knack

gin'nasio *nm* (scuola) grammar school

gin'nasta *nmf* gymnast

gin'nastica *nf* gymnastics *sg*; (esercizi) exercises *pl*
■ ginnastica ritmica eurhythmics

ginocchi'ata *nf* prendere una ~ bang one's knee

ginocchi'era *nf* knee-pad

◆ **gi'nocchio** *nm* (*pl m* **ginocchi** *o f* **ginocchia**) knee; in ~ on one's knees, kneeling; **mettersi in** ~ kneel down; (per supplicare) go down on one's knees; **al** ~ ‹gonna› knee-length

ginocchi'oni *adv* kneeling

◆ **gio'care** *vt/i* play; (giocherellare) toy; (d'azzardo) gamble; (puntare) stake; (ingannare) trick; ~ **a calcio/a pallavolo** play football/volleyball; ~ **d'astuzia** be crafty; ~ **d'azzardo** gambling; ~ **in Borsa** speculate on the Stock Exchange; ~ **in casa** Sport *fig* play at home

gio'carsi *vr* ~ **la carriera** throw one's career away

gioca|'tore, -trice *nmf* player; (d'azzardo) gambler

gio'cattolo *nm* toy

giocherel'lare *vi* toy; (nervosamente) fiddle

giocherel'lone *adj* skittish

◆ **gi'oco** *nm* game; (di bambini, Techn) play; (d'azzardo) gambling; (scherzo) joke; (insieme di pezzi ecc) set; **essere in** ~ be at stake; **fare il doppio** ~ **con qualcuno** double-cross somebody; **è un** ~ **da ragazzi** *fam* it's a cinch
■ gioco elettronico computer game; giochi *pl* della gioventù nation-wide sports tournament for children; gioco dell'oca snakes and ladders; Giochi *pl* Olimpici Olympic Games; giochi *pl* online on-line gaming; gioco di parole play on words; gioco di pazienza game of manual skill; gioco di prestigio conjuring trick; gioco di società board game

giocoli'ere *nm* juggler

gio'coso *adj* playful

gi'ogo *nm* yoke

◆ **gi'oia** *nf* joy; (gioiello) jewel; (appellativo) sweetie

gioielle'ria *nf* jeweller's [shop]

gioi'elli *nmpl* jewellery

gioielli'ere, -a *nmf* jeweller; (negozio) jeweller's

gioi'ello *nm* jewel

gioiosa'mente *adv* joyfully

gioi'oso *adj* joyful

gioi're *vi* ~ **per** rejoice at

Gior'dania *nf* Jordan

gior'dano, -a *adj & nmf* Jordanian

giorna'laio, -a *nmf* newsagent, newsdealer

◆ **gior'nale** *nm* [news]paper; (diario) journal
■ giornale di bordo logbook; giornale gratuito freebie; giornale del mattino morning paper; giornale radio radio news; giornale della sera evening paper

giornali'ero ❶ *adj* daily
❷ *nm* (per sciare) day pass

giorna'lino *nm* comic

giorna'lismo *nm* journalism

giorna'lista *nmf* journalist

giornal'mente *adv* daily

◆ **gior'nata** *nf* day; **buona** ~! have a good day!; **in** ~ today; **a** ~ ‹essere pagato› on a day-to-day basis; **vivere alla** ~ live from day to day
■ giornata lavorativa working day

◆ **gi'orno** *nm* day; **al** ~ per day; **al** ~ **d'oggi** nowadays; **di** ~ by day; **in pieno** ~ in broad daylight; **un** ~ **sì, un** ~ **no** every other day; ~ **per** ~ day by day
■ giorno di chiusura closing day; giorno delle elezioni polling day; giorno fatidico (importante) D-day; giorno feriale weekday; giorno festivo public holiday; giorno del giudizio Judgement Day; giorno dei morti All Souls' day; giorno di paga payday

gi'ostra *nf* merry-go-round

gio'strarsi *vr* manage

giova'mento *nm* trarre ~ **da** derive benefit from

◆ **gi'ovane** ❶ *adj* young; (giovanile) youthful
❷ *nm* youth; young man; **giovani** *pl* young people
❸ *nf* girl, young woman

giova'nile *adj* youthful; ‹scritto› early

◆ **giova'notto** *nm* young man

gio'vare *vi* ~ **a** be useful to; (far bene a) be good for

gio'varsi *vr* ~ **di** avail oneself of

Gi'ove *nm* Jupiter, Jove

giovedì *nm inv* Thursday; **di** ~ on Thursdays
■ giovedì grasso *last Thursday before Lent*; giovedì santo Maundy Thursday

gioventù *nf* youth; (i giovani) young people *pl*; ~ **bruciata** young drop-outs *pl*

giovi'ale *adj* jovial

giovi'nezza *nf* youth

gi'rabile *adj* ‹assegno› endorsable

gira'dischi *nm inv* record-player

gi'raffa *nf* giraffe; Cinema boom

gira'mondo *nmf inv* globetrotter; **da** ~ globetrotting

gi'randola *nf* (fuoco d'artificio) Catherine wheel; (giocattolo) windmill; (banderuola) weathercock

---

◆ indicates a very frequent word

gi'rare ① *vt* turn; (andare intorno, visitare) go round; Comm endorse; Cinema shoot ② *vi* turn; *⟨aerei, uccelli⟩* circle; (andare in giro) wander; **~ sotto…** Comput run under …; **mi gira la testa** I feel dizzy; **far ~ la testa a qualcuno** make somebody's head spin; **far ~ le scatole a qualcuno** fam drive somebody round the twist; **~ al largo** steer clear

girar'rosto *nm* spit

gi'rarsi *vr* turn [round]

gira'sole *nm* sunflower

gi'rata *nf* turn; Comm endorsement; (in macchina ecc) ride; **fare una ~** (a piedi) go for a walk; (in macchina) go for a ride

gira'volta *nf* spin; fig U-turn

gi'rello *nm* (per bambini) babywalker; Culin topside

gi'revole *adj* revolving; **ponte girevole** swing bridge

gi'rino *nm* tadpole

'giro *nm* turn; (circolo) circle; (percorso) round; (viaggio) tour; (passeggiata) short walk; (in macchina) drive; (in bicicletta) ride; (circolazione di denaro) circulation; **andare a fare un ~** (a piedi) go for a stroll; (in macchina) go for a drive; (in bicicletta) go for a cycle ride; **fare il ~ di** go round; **nel ~ di un mese/anno** within a month/year; **prendere in ~ qualcuno** pull somebody's leg; **sentir dire in ~ qualcosa** hear something on the grapevine; **a ~ di posta** by return mail ▪ **giro d'affari** Comm turnover; **giro in barca** boat trip; **giro guidato** guided tour; **giro [della] manica** armhole; **giri** *pl* **al minuto** revs per minute, rpm; **giro d'onore** lap of honour; **giri** *pl* **di parole** beating about the bush; **giro di pista** lap; **giro di prova** trial lap; **giro turistico** sightseeing tour; **giro vita** waist measurement; **giro di vite** fig clampdown

giro'collo *nm* choker; **a ~** roundneck

gi'rone *nm* round ▪ **girone di andata** first half of the season; **girone di ritorno** second half of the season

gironzo'lare *vi* wander about

giro'tondo *nm* ring-a-ring-o'-roses

girova'gare *vi* wander about

gi'rovago *nm* wanderer

'gita *nf* trip; **andare in ~** go on a trip ▪ **gita didattica** field trip; **gita organizzata** package tour; **gita in pullman** coach trip; **gita scolastica** school trip

gi'tano, -a *nmf* gipsy

gi'tante *nmf* tripper

giù *adv* down; (sotto) below; (dabbasso) downstairs; **a testa in ~** (a capofitto) headlong; **essere ~** (di morale) be down, be depressed; (di salute) be run down; **~ di corda** down; **~ di lì, su per ~** more or less; **non andare ~ a qualcuno** stick in somebody's craw

gi'ubba *nf* jacket; Mil tunic

giub'botto *nm* bomber jacket, jerkin ▪ **giubbotto antiproiettile** bulletproof vest; **giubbotto di pelle** leather jacket; **giubbotto di salvataggio** lifejacket

gi'ubilo *nm* rejoicing

giudi'care *vt* judge; (ritenere) consider

gi'udice *nm* judge ▪ **giudice conciliatore** Justice of the Peace, JP; **giudice di gara** umpire; **giudice di linea** linesman; **giudice di pace** Justice of the Peace, JP

giudizi'ario *adj* legal, judicial

giu'dizio *nm* judg[e]ment; (opinione) opinion; (senno) wisdom; (processo) trial; (sentenza) sentence; **mettere ~** become wise ▪ **giudizio universale** Last Judgement

giudizi'oso *adj* sensible

gi'ugno *nm* June

giugu'lare *nf* jugular

giul'lare *nm* jester

giu'menta *nf* mare

giun'chiglia *nf* jonquil

gi'unco *nm* reed

gi'ungere ① *vi* arrive; **~ a** (riuscire) succeed in; **mi giunge nuovo** it's news to me ② *vt* (unire) join

gi'ungla *nf* jungle ▪ **giungla d'asfalto** concrete jungle

gi'unta *nf* addition; **per ~** in addition ▪ **giunta comunale** district council; **giunta [militare]** [military] junta

gi'unto ① *pp di* GIUNGERE ② *nm* Mech joint ▪ **giunto sferico** ball-and-socket joint

giun'tura *nf* joint

gluo'care, gluoco = GIOCARE, GIOCO

giura'mento *nm* oath; **sotto ~** under oath; **prestare ~** take the oath ▪ **giuramento d'Ippocrate** Hippocratic oath

giu'rare *vt/i* swear

giu'rato, -a ① *adj* sworn ② *nmf* juror

giu'ria *nf* jury

giu'ridico *adj* legal

giurisdizi'one *nf* jurisdiction

giurispru'denza *nf* jurisprudence

giu'rista *nmf* jurist

giu'stezza *nf* justness

giustifi'care *vt* justify

giustifi'carsi *vr* justify oneself; **~ di** *o* **per qualcosa** give an explanation for something

giustificazi'one *nf* justification

giu'stizia *nf* justice; **farsi ~ da sé** take the law into one's own hands

giustizi'are *vt* execute

giustizi'ere *nm* executioner

gi'usto ① *adj* just, fair; (adatto) right; (esatto) exact ····⟶

2 *nm* (uomo retto) just man; (cosa giusta) right
3 *adv* exactly; ∼ **ora** just now

glaci'ale *adj* glacial

gladia'tore *nm* gladiator

gla'diolo *nm* gladiolus

'glassa *nf* Culin icing

glau'coma *nm* glaucoma

🔑 **gli** 1 (def art) *m pl*, the; ▶ IL
2 *pers pron* (a lui) [to] him; (a esso) [to] it; (a loro) [to] them; **non** ∼ **credo** I don't believe him/them

glice'mia *nf* glycaemia

glice'rina *nf* glycerine

'glicine *nm* wisteria

gli'elo *pron* (a lui) to him; (a lei) to her; (a loro) to them; (a Lei, forma di cortesia) to you; ∼ **prestai** I lent it to him/her etc; **gliel'ho chiesto** I've asked him/her etc

glie'ne *pron* (di ciò) of it; ∼ **ho dato un po'** I gave him/her/them/you some [of it]; ∼ **ho parlato** I've talked to him/her etc about it

glis'sare *vi* avoid the issue; ∼ **su qualcosa** skate over something

glo'bale *adj* global; fig overall

globalizzazi'one *nf* globalization

global'mente *adv* globally

'globo *nm* globe
■ **globo oculare** eyeball; **globo terrestre** globe

'globulo *nm* globule; Med corpuscle
■ **globulo bianco** white cell, white corpuscle; **globulo rosso** red cell, red corpuscle

🔑 **'gloria** *nf* glory

glori'arsi *vr* ∼ **di** be proud of

glorifi'care *vt* glorify

gloriosa'mente *adv* gloriously

glori'oso *adj* glorious

'glossa *nf* gloss

glos'sario *nm* glossary

glottolo'gia *nf* linguistics *sg*

glu'cosio *nm* glucose

glutam'mato *nm*
■ **glutammato di sodio** monosodium glutamate

'gluteo *nm* buttock

'gnocchi *nmpl* (di patate) *small flour and potato dumplings*

'gnomo *nm* gnome

'gnorri *nm* **fare lo** ∼ play dumb

goal *nm inv* goal; **fare un** ∼ score *or* get a goal

'gobba *nf* hump

'gobbo, -a 1 *adj* hunchbacked
2 *nmf* hunchback

goc'cetto *nm* pick-me-up

🔑 **'goccia** *nf* drop; (di sudore) bead; **è stata l'ultima** ∼ it was the last straw
■ **goccia di pioggia** raindrop; **goccia di rugiada** dewdrop

goccio'lare *vi* drip

goccio'lio *nm* dripping

🔑 **go'dere** *vi* sl (sessualmente) come; ∼ **di qualcosa** enjoy something, make the most of something

go'dersi *vr* ∼ **qualcosa** enjoy something; **godersela** have a good time

godi'mento *nm* enjoyment

gof'faggine *nf* awkwardness

goffa'mente *adv* awkwardly

'goffo *adj* awkward

go-'kart *nm inv* go-kart

🔑 **'gola** *nf* throat; (ingordigia) gluttony; Geog gorge; (di camino) flue; **avere mal di** ∼ have a sore throat; **far** ∼ **a qualcuno** tempt somebody

go'letta *nf* schooner

golf *nm inv* jersey; Sport golf

gol'fino *nm* jumper

'golfo *nm* gulf

goli'ardico *adj* student *attrib*

golosità *nf inv* greediness; (cibo) tasty morsel

go'loso *adj* greedy

'golpe *nm inv* coup

go'mena *nf* painter

gomi'tata *nf* nudge; **dare una** ∼ **a qualcuno** elbow somebody

'gomito *nm* elbow; **alzare il** ∼ fam (bere) raise one's elbow; ∼ **a** ∼ (lavorare) side by side

go'mitolo *nm* ball

🔑 **'gomma** *nf* rubber; (colla) gum; (pneumatico) tyre; **avere una** ∼ **a terra** have a flat
■ **gomma arabica** gum arabic; **gomma da masticare** chewing gum; **gomma di scorta** spare tyre

gommapi'uma® *nf* foam rubber

gom'mino *nm* rubber tip

gom'mista *nm* tyre specialist

gom'mone *nm* [rubber] dinghy

gom'moso *adj* chewy

'gondola *nf* gondola

gondoli'ere *nm* gondolier

gonfa'lone *nm* banner

gonfi'abile *adj* inflatable

gonfi'are 1 *vi* swell
2 *vt* blow up; pump up ‹pneumatico›; (esagerare) exaggerate

gonfi'arsi *vr* swell; ‹acque› rise

🔑 **'gonfio** *adj* swollen; ‹pneumatico› inflated

gonfi'ore *nm* swelling

gongo'lante *adj* overjoyed

gongo'lare *vi* be overjoyed

goni'ometro *nm* protractor

🔑 **'gonna** *nf* skirt
■ **gonna pantalone** culottes *pl*; **gonna a pieghe** pleated skirt; **gonna a portafoglio** wrapover skirt

---

🔑 indicates a very frequent word

gonor'rea *nf* gonorrh[o]ea

'gonzo *nm* simpleton

gorgheggi'are *vi* warble

gor'gheggio *nm* warble

'gorgo *nm* whirlpool

gorgogli'ante *adj* burbling, gurgling

gorgogli'are *vi* gurgle

gor'goglio *nm* burble

gorgon'zola *nf* strong, soft blue cheese

go'rilla *nm inv* gorilla; (guardia del corpo) bodyguard, minder

'gota *nf* cheek

'gotico *adj & nm* Gothic

'gotta *nf* gout

gover'nante *nf* housekeeper

gover'nare *vt* govern; (dominare) rule; (dirigere) manage; (curare) look after

governa'tivo *adj* government

governa'tore *nm* governor

⚓ **go'verno** *nm* government; (dominio) rule; **al ∼** in power
■ **governo ombra** shadow cabinet

'gozzo *nm* (di animale) crop; Med goitre; fam throat

gozzovigli'are *vi* eat, drink and be merry

gr, GR *nm abbr* (**giornale radio**) radio news

gracchi'are *vi* caw; fig ‹persona› screech

'gracchio *nm* caw

graci'dare *vi* croak

'gracile *adj* delicate

gra'dasso *nm* braggart

gradata'mente *adv* gradually

gradazi'one *nf* gradation
■ **gradazione alcolica** alcohol[ic] content; **a bassa gradazione alcolica** ‹birra› low-alcohol

gra'devole *adj* agreeable

gradevol'mente *adv* pleasantly, agreeably

gradi'ente *nm* gradient

gradi'mento *nm* liking; **indice di gradimento** Radio, TV popularity rating; **non è di mio ∼** it's not to my liking

gradi'nata *nf* flight of steps; (di stadio, teatro) tiers *pl*

gra'dino *nm* step

⚓ **gra'dire** *vt* like; (desiderare) wish

gra'dito *adj* pleasant; (bene accetto) welcome

⚓ **'grado** *nm* degree; (rango) rank; **di buon ∼** willingly; **essere in ∼ di fare qualcosa** be in a position to do something; (essere capace a) be able to do something; **per gradi** ‹procedere› by degrees

gradu'ale *adj* gradual

gradual'mente *adv* gradually

gradu'are *vt* graduate

gradu'ato 1 *adj* graded; (provvisto di scala graduata) graduated

2 *nm* Mil noncommissioned officer

gradua'toria *nf* list

graduazi'one *nf* graduation

'graffa *nf* clip; (segno grafico) brace

graf'fetta *nf* staple

graffi'are *vt* scratch

graffia'tura *nf* scratch

'graffio *nm* scratch

gra'fia *nf* [hand]writing; (ortografia) spelling

'grafica *nf* graphics *sg*; (disciplina) graphics *sg*, graphic design
■ **grafica pubblicitaria** commercial art

grafica'mente *adv* in graphics , graphically

'grafico 1 *adj* graphic
2 *nm* graph; (persona) graphic designer
■ **grafico a torta** pie chart

gra'fite *nf* graphite

gra'fologo, -a *nmf* graphologist

gra'migna *nf* weed

gram'matica *nf* grammar

grammati'cale *adj* grammatical

grammatical'mente *adv* grammatically

gram'matico *nm* grammarian

'grammo *nm* gram[me]

gram'mofono *nm* gramophone

gran ▶ GRANDE

'grana *nf* grain; (formaggio) parmesan; fam (seccatura) trouble; fam (soldi) readies *pl*

gra'naio *nm* barn

gra'nata *nf* Mil grenade; (frutto) pomegranate

granati'ere *nm* Mil grenadier

gra'nato *nm* garnet

Gran Bre'tagna *nf* Great Britain

gran'cassa *nf* bass drum

gran'cevola *nf* spiny spider crab

'granchio *nm* crab; fig (errore) blunder; **prendere un ∼** make a blunder

grandango'lare *nm* wide-angle lens

gran'dangolo *nm* wide-angle lens

⚓ **'grande** 1 (*a volte* **gran**) *adj* (ampio) large; (grosso) big; (alto) tall; (largo) wide; fig (senso morale) great; (grandioso) grand; (adulto) grown-up; **∼ e grosso** beefy; **ho una gran fame** I'm very hungry; **fa un gran caldo** it's very hot; **in ∼** on a large scale; **in gran parte** to a great extent; **non è un gran che** it is nothing much; **di gran carriera** hotfoot; **un gran ballo** a grand ball; **alla ∼** sl in a big way
2 *nmf* (persona adulta) grown-up; (persona eminente) great man/woman

grandeggi'are *vi* **∼ su** tower over; (darsi arie) show off

gran'dezza *nf* greatness; (ampiezza) largeness; (larghezza) width, breadth;

⋯∴

(dimensione) size; (fasto) grandeur; (prodigalità) lavishness; **a ~ naturale** life-size

grandi'nare *vi* hail; **grandina** it's hailing

'grandine *nf* hail

grandiosità *nf* grandeur

grandi'oso *adj* grand

gran'duca *nm* grand duke

grandu'cato *nm* grand duchy

grandu'chessa *nf* grand duchess

gra'nello *nm* grain; (di frutta) pip

gra'nita *nf crushed ice drink*

gra'nito *nm* granite

✧ **'grano** *nm* grain; (frumento) wheat
■ **grano di pepe** peppercorn; **grano saraceno** buckwheat

gran[o]'turco *nm* corn

'granulo *nm* granule

'grappa *nf very strong, clear spirit distilled from grapes*; (morsa) cramp

'grappolo *nm* bunch
■ **grappolo d'uva** bunch of grapes

gras'setto *nm* bold [type]

gras'sezza *nf* fatness; (untuosità) greasiness

'grasso [1] *adj* fat; ‹cibo› fatty; (unto) greasy; ‹terreno› rich; (grossolano) coarse [2] *nm* fat; (sostanza) grease; **a basso contenuto di grassi** low-fat; **senza grassi** nonfat, fat-free

gras'soccio *adj* plump

gras'sone, -a *nmf* dumpling

'grata *nf* grating

gra'tella *nf* Culin grill

gra'ticcio *nm* (per piante) trellis; (stuoia) rush matting

gra'ticola *nf* Culin grill

gra'tifica *nf* bonus

gratificazi'one *nf* satisfaction

gra'tin *nm inv* gratin
■ **gratin di patate** potatoes with grated cheese

grati'nare *vt* cook au gratin

grati'nato *adj* au gratin

'gratis *adv* free

grati'tudine *nf* gratitude

'grato *adj* grateful; (gradito) pleasant

gratta'capo *nm* trouble

grattaci'elo *nm* skyscraper

'gratta e 'vinci *nm inv* scratch card

grat'tare [1] *vt* scratch; (raschiare) scrape; (grattugiare) grate; fam (rubare) pinch [2] *vi* grate

grat'tarsi *vr* scratch oneself

grat'tugia *nf* grater

grattugi'are *vt* grate

gratuita'mente *adv* free [of charge]

gra'tuito *adj* free [of charge]; (ingiustificato) gratuitous

✧ indicates a very frequent word

gra'vare [1] *vt* burden [2] *vi* **~ su** weigh on

✧ **'grave** *adj* (pesante) heavy; (serio) serious; (difficile) hard; ‹voce, suono› low; (fonetica) grave; **essere ~** (gravemente ammalato) be seriously ill

grave'mente *adv* seriously, gravely

gravi'danza *nf* pregnancy
■ **gravidanza extrauterina** ectopic pregnancy; **gravidanza indesiderata** unwanted pregnancy

'gravido *adj* pregnant

gravità *nf* seriousness; Phys gravity

gravi'tare *vi* gravitate

gra'voso *adj* onerous

✧ **'grazia** *nf* grace; (favore) favour; Jur pardon; **entrare nelle grazie di qualcuno** get into somebody's good books; **ministero di grazia e giustizia** Ministry of Justice

grazi'are *vt* pardon

'grazie *int* thank you!, thanks!; **~ mille!** many thanks!, thanks a lot!; **~ a Dio/al cielo!** thank God/goodness!; **~ a** thanks to

grazi'oso *adj* charming; (carino) pretty

'Grecia *nf* Greece

✧ **'greco, -a** *adj & nmf* Greek
■ **greco antico** (lingua) classical Greek

gre'gario [1] *adj* gregarious [2] *nm* (ciclismo) supporting rider

'gregge *nm* flock

'greggio [1] *adj* raw [2] *nm* (petrolio) crude [oil]

grembi'ale, **grembiule** *nm* apron

'grembo *nm* lap; (utero) womb; fig bosom

gre'mire *vt* pack

gre'mirsi *vr* become crowded (**di** with)

gre'mito *adj* packed

'gretto *adj* stingy; (di vedute ristrette) narrow-minded

'greve *adj* heavy

'grezzo *adj* = GREGGIO

✧ **gri'dare** [1] *vi* shout; (di dolore) scream; ‹animale› cry [2] *vt* shout; **~ qualcosa ai quattro venti** shout something from the rooftops

✧ **'grido** *nm* (*pl m* **gridi** *o pl f* **grida**) shout, cry; (di animale) cry; **all'ultimo ~** the latest fashion; **scrittore di ~** celebrated writer
■ **grido d'aiuto** cry for help; **grido di battaglia** battle cry

✧ **'grigio** *adj & nm* grey
■ **grigio perla** pearl grey

'griglia *nf* grill; **alla ~** grilled; **cuocere alla ~** grill

grigli'ata *nf* barbecue
■ **grigliata mista** mixed grill; **grigliata di pesce** grilled fish

gril'letto *nm* trigger

'grillo *nm* cricket; fig (capriccio) whim

grimal'dello *nm* picklock

'grinfia *nf* fig clutch

'grinta *nf* grit

grin'toso *adj* determined

'grinza *nf* wrinkle; (di stoffa) crease; **non fare una** ∼ fig ‹*ragionamento*› be flawless

grip'pare *vi* Mech seize up

gri'sou *nm* firedamp

gris'sino *nm* bread-stick

'grizzly *nm inv* grizzly

groenlan'dese ① *adj* of Greenland ② *nmf* Greenlander

Groen'landia *nf* Greenland

'groggy *adj inv* punch-drunk

'gronda *nf* eaves *pl*

gron'daia *nf* gutter

gron'dare *vi* pour; (essere bagnato fradicio) be dripping wet

'groppa *nf* back

'groppo *nm* knot; **avere un** ∼ **alla gola** have a lump in one's throat

gros'sezza *nf* size; (spessore) thickness

gros'sista *nmf* wholesaler

'grosso ① *adj* big, large; (spesso) thick; (grossolano) coarse; (grave) serious ② *nm* big part; (massa) bulk; **farla grossa** do a stupid thing

grossolanità *nf inv* (qualità) coarseness; (di errore) grossness; (gesto) boorishness

grosso'lano *adj* coarse; ‹*errore*› gross; ‹*comportamento*› boorish

grosso'modo *adv* roughly

'grotta *nf* cave, grotto

grot'tesco *adj & nm* grotesque

grovi'era *nmf* Gruyère

gro'viglio *nm* tangle; fig muddle

gru *nf inv* (uccello, edilizia) crane

'gruccia *nf* (stampella) crutch; (per vestito) hanger
■ **gruccia appendiabiti** clotheshanger

grufo'lare *vi* root

gru'gnire *vi* grunt

gru'gnito *nm* grunt

'grugno *nm* snout

'grullo *adj* silly

'grumo *nm* clot; (di farina ecc) lump

gru'moso *adj* lumpy

grunge *nm inv* grunge

'gruppo *nm* group; (comitiva) party
■ **gruppo d'azione** action group; **gruppo pop** pop group; **gruppo sanguigno** blood group; **gruppo di sostegno** support group; **gruppo di utenti** user group

gruvi'era *nmf* = GROVIERA

'gruzzolo *nm* nest-egg

guada'gnare *vt* earn; gain ‹*tempo, forza ecc*›

guada'gnarsi *vr* ∼ **da vivere** earn a living

gua'dagno *nm* gain; (profitto) profit; (entrate) earnings *pl*; **guadagni** *pl* **illeciti** ill-gotten gains

gu'ado *nm* ford; **passare a** ∼ ford

gua'ina *nf* sheath; (busto) girdle

gu'aio *nm* trouble; **che** ∼**!** that's just brilliant!; **essere nei guai** be in a fix; **guai a te se lo tocchi!** don't you dare touch it!

gua'ire *vi* yelp

gua'ito *nm* yelp; **guaiti** *pl* yelping

gu'ancia *nf* cheek

guanci'ale *nm* pillow

gu'anto *nm* glove
■ **guanto da forno** oven glove; **guanto di spugna** face cloth

guan'tone *nm* mitt; **guantoni** *pl* **[da boxe]** boxing gloves

guarda'boschi *nm inv* forester

guarda'caccia *nm inv* gamekeeper

guarda'coste *nm inv* coastguard

guarda'linee *nm inv* Sport linesman

guarda'macchine *nmf* car-park attendant

guarda'parco *nm inv* park ranger

guar'dare ① *vt* look at; (osservare) watch; (badare a) look after; ‹*finestra*› look out on; ∼ **la televisione** watch television ② *vi* look; (essere orientato verso) face; ∼ **in su** look up

guarda'roba *nm inv* wardrobe; (di locale pubblico) cloakroom

guardarobi'ere, -a *nmf* cloakroom attendant

guar'darsi *vr* look at oneself: ∼ **da** beware of; (astenersi) refrain from

gu'ardia *nf* guard; (poliziotto) policeman; (vigilanza) watch; **essere di** ∼ be on guard; ‹*medico*› be on duty; **fare la** ∼ **a** keep guard over; **mettere in** ∼ **qualcuno** warn somebody; **stare in** ∼ be on one's guard
■ **guardia carceraria** prison warder, prison officer; **guardia del corpo** bodyguard, minder; **Guardia di finanza** *body of police officers responsible for border control and for investigating fraud*; **guardia forestale** forest ranger; **guardia medica** duty doctor

guardi'ano, -a *nmf* caretaker
■ **guardiano notturno** night watchman; **guardiano dello zoo** zoo keeper

guar'dingo *adj* cautious

guardi'ola *nf* gatekeeper's lodge

guarigi'one *nf* recovery

gua'rire ① *vt* cure ② *vi* recover; ‹*ferita*› heal [up]

gua'rito *adj* cured

guari|'tore, -trice *nmf* healer

guarnigi'one *nf* garrison

guar'nire *vt* trim; Culin garnish

guarnizi'one *nf* trimming; Culin garnish; Mech gasket
- guarnizione del freno brake lining

guasta'feste *nmf inv* spoilsport

gua'stare *vt* spoil; (rovinare) ruin; break ‹*meccanismo*›

gua'starsi *vr* spoil; (andare a male) go bad; ‹*tempo*› change for the worse; ‹*meccanismo*› break down

⚜ **gu'asto** ⓵ *adj* broken; ‹*ascensore, telefono*› out of order; ‹*auto*› broken down; ‹*cibo, dente*› bad
  ⓶ *nm* breakdown; (danno) damage; **ho un ~ alla macchina** my car's not working
- guasto al motore engine failure

Guate'mala *nm* Guatemala

guazza'buglio *nm* muddle

guaz'zare *vi* wallow

gu'ercio *adj* cross-eyed

⚜ **gu'erra** *nf* war; (tecnica bellica) warfare; **la grande ~** the Great War, World War I
- guerra batteriologica germ warfare; guerra biologica biological warfare; guerra civile civil war; guerra fredda Cold War; guerra del Golfo Gulf War; guerra lampo blitzkrieg; guerra mondiale world war; prima guerra mondiale World War I, WW1; seconda guerra mondiale World War II, WW2; guerra dei prezzi price war; guerra di secessione American Civil War

guerrafon'daio, -a *nmf* warmonger

guerreggi'are *vi* wage war

guer'resco *adj* (di guerra) war; (bellicoso) warlike

guerri'ero *nm* warrior

guer'riglia *nf* guerrilla warfare

guerrigli'ero, -a *nmf* guerrilla

'gufo *nm* owl

'guglia *nf* spire

⚜ **gu'ida** *nf* guide; (direzione) guidance; (comando) leadership; (elenco) directory; Auto driving; (tappeto) runner; **chi era alla ~?** who was driving?; **essere alla ~ di** fig be the head of; **fare da ~** be a guide (**a** to)
- guida commerciale trade directory; guida a destra right-hand drive; guida a sinistra left-hand drive; guida telefonica phone book, telephone directory; guida turistica tourist guide

⚜ **gui'dare** *vt* guide; Auto drive; steer ‹*nave*›; **~ a passo d'uomo** drive at walking speed

guida'tore, -trice *nmf* driver
- guidatore della domenica Sunday driver

Gui'nea *nf* Guinea

Gui'nea-Bis'sau *nf* Guinea-Bissau

Gui'nea Equato'riale *nf* Equatorial Guinea

guin'zaglio *nm* leash

gu'isa *nf* **a ~ di** like

guiz'zare *vi* dart; ‹*luce*› flash

gu'izzo *nm* dart; (di luce) flash

'gulag *nm inv* Gulag

'gulasch *nm inv* goulash

'guru *nm inv* high priest

'guscio *nm* shell; (di cellulare) fascia

gu'stare ⓵ *vt* taste
  ⓶ *vi* like

⚜ **'gusto** *nm* taste; (piacere) liking; **mangiare di ~** eat heartily; **prenderci ~** come to enjoy it, develop a taste for it; **al ~ di pistacchio** pistachio flavoured; **buon ~** good taste

gu'stoso *adj* tasty; fig delightful

guttu'rale *adj* guttural

Gu'yana *nf* Guyana

H h

'habitat *nm inv* habitat

habitué *nmf inv* regular [customer]

'hacker *nmf inv* Comput hacker

Ha'iti *nf* Haiti

haiti'ano, -a *adj & nmf* Haitian

'halal *adj* halal

hall *nf inv* foyer; (di stazione) concourse

ham'burger *nm inv* hamburger
- hamburger vegetariano veggie burger

'handicap *nm inv* handicap

handicap'pare *vt* handicap

handicap'pato, -a ⓵ *adj* disabled

  ⓶ *nmf* disabled person
- ~ mentale mentally handicapped person

'hangar *nm inv* hangar

'hard[-core] *adj* hard core

hard 'disk *nm inv* hard disk

hard 'rock *nm inv* hard rock

'hardware *nm inv* Comput hardware

'harem *nm inv* harem

'hashish *nm* hashish

hawa'iano, -a *adj & nmf* Hawaiian

'Hawaii *nfpl* **le ~** Hawaii

'heavy metal *nm* Mus heavy metal

henné *nm* henna

⚜ indicates a very frequent word

'herpes *nm inv* herpes; (su labbra) cold sore
■ **herpes zoster** shingles
'hi-fi *nm inv* hi-fi
high 'tech *nf* high tech
'Himalaia *nm* Himalayas *pl*
'hinterland *nm inv* hinterland
'hippy *adj & nmf inv* hippy
'hit parade *nf* hit parade, charts *pl*
HIV *nm* HIV
'hockey *nm* hockey

■ **hockey su ghiaccio** ice hockey; **hockey su prato** field hockey
'holding *nf inv* holding company
hollywoo'diano *adj* Hollywood
Hong 'Kong *nf* Hong Kong
'hostess *nf inv* (air) stewardess
hot 'dog *nm inv* hot dog
'hotel *nm inv* hotel
'humus *nm* humus

Ii

i *def art mpl* the; ▶ **IL**
i'ato *nm* hiatus
i'berico *adj* Iberian
Iber'nare *vt* hibernate
ibernazi'one *nf* hibernation
i'bisco *nm* hibiscus
Ibri'dare *vt* interbreed
ibridazi'one *nf* interbreeding
'ibrido *adj & nm* hybrid
'iceberg *nm inv* iceberg; **la punta dell'~** *fig* the tip of the iceberg
i'cona *nf* icon
iconiz'zare *vt* iconize
icono'clasta *adj & nmf* iconoclast
icono'clastico *adj* iconoclastic
id'dio *nm* God
⚜ **l'dea** *nf* idea; (opinione) opinion; (ideale) ideal; (indizio) inkling; (piccola quantità) hint; (intenzione) intention; **cambiare ~** change one's mind; **neanche per ~!** not on your life!; **chiarirsi le idee** get one's ideas straight; **dare l'~ di …** give the impression that …; **essere dell'~ che …** be of the opinion that …; **non ne ho ~!** I've no idea!
■ **idea fissa** obsession
⚜ **ide'ale** *adj & nm* ideal
idea'lista *nmf* idealist
idealiz'zare *vt* idealize
ide'are *vt* conceive
idea|'tore, -trice *nmf* originator
'idem *adv* the same
identica'mente *adv* identically
i'dentico *adj* identical
identifi'cabile *adj* identifiable
identifi'care *vt* identify
identifica'tivo *nm*
■ **identificativo del chiamante** caller identification
identificazi'one *nf* identification
identi'kit® *nm inv* identikit

■ **identikit elettronico** e-fit
identità *nf inv* identity
ideo'gramma *nm* ideogram
ideolo'gia *nf* ideology
ideologica'mente *adv* ideologically
ideo'logico *adj* ideological
idillica'mente *adv* idyllically
i'dillico *adj* idyllic
i'dillio *nm* idyll
idi'oma *nm* language
idio'matico *adj* idiomatic; **espressione idiomatica** idiom, idiomatic expression
idiosincra'sia *nf* *fig* aversion; Med allergy
idi'ota ① *adj* idiotic
② *nmf* idiot
idio'zia *nf* idiocy; **dire/fare un'~** do/say something stupid; **dire idiozie** talk nonsense; **non fare idiozie!** don't act daft!
idola'trare *vt* worship
idoleggi'are *vt* idolize
'idolo *nm* idol
idoneità *nf* suitability; Mil fitness; **esame di idoneità** qualifying examination
i'doneo *adj* **~ a** suitable for; Mil fit for
i'drante *nm* hydrant; (tubo) hose; (usato dalla polizia) water cannon
idra'tante *adj* ‹crema› moisturizing
idra'tare *vt* hydrate; ‹cosmetico› moisturize
idratazi'one *nf* moisturizing
i'draulico ① *adj* hydraulic
② *nm* plumber
'idrico *adj* water *attrib*
idrocar'buro *nm* hydrocarbon
idroelettricità *nf* hydroelectricity
idroe'lettrico *adj* hydroelectric
i'drofilo *adj* **cotone ~** cotton wool, absorbent cotton Am
idrofo'bia *nf* rabies *sg*
i'drofobo *adj* rabid; fig furious

i'drofugo adj water-repellent

i'drogeno nm hydrogen

idrogra'fia nf hydrography

i'drolisi nf hydrolysis

idromas'saggio nm (sistema) whirlpool bath; **vasca con** ~ jacuzzi®

idro'mele nm mead

idrorepel'lente adj & nm water-repellent

idroso'lubile adj water-soluble

idrotera'pia nf hydrotherapy

idrovo'lante nm seaplane

i'druro nm hydride

i'ella nf fam bad luck; **portare** ~ be bad luck

iel'lato adj fam jinxed, plagued by bad luck

i'ena nf hyena

◆ **i'eri** adv yesterday; ~ **l'altro, l'altro** ~ the day before yesterday; **il giornale di** ~ yesterday's paper; ~ **mattina** yesterday morning

ietta|'tore, -trice nmf jinx

ietta'tura nf (sfortuna) bad luck

igi'ene nf hygiene; **ufficio d'igiene** ≈ Public Health Service
- **igiene mentale** mental health; **igiene personale** personal hygiene; **igiene pubblica** public health

igienica'mente adv hygienically

igi'enico adj hygienic

igie'nista nmf hygienist

ig'loo nm inv igloo

i'gname nm yam

i'gnaro adj unaware

i'gnifugo adj flame-retardant, fire-retardant

i'gnobile adj despicable

ignobil'mente adv despicably

igno'minia nf disgrace

igno'rante [1] adj ignorant [2] nmf ignoramus

igno'ranza nf ignorance; **ignoranza crassa** crass ignorance

igno'rare vt (non sapere) be unaware of; (trascurare) ignore; **essere ignorato** go unheeded

i'gnoto adj unknown

i'guana nf iguana

◆ **il** def art m, the; **il latte fa bene** milk is good for you; **il signor Magnetti** Mr Magnetti; **il dottor Piazza** Doctor Piazza; **ha il naso grosso** he's got a big nose; **ha gli occhi azzurri** he's got blue eyes; **mettiti il cappello** put your hat on; **il lunedì** on Mondays; **il 2010** 2010; **costa 5 euro il chilo** it costs 5 euros a kilo

'ilare adj merry

ilarità nf hilarity

---

i'leo nm hipbone

illangui'dire vi grow weak

illazi'one nf inference

illecita'mente adv illicitly

il'lecito adj illicit

ille'gale adj illegal

illegalità nf illegality

illegal'mente adv illegally

illeg'gibile adj illegible; ‹libro› unreadable

illegittimità nf illegitimacy

ille'gittimo adj illegitimate

il'leso adj unhurt, uninjured

illette'rato, -a adj & nmf illiterate

illi'bato adj chaste

illimita'mente adv indefinitely

illimi'tato adj unlimited

illivi'dire [1] vt bruise [2] vi (per rabbia) turn livid

illogica'mente adv illogically

il'logico adj illogical

◆ **il'ludere** vt deceive

il'ludersi vr deceive oneself

◆ **illumi'nare** vt light up; fig enlighten; ~ **a giorno** floodlight

illumi'narsi vr light up

illuminazi'one nf lighting; fig enlightenment
- **illuminazione a gas** gas lighting; **illuminazione al neon** strip lighting

Illumi'nismo nm Enlightenment

◆ **illusi'one** nf illusion; **farsi illusioni** delude oneself
- **illusione ottica** optical illusion

illusio'nismo nm conjuring

illusio'nista nmf conjurer

il'luso, -a [1] pp di ILLUDERE [2] adj deluded [3] nmf day-dreamer

illu'sorio adj illusory

illu'strare vt illustrate

illustra'tivo adj illustrative

illustra|'tore, -trice nmf illustrator

illustrazi'one nf illustration
- **illustrazione a colori/in bianco e nero** colour/black and white illustration

il'lustre adj distinguished

imbacuc'care vt wrap up

imbacuc'carsi vr wrap up

imbacuc'cato adj wrapped up

imbal'laggio nm packing

imbal'lare vt pack; Auto race

imballa|'tore, -trice nmf packer

imbalsa'mare vt embalm; stuff ‹animale›

imbalsa'mato adj embalmed; ‹animale› stuffed

imbambo'lato adj vacant

imban'dito adj ‹tavola› covered with food

imbaraz'zante adj embarrassing

---

imbaraz'zare *vt* embarrass; (ostacolare)
encumber

imbaraz'zato *adj* embarrassed

imba'razzo *nm* embarrassment; (ostacolo)
hindrance; **trarre qualcuno d' ∼** help
somebody out of a difficulty; **avere l' ∼ della
scelta** be spoilt for choice

■ **imbarazzo di stomaco** indigestion

imbarba'rire *vt* barbarize

imbarba'rirsi *vr* become barbarized

imbarca'dero *nm* landing-stage

imbar'care *vt* embark; fam (rimorchiare)
score; **∼ acqua** ship water

imbar'carsi *vr* go on board; fig embark
(**in** on)

imbarcazi'one *nf* boat

■ **imbarcazione da pesca** fishing boat;
imbarcazione di salvataggio lifeboat

im'barco *nm* boarding; (banchina) landing-
stage; '**∼ immediato**' 'now boarding'

imbastar'dire *vt* debase

imbastar'dirsi *vr* become debased

imba'stire *vt* tack, baste; fig sketch

imbasti'tura *nf* tacking, basting

im'battersi *vr* **∼ in** run into

imbat'tibile *adj* unbeatable

imbat'tuto *adj* unbeaten

imbavagli'are *vt* gag

imbec'cata *nf* Theat prompt

imbe'cille [1] *adj* stupid
[2] *nmf* Med imbecile

imbellet'tarsi *vr* hum doll oneself up

imbel'lire *vt* embellish

im'berbe *adj* beardless; fig inexperienced

imbestia'lire *vi* fly into a rage; **far ∼
qualcuno** drive somebody crazy

imbestia'lirsi *vr* fly into a rage

imbestia'lito *adj* enraged

im'bevere *vt* imbue (**di** with)

im'beversi *vr* absorb

imbe'vibile *adj* undrinkable

imbe'vuto *adj* **∼ di** ⟨acqua⟩ soaked in;
⟨nozioni⟩ imbued with

imbian'care [1] *vt* whiten
[2] *vi* turn white

imbian'chino *nm* [house] painter

imbion'dire [1] *vt* bleach
[2] *vi* become bleached

imbion'dirsi *vr* become bleached

imbizzar'rire *vr* become restless;
(arrabbiarsi) become angry

imbizzar'rirsi *vi* become restless;
(arrabbiarsi) become angry

imboc'care *vt* feed; (entrare) enter; fig
prompt

imbocca'tura *nf* opening; (ingresso)
entrance; Mus (di strumento) mouthpiece

im'bocco *nm* entrance

imboni'mento *nm* spiel

imboni'tore *nm* clever talker

imborghe'sire *vi* become middle class

imborghe'sirsi *vr* become middle class

imbo'scare *vt* hide

imbo'scarsi *vr* Mil shirk military service

imbo'scata *nf* ambush

imbo'scato *nm* draft dodger

imbottiglia'mento *nm* traffic jam

imbottigli'are *vt* bottle

imbottigli'arsi *vr* get snarled up in a
traffic jam

imbottigli'ato *adj* (vino, acqua) bottled;
⟨auto⟩ stuck in a traffic jam, snarled up; **nave
imbottigliata** ship in a bottle

imbot'tire *vt* stuff; pad ⟨giacca⟩; Culin fill

imbot'tirsi *vr* **∼ di** fig (di pasticche) stuff
oneself with

imbot'tita *nf* quilt

imbot'tito *adj* ⟨spalle⟩ padded; ⟨cuscino⟩
stuffed; ⟨panino⟩ filled

imbotti'tura *nf* stuffing; (di giacca)
padding; Culin filling

imbraca'tura *nf* harness

imbracci'are *vt* shoulder ⟨fucile⟩; grasp
⟨scudo⟩

imbra'nato *adj* clumsy

imbrat'tare *vt* mark

imbrat'tarsi *vr* dirty oneself

imbrigli'are *vt* bridle ⟨cavallo⟩; dam
⟨acque⟩

imbroc'care *vt* hit; **imbroccarla giusta** hit
the nail on the head

imbrogli'are *vt* muddle; (raggirare) cheat;
∼ le carte fig confuse the issue

imbrogli'arsi *vr* get tangled; (confondersi)
get confused

im'broglio *nm* tangle; (pasticcio) mess;
(inganno) trick

imbrogli'one, -a *nmf* cheat

imbronci'are *vi* sulk

imbronci'arsi *vr* sulk

imbronci'ato *adj* sulky

imbru'nire *vi* get dark; **all'∼** at dusk

imbrut'tire [1] *vt* make ugly
[2] *vi* become ugly

imbu'care *vt* post, mail; (nel biliardo) pot

imbu'cato *adj* fam **è ∼** he only got the job
because of who he knows

imbufa'lirsi *vr* hit the roof

imbur'rare *vt* butter

im'buto *nm* funnel

i'mene *nm* hymen

imi'tare *vt* imitate

imita|'tore, -trice *nmf* imitator,
impersonator

imitazi'one *nf* imitation; '**diffidare delle
imitazioni**' 'beware of imitations'

immaco'lato *adj* spotless, immaculate; **l'immacolata Concezione** the Immaculate Conception

immagazzi'nare *vt* store

ꚍ **immagi'nare** *vt* imagine; (supporre) suppose; (formula di cortesia) **s'immagini!** don't mention it!

immagi'nario *adj* imaginary

immaginazi'one *nf* imagination; **è frutto della tua ~** it's a figment of your imagination

ꚍ **im'magine** *nf* image; (rappresentazione, idea) picture
- **immagine aziendale** corporate image; **immagine della marca** brand image; **immagine speculare** mirror image

immagi'noso *adj* full of imagery

immalinco'nire *vt* sadden

immalinco'nirsi *vr* grow melancholy

imman'cabile *adj* unfailing

immancabil'mente *adv* without fail

im'mane *adj* huge; (orribile) terrible

imma'nente *adj* immanent

immangi'abile *adj* inedible

immatrico'lare *vt* register

immatrico'larsi *vr* ⟨studente⟩ matriculate

immatrico'lato *adj* registered

immatricolazi'one *nf* registration; (di studente) matriculation

immaturità *nf* immaturity

imma'turo *adj* unripe; ⟨persona⟩ immature; (precoce) premature

immedesi'marsi *vr* **~ in** identify oneself with

immedesimazi'one *nf* identification

immediata'mente *adv* immediately

immedia'tezza *nf* immediacy

immedi'ato *adj* immediate; **nell'~ futuro** in the immediate future

immemo'rabile *adj* immemorial

im'memore *adj* oblivious

immensa'mente *adv* enormously

immensità *nf* immensity

ꚍ **im'menso** *adj* immense

immensu'rabile *adj* immeasurable

ꚍ **im'mergere** *vt* immerse

im'mergersi *vr* plunge; ⟨sommergibile⟩ dive; **~ in** immerse oneself in

immeritata'mente *adv* undeservedly

immeri'tato *adj* undeserved

immeri'tevole *adj* undeserving

immersi'one *nf* immersion; (di sommergibile, palombaro) dive
- **immersione [subacquea]** skin diving, scuba diving

im'merso *pp di* IMMERGERE

im'mettere *vt* introduce

im'mettersi *vr* introduce oneself

immi'grante *adj* & *nmf* immigrant

immi'grare *vi* immigrate

immi'grato, -a *nmf* immigrant

immigrazi'one *nf* immigration
- **immigrazione interna** migration

immi'nente *adj* imminent

immi'nenza *nf* imminence

immischi'are *vt* involve

immischi'arsi *vr* **~ in** meddle in

immi'scibile *adj* immiscible

immis'sario *nm* tributary

immissi'one *nf* insertion; Techn intake; (introduzione) introduction
- **immissione [di] dati** data entry

im'mobile *adj* motionless

im'mobili *nmpl* real estate

immobili'are *adj* **società ~** building society, savings and loan *Am*

immobilità *nf* immobility

immobiliz'zare *vt* immobilize; *Comm* tie up

immobiliz'zato *adj* immobilized
- **immobilizzato a letto** confined to bed

immobilizza'tore *nm*
- **immobilizzatore elettronico** *Auto* immobilizer

immobilizzazi'one *nf* immobilization; *Fin* fixed asset; **spese d'~** capital expenditure

immoderata'mente *adv* immoderately

immode'rato *adj* immoderate

immo'destia *nf* immodesty

immo'desto *adj* immodest

immo'lare *vt* sacrifice

immo'larsi *vr* sacrifice oneself

immondez'zaio *nm* rubbish tip

immon'dizia *nf* filth; (spazzatura) rubbish

im'mondo *adj* filthy

immo'rale *adj* immoral

immoral'mente *adv* immorally

immorta'lare *vt* immortalize

immor'tale *adj* immortal

immortalità *nf* immortality

immoti'vato *adj* unjustified, unmotivated

im'moto *adj* motionless

im'mune *adj* exempt; *Med* immune

immunità *nf* immunity
- **immunità diplomatica** diplomatic immunity; **immunità parlamentare** parliamentary privilege

immuniz'zare *vt* immunize

immunizzazi'one *nf* immunization

immunodefici'enza *nf* immunodeficiency

immunodepres'sivo *adj* & *nm* immunodepressant

immunolo'gia *nf* immunology

immuno'logico *adj* immunological

ꚍ indicates a very frequent word

immuso'nirsi *vr* sulk
immuso'nito *adj* sulky
immu'tabile *adj* unchangeable
immu'tato *adj* unchanging
impacchet'tare *vt* wrap up
impacci'are *vt* hamper; (disturbare) inconvenience; (imbarazzare) embarrass
impacciata'mente *adv* awkwardly
impacci'ato *adj* embarrassed; (goffo) awkward
im'paccio *nm* embarrassment; (ostacolo) hindrance; (situazione difficile) awkward situation; **trarsi d'~** get out of an awkward situation
im'pacco *nm* compress
impadro'nirsi *vr* **~ di** take possession of; fig (imparare) master
impa'gabile *adj* priceless
impagi'nare *vt* paginate
impaginazi'one *nf* pagination
impagli'are *vt* stuff ‹animale›
impa'lare *vt* impale
impa'lato *adj* fig stiff
impalca'tura *nf* scaffolding; fig structure
impal'lare *vt* snooker
impalli'dire *vi* turn pale; fig (perdere d'importanza) pale into insignificance
impalli'nare *vt* riddle with bullets
impal'pabile *adj* impalpable; ‹tessuto› gossamer-like
impa'nare *vt* Culin bread
impa'nato *adj* breaded
impanta'narsi *vr* get bogged down
impape'rarsi *vr* falter, stammer
impappi'narsi *vr* falter, stammer
⚔ **impa'rare** *vt* learn; **~ a proprie spese** learn to one's cost
impara'ticcio *nm* half-baked
impareggi'abile *adj* incomparable
imparen'tarsi *vr* **~ con** become related to
imparen'tato *adj* related
'impari *adj* unequal; (dispari) odd
impar'tire *vt* impart
imparzi'ale *adj* impartial
imparzialità *nf* impartiality
im'passe *nf inv* impasse
impas'sibile *adj* impassive; **con aria ~** impassively
impa'stare *vt* Culin knead; blend ‹colori›
impasta'tura *nf* kneading
impastic'carsi *vr* pop pills
impasticci'are *vt* make a mess of
im'pasto *nm* Culin dough; (miscuglio) mixture
im'patto *nm* impact
■ **impatto ambientale** environmental impact
impau'rire *vt* frighten

impau'rirsi *vr* get frightened
im'pavido *adj* fearless
impazi'ente *adj* impatient; **~ di fare qualcosa** eager to do something
impazien'tirsi *vr* lose patience
impazi'enza *nf* impatience
impaz'zata *nf* **all'~** at breakneck speed
⚔ **impaz'zire** *vi* go mad; ‹maionese› separate; **far ~ qualcuno** drive somebody mad; **~ per** be crazy about; **da ~** ‹mal di testa› blinding
impaz'zito *adj* crazed
impec'cabile *adj* impeccable
impeccabil'mente *adv* impeccably
impedi'mento *nm* hindrance; (ostacolo) obstacle
⚔ **impe'dire** *vt* (impacciare) hinder; (ostruire) obstruct; **~ di** prevent from; **~ a qualcuno di fare qualcosa** prevent somebody [from] doing something
⚔ **impe'gnare** *vt* (dare in pegno) pawn; (vincolare) bind; (prenotare) reserve; (assorbire) take up
impe'gnarsi *vr* apply oneself; **~ a fare qualcosa** commit oneself to doing something
impegna'tiva *nf* referral
impegna'tivo *adj* binding; ‹lavoro› demanding
impe'gnato *adj* politically committed
⚔ **im'pegno** *nm* engagement; Comm commitment; (zelo) care; **con ~** with dedication; **ho un ~** I'm doing something
impego'larsi *vr* **~ in** become enmeshed in
impel'lente *adj* pressing
impene'trabile *adj* impenetrable
impen'narsi *vr* ‹cavallo› rear; fig bristle
impen'nata *nf* (di prezzi) sharp rise; (di cavallo) rearing; (di moto) wheelie; (di aereo) climb
impen'sabile *adj* unthinkable
impen'sato *adj* unexpected
impensie'rire *vt* worry
impensie'rirsi *vr* worry
impe'rante *adj* prevailing
impe'rare *vi* reign
impera'tivo *adj & nm* imperative
impera|'tore, -trice **1** *nm* emperor **2** *nf* empress
impercet'tibile *adj* imperceptible
impercettibil'mente *adv* imperceptibly
imperdo'nabile *adj* unforgivable
imperfetta'mente *adv* imperfectly
imper'fetto *adj & nm* imperfect
imperfezi'one *nf* imperfection
imperi'ale *adj* imperial
imperia'lismo *nm* imperialism
imperia'lista *adj & nmf* imperialist

imperia'listico *adj* imperialistic
imperi'oso *adj* imperious; (impellente) urgent
imperi'turo *adj* immortal
impe'rizia *nf* lack of skill
imper'lare *vt* bead
imperma'lire *vt* offend
imperma'lirsi *vr* take offence
imperme'abile [1] *adj* ‹orologio› waterproof; ‹terreno› impermeable [2] *nm* raincoat
imperni'are *vt* pivot; (fondare) base
imperni'arsi *vr* ~ **su** be based on
im'pero *nm* empire; (potere) rule; **stile impero** empire style
imperscru'tabile *adj* inscrutable
imperso'nale *adj* impersonal
imperso'nare *vt* personify; (interpretare) act [the part of]
imper'territo *adj* undaunted, undeterred
imperti'nente *adj* impertinent
imperti'nenza *nf* impertinence
impertur'babile *adj* imperturbable
impertur'bato *adj* unperturbed
imperver'sare *vi* rage
im'pervio *adj* inaccessible
'impeto *nm* impetus; (impulso) impulse; (slancio) transport
impet'tito *adj* stiff
impetuosa'mente *adv* impetuously
impetu'oso *adj* impetuous; ‹vento› blustering
impiallacci'are *vt* veneer
impiallacci'ato *adj* veneered
impian'tare *vt* install; set up ‹azienda›
impi'anto *nm* plant; (sistema) system; (operazione) installation
■ **impianto di amplificazione** public address system, PA system; **impianto audio** sound system; **impianto elettrico** electrical system; **impianti** *pl* **fissi** fixtures and fittings; **impianto radio** Auto car stereo system; **impianto di rilavorazione [di scorie nucleari]** reprocessing plant; **impianto di riscaldamento** heating system; **impianto stereo** hi-fi
impia'strare *vt* plaster; (sporcare) dirty
impia'strarsi *vr* get dirty; ~ **le mani** get one's hands dirty
impi'astro *nm* poultice; ‹persona noiosa› bore; (pasticcione) cack-handed person
impiccagi'one *nf* hanging
impic'care *vt* hang
impic'carsi *vr* hang oneself
impic'cato, -a [1] *nm* hanged man [2] *nf* hanged woman
impicci'arsi *vr* meddle
im'piccio *nm* hindrance; (seccatura) bother

impicci'one, -a *nmf* nosey parker
impie'gare *vt* employ; (usare) use; spend ‹tempo, denaro›; Fin invest; **l'autobus ha impiegato un'ora** it took the bus an hour
impie'garsi *vr* get [oneself] a job
impiega'tizio *adj* clerical
impie'gato, -a *nmf* employee; (di ufficio) office worker
■ **impiegato di banca** bank clerk; **impiegato di concetto** administrative employee; **impiegato in prova** probationer; **impiegato statale** civil servant
impi'ego *nm* employment; (posto) job; Fin investment; **pubblico impiego** public sector; **impiego fisso** permanent job; **impieghi** *pl* **saltuari** odd jobs, casual employment
■ **impiego temporaneo** temporary job
impieto'sire *vt* move to pity
impieto'sirsi *vr* be moved to pity
impie'toso *adj* pitiless
impie'trito *adj* petrified
impigli'are *vt* entangle
impigli'arsi *vr* get entangled
impi'grire *vt* make lazy
impi'grirsi *vr* get lazy
impi'lare *vt* stack
impingu'are *vt* fig fill
impiom'bare *vt* seal ‹cassa, porta›
impla'cabile *adj* implacable
implemen'tare *vt* implement
impli'care *vt* implicate; (sottintendere) imply
impli'carsi *vr* become involved
implicazi'one *nf* implication
implicita'mente *adv* implicitly
im'plicito *adj* implicit
implo'rante *adj* imploring
implo'rare *vt* implore
implorazi'one *nf* entreaty
implosi'one *nf* implosion
impolli'nare *vt* pollinate
impollinazi'one *nf* pollination
impoltro'nire *vt* make lazy
impoltro'nirsi *vr* become lazy
impolve'rare *vt* cover with dust
impolve'rarsi *vr* get covered with dust
impolve'rato *adj* dusty
impoma'tare *vt* put brilliantine on ‹capelli›
impoma'tarsi *vr* put brilliantine on
imponde'rabile *adj* imponderable; ‹causa, evento› unpredictable
impo'nente *adj* imposing
impo'nenza *nf* impressiveness
impo'nibile [1] *adj* taxable [2] *nm* taxable income
impopo'lare *adj* unpopular
impopolarità *nf* unpopularity
imporpo'rarsi *vr* turn red

⚬ **im'porre** *vt* impose; (ordinare) order

im'porsi *vr* assert oneself; (aver successo) be successful; **~ di** (prefiggersi di) set oneself the task of

⚬ **impor'tante** 1 *adj* important
2 *nm* important thing

⚬ **impor'tanza** *nf* importance; **di vitale ~** crucially important

⚬ **impor'tare** 1 *vt* Comm, Comput import; (comportare) cause
2 *vi* matter; (essere necessario) be necessary; **non importa!** it doesn't matter!; **non me ne importa niente!** I couldn't care less!

importa|'tore, -trice 1 *adj* importing
2 *nmf* importer

importazi'one *nf* importation; (merce importata) import

import-'export *nm inv* import-export

im'porto *nm* amount

importu'nare *vt* pester; **~ qualcuno per qualcosa** pester somebody for something

impor'tuno *adj* troublesome; (inopportuno) untimely

imposizi'one *nf* imposition; (imposta) tax

imposses'sarsi *vr* **~ di** seize

⚬ **impos'sibile** 1 *adj* impossible
2 *nm* **fare l'~** do absolutely all one can

impossibilità *nf* impossibility

im'posta¹ *nf* tax
■ **imposta fondiaria** land tax; **imposta patrimoniale** property tax; **imposta sul reddito** income tax; **imposta sui redditi di capitale** capital gains tax; **imposta sulle società** corporation tax; **imposta supplementare** surtax; **imposta sul valore aggiunto** value added tax

im'posta² *nf* (di finestra) shutter

impo'stare *vt* (progettare) plan; (basare) base; Mus pitch; (imbucare) post, mail; set out (domanda, problema)

impostazi'one *nf* planning; (di voce) pitching; **impostazioni** *pl* Comput, Teleph settings

im'posto *pp di* IMPORRE

impo'store, -a *nmf* impostor

impo'stura *nf* imposture

impo'tente *adj* powerless; Med impotent

impo'tenza *nf* powerlessness; Med impotence

impoveri'mento *nm* impoverishment

impove'rire *vt* impoverish

impove'rirsi *vr* become poor; (risorse) become depleted; (linguaggio) become impoverished

imprati'cabile *adj* impracticable; (strada) impassable

impraticabilità *nf* **per ~ del terreno/ delle strade** because of the state of the pitch/ roads

imprati'chire *vt* train

imprati'chirsi *vr* **~ in, ~ a** get practice in

impre'care *vi* curse

imprecazi'one *nf* curse

impreci'sabile *adj* indeterminable

impreci'sato *adj* indeterminate

imprecisi'one *nf* inaccuracy

impre'ciso *adj* inaccurate

impre'gnare *vt* impregnate; (imbevere) soak; fig imbue

impre'gnarsi *vr* become impregnated with

imprendi|'tore, -trice *nmf* entrepreneur

imprenditori'ale *adj* entrepreneurial

imprepa'rato *adj* unprepared

⚬ **im'presa** *nf* undertaking; (gesta) exploit; (azienda) firm
■ **impresa edile** property developer; **impresa familiare** family business; **impresa di pompe funebri** undertakers, funeral directors; **impresa pubblica** state-owned company; **impresa di traslochi** removals firm Br

impre'sario *nm* impresario; (appaltatore) contractor
■ **impresario di pompe funebri** undertaker, funeral director, mortician Am; **impresario teatrale** theatre manager

imprescin'dibile *adj* inescapable

impressio'nabile *adj* impressionable

impressio'nante *adj* impressive; (spaventoso) frightening

impressio'nare *vt* impress; (spaventare) frighten; expose (foto)

impressio'narsi *vr* be affected; (spaventarsi) be frightened

⚬ **impressi'one** *nf* impression; (sensazione) sensation; (impronta) mark; **far ~ a qualcuno** upset somebody; **dare l'~ di essere ...** give the impression of being ...

impressio'nismo *nm* impressionism

impressio'nista *adj* & *nmf* impressionist

impressio'nistico *adj* impressionistic

im'presso 1 *pp di* IMPRIMERE
2 *adj* printed

impre'stare *vt* lend

impreve'dibile *adj* unforeseeable; (persona) unpredictable

imprevedibil'mente *adv* unexpectedly

imprevi'dente *adj* improvident

impre'visto 1 *adj* unforeseen
2 *nm* unforeseen event; **salvo imprevisti** all being well

imprigiona'mento *nm* imprisonment

imprigio'nare *vt* imprison

im'primere *vt* impress; (stampare) print; (comunicare) impart; **rimanere impresso a qualcuno** stick in somebody's mind

impro'babile *adj* unlikely, improbable; **è ~ che ci sia** he is unlikely to be there

improbabilità *nf* improbability

improdut'tivo *adj* unproductive

im'pronta *nf* impression; (di dito) print; fig mark
- impronta digitale fingerprint; **impronta ecologica** ecological footprint; **impronte** *pl* **genetiche** genetic fingerprinting; **impronta del piede** footprint

impron'tato *adj* ~ all'ironia tinged with irony

impronunci'abile *adj* unpronounceable

impro'perio *nm* insult; **improperi** *pl* abuse *sg*

impropo'nibile *adj* unrealistic

im'proprio *adj* improper

improro'gabile *adj* which cannot be extended

improvvisa'mente *adv* suddenly

improvvi'sare *vt/i* improvise

improvvi'sarsi *vr* turn oneself into a

improvvi'sata *nf* surprise

improvvi'sato *adj* ‹discorso› unrehearsed

improvvisazi'one *nf* improvisation

✸ **improv'viso** *adj* unexpected, sudden; all'~ unexpectedly, suddenly

impru'dente *adj* imprudent

imprudente'mente *adv* imprudently

impru'denza *nf* imprudence

impu'dente *adj* impudent

impudente'mente *adv* impudently

impu'denza *nf* impudence

impu'dico *adj* immodest

impu'gnare *vt* grasp; Jur contest

impugna'tura *nf* grip; (manico) handle
- impugnatura a due mani two-handed grip

impulsiva'mente *adv* impulsively

impulsività *nf* impulsiveness

impul'sivo *adj* impulsive

im'pulso *nm* impulse; **agire d'**~ act on impulse

impune'mente *adv* with impunity

impunità *nf* impunity

impu'nito *adj* unpunished

impun'tarsi *vr* fig dig one's heels in

impun'tura *nf* stitching

impuntu'rare *vt* backstitch

impurità *nf inv* impurity

im'puro *adj* impure

impu'tabile *adj* attributable (**a** to); Jur indictable

impu'tare *vt* attribute; Jur charge

impu'tato, -a *nmf* accused

imputazi'one *nf* charge
- imputazione di omicidio murder charge

imputri'dire *vi* putrefy

imputri'dito *adj* putrefied

✸ **in** *prep* in; (moto a luogo) to; (su) on; (dentro) within; (mezzo) by; (con materiale) made of; **essere in casa/ufficio** be at home/at the office; **in mano/tasca** in one's hand/pocket; **in fondo alla strada/borsa** at the bottom of the street/bag; **andare in Francia/campagna** go to France/the country; **salire in treno** get on the train; **versa la birra nel bicchiere** pour the beer into the glass; **in alto** up there; **in giornata** within the day; **nel 2011** in 2011; **una borsa in pelle** a bag made of leather, a leather bag; **in macchina** ‹viaggiare, venire› by car; **in contanti [in]** cash; **in vacanza** on holiday; **di giorno in giorno** from day to day; **se fossi in te** if I were you; **siamo in sette** there are seven of us

inabbor'dabile *adj* unapproachable

i'nabile *adj* incapable; (fisicamente) unfit

inabilità *nf* incapacity

inabi'tabile *adj* uninhabitable

inacces'sibile *adj* inaccessible; ‹persona› unapproachable

inaccet'tabile *adj* unacceptable

inaccettabilità *nf* unacceptability

inacer'barsi *vr* grow bitter

inacer'bire *vt* embitter; exacerbate ‹rapporto›

inaci'dire *vt* turn sour

inaci'dirsi *vr* go sour; ‹persona› become embittered

ina'datto *adj* unsuitable

inadegua'tezza *nf* inadequacy

inadegu'ato *adj* inadequate

inadempi'ente *nmf* defaulter

inadempi'enza *nf* nonfulfilment (**a** of)
- inadempienza contrattuale breach of contract

inadempi'mento *nm* nonfulfilment

inaffer'rabile *adj* elusive

inaffi'dabile *adj* untrustworthy

inaffon'dabile *adj* unsinkable

ina'lare *vt* inhale

inala'tore *nm* inhaler

inalazi'one *nf* inhalation

inalbe'rare *vt* hoist

inalbe'rarsi *vr* ‹cavallo› rear [up]; (adirarsi) lose one's temper

inalie'nabile *adj* inalienable

inalte'rabile *adj* unchanging; ‹colore› fast

inalte'rato *adj* unchanged

inami'dare *vt* starch

inami'dato *adj* starched

inammis'sibile *adj* inadmissible

inamo'vibile *adj* ‹disco ecc› non-removable

inanel'lato *adj* bejewelled

inani'mato *adj* inanimate; (senza vita) lifeless

inappa'gabile *adj* unsatisfiable

inappaga'mento *nm* nonfulfilment
inappa'gato *adj* unfulfilled
inappel'labile *adj* final
inappe'tenza *nf* lack of appetite
inappli'cabile *adj* inapplicable
inappropri'ato *adj* inapt
inappun'tabile *adj* faultless
inar'care *vt* arch; raise ‹sopracciglia›
inar'carsi *vr* ‹legno› warp; ‹ripiano› sag; (linea) curve
inari'dire *vt* parch; empty of feelings ‹persona›
inari'dirsi *vr* dry up; ‹persona› become empty of feelings
inarre'stabile *adj* unstoppable
inartico'lato *adj* inarticulate
inascol'tato *adj* unheard
inaspettata'mente *adv* unexpectedly
inaspet'tato *adj* unexpected
inaspri'mento *nm* (di carattere) embitterment; (di conflitto) worsening
ina'sprire *vt* embitter
ina'sprirsi *vr* become embittered
inattac'cabile *adj* unassailable; (irreprensibile) irreproachable
inatten'dibile *adj* unreliable
inat'teso *adj* unexpected
inattività *nf* inactivity
inat'tivo *adj* inactive
inattu'abile *adj* impracticable
inau'dito *adj* unheard of
inaugu'rale *adj* inaugural; **cerimonia inaugurale** official opening; **viaggio inaugurale** maiden voyage
inaugu'rare *vt* inaugurate, open ‹mostra›; unveil ‹statua›; christen ‹lavastoviglie ecc›
inaugurazi'one *nf* inauguration; (di mostra) opening, (di statua) unveiling
inavve'duto *adj* inadvertent; (sbadato) careless
inavver'tenza *nf* inadvertence
inavvertita'mente *adv* inadvertently
inavvici'nabile *adj* unapproachable
in'breeding *nm inv* inbreeding
'inca *adj & nmf* (*pl* **inca** *o* **incas**) Inca
incagli'are ⓵ *vi* ground ⓶ *vt* hinder
incagli'arsi *vr* run aground
in'caglio *nm* running aground; fig obstacle
incalco'labile *adj* incalculable
incal'lirsi *vr* grow callous; (abituarsi) become hardened
incal'lito *adj* callous; (abituato) hardened
incal'zante *adj* ‹ritmo› driving; ‹richiesta› urgent; ‹crisi› imminent
incal'zare *vt* pursue; fig press
iname'rare *vt* appropriate

incammi'nare *vt* get going; fig (guidare) set off
incammi'narsi *vr* set out
incanala'mento *nm* canalization; fig channelling
incana'lare *vt* canalize; fig channel
incana'larsi *vr* converge on
incancel'labile *adj* indelible
incande'scente *adj* incandescent; ‹discussione› burning
incande'scenza *nf* incandescence
incan'tare *vt* enchant
incan'tarsi *vr* stand spellbound; (incepparsi) jam
incanta'tore, -trice *nmf* enchanter; enchantress
■ **incantatore di serpenti** snake charmer
incan'tesimo *nm* spell
incan'tevole *adj* enchanting
in'canto *nm* spell; fig delight; (asta) auction; **come per ∼** as if by magic
incanu'tire *vt* turn white
incanu'tito *adj* white
inca'pace *adj* incapable; **incapace d'intendere e di volere** Jur unfit to plead
incapacità *nf* incapability
incapo'nirsi *vr* be set
incap'pare *vi* ∼ **in** run into
incappucci'arsi *vr* wrap up
incapretta'mento *nm* method of trussing up a victim by the ankles
incapricci'arsi *vr* ∼ **di** take a fancy to
incapsu'lare *vt* seal; crown ‹dente›
incarce'rare *vt* imprison
incarcerazi'one *nf* imprisonment
incari'care *vt* charge
incari'carsi *vr* take upon oneself; **me ne incarico io** I will see to it
incari'cato, -a ⓵ *adj* in charge ⓶ *nmf* representative
■ **incaricato d'affari** chargé d'affaires
in'carico *nm* charge; **per ∼ di** on behalf of
incar'nare *vt* embody
incar'narsi *vr* become incarnate
incarnazi'one *nf* incarnation
incarta'mento *nm* documents *pl*
incartapeco'rito *adj* shrivelled up
incar'tare *vt* wrap [in paper]
incasel'lare *vt* pigeonhole
incasi'nato *adj* fam ‹vita› screwed up; ‹stanza› messed up
incas'sare *vt* pack; Mech embed; (incastonare) set; (riscuotere) cash; take ‹colpo›
incas'sato *adj* set; ‹fiume› deeply embanked
in'casso *nm* collection; (introito) takings *pl*
incasto'nare *vt* set

incasto'nato *adj* embedded; ‹anello› inset (di with)

incastona'tura *nf* setting

inca'strare *vt* fit in; fam (in situazione) corner

inca'strarsi *vr* fit, interlock

in'castro *nm* joint; a ~ ‹pezzi› interlocking
  ■ incastro a coda di rondine dovetail joint

incate'nare *vt* chain

incatra'mare *vt* tar

incatti'vire *vt* turn nasty

incauta'mente *adv* imprudently

in'cauto *adj* imprudent

inca'vare *vt* hollow out

inca'vato *adj* hollow

incava'tura *nf* hollow

in'cavo *nm* hollow; (scanalatura) groove

incavo'larsi *vr* fam get shirty

incavo'lato *adj* fam shirty

in'cedere *fml* [1] *vi* advance solemnly [2] *nm* solemn gait

incendi'are *vt* set fire to; fig inflame

incendi'ario, -a [1] *adj* incendiary; fig ‹discorso› inflammatory; fig ‹bellezza› sultry [2] *nmf* arsonist

incendi'arsi *vr* catch fire

in'cendio *nm* fire
  ■ incendio doloso arson; incendi *pl* dolosi cases of arson

inceneri'mento *nm* incineration; (cremazione) cremation

incene'rire *vt* burn to ashes; (cremare) cremate

incene'rirsi *vr* be burnt to ashes

inceneri'tore *nm* incinerator

in'censo *nm* incense

incensu'rabile *adj* irreproachable

incensu'rato *adj* blameless; essere ~ Jur have a clean record

incenti'vare *vt* motivate

incen'tivo *nm* incentive
  ■ incentivo fiscale tax incentive

incen'trarsi *vr* ~ su centre on

incep'pare *vt* block; fig hamper

incep'parsi *vr* jam

ince'rata *nf* oilcloth

incerot'tato *adj* with a plaster on

incer'tezza *nf* uncertainty

in'certo [1] *adj* uncertain, unsure [2] *nm* uncertainty; sono gli incerti del mestiere that's the way it goes in this business

incespi'care *vi* (inciampare) stumble

inces'sante *adj* unceasing

incessante'mente *adv* incessantly

in'cesto *nm* incest

incestu'oso *adj* incestuous

in'cetta *nf* buying up; fare ~ di stockpile

inchi'esta *nf* investigation; fare un'~ conduct an inquiry
  ■ inchiesta giudiziaria criminal investigation; inchiesta parlamentare parliamentary inquiry

inchi'nare *vt* bow

inchi'narsi *vr* bow

in'chino *nm* bow; (di donna) curtsy

inchio'dare *vt* nail; nail down ‹coperchio›; ~ a letto ‹malattia› confine to bed

inchi'ostro *nm* ink
  ■ inchiostro di china Indian ink; inchiostro simpatico invisible ink; inchiostro di stampa newsprint

inciam'pare *vi* stumble; ~ in trip over; (imbattersi) run into

inci'ampo *nm* hindrance

inciden'tale *adj* incidental

✓ **inci'dente** *nm* (episodio) incident; (infortunio) accident
  ■ incidente aereo plane crash; incidente d'auto car accident; incidente sul lavoro industrial accident; incidente stradale road accident

inci'denza *nf* incidence

in'cidere [1] *vt* cut; (arte) engrave; (registrare) record [2] *vi* ~ su (gravare) weigh upon

in'cinta *adj* pregnant

incipi'ente *adj* incipient

incipri'are *vt* powder

incipri'arsi *vr* powder one's face

in'circa *adv* all'~ more or less

incisi'one *nf* incision; (arte) engraving; (acquaforte) etching; (registrazione) recording

inci'sivo [1] *adj* incisive [2] *nm* (dente) incisor

in'ciso *nm* per ~ incidentally

inci'sore *nm* engraver

incita'mento *nm* incitement

inci'tare *vt* incite

inci'vile *adj* uncivilized; (maleducato) impolite

incivil'tà *nf* barbarism; (maleducazione) rudeness

inclassifi'cabile *adv* unclassifiable

incle'mente *adj* harsh

incle'menza *nf* harshness

incli'nabile *adj* reclining

incli'nare [1] *vt* tilt [2] *vi* ~ a be inclined to

incli'narsi *vr* (torre) lean; (aereo) tilt

incli'nato *adj* tilted; ‹terreno› sloping

inclinazi'one *nf* slope, inclination

in'cline *adj* inclined

in'cludere *vt* include; (allegare) enclose

inclusi'one *nf* inclusion

inclu'sivo *adj* inclusive

in'cluso [1] pp di INCLUDERE

2 *adj* included; (compreso) inclusive; (allegato) enclosed

incoe'rente *adj* (contraddittorio) inconsistent

incoerente'mente *adv* inconsistently

incoe'renza *nf* inconsistency

in'cognita *nf* unknown quantity

in'cognito **1** *adj* unknown

2 *nm* in ∼ incognito

incol'lare *vt* stick; (con colla liquida) glue; Comput paste

incol'larsi *vr* stick to; ∼ **a qualcuno** stick close to somebody

incolla'tura *nf* (nell'ippica) neck

incolle'rirsi *vr* lose one's temper

incolle'rito *adj* enraged

incol'mabile *adj* ‹differenza› unbridgeable; ‹vuoto› unfillable

incolon'nare *vt* line up

inco'lore *adj* colourless

incol'pare *vt* blame

in'colto *adj* uncultivated; ‹persona› uneducated

in'colume *adj* unhurt

incom'bente *adj* impending

incom'benza *nf* task

in'combere *vi* ∼ **su** hang over; ∼ **a** (spettare) be incumbent on

incombu'stibile *adj* noncombustible

✎ **incominci'are** *vt/i* begin, start

incommensu'rabile *adj* immeasurable

incomo'dare *vt* inconvenience

incomo'darsi *vr* trouble

in'comodo **1** *adj* uncomfortable; (inopportuno) inconvenient

2 *nm* inconvenience; **fare il terzo** ∼ play gooseberry

incompa'rabile *adj* incomparable

incompa'tibile *adj* incompatible

incompatibilità *nf inv* incompatibility

■ incompatibilità di carattere incompatibility

incompe'tente *adj* incompetent

incompe'tenza *nf* incompetence

incompi'uto *adj* unfinished

incom'pleto *adj* incomplete

incompren'sibile *adj* incomprehensible, unintelligible

incomprensibil'mente *adv* incomprehensibly

incomprensi'one *nf* lack of understanding; (malinteso) misunderstanding

incom'preso *adj* misunderstood

inconce'pibile *adj* inconceivable

inconcili'abile *adj* irreconcilable

inconclu'dente *adj* inconclusive; ‹persona› ineffectual

incondizionata'mente *adv* unconditionally

incondizio'nato *adj* unconditional

inconfes'sabile *adj* unmentionable

inconfon'dibile *adj* unmistakable

inconfondibil'mente *adv* unmistakably

inconfu'tabile *adj* irrefutable

inconfutabil'mente *adv* irrefutably

incongru'ente *adj* inconsistent

incongru'enza *nf* incongruity

in'congruo *adj* inadequate

inconsa'pevole *adj* unaware; (inconscio) unconscious

inconsapevol'mente *adv* unwittingly

inconscia'mente *adv* unconsciously

in'conscio *adj & nm* Psych unconscious

inconsegu'ente *adj* essere ∼ be a non sequitur

inconside'rabile *adj* negligible

inconside'rato *adj* inconsiderate

inconsi'stente *adj* insubstantial; ‹notizia ecc› unfounded

inconsi'stenza *nf* (di ragionamento, prove) flimsiness

inconso'labile *adj* inconsolable

inconsu'eto *adj* unusual

incon'sulto *adj* rash

incontami'nato *adj* uncontaminated

inconte'nibile *adj* irrepressible

inconten'tabile *adj* insatiable; (esigente) hard to please

inconte'stabile *adj* indisputable

inconte'stato *adj* unchallenged

inconti'nente *adj* incontinent

inconti'nenza *nf* incontinence

✎ **incon'trare** *vt* meet; encounter, meet with ‹difficoltà›

incon'trario: all'∼ *adv* the other way around; (in modo sbagliato) the wrong way around

incon'trarsi *vr* meet; ∼ **con qualcuno** meet somebody

incontra'stabile *adj* incontrovertible

incontra'stato *adj* undisputed

✎ **in'contro** **1** *nm* meeting; (casuale) encounter; (di calcio, rugby) match; (di tennis) game; (di pugilato) fight

■ incontro al vertice summit meeting

2 *prep* ∼ **a** towards; **andare** ∼ **a qualcuno** go to meet somebody; fig meet somebody half way

incontrol'labile *adj* uncontrollable

incontrollata'mente *adv* uncontrollably

inconveni'ente *nm* drawback

incoraggia'mento *nm* encouragement

incoraggi'ante *adj* encouraging

incoraggi'are *vt* encourage

incor'nare *vt* gore

incornici'are *vt* frame

incornicia'tura *nf* framing
incoro'nare *vt* crown
incoronazi'one *nf* coronation
incorpo'rare *vt* incorporate; (mescolare) blend
incorpo'rarsi *vr* blend; ‹territori› merge
incorreg'gibile *adj* incorrigible
in'correre *vt* ~ **in** incur; ~ **nel pericolo di** ... run the risk of ...
incorrut'tibile *adj* incorruptible
incosci'ente ① *adj* unconscious; (irresponsabile) reckless
② *nmf* irresponsible person
incosci'enza *nf* unconsciousness; (irresponsabilità) recklessness
inco'stante *adj* changeable; ‹persona› fickle
inco'stanza *nf* changeableness; (di persona) fickleness
incostituzio'nale *adj* unconstitutional
incostituzionalità *nf* unconstitutionality
⚡ **incre'dibile** *adj* incredible, unbelievable
incredibil'mente *adv* incredibly, unbelievably
incredulità *nf* incredulity
in'credulo *adj* incredulous
incremen'tale *adj* Comput, Math incremental
incremen'tare *vt* increase; (intensificare) step up
incre'mento *nm* increase
■ **incremento demografico** population growth; **incremento produttivo** increase in production
incresci'oso *adj* regrettable
incre'spare *vt* ruffle; wrinkle ‹tessuto›; make frizzy ‹capelli›; ~ **la fronte** frown
incre'sparsi *vr* ‹acqua› ripple; ‹tessuto› wrinkle; ‹capelli› go frizzy
incrimi'nabile *adj* indictable
incrimi'nante *adj* incriminating
incrimi'nare *vt* indict; fig incriminate
incriminazi'one *nf* indictment
incri'nare *vt* crack; fig affect ‹amicizia›
incri'narsi *vr* crack; ‹amicizia› be affected
incrina'tura *nf* crack
incroci'are ① *vt* cross
② *vi* Naut, Aeron cruise
incroci'arsi *vr* cross; ‹razze› interbreed
incroci'ato *adj* crossover
incrocia'tore *nm* cruiser
in'crocio *nm* crossing; (di strade) crossroads *sg*
incrol'labile *adj* indestructible
incro'stare *vt* encrust
incrostazi'one *nf* encrustation
incuba'trice *nf* incubator

incubazi'one *nf* incubation
'incubo *nm* nightmare; **da** ~ nightmarish
in'cudine *nf* anvil
incul'care *vt* inculcate
incune'are *vt* wedge
incune'arsi *vr* slot in
incune'ato *adj* Med impacted
incu'pirsi *vr* fig darken
incu'rabile *adj* incurable
incu'rante *adj* careless
in'curia *nf* negligence
incurio'sire *vt* make curious
incurio'sirsi *vr* become curious
incursi'one *nf* raid
■ **incursione aerea** air raid, airstrike
incurva'mento *nm* bending
incur'vare *vt* bend
incur'varsi *vr* bend
incurva'tura *nf* bending
in'cusso *pp di* INCUTERE
incusto'dito *adj* unguarded
in'cutere *vt* arouse; ~ **spavento a qualcuno** strike fear into somebody
'indaco *nm* indigo
indaffa'rato *adj* busy
inda'gare *vt/i* investigate
indaga'tore *adj* ‹sguardo› enquiring
in'dagine *nf* research; (giudiziaria) investigation
■ **indagine demoscopica** public opinion poll; **indagine di mercato** market survey
indebi'tare *vt* get into debt
indebi'tarsi *vr* get into debt
in'debito *adj* undue
indeboli'mento *nm* weakening
indebo'lire *vt* weaken
indebo'lirsi *vr* weaken
inde'cente *adj* indecent
indecente'mente *adv* indecently
inde'cenza *nf* indecency; (vergogna) disgrace
indeci'frabile *adj* indecipherable
indecisi'one *nf* indecision
inde'ciso *adj* undecided
indecli'nabile *adj* indeclinable
indeco'roso *adj* indecorous
inde'fesso *adj* tireless
indefi'nibile *adj* indefinable
indefi'nito *adj* indefinite
indefor'mabile *adj* crushproof
in'degno *adj* unworthy
inde'lebile *adj* indelible
indelebil'mente *adv* indelibly
indelicata'mente *adv* indiscreetly
indelica'tezza *nf* indelicacy; (azione) tactless act

⚡ indicates a very frequent word

indeli'cato *adj* indiscreet; (grossolano) indelicate

indemagli'abile *adj* ladderproof

indemoni'ato *adj* possessed

in'denne *adj* uninjured; (da malattia) unaffected

inden'nità *nf inv* allowance; (per danni) compensation
■ **indennità di accompagnamento** mobility allowance; **indennità di contingenza** cost-of-living allowance; **indennità di disoccupazione** job seeker's allowance; **indennità di fine rapporto** severance payment; **indennità di malattia** sickpay; **indennità parlamentare** MP's salary; **indennità di trasferimento** relocation allowance; **indennità di trasferta** travel allowance

indenniz'zare *vt* compensate

inden'nizzo *nm* compensation

indero'gabile *adj* binding

indescri'vibile *adj* indescribable

indescrivibil'mente *adv* indescribably

indeside'rabile *adj* undesirable

indeside'rato *adj* ‹figlio, ospite› unwanted

indetermi'nabile *adj* indeterminable

indetermina'tezza *nf* vagueness

indetermina'tivo *adj* indefinite

indetermi'nato *adj* indeterminate

'India *nf* India

indi'ano, -a *adj & nmf* Indian; **in fila indiana** in single file
■ **indiano d'America** American Indian

indiavo'lato *adj* possessed; (vivace) wild

⚡ **indi'care** *vt* show, indicate; (col dito) point at; (far notare) point out; (consigliare) advise

indicativa'mente *adv* as an idea; **può dirmi quanto costa ∼?** can you give me an idea of the price?

indica'tivo ① *adj* indicative; ‹prezzo, cifra› rough
② *nm* Gram indicative

indica'tore *nm* indicator; Techn gauge; (prontuario) directory
■ **indicatore di direzione** indicator light; **indicatore economico** economic indicator; **indicatore [del livello] dell'olio** oil gauge; **indicatore di velocità** speedometer

indicazi'one *nf* indication; (istruzione) direction
■ **indicazione stradale** road sign

'indice *nm* (dito) forefinger; (lancetta) pointer; (di libro, statistica) index; fig (segno) sign
■ **indice di ascolto** audience rating; **indice azionario** share index; **indice di gradimento** popularity rating; **indice di massa corporea** body mass index; **indice di mortalità** death rate; **indice di natalità** birth rate

indi'cibile *adj* inexpressible

indiciz'zare *vt* index-link

indiciz'zato *adj* index-linked

indicizzazi'one *nf* indexing

indietreggi'are *vi* draw back; Mil withdraw

⚡ **indi'etro** *adv* back, behind; **all' ∼** backwards; **essere ∼** be behind; (mentalmente) be backward; (con pagamenti) be in arrears; (di orologio) be slow; **fare marcia ∼** reverse; **rimandare ∼** send back; **rimanere ∼** be left behind; **torna ∼!** come back!

indifen'dibile *adj* indefensible

indi'feso *adj* undefended; (inerme) helpless

⚡ **indiffe'rente** *adj* indifferent; **mi è ∼** it's all the same to me

indifferente'mente *adv* (senza fare distinzioni) without distinction; (con indifferenza) indifferently; **funziona ∼ con i due programmi** it works equally well with either program

indiffe'renza *nf* indifference

in'digeno, -a ① *adj* indigenous
② *nmf* native

indi'gente *adj* needy, poverty-stricken

indi'genza *nf* poverty

indigesti'one *nf* indigestion

indi'gesto *adj* indigestible

indi'gnare *vt* make indignant

indi'gnarsi *vr* be indignant

indi'gnato *adj* indignant

indignazi'one *nf* indignation

indimenti'cabile *adj* unforgettable

'indio, -a ① *adj* Indian
② *nmf* (mpl **indii** o **indios**) Indian

indipen'dente *adj* independent; ‹economicamente› self-supporting

indipendente'mente *adv* independently; **∼ da** regardless of

⚡ **indipen'denza** *nf* independence

in'dire *vt* announce

indiretta'mente *adv* indirectly

indi'retto *adj* indirect

indiriz'zare *vt* address; (mandare) send; (dirigere) direct

indiriz'zario *nm* mailing list

indiriz'zarsi *vr* direct one's steps

⚡ **indi'rizzo** *nm* address; (direzione) direction
■ **indirizzo di consegna** delivery address; **'indirizzo del destinatario'** 'addressee'; **indirizzo di memoria** Comput memory address; **'indirizzo del mittente'** 'sender's address'; **indirizzo di posta elettronica** e-mail address

indisci'plina *nf* lack of discipline

indiscipli'nato *adj* undisciplined

indi'screto *adj* indiscreet; **in modo ∼** indiscreetly

indiscrezi'one *nf* indiscretion

indiscriminata'mente *adv* indiscriminately

indiscrimi'nato *adj* indiscriminate

indi'scusso *adj* unquestioned

indiscu'tibile *adj* unquestionable

indiscutibil'mente *adv* unquestionably

indispen'sabile *adj* essential; ‹persona› indispensable

indispet'tire *vt* irritate

indispet'tirsi *vr* get irritated

indi'sporre *vt* anger

indisposizi'one *nf* indisposition

indi'sposto ① *pp di* INDISPORRE ② *adj* indisposed

indisso'lubile *adj* indissoluble

indissolubil'mente *adv* indissolubly

indistin'guibile *adj* indiscernible

indistinta'mente *adv* without exception

indi'stinto *adj* indistinct

indistrut'tibile *adj* indestructible

indistur'bato *adj* undisturbed

in'divia *nf* endive

individu'abile *adj* detectable

individu'ale *adj* individual

individua'lista *nmf* individualist

individua'listico *adj* individualistic

individualità *nf* individuality

individu'are *vt* individualize; (localizzare) locate; (riconoscere) single out

indi'viduo *nm* individual

indivi'sibile *adj* indivisible

indivisibilità *nf* indivisibility

indi'viso *adj* undivided

indizi'are *vt* throw suspicion on

indizi'ario *adj* circumstantial

indizi'ato, -a ① *adj* suspected ② *nmf* suspect

in'dizio *nm* sign; Jur circumstantial evidence

Indo'cina *nf* Indochina

indoeuro'peo *adj* Indo-European

'indole *nf* nature

indo'lente *adj* indolent

indo'lenza *nf* indolence

indolenzi'mento *nm* stiffness, ache

indolen'zire *vt* stiffen up

indolen'zirsi *vr* stiffen up, go stiff

indolen'zito *adj* stiff

indo'lore *adj* painless

indo'mabile *adj* untameable

indo'mani *nm* l'~ the following day

in'domito *adj* untamed

Indo'nesia *nf* Indonesia

indonesi'ano, -a *adj & nmf* Indonesian

indo'rare *vt* gild; ~ **la pillola** sugar the pill

✔ **indos'sare** *vt* wear; (mettere addosso) put on

indossa|'tore, -trice ① *nm* [male] model ② *nf* model

in'dotto *pp di* INDURRE

indottri'nare *vt* indoctrinate

indovi'nare *vt* guess; (predire) foretell

indovi'nato *adj* successful; (scelta) well-chosen

indovi'nello *nm* riddle

indo'vino, -a *nmf* fortune-teller

indù *adj inv & nmf inv* Hindu

indubbia'mente *adv* undoubtedly

in'dubbio *adj* undoubted

indubi'tabile *adj* indubitable

indubitabil'mente *adv* indubitably

indugi'are *vi* linger

indugi'arsi *vr* linger

in'dugio *nm* delay

indu'ismo *nm* Hinduism

indul'gente *adj* indulgent

indul'genza *nf* indulgence

in'dulgere *vi* ~ a indulge in

in'dulto ① *pp di* INDULGERE ② *nm* Jur pardon

indu'mento *nm* garment; **indumenti** *pl* clothes
  ■ **indumenti intimi** *pl* underwear

induri'mento *nm* hardening

indu'rire *vt* harden

indu'rirsi *vr* harden

in'durre *vt* induce; ~ **qualcuno a fare** induce somebody to do; ~ **in tentazione** lead into temptation

✔ **in'dustria** *nf* industry
  ■ **industria dell'abbigliamento** clothing industry, fam rag trade; **industria leggera** light industry; **industria pesante** heavy industry; **industria dello spettacolo** show business, entertainment industry, fam showbiz; **industria terziaria** service industry; **industria tessile** textile industry, textiles

✔ **industri'ale** ① *adj* industrial; **zona industriale** industrial estate ② *nmf* industrialist

industrializ'zare *vt* industrialize

industrializ'zato *adj* industrialized

industrializzazi'one *nf* industrialization

industrial'mente *adv* industrially

industri'arsi *vr* ~ **per guadagnare qualcosa** set to and earn some money

industriosa'mente *adv* industriously

industri'oso *adj* industrious

indut'tivo *adj* inductive

indut'tore *nm* inductor

induzi'one *nf* induction

inebe'tire *vt* daze

inebe'tito *adj* stunned

inebri'ante *adj* intoxicating, exciting

✔ indicates a very frequent word

inebri'are *vt* intoxicate
inebri'arsi *vr* become inebriated
inecce'pibile *adj* unexceptionable
i'nedia *nf* starvation
i'nedito *adj* unpublished
inedu'cato *adj* impolite
inef'fabile *adj* inexpressible
ineffi'cace *adj* ineffective
ineffici'ente *adj* inefficient
ineffici'enza *nf* inefficiency
ineguagli'abile *adj* incomparable
ineguaglianza *nf* inequality
ineguagli'ato *adj* unequalled
inegu'ale *adj* unequal; ‹superficie› uneven
inelut'tabile *adj* inescapable
inenar'rabile *adj* indescribable
inequivo'cabile *adj* unequivocal
inequivocabil'mente *adv* unequivocally
ine'rente *adj* ∼ a inherent in
inerente'mente *adv* ∼ a concerning
i'nerme *adj* unarmed; fig defenceless
inerpi'carsi *vr* ∼ su clamber up
i'nerte *adj* inactive; Phys inert
i'nerzia *nf* inactivity; Phys inertia
inesat'tezza *nf* inaccuracy
ine'satto *adj* inaccurate; (erroneo) incorrect; (non riscosso) uncollected
inesau'ribile *adj* inexhaustible
inesi'stente *adj* non-existent
inesi'stenza *nf* non-existence
ineso'rabile *adj* inexorable
inesorabil'mente *adv* inexorably
inesperi'enza *nf* inexperience
ine'sperto *adj* inexperienced
inespli'cabile *adj* inexplicable
inesplicabil'mente *adv* inexplicably
inesplo'rato *adj* undiscovered
ine'sploso *adj* unexploded
inespres'sivo *adj* expressionless
inespri'mibile *adj* inexpressible
inespu'gnabile *adj* impregnable
ineste'tismo *nm* blemish
inesti'mabile *adj* inestimable
inestin'guibile *adj* ‹sete› insatiable; ‹odio› undying
inestir'pabile *adj* impossible to eradicate
inestri'cabile *adj* inextricable
inestricabil'mente *adv* inextricably
inetti'tudine *nf* ineptitude
i'netto *adj* inept; ∼ a unsuited to
ine'vaso *adj* ‹pratiche, corrispondenza› pending
inevi'tabile *adj* inevitable
inevitabil'mente *adv* inevitably
in ex'tremis *adv* ‹segnare un gol› in the nick of time; (prima di morire) in extremis

i'nezia *nf* trifle
infagot'tare *vt* wrap up
infagot'tarsi *vr* wrap [oneself] up
infal'libile *adj* infallible
infa'mante *adj* defamatory
infa'mare *vt* defame
infama'torio *adj* defamatory
in'fame *adj* infamous; fam (orrendo) awful, shocking
in'famia *nf* infamy
infan'gare *vt* cover with mud; fig sully
infan'garsi *vr* get muddy
infanti'cida *nmf* infanticide
infanti'cidio *nm* infanticide
infan'tile *adj* ‹letteratura, abbigliamento› children's *attrib*; ‹ingenuità› childlike; pej childish
✧ **in'fanzia** *nf* childhood; (bambini) children *pl*; prima Infanzia infancy
infar'cire *vt* stuff (di with)
infari'nare *vt* flour; ∼ di sprinkle with
infarina'tura *nf* fig smattering
in'farto *nm* heart attack
infasti'dire *vt* irritate
infasti'dirsi *vr* get irritated
infati'cabile *adj* untiring
infaticabil'mente *adv* tirelessly
✧ **in'fatti** *conj* as a matter of fact; (veramente) indeed
infatu'arsi *vr* ∼ di become infatuated with
infatu'ato *adj* infatuated
infatuazi'one *nf* infatuation
in'fausto *adj* ill-omened
infecondità *nf* infertility
infe'condo *adj* infertile
infe'dele *adj* unfaithful
infedeltà *nf* unfaithfulness
✧ **infe'lice** *adj* unhappy; (inappropriato) unfortunate; (cattivo) bad
infelicità *nf* unhappiness
infel'trire *vi* matt
infel'trirsi *vr* matt
infel'trito *adj* matted
✧ **inferi'ore** [1] *adj* (più basso) lower; ‹qualità› inferior
   [2] *nmf* inferior
inferiorità *nf* inferiority
infe'rire *vt* infer; strike ‹colpo›
inferme'ria *nf* infirmary; (di nave, scuola) sickbay
infermi'ere, -a [1] *nm* [male] nurse
   [2] *nf* nurse
infermità *nf* sickness
■ infermità mentale mental illness
in'fermo, -a [1] *adj* sick
   [2] *nmf* invalid
infer'nale *adj* infernal; (spaventoso) hellish
✧ **in'ferno** *nm* hell; va' all'∼! go to hell!

I

infero'cirsi vr become fierce

inferri'ata nf grating

infervo'rare vt arouse enthusiasm in

infervo'rarsi vr get excited

infe'stare vt infest

infestato adj infested; ~ **dai fantasmi** haunted

infestazi'one nf infestation

infet'tare vt infect

infet'tarsi vr become infected

infet'tivo adj infectious

in'fetto adj infected

infezi'one nf infection

infiac'chire vt/i weaken

infiac'chirsi vr weaken

infiam'mabile adj [in]flammable

infiam'mare vt set on fire; Med, fig inflame

infiam'marsi vr catch fire; Med become inflamed

infiammazi'one nf Med inflammation

infia'scare vt bottle

infici'are vt Jur invalidate

in'fido adj treacherous

infie'rire vi (imperversare) rage; ~ **su** attack furiously

in'figgere vt drive

in'figgersi vr ~ **in** penetrate

⚡ **infi'lare** vt thread; (mettere) insert; (indossare) put on

infi'larsi vr slip on ‹vestito›; ~ **in** (introdursi) slip into

infil'trarsi vr infiltrate

infil'trato, -a nmf infiltrator

infiltrazi'one nf infiltration; (d'acqua) seepage; Med (iniezione) injection

infil'zare vt pierce; (infilare) string; (conficcare) stick

'infimo adj lowest

⚡ **in'fine** adv finally; (insomma) in short

infin'gardo adj slothful

infinità nf infinity; **un'**~ **di** masses of

infinita'mente adv infinitely

infinitesi'male adj infinitesimal

⚡ **infi'nito** [1] adj infinite; Gram infinitive [2] nm infinite; Gram infinitive; Math infinity; **all'**~ endlessly

infinocchi'are vt fam hoodwink

infiocchet'tare vt tie up with ribbons

infiore'scenza nf inflorescence

infischi'arsi vr ~ **di** not care about; **me ne infischio** fam I couldn't care less

in'fisso [1] pp di INFIGGERE [2] nm fixture; (di porta, finestra) frame

infit'tire vt/i thicken

infit'tirsi vr thicken

inflazi'one nf inflation

■ **inflazione galoppante** galloping inflation; inflazione striscante creeping inflation

inflazio'nistico adj inflationary

infles'sibile adj inflexible

inflessibilità nf inflexibility

inflessi'one nf inflection, inflexion

in'fliggere vt inflict

in'flitto pp di INFLIGGERE

influ'ente adj influential

influ'enza nf influence; Med influenza; **prendere l'**~ catch the flu

■ **influenza A** swine flu; **influenza aviaria** o **dei polli** bird flu; **influenza gastrointestinale** gastric flu

influen'zabile adj ‹mente, opinione› impressionable

influen'zare vt influence

influen'zato adj essere ~ (con febbre) have the flu

influ'ire vi ~ **su** influence

in'flusso nm influence

info'carsi vr catch fire; ‹viso› go red; ‹discussione› become heated

info'gnarsi vr fam get into a mess

infol'tire vt/i thicken

infon'dato adj unfounded

in'fondere vt instil

infor'care vt fork ‹fieno›; get on ‹bici›; put on ‹occhiali›

inforca'tura nf crotch

infor'male adj informal

⚡ **infor'mare** vt inform

infor'marsi vr inquire (**di** about)

infor'matica nf information technology

infor'matico adj computer attrib

informa'tivo adj informative

infor'mato adj informed; **male** ~ ill-informed

informa|'tore, -trice nmf (di polizia) informer

■ **informatore medico scientifico** representative of a pharmaceutical company

⚡ **informazi'one** nf information; **un'**~ a piece of information; **informazioni** pl information; **servizio informazioni** enquiries

■ **informazione genetica** genetic code; **informazione riservata** confidential information; **informazioni** pl **sbagliate** misinformation; **informazioni** pl **sulla viabilità** travel news

in'forme adj shapeless

infor'nare vt put into the oven

infortu'narsi vr have an accident

infortu'nato, -a [1] adj injured [2] nmf injured person; **gli infortunati** the injured

infor'tunio nm accident

■ **infortunio sul lavoro** industrial accident

⚡ indicates a very frequent word

infortu'nistica *nf* study of industrial accidents

infos'sarsi *vr* sink; ‹*guance, occhi*› become hollow

infos'sato *adj* sunken, hollow

infradici'are *vt* drench

infradici'arsi *vr* get drenched; (diventare marcio) rot

infra'dito *nmpl* (scarpe) flip-flops

in'frangere *vt* break; (in mille pezzi) shatter

in'frangersi *vr* break; (in mille pezzi) shatter

infran'gibile *adj* unbreakable

in'franto ⓵ *pp di* INFRANGERE
⓶ *adj* shattered; fig ‹*cuore*› broken

infra'rosso *adj* infra-red

infrasettima'nale *adj* midweek

infrastrut'tura *nf* infrastructure

infrazi'one *nf* offence
■ infrazione al codice della strada traffic offence

infredda'tura *nf* cold

infreddo'lirsi *vr* feel cold

infreddo'lito *adj* cold

infre'quente *adj* infrequent

infruttu'oso *adj* fruitless

infuo'care *vt* make red-hot

infuo'cato *adj* burning

infu'ori *adv* all'~ outwards; all'~ di except; denti ~ buck teeth

infuri'are *vi* rage

infuri'arsi *vr* fly into a rage

infuri'ato *adj* blustering

infusi'one *nf* infusion

in'fuso ⓵ *pp di* INFONDERE
⓶ *nm* infusion

Ing. *abbr* (**ingegnere**)

ingabbi'are *vt* cage; fig (mettere in prigione) jail

ingaggi'are *vt* engage; sign up ‹*calciatori ecc*›; begin ‹*lotta, battaglia*›

in'gaggio *nm* engagement; (di calciatore) signing [up]

ingan'nare *vt* deceive; (essere infedele a) be unfaithful to; ~ l'attesa kill time

ingan'narsi *vr* deceive oneself; se non m'inganno if I am not mistaken

ingan'nevole *adj* deceptive

in'ganno *nm* deceit; (frode) fraud; trarre in ~ deceive

ingarbugli'are *vt* entangle; (confondere) confuse

ingarbugli'arsi *vr* get entangled; (confondersi) become confused

ingarbu'gliato *adj* confused

inge'gnarsi *vr* do one's best; ~ per vivere try to scrape a living

⚲ **inge'gnere** *nm* engineer
■ ingegnere aeronautico aeronautical engineer; ingegnere civile civil engineer;

ingegnere edile structural engineer; ingegnere meccanico mechanical engineer; ingegnere minerario mining engineer; ingegnere navale marine engineer

ingegne'ria *nf* engineering
■ ingegneria aeronautica aeronautical engineering; ingegneria civile civil engineering; ingegneria edile structural engineering; ingegneria genetica genetic engineering; ingegneria meccanica mechanical engineering

in'gegno *nm* brains *pl*; (genio) genius; (abilità) ingenuity

ingegnosa'mente *adv* ingeniously

ingegnosità *nf* ingenuity

inge'gnoso *adj* ingenious

ingelo'sire *vt* make jealous

ingelo'sirsi *vr* become jealous

in'gente *adj* huge

ingenua'mente *adv* artlessly

ingenuità *nf* ingenuousness

in'genuo *adj* ingenuous; (credulone) naïve

inge'renza *nf* interference

inge'rire *vt* swallow

inges'sare *vt* put in plaster

inges'sato *adj* fig (rigidamente formale) stilted, stiff

ingessa'tura *nf* plaster, plaster cast

Inghil'terra *nf* England

inghiot'tire *vt* swallow

in'ghippo *nm* trick

ingial'lire *vi* turn yellow

ingial'lirsi *vr* turn yellow

ingial'lito *adj* yellowed

ingigan'tire ⓵ *vt* magnify; blow up out of proportion ‹*problema*›
⓶ *vi* take on gigantic proportions

ingigan'tirsi *vr* take on gigantic proportions

inginocchi'arsi *vr* kneel [down]

inginocchi'ato *adj* kneeling

inginocchia'toio *nm* prie-dieu

ingioiel'larsi *vr* put on one's jewels

ingioiel'lato *adj* bejewelled

ingiù *adv* down; all'~ downwards; a testa ~ head downwards

Ingl'ungere *vt* order

ingiunzi'one *nf* injunction, court order
■ ~ di pagamento final demand

ingi'uria *nf* insult; (torto) wrong; (danno) damage

ingiuri'are *vt* insult; (fare un torto a) wrong

ingiuri'oso *adj* insulting

ingiusta'mente *adv* unjustly

ingiustifi'cabile *adj* unjustifiable; ‹*comportamento*› indefensible

ingiustifi'cato *adj* unjustified

ingiu'stizia *nf* injustice

ingi'usto *adj* unjust

◦ **in'glese** ☐1 *adj* English
☐2 *nm* Englishman; (lingua) English; **gli inglesi** the English
☐3 *nf* Englishwoman

inglori'oso *adj* inglorious

ingob'bire *vi* become stooped

ingoi'are *vt* swallow

ingol'fare *vt* flood ‹motore›

ingol'farsi *vr* fig get involved; ‹motore› flood

ingol'lare *vt* gulp down

ingom'brante *adj* cumbersome

ingom'brare *vt* clutter up; fig cram ‹mente›

in'gombro *nm* encumbrance; **essere d'∼** be in the way

ingor'digia *nf* greed

in'gordo *adj* greedy

ingor'gare *vt* block

ingor'garsi *vr* be blocked [up]

in'gorgo *nm* blockage; (del traffico) jam

ingoz'zare *vt* gobble up; (nutrire eccessivamente) stuff; fatten ‹animali›

ingoz'zarsi *vr* stuff oneself (**di** with)

ingra'naggio *nm* gear; fig mechanism

ingra'nare ☐1 *vt* engage
☐2 *vi* be in gear

ingrandi'mento *nm* enlargement

ingran'dire *vt* enlarge; (esagerare) magnify

ingran'dirsi *vr* become larger; (aumentare) increase

ingrandi'tore *nm* Phot enlarger

ingras'saggio *nm* greasing, lubrication

ingras'sare ☐1 *vt* fatten [up]; Mech lubricate, grease
☐2 *vi* put on weight

ingras'sarsi *vr* put on weight

in'grasso *nm* **mettere all'∼** force-feed

ingrati'tudine *nf* ingratitude

in'grato *adj* ungrateful; (sgradevole) thankless

ingrazi'arsi *vr* ingratiate oneself with

ingredi'ente *nm* ingredient

◦ **in'gresso** *nm* entrance; (accesso) admittance; (sala) hall; Comput input
■ **ingresso gratuito** *o* **libero** admission free; **'vietato l'∼'** 'no entry', 'no admittance'; **ingresso degli artisti** stage door; **ingresso principale** main entrance; **ingresso di servizio** tradesmen's entrance; **ingresso/uscita** Comput input/output; **ingresso video** Techn video input

ingros'sare ☐1 *vt* make big; (gonfiare) swell
☐2 *vi* grow big; (gonfiare) swell

ingros'sarsi *vr* grow big; (gonfiare) swell

in'grosso: all'∼ *adv* wholesale; (pressappoco) roughly

inguai'arsi *vr* get into trouble

inguai'nare *vt* sheathe

ingual'cibile *adj* crease-resistant

ingua'ribile *adj* incurable

inguaribil'mente *adv* incurably

'inguine *nm* groin

ingurgi'tare *vt* gulp down

ini'bire *vt* inhibit; (vietare) forbid

ini'bito *adj* inhibited

inibi'tore *nm* suppressant

inibizi'one *nf* inhibition; (divieto) prohibition

iniet'tare *vt* inject

iniet'tarsi *vr* **∼ di sangue** ‹occhi› become bloodshot

iniezi'one *nf* injection
■ **iniezione endovenosa** intravenous injection; **iniezione intramuscolare** intramuscular injection

inimic'arsi *vr* **∼ qualcuno** make an enemy of somebody

inimi'cizia *nf* enmity

inimi'tabile *adj* inimitable

inimmagi'nabile *adj* unimaginable

ininfiam'mabile *adj* nonflammable

intelli'gibile *adj* unintelligible

ininterrotta'mente *adv* continuously

ininter'rotto *adj* continuous

iniquità *nf inv* iniquity

i'niquo *adj* iniquitous

inizi'ale *adj* & *nf* initial

inizial'mente *adv* initially

◦ **inizi'are** ☐1 *vt* begin; (avviare) open; **∼ a fare qualcosa** begin doing something; **∼ qualcuno a qualcosa** initiate somebody in something
☐2 *vi* begin

inizia'tiva *nf* initiative; **prendere l'∼** take the initiative
■ **iniziativa privata** private enterprise

inizi'ato, -a *nmf* initiated

inizia|'tore, -trice *nmf* initiator

iniziazi'one *nf* initiation

◦ **i'nizio** *nm* beginning, start; **dare ∼ a** start; **avere ∼** get under way

innaffi'are *vt* water

innaffia'toio *nm* watering-can

innal'zare *vt* raise; (erigere) erect

innal'zarsi *vr* rise

◦ **innamo'rarsi** *vr* fall in love (**di** with)

innamo'rato, -a ☐1 *adj* in love
☐2 *nm* boyfriend
☐3 **innamorata** *nf* girlfriend

in'nanzi ☐1 *adv* (stato in luogo) in front; (di tempo) ahead; (avanti) forward; (prima) before; **d'ora ∼** from now on
☐2 *prep* (prima) before; **∼ a** in front of; **∼ tutto** = INNANZITUTTO

innanzi'tutto *adv* (soprattutto) above all; (per prima cosa) first of all

in'nato *adj* innate
innatu'rale *adj* unnatural
inne'gabile *adj* undeniable
innegabil'mente *adv* undeniably
inneggi'are *vi* praise
innervo'sire *vt* make nervous
innervo'sirsi *vr* get irritated
inne'scare *vt* prime
in'nesco *nm* primer
inne'stare *vt* graft; Mech engage; (inserire) insert
in'nesto *nm* graft; Mech clutch; Electr connection
inneva'mento *nm* snowfall
■ innevamento artificiale snow-making
inne'vato *adj* covered in snow
'inno *nm* hymn
■ inno nazionale national anthem
✓ **inno'cente** *adj* innocent; Jur not guilty
innocente'mente *adv* innocently
inno'cenza *nf* innocence
in'nocuo *adj* innocuous
inno'vare *vt* update
innova'tivo *adj* innovative
innova'tore *adj* trail-blazing
innovazi'one *nf* innovation
innume'revole *adj* innumerable
+ino *suff* fratellino *nm* little brother; sorellina *nf* little sister; freddino *adj* (piuttosto freddo) chilly; bellino *adj* (abbastanza bello) pretty; benino *adv* (cosi cosi) not bad; pochino *adv* (troppo poco) not enough; un pochino a little bit
inocu'lare *vt* inoculate
ino'doro *adj* odourless
inoffen'sivo *adj* inoffensive, harmless; ‹animale› harmless
inol'trare *vt* forward
inol'trarsi *vr* advance
inol'trato *adj* late
✓ **i'noltre** *adv* besides
i'noltro *nm* forwarding
inon'dare *vt* flood
inondazi'one *nf* flood
inope'roso *adj* idle
inopi'nabile *adj* unimaginable
inoppor'tuno *adj* untimely
inor'ganico *adj* inorganic
inorgo'glire *vt* make proud
inorgo'glirsi *vr* become proud
inorri'dire [1] *vt* horrify
[2] *vi* be horrified
inospi'tale *adj* inhospitable
inosser'vato *adj* unobserved; (non rispettato) disregarded; passare ~ go unnoticed
inossi'dabile *adj* stainless

'inox *adj inv* ‹acciaio› stainless; ‹pentole› stainless steel
'input *nm inv*
■ input dati data input
inqua'drare *vt* frame; fig set
inqua'drarsi *vr* ~ in fit into
inquadra'tura *nf* framing
inqualifi'cabile *adj* unspeakable
inquie'tante *adj* unnerving
inquie'tare *vt* worry
inquie'tarsi *vr* get worried; (impazientirsi) get cross
inqui'eto *adj* restless; (preoccupato) worried
inquie'tudine *nf* anxiety
inqui'lino, -a *nmf* tenant
inquina'mento *nm* pollution
■ inquinamento acustico noise pollution; inquinamento atmosferico air pollution; inquinamento luminoso light pollution; inquinamento delle prove Jur tampering with the evidence
inqui'nare *vt* pollute
inqui'nato *adj* polluted
inqui'rente *adj* Jur ‹magistrato› examining; ‹commissione› of investigation
inqui'sire *vt/i* investigate
inqui'sito [1] *adj* under investigation
[2] *nm* person under investigation
inquisi'tore, -trice [1] *adj* inquiring
[2] *nmf* inquisitor
inquisi'torio *adj* questioning
inquisizi'one *nf* inquisition
insabbi'are *vt* bury
insabbi'arsi *vr* run aground
insa'lata *nf* salad
■ insalata belga Belgian endive; insalata di mare seafood salad; insalata mista mixed salad; insalata di riso rice salad; insalata russa Russian salad
insalati'era *nf* salad bowl
insa'lubre *adj* unhealthy
insa'nabile *adj* incurable
insangui'nare *vt* stain with blood
insangui'nato *adj* blood-stained
insapo'nare *vt* soap
insapo'narsi *vr* soap oneself
insapo'nata *nf* soaping
insa'pore *adj* tasteless
insapo'rire *vt* flavour
insa'puta *nf* all'~ di unknown to
in'saturo *adj* unsaturated
insazi'abile *adj* insatiable
inscato'lare *vt* can
inscatola'trice *nf* canning machine
insce'nare *vt* stage
inscin'dibile *adj* inseparable
in'scrivere *vt* Math inscribe
insec'chire *vt/i* wither

insedia'mento nm installation
insedi'are vt install
insedi'arsi vr install oneself
in'segna nf sign; (bandiera) flag; (decorazione) decoration; (emblema) insignia pl; (stemma) symbol
■ insegna luminosa neon sign
insegna'mento nm teaching
inse'gnante [1] adj teaching
[2] nmf teacher
■ insegnante di matematica maths teacher; insegnante di sostegno tutor; insegnante tirocinante student teacher
◦' **inse'gnare** vt/i teach; ~ qualcosa a qualcuno teach somebody something
insegui'mento nm pursuit
insegu'ire vt pursue
insegui|'tore, -trice nmf pursuer
inselvati'chire [1] vt make wild
[2] vi grow wild
inselvati'chirsi vr grow wild
insemi'nare vt inseminate
inseminazi'one nf insemination
■ inseminazione artificiale artificial insemination
insena'tura nf inlet
insensata'mente adv senselessly
insen'sato adj senseless; (folle) crazy
insen'sibile adj fig insensitive; avere le gambe insensibili have no feeling in one's legs
insensibilità nf lack of feeling; fig insensitivity
insepa'rabile adj inseparable
inseri'mento nm insertion
inse'rire vt insert, place ‹annuncio›; Electr connect
inse'rirsi vr ~ in get into
inseri'tore nm
■ inseritore fogli (singoli) (single) sheetfeed
in'serto nm file; (in un giornale) supplement; (in un film ecc) insert
inservi'ente nmf attendant
inserzi'one nf insertion; (avviso) advertisement; inserzioni pl classified ads
inserzio'nista nmf advertiser
insetti'cida nm insecticide
insetti'fugo nm insect repellent
in'setto nm insect
insicu'rezza nf insecurity
insi'curo adj insecure
in'sidia nf trick; (tranello) snare
insidi'are vt/i lay a trap for
insidi'oso adj insidious
◦' **insi'eme** [1] adv together; (contemporaneamente) at the same time
[2] prep ~ a [together] with
[3] nm whole; (completo) outfit; Theat

ensemble; Math set; nell'~ as a whole; tutto ~ (in una volta) at one go
insie'mistica nf set theory
in'signe adj renowned
insignifi'cante adj insignificant
insi'gnire vt decorate
insin'cero adj insincere
insinda'cabile adj final
insinu'ante adj insinuating
insinu'are vt insinuate
insinu'arsi vr penetrate; ~ in fig creep into
insinuazi'one nf insinuation
in'sipido adj insipid
insi'stente adj insistent
insistente'mente adv repeatedly
insi'stenza nf insistence
◦' **in'sistere** vi insist; (perseverare) persevere
'insito adj inherent
insoddisfa'cente adj unsatisfactory
insoddi'sfatto adj unsatisfied; (scontento) dissatisfied
insoddisfazi'one nf dissatisfaction
insoffe'rente adj intolerant
insoffe'renza nf intolerance
insolazi'one nf sunstroke
inso'lente adj rude, insolent
insolente'mente adv insolently
inso'lenza nf rudeness, insolence; (commento) insolent remark
insolita'mente adv unusually
in'solito adj unusual
inso'lubile adj insoluble
inso'luto adj unsolved; (non pagato) unpaid
insol'vente adj Jur insolvent
insol'venza nf insolvency
insol'vibile adj insolvent
◦' **in'somma** adv in short; ~! well!
inson'dabile adj unfathomable
in'sonne adj sleepless
in'sonnia nf insomnia
insonno'lito adj sleepy
insonoriz'zare vt soundproof
insonoriz'zato adj soundproofed
insoppor'tabile adj unbearable
insoppri'mibile adj unsuppressible
insor'genza nf onset
in'sorgere vi revolt, rise up; ‹problema› arise
insormon'tabile adj ‹ostacolo, difficoltà› insurmountable
in'sorto [1] pp di INSORGERE
[2] adj rebellious
[3] nm rebel
insospet'tabile adj unsuspected
insospet'tire [1] vt make suspicious
[2] vi become suspicious
insospet'tirsi vr becomes suspicious

◦' indicates a very frequent word

insoste'nibile *adj* untenable; (insopportabile) unbearable

insostitu'ibile *adj* irreplaceable

insoz'zare *vt* dirty

inspe'rabile *adj* hopeless; (insperato) unhoped-for

inspe'rato *adj* unhoped-for

inspie'gabile *adj* inexplicable

inspiegabil'mente *adv* inexplicably

inspi'rare *vt* breathe in

in'stabile *adj* unstable; (variabile) unsettled

instabilità *nf* instability; (di tempo) changeability

instal'lare *vt* install

instal'larsi *vr* (in casa, lavoro) settle in

installa|'tore, -trice *nmf* fitter

installazi'one *nf* installation; installazioni *pl* di bordo on-board equipment

instan'cabile *adj* untiring

instancabil'mente *adv* tirelessly

instau'rare *vt* found

instau'rarsi *vr* become established

instaurazi'one *nf* foundation

instra'dare *vt* direct

insù: all'∼ *adv* upwards; naso all'∼ turned-up nose

insubordi'nato *adj* insubordinate

insubordinazi'one *nf* insubordination

insuc'cesso *nm* failure

insudici'are *vt* dirty

insudici'arsi *vr* get dirty

insuffici'ente [1] *adj* insufficient; (inadeguato) inadequate [2] *nf* Sch fail

insufficiente'mente *adv* insufficiently

insuffici'enza *nf* insufficiency; (inadeguatezza) inadequacy; Sch fail ■ insufficienza cardiaca cardiac insufficiency; insufficienza di prove lack of evidence

insu'lare *adj* insular

insu'lina *nf* insulin

in'sulso *adj* insipid; (sciocco) silly

insul'tare *vt* insult

in'sulto *nm* insult; coprire qualcuno di insulti heap abuse on somebody

insupe'rabile *adj* insuperable; (eccezionale) incomparable

insurrezi'one *nf* insurrection

insussi'stente *adj* groundless

intac'cabile *adj* subject to corrosion; fig open to criticism

intac'care *vt* nick; (corrodere) corrode; draw on ‹capitale›; (danneggiare) damage

intagli'are *vt* carve

in'taglio *nm* carving

intan'gibile *adj* untouchable

✔ in'tanto *adv* meanwhile; (per ora) for the moment; (avversativo) but; ∼ che while

intarsi'are *vt* inlay

intarsi'ato *adj* ∼ di inset with

in'tarsio *nm* inlay

intasa'mento *nm* (ostruzione) blockage; (ingorgo) traffic jam

inta'sare *vt* block, clog

inta'sarsi *vr* become blocked

inta'sato *adj* blocked

inta'scare *vt* pocket

in'tatto *adj* intact

intavo'lare *vt* start

inte'gerrimo *adj* of integrity

inte'grale *adj* whole; edizione integrale unabridged edition; pane integrale wholemeal bread; versione integrale (di film) uncut version; (di romanzo) unabridged version

integra'lista *nmf* fundamentalist

integral'mente *adv* fully

inte'grante *adj* integral

inte'grare *vt* integrate; (aggiungere) supplement

inte'grarsi *vr* integrate

integra'tivo *adj* supplementary, additional; esame integrativo *test taken by pupil wishing to transfer from arts to a scientific stream etc*

integra'tore *nm* ■ integratore alimentare dietary supplement

integrazi'one *nf* integration

integrità *nf* integrity

'integro *adj* complete; (retto) upright

intelaia'tura *nf* framework

intellet'tivo *adj* intellectual

intel'letto *nm* intellect

intellettu'ale *adj & nmf* intellectual

intellettual'mente *adv* intellectually

✔ intelli'gente *adj* intelligent

intelligente'mente *adv* intelligently

✔ intelli'genza *nf* intelligence ■ intelligenza artificiale artificial intelligence

intelli'ghenzia *nf* intelligentsia

intelli'gibile *adj* intelligible

intelligibil'mente *adv* intelligibly

intelligi'oco *nm* computer game

intempe'rante *adj* intemperate

intempe'ranza *nf* intemperance; intemperanze *pl* excesses

intem'perie *nfpl* bad weather

intempe'stivo *adj* untimely

inten'dente *nm* superintendent

inten'denza *nf* ■ intendenza di finanza inland revenue office

✔ in'tendere *vt* (comprendere) understand; (udire) hear; (avere intenzione) intend; (significare) mean; [siamo] intesi? is that clear?

in'tendersi *vr* (capirsi) understand each other; ~ **di** (essere esperto in) have a good knowledge of; **intendersela con** fam (avere una relazione con) have it off with

intendi'mento *nm* understanding; (intenzione) intention

intendi|'tore, -trice *nmf* connoisseur; **intenditori** *pl* cognoscenti

intene'rire *vt* soften; (commuovere) touch

intene'rirsi *vr* be touched

intensa'mente *adv* intensely

intensifi'care *vt* intensify

intensifi'carsi *vr* intensify

intensità *nf* intensity

intensiva'mente *adv* intensively

inten'sivo *adj* intensive
■ **terapia intensiva** intensive care

in'tenso *adj* intense

inten'tare *vt* start up; ~ **causa contro qualcuno** bring *or* institute proceedings against somebody

inten'tato *adj* **non lasciare nulla di** ~ try everything

in'tento [1] *adj* engrossed (**a** in)
[2] *nm* purpose

intenzio'nale *adj* intentional

intenzio'nato *adj* **essere** ~ **a fare qualcosa** have the intention of doing something

♂ **intenzi'one** *nf* intention; **senza** ~ unintentionally; **avere** ~ **di fare qualcosa** intend to do something, have the intention of doing something

intera'gire *vi* interact

intera'mente *adv* completely, entirely

interat'tivo *adj* interactive

interazi'one *nf* interaction

interca'lare [1] *nm* stock phrase
[2] *vt* insert ‹esclamazione›

intercambi'abile *adj* interchangeable

interca'pedine *nf* cavity

inter'cedere *vi* intercede

intercessi'one *nf* intercession

intercet'tare *vt* intercept; tap ‹telefono›

intercettazi'one *nf* interception
■ **intercettazione telefonica** telephone tapping

inter'city *nm inv* inter-city

intercomuni'cante *adj* [inter]communicating

interconfessio'nale *adj* interdenominational

intercon'nettere *vt* interconnect

intercontinen'tale *adj* intercontinental

inter'correre *vi* ‹tempo› elapse; (esistere) exist

interco'stale *adj* intercostal

♂ indicates a very frequent word

interden'tale *adj* between the teeth; **filo interdentale** dental floss

inter'detto [1] pp di INTERDIRE
[2] *adj* astonished; (proibito) forbidden; **rimanere** ~ be taken aback; **lasciare qualcuno** ~ astonish somebody, dumbfound somebody
[3] *nm* Relig interdict

interdipartimen'tale *adj* interdepartmental

interdipen'dente *adj* interdependent

interdipen'denza *nf* interdependence

inter'dire *vt* ban; (nel calcio) intercept; Jur deprive of civil rights; Relig interdict; ~ **a qualcuno di fare qualcosa** forbid somebody to do something

interdiscipli'nare *adj* interdisciplinary

interdizi'one *nf* ban; (nel calcio) interception; Relig interdict
■ **interdizione giudiziale** *appointment of a legal guardian to a person of unsound mind*; **interdizione legale** *legally imposed ban*; **interdizione dai pubblici uffici** *ban on taking public office*

interessa'mento *nm* interest

interes'sante *adj* interesting; **essere in stato** ~ be pregnant

♂ **interes'sare** [1] *vt* interest; (riguardare) concern
[2] *vi* ~ **a** interest; **non mi interessa** I'm not interested; (non mi importa) I don't care, it doesn't matter to me

interes'sarsi *vr* ~ **a** take an interest in; ~ **di** take care of

interes'sato *adj* (attento) interested; pej self-interested; **diretto** ~ person concerned

♂ **inte'resse** *nm* interest; **fare qualcosa per** ~ do something out of self-interest; **essere nell'**~ **di qualcuno** be in somebody's interest; **un** ~ **del 4%** 4% interest
■ **interesse attivo** interest charge; **interesse maturato** accrued interest; **interesse privato in atti di ufficio** abuse of public office; **interesse a tasso variabile** floating rate interest

interes'senza *nf* Econ profit-sharing

inter'faccia *nf* interface
■ **interfaccia grafica** graphics interface; **interfaccia uomo/macchina** man/machine interface; **interfaccia utente** user interface

interfacci'are *vt* interface

interfacci'arsi *vr* interface

interfe'renza *nf* interference

interfe'rire *vi* interfere

inter'fono *nm* intercom

interga'lattico *adj* intergalactic

interiet'tivo *adj* interjectory

interiezi'one *nf* interjection

'interim *nm inv* (incarico) temporary appointment; (periodo) interim; **ad** ~ on a temporary basis; ‹presidente› acting

interi'ora *nfpl* entrails

interi'ore *adj* inner
interioriz'zare *vt* internalize
interior'mente *adv* (nella parte interiore) internally; (emotivamente) inwardly
inter'linea *nf* line spacing; Typ leading
■ **interlinea doppia** double spacing
interline'are ① *vt* space out
② *adj* line *attrib*
interlocu|'tore, -trice *nmf* speaker, interlocutor fml; **il mio ~** the person I am/was speaking to
inter'ludio *nm* interlude
intermedi'ario, -a *adj & nmf* intermediary; Econ middleman
intermediazi'one *nf* (intervento) mediation
inter'medio *adj* in-between
inter'mezzo *nm* Theat, Mus intermezzo
intermi'nabile *adj* interminable
interministeri'ale *adj* interdepartmental
intermissi'one *nf* intermission
intermit'tente *adj* intermittent; ‹vulcano› dormant
intermit'tenza *nf* **a ~** intermittent
interna'mente *adv* internally
interna'mento *nm* internment; (in manicomio) committal
inter'nare *vt* intern; (in manicomio) commit [to a mental institution]
inter'nato, -a ① *adj* interned
② *nmf* internee
③ *nm* boarding school
✶ **internazio'nale** *adj* international
internazional'mente *adv* internationally
'Internet *nf* Internet; **in ~** on the Internet; **via ~** through the Internet
■ **Internet point** Internet kiosk
inter'nista *nmf* internist
✶ **in'terno** ① *adj* internal; Geog inland; (interiore) inner; ‹politica› national; **alunno ~** boarder
② *nm* interior; (di condominio) flat; Teleph extension; Cinema interior shot; **all'~** inside; **ministero degli interni** Ministry of the Interior, ≈ Home Office
✶ **in'tero** ① *adj* whole, entire; Math whole; (intatto) intact; (completo) complete; **per ~** in full
② *nm* (totalità) whole
interparlamen'tare *adj* interparliamentary
interpar'titico *adj* cross-party
interpel'lanza *nf* parliamentary question
interpel'lare *vt* consult
interpel'lato, -a *nmf* person being questioned
interperso'nale *adj* interpersonal
interplane'tario *adj* interplanetary

interpo'lare *vt* interpolate
inter'porre *vt* interpose; use ‹influenza›; **~ ostacoli a** put obstacles in the way of
inter'porsi *vr* intervene; **~ tra** come between
inter'posto *adj* **per interposta persona** through a third party
interpre'tare *vt* interpret; Mus perform; **~ male** misinterpret
interpretari'ato *nm* interpreting
interpretazi'one *nf* interpretation; Mus performance
in'terprete *nmf* interpreter; Mus performer
interpunzi'one *nf* punctuation
inter'rare *vt* (seppellire) bury; (riempire) fill in; lay underground ‹cavo, tubo›; plant ‹pianta, seme›
inter'rato *nm* basement
interregio'nale *nm* long-distance train, stopping at most stations
interro'gante *nmf* questioner
interro'gare *vt* question; Sch examine
interrogativa'mente *adv* ‹guardare› inquiringly
interroga'tivo ① *adj* interrogative; (sguardo) questioning; **punto ~** question mark
② *nm* question
interro'gato *adj* ‹studente› examinee; Jur person questioned
interroga'torio *adj & nm* questioning
interrogazi'one *nf* question; Sch oral [test]
■ **interrogazione ciclica** polling; **interrogazione parlamentare** parliamentary question
✶ **inter'rompere** *vt* interrupt; (sospendere) stop; cut off ‹collegamento›
inter'rompersi *vr* break off
interrut'tore *nm* switch
■ **interruttore a reostato** dimmer
interruzi'one *nf* interruption; **senza ~** non-stop
■ **interruzione della corrente** power cut; **interruzione di gravidanza** termination of pregnancy
interscambi'abile *adj* interchangeable
inter'scambio *nm* import-export trade
interse'care *vt* intersect
interse'carsi *vr* intersect
intersezi'one *nf* intersection
inter'stizio *nm* interstice
interur'bana *nf* long-distance call
interur'bano *adj* inter-city; **telefonata interurbana** long-distance call
interval'lare *vt* space out
inter'vallo *nm* interval; (spazio) space; (in ufficio) tea/coffee break; TV, Sch break; **fare un ~** have a break; **a intervalli regolari** at regular intervals
■ **intervallo del pranzo** lunch hour, lunch

break; **intervallo pubblicitario** commercial break

✔ **interve'nire** *vi* intervene; Med (operare) operate; ~ **a** take part in

inter'vento *nm* intervention; (presenza) presence; (chirurgico) operation; **pronto intervento** emergency services; **un** ~ **a cuore aperto** open-heart surgery

inter'vista *nf* interview
■ **intervista esclusiva** exclusive interview

intervi'stare *vt* interview

intervi'stato, -a *nmf* interviewee

intervista|'tore, -trice *nmf* interviewer

in'tesa *nf* understanding; **d'**~ ‹cenno› of acknowledgement

in'teso, -a ① pp di INTENDERE
② *adj* **resta** ~ **che ...** needless to say, ...; ~ **a** meant to; **[siamo] intesi!** agreed!
③ *nf* understanding

in'tessere *vt* weave together

inte'stare *vt* head; write one's name and address at the top of ‹lettera›; Comm register

inte'starsi *vr* ~ **a fare qualcosa** take it into one's head to do something

intesta'tario, -a *nmf* holder

intestazi'one *nf* heading; (su carta da lettere) letterhead

intesti'nale *adj* intestinal

inte'stino ① *adj* ‹lotte› internal
② *nm* intestine
■ **intestino crasso** large intestine; **intestino tenue** small intestine

intiepi'dire *vt* (scaldare) warm; cool ‹passione, desiderio›

intiepi'dirsi *vr* cool [down]; (scaldarsi) warm [up]; ‹fede› wane

intima'mente *adv* ‹conoscere› intimately

inti'mare *vt* order; ~ **l'alt** give the order to halt; ~ **l'alt a qualcuno** order somebody to stop

intimazi'one *nf* order
■ **intimazione di sfratto** eviction notice

intimida'torio *adj* threatening, intimidating

intimidazi'one *nf* intimidation

intimi'dire *vt* intimidate

intimi'dirsi *vr* be overwhelmed with shyness

intimità *nf* intimacy, togetherness

'intimo ① *adj* intimate; (interno) innermost; ‹amico› close
② *nm* (amico) close friend; (dell'animo) heart

intimo'rire *vt* frighten

intimo'rirsi *vr* get frightened

intimo'rito *adj* frightened

in'tingere *vt* dip

in'tingolo *nm* sauce; (pietanza) stew

intiriz'zire *vt* numb

intiriz'zirsi *vr* grow numb

intiriz'zito *adj* **essere** ~ (dal freddo) be perished

intito'lare *vt* entitle; (dedicare) dedicate

intito'larsi *vr* be called

intolle'rabile *adj* intolerable

intolle'rante *adj* intolerant

intona'care *vt* plaster

intonaca'tore *nm* plasterer

in'tonaco *nm* plaster
■ **intonaco a pinocchino** pebbledash

into'nare *vt* start to sing; tune ‹strumento›; (accordare) match ‹colori›

into'narsi *vr* match

into'nato *adj* ‹persona› able to sing in tune; ‹voce, strumento› in tune; ‹colore› matching

intonazi'one *nf* (inflessione) intonation; ‹ironica› tone; (cantando) ability to sing in tune

in'tonso *adj* ‹libro› untouched

inton'tire ① *vt* ‹botta› stun, daze; ‹gas› make dizzy; fig stun
② *vi* go ga-ga

inton'tito *adj* dazed; fig stunned; ‹con l'età› ga-ga

intop'pare *vi* ~ **in** run into

in'toppo *nm* **c'è un** ~ something's come up

✔ **in'torno** ① *adv* around
② *prep* ~ **a** around; (circa) about; ~ **al mondo** round-the-world

intorpi'dire *vt* numb

intorpi'dirsi *vr* become numb

intorpi'dito *adj* torpid

intossi'care *vt* poison

intossi'carsi *vr* be poisoned

intossicazi'one *nf* poisoning
■ **intossicazione alimentare** food poisoning

intra-azien'dale *adj* in-house

intradu'cibile *adj* untranslatable

intralci'are *vt* hamper

in'tralcio *nm* hitch; **essere d'**~ (a qualcuno/qualcosa) be a hindrance (to somebody/something)

intrallaz'zare *vi* intrigue

intral'lazzo *nm* racket

intramon'tabile *adj* timeless

intramusco'lare *adj* intramuscular

intra'net *nf inv* intranet

intransi'gente *adj* intransigent, uncompromising

intransi'genza *nf* intransigence

intransi'tivo *adj* intransitive

intrappo'lato *adj* **rimanere** ~ be trapped

intrapren'dente *adj* enterprising

intrapren'denza *nf* initiative

intra'prendere *vt* undertake

intrat'tabile *adj* very difficult

intratte'nere *vt* entertain

intratte'nersi *vr* linger
intratteni'mento *nm* entertainment
intrave'dere *vt* catch a glimpse of; (presagire) foresee
intrecci'are *vt* interweave; plait ‹capelli, corda›; ~ **le mani** clasp one's hands
intrecci'arsi *vr* intertwine; (aggrovigliarsi) become tangled
in'treccio *nm* (trama) plot; (di nastri, strade) tangle
in'trepido *adj* intrepid
intri'cato *adj* tangled
intri'gante ① *adj* intriguing ② *nmf* schemer
intri'gare ① *vt* entangle; (incuriosire) intrigue ② *vi* be intriguing
intri'garsi *vr* become entangled; (immischiarsi) meddle
in'trigo *nm* plot; **intrighi** *pl* plotting; (di corte) intrigues
intrinseca'mente *adv* intrinsically
in'trinseco *adj* intrinsic
in'triso *adj* ~ **di** soaked with; *fig* imbued with
intri'stire *vt* sadden
intri'stirsi *vr* grow sad
⚔ **intro'durre** *vt* introduce; (inserire) insert; ~ **a** (iniziare a) introduce to
intro'dursi *vr* get in; ~ **in** get into
introdut'tivo *adj* ‹pagine, discorso› introductory
introduzi'one *nf* introduction
in'troito *nm* income, revenue; (incasso) takings *pl*
intro'mettere *vt* introduce
intro'mettersi *vr* interfere; (interporsi) intervene
intromissi'one *nf* intervention
introspet'tivo *adj* introspective
intro'vabile *adj* unobtainable
intro'verso, -a ① *adj* introverted ② *nmf* introvert
intrufo'larsi *vr* sneak in
in'truglio *nm* concoction
intrusi'one *nf* intrusion
in'truso, -a *nmf* intruder
intu'ibile *adj* deducible
intu'ire *vt* perceive
intuitiva'mente *adv* intuitively
intui'tivo *adj* intuitive
in'tuito *nm* intuition
intuizi'one *nf* intuition
inu'mano *adj* inhuman
inu'mare *vt* inter
inumi'dire *vt* dampen; moisten ‹labbra›
inumi'dirsi *vr* become damp
⚔ **i'nutile** *adj* useless; (superfluo) unnecessary

inutilità *nf* uselessness
inutiliz'zabile *adj* unusable
inutiliz'zato *adj* unused
inutil'mente *adv* fruitlessly
inva'dente *adj* intrusive
⚔ **in'vadere** *vt* invade; (affollare) overrun
inva'ghirsi *vr* ~ **di** take a fancy to
invali'cabile *adj* impassable; '**limite** ~' Mil 'no access beyond this point'
invali'dare *vt* invalidate
invalidità *nf* disability; Jur invalidity
in'valido, -a ① *adj* invalid; (handicappato) disabled ② *nmf* disabled person; **gli invalidi** the handicapped
■ **invalido di guerra** disabled ex-serviceman; **invalido del lavoro** industrial accident victim
in'vano *adv* in vain
invari'abile *adj* invariable
invariabil'mente *adv* invariably
invari'ato *adj* unchanged
invasi'one *nf* invasion
in'vaso *pp di* INVADERE
inva'sore ① *adj* invading ② *nm* invader
invecchia'mento *nm* (di vino) maturation
⚔ **invecchi'are** *vt/i* age
⚔ **in'vece** *adv* instead; (anzi) but; ~ **di** instead of
inve'ire *vi* ~ **contro** inveigh against
invele'nito *adj* embittered
inven'dibile *adj* unsaleable
inven'duto *adj* unsold
⚔ **inven'tare** *vt* invent
inventari'are *vt* make an inventory of
inven'tario *nm* inventory
inven'tato *adj* made-up
inven'tiva *nf* inventiveness
inven'tivo *adj* inventive
inven|'tore, -trice *nmf* inventor
invenzi'one *nf* invention
inver'nale *adj* wintry; **sport** *pl* **invernali** winter sports
⚔ **in'verno** *nm* winter
invero'simile *adj* improbable
inverosimil'mente *adv* incredibly
inversa'mente *adv* inversely; ~ **proporzionale** in inverse proportional
inversi'one *nf* inversion; Mech reversal; **fare un'**~ **a U** do a U-turn
■ **inversione di fondo** Comput reverse video; **inversione di tendenza** turnaround
in'verso ① *adj* inverse; (opposto) opposite ② *nm* opposite
inverte'brato *adj & nm* invertebrate
inver'tire *vt* reverse; (capovolgere) turn upside-down

investi'gare *vt* investigate

investiga|'tore, -trice *nmf* investigator
- **investigatore privato** private investigator, private eye

investigazi'one *nf* investigation

investi'mento *nm* investment; (incidente) crash

inve'stire *vt* invest; (urtare) collide with; (travolgere) run over; **~ qualcuno di** invest somebody with

investi'tura *nf* investiture

invete'rato *adj* inveterate

invet'tiva *nf* invective

⚘ **invi'are** *vt* send

invi'ato, -a *nmf* envoy; (di giornale) correspondent
- **inviato di pace** peace envoy

in'vidia *nf* envy

invidi'are *vt* envy

invidi'oso *adj* envious

invigo'rire *vt* invigorate

invigo'rirsi *vr* become strong

invin'cibile *adj* invincible

in'vio *nm* dispatch; Comput enter

invio'labile *adj* inviolable

invipe'rirsi *vr* get nasty

invipe'rito *adj* furious

invischi'arsi *vr* get involved (**in** in)

invi'sibile *adj* invisible

invisibilità *nf* invisibility

invi'tante *adj* ‹piatto, profumo› enticing

⚘ **invi'tare** *vt* invite

invi'tato, -a *nmf* guest

⚘ **in'vito** *nm* invitation

invo'care *vt* invoke; (implorare) beg

invocazi'one *nf* invocation

invogli'are *vt* tempt; (indurre) induce

invogli'arsi *vr* **~ di** take a fancy to

involga'rire *vt* vulgarize

involontaria'mente *adv* involuntarily

involon'tario *adj* involuntary

invol'tini *nmpl* stuffed rolls (*of meat, pastry*)

in'volto *nm* parcel; (fagotto) bundle

in'volucro *nm* wrapping

invo'luto *adj* involved

invulne'rabile *adj* invulnerable

inzacche'rare *vt* splash with mud

inzup'pare *vt* soak; (intingere) dip

inzup'parsi *vr* get soaked

⚘ **'io** ① *pers pron* I; **sono io** it's me; **l'ho fatto io [stesso]** I did it myself
  ② *nm* **l'io** the ego

i'odio *nm* iodine

i'one *nm* ion

i'onico *adj* Ionic

I'onio *nm* **lo ~** the Ionian [Sea]

iono'sfera *nf* ionosphere

i'osa: a ~ *adv* in abundance

iperattività *nf* hyperactivity

iperat'tivo *adj* hyperactive

i'perbole *nf* hyperbole

iper'critico *adj* hypercritical

ipermer'cato *nm* hypermarket

iper'metrope *adj* long-sighted

ipersen'sibile *adj* hypersensitive

ipertensi'one *nf* high blood pressure

iper'testo *nm* Comput hypertext

iperte'stuale *adj*
- **collegamento ipertestuale** hyperlink

iperventi'lare *vi* hyperventilate

ip'nosi *nf* hypnosis

ipnotera'pia *nf* hypnotherapy

ip'notico *adj* hypnotic

ipno'tismo *nm* hypnotism

ipnotiz'zare *vt* hypnotize

ipoaller'genico *adj* hypoallergenic

ipoca'lorico *adj* low-calorie

ipo'centro *nm* focus

ipocon'dria *nf* hypochondria

ipocon'driaco, -a *adj & nmf* hypochondriac

ipocri'sia *nf* hypocrisy

i'pocrita ① *adj* hypocritical
  ② *nmf* hypocrite

ipocrita'mente *adv* hypocritically

ipo'dermico *adj* hypodermic

i'pofisi *nf inv* pituitary gland

ipo'teca *nf* mortgage

ipote'cabile *adj* mortgageable

ipote'care *vt* mortgage

ipote'cario *adj* mortgage *attrib*

ipote'nusa *nf* hypotenuse

ipo'termia *nf* hypothermia

i'potesi *nf inv* hypothesis; (caso, eventualità) eventuality; **nella migliore delle ~** at best; **nella peggiore delle ~** if the worst comes to the worst

ipo'tetico *adj* hypothetical

ipotiz'zare *vt* hypothesize

'ippico, -a ① *adj* horse *attrib*
  ② *nf* riding

ippoca'stano *nm* horse-chestnut

ip'podromo *nm* racecourse

ippo'potamo *nm* hippopotamus

'ipsilon *nf inv* [the letter] y

'ira *nf* anger

ira'scibile *adj* irascible

i'rato *adj* irate

'iride *nf* Anat iris; (arcobaleno) rainbow

'iris *nm inv* Bot iris

Ir'landa *nf* Ireland
- **Irlanda del Nord** Northern Ireland

⚘ indicates a very frequent word

irlan'dese [1] *adj* Irish
  [2] *nm* Irishman; (lingua) Irish
  [3] *nf* Irishwoman
iro'nia *nf* irony
i'ronico *adj* ironic[al]
irradi'are *vt/i* radiate
irradiazi'one *nf* radiation
irraggiun'gibile *adj* unattainable
irragio'nevole *adj* unreasonable;
  ‹speranza, timore› irrational; (assurdo)
  absurd
irranci'dire *vi* go rancid
irrazio'nale *adj* irrational
irrazionalità *adj* irrationality
irrazional'mente *adv* irrationally
irre'ale *adj* unreal
irrea'listico *adj* unrealistic
irrealiz'zabile *adj* unattainable
irrealtà *nf* unreality
irrecupe'rabile *adj* irrecoverable
irrecu'sabile *adj* incontrovertible
irredi'mibile *adj* irredeemable
irrefre'nabile *adj* uncontrollable
irrefu'tabile *adj* irrefutable
irrego'lare *adj* irregular
irregolarità *nf inv* irregularity; (di terreno)
  unevenness; Sport foul
irregolar'mente *adv* ‹frequentare›
  irregularly; ‹comportarsi› erratically;
  ‹disporre› unevenly
irremo'vibile *adj* fig adamant
irrepa'rabile *adj* irreparable
irrepe'ribile *adj* ‹persona› not to be
  found; **sarò irreperibile** I'm not going to be
  contactable
irrepren'sibile *adj* irreproachable
irrepri'mibile *adj* irrepressible
irrequi'eto *adj* restless
irresi'stibile *adj* irresistible
irresistibil'mente *adv* irresistibly
irreso'luto *adj* irresolute
irrespon'sabile *adj* irresponsible
irresponsabilità *nf* irresponsibility
irrestrin'gibile *adj* preshrunk
irre'tire *vt* seduce
irrever'sibile *adj* irreversible
irreversibil'mente *adv* irrevocably
irrevo'cabile *adj* irrevocable
irrevocabil'mente *adv* irreversibly
irricono'scibile *adj* unrecognizable
irridu'cibile *adj* irreducible
irri'gare *vt* irrigate; ‹fiume› flow through
☞ **irrigazi'one** *nf* irrigation
irrigidi'mento *nm* (di muscoli) stiffening;
  (di disciplina) tightening
irrigi'dire *vt* stiffen up
irrigi'dirsi *vr* stiffen up
irrile'vante *adj* unimportant

irrimedi'abile *adj* irreparable
irrimediabil'mente *adv* irreparably
irripe'tibile *adj* unrepeatable
irri'solto *adj* unresolved
irri'sorio *adj* derisive; (insignificante)
  derisory
irri'tabile *adj* irritable
irri'tante *adj* aggravating, annoying
irri'tare *vt* irritate, annoy
irri'tarsi *vr* get annoyed
irri'tato *adj* irritated, annoyed; ‹gola› sore
irritazi'one *nf* irritation
irrive'renza *nf* (qualità) irreverence;
  (azione) irreverent action
irrobu'stire *vt* fortify
irrobu'stirsi *vr* get stronger
ir'rompere *vi* burst (in into)
irro'rare *vt* sprinkle
irrorazi'one *nf* (di piante) crop spraying
irru'ente *adj* impetuous
irruvi'dire *vt* roughen
irruvi'dirsi *vr* become rough
irruzi'one *nf* raid; fig eruption; **fare ∼ in**
  burst into
ir'suto *adj* shaggy
'irto *adj* bristly
i'scritto, -a [1] *pp di* ISCRIVERE
  [2] *adj* registered
  [3] *nmf* member; **per ∼** in writing
☞ **i'scrivere** *vt* register
i'scriversi *vr* **∼ a** register at, enrol at
  ‹scuola›; join ‹circolo ecc›
iscrizi'one *nf* registration; (epigrafe)
  inscription
i'slamico *adj* Islamic
isla'mismo *nm* Islam
isla'mista *nmf* Islamist
l'slanda *nf* Iceland
islan'dese [1] *adj* Icelandic
  [2] *nmf* Icelander
'ismi *nmpl* isms
i'sobara *nf* isobar
☞ **'isola** *nf* island; **le isole britanniche** the
  British Isles; **l'∼ di Man** Isle of Man
  ■ **isola deserta** desert island; **isola pedonale**
  traffic island; **isola spartitraffico** traffic island
iso'lano, -a [1] *adj* insular
  [2] *nmf* islander
iso'lante [1] *adj* insulating
  [2] *nm* insulator
☞ **iso'lare** *vt* isolate; Mech, Electr insulate;
  (acusticamente) soundproof
iso'lato [1] *adj* isolated
  [2] *nm* (di appartamenti) block
isolazio'nismo *nm* isolationism
iso'metrico *adj* isometric
i'soscele *adj* isosceles
is'panico *adj* Hispanic**

ispessi'mento *nm* thickening

ispes'sire *vt* thicken

ispes'sirsi *vr* thicken

ispetto'rato *nm* inspectorate

ispet'tore *nm* inspector
- ispettore capo chief inspector; **ispettore di polizia** police inspector; **ispettore scolastico** inspector of schools; **ispettore delle tasse** tax inspector; **ispettore di zona** Comm area manager

ispezio'nare *vt* inspect

ispezi'one *nf* inspection; (di nave) boarding

'ispido *adj* bristly

ispi'rare *vt* inspire; suggest ‹idea, soluzione›

ispi'rarsi *vr* ~ a be based on

ispi'rato *adj* inspired

ispirazi'one *nf* inspiration; (idea) idea

Isra'ele *nm* Israel

israeli'ano, -a *adj & nmf* Israeli

is'sare *vt* hoist

ist. *abbr* (**istituto**) dept

istan'taneo, -a ① *adj* instantaneous ② *nf* snapshot

❧ **i'stante** *nm* instant; **all'**~ instantly

i'stanza *nf* petition
- istanza di divorzio petition for divorce

isterecto'mia *nf* hysterectomy

i'sterico *adj* hysterical; **attacco isterico** hysterics *pl*

iste'rismo *nm* hysteria
- isterismo di massa mass hysteria

isti'gare *vt* instigate; ~ **qualcuno al male** incite somebody to evil

istiga|'tore, -trice *nmf* instigator

istigazi'one *nf* instigation; ~ **a delinquere** incitement to crime

istintiva'mente *adv* instinctively

istin'tivo *adj* instinctive

i'stinto *nm* instinct; **d'**~ instinctively
- istinto di conservazione instinct of self-preservation; **istinto materno** maternal instinct

istitu'ire *vt* institute; (fondare) found; initiate ‹manifestazione›

isti'tuto *nm* institute; Sch secondary school; Univ department
- istituto di bellezza beauty salon; **istituto commerciale** business college; **istituto di credito** bank; **istituto per l'infanzia** children's home; **istituto tecnico professionale** technical college

istitu|'tore, -trice *nmf* (insegnante) tutor; (fondatore) founder

istituzio'nale *adj* institutional

istituzionaliz'zare *vt* institutionalize

istituzionaliz'zarsi *vr* become an institution

istituzionalizzazi'one *nf* institutionalization

istituzi'one *nf* institution; **le istituzioni** state institutions

'istmo *nm* isthmus

isto'gramma *nm* bar chart

istolo'gia *nf* histology

istra'dare *vt* divert; fig guide (a towards)

'istrice *nm* porcupine

istri'one *nm* clown; Theat sl ham

istru'ire *vt* instruct; (addestrare) train; (informare) inform; Jur prepare

istru'ito *adj* well-educated

istrut'tivo *adj* instructive, enlightening

istrut|'tore, -trice *nmf* instructor
- giudice istruttore examining magistrate; **istruttore di guida** driving instructor; **istruttore di nuoto** swimming instructor

istrut'toria *nf* Jur investigation

istruzi'one *nf* instruction; Sch education; **ministero della pubblica istruzione** Department of Education
- istruzioni *pl* per l'uso instructions for use

istupi'dire *vt* stupefy

I'talia *nf* Italy

❧ **itali'ano, -a** *adj & nmf* Italian

italoameri'cano *adj* Italian-American

itine'rante *adj* wandering; ‹mostra› touring; ‹spettacolo› travelling

itine'rario *nm* route, itinerary
- itinerario turistico tourist route

itte'rizia *nf* jaundice

'ittico *adj* fishing *attrib*

i'uta *nf* jute

I.V.A. *nf abbr* (**imposta sul valore aggiunto**) VAT; **I.V.A. compresa** inclusive of VAT, VAT inclusive

'ivi *adv* (linguaggio burocratico) therein

Jj

ja'bot *nm inv* jabot
jack *nm inv* jack
ja'cquard *adj inv* (nella maglia) jacquard
'jais *nm* jet
'jam-session *nf inv* jam-session
jazz *nm* jazz
jaz'zista *nmf* jazz player
jeep® *nf inv* jeep®
'jersey *nm* jersey
jet *nm inv* jet
■ jet privato private jet
jet-'set *nm* jet set
'jingle *nm inv* jingle
'jodel *nm inv* yodel
'jogging *nm* jogging

joint 'venture *nf inv* Comm joint venture
'jolly 1 *nm inv* (carta da gioco) joker
2 *adj* Comput
■ carattere jolly wildcard [character]
'joystick *nm inv* joystick
Jugo'slavia *nf* Hist Yugoslavia
jugo'slavo, -a *adj & nmf* Hist Yugoslav[ian]
ju'jitsu *nm* ju-jitsu
juke'box *nm inv* juke box
jumbo-jet *nm inv* jumbo jet
junghi'ano, -a *adj & nmf* Jungian
'junior 1 *adj inv* junior
2 *nm* (*pl* **juniores**) junior
'juta *nf* jute

Kk

kafki'ano *adj* Kafkan, Kafkaesque
ka'jal *nm inv* kohl
'kaki 1 *adj inv* khaki
2 *nm inv* persimmon
ka'pok *nm* kapok
ka'putt *adj inv* kaput
kara'kiri *nm* fare ~ commit hara-kiri
kara'oke *nm inv* karaoke; apparecchio per ~ karaoke machine
kara'te *nm* karate
kart *nm inv* go-kart
kar'tismo *nm* go-karting; fare del ~ go go-karting
'kasher *adj inv* kosher
'Kashmir *nm* Kashmir
ka'yak *nm inv* kayak
Ka'zakistan *nm* Kazakhstan
KB Comput *abbr* (**kilobyte**) K, KB
Kbyte Comput *abbr* (**kilobyte**) kbyte
ke'bab *nm inv* kebab
'Kenya *nm* Kenya
ker'messe *nf inv* fair; fig rowdy celebration
kero'sene *nm* paraffin
'ketchup *nm* ketchup
kg *abbr* (**chilogrammo**) kg

kib'butz *nm inv* kibbutz
'killer *nmf inv* assassin, hit man
'kilo *nm* kilo
kilt *nm inv* kilt
ki'mono *nm inv* kimono
kinesitera'pia *nf* physiotherapy
Kir'ghizistan *nm* Kyrgyzstan
kit *nm inv*
■ kit di aggiornamento upgrade kit; kit multimediale multimedia kit
kitsch *adj inv* kitschy
'kiwi *nm inv* kiwi
'kleenex® *nm inv* Kleenex
km *abbr* (**chilometro**) km
km/h *abbr* (**chilometri all'ora**) kph
kmq *abbr* (**chilometro quadrato**) km²
ko'ala *nm inv* koala
koso'varo, -a *adj & nmf* Kosovan
'Kosovo *nm* Kosovo
'krapfen *nm inv* doughnut
'kripton *nm* krypton
'Kurdistan *nm* Kurdistan
kuwaiti'ano *nm* Kuwaiti
kW *abbr* (**kilowatt**) kW
K-'way® *nm inv* cagoule
kWh *abbr* (**kilowatt all'ora**) kWh

L l

l' *def art mf (before vowel)* the; ▶ IL

🗡 **la** 1 *def art f* the; ▶ IL
2 *pron* (oggetto, riferito a persona) her; (riferito a cosa, animale) it; (forma di cortesia) you
3 *nm inv* Mus (chiave, nota) A

🗡 **là** *adv* there; **di là** (in quel luogo) in there; (da quella parte) that way; **eccolo là!** there he is!; **farsi più in là** (far largo) make way; **là dentro** in there; **là fuori** out there; **[ma] va' là!** come off it!; **più in là** (nel tempo) later on; (nello spazio) further on

🗡 **'labbro** *nm* (*pl nf* **labbra**) lip; **pendere dalle labbra di qualcuno** hang on somebody's every word
■ **labbro leporino** harelip

labi'ale *adj & nf* labial

'labile *adj* fleeting

labiolet'tura *nf* lip-reading

labi'rinto *nm* labyrinth; (di sentieri ecc) maze

🗡 **labora'torio** *nm* laboratory; (di negozio, officina ecc) workshop
■ **laboratorio linguistico** language lab

laboriosa'mente *adv* laboriously

labori'oso *adj* (operoso) industrious; (faticoso) laborious

labra'dor *nm inv* labrador

labu'rista 1 *adj* Labour
2 *nmf* member of the Labour Party

'lacca *nf* lacquer; (per capelli) hairspray

lac'care *vt* lacquer

lacchè *nm inv* lackey

'laccio *nm* noose; (lazo) lasso; (trappola) snare; (stringa) lace
■ **laccio emostatico** tourniquet

lace'rante *adj* ‹grido› earsplitting

lace'rare *vt* tear; lacerate ‹carne›

lace'rarsi *vr* tear

lacerazi'one *nf* laceration

'lacero *adj* torn; (cencioso) ragged

la'conico *adj* laconic

🗡 **'lacrima** *nf* tear; (goccia) drop

lacri'male *adj* ‹condotto, ghiandola› tear *attrib*

lacri'mare *vi* weep

lacri'mevole *adj* tear-jerking

lacri'mogeno *adj* gas ∼ tear gas

lacri'moso *adj* tearful

la'cuna *nf* gap

lacu'noso *adj* ‹preparazione, resoconto› incomplete

la'custre *adj* lake *attrib*

lad'dove *conj* whereas

🗡 **'ladro, -a** 1 *adj* thieving
2 *nmf* thief; **al ∼!** stop thief!

ladro'cinio *nm* theft

la'druncolo *nm* petty thief

'lager *nm inv* concentration camp

🗡 **laggiù** *adv* down there; (lontano) over there

'lagna *nf* fam (persona) moaning Minnie; (film) bore

la'gnanza *nf* complaint

la'gnarsi *vr* moan, whinge; (protestare) complain (**di** about)

la'gnoso *adj* ‹persona› moaning, whining; ‹film› weepy

🗡 **'lago** *nm* lake
■ **lago di Garda** Lake Garda; **lago di sangue** pool of blood

la'guna *nf* lagoon

lagu'nare *adj* lagoon *attrib*

laiciz'zare *vt* laicize

'laico, -a 1 *adj* lay; ‹vita› secular
2 *nm* layman
3 *nf* laywoman

'lama 1 *nf* blade; **a doppia ∼** ‹rasoio› twin-blade
2 *nm inv* (animale) llama

lambic'carsi *vr* ∼ **il cervello** rack one's brains

lam'bire *vt* lap

lamé *nm inv* lamé

la'mella *nf* (di fungo) lamella; (di metallo, plastica) sheet

🗡 **lamen'tare** *vt* lament

lamen'tarsi *vr* moan; ∼ **di** (lagnarsi) complain about

lamen'tela *nf* complaint

lamen'tevole *adj* mournful; (pietoso) pitiful

la'mento *nm* moan

la'metta *nf*
■ **lametta, [da barba]** razor blade

lami'era *nf* sheet metal
■ **lamiera ondulata** corrugated iron

'lamina *nf* foil
■ **lamina d'oro** gold leaf

lami'nare *vt* laminate

lami'naria *nf* kelp

lami'nato 1 *adj* laminated
2 *nm* laminate; (tessuto) lamé

'lampada *nf* lamp
■ **lampada abbronzante** sunlamp; **lampada**

🗡 indicates a very frequent word

alogena halogen lamp; **lampada da comodino** beside lamp; **lampada a gas** gas lamp; **lampada a olio** oil lamp; **lampada a pila** torch; **lampada da soffitto** overhead light; **lampada da tavolo** table lamp

lampa'dario *nm* chandelier

lampa'dato *nm* sl sun-bed freak

lampa'dina *nf* light bulb

lam'pante *adj* clear

lam'para *nf light used when fishing at night*

lampeg'giante *adj* flashing

lampeggi'are *vi* flash

lampeggia'tore *nm* Auto indicator

lampi'one *nm* street lamp

'lampo *nm* flash of lightning; (luce) flash; **lampi** *pl* lightning *sg*

■ **cerniera lampo** zip [fastener], zipper Am; **lampo di genio** stroke of genius; **lampo al magnesio** magnesium flash

lam'pone *nm* raspberry

'lana *nf* wool; **di ~** woollen

■ **lana d'acciaio** steel wool; **lana grossa** double knitting [wool]; **lana merino** botany wool; **lana vergine** new wool; **lana di vetro** glass wool

lan'cetta *nf* pointer; (di orologio) hand

■ **lancetta dei minuti** minute hand; **lancetta delle ore** hour hand; **lancetta dei secondi** second hand

'lancia *nf* (arma) spear, lance; Naut launch

■ **lancia di salvataggio** lifeboat

lanciafi'amme *nm inv* flamethrower

lancia'missili *nm inv* missile launcher

lancia'palle *adj inv* **macchina ~** ball launcher for tennis practice ① *adj inv* **pistola lanciarazzi** Very pistol
② *nm inv* rocket launcher

✔ **lanci'are** *vt* throw; (da un aereo) drop; launch ‹missile, prodotto, attacco›; give ‹grido›; Comput run ‹file›; **~ uno sguardo a** glance at; **~ in alto** throw up

lanci'arsi *vr* fling oneself; (intraprendere) launch out

lanci'nante *adj* piercing

'lancio *nm* throwing; (da aereo) drop; (di missile, prodotto) launch; Comput (di file) running

■ **lancio del disco** discus [throwing]; **lancio del giavellotto** javelin [throwing]; **lancio col paracadute** (di persona) parachute jump; (di pacco) airdrop, parachute drop; **lancio del peso** putting the shot, shot put

'landa *nf* moor

languida'mente *adv* languidly

'languido *adj* languid; (debole) feeble

langu'ore *nm* languor; (spossatezza) listlessness

■ **languore di stomaco** hunger pangs *pl*

lani'ero *adj* wool; **industria laniera** wool industry

lani'ficio *nm* woollen mill

lano'lina *nf* lanolin

la'noso *adj* woolly

lan'terna *nf* lantern; (faro) lighthouse

la'nugine *nf* down

'Laos *nm* Laos

lapalissi'ano *adj* obvious

laparosco'pia *nf* laparoscopy

lapi'dare *vt* stone; fig demolish

lapi'dario *adj* (conciso) terse; **arte lapidaria** stone carving

'lapide *nf* tombstone; (commemorativa) memorial tablet

'lapis *nm inv* pencil

lapi'slazzuli *nm inv* lapis lazuli

'lappa *nf* Bot burr

Lap'ponia *nf* Lapland

'lapsus *nm inv* lapse, error

■ **lapsus freudiano** Freudian slip

'laptop *nm inv* laptop

lardel'lare *vt* Culin lard

'lardo *nm* lard

larga'mente *adv* (ampiamente) widely

largheggi'are *vi* **~ in** be free with

lar'ghezza *nf* width; (di spalle) breadth; fig liberality

■ **larghezza di vedute** broad-mindedness

✔ **'largo** ① *adj* wide; (ampio) broad; ‹abito› loose; (liberale) liberal; (abbondante) generous; **stare alla larga** keep away; **~ di manica** fig generous; **~ di spalle/vedute** broad-shouldered/-minded; **a gambe larghe** with one's legs wide apart; **di larghe vedute** broad-minded
② *nm* width; **andare al ~** Naut go out to sea; **fare ~** make room; **farsi ~** make one's way; **al ~ di** off the coast of

'larice *nm* larch

la'ringe *nf* larynx

larin'gite *nf* laryngitis

'larva *nf* larva; (persona emaciata) shadow

■ **larva di pidocchio** nit

la'sagne *nfpl* lasagne

'lasca *nf* roach

lasciapas'sare *nm inv* pass

✔ **lasci'are** *vt* leave; (rinunciare) give up; (rimetterci) lose; (smettere di tenere) let go [of]; (concedere) let; **~ a desiderare** leave a lot to be desired; **~ di fare qualcosa** (smettere) stop doing something; **lascia perdere!** forget it!; **lascialo venire, lascia che venga** let him come

lasci'arsi *vr* (reciproco) leave each other, split up; **~ andare** let oneself go

'lascito *nm* legacy

la'scivo *adj* lascivious

'laser *adj & nm inv*

■ **[raggio] laser** laser [beam]

lasertera'pia *nf* laser treatment
lassa'tivo *adj & nm* laxative
las'sismo *nm* laxity
'lasso *nm*
■ lasso di tempo period of time
⚹ **lassù** *adv* up there
'lastra *nf* slab; (di ghiaccio) sheet; (di metallo, Phot) plate; (radiografia) X-ray [plate]
■ lastra di pietra paving slab, paving stone; lastra di vetro plate glass
lastri'care *vt* pave
lastri'cato *nm* pavement
'lastrico *nm* paving; sul ∼ on one's beam-ends
la'tente *adj* latent
late'rale *adj* side *attrib*; Med, Techn ecc lateral; via ∼ side street
lateral'mente *adv* sideways
late'rizi *nmpl* bricks
'latice *nm* latex
latifon'dista *nm* big landowner
lati'fondo *nm* large estate
lati'nismo *nm* Latinism
⚹ **la'tino** *adj & nm* Latin
latino-ameri'cano, **-a** *adj & nmf* Latin American
lati'tante ① *adj* in hiding ② *nmf* fugitive [from justice]
lati'tanza *nf* darsi alla ∼ go into hiding
⚹ **lati'tudine** *nf* latitude
⚹ **'lato** ① *adj* (ampio) broad; in senso ∼ broadly speaking ② *nm* side; (aspetto) aspect; a ∼ di beside; dal ∼ mio (punto di vista) for my part; d'altro ∼ fig on the other hand
■ lato B B side
la'|tore, **-trice** *nmf* Comm bearer
la'trare *vi* bark
la'trato *nm* barking
la'trina *nf* latrine
'latta *nf* tin, can
lat'taio, **-a** ① *nm* milkman ② *nf* milkwoman
lat'tante ① *adj* breast-fed ② *nmf* suckling
⚹ **'latte** *nm* milk
■ latte acido sour milk; latte condensato condensed milk, evaporated milk; latte detergente cleansing milk; latte di gallina eggnog; latte intero whole milk, full-cream milk; latte a lunga conservazione long-life milk; latte materno mother's milk, breast milk; latte parzialmente scremato semi-skimmed milk; latte in polvere powdered milk; latte scremato skimmed milk; latte di soia soya milk
lat'teo *adj* milky; dieta lattea milk diet; la Via Lattea the Milky Way

latte'ria *nf* dairy
'lattice *nm* latex
latti'cello *nm* buttermilk
latti'cini *nmpl* dairy products
latti'era *nf* milk jug
lattigi'noso *adj* milky
lat'tina *nf* can, tin can
lat'tosio *nm* lactose
lat'tuga *nf* lettuce
■ lattuga romana cos lettuce
'laudano *nm* laudanum
'laurea *nf* degree; prendere la ∼ graduate
■ laurea breve *degree that takes less than the standard period of time*; laurea in Lettere arts degree; laurea specialistica *Italian degree similar to a master's degree*; laurea triennale
▶ LAUREA BREVE
laure'ando, **-a** *nmf* final-year student
⚹ **laure'are** *vt* confer a degree on
laure'arsi *vr* graduate
laure'ato, **-a** *adj & nmf* graduate
'lauro *nm* laurel
'lauto *adj* lavish; ∼ guadagno handsome profit
'lava *nf* lava
la'vabile *adj* washable
■ lavabile in lavastoviglie dishwasher-safe
la'vabo *nm* wash-basin
lavacri'stallo *nm* windscreen wiper
la'vaggio *nm* washing
■ lavaggio automatico (per auto) carwash; lavaggio del cervello brainwashing; lavaggio a secco dry-cleaning
la'vagna *nf* slate; Sch blackboard
■ lavagna a fogli mobili flipchart; lavagna luminosa overhead projector, OHP
lava'macchine *nmf inv* car washer
la'vanda *nf* wash; Bot lavender; gli hanno fatto la ∼ gastrica he had his stomach pumped
lavan'daia *nf* washerwoman
lavande'ria *nf* laundry
■ lavanderia automatica launderette
lavan'dino *nm* sink; hum (persona) bottomless pit
lavapi'atti *nmf inv* dishwasher
⚹ **la'vare** *vt* wash; ∼ i piatti wash up; ∼ a secco dry-clean; ∼ a mano wash by hand; ∼ i panni do the washing
la'varsi *vr* wash, have a wash; ∼ i denti brush one's teeth; ∼ le mani/il viso wash one's hands/face; ∼ la testa o i capelli wash one's hair
lava'secco *nmf inv* dry-cleaner's
lavasto'viglie *nf inv* dishwasher
la'vata *nf* wash; darsi una ∼ have a wash
■ lavata di capo fig scolding
lava'tivo, **-a** *nmf* idler
lava'trice *nf* washing-machine

⚹ indicates a very frequent word

lava'vetri *nm inv* squeegee

la'vello *nm* kitchen sink

'lavico *adj* formed by lava

la'vina *nf* snowslide

lavo'rante *nmf* worker

lavo'rare [1] *vi* work; ~ **di fantasia** (sognare) day-dream
[2] *vt* work; knead ‹*pasta ecc*›; till ‹*la terra*›; ~ **a maglia** knit; ~ **troppo** overwork

lavora'tivo *adj* working; **giorno lavorativo** workday; **settimana lavorativa** working week

lavo'rato *adj* ‹*pietra, legno*› carved; ‹*cuoio*› tooled; ‹*metallo*› wrought; ‹*golf*› patterned; ‹*terra*› cultivated

lavora|'tore, -trice [1] *nmf* worker
■ **lavora|tore a domicilio** outworker, homeworker
[2] *adj* working

lavorazi'one *nf* manufacture; (di terra) working; (del terreno) cultivation
■ **lavorazione [artigianale]** workmanship; **lavorazione del metallo** metalwork; **lavorazione in serie** mass production

lavo'rio *nm* intense activity

la'voro *nm* work; (faticoso, sociale) labour; (impiego) job; Theat play; **andare al** ~ go to work; **essere senza** ~ be out of work; **mettersi al** ~ **(su qualcosa)** set to work (on something); **ministero dei lavori pubblici** Department of Public Works; **lavori** *pl* **di casa** housework; **lavori** *pl* **in corso** roadworks; **lavori** *pl* **forzati** hard labour *sg*; **lavori** *pl* **stradali** roadworks
■ **lavoro atipico** *employment relationship not conforming to the usual model of full-time, continuous employment with a single employer over a long time span*; **lavoro a domicilio** homeworking; **lavoro di gruppo** Sch working in groups, group work; **lavoro interinale** temping; **lavoro a maglia** knitting; **lavoro nero** moonlighting; **lavoro part time** part-time job; **lavoro straordinario** overtime; **lavoro teatrale** play; **lavoro a tempo pieno** full-time job

lazza'rone *nm* rascal

le [1] *def art fpl* the; ▶ IL
[2] *pers pron* (oggetto) them; (a lei) her; **le hai parlato?** did you talk to her?; (forma di cortesia) you

'leader [1] *nm inv* leader
■ **leader della marca** brand leader
[2] *adj inv* leading; **prodotto leader** market leader

le'ale *adj* loyal

leal'mente *adv* loyally

lealtà *nf* loyalty

'leasing *nm inv* lease-purchase, leasing

'lebbra *nf* leprosy

lecca 'lecca *nm inv* lollipop

leccapi'edi *nmf inv* pej bootlicker

lec'care *vt* lick; fig suck up to

lec'carsi *vr* lick; fig (agghindarsi) doll oneself up; **da** ~ **i baffi** mouth-watering

lec'cata *nf* lick

lec'cato *adj* ‹*persona*› dressed to kill

'leccio *nm* holm oak

leccor'nia *nf* delicacy

lecita'mente *adv* lawfully

'lecito *adj* lawful; (permesso) permissible

'ledere *vt* damage; Med injure

'lega *nf* league; (di metalli) alloy; **far** ~ **con qualcuno** take up with somebody
■ **lega doganale** customs union

le'gaccio *nm* string; (delle scarpe) shoelace

le'gale [1] *adj* legal
[2] *nm* lawyer

legalità *nf* legality

legaliz'zare *vt* authenticate; (rendere legale) legalize

legalizzazi'one *nf* legalization

legal'mente *adv* legally

Legam'biente *nf Italian association for environmental protection*

le'game *nm* tie; (amoroso) liaison; (connessione) link
■ **legame di parentela** family relationship; **legame di sangue** blood relationship; **legame sentimentale** emotional relationship

lega'mento *nm* Med ligament

le'gare [1] *vt* tie; tie up ‹*persona*›; tie together ‹*due cose*›; (unire, rilegare) bind; alloy ‹*metalli*›; (connettere) connect; **legarsela al dito** fig bear a grudge
[2] *vi* (far lega) get on well

le'garsi *vr* bind oneself; ~ **a qualcuno** become attached to somebody

lega'tario, -a *nmf* legatee

le'gato *nm* legacy; Relig legate

lega'tura *nf* tying; (di libro) binding

legazi'one *nf* legation

le'genda *nf* legend

'legge *nf* law; (parlamentare) act; **a norma di** ~ by law
■ **legge marziale** martial law

leg'genda *nf* legend; (didascalia) caption
■ **leggenda metropolitana** urban myth

leggen'dario *adj* legendary

'leggere *vt/i* read; ~ **male** (sbagliato) misread

legge'rezza *nf* lightness; (frivolezza) frivolity; (incostanza) fickleness

legger'mente *adv* slightly

leg'gero *adj* light; ‹*bevanda*› weak; (lieve) slight; (frivolo) frivolous; (incostante) fickle; ~ **come una piuma** [as] light as a feather; **alla leggera** lightly

leggi'adro *adj* (liter) graceful

leg'gibile *adj* ‹*scrittura*› legible; ‹*stile*› readable

leg'gio *nm* lectern; Mus music stand

legife'rare *vi* legislate
legio'nario *nm* legionary
legi'one *nf* legion
legisla'tivo *adj* legislative
legisla'tore *nm* legislator
legisla'tura *nf* legislature
legislazi'one *nf* legislation
legittima'mente *adv* legitimately
legittimità *nf* legitimacy
le'gittimo *adj* legitimate; (giusto) proper; legittima difesa self-defence
'legna *nf* firewood
le'gnaia *nf* woodshed
le'gname *nm* timber
le'gnata *nf* blow with a stick
◆ **'legno** *nm* wood; di ∼ wooden; legni *pl* Mus woodwind
■ legno compensato plywood
le'gnoso *adj* woody; (di legno) wooden; ‹gambe› stiff; ‹movimento› wooden
le'gume *nm* pod
◆ **'lei** *pers pron* (soggetto) she; (oggetto, con prep) her; (forma di cortesia) you; lo ha fatto ∼ stessa she did it herself
'lembo *nm* edge; (di terra) strip
'lemma *nm* headword
'lemming *nm inv* lemming
'lena *nf* vigour
'lendine *nm* nit
le'nire *vt* soothe
lenta'mente *adv* slowly
'lente *nf* lens
■ lente a contatto contact lens; mettersi le lenti a contatto put in one's contact lenses; lente a contatto morbida soft lens; lente a contatto rigida hard lens; lente d'ingrandimento magnifying glass; lente semi-rigida gas-permeable lens
len'tezza *nf* slowness
len'ticchia *nf* lentil
len'tiggine *nf* freckle
◆ **'lento** *adj* slow; (allentato) slack; ‹abito› loose
'lenza *nf* fishing-line
len'zuolo *nm* sheet; le lenzuola the sheets
■ lenzuolo con gli angoli fitted sheet; lenzuolo funebre shroud
leon'cino *nm* lion cub
le'one *nm* lion; Astr Leo
■ leone marino sea lion
leo'nessa *nf* lioness
leo'pardo *nm* leopard
lepo'rino *adj* labbro ∼ harelip
'lepre *nf* hare
le'protto *nm* leveret
'lercio *adj* filthy
lerci'ume *nm* filth

'lesbica *nf* lesbian
'lesbico *adj* lesbian
lesi'nare ① *vt* grudge
② *vi* be stingy
lesio'nare *vt* damage
lesi'one *nf* lesion; (danno) damage
■ lesione cerebrale brain damage; lesione interna internal injury; lesioni personali *pl* grievous bodily harm, GBH
'leso ① pp di LEDERE
② *adj* injured; lesa maestà high treason
les'sare *vt* boil
lessi'cale *adj* lexical
'lessico *nm* vocabulary
lessicogra'fia *nf* lexicography
lessi'cografo, -a *nmf* lexicographer
'lesso ① *adj* boiled
② *nm* boiled meat
'lesto *adj* quick; ‹mente› sharp
■ lesto di mano light-fingered
le'tale *adj* lethal
leta'maio *nm* dunghill; fig pigsty
le'tame *nm* dung
le'targico *adj* lethargic
le'targo *nm* lethargy; (di animali) hibernation
le'tizia *nf* joy
◆ **'lettera** *nf* letter; alla ∼ literally; eseguire qualcosa alla ∼ carry out something to the letter; lettere *pl* (letteratura) literature sg; Univ Arts; dottore in lettere BA, Bachelor of Arts
■ lettera d'accompagnamento covering letter; lettera d'amore love letter; lettera assicurata registered letter; lettera di cambio bill of exchange; lettera di credito letter of credit; lettera maiuscola capital [letter]; lettera minuscola small letter; lettera di presentazione letter of introduction; lettera raccomandata recorded delivery letter; lettera di scuse letter of apology; lettera di trasporto aereo air waybill
lette'rale *adj* literal
letteral'mente *adv* literally
lette'rario *adj* literary
lette'rato ① *adj* well-read
② *nm* scholar; letterati *pl* literati
lettera'tura *nf* literature
■ letteratura pulp pulp fiction
letti'era *nf* (per gatto) litter
let'tiga *nf* stretcher
let'tino *nm* cot; Med couch
■ lettino [pieghevole] camp bed
◆ **'letto** *nm* bed; andare a ∼ go to bed; [ri]fare il ∼ make the bed
■ letto a castello bunkbed; letto di fiume river bed; letti gemelli *pl* twin beds; letto matrimoniale double bed; letto a una piazza single bed; letto a due piazze double bed; letto singolo single bed

Let'tonia *nf* Latvia

letto'rato *nm* (corso) tutorial

let|'tore, -trice 1 *nmf* reader; Univ language assistant
2 *nm* Comput disk drive
■ **lettore di CD** CD player, CD system; **lettore [di] CD-ROM** CD-Rom drive; **lettore di codice a barre** barcode reader, scanner; **lettore di compact disc** compact disc player; **lettore di disco** disk drive; **lettore di floppy** floppy [disk] drive; **lettore di minidisc** minidisc player; **lettore [di] MP3** MP3 player

let'tura *nf* reading

leuce'mia *nf* leukaemia

'leva *nf* lever; Mil call-up; **nuove leve** *pl* new blood, young blood; **far ∼ lever**
■ **leva del cambio** gear lever; **leva di comando** control lever

le'vante *nm* East; (vento) east wind

leva'punti *nm inv* staple remover

⚔ **le'vare** *vt* (alzare) raise; (togliere) take away; (rimuovere) take off; (estrarre) pull out, lift, abolish ⟨divieto, tassa⟩; **∼ di mezzo qualcosa** get something out of the way

le'varsi *vr* move (da away from); ⟨vento⟩ get up; ⟨sole⟩ rise; **∼ di mezzo** get out of the way

le'vata *nf* rising; (di posta) collection

leva'taccia *nf* **fare una ∼** get up at the crack of dawn

leva'toio *adj* **ponte ∼** drawbridge

leva'trice *nf* midwife

leva'tura *nf* intelligence

levi'gare *vt* smooth; (con carta vetro) rub down

levi'gato *adj* ⟨superficie⟩ polished; ⟨pelle⟩ smooth

leviga'trice *nf* sander

levi'tare *vi* levitate

levitazi'one *nf* levitation

Le'vitico *nm* Leviticus

levri'ero *nm* greyhound
■ **levriero afgano** Afghan hound

⚔ **lezi'one** *nf* lesson; Univ lecture; (rimprovero) rebuke
■ **lezione di guida** driving lesson; **lezione di italiano** Italian lesson, Italian class

lezi'oso *adj* ⟨stile, modi⟩ affected

'lezzo *nm* stench

⚔ **li** *pers pron mpl* them

⚔ **lì** *adv* there; **fin lì** as far as there; **giù di lì** thereabouts; **lì per lì** there and then; **la cosa è finita lì** that was the end of it

li'ana *nf* liana

liba'nese *adj & nmf* Lebanese

Li'bano *nm* Lebanon

'libbra *nf* (peso) pound

li'beccio *nm* south-west wind

li'bello *nm* libel

li'bellula *nf* dragon-fly

libe'rale 1 *adj* liberal; (generoso) generous
2 *nmf* liberal

libera'lismo *nm*
■ **liberalismo [economico]** economic liberalism

liberalità *nf* generosity

liberal'mente *adv* liberally

⚔ **libe'rare** *vt* free, release ⟨prigioniero⟩; vacate ⟨stanza⟩; (salvare) rescue

libe'rarsi *vr* ⟨stanza⟩ become vacant; Teleph become free; (da impegno) get out of it; **∼ di** get rid of

libera|'tore, -trice 1 *adj* liberating
2 *nmf* liberator

libera'torio *adj* liberating
■ **pagamento liberatorio** full and final payment

liberazi'one *nf* liberation; **la Liberazione** (ricorrenza) Liberation Day
■ **liberazione della donna** women's liberation, women's lib

Li'beria *nf* Liberia

libe'rismo *nm* free trade

⚔ **'libero** *adj* free; ⟨strada⟩ clear; **∼ come l'aria** free as a bird
■ **libero arbitrio** *nm* free will; **libero docente** *nm* qualified university lecturer; **libero professionista** *nm* self-employed person

⚔ **libertà** *nf* freedom; (di prigioniero) release; **∼ pl** (confidenze) liberties; **prendersi la ∼ di fare qualcosa** take the liberty of doing something
■ **libertà di espressione** freedom of speech; **libertà di parola** free speech; **libertà di pensiero** freedom of thought; **libertà provvisoria** Jur bail; **libertà di stampa** freedom of the press; **libertà vigilata** probation

liber'tino, -a 1 *adj* dissolute, libertine
2 *nmf* libertine

'liberty *nm & adj inv* Art Nouveau

'Libia *nf* Libya

'libico, -a *adj & nmf* Libyan

li'bidine *nf* lust

libidi'noso *adj* lustful

li'bido *nf* libido

libra'io *nm* bookseller

libre'ria *nf* (negozio) bookshop; (mobile) bookcase; (biblioteca) library

li'bretto *nm* booklet; Mus libretto
■ **libretto degli assegni** cheque book; **libretto di circolazione** logbook; **libretto d'istruzioni** instruction booklet; **libretto di risparmio** savings account; (documento) passbook, savings book; **libretto universitario** *book held by students which records details of their exam performances*

⚔ **'libro** *nm* book
■ **libro bianco** White Paper; **libro dei canti** hymn-book; **libro contabile** account book; **libro di esercizi** workbook; **libro giallo** crime ⋯▶

novel; **libro mastro** Comm ledger; **libro paga** payroll; **libro di ricette** cookbook, recipe book; **libri** *pl* **sociali** company's books; **libro tascabile** paperback; **libro di testo** course book

li'cantropo *nm* werewolf

lice'ale ⚊1⚊ *nmf* secondary-school student ⚊2⚊ *adj* secondary-school *attrib*

li'cenza *nf* licence; (permesso) permission; Mil leave; Sch school-leaving certificate; **essere in** ∼ be on leave
■ **licenza di caccia** hunting licence; **licenza di esportazione** export licence; **licenza matrimoniale** marriage licence; **licenza di pesca** fishing licence; **licenza poetica** poetic licence; **licenza di porto d'armi** gun licence

licenzia'mento *nm* dismissal, lay-off

licenzi'are *vt* dismiss, sack fam; (conferire un diploma) grant a school-leaving certificate to

licenzi'arsi *vr* (da un impiego) resign; (accomiatarsi) take one's leave

licenzi'oso *adj* licentious

li'ceo *nm* secondary school, high school
■ **liceo classico** *secondary school with an emphasis on humanities*; **liceo scientifico** *secondary school with an emphasis on sciences*

li'chene *nm* lichen

'lido *nm* beach

'Liechtenstein *nm* Liechtenstein

lieta'mente *adv* happily

⚘ **li'eto** *adj* glad; ‹evento› happy; **molto** ∼**!** pleased to meet you!
■ **lieto fine** happy ending

li'eve *adj* light; (debole) faint; (trascurabile) slight

lievi'tare ⚊1⚊ *vi* rise ⚊2⚊ *vt* leaven

li'evito *nm* yeast
■ **lievito in polvere** baking powder

lift *nm inv* liftboy

'lifting *nm inv* face-lift

'ligio *adj* **essere** ∼ **al dovere** have a sense of duty

li'gnaggio *nm* lineage

'ligneo *adj* wooden

'lilla *nm* (colore) lilac

lillà *nm* Bot lilac

'lima *nf* file

limacci'oso *adj* slimy

li'manda *nf* dab

li'mare *vt* file

lima'tura *nf* (atto) filing; (residui) filings *pl*

'limbo *nm* limbo

li'metta *nf* limetta [da unghie] nail file; (di carta) emery board

⚘ **limi'tare** ⚊1⚊ *nm* threshold ⚊2⚊ *vt* limit

limi'tarsi *vr* ∼ **a fare qualcosa** restrict oneself to doing something; ∼ **in qualcosa** cut down on something

limitata'mente *adv* to a limited extent

limita'tivo *adj* limiting

limi'tato *adj* limited

limitazi'one *nf* limitation

⚘ **'limite** ⚊1⚊ *adj* ‹caso› extreme ⚊2⚊ *nm* limit; (confine) boundary; **entro certi limiti** within certain limits
■ **limite di credito** credit limit, credit ceiling; **limite di sopportazione** breaking point; 'limite di sosta' 'restricted parking'; **limite di tempo** time limit; **limite di velocità** speed limit; **rispettare il** ∼ **di velocità** keep to the speed limit

li'mitrofo *adj* neighbouring

'limo *nm* slime

limo'nata *nf* (bibita) lemonade; (succo) lemon juice
■ **limonata amara** bitter lemon

li'mone *nm* lemon; (albero) lemon tree

'limpido *adj* clear; ‹occhi› limpid

'lince *nf* lynx

linci'are *vt* lynch

'lindo *adj* neat; (pulito) clean

⚘ **'linea** *nf* line; (di autobus, aereo) route; (di metropolitana) line; (di abito) cut; (di auto, mobile) design; (fisico) figure; **in** ∼ **d'aria** as the crow flies; **è caduta la** ∼ I've been cut off; **in** ∼ **di massima** as a rule; **a grandi linee** in outline; **mantenere la** ∼ keep one's figure; **in** ∼ Comput on-line; **in prima** ∼ in the front line; **mettersi in** ∼ line up
■ **nave di linea** liner; **volo di linea** scheduled flight; **linea aerea** airline; **linea d'arrivo** Sport finishing line; **linea commutata** Teleph switched line; **linea di confine** boundary; **linea continua** unbroken line; **linea dedicata** dedicated line; **linea di demarcazione** border line; **linea ferroviaria** railway line; **linea di fondo** baseline; **linea d'immersione** water line; **linea laterale** Sport touch line; **linee della mano** *pl* lines of the hand; **linea di marea** tidemark; **linea mediana** Sport halfway line; **linea di partenza** Sport starting line; **linea principale** Rail main line; **linea punteggiata** dotted line; **linea secondaria** Rail branch line; **linea di tiro** line of fire; **linea tratteggiata** broken line

linea'menti *nmpl* features

line'are *adj* linear; ‹discorso› to the point; ‹ragionamento› consistent

line'etta *nf* (tratto lungo) dash; (d'unione) hyphen

'linfa *nf* Anat lymph; Bot sap
■ **linfa vitale** fig life blood

lin'fatico *adj* Anat lymphatic

linfoghi'andola *nf* lymph gland

linfo'nodo *nm* lymph node

linge'rie *nf* lingerie

⚘ indicates a very frequent word

lin'gotto *nm* ingot

⚡ **'lingua** *nf* tongue; (linguaggio) language; avere la ∼ lunga fig have a big mouth ■ lingua d'arrivo target language; lingua moderna modern language; lingua morta dead language; lingua di partenza source language; lingua straniera foreign language

lingu'accia *nf* (persona) backbiter; fare le linguacce put one's tongue out (a at)

lingu'aggio *nm* language ■ linguaggio infantile baby-talk; linguaggio per la marcatura di ipertesti Comput hypertext markup language; linguaggio dei segni sign language

lingu'etta *nf* (di scarpa) tongue; (di strumento) reed; (di busta) flap; Mus reed; (da tirare) tab

lingu'ista *nmf* linguist

lingu'istica *nf* linguistics *sg*

lingu'istico *adj* linguistic

lln'kare *vt* Comput link ‹sti Web›

'lino *nm* Bot flax; (tessuto) linen

li'noleum *nm* linoleum

liofiliz'zare *vt* freeze-dry

liofiliz'zato *adj* freeze dried

li'pide *nm* lipid

liposuzi'one *nf* liposuction

li'quame *nm* slurry

lique'fare *vt* liquefy; (sciogliere) melt

lique'farsi *vr* liquefy; (sciogliersi) melt

liqui'dare *vt* liquidate; settle ‹conto›; pay off ‹debiti›; clear ‹merce›; fam (uccidere) get rid of

liquida'tore *nm* liquidator

liquidazi'one *nf* liquidation; (di conti) settling; (di merce) clearance sale ■ liquidazione totale [per cessata attività] closing-down sale

'liquido *adj & nm* liquid ■ liquido dei freni brake fluid; liquido scongelante Auto de-icer; liquido tergicristallo screen wash

liqui'gas® *nm inv* Calor gas®

liquirizia *nf* liquorice

li'quore *nm* liqueur; liquori *pl* (superalcolici) liquors

'lira *nf* (ex moneta italiana) lira; (moneta di vari paesi) pound; Mus lyre ■ lira sterlina pound sterling

'lirico, -a ⨎1⨎ *adj* lyrical; ‹poesia› lyric; ‹cantante› (musica) opera *attrib* ⨎2⨎ *nf* lyric poetry; Mus opera

li'rismo *nm* lyricism

'lisca *nf* fishbone; avere la ∼ fam (nel parlare) have a lisp

lisci'are *vt* smooth; (accarezzare) stroke

'liscio *adj* smooth; ‹capelli› straight; ‹liquore› neat, straight; ‹acqua minerale› still; passarla liscia get away with it

li'seuse *nf inv* bed jacket

'liso *adj* worn [out]

⚡ **'lista** *nf* list; (striscia) strip; fare una ∼ make out a list ■ lista di attesa waiting list; in ∼ di attesa on the waiting list; Aeron on stand-by; lista elettorale list of candidates; lista degli invitati guest list; lista nera blacklist; lista di nozze wedding list; lista della spesa shopping list; lista dei vini wine list

li'stare *vt* edge; Comput list

li'stino *nm* list ■ listino di borsa Stock-Exchange list; listino dei cambi exchange rates *pl*; listino [dei] prezzi price list

Lit. *abbr* (**lire italiane**) Italian lire

lita'nia *nf* litany

'litchi *nm inv* lychee

'lite *nf* quarrel; (baruffa) row; Jur lawsuit

liti'gante *nmf* Jur litigant

⚡ **liti'gare** *vi* quarrel; Jur litigate

li'tigio *nm* quarrel

litigi'oso *adj* quarrelsome

'litio *nm* lithium

litogra'fia *nf* (procedimento) lithography; (stampa) lithograph

li'tografo, -a *nmf* lithographer

lito'rale ⨎1⨎ *adj* coastal ⨎2⨎ *nm* coast

lito'raneo *adj* coastal

'litro *nm* litre

Litu'ania *nf* Lithuania

litu'ano, -a *adj & nmf* Lithuanian

litur'gia *nf* liturgy

li'turgico *adj* liturgical

li'uto *nm* lute

li'vella *nf* level ■ livella a bolla d'aria spirit level

livella'mento *nm* levelling out, levelling off

livel'lare *vt* level

livel'larsi *vr* level out

livella'tore *adj* levelling

livella'trice *nf* bulldozer

li'vello *nm* level; passaggio a livello level crossing; sotto/sul ∼ del mare below/above sea level; ad alto ∼ ‹conferenza, trattative› top-level, high-level; a più livelli multilevel ■ livello di guardia danger level; livello di magazzino stock level; livello occupazionale level of employment

'livido ⨎1⨎ *adj* livid; (per il freddo) blue; (per una botta) black and blue ■ livido di rabbia livid ⨎2⨎ *nm* bruise

li'vore *nm* spite

Li'vorno *nf* Leghorn

li'vrea *nf* livery

'lizza *nf* lists *pl*; essere in ∼ per qualcosa be in the running for something

⚡ **lo** [1] *def art m before s + consonant, gn, ps, z,* the; ▶ IL

[2] *pron* (riferito a persona) him; (riferito a cosa) it; **non lo so** I don't know

'lobbia *nf* Homburg [hat]

lob'bismo *nm* lobbying

lob'bista *nmf* lobbyist

'lobby *nf inv* lobby

lo'belia *nf* lobelia

'lobo *nm* lobe

loboto'mia *nf* lobotomy

lo'cale [1] *adj* local

[2] *nm* (stanza) room; (treno) local train; **locali** *pl* (edifici) premises

■ **locale notturno** nightclub

⚡ **località** *nf* locality

■ **località balneare** seaside resort; **località turistica** tourist resort; **località di villeggiatura** holiday resort

localiz'zare *vt* localize; (reperire) locate

localiz'zarsi *vr* ~ **in** be located in

localiz'zato *adj* localized

localizzazi'one *nf* localization; (reperimento) location

local'mente *adv* locally

lo'canda *nf* inn

locandi'ere, -a *nmf* innkeeper

locan'dina *nf* bill, poster

loca'tario, -a *nmf* tenant

■ **locatario residente** sitting tenant

loca'tivo *adj* Gram locative; Jur rental

loca|'tore, -trice [1] *nm* landlord

[2] *nf* landlady

locazi'one *nf* tenancy

locomo'tiva *nf* locomotive

■ **locomotiva a vapore** steam engine

locomo'tore *nm* locomotive, engine

locomozi'one *nf* locomotion; **mezzi di locomozione** means of transport

'loculo *nm* burial niche

lo'custa *nf* locust

locuzi'one *nf* expression

lo'dare *vt* praise

'lode *nf* praise; **degno di lode** praiseworthy; **laurea con lode** first-class degree

'loden *nm inv* (cappotto) loden [coat]; (stoffa) loden

lo'devole *adj* praiseworthy

'lodola *nf* lark

loga'ritmo *nm* logarithm

'loggia *nf* loggia; (massonica) lodge

loggi'one *nm* gallery, gods *pl*

'logica *nf* logic

logica'mente *adv* (in modo logico) logically; (ovviamente) of course

logicità *nf* logic

'logico *adj* logical

lo'gistica *nf* logistics

lo'gistico *adj* logistic[al]

'logo *nm inv* logo

logope'dia *nf* speech therapy

logope'dista *nmf* speech therapist

logo'rante *adj* ‹attesa, esperienza› wearing

logo'rare *vt* wear out; (sciupare) waste

logo'rarsi *vr* wear out; ‹persona›; wear oneself out

logo'rio *nm* wear and tear; (stress) stress

'logoro *adj* worn-out

logor'roico *adj* loquacious

lom'baggine *nf* lumbago

Lombar'dia *nf* Lombardy

lom'bardo *adj* Lombardy *attrib*

lom'bare *adj* lumbar

lom'bata *nf* loin

■ **lombata di manzo** sirloin

'lombo *nm* Anat loin

lom'brico *nm* earthworm

londi'nese [1] *adj* London *attrib*

[2] *nmf* Londoner

'Londra *nf* London

long-'drink *nm inv* long drink

longevità *nf* longevity

lon'gevo *adj* long-lived

longhe'rone *nm* strut

longi'lineo *adj* rangy

longitudi'nale *adj* lengthwise

longitudinal'mente *adv* lengthwise

longi'tudine *nf* longitude

long 'playing *nm inv* LP, long-playing record

lontana'mente *adv* distantly; (vagamente) vaguely; **neanche** ~ not for a moment

lonta'nanza *nf* distance; (separazione) separation; **in** ~ in the distance

⚡ **lon'tano** [1] *adj* far; (distante) distant; (nel tempo) far-off, distant; ‹parente› distant; (vago) vague; (assente) absent; **più** ~ further; **è** ~ **un paio di chilometri** it is a couple of kilometres away

[2] *adv* far [away]; **da** ~ from a distance; **tenersi** ~ **da** keep away from; **andare** ~ (allontanarsi) go away; (avere successo) go far

'lontra *nf* otter

'lonza *nf* (lombata) loin

lo'quace *adj* talkative

'lordo *adj* dirty; ‹somma, peso› gross; **al** ~ **di imposte** pre-tax

⚡ **'loro¹** *pers pron pl* (soggetto) they; (oggetto) them; (forma di cortesia) you; **sta a** ~ it is up to them

'loro² [1] (**il** ~ *m,* **la** ~ *f,* **i** ~ *mpl,* **le** ~ *fpl*) *poss adj* their; (forma de cortesia) your; **un** ~ **amico** a friend of theirs; (forma di cortesia) a friend of yours

[2] *poss pron* theirs; (forma di cortesia) yours; **i** ~ (famiglia) their folk

---

⚡ indicates a very frequent word

lo'sanga *nf* lozenge; **a losanghe** diamond-shaped

losca'mente *adv* suspiciously

'losco *adj* suspicious

'loto *nm* lotus

♂ **'lotta** *nf* fight, struggle; (contrasto) conflict; Sport wrestling
  ■ **lotta di classe** class struggle; **lotta libera** all-in wrestling

♂ **lot'tare** *vi* fight, struggle; Sport fig wrestle

lotta|'tore, -trice *nmf* wrestler

lotte'ria *nf* lottery
  ■ **Lotteria di Stato** National Lottery

lottiz'zare *vt* divide up ‹terreno›; fig parcel out

lottizzazi'one *nf* (di terreno) division into lots; fig parcelling out

'lotto *nm* [state] lottery; (porzione) lot; (di terreno) plot

lozi'one *nf* lotion
  ■ **lozione idratante** moisturizer; **lozione solare** suntan lotion

lubrifi'cante ⨯1⨯ *adj* lubricating
  ⨯2⨯ *nm* lubricant

lubrifi'care *vt* lubricate

luc'chetto *nm* padlock

lucci'cante *adj* sparkling

lucci'care *vi* sparkle

lucci'chio *nm* sparkle

lucci'cone *nm* **far venire i lucciconi** bring tears to the eyes

'luccio *nm* pike

'lucciola *nf* glow-worm; fam (prostituta) lady of the night

♂ **'luce** *nf* light; **accendere/spegnere la ∼** switch the light on/off; **far ∼ su** fig shed light on; **dare alla ∼** give birth to; **venire alla ∼** come to light
  ■ **luci** *pl* **di arresto** Auto stop lights; **luci** *pl* **d'atterraggio** landing lights; **luci** *pl* **d'emergenza** Auto hazard [warning] lights, hazards; **luce della luna** moonlight; **luci** *pl* **di posizione** Auto sidelights; **luci** *pl* **posteriori** Auto rear-lights; **luci** *pl* **di retromarcia** Auto reversing lights; **luce del sole** sunlight; **luce stroboscopica** strobe

lu'cente *adj* shining

lucen'tezza *nf* shine

lucer'nario *nm* skylight

lu'certola *nf* lizard

lucida'labbra *nm inv* lip gloss

luci'dare *vt* polish

lucida'trice *nf* [floor-]polisher

♂ **'lucido** ⨯1⨯ *adj* shiny; ‹pavimento, scarpe› polished; (chiaro) clear; ‹persona, mente› lucid; ‹occhi› watery
  ⨯2⨯ *nm* shine
  ■ **lucido [da scarpe]** [shoe] polish

lucra'tivo *adj* lucrative

'lucro *nm* lucre; **senza fini di ∼** non-profit-making, not-for-profit Am

luculli'ano *adj* ‹pranzo› lavish

ludo'teca *nf* playroom

♂ **'luglio** *nm* July

'lugubre *adj* gloomy

♂ **'lui** *pers pron* (soggetto) he; (oggetto, con prep) him; **lo ha fatto ∼ stesso** he did it himself

lu'maca *nf* (mollusco) snail; fig slowcoach

'lume *nm* lamp; (luce) light; **a ∼ di candela** by candlelight; **perdere il ∼ della ragione** be beside oneself with rage

lumi'nare *nmf* luminary

lumi'narie *nfpl* illuminations

lumine'scente *adj* luminescent

lumine'scenza *nf* luminescence

lu'mino *nm*
  ■ **lumino da notte** nightlight

luminosa'mente *adv* luminously

luminosità *nf* brightness

lumi'noso *adj* luminous; ‹stanza, cielo ecc› bright; **idea luminosa** brain wave

♂ **'luna** *nf* moon; **chiaro di luna** moonlight; **avere la ∼ storta** be in a bad mood
  ■ **luna di miele** honeymoon; **luna piena** full moon

'luna park *nm inv* fairground

lu'nare *adj* lunar

lu'naria *nf* moonstone

lu'nario *nm* almanac; **sbarcare il ∼** make [both] ends meet

lu'natico *adj* moody

lunedì *nm inv* Monday; **di ∼** on Mondays

lu'netta *nf* half-moon [shape]

lun'gaggine *nf* slowness

lunga'mente *adv* at great length

lun'ghezza *nf* length; **di ∼ media** medium-length
  ■ **lunghezza d'onda** wavelength

'lungi *adv* **ero [ben] ∼ dall'immaginare che…** I never dreamt for a moment that…

lungimi'rante *adj* far-seeing

lungimi'ranza *nf* far-sightedness

♂ **'lungo** ⨯1⨯ *adj* long; (diluito) weak; (lento) slow; **a ∼ andare** in the long run; **saperla lunga** be shrewd; **andare per le lunghe** drag on
  ⨯2⨯ *nm* length; **di gran lunga** by far; **di lunga data** long-term
  ⨯3⨯ *prep* (durante) throughout; (per la lunghezza di) along

lungofi'ume *nm* riverside

lungo'lago *nm* lakeside

lungo'mare *nm inv* seafront

lungome'traggio *nm* feature film

lu'notto *nm* rear window
  ■ **lunotto termico** heated rear window

'lunula *nf* half-moon

♂ **lu'ogo** *nm* place; (punto preciso) spot; (passo d'autore) passage; **aver ∼** take place; **dar ∼** ⋯⋮➤

a give rise to; **fuori ~** out of place; **del ~** ‹usanze› local

■ **luogo comune** cliché; **luogo di nascita** birthplace; **luogo natale** birthplace; **luogo pubblico** public place; **luogo di villeggiatura** holiday resort

luogote'nente *nm* Mil lieutenant

'lupa *nf* she-wolf

lu'para *nf* sawn-off shotgun

lu'petto *nm* Cub [Scout]

⚜ **'lupo** *nm* wolf

■ **lupo mannaro** werewolf

'luppolo *nm* hop

'lurido *adj* filthy

luri'dume *nm* filth

lu'singa *nf* flattery

lusin'gare *vt* flatter

lusin'garsi *vr* flatter oneself; (illudersi) fool oneself

lusinghi'ero *adj* flattering

lus'sare *vt* dislocate

lus'sarsi *vr* dislocate

lussazi'one *nf* dislocation

Lussem'burgo *nm* Luxembourg

⚜ **'lusso** *nm* luxury; **di ~** luxury *attrib*

lussuosa'mente *adv* luxuriously

lussu'oso *adj* luxurious

lussureggi'ante *adj* luxuriant

lus'suria *nf* lust

lussuri'oso *adj* dissolute

lu'strare *vt* polish

lu'strino *nm* sequin

'lustro ① *adj* shiny

② *nm* sheen; fig prestige; (quinquennio) five-year period

lute'rano *adj* & *nmf* Lutheran

'lutto *nm* mourning; **parato a ~** draped in black

■ **lutto stretto** deep mourning

luttu'oso *adj* mournful

M m

m *abbr* (**metro**) m

⚜ **ma** *conj* but; (eppure) yet; **ma!** (dubbio) I don't know; (indignazione) really!; **ma davvero? really?**; **ma va'?** really?; **ma sì!** why not!; (certo che sì) of course!

'macabro *adj* macabre

macché *int* of course not!

macche'roni *nmpl* macaroni *sg*

macche'ronico *adj* ‹italiano› broken

⚜ **'macchia¹** *nf* stain; (di diverso colore) spot; (piccola) speck; **senza ~** spotless; **spargersi a ~ d'olio** spread rapidly

■ **macchia di colore** splash of colour; **macchia d'inchiostro** ink stain; **macchia di sangue** bloodstain

'macchia² *nf* (boscaglia) scrub; **darsi alla ~** take to the woods

macchi'are *vt* stain

macchi'arsi *vr* stain

macchi'ato ① *adj* ‹caffè› with a dash of milk; ‹pelo› spotted; **~ di** (sporco) stained with; **~ d'inchiostro** ink-stained, inky

② *nm* (caffè) espresso with a dash of milk

macchi'etta *nf* spot

⚜ **'macchina** *nf* machine; (motore) engine; (automobile) car; **in ~** by car; **giro in ~** drive; **cimitero delle macchine** scrapyard

■ **macchina del caffè** coffee-maker; **macchina da cucire** sewing machine; **macchina per l'espresso** coffee machine; **macchina fotografica** camera; **macchina fototessere** photo booth; **macchina obliteratrice** ticket-stamping machine; **macchina da presa** cine camera; **macchina da scrivere** typewriter; **macchina sverniciante** paint stripper; **macchina utensile** machine tool; **macchina della verità** lie detector

macchinal'mente *adv* mechanically

macchi'nare *vt* plot

macchi'nario *nm* machinery

macchinazi'oni *nfpl* machinations, scheming

macchi'netta *nf* (per i denti) brace; (per il caffè) espresso coffee maker; (accendino) lighter

macchi'nista *nm* Rail engine driver; Naut engineer; Theat stagehand

macchi'noso *adj* complicated

mace'donia *nf* fruit salad

Mace'donia *nf* Macedonia

macel'laio, -a *nmf* butcher

macel'lare *vt* slaughter

macellazi'one *nf* slaughtering

macelle'ria *nf* butcher's [shop]

ma'cello *nm* (mattatoio) slaughterhouse; fig shambles *sg*; **andare al ~** fig go to the slaughter; **mandare al ~** fig send to his/her death

mace'rare *vt* macerate; fig distress

⚜ indicates a very frequent word

mace'rarsi *vr* be consumed

macerazi'one *nf* maceration

ma'cerie *nfpl* rubble *sg*; (rottami) debris *sg*

'macero *nm* pulping; (stabilimento) pulping mill

Mach *nm inv* Mach

ma'chete *nm inv* machete

machia'vellico *adj* Machiavellian

ma'chismo *nm* machismo

'macho *adj* macho

ma'cigno *nm* boulder

maci'lento *adj* emaciated

'macina *nf* millstone

macinacaffè *nm inv* coffee mill

macina'pepe *nm inv* pepper mill

maci'nare *vt* mill

maci'nato [1] *adj* ground [2] *nm* (carne) mince

maci'nino *nm* mill; hum (macchina) old banger

maciul'lare *vt* (stritolare) crush

'macro *nf inv* Comput macro

macrobi'otica *nf*
■ negozio di macrobiotica health-food shop

macrobi'otico *adj* macrobiotic

macro'clima *nm* macroclimate

macro'cosmo *nm* macrocosm

macrofotogra'fia *nf* macrophotography

macro'scopico *adj* macroscopic

macu'lato *adj* spotted

Madaga'scar *nm* Madagascar

madami'gella *nf* young lady

'madia *nf* cupboard with a covered trough on top for making bread

'madido *adj* ~ di damp with ‹sudore›

Ma'donna *nf* Our Lady

mador'nale *adj* gross

⚡ **'madre** *nf* mother
■ madre biologica birth mother; madre single single mother

madre'lingua *adj inv* inglese ~ English native speaker

madre'patria *nf* native land

madre'perla *nf* mother-of-pearl

ma'drepora *nf* madrepore

madri'gale *nm* madrigal

ma'drina *nf* godmother

maestà *nf* majesty

maestosa'mente *adv* majestically

maestosità *nf* majesty

mae'stoso *adj* majestic

ma'estra *nf* teacher; Sch primary school teacher
■ maestra d'asilo kindergarten teacher; maestra di canto singing teacher; maestra di piano piano teacher; maestra di sci ski instructor

mae'strale *nm* northwest wind

mae'stranza *nf* workers *pl*

mae'stria *nf* mastery

⚡ **ma'estro** [1] *nm* teacher; Sch primary school teacher; Mus maestro; (esperto) master; colpo da maestro masterstroke
■ maestro d'asilo kindergarten teacher; maestro di canto singing teacher; maestro di cerimonie master of ceremonies; maestro di piano piano teacher; maestro di sci ski instructor
[2] *adj* (principale) main; (di grande abilità) skilful

'mafia *nf* Mafia

mafi'oso [1] *adj* of the Mafia [2] *nm* member of the Mafia, Mafioso

'maga *nf* sorceress, magician

ma'gagna *nf* fault

⚡ **ma'gari** [1] *adv* (forse) maybe [2] *int* I wish! [3] *conj* (per esprimere desiderio) if only; (anche se) even if

magazzini'ere *nm* storeman, warehouseman

magaz'zino *nm* (deposito) warehouse; (in negozio) stockroom; (emporio) shop; grande magazzino department store
■ magazzini *pl* portuali naval stores

Magg. *abbr* (**maggiore**) Maj

mag'gese *nm* field lying fallow

⚡ **'maggio** *nm* May

maggio'lino *nm* May bug

maggio'rana *nf* marjoram

maggio'ranza *nf* majority

maggio'rare *vt* increase

maggior'domo *nm* butler

⚡ **maggi'ore** [1] *adj* (di dimensioni, numero) bigger, larger; (superlativo) biggest, largest; (di età) older; (superlativo) oldest; (di importanza, Mus) major; (superlativo) greatest; la maggior parte di most; la maggior parte del tempo most of the time
[2] *pron* (di dimensioni) the bigger, the larger; (superlativo) the biggest, the largest; (di età) the older; (superlativo) the oldest; (di importanza) the major; (superlativo) the greatest
[3] *nm* Mil major; Aeron squadron leader

maggio'renne [1] *adj* of age [2] *nmf* adult

maggiori'tario *adj* (della maggioranza) majority; ‹sistema› first-past-the-post *attrib*

maggior'mente *adv* [all] the more; (più di tutto) most

'Magi *nmpl* i re ~ the Magi

ma'gia *nf* magic; (trucco) magic trick

magica'mente *adv* magically

'magico *adj* magic

magi'stero *nm* (insegnamento) teaching; (maestria) skill; facoltà di magistero arts faculty

magi'strale *adj* masterly; **istituto magistrale** teacher-training college

magistral'mente *adv* in a masterly fashion

magi'strato *nm* magistrate

magistra'tura *nf* magistrature; **la ∼** the Bench

✧ **'maglia** *nf* stitch; (lavoro ai ferri) knitting; (tessuto) jersey; (di rete) mesh; (indumento intimo) vest; (esterno) top; (di calciatore) shirt; **fare la ∼** knit
- **maglia con cappuccio** fam hoody; **maglia diritta** knit; **maglia rosa** (ciclismo) yellow jersey; **maglia rovescia** purl

magli'aia *nf* knitter

maglie'ria *nf* knitwear

magli'etta *nf*
- **maglietta [a maniche corte]** tee-shirt

magli'ficio *nm* knitwear factory

ma'glina *nf* (tessuto) jersey

'maglio *nm* mallet

magli'one *nm* sweater, jumper
- **maglione dolcevita** polo neck [jumper]; **maglione a girocollo** crew neck [sweater]; **maglione a V** V-neck [sweater]

'magma *nm* magma

ma'gnaccia *nm inv* fam pimp

ma'gnanimo *adj* magnanimous

ma'gnate *nm* magnate

ma'gnesia *nf* magnesia

ma'gnesio *nm* magnesium

ma'gnete *nm* magnet

magnetica'mente *adv* magnetically

ma'gnetico *adj* magnetic

magne'tismo *nm* magnetism

magne'tofono *nm* tape recorder

magnifica'mente *adv* magnificently

magnifi'cenza *nf* magnificence; (generosità) munificence

✧ **ma'gnifico** *adj* magnificent; (generoso) munificent

magni'tudine *nf* Astr magnitude

'magno *adj* **aula magna** main hall

ma'gnolia *nf* magnolia

'magnum *nf inv* (bottiglia, pistola) magnum

'mago *nm* magician

ma'gone *nm* **avere il ∼** be down; **mi è venuto il ∼** I've got a lump in my throat

'magra *nf* low water

ma'grezza *nf* thinness

✧ **'magro** *adj* thin; ‹carne› lean; (scarso) meagre; **magra consolazione** cold comfort

✧ **'mai** *adv* never; (inter, talvolta) ever; **caso ∼** if anything; **caso ∼ tornasse** in case he comes back; **come ∼?** why?; **cosa ∼?** what on earth?; **∼ più** never again; **più che ∼** more than ever; **quando ∼?** whenever?; **quasi ∼**

hardly ever

mai'ale *nm* pig; (carne) pork
- **maiale arrosto** roast pork

maia'lino *nm* piglet

'mailing *nm* direct mail, mailing

mai'olica *nf* majolica

maio'nese *nf* mayonnaise

'mais *nm* maize

mai'uscola *nf* capital [letter]; **bloc maiusc** (tasto) caps lock

mai'uscolo *adj* capital

mai'zena® *nf* cornflour

mal ▸ MALE

'mala *nf sl* **la ∼** the underworld

malac'corto *adj* unwise

mala'fede *nf* bad faith

malaf'fare *nm*
- **gente di malaffare** shady characters *pl*

mala'lingua *nf* backbiter

mala'mente *adv* ‹ridotto› badly; ‹rispondere› rudely

malan'dato *adj* in bad shape; (di salute) in poor health

ma'lanimo *nm* ill will

ma'lanno *nm* misfortune; (malattia) illness; **prendersi un ∼** catch something

mala'pena *adv* **a ∼** hardly

ma'laria *nf* malaria

mala'ticcio *adj* sickly

✧ **ma'lato, -a** ① *adj* ill, sick; ‹pianta› diseased
  ② *nmf* sick person
- **malato di Aids** AIDS sufferer; **malato di cancro** cancer patient; **malato di mente** mentally ill person

✧ **malat'tia** *nf* disease, illness; **ho preso due giorni di ∼** I had two days off sick; **essere in ∼** be on sick leave
- **malattia nervosa** nervous disease; **malattia venerea** venereal disease, VD

malaugurata'mente *adv* unfortunately

malaugu'rato *adj* ill-omened

malau'gurio *nm* bad *or* ill omen

mala'vita *nf* underworld

malavi'toso, -a *nmf* gangster

mala'voglia *nf* unwillingness; **di ∼** unwillingly

Ma'lawi *nm* Malawi

malcapi'tato *adj* wretched

malce'lato *adj* ill-concealed

mal'concio *adj* battered

malcon'tento *nm* discontent

malco'stume *nm* immorality

mal'destro *adj* awkward; (inesperto) inexperienced

maldi'cente *adj* slanderous

maldi'cenza *nf* slander

maldi'sposto *adj* ill-disposed

✧ indicates a very frequent word

Mal'dive *nfpl* Maldives

⚡ **'male** ① *adv* badly; **funzionare ~** not work properly; **star ~** be ill; **star ~ a qualcuno** ‹vestito ecc› not suit somebody; **rimanerci ~** be hurt; **ho dormito ~** I didn't sleep well; **non c'è ~!** not bad at all!

② *nm* evil; (dolore) pain, ache; (malattia) illness; (danno) harm; **distinguere il bene dal ~** know right from wrong; **andare a ~** go off; **aver ~ a** have a pain in; **dove hai ~?** where does it hurt?, where is the pain?; **far ~ a qualcuno** (provocare dolore) hurt somebody; ‹cibo› be bad for somebody; **le cipolle mi fanno ~** onions don't agree with me; **mi fa ~ la schiena** my back is hurting; **farsi ~ alla schiena** hurt one's back

■ **mal d'aereo** airsickness; **mal d'aria** airsickness; **soffrire il mal d'aria** be airsick; **mal d'auto** carsickness; **mal di denti** toothache; **mal di gola** sore throat; **mal di mare** seasickness; **avere il mal di mare** be seasick; **mal d'orecchi** earache; **mal di pancia** lit stomach-ache; fig fam trouble; **mal di schiena** backache, **mal di testa** headache

maledetta'mente *adv* flipping

male'detto *adj* cursed; (orribile) awful

male'dire *vt* curse

maledizi'one *nf* curse; **~!** damn!

maleducata'mente *adv* rudely

maledu'cato *adj* ill-mannered

maleducazi'one *nf* rudeness

male'fatta *nf* misdeed

male'ficio *nm* witchcraft

ma'lefico *adj* ‹azione› evil; (nocivo) harmful

maleodo'rante *adj* foul-smelling

ma'lese *adj & nmf* Malaysian

Ma'lesia *nf* Malaysia

ma'lessere *nm* indisposition; fig uneasiness

ma'levolo *adj* malevolent

malfa'mato *adj* of ill repute

mal'fatto *adj* badly done; (malformato) ill-shaped

malfat'tore *nm* wrongdoer

mal'fermo *adj* unsteady; ‹salute› poor

malfor'mato *adj* misshapen

malformazi'one *nf* malformation

mal'gascio, -a *adj & nmf* Malagasy

malgo'verno *nm* misgovernment

mal'grado ① *prep* in spite of ② *conj* although

'Mali *nm* Mali

ma'lia *nf* spell

maligna'mente *adv* maliciously

mali'gnare *vi* malign

malignità *nf* malice; Med malignancy

ma'ligno *adj* malicious; (perfido) evil; Med malignant

malinco'nia *nf* melancholy

malinconica'mente *adv* melancholically

malin'conico *adj* melancholy

malincu'ore: **a ~** *adv* unwillingly, reluctantly

malinfor'mato *adj* misinformed

malintenzio'nato, -a *nmf* miscreant

malin'teso ① *adj* mistaken ② *nm* misunderstanding

ma'lizia *nf* malice; (astuzia) cunning; (espediente) trick

maliziosa'mente *adv* mischievously, naughtily

maliziosità *nf* naughtiness

malizi'oso *adj* (birichino) mischievous, naughty

malle'abile *adj* malleable

mal'leolo *nm* Anat malleolus

malleva'dore *nm* guarantor

'mallo *nm* husk

mal'loppo *nm* fam loot

malme'nare *vt* ill-treat

mal'messo *adj* (vestito male) shabbily dressed; ‹casa› poorly furnished; fig (senza soldi) hard up

malnu'trito *adj* undernourished

malnutrizi'one *nf* malnutrition

'malo *adj* in **~ modo** badly

ma'locchio *nm* evil eye

ma'lora *nf* ruin; **della ~** awful; **andare in ~** go to ruin

ma'lore *nm* illness; **essere colto da ~** be suddenly taken ill

malri'dotto *adj* ‹persona› in a sorry state; (auto, casa) dilapidated, in a sorry state

mal'sano *adj* unhealthy

malsi'curo *adj* unsafe; (incerto) uncertain

'malta *nf* mortar

mal'tempo *nm* bad weather

mal'tese *adj & nmf* Maltese

'malto *nm* malt

mal'tosio *nm* maltose

maltratta'mento *nm* ill-treatment

maltrat'tare *vt* ill-treat

malu'more *nm* bad mood; **di ~** in a bad mood

'malva *adj inv* mauve

mal'vagio *adj* wicked

malvagità *nf* wickedness

malva'sia *nf* type of dessert wine

malversazi'one *nf* embezzlement

mal'visto *adj* unpopular (da with)

malvi'vente *nm* criminal

malvolenti'eri *adv* unwillingly

malvo'lere *vt* **farsi ~** make oneself unpopular; **prendere qualcuno a ~** take a dislike to somebody

m

⚲ '**mamma** *nf* mummy, mum; ∼ **mia!** good gracious!

mam'mario *adj* mammary

mam'mella *nf* breast

mam'mifero *nm* mammal

mam'mismo *nm* (del figlio) dependency on the mother figure; (della madre) excessive motherliness

mammogra'fia *nf* mammograph

'**mammola** *nf* violet

mammo'letta *nf* shrinking violet

mam'mone *nm* mummy's boy

mam'mut *nm inv* mammoth

ma'nata *nf* handful; (colpo) slap

'**manca** *nf* ▶ MANCO

manca'mento *nm* **avere un** ∼ faint

man'cante *adj* missing

⚲ **man'canza** *nf* lack; (assenza) absence; (insufficienza) shortage; (fallo) fault; (imperfezione) defect; **in** ∼ **d'altro** failing all else; **sento la sua** ∼ I miss him

■ **mancanza di tatto** lack of tact, indelicacy

⚲ **man'care** 1 *vi* be lacking; (essere assente) be missing; (venir meno) fail; (morire) pass away; ∼ **di** be lacking in; ∼ **a** fail to keep ⟨promessa⟩; **mi manca casa** I miss home; **mi manchi** I miss you; **mi è mancato il tempo** I didn't have [the] time; **mi mancano 10 euro** I'm 10 euros short; **quanto manca alla partenza?** how long before we leave?; ∼**è mancata la corrente** there was a power failure; **sentirsi** ∼ feel faint; **sentirsi** ∼ **il respiro** be unable to breathe [properly] 2 *vt* miss ⟨bersaglio⟩; **è mancato poco che cadesse** he nearly fell

man'cato *adj* ⟨appuntamento⟩ missed; ⟨tentativo⟩ unsuccessful; ⟨occasione⟩ wasted

'**manche** *nf inv* heat

man'chevole *adj* defective

'**mancia** *nf* tip

■ ∼ **competente** reward

manci'ata *nf* handful

man'cino *adj* left-handed

'**manco, -a** 1 *adj* left 2 *nf* left hand 3 *adv* (nemmeno) not even

⚲ **man'dante** *nmf* (di delitto) instigator; Jur principal

manda'rancio *nm* clementine

man'dare *vt* send; (emettere) give off; utter ⟨suono⟩; ∼ **a chiamare** send for; ∼ **avanti la casa** run the house; ∼ **giù** (ingoiare) swallow

manda'rino *nm* Bot mandarin

man'data *nf* consignment; (di serratura) turn; **chiudere a doppia** ∼ double lock

manda'tario *nm* Jur agent

man'dato *nm* (incarico) mandate; Jur warrant

■ **mandato di comparizione [in giudizio]** subpoena; **mandato di pagamento** money order; **mandato di perquisizione** search warrant

man'dibola *nf* jaw

mando'lino *nm* mandolin

'**mandorla** *nf* almond; **a** ∼ ⟨occhi⟩ almond-shaped

■ **mandorla amara** bitter almond

mandor'lato *nm* nut brittle (type of nougat)

'**mandorlo** *nm* almond [tree]

man'dragola *nf* mandrake

'**mandria** *nf* herd

mandri'ano *nm* cowherd

man'drillo *nm* (scimmia) mandrill; (attrezzo) mandrel; fig fam goat

maneg'gevole *adj* easy to handle

maneggi'are *vt* handle

ma'neggio *nm* handling; (intrigo) plot; (scuola di equitazione) riding school

ma'nesco *adj* quick to hit out

ma'netta *nf* lever; **a tutta** ∼ flat out; **manette** *pl* handcuffs

man'forte *nm* **dare** ∼ **a qualcuno** support somebody

manga'nello *nm* truncheon

manga'nese *nm* manganese

mange'reccio *adj* edible

mangiacas'sette *nm inv* cassette player

mangia'dischi® *nm inv* portable record player

mangia'fumo *adj inv* **candela** ∼ air-purifying candle

mangia'nastri *nm inv* cassette player

⚲ **mangi'are** 1 *vt/i* eat; (consumare) eat up; (corrodere) eat away; take ⟨scacchi, carte ecc⟩; **dar da** ∼ **al gatto/cane** feed the cat/dog 2 *nm* eating; (cibo) food; (pasto) meal

mangi'arsi *vr* ∼ **le parole** mumble; ∼ **le unghie** bite one's nails

mangia'soldi *adj inv* **macchinetta** ∼ one-armed bandit

mangi'ata *nf* big meal; **farsi una bella** ∼ **di...** feast on...

mangia'toia *nf* manger

mangia|'tore, -trice *nmf* eater

■ **mangiatore di fuoco** fire-eater; **mangiatrice di uomini** maneater

man'gime *nm* fodder

■ **mangime per i polli** chicken feed

mangi'one, -a *nmf* fam glutton

mangiucchi'are *vt* nibble

'**mango** *nm* mango

man'grovia *nf* mangrove

man'gusta *nf* mongoose

ma'nia *nf* mania

■ **mania di grandezza** delusions of grandeur; **mania di persecuzione** persecution complex

m

mania'cale *adj* manic

ma'niaco, -a [1] *adj* maniacal
[2] *nmf* maniac
■ **maniaco sessuale** sex maniac

ma'niaco-depres'sivo *adj & nmf* manic-depressive

'manica *nf* sleeve; fam (gruppo) band; **a maniche lunghe** long-sleeved; **senza maniche** sleeveless; **essere in maniche di camicia** be in shirt sleeves; **essere di ∼ larga** be generous; **essere di ∼ stretta** be strict
■ **manica a vento** wind sock

'Manica *nf* **la ∼** the [English] Channel

manica'retto *nm* tasty dish

maniche'ismo *nm* Manicheism

mani'chetta *nf* hose

mani'chino *nm* (da sarto, vetrina) dummy

'manico *nm* handle; Mus neck
■ **manico di scopa** broom handle

mani'comio *nm* mental home; fam (confusione) tip

mani'cotto *nm* muff; Mech sleeve

mani'cure [1] *nf* manicure
[2] *nmf inv* (persona) manicurist

⚘ **mani'era** *nf* manner; **in ∼ che** so that

manie'rato *adj* affected; ⟨stile⟩ mannered

manie'rismo *nm* mannerism

mani'ero *nm* manor

manifat'tura *nf* manufacture; (fabbrica) factory

manifatturi'ero *adj* manufacturing

manifesta'mente *adv* demonstrably, manifestly

manife'stante *nmf* demonstrator

⚘ **manife'stare** [1] *vt* show; (esprimere) express
[2] *vi* demonstrate

manifes'tarsi *vr* show oneself

manifestazi'one *nf* show; (espressione) expression; (sintomo) manifestation; (dimostrazione pubblica) demonstration

mani'festo [1] *adj* evident
[2] *nm* poster; (dichiarazione pubblica) manifesto

ma'niglia *nf* handle; (sostegno, in autobus ecc) strap

manipo'lare *vt* handle; (massaggiare) massage; (alterare) adulterate; fig manipulate

manipola|'tore, '-trice [1] *nmf* manipulator
[2] *adj* manipulative

manipolazi'one *nf* handling; (massaggio) massage; (alterazione) adulteration; fig manipulation

mani'scalco *nm* smith

'manna *nf*
■ **manna dal cielo** manna from heaven

man'naia *nf* (scure) axe; (da macellaio) cleaver

man'naro *adj* **lupo ∼** werewolf

⚘ **'mano** *nf* hand; (strato di vernice ecc) coat; **alla ∼** informal; **fuori ∼** out of the way; **man ∼** little by little; **man ∼ che** as; **sotto ∼** to hand; **di seconda ∼** secondhand; **a mani vuote** empty-handed; **a ∼** ⟨scritto, ricamato, fatto⟩ by hand; ⟨trapano ecc⟩ hand[-held]; **dare una ∼ a qualcuno** give *or* lend somebody a hand; **ha le mani di pastafrolla** he is a butterfingers

mano'dopera *nf* labour

ma'nometro *nm* manometer, pressure gauge

mano'mettere *vt* tamper with; (violare) violate

ma'nopola *nf* (di apparecchio) knob; (guanto) mitten; (su pullman) handle

mano'scritto [1] *adj* handwritten
[2] *nm* manuscript

mano'vale *nm* labourer

mano'vella *nf* handle; Techn crank
■ **manovella alzacristalli** winder

ma'novra *nf* manoeuvre; Rail shunting; **fare le manovre** Auto manoeuvre; **manovre** *pl* **di corridoio** lobbying

mano'vrabile *adj* manoeuvrable; fig ⟨persona⟩ easy to manipulate

mano'vrare [1] *vt* (azionare) operate; fig manipulate ⟨persona⟩
[2] *vi* manoeuvre

manro'vescio *nm* slap

man'sarda *nf* attic

mansio'nario *nm* job description

mansi'one *nf* task; (dovere) duty

mansu'eto *adj* meek; ⟨animale⟩ docile

'manta *nf* Zool manta

mante'cato [1] *nm* soft ice cream
[2] *adj* creamy

man'tella *nf* cape

man'tello *nm* cloak; (soprabito, di animale) coat; (di neve) mantle

⚘ **mante'nere** *vt* (conservare) keep; (in buono stato, sostentare) maintain

mante'nersi *vr* **∼ in forma** keep fit

manteni'mento *nm* maintenance
■ **mantenimento dell'ordine pubblico** policing; **mantenimento della pace** Mil, Pol peacekeeping

mante'nuta *nf* kept woman

'mantice *nm* bellows *pl*; (di automobile) hood, top

'mantide *nf* mantis

man'tiglia *nf* mantilla

'manto *nm* cloak; (coltre) mantle

'Mantova *nf* Mantua

manto'vana *nf* (di tende) pelmet

manu'ale *adj & nm* manual
■ **manuale di conversazione** phrasebook; **manuale d'uso** user manual

manual'mente *adv* manually

ma'nubrio *nm* handle; (di bicicletta) handlebars *pl*; (per ginnastica) dumb-bell

m

manu'fatto *adj* manufactured

manutenzi'one *nf* maintenance; **un giardino che richiede poca ~** a low-maintenance garden

'**manzo** *nm* steer; (carne) beef

maomet'tano *adj & nm* Muslim

Mao'metto *nm* Mohammed, Muhammad

ma'ori *adj inv & nm inv* Maori

'**mappa** *nf* map

mappa'mondo *nm* globe

mar ▶ MARE

mara'chella *nf* prank

maragià *nm inv* maharajah

maran'tacea *nf* Bot arrowroot

mara'schino *nm* maraschino (*sweet liqueur*)

ma'rasma *nm* fig decline

mara'tona *nf* marathon

marato'neta *nmf* marathon runner

'**marca** *nf* mark; Comm brand; (fabbricazione) make; (scontrino) ticket; **di ~** branded
■ **marca da bollo** *stamp showing that the necessary duties have been paid*

mar'care *vt* mark; Sport score

marcata'mente *adv* markedly

mar'cato *adj* ‹tratto, accento› strong, marked

marca'tore *nm* (chi segna un gol) scorer; (chi marca un avversario) marker; (pennarello) marker pen

'**Marche** *nfpl* Marches

mar'chese, -a ① *nm* marquis ② *nf* marchioness

mar'chetta *nf* (assicurativa) National Insurance stamp; **fare marchette** fam be on the game

marchi'are *vt* brand

'**marchio** *nm* brand; (caratteristica) mark
■ **marchio depositato** registered trademark; **marchio di fabbrica** trademark, TM; **marchio registrato** registered trademark

◆ '**marcia** *nf* march; Auto gear; Sport walk; **mettere in ~** put into gear; **mettersi in ~** start off; **cambiare ~** change gear
■ **marcia a senso unico alternato** temporary one way system in operation; **marcia forzata** forced march; **marcia funebre** funeral march; **marcia indietro** reverse gear; **fare ~ indietro** reverse; fig back-pedal; **marcia nuziale** wedding march

marcia'longa *nf* (di sci) cross-country skiing race; (a piedi) long-distance race

marciapi'ede *nm* pavement, sidewalk Am; (di stazione) platform

marci'are *vi* march; (funzionare) go, work

marcia|'tore, -trice *nmf* walker

'**marcio** ① *adj* rotten ② *nm* rotten part; fig corruption

◆ indicates a very frequent word

mar'cire *vi* go bad, rot

mar'cita *nf* water meadow

'**marco** *nm* (moneta) mark

marco'nista *nmf* radio operator

◆ '**mare** *nm* sea; (luogo di mare) seaside; **sul ~** ‹casa› at the seaside; ‹città› on the sea; **andare al ~** go to the sea; **in alto ~** on the high seas; **d'alto ~** ocean-going; **essere in alto ~** fig not know which way to turn
■ **mare Adriatico** Adriatic Sea; **mar Cinese** China Sea; **mar Ionio** Ionian Sea; **mare d'Irlanda** Irish Sea; **mar Mediterraneo** Mediterranean; **mar Morto** Dead Sea; **mar Nero** Black Sea; **mare del Nord** North Sea; **mar Tirreno** Tyrrhenian Sea

ma'rea *nf* tide; **una ~ di** hundreds of; **alta/bassa marea** high/low tide
■ **marea montante** flood tide

mareggi'ata *nf* [sea] storm

mare'moto *nm* tidal wave, seaquake

◆ **maresci'allo** *nm* (ufficiale) marshal; (sottufficiale) warrant officer

ma'retta *nf* choppiness; fig tension

marga'rina *nf* margarine

marghe'rita *nf* marguerite
■ **margherita settembrina** Michaelmas daisy

margheri'tina *nf* daisy

margi'nale *adj* marginal

marginaliz'zare *vt* marginalize

marginal'mente *adv* marginally

'**margine** *nm* margin; (orlo) brink; (bordo) border
■ **margine di errore** margin of error; **margine di sicurezza** safety margin; **margine di vendita** mark-up

mari'ano *adj* Relig Marian

ma'rina *nf* navy; (costa) seashore; (quadro) seascape
■ **marina mercantile** merchant navy; **marina militare** navy

mari'naio *nm* sailor
■ **marinaio d'acqua dolce** landlubber

mari'nare *vt* marinate; **~ la scuola** play truant

mari'naro *adj* seafaring

mari'nata *nf* marinade

mari'nato *adj* Culin marinated

ma'rino *adj* sea *attrib*, marine

mario'netta *nf* puppet

mari'tare *vt* marry

mari'tarsi *vr* get married

◆ **ma'rito** *nm* husband

mari'tozzo *nm* currant bun

ma'rittimo *adj* maritime

mar'maglia *nf* rabble

marmel'lata *nf* jam; (di agrumi) marmalade

mar'mitta *nf* pot; Auto silencer
■ **marmitta catalitica** catalytic converter

◆ '**marmo** *nm* marble

mar'mocchio *nm* fam brat
mar'moreo *adj* marble
marmoriz'zato *adj* marbled
mar'motta *nf* marmot
maroc'chino *adj & nmf* Moroccan
Ma'rocco *nm* Morocco
ma'roso *nm* breaker
mar'rone [1] *adj* brown
　[2] *nm* brown; (castagna) chestnut; **marroni** *pl* **canditi** marrons glacés
'Marshall *nfpl* **le isole ~** Marshall Islands
mar'sina *nf* tails *pl*
marsupi'ale *nm* marsupial
mar'supio *nm* (borsa) bumbag
'Marte *nm* Mars
martedì *nm* Tuesday; **di ~** on Tuesdays
　■ **martedì grasso** Shrove Tuesday
martel'lante *adj* ‹mal di testa› pounding, throbbing; **hanno fatto una pubblicità ~** they hyped the product, they bombarded the market with publicity
martel'lare [1] *vt* hammer
　[2] *vi* throb
martel'lata *nf* hammer blow
martel'letto *nm* (di giudice) gavel; (di pianoforte) hammer; (di medico) percussion hammer
martel'lio *nm* hammering
mar'tello *nm* hammer; (di battente) knocker
　■ **~ pneumatico** pneumatic drill
marti'netto *nm* Mech jack
martin pesca'tore *nm inv* kingfisher
'martire *nmf* martyr
mar'tirio *nm* martyrdom
'martora *nf* marten
martori'are *vt* torment
mar'xismo *nm* Marxism
mar'xista *adj & nmf* Marxist
marza'pane *nm* marzipan
marzi'ale *adj* martial
marzi'ano, -a *adj & nmf* Martian
'marzo *nm* March
mascal'zone *nm* rascal
ma'scara *nm inv* mascara
mascar'pone *nm full-fat cream cheese often used for desserts*
ma'scella *nf* jaw
'maschera *nf* mask; (costume) fancy dress; Cinema, Theat usher (*m*), usherette (*f*); (nella commedia dell'arte) stock character
　■ **maschera antigas** gas mask; **maschera di bellezza** face pack; **maschera mortuaria** death mask; **maschera ad ossigeno** oxygen mask
maschera'mento *nm* masking; Mil camouflage
masche'rare *vt* mask; fig camouflage
masche'rarsi *vr* put on a mask; **~ da** dress up as
masche'rata *nf* masquerade

maschi'accio *nm* (ragazza) tomboy
ma'schile [1] *adj* masculine; ‹sesso› male
　[2] *nm* masculine [gender]
maschi'lismo *nm* male chauvinism
maschi'lista [1] *adj* sexist
　[2] *nm* male chauvinist
'maschio [1] *adj* male; (virile) manly
　[2] *nm* male; (figlio) son
　■ **maschio dominante** alpha male
masco'lino *adj* masculine
ma'scotte *nf inv* mascot
maso'chismo *nm* masochism
maso'chista *adj & nmf* masochist
'massa *nf* mass; Electr earth, ground Am; **una ~ [di gente]** a crowd [of people]
massa'crante *adj* gruelling
massa'crare *vt* massacre
mas'sacro *nm* massacre; fig mess
massaggi'are *vt* massage
massaggia|'tore, -trice [1] *nm* masseur
　[2] *nf* masseuse
mas'saggio *nm* massage
　■ **massaggio cardiaco** heart massage
mas'saia *nf* housewife
mas'sello [1] *nm* (metallo) ingot
　[2] *adj* ‹legno› solid
masse'rizie *nfpl* household effects
massiccia'mente *adv* on a big scale
massicci'ata *nf* hard core
mas'siccio [1] *adj* massive; ‹oro ecc› solid; ‹corporatura› heavy
　[2] *nm* massif
massifi'care *vt* de-individualize ‹società›
massificazi'one *nf* de-individualization
'massima *nf* maxim; (temperatura) maximum
massi'male *nm* (assicurazione) limit of indemnity
massimiz'zare *vt* maximize
massimizzazi'one *nf* maximization
'massimo [1] *adj* greatest; ‹quantità› maximum, greatest
　[2] *nm* **il ~** the maximum; **al ~** at [the] most, as a maximum
　■ **massimo storico** all-time high
'masso *nm* rock
mas'sone *nm* [Free]mason
masso'neria *nf* Freemasonry
mastecto'mia *nf* mastectomy
ma'stello *nm wooden box for the grape or olive harvest*
masteriz'zare *vt* ‹CD, DVD› burn
masterizza'tore *nm*
　■ **masterizzatore di CD/DVD** CD/DVD burner
masti'care *vt* chew; (borbottare) mumble
'mastice *nm* mastic, filler; (per vetri) putty
ma'stino *nm* mastiff
masto'dontico *adj* gigantic

ma'stoide *nm* mastoid

'**mastro** *nm* master; **libro mastro** ledger

mastur'barsi *vr* masturbate

masturbazi'one *nf* masturbation

ma'tassa *nf* skein

match 'point *nm inv* Tennis match point

matelassé *nm inv* quilting

mate'matica *nf* mathematics, maths *both sg*, math *Am*
■ **matematica pura** pure mathematics

mate'matico, -a [1] *adj* mathematical [2] *nmf* mathematician

materas'sino *nm* small mattress
■ **materassino gonfiabile** air bed, lilo®

mate'rasso *nm* mattress
■ **materasso ad acqua** water bed; **materasso di gommapiuma** foam mattress; **materasso a molle** spring mattress

🗲 **ma'teria** *nf* matter; (materiale) material; (di studio) subject
■ **materia grigia** grey matter; **materia oscura** dark matter; **materia prima** raw material

materi'ale [1] *adj* material; (grossolano) coarse [2] *nm* material
■ **materiale da costruzione** building material; **materiale pubblicitario** publicity material; **materiale di scarto** waste material

materia'lismo *nm* materialism

materia'lista [1] *adj* materialistic; **non** ∼ unworldly [2] *nmf* materialist

materializ'zarsi *vr* materialize

material'mente *adv* physically

materna'mente *adv* maternally

maternità *nf* motherhood; **è alla prima** ∼ it's her first baby; **ospedale di maternità** maternity hospital

ma'terno *adj* maternal; **lingua materna** mother tongue

ma'tita *nf* pencil; **matite** *pl* **colorate** colour[ed] pencils
■ **matita emostatica** styptic pencil; **matita per gli occhi** eyeliner pencil

matriar'cale *adj* matriarchal

ma'trice *nf* matrix; (origini) roots *pl*; Comm counterfoil
■ **matrice attiva** Comput active matrix; **matrice passiva** Comput passive matrix

ma'tricola *nf* (registro) register; Univ fresher; **numero di matricola** (di studente) matriculation number

ma'trigna *nf* stepmother

matrimoni'ale *adj* matrimonial; **vita matrimoniale** married life

🗲 **matri'monio** *nm* marriage; (cerimonia) wedding
■ **matrimonio in bianco** white wedding;

matrimonio civile civil wedding; **matrimonio di convenienza** marriage of convenience; **matrimonio di fatto** common-law marriage; **matrimonio omosessuale** gay marriage

ma'trona *nf* matron

'**matta** *nf* (nelle carte) joker

mattacchi'one, -a *nmf* rascal

mat'tanza *nf* (di tonni) tuna fishing; fig killings *pl*

matta'toio *nm* slaughterhouse

matta'tore *nm* (artista) star performer

matte'rello *nm* rolling-pin

🗲 **mat'tina** *nf* morning; **la** ∼, **alla** ∼ in the morning; **domani** ∼ tomorrow morning; **ieri** ∼ yesterday morning

matti'nata *nf* morning; Theat matinée

mattini'ero *adj* **essere** ∼ be an early riser

🗲 **mat'tino** *nm* morning

🗲 '**matto, -a** [1] *adj* mad, crazy; Med insane; (falso) false; (opaco) matt; **avere una voglia matta di...** be dying for...
■ **matto da legare** barking mad [2] *nm* madman [3] *nf* madwoman

mat'tone *nm* brick; (libro) bore

matto'nella *nf* tile
■ **mattonella grezza** quarry tile

mattu'tino *adj* morning *attrib*

matu'rare *vt* ripen; Fin mature

maturazi'one *nf* ripening; Fin maturity; fig (di idea ecc) gestation; **arrivare a** ∼ ‹frutta› ripen; ‹polizza› mature

maturità *nf* maturity; Sch school-leaving certificate

ma'turo *adj* mature; ‹frutto› ripe

ma'tusa *nm* old fogey

Mauri'tania *sf* Mauritania

Mau'rizio *nf* [isola di] ∼ Mauritius

mauso'leo *nm* mausoleum

maxis'chermo *nm* wide screen

'**mayday** *nm inv* Radio Mayday

'**mazza** *nf* club; (martello) hammer; (da baseball, cricket) bat
■ **mazza da golf** golf-club

maz'zata *nf* blow

maz'zetta *nf* (di banconote) bundle; (tangente) bribe

'**mazzo** *nm* bunch; (carte da gioco) pack

Mb *nm abbr* (**megabyte**) Comput Mb

🗲 **me** *pers pron* me; **me lo ha dato** he gave it to me; **secondo me** in my opinion; **fai come me** do as I do; **è più veloce di me** he is faster than me *or* faster than I am

me'andro *nm* meander

'**Mecca** *nf* **la** ∼ Mecca

mec'canica *nf* mechanics *sg*
■ **meccanica quantistica** quantum mechanics

meccanica'mente *adv* mechanically

🗲 indicates a very frequent word

mec'canico [1] *adj* mechanical
[2] *nm* mechanic

mecca'nismo *nm* mechanism

meccanizza'zione *nf* mechanization

meccanogra'fia *nf* data processing

meccano'grafico *adj* data processing *attrib*

mece'nate *nmf* patron

mèche *nfpl* highlights; **farsi [fare] le ∼** have highlights put in, have one's hair streaked

me'daglia *nf* medal
■ **medaglia d'oro** (premio) gold medal; (atleta) gold medallist; **medaglia al valore** medal for valour

medagli'ere *nm* medal collection

medagli'one *nm* medallion; (gioiello) locket; **medaglioni** *pl* **di vitello** Culin medallions of veal

✧ **me'desimo** *adj* same

'media *nf* average; Sch average mark; Math mean; **essere nella ∼** be in the mid-range

medi'ano [1] *adj* middle
[2] *nm* (calcio) half-back
■ **mediano di mischia** scrum half

medi'ante *prep* by

medi'are *vt* act as intermediary in

media|'tore, -trice *nmf* mediator; Comm middleman
■ **mediatore d'affari** business agent; **mediatore culturale** *voluntary or professional worker who helps immigrants integrate into Italian daily life*

mediazi'one *nf* mediation

medica'mento *nm* medicine

medi'care *vt* treat; dress ‹ferita›

medi'cato *adj* ‹shampoo› medicated

medicazi'one *nf* medication; (di ferita) dressing

me'diceo *adj* from the period of the Medici, Medicean

✧ **medi'cina** *nf* medicine
■ **medicina alternativa** alternative medicine, complementary medicine; **medicina del lavoro** occupational health; **medicina legale** forensic medicine, forensic science; **medicina popolare** folk medicine

medici'nale [1] *adj* medicinal
[2] *nm* medicine

✧ **'medico** [1] *adj* medical
[2] *nm* doctor
■ **medico di base** general practitioner, GP; **medico di famiglia** family doctor; **medico generico** general practitioner, GP; **medico legale** forensic scientist; **medico di turno** duty doctor

medie'vale *adj* medieval

'medio [1] *adj* average; ‹punto› middle; ‹statura› medium; **scuola media** secondary school

[2] *nm* (dito) middle finger
■ **Medio Oriente** Middle East

medi'ocre *adj* mediocre; (scadente) poor

mediocre'mente *adv* indifferently

medio'evo *nm* Middle Ages *pl*

mediorien'tale *adj* middle-eastern

medita'bondo *adj* meditative

medi'tare [1] *vt* meditate; (progettare) plan; (considerare attentamente) think over
[2] *vi* meditate

medita'tivo *adj* meditative

meditazi'one *nf* meditation

mediter'raneo *adj* Mediterranean; **il** [mar] **Mediterraneo** the Mediterranean [Sea]

me'dusa *nf* jellyfish

'megabyte *nm inv* Comput megabyte

me'gafono *nm* megaphone

megaga'lattico *adj* gigantic

mega'lite *nm* megalith

mega'lomane *nmf* megalomaniac

me'gera *nf* hag

'meglio [1] *adv* better; **tanto ∼, ∼ così** so much the better
[2] *adj* better; (superlativo) best
[3] *nmf* best
[4] *nf* **avere la ∼ su** have the better of; **fare qualcosa alla [bell'e] ∼** do something as best one can
[5] *nm* **fare del proprio ∼** do one's best; **fare qualcosa il ∼ possibile** make an excellent job of something; **al ∼** to the best of one's ability; **per il ∼** for the best

✧ **'mela** *nf* apple; **succo di mela** apple juice
■ **mela cotogna** quince

mela'grana *nf* pomegranate

mè'lange [1] *nm inv* flecked wool
[2] *adj inv* ‹lana› flecked

mela'nina *nf* melanin

melan'zana *nf* aubergine, eggplant Am; **melanzane** *pl* **alla parmigiana** *baked layers of aubergine, tomato and cheese*

me'lassa *nf* molasses *sg*

me'lenso *adj* ‹persona, film› dull

me'leto *nm* apple orchard

mel'lifluo *adj* ‹parole› honeyed; ‹voce› sugary

'melma *nf* slime

mel'moso *adj* slimy

'melo *nm* apple [tree]

melo'dia *nf* melody

me'lodico *adj* melodic

melodi'oso *adj* melodious

melo'dramma *nm* melodrama

melodrammatica'mente *adv* melodramatically

melodram'matico *adj* melodramatic

melo'grano *nm* pomegranate tree

me'lone *nm* melon

mem'brana *nf* membrane

⚜ **'membro** *nm* member (*pl nf* **membra**) Anat limb

memo'rabile *adj* memorable

'memore *adj* mindful; (riconoscente) grateful

⚜ **me'moria** *nf* memory; (oggetto ricordo) souvenir; **imparare a** ∼ learn by heart; **memorie** *pl* (biografiche) memoirs
■ **memoria cache** Comput cache memory; **memoria collettiva** folk memory; **memoria dinamica** Comput RAM; **memoria di massa** Comput mass storage; **memoria permanente** Comput non-volatile memory; **memoria di sola lettura** Comput read-only memory, ROM; **memoria a tampone** Comput buffer [memory]; **memoria volatile** Comput volatile memory

memori'ale *nm* memorial

memoriz'zare *vt* memorize; Comput save, store

mena'dito: **a** ∼ *adv* perfectly

me'nare *vt* lead; fam (picchiare) hit; ∼ **la coda** ‹*cane*› wag its tail; ∼ **qualcuno per il naso** pull somebody's leg

mendi'cante *nmf* beggar, panhandler Am fam

mendi'care *vt/i* beg

menefre'ghista *adj* devil-may-care

mene'strello *nm* minstrel

me'ningi *nfpl* **spremersi le** ∼ rack one's brains

menin'gite *nf* meningitis

me'nisco *nm* meniscus

⚜ **'meno** ① *adv* less; (superlativo) least; (in operazioni, con temperatura) minus; ∼ **di** less than; **di** ∼ less; ∼ **moderno** less modern; **il** ∼ **moderno di tutti** the least modern of all; **far qualcosa alla** ∼ **peggio** do something as best one can; **fare a** ∼ **di qualcosa** do without something; **non posso fare a** ∼ **di ridere** I can't help laughing; ∼ **male!** thank goodness!; **sempre** ∼ less and less; **venir** ∼ (svenire) faint; **venir** ∼ **a qualcuno** ‹*coraggio*› fail somebody; **sono le tre** ∼ **un quarto** it's a quarter to three; **che tu venga o** ∼ whether you're coming or not; **quanto** ∼ at least ② *adj inv* less; (con nomi plurali) fewer ③ *nm* least; Math minus sign; **il** ∼ **possibile** as little as possible; **per lo** ∼ at least ④ *prep* except [for] ⑤ *conj* **a** ∼ **che** unless

meno'mare *vt* ‹*incidente*› maim

meno'mato ① *adj* disabled ② *nmf* disabled person

meno'pausa *nf* menopause

'mensa *nf* table; Mil mess; Sch, Univ canteen

men'sile ① *adj* monthly ② *nm* (stipendio) [monthly] salary; (rivista) monthly

mensilità *nf inv* monthly salary

mensil'mente *adv* monthly

'mensola *nf* bracket; (scaffale) shelf

'menta *nf* mint; **al gusto di** ∼ mint-flavoured
■ **menta piperita** peppermint; **menta verde** spearmint

men'tale *adj* mental

mentalità *nf inv* mentality
■ **mentalità ristretta** bigotry

⚜ **'mente** *nf* mind; **a** ∼ **fredda** in cold blood; **cosa ti è saltato in** ∼? what possessed you?; **venire in** ∼ **a qualcuno** occur to somebody

men'tina *nf* mint

⚜ **men'tire** *vi* lie

'mento *nm* chin

men'tolo *nm* menthol; **al** ∼ mentholated

⚜ **'mentre** *conj* (temporale) while; (invece) whereas

me'nu *nm inv* menu
■ **menu a discesa** Comput pull-down menu; **menu fisso** set menu; **menu a tendina** Comput pull-down menu, drop-down menu; **menu turistico** tourist menu

menzio'nare *vt* mention

menzi'one *nf* mention
■ **menzione speciale** special mention

men'zogna *nf* lie

⚜ **mera'viglia** *nf* wonder; **a** ∼ marvellously; **che** ∼! how wonderful!; **con mia grande** ∼ much to my amazement; **mi fa** ∼ **che…** I am surprised that…

meravigli'are *vt* surprise

meravigli'arsi *vr* ∼ **di** be surprised at

meravigliosa'mente *adv* marvellously

⚜ **meravigli'oso** *adj* marvellous, wonderful

mer'cante *nm* merchant
■ **mercante d'arte** art dealer; **mercante di schiavi** slave trader

mercanteggi'are *vi* trade; (sul prezzo) bargain

mercan'tile ① *adj* mercantile ② *nm* merchant ship

mercan'zia *nf* merchandise, goods *pl*

merca'tino *nm* (di quartiere) local street market; Fin unlisted securities market

⚜ **mer'cato** *nm* market; Fin market[place]; **a buon** ∼ ‹*comprare*› cheap[ly]; ‹*articolo*› cheap
■ **mercato all'aperto** street market; **mercato aperto** Econ open market; **mercato azionario** Fin equity market, share market; **mercato dei cambi** foreign exchange market; **Mercato Comune [Europeo]** [European] Common Market; **mercato coperto** covered market, indoor market; **mercato dell'eurovaluta** eurocurrency market; **mercato immobiliare** property market; **mercato del lavoro** job market; **mercato libero** free market; **mercato di massa** mass market; **mercato nero** black market; **mercato del pesce** fish market; **mercato di prova** test market; **mercato al rialzo** Fin bull market; **mercato al ribasso** Fin

---

bear market; **mercato specializzato** niche market; **mercato unico** Single Market

'merce *nf* goods *pl*, merchandise; **la ~ venduta non si cambia senza lo scontrino** goods will not be exchanged without a receipt
■ **merce in conto vendita** sale or return goods; **merce deperibile** perishable goods

mercé *nf* **alla ~ di** at the mercy of

merce'nario *adj & nm* mercenary

merceolo'gia *nf* study of commodities

merce'ria *nf* haberdashery; (negozio) haberdasher's

mercifi'care *vt* commercialize

mercificazi'one *nf* commercialization

mercoledì *nm inv* Wednesday; **di ~ on** Wednesdays
■ **mercoledì delle Ceneri** Ash Wednesday

mer'curio *nm* mercury

me'renda *nf* afternoon snack; **far ~** have an afternoon snack

meridi'ana *nf* sundial

meridi'ano ① *adj* midday ② *nm* meridian

meridio'nale ① *adj* southern ② *nmf* southerner

meridi'one *nm* south

me'ringa *nf* meringue

merin'gata *nf* meringue pie

⚬ **meri'tare** *vt* deserve

meri'tato *adj* deserved

meri'tevole *adj* deserving

⚬ **'merito** *nm* merit; (valore) worth; **in ~ a** as to; **per ~ di** thanks to

merito'cratico *adj* meritocratic

meri'torio *adj* meritorious

merla'tura *nf* battlements *pl*

merlet'taia *nf* lacemaker

mer'letto *nm* lace

'merlo *nm* blackbird; **bravo ~!** you fool!

mer'luzzo *nm* cod

'mero *adj* mere

mesca'lina *nf* mescaline

'mescere *vt* pour out

meschine'ria *nf* meanness

me'schino ① *adj* wretched; (gretto) mean ② *nm* wretch

'mescita *nf* wine shop

mescola'mento *nm* mixing

mesco'lanza *nf* mixture

mesco'lare *vt* mix; shuffle ‹carte›; (confondere) mix up; blend ‹tè, tabacco ecc›

mesco'larsi *vr* mix; (immischiarsi) meddle

mesco'lata *nf* (a carte) shuffle; Culin stir

⚬ **'mese** *nm* month
■ **mese civile** calendar month

me'setto *nm* **un ~** about a month, a month or so

⚬ **'messa¹** *nf* Mass
■ **messa nera** black mass; **messa da requiem** requiem mass; **messa solenne** High Mass

'messa² *nf* (il mettere) putting
■ **messa in moto** Auto starting; **messa in piega** (di capelli) set; **farsi fare la ~ in piega** have one's hair set; **messa a punto** adjustment; **messa in scena** production; fig production number; **messa a terra** earthing, grounding Am

messagge'ria *nf*
■ **messaggeria elettronica** Comput messaging

messag'gero *nm* messenger

messa'ggiare *vi* Teleph text

messa'ggino *nm* text message

mes'saggio *nm* message
■ **messaggio di errore** Comput error message; **messaggio di testo** Teleph text message

mes'sale *nm* missal

'messe *nf* harvest

Mes'sia *nm* Messiah

messi'cano, -a *adj & nmf* Mexican

'Messico *nm* Mexico

messin'scena *nf* staging; fig act

'messo ① *pp di* METTERE ② *nm* messenger

⚬ **mesti'ere** *nm* trade; ‹lavoro› job; **essere del ~** be an expert, know one's trade

'mesto *adj* sad

'mestola *nf* (di cuoco) ladle; (di muratore) trowel

mestru'ale *adj* menstrual

mestruazi'one *nf* menstruation; **mestruazioni** *pl* period

'meta *nf* destination; fig aim

⚬ **metà** *nf inv* half; (centro) middle; **a ~ prezzo** half price; **a ~ strada** halfway; **a ~ serata** halfway through the evening; **fare a ~ con qualcuno** go halves with somebody, go fifty-fifty with somebody; **fare [a] ~ e ~** go fifty-fifty, go halves

metabo'lismo *nm* metabolism

meta'carpo *nm* metacarpus

meta'done *nm* methadone

meta'fisica *n* metaphysics *sg*

meta'fisico *adj* metaphysical

me'tafora *nf* metaphor

metaforica'mente *adv* metaphorically

meta'forico *adj* metaphorical

me'tallico *adj* metallic

metalliz'zato *adj* ‹grigio› metallic

me'tallo *nm* metal
■ **metallo vile** base metal

metal'loide *nm* metalloid

metallur'gia *nf* metallurgy

metal'lurgico *adj* metallurgical

metalmec'canico ① *adj* engineering ② *nm* engineering worker

meta'morfosi *nf* metamorphosis

me'tano *nm* methane

metano'dotto *nm* methane pipeline

meta'nolo *nm* methanol

me'tastasi *nf inv* metastasis

meta'tarso *nm* metatarsus

me'teora *nf* meteor

meteo'rite *nm* meteorite

meteorolo'gia *nf* meteorology

meteoro'logico *adj* meteorological

meteo'rologo *nm* meteorologist

me'ticcio, -a *nmf* half-caste

meticolosa'mente *adv* meticulously

metico'loso *adj* meticulous

me'tile *nm* methyl

me'todico *adj* methodical

meto'dista *adj & nmf* Methodist

'metodo *nm* method

metodolo'gia *nf* methodology

metodo'logico *adj* methodological

me'traggio *nm* length (*in metres*); **vendere a ~** sell by the metre

'metrica *nf* metrics

'metrico *adj* metric; (*in poesia*) metrical

✦ **'metro¹** *nm* metre; (*nastro*) tape measure
■ **metro cubo** cubic metre; **metro quadrato** square metre

'metro² *nf inv* fam underground, subway Am

me'tronomo *nm* metronome

metro'notte *nmf inv* night security guard

me'tropoli *nf inv* metropolis

metropoli'tana *nf* underground, subway Am

metropoli'tano *adj* metropolitan

✦ **'mettere** *vt* put; (*indossare*) put on; fam (*installare*) put in; **~ al mondo** bring into the world; **~ da parte** set aside; **~ fiducia** inspire trust; **~ qualcosa in chiaro** make something clear; **~ in mostra** display; **~ a posto** tidy up; **~ in vendita** put up for sale; **~ su** set up ‹*casa, azienda*›; **metter su famiglia** start a family; **ci ho messo un'ora** it took me an hour; **mettiamo che...** let's suppose that...

'mettersi *vr* (*indossare*) put on; (*diventare*) turn out; **~ a** start to; **~ con qualcuno** fam (*formare una coppia*) start to go out with somebody; **~ a letto** go to bed; **~ a sedere** sit down; **~ in viaggio** set out

metti'foglio *nm* feeder

'mezza *nf* **è la ~** it's half past twelve; **sono le quattro e ~** it's half past four

mez'zadria *nf* sharecropping

mezza'luna *nf* half moon; (*simbolo islamico*) crescent; (*coltello*) two-handled chopping knife; **a ~** half-moon

mezza'manica *nf* **a ~** ‹*maglia*› short-sleeved; **mezzemaniche** *pl* pej lowest grade of clerks, pen-pushers

mezza'nino *nm* mezzanine

mez'zano, -a *adj* middle

mezza'notte *nf* midnight; **aspettare la ~** see in the New Year

mezz'asta: **a ~** *adv* at half mast

mezze'ria *nf* centre line

✦ **'mezzo** ① *adj* half; **di mezza età** middle aged; **~ bicchiere** half a glass; **una mezza idea** a vague idea; **siamo mezzi morti** we're half dead; **sono le quattro e ~** it's half past four
■ **mezza cartuccia** *nf* runt; **mezza dozzina** *nf* half-dozen; **mezza età** *nf* midlife; **mezza giornata** *nf* half day; **mezzo guanto** *nm* mitt; **mezzo litro** *nm* half a litre; **mezz'ora** *nf* half an hour; **mezza pensione** *nf* half board; **mezza stagione** *nf* demi-season; **una giacca di ~ stagione** a spring/autumn jacket; **mezza verità** *nf* half-truth
② *adv* (*a metà*) half; **~ addormentato** half asleep; **~ morto** half-dead; **~ morto di paura** petrified; **~ e ~** (*così così*) so so
③ *nm* (*metà*) half; (*centro*) middle; (*per raggiungere un fine*) means *sg*; **uno e ~** one and a half; **tre anni e ~** three and a half years; **in ~ a** in the middle of; **il giusto ~** the happy medium; **levare di ~** clear away; **per ~ di** by means of; **a ~ posta** by mail; **via di ~** fig halfway house; (*soluzione*) middle way; **mezzi** *pl* (*denaro*) means *pl*; **mezzi** *pl* **di comunicazione di massa** mass media; **mezzi** *pl* **pubblici** public transport; **mezzi** *pl* **di trasporto** [means of] transport

mezzo'busto *nm* (*statua*) bust; TV talking head; **a ~** ‹*foto, ritratto*› half-length

mezzo'fondo *nm* middle-distance running

✦ **mezzogi'orno** *nm* midday, noon; (*sud*) South; **il Mezzogiorno** Southern Italy
■ **mezzogiorno in punto** high noon

mezzo'sangue *nmf* crossbreed

mezzo'servizio *nm* **lavorare a ~** do part-time cleaning work

✦ **mi** ① *pers pron* me; *refl*, myself; **mi ha dato un libro** he gave me a book; **non mi parla** he doesn't talk to me; **mi lavo le mani** I wash my hands; **eccomi** here I am
② *nm* Mus (*chiave, nota*) E

'mia ▶ MIO

miago'lare *vi* miaow

miago'lio *nm* miaowing

mi'ao *nm* miaow

'mica¹ *nf* mica

✦ **'mica²** *adv* fam (*per caso*) by any chance; **hai ~ visto Paolo?** have you seen Paul, by any chance?; **non è ~ bello** it is not at all nice; **~ male** not bad

'miccia *nf* fuse

micidi'ale *adj* deadly

'micio *nm* pussy cat

mi'cosi *nf* athlete's foot

✦ indicates a very frequent word

mi'cotico *adj* fungal
microbiolo'gia *nf* microbiology
'microbo *nm* microbe
microchirur'gia *nf* microsurgery
micro'clima *nm* microclimate
microcom'puter *nm inv* microcomputer
micro'cosmo *nm* microcosm
micro'fiche *nf inv* microfiche
micro'film *nm inv* microfilm
micro'fisica *nf* microphysics *sg*
mi'crofono *nm* microphone
- microfono con la clip clip-on microphone; microfono spia bugging device, bug; microfono a stelo boom microphone

microfotogra'fia *nf* Phot micrograph; (tecnica) micrography
microinfor'matica *nf* microcomputing
micro'onda *nf* microwave
microorga'nismo *nm* microorganism
microproces'sore *nm* microprocessor
micro'scheda *nf* microfiche
micro'scopico *adj* microscopic
micro'scopio *nm* microscope; **passare qualcosa a** ~ *fig* examine something in microscopic detail
microse'condo *nm* microsecond
micro'solco *nm* (disco) long-playing record
micro'spia *nf* bug
mi'dollo Anat *nm* (*pl nf* **midolla**) marrow; **fino al** ~ ‹bagnato› through and through; ‹corrotto› to the core
- midollo osseo bone marrow; midollo spinale spinal cord

'mie ▶ MIO
mi'ei ▶ MIO
mi'ele *nm* honey
- miele d'acacia acacia honey

mi'etere *vt* reap
mietitrebbia'trice *nf* combine harvester
mieti'trice *nf* harvester
mieti'tura *nf* harvest
migli'aia *nfpl* thousands
✓ **migli'aio** *nm* (*pl nf* **migliaia**) thousand; **a migliaia** in thousands
'miglio *nm* Bot millet (misura: *pl f* **miglia**) mile
- miglia aeree *pl* Br Air Miles Am, frequent-flyer miles; miglio nautico nautical mile; miglia all'ora *pl* miles per hour, mph; miglio terrestre mile

migliora'mento *nm* improvement
miglio'rare *vt/i* improve
✓ **migli'ore** [1] *adj* better; (superlativo) the best; ~ **amico** best friend; **i migliori auguri** best wishes
   [2] *nmf* **il/la** ~ the best
miglio'ria *nf* improvement

mi'gnatta *nf* leech
'mignolo *nm* little finger, pinkie fam; (del piede) little toe
mi'gnon *adj inv* (bottiglie) miniature
mi'grante *nmf* (persona) migrant
mi'grare *vi* migrate
migra'tore *adj* migratory
migra'torio *adj* migratory
migrazi'one *nf* migration
'mila ▶ MILLE
✓ **mila'nese** *adj & nmf* Milanese
Mi'lano *nf* Milan
miliar'dario, -a [1] *nm* millionaire; (pluri-miliardario) billionaire
   [2] *nf* millionaires; billionairess
✓ **mili'ardo** *nm* billion
mili'are *adj* **pietra** ~ milestone
milio'nario, -a [1] *nm* millionaire
   [2] *nf* millionairess
✓ **mili'one** *nm* million
milio'nesimo *adj & nm* millionth
mili'tante *adj & nmf* militant
mili'tanza *nf* militancy
✓ **mili'tare** [1] *vi* ~ **in** be a member of ‹un partito ecc›
   [2] *adj* military
   [3] *nm* soldier; **fare il** ~ do one's military service
- militare di carriera regular [soldier]; militare di leva National Serviceman

milita'rismo *nm* militarism
milita'rista *adj* militaristic
militariz'zare *vt* militarize
militas'solto *adj* having done National Service
'milite *nm* soldier
milite'sente *adj* exempt from National Service
mil'izia *nf* militia
millanta|'tore, -trice *nmf* boaster
✓ **'mille** *adj & nm* (*pl* **mila**) a *or* one thousand; **due/tre mila** two/three thousand; ~ **grazie!** thanks a lot!; **millenovecentonovantaquattro** *nm* nineteen ninety-four
mille'foglie *nm inv* Culin vanilla slice
mil'lennio *nm* millennium
millepi'edi *nm inv* centipede
mil'lesimo *adj & nm* thousandth
milli'bar *nm inv* millibar
milli'grammo *nm* milligram
mil'lilitro *nm* millilitre
mil'limetro *nm* millimetre
'milza *nf* spleen
mi'mare [1] *vt* mimic ‹persona›
   [2] *vi* mime
mi'metico *adj* **tuta** *f* **mimetica** camouflage; **animale mimetico** animal which has ····>

m

the ability to camouflage itself; **vernice mimetica** camouflage paint

mime'tismo *nm* ability to camouflage itself

■ **mimetismo politico** chameleon-like political traits

mimetiz'zare *vt* camouflage

mimetiz'zarsi *vr* camouflage oneself

'mimica *nf* mime

■ **mimica facciale** facial expressions *pl*

'mimico *adj* mimic

'mimo *nm* mime

mi'mosa *nf* mimosa

'mina *nf* mine; (di matita) lead

mi'naccia *nf* threat; **avere una ∼ di aborto** come close to having a miscarriage

■ **minaccia di morte** death threat

⚜ **minacci'are** *vt* threaten

minacciosa'mente *adv* threateningly, menacingly

minacci'oso *adj* threatening; ‹onde› menacing

mi'nare *vt* mine; fig undermine

mina'reto *nm* minaret

mina'tore *nm* miner

mina'torio *adj* threatening

⚜ **mine'rale** *adj & nm* mineral

mineralo'gia *nf* mineralogy

mine'rario *adj* mining *attrib*

mi'nestra *nf* soup

■ **minestra in brodo** noodle soup; **minestra di verdure** vegetable soup

mine'strone *nm* minestrone (*vegetable soup*); fam (insieme confuso) hotchpotch

mingher'lino *adj* skinny

'mini ① *nf inv* (gonna) mini ② *adj inv* mini

mini+ *pref* mini+

miniapparta'mento *nm* studio flat Br, studio apartment

minia'tura *nf* miniature

miniaturiz'zato *adj* miniaturized

mini'bus *nm inv* minibus

mini'disc *nm inv* minidisc

mini'disco *nm* minidisc

mini'era *nf* mine; **una ∼ di notizie** a mine of information; **è una ∼ di idee** he's full of ideas

■ **miniera a cielo aperto** opencast mine; **miniera d'oro** gold mine

mini'golf *nm* minigolf, miniature golf

mini'gonna *nf* miniskirt, mini

'minima *nf* (atmosferica) minimum temperature; Med diastolic blood-pressure level; Mus minim

minima'lista *nmf* minimalist

minima'mente *adv* minimally

mini'market *nm inv* minimarket

minimiz'zare *vt* minimize, downplay

⚜ **'minimo** ① *adj* least, slightest; (il più basso) lowest; ‹salario, quantità ecc› minimum ② *nm* minimum; **girare al ∼** Auto idle; **toccare il ∼ storico** be at an all-time low; **come ∼** at least, as a minimum

mini'moto *nf inv* pocket bike

'minio *nm* red lead

ministeri'ale *adj* (di ministero) ministerial; (di governo) government

mini'stero *nm* ministry; (governo) government

■ **ministero dell'Ambiente e della Tutela del Territorio** Department of Natural Resources Am, Department for Environment, Food, and Rural Affairs Br; **ministero degli [affari] Esteri** Foreign Office Br, State Department Am; **ministero della Difesa** Ministry of Defence Br, Department of Defense Am; **ministero di Grazia e Giustizia** Justice Department Am; **ministero degli Interni** Ministry of the Interior, Home Office; **ministero dell'Istruzione** Department for Education and Skills Br; **ministero del Lavoro e delle Politiche Sociali** Department for Work and Pensions; **ministero per le Politiche Agricole e Forestali** Department for Environment, Food, and Rural Affairs Br; **ministero della Salute** Department of Health

⚜ **mi'nistro** *nm* minister

■ **ministro della Difesa** Defence Minister Br, Defense Secretary Am; **ministro degli Esteri** Foreign Secretary Br, Secretary of State Am, foreign minister; **ministro di Grazia e Giustizia** Attorney General; **ministro dell'Interno** Home Secretary Br, Secretary of the Interior Am; **ministro del Lavoro** Secretary of State for Work and Pensions Br, Secretary of Labor Am; **ministro del Tesoro** Chancellor of the Exchequer Br, Secretary of the Treasury Am

mini'tower *nm* Comput minitower

mino'ranza *nf* minority

■ **minoranza etnica** ethnic minority

mino'rato, -a ① *adj* disabled ② *nmf* disabled person

Mi'norca *nf* Menorca

⚜ **mi'nore** ① *adj* ‹gruppo, numero› smaller; (superlativo) smallest; ‹distanza› shorter; (superlativo) shortest; ‹prezzo› lower; (superlativo) lowest; (di età) younger; (superlativo) youngest; (di importanza) minor; (superlativo) least important ② *nmf* younger; (superlativo) youngest; Jur minor; **il ∼ dei mali** the lesser of two evils; **i minori di 14 anni** children under 14

mino'renne ① *adj* under age ② *nmf* minor

minori'tario *adj* minority *attrib*

minu'etto *nm* minuet

mi'nuscolo, -a ① *adj* tiny, minuscule ② *nf* small letter

⚜ indicates a very frequent word

mi'nuta *nf* rough copy

minuta'mente *adv* ‹*esaminato*› in minute detail, minutely; ‹*lavorato, tritato*› finely

mi'nuto[1] *adj* minute; (persona) delicate; (ricerca) detailed; ‹*pioggia, neve*› fine; **al ~** Comm retail

mi'nuto[2] *nm* ‹*di tempo*› minute; **spaccare il ~** be dead on time; **minuti** *pl* **di recupero** Sport injury time

mi'nuzia *nf* trifle; **minuzie** *pl* minutiae

minuziosa'mente *adv* minutely

minuzi'oso *adj* minute, detailed; ‹*persona*› meticulous

'mio [1] (**il mio** *m*, **la mia** *f*, **i miei** *mpl*, **le mie** *fpl*) *poss adj* my; **questa macchina è mia** this car is mine; **~ padre** my father; **un ~ amico** a friend of mine
[2] *poss pron* mine; **i miei** (genitori ecc) my folks

'miope *adj* short-sighted

mio'pia *nf* short-sightedness

'mira *nf* aim; (bersaglio) target; **prendere la ~** take aim; **prendere di ~ qualcuno** fig have it in for somebody

mi'rabile *adj* admirable

miraco'lato *adj* ‹*malato*› miraculously cured

mi'racolo *nm* miracle

miracolosa'mente *adv* miraculously

miraco'loso *adj* miraculous

mi'raggio *nm* mirage

mi'rare *vi* [take] aim; **~ alto** aim high

mi'rarsi *vr* (guardarsi) look at oneself

mi'riade *nf* myriad

mi'rino *nm* sight; Phot view-finder

'mirra *nf* myrrh

mir'tillo *nm* blueberry

'mirto *nm* myrtle

mi'santropo, -a *nmf* misanthropist

mi'scela *nf* mixture; ‹*di caffè, tabacco ecc*› blend

misce'lare *vt* mix

miscela'tore *nm* ‹*apparecchio*› blender; (di acqua) mixer tap

miscel'lanea *nf* miscellany

'mischia *nf* scuffle; (nel rugby) scrum

mischi'are *vt* mix; shuffle ‹*carte da gioco*›

mischi'arsi *vr* mix; (immischiarsi) interfere

misco'noscere *vt* not appreciate

miscre'dente *nmf* heretic

mi'scuglio *nm* mixture; fig medley

mise'rabile *adj* wretched

misera'mente *adv* ‹*finire*› miserably; ‹*vivere*› in abject poverty; ‹*vestito*› shabbily

mi'seria *nf* misery; (infelicità) misery; **guadagnare una ~** earn a pittance; **miserie** *pl* (disgrazie) misfortunes; **porca ~!** fam hell!

miseri'cordia *nf* mercy

misericordi'oso *adj* merciful

'misero *adj* (miserabile) wretched; (povero) poor; (scarso) paltry

mi'sfatto *nm* misdeed

mi'sogino *nm* misogynist

mis'saggio *nm* vision mixer

'missile *nm* missile

■ **missile cruise** cruise missile; **missile terra-aria** surface-to-air missile

missi'listico *adj* missile *attrib*

missio'nario, -a *nmf* missionary

missi'one *nf* mission

■ **missione di pace** peace mission

misteriosa'mente *adv* mysteriously

misteri'oso *adj* mysterious

mi'stero *nm* mystery

'mistica *nf* mysticism

misti'cismo *nm* mysticism

'mistico [1] *adj* mystic[al]
[2] *nm* mystic

mistifi'care *vt* distort ‹*verità*›

mistificazi'one *nf* (della verità) distortion

'misto [1] *adj* mixed; **scuola mista** mixed or co-educational school
[2] *nm* mixture; (di oggetti) miscellany

■ **misto lana** wool mixture; **misto lana/cotone** wool/cotton mix

mi'sura *nf* measure; (dimensione) measurement; (taglia) size; (limite) limit; **su ~** ‹*abiti*› made to measure; ‹*mobile*› custom-made; **a ~** ‹*andare, calzare*› perfectly; **a ~ che** as; **nella ~ in cui** insofar as

■ **misura di capacità** unit of capacity; **misura di lunghezza** unit of length; **misura profilattica** prophylactic; **misura di sicurezza** safety measure; **misure antidiscriminatorie** *pl* positive discrimination

misu'rare *vt* measure; try on ‹*indumenti*›; (limitare) limit

misu'rarsi *vr* **~ con** (gareggiare) compete with

misu'rato *adj* measured

misu'rino *nm* measuring spoon

'mite *adj* mild; ‹*prezzo*› moderate

'mitico *adj* mythical

miti'gare *vt* mitigate

miti'garsi *vr* calm down; ‹*clima*› become mild

'mitilo *nm* mussel

mitiz'zare *vt* mythicize

'mito *nm* myth

mitolo'gia *nf* mythology

mito'logico *adj* mythological

mi'tomane *nmf* compulsive liar

'mitra [1] *nf* Relig mitre
[2] *nm* *inv* Mil machine-gun

mitragli'are *vt* machine-gun; **~ di domande** fire questions at

mitraglia'trice *nf* machine-gun

mitt. *abbr* (**mittente**) sender

mitteleuro'peo *adj* Central European

mit'tente *nmf* sender

'mixer *nm inv* mixer

mne'monico *adj* mnemonic; **frase mnemonica** mnemonic

mo' *nm* **a mo' di** by way of *‹esempio, consolazione›*

♂ **'mobile¹** *adj* mobile; *‹volubile›* fickle; (che si può muovere) movable; **beni** *pl* **mobili** movable personal estate; **squadra mobile** flying squad

♂ **'mobile²** *nm* piece of furniture; **mobili** *pl* furniture *sg*
  ■ **mobile bar** drinks cabinet; **mobili** *pl* **da giardino** garden furniture; **mobili** *pl* **in stile** reproduction furniture

mo'bilia *nf* furniture

mobili'are *adj ‹capitale›* movable; *‹credito›* medium-term; *‹mercato›* share *attrib*; **patrimonio mobiliare** non-property assets

mobili'ere *nm* furniture dealer

mobili'ficio *nm* furniture factory

mo'bilio *nm* furniture

mobilità *nf* mobility
  ■ **mobilità del lavoro** labour mobility; **mobilità sociale** social mobility

mobili'tare *vt* mobilize

mobilitazi'one *nf* mobilization

'moca *nm inv* mocha

mocas'sino *nm* moccasin

mocci'coso, -a ⓵ *adj* snotty
  ⓶ *nmf* snottynosed kid; brat

'moccolo *nm* (di candela) candle-end; (moccio) snot

♂ **'moda** *nf* fashion; **di ~** in fashion; **andare di ~** be in fashion; **alla ~** *‹musica, vestiti›* up to-date; **fuori ~** unfashionable

mo'dale *adj ‹verbo›* modal

modalità *nf inv* formality
  ■ **modalità d'uso** instruction

modana'tura *nf* moulding

mo'della *nf* model

model'lante *adj ‹gel per capelli›* styling

model'lare *vt* model

model'lino *nm* model

model'lismo *nm* model-making; (collezionismo) collecting models

model'lista *nmf* model-maker; (moda) [fashion] designer

♂ **mo'dello** *nm* model; *‹stampo›* mould; (di carta) pattern; (modulo) form; (moda) male model
  ■ **modello CUD** P45; **modello in scala** scale model

'modem *nm inv* modem; **mandare per ~** modem, send by modem

'modem-fax *nm* fax-modem

mode'rare *vt* moderate; (diminuire) reduce

mode'rarsi *vr* control oneself

moderata'mente *adv* moderately

mode'rato *adj* moderate

modera|'tore, -trice ⓵ *nmf* (in tavola rotonda) moderator
  ⓶ *adj* moderating

moderazi'one *nf* moderation

moderna'mente *adv* (in modo moderno) in a modern style

modernari'ato *nm* collecting 20th-century art and products

moder'nismo *nm* modernism

modernità *nf* modernity

moderniz'zare *vt* modernize

modernizzazi'one *nf* modernization

♂ **mo'derno** *adj* modern

mo'destia *nf* modesty

♂ **mo'desto** *adj* modest

'modico *adj* reasonable

mo'difica *nf* modification

modifi'care *vt* modify

modifi'cato *adj* modified
  ■ **modificato geneticamente** genetically modified

modifica'tore *nm* modifier

modificazi'one *nf* modification

mo'dista *nf* milliner

♂ **'modo** *nm* way; (garbo) manners *pl*; (occasione) chance; Gram mood; **ad ogni ~** anyhow; **di ~ che** so that; **fare in ~ di** try to; **in che ~** (inter) how; **in qualche ~** somehow; **in questo ~** like this; **in ~ ottmistico/ pessimistico/anormale** optimistically/ pessimistically/abnormally
  ■ **modo di dire** idiom; **per ~ di dire** so to speak

modu'lare *vt* modulate

modula'tore *nm* modulator
  ■ **modulatore di frequenza** frequency modulator

modulazi'one *nf* modulation
  ■ **modulazione di frequenza** frequency modulation

'modulo *nm* form; *‹lunare, di comando›* module
  ■ **modulo continuo** continuous paper; **modulo di domanda** application form; **modulo di iscrizione** enrolment form; **modulo di ordinazione** order form; **modulo di richiesta** claim form

'modus ope'randi *nm inv* modus operandi

'modus vi'vendi *nm inv* modus vivendi

mof'fetta *nf* skunk

'mogano *nm* mahogany

'mogio *adj* dejected

♂ **'moglie** *nf* wife

moi'cano *adj* **taglio [di capelli] alla moicana** mohican [haircut]

mo'ine *nfpl* **fare le ~** behave in an affected way

♂ indicates a very frequent word

'**mola** *nf* millstone; Mech grindstone

mo'**lare** *nm* molar

mo'**lato** *adj* ‹vetro› cut

mola'**trice** *nf* Mech grinder

Mol'**davia** *nf* Moldavia

'**mole** *nf* mass; (dimensione) size

mo'**lecola** *nf* molecule

moleco'**lare** *adj* molecular

mole'**stare** *vt* bother; (più forte) molest

molesta|'**tore, -trice** *nmf* molester

mo'**lestia** *nf* nuisance; **molestie** *pl* sessuali sexual harassment *sg*

mo'**lesto** *adj* bothersome

Mo'**lise** *nm* Molise

'**molla** *nf* spring; **molle** *pl* tongs; **prendere qualcuno con le molle** handle somebody with kid gloves

mol'**lare** [1] *vt* let go; fam (lasciare) leave; fam give ‹ceffone›; Naut cast off [2] *vi* cease; **mollala!** fam stop that!

'**molle** *adj* soft; (bagnato) wet

molleggi'**are** [1] *vi* be springy [2] *vt* spring

molleggi'**arsi** *vr* bend at the knees

molleg'**giato** *adj* bouncy, springy

mol'**leggio** *nm* (di auto) suspension; (di letto) springs *pl*; (esercizio) knee-bends *pl*

mol'**letta** *nf* (per capelli) hairgrip, barrette Am; **mollette** *pl* (per ghiaccio ecc) tongs

▪ **molletta da bucato** clothes peg

mollet'**tone** *nm* (per tavolo) padded table cloth

mol'**lezza** *nf* softness; **mollezze** *pl* fig luxury

mol'**lica** *nf* crumb

mol'**liccio** *adj* squidgy

mol'**lusco** *nm* mollusc

'**molo** *nm* pier; (banchina) dock

'**molotov** *adj inv* **bottiglia** ~ Molotov cocktail

mol'**teplice** *adj* manifold; (numeroso) numerous

molteplici'**tà** *nf* multiplicity

mol'**tiplica** *nf* (di bicicletta) gear ratio, gear wheel

moltipli'**care** *vt* multiply

moltipli'**carsi** *vr* multiply

moltiplica'**tore** *nm* multiplier

moltiplica'**trice** *nf* calculating machine

moltiplicazi'**one** *nf* multiplication

molti'**tudine** *nf* multitude

⚓ '**molto** [1] *adj* a lot of; (con negazione e interrogazione) much, a lot of; (con nomi plurali) many, a lot of; **non** ~ **tempo** not much time, not a lot of time; **molte grazie** thank you very much [2] *adv* very; (con verbi) a lot; (con avverbi) much; ~ **stupido** very stupid; ~ **bene,**

grazie very well, thank you; **mangiare** ~ eat a lot; ~ **più veloce** much faster; **non mangiare** ~ not eat a lot, not eat much [3] *pron* a lot; (molto tempo) a lot of time; (con negazione e interrogazione) much, a lot; (plurale) many; **non ne ho** ~ I don't have much, I don't have a lot; **non ne ho molti** I don't have many, I don't have a lot; **non ci metterò** ~ I won't be long; **fra non** ~ before long; **molti** (persone) a lot of people; **eravamo in molti** there were a lot of us

momentanea'**mente** *adv* momentarily; **è** ~ **assente** he's not here at the moment

momen'**taneo** *adj* momentary

⚓ mo'**mento** *nm* moment; **a momenti** (a volte) sometimes; (fra un momento) in a moment; **dal** ~ **che** since; **per il** ~ for the time being; **al** ~ at the moment; **da un** ~ **all'altro** ‹cambiare idea ecc› from one moment to the next; ‹aspettare l'arrivo di qualcuno ecc› at any moment

'**monaca** *nf* nun

'**monaco** *nm* monk

'**Monaco** *nf* (di Baviera) Munich; **Principato di Monaco** Monaco

mo'**narca** *nm* monarch

monar'**chia** *nf* monarchy

mo'**narchico, -a** [1] *adj* monarchic [2] *nmf* monarchist

mona'**stero** *nm* (di monaci) monastery; (di monache) convent

mo'**nastico** *adj* monastic

monche'**rino** *nm* stump

'**monco** *adj* maimed; fig (troncato) truncated; ~ **di un braccio** one-armed

mon'**dana** *nf* lady of the night

monda'**nità** *nf* (gente) beau monde; ~ *pl* pleasures of the world

mon'**dano** *adj* worldly; **vita mondana** social life

mon'**dare** *vt* (sbucciare) peel; shell ‹piselli›; (pulire) clean

⚓ mondi'**ale** *adj* world *attrib*; ‹scala› worldwide; fam (fantastico) fantastic; **di fama** ~ world-famous

mondi'**ali** *nmpl* World Cup

mondial'**mente** *adv* ‹operare› worldwide; ~ **noto** world-famous

mon'**dina** *nf* seasonal worker in the rice fields

⚓ '**mondo** *nm* world; **il bel** ~ fashionable society; **un** ~ (molto) a lot; **non è la fine del** ~ it's not the end of the world; **è la fine del** ~ fam (fantastico) it's out of this world; ~ **cane!** fam damn!

▪ **mondo accademico** academia; **mondo del lavoro** world of work; **mondo dei sogni** never-never land; **mondo dello spettacolo** show biz

mondovisi'**one** *nf* **in** ~ transmitted worldwide

monelle'**ria** *nf* prank

m

mo'nello, -a *nmf* urchin

mo'neta *nf* coin; (denaro) money; (denaro spicciolo) [small] change
■ **moneta estera** foreign currency; **moneta [a corso] legale** legal tender; **moneta unica** single currency

mone'tario *adj* monetary

mongolfi'era *nf* hot air balloon

Mon'golia *nf* Mongolia

'mongolo *adj* Mongol

mo'nile *nm* jewel

'monito *nm* warning

'monitor *nm inv* monitor

monito'raggio *nm* monitoring

moni'tore *nm* monitor

mono'albero *adj inv* single-camshaft *attrib*

mono'blocco 1 *nm* Auto cylinder block 2 *adj inv* «cucina» fitted

mo'nocolo *nm* monocle

monoco'lore *adj* Pol one-party

monocro'matico *adj* monochrome

mono'dose *adj inv* individually packaged

monoga'mia *nf* monogamy

mo'nogamo *adj* monogamous

monogra'fia *nf* monograph

mono'gramma *nm* monogram

mono'kini *nm inv* monokini

mono'lingue *adj* monolingual

mono'lito *nm* monolith

monolo'cale *nm* studio flat Br, studio apartment

mo'nologo *nm* monologue

monoma'nia *nf* monomania

mononucle'osi *nf inv*
■ **mononucleosi infettiva** glandular fever

monoparen'tale *adj* single-parent *attrib*

mono'pattino *nm* [child's] scooter

mono'petto *adj* single-breasted

mono'plano *nm* monoplane

mono'polio *nm* monopoly
■ **monopolio di Stato** state monopoly

monopoliz'zare *vt* monopolize

mono'posto *nm* single-seater

mono'reddito *adj* single-income *attrib*

monosac'caride *nm* monosaccharide

mono'sci *nm inv* monoski

monosil'labico *adj* monosyllabic

mono'sillabo 1 *nm* monosyllable 2 *adj* monosyllabic

mo'nossido *nm*
■ **monossido di carbonio** carbon monoxide

monote'istico *adj* monotheistic

monotona'mente *adv* monotonously

monoto'nia *nf* monotony

mo'notono *adj* monotonous

mono'uso *adj* disposable

monou'tente *adj inv* single-user *attrib*

monovo'lume *nf* people carrier, multi-purpose vehicle

monsi'gnore *nm* monsignor

mon'sone *nm* monsoon

'monta *nf* Zool covering; (modo di cavalcare) riding style; **stallone da monta** stud horse

monta'carichi *nm inv* hoist

mon'taggio *nm* Mech assembly; Cinema editing; **scatola di montaggio** assembly kit; **catena di montaggio** production line

✓ **mon'tagna** *nf* mountain; (zona) mountains *pl*
■ **Montagne** *pl* **Rocciose** Rocky Mountains; **montagne** *pl* **russe** roller coaster, big dipper

monta'gnoso *adj* mountainous

monta'naro, -a *nmf* highlander

mon'tano *adj* mountain *attrib*

mon'tante *nm* (di finestra, porta) upright; Fin total amount; (nel pugilato) upper cut

✓ **mon'tare** *vt/i* mount; get on «veicolo»; (aumentare) rise; Mech assemble; frame «quadro»; Culin whip; edit «film»; (a cavallo) ride; fig blow up
mon'tarsi *vr* ~ **la testa** get big-headed

monta'scale *nm inv* stairlift

mon'tato, -a *nmf* fam poser

monta|'tore, -trice *nmf* assembler

monta'tura *nf* Mech assembling; (di occhiali) frame; (di gioiello) mounting; fig exaggeration

✓ **'monte** *nm* anche fig mountain; **a** ~ up stream; **andare a** ~ be ruined; **mandare a** ~ **qualcosa** ruin something
■ **Monte Bianco** Mont Blanc; **monte di pietà** pawnshop

Monte'negro *nm* Montenegro

monte'premi *nm inv* jackpot

mont'gomery *nm inv* duffel coat

mon'tone *nm* ram; **carne di montone** mutton

montu'oso *adj* mountainous

monumen'tale *adj* monumental

✓ **monu'mento** *nm* monument
■ **monumento ai caduti** war memorial; **monumento commemorativo** memorial; **monumento nazionale** national monument

mo'plen® *nm* moulded plastic

mo'quette *nf* (tappeto) fitted carpet

'mora *nf* (di gelso) mulberry; (di rovo) blackberry

✓ **mo'rale** 1 *adj* moral 2 *nf* morals *pl*; (di storia) moral 3 *nm* morale

mora'lista *nmf* moralist

mora'listico *adj* moralistic

moralità *nf inv* morality; (condotta) morals *pl*

✓ indicates a very frequent word

moraliz'zare *vt/i* moralize
moral'mente *adv* morally
mora'toria *nf* moratorium
morbida'mente *adv* softly
morbi'dezza *nf* softness
'morbido *adj* soft
mor'billo *nm* measles *sg*
'morbo *nm* disease
- morbo di Alzheimer Alzheimer's disease; morbo di Creutzfeldt Jakob Creutzfeldt-Jakob disease, CJD; morbo della mucca pazza mad cow disease

morbosa'mente *adv* morbidly
morbosità *nf* (qualità) morbidity
mor'boso *adj* morbid
'morchia *nf* sludge
mor'dace *adj* cutting
mor'dente *adj* biting
'mordere *vt* bite; (corrodere) bite into
mordicchi'are *vt* gnaw
mordi e fuggi *adj* ‹vacanza› very short
mo'rello ⌐1⌐ *nm* black horse
  ⌐2⌐ *adj* blackish
mo'rena *nf* moraine
mo'rente *adj* dying
mo'resco *adj* Moorish
mor'fina *nf* morphine
morfi'nomane *nmf* morphine addict
morfolo'gia *nf* morphology
morfo'logico *adj* morphological
mori'bondo *adj* dying; ‹istituzione› moribund
morige'rato *adj* moderate
⚐ **mo'rire** *vi* die; fig die out; fa un freddo da ∼ it's freezing cold, it's perishing; ∼ di noia be bored to death; c'era da ∼ dal ridere it was hilariously funny; morir di fame starve to death; fig starve
mor'mone *nmf* Mormon
mormo'rare *vt/i* murmur; ‹brontolare› mutter
mormo'rio *nm* murmuring; (lamentela) grumbling
'moro ⌐1⌐ *adj* dark
  ⌐2⌐ *nm* Moor
morosità *nf* default
mo'roso *adj* in arrears
'morra *nf* game for two players where each shouts a number at the same time as showing a number of fingers
'morsa *nf* vice; fig grip
'morse *adj* alfabeto ∼ Morse code
mor'setto *nm* clamp; (stringinaso) nose clip
- morsetto per batteria battery lead connection

morsi'care *vt* bite
morsica'tura *nf* [snake] bite

'morso *nm* bite; (di cibo, briglia) bit; i morsi della fame hunger pangs
morta'della *nf* mortadella (*type of salted pork*)
mor'taio *nm* mortar
⚐ **mor'tale** *adj* mortal; (simile a morte) deadly; di una noia ∼ deadly
mortalità *nf* mortality
mortal'mente *adv* ‹ferito› fatally; ‹offeso› mortally; ‹annoiato› to death; ∼ stanco fam dead tired
morta'retto *nm* firecracker
⚐ **'morte** *nf* death; non è la ∼ di nessuno it's not the end of the world; lo odia a ∼ fam she can't stand the sight of him; annoiarsi a ∼ fam be bored to death
- ∼ cerebrale brain death

mortifi'cante *adj* mortifying
mortifi'care *vt* mortify
mortifi'carsi *vr* be mortified
mortifi'cato *adj* mortified
mortificazi'one *nf* mortification
⚐ **'morto, -a** ⌐1⌐ *pp di* MORIRE
  ⌐2⌐ *adj* dead; ∼ di freddo frozen to death; stanco ∼ dead tired
  ⌐3⌐ *nm* dead man
  ⌐4⌐ *nf* dead woman
mor'torio *nm* funeral
mo'saico *nm* mosaic
'mosca *nf* fly; (barba) goatee; cadere come le mosche be dropping like flies; essere una ∼ bianca be a rarity; non si sentiva volare una ∼ you could have heard a pin drop
- mosca cieca blindman's buff

'Mosca *nf* Moscow
mo'scato ⌐1⌐ *adj* muscat; noce moscata nutmeg
  ⌐2⌐ *nm* muscatel
mosce'rino *nm* midge; fam (persona) midget
mo'schea *nf* mosque
moschetti'ere *nm* musketeer
mo'schetto *nm* musket
moschet'tone *nm* (in alpinismo) snaplink; (gancio) spring clip
moschi'cida ⌐1⌐ *adj inv* carta ∼ fly paper
  ⌐2⌐ *nm* fly spray
'moscio *adj* limp; avere l'erre moscia not be able to say one's r's properly
mo'scone *nm* bluebottle; (barca) pedalo
Mosè *nm* Moses
'mossa *nf* movement; (passo) move
'mosso ⌐1⌐ *pp di* MUOVERE
  ⌐2⌐ *adj* ‹mare› rough; ‹capelli› wavy; ‹fotografia› blurred
mo'starda *nf* mustard
- mostarda di Cremona preserve made from candied fruit in grape must or sugar with mustard

'mostra *nf* show; (d'arte) exhibition; **far ~ di** pretend; **in ~** on show; **mettersi in ~** make oneself conspicuous; **far ~ di sé** show off; **far bella ~ di sé** look impressive
■ **mostra dell'artigianato** craft fair

'mostra-mer'cato *nf* trade fair

⚐ **mo'strare** *vt* show; (indicare) point out; (spiegare) explain; **~ di** (sembrare) seem; (fingere) pretend

mos'trarsi *vr* show oneself; (apparire) appear

mo'strina *nf* flash

⚐ **'mostro** *nm* monster; fig (persona) genius
■ **mostro sacro** fig sacred cow

mostruosa'mente *adv* tremendously

mostru'oso *adj* monstrous; (incredibile) enormous

mo'tel *nm inv* motel

moti'vare *vt* cause; Jur justify

moti'vato *adj* ⟨persona⟩ motivated; ⟨azione⟩ justified

motivazi'one *nf* motivation; (giustificazione) justification

⚐ **mo'tivo** *nm* reason; (movente) motive; (in musica, letteratura) theme; (disegno) pattern, motif; **senza ~** for no reason; (senza giustificazione) unjustifiably
■ **motivo cachemire** paisley; **motivo a scacchi** chequered pattern

⚐ **'moto** ① *nm* motion; (esercizio) exercise; (gesto) movement; (sommossa) rising; **mettere in ~** start ⟨motore⟩
■ **moto ondoso** swell; **moto perpetuo** perpetual motion
② *nf inv* (motocicletta) motor bike

moto'carro *nm* three-wheeler

⚐ **motoci'cletta** *nf* motorcycle, motorbike
■ **motocicletta da corsa** racing motorbike, racer

motoci'clismo *nm* motorcycling

motoci'clista *nmf* motorcyclist, biker

moto'cross *nm* motocross, scrambling

motocros'sista *nmf* scrambler

moto'lancia *nf* motor launch

moto'nautica *nf* speedboat racing

moto'nave *nf* motor vessel

⚐ **mo'tore** ① *adj* motor *attrib*
② *nm* motor, engine; **con ~ turbo** turbocharged
■ **motore diesel** diesel engine; **motore a iniezione** fuel injection engine; **motore raffreddato ad aria** air-cooled engine; **motore a reazione** jet [engine]; **motore di ricerca** Comput search engine; **motore a scoppio** internal combustion engine

moto'retta *nf* motor scooter

moto'rino *nm* moped
■ **motorino d'avviamento** starter motor

mo'torio *adj* motor *attrib*

⚐ indicates a very frequent word

moto'rista *nmf*
■ **motorista di bordo** flight engineer

motoriz'zare *vt* motorize

motoriz'zato *adj* Mil motorized

motorizzazi'one *nf* (ufficio) vehicle licensing office

moto'scafo *nm* motorboat

moto'sega *nf* chain saw

motove'detta *nf* patrol vessel, patrol boat

mo'trice *nf* engine

'motto *nm* motto; (facezia) witticism; (massima) saying

'mountain bike *nf inv* mountain bike

mouse *nm inv* Comput mouse

mousse *nf inv* Culin mousse
■ **mousse al cioccolato** chocolate mousse

mo'vente *nm* motive

mo'venze *nfpl* movements

movimen'tare *vt* enliven

movimen'tato *adj* lively

⚐ **movi'mento** *nm* movement; **essere sempre in ~** be always on the go
■ **movimento passeggeri e merci** passenger and freight traffic

Mozam'bico *nm* Mozambique

mozi'one *nf* motion
■ **mozione d'ordine** point of order

mozzafi'ato *adj inv* nail-biting

moz'zare *vt* cut off; dock ⟨coda⟩; **~ il fiato a qualcuno** take somebody's breath away

mozza'rella *nf* mozzarella (*mild, white cheese*)
■ **mozzarella di bufala** buffalo mozzarella

mozzi'cone *nm* (di sigaretta) stub

'mozzo ① *nm* Mech hub; Naut ship's boy
② *adj* ⟨coda⟩ truncated; ⟨testa⟩ severed

ms *abbr* (**manoscritto**) MS

'mucca *nf* cow; **morbo della mucca pazza** mad cow disease

⚐ **'mucchio** *nm* heap, pile; **un ~ di** fig lots of

mucil'lagine *nf* Bot mucilage

'muco *nm* mucus

'muffa *nf* mould; **fare la ~** go mouldy

muf'fire *vi* go mouldy

muf'fola *nf* mitt

mu'flone *nm* Zool mouflon

mugghi'are *vi* ⟨vento, mare⟩ roar

mug'gire *vi* ⟨mucca⟩ moo, low; ⟨toro⟩ bellow

mug'gito *nm* moo; (di toro) bellow; (azione) mooing; bellowing

mu'ghetto *nm* lily of the valley

mugo'lare *vi* whine; ⟨persona⟩ moan

mugo'lio *nm* whining

mugu'gnare *vt* fam mumble

mulatti'era *nf* mule track

mu'latto, -a *nmf* mulatto

mu'leta *nf inv* muleta

muli'ebre *adj* (liter) feminine

muli'nare *vi* spin

muli'nello *nm* (d'acqua) whirlpool; (di vento) eddy; (giocattolo) windmill

mu'lino *nm* mill
■ mulino a vento windmill

'**mulo** *nm* mule

'**multa** *nf* fine
■ multa per divieto di sosta parking ticket

mul'tare *vt* fine

multico'lore *adj* multicoloured

multicultu'rale *adj* multicultural

multi'etnico *adj* multi-ethnic

multifo'cale *adj* ‹lente› varifocal
■ occhiali multifocali varifocals

multifunzio'nale *adj* multifunction[al]

multilate'rale *adj* multilateral

multi'lingue *adj* multilingual

multi'media *mpl* multimedia

multimedi'ale *adj* multimedia *attrib*

multimedialità *nf* multimedia

multimiliar'dario, -a *nmf* multi-millionaire

multinazio'nale *adj & nf* multinational

'**multiplo** *adj & nm* multiple

multiproprietà *nf nv* time-share; una casa in ~ a time-share

multiraz'ziale *adj* multi-racial

multi'sale *adj inv* cinema ~ multiplex [cinema]

multi'tasking *nm* Comput multitasking

multi'uso *adj* ‹utensile› all purpose

'**mummia** *nf* mummy; fig (persona) old fogey

mummifi'care *vt* mummify

'**mungere** *vt* milk

mungi'tura *nf* milking

munici'pale *adj* municipal

municipalità *nf inv* town council

muni'cipio *nm* town hall

munifi'cenza *nf* munificence, bounty

mu'nifico *adj* munificent

mu'nire *vt* fortify; ~ di (provvedere) supply with; munitevi di un carrello/cestino please take a trolley/basket

munizi'oni *nfpl* ammunition *sg*

'**munto** pp di MUNGERE

☞ **mu'overe** *vt* move; (suscitare) arouse

mu'oversi *vr* move; muoviti! hurry up!, come on!

'**mura** *nfpl* (cinta di città) walls

mu'raglia *nf* wall

mu'rale *adj* mural; ‹pittura› wall *attrib*

mur'are *vt* wall up

mu'rario *adj* masonry *attrib*; cinta muraria walls *pl*; opera muraria masonry

mura'tore *nm* bricklayer; (con pietre) mason; (operaio edile) builder

mura'tura *nf* (di pietra) masonry, stonework; (di mattoni) brickwork

mu'rena *nf* moray eel

☞ '**muro** *nm* wall; (di nebbia) bank; a ~ ‹armadio› built-in
■ muro divisorio partition wall; muro di gomma fig wall of indifference; fare ~ di gomma stonewall; muro a intercapedine cavity wall; Muro del pianto Wailing Wall; muro portante load-bearing wall; muro del suono sound barrier

'**musa** *nf* anche fig muse

muschi'ato *adj* musky

'**muschio** *nm* musk; Bot moss

musco'lare *adj* muscular

muscola'tura *nf* muscles *pl*

'**muscolo** *nm* muscle

musco'loso *adj* muscular

☞ **mu'seo** *nm* museum

museru'ola *nf* muzzle

☞ '**musica** *nf* music
■ musica gospel gospel music; musica folk folk [music]

'**musical** *nm inv* musical

musi'cale *adj* musical

musi'care *vt* set to music

musicas'setta *nf* cassette

musi'cista *nmf* musician

musicolo'gia *nf* musicology

'**muso** *nm* muzzle; pej (di persona) mug; (di aeroplano) nose; fare il ~ sulk

mu'sone, -a *adj & nmf* sulker

'**mussola** *nf* muslin

mussul'mano, -a *adj & nmf* Muslim, Moslem

'**muta** *nf* (cambio) change; (di penne) moult; (di cani) pack; (per immersione subacquea) wetsuit

muta'mento *nm* change

mu'tande *nfpl* pants

mutan'dine *nfpl* panties
■ mutandine da bagno bathing trunks; (da donna) bikini bottom

mutan'doni *nmpl* (da uomo) long johns; (da donna) bloomers

mu'tante *nmf* mutant

mu'tare *vt* change

mutazi'one *nf* mutation

mu'tevole *adj* changeable

muti'lare *vt* mutilate

muti'lato, -a 1 *adj* crippled 2 *nmf* disabled person
■ mutilato di guerra disabled ex-serviceman; mutilato del lavoro person disabled at work

mutilazi'one *nf* mutilation

mu'tismo *nm* dumbness; fig obstinate silence

☞ '**muto** *adj* dumb; (silenzioso) silent; (fonetica) mute

'mutua *nf*
■ [cassa] mutua sickness benefit fund
mutu'abile *adj* ‹farmaco› prescribable on the NHS
mutu'are *vt* borrow ‹teoria, parola›
mutua'tario, -a *nmf* Fin borrower

mutu'ato, -a *nmf* NHS patient
'mutuo¹ *adj* mutual
'mutuo² *nm* loan; (per la casa) mortgage; **fare un** ∼ take out a mortgage; **società di mutuo soccorso** friendly society
■ **mutuo ipotecario** mortgage

N n

N° *abbr* (**numero**) No.
na'babbo *nm* nabob; **vivere da** ∼ live in the lap of luxury
'nacchera *nf* castanet
na'dir *nm* nadir
'nafta *nf* naphtha; (per motori) diesel oil; **a** ∼ ‹bruciatore› oil-burning
'naia *nf* cobra; sl (servizio militare) national service
'nailon *nm* nylon
Na'mibia *nf* Namibia
na'nismo *nm* dwarfism
'nanna *nf* sl (infantile) bye-byes; **andare a** ∼ go bye-byes; **fare la** ∼ sleep
'nano, -a *adj* & *nmf* dwarf
nanose'condo *nm* nanosecond
'napalm *nm* napalm
napole'tana *nf* (caffettiera) Neapolitan coffee maker
napole'tano, -a *adj* & *nmf* Neapolitan
'Napoli *nf* Naples
'nappa *nf* tassel; (pelle) soft leather
narci'sismo *nm* narcissism
narci'sista *adj* & *nmf* narcissist
nar'ciso *nm* narcissus
nar'cosi *nf* general anaesthesia
nar'cotici *nf* Drug Squad
nar'cotico *adj* & *nm* narcotic
na'rice *nf* nostril
nar'rare *vt* tell
narra'tivo, -a [1] *adj* narrative [2] *nf* fiction
narra|'tore, -trice *nmf* narrator
narrazi'one *nf* narration; (racconto) story
na'sale *adj* nasal
na'scente *adj* budding
⚦ **'nascere** *vi* (venire al mondo) be born; (germogliare) sprout; (sorgere) rise; ∼ **da** fig arise from
⚦ **'nascita** *nf* birth
nasci'turo *nm* unborn child
⚦ **na'scondere** *vt* hide

na'scondersi *vr* hide
nascon'diglio *nm* hiding place
nascon'dino *nm* hide-and-seek
na'scosto [1] *pp di* NASCONDERE [2] *adj* hidden; **di** ∼ secretly; **ascoltare di** ∼ listen in on ‹conversazione›
na'sello *nm* (pesce) hake
⚦ **'naso** *nm* nose
na'sone *nm* big nose, hooter fam
'nassa *nf* lobster pot
'nastro *nm* ribbon; (di registratore ecc) tape
■ **nastro adesivo** adhesive tape, sticky tape; **nastro isolante** insulating tape; **nastro magnetico** magnetic tape, magtape fam; **nastro trasportatore** conveyor belt
⚦ **na'tale** *adj* ‹giorno, paese› of one's birth
⚦ **Na'tale** *nm* Christmas
na'tali *nmpl* parentage
natalità *nf* [number of] births, birthrate
nata'lizio *adj* ‹del Natale› Christmas *attrib*
na'tante [1] *adj* floating [2] *nm* craft
'natica *nf* buttock
na'tio *adj* native
Nativ ità *nf* Nativity
na'tivo, -a *adj* & *nmf* native
'nato [1] *pp di* NASCERE [2] *adj* born; **uno scrittore** ∼ a born writer; **nata Rossi** née Rossi
'NATO *nf* Nato, NATO
⚦ **na'tura** *nf* nature; **pagare in** ∼ pay in kind; **di** ∼ **politica** of a political nature
■ **natura morta** still life
⚦ **natu'rale** *adj* natural; **al** ∼ ‹alimento› plain, natural; ∼**!** naturally, of course
natura'lezza *nf* naturalness
naturaliz'zare *vt* naturalize
natural'mente *adv* (ovviamente) naturally, of course
natu'rista *nmf* naturalist
natu'ristico *adj* naturist
naufra'gare *vi* be wrecked; ‹persona› be shipwrecked
nau'fragio *nm* shipwreck; fig wreck

⚦ indicates a very frequent word

'naufrago, -a *nmf* survivor

'nausea *nf* nausea; **avere la ~** feel sick

nausea'bondo *adj* nauseating

nause'are *vt* nauseate

'nautica *nf* navigation

'nautico *adj* nautical

na'vale *adj* naval

na'vata *nf* (centrale) nave; (laterale) aisle

✓ 'nave *nf* ship
  ■ **nave ammiraglia** flagship; **nave da carico** cargo boat; **nave cisterna** tanker; **nave da crociera** cruise liner; **nave fattoria** factory ship; **nave da guerra** warship; **nave di linea** liner; **nave passeggeri** passenger ship; **nave portacontainer** container ship; **nave spaziale** spaceship; **nave traghetto** ferry

na'vetta *nf* shuttle

navi'cella *nf*
  ■ **navicella spaziale** nose cone

navi'gabile *adj* navigable

navi'gare *vi* sail; **~ in Internet** surf the Net, browse

naviga|'tore, -trice *nmf* navigator; (in Internet) surfer
  ■ **navigatore solitario** lone yachtsman; **navigatore spaziale** spaceman

navigazi'one *nf* navigation; **della ~** navigational

na'viglio *nm* fleet; (canale) canal

nazifa'scismo *nm* Nazi fascism

nazifa'scista *nmf* Nazi fascist

✓ nazio'nale ① *adj* national
  ② *nf* Sport national team

naziona'lismo *nm* nationalism

naziona'lista *nmf* nationalist

nazionalità *nf inv* nationality

nazionaliz'zare *vt* nationalize

✓ nazi'one *nf* nation; **Nazioni** *pl* **Unite** United Nations

na'zista *adj & nmf* Nazi

N.B. *abbr* (**nota bene**) NB

n.d.r. *abbr* (**nota del redattore**) editor's note

'n 'drangheta *nf* Calabrian Mafia

n.d.t. *abbr* (**nota del traduttore**) translator's note

✓ ne ① *pron* (di lui) about him; (di lei) about her; (di loro) about them; (di ciò) about it; (da ciò) from that; (di un insieme) of it; (di un gruppo) of them; **ne sono contento** I'm happy about it; **non ne conosco nessuno** I don't know any of them; **ne ho** I have some; **non ne ho più** I don't have any left
  ② *adv* from there; **ne vengo ora** I've just come from there; **me ne vado** I'm off; **ne va della mia reputazione** my reputation is at stake

NE *abbr* (**nord-est**) NE

✓ né *conj* **né... né...** neither... nor...; **non ne ho il tempo né la voglia** I don't have either the

time or the inclination; **né tu né io vogliamo andare** neither you nor I want to go; **né l'uno né l'altro** neither [of them/us]

✓ ne'anche ① *adv* (neppure) not even; (senza neppure) without even
  ② *conj* (e neppure) neither...nor; **io non parlo inglese e lui ~** I don't speak English, neither does he *or* and he doesn't either

✓ 'nebbia *nf* mist; (in città, autostrada) fog

nebbi'oso *adj* misty; (in città, autostrada) foggy

nebuliz'zare *vt* atomize

nebulizza'tore *nm* atomizer; (per il naso) nasal spray

nebulizzazi'one *nf* atomizing; **fare delle nebulizzazioni** take nasal sprays

nebulosità *nf* vagueness

nebu'loso *adj* hazy; ‹teoria› nebulous; ‹discorso› woolly

necessaria'mente *adv* necessarily

✓ neces'sario ① *adj* necessary
  ② *nm* **fare il ~** do the necessary, do the needful

✓ necessità *nf inv* necessity; (bisogno) need

necessi'tare *vi* **~ di** need; (essere necessario) be necessary

necro'logio *nm* obituary

ne'cropoli *nf inv* necropolis

ne'crosi *nf* necrosis

ne'fando *adj* wicked

ne'fasto *adj* ill omened

ne'frite *nf* nephritis

nefrolo'gia *nf* nephrology

ne'frologo, -a *nmf* nephrologist

ne'gabile *adj* deniable

✓ ne'gare *vt* deny; (rifiutare) refuse; **essere negato per qualcosa** be no good at something

nega'tiva *nf* negative

nega'tivo *adj* negative

negazi'one *nf* negation; (diniego) denial; Gram negative

ne'gletto *adj* neglected

'negli = IN + GLI

negli'gente *adj* negligent

negli'genza *nf* negligence

negozi'abile *adj* negotiable

negozi'ante *nmf* dealer; (bottegaio) shopkeeper

negozi'are ① *vt* negotiate
  ② *vi* **~** in trade in, deal in

negozi'ati *nmpl* negotiations

✓ ne'gozio *nm* shop
  ■ **negozio di abbigliamento** clothes shop; **negozio di alimentari** grocer's; **negozio di antiquariato** antique shop; **negozio duty free** duty-free shop; **negozio di ferramenta** hardware shop; **negozio giuridico** legal transaction; **negozio di souvenir** gift shop

n

'negro, -a [1] *adj* Negro, black
[2] *nmf* Negro, black; (scrittore) ghost writer; **come un ~** ‹lavorare› like a slave
negro'mante *nmf* necromancer
'nei = IN + I
nel = IN + IL
'nella = IN + LA
'nelle = IN + LE
'nello = IN + LO
'nembo *nm* nimbus
ne'mesi *nf* nemesis
✣ **ne'mico, -a** [1] *adj* hostile
[2] *nmf* enemy
✣ **nem'meno** *conj* not even
'nenia *nf* dirge; (per bambini) lullaby; (piagnucolio) wail
'neo *nm* mole; (applicato) beauty spot
neo+ *pref* neo+
neo'classico *adj* neoclassical
neocolonia'lismo *nm* neocolonialism
neofa'scismo *nm* neofascism
neola'tino *adj* Romance
neolaure'ato, -a *nmf* recent graduate
neo'litico *adj* Neolithic
neolo'gismo *nm* neologism
'neon *nm* neon
neo'nato, -a [1] *adj* new born
[2] *nmf* newborn baby
neona'zismo *nm* Neonazism
neona'zista *adj & nmf* Neonazi
neozelan'dese [1] *adj* New Zealand *attrib*
[2] *nmf* New Zealander
'Nepal *nm* Nepal
✣ **nep'pure** *conj* not even
ne'rastro *adj* blackish
'nerbo *nm* (forza) strength; fig backbone; **senza ~** effete
nerbo'ruto *adj* brawny
ne'retto *nm* Typ bold [type]
✣ **'nero** [1] *adj* black; fam (arrabbiato) fuming
[2] *nm* black; **l'ho visto ~ su bianco** I've seen it in black and white; **mettere ~ su bianco** put in writing
■ **nero pieno** Typ solid; **nero di seppia** sepia
nerva'tura *nf* nerves *pl*; Bot veining; (di libro) band
ner'vetti *nmpl* chopped beef and veal with onions
ner'vino *adj* ‹gas› nerve *attrib*
✣ **'nervo** *nm* nerve; Bot vein; **avere i nervi** be bad-tempered; **dare ai o sui nervi a qualcuno** get on somebody's nerves
nervo'sismo *nm* nerviness
✣ **ner'voso** *adj* nervous, edgy; (irritabile) bad-tempered; **avere il ~** be irritable; **esaurimento nervoso** nervous breakdown

'nespola *nf* medlar
'nespolo *nm* medlar[-tree]
'nesso *nm* link, connection
✣ **nes'suno** [1] *adj* no, not... any; (qualche) any; **non ho nessun problema** I don't have any problems, I have no problems; **non ha nessun valore** it hasn't any value, it has no value; **da nessuna parte** nowhere; **non lo trovo da nessuna parte** I can't find it anywhere; **in nessun modo** on no account; **per nessun motivo** for no reason; **nessuna notizia?** any news?
[2] *pron* nobody, no one, not... anybody, not... anyone; (qualcuno) anybody, anyone; **hai delle domande? – nessuna** do you have any questions? – none; **~ di voi** none of you; **~ dei due** (di voi due) neither of you; **non ho visto ~ dei tuoi amici** I haven't seen any of your friends; **c'è ~?** is anybody there?
'nesting *nm inv* Comput nesting
net *nm inv* Tennis net cord
net'tare *vt* clean
'nettare *nm* nectar
netta'rina *nf* nectarine
net'tezza *nf* cleanliness
■ **nettezza urbana** cleansing department
'netto *adj* clean; (chiaro) clear; Comm net; **di ~** just like that
Net'tuno *nm* Neptune
nettur'bino *nm* dustman
'network *nm inv* network
■ **network televisivo** network television
'neuro *nf* neurological clinic
neuro+ *pref* neuro+
neurochirur'gia *nf* brain surgery
neurochi'rurgo *nm* brain surgeon
neurolo'gia *nf* neurology
neuro'logico *adj* neurological
neuropsichi'atra *nmf* neuropsychiatrist
neuropsichia'tria *nf* neuropsychiatry
neu'trale *adj & nm* neutral
neutralità *nf* neutrality
neutraliz'zare *vt* neutralize
'neutro [1] *adj* neutral; Gram neuter
[2] *nm* Gram neuter
neu'trone *nm* neutron
ne'vaio *nm* snow-field
✣ **'neve** *nf* snow
nevi'care *vi* snow; **nevica** it is snowing
nevi'cata *nf* snowfall
ne'vischio *nm* sleet
ne'voso *adj* snowy
nevral'gia *nf* neuralgia
ne'vralgico *adj* neuralgic; **punto nevralgico** nerve centre; (di questione ecc) crucial point
nevraste'nia *nf* neurasthenia
nevra'stenico *adj* neurasthenic; (irritabile) hot tempered

✣ indicates a very frequent word

ne'vrite *nf* neuritis
ne'vrosi *nf inv* neurosis
ne'vrotico *adj* neurotic
'**nibbio** *nm* kite
Nica'ragua *nm* Nicaragua
nicara'guense *adj & nmf* Nicaraguan
'**nicchia** *nf* niche
nicchi'are *vi* shilly-shally
'**nichel** *nm* nickel
nichi'lista [1] *nmf* nihilist
  [2] *adj* nihilistic
nico'tina *nf* nicotine
nidi'ace *nm* nestling
nidi'ata *nf* brood
nidifi'care *vi* nest
nidifi'cato *adj* Comput nested
nidificazi'one *nf* Zool nesting
'**nido** *nm* nest; (giardino d'infanzia) crèche; **a ~ d'ape** ‹tessuto› honeycomb
■ **nido di uccello** bird's nest; **nido di vipere** fig nest of vipers
⚡ **ni'ente** [1] *pron* nothing, not… anything; (qualcosa) anything; **non ho fatto ~ di male** I didn't do anything wrong, I did nothing wrong; **nient'altro?** anything else?; **grazie! – di ~!** thank you! – don't mention it!; **non serve a ~** it is no use; **vuoi ~?** do you want anything?; **dal ~** ‹venire su› from nothing; **da ~** (poco importante) minor; (di poco valore) worthless
  [2] *adj inv* fam **~ pesci oggi** no fish today; **non ho ~ fame** I'm not the slightest bit hungry
  [3] *adv* **non fa ~** (non importa) it doesn't matter; **per ~** at all; ‹litigare› over nothing; **~ affatto!** no way!
  [4] *nm* **un bel ~** absolutely nothing, damn all fam; **basta un ~ per spaventarlo** it doesn't take much to scare him
  [5] *inter* **"cos'è successo?" – "niente… mi hanno rubato l'auto"** fam "what happened?" – "well, er… I had my car stolen"
nientedi'meno, nientemeno [1] *adv* **~ che** no less than
  [2] *int* fancy that!
'**Niger** *nm* Niger
Ni'geria *nf* Nigeria
night *nm inv* night club
'**Nilo** *nm* Nile
'**ninfa** *nf* nymph
nin'fea *nf* water lily
nin'fomane *nf* nymphomaniac; **da ~** nymphomaniac
ninna'nanna *nf* lullaby
'**ninnolo** *nm* plaything; (fronzolo) knick-knack
⚡ **ni'pote** [1] *nm* (di zii) nephew; (di nonni) grandson, grandchild; **nipoti** *pl* (collettivo) grandchildren, nephews and nieces
  [2] *nf* (di zii) niece; (di nonni) granddaughter, grandchild
nip'ponico *adj* Japanese

'**nisba** *pron* sl (niente) zilch
'**nitido** *adj* neat; (chiaro) clear
ni'trato *nm* nitrate
'**nitrico** *adj* nitric
ni'trire *vi* neigh
ni'trito *nm* (di cavallo) neigh; Chem nitrite
nitro+ *pref* nitro+
nitroglice'rina *nf* nitroglycerine
'**niveo** *adj* snow-white
N.N. *abbr* (numeri) Nos
⚡ **no** [1] *adv* no; **credo di no** I don't think so; **perché no?** why not?; **io no** not me; **sì o no?** yes or no?; **ha detto così, no?** he said so, didn't he?; **fa freddo, no?** it's cold, isn't it?; **se no** otherwise
  [2] *nm* no; (nelle votazioni) nay
NO *abbr* (nord-ovest) NW
nobil'donna *nf* noblewoman
⚡ '**nobile** [1] *adj* noble; **metallo ~** noble metal; **di animo ~** noble-minded
  [2] *nm* noble, nobleman
  [3] *nf* noble, noblewoman
nobili'are *adj* noble
nobiltà *nf* nobility
nobilu'omo *nm* nobleman
'**nocca** *nf* knuckle
nocci'ola *nf* hazelnut
nocci'oline [americane] *nfpl* peanuts
'**nocciolo** *nm* stone; Phys core; fig heart; **il ~ della questione** the heart of the matter
nocci'olo *nm* (albero) hazel
'**noce** [1] *nf* walnut
■ **noce moscata** nutmeg; **noce pecan** pecan; **noce di vitello** veal with mushrooms
  [2] *nm* (legno) walnut; (albero) walnut [tree]
noce'pesca *nf* nectarine
no'cino *nm* walnut liqueur
no'civo *adj* harmful
no'dino *nm* veal chop
⚡ '**nodo** *nm* knot; fig lump; Comput node; **fare il ~ della cravatta** do up one's tie
■ **nodo alla gola** lump in the throat; **nodo della questione** crux of the matter; **nodo ferroviario** railway junction; **nodo piano** reef knot; **nodo scorsoio** slipknot
no'doso *adj* knotty
'**nodulo** *nm* nodule
Noè *nm* Noah
no-'global *adj* anti-globalization
⚡ '**noi** *pers pron* (soggetto) we; (oggetto, con prep) us; **chi è? – siamo ~** who is it? – it's us; **~ due** the two of us
⚡ '**noia** *nf* boredom; (fastidio) bother; (persona) bore; **dar ~** annoy
noi'altri *pers pron* we
⚡ **noi'oso** *adj* boring; (fastidioso) tiresome
noleggi'are *vt* hire; (dare a noleggio) hire out; charter ‹nave, aereo›
no'leggio *nm* hire; (di nave, aereo) charter   ⸱⸱⸱⧐

■ **noleggio barche/biciclette/sci** boat/cycle/ski hire

'**nolo** *nm* hire; Naut freight; **a ~** for hire

'**nomade** ❶ *adj* nomadic
❷ *nmf* nomad

◆ '**nome** *nm* name; Gram noun; **a ~ di** ‹da parte di› on behalf of; **di ~** by name; **farsi un ~** make a name for oneself; **nel ~ di...** in the name of....

■ **nome d'arte** professional name; **nome di battaglia** nom de guerre; **nome di battesimo** first name, Christian name, given name; **nome in codice** code name; **nome depositato** trade-name; **nome di dominio** Comput domain name; **nome per esteso** full name; **nome di famiglia** surname, family name; **nome del file** filename; **nome proprio** proper name, proper noun; **nome da ragazza** maiden name; **nome da sposata** married name; **nome utente** username

no'mea *nf* reputation

nomencla'tura *nf* nomenclature

no'mignolo *nm* nickname

'**nomina** *nf* appointment; **di prima ~** newly appointed

nomi'nale *adj* nominal; Gram noun *attrib*

◆ **nomi'nare** *vt* name; (menzionare) mention; (eleggere) appoint

nomina'tivo ❶ *adj* nominative; Comm registered
❷ *nm* nominative; (nome) name; **caso nominativo** nominative case

◆ **non** *adv* not; **~ ti amo** I do not *or* don't love you; **~ c'è di che** not at all; **~ più** no longer

nonché *conj* (tanto meno) let alone; (e anche) as well as

nonconfor'mista *adj* & *nmf inv* nonconformist

nonconformità *nf* noncompliance

noncu'rante *adj* nonchalant; (negligente) indifferent

noncu'ranza *nf* nonchalance; (negligenza) indifference

nondi'meno *conj* nevertheless

◆ '**nonna** *nf* grandmother, grandma fam, gran fam

◆ '**nonno** *nm* grandfather, grandpa fam; **nonni** *pl* grandparents

non'nulla *nm inv* trifle

'**nono** *adj* & *nm* ninth

◆ **nono'stante** ❶ *prep* in spite of
❷ *conj* although

non stop *adj inv* & *adv* nonstop

nontiscordardimé *nm inv* forget-me-not

nonvio'lento *adj* nonviolent

nonvio'lenza *nf* nonviolence

no 'profit *adj* non profit

nor'cino *nm* pig butcher

◆ **nord** *nm* north; **del ~** northern

nord-'est *nm* northeast; **a ~** northeasterly; **del ~** northeastern; **vento di nord-est** northeasterly [wind]

'**nordico** *adj* northern

nor'dista *adj* & *nmf* Yankee

nordocciden'tale *adj* northwestern

nordorien'tale *adj* northeastern

nord-'ovest *nm* northwest; **a ~** northwesterly; **del ~** northwestern; **vento di nord-ovest** northwesterly [wind]

'**norma** *nf* norm; (regola) rule; (per l'uso) instruction; **a ~ di legge** according to law; **è buona ~** it's advisable; **di ~** as a rule, normally

◆ **nor'male** ❶ *adj* normal
❷ *nm* **fuori del ~** out of the ordinary; **superiore al ~** above average

normalità *nf* normality; **rientrare nella ~** be quite normal

normaliz'zare *vt* normalize

normal'mente *adv* normally

Norman'dia *nf* Normandy

nor'manno *adj* from Normandy; (storico) Norman

normativa *nf* regulations *pl*, laws *pl*

norma'tivo *adj* normative, prescriptive

nor'mografo *nm* stencil

nor'reno *adj* Norse

norve'gese *adj* & *nmf* Norwegian

Nor'vegia *nf* Norway

noso'comio *nm fml* hospital

nossi'gnore *adv* (assolutamente no) no way

nostal'gia *nf* (di casa, patria) homesickness; (del passato) nostalgia; **aver ~** be homesick; **aver ~ di qualcuno** miss somebody

no'stalgico, -a ❶ *adj* nostalgic
❷ *nmf* reactionary

nostra ▶ NOSTRO

no'strale *adj* local

no'strano *adj* local; (fatto in casa) home-made

'**nostre** ▶ NOSTRO

'**nostri** ▶ NOSTRO

◆ '**nostro** ❶ (**il nostro** *m*, **la nostra** *f*, **i nostri** *mpl*, **le nostre** *fpl*) *poss adj* our; **quella macchina è nostra** that car is ours; **~ padre** our father; **un ~ amico** a friend of ours
❷ *poss pron* ours

no'stromo *nm* bo's'n, boatswain

'**nota** *inf* (segno) sign; (comunicazione, commento, Mus) note; (conto) bill; (lista) list; **degno di ~** noteworthy; **prendere ~** take note; **una ~ di colore** a touch of colour; **mettere in ~ qualcosa** add something to the list

■ **nota di accredito** Comm credit note; **note** *pl* **caratteristiche** distinguishing marks; **nota spese** expense account

---

◆ indicates a very frequent word

no'tabile *adj & nm* notable

no'taio *nm* notary

no'tare *vt* (segnare) mark; (annotare) note down; (osservare) notice; **far ∼ qualcosa** point something out; **farsi ∼** get oneself noticed; **nota bene che…** please note that…

notazi'one *nf* marking; (annotazione) notation

'notebook *nm inv* Comput notebook (PC)

'notes *nm inv* notepad

no'tevole *adj* (degno di nota) remarkable; (grande) considerable

no'tifica *nf* notification

notifi'care *vt* notify; Comm advise; **∼ un ordine di comparizione [in giudizio]** subpoena

notificazi'one *nf* notification

no'tizia *nf* **una ∼** a piece of news, some news; (informazione) a piece of information, some information; **le notizie** the news *sg*; **per avere ∼ di** ⟨telefonare⟩ for news of; **non ha più dato notizie di sè** he hasn't been in touch since

■ **notizia di attualità** news item

notizi'ario *nm* news *sg*

'noto *adj* [well-]known; **rendere ∼** (far sapere) announce

notorietà *nf* fame; **raggiungere la ∼** become famous

no'torio *adj* well-known; *pej* notorious

not'tambulo *nm* night-bird

not'tata *nf* night; **far ∼** stay up all night

'notte *nf* night; **di ∼** at night; **a ∼ fatta** when night had fallen; **la ∼** (durante la notte) at night; **buona ∼** good night; **fermarsi per la ∼** stay overnight; **peggio che andar di ∼** worse than ever; **prima ∼ di nozze** wedding night

■ **notte bianca** (notte insonne) sleepless night; (manifestazione) all-night cultural festival, Light Night *Br*

notte'tempo *adv* at night[-time]

not'turno *adj* nocturnal; ⟨servizio ecc⟩ night *attrib*; **in notturna** ⟨partita⟩ under flood-lights

'notula *nf* (conto) fee note

no'vanta *adj & nm* ninety

novan'tenne *adj & nmf* ninety year old

novan'tesimo *adj & nm* ninetieth

novan'tina *nf* about ninety

'nove *adj & nm* nine; **prova del ∼** Math casting out nines

nove'cento *adj & nm* nine hundred; **il Novecento** the twentieth century; **stile novecento** twentieth-century

no'vella *nf* short story

novelli'ere *nm* short-story writer

novel'lino, -a 1 *adj* inexperienced 2 *nmf* novice, beginner

no'vello *adj* new

■ **patate novelle** new potatoes

no'vembre *nm* November

nove'mila *adj & nm* nine thousand

no'vena *nf* novena

novi'lunio *nm* new moon

novità *nf inv* novelty; (notizie) news *sg*; **l'ultima ∼** (moda) the latest fashion

novizi'ato *nm* Relig novitiate; (tirocinio) apprenticeship

nozi'one *nf* notion; **perdere la ∼ del tempo** lose track of time; **non avere la ∼ del tempo** have no sense of time; **nozioni** *pl* rudiments; **poche nozioni di inglese** very basic English

nozio'nismo *nm* accumulation of facts

'nozze *nfpl* marriage *sg*; (cerimonia) wedding *sg*; **andare a ∼** (godersela) have a field day

■ **nozze d'argento** silver wedding [anniversary]; **nozze di diamante** diamond wedding [anniversary]; **nozze d'oro** golden wedding [anniversary]

'nube *nf* cloud

■ **nube di mistero** shroud of mystery; **nube tossica** toxic cloud

nubi'fragio *nm* cloudburst

'nubile 1 *adj* unmarried 2 *nf* unmarried woman

'nuca *nf* nape

nucle'are *adj* nuclear

'nucleo *nm* nucleus; (unità) unit

■ **nucleo familiare** family unit

nu'dismo *nm* nudism

nu'dista *nmf* nudist

nudità *nf* nudity, nakedness

'nudo *adj* naked; ⟨spoglio, terra⟩ bare; **a occhio ∼** to the naked eye; **verità nuda e cruda** naked truth; **a piedi nudi** barefoot

'nugolo *nm* large number

'nulla 1 *pron* = NIENTE 2 **da ∼** worthless; **per ∼** for nothing

nulla'osta *nm inv* permit

nullate'nente *nm* **i nullatenenti** the have-nots

nullità *nf inv* (persona) nonentity

'nullo *adj* Jur null and void

'nume *nm* numen

nume'rabile *adj* countable

nume'rale *adj & nm* numeral

nume'rare *vt* number

numera'tore *nm* Math numerator

numerazi'one *nf* numbering

nu'merico *adj* numerical

'numero *nm* number; (romano, arabo) numeral; (di scarpe ecc) size; **fare o comporre il ∼** dial [the number]; **dare i numeri** *fam* be off one's head; **avere tutti i numeri per** have what it takes to

■ **numero arretrato** back issue; **numero cardinale** cardinal [number]; **numero di conto** account number; **numero decimale** ⋯⟩

decimal; **numero di fax** fax number; **numero intero** whole number; **numero ordinale** ordinal [number]; **numero d'ordine** Comm order number; **numero di previdenza sociale** National Insurance number; **numero di protocollo** reference number; **numero di scarpa** shoe size; **numero di telefono** phone number; **numero uno** number one; **numero verde** ≈ Freephone® number, toll-free number Am; **numero di volo** flight number

nume'roso *adj* numerous

numi'smatico *adj* numismatic

'nunzio *nm* nuncio

nu'ocere *vi* ~ **a** harm

nu'ora *nf* daughter-in-law

nuo'tare *vi* swim; fig wallow; ~ **come un pesce** swim like a fish; ~ **nell'oro** be stinking rich, be rolling in it

nuo'tata *nf* swim; **fare una** ~ have a swim

nuota|'tore, -trice *nmf* swimmer

nu'oto *nm* swimming; **stili** *mpl* **di** ~ swimming strokes

nu'ova *nf* piece of news; **buone nuove** good news; **nessuna** ~**, buona** ~ no news is good news

Nu'ova Cale'donia *nf* New Caledonia

Nu'ova Gui'nea *nf* New Guinea

nuova'mente *adv* again

Nu'ova Ze'landa *nf* New Zealand

nu'ovo *adj* new; **di** ~ again; **uscire di** ~ go/come back out, go/come out again; **mi risulta** ~ that's news to me; ~ **di pacca** *o* **zecca** brand new; **rimettere a** ~ give a new lease of life to; ~ **del mestiere** new to the job; **il** ~ **anno** [the] New Year
 ■ **nuova linfa** *nf* new blood; **nuovo stile** *nm* new look; **Nuovo Testamento** *nm* New Testament

'nursery *nf* nursery

nutri'ente *adj* nourishing

nutri'mento *nm* nourishment

nu'trire 1 *vt* feed ‹animale, malato, pianta›; harbour ‹sentimenti›; cherish ‹sogno›
 2 *vi* (essere nutriente) be nourishing

nu'trirsi *vr* eat; ~ **di** fig live on

nutri'tivo *adj* nourishing, nutritional

nutrizi'one *nf* nutrition

'nuvola *nf* cloud; **avere la testa fra le nuvole** have one's head in the clouds; **vivere fra le nuvole** live in cloud cuckoo land; **cadere dalle nuvole** be astounded

nuvo'loso *adj* cloudy

nuzi'ale *adj* nuptial; ‹vestito, anello ecc› wedding *attrib*; **pranzo nuziale** wedding breakfast

O o

n
o

o *conj* or; **o l'uno o l'altro** one or the other; either; **o... o...** either...or...

O *abbr* (**ovest**) W

'oasi *nf inv* oasis

obbedi'ente = UBBIDIENTE

obbedi'enza = UBBIDIENZA

obbe'dire = UBBIDIRE

obbli'gare *vt* force, oblige

obbli'garsi *vr* ~ **a** undertake to

obbli'gato *adj* obliged

obbligatoria'mente *adv* fare qualcosa ~ be obliged to do something; bisogna ~ farlo you absolutely have to do it

obbliga'torio *adj* compulsory

obbligazi'one *nf* obligation; Comm bond
 ■ **obbligazione a premio** premium bond

'obbligo *nm* obligation; (dovere) duty; **avere obblighi verso** be under an obligation to; **d'**~ obligatory

ob'brobrio *nm* disgrace

obbrobri'oso *adj* disgraceful

❖ indicates a very frequent word

obe'lisco *nm* obelisk

obe'rare *vt* overburden

obesità *nf* obesity

o'beso *adj* obese

obiet'tare *vt/i* object; ~ **su** object to

obiettiva'mente *adv* objectively

obiettività *nf* objectivity

obiet'tivo 1 *adj* objective
 2 *nm* objective; (scopo) object

obiet'tore *nm* objector
 ■ **obiettore di coscienza** conscientious objector

obiezi'one *nf* objection; **fare** ~ **di coscienza** be a conscientious objector

obi'torio *nm* mortuary

o'blio *nm* oblivion

o'bliquo *adj* oblique; fig underhand

oblite'rare *vt* obliterate

oblò *nm inv* porthole

ob'lungo *adj* oblong

'oboe *nm* oboe

obsole'scenza *nf* obsolescence

obso'leto *adj* obsolete

'oca *nf* (*pl* **oche**) goose; (donna) silly girl

occasio'nale *adj* occasional

occasional'mente *adv* occasionally

⚘ **occasi'one** *nf* occasion; (buon affare) bargain; (motivo) cause; (opportunità) chance; **d'~** secondhand

occhi'aia *nf* eye socket; **occhiaie** *pl* shadows under the eyes

occhi'ali *nmpl* glasses, spectacles

■ **occhiali multifocali** varifocals; **occhiali scuri** dark glasses; **occhiali da sole** sunglasses; **occhiali da sole avvolgenti** wraparound sunglasses; **occhiali da vista** glasses, spectacles

occhia'luto *adj* wearing glasses

⚘ **occhi'ata** *nf* look; **dare un'~ a** have a look at

occhieggi'are **1** *vt* ogle **2** *vi* (far capolino) peep

occhi'ello *nm* buttonhole; (asola) eyelet

⚘ **'occhio** *nm* eye; **~!** watch out!; **~ ai falsi** beware of imitations; **a quattr'occhi** in private; **abbassare gli occhi** look down, lower one's eyes; **sollevare gli occhi** look up, raise one's eyes; **tenere d'~ qualcuno** keep an eye on somebody; **perdere d'~** lose sight of; **a ~ [e croce]** roughly; **chiudere un ~ (su qualcosa)** turn a blind eye (to something); **dare nell'~** attract attention; **pagare o spendere un ~ [della testa]** pay an arm and a leg; **saltare agli occhi** be blindingly obvious

■ **occhio di falco** eagle eye; **occhio nero** (pesto) black eye; **occhio di pernice** (callo) corn

occhio'lino *nm* faro l'~ **a qualcuno** wink at somebody, give somebody a wink

⚘ **occiden'tale** **1** *adj* western **2** *nmf* westerner

occidentaliz'zare *vt* westernize

occidentaliz'zarsi *vr* become westernized

occi'dente *nm* west; (paesi capitalisti) West

oc'cludere *vt* obstruct

occlusi'one *nf* occlusion

occor'rente **1** *adj* necessary **2** *nm* the necessary

occor'renza *nf* need; **all'~** if need be

⚘ **oc'correre** *vi* be necessary; **non occorre farlo** there is no need to do it

occulta'mento *nm*

■ **occultamento di prove** concealment of evidence

occul'tare *vt* hide

occul'tismo *nm* occult

oc'culto *adj* hidden; (magico) occult

occu'pante *nmf* occupier; (abusivo) squatter

⚘ **occu'pare** *vt* occupy; spend ‹tempo›; take up ‹spazio›; (dar lavoro a) employ

occu'parsi *vr* occupy oneself; (trovare lavoro) find a job; **~ di** (badare) look after; **occupati dei fatti tuoi!** mind your own business!

occu'pato *adj* engaged; ‹persona› busy; ‹posto› taken; **casa occupata** (alloggio abusivo) squat

⚘ **occupazi'one** *nf* occupation; Comm employment; (passatempo) pastime; **trovarsi un'~** (interesse) find oneself something to do

o'ceano *nm* ocean

■ **oceano Atlantico** Atlantic [Ocean]; **oceano Indiano** Indian Ocean; **oceano Pacifico** Pacific [Ocean]

'ocra *nf* ochre

'OCSE *nf abbr* (**Organizzazione per la Cooperazione e lo Sviluppo Economico**) OECD

ocu'lare *adj* ocular; ‹testimone, bagno› eye *attrib*

ocula'tezza *nf* care

ocu'lato *adj* ‹scelta, persona› prudent

ocu'lista *nmf* optician; (per malattie) ophthalmologist

od *conj* (davanti alla vocale o) or

'ode *nf* ode

⚘ **odi'are** *vt* hate; **~ a morte** not be able to stand

odi'erno *adj* of today; (attuale) present

⚘ **'odio** *nm* hatred; **avere in ~** hate

odi'oso *adj* hateful

odis'sea *nf* odyssey

o'dometro *nm* Auto milometer, odometer Am

odo'rare **1** *vt* smell; (profumare) perfume **2** *vi* **~ di** smell of

odo'rato *nm* sense of smell

⚘ **o'dore** *nm* smell; (profumo) scent; **c'è ~ di...** there's a smell of...; **avere un buon/cattivo ~** smell nice/awful; **sentire ~ di** smell; **odori** *pl* Culin herbs

odo'roso *adj* fragrant

⚘ **of'fendere** *vt* offend; (ferire) injure

of'fendersi *vr* take offence

offen'siva *nf* Mil fig offensive

offen'sivo *adj* offensive

offen'sore *nm* offender

offe'rente *nmf* offerer; (in aste) bidder; **il miglior ~** the highest bidder

of'ferta *nf* offer; (donazione) donation; Comm supply; (nelle aste) bid; (di appalto) tender; **in ~ speciale** on special offer; **"offerte d'impiego"** "situations vacant"

■ **offerta pubblica di acquisto** takeover bid

of'ferto *pp di* OFFRIRE

offer'torio *nm* offertory

of'fesa *nf* offence

of'feso **1** *pp di* OFFENDERE **2** *adj* offended

offi'ciare vt officiate

offi'cina nf workshop
■ officina [meccanica] garage

officinale adj ‹pianta› medicinal

✓ **of'frire** vt offer

of'frirsi vr offer oneself; ‹occasione›
present itself; ~ **di fare qualcosa** offer to do
something

off'set nm inv offset printing

off'shore nm inv (motoscafo) speedboat

offu'scare vt darken; fig dull ‹memoria,
bellezza›; blur ‹vista›

offu'scarsi vr darken; fig ‹memoria,
bellezza› fade away; ‹vista› become blurred

of'talmico adj ophthalmic

ogget'tistica nf manufacture and
selling of household and gift items; (oggetti)
household and gift items; **negozio di
oggettistica** gift shop

oggettività nf objectivity

ogget'tivo adj objective

✓ **og'getto** nm object; (argomento) subject
■ oggetto sessuale sex object; **oggetti** pl
smarriti lost property, lost and found Am

✓ **'oggi** adv & nm today; (al giorno d'oggi)
nowadays; **da ~ in poi** from today on;
~ **[a] otto** a week today; **dall'~ al domani**
overnight; **il giornale di ~** today's paper; **al
giorno d'~** these days, nowadays

✓ **oggigi'orno** adv nowadays

o'giva nf Mil warhead

'ogni adj inv every; (qualsiasi) any; ~ **tre
giorni** every three days; **ad ~ costo** at any
cost; **ad ~ modo** anyway; ~ **ben di Dio** all
sorts of good things; ~ **cosa** everything;
~ **tanto** now and then; ~ **volta che** every
time, whenever

✓ **o'gnuno** pron everyone, everybody; ~ **di
voi** each of you

ohibò int oh dear!

ohimè int oh dear!

o'kay nm **dare l'~ a qualcuno/qualcosa**
give somebody/something the OK

'ola nf inv Mexican wave

O'landa nf Holland

olan'dese [1] adj Dutch
[2] nm Dutchman; (lingua) Dutch; (formaggio)
Edam
[3] nf Dutchwoman

ole'andro nm oleander

ole'ato adj oiled; **carta oleata** greaseproof
paper

oleo'dotto nm oil pipeline

ole'oso adj oily

ol'fatto nm sense of smell

oli'are vt oil

olia'tore nm oilcan

oli'era nf cruet

✓ indicates a very frequent word

olim'piadi nfpl Olympic games, Olympics

o'limpico adj Olympic

olim'pionico adj ‹primato, squadra›
Olympic; **costume** ~ Olympic swimming
costume

+olino suff **bestiolina** nf (affettuoso) little
creature; **macchiolina** nf spot; **pesciolino** nm
little fish; **risolino** nm giggle; **sassolino** nm
pebble; **strisciolina** nf thin strip; **magrolino**
adj skinny

✓ **'olio** nm oil; **sott'~** in oil; **colori a ~** oils;
quadro a ~ oil painting
■ olio [di semi] di arachidi groundnut oil; olio
essenziale essential oil; olio extravergine di
oliva extra-virgin olive oil; olio di fegato di
merluzzo cod-liver oil; olio di gomito elbow
grease; olio lubrificante lubricating oil; olio
di mais corn oil; olio minerale mineral oil;
olio [del] motore engine oil; olio d'oliva olive
oil; olio di semi vegetable oil; olio [di semi] di
lino linseed oil; olio solare suntan oil; olio [di
semi] di vinaccioli grapeseed oil

✓ **o'liva** nf olive

oli'vastro adj olive

oli'veto nm olive grove

oli'vetta nf toggle

o'livo nm olive tree

'olmo nm elm

olo'causto nm holocaust; **l'Olocausto** the
Holocaust

o'lografo adj holograph

olo'gramma nm hologram

oltraggi'are vt offend

ol'traggio nm offence
■ oltraggio al pudore Jur gross indecency

oltraggi'oso adj offensive

ol'tranza nf **ad ~** to the bitter end

✓ **'oltre** [1] adv (di luogo) further; (di tempo)
longer
[2] prep (nello spazio) beyond; (di tempo) later
than; (più di) more than; (in aggiunta) besides;
~ **a** (eccetto) except, apart from; **per ~ due
settimane** for more than two weeks; **una
settimana e ~** a week and more

oltrecon'fine adj cross-border

oltre'mare adv overseas

oltre'modo adv extremely

oltrepas'sare vt go beyond; (eccedere)
exceed; **oltrepassi il semaforo** go past the
traffic lights; ~ **il limite di velocità** break the
speed limit; **'non ~'** 'no trespassing'

OM abbr Radio (**onde medie**) MW

omacci'one nm bruiser

o'maggi nmpl (saluti) respects

o'maggio nm homage; (dono) gift; **in ~ con**
free with

'Oman nm Oman

ombeli'cale adj umbilical; **cordone
ombelicale** umbilical cord

ombe'lico nm navel

ꜰ 'ombra *nf* (zona) shade; (immagine oscura) shadow; all'~ in the shade

ombreggi'are *vt* shade

ombreggia'ture *nfpl* shading

om'brello *nm* umbrella

ombrel'lone *nm* beach umbrella

om'bretto *nm* eye-shadow

om'broso *adj* shady; ‹cavallo› skittish; ‹persona› touchy

ome'lette *nf inv* omelette

ome'lia *nf* Relig sermon

omeopa'tia *nf* homeopathy

omeo'patico [1] *adj* homeopathic [2] *nm* homeopath

omertà *nf inv* conspiracy of silence

o'messo *pp di* OMETTERE

o'mettere *vt* omit

'OMG *nm abbr* (**Organismo Modificato Geneticamente**) GMO

omi'cida [1] *adj* murderous, homicidal [2] *nmf* murderer

omi'cidio *nm* murder
■ omicidio colposo manslaughter; omicidio di massa mass murder; omicidio volontario Jur culpable homicide

omissi'one *nf* omission

'omnibus *nm inv* omnibus

omofo'bia *nf* homophobia

omogeneiz'zare *vt* homogenize

omogeneiz'zato *adj* homogenized

omo'geneo *adj* homogeneous

o'mografo *nm* homograph

omolo'gare *vt* approve; fare ~ un testamento prove a will

omologazi'one *nf* probate

o'monimo, -a [1] *nmf* namesake [2] *nm* (parola) homonym [3] *adj* of the same name

omosessu'ale *adj & nmf* homosexual

omosessualità *nf* homosexuality

'OMS *nf abbr* (**Organizzazione Mondiale della Sanità**) WHO

On. *abbr* (**onorevole**) MP, Hon.

'oncia *nf* ounce
■ oncia fluida fluid ounce

ꜰ 'onda *nf* wave; andare in ~ TV, Radio go on the air; seguire l'~ go with the crowd; onde *pl* corte short wave; onde *pl* lunghe long wave
■ onda di maremoto tidal wave; onde *pl* medie medium wave; onde *pl* radio radio waves; onda d'urto shock wave

on'data *nf* wave; a ondate in waves
■ ondata di freddo cold snap

'onde *conj fml* so that

ondeggi'are *vi* wave; ‹barca› roll

ondu'lato *adj* wavy

ondula'torio *adj* undulating

ondulazi'one *nf* undulation; (di capelli) wave

+one *suff* cucchiaione *nm* big spoon; gattone *nm* fat cat; bacione *nm* smacker; bacioni *pl* (in lettera) love and kisses; omone *nm* big guy; nasone *nm* big nose; nebbione *nm* dense fog, peasouper fam; simpaticone *nm* very friendly person; lumacone *nm* slowcoach; testone *nm* mule; facilone *nm pej* over-casual sort of person; grassone *nm pej* fat slob; pigrone *nm* lazy-bones *sg*; chiacchierone *nm* chatterbox; criticone *nm* nit-picker; pasticcione *nm* bungler

'onere *nm* burden

oner'oso *adj* onerous

onestà *nf* honesty; (rettitudine) integrity, honesty

ꜰ o'nesto *adj* honest; (giusto) just

'ONG *nf abbr* (**organizzazione non governativa**) non-governmental organization, NGO

'onice *nf* onyx

o'nirico *adj* dream *attrib*

o'nisco *nm* slater

ONLUS *nf abbr* (**organizzazione non lucrativa di utilità sociale**) non-profit organization

onnipo'tente *adj* omnipotent

onnipre'sente *adj* ubiquitous; Rel omnipresent

onnisci'ente *adj* omniscient

ono'mastico *nm* name day

onomato'pea *nf* onomatopoeia

onomato'peico *adj* onomatopoeic

ono'rabile *adj* honourable

ono'rare *vt* (fare onore a) be a credit to; honour ‹promessa›

ono'rario [1] *adj* honorary [2] *nm* fee

ono'rarsi *vr* ~ di be proud of

ono'rato *adj* ‹famiglia, professione› respectable; considerarsi ~ da qualcosa consider oneself honoured by something; l'onorata società *nf* the Mafia

ꜰ o'nore *nm* honour; in ~ di ‹festa, ricevimento› in honour of; fare ~ a do justice to ‹pranzo›; farsi ~ in excel in; a onor del vero to tell the truth; fare gli onori di casa do the honours

ono'revole [1] *adj* honourable [2] *nmf* Member of Parliament

onorifi'cenza *nf* honour; (decerazione) decoration

ono'rifico *adj* honorary

'onta *nf* shame

on'tano *nm* alder

'O.N.U. *nf abbr* (**Organizzazione delle Nazioni Unite**) UN

opacità *nf* opaqueness, opacity

⬤ **O**

o'paco adj opaque; ‹colori ecc› dull; ‹fotografia, rossetto› matt

o'pale nf opal

'OPEC nf inv Opec, OPEC

⚹ **'opera** nf (lavoro) work; (azione) deed; Mus opera; (teatro) opera house; (ente) institution; **mettere in** ∼ put into effect; **mettersi all'**∼ get to work
■ **opera d'arte** work of art; **opera lirica** opera; **opere** pl **pubbliche** public works

ope'rabile adj operable

⚹ **ope'raio, -a** [1] adj working
[2] nmf worker
■ **operaio edile** building worker; **operaio specializzato** skilled worker

⚹ **ope'rare** [1] vt Med operate on; ∼ **qualcuno al cuore** operate on somebody's heart; **farsi** ∼ have an operation
[2] vi operate; (agire) work

opera'tivo, operatorio adj operating attrib

opera|'tore, -trice nmf operator; TV cameraman
■ **operatore ecologico** refuse collector; **operatore sanitario** health worker; **operatore turistico** tour operator

⚹ **operazi'one** nf operation; Comm transaction
■ **operazione antidroga** anti-drug operation; **operazioni** pl **di soccorso** rescue operations; **operazione d'urgenza** emergency operation

ope'retta nf operetta

ope'roso adj industrious

⚹ **opini'one** nf opinion; **rimanere della propria** ∼ still feel the same way
■ **opinione pubblica** public opinion, vox pop

oplà int oops

o'possum nm inv possum

'oppio nm opium

oppo'nente [1] adj opposing
[2] nmf opponent

⚹ **op'porre** vt oppose; (obiettare) object; ∼ **resistenza** offer resistance

op'porsi vr ∼ **a** oppose

opportu'nismo nm expediency

opportu'nista nmf opportunist

opportunità nf inv opportunity; (l'essere opportuno) timeliness; **avere il senso dell'**∼ have a sense of what is appropriate

oppor'tuno adj opportune; (adeguato) appropriate; **ritenere** ∼ **fare qualcosa** think it appropriate to do something; **il momento** ∼ the right moment

opposi'tore nm opposer

opposizi'one nf opposition; **d'**∼ ‹giornale, partito› opposition attrib; **in** ∼ in opposition

op'posto [1] pp di OPPORRE
[2] adj opposite; ‹opinioni› opposing

[3] nm opposite; **all'**∼ on the contrary

oppressi'one nf oppression

oppres'sivo adj oppressive

op'presso [1] pp di OPPRIMERE
[2] adj oppressed

oppres'sore nm oppressor

oppri'mente adj oppressive

op'primere vt oppress; (gravare) weigh down

⚹ **op'pure** conj otherwise, or [else]; **lunedì** ∼ **martedì** Monday or Tuesday

ops int oops

op'tare vi ∼ **per** opt for

'optional nm inv optional extra

opu'lento adj opulent

opu'lenza nf opulence

o'puscolo nm booklet; (pubblicitario) brochure

opzio'nale adj optional

opzi'one nf option

⚹ **'ora¹** nf time; (unità) hour; **di buon'**∼ early; **che** ∼ **è?, che ore sono?** what time is it?; **a che** ∼**?** at what time?; **mezz'**∼ half an hour; **a ore** ‹lavorare, pagare› by the hour; **50 km all'**∼ 50 km an hour; **è** ∼ **di finirla!** that's enough now!; **a un'**∼ **di macchina** one hour by car; **non vedo l'**∼ **di vederti** I can't wait to see you; **fare le ore piccole** stay up until the small hours
■ ∼ **d'arrivo** arrival time; **ora di cena** dinnertime; **l'ora esatta** Teleph speaking clock; **ora legale** daylight saving time; **ora locale** local time; **ora di pranzo** dinnertime; **ora di punta, ore di punta** pl peak time; (per il traffico) rush hour; **ora solare** Greenwich Mean Time, GMT; **ora zero** Mil fig zero hour

⚹ **'ora²** [1] adv now; (tra poco) presently; ∼ **come** ∼ just now, at the moment; **d'**∼ **in poi** from now on; **per** ∼ for the time being, for now
[2] conj (dunque) now [then]; ∼ **che ci penso, ...** now that I [come to] think about it...

o'racolo nm oracle

'orafo nm goldsmith

o'rale adj & nm oral; **per via** ∼ by mouth

⚹ **ora'mai** = ORMAI

o'rario [1] adj ‹tariffa› hourly; ‹segnale› time attrib; ‹velocità› per hour; **in senso** ∼ clockwise
[2] nm time; (tabella dell'orario) timetable, schedule Am; **essere in** ∼ be on time; **partire in** ∼ leave on time; **lavorare fuori** ∼ work outside normal hours
■ **orario di apertura** opening hours pl; **orario di chiusura** closing time; **orario estivo** summer timetable; **orario ferroviario** railway timetable, railroad schedule Am; **orario flessibile** flexitime; **orario invernale** winter timetable; **orario di lavoro** working hours pl; **orario degli spettacoli** performance times pl;

⚹ indicates a very frequent word

orario di sportello banking hours *pl*; **orario d'ufficio** business hours *pl*; **orario di visita** visiting hours *pl*, visiting time; (del medico) consulting hours *pl*; **orario di volo** flight time

o'rata *nf* gilthead

ora|'tore, -trice *nmf* orator; (conferenziere) speaker

ora'torio, -a [1] *adj* oratorical
[2] *nm* Mus oratorio
[3] *nmf* oratory

orazi'one *nf* Relig prayer

'orbita *nf* orbit; Anat [eye-]socket

'Orcadi *nfpl* Orkneys

or'chestra *nf* orchestra; (parte del teatro) pit
■ **orchestra da camera** chamber orchestra; **orchestra sinfonica** symphony orchestra

orche'strale [1] *adj* orchestral
[2] *nmf* member of an/the orchestra

orche'strare *vt* orchestrate

orchi'dea *nf* orchid

'orco *nm* ogre

'orda *nf* horde

or'digno *nm* device; (arnese) tool
■ **ordigno esplosivo** explosive device; **ordigno incendiario** incendiary device, firebomb

ordi'nale *adj & nm* ordinal

ordina'mento *nm* order; (leggi) rules *pl*

ordi'nanza *nf* (del sindaco) bylaw; **d'~** ‹soldato› on duty

◆ **ordi'nare** *vt* (sistemare) arrange; (comandare) order; (prescrivere) prescribe; Relig ordain

ordi'nario [1] *adj* ordinary; ‹grossolano› common; (professore) with a permanent position; **di ordinaria amministrazione** routine
[2] *nm* ordinary; Univ professor; **fuori dell'~** out of the ordinary

ordi'nato *adj* (in ordine) tidy

ordinazi'one *nf* order; **fare un'~** place an order

◆ **'ordine** *nm* order; (di avvocati, medici) association; **mettere in ~** put in order; tidy up ‹appartamento ecc›; **di prim'~** first-class; **di terz'~** ‹film, albergo› third-rate; **di ~ pratico/economico** ‹problema› of a practical/economic nature; **fino a nuovo ~** until further notice; **parola d'ordine** password
■ **ordine di acquisto** Comm purchase order; **ordine del giorno** agenda; **ordine di pagamento** banker's order; **ordine permanente** Fin standing order; **ordine pubblico** law and order; **ordini** *pl* **sacri** Holy Orders

or'dire *vt* (tramare) plot

orecchi'ette *nfpl* small pasta shells

orec'chino *nm* ear-ring; **orecchini** *pl* **con le clip** clip-ons

◆ **o'recchio** *nm* (*pl nf* **orecchie**) ear; **avere ~** have a good ear; **esser duro d'~** be hard of hearing; **mi è giunto all'~ che…** I've heard that…; **parlare all'~ a qualcuno**

whisper in somebody's ear; **suonare a ~** play by ear

orecchi'oni *nmpl* Med mumps *sg*

o'refice *nm* jeweller

orefice'ria *nf* (arte) goldsmith's art; (negozio) goldsmith's [shop]

'orfano, -a [1] *adj* orphan
[2] *nmf* orphan

orfano'trofio *nm* orphanage

orga'netto *nm* barrel-organ; (a bocca) mouth-organ; (fisarmonica) accordion

or'ganico [1] *adj* organic
[2] *nm* personnel

orga'nino *nm* hurdy-gurdy

orga'nismo *nm* organism; (corpo umano) body

orga'nista *nmf* organist

◆ **organiz'zare** *vt* organize

organiz'zarsi *vr* get organized

organizza'tivo *adj* organizational

organizza|'tore, -trice *nmf* organizer

organizzazi'one *nf* organization
■ **organizzazione del servizio d'ordine** policing; **organizzazione studentesca** student union; **organizzazione umanitaria** relief agency, aid agency

'organo *nm* organ

or'gasmo *nm* orgasm; fig agitation

'orgia *nf* orgy

or'goglio *nm* pride

orgogli'oso *adj* proud

orien'tale *adj* eastern; (cinese ecc) oriental

orienta'mento *nm* orientation; **perdere l'~** lose one's bearings; **senso dell'~** sense of direction
■ **orientamento professionale** careers guidance; **orientamento scolastico** educational guidance

orien'tare *vt* orientate

orien'tarsi *vr* find one's bearings; (tendere) tend

ori'ente *nm* east
■ **l'Estremo Oriente** the Far East; **il Medio Oriente** the Middle East

orien'teering *nm inv* orienteering

o'rigano *nm* oregano

origi'nale [1] *adj* original; (eccentrico) odd
[2] *nm* original

originalità *nf* originality

origi'nare *vt/i* originate

origi'nario *adj* (nativo) native

o'rigine *nf* origin; **in ~** originally; **aver ~ da** originate from; **dare ~ a** give rise to

origli'are *vi* eavesdrop

o'rina *nf* urine

ori'nale *nm* chamber-pot

ori'nare *vi* urinate

ori'undo *adj* native

orizzon'tale *adj* horizontal

orizzon'tare = ORIENTARE

oriz'zonte nm horizon

or'lare vt hem

orla'tura nf hem

'orlo nm edge; (di vestito ecc) hem

'orma nf track; (di piede) footprint; (impronta) mark

⚡ **or'mai** adv by now; (passato) by then; (quasi) almost

ormegg'iare vt moor

or'meggio nm mooring

ormo'nale adj hormonal

or'mone nm hormone

ornamen'tale adj ornamental

orna'mento nm ornament; d'∼ ⟨oggetto⟩ ornamental

or'nare vt decorate

or'narsi vr deck oneself

or'nato adj ⟨stile⟩ ornate

ornitolo'gia nf ornithology

orni'tologo, -a nmf ornithologist

ornito'rinco nm platypus

⚡ **'oro** nm gold; d'∼ gold; fig golden; una persona d'∼ a wonderful person

■ oro nero black gold

orologe'ria nf watchmaker

orologi'aio, -a nmf clockmaker, watchmaker

⚡ **oro'logio** nm (da polso, tasca) watch; (da tavolo, muro ecc) clock

■ orologio biologico biological clock; orologio a carica automatica self-winding watch; orologio a cucù cuckoo clock; orologio digitale digital clock; orologio a pendolo grandfather clock; orologio da polso wristwatch; orologio al quarzo quartz watch; orologio a sveglia alarm clock

o'roscopo nm horoscope

or'rendo adj awful, dreadful

or'ribile adj horrible

orribil'mente adv horribly

orripi'lante adj horrifying

⚡ **or'rore** nm horror; avere qualcosa in ∼ hate something; ∼! heck!; film/romanzo dell'orrore horror film/story

orsacchi'otto nm teddy bear

or'setto nm

■ orsetto lavatore raccoon

'orso nm bear; (persona scontrosa) hermit

■ orso bianco polar bear; orso bruno brown bear

orsù int come now!

or'taggio nm vegetable

or'tensia nf hydrangea

or'tica nf nettle; buttare qualcosa alle ortiche fig fam chuck in

orti'caria nf nettle rash

orticol'tura nf horticulture

⚡ **'orto** nm vegetable plot

orto'dontico adj orthodontic

ortodon'zia nf orthodontics sg

ortodos'sia nf conformity

orto'dosso adj orthodox

ortofrut'ticolo adj mercato ∼ fruit and vegetable market

ortofrutticol'tore nm market gardener, truck farmer Am

ortofrutticol'tura nf market gardening

ortogo'nale adj perpendicular

ortogra'fia nf spelling

orto'grafico adj spelling attrib

orto'lano nm market gardener, truck farmer Am; (negozio) greengrocer's

ortope'dia nf orthopaedics sg

orto'pedico ① adj orthopaedic ② nm orthopaedic specialist

orzai'olo nm sty

or'zata nf barley-water

'orzo nm barley

■ orzo perlato pearl barley

osan'nato adj (esaltato) praised to the skies

⚡ **o'sare** vt/i dare; (avere audacia) be daring

oscenità nf inv obscenity

o'sceno adj obscene

oscil'lare vi swing; ⟨prezzi ecc⟩ fluctuate; Tech oscillate; fig (essere indeciso) vacillate

oscillazi'one nf swinging; (di prezzi) fluctuation; Tech oscillation

oscura'mento nm darkening; fig (di vista, mente) dimming; (totale) black-out

oscu'rare vt darken; fig obscure

oscu'rarsi vr get dark

oscurità nf darkness; (incomprensibilità) obscurity; uscire dall'∼ fig emerge from obscurity; morire nell'∼ fig die in obscurity

⚡ **o'scuro** adj dark; (triste) gloomy; (incomprensibile) obscure

o'smosi nf inv osmosis

⚡ **ospe'dale** nm hospital

■ ospedale universitario teaching hospital

ospedali'ero adj hospital attrib

ospi'tale adj hospitable

ospitalità nf hospitality; non voglio abusare della tua ∼ I don't want to outstay my welcome

ospi'tare vt give hospitality to

⚡ **'ospite** ① nm (chi ospita) host; (chi viene ospitato) guest ② nf hostess; guest

o'spizio nm (per anziani) [old people's] home

ossa'tura nf bone structure; (di romanzo) structure, framework

'osseo adj bone attrib

osse'quente adj deferential; ∼ alla legge law-abiding

⚡ indicates a very frequent word

ossequi'are *vt* pay one's respects to

os'sequio *nm* homage; **ossequi** *pl* respects

ossequi'oso *adj* obsequious

osser'vabile *adj* observable

osser'vante *adj* ‹cattolico› practising

osser'vanza *nf* observance

⚲ osser'vare *vt* observe; (notare) notice; keep ‹ordine, silenzio›

osserva|'tore, -trice *nmf* observer

osserva'torio *nm* Astr observatory; Mil observation post

osservazi'one *nf* observation; (rimprovero) reproach

ossessio'nante *adj* haunting; ‹persona› nagging

ossessio'nare *vt* obsess; (infastidire) nag

ossessi'one *nf* obsession; (assillo) pain in the neck

osses'sivo *adj* obsessive; ‹paura› neurotic

os'sesso *adj* obsessed

⚲ os'sia *conj* that is

ossi'dabile *adj* liable to tarnish

ossi'dante *adj* tarnishing

ossi'dare *vt* oxidize

ossi'darsi *vr* oxidize

'ossido *nm* oxide
- **ossido di carbonio** carbon monoxide; **ossido di zinco** zinc oxide

os'sidrico *adj* **fiamma ossidrica** blowlamp

ossige'nare *vt* oxygenate; (decolorare) bleach

ossige'narsi *vr* put back on its feet ‹azienda›; **∼ i capelli** dye one's hair blonde

os'sigeno *nm* oxygen

⚲ 'osso *nm* Anat (*pl nf* **ossa**) bone; (di frutto) stone; **senz'∼** boneless
- **osso mascellare** jawbone

osso'buco *nm* marrowbone

os'suto *adj* bony

ostaco'lare *vt* hinder, obstruct

ostaco'lista *nmf* hurdler

o'stacolo *nm* obstacle; Sport hurdle

o'staggio *nm* hostage; **prendere in ∼** take hostage

o'stello *nm*
- **ostello della gioventù** youth hostel

osten'tare *vt* show off; **∼ indifferenza** pretend to be indifferent

ostentata'mente *adv* ostentatiously

ostentazi'one *nf* ostentation

osteopo'rosi *nf inv* osteoporosis

oste'ria *nf* inn

oste'tricia *nf* obstetrics *sg*

o'stetrico, -a [1] *adj* obstetric [2] *nmf* obstetrician

'ostia *nf* host; (cialda) wafer

'ostico *adj* tough

o'stile *adj* hostile

ostilità *nf inv* hostility

osti'narsi *vr* **∼** persist (**a** in)

osti'nato *adj* obstinate

ostinazi'one *nf* obstinacy

ostra'cismo *nm* ostracism

'ostrica *nf* oyster

ostro'goto *nm* **parlare ∼** talk double Dutch

ostru'ire *vt* obstruct

ostruzi'one *nf* obstruction

ostruzio'nismo *nm* obstructionism; Sport obstruction
- **ostruzionismo sindacale** work-to-rule

oto'rino *nm* ear, nose and throat *attrib*

otorinolaringoi'atra *nmf* ear, nose and throat specialist

'otre *nm* leather bottle

ottago'nale *adj* octagonal

ot'tagono *nm* octagon

ot'tanta *adj & nm* eighty

ottan'tenne *adj & nmf* eighty-year-old

ottan'tesimo *adj & nm* eightieth

ottan'tina *nf* about eighty

ot'tava *nf* octave

ot'tavo *adj & nm* eighth

⚲ otte'nere *vt* obtain; (più comune) get; (conseguire) achieve

ot'tetto *nm* Mus octet

'ottico, -a [1] *adj* optic[al] [2] *nmf* optician [3] *nf* (scienza) optics *sg*; (di lenti ecc) optics *pl*

otti'male *adj* optimum

ottima'mente *adv* very well

otti'mismo *nm* optimism

otti'mista *nmf* optimist

otti'mistico *adj* optimistic

ottimiz'zare *vt* optimize

⚲ 'ottimo [1] *adj* very good [2] *nm* optimum; **essere all'∼ della forma** be on top form

⚲ 'otto *adj & nm* eight

+otto *suff* **bassotto** *adj* (piuttosto basso) quite short; **contadinotto** *nm* pej (semplicione) country bumpkin; **paesotto** *nm* hamlet; **leprotto** *nm* leveret; (affettuoso) baby hare; **pienotto** *adj* ‹viso› chubby

⚲ ot'tobre *nm* October

otto'cento *adj & nm* eight hundred; **l'Ottocento** the nineteenth century

ot'tone *nm* brass; **gli ottoni** Mus the brass

ottuage'nario, -a *adj & nmf* octogenarian

ot'tundere *vt* blunt

ottu'rare *vt* block; fill ‹dente›

ottu'rarsi *vr* clog

ottura'tore *nm* Phot shutter

otturazi'one *nf* stopping; (di dente) filling

O

ot'tuso [1] pp di OTTUNDERE
[2] adj obtuse

ouver'ture nf inv overture

o'vaia nf ovary

o'vale adj & nm oval

o'vatta nf cotton wool, absorbent cotton Am

ovat'tato adj ‹suono, passi› muffled

ovazi'one nf ovation

'ove adv (liter) where

over'dose nf inv overdose

'overdrive nm inv Auto overdrive

'ovest nm west

o'vile nm sheep-fold, pen

o'vino adj sheep attrib

ovoi'dale adj egg-shaped

ovo'via nf two-seater cable car

ovulazi'one nf ovulation

o'vunque = DOVUNQUE

ov'vero conj or; (cioè) that is

ovvia'mente adv obviously

ovvi'are vi ~ a qualcosa counter something

'ovvio adj obvious

ozi'are vi laze around

'ozio nm idleness; **stare in** ~ idle about

ozi'oso adj idle; ‹questione› pointless

o'zono nm ozone; **buco nell'ozono** hole in the ozone layer

Pp

pacare vt calm

paca'tezza nf calm[ness]

pa'cato adj calm

'pacca nf slap

pac'chetto nm packet; (postale) parcel, package; (di sigarette) pack, packet
■ **pacchetto informativo** information pack; **pacchetto integrato** Comput integrated package; **pacchetto software** software package

'pacchia nf fam (situazione) bed of roses

pacchia'nata nf è una ~ it's so garish

pacchi'ano adj garish

⚬ **'pacco** nm parcel; (involto) bundle; **disfare un** ~ unwrap a parcel; **fare un** ~ make up a parcel; **pacchi postali** pl parcels, packages
■ **pacco bomba** parcel bomb; **pacco regalo** gift-wrapped package; **le faccio un** ~ **regalo?** would you like it gift-wrapped?; **pacco umanitario** aid package

paccot'tiglia nf (roba scadente) junk, rubbish

⚬ **'pace** nf peace; **darsi** ~ forget it; **fare** ~ **con qualcuno** make it up with somebody; **lasciare in** ~ **qualcuno** leave somebody in peace; **mettere** ~ **fra** pacify, make [the] peace between; **andate in** ~ Relig peace be with you; **in tempo di** ~ in peacetime; **del tempo di** ~ peacetime; **di** ~ ‹milizia› peacekeeping; **firmare la** ~ sign a peace treaty; **per amor di** ~ for a quiet life

pace-'maker nm (apparecchio) pacemaker

pachi'derma nm (animale) pachyderm; fig thick-skinned person

pachi'stano, -a nmf & adj Pakistani

paci'ere nm peacemaker

pacifi'care vt reconcile; (mettere pace) pacify

pacificazi'one nf reconciliation

pa'cifico [1] adj pacific; (calmo) peaceful; **è** ~ **che…** (comunemente accettato) it is clear that…
[2] nm il **Pacifico** the Pacific

paci'fismo nm pacifism

paci'fista adj & nmf pacifist

pacioc'cone, -a nmf fam chubby-chops

paci'ugo nm (poltiglia) mush

pa'dano adj pianura padana Po Valley

pa'della nf frying-pan; (per malati) bedpan; **cuocere in** ~ fry; **della** ~ **alla brace** out of the frying pan into the fire

padel'lata nf una ~ di a frying-panful of

padigli'one nm pavilion
■ **padiglione auricolare** auricle

'Padova nf Padua

⚬ **'padre** nm father; **padri** pl (antenati) forefathers; **i padri della chiesa** the Church Fathers; **di** ~ **in figlio** from father to son
■ **padre adottivo** (marito della madre) stepfather; **padre di famiglia** father, paterfamilias; **sono** ~ **di famiglia** I have a family to look after; **padre spirituale** spiritual father

padre'nostro nm il ~ the Lord's Prayer

padre'terno nm God Almighty

pa'drino nm godfather; ~ **e madrina** godparents

padro'nale adj principal

padro'nanza nf mastery
■ **padronanza di sé** self-control

⚬ indicates a very frequent word

pa'drone, **-a** *nmf* master; mistress; (datore di lavoro) boss; (proprietario) owner
■ **padrone di casa** (di inquilini) landlord; landlady; (in ricevimento) master of the house; lady of the house

padroneggi'are *vt* master

padro'nesco *adj* domineering

padro'nissimo *adj* **essere ∼ di fare qualcosa** be quite at liberty to do something

pae'saggio *nm* scenery; (pittura) landscape
■ **paesaggio marino** seascape; **paesaggio montano** mountain landscape

paesag'gista *nmf* landscape architect

paesag'gistico *adj* landscape *attrib*

pae'sano, **-a** ① *adj* country *attrib* ② *nmf* villager

pa'ese *nm* (nazione) country; (territorio) land; (villaggio) village; **il Bel Paese** Italy; **va' a quel ∼!** get lost!; **il mio ∼ natio** where I was born; **Paesi Bassi** *pl* Netherlands; **paesi dell'est** *pl* Eastern Bloc countries

paf'futo *adj* plump

pag. *abbr* (**pagina**) p.

'paga *nf* pay, wages *pl*

pa'gabile *adj* payable

pa'gaia *nf* paddle

paga'mento *nm* payment; **a ∼** (parcheggio) which you have to pay to use.
■ **pagamento anticipato** Comm advance payment; **pagamento alla consegna** cash on delivery, COD; **pagamento pedaggio** toll

paga'nesimo *nm* paganism

pa'gano, **-a** *adj* & *nmf* pagan

pa'gante *nmf* payer

pa'gare *vt/i* pay; **∼ da bere a qualcuno** buy somebody a drink; **pagato in anticipo** prepaid, paid in advance; **te la faccio ∼** you'll pay for this; **quanto pagherei per poter venire!** what I wouldn't give to be able to come!

pa'gella *nf* [school] report

pagg. *abbr* (**pagine**) pp

pag'gio *nm* pageboy

'pagina *nf* page; **prima ∼** Journ front page; **∼ economica** financial news, financial pages; **pagine gialle** *pl* Yellow Pages
■ **pagina mastra** master page; **pagina web** Comput web page

pagi'none *nm* centrefold

'paglia *nf* straw
■ **paglia e fieno** Culin *mixture of ordinary and green tagliatelle*

pagliac'cesco *adj* farcical

pagliac'cetto *nm* (per bambini) rompers *pl*; (da donna) camiknickers

pagliac'ciata *nf* farce

pagli'accio *nm* clown; **fare il ∼** act *or* play the clown

pagli'aio *nm* haystack

paglie'riccio *nm* straw mattress

pagli'etta *nf* (cappello) boater; (per pentole) steel wool

pagli'uzza *nf* wisp of straw; (di metallo) particle

pa'gnotta *nf* [round] loaf

'pago *adj* satisfied

pa'goda *nf* pagoda

pa'guro *nm* hermit crab

pail'lard *nf inv* slice of grilled veal

pail'lette *nf inv* sequin

'paio *nm* (*pl* **paia**) pair; **un ∼** (circa due) a couple; **un ∼ di** ‹scarpe, forbici› a pair of; **è un altro ∼ di maniche** fig that's a different kettle of fish

pai'olo *nm* copper pot

'Pakistan *nm* Pakistan

paki'stano, **-a** *adj* & *nmf* Pakistani

'pala *nf* shovel; (di remo, elica) blade; (di ruota) paddle; (di mulino) blade, vane
■ **pala d'altare** altar piece; **pala da fornaio** shovel; **pala meccanica** mechanical digger

pala'dino *nm* paladin; fig champion

pala'fitta *nf* pile-dwelling

palan'drana *nf* (abito largo) big long coat

pala'sport *nm inv* indoor sports arena

pa'late *nfpl* **a ∼** ‹fare soldi› hand over fist

pa'lato *nm* palate

palaz'zetto *nm*
■ **palazzetto dello sport** indoor sports arena

palaz'zina *nf* villa

pa'lazzo *nm* palace; (edificio) building
■ **∼ comunale** town hall; **Palazzo Ducale** Doge's Palace; **palazzo delle esposizioni** exhibition centre; **palazzo di giustizia** law courts *pl*, courthouse; **palazzo dello sport** indoor sports arena

'palco *nm* (pedana) platform; Theat box; (palcoscenico) stage

palco'scenico *nm* stage

paleogra'fia *nf* palaeography

paleo'grafico *adj* palaeographical

pale'ografo, **-a** *nmf* palaeographer

paleo'litico *adj* palaeolithic

pale'sare *vt* disclose

pale'sarsi *vr* reveal oneself

pa'lese *adj* evident

Pale'stina *nf* Palestine

palesti'nese *adj* & *nmf* Palestinian

pa'lestra *nf* gymnasium, gym; (ginnastica) gymnastics *pl*

pa'letta *nf* spade; (per focolare) shovel
■ **paletta [della spazzatura]** dustpan

palet'tata *nf* shovelful

pa'letto *nm* peg

palin'sesto *nm* (documento) palimpsest; TV programme schedule

'palio *nm* (premio) prize; **il Palio** *horse-race held at Siena*

palis'sandro *nm* rosewood

paliz'zata nf fence

ℰ **'palla** nf ball; (proiettile) bullet; fam (bugia) porkie; **prendere la ~ al balzo** seize an opportunity; **essere una ~** sl be a drag; **che palle!** vulg this is a pain in the arse!, what a drag!
■ **palla da biliardo** billiard ball; **palla medica** medicine ball; **palla di neve** snowball; **palla al piede** fig millstone round one's neck

pallaca'nestro nf basketball

palla-'goal nf **hanno avuto molte palle-goal** they had a lot of goal-scoring opportunities

palla'mano nf handball

pallanuo'tista nmf water polo player

pallanu'oto nf water polo

pallavo'lista nmf volleyball player

palla'volo nf volleyball

palleggi'are vi (calcio) practise ball control; Tennis knock up

pal'leggio nm Sport warm-up

'pallet nm inv pallet

pallet'toni nmpl buckshot

pallia'tivo nm palliative

ℰ **'pallido** adj pale; **non ne ho la più pallida idea** I don't have the faintest or foggiest idea

pal'lina nf (di vetro) marble

pal'lino nm **avere il ~ del calcio** be crazy about football, be football crazy

pallon'cino nm balloon; (lanterna) Chinese lantern; fam (etilometro) Breathalyzer®

pal'lone nm ball; (calcio) football; (aerostato) balloon; **essere/andare nel ~** be/become confused
■ **pallone da calcio** football; **pallone gonfiato: è un ~ gonfiato** he's so puffed-up; **pallone sonda** weather balloon

pallo'netto nm lob

pal'lore nm pallor

pal'loso adj sl boring

pal'lottola nf pellet; (proiettile) bullet
■ **pallottola dum-dum** dumdum bullet

pallottoli'ere nm abacus

'palma nf Bot palm
■ **palma da cocco** coconut palm; **palma da datteri** date palm

palmarès nm inv (di festival) award winners pl; fig (i migliori) top names pl

pal'mato adj ‹piede› webbed

pal'mento nm **mangiava a quattro palmenti** he was really tucking in

pal'meto nm palm grove

palmi'pede nm web-footed animal

'palmo nm Anat palm; (misura) hand's breadth; **restare con un ~ di naso** feel disappointed

'palo nm pole; (di sostegno) stake; (in calcio) goalpost; **fare il ~** ‹ladro› keep a lookout

■ **palo d'arrivo** (in ippica) finishing post; **palo della luce** lamppost; **palo di partenza** (in ippica) starting post

palom'baro nm diver

pa'lombo nm dogfish

pal'pare vt feel

pal'pata nf **dare una ~ a qualcosa** give something a feel

'palpebra nf eyelid

palpeggi'are vt feel

palpi'tare vi throb; (fremere) quiver

palpitazi'one nf palpitation; **avere le palpitazioni** have palpitations

'palpito nm throb; (del cuore) beat

paltò nm inv overcoat

pa'lude nf marsh, swamp

palu'doso adj marshy

pa'lustre adj marshy; ‹piante, uccelli› marsh attrib

'pampas nfpl pampas

'pamphlet nm inv pamphlet

pamphlet'tista nmf pamphleteer

'pampino nm vine leaf

pan nm ▶ PANE

pana'cea nf panacea

pa'nache nm inv far **~** (in ippica) fall

'Panama nm Panama; **il canale di ~** the Panama Canal

'panca nf bench; (in chiesa) pew

pancarré nm sliced bread

pan'cetta nf Culin bacon; (ciccia) paunch
■ **pancetta affumicata** smoked bacon

pan'chetto nm [foot]stool

pan'china nf garden seat; (in calcio) bench

ℰ **'pancia** nf belly, tummy fam; (di bottiglia, vaso) body; **di pancia** fam gut-level; **mal di pancia** stomach-ache; **a ~ piena/vuota** on a full/empty stomach; **metter su ~** develop a paunch; **a ~ in giù** lying face down

panci'ata nf **prendere una ~** (in tuffo) do a belly flop

panci'era nf corset

panci'olle:, in panciolle adv **stare in ~** lounge about

panci'one nm (persona) pot belly

panci'otto nm waistcoat

panci'uto adj potbellied

'pancreas nm inv pancreas

pancre'atico adj pancreatic

'panda nm inv panda

pande'monio nm pandemonium

pan'dolce nm Christmas cake similar to panettone

pan'doro nm kind of sponge cake traditionally eaten at Christmas time

ℰ **'pane** nm bread; (pagnotta) loaf; (di burro) block
■ **pane casereccio** home-made bread; **pane a cassetta** sliced bread; **pan grattato**

ℰ indicates a very frequent word

breadcrumbs *pl*; **pane integrale** wholemeal bread, granary bread; **pane nero** blackbread; **pane di segale** rye bread; **pan di Spagna** sponge cake; **pane tostato** toast

'**panel** *nm inv* (gruppo) panel

panette'ria *nf* bakery; (negozio) baker's [shop]

panetti'ere, -a *nmf* baker

panet'tone *nm dome-shaped cake with sultanas and candied fruit eaten at Christmas*

'**panfilo** *nm* yacht

pan'forte *nm nougat-like spicy delicacy from Siena*

'**panico** *nm* panic; **farsi prendere dal ∼** panic

pani'ere *nm* basket; (cesta) hamper

pani'ficio *nm* bakery; (negozio) baker's [shop]

pani'naro, -a *nmf* preppie

pa'nino *nm* [bread] roll
■ **panino imbottito** filled roll; **panino al prosciutto** ham roll

panino'teca *nf* sandwich bar

'**panna** *nf* cream
■ **panna cotta** *kind of creme caramel*; **panna da cucina** [single] cream; **panna montata** whipped cream

'**panne** *nf inv* Mech; **in panne** broken down; **restare in ∼** break down

panneggi'ato *adj* draped

pan'neggio *nm* drapery

pan'nello *nm* panel
■ **pannello di controllo** control panel; **pannello solare** solar panel

'**panno** *nm* cloth; (di tavolo da gioco) baize; **panni** *pl* (abiti) clothes; **mettersi nei panni di qualcuno** fig put oneself in somebody's shoes

pan'nocchia *nf* (di granturco) cob

panno'lenci® *nm inv* brightly coloured felt

panno'lino *nm* (per bambini) nappy; (da donna) sanitary towel

pano'rama *nm* panorama; fig overview

pano'ramica *nf* (rassegna) overview

pano'ramico *adj* panoramic

panpe'pato *nm type of gingerbread*

pantacol'lant *nmpl* leggings

pantagru'elico *adj* ‹pranzo› gargantuan

pantalon'cini *nmpl* shorts
■ **pantaloncini da ciclista** cycling shorts; **pantaloncini corti** shorts

panta'loni *nmpl* trousers, pants Am
■ **pantaloni da sci** ski pants; **pantaloni della tuta** sweat pants; **pantaloni a tubo** drain-pipe trousers; **pantaloni a zampa d'elefante** bell-bottoms, flares

pan'tano *nm* bog

panta'noso *adj* marshy

pan'tera *nf* panther; (auto della polizia) high-speed police car
■ **pantera nera** black panther

pan'tofola *nf* slipper

pantofo'laio, -a *nmf* fig stay-at-home

panto'mima *nf* pantomime; fig act

pan'zana *nf* fib

'**panzer** *nm inv* Mil tank

pao'nazzo *adj* purple

✎ '**papa** *nm* Pope; **a ogni morte di ∼** fig once in a blue moon

✎ **papà** *nm inv* dad[dy]

pa'paia *nf* pawpaw, papaya

pa'pale *adj* papal

papa'lina *nf* skull-cap

papa'razzo *nm* paparazzo

pa'pato *nm* papacy

pa'pavero *nm* poppy

'**papera** *nf* (errore) slip of the tongue

'**papero** *nm* gosling

papi *nm* fam daddy

pa'pilla *nf*
■ **papilla gustativa** taste bud

papil'lon *nm inv* bow tie

pa'piro *nm* papyrus

'**pappa** *nf* (per bambini) baby food; **trovare la ∼ pronta** fig have everything ready and waiting

pappagal'lino *nm* budgerigar, budgie

pappa'gallo *nm* parrot

pappa'gorgia *nf* double chin

pappa'molle *nmf* wimp

pappar'delle *nfpl strips of pasta with a meat sauce*

pap'parsi *vr* fam tuck away

pap'pone *nm* sl (mangione) pig; (sfruttatore) pimp

'**paprica** *nf* paprika

Pap test *nm inv* smear test, cervical smear

'**Papua 'Nuova Gui'nea** *nf* Papua New Guinea

'**para** *nf* **suole di ∼** crepe soles

parà *nm inv* para

pa'rabola *nf* parable; (curva) parabola

para'bolico *adj* parabolic

para'brezza *nm inv* windscreen, windshield Am

paracadu'tare *vt* parachute

paracadu'tarsi *vr* parachute

paraca'dute *nm inv* parachute

paracadu'tismo *nm* parachuting
■ **paracadutismo ascensionale** parascending

paracadu'tista *nmf* parachutist

para'carro *nm* roadside post

para'digma *nm* Gram paradigm

paradi'siaco *adj* heavenly

para'diso *nm* paradise

···⊱

■ **paradiso fiscale** tax haven; **paradiso terrestre** Eden, earthly paradise

parados'sale *adj* paradoxical

para'dosso *nm* paradox

para'fango *nm* mudguard

parafarma'cia *nf* over-the-counter products

paraf'fina *nf* paraffin

parafra'sare *vt* paraphrase

pa'rafrasi *nf inv* paraphrase

para'fulmine *nm* lightning conductor

para'fuoco *nm inv* fireguard

pa'raggi *nmpl* neighbourhood *sg*

parago'nabile *adj* comparable (**a** to)

parago'nare *vt* compare

parago'narsi *vr* compare oneself

para'gone *nm* comparison; **a ~ di** in comparison with; **non c'è ~!** there's no comparison!

paragra'fare *vt* paragraph

pa'ragrafo *nm* paragraph

paraguai'ano, -a *adj & nmf* Paraguayan

Paragu'ay *nm* Paraguay

pa'ralisi *nf inv* paralysis

para'litico, -a *adj & nmf* paralytic

paraliz'zante *adj* crippling

paraliz'zare *vt* paralyse

paraliz'zato *adj* (dalla paura) transfixed

paral'lela *nf* parallel line; **è una ~ di…** ‹strada› it runs parallel to…; **parallele** *pl* parallel bars

parallela'mente *adv* in parallel

paralle'lismo *nm* parallelism

paral'lelo *adj & nm* parallel; **fare un ~ tra** draw a parallel between

parallelo'gramma *nm* parallelogram

para'lume *nm* lampshade

para'medico *nm* paramedic

para'mento *nm* hangings *pl*

pa'rametro *nm* parameter

paramili'tare *adj* paramilitary

pa'ranco *nm* block and tackle

para'noia *nf* paranoia

para'noico, -a *adj & nmf* paranoid

paranor'male *adj & nm* paranormal

para'occhi *nmpl* blinkers

parao'recchie *nm* earmuffs

parapen'dio *nm* paragliding

para'petto *nm* parapet

para'piglia *nm* turmoil

para'plegico, -a *adj & nmf* paraplegic

pa'rare ① *vt* (addobbare) adorn; (riparare) shield; save ‹tiro, pallone›; ward off, parry ‹schiaffo, pugno›
② *vi* (mirare) lead up to

pa'rarsi *vr* (abbigliarsi) dress up; (da pioggia, pugni) protect oneself; **~ dinanzi a qualcuno** appear in front of somebody

parasco'lastico *adj* ‹attività› extracurricular

para'sole *nm inv* parasol

paras'sita ① *adj* parasitic
② *nm* parasite

parassi'tario *adj* anche fig parasitic

parassi'tismo *nm* parasitism

parasta'tale *adj* government-controlled

para'stinchi *nm inv* shinpad, shinguard

pa'rata *nf* parade; (in calcio) save; (in scherma, pugilato) parry
■ **parata aerea** flypast

para'tia *nf* bulkhead

parauniversi'tario *adj* at university level

para'urti *nm inv* Auto bumper, fender Am
■ **paraurti** *pl* **tubolari rigidi** bull bars

para'vento *nm* screen

par'boiled *adj* **riso ~** parboiled rice

par'cella *nf* bill

parcheggi'are *vt* anche fig park; **~ in doppia fila** double-park

parcheggia|'tore, -trice *nmf* parking attendant
■ **parcheggiatore abusivo** *person who illegally earns money by looking after parked cars*

par'cheggio *nm* parking; (posteggio) car park, parking lot Am
■ **parcheggio carta** Comput paper park; **parcheggio custodito** car park with attendant; **parcheggio incustodito** unattended car park; **parcheggio a pagamento** paying car park; **parcheggio sotterraneo** underground car park, underground parking garage Am

par'chimetro *nm* parking meter

'parco¹ *adj* sparing; (moderato) moderate; **essere ~ nel mangiare** eat sparingly

⚷ **'parco²** *nm* park
■ **parco di divertimenti** fun fair; **parco giochi** playground; **parco macchine** Auto fleet of cars; **parco naturale** wildlife park; **parco nazionale** national park; **parco regionale** [regional] wildlife park

par'cometro *nm* (pay-and-display) ticket machine

⚷ **pa'recchio** ① *adj* quite a lot of; **parecchi** *pl* several, quite a lot of
② *pron* quite a lot; **parecchi** *pl* several, quite a lot
③ *adv* rather; (parecchio tempo) quite a time

pareggi'are ① *vt* level; (eguagliare) equal; Comm balance; **~ il bilancio** balance the scales
② *vi* draw; **hanno pareggiato nel secondo tempo** they equalized in the second half

---

⚷ indicates a very frequent word

pa'reggio *nm* Comm balance; Sport draw; **il gol del** ~ the equalizer

paren'tado *nm* relatives *pl*; (vincolo di sangue) relationship

⚹ **pa'rente** *nmf* relative, relation
- **parente acquisito** relation by marriage; **parente alla lontana** distant relation; **parente stretto** close relation

paren'tela *nf* relatives *pl*; (vincolo di sangue) relationship; **grado di parentela** degree of kinship

pa'rentesi *nf inv* parenthesis; (segno grafico) bracket; fig (pausa) break; **aprire una** ~ fig digress; ~ *pl* **graffe** curly brackets; ~ *pl* **quadre** square brackets; **tra** ~ **quadre** in square brackets; ~ *pl* **tonde** round brackets; **fra** ~,... (a proposito) by the way,...

pa'reo *nm* (copricostume) sarong; **a** ~ ‹gonna› wrap-around

pa'rere¹ *nm* opinion; **a mio** ~ in my opinion; **essere del** ~ **che** be of the opinion that

⚹ **pa'rere²** *vi* seem; (pensare) think; **che te ne pare?** what do you think of it?; **pare di sì** it seems so; **mi pare che...** I think that...; **non mi par vero** I can't believe it; **mi pareva bene!** I thought as much!

⚹ **pa'rete** *nf* wall; (in alpinismo) face
- **parete divisoria** partition wall

'pargolo *nf* (liter) child

⚹ **'pari** ① *adj inv* equal; ‹numero› even; **andare di** ~ **passo** keep pace; **essere** ~ be even *or* quits; **arrivare** ~ draw; ~ ~ ‹copiare, ripetere› word for word; **fare** ~ **o dispari** toss a coin
② *nmf inv* equal, peer; **ragazza alla** ~ au pair [girl]; **lavorare alla** ~ work [as an] au pair; **mettersi in** ~ **con qualcosa** catch up with something
③ *nm* (titolo nobiliare) peer

'paria *nm inv* pariah

parifi'cato *adj* ‹scuola› state-recognized

Pa'rigi *nf* Paris

pari'gino, -a *adj & nmf* Parisian

pa'riglia *nf* pair; **rendere la** ~ **a qualcuno** give somebody tit for tat

parità *nf* equality; Tennis deuce; **a** ~ **di condizioni/voti** if all circumstances/the votes are equal; **finire in** ~ ‹partita› end in a draw
- **parità dei diritti** equal rights; **parità monetaria** monetary parity; **parità dei sessi** sexual equality, equality of the sexes

pari'tario *adj* parity *attrib*

'parka *nm inv* parka

parlamen'tare ① *adj* parliamentary
② *nmf* Member of Parliament
③ *vi* negotiate

parla'mento *nm* Parliament; **il Parlamento europeo** the European Parliament

par'lante *adj* ‹bambola, pappagallo› talking

parlan'tina *nf* **avere la** ~ be a chatterbox

⚹ **par'lare** *vt/i* speak, talk; speak ‹inglese, italiano›; (confessare) talk; ~ **bene/male di qualcuno** speak well/ill of somebody; ~ **da solo** speak to oneself; **chi parla?** Teleph who's speaking?; **senti chi parla!** look who's talking!; **non parliamone più** let's forget about it; **non se ne parla memmeno!** don't even mention it!; ~ **a braccio** speak off the top of one's head; **far** ~ **qualcuno** make somebody talk

par'lato *adj* ‹lingua› spoken

parla|'tore, -trice *nmf* speaker

parla'torio *nm* parlour; (in prigione) visiting room

parlot'tare *vi* mutter

parlot'tio *nm* muttering

parlucchi'are *vt* speak a little, have a smattering of ‹lingua›

parmigi'ano *nm* Parmesan

paro'dia *nf* parody, send up; **fare la** ~ **di qualcuno** take somebody off

parodi'are *vt* parody, mimic

paro'distico *adj* ‹tono› parodying; **programma parodistico** take-off show

⚹ **pa'rola** *nf* word; (facoltà) speech; **è una** ~! it is easier said than done!; **parole** *pl* (di canzone) words, lyrics; **rivolgere la** ~ **a** address; **passare** ~ spread the word; **non fare** ~ **di qualcosa con nessuno** not breathe a word of something to anybody; **ti credo sulla** ~ I'll take your word for it; **togliere la** ~ **di bocca a qualcuno** take the words [right] out of somebody's mouth; **voler sempre l'ultima** ~ always want to have the last word; **dire due parole a qualcuno** have a word *or* chat with somebody; **di poche parole** ‹persona› of few words; **dare a qualcuno la propria** ~ give somebody one's word; ~ **per** ~ word for word; **in parole povere** crudely speaking
- **parola chiave** *inv* keyword; **parole** *pl* **incrociate** crossword [puzzle]; **parola di moda** buzzword; **parola d'onore** word of honour; **parola d'ordine** password

paro'laccia *nf* swearword

paro'liere *nm* lyricist

paro'lina *nf* **dire due paroline a qualcuno** have a word *or* chat with somebody

paro'loni *nmpl* mumbo jumbo

paros'sismo *nm* paroxysm

paros'sistico *adj* Med paroxysmal

par'quet *nm inv* (pavimento) parquet flooring

parri'cida *nmf* parricide

parri'cidio *nm* parricide

par'rocchia *nf* parish

parrocchi'ale *adj* parish *attrib*

parrocchi'ano, -a *nmf* parishioner

'parroco *nm* parish priest

par'rucca *nf* wig

parrucchi'ere, **-a** *nmf* hairdresser

parruc'chino *nm* toupée, hairpiece

parsi'monia *nf* thrift

parsimoni'oso *adj* thrifty

'parso *pp di* PARERE²

✧ **'parte** *nf* part; (lato) side; (partito) party; (porzione) share; (fazione) group; **a ∼** apart from; **in ∼** in part; **la maggior ∼ di** the majority of; **d'altra ∼** on the other hand; **da ∼** aside; (in disparte) to one side; **farsi da ∼** stand aside; **da ∼ di** from; (per conto di) on behalf of; **è gentile da ∼ tua** it is kind of you; **fare una brutta ∼ a qualcuno** behave badly towards somebody; **da che ∼ è...?** whereabouts is...?; **da una parte..., dall'altra...** on the one hand..., on the other hand...; **dall'altra ∼ di** on the other side of; **da nessuna ∼** nowhere; **da qualche ∼** somewhere; **da qualche altra ∼** somewhere else, elsewhere; **da tutte le parti** (essere) everywhere; **da questa ∼** (in questa direzione) this way; **da queste parti** hereabouts; **da un anno a questa ∼** for about a year now; **mettere qualcosa da ∼** put something aside; **essere dalla ∼ di qualcuno** be on somebody's side; **prendere le parti di qualcuno** take somebody's side; **dalla ∼ della ragione/del torto** in the right/ the wrong; **essere ∼ in causa** be involved; **fare ∼ di** (appartenere a) be a member of; **fare la propria ∼** do one's share *or* bit; **mettere qualcuno a ∼ di qualcosa** inform somebody of something; **prendere ∼ a qualcosa** take part in something

■ **parte civile** plaintiff; **parte del discorso** part of speech

parteci'pante *nmf* participant

✧ **parteci'pare** *vi* **∼ a** participate in, take part in; (condividere) share in

partecipazi'one *nf* participation; (annuncio) announcement; Fin shareholding; (presenza) presence; **con la ∼ [straordinaria] di...** featuring...

■ **partecipazione statale** (quota) state interest

par'tecipe *adj* participating

parteggi'are *vi* **∼ per** side with

✧ **par'tenza** *nf* departure; Sport start; **in ∼ per** leaving for; **falsa partenza** false start

parti'cella *nf* particle

parti'cina *nf* bit part

parti'cipio *nm* participle

■ **participio passato** past participle; **participio presente** present participle

✧ **partico'lare** ⟨1⟩ *adj* particular; (privato) private; (speciale) special, particular ⟨2⟩ *nm* detail, particular; **fin nei minimi particolari** down to the smallest detail; **in ∼** (particolarmente) in particular

---

✧ indicates a very frequent word

---

particolareggi'ato *adj* detailed

particolarità *nf inv* particularity; (dettaglio) detail

particolar'mente *adv* particularly

✧ **partigi'ano**, **-a** *adj & nmf* partisan

✧ **par'tire** *vi* leave; (aver inizio) start; fam (rompersi) break; **a ∼ da** [beginning] from; **∼ in quarta** go off at half cock; **è partito** fam (ubriaco) he's away

✧ **par'tita** *nf* game; (incontro) match; Comm lot; (contabilità) entry; **dare ∼ vinta a qualcuno** fig give in to somebody

■ **partita amichevole** friendly [match]; **partita di calcio** football match; **partita a carte** game of cards; **partita doppia** Comm double-entry book keeping; **partita di ritorno** Sport return match, rematch; **partita semplice** Comm single-entry book keeping

parti'tario *nm* Comm ledger

■ **partitario vendite** sales ledger

✧ **par'tito** *nm* party; (scelta) choice; (occasione di matrimonio) match; **per ∼ preso** out of sheer pig-headedness

■ **partito di governo** governing party; **partito di maggioranza** majority party; **partito politico** political party

partitocra'zia *nf concentration of power in the hands of political parties to the detriment of parliamentary democracy*

partizi'one *nf* (divisione) division; Comput (di disco) partition

'partner *nmf inv* (in affari, coppia) partner

'parto *nm* childbirth; **un ∼ facile** an easy birth *or* labour; **dolori del ∼** *pl* labour pains; **morire di ∼** die in childbirth

■ **parto cesareo** Caesarean; **parto in acqua** water birth; **parto indolore** natural childbirth; **parto pilotato** induction, induced labour; **parto prematuro** premature birth

partori'ente *nf* woman in labour

parto'rire *vt* anche fig give birth to

part-'time ⟨1⟩ *adj* part-time ⟨2⟩ *nm* **chiedere il ∼** ask to work part-time

pa'rure *nf inv* (di gioielli) set of jewellery; (di biancheria intima) set of matching lingerie

par'venza *nf* appearance

parzi'ale *adj* partial

parzialità *nf inv* partiality; **fare ∼ per qualcuno** be biased towards somebody

parzial'mente *adv* partially; (con parzialità) with bias; **parzialmente cieco** partially sighted; **parzialmente scremato** semi-skimmed

'pascere ⟨1⟩ *vi* ⟨mucche⟩ graze ⟨2⟩ *vt* graze on ⟨erba⟩

pasci'uto *adj* **ben ∼** plump

pasco'lare *vt* graze

'pascolo *nm* pasture

'Pasqua *nf* Easter; **l'isola di Pasqua** Easter Island

pa'squale *adj* Easter *attrib*

pa'squetta *nf* (lunedì di Pasqua) Easter Monday

'passa *adv* e ~ (e oltre) plus

pas'sabile *adj* passable

pas'saggio *nm* passage; (traversata) crossing; Sport pass; (su veicolo) lift, ride; **essere di ~** be passing through; **è stato un ~ obbligato** fig it was something essential, it had to be done

■ **passaggio a livello** level crossing, grade crossing Am; **passaggio pedonale** pedestrian crossing, crosswalk Am; **passaggio di proprietà** transfer of ownership, conveyancy

passamane'ria *nf* braid

passamon'tagna *nm inv* balaclava

pas'sante [1] *nmf* passer-by
[2] *nm* (di cintura) loop
[3] *adj* Tennis passing

passa'porto *nm* anche fig passport
■ **passaporto europeo** European passport, Europassport

pas'sare [1] *vi* pass; (attraversare) pass through; (far visita) call; (andare) go; (essere approvato) be passed; ~ **davanti a qualcuno** go in front of somebody; ~ **alla storia** go down in history; ~ **di moda** go out of fashion; **mi è passato di mente** it slipped my mind; ~ **sopra a qualcosa** pass over something; ~ **per un genio/idiota** be taken for a genius/an idiot; **farsi ~ per qualcuno** pass oneself off as somebody; **passo!** (nelle carte) pass!; (per radio) over!
[2] *vt* (far scorrere) pass over; (sopportare) go through; (al telefono) put through; Culin strain; **pass** ‹*esame, visita*›; ~ **in rivista** review; ~ **qualcosa a qualcuno** pass something to somebody; **le passo il signor Rossi** Teleph I'll put you through to Mr Rossi; ~ **qualcosa su qualcosa** ‹*crema, cera ecc*› give something a coat of something; ~ **il limite** go over the limit; **passarsela bene** be well off; **come te la passi?** how are you doing?
[3] *nm* **col ~ del tempo** with the passing *or* passage of time

pas'sata *nf* (di vernice) coat; (spolverata) dusting; (occhiata) look

passa'tempo *nm* pastime

pas'sato [1] *adj* past; **l'anno ~** last year; **sono le tre passate** it's past *or* after three o'clock
[2] *nm* past; Culin purée; Gram past tense; **in ~** in the past; **la musica del ~** the music of yesteryear
■ **passato di moda** old-fashioned; **passato prossimo** present perfect; **passato remoto** [simple] past; **passato di verdure** cream of vegetable soup

passaver'dure *nm inv* food mill

passavi'vande *nm inv* serving hatch

passeg'gero, -a [1] *adj* passing
[2] *nmf* passenger

■ **passeggero in transito** transit passenger

passeggi'are *vi* walk, stroll

passeg'giata *nf* walk, stroll; (luogo) public walk; (in bicicletta) ride; **fare una ~** go for a walk

passeggia'trice *nf* streetwalker

passeg'gino *nm* pushchair, stroller Am

pas'seggio *nm* walk; (luogo) promenade; **andare a ~** go for a walk; **scarpe da passeggio** walking shoes

passe-par'tout *nm inv* master-key

passe'rella *nf* gangway; Aeron boarding bridge; (per sfilate) catwalk

'passero *nm* sparrow

passe'rotto *nm* (passero) sparrow

pas'sibile *adj* ~ **di** liable to

passio'nale *adj* passionate; **delitto passionale** crime of passion

passi'one *nf* passion; **avere la ~ del gioco** have a passion for gambling

passiva'mente *adv* passively

passività *nf* (inerzia) passiveness, passivity; Fin liabilities *pl*; ~ *pl* **correnti** current liabilities

pas'sivo [1] *adj* passive
[2] *nm* passive; Fin liabilities *pl*; **in ~** ‹*azienda*› in deficit; ‹*bilancio*› debit, in deficit

'passo *nm* step; (orma) footprint; (andatura) pace, step; (di libro) passage; (valico) pass; **a due passi da qui** a stone's throw away; **a ~ d'uomo** at walking pace; **di buon ~** at a spanking pace, at a cracking pace; **a passi felpati** stealthily; **di questo ~** at this rate; ~ ~ step by step; **fare due passi** go for a stroll; **allungare il ~** quicken one's pace, step out; **tornare sui propri passi** retrace one's steps; **fare un ~ avanti** anche fig take a step forward; **fare un ~ falso** fig make a wrong move; **di pari ~** fig hand in hand; **stare al ~ con i tempi** keep up with the times, keep abreast of the times; **tenere il ~** keep up

■ **passo carrabile, passo carraio** driveway; **passo dell'oca** goose-step

'pasta *nf* (impasto per pane ecc) dough; (per dolci, pasticcino) pastry; (pastasciutta) pasta; (massa molle) paste; fig nature; **sono fatti della stessa ~** they're birds of a feather
■ **pasta e fagioli** *very thick soup with blended borlotti beans and small pasta*; **pasta al forno** *pasta baked in white sauce with grated cheese*; **pasta frolla** shortcrust pastry; **pasta al ragù** pasta with Bolognese sauce

pastasci'utta *nf* pasta

pa'stella *nf* batter

pa'stello *nm* pastel

pa'sticca *nf* pastille; fam (pastiglia) pill

pasticce'ria *nf* cake shop, patisserie; (pasticcini) pastries *pl*; (arte) confectionery

pasticci'are [1] *vi* make a mess
[2] *vt* make a mess of

pasticci'ere, **-a** *nmf* confectioner

pastic'cino *nm* little cake

pa'sticcio *nm* Culin pie; (lavoro disordinato) mess; **mettersi nei pasticci** get into trouble

pasticci'one, **-a** ① *nmf* bungler ② *adj* bungling

pasti'ficio *nm* pasta factory

pa'stiglia *nf* Med pill, tablet; (di menta) sweet

■ **pastiglia dei freni** Auto brake pad; **pastiglia per la gola** throat pastille; **pastiglia per la tosse** cough sweet

pa'stina *nf* small pasta shape

■ **pastina in brodo** noodle soup

'pasto *nm* meal; **fuori** ~ between meals; **dare qualcosa in** ~ **a** fig serve something up on a platter to ⟨pubblico, stampa⟩

■ **pasto pronto** TV dinner

pa'stora *nf* shepherdess

pasto'rale *adj* pastoral

⚘ **pa'store** *nm* shepherd; Relig pastor, vicar

■ **pastore scozzese** collie; **pastore tedesco** German shepherd, Alsatian

pasto'rizio *adj* sheep farming *attrib*

pastoriz'zare *vt* pasteurize

pastoriz'zato *adj* pasteurized

pastorizzazi'one *nf* pasteurization

pa'stoso *adj* doughy; fig mellow

pa'strocchio *nm* mess

pa'stura *nf* pasture; (per pesci) bait

pa'tacca *nf* (macchia) stain; fig (oggetto senza valore) piece of junk

pa'tata *nf* potato

■ **patata americana** sweet potato; **patate** *pl* **arrosto** roast potatoes; **patate** *pl* **al cartoccio** jacket potatoes; **patate** *pl* **fritte** chips Br, French fries; **patate** *pl* **in insalata** potato salad; **patate** *pl* **lesse** boiled potatoes

pata'tine *nfpl* [potato] crisps, [potato] chips Am

pata'trac *nm inv* (crollo) crash

patch'work *nm inv* patchwork

pâté *nm inv* pâté

■ **pâté di fegato** liver pâté

pa'tella *nf* limpet

pa'tema *nm* anxiety

pa'tente *nf* licence; **prendere la** ~ get one's driving licence

■ **patente di guida** driving licence, driver's license Am

pater'nale *nf* scolding

paterna'lismo *nm* paternalism

paterna'lista *nm* paternalist

paterna'listico *adj* paternalistic

paternità *nf inv* paternity

pa'terno *adj* paternal; ⟨affetto ecc⟩ fatherly

pa'tetico *adj* pathetic; **cadere nel** ~ become over-sentimental

'pathos *nm* pathos

pa'tibolo *nm* gallows *sg*

pati'mento *nm* suffering

'patina *nf* patina; (sulla lingua) coating

'patio *nm* patio garden

⚘ **pa'tire** *vt/i* suffer

pa'tito, **-a** ① *adj* suffering ② *nmf* fanatic

■ **patito della musica** music lover

patolo'gia *nf* pathology

■ **patologia da radiazioni** radiation sickness; **patologia da sforzo ripetuto** repetitive strain injury, RSI

pato'logico *adj* pathological

pa'tologo, **-a** *nmf* pathologist

⚘ **'patria** *nf* native land; **amor di** ~ love of one's country

patri'arca *nm* patriarch

patriar'cale *adj* patriarchal

patriar'cato *nm* patriarchy

pa'trigno *nm* stepfather

patrimoni'ale *adj* property *attrib*

patri'monio *nm* estate

patri'ota *nmf* patriot

patri'ottico *adj* patriotic

patriot'tismo *nm* patriotism

pa'trizio, **-a** *adj* & *nmf* patrician

patroci'nante *adj* sponsoring

patroci'nare *vt* support

patro'cinio *nm* support; **sotto il** ~ **di** under the sponsorship of; Jur defended by

■ **patrocinio gratuito** legal aid

patro'nato *nm* patronage

pa'trono *nm* Relig patron saint; Jur counsel

'patta¹ *nf* (di tasca) flap

'patta² *nf* (pareggio) draw

patteggia'mento *nm* bargaining

patteggi'are *vt/i* negotiate

patti'naggio *nm* skating

■ **pattinaggio artistico** figure skating; **pattinaggio su ghiaccio** ice skating; **pattinaggio a rotelle** roller-skating

patti'nare *vi* skate; (auto) skid

pattina|'tore, **-trice** *nmf* skater

'pattino *nm* skate; Aeron skid

■ **pattino da ghiaccio** ice skate; **pattino a rotelle** roller skate

⚘ **'patto** *nm* deal; Pol pact; **a** ~ **che** on condition that; **scendere a patti**, **venire a patti** reach a compromise

pat'tuglia *nf* patrol; **essere di** ~ be on patrol

■ **pattuglia stradale** highway patrol Am, ≈ patrol car; police motorbike

pattu'ire *vt* negotiate

pat'tume *nm* rubbish

pattumi'era *nf* dustbin, trashcan Am

⚘ **pa'ura** *nf* fear; (spavento) fright; **aver** ~ be afraid; **mettere** ~ **a** frighten; **per** ~ **di** for fear of; **da** ~ sl (libro, film) brilliant

---

⚘ indicates a very frequent word

pau'roso *adj* (che fa paura) frightening; (che ha paura) fearful; fam (enorme) awesome

'pausa *nf* pause; (nel lavoro) break; **fare una ~** pause; (nel lavoro) have a break
■ **pausa [per il] caffè** coffee break; **pausa [per il] pranzo** lunchbreak, lunch hour

pavida'mente *adv* timidly

'pavido ①️ *adj* cowardly
②️ *nm* coward

pavimen'tare *vt* pave ‹strada›

pavimentazi'one *nf* paving

pavi'mento *nm* floor

pa'vone *nm* peacock

pavoneggi'arsi *vr* strut

pay tv *nf inv* pay TV

pazien'tare *vi* be patient

pazi'ente *adj & nmf* patient

paziente'mente *adv* patiently

✂ **pazi'enza** *nf* patience; **~!** never mind!; **perdere la ~** lose one's patience

'pazza *nf* madwoman

pazza'mente *adv* madly

pazzerel'lone, -a *nmf* madcap

paz'zesco *adj* foolish; (esagerato) crazy

paz'zia *nf* madness; (azione) [act of] folly

✂ **'pazzo** ①️ *adj* mad; fig crazy; **sei ~?** you must be crazy!, are you crazy? **essere ~ di/per** be crazy about; **~ di gioia** mad with joy; **da pazzi** fam crackpot; **darsi alla pazza gioia** live it up
②️ *nm* madman

paz'zoide *adj* fam whacky

P.C.I. *nm abbr* (**Partito Comunista Italiano**) Italian Communist Party

PD, pd *nm abbr* (**Partito Democratico**) Democratic Party

PdL *nm abbr* (**Popolo della Libertà**) *Italian political party*

'pecan *nm inv* pecan

'pecca *nf* fault; **senza ~** flawless

peccami'noso *adj* sinful

pec'care *vi* sin; **~ di** be guilty of ‹ingratitudine›

✂ **pec'cato** *nm* sin; **~ che...** it's a pity that...; **[che] ~!** [what a] pity!
■ **peccato di gioventù** youthful folly

pecca|'tore, -trice *nmf* sinner

'pece *nf* pitch; **nero come la ~** black as pitch

pechi'nese *nm* Pekin[g]ese

Pe'chino *nf* Peking

'pecora *nf* sheep
■ **pecora nera** black sheep

peco'raio *nm* shepherd

peco'rella *nf* **cielo a pecorelle** sky full of fluffy white clouds
■ **pecorella smarrita** lost sheep

peco'rino *nm* (formaggio) sheep's milk cheese

peculi'are *adj* **~ di** peculiar to

peculiarità *nf inv* peculiarity

pecuni'ario *adj* money *attrib*

pe'daggio *nm* toll

pedago'gia *nf* pedagogy

peda'gogico *adj* pedagogical

peda'gogo, -a *nmf* pedagogue

peda'lare *vi* pedal

peda'lata *nf* push on the pedals

pe'dale *nm* pedal
■ **pedale dell'acceleratore** gas pedal; **pedale del freno** brake pedal

pedalò *nm inv* pedalo

pe'dana *nf* footrest; Sport springboard

pe'dante *adj* pedantic

pedante'ria *nf* pedantry

pedan'tesco *adj* pedantic

pe'data *nf* (calcio) kick; (impronta) footprint

pede'rasta *nm* pederast

pe'destre *adj* pedestrian

pedi'atra *nmf* paediatrician

pedia'tria *nf* paediatrics *sg*

pedi'atrico *adj* paediatric

pedi'cure ①️ *nmf inv* chiropodist, podiatrist Am
②️ *nm* (cura dei piedi) pedicure

pedi'gree *nm inv* pedigree

pedi'luvio *nm* footbath

pe'dina *nf* (alla dama) piece; fig pawn

pedina'mento *nm* shadowing

pedi'nare *vt* shadow

pedofi'lia *nf* paedophilia

pe'dofilo, -a *nmf* paedophile

pedo'nale *adj* pedestrian

pe'done, -a *nmf* pedestrian

'pedule *nf pl* hiking boots

'peeling *nm inv* exfoliation treatment

✂ **'peggio** ①️ *adv* worse; **~ per te!** too bad!, tough!; **tanto ~** too bad; **~ di così** any worse; **la persona ~ vestita** the worst dressed person
②️ *adj* worse; **niente di ~** nothing worse; **stare ~** di be worse off than
③️ *nm* **il ~ è che...** the worst of it is that...; **pensare al ~** think the worst
④️ *nf* **alla ~** at worst; **avere la ~** get the worst of it; **alla meno ~** as best I can

peggiora'mento *nm* worsening

peggio'rare ①️ *vt* make worse, worsen
②️ *vi* get worse, worsen

peggiora'tivo *adj* pejorative

peggi'ore ①️ *adj* worse; (superlativo) worst; **nella ~ delle ipotesi** if the worst comes to the worst
②️ *nmf* **il/la ~** the worst

'pegno *nm* pledge; (nei giochi di società) forfeit; fig token; **dare qualcosa in ~** pawn something; **in ~ d'amicizia** as a token of friendship

pelan'drone *nm* slob

p

pe'lare *vt* (spennare) pluck; (spellare) skin; (sbucciare) peel; fam (spillare denaro) fleece

pe'larsi *vr* fam lose one's hair

pe'lati *nmpl* (pomodori) peeled tomatoes

pe'lato *adj* (calvo) bald

pel'lame *nm* skins *pl*

✧ **'pelle** *nf* skin; (cuoio) leather; (buccia) peel; **avere la ~ d'oca** have goose-flesh; **non stare più nella ~** be beside oneself; **salvare la ~** save one's skin; **lasciarci la ~** buy it; **essere ~ e ossa** be all skin and bones; **avere la ~ dura** be tough; **borsa di pelle** leather bag
■ **pelle scamosciata** suede

pellegri'naggio *nm* pilgrimage

pelle'grino, -a *nmf* pilgrim

pelle'rossa *nmf* Red Indian, Redskin

pellette'ria *nf* leather goods *pl*

pelli'cano *nm* pelican

pellicce'ria *nf* furrier's [shop]

pel'liccia *nf* fur; (indumento) fur [coat]

pellicci'aio, -a *nmf* furrier

pel'licola *nf* Phot, Cinema film
■ **pellicola a colori** colour film; **pellicola trasparente** Culin cling film

✧ **'pelo** *nm* hair; (di animale) coat; (di lana) pile; **per un ~** by the skin of one's teeth; **cavarsela per un ~** have a narrow escape; **cercare il ~ nell'uovo** nitpick

pe'loso *adj* hairy

'peltro *nm* pewter

pe'luche *nm*
■ **giocattolo di peluche** soft toy; **orsetto di peluche** teddy bear

pe'luria *nf* down

'pelvico *adj* pelvic

✧ **'pena** *nf* (punizione) punishment; (sofferenza) pain; (dispiacere) sorrow; (disturbo) trouble; **a mala ~** hardly; **mi fa ~** I pity him; **vale la ~ andare** it is worth [while] going; **pene** *pl* **dell'inferno** hellfire
■ **pena di morte** death sentence

pe'nale *adj* criminal; **diritto penale** criminal law

pena'lista *nmf* criminal lawyer

penalità *nf inv* penalty

penaliz'zare *vt* penalize

penalizzazi'one *nf* (penalità) penalty

pe'nare *vi* suffer; (faticare) find it difficult

pen'daglio *nm* pendant

pen'dant *nm inv* **fare ~ [con]** match

pen'dente [1] *adj* hanging; Comm outstanding
[2] *nm* (ciondolo) pendant; **pendenti** *pl* drop earrings

pen'denza *nf* slope; Comm outstanding account

'pendere *vi* hang; (superficie) slope; (essere inclinato) lean

pen'dio *nm* slope; **in ~** sloping

'pendola *nf* grandfather clock

pendo'lare [1] *adj* pendulum
[2] *nmf* commuter

pendo'lino *nm* (treno) *special, first class only, fast train*

'pendolo *nm* pendulum; **orologio a pendolo** grandfather clock

'pene *nm* penis

pene'trante *adj* penetrating; (freddo) biting

pene'trare [1] *vt/i* penetrate; (trafiggere) pierce
[2] *vt* (odore) get into
[3] *vi* (entrare furtivamente) steal in

penetrazi'one *nf* penetration

penicil'lina *nf* penicillin

pe'nisola *nf* peninsula

peni'tente *adj & nmf* penitent

peni'tenza *nf* penitence; (punizione) penance; (in gioco) forfeit

penitenzi'ario *nm* penitentiary

'penna *nf* (da scrivere) pen; (di uccello) feather
■ **penna a feltro** felt-tip[ped pen]; **penna ottica** light pen; **penna a sfera** ball-point [pen]; **penna stilografica** fountain-pen; **penna USB** pendrive

pen'nacchio *nm* plume

penna'rello *nm* felt-tip[ped pen]

'penne *nfpl* pasta quills

pennel'lare *vt* paint

pennel'lata *nf* brushstroke

pen'nello *nm* brush; **a ~** (a perfezione) perfectly
■ **~ da barba** shaving brush

pen'nino *nm* nib

pen'none *nm* (di bandiera) flagpole

pen'nuto *adj* feathered

pe'nombra *nf* half-light

pe'noso *adj* fam (pessimo) painful

pen'sabile *adj* **non è ~** it's unthinkable

✧ **pen'sare** [1] *vi* think; **penso di sì** I think so; **~ a** think of; remember to (chiudere il gas ecc); **pensa ai fatti tuoi!** mind your own business!; **ci penso io** I'll take care of it; **~ di fare qualcosa** think of doing something; **a pensarci bene** on second thoughts; **~ tra sé e sé** think to oneself; **pensarci su** think it over
[2] *vt* think

pen'sata *nf* idea

pensa|'tore, -trice *nmf* thinker

✧ **pensi'ero** *nm* thought; (mente) mind; (preoccupazione) worry; **stare in ~ per** be anxious about; **levarsi il ~** to get something out of the way

pensie'roso *adj* pensive

'pensile [1] *adj* hanging; **giardino pensile** roof-garden
[2] *nm* (mobile) wall unit

✧ indicates a very frequent word

pensi'lina *nf* (di fermata d'autobus) bus shelter

pensio'nante *nmf* boarder; (ospite pagante) lodger

pensio'nato, -a [1] *nmf* pensioner [2] *nm* (per anziani) [old folks'] home; (per studenti) hostel

⚘ **pensi'one** *nf* pension; (albergo) boarding house; (vitto e alloggio) board and lodging; (da lavoro) retirement; **andare in** ∼ retire; **essere in** ∼ be retired; **mezza pensione** half board
 ■ **pensione di anzianità** old-age pension; **pensione completa** full board; **pensione di invalidità** disability pension

pen'soso *adj* pensive

pen'tagono *nm* pentagon; **il Pentagono** the Pentagon

pen'tathlon *nm inv* pentathlon

Pente'coste *nf* Whitsun, Whit Sunday

penti'mento *nm* repentance

pen'tirsi *vr* ∼ **di** repent of; (rammaricarsi) regret

penti'tismo *nm* turning informant

pen'tito *nm* terrorist or Mafioso turned informant

'pentola *nf* saucepan; (contenuto) potful
 ■ **pentola a pressione** pressure cooker

pento'lino *nf* saucepan

pe'nultimo *adj* last but one, penultimate

pe'nuria *nf* shortage

penzo'lare *vi* dangle

penzo'loni *adv* dangling

pe'onia *nf* peony

pepai'ola *nf* pepper pot

pe'pare *vt* pepper

pe'pato *adj* peppery

'pepe *nm* pepper; **grano di pepe** peppercorn
 ■ **pepe di Caienna** cayenne pepper; **pepe in grani** whole peppercorns; **pepe macinato** ground pepper; **pepe nero** black pepper

pepero'nata *nf* dish of peppers and tomatoes

peperon'cino *nm* chilli pepper

pepe'rone *nm* [sweet] pepper; **rosso come un** ∼ red as a beetroot; **peperoni** *pl* **ripieni** stuffed peppers
 ■ **peperone rosso** red pepper; **peperone verde** green pepper

pepi'era *nf* pepper pot; (macinino) pepper mill

pe'pita *nf* nugget

'peptico *adj* peptic

⚘ **'per** *prep* for; (attraverso) through; (stato in luogo) in, on; (distributivo) per; (mezzo, entro) by; (causa) with; (in qualità di) as; **mi è passato per la mente** it crossed my mind; ∼ **strada** on the street; ∼ **la fine del mese** by the end of the month; **in fila** ∼ **due** in double file; **l'ho sentito** ∼ **telefono** I spoke to him on the phone; ∼ **iscritto** in writing; ∼ **caso** by chance; ∼ **esempio** for example; **ho aspettato** ∼ **ore** I've been waiting for hours; ∼ **tutta la durata del viaggio** for the entire journey; ∼ **tempo** in time; ∼ **sempre** forever; ∼ **scherzo** as a joke; **gridare** ∼ **il dolore** scream with pain; **vendere** ∼ **10 milioni** sell for 10 million; **uno** ∼ **volta** one at a time; **uno** ∼ **uno** one by one; **venti** ∼ **cento** twenty per cent; ∼ **fare qualcosa** [in order to] do something; **stare** ∼ be about to; **è troppo bello** ∼ **essere vero** it's too good to be true

'pera *nf* pear; **farsi una** ∼ *sl* (di eroina) shoot up

perbe'nismo *nm* prissiness

perbe'nista *adj inv* prissy

per'calle *nm* gingham

per'cento *adv* per cent

percentu'ale *nf* percentage

perce'pibile *adj* perceivable; (somma) payable

perce'pire *vt* perceive; (riscuotere) cash

percet'tibile *adj* perceptible

percettibil'mente *adv* perceptibly

percezi'one *nf* perception

⚘ **perché** [1] *conj* (in interrogazioni) why; (per il fatto che) because; (affinché) so that; ∼ **non vieni?** why don't you come?; **dimmi** ∼ tell me why; ∼ **no/sì!** because!; **è troppo difficile** ∼ **lo possa capire** it's too difficult for him to understand [2] *nm inv* reason [why]; **senza un** ∼ without any reason

⚘ **perciò** *conj* so

per'correre *vt* cover ‹distanza›; (viaggiare) travel

percor'ribile *adj* (strada) drivable, passable

percorribilità *nf*
 ■ **percorribilità delle strade** road conditions *pl*

per'corso [1] pp di PERCORRERE [2] *nm* (tragitto) course, route; (distanza) distance; (viaggio) journey
 ■ **percorso ecologico** nature trail; **percorso di guerra** assault course; **percorso a ostacoli** obstacle course; **percorso vascolare** cardiovascular circuit

per'cossa *nf* blow; **percosse** *pl* Jur assault and battery

per'cosso pp di PERCUOTERE

percu'otere *vt* strike

percussi'one *nf* percussion; **strumenti a** ∼ percussion instruments

percussio'nista *nmf* percussionist

per'dente *nmf* loser

⚘ **'perdere** [1] *vt* lose; (sprecare) waste; (non prendere) miss; fig (vizio) ruin; ∼ **tempo** waste time; **lascia** ∼! forget it!; ∼ **di vista** lose touch [with each other] [2] *vi* lose; (recipiente) leak; **a** ∼ (vuoto) nonreturnable; **non avere niente da** ∼ have nothing to lose

'perdersi *vr* get lost; (reciproco) lose touch

perdifi'ato: a ∼ *adv* ⟨gridare⟩ at the top of one's voice

perdigi'orno *nmf inv* idler

⚘ **'perdita** *nf* loss; (spreco) waste; (falla) leak; a ∼ **d'occhio** as far as the eye can see; **chiudere in** ∼ (azienda) show a loss
■ **perdita di gas** gas leak; **perdita di sangue** loss of blood, bleeding; **perdita di tempo** waste of time

perdi'tempo *nm* waste of time

perdizi'one *nf* perdition

⚘ **perdo'nare** ① *vt* forgive; (scusare) excuse; **mi perdoni se interrompo** sorry to interrupt, excuse me for interrupting; **per farsi** ∼ as an apology
② *vi* ∼ **a qualcuno** forgive somebody; **un male che non perdona** an incurable disease

per'dono *nm* forgiveness; Jur pardon; **chiedere** ∼ ask for forgiveness; (scusarsi) apologize

perdu'rare *vi* last; (perseverare) persist

perduta'mente *adv* hopelessly

per'duto ① *pp di* PERDERE
② *adj* lost; (rovinato) ruined

pe'renne *adj* everlasting; Bot perennial; **nevi perenni** perpetual snow

perenne'mente *adv* perpetually

peren'torio *adj* peremptory

⚘ **per'fetto** ① *adj* perfect
② *nm* Gram perfect [tense]

perfezio'nare *vt* perfect; (migliorare) improve

perfezio'narsi *vr* improve oneself; (specializzarsi) specialize

perfezi'one *nf* perfection; **alla** ∼ to perfection

perfezio'nismo *nm* perfectionism

perfezio'nista *nmf* perfectionist

per'fidia *nf* wickedness; (atto) wicked act

'perfido *adj* treacherous; (malvagio) perverse

⚘ **per'fino** *adv* even

perfo'rare *vt* pierce; punch ⟨schede⟩; Mech drill

perfora|'tore, -trice *nmf* punch-card operator

perfora'tore *nm* (apparecchio) punch
■ **perforatore di schede** card punch

perforazi'one *nf* perforation; (di schede) punching

per'formance *nf inv* Theat performance

perga'mena *nf* parchment

'pergola *nf* pergola

pergo'lato *nm* bower

periar'trite *nf* rheumatoid arthritis

perico'lante *adj* precarious; ⟨azienda⟩ shaky

⚘ *indicates a very frequent word*

⚘ **pe'ricolo** *nm* danger; (rischio) risk; **mettere in** ∼ endanger; **essere fuori** ∼ be out of danger
■ **pericolo pubblico** danger to society; **pericolo di valanghe** danger of avalanches

pericolosa'mente *adv* dangerously

pericolosità *nf* danger

⚘ **perico'loso** *adj* dangerous

peridu'rale *nf* epidural

perife'ria *nf* periphery; (di città) outskirts *pl*; fig fringes *pl*

peri'ferica *nf* peripheral; ⟨strada⟩ ring road
■ **periferica di input** Comput input device

peri'ferico *adj* peripheral; ⟨quartiere⟩ outlying

pe'rifrasi *nf inv* circumlocution

perime'trale *adj* ⟨muro⟩ perimeter *attrib*

pe'rimetro *nm* perimeter

peri'odico ① *nm* periodical
② *adj* periodical; ⟨vento, mal di testa⟩ Math recurring

⚘ **pe'riodo** *nm* period; Gram sentence
■ **periodo nero** bad patch; **periodo di prova** trial period; **periodo di ripensamento** cooling-off period; **periodo di riposo** breathing space; **periodo di transizione** transitional period, interim; **periodo di validità** period of validity

peripe'zie *nfpl* misadventures

pe'rire *vi* perish

peri'scopio *nm* periscope

pe'rito, -a ① *adj* skilled
② *nmf* expert
■ **perito agrario** agriculturalist; **perito di assicurazione** Comm loss adjuster; **perito edile** chartered surveyor; **perito elettronico** electronics engineer

perito'nite *nf* peritonitis

pe'rizia *nf* skill; (valutazione) survey
■ **perizia medico-legale** forensic tests

peri'zoma *nm inv* loincloth

'perla *nf* pearl
■ **perla coltivata** cultured pearl

per'lina *nf* bead

perli'nato *nm* matchboard

perlo'meno *adv* at least

perlu'strare *vt* patrol

perlustrazi'one *nf* patrol; **andare in** ∼ go on patrol

perma'loso *adj* touchy

perma'nente ① *adj* permanent
② *nf* perm; **farsi [fare] la** ∼ have a perm

perma'nenza *nf* permanence; (soggiorno) stay; **in** ∼ permanently
■ **permanenza in carica** tenure

perma'nere *vi* remain

perme'are *vt* permeate

perme'ato *adj* ∼ **di** fig permeated with

⚘ **per'messo** ① *pp di* PERMETTERE
② *nm* permission; (autorizzazione) permit,

licence; Mil leave; **[è]** ~**?, con** ~ (posso entrare?) may I come in?; (posso passare?) excuse me
■ **permesso di lavoro** work permit; **permesso di soggiorno** residence permit
◆ **per'mettere** *vt* allow, permit; **potersi** ~ **qualcosa** (finanziariamente) be able to afford something
per'mettersi *vr* ~ **di fare qualcosa** allow oneself to do something; **come si permette?** how dare you?
permis'sivo *adj* permissive
permutazi'one *nf* exchange; Math permutation
per'nacchia *nf fam* raspberry fam
per'nice *nf* partridge
pernici'oso *adj* pernicious
'perno *nm* pivot
pernot'tare *vi* stay overnight
'pero *nm* pear-tree
◆ **però** *conj* but; (tuttavia) however
pe'rone *nm* Anat fibula
pero'rare *vt* plead
perpendico'lare *adj & nf* perpendicular
perpe'trare *vt* perpetrate
per'petua *nf* (di prete) priest's housekeeper
perpetu'are *vt* perpetuate
per'petuo *adj* perpetual
perplessità *nf inv* perplexity; (dubbio) doubt
per'plesso *adj* perplexed, puzzled
perqui'sire *vt* search
perquisizi'one *nf* search
■ **perquisizione domiciliare** search of the premises
persecu|'tore, -trice *nmf* persecutor
persecuzi'one *nf* persecution
persegu'ire *vt* pursue
persegui'tare *vt* persecute
persegui'tato, -a *nmf* victim of persecution
perseve'rante *adj* persevering
perseve'ranza *nf* perseverance
perseve'rare *vi* persevere
'Persia *nf* Persia
persi'ana *nf* shutter
■ **persiana avvolgibile** roller shutter
persi'ano, -a *adj & nmf* Persian
'persico *adj* Persian
per'sino = PERFINO
persi'stente *adj* persistent; ‹dubbio› nagging
persi'stenza *nf* persistence
per'sistere *vi* persist; ~ **nel fare qualcosa** persist in doing something
'perso [1] *pp di* PERDERE
[2] *adj* lost; **a tempo** ~ in one's spare time
◆ **per'sona** *nf* person; (un tale) somebody; **di** ~, **in** ~ in person, personally; **per** ~ per

person, a head; **per interposta** ~ through an intermediary; **curare la propria** ~ look after oneself, look after number one; **persone** *pl* people
■ **persona a carico** dependant; **persona di colore** black person; **persona giuridica** legal person; **persona di servizio** domestic
◆ **perso'naggio** *nm* (persona di riguardo) personality; Theat ecc character
◆ **perso'nale** [1] *adj* personal
[2] *nm* staff; (aspetto) build
■ **personale di terra** ground crew
personalità *nf inv* personality
personaliz'zare *vt* customize ‹auto ecc›; personalize ‹penna ecc›
personifi'care *vt* personify
personificazi'one *nf* personification
perspi'cace *adj* shrewd
perspi'cacia *nf* shrewdness
persua'dere *vt* convince; impress ‹critici›; ~ **qualcuno a fare qualcosa** persuade somebody to do something
persuasi'one *nf* persuasion; **fare opera di** ~ **su qualcuno** try to persuade somebody
persuasivltà *nf* persuasiveness
persua'sivo *adj* persuasive
persu'aso *pp di* PERSUADERE
persua'sore *nm* persuader
per'tanto *conj* therefore
'pertica *nf* pole
perti'nace *adj* pertinacious
perti'nente *adj* relevant
per'tosse *nf* whooping cough
per'tugio *nm* opening
pertur'bare *vt* perturb
perturbazi'one *nf* disturbance
■ **perturbazione atmosferica** atmospheric disturbance
Perù *nm* Peru
peruvi'ano, -a *adj & nmf* Peruvian
per'vadere *vt* pervade
perva'sivo *adj* pervasive
per'vaso *pp di* PERVADERE
perven'ire *vi* reach; **far** ~ **qualcosa a qualcuno** send something to somebody
perversa'mente *adv* perversely
perversi'one *nf* perversion
perversità *nf* perversity
per'verso *adj* perverse
perver'tire *vt* pervert
perver'tirsi *vr* (gusti, costumi) become debased
perver'tito [1] *adj* perverted
[2] *nm* pervert
pervi'cace *adj* obstinate
pervicace'mente *adv* obstinately
pervi'cacia *nf* obstinacy
per'vinca¹ *nm* (colore) blue with a touch of purple

per'vinca² *nf* Bot periwinkle

p.es. *abbr* (**per esempio**) e.g.

'pesa *nf* weighing; (bilancia) weighing machine; (per veicoli) weighbridge

❖ **pe'sante** ① *adj* heavy; ‹stomaco› overfull; ‹accusa, ingiuria› serious; (noioso) boring; **andarci ∼ con qualcuno** be heavy-handed with somebody
② *adv* ‹vestirsi› warmly

pesante'mente *adv* ‹cadere› heavily; ‹insultare› seriously

pesan'tezza *nf* heaviness

pesaper'sone *nm inv* scales

❖ **pe'sare** ① *vt* weigh; ∼ **le parole** weigh one's words
② *vi* weigh; (essere pesante) be heavy; ∼ **su** fig lie heavy on

pe'sarsi *vr* weigh oneself

'pesca¹ *nf* (frutto) peach

'pesca² *nf* fishing; **andare a ∼** go fishing
■ **pesca di beneficenza** lucky dip; **pesca con la lenza** angling; **pesca subacquea** underwater fishing

pe'scare *vt* (andare a pesca di) fish for; (prendere) catch; (pigliare) fam (trovare) dig up, find; **guai se ti pesco!** there will be trouble if I catch you!

pesca'tore *nm* fisherman
■ **pescatore di frodo** poacher; **pescatore di perle** pearl diver

❖ **'pesce** *nm* fish; **non sapere che pesci pigliare** fig not know which way to turn; **prendere qualcuno a pesci in faccia** fig treat somebody like dirt; **sentirsi un ∼ fuor d'acqua** feel like a fish out of water
■ **pesce d'aprile!** April Fool!; **pesce in carpione** soused fish; **pesce al cartoccio** fish baked in foil; **pesce gatto** catfish; **pesce grosso** fig big fish; **pesce persico** perch; **pesce piccolo** fig small fry; **pesce rosso** goldfish; **pesce spada** swordfish

pesce'cane *nm* shark

pesche'reccio *nm* fishing boat

pesche'ria *nf* fishmonger's [shop]

peschi'era *nf* fish-pond

'Pesci *nmpl* Astr Pisces

pescio'lino *nm*
■ **pesciolino d'acqua dolce** minnow

pesci'vendolo *nm* fishmonger

'pesco *nm* peach tree

pe'scoso *adj* teeming with fish

pe'seta *nf* peseta

pe'sista *nm* (in sollevamento pesi) weight-lifter; (in lancio del peso) shot-putter

❖ **'peso** *nm* weight; **essere di ∼ per qualcuno** be a burden to somebody; **alzare di ∼** lift up in one go; **avere un ∼ sullo stomaco** have a lead weight on one's stomach; **di poco ∼** (senza importanza) not very important;

non dare ∼ a qualcosa not attach any importance to something
■ **peso massimo** (nel pugilato) heavy weight; **peso medio** (nel pugilato) middleweight; **peso morto** dead weight; **peso netto** net weight; **peso piuma** (nel pugilato) featherweight; **peso specifico** specific gravity; **peso welter** (nel pugilato) welterweight

pessi'mismo *nm* pessimism

pessi'mista ① *nmf* pessimist
② *adj* pessimistic

pessimistica'mente *adv* pessimistically

'pessimo *adj* very bad

pe'staggio *nm* beating-up

pe'stare *vt* tread on; (picchiare) beat; crush ‹aglio, prezzemolo, uva›; ∼ **i piedi [per terra]** stamp one's feet [on the ground]; ∼ **un piede a qualcuno** tread on somebody's foot

pe'stata *nf* bash; **dare una ∼ a un piede a qualcuno** tread on somebody's foot

'peste *nf* plague; (persona) pest; **dire ∼ e corna di qualcuno** tear somebody to bits
■ **peste bubbonica** bubonic plague

pe'stello *nm* pestle

pesti'cida *nm* pesticide

pe'stifero *adj* (fastidioso) pestilential

pesti'lenza *nf* pestilence; (fetore) stench, stink

pestilenzi'ale *adj* ‹odore, aria› noxious

'pesto ① *adj* ground; **occhio pesto** black eye
② *nm* basil and garlic sauce

'petalo *nm* petal

pe'tardo *nm* banger

petizi'one *nf* petition; **fare una ∼** draw up a petition

petrol'chimico *adj* petrochemical

petro'dollaro *nm* petrodollar

petroli'era *nf* [oil] tanker

petroli'ere *nm* oilman

petro'lifero *adj* oil-bearing

❖ **pe'trolio** *nm* oil

pettego'lare *vi* gossip

pettego'lezzo *nm* piece of gossip; **pettegolezzi** *pl* gossip *sg*; **far pettegolezzi** gossip

pet'tegolo, -a ① *adj* gossipy
② *nmf* gossip

petti'nare *vt* comb

petti'narsi *vr* comb one's hair

pettina'tura *nf* combing; (acconciatura) hairstyle; ∼ **a caschetto** bob

'pettine *nm* comb

'petting *nm* petting

petti'nino *nm* (fermaglio) comb

petti'rosso *nm* robin [redbreast]

❖ **'petto** *nm* chest; (seno) breast; **a doppio ∼** double-breasted; **prendere qualcosa/**

❖ indicates a very frequent word

p

qualcuno di ∼ face up to something/
somebody; **petti** *pl* **di pollo** chicken breasts
petto'rale **1** *nm* Sport number; **pettorali**
pecs
2 *adj* pectoral
petto'rina *nf* (di salopette) bib
petto'ruto *adj* ‹donna› full-breasted;
‹uomo› broad-chested
petu'lante *adj* impertinent
petu'lanza *nf* impertinence
pe'tunia *nf* petunia
'pezza *nf* cloth; (toppa) patch; (rotolo di tessuto)
roll; **trattare qualcuno come una ∼ da piedi**
walk all over somebody
■ **pezza d'appoggio** voucher; **pezza
giustificativa** voucher
pez'zato *adj* ‹cavallo, mucca› piebald
pez'zente *nmf* tramp; (avaro) miser
'pezzo *nm* piece; (parte) part; Mus piece; **un
bel ∼ d'uomo** a fine figure of a man; **un ∼**
(di tempo) some time; (di spazio) a long way;
al ∼ ‹costare› each; **essere a pezzi** (stanco) be
shattered; **fare a pezzi** tear to shreds; **andare
in mille pezzi** break into a thousand pieces;
cadere a pezzi fall to pieces, fall to bits
■ **pezzo forte** centre-piece; **pezzi** *pl* **grossi** top
brass; **pezzo grosso** bigwig, big shot; **pezzi**
pl **grossi** top brass; **pezzo di imbecille** stupid
idiot; **pezzo di ricambio** spare [part]
pezzu'ola *nf* scrap of material
photo'fit® *nm inv* Photofit
pia'cente *adj* attractive
pia'cere **1** *nm* pleasure; (favore) favour;
a ∼ as much as one likes; **per ∼!** please!;
∼ [di conoscerla]! (nelle presentazioni) pleased
to meet you!; **con ∼** with pleasure; **fare un
∼ a qualcuno** do somebody a favour
2 *vi* **la Scozia mi piace** I like Scotland; **mi
piacciono i dolci** I like sweets; **mi piacerebbe
venire** I'd like to come; **faccio come mi pare
e piace** I do as I please; **ti piace?** do you like
it?; **lo spettacolo è piaciuto** the show was a
success
pia'cevole *adj* pleasant
piacevol'mente *adv* agreeably
piaci'mento *nm* **a ∼** as much as you like
pia'dina *nf unleavened focaccia bread*
pi'aga *nf* sore; fig scourge; fig (persona noiosa)
pain; fig (ricordo doloroso) wound
pia'gato *adj* covered with sores
piagni'steo *nm* whining
piagnuco'lare *vi* whimper
piagnuco'lio *nm* whimpering
piagnuco'loso *adj* maudlin
pi'alla *nf* plane
pial'lare *vt* plane
pialla'tura *nf* planing
pi'ana *nf* (pianura) plane
pianeggi'ante *adj* level
piane'rottolo *nm* landing

pia'neta *nm* planet
pi'angere **1** *vi* cry; (disperatamente) weep;
mi piange il cuore my heart bleeds; **mettersi
a ∼ come una fontana** turn the waterworks
on; **∼ sul latte versato** cry over spilt milk
2 *vt* (lamentare) lament; (per un lutto) mourn;
∼ la morte di qualcuno mourn somebody's
death
pianifi'care *vt* plan
pianificazi'one *nf* planning
■ **pianificazione aziendale** corporate planning;
pianificazione familiare family planning;
pianificazione territoriale town-and-country
planning
pia'nista *nmf* Mus pianist
pi'ano **1** *adj* flat; (a livello) flush; (regolare)
smooth; (facile) easy; **i 400 metri piani** the
400 metres flat race
2 *adv* slowly; (con cautela) gently; (sottovoce)
quietly; **andarci ∼** go carefully
3 *nm* plain; (di edificio) floor, storey; (livello)
plane; (progetto) plan; Mus piano; **di primo ∼**
first-rate; **primo piano** Phot close-up; **in
primo ∼** in the foreground; **essere/mettersi
in primo ∼** fig take/occupy centre-stage;
secondo piano middle distance
■ **piano d'azione** action plan; **piano bar** piano
bar; **piano d'emergenza** contingency plan;
piano di incentivi incentive scheme; **piano
di lavoro** work surface; (programma) work
schedule; **piano di pensionamento** pension
plan, pension scheme; **piano regolatore** town
plan; **piano di sopra** upstairs; **piano di sotto**
downstairs; **piano di studi** syllabus; **piano
superiore** upper floor
piano'forte *nm* piano
■ **pianoforte a coda** grand [piano]; **pianoforte
verticale** upright [piano]
pia'nola® *nf* pianola
piano'terra *nm inv* ground floor, first
floor Am
pi'anta *nf* plant; (del piede) sole; (disegno)
plan; (di città) map; **di sana ∼** (totalmente)
entirely; **in ∼ stabile** permanently
■ **pianta da appartamento** house-plant; **pianta
stradale** road map
piantagi'one *nf* plantation
pianta'grane *nmf* fam **è un/una ∼** he's/
she's bolshy
pian'tare *vt* plant; (conficcare) drive; pitch
‹tenda›; fam (abbandonare) dump; **piantala!** fam
stop it!; **piantato in** ‹spina, chiodo› embedded
in; **∼ baracca e burattini** drop everything;
(per sempre) chuck everything in
pian'tarsi *vr* plant oneself; fam (lasciarsi)
leave each other
pianta|'tore, -trice *nmf* planter
pianter'reno *nm* ground floor, first floor
Am
pi'anto **1** *pp di* PIANGERE
2 *nm* crying; (disperato) weeping; (lacrime)
tears *pl*

p

pianto'nare *vt* guard

pian'tone *nm* guard; **stare di ~** stand guard; **mettere di ~** put on guard
■ piantone dello sterzo Auto steering column

✧ **pia'nura** *nf* plain
■ pianura padana Po valley

pi'astra *nf* plate; (lastra) slab; Culin griddle
■ piastra elettronica circuit board; **piastra madre** Comput motherboard; **piastra di registrazione** cassette deck

pia'strella *nf* tile

pia'strina *nf* Mil identity disc; Med platelet; Comput chip
■ piastrina di riconoscimento identity tag; **piastrina di silicio** silicon chip

piatta'forma *nf* platform
■ piattaforma di lancio launch pad; **piattaforma petrolifera** oil platform, offshore rig; **piattaforma rivendicativa** *o* **sindacale** union claims *pl*

piat'tino *nm* (di tazzina) saucer; (piatto piccolo) side plate

✧ **pi'atto** ① *adj* flat; (monotono) dull
② *nm* plate; (da portata, vivanda) dish; (portata) course; (parte piatta) flat; (di giradischi) turntable; (di bilancia) pan; **piatti** *pl* Mus cymbals; **lavare i piatti** do the dishes, do the washing-up; **piatti** *pl* **da asporto** takeaway, carryout *Am*; **piatti** *pl* **caldi** hot dishes; **piatti** *pl* **di carne** meat dishes
■ piatto fondo soup plate; **piatto del giorno** dish of the day; **piatto piano** [ordinary] plate; **piatto di portata** serving dish, server; **piatto pronto** ready meal; **piatto unico** complete meal

✧ **pi'azza** *nf* square; Comm market; **letto a una piazza** single bed; **letto a due piazze** double bed; **far ~ pulita** make a clean sweep; **mettere qualcosa in ~** fig make something public; **scendere in ~** fig take to the streets
■ piazza d'armi parade ground; **piazza del mercato** market square; **Piazza San Pietro** St Peter's Square

piazza'forte *nf* stronghold

piaz'zale *nm* large square

piazza'mento *nm* (in classifica) placing

piaz'zare *vt* place

piaz'zarsi *vr* Sport be placed; **~ secondo** come second, be placed second

piaz'zato *adj* ‹cavallo› placed; **ben ~** (robusto) well-built

piaz'zista ① *nm* salesman
② *nf* saleswoman

piaz'z[u]ola *nf*
■ piazz[u]ola di partenza (nel golf) tee; **piazz[u] ola di sosta** pull-in

pic'cante *adj* hot; (pungente) sharp; (salace) spicy

pic'carsi *vr* (risentirsi) take offence; **~ di** (vantarsi di) claim to

pic'cata *nf* veal in sour lemon sauce

'picche *nfpl* (in carte) spades

picchet'taggio *nm* picketing

picchet'tare *vt* stake; ‹scioperanti› picket

pic'chetto *nm* picket

✧ **picchi'are** ① *vt* hit; **~ la testa (contro qualcosa)** bang *or* hit one's head (against something)
② *vi* (bussare) knock; Aeron nosedive; **~ in testa** (motore) knock

picchi'arsi *vr* **~ il petto** beat one's breast

picchi'ata *nf* beating; Aeron nosedive; **scendere in ~** nosedive

picchi'ato *adj* (matto) touched

picchia'tore *nm* goon

picchiet'tare *vt* tap; (punteggiare) spot

picchiet'tato *adj* spotted

picchiet'tio *nm* tapping

'picchio *nm* woodpecker

pic'cino ① *adj* tiny; (gretto) mean; (di poca importanza) petty
② *nm* little one, child

piccion'cini *nmpl* fam lovebirds; **fare i ~** get all lovey-dovey

picci'one *nm* pigeon; **prendere due piccioni con una fava** kill two birds with one stone
■ piccione viaggiatore carrier pigeon

'picco *nm* peak; **a ~** vertically; **colare a ~** sink

picco'lezza *nf* (di persona, ambiente) smallness; (grettezza) meanness; (inezia) trifle

✧ **'piccolo, -a** ① *adj* small, little; ‹vacanza, pausa› little, short; (di statura) short; (gretto) petty
② *nmf* child, little one; **da ~** as a child; **in ~** in miniature; **nel mio ~** in my own small way

pic'cone *nm* pickaxe
■ piccone da ghiaccio ice pick

pic'cozza *nf* ice axe

pic'nic *nm inv* picnic

pi'docchio *nm* louse

pidocchi'oso ① *adj* flea-bitten; fam (avaro) stingy
② *nm* fam miser

piè *nm inv* **a ~ di pagina** at the foot of the page; **saltare a ~ pari** skip; **ad ogni ~ sospinto** all the time, endlessly

✧ **pi'ede** *nm* foot; (di armadio, letto) leg; **a piedi** on foot; **andare a piedi** walk; **a piedi nudi** barefoot; **avere i piedi piatti** have flat feet, be flat-footed; **a ~ libero** free; **in piedi** standing; **alzarsi in piedi** stand up; **in punta di piedi** on tiptoe; **ai piedi di** ‹montagna› at the foot of; **avere qualcuno ai propri piedi** have somebody at one's feet; **essere sul ~ di guerra** be ready for action; (nazione) be on

p

a war footing; **prendere** ∼ fig gain ground; ‹*moda*› catch on; **partire col** ∼ **sbagliato** get off on the wrong foot; **mettere in piedi** (allestire) set up; **togliti dai piedi!** get out of the way!
■ **piede di insalata** head of lettuce; **piede di porco** (strumento) jemmy

pie'dino *nm* **fare** ∼ **a qualcuno** fam play footsie with somebody

piedi'stallo *nm* pedestal

pi'ega *nf* (piegatura) fold; (di gonna) pleat; (di pantaloni) crease; (grinza) wrinkle; (andamento) turn; **a pieghe** with pleats, pleated; **non fare una** ∼ (ragionamento) be flawless; (persona) not bat an eyelid; **prendere una brutta** ∼ get into bad ways

⚡ **pie'gare** [1] *vt* fold; (flettere) bend
[2] *vi* bend

pie'garsi *vr* bend; ∼ **a** fig yield to

piega'tura *nf* folding; (piega) fold

pieghet'tare *vt* pleat

pieghet'tato *adj* pleated

ple'ghevole [1] *adj* pliable; (tavolo) folding
[2] *nm* leaflet

Pie'monte *nm* Piedmont

piemon'tese *adj & nmf* Piedmontese

pi'ena *nf* (di fiume) flood; (folla) crowd

⚡ **pi'eno** [1] *adj* full; (massiccio) solid; **in piena estate** in the middle of summer; **a pieni voti** (diplomarsi) ≈ with A-grades, with first class honours
[2] *nm* (colmo) height; (carico) full load; **in** ∼ (completamente) fully; **fare il** ∼ (di benzina) fill up; **nel** ∼ **delle forze** in top physical form

pie'none *nm* **c'era il** ∼ the place was packed

'piercing *nm inv* body piercing
■ **piercing all'ombelico** navel ring; **piercing nella lingua** tongue stud

⚡ **pietà** *nf* pity; (misericordia) mercy; **senza** ∼ (persona) pitiless; (spietatamente) pitilessly; **avere** ∼ **di qualcuno** take pity on somebody; **far** ∼ (far pena) be pitiful; fam (essere orrendo) be useless

pie'tanza *nf* dish

pie'toso *adj* pitiful, merciful; fam (pessimo) terrible

⚡ **pi'etra** *nf* stone
■ **pietra dura** semiprecious stone; **pietra preziosa** precious stone; **pietra dello scandalo** cause of the scandal

pie'traia *nf* scree

pie'trame *nm* stones *pl*

pietrifi'care *vt* petrify

pie'trina *nf* (di accendino) flint

pie'troso *adj* stony

'piffero *nm* fife

pigi'ama *nm* pyjamas *pl*, pajamas Am

'pigia 'pigia *nm inv* crowd, crush

pigi'are *vt* press

pigia'trice *nf* winepress

pigi'one *nf* rent; **dare a** ∼ let, rent out; **prendere a** ∼ rent

⚡ **pigli'are** *vt* fam (afferrare) catch

'piglio *nm* air

pig'mento *nm* pigment

pig'meo, -a *adj & nmf* pygmy

'pigna *nf* cone
■ **pigna di abete** fir cone

pi'gnolo *adj* pedantic

pignora'mento *nm* Jur distraint

pigno'rare *vt* Jur distrain upon

pigo'lare *vi* chirp

pigo'lio *nm* chirping

pigra'mente *adv* lazily

pi'grizia *nf* laziness

'pigro *adj* lazy, (intelletto) slow

PIL *abbr* (**prodotto interno lordo**) GDP

'pila *nf* pile; Electr battery; fam (lampadina tascabile) torch; (vasca) basin; **a pile** battery operated, battery powered

pi'lastro *nm* pillar

'pillola *nf* pill; **prendere la** ∼ be on the pill
■ **pillola del giorno dopo** morning-after pill

pi'lone *nm* pylon; (di ponte) pier

pi'lota [1] *nmf* pilot; Auto driver
■ **pilota automatico** automatic pilot; **pilota di caccia** fighter pilot
[2] *adj inv* **progetto** ∼ pilot project

pilo'taggio *nm* flying; **cabina di pilotaggio** flight deck

pilo'tare *vt* pilot; drive ‹*auto*›

pinaco'teca *nf* art gallery

'Pinco Pal'lino *nm* so-and-so

pi'neta *nf* pine-wood

ping-'pong *nm* table tennis, ping-pong fam

'pingue *adj* fat

pingu'edine *nf* fatness

pingu'ino *nm* penguin; (gelato) choc ice on a stick

'pinna *nf* fin; (per nuotare) flipper

pin'nacolo *nm* pinnacle

'pino *nm* pine[-tree]
■ **pino marittimo** cluster pine, maritime pine

pi'nolo *nm* pine kernel

'pinta *nf* pint

pin-'up *nf inv* pin-up [girl]

'pinza *nf* pliers *pl*; Med forceps *pl*; **prendere qualcosa con le pinze** fig treat something cautiously

pin'zare *vt* (con pinzatrice) staple

pinza'trice *nf* stapler

pin'zette *nfpl* tweezers

pinzi'monio *nm* sauce for crudités

'pio *adj* pious; (benefico) charitable

piogge'rella *nf* drizzle

pi'oggia *nf* rain; *fig* (di pietre, insulti) hail, shower; **sotto la ∼** in the rain
■ **pioggia acida** acid rain; **pioggia radioattiva** radioactive fallout

pi'olo *nm* (di scala) rung

piom'bare ① *vi* fall heavily; **∼ su** fall upon; **∼ all'improvviso nella stanza** suddenly burst into the room
② *vt* **∼ qualcuno nella disperazione** plunge somebody into despair

piom'bino *nm* (sigillo) [lead] seal; (da pesca) sinker; (in tende) weight

pi'ombo *nm* lead; (sigillo) [lead] seal; **a ∼** plumb; **senza ∼** (benzina) lead-free; **avere un sonno di ∼** be a very heavy sleeper; **andare con i piedi di ∼** tread carefully; **anni di ∼** *years when terrorism was at its height*

pioni'ere, -a *nmf* pioneer

pi'oppo *nm* poplar

pior'rea *nf* pyorrhoea

pio'vano *adj* **acqua piovana** rainwater

pi'overe *vi* rain; **∼** it's raining; **∼ addosso a qualcuno** (guai, debiti) rain down on somebody; **[su questo] non ci piove** *fam* that's for sure

pioviggi'nare *vi* drizzle

pio'voso *adj* rainy

pi'ovra *nf* octopus

pio'vuto *adj* **∼ dal cielo** fallen into one's lap

'pipa *nf* pipe

pipe'rito *adj* **menta piperita** peppermint

pipì *nf* **fare [la] ∼** pee, piddle; **andare a fare [la] ∼** go for a pee

pipi'strello *nm* bat

piqué *nm inv* piqué

'pira *nf* pyre

pi'ramide *nf* pyramid

pi'ranha *nm inv* piranha

pi'rata ① *nm* pirate
■ **pirata dell'aria** skyjacker; **pirata della strada** hit-and-run driver; (prepotente) road-hog
② *adj inv* pirate

pirate'ria *nf* piracy
■ **pirateria informatica** software piracy

pi'rite *nf* pyrite

piro'etta *nf* pirouette

pi'rofila *nf* (tegame) oven-proof dish

pi'rofilo *adj* heat-resistant

pi'romane *nmf* pyromaniac

piroma'nia *nf* pyromania

pi'roscafo *nm* steamer
■ **piroscafo di linea** liner

'piscia *nf vulg* piss

pisci'are *vi vulg* piss

pisci'ata *nf vulg* piss

pi'scina *nf* [swimming] pool

■ **piscina coperta** indoor [swimming] pool; **piscina gonfiabile** [inflatable] paddling pool; **piscina olimpionica** Olympic [swimming] pool; **piscina per il parto** birthing pool; **piscina scoperta** outdoor [swimming] pool, lido

pi'sello *nm* pea; *fam* (pene) willie; **piselli** *pl* **odorosi** sweetpeas

piso'lino *nm* nap; **fare un ∼** have a nap

'pista *nf* track; *Aeron* runway, tarmac; (orma) footprint; (sci) slope, piste
■ **pista d'atterraggio** runway; **pista da ballo** dance floor; **pista ciclabile** cycle track; **pista da fondo** cross-country ski track; **pista di pattinaggio** ice rink; **pista per principianti** nursery slope; **pista da sci** ski slope, ski run, piste; **pista per slitte** toboggan run

pi'stacchio *nm* pistachio

pi'stola *nf* pistol; (per spruzzare) spray-gun
■ **pistola a capsule** cap gun; **pistola a spruzzo** paint spray; **pistola a tamburo** revolver

pisto'lero *nm* gunslinger

pi'stone *nm* piston

'pitbull *nm inv* pitbull (terrier)

pi'tocco *nm* miser

pi'tone *nm* python

pitto'gramma *nm* pictogram

pit|'tore, -trice *nmf* painter

pitto'resco *adj* picturesque

pit'torico *adj* pictorial

pit'tura *nf* painting; **pitture** *pl* **di guerra** warpaint
■ **pittura a guazzo** poster paint; **pittura rupestre** cave painting

pittu'rare *vt* paint

pitui'tario *adj* pituitary

più ① *adv* more; (superlativo) most; *Math* plus; **∼ importante** more important; **il ∼ importante** the most important; **∼ caro/grande** dearer/bigger; **il ∼ caro/grande** the dearest/biggest; **di ∼** more; **una coperta in ∼** an extra blanket; **non ho ∼ soldi** I don't have any more money; **non vive ∼ a Milano** he no longer lives in Milan; **∼ o meno** more or less; **il ∼ lentamente possibile** as slowly as possible; **al ∼ presto** as soon as possible; **per di ∼** what's more; **mai ∼!** I never again!; **∼ di** more than; **sempre ∼** more and more
② *adj* more; (superlativo) most; **∼ tempo** more time; **la classe con ∼ alunni** the class with most pupils; **∼ volte** several times ③ *nm* most; *Math* plus sign; **il ∼ è fatto** the worst is over; **parlare del ∼ e del meno** make small talk; **i ∼** the majority

piuccheper'fetto *nm* pluperfect

pi'uma *nf* feather

piu'maggio *nm* plumage

piu'mato *adj* plumed

piu'mino *nm* (di cigni) down; (copriletto) eiderdown; (per cipria) powder-puff; (per spolverare) feather duster; (giacca) down jacket

---

piu'mone® *nm* duvet, continental quilt

⚐ **piut'tosto** *adv* rather; (invece) instead

'**piva** *nf* **con le pive nel sacco** emptyhanded

pi'vello *nm* fam greenhorn

'**pivot** *nm inv* (in pallacanestro) centre

'**pizza** *nf* pizza; Cinema reel; fam (noia) bore

∎ **pizza margherita** *tomato and mozzarella pizza*; **pizza marinara** *pizza with tomato, oregano, garlic and anchovies*; **pizza napoletana** *pizza with tomato, mozzarella and anchovies*; **pizza quattro stagioni** *pizza with tomato, mozzarella, ham, mushrooms and artichokes*

pizzai'ola: alla ∼ *adj* with tomatoes, garlic, and oregano

pizze'ria *nf* pizza restaurant, pizzeria

piz'zetta *nf* small pizza

piz'zetto *nm* (barba) goatee

pizzi'care ① *vt* pinch; (pungere) sting; (di sapore) taste sharp; fam (sorprendere) catch; Mus pluck

② *vi* scratch; ‹cibo› be spicy

'**pizzico**, **pizzicotto** *nm* pinch

'**pizzo** *nm* lace; (di montagna) peak

pla'care *vt* placate; assuage ‹fame, dolore›

pla'carsi *vr* calm down

'**placca** *nf* plate; (commemorativa, dentale) plaque; Med patch

∎ **placca batterica** plaque

plac'care *vt* plate

plac'cato *adj* ∼ **d'argento** silver-plated; ∼ **d'oro** gold-plated

placca'tura *nf* plating

pla'cebo *nm inv* placebo; **effetto placebo** placebo effect

pla'centa *nf* placenta, afterbirth

'**placido** *adj* placid

pla'fond *nm inv* Comm ceiling

plafoni'era *nf* ceiling light

plagi'are *vt* plagiarize; pressure ‹persona›

'**plagio** *nm* plagiarism

plaid *nm inv* tartan rug

pla'nare *vi* glide

'**plancia** *nf* Naut bridge; (passerella) gangplank

'**plancton** *nm* plankton

plane'tario ① *adj* planetary

② *nm* planetarium

pla'smare *vt* mould

'**plastica** *nf* (materia) plastic; Med plastic surgery; (arte) plastic art; **sacchetto di** ∼ plastic bag

'**plastico** ① *adj* plastic; (rappresentazione) three-dimensional

② *nm* plastic model

'**platano** *nm* plane tree

pla'tea *nf* stalls *pl* (pubblico) audience

'**platino** *nm* platinum

pla'tonico *adj* platonic

plau'sibile *adj* plausible; **poco** ∼ implausible

plausibilità *nf* plausibility

'**plauso** *nm* (consenso) approval

play'back *nm* **cantare in** ∼ **mime**

play'boy *nm inv* playboy

play'maker *nm inv* Sport playmaker

p.le *abbr* (**piazzale**) Sq

ple'baglia *nf* pej mob

'**plebe** *nf* common people

ple'beo, -a *adj & nmf* plebeian

plebi'scito *nm* plebiscite

ple'nario *adj* plenary

pleni'lunio *nm* full moon

'**plettro** *nm* plectrum

pleu'rite *nf* pleurisy

'**plico** *nm* packet; **in** ∼ **a parte** under separate cover

plissé *adj inv* plissé; (gonna) accordeon pleated

plop *nm inv* plop; **fare** ∼ plop

plo'tone *nm* platoon; (di ciclisti) group

∎ **plotone d'esecuzione** firing squad

'**plotter** *nm inv* Comput plotter

∎ **plotter da tavolo** flatbed plotter

'**plumbeo** *adj* leaden

plum-'cake *nm inv* fruit cake

plu'rale *adj & nm* plural; **al** ∼ in the plural

pluralità *nf* (maggioranza) majority

pluridiscipli'nare *adj* multidisciplinary

plurien'nale *adj* ∼ **esperienza** many years' experience

plurigemel'lare *adj* (parto) multiple

pluripar'titico *adj* Pol multi-party

Plu'tone *nm* Pluto

plu'tonio *nm* plutonium

pluvi'ale *adj* rain *attrib*

pluvi'ometro *nm* rain gauge

pneu'matico ① *adj* pneumatic

② *nm* tyre

∎ **pneumatico radiale** radial [tyre]

pneu'monia *nf* pneumonia

PNL *abbr* (**prodotto nazionale lordo**) GNP

Po *nm* Po

po' ▶ POCO

po'chette *nf inv* clutch bag

po'chino *nm* **un** ∼ a little bit

⚐ '**poco** ① *adj* little; (tempo) short; (con nomi plurali) few

② *pron* little; (poco tempo) a short time; (plurale) few

③ *nm* little; **un po'** a little [bit]; **un po' di** a little, some; (con nomi plurali) a few; **a** ∼ **a** ∼ little by little; **fra** ∼ soon; **per** ∼ (a poco prezzo) cheap; (quasi) nearly; ∼ **fa** a little while ago; **sono arrivato da** ∼ I have just arrived; **un bel po'** quite a lot; **un bel po'** ⋯⋗

di più/meno quite a lot more/less; **un ~ di buono** a shady character

[4] *adv* (con verbi) not much; (con avverbi, aggettivi) not very; **parla ~** he doesn't speak much; **lo conosco ~** I don't know him very well; **~ spesso** not very often

podcas'tare *vi* podcast

po'dere *nm* farm

pode'roso *adj* powerful

'podio *nm* dais; Mus podium

po'dismo *nm* walking

po'dista *nmf* walker

po'ema *nm* poem
■ **poema epico** epic [poem]; **poema sinfonico** symphonic poem

✓ **poe'sia** *nf* poetry; (componimento) poem

✓ **po'eta** *nm* poet

poe'tessa *nf* poetess

po'etico *adj* poetic

poggiapi'edi *nm inv* footrest

poggi'are [1] *vt* lean; (posare) place
[2] *vi* **~ su** be based on

poggia'testa *nm inv* head-rest

'poggio *nm* hillock

poggi'olo *nm* balcony

✓ **'poi** [1] *adv* (dopo) then; (più tardi) later [on]; (finalmente) finally; **d'ora in ~** from now on; **questa ~!** well!
[2] *nm* **pensare al ~** think of the future

✓ **poiché** *conj* since

pois *nm inv* **a ~** polka-dot

'poker *nm* poker

po'lacco, -a [1] *adj* Polish
[2] *nmf* Pole
[3] *nm* (lingua) Polish

po'lare *adj* polar

polarità *nf inv* polarity

polariz'zare *vt* polarize

pola'roid® *nf inv* instant camera

'polca *nf* polka

po'lemica *nf* controversy

polemica'mente *adv* controversially

polemiciz'zare *vi* engage in controversy

po'lemico *adj* controversial

po'lenta *nf* cornmeal porridge

poli'clinico *nm* general hospital

policro'mia *nf* polychromy

po'licromo *adj* polychrome

poli'estere *nm* polyester

polieti'lene *nm* polyethylene

poliga'mia *nf* polygamy

poli'gamico *adj* polygamous

po'ligamo *adj* polygamous

poli'glotta *nmf* polyglot

po'ligono *nm* polygon; (di tiro) rifle range

po'limero *nm* polymer

───────────

✓ indicates a very frequent word

Poli'nesia *nf* Polynesia

polinesi'ano *adj & nmf* Polynesian

'polio[mie'lite] *nf* polio[myelitis]

'polipo *nm* polyp

polisti'rolo *nm* polystyrene

poli'tecnico *nm* polytechnic

✓ **po'litica** *nf* politics *sg*; (linea di condotta) policy; **fare ~** be in politics; **darsi alla ~** go into politics
■ **politica energetica** energy policy; **politica estera** foreign policy; **politica monetaria** monetary policy

politica'mente *adv* politically; **~ corretto** politically correct, pc

politi'chese *nm* political jargon

politiciz'zare *vt* politicize

✓ **po'litico, -a** [1] *adj* political
[2] *nmf* politician

poliva'lente *adj* all-purpose

✓ **poli'zia** *nf* police, police force
■ **polizia giudiziaria** Criminal Investigation Department, CID; **polizia scientifica** forensics; **polizia stradale** traffic police

polizi'esco *adj* police *attrib*; (romanzo, film) detective *attrib*

✓ **polizi'otto** [1] *nm* policeman
■ **poliziotto in borghese** plain clothes policeman; **poliziotto privato** private detective
[2] *adj* police *attrib*

'polizza *nf* policy
■ **polizza di assicurazione** insurance policy

pol'laio *nm* chicken run; fam (luogo chiassoso) mad house

pol'lame *nm* poultry

polla'strella *nf* spring chicken; fig fam bird

polla'strello *nm* spring chicken

pol'lastro *nm* cockerel

polle'ria *nf* poultry butcher, poulterer

'pollice *nm* thumb; (unità di misura) inch

'polline *nm* pollen; **allergia al polline** hay fever

polli'vendolo, -a *nmf* poulterer

'pollo *nm* chicken; fam (semplicione) simpleton; **far ridere i polli** be ridiculous
■ **pollo allevato a terra** free-range chicken; **pollo arrosto** roast chicken; **pollo di batteria** battery chicken; **pollo alla cacciatora** chicken chasseur

polmo'nare *adj* pulmonary

pol'mone *nm* lung
■ **polmone d'acciaio** iron lung

polmo'nite *nf* pneumonia

'polo *nm* pole; Sport polo; (maglietta) polo top; Pol party; (conservatori) Italian Conservatives
■ **polo magnetico** magnetic pole; **polo nord** North Pole; **polo sud** South Pole

Po'lonia *nf* Poland

'polpa *nf* pulp

pol'paccio *nm* calf

polpa'strello *nm* fingertip

pol'petta *nf* meatball

polpet'tone *nm* meatloaf
- polpettone sentimentale *fam* hokum

'polpo *nm* octopus

pol'poso *adj* fleshy

pol'sino *nm* cuff

'polso *nm* pulse; *Anat* wrist; *fig* authority;
avere ∼ be strict; essere privo di ∼ be soft

pol'tiglia *nf* mush

pol'trire *vi* lie around

✧ **pol'trona** *nf* armchair; *Theat* seat in the
stalls

pol'trone *adj* lazy

✧ **'polvere** *nf* dust; (sostanza polverizzata)
powder; in ∼ powdered; sapone in polvere
soap powder
- polvere da sparo gun powder

polveri'era *nf* gunpowder magazine; *fig*
tinderbox

polve'rina *nf* (medicina) powder

polvoriz'zare *vt* pulverize; (nebulizzare)
atomize; smash, shatter ‹record›;
∼ qualcuno pulverize somebody

polve'rone *nm* cloud of dust

polve'roso *adj* dusty

po'mata *nf* ointment, cream
- pomata cicatrizzante healing cream for cuts

pomel'lato *adj* dappled

po'mello *nm* knob; (guancia) cheek

pomeridi'ano *adj* afternoon *attrib*; alle
tre pomeridiane at three in the afternoon, at
three p.m.

✧ **pome'riggio** *nm* afternoon; buon ∼! have
a good afternoon!; oggi ∼ this afternoon;
questo ∼ this afternoon

'pomice *nf* pumice

pomici'are *vi fam* snog, neck

pomici'ata *nf fam* snogging, necking

'pomo *nm* (oggetto) knob
- pomo d'Adamo Adam's apple

✧ **pomo'doro** *nm* tomato

'pompa *nf* pump; (sfarzo) pomp
- pompa della benzina petrol pump, gas pump
Am; pompe *pl* funebri (funzione) funeral

pom'pare *vt* pump; (gonfiare d'aria) pump up;
fig (esagerare) exaggerate; ∼ fuori pump out

pompei'ano, -a *adj & nmf* Pompeian

pom'pelmo *nm* grapefruit

pompi'ere *nm* fireman; i pompieri the fire
brigade

pom'pon *nm inv* pompom

pom'poso *adj* pompous

'poncho *nm inv* poncho

ponde'rare *vt* ponder

ponde'roso *adj* ponderous

po'nente *nm* west

✧ **'ponte** *nm* bridge; *Naut* deck; (impalcatura)
scaffolding; fare il ∼ *fig* make a long weekend

of it; governo ∼ interim government; legge
∼ interim or bridging law
- ponte aereo airlift; ponte auto car deck;
ponte di coperta main deck; ponte levatoio
drawbridge; ponte radio radio link; ponte
dei Sospiri Bridge of Sighs; ponte di volo
flight deck

pon'tefice *nm* pontiff

pontifi'care *vi* pontificate

pontifi'cato *nm* pontificate

ponti'ficio *adj* papal

pon'tile *nm* jetty

'pony *nm inv* pony
- pony express express delivery service

pool *nm inv Comm* consortium; (di giornalisti)
team; (di esperti) pool, team
- ∼ genico gene pool

pop'corn *nm inv* popcorn

'popelin *nm* poplin

popò¹ *nf inv fam* pooh

popò² *nm inv fam* bottie, bum

popo'lano *adj* of the [common] people

popo'lare ⃞1 *adj* popular; (comune)
common
⃞2 *vt* populate; essere popolato da (pieno di)
be full of

popolarità *nf* popularity

popo'larsi *vr* get crowded

popolazi'one *nf* population

✧ **'popolo** *nm* people

popo'loso *adj* populous

'poppa *nf Naut* stern; (mammella) breast; a ∼
astern

pop'pare *vt* suck

pop'pata *nf* (pasto) feed

poppa'tolo *nm* [feeding-]bottle

popu'lista *nmf* populist

por'caio *nf* anche *fig* pigsty; fare un ∼ *fam*
make a mess

por'cata *nf* load of rubbish; porcate *pl fam*
(cibo) junk food; fare una ∼ a qualcuno play
a dirty trick on somebody

porcel'lana *nf* porcelain, china
- porcellana fine bone china

porcel'lino *nm* piglet
- porcellino d'India guinea-pig

porche'ria *nf* dirt; *fig* (cosa orrenda) piece of
filth; *fam* (robaccia) rubbish

por'chetta *nf* roast sucking pig

por'cile *nm* pigsty

por'cino ⃞1 *adj* pig *attrib*
⃞2 *nm* (fungo) cep (edible mushroom)

'porco *nm* pig; (carne) pork

porco'spino *nm* porcupine

'porfido *nm* porphyry

'porgere *vt* give; (offrire) offer; ∼ orecchio
lend an ear; porgo distinti saluti (in lettera)
I remain, yours sincerely

'porno adj inv porn

pornogra'fia nf pornography

porno'grafico adj pornographic

'poro nm pore

po'roso adj porous

'porpora nf purple

♂ **'porre** vt put; (collocare) place; (supporre) suppose; ask ‹domanda›; present ‹candidatura›; ～ **una domanda a qualcuno** ask somebody a question; **poniamo [il caso] che…** let us suppose that…; ～ **fine** o **termine a** put an end to

'porro nm Bot leek; (verruca) wart

'porsi vr put oneself; ～ **a sedere** sit down; ～ **in cammino** set out

♂ **'porta** nf door; Sport goal; (di città) gate; Comput port; ～ **a** ～ door-to-door; **mettere alla** ～ show somebody the door; **a porte chiuse** (riunione, processo) behind closed doors, in camera; **essere alle porte** (vicino) be on the doorstep

■ **porta a due battenti** double door[s]; **porta d'ingresso** front door; **porta parallela** Comput parallel port; **porta seriale** Comput serial port; **porta di servizio** tradesman's entrance; **porta di sicurezza** emergency exit; **porta per la stampante** Comput printer port; **porta a vento** swing-door

portaba'gagli nm inv (facchino) porter; (di treno ecc) luggage-rack; Auto boot, trunk Am; (sul tetto di un'auto) roof-rack

portabandi'era nmf inv standard-bearer

portabici'clette nm inv cycle rack

portabot'tiglie nm inv bottle rack, wine rack

porta'burro nm inv butter dish

porta'cenere nm inv ashtray

portachi'avi nm inv keyring

porta'cipria nm inv compact

portacon'tainer nm inv container truck

portadocu'menti nm inv document wallet

porta'erei nf inv aircraft carrier

portafi'nestra nf French window

porta'foglio nm wallet; (per documenti) portfolio; (ministero) ministry; **a** ～ ‹gonna› wrap-over

portafor'tuna 1 nm inv lucky charm 2 adj inv lucky

portagi'oie nm inv jewellery box

por'tale nm door; Comput portal

portama'tite nm inv pencil case

porta'mento nm carriage; (condotta) behaviour

porta'mina nm inv propelling pencil

portamo'nete nm inv purse

por'tante adj bearing attrib

portan'tina nf sedan-chair

portaom'brelli nm inv umbrella stand

porta'pacchi nm inv roof rack; (su bicicletta) luggage rack

porta'penne nm inv pencil case

♂ **por'tare** vt (verso chi parla) bring; (lontano da chi parla) take; (sorreggere, Math) carry; (condurre) lead; (indossare) wear; (avere) bear; ～ **a spasso il cane** take the dog for a walk; ～ **a termine** bring to a close; ～ **avanti** carry on; ～ **bene/male** bring good/bad luck; ～ **bene/male gli anni** look young/old for one's age; ～ **fortuna** be lucky; ～ **rancore** bear a grudge; ～ **via** take away

portari'viste nm inv magazine rack

por'tarsi vr (trasferirsi) move; (comportarsi) behave

porta'sci nm inv ski rack

portasciuga'mano nm towel rail

portasiga'rette nm inv cigarette-case

porta'spilli nm inv pin-cushion

por'tata nf (di pranzo) course; Auto carrying capacity; (di arma) range; fig (abilità) capability; **a** ～ **di mano** within reach; **alla** ～ **di tutti** accessible to all; (finanziariamente) within everybody's reach; **di grande** ～ (scoperta) with far-reaching consequences

por'tatile 1 adj, portable 2 nm Comput laptop

por'tato adj (indumento) worn; (dotato) gifted; **essere** ～ **per qualcosa** have a gift for something; **essere** ～ **a** (tendere a) be inclined to

porta|'tore, -trice nmf bearer; **al** ～ to the bearer

■ **portatore di handicap** disabled person

portatovagli'olo nm napkin ring

portau'ovo nm inv egg-cup

porta'voce nmf inv spokesperson

por'tello nm hatch

■ **portello di sicurezza** escape hatch

por'tento nm marvel; (persona dotata) prodigy

porten'toso adj wonderful

port'folio nm inv (di fotografie ecc) portfolio

porti'cato nm portico

'portico nm portico

porti'era nf door; (tendaggio) door curtain

porti'ere nm porter, doorman; Sport goalkeeper

■ **portiere di notte** night porter

porti'naio, -a nmf caretaker, concierge

portine'ria nf concierge's room; (di ospedale) porter's lodge

♂ **'porto** 1 pp di PORGERE 2 nm harbour; (complesso) port; (vino) port [wine]; (spesa di trasporto) carriage; **andare in** ～ succeed

■ **porto d'armi** gun licence; **porto container** container port; **porto fluviale** river port; **porto franco** free port; **porto marittimo** seaport

---

♂ indicates a very frequent word

Porto'gallo *nm* Portugal

porto'ghese *adj & nmf* Portuguese

por'tone *nm* main door

portori'cano, -a *adj & nmf* Puerto Rican

Porto'rico *nm* Puerto Rico

portu'ale *nm* dock worker, docker

porzi'one *nf* portion

'posa *nf* laying; (riposo) rest; Phot exposure; (atteggiamento) pose; **mettersi in ~** pose; **senza ~** without rest

po'sare [1] *vt* put; (giù) put [down]
[2] *vi* (poggiare) rest; (per un ritratto) pose

po'sarsi *vr* alight; (sostare) rest; Aeron land

po'sata *nf* piece of cutlery; **posate** *pl* cutlery *sg*, flatware *sg* Am

po'sato *adj* sedate

po'scritto *nm* postscript

posi'tivo *adj* positive

posizio'nare *vt* position

posizi'one *nf* position; **farsi una ~** get ahead; **prendere ~** take a stand

posolo'gia *nf* dosage

po'sporre *vt* place after; (posticipare) postpone

po'sposto pp di POSPORRE

posse'dere *vt* possess, own

possedi'mento *nm* possession

posses'sivo *adj* possessive

pos'sesso *nm* possession, ownership; (bene) possession; **entrare in ~ di** come into possession of; **essere in ~ di** be in possession of; **prendere ~ di** take possession of

posses'sore *nm* owner

pos'sibile [1] *adj* possible; **il più presto ~** as soon as possible
[2] *nm* **fare [tutto] il ~** do one's best

possibilità [1] *nf inv* possibility; (occasione) chance; **avere la ~ di fare qualcosa** have the chance *or* opportunity to do something
[2] *nfpl* (mezzi) means

possi'dente *nmf* land-owner

'posso ▶ POTERE

'posta *nf* post, mail; (ufficio postale) post office; (al gioco) stake; **spese di ~** postage; **per ~** by post, by mail; **la ~ in gioco è…** fig what's at stake is…; **a bella ~** on purpose; **Poste e Telecomunicazioni** [Italian] Post Office
■ **posta aerea** airmail; **posta centrale** main post office, central post office; **posta del cuore** agony column; **posta elettronica** electronic mail, e-mail; **spedire per ~ elettronica** e-mail; **posta elettronica vocale** voicemail; **posta in arrivo** inbox; **posta prioritaria** first-class mail

posta'giro *nm* postal giro

po'stale *adj* postal

pos'tare *vt* Comput sl (in un blog) post

postazi'one *nf* position; Mil emplacement

post'bellico *adj* postwar

postda'tare *vt* postdate ‹assegno›

posteggi'are *vt/i* park

posteggia'tore, -trice *nmf* parking attendant

po'steggio *nm* car-park, parking lot Am; (di taxi) taxi-rank

'posteri *nmpl* descendants

posteri'ore [1] *adj* back *attrib*, rear *attrib*; (nel tempo) later
[2] *nm* fam posterior; behind

posterità *nf* posterity

po'sticcio [1] *adj* artificial; (baffi, barba) false
[2] *nm* hair-piece

postici'pare *vt* postpone

po'stilla *nf* note; Jur rider

po'stino *nm* postman, mailman Am

postmo'derno *adj* postmodern

'posto [1] pp di PORRE
[2] *nm* place; (spazio) room; (impiego) job; Mil post; (sedile) seat; **a/fuori ~** in/out of place; **prendere ~** take up room; **sul ~** on-site; **essere a ~** ‹casa, libri› be tidy; **non grazie, sono a ~** no thanks, I'm all right; **mettere a ~** tidy ‹stanza›; **fare ~** make room for; **al ~ di** (invece di) in place of, instead of
■ **posto di blocco** checkpoint; **posto di guardia** guard post; **posto di guida** driving seat; **posto di lavoro** job; Comput workstation; **posti** *pl* **in piedi** standing room; **posto di polizia** police station; **posti** *pl* **a sedere** seating, seats

post-'partum *adj* post-natal

'postumo [1] *adj* posthumous
[2] *nm* after-effect; **postumi** *pl* **della sbornia** hangover

po'tabile *adj* drinkable; **acqua potabile** drinking water; **non ~** undrinkable

po'tare *vt* prune

po'tassa *nf* potash

po'tassio *nm* potassium

po'tente *adj* powerful; (efficace) potent

po'tenza *nf* power; (efficacia) potency
■ **potenza mondiale** world power; **potenza nucleare** nuclear power

potenzi'ale *adj & nm* potential

po'tere [1] *nm* power; **al ~** in power
■ **potere d'acquisto** purchasing power, spending power; **il quarto potere** the fourth estate
[2] *vi* can, be able to; **posso entrare?** can I come in?; (formale) may I come in?; **mi spiace, non posso venire alla festa** I'm sorry, I can't come to the party *or* I won't be able to come to the party; **posso fare qualcosa?** can I do something?; **che tu possa essere felice!** may you be happy!; **non ne posso più** (sono stanco) I can't go on; (sono stufo) I can't take any more; **può darsi** perhaps; **può darsi che sia vero** perhaps it's true; **potrebbe aver ragione** he could be right, he might be ⋯▸

p

right; **avresti potuto telefonare** you could have phoned, you might have phoned; **spero di poter venire** I hope to be able to come; **senza poter telefonare** without being able to phone; **spero che potremo incontrarci presto** I hope we can meet soon

potestà *nf* power

pot-pour'ri *nm inv* medley

✓ **'povero, -a** [1] *adj* poor; (semplice) plain; ∼ **di** (paese, terreno) lacking in; **in parole povere** in a few words
[2] *nf* poor woman
[3] *nm* poor man; **i poveri** the poor

povertà *nf* poverty

pozi'one *nf* potion

'pozza *nf* pool

poz'zanghera *nf* puddle

✓ **'pozzo** *nm* well; (minerario) pit
■ **pozzo petrolifero** oil well; **pozzo di petrolio** oil well; **pozzo di ventilazione** air shaft

pp. *abbr* (**pagine**) pp

PP.TT. *abbr* (**Poste e Telecomunicazioni**) [Italian] Post Office

PR *nfpl abbr* PR

'Praga *nf* Prague

prag'matico *adj* pragmatic

prali'nato *adj* (mandorla, gelato) praline-coated

pram'matica *nf* **essere di** ∼ be customary

pranotera'pia *nf* laying on of hands

pran'zare *vi* dine; (a mezzogiorno) lunch

✓ **'pranzo** *nm* dinner; (a mezzogiorno) lunch
■ **pranzo di lavoro** business lunch, working lunch; **pranzo della mensa scolastica** school lunch; **pranzo di nozze** wedding breakfast

'prassi *nf* standard procedure

prate'ria *nf* grassland, prairie

✓ **'pratica** *nf* practice; (esperienza) experience; (documentazione) file; **avere** ∼ **di qualcosa** be familiar with something, have experience of something; **mettere qualcosa in** ∼ put something into practice; **far** ∼ gain experience; **fare le pratiche per** gather the necessary papers for

prati'cabile *adj* practicable; (strada) passable

pratica'mente *adv* practically

prati'cante *nmf* apprentice; Relig [regular] churchgoer

prati'care *vt* practise; (frequentare) associate with; (fare) make

praticità *nf* practicality

✓ **'pratico** *adj* practical; (esperto) experienced, knowledgeable; (comodo) convenient; **essere** ∼ **di qualcosa** know about something; **all'atto** ∼ in practice

✓ indicates a very frequent word

✓ **'prato** *nm* meadow; (di giardino) lawn
■ **prato all'inglese** lawn

preaccensi'one *nf* Auto pre-ignition

pre'ambolo *nm* preamble

preannunci'are *vt* give advance notice of

prean'nuncio *nm* advance notice

preavvi'sare *vt* forewarn

preav'viso *nm* warning

precari'cato *adj* preloaded

precarietà *nf inv* frailty

pre'cario *adj* precarious

precauzi'one *nf* precaution; (cautela) care

✓ **prece'dente** [1] *adj* previous
[2] *nm* precedent; **avere dei precedenti penali** have a police record; **senza precedenti** (successo) unprecedented

precedente'mente *adv* previously

prece'denza *nf* precedence; (di veicoli) right of way; **dare la** ∼ **a** give priority to; Auto give way to; **avere la** ∼ have priority; Auto have right of way; ∼ **assoluta** top priority

✓ **pre'cedere** *vt* precede

pre'cetto *nm* precept

precet|'tore, -trice *nmf* tutor

✓ **precipi'tare** [1] *vt* ∼ **le cose** precipitate events; ∼ **qualcuno nella disperazione** cast somebody into a state of despair
[2] *vi* fall headlong; (situazione, eventi) come to a head

precipi'tarsi *vr* (gettarsi) throw oneself; (affrettarsi) rush; ∼ **a fare qualcosa** rush to do something

precipitazi'one *nf* (fretta) haste; (atmosferica) precipitation

precipi'toso *adj* hasty; (avventato) reckless; (caduta) headlong

preci'pizio *nm* precipice; **a** ∼ headlong

preci'sabile *adj* specifiable

precisa'mente *adv* precisely

preci'sare *vt* specify; (spiegare) clarify; **ci tengo a** ∼ **che…** I want to make the point that…

precisazi'one *nf* clarification

precisi'one *nf* precision

✓ **pre'ciso** *adj* precise; (calcolo, risposta) accurate; (ore) sharp; (identico) identical

pre'cludere *vt* preclude

pre'cludersi *vr* ∼ **ogni possibilità** preclude every possibility

pre'cluso *pp di* PRECLUDERE

pre'coce *adj* precocious; (prematuro) premature

precocità *nf* precociousness

precon'cetto [1] *adj* preconceived
[2] *nm* prejudice

preconfezio'nato *adj* pre-packed

preconfigu'rato *adj* preconfigured

pre'correre *vt* (anticipare) anticipate; ~ **i tempi** be ahead of one's time

precorri|'tore, -trice *nmf* precursor, forerunner

pre'cotto *adj* ready-cooked
■ **precotto e surgelato** cook-chill

precur'sore *nm* forerunner, precursor

'preda *nf* prey; (bottino) booty; **essere in ~ al panico** be panic-stricken; **in ~ alle fiamme** engulfed in flames

pre'dare *vt* plunder

preda'tore *nm* predator

predeces'sore *nmf* predecessor

pre'della *nf* platform

predel'lino *nm* step

predesti'nare *vt* predestine

predesti'nato *adj* predestined, preordained

predestinazi'one *nf* predestination

predetermi'nare *vt* predetermine

predetermi'nato *adj* predetermined, preordained

pre'detto pp di PREDIRE

'predica *nf* sermon; fig lecture

predi'care *vt* preach

predi'cato *nm* predicate

predige'rito *adj* predigested

predi'letto, -a [1] pp di PREDILIGERE
[2] *adj* favourite
[3] *nmf* pet fam

predilezi'one *nf* predilection; **avere una ~ per** have a predilection for, be partial to

predi'ligere *vt* prefer

prediposizi'one *nf* predisposition; (al disegno ecc) bent (a for)

pre'dire *vt* foretell

predi'sporre *vt* arrange; ~ **qualcuno a qualcosa** Med predispose somebody to something; (preparare) prepare somebody for something

predi'sporsi *vr* ~ **a** prepare oneself for

predi'sposto, -a [1] pp di PREDISPORRE
[2] *adj* arranged
■ **predisposto per la TV via cavo** cable-ready

predizi'one *nf* prediction

predomi'nante *adj* predominant

predomi'nare *vi* predominate

predo'minio *nm* predominance

pre'done *nm* robber

prefabbri'cato [1] *adj* prefabricated
[2] *nm* prefabricated building

prefazi'one *nf* preface

prefe'renza *nf* preference; **di ~** preferably

preferenzi'ale *adj* preferential; **corsia preferenziale** bus and taxi lane

prefe'ribile *adj* preferable

preferibil'mente *adv* preferably

☞ **prefe'rire** *vt* prefer

prefe'rito, -a *adj & nmf* favourite

pre'fetto *nm* prefect

prefet'tura *nf* prefecture

pre'figgere *vt* decide in advance, pre-arrange ‹termine›

pre'figgersi *vr* ~ **uno scopo** set oneself an objective

prefigu'rare *vt* (anticipare) foreshadow

prefinanzia'mento *nm* bridging loan

prefis'sare *vt* pre-arrange ‹data, appuntamento›

pre'fisso [1] pp di PREFIGGERE
[2] *nm* prefix; Teleph [dialling] code

☞ **pre'gare** [1] *vi* Relig pray
[2] *vt* Relig pray to; (supplicare) beg; **farsi ~** need persuading; ~ **qualcuno di fare qualcosa** ask somebody to do something; **si prega di... please...; si prega di non... please do not...; si prega di non fumare** please refrain from smoking

pre'gevole *adj* valuable

preghi'era *nf* prayer; (richiesta) request

pregi'arsi *vr* **si pregia di non essere mai in ritardo** he prides himself on never being late

pre'giato *adj* esteemed; (prezioso) valuable

'pregio *nm* esteem; (valore) value; (di persona) good point; **di ~** valuable

pregiudi'care *vt* prejudice; (danneggiare) harm

pregiudi'cato [1] *adj* prejudiced
[2] *nm* Jur previous offender

pregiu'dizio *nm* prejudice; (danno) detriment

pre'gnante *adj* (parola) pregnant, pregnant with meaning

'pregno *adj* (parola) pregnant, (pieno) full; ~ **di** (umidità) saturated with; (significato) pregnant with

'prego *int* (non c'è di che) don't mention it!; (per favore) please; **~?** I beg your pardon?; **posso? – ~** may I? – please do

pregu'stare *vt* look forward to

preinstal'lato *adj* preinstalled

prei'storia *nf* prehistory

prei'storico *adj* prehistoric

pre'lato *nm* prelate

prela'vaggio *nm* prewash

preleva'mento *nm* withdrawal

prele'vare *vt* withdraw ‹soldi›; collect ‹merci›; Med take

preli'evo *nm* (di soldi) withdrawal
■ **prelievo di sangue** blood sample

prelimi'nare [1] *adj* preliminary
[2] *nm* **preliminari** *pl* preliminaries

pre'ludere *vi* ~ **a** a herald

pre'ludio *nm* prelude

prema'man [1] *nm inv* maternity dress
[2] *adj* maternity *attrib*

prematrimoni'ale *adj* premarital

p

prematura'mente *adv* prematurely

prema'turo, -a [1] *adj* premature
[2] *nmf* premature baby

premedi'tare *vt* premeditate

premeditazi'one *nf* premeditation; **con**
∼ (omicidio) premeditated

'premere [1] *vt* press; Comput hit ‹*tasto*›
[2] *vi* **∼ a** (importare) matter to; **mi preme**
sapere I need to know; **∼ su** press on; push
‹*pulsante*›; fig (fare pressione su) put pressure
on, pressure; **∼ per ottenere qualcosa** push
for something

pre'messa *nf* introduction; **senza tante**
premesse without further ado

pre'messo (pp di PREMETTERE); **∼ che**
bearing in mind that

pre'mettere *vt* (mettere prima) put before;
premetto che... I want to make it clear first
that...; **∼ un'introduzione a un libro** put an
introduction at the beginning of a book

premi'are *vt* give a prize to; (ricompensare)
reward

premi'ato *adj* award-winning

premiazi'one *nf* prize giving

premi'nente *adj* pre-eminent

premi'nenza *nf* pre-eminence

⚹ **'premio** *nm* prize; (ricompensa) reward; (di
produzione ecc) bonus; Fin premium
■ **premio di assicurazione** insurance premium;
premio di consolazione consolation prize;
(ridicolo) booby prize; **premio di ingaggio**
Sport signing fee; **premio di produzione**
productivity bonus

premoni'tore *adj* ‹*sogno, segno*›
premonitory

premonizi'one *nf* premonition

premu'nire *vt* fortify

premu'nirsi *vr* take protective measures;
∼ di provide oneself with; **∼ contro** protect
oneself against

pre'mura *nf* (fretta) hurry; (cura) care; **far ∼**
a qualcuno hurry somebody up

premu'roso *adj* thoughtful

prena'tale *adj* antenatal

⚹ **'prendere** [1] *vt* take; (afferrare) seize;
catch ‹*treno, malattia, ladro, pesce*›;
have ‹*cibo, bevanda*›; (far pagare) charge;
‹*assumere*› take on; (ottenere) get; (occupare)
take up; (guadagnare) earn; **∼ informazioni**
make inquiries; **∼ in giro qualcuno** pull
somebody's leg; **∼ a calci/pugni** kick/
punch; **che ti prende?** what's got into you?;
quanto prende? what do you charge?; **∼ una**
persona per un'altra mistake a person for
somebody else; **passare a ∼ qualcuno**
collect somebody, pick somebody up
[2] *vi* (voltare) turn; (attecchire) take root;
(rapprendersi) set; ‹*fuoco*› catch, take; **∼ a**
destra/sinistra turn right/left; **∼ a fare**

⚹ indicates a very frequent word

qualcosa start doing something; **la colla non**
ha preso the glue didn't take

'prendersi *vr* **∼ a pugni** come to
blows; **∼ cura di** take care of ‹*ammalato*›;
prendersela take it to heart; **si prende troppo**
sul serio he takes himself too seriously

prendi'sole *nm* sundress

preno'tare *vt* book, reserve

preno'tarsi *vr* **∼ per** put one's name
down for

preno'tato *adj* booked, reserved

prenotazi'one *nf* booking, reservation
■ **prenotazione di gruppo** group booking

'prensile *adj* prehensile

preoccu'pante *adj* alarming

⚹ **preoccu'pare** *vt* worry

preoccu'parsi *vr* **∼** worry (**di** about);
∼ di fare qualcosa take the trouble to do
something

preoccu'pato *adj* worried; (apprensivo)
concerned

⚹ **preoccupazi'one** *nf* worry; (apprensione)
concern

preopera'torio *adj* preoperative

prepagato, -a [1] *adj* prepaid
[2] *nm* Teleph pay-as-you-go

⚹ **prepa'rare** *vt* prepare; study for ‹*esame*›;
∼ da mangiare prepare a meal

prepa'rarsi *vr* get ready

prepara'tivi *nmpl* preparations

prepa'rato *nm* (prodotto) preparation

prepara'torio *adj* preparatory

preparazi'one *nf* preparation;
(competenza) knowledge

prepensiona'mento *nm* early
retirement

preponde'rante *adj* predominant,
preponderant

preponde'ranza *nf* preponderance,
prevalence

pre'porre *vt* place before

preposizi'one *nf* preposition

pre'posto [1] pp di PREPORRE
[2] *adj* **∼ a** (addetto a) in charge of

prepo'tente [1] *adj* overbearing
[2] *nmf* bully; **fare il/la ∼ con qualcuno**
bully somebody

prepo'tenza *nf* high-handedness

preprogram'mato *adj* Comput
preprogrammed

pre'puzio *nm* foreskin, prepuce

preroga'tiva *nf* prerogative

'presa *nf* taking; (conquista) capture; (stretta)
hold; (di cemento ecc) setting; Electr socket; (di
gas, acqua) inlet, connection; (pizzico) pinch;
essere alle prese con be struggling *or*
grappling with; **a ∼ rapida** ‹*cemento, colla*›
quick-setting; **fare ∼ su qualcuno** influence
somebody
■ **macchina da presa** cine camera; **presa d'aria**

air vent; **presa in giro** leg-pull; **presa multipla** adaptor; **presa scart** scart connector

pre'sagio *nm* omen

presa'gire *vt* foretell

presa'lario *nm* maintenance grant

'presbite *adj* long-sighted

presbiteri'ano, -a *adj & nmf* Presbyterian

presbi'terio *nm* presbytery

pre'scelto *adj* selected

pre'scindere *vi* ∼ **da** leave aside; **a** ∼ **da** apart from

presco'lare *adj* pre-school; **in età** ∼ pre-school

pre'scritto pp di PRESCRIVERE

pre'scrivere *vt* prescribe

prescrizi'one *nf* prescription; (norma) rule; **cadere in** ∼ cease to be valid as a result of the statute of limitations

preselezi'one *nf* preliminary selection; (per il traffico) advance lane markings; Sport [qualifying] heats *pl*

⚬ **presen'tare** *vt* present; (far conoscere) introduce; show ‹*documento*›; (inoltrare) submit

presen'tarsi *vr* present oneself; (farsi conoscere) introduce oneself; (a ufficio) attend; (alla polizia ecc) report; (come candidato) stand, run (**a** for); ‹*occasione*› occur; ∼ **bene/male** ‹*persona*› make a good/ bad impression; ‹*situazione*› look good/bad

presenta|'tore, -trice *nmf* presenter; (di notiziario) announcer

■ **presentatore di talk show** chatshow host

presentazi'one *nf* presentation; (per conoscersi) introduction; **fare le presentazioni** do the introductions; **dietro** ∼ **di ricetta medica** on doctor's prescription only

⚬ **pre'sente** [1] *adj* present; (attuale) current; (questo) this; **aver** ∼ remember

[2] *nm* present; **i presenti** those present

[3] *nf* **allegato alla** ∼ (in lettera) enclosed

presenti'mento *nm* foreboding

⚬ **pre'senza** *nf* presence; (aspetto) appearance; **in** ∼ **di, alla** ∼ **di** in the presence of; **di bella** ∼ personable

■ **presenza di spirito** presence of mind

presenzi'are *vi* ∼ **a** attend

pre'sepe, presepio *nm* crib

preser'vare *vt* preserve; (proteggere) protect (**da** from)

preserva'tivo *nm* condom

preservazi'one *nf* preservation

'preside [1] *nm* headmaster; Univ dean

[2] *nf* headmistress; Univ dean

⚬ **presi'dente** [1] *nm* chairman; Pol president

[2] *nf* chairwoman; Pol president

■ **presidente del consiglio [dei ministri]** Prime Minister; **presidente della repubblica** President of the Republic

presiden'tessa *nf* chairwoman

presi'denza *nf* presidency; (di assemblea) chairmanship

presidenzi'ale *adj* presidential

presidi'are *vt* garrison

pre'sidio *nm* garrison

presi'edere *vt* preside over

'preso pp di PRENDERE

'pressa *nf* Mech press

press-'agent *mf inv* publicist, press agent

pres'sante *adj* urgent

pressap'poco *adv* about

pres'sare *vt* press

pressi'one *nf* pressure; **far** ∼ **su** put pressure on; **essere sotto** ∼ fig be under pressure; **esercitare pressioni su qualcuno** put pressure on somebody; **a/di alta** ∼ high pressure

■ **pressione fiscale** tax burden; **pressione [delle] gomme** tyre pressure; **pressione del sangue** blood pressure

⚬ **'presso** [1] *prep* near; (a casa di) with; (negli indirizzi) care of, c/o; ‹*lavorare*› for; **richiedere qualcosa** ∼ **una società** request something from a company

[2] *nmpl* **pressi: nei pressi di...** in the neighbourhood *or* vicinity of...

pressoché *adv* almost

pressuriz'zare *vt* pressurize

pressuriz'zato *adj* pressurized

prestabi'lire *vt* arrange in advance

prestabi'lito *adj* agreed, predetermined

prestam'pato [1] *adj* printed

[2] *nm* (modulo) form

pre'stante *adj* good-looking

pre'stanza *nf* good looks *pl*

⚬ **pre'stare** *vt* lend; ∼ **attenzione** pay attention; ∼ **aiuto** lend a hand; ∼ **ascolto** lend an ear; ∼ **fede a** give credence to; ∼ **giuramento** take the oath; **farsi** ∼ borrow (**da** from)

pre'starsi *vr* ‹*frase*› lend itself; ‹*persona*› offer

prestazi'one *nf* performance; **prestazioni** *pl* (servizi) services

prestigia|'tore, -trice *nmf* conjuror, conjurer

pre'stigio *nm* prestige; **gioco di prestigio** conjuring trick

prestigi'oso *nm* prestigious

⚬ **pre'stito** *nm* loan; **dare in** ∼ lend; **prendere in** ∼ borrow

■ **prestito bancario** bank loan; **prestito con garanzia collaterale** collateral loan

⚬ **'presto** *adv* soon; (di buon'ora) early; (in fretta) quickly; **a** ∼ see you soon; **al più** ∼ as soon as possible; ∼ **o tardi** sooner or later; **far** ∼ be quick

pre'sumere *vt* presume; (credere) think

p

presu'mibile *adj* è ~ che...
presumably, ...

pre'sunto *adj* ‹colpevole› presumed

presuntu'oso ⓵ *adj* presumptuous
⓶ *nmf* presumptuous person

presunzi'one *nf* presumption

presup'porre *vt* suppose; (richiedere)
presuppose

presupposizi'one *nf* presupposition

presup'posto *nm* essential requirement

prêt-à-por'ter *nm* ready-to-wear clothing

✧ **'prete** *nm* priest

preten'dente ⓵ *nmf* pretender
⓶ *nm* (corteggiatore) suitor

✧ **pre'tendere** ⓵ *vt* (sostenere) claim;
(esigere) demand
⓶ *vi* ~ a claim to; ~ di (esigere) demand to

pretensi'one *nf* pretension

pretenzi'oso *adj* pretentious

preterintenzio'nale *adj* omicidio ~
manslaughter

pre'terito *nm* preterite

pre'tesa *nf* pretension; (esigenza) claim;
senza pretese unpretentious

pre'teso *pp di* PRETENDERE

pre'testo *nm* pretext

pre'tore *nm* magistrate

pretta'mente *adv* decidedly

'pretto *adj* pure

pre'tura *nf* magistrate's court

preva'lente *adj* prevalent

prevalente'mente *adv* primarily,
predominantly

preva'lenza *nf* prevalence

preva'lere *vi* prevail

pre'valso *pp di* PREVALERE

✧ **preve'dere** *vt* foresee; forecast ‹tempo›;
(legge ecc) provide for

preve'nire *vt* precede; (evitare) prevent;
(avvertire) forewarn

preventi'vare *vt* estimate; (aspettarsi)
budget for

preven'tivo ⓵ *adj* preventive; bilancio
preventivo budget
⓶ *nm* Comm estimate

preve'nuto *adj* forewarned; (maldisposto)
prejudiced

prevenzi'one *nf* prevention; (preconcetto)
prejudice

previ'dente *adj* provident

previ'denza *nf* foresight
■ previdenza integrativa supplementary
social security, supplementary welfare Am;
previdenza sociale social security, welfare Am

previdenzi'ale *adj* provident

'previo *adj* ~ pagamento on payment

previsi'one *nf* forecast; in ~ di in
anticipation of; previsioni *pl* del tempo
weather forecast

pre'visto ⓵ *pp di* PREVEDERE
⓶ *adj* foreseen
⓷ *nm* più/meno/prima del ~ more/less/
earlier than expected

✧ **prezi'oso** *adj* precious

prez'zemolo *nm* parsley

✧ **'prezzo** *nm* price; [a] metà ~ half price; a
~ ribassato at a reduced price; non aver ~
fig be priceless
■ prezzo d'acquisto purchase price; prezzo
di costo cost price; prezzo al dettaglio retail
price; prezzo di fabbrica factory price; prezzo
di favore special price; prezzo all'ingrosso
wholesale price; prezzo intero full price;
prezzo di listino list price; prezzo di mercato
market price; prezzo al minuto retail price;
prezzo d'offerta offer price; prezzo politico
subsidized price; prezzo di riferimento
benchmark price; prezzo scontato sale price;
prezzo sorvegliato controlled price; prezzo
stracciato slashed price, drastically reduced
price; prezzo trattabile price negotiable;
prezzo unitario unit price; prezzo di vendita
selling price

✧ **prigi'one** *nf* prison; (pena) imprisonment;
mettere in ~ imprison, put in prison

prigio'nia *nf* imprisonment

✧ **prigioni'ero, -a** ⓵ *adj* imprisoned
⓶ *nmf* prisoner; tenere ~ qualcuno keep
somebody prisoner
■ prigioniero di guerra prisoner of war, POW;
prigioniero politico political prisoner

✧ **'prima** ⓵ *adv* before; (più presto) earlier;
(in anticipo) beforehand; (in primo luogo) first;
finiamo questo, ~ let's finish this first;
puoi venire ~? (di giorni) can't you come any
sooner?; (di ore) can't you come any earlier?;
~ o poi sooner or later; quanto ~ as soon
as possible
⓶ *prep* ~ di before; ~ di mangiare before
eating; ~ d'ora before now
⓷ *conj* ~ che before; ~ che posso as soon
as I can; ~ possibile asap
⓸ *nf* first class; Theat first night; Auto first
[gear]
■ prima elementare first grade

pri'mario *adj* primary; (principale) principal

pri'mate *nm* primate

prima'tista *nmf* record-holder

pri'mato *nm* supremacy; Sport record

✧ **prima'vera** *nf* spring

primave'rile *adj* spring *attrib*

primeggi'are *vi* excel

primi'tivo *adj* primitive; (originario) original

pri'mizie *nfpl* early produce *sg*

✧ **'primo** ⓵ *adj* first; (fondamentale) principal;
(in importanza) main; (precedente di due) former;
(iniziale) early; (migliore) best

✧ indicates a very frequent word

2 *nm* first; **il ~ d'aprile** April the first, April Fools' Day; **primi** *pl* **tempi** (i primi giorni) the beginning; **in un ~ tempo** at first
■ **prima colazione** *nf* breakfast; **prima copia** *nf* master copy; **prima linea** *nf* Mil front line; **prima serata** *nf* prime time; **in prima serata trasmetteremo...** in the early evening slot we're bringing you...

primo'genito, -a *adj & nmf* first-born

primogeni'tura *nf* primogeniture; **vendere la ~** sell one's birthright

primordi'ale *adj* primordial

'primula *nf* primrose

⚜ **princi'pale 1** *adj* main
  2 *nm* head, boss *fam*

princi'pato *nm* principality
■ **il Principato di Monaco** Monaco

⚜ **'principe** *nm* prince; **da ~** princely
■ **principe ereditario** crown prince; **principe del foro** *famous lawyer*

princi'pesco *adj* princely

⚜ **princi'pessa** *nf* princess

principi'ante *nmf* beginner

principi'are *vt/i* begin, start

⚜ **prin'cipio** *nm* beginning; (concetto) principle; (causa) cause; **per ~** on principle; **una questione di ~** a matter of principle
■ **principio attivo** active ingredient

pri'ore *nm* prior

pri'ori: a ~ 1 *adv* ‹decidere› a priori; **farsi a ~ un'opinione di** prejudge
  2 *adj* a priori

priorità *nf inv* priority

priori'tario *adj* having priority; ‹obiettivo› priority *attrib*; **la nostra scelta prioritaria** our decision, which must take priority

'prisma *nm* prism

'privacy *nf* privacy

pri'vare *vt* deprive

pri'varsi *vr* deprive oneself

privatiz'zare *vt* privatize

privatizzazi'one *nf* privatization

⚜ **pri'vato, -a 1** *adj* private
  2 *nmf* private citizen; **in ~** in private; **ritirarsi a vita privata** withdraw from public life

privazi'one *nf* deprivation

privilegi'are *vt* privilege; (considerare più importante) favour

privi'legio *nm* privilege; **avere il ~ di** have the privilege of; **questo dizionario ha il ~ della chiarezza** this dictionary has the merit of clarity

⚜ **'privo** *adj* **~ di** devoid of; (mancante) lacking in

pro 1 *prep* for
  2 *nm* advantage; **a che ~?** what's the point?; **il ~ e il contro** the pros and cons

pro'babile *adj* probable

probabilità *nf inv* probability; **avere buone ~** have a fighting chance; **~ di riuscita** chances of success

probabil'mente *adv* probably

pro'bante *adj* convincing

probità *nf* probity

⚜ **pro'blema** *nm* problem; **non c'è ~** no problem

proble'matico *adj* problematic

pro'boscide *nf* trunk

procacci'are *vt* obtain

procacci'arsi *vr* obtain

pro'cace *adj* ‹ragazza› provocative

⚜ **pro'cedere** *vi* (in percorso, discorso) go on, proceed fml; (iniziare) start; **il lavoro procede bene** the work is going well; **~ contro** Jur start legal proceedings against

procedi'mento *nm* process; Jur proceedings *pl*
■ **procedimento giudiziario** legal proceedings

proce'dura *nf* procedure
■ **procedura civile** civil proceedings *pl*; **procedura fallimentare** bankruptcy proceedings *pl*

procedu'rale *adj* procedural

proces'sare *vt* Jur try

processi'one *nf* procession

⚜ **pro'cesso** *nm* process; Jur trial; **essere sotto ~** be on trial; **mettere sotto ~** put on trial
■ **processo di pace** peace process

proces'sore *nm* Comput processor

processu'ale *adj* trial *attrib*

pro'cinto *nm* **essere in ~ di** be about to

proci'one *nm* raccoon

pro'clama *nm* proclamation

procla'mare *vt* proclaim

proclamazi'one *nf* proclamation

procrasti'nare *vt* (ltter) postpone

procre'are *vt* procreate

procreazi'one *nf* procreation

pro'cura *nf* power of attorney; **per ~** by proxy
■ **Procura [della Repubblica]** Public Prosecutor's office

⚜ **procu'rare** *vt/i* procure; (causare) cause; (cercare) try

procura'tore *nm* attorney
■ **Procuratore Generale** Attorney General; **procuratore legale** lawyer; **procuratore della repubblica** public prosecutor

'prode *adj* brave

pro'dezza *nf* bravery

prodi'gare *vt* lavish

prodi'garsi *vr* do one's best

pro'digio *nm* prodigy

prodigi'oso *adj* prodigious

'prodigo *adj* prodigal

prodi'torio *adj* treasonable

✓ **pro'dotto** ① pp di PRODURRE
　② nm product
　■ prodotti pl agricoli farm produce sg; prodotto artigianalmente adj made by craftsmen; prodotti pl di bellezza cosmetics; prodotto derivato by-product; prodotto in fabbrica adj factory-made; prodotto finito end product, finished product; prodotto interno lordo gross domestic product; prodotto nazionale lordo gross national product

✓ **pro'durre** vt produce

pro'dursi vr ⟨attore⟩ play; (accadere) happen, occur

produttività nf productivity

produt'tivo adj productive; poco ~ unproductive

produt|'tore, -trice ① adj producing
　■ produttore di petrolio oil-producing
　② nmf producer

✓ **produzi'one** nf production
　■ produzione in serie mass production

Prof. abbr (**professore**) Prof

profa'nare vt desecrate

profanazi'one nf desecration

pro'fano ① adj profane
　② nm i profani pl the uninitiated

profe'rire vt utter

Prof.essa abbr (**Professoressa**) Prof

profes'sare vt profess; practise ⟨professione⟩

professio'nale adj professional; istituto professionale training college

professionalità nf professionalism

✓ **professi'one** nf profession; libera professione profession

professio'nismo nm professionalism

professio'nista nmf professional

professo'rale adj professorial

✓ **profes'sor|e, -essa** nmf Sch teacher; Univ lecturer; (titolare di cattedra) professor

pro'feta nm prophet

pro'fetico adj prophetic

profetiz'zare vt prophesy

profe'zia nf prophecy

pro'ficuo adj profitable

profi'lare vt outline; (ornare) border; Aeron streamline

profi'larsi vr stand out

profi'lattico ① adj prophylactic
　② nm condom

pro'filo nm profile; (breve studio) outline; di ~ in profile
　■ profilo genetico genetic profiling

profite'roles nmpl profiteroles

profit'tare vi ~ di (avvantaggiarsi) profit by; (approfittare) take advantage of

pro'fitto nm profit; (vantaggio) advantage; mettere qualcosa a ~ turn something to

one's advantage; trarre ~ da (vantaggio) derive benefit from

profonda'mente adv deeply, profoundly

profondità nf inv depth; (del pensiero ecc) depth, profundity; in ~ in depth; passaggio in ~ Sport deep pass [down the field]
　■ profondità di campo Phot depth of field

✓ **pro'fondo** adj deep; ⟨pensiero ecc⟩ profound; ⟨cultura⟩ great

pro 'forma ① adj routine; fattura pro forma pro forma [invoice]
　② adv as a formality
　③ nm formality

'profugo, -a nmf refugee

profu'mare ① vi smell good; ~ di smell of
　② vt perfume

profu'marsi vr put on perfume

profumata'mente adv pagare ~ pay through the nose

profu'mato adj ⟨fiore⟩ fragrant; ⟨fazzoletto ecc⟩ scented

profume'ria nf perfumery

✓ **pro'fumo** nm perfume, scent

profusi'one nf profusion; a ~ in profusion

pro'fuso adj profuse

pro'genie nf progeny

progeni|'tore, -trice nmf ancestor

proget'tare vt plan; plan, design ⟨costruzione⟩

progettazione nf planning, design
　■ progettazione assistita da computer computer-aided design, CAD

proget'tista nmf designer

✓ **pro'getto** nm plan; (di lavoro importante) project
　■ progetto di legge bill; progetto pilota pilot scheme

prog'nosi nf inv prognosis; in ~ riservata on the danger list

✓ **pro'gramma** nm programme; Comput program; avere qualcosa in ~ have something planned, have something on; programmi pl televisivi del mattino breakfast TV
　■ programma antivirus Comput antivirus program, antivirus software; programma assemblatore Comput assembler; programma aziendale business plan; programma per la gestione dei file Comput file manager; programma di grafica Comput graphics program; programma politico manifesto; programma scolastico syllabus; programma di setup Comput setup program; programma di utilità Comput utility

program'mare vt programme; Comput program

program'mato adj (sviluppo) planned

programma|'tore, -trice nmf [computer] programmer

---

programmazi'one *nf* programming
progre'dire *vi* [make] progress
progres'sione *nf* progression
progres'sista *nmf* progressive
progres'sivo *adj* progressive
pro'gresso *nm* progress; **fare progressi** make progress
⚡ **proi'bire** *vt* forbid
proibi'tivo *adj* prohibitive
proibito *adj* forbidden; **è ~ fumare qui** it's no smoking here
proibizi'one *nf* prohibition
proibizio'nismo *nm* prohibition
proiet'tare *vt* project; show ‹film›
proi'ettile *nm* bullet
proiet'tore *nm* projector; Auto headlight
■ **proiettore per diapositive** slide projector
proiezi'one *nf* projection
■ **proiezione di diapositive** slide show
'prole *nf* offspring
proletari'ato *nm* proletariat
prole'tarlo *adj & nm* proletarian
prolife'rare *vi* proliferate
pro'lifico *adj* prolific
prolissità *nf* prolixity, diffuseness
pro'lisso *adj* verbose, prolix
pro 'loco *nf* tourist office (*in small towns*)
'prologo *nm* prologue
pro'lunga *nf* extension
prolunga'mento *nm* extension
prolun'gare *vt* extend ‹contratto, scadenza, strada›; prolong ‹vita›; lengthen ‹vita, strada›
prolun'garsi *vr* continuo, go on; **~ su** (dilungarsi) dwell upon
prome'moria *nm* memo; (per se stessi) reminder; note; (formale) memorandum
⚡ **pro'messa** *nf* promise; **era già una ~ del...** he was already a promising new talent in...
pro'messo 1 *pp di* PROMETTERE
2 *adj* ‹terra› promised
■ **promesso sposo, promessa sposa** *nm,f* betrothed
promet'tente *adj* promising
⚡ **pro'mettere** *vt/i* promise
promi'nente *adj* prominent
promi'nenza *nf* prominence
promiscuità *nf* promiscuity
pro'miscuo *adj* promiscuous
promon'torio *nm* promontory
pro'mosso 1 *pp di* PROMUOVERE
2 *adj* Sch who has gone up a year; Univ who has passed an exam
promo|'tore, -trice *nmf* promoter
promozio'nale *adj* promotional; **vendita promozionale** special offer
promozi'one *nf* promotion

promul'gare *vt* promulgate
promulgazi'one *nf* promulgation
promu'overe *vt* promote; Sch move up a class; **essere promosso** Sch, Univ pass one's exams
proni'pote 1 *nm* (di bisnonno) great-grandson; (di prozio) great-nephew; **pronipoti** *pl* great-grandchildren
2 *nf* (di bisnonno) great-granddaughter; (di prozio) great-niece
pro'nome *nm* pronoun
pronomi'nale *adj* pronominal
pronosti'care *vt* forecast, predict
pronostica|'tore, -trice *nmf* forecaster
pro'nostico *nm* forecast
pron'tezza *nf* readiness; (rapidità) quickness; **con ~ di spirito** quick-wittedly
■ **prontezza di riflessi** quick reflexes *pl*
⚡ **'pronto** *adj* ready; (rapido) quick; **~!** Teleph hello!; **tenersi ~ (per qualcosa)** be ready (for something); **pronti, via!** (in gare) ready! steady! go!; **a pronta cassa** cash on delivery
■ **pronto intervento** *nm* emergency service; **pronto soccorso** *nm* first aid; (in ospedale) accident and emergency, A&E
prontu'ario *nm* handbook
pro'nuncia *nf* pronunciation
⚡ **pronunci'are** *vt* pronounce; (dire) utter; deliver ‹discorso›
pronunci'arsi *vr* (su un argomento) give one's opinion; **~ a favore/contro qualcosa** pronounce oneself in favour of/against something
pronunci'ato *adj* pronounced; (prominente) prominent
pro'nunzia = PRONUNCIA
pronunzi'are = PRONUNCIARE
propa'ganda *nf* propaganda
■ **propaganda elettorale** electioneering; **propaganda di partito** party political propaganda
propa'gare *vt* propagate
propa'garsi *vr* spread
propagazi'one *nf* propagation
prope'deutico *adj* introductory
propel'lente *nm* propellant
pro'pendere *vi* **~ per** be in favour of
propensi'one *nf* inclination, propensity
pro'penso 1 *pp di* PROPENDERE
2 *adj* essere **~ a fare qualcosa** be inclined to do something
propi'nare *vt* administer
pro'pizio *adj* favourable
proponi'mento *nm* resolution
⚡ **pro'porre** *vt* propose; (suggerire) suggest
pro'porsi *vr* set oneself ‹obiettivo, meta›; **~ di** intend to
proporzio'nale *adj* proportional
proporzio'nare *vt* proportion

proporzio'nato adj proportioned

proporzi'one nf proportion

✧ **pro'posito** nm intention; **ho fatto il ~ di…** I have made the decision to…; **a ~** by the way; **a ~ di** with regard to; **di ~** (apposta) on purpose; **capitare a ~, giungere a ~** come at just the right time; **propositi** pl **per l'anno nuovo** New Year's resolutions

proposizi'one nf clause; (frase) sentence

✧ **pro'posta** nf proposal, suggestion
  ■ **proposta di legge** bill; **proposta di matrimonio** [marriage] proposal

pro'posto pp di PROPORRE

propria'mente adv **~ detto** in the strict sense of the word

proprietà nf inv property; (diritto) ownership; (correttezza) propriety; **essere di ~ di qualcuno** be somebody's property
  ■ **proprietà collettiva** collective ownership; **proprietà immobiliare** property; **proprietà di linguaggio** correct use of language; **proprietà privata** private property

proprie'taria nf owner; (di casa affittata) landlady

proprie'tario nm owner; (di casa affittata) landlord

✧ **'proprio** [1] adj one's [own]; (caratteristico) typical; (appropriato) proper
  [2] adv just; (veramente) really; **non ~** not really, not exactly; (affatto) not… at all
  [3] pron one's own
  [4] nm one's own; **lavorare in ~** be one's own boss; **mettersi in ~** set up on one's own

propu'gnare vt support

propulsi'one nf propulsion; **a ~ atomica** atomic[-powered]
  ■ **propulsione a getto** jet propulsion

propul'sore nm propeller

'prora nf Naut prow

'proroga nf extension

proro'gabile adj extendable

proro'gare vt extend

pro'rompere vi burst out

'prosa nf prose

pro'saico adj prosaic

pro'sciogliere vt release; Jur acquit

prosciogli'mento nm release

pro'sciolto pp di PROSCIOGLIERE

prosciu'gare vt dry up; (bonificare) reclaim

prosciu'garsi vr dry up

prosci'utto nm ham
  ■ **prosciutto cotto** cooked ham; **prosciutto crudo** type of dry-cured ham, Parma ham

pro'scritto, -a [1] pp di PROSCRIVERE
  [2] nmf exile

pro'scrivere vt exile, banish

proscrizi'one nf exile, banishment

prosecuzi'one nf continuation

✧ indicates a very frequent word

prosegui'mento nm continuation; **buon ~!** (viaggio) have a good journey!; (festa) enjoy the rest of the party!

prosegu'ire [1] vt continue
  [2] vi go on, continue

pro'selito nm convert

prospe'rare vi prosper

prosperità nf prosperity

'prospero adj prosperous; (favorevole) favourable

prospe'roso adj flourishing; (ragazza) buxom

prospet'tare vt show

prospet'tarsi vr seem

prospet'tiva nf perspective; (panorama) view; fig prospect

pro'spetto nm (vista) view; (facciata) façade; (tabella) table

prospici'ente adj facing

prossima'mente adv soon

prossimità nf proximity; **in ~ di** near

✧ **'prossimo, -a** [1] adj near; (seguente) next; (molto vicino) close; **l'anno ~** next year; **~ venturo** next; **essere ~ a fare qualcosa** be about to do something
  [2] nmf neighbour

'prostata nf prostate

prostitu'irsi vr prostitute oneself

prosti'tuta nf prostitute

prostituzi'one nf prostitution

pro'strare vt prostrate

pro'strarsi vr prostrate oneself

pro'strato adj prostrate

protago'nista nmf protagonist; **ruolo/ attore non ~** supporting role/actor

✧ **pro'teggere** vt protect; (favorire) favour; **~ da sovrascrittura** write-protect

pro'teico adj protein attrib; **molto ~** rich in protein

prote'ina nf protein

pro'tendere vt stretch out

pro'tendersi vr (in avanti) lean out

pro'teso pp di PROTENDERE

pro'testa nf protest; (dichiarazione) protestation

prote'stante adj & nmf Protestant

prote'stare vt/i protest

prote'starsi vr **~ innocente** protest one's innocence

protet'tivo adj protective

pro'tetto, -a [1] pp di PROTEGGERE
  [2] adj protected; **non ~** unprotected
  ■ **protetto da password** password-protected

protetto'rato nm protectorate

protet|'tore, -trice [1] nmf protector; (sostenitore) patron
  [2] nm (di prostituta) pimp

protezi'one nf protection
  ■ **protezione aerea** air cover; **protezione**

dell'ambiente environmental protection;
protezione antivirus virus protection;
protezione civile civil defence
protocol'lare ☐1☐ *adj* (visita) protocol
☐2☐ *vt* register
proto'collo *nm* protocol; (registro) register;
carta protocollo official stamped paper
■ protocollo di gestione remota della posta
elettronica IMAP; protocollo Internet Internet
protocol; protocollo per il trasferimento di
file file transfer protocol; protocollo per il
trasferimento di ipertesti hypertext transfer
protocol
pro'totipo *nm* prototype
pro'trarre *vt* protract; (differire) postpone
pro'trarsi *vr* go on, continue
pro'tratto *pp di* PROTRARRE
protube'rante *adj* protuberant
protube'ranza *nf* protuberance
'prova *nf* test; (dimostrazione) proof; (tentativo)
try, attempt; (di abito) fitting; Sport heat;
Theat rehearsal; (bozza) proof; **prove** *pl*
evidence; **fino a ~ contraria** until I'm told
otherwise; **in ~** (assumere) for a trial period;
mettere alla ~ put to the test; **a ~ di bomba**
bombproof; **a ~ di ladro** burglarproof
■ prova del fuoco fig acid test; prova generale
dress rehearsal; prova medico-legale forensic
evidence
pro'vare *vt* test; (dimostrare) prove; (tentare)
try; try on ‹abiti ecc›; (sentire) feel; Theat
rehearse; **prova!** just try!
pro'varsi *vr* try
proveni'enza *nf* origin
prove'nire *vi* **~ da** come from
pro'vento *nm* proceeds *pl*
prove'nuto *pp di* PROVENIRE
pro'verbio *nm* proverb
pro'vetta *nf* test-tube; **bambino in provetta**
test-tube baby
pro'vetto *adj* skilled
pro'vincia *nf* province
provinci'ale *adj* provincial; **strada**
provinciale B road, secondary road
pro'vino *nm* specimen; Cinema screen test
provo'cante *adj* provocative
provo'care *vt* provoke; (causare) cause
provoca|'tore, -trice *nmf* trouble-maker
provoca'torio *adj* provocative,
confrontational
provocazi'one *nf* provocation
provo'lone *nm* type of cheese with a
slightly smoked flavour
provve'dere *vi* **~ a** provide for
provvedi'mento *nm* measure; (previdenza)
precaution
■ provvedimento disciplinare disciplinary
measure
provvedito'rato *nm*

■ provveditorato agli studi education
department
provvedi'tore *nm*
■ provveditore agli studi director of education
provvi'denza *nf* providence
provvidenzi'ale *adj* providential
provvigi'one *nf* Comm commission;
lavorare a **~** work on commission
provvi'sorio *adj* provisional; **in via**
provvisoria provisionally, for the time being
prov'vista *nf* supply
pro'zia *nf* great-aunt
pro'zio *nm* great-uncle
'prua *nf* Naut prow
pru'dente *adj* prudent
pru'denza *nf* prudence; **per ~** as a
precaution
prudenzi'ale *adj* prudential
'prudere *vi* itch
'prugna *nf* plum
■ prugna secca prune; prugna selvatica
damson
'prugno *nm* plum[-tree]
'prugnolo *nm* sloe
pruri'gi'noso *adj* itchy
pru'rito *nm* itch
P.S. *abbr* (**Pubblica Sicurezza**) police
pseu'donimo *nm* pseudonym
psica'nalisi *nf* psychoanalysis
psicana'lista *nmf* psychoanalyst
psicanaliz'zare *vt* psychoanalyse
'psiche *nf* psyche
psiche'delico *adj* psychedelic
psichi'atra *nmf* psychiatrist
psichia'tria *nf* psychiatry
psichi'atrico *adj* psychiatric
'psichico *adj* mental
psico'farmaco *nm* drug that affects the
mind
psicolo'gia *nf* psychology
psico'logico *adj* psychological
psi'cologo, -a *nmf* psychologist
psico'patico, -a ☐1☐ *adj* psychopathic
☐2☐ *nmf* psychopath
psicopedago'gia *nf* educational
psychology
psi'cosi *nf inv* psychosis
psicoso'matico *adj* psychosomatic
psicotera'peuta *nmf* psychotherapist
psicotera'pista *nmf* psychotherapist
psi'cotico, -a *adj & nmf* psychotic
PT *abbr* (**Posta e Telegrafi**) PO
puàh *int* yuck!
pub *nm* pub
pubbli'care *vt* publish
pubblicazi'one *nf* publication;
pubblicazioni *pl* (di matrimonio) banns
■ pubblicazione periodica periodical

p

pubbli'cista *nmf* Journ correspondent

pubblicità *nf inv* publicity, advertising; (annuncio) advertisement, advert; **fare ~ a qualcosa** advertise something; **piccola pubblicità** small advertisements

pubblici'tario *adj* advertising

⚡ **'pubblico** [1] *adj* public; **scuola pubblica** state school
[2] *nm* public; (spettatori) audience; **in ~** in public; **grande ~** general public; **Pubblica Sicurezza** police
■ **pubblico ministero** public prosecutor; **pubblico ufficiale** civil servant

'pube *nm* pubis

pubertà *nf* puberty

pu'dico *adj* modest

pu'dore *nm* modesty

pue'rile *adj* children's; pej childish

'puerpera *nf* new mother

puerpe'rale *adj* of childbirth, puerperal fml; (depressione) postnatal

puer'perio *nm* postnatal period

pugi'lato *nm* boxing

'pugile *nm* boxer

'Puglia *nf* Apulia

pugli'ese *adj* & *nmf* Apulian

pugna'lare *vt* stab

pugna'lata *nf* stab

pu'gnale *nm* dagger

⚡ **'pugno** *nm* fist; (colpo) punch; (manciata) fistful; fig (numero limitato) handful; **dare un ~** a punch; **di proprio ~** (scrivere) in one's own hand; **fare a pugni** (colori) clash; **tenere in ~** (situazione) have under control; **have in the palm of one's hand** (persona); **un ~ in un occhio** fig an eyesore
■ **pugno di ferro** iron fist

'pula *nf* s| **la ~** the fuzz

'pulce *nf* flea; (microfono) bug; **mettere la ~ nell'orecchio a qualcuno** sow a doubt in somebody's mind

pul'cino *nm* chick; (nel calcio) junior

pu'ledra *nf* filly

pu'ledro *nm* foal, colt

pu'leggia *nf* pulley

⚡ **pu'lire** *vt* clean; **~ a secco** dry-clean; **far ~ qualcosa** have something cleaned

puliscipi'edi *nm inv* boot scraper

pu'lito *adj* clean

puli'tura *nf* cleaning

puli'zia *nf* (il pulire) cleaning; (l'essere pulito) cleanliness; **pulizie** *pl* housework; **fare le pulizie** do the cleaning
■ **pulizia personale** personal hygiene

'pullman *nm inv* coach, bus; (urbano) bus; **gita in ~** coach trip

pull'over *nm* pullover

pul'mino *nm* minibus

'pulpito *nm* pulpit

pul'sante *nm* button; Electr [push-]button
■ **pulsante di accensione** on/off switch; **pulsante di alimentazione** power switch

pul'sare *vi* pulsate

pulsazi'one *nf* pulsation

pul'viscolo *nm* dust

'puma *nm inv* puma

'punching 'bag *nf inv* punchbag

pun'gente *adj* prickly; (insetto) stinging; (odore ecc) sharp

'pungere *vt* prick; (insetto) sting; **~ qualcuno sul vivo** cut somebody to the quick

pungersi *vr* prick oneself; **~ un dito** prick one's finger

pungigli'one *nm* sting

pungo'lare *vt* goad

pu'nire *vt* punish

puni'tivo *adj* punitive

punizi'one *nf* punishment; Sport penalty; (in calcio) free kick
■ **punizione corporale** corporal punishment

⚡ **'punta** *nf* point; (estremità) tip; (di monte) peak, top; (un po) pinch; Sport forward; **doppie punte** (di capelli) split ends; **di ~** (ore) peak; (personaggio) leading

⚡ **pun'tare** [1] *vt* point; (spingere con forza) push; (scommettere) bet; fam (appuntare) fasten
[2] *vi* **~ su** fig rely on; (scommettere) bet on; **~ verso** (dirigersi) head for; **~ a** aspire to; **punta e clicca** Comput point and click

punta'spilli *nm inv* pincushion

pun'tata *nf* (di una storia) instalment; (televisiva) episode; (al gioco) stake, bet; (breve visita) flying visit; **a puntate** serialized, in instalments; **fare una ~ a/in** pop over to (luogo)

punteggia'tura *nf* punctuation

pun'teggio *nm* score

puntel'lare *vt* prop

pun'tello *nm* prop

punteru'olo *nm* awl

pun'tiglio *nm* spite; (ostinazione) obstinacy

puntigli'oso *adj* punctilious, pernickety pej

pun'tina *nf* (da disegno) drawing pin, thumb tack Am; (di giradischi) stylus
■ **puntina da disegno** drawing pin, thumb tack Am

pun'tine *nfpl* Aut puntine [platinate] points

pun'tino *nm* dot; **a ~** perfectly; (cotto) to a T; **puntini** *pl* [di sospensione] suspension points

⚡ **'punto** *nm* point; (in cucito, Med) stitch; (in punteggiatura) full stop; **in che ~?** where, exactly?; **di ~ in bianco** all of a sudden; **essere sul ~ di fare qualcosa** be on the point of doing something, be about to do something; **in ~** sharp; **mettere a ~** put right; fig fine-tune; tune up ‹*motore*›; **messa a ~** fine tuning; **due punti** colon; **punti** *pl* **cardinali** points of the compass

■ **punto cieco** blind spot; **punto di congelamento** freezing point; **punto croce** cross-stitch; **punto debole** weak spot; **punto di domanda** question mark; **punto di ebollizione** boiling point; **punto esclamativo** exclamation mark; **punto di fuga** vanishing point; **punto di fusione** melting point; **punto d'incontro** meeting-point; **punto di infiammabilità** flashpoint; **punto interrogativo** question mark; **punto morto** fig stand-off; **punto nero** (comedone) blackhead; **punto di pareggio** Fin breakeven point; **punto di partenza** starting point; **punto di riferimento** landmark; (per la qualità) benchmark; **punto di rottura** breaking point; **punto a smerlo** blanket stitch; **punto [di] vendita** point of sale, outlet; **pubblicità al ~ [di] vendita** point-of-sale publicity; **punto e virgola** semicolon; **punto di vista** point of view

puntu'ale *adj* punctual; **essere ~** be punctual, be on time

puntualità *nf* punctuality

puntualiz'zare *vt* make clear, clarify

puntual'mente *adv* punctually, on time; (come al solito) as usual

pun'tura *nf* (di insetto) sting; (di ago ecc) prick; Med puncture; (iniezione) injection; (fitta) stabbing pain

■ **puntura d'ape** bee sting; **puntura d'insetto** insect bite; **puntura di spillo** pinprick; **puntura di zanzara** mosquito bite

punzecchi'are *vt* prick; fig tease

punzo'nare *vt* Techn punch, stamp

pun'zone *nm* punch

può ▶ POTERE; **~ darsi** maybe, perhaps

'pupa *nf* doll

pu'pazzo *nm* puppet

■ **pupazzo di neve** snowman

pup'illa *nf* Anat pupil

pu'pillo, -a *nmf* Jur ward; (di professore) favourite

⚘ **purché** *conj* provided

⚘ **'pure** 1 *adv* too, also; (concessivo) fate ~! please do!; **io ~** me too; **è venuto ~ lui** he

came too, he also came 2 *conj* (tuttavia) yet; (anche se) even if; **pur di** just to

⚘ **purè** *nm inv* purée

■ **purè di patate** mashed potatoes, creamed potatoes

pu'rezza *nf* purity

'purga *nf* purge

pur'gante *nm* laxative

pur'gare *vt* purge

purga'torio *nm* purgatory

purifi'care *vt* purify

purificazi'one *nf* purification

pu'rista *nmf* purist

puri'tano, -a *adj & nmf* Puritan

⚘ **'puro** *adj* pure; ‹*vino ecc*› undiluted; **per ~ caso** by sheer chance, purely by chance

■ **puro cotone** *nm* pure cotton, 100% cotton; **pura lana vergine** *nf* pure new wool; **pura seta** *nf* pure silk

puro'sangue *adj & nm* thoroughbred

⚘ **pur'troppo** *adv* unfortunately

'pus *nm* pus

'pustola *nf* pimple

puti'ferio *nm* uproar

putre'fare *vi* putrefy

putre'farsi *vr* putrefy

putre'fatto *adj* rotten

putrefazi'one *nf* putrefaction

'putrido *adj* putrid

putt *nm inv* putt

put'tana *nf* vulg whore

'puzza *nf* stink; **avere la ~ sotto il naso** be sniffy

puz'zare *vi* anche fig stink; **~ di bruciato** fig smell fishy; **~ d'imbroglio** stink; **~ di corruzione** stink of corruption; **questa storia mi puzza** the story stinks

⚘ **'puzzo** *nm* stink

'puzzola *nf* polecat

puzzo'lente *adj* stinking

puz'zone *nm* fam bastard

p.zza *abbr* (**piazza**) Sq.

Qq

Qatar *nm* Qatar

QI *abbr* (**quoziente di intelligenza**) IQ

⚘ **qua** *adv* here; **da un anno in ~** for the last year; **da quando in ~?** since when?; **di ~** this way; **di ~ di** on this side of; **~ dentro** in here; **~ sotto** under here; **~ vicino** near

here; **~ e là** here and there

'quacchero, -a *nmf* Quaker

qua'derno *nm* exercise book; (per appunti) notebook

■ **quaderno a quadretti** maths exercise book; **quaderno a righe** lined exercise book

quadrango'lare *adj* ‹forma›
quadrangular; **incontro quadrangolare** Sport
four-sided tournament

qua'drangolo *nm* quadrangle

qua'drante *nm* quadrant; (di orologio) dial

qua'drare ① *vt* square; (contabilità)
balance
② *vi* fit in

qua'drato ① *adj* square; (equilibrato)
level-headed
② *nm* square; (nel pugilato) ring; **al ~**
squared

quadra'tura *nf* Math squaring; (di bilancio)
balancing

quadret'tare *vt* divide into small squares

quadret'tato *adj* squared; ‹carta› graph
attrib; ‹tessuto› check, checked

qua'dretto *nm* square; (piccolo quadro)
small picture; **a quadretti** ‹tessuto› check

quadricro'mia *nf* four-colour printing

quadrien'nale *adj* (che dura quattro anni)
four-year; (ogni quattro anni) four-yearly

quadri'foglio *nm* four-leaf clover

qua'driglia *nf* square dance

quadri'latero *nm* quadrilateral

quadri'mestre *nm* (periodo) four-month
period; Sch term

quadrimo'tore *nm* four-engined plane

quadri'nomio *nm* Math quadrinomial

quadripar'tito ① *adj* four-party
② *nm* (politica) four-party government

quadri'plegico *adj* quadriplegic

ʃ **'quadro** *nm* picture, painting; (quadrato)
square; fig (scena) sight; (tabella) table; Theat
scene; (dirigente) executive; **fare il ~ della
situazione** outline the situation; **fuori ~**
Cinema, TV out of shot; **quadri** *pl* (carte)
diamonds; **a quadri** ‹tessuto, giacca, motivo›
check, checked

  ■ **quadro clinico** case history; **quadro di
  comando** control panel; **quadri** *pl* **direttivi**
  senior management; **quadro di distribuzione**
  Electr switchboard; **quadri** *pl* **intermedi** middle
  management; **quadro degli interruttori** switch
  panel; **quadro degli strumenti** instrument
  panel

qua'drupede *nm* quadruped

quadrupli'care *vt* quadruple

quadrupli'carsi *vr* quadruple

qua'druplice *adj* quadruple

'quadruplo *adj & nm* quadruple

quaggiù *adv* down here

'quaglia *nf* quail

ʃ **'qualche** *adj* (alcuni) a few, some; (un certo)
some; (in interrogazioni) any; **ho ~ problema** I
have a few problems, I have some problems;
~ tempo fa some time ago; **hai ~ libro
italiano?** have you any Italian books?; **posso**

prendere ~ libro? can I take some books?; **in
~ modo** somehow; **in ~ posto** somewhere;
~ volta sometimes; **~ cosa** = QUALCOSA

qualche'duno *pron* somebody, someone

ʃ **qual'cosa** *pron* something; (in interrogazioni)
anything; **qualcos'altro** something else;
vuoi qualcos'altro? would you like anything
else?; **~ di strano** something strange; **vuoi
~ da mangiare?** would you like something
to eat?; **vuoi ~ da bere?** would you like a
drink?, would you like something to drink?

ʃ **qual'cuno** *pron* someone, somebody; (in
interrogazioni) anyone, anybody; (alcuni) some;
(in interrogazioni) any; **c'è ~?** is anybody in?;
qualcun altro someone else, somebody else;
c'è qualcun altro che aspetta? is anybody
else waiting?; **ho letto ~ dei suoi libri** I've
read some of his books; **conosci ~ dei suoi
amici?** do you know any of his friends?

ʃ **'quale** ① *adj* which; (indeterminato) what;
(come) as, like; **~ macchina è la tua?** which
car is yours?; **~ motivo avrà di parlare così?**
what reason would he have to speak like
that?; **~ onore!** what an honour!; **città quali
Venezia** towns like Venice; **~ che sia la tua
opinione** whatever you may think
② *pron* (inter) which [one]; **~ preferisci?**
which [one] do you prefer?
③ *pron rel* **il/la ~** (persona) who; (animale,
cosa) that, which; (oggetto: con prep) whom;
(oggetto: animale, cosa) which; **ho incontrato
tua madre, la ~ mi ha detto…** I met your
mother who told me…; **l'ufficio nel ~ lavoro**
the office in which I work; **l'uomo con il ~
parlavo** the man to whom I was speaking
④ *adv* (come) as

qua'lifica *nf* qualification; (titolo) title

qualifi'cabile *adj* qualifiable

qualifi'care *vt* qualify; (definire) define

qualifi'carsi *vr* be placed

qualifica'tivo *adj* qualifying

qualifi'cato *adj* ‹operaio› semi-skilled

qualificazi'one *nf* qualification

ʃ **qualità** *nf inv* quality; (specie) kind; **in ~
di** in one's capacity as; **di prima ~** high
quality; **di ottima/cattiva ~** top/poor quality

qualitativa'mente *adv* qualitatively

qualita'tivo *adj* qualitative

qua'lora *conj* in case

ʃ **qualsiasi, qualunque** *adj* any; (non
importa quale) whatever; (ordinario) ordinary;
dammi una penna ~ give me any pen
[whatsoever]; **farei ~ cosa** I would do
anything; **~ cosa io faccia** whatever I do;
~ persona anyone, anybody; **in ~ caso** in
any case; **uno ~** any one, whichever; **l'uomo
qualunque** the man in the street; **vivo in una
casa ~** I live in an ordinary house

qualunqu'ismo *nm* lack of political
views

qualunqu'ista *nmf* (menefreghista) person
with no political views

ʃ indicates a very frequent word

q

⚡ **'quando** *conj & adv* when; **da ~ ti ho visto** since I saw you; **da ~ esci con lui?** how long have you been going out with him?; **da ~ in qua?** since when?; **~... ~...** sometimes..., sometimes...; **continua ad insistere ~ sa di avere torto** he keeps on insisting even when he knows he's wrong

quantifi'cabile *adj* quantifiable

quantifi'care *vt* quantify

⚡ **quantità** *nf inv* quantity, amount; **una ~ di** (gran numero) a great deal of

quantitativa'mente *adv* quantitatively

quantita'tivo 1 *nm* amount
2 *adj* quantitative

⚡ **'quanto** 1 *adj inter* how much; (con nomi plurali) how many; (in esclamazione) what a lot of; (tempo) how long; **quanti anni hai?** how old are you?
2 *adj* (rel) as much... as; (tempo) as long as; (con nomi plurali) as many... as; **prendi ~ denaro ti serve** take as much money as you need; **prendi quanti libri vuoi** take as many books as you like; **e quant'altro** and whatever, and so on
3 *pron* (inter) how much; (quanto tempo) how long; (plurale) how many; **quanti ne abbiamo oggi?** what date is it today?
4 *pron* (rel) as much as; (quanto tempo) as long as; (plurale) as many as; **prendine ~/ quanti ne vuoi** take as much/as many as you like; **stai ~ vuoi** stay as long as you like; **questo è ~** that's it
5 *adv* (inter) how much; (quanto tempo) how long; **~ sei alto?** how tall are you?; **~ hai aspettato?** how long did you wait for?; **~ costa?** how much is it?; **~ mi dispiace!** I'm so sorry!; **quant'è bello!** how nice!
6 *adv rel* as much as; **lavoro ~ posso** I work as much as I can; **è tanto intelligente ~ bello** he's as intelligent as he's good-looking; **in ~** (in qualità di) as; (poiché) since; **~ a** as for; **in ~ a me** as far as I'm concerned; **per ~** however; **per ~ ne sappia** as far as I know; **per ~ mi riguarda** as far as I'm concerned; **per ~ mi sia simpatico** much as I like him; **~ prima** (al più presto) as soon as possible

quan'tunque *conj* although

⚡ **qua'ranta** *adj & nm* forty

quaran'tena *nf* quarantine

quaran'tenne 1 *adj* forty-year-old; (sulla quarantina) in his/her forties
2 *nmf* forty-year-old; (sulla quarantina) person in his/her forties

quaran'tennio *nm* period of forty years

quaran'tesimo *adj & nm* fortieth

quaran'tina *nf* **una ~** about forty

qua'resima *nf* Lent

quar'tetto *nm* quartet

⚡ **quarti'ere** *nm* district, area; Mil quarters *pl*; **quartieri** *pl* **alti** smart districts; **quartieri** *pl* **bassi** poor areas
■ **quartiere cinese** China-town; **quartiere**

dormitorio dormitory town; **quartiere generale** headquarters; **quartiere a luci rosse** red light area; **quartiere residenziale** residential area

quar'tino *nm* (strumento musicale) *instrument similar to a clarinet*; Typ quarto; (di vino) quarter litre

⚡ **'quarto** 1 *adj* fourth
2 *nm* fourth; (quarta parte) quarter; **le sette e un ~** [a] quarter past seven, [a] quarter after seven Am; **a tre quarti** (giacca, maniche) three-quarter length; **quarti** *pl* **di finale** quarter-finals
■ **quarto d'ora** quarter of an hour
3 *nf* (marcia) fourth [gear]

quarto'genito, -a *nmf* fourth child

quar'tultimo, -a *adj & nmf* fourth last

'quarzo *nm* quartz; **al ~** quartz
■ **quarzo rosa** rose quartz

⚡ **'quasi** 1 *adv* almost, nearly; **~ mai** hardly ever
2 *conj* (come se) as if; **~ ~ sto a casa** I'm tempted to stay home

quassù *adv* up here

qua'terna *nf* (lotto, tombola) set of four winning numbers

quater'nario *nm* (era) Quaternary

'quatto *adj* crouching; (silenzioso) silent; **starsene ~ ~** keep very quiet

quattordi'cenne *adj & nmf* fourteen-year-old

quattordi'cesimo *adj & nm* fourteenth

quat'tordici *adj & nm* fourteen

quat'trini *nmpl* money *sg*, dosh *sg* fam

⚡ **'quattro** *adj & nm* four; **dirne ~ a qualcuno** give somebody a piece of one's mind; **farsi in ~** (per qualcuno/per fare qualcosa) go to a lot of trouble (for somebody/to do something); **in ~ e quattr'otto** in a flash; **a ~ tempi** Auto four-stroke
■ **~ per ~** *nf inv* Auto four-wheel drive [vehicle], four-by-four

quat'trocchi *adv* **a ~** in private

quattrocen'tesco *adj* fifteenth-century

quattro'cento *adj & nm* four hundred; **il Quattrocento** the fifteenth century

quattro'mila *adj & nm* four thousand

Qué'bec *nm* Quebec

⚡ **'quello** 1 *adj* that *pl*, those; **quell'albero** that tree; **quegli alberi** those trees; **quel cane** that dog; **quei cani** those dogs
2 *pron* that [one] *pl*, those [ones]; **~ lì** that one over there; **~ che** the one that; (ciò che) what; **quelli che** the ones that, those that; **~ a destra** the one on the right

'quercia *nf* oak; **di ~** oak

que'rela *nf* [legal] action

quere'lante *nmf* plaintiff

quere'lare *vt* bring an action against

quere'lato, -a *nmf* defendant

q

que'sito *nm* question

questio'nare *vi* dispute

questio'nario *nm* questionnaire

quest'ione *nf* question; (faccenda) matter; (litigio) quarrel; **in ~** in doubt; **è fuori ~** it's out of the question; **è ~ di vita o di morte** it's a matter of life and death; **mettere qualcosa in ~** cast doubt on something; **una ~ personale** a personal matter

'questo [1] *adj* this *pl*, these
[2] *pron* this [one] *pl*, these [ones]; **~ qui, ~ qua** this one here; **è quello che ha detto** that's what he said; **per ~** for this *or* that reason; **quest'oggi** today

que'store *nm* chief of police

'questua *nf* collection

que'stura *nf* police headquarters

qui [1] *adv* here; **da ~ in poi, da ~ in avanti** from now on; **di ~ a una settimana** in a week's time; **fin ~** (di tempo) up till now, until now; **~ dentro** in here; **~ sotto** under here; **~ vicino** *adv* near here
[2] *nm* **~ pro quo** misunderstanding

quie'scenza *nf* (di vuicano) dormancy; (pensione) retirement; **trattamento di quiescenza** retirement package

quie'tanza *nf* receipt

quie'tare *vt* calm

quie'tarsi *vr* calm down

qui'ete *nf* quiet; **disturbo della quiete pubblica** breach of the peace; **stato di quiete** Phys state of rest

qui'eto *adj* quiet

'quindi [1] *adv* then
[2] *conj* therefore

quindi'cenne *adj & nmf* fifteen-year-old

quindi'cesimo *adj & nm* fifteenth

'quindici *adj & nm* fifteen; **~ giorni** a fortnight Br, two weeks *pl*

quindi'cina *nf* **una ~** about fifteen; **una ~ di giorni** a fortnight Br, two weeks *pl*

quindici'nale [1] *adj* fortnightly Br, twice-monthly

[2] *nm* fortnightly magazine Br, twice-monthly magazine

quinquen'nale *adj* (che dura cinque anni) five-year; (ogni cinque anni) five-yearly

quin'quennio *nm* [period of] five years

'quinta *nf* Auto fifth [gear], overdrive

quin'tale *nm* a hundred kilograms

'quinte *nfpl* Theat wings

quintes'senza *nf* quintessence

quin'tetto *nm* quintet

'quinto *adj & nm* fifth

quintupli'care *vt* quintuple

quin'tuplo *adj* quintuple

qui'squilia *nf* trifle; **perdersi in quisquilie** get bogged down in details

quiz *nm inv*
■ [gioco a] quiz quiz game; quiz radiofonico radio quiz

'quota *nf* quota; (rata) instalment; (altitudine) height; Aeron altitude, height; (ippica) odds *pl*; **perdere/prendere ~** lose/gain altitude *or* height; **da alta ~** high-flying
■ quota fissa fixed amount; quota non imponibile personal allowance; quota di iscrizione entry fee; (di club) membership fee; quota di mercato market share; quota zero sea level

quo'tare *vt* Comm quote

quo'tato *adj* quoted; **essere ~ in Borsa** be quoted on the Stock Exchange

quotazi'one *nf* quotation
■ quotazione d'acquisto buying rate; quotazione ufficiale (in Borsa) official quotation; quotazione di vendita selling rate

quotidiana'mente *adv* daily

quotidi'ano [1] *adj* daily; (ordinario) everyday
[2] *nm* daily [paper]

'quoto *nm* Math quotient

quozi'ente *nm* quotient
■ quoziente d'intelligenza intelligence quotient, IQ; quoziente di purezza purity

Rr

ra'barbaro *nm* rhubarb

'rabbia *nf* rage; (ira) anger; Med rabies *sg*; **che ~!** what a nuisance!; **mi fa ~** it makes me angry

'rabbico *adj* ‹virus› rabies *attrib*

rab'bino *nm* rabbi

⎯⎯⎯⎯⎯⎯⎯⎯⎯⎯⎯⎯⎯⎯⎯⎯
*indicates a very frequent word

rabbiosa'mente *adv* furiously

rabbi'oso *adj* hot-tempered; Med rabid; (violento) violent

rabboc'care *vt* top up ‹fiasco›

rabbo'nire *vt* pacify

rabbo'nirsi *vr* calm down

rabbrivi'dire *vi* shudder; (di freddo) shiver

rabbuf'fare *vt* reprimand; ruffle ‹capelli›

q
r

rab'buffo *nm* reprimand

rabbui'arsi *vr* get dark; ‹*viso*› darken

rabdo'mante *nmf* water diviner

rabdoman'zia *nf* water divining

raccapez'zare *vt* put together

raccapez'zarsi *vr* see one's way ahead

raccapricci'ante *adj* horrifying

raccatta'palle [1] *nm inv* ball boy
[2] *nf inv* ball girl

raccat'tare *vt* pick up

rac'chetta *nf* racket
■ racchetta da neve snowshoe; racchetta da ping pong table-tennis bat; racchetta da sci ski stick, ski pole; racchetta da tennis tennis racket

'racchio *adj* fam ugly

racchi'udere *vt* contain

⚬ **rac'cogliere** *vt* pick; (da terra) pick up; (mietere) harvest; (collezionare) collect; (radunare) gather; win ‹*voti ecc*›; (dare asilo a) take in

rac'cogliersi *vr* gather; (concentrarsi) collect one's thoughts

raccogli'mento *nm* concentration

raccogli|'tore, -trice *nmf* collector
■ raccoglitore a fogli mobili ring-binder

rac'colta *nf* collection; (di scritti) compilation; (del grano ecc) harvesting; (adunata) gathering; chiamare a ∼ call *or* gather together
■ raccolta differenziata *collection of items for recycling*; raccolta di fondi fund-raising

rac'colto, -a [1] *pp di* RACCOGLIERE
[2] *adj* (rannicchiato) hunched; (intimo) cosy; (concentrato) engrossed
[3] *nm* (mietitura) harvest

raccoman'dabile *adj* advisable; poco ∼ ‹*persona*› shady

⚬ **raccoman'dare** *vt* recommend; (affidare) entrust

raccoman'darsi *vr* (implorare) beg

raccoman'data *nf* letter sent by recorded delivery, certified mail Am; per ∼ by recorded delivery
■ raccomandata con ricevuta di ritorno *letter sent by recorded delivery with acknowledgement of receipt*

raccoman'data-e'spresso *nf express recorded delivery service*

raccomandazi'one *nf* recommendation

raccomo'dare *vt* repair

⚬ **raccon'tare** *vt* tell

rac'conto *nm* story
■ racconto dell'orrore horror story

raccorci'are *vt* shorten

raccorci'arsi *vr* become shorter; ‹*giorni*› draw in

raccor'dare *vt* join

rac'cordo *nm* connection; (stradale) feeder
■ raccordo anulare ring road; raccordo

autostradale motorway junction Br, intersection; raccordo ferroviario siding; raccordo a gomito elbow

ra'chitico *adj* rickety; (poco sviluppato) stunted

racimo'lare *vt* scrape together

'racket *nm inv* racket

'rada *nf* Naut roads *pl*

'radar *nm* radar; uomo radar air traffic controller

radden'sare *vt* thicken

radden'sarsi *vr* thicken

raddob'bare *vt* refit

rad'dobbo *nm* refit

raddol'cire *vt* sweeten; fig soften

raddol'cirsi *vr* become milder; ‹*carattere*› mellow

raddoppia'mento *nm* doubling

raddoppi'are *vt* double; increase twofold

rad'doppio *nm* doubling, twofold increase; (equitazione) gallop; (biliardo) double

raddriz'zabile *adj* which can be straightened

raddriz'zare *vt* straighten

raddrizza'tore *nm* (di corrente) rectifier

ra'dente *adj* grazing, shaving; tiro radente Mil grazing fire; Sport low shot just skimming the surface; volo radente Aeron hedge-hopping

'radere *vt* shave; graze ‹*muro*›; ∼ al suolo raze [to the ground]

'radersi *vr* shave

radi'ale *adj* radial

radi'ante [1] *adj* radiant
[2] *nm* Math radian

radi'are *vt* strike off; ∼ dall'albo strike off ‹*medico*›; debar ‹*avvocato*›

radia'tore *nm* radiator

radiazi'one *nf* radiation
■ radiazione nucleare nuclear radiation

'radica *nf* briar

radi'cale [1] *adj* radical
[2] *nm* Gram root; Pol radical

radical'mente *adv* radically

radi'carsi *vr* ∼ in be rooted in

radi'cato *adj* deep-seated

ra'dicchio *nm* chicory

ra'dice *nf* root; mettere [le] radici ‹*pianta*› take root; fig put down roots
■ radice quadrata square root

⚬ **'radio** [1] *nf inv* radio; via ∼ by radio; contatto radio radio contact; ponte radio radio link
■ radio pirata pirate radio; radio portatile portable radio; radio ricevente receiver; radio [a] transistor transistor radio; radio trasmittente transmitter
[2] *nm* Chem radium

radioama|'tore, -trice *nmf* radio ham

radioascolta|'tore, -trice *nmf* listener

radioassi'stito *adj* radio-assisted

radioattività *nf* radioactivity

radioat'tivo *adj* radioactive

radiobiolo'gia *nf* radiobiology

radio'bussola *nf* radio compass

radiocoman'dare *vt* operate by remote control

radiocoman'dato *adj* remote-controlled, radio-controlled

radio'cronaca *nf* radio commentary; **fare la ~ di** commentate on

radiocro'nista *nmf* radio reporter

radiodiffusi'one *nf* broadcasting

radio'faro *nm* radio beacon

radio'fonico *adj* radio *attrib*

radiofre'quenza *nf* radio frequency

radiogo'niometro *nm* direction finder, radiogoniometer

radiogra'fare *vt* X-ray

radiogra'fia *nf* X-ray [photograph]; (radiologia) radiography; **fare una ~** ‹paziente› have an X-ray; ‹dottore› take an X-ray

radio'lina *nf* transistor

radiolocaliz'zare *vt* locate by radar

radiolo'gia *nf* radiology

radi'ologo, -a *nmf* radiologist

radio'onda *nf* radio wave

radioregistra'tore *nm*
■ **radioregistratore portatile** portable radio cassette recorder

radiosco'pia *nf* Med radioscopy

radio'scopico *adj* radioscopic

radi'oso *adj* radiant

radio'spia *nf* bug

radio'sveglia *nf* radio alarm, clock radio

radio'taxi *nm inv* radio taxi

radiote'lefono *nm* radio-telephone; (privato) cordless [phone]

radiotelevi'sivo *adj* broadcasting *attrib*

radiotera'pia *nf* radiotherapy

radiotra'smettere *vt* radio

radiotrasmetti'tore *nm* radio

radiotrasmit'tente *nf* radio station

'rado *adj* sparse; (non frequente) rare; **di ~** seldom

radu'nare *vt* gather [together]

radu'narsi *vr* gather [together]

radu'nata *nf* gathering
■ **radunata sediziosa** seditious assembly

ra'duno *nm* meeting; Sport rally

ra'dura *nf* clearing

'rafano *nm* horseradish

raffazzo'nato *adj* ‹discorso, lavoro› botched

raf'fermo *adj* stale

'raffica *nf* gust; (di armi da fuoco) burst; (di domande, insulti) barrage

raffigu'rare *vt* represent

raffigurazi'one *nf* representation

raffi'nare *vt* refine

raffinata'mente *adv* elegantly

raffina'tezza *nf* refinement

raffi'nato *adj* refined

raffine'ria *nf* refinery
■ **raffineria di petrolio** oil refinery

rafforza'mento *nm* reinforcement; (di muscolatura, carattere) strengthening

raffor'zare *vt* reinforce

rafforza'tivo **1** *adj* Gram intensifying **2** *nm* Gram intensifier

raffredda'mento *nm* (processo) cooling; **di ~** cooling
■ **raffreddamento ad acqua** water-cooling; **raffreddamento ad aria** air-cooling

raffred'dare *vt* cool

raffred'darsi *vr* get cold; (prendere un raffreddore) catch a cold; ‹sentimento, passione› cool [off]

raffred'dato *adj* **essere ~** ‹persona› have a cold

raffred'dore *nm* cold; **avere il ~** have a cold
■ **raffreddore da fieno** hay fever

raf'fronto *nm* comparison

'rafia *nf* raffia

Rag. *abbr* = **ragioniere**

♂ **ra'gazza** *nf* girl; (fidanzata) girlfriend; **nome da ragazza** maiden name
■ **ragazza copertina** cover girl; **ragazza madre** unmarried mother; **ragazza alla pari** au pair [girl]; **ragazza squillo** call girl

ragaz'zata *nf* prank

♂ **ra'gazzo** *nm* boy; (fidanzato) boyfriend; **da ~** (da giovane) as a boy
■ **ragazzo padre** unmarried father; **ragazzo di strada** guttersnipe; **ragazzo di vita** rent boy

ragge'lare *vt* fig freeze

ragge'larsi *vr* fig turn to ice

raggi'ante *adj* radiant

raggi'era *nf* (di ruota) spokes *pl*; **a ~** with a pattern like spokes radiating from a centre

♂ **'raggio** *nm* ray; Math radius; (di ruota) spoke; **a raggi infrarossi** infrared
■ **raggio d'azione** range; **raggio laser** laser beam; **raggio di luna** moonbeam; **raggio di sole** ray of sunshine, sunbeam; **raggio di speranza** ray of hope; **raggio ultravioletto** ultraviolet ray; **raggi** *pl* **X** X-rays

raggi'rare *vt* trick, deceive

rag'giro *nm* trick, con trick

♂ **raggi'ungere** *vt* reach; (conseguire) achieve

r

raggiun'gibile *adj* ‹luogo› within reach
raggiungi'mento *nm* attainment
raggomito'lare *vt* wind
raggomito'larsi *vr* curl up
raggranel'lare *vt* scrape together
raggrin'zire *vt* wrinkle
raggrin'zirsi *vr* wrinkle
raggru'mare *vt* curdle ‹latte›
raggru'marsi *vr* ‹latte› curdle
raggruppa'mento *nm* (gruppo) group; (azione) grouping; Comm groupage
raggrup'pare *vt* group together
ragguagli'are *vt* compare; (informare) inform
raggu'aglio *nm* comparison; (informazione) information
ragguar'devole *adj* considerable
'ragia *nf* resin; **acqua ~** turpentine
ragià *nm inv* rajah
ragiona'mento *nm* reasoning; (discussione) discussion
■ **ragionamento per assurdo** reductio ad absurdum
ragio'nare *vi* reason; (discutere) discuss
ragio'nato *adj* ‹argomento› reasoned; ‹cruciverba› cryptic
◢ **ragi'one** *nf* reason; (ciò che è giusto) right; **a ~ o a torto** rightly or wrongly; **aver ~** be right; **perdere la ~** go out of one's mind; **a ragion veduta** after due consideration; **prenderle/darle di santa ~** get/give a good walloping
■ **ragion d'essere** raison d'être; **ragione di scambio** terms of trade; **ragione sociale** company name; **ragion di Stato** reasons of State
ragione'ria *nf* accountancy; (scuola) *secondary school which provides training in accountancy*
ragio'nevole *adj* reasonable
ragionevol'mente *adv* reasonably
ragioni'ere, -a *nmf* accountant
ra'glan *adj inv* ‹manica› raglan
ragli'are *vi* bray
'raglio *nm* bray
ragna'tela *nf* cobweb, web, spider web
'ragno *nm* spider
ragù *nm inv* meat sauce
RAI *nf abbr* (**Radio Audizioni Italiane**) Italian public broadcasting company
'raid *nm inv* raid
'raion® *nm* rayon®
ra'lenti *nm* **al ~** in slow motion
rallegra'menti *nmpl* congratulations
ralle'grare *vt* gladden
ralle'grarsi *vr* rejoice; **~ con qualcuno** congratulate somebody
rallenta'mento *nm* slowing down
rallen'tare *vt/i* slow down; (allentare) slacken

rallen'tarsi *vr* slow down
rallenta'tore *nm* (su strada) speed bump; **al ~** in slow motion
'rally *nm inv* rally
RAM *nf inv* RAM
ramai'olo *nm* ladle
raman'zina *nf* reprimand
ra'mare *vt* stake ‹pianta›
ra'marro *nm* (animale) type of lizard
ra'mato *adj* ‹capelli› copper[-coloured], coppery
'rame *nm* copper; **color ~** copper-coloured
ramifi'care *vi* ‹pianta› put out branches
ramifi'carsi *vr* ‹pianta› put out branches; ‹strada, fiume ecc› branch; ‹teoria› ramify, branch
ramificazi'one *nf* ramification
ra'mino *nm* rummy
rammari'carsi *vr* **~ di** regret; (lamentarsi) complain (**di** about)
ram'marico *nm* regret
rammen'dare *vt* darn
ram'mendo *nm* darning
rammen'tare *vt* remember; **~ qualcosa a qualcuno** (richiamare alla memoria) remind somebody of something
rammen'tarsi *vr* remember
rammol'lire *vt* soften
rammol'lirsi *vr* go soft
rammol'lito, -a *nmf* wimp
◢ **'ramo** *nm* branch
ramo'scello *nm* twig
'rampa *nf* (di scale) flight
■ **rampa d'accesso** slip road; **rampa di carico** loading ramp; **rampa di lancio** launch[ing] pad
ram'pante *adj* ‹leone, cavallo› rampant; **giovane ~** yuppie
rampi'cante ① *adj* climbing ② *nm* Bot creeper
ram'pino *nm* hook; fig pretext
ram'pollo *nm* (hum) brat; (discendente) descendant
ram'pone *nm* harpoon; (per scarpe) crampon
'rana *nf* frog; (nel nuoto) breaststroke; **uomo rana** frogman
ranch *nm inv* ranch
'rancido *adj* rancid
'rancio *nm* rations *pl*
◢ **ran'core** *nm* rancour, resentment; **serbare ~ verso qualcuno** bear somebody a grudge
'randa *nf* mainsail
ran'dagio *adj* stray
randel'lata *nf* blow with a club
ran'dello *nm* club
'rango *nm* rank
rannicchi'arsi *vr* huddle up

rannuvola'mento *nm* clouding over

rannuvo'larsi *vr* cloud over

ra'nocchio *nm* frog

ranto'lare *vi* wheeze

'**rantolo** *nm* wheeze; (di moribondo) death rattle

ra'nuncolo *nm* buttercup

'**rapa** *nf* turnip

ra'pace *adj* rapacious; ‹*uccello*› predatory

rapa'nello *nm* radish

ra'pare *vt* crop

ra'parsi *vr* fam have one's head shaved

'**rapida** *nf* rapids *pl*

rapida'mente *adv* quickly, rapidly

rapidità *nf* speed

✍ '**rapido** [1] *adj* fast, quick; ‹*guarigione, sviluppo*› rapid
  [2] *nm* (treno) express [train]

rapi'mento *nm* (crimine) kidnapping

ra'pina *nf* robbery, hold-up fam
  ■ **rapina a mano armata** armed robbery; **rapina in banca** bank robbery

rapi'nare *vt* rob

rapina'tore *nm* robber
  ■ **rapinatore di banca** bank robber

ra'pire *vt* abduct; (per riscatto) kidnap; fig (estasiare) ravish

ra'pito, -a [1] *adj* abducted; (per riscatto) kidnapped; (estasiato) rapt
  [2] *nmf* kidnap victim

rapi|'tore, -trice *nmf* kidnapper

rappacifi'care *vt* pacify

rappacifi'carsi *vr* be reconciled, make it up

rappacificazi'one *nf* reconciliation

'**rapper** *nmf inv* Mus rapper

rappez'zare *vt* patch up

rappor'tare *vt* reproduce ‹*disegno*›; (confrontare) compare

✍ **rap'porto** *nm* report; (connessione) relation; (legame) relationship; Math, Techn ratio; **rapporti** *pl* relations, relationship; **essere in buoni rapporti** be on good terms
  ■ **rapporti** *pl* **d'affari** business relations; **rapporto di amicizia** friendship; **avere un ~ di amicizia con qualcuno** be friends with somebody; **rapporto di lavoro** working relationship; **rapporto di parentela** family relationship; **aver un ~ di parentela con qualcuno** be related to somebody; **rapporti** *pl* **prematrimoniali** premarital sex; **rapporto prezzo-prestazioni** price/performance ratio; **rapporto prezzo-qualità** value for money; **rapporti** *pl* **sessuali** sexual intercourse; **rapporto di trasmissione** Auto gear

rap'prendersi *vr* set; ‹*latte*› curdle

rappre'saglia *nf* reprisal

✍ **rappresen'tante** *nmf* representative

■ **rappresentante di classe** class representative; **rappresentante di commercio** sales representative, [sales] rep fam; **rappresentante sindacale** trade union representative

rappresen'tanza *nf* delegation; Comm agency; **spese di rappresentanza** entertainment expenses; **di ~** ‹*appartamento, macchina*› company *attrib*
  ■ **rappresentanza esclusiva** sole agency; **rappresentanza legale** legal representation; **rappresentanza proporzionale** proportional representation, PR

✍ **rappresen'tare** *vt* represent; Theat perform

rappresenta'tiva *nf* representatives *pl*

rappresenta'tivo *adj* representative

rappresentazi'one *nf* representation; (spettacolo) performance

rap'preso *pp di* RAPPRENDERSI

rapso'dia *nf* rhapsody

'**raptus** *nm inv* fit of madness

rara'mente *adv* rarely, seldom

rare'fare *vt* rarefy

rare'farsi *vr* rarefy

rare'fatto *adj* rarefied

rarità *nf inv* rarity

'**raro** *adj* rare

ra'sare *vt* shave; trim ‹*siepe ecc*›

ra'sarsi *vr* shave

ra'sato *adj* shaved

rasa'tura *nf* shaving

raschia'mento *nm* Med curettage

raschi'are *vt* scrape; (togliere) scrape off

raschi'arsi *vr* **~ la gola** clear one's throat

rasen'tare *vt* go close to

ra'sente *prep* very close to

'**raso** [1] *pp di* RADERE
  [2] *adj* smooth; (colmo) full to the brim; ‹*barba*› close-cropped; **~ terra** close to the ground; **un cucchiaio ~** a level spoonful
  [3] *nm* satin

ra'soio *nm* razor
  ■ **rasoio elettrico** electric shaver; **rasoio a mano libera** cut-throat razor

'**raspa** *nf* rasp

'**raspo** *nm* (di uva) small bunch

ras'segna *nf* review; (mostra) exhibition; (musicale, cinematografica) festival; **passare in ~** review; Mil inspect

✍ **rasse'gnare** *vt* present

rasse'gnarsi *vr* resign oneself

rassegnata'mente *adv* with resignation

rasse'gnato *adj* ‹*persona, aria, tono*› resigned

rassegnazi'one *nf* resignation

rassere'nare *vt* clear; fig cheer up

✍ indicates a very frequent word

rassere'narsi *vr* become clear; fig cheer up

rasset'tare *vt* tidy up; (riparare) mend

rassicu'rante *adj* ⟨persona, parole, presenza⟩ reassuring

rassicu'rare *vt* reassure

rassicurazi'one *nf* reassurance

rasso'dare *vt* harden; fig strengthen

rassomigli'ante *adj* similar

rassomigli'anza *nf* resemblance

rassomigli'are *vi* ~ a resemble

rastrella'mento *nm* (di fieno) raking; (perlustrazione) combing

rastrel'lare *vt* rake; (perlustrare) comb

rastrelli'era *nf* rack; (per biciclette) bicycle rack; (scolapiatti) [plate] rack

ra'strello *nm* rake

'rata *nf* instalment; (di mutuo) mortgage repayment; **pagare a rate** pay by instalments; **comprare qualcosa a rate** buy something on hire purchase, buy something on the installment plan Am

rate'ale *adj* by instalments; **pagamento rateale** payment by instalments; **vendita rateale** hire purchase

rate'are, **rateizzare** *vt* divide into instalments

ra'tifica *nf* Jur ratification

ratifi'care *vt* Jur ratify

'ratto¹ *nm* (rapimento) abduction

'ratto² *nm* (roditore) rat
- **ratto comune** black rat

rattop'pare *vt* patch

rat'toppo *nm* patch

rattrap'pire *vt* make stiff

rattrap'pirsi *vr* become stiff

rattri'stare *vt* sadden

rattri'starsi *vr* become sad

rau'cedine *nf* hoarseness

'rauco *adj* hoarse

rava'nello *nm* radish

ravi'oli *nmpl* ravioli *sg*

ravve'dersi *vr* mend one's ways

ravvi'are *vt* tidy ⟨capelli, stanza⟩

ravvicina'mento *nm* (tra persone) reconciliation; Pol rapprochement

ravvici'nare *vt* bring closer; (riconciliare) reconcile

ravvici'narsi *vr* be reconciled

ravvi'sare *vt* recognize

ravvi'vare *vt* revive; fig brighten up

ravvi'varsi *vr* revive

rav'volgere *vt* roll up

rav'volgersi *vr* wrap oneself up

'rayon® *nm* rayon

razio'cinio *nm* rational thought; (buon senso) common sense

razio'nale *adj* rational

razionalità *nf* (raziocinio) rationality; (di ambiente) functional nature

razionaliz'zare *vt* rationalize ⟨programmi, metodi, spazio⟩

razional'mente *adv* (con raziocinio) rationally

raziona'mento *nm* rationing

razio'nare *vt* ration

razi'one *nf* ration

✧ **'razza** *nf* race; (di cani ecc) breed; (genere) kind; **che ~ di idiota!** fam what an idiot!

raz'zia *nf* raid

razzi'ale *adj* racial

raz'zismo *nm* racism

raz'zista *adj* & *nmf* racist

'razzo *nm* rocket
- **razzo da segnalazione** flare

razzo'lare *vi* ⟨polli⟩ scratch about

✧ **re** *nm inv* king; Mus (chiave, nota) D; **Re** *pl* **Magi** Wise Men

rea'gente *adj* & *nm* reactant

rea'gire *vi* react

✧ **re'ale** *adj* real; (di re) royal

rea'lismo *nm* realism

rea'lista *nmf* realist; (fautore del re) royalist

realistica'mente *adv* realistically

rea'listico *adj* realistic

realiz'zabile *adj* feasible

✧ **realiz'zare** *vt* (attuare) carry out, realize; Comm make; score ⟨gol, canestro⟩; (rendersi conto di) realize

realiz'zarsi *vr* come true; (nel lavoro ecc) fulfil oneself

realiz'zato *adj* ⟨persona⟩ fulfilled

realizzazi'one *nf* realization; (di sogno, persona) fulfilment
- **realizzazione scenica** production

rea'lizzo *nm* (vendita) proceeds *pl*; (riscossione) yield

real'mente *adv* really

✧ **realtà** *nf inv* reality; **in ~** in reality; (a dire il vero) actually
- **realtà virtuale** virtual reality

re'ame *nm* realm

re'ato *nm* crime, criminal offence; **reati** *pl* **informatici** computer crime
- **reato minore** minor offence

reattività *nf* reactivity; (a farmaco) reaction

reat'tivo *adj* reactive

reat'tore *nm* reactor; Aeron jet [aircraft]
- **reattore nucleare** atomic reactor

reazio'nario, **-a** *adj* & *nmf* reactionary

reazi'one *nf* reaction; **a ~** ⟨motore, aereo⟩ jet
- **reazione a catena** chain reaction; **reazione chimica** chemical reaction

'rebus *nm inv* rebus; (enigma) puzzle

recapi'tare *vt* deliver

r

re'capito *nm* address; (consegna) delivery; **in caso di mancato ~...** if undelivered...
∎ **recapito a domicilio** home delivery; **recapito telefonico** contact telephone number

re'care *vt* bear; (produrre) cause

re'carsi *vr* go

re'cedere *vi* recede; fig give up

recensi'one *nf* review

recen'sire *vt* review

recen'sore *nm* reviewer

𝄞 **re'cente** *adj* recent; **di ~** recently

recente'mente *adv* recently

re'ception *nf inv* reception [desk]

re'ceptionist *nmf* receptionist

recessi'one *nf* recession

reces'sivo *adj* Biol recessive; Econ recessionary

re'cesso *nm* recess

re'cidere *vt* cut off

reci'diva *nf* Jur recidivism; Med relapse; **furto con ~** repeat offence of theft

recidività *nf inv* recidivism

reci'divo, -a [1] *adj* Med recurrent
[2] *nmf* repeat offender, persistent offender, recidivist fml; **è ~** fig he's lapsed back into his old ways

recin'tare *vt* close off

re'cinto *nm* enclosure; (per animali) pen; (per bambini) playpen
∎ **recinto delle grida** Fin [trading] floor; **recinto del peso** (ippica) weigh-in room

recinzi'one *nf* (azione) enclosure; (muro) wall; (rete) wire fence; (cancellata) railings *pl*

recipi'ente *nm* container

re'ciproco *adj* reciprocal

re'ciso [1] pp di RECIDERE
[2] *adj* (risoluto) definite

'recita *nf* performance
∎ **recita scolastica** school play

re'cital *nm inv* recital

𝄞 **reci'tare** [1] *vt* recite; Theat act; play ⟨*ruolo*⟩
[2] *vi* act; **~ a soggetto** improvise

recitazi'one *nf* recitation; Theat acting; **scuola di ~** drama school

recla'mare [1] *vi* protest
[2] *vt* claim

ré'clame *nf inv* advertising; (avviso pubblicitario) advertisement

reclamiz'zare *vt* advertise

re'clamo *nm* complaint; **ufficio reclami** complaints department

recli'nabile *adj* reclining; **sedile reclinabile** reclining seat

recli'nare *vt* tilt ⟨*sedile*⟩; lean ⟨*capo*⟩

reclusi'one *nf* imprisonment

re'cluso, -a [1] *adj* secluded
[2] *nmf* prisoner

'recluta *nf* recruit

recluta'mento *nm* recruitment

reclu'tare *vt* recruit

re'condito *adj* secluded; (intimo) secret

'record [1] *nm inv* record; **a tempo di ~** in record time
[2] *adj inv* ⟨*cifra*⟩ record *attrib*

recrimi'nare *vi* recriminate

recriminazi'one *nf* recrimination

recrude'scenza *nf* Med fresh outbreak; fig (di violenza) renewed outbreak; (di criminalità) upsurge

recupe'rare [1] *vt* recover; rehabilitate ⟨*tossicodipendente*⟩; make up ⟨*ore di assenza*⟩; **~ il tempo perduto** make up for lost time
[2] *vi* catch up

re'cupero *nm* recovery; (di tossicodipendenti) rehabilitation; (salvataggio) rescue; **corso di recupero** additional classes *pl*; **materiali di recupero** recycled material; (che possono essere recuperati) recyclable material; **[minuti di] recupero** Sport injury time; **partita di recupero** rematch
∎ **recupero crediti** debt collection; **recupero [dei] dati** data recovery

redargu'ire *vt* rebuke

re'datto pp di REDIGERE

redat|'tore, -trice *nmf* editor; (di testo) writer
∎ **redattore capo** editor in chief

redazi'one *nf* (ufficio) editorial office; (di testi) editing

redditività *nf* earning power

reddi'tizio *adj* profitable

'reddito *nm* income; **a basso ~** ⟨*famiglia*⟩ low income
∎ **imposta sul reddito** income tax; **reddito complessivo** gross income; **reddito imponibile** taxable income; **reddito non imponibile** non-taxable income; **reddito da lavoro** earned income; **redditi** *pl* **occasionali** casual earnings; **reddito pubblico** government revenue

re'dento pp di REDIMERE

reden'tore *nm* redeemer

redenzi'one *nf* redemption

re'digere *vt* write; draw up ⟨*documento*⟩

re'dimere *vt* redeem

re'dimersi *vr* redeem oneself

redi'mibile *adj* ⟨*titoli*⟩ redeemable

'redine *nf* rein

redin'gote *nf inv* frock-coat; **abito a redingote** fitted button-through dress

'redini *nfpl* reins

redi'vivo *adj* restored to life

'reduce [1] *adj* **~ da** back from
[2] *nmf* survivor

refe'rendum *nm inv* referendum

𝄞 indicates a very frequent word

refe'renza *nf* reference
referenzi'ato *adj* with references
re'ferto *nm* report
■ **referto medico** medical report
refet'torio *nm* refectory
reflazio'nare *vt* Econ reflate
reflazi'one *nf* Econ reflation
'reflex *nm inv* reflex camera
'refluo *nm* effluent
refrat'tario *adj* refractory; **essere** ∼ **a** fig be insensitive to ‹*sentimenti*›; **sono** ∼ **alla matematica** maths are a closed book to me
refrige'rante *adj* cooling *attrib*
refrige'rare *vt* refrigerate
refrigerazi'one *nf* refrigeration
refur'tiva *nf* stolen goods *pl*
re'fuso *nm* Typ literal, typo
◢ **rega'lare** *vt* give
re'gale *adj* regal
◢ **re'galo** *nm* present, gift; **articoli da regalo** gifts
■ **confezione regalo** gift set
re'gata *nf* regatta
'reggae *nm inv* Mus reggae
reg'gente *nmf* regent
reg'genza *nf* regency
◢ **'reggere** ① *vt* (sorreggere) bear; (tenere in mano) hold; (dirigere) run; (governare) govern; Gram take
② *vi* (resistere) hold out; (durare) last; fig stand
'reggersi *vr* stand
'reggia *nf* royal palace
reggi'calze *nm inv* suspender bolt
reggi'mento *nm* regiment; fig (molte persone) army
reggi'petto, **reggiseno** *nm* bra
re'gia *nf* Cinema direction; Theat production
re'gime *nm* regime; (dieta) diet; (di fiume) rate of flow; **a** ∼ **torrentizio** in spate; **a pieno** ∼ ‹*funzionare*› at full speed
■ **regime alimentare** diet; **regime fiscale** tax system; **regime di giri** (di motore) revs per minute, rpm; **regime militare** military regime; **regime monetario aureo** gold standard; **regime di vita** lifestyle
◢ **re'gina** *nf* queen; **ape regina** queen bee
■ **regina madre** queen mother
'regio *adj* royal
regio'nale *adj* regional
regiona'lismo *nm* (parola) regionalism
regional'mente *adv* regionally
regi'one *nf* region
re'gista *nmf* Cinema, TV director; Theat producer
regi'strare *vt* register; Comm enter; (incidere su nastro) tape, record; (su disco) record

registra'tore *nm* recorder; (magnetofono) tape-recorder
■ **registratore di cassa** cash register; **registratore a cassette** tape recorder, cassette recorder; **registratore di volo** flight recorder
registrazi'one *nf* registration; Comm entry; (di programma) recording; **sala di registrazione** recording studio
■ **registrazione [dei] dati** data capture
re'gistro *nm* register; (ufficio) registry
■ **registro di bordo** log; **registro di cassa** ledger; **registro di classe** class register; **registro linguistico** register
re'gnare *vi* reign
◢ **'regno** *nm* kingdom; (sovranità) reign
■ **regno animale** animal kingdom; **Regno Unito** United Kingdom; **regno vegetale** plant kingdom
◢ **'regola** *nf* rule; **essere in** ∼ be in order; ‹*persona*› have one's papers in order; **a** ∼ **d'arte** in a workmanlike fashion
rego'labile *adj* ‹*velocità, luminosità*› adjustable
regola'mento *nm* regulation; Comm settlement
■ **regolamento di conti** settling of scores
◢ **rego'lare** ① *adj* regular
② *vt* regulate; (ridurre, moderare) limit; (sistemare) settle
regolarità *nf inv* regularity
regolariz'zare *vt* settle ‹*debito*›; regularize ‹*situazione*›
rego'larsi *vr* (agire) act; (moderarsi) control oneself
rego'lata *nf* **darsi una** ∼ pull oneself together
regola'tore, **-trice** ① *adj*
■ **piano regolatore** urban development plan
② *nmf* regulator
'regolo *nm* ruler
■ **regolo calcolatore** slide-rule
regre'dire *vi* Biol, Psych regress
regressi'one *nf* regression
regres'sivo *adj* regressive
re'gresso *nm* decline
reincar'narsi *vr* ∼ **in…** be reincarnated as…
reincarnazi'one *nf* reincarnation
reinseri'mento *nm* (di persona) reintegration
reinser'irsi *vr* (in ambiente) reintegrate
reinstal'lare *vt* reinstall
reinte'grare *vt* restore
reinven'tare *vt* reinvent
reinvesti'mento *nm* reinvestment
reinve'stire *vt* reinvest ‹*soldi*›
reite'rare *vt* reiterate
reiterazi'one *nf* reiteration
re'lais *nm inv* relay

r

relativa'mente *adv* relatively; ~ **a** as regards

relatività *nf* relativity

rela'tivo *adj* relative

rela|'tore, **-trice** *nmf* (in una conferenza) speaker; (di tesi) supervisor

re'lax *nm* relaxation

☞ **relazi'one** *nf* relation; (di lavoro ecc) relationship; (rapporto amoroso) [love] affair; (resoconto) report; **pubbliche relazioni** *pl* public relations

■ **relazione extraconiugale** extramarital relationship; **relazioni** *pl* **industriali** industrial relations

rele'gare *vt* relegate

relegazi'one *nf* relegation

religi'one *nf* religion

religi'oso, **-a** ① *adj* religious
② *nm* monk
③ *nf* nun

re'liquia *nf* relic

reliqui'ario *nm* reliquary

re'litto *nm* wreck

re'mainder *nm inv* (libro) remainder

re'make *nm inv* remake

re'mare *vi* row

rema|'tore, **-trice** *nmf* rower

remini'scenza *nf* reminiscence

remissi'one *nf* remission; (sottomissione) submissiveness

■ **remissione del debito** remission of debt; **remissione di querela** withdrawal of an action

remissiva'mente *adv* submissively

remis'sivo *adj* submissive

re'mix *nm inv* Mus remix

'remo *nm* oar

'remora *nf* **senza remore** without hesitation

re'moto *adj* remote

remo'vibile *adj* removable

remune'rare *vt* remunerate

remunera'tivo *adj* remunerative

remunerazi'one *nf* remuneration

re'nale *adj* renal, kidney *attrib*

☞ **'rendere** *vt* (restituire) return; (esprimere) render; (fruttare) yield; (far diventare) make

'rendersi *vr* become; ~ **conto di qualcosa** realize something; ~ **utile** make oneself useful

rendi'conto *nm* report

rendi'mento *nm* rendering; (produzione) yield

'rendita *nf* income; (dello Stato) revenue; **vivere di** ~ *fig* rest on one's laurels

■ **rendita vitalizia** life annuity

'rene *nm* kidney

■ **rene artificiale** kidney machine

'reni *nfpl* (schiena) back

reni'tente ① *adj* essere ~ **a** ‹consigli di qualcuno› be loath to accept; refuse to obey ‹legge›
② *nm* ■ **renitente alla leva** person who fails to report for military service after being called up, draft dodger Am

'renna *nf* reindeer *pl inv*; (pelle) buckskin

'Reno *nm* Rhine

'reo, **-a** ① *adj* guilty
② *nmf* criminal

■ **reo confesso** self-confessed criminal

Rep. *abbr* (**repubblica**) Rep.

re'parto *nm* department; Mil unit; **reparti** *pl* **d'assalto** Mil assault troops

■ **reparto d'attacco** Sport attack; **reparto difensivo** Sport defence; **reparto grandi ustionati** Med burns unit; **reparto di massima sicurezza** secure unit; **reparto maternità** obstetrics [department]; **reparto radiologia** X-ray unit

repel'lente *adj* repulsive

repen'taglio *nm* mettere a ~ risk

repentina'mente *adv* suddenly

repen'tino *adj* sudden

reper'ibile *adj* available; **non è** ~ (perduto) it's not to be found

reperibilità *nf* availability

repe'rire *vt* trace ‹fondi›

re'perto: *nm*

■ **reperto archeologico** find; **reperto giudiziario** exhibit

reper'torio *nm* repertory; (elenco) index; **immagini** *pl* **di repertorio** archive footage

re'play *nm inv* [instant] replay

'replica *nf* reply; (obiezione) objection; (copia) replica; Theat repeat performance

repli'care *vt* reply; Theat repeat

repor'tage *nm inv* report

repressi'one *nf* repression

repres'sivo *adj* repressive

re'presso *pp di* REPRIMERE

re'primere *vt* repress

☞ **re'pubblica** *nf* republic

■ **Repubblica Ceca** Czech Republic; **Repubblica Centrafricana** Central African Repblic; **Repubblica Dominicana** Dominican Republic; **Repubblica d'Irlanda** Republic of Ireland, Irish Republic; **repubblica parlamentare** parliamentary republic; **Repubblica Popolare cinese** People's Republic of China; **repubblica presidenziale** presidential-style republic; **Repubblica Slovacca** Slovakia

repubbli'cano, **-a** *adj & nmf* republican

repu'tare *vt* consider

repu'tarsi *vr* consider oneself

reputazi'one *nf* reputation

'requiem *nm inv* requiem

requi'sire *vt* requisition

requi'sito *nm* requirement
- **requisiti di sistema** Comput system requirements

requisi'toria *nf* (arringa) closing speech

requisizi'one *nf* requisition

'resa *nf* surrender; Comm rendering
- **resa dei conti** rendering of accounts; **resa incondizionata** unconditional surrender

re'scindere *vt* cancel

'residence *nm inv* residential hotel

resi'dente *adj & nmf* resident

resi'denza *nf* residence; (soggiorno) stay
- **residenza protetta** sheltered accomodation

residenzi'ale *adj* residential; **zona residenziale** residential district

re'siduo ⊡ *adj* residual
⊡ *nm* remainder; **residui** *pl* **industriali** industrial waste

'resina *nf* resin

✧ **resi'stente** *adj* resistant
- **resistente all'acqua** water resistant

resi'stenza *nf* resistance; (fisica) stamina; Electr resistor, **la Resistenza** the Resistance
- **resistenza passiva** passive resistance; **resistenza a pubblico ufficiale** resisting arrest

✧ **re'sistere** *vi* ~ **[a]** resist; (a colpi, scosse) stand up to; ~ **alla pioggia/al vento** be rain/wind-resistant

'reso *pp di* RENDERE

reso'conto *nm* report
- **resoconto annuale** annual report

respin'gente *nm* Rail buffer

✧ **re'spingere** *vt* repel; (rifiutare) reject; (bocciare) fail

respingi'mento *nm* repatriation

re'spinto *pp di* RESPINGERE

✧ **respi'rare** *vt/i* breathe

respira'tore *nm* respirator
- **respiratore artificiale** life support machine; **respiratore [a tubo]** snorkel

respira'torio *adj* respiratory

respirazi'one *nf* breathing; Med respiration
- **respirazione artificiale** artificial respiration; **respirazione assistita** life support; **respirazione bocca a bocca** mouth-to-mouth resuscitation, kiss of life

re'spiro *nm* breath; (il respirare) breathing; fig respite
- **respiro di sollievo** sigh of relief

✧ **respon'sabile** ⊡ *adj* responsible (**di** for); Jur liable
⊡ *nmf* person responsible
- **responsabile della gestione del portafoglio fondi di investimento** investment manager; **responsabile della produzione** production manager; **responsabile delle risorse umane** human resources manager

✧ **responsabilità** *nf inv* responsibility; Jur liability
- **responsabilità civile** Jur civil liability; **responsabilità limitata** limited liability; **responsabilità penale** criminal liability

responsabiliz'zare *vt* give responsibility to ‹*dipendente*›; give a sense of responsibility to ‹*gente*›

responsabil'mente *adv* responsibly

re'sponso *nm* response

'ressa *nf* crowd

re'stante ⊡ *adj* remaining
⊡ *nm* remainder

✧ **re'stare** = RIMANERE

restau'rare *vt* restore

restaura|'tore, -trice *nmf* restorer

restaurazi'one *nf* restoration

re'stauro *nm* (riparazione) repair

re'stio *adj* restive; ~ **a** reluctant to

restitu'ibile *adj* returnable

restitu'ire *vt* return; (reintegrare) restore

restituzi'one *nf* return; Jur restitution

✧ **'resto** *nm* rest, remainder; (saldo) balance; (denaro) change; **resti** *pl* (avanzi) remains; **del** ~ besides

re'stringere *vt* contract; take in ‹*vestiti*›; (limitare) restrict; shrink ‹*stoffa*›

re'stringersi *vr* contract; (farsi più vicini) close up; ‹*stoffa*› shrink

restringi'mento *nm* (di tessuto) shrinkage
- **restringimento del campo visivo** Med tunnel vision

restrit'tivo *adj* restrictive

restrizi'one *nf* restriction

resurrezi'one *nf* resurrection

resusci'tare ⊡ *vt* revive; resuscitate ‹*moribondo*›
⊡ *vi* ‹*Cristo*› rise again; fig revive

re'taggio *nm* legacy

re'tata *nf* round-up

✧ **'rete** *nf* net; (sistema) network; (televisiva) channel; (in calcio, hockey) goal; fig trap; (per la spesa) string bag; **la Rete** (Internet) the net, the web
- **rete commutata pubblica** Teleph switched public network; **rete di distribuzione** Comm distribution network; **rete fissa** Teleph fixed telephone network; **rete locale** Comput local [area] network, LAN; **rete mobile** Teleph mobile telephone network; **rete di protezione** (per acrobata) safety net; **rete sociale** social network; **rete stradale** road network; **rete telematica** communications network; **rete televisiva** television channel; **rete televisiva satellitare** satellite channel; **rete televisiva via cavo** cable company

reti'cente *adj* reticent

reti'cenza *nf* reticence

retico'lato *nm* grid; (rete metallica) wire netting

re'ticolo *nm* network
■ **reticolo geografico** grid
'retina *nf* Anat retina
re'tina *nf* (per capelli) hair net
re'tino *nm* net
retorica'mente *adv* rhetorically
re'torico, -a ① *adj* rhetorical; **domanda retorica** rhetorical question; **figura retorica** figure of speech
② *nf* rhetoric
re'trattile *adj* ⟨punta⟩ retractable
retribu'ire *vt* remunerate
retribu'tivo *adj* salary *attrib*
retribuzi'one *nf* remuneration
'retro ① *adv* behind; **vedi** ~ see over
② *nm inv* back
■ **retro di copertina** outside back cover
retroat'tivo *adj* retroactive
retrobot'tega *nm inv* back shop
retro'cedere ① *vi* retreat
② *vt* Mil demote; Sport relegate
retrocessi'one *nf* Sport relegation
retroda'tare *vt* backdate, predate
retro'fit *nm inv* Auto retrofitted catalytic converter
re'trogrado *adj* retrograde; fig old-fashioned; Pol reactionary
retrogu'ardia *nf* Mil rearguard
retro'gusto *nm* after-taste
retro'marcia *nf* reverse [gear]
retro'scena *nm inv* Theat backstage; **i** ~ fig the real story
retrospettiva'mente *adv* retrospectively
retrospet'tivo *adj* retrospective
retro'stante *adj* **il palazzo** ~ the building behind
retro'via *nf* Mil area behind the front lines
retro'virus *nm inv* retrovirus
retrovi'sore *nm* rear-view mirror
'retta¹ *nf* Math straight line; (di collegio, pensionato) fee
'retta² *nf* **dar** ~ **a qualcuno** take somebody's advice
rettango'lare *adj* rectangular
ret'tangolo ① *adj* right-angled
② *nm* rectangle
ret'tifica *nf* rectification
rettifi'care *vt* rectify
'rettile *nm* reptile
retti'lineo ① *adj* rectilinear; (retto) upright
② *nm* Sport back straight
retti'tudine *nf* rectitude
'retto ① pp di REGGERE
② *adj* straight; fig upright; (giusto) correct;

angolo retto right angle
③ *nm* rectum
ret'tore *nm* Relig rector; Univ chancellor
reu'matico *adj* rheumatic
reuma'tismi *nmpl* rheumatism
reve'rendo *adj* reverend
rever'sibile *adj* reversible
revisio'nare *vt* revise; Comm audit; Auto overhaul
revisi'one *nf* revision; Comm audit; Auto overhaul
revisio'nismo *nm* Pol revisionism
revisio'nista *adj* ⟨politica⟩ revisionist
revi'sore *nm* (di conti) auditor; (di bozze) proofreader; (di traduzioni) reviser
■ **revisore di bozze** proofreader; **revisore dei conti** auditor
re'vival *nm inv* revival
'revoca *nf* repeal
revo'care *vt* repeal
revolve'rata *nf* revolver shot
rhythm and blues *nm* rhythm and blues, R & B
riabbas'sare *vt* lower again
riabbas'sarsi *vr* ⟨acque⟩ recede; ⟨temperatura⟩ fall again
riabbotto'nare *vt* button up again
riabbracci'are *vt* (abbracciare di nuovo) embrace again; fig (rivedere) see again
riabili'tare *vt* rehabilitate
riabilitazi'one *nf* rehabilitation; **centro di riabilitazione** rehabilitation centre
riabitu'are *vt* ~ **qualcuno a qualcosa** reaccustom somebody to something, get somebody used to something again
riabitu'arsi *vr* ~ **a qualcosa** get used to something again, reaccustom oneself to something
riac'cendere *vt* switch on again ⟨luce, TV⟩; rekindle, revive ⟨interesse, passione⟩; rekindle ⟨fuoco⟩
riac'cendersi *vr* ⟨luce⟩ come back on; ⟨interesse, passione⟩ rekindle, revive
riaccensi'one *nf* **la continua** ~ continual switching on and off
riaccer'tare *vt* reassess
riacqui'stare *vt* buy back; regain ⟨libertà, prestigio⟩; recover ⟨vista, udito⟩
riacutiz'zarsi *vr* get worse again
riadatta'mento *nm* readjustment
riadat'tare *vt* convert ⟨stanza⟩; alter ⟨indumento⟩
riadat'tarsi *vr* readjust
riaddormen'tare *vt* get [back] to sleep again
riaddormen'tarsi *vr* fall asleep again
riadope'rare *vt* reuse

ꝺ indicates a very frequent word

riaffacci'arsi *vr* (alla finestra) appear again; ‹*idea*› surface again

riaffermare *vt* reaffirm, reassert

riaffon'dare *vi* sink again

riaffron'tare *vt* deal with again ‹*situazione*›; take up again ‹*argomento*›

riagganci'are ① *vt* replace ‹*ricevitore*›; ∼ **la cornetta** hang up ② *vi* hang up

riaggre'garsi *vr* regroup

riallac'ciare *vt* refasten; reconnect ‹*corrente*›; renew ‹*amicizia*›

riallar'gare *vt* widen again ‹*tunnel, strada*›

riallinea'mento *nm* realignment

rialline'are *vt* realign

rialloggi'are *vt* rehouse

rial'zare ① *vt* raise ② *vi* rise

rial'zarsi *vr* get up again

rial'zato *adj* **piano** ∼ mezzanine

ri'alzo *nm* rise; **al** ∼ Fin bullish ▪ **rialzo dei prezzi** price rise

ria'mare *vt* ∼ **qualcuno** reciprocate somebody's love, love somebody back

riamma'larsi *vr* fall ill again

riam'mettere *vt* readmit ‹*socio, studente*›

rian'dare *vi* return

riani'mare *vt* Med resuscitate; (ridare forza a) revive; (ridare coraggio a) cheer up

riani'marsi *vr* regain consciousness; (riprendere forza) revive; (riprendere coraggio) cheer up

rianimazi'one *nf* intensive care [unit]; **sala di rianimazione** intensive care unit

rianno'dare *vt* retie ‹*filo*›; renew ‹*rapporti*›

riaper'tura *nf* reopening

riappa'rire *vi* reappear

riap'pendere *vt* replace ‹*cornetta*›; ∼ [il telefono] hang up

riappiso'larsi *vr* doze off again

riappropri'arsi *vr* ∼ **di** take back

ria'prire *vt* reopen

ria'prirsi *vr* reopen

ri'armo *nm* rearmament

ri'arso *adj* parched

riascol'tare *vt* listen to again

riasse'gnare *vt* reallocate

riassicu'rare *vt* reinsure

riassicurazi'one *nf* reinsurance

riassorbi'mento *nm* reabsorption

riassor'bire *vt* reabsorb

rias'sumere *vt* re-employ, take on again ‹*impiegato*›; ‹*ricapitolare*› resume

riassu'mibile *adj* (riepilogabile) which can be summarized, summarizable

riassun'tivo *adj* summarizing

rias'sunto ① *pp di* RIASSUMERE ② *nm* summary

riattac'care ① *vt* ∼ **il telefono** hang up ② *vi* (al telefono) hang up

riatti'vare *vt* reactivate ‹*processo*›; reintroduce, bring back ‹*servizio*›; start up again, restart ‹*congegno*›; stimulate ‹*circolazione sanguigna*›

ria'vere *vt* get back; regain ‹*salute, vista*›

ria'versi *vr* recover

riavvicina'mento *nm* (tra persone) reconciliation; (tra paesi) rapprochement

riavvici'nare *vt* fig reconcile ‹*paesi, persone*›

riavvici'narsi *vr* (riconciliarsi) be reconciled, make it up fam

riav'volgere *vt* rewind

riba'dire *vt* (confermare) reaffirm

ri'balta *nf* flap; Theat footlights *pl*; fig limelight

ribal'tabile *adj* tip-up

ribal'tare *vt/i* tip over; Naut capsize

ribal'tarsi *vr* tip over; Naut capsize

ribas'sare ① *vt* lower ② *vi* fall

ribas'sato *adj* reduced

ri'basso *nm* fall; (sconto) discount

ri'battere ① *vt* (a macchina) retype; (controbattere) deny ② *vi* answer back

ribattez'zare *vt* rename

✓ **ribel'larsi** *vr* rebel

ri'belle ① *adj* rebellious ② *nmf* rebel

ribelli'one *nf* rebellion

'ribes *nm inv* (rosso) redcurrant; (nero) blackcurrant

ribol'lire *vi* (fermentare) ferment; fig seethe

ri'brezzo *nm* disgust; **far** ∼ **a** disgust

ribut'tante *adj* repugnant

ribut'tare *vt* (buttare di nuovo) throw back

rica'dere *vi* fall back; (nel peccato ecc) lapse; (pendere) hang [down]; ∼ **su** (riversarsi) fall on

rica'duta *nf* relapse; **avere una** ∼ to have a relapse

rical'care *vt* trace

ricalci'trante *adj* recalcitrant

ricalco'lare *vt* recalculate

rica'mare *vt* embroider

rica'mato *adj* embroidered

ri'cambi *nmpl* spare parts

ricambi'are *vt* return; reciprocate ‹*sentimento*›; ∼ **qualcosa a qualcuno** repay somebody for something

ri'cambio *nm* replacement; Biol metabolism; **pezzo di ricambio** spare [part]

ri'camo *nm* embroidery

ricandi'dare *vt* (a elezioni) put forward as a candidate again

r

ricandi'darsi vr (a elezioni) stand again

ricapito'lare vt sum up; **ricapitoliamo** let's recap

ricapitolazi'one nf summary, recap fam

ri'carica nf (di sveglia) winder; (di batteria) recharging; (di penna) refill; (di fucile) reloading; Teleph top-up card

ricari'cabile adj rechargeable

ricari'care vt reload ‹macchina fotografica, fucile, camion›; recharge ‹batteria›; Comput reboot; rewind ‹orologio›; top up ‹cellulare›

ricat'tare vt blackmail

ricatta|'tore, **-trice** nmf blackmailer

ricatta'torio adj blackmail attrib

ri'catto nm blackmail
■ **ricatto morale** moral blackmail, emotional blackmail

rica'vare vt get; (ottenere) obtain; (dedurre) draw

rica'vato nm proceeds pl

ri'cavo nm proceeds pl

ricca'mente adv lavishly

ric'chezza nf wealth; fig richness; **ricchezze** pl riches

'riccio 1 adj curly
2 nm curl; (animale) hedgehog
■ **riccio di mare** sea-urchin

'ricciolo nm curl

riccio'luto adj curly

ricci'uto adj ‹barba› curly; ‹persona› curly-haired

ꞓ **'ricco**, **-a** 1 adj rich
■ **ricco sfondato** fam filthy rich
2 nmf rich person; **i ricchi** the rich

ꞓ **ri'cerca** nf search; (indagine) investigation; (scientifica) research; Sch project
■ **ricerca avanzata** Comput advanced search; **ricerca sul campo** field work; **ricerca di mercato** market research; **ricerca operativa** operational research

ricer'care vt search for; (fare ricerche su) research

ricer'cata nf wanted woman

ricercata'mente adv ‹vestire› with refinement; ‹parlare› in a refined way

ricerca'tezza nf refinement

ricer'cato 1 adj sought-after; (raffinato) refined
2 nm (dalla polizia) wanted man

ricerca|'tore, **-trice** nmf researcher

ricetrasmit'tente nf transceiver, two-way radio

ri'cetta nf Culin recipe; Med prescription

ricet'tacolo nm receptacle

ricet'tario nm (di cucina) recipe book; (di medico) prescription pad

ricetta|'tore, **-trice** nmf receiver of stolen goods, fence fam

ricettazi'one nf receiving [stolen goods]

rice'vente 1 adj ‹apparecchio, stazione› receiving
2 nmf receiver

ꞓ **ri'cevere** vt receive; (dare il benvenuto) welcome; (di albergo) accommodate

ricevi'mento nm receiving; (accoglienza) welcome; (trattenimento) reception

ricevi'tore nm receiver
■ **ricevitore delle imposte** tax man; **ricevitore del lotto** lottery ticket agent

ricevito'ria nf
■ **ricevitoria delle imposte** ≈ Inland Revenue; **ricevitoria del lotto** agency authorized to sell lottery tickets

rice'vuta nf receipt
■ **ricevuta d'acquisto** proof of purchase; **ricevuta doganale** docket; **ricevuta fiscale** tax receipt; **ricevuta di ritorno** acknowledgement of receipt; **ricevuta di versamento** receipt (given for bills etc paid at the Post Office)

rice'vuto int roger

ricezi'one nf Radio, TV reception

ꞓ **richia'mare** vt (al telefono) call back; (far tornare) recall; (rimproverare) rebuke; (attirare) draw; ∼ **alla mente** call to mind

richi'amo nm recall; (attrazione) call

richie'dente nmf applicant

ꞓ **richi'edere** vt ask for; (di nuovo) ask again for; ∼ **a qualcuno di fare qualcosa** ask or request somebody to do something

richi'esta nf request; Comm demand
■ **richiesta di indennizzo** claim for damages

richi'esto adj sought-after

ri'chiudere vt shut again, close again

ri'chiudersi vr ‹ferita› heal; ‹porta› shut again, close again

rici'clabile adj recyclable

rici'claggio nm recycling; (di denaro) laundering

rici'clare vt recycle ‹carta, vetro›; launder ‹denaro sporco›

rici'clarsi vr retrain; (cambiare lavoro) change one's line of work

rici'clato adj recycled

'ricino nm
■ **olio di ricino** castor oil

ricogni'tore nm reconnaissance plane

ricognizi'one nf Mil reconnaissance

ricolle'gare vt (collegare di nuovo) reconnect

ricolle'garsi vr ∼ **a** ‹evento, fatto› relate to, tie up with

ricol'mare vt fill to the brim

ri'colmo adj full

ꞓ **ricominci'are** vt/i start again; ∼ **da capo** start all over again

ricompa'rire vi reappear

ricom'parsa nf reappearance

r

ricom'pensa *nf* reward
ricompen'sare *vt* reward
ricom'porre *vt* (riscrivere) rewrite; (ricostruire) reform; Teleph redial; Typ reset
ricom'porsi *vr* regain one's composure
ricomposi'zione *nf* Teleph
■ ricomposizione automatica dell'ultimo numero redial facility
riconcili'are *vt* reconcile
riconcili'arsi *vr* be reconciled
riconciliazi'one *nf* reconciliation
riconfer'mare *vt* reappoint
ricongi'ungere *vt* reunite
ricongi'ungersi *vr* become reunited
ricono'scente *adj* grateful
ricono'scenza *nf* gratitude
✦ **rico'noscere** *vt* recognize; (ammettere) acknowledge
ricono'scibile *adj* recognizable
riconosci'mento *nm* recognition; (ammissione) acknowledgement; (per la polizia) identification
■ riconoscimento vocale Comput voice recognition
riconosci'uto *adj* recognized
ricon'quista *nf* reconquest
riconqui'stare *vt* Mil reconquer
ricon'segna *nf* return
riconse'gnare *vt* return
riconside'rare *vt* rethink
ricontrol'lare *vt* double-check
riconversi'one *nf* Econ restructuring
ricopi'are *vt* copy again
✦ **rico'prire** *vt* re-cover; (rivestire) coat; (di insulti) shower (di with); hold ‹carica›; ~ qualcuno di attenzioni lavish attention on somebody
✦ **ricor'dare** *vt* remember; (richiamare alla memoria) recall; (far ricordare) remind; (rassomigliare) look like
ricor'darsi *vr* ~ [di] remember; ~ di fare qualcosa remember to do something
✦ **ri'cordo** *nm* memory; (oggetto) memento; (di viaggio) souvenir; ricordi *pl* (memorie) memoirs
■ ~ di famiglia family heirloom
ricor'reggere *vt* correct again
ricor'rente *adj* recurrent
ricor'renza *nf* recurrence; (anniversario) anniversary
✦ **ri'correre** *vi* recur; (accadere) occur; ‹data› fall; ~ a have recourse to; (rivolgersi a) turn to
ri'corso ① *pp di* RICORRERE
② *nm* recourse; Jur appeal
ricostitu'ente *nm* tonic
ricostitu'ire *vt* re-establish
ricostru'ire *vt* reconstruct
ricostruzi'one *nf* reconstruction

ricove'rare *vt* give shelter to; ~ in ospedale admit to hospital, hospitalize
ricove'rato, -a *nmf* hospital patient
ri'covero *nm* shelter; (ospizio) home
ricreare *vt* recreate; (ristorare) restore
ricre'arsi *vr* amuse oneself
ricrea'tivo *adj* recreational
ricreazione *nf* recreation; Sch break, playtime
ri'credersi *vr* change one's mind
ri'crescere *vi* grow again
ricu'cire *vt* sew up; stitch up ‹ferita›
ricupe'rare, ricupero = RECUPERARE, RECUPERO
ri'curvo *adj* bent
ricu'sare *vt* refuse
ridacchi'are *vi* giggle
✦ **ri'dare** *vt* give back, return
rida'rella *nf* giggles *pl*
ridefi'nire *vt* redefine
ri'dente *adj* (piacevole) pleasant
✦ **'ridere** *vi* laugh; ~ di (deridere) laugh at
ride'stare *vt* reawaken ‹ricordo, sentimento›
ri'detto *pp di* RIDIRE
ridicoliz'zare *vt* ridicule
✦ **ri'dicolo** *adj* ridiculous
ridimensiona'mento *nm* restructuring
ridimensio'nare *vt* restructure ‹azienda›, fig get into perspective
ridi'pingere *vt* repaint
ri'dire *vt* repeat; trova sempre da ~ he's always finding fault; hai qualcosa da ~? do you have something to say?; se non hai niente da ~, ... if you've no objection...
ridi'scendere *vi* go back down
ridistribu'ire *vt* redistribute
ridistribuzi'one *nf* redistribution
ridon'dante *adj* redundant
ri'dosso: a ~ di *adv* behind
ri'dotto ① *pp di* RIDURRE
② *adj* reduced; essere ~ male be worn out
③ *nm* Theat foyer
✦ **ri'durre** *vt* reduce
ri'dursi *vr* diminish; ~ a fare qualcosa be reduced to doing something; ~ a ‹problema› come down to
ridut'tivo *adj* reductive
ridut'tore *nm* Electr adaptor
riduzi'one *nf* reduction; (per cinema, teatro) adaptation
■ riduzione cinematografica film adaptation; riduzione della pena reduced sentence; riduzione di prezzo price cut; riduzione teatrale adaptation for the theatre
riedifi'care *vt* rebuild
rieducazi'one *nf* (di malato) rehabilitation
rie'leggere *vt* re-elect

r

rielezi'one *nf* re-election
rie'mergere *vi* resurface
◆ **riem'pire** *vt* fill [up]; fill in ‹moduli ecc›
riem'pirsi *vr* fill [up]
riempi'tivo ① *adj* filling
② *nm* filler
rien'tranza *nf* recess
◆ **rien'trare** *vi* go/come back in; (tornare) return; (piegare indentro) recede; ~ **in** (far parte) fall within
ri'entro *nm* return; (di astronave) re-entry; **grande ~** mass return home after the holidays
riepilo'gare *vt* recapitulate
rie'pilogo *nm* summing-up
rie'same *nm* reassessment
riesami'nare *vt* reappraise
ri'essere *vi* ci risiamo! here we go again!
riesu'mare *vt* exhume
rievo'care *vt* (commemorare) commemorate; recall ‹passato›
rievocazi'one *nf* (commemorazione) commemoration; (ricordo) recollection
rifaci'mento *nm* remake
◆ **ri'fare** *vt* do again; (creare) make again; (riparare) repair; (imitare) imitate; make ‹letto›
ri'farsi *vr* (rimettersi) recover; (vendicarsi) get even; ~ **una vita/carriera** make a new life/career for oneself; ~ **il trucco** touch up one's makeup; ~ **di** make up for
ri'fatto *pp di* RIFARE
riferi'mento *nm* reference
◆ **rife'rire** ① *vt* report; ~ **a** attribute to
② *vi* make a report
rife'rirsi *vr* ~ **a** refer to
rifi'lare *vt* (tagliare a filo) trim; fam (affibbiare) saddle
rifi'nire *vt* finish off
rifini'tura *nf* finish
rifio'rire *vi* blossom again; fig flourish again
◆ **rifiu'tare** *vt* refuse; ~ **di fare qualcosa** refuse to do something
rifi'uto *nm* refusal; **acque** *pl* **di ~** waste water; **rifiuti** *pl* (immondizie) rubbish; **rifiuti** *pl* **industriali** industrial waste; **rifiuti** *pl* **urbani** urban *or* municipal waste
riflessi'one *nf* reflection; (osservazione) remark
rifles'sivo *adj* thoughtful; Gram reflexive
◆ **ri'flesso** ① *pp di* RIFLETTERE
② *nm* (luce) reflection; Med reflex; **per ~** indirectly
◆ **ri'flettere** ① *vt* reflect
② *vi* think (**su** about)
ri'flettersi *vr* be reflected

◆ indicates a very frequent word

riflet'tore *nm* reflector; (proiettore) search-light
ri'flusso *nm* ebb
rifocil'lare *vt* restore
rifocil'larsi *vr* (liter, hum) take some refreshment
rifondazi'one *nf* refounding
■ **Rifondazione Comunista** *diehard Communist party*
ri'fondere *vt* (rimborsare) refund
ri'forma *nf* reform; Relig reformation; Mil exemption on medical grounds
rifor'mare *vt* re-form; (migliorare) reform; Mil declare unfit for military service
rifor'mato *adj* ‹chiesa› Reformed; ‹recluta, soldato› unfit for military service
riforma|'tore, -trice *nmf* reformer
riforma'torio *nm* reformatory
riformat'tare *vt* Comput reformat
rifor'mista *adj & nmf* reformist
riformu'lare *vt* recast
riforni'mento *nm* supply; (scorta) stock; (di combustibile) refuelling; **stazione di rifornimento** petrol station
◆ **rifor'nire** *vt* restock; ~ **di** provide with
rifor'nirsi *vr* restock, stock up (**di** with)
ri'frangere *vt* refract
ri'fratto *pp di* RIFRANGERE
rifrazi'one *nf* refraction
rifug'gire ① *vt* shun ‹gloria, celebrità›
② *vi* escape again; ~ **da** fig shun
rifugi'arsi *vr* take refuge
rifugi'ato, -a *nmf* refugee
ri'fugio *nm* shelter; (nascondiglio) hideaway, safe house
■ **rifugio antiaereo** bomb shelter; **rifugio antiatomico** fallout shelter
'riga *nf* line; (fila) row; (striscia) stripe; (scriminatura) parting; (regolo) rule; **a righe** (stoffa) striped; ‹quaderno› ruled; **mettersi in ~** line up
ri'gaglie *nfpl* (interiora) giblets
ri'gagnolo *nm* rivulet
ri'gare ① *vt* rule ‹foglio›
② *vi* ~ **dritto** behave well
riga'toni *nmpl* small ridged pasta tubes
rigatti'ere *nm* junk dealer
rigene'rante *adj* regenerative
rigene'rare *vt* regenerate
riget'tare *vt* (gettare indietro) throw back; (respingere) reject; (vomitare) throw up
ri'getto *nm* rejection
ri'ghello *nm* ruler
rigida'mente *adv* rigidly
rigidità *nf* rigidity; (di clima) severity; (severità) strictness
■ **rigidità cadaverica** rigor mortis
'rigido *adj* rigid; (freddo) severe; (severo) strict

rigi'rare [1] *vt* turn again; (ripercorrere) go round; fig twist ‹argomentazione›
[2] *vi* walk about

rigi'rarsi *vr* turn round; (nel letto) turn over

ri'giro *nm* (imbroglio) trick

'rigo *nm* line; Mus staff

ri'goglio *nm* bloom

rigogliosa'mente *adv* luxuriantly

rigogli'oso *adj* luxuriant

rigonfia'mento *nm* swelling

rigonfi'are *vt* reinflate

ri'gonfio *adj* swollen

ri'gore *nm* rigours *pl*; **a rigor di logica** strictly speaking; **calcio di rigore** penalty [kick]; **area di rigore** penalty area; **essere di** ∼ be compulsory

rigorosa'mente *adv* ‹giudicare› severely; (seguire istruzioni) exactly; **vestito** ∼ **in giacca e cravatta** wearing the obligatory jacket and tie

rigo'roso *adj* (severo) strict; (scrupoloso) rigorous

rigover'nare *vt* wash up

riguada'gnare *vt* regain, win back ‹stima›; win more ‹tempo, punti›

⚡ **riguar'dare** *vt* look at again; (considerare) regard; (concernere) concern; **per quanto riguarda...** with regard to...

riguar'darsi *vr* take care of oneself

⚡ **rigu'ardo** *nm* care; (considerazione) consideration; **nei riguardi di** towards; ∼ **a** with regard to

rigurgi'tante *adj* ∼ **di** swarming with

rigurgi'tare [1] *vt* regurgitate
[2] *vi* ∼ **di** fig be swarming with

ri'gurgito *nm* regurgitation; fig (di xenofobia, nazionalismo ecc) resurgence

rilanci'are [1] *vt* throw back ‹palla›; (di nuovo) throw again; increase ‹offerta›; revive ‹moda›; relaunch ‹prodotto›
[2] *vi* (a carte) raise the stakes; **rilancio di dieci** I'll raise you ten

ri'lancio *nm* (di offerta) increase; (di prodotto) re-launch

rilasci'are *vt* (concedere) grant; (liberare) release; issue ‹documento›

rilasci'arsi *vr* relax

ri'lascio *nm* release; (di documento) issue

rilassa'mento *nm* relaxation
▪ **rilassamento cutaneo** sagging of the skin

rilas'sare *vt* relax

rilas'sarsi *vr* relax

rilas'sato *adj* relaxed

rile'gare *vt* bind ‹libro›

rile'gato *adj* bound

rilega|'tore, -trice *nmf* bookbinder

rilega'tura *nf* binding

ri'leggere *vt* reread

ri'lento: a ∼ *adv* slowly

rileva'mento *nm* survey; Comm buyout
▪ **rilevamento dirigenti** management buyout, MBO

rile'vante *adj* considerable

rile'vanza *nf* significance

rile'vare *vt* (trarre) get; (mettere in evidenza) point out; (notare) notice; (topografia) survey; Comm take over; Mil relieve

rilevazi'one *nf* (statistica) survey

rili'evo *nm* relief; Geog elevation; (topografia) survey; (importanza) importance; (osservazione) remark; **mettere in** ∼ **qualcosa** point something out

rilut'tante *adj* reluctant

rilut'tanza *nf* reluctance, unwillingness

'rima *nf* rhyme; **far** ∼ **con qualcosa** rhyme with something; **rispondere a qualcuno per le rime** give somebody as good as one gets
▪ **rima alternata** alternate rhyme; **rima baciata** rhyming couplet

⚡ **riman'dare** *vt* (posporre) postpone; (mandare indietro) send back; (mandare di nuovo) send again; (far ridare un esame) make resit an examination

ri'mando *nm* return; (in un libro) cross-reference

rimaneggia'mento *nm* rejig

rimaneggi'are *vt* rejig, recast

rima'nente [1] *adj* remaining
[2] *nm* remainder

rima'nenza *nf* remainder; **rimanenze** *pl* remnants; **rimanenze** *pl* **di magazzino** unsold stock

⚡ **rima'nere** *vi* stay, remain; (essere d'avanzo) be left; (venirsi a trovare) be; (restare stupito) be astonished; (restare d'accordo) agree; ∼ **senza parole** be speechless

rimangi'are *vt* (mangiare di nuovo) have again, eat again

rimangi'arsi *vr* ∼ **la parola** break one's promise

rimar'care *vt* remark

rimar'chevole *adj* remarkable

ri'mare *vt/i* rhyme

rimargi'nare *vt* heal

rimargi'narsi *vr* heal

ri'masto *pp di* RIMANERE

rima'sugli *nmpl* (di cibo) leftovers

rimbal'zare *vi* rebound; (proiettile) ricochet; **far** ∼ bounce

rim'balzo *nm* rebound; (di proiettile) ricochet

rimbam'bire [1] *vi* be in one's dotage
[2] *vt* stun

rimbam'bito *adj* in one's dotage

rimbec'care *vi* retort

rimbecil'lire *vt* make brain-dead

rimbecil'lito *adj* (stupido) brain-dead; (frastornato) stunned

rimboc'care *vt* turn up; roll up ‹maniche›; tuck in ‹coperte›; ∼ **le coperte a qualcuno** tuck somebody into bed

r

rimboc'carsi *vr* ∼ **le maniche** roll up one's sleeves

rimbom'bare *vi* boom, resound

rim'bombo *nm* boom

rimbor'sabile *adj* reclaimable

rimbor'sare *vt* reimburse, repay

rim'borso *nm* reimbursement, repayment
■ **rimborso d'imposta** tax rebate; **rimborso spese** reimbursement of expenses

rimboschi'mento *nm* reafforestation Br, reforestation

rim'brotto *nm* reproach

rimedi'abile *adj* ‹errore› which can be remedied

rimedi'are *vi* ∼ **a** remedy; make up for ‹errore›; (procurare) scrape up

ri'medio *nm* remedy

rimesco'lare *vt* mix [up]; shuffle ‹carte›; (rivangare) rake up; **mi fa** ∼ **il sangue** it makes my blood boil

rimesco'lio *nm* (turbamento) shock

ri'messa *nf* (per veicoli) garage; (per aerei) hangar; (per autobus) depot; (di denaro) remittance; (di merci) consignment
■ **rimessa laterale** Sport throw-in

ri'messo *pp di* RIMETTERE

rime'stare *vt* stir well

✧ **ri'mettere** *vt* (a posto) put back; (restituire) return; (affidare) entrust; (perdonare) remit; (rimandare) put off; (vomitare) bring up; ∼ **in gioco** (nel calcio) throw in; ∼ **in moto** restart; **rimetterci** fam (perdere) lose [out]

ri'mettersi *vr* (ristabilirsi) recover; ‹tempo› clear up; ∼ **a** start again

'rimmel® *nm inv* mascara

rimoder'nare *vt* modernize

ri'monta *nf* Sport recovery

rimon'tare 1 *vt* (risalire) go up; Mech reassemble
2 *vi* remount; ∼ **a** (risalire) go back to

rimorchi'are *vt* tow; fam pick up ‹ragazza›

rimorchia'tore *nm* tug[boat]

ri'morchio *nm* tow; (veicolo) trailer

ri'mordere *vt* **mi rimorde la coscienza** fig it's preying on my conscience

ri'morso *nm* remorse

rimo'stranza *nf* complaint

rimo'vibile *adj* removable

rimozi'one *nf* removal; (da un incarico) dismissal
■ **rimozione forzata** *illegally parked vehicles removed at owner's expense*

rim'pallo *nm* bounce

rim'pasto *nm* Pol reshuffle

rimpatri'are 1 *vt* repatriate
2 *vi* return home

rimpatri'ata *nf* reunion

✧ indicates a very frequent word

rim'patrio *nm* repatriation

rim'piangere *vt* regret

rimpiangi'mento 1 *pp di* RIMPIANGERE
2 *nm* regret

rimpiat'tino *nm* hide-and-seek

rimpiaz'zare *vt* replace

rimpi'azzo *nm* replacement

rimpiccioli'mento *nm* shrinkage

rimpiccio'lire 1 *vt* make smaller
2 *vi* become smaller

rimpinz'are *vt* ∼ **di** stuff with

rimpin'zarsi *vr* stuff oneself

rimpol'pare *vt* (ingrassare) fatten up; fig pad out ‹scritto›

rimprove'rare *vt* reproach; ∼ **qualcosa a qualcuno** reproach somebody for something

rim'provero *nm* reproach

rimugi'nare *vt* liter rummage; fig ∼ **su** brood over

rimune'rare *vt* remunerate

rimunera'tivo *adj* remunerative

rimunerazi'one *nf* remuneration

ri'muovere *vt* remove

ri'nascere *vi* be reborn, be born again

rinascimen'tale *adj* Renaissance

Rinasci'mento *nm* Renaissance

ri'nascita *nf* rebirth

rincal'zare *vt* (sostenere) support; (rimboccare) tuck in

rin'calzo *nm* support; **rincalzi** *pl* Mil reserves

rincantucci'arsi *vr* hide oneself away in a corner

rinca'rare 1 *vt* increase the price of
2 *vi* become more expensive

rin'caro *nm* price increase

rincar'tare *vt* rewrap

rinca'sare *vi* return home

rinchi'udere *vt* shut up

rinchi'udersi *vr* shut oneself up

rincon'trare *vt* meet again

rincon'trarsi *vr* meet [each other] again

rin'correre *vt* run after

rin'corsa *nf* run-up

rin'corso *pp di* RINCORRERE

rin'crescere *vi* **mi rincresce di non...** I'm sorry *or* I regret that I can't...; **se non ti rincresce** if you don't mind; **rincresce vedere...** it's sad to see...

rincresci'mento *nm* regret

rincresci'uto *pp di* RINCRESCERE

rincreti'nire 1 *vt* make brain-dead
2 *vi* go brain-dead

rincu'lare *vi* ‹arma› recoil; ‹cavallo› shy

rin'culo *nm* recoil

rincuo'rare *vt* encourage

rincuo'rarsi *vr* take heart

rinfacci'are *vt* ~ qualcosa a qualcuno throw something in somebody's face

rinfode'rare *vt* sheathe

rinfor'zare *vt* strengthen; (rendere più saldo) reinforce

rinfor'zarsi *vr* become stronger

rin'forzo *nm* reinforcement; fig support; **rinforzi** *pl* Mil reinforcements

rinfran'care *vt* reassure

rinfre'scante *adj* cooling

rinfre'scare ① *vt* cool; (rinnovare) freshen up
② *vi* get cooler

rinfre'scarsi *vr* freshen [oneself] up

rin'fresco *nm* light refreshment; (ricevimento) party

rin'fusa *nf* alla ~ at random

ringalluz'zire ① *vt* make cocky
② *vi* get cocky

ringhi'are *vi* snarl

ringhi'era *nf* railing; (di scala) banisters *pl*

ringhi'oso *adj* snarling

ringiova'nire ① *vt* rejuvenate ‹pelle, persona›; ‹vestito› make look younger
② *vi* become young again; (sembrare) look young again

ringrazia'mento *nm* thanks *pl*

꙳ **ringrazi'are** *vt* thank

rinne'gare *vt* disown

rinne'gato, -a *nmf* renegade

rinno'vabile *adj* renewable; ‹risorsa, foresta› sustainable

rinnova'mento *nm* renewal; (di edifici) renovation

rinno'vare *vt* renew; renovate ‹edifici›

rinno'varsi *vr* be renewed; (ripetersi) recur, happen again

rin'novo *nm* renewal

rinoce'ronte *nm* rhinoceros

rino'mato *adj* renowned

rinsal'dare *vt* consolidate

rinsa'vire *vi* come to one's senses

rinsec'chire *vi* shrivel up

rinsec'chito *adj* shrivelled up

rinta'narsi *vr* hide oneself away; ‹animale› retreat into its den

rintoc'care *vi* ‹compana› toll; ‹orologio› strike

rin'tocco *nm* toll; (di orologio) stroke

rinton'tire *vt* anche fig stun

rinton'tito *adj* (stordito) dazed

rintracci'are *vt* trace

rintro'nare ① *vt* stun
② *vi* boom

rintuz'zare *vt* blunt; (ribattere) retort; (reprimere) repress

ri'nuncia *nf* renunciation

꙳ **rinunci'are** *vi* ~ a renounce, give up

rinuncia'tario *adj* defeatist

ri'nunzia, rinunziare = RINUNCIA, RINUNCIARE

rinveni'mento *nm* (di reperti) discovery; (di refurtiva) recovery

rinve'nire ① *vt* find
② *vi* (riprendere i sensi) come round; (ridiventare fresco) revive

rinvi'are *vt* put off; (mandare indietro) return; (in libro) refer; ~ a giudizio indict

rinvigo'rire *vt* strengthen

rin'vio *nm* Sport goal kick; (in libro) cross-reference; (di appuntamento) postponement; (di merce) return

∎ **rinvio a giudizio** indictment

rioccu'pare *vt* reoccupy

rio'nale *adj* local

ri'one *nm* district

riordina'mento *nm* reorganization

riordi'nare *vt* tidy [up]; (ordinare di nuovo) reorder

riorganiz'zare *vt* reorganize

riorganizzazi'one *nf* reorganization

R.I.P. *abbr* (**riposi in pace**) RIP

ripa'gare *vt* repay

꙳ **ripa'rare** ① *vt* (proteggere) shelter, protect; (aggiustare) repair; (porre rimedio) remedy
② *vi* ~ a make up for

ripa'rarsi *vr* take shelter

ripa'rato *adj* ‹luogo› sheltered

riparazi'one *nf* repair; fig reparation

ripar'lare *vi* ne riparliamo stasera we'll talk about it again tonight

ri'paro *nm* shelter; (rimedio) remedy

ripar'tire ① *vt* (dividere) divide
② *vi* leave again

ripartizi'one *nf* division

ripas'sare ① *vt* recross; (rivedere) revise
② *vi* pass again

ripas'sata *nf* (spolverata) quick dust; (stirata) quick iron; (di vernice) second coat; fam (rimprovero) telling-off; **dar una** ~ **a** (lezione) revise

ri'passo *nm* (di lezione) revision

ripensa'mento *nm* second thoughts *pl*

꙳ **ripen'sare** *vi* ~ a think back to; **ripensarci** (cambiare idea) change one's mind; **ripensaci!** think again!

riper'correre *vt* (con la memoria) go back over; trace ‹storia›; ~ **la strada fatta** go back the way one came

riper'cosso *pp* di RIPERCUOTERE

ripercu'otere *vt* strike again

ripercu'otersi *vr* ‹suono› reverberate; ~ **su qualcosa** fig (avere conseguenze) impact on something

ripercussi'one *nf* repercussion

ripe'scare *vt* (recuperare) fish out; (ritrovare) find again

ripe'tente *nmf student who is repeating a year*

✔ **ri'petere** *vt* repeat

ri'petersi *vr* ‹evento› recur; ‹persona› repeat oneself

ripeti'tore *nm* TV relay

ripetizi'one *nf* repetition; (di lezione) revision; (lezione privata) private lesson

ripetuta'mente *adv* repeatedly

ri'piano *nm* (di scaffale) shelf; (terreno pianeggiante) terrace

ri'picca *nf* spite; **fare qualcosa per ∼** do something out of spite

ri'picco = RIPICCA

ripida'mente *adv* steeply

'ripido *adj* steep

ripie'gare ① *vt* refold; (abbassare) lower ② *vi* (indietreggiare) retreat

ripie'garsi *vr* bend; ‹sedile› fold

ripi'ego *nm* expedient; (via d'uscita) way out

ripi'eno ① *adj* full; Culin stuffed ② *nm* filling; Culin stuffing

ripiom'bare *vi* (per terra) fall down again; **∼ nella disperazione** sink back into despair

ripopo'lare *vt* repopulate

ripopo'larsi *vr* be repopulated

ri'porre *vt* put back; (mettere da parte) put away; (collocare) place; repeat ‹domanda›

✔ **ripor'tare** *vt* (restituire) bring/take back; (riferire) report; (subire) suffer; Math carry; win ‹vittoria›; transfer ‹disegno›

ripor'tarsi *vr* go back; (riferirsi) refer

✔ **ri'porto** *nm* (su abito, scarpa) appliqué; **∼ di 4** Math carry 4; **cane da riporto** gun dog, retriever; **nascondere la calvizie con un ∼** comb one's hair over a bald spot

ripo'sante *adj* restful

ripo'sare ① *vi* rest ② *vt* put back

ripo'sarsi *vr* rest

ripo'sato *adj* ‹mente› fresh; ‹viso› rested

✔ **ri'poso** *nm* rest; **andare a ∼** retire; **∼!** Mil at ease!; **giorno di riposo** day off

ripo'stiglio *nm* cupboard

ri'posto *pp di* RIPORRE

✔ **ri'prendere** *vt* take again; (prendere indietro) take back; (riconquistare) recapture; (ricuperare) recover; (ricominciare) resume; (rimproverare) reprimand; take in ‹cucitura›; Cinema shoot

ri'prendersi *vr* recover; (correggersi) correct oneself

ri'presa *nf* resumption; (ricupero) recovery; Theat revival; Cinema shot; Auto acceleration; Mus repeat; **riprese** *pl* Cinema filming ■ **ripresa aerea** bird's-eye view

ripresen'tare *vt* resubmit ‹domanda, certificato›; reintroduce ‹problema, persona›

ripresen'tarsi *vr* (a ufficio) go/come back again; (come candidato) stand again, run again; ‹occasione› arise again; ‹problema› come up again, reappear; (a esame) resit

ri'preso *pp di* RIPRENDERE

ripristi'nare *vt* restore

ripro'dotto *pp di* RIPRODURRE

ripro'durre *vt* reproduce

ripro'dursi *vr* Biol reproduce; ‹fenomeno› happen again, recur

riprodut'tivo *adj* reproductive

riproduzi'one *nf* reproduction ■ **'riproduzione vietata'** 'copyright'

ripro'mettersi *vr* (intendere) intend

ripro'porre *vt* put forward again

ripro'porsi *vr* **∼ di fare qualcosa** intend to do something; (come candidato) stand again; ‹problema› come up again, reappear

ri'prova *nf* confirmation; **a ∼ di** as confirmation of

ripro'vare *vt/i* retry

riprovazi'one *nf* ■ **riprovazione generale** outcry

riprove'vole *adj* reprehensible

ripubbli'care *vt* republish

ripudi'are *vt* repudiate

ripu'gnante *adj* repugnant

ripu'gnanza *nf* disgust

ripu'gnare *vi* **∼ a** disgust

ripu'lire *vt* clean [up]; fig polish

ripu'lita *nf* quick clean; **darsi una ∼** have a wash and brushup

ripulsi'one *nf* repulsion

ripul'sivo *adj* repulsive

ri'quadro *nm* square; (pannello) panel

riqualifi'care *vt* reskill ‹lavoratori›

riqualifica'zione *nf* retraining

ri'sacca *nf* undertow

ri'saia *nf* rice field, paddy field

✔ **risa'lire** ① *vt* go back up ② *vi* **∼ a** (nel tempo) date back to; (individuare) trace ‹colpevole›

risa'lita *nf* ascent; **impianto di risalita** ski lift

risal'tare *vi* (emergere) stand out

ri'salto *nm* prominence; (rilievo) relief

risana'mento *nm* reclamation, redevelopment

risa'nare *vt* heal; (bonificare) reclaim; redevelop ‹area, quartiere›

risa'puto *adj* well-known

risar'cibile *adj* refundable

risarci'mento *nm* compensation

risar'cire *vt* indemnify; **mi hanno risarcito i danni** they compensated me for the damage

ri'sata *nf* laugh

riscalda'mento *nm* heating ■ **riscaldamento autonomo** central heating *(for one flat)*; **riscaldamento centralizzato** *central heating system for whole block of flats*

riscal'dare vt heat; warm ⟨persona⟩

riscal'darsi vr warm up

riscat'tabile adj redeemable

riscat'tare vt ransom

riscat'tarsi vr redeem oneself

ri'scatto nm ransom; (morale) redemption

rischia'rare vt light up; brighten ⟨colore⟩

rischia'rarsi vr light up; ⟨cielo⟩ clear up

rischi'are ① vt risk
② vi run the risk; ~ **inutilmente** take needless risks

'rischio nm risk; **a ~** ⟨soggetti⟩ at-risk; **a basso ~** low-risk

rischi'oso adj risky

risciac'quare vt rinse

risci'acquo nm rinse

risciò nm inv rickshaw

riscon'trare vt (confrontare) compare; (verificare) verify; (rilevare) find

ri'scontro nm comparison; (verifica) verification; Comm (risposta) reply

risco'prire vt rediscover

ri'scossa nf revolt; (riconquista) recovery

riscossi'one nf collection

ri'scosso pp di RISCUOTERE

ri'scrivere vt (scrivere di nuovo) rewrite; (rispondere) write back

riscri'vibile adj rewritable

riscu'otere vt shake; (percepire) draw; (ottenere) gain; cash ⟨assegno⟩

riscu'otersi vr rouse oneself

risen'tire ① vt hear again; (provare) feel
② vi ~ **di** feel the effect of

risen'tirsi vr (offendersi) take offence

risentita'mente adv resentfully

risen'tito adj resentful

ri'serbo nm reserve; **mantenere il ~** remain tight-lipped

ri'serva nf reserve; (di caccia, pesca) preserve; Sport substitute, reserve; **di ~** spare; **senza riserve** wholeheartedly ⟨accettare, appoggiare⟩
■ **riserva di caccia** game reserve; **riserva indiana** Indian reservation; **riserva naturale** wildlife reserve

riser'vare vt reserve; (prenotare) book; (per occasione) keep

riser'varsi vr (ripromettersi) plan for oneself ⟨cambiamento⟩; **mi riservo la sorpresa** I want it to be a surprise

riserva'tezza nf reserve

riser'vato adj reserved; (confidenziale) classified; '~ **ai clienti dell'albergo** 'for hotel guests only'; '~ **carico** 'loading only'

ri'sguardo nm endpaper

ri'siedere vi ~ **a** reside in

'risma nf ream; fig kind

'riso¹ ① pp di RIDERE
② nm (pl nf **risa**) laughter; (singolo) laugh

'riso² nm (cereale) rice
■ **riso integrale** brown rice

riso'lino nm giggle

risolle'vare vt raise again; raise ⟨il morale⟩; raise again, bring up again ⟨problema, questione⟩; increase, improve ⟨le sorti⟩

risolle'varsi vr (da terra) rise again; fig pick up

ri'solto pp di RISOLVERE

risoluta'mente adv energetically

risolu'tezza nf determination

risolu'tivo adj (determinante) decisive; **scelta risolutiva** solution

riso'luto adj resolute, determined

risoluzi'one nf resolution

ri'solvere vt resolve; Math solve

ri'solversi vr (decidersi) decide; ~ **in** turn into

riso'nanza nf resonance; **aver ~** fig arouse great interest
■ **risonanza magnetica** magnetic resonance, magnetic resonance imaging

riso'nare vi resound; (rimbombare) echo

ri'sorgere vi rise again

risorgi'mento nm revival; **il Risorgimento** the Risorgimento

ri'sorsa nf resource; (espediente) resort; **risorse** pl **energetiche** energy resources; **risorse** pl **naturali** natural resources; **risorse** pl **umane** human resources

ri'sorto pp di RISORGERE

ri'sotto nm risotto
■ **risotto alla marinara** sea-food risotto; **risotto alla milanese** risotto with saffron

ri'sparmi nmpl (soldi) savings

risparmi'are vt save; (salvare) spare

risparmia|'tore, -trice nmf saver

ri'sparmio nm saving
■ **risparmio di carburante** fuel economy; **risparmio energetico** energy saving

rispecchi'are vt reflect

rispe'dire vr send back, return

rispet'tabile adj respectable

rispettabilità nf respectability

rispet'tare vt respect; **farsi ~** command respect

rispet'tivo adj respective

ri'spetto nm respect; ~ **a** as regards; (a paragone di) compared to

rispettosa'mente adv respectfully

rispet'toso adj respectful

risplen'dente adj shining

ri'splendere vi shine

rispon'dente adj ~ **a** in keeping with

rispon'denza nf correspondence

ri'spondere vi answer; (rimbeccare) answer back; (obbedire) respond; ~ **a** reply to; ~ **di** (rendersi responsabile) answer for

r

rispo'sare vt remarry

rispo'sarsi vr remarry

◆ **ri'sposta** nf answer, reply; (reazione) response; **senza risposta** unanswered ‹domanda, lettera›

ri'sposto pp di RISPONDERE

rispun'tare vi ‹persona, sole› reappear

'rissa nf brawl

ris'soso adj pugnacious

ristabi'lire vt re-establish

ristabi'lirsi vr (in salute) recover

rista'gnare vi stagnate; (sangue) coagulate

ri'stagno nm stagnation

ri'stampa nf reprint; (azione) reprinting

ristam'pare vt reprint

◆ **risto'rante** nm restaurant

risto'rare vt refresh

risto'rarsi vr liter take some refreshment; (riposarsi) take a rest

ristora|'tore, -trice 1 nmf (proprietario di ristorante) restaurateur; (fornitore) caterer 2 adj refreshing

ri'storo nm refreshment; (sollievo) relief; **servizio di ristoro** refreshments pl

ristret'tezza nf narrowness; (povertà) poverty; **vivere in ristrettezze** live in straitened circumstances

ri'stretto 1 pp di RESTRINGERE 2 adj narrow; (condensato) condensed; (limitato) restricted; **di idee ristrette** narrow-minded

ristruttu'rante adj ‹cosmetico› conditioning

ristruttu'rare vt Comm restructure; renovate ‹casa›; repair ‹capelli›

ristrutturazi'one nf Comm restructuring; (di casa) renovation

risucchi'are vt suck in

ri'succhio nm whirlpool; (di corrente) undertow

◆ **risul'tare** vi result; (riuscire) turn out

◆ **risul'tato** nm result; **risultati** pl **parziali** (di elezioni) preliminary results; (di partite) half-time results

risuo'nare 1 vt play again ‹pezzo musicale›; ring again ‹campanello› 2 vi ‹grida, parola› echo; Phys resonate

risurrezi'one, risuscitare = RESURREZIONE, RESUSCITARE

risvegli'are vt reawaken ‹interesse›

risvegli'arsi vr wake up; ‹natura› awake; ‹desiderio› be aroused

ri'sveglio nm waking up; (dell'interesse) revival; (del desiderio) arousal

ri'svolto nm (di giacca) lapel; (di pantaloni) turn-up, cuff Am; (di manica) cuff; (di tasca) flap; (di libro) inside flap

ritagli'are vt cut out

◆ indicates a very frequent word

ri'taglio nm cutting; (di stoffa) scrap

ritar'dare 1 vi be late; ‹orologio› be slow 2 vt delay; slow down ‹progresso›; (differire) postpone

ritarda'tario, -a nmf latecomer

ritar'dato 1 pp di RITARDARE 2 adj delayed; **a scoppio ~** delayed action attrib; Psych retarded

◆ **ri'tardo** nm delay; **essere in ~** be late; ‹volo› be delayed

ri'tegno nm reserve

ritem'prare vt restore

◆ **rite'nere** vt retain; deduct ‹somma›; (credere) believe

riten'tare vt try again

rite'nuta nf (sul salario) deduction ■ **ritenuta d'acconto** tax deducted in advance from payments made to self-employed people; **ritenuta diretta** taxation at source; **ritenuta alla fonte** taxation at source, deduction at source

ritenzi'one nf Med retention

◆ **riti'rare** vt throw back ‹palla›; (prelevare) withdraw; (riscuotere) draw; collect ‹pacco›

riti'rarsi vr withdraw; ‹stoffa› shrink; (da attività) retire; ‹marea› recede

riti'rata nf retreat; (WC) toilet

ri'tiro nm withdrawal; Relig retreat; (da attività) retirement ■ **ritiro bagagli** baggage reclaim

'ritmica nf rhythmic gymnastics

ritmica'mente adv rhythmically

'ritmico adj rhythmic[al]

'ritmo nm rhythm; **a ~ serrato** at a cracking pace

'rito nm rite; **di ~** customary ■ **rito funebre** funeral service

ritoc'care vt (correggere) touch up

ri'tocco nm alteration; **ritocchi** pl Phot retouching

ri'torcersi vr **~ contro qualcuno** boomerang on somebody

◆ **ritor'nare** vi return; (andare/venire indietro) go/come back; (ricorrere) recur; (ridiventare) become again

ritor'nello nm refrain

◆ **ri'torno** nm return

ritorsi'one nf retaliation

ri'torto adj ‹filo, cavo› twisted

ritra'durre vt (tradurre di nuovo) retranslate

ri'trarre vt (ritirare) withdraw; (distogliere) turn away; (rappresentare) portray

ritra'smettere vt TV show again, re-broadcast

ritrat'tabile adj ‹accusa› which can be withdrawn

ritrat'tare vt retract, withdraw ‹dichiarazione›

ritrattazi'one nf withdrawal, retraction

ritrat'tista *nmf* portrait painter

✓ **ri'tratto** 1 *pp di* RITRARRE
2 *nm* portrait

ritrazi'one *nf* retraction

ritrosa'mente *adv* shyly

ritro'sia *nf* shyness

ri'troso *adj* (timido) shy; **a** ∼ backwards; ∼ **a reluctant to**

ritrova'mento *nm* (azione) finding; (cosa) find

✓ **ritro'vare** *vt* find [again]; regain ‹salute›

ritro'varsi *vr* meet; (di nuovo) meet again; (capitare) find oneself; (raccapezzarsi) see one's way

ritro'vato *nm* discovery

ri'trovo *nm* meeting-place
■ **ritrovo notturno** night club

'ritto *adj* upright; (diritto) straight

ritu'ale *adj & nm* ritual

ritual'mente *adv* ritually

riunifi'care *vt* reunify

riunifi'carsi *vr* be reunited

riunificazi'one *nf* reunification

✓ **riuni'one** *nf* meeting; (dopo separazione) reunion
■ **riunione del corpo insegnante** staff meeting; **riunione dei genitori (degli alunni)** parents' evening

✓ **riu'nire** *vt* (unire) join together; (radunare) gather

riu'nirsi *vr* be reunited; (adunarsi) meet

riu'sare *vt* reuse

✓ **riusc'ire** *vi* (aver successo) succeed; (in matematica ecc) be good (**in** at); (aver esito) turn out; **le è riuscito simpatico** she found him likeable

riu'scita *nf* (esito) result; (successo) success

ri'uso *nm* reuse

riutiliz'zare *vt* reuse

✓ **'riva** *nf* (di mare, lago) shore; (di fiume) bank; **in** ∼ **al mare** on the seashore

rivacci'nare *vt* revaccinate

ri'vale *nmf* rival

rivaleggi'are *vi* compete (**con** with)

rivalità *nf inv* rivalry

ri'valsa *nf* revenge; **prendersi una** ∼ **su qualcuno** take revenge on somebody

rivalu'tare *vt* reappraise

rivalutazi'one *nf* revaluation

rivan'gare *vt* dig up again

✓ **rive'dere** *vt* see again; revise ‹lezione›; review ‹accordo›; verificare ‹check›

rive'dibile *adj* ‹accordo› reviewable; ‹recluta› temporarily unfit

✓ **rive'lare** *vt* reveal

rive'larsi *vr* (dimostrarsi) turn out

rivela'tore 1 *adj* revealing
2 *nm* Techn detector
■ **rivelatore di mine** mine detector

rivelazi'one *nf* revelation

ri'vendere *vt* resell

rivendi'care *vt* claim

rivendicazi'one *nf* claim

ri'vendita *nf* (negozio) shop
■ **rivendita autorizzata** authorized retailer

rivendi'tore, -trice *nmf* retailer
■ **rivenditore autorizzato** authorized retailer

riverbe'rare *vt* reflect ‹luce›

ri'verbero *nm* reverberation; (bagliore) glare

rive'renza *nf* reverence; (inchino) curtsy; (di uomo) bow

rive'rire *vt* respect; (ossequiare) pay one's respects to

rivernici'are *vt* repaint; (con smalto) revarnish

river'sare *vt* pour

river'sarsi *vr* ‹fiume› flow

river'sibile *adj* reversible

rivesti'mento *nm* covering

✓ **rive'stire** *vt* (rifornire di abiti) clothe; (ricoprire) cover; (internamente) line; hold ‹carica›

rive'stirsi *vr* get dressed again

rive'stito *adj* ∼ **di** covered with

rivi'era *nf* coast; (in corsa a ostacoli) water jump; **la** ∼ **ligure** the Italian Riviera

ri'vincita *nf* Sport return match; (vendetta) revenge

rivis'suto *pp di* RIVIVERE

ri'vista *nf* review; (pubblicazione) magazine; Theat revue; **passare in** ∼ review
■ **rivista patinata** glossy magazine

rivitaliz'zare *vt* revitalize

rivitalizzazi'one *nf* revitalization

ri'vivere 1 *vi* come to life again; (riprendere le forze) revive
2 *vt* relive

'rivo *nm* stream

rivo'lere *vt* (volere di nuovo) want again; (volere indietro) want back

✓ **ri'volgere** *vt* turn; (indirizzare) address

ri'volgersi *vr* turn round; ∼ **a** (indirizzarsi) turn to

rivolgi'mento *nm* upheaval

ri'volta *nf* revolt

rivol'tante *adj* revolting, disgusting

rivol'tare *vt* turn [over]; (mettendo l'interno verso l'esterno) turn inside out; (sconvolgere) upset

rivol'tarsi *vr* (ribellarsi) revolt

rivol'tella *nf* revolver

ri'volto *pp di* RIVOLGERE

rivol'toso, -a *nmf* rebel, insurgent

rivoluzio'nare *vt* revolutionize

rivoluzio'nario, -a *adj & nmf* revolutionary

✓ **rivoluzi'one** *nf* revolution; fig (disordine) chaos

⋯⟩

■ **rivoluzione francese** French Revolution; **rivoluzione industriale** Industrial Revolution

riz'zare *vt* raise; (innalzare) erect; prick up ‹orecchie›

riz'zarsi *vr* stand up; ‹capelli› stand on end; ‹orecchie› prick up

'roaming *nm* Teleph
■ **roaming internazionale** roaming

'roast-beef *nm inv* roast beef

⚘ **'roba** *nf* stuff; (personale) belongings *pl*, stuff; (faccenda) thing; sl (droga) drugs *pl*; ~ **da matti!** absolute madness!
■ **roba da bere** drink; **roba da lavare** washing; **roba da mangiare** food, things to eat; **roba da stirare** ironing

ro'baccia *nf* rubbish

robi'vecchi *nm inv* second-hand dealer

ro'bot *nm inv* robot; (da cucina) food processor

ro'botica *nf* robotics *sg*

ro'botico *adj* robotic

robotiz'zato *adj* robotic, robotized

robu'stezza *nf* sturdiness, robustness; (forza) strength

⚘ **ro'busto** *adj* sturdy, robust; (forte) strong

rocambo'lesco *adj* incredible

'rocca *nf* fortress

rocca'forte *nf* stronghold

rocchetti'era *nf* winder

roc'chetto *nm* reel

'roccia *nf* rock; (sport) rock-climbing

rock *nm* rock [music]
■ **rock acrobatico** rock 'n' roll

'roco *adj* throaty

ro'daggio *nm* running in

'Rodano *nm* Rhone

ro'dare *vt* run in

ro'deo *nm* rodeo

'rodere *vt* gnaw; (corrodere) corrode

'rodersi *vr* ~ **da** (logorarsi) be consumed with

rodi'tore *nm* rodent

rodo'dendro *nm* rhododendron

'rogito *nm* Jur deed

'rogna *nf* scabies *sg*; fig nuisance

ro'gnone *nm* Culin kidney

ro'gnoso *adj* scabby

'rogo *nm* (supplizio) stake; (per cadaveri) pyre

rol'lare ① *vt* roll ‹sigaretta›
② *vi* ‹aereo, nave› roll

'rom *adj inv & nmf inv* (zingaro) Roma, Romany

ROM *nf inv* Comput ROM

'Roma *nf* Rome

Roma'nia *nf* Romania

ro'manico *adj* Romanesque

⚘ **ro'mano, -a** *adj & nmf* Roman

romantica'mente *adv* romantically

romanti'cismo *nm* romanticism

ro'mantico *adj* romantic

ro'manza *nf* romance

roman'zare *vt* fictionalize

roman'zato *adj* romanticized, fictionalized

roman'zesco *adj* fictional; (stravagante) wild, unrealistic

roman'zetto *nm*
■ **romanzetto rosa** novelette

romanzi'ere *nm* novelist

ro'manzo ① *adj* Romance
② *nm* novel; (storia incredibile romantica) romance
■ **romanzo d'appendice** serial story; **romanzo giallo** thriller; **romanzo sceneggiato** novel adapted for television/radio

rom'bare *vi* rumble

'rombo *nm* rumble; Math rhombus; (pesce) turbot

romboi'dale *adj* rhomboid, diamond-shaped

⚘ **'rompere** *vt* break; break off ‹relazione›; **non** ~ **[le scatole]!** fam (seccare) don't be a pain [in the neck]!

'rompersi *vr* break; ~ **una gamba** break one's leg

rompi'capo *nm* nuisance; (indovinello) puzzle

rompi'collo *nm* daredevil; **a** ~ at breakneck speed

rompighi'accio *nm* ice-breaker

rompi'mento *nm* fam pain

rompi'scatole *nmf inv* fam pain

'ronda *nf* rounds *pl*

ron'della *nf* Mech washer

'rondine *nf* swallow

ron'done *nm* swift

ron'fare *vi* (russare) snore; (fare le fusa) purr

ron'zare *vi* buzz; ~ **attorno a qualcuno** fig hang about somebody

ron'zino *nm* jade

ron'zio *nm* buzz

⚘ **'rosa** ① *nf* rose
■ **rosa rampicante** rambler, rambling rose; **rosa selvatica** wild rose; **rosa dei venti** wind rose
② *adj & nm* (colore) pink

ro'saio *nm* rosebush

ro'sario *nm* rosary

ro'sato ① *adj* rosy
② *nm* (vino) rosé

'rosbif = ROAST-BEEF

rosé *nm inv* rosé

'roseo *adj* pink

ro'seto *nm* rose garden

ro'setta *nf* (coccarda) rosette; Mech washer

⚘ indicates a very frequent word

rosicchi'are *vt* nibble; (rodere) gnaw

rosma'rino *nm* rosemary

'roso *pp di* RODERE

roso'lare *vt* brown

roso'lato *adj* sauté

roso'lia *nf* German measles *sg*

ro'sone *nm* rosette; (apertura) rose window

'rospo *nm* toad

ros'setto *nm* lipstick

'rosso *adj & nm* red; **diventare ~** go red; **ha i capelli rossi** she's a redhead; **passare col ~** go through a red light, jump a red light
■ **rosso mattone** *adj* brick red; **rosso sangue** *adj* blood red; **rosso scarlatto** *adj* scarlet; **rosso d'uovo** [egg] yolk; **rosso vermiglio** *adj* vermilion

ros'sore *nm* redness; (della pelle) flush

rosticce'ria *nf* shop selling cooked meat and other prepared food

'rostro *nm* rostrum; (becco) bill

ro'tabile *adj* **strada ~** carriageway

ro'taia *nf* rail; (solco) rut

ro'tante *adj* rotating

ro'tare *vt/i* rotate

rota'tiva *nf* rotary press

rota'torio *adj* rotary

rotazi'one *nf* rotation; (di personale) turnover
■ **rotazione delle colture** crop rotation

rote'are *vt/i* roll

ro'tella *nf* small wheel; (di mobile) castor

roto'calco *nm* (sistema) rotogravure; ‹rivista› illustrated magazine

roto'lare *vt/i* roll

roto'larsi *vr* roll [about]

roto'lio *nm* rolling

'rotolo *nm* roll; (di pergamena) scroll; **andare a rotoli** go to rack and ruin
■ **rotolo di carta igienica** toilet roll

roto'loni *adv* **cadere ~** tumble

ro'tonda *nf* roundabout, traffic circle Am

rotondità *nf inv* (qualità) roundness; **~** *pl* (curve femminili) curves *pl*, curvaceousness

ro'tondo, -a ① *adj* round
② *nf* (spiazzo) terrace

ro'tore *nm* rotor

'rotta¹ *nf* Naut, Aeron course; **far ~ per** set a course for; **fuori ~** off course; **in ~ di collisione** on a collision course

'rotta² *nf* **a ~ di collo** at breakneck speed; **essere in ~ con** be on bad terms with

rotta'maio *nm* junkyard

rot'tame *nm* scrap; fig wreck

'rotto ① *pp di* ROMPERE
② *adj* broken; (stracciato) torn

rot'tura *nf* break; **che ~ di scatole!** fam what a pain!

'rotula *nf* kneecap

rou'lette *nf inv* roulette
■ **roulette russa** Russian roulette

rou'lotte *nf inv* caravan, trailer Am

rou'tine *nf inv* routine; **di ~** ‹operazioni, controlli› routine

ro'vente *adj* scorching

'rovere *nm* (legno) oak

rovescia'mento *nm* overthrow

rovesci'are *vt* (buttare a terra) knock over; (sottosopra) turn upside down; (rivoltare) turn inside out; spill ‹liquido›; overthrow ‹governo›; reverse ‹situazione›

rovesci'arsi *vr* (capovolgersi) overturn; (riversarsi) pour

ro'vescio ① *adj* (contrario) reverse; **alla rovescia** (capovolto) upside down; (con l'interno all'esterno) inside out
② *nm* reverse; (nella maglia) purl; (di pioggia) downpour; Tennis backhand

ro'vina *nf* ruin; (crollo) collapse; **in ~** in ruins

rovi'nare ① *vt* ruin; (guastare) spoil
② *vi* crash

rovi'narsi *vr* be ruined; ‹persona› ruin oneself

rovi'nato *adj* ruined

ro'vine *nfpl* ruins

rovi'noso *adj* ruinous

rovi'stare *vt* ransack

'rovo *nm* bramble

rozza'mente *adv* crudely

roz'zezza *nf* indelicacy

'rozzo *adj* rough

R.R. *abbr* (**ricevuta di ritorno**) acknowledgement of receipt

R.U. *abbr* (**Regno Unito**) UK

'ruba *nf* **andare a ~** sell like hot cakes

rubacchi'are *vt* pilfer

rubacu'ori *nm inv* heart-throb

ru'bare *vt* steal

rubi'condo *adj* ruddy

rubi'netto *nm* tap, faucet Am

ru'bino *nm* ruby

ru'bizzo *adj* spry

'rublo *nm* rouble

ru'brica *nf* (in giornale) column; (in programma televisivo) TV report; (quaderno con indice) address book
■ **rubrica degli annunci personali** personal column; **rubrica dei cuori solitari** lonely hearts' column; **rubrica sportiva** sports column; **rubrica degli spettacoli** listings; **rubrica telefonica** telephone and address book

'rucola *nf* rocket

'rude *adj* rough

'rudere *nm* ruin

ru'dezza *nf* bluntness

rudimen'tale *adj* rudimentary

rudi'menti *nmpl* rudiments
ruffi'ana *nf* procuress
ruffi'ano *nm* pimp; (adulatore) bootlicker
'ruga *nf* wrinkle
'ruggine *nf* rust; **fare la** ∼ go rusty
ruggi'noso *adj* rusty
rug'gire *vi* roar
rug'gito *nm* roar
rugi'ada *nf* dew
ru'goso *adj* wrinkled
rul'lare *vi* roll; Aeron taxi
rul'lino *nm* film
rul'lio *nm* rolling; Aeron taxiing
'rullo *nm* roll; Techn roller
rum *nm inv* rum
ru'meno, -a *adj & nmf* Romanian
rumi'nante *nm* ruminant
rumi'nare *vt* ruminate
⚡ **ru'more** *nm* noise; fig rumour
rumoreggi'are *vi* rumble
rumorosa'mente *adv* noisily
rumo'roso *adj* noisy; (sonoro) loud
ru'olo *nm* roll; Theat role; **di** ∼ on the staff
   ■ **ruolo delle imposte** tax notice; **ruolo primario/secondario** major/minor role

⚡ **ru'ota** *nf* wheel; **andare a** ∼ **libera** free-wheel; **fare la** ∼ do a cartwheel
   ■ **ruota dentata** cogwheel; **ruota di scorta** spare wheel; **ruota di stampa** (di stampante) print wheel; **ruota del timone** helm
'rupe *nf* cliff
ru'pestre *adj* ⟨pittura⟩ rock *attrib*
ru'pia *nf* rupee
ru'rale *adj* rural
ru'scello *nm* stream
'ruspa *nf* bulldozer
ru'spante *adj* free-range
rus'sare *vi* snore
'Russia *nf* Russia
⚡ **'russo, -a** 1 *adj & nmf* Russian
   2 *nm* (lingua) Russian
'rustico *adj* rural; ⟨carattere⟩ rough
'ruta *nf* Bot rue
rut'tare *vi* belch, burp
rut'tino *nm* (di bambino) burp
'rutto *nm* belch, burp
'ruvido *adj* coarse
ruzzo'lare *vi* tumble down
ruzzo'lone *nm* tumble; **cadere ruzzoloni** tumble down, tumble [helter-skelter]
'Rwanda *nf* Rwanda

Ss

S. (a) *abbr* (**santo, santa**) St.
   (b) *abbr* (**sud**) south
⚡ **'sabato** *nm* Saturday; **di** ∼ on Saturdays
sab'batico *adj* sabbatical; **anno sabbatico** sabbatical [year]
⚡ **'sabbia** *nf* sand; **sabbie** *pl* **mobili** quicksand
sabbi'are *vt* sandblast
sabbia'tura *nf* (di vetro, metallo) sandblasting; (terapeutica) sand-bath
sabbi'oso *adj* sandy
sabo'taggio *nm* sabotage
sabo'tare *vt* sabotage
sabota'|tore, -trice *nmf* saboteur
'sacca *nf* bag
   ■ **sacca di resistenza** pocket of resistance; **sacca da viaggio** travel[ling]-bag, duffel bag
sacca'rina *nf* saccharin
sac'cente 1 *adj* conceited
   2 *nmf* know-all, know-it-all Am
saccente'ria *nf* conceit
saccheggi'are *vt* sack; (hum) plunder ⟨frigo⟩

saccheggia'|tore, -trice *nmf* plunderer
sac'cheggio *nm* sack
sac'chetto *nm* bag
   ■ **sacchetto di plastica** plastic bag; **sacchetto per la spazzatura** bin liner, bin bag
⚡ **'sacco** *nm* sack; Anat sac; (contenuto) sack[ful]; **mettere nel** ∼ fig swindle; **un** ∼ (moltissimo) a lot; **un** ∼ **di** (gran quantità) lots of; **un** ∼ **di soldi** shedloads of money fam
   ■ **sacco a pelo** sleeping-bag; **sacco postale** mail-bag
saccope'lista *nmf* backpacker
sacer'dote *nm* priest
sacer'dozio *nm* priesthood
sacra'mento *nm* sacrament
sacrifi'cale *adj* sacrificial
sacrifi'care *vt* sacrifice
sacrifi'carsi *vr* sacrifice oneself
sacrifi'cato *adj* sacrificed; (non valorizzato) wasted
⚡ **sacri'ficio** *nm* sacrifice
sacri'legio *nm* sacrilege
sa'crilego *adj* sacrilegious

⚡ indicates a very frequent word

r
s

ꞩ '**sacro** [1] *adj* sacred; **la Sacra Bibbia** the Holy Bible
　[2] *nm* Anat sacrum

sacro'santo *adj* sacrosanct; (verità) gospel; (diritto) sacred

'**sadico, -a** [1] *adj* sadistic
　[2] *nmf* sadist

sa'dismo *nm* sadism

sa'etta *nf* arrow; (fulmine) thunderbolt; **correre come una ～** run like the wind

sa'fari *nm inv* safari

'**saga** *nf* saga

sa'gace *adj* shrewd

sa'gacia *nf* sagacity

sag'gezza *nf* wisdom

saggia'mente *adv* sagely

saggi'are *vt* test

'**saggio¹** *nm* (scritto) essay; (prova) proof; (di metallo) assay; (campione) sample; (esempio) example

'**saggio²** [1] *adj* wise
　[2] *nm* (persona) sage

sag'gista *nmf* essayist

sag'gistica *nf* non-fiction

Sagit'tario *nm* Astr Sagittarius

'**sago** = ᴤᴀɢÙ

'**sagoma** *nf* shape; (profilo) outline; (in falegnameria) template; **che ～!** fam what a character!

sago'mare *vt* make according to a template

'**sagra** *nf* festival

sa'grato *nm* churchyard

sagre'stano *nm* sacristan

sagre'stia *nf* sacristy

sagù *nm inv* sago

Sa'hara *nm* Sahara

ꞩ '**sala** *nf* hall; (salotto) living room; (per riunioni ecc) room; (di cinema) cinema
　■ **sala arrivi** arrivals lounge; **sala d'aspetto** waiting room; **sala d'attesa** waiting room; **sala da ballo** ballroom; **sala di comando** control room; **sala conferenze** conference hall; **sala giochi** amusement arcade, games room; **sala d'imbarco** departure lounge; **sala di lettura** reading room; **sala macchine** engine room; **sala operatoria** operating theatre Br, operating room Am; **sala parto** delivery room; **sala da pranzo** dining room; **sala professori** staff room, common room; **sala di regia** Radio, TV control room; **sala di ricevimento** function room; **sala riunioni** conference room; **sala da tè** tea shop

sa'lace *adj* salacious

sa'lame *nm* salami

salame'lecchi *nmpl* **fare ～** bow and scrape; **prendi quello che vuoi senza tanti ～** don't stand on ceremony, take what you want

sala'moia *nf* brine

sa'lare *vt* salt

salari'ato *nm* wage earner

sa'lario *nm* wages *pl*

salas'sare *vt* Med bleed; fig bleed dry

sa'lasso *nm* bleeding; **essere un ～** fig cost a fortune

sala'tini *nmpl* savouries (*eaten with aperitifs*)

sa'lato *adj* salty; (costoso) dear; **acqua salata** salt water

sal'ciccia = ᴤᴀʟᴤɪᴄᴄɪᴀ

sal'dare *vt* weld; set ‹osso›; pay off ‹debito›; settle ‹conto›; **～ a stagno** solder

sal'darsi *vr* ‹osso› knit; ‹ferita› heal

saldat'rice *nf* soldering iron

salda'tura *nf* soldering; (giunzione) join

'**saldo** [1] *adj* firm, unshaken; (resistente) strong; **～ come una roccia** solid as a rock; **essere ～ nei propri principi** stick to one's principles
　[2] *nm* (pagamento) settlement; Comm balance; ‹di conto corrente› bank balance; **saldi** *pl* sale; **i ～ di fine stagione** the end of season sales; **in ～** ‹essere› on sale; ‹comprato› in a sale
　■ **saldo iniziale** opening balance

ꞩ '**sale** *nm* salt; **non ha ～ in zucca** fam he hasn't got an ounce of common sense; **restare di ～** be struck dumb [with astonishment]; **sali** *pl* Med smelling salts; **sali da bagno** *pl* bath salts
　■ **sale da cucina** cooking salt; **sale fino** table salt; **sale grosso** cooking salt; **sale marino** sea salt; **sali e tabacchi** *pl* (negozio) tobacconist's shop

'**salice** *nm* willow
　■ **salice piangente** weeping willow

sali'ente *adj* outstanding; **i punti salienti** the main points, the highlights

sali'era *nf* salt-cellar

sa'lina *nf* salt-works *sg*

salinità *nf* saltiness

sa'lino *adj* saline

ꞩ **sa'lire** [1] *vi* go/come up; (levarsi) rise; (su treno ecc) get on; (in macchina) get in
　[2] *vt* go/come up ‹scale›

sa'lita *nf* climb; (aumento) rise; **in ～** uphill

sa'liva *nf* saliva

sali'vare [1] *vt* salivate
　[2] *adj* ‹ghiandola› salivary

'**salma** *nf* corpse

sal'mastro [1] *adj* brackish
　[2] *nm* salt air

salmì *nm* **in ～** marinated and slowly cooked in the marinade

salmi'strare *vt* Culin cure

'**salmo** *nm* psalm

sal'mone *nm & adj inv* salmon
　■ **salmone affumicato** smoked salmon

salmo'nella *nf* salmonella

S

sa'lone nm (salotto) living room; (di parrucchiere) salon
■ salone dell'automobile motor show; **salone di bellezza** beauty parlour; **salone del libro** book fair

salo'pette nf inv dungarees pl

salotti'ero adj pej mundane; **discorso salottiero** small talk

salot'tino nm bower

sa'lotto nm drawing room; (soggiorno) sitting room; (mobili) [three-piece] suite; **fare ~** chat
■ salotto letterario literary salon

sal'pare ① vi sail
② vt ~ l'ancora weigh anchor

'salsa nf sauce; Mus salsa
■ salsa di pomodoro tomato sauce; **salsa di rafano** horseradish sauce; **salsa di soia** soy sauce; **salsa tartara** tartar sauce

sal'sedine nf saltiness

sal'siccia nf sausage

salsi'era nf sauce-boat, gravy boat

✧ **sal'tare** ① vi jump; (venir via) come off; (balzare) leap; (esplodere) blow up; **saltar fuori** spring from nowhere; ‹oggetto cercato› turn up; **è saltato fuori che …** it emerged that …; **~ fuori con …** come out with …; **salta agli occhi** (è evidente) it hits you; **~ in aria** blow up; **~ in mente** spring to mind
② vt jump [over]; skip ‹pasti, lezioni›; Culin sauté

sal'tato adj Culin sautéed

saltel'lare vi hop; (di gioia) skip

saltim'banco nm acrobat

saltim'bocca nm inv slice of veal rolled with ham and sage and shallow-fried

✧ **'salto** nm jump; (balzo) leap; (dislivello) drop; fig (omissione, lacuna) gap; **fare un ~ da** ‹visitare› drop in on; **in un ~** in a jiffy; **fare i salti mortali** fig go to great lengths; **fare quattro salti** fam go dancing; **fare un ~ nel buio** fig take a leap in the dark
■ salto in alto high jump; salto con l'asta pole-vault; **salto con l'elastico** bungee jump; **salto con la corda** skipping; **salto in lungo** long jump; **salto pagina** Comput page down; **salto di qualità** quality leap

saltuaria'mente adv occasionally, from time to time

saltu'ario adj desultory
■ lavoro saltuario casual work

sa'lubre adj healthy

salume'ria nf delicatessen

sa'lumi nmpl cold cuts

salumi'ere nm person who sells cold meat

✧ **salu'tare** ① vt greet; (congedandosi) say goodbye to; (portare i saluti a) give one's regards to; Mil salute; **ti saluto!** fam cheerio!
② adj healthy

salu'tarsi vr (all'arrivo) greet each other; (in partenza) say goodbye to each other

✧ **sa'lute** nf health; **godere di ottima ~** be in the best of health, enjoy excellent health; **in ~** in good health; **~!** (dopo uno starnuto) bless you!; (a un brindisi) cheers!
■ salute di ferro iron constitution

salu'tista nmf health fanatic; (dell'Esercito della Salvezza) Salvationist

✧ **sa'luto** nm greeting; (di addio) goodbye; Mil salute; **saluti** pl (ossequi) regards

'salva nf salvo; **sparare a salve** shoot blanks; **a salve** ‹pistola› loaded with blank cartridges

salvacon'dotto nm safe-conduct

salvada'naio nm money box

salva'gente nm lifebelt; (a giubbotto) lifejacket; (ciambella) rubber ring; (spartitraffico) traffic island

salvaguar'dare vt protect, safeguard

salvaguar'darsi vr protect oneself

salvagu'ardia nf safeguard

✧ **sal'vare** vt save; (proteggere) protect; **~ la faccia** save face; **~ la pelle** save one's skin

sal'varsi vr save oneself

salva'schermo nm Comput screen saver

salva'slip nm inv panty-liner

salva'taggio nm rescue; Naut salvage; Comput saving; **battello di salvataggio** lifeboat

salva|'tore, -'trice nmf saviour

salva'vita nm inv Electr circuit breaker

'salve ▶ SALVA

sal'vezza nf safety; Relig salvation
■ ancora di salvezza fig salvation

'salvia nf sage

salvi'etta nf serviette

✧ **'salvo** ① adj safe
② nm trarre in ~ rescue
③ prep except [for]
④ conj ~ che (a meno che) unless; (eccetto che) except that

samari'tano, -a adj & nmf Samaritan; **un buon ~** a good Samaritan

'samba nf samba

sam'buca nf sambuca

sam'buco nm elder

Sa'moa nfpl
■ Samoa Occidentali Western Samoa

san nm (before proper names starting with a consonant) saint; ▶ SANTO

sa'nabile adj curable

sa'nare vt heal; (bonificare) reclaim; **~ il bilancio** balance the books

sana'toria nf decree legitimizing a situation which is in principle illegal

sana'torio nm sanatorium

san'cire vt sanction

'sandalo nm sandal; Bot sandalwood

✧ indicates a very frequent word

sandi'nista *adj & nmf* Sandinista

'sandwich *nm inv* sandwich
- **uomo sandwich** sandwich-man

san'gallo *nm* (tessuto) broderie anglaise

san'gria *nf* sangria

⚔ **'sangue** *nm* blood; **a ~ freddo** in cold blood; **al ~** Culin rare; **appena al ~** Culin medium-rare; **farsi cattivo ~ per** worry about; **iniettato di ~** ‹occhio› bloodshot; **all'ultimo ~** ‹lotta› to the death; **di ~ blu** blue-blooded; **perdere ~ dal naso** have a nose bleed; **sudare ~** sweat blood
- **sangue freddo** composure

sangue'misto *nm* half-caste

sangu'igno *adj* blood *attrib*

sangui'naccio *nm* Culin black pudding

sangui'nante *adj* bleeding

sangui'nare *vi* bleed

sangui'nario *adj* bloodthirsty

sangui'noso *adj* bloody

sangui'suga *nf* leech

sanità *nf* soundness; (salute) health; **ministero della sanità** Department of Health
- **sanità di costumi** morality; **sanità mentale** sanity, mental health

sani'tario [1] *adj* sanitary; **servizio sanitario** health service
[2] *nm* doctor

San Ma'rino *nm* San Marino

⚔ **'sano** *adj* sound; (salutare) healthy; **~ come un pesce** as fit as a fiddle
- **sano di mente** sane

'sansa *nf* husk

San Sil'vestro *nm* New Year's Eve

santifi'care *vt* sanctify

santità *nf* sainthood

⚔ **'santo, -a** [1] *adj* holy; (con nome proprio) saint; **Sant'Antonio** St Anthony; **San Francesco d'Assisi** St Francis of Assisi; **di santa ragione** in no uncertain terms
[2] *nmf* saint
- **santo patrono, santa patrona** patron saint

san'tone *nm* guru

santo'reggia *nf* Bot savory

santu'ario *nm* sanctuary

san Valen'tino *nm* St Valentine's Day; **giorno di san Valentino** Valentine's Day

sanzio'nare *vt* sanction

sanzi'one *nf* sanction
- **sanzione amministrativa** administrative sanction; **sanzione penale** legal sanction

⚔ **sa'pere** [1] *vt* know; (essere capace di) be able to; (venire a sapere) hear; **saperla lunga** know a thing or two; **non lo so** I don't know; **non so che farci** there's nothing I can do about it; **~ a memoria** know by heart; **~ il fatto proprio** know what one is talking about; **per quanto ne sappia** insofar as I know
[2] *vi* **~ di** know about; (aver sapore di)

taste of; (aver odore di) smell of; **saperci fare** know how to go about it; **saperci fare con i bambini** be good with children
[3] *nm* knowledge

sapi'ente [1] *adj* wise; (esperto) expert
[2] *nm* sage

sapiente'mente *adv* wisely; (abilmente) skilfully

sapien'tone *nm* smart alec[k]

sapi'enza *nf* wisdom

sa'pone *nm* soap; **bolla di ~** soap bubble; **finire in una bolla di ~** fig come to nothing
- **sapone da barba** shaving soap; **sapone da bucato** washing soap

sapo'netta *nf* bar of soap

sapo'noso *adj* soapy

⚔ **sa'pore** *nm* taste; **sentire ~ di** detect a hint of

saporita'mente *adv* ‹condire› skilfully; ‹mangiare› appreciatively; ‹dormire› soundly

sapo'rito *adj* tasty

sapu'tello, -a *adj & nm* sl know-all, know-it-all Am

sara'banda *nf* fig uproar

sara'ceno, -a *adj & nmf* Saracen; **grano saraceno** buckwheat

saraci'nesca *nf* roller shutter; (di chiusa) sluice gate

'sarago *nm* white bream

sar'casmo *nm* sarcasm

sarcastica'mente *adv* sarcastically

sar'castico *adj* sarcastic

sar'cofago *nm* sarcophagus

Sar'degna *nf* Sardinia

sar'dina *nf* sardine

'sardo, -a *adj & nmf* Sardinian

sar'donico *adj* sardonic

SARS *nf* SARS

sar'tiame *nm* rigging

'sarto, -a [1] *nm* tailor
[2] *nf* dressmaker

sarto'ria *nf* (da uomo) tailor's; (da donna) dressmaker's; (arte) couture

s.a.s. *abbr* (**società in accomandita semplice**) limited partnership

sas'saia *nf* stony ground

sassai'ola *nf* hail of stones

sas'sata *nf* blow with a stone; **una ~ ha rotto il vetro** a stone broke the window; **prendere a sassate** throw stones at, stone

⚔ **'sasso** *nm* stone; (ciottolo) pebble; **sono rimasto di ~** I was struck dumb [with astonishment]

sassofo'nista *nmf* saxophonist

sas'sofono *nm* saxophone

'sassone *nmf* Saxon; **genitivo sassone** Saxon genitive

sas'soso *adj* stony

S

'Satana *nm* Satan

sa'tanico *adj* satanic

sa'tellite *adj inv & nm* satellite; **città satellite** satellite town

sati'nare *vt* glaze; polish ‹*metallo*›

sati'nato *adj* glazed; ‹*metallo*› polished

'satira *nf* satire

sa'tirico *adj* satirical

satol'lare *vt* (hum) stuff

sa'tollo *adj* (hum) replete, full

satu'rare *vt* saturate

saturazi'one *nf* saturation

satur'nismo *nm* lead poisoning

Sa'turno *nm* Saturn

'saturo *adj* saturated; (pieno) full

S.A.U.B. *nf abbr* (**Struttura Amministrativa Unificata di Base**) *Italian national health service*

'sauna *nf* sauna

sa'vana *nf* savannah

savoi'ardo *nm* (biscotto) sponge finger

savoir-'faire *nm inv* expertise, know-how

sazi'are *vt* satiate

sazi'arsi *vr* ~ **di** fig weary of, grow tired of

sazi'età *nf* **mangiare a** ~ eat one's fill

'sazio *adj* satiated

sbaciucchi'are *vt* smother with kisses

sbaciucchi'arsi *vr* kiss and cuddle

sbada'taggine *nf* carelessness; **è stata una** ~ it was careless

sbadata'mente *adv* carelessly

sba'dato *adj* careless

sbadigli'are *vi* yawn

sba'diglio *nm* yawn

sba'fare *vt* sponge

sba'fata *nf* fam nosh; **farsi una** ~ fam have a nosh-up

'sbaffo *nm* smear

'sbafo *nm* sponging; **a** ~ (gratis) without paying

⚜ **sbagli'are** ① *vi* make a mistake; (aver torto) be wrong
② *vt* make a mistake in; ~ **strada** go the wrong way; ~ **numero** get the number wrong; Teleph dial a wrong number; **sbagliando s'impara** practice makes perfect

sbagli'arsi *vr* make a mistake; **ti sbagli** you're mistaken, you're wrong; ~ **di grosso** be totally wrong

sbagli'ato *adj* wrong

'sbaglio *nm* mistake; **per** ~ by mistake

sbale'strare *vt* fig disconcert

sbale'strato *adj* disconcerted

sbal'lare ① *vt* unpack; fam screw up ‹*conti*›
② *vi* fam go crazy

sbal'lato *adj* (squilibrato) unbalanced

'sballo *nm* fam scream; (per droga) trip; **da** ~ sl terrific

sballot'tare *vt* toss about

sbalordi'mento *nm* amazement

sbalor'dire ① *vt* stun
② *vi* be stunned

sbalordi'tivo *adj* amazing

sbalor'dito *adj* stunned; **restare** ~ be stunned

sbal'zare ① *vt* throw; (da una carica) dismiss
② *vi* bounce; (saltare) leap

'sbalzo *nm* bounce; (sussulto) jolt; (di temperatura) sudden change; **a sbalzi** in spurts; **a** ~ (a rilievo) embossed

sban'care *vt* bankrupt; excavate ‹*terreno*›; ~ **il banco** break the bank

sbanda'mento *nm* Auto skid; Naut list; fig going off the rails

sban'dare *vi* Auto skid; Naut list

sban'darsi *vr* (disperdersi) disperse

sban'data *nf* skid; Naut list; **prendere una** ~ **per** get a crush on

sban'dato, -a ① *adj* mixed-up
② *nmf* mixed-up person

sbandie'rare *vt* wave; fig display

sbarac'care *vt/i* clear up

sbaragli'are *vt* rout

sba'raglio *nm* rout; **mettere allo** ~ rout

sbaraz'zare *vt* clear

sbaraz'zarsi *vr* ~ **di** get rid of

sbaraz'zino, -a ① *adj* mischievous
② *nmf* scamp

sbar'bare *vt* shave

sbar'barsi *vr* shave

sbarba'tello, -a *adj & nmf* novice

sbar'care *vt/i* disembark; ~ **il lunario** make ends meet

'sbarco *nm* landing; (di merci) unloading

'sbarra *nf* bar; (di passaggio a livello) barrier
■ **sbarra spaziatrice** space bar

sbarra'mento *nm* barricade

sbar'rare *vt* bar; (ostruire) block; cross ‹*assegno*›; (spalancare) open wide

sbar'retta *nf* oblique

sbatacchi'are *vt/i* sl bang, slam

⚜ **'sbattere** ① *vt* bang; slam, bang ‹*porta*›; (urtare) knock; Culin beat; flap ‹*ali*›; shake ‹*tappeto*›; ~ **le palpebre** blink
② *vi* bang; ‹*porta*› slam, bang; ~ **contro** knock against; **andare a** ~ **contro** run into

sbat'tersi *vr* sl rush around; **sbattersene di qualcosa** not give a toss about something

sbat'tuto *adj* tossed; Culin beaten; fig run down

sba'vare *vi* dribble; ‹*colore*› smear

sbava'tura *nf* smear; **senza sbavature** fig faultless

sbec'care *vt* chip

⚜ indicates a very frequent word

sbec'cato *adj* chipped

sbeffeggi'are *vt* mock

sbelli'carsi *vr* ∼ **dalle risa** split one's sides [with laughter]

sben'dare *vt* unbandage

'sberla *nf* slap

sbevaz'zare *vi* fam tipple

sbia'dire *vt/i* fade

sbia'dirsi *vr* fade

sbia'dito *adj* faded; fig colourless

sbian'cante *nm* whitener

sbian'care *vt/i* whiten

sbian'carsi *vr* whiten

sbi'eco *adj* slanting; **di** ∼ on the slant; ⟨*guardare*⟩ sidelong; **guardare qualcuno di** ∼ look askance at somebody; **tagliare di** ∼ cut on the bias

sbigot'tire 1 *vt* dismay
  2 *vi* be dismayed

sbigot'tirsi *vr* be dismayed

sbigot'tito *adj* dismayed

sbilanci'are 1 *vt* unbalance
  2 *vi* (perdere l'equilibrio) overbalance

sbilanci'arsi *vr* lose one's balance

sbi'lancio *nm* lack of balance; Comm deficit

sbirci'are *vt* cast sidelong glances at

sbirci'ata *nf* furtive glance

sbircia'tina *nf* **dare una** ∼ a sneak a glance at

'sbirro *nm* pej cop

sbizzar'rirsi *vr* satisfy one's whims

sbloc'care *vt* unblock; Mech release; decontrol ⟨*prezzi*⟩

'sbobba *nf* fam pigswill

sboc'care *vi* ∼ **in** ⟨*fiume*⟩ flow into; ⟨*strada*⟩ lead to; ⟨*folla*⟩ pour into

sboc'cato *adj* foul-mouthed

sbocci'are *vi* blossom

'sbocco *nm* flowing; (foce) mouth; Comm outlet

sbolo'gnare *vt* fam get rid of

'sbornia *nf* **prendere una** ∼ get drunk; **smaltire la** ∼ sober up

sbor'sare *vt* pay out

sbot'tare *vi* burst out

sbotto'nare *vt* unbutton

sbotto'narsi *vr* fam (confidarsi) open up; ∼ **la camicia** unbutton one's shirt

sboz'zare *vt* draft; sketch out ⟨*dipinto*⟩

sbra'carsi *vr* put on something more comfortable; ∼ **dalle risate** fam kill oneself laughing

sbracci'arsi *vr* wave one's arms

sbracci'ato *adj* bare-armed; ⟨*abito*⟩ sleeveless

sbrai'tare *vi* bawl

sbra'nare *vt* tear to shreds *or* pieces

sbra'narsi *vr* tear each other to shreds

sbrat'tare *vt* clean up

sbrec'cato *adj* chipped

sbricio'lare *vt* crumble

sbricio'larsi *vr* crumble

⚘ **sbri'gare** *vt* expedite; (occuparsi di) attend to

sbri'garsi *vr* hurry up, be quick

sbriga'tivo *adj* hurried, quick

sbrigli'ato *adj* ⟨*fantasia*⟩ unbridled

sbri'nare *vt* defrost; Auto de-ice

sbrina'tore *nm* Auto de-icer; (di frigo) defrost button

sbrindel'lare *vt* tear to shreds

sbrindel'lato *adj* in rags

sbrodo'lare *vt* stain

sbrodo'lone, -a *nmf* messy eater

sbrogli'are *vt* disentangle

'sbronza *nf* fam **prendersi una** ∼ get drunk, get hammered fam

sbron'zarsi *vr* get drunk, get hammered fam

'sbronzo *adj* (ubriaco) drunk, hammered fam

sbruffo'nata *nf* boast

sbruf'fone, -a *nmf* boaster

sbu'care *vi* come out

sbucci'are *vt* peel; shell ⟨*piselli*⟩

sbucci'arsi *vr* graze oneself

sbuccia'tore *nm* parer

sbuccia'tura *nf* graze

sbudel'lare *vt* gut ⟨*pesce*⟩; draw ⟨*pollo*⟩; disembowel ⟨*persona*⟩

sbudel'larsi *vr* ∼ **dal ridere** die laughing

sbuf'fare *vi* snort; (per impazienza) fume

'sbuffo *nm* puff; **a** ∼ ⟨*maniche*⟩ puff *attrib*

sbugiar'dare *vt* show to be a liar

sbuz'zare *vt* fam gut ⟨*pesce*⟩; draw ⟨*pollo*⟩; disembowel ⟨*persona*⟩

'scabbia *nf* scabies *sg*

'scabro *adj* rough; ⟨*terreno*⟩ uneven; ⟨*stile*⟩ bald

sca'broso *adj* rough; ⟨*terreno*⟩ uneven; fig ⟨*question*⟩ difficult; ⟨*scena*⟩ offensive

scacchi'era *nf* chessboard

scacciapensi'eri *nm inv* Mus Jew's harp

scacci'are *vt* chase away

'scacco *nm* check; **scacchi** *pl* (gioco) chess; (pezzi) chessmen; **dare** ∼ **matto a** a checkmate; **a scacchi** ⟨*tessuto*⟩ checked; **subire uno** ∼ fig suffer a humiliating defeat

sca'dente *adj* shoddy, low-quality

sca'denza *nf* (di contratto) expiry; (di progetto, candidatura) deadline; Comm maturity; **a breve/lunga** ∼ short-/long-term

scaden'zario *nm* schedule

sca'dere *vi* expire; ⟨*valore*⟩ decline; ⟨*debito*⟩ be due

sca'duto *adj* ⟨*biglietto*⟩ out-of-date

sca'fandro *nm* diving suit

scaffala'tura *nf* shelves *pl*, shelving

scaf'fale *nm* shelf; (libreria) bookshelf

S

sca'fista *nmf person who ferries illegal immigrants to Italy by boat for a high fee*

'scafo *nm* hull

scagion'are *vt* exonerate

'scaglia *nf* scale; (di sapone) flake; (scheggia) chip

scagli'are *vt* fling

scagli'arsi *vr* fling oneself; ∼ **contro** fig rail against

scaglio'nare *vt* space out

scagli'one *nm* group; **a scaglioni** in groups
■ **scaglione di reddito** tax bracket

sca'gnozzo *nm* henchman

⚡ **'scala** *nf* staircase; (portatile) ladder; Mus (misura) scale; **scale** *pl* stairs; **in** ∼ to scale; **su larga** ∼ large-scale *attrib*
■ **scala allungabile** extension ladder; **scala antincendio** fire escape; **scala Beaufort** Beaufort scale; **scala a chiocciola** spiral staircase; **scala mobile** escalator; (dei salari) cost of living index; **scala Richter** Richter scale; **scala di servizio** backstairs; **scala di sicurezza** fire escape

sca'lare 1 *adj* scalar
2 *vt* climb; layer ‹*capelli*›; (detrarre) deduct

sca'lata *nf* climb; (dell'Everest ecc) ascent; **fare delle scalate** go climbing

scala|'tore, -trice *nmf* climber

scalca'gnato *adj* down at heel

scalci'are *vi* kick

scalci'nato *adj* shabby

scalda'acqua *nm inv* water-heater

scalda'bagno *nm* water-heater

scalda'muscoli *nm inv* legwarmer

scal'dare *vt* heat

scal'darsi *vr* warm up; (eccitarsi) get excited

sca'leno *adj* scalene

sca'leo *nm* step-ladder

scal'fire *vt* scratch

scalfit'tura *nf* scratch

scali'nata *nf* flight of steps
■ **scalinata di piazza di Spagna** Spanish Steps

sca'lino *nm* step; (di scala a pioli) rung

scalma'narsi *vr* rush about; (nel parlare) get worked up

scalma'nato *adj* worked up; **è** ∼ (vivace) he can't sit still

'scalmo *nm* rowlock

'scalo *nm* slipway; Naut port of call; **fare** ∼ a call at; Aeron land at; **senza scalo** nonstop
■ **scalo merci** freight depot, goods yard; **scalo passeggeri** stopover

sca'logna *nf* fam bad luck

scalo'gnato *adj* fam unlucky

sca'logno *nm* Bot scallion

scalop'pina *nf* escalope

scal'pare *vt* scalp

scalpel'lare *vt* chisel

scalpel'lino *nm* stone-cutter

scal'pello *nm* chisel

scalpi'tare *vi* paw the ground; fig champ at the bit

scalpi'tio *nm* pawing of the ground

'scalpo *nm* scalp

scal'pore *nm* noise; **far** ∼ fig cause a sensation

scal'trezza *nf* shrewdness

scal'trirsi *vr* get shrewder

'scaltro *adj* shrewd

scal'zare *vt* bare the roots of ‹*albero*›; fig undermine; (da una carica) oust

'scalzo *adj & adv* barefoot

scambi'are *vt* exchange; ∼ **qualcuno per qualcun altro** mistake somebody for somebody else

scambi'arsi *vr* exchange; ∼ **i saluti** exchange greetings

scambi'evole *adj* reciprocal

⚡ **'scambio** *nm* exchange; Comm trade
■ **libero scambio** free trade; **scambio di persona** mistaken identity

scamici'ato *nf* pinafore [dress]

sca'morza *nf* soft cheese

scamosci'ato *adj* suede *attrib*

scampa'gnata *nf* trip to the country

scampa'nato *adj* ‹*gonna*› flared

scampanel'lata *nf* [loud] ring

scampanel'lio *nm* ringing

scampan'io *nm* peal[ing]

scam'pare *vt* save; (evitare) escape; **scamparla bella** have a lucky escape

scam'pato 1 *adj* **lo** ∼ **pericolo** the escape from danger
2 *nmf* survivor

'scampi *nmpl* (crostaceo) scampi

'scampo *nm* escape; **non c'è** ∼ there's no way out

'scampolo *nm* remnant

scanala'tura *nf* groove

scandagli'are *vt* sound

scanda'lismo *nm* muckraking

scanda'listico *adj* sensational; ‹*giornale*› sensationalist

scandaliz'zare *vt* scandalize

scandaliz'zarsi *vr* be scandalized

'scandalo *nm* scandal

scanda'loso *adj* scandalous; ‹*somma ecc*› scandalous; ‹*fortuna*› outrageous

Scandi'navia *nf* Scandinavia

scan'dinavo, -a *adj & nmf* Scandinavian

scan'dire *vt* scan ‹*verso*›; pronounce clearly ‹*parole*›; ∼ **il tempo** beat time

---
⚡ indicates a very frequent word

scandi'tore *nm*
■ scanditore ottico Comput optical scanner
scan'nare *vt* slaughter
scan'nello *nm* lectern
'scanner *nm inv* scanner
■ scanner manuale Comput handheld scanner; scanner piatto flatbed scanner
scanneriz'zare *vt* Comput scan
scansafa'tiche *nmf inv* lazybones *sg*
scan'sare *vt* shift; (evitare) avoid
scan'sarsi *vr* get out of the way
scan'sia *nf* shelves *pl*
scansi'one *nf* Comput scanning
'scanso *nm* a ∼ di in order to avoid; a ∼ di equivoci to avoid any misunderstanding
scanti'nato *nm* basement
scanto'nare *vi* turn the corner; (svignarsela) sneak off
scanzo'nato *adj* easy-going
scapacci'one *nm* smack
scape'strato *adj* dissolute
scapigli'ato *adj* dishevelled
'scapito *nm* loss; a ∼ di to the detriment of
'scapola *nf* shoulder-blade
'scapolo *nm* bachelor
scappa'mento *nm* Auto exhaust
scap'pare *vi* escape; (andarsene) dash [off]; (sfuggire) slip; mi scappa da ridere! I want to burst out laughing; mi scappa la pipì I'm bursting, I need a pee; mi ha fatto ∼ la pazienza he tried my patience a bit too far; lasciarsi ∼ l'occasione let the opportunity slip; scappar via run off *or* away
scap'pata *nf* fam short visit
scappa'tella *nf* escapade; (infedeltà) fling
scappa'toia *nf* way out
scappel'lotto *nm* cuff
scarabeo¹ *nm* scarab beetle
scarabeo®² *nm* Scrabble®
scarabocchi'are *vt* scribble
scara'bocchio *nm* scribble
scara'faggio *nm* cockroach
scara'mantico *adj* ⟨gesto⟩ to ward off the evil eye
scaraman'zia *nf* superstition
scara'mazzo *adj* ⟨perla⟩ baroque
scara'muccia *nf* skirmish
scaraven'tare *vt* hurl
scarcas'sato *adj* ⟨fam: macchina⟩ beat-up
scarce'rare *vt* release [from prison]
scardi'nare *vt* unhinge
'scarica *nf* discharge; (di arma da fuoco) volley; fig shower; una ∼ di botte a hail of blows
scaricaba'rili *nm* fare a ∼ blame each other
scari'care *vt* discharge; Comput download; unload ⟨arma, merci, auto⟩; fig unburden

scari'carsi *vr* ⟨fiume⟩ flow; ⟨orologio, batteria⟩ run down; fig unwind
scarica'tore *nm* loader; (di porto) docker
'scarico ① *adj* unloaded; (vuoto) empty; ⟨orologio⟩ run-down; ⟨batteria⟩ flat; fig untroubled
② *nm* unloading; (di rifiuti) dumping; (di acqua) draining; (di sostanze inquinanti) discharge; (luogo) [rubbish] dump; Auto exhaust; (idraulico) drain; (tubo) waste pipe
■ 'divieto di scarico' 'no dumping'; tubo di scarico waste pipe
scarlat'tina *nf* scarlet fever
scar'latto *adj* scarlet
scarmigli'ato *adj* ruffled
scar'nire *vt* fig simplify
'scarno *adj* thin; fig ⟨stile⟩ bare
sca'rogna, scarognato = SCALOGNA, SCALOGNATO
sca'rola *nf* curly endive
'scarpa *nf* shoe; fam (persona) dead loss; fare le scarpe a qualcuno fig double-cross somebody; scarpe *pl* basse flat shoes, flats; scarpe *pl* da danza ballet shoes; scarpe *pl* da ginnastica trainers, gym shoes; scarpe *pl* col tacco high heels; scarpe *pl* col tacco a spillo stilettos; scarpe *pl* con la zeppa platform shoes
scar'pata *nf* slope; (burrone) escarpment
scarpi'era *nf* shoe rack
scarpi'nare *vi* hike
scarpon'cino *nm* ankle boot
■ scarponcino Clark® desert boot
scar'pone *nm* boot
■ scarpone da alpinismo climbing boot; scarponi da sci *pl* ski boots; scarponi da trekking *pl* walking boots
scarroz'zare *vt/i* drive around
scarroz'zata *nf* fam trip
scarruf'fato *adj* ruffled
scarseggi'are *vi* be scarce; ∼ di (mancare) be short of
scar'sezza *nf* scarcity, shortage
scarsità *nf* shortage
'scarso *adj* scarce; (manchevole) short
scartabel'lare *vt* skim through
scarta'mento *nm* Rail gauge
■ scartamento ridotto narrow gauge
scar'tare ① *vt* discard; unwrap ⟨pacco⟩; (respingere) reject
② *vi* (deviare) swerve
scartave'trare *vt* sand
'scarto *nm* scrap; (in carte) discard; (deviazione) swerve; (distacco) gap
scartocci'are *vt* unwrap
scar'toffie *nfpl* bumf, bumph
scas'sare *vt* break
scas'sato *adj* fam clapped out
scassi'nare *vt* force open; pick ⟨serratura⟩

S

scassina|'tore, -trice *nmf* burglar

'scasso *nm* (furto) house-breaking

scata'fascio = CATAFASCIO

scate'nare *vt* fig stir up ‹folla›; arouse ‹sentimenti›

scate'narsi *vr* break out; fig ‹temporale› break; fam (darsi alla pazza gioia) go crazy, go wild; fam (infiammarsi) get excited

scate'nato *adj* crazy, wild; **pazzo** ∼ fam off his head

♂ **'scatola** *nf* box; (di latta) can, tin Br; **in** ∼ ‹cibo› canned, tinned Br; **rompere le scatole a qualcuno** fam get on somebody's nerves; **a** ∼ **chiusa** ‹comprare› sight unseen
 ■ **scatola del cambio** gearbox; **scatola nera** Aeron black box

scato'lame *nm* (cibo) canned food

scato'letta *nf* small box; (di cibo) tin

scato'logico *adj* scatological

scat'tante *adj* zippy

♂ **scat'tare** *vi* go off; (balzare) spring up; (adirarsi) lose one's temper; take ‹foto›

'scatto *nm* (balzo) spring; (d'ira) outburst; (di telefono) unit; (dispositivo) release; **a scatti** jerkily; **di** ∼ suddenly

scatu'rire *vi* spring

scaval'care *vt* jump over ‹muretto›; climb over ‹muro›; fig (superare) overtake

sca'vare *vt* dig ‹buca›; dig up ‹tesoro›; excavate ‹città sepolta›

scava'trice *nf* excavator

scavezza'collo *nm* daredevil

'scavo *nm* excavation

scazzot'tare *vt* fam beat up

scazzot'tata *nf* fam punch-up; **prendersi una** ∼ get beaten up

♂ **'scegliere** *vt* choose, select

sce'icco *nm* sheikh

scelle'rato *adj* wicked

♂ **'scelta** *nf* choice; (di articoli) range; **... a** ∼ (in menù) choice of ...; **prendine uno a** ∼ take your choice *or* pick; **di prima** ∼ top-grade, choice; ‹albergo› first-rate; **di seconda** ∼ second grade; pej second-rate
 ■ **scelta multipla** multiple choice

'scelto ① pp di SCEGLIERE
 ② *adj* select; ‹merce ecc› choice
 ■ **tiratore scelto** marksman

sce'mare *vt/i* diminish

sce'menza *nf* silliness; (azione) silly thing to do/say; **non diciamo scemenze!** let's not be silly!

♂ **'scemo** ① *adj* idiotic
 ② *nm* idiot

scempi'aggine *nf* foolish thing to do/say

'scempio *nm* havoc; fig (di paesaggio) ruination; **fare** ∼ **di** play havoc with

---

♂ indicates a very frequent word

♂ **'scena** *nf* scene; (palcoscenico) stage; **entrare in** ∼ Theat go/come on [stage]; fig come on the scene; **fare** ∼ put on an act; **fare una** ∼ make a scene; **fare scene** make a fuss; **andare in** ∼ ‹Theat: spettacolo› be staged, be put on; **fare** ∼ **muta** not open one's mouth; **scomparire dalla** ∼ fig vanish from the scene; **mettere in** ∼ produce, stage; **messa in** ∼ production, staging; fig set-up

sce'nario *nm* scenery

sce'nata *nf* row, scene

♂ **'scendere** ① *vi* go/come down; (da treno, autobus) get off; (da macchina) get out; ‹strada› slope; ‹notte, prezzi› fall
 ② *vt* go/come down ‹scale›

scendi'letto *nm* bedside rug

sceneggi'are *vt* dramatize

sceneggi'ato *nm* television serial

sceneggia'tura *nf* screenplay

'scenico *adj* scenic

sceno'grafia *nf* set design

sce'nografo, -a *nmf* set designer

sce'riffo *nm* sheriff

scervel'larsi *vr* rack one's brains

scervel'lato *adj* brainless

'sceso pp di SCENDERE

scespi'riano *agg.* Shakespearean

scetti'cismo *nm* scepticism

'scettico, -a ① *adj* sceptical
 ② *nmf* sceptic

'scettro *nm* sceptre

'scheda *nf* card
 ■ **scheda audio** Comput sound card; **scheda elettorale** ballot-paper; **scheda di espansione** Comput expansion card; **scheda grafica** Comput graphics card; **scheda madre** Comput motherboard; **scheda magnetica** card key; **scheda perforata** punch card; **scheda di rete** Comput network card; **scheda sonora** Comput sound card; **scheda telefonica** phonecard; **scheda di valutazione scolastica** report card, school report; **scheda video** Comput video card

sche'dare *vt* file

sche'dario *nm* file; (mobile) filing cabinet

sche'dato, -a ① *adj* with a police record
 ② *nmf* person with a police record

sche'dina *nf* pools coupon; **giocare la** ∼ do the pools

'scheggia *nf* fragment; (di legno) splinter

scheggia're *vt* splinter

scheggi'arsi *vr* chip; ‹legno› splinter

sche'letrico *adj* skeletal

'scheletro *nm* skeleton; **essere ridotto ad uno** ∼ be all skin and bones

'schema *nm* diagram; (abbozzo) outline; **uscire dagli schemi** break with tradition

schematica'mente *adv* schematically

sche'matico *adj* schematic

schematiz'zare *vt* present schematically

'scherma *nf* fencing

scher'maglia *nf* skirmish

scher'mirsi *vr* protect oneself

'schermo *nm* screen; **sul grande** ∼ on the big screen; **farsi** ∼ **con** shield oneself with
■ **schermo panoramico** wide screen; **schermo al plasma** plasma screen; **schermo a sfioramento** Comput touch screen

scher'nire *vt* mock

'scherno *nm* mockery

⚡ **scher'zare** *vi* joke; (giocare) play; **c'è poco da** ∼! it's nothing to laugh about!

⚡ **'scherzo** *nm* joke; (trucco) trick; (effetto) play; Mus scherzo; **fare uno** ∼ **a qualcuno** play a joke on somebody; **giocare brutti scherzi (a qualcuno)** ‹memoria, vista› play tricks on somebody); **per** ∼ for fun; **scherzi a parte** joking apart, seriously; **stare allo** ∼ take a joke
■ **scherzo di natura** freak of nature

scher'zoso *adj* playful

schiaccia'noci *nm inv* nutcrackers *pl*

schiacci'ante *adj* damning; ‹vittoria› crushing

⚡ **schiacci'are** *vt* crush; (in tennis ecc) smash; press ‹pulsante›; crack ‹noce›; ∼ **un pisolino** grab forty winks

schiacci'arsi *vr* get crushed

schiaccia'sassi *nf inv* steamroller

schiaf'fare *vt* fam shove

schiaffeggi'are *vt* slap

schi'affo *nm* slap; **dare uno** ∼ **a** slap; **avere una faccia da schiaffi** have the kind of face you'd love to take a swipe at
■ **schiaffo morale** slap in the face

schiamaz'zare *vi* make a racket; ‹galline› cackle

schia'mazzo *nm* din; **schiamazzi** *pl* **notturni** disturbing the peace

schian'tare ① *vt* break
② *vi* **schianto dalla fatica** I'm wiped out

schian'tarsi *vr* crash

'schianto *nm* crash; fam knock-out; (divertente) scream

schia'rire ① *vt* clear; (sbiadire) fade
② *vi* brighten up

schia'rirsi *vr* brighten up; ∼ **la gola** clear one's throat; ∼ **le idee** get things clear in one's head; (dopo aver bevuto) clear one's head

schia'rita *nf* sunny interval

schiat'tare *vi* burst; ∼ **di invidia** be green with envy

schia'vista *nmf* slave-driver

schiavitù *nf* slavery

schi'avo, -a *nmf* slave

⚡ **schi'ena** *nf* back
■ **mal di schiena** backache

schie'nale *nm* (di sedia) back

schi'era *nf* Mil rank; (moltitudine) crowd

schiera'mento *nm* lining up; Mil battle line
■ **schieramento di forze** rallying of the troops

schie'rare *vt* draw up; rally ‹forze›

schie'rarsi *vr* draw up; ‹forze› rally; ∼ **dalla parte di qualcuno**, ∼ **con qualcuno** rally [in support] to somebody; ∼ **contro qualcuno** rally in opposition to somebody

schiet'tezza *nf* frankness

schi'etto *adj* frank; (puro) pure

schi'fezza *nf* **è una** ∼ it's disgusting; ‹film, libro› it's rubbish

⚡ **'schifo** *nm* disgust; **fare** ∼ be disgusting; **è uno** ∼! it's disgusting!

schi'foso *adj* disgusting, yucky fam; (di cattiva qualità) rubbishy

schioc'care ① *vt* crack ‹frusta›; snap, click ‹dita›; click ‹lingua›
② *vi* crack

schi'occo *nm* (di frusta) crack; (di bacio) smack; (di dita, lingua) click

schioppet'tata *nf* shot

schi'oppo *nm* fam rifle; **a un tiro di** ∼ fig a stone's throw away

schiri'bizzo *nm* fam fancy; **se mi salta lo** ∼ … if it takes my fancy …

schi'udere *vt* open

schi'udersi *vr* open

schi'uma *nf* foam; (di sapone) lather; (di bucato) suds; (feccia) scum
■ **schiuma da barba** shaving foam

schiu'mare ① *vt* skim
② *vi* foam

schiuma'rola *nf* Culin skimmer

schiu'mogeno *adj* foaming

schiu'moso *adj* ‹birra, crema› frothy, foamy; ‹liquido› scummy

schi'uso *pp di* SCHIUDERE

schi'vare *vt* avoid

'schivo *adj* bashful

schizofre'nia *nf* schizophrenia

schizo'frenico, -a *adj & nmf* schizophrenic

schiz'zare ① *vt* squirt; (inzaccherare) splash; (abbozzare) sketch; ∼ **qualcuno/ qualcosa di qualcosa** splatter somebody/ something with something
② *vi* spurt; ∼ **via** fig scurry away

schiz'zato, -a *adj & nmf* fam loony

schizzi'noso *adj* squeamish

'schizzo *nm* squirt; (di fango) splash; (abbozzo) sketch

sci *nm inv* ski; (sport) skiing
■ **sci d'acqua, sci acquatico** water-skiing; **sci acrobatico** hot dogging; **sci di fondo** cross-country skiing

'scia *nf* wake; (di fumo ecc) trail; **sulla** ∼ **di qualcuno** following in somebody's footsteps

sci'abola *nf* sabre

sciabor'dare vt/i lap
sciabor'dio nm lapping
sciacal'laggio nm profiteering
scia'callo nm jackal; fig profiteer
sciac'quare vt rinse
sciac'quarsi vr rinse oneself
sci'acquo nm mouthwash
scia'gura nf disaster
sciagu'rato adj unfortunate; (scellerato) wicked
scialac'quare vt squander
scialacqua|'tore, -trice nmf squanderer
scia'lare vi spend money like water
sci'albo adj pale; fig dull
sci'alle nm shawl
scia'luppa nf dinghy
■ **scialuppa di salvataggio** lifeboat
sciaman'nato adj good-for-nothing
scia'mano n shaman
scia'mare vi swarm
sci'ame nm swarm; **a sciami** in swarms
sci'ampo nm shampoo
scian'cato adj lame
sci'are vi ski; **andare a ∼** go skiing
sci'arpa nf scarf
sci'atica nf Med sciatica
scia|'tore, -trice nmf skier
sciatte'ria nf slovenliness
sci'atto adj slovenly; ⟨stile⟩ careless
sciat'tone, -a nmf slovenly person
'scibile nm knowledge; **lo ∼ umano** the sum of human knowledge
scic'coso adj fam snazzy
scienti'fico adj scientific
⟋ **sci'enza** nf science; (sapere) knowledge; **avere la ∼ infusa** be naturally talented; **scienze** pl **sociali** social science
scienzi'ato, -a nmf scientist
sci'ita adj & nmf Shiite
scilin'guagnolo nm fig **avere lo ∼** be a chatterbox
'scimmia nf monkey
scimmiot'tare vt ape
scimpanzé nm inv chimpanzee, chimp
scimu'nito adj idiotic
'scindere vt separate; **∼ in** break down into
'scindersi vr divide; **∼ in** divide into
scin'tilla nf spark
scintil'lante adj sparkling
scintil'lare vi sparkle
scintil'lio nm sparkle
sciò int shoo!
scioc'cante adj shocking
scioc'care vt shock

⟋ **scioc'chezza** nf foolishness; (assurdità) foolish thing; **sciocchezze!** nonsense!
sci'occo adj foolish
⟋ **sci'ogliere** vt untie; undo, untie ⟨nodo⟩; (liberare) release; (liquefare) melt; dissolve ⟨contratto, qualcosa nell'acqua⟩; loosen up ⟨muscoli⟩
sci'ogliersi vr ⟨nodo⟩ come undone; (liquefarsi) melt; ⟨contratto⟩ be dissolved; ⟨pastiglia⟩ dissolve
sciogli'lingua nm inv tongue-twister
scio'lina nf ski wax
sciol'tezza nf agility; (disinvoltura) ease
sci'olto [1] pp di SCIOGLIERE
[2] adj loose; (agile) agile; (disinvolto) easy; **versi** pl **sciolti** blank verse
sciope'rante nmf striker
sciope'rare vi go on strike, strike
sci'opero nm strike, industrial action; **in ∼** on strike
■ **sciopero bianco** work-to-rule; **sciopero generale** general strike; **sciopero a singhiozzo** on-off strike
sciori'nare vt fig show off
sciovi'nismo nm chauvinism
sciovi'nista nmf Pol chauvinist
sciovi'nistico adj Pol chauvinistic
sci'pito adj insipid
scip'pare vt fam snatch; **∼ qualcuno** snatch somebody's bag/bracelet etc
scippa|'tore, -trice nmf bag-snatcher
'scippo nm bag-snatching
sci'rocco nm sirocco
scirop'pato adj ⟨frutta⟩ in syrup
sci'roppo nm syrup
scirop'poso adj syrupy
'scisma nm schism
scissi'one nf division
scissio'nista adj breakaway attrib
'scisso pp di SCINDERE
sciupacchi'are vt spoil
sciupacchi'ato adj spoilt
sciu'pare vt spoil; (sperperare) waste
sciu'parsi vr get spoiled; (deperire) wear oneself out
sciu'pio nm waste
⟋ **scivo'lare** vi slide; (involontariamente) slip
'scivolo nm slide; Techn chute
scivo'lone nm fall; fig (errore) blunder
scivo'loso adj slippery
scle'rosi nf sclerosis
■ **sclerosi multipla, sclerosi a placche** multiple sclerosis, MS
scoc'care [1] vt fire ⟨freccia⟩; strike ⟨ore⟩
[2] vi ⟨scintilla⟩ shoot out; **sono scoccate le cinque** five o'clock has just struck
scocci'are vt fam (dare noia a) bother
scocci'arsi vr fam be bored; **mi sono scocciato di aspettare** I'm fed up with waiting

---

⟋ indicates a very frequent word

s

scocci'ato *adj* fam fed up

scoccia'tore, -trice *nmf* nuisance

scoccia'tura *nf* fam nuisance

sco'della *nf* bowl

scodel'lare *vt* dish out, dish up

scodinzo'lare *vi* wag its tail

scogli'era *nf* cliff; (a fior d'acqua) reef

'scoglio *nm* rock; fig (ostacolo) stumbling block

scoglio'nato *adj* vulg pissed off

scoi'attolo *nm* squirrel

scola'pasta *nm inv* colander

scolapi'atti *nm inv* dish drainer

sco'lara *nf* schoolgirl

sco'lare¹ [1] *vt* drain; strain ⟨pasta, verdura⟩
[2] *vi* drip

sco'lare² *adj* school *attrib*; in età ∼ ⟨bambino⟩ school-age

scola'resca *nf* pupils *pl*

sco'laro *nm* schoolboy

sco'lastico *adj* school *attrib*; gita scolastica school trip

scoli'osi *nf* curvature of the spine

scollacci'ato *adj* low-cut

scol'lare *vt* cut away the neck of ⟨abito⟩; (staccare) unstick

scol'lato *adj* ⟨abito⟩ low-necked

scolla'tura *nf* neckline; ∼ profonda plunging neckline

scolle'gare *vt* disconnect

'scollo *nm* neckline
■ scollo a V V-neck

'scolo *nm* drainage

scolo'rare *vt* fade

scolori'mento *nm* fading

scolo'rire *vt* fade

scolo'rirsi *vr* fade

scolo'rito *adj* faded

scol'pire *vt* carve; (imprimere) engrave

scombi'nare *vt* upset

scombusso'lare *vt* muddle up

scom'messa *nf* bet

scom'messo pp di SCOMMETTERE

scom'mettere *vt* bet; ci puoi ∼! you bet!

scomo'dare *vt* trouble

scomo'darsi *vr* trouble

scomodità *nf inv* discomfort

'scomodo [1] *adj* uncomfortable
[2] *nm* essere di ∼ a qualcuno be a trouble to somebody

scompagin'are *vt* mess up

scompa'gnare *vt* split

scompa'gnato *adj* odd

⚹ scompa'rire *vi* disappear; (morire) pass away

scom'parsa *nf* disappearance; (morte) death, passing

scom'parso, -a [1] pp di SCOMPARIRE
[2] *adj* missing; (morto) departed
[3] *nmf* missing person; (morto) departed

scomparti'mento *nm* compartment

scom'parto *nf* compartment
■ scomparto freezer freezer compartment

scompen'sare *vt* throw off balance

scom'penso *nm* imbalance
■ scompenso cardiaco cardiac insufficiency

scompigli'are *vt* disarrange

scom'piglio *nm* confusion

scompisci'arsi *vr* fam ∼ [dalle risa] wet oneself, split one's sides laughing fam

scom'porre *vt* break down; ruffle ⟨capelli⟩; fig (turbare) upset

scom'porsi *vr* lose one's composure

scomposizi'one *nf* breaking down

scom'posto [1] pp di SCOMPORRE
[2] *adj* ⟨sguaiato⟩ unseemly; (disordinato) untidy

sco'munica *nf* excommunication

scomuni'care *vt* excommunicate

sconcer'tante *adj* disconcerting; (che rende perplesso) bewildering, baffling

sconcer'tare *vt* disconcert; (rendere perplesso) bewilder; baffle

sconcer'tato *adj* disconcerted; (perplesso) bewildered, baffled

scon'cezza *nf* indecency

'sconcio [1] *adj* indecent
[2] *nm* è uno ∼ che … it's a disgrace that …

sconclusio'nato *adj* incoherent

scon'dito *adj* unseasoned; (insalata) with no dressing

sconfes'sare *vt* disown

scon'figgere *vt* defeat

sconfi'nare *vi* cross the border; (in proprietà privata) trespass

sconfi'nato *adj* unlimited

scon'fitta *nf* defeat; subire una ∼ be defeated, suffer defeat

scon'fitto pp di SCONFIGGERE

sconfor'tante *adj* disheartening, discouraging

scon'forto *nm* discouragement; farsi prendere dallo ∼ get discouraged, get disheartened

sconge'lare *vt* thaw out ⟨cibo⟩; defrost ⟨frigo⟩

scongiu'rare *vt* beseech; (evitare) avert

scongi'uro *nm* fare gli scongiuri ≈ touch wood, knock on wood Am

scon'nesso [1] pp di SCONNETTERE
[2] *adj* fig incoherent

scon'nettere *vt* disconnect

⚹ sconosci'uto, -a [1] *adj* unknown
[2] *nmf* stranger

sconquas'sare *vt* smash; (sconvolgere) upset

sconsa'crare *vt* deconsecrate

sconsiderata'mente *adv* inconsiderately

sconsidera'tezza *nf* lack of consideration, thoughtlessness

sconside'rato *adj* inconsiderate, thoughtless

sconsigli'abile *adj* not advisable

sconsigli'are *vt* advise against

sconso'lato *adj* disconsolate

scon'tare *vt* discount; (dedurre) deduct; (pagare) pay off; serve ‹pena›; ~ **la propria colpa** pay for one's sins

scon'tato *adj* discounted; (ovvio) expected; ~ **del 10%** with 10% discount; **era** ~ **it** it was to be expected; **dare qualcosa per** ~ take something for granted

scon'tento 1 *adj* displeased 2 *nm* discontent

'sconto *nm* discount; **fare uno** ~ give a discount
■ **sconto commerciale** trade discount

scon'trarsi *vr* clash; (urtare) collide

scon'trino *nm* ticket; (di cassa) receipt; '**munirsi dello** ~ **alla cassa**' sign reminding customers that payment must be made at the cash desk beforehand

'scontro *nm* clash; (urto) collision
■ **scontro automobilistico** car crash; **scontro di civiltà** clash of civilizations; **scontro frontale** head-on collision; **scontro a fuoco** shootout

scontrosità *nf* surliness

scon'troso *adj* surly

sconveni'ente *adj* unprofitable; (scorretto) unseemly

sconvol'gente *adj* (sorprendente) mind-blowing; (inquietante) upsetting

scon'volgere *vt* upset; (mettere in disordine) disarrange

sconvolgi'mento *nm* upheaval

scon'volto 1 *pp di* SCONVOLGERE 2 *adj* distraught, upset

'scooter *nm inv* scooter

'scopa *nf* broom; (gioco di carte) type of card game

sco'pare *vt* sweep; vulg shag

sco'pata *nf* sweep; vulg shag; **dare una** ~ **per terra** give the floor a sweep

scoperchi'are *vt* take the lid off ‹pentola›; take the roof off ‹casa›

sco'perta *nf* discovery

sco'perto 1 *pp di* SCOPRIRE 2 *adj* uncovered; (senza riparo) exposed; (conto) overdrawn; (spoglio) bare

⚜ **'scopo** *nm* aim; **a** ~ **di** for the sake of; **allo** ~ **di** in order to

sco'pone *nm* (gioco di carte) type of card game

⚜ **scoppi'are** *vi* burst; fig break out

⚜ indicates a very frequent word

scoppiet'tare *vi* crackle

⚜ **'scoppio** *nm* burst; (di guerra) outbreak; (esplosione) explosion; **a** ~ **ritardato** ‹bomba› delayed action; **ha reagito a** ~ **ritardato** he did a double take

⚜ **sco'prire** *vt* discover; (togliere la copertura a) uncover; unveil ‹statua›; ~ **gli altarini** fam reveal his/her etc guilty secrets

scoraggia'mento *nm* discouragement

scoraggi'ante *adj* discouraging

scoraggi'are *vt* discourage

scoraggi'arsi *vr* lose heart

scor'butico *adj* Med suffering from scurvy; fig (scontroso) disagreeable

scor'buto *nm* Med scurvy

scorci'are *vt* shorten

scorcia'toia *nf* short cut

'scorcio *nm* (di cielo) patch; (in arte) foreshortening; **di** ~ (vedere) from an angle
■ **scorcio panoramico** panoramic view; **scorcio del secolo** end of the century

scor'dare *vt* forget; ~ **qualcosa a casa** leave something at home

scor'darsi *vr* forget; ~ **di qualcosa** forget something

scor'dato *adj* Mus out of tune

scorda'tura *nf* Mus going out of tune

sco'reggia *nf* fam fart

scoreggi'are *vi* fam fart

'scorfano *nm* scorpion fish

'scorgere *vt* make out; (notare) notice

'scoria *nf* waste; (di carbone) slag; **scorie** *pl* **nucleari** nuclear waste

scor'nare *vt* fig humiliate

scor'narsi *vr* fig come a cropper

scor'nato *adj* fig hangdog

'scorno *nm* humiliation

scorpacci'ata *nf* bellyful; **fare una** ~ **di** stuff oneself with

scorpi'one *nm* scorpion; Astr Scorpio

scorraz'zare *vi* run about

⚜ **'scorrere** 1 *vt* (dare un'occhiata) glance through 2 *vi* run; (scivolare) slide; (fluire) flow; Comput scroll; (attorno a un oggetto) wrap

scorre'ria *nf* raid

scorret'tezza *nf* (mancanza di educazione) bad manners *pl*

scor'retto *adj* incorrect; (sconveniente) improper

scor'revole *adj* porta ~ sliding door

scorri'banda *nf* raid; fig excursion

scorri'mento *nm* Comput scrolling; (attorno a un oggetto) wrapping

'scorsa *nf* glance; **dare una** ~ **a** glance through

'scorso 1 *pp di* SCORRERE 2 *adj* last; **l'anno** ~ last year

scor'soio adj nodo ∼ noose

'scorta nf escort; (provvista) supply

scor'tare vt escort

scortecci'are vt debark ‹albero›; strip ‹muro›

scor'tese adj rude

scorte'sia nf rudeness

scorti'care vt skin

scortica'tura nf graze

'scorto pp di SCORGERE

'scorza nf peel; (crosta) crust; (corteccia) bark; fig exterior
■ **scorza d'arancia** orange peel

scorzo'nera nf salsify

sco'sceso adj steep

'scossa nf shake; Electr fig shock; **prendere la ∼** get an electric shock
■ **scossa elettrica** electric shock; **scossa sismica** earth tremor

'scosso 1 pp di SCUOTERE
2 adj shaken; (sconvolto) upset

scos'sone nm jolt

sco'stante adj off-putting

sco'stare vt push away

sco'starsi vr stand aside

scostu'mato adj dissolute; (maleducato) ill-mannered

scotch® nm Scotch tape

scoten'nare vt skin ‹maiale›; scalp ‹persona›

scot'tante adj ‹argomento› burning; fig ‹notizia› sensational

scot'tare 1 vt burn; (con liquido, vapore) scald; Culin blanch
2 vi ‹bevanda, cibo› be too hot; ‹sole, pentola› be very hot

scot'tarsi vr burn oneself; (con liquido, vapore) scald oneself; (al sole) get sunburnt; fig get one's fingers burnt

scot'tato adj Culin blanched

scotta'tura nf burn; (da liquido) scald; fig painful experience
■ **scottatura solare** sunburn

'Scottex® nm paper towel

'scotto¹ adj overcooked

'scotto² nm score; **pagare lo ∼ di qualcosa** pay for something

scout 1 adj inv scout attrib
2 nmf inv scout

scou'tismo nm scout movement

sco'vare vt (scoprire) discover

scovo'lino nm bottle brush; (per pipa) pipe cleaner

'Scozia nf Scotland

scoz'zese 1 adj Scottish
2 nmf Scot

'scrambler nm inv Radio, Teleph scrambler

screan'zato adj rude

scredi'tare vt discredit

scre'mare vt skim

screpo'lare vt chap

screpo'larsi vr get chapped; ‹intonaco› crack

screpo'lato adj chapped; ‹intonaco› cracked

screpola'tura nf crack

screzi'ato adj speckled

'screzio nm disagreement

scribacchi'are vt scribble

scribac'chino, -a nmf scribbler; ‹impiegato› penpusher

scricchio'lante adj creaky

scricchio'lare vi creak

scricchio'lio nm creaking

'scricciolo nm wren; fig delicate-looking creature

'scrigno nm casket

scrimina'tura nf parting

scriteri'ato adj empty-headed

'scritta nf writing; (su muro) graffiti

'scritto 1 pp di SCRIVERE
2 adj written; ∼ **col computer** word-processed; ∼ **a macchina** typed; ∼ **a mano** handwritten
3 nm writing; (lettera) letter

scrit'toio nm writing-desk

scrit|'tore, -trice nmf writer

scrit'tura nf writing; Relig scripture; (calligrafia) handwriting; **scritture** pl contabili account books
■ **scrittura privata** Jur legal document drawn up by an individual

scrittu'rare vt engage

scriva'nia nf desk

scri'vente nmf writer

'scrivere vt write; (descrivere) write about; ∼ **a macchina** type

scroc'care vt fam

scrocchi'are vi crack

'scrocco¹ nm fam **a ∼** without paying; **vivere a ∼** sponge off other people

'scrocco² nm
■ **coltello a scrocco** pocket knife; **serratura a scrocco** spring lock

scroc'cone, -a nmf fam sponger

'scrofa nf sow

scrol'lare vt shake; ∼ **le spalle** shrug one's shoulders; ∼ **la testa** shake one's head

scrol'larsi vr shake oneself; ∼ **qualcosa di dosso** shake something off

'scrolling nm Comput scrolling

scrosci'ante adj pouring; ‹applausi› thunderous

scrosci'are vi roar; ‹pioggia›; pelt down

'scroscio nm roar; (di pioggia) pelting; **uno ∼ di applausi** thunderous applause; **piovere a ∼** lash down

S

scro'stare vt scrape

scro'starsi vr flake

scro'stato adj flaky

'scroto nm scrotum

'scrupolo nm scruple; (diligenza) care; **senza scrupoli** unscrupulous, without scruples; **farsi scrupoli per qualcosa** have scruples about something

scrupo'loso adj scrupulous

scru'tare vt scan; (indagare) search

scruta'tore nm (di voti) returning officer

scruti'nare vt scrutinize

scru'tinio nm (di voti) poll; Sch assessment of progress; **scrutini** pl Sch meeting of teachers to discuss pupils' work and assign marks

■ **scrutinio segreto** secret ballot

scu'cire vt unstitch; **scuci i soldi!** fig fam cough up [the money]!

scu'cirsi vr come unstitched; fig (parlare) talk; **non si scuce** he won't talk

scuci'tura nf unstitching

scude'ria nf stable; **scuderie** pl mews

scu'detto nm Sport championship shield; (campionato) national championship

scudi'ero nm squire

scudisci'ata nf whipping

'scudo nm shield; **farsi ~ con qualcosa** shield oneself with something

scuffi'are vi capsize

scu'gnizzo nm street urchin

sculacci'are vt spank

sculacci'ata nf spanking; **prendere a sculacciate** spank

sculacci'one nm spanking

sculet'tare vi wiggle one's hips

scul|'tore, -trice [1] nm sculptor [2] nf sculptress

scul'tura nf sculpture

⚘ **scu'ola** nf school

■ **scuola allievi ufficiali** cadet school; **scuola per bambini con difficoltà d'apprendimento** special school; **scuola elementare** primary school, grade school Am; **scuola guida** driving school; **scuola materna** day nursery; **scuola media** secondary school; **scuola media inferiore** secondary school (10-13); junior high school Am; **scuola media superiore** secondary school (13-18); **scuola dell'obbligo** compulsory education; **scuola privata** private school, public school Br; **scuola di sci** ski school; **scuola serale** evening school; **scuola statale** state school; **scuola superiore** high school

scu'otere vt shake

scu'otersi vr (destarsi) rouse oneself; **~ qualcosa di dosso** fig shake something off

'scure nf axe

scu'rire vt/i darken

⚘ **'scuro** [1] adj dark [2] nm darkness; (imposta) shutter

scur'rile adj scurrilous

⚘ **'scusa** nf excuse; (giustificazione) apology; (pretesto) pretext; **chiedere ~** apologize; **chiedo] ~!** [I'm] sorry!

⚘ **scu'sare** vt excuse

scu'sarsi vr apologize (**di** for); **[mi] scusi!** excuse me!; (chiedendo perdono) [I'm] sorry!

sdebi'tarsi vr repay the kindness

sde'gnare vt despise; (fare arrabbiare) enrage

sde'gnarsi vr become angry

sde'gnato adj indignant

'sdegno nm disdain; (ira) indignation

sde'gnoso adj disdainful

sden'tato adj toothless

sdipa'nare vt wind

sdogana'mento nm customs clearance

sdoga'nare vt clear through customs

sdolci'nato adj sentimental, schmaltzy

sdoppia'mento nm splitting

■ **sdoppiamento della personalità** split personality

sdoppi'are vt halve

sdrai'arsi vr lie down

'sdraio nf [sedia a] ~ deckchair

sdrammatiz'zare [1] vt take the heat out of [2] vi take the heat out of the situation

sdruccio'lare vi slither

sdruccio'levole adj slippery

sdruccio'lone nm slip

⚘ **se** [1] conj if; (interrogativo) whether, if; **se mai** (caso mai) if need be; **se mai telefonasse,...** should he call,..., if he calls,...; **se no** otherwise, or else; **se non altro** at least, if nothing else; **se pure** (sebbene) even though; (anche se) even if; **non so se sia vero** I don't know whether it's true, I don't know if it's true; **come se** as if; **se lo avessi saputo prima!** if only I had known before!; **e se andassimo fuori a cena?** how about going out for dinner? [2] nm inv if; **non voglio né se né ma** I don't want any ifs or buts

SE abbr (**sud-est**) SE

⚘ **sé** pers pron oneself; (lui) himself; (lei) herself; (esso, essa) itself; (loro) themselves; **l'ha fatto da sé** he did it himself; **ha preso i soldi con sé** he took the money with him; **si sono tenuti le notizie per sé** they kept the news to themselves

se'baceo adj sebaceous

seb'bene conj although

'sebo nm sebum

sec. abbr (**secolo**) c.

⚘ **'secca** nf shallows pl; **in ~** (nave) grounded

sec'cante adj annoying

⚘ indicates a very frequent word

sec'care ⒈ *vt* dry; (importunare) annoy
⒉ *vi* dry up

sec'carsi *vr* dry up; (irritarsi) get annoyed

secca|'**tore**, **-trice** *nmf* nuisance

secca'tura *nf* bother; **dare una ∼ a
qualcuno** trouble somebody, bother
somebody; **non voglio seccare!** I don't
want the bother!

secchi'ata *nf* bucketful

secchi'ello *nm* bucket
■ **secchiello del ghiaccio** ice bucket

'**secchio** *nm* bucket
■ **secchio della spazzatura** rubbish bin, trash
can Am

sec'chione, **-a** *nmf* fam dweeb

♂ '**secco**, **-a** ⒈ *adj* dry; (disseccato) dried;
(magro) thin; (brusco) curt; (preciso) sharp;
restare a ∼ be left penniless; **restarci ∼** fam
(morire di colpo) be killed on the spot; **frutta
secca** nuts *pl*
⒉ *nm* (siccità) drought; **lavare a ∼** dry-clean

secessi'one *nf* secession
■ **guerra di secessione** War of Secession

seco'lare *adj* age-old; (laico) secular

♂ '**secolo** *nm* century; (epoca) age; **è un ∼ che
non lo vedo** fam I haven't seen him for ages
o yonks

se'conda ⒈ *nf* Sch, Rail second class; Auto
second [gear]
⒉ *prep* **a ∼ di** according to

secon'dario *adj* Jur collateral; **effetto ∼**
side effect

♂ **se'condo** ⒈ *adj* second
⒉ *nm* second, sec fam; (secondo piatto) main
course; **un ∼!** just a sec[ond]!
⒊ *prep* according to; **∼ me** in my opinion

secondo'genito, **-a** *adj* & *nm* second-
born

secrezi'one *nf* secretion

'**sedano** *nm* celery
■ **sedano rapa** celeriac

se'dare *vt* put down, suppress ⟨*rivolta*⟩; fig
soothe

seda'tivo *adj* & *nm* sedative;
somministrare sedativi a sedate

♂ '**sede** *nf* seat; (centro) centre; Relig see; Comm
head office; **in ∼ di esami** during the exams;
in separata ∼ in private
■ **sede centrale** head office; **sede sociale**
registered office

seden'tario *adj* sedentary

♂ **se'dere** ⒈ *vi* sit
⒉ *nm* (deretano) bottom

se'dersi *vr* sit down

♂ '**sedia** *nf* chair
■ **sedia a dondolo** rocking chair; **sedia
elettrica** electric chair; **sedia da giardino**
garden seat; **sedia girevole** swivel chair;
sedia a rotelle wheelchair; **sedia a sdraio**
deckchair

sedi'cenne *adj* & *nmf* sixteen-year-old

sedi'cente *adj* self-styled

sedi'cesimo, **-a** *adj* & *nm* sixteenth

'**sedici** *adj* & *nm* sixteen

se'dile *nm* seat

sedimen'tare *vi* leave a sediment

sedi'mento *nm* sediment

sedizi'one *nf* sedition

sedizi'oso *adj* seditious

se'dotto pp di SEDURRE

sedu'cente *adj* seductive; (allettante)
enticing

se'durre *vt* seduce

se'duta *nf* session; (di posa) sitting;
∼ stante *adv* here and now

se'duto *adj* sitting

sedut|'**tore**, **-trice** ⒈ *nm* charmer
⒉ *nf* temptress

seduzi'one *nf* seduction

seg. *abbr* (**seguente**) foll

♂ '**sega** *nf* saw; vulg wank; **mezza ∼** vulg
tosser; **non capire una ∼** understand damn
all
■ **sega circolare** circular saw; **sega a mano**
handsaw; **sega a nastro** band saw

'**segale** *nf* rye
■ **pane di segale** rye bread

sega'ligno *adj* wiry

se'gare *vt* saw

sega'trice *nf* saw
■ **segatrice a nastro** band saw

sega'tura *nf* sawdust

'**seggio** *nm* seat
■ **seggio elettorale** polling station

seg'giola *nf* chair

seggio'lino *nm* seat; (da bambino) child seat
■ **seggiolino per auto** car seat; **seggiolino
regolabile** adjustable seat

seggio'lone *nm* (per bambini) high chair

seggio'via *nf* chair lift

seghe'ria *nf* sawmill

se'ghetto *nm* hacksaw

segmen'tare *vt* segment

seg'mento *nm* segment

segna'carte *nm* bookmark

segna'lare *vt* signal; (annunciare)
announce; (indicare) point out

segna'larsi *vr* distinguish oneself

segnalazi'one *nf* signals *pl*; (di candidato)
recommendation
■ **segnalazione stradale** road signs *pl*

se'gnale *nm* signal; (stradale) sign
■ **segnale acustico** beep; **segnale d'allarme**
alarm; (in treno) communication cord Br,
emergency brake; fig warning sign; **segnale
digitale** Comput digital signal; **segnale di
libero** Teleph dialling tone; **segnale orario** time
signal, speaking clock

segna'letica *nf* signals *pl*; '**∼ in
rifacimento**' 'road signs being repainted' ⸱⸱⸱⸹

■ **segnaletica orizzontale** painted road markings *pl*; **segnaletica stradale** road signs *pl*

segna'letico *adj* dati segnaletici description; **foto segnaletica** *photograph used for identification purposes*

segna'libro *nm* bookmark

segna'punti *nm inv* pegboard

⚘ **se'gnare** *vt* mark; (prendere nota) note; (indicare) indicate; Sport score; ∼ **la fine di qualcosa** sound the death knell for something; ∼ **il passo** mark time

se'gnarsi *vr* cross oneself

se'gnato *adj* marked

⚘ **'segno** *nm* sign; (traccia, limite) mark; (bersaglio) target; **far** ∼ (col capo) nod; (con la mano) beckon; **fare** ∼ **di no** (con la testa) shake one's head; **fare** ∼ **di sì** (con la testa) nod [one's head]; **lasciare il** ∼ leave a mark; **non dare segni di vita** give no sign of life; **oltrepassare il** ∼ *fig* overstep the mark
■ **segno della croce** sign of the cross; **segno premonitore** early warning; **segno di sottolineatura** underscore; **segno più** plus sign; **segno zodiacale** sign of the Zodiac, birth sign, star sign

segre'gare *vt* segregate

segre'garsi *vr* cut oneself off

segre'gato *adj* in isolation

segregazi'one *nf* segregation

segregazio'nistico *adj* segregated

segretari'ato *nm* secretariat

segre'tario, -a *nmf* secretary; **fare da** ∼ **a qualcuno** be somebody's secretary; **segretaria tuttofare** girl Friday
■ **segretario bilingue** bilingual secretary; **segretario comunale** town clerk; **segretario di direzione** executive secretary; **segretario personale** personal assistant, PA; **Segretario di Stato** Secretary of State

segrete'ria *nf* (ufficio) administrative office; (segretariato) secretariat
■ **segreteria studenti** Univ admissions office; **segreteria telefonica** answering machine, answerphone

segre'tezza *nf* secrecy

⚘ **se'greto** *adj & nm* secret; **in** ∼ in secret

segu'ace *nmf* follower; **avere molti seguaci** have a large following

segu'ente *adj* following, next

se'gugio *nm* bloodhound

⚘ **segu'ire** *vt/i* follow; (continuare) continue; ∼ **con lo sguardo** follow with one's eyes; ∼ **le orme di qualcuno** follow in somebody's footsteps; ∼ **un corso** take a course

segui'tare *vt/i* continue

⚘ **'seguito** *nm* retinue; (sequela) series; (continuazione) continuation; **di** ∼ in succession; **in** ∼ later on; **in** ∼ **a** following;

(a causa di) owing to; **al** ∼ in his/her wake; **fare** ∼ **a** Comm follow up

⚘ **'sei** *adj & nm* six

sei'cento *adj & nm* six hundred; **il Seicento** the seventeenth century

sei'mila *adj & nm* six thousand

'selce *nf* flint

sel'ciato *nm* paving

se'lenio *nm* selenium

selettività *nf* selectivity

selet'tivo *adj* selective; **memoria selettiva** selective memory

selet'tore *nm* selector

selezio'nare *vt* select; '∼ **il numero**' 'dial [the number]'

selezi'one *nf* selection
■ **selezione naturale** natural selection

self-con'trol *nm* self-control

self-'service *adj & nm inv* self-service

'sella *nf* saddle

sel'lare *vt* saddle

seltz *nm inv* soda water

'selva *nf* forest; *fig* (di errori, capelli) mass; (di ammiratori) horde

selvag'gina *nf* game

sel'vaggio, -a ① *adj* wild; (primitivo) savage
② *nmf* savage

sel'vatico *adj* wild

selvicol'tura *nf* forestry

se'maforo *nm* traffic lights *pl*

se'mantica *nf* semantics *sg*

se'mantico *adj* semantic

sembi'anza *nf* semblance; **sembianze** *pl* (di persona) appearance

⚘ **sem'brare** *vi* seem; (assomigliare) look like; **che te ne sembra?** what do you think?; **mi sembra che …** I think …; **sembra che vada bene** it's fine, seemingly *or* apparently

'seme *nm* seed; (di mela) pip; (di carte) suit; (sperma) semen
■ **seme della discordia** seeds *pl* of discord

se'mente *nf* seed

seme'strale *adj* ‹corso› six-month; ‹pagamento› six-monthly, half-yearly

se'mestre *nm* six months; Univ term, semester Am

semia'perto *adj* half-open

semi'asse *nm* axle

semiauto'matico *adj* semiautomatic

semi'breve *nf* Mus semibreve

semi'cerchio *nm* semicircle

semicirco'lare *adj* semicircular

semicirconfe'renza *nf* semicircle

semicondut'tore *adj & nm* semiconductor

semicon'vitto *nm*
■ **scuola a semiconvitto** *school for dayboarders*

⚘ indicates a very frequent word

semicosci'ente *adj* semi-conscious; half-conscious

semi'croma *nf* Mus semiquaver

semifi'nale *nf* semifinal

semifina'lista *nmf* semifinalist

semi'freddo *nm* cold dessert resembling ice cream

semilavo'rato 1 *adj* semi-finished 2 *nm* semilavorati *pl* semi-finished goods

semi'minima *nf* Mus crotchet

'semina *nf* sowing

semi'nare *vt* sow; fam shake off ‹inseguitori›; ~ **zizzania** cause trouble

semi'nario *nm* seminar; Relig seminary

semina'rista *nm* seminarist

seminfermità *nf* partial disability
■ **seminfermità mentale** diminished responsibility

scminter'rato *nm* basement

semi'nudo *adj* half-naked

semioscurità *nf* semi-darkness

semiprezi'oso *adj* semiprecious

semi'secco *adj* medium-dry

scmi'serio *adj* semi-serious

se'mitico *adj* Semitic

semi'tono *nm* Mus semitone

sem'mai 1 *conj* in case 2 *adv* è lui, ~, che ... if anyone, it's him who...

'semola *nf* bran

semo'lato *adj* ‹zucchero› caster *attrib*

semo'lino *nm* semolina

'semplice *adj* simple; **in parole semplici** in plain words

semplice'mente *adv* simply

semplici'otto, -a *nmf* simpleton

sempli'cistico *adj* simplistic

semplicità *nf* simplicity

semplifi'care *vt* simplify

'sempre *adv* always; (ancora) still; **di ~** ever; **per ~** for ever; ~ **più** more and more; **pur ~** still, nevertheless

sempre'verde *adj & nm* evergreen

'senape *nf* mustard

se'nato *nm* senate

sena|'tore, -trice *nmf* senator

'Senegal *nm* Senegal

se'nile *adj* senile

senilità *nf* senility

'senior 1 *adj* senior 2 *nmf* (*pl* **seniores**); Sport senior

'senno *nm* sense; **giudicare col ~ del poi** use hindsight

sennò *adv* otherwise, or else

sennonché *conj* but, except that; (fuorché) but, except

'seno *nm* (petto) breast; Math sine; **in ~ a** in the bosom of

sen'sale *nm* broker

sen'sato *adj* sensible

sensazio'nale *adj* sensational

sensaziona'listico *adj* sensationalist

sensazi'one *nf* sensation; **fare ~** ‹notizia, scoperta› cause a sensation

sen'sibile *adj* sensitive; (percepibile) perceptible; (notevole) considerable; **mondo ~** tangible world

sensibilità *nf* sensitivity

sensibiliz'zare *vt* make more aware (a

sensibil'mente *adv* appreciably

sensi'tivo 1 *adj* sensory 2 *nmf* sensitive person; (medium) medium

'senso *nm* sense; (significato) meaning; (direzione) direction; **far ~ a qualcuno** make somebody shudder; **in ~ orario/antiorario** clockwise/anticlockwise; **ai sensi della legge** in accordance with the law; **non ha ~** it doesn't make sense; **avere il ~ degli affari** have good business sense; **di buon ~** ‹persona› sensible; **senza ~** meaningless; **in un certo ~ ...** in a sense *o* way ...; **perdere i sensi** lose consciousness; **a ~** ‹ripetere, tradurre› in general terms; **in ~ opposto** in the opposite direction; **a ~ unico** ‹strada› one-way; **a doppio ~ [di marcia]** ‹strada› two-way; **a doppio ~** ‹parola, espressione› with a double meaning
■ **senso dell'umorismo** sense of humour; **'senso vietato'** 'no entry'

sen'sore *nm* sensor

sensu'ale *adj* sensual

sensualità *nf* sensuality

sen'tenza *nf* sentence; (massima) saving; **pronunciare una ~** hand down a sentence; **pronunciare la ~** pronounce sentence

sentenzi'are *vi* pass judgment

senti'ero *nm* path
■ **sentiero luminoso di avvicinamento** Aeron approach lights

sentimen'tale *adj* sentimental

sentimenta'lista *nmf* sentimentalist

sentimental'mente *adv* sentimentally

senti'mento *nm* feeling; **essere fuori di ~** be out of one's mind

sen'tina *nf* Naut bilge

senti'nella *nf* sentry; **essere di ~** be on guard

sen'tire 1 *vt* feel; (udire) hear; (ascoltare) listen to; (gustare) taste; (odorare) smell 2 *vi* feel; (udire) hear; ~ **caldo/freddo** feel hot/cold

sen'tirsi *vr* feel; ~ **di fare qualcosa** feel like doing something; ~ **bene/male** feel well/ill; **sentirsela di fare qualcosa** feel up to doing something

sen'tito *adj* (sincero) sincere; **per ~ dire** by hearsay

sen'tore *nm* inkling

S

⚡ **'senza** *prep* without; ~ **ombrello** without an umbrella; ~ **correre** without running; **senz'altro** certainly; ~ **un soldo** penniless; '~ **conservanti**' 'no preservatives'; **fare** ~ do without

senza'tetto *nm inv* i ~ the homeless

'sepalo *nm* sepal

⚡ **sepa'rare** *vt* separate

sepa'rarsi *vr* separate; ‹*prendere commiato*› part; ~ **da** be separated from

separata'mente *adv* separately

separa'tista *nmf* separatist

sepa'rato *adj* separate

separazi'one *nf* separation

■ **separazione consensuale** separation by mutual consent; **separazione legale** legal separation

sepol'crale *adj* (liter) sepulchral

se'polcro *nm* sepulchre

se'polto ① *pp di* SEPPELLIRE ② *adj* buried; **morto e** ~ fig dead and buried

sepol'tura *nf* burial; **dare** ~ **a qualcuno** bury somebody

⚡ **seppel'lire** *vt* bury

seppel'lirsi *vr* fig cut oneself off

'seppia ① *nf* cuttle fish ② *adj inv* sepia

sep'pure *conj* even if

se'quela *nf* series, succession; (di insulti) string

se'quenza *nf* sequence

sequenzi'ale *adj* sequential

seque'strare *vt* (rapire) kidnap; (confiscare) confiscate; Jur impound

sequestra|'tore, -trice *nmf* kidnapper

se'questro *nm* Jur impounding; (di persona) kidnap[ping]

se'quoia *nf* sequoia

⚡ **'sera** *nf* evening, night; **di** ~, **la** ~ in the evening; **da** ~ ‹*abito*› evening *attrib*; **alle 8 di** ~ at 8 o'clock in the evening, at 8 o'clock at night; **buona** ~! good evening!; **dalla mattina alla** ~ from morning to night; **ieri** ~ yesterday evening, last night; **questa** ~ this evening, tonight

se'rale *adj* evening *attrib*

seral'mente *adv* every evening, every night

se'rata *nf* evening; (ricevimento) party

■ **serata danzante** dance; **serata di gala** gala night

ser'bare *vt* keep; harbour ‹*odio*›; cherish ‹*speranza*›

serba'toio *nm* tank

■ **serbatoio d'acqua** water tank; **serbatoio della benzina** petrol tank, gas tank Am

'Serbia *nf* Serbia

'serbo¹, -a ① *adj & nmf* Serbian ② *nm* (lingua) Serbian

'serbo² *nm* **mettere in** ~ put aside

serbo-cro'ato *nmf* Serbo-Croat[ian]

sere'nata *nf* serenade

serenità *nf* serenity

⚡ **se'reno** *adj* serene; ‹*cielo*› clear; **un fulmine a ciel** ~ fam bolt from the blue

ser'gente *nm* sergeant

'serial *nm inv*

■ **serial [televisivo]** television serial

seri'ale *adj* serial

seria'mente *adv* seriously

'serico *adj* silk

⚡ **'serie** *nf inv* series; (complesso) set; Sport division; **fuori** ~ custom-built; **produzione in** ~ mass production

■ **serie A** (di calcio) Premier League; **serie B** (di calcio) First Division; **di** ~ **B** fig second-rate; **serie numerica** numerical series

serietà *nf* seriousness

⚡ **'serio** *adj* serious; (degno di fiducia) reliable; **sul** ~ seriously; (davvero) really

ser'mone *nm* sermon

seroto'nina *nf* serotonin

'serpe *nf* (liter) viper

serpeggi'ante *adj* ‹*strada*› twisting, winding

serpeggi'are *vi* ‹*strada*› twist, wind; fig (diffondersi) spread

ser'pente *nm* snake

■ **serpente a sonagli** rattlesnake; **serpente velenoso** poisonous snake

serpen'tina *nf* **a** ~ twisting and turning, winding; **fare una** ~ weave

'serra *nf* greenhouse

■ **effetto serra** greenhouse effect

ser'raglio *nm* harem

ser'randa *nf* shutter

ser'rare *vt* shut; (stringere) tighten; (incalzare) press on

ser'rata *nf* lockout

serra'tura *nf* lock

'server *nm inv* server

■ **server di posta** mail server; **server web** web server

ser'vibile *adj* usable

ser'vile *adj* servile

servi'lismo *nm* servility

⚡ **ser'vire** ① *vt* serve; (al ristorante) wait on ② *vi* serve; (essere utile) be of use; **non serve** it's no good; '~ **freddo**' 'serve chilled'

ser'virsi *vr* (di cibo) help oneself; ~ **da** buy from; ~ **di** use

servi|'tore, -trice *nmf* retainer

servitù *nf* servitude; (personale di servizio) servants *pl*

servizi'evole *adj* obliging

S

⚡ indicates a very frequent word

ser'vizio *nm* service; (da caffè ecc) set; (di cronaca, sportivo) report; (in tennis) serve; **servizi** *pl* bathroom; **essere di** ~ be on duty; **fare** ~ ‹*autobus ecc*› run; **fuori servizio** ‹*bus*› not in service; ‹*ascensore*› out of order; **servizi** *pl* (terziario) services; **servizi** *pl* **bancari a domicilio** home banking; **servizi** *pl* **bancari via telefono** telephone banking; **servizi** *pl* **igienici** toilet block; **servizi** *pl* **di pronto intervento** emergency services; **servizi** *pl* **pubblici** (bagni) public toilets; **servizi** *pl* **sociali** welfare services

■ **donna di servizio** maid; **servizio bus navetta** courtesy bus; **servizio compreso** service charge included; **servizio escluso** not including service charge; **area di servizio** service station; **servizio in camera** room service; **servizio civile** *civilian duties done instead of national service*; **servizio filmato** film report; **servizio di linea** passenger service; **servizio militare** military service; **servizio pubblico** utility company; **servizio al tavolo** waiter service; **servizio da tavola** dinnerware; **servizio traghetto** passenger ferry

'servo, -a *nmf* servant

servo'freno *nm* servo brake

servo'sterzo *nm* power steering

'sesamo *nm* sesame

ses'santa *adj & nm* sixty

sessan'tenne *adj & nmf* sixty-year-old

sessan'tesimo *adj & nm* sixtieth

sessan'tina *nf* **una** ~ **di** about sixty

Sessan'totto *nm* *protest movement of 1968*

sessi'one *nf* session

ses'sista *adj* sexist

'sesso *nm* sex; **fare** ~ si have sex

■ **sesso forte** stronger sex; **gentil sesso** fair sex; **sesso sicuro** safe sex

sessu'ale *adj* sexual

sessualità *nf* sexuality

'sesto¹ *adj & nm* sixth

sesto² *nm* **rimettere in** ~ put back on its feet ‹*azienda*›; restore ‹*vestito*›; recondition ‹*motore, auto*›

set *nm inv* set

'seta *nf* silk; **di** ~ silk *attrib*

setacci'are *vt* sieve

se'taccio *nm* sieve; **passare qualcosa al** ~ fig go through something with a fine-tooth comb

'sete *nf* thirst; **avere** ~ be thirsty

■ **sete di sangue** blood lust

'setola *nf* bristle

'setta *nf* sect

set'tanta *adj & nm* seventy

settan'tenne *adj & nmf* seventy-year-old

settan'tesimo *adj & nm* seventieth

settan'tina *nf* **una** ~ **di** about seventy

set'tario *adj* sectarian

'sette *adj & nm* seven

sette'cento *adj & nm* seven hundred; **il Settecento** the eighteenth century

set'tembre *nm* September

settentrio'nale **1** *adj* northern **2** *nmf* northerner

settentri'one *nm* north

'setter *nm inv* setter

'settico *adj* septic

setti'mana *nf* week; **alla** ~ per week; **a metà** ~ midweek, half-way through the week

■ **settimana corta** five-day week; **settimana lavorativa** working week

settima'nale *adj & nm* weekly

setti'mino, -a **1** *adj* born two months premature **2** *nmf* baby born two months premature

'settimo *adj & nm* seventh

set'tore *nm* sector

settori'ale *adj* sector-based

severità *nf* severity

se'vero *adj* severe; (rigoroso) strict

se'vizia *nf* torture; **sevizie** *pl* torture *sg*

sevizi'are *vt* torture

Sey'chelles *nfpl* Seychelles

sezio'nare *vt* divide; Med dissect

sezi'one *nf* section; (reparto) department; Med dissection

sfaccen'dare *vi* bustle about

sfaccen'dato *adj* idle

sfacet'tare *vt* cut

sfacet'tato *adj* cut; fig many-sided, multifaceted

sfacetta'tura *nf* cutting; fig facet

sfacchi'nare *vi* toil

sfacchi'nata *nf* drudgery

sfaccia'taggine *nf* cheek

sfacciata'mente *adv* cheekily

sfacci'ato *adj* cheeky, fresh Am

sfa'celo *nm* ruin; **in** ~ in ruins

sfagio'lare *vi* fam **non mi sfagiola** it's/ he's/she's not my cup of tea

sfal'darsi *vr* flake off

sfal'sare *vt* stagger; ~ **il tiro** shoot wide

sfa'mare *vt* feed

sfa'marsi *vt* satisfy one's hunger, eat one's fill

sfarfal'lio *nm* (di schermo, luce) flicker

'sfarzo *nm* pomp

sfar'zoso *adj* sumptuous

sfa'sato *adj* fam confused; ‹*motore*› which needs tuning; **sentirsi** ~ fam be out of sync[h]

sfasci'are *vt* unbandage; (fracassare) smash

sfasci'arsi *vr* fall to pieces

sfasci'ato *adj* beat-up

'**sfascio** *nm* ruin; **andare allo** ∼ go to rack and ruin
sfa'tare *vt* explode
sfati'cato *adj* lazy
'**sfatto** *adj* unmade
sfavil'lante *adj* sparkling
sfavil'lare *vi* sparkle
sfavo'revole *adj* unfavourable
sfavo'rire *vt* disadvantage, put at a disadvantage
sfeb'brare *vi* **comincia a** ∼ his temperature is starting to come down
'**sfera** *nf* sphere
■ **sfera affettiva** area of feelings and emotions; **sfera celeste** celestial sphere; **sfera di cristallo** crystal ball; **sfera di influenza** sphere of influence
'**sferico** *adj* spherical
sfer'rare *vt* unshoe ‹*cavallo*›; give ‹*calcio, pugno*›
sferruz'zare *vi* knit
sfer'zare *vt* whip
sfer'zata *nf* whip; fig telling-off
sfian'cante *adj* wearing
sfian'care *vt* wear out
sfian'carsi *vr* wear oneself out
sfiata'toio *nm* blowhole
sfi'brare *vt* exhaust
sfi'brato *adj* exhausted
'**sfida** *nf* challenge
sfi'dare *vt* challenge
sfi'ducia *nf* mistrust
sfiduci'ato *adj* discouraged
'**sfiga** *nf* sl bloody bad luck; **avere** ∼ be bloody unlucky
sfi'gato, -a sl ① *adj* bloody unlucky
  ② *nmf* unlucky beggar
sfigu'rare ① *vt* disfigure
  ② *vi* (far cattiva figura) look out of place
sfilacci'are *vt* fray
sfilacci'arsi *vr* fray
sfi'lare ① *vt* unthread; (togliere di dosso) take off
  ② *vi* ‹*truppe*› march past; (in parata) parade
sfi'larsi *vr* come unthreaded; ‹*collant*› ladder; take off ‹*pantaloni*›
sfi'lata *nf* parade; (sfilza) series
■ **sfilata di moda** fashion show
sfila'tino *nm* long, thin loaf
'**sfilza** *nf* string
'**sfinge** *nf* sphinx
sfi'nire *vt* wear out
sfi'nito *adj* worn out
sfio'rare *vt* skim; touch on ‹*argomento*›
sfio'rire *vi* wither; ‹*bellezza*› fade
sfis'sare *vt* cancel
'**sfitto** *adj* vacant

───────────────────
⚡ indicates a very frequent word

'**sfizio** *nm* whim, fancy; **togliersi uno** ∼ satisfy a whim
sfizi'oso *adj* nifty
sfo'cato *adj* out of focus
sfoci'are *vi* ∼ **in** flow into
sfode'rare *vt* draw ‹*pistola, spada*›; fig show off ‹*cultura*›; ∼ **un sorriso** smile insincerely
sfode'rato *adj* ‹*giacca*› unlined
sfo'gare *vt* vent
sfo'garsi *vr* give vent to one's feelings
sfoggi'are *vt/i* show off
'**sfoggio** *nm* show, display; **fare** ∼ **di** show off
'**sfoglia** *nf* sheet of pastry
■ **pasta sfoglia** puff pastry
sfogli'are *vt* leaf through
sfogli'ata¹ *nf* flaky pastry with filling
sfogli'ata² *nf* **dare una** ∼ **a** ‹*libro, giornale*› flick through
'**sfogo** *nm* outlet; fig outburst; Med rash; **dare** ∼ **a** give vent to
sfolgo'rante *adj* blazing
sfolgo'rare *vi* blaze
sfolla'gente *nm* truncheon, billy Am
sfol'lare ① *vt* clear
  ② *vi* Mil be evacuated
sfol'lato, -a *nmf* evacuee
sfol'tire *vt* thin [out]; **farsi** ∼ **i capelli** have one's hair thinned
sfon'dare ① *vt* break down
  ② *vi* (aver successo) make a name for oneself
'**sfondo** *nm* background; **un'aggressione a** ∼ **politico/razziale** a politically/racially motivated attack
sfon'done *nm* fam blunder
sfor'mare *vt* pull out of shape ‹*tasche*›
sfor'marsi *vi* lose its shape; ‹*persona*› lose one's figure
sfor'mato *nm* Culin flan
sfor'nito *adj* ∼ **di** ‹*negozio*› out of
sfor'tuna *nf* bad luck
sfortunata'mente *adv* unfortunately, unluckily
sfortu'nato *adj* unlucky
sfor'zare *vt* force
sfor'zarsi *vr* try hard
sfor'zato *adj* forced
⚡ '**sforzo** *nm* effort; (tensione) stress
'**sfottere** *vt* sl tease
sfracel'larsi *vr* smash; ∼ **al suolo** crash to the ground
sfrangi'ato *adj* fringed
sfrat'tare *vt* evict
'**sfratto** *nm* eviction
sfrecci'are *vi* flash past
sfrega'mento *nm* crackling
sfre'gare *vt* rub

sfregi'are *vt* slash

sfregi'ato, -a [1] *adj* scarred [2] *nmf* scarface

'sfregio *nm* slash

sfre'narsi *vr* run wild

sfre'nato *adj* wild

sfrigo'lio *nm* crackling

sfron'dare *vt* prune

sfron'tato *adj* shameless, brazen

sfrutta'mento *nm* exploitation

⚘ **sfrut'tare** *vt* exploit; take advantage of, make the most of ‹*occasione*›

sfug'gente *adj* elusive; ‹*mento*› receding

⚘ **sfug'gire** [1] *vi* escape; ~ **a** escape [from]; **mi sfugge** it escapes me; **mi è sfuggito [di mente]** it [completely] slipped my mind; **mi è sfuggito di mano** I lost hold of it; **lasciarsi ~ un'occasione** let an opportunity slip; **mi è sfuggito un rutto** I just came out with a belch; **gli è sfuggito un colpo dal fucile** the rifle just went off in his hands [2] *vt* avoid

sfug'gita *nf* **di ~** in passing

sfu'mare [1] *vi* (svanire) vanish; ‹*colore*› shade off [2] *vt* soften ‹*colore*›

sfuma'tura *nf* shade

sfuri'ata *nf* outburst [of anger]

sga'bello *nm* stool

sgabuz'zino *nm* cupboard

sgam'bato *adj* ‹*costume da bagno*› high cut

sgambet'tare *vi* kick one's legs; (camminare) trot

sgam'betto *nm* **fare lo ~ a qualcuno** trip somebody up

sganasci'arsi *vr* ~ **dalle risa** roar with laughter

sganci'are *vt* unhook; Rail uncouple; drop ‹*bombe*›; fam cough up ‹*denaro*›

sganci'arsi *vr* become unhooked; fig get away

sganghe'rato *adj* ramshackle

sgar'bato *adj* rude

'sgarbo *nm* discourtesy; **fare uno ~ a qualcuno** be rude to somebody; **ricevere uno ~** be treated rudely

sgargi'ante *adj* garish

sgar'rare *vi* be wrong; (da regola) stray from the straight and narrow

'sgarro *nm* mistake, slip

sga'sato *adj* flat

sgattaio'lare *vi* sneak away; ~ **via** decamp

sge'lare *vt/i* thaw

'sghembo *adj* slanting; **a ~** obliquely

sghiacci'are *vt* defrost; thaw out ‹*carne*›

sghignaz'zare *vi* laugh scornfully

sghiri'bizzo *nm* whim, fancy

sgob'bare *vi* slog; ‹*fam: studente*› swot

sgob'bone, -a *nmf* slogger; fam (studente) swot

sgoccio'lare *vi* drip

'sgocciolo *nm* dripping

sgo'larsi *vr* shout oneself hoarse

sgombe[r]'rare *vt* clear [out]

'sgombro [1] *adj* clear [2] *nm* (trasloco) removal; (pesce) mackerel

sgomen'tare *vt* dismay

sgomen'tarsi *vr* be dismayed

sgo'mento *nm* dismay

sgomi'nare *vt* defeat

sgom'mare *vi* make the tyres screech

sgom'mata *nf* screech of tyres

sgonfi'are *vt* deflate

sgonfi'arsi *vr* go down

'sgonfio *adj* flat

'sgorbio *nm* scrawl; fig (vista sgradevole) sight

sgor'gare [1] *vi* gush [out] [2] *vt* flush out, unblock ‹*lavandino*›

sgoz'zare *vt* ~ **qualcuno** cut somebody's throat

sgra'devole *adj* disagreeable

sgra'dito *adj* unwelcome

sgraffi'are *vt* scratch

'sgraffio *nm* scratch

sgrammaticata'mente *adv* ungrammatically

sgrammati'cato *adj* ungrammatical

sgra'nare *vt* shell ‹*piselli*›; open wide ‹*occhi*›

sgra'nato *adj* grainy; ‹*fagioli*› shelled; ‹*occhi*› wide-open

sgran'chire *vt* stretch

sgran'chirsi *vr* stretch

sgranocchi'are *vt* munch

sgras'sare *vt* remove the grease from

'sgravio *nm* relief
∎ **sgravio fiscale** tax relief

sgrazi'ato *adj* ungainly

sgreto'lare *vt* crumble

sgreto'larsi *vr* crumble

sgri'dare *vt* scold

sgri'data *nf* scolding

sgron'dare *vt* drain

sgros'sare *vt* rough-hew ‹*marmo*›; fig polish

sguai'ato *adj* coarse

sgual'cire *vt* crumple

sgual'drina *nf* slut

⚘ **sgu'ardo** *nm* look; (breve) glance; **dare uno ~ a** a glance at ‹*giornale, testo*›
∎ **sguardo di insieme** overview

sguar'nito *adj* unadorned; (privo di difesa) undefended

'sguattero, -a *nmf* skivvy

sguaz'zare *vi* splash; (nel tango) wallow

S

'sguincio nm sidelong glance
sguinzagli'are vt unleash
sgusci'are [1] vt shell
[2] vi (sfuggire) slip away; ~ **fuori** slip out
'shaker nm inv shaker
shake'rare vt shake
'shampoo nm inv shampoo; ~ **e messa in piega** shampoo and set
'shopper nm inv carrier bag
'shuttle nm inv [space] shuttle
⚬ **si¹** pers pron (riflessivo) oneself; (lui) himself; (lei) herself; (esso, essa) itself; (loro) themselves; (reciproco) each other; (tra più di due) one another; (impersonale) you, one fml; lavarsi wash [oneself]; **si è lavata** she washed [herself]; **lavarsi le mani** wash one's hands; **si è lavata le mani** she washed her hands; **si è mangiato un pollo intero** he ate an entire chicken by himself; **incontrarsi** meet each other; **la gente si aiuta a vicenda** people help one another; **si potrebbe pensare che ...** you might think that ..., one might think that ... fml; **non si sa mai** you never know, one never knows; **queste cose si dimenticano facilmente** these things are easily forgotten
si² nm Mus (chiave, nota) B
⚬ **sì** adv yes; **credo di sì** I believe so; **penso di sì** I think so; **ha detto di sì** she said yes; **sì?** really?; **sì che mi piace!** yes I do like it!
sia¹ ▶ ESSERE
⚬ **sia²** conj ~... ~... (entrambi) both...and...; (o l'uno o l'altro) either...or...; ~ **che venga**, ~ **che non venga** whether he comes or not; **scegli** ~ **questo** o ~ **quello** choose either this one or that one; **voglio** ~ **questo che quello** I want both this one and that one; **verranno** ~ **Giuseppe** ~ **Giacomo** both Giuseppe and Giacomo are coming
sia'mese adj Siamese
Si'beria nf Siberia
sibi'lare vi hiss
sibil'lino adj sibylline
'sibilo nm hiss
si'cario nm hired killer
sicché conj (perciò) so [that]; (allora) then
siccità nf drought
⚬ **sic'come** conj as
Si'cilia nf Sicily
sicili'ano, -a adj & nmf Sicilian
sico'moro nm sycamore
si'cura nf safety catch; (di portiera) childproof lock
sicura'mente adv definitely; ~ **sarà arrivato** he must have arrived by now
⚬ **sicu'rezza** nf (certezza) certainty; (salvezza) safety; (personale di sorveglianza e protezione) security, security guards; **chiamare la** ~ call security; **di** ~ ‹dispositivo› safety attrib; **di**

massima ~ top security
■ **uscita di sicurezza** emergency exit
⚬ **si'curo** [1] adj (non pericoloso) safe; (certo) sure; ‹saldo› steady; Comm sound
[2] adv certainly
[3] nm safety; **al** ~ safe; **andare sul** ~ play [it] safe; **di** ~ definitely; **di** ~ **sarà arrivato** he must have arrived; ~**!** sure!
'sidecar nm inv sidecar
siderur'gia nf iron and steel industry
side'rurgico adj iron and steel attrib
'sidro nm cider
si'epe nf hedge
si'ero nm serum
sieronega'tivo, -a [1] adj HIV negative
[2] nmf person who is HIV negative
sieroposi'tivo, -a [1] adj HIV positive
[2] nmf person who is HIV positive
Si'erra Le'one nf Sierra Leone
si'esta nf afternoon nap, siesta; **fare la** ~ have an afternoon nap
si'fone nm siphon
Sig. abbr (**signore**) Mr
Sig.a abbr (**signora**) Mrs, Ms
⚬ **siga'retta** nf cigarette; **pantaloni** pl a ~ drainpipes
'sigaro nm cigar
Sigg. abbr (**signori**) Messrs
sigil'lare vt seal
si'gillo nm seal
'sigla nf initials pl
■ **sigla musicale** signature tune
si'glare vt initial
Sig.na abbr (**signorina**) Miss, Ms
⚬ **signifi'care** vt mean
significa'tivo adj significant
signifi'cato nm meaning
⚬ **si'gnora** nf lady; (davanti a nome proprio) Mrs; (non sposata) Miss; (in lettere ufficiali) Dear Madam; **la** ~ **Rossi** Mrs Rossi; **il signor Vené e** ~ Mr and Mrs Vené
⚬ **si'gnore** nm gentleman; Relig lord; (davanti a nome proprio) Mr; **il signor Rossi** Mr Rossi
signo'rile adj gentlemanly; (di lusso) luxury
signo'rina nf young lady; (seguito da nome proprio) Miss; **la** ~ **Rossi** Miss Rossi
silenzia'tore nm silencer
⚬ **si'lenzio** nm silence
■ **silenzio di tomba** deathly hush
silenzi'oso adj silent
'silfide nf sylph
silhou'ette nf inv silhouette, outline; **che** ~**!** you're so slim!
si'licio nm
■ **piastrina di silicio** silicon chip
sili'cone nm silicone
'sillaba nf syllable
silla'bario nm primer

⚬ indicates a very frequent word

sillaba'tore *nm* Comput hyphenation program

sillo'gismo *nm* syllogism

silu'rare *vt* torpedo

si'luro *nm* torpedo

simbi'osi *nf* symbiosis; **vivere in ~** need each other, have a symbiotic relationship

simboleggi'are *vt* symbolize

sim'bolico *adj* symbolic[al]

simbo'lismo *nm* symbolism

simbo'lista *nmf* symbolist

'simbolo *nm* symbol

similarità *nf inv* similarity

'simile ⟦1⟧ *adj* similar; (tale) such; **è ~ a...** it's like..., it's similar to...; **qualcosa di ~** something similar
⟦2⟧ *nm* (il prossimo) fellow human being, fellow man

simili'tudine *nf* Gram simile

simil'mente *adv* similarly

simil'pelle *nf* Leatherette®

simme'tria *nf* symmetry

sim'metrico *adj* symmetric[al]

simpa'tia *nf* liking; (compenetrazione) sympathy; **prendere qualcuno in ~** take a liking to somebody; **provare ~ per** like

sim'patico *adj* nice
■ **inchiostro simpatico** invisible ink

simpatiz'zante *nmf* well-wisher

simpatiz'zare *vt* **~ con** take a liking to; **~ per qualcosa/qualcuno** lean towards something/somebody

sim'posio *nm* symposium

simu'lare *vt* simulate; feign ⟨amicizia, interesse⟩

simula'tore *nm* simulator

simulazi'one *nf* simulation
■ **simulazione di reato** Jur *making of false accusations*

simul'tanea *nf* **in ~** simultaneously

simul'taneo *adj* simultaneous

sina'goga *nf* synagogue

sincera'mente *adv* sincerely; (a dire il vero) honestly

since'rarsi *vr* make sure

sincerità *nf* sincerity

sin'cero *adj* sincere

'sincope *nf* syncopation; Med fainting fit

sincron'ia *nf* sync[h]

sincro'nismo *nm* synchronism

sincroniz'zare *vt* synchronize

sincroniz'zato *adj* synchronized; **essere ben ~ con** be in sync[h] with

sincronizzazi'one *nf* synchronization

'sincrono *adj* synchronous

sinda'cabile *adj* arguable

sinda'cale *adj* [trade] union *attrib*, [labor] union Am

sindaca'lista *nmf* trade unionist, labor union member Am

sinda'care *vt* inspect

sinda'cato *nm* [trade] union, [labor] union Am; (associazione) syndicate
■ **sindacato di categoria** trade union

'sindaco *nm* mayor

'sindrome *nf* syndrome
■ **sindrome da colon irritabile** irritable bowel syndrome; **sindrome di Down** Down's syndrome; **sindrome da edifici malsani** sick building syndrome; **sindrome premestruale** premenstrual syndrome, PMS; **sindrome respiratoria acuta severa** severe acute respiratory syndrome, SARS

sinfo'nia *nf* symphony

sin'fonico *adj* symphonic

Singa'pore *nf* Singapore

singhioz'zare *vt* (di pianto) sob

singhi'ozzo *nm* hiccup; (di pianto) sob; **avere il ~** have the hiccups

'single *nmf inv* single

singo'lare ⟦1⟧ *adj* singular; (strano) peculiar
⟦2⟧ *nm* Gram singular

singolar'mente *adv* individually; (stranamente) peculiarly

'singolo ⟦1⟧ *adj* single
⟦2⟧ *nm* individual; Mus single; Tennis singles *pl*; **un ~ di successo** a hit single

si'nistra *nf* left; **a ~** on the left; **girare a ~** turn to the left, **la seconda a ~** the second on the left; **con la guida a ~** ⟨auto⟩ with left-hand drive; **la ~** Pol the left; **di ~** Pol left wing

sini'strare *vt* injure; damage ⟨cosa⟩

sini'strato *adj* injured; ⟨casa⟩ damaged

si'nistro ⟦1⟧ *adj* left[-hand]; (avverso) sinister
⟦2⟧ *nm* accident

sini'strorso, -a *nmf* pej leftie

'sino *prep* = FINO¹

si'nonimo ⟦1⟧ *adj* synonymous
⟦2⟧ *nm* synonym

sin'tassi *nf* syntax

sin'tattico *adj* syntactic[al]

'sintesi *nf* synthesis; (riassunto) summary

sin'tetico *adj* synthetic; (conciso) summary

sintetiz'zare *vt* summarize

sintetizza'tore *nm* synthesizer

sinto'matico *adj* symptomatic

'sintomo *nm* symptom

sinto'nia *nf* tuning; **in ~** on the same wavelength; **in ~ con** in harmony with, in tune with

sintonizza'tore *nm* tuner

sinu'oso *adj* ⟨strada⟩ winding

sinu'site *nf* sinusitis

sio'nismo *nm* Zionism

sio'nista *adj & nmf* Zionist

si'pario *nm* curtain

si'rena *nf* siren; (di nave) hooter

'Siria *nf* Syria

siri'ano, -a *adj & nmf* Syrian

si'ringa *nf* syringe

'sismico *adj* seismic

si'smografo *nm* seismograph

sismolo'gia *nf* seismology

✧ **si'stema** *nm* system; **non è ~!** that's no way to behave!
  ▪ **sistema di amplificazione sonora** induction loop; **sistema di gestione banca dati** database management system, DBMS; **sistema immunitario** immune system; **Sistema Monetario Europeo** European Monetary System; **sistema nervoso** nervous system; **sistema operativo** Comput operating system; **sistema solare** solar system; **sistema di vita** way of life

✧ **siste'mare** *vt* (mettere) put; tidy up ‹casa, camera›; (risolvere) sort out; (procurare lavoro a) fix up with a job; (trovare alloggio a) find accommodation for; (sposare) marry off; fam (punire) sort out

siste'marsi *vr* settle down; (trovare un lavoro) find a job; (trovare alloggio) find accommodation; (sposarsi) marry

sistematica'mente *adv* systematically

siste'matico *adj* systematic

sistemazi'one *nf* arrangement; (di questione) settlement; ‹lavoro› job; (alloggio) accommodation; (matrimonio) marriage

siste'mista *nmf* Comput systems engineer

'sistole *nf* systole

'sit-in *nm inv* sit-in

'sito *nm* site
  ▪ **sito web** Comput web site

situ'are *vt* place

✧ **situazi'one** *nf* situation; **essere all'altezza della ~** be equal to the situation, be up to the situation

'skai *nm* Leatherette®

'skateboard *nm inv* skateboard

sketch *nm inv* sketch

ski-'lift *nm* ski tow

'skipper *nmf inv* skipper

slab'brare *vt* stretch out of shape ‹maglia, tasca›

slab'brato *adj* ‹maglia, tasca› shapeless

slacci'are *vt* unfasten; unlace ‹scarpe›

'slalom *nm inv* slalom; **a ~** slalom *attrib*

slanci'arsi *vr* hurl oneself

slanci'ato *adj* slender

'slancio *nm* impetus; (impulso) impulse; **agire di ~** act on impulse

sla'vato *adj* ‹carnagione, capelli› fair

'slavo *adj* Slav[onic]

sle'ale *adj* disloyal; **concorrenza sleale** unfair competition

slealtà *nf* disloyalty

sle'gare *vt* untie

sle'garsi *vr* untie oneself

slip *nmpl* underpants

'slitta *nf* sledge; (trainata) sleigh

slitta'mento *nm* (di macchina) skid; fig (di riunione) postponement

slit'tare *vi* Auto skid; ‹riunione› be put off

slit'tata *nf* skid

slit'tino *nm* toboggan

'slogan *nm inv* slogan, rallying cry

slo'gare *vt* dislocate

slo'garsi *vr* ~ **una caviglia** sprain one's ankle

slo'gato *adj* sprained

sloga'tura *nf* sprain

sloggi'are ① *vt* dislodge ② *vi* move out

slot *nm*
  ▪ **slot di espansione** Comput expansion slot

slot-ma'chine *nf inv* slot-machine, one-armed bandit

Slo'vacchia *nf* Slovakia

slo'vacco, -a *adj & nmf* Slovak

Slo'venia *nf* Slovenia

smacchi'are *vt* clean

smacchia'tore *nm* stain remover

'smacco *nm* humiliating defeat

smagli'ante *adj* dazzling

smagli'arsi *vr* ‹calza› ladder (*Br*), run

smaglia'tura *nf* ladder (*Br*), run

smagnetiz'zare *vt* demagnetize

smagnetiz'zatore *nm* demagnetizer

sma'grito *adj* thinner

smalizi'ato *adj* cunning

smal'tare *vt* enamel; glaze ‹ceramica›; varnish ‹unghie›

smal'tato *adj* enamelled; ‹ceramica› glazed; ‹unghie› varnished

smalta'tura *nf* enamelling; (di ceramica) glazing

smalti'mento *nm* disposal; (di merce) selling off; (di grassi) burning off
  ▪ **smaltimento [dei] rifiuti** waste disposal

smal'tire *vt* burn off; (merce) sell off; fig get through ‹corrispondenza›; ~ **la sbornia** sober up

'smalto *nm* enamel; (di ceramica) glaze; (per le unghie) nail varnish, nail polish

smance'ria *nf* **fare smancerie** be overpolite

smance'roso *adj* simpering

s

'smania *nf* fidgets *pl*; (desiderio) longing; avere la ∼ **di** have a craving for

smani'are *vi* have the fidgets; ∼ **per** long for

smani'oso *adj* restless

smantella'mento *nm* dismantling

smantel'lare *vt* dismantle

smarri'mento *nm* loss; (psicologico) bewilderment

smar'rire *vt* lose; (temporaneamente) mislay

smar'rirsi *vr* get lost; (turbarsi) be bewildered

smar'rito *adj* lost; ‹sguardo› bewildered, lost

smasche'rare *vt* unmask

smasche'rarsi *vr* fig reveal oneself

SME *nm abbr* (**Sistema Monetario Europeo**) EMS

smem'brare *vt* dismember

smemo'rato, -a [1] *adj* forgetful [2] *nmf* scatterbrain

smen'tire *vt* deny

smen'tita *nf* denial

sme'raldo *nm & adj inv* emerald

smerci'are *vt* sell off

'smercio *nm* sale

smerigli'ato *adj* emery
■ **vetro smerigliato** frosted glass

sme'riglio *nm* emery

smer'lare *vt* scallop

'smerlo *nm* scallop

'smesso [1] *pp di* SMETTERE [2] *adj* ‹abiti› cast-off

✓ **'smettere** *vt* stop; stop wearing ‹abiti›; smettila! stop it!

smidol'lato *adj* spineless

smilitariz'zare *vt* demilitarize

'smilzo *adj* thin

sminu'ire *vt* diminish

sminu'irsi *vr* fig belittle oneself

sminuz'zare *vt* crumble; fig (analizzare) analyse in detail

smista'mento *nm* clearing; (postale) sorting; **stazione di** ∼ shunting yard, marshalling yard
■ **smistamento rifiuti** sorting of waste

smi'stare *vt* sort; Mil post; Rail marshall

smisu'rato *adj* boundless; (esorbitante) excessive

smitiz'zare *vt* demythologize

smobili'tare *vt* demobilize

smobilitazi'one *nf* demobilization

smo'dato *adj* immoderate

smog *nm* smog

'smoking *nm inv* dinner jacket, tuxedo Am

smon'tabile *adj* jointed

smon'taggio *nm* disassembly

smon'tare [1] *vt* take to pieces; (scoraggiare) dishearten; take down ‹tenda› [2] *vi* (da veicolo) get off; (da cavallo) dismount; (dal servizio) go off duty

smon'tarsi *vr* lose heart

'smorfia *nf* grimace; (moina) simper; **fare smorfie** make faces

smorfi'oso *adj* affected

'smorto *adj* pale; ‹colore› dull

smor'zare *vt* dim ‹luce›; tone down ‹colori›; deaden ‹suoni›; quench ‹sete›

smor'zata *nf* Sport drop shot

'smosso *pp di* SMUOVERE

smotta'mento *nm* landslide

SMS *nm abbr* SMS message, text message; mandare un ∼ **a qualcuno** text somebody

'smunto *adj* emaciated

smu'overe *vt* shift; (commuovere) move

smu'oversi *vr* move; (commuoversi) be moved

smus'sare *vt* round off; fig (attenuare) tone down

smus'sarsi *vr* go blunt

smussa'tura *nf* bevel

snack bar *nm inv* snack bar

snatu'rato *adj* inhuman

snazionaliz'zare *vt* denationalize

S.N.C. *abbr* (**società in nome collettivo**)

snel'lire *vt* slim down

snel'lirsi *vr* slim [down]

'snello *adj* slim

sner'vante *adj* enervating

sner'vare *vt* enervate

sner'varsi *vr* get exhausted

sni'dare *vt* drive out

snif'fare *vt* snort

snob'bare *vt* snub

sno'bismo *nm* snobbery

snoccio'lare *vt* stone; fig blurt out

snoccio'lato *adj* ‹olive› pitted, with the stones removed

sno'dabile *adj* jointed

sno'dare *vt* untie; (sciogliere) loosen

sno'darsi *vr* come untied; ‹strada› wind

sno'dato *adj* ‹persona› double-jointed; ‹dita› flexible

'snodo *nm* coupling
■ **snodo ferroviario** coupling

'snowboard *nm inv* snowboard; **fare** ∼ snowboard

SO *abbr* (**sud-ovest**) SW

soap 'opera *nf inv* soap [opera]

so'ave *adj* gentle

sobbal'zare *vi* jerk; (trasalire) start

sob'balzo *nm* jerk; (trasalimento) start

sobbar'carsi *vr* ∼ **a** undertake

sobbol'lire *vi* simmer

S

sob'borgo nm suburb
sobil'lare vt stir up
sobilla|'tore, -trice nm instigator
sobrietà nf inv sobriety
'sobrio adj sober
soc'chiudere vt half-close
socchi'uso ① pp di SOCCHIUDERE
② adj ‹occhi› half-closed; ‹porta› ajar
soc'combere vi succumb
soc'correre vt assist
soccorri'tore, -trice nmf rescue worker
soc'corso ① pp di SOCCORRERE
② nm assistance, help; **venire in ~ come
to help, come to the rescue; venire in ~
a qualcuno** come to somebody's rescue;
soccorsi pl help; (persone) rescuers; (dopo
disastro) relief workers
■ **soccorso alpino** mountain rescue; **soccorso
disastri** disaster relief; **soccorso stradale**
breakdown service, wrecking service Am
sociademo'cratico, -a ① adj Social
Democratic
② nmf Social Democrat
socialdemocra'zia nf Social
Democracy
⚜ **soci'ale** adj social
socia'lismo nm Socialism
⚜ **socia'lista** adj & nmf Socialist
socializ'zare vi socialize
⚜ **società** nf inv society; Comm company
■ **società in accomandita semplice** limited
partnership; **società per azioni** public
limited company, plc; **società dei consumi**
consumer society; **società in nome collettivo**
commercial partnership; **società fiduciaria**
trust company; **società a responsabilità
limitata** limited liability company; **società di
telecomunicazioni** communications company
soci'evole adj sociable
'socio, -a nmf member; Comm partner
socioeco'nomico adj socio-economic
soci'ologa nf sociologist
sociolo'gia nf sociology
socio'logico adj sociological
soci'ologo nm sociologist
'soda nf soda
■ **soda da bucato** washing soda
soda'lizio nm association, society
soddisfa'cente adj satisfactory
⚜ **soddi'sfare** vt/i satisfy; meet ‹richiesta›;
make amends for ‹offesa›
soddi'sfatto ① pp di SODDISFARE
② adj satisfied
⚜ **soddisfazi'one** nf satisfaction
'sodo ① adj hard; fig firm; ‹uovo› hard-
boiled
② adv hard; **dormire ~** sleep soundly
③ nm **venire al ~** get to the point

sofà nm inv sofa
soffe'rente adj (malato) ill
⚜ **soffe'renza** nf suffering
soffer'marsi vr pause; **~ su** dwell on
sof'ferto pp di SOFFRIRE
soffi'are ① vt blow; reveal ‹segreto›;
(rubare) pinch fam
② vi blow
soffi'ata nf **datti una ~ al naso** blow
your nose; **fare una ~ a qualcuno** fig sl tip
somebody off, give somebody a tip-off
'soffice adj soft
soffi'etto nm bellows; **a ~** ‹borsa›
expanding
■ **soffietto editoriale** blurb
'soffio nm puff; Med murmur
sof'fitta nf attic
sof'fitto nm ceiling
soffoca'mento nm suffocation
soffo'cante adj suffocating
⚜ **soffo'care** vt/i choke; fig stifle
sof'friggere vt fry lightly
⚜ **sof'frire** vt/i suffer; (sopportare) bear; **~ di**
suffer from; **~ di [mal di] cuore** suffer from
or have a heart condition; **~ la fame/il
freddo** be hungry/cold
sof'fritto ① pp di SOFFRIGGERE
② nm fried ingredients pl
sof'fuso adj ‹luce› soft, suffused
sofisti'care ① vt (adulterare) adulterate
② vi (sottilizzare) quibble
sofisti'cato adj sophisticated
soft adj soft
'softcopy nf Comput soft copy
'soft-core ① nm soft-core, soft porn
② adj **pornografia ~** soft porn
'software nm inv software; **dei ~** software
packages
■ **software di accesso** access software;
software applicativo application software;
software di autoapprendimento tutorial
package, tutorial software; **software di
comunicazione** communications software,
comms software; **software didattico**
educational software; **software di gestione
errori** error correction software; **software
di OCR** OCR software; **software di sistema**
system software
softwa'rista nm Comput software engineer
soggettiva'mente adv subjectively
sogget'tivo adj subjective
⚜ **sog'getto** ① nm subject; **cattivo ~** bad
sort
② adj subject; **essere ~ a** be subject to
soggezi'one nf subjection; (rispetto) awe
sogghi'gnare vi sneer
sog'ghigno nm sneer
soggio'gare vt subdue
soggior'nare vi stay

soggi'orno *nm* stay; (stanza) living room
- **permesso di soggiorno** residence permit

soggi'ungere *vt* add

'soglia *nf* threshold; **alle soglie di qualcosa** on the threshold of something
- **soglia del dolore** pain threshold; **soglia di povertà** poverty line

'sogliola *nf* sole
- **sogliola limanda** lemon sole

✔ **so'gnare** *vt/i* dream; ~ **a occhi aperti** daydream

so'gnarsi *vr* dream; **non te lo sogni neppure!** forget it!, don't even think of it!

sogna|'tore, -trice *nmf* dreamer

✔ **'sogno** *nm* dream; **fare un** ~ have a dream; **neanche per** ~! not on your life!; **essere un** ~ (bellissimo) be a dream; **una casa da** ~ a dream house; **il mio** ~ **nel cassetto** my secret dream

'soia *nf* soya

sol *nm* Mus (chiave, nota) G

so'laio *nm* attic

sola'mente *adv* only

so'lare *adj* ⟨energia, raggi⟩ solar; ⟨crema⟩ sun *attrib*

so'larium *nm inv* solarium

sol'care *vt* plough

'solco *nm* furrow; (di ruota) track; (di nave) wake; (di disco) groove

solda'tessa *nf* servicewoman

✔ **sol'dato** *nm* soldier
- **soldato semplice** private

✔ **'soldo** *nm* **non ha un** ~ he hasn't got a penny to his name; **senza un** ~ penniless; **al** ~ **di** in the pay of; **soldi** *pl* (denaro) money *sg*; **fare [i] soldi** make money; **prelevare dei soldi** withdraw money; **da quattro soldi** cheapo, nickel-and-dime Am

✔ **'sole** *nm* sun; (luce del sole) sun[light]; **al** ~ in the sun; **prendere il** ~ sunbathe

sole'cismo *nm* solecism

soleggi'ato *adj* sunny

so'lenne *adj* solemn

solennità *nf* solemnity

so'lere *vi* be in the habit of; **come si suol dire** as they say

so'letta *nf* insole

sol'fato *nm* sulphate

sol'feggio *nm* sol-fa

'solfuro *nm* sulphur

soli'dale *adj* in agreement

solidarietà *nf* solidarity

solidifi'care *vt/i* solidify

solidifi'carsi *vr* solidify

solidità *nf* solidity; (di colori) fastness

✔ **'solido** [1] *adj* solid; (robusto) sturdy; ⟨colore⟩ fast; **in** ~ Jur jointly and severally [2] *nm* solid

soli'loquio *nm* soliloquy

so'lista [1] *adj* solo [2] *nmf* soloist

solita'mente *adv* usually

soli'tario [1] *adj* solitary; (isolato) lonely [2] *nm* (brillante) solitaire; (gioco di carte) patience, solitaire

✔ **'solito** [1] *adj* usual; **essere** ~ **fare qualcosa** be in the habit of doing something [2] *nm* the usual; **di** ~ usually

✔ **soli'tudine** *nf* solitude

solleci'tare *vt* speed up; urge ⟨persona⟩

sollecitazi'one *nf* (richiesta) request; (preghiera) entreaty

sol'lecito [1] *adj* prompt [2] *nm* reminder

solleci'tudine *nf* promptness; (interessamento) concern; **con la massima** ~ Comm as soon as possible

solle'one *nm* noonday sun; (periodo) dog days of summer

solleti'care *vt* tickle

sol'letico *nm* tickling; **fare il** ~ **a qualcuno** tickle somebody; **soffrire il** ~ be ticklish

solleva'mento *nm*
- **sollevamento pesi** weightlifting

solle'vare *vt* lift; (elevare) raise; (confortare) comfort; ~ **una questione** raise a question; ~ **qualcuno da un incarico** relieve somebody of a responsibility

solle'varsi *vr* rise; (riaversi) recover

solle'vato *adj* relieved

solli'evo *nm* relief; **che** ~! what a relief!

✔ **'solo, -a** [1] *adj* alone; (isolato) lonely; (unico) only; Mus solo; **da** ~ by myself/yourself/ himself *etc* [2] *nmf* **il** ~, **la sola** the only one [3] *nm* Mus solo [4] *adv* only; ~ **il sabato/la domenica** Saturdays/Sundays only, only on Saturdays/Sundays

sol'stizio *nm* solstice

✔ **sol'tanto** *adv* only

so'lubile *adj* soluble; ⟨caffè⟩ instant

✔ **soluzi'one** *nf* solution; Comm payment; **senza** ~ **di continuità** without interruption; **in unica** ~ Comm as a lump sum
- **soluzione salina per lenti** soaking solution

sol'vente [1] *nm* solvent
- **solvente per lo smalto** nail varnish remover; **solvente per unghie** nail polish remover [2] *adj* solvent
- **reparto solvente** pay ward

solvibilità *nf* Fin solvency

'soma *nf* load
- **bestia da soma** beast of burden

'somalo, -a *adj* & *nmf* Somali

so'maro *nm* ass, donkey; Sch dunce

so'matico *adj* somatic; **tratti somatici** physical features

S

somatiz'zare *vt* react psychosomatically to

som'brero *nm* sombrero

somigli'ante *adj* similar

somigli'anza *nf* resemblance

somigli'are *vi* ~ a look like, resemble

somigli'arsi *vr* be alike; **chi si somiglia si piglia** birds of a feather flock together

❧ **'somma** *nf* sum; Math addition

som'mare *vt* add; (totalizzare) add up

sommaria'mente *adv* summarily

som'mario *adj & nm* summary

som'mato *adj* **tutto** ~ all things considered

somme'lier *nm inv* wine waiter

som'mergere *vt* submerge

sommer'gibile *nm* submarine

som'merso 1 *pp di* SOMMERGERE 2 *nm* Econ black economy

som'messo *adj* soft

sommini'strare *vt* administer

somministrazi'one *nf* administration; ~ **per via orale** to be taken orally

sommità *nf inv* summit

'sommo 1 *adj* highest; fig supreme 2 *nm* summit

som'mossa *nf* rising

sommozza'tore *nm* frogman

so'naglio *nm* bell

'sonar *nm* sonar

so'nata *nf* sonata; fig fam beating

'sonda *nf* Mech drill; (spaziale, Med) probe

son'daggio *nm* drilling; (spaziale, Med) probe; (indagine) survey

■ **sondaggio d'opinione** opinion poll

son'dare *vt* sound; (investigare) probe

so'netto *nm* sonnet

sonnambu'lismo *nm* sleepwalking

son'nambulo, -a *nmf* sleepwalker

sonnecchi'are *vi* doze

son'nifero *nm* sleeping-pill

❧ **'sonno** *nm* sleep; **aver** ~ be sleepy; **morire di** ~ be dead tired, be dead on one's feet; **morto di** ~ fam (stupido) zombie; **perdere il** ~ anche fig lose sleep

■ **sonno eterno** Relig eternal rest

sonno'lenza *nf* sleepiness

'sono ▶ ESSERE

sonoriz'zare *vt* add a soundtrack to

so'noro 1 *adj* resonant; (rumoroso) loud; ‹onde, scheda› sound *attrib* 2 *nm* Tech (di film) soundtrack

sontu'oso *adj* sumptuous

sopo'rifero *adj* soporific

sop'palco *nm* platform

■ **soppalco abitabile** loft conversion

---

soppe'rire *vi* ~ a qualcosa provide for something

soppe'sare *vt* weigh up ‹situazione›

soppi'atto: **di** ~ *adv* furtively

❧ **soppor'tare** *vt* support; (tollerare) stand; bear ‹dolore›

sopportazi'one *nf* patience

soppressi'one *nf* removal; (di legge) abolition; ‹di diritti, pubblicazione› suppression; (annullamento) cancellation

sop'presso *pp di* SOPPRIMERE

sop'primere *vt* get rid of: abolish ‹legge›; suppress ‹diritti, pubblicazione›; (annullare) cancel

❧ **'sopra** 1 *adv* on top; (più in alto) higher [up]; (al piano superiore) upstairs; (in testo) above; **mettilo lì** ~ put it up there; **di** ~ upstairs; **dormirci** ~ fig sleep on it; **pensarci** ~ think about it; **vedi** ~ see above 2 *prep* ~ [a] on; (senza contatto, oltre) over; (riguardo a) about; **è** ~ **al tavolo**, **è** ~ **il tavolo** it's on the table; **il quadro è appeso** ~ **al camino** the picture is hanging over the fireplace; **il ponte passa** ~ **all'autostrada** the bridge crosses over the motorway; **è caduto** ~ **il tetto** it fell on the roof; **l'uno** ~ **l'altro** one on top of the other; (senza contatto) one above the other; **abita** ~ **di me** he lives upstairs from me; **i bambini** ~ **i dieci anni** children over ten; **20°** ~ **lo zero** 20 above zero; ~ **il livello del mare** above sea level; **rifletti** ~ **quello che è successo** think about what happened; **prendere** ~ **di sé la responsabilità di qualcosa** assume responsibility for something; **scaricare la colpa** ~ **qualcuno** put the blame on somebody; **non ha nessuno** ~ **di sé** he has nobody above him; **al di** ~ **di** over; **al di** ~ **di ogni sospetto** beyond suspicion 3 *nm* **il [di]** ~ the top

so'prabito *nm* overcoat

soprac'ciglio *nm* (*pl nf* **sopracciglia**) eyebrow

soppracco'perta *nf* (di letto) bedspread

sopraccoper'tina *nf* book jacket, dust jacket

soprad'detto *adj* above-mentioned

sopraele'vare *vt* raise

sopraele'vata *nf* elevated railway

sopraele'vato *adj* raised

sopraf'fare *vt* overwhelm

sopraf'fatto *pp di* SOPRAFFARE

sopraffazi'one *nf* abuse of power

sopraf'fino *adj* excellent; ‹gusto, udito› highly refined

sopraggi'ungere *vi* ‹persona› turn up; (accadere) happen; **è sopraggiunta la pioggia** and then it started to rain

soprallu'ogo *nm* inspection

sopram'mobile *nm* ornament

soprannatu'rale *adj & nm* supernatural

sopran'nome *nm* nickname
soprannomi'nare *vt* nickname
sopran'numero *adv* sono in ∼ there are
too many of them; **ce ne sono 15 in** ∼ there
are 15 too many of them, there are 15 of
them too many
so'prano *nmf* soprano
soprappensi'ero *adv* lost in thought
sopras'salto *nm* di ∼ with a start
soprasse'dere *vi* ∼ a postpone
soprat'tassa *nf* surtax
■ **soprattassa postale** excess postage
soprat'tetto *nm* fly sheet
soprat'tutto *adv* above all
sopravvalu'tare *vt* overvalue;
overestimate ‹forze›
sopravvalutazi'one *nf* overvaluation;
(di forze) overestimation
sopravve'nire *vi* turn up; (accadere)
happen
soprav'vento *nm* fig upper hand;
prendere il ∼ take the upper hand
sopravvis'suto, -a ① pp di
SOPRAVVIVERE
② *adj* surviving
③ *nmf* survivor
sopravvi'venza *nf* survival
soprav'vivere *vi* survive; ∼ a outlive
‹persona›
soprinten'dente *nmf* supervisor; (di
museo ecc) keeper
soprinten'denza *nf* supervision; (ente)
board
so'pruso *nm* abuse of power
soq'quadro *nm* mettere a ∼ turn upside
down
sor'betto *nm* sorbet
sor'bire *vt* sip; fig put up with
'sorcio *nm* mouse; far vedere i sorci verdi a
qualcuno give somebody a rough time
'sordido *adj* sordid; (avaro) stingy
sor'dina *nf* mute; **in** ∼ fig on the quiet
sordità *nf* deafness
'sordo, -a ① *adj* deaf; ‹rumore, dolore› dull
② *nmf* deaf person
sordo'muto, -a ① *adj* deaf-and-dumb,
deaf without speech
② *nmf* deaf mute
so'rella *nf* sister
■ **sorella gemella** twin sister
sorel'lastra *nf* stepsister, half-sister
sor'gente *nf* spring; (fonte) source
■ **programma sorgente** Comput source program
'sorgere *vi* rise; fig arise
sormon'tare *vt* surmount
sorni'one *adj* sly
sorpas'sare *vt* surpass; (eccedere) exceed;
overtake, pass Am ‹veicolo›
sorpas'sato *adj* old-fashioned

sor'passo *nm* overtaking, passing Am
sorpren'dente *adj* surprising;
(straordinario) remarkable
sorprendente'mente *adv* surprisingly
sor'prendere *vt* surprise; (cogliere in
flagrante) catch
sor'prendersi *vr* be surprised; ∼ a fare
qualcosa catch oneself doing something;
non c'è da ∼ it's hardly surprising
sor'presa *nf* surprise; **di** ∼ by surprise;
provare ∼ feel surprised
sor'preso pp di SORPRENDERE
sor'reggere *vt* support; (tenere) hold up
sor'reggersi *vr* support oneself
sor'retto pp di SORREGGERE
sorri'dente *adj* smiling
sor'ridere *vi* smile; **la fortuna mi ha
sorriso** fortune smiled on me
sor'riso ① pp di SORRIDERE
② *nm* smile
sorseggi'are *vt* sip
'sorso *nm* sip, (piccola quantità) drop
'sorta *nf* sort; **di** ∼ whatever; **ogni** ∼ **di** all
sorts of
'sorte *nf* fate; (caso imprevisto) chance; **tirare
a** ∼ draw lots; **per buona** ∼ (liter) by good
fortune
sorteggi'are *vt* draw lots for
sor'teggio *nm* draw
sorti'legio *nm* witchcraft
sor'tire ① *vi* come out
② *vt* bring about ‹effetto›
sor'tita *nf* Mil sortie; (battuta) witticism
'sorto pp di SORGERE
sorvegli'ante *nmf* keeper; (controllore)
overseer
sorvegli'anza *nf* watch; Mil ecc
surveillance
■ **sorveglianza tramite braccialetto elettronico**
electronic tagging
sorvegli'are *vt* watch over; (controllare)
oversee; ‹polizia› watch, keep under
surveillance
sorvegli'ato, -a ① *adj* under surveillance
② *nmf* ∼ speciale person kept under special
surveillance
sorvo'lare *vt* fly over; fig skip
SOS *nm* SOS
'sosia *nm inv* double
so'spendere *vt* hang; (interrompere) stop;
(privare di una carica) suspend
sospensi'one *nf* suspension
■ **sospensione condizionale [della pena]**
suspended sentence
sospen'sorio *nm* Sport jockstrap
so'speso ① pp di SOSPENDERE
② *adj* ‹impiegato, alunno› suspended; ∼ a
hanging from; ∼ a un filo fig hanging by a
thread ⋯⟶

[3] *nm* in ∼ pending; (emozionato) in suspense

✧ **sospet'tare** *vt* suspect

✧ **so'spetto** [1] *adj* suspicious
[2] *nm* suspicion; (persona) suspect; **al di sopra di ogni** ∼ above suspicion

sospet'toso *adj* suspicious

so'spingere *vt* drive

so'spinto pp di SOSPINGERE

sospi'rare [1] *vi* sigh
[2] *vt* long for

so'spiro *nm* sigh

'sosta *nf* stop, stop-off; (pausa) pause; **senza** ∼ nonstop; **'∼ autorizzata ...'** 'parking permitted for ...'
■ **'divieto di sosta'** 'no parking'

sostan'tivo *nm* noun

✧ **so'stanza** *nf* substance; **sostanze** *pl* (patrimonio) property *sg*; **in** ∼ to sum up; **la** ∼ **della questione** the nub of the matter

sostanzi'oso *adj* substantial; ‹cibo› nourishing; **poco** ∼ insubstantial

so'stare *vi* stop; (fare una pausa) pause

so'stegno *nm* support
■ **sostegno morale** moral support

✧ **soste'nere** *vt* support; (sopportare) bear; (resistere) withstand; (affermare) maintain; (nutrire) sustain: sit ‹esame›; ∼ **le spese** meet the costs; ∼ **delle spese** incur expenditure; ∼ **una carica** hold a position; ∼ **una parte** play a role

soste'nersi *vr* support oneself

soste'nibile *adj* ‹sviluppo, crescita› sustainable

sosteni|'tore, -trice *nmf* supporter

sostenta'mento *nm* maintenance

soste'nuto [1] *adj* ‹stile› formal; ‹velocità› high; ‹mercato, prezzi› steady
[2] *nm* fare il ∼ be stand-offish

✧ **sostitu'ire** *vt* substitute (**a** for), replace (**con** with)

sostitu'irsi *vr* ∼ **a** replace

sosti'tuto, -a [1] *nmf* replacement, stand-in
[2] *nm* (surrogato) substitute

sostituzi'one *nf* substitution

sotta'ceto *adj* pickled; **sottaceti** *pl* pickles

sot'tacqua *adv* underwater

sot'tana *nf* petticoat; (di prete) cassock

sotter'fugio *nm* subterfuge; **di** ∼ secretly

sotter'raneo [1] *adj* underground
[2] *nm* cellar

sotter'rare *vt* bury

sottigli'ezza *nf* slimness; fig subtlety

✧ **sot'tile** *adj* thin; ‹udito, odorato› keen; ‹osservazione, distinzione› subtle

sotti'letta® *nf* cheese slice

sottiliz'zare *vi* split hairs

----

sottin'tendere *vt* imply

sottin'teso [1] pp di SOTTINTENDERE
[2] *nm* allusion; **senza sottintesi** openly
[3] *adj* implied

✧ **'sotto** [1] *adv* below; (più in basso) lower [down]; (al di sotto) underneath; (al piano di sotto) downstairs; **è lì** ∼ it's underneath; ∼ ∼ deep down; (di nascosto) on the quiet; **di** ∼ downstairs; **mettersi** ∼ fig get down to it; **mettere** ∼ fam (investire) knock down; **fatti** ∼! fam get stuck in!
[2] *prep* ∼ **[a]** under; (al di sotto di) under[neath]; **il fiume passa** ∼ **un ponte** the river passes under[neath] a bridge; **è** ∼ **il tavolo, è** ∼ **al tavolo** it's under[neath] the table; **abita** ∼ **di me** he lives downstairs from me; **i bambini** ∼ **i dieci anni** children under ten; **20°** ∼ **zero** 20 below zero; ∼ **il livello del mare** below sea level; ∼ **la pioggia** in the rain; ∼ **Elisabetta I** under Elizabeth I; ∼ **calmante** under sedation; ∼ **chiave** under lock and key; ∼ **condizione che ...** on condition that ...; ∼ **giuramento** under oath; ∼ **sorveglianza** under surveillance; ∼ **Natale/gli esami** around Christmas/exam time; **al di** ∼ **di** under; **andare** ∼ **i 50 all'ora** do less than 50km an hour
[3] *nm* il **[di]** ∼ the bottom

sotto'banco *adv* ‹vendere, comprare› under the counter

sottobicchi'ere *nm* coaster

sotto'bosco *nm* undergrowth

sotto'braccio *adv* arm in arm

sottoccu'pato *adj* underemployed

sottochi'ave *adv* under lock and key

sotto'costo *adj & adv* at less than cost price

sottodi'rectory *nf* Comput subdirectory

sottoe'sporre *vt* underexpose

sotto'fondo *nm* background

sotto'gamba *adv* prendere qualcosa ∼ take something lightly

sotto'gonna *nf* underskirt

sottoindi'cato *adj* undermentioned

sottoinsi'eme *nm* Math subset

sottoline'are *vt* underline; fig underline ‹importanza›; emphasize ‹forma degli occhi ecc›

sot'tolio *adv* in oil

sotto'mano *adv* within reach

sottoma'rino *adj & nm* submarine

sotto'messo [1] pp di SOTTOMETTERE
[2] *adj* (remissivo) submissive

sotto'mettere *vt* submit; subdue ‹popolo›

sotto'mettersi *vr* submit

sottomissi'one *nf* submission

sottopa'gare *vt* underpay

sottopas'saggio *nm* underpass; (pedonale) subway

sottopi'atto *nm* place mat, table mat

sotto'porre vt submit; (costringere) subject

sotto'porsi vr submit oneself; ~ **a** undergo

sotto'posto pp di SOTTOPORRE

sottoproletari'ato nm underclass

sotto'scala nm cupboard under the stairs

sotto'scritto [1] pp di SOTTOSCRIVERE [2] nm undersigned

sotto'scrivere vt sign; (approvare) sanction, subscribe to

sottoscrizi'one nf (petizione) petition; (approvazione) sanction; (raccolta di denaro) appeal

sottosegre'tario nm undersecretary

sotto'sopra adv upside-down

sotto'stante adj **la strada** ~ the road below

sottosu'olo nm subsoil

sottosvilup'pato adj underdeveloped

sottosvi'luppo nm underdevelopment

sottote'nente nm second lieutenant; Naut sub lieutenant

sotto'terra adv underground

sottotito'lato adj subtitled

sotto'titolo nm (di film, programma) subtitle; (in libro, giornale) subheading

sottovalu'tare vt underestimate

sotto'vento adv downwind

sotto'veste nf slip

sotto'voce adv in a low voice

sottovu'oto adj vacuum-packed

sotto'zero adj inv subzero

sot'trarre vt remove; embezzle (fondi); Math subtract

sot'trarsi vr ~ **a** escape from; avoid (responsabilità)

sot'tratto pp di SOTTRARRE

sottrazi'one nf removal; (di fondi) embezzlement; Math subtraction

sottuffici'ale nm non-commissioned officer; Naut petty officer

sou'brette nf showgirl

souf'flé nm inv soufflé

souve'nir nm inv souvenir
■ **negozio di souvenir** souvenir shop

so'vente adv (liter) often

soverchie'ria nf bullying; **fare soverchierie a** bully

so'vietico, -a adj & nmf Soviet

sovrabbon'danza nf overabundance

sovraccari'care vt overload

sovrac'carico [1] adj overloaded (di with)
[2] nm overload

sovraffati'carsi vr overexert oneself

sovraffolla'mento nm overcrowding

sovralimen'tare vt overfeed

sovrannatu'rale adj & nm = SOPRANNATURALE

sovrannazio'nale adj supranational

so'vrano, -a [1] adj sovereign; fig supreme [2] nmf sovereign

sovrappopo'lato adj overpopulated

sovrap'porre vt superimpose

sovrap'porsi vr overlap

sovrapposizi'one nf superimposition

sovrapro'fitto nm excess profits

sovra'stare vt dominate; fig (pericolo) hang over

sovrastrut'tura nf superstructure

sovratensi'one nf Electr overload, overvoltage

sovrecci'tarsi vr get overexcited

sovrecci'tato adj overexcited

sovresposizi'one nf Phot overexposure

sovrimpressi'one nf Phot double exposure

sovrinten'dente, sovrintendenza = SOPRINTENDENTE, SOPRINTENDENZA

sovru'mano adj superhuman

sovvenzio'nare vt subsidize

sovvenzio'nato [1] pp di SOVVENZIONARE [2] adj subsidized; ~ **dallo Stato** state-funded

sovvenzi'one nf subsidy

sovver'sivo, -a adj & nmf subversive

sovver'tire vt subvert

'sozzo adj filthy

SP nf abbr (**strada provinciale**) secondary road

S.p.A. abbr (**società per azioni**) plc

spac'care vt split; chop (legna); ~ **il minuto** keep perfect time; ~ **il muso a qualcuno** sl smash somebody's face in; **o la va o la spacca** it's all or nothing; **un sole che spacca le pietre** a sun hot enough to fry an egg

spac'carsi vr split

spacca'tura nf split

spacci'are vt deal in, push (droga); ~ **qualcosa per qualcosa** pass something off as something; **essere spacciato** be done for, be a goner

spacci'arsi vr ~ **per** pass oneself off as

spaccia|'tore, -trice nmf (di droga) dealer, pusher; (di denaro falso) distributor of forged bank notes

'spaccio nm (di droga) dealing; (negozio) shop

'spacco nm split

spacco'nate nfpl blustering

spac'cone, -a nmf boaster

'spada nf sword

spadac'cino nm swordsman

spadroneggi'are vi act the boss

spae'sato adj disorientated

spa'ghetti nmpl spaghetti sg ⋯⟶

■ spaghetti in bianco *spaghetti with butter, oil and cheese*; spaghetti alla carbonara *spaghetti with egg, cheese and diced bacon*; spaghetti al sugo *spaghetti with a sauce*

spa'ghetto *nm* fam (spavento) fright

'Spagna *nf* Spain

spagno'letta *nf* spool

spa'gnolo, -a ① *adj* Spanish
② *nmf* Spaniard
③ *nm* (lingua) Spanish

'spago *nm* string; fam (spavento) fright; dare ∼ a qualcuno encourage somebody

spai'ato *adj* odd

spalan'care *vt* open wide

spalan'carsi *vr* open wide

spalan'cato *adj* wide open

spa'lare *vt* shovel

✱ 'spalla *nf* shoulder; (di comico) straight man; spalle *pl* (schiena) back; alzata di spalle shrug [of the shoulders]; alle spalle di behind; alle spalle di qualcuno ‹ridere› behind somebody's back; avere qnco/qualcosa alle spalle have somebody/something behind one; di ∼ ‹violino ecc› second; vivere alle spalle di qualcuno live off somebody; con le spalle al muro anche fig with one's back to the wall; voltare le spalle turn one's back

spal'lata *nf* push with the shoulder; (alzata di spalle) shrug [of the shoulders]

spalleggi'are *vt* back up

spal'letta *nf* parapet

spalli'era *nf* back; (di letto) headboard; (ginnastica) wall bars *pl*

spal'lina *nf* strap; (imbottitura) shoulder pad; senza spalline strapless

spal'mare *vt* spread

spal'marsi *vr* cover oneself

spa'nato *adj* ‹vite› threadless

spanci'ata *nf* belly flop

'spandere *vt* spread; (versare) spill; spendere e ∼ spend and spend

'spandersi *vr* spread

spandighi'aia *nm inv* gritter

'spaniel *nm inv* spaniel

spappo'lare *vt* crush

✱ spa'rare *vt/i* shoot; spararle grosse talk big; ∼ fandonie talk nonsense

spa'rarsi *vr* shoot oneself; si è sparato un colpo alla tempia he shot himself in the temple

spa'rata *nf* fam tall story

spa'rato *nm* (della camicia) dicky

spara'toria *nf* shooting
■ sparatoria da auto in corsa drive-by shooting

sparecchi'are *vt* clear

spa'reggio *nm* Comm deficit; Sport play-off

'spargere *vt* scatter; (diffondere) spread; shed ‹lacrime, sangue›

'spargersi *vr* spread

✱ spargi'mento *nm* scattering; (di lacrime, sangue) shedding
■ spargimento di sangue bloodshed

spa'rire *vi* disappear; sparisci! get lost!, scram!

sparizi'one *nf* disappearance

spar'lare *vi* ∼ di run down

'sparo *nm* shot
■ sparo d'avvertimento warning shot

sparpagli'are *vt* scatter

sparpagli'arsi *vr* scatter

sparpagli'ato *adj* far-flung

'sparso ① pp di SPARGERE
② *adj* scattered; (sciolto) loose

sparti'neve *nm inv* snowplough

spar'tire *vt* share out; (separare) separate

spar'tirsi *vr* share

spar'tito *nm* Mus score

sparti'traffico *nm inv* traffic island; (di autostrada) central reservation, median strip Am

spartizi'one *nf* division

spa'ruto *adj* gaunt; ‹gruppo› small; ‹peli, capelli› sparse

sparvi'ero *nm* sparrow-hawk

spasi'mante *nm* (hum) admirer

spasi'mare *vi* suffer agonies; ∼ per be madly in love with

'spasimo *nm* spasm

spa'smodico *adj* spasmodic

spas'sarsi *vr* amuse oneself; spas'sarsela have a good time

spassio'nato *adj* ‹osservatore› dispassionate, impartial

'spasso *nm* fun; essere uno ∼ be hilarious; andare a ∼ go for a walk; essere a ∼ be out of work

spas'soso *adj* hilarious

'spastico *adj* spastic

'spatola *nf* spatula

spau'racchio *nm* scarecrow; fig bugbear

spau'rire *vt* frighten

spa'valdo *adj* defiant

spaventa'passeri *nm inv* scarecrow

✱ spaven'tare *vt* frighten, scare

spaven'tarsi *vr* be frightened, be scared

spa'vento *nm* fright; brutto da fare ∼ incredibly ugly

spaven'toso *adj* frightening; fam (enorme) incredible

spazi'ale *adj* spatial; (cosmico) space *attrib*

spazi'are ① *vt* space out
② *vi* range

spazien'tirsi *vr* lose [one's] patience

✱ 'spazio *nm* space
■ spazio aereo airspace; spazio indietro Comput backspace; spazio di tempo period of time;

---

spazio vitale elbowroom; **spazio web** web space

spazi'oso *adj* spacious

spazio-tempo'rale *adj* spatiotemporal

spazzaca'mino *nm* chimney sweep

spazza'neve *nm inv* (anche sci) snowplough

spaz'zare *vt* sweep; ~ **via** sweep away; *fam* (mangiare) devour

spazza'trice *nf* sweeper

spazza'tura *nf* (immondizia) rubbish

spaz'zino *nm* road sweeper; (netturbino) dustman, refuse collector

'spazzola *nf* brush; (di tergicristallo) blade; **capelli a** ~ crew cut

spazzo'lare *vt* brush

spazzo'larsi *vr* ~ **i capelli** brush one's hair

spazzo'lino *nm* small brush
■ **spazzolino da denti** toothbrush; **spazzolino per le unghie** nailbrush

spazzo'lone *nm* scrubbing brush

'speaker *nm inv* Radio, TV announcer

specchi'arsi *vr* look at oneself in a/the mirror; (riflettersi) be mirrored; ~ **in qualcuno** model oneself on somebody

specchi'ato *adj* **di specchiata onestà** of spotless integrity

specchi'etto *nm* small mirror
■ **specchietto laterale** wing mirror; **specchietto retrovisore** driving mirror; rear-view mirror

⚔ **'specchio** *nm* mirror
■ **specchio unilaterale** two-way mirror

⚔ **speci'ale** [1] *adj* special
[2] *nm* TV special [programme]

specia'lista *nmf* specialist

specialità *nf inv* speciality, specialty

specializ'zare *vt* specialize

specializ'zarsi *vr* specialize

specializ'zato *adj* ‹operaio› skilled; **siamo specializzati in …** we specialize in …

special'mente… *adv* especially

⚔ **'specie** *nf* (scientifico) species; (tipo) kind; **fare** ~ **a** surprise; **in** ~ especially
■ **specie a rischio** endangered species

specifi'care *vt* specify

specificata'mente *adv* specifically

spe'cifico *adj* specific

speci'oso *adj* specious

specu'lare[1] *vi* speculate; ~ **su** (indagare) speculate on; Fin speculate in

specu'lare[2] *adj* mirror *attrib*

specula'tivo *adj* speculative

specula'tore *nm* speculator

speculazi'one *nf* speculation

⚔ **spe'dire** *vt* send; ~ **per posta** mail, post *Br*; ~ **qualcuno all'altro mondo** send somebody to meet his/her maker

spe'dito [1] pp di SPEDIRE
[2] *adj* quick; ‹parlata› fluent

spedizi'one *nf* (di lettere ecc) dispatch; Comm consignment, shipment; ‹scientifica› expedition

spedizioni'ere *nm* Comm freight forwarder

⚔ **'spegnere** *vt* put out; turn off, switch off ‹motore, luce, televisione›; turn off ‹gas›; quench, slake ‹sete›

'spegnersi *vr* go out; (morire) pass away

spegni'mento *nm* standby

spelacchi'ato *adj* ‹tappeto› threadbare; ‹cane› mangy

spe'lare *vt* remove the fur of ‹coniglio›

spe'larsi *vr* ‹cane, tappeto› moult

speleolo'gia *nf* potholing, speleology

spel'lare *vt* skin; *fig* fleece

spel'larsi *vr* ‹serpente› shed its skin; (per il sole) peel; **mi sono spellato un ginocchio** I grazed *or* skinned my knee

spe'lonca *nf* cave; *fig* dingy hole

spendacci'one, -a *nmf* spendthrift

⚔ **'spendere** *vt* spend; ~ **fiato** waste one's breath

spen'nare *vt* pluck; *fam* fleece ‹cliente›

spennel'lare [1] *vt* brush
[2] *vi* paint

spensierata'mente *adv* blithely

spensiera'tezza *nf* lightheartedness

spensie'rato *adj* lighthearted, carefree

'spento [1] pp di SPEGNERE
[2] *adj* off; ‹gas› out; (smorto) dull; ‹vulcano› extinct

spenzo'lare *vt* dangle

⚔ **spe'ranza** *nf* hope; **pieno di** ~ hopeful; **senza** ~ hopeless

⚔ **spe'rare** [1] *vt* hope for; (aspettarsi) expect
[2] *vi* ~ **in** trust in; **spero di sì** I hope so

'sperdersi *vr* get lost

sper'duto *adj* lost; (isolato) secluded

spergiu'rare *vi* commit perjury

spergi'uro, -a [1] *nmf* perjurer
[2] *nm* perjury

sperico'lato *adj* swashbuckling

sperimen'tale *adj* experimental

sperimen'tare *vt* experiment with; test ‹resistenza, capacità, teoria›

sperimen'tato *adj* ‹metodo› tried and tested

sperimentazi'one *nf* experimentation; ~ **sugli animali** animal testing

'sperma *nm* sperm

spermi'cida [1] *adj* spermicidal
[2] *nm* spermicide

spero'nare *vt* ram

spe'rone *nm* spur

sperpe'rare *vt* squander

'sperpero *nm* waste, squandering

spersonaliz'zare *vt* depersonalize

spersonaliz'zarsi *vr* become depersonalized

spersonalizzazi'one *nf* depersonalization

⚘ **'spesa** *nf* expense; (acquisto) purchase; **andare a far spese** go shopping; **darsi a spese folli** go on a shopping spree; **fare la ~** do the shopping; **fare le spese di** pay for; **a proprie spese** at one's own expense; **spese** *pl* **di amministrazione** handling charge; **spese** *pl* **bancarie** bank charges; **spese** *pl* **di capitale** capital expenditure; **spese** *pl* **a carico del destinatario** carriage forward; **spese** *pl* **di esercizio** business expenses; **spese** *pl* **extra** out-of-pocket expenses; **spese** *pl* **di gestione** operating costs; **spese** *pl* **di movimentazione** handling charge; **spese** *pl* **di spedizione** shipping costs; **spese** *pl* **di viaggio** travel expenses

spe'sare *vt* pay expenses for; **spesato della ditta** paid for by the company, on the company

spe'sato *adj* all-expenses-paid

'speso *pp di* SPENDERE

'spesso¹ *adj* thick

⚘ **'spesso²** *adv* often

spes'sore *nm* thickness; fig (consistenza) substance

spet'tabile *adj* (comm abbr **Spett.**) **Spettabile ditta Rossi** Messrs Rossi

spettaco'lare *adj* spectacular

⚘ **spet'tacolo** *nm* spectacle; (rappresentazione) show; **dare ~ di sé** make a spectacle *or* an exhibition of oneself; **il mondo dello ~** show business

  ■ **spettacolo di burattini** Punch-and-Judy show; **spettacolo di varietà** variety show

spettaco'loso *adj* spectacular

spet'tanza *nf* concern

spet'tare *vi* **~ a** be up to; ‹diritto› be due to

spetta|'tore, -trice *nmf* spectator; **spettatori** *pl* (di cinema ecc) audience *sg*

spettego'lare *vi* gossip

spetti'nare *vt* **~ qualcuno** ruffle somebody's hair

spetti'narsi *vr* ruffle one's hair

spet'trale *adj* ghostly

'spettro *nm* ghost; fig (della fame) spectre; Phys spectrum; **ad ampio ~** ‹medicina› broad-spectrum

spezi'are *vt* add spices to, spice

spezi'ato *adj* spicy

'spezie *nfpl* spices

⚘ **spez'zare** *vt* break

spez'zarsi *vr* break

spezza'tino *nm* stew

spez'zato ⓵ *adj* broken

⚘ indicates a very frequent word

⓶ *nm* coordinated jacket and trousers

spezzet'tare *vt* break into small pieces

spez'zone *nm* Cinema clip, footage *no pl*; (bomba) cluster bomb

⚘ **'spia** *nf* spy; (della polizia) informer; (di porta) peep-hole; **fare la ~** sneak

  ■ **spia di accensione** power-on light; **spia di attività dell'hard disk** Comput hard disk activity light; **spia della benzina** petrol gauge; **spia luminosa** warning light; **spia dell'olio** oil [warning] light

spiacci'care *vt* squash

spia'cente *adj* sorry

spia'cevole *adj* unpleasant

⚘ **spi'aggia** *nf* beach

spiag'giare *vi* [balena] strand, beach

spiag'giarsi *vr* strand oneself, beach oneself

spia'nare *vt* level; (rendere liscio) smooth; roll out ‹pasta›; raze to the ground ‹edificio›

spia'nata *nf* flat ground

spi'ano *nm* **a tutto ~** flat out

spian'tato *adj* fig penniless

spi'are *vt* spy on; wait for ‹occasione ecc›

spiattel'lare *vt* blurt out; shove ‹oggetto›

spiaz'zare *vt* wrong-foot

spi'azzo *nm* (radura) clearing

spic'care ⓵ *vt* **~ un salto** jump; **~ il volo** take flight
  ⓶ *vi* stand out

spic'cato *adj* marked

'spicchio *nm* (di agrumi) segment; (di aglio) clove

spicci'arsi *vr* hurry up

spiccia'tivo *adj* speedy

'spiccio *adj* no-nonsense

'spiccioli *nmpl* change

'spicciolo *adj* (comune) banal; ‹denaro› in change

'spicco *nm* relief; **fare ~** stand out; **di ~** high-profile

'spider *nmf inv* open-top sports car

spie'dino *nm* kebab

spi'edo *nm* spit; **allo ~** on a spit, spitroasted

spiega'mento *nm* deployment

⚘ **spie'gare** *vt* explain; open out ‹cartina›; unfurl ‹vele›

spie'garsi *vr* explain oneself; ‹vele, bandiere› unfurl; **non so se mi spiego** need I say more?; **mi sono spiegato?** (minaccia) do I make myself clear?; **non riesco a spiegarmi come ...** I can't understand how ...

spie'gato *adj* ‹ali› outspread; **a sirene spiegate** with sirens blaring; **a voce spiegata** at the top of one's voice; **a vele spiegate** under full sail, with all sails in the wind

spiegazi'one *nf* explanation; **venire a una ~ con qualcuno** sort things out with somebody

spiegaz'zare *vt* crumple

spiegaz'zato *adj* crumpled

spiela'tezza *nf* ruthlessness

spie'tato *adj* ruthless

spiffe'rare [1] *vt* blurt out [2] *vi ‹vento›* whistle

'spiffero *nm* (corrente d'aria) draught

'spiga *nf* spike; Bot ear

spi'gato *adj* herringbone

spigli'ato *adj* self-possessed

'spigola *nf* sea bass

spigo'lare *vt* glean

'spigolo *nm* edge; (angolo) corner

'spilla *nf* (gioiello) brooch
■ **spilla da balia** safety pin; **spilla di sicurezza** safety pin

spil'lare *vt* tap

'spillo *nm* pin
■ **spillo di sicurezza** safety pin

spil'lone *nm* hatpin

spilluzzi'care *vt* pick at

spi'lorcio, -a [1] *adj* stingy [2] *nm* miser, skinflint

spilun'gone, -a *nmf* beanpole

'spina *nf* thorn; (di pesce) bone; Electr plug; **a ~ di pesce** ‹tessuto, disegno› herringbone; ‹parcheggio› in two angled rows; **stare sulle spine** be on tenterhooks; **una ~ nel fianco** a thorn in one's side
■ **spina dorsale** spine

spi'naci *nmpl* spinach

spi'nale *adj* spinal

spi'nato [1] *adj ‹filo›* barbed [2] *nm* (tessuto) herringbone

spi'nello *nm* fam (droga) joint

'spingere *vt* push; fig drive

'spingersi *vr* (andare) proceed

'spinnaker *nm* spinnaker

spi'noso *adj* thorny

spi'notto *nm* Electr plug

'spinta *nf* push; (violenta) thrust; fig spur; **dare una ~ a qualcosa/qualcuno** give somebody/something a push; **farsi largo a spinte** push one's way through

spinta'rella *nf* fam (raccomandazione) **ha ottenuto il lavoro grazie alla ~ dello zio** his uncle got him the job by pulling a few strings

'spinto [1] *pp di* SPINGERE [2] *adj ‹barzelletta, spettacolo›* risqué

spin'tone *nm* shove

spio'naggio *nm* espionage, spying

spi'one, -a *nmf* tell-tale

spio'vente [1] *adj ‹tetto›* sloping [2] *nm* slope

spi'overe *vi* (liter) stop raining; (ricadere) fall; (scorrere) flow down

'spira *nf* coil

spi'raglio *nm* small opening; (soffio d'aria) breath of air; (raggio di luce) gleam of light

spi'rale [1] *adj* spiral [2] *nm* spiral; (negli orologi) hairspring; (anticoncezionale) coil; **a ~** spiral-shaped

spi'rare *vi* (soffiare) blow; (morire) pass away

spiri'tato *adj* possessed; ‹espressione› wild

spiri'tismo *nm* spiritualism

spiri'tista *nmf* spiritualist

spiri'tistico *adj* spiritualist

'spirito *nm* spirit; (arguzia) wit; (intelletto) mind; **fare dello ~** be witty; **persona di ~** witty person; **sotto ~** in brandy
■ **spirito civico** community spirit; **spirito di contraddizione** contrariness; **Spirito Santo** Holy Spirit, Holy Ghost

spirito'saggine *nf* witticism

spiri'toso *adj* witty

spiritu'ale *adj* spiritual

spiritual'mente *adv* spiritually

splen'dente *adj* shining; **denti bianchi splendenti** gleaming white teeth

'splendere *vi* shine

'splendido *adj* splendid

splen'dore *nm* splendour

'spocchia *nf* conceit

spocchi'oso *adj* conceited

spode'stare *vt* dispossess; depose ‹re›

spoetiz'zare *vt* disenchant

'spoglia *nf* (di animale) skin; **spoglie** *pl* (salma) mortal remains; (bottino) spoils; **sotto false spoglie** under false pretences

spogli'are *vt* strip; (svestire) undress; (fare lo spoglio di) go through; **~ qualcuno di un diritto** divest somebody of a right

spogliarel'lista *nf* strip-tease artist, stripper

spoglia'rello *nm* strip-tease

spogli'arsi *vr* strip, undress

spoglia'toio *nm* (in piscina, palestra) locker room; Sport changing room; (guardaroba) cloakroom, checkroom Am

'spoglio [1] *adj* undressed; ‹albero, muro› bare; **~ di** (privo) stripped of [2] *nm* (scrutinio) perusal

'spoiler *nm inv* Auto spoiler

'spola *nf* shuttle; **fare la ~** shuttle

spo'letta *nf* spool

spolmo'narsi *vr* shout oneself hoarse

spol'pare *vt* take the flesh off; fig fleece

spolve'rare *vt* dust; fam devour ‹cibo›

'sponda *nf* (di mare, lago) shore; (di fiume) bank; (bordo) edge
■ **sponda posteriore ribaltabile** Auto tailgate

sponsoriz'zare *vt* sponsor

sponsorizzazi'one *nf* sponsorship

spontaneità *nf* spontaneity
spon'taneo *adj* spontaneous
'spooling *nm* Comput spooling
spopola'mento *nm* depopulation
spopo'lare ⟨1⟩ *vt* depopulate
⟨2⟩ *vi* (avere successo) draw the crowds
spopo'larsi *vr* become depopulated
'spora *nf* spore
sporadica'mente *adv* sporadically
spo'radico *adj* sporadic
sporcacci'one, -a *nmf* dirty pig
spor'care *vt* dirty; (macchiare) soil
spor'carsi *vr* get dirty
spor'cizia *nf* dirt
✈ **'sporco** ⟨1⟩ *adj* dirty; (macchiato) soiled; avere la coscienza sporca have a guilty conscience
⟨2⟩ *nm* dirt
spor'gente *adj* jutting, protruding; ha i denti sporgenti fam she has goofy teeth
spor'genza *nf* projection
'sporgere ⟨1⟩ *vt* stretch out; ~ querela contro take legal action against
⟨2⟩ *vi* jut out
'sporgersi *vr* lean out
✈ **sport** *nm inv* sport; fare qualcosa per ~ do something for fun
■ sport estremi *pl* extreme sports; sport invernali *pl* winter sports
'sporta *nf* shopping basket
spor'tello *nm* door; (di banca ecc) window
■ sportello automatico cash dispenser, cash point, cash machine, hole-in-the-wall; sportello della biglietteria ticket window; sportello pacchi parcels counter
✈ **spor'tivo, -a** ⟨1⟩ *adj* sports *attrib*; ⟨persona⟩ sporty
⟨2⟩ *nm* sportsman
⟨3⟩ *nf* sportswoman
'sporto *pp di* SPORGERE
✈ **'sposa** *nf* bride; dare in ~ give in marriage, give away; prendere in ~ marry
sposa'lizio *nm* wedding
✈ **spo'sare** *vt* marry; fig espouse
spo'sarsi *vr* get married; ⟨vino⟩ go (con with)
spo'sato *adj* married
spo'sini *nmpl* newly-weds
'sposo *nm* bridegroom; sposi *pl* [novelli] newlyweds
spossa'tezza *nf* exhaustion
spos'sato *adj* exhausted, worn out
sposses'sato *adj* dispossessed
sposta'mento *nm* displacement
■ spostamento d'aria airflow
✈ **spo'stare** *vt* move; (differire) postpone; (cambiare) change
spo'starsi *vr* move
spo'stato, -a ⟨1⟩ *adj* ill-adjusted

⟨2⟩ *nmf* (disadattato) misfit
spot *nm inv*
■ spot [pubblicitario] commercial
S.P.R. *abbr* (si prega rispondere) RSVP
'spranga *nf* bar
spran'gare *vt* bar
'sprazzo *nm* (di colore) splash; (di luce) flash; fig glimmer
spre'care *vt* waste
'spreco *nm* waste
spre'cone *adj* spendthrift
spre'gevole *adj* despicable
spregia'tivo *adj* pejorative
'spregio *nm* contempt; fare uno ~ a qualcuno offend somebody
spregiudi'cato *adj* unprejudiced; pej unscrupulous
'spremere *vt* squeeze
'spremersi *vr* ~ le meningi rack one's brains
spremi'aglio *nm inv* garlic press
spremia'grumi *nm inv* lemon squeezer
spremili'moni *nm inv* lemon squeezer
spre'muta *nf* juice
■ spremuta d'arancia fresh orange [juice], freshly squeezed orange juice
spre'tato *nm* former priest
sprez'zante *adj* contemptuous
sprigio'nare *vt* emit
sprigio'narsi *vr* burst out
sprint *nm* sprint; fare uno ~ put on a spurt
spriz'zare *vt/i* spurt; be bursting with ⟨salute, gioia⟩
sprofon'dare *vi* sink; (crollare) collapse
sprofon'darsi *vr* ~ in sink into; fig be engrossed in
spron *nm* ▶ SPRONE
spro'nare *vt* spur on
'sprone *nm* spur; (sartoria) yoke; a spron battuto instantly; andare a spron battuto go hell-for-leather
sproporzio'nato *adj* disproportionate
sproporzi'one *nf* disproportion
spropo'sitato *adj* full of blunders; (enorme) huge
spro'posito *nm* blunder; (eccesso) excessive amount; a ~ inopportunely
sprovve'duto *adj* unprepared; ~ di lacking in
sprov'visto *adj* ~ di out of; lacking in ⟨fantasia, pazienza⟩; alla sprovvista unexpectedly
spruz'zare *vt* sprinkle; (vaporizzare) spray; (inzaccherare) spatter
spruzza'tore *nm* spray
'spruzzo *nm* spray; (di fango) splash
spudorata'mente *adv* shamelessly
spudora'tezza *nf* shamelessness

✈ indicates a very frequent word

spudo'rato *adj* shameless

'spugna *nf* sponge; (tessuto) towelling

spu'gnoso *adj* spongy

'spuma *nf* foam; (schiuma) froth; Culin mousse

spu'mante *nm* sparkling wine, spumante

spumeggi'ante *adj* bubbly; ‹mare› foaming

spumeggi'are *vi* ‹champagne› bubble; ‹birra› foam

'spunta *nf*
■ segno di spunta tick

⚔ **spun'tare** [1] *vt* (rompere la punta di) break the point of; trim ‹capelli›; ‹lista, elenco› check off; **spuntarla** fig win
[2] *vi* ‹pianta› sprout; ‹capelli› begin to grow; (sorgere) rise; (apparire) appear

spun'tarsi *vr* get blunt

spun'tata *nf* trim

spun'tino *nm* snack

'spunto *nm* cue; fig starting point; **dare ~ a** give rise to

spur'gare *vt* purge

spur'garsi *vr* Med expectorate

'spurio *adj* spurious

spu'tacchio *nm* spittle

spu'tare *vt/i* spit; spit out ‹cibo›; **~ sentenze** pass judgement; **~ l'osso** *sl* spit it out

'sputo *nm* spit

⚔ **'squadra** *nf* (gruppo) team, squad; (di polizia ecc) squad; (da disegno) square; **lavoro di squadra** teamwork
■ squadra del buoncostume Vice Squad; squadra mobile Flying Squad; squadra narcotici Drug Squad; squadra di soccorso rescue team

squa'drare *vt* square; (guardare) look up and down

squa'driglia *nf*, **squadriglione** *nm* squadron

squa'drone *nm* squadron

squagli'are *vt* melt

squagli'arsi *vr* melt; **squagliarsela** fam (svignarsela) steal out

squa'lifica *nf* disqualification

squalifi'care *vt* disqualify

'squallido *adj* squalid

squal'lore *nm* squalor

'squalo *nm* shark

'squama *nf* scale; (di pelle) flake

squa'mare *vt* scale

squa'marsi *vr* ‹pelle› flake off

squa'moso *adj* scaly; ‹pelle› flaky

squarcia'gola: **a ~** *adv* at the top of one's voice

squarci'are *vt* rip

'squarcio *nm* rip; (di ferita, in nave) gash; (di cielo) patch

squar'tare *vt* quarter; dismember ‹animale›

squarta'tore *nm* **Jack lo ~** Jack the Ripper

squash *nm inv* squash

squas'sare *vt* shake

squattri'nato *adj* penniless

squaw *nf inv* squaw

squilib'rare *vt* unbalance

squili'brato, -a [1] *adj* unbalanced [2] *nmf* lunatic

squi'librio *nm* imbalance

squil'lante *adj* shrill

squil'lare *vi* ‹campana› peal; ‹tromba› blare; ‹telefono› ring

'squillo *nm* blare; Teleph ring

squinter'nato *adj* anche fig crazy

squisi'tezza *nf* refinement

squi'sito *adj* exquisite; fam (pietanza) yummy

squit'tire *vi* fig ‹pappagallo› squawk; ‹topo› squeak

sradi'care *vt* uproot; eradicate ‹vizio, male›

sragio'nare *vi* rave

sregola'tezza *nf* dissipation

srego'lato *adj* inordinate; (dissoluto) dissolute

s.r.l. *abbr* (**società a responsabilità limitata**) Ltd

sroto'lare *vt* uncoil

ss *abbr* (**seguenti**) following

SS (a) *abbr* (**strada statale**) national road (b) *abbr* (**Santissimo**) Most Holy

sst *int* sh!

'stabile [1] *adj* stable; (permanente) lasting; ‹saldo› steady
■ compagnia stabile Theat repertory company
[2] *nm* (edificio) building

stabili'mento *nm* factory; (industriale) plant; (edificio) establishment
■ stabilimento balneare lido

⚔ **stabi'lire** *vt* establish; (decidere) decide

stabi'lirsi *vr* settle

stabilità *nf* stability

stabi'lito *adj* established

stabiliz'zare *vt* stabilize

stabiliz'zarsi *vr* stabilize

stabilizza'tore *nm* stabilizer

stacano'vista *nmf* workaholic

⚔ **stac'care** [1] *vt* detach; pronounce clearly ‹parole›; (separare) separate; turn off ‹corrente›; **~ gli occhi da** take one's eyes off [2] *vi* fam (finire di lavorare) knock off

stac'carsi *vr* come off; **~ da** break away from ‹partito, famiglia›; **si stacca alle cinque** knocking off time is five o'clock

staccata'mente *adv* staccato

stac'cato *adj* Mus staccato

staccio'nata nf fence

'stacco nm gap

'stadio nm stadium, sports ground

'staffa nf stirrup; **perdere le staffe** fig fly off the handle

staf'fetta nf Sport relay [race], Mil dispatch rider

staffet'tista nmf Sport relay runner

stagio'nale adj seasonal

stagio'nare vt season ‹legno›; mature ‹formaggio›

stagio'nato adj ‹legno› seasoned; ‹formaggio› matured

stagiona'tura nf (di legno) seasoning; (di formaggio) maturation, maturing

◆ **stagi'one** nf season; **di** ~ in season; **fuori** ~ out of season
  ■ **alta/bassa stagione** high/low season; **stagione lirica** opera season; **stagione delle piogge** rainy season

stagli'arsi vr stand out

sta'gnante adj stagnant

sta'gnare ① vt (saldare) solder; (chiudere ermeticamente) seal
  ② vi ‹acqua› stagnate

'stagno ① adj (a tenuta d'acqua) watertight
  ② nm (acqua ferma) pond; (metallo) tin

sta'gnola nf tinfoil

stalag'mite nf stalagmite

stalat'tite nf stalactite

◆ **'stalla** nf stable; (per buoi) cowshed

stalli'ere nm groom

stal'lone nm stallion

◆ **sta'mani, stamat'tina** adv this morning

stam'becco nm ibex

stam'berga nf hovel

◆ **'stampa** nf Typ printing; (giornali, giornalisti) press; (riproduzione) print; **stampe** (postale) printed matter
  ■ **stampa fronte retro** two-sided printing, duplex printing; **stampa scandalistica** gutter press, tabloid press

stam'pante nf printer
  ■ **stampante ad aghi** dot matrix printer; **stampante a getto d'inchiostro** inkjet printer; **stampante laser** laser printer; **stampante a matrice di punti** dot matrix printer; **stampante seriale** serial printer; **stampante termica** thermal printer

stam'pare vt print

stampa'tello nm block letters pl, block capitals pl

stam'pato ① adj printed
  ② nm leaflet; Comput hard copy, printout; (modulo) print; **stampati** (pubblicità) promotional literature

stam'pella nf crutch

stampigli'are vt stamp

◆ indicates a very frequent word

stampiglia'tura nf stamping; (dicitura) stamp

stam'pino nm stencil

'stampo nm mould; **di vecchio** ~ ‹persona› of the old school

sta'nare vt drive out

stan'care vt tire; (annoiare) bore

stan'carsi vr get tired

stan'chezza nf tiredness

◆ **'stanco** adj tired; ~ **di** (stufo) fed up with; ~ **morto** dead tired, knackered fam

stand nm inv stand

'standard adj & nm inv standard

standardiz'zare vt standardize

standardizzazi'one nf standardization

'stand-by adj inv stand-by

'stanga nf bar; (persona) beanpole

stan'gare vt fam fail ‹studente›; (con le tasse ecc) clobber

stan'gata nf fig blow; fam (nel calcio) big kick; **prendere una** ~ fam (agli esami, economica) come a cropper

stan'ghetta nf (di occhiali) leg

◆ **sta'notte** nf tonight; (la notte scorsa) last night

'stante prep on account of; **a sé** ~ separate

stan'tio adj stale

stan'tuffo nm piston

◆ **'stanza** nf room; (metrica) stanza
  ■ **stanza dei giochi** games room; **stanza da pranzo** dining room

stanzia'mento nm allocation

stanzi'are vt allocate

stan'zino nm walk-in cupboard

stap'pare vt uncork

star nf inv (del cinema, dello sport) star

◆ **'stare** vi (rimanere) stay; (abitare) live; (con gerundio) be; **sto solo cinque minuti** I'll stay only five minutes; **sto in piazza Peyron** I live in Peyron Square; **sta dormendo** he's sleeping; ~ **a** (attenersi) keep to; (spettare) be up to; ~ **bene** (economicamente) be well off; (di salute) be well; (addirsi) suit; **sta bene!** that's fine!; ~ **dietro a** (seguire) follow; (sorvegliare) keep an eye on; (corteggiare) run after; ~ **in piedi** stand; ~ **per** be about to; ~ **sempre a fare qualcosa** be always doing something; **ben ti sta!** it serves you right!; **come stai/ sta?** how are you?; **lasciar** ~ leave alone; **starci** (essere contenuto) go into; (essere d'accordo) agree; **il 3 nel 12 ci sta 4 volte** 3 into 12 goes 4; **non sa** ~ **agli scherzi** he can't take a joke; ~ **su** (con la schiena) sit up straight; ~ **sulle proprie** keep oneself to oneself

'starna nf partridge

starnaz'zare vi quack; fig shriek

starnu'tire vi sneeze

star'nuto nm sneeze

◆ **'starsene** vr (rimanere) stay

'starter *nm inv* choke

sta'sera *adv* this evening, tonight

'stasi *nf* stasis

sta'tale [1] *adj* state *attrib*
[2] *nmf* state employee, civil servant
[3] *nf* (strada) main road, trunk road

'statico *adj* static

sta'tista *nm* statesman

sta'tistica *nf* statistics *sg*

sta'tistico *adj* statistical

'Stati 'Uniti [d'America] *nmpl* gli ∼ ∼ the United States [of America]

'stato [1] *pp di* ESSERE, STARE
[2] *nm* state; (posizione sociale) position; Jur status; **lo Stato** Pol the state
■ **stato d'animo** frame of mind; **stato di attesa** Comput wait state; **stato canaglia** rogue state; **stato civile** marital status; **stato cuscinetto** buffer state; **Stato Maggiore** Mil General Staff; **stato di salute** state of health

stato-nazi'one *nm* nation-state

'statua *nf* statue
■ **statua di cera** waxwork

statu'ario *adj* statuesque

statuni'tense [1] *adj* United States *attrib*, US *attrib*
[2] *nmf* citizen of the United States, US citizen

sta'tura *nf* height; **di alta ∼** tall; **di bassa ∼** short; **di media ∼** of average height
■ **statura morale** moral stature

sta'tuto *nm* statute

sta'volta *adv* this time

stazio'nario *adj* stationary

stazi'one *nf* station; (città) resort
■ **stazione degli autobus** bus station; **stazione balneare** seaside resort; **stazione climatica** health resort; **stazione ferroviaria** railway station (*Br*), train station; **stazione marittima** ferry terminal; **stazione master** Comput master station; **stazione multimediale** Comput multimedia station; **stazione dei pullman** coach station (*Br*), bus station; **stazione radiofonica** radio station; **stazione di servizio** petrol station (*Br*), service station; **stazione slave** Comput slave station; **stazione spaziale** space station; **stazione termale** spa, health resort

'stecca *nf* stick; (di ombrello) rib; (da biliardo) cue; Med splint; (di sigarette) carton; (di reggiseno) stiffener; **fare una ∼** Mus fluff a note

stec'cato *nm* fence

stec'chino *nm* cocktail stick

stec'chito *adj* skinny; (rigido) stiff; (morto) stone cold dead

'stele *nf* stele

'stella *nf* star; **salire alle stelle** (prezzi) rise sky-high, rocket
■ **stella alpina** edelweiss; **stella cadente** shooting star; **stella del cinema** movie star; **stella cometa** comet; **stella filante** streamer; **stella di mare** starfish; **stella polare** Pole Star, North Star

stel'lare *adj* star *attrib*; (grandezza) stellar

stel'lato *adj* starry

stel'lina *nf* starlet

'stelo *nm* stem
■ **lampada a stelo** standard lamp (*Br*), floor lamp

'stemma *nm* coat of arms

stempe'rare *vt* dilute

stempi'ato *adj* bald at the temples

sten'dardo *nm* standard

'stendere *vt* spread out; (appendere) hang out; (distendere) stretch [out]; (scrivere) write down

'stendersi *vr* stretch out

stendibianche'ria *nm inv* clothes horse

stendi'toio *nm* clothes horse

stenodattilogra'fia *nf* shorthand typing

stenodatti'lografo, -a *nmf* shorthand typist

stenogra'fare *vt* take down in shorthand

stenogra'fia *nf* shorthand

sten'tare *vi* ∼ **a** find it hard to

sten'tato *adj* laboured

'stento *nm* (fatica) effort; **a ∼** with difficulty; **stenti** *pl* hardships, privations

'step *nm inv* step aerobics *sg*

'steppa *nf* steppe

'sterco *nm* dung

stereo[fonico] *adj* stereo[phonic]

stereo'scopico *adj* stereoscopic

stereoti'pato *adj* stereotyped; (sorriso) insincere

stere'otipo *nm* stereotype

'sterile *adj* sterile; (terreno) barren

sterilità *nf* sterility

steriliz'zare *vt* sterilize

sterilizzazi'one *nf* sterilization

ster'lina *nf* pound
■ **lira sterlina** [pound] sterling

stermi'nare *vt* exterminate

stermi'nato *adj* immense

ster'minio *nm* extermination

'sterno *nm* breastbone

sternu'tire, sternuto = STARNUTIRE, STARNUTO

ste'roide *nm* steroid

ster'paglia *nf* brushwood

ster'rare *vt* excavate; dig up (strada)

ster'rato [1] *adj* (strada) dug up
[2] *nm* excavation; (di strada) digging up

ster'zare *vi* steer

'sterzo *nm* steering; (volante) steering wheel

S

'steso pp di STENDERE

♂ **'stesso** ⓵ *adj* same; **io** ~ myself; **tu** ~ yourself; **me** ~ myself; **se** ~ himself; **in quel momento** ~ at that very moment; **è stato ricevuto dalla stessa regina** (in persona) he was received by the Queen herself; **tuo fratello** ~ **dice che hai torto** even your brother says you're wrong; **l'ho visto coi miei stessi occhi** I saw it with my own eyes; **con le mie stesse mani** with my own hands; **è venuto il giorno** ~ he came the same day, he came that very day; **lo farò oggi** ~ I'll do it straight away today

⓶ *pron* **lo** ~ the same one; (la stessa cosa) the same; **fa lo** ~ it's all the same; **ci vado lo** ~ I'll go just the same

ste'sura *nf* drawing up; (documento) draft

steto'scopio *nm* stethoscope

'steward *nm inv* steward, air steward

stick *nm inv*
■ **colla a stick** glue stick; **deodorante in stick** stick deodorant

stiepi'dire *vt* warm

'stigma *nm* stigma

'stigmate *nfpl* stigmata

sti'lare *vt* draw up

'stile *nm* style; **in grande** ~ in style; **essere nello** ~ **di qualcuno** be typical of somebody, be just like somebody
■ **stile libero** (nel nuoto) freestyle, crawl; **stile di vita** life style

sti'lista *nmf* [fashion] designer; (parrucchiere) stylist

stiliz'zato *adj* stylized

'stilla *nf* drop

stil'lare *vi* ooze

stilo'grafica *nf* fountain pen

stilo'grafico *adj* **penna stilografica** fountain pen

'stima *nf* esteem; (valutazione) estimate

sti'mare *vt* esteem; (valutare) estimate; (ritenere) consider

sti'marsi *vr* consider oneself

sti'mato *adj* well-thought-of

stimo'lante ⓵ *adj* stimulating
⓶ *nm* stimulant

stimo'lare *vt* stimulate; (incitare) incite

'stimolo *nm* stimulus; (fitta) pang

'stinco *nm* shin; **non è uno** ~ **di santo** fam he's no saint

'stingere *vt/i* fade

'stingersi *vr* fade

'stinto pp di STINGERE

sti'pare *vt* cram

sti'parsi *vr* crowd together

stipendi'are *vt* pay a salary to

stipendi'ato ⓵ *adj* salaried
⓶ *nm* salaried worker

sti'pendio *nm* salary
■ **stipendio base** basic salary; **stipendio iniziale** starting salary

'stipite *nm* doorpost

stipu'lare *vt* stipulate

stipulazi'one *nf* stipulation; (accordo) agreement

stira'mento *nm* sprain

sti'rare *vt* iron; (distendere) stretch

sti'rarsi *vr* (distendersi) stretch; pull ‹muscolo›

stira'tura *nf* ironing

'stiro *nm*
■ **ferro da stiro** iron

'stirpe *nf* stock

stiti'chezza *nf* constipation

'stitico *adj* constipated

'stiva *nf* Naut hold

sti'vale *nm* boot; **lo Stivale** (Italia) Italy; **stivali** *pl* **di gomma** Wellington boots, Wellingtons; **poeta dei miei stivali!** fam poet my eye!, poet my foot!

stiva'letto *nm* ankle boot

stiva'lone *nm* high boot; **stivaloni** *pl* **da caccia** hunting boots; **stivaloni** *pl* **di gomma** waders

sti'vare *vt* load

'stizza *nf* anger

stiz'zire *vt* irritate

stiz'zirsi *vr* become irritated

stiz'zito *adj* irritated

stiz'zoso *adj* peevish

stocca'fisso *nm* stockfish

stoc'cata *nf* stab; (battuta pungente) gibe

Stoc'colma *nf* Stockholm

stock *nm* Comm stock

'stock-car *nm inv* stock car

♂ **'stoffa** *nf* material; fig stuff; **avere** ~ have what it takes

stoi'cismo *nm* stoicism

'stoico *adj & nm* stoic

sto'ino *nm* doormat

'stola *nf* stole

'stolido *adj* stolid

'stolto *adj* foolish

stoma'chevole *adj* revolting

♂ **'stomaco** *nm* stomach
■ **mal di stomaco** stomachache

stoma'tite *nf* stomatitis

sto'nare ⓵ *vt/i* sing/play out of tune
⓶ *vi* (non intonarsi) clash

sto'nato *adj* out of tune; (discordante) clashing; (confuso) bewildered

stona'tura *nf* false note; (discordanza) clash

stop *nm inv* (segnale stradale) stop sign; (in telegramma) stop

stop'pare *vt* stop

'stopper *nm* Sport fullback

'stoppia *nf* stubble
stop'pino *nm* wick
stop'poso *adj* tough
'storcere *vt* twist
'storcersi *vr* twist
stor'dire *vt* stun; (intontire) daze
stor'dirsi *vr* dull one's senses
stor'dito *adj* stunned; (intontito) dazed; (sventato) heedless
⚜ **'storia** *nf* history; (racconto, bugia) story; (pretesto) excuse; **senza storie!** no fuss!; **fare [delle] storie** make a fuss
 ■ **storia d'amore** love story; **storia di vita vissuta** human interest story
⚜ **'storico** ① *adj* historical; (di importanza storica) historic
 ② *nm* historian
stori'ella *nf* fam little story
storiogra'fia *nf* historiography
stori'ografo *nm* historiographer
stori'one *nm* sturgeon
'stormo *nm* flock
stor'nare *vt* avert; transfer ‹somma›
'storno *nm* starling
storpi'are *vt* cripple; mangle ‹parole›
storpia'tura *nf* deformation
'storpio, -a ① *adj* crippled
 ② *nmf* cripple
'storta *nf* (distorsione) sprain; **prendere una ~ alla caviglia** sprain one's ankle
'storto ① pp di STORCERE
 ② *adj* crooked; (ritorto) twisted; ‹gambe› bandy; fig wrong
stor'tura *nf* deformity; **~ mentale** twisted way of thinking
sto'viglie *nfpl* crockery *sg*, flatware Am
'strabico *adj* cross-eyed; **essere ~** be cross-eyed, [have a] squint
strabili'ante *adj* astonishing
strabili'are *vt* astonish
stra'bismo *nm* squint
straboc'care *vi* overflow
strabuz'zare *vt* **~ gli occhi** goggle; **ha strabuzzato gli occhi** his eyes popped out of his head
straca'narsi *vr* fam work like a slave, slave away
stra'carico *adj* overloaded
strac'chino *nm* soft cheese from Lombardy
stracci'are *vt* tear; fam (vincere) thrash
straccia'tella *nf* vanilla ice cream with chocolate chips
stracci'ato *adj* torn; ‹persona› in rags; ‹prezzi› slashed; **a un prezzo ~** at a knock-down price, dirt cheap
'straccio ① *adj* torn
 ② *nm* rag; (strofinaccio) cloth; **essere ridotto ad uno ~** feel like a wet rag
stracci'one *nm* tramp

stracci'vendolo *nm* ragman
stracol'larsi *vr* sprain
stra'cotto ① *adj* overdone; fam (innamorato) head over heels
 ② *nm* stew
⚜ **'strada** *nf* road; (di città) street; fig (cammino) way; **essere fuori ~** be on the wrong track; **fare ~** lead the way; **tener la macchina in ~** keep the car on the road; (parcheggiare) keep the car on the street; **su ~** ‹trasportare› by road; **farsi ~** (aver successo) make one's way [in the world]
 ■ **strada d'accesso** approach road; **strada camionabile** road for heavy vehicles; **strada maestra** main road; **strada pedonale** pedestrianized street; **strada principale** main road; **strada privata** private road; **strada secondaria** secondary road; **strada a senso unico** one-way street; **strada senza uscita** dead end, cul-de-sac; **strada di terra battuta** dirt track
⚜ **stra'dale** ① *adj* road *attrib*
 ② *nf* **la Stradale** fam traffic police
stra'dario *nm* street plan
stra'dina *nf* little street; (in campagna) little road
strafalci'one *nm* blunder
stra'fare *vi* overdo it, overdo things
stra'foro: **di ~** *adv* on the sly
strafot'tente *adj* arrogant
strafot'tenza *nf* arrogance
'strage *nf* slaughter
stra'grande *adj* vast
stralci'are *vt* remove
'stralcio *nm* removal; (parte) extract
stralu'nare *vt* **~ gli occhi** open one's eyes wide
stralu'nato *adj* ‹occhi› staring; ‹persona› distraught
stramaz'zare *vi* fall heavily; **~ al suolo** crash to the ground
strambe'ria *nf* oddity
'strambo *adj* strange
strampa'lato *adj* odd
stra'nezza *nf* strangeness
strango'lare *vt* strangle
⚜ **strani'ero, -a** ① *adj* foreign
 ② *nmf* foreigner
⚜ **'strano** *adj* strange; **~ ma vero** surprisingly enough, funnily enough
straordinaria'mente *adv* extraordinarily
⚜ **straordi'nario** *adj* extraordinary; (notevole) remarkable; ‹edizione› special
 ■ **lavoro straordinario** overtime; **treno straordinario** special [train]
strapaz'zare *vt* ill-treat; scramble ‹uova›
strapaz'zarsi *vr* tire oneself out
stra'pazzo *nm* strain; **da ~** fig worthless
strapi'eno *adj* overflowing

S

strapi'ombo *nm* projection; **a ∼** sheer

strapo'tere *nm* overwhelming power

strappa'lacrime *adj inv* weepy

♂ **strap'pare** *vt* tear; (per distruggere) tear up; pull out ‹*dente, capelli*›; (sradicare) pull up; (estorcere) wring

strap'parsi *vr* get torn; (allontanarsi) tear oneself away; **∼ i capelli** fig be tearing one's hair out

'strappo *nm* tear; (strattone) jerk; fam (passaggio) lift; **fare uno ∼ alla regola** make an exception to the rule
■ **strappo muscolare** muscle strain

strapun'tino *nm* folding seat

strari'pare *vi* flood

strasci'care *vt* trail; shuffle ‹*piedi*›; drawl ‹*parole*›

'strascico *nm* train; fig after-effect

strasci'coni: **a ∼** *adv* dragging one's feet

straseco'lare *vi* be amazed

strass *nm inv* rhinestone

strata'gemma *nm* stratagem

stra'tega *nmf* strategist

strate'gia *nf* strategy

stra'tegico *adj* strategic; **mossa strategica** strategic move

stratifi'care *vt* stratify

stratigra'fia *nf* Geol stratigraphy

'strato *nm* layer; (di vernice ecc) coat, layer; (roccioso, sociale) stratum
■ **strato di nuvole** cloud layer

strato'sfera *nf* stratosphere

strato'sferico *adj* stratospheric; fig sky-high

stravac'carsi *vr* fam slouch

stravac'cato *adj* fam slouching

strava'gante *adj* extravagant; (eccentrico) eccentric

strava'ganza *nf* extravagance; (eccentricità) eccentricity

stra'vecchio *adj* ancient

strave'dere *vt* **∼ per** worship

stravizi'are *vi* indulge oneself

stra'vizio *nm* excess

stra'volgere *vt* twist; (turbare) upset

stravolgi'mento *nm* twisting

stra'volto *adj* distraught; fam (stanco) done in

strazi'ante *adj* heartrending; ‹*dolore*› agonizing

strazi'are *vt* grate on ‹*orecchie*›; break ‹*cuore*›

'strazio *nm* agony; **essere uno ∼** be agony; **che ∼!** fam it's awful!; **fare ∼ di qualcosa** ‹*fam: attore, cantante*› murder something

'streamer *nm inv* Comput streamer

'strega *nf* witch

---

stre'gare *vt* bewitch

stre'gone *nm* wizard

stregone'ria *nf* witchcraft

'stregua *nf* **alla ∼ di** in the same way as; **alla stessa ∼** ‹*giudicare*› by the same yardstick; **a questa ∼** at this rate

stre'mare *vt* exhaust

stre'mato *adj* exhausted

'stremo **1** *adj* extreme
2 *nm* **ridotto allo ∼** at the end of one's tether

'strenna *nf* present

'strenuo *adj* strenuous

strepi'tare *vi* make a din

strepi'tio *nm* din, uproar

strepi'toso *adj* noisy; fig resounding

strepto'cocco *nm* Med streptococcus

streptomi'cina *nf* Med streptomycin

stress *nm inv* stress

stres'sante *adj* ‹*lavoro, situazione*› stressful

stres'sare *vt* put under stress, be stressful for

stres'sarsi *vr* get stressed

stres'sato *adj* stressed [out]

'stretta *nf* grasp, squeeze; (dolore) pang; **essere alle strette** be in dire straits; **mettere alle strette qualcuno** have somebody's back up against the wall; **provare una ∼ al cuore** feel a pang
■ **stretta creditizia** credit crunch; **stretta di mano** handshake

stret'tezza *nf* narrowness; **stret'tezze** *pl* (difficoltà finanziarie) financial difficulties

'stretto **1** *pp di* STRINGERE
2 *adj* narrow; (serrato) tight; (vicino) close; ‹*dialetto*› broad; (rigoroso) strict; **lo ∼ necessario** the bare minimum
3 *nm* Geog strait
■ **stretto di Messina** Straits of Messina

stret'toia *nf* bottleneck; fam (difficoltà) tight spot

stri'ato *adj* striped

stria'tura *nf* streak

stri'dente *adj* strident

'stridere *vi* squeak; fig clash

stri'dore *nm* screech

'stridulo *adj* shrill

strigli'are *vt* groom

strigli'ata *nf* grooming; fig dressing down

stril'lare *vi/t* scream

'strillo *nm* scream

stril'lone *nm* newspaper seller

strimin'zito *adj* skimpy; (magro) skinny

strimpel'lare *vt* strum

stri'nare *vt* singe, scorch

'stringa *nf* lace; Comput string

strin'gato *adj* fig terse

♂ **'stringere** ⃞1 *vt* press; (serrare) squeeze; (tenere stretto) hold tight; take in ‹abito›; (comprimere) be tight; (restringere) tighten; ∼ **la mano a** shake hands with
⃞2 *vi* (premere) press

'stringersi *vr* (accostarsi) draw close (**a** to); (avvicinarsi) squeeze up

strip'pata *nf* fam nosh-up; **farsi una** ∼ have a nosh-up

strip-'tease *nm* striptease

'striscia *nf* strip; (riga) stripe; **a strisce** striped; **strisce** *pl* **di mezzeria** Auto lane markings; **strisce** *pl* **[pedonali]** zebra crossing *sg*, crosswalk Am

strisci'are ⃞1 *vi* crawl; (sfiorare) graze
⃞2 *vt* drag ‹piedi›

strisci'arsi *vr* ∼ **a** rub against

strisci'ata *nf* scratch

'striscio *nm* graze; Med smear; **colpire di** ∼ graze

strisci'one *nm* banner

strito'lare *vt* grind

strizzacer'velli *nmf* sl shrink

striz'zare *vt* squeeze; (torcere) wring [out]; ∼ **l'occhio** wink

'strofa *nf* strophe

strofi'naccio *nm* cloth; (per spolverare) duster
■ **strofinaccio da cucina** tea towel; **strofinaccio per i piatti** dishtowel

strofi'nare *vt* rub

strofi'nio *nm* rubbing

strom'bare *vt* splay

strombaz'zare ⃞1 *vt* boast about
⃞2 *vi* hoot

strombaz'zata *nf* (di clacson) hoot

stron'care *vt* cut off; (reprimere) crush; (criticare) tear to shreds

stron'zate *nfpl* vulg crap

'stronzo *nm* vulg shit

stropicci'are *vt* rub; crumple ‹vestito›

stropicci'ata *nf* rub

stro'piccio *nm* rubbing

stroppi'are *vt* **il troppo stroppia** enough is as good as a feast

stroz'zare *vt* strangle

strozza'tura *nf* strangling; (di strada) narrowing

strozzi'naggio *nm* loan-sharking

stroz'zino *nm* pej usurer; (truffatore) shark

struc'cante *nm* make-up remover

struc'carsi *vr* remove one's make-up

strug'gente *adj* all-consuming

'struggersi *vr* (liter) pine [away]; ∼ **di invidia/desiderio** be consumed with envy/ desire

strugg'mento *nm* yearning

strumen'tale *adj* instrumental

strumentaliz'zare *vt* make use of

strumen'tario *nm* instruments *pl*

strumentazi'one *nf* instrumentation

strumen'tista *nm* instrumentalist

stru'mento *nm* instrument; (arnese) tool
■ **strumento a corda/fiato** string/wind instrument; **strumento musicale** musical instrument; **strumento a percussione** percussion instrument

strusci'are *vt* rub

strusci'arsi *vr* ‹gatto› rub itself; ‹due innamorati› caress each other; ∼ **intorno a qualcuno** fam suck up to somebody

'strutto *nm* lard

strut'tura *nf* structure

struttu'rale *adj* structural

struttura'lismo *nm* structuralism

struttural'mente *adv* structurally

struttu'rare *vt* structure

strutturazi'one *nf* structuring

'struzzo *nm* ostrich

stuc'care *vt* plaster; (per decorazione) stucco; put putty in ‹vetri›

stucca'tore *nm* plasterer; (decorativo) stucco worker

stucca'tura *nf* plastering; (decorativo) stucco work

stuc'chevole *adj* nauseating

'stucco *nm* plaster; (decorativo) stucco; (per vetro) putty; **rimanere di** ∼ be thunder-struck

♂ **stu'dente, studentessa** *nmf* student; (di scuola) schoolboy; schoolgirl

studen'tesco *adj* student; (di scolaro) school *attrib*

♂ **studi'are** *vt* study

studi'arsi *vr* ∼ **di** try to

♂ **'studio** *nm* studying; (stanza, ricerca) study; (di artista, TV ecc) studio; (di professionista) office
■ **studio cinematografico** film studio; **studio dentistico** dental surgery

studi'oso, -a ⃞1 *adj* studious
⃞2 *nmf* scholar

'stufa *nf* stove
■ **stufa elettrica** electric fire; **stufa a gas** gas fire; **stufa a legna** wood-[burning] stove

stu'fare *vt* Culin stew; (dare fastidio) bore

stu'farsi *vr* get bored

stu'fato *nm* stew

'stufo *adj* bored; **essere** ∼ **di** be bored with, be fed up with

stu'oia *nf* mat

stu'olo *nm* crowd

stupefa'cente ⃞1 *adj* amazing
⃞2 *nm* drug

stupe'fare *vt* stun

♂ **stu'pendo** *adj* stupendous; ∼ **!** brilliant!

stupi'daggine *nf* (azione) stupid thing; (cosa da poco) nothing; **non dire stupidaggini!** don't talk stupid!

stupi'data *nf* stupid thing

S

stupidità *nf* stupidity

✔ **'stupido** *adj* stupid

stu'pire [1] *vt* astonish
[2] *vi* be astonished

stu'pirsi *vr* be astonished

stu'pore *nm* amazement

stu'prare *vt* rape

stupra'tore *nm* rapist

'stupro *nm* rape

sturabot'tiglie *nm inv* corkscrew

sturalavan'dini *nm inv* plunger

stu'rare *vt* uncork; unblock ‹*lavandino*›

stuzzica'denti *nm inv* toothpick

stuzzi'care *vt* prod [at]; pick ‹*denti*›; poke ‹*fuoco*›; (molestare) tease; whet ‹*appetito*›

stuzzi'chino *nm* Culin appetizer

✔ **su** [1] *prep* on; (senza contatto) over; (riguardo a) about; (circa, intorno a) about, around; **le chiavi sono sul tavolo** the keys are on the table; **il quadro è appeso sul camino** the picture is hanging over the fireplace; **un libro sull'antico Egitto** a book on *or* about Ancient Egypt; **sarò lì sulle cinque** I'll be there about five, I'll be there around five; **è durato sulle tre ore** it lasted for about three hours; **costa sui 75 euro** it costs about 75 euros; **decidere sul momento** decide at the time; **su commissione** on commission; **su due piedi** on the spot; **su misura** made to measure; **uno su dieci** one out of ten; **stare sulle proprie** keep oneself to oneself; **sul mare** ‹*casa*› by the sea
[2] *adv* (sopra) up; (al piano di sopra) upstairs; (addosso) on; **andare su** go up; (al piano di sopra) go upstairs; **ho su il cappotto** I've got my coat on; **in su** ‹*guardare*› up; **dalla vita in su** from the waist up; **su!** come on!

sua'dente *adj* persuasive

sub *nmf inv* skin-diver

sub+ *pref* sub+

su'bacqueo, -a [1] *adj* underwater
[2] *nmf* skin-diver

subaffit'tare *vt* sublet

subaf'fitto *nm* sublet; **in ~** sublet

suba'gente *nm* subagent

subal'terno *adj & nm* subordinate

subappal'tare *vt* subcontract

subappalta|'tore, -trice *nmf* subcontractor

subap'palto *nm* subcontract; **in ~** subcontracted; **dare in ~** subcontract; **prendere in ~** take on a subcontract basis

sub'buglio *nm* turmoil

sub'conscio *adj & nm* subconscious

subconti'nente *nm* subcontinent

subcosci'ente *adj & nm* subconscious

subdi'rectory *nf* Comput subdirectory

subdola'mente *adv* deviously

'subdolo *adj* devious, underhand

suben'trare *vi* ‹*circostanze*› come up; **~ a** take the place of

su'bentro *nm* changeover

subequatori'ale *adj* subequatorial

✔ **su'bire** *vt* undergo; (patire) suffer

subis'sare *vt* fig **~ di** overwhelm with

subi'taneo *adj* sudden

✔ **'subito** *adv* at once, immediately, right away; **~ dopo** straight after; **vengo ~** I'll be right there

subli'mare *vt* sublimate

su'blime *adj* sublime

sublimi'nale *adj* subliminal

sublingu'ale *adj* sublingual

sublo'care *vt* sublease

subloca'tario *nm* sublessor

sublocazi'one *nf* sublease

subnor'male *adj* subnormal

subodo'rare *vt* suspect

subordi'nare *vt* subordinate

subordi'nato, -a *adj & nmf* subordinate

su'bordine *nm* **in ~** second in order of importance

subrou'tine *nf* Comput subroutine

subsi'denza *nf* Geol subsidence

sub'strato *nm* substratum, substrate

subto'tale *nm* subtotal

subtropi'cale *adj* subtropical

subu'mano *adj* subhuman

subur'bano *adj* suburban

✔ **suc'cedere** *vi* (accadere) happen; **~ a** (in carica) succeed; (venire dopo) follow; **~ al trono** succeed to the throne

suc'cedersi *vr* happen one after the other; **si sono succeduti molti …** there was a series of …

successi'one *nf* succession; **in ~** in succession

successiva'mente *adv* subsequently

succes'sivo *adj* successive; ‹*mese, giorno*› following

✔ **suc'cesso** [1] *pp di* SUCCEDERE
[2] *nm* success; (esito) outcome; (disco ecc) hit

succes'sone *nm* huge success

succes'sore *nm* successor

succhi'are *vt* suck [up]; **~ il sangue a qualcuno** fig bleed somebody dry

succhi'ello *nm* gimlet

succinta'mente *adv* succinctly

suc'cinto *adj* (conciso) concise; ‹*abito*› scanty

'succo *nm* juice; fig essence
■ **succo d'arancia** orange juice; **succo di frutta** fruit juice; **succo di limone** lemon juice

suc'coso *adj* juicy

'succube *nm* essere **~ di qualcuno** be totally dominated by somebody

---

✔ indicates a very frequent word

s

succu'lento *adj* succulent

succur'sale *nf* branch [office]

⚔ **sud** *nm* south; **del ∼** southern; **a ∼ di** [to the] south of

Sud'africa *nm* South Africa

sudafri'cano *adj & nmf* South African

Suda'merica *nf* South America

sudameri'cano, -a *adj & nmf* South American

Su'dan *nm* **il ∼** the Sudan

suda'nese *adj & nmf* Sudanese

su'dare *vi* sweat, perspire; (faticare) sweat blood; **∼ freddo** be in a cold sweat; **∼ sangue** sweat blood; **mi fa ∼ freddo** it brings me out in a cold sweat; **∼ sette camicie** sweat blood

su'data *nf* anche fig sweat

suda'ticcio *adj* sweaty

su'dato *adj* sweaty; ‹vittoria› hard-won; ‹pane› hard-earned

sud'detto *adj* above-mentioned

'suddito, -a *nmf* subject

suddi'videre *vt* subdivide

suddivisi'one *nf* subdivision

su'd-est *nm* southeast

'sudicio *adj* dirty, filthy

sudici'ume *nm* dirt, filth

sudocciden'tale *adj* southwestern

su'doku *nm inv* sudoku, sudoku puzzle

sudorazi'one *nf* perspiring

su'dore *nm* sweat, perspiration; fig sweat; **in un bagno di ∼** bathed in sweat; **con il ∼ della fronte** fig by the sweat of one's brow
■ **sudore freddo** cold sweat

sudo'riparo *adj* sweat *attrib*

su'd-ovest *nm* southwest

'sue ▶ SUO

⚔ **suffici'ente** 1 *adj* sufficient; (presuntuoso) conceited
2 *nm* bare essentials *pl*; Sch pass mark

suffici'enza *nf* sufficiency; (presunzione) conceit; Sch pass; **a ∼** enough; **prendere la ∼** get the pass-mark

suf'fisso *nm* suffix

sufflè *nm* Culin soufflé

suffra'getta *nf* suffragette

suf'fragio *nm* (voto) vote; **in ∼ di qualcuno** in homage to
■ **suffragio universale** universal suffrage

suffu'migio *nm* inhalation

suggel'lare *vt* seal

suggeri'mento *nm* suggestion

sugge'rire *vt* suggest; Theat prompt

suggeri|'tore, -trice *nmf* Theat prompter

suggestio'nabile *adj* suggestible

suggestio'nare *vt* influence

suggestio'nato *adj* influenced

suggesti'one *nf* influence

sugge'stivo *adj* suggestive; ‹musica ecc› evocative

'sughero *nm* cork

'sugli = SU + GLI

'sugo *nm* (di frutta) juice; (di carne) gravy; (salsa) sauce; (sostanza) substance

'sui = SU + I

sui'cida 1 *adj* suicidal
2 *nmf* suicide

suici'darsi *vr* commit suicide

sui'cidio *nm* anche fig suicide; **commettere ∼** commit suicide; **tentato ∼** attempted suicide

su'ino 1 *adj* **carne suina** pork
2 *nm* swine

suite *nf* suite

sul = SU + IL

sulfa'midico *nm* sulphonamide/sulpha drug

sul'fureo *adj* sulphuric

'sulla = SU + LA

'sulle = SU + LE

'sullo = SU + LO

sul'tana *nf* (persona) sultana

sulta'nina *adj* **uva ∼** sultana

sul'tano *nm* sultan

'sunto *nm* summary

⚔ **'suo, -a** 1 *poss adj* **il suo, i suoi, la sua, le sue** (di lui) his; (di lei) her; (di cosa o animale) its; (forma di cortesia) your; **questa macchina è sua** this car is his/hers; **∼ padre** his/her/your father; **un ∼ amico** a friend of his/hers/yours
2 *poss pron*; **il suo, i suoi, la sua, le sue** (di lui) his; (di lei) hers; (di cosa o animale) its; (forma di cortesia) yours; **i suoi** his/her folk[s]

su'ocera *nf* mother-in-law

su'ocero *nm* father-in-law

su'oi ▶ SUO

su'ola *nf* sole; **suole** *pl* **di para** crepe soles

su'olo *nm* ground; (terreno) soil
■ **suolo pubblico** public land

⚔ **suo'nare** 1 *vt* Mus play; ring ‹campanello›; sound ‹allarme, clacson›; ‹orologio› strike ‹ore›; **∼ il clacson** sound the horn, hoot the horn; fam (imbrogliare) do
2 *vi* ‹campanello, telefono, sveglia› ring; ‹clacson› hoot; ‹sirena› go [off]; ‹giradischi› play

suo'nato *adj* fam bonkers

suona|'tore, -trice *nmf* player

suone'ria *nf* alarm; (di cellulare) ringtone

⚔ **su'ono** *nm* sound

su'ora *nf* nun; **Suor Maria** Sister Maria

'super *nf* 4-star [petrol], premium [gas] Am

super+ *pref* super+

supe'rabile *adj* surmountable

superal'colico 1 *nm* spirit
2 *adj* **bevande superalcoliche** spirits

S

supera'mento *nm* (di timidezza) overcoming; (di esame) success (**di** in)

🗸 **supe'rare** *vt* surpass; (eccedere) exceed; (vincere) overcome; overtake, pass Am ‹*veicolo*›; pass ‹*esame*›; **~ la barriera del suono** break the sound barrier; **~ se stessi** surpass oneself; **ha superato la trentina** he's over thirty

su'perbia *nf* haughtiness

su'perbo *adj* haughty; (magnifico) superb

super'donna *nf* superwoman

superdo'tato *adj* highly gifted, super-talented

superfici'ale [1] *adj* superficial
[2] *nmf* superficial person

superficialità *nf* superficiality

🗸 **super'ficie** *nf* surface; (area) area; **in ~** on the surface; fig ‹*esaminare*› superficially

su'perfluo *adj* superfluous

Super-'Io *nm* Psych superego

superi'ora *nf* superior; Relig mother superior

🗸 **superi'ore** [1] *adj* superior; (di grado) senior; (più elevato) higher; (sovrastante) upper; (al di sopra) above
[2] *nm* superior

superiorità *nf* superiority

superla'tivo *adj* & *nm* superlative

supermer'cato *nm* supermarket

supermo'della *nf* supermodel

super'nova *nf* Astr supernova

superpetroli'era *nf* Naut supertanker

superpo'tenza *nf* superpower

super'sonico *adj* supersonic

su'perstite [1] *adj* surviving
[2] *nmf* survivor

superstizi'one *nf* superstition

superstizi'oso *adj* superstitious

super'strada *nf* toll-free motorway
■ **superstrada informatica** information superhighway

superu'omo *nm* superman

superu'tente *nm* Comput superuser

supervalu'tare *vt* overvalue

supervalutazi'one *nf* overvaluation

supervisi'one *nf* supervision

supervi'sore *nm* supervisor

su'pino *adj* supine

suppel'lettili *nfpl* furnishings

suppergiù *adv* about

supplemen'tare *adj* additional, supplementary

supple'mento *nm* supplement
■ **supplemento illustrato** colour supplement; **supplemento rapido** express train supplement

sup'plente [1] *adj* temporary

[2] *nmf* Sch supply teacher

sup'plenza *nf* temporary post

'supplica *nf* plea; (domanda) petition

🗸 **suppli'care** *vt* beg

suppli'chevole *adj* imploring

sup'plire [1] *vt* replace
[2] *vi* **~ a** (compensare) make up for

sup'plizio *nm* torture

sup'porre *vt* suppose

supportare *vt* Comput support

sup'porto *nm* support
■ **supporto di sistema** Comput system support

supposizi'one *nf* supposition

sup'posta *nf* suppository

sup'posto *pp di* SUPPORRE

suppu'rare *vi* fester

suppurazi'one *nf* suppuration; **andare in ~** fester

suprema'zia *nf* supremacy

su'premo *adj* supreme

surclas'sare *vt* outclass

surf *nm* surfboard; (sport) surfboarding

sur'fista *nmf* surfer

surge'lare *vt* deep-freeze

surge'lato [1] *adj* frozen
[2] *nm* **surgelati** *pl* frozen food *sg*

Suri'name *nm* Surinam

'surplus *nm* surplus

surre'ale *adj* surreal

surrea'lismo *nm* surrealism

surrea'lista *nmf* surrealist

surrea'listico *adj* surrealist

surre'nale *adj* adrenal

surriscal'dare *vt* overheat

surriscal'darsi *vr* overheat

surro'gato *nm* substitute

suscet'tibile *adj* touchy

suscettibilità *nf* touchiness

🗸 **susci'tare** *vt* stir up; arouse ‹*ammirazione ecc*›

su'sina *nf* plum
■ **susina selvatica** damson

su'sino *nm* plumtree

su'spense *nf* suspense

sussegu'ente *adj* subsequent

sussegu'irsi *vr* follow one after the other

sussidi'are *vt* subsidize

sussidi'ario *adj* subsidiary

sus'sidio *nm* subsidy; (aiuto) aid
■ **sussidio didattico** study aid; **sussidio di disoccupazione** unemployment benefit; **sussidio di malattia** sickness benefit

sussi'ego *nm* haughtiness; **con ~** haughtily

sussi'stenza *nf* subsistence

sus'sistere *vi* subsist; (essere valido) hold good

s

🗸 indicates a very frequent word

sussul'tare *vi* start; **far ~ qualcuno** give somebody a start

sus'sulto *nm* start

sussur'rare *vt/i* whisper; **si sussurra che …** it is rumoured that …

sussur'rio *nm* murmur

sus'surro *nm* whisper

su'tura *nf* suture

sutu'rare *vt* suture

suv, SUV *nm inv* SUV

suv'via *int* come on!

sva'gare *vt* amuse

sva'garsi *vr* amuse oneself

'svago *nm* relaxation; (divertimento) amusement; **prendersi un po' di ~** have a break

svaligi'are *vt* rob; burgle ‹casa›

svalu'tare *vt* devalue; fig underestimate

svalu'tarsi *vr* lose value

svalutazi'one *nf* devaluation

svam'pito, -a *nmf* airhead

sva'nire *vi* vanish

sva'nito, -a [1] *adj* ‹persona› absent-minded; ‹sapore, sogno› faded [2] *nmf* absent-minded person

svantaggi'ato *adj* at a disadvantage; ‹bambino, paese› disadvantaged

svan'taggio *nm* disadvantage; **essere in ~** Sport be losing; **in ~ di tre punti** three points down; **in ~ rispetto a qualcuno** at a disadvantage compared with somebody

svantaggi'oso *adj* disadvantageous

svapo'rare *vi* evaporate

svari'ato *adj* varied

svari'one *nm* blunder

sva'sare *vt* splay; flare ‹gonna›

sva'sato *adj* ‹gonna› flared

svasa'tura *nf* flare

'svastica *nf* swastika

sve'dese [1] *adj & nm* (lingua) Swedish [2] *nmf* Swede

'sveglia *nf* ‹orologio› alarm [clock]; **~!** get up!; **mettere la ~** set the alarm [clock] ■ **sveglia automatica** alarm call; **sveglia telefonica** wake-up call

✎ **svegli'are** *vt* wake up; fig awaken; **~ l'appetito a qualcuno** whet somebody's appetite

svegli'arsi *vr* wake up

'sveglio *adj* awake; (di mente) alert, sharp

sve'lare *vt* reveal

svel'tezza *nf* speed; fig quick-wittedness

svel'tire *vt* quicken

svel'tirsi *vr* ‹persona› liven up

✎ **'svelto** *adj* quick; (slanciato) svelte; **alla svelta** quickly; **a passo ~** quickly

sve'narsi *vr* slash one's wrists; fig reduce oneself to poverty

'svendere *vt* undersell

'svendita *nf* [clearance] sale

sve'nevole *adj* sentimental

sveni'mento *nm* fainting fit

sve'nire *vi* faint; **da ~** incredibly

sven'tare *vt* foil

sven'tato [1] *adj* thoughtless [2] *nmf* thoughtless person

'sventola *nf* slap ■ **orecchie a sventola** protruding ears, jug-handle ears fam

svento'lare *vt/i* wave

svento'larsi *vr* fan oneself

svento'lio *nm* flutter

sventra'mento *nm* disembowelment; (di pollo) gutting; fig (di edificio) demolition ‹edificio›

sven'trare *vt* disembowel; gut ‹pollo›; fig demolish ‹edificio›

sven'tura *nf* misfortune

sventu'rato *adj* unfortunate

sve'nuto *pp* di SVENIRE

svergi'naro *vt* deflower

svergo'gnato *adj* shameless

sver'nare *vi* winter

svernici'ante *nm* paint stripper

svernici'are *vt* strip

sve'stire *vt* undress

sve'stirsi *vr* undress, get undressed

svet'tare *vi* ‹albero, torre› stand out; **~ verso il cielo** stretch skywards

'Svezia *nf* Sweden

svezza'mento *nm* weaning

svez'zare *vt* wean

svi'are *vt* divert; (corrompere) lead astray

svi'arsi *vr* fig go astray

svico'lare *vi* turn down a side street; fig (dalla questione ecc) evade the issue; fig (da una persona) dodge out of the way

svi'gnarsela *vr* slip away

svigo'rire *vt* emasculate

svili'mento *nm* debasement

svi'lire *vt* debase

✎ **svilup'pare** *vt* develop

svilup'parsi *vr* develop

sviluppa|'tore, -trice *nmf* developer ■ **sviluppatore web** web developer

✎ **svi'luppo** *nm* development ■ **paese in via di sviluppo** developing country

svinco'lare *vt* release; clear ‹merce›; redeem ‹deposito›

svinco'larsi *vr* free oneself

'svincolo *nm* clearance; (di autostrada) exit; **~ di un deposito cauzionale** redemption of a deposit

svioli'nata *nf* fawning

svisce'rare *vt* gut; fig dissect

svisce'rato *adj* ‹amore› passionate; (ossequioso) obsequious

'svista *nf* oversight

svi'tare *vt* unscrew

svi'tato *adj* fam (matto) cracked, nutty

'svizzera *nf* hamburger

'Svizzera *nf* Switzerland

↙ **'svizzero, -a** *adj & nmf* Swiss

svoglia'taggine *nf* laziness; (riluttanza) unwillingness

svogli'atamente *adv* half-heartedly; (senza energia) listlessly

svoglia'tezza *nf* half-heartedness; (mancanza di energia) listlessness

svogli'ato *adj* half-hearted; (senza energic) listless

svolaz'zante *adj* ‹capelli› wind-swept

svolaz'zare *vi* flutter

svolaz'zio *nm* flutter

↙ **'svolgere** *vt* unwind; unwrap ‹pacco›; (risolvere) solve; (portare a termine) carry out; (sviluppare) develop

'svolgersi *vr* (accadere) take place

svolgi'mento *nm* course; (sviluppo) development

'svolta *nf* turning; fig turning-point

svol'tare *vi* turn

'svolto pp di SVOLGERE

svuo'tare *vt* empty [out]; fig (di significato) deprive

'Swaziland *nm* Swaziland

swing *nm* Mus swing

switch *nm* Comput switch

Tt

T *abbr* (**tabaccheria**) tobacconist's

tabac'caio, -a *nmf* tobacconist

tabacche'ria *nf* tobacconist's (which also sells stamps, postcards etc)

↙ **ta'bacco** *nm* tobacco; **tabacchi** *pl* cigarettes and tobacco

taba'gismo *nm* nicotine addiction

ta'bella *nf* table; (lista) list

■ **tabella di conversione** conversion table; **tabella di marcia** fig schedule; **tabella dei prezzi** price list; **tabella retributiva** salary scale

tabel'lina *nf* Math multiplication table

tabel'lone *nm* wall chart

■ **tabellone degli arrivi** arrivals board; **tabellone del canestro** backboard; **tabellone delle partenze** departures board; **tabellone segnapunti** scoreboard

taber'nacolo *nm* tabernacle

tabù *adj & nm inv* taboo

tabu'lare *vt* tabulate

tabu'lato *nm* Comput [data] printout

tabula'tore *nm* tabulator

tabulazi'one *nf* tabulation

TAC *nf abbr* (**tomografia assiale computerizzata**) CAT scan

'tacca *nf* notch; **di mezza ~** ‹attore› (giornalista) second-rate

taccagne'ria *nf* penny-pinching

tac'cagno *adj* fam stingy

taccheggia|'tore, -trice *nmf* shoplifter

tac'cheggio *nm* shoplifting

tac'chetto *nm* Sport stud

tac'chino *nm* turkey

tacci'are *vt* **~ qualcuno di qualcosa** accuse somebody of something

'tacco *nm* heel; **alzare i tacchi** take to one's heels; **scarpe senza ~** flat shoes, flats; **colpo di tacco** backheel

■ **tacchi a spillo** *pl* stiletto heels, stilettos

taccu'ino *nm* notebook

↙ **ta'cere** ⊞ *vi* be silent ⊡ *vt* say nothing about; **mettere a ~** qualcosa ‹scandalo› hush something up; **mettere a ~ qualcuno** silence somebody

tachicar'dia *nf* tachycardia

ta'chigrafo *nm* tachograph

ta'chimetro *nm* speedometer

tacita'mente *adv* tacitly; (in silenzio) silently

'tacito *adj* tacit, unspoken; (silenzioso) silent

taci'turno *adj* taciturn

ta'fano *nm* horsefly

taffe'ruglio *nm* scuffle

taffettà *nm* taffeta

'taglia *nf* (riscatto) ransom; (ricompensa) reward; (statura) height; (di abiti) size; **per taglie forti** outsize, OS

■ **taglia unica** one size

taglia'carte *nm inv* paperknife

'taglia e in'colla *nm inv* cut and paste; **fare un ~** cut and paste

taglia'erba *nm inv* lawnmower

tagliafu'oco ⊞ *adj inv* ■ **porta ~** fire door; **striscia ~** fire break ⊡ *nm inv* (in bosco) fire break

tagli'ando *nm* coupon; **fare il ∼** put one's car in for its MOT

■ **tagliando di controllo** manufacturer's sticker; (da raccogliere) token; **tagliando controllo bagaglio** baggage claim sticker; **tagliando di garanzia** warranty

taglia'pasta ⟦1⟧ *adj inv* **rotella ∼** pastry cutter

⟦2⟧ *nm inv* pastry cutter

tagliapa'tate *nm inv* potato peeler

⚔ **tagli'are** ⟦1⟧ *vt* cut; (attraversare) cut across; cut off ⟨telefono, elettricità⟩; carve ⟨carne⟩; mow ⟨erba⟩; **farsi ∼ i capelli** have a haircut, have one's hair cut; **∼ i viveri a qualcuno** stop somebody's allowance

⟦2⟧ *vi* cut

tagli'arsi *vr* cut oneself; **∼ il dito** cut one's finger; **∼ i capelli** have a haircut, have one's hair cut

taglia'sigari *nm inv* cigar cutter

tagll'ata *nf* finely-cut beef fillet; **dare una ∼ a qualcosa** give something a cut, cut something

tagli'ato *adj* (a pezzi) jointed; **essere ∼ per qualcosa** fig be cut out for something

taglia'unghie *nm inv* nail clippers *pl*

taglieggi'are *vt* extort money from

tagli'ente ⟦1⟧ *adj* sharp

⟦2⟧ *nm* cutting edge

tagli'ere *nm* chopping board

■ **∼ per il pane** breadboard

taglie'rina *nf* (per carta) guillotine; (per foto) trimmer; (per metallo, vetro) cutter

'taglio *nm* cut; (di stoffa) length; (di capelli) [hair-]cut; (parte tagliente) cutting edge; **di ∼** edgeways; **a doppio ∼** fig double-edged; **dacci un ∼!** fam put a sock in it!

■ **taglio e cucito** dressmaking; **taglio di carne** cut of meat; **taglio cesareo** Caesarean section; **taglio di personale** personnel cut; **taglio dei prezzi** price cutting; **taglio alla spesa** spending cut

tagli'ola *nf* trap

taglio'lini *nmpl* thin soup noodles

tagli'one *nm*

■ **legge del taglione** an eye for an eye and a tooth for a tooth

tagliuz'zare *vt* cut into small pieces

tail'leur *nm inv* [lady's] suit

Tai'wan *nf* Taiwan

ta'lare *adj* **prendere la veste ∼** take holy orders

talassotera'pia *nf therapy based on seawater*

'talco *nm* talcum powder, talc

⚔ **'tale** ⟦1⟧ *adj* such a; (con nomi plurali) such; **c'è un ∼ disordine** there is such a mess; **non accetto tali scuse** I won't accept such excuses; **è un ∼ bugiardo!** he's such a liar!; **il rumore era ∼ che non si sentiva nulla** there was so much noise you couldn't hear

yourself think; **il ∼ giorno** on such and such a day; **vai il tal giorno alla tal ora** go on such a day at such a time; **quel tal signore** that gentleman; **∼ padre ∼ figlio** like father like son; **∼ quale** just like

⟦2⟧ *pron* **un ∼** someone; **quel ∼** that man; **il tal dei tali** such and such a person

ta'lea *nf* cutting

tale'bano *adj & nm* Taliban

ta'lento *nm* talent

'talent scout *nmf inv* talent scout

tali'smano *nm* talisman

tallo'nare *vt* be hot on the heels of

tallon'cino *nm* coupon

■ **talloncino del prezzo** price tag

tal'lone *nm* heel

■ **tallone di Achille** fig Achilles' heel; **tallone aureo** Econ gold standard

⚔ **tal'mente** *adv* so

ta'lora *adj* – TALVOLTA

'talpa *nf* mole

tal'volta *adv* sometimes

tamburel'lare *vi* (con le dita) drum; (pioggia) beat, drum

tambu'rello *nm* tambourine

tambu'rino *nm* drummer

tam'buro *nm* drum

■ **tamburo del freno** brake drum

tame'rice *nf* tamarisk

'tamia *nm inv* chipmunk

Ta'migi *nm* Thames

tampona'mento *nm* Auto collision; (di ferita) dressing, (di falla) plugging

■ **tamponamento a catena** pile-up

tampo'nare *vt* (urtare) crash into, plug ⟨falla⟩; dress ⟨ferita⟩

tam'pone *nm* swab; (per timbri) pad; (per mestruazioni) tampon; (per treni, Comput) buffer

tam'tam *nm inv* bush telegraph

TAN *abbr* (**tasso annuale nominale**) Fin AER

'tana *nf* den

'tandem *nm inv* tandem; **in ∼** (lavorare) in tandem

'tanfo *nm* stench

'tanga *nm inv* tanga

tan'gente ⟦1⟧ *adj* tangent

⟦2⟧ *nf* tangent; (somma) bribe

tangen'topoli *nf widespread corruption in Italy in the early 90s*

tangenzi'ale *nf* orbital road

tan'gibile *adj* tangible

tangibil'mente *adv* tangibly

'tango *nm inv* tango

ta'nica *nf* (contenitore) jerry can; (serbatoio di nave) tank

■ **tanica di benzina** petrol can

tan'nino *nm* tannin

tan'tino: **un ∼** *adv* a little [bit]

✓ **'tanto** ☐1 *adj* [so] much; (con nomi plurali) [so] many, [such] a lot of; ∼ **tempo** [such] a long time; **non ha tanta pazienza** he doesn't have much patience; ∼ **tempo quanto ti serve** as much time as you need; **tanti amici quanti parenti** as many friends as relatives
☐2 *pron* much; (plurale) many; (tanto tempo) much time; **è un uomo come tanti** he's just an ordinary man; **tanti** (molte persone) many people; **non ci vuole così** ∼ it doesn't take that long; ∼ **quanto** as much as; **tanti quanti** as many as
☐3 *conj* (comunque) anyway, in any case
☐4 *adv* (così) so; (con verbi) so much; **è** ∼ **debole che non sta in piedi** he's so weak that he can't stand; **è** ∼ **ingenuo da crederle** he's naive enough to believe her; **di** ∼ **in** ∼ every now and then; ∼ **l'uno come l'altro** both; ∼ **quanto** as much as; **non è** ∼ **intelligente quanto suo padre** he's not as intelligent as his father; **tre volte** ∼ three times as much; **una volta** ∼ once in a while; ∼ **meglio così!** so much the better!; **tant'è** so much so; ∼ **vale che andiamo a casa** we might as well go home; ∼ **per cambiare** for a change

Tan'zania *nf* Tanzania

tapi'oca *nf* tapioca

ta'piro *nm* tapir

ta'pis rou'lant *nm inv* conveyor belt

'tappa *nf* (parte di viaggio) stage; **fare** ∼ **a** break one's journey in

tappa'buchi *nm inv* stopgap

tap'pare *vt* plug; cork ‹bottiglia›; ∼ **la bocca a qualcuno** fam shut somebody up

tappa'rella *nf* fam roller blind; **tirar su la** ∼ pull the blind up

tap'parsi *vr* ∼ **gli occhi** cover one's eyes; ∼ **il naso** hold one's nose; ∼ **le orecchie** put one's fingers in one's ears

tappe'tino *nm* mat; Comput mouse mat
■ **tappetino antiscivolo** [anti-slip] safety bathmat; **tappetino da bagno** bathmat

tap'peto *nm* carpet; (piccolo) rug; **andare al** ∼ (pugilato) hit the canvas; **mandare qualcuno al** ∼ knock somebody down; **bombardamento a tappeto** carpet bombing
■ **tappeto erboso** lawn; **tappeto persiano** Persian carpet; **tappeto stradale** road surface; **tappeto verde** (tavolo) card table; **tappeto volante** magic carpet

tappez'zare *vt* paper ‹pareti›; (con manifesti) cover

tappezze'ria *nf* tapestry; (di carta) wallpaper; (arte) upholstery; **fare da** ∼ fig be a wallflower

tappezzi'ere *nm* upholsterer; (imbianchino) decorator

'tappo *nm* plug; (di sughero) cork; (di metallo, per penna) top; fam (persona piccola) dwarf

---

■ **tappo di bottiglia** bottle top; **tappo a corona** crown cap; **tappi per le orecchie** *pl* earplugs; **tappo salvagocce** anti-drip top; **tappo di scarico** [della coppa] sump drain plug; **tappo a strappo** ring-pull; **tappo di sughero** cork; **tappo a vite** screw top

'tara *nf* (difetto) flaw; (ereditaria) hereditary defect; (peso) tare

taran'tella *nf* tarantella

ta'rantola *nf* tarantula

ta'rare *vt* Techn calibrate; Comm discount

ta'rato *adj* Comm discounted; Techn calibrated; Med with a hereditary defect; fam crazy

tarchi'ato *adj* stocky

tar'dare ☐1 *vi* be late
☐2 *vt* delay

✓ **'tardi** *adv* late; **al più** ∼ at the latest; **più** ∼ later [on]; **sul** ∼ late in the day; **far** ∼ (essere in ritardo) be late; (con gli amici) stay up late; **a più** ∼ see you later; **svegliarsi troppo** ∼ oversleep

tardiva'mente *adv* late

tar'divo *adj* late; (bambino) retarded

'tardo *adj* slow; (pomeriggio, mattinata) late

'targa *nf* plate; Auto numberplate

tar'gato *adj* **un'auto targata...** a car with the registration number...

targ'hetta *nf* (su porta) nameplate; (sulla valigia) name tag
■ **targhetta di circolazione** numberplate; **targhetta commemorativa** memorial plaque; **targhetta stradale** street sign

ta'riffa *nf* rate, tariff; **a** ∼ **ridotta** Teleph offpeak
■ **tariffa aerea** airfare; **tariffa doganale** customs tariff; **tariffa ferroviaria** [rail] fares; **tariffa interna** inland postage; **tariffa ore di punta** peak rate; **tariffa professionale** [professional] fee; **tariffa telefonica** telephone charges; **tariffa unica** flat rate

tarif'fario ☐1 *adj* tariff (adv)
☐2 *nm* price list

tar'larsi *vr* get worm-eaten

tar'lato *adj* worm-eaten

'tarlo *nm* woodworm

'tarma *nf* moth

tar'marsi *vr* get moth-eaten

tarmi'cida *nm* moth-repellent

ta'rocco *nm* tarot; **tarocchi** *pl* tarot

tar'pare *vt* clip

tartagli'are *vi* stutter

'tartaro *adj & nm* tartar; **salsa tartara** tartar[e] sauce

tarta'ruga *nf* tortoise; (di mare) turtle; (per pettine ecc) tortoiseshell

tartas'sare *vt* (angariare) harass

tar'tina *nf* canapé

tar'tufo *nm* truffle

'tasca *nf* pocket; (in borsa) compartment; **da ~** pocket *attrib*; **avere le tasche piene di qualcosa** fam have had a bellyful of something; **se ne è stato con le mani in ~** fig he didn't lift a finger [to help]
- **tasca a battente** flap pocket; **tasca del nero** (di polpo, seppia) ink sac; **tasca da pasticciere** icing bag; **tasca tagliata** slit pocket; **tasca a toppa** patchpocket

ta'scabile ① *adj* pocket *attrib* ② *nm* paperback

tasca'pane *nm inv* haversack

ta'schino *nm* breast pocket

'tassa *nf* tax; (d'iscrizione ecc) fee; (doganale) duty
- **tassa di circolazione** road tax; **tassa di esportazione** export duty; **tassa d'iscrizione** registration fee; **tassa di soggiorno** tourist tax, visitors' tax; **tasse** *pl* **scholastiche** school fees; **tasse** *pl* **universitarie** tuition fees

tas'sabile *adj* taxable

tas'sametro *nm* meter

tas'sare *vt* tax

tassativa'mente *adv* without fail

tassa'tivo *adj* strict

tassazi'one *nf* taxation

tas'sello *nm* wedge; (di stoffa) gusset; (per legno, parete) rawlplug

tassì *nm inv* taxi

tas'sista *nmf* taxi driver

'tasso¹ *nm* Bot yew; (animale) badger

'tasso² *Comm* rate
- **tasso agevolato** cut rate; **prestito a ~ agevolato** soft loan; **tasso base** base rate; **tasso base di interesse** base lending rate; **tasso di cambio** exchange rate; **tasso di crescita** growth rate; **tasso di disoccupazione** unemployment rate; **tasso d'inquinamento** pollution level; **tasso di interesse** interest rate; **tasso di mortalità** death rate; **tasso di sconto** discount rate

ta'stare *vt* feel; **~ il terreno** fig test the water *or* ground

tasti'era *nf* keyboard
- **tastiera numerica** Comput numeric keypad; **telefono a tastiera** touch-tone telephone

tastie'rino *nm*
- **tastierino numerico** numeric keypad

tastie'rista *nmf* keyboarder

'tasto *nm* key; (tatto) touch
- **tasto Alt** Alt key; **tasto di cancellazione** delete key; **tasto control** Comput control key; **tasto cursore** Comput cursor key; **tasto delicato** fig touchy subject; **tasto eject** eject button; **tasto escape** escape key; **tasto funzione** Comput function key; **tasto numerico** Comput numeric[al] key; **tasto di ritorno a margine** return key; **tasto tabulatore** tab [key]

ta'stoni: a ~ *adv* gropingly; **camminare a ~** grope around; **cercare qualcosa a ~** grope for something

'tattica *nf* tactics *pl*

'tattico *adj* tactical

'tattile *adj* tactile

'tatto *nm* (senso) touch; (accortezza) tact; **aver ~** be tactful

tatu'aggio *nm* tattoo

tatu'are *vt* tattoo

tautolo'gia *nf* tautology

tauto'logico *adj* tautological

'tavola *nf* table; (illustrazione) plate; (asse) plank; **saper stare a ~** have good table manners; **calmo come una ~** (mare) like a mill pond
- **tavola calda** snackbar; **tavola fredda** salad bar; **tavola periodica degli elementi** periodic table; **tavola pitagorica** multiplication table; **tavola rotonda** fig round table; **tavola a vela** sailboard; **fare ~ a vela** sailboard, windsurf

tavo'lato *nm* (pavimento) wooden flooring

tavo'letta *nf* bar; (medicinale) tablet; **andare a ~** Auto drive flat out
- **tavoletta di cioccolata** chocolate bar; **tavoletta grafica** Comput digitizing tablet

tavo'lino *nm* [small] table; (da salotto) coffee table

'tavolo *nm* table
- **tavolo anatomico** mortuary table, slab fam; **tavolo da biliardo** pool table; **tavolo da cucina** kitchen table; **tavolo da gioco** card table; **tavolo operatorio** Med operating table; **tavolo da pranzo** dining-table

tavo'lozza *nf* palette

taxi *nm inv* taxi

'tazza *nf* cup; (del water) bowl
- **tazza da caffè/tè** coffee-cup/teacup

taz'zina *nf*
- **tazzina da caffè** espresso coffee cup

TBC *nf abbr* (**tubercolosi**) TB

T.C.I. *abbr* (**Touring Club Italiano**) *association promoting tourism nationally and internationally*

te *pers pron* you; **te l'ho dato** I gave it to you

tè *nm inv* tea
- **tè al latte** tea with milk; **tè al limone** lemon tea

TEAM *nf abbr* (**Tessera Europea di Assicurazione Malattia**) EHIC

tea'trale *adj* theatre *attrib*; (affettato) theatrical

te'atro *nm* theatre
- **teatro all'aperto** open-air theatre; **teatro lirico** opera [house]; **teatro neorealista** kitchen sink drama; **teatro di posa** Cinema set; **teatro tenda** *marquee for fashions shows, concerts etc.*

'techno *nf inv* techno (music)

'tecnico, -a ① *adj* technical ② *nmf* technician
- **tecnico elettronico** electronics engineer; **tecnico informatico** computer engineer;

⋯⟫

tecnico delle luci Cinema, TV gaffer; **tecnico delle riparazioni** repairman; **tecnico del suono** sound technician

③ *nf* technique

tec'nigrafo *nm* drawing board

tec'nocrate *nmf* technocrat

tec'nofobo *adj* technophobe

tecnolo'gia *nf* technology

tecno'logico *adj* technological

✦ **te'desco, -a** *adj & nmf* German

'tedio *nm* tedium

tedi'oso *adj* tedious

'TEE *nm abbr* (**treno espresso transeuropeo**) Trans-Europe-Express [train]

te'game *nm* saucepan; **uova al tegame** fried eggs

'teglia *nf* baking tin

'tegola *nf* tile; *fig* blow

tei'era *nf* teapot

te'ina *nf* theine

tek *nm* teak

tel. *abbr* (**telefono**) tel

'tela *nf* cloth; (per quadri, vele) canvas; Theat curtain

■ **tela cerata** oilcloth; **tela indiana** cheesecloth; **tela di iuta** hessian; **tela di lino** linen; **tela rigida** buckram

te'laio *nm* (di bicicletta, finestra) frame; Auto chassis; (per tessere) loom

'tele *nf* fam telly, TV

tele'camera *nf* television camera

telecoman'dato *adj* remote-controlled, remote control *attrib*

teleco'mando *nm* remote control

'Telecom I'talia *nf* Italian State telephone company

telecomunicazi'oni *nfpl* telecommunications, telecomms

teleconfe'renza *nf* teleconference

tele'cronaca *nf* [television] commentary; **fare la ∼ di** commentate on

■ **telecronaca diretta** live [television] coverage; **telecronaca registrata** recording

telecro'nista *nmf* television commentator

tele'ferica *nf* cableway

tele'film *nm inv* film [made] for television

■ **telefilm a episodi** series

✦ **telefo'nare** *vt/i* [tele]phone, ring

telefo'nata *nf* call, [tele]phone call; **fare una ∼** make a phone call

■ **telefonata anonima** nuisance call; **telefonata a carico del destinatario** reverse charge [phone] call; **fare una ∼ a carico [del destinatario]** reverse the charges; **telefonata interurbana** long-distance call; **telefonata di lavoro** business call; **telefonata in teleselezione** ≈ STD call; **telefonata urbana** local call

telefonica'mente *adv* by [tele]phone

tele'fonico *adj* [tele]phone *attrib*

telefo'nino *nm* mobile [phone]

telefo'nista *nmf* operator

✦ **te'lefono** *nm* [tele]phone; **numero di telefono** [tele]phone number

■ **telefono amico** the Samaritans; **telefono azzurro** children in need help line; **telefono cellulare** cell[ular] [tele]phone, mobile; **telefono cordless** cordless [phone]; **telefono interno** intercom; **telefono a monete** pay phone; **telefono pubblico** public telephone; **telefono rosso** Mil, Pol hotline; **telefono satellitare** satellite phone; **telefono a scatti** *telephone with call charges based on time-units*; **telefono a scheda** cardphone; **telefono a tastiera** push-button phone

tele'genico *adj* telegenic

telegior'nale *nm* television news

telegra'fare *vt* telegraph

telegra'fia *nf* telegraphy

telegrafica'mente *adv* (con telegrafo) by telegram

tele'grafico *adj* telegraphic; (risposta) monosyllabic; **sii ∼** keep it brief

te'legrafo *nm* telegraph

tele'gramma *nm* telegram

telela'voro *nm* teleworking

tele'matica *nf* data communications, telematics *sg*

teleno'vela *nf* soap opera

teleobiet'tivo *nm* telephoto lens

telepa'tia *nf* telepathy

tele'patico *adj* telepathic

tele'quiz *nm inv* TV quiz programme

teleradiotra'smettere *vt* simulcast

telero'manzo *nm* television serial

tele'schermo *nm* television screen

tele'scopio *nm* telescope

telescri'vente *nf* telex [machine]

teleselet'tivo *adj* direct dialling

teleselezi'one *nf* subscriber trunk dialling, STD; **chiamare in ∼** call direct, dial direct

■ **teleselezione internazionale** international direct dialling

telespetta|'tore, -trice *nmf* viewer; **i telespettatori** the viewing public

tele'text *nm* Teletext

'telethon *nm inv* telethon

Tele'video *nm* Teletext, Ceefax

televisi'one *nf* television; **guardare la ∼** watch television; **alla ∼** on television

■ **televisione ad alta definizione** high-definition television; **televisione in bianco e nero** black and white television; **televisione via cavo** cable TV; **televisione a circuito chiuso** closed-circuit television, CCTV; **televisione a colori** colour television; **televisione satellitare** satellite television

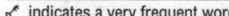

televi'sivo *adj* television, TV *attrib*; **apparecchio televisivo** television set; **operatore televisivo** television cameraman

televi'sore *nm* television [set], TV [set]
■ **televisore portatile** portable [TV], portable [television set]; **televisore con schermo panoramico** wide-screen TV

'telex ⒈ *nm inv* telex
⒉ *adj inv* telex *attrib*

tel'lurico *adj* telluric

'telo *nm* [piece of] cloth
■ **telo da bagno** beach towel; **telo di salvataggio** rescue blanket

'tema *nm* theme; Sch essay

te'matica *nf* main theme

teme'rario *adj* reckless

⚘ **te'mere** ⒈ *vt* be afraid of
⒉ *vi* be afraid

tem'paccio *nm* filthy weather

'tempera *nf* tempera; (pittura) painting in tempera

temperama'tite *nm inv* pencil-sharpener

tempera'mento *nm* temperament

tempe'rare *vt* temper; sharpen ‹matita›

tempe'rato *adj* temperate

⚘ **tempera'tura** *nf* temperature
■ **temperatura ambiente** room temperature

tempe'rino *nm* penknife

tem'pesta *nf* storm
■ **tempesta magnetica** magnetic storm; **tempesta di neve** snowstorm; **tempesta di sabbia** sandstorm

tempe'stare *vt* ~ qualcuno di colpi rain blows on somebody; ~ qualcuno di domande bombard somebody with questions

tempe'stato *adj* (anello, diadema) encrusted (di with)

tempestiva'mente *adv* quickly, in a short space of time

tempe'stivo *adj* timely, well-timed

tempe'stoso *adj* stormy

'tempia *nf* Anat temple

'tempio *nm* Relig temple

tem'pismo *nm* timing

⚘ **'tempo** *nm* time; (atmosferico) weather; Mus tempo; Gram tense; (di film) part; (di partita) half; **a suo ~** in due course; **~ fa** some time ago; **per molto ~, per tanto ~** for a long time; **tanto ~ fa** a long time ago; **un ~** once; **ha fatto il suo ~** it's out of date; **a ~ indeterminato** (contratto) permanent; **primo tempo** (di film, partita) first half
■ **tempo di accesso** Comput access time; **tempo di cottura** cooking time; **tempo di esposizione** Phot exposure time; **tempo libero** free time, leisure time; **tempo limite di accettazione** latest check-in time; **tempo di pace** peacetime; **tempo reale** Comput real time; **in tempo reale** real-time *attrib*; **tempo**

supplementare extra time; Sport extra time, overtime Am; **andare ai tempi supplementari** Sport go into extra time

tempo'rale ⒈ *adj* temporal
⒉ *nm* [thunder]storm

temporanea'mente *adv* temporarily

tempo'raneo *adj* temporary

temporeggi'are *vi* play for time

tem'prare *vt* form

te'nace *adj* tenacious, strong-willed

tenace'mente *adv* tenaciously

te'nacia *nf* tenacity

te'naglia *nf* pincers *pl*

'tenda *nf* curtain; (per campeggio) tent; (tendone) awning; **tirare le tende** draw the curtains
■ **tenda della doccia** shower curtain; **tenda a igloo** dome tent; **tenda a ossigeno** oxygen tent

ten'denza *nf* tendency
■ **tendenza al rialzo/ribasso** Fin bull/bear market

tendenzial'mente *adv* by nature

tendenzi'oso *adj* tendentious

⚘ **'tendere** ⒈ *vt* (allargare) stretch [out]; (tirare) tighten; (porgere) hold out; fig lay ‹trappola›
⒉ *vi* ~ a aim at; (essere portato a) tend to

'tendersi *vr* tauten

'tendine *nm* tendon
■ **tendine d'Achille** Achille's tendon; **tendine del garretto** hamstring; **tendine del ginocchio** hamstring

ten'done *nm* awning; (di circo) tent
■ **tendone del circo** big top

ten'dopoli *nf inv* tent city

'tenebre *nfpl* darkness

tene'broso ⒈ *adj* gloomy
⒉ *nm* **bel ~** dark and handsome man

⚘ **te'nente** *nm* lieutenant
■ **tenente colonnello** wing commander

tenera'mente *adv* tenderly

⚘ **te'nere** ⒈ *vt* hold; (mantenere) keep; (gestire) run; (prendere) take; (seguire) follow; (considerare) consider
⒉ *vi* hold; ~ **stretto** hold tight; ~ **a qualcosa** (oggetto) be fond of something; **tengo alla sua presenza** I very much want him to be there; ~ **per** (squadra) support

⚘ **te'rezza** *nf* tenderness

⚘ **'tenero** *adj* tender

tene'rone, -a *nmf* softie

te'nersi *vr* hold on (a to); (in una condizione) keep oneself; ~ **indietro** stand back

'tenia *nf* tapeworm

'tennis *nm* tennis
■ **tennis da tavolo** table tennis

ten'nista *nmf* tennis player

te'nore *nm* standard; Mus tenor; **a ~ di legge** by law

■ **tenore di vita** standard of living

tensi'one *nf* tension; Electr voltage; **mettere sotto ~** energize; **in ~** under stress

■ **alta tensione** high voltage; **tensione premestruale** premenstrual tension, PMT

ten'tacolo *nm* tentacle

⚘ **ten'tare** *vt* attempt; (sperimentare) try; (indurre in tentazione) tempt; **~ la strada di** make a foray *or* venture into

⚘ **tenta'tivo** *nm* attempt

ten'tato *adj* **~ suicidio** suicide attempt

tentazi'one *nf* temptation

tentenna'mento *nm* wavering; **ha avuto dei tentennamenti** he wavered a bit

tenten'nare *vi* waver

ten'toni *adv* **cercare qualcosa a ~** grope for something

'**tenue** *adj* fine; (debole) weak; (esiguo) small; (leggero) slight

te'nuta *nf* (capacità) capacity; Sport; (resistenza) stamina; (possedimento) estate; (divisa) uniform; (abbigliamento) clothes *pl*; **a ~ d'aria** airtight

■ **tenuta di strada** road holding

teolo'gia *nf* theology

teo'logico *adj* theological

te'ologo *nm* theologian

teo'rema *nm* theorem

teo'ria *nf* theory

■ **teoria del complotto** conspiracy theory

teorica'mente *adv* theoretically

te'orico *adj* theoretical

te'pore *nm* warmth

'**teppa** *nf* mob

tep'pismo *nm* hooliganism

tep'pista *nm* hooligan, yob fam

te'quila *nf inv* tequila

tera'peutico *adj* therapeutic

tera'pia *nf* therapy; **in ~** in therapy

■ **terapia genica** gene therapy; **terapia di gruppo** group therapy; **terapia intensiva** critical care; **terapia ormonale sostitutiva** hormone replacement therapy, HRT; **terapia d'urto** shock treatment

tergicri'stallo *nm* windscreen wiper, windshield wiper Am

tergilu'notto *nm* rear windscreen wiper

tergiver'sante *adj* equivocating, pussyfooting fam

tergiver'sare *vi* equivocate, pussyfoot around fam

'**tergo** *nm* **a ~** behind; **segue a ~** please turn over, PTO

teri'lene® *nm* Terylene®

'**terital**® *nm* Terylene®

ter'male *adj* thermal; **stazione termale** spa

'**terme** *nfpl* thermal baths

'**termico** *adj* thermal; **borsa termica** cool bag

'**terminal** *nm inv* air terminal

termi'nale *adj* & *nm* terminal; **malato terminale** terminally ill person

termina'lista *nmf* computer operator

⚘ **termi'nare** *vt/i* end, finish

terminazi'one *nf* (fine) termination; Gram ending

■ **terminazione nervosa** nerve ending

⚘ '**termine** *nm* (limite) limit; (fine) end; (condizione, parola) term; (scadenza) deadline; **ai termini della legge...** under the terms of act...; **contratto a termine** fixed-term contract

■ **termine di paragone** Gram term of comparison; **termine ultimo** final deadline

terminolo'gia *nf* terminology

'**termite** *nf* termite

termoco'perta *nf* electric blanket

termogra'fia *nf* thermal imaging

ter'mometro *nm* thermometer

'**termos** *nm inv* thermos®

termosi'fone *nm* radiator; (sistema) central heating

ter'mostato *nm* thermostat

termotera'pia *nf* Med heat treatment

termovalorizza'tore *nm* waste-to-energy plant

termoventila'tore *nm* fan heater

⚘ '**terra** *nf* earth; (regione) land; (terreno) ground; (argilla) clay; (cosmetico) bronzing powder; **a ~** (sulla costa) ashore; (installazioni) onshore; **essere a ~** (gomma) be flat; fig be at rock bottom; **per ~** on the ground; (su pavimento) on the floor; **sotto ~** underground; **far ~ bruciata** carry out a scorched earth policy

■ **terra promessa** Promised Land; **Terra Santa** Holy Land; **terra di Siena** sienna

terra'cotta *nf* terracotta; **vasellame di ~** earthenware

terra'ferma *nf* dry land

Terra'nova *nf* Newfoundland

terrapi'eno *nm* embankment

ter'razza *nf*, **terrazzo** *nm* balcony

terremo'tato, -a [1] *adj* (zona) affected by an earthquake

    [2] *nmf* earthquake victim

terre'moto *nm* earthquake

⚘ **ter'reno** [1] *adj* earthly

    [2] *nm* ground; (suolo) soil; (proprietà terriera) land; **perdere/guadagnare ~** lose/gain ground

■ **terreno alluvionale** alluvial soil; **terreno di bonifica** reclaimed land; **terreno boschivo** woodland; **terreno edificabile** building land; **terreno di gioco** playing field; **terreno di scontro** battlefield

ter'restre *adj* terrestrial; (superficie, diametro) of the earth; **esercito terrestre** land forces *pl*

⚘ **ter'ribile** *adj* terrible

terribil'mente *adv* terribly

⚘ indicates a very frequent word

ter'riccio *nm* potting compost

'terrier *nm inv* terrier

terri'ero *adj* (proprietario) land *attrib*; (aristocrazia) landed; **proprietà** *pl* **terriere** landed property

terrifi'cante *adj* terrifying

territori'ale *adj* territorial; **acque territoriali** territorial waters

terri'torio *nm* territory

ter'rone, -a *nmf* pej bloody Southerner

ter'rore *nm* terror

terro'rismo *nm* terrorism

terro'rista *nmf* terrorist

terroriz'zare *vt* terrorize

'terso *adj* clear

'terza *nf* (marcia) third [gear]

ter'zetto *nm* trio

terzi'ario ⒈ *adj* tertiary
⒉ *nm* service sector, tertiary sector

ℐ **'terzo** ⒈ *adj* third; **di terz'ordine** (locale, servizio) third-rate; **fare il ∼ grado a qualcuno** give somebody the third degree; **la terza età** the third age; **il ∼ mondo** the Third World
■ **terzo settore** voluntary sector
⒉ *nm* third; **terzi** *pl* Jur third party

terzo'genito, -a *nmf* third-born

ter'zultimo, -a *adj & n* third from last

'tesa *nf* brim

'teschio *nm* skull

'tesi *nf inv* thesis

'teso ⒈ *pp di* TENDERE
⒉ *adj* taut; fig tense

tesore'ria *nf* treasury

tesori'ere *nm* treasurer

ℐ **te'soro** *nm* treasure; (tesoreria) treasury; **ministro del Tesoro** Finance Minister; Chancellor of the Exchequer Br

'tessera *nf* card; (abbonamento all'autobus) season ticket; (di club) membership card
■ **tessera magnetica** swipe card; **tessera dei trasporti pubblici** travel card; **tessera di sconto** discount card

'tessere *vt* weave; hatch «complotto»; **∼ le lodi di qualcosa** sing the praises of something

tesse'rino *nm* travel card

'tessile ⒈ *adj* textile
⒉ *nm* **tessili** *pl* textiles; (operai) textile workers

tessi|'tore, -trice *nmf* weaver

tessi'tura *nf* weaving

tes'suto ⒈ *pp di* TESSERE
⒉ *adj* woven; **∼ a mano** hand-woven
⒊ *nm* fabric, material; Anat tissue
■ **tessuto sintetico** synthetic material; **tessuto di spugna** terry towelling

'test *nm inv* test; **test genetici** *pl* genetic testing
■ **test alcolimetrico** alcohol test; **test del DNA** DNA test

ℐ **'testa** *nf* head; (cervello) brain; **essere in ∼** a be ahead of; **in ∼** Sport in the lead; **∼ o croce?** heads or tails?; **fare a ∼ o croce** spin a coin, toss a coin; **andare a ∼ alta** hold one's head up
■ **testa di rapa** fam pinhead; **testa di sbarco** beachhead; **testa di serie** (squadra) seeded team; **testa del treno** front of the train

testa-'coda *nm inv* **fare un ∼** spin right round

testa'mento *nm* will
■ **testamento biologico** living will; **Antico Testamento** Relig Old Testament; **Nuovo Testamento** Relig New Testament

testar'daggine *nf* stubbornness

testarda'mente *adv* stubbornly

te'stardo *adj* stubborn

te'stare *vt* test

te'stata *nf* head; (intestazione) heading; (colpo) [head]butt
■ **testata nucleare** nuclear warhead

'teste *nmf* witness

'tester *nm inv* tester

te'sticolo *nm* testicle

testi'mone *nmf* witness; **essere ∼ di qualcosa** witness something
■ **testimone di Geova** Jehovah's Witness; **testimone oculare** eye witness

testi'monial *nmf inv* celebrity who endorses a product

testimoni'anza *nf* testimony; **falsa testimonianza** Jur perjury

testimoni'are ⒈ *vt* testify to
⒉ *vi* testify, give evidence

te'stina *nf* head; (di stampante) printhead
■ **testina di cancellazione** Comput erase head; **testina di lettura** Comput read head; **testina rotante** (di macchina da scrivere) golf-ball; **testina di vitello** Culin calf's head

'testo *nm* text; **far ∼** be authoritative; **con ∼ a fronte** (traduzione) with the original text on the opposite page

te'stone, -a *nmf* blockhead

testoste'rone *nm* testosterone

testu'ale *adj* textual

'tetano *nm* tetanus

te'traggine *nf* bleakness

tetra'pak® *nm inv* tetrapak

'tetro *adj* bleak

tetta'rella *nf* teat

ℐ **'tetto** *nm* roof; **abbandono del ∼ coniugale** Jur desertion
■ **tetto apribile** (di auto) sun[shine] roof; **tetto a terrazza** flat roof

tet'toia *nf* roofing

tet'tuccio *nm*
■ **tettuccio apribile** sun-roof

teu'tonico *adj* Teutonic

'Tevere *nm* Tiber

TFR *nm abbr* (**trattamento di fine rapporto**) severance pay

tg, TG *nm abbr* (**telegiornale**) (television) news

✐ **ti** *pers pron* you; (riflessivo) yourself; **ti ha dato un libro** he gave you a book; **lavati le mani** wash your hands; **eccoti!** here you are!; **sbrigati!** hurry up!

ti'ara *nf* tiara

'Tibet *nm* Tibet

tic *nm inv* tic

ticchet'tare *vi* tick

ticchet'tio *nm* ticking

'ticchio *nm* tic; (ghiribizzo) whim

'ticket *nm inv* (per farmaco, analisi) prescription charges (*amount paid by National Health patients*)

tie-break *nm inv* tie break[er]

tiepida'mente *adv* half-heartedly

ti'epido *adj* lukewarm; fig half-hearted

ti'fare *vi* ~ **per** be a fan of

'tifo *nm* Med typhus; **fare il** ~ **per** (appoggiare) be a fan of

tifoi'dea *nf* typhoid

ti'fone *nm* typhoon

ti'foso, -a *nmf* fan

tight *nm inv* morning dress

'tiglio *nm* lime

'tigna *nf* ringworm

ti'grato *adj* gatto ~ tabby [cat]

'tigre *nf* tiger

'tilde *nmf* tilde

tim'ballo *nm* Culin pie

tim'brare *vt* stamp; ~ **il cartellino** (all'entrata) clock in; (all'uscita) clock out

'timbro *nm* stamp; (di voce) tone
■ **timbro a secco** embossing stamp

time out *nm inv* Sport time-out

'timer *nm inv* timer

timida'mente *adv* timidly, shyly

timi'dezza *nf* timidity, shyness

'timido *adj* timid, shy

'timo *nm* thyme

ti'mone *nm* rudder
■ **timone di direzione** (di aereo) rudder; **timone di quota** (di aereo) elevator

timoni'ere *nm* helmsman

timo'rato *adj* ~ **di Dio** God-fearing

✐ **ti'more** *nm* fear; (soggezione) awe

'Timor 'Est *nm* East Timor

timo'roso *adj* timorous

'timpano *nm* eardrum; Mus kettledrum; **timpani** *pl* Mus timpani, kettledrums; **rompere i timpani a qualcuno** fig shatter somebody's eardrums

ti'nello *nm* dining-room

'tingere *vt* dye; (macchiare) stain

'tingersi *vr* (viso, cielo) be tinged (**di** with); ~ **i capelli** have one's hair dyed; (da solo) dye one's hair

'tino *nm*, **'tinozza** *nf* tub

'tinta *nf* dye; (colore) colour; **in** ~ **unita** plain, self-coloured

tinta'rella *nf* fam suntan

tintin'nare *vi* tinkle

'tinto *pp di* TINGERE

tinto'ria *nf* (negozio) cleaner's

tin'tura *nf* dyeing; (colorante) dye
■ **tintura di iodio** iodine

tipica'mente *adv* typically

'tipico *adj* typical

✐ **'tipo** *nm* type; fam (individuo) chap, guy

tipogra'fia *nf* printer's; (arte) typography

tipo'grafico *adj* typographic[al]

ti'pografo *nm* printer

tip tap *nm inv* tap dancing

ti'raggio *nm* draught

tiranneggi'are *vt* tyrannize

tiran'nia *nf* tyranny

ti'ranno, -a ① *adj* tyrannical
② *nmf* tyrant

tiranno'sauro *nm* tyrannosaurus

ti'rante *nm* rope

tirapi'edi *nm inv* pej hanger-on

tira'pugni *nm inv* knuckle-duster

✐ **ti'rare** ① *vt* pull; (gettare) throw; (nel calcio) kick; (tracciare) draw; (stampare) print; fam land ‹calci, pugni›
② *vi* pull; (vento) blow; (abito) be tight; (sparare) fire; ~ **avanti** fig get by; ~ **su** bring up ‹figli›; (da terra) pick up; **tirar su [col naso]** sniffle

ti'rarsi *vr* ~ **indietro** fig back out, pull out

tiras'segno *nm* target shooting; (alla fiera) rifle range

ti'rata *nf* (strattone) pull, tug; **in una** ~ in one go; **dare a qualcuno una** ~ **d'orecchi** fig give somebody a telling off

tira'tore *nm* shot
■ **tiratore scelto** marksman

tira'tura *nf* printing; (di giornali) circulation; (di libri) [print] run

tirchie'ria *nf* meanness

'tirchio *adj* mean

tiri'tera *nf* spiel

'tiro *nm* (lancio) throw; (azione) throwing; (sparo) shot; (azione) shooting; (scherzo) trick; **cavallo da tiro** draught horse
■ **tiro con l'arco** archery; **tiro al bersaglio** target practice; **tiro alla fune** tug-of-war; **tiro al piattello** clay pigeon shooting; **tiro in porta** shot at goal; **tiro a segno** rifle-range

tiroci'nante *nmf* trainee

tiro'cinio *nm* training

ti'roide *nf* thyroid

Tir'reno *nm* il [mar] ~ the Tyrrhenian Sea

✐ indicates a very frequent word

ti'sana *nf* herb[al] tea

'tisi *nf* consumption

ti'tanio *nm* titanium

tito'lare [1] *adj* permanent
[2] *nmf* (proprietario) owner; (calcio) regular player; Jur (di diritto) holder

◦ **'titolo** *nm* title; (accademico) qualification; Comm security; a ∼ di as; a ∼ di favore as a favour; **titoli** *pl* (di giornale, telegiornale) headlines
■ titoli di coda closing credits; titolo di credito credit instrument; titolo mondiale world title; titolo obbligazionario bond; titoli delle principali notizie *pl* news headlines; titolo in sovrimpressione superimposed title; titolo di Stato government security; titoli di studio *pl* qualifications; titoli di testa *pl* Cinema, TV opening credits; titolo a tutta pagina banner headline

titu'bante *adj* hesitant

titu'banza *nf* hesitation

titu'bare *vi* hesitate

tivù *nf inv* fam TV, telly

'tizio, -a [1] *nm* so-and-so; un ∼ some man
[2] *nf* una tizia some woman

tiz'zone *nm* brand

toc'cante *adj* touching

◦ **toc'care** [1] *vt* touch; touch on ‹argomento›; (tastare) feel; (riguardare) concern
[2] *vi* ∼ a (capitare) happen to; mi tocca aspettare I'll have to wait; tocca a te it's your turn; (a pagare da bere) it's your round; 'non ∼' 'please do not touch'

tocca'sana *nm inv* panacea

toc'cato *adj* fam (matto) touched

'tocco [1] *nm* touch; (di pennello, orologio) stroke; (di pane ecc) chunk; il ∼ finale the finishing touches
[2] *adj* fam crazy, touched

toc 'toc *nm inv* knock, knock

'toga *nf* toga; (accademica, di magistrato) gown

◦ **'togliere** *vt* take off ‹coperta›; Math (da scuola) take away; quench ‹sete›; take out, remove ‹tonsille, dente ecc›; ∼ qualcosa di mano a qualcuno take something away from somebody; ∼ qualcuno dai guai get somebody out of trouble; ciò non toglie che… nevertheless…, the fact remains that…; farsi ∼ le tonsille have one's tonsils [taken] out

'togliersi *vr* take off ‹abito›; ∼ la vita take one's [own] life; ∼ di mezzo get out of the way; togliti dai piedi! get out of the way!

'Togo *nm* Togo

toi'lette *nf inv* toilet; (mobile) dressing table

to'letta *nf* toilet; (mobile) dressing table

tolle'rante *adj* tolerant

tolle'ranza *nf* tolerance; casa di tolleranza brothel

tolle'rare *vt* tolerate

'tolto *pp di* TOGLIERE

to'maia *nf* upper

◦ **'tomba** *nf* grave

tom'bino *nm* manhole cover

'tombola *nf* bingo; (caduta) tumble

to'mino *nm* goat-cheese

'tomo *nm* tome

tomogra'fia *nf* Med tomography
■ tomografia assiale computerizzata computerized axial tomography, CAT

'tonaca *nf* habit

to'nale *adj* tonal

tonalità *nf inv* Mus tonality

to'nante *adj* booming

'tondo [1] *adj* (cifra) round
[2] *nm* circle

'toner *nm inv* toner

'tonfo *nm* thud; (in acqua) splash

'Tonga *nf* Tonga

'tonica *nf* Mus keynote

'tonico [1] *adj* (sillaba) stressed; (muscoli) well toned
[2] *nm* tonic

tonifi'care *vt* tone up ‹muscoli›

ton'nara *nf* tuna-fishing net

ton'nato *adj* vitello ∼ veal with a tuna and mayonnaise sauce

tonnel'laggio *nm* tonnage

tonnel'lata *nf* ton
■ tonnellata corta americana short ton, net ton

'tonno *nm* tuna [fish]

◦ **'tono** *nm* tone

ton'sille *nfpl* tonsils

tonsil'lite *nf* tonsillitis

'tonto *adj* fam thick

top *nm inv* (indumento) sun-top

to'pazio *nm* topaz

'topless *nm inv* in ∼ topless

top 'model *nf inv* supermodel, top model

'topo *nm* mouse
■ topo di albergo/appartamento *thief in a hotel/block of flats*; topo di biblioteca bookworm; topo domestico domestic mouse

topogra'fia *nf* topography

topo'grafico *adj* topographic[al]

to'ponimo *nm* place name

topo'ragno *nm* shrew

'toppa *nf* (rattoppo) patch; (serratura) keyhole

to'race *nm* chest

to'racico *adj* thoracic; gabbia toracica rib cage

'torba *nf* peat

'torbido *adj* cloudy; fig troubled

'torcere *vt* twist; wring [out] ‹biancheria›

'torcersi *vr* twist

'torchio *nm* press

'torcia *nf* torch
■ torcia elettrica torch

t

torci'collo *nm* stiff neck

'tordo *nm* thrush

to'rero *nm* bullfighter

To'rino *nf* Turin

tor'menta *nf* snowstorm

⚐ **tormen'tare** *vt* torment

tormen'tato *adj* tormented

tor'mento *nm* torment

tormen'tone *nm* (frase) catchphrase; (argomento) *constantly repeated topic*; (canzone) *catchy song that is constantly played on the radio*

torna'conto *nm* benefit

tor'nado *nm* tornado

tor'nante *nm* hairpin bend

⚐ **tor'nare** *vi* return, go/come back; (ridiventare) become again; ‹conto› add up; **~ a sorridere** smile again; **~ su** go back up

tor'neo *nm* tournament

'tornio *nm* lathe

'torno *nm* **togliersi di ~** get out of the way

'toro *nm* bull; Astr Taurus

tor'pedine *nf* torpedo

torpedini'era *nf* torpedo boat

tor'pore *nm* torpor

⚐ **'torre** *nf* tower; (scacchi) castle
■ **torre d'avorio** ivory tower; **torre di controllo** control tower; **torre di osservazione** observation tower; **torre pendente, torre di Pisa** Leaning Tower of Pisa

torrefazi'one *nf* roasting; (negozio) coffee retailer

tor'rente *nm* torrent, mountain stream; fig (di lacrime) flood; fig (di parole) torrent

torrenzi'ale *adj* torrential; **in regime ~** in spate

tor'retta *nf* turret

'torrido *adj* torrid, sweltering

torri'one *nm* keep

tor'rone *nm* nougat

torsi'one *nf* twisting; (in ginnastica) twist

'torso *nm* torso; (di mela, pera) core; **a ~ nudo** bare-chested

'torsolo *nm* core

'torta *nf* cake; (crostata) tart
■ **torta di compleanno** birthday cake; **torta di mele** apple tart; **torta nuziale** wedding cake; **torta pasqualina** spinach pie

torti'era *nf* cake tin

tor'tino *nm* pie

⚐ **'torto** ① pp di TORCERE
② *adj* twisted
③ *nm* wrong; (colpa) fault; **aver ~** be wrong; **a ~** wrongly; **far ~ a qualcuno** wrong somebody; fig not do somebody justice; **non hai tutti i torti** you're not altogether wrong

'tortora *nf* turtle-dove

⚐ indicates a very frequent word

tortuosa'mente *adv* tortuously

tortu'oso *adj* winding; (ambiguo) tortuous

tor'tura *nf* torture

tortu'rare *vt* torture

'torvo *adj* (sguardo) menacing

tosa'erba *nm inv* lawnmower

to'sare *vt* shear

tosasi'epi *nm inv* hedge trimmer

tosa'tura *nf* shearing

To'scana *nf* Tuscany

to'scano, -a *adj & nmf* Tuscan

'tosse *nf* cough

'tossico ① *adj* toxic
② *nm* poison

tossicodipen'denza *nf* drug addiction, drug habit

tossi'comane *nmf* drug addict, drug user

tos'sire *vi* cough

tosta'pane *nm inv* toaster
■ **tostapane a espulsione automatica** pop-up toaster

to'stare *vt* toast ‹pane›; roast ‹caffe›

'tosto ① *adv* (subito) soon
② *adj* fam cool; **faccia tosta** cheek

tot ① *adj inv* **una cifra ~** such and such a figure
② *nm* **un ~** so much

to'tale *adj & nm* total
■ **totale complessivo** grand total; **totale parziale** subtotal

totalità *nf* entirety; **la ~ dei presenti** all those present

totali'tario *adj* totalitarian

totaliz'zare *vt* total; score ‹punti›

totalizza'tore *nm* (per scommesse) totalizer, tote

total'mente *adv* totally

'totano *nm* squid

'totem *nm inv* totem pole

toto'calcio *nm* [football] pools *pl*

'touche *nf inv* touch line

tou'pet *nm inv* toupee

tour'née *nf inv* tour

to'vaglia *nf* tablecloth

tovagli'etta *nf*
■ **tovaglietta [all'americana]** place mat

tovagli'olo *nm* napkin
■ **tovagliolo di carta** paper napkin

'tozzo *adj* squat
■ **tozzo di pane** stale piece of bread

⚐ **tra** = FRA

trabal'lante *adj* staggering; (sedia) rickety, wonky

trabal'lare *vi* stagger; (veicolo) jolt

tra'biccolo *nm* fam contraption; (auto) jalopy

traboc'care *vi* overflow

traboc'chetto *nm* trap

traca'gnotto *adj* dumpy

tracan'nare *vt* gulp down

'traccia *nf* track; (orma) footstep; (striscia) trail; (residuo) trace; fig sign

tracci'are *vt* trace; sketch out ‹schema›; draw ‹linea›

tracci'ato *nm* (schema) layout

■ tracciato di gara circuit

tra'chea *nf* windpipe, trachea

tra'colla *nf* shoulder-strap; **borsa a tracolla** shoulder-bag

tra'collo *nm* collapse

tradi'mento *nm* betrayal; Pol treason; **alto tradimento** high treason

⚡ **tra'dire** *vt* betray; be unfaithful to ‹moglie, marito›

tradi|'tore, -trice *nmf* traitor

tradizio'nale *adj* traditional

tradiziona'lista *nmf* traditionalist

tradizional'mente *adv* traditionally

tradizi'one *nf* tradition

tra'dotto pp di TRADURRE

tra'durre *vt* translate

tradut|'tore, -trice *nmf* translator

■ traduttore elettronico electronic phrasebook

traduzi'one *nf* translation

■ traduzione consecutiva consecutive interpreting; **traduzione simultanea** simultaneous interpreting

tra'ente *nmf* Comm drawer

trafe'lato *adj* breathless

traffi'cante *nmf* dealer, trafficker

■ trafficante d'armi arms dealer; **trafficante di droga** drug dealer

traffi'care *vi* (affaccendarsi) busy oneself; ~ in pej traffic in

'traffico *nm* traffic; Comm trade

■ traffico aereo air traffic; **traffico della droga** drug trafficking; **traffico ferroviario** rail traffic; **traffico di stupefacenti** drug trafficking

traffi'cone, -a *nmf* fam wheeler dealer

tra'figgere *vt* penetrate, pierce; fig pierce

tra'fila *nf* fig rigmarole

trafi'letto *nm* minor news item

trafo'rare *vt* bore, drill

tra'foro *nm* boring, drilling; (galleria) tunnel; **lavoro di traforo** fretwork

trafu'gare *vt* steal

tra'gedia *nf* tragedy

traghet'tare *vt* ferry

tra'ghetto *nm* ferrying; (nave) ferry

tragica'mente *adv* tragically

'tragico ① *adj* tragic
② *nm* (autore) tragedian

tra'gitto *nm* journey; (per mare) crossing

tragu'ardo *nm* finishing post; (meta) goal

traiet'toria *nf* trajectory

trai'nare *vt* drag; (rimorchiare) tow

tralasci'are *vt* interrupt; (omettere) leave out; ~ **di fare qualcosa** fail to do something, omit to do something

'tralcio *nm* Bot shoot

tra'liccio *nm* (tela) ticking; (graticcio) trellis

tra'lice: in ~ *adv* (tagliare) on the slant; (guardare) sideways

tralu'cente *adj* shining

tram *nm inv* tram, streetcar Am

'trama *nf* weft; (di film ecc) plot

traman'dare *vt* hand down

tra'mare *vt* weave; (macchinare) plot

tram'busto *nm* turmoil

trame'stio *nm* bustle

tramez'zino *nm* sandwich

tra'mezzo *nm* partition

'tramite ① *prep* through
② *nm* link; **con il** ~ **di** by means of; **fare da** ~ act as go-between

tramon'tana *nf* north wind

tramon'tare *vi* set; (declinare) decline

⚡ **tra'monto** *nm* sunset; (declino) decline

tramor'tire ① *vt* stun
② *vi* faint

trampoli'ere *nm* wader

trampo'lino *nm* springboard; (per lo sci) ski-jump

■ trampolino di lancio fig launch pad

'trampolo *nm* stilt

tramu'tare *vt* transform

trance *nf inv* trance; **essere in** ~ be in a trance

'trancia *nf* shears *pl*; (fetta) slice

tra'nello *nm* trap

trangugi'are *vt* gulp down

'tranne *prep* except

tranquilla'mente *adv* peacefully

tranquil'lante *nm* tranquillizer

tranquillità *nf* calm; (di spirito) tranquillity

tranquilliz'zare *vt* reassure

⚡ **tran'quillo** *adj* quiet; (pacifico) peaceful; (coscienza) easy; **stai** ~ ! (non preoccuparti) don't worry!

transa'tlantico ① *adj* transatlantic
② *nm* ocean liner

tran'satto pp di TRANSIGERE

transazi'one *nf* Comm transaction; Jur settlement

tran'senna *nf* (barriera) barrier

transessu'ale *nmf* transsexual

tran'setto *nm* transept

'transfert *nm inv* Psych transference

tran'sigere *vi* Jur reach a settlement; (cedere) compromise

tran'sistor *nm inv* fam transistor [radio]

transi'tabile *adj* passable

transi'tare *vi* pass

transi'tivo *adj* transitive

t

'transito nm transit; **'divieto di ~'** 'no thoroughfare'; **diritto di transito** right of way ■ **'transito alterno'** 'temporary one-way system'

transi'torio adj transitory

transizi'one nf transition; **di ~** transitional

tran'tran nm fam routine

tranvi'ere nm tram driver, streetcar driver Am

'trapano nm drill ■ **trapano elettrico** electric drill

trapas'sare ① vt pierce, penetrate ② vi (morire) pass away

trapas'sato nm pluperfect

tra'passo nm passage

trape'lare vi anche fig leak out

tra'pezio nm trapeze; Math trapezium

trapian'tare vt transplant

trapi'anto nm transplant ■ **trapianto di cuore** heart transplant

'trappola nf trap

tra'punta nf quilt

'trarre vt draw; (ricavare) obtain; **~ in inganno** deceive

trasa'lire vi start

trasan'dato adj shabby

trasbor'dare ① vt transfer; Naut tran[s]ship ② vi change

tra'sbordo nm trans[s]hipment

trascenden'tale adj transcendental

tra'scendere ① vt transcend ② vi (eccedere) go too far

❖ **trasci'nare** vt drag; fig (entusiasmo) carry away; **~ e rilasciare** Comput drag and drop

trasci'narsi vr drag oneself; (camminare piano) dawdle

❖ **tra'scorrere** ① vt spend ② vi pass

tra'scritto pp di TRASCRIVERE

tra'scrivere vt transcribe

trascrizi'one nf transcription

trascu'rabile adj negligible

trascu'rare vt neglect; (non tenere conto di) disregard

trascurata'mente adv carelessly

trascura'tezza nf negligence

trascu'rato adj negligent; (curato male) neglected; (nel vestire) slovenly

traseco'lato adj amazed

trasferi'mento nm transfer; (trasloco) move ■ **trasferimento automatico** direct debit; **trasferimento bancario** bank transfer

❖ **trasfe'rire** vt transfer

trasfe'rirsi vr move

tra'sferta nf transfer; (indennità) subsistence allowance; Sport away match; **in ~** (impiegato) on secondment; **giocare in ~** play away

trasfigu'rare vt transfigure

❖ **trasfor'mare** vt transform; (in rugby) convert

trasfor'marsi vr be transformed; **~ in** turn into

trasforma'tore nm transformer

trasformazi'one nf transformation; (in rugby) conversion

trasfor'mista nmf (artista) quick-change artist

trasfusi'one nf transfusion

trasgre'dire vt disobey; Jur infringe

trasgredi'trice nf transgressor

trasgressi'one nf infringement; (di ordine) failure to obey

trasgres'sivo adj intended to shock

trasgres'sore nm transgressor

tra'slato adj metaphorical

traslitte'rare vt transliterate

traslo'care ① vt move ② vi move [house]

traslo'carsi vr move [house]

tra'sloco nm move; **compagnia di trasloco** removal company

tra'smesso pp di TRASMETTERE

❖ **tra'smettere** vt pass on; TV, Radio broadcast; Techn, Med transmit

trasmetti'tore nm transmitter

trasmis'sibile adj transmissible

trasmissi'one nf transmission; TV, Radio programme ■ **trasmissione dati** data transmission; **trasmissione via fax** fax transmission; **trasmissione radiofonica** radio programme; **trasmissione remota** remote transmission; **trasmissione televisiva** television programme

trasmit'tente ① nm transmitter ② nf broadcasting station

traso'gnare vi day-dream

traso'gnato adj dreamy

traspa'rente adj transparent

traspa'renza nf transparency; **in ~** against the light

traspa'rire vi show [through]

traspi'rare vi perspire; fig transpire

traspirazi'one nf perspiration

tra'sporre vt transpose

traspor'tare vt transport; **lasciarsi ~ da** get carried away by; **~ con ponte aereo** airlift

traspor'tato adj transported; **~ dall'aria** airborne

trasporta'tore nm conveyor; (società) transport company, road haulier

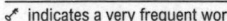

tra'sporto nm transport; fig (passione) passion; **ministro dei trasporti** Ministry of Transport
- **trasporto aereo** air freight; **trasporto ferroviario** rail transport; **trasporto pesante** heavy goods transport; **trasporti pubblici** pl public transport; **trasporto stradale** road transport, road haulage

trastul'lare vt amuse

trastul'larsi vr amuse oneself; (perdere tempo) fool around

trasu'dare ① vt ooze [with]
② vi ooze

trasver'sale adj transverse; **strada trasversale** cross street

trasversal'mente adv widthways

trasvo'lare ① vt fly over
② vi ~ **su** fig skim over

trasvo'lata nf crossing [by air]

'tratta nf (traffico illegale) trade; Comm draft
- **tratta bancaria** Fin banker's draft; **tratta delle bianche** white slave trade; **tratta documentaria** documentary bill

trat'tabile adj or nearest offer, o.n.o.

tratta'mento nm treatment
- **trattamento automatico delle informazioni** electronic data processing, EDP; **trattamento di bellezza** beauty treatment; **trattamento di fine rapporto** severance pay; **trattamento dell'immagine** image processing; **trattamento di riguardo** special treatment

trat'tante adj conditioning

⚘ **trat'tare** ① vt treat; (commerciare in) deal in; (negoziare) negotiate
② vi ~ **di** deal with

trat'tario nm Comm drawee

trat'tarsi vr **di che si tratta?** what's it about?; **si tratta di...** it's about...

tratta'tive nfpl negotiations; **il tavolo delle ~** the negotiating table

trat'tato nm treaty; (opera scritta) treatise
- **trattato di pace** peace treaty

tratteggi'are vt outline; (descrivere) sketch

⚘ **tratte'nere** vt (far restare) keep; hold ‹respiro, in questura›; hold back ‹lacrime, riso›; (frenare) restrain; (da paga) withhold; **sono stato trattenuto** (ritardato) I got held up

tratte'nersi vr restrain oneself; (fermarsi) stay; ~ **su** (indugiare) dwell on

tratteni'mento nm entertainment; (ricevimento) party

tratte'nuta nf deduction

trat'tino nm dash; (in parole composte) hyphen

⚘ **'tratto** ① pp di TRARRE
② nm (di spazio, tempo) stretch; (di penna) stroke; (linea) line; (brano) passage; **tratti** pl (lineamenti) features; **a tratti** at intervals; **ad un ~** suddenly

trat'tore nm tractor

tratto'ria nf restaurant

'trauma nm trauma

trau'matico adj traumatic

traumatiz'zante adj traumatic

traumatiz'zare vt traumatize

tra'vaglio nm labour; (angoscia) anguish

trava'sare vt decant

tra'vaso nm decanting

trava'tura nf beams pl

'trave nf beam
- **trave a sbalzo** cantilever

tra'veggole nfpl **avere le ~** be seeing things

'travellers cheque nm inv traveller's cheque

tra'versa nf (nel calcio) crossbar; **è una ~ di via Roma** it's off via Roma, it crosses via Roma

traver'sare vt cross

traver'sata nf crossing

traver'sie nfpl misfortunes

traver'sina nf Rail sleeper

tra'verso ① adj crosswise
② adv **di ~** crossways; **andare di ~** (cibo) go down the wrong way; **camminare di ~** not walk in a straight line; **guardare qualcuno di ~** look askance at somebody; **sapere per vie traverse** fam find out indirectly

traver'sone nm (in calcio) cross

travesti'mento nm disguise

trave'stire vt disguise

trave'stirsi vr disguise oneself

travesti'tismo nm transvestism, crossdressing

trave'stito ① adj disguised
② nm transvestite

travi'are vt lead astray

travisa'mento nm distortion

travi'sare vt distort

travol'gente adj overwhelming

tra'volgere vt sweep away; (sopraffare) overwhelm

tra'volto pp di TRAVOLGERE

trazi'one nf traction
- **trazione anteriore/posteriore** front-/rear-wheel drive

⚘ **tre** adj & nm three

tre'alberi nm inv three-masted ship, three-master

trebbi'are vt thresh

trebbia'trice nf threshing machine

'treccia nf plait, braid; (in maglia) cable; **a trecce** cable attrib

tre'cento adj & nm three hundred; **il Trecento** the fourteenth century

tredi'cesima nf extra month's salary paid as a Christmas bonus

tredi'cesimo, -a adj & nm thirteenth

⚘ **'tredici** adj & nm thirteen

t

'tregua nf truce; fig respite

'trekking nm trekking

tre'mante adj trembling, quivering; (per il freddo) shivering

⚜ **tre'mare** vi tremble, quiver; (di freddo) shiver

trema'rella nf fam jitters pl

tremenda'mente adv terribly, tremendously

tre'mendo adj terrible, tremendous; **ho una fame tremenda** I'm terribly hungry

tremen'tina nf turpentine

tre'mila adj & nm three thousand

'tremito nm tremble, quiver; (per il freddo) shiver

tremo'lare vi shake; (luce) flicker

tre'more nm trembling

'tremulo adj tremulous

tre'nino nm miniature railway

⚜ **'treno** nm train
  ■ treno merci freight train, goods train; **treno navetta** shuttle; **treno passeggeri** passenger train; **treno postale** mail train; **treno straordinario** special train

⚜ **'trenta** adj & nm thirty
  ■ trenta e lode Univ first-class honours

trentatré 'giri nm inv LP

tren'tenne adj & nmf thirty-year-old

tren'tesimo adj & nm thirtieth

tren'tina nf una ∼ di about thirty

trepi'dare vi be anxious

'trepido adj anxious

treppi'ede nm tripod

'tresca nf intrigue; (amorosa) affair

'trespolo nm perch

triango'lare adj triangular

tri'angolo nm triangle
  ■ triangolo delle Bermude Bermuda Triangle; **triangolo equilatero** equilateral triangle; **triangolo isoscele** isosceles triangle; **triangolo rettangolo** right-angled triangle; **triangolo di segnalazione** warning triangle

tri'bale adj tribal

tribo'lare vi (soffrire) suffer; (fare fatica) go to a lot of trouble

tribolazi'one nf suffering

tri'bordo nm starboard

tribù nf inv tribe

tri'buna nf podium, dais; (per uditori) gallery; Sport stand
  ■ tribuna coperta stand; **tribuna riservata al pubblico** public gallery; **tribuna della stampa** press gallery

tribu'nale nm court
  ■ tribunale fallimentare bankruptcy court; **tribunale minorile** juvenile court; **tribunale penale internazionale** international criminal court, ICC

tribu'tare vt bestow, confer

tribu'tario adj tax attrib

tri'buto nm tribute; (tassa) tax

tri'checo nm walrus

tri'ciclo nm tricycle

trico'lore ⓵ adj three-coloured
  ⓶ nm (bandiera) Italian flag

tri'dente nm trident

tridimensio'nale adj three-dimensional

trien'nale adj (ogni tre anni) three-yearly; (lungo tre anni) three-year

tri'ennio nm three-year period

tri'fase adj three-phase

tri'foglio nm clover

trifo'lato adj sliced thinly and cooked with olive oil, parsley and garlic

tri'gemino adj parto ∼ birth of triplets

'triglia nf mullet

trigonome'tria nf trigonometry, trig fam

tri'lingue adj trilingual

tril'lare vi trill

'trillo nm trill

trilo'gia nf trilogy

trime'strale adj quarterly

tri'mestre nm quarter

'trina nf lace

trin'cea nf trench

trince'rare vt entrench

trincia'pollo nm inv poultry shears pl

trinci'are vt cut up

trincia'trice nf
  ■ trinciatrice di documenti document shredder

Trini'dad e To'bago nm Trinidad and Tobago

Trinità nf Trinity

'trio nm trio

trion'fale adj triumphal

trionfal'mente adv triumphantly

trion'fante adj triumphant

trion'fare vi triumph (**su** over)

tri'onfo nm triumph

tri'pletta nf Sport hat trick

tripli'care vt triple

'triplice adj triple; **in** ∼ [copia] in triplicate

'triplo ⓵ adj treble, triple; **una somma tripla del previsto** an amount three times as much as forecast
  ⓶ nm il ∼ **(di)** three times as much (as)

'trippa nf tripe; fam (pancia) belly

tripudi'are vi rejoice

tri'pudio nm jubilation

tris nm (gioco) noughts and crosses, ticktack-toe Am

⚜ **'triste** adj sad; (luogo) gloomy

tri'stezza nf sadness; (di luogo) gloominess

'tristo adj nasty

⚜ indicates a very frequent word

trita'carne *nm inv* mincer
tritaghi'accio *nm inv* ice-crusher
tri'tare *vt* mince
trita'tutto *nm inv* (elettrico) [food] processor
'**trito** *adj* ~ **e ritrito** well-worn, trite
tri'tolo *nm* TNT
tri'tone *nm* (mitologia) Triton; Zool newt
'**trittico** *nm* triptych
trit'tongo *nm* triphthong
tritu'rare *vt* chop finely
triumvi'rato *nm* triumvirate
tri'vella *nf* drill
trivel'lare *vt* drill
trivi'ale *adj* vulgar
tro'feo *nm* trophy
troglo'dita *nmf* (preistoria) cave-dweller; fig Neanderthal
'**trogolo** *nm* (per maiali) trough
'**troia** *nf* sow; vulg bitch; (sessuale) whore
'**tromba** *nf* trumpet; Auto horn; (delle scale) well; **partire in** ~ dive in head first
 ■ **tromba d'aria** whirlwind; **tromba di Eustachio** Eustachian tube; **tromba di Falloppio** Fallopian tube; **tromba delle scale** stairwell
trom'bare ① *vt* vulg bonk; fam (in esame) fail
 ② *vi* vulg bonk
trom'betta *nm* toy trumpet
trombetti'ere *nm* bugler
trombet'tista *nmf* trumpet-player
trom'bone *nm* trombone
trom'bosi *nf* thrombosis
 ■ **trombosi coronarica** coronary thrombosis; **trombosi venosa profonda** deep-vein thrombosis, DVT
tron'care *vt* sever; truncate ‹parola›
tron'chese *nm* wire cutters *pl*
tronche'sino *nm* (per le unghie) nail clippers *pl*
tron'chetto *nm*
 ■ **tronchetto natalizio** Yule log
⚹ '**tronco** ① *adj* truncated; **licenziare in** ~ fire on the spot
 ② *nm* trunk; (di strada) section
 ■ **tronco d'albero** tree trunk; **tronco di cono** truncated cone
tron'cone *nm* stump
troneggi'are *vi* ~ **su** tower over
'**trono** *nm* throne
tropi'cale *adj* tropical
'**tropici** *nmpl* Tropics
'**tropico** *nm* tropic
 ■ **tropico del Cancro** Tropic of Cancer; **tropico del Capricorno** Tropic of Capricorn
⚹ '**troppo** ① *adj* too much; (con nomi plurali) too many
 ② *pron* too much; (plurale) too many; (troppo tempo) too long; **troppi** (troppa gente) too many

people; **me ne hai dato** ~ you gave me too much
 ③ *adv* too; (con verbi) too much; ~ **stanco** too tired; **ho mangiato** ~ I ate too much; **hai fame? – non** ~ are you hungry? – not very; **sentirsi di** ~ feel unwanted
'**trota** *nf* trout
 ■ **trota di mare** sea trout; **trota salmonata** salmon trout
trot'tare *vi* trot
trotterel'lare *vi* trot along; (bambino) toddle
'**trotto** *nm* trot; **andare al** ~ trot
'**trottola** *nf* [spinning] top; (movimento) spin
troupe *nf inv*
 ■ **troupe televisiva** camera crew
trousse *nf inv* (per trucco) make-up bag
⚹ **tro'vare** *vt* find; (scoprire) find out; (incontrare) meet; (ritenere) think; **andare a** ~ go to see
trova'robe *nmf* (persona) props *sg*
tro'varsi *vr* find oneself; (luogo) be; (sentirsi) feel
tro'vata *nf* bright idea
 ■ **trovata pubblicitaria** advertising gimmick, publicity stunt
trova'tello, -a *nmf* foundling
truc'care *vt* make up; cook ‹libri contabili›; soup up ‹motore›; rig ‹partita, elezioni›
truc'carsi *vr* put one's make-up on
truc'cato *adj* made-up; (libri contabili) cooked; (partita, elezioni) rigged; (motore) souped up
trucca|'tore, -trice *nmf* make-up artist
⚹ '**trucco** *nm* (cosmetici) make-up; (imbroglio) trick; **trucchi** *pl* **del mestiere** tricks of the trade
'**truce** *adj* fierce; (delitto) savage
truci'dare *vt* slay
trucio'lato *nm* chipboard
'**truciolo** *nm* shaving
trucu'lento *adj* (delitto) savage; (film) violent
'**truffa** *nf* fraud
truf'fare *vt* defraud
truffa|'tore, -trice *nmf* fraudster
'**trullo** *nm* traditional house with a conical roof found in Apulia
⚹ '**truppa** *nf* troops *pl* (gruppo) group; **truppe** *pl* **d'assalto** assault troops; **truppe** *pl* **di terra** ground troops
T-shirt *nf inv* tee-shirt, T-shirt
tsu'nami *nm* tsunami
⚹ **tu** *pers pron* you; **sei tu?** is that you?; **l'hai fatto tu?** did you do it yourself?; **a tu per tu** in private; **darsi del tu** use the familiar tu to each other
'**tua** ▶ TUO
'**tuba** *nf* Mus tuba; (cappello) top hat
tu'bare *vi* coo; (innamorati) bill and coo
tuba'tura *nf* piping

tubazi'one *nf* piping; **tubazioni** *pl* piping *sg*, pipes

tuberco'lina *nf* tuberculin

tuberco'losi *nf* tuberculosis

'tubero *nm* tuber

tube'rosa *nf* tuberose

tu'betto *nm* tube

■ **tubetto di colore** tube of paint

tu'bino *nm* (vestito) shift; (cappello) bowler; derby Am

'tubo *nm* pipe; Anat canal; **non ho capito un ~ fam** I understood zilch

■ **tubo digerente** alimentary canal; **tubo a raggi catodici** cathode-ray tube; **tubo di scappamento** exhaust [pipe]; **tubo di scarico** waste pipe

tubo'lare *adj* tubular

'tue ▶ TUO

tuf'fare *vt* plunge

tuf'farsi *vr* dive; **'vietato ~'** 'no diving'

tuffa|'tore, -trice *nmf* diver

'tuffo *nm* dive; (bagno) dip; **ho avuto un ~ al cuore** my heart leapt into my mouth

■ **tuffo di testa** dive

'tufo *nm* tufa

tu'gurio *nm* hovel

tuli'pano *nm* tulip

'tulle *nm* tulle

tume'fatto *adj* swollen

tumefazi'one *nf* swelling

'tumido *adj* swollen

tu'more *nm* tumour

■ **tumore benigno** benign tumour; **tumore del collo dell'utero** cevical cancer; **tumore maligno** malignant tumour

tumulazi'one *nf* burial

'tumulo *nm* (di pietre) cairn

tu'multo *nm* turmoil; (sommossa) riot

tumultu'oso *adj* tumultuous

tung'steno *nm* tungsten

'tunica *nf* tunic

Tuni'sia *nf* Tunisia

tuni'sino *adj & nmf* Tunisian

'tunnel *nm inv* tunnel

■ **tunnel sotto la Manica** Channel Tunnel

ᵈ **'tuo** ① (**il ~ m**, **la tua** *f*, **i tuoi** *mpl*, **le tue** *fpl*) *poss adj* your; **è tua questa macchina?** is this car yours?; **un ~ amico** a friend of yours; **~ padre** your father ② *poss pron* yours; **i tuoi** your folk

tu'oi ▶ TUO

tuo'nare *vi* thunder

tu'ono *nm* thunder

tu'orlo *nm* yolk

tu'racciolo *nm* stopper; (di sughero) cork

tu'rare *vt* block; cork ‹*bottiglia*›

tu'rarsi *vr* become blocked; **~ le orecchie** stick one's fingers in one's ears; **~ il naso** hold one's nose

'turba *nf* (folla) rabble

■ **turba psichica** mental illness

turba'mento *nm* disturbance; (sconvolgimento) upsetting

■ **turbamento della quiete pubblica** breach of the peace

tur'bante *nm* turban

tur'bare *vt* upset

tur'barsi *vr* get upset

tur'bato *adj* upset

tur'bina *nf* turbine

turbi'nare *vi* whirl

'turbine *nm* whirl

■ **turbine di polvere** dust storm; **turbine di vento** whirlwind

'turbo *nm inv* turbo

turbocompres'sore *nm* Tech turbocharger

turbo'lento *adj* turbulent

turbo'lenza *nf* turbulence

turboreat'tore *nm* turbo-jet

tur'chese *adj & nmf* turquoise

Tur'chia *nf* Turkey

tur'chino *adj & nm* deep blue

'turco, -a ① *adj* Turkish ② *nmf* Turk; **fumare come un ~** smoke like a chimney; **bestemmiare come un ~** swear like a trooper ③ *nm* (lingua) Turkish; fig double Dutch

'turgido *adj* turgid

tu'rismo *nm* tourism

tu'rista *nmf* tourist

tu'ristico *adj* tourist *attrib*

tur'nista *nmf* shift-worker

'turno *nm* turn; **a ~** in turn; **fare a ~** take turns; **fare i turni** work shifts; **di ~** on duty

■ **turno eliminatorio** heat; **turno di giorno** day shift; **turno di guardia** guard duty; **turno di lavoro** shift; **turno di notte** night shift; **del turno di notte** night shift *attrib*; **fare il turno di notte** be on night shift

'turpe *adj* base

turpi'loquio *nm* foul language

'tuta *nf* overalls *pl*; Sport tracksuit

■ **tuta da ginnastica** tracksuit; **tuta da lavoro** overalls *pl*; **tuta mimetica** camouflage; **tuta da sci** ski suit; **tuta spaziale** spacesuit; **tuta subacquea** wetsuit

tu'tela *nf* Jur guardianship; (protezione) protection

■ **tutela dell'ambiente** environmental protection

tute'lare *vt* protect

tu'tina *nf* sleepsuit; (da danza) leotard

tu|'tore, -trice *nmf* guardian

'tutta *nf* **mettercela ~ per fare qualcosa** go flat out for something

ᵈ **tutta'via** *conj* nevertheless, still

ᵈ indicates a very frequent word

'tutto ⟨1⟩ *adj* whole; (con nomi plurali) all; (ogni) every; **tutta la classe** the whole class, all the class; **tutti gli alunni** all the pupils; **a tutta velocità** at full speed; **ho aspettato ∼ il giorno** I waited all day [long]; **vestito di ∼ punto** all kitted out; **in ∼ il mondo** all over the world; **noi tutti** all of us; **era tutta contenta** she was delighted; **tutti e due** both; **tutti e tre** all three

⟨2⟩ *pron* all; (tutta la gente) everybody; (tutte le cose) everything; (qualunque cosa) anything; **c'è ancora del dolce? – no, l'ho mangiato ∼** is there still some cake? – no, I ate it all; **le finestre sono pulite, le ho lavate tutte** the windows are clean, I washed them all; **raccontami ∼** tell me everything; **lo sanno tutti** everybody knows; **è capace di ∼** he's capable of anything; **∼ compreso** all in; **del ∼** quite; **in ∼** altogether

⟨3⟩ *adv* completely; **tutt'a un tratto** all at once; **tutt'altro** not at all; **tutt'altro che** anything but

⟨4⟩ *nm* whole; **tentare il ∼ per ∼** go for broke; **∼ compreso** all-inclusive; **∼ esaurito** *Theat* full house

tutto'fare *adj inv & nmf inv* [impiegato] **∼** general handyman

tut'tora *adv* still

tutù *nm inv* tutu; (lungo) ballet dress

tv *nf inv* TV

■ **tv via cavo** cable TV; **tv digitale** digital (television); **tv interattiva** interactive TV

tweed *nm inv* tweed

U u

ubbidi'ente *adj* obedient

ubbidiente'mente *adv* obediently

ubbidi'enza *nf* obedience

ubbi'dire *vi* **∼ (a)** obey

ubi'cato *adj* located

ubicazi'one *nf* location

ubiquità *nf* **non ho il dono dell'∼** I can't be in two places at once

ubria'care *vt* get drunk

ubria'carsi *vr* get drunk; **∼ di** *fig* become intoxicated with

ubria'chezza *nf* drunkenness; **in stato di ∼** inebriated; **in stato di ∼ molesta** drunk and disorderly

ubri'aco, -a ⟨1⟩ *adj* drunk

■ **ubriaco fradicio** dead *or* blind drunk

⟨2⟩ *nmf* drunk

ubria'cone ⟨1⟩ *nm* drunkard

⟨2⟩ *adj* **un marito ∼** a drunkard of a husband

uccelli'era *nf* aviary

uccel'lino *nm* baby bird

uc'cello *nm* bird; *vulg* (pene) cock

■ **uccello acquatico** water fowl; **uccello da cacciagione** game bird; **uccello del malaugurio** bird of ill omen; **uccello notturno** night *or* nocturnal bird; **uccello del paradiso** bird of paradise; **uccello di passo** bird of passage; **uccello rapace** bird of prey

uc'cidere *vt* kill

uc'cidersi *vr* kill oneself; (morire) be killed

+uccio *suff* **boccuccia** *nf* pretty little mouth; **calduccio** *nm* cosy warmth; **c'è un bel calduccio** it's nice and cosy; **tesoruccio** *nm* sweetie; **avvocatuccio** *nm pej* small town lawyer; **cosuccia** *nf* trifle; **è una cosuccia da niente** it's nothing; **doloruccio** *nm* twinge; **vestituccio** *nm pej* skimpy little dress

uccisi'one *nf* killing

uc'ciso *pp di* UCCIDERE

ucci'sore *nm* killer

U'craina *nf* **l' ∼** the Ukraine

u'craino, -a *adj & nmf* Ukrainian

u'dente *adj* **i non udenti** the hearing-impaired

u'dibile *adj* audible

udi'enza *nf* audience; (colloquio) interview; *Jur* hearing

■ **udienza a porte chiuse** hearing in camera

u'dire *vt* hear

udi'tivo *adj* auditory

u'dito *nm* hearing

udi|'tore, -trice *nmf* listener; *Sch* unregistered student (*allowed to sit in on lectures*)

udi'torio *nm* audience

UE *abbr* (**Unione Europea**) EU

uff *int* phew!

'uffa *int* (con impazienza) come on!; (con tono seccato) damn!

uffici'ale ⟨1⟩ *adj* official

⟨2⟩ *nm* officer; (funzionario) official; **pubblico ufficiale** public official

■ **ufficiale dell'esercito** army officer; **ufficiale giudiziario** clerk of the court; **ufficiale sanitario** health officer; **ufficiale dello Stato civile** registrar

ufficialità *nf* official status

ufficializ'zare *vt* make official, officialize

ufficial'mente *adv* officially

uf'ficio nm office; (dovere) duty; (reparto) department; **andare in** ~ go to the office
■ **ufficio acquisti** purchasing department; **ufficio cambi** bureau de change, exchange bureau; **ufficio di collocamento** employment office, jobcentre Br; **Ufficio Dazi e Dogana** Customs and Excise; **ufficio funebre** Relig funeral service; **ufficio delle imposte** tax office; **ufficio informazioni** information office; **ufficio di informazioni turistiche** tourist information office or centre; **ufficio oggetti smarriti** lost property office, lost and found Am; **ufficio del personale** personnel department; **ufficio postale** post office; **ufficio prenotazioni** advance booking office; **ufficio della redazione** newspaper office; **ufficio del turismo** tourist office; **ufficio turistico** tourist office

ufficiosa'mente adv unofficially
uffici'oso adj unofficial, off-the-record
'ufo¹ nm inv UFO
'ufo²: a ~ adv without paying
ufolo'gia nf ufology
U'ganda nf Uganda
ugan'dese adj & nmf Ugandan
uggiosità nf dullness
uggi'oso adj boring
uguagli'anza nf equality
uguagli'are vt make equal; (essere uguale) equal; (livellare) level
uguagli'arsi vr ~ a compare oneself to
⚜ **ugu'ale** ⚊1⚊ adj equal; (lo stesso) the same; (simile) like; **due più due è** ~ **a quattro** two plus two equals four
 ⚊2⚊ nm Math equals sign; **che non ha** ~ unequalled
ugual'mente adv equally; (malgrado tutto) all the same
'ulcera nf ulcer
■ **ulcera gastrica** gastric ulcer; **ulcera peptica** peptic ulcer
u'liva nf ▶ OLIVA
uli'veto nm olive grove
u'livo nm olive[-tree]
'ulna nf Anat ulna
ulteri'ore adj further
ulterior'mente adv further
ultima'mente adv lately
ulti'mare vt complete
ulti'matum nm inv ultimatum
ulti'missime nfpl Journ stop press, latest news sg
⚜ **'ultimo** ⚊1⚊ adj last; (notizie ecc) latest; (più lontano) farthest; fig ultimate; ‹prezzo› rockbottom; **l'** ~ **piano** the top floor
 ⚊2⚊ nm last; **fino all'** ~ to the last; **per** ~ at the end
ultimo'genito, -a nmf last-born

⚜ indicates a very frequent word

ultrà nmf inv Sport fanatical supporter
ultraleg'gero nm (aereo) microlight
ultrapi'atto adj ultra-thin
ultrapo'tente adj extra-strong
ultra'rapido adj extra-fast
ultraresi'stente adj extra-strong
ultrasen'sibile adj ultrasensitive
ultrasessan'tenne nm gli ultrasessantenni the over-60s
ultra'sonico adj ultrasonic
ultrasu'ono nm ultrasound
ultrater'reno adj ‹vita› after death
ultravio'letto adj ultraviolet
ulu'lare vi howl
ulu'lato nm howling; **gli ululati** the howls, the howling
umana'mente adv ‹trattare› humanely; ~ **impossibile** not humanly possible
uma'nesimo nm humanism
uma'nista nmf humanist
⚜ **umanità** nf humanity
umani'tario adj humanitarian
⚜ **u'mano** adj human; (benevolo) humane
'Umbria nf Umbria
'umbro, -a adj & nmf Umbrian
umet'tare vt moisten
umidifica'tore nm humidifier
umidità nf dampness; (di clima) humidity
'umido ⚊1⚊ adj damp; ‹clima› humid; ‹mani, occhi› moist
 ⚊2⚊ nm dampness; **in** ~ Culin stewed
⚜ **'umile** adj humble
umili'ante adj humiliating
⚜ **umili'are** vt humiliate
umili'arsi vr humble oneself
umiliazi'one nf humiliation
umil'mente adv humbly
umiltà nf humility
u'more nm humour; (stato d'animo) mood; **di cattivo/buon** ~ in a bad/good mood
umo'rismo nm humour
umo'rista nmf humorist
umoristica'mente adv humorously
umo'ristico adj humorous
un ▶ UNO
un' ▶ UNO
'una ▶ UNO
u'nanime adj unanimous
unanime'mente adv unanimously
unanimità nf unanimity; **all'** ~ unanimously
unci'nare vt hook
unci'nato adj hooked; ‹parentesi› angle attrib
unci'netto nm crochet hook
un'cino nm hook
undi'cenne adj & nmf eleven-year-old

undi'cesimo *adj & nm* eleventh

✓ '**undici** *adj & nm* eleven

'**ungere** *vt* grease; (sporcare) get greasy; Relig anoint; (blandire) flatter

'**ungersi** *vr* (con olio solare) oil oneself; ~ **le mani** get one's hands greasy

unghe'rese [1] *adj & nmf* Hungarian [2] *nm* (lingua) Hungarian

Unghe'ria *nf* Hungary

✓ '**unghia** *nf* nail; (di animale) claw; **cadere sotto le unghie di qualcuno** fall into somebody's clutches

■ **unghia fessa** cloven hoof

unghi'ata *nf* (graffio) scratch

ungu'ento *nm* ointment

unica'mente *adv* only

unicellu'lare *adj* single-cell, unicellular

unicità *nf* uniqueness

✓ '**unico** *adj* only; (singolo) single; (incomparabile) unique

uni'corno *nm* unicorn

unidimensio'nale *adj* one-dimensional

unidirezio'nale *adj* unidirectional

unifamili'are *adj* one-family

unifi'care *vt* unify

unificazi'one *nf* unification

unifor'mare *vt* level

unifor'marsi *vr* conform (a to)

uni'forme [1] *adj* uniform [2] *nf* uniform

■ **uniforme di gala** Mil mess dress

uniformità *nf* uniformity

unilate'rale *adj* unilateral

unilateral'mente *adv* unilaterally

uninomi'nale *adj* Pol single-candidate

uni'one *nf* union; (armonia) unity, **Unione economica e monetaria** Economic and Monetary Union

■ **unione di fatto** registered partnership; **Unione Europea** European Union; **Unione Monetaria Europea** European Monetary Union; **unione sindacale** trade union, labor union Am; **Unione Sovietica** Soviet Union

unio'nista *nmf* Pol Unionist

✓ **u'nire** *vt* unite; (collegare) join; blend «*colori ecc*»

u'nirsi *vr* unite; (collegarsi) join

'**unisex** *adj inv* unisex

u'nisono *nm* all'~ in unison

unità *nf inv* unity; Math, Mil (reparto ecc) unit; Comput drive

■ **unità di archivio dati** data storage device; **unità di backup a nastro** Comput tape backup drive; **unità centrale di elaborazione** Comput central processing unit, CPU; **unità floppy disk** Comput floppy disk drive; **unità di inizializzazione** Comput boot drive; **unità di memoria di massa** Comput mass storage device; **unità di misura** unit of measurement; **unità a nastro magnetico** Comput tapedrive; **unità periferica** Comput peripheral; **unità di produzione** factory

unit; **unità socio-sanitaria locale** local health centre; **unità di visualizzazione** Comput visual display unit, VDU

uni'tario *adj* unitary; **prezzo unitario** unit price

u'nito *adj* united; «*tinta*» plain; «*comunità*» tight-knit

univer'sale *adj* universal

universaliz'zare *vt* universalize

universal'mente *adv* universally

✓ **università** *nf inv* university

universi'tario, -a [1] *adj* university *attrib* [2] *nmf* (docente) university lecturer; (studente) undergraduate

uni'verso *nm* universe

u'nivoco *adj* unambiguous

✓ **uno, -a** [1] *art indef* a; (davanti a vocale o h muta) an; **un esempio** an example [2] *pron* one; **a ~ a ~** one by one; ~ **alla volta** one at a time; **l'~ e l'altro** both [of them]; **né l'~ né l'altro** neither [of them]; ~ **di noi** one of us; ~ **fa quello che può** you do what you can [3] *adj* a, one [4] *nm* (numerale) one; (un tale) some man [5] *nf* some woman

'**unto** [1] *pp di* UNGERE [2] *adj* greasy [3] *nm* grease

untu'oso *adj* greasy

unzi'one *nf*

■ **l'Estrema Unzione** Extreme Unction, last rites

✓ **u'omo** *nm* (*pl* **uomini**) man; '**uomini**' (bagni) 'gents', 'men's room'

■ **uomo d'affari** business man; **uomo di colore** black man; **uomo di fiducia** right-hand man; **uomo di mondo** man of the world; **uomo-oggetto** toy boy; **uomo delle pulizie** cleaner; **uomo sandwich** sandwich man; **uomo di Stato** statesman; **uomo della strada** man on the street

✓ **u'ovo** *nm* (*pl f* **uova**) egg; **uova** *pl* **al bacon** bacon and eggs

■ **uovo barzotto** *o* **bazzotto** soft-boiled egg; **uovo in camicia** poached egg; **uovo di Colombo** obvious simple solution; **uovo all'occhio di bue** fried egg; **uovo all'ostrica** raw egg; **uovo di Pasqua** Easter egg; **uova al prosciutto** *pl* ham and eggs; **uovo sodo** hard-boiled egg; **uovo strapazzato** scrambled egg; **uovo al tegamino** fried egg

upgra'dabile *adj* upgradeable

'**upupa** *nf* hoopoe

ura'gano *nm* hurricane

u'ranio *nm* uranium

U'rano *nm* Urano

urba'nesimo *nm* urbanization

urba'nista *nmf* town planner

urba'nistica *nf* town planning

urba'nistico *adj* urban

urbaniz'zare *vt* urbanize

urbanizzazi'one *nf* urbanization

u

ur'bano *adj* urban; (cortese) urbane

u'rea *nf* urea

u'retra *nf* Anat urethra

✓ **ur'gente** *adj* urgent

urgente'mente *adv* urgently

ur'genza *nf* urgency; **in caso d'~** in an emergency; **d'~** ‹misura, chiamata› emergency *attrib*; **operare d'~** perform an emergency operation on

'urgere *vi* be urgent

u'rina *nf* urine

uri'nare *vi* urinate

✓ **ur'lare** *vi* shout, yell; ‹cane, vento› howl

'urlo *nm* (*pl m* **urli**, *pl f* **urla**) shout; (di cane, vento) howling

'urna *nf* urn; (elettorale) ballot box; **andare alle urne** go to the polls

urrà *int* hurrah!

URSS *nf abbr* (**Unione delle Repubbliche Socialiste Sovietiche**) USSR

ur'tare *vt* knock against; (scontrarsi) bump into; fig irritate

ur'tarsi *vr* collide; fig clash

'urto *nm* knock; (scontro) crash; (contrasto) conflict; fig clash; **d'~** ‹misure, terapia› shock

Uru'guay *nm* Uruguay

U.S.A. *nmpl* US[A] *sg*

usa e getta *adj inv* ‹rasoio, siringa› throw-away, disposable

u'sanza *nf* custom; (moda) fashion

✓ **u'sare** ① *vt* use; (impiegare) employ; (esercitare) exercise; **~ fare qualcosa** be in the habit of doing something
② *vi* (essere di moda) be fashionable; **non si usa più** it is out of fashion; ‹attrezzatura, espressione› it's not used any more

u'sato ① *adj* used; (non nuovo) second-hand
② *nm* second-hand goods *pl*; **dell'~** second-hand; **fuori dell'~** unusual

u'sbeco, -a *adj & nmf* Uzbekistani

u'scente *adj* ‹presidente› outgoing

usci'ere *nm* usher

'uscio *nm* door

✓ **u'scire** *vi* come out; (andare fuori) go out; (sfuggire) get out; (essere sorteggiato) come up; ‹giornale› come out; **~ da** Comput exit from, quit; **~ di strada** leave the road

✓ **u'scita** *nf* exit, way out; (spesa) outlay; (di autostrada) junction; (battuta) witty remark; (in ginnastica artistica) dismount; **uscite** *pl* Fin outgoings; **essere in libera ~** be off duty
■ **uscita di servizio** back door; **uscita di sicurezza** emergency exit, fire exit

usi'gnolo *nm* nightingale

✓ **'uso** *nm* use; (abitudine) custom; (usanza) usage; **fuori ~** out of use; **per ~ esterno** ‹medicina› for external use only

───────────────

✓ indicates a very frequent word

■ **uso e dosi** use and dosage

us'saro *nm* hussar

U.S.S.L. *nf abbr* (**Unità Socio-Sanitaria Locale**) local health centre

ustio'narsi *vr* burn oneself

ustio'nato, -a ① *nmf* burns case
② *adj* burnt

usti'one *nf* burn; **ustioni di primo grado** first-degree burns

usu'ale *adj* usual

usual'mente *adv* usually

usucapi'one *nf* Jur usucaption

usufru'ire *vi* **~ di** take advantage of, make use of

usu'frutto *nm* Jur use, usufruct fml

usufruttu'ario, -a *nmf* user, usufructuary fml

u'sura *nf* usury

usu'raio *nm* usurer

usur'pare *vt* usurp

usurpa|'tore, -trice *nmf* usurper

u'tensile *nm* tool; Culin utensil; **cassetta degli utensili** tool box; **utensili** *pl* **da cucina** kitchen utensils

u'tente *nmf* user
■ **utente finale** end user; **utenti della strada** *pl* road users

u'tenza *nf* use; (utenti) users *pl*
■ **utenza finale** end users *pl*

ute'rino *adj* uterine

'utero *nm* womb

✓ **'utile** ① *adj* useful
② *nm* Comm profit; **unire l'~ al dilettevole** combine business with pleasure
■ **utile su cambi** foreign exchange gain; **utile sul capitale investito** return on investment

utilità *nf* usefulness, utility; Comput utility

utili'tario, -a ① *adj* utilitarian
② *nf* Auto small car

utilita'ristico *adj* utilitarian

u'tility *nm* utility

utiliz'zare *vt* utilize

utilizzazi'one *nf* utilization

uti'lizzo *nm* use

util'mente *adv* usefully

Uto'pia *nf* Utopia

uto'pista *nmf* Utopian

uto'pistico *adj* Utopian

'uva *nf* grapes *pl*; **chicco d'uva** grape
■ **uva bianca** white grapes; **uva nera** black grapes; **uva passa** raisins *pl*; **uva sultanina** currants *pl*; **uva da tavola** [eating] grapes; **uva da vino** wine grapes

UVA *nmpl abbr* (**ultravioletto prossimo**) UV

u'vetta *nf* raisins *pl*

uxori'cida ① *nm* wife-killer, uxoricide fml
② *nf* husband-killer

Uzbeki'stan *nm* Uzbekistan

Vv

va' ▶ ANDARE
va'cante *adj* vacant
va'canza *nf* holiday, vacation Am; **[giorno di]** ~ holiday; (posto vacante) vacancy; **vacanze** *pl* holidays, vacation Am; Univ vacation, vac *fam*; **essere in** ~ be on holiday/vacation; **prendersi una** ~ take a holiday/vacation; **andare in** ~ go on holiday/vacation; **è** ~ it's a holiday
■ **vacanza avventura** adventure holiday; **vacanze** *pl* **estive** summer holidays/vacation; **vacanze** *pl* **di Natale** Christmas holidays/ vacation; **vacanze** *pl* **di Pasqua** Easter holidays/vacation; **vacanze** *pl* **scolastiche** school holidays/vacation
vacan'ziere, -a *nmf* vacationer Am, holidaymaker Br
'vacca *nf* cow
■ **vacca da latte** dairy cow
vac'caro, -a *nf* cowherd
vacci'nare *vt* vaccinate; **farsi** ~ get vaccinated
vaccinazi'one *nf* vaccination
vac'cino *nm* vaccine
vacil'lante *adj* tottering; ‹oggetto› wobbly; ‹luce› flickering; *fig* wavering, faltering
vacil'lare *vi* totter; ‹oggetto› wobble; ‹luce› flicker; *fig* waver
'vacuo [1] *adj* (vano) vain; *fig* empty [2] *nm* vacuum
'vado ▶ ANDARE
vaffan'culo *int* vulg fuck off!
vagabon'daggio *nm* Jur vagrancy
vagabon'dare *vi* wander
vaga'bondo [1] *adj* ‹cane› stray [2] *nmf* tramp
vaga'mente *adv* vaguely
va'gante *adj* wandering; **mina vagante** floating mine; **proiettile vagante** stray bullet
va'gare *vi* wander
vagheggi'are *vt* long for
va'ghezza *nf* vagueness
va'gina *nf* vagina
vagi'nale *adj* vaginal
va'gire *vi* whimper
va'gito *nm* whimper
'vaglia *nm inv* money order
■ **vaglia bancario** bank draft; **vaglia cambiario** promissory note; **vaglia internazionale** international money order; **vaglia postale** postal order
vagli'are *vt* sift; *fig* weigh
'vaglio *nm* sieve

'vago *adj* vague
vagon'cino *nm* (di funivia) car
■ **vagoncino a piattaforma** flat[bed] wagon
va'gone *nm* (per passeggeri) carriage, car; (per merci) truck, wagon
■ **vagone bagagliaio** luggage van, baggage car Am; **vagone ferroviario** railway carriage Br, railroad car Am; **vagone frigorifero** refrigerator van; **vagone letto** sleeper; **vagone postale** mail coach; **vagone ristorante** restaurant car, dining car
vai'olo *nm* smallpox
va'langa *nf* avalanche
val'chiria *nf* Valkyrie
val'dese *adj* & *nmf* Waldensian
va'lente *adj* skilful
va'lenza *nf* Chem valency; *fig* (valore) value
va'lere [1] *vi* be worth; (contare) count; ‹regola› apply (**per** to); (essere valido) be valid; **far** ~ **i propri diritti** assert one's rights; **farsi** ~ assert oneself; **non vale!** that's not fair!; **tanto vale che me ne vada** I might as well go [2] *vt* ~ **qualcosa a qualcuno** (procurare) earn somebody something; **valerne la pena** be worth it; **vale la pena di vederlo** it's worth seeing; **valersi di** avail oneself of
valeri'ana *nf* valerian
va'levole *adj* valid
'valgo *adj* **ginocchia** *pl* **valghe** knock knees
■ **alluce valgo** hallux valgus
vall'care *vt* cross
'valico *nm* pass
valida'mente *adv* validly; (efficacemente) efficiently; ‹contribuire› effectively
validità *nf inv* validity; **con** ~ **illimitata** valid indefinitely
'valido *adj* valid; (efficace) efficient; ‹contributo› valuable
valige'ria *nf* (fabbrica) leather factory; (negozio) leather goods shop
vali'getta *nf* small case; (per attrezzi) box
■ **valigetta del pronto soccorso** first aid kit; **valigetta ventiquattrore** overnight bag
va'ligia *nf* suitcase; **fare le valigie** pack; *fig* pack one's bags
■ **valigia diplomatica** diplomatic bag
val'lata *nf* valley
'valle *nf* valley; **a** ~ downstream
val'letta *nf* TV assistant
val'letto *nm* valet; TV assistant
'vallo *nm* wall; **il** ~ **Adriano** Hadrian's Wall
val'lone¹ *nm* (valle) deep valley
val'lone², -a *adj* & *nmf* Walloon

ꝓ **va'lore** *nm* value, worth; (merito) merit; (coraggio) valour; **valori** *pl* Comm securities; **di ~** (oggetto) valuable; **oggetti di valore** valuables; **di grande ~** of great value; ‹*medico, scienziato*› top *attrib*; **senza ~** worthless; **a ~ aggiunto** value-added
■ **valore bollato** revenue stamp; **valore contabile** book value; **valore effettivo** real value; **valore di mercato** market value, street value; **valore mobiliare** security; **valore nominale** nominal value; **valore di realizzo** break-up value; **valore di riscatto** surrender value

valoriz'zare *vt* (mettere in valore) use to advantage; (aumentare di valore) increase the value of; (migliorare l'aspetto di) enhance

valoriz'zarsi *vr* **il paese ha bisogno di ~ migliorando...** the country needs to enhance the value of its assets by improving...

valorosa'mente *adv* courageously

valo'roso *adj* courageous

'valso *pp di* VALERE

va'luta *nf* currency
■ **valuta a corso legale** legal tender; **valuta estera** foreign currency

valu'tare *vt* value; weigh up ‹*situazione*›

valu'tario *adj* ‹*mercato, norme*› currency *attrib*

valuta'tivo *adj* for evaluation, evaluative

valutazi'one *nf* valuation

'valva *nf* valve

'valvola *nf* valve; Electr fuse
■ **valvola a farfalla** butterfly valve; **valvola pneumatica** air valve; **valvola di sicurezza** *anche fig* safety valve

'valzer *nm inv* waltz

vamp *nf inv* vamp

vam'pata *nf* blaze; (di calore) blast; (al viso) flush

vam'piro *nm* vampire; *fig* bloodsucker

va'nadio *nm* vanadium

vanaglori'oso *adj* vainglorious

vana'mente *adv* (inutilmente) in vain; (con vanità) vainly

van'dalico *adj* **atto ~** act of vandalism

vanda'lismo *nm* vandalism

vandaliz'zare *vt* vandalize

vandalizzazi'one *nf* vandalizing

'vandalo, -a *nmf* vandal

vaneggia'mento *nm* delirium

vaneggi'are *vi* rave

va'nesio *adj* conceited

'vanga *nf* spade

van'gare *vt* dig

van'gata *nf* (quantità) spadeful; (azione) blow with a spade

van'gelo *nm* Gospel; *fam*; (verità) gospel [truth]

vanifi'care *vt* nullify

va'niglia *nf* vanilla

vanigli'ato *adj* ‹*zucchero*› vanilla

vanil'lina *nf* vanillin

vanità *nf* vanity

vanitosa'mente *adv* vainly

vani'toso *adj* vain

'vano ① *adj* vain
② *nm* (stanza) room; (spazio vuoto) hollow
■ **vano doccia** shower room; **vano portabagagli** Auto boot, trunk Am

ꝓ **van'taggio** *nm* advantage; Sport lead; Tennis advantage; **trarre ~ da qualcosa** derive benefit from something

vantaggiosa'mente *adv* advantageously

vantaggi'oso *adj* advantageous

van'tare *vt* praise; (possedere) boast

van'tarsi *vr* boast

vante'ria *nf* boasting; **vanterie** *pl* boasting

'vanto *nm* boast

'vanvera *nf* **a ~** at random; **parlare a ~** talk nonsense

va'pore *nm* steam; (di benzina, cascata) vapour; **a ~** steam *attrib*; **al ~** Culin steamed; **battello a vapore** steamboat
■ **vapore acqueo** steam, water vapour

vapo'retto *nm* ferry

vapori'era *nf* steam engine

vaporiz'zare *vt* vaporize

vaporizza'tore *nm* spray

vapo'roso *adj* ‹*vestito*› filmy; **capelli** *pl* big hair

va'rano *nm* monitor [lizard]

va'rare *vt* launch

var'care *vt* cross

'varco *nm* passage; **aspettare al ~** lie in wait

vare'china *nf* bleach

vari'abile ① *adj* changeable, variable
② *nf* Math variable

variabilità *nf* changeableness, variability

varia'mente *adv* variously

vari'ante *nf* variant

vari'are *vt/i* vary; **~ di umore** change one's mood

vari'ato *adj* varied

variazi'one *nf* variation

va'rice *nf* varicose vein

vari'cella *nf* chickenpox

vari'coso *adj* varicose

varie'gato *adj* variegated

varietà ① *nf inv* variety
② *nm inv* variety show

ꝓ **'vario** *adj* varied; (al pl, parecchi) various; **varie** *pl* (molti) several; **varie ed eventuali** any other business

vario'pinto *adj* multicoloured

'varo *nm* launch

Var'savia *nf* Warsaw

ꝓ indicates a very frequent word

vasaio *nm* potter

'vasca *nf* tub; (piscina) pool; (lunghezza) length
■ **vasca da bagno** bath; **vasca con idromassaggio** whirlpool bath; **vasca di sviluppo** Phot developing tank

va'scello *nm* vessel; **capitano di vascello** captain

va'schetta *nf* tub; Phot tray
■ **vaschetta per il ghiaccio** ice-tray

vasco'lare *adj* Anat, Bot vascular

vasecto'mia *nf* vasectomy

vase'lina *nf* Vaseline®

vasel'lame *nm* china
■ **vasellame d'oro/d'argento** gold/silver plate

va'setto *nm* small pot; (per marmellata) jam jar

⚘ **'vaso** *nm* pot; (da fiori) vase; Anat vessel; (per cibi) jar
■ **vaso da notte** chamberpot; **vaso sanguigno** blood vessel

vasocostrit'tore *adj* vasoconstrictor

vasodilata'tore *adj* vasodilator

vas'sallo *nm* vassal

vas'coio *nm* tray

vastità *nf* vastness

⚘ **'vasto** *adj* vast; **di vaste vedute** broadminded

Vati'cano *nm* Vatican

vati'cinio *nm* prophecy

vattela'pesca *adv* fam God knows

'vattene! go away!; ▶ ANDARE

VCR *abbr* (**videoregistratore**) VCR

⚘ **ve** *pers pron* you; **ve l'ho dato** I gave it to you

'vecchia *nf* old woman

vecchi'aia *nf* old age

⚘ **'vecchio, -a** [1] *adj* old
[2] *nmf* old man; old woman; **i vecchi** old people; ~ **mio** old man

'veccia *nf* vetch

'vece *nf* **in** ~ **di** in place of; **fare le veci di qualcuno** take somebody's place

ve'dente *adj* **i non** ~ the visually handicapped

⚘ **ve'dere** [1] *vt* see; see, watch ‹film, partita›; **farsi** ~ show one's face; **non si vede** ‹macchia, imperfezione› it doesn't show; **non veder l'ora di fare qualcosa** be raring to go; **non poter** ~ **qualcuno** not be able to stand the sight of somebody; **vederci doppio** have double vision; **ne ho viste di tutti i colori** fig I've really seen life; **da** ~ ‹film, spettacolo› not to be missed; **questo è da** ~! that remains to be seen!; **chi si vede!** fam look who it is!
[2] *vi* see

ve'dersi *vr* see oneself; (reciproco) see each other; **vedersela brutta** have a narrow escape

ve'detta *nf* (luogo) lookout; (*Naut*), patrol vessel

'vedova *nf* widow
■ **vedova nera** Zool black widow [spider]

'vedovo *nm* widower

ve'duta *nf* view

vee'mente *adj* vehement

vege'tale *adj & nm* vegetable

vegetali'ano *adj & nmf* vegan

vegeta'lismo *nm* veganism

vege'tare *vi* vegetate

vegetaria'nismo *nm* vegetarianism

vegetari'ano, -a *adj & nmf* vegetarian

vegeta'tivo *adj* vegetative

vegetazi'one *nf* vegetation

'vegeto *adj* ▶ VIVO

veg'gente *nmf* clairvoyant

'veglia *nf* watch; **fare la** ~ keep watch
■ **veglia funebre** vigil

vegli'are *vi* be awake; ~ **su** watch over

vegli'one *nm*
■ **veglione di capodanno** New Year's Eve celebration

veico'lare [1] *vt* carry ‹malattia›
[2] *adj* ‹traffico› vehicular

ve'icolo *nm* vehicle
■ **veicolo pesante** heavy goods vehicle, HGV; **veicolo spaziale** spacecraft

⚘ **'vela** *nf* sail; Sport sailing; **andare a gonfie vele** fig go beautifully; ‹affari› be booming; **far** ~ set sail
■ **vela di taglio** mainsail

ve'lare *vt* veil; fig (nascondere) hide

ve'larsi *vr* ‹vista› mist over; ‹voce› go husky

velata'mente *adv* indirectly

ve'lato *adj* veiled; ‹occhi› misty; ‹collant› sheer

vela'tura *nf* sails *pl*

'velcro® *nm* velcro®

veleggi'are *vi* sail

ve'leno *nm* poison

velenosa'mente *adv* ‹rispondere› venomously

vele'noso *adj* poisonous; ‹frase› venomous

ve'letta *nf* (di cappello) veil

'velico *adj* ‹circolo› sailing attrib; **superficie velica** sail area

veli'ero *nm* sailing ship

ve'lina *nf* young female assistant on some entertainment programmes who dances around and looks pretty
■ **(carta) velina** tissue paper; (copia) carbon copy

ve'lista [1] *nm* yachtsman
[2] *nf* yachtswoman

ve'livolo *nm* aircraft

velleità *nf inv* foolish ambition

vellei'tario *adj* unrealistic

'vello *nm* fleece

vellu'tato *adj* velvety

vel'luto *nm* velvet
■ **velluto a coste** corduroy

'velo *nm* veil; (di zucchero, cipria) dusting; (tessuto) voile

⚘ **ve'loce** *adj* fast

veloce'mente *adv* quickly
velo'cipede *nm* penny-farthing
velo'cista *nmf* Sport sprinter
velocità *nf inv* speed; Auto (marcia) gear;
a due ∼ fig two-tier
■ velocità di clock Comput clock speed; velocità
di crociera cruising speed; velocità di stampa
print speed
velociz'zare *vt* speed up
ve'lodromo *nm* cycle track
'vena *nf* vein; essere in ∼ di be in the mood
for
■ vena poetica poetic mood
ve'nale *adj* venal; ‹persona› mercenary,
venal
ve'nato *adj* grainy
vena'torio *adj* hunting *attrib*
vena'tura *nf* (di legno) grain; (di foglia, marmo)
vein
ven'demmia *nf* grape harvest
vendemmi'are *vt* harvest
vendemmia|'tore, -trice *nmf*
grapepicker
◊ **'vendere** *vt* sell; 'vendesi' 'for sale'
'vendersi *vr* sell oneself
◊ **ven'detta** *nf* revenge
■ vendetta trasversale vendetta
vendi'care *vt* avenge
vendi'carsi *vr* take revenge, get one's
revenge; ∼ di qualcuno take one's
vengeance on somebody; ∼ di qualcosa take
revenge for something
vendicativa'mente *adv* vindictively
vendica'tivo *adj* vindictive
vendica|'tore, -trice *nmf* avenger
'vendita *nf* sale; in ∼ on sale
■ vendita all'asta sale by auction; vendita di
beneficenza bring and buy sale; vendita per
corrispondenza mail-order; azienda di ∼
per corrispondenza mail-order company;
catalogo di ∼ per corrispondenza mail-order
catalogue; vendita al dettaglio retailing;
vendite *pl* al dettaglio retail sales; vendita
all'ingrosso wholesaling; vendita al minuto
retailing; vendita porta a porta door-to-
door selling; vendita a rate hire purchase,
installment plan Am
vendi|'tore, -trice *nmf* seller
■ venditore ambulante hawker, pedlar;
venditore al dettaglio retailer; venditore
all'ingrosso wholesaler; venditore al mercato
market trader; venditore al minuto retailer
ven'duto *adj* ‹merce› sold; fig ‹arbitro› bent;
arbitro ∼! whose side are you on, ref!
vene'rabile, vene'rando *adj* venerable
vene'rare *vt* revere
venerazi'one *nf* reverence
venerdì *nm inv* Friday; di ∼ on Fridays

◊ indicates a very frequent word

■ Venerdì Santo Good Friday
'Venere *nf* Venus
ve'nereo *adj* venereal
'veneto *adj* from the Veneto
'Veneto *nm* Veneto
Ve'nezia *nf* Venice
venezi'ano, -a ① *adj & nmf* Venetian
② *nf* (persiana) Venetian blind; Culin sweet bun
Vene'zuela *nm* Venezuela
venezue'lano, -a *adj & nmf* Venezuelan
'vengo ▶ VENIRE
veni'ale *adj* venial
◊ **ve'nire** *vi* come; (riuscire) turn out; (costare)
cost; (in passivi) be; quanto viene? how much
is it?; viene prodotto in serie it's mass-
produced; ∼ a sapere learn; ∼ in mente
occur; mi è venuto un dubbio I've just had
a doubt; gli è venuta la febbre he's got a
temperature; ∼ meno (svenire) faint; ∼ meno
a un contratto go back on a contract, renege
on a contract; ∼ via come away; (staccarsi)
come off; mi viene da piangere I feel like
crying; vieni a prendermi come and pick me
up; vieni a trovarmi come and see me; nei
giorni a ∼ in [the] days to come
ve'noso *adj* venous
ven'taglio *nm* fan
ven'tata *nf* gust [of wind]; fig breath
ven'tenne *adj & nmf* twenty-year-old
ven'tesimo *adj & nm* twentieth
◊ **'venti** *adj & nm* twenty
venti'lare *vt* ventilate, air; ∼ un'idea give an
idea an airing; poco ventilato ‹stanza› airless
ventila'tore *nm* fan
ventilazi'one *nf* ventilation
ven'tina *nf* una ∼ (circa venti) about twenty
ventiquat'trore ① *nf inv* (valigetta)
overnight bag
② *adv* ∼ su ventiquattro ‹lavorare› round-
the-clock; ‹aperto› 24 hours
◊ **'vento** *nm* wind; c'è molto ∼ it's very
windy; farsi ∼ fan oneself
■ vento contrario headwind; vento di prua
headwind; vento di traverso crosswind
'ventola *nf* fan
vento'lina *nf* fan
■ ventolina di raffreddamento Comput cooling fan
ven'tosa *nf* sucker, suction pad
ven'toso *adj* windy
'ventre *nm* stomach; fig (di terra) bowels *pl*;
basso ∼ lower abdomen
ventrico'lare *adj* Med ventricular
ven'tricolo *nm* ventricle
ven'triloquo *nm* ventriloquist
ventu'nesimo *adj & nm* twenty-first
ven'tuno *adj & nm* twenty-one
ven'tura *nf* fortune; andare alla ∼ trust
to luck
ven'turo *adj* next

ve'nuta *nf* coming; ∼ **meno a** breaking

'vera *nf* (anello) wedding ring

⚘ **vera'mente** *adv* really

ve'randa *nf* veranda

ver'bale [1] *adj* verbal
[2] *nm* (di riunione) minutes *pl*
■ **verbale di contravvenzione** fine

verbal'mente *adv* verbally

ver'bena *nf* verbena

'verbo *nm* verb; **il Verbo** Relig the Word
■ **verbo ausiliare** auxiliary [verb]; **verbo modale** modal auxiliary; **verbo riflessivo** reflexive verb

ver'boso *adj* verbose

ver'dastro *adj* greenish

⚘ **'verde** [1] *adj* green; ∼ **d'invidia** green with envy
[2] *nm* green; (vegetazione) greenery; (semaforo) green light; **essere al** ∼ be broke
■ **verde bottiglia** bottle green; **verde oliva** olive green; **verde pisello** pea green; **verde pubblico** public parks *pl*

verdeggi'ante *adj* (liter) verdant

verde'mare *adj* & *nm inv* sea-green

verde'rame *nm* verdigris

ver'detto *nm* verdict
■ **verdetto di assoluzione** not guilty verdict; **verdetto di condanna** guilty verdict

ver'done *nm* greenfinch

ver'dura *nf* vegetables *pl*; **una** ∼ a vegetable; **verdure** *pl* **miste** mixed vegetables

'verga *nf* rod

ver'gato *adj* lined

vergi'nale *adj* virginal

'vergine [1] *nf* virgin; Astr Virgo
[2] *adj* virgin; ‹cassetta› blank

vergi'nità *nf* virginity

⚘ **ver'gogna** *nf* shame; (timidezza) shyness

⚘ **vergo'gnarsi** *vr* feel ashamed; (essere timido) feel shy

vergognosa'mente *adv* shamefully

vergo'gnoso *adj* ashamed; (timido) shy; (disonorevole) shameful

veridicità *nf* veracity

ve'rifica *vt* check
■ **verifica dei bilanci** audit; **verifica di cassa** cash check

verifi'cabile *adj* verifiable

verifi'care *vt* check; verify ‹teoria›

verifi'carsi *vr* come true

verifica|'tore, -trice *nmf* checker

ve'rismo *nm* realism

⚘ **verità** *nf inv* truth

veriti'ero *adj* truthful

'verme *nm* worm
■ **verme solitario** tapeworm

vermi'celli *nmpl* vermicelli *sg* (*pasta thinner than spaghetti*)

ver'mifugo [1] *adj* vermifugal

[2] *nm* vermifuge

ver'miglio *adj* & *nm* vermilion

'vermut *nm inv* vermouth

ver'nacolo *nm* vernacular

ver'nice *nf* paint; (trasparente) varnish; (pelle) patent leather; fig veneer; '∼ **fresca**' 'wet paint'
■ **vernice a spirito** spirit varnish

vernici'are *vt* paint; (con vernice trasparente) varnish

vernicia'tura *nf* painting; (con vernice trasparente) varnishing; (strato) paintwork; fig veneer

vernis'sage *nm inv* vernissage

⚘ **'vero** [1] *adj* true; (autentico) real; (perfetto) perfect; **è** ∼**?** is that so?; ∼ **e proprio** full-blown; **sei stanca,** ∼**?** you're tired, aren't you; **non ti piace,** ∼**?** you don't like it, do you?
■ **vero cuoio** real leather
[2] *nm* truth; (realtà) life

verosimigli'anza *nf* plausibility

vero'simile *adj* probable, likely

verosimil'mente *adv* probably

ver'ruca *nf* wart; (sotto la pianta del piede) verruca

versa'mento *nm* (pagamento) payment; (in banca) deposit

ver'sante *nm* slope

⚘ **ver'sare** [1] *vt* pour; (spargere) shed; (rovesciare) spill; pay ‹denaro›; (in banca) pay in
[2] *vi* (trovarsi) be

ver'sarsi *vr* spill; (sfociare) flow

ver'satile *adj* versatile

versatilità *nf* versatility

ver'sato *adj* (pratico) versed

ver'setto *nm* verse

versifica|'tore, -trice *nmf* versifier

versi'one *nf* version; (traduzione) translation
■ '**versione integrale**' (libro) 'unabridged version'; (film) 'uncut'; **versione originale** original version; '**versione ridotta**' 'abridged version'; **versione teatrale** dramatization

'verso[1] *nm* verse; (grido) cry; (gesto) gesture; (senso) direction; (modo) manner; **fare il** ∼ **a qualcuno** ape somebody; **non c'è** ∼ **di** there is no way of; **versi** *pl* **sciolti** blank verse

⚘ **'verso**[2] *prep* towards; (nei pressi di) round about; ∼ **dove?** which way?

'vertebra *nf* vertebra

verte'brale *adj* vertebral

verte'brato *nm* vertebrate

ver'tenza *nf* dispute
■ **vertenza sindacale** industrial dispute

'vertere *vi* ∼ **su** focus on

verti'cale [1] *adj* vertical; (in parole crociate) down
[2] *nm* vertical
[3] *nf* handstand; **fare la** ∼ do a handstand

vertical'mente *adv* vertically

v

'vertice *nm* summit; Math vertex;
  conferenza al vertice summit conference;
  incontro al vertice summit meeting
ver'tigine *nf* dizziness; Med vertigo;
  vertigini *pl* giddy spells; **avere le vertigini**
  feel dizzy
vertiginosa'mente *adv* dizzily
vertigi'noso *adj* dizzy; ⟨velocità⟩ breakneck;
  ⟨prezzi⟩ sky-high; ⟨scollatura⟩ plunging
'vescia *nf* puffball
ve'scica *nf* bladder; (sulla pelle) blister
'vescovo *nm* bishop
'vespa *nf* wasp
'Vespa® *nf* scooter, Vespa®
vespasi'ano *nm* urinal
'vespro *nm* vespers *pl*
ves'sare *vt fml* oppress
ves'sillo *nm* standard
ve'staglia *nf* dressing gown, robe Am
'veste *nf* dress; (rivestimento) covering; **in**
  ∼ di in the capacity of; **in ∼ ufficiale** in an
  official capacity
  ■ **veste da camera** dressing gown, robe Am;
  veste editoriale layout; **veste tipografica**
  typographical design
vesti'ario *nm* clothing
ve'stibolo *nm* hall
ve'stigio *nm* (*pl m* **vestigi**, *pl f*
  vestigia) trace
ᕀ **ve'stire** *vt* dress
ve'stirsi *vr* get dressed; **∼ da** dress up as a
ᕀ **ve'stito** ① *adj* dressed
  ② *nm* (da uomo) suit; (da donna) dress; **vestiti**
  pl clothes
  ■ **vestito da sposa** wedding dress; **vestito da**
  uomo suit
vete'rano, -a *adj & nmf* veteran
veteri'nario, -a ① *adj* veterinary
  ② *nm* veterinary surgeon
  ③ *nf* veterinary science
'veto *nm inv* veto
ve'traio *nm* glazier
ve'trato, -a ① *adj* glazed
  ② *nf* big window; (in chiesa) stained-glass
  window; (porta) glass door
vetre'ria *nf* glass works
ve'trina *nf* [shop-]window; (mobile) display
  cabinet
vetri'nista *nmf* window dresser
ve'trino *nm* (di microscopio) slide
vetri'olo *nm* vitriol
ᕀ **'vetro** *nm* glass; (di finestra, porta) pane
  ■ **∼ di sicurezza** safety glass
vetro'resina *nf* fibreglass
ve'troso *adj* vitreous
'vetta *nf* peak
vet'tore *nm* vector
vetto'vaglie *nfpl* provisions

vet'tura *nf* coach; (ferroviaria) coach,
  carriage; Auto car
  ■ **vettura di cortesia** courtesy car; **vettura**
  d'epoca vintage car
vettu'rino *nm* coachman
vezzeggi'are *vt* fondle
vezzeggia'tivo *nm* pet name
'vezzo *nm* habit; (attrattiva) charm; **vezzi** *pl*
  (moine) affectation
vez'zoso *adj* charming; pej affected
VF *abbr* (**Vigili del Fuoco**) fire brigade,
  fire department Am
ᕀ **vi** ① *pers pron* you; (riflessivo) yourselves;
  (reciproco) each other; (tra più persone) one
  another; **vi ho dato un libro** I gave you a
  book; **lavatevi le mani** wash your hands;
  eccovi! here you are!
  ② *adv* = CI
ᕀ **via¹** *nf* street, road; fig way; Anat tract; **in ∼**
  di in the course of; **per ∼ di** on account of;
  per ∼ aerea by airmail
  ■ **Via Lattea** Astr Milky Way; **via di mezzo**
  halfway house; **via respiratoria** Anat airway;
  via d'uscita let-out
ᕀ **via²** ① *adv* away; (fuori) out; **andar ∼** go
  away; ⟨macchia⟩ come off, come out; **e**
  così ∼ and so on; **e ∼ dicendo** and whatnot;
  ∼ ∼ che as
  ② *int* ∼! go away!; Sport go!; (andiamo) come
  on!; **∼, non ci credo** come off it *or* come on,
  I don't believe it
  ③ *nm* starting signal
viabilità *nf* road conditions *pl*; (rete) road
  network; (norme) road and traffic laws *pl*
via'card *nf inv* motorway card
vi'ado *nm* (*pl* **viados**) rent boy
via'dotto *nm* viaduct
ᕀ **viaggi'are** *vi* travel; **il treno viaggia con**
  20 minuti di ritardo the train is 20 minutes late
viaggia|'tore, trice *nmf* traveller
ᕀ **vi'aggio** *nm* journey; (breve) trip; **buon ∼!**
  safe journey!, have a good trip!; **fare un ∼**
  go on a journey; **essere in ∼** be underway;
  mettersi in ∼ get underway
  ■ **viaggio d'affari** business trip; **viaggio**
  di lavoro working trip; **viaggio di nozze**
  honeymoon; **viaggio organizzato** package tour
vi'ale *nm* avenue; (privato) drive
via'letto *nm* path
via'vai *nm* coming and going
vi'brante *adj* vibrant
vi'brare *vi* vibrate; (fremere) quiver
vibra'tore *nm* vibrator
vibra'torio *adj* vibratory
vibrazi'one *nf* vibration
vi'cario *nm* vicar
'vice *nmf* deputy
vice+ *pref* vice+
vicecoman'dante *nm* Mil second in
  command

vicediret|'tore, -trice 1 *nm* assistant manager

2 *nf* assistant manageress

⚬ **vi'cenda** *nf* event; **a ~** (fra due) each other; (a turno) in turn[s]

vicendevol'mente *adv* each other

vice'preside *nmf* vice-principal

vicepresi'dente *nm* vice-president; Comm vice-chairman, vice-president Am

vicepresi'denza *nf* vice-presidency; Sch deputy head's office

vicerè *nm inv* viceroy

viceret'tore *nm* vice-chancellor

vice'versa *adv* vice versa

vi'chingo, -a *adj & nmf* Viking

vi'cina *nf* neighbour

vici'nanza *nf* nearness; *pl* **vicinanze** (paraggi) neighbourhood

vici'nato *nm* neighbourhood; (vicini) neighbours *pl*

⚬ **vi'cino, -a** 1 *adj* near; (accanto) next

2 *adv* near, close

3 *prep* **~ a** near [to]

4 *nmf* neighbour

■ **vicino di casa** nextdoor neighbour

vicissi'tudine *nf* vicissitude

'vicolo *nm* alley

■ **vicolo cieco** anche fig blind alley

'video *nm* (musicale) video; (schermo) screen

■ **video interattivo** interactive video

video'camera *nf* camcorder

videocas'setta *nf* video, video cassette

videoci'tofono *nm* video entry phone, videophone

video'clip *nm inv* video clip

videoconfe'renza *nf* videoconference

video'disco *nm* videodisc

videofo'nino® *n* videophone, camera phone

videogi'oco *nm* video game

video'leso, -a 1 *adj* visually handicapped, visually impaired

2 *nmf* visually handicapped person

videoregistra'tore *nm* videorecorder

videoscrit'tura *nf* word processing

videosorvegli'anza *nf* video surveillance

video'teca *nf* video library

video'tel® *nm* Videotex®

videote'lefono *nm* view phone

videotermi'nale *nm* visual display unit, VDU

vidi'mare *vt* authenticate

vi'eni ▶ VENIRE

Vi'enna *nf* Vienna

vien'nese *adj & nmf* Viennese

⚬ **vie'tare** *vt* forbid; **~ qualcosa a qualcuno** forbid somebody something

vie'tato *adj* forbidden; **sosta vietata** no parking; **~ fumare** no smoking; **~ ai minori di 18 anni** ‹film› for over 18-year-olds only, X-rated

Vi'etnam *nm* Vietnam

vietna'mita *adj & nmf* Vietnamese

vi'gente *adj* in force

'vigere *vi* be in force

vigi'lante *adj* vigilant

vigi'lanza *nf* vigilance; (sorveglianza) (a scuola) supervision; (di polizia) surveillance

■ **vigilanza notturna** night security guards *pl*; **vigilanza urbana** traffic police (*in towns*)

vigi'lare 1 *vt* keep an eye on

2 *vi* keep watch

vigi'lato, -a 1 *adj* under surveillance

2 *nmf* person under police surveillance

■ **vigilato speciale** person under special police surveillance

'vigile 1 *adj* watchful

2 *nm* **~ [urbano]** traffic policeman

■ **vigile del fuoco** fireman, firefighter; **vigili del fuoco** *pl* firemen, fire brigade, fire service; **vigili urbani** *pl* traffic police (*in towns*)

vi'gilia *nf* eve; Relig fast

■ **vigilia di Natale** Christmas Eve

vigliacca'mente *adv* in a cowardly way

vigliacche'ria *nf* cowardice

⚬ **vigli'acco, -a** 1 *adj* cowardly

2 *nmf* coward

'vigna *nf*, **vi'gneto** *nm* vineyard

vi'gnetta *nf* cartoon

vignet'tista *nm* cartoonist

vi'gogna *nf* (tessuto) vicuña

vi'gore *nm* vigour; **entrare in ~** come into force; **essere in ~** be in force

vigorosa'mente *adv* energetically

vigo'roso *adj* vigorous

'vile *adj* cowardly; (abietto) vile

vili'pendio *nm* scorn, contempt

⚬ **'villa** *nf* villa

vil'laggio *nm* village

■ **villaggio olimpico** Olympic village; **villaggio residenziale** commuter town; **villaggio satellite** satellite village; **villaggio turistico** holiday village

villa'nia *nf* rudeness

vil'lano 1 *adj* rude

2 *nm* boor; (contadino) peasant

villeggi'ante *nmf* holidaymaker

villeggi'are *vi* spend one's holidays

villeggia'tura *nf* holiday[s] *pl*

vil'letta *nf* small detached house

■ **villetta bifamiliare** semi-detached house; **villette a schiera** *pl* terraced houses

vil'lino *nm* detached house

vil'loso *adj* hairy

vil'mente *adv* in a cowardly way; (in modo spregevole) contemptibly

viltà *nf* cowardice

'vimine *nm* wicker; **sedia di vimini** wicker chair

vi'naio, **-a** *nmf* wine merchant

ꝭ **'vincere** *vt* win; (sconfiggere) beat; (superare) overcome

'vincita *nf* win; (somma vinta) winnings *pl*

vinci'tore, **-trice** ① *nmf* winner; (di battaglia) victor, winner ② *adj* winning, victorious

vinco'lante *adj* binding

vinco'lare *vt* bind; Comm tie up

vinco'lato *adj* Fin nonredeemable; **deposito vincolato** fixed deposit, term deposit

'vincolo *nm* bond

vi'nicolo *adj* wine *attrib*

vi'nile *nm* vinyl

vi'nilico *adj* vinyl

vinil'pelle® *nm* Leatherette®

ꝭ **'vino** *nm* wine
■ **vino d'annata** vintage wine; **vino bianco** white wine; **vino della casa** house wine; **vino da dessert** dessert wine; **vino nuovo** new wine; **vino rosato** rosé [wine]; **vino rosé** rosé [wine]; **vino rosso** red wine; **vino spumante** sparkling wine; **vino da taglio** blending wine; **vino da tavola** table wine

vin'santo *nm dessert wine from Tuscany*

'vinto *pp di* VINCERE

vi'ola *nf* Bot violet; Mus viola
■ **viola del pensiero** Bot pansy

vio'laceo *adj* purplish; ⟨labbra⟩ blue

vio'lare *vt* violate

violazi'one *nf* violation
■ **violazione di contratto** breach of contract; **violazione di domicilio** breaking and entering

violen'tare *vt* rape

violente'mente *adv* violently

ꝭ **vio'lento** *adj* violent

ꝭ **vio'lenza** *nf* violence
■ **violenza carnale** rape

vio'letto, **-a** ① *adj & nm* (colore) violet ② *nf* violet

violi'nista *nmf* violinist

vio'lino *nm* violin

violon'cello *nm* cello

vi'ottolo *nm* path

'vipera *nf* viper

vi'raggio *nm* Phot toning; Naut, Aeron turn

vi'rale *adj* viral

vi'rare *vi* turn; ⟨nave⟩ put about; **virare di bordo** change course

vi'rata *nf* (di aereo) turning; (di nave) coming about; (nel nuoto) turn; fig change of direction

'virgola *nf* comma; Math [decimal] point; **punto e virgola** semicolon; **quattro ∼ due (4,2)** (decimali) four point two (4.2)

virgo'lette *nfpl* inverted commas, quotation marks

vi'rile *adj* virile; (da uomo) manly

virilità *nf* virility; manliness

viril'mente *adv* in a manly way

vi'rologo *nm* virologist

virtù *nf inv* virtue; **in ∼ di** ⟨legge⟩ under

virtu'ale *adj* virtual

virtual'mente *adv* virtually

virtuo'sismo *nm* bravura

virtu'oso ① *adj* virtuous ② *nm* virtuoso

viru'lento *adj* virulent

'virus *nm* virus

visa'gista *nmf* beautician

visce'rale *adj* visceral; ⟨odio⟩ deep-seated; ⟨reazione⟩ gut

'viscere ① *nm* internal organ ② *nfpl* guts

'vischio *nm* mistletoe

vischi'oso *adj* viscous; (appiccicoso) sticky

'viscido *adj* slimy

vi'sconte *nm* viscount

viscon'tessa *nf* viscountess

vi'scoso *adj* viscous

vi'sibile *adj* visible

visi'bilio *nm* profusion; **andare in ∼** go into ecstasies

visibilità *nf* visibility; **scarsa visibilità** poor visibility

visi'era *nf* (di elmo) visor; (di berretto) peak

visio'nare *vt* examine; Cinema screen

visio'nario, **-a** *adj & nmf* visionary

visi'one *nf* vision; **prima visione** Cinema first showing; **seconda visione** re-release, second showing
■ **visione notturna** night vision

ꝭ **'visita** *nf* visit; (breve) call; Med examination; **fare ∼ a qualcuno** pay somebody a visit
■ **visita di controllo** Med checkup; **visita di cortesia** courtesy visit; **visita doganale** customs inspection; **visita a domicilio** home visit, call-out, house call; **visita fiscale** tax inspection; **visita guidata** guided tour; **visita lampo** flying visit; **visita di leva** medical examination (*for military service*)

ꝭ **visi'tare** *vt* visit; (brevemente) call on; Med examine

visita'tore, **-trice** *nmf* visitor

visiva'mente *adv* visually

vi'sivo *adj* visual

ꝭ **'viso** *nm* face
■ **viso pallido** paleface

vi'sone *nm* mink

'vispo *adj* lively

vis'suto ① *pp di* VIVERE ② *adj* experienced

ꝭ **'vista** *nf* sight; (veduta) view; **a ∼ d'occhio** ⟨crescere⟩ visibly; ⟨estendersi⟩ as far as the eye can see; **in ∼ di** in view of; **perdere di ∼ qualcuno** lose sight of somebody; fig lose

---

ꝭ indicates a very frequent word

touch with somebody; **a prima ∼** at first sight
■ **vista sul mare** sea view

'visto ① *pp di* VEDERE
② *nm* visa
■ **visto di entrata** *o* **di ingresso** entry visa, entry permit; **visto d'uscita** exit visa
③ *conj* ∼ **che...** seeing that...

vistosa'mente *adv* conspicuously

vi'stoso *adj* showy; (notevole) considerable

visu'ale *adj* visual

visualiz'zare *vt* visualize; Comput display

visualizza'tore *nm* Comput display, VDU
■ **visualizzatore a cristalli liquidi** Comput liquid crystal display

visualizzazi'one *nf* Comput display

'vita *nf* life; (durata della vita) lifetime; Anat waist; **a ∼** for life; **essere in fin di ∼** be at death's door; **essere in ∼** be alive; **fare la bella ∼** lead the good life; **costo della vita** cost of living
■ **vita eterna** eternal life; **vita media** Biol life expectancy; **vita mondana** high life; **fare ∼ mondana** lead the high life; **vita notturna** night life; **vita terrena** Relig life on earth

vi'taccia *nf* slog

vi'tale *adj* vital

vitalità *nf* vitality

vita'lizio ① *adj* life attrib
② *nm* [life] annuity

vita'mina *nf* vitamin

vita'minico *adj* vitamin-enriched

vitaminiz'zato *adj* vitamin-enriched

'vite *nf* Mech screw; Bot vine; **giro di vite** fig clampdown
■ **vite canadese** Virginia creeper; **vite di coda** Aeron tailspin; **vite perpetua** endless screw

vi'tella *nf* (animale) calf; (carne) veal

vi'tello *nm* calf; (carne) veal; (pelle) calfskin
■ **vitello di latte** milk-fed veal; **vitello tonnato** *sliced veal with tuna, anchovy, oil and lemon sauce*

vi'ticcio *nm* tendril

viticol'tore *nm* wine grower

viticol'tura *nf* wine growing

vi'tino *nm* narrow waist
■ **vitino di vespa** slender little waist

'vitreo *adj* vitreous; (sguardo) glassy

'vittima *nf* victim

'vitto *nm* food; (pasti) board
■ **vitto e alloggio** board and lodging

vit'toria *nf* victory

vittori'ano *adj* Victorian

vittoriosa'mente *adv* victoriously, triumphantly

vittori'oso *adj* victorious

vitupe'rare *vt* vituperate

vitu'perio *nm* insult

vi'uzza *nf* narrow lane

'viva *int* hurrah!; **∼ la Regina!** long live the Queen!

vi'vace *adj* vivacious; (mente) lively; (colore) bright

vivace'mente *adv* vivaciously

vivacità *nf* vivacity; (di mente) liveliness; (di colore) brightness

vivaciz'zare *vt* liven up

vi'vaio *nm* nursery; (per pesci) pond; fig breeding ground

viva'mente *adv* (ringraziare) warmly

vi'vanda *nf* food; (piatto) dish

vi'vente ① *adj* living
② *nmpl* **i viventi** the living

'vivere ① *vi* live; **∼ di** live on; **vive** Typ stet
② *vt* (passare) go through
③ *nm* life; **modo di vivere** way of life

'viveri *nmpl* provisions

vivida'mente *adv* vividly

'vivido *adj* vivid

vi'viparo *adj* viviparous

vivisezio'nare *vt* vivisect

vivisezi'one *nf* vivisection

'vivo ① *adj* alive; (vivente) living; (vivace) lively; (colore) bright; **farsi ∼** keep in touch; (arrivare) turn up
② *nm* **colpire qualcuno sul ∼** cut somebody to the quick; **dal ∼** (trasmissione) live; (disegnare) from life; **i vivi** the living
■ **vivo e vegeto** alive and kicking

vizi'are *vt* spoil (bambino ecc); (guastare) vitiate

vizi'ato *adj* spoilt; (aria) stale

'vizio *nm* vice; (cattiva abitudine) bad habit; (difetto) flaw
■ **vizio capitale** deadly sin; **vizio di forma** legal technicality; **vizio procedurale** procedural error

vizi'oso *adj* dissolute; (difettoso) faulty; **circolo vizioso** vicious circle

'vizzo *adj* (pelle) wrinkled; (pianta) withered

V.le *abbr* (**viale**) Ave

vocabo'lario *nm* dictionary; (lessico) vocabulary

vo'cabolo *nm* word

vo'cale ① *adj* vocal
② *nf* vowel

vo'calico *adj* (corde) vocal; (suono) vowel attrib

vocazi'one *nf* vocation

'voce *nf* voice; (diceria) rumour; (di bilancio, dizionario) entry
■ **voce bianca** Mus treble voice; **voce fuori campo** voiceover

voci'are ① *vi* (spettegolare) gossip
② *nm* buzz of conversation

vocife'rare *vi* shout; **si vocifera che...** it is rumoured that...

'vodka *nf inv* vodka

'voga *nf* rowing; (lena) enthusiasm; (moda) vogue; **essere in ∼** be in vogue

vo'gare *vi* row; ~ **a bratto** scull; ~ **di coppia** scull

voga'tore *nm* oarsman; (attrezzo) rowing machine

⚔ **'voglia** *nf* desire; (volontà) will; (della pelle) birthmark; **aver** ~ **di fare qualcosa** feel like doing something; **morire dalla** ~ **di qualcosa** be dying for something; **di buona** ~ willingly

'voglio ▶ VOLERE

vogli'oso *adj* ⟨occhi, persona⟩ covetous; **essere** ~ **di qualcosa** want something

⚔ **'voi** *pers pron* you; **siete** ~? is that you?; **l'avete fatto** ~? did you do it yourselves?

voia'ltri *pers pron* you

vo'lano *nm* shuttlecock; Mech flywheel

vo'lant *nm inv* valance

vo'lante ① *adj* flying; ⟨foglio⟩ loose ② *nm* steering-wheel

volanti'nare *vi* hand out leaflets

volan'tino *nm* leaflet

⚔ **vo'lare** *vi* fly

vo'lata *nf* Sport final sprint; **di** ~ in a rush

vo'latile ① *adj* ⟨liquido⟩ volatile ② *nm* bird

volatiliz'zarsi *vr* vanish

vol-au-'vent *nm inv* vol-au-vent

vo'lée *nf inv* Tennis volley

vo'lente *adj* ~ **o nolente** whether you like it or not

volente'roso *adj* willing

⚔ **volenti'eri** *adv* willingly; ~! with pleasure!

⚔ **vo'lere** ① *vt* want; (chiedere di) ask for; (aver bisogno di) need; **non voglio** I don't want to; **vuole che lo faccia** io he wants me to do it; **fai come vuoi** do as you like; **se tuo padre vuole, ti porto al cinema** if your father agrees, I'll take you to the cinema; **questa pianta vuole molte cure** this plant needs a lot of care; **vorrei un caffè** I'd like a coffee; **la leggenda vuole che…** legend has it that…; **la vuoi smettere?** will you stop that!; **senza** ~ without meaning to; **voler bene/male a qualcuno** love/have something against somebody; **voler dire** mean; **ci vuole il latte** we need milk; **ci vuole tempo/pazienza** it takes time/patience; **volerne a** have a grudge against; **vuoi… vuoi…** either… or… ② *nm* will; **voleri** *pl* wishes

⚔ **vol'gare** *adj* vulgar; (popolare) common

volgarità *nf* vulgarity; **dire** ~ use vulgar language, be vulgar

volgariz'zare *vt* popularize

volgarizzazi'one *nf* popularization

volgar'mente *adv* (grossolanamente) vulgarly; (comunemente) commonly, popularly

⚔ **'volgere** *vt/i* turn

'volgersi *vr* turn [round]; ~ **a** (dedicarsi) take up

'volgo *nm* common people

⚔ indicates a very frequent word

---

voli'era *nf* aviary

voli'tivo *adj* strong-minded

⚔ **'volo** *nm* flight; **al** ~ ⟨fare qualcosa⟩ quickly; ⟨prendere qualcosa⟩ in mid-air; **alzarsi in** ~ ⟨uccello⟩ take off; **in** ~ airborne

◾ **volo di andata** outward flight; **volo charter** charter flight; **volo diretto** direct flight; **volo di linea** scheduled flight; **volo nazionale** domestic flight; **volo di ritorno** return flight; **volo strumentale** flying on instruments; **volo a vela** gliding

⚔ **volontà** *nf inv* will; (desiderio) wish; **a** ~ ⟨mangiare⟩ as much as you like

volontaria'mente *adv* voluntarily

volon'tario ① *adj* voluntary ② *nm* volunteer

volonte'roso *adj* willing

'volpe *nf* fox

vol'pino ① *adj* ⟨astuzia⟩ fox-like ② *nm* (cane) Pomeranian

volt *nm inv* volt

⚔ **'volta** *nf* time; (turno) turn; (curva) bend; Archit vault; **4 volte 4** 4 times 4; **a volte, qualche** ~ sometimes; **c'era una** ~… once upon a time there was…; **una** ~ once; **due volte** twice; **tre/quattro volte** three/four times; **una** ~ **per tutte** once and for all; **una** ~ **ogni tanto** every so often; **uno alla** ~ one at a time; **alla** ~ **di** in the direction of

◾ **volta a botte** barrel vault; **volta celeste** vault of heaven; **volta cranica** cranial vault; **volta a crociera** groin vault; **volta a vela** ribbed vault; **volta a ventaglio** fan vault

volta'faccia *nm inv* volte-face

voltagab'bana *nmf inv* turncoat

vol'taggio *nm* voltage

⚔ **vol'tare** *vt/i* turn; (rigirare) turn round; (rivoltare) turn over; ~ **pagina** fig turn over a new leaf

vol'tarsi *vr* turn [round]

volta'stomaco *nm* nausea; fig disgust

volteggi'are *vi* circle; (ginnastica) vault

⚔ **'volto** ① *pp di* VOLGERE ② *nm* face; **ha mostrato il suo vero** ~ he revealed his true colours

vol'tura *nf* (catastale) transfer of property

◾ ~ **di contratto** transfer of contract

vo'lubile *adj* fickle

volubil'mente *adv* in a fickle way, inconstantly

vo'lume *nm* volume

◾ **volume di gioco** Sport possession

volumi'noso *adj* voluminous

vo'luta *nf* (spirale) spiral; (di capitello) volute

voluta'mente *adv* deliberately

vo'luto *adj* deliberate, intended

voluttà *nf* voluptuousness

voluttu'ario *adj* non-essential; **beni** *pl* **voluttuari** non-essentials

voluttu'oso *adj* voluptuous

vomi'tare *vt* vomit, be sick

vomi'tevole *adj* nauseating

'vomito *nm* vomit

'vongola *nf* clam

vo'race *adj* voracious

vorace'mente *adv* voraciously

vo'ragine *nf* abyss

vor'rei ▸ VOLERE

'vortice *nm* whirl; (gorgo) whirlpool; (di vento) whirlwind

vorticosa'mente *adv* in whirls

⚥ **'vostro** ① (il ∼ *m*, la vostra *f*, i vostri *mpl*, le vostre *fpl*) *poss adj* your; è vostra questa macchina? is this car yours?; un ∼ amico a friend of yours; ∼ padre your father ② *poss pron* yours; i vostri your folks

vo'tante *nmf* voter

⚥ **vo'tare** *vi* vote

votazi'one *nf* voting; Sch marks *pl*
  ■ votazione di fiducia Pol fig vote of confidence; votazione per alzata di mano show of hands; votazione a scrutinio segreto secret ballot

⚥ **'voto** *nm* vote; Sch mark; Relig vow
  ■ voto decisivo casting vote; voto per alzata di mano show of hands

vs. *abbr* Comm (**vostro**) yours

'vudu *nm inv* voodoo

vul'canico *adj* volcanic

vul'cano *nm* volcano
  ■ vulcano intermittente dormant volcano; vulcano spento extinct volcano

vulne'rabile *adj* vulnerable

vulnerabilità *nf* vulnerability

'vulva *nf* vulva

vuo'tare *vt* empty

vuo'tarsi *vr* empty

⚥ **vu'oto** ① *adj* empty; (non occupato) vacant; ∼ di (sprovvisto) devoid of ② *nm* empty space; Phys vacuum; fig void; assegno a ∼ dud cheque; sotto ∼ ‹prodotto› vacuum-packed
  ■ vuoto d'aria air pocket; vuoto a perdere no deposit; vuoto a rendere ‹bottiglia› returnable

W w

W *abbr* (**viva**) long live

'wafer *nm inv* (biscotto) wafer

wagon-'lit *nm inv* sleeping car

walkie-'talkie *nm inv* walkie-talkie

'water *nm inv* toilet, loo fam

watt *nm inv* watt

wat'tora *nm inv* Phys watt-hour

WC *nm* WC

'web *nm inv* Web

web'cam *nf inv* web cam

web'master *nm inv* webmster

wee'kend *nm inv* weekend

'welter *adj & nm inv* (in pugilato) welterweight

'western ① *adj inv* cowboy *attrib* ② *nm inv* Cinema western

'whisky *nm inv* whisky
  ■ whisky di malto malt [whisky]

wind'surf *nm inv* (tavola) windsurf; (sport) windsurfing; fare ∼ windsurf

windsur'fista *nmf* sailboarder, windsurfer

'würstel *nm inv* frankfurter

X x

xenofo'bia *nf* xenophobia

xe'nofobo, -a ① *adj* xenophobic ② *nmf* xenophobe

'xeres *nm inv* sherry

xero'copia *nf* xerox

xeroco'piare *vt* photocopy

xerocopia'trice *nf* photocopier

xilofo'nista *nmf* xylophone player

'xilofono *nm* xylophone

Y y

yacht *nm inv* yacht
yak *nm inv* Zool yak
'yankee *nmf inv* Yank
'Yemen *nm* Yemen
yeme'nita *nmf* Yemeni
yen *nm inv* yen
'yeti *nm* yeti
'yiddish *adj inv & nm* Yiddish

'yoga 1 *nm* yoga
   2 *adj inv* yoga *attrib*
'yogurt *nm inv* yoghurt
yogurti'era *nf* yoghurt-maker
'yorkshire *nm inv* (cane) Yorkshire terrier
yo-'yo® *nm inv* yo-'yo®
yup'pismo *nm* yuppiedom

Z z

zaba[gl]ione *nm* zabaglione (*dessert made from eggs, wine or marsala and sugar*)
'zacchera *nf* (schizzo) splash of mud
zaf'fata *nf* whiff; (di fumo) cloud
zaffe'rano *nm* saffron
zaf'firo *nm* sapphire
'zagara *nf* orange-blossom
'zaino *nm* rucksack
Za'ire *nm* Zaire
'Zambia *nm* Zambia
'zampa *nf* leg; **a quattro zampe** (animale) four-legged; (carponi) on all fours; **zampe** *pl* **di gallina** fig crow's feet; **zampe** *pl* **posteriori** hind legs
zam'pata *nf* paw; **dare una ∼ a** hit with its paw
zampet'tare *vi* scamper
zam'petto *nm* Culin knuckle
zampil'lante *adj* spurting
zampil'lare *vi* spurt
zam'pillo *nm* spurt
zam'pino *nm* paw; **mettere lo ∼ in** fig have a hand in
zam'pogna *nf* bagpipe
zampo'gnaro *nm* piper
zam'pone *nfpl* stuffed pigs trotter with lentils
'zangola *nf* churn
'zanna *nf* fang; (di elefante) tusk
zan'zara *nf* mosquito
zanzari'era *nf* (velo) mosquito net; (su finestra) insect screen

'zappa *nf* hoe; **darsi la ∼ sui piedi** fig shoot oneself in the foot
zap'pare *vt* hoe
zap'pata *nf* **dare una ∼ a** a hit with a hoe
zappet'tare *vt* hoe
'zapping *nm inv* channel-hopping Br, channel-surfing Am; **fare lo ∼** channel-hop Br, channel-surf Am
zar *nm inv* tzar
za'rina *nf* tzarina
za'rista *adj & nmf* tzarist
'zattera *nf* raft
zatte'roni *nmpl* (scarpe) wedge shoes
za'vorra *nf* ballast; fig dead wood
zavor'rare *vt* load with ballast
'zazzera *nf* mop of hair
'zebra *nf* zebra; **zebre** *pl* (passaggio pedonale) zebra crossing, crosswalk Am
ze'brato *adj* ‹tessuto› with black and white stripes
'zecca¹ *nf* mint; **nuovo di ∼** brand-new
'zecca² *nf* (parassita) tick
zec'chino *nm* sequin; **oro zecchino** pure gold
ze'lante *adj* zealous
'zelo *nm* zeal
'zenit *nm* zenith
'zenzero *nm* ginger
'zeppa *nf* wedge
'zeppo *adj* packed full; **pieno ∼ di** crammed *or* packed with
zer'bino *nm* doormat
'zero *nm* zero, nought; (in calcio) nil; Tennis love; **due a ∼** (in partite) two nil; **ricominciare da ∼** fig start again from scratch; **sparare a**

⚜ indicates a very frequent word

y
z

~ su qualcuno fig lay into somebody; avere il morale sotto ~ fig be down in the dumps

'zeta nf zed, zee Am

♂ **'zia** nf aunt

zibel'lino nm sable

zi'gano, -a adj & nmf gypsy

'zigolo nm Zool bunting

'zigomo nm cheekbone

zigri'nato adj ‹pelle› grained; ‹metallo› milled

zig'zag nm inv zigzag; andare a ~ zigzag

Zim'babwe nm Zimbabwe

zim'bello nm decoy; (oggetto di scherno) laughing-stock

'zinco nm zinc

zinga'resco adj gypsy attrib

'zingaro, -a nmf gypsy

♂ **'zio** nm uncle

'zippo nm sl lighter

zi'tella nf spinster; pej old maid

zitel'lona nf pej old maid

zit'tire [1] vi fall silent [2] vt silence

♂ **'zitto** adj silent; sta' ~! keep quiet!

ziz'zania nf (discordia) discord; seminare ~ cause trouble

'zoccola nf vulg whore

'zoccolo nm clog; (di cavallo) hoof; (di terra) clump; (di parete) skirting board, baseboard Am; (di colonna) base

■ zoccolo duro Pol hard core; zoccolo fesso cloven foot, cloven hoof

zodia'cale adj of the zodiac; segno zodiacale sign of the zodiac, birth sign

zo'diaco nm zodiac

zolfa'nello nm match

'zolfo nm sulphur

'zolla nf clod

zol'letta nf sugar cube, sugar lump

'zombi nmf inv fig zombie

zom'pare vi sl bonk

♂ **'zona** nf zone; (area) area

■ zona calda fig hot spot; zona denuclearizzata nuclear-free zone; zona di depressione area of low pressure; zona disastrata disaster area; zona disco area for parking discs only; zona erogena erogenous zone; zona di esclusione aerea air exclusion zone; zona euro Eurozone; zona giorno living area; zona industriale industrial estate; zona notte sleeping area; zona d'ombra fig twilight zone; zona pedonale pedestrian precinct; zona a traffico limitato restricted traffic area; zona verde green belt

zonizzazi'one nf zoning

'zonzo:, a zonzo adv andare a ~ stroll about

'zoo nm inv zoo

zoolo'gia nf zoology

zoo'logico adj zoological

zo'ologo, -a nmf zoologist

zoosa'fari nm inv safari park

zootec'nia nf animal husbandry

zoo'tecnico adj ‹progresso› in animal husbandry; patrimonio zootecnico livestock

zoppi'cante adj limping; fig shaky

zoppi'care vi limp; (essere debole) be shaky

'zoppo, -a [1] adj lame [2] nmf cripple

'zotico adj uncouth

zoti'cone nm boor

zu'ava nf calzoni pl alla ~ plus-fours

'zucca nf marrow; fam (testa) head; fam (persona) thickie; cos'hai in quella ~? haven't you got anything between your ears?

zuc'cata nf prendere una ~ fam hit one's head

zucche'rare vt sugar

zucche'rato adj sugared; non ~ ‹succo d'arancia ecc› unsweetened

zuccheri'era nf sugar bowl

zuccheri'ficio nm sugar refinery

zucche'rino [1] adj sugary [2] nm sugar cube, sugar lump; fig sweetener; essere uno ~ fig ‹persona› be a softy; ‹cosa› be a cinch

'zucchero nm sugar

■ zucchero di canna cane sugar; zucchero filato candyfloss; zucchero greggio brown sugar; zucchero vanigliato vanilla sugar; zucchero a velo icing sugar, confectioners' sugar Am

zucche'roso adj fig honeyed

zuc'chetto nm (cappello) beanie

zuc'china nf courgette, zucchini Am

zuc'chino nm courgette, zucchini Am

zuc'cone nm fam blockhead

zuc'cotto nm dessert made with sponge, cream, chocolate and candied fruit

'zuffa nf scuffle

zufo'lare vt/i whistle

'zufolo nm penny whistle

zu'mare vi zoom

zu'mata nf zoom

'zuppa nf soup

■ zuppa inglese trifle

zup'petta nf fare ~ [con] dunk

zuppi'era nf soup tureen

'zuppo adj soaked

Contents

Culture / Cultura
Letters / Lettere
Calendar

Italian traditions, festivals, and holidays

1 January
Capodanno (New Year's Day).
A public holiday often spent getting over the excesses of New Year's Eve.

6 January
Epifania (Twelfth Night).
A public holiday and religious festival celebrating the adoration of Jesus by the three kings. By popular tradition it is also the day when Befana, a legendary old woman on a broomstick, brings children gifts: they are supposed to hang up their stockings the night before and in the morning should find them full of sweets, cakes, and little presents or, if they have been naughty, coal (though nowadays it is usually a sugary substitute).

14 February
San Valentino (St Valentine's Day).
As in other countries, this day is for lovers, marked by flowers, chocolates, and candlelit dinners.

8 March
Festa delle donne (Women's Day).
Since the 1970s, Women's Day has been celebrated with sprays of mimosa and discussions on women's issues.

19 March
Festa del papà (Father's Day).
St Joseph's Day is the day on which Italian fathers are celebrated.

1 April
Pesce d'aprile.
This is April Fool's Day, when it is traditional to play jokes and tricks on people. Children have fun trying to stick a little paper fish (*pesciolino*) onto people's backs without their noticing, and then calling, '*Il pesce d'aprile!*' (literally, 'April fish').

25 April
Anniversario della Liberazione (Anniversary of the Liberation).
A public holiday, this is a day of official ceremonies. It commemorates the day in 1945 when Italy was liberated from Nazi German occupation by invading Allied forces.

1 May
Festa del lavoro (International Labour Day) is a public holiday. This is a civil festival celebrating the workers of the world.

2 June
Festa della Repubblica is a public holiday, a civil festival to commemorate the referendum of 2 June 1946 which led to the proclamation of the Italian Republic.

15 August
L'Assunzione (Feast of the Assumption) is a public holiday – a religious festival that celebrates the Assumption of the Virgin Mary to heaven. Also known as *ferragosto*, it marks the peak of the summer holidays. The factories in the north are closed, as are many shops, except for those in tourist areas.

1 November
I Santi/Ognissanti (All Saints' Day).
Public holiday and religious festival celebrating all the saints. Typically, cakes made with nuts and raisins, which vary from region to region, are eaten during this festival. People go to the cemetery to take flowers for their dead loved ones, although the Festival of the Dead (I Morti) is the following day, 2 November, which is not a public holiday.

8 December
L'immacolata Concezione (Feast of the Immaculate Conception).
Public holiday and religious festival that celebrates the purity of the Virgin Mary.

24 December
La vigilia di Natale (Christmas Eve) is not a public holiday, although the schools are usually closed. Families get together, and often a large dinner is prepared. Afterwards people open their Christmas presents from under the tree. The faithful go to midnight Mass.

25 December
Natale (Christmas Day) is a public holiday and one of the most important religious festivals for Italians. Families

who did not open their presents the night before do so on Christmas morning. Children who believe in Father Christmas think that he has come down the chimney to bring their presents during the night. Families get together to eat a big dinner, typically including a capon and ending with *panettone* (a dome-shaped cake with sultanas and candied fruit) and a glass of spumante, Italian sparkling wine.

26 December
Santo Stefano (St Stephen's Day). A public and religious holiday during which Christmas celebrations continue.

31 December
San Silvestro (New Year's Eve). The celebration of the end of the old year and beginning of the new. It is a working day for many people, although students are on holiday, but in the evening there is usually a big meal and a party, either at home or in a restaurant. Typical dishes are lentils (which are said to bring wealth) and *cotechino* (a large pork sausage), and a great deal of champagne and spumante is drunk. On the stroke of midnight, fireworks are set off. In days gone by, it was traditional to throw crockery and other belongings out of the window to mark the rejection of the old in readiness for the New Year, but this no longer happens, to avoid damage to cars and injury to passers-by.

Movable holidays

Giovedì grasso (the Thursday before Lent). Fancy dress parties are held and people traditionally eat pancakes and fried pastries.

Martedì grasso (Shrove Tuesday). In some regions schools are closed.

Mercoledì delle ceneri (Ash Wednesday) is a religious occasion that marks the beginning of Lent. Some people fast on this day.

Venerdì santo (Good Friday).

A religious occasion. It is not a public holiday, though some schools are closed.

Pasqua (Easter) is the most important Catholic festival, celebrating the resurrection of Christ. A popular saying goes: '*Natale con i tuoi, Pasqua con chi vuoi*' (Christmas with your family, Easter with whoever you want), and in fact Italians often take the opportunity of the holiday period to go away on holiday. Those who stay at home cook a big meal, usually of lamb because of its symbolic meaning. A *colomba* (dove-shaped cake) is the traditional Easter cake.

Pasquetta (Easter Monday) is a public holiday when people often go out for the day, to the sea, the mountains, or the countryside.

L'Ascensione (Ascension). A religious festival celebrating the ascension of Christ to heaven. It falls on the Thursday forty days after Easter.

Pentecoste (Whitsun) is a religious festival celebrating the descent of the holy spirit to the apostles. It falls fifty days after Easter.

Festa della Mamma (Mothers' Day) is on the second Sunday in May. Cards are sent and sometimes a present: perfume, chocolates, or flowers, especially roses.

Festival dei Due Mondi or Festival di Spoleto (in the province of Perugia) takes place each year from late June to mid-July. It hosts dance, theatre, opera, and music events, to which the biggest world names are invited.

Festival di Sanremo This Ligurian tourist resort has hosted the festival of Italian music every year since 1951. After a period of decline in the 1970s, the festival has recently regained its popularity. Established singers take part, but it is also often the launch pad for new talent.

Calendar

Giorni festivi nei paesi anglofoni

1 gennaio
New Year's Day (Capodanno).
Giorno festivo, generalmente trascorso a riprendersi dai festeggiamenti della notte precedente.

2 gennaio
Giorno festivo in Scozia.

6 gennaio
Epiphany o **Twelfth Night** (Epifania).
Non ci sono particolari tradizioni legate a questa giornata, ma molti in questo giorno disfano l'albero di Natale e mettono via le decorazioni natalizie.

25 gennaio
Burns Night.
Ricorrenza della nascita del poeta scozzese Robert Burns (XVIII secolo). Gli scozzesi festeggiano con una cena detta *Burns Supper* il cui piatto forte si chiama *haggis* (intestino di pecora farcito con una miscela di avena, frattaglie, cipolle e spezie). Tradizionalmente, durante la cena accompagnata dal suono delle cornamuse, si beve whisky e si leggono ad alta voce brani delle poesie di Robert Burns.

2 febbraio
Groundhog Day.
Giorno in cui, secondo la tradizione statunitense, la marmotta (*groundhog*) esce dalla sua tana sotterranea alla fine del letargo. Se c'è il sole e la marmotta vede la propria ombra si nasconderà nella tana e ci saranno altre sei settimane di cattivo tempo. Se non vede la propria ombra, si crede che la primavera comincerà presto.

14 febbraio
St Valentine's Day (San Valentino).
Nel giorno di San Valentino gli innamorati si scambiano fiori e regali. Esiste inoltre la tradizione di inviare un biglietto anonimo alla persona per cui si prova una tenera simpatia.

1 marzo
St David's Day.
Giorno di festa nazionale in Galles, di cui San Davide è il santo protettore.

17 marzo
St Patrick's Day.
La festa di San Patrizio, patrono d'Irlanda, viene celebrata dagli irlandesi in tutto il mondo con musica, canti e grandi bevute.

1 aprile
April Fools' Day (Pesce d'Aprile).
Giornata in cui si fanno numerosi scherzi: le vittime di tali scherzi sono dette *April Fools*.

23 aprile
St George's Day.
San Giorgio è il patrono d'Inghilterra.

1 luglio
Canada Day.
Festa nazionale che commemora l'unificazione delle colonie britanniche nordamericane del 1° luglio 1867.

4 luglio
Independence Day.
In questo giorno di festa nazionale negli Stati Uniti si celebra l'approvazione della Dichiarazione d'Indipendenza (1776) con parate, spettacoli di fuochi artificiali e picnic. In moltissime case viene esposta la bandiera americana.

12 ottobre
Columbus Day.
Giorno festivo negli Stati Uniti, ricorrenza della scoperta dell'America da parte di Cristoforo Colombo nel 1492.

31 ottobre
Hallowe'en (vigilia d'Ognissanti).
La notte della vigilia d'Ognissanti in cui, secondo un'antica credenza anglosassone, è possibile vedere i fantasmi. Oggi è festeggiata per lo più dai bambini, che ricavano lanterne dalle zucche svuotate, si mascherano e fanno

il giro del vicinato per chiedere dolci e regalini con il *trick or treat* ('dolcetto o scherzetto').

5 novembre
Bonfire Night/Guy Fawkes Night.
In Gran Bretagna si festeggia il fallimento della Congiura delle Polveri per far saltare in aria il Parlamento nel 1605. Ovunque si organizzano spettacoli di fuochi d'artificio e falò in cui viene bruciato un pupazzo rudimentale detto *guy* che rappresenta Guy Fawkes, uno dei cospiratori.

11 novembre
Remembrance Day,
Veteran's Day negli USA.
Giornata in cui si commemorano i caduti di tutte le guerre e la firma dell'armistizio (1918) che mise fine alla prima guerra mondiale.

In Gran Bretagna la ricorrenza è anche nota come Poppy Day (giorno del papavero), per l'usanza di portare un papavero rosso di stoffa o carta sul petto (dai campi di papaveri in cui morirono migliaia di soldati sui fronti francese e belga).

30 novembre
St Andrew's Day.
Sant'Andrea è il patrono della Scozia.

25 dicembre
Christmas Day (giorno di Natale).
Giorno festivo. Per tradizione i familiari si scambiano i doni intorno all'albero la mattina di Natale e i bambini spesso trovano, al risveglio, una calza (*Christmas stocking*) piena di dolci e regalini lasciata da Father Christmas, anche chiamato Santa Claus.

26 dicembre
Boxing Day in Gran Bretagna,
St Stephen's Day in Irlanda.
Giorno festivo.

31 dicembre
New Year's Eve (la notte di San Silvestro).
In Scozia si chiama **Hogmanay** ed è tradizione andare a trovare amici e vicini di casa per augurare loro pace e prosperità portando in dono un pezzo di carbone o del whisky o qualcosa da mangiare.

A–Z of Italian life and culture

Accademia della Crusca An academy for the study of the Italian language, founded in Florence in 1583, with the original aim of establishing the supremacy of the literary dialect in Florence – or of separating the 'flour' of pure language from the 'bran' (*crusca* – hence its name) of vulgarity. From 1612 it published the *Vocabolario degli accademici della Crusca* (Dictionary of the Members of the Accademia della Crusca), which became a model for similar works on the major European languages, and was printed in various editions until 1923. With only one interruption, from 1783 to 1811, the Academy has continued its work down to the present day. Currently based in the Villa di Castello near Florence, it is a centre for linguistic, philological, and lexicographical research. Unlike the French Académie Française or the Spanish Real Academia, however, it does not have the last word on what is correct or incorrect in Italian.

acqua alta An exceptionally high tide that sometimes affects the lagoon of Venice during the winter months. It is caused by particular wind conditions, but exacerbated by human interference with the environment. When the level of the lagoon rises, peaking sometimes at 1.4 metres (4.6 feet) and over, many of the streets and piazzas of Venice disappear under centimetres of water. Sirens are sounded three or four hours before the *acqua alta* reaches full height, and footbridges are put up to allow pedestrians to continue to use the busiest routes.

agriturismo A holiday based on a farm. It was originally intended that the holiday-makers would help with work on the farm in some capacity, but nowadays this virtually never happens. The word *agriturismo* is also used for the venue – the farmhouse, often renovated and refurbished specially for tourists. This type of holiday offers activities such as walking, horse-riding, etc. Good food and the open-air lifestyle are the main attractions. It is becoming much more popular and more expensive than it was at first.

Alto Adige The northern part of the Trentino-Alto Adige region, consisting of the province of Bolzano (called Südtirol [South Tirol] in German), ceded to Italy after the First World War. The majority of the population are German-speaking and of German descent. Since 1948 it has had a degree of autonomy, reinforced in 1972; place names are shown in Italian and German and holders of public offices have to pass an exam to show they are bilingual. Teaching in schools, however, is in German only for those of German descent, or Italian only for those of Italian descent. In future, this system is to be replaced by genuine bilingualism.

anno scolastico The Italian school year usually begins in mid-September and ends at the beginning of June (except for students who are taking exams). As well as a few days' holiday for the various civil and religious festivals, there are about ten days' holiday over Christmas, New Year, and Twelfth Night, plus a few days at Easter. *See also* SCUOLA.

aperitivo It is an Italian tradition to have an aperitif, which may or may not be alcoholic and is served with a few peanuts, olives, or other appetizers, before lunch or dinner. Many bars have their own, homemade *aperitivo*, based on liqueurs and fruit juices. Taking time for a pre-meal drink also provides a chance to catch up with friends.

ASL – Azienda Sanitaria Locale The Servizio Nazionale di Assistenza Sanitaria (or National Health Service) provides care for citizens through these local health authorities.

autoricarica A mobile phone scheme available in Italy where customers are rewarded by having their accounts re-credited according to either how long they have spent on incoming (or outgoing) calls, or how many text messages they have received (or sent).

autostrade Italy has a network of motorways – toll roads with two or more lanes on each carriageway. The tolls paid for using motorways finance their construction, management, and maintenance. The tariff depends on the vehicle in which you are travelling and the stretch of motorway concerned, the relative costs of construction and maintenance being taken into account (e.g. mountain stretches can be more expensive). Usually you take a ticket from the booth when joining the motorway and hand it in for payment at the other end. The maximum speed limit for cars is 130 km/h (80 mph), or up to 150 km/h (94 mph) on some stretches.

Azzurri A popular name for the Italian national team in sports such as football, rugby, and hockey, from the blue shirts worn by the players.

Banca d'Italia The Italian central bank, founded in 1893. Since 1926 it has had a monopoly on the issue of currency, and supervisory jurisdiction over the Italian banking system. It also acts as the state treasury. Its central offices are located in the Via Nazionale in Rome. In the media, Via Nazionale is often used to mean the Bank of Italy.

Bancomat This is the name of the system of automatic cash withdrawal, of the actual cash machine, and of the card itself. The same card is often used as both a credit card and a bancomat card, so when you pay with the card in a shop you can use it as a credit card, or – by keying in your PIN on a special keypad – as a debit card.

Culture

bandiera arancione The orange flag is the mark of environmental quality awarded by the Italian Touring Club in inland areas. The criteria for the awarding of the orange flag are the development of cultural heritage, protection of the environment, standards of hospitality, and quality both of restoration and of local products.

bandiera blu The blue flag is an award given to beaches and ports in the member countries of the FEE (Federation for Environmental Education). The criteria that have to be met are, for beaches, the quality of the water and the coast, safety measures and services, and the promotion of environmental education. For ports, it is the quality of the water in the harbour, safety and disposal services, and environmental information.

bar A real institution of Italian life and culture, the bar is the place where you can have snacks, sandwiches, coffees, soft and alcoholic drinks, etc. Usually drinks are taken standing at the bar. In many bars there are also tables where you can sit and read the newspapers. Bars also play an important role in the lives of sports fans, as they meet there to watch football matches or other events on the television.

bel canto A style of singing, still practised today, that combines a light, bright quality of voice with the ability to sustain a beautifully clear and even tone through complicated passages. It emerged in Italy in the 15th and 16th centuries and was at its height in the early 19th century, when the composers Rossini, Bellini, and Donizetti exploited it to the full in their operas.

Biennale di Venezia An international show for the visual arts, cinema, architecture, dance, music, and theatre. The visual arts section still takes place every two years and often welcomes avant-garde artists. *See also* MOSTRA INTERNAZIONALE D'ARTE CINEMATOGRAFICA.

Bocconi With its headquarters in Milan, the Bocconi commercial university is an extremely prestigious private university, with only one faculty – economics.

caffè Coffee is a favourite Italian drink. Outside the home it can be drunk quickly standing at a bar counter, or in a more leisurely fashion while chatting at a table. In bars or restaurants you can order *un caffè* (normal), *ristretto* or *lungo* (weaker or stronger), *macchiato* (hot or cold, with a drop of milk), or *corretto* (with a drop of spirits). Also on offer are decaff and hot malt drinks (*caffè d'orzo*).

calcio Football is the sport that Italians love most, and of course it is a sport in which Italian teams have always excelled. The national league is divided into Serie A, Serie B, and Serie C. Some of the most famous Italian teams are Juventus, Milan, Inter (also in Milan), Roma, and Lazio. *See also* AZZURRI.

Culture

Camera dei Deputati The legislative assembly that, along with the SENATO, makes up the Italian Parliament. It is composed of 630 deputies, elected by universal direct suffrage by citizens over 18 years of age.

Camicie rosse ▸ I MILLE

Camorra An organized-crime network operating in Naples and the Campania. The Camorra is not a single organization but made up of groups (families) who often fight for control of criminal activities. Emerging in the 1500s, it has for centuries practised blackmail and extortion on small businesses in Naples. After the Second World War, and particularly from the 1980s, it began to control drugs and arms trafficking, prostitution, and the allocation of public contracts, developing political links and assuming ever greater control of the Naples area.

Canton Ticino This is the only canton of the Swiss Confederation which has Italian as its official language. It is also the only Swiss region located south of the Alps. The history, culture, and language of this area are intermingled with those of the neighbouring Italian regions.

Capitoline One of the SEVEN HILLS OF ROME, the Capitoline was the acropolis and religious centre of the ancient city, and is now the headquarters of the City of Rome. The Piazza del Campidoglio at its top was designed by Michelangelo; the square is flanked by three palazzi now housing the Capitoline Museums. In the centre of the piazza stands a statue of Roman emperor, Marcus Aurelius, on horseback.

Caporetto A First World War battle in which Italian troops were heavily defeated. On 24 October 1917, Austrian and German troops launched a major offensive on the Italian front, breaking through near the small town of Caporetto (now Kobarid in Slovenia). The Italians retreated in disorder with very heavy losses. The name Caporetto entered the language as a byword for a total defeat or failure.

Capri An island close to the southern entrance to the Bay of Naples, and favourite tourist destination. Capri is chiefly famous for its romantic setting, for the Blue Grotto – a sea cave with a low entrance, which gets its name from the colour of the light filtered through the water, and for the remains of Roman villas built by the Emperor Tiberius, who made Capri his headquarters from AD 27–37.

carabinieri A corps of the Italian army that has the task of guaranteeing the safety of citizens and their property and ensuring that state laws are observed. As well as being a military police force and responsible for public safety, the *carabinieri* also function as judiciary police. *See also* POLIZIA DI STATO.

Carnevale This is the period before Lent running from Twelfth Night to Ash Wednesday. It is celebrated with fancy dress parties, confetti, and streamers, especially during the weekend running from '*giovedì grasso*' (the last Thursday) to '*martedì grasso*' (Shrove Tuesday), which is the final day. The Venice Carnival is one of the most famous, with its open-air shows and fancy-dress balls, and the Viareggio Carnival is also well known.

carta d'identità An identity document issued to all citizens aged 15 and over. It is valid for foreign travel within the countries of the European Union, and for trips to some other countries with which there is an agreement. It is renewed every five years at the town hall. An electronic card, the same size as a credit card, can be requested.

Cassa integrazione or **Cassa integrazione guadagni** The benefit system for employees who are temporarily laid off because of a crisis in the company they work for. It is run by the INPS, which undertakes to pay 80 per cent of normal salary for a period of one or two years.

Cattolica The 'Catholic university' is a prestigious private institute with humanities and science faculties, spread over five different campuses throughout Italy.

Cavaliere – short for *Cavaliere al merito del lavoro* (Knight for services to industry) – is an official title, conferred since 1901 on those who make a major contribution to economic development. However, it is not uncommon for successful entrepreneurs to give their surnames the prefix *cavaliere* unofficially. Another frequently encountered title is that of *commendatore*, in common use over the past few decades as an honorific for any wealthy person.

Cavallino rampante The 'prancing horse' symbol of Ferrari. Enzo Ferrari adopted the symbol from a coat of arms belonging to a First World War flying ace. He first used it on the Alfa Romeo cars in his racing stable, then on the cars he began to produce himself in 1947 in Maranello (near Modena). Today it is synonymous with Ferrari both as a car-maker and as a Formula 1 team.

Cinecittà A complex of all of the different cinematographic studios set up on the outskirts of Rome in 1937. It includes a large number of film studios as well as studios for soundtracking.

CNR The Consiglio Nazionale delle Ricerche (National Research Council) is a national public body which carries out and promotes research activities for the scientific, technological, economic, and social development of the country.

codice civile e penale The civil and penal codes. The Italian codes, like those of other continental European countries, were modelled on the Code Napoléon, the French civil code first introduced in 1804. These superseded the common law, restructuring it on the enlightened principles of the French Revolution. The unified Italian state, founded in 1861, brought together the codes of the various states that made it up to constitute the civil code, the code of civil procedure, and the code of criminal procedure (on the French model) in 1865, and the criminal code in 1889. The new codes drawn up in the 20th century followed the same lines, with some modifications.

codice fiscale A combination of letters and numbers, based on the holder's particulars, which identifies every citizen or resident of Italy for tax purposes and other dealings with the authorities. It is indispensable if a person wishes to work, open a bank account, use the health service, etc. In current usage the term *codice fiscale* (tax code) also refers to the plastic card, similar in size to a credit card, issued to everybody by the Ministry of the Economy and Finance and bearing the holder's code and personal details.

Colosseo The name given in the Middle Ages to the 'colossal' Flavian Amphitheatre, the most famous monument of Ancient Rome, which was begun by Vespasian in about 75 AD and inaugurated by Titus in 80 AD. It is oval in shape and up to 50,000 spectators could attend the bloody battles between gladiators and beasts that were staged there.

comuni Each province is subdivided into municipalities (*comuni*), each of which is run by a council and municipal committee headed by a SINDACO (mayor). The functions of the *comuni* are mainly administrative.

confederazioni sindacali The three large Italian trade union organizations that represent workers in all categories and sectors: the formerly Communist-oriented CGIL (Confederazione generale italiana del lavoro); the Christian-oriented CISL (Confederazione italiana sindacati lavoratori) and the social-democrat-oriented UIL (Unione italiana del lavoro). During the 1970s and 1980s they formed an alliance and collaborated to play a central role in politics and in the Italian economy. However, recent transformations in the economy and the labour market have reduced their unity of action, and their role has been partly reshaped by the rise of autonomous sectoral unions.

consiglio dei ministri A body composed of ministers and headed by the PRESIDENTE DEL CONSIGLIO: it forms the government.

consultorio familiare Social-health service set up in the mid-1970s. It provides health education (including preventive medicine) in the fields of gynaecology and paediatrics, as well as advice and support for people with mental health or legal problems.

Culture

Corte Costituzionale The constitutional court, in operation since 1955, which has the duty of ensuring that laws passed by parliament do not conflict with the COSTITUZIONE and of ruling on conflicts between the powers of the state and those of the regions. It is made up partly of magistrates and partly of jurists chosen by the parliament and the PRESIDENTE DELLA REPUBBLICA. It is based in Rome, in the Palazzo della Consulta (the Consulta being a former papal institution) next door to the QUIRINALE, and is often referred to as La Consulta.

costituzione The constitution of the Italian Republic, which came into force on 1 January 1948. It was drawn up by a constituent assembly, elected by the people, and based on the principles of liberty, equality, and democracy. A constitutional court (CORTE COSTITUZIONALE) ensures that any individual laws passed by parliament conform to the constitution.

denominazione di origine controllata (*DOC*) The state-certified mark of quality awarded to Italian wines that possess certain verified characteristics, such as origin within a defined zone of production, derivation from particular types of vines and soils, ratio between the quantity of grapes used and quantity of wine obtained, and methods used in production. *DOC* wines that have become particularly famous for their special qualities are now certified as *DOCG* (*denominazione di origine controllata e garantita*), a mark based on even stricter standards of verification. *See also* VINO.

Divina Commedia The most celebrated and important work in Italian literature, written by Dante Alighieri between 1306 and 1321. *The Divine Comedy* is divided into three parts, *Inferno* (Hell), *Purgatorio* (Purgatory), and *Paradiso* (Heaven), each containing thirty-three cantos (plus one introductory canto to make 100). It describes a journey through the Christian afterlife and is probably best known and loved for its retelling of the stories of the characters Dante discovers in the three realms. Part of Dante's purpose was to prove that the Italian language could be used for serious works of literature. In his writing, he blended the language of court with the most expressive elements of his native Tuscan and other dialects, helping to lay the foundations of modern Italian.

Dolce Vita, La A film, whose title literally means 'The Sweet Life', made by the director Federico Fellini and released in 1960. It depicted the emptiness and squalor of high society in Rome. Its title very quickly became a cliché for a worldly Italian lifestyle that perhaps never even existed, and it ended up as banal slogan for mass tourism.

dottore The legally recognized title in Italy for a person who receives a degree after completing a university course lasting at least four years. It is widely used both in writing (on letters or on business cards) or as a form of address to refer formally to all graduates, not simply graduates in medicine. There is a saying in Italy that 'no one ever denies being doctor', meaning that anyone – with or without a degree – is happy to accept *dottore* as a term of deference from waiters, parking attendants, and so on. *See also* LAUREA.

enoteca A place where good local wines are offered for sale and often for tasting. In many *enoteche* you can also eat while tasting the wines.

extracomunitari The Italian term used to refer to immigrants from Third World countries (black Africa, the Arab countries of North Africa, the Philippines, Sri Lanka, and China) or European countries that are not yet members of the European Union (such as Albania). Though the term may seem purely bureaucratic, *extracomunitario* (literally, 'outside the community') is a discriminatory word in common speech reflecting deep-seated prejudices; it is used with mistrust or fear, sometimes with scorn or hostility, as a label for poor immigrants, exploited as underpaid labour, often staying illegally without a residence permit, and involved in illegal trafficking or criminal activities.

FAI The Fondo per l'Ambiente Italiano (Fund for the Italian Environment), set up in 1975 with the aim of contributing to the protection, conservation, and use of Italy's artistic and environmental heritage. It has acquired, mostly through donations, many important buildings and sites (villas, palaces, castles, parks, and gardens) that it has subsequently restored and opened to the public.

farmaci Following a change in the law, it is now possible to buy over-the-counter medicines in the "health corner" of supermarkets, where a pharmacist must be present by law. They can also be bought from the so-called *parafarmacie*, which are similar to traditional pharmacies except that a doctor's prescription is not necessary.

Farnesina A term used in the media to refer to the Italian Ministry of Foreign Affairs which, since 1959, has been housed in the Palazzo della Farnesina, a vast building constructed in a functional style between 1938 and the 1950s outside the historic centre of Rome.

Fascism A movement, based on an ultra-conservative, anti-socialist, nationalist, racist, and authoritarian ideology, which controlled Italy from 1922 to 1943. The name comes from the *fasces*, an axe with its handle encased in a bundle of rods, which was a symbol of power and unity in Roman times. The Fascists, led by Benito Mussolini (known as *il duce*, the leader), were both a political party and a paramilitary organization. They ruled dictatorially, intimidating, imprisoning, and sometimes murdering, their political opponents. Under the Fascist regime Italian armies conquered Abyssinia and Albania, but military failures during World War II, in which Italy was initially allied with Germany and Japan, led to the Fascists' downfall.

Fiamme Gialle The nickname (literally meaning 'Yellow Flames') for the *guardia di finanza*, an Italian police force organized along military lines, which specializes in combating economic, financial, and fiscal crime (fraud, tax evasion, and money laundering) and guarding Italy's land and sea borders (against smuggling, drug trafficking, and illegal immigration). It was set up in 1881 and its members wear uniforms with yellow insignia, hence the nickname.

foglio rosa This is the provisional driving licence, which can be applied for after passing the theory test and is valid for six months.

Fratelli d'Italia The name by which Italy's national anthem is commonly known. Its official name is the *Inno di Mameli* (Mameli's hymn), after its author, the poet and patriot Goffredo Mameli, who died in 1849, aged 22, fighting with Garibaldi for the defence of the Roman Republic (*see* I MILLE). It was adopted as the national anthem in 1946. The common name comes from the opening lines of the first verse: *Fratelli d'Italia, l'Italia s'è desta, / dell'elmo di Scipio s'è cinta la testa* (Brothers of Italy, Italy has awoken / It has circled its head with the helmet of Scipio). All Italians know the tune (composed by Mameli's friend, the choirmaster Michele Novaro), but very few know the rest of the words (it has five verses) by heart.

Gazzetta dello Sport This is the sports daily, printed on its characteristic pink paper. It was founded in Milan in 1896 and is the most widely read sports newspaper in Italy. It organizes the GIRO D'ITALIA.

Gazzetta Ufficiale The official newspaper of the Italian state, which publishes approved laws, decrees, and various official announcements.

gelato Made with milk, sugar, eggs, and various other ingredients, this is an Italian speciality. The hand-made variety, bought in *gelaterie*, can be served in a dish or in a cone. There are dozens of flavours to choose from.

giornali Among the main Italian dailies are *Repubblica* and *Corriere della Sera*. The daily financial paper is *il Sole 24 ore*. The weekly magazines *L'Espresso* and *Panorama* deal with current affairs, politics, and culture. As well as Italian versions of international titles, the weekly magazines *Grazia*, *A*, and *Donna Moderna* cater for women. *Famiglia Cristiana* is the Catholic weekly. Of the gossip magazines, *Novella 2000* and *Chi* are the most popular.

giro d'Italia Like the Tour de France, one of the most famous cycling races in the world. It takes place from mid-May to the beginning of June. The route changes every year, but the last stage always ends in Milan. The winner is awarded the pink jersey. *See also* GAZZETTA DELLO SPORT.

gondola A low narrow boat with a raised curved prow, used on the canals of Venice. The gondola is propelled by a *gondoliere* (gondolier) using a single oar that pivots on a small post attached to the starboard side. The gondoliers usually dress in traditional striped tops and a straw hat. A 17th-century *doge* (*see* VENETIAN REPUBLIC) ordered that all gondolas should be painted black, so as not to glorify worldly wealth. They remain black, but are now used almost exclusively for tourists.

Herculaneum ▸ VESUVIUS

Informagiovani As the name suggests, this is a service of information and guidance for young people. Promoted by local bodies, the various centres (and their web sites) provide information about all areas of interest to young people: courses and training, jobs, culture, politics, voluntary work, travel, etc. The first centres opened in Turin and Milan in the early 1980s; now there are about 600 centres throughout Italy. In addition to supplying information, they carry out a role of 'listening' to young people and also promote projects created by young people for young people.

INPS – Istituto Nazionale per la Previdenza Sociale (National Institute of Social Security). This is the major public body in Italy that pays workers' old-age pensions after receiving contributions from them during their working lives. It also manages the various kinds of assistance provided by the welfare state, such as the CASSA INTEGRAZIONE, sickness, maternity, unemployment, and invalidity benefit.

Internet The World Wide Web is much used in Italy, as elsewhere. All major Italian newspapers and television stations have their own websites, as do councils, museums, etc. The suffix for Italian sites is '.it'.

laghi The north of Italy is the area with the highest concentration of lakes, which includes the three largest and most famous: Lake Garda (the largest of all), Lake Maggiore, and Lake Como. The area's mild climate and abundant greenery have always held a great attraction for both Italians and foreigners. Some lakes are equipped for water sports; others offer luxurious hotels and health farms.

laurea The title, meaning 'graduate', that is traditionally awarded in Italy to people who complete a course of study at a university, usually lasting four years. Recently a *laurea triennale* (or *breve*) was introduced; this 'three-year' or 'short degree' gives immediate access to the labour market. In contrast the *laurea specialistica*, 'specialist degree', requires a further two years of study and entitles the holder to be known as DOTTORE.

Leaning Tower of Pisa The eight-storey bell tower of the cathedral of Pisa. Building work began in 1183, but the tower started to lean noticeably to the north, as the ground beneath it was unstable. Work continued on and off on the tower for the next 200 years, and by 1360 it was complete – it was now leaning to the south, however. Over the centuries, the problem worsened. Finally, in the late 1990s, engineers removed rock and soil from under the north side of the tower and succeeded in reducing the angle of tilt from 10 per cent to 5 per cent. The tower is now said to be safe for the next 300 years.

Liberazione, La The effective end of the Second World War in Italy in late April 1945, when a general uprising staged by the RESISTENZA in the northern cities (Turin, Milan, and Genoa) led to the surrender or retreat of German troops before the arrival of the victorious Anglo-American forces. It is celebrated by the Festa della Liberazione (Liberation Day holiday) on 25 April each year.

liceo A type of secondary school, similar to a grammar school, which aims to form students' characters, pass on theoretical rather than applied knowledge, and develop the capacity for independent judgement and

criticism. These aims are fully embodied in the more traditional type of *liceo*, the *liceo classico*, focused on the study of ancient languages (Latin and Greek). In the *liceo scientifico*, a more recent type, mathematics and the sciences are strongly represented in the curriculum along with Latin and philosophy, the latter being trademark subjects of *liceo* teaching whatever the school's specialism, whether science, modern languages, or art, etc. The evolution of the Italian school system is leading to the term *liceo* also being applied to schools that specialize in technical or business subjects.

Lotto The lottery game first appeared in Italy in Genoa during the 16th century, and during the following century spread to the other Italian states. From the 19th century it has been run directly by the state, and since 1871 there have been weekly Saturday draws in ten cities (known as *ruote*). Over the centuries a popular myth has grown up that the interpretation of dreams can help in the selection of winning numbers. The principles, a mixture of esotericism and cabbalism, are set out in the book of *Smorfia* (a corruption of Morpheus, the name of the Greek and Roman god of sleep and dreams). This ancient game still has great potential, as the development of recent variants such as the hugely popular Superenalotto has shown.

Mafia Since the Second World War, the Sicilian Mafia (also called Cosa Nostra) has expanded and developed substantially, creating an alternative power that is partly complementary to that of the state. Starting from illegal activities such as extortion and usury, it then assumed control of the building trade and the award of public contracts, and finally took over the traffic in illegal drugs, which brought in enormous profits. The Mafia has a vertical structure (a strict hierarchy of 'families'), but it is distinguished from other criminal organizations above all by its close relationships and complicity with political authorities.

Culture

Mani pulite The name (meaning 'clean hands') given to the landmark judicial inquiry, which, beginning in 1992 in Milan, brought to light the system of *tangenti* (payments on the side) and corruption in which the governing parties were involved. It resulted in their dissolution and the end of the so-called 'first republic' (PRIMA REPUBBLICA).

Manifesti funebri Small posters printed by the family of someone who has died, announcing the death, saying a few words about the deceased, and giving the date and time of the funeral. These are put up on special boards – or indeed on any available surface – to inform local people of what has happened and to ensure a large attendance at the funeral.

matrimoni Traditionally, marriages in Italy were arranged by the couple's families, and it is still not uncommon for a male relative of the groom to visit the bride's father or uncle to ask formally for the girl's hand on the groom's behalf. Traditionally, too, the bride would be given a dowry – nowadays her family and friends will usually arrange bridal showers before the wedding to provide her with household goods, and she carries a satin bag at the reception into which guests put money. Weddings in Italy do not usually take place during the solemn church seasons of Advent and Lent, or during the months of May and August. Other customs include the throwing of confetti (not scraps of paper, but small bags of sugared almonds) and the breaking of a glass or vase at the end of the wedding feast, which is usually sumptuous. The number of pieces into which the object breaks is supposed to represent the number of years the couple will live together.

maturità This is the exam that students take at the end of the five years of secondary school, between the ages of 18 and 19. It consists of three written tests (one of which is Italian language) and one oral. Marks (the minimum is 60 out of 100) depend on both the result of the tests and the number of credits gained by the student over the previous three years. The diploma is a requirement for university entrance and, depending on the type of secondary school attended, it can be in science, classics, arts, or technology, etc.

mercati Every Italian town and city has its own market, either open-air or covered, where fruit, vegetables, cheeses, cooked meats, and a range of other produce is sold. There is also a weekly market where it is possible to buy clothes, bags, household goods, and other items. The prices are cheaper than in the shops, and people often haggle over the goods displayed on the stalls.

Mezzogiorno A term referring to southern Italy, including Sicily and Sardinia, which is less economically developed than the north. The name literally means 'midday', i.e. siesta time, indicating that – though it has a wealth of artistic treasures and beautiful countryside – the pace of life here is markedly less frenetic than in northern Italy.

Culture

Culture

I Mille In 1860, soldier Giuseppe Garibaldi (1807–82) set sail from Genoa with two ships and just over 1,000 volunteers (*i mille*), known as the *Camicie rosse* (Red Shirts). Garibaldi and his followers managed to wrest Sicily and Naples from Bourbon hands, territory which he then handed over to King Victor Emmanuel II of Sardinia-Piedmont. In the following year, Victor Emmanuel was declared king of the newly unified Italy. The original 1,000 volunteers remained a symbol of the most notable event of the Italian RISORGIMENTO, and are commemorated in street names in many Italian cities.

Mole Antonelliana The Mole Antonelliana, an extremely unusual monument (167 m – 548 ft – high), is the symbol of Turin. Destined to be a synagogue, the building was begun in 1863 but, following financial problems and arguments about its stability, it was not finished until 1889. Subsequently acquired by the city, it is now the home of the New Museum of the Cinema. A glass lift provides access to the steeple.

Montecitorio A palace, built between 1650 and 1697, to house papal courts. It is situated in a piazza of the same name in the centre of Rome. Since 1871 it has been home to the lower house of the Italian parliament, the CAMERA DEI DEPUTATI (Chamber of Deputies). The term Montecitorio is used in the media to refer to the Chamber itself.

Monza A small city north of Milan, best known as the site of Autodromo nazionale, the motor-racing circuit where the Italian Grand Prix is held.

Mostra Internazionale d'Arte Cinematografica Also known as the Venice Film Festival, this is the film section of the BIENNALE DI VENEZIA. It was started in the 1930s and takes place every year at the end of August at the Palazzo del Cinema on the Venice Lido. One of the largest film festivals in Europe (and indeed the world), it attracts films, actors, directors, and other technicians from around the world. The festival winners are awarded the Golden Lion.

negozi The hours of opening for shops vary according to the type of shop and where it is located. In general, food shops open at about 8 a.m. and close at 7.30 p.m. with a lunch break from 12.30 to 3.30 p.m. Clothes shops, bookshops, etc. open from 9 a.m. until 12.30 or 1 p.m. and then again from 3.30 to 7.30 p.m. In summer the lunch break is longer and shops stay open until 8.00 p.m. Some supermarkets and department stores in the big cities are open all day. Weekly closing also varies according to the type of shop. Some shops close for two to three weeks in August, after the summer sales, then reopen with the new autumn-season stock.

Nordest The northeast, the area comprising the regions Veneto, Trentino, and Friuli, where a highly successful model of industrial development was applied during the 1990s. This led to the rapid emergence of many small and medium-sized companies, producing mainly textiles, footwear, and mechanical goods, and to strong export growth. Since then, however, the 'northeastern model' has been discussed mainly in terms of its downsides (damage to the environment, absence of general social development, lack of professional training for workers). Today it is in difficulties because of globalized competition; it no longer appears to be a more successful alternative to the traditional industrial area of the northwest, the TRIANGOLO INDUSTRIALE.

Normale The Scuola Normale Superiore di Pisa was set up in the early 1800s as a branch of the Paris Ecole Normale. Today, it is an extremely prestigious institute offering first degree courses and research doctorates in science and the humanities.

onomastico This is the feast day of the saint whose name a person bears. Although less important than his or her birthday, a saint's day is always celebrated, sometimes with a small gift.

oratorio In Italy there are thousand of *oratorios* (usually buildings with courtyards and playing fields attached to Catholic parishes), which are used by pupils – on afternoons when they are not in school – as meeting places and for recreation (typically for ball games, but also for many other sporting or theatrical activities, etc.) and educational purposes. They are supervised by priests or their lay assistants. Created in the 19th century to rescue poor boys from immorality and crime, they have become a typical feature of young people's lives at all social levels in Italy.

Padania A term used by the political party Lega Nord (the Northern League) to refer to the whole of northern Italy, roughly the area falling within the basin of the River Po and the Venetian regions, supposed to be inhabited by a population of Celtic rather than Latin origin. According to its more extreme proponents, Padania should aim to secede from the rest of Italy (dominated by a 'corrupt' Rome), and especially from the uncivilized and backward south. But, for critics and opponents of the League, Padania is a meaningless term, because it does not correspond to a unified area that can be defined geographically, historically, or linguistically – and because the idea that the Padanians are direct descendants of the ancient Celts is mythical nonsense.

Palazzo Chigi The seat of the Italian government since 1961. The Palazzo Chigi, built in the 16th and 17th centuries, is situated in Piazza Colonna in the heart of Rome near the MONTECITORIO palace. In the media, the term Palazzo Chigi means the Italian government or PRESIDENTE DELLA REPUBBLICA.

Culture

Palio di Siena A popular event that takes place every year in Siena on 2 July and 16 August. The *contrade*, or districts of the city, fight for the *palio*, a banner, in a frantic race on horseback around the medieval Piazza del Campo. It has deep historical roots but is still passionately followed by the Sienese and is a huge attraction for tourists from all over the world. There is a spectacular historical procession in brightly coloured Renaissance costumes before the race.

Papal States Areas of central Italy owned and governed by the Pope from the early Middle Ages until the 19th century, including Latium, Umbria, Marche, and the city of Rome itself. The process of transferring these areas to secular government began with the conquest of Italy by Napoleon Bonaparte, but was not completed until 1870, when the Pope was forced to relinquish control of Rome, enabling it to become the capital of a united Italy.

parchi nazionali In Italy there are about twenty national parks covering 5 per cent of the territory. Controlled by the Ministry of the Environment, their objective is the protection and development of large areas that are of particular importance in terms of environment and landscape. The best-known are 'Gran Paradiso', the national parks in Abruzzi, Lazio, and Molise, and the National Park of the Maddalena Archipelago. The marine parks, which aim to protect stretches of sea, coast, and sometimes whole islands and archipelagos, are becoming increasingly important.

partiti politici While political parties have always been numerous in Italy, particularly at a local level, nationally there has been a gradual polarization between the centre-right – whose main party is the Popolo della Libertà (PdL, formed by a merger of Forza Italia and Alleanza Nazionale) – and the centre-left, dominated by the Partito Democratico (PD, the result of a merger between the Unione dei Democratici di Sinistra and la Margherita). The other three most important political parties in Italy are Italia dei Valori (IdV, founded by Antonio di Pietro, the judge who led the MANI PULITE inquiry), the Lega Nord (sometimes known as just Lega), and the Unione di Centro (UDC).

passeggiata This typical Italian custom involves walking with family or friends in the square or main street, or along the promenade. It usually takes place before eating, on Saturday afternoon or Sunday morning, and in the summer it can also take place in the evening after dinner. Depending on the time and the weather, people might have an aperitif or an ice cream. The purpose is to stretch one's legs, chat, see who is around, and be seen.

pasta The basic ingredient of many Italian dishes, which is made by mixing flour from durum (hard) wheat with water, and sometimes adding other ingredients such as beaten egg or cooked spinach. Fresh pasta is soft and can be moulded into a variety of different forms, such as flat sheets (lasagne), long thin sticks (spaghetti), tubes (macaroni, cannelloni), or small square pillow shapes (ravioli). Commercially made pasta is dried after shaping until hard. In this form it will keep for a long time. Pasta is also a healthy food as it contains very little fat.

patente a punti Following reform of the Italian highway code, each driving licence is now given an initial value of twenty points, which are reduced if traffic offences are committed. For example, for the more serious offences (overtaking on a bend, drink driving, or driving while under the effect of drugs), ten points are deducted; passing a red light costs you six points, while parking in an area reserved for public transport costs two points. Once the number of infringements committed has reduced the initial number of points to zero, the licence is withdrawn and the driving test has to be retaken. Drivers with the worst records are required to undergo courses of 're-education'. The points system is also applied to foreign citizens who are passing though Italy: the penalties are totted up and filed in a special register.

permesso di soggiorno Foreigners who enter Italy with a passport and visa, especially for work or study, have to apply for this residence permit from the state police – that is from a QUESTURA or a *commissariato* (police headquarters or local police station) – within eight days of arrival. The permit is valid for between three months and two years, depending on the circumstances, and is renewable. It entitles the holder to be issued with an identity card (CARTA D'IDENTITÀ) and a tax code (CODICE FISCALE). *See also* POLIZIA DI STATO.

Piazza Affari A term commonly used in the media to refer to the Milan stock exchange, the most important in Italy. The stock exchange came into existence in 1808 and is now housed in the Palazzo della Borsa (built between 1928 and 1931), situated in the centre of the city in the Piazza degli Affari.

Pinocchio The hero of the children's book, *Le Avventure di Pinocchio* (The Adventures of Pinocchio) by Carlo Collodi (1826–90), Pinocchio is a wooden puppet whose nose grows whenever he tells a lie. After various tribulations, accompanied by such famous characters as Geppetto (the puppetmaker), the Blue Fairy, the Fire-Eater, Lucignolo, and the whale, etc., Pinocchio is turned into a real boy. Adapted for television and as a cartoon, the story has also been reinterpreted from a sociological and psychoanalytical point of view.

pizza Now a 'global food', pizza was for centuries a speciality of the city of Naples, and many people still think that it cannot be properly appreciated elsewhere. Pizze (flattened pieces of bread dough) were eaten in Naples in the late Middle Ages with garlic and lard, cheese and basil, or small fish. The modern pizza, with tomato, appeared in the late 1700s. The first pizzeria was opened in Naples in 1830 (before that, pizza was sold and eaten in the street). In 1889 the *pizzaolo* (pizza-maker) Raffaele Esposito made a pizza topped with

Culture (vertical text in right margin)

tomato, ricotta, and some leaves of basil (thus red, white, and green, the colours of the Italian flag) for Queen Margherita, the wife of Umberto I. Since then, this, the most widespread type of pizza, has been known as pizza margherita.

politecnico A scientific and technological university that includes faculties of engineering and architecture among its specializations. There are three in Italy. The oldest and most famous are those of Turin (1859) and Milan (1863); the latest is in Bari.

polizia di stato The name, meaning 'state police', of the Italian civil police force. The force was organized along military lines from 1919 to 1981 and called the Corpo delle Guardie di Pubblica Sicurezza (PS), Guards of Public Safety. It had headquarters (QUESTURE) in the capital city of each province, and police stations (*commissariati*) in city districts and minor centres. The reform of 1981 demilitarized and democratized it, and many of its officers and staff are now women. It continues to assist the CARABINIERI (who cover a wider area) in the task of maintaining law and order.

Pompeii ▶ VESUVIUS

Ponte Vecchio The ancient bridge in Florence that spans the River Arno. It carries a roadway lined with goldsmiths' and jewellers' shops.

popular music In Italy the popular and classical traditions of vocal music tend to merge. The repertoires of star singers such as Luciano Pavarotti and Andrea Boccelli include popular Italian, especially Neapolitan songs, alongside operatic arias. Italian pop singers are less well known abroad. Singers such as Mina, Lucio Battisti, and Eros Ramazzotti tend to specialize in romantic songs. Italy does, however, have its share of rock, hip-hop, etc, artists and groups.

Premio Strega The most famous literary prize in Italy, instituted in 1947 and sponsored by a wealthy liquor manufacturer (producer of the Strega liqueur). Previous winners have included Edoardo De Filippo, Pierpaolo Pasolini, and Umberto Eco. The prize is awarded annually, in July, in the 16th-century Ninfeo (a garden with monumental fountain) of the Villa Giulia in Rome.

presepio (or *presepe*) A 'crib', a representation of the Nativity and the Adoration of the Magi in the form of wood or terracotta statues against a painted landscape. Cribs first appeared in Tuscany in the 13th and 14th centuries, but it was in Naples in the 17th and 18th centuries, during the baroque and rococo periods, that churches began to display magnificent examples. Scenes of everyday life were reproduced down to the smallest detail. During the 19th century, families began to build their own cribs for the

Culture

Christmas season, with terracotta, plaster, or papier-mâché figurines. In
recent years this custom has become a little less common with the
introduction of the Christmas tree from northern Europe.

presidente del consiglio This is the title of the Italian prime minister, the
head of the government and of the CONSIGLIO DEI MINISTRI. Nominated by the
PRESIDENTE DELLA REPUBBLICA, he proposes the ministers. He controls and is
responsible for government policy.

presidente della repubblica The head of state who represents the nation.
He/she is elected by parliament and remains in office for seven years. As Italy
is a parliamentary republic, the duties of the president are: to enact laws, to
dissolve parliament and call new elections when necessary, to nominate the
prime minister and ratify his choice of the ministers, and to grant pardons.
He/she also chairs the body which oversees the appointment of judges.

Prima repubblica The name (meaning 'first republic') given to the
political system that collapsed in 1992–93 in the wake of
scandals revealed by the MANI PULITE (Clean Hands) inquiry
and the weakening of the opposing ideological positions
associated with the Cold War. The big governing parties of
those days – especially the Christian Democrats and the
Socialist Party – disbanded, and new parties emerged; these
are still active today (*see also* PARTITI POLITICI).

provincia In Italy's system of local government, each
province is made up of neighbouring municipalities, the most
important of which acts as the provincial capital. Each
province is served by a provincial council, a committee, and a
president.

quadrilatero della moda The 'fashion quadrilateral' is an area in the
centre of Milan defined by the Via Montenapoleone, Via della Spiga, Via
Manzoni, and Via Sant'Andrea, where the biggest names in Italian fashion,
such as Armani, Trussardi, Coveri, Versace, Prada, Missoni, and Dolce &
Gabbana, have their boutiques and showrooms.

questura Provincial headquarters of the police force. Thefts are reported to
the *questura* and passports renewed there.

Quirinale A 16th-century building on the hill of the same name in Rome,
now the residence of the PRESIDENTE DELLA REPPUBLICA. It was formerly the
summer residence of the popes and then of the kings of Italy.

RAI The state radio and television company. There are three television
channels, RAI 1, RAI 2, and RAI 3, and three radio stations, Radio 1, Radio 2, and
Radio 3, which tend to be supportive of the government.

reality TV Reality television has become as popular in Italy as in other countries. Most Italian shows follow the same formats used elsewhere. Italy has its own version of 'Big Brother' (*Il Grande Fratello*), of 'Survivor' (*L'isola dei Famosi*) and various talent shows such as *X Factor* and *Ballando con le stelle* (*Strictly Come Dancing*).

regione Italy is subdivided into twenty regions, five of which have a certain amount of political autonomy. Each region is subdivided in its turn into provinces (*see* PROVINCIA) and municipalities. The regions can issue legislative standards. They also have administrative duties which can be delegated to the provinces and the municipalities. Each region is served by a council, a committee, and a regional president.

repubblica The Italian republic was founded after the Second World War, based on the results of the referendum of 2 June 1946, which abolished the monarchy in favour of a republican form of government. The COSTITUZIONE published in 1948 established its parliamentary character.

Resistenza On 8 September 1943, Italy, which had been allied to Hitler's Germany, surrendered to British and US forces. The Germans reacted immediately by invading the greater part of the peninsula, which was not yet occupied by allied forces, and by imposing a harshly oppressive regime on their former ally. Soldiers from the disbanded army and antifascist civilians organized themselves into groups of partisans to fight the Germans and their Fascist collaborators behind the lines, leading to the Liberation in 1945. The ideals of liberty and democracy that inspired the partisans and their unity of action in spite of differing political views were the foundation of the new post-war Italian republic. For this reason, the Resistance still carries considerable political weight in present-day Italy.

Risorgimento The name, meaning 'the Resurgence', given to the historical period marked by the struggles for Italian independence and unification. After its beginnings in 1820–21 and 1831 and the uprisings of 1848–49, its principal events were the three wars of independence against Austria-Hungary (1848–49, 1859, and 1866) and the expedition of Garibaldi and I MILLE (the 1,000) in 1860. The moderate monarchical movement prevailed against the republican and revolutionary tendency of Giuseppe Mazzini, so that the House of Savoy (under Victor Emmanuel II) obtained the Italian crown in 1861. Rome became the capital city in 1871 (*see also* PAPAL STATES).

riviera The Italian word *riviera* means a 'coastal region'. It has been borrowed by many other languages and come to mean an area with a warm climate, fashionable resorts, and beaches for holidaymakers. The Italian, or Ligurian, Riviera is the stretch of coastline that begins at the French border and extends as far as Tuscany. The main city and port in the region is Genoa – popular holiday towns include Portofino, San Remo, and Rapallo.

rugby Both rugby union and rugby league are played in Italy, mainly in northern regions. There has been a national championship in rugby union since 1929, and in 2000 Italy joined England, Wales, Scotland, Ireland, and France to make up the Six Nations competition.

sagra A popular festival with a fair and market, which takes place in many villages once a year, sometimes more frequently. *Sagre* usually have a theme such as wine, sausages, fish, or truffles – depending on what the local speciality is.

St Peter's The largest Christian church in the world, situated in the VATICANO in Rome. The Basilica of St Peter's is not a cathedral; its importance lies in its closeness to the papal residence and its use for most papal ceremonies, as well as in its size and architectural magnificence. The present building was designed by Bramante – various other famous artists participated, including Michelangelo, who designed the dome – and it was constructed between 1506 and 1615.

San Marino The republic of San Marino forms an enclave within Italian territory, but is an independent sovereign state completely surrounded by Italian soil, lying between Emilia-Romagna and the Marche, not far from the Adriatic coast. At just over 60 sq. km (23 sq. miles) in area, it is one of the smallest states in the world.

santo patrono In Italy the worship of saints is widespread. The patron saint of a town or community is considered to be its protector. His or her saint's day is a religious holiday on which schools, offices, and most shops are closed. It is celebrated with a special mass and processions. In towns and cities, illuminations are put up and there are stalls and sometimes a fair, in a mixture of the sacred and the secular.

Scala, La The Teatro alla Scala, the Milan opera house, is one of the most famous opera houses in the world. Built in 1776–78, it has recently undergone a programme of restoration, during which the Teatro degli Arcimboldi, outside the city, staged its productions.

scuola The Italian system provides for primary schools, middle schools, and secondary schools. Primary school lasts for five years from the age of six, middle school lasts for three years, and secondary school for five. Primary and middle schools all follow the same curriculum but there are a number of different types of secondary schools: scientific, classical, linguistic, and artistic grammar schools, various technical and commercial institutes, and schools for training nursery school teachers (*see also* LICEO).

Senato The upper house of the Italian Parliament. Three hundred and fifteen senators are elected by universal suffrage by citizens over 25 years of age. Senators must be at least 40 years old. These 315 seats are elected on a regional basis, i.e. they are split between the regions in proportion to population. The elected senators are joined by ex-heads of state and life senators. These are nominated by the PRESIDENTE DELLA REPUBBLICA from people who have given exceptional service to the country in the scientific, social, artistic, or literary fields.

settimana bianca A winter holiday spent with family or schoolfriends in a ski resort.

Seven Hills of Rome A group of seven small hills lying east of the River Tiber. According to tradition, the ancient city of Rome was founded by Romulus on the Palatine hill. The city gradually spread to cover the other six, the CAPITOLINE, Quirinal (QUIRINALE), Viminal (VIMINALE), Esquiline, Caelian, and Aventine hills. The hills are no longer a prominent geographical feature in modern Rome, but some are still associated with districts that have a distinctive character. The Capitoline hill, for instance, remains a seat of government, just as it was in Roman times.

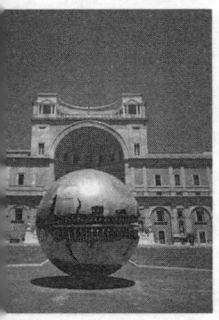

sindaco The mayor is the head of local government and holds power for four years. He chairs and represents the council and municipal committee.

Sistine Chapel A chapel in the Vatican, built by Pope Sixtus IV. In 1505, Pope Julius II commissioned Michelangelo to decorate the ceiling with a series of scenes from the book of Genesis. Michelangelo also painted his vision of the *Last Judgement* on the east wall.

spaghetti western A low-budget western made in Europe by an Italian director or production company, often in English and with an American star, usually featuring lots of explicit violence. The best and most famous of these films are *A Fistful of Dollars, For a Few Dollars More*, and *The Good, the Bad and the Ugly*, directed by Sergio Leone.

spumante A sparkling white wine, sometimes seen as the poor relation of French champagne but also often greatly prized. It can be dry or sweet and always features on Italian Christmas, New Year, and party menus.

stabilimento balneare A stretch of beach equipped with parasols, loungers, showers, huts, perhaps a swimming-pool, and a bar. There is a charge for using it. These beach clubs vary from large and crowded to very chic and exclusive, and from fairly basic to luxurious. Many of them organize sports tournaments, card games, beauty contests, and dances.

stellone A big star, *stellone d'Italia* or *stellone italico* (star of Italy) which, since the RISORGIMENTO, has been associated with the personification of Italy (a woman with a star on her forehead or in her crown). Representing a beacon of hope in times of difficulty, it became part of the coat of arms of the unified kingdom and was then incorporated into the emblem of the

Republic. Today it is mainly used ironically or polemically to criticize the tendency of Italians – a sign both of their vitality and of their happy-go-lucky attitude and fatalism – to trust to good luck rather than to hard work to get them through times of national crisis.

tabaccaio The tobacconist sells cigarettes and tobacco and is also the only shop apart from the post office where you can buy revenue stamps and postage stamps. It also sells bus tickets and other products. Sometimes there is also a bar. Its sign features a white 'T' on a black background.

Tangentopoli A name ('kick-back city') widely used in the Italian media to refer first to Milan, where the judiciary investigated a series of episodes of corruption, and then extended to mean the whole system of illicit financing used by the governing parties, unmasked by the famous MANI PULITE inquiry in 1992–93.

Telecom Italia One of the largest telephone companies supplying both land lines and mobile phones.

terrone A pejorative, racist term typically applied by northern Italians to southern Italians, and usually accompanied by equally disparaging adjectives such as 'ignorant', 'filthy', and 'uncivilized'. The word derives from *terra* (earth, land), depicting the typical southerner as an argicultural labourer. It became widespread in the 1960s and 1970s when large-scale immigration from the south to the industrial northwest took place. In present-day Italy, racist insults are mainly reserved for despised foreign immigrants (EXTRACOMUNITARI), while the term *terrone* is less widely used and has even acquired a jocular tone (the more so since it is used by southerners themselves). The pejorative sense has, however, been given a new lease of life in the anti-southern polemics of the Northern League (*see* PARTITI POLITICI).

trattoria A trattoria used to be distinguishable from a restaurant because it was simpler, often family-run, and less expensive. Nowadays it is merely a 'typical' local restaurant, serving traditional local dishes in a country-style setting. It can also be very sophisticated, and sometimes quite expensive.

triangolo industriale A name for the industrial zone of northwestern Italy, a triangle with the cities of Milan, Turin, and Genoa at its corners, where modern industry began to develop at the end of the 19th century. It has been the major productive centre in Italy, attracting large-scale internal immigration from the south, especially between the 1950s and 1970s. The subsequent decline of heavy industry has transformed the industrial triangle into an area where small and medium-sized enterprises and the tertiary sector now predominate. Other models of strong development have emerged elsewhere, particularly in the areas around Venice (*see* NORDEST).

Tricolore The Italian national flag: green, white, and red in vertical bands of equal width. It was designed at the end of 1700s and adopted as the flag of the republic after the Second World War.

Uffizi A vast art gallery in Florence, famous for its collection of works by Italian Renaissance painters such as Botticelli, Piero della Francesca, Leonardo, and Raphael. The building containing the gallery was built in the late 15th century to house government administration – hence its name, which means 'offices'.

Ultima cena *The Last Supper*, one of Leonardo da Vinci's most famous works, painted on the wall of the refectory of the monastery of St Maria della Grazia in Milan. Leonardo was experimenting with a new technique for fresco (painting directly onto fresh plaster), which was not altogether successful. As a result, the painting has deteriorated badly over the centuries and been restored several times.

Valle dei Templi An archaeological zone in the province of Agrigento that provides the most glorious evidence of Ancient Greek civilization in Sicily. The remains of many temples are to be found on a ridge (not a valley as the name suggests), among the almond trees. Built in the Doric style in the 5th century BC, the temples were burnt down by the Carthaginians, restored by the Romans in the 1st century AD, then half-destroyed by earthquakes and plundered over the following centuries, so that the only one that now remains intact is the magnificent Tempio della Concordia.

Vaticano The Vatican (also called Vatican City) has been an independent state within the city of Rome and the seat of the Pope since 1929. The Vatican Palace, which surrounds ST PETER'S, is the Pope's residence and houses artistic treasures such as the SISTINE CHAPEL and Raphael's frescos, as well as museums.

Venetian Republic For over a thousand years, from 697 to 1797, the island city of Venice and the mainland territory surrounding it formed an independent republic ruled by an elected chief magistrate (the *doge*) and a council of ten (the *dieci*). From the time of the Crusades to the late 15th century, Venice was the major power in the eastern Mediterranean and became enormously wealthy thanks to its trade with the Muslim world and Asia. From the 16th century, however, its power began to wane. It lost its independence when conquered by Napoleon, and eventually became part of Italy in 1866.

Vespa A motor scooter designed by aeronautical engineer, Corradino D'Ascanio, for the Piaggio company just after World War II. D'Ascanio's brief was to design a vehicle that would be affordable, easy to drive, carry a passenger, and not get the driver's clothes dirty – hence the trademark

Culture

upswept mudguard behind the handlebars. The Vespa is particularly associated with the 1950s and 1960s in Italy, but it remains a popular means of transport to this day.

Vesuvius An active volcano, near Naples, that has erupted many times, most notably in AD 79, when it overwhelmed the ancient Roman cities of Pompeii and Herculaneum. The explosion buried the area under volcanic ash, preserving many of the buildings, as well as the bodies of those who did not flee, virtually intact. The towns were only rediscovered in the 18th century; excavations have revealed a stunning record of daily life in Roman times.

vigile urbano This policeman is responsible for controlling traffic and levying fines for traffic offences, for environmental protection, and for ensuring that municipal regulations and town laws are observed. He also deals with social problems, such as abandoned children, and the monitoring of refugees' and travellers' camps.

Viminale A media name for the Italian Ministry of Internal Affairs (or Home Office), which since 1961 has been housed in the Palazzo del Viminale, a vast Renaissance-style building erected in the early 20th century on the Viminal hill in Rome (*see* SEVEN HILLS OF ROME).

vino Wine is produced in every region of Italy, and the Italian wine-making tradition dates back 4,000 years to prehistoric times. Italy produces some white wine, but is mainly renowned for its red wines. The most internationally famous of these is Chianti, produced in Tuscany. Other famous varieties include Valpolicella, Barolo, Marsala, and Soave. High-quality Italian wines are labelled *DOC* (DENOMINAZIONE DI ORIGINE CONTROLLATA) or *DOCG* (*denominazione di origine controllata e garantita*).

Culture

Vita e cultura nel mondo anglofono dalla A alla Z

Cultura

ABC 1. American Broadcasting Company Una delle principali reti televisive statunitensi, attualmente di proprietà della Walt Disney.
2. Australian Broadcasting Corporation Rete radiotelevisiva statale australiana.

ACT – American College Test Esame che gli studenti nordamericani devono superare per l'ammissione all'università. Generalmente ha luogo al termine della HIGH SCHOOL e copre alcune delle principali materie, come ad es. inglese e matematica.

Advance Australia Fair Inno nazionale australiano.

A level ▶ EXAMINATIONS

Alliance Party ▶ NORTHERN IRELAND

American Dream Il sogno americano è la convinzione che negli Stati Uniti chiunque sia disposto a lavorare sodo possa migliorare la propria posizione economica e sociale. Per gli immigrati e le minoranze il concetto significa anche libertà e uguaglianza di diritti.

American Football Il football americano è un gioco simile al rugby. Si gioca con una palla ovale e le due squadre in campo sono composte da undici giocatori ciascuna. È uno sport spettacolare ma molto violento e i giocatori indossano pertanto caschi e imbottiture protettive. L'evento principale della stagione è il Super Bowl, la finale di campionato della National Football League.

American Indian ▶ NATIVE AMERICAN

Anglican Church ▶ CHURCH OF ENGLAND

Anzac Soldato dell'Australian and New Zealand Army Corps. Questo contingente partecipò alla prima e alla seconda guerra mondiale e viene ricordato in particolare per l'eroismo con cui si distinse durante la disastrosa campagna di Gallipoli (in Turchia), nel 1915–16. Il valore degli *Anzacs* giocò un ruolo importante nel consolidare il sentimento di coscienza nazionale in Australia e Nuova Zelanda; viene commemorato annualmente il 25 aprile, l'Anzac Day.

April Fool's Day ▶ GIORNI FESTIVI NEI PAESI ANGLOFONI

Armistice Day ▶ POPPY DAY

A/S Level ► EXAMINATIONS

Australia Day Festa nazionale australiana celebrata il primo lunedì dopo il 26 gennaio. Commemora l'arrivo dei primi coloni britannici nell'allora Port Jackson, oggi la baia di Sydney, nel 1788.

Australian Rules Gioco australiano simile al rugby, giocato in un campo ovale da squadre di 18 giocatori che si disputano un pallone ovale. È lo sport invernale più popolare in gran parte dell'Australia.

Authorized Version Traduzione inglese della Bibbia pubblicata per la prima volta nel 1611. Realizzata da un gruppo di eruditi e commissionata da Giacomo I d'Inghilterra, per cui è anche chiamata la Bibbia di re Giacomo (*King James Bible*). Dal XVII al XX secolo è stata l'unica versione della Bibbia autorizzata per l'uso nell'ambito della Chiesa Anglicana (CHURCH OF ENGLAND). Il testo ha profondamente influenzato la letteratura e la lingua inglese.

bank holiday Termine che nel Regno Unito indica alcuni giorni festivi, nei quali si ha la chiusura di banche, poste, uffici e scuole. Cade sempre di lunedì.

barrister ► LAWYER

baseball È lo sport nazionale degli Stati Uniti. Il torneo annuale più importante è la *World Series*.

B & B ► BED AND BREAKFAST

BBC – British Broadcasting Corporation Uno dei principali enti radiotelevisivi britannici. Non è finanziato dalla pubblicità commerciale ma attraverso un canone di abbonamento che chiunque abbia la televisione deve pagare. Ha l'obbligo di fornire un servizio di informazione imparziale.

bed and breakfast I *bed & breakfast* o *B&B* sono piccole pensioni o case di privati che offrono camera e colazione a prezzi generalmente abbastanza convenienti.

Big Apple Significa letteralmente 'la grande mela' ed è l'appellativo di New York.

Bill of Rights I primi dieci emendamenti alla Costituzione degli Stati Uniti d'America. Tra i diritti che essi garantiscono ai cittadini statunitensi ci sono la libertà di culto, di parola, di stampa e vari diritti nel caso una persona venga accusata di un qualche reato. Il celebre Quinto Emendamento (*Fifth Amendment*) stabilisce tra l'altro che nessuno è obbligato a deporre contro se stesso. Il Secondo Emendamento tutela invece il diritto di portare armi.

Bonfire Night ► GIORNI FESTIVI NEI PAESI ANGLOFONI

Boxing Day ▸ GIORNI FESTIVI NEI PAESI ANGLOFONI

British Isles Le Isole Britanniche comprendono la Gran Bretagna (GREAT BRITAIN), l'Irlanda – sia l'Irlanda del Nord (NORTHERN IRELAND) che la Repubblica d'Irlanda (Republic of Ireland) – e le isole più piccole quali le Shetlands, l'Isola di Man (Isle of Man), e le Isole Anglo-Normanne o del Canale (CHANNEL ISLANDS).

Broadway Strada nel quartiere newyorkese di Manhattan, celebre per i numerosi teatri. Il termine Broadway si usa infatti anche per indicare il teatro e il mondo dello spettacolo americano in generale. Prima della nascita dell'industria cinematografica era il luogo principale dove attori e artisti potevano esibirsi e diventare famosi.

Buckingham Palace Residenza ufficiale del sovrano britannico a Londra. Il cambio della guardia, accompagnato dalla banda del reggimento, ha luogo quasi tutte le mattine davanti al palazzo reale.

Burns Night ▸ GIORNI FESTIVI NEI PAESI ANGLOFONI

Cabinet È il Gabinetto del governo britannico, equivalente al nostro Consiglio dei Ministri. Formato da una ventina di ministri nominati dal Primo Ministro, ciascuno dei quali è responsabile di un settore specifico. Il Cabinet al completo si riunisce regolarmente per discutere e decidere la politica del governo. Il leader del principale partito all'opposizione nomina lo Shadow Cabinet, un Gabinetto ombra omologo al governo.

Canada Situato a nord degli Stati Uniti e secondo al mondo per superficie, il Canada è uno stato federale costituito da dieci province e tre territori. Storicamente legato alla Gran Bretagna ed appartenente al Commonwealth, è una monarchia costituzionale (il capo dello stato è la regina Elisabetta II) e democrazia parlamentare, con Parlamento a Ottawa, la capitale. Le lingue ufficiali sono l'inglese e il francese; quanto alla religione circa il 42% della popolazione canadese è cattolica, mentre il 23% è protestante. Florida nazione industriale, il Canada è molto ricco di risorse naturali; possiede oltre il 60% dei laghi mondiali: i Grandi Laghi (Superiore, Michigan, Huron, Erie e Ontario) si trovano al confine con gli Stati Uniti, come pure le spettacolari Cascate del Niagara; vanta inoltre ampie foreste da legname e catene montuose (tra cui le Montagne Rocciose canadesi). Una istituzione tipica del paese è infine la Royal Canadian Mounted Police, le leggendarie Giubbe Rosse che vantano la reputazione di acciuffare immancabilmente il loro uomo.

Capitol Il Campidoglio è la sede del Congresso degli Stati Uniti d'America (CONGRESS) situata sul Capitol Hill, nella città di Washington. The Capitol indica anche il Congresso stesso.

CBS – Columbia Broadcasting System Uno dei tre principali enti radiotelevisivi nazionali degli Stati Uniti.

Central Park Vasto parco nel quartiere di Manhattan a New York, caro ai newyorkesi in quanto costituisce un'oasi di verde in una zona fortemente urbanizzata.

Channel Islands Le Isole Anglo-Normanne (o Isole del Canale) sono un arcipelago situato nella Manica, vicino alla costa francese. Non fanno parte del Regno Unito ma sono dipendenze autonome della corona britannica. Jersey e Guernsey sono le isole più grandi.

Christmas Day ▶ GIORNI FESTIVI NEI PAESI ANGLOFONI

Church of England Il termine Chiesa d'Inghilterra indica la Chiesa Anglicana, chiesa protestante ufficiale in Inghilterra. Fu creata nel 1534 da Enrico VIII, il quale con l'Atto di supremazia (Act of Supremacy) si sostituì al Papa come capo della chiesa in Inghilterra. Ancora oggi il sovrano è il governatore supremo della Chiesa Anglicana; i vescovi e gli arcivescovi sono nominati dalla Corona su proposta del Primo Ministro. Il capo spirituale è invece l'Arcivescovo di Canterbury. L'Inghilterra è suddivisa in 44 diocesi e da 13.000 parrocchie (*parishes*), ciascuna con a capo un parroco (*vicar*). Nel 1992, il Sinodo Generale (General Synod) ha approvato l'ordinazione di sacerdoti donna. Fuori dall'Inghilterra si hanno altre comunioni anglicane: la Chiesa Episcopale in Scozia e negli Stati Uniti (Episcopalian Church), la Chiesa d'Irlanda (Church of Ireland), la Chiesa gallese (Church of Wales).

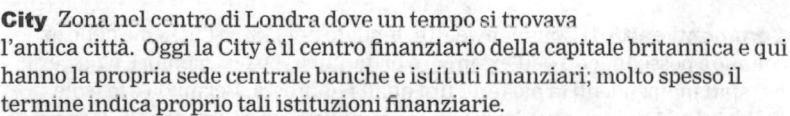

City Zona nel centro di Londra dove un tempo si trovava l'antica città. Oggi la City è il centro finanziario della capitale britannica e qui hanno la propria sede centrale banche e istituti finanziari; molto spesso il termine indica proprio tali istituzioni finanziarie.

Civil War 1. (negli Stati Uniti) La Guerra di Secessione (1861–65), combattuta tra gli stati del nord e quelli del sud, scoppiata principalmente per la questione della schiavitù. Gli stati del sud, la cui economia agricola dipendeva dalla manodopera fornita dagli schiavi neri, nel 1861 costituirono la Confederazione degli Stati d'America separandosi così dall'Unione. Il conflitto tra sudisti e nordisti ebbe inizio il 12 aprile 1861 e il 9 aprile 1865 gli stati della Confederazione si arresero. La conclusione della guerra segnò l'abolizione della schiavitù; il 13° emendamento della Costituzione e successivamente il 14° (del 1868) e il 15° (del 1870) garantirono ai neri gli stessi diritti dei cittadini bianchi, almeno sulla carta. **2. (in Inghilterra)** Conflitto tra la Corona e il Parlamento (1642–51). Da un lato erano schierati i Royalists o Cavaliers (i monarchici sostenitori di Carlo I Stuart) e dall'altro le forze parlamentari, le cosiddette Teste rotonde

(Roundheads) per il taglio corto dei capelli, capeggiate da Oliver Cromwell.
Molti dei fattori all'origine della guerra civile avevano a che vedere con i
problemi religiosi ed economici dell'epoca. Il Parlamento si opponeva a
concedere fondi a Carlo I per finanziare il suo assolutismo; il tentativo del
sovrano di arrestare alcuni parlamentari portò infine allo scoppio della guerra.
Sconfitto nelle battaglie di Marston Moor (1644) e di Naseby (1645), il re si arrese
all'esercito scozzese un anno più tardi. Processato e condannato a morte da
una commissione parlamentare sotto Cromwell, fu decapitato nel 1649.
L'Inghilterra si dette un ordinamento repubblicano e Cromwell la governò per
anni con pieni poteri, sciogliendo in varie occasioni il Parlamento. La
monarchia fu restaurata nel 1660, due anni dopo la morte di Cromwell, quando
il figlio di Carlo I, Carlo II, salì al trono.

CNN – Cable News Network Emittente televisiva statunitense che
trasmette programmi di informazione via satellite 24 ore su 24.

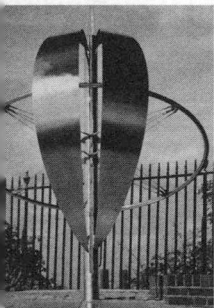

Cockney Una persona nata e cresciuta nei quartieri popolari
della zona est (EAST END) londinese. È anche il nome del
dialetto tipico della zona, caratterizzato dalla sostituzione di
parole con altre che vi fanno rima, ad esempio '*apples and
pears*' significa '*stairs*' e '*trouble and strife*' sta per '*wife*'.

common law Sistema giuridico anglosassone basato sulla
consuetudine e sulle sentenze delle corti di giustizia
(rispettivamente diritto consuetudinario e giurisprudenza) e
non sulle leggi create dal Parlamento e quindi sulla
codificazione del diritto. Si ricorre alla *common law* soltanto
per quelle questioni su cui il diritto scritto (*statute law*) non si
pronuncia.

Commonwealth Il Commonwealth, fondato nel 1931, è l'insieme delle ex
colonie e possedimenti dell'ex impero britannico. I paesi membri, oggi per lo
più stati indipendenti (a parte alcuni quali Gibilterra, Bermuda e le Isole
Falkland o Malvine), sono legati da rapporti economici e culturali. I vari capi
di stato si incontrano con scadenza biennale (the Commonwealth Conference)
e progetti educativi internazionali vengono promossi regolarmente. Ogni
quattro anni, inoltre, si tengono i Commonwealth Games, manifestazioni
sportive cui partecipano atleti dei vari paesi.

community college Istituto statunitense che offre corsi biennali indirizzati
alla comunità locale, per lo più di carattere pratico.

comprehensive school Tipo di scuola secondaria britannica per studenti
dagli 11 ai 18 anni, di tutti i livelli di rendimento. Le *comprehensive schools*
vennero istituite negli anni Sessanta allo scopo di creare un sistema educativo
più ugualitario, contrapposto al sistema selettivo operante all'epoca. *Vedi
anche* GRAMMAR SCHOOL.

Cultura

Congress L'organo legislativo nazionale degli Stati Uniti. Si riunisce al Campidoglio (CAPITOL) ed è formato da due Camere: il Senato (SENATE) e la Camera dei Rappresentanti (HOUSE OF REPRESENTATIVES). Si rinnova ogni due anni e ha il compito di redigere e approvare le leggi. Ogni nuova legge deve essere approvata prima dalle due Camere e poi dal Presidente (PRESIDENT).

Conservative Party Uno dei maggiori partiti politici britannici. È un partito di centrodestra che appoggia il sistema capitalista, la libera impresa e la privatizzazione dell'industria e dei servizi pubblici. Il Partito Conservatore nacque intorno al 1830–40 dall'evoluzione del Partito Tory, nome col quale ancora oggi viene spesso indicato.

constituency Una delle ripartizioni in cui sono suddivisi Regno Unito, Canada, e Australia a fini elettorali.

Constitution La Costituzione americana, redatta dopo l'indipendenza dalla Gran Bretagna e ratificata nel 1789 dai rappresentanti di ciascuna delle tredici ex colonie che formavano gli Stati Uniti d'America, inclusi alcuni dei padri fondatori della nazione (FOUNDING FATHERS). La Costituzione stabiliva la suddivisione dei tre poteri dello stato: quello legislativo affidato al Congresso (CONGRESS), quello esecutivo al Presidente (PRESIDENT) e quello giudiziario alle Corti federali con al vertice la Corte Suprema di giustizia (SUPREME COURT). La spartizione dei poteri tra diversi organi dello Stato si ispirava alle idee degli Illuministi francesi e aveva lo scopo di garantire maggiore democrazia. Il testo della Costituzione resta essenzialmente in vigore ancora oggi. Dal 1789 ci sono stati tuttavia 27 emendamenti, di cui i primi dieci prendono il nome di BILL OF RIGHTS.

council Ai fini amministrativi la Gran Bretagna è suddivisa in varie aree. Le più grandi sono le COUNTIES, e in Scozia le *regions*, ripartite a loro volta in *districts*. I *parish councils*, e i *community councils* in Scozia e Galles, rappresentano le ripartizioni amministrative più piccole. A capo delle varie unità vi sono i consigli (*councils*). Tali autorità locali hanno poteri conferiti dal governo centrale e sono formate da consiglieri (*councillors*) eletti dai cittadini nelle elezioni amministrative (*local elections*). I *councils* sono responsabili dell'educazione, dei servizi sociali, di polizia e vigili del fuoco, degli alloggi popolari, delle biblioteche, e di altri servizi a livello locale.

county Principale unità amministrativa in Inghilterra, suddivisa a sua volta in *districts*. I confini delle contee hanno spesso radici storiche e risalgono a molti anni fa. Tuttavia, negli ultimi decenni sia l'estensione che i nomi delle *counties* sono cambiati, e il termine stesso è meno usato. Anche negli Stati Uniti la maggior parte degli stati è suddivisa in contee, per un totale di circa 3.000.

courts Negli Stati Uniti la giustizia è amministrata nei vari stati tramite organi giudiziari indipendenti, ma esistono anche tribunali federali che si occupano tra le altre cose di controversie tra stati e tra cittadini di stati diversi. La Corte Suprema (SUPREME COURT) è un tribunale federale. Nella maggior parte degli stati esistono sia tribunali civili che penali e anche una sorta di corti d'appello. Un tipico procedimento penale viene giudicato in un tribunale distrettuale, dove il procuratore distrettuale (*district attorney*) sostiene l'accusa. Il giudice indossa la toga nera mentre gli avvocati (*counsels*) indossano abbigliamento normale. In Inghilterra e in Galles i tribunali locali sono detti *magistrates' courts* e si occupano di cause civili e reati minori. I reati più gravi competono alle *crown courts*, dove i *barristers* (avvocati abilitati ad esercitare in corti di livello superiore) sostengono l'accusa e la difesa. Il tribunale di ultima istanza è la Camera dei Lords (HOUSE OF LORDS). In Scozia, dove esiste un sistema giuridico diverso, le cause per reati minori sono giudicate dalle *magistrates' courts* o da tribunali di polizia. I reati più gravi vengono giudicati dallo *sheriff* (il giudice di grado più alto in un distretto). I tribunali di massimo livello sono la High Court of Justiciary e la Court of Session, rispettivamente per le cause penali e civili. Nelle aule dei tribunali d'Inghilterra, Galles e Scozia sia giudici che avvocati portano toga e parrucca.

Cup final ▶ FOOTBALL

degree Diploma di laurea assegnato alla fine di un corso universitario. Esistono due livelli di laurea e due qualifiche corrispondenti: *bachelor's degree* e *master's degree*; il livello ancora superiore è il *doctorate*, che equivale al dottorato di ricerca. Una laurea di primo livello in lettere e filosofia o altre discipline umanistiche si chiama *Bachelor of Arts* (*BA* e negli Stati Uniti anche *AB*); una laurea di secondo livello in discipline scientifiche è un *Master of Sciences* (*MSc*, in America detto anche *ScM*); il *doctorate* è il *PhD*. *BA*, *MSc*, ecc. indicano il titolo ma anche il titolare della qualifica, ad es. Patricia Ramsay, *MA* (*Master of Arts*).

Democratic Party Fondato nel 1792, è uno dei due principali partiti politici statunitensi. L'altro è il Partito Repubblicano (REPUBLICAN PARTY). Il Partito Democratico è considerato fautore di una politica più liberale, particolarmente rispetto alle questioni sociali. Per questo motivo ha l'appoggio dei sindacati e delle minoranze.

devolution Nel Regno Unito il termine *devolution* indica il trasferimento di alcune competenze del governo centrale a enti regionali della Scozia, del Galles, dell'Irlanda del Nord e di altre regioni periferiche dello stato britannico. Dopo la vittoria del partito laburista nelle elezioni del 1997, il processo di decentramento fu attuato con il riconoscimento del Parlamento Scozzese, dell'Assemblea dell'Irlanda del Nord e di quella gallese. *Vedi anche* SCOTLAND, NORTHERN IRELAND, WALES.

District Attorney ► COURTS

Dow Jones Averages Detto anche Dow Jones Index (indice Dow Jones), indica il prezzo medio espresso in punti delle trenta azioni industriali principali quotate alla Borsa di New York ogni giorno di transazioni. Viene utilizzato per prevedere le tendenze generali del mercato azionario statunitense.

Downing Street Strada nel centro di Londra, nel quartiere di Westminster. Al numero 10 si trova la residenza ufficiale del Primo Ministro (Prime Minister) britannico e al numero 11 quella del Chancellor of the Exchequer (il Cancelliere dello Scacchiere, equivalente del Ministro delle Finanze e del Tesoro). Le espressioni 'Downing Street' e 'Number 10' sono spesso usate dalla stampa per indicare il Primo Ministro.

driving Nel Regno Unito, in Australia, in Nuova Zelanda e in Sudafrica si ha la guida a sinistra, ossia i veicoli procedono sul lato sinistro della strada. Negli Stati Uniti e in Canada si ha invece la guida a destra, come in Italia e nel resto d'Europa.

East End Quartieri nella zona est di Londra, tradizionalmente abitati dalla classe operaia e sede della zona del porto londinese (Docklands), oggi quasi completamente chiuso alle navi. La zona portuale dei Docklands negli ultimi anni è stata profondamente riurbanizzata e adesso ospita complessi residenziali di lusso e numerose strutture commerciali, quali l'imponente grattacielo di Canary Wharf, sedi di quotidiani e istituti finanziari. La zona è collegata al resto di Londra tramite il servizio ferroviario dei DLR (Docklands Light Railway).

East Side A New York, è la zona a est di Central Park, tradizionalmente più ricca e moderna del West Side, la parte ovest della città.

Edinburgh Festival La più importante manifestazione culturale britannica, istituita nel 1947. Si tiene annualmente nella capitale scozzese ad agosto, per tre settimane. Il festival offre spettacoli di musica, teatro, danza, cabaret e attira ogni anno moltissimi visitatori. Un settore sempre molto interessante è quello del cosiddetto the Edinburgh Fringe, ossia degli eventi fuori dal programma ufficiale.

education Negli Stati Uniti l'insegnamento primario e secondario è fornito gratuitamente dal governo federale. A cinque anni i bambini iniziano a frequentare il *kindergarten* che insieme ai successivi cinque o sei anni di scuola costituisce le elementari (ELEMENTARY SCHOOL). Seguono poi due anni di *junior high school* o tre anni di *middle school* e infine gli ultimi anni di educazione superiore nella HIGH SCHOOL che termina intorno ai 18 anni. Dopodiché l'educazione non è più gratuita, ma i vari stati in qualche modo la sussidiano. Circa il 45% degli americani continua gli studi dopo le superiori e oltre il 20% consegue un diploma presso istituti o università.

Cultura

Nel Regno Unito la scuola obbligatoria va dai cinque ai 16 anni. I bambini iniziano frequentando l'*infant school* e poi la *primary school* (educazione elementare). A partire dagli 11 anni ha inizio la scuola secondaria, che si tratta nella maggioranza dei casi di una COMPREHENSIVE SCHOOL. Un numero ridotto di ragazzi frequenta le più selettive GRAMMAR SCHOOLS. Dopo i 16 anni alcuni alunni lasciano la scuola, mentre altri proseguono gli studi in istituti a carattere più professionale quali i *colleges of further education* o per preparare gli *A levels*. Se desiderano accedere all'università gli studenti devono pagarsi sia le tasse universitarie che le spese di vitto e alloggio, per cui molti devono chiedere prestiti in banca. Nel complesso la maggioranza dei ragazzi frequenta la scuola pubblica e soltanto una minoranza è iscritta alle INDEPENDENT SCHOOLS che sono a pagamento.

elections Negli Stati Uniti si indicono elezioni per la carica di Presidente (PRESIDENT), per i seggi nelle due Camere del Congresso (CONGRESS) e per cariche a livello statale e locale. I candidati si presentano per il Partito Repubblicano (REPUBLICAN PARTY) o per il Partito Democratico (DEMOCRATIC PARTY). I candidati indipendenti possono presentarsi avendo fatto una petizione con le firme dei propri sostenitori. Le elezioni presidenziali hanno luogo ogni quattro anni. I partiti selezionano i propri candidati nelle elezioni primarie (PRIMARY) indette nei singoli stati. La selezione finale dei candidati alla presidenza e vicepresidenza si effettua in occasione della *party convention*, il congresso che ciascun partito tiene nei mesi di luglio e agosto. Il presidente viene eletto a novembre col sistema dell'ELECTORAL COLLEGES. Nel Regno Unito, le elezioni politiche (*general elections*) vengono indette per legge ogni cinque anni. Tuttavia il Primo Ministro può indire elezioni anticipate se ritiene di avere buone probabilità di vittoria. Nel Regno Unito ci sono 659 CONSTITUENCIES, ciascuna delle quali elegge un rappresentante in Parlamento (MP). Il sistema elettorale è il *first-past-the-post system*, vale a dire quello della maggioranza relativa. Il leader del partito che ottiene il maggior numero di seggi diventa Primo Ministro e forma il nuovo governo.

electoral college Sistema adottato negli Stati Uniti per l'elezione del Presidente e del Vicepresidente. In ciascuno stato gli elettori eleggono dei delegati (*electors*), i quali formano l'assemblea dell'*electoral college* e a loro volta si impegnano a votare per un determinato candidato. Tutti i voti di uno stato vanno a un candidato. Bastano 270 voti (*electoral college votes*) per vincere le elezioni, il che significa che il Presidente può essere eletto anche senza ottenere la maggioranza del voto popolare.

elementary school Negli Stati Uniti è una scuola elementare per bambini tra i 6 e i 12 anni. Detta anche *grade school*.

England L'Inghilterra è il più esteso e popolato dei paesi che costituiscono il

Regno Unito. Nel corso dei secoli affermò il predominio militare, politico ed economico sulla Scozia, il Galles e gli altri paesi che formano le Isole Britanniche (BRITISH ISLES). Tale processo è oggi parzialmente invertito (*vedi* DEVOLUTION) e Scozia, Galles e Irlanda del Nord hanno organi legislativi distinti con poteri più o meno autonomi. L'Inghilterra è invece governata esclusivamente dal Parlamento Britannico.

examinations In Inghilterra, Galles e Irlanda del Nord al termine del quinto anno di scuola secondaria si sostengono gli esami del *General Certificate of Secondary Education* (*GCSE*), in varie combinazioni di materie. I ragazzi che proseguono gli studi sostengono, in un numero minore di materie, gli esami dell'*Advanced Supplementary* (*A/S*) *Level* alla fine del sesto anno, e poi gli esami dell'*Advanced Level* (*A Level*) l'ultimo anno delle superiori. Per l'accesso all'università è necessario passare almeno due *A levels*. I ragazzi che invece preferiscono compiere studi presso scuole professionali e istituti tecnici sostengono gli esami per le *General National Vocational Qualifications* (*GNVQs*). In Scozia, invece, si sostengono gli esami dello *Standard Grade* al termine del quarto anno di superiori e gli *Higher* e *Advanced Higher* per accedere all'università. Negli Stati Uniti il sistema scolastico non prevede esami ufficiali. Gli alunni conseguono un diploma di scuola secondaria al termine della HIGH SCHOOL, per cui ci si basa principalmente sui voti assegnati dai professori delle varie materie. Per l'accesso ad alcuni istituti universitari è richiesto il *College Test* (*vedi* ACT), un esame in inglese, matematica o scienze. *Vedi anche* EDUCATION.

Cultura

Fifth Amendment ▶ BILL OF RIGHTS

Flower of Scotland Inno nazionale scozzese.

football Il calcio è lo sport più popolare del Regno Unito. Molte delle squadre più celebri sono a Londra (Arsenal, Chelsea, Tottenham Hotspur) e in città dell'Inghilterra centrale e del nord (Manchester United, Newcastle United, Aston Villa). Le squadre scozzesi giocano in campionati separati; le squadre principali (Celtic e Rangers) hanno sede a Glasgow. Negli Stati Uniti il calcio si chiama *soccer* in quanto per football si intende football americano.

Founding Fathers I padri fondatori che nel 1787 contribuirono a fondare gli Stati Uniti d'America in occasione nella *Federal Constitution Convention*, durante la quale venne redatta la costituzione americana (CONSTITUTION). I più noti sono George Washington, Thomas Jefferson e Benjamin Franklin.

fraternity Associazione studentesca maschile presso molte università americane. Il nome delle varie *fraternities* è formato da due o tre lettere dell'alfabeto greco, ad es. '*Lambda Delta Chi*'. Di solito i soci di una *fraternity* dividono gli alloggi della *fraternity house*. Alcune confraternite si occupano di opere di beneficenza, mentre altre approfondiscono argomenti di carattere accademico. Le *fraternities* sono state spesso criticate perché considerate istituzioni elitarie e discriminatorie, ma attualmente sono più accettate: oggi che l'educazione è sempre più cara, la loro essenza comunitaria aiuta a ridurre il costo della vita degli studenti. *Vedi anche* SORORITY.

FTSE-100 (pronunciato *Footsie one hundred*) La media del valore dei 100 principali titoli che compaiono nel listino della Borsa di Londra, pubblicato giornalmente sul quotidiano finanziario, *the Financial Times*. Fornisce importanti indicazioni sulla situazione economica in Gran Bretagna.

further education In Gran Bretagna il termine indica qualunque tipo di educazione per studenti oltre i 16 anni di età (la fine della scuola dell'obbligo) ad esclusione dell'educazione universitaria, nel qual caso si parla di *higher education*. Negli Stati Uniti, invece, *further education* si usa spesso anche per riferirsi all'educazione universitaria.

gap year In Gran Bretagna il *gap year* è l'anno di intervallo che molti studenti si prendono tra la fine delle superiori e l'università. Molti studenti utilizzano questo periodo sabbatico per fare esperienza nel mondo del lavoro e mettere da parte qualche risparmio, altri invece ne approfittano per viaggiare all'estero e conoscere il mondo.

GCSE ▸ EXAMINATIONS

Gettysburg Address Il discorso tenuto da Abraham Lincoln nel 1863, per l'inaugurazione del cimitero per i caduti nella battaglia di Gettysburg durante la Guerra di Secessione (CIVIL WAR). Contiene la storica definizione di democrazia come 'governo di popolo, dal popolo e per il popolo'.

GNVQ ▸ EXAMINATIONS

God Save the Queen Inno nazionale britannico. Non si sa chi ne compose il testo o la musica, ma si cantava già nel XVIII secolo.

grade school ▸ ELEMENTARY SCHOOL

grammar school In alcune zone dell'Inghilterra e del Galles è un tipo di scuola secondaria (*secondary school*) cui accedono alunni che hanno superato una prova d'ammissione. Dal 1965 le *grammar schools* sono state sostituite per la maggioranza dalle COMPREHENSIVE SCHOOLS.

Grand National In Gran Bretagna, la corsa di cavalli a ostacoli più importante, tenuta annualmente a Aintree, presso Liverpool. È un evento di portata nazionale che attira puntualmente un forte interesse. Sono molte le persone che puntano sui cavalli solo in occasione di questa corsa.

Great Britain La Gran Bretagna è la più grande delle Isole Britanniche (BRITISH ISLES). Include l'Inghilterra, la Scozia e il Galles. Spesso si usa erroneamente il termine *'Britain'* per indicare il Regno Unito (UNITED KINGDOM) o l'Inghilterra.

green card Negli Stati Uniti è un documento ufficiale che concede a qualsiasi persona priva della cittadinanza americana il permesso di risiedere e lavorare indefinitivamente negli Stati Uniti. Nel Regno Unito, invece, è un documento che i conducenti o proprietari di autoveicoli devono richiedere alla propria compagnia di assicurazione per convalidare la polizza in occasione di viaggi all'estero.

Greyhound bus Veicolo della più grande compagnia di pulmann statunitense (The Greyhound Lines Company) che collegando le maggiori città copre tutto il paese. È il mezzo di trasporto più usato dai giovani e dai turisti con budget limitato per percorrere grandi distanze.

Groundhog Day ▸ GIORNI FESTIVI NEI PAESI ANGLOFONI

gun control Il controllo sulle armi da fuoco è al momento un tema molto controverso negli Stati Uniti. Molti ritengono che il porto d'armi dovrebbe essere vietato ai comuni cittadini, dato il gran numero di omicidi e altri reati commessi. Altri sostengono invece che l'abolizione del porto d'armi contravverrebbe alla Costituzione (CONSTITUTION), la quale con il *'right to bear arms'* ne sancisce il diritto. La NATIONAL RIFLE ASSOCIATION si oppone a ogni legge al riguardo. Nel 1993 il congresso ha tuttavia approvato la Brady Bill che limita la vendita e l'uso di alcuni tipi di arma.

Gunpowder Plot ▸ BONFIRE NIGHT

Guy Fawkes' Night ▸ BONFIRE NIGHT

haka Il rituale urlo di guerra dei Maori neozelandesi, cantato battendo energicamente i piedi per terra e muovendo le braccia. La nazionale neozelandese di rugby esegue l'*haka* prima di ogni partita.

Halloween ▸ GIORNI FESTIVI NEI PAESI ANGLOFONI

high school Negli Stati Uniti indica la scuola secondaria, generalmente per alunni di età compresa tra i 14 e i 18 anni. In Gran Bretagna, il termine si ritrova solo nel nome di alcune scuole.

holidays ▸ GIORNI FESTIVI NEI PAESI ANGLOFONI

homecoming Incontro annuale degli ex studenti di istituti universitari o HIGH SCHOOLS statunitensi. In genere ha luogo in autunno quando i vecchi studenti fanno una rimpatriata e partecipano a varie attività, tra cui una partita di football americano, la *homecoming parade* e la *homecoming dance*. In questa occasione viene anche eletta la *homecoming queen*.

House of Commons La Camera dei Comuni è la camera bassa del Parlamento britannico HOUSES OF PARLIAMENT. I deputati eletti si chiamano MPS (*members of Parliament*). La Camera dei Comuni è anche la camera bassa del Parlamento canadese, con 308 membri, eletti per cinque anni a suffragio diretto.

House of Lords La Camera dei Lord è la camera alta del Parlamento britannico (HOUSES OF PARLIAMENT). La sua funzione è discutere e poi approvare alcuni disegni di legge della HOUSE OF COMMONS o suggerire dei cambiamenti. La Camera dei Lord ha anche la funzione nel sistema giudiziario come corte di ultima istanza. I Lord sono per la maggioranza nominati (non eletti), e fino al 1999 un certo numero di cariche erano ereditarie. Sono state proposte alcune riforme per far sì che una percentuale di loro siano eletti direttamente dal popolo.

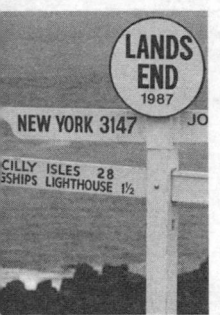

House of Representatives La camera bassa del Congresso degli Stati Uniti (CONGRESS). È costituita da 435 rappresentanti (REPRESENTATIVES) eletti ogni due anni; a ciascuno stato spetta un numero di rappresentanti proporzionale alla propria popolazione. La House of Representatives è incaricata dell'approvazione di ogni nuova legge.

Houses of Parliament Sono le due camere del Parlamento britannico, la Camera dei Comuni (HOUSE OF COMMONS) e la Camera dei Lord (HOUSE OF LORDS). Il termine indica anche la sede del Parlamento, il Palazzo di Westminster situato in riva al Tamigi nel centro di Londra.

Inauguration Day Negli Stati Uniti è il giorno in cui il neoeletto Presidente assume ufficialmente il potere. La cerimonia di insediamento ha sempre luogo il 20 gennaio, a Washington DC.

Independence Day ▸ GIORNI FESTIVI NEI PAESI ANGLOFONI

independent school Tipo di scuola britannica privata che si autofinanzia tramite il pagamento di quote da parte dei genitori degli alunni, anziché ricevere finanziamenti statali. Le PUBLIC SCHOOLS e le PREPARATORY SCHOOLS rientrano in questa categoria.

infant school ▸ EDUCATION

IRA (Irish Republican Army) L'IRA (Esercito Repubblicano Irlandese) è un'organizzazione paramilitare clandestina il cui obiettivo è l'unificazione della Repubblica d'Irlanda e dell'Irlanda del Nord. Nel 1970, come reazione a una politica considerata repressiva nei confronti delle minoranze cattoliche dell'Irlanda del Nord, una fazione dell'IRA (Provisional IRA) portò avanti atti terroristici in Irlanda del Nord e in Inghilterra. Nel 1998, l'accordo del Venerdì Santo (Good Friday Agreement) ha dato inizio a un periodo di relativa pace tra le comunità contrapposte dell'Irlanda del Nord. *Vedi anche* SINN FEIN.

ITV – Independent Television Gruppo di enti televisivi privati che offrono una programmazione diversificata in 15 diverse zone del Regno Unito.

Ivy League Il gruppo delle più antiche e rinomate università statunitensi, situate nel nordest del paese: Harvard, Yale, Columbia University, Cornell University, Dartmouth College, Brown University, Princeton University e la University of Pennsylvania. Il nome deriva dall'edera che cresce sugli antichi edifici universitari.

junior high school ► EDUCATION

junior school Scuola statale britannica per alunni di età compresa tra i 7 e gli 11 anni.

King James Bible ► AUTHORIZED VERSION

kirk In scozzese significa chiesa. 'The Kirk' indica the Church of Scotland (la Chiesa Episcopale scozzese).

kiwi Uccello privo di ali e coda originario della Nuova Zelanda. Il termine Kiwis viene anche usato per indicare i neozelandesi e le squadre sportive di questo paese.

Labor Day Festa del Lavoro. Negli Stati Uniti questa festività in onore dei lavoratori viene celebrata a livello nazionale il primo lunedì di settembre.

Labor Party In Australia è uno dei principali partiti politici. Rappresenta il centro-sinistra moderato.

Labour Party In Gran Bretagna il Partito Laburista è uno dei maggiori partiti politici. Andò per la prima volta al potere nel 1924, con l'obiettivo di farsi portavoce degli interessi dei lavoratori e dei sindacati. Negli ultimi anni il partito ha abbandonato alcune posizioni della sinistra storica, ad es. riguardo alla privatizzazione dell'industria e dei servizi pubblici. I suoi leader preferiscono oggi il termine 'New Labour'.

lawyer Termine generico per avvocato. Nel Regno Unito si ha il *solicitor* e il *barrister*. Il primo offre consulenza legale ai cittadini riguardo a questioni minori (è una figura tra l'avvocato e il notaio). Il secondo rappresenta i clienti davanti a corti di livello più alto; quando un *barrister* è ammesso ad esercitare l'avvocatura si dice che '*has been called to the Bar*'. Negli Stati Uniti non si ha questa distinzione. Sia nel Regno Unito che negli Stati Uniti si usa il termine *counsel* per indicare un avvocato o un gruppo di avvocati che presentano una causa in tribunale.

Cultura

Liberal Democratic Party Il Partito Liberaldemocratico, familiarmente abbreviato in 'Lib Dems'. È per importanza il terzo partito della Gran Bretagna. Si è costituito nel 1988 dalla fusione del Partito Liberale (Liberal Party) e del Partito Socialdemocratico (Social Democratic Party).

Liberal Party Importante partito australiano, fautore di una politica essenzialmente conservatrice.

L-plates Nel Regno Unito è un cartello di plastica bianco, con la lettera 'L' in rosso. Va applicato sul davanti e sul retro di un veicolo per segnalare che il conducente si sta preparando all'esame di guida.

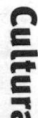

mayor Negli Stati Uniti il sindaco di una città viene eletto dagli abitanti. In Inghilterra e Galles è il capo del consiglio comunale (*council*), tradizionalmente eletto dagli altri consiglieri (*councillors*), ma ha prevalentemente incarichi di rappresentanza nelle cerimonie ufficiali, senza reale autorità politica. Talvolta ha il titolo di *lord mayor* (in Scozia *provost* o *lord provost*). Recentemente in alcune grandi città è stata creata la figura di un *mayor* eletto dal popolo.

member of Parliament ▸ MP

Memorial Day Festività statunitense che commemora gli americani caduti in guerra. Generalmente ricorre l'ultimo lunedì di maggio.

middle school ▸ EDUCATION

midterms (*midterm elections*) Negli Stati Uniti sono le elezioni per la Camera dei Rappresentanti (HOUSE OF REPRESENTATIVES) indette a metà del mandato presidenziale.

Mormon La Chiesa di Gesù Cristo dei Santi dell'Ultimo Giorno (Church of Jesus Christ of Latter-Day Saints) conta oggi circa 10 milioni di fedeli, meglio conosciuti come Mormoni. Fu fondata negli Stati Uniti nel 1830 da Joseph Smith. Successivamente, sotto la guida di Brigham Young, i membri si spostarono nella parte ovest del paese, dove fondarono Salt Lake City nello stato dello Utah, i cui abitanti sono ancora oggi Mormoni. Hanno regole morali molto rigide e non bevono né alcolici né caffè.

Morris dancing Una danza folkloristica originaria del Regno Unito, eseguita solitamente da gruppi di soli uomini (*Morris men*) disposti in file. I danzatori, che indossano una camicia bianca, un cappello di paglia e pantaloni con applicati campanelli, agitano bastoni o fazzoletti.

Mother's Day (Mothering Sunday) ▸ GIORNI FESTIVI NEI PAESI ANGLOFONI

motorways La Gran Bretagna ha un'ampia rete di autostrade a tre corsie, segnalate dalla lettera 'M' seguita da un numero. Il limite di velocità sulla motorway è di 70 miglia all'ora, che equivale a 112 km/h. A differenza dell'Italia non si deve in genere pagare il pedaggio. Attualmente una sola *motorway* è a pagamento.

MP (*member of Parliament*) Un membro della Camera dei Comuni che rappresenta una delle 659 'CONSTITUENCIES' in cui è suddiviso il Regno Unito. *Vedi anche* HOUSE OF COMMONS.

National Guard Un corpo militare statunitense la cui origine risale all'epoca coloniale, composto di volontari reclutati in ciascun stato. In caso di catastrofi naturali o di emergenze civili può passare sotto il comando federale. Oggi la National Guard è considerata parte dell'esercito nazionale.

National Health Service (NHS) È il servizio di assistenza sanitaria britannico, finanziato in gran parte dal governo, per cui l'assistenza è per lo più gratuita. I medicinali prescritti e le cure dentistiche sono a pagamento, eccetto per alcune categorie di persone, quali i bambini e i pensionati.

National Insurance È il servizio di previdenza sociale in Gran Bretagna. Lavoratori e datori di lavoro versano dei contributi fiscali (*National Insurance contributions*) da cui dipendono i diversi servizi che offre lo stato, quali la pensione, l'assistenza sanitaria, i sussidi di disoccupazione. Chiunque lavori o faccia domanda per i sussidi deve richiedere un numero di identificazione (*National Insurance number*).

National Lottery È regolata dalla National Lottery Commission, ente pubblico non governativo che dipende dal Ministero della Cultura, Media e Spettacolo. Parte dei proventi viene destinata a iniziative culturali e sportive, alla conservazione del patrimonio culturale e ambientale e a organizzazioni no-profit.

National Party Importante partito politico neozelandese, fautore di una politica fondamentalmente conservatrice.

National Rifle Association (NRA) Una organizzazione statunitense favorevole al possesso di armi da fuoco da usare nella caccia, gli sport e la legittima difesa. Secondo i suoi 3,4 milioni di iscritti il diritto di ogni cittadino a possedere armi è garantito dalla Costituzione americana (CONSTITUTION).

National Trust Una fondazione britannica senza scopo di lucro finalizzata alla conservazione dei luoghi di interesse storico e del patrimonio ambientale. Finanziato da donazioni e sovvenzioni private, il National Trust è il maggiore proprietario terriero del Regno Unito. Nel corso degli anni ha acquisito enormi estensioni di terreni (circa 248.000 ettari) e di litorali (circa 960 km), come pure edifici, borghi e giardini, molti dei quali vengono aperti al pubblico in certi periodi dell'anno. In Scozia esiste una fondazione analoga ma indipendente, il National Trust for Scotland.

Native American È il termine più ampiamente accettato per indicare i

Cultura

popoli indigeni di tutto il continente americano. Secondo il Bureau of Indian Affairs, l'organizzazione governativa statunitense che si occupa delle questioni indiane, esistono circa 562 tribù per un totale di 1,9 milioni di persone. Circa un milione di indiani vive nelle riserve e di questi il 49% è disoccupato. Molte riserve aprono case da gioco grazie all'autonomia di cui godono.

NBC – National Broadcasting Company Il primo ente radiofonico istituito negli Stati Uniti (1926). Il primo canale televisivo della NBC cominciò a trasmettere nel 1940.

Newspapers Negli Stati Uniti il 95% della popolazione legge la stampa locale. Esiste un unico quotidiano nazionale, *USA Today*, gli altri sono locali. I quotidiani di alcune grandi città, quali il *New York Times*, il *Los Angeles Times*, e il *Washington Post*, sono comunque diffusi in tutto il paese. Anche l'*International Herald Tribune*, pubblicato fuori dagli Stati Uniti, viene letto

da molti americani all'estero. Il *Wall Street Journal*, che pubblica il DOW JONES AVERAGE, è il quotidiano di economia e finanza più importante degli Stati Uniti. La stampa americana è nel complesso piuttosto conservatrice, in modo da garantirsi una più alta distribuzione. Nel Regno Unito i quotidiani escono in due formati: quello grande dei *broadsheets* e quello più piccolo e compatto dei *tabloids*. Fino a poco tempo fa i quotidiani nazionali più seri erano tutti *broadsheets*. Il *Daily Telegraph* e il *Financial Times* (stampato sull'inconfondibile carta color salmone) hanno conservato questo formato, ma recentemente il *Times*, l'*Independent* e il *Guardian* hanno ridotto il formato. Del gruppo dei popolarissimi quotidiani più sensazionalistici (tutti in formato tabloid), fanno parte il *Sun*, il *Mirror*, l'*Express* e il *Mail*. Questi giornali sono rinomati per enfatizzare l'aspetto umano e spesso puramente scandalistico delle notizie. Sia negli Stati Uniti che nel Regno Unito i quotidiani che escono il sabato o la domenica hanno un gran numero di supplementi di sport, viaggi, cultura ecc.

Northern Ireland È una provincia del Regno Unito, situata nella parte nordorientale dell'Irlanda. Rimase a far parte del Regno Unito, con autonomia limitata, quando, nel 1920, il resto dell'isola divenne indipendente. La vita in Irlanda del Nord è stata a lungo dominata dal conflitto tra la maggioranza protestante che vuole restare vincolata al Regno Unito e la minoranza cattolica che vorrebbe unirsi alla Repubblica d'Irlanda. Gli anni dal 1969 al 1998 sono stati anni di sanguinosa violenza, sia in Irlanda nel Nord sia nei territori della Gran Bretagna; mentre i cattolici erano impegnati nella campagna per i diritti civili, organizzazioni paramilitari di ambo le parti hanno portato avanti assassinii, rapresaglie e atti terroristici. Durante gran parte di questo periodo la provincia è tornata sotto il diretto governo britannico e truppe britanniche vi erano stanziate stabilmente. L'accordo del Venerdì Santo (Good Friday Agreement) del 1998 ha messo fine alla violenza e la semiautonomia è stata restaurata sulla base di un accordo sulla spartizione del potere. Il Parlamento dell'Irlanda del Nord è stato tuttavia sospeso più volte, in quanto la cooperazione tra i partiti non è sempre attuabile. I singoli partiti sono spesso divisi in fazioni. Il Partito Democratico Unionista (Democratic Unionist Party) e il più moderato Partito Unionista dell'Ulster (Ulster Unionist Party) rappresentano la comunità protestante, mentre SINN FEIN e i più moderati Partito Social-democratico e laburista (SDLP, Social Democratic and Labour Party) rappresentano i cattolici. Il piccolo Partito dell'Alleanza (Alliance Party) si oppone invece alla divisione religiosa. *Vedi anche* IRA.

Number Ten ► DOWNING STREET

NVQ ► EXAMINATIONS

Old Glory ► STARS AND STRIPES

Open University (OU) Università a distanza britannica fondata nel 1969.

Oxbridge Termine che indica nel loro insieme le università più antiche e prestigiose del Regno Unito: Oxford e Cambridge.

Pancake Day ► SHROVE TUESDAY

Parliament Il Parlamento britannico è l'organo legislativo del Regno Unito ed è suddiviso in due Camere: la Camera dei Comuni (HOUSE OF COMMONS) e la Camera dei Lord (HOUSE OF LORDS). Il Parlamento canadese è costituito dal Senato (SENATE) e dalla Camera dei Comuni. *Vedi anche* MP.

PBS – Public Broadcasting Service Servizio radiotelevisivo statunitense, finanziato dal governo e rinomato per i programmi di qualità. È costituito dall'associazione di emittenti locali che trasmettono senza scopo di lucro e senza pubblicità.

Peace Corps Agenzia federale statunitense fondata nel 1961. I Corpi di Pace, composti da volontari, operano principalmente nei paesi in via di sviluppo in settori quali l'insegnamento, la sanità, l'agricoltura e l'ambiente.

Pentagon L'edificio a pianta ottagonale situato a Washington dove hanno sede gli uffici centrali del ministero della Difesa e delle forze armate americani. Talvolta la stampa utilizza il termine per riferirsi allo Stato Maggiore.

Pledge of Allegiance Giuramento di fedeltà che i cittadini degli Stati Uniti prestano alla bandiera e alla patria. In molte scuole gli studenti lo ripetono tutte le mattine davanti alla bandiera tenendo una mano sul petto.

Cultura

Poppy Day ▸ GIORNI FESTIVI NEI PAESI ANGLOFONI

preparatory school Negli Stati Uniti è un tipo di scuola secondaria in cui viene offerta una speciale preparazione preuniversitaria. In Gran Bretagna, dov'è anche detta *prep school*, è una scuola privata per alunni dai 7 ai 13 anni. Generalmente non è un istituto misto e in molte *preparatory schools* parte degli alunni stanno a convitto. La maggioranza degli alunni prosegue poi gli studi in una scuola privata (PUBLIC SCHOOL).

President Negli Stati Uniti il Presidente può restare in carica per un massimo di due mandati (*terms*) ciascuno di durata quadriennale. Poiché il paese è una repubblica federale di tipo presidenziale, egli è il capo dello stato e allo stesso tempo il capo del governo. È responsabile della politica estera e il comandante in capo delle forze armate.

President's Day ▸ GIORNI FESTIVI NEI PAESI ANGLOFONI

primary (primary election) Negli Stati Uniti le elezioni primarie (*primaries*) vengono indette per selezionare i candidati prima delle elezioni principali, specialmente nel caso delle presidenziali. I candidati alla carica di presidente (PRESIDENT) vengono eletti dopo una serie di primarie a livello statale. *Vedi anche* ELECTIONS.

primary school ▸ EDUCATION

Provost ▸ MAYOR

pub (*public house*) Letteralmente 'casa aperta al pubblico', il *pub* è il tipico locale dove in Gran Bretagna e Irlanda si va per bere birra e altre bevande, alcoliche e non. Le origini dei *pub* risalgono all'epoca dei Romani. Alla fine del XIV secolo chiunque producesse e vendesse birra (*ale*) doveva esporre un cartello e le caratteristiche insegne colorate contraddistinguono i *pub* ancora oggi. Il *pub* è spesso al centro della vita sociale e culturale del quartiere o del paese.

public access channel Negli Stati Uniti è un canale televisivo riservato a programmi di persone e organizzazioni che operano senza fini di lucro.

public house ▸ PUB

public school In Gran Bretagna sono, al contrario di quanto farebbe pensare il nome, scuole private a pagamento, per alunni tra i 13 e i 18 anni. Spesso si tratta di scuole miste e nella maggior parte di esse gli allievi sono a convitto. In Scozia e negli Stati Uniti il termine *public school* indica invece una scuola statale. *Vedi anche* PREPARATORY SCHOOL.

Remembrance Sunday ▸ POPPY DAY

Representative Un membro della Camera dei Rappresentanti (HOUSE OF REPRESENTATIVES) americana.

'Republican Party Uno dei maggiori partiti politici statunitensi. Sebbene sia stato fondato nel 1854 da chi appoggiava l'abolizione della schiavitù, viene considerato più conservatore del Partito Democratico (DEMOCRATIC PARTY), l'altro principale partito americano.

rugby Il gioco della palla ovale, originario della Gran Bretagna. Esistono due varianti di questo sport, il rugby a 13 (*rugby league*) con squadre composte di 13 giocatori e il rugby a 15 (*rugby union*) con 15 giocatori. Il *rugby league* è stato fin dagli inizi giocato a livello professionale, mentre il *rugby union* lo è divenuto nel 1995.

SAT Negli Stati Uniti indica lo *Scholastic Aptitude Test*, una prova attitudinale sostenuta generalmente l'ultimo anno della HIGH SCHOOL. È necessario superare il *SAT* per accedere alla maggior parte delle università. In Inghilterra e Galles indica invece lo *Standard Assessment Test* o *Task*, una prova sostenuta a 7, 11 e 14 anni dagli alunni di tutte le scuole allo scopo di valutarne i progressi.

Scotland La parte più settentrionale del Regno Unito, la cui popolazione è concentrata in una cintura centrale intorno alle due città principali, Glasgow e Edimburgo, la capitale. La Scozia è particolarmente rinomata per la bellezza delle montagne, dei laghi (in scozzese '*loch*') e delle Highlands, la zona a nordest di Edimburgo. Fino al secolo XVI la Scozia era frequentemente in guerra con l'Inghilterra. Nel 1603, re Giacomo IV (James) di Scozia diventò anche re d'Inghilterra (regnandovi come James I) e l'unione dei due paesi venne finalizzata nel 1707 quando il Parlamento scozzese si sciolse. La Scozia tuttavia conserva molte delle proprie istituzioni. Il sistema scolastico, ad esempio, è diverso dal resto del Regno Unito. Tra gli scozzesi ci sono sempre stati coloro che pensano che la Scozia dovrebbe essere completamente indipendente. Reinstaurato nel 1999 (*vedi* DEVOLUTION), lo Scottish Parliament ha sede a Edimburgo. A differenza dell'Assemblea gallese, esso ha pieni poteri sul piano legislativo e esecutivo riguardo alle questioni scozzesi, mentre ha autorità limitata relativamente al sistema fiscale. *Vedi anche* WALES.

SDLP ► NORTHERN IRELAND

Senate Negli Stati Uniti il Senato è la camera alta del Congresso (CONGRESS). È formato da 100 senatori (*senators*), due per ciascuno stato, eletti con mandato di sei anni. Le nuove leggi devono essere approvate sia dal Senato che dalla Camera dei Rappresentanti (HOUSE OF REPRESENTATIVES). Il Parlamento canadese è costituito dal Senato e dalla Camera dei Comuni (HOUSE OF COMMONS).

Shadow Cabinet ► CABINET

Cultura

Shrove Tuesday ▶ GIORNI FESTIVI NEI PAESI ANGLOFONI

Sinn Fein Partito politico irlandese fondato nel 1905 con l'obiettivo di unificare le 32 contee dell'Irlanda nella Repubblica d'Irlanda creata nel 1949. Viene considerato l'ala politica dell'IRA, anche se nega qualunque legame con l'organizzazione paramilitare.

Smithsonian Institution Rinomato istituto statunitense che raccoglie vari musei e centri di ricerca. Situato a Washington DC, è familiarmente soprannominato '*the nation's attic*', la soffitta della nazione.

social security number Un numero di identificazione che negli Stati Uniti tutti devono avere. Inizialmente veniva richiesto per poter lavorare ed essere coperti dalla sicurezza sociale. Tuttavia nel 1987 il governo ha deciso di assegnarlo anche ai bambini. Attualmente viene usato in molte occasioni diverse: compare sugli assegni, sulla patente, ed è il numero con cui vengono identificati gli alunni degli istituti superiori.

sorority Una delle associazioni studentesche femminili presenti in molti istituti universitari. *Vedi anche* FRATERNITY.

Speaker La persona che presiede i dibattiti nella Camera dei Comuni (HOUSE OF COMMONS), eletta dai deputati (MPS) dei vari partiti.

Speaker of the House Negli Stati Uniti è la persona incaricata di presiedere la maggior parte delle attività della Camera dei Rappresentanti (HOUSE OF REPRESENTATIVES). È responsabile di mantenere l'ordine durante i dibattiti, di nominare i comitati e di presentar loro le proposte di legge. È un rappresentante del partito di maggioranza alla Camera dal quale viene eletto. È la persona che segue al vicepresidente nella successione per la presidenza.

Stars and Stripes La bandiera degli Stati Uniti. Le cinquanta stelle (*stars*) rappresentano i cinquanta stati e le tredici strisce (*stripes*) orizzontali rappresentano le prime tredici colonie che formarono gli Stati Uniti all'epoca dell'indipendenza. Viene anche chiamata Old Glory o STAR-SPANGLED BANNER.

Star-Spangled Banner Uno dei nomi con cui si indica la bandiera degli Stati Uniti. È anche il titolo dell'inno nazionale statunitense, composto nel 1814 ma adottato come tale soltanto nel 1931.

state school In Gran Bretagna indica una scuola statale che è finanziata direttamente o indirettamente dallo stato e offre istruzione gratuita. La maggior parte dei ragazzi frequenta questo tipo di scuole.

State of the Union Address Tradizionale discorso che il Presidente degli Stati Uniti (PRESIDENT) tiene annualmente al Congresso (CONGRESS) per metterlo al corrente della 'situazione dell'Unione', come previsto dalla

Costituzione (CONSTITUTION). Il discorso è l'occasione per parlare dei progressi del governo, dei suoi progetti e della politica per il futuro. Viene trasmesso in diretta alla televisione.

Statue of Liberty La celebre statua situata sulla Liberty Island nella baia di New York. Donata dal popolo francese come omaggio al popolo americano, raffigura una donna che innalza la fiaccola della libertà. È ormai l'inconfondibile simbolo di New York e dell'America.

summer camp Negli Stati Uniti indica il campeggio estivo cui moltissimi ragazzi si recano per socializzare e praticare attività ricreative e sportive all'aria aperta; tra queste il nuoto, il canottaggio, l'arrampicata e i corsi di sopravvivenza.

Super Bowl ▸ AMERICAN FOOTBALL

Supreme Court È l'organo più importante del sistema giudiziario statunitense, composto da nove giudici, nominati a vita dal Presidente (PRESIDENT) con l'approvazione del Congresso (CONGRESS). La Corte Suprema decide riguardo alla costituzionalità delle leggi e ha inoltre la facoltà di impedire l'approvazione delle leggi, tanto federali quanto statali o locali. È anche la corte di ultima istanza, che riesamina i casi già passati davanti ai tribunali di grado inferiore. Le sentenze della Corte Suprema costituiscono giurisprudenza, vale a dire possono essere usate come precedenti in altri processi.

tabloid ▸ NEWSPAPERS

Teamsters Teamsters Union è il più grosso sindacato degli Stati Uniti, con circa 1 milione e mezzo di iscritti. Sebbene inizialmente rappresentasse i camionisti (*teamsters*), oggi ne fanno parte lavoratori di molti altri settori.

Thanksgiving ▸ GIORNI FESTIVI NEI PAESI ANGLOFONI

TOEFL (*Test of English as a Foreign Language*) Un esame che valuta il livello di conoscenza dell'inglese degli studenti che fanno domanda d'iscrizione in un'università americana ma non sono di madrelingua inglese.

Tory ▸ CONSERVATIVE PARTY

trick or treat ▸ HALLOWEEN

Uncle Sam Personaggio immaginario che rappresenta gli Stati Uniti, il suo governo e i suoi cittadini. Nell'iconografia è tradizionalmente rappresentato con la barba bianca, vestito dei colori nazionali bianco, rosso e azzurro, con un gran cappello a cilindro con le stelle della bandiera statunitense. Spesso utilizzato quando si fa appello al patriottismo americano.

Cultura

Union Jack o **Union Flag** Il nome della bandiera del Regno Unito. È formata da tre croci: quella di San Giorgio (St George), patrono d'Inghilterra, quella di Sant'Andrea (St Andrew), patrono di Scozia, e quella di San Patrizio (St Patrick), patrono d'Irlanda. Il Galles e San David suo patrono non vi sono rappresentati.

United Kingdom Il Regno Unito di Gran Bretagna e Irlanda del Nord (United Kingdom of Great Britain and Northern Ireland) comprende l'Inghilterra, la Scozia, il Galles e l'Irlanda del Nord. Fa parte del COMMONWEALTH e dell'Unione Europea.

Veterans Day ▸ GIORNI FESTIVI NEI PAESI ANGLOFONI

Cultura

Wales Parte del Regno Unito confinante con l'Inghilterra centro-occidentale. La maggior parte dei centri abitati sono situati sulla costa (l'interno del paese è montuoso e poco popolato), in particolare lungo la costa meridionale, intorno alle due maggiori città, Cardiff, la capitale, e Swansea. Nel nord del

Galles il sentimento nazionalistico è più sentito e la lingua gallese (WELSH) è maggiormente diffusa. L'occupazione inglese del Galles ebbe inizio poco dopo la conquista normanna del 1066. Nel XVI secolo il Galles fu integrato all'Inghilterra ai fini legali, amministrativi e parlamentari. Nel 1999, in seguito al processo di decentramento (DEVOLUTION) è stata istituita l'Assemblea Nazionale del Galles, anche detta Assemblea Gallese (Welsh Assembly). Relativamente agli affari gallesi ha poteri legislativi secondari limitati.

Wall Street Via di Manhattan, a New York, dove hanno sede la Borsa e molti altri istituti finanziari. Quando si parla di Wall Street ci si riferisce spesso a tali istituti.

Weddings Nei paesi anglosassoni il matrimonio tradizionale si svolge in chiesa. La sposa (*bride*) indossa l'abito bianco ed ha al seguito una o più damigelle d'onore (*bridesmaids*). Il padre accompagna la sposa all'altare, mentre lo sposo (*bridegroom*) è affiancato dal *best man*, un parente o amico. Gli sposi si scambiano gli anelli (*wedding rings* o *bands*). Nel caso di matrimonio civile la cerimonia si svolge in comune. Dopo la cerimonia ha luogo il rinfresco nuziale (*wedding reception*) durante il quale il padre della sposa e il *best man* tengono un discorso. Alla fine del rinfresco gli sposi vanno in luna di miele (*honeymoon*). La sera prima del matrimonio, religioso o civile, è tradizione che il promesso sposo esca con gli amici per dare l'addio al celibato (la serata è detta *stag night* o negli Stati Uniti *bachelor party*). Oggi anche la sposa festeggia con le amiche l'addio al nubilato (*hen night*, e negli Stati Uniti *bachelorette party*). Negli Stati Uniti un'amica o una parente della sposa (di solito la damigella d'onore) organizza anche la cosiddetta *shower*, una festicciola in occasione della quale si danno alla sposa dei regali.

Welfare Negli Stati Uniti il termine *welfare* e *welfare programs* indicano le diverse misure di sicurezza sociale prese dal governo per garantire il benessere dei cittadini, in particolare in caso di povertà, malattia, disoccupazione. Fanno parte di questo sistema Medicare, Medicaid e i buoni per l'acquisto di viveri (*food stamps*).

Welsh È il gallese (*Cymraeg*), lingua di origine celtica, come il bretone e il cornico. È la lingua madre del 20% della popolazione gallese e negli ultimi quarant'anni ha vissuto una certa rinascita. In Galles oggi è usata insieme all'inglese in certi contesti ufficiali ed è materia obbligatoria nella maggior parte delle scuole.

Westminster Un quartiere del centro di Londra dove sono situati alcuni dei principali edifici governativi, quali il Parlamento (HOUSES OF PARLIAMENT) e la residenza del Primo Ministro in DOWNING STREET, ed anche l'Abbazia di Westminster (Westminster Abbey). Oggi la stampa usa il termine 'Westminster' per indicare il Parlamento britannico.

West Side ▸ EAST SIDE

whip Nella Camera dei Comuni britannica (HOUSE OF COMMONS), *whips* sono i deputati (MPS) incaricati di far rispettare la disciplina parlamentare ai colleghi del proprio partito, di assicurarsi che siano presenti alle sessioni e che votino. Negli Stati Uniti sono membri del Congresso (CONGRESS) con simili responsabilità.

Whitehall Una via nel centro di Londra dove hanno sede vari uffici governativi. La stampa usa il termine per indicare il governo e l'amministrazione statale.

White House La Casa Bianca, situata a Washington, è la residenza ufficiale del Presidente degli Stati Uniti. La stampa usa il termine per indicare il Presidente e i suoi collaboratori.

World Series ▸ BASEBALL

Yankee Termine spregiativo con cui durante la Guerra di Secessione i sudisti chiamavano i nordisti. Oggi è usato in tutto il mondo per indicare gli americani in generale. Negli Stati Uniti del sud ha ancora il significato originario, mentre in quelli del nord è utilizzato per indicare gli oriundi del New England.

yearbook Negli Stati Uniti è l'album che annualmente viene pubblicato per gli studenti dell'ultimo anno della HIGH SCHOOL. Contiene un profilo di ciascun studente con notizie sulle sue attività accademiche, sportive e ricreative, accompagnato da una fotografie e da una dedica.

Letter-writing / Redazione di lettere

Christmas and New Year wishes (informal)

> Natale 2010
>
> Cari Teresa e Federico,
>
> Buon Natale e Felice Anno Nuovo
>
> Vi auguro con tutto il cuore un anno pieno di belle sorprese e spero che ci sia al più presto l'occasione di rivederci.
>
> Un abbraccio a tutti e due,
>
> Paola

- You write the date like this on greetings cards. For Easter you write Pasqua and the year. For other occasions (birthdays, etc.) you can write the date in full: 6 febbraio 2010 with the number, the month without a capital letter, then the year, or as a number: 6/2/10.

- Standard greeting for Christmas and New Year cards.

Christmas and New Year wishes (formal)

On the envelope:

> Gentile Dott. Bossi e famiglia

- In Italy fewer people send Christmas cards than in Great Britain. Young people don't send them; it's considered slightly formal. If you send a present to someone you might attach a card, but if you exchange presents in person you don't normally give them a card, just wish them Buon Natale. The same goes for birthdays.

> Monza, Natale 2010
>
> BUON NATALE E FELICE ANNO NUOVO
>
> I miei più sentiti auguri a Lei ① e alla famiglia
>
> Fausto Mameli

- Inside greetings cards you can write the place you are writing from in front of the date.

① Lei is written with a capital letter in more formal letters.

Letter-writing / Redazione di lettere

Auguri di Buon Natale e Buon Anno

Su un biglietto:

[Best wishes for a] Happy ① Christmas and a Prosperous New Year

Best wishes for Christmas and the New Year

Wishing you every happiness this Christmas and in the New Year

① *Oppure:* Merry.

In una lettera:

44 Louis Gardens
London NW6 4GM

December 20th 2009

Dear Peter and Claire,

First of all, a very happy Christmas and all the best for the New Year to you and the children. ② We hope you're all well ③ and that we'll see you again. It seems ages since we last met up.

We've had a very eventful year. Last summer Gavin came off his bike and broke his arm and collarbone. Kathy scraped through her A Levels and is now at Sussex doing European Studies. Poor Tony was made redundant in October and is still looking for a job.

Do come and see us next time you are over this way. Just give us a ring a couple of days before so we can fix something.

All best wishes

Tony and Ann

② *Oppure (se i figli sono adulti):* to you and your family.

③ *Oppure (informale):* flourishing.

. . . .

Invitation to a wedding and wedding reception

Filippo Bartolini	*Cristiana Tedeschi*

Annunciano il loro matrimonio

Chiesa di S. Jacopo – Siena

Sabato 22 maggio 2010 – ore 16.30

Siena –	*Volterra –*
Via della Salute, 50	*Via A. Diaz, 6*

■ *Invitations to weddings are called 'partecipazioni' and are written or printed.*

■ *Very formal invitations are sent out by the parents who are announcing their son's or daughter's wedding.*

Filippo e Cristiana

*dopo la cerimonia saranno lieti di salutare
parenti ed amici presso la
Villa 'Il Poggio'
Via Marradi 45 – Siena*

R.S.V.P.

Invitation to a christening

Invitations to parties are usually by word of mouth, while for weddings announcements are usually sent out.

*Fabrizio Castelli e Katherine Ferguson
partecipano la nascita di Luigi*

*Vi invitano al suo battesimo nel Duomo di Barga
il 15 febbraio 2010 alle ore 12.00
e al rinfresco che seguirà alla Locanda da Gabriele
in località la Mocchia di Barga*

RSVP tel. 0583 – 861042

■ *When a phone number is given after RSVP you reply to the invitation by phone.*

Invito (informale)

- La data si può anche scrivere nei modi seguenti: April 10, 10 April, 10th April. Il nome del mese è in maiuscolo.

- In alto a destra si indica il nome e l'indirizzo del mittente, e sotto si scrive la data.

35 Winchester Drive
Stoke Gifford
Bristol
BS34 8PD

April 22nd 2009

Dear Luca,

Is there any chance of your coming to stay with us in the summer holidays? Roy and Debbie would be delighted if you could (as well as David and me, of course). We hope to go to North Wales at the end of July / beginning of August, and you'd be very welcome to come too. It's really beautiful up there. We'll probably take tents – I hope that's OK by you.

Let me know as soon as possible if you can manage it.

All best wishes

Rachel Hemmings

Letters / Lettere

Invito (formale)

Invito a un matrimonio e al rinfresco

Mr and Mrs Peter Thompson
request the pleasure of your company
at the marriage of their daughter
Hannah Louise
to
Steven David Warner
at St Mary's Church, Little Bourton
on Saturday 22nd July 2010 at 2 p.m.
And afterwards at the Golden Cross Hotel, Billing

R.S.V.P

23 Santers Lane
Little Bourton
Northampton
NN6 1AZ

Letters / Lettere

Accepting an invitation (formal)

CARLO E BEATRICE BUOZZI

*ringraziano calorosamente per il gentile invito
e sono lieti di poter partecipare.*

Invitation (informal)

Cara Claudia

È un po' che non ci sentiamo ma spero che tutto vada bene, sia con Andrea che con l'università. Il 7 agosto è il mio compleanno e pensavo di fare una festa. Che ne dici ① di venire qui a Napoli? Naturalmente sei invitata a casa mia per qualche giorno e ne approfitteremo per fare un po' di chiacchiere e un po' di mare. Fammi sapere al più presto! Spero tanto che tu venga, da sola o accompagnata, se tu e Andrea state ancora insieme. Il mio indirizzo email è grazia@hotmail.com.

Un bacione ② e a prestissimo,

Grazia

- Invitations to parties are usually made in person or on the phone, unless it's a really formal occasion.

① For a letter to a friend you use the 'tu' form.

② This affectionate ending is used with close friends or relatives. Other informal endings are Baci or Un abbraccio.

Accepting an invitation (informal)

24 aprile 2009

Cara Grazia

Quanto tempo! Scusa se non mi sono fatta più viva ma tra gli esami e altre storie il tempo è volato. Certo che vengo giù a Napoli. L'ultimo esame lo dovrei avere a fine luglio e non ho ancora programmato niente per le vacanze, tanto più che adesso sono sola (mollata da Andrea due mesi fa, ma senza troppi drammi). Ora che ci siamo rimesse in contatto prometto di non sparire e non vedo l'ora di rivederti di persona. Torno a studiare.

Un abbraccio,

Claudia

- In informal letters you write the date at the top but not your address.

- In replies to informal invitations you also use only the Christian name, the 'tu' form and an affectionate ending.

Per accettare un invito (informale)

> Luca Vallerini
> viale Italia 78
> 20162 Milano
>
> 2 May 2009
>
> Dear Mrs Hemmings ①,
>
> Many thanks for your letter and kind invitation. Since I don't have anything fixed yet for the summer holidays, I'd be delighted to come. However I mustn't be away for more than four or five days since my mother hasn't been very well.
>
> You must let me know what I should bring. How warm is it in North Wales? Can you swim in the sea? Camping is fine as far as I'm concerned, we take our tents everywhere.
>
> Looking forward to seeing you soon,
>
> Yours ②,
>
> Luca

① Questa è la lettera che un ragazzo scrive alla madre di un amico e quindi, anche se il tono generale è informale, si apre in modo piuttosto formale.

② Altre formule per questo tipo di lettera: With best wishes, Yours sincerely, Kind/Kindest regards.

Risposta a un invito (formale)

> Per accettare: Richard Willis has great pleasure in accepting Mr and Mrs Peter Thompson's kind invitation to the marriage of their daughter Hannah Louise to Steven Warner at St Mary's Church, Little Bourton, on Saturday 22nd July.

■ Si ripetono i particolari dell'invito, ma in modo meno dettagliato.

> Per declinare: Richard Willis regrets that he is unable to accept Mr and Mrs Peter Thompson's kind invitation to ...., owing to a prior engagement.

■ Nel caso non si possa accettare l'invito è consigliabile scrivere una lettera ai genitori della sposa, specialmente se si conoscono di persona.

Letters / Lettere

Replying to a job advertisement

■ *When you don't know the name of the person use this style. If you are writing to a company you can also use Spett.le Ditta.*

■ *In letters written in reply to an advertisement you should make specific reference to the advert: under oggetto you put the position you are applying for with the reference number or abbreviation, as well as the newspaper and date that the advert appeared.*

Bristol, 25 settembre 2010

Grifoni S.p.a.
viale Marconi, 67
20100 Milano

Oggetto: ricerca programmatore
Rif. AB 067
Corriere della Sera 12.09.2010

Gentili Signori

Ho letto con molto interesse il Vostro annuncio apparso sul Corriere della Sera del 12 settembre scorso e Vi sarei grato se poteste inviarmi ulteriori informazioni riguardo la posizione in oggetto.

Attualmente sono impiegato presso un'azienda di Bristol ma il mio contratto termina alla fine del mese e vorrei approfittare di questa opportunità per lavorare a Milano. Come risulta dal curriculum vitae che allego alla presente, oltre a possedere i titoli e l'esperienza richiesti, ho vissuto per qualche tempo in Italia ed ho un'ottima conoscenza della lingua italiana.

Resto a disposizione per un eventuale colloquio nel momento che riterrete più opportuno e faccio presente che dal 6 ottobre prossimo sarò raggiungibile a Milano al seguente indirizzo:

via Indipendenza 7
20100 Milano
tel. 02 429.96.67

In attesa di un Vostro cortese riscontro porgo cordiali saluti

David Baker
67 Whiteley Avenue
Bristol, BS5 6TW
UK

■ *When you are writing you should always include your own address after the signature either on the right or on the left.*

· ·

Risposta a un annuncio di lavoro

---

via Giolitti 32
00100 Rome

26 September 2010

The Personnel Manager ①
Patterson Software plc
Milton State
Bath BA6 8YZ

Dear Sir or Madam ①,

I am interested in the post of programmer advertised in The Guardian of
12 September and would be very grateful if you could send me further
particulars. ②

I am currently working for the Sempo Corporation, but my contract
finishes at the end of the month, and I would like ③ to come and work in
England. As you can see from my CV (enclosed), I have an excellent
command of English and also the required qualifications and experience.

I will be available for interview any time after 6th October, from which date
I can be contacted at the following address in the UK:

c/o Lewis
51 Dexter Road
London N7 6BW
Tel. 0208 607 5512

I look forward to hearing from you. ④

Yours sincerely

Maria Luisa Bianchi

Encl.

---

① *Oppure:* Ms Angela Summers, … *se nell'inserzione compare* Reply to Angela Summers;
oppure Dear Ms Summers, Dear Mrs Wright *se compare solo il cognome.*

② *Oppure:* and would like to apply for this position, *se l'annuncio è ben dettagliato.*

③ *Se al momento si è disoccupati si scrive invece:* I am currently looking for work and I would like…

④ *Oppure:* Thanking you in anticipation/advance.

Curriculum Vitae

CURRICULUM VITAE

Nome e cognome	Gina Allen
Luogo e data di nascita	Birmingham, 21 settembre 1987
Residenza	127 Chatterton Terrace
	Londra W10 4RT, Gran Bretagna
Telefono abitazione	+44 (0)20 8741390
Telefono cellulare	+44 776 63294031
Indirizzo di posta elettronica	gina.allen@aol.com
Stato civile	Nubile ①
Nazionalità	Britannica ②

FORMAZIONE

2003–2004	'A Levels' (equivalente al diploma di scuola secondaria superiore) in italiano, storia e storia dell'arte, presso il Fulham Sixth Form College
2004–2005	Soggiorno in Italia durante il quale ho seguito un corso di italiano per stranieri a Bologna.
2005–2008	Laurea in storia dell'arte, University of Westminster di Londra, con tesi sul Mantegna.
	Durante l'ultimo anno di corso ho fatto uno stage presso la casa d'aste Sotheby's.
autunno 2008	Corso trimestrale di ricerca fotografica.

ESPERIENZE LAVORATIVE

dal luglio 2010	Ricercatrice fotografica presso la casa editrice Zoom. Mi occupo della ricerca iconografica per le pubblicazioni d'arte.
2009–2010	Assistente presso l'archivio fotografico 'PhotoArt' di Londra, specializzato in immagini di Belle Arti.
2004–2005	Impiego part-time presso un'agenzia di viaggi di Bologna.
Conoscenze linguistiche	Inglese madrelingua - Italiano buono parlato e scritto
Conoscenze informatiche	Buone conoscenze. Esperienza di ISDN/Photoshop
Interessi	Fotografia, cinema, yoga, ciclismo

① *A single man would put* celibe. *Otherwise you could put* coniugato/a *(you can add, if it is relevant,* senza figli *or* un figlio *etc.),* divorziato/a, vedovo/a.

② *Italian men also have to add whether they have completed their military service.*

• •

Curriculum Vitae

CURRICULUM VITAE ①

Name:	Maria Luisa Bianchi
Address:	via Giolitti 32
	00100 Rome
	Italy
Telephone:	(+39) 06 243 53 94
Nationality:	Italian
Date of Birth:	11/3/79

EDUCATION:

1996–2001	Degree Course in Information Technology and English at Università degli Studi of Rome.
1993–1997	Diploma di Maturità Scientifica (equivalent to A levels) at the Liceo Scientifico in Rome.

EMPLOYMENT:

2002–present	Program development engineer with Sempo Informatica, Rome, specializing in computer graphics.
2001–2002	Trainee programmer with Oregon-Italia, Rome.

FURTHER SKILLS:

Languages:	Italian (mother tongue),
	English (fluent, spoken and written),
	French (good).
Interests:	Travel, fashion, tennis.

---

① *Oppure:* Resumé *(inglese americano)*

Letter-writing / Redazione di lettere

Booking a hotel room

18 giugno 2010

Hotel La rosa
Corso del Partigiano, 56
22100 Como

Gentile Signora Pacini ①
In seguito alla conversazione telefonica di stamattina, le scrivo
per confermare la prenotazione di una camera doppia con bagno
② dall'8 al 12 luglio. Mia moglie ed io arriveremo nel tardo
pomeriggio di giovedì 8. Per ogni comunicazione urgente il mio
numero di telefono è +44 031 5790 3352.

Cordiali saluti
P. Bromfield
Cardross Gardens
Edinburgh
EH2 5EG
Gran Bretagna

① *Alternatively you
can write* Gentili
Signori *if you
don't know the
name of the
person you are
writing to.*

② *Or:* una camera
singola/con
doccia

Prenotazione di una camera d'albergo

The Manager   35 Prince Edward Road
Torbay Hotel   Oxford OX7 3AA
Dawlish
Devon   Tel. 01865 322435
EX37 2LR

                                23rd April 2009

Dear Sir or Madam,

I saw your hotel listed in the Inns of Devon guide for last year, and
wish to reserve a double (or twin-bedded) room with
shower ① in a quiet position from August 2nd-11th (nine
nights), also a single room for my son.

If you have anything suitable for this period please let me know
the price and whether you require a deposit.

Yours faithfully,

Charles Fairhurst

① *Oppure:*
with bath/with
ensuite.

• •

Sending an e-mail

The illustration shows a typical interface for sending e-mail.

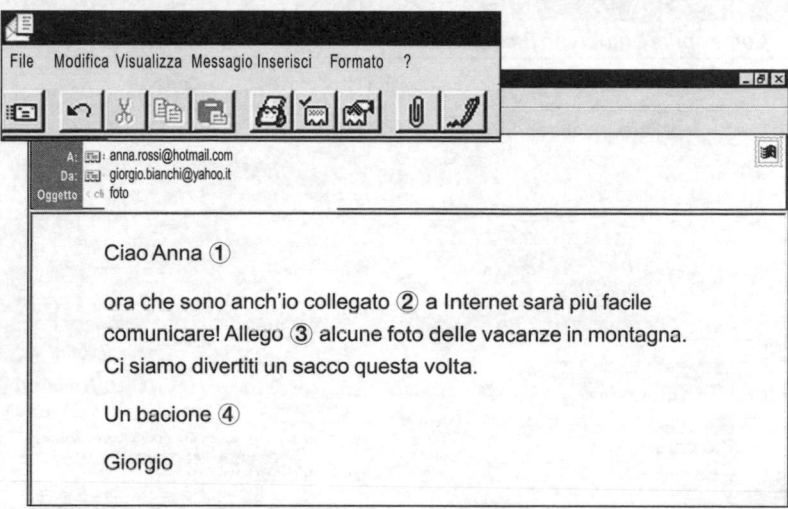

① *The beginning changes according to how formal it is. You can use caro/cara or leave it out.*

② *Collegata if the person writing is a girl or woman.*

③ *Allegare means to enclose and also to attach in e-mails.*

④ *In more formal e-mails you can end with 'Distinti saluti' like in letters.*

E-mail

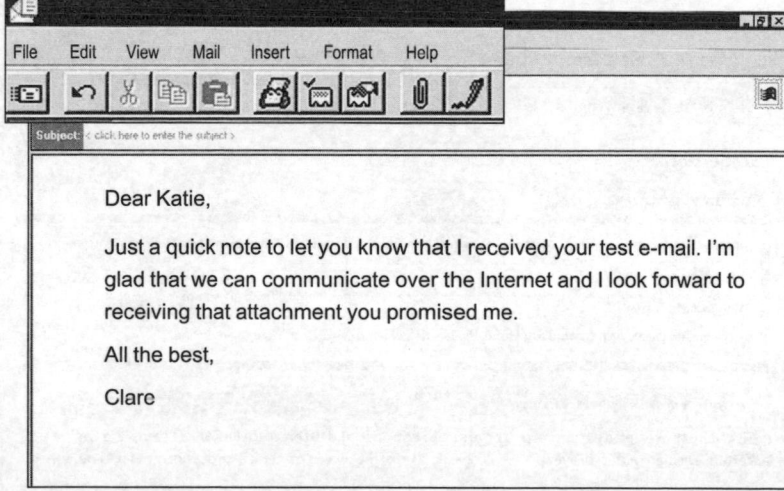

Internet

Opening an online bank account

Banca Esemplare Online

Come aprire il tuo conto Esemplare online

Inserisci i tuoi dati e clicca su '**Invia**'. I campi contrassegnati con il simbolo * sono obbligatori.
Clicca qui per accedere all'**Aiuto?**
Guarda la **demo interattiva** o leggi le domande più frequenti **FAQ**.

Dati anagrafici

* Nome

* Cogome

* Data di nascita
gg   mm   aaaa

* Codice fiscale

Telefono fisso

Cellulare

* Indirizzo

* Comune

* Cap

Indirizzo email

*La Banca Esemplare Online, e altre società del Gruppo Esemplare, vorrebbero contattarti via email per informarti su prodotti e servizi che potrebbero interessarti. Seleziona la casella se **non** vuoi ricevere tali informazioni.* ☐

Documento d'identità

* Tipologia

* Numero

* Data di rilascio
gg   mm   aaaa

* Riferimenti bancari – obbligatori

Inserisci l'IBAN relativo al tuo conto corrente in essere presso la Banca Esemplare. Puoi trovare il tuo IBAN in alto a destra nel tuo estratto conto Banca Esemplare. Se non sei intestatario di un conto presso la Banca Esemplare inserisci il numero della tua carta di credit.

◉ IBAN

o

◯ Numero carta di credito

Codice di sicurezza

Cos'è il codice di sicurezza?

* Sei intestatario di altri conti con la Banca Esemplare o altre società del Gruppo Banca Esemplare?
S ☐ N ☐

Cos'è questo?

* La tua password

Inserisci la tua password per l'accesso al servizio di internet banking con la Banca Esemplare Online

Inserisci la password

Conferma la password

(tra 8 e 16 caratteri – solo caratteri minuscoli e numeri)

Non rivelare mai la tua password a nessuno. Usala solo per il tuo conto Banca Esemplare Online.

* Termini e condizioni di utilizzo

☐ Dichiaro di aver letto e compreso i **termini e le condizioni di utilizzo** della Banca Esemplare Online e di accettarli. Dichiaro altresì di aver preso visione dell'**informativa** in materia di protezione dei dati personali.

Aprire un conto online

Exemplary Bank Online

Application for Internet banking

Fill in your details below and click '**Send**'.
Boxes marked * are obligatory.

Click here for **Help?**

View our **interactive demo** or read our customers' most frequently asked questions **FAQ**.

Your details

* Title   * First name   * Surname

* Date of birth   Telephone Number   Mobile/Cell phone
dd   mm   yyyy

* Home address   * Postcode/Zip code

Email address   *Exemplary Bank Online, and other Exemplary Group companies, would like to email you about our products and services that may interest you. Please check this box if you do **not** want to receive this information.* ☐

* Account details – mandatory

Please provide details of the current/checking account you already have with the Exemplary Bank.
Give your credit card number if you do not have an Exemplary Bank current/checking account.

◉   Sort code   ▼   Account number

or

○   Credit Card Number   Security Code   **What is my security code?**

* Do you have any other accounts with Exemplary Bank or Exemplary Bank Group companies?
Y ☐ N ☐

What's this?

* Your password

Please enter your password for your Exemplary Bank Online internet banking service

Enter password   *(between 8 and 16 characters – lower case letters and numbers only)*

Confirm password

Do not reveal your password to others. Use it only for your Exemplary Bank Online **account.**

* Legal conditions

☐ I have read the Exemplary Bank Online **terms and conditions** and confirm that I have understood them and agree to be bound by them.

Booking train tickets online

Internet

Acquista il tuo biglietto online con **Europtrains**

| **Biglietti** | Orari | Mappe, destinazioni e itinerari |

Partenza
Seleziona la stazione ▶ **Tutte le stazioni**

Arrivo
Seleziona la stazione ▶ **Tutte le stazioni**

Andata
Giu ▶ 17 ▶ 2010 ▶   Ore Qualunque ▶
calendario

Ritorno
(non selezionare per viaggio di sola andata)
Giu ▶ 18 ▶ 2010 ▶   Ore Qualunque ▶
calendario

Le date del mio viaggio sono flessibili ☐

Numero di passeggeri Adulti ▶ Bambini ▶ Studenti ▶ Ultrasessantenni ▶

Prima classe ☐
Seconda classe ☐

RICERCA

Offerte speciali

Risparmia il 25%
quando prenoti online
a partire dal 1 luglio 2010

• Milano–Bruxelles solo andata
a metà prezzo

Clicca qui per saperne di più

• Milano–Londra andata e ritorno
a soli € 50,00

Clicca qui per maggiori dettagli

Studenti: come risparmiare
viaggiando con la pass card
**Telefona per scoprire tutti i
vantaggi e le condizioni.**

Area clienti

Nome utente
Password
Ricorda la mia password ☐
Hai scordato la password?
Registrati ora!

Altre opzioni

In viaggio per lavoro
Viaggiare in gruppo
Assistenza per disabili
Treno e bici

Cambiare una prenotazione
Cancellare una prenotazione
Ricevere i biglietti a domicilio

Altre offerte speciali
Abbonamenti
Hotels
Assicurazione

mappa del sito | chi siamo | FAQ | contatti

Comprare i biglietti su Internet

Buy tickets online with **Europtrains**

| Tickets | Timetables | Maps, destinations & route planner |

From
Select station ▶ See all stations

To
Select station ▶ See all stations

Departure date
June ▶ 17 ▶ 2010 ▶   Time
Anytime ▶
Calendar

Return date
(leave blank for one-way travel)
June ▶ 18 ▶ 2010 ▶   Time
Anytime ▶
Calendar

Flexible dates? ☐

Number of   Adults   Children   Students   Seniors
passengers ▶   ▶   ▶   ▶

First class ☐
Second classe ☐

(SEARCH)

Special offer

Save 25%
when you book online
from 1st July 2010 onwards

● London to Brussels one way
half-price
To find out more, click here

● London to Milan round trip
from just €50
Click here for details

Students: buy your pass card and
save money on travel
Call for details.
Conditions apply

My account

Username [ ]
Password [ ]

Remember my password ☐
Forgotten your password?
Register here

More options

Business travellers
Group travellers
Travelling with a wheelchair
Travelling with a bicycle

Changing a reservation
Cancelling a reservation
Receiving your tickets

More special offers
Rail passes
Hotels
Travel Insurance

Internet

site map | about us | FAQ | contact us

SMS (electronic text-messaging)

The basic principles governing Italian SMS abbreviations are similar to those governing English SMS. Certain words or syllables can be represented by letters or numbers that sound the same but take up less space. The word 'sei', for example, can be replaced by '6', and the word 'che' shortened to 'ke'. Another way of shortening words and phrases is simply to omit certain letters, especially vowels. For example, 'comunque' becomes 'cmq' and 'ci vediamo dopo' becomes 'cvd'.

As in English, 'faccine' (emoticons) are very popular, and some of the more established ones are included in the table below.

Glossary of Italian SMS abbreviations

Abbreviation	Full word
"xxx"	tanti baci
+o-	più o meno
6 la +	sei la migliore
6 sxme	sei speciale per me
amò	amore
ap	a presto
axitivo	aperitivo
ba	bacio
cel	cellulare
cmq	comunque
cvd	ci vediamo dopo
dom	domani
dx	destra
ke	che
-male	meno male
midi	mi dispiace
MMT+	mi manchi tantissimo
msg	messaggio
Nm	numero
Nn	non
qlc	qualcuno
qls	qualcosa
risp	rispondimi
sx	sinistra
t tel + trd	ti telefono + tardi
tat	ti amo tanto
tel	telefono
tipe	ti penso
to	ti odio
ttp	torno tra un pò
tu6	tu sei

Abbreviation	Full word
tvb	ti voglio bene
tvtb	ti voglio tanto bene
vng dp	vengo dopo
x	per
x fv	per favore
x me	per me
xdere	perdere
xh	per ora
xké	perché

Emoticons*

:-)	sorriso
:-(	tristezza
:-D	risata
;-)	strizzare l'occhio
:-*	baciare
!(	occhio nero
:-/	scettico
:'(	piangere
#:-o	traumatizzato
:-i	penso
:-o	sorpreso
:-q	nauseato
:-P	linguaccia
$)	felice di aver vinto la lotteria
:*)	pagliaccio
*<:-)	Babbo Natale

*NB: the '-' which depicts the nose is often omitted or replaced by an 'o' e.g. :) or :o)

SMS

SMS (messaggi elettronici)

Poiché lo spazio per gli SMS è limitato (solitamente 160 caratteri al massimo), anche in inglese quando si scrive un messaggino si ricorre a molte abbreviazioni. Spesso si accorciano le parole eliminando alcune lettere, ad esempio 'please' è in genere abbreviato con 'pls'. Un altro metodo consiste nel sostituire alcune parole o suoni con numeri o lettere. Un tipico esempio è l'uso di '2' invece della parola 'to' e della lettera 'U' al posto di 'you'.

Anche gli 'emoticons' (le faccine) sono popolari e alcuni dei più usati si trovano nel glossario qui sotto.

Glossario di abbreviazioni SMS inglesi

Abbreviazione	Senso	Abbreviazione	Senso
afaik	as far as I know	**ruok**	are you OK?
atb	all the best	**som1**	someone
b4	before	**thkq**	thank you
bbl	be back late(r)	**tx**	thanks
brb	be right back	**ur**	you are
btw	by the way	**wan2**	want to
cu	see you	**wot**	what
cul8r	see you later	**xlnt**	excellent
f2f	face to face	**2moro**	tomorrow
fwiw	for what it's worth		
fyi	for your information	*Faccina**	
gr8	great		
h8	hate	**:-)**	happy face
hand	have a nice day	**:-(**	sad face
hth	hope this helps	**:-D**	laughing
ic	I see	**;-)**	winking
imho	in my humble opinion	**:-***	big kiss!
imo	in my opinion	**!(**	black eye
iow	in other words	**:-/**	sceptical
jk	just kidding	**:'(**	crying
lol	laughing out loud/lots of luck	**#:-o**	traumatized
msg	message	**:-i**	I'm thinking
myob	mind your own business	**:-o**	surprised
ne1	anyone	**:-q**	feeling sick
no1	no one	**:-P**	tongue sticking out
oic	oh I see	**\$)**	I've just won the lottery
otoh	on the other hand	**:*)**	clown
pls	please	**@}-,-'--**	a rose
ppl	people		
r	are	*NB: il '-' che rappresenta il naso è spesso	
rofl	rolling on the floor, laughing	sostituito con 'o' ad es. :) o :o)	

SMS

Aa

a¹, A /eɪ/ (letter) a, A *f inv*; Mus la *m inv*

a² ⓵ /ə/ *accentato* /eɪ/ (*before a vowel* **an**) *indef art* un *m*, una *f*; (before s + consonant, gn, ps, z) uno; (before nf starting with vowel) un'; (each) a; **I am a lawyer** sono avvocato; **a tiger is a feline** la tigre è un felino; **a knife and fork** un coltello e una forchetta; **a Mr Smith is looking for you** un certo signor Smith ti sta cercando; **£2 a kilo/a head** due sterline al chilo/a testa
⓶ /eɪ/ *n* Mus la *m inv*

A & E *n abbr* Br (**Accident and Emergency**) pronto soccorso *m*

A2 *n* ‹exam/course› esame (m) sostenuto al termine del secondo anno del biennio di preparazione agli A-Level

A4 *adj* A4

AA *n abbr* 1 Br (**Automobile Association**) ≈ A.C.I. *m*
2 (**Alcoholics Anonymous**)

AAA *n abbr* Am (**American Automobile Association**) ≈ A.C.I. *m*

aback /ə'bæk/ *adv* **be taken** ∼ essere preso in contropiede

abacus /'æbəkəs/ *n* (*pl* **-cuses**) abaco *m*

abandon /ə'bændən/ ⓵ *vt* abbandonare; (give up) rinunciare a
⓶ *n* abbandono *m*

abandoned /ə'bændɪnd/ *adj* abbandonato, ‹behaviour› dissoluto

abandonment /ə'bændənmənt/ *n* (of strike, plan etc) rinuncia *f*

abashed /ə'bæʃt/ *adj* imbarazzato

abate /ə'beɪt/ *vi* calmarsi

abattoir /'æbətwɑː(r)/ *n* mattatoio *m*

abbess /'æbes/ *n* badessa *f*

abbey /'æbɪ/ *n* abbazia *f*

abbot /'æbət/ *n* abate *m*

abbreviate /ə'briːvɪeɪt/ *vt* abbreviare

abbreviation /əbriːvɪ'eɪʃn/ *n* abbreviazione *f*

ABC ⓵ *n* (alphabet) alfabeto *m*; **the** ∼ **of** (basics) l'ABC *m inv* di
⓶ *n abbr* (**American Broadcasting Company**) rete (*f*) televisiva americana

abdicate /'æbdɪkeɪt/ ⓵ *vi* abdicare
⓶ *vt* rinunciare a

abdication /æbdɪ'keɪʃn/ *n* abdicazione *f*

abdomen /'æbdəmən/ *n* addome *m*

abdominal /əb'dɒmɪnl/ *adj* addominale

abduct /əb'dʌkt/ *vt* rapire

abduction /əb'dʌkʃn/ *n* rapimento *m*

abductor /əb'dʌktə(r)/ *n* rapitore, -trice *mf*

aberrant /ə'berənt/ *adj* ‹behaviour, nature› aberrante

aberration /æbə'reɪʃn/ *n* aberrazione *f*

abet /ə'bet/ *vt* (*pt/pp* **abetted**) **aid and** ∼ Jur *essere complice di*

abeyance /ə'beɪəns/ *n* **in** ∼ in sospeso; **fall into** ∼ cadere in disuso

abhor /əb'hɔː(r)/ *vt* (*pt/pp* **abhorred**) aborrire

abhorrence /əb'hɒrəns/ *n* orrore *m*

abhorrent /əb'hɒrənt/ *adj* ripugnante

abide /ə'baɪd/ ⓵ *vt* (*pt/pp* **abided**) (tolerate) sopportare
⓶ *vt* **abide by** rispettare

abiding /ə'baɪdɪŋ/ *adj* perpetuo

ability /ə'bɪlətɪ/ *n* capacità *f inv*

abject /'æbdʒekt/ *adj* ‹poverty› degradante; ‹apology› umile; ‹coward› abietto

ablative /'æblətɪv/ *n* ablativo *m*

ablaze /ə'bleɪz/ *adj* in fiamme; **be** ∼ **with light** risplendere di luci

able /'eɪbl/ *adj* capace, abile; **be** ∼ **to do something** poter fare qualcosa; **were you** ∼ **to...?** sei riuscito a...?

able-bodied /-'bɒdɪd/ *adj* robusto; Mil abile

able seaman *n* marinaio *m* scelto

ably /'eɪblɪ/ *adv* abilmente

abnegation /æbnɪ'geɪʃn/ *n* (of rights, privileges) rinuncia *f*; (self-abnegation) abnegazione *f*

abnormal /æb'nɔːml/ *adj* anormale

abnormality /æbnɔː'mælətɪ/ *n* anormalità *f inv*

abnormally /æb'nɔːməlɪ/ *adv* in modo anormale

aboard /ə'bɔːd/ *adv & prep* a bordo

abode /ə'bəʊd/ *n* dimora *f*

abolish /ə'bɒlɪʃ/ *vt* abolire

abolition /æbə'lɪʃn/ *n* abolizione *f*

abominable /ə'bɒmɪnəbl/ *adj* abominevole

abominably /ə'bɒmɪnəblɪ/ *adv* disgustosamente

abominate /ə'bɒmɪneɪt/ *vt* abominare

aboriginal /æbə'rɪdʒɪnl/ *adj & n* (native) aborigeno, a *mf*, indigeno, a *mf*

Aborigine /æbə'rɪdʒəniː/ *n* aborigeno, -a *mf* d'Australia

abort /ə'bɔːt/ *vt* fare abortire; fig annullare

a

abortion /əˈbɔːʃn/ n aborto m; **have an ∼** abortire

abortionist /əˈbɔːʃnɪst/ n persona (f) che pratica aborti, specialmente clandestini

abortive /əˈbɔːtɪv/ adj ‹attempt› infruttuoso

abound /əˈbaʊnd/ vi abbondare (**in** di)

❖ **about** /əˈbaʊt/ **1** adv (here and there) [di] qua e [di] là; (approximately) circa; **be ∼** ‹illness, tourists› essere in giro; **be up and ∼** essere alzato; **leave something lying ∼** lasciare in giro qualcosa

2 prep (concerning) su; (in the region of) intorno a; (here and there in) per; **what is the book/the film ∼?** di cosa parla il libro/il film?; **he wants to see you — what ∼?** ti vuole vedere — a che proposito?; **talk/know ∼** parlare/sapere di; **I know nothing ∼ it** non ne so niente; **∼ 5 o'clock** intorno alle 5; **travel ∼ the world** viaggiare per il mondo; **be ∼ to do something** stare per fare qualcosa; **how ∼ going to the cinema?** e se andassimo al cinema?

about-face, about-turn n dietro front m inv

❖ **above** /əˈbʌv/ adv & prep sopra; **∼ all** soprattutto

above-board adj onesto

above-ground adv in superficie

above-mentioned /-menʃnd/ adj suddetto

above-named /-neɪmd/ adj suddetto

abrasion /əˈbreɪʒn/ n (injury) abrasione f

abrasive /əˈbreɪsɪv/ **1** adj abrasivo; (remark) caustico

2 n abrasivo m

abreast /əˈbrest/ adv fianco a fianco; **come ∼ of** allinearsi con; **keep ∼ of** tenersi al corrente di

abridged /əˈbrɪdʒd/ adj ridotto

abridg[e]ment /əˈbrɪdʒmnt/ n (version) edizione f ridotta

abroad /əˈbrɔːd/ adv all'estero

abrupt /əˈbrʌpt/ adj brusco

abruptly /əˈbrʌptlɪ/ adv bruscamente

ABS n abbr (**anti-lock braking system**) ABS m inv

abscess /ˈæbsɪs/ n ascesso m

abscond /əbˈskɒnd/ vi fuggire

abseiling /ˈæbseɪlɪŋ/ n Br discesa f a corda doppia; **to go ∼** fare discesa a corda doppia

❖ **absence** /ˈæbsəns/ n assenza f; (lack) mancanza f

absent¹ /ˈæbsənt/ adj assente

absent² /æbˈsent/ vt **∼ oneself** essere assente

absentee /æbsənˈtiː/ n assente mf

absenteeism /æbsənˈtiːɪzm/ n assenteismo m

absentee landlord n proprietario (m) che affitta una casa in cui non abita

absently /ˈæbsəntlɪ/ adv ‹say, look› distrattamente

absent-minded /-ˈmaɪndɪd/ adj distratto

absent-mindedly /-ˈmaɪndɪdlɪ/ adv distrattamente

absent-mindedness /-ˈmaɪndɪdnɪs/ n distrazione f

absolute /ˈæbsəluːt/ adj assoluto; **an ∼ idiot** un perfetto idiota

❖ **absolutely** /ˈæbsəluːtlɪ/ adv assolutamente; fam (indicating agreement) esattamente; **∼ not** assolutamente no

absolution /æbsəˈluːʃn/ n assoluzione f

absolve /əbˈzɒlv/ vt assolvere

absorb /əbˈsɔːb/ vt assorbire; **∼ed in** assorto in

absorbency /əbˈsɔːbənsɪ/ n capacità f d'assorbimento

absorbent /əbˈsɔːbənt/ adj assorbente

absorbent cotton n Am cotone m idrofilo, ovatta f

absorbing /əbˈsɔːbɪŋ/ adj avvincente

absorption /əbˈsɔːpʃn/ n assorbimento m; (in activity) concentrazione f

abstain /əbˈsteɪn/ vi astenersi (**from** da)

abstemious /əbˈstiːmɪəs/ adj moderato

abstention /əbˈstenʃn/ n Pol astensione f

abstinence /ˈæbstɪnəns/ n astinenza f

abstract /ˈæbstrækt/ **1** adj astratto

2 n astratto m; (summary) estratto m

abstraction /əbˈstrækʃn/ n **an air of ∼** un'aria distratta

absurd /əbˈsɜːd/ adj assurdo

absurdity /əbˈsɜːdətɪ/ n assurdità f inv

absurdly /əbˈsɜːdlɪ/ adv assurdamente

abundance /əˈbʌndəns/ n abbondanza f

abundant /əˈbʌndənt/ adj abbondante

abundantly /əˈbʌndəntlɪ/ adv **∼ clear** più che chiaro

abuse¹ /əˈbjuːz/ vt (misuse) abusare di; (insult) insultare; (ill-treat) maltrattare

❖ **abuse²** /əˈbjuːs/ n abuso m; (verbal) insulti mpl; (ill-treatment) maltrattamento m; **∼ of power** sopraffazione f

abusive /əˈbjuːsɪv/ adj offensivo

abut /əˈbʌt/ vi (pt/pp **abutted**) confinare (**onto** con)

abysmal /əˈbɪzml/ adj fam pessimo; ‹ignorance› abissale

abyss /əˈbɪs/ n abisso m

a/c abbr (**account**) c/c

academia /ækəˈdiːmɪə/ n mondo m accademico

❖ **academic** /ækəˈdemɪk/ **1** adj teorico; ‹qualifications, system› scolastico; **be ∼**

❖ indicates a very frequent word

⟨person⟩ avere predisposizione allo studio
2 n docente mf universitario, -a

academically /ækæˈdemɪklɪ/ adv ⟨gifted⟩
accademicamente

academician /əkædəˈmɪʃn/ n
accademico, -a mf

academy /əˈkædəmɪ/ n accademia f; (of
music) conservatorio m

ACAS /ˈeɪkæs/ n abbr Br (**Advisory
Conciliation and Arbitration
Service**) organismo (m) pubblico di
mediazione tra i lavoratori e i datori di
lavoro

accede /əkˈsiːd/ vi ~ to accedere a
⟨request⟩; salire a ⟨throne⟩

accelerate /əkˈseləreɪt/ vt/i accelerare

acceleration /əksələˈreɪʃn/ n
accelerazione f

accelerator /əkˈseləreɪtə(r)/ n Auto,
Comput acceleratore m

accent¹ /ˈæksənt/ n accento m

accent² /ækˈsent/ vt accentare

accented /ˈæksəntɪd/ adj ⟨speech⟩ con
accento marcato

accentuate /əkˈsentjʊeɪt/ vt accentuare

⚔ **accept** /əkˈsept/ vt accettare

acceptability /əkseptəˈbɪlɪtɪ/ n
ammissibilità f

acceptable /əkˈseptəbl/ adj accettabile

acceptance /əkˈseptəns/ n accettazione f

⚔ **access** /ˈækses/ **1** n accesso m
2 vt Comput accedere a

accessible /əkˈsesəbl/ adj accessibile

accession /əkˈseʃn/ n ⟨to throne⟩ ascesa
f al trono

accessory /əkˈsesərɪ/ n accessorio m; Jur
complice mf

⚔ **accident** /ˈæksɪdənt/ n incidente m;
(chance) caso m; by ~ per caso; (unintentionally)
senza volere; I'm sorry, it was an ~ mi
dispiace, non l'ho fatto apposta

accidental /æksɪˈdentl/ adj ⟨meeting⟩
casuale; ⟨death⟩ incidentale; (unintentional)
involontario

accidentally /æksɪˈdentəlɪ/ adv per caso;
(unintentionally) inavvertitamente

accident-prone /ˌæksɪdəntˈprəʊn/ adj
soggetto a incidenti

acclaim /əˈkleɪm/ **1** n acclamazione f
2 vt acclamare (as come)

acclimatization /əklaɪmətaɪˈzeɪʃn/ n
acclimatazione f

acclimatize /əˈklaɪmətaɪz/ vt become ~d
acclimatarsi

accolade /ˈækəleɪd/ n riconoscimento m

accommodate /əˈkɒmədeɪt/ vt ospitare;
(oblige) favorire

accommodating /əˈkɒmədeɪtɪŋ/ adj
accomodante

accommodation Br,
accommodations Am
/əkɒməˈdeɪʃn(z)/ n (place to stay) sistemazione
f; look for ~ cercare una sistemazione

accompaniment /əˈkʌmpənɪmənt/ n
accompagnamento m

accompanist /əˈkʌmpənɪst/ n Mus
accompagnatore, -trice mf

⚔ **accompany** /əˈkʌmpənɪ/ vt (pt/pp -ied)
accompagnare

accomplice /əˈkʌmplɪs/ n complice mf

accomplish /əˈkʌmplɪʃ/ vt (achieve)
concludere; realizzare ⟨aim⟩

accomplished /əˈkʌmplɪʃt/ adj dotato;
⟨fact⟩ compiuto

accomplishment /əˈkʌmplɪʃmənt/ n
realizzazione f; (achievement) risultato m;
(talent) talento m

accord /əˈkɔːd/ **1** n (treaty) accordo m;
with one ~ tutti d'accordo; of his own ~ di
sua spontanea volontà
2 vt accordare

accordance /əˈkɔːdəns/ n in ~ with in
conformità di o a

according /əˈkɔːdɪŋ/ adv ~ to secondo

accordingly /əˈkɔːdɪŋlɪ/ adv di
conseguenza

accordion /əˈkɔːdɪən/ n fisarmonica f

accost /əˈkɒst/ vt abbordare

⚔ **account** /əˈkaʊnt/ n conto m; (report)
descrizione f; (of eyewitness) resoconto m; ~s
pl Comm conti mpl; on ~ of a causa di; on no
~ per nessun motivo; on this ~ per questo
motivo; on my ~ per causa mia; of no ~
di nessuna importanza; take into ~ tener
conto di

■ **account for** vt (explain) spiegare; ⟨person⟩
render conto di; (constitute) costituire; (destroy)
distruggere

accountability /əkaʊntəˈbɪlɪtɪ/ n
responsabilità f

accountable /əˈkaʊntəbl/ adj
responsabile (for di)

accountancy /əˈkaʊntənsɪ/ n ragioneria
f, contabilità f

accountant /əˈkaʊntənt/ n (bookkeeper)
contabile mf; ragioniere, -a mf; (consultant)
commercialista mf

account book n libro m contabile

account director n account director
mf inv

account holder /əˈkaʊnthəʊldə(r)/ n
(with bank, credit company) titolare mf del conto

accounting /əˈkaʊntɪŋ/ n (field) ragioneria
f; (auditing) contabilità f

accounting period n periodo m
contabile

account manager n account manager
mf

account number n numero m di conto

a

accounts department n [ufficio m] contabilità f

accounts payable npl conto m creditori diversi

accounts receivable npl conto m creditori diversi

accoutrements /ə'ku:trəmənts/ npl equipaggiamento msg

accredited /ə'kredɪtɪd/ adj accreditato

accretion /ə'kri:ʃn/ n accrescimento m

accrue /ə'kru:/ vi ‹interest› maturare

accumulate /ə'kju:mjʊleɪt/ ① vt accumulare
② vi accumularsi

accumulation /əkju:mjʊ'leɪʃn/ n accumulazione f

accumulator /ə'kju:mjʊleɪtə(r)/ n Electr accumulatore m

accuracy /'ækjʊrəsɪ/ n precisione f

accurate /'ækjʊrət/ adj preciso

accurately /'ækjʊrətlɪ/ adv con precisione

accusation /ækjʊ'zeɪʃn/ n accusa f

accusative /ə'kju:zətɪv/ adj & n ∼ [case] Gram accusativo m

✦ **accuse** /ə'kju:z/ vt accusare; ∼ somebody of doing something accusare qualcuno di fare qualcosa

accused /ə'kju:zd/ n the ∼ l'accusato m, l'accusata f

accuser /ə'kju:zə(r)/ n accusatore, trice mf

accusing /ə'kju:zɪŋ/ adj accusatore

accusingly /ə'kju:zɪŋlɪ/ adv ‹say, point› in modo accusatorio

accustom /ə'kʌstəm/ vt abituare (to a)

accustomed /ə'kʌstəmd/ adj abituato; grow or get ∼ to abituarsi a

ace /eɪs/ n (in cards) asso m; Tennis ace m inv

acerbic /ə'sɜ:bɪk/ adj acido

acetate /'æsɪteɪt/ n acetato m

ache /eɪk/ ① n dolore m
② vi dolere, far male; ∼ all over essere tutto indolenzito

✦ **achieve** /ə'tʃi:v/ vt ottenere ‹success›; realizzare ‹goal, ambition›

✦ **achievement** /ə'tʃi:vmənt/ n (feat) successo m

achiever /ə'tʃi:və(r)/ n persona f di successo

Achilles' heel /əkɪli:z'hi:l/ n tallone m di Achille

aching /'eɪkɪŋ/ adj ‹body, limbs› dolorante; an ∼ void un vuoto incolmabile

acid /'æsɪd/ ① adj acido
② n acido m

acid drop n caramella f agli agrumi

acidic /ə'sɪdɪk/ adj acido

acidity /ə'sɪdətɪ/ n acidità f

acid rain n pioggia f acida

acid stomach n Med acidità f di stomaco

acid test n fig prova f del fuoco

✦ **acknowledge** /ək'nɒlɪdʒ/ vt riconoscere; rispondere a ‹greeting›; far cenno di aver notato ‹sb's presence›; ∼ receipt of accusare ricevuta di; ∼ defeat dichiararsi vinto

acknowledgement /ək'nɒlɪdʒmənt/ n riconoscimento m; send an ∼ of a letter confermare il ricevimento di una lettera

acme /'ækmɪ/ n the ∼ of l'apice m di

acne /'æknɪ/ n acne f

acorn /'eɪkɔ:n/ n ghianda f

acoustic /ə'ku:stɪk/ adj acustico

acoustically /ə'ku:stɪklɪ/ adv acusticamente

acoustic guitar n chitarra f acustica

acoustics /ə'ku:stɪks/ npl acustica fsg

acquaint /ə'kweɪnt/ vt ∼ somebody with metter qualcuno al corrente di

acquaintance /ə'kweɪntəns/ n ‹person› conoscente mf; make sb's ∼ fare la conoscenza di qualcuno

acquainted adj be ∼ with conoscere ‹person›; essere a conoscenza di ‹fact›; get or become ∼ with somebody fare conoscenza con qualcuno; get or become ∼ with something familiarizzare con qualcosa

acquiesce /ækwɪ'es/ vi acconsentire (to, in a)

acquiescence /ækwɪ'esəns/ n acquiescenza f

acquiescent /ækwɪ'esənt/ adj arrendevole

✦ **acquire** /ə'kwaɪə(r)/ vt acquisire

acquired /ə'kwaɪəd/ adj ‹characteristic› acquisito; it's an ∼ taste una cosa che si impara ad apprezzare

acquisition /ækwɪ'zɪʃn/ n acquisizione f

acquisitive /ə'kwɪzətɪv/ adj avido

acquit /ə'kwɪt/ vt (pt/pp acquitted) assolvere; ∼ oneself well cavarsela bene

acquittal /ə'kwɪtəl/ n assoluzione f

acre /'eɪkə(r)/ n acro m (= 4 047 m²)

acreage /'eɪkərɪdʒ/ n superficie f in acri

acrid /'ækrɪd/ adj acre

acrimonious /ækrɪ'məʊnɪəs/ adj aspro

acrimony /'ækrɪmənɪ/ n asprezza f

acrobat /'ækrəbæt/ n acrobata mf

acrobatic /ækrə'bætɪk/ adj acrobatico

acrobatics /ækrə'bætɪks/ npl acrobazie fpl

acronym /'ækrənɪm/ n acronimo m

✦ **across** /ə'krɒs/ ① adv dall'altra parte; (wide) in larghezza; (not lengthwise) attraverso; (in crossword) orizzontale; come ∼ something imbattersi in qualcosa; go ∼ attraversare
② prep (crosswise) di traverso su; (on the other side of) dall'altra parte di

---

✦ indicates a very frequent word

across-the-board ① *adj* generale
② *adv* in generale

acrylic /əˈkrɪlɪk/ ① *n* acrilico *m*
② *attrib* ‹garment› acrilico

⚹ **act** /ækt/ ① *n* atto *m*; (in variety show) numero *m*; **put on an ~** fam fare scena
② *vi* agire; (behave) comportarsi; Theat recitare; (pretend) fingere; **~ as** fare da
③ *vt* recitare ‹role›
■ **act for** *vi* agire per conto di
■ **act out** *vt* ‹part› recitare; ‹fantasy› mettere in atto
■ **act up** *vi* ‹child, photocopier› fare i capricci

acting /ˈæktɪŋ/ ① *adj* ‹deputy› provvisorio
② *n* Theat recitazione *f*; (profession) teatro *m*; **~ profession** professione *f* dell'attore

⚹ **action** /ˈækʃn/ *n* azione *f*; Mil combattimento *m*; Jur azione *f* legale; **out of ~** ‹machine› fuori uso; **take ~** agire; **~!** Cinema ciac si gira!

action group *n* gruppo *m* d'azione

action-packed *adj* ‹film› d'azione

action painting *n* pittura *f* d'azione

action plan *n* piano *m* d'azione

action replay *n* replay *m inv*

activate /ˈæktɪveɪt/ *vt* attivare; Chem, Phys rendere attivo

⚹ **active** /ˈæktɪv/ *adj* attivo

active duty, active service *n* Mil **be on ~** prestare servizio in zona di operazioni

actively /ˈæktɪvlɪ/ *adv* attivamente

activist /ˈæktɪvɪst/ *n* attivista *mf*

⚹ **activity** /ækˈtɪvɪtɪ/ *n* attività *f inv*

activity holiday *n* Br vacanza *f* con attività ricreative

act of God *n* causa *f* di forza maggiore

⚹ **actor** /ˈæktə(r)/ *n* attore *m*

actress /ˈæktrəs/ *n* attrice *f*

⚹ **actual** /ˈæktʃʊəl/ *adj* (real) reale

⚹ **actually** /ˈæktʃʊəlɪ/ *adv* in realtà

actuary /ˈæktʃʊərɪ/ *n* attuario, -a *mf*

acumen /ˈækjʊmən/ *n* acume *m*

acupuncture /ˈækjʊpʌŋktʃə(r)/ *n* agopuntura *f*

acupuncturist /ˈækjʊˈpʌŋktʃərɪst/ *n* agopuntore, -trice *mf*

acute /əˈkjuːt/ *adj* acuto; ‹shortage, hardship› estremo

acute accent *n* accento *m* acuto

acute angle *n* angolo *m* acuto

acutely /əˈkjuːtlɪ/ *adv* acutamente; ‹embarrassed, aware› estremamente

AD *abbr* (**Anno Domini**) d.C.

⚹ **ad** /æd/ *n* pubblicità *f inv*; (in paper) inserzione *f*, annuncio *m*

adage /ˈædɪdʒ/ *n* detto *m*, adagio *m*

adamant /ˈædəmənt/ *adj* categorico (**that** sul fatto che)

Adam's apple /ˈædəmz/ *n* pomo *m* di Adamo

adapt /əˈdæpt/ ① *vt* adattare ‹play›
② *vi* adattarsi

adaptability /ədæptəˈbɪlətɪ/ *n* adattabilità *f*

adaptable /əˈdæptəbl/ *adj* adattabile

adaptation /ædæpˈteɪʃn/ *n* Theat adattamento *m*

adapter, adaptor /əˈdæptə(r)/ *n* adattatore *m*; (two-way) presa *f* multipla

⚹ **add** /æd/ ① *vt* aggiungere; Math addizionare
② *vi* addizionare
■ **add in** *vt* (include) includere
■ **add on** *vt* aggiungere
■ **add to** *vi* fig (increase) aggravave
■ **add up** ① *vt* addizionare ‹figures›
② *vi* addizionare; **it doesn't ~ up** fig non quadra; **~ up to** ammontare a

added /ˈædɪd/ *adj* maggiore

adder /ˈædə(r)/ *n* vipera *f*

addict /ˈædɪkt/ *n* tossicodipendente *mf*; fig fanatico, -a *mf*

addicted /əˈdɪktɪd/ *adj* assuefatto (**to** a); **~ to drugs** tossicodipendente; **he's ~ to television** è videodipendente

addiction /əˈdɪkʃn/ *n* dipendenza *f*; (to drugs) tossicodipendenza *f*

addictive /əˈdɪktɪv/ *adj* **be ~** dare assuefazione

⚹ **addition** /əˈdɪʃn/ *adj* Math addizione *f*; (thing added) aggiunta *f*; **in ~** in aggiunta

⚹ **additional** /əˈdɪʃnəl/ *adj* supplementare

additionally /əˈdɪʃnəlɪ/ *adv* in più

additive /ˈædɪtɪv/ *n* additivo *m*

addled /ˈædld/ *adj* ‹thinking› confuso

add-on *adj* accessorio

⚹ **address** /əˈdrɛs/ ① *n* indirizzo *m*; (speech) discorso *m*; **form of ~** formula *f* di cortesia
② *vt* indirizzare; (speak to) rivolgersi a ‹person›; tenere un discorso a ‹meeting›

address book *n* rubrica *f*

addressee /ædrɛˈsiː/ *n* destinatario, -a *mf*

adenoids /ˈædənɔɪdz/ *npl* adenoidi *fpl*

adept /ˈædept/ *adj* esperto, -a *mf* (**at** in)

adequate /ˈædɪkwət/ *adj* adeguato

adequately /ˈædɪkwətlɪ/ *adv* adeguatamente

ADHD *abbr* (**Attention Deficit and Hyperactivity Disorder**) disturbo *m* da deficit dell'attenzione con iperattività

adhere /ədˈhɪə(r)/ *vi* aderire; **~ to** attenersi a ‹principles, rules›

adherence /ədˈhɪərəns/ *n* fedeltà *f*

adherent /ədˈhɪərənt/ *n* (of doctrine) adepto, -a *mf*; (of policy) sostenitore, -trice *mf*; (of cult) seguace *mf*

adhesion /ədˈhiːʒn/ *n* adesione *f*

adhesive /ədˈhiːsɪv/ ① *adj* adesivo
② *n* adesivo *m*

ad hoc /æd'hɒk/ *adj ‹alliance, arrangement›* ad hoc; *‹committee, legislation›* apposito; **on an ∼ basis** secondo le esigenze del momento

adieu /ə'dju:/ *n* **bid somebody ∼** dire addio a qualcuno

ad infinitum /ædɪnfɪ'naɪtəm/ *adv ‹continue›* all'infinito

adjacent /ə'dʒeɪsənt/ *adj* adiacente

adjective /'ædʒɪktɪv/ *n* aggettivo *m*

adjoin /ə'dʒɔɪn/ *vt* essere adiacente a

adjoining /ə'dʒɔɪnɪŋ/ *adj* adiacente

adjourn /ə'dʒɜːn/ *vt* aggiornare **(until a)**

adjournment /ə'dʒɜːnmənt/ *n* aggiornamento *m*

adjudge /ə'dʒʌdʒ/ *vt* Jur (decree) giudicare; aggiudicare *‹costs, damages›*

adjudicate /ə'dʒuːdɪkeɪt/ *vi* decidere; (in competition) giudicare

adjudicator /ə'dʒuːdɪkeɪtə(r)/ *n* giudice *m*, arbitro *m*

adjunct /'ædʒʌnkt/ *n* aggiunta *f*; hum (person) appendice *f*

adjust /ə'dʒʌst/ **1** *vt* modificare; regolare *‹focus, sound etc›*
2 *vi* adattarsi

adjustable /ə'dʒʌstəbl/ *adj* regolabile

adjustable spanner *n* chiave *f* [inglese] a rullino

adjustment /ə'dʒʌstmənt/ *n* adattamento *m*; Techn regolamento *m*

adjutant /'ædʒʊtənt/ *n* Mil aiutante *mf*

ad lib /æd'lɪb/ **1** *adj* improvvisato
2 *adv* a piacere
3 *vi* (*pt/pp* **ad libbed**) fam improvvisare

adman /'ædmæn/ *n* fam pubblicitario *m*

admin /'ædmɪn/ *n* Br fam amministrazione *f*

administer /əd'mɪnɪstə(r)/ *vt* amministrare; somministrare *‹medicine›*

❖ **administration** /ədmɪnɪ'streɪʃn/ *n* amministrazione *f*; Pol governo *m*

administration costs *n* costi *mpl* di gestione

administrative /əd'mɪnɪstrətɪv/ *adj* amministrativo

administrator /əd'mɪnɪstreɪtə(r)/ *n* amministratore, -trice *mf*

admirable /'ædmərəbl/ *adj* ammirevole

admiral /'ædmərəl/ *n* ammiraglio *m*

admiralty /'ædmɪrəltɪ/ *n* Br ministero (*m*) *della marina militare britannica*

admiration /ædmə'reɪʃn/ *n* ammirazione *f*

admire /əd'maɪə(r)/ *vt* ammirare

admirer /əd'maɪrə(r)/ *n* ammiratore, -trice *mf*

admiring /əd'maɪrɪŋ/ *adj ‹person›* pieno d'ammirazione; *‹look›* ammirativo

admiringly /əd'maɪrɪŋlɪ/ *adv ‹look, say›* con ammirazione

admissible /əd'mɪsəbl/ *adj* ammissibile

admission /əd'mɪʃn/ *n* ammissione *f*; (to hospital) ricovero *m*; (entry) ingresso *m*

admissions office *n* Univ segreteria *f* studenti

❖ **admit** /əd'mɪt/ **1** *vt* (*pt/pp* **admitted**) (let in) far entrare; (to hospital) ricoverare; (acknowledge) ammettere
2 *vi* ∼ **to something** ammettere qualcosa

admittance /əd'mɪtəns/ *n* ammissione *f*; **'no ∼'** 'vietato l'ingresso'

admittedly /əd'mɪtɪdlɪ/ *adv* bisogna riconoscerlo

admonish /əd'mɒnɪʃ/ *vt* ammonire

admonition /ædmə'nɪʃn/ *n* ammonimento *m*

ad nauseam /æd'nɔːzɪæm/ *adv ‹discuss, repeat›* fino alla nausea

ado /ə'du:/ *n* **without more ∼** senza ulteriori indugi

adolescence /ædə'lesns/ *n* adolescenza *f*

adolescent /ædə'lesnt/ *adj & n* adolescente *mf*

❖ **adopt** /ə'dɒpt/ *vt* adottare; Pol scegliere *‹candidate›*

adopted /ə'dɒptɪd/ *adj ‹son, daughter›* adottivo

adoption /ə'dɒpʃn/ *n* adozione *f*

adoption agency *n* agenzia *f* di adozioni

adoptive /ə'dɒptɪv/ *adj* adottivo

adorable /ə'dɔːrəbl/ *adj* adorabile

adoration /ædə'reɪʃn/ *n* adorazione *f*

adore /ə'dɔː(r)/ *vt* adorare

adoring /ə'dɔːrɪŋ/ *adj ‹fan›* in adorazione; **she has an ∼ husband** ha un marito che la adora

adoringly /ə'dɔːrɪŋlɪ/ *adv* con adorazione

adorn /ə'dɔːn/ *vt* adornare

adornment /ə'dɔːnmənt/ *n* ornamento *m*

adrenalin /ə'drenəlɪn/ *n* adrenalina *f*

Adriatic /eɪdrɪ'ætɪk/ *adj & n* **the ∼ [Sea]** il mare Adriatico, l'Adriatico *m*

adrift /ə'drɪft/ *adj* alla deriva; **be ∼** andare alla deriva; **come ∼** staccarsi

adroit /ə'drɔɪt/ *adj* abile

adroitly /ə'drɔɪtlɪ/ *adv* abilmente

ADSL *abbr* (**Asymmetric Digital Subscriber Line**) ADSL *f*

adulation /ædjʊ'leɪʃn/ *n* adulazione *f*

❖ **adult** /'ædʌlt/ *n* adulto, -a *mf*

Adult Education *n* Br ≈ corsi *mpl* serali

adulterate /ə'dʌltəreɪt/ *vt* adulterare *‹wine›*

adulterated /ə'dʌltəreɪtɪd/ *adj ‹wine›* adulterato

❖ indicates a very frequent word

adulterous /ə'dʌltərəs/ *adj ‹relationship›*
adulterino; *‹person›* adultero

adultery /ə'dʌltərɪ/ *n* adulterio *m*

adulthood /'ædʌlthʊd/ *n* età *f* adulta

adult literacy classes *n* Br corso *m* di
alfabetizzazione per adulti

advance /əd'vɑːns/ ① *n* avanzamento *m*;
Mil avanzata *f*; (payment) anticipo *m*; **in ∼** in
anticipo
② *vi* avanzare; (make progress) fare
progressi
③ *vt* promuovere *‹cause›*; avanzare *‹theory›*;
anticipare *‹money›*

advance booking *n* prenotazione *f* [in
anticipo]

advance booking office *n* ufficio *m*
prenotazioni

advanced /əd'vɑːnst/ *adj* avanzato

Advanced Level *n* Br Sch = A-LEVEL

advanced search *n* Comput ricerca
f avanzata; **∼ option** opzione *f* ricerca
avanzata

advancement /əd'vɑːnəmənt/ *n*
promozione *f*

advance notice *n* preannuncio *m*

advance party *n* Mil avanguardia *f*

advance payment *n* Comm pagamento
m anticipato

advance warning *n* preavviso *m*

✔ **advantage** /əd'vɑːntɪdʒ/ *n* vantaggio *m*;
take ∼ of approfittare di

advantageous /ædvən'teɪdʒəs/ *adj*
vantaggioso

advent /'ædvent/ *n* avvento *m*; **A∼** Relig
Avvento *m*

adventure /əd'ventʃə(r)/ *n* avventura *f*

adventure holiday *n* vacanza *f*
avventura

adventure playground *n* Br parco *m*
giochi

adventurer /əd'ventʃərə(r)/ *n*
avventuriero, -a *mf*

adventuress /əd'ventʃərɪs/ *n*
avventuriera *f*

adventurous /əd'ventʃərəs/ *adj*
avventuroso

adverb /'ædvɜːb/ *n* avverbio *m*

adversary /'ædvəsərɪ/ *n* avversario, -a *mf*

adverse /'ædvɜːs/ *adj* avverso

adversity /əd'vɜːsətɪ/ *n* avversità *f*

advert /'ædvɜːt/ *n* fam = ADVERTISEMENT

advertise /'ædvətaɪz/ ① *vt* reclamizzare;
mettere un annuncio per *‹job, flat›*
② *vi* fare pubblicità; (for job, flat) mettere un
annuncio

advertisement /əd'vɜːtɪsmənt/ *n*
pubblicità *f inv*; (in paper) inserzione *f*,
annuncio *m*

advertiser /'ædvətaɪzə(r)/ *n* (in newspaper)
inserzionista *mf*

advertising /'ædvətaɪzɪŋ/ ① *n*
pubblicità *f*
② *attrib* pubblicitario

advertising agency *n* agenzia *f*
pubblicitaria

advertising campaign *n* campagna *f*
pubblicitaria

advertising executive *n* dirigente *mf*
pubblicitario, -a

advertising industry *n* settore *m*
pubblicitario

Advertising Standards Authority
n Br *organo (m) di controllo sulla pubblicità*

✔ **advice** /əd'vaɪs/ *n* consigli *mpl*; **piece of ∼**
consiglio *m*

advice centre *n* centro *m* di consulenza

advice note *n* avviso *m*

advice slip *n* avviso *m* di accreditamento

advisability /ədvaɪzə'bɪlətɪ/ *n*
opportunità *f*

advisable /əd'vaɪzəbl/ *adj* consigliabile

✔ **advise** /əd'vaɪz/ *vt* consigliare; (inform)
avvisare; **∼ somebody to do something**
consigliare a qualcuno di fare qualcosa;
∼ somebody against something
sconsigliare qualcosa a qualcuno

advisedly /əd'vaɪzɪdlɪ/ *adv ‹say›*
deliberatamente

adviser /əd'vaɪzə(r)/ *n* consulente *mf*

advisory /əd'vaɪzərɪ/ *adj* consultivo

advisory committee *n* comitato *m*
consultivo

advisory service *n* servizio *m* di
consulenza; **pensions/immigration/
pregnancy ∼** servizio di consulenza
in materia di pensioni/immigrazione/
gravidanza

advocacy /'ædvəkəsɪ/ *n* appoggio *m*

advocate¹ /'ædvəkət/ *n* (supporter) fautore,
-trice *mf*

advocate² /'ædvəkeɪt/ *vt* propugnare

Aegean /ɪ'dʒiːən/ *n* **the ∼** l'Egeo *m*

aegis /'iːdʒɪs/ *n* **under the ∼ of** sotto l'egida
di

aeon /'iːən/ *n* **∼s ago** milioni *mpl* e milioni
di anni fa

AER *n abbr* (**Annual Equivalence
Rate**) TAN *m*

aerate /'eəreɪt/ *vt* aerare; addizionare
anidride carbonica a *‹water›*

aerial /'eərɪəl/ ① *adj* aereo
② *n* antenna *f*

aerial camera *n* macchina *f* fotografica
per fotografie aeree

aerial photography *n* fotografia *f* aerea

aerial warfare *n* guerra *f* aerea

aerie /'eərɪ/ *n* Am (eyrie) nido *m* [d'aquila]

aerobatics /eərə'bætɪks/ *npl* (manoeuvres)
acrobazie *fpl* aeree

aerobics /eə'rəʊbɪks/ *n* aerobica *fsg*

a

aerodrome /'eərədrəum/ n aerodromo m

aerodynamic /eərəudaɪ'næmɪk/ adj aerodinamico

aerodynamics /eərəudaɪ'næmɪks/ n aerodinamica f

aerogram[me] /'eərəugræm/ n aerogramma m

aeronautic[al] /eərə'nɔːtɪk[əl]/ adj aeronautico

aeronautic[al] engineer n ingegnere m aeronautico

aeronautic[al] engineering n ingegneria f aeronautica

aeronautics /eərə'nɔːtɪks/ n aeronautica f

aeroplane /'eərəpleɪn/ n aeroplano m

aerosol /'eərəsɒl/ n bomboletta f spray

aerospace /'eərəspeɪs/ [1] n (industry) industria f aerospaziale
[2] attrib ‹engineer, company› aerospaziale

aesthete /'iːsθiːt/ n esteta mf

aesthetic /iːs'θetɪk/ adj estetico

aesthetically /iːs'θetɪklɪ/ adv ‹restore› con gusto; ‹satisfying› esteticamente

aestheticism /iːs'θetɪsɪzm/ n (taste) estetica f; (doctrine, quality) estetismo m

aesthetics /iːs'θetɪks/ n estetica f

afar /ə'fɑː(r)/ adv from ∼ da lontano

affable /'æfəbl/ adj affabile

affably /'æfəblɪ/ adv affabilmente

⚘ **affair** /ə'feə(r)/ n affare m; (scandal) caso m; (sexual) relazione f

⚘ **affect** /ə'fekt/ vt influire su; (emotionally) colpire; (concern) riguardare; (pretend) affettare

affectation /æfek'teɪʃn/ n affettazione f

affected /ə'fektɪd/ adj affettato

affectedly /ə'fektɪdlɪ/ adv ‹talk› con affettazione

affection /ə'fekʃn/ n affetto m

affectionate /ə'fekʃnət/ adj affettuoso

affectionately /ə'fekʃnətlɪ/ adv affettuosamente

affidavit /æfr'deɪvɪt/ n affidavit m inv (dichiarazione scritta e giurata davanti a un pubblico ufficiale)

affiliated /ə'fɪlɪeɪtɪd/ adj affiliato

affiliation /ə'fɪlɪ'eɪʃn/ n (process, state) affiliazione f; (link) legame m

affinity /ə'fɪnətɪ/ n affinità f inv

affinity card n carta (f) di credito destinata ad una causa sociale

affirm /ə'fɜːm/ vt affermare; Jur dichiarare solennemente

affirmative /ə'fɜːmətɪv/ [1] adj affermativo
[2] n in the ∼ affermativamente

affix /ə'fɪks/ vt affiggere; apporre ‹signature›

⚘ indicates a very frequent word

afflict /ə'flɪkt/ vt affliggere

affliction /ə'flɪkʃn/ n afflizione f

affluence /'æfluəns/ n agiatezza f

affluent /'æfluənt/ adj agiato

⚘ **afford** /ə'fɔːd/ vt (provide) fornire; **be able to ∼ something** potersi permettere qualcosa

affordable /ə'fɔːdəbl/ adj abbordabile

affray /ə'freɪ/ n rissa f

affront /ə'frʌnt/ [1] n affronto m
[2] vt fare un affronto a

Afghan /'æfgæn/ n (person) afgano, -a mf; (language) afgano m; (coat) pelliccotto m afgano

Afghan hound n levriero m afgano

Afghanistan /æf'gænɪstæn/ n Afganistan m

aficionado /æfɪsjə'nɑːdəu/ n aficionado, -a mf

afield /ə'fiːld/ adv **further ∼** più lontano

aflame /ə'fleɪm/ adj & adv liter in fiamme, sfolgorante; **be ∼** ‹cheek› essere in fiamme; **be ∼ with desire** ardere dal desiderio

afloat /ə'fləut/ adj a galla

afoot /ə'fut/ adj **there's something ∼** si sta preparando qualcosa

aforesaid /ə'fɔːsed/ adj Jur suddetto

⚘ **afraid** /ə'freɪd/ adj **be ∼** aver paura; **I'm ∼ not** purtroppo no; **I'm ∼ so** temo di sì; **I'm ∼ I can't help you** mi dispiace ma non posso esserle d'aiuto

afresh /ə'freʃ/ adv da capo

Africa /'æfrɪkə/ n Africa f

⚘ **African** /'æfrɪkən/ adj & n africano, -a mf

African-American n afroamericano, -a mf

Afrikaans /æfrɪ'kɑːns/ n afrikaans m

Afrikaner /æfrɪ'kɑːnə(r)/ n boero, -a mf

Afro-American /æfrəuə'merɪkən/ adj & n afroamericano, -a mf

Afro-Caribbean /æfrəukærə'bɪən/ adj & n afrocaraibico, -a mf

aft /ɑːft/ adv Naut a poppa; (towards the stern) verso poppa

⚘ **after** /'ɑːftə(r)/ [1] adv dopo; **the day ∼** il giorno dopo; **be ∼** cercare
[2] prep dopo; **∼ all** dopotutto; **the day ∼ tomorrow** dopodomani
[3] conj dopo che

afterbirth n residui mpl di placenta

aftercare n Med ospedalizzazione f domiciliare

after-dinner speaker n persona (f) invitata a tenere un discorso dopo una cena o un ricevimento

after-effect n conseguenza f

afterlife n vita f nell'aldilà

aftermath /'ɑːftəmɑːθ/ n conseguenze fpl; **the ∼ of war** il dopoguerra; **in the ∼ of** nel periodo successivo a

afternoon n pomeriggio m; **good ~!** buon giorno!

afternoon tea n merenda f

afterpains npl dolori mpl post-parto

after-sales service n servizio m assistenza clienti

after-school adj doposcuola; **~ club/activities** club/attività doposcuola

aftershave n [lozione f] dopobarba m inv

aftershock n fig effetti mpl

aftersun n & adj doposole m inv.

aftertaste n retrogusto m

after-tax adj ‹profits, earnings› al netto

afterthought n added as an ~ aggiunto in un secondo momento; **as an ~, why not...?** ripensandoci bene, perché non...?

afterwards /'ɑːftəwədz/ adv in seguito

✐ **again** /ə'geɪn/ adv di nuovo; [then] ~ (besides) inoltre; (on the other hand) d'altra parte; **~ and ~** continuamente

✐ **against** /ə'geɪnst/ prep contro

✐ **age** /eɪdʒ/ [1] n età f inv; (era) era f; **~ s** fam secoli; **~s ago** fam secoli fa; **what ~ are you?** quanti anni hai?; **be under ~** non avere l'età richiesta; **he's two years of ~** ha due anni [2] vt/i (pres p **ageing**) invecchiare

age bracket, age group n fascia f d'età

aged¹ /eɪdʒd/ adj ~ **two** di due anni

aged² /'eɪdʒɪd/ [1] adj anziano [2] n the ~ pl gli anziani

aged debt n Fin somma f in scadenza

age discrimination n discriminazione f in base all'età

ageing /'eɪdʒɪŋ/ [1] n invecchiamento m [2] adj ‹person, population› che sta invecchiando

ageism /'eɪdʒɪzm/ n discriminazione f contro chi non è più giovane

ageless /'eɪdʒlɪs/ adj senza età

✐ **agency** /'eɪdʒənsɪ/ n agenzia f; **have the ~ for** essere un concessionario di

agency-fee n commissione f

agency-nurse n infermiere, -a mf privato, -a

✐ **agenda** /ə'dʒendə/ n ordine m del giorno; **on the ~** all'ordine del giorno; fig in programma

✐ **agent** /'eɪdʒənt/ n agente mf

age-old adj secolare

age range n fascia f d'età

aggravate /'ægrəveɪt/ vt aggravare; (annoy) esasperare

aggravating /'ægrəveɪtɪŋ/ adj Jur aggravante; fam (irritating) irritante

aggravation /ægrə'veɪʃn/ n aggravamento m; (annoyance) esasperazione f

aggregate /'ægrɪgət/ [1] adj totale

[2] n totale m; **on ~** nel complesso

aggression /ə'greʃn/ n aggressione f

aggressive /ə'gresɪv/ adj aggressivo

aggressively /ə'gresɪvlɪ/ adv aggressivamente

aggressiveness /ə'gresɪvnɪs/ n aggressività f

aggressor /ə'gresə(r)/ n aggressore m

aggrieved /ə'griːvd/ adj risentito

aggro /'ægrəʊ/ n fam aggressività f; (problems) grane fpl

aghast /ə'gɑːst/ adj inorridito

agile /'ædʒaɪl/ adj agile

agility /ə'dʒɪlətɪ/ n agilità f

agitate /'ædʒɪteɪt/ [1] vt mettere in agitazione; (shake) agitare [2] vi fig ~ **for** creare delle agitazioni per

agitated /'ædʒɪteɪtɪd/ adj agitato

agitation /ædʒɪ'teɪʃn/ n agitazione f

agitator /'ædʒɪteɪtə(r)/ n agitatore, -trice mf

AGM n abbr (**annual general meeting**) assemblea f generale annuale

agnostic /æg'nɒstɪk/ adj & n agnostico, -a mf

✐ **ago** /ə'gəʊ/ adv fa; **a long time/a month ~** molto tempo/un mese fa; **how long ~ was it?** quanto tempo fa è successo?

agog /ə'gɒg/ adj eccitato

agonize /'ægənaɪz/ vi angosciarsi (**over** per)

agonized /'ægənaɪzd/ adj ‹expression, cry› angosciato

agonizing /'ægənaɪzɪŋ/ adj angosciante

agony /'ægənɪ/ n agonia f; (mental) angoscia f; **be in ~** avere dei dolori atroci

agony aunt n persona (f) chi tiene la posta del cuore in una rivista

agoraphobia /ægərə'fəʊbɪə/ n agorafobia f

agoraphobic /ægərə'fəʊbɪk/ adj agorafobo, -a mf

✐ **agree** /ə'griː/ [1] vt accordarsi su; **~ to do something** accettare di fare qualcosa; **~ that** essere d'accordo [sul fatto] che [2] vi essere d'accordo; ‹figures› concordare; (reach agreement) mettersi d'accordo; (get on) andare d'accordo; (consent) acconsentire (**to** a); **it doesn't ~ with me** mi fa male; **~ with something** (approve of) approvare qualcosa

agreeable /ə'griːəbl/ adj gradevole; (willing) d'accordo

agreeably /ə'griːəblɪ/ adv (pleasantly) piacevolmente; (amicably) in modo amichevole

agreed /ə'griːd/ adj convenuto

✐ **agreement** /ə'griːmənt/ n accordo m; **in ~** d'accordo; **reach ~** arrivare ad un accordo

agricultural /ægrɪ'kʌltʃərəl/ adj agricolo

agriculturalist /ægrɪ'kʌltʃərəlɪst/ n
agronomo, -a mf

agricultural show n fiera f agricola

agriculture /'ægrɪkʌltʃə(r)/ n agricoltura
f

agritourism /ægrɪ'tʊərɪzəm/ n
agriturismo m

agronomy /ə'grɒnəmɪ/ n agronomia f

aground /ə'graʊnd/ adv run ∼ ‹ship›
arenarsi

ah /ɑː/ int ∼ well! (resignedly) va bene!

⚐ **ahead** /ə'hed/ adv essere ∼ of essere
davanti a; fig essere avanti rispetto a;
draw ∼ passare davanti (of a); go on
∼ cominciare ad andare; get ∼ ‹in life›
riuscire; go ∼! fai pure!; look ∼ pensare
all'avvenire; plan ∼ fare progetti per
l'avvenire

⚐ **aid** /eɪd/ ① n aiuto m; in ∼ of a favore di
② vt aiutare

aid agency n organizzazione f
umanitaria

aide n assistente mf

aid package n pacco m umanitario

Aids /eɪdz/ n AIDS m

Aids awareness n sensibilizzazione f
all'AIDS

aid worker n cooperante mf

ailing /'eɪlɪŋ/ adj malato

ailment /'eɪlmənt/ n disturbo m

aim /eɪm/ ① n mira f; fig scopo m; take ∼
prendere la mira
② vt puntare ‹gun› (at su)
③ vi mirare; ∼ to do something aspirare a
fare qualcosa

aimless /'eɪmlɪs/ adj senza scopo

aimlessly /'eɪmlɪslɪ/ adv senza scopo

ain't /eɪnt/ fam am not; are not; have not;
has not

⚐ **air** /eə(r)/ ① n aria f; be on the ∼
‹programme› essere in onda; put on ∼s
darsi delle arie; by ∼ in aereo; (airmail) per
via aerea
② vt arieggiare; far conoscere ‹views›; pej
sfoggiare ‹knowledge›

air ambulance n aereo m ambulanza;
(helicopter) eliambulanza f

air attack n attacco m aereo

air bag n Auto air bag m inv

air bed n materassino m [gonfiabile]

airborne /'eəbɔːn/ adj (plane) in volo;
‹troops› aerotrasportato

airbrush n aerografo m

air bubble n (in liquid, plastic, wallpaper) bolla
f d'aria

air-conditioned adj con aria
condizionata

air conditioner n condizionatore m

air-conditioning n aria f condizionata

air-cooled adj ‹engine› raffreddato ad aria

air cover n protezione f aerea

⚐ **aircraft** n aereo m

aircraft carrier n portaerei f inv

aircraft[s]man n Br aviere m

air crash n disastro m aereo

aircrew n equipaggio m di volo

air cushion n (inflatable cushion) cuscino m
gonfiabile; (of hovercraft) cuscino m d'aria

air disaster n disastro m aereo

air display n esibizione f in volo

airdrop n lancio m con paracadute

air duct n condotto m dell'aria

air exclusion zone n zona f di
esclusione aerea

airfare n tariffa f aerea

airfield n campo m d'aviazione

airflow n spostamento m d'aria

air force n aviazione f

airfreight n (goods) merce f spedita via
aerea; (method of transport) trasporto m aereo;
(charge) costo m per trasporto aereo

air-freshener n deodorante m per
ambienti

air gun n fucile m ad aria compressa

airhead n fam svampito, -a mf

air hole n sfiatatoio m

air hostess n hostess f inv

airing /'eərɪŋ/ n give a room an ∼
arieggiare una stanza; give an idea an ∼ fig
ventilare un'idea

airing cupboard n Br sgabuzzino (m) del
boiler dove viene riposta la biancheria ad
asciugare

airless /'eəlɪs/ adj ‹evening› senza vento;
‹room› poco ventilato

air letter n aerogramma m

airlift ① vt trasportare con ponte aereo
② n ponte m aereo

airline n compagnia f aerea

airliner n aereo m di linea

airlock n bolla f d'aria

airmail n posta f aerea

air marshal n Br maresciallo m
d'aviazione

Air Miles® npl Br miglia fpl aeree

airplane n Am aereo m

air pocket n vuoto m d'aria

⚐ **airport** n aeroporto m

air power n potenza f aerea

air raid n incursione f aerea

air-raid shelter n rifugio m antiaereo

air-raid siren n allarme m aereo

air-raid warning n allarme m aereo

air rifle n fucile m ad aria compressa

air-sea rescue n salvataggio (m) dal
mare con impiego di mezzi aerei

⚐ indicates a very frequent word

air shaft n (in mine) pozzo m di ventilazione

airship n dirigibile m

air show n (trade exhibition) salone m dell'aviazione; (flying show) manifestazione f aerea

airsickness n mal m d'aereo

air sock n manica f a vento

airspeed n velocità f relativa all'aria

airspeed indicator n indicatore m di velocità (su un aereo)

air steward n steward m inv

air stewardess n hostess f inv

airstream n corrente f d'aria

airstrike n incursione f aerea

airstrip n pista f d'atterraggio

air terminal n (in town, terminus) [air-] terminal m inv

airtight adj ermetico

airtime n Radio, TV spazio m radiofonico/ televisivo

air-to-air adj ‹missile› aria-aria; ‹refuelling› in volo

air traffic n traffico m aereo

air-traffic controller n controllore m di volo

air travel n viaggi mpl in aereo

air valve n valvola f pneumatica

air vent n presa f d'aria

air vice-marshal n Br vice-maresciallo m dell'aviazione

air war n conflitto m aereo

airwaves npl Radio, TV onde fpl radio

airway n (route) rotta f aerea; (airline) compagnia f aerea; Anat via f respiratoria; (ventilating passage) pozzo m di ventilazione

air waybill n polizza f di carico aerea

airworthiness n idoneità f di volo

airworthy adj idoneo al volo

airy /'eərɪ/ adj (-ier, -iest) arieggiato; ‹manner› noncurante

airy-fairy /eərɪ'feərɪ/ adj Br fam ‹plan, person› fuori dalla realtà

aisle /aɪl/ n corridoio m; (in supermarket) corsia f; (in church) navata f

ajar /ə'dʒɑː(r)/ adj socchiuso

aka abbr (**also known as**) alias

akin /ə'kɪn/ adj ∼ to simile a

AI n abbr (**artificial intelligence**) I.A. f

alabaster /'æləbɑːstə(r)/ n alabastro m

alacrity /ə'lækrətɪ/ n alacrità f inv

alarm /ə'lɑːm/ [1] n allarme m; **set the** ∼ (of alarm clock) mettere la sveglia; **in** ∼ in stato di allarme
[2] vt allarmare; **don't be** ∼**ed!** non si allarmi!

alarm bell n campanello m d'allarme; **set the** ∼**s ringing** n Br fig far scattare il campanello d'allarme

alarm call n Teleph sveglia f automatica

alarm clock n sveglia f

alarmed /ə'lɑːmd/ adj allarmato

alarming /ə'lɑːmɪŋ/ adj allarmante, preoccupante

alarmist /ə'lɑːmɪst/ adj & n allarmista mf

alas /ə'læs/ int ahimè

Albania /æl'beɪnɪə/ n Albania f

Albanian /æl'beɪnɪən/ [1] n (person) albanese mf; (language) albanese m
[2] adj albanese

albatross /'ælbətrɒs/ n (also in golf) albatro m

albeit /ɔːl'biːɪt/ adv & conj benché

albino /æl'biːnəʊ/ adj & n albino, -a mf

✎ **album** /'ælbəm/ n album m inv

albumen /'ælbjʊmɪn/ n Biol, Bot albume m

alchemist /'ælkɪmɪst/ n alchimista m

alchemy /'ælkɪmɪ/ n Chem fig alchimia f

✎ **alcohol** /'ælkəhɒl/ n alcol m

alcoholic /ælkə'hɒlɪk/ [1] adj alcolico
[2] n alcolizzato, -a mf

Alcoholics Anonymous n Anonima f Alcolisti

alcoholism /'ælkəhɒlɪzm/ n alcolismo m

alcohol-related adj ‹illness, disease› legato al consumo di alcol

alcopop /'ælkəʊpɒp/ n bibita f alcolica

alcove /'ælkəʊv/ n alcova f

alder /'ɔːldə(r)/ n (tree, wood) ontano m

ale /eɪl/ n birra f

alert /ə'lɜːt/ [1] adj attento; (watchful) vigile
[2] n segnale m d'allarme; **be on the** ∼ stare allerta
[3] vt allertare

alertness /ə'lɜːtnɪs/ n (attentiveness) attenzione f; (liveliness) vivacità f

A-level n Br Sch ∼s ≈ esami mpl di maturità; **he got an** ∼ **in history** ha portato storia alla maturità

Alexandria /ælɪg'zændrɪə/ n Alessandria f [d'Egitto]

alfalfa /æl'fælfə/ n erba f medicinale

alfresco /æl'freskəʊ/ adj & adv all'aperto

algae /'ældʒiː/ npl alghe fpl

algebra /'ældʒɪbrə/ n algebra f

Algeria /æl'dʒɪərɪə/ n Algeria f

Algerian /æl'dʒɪərɪən/ adj & n algerino, -a mf

Algiers /æl'dʒɪəz/ n Algeri f

algorithm /'ælgərɪðm/ n algoritmo m

alias /'eɪlɪəs/ [1] n pseudonimo m
[2] adv alias

alibi /'ælɪbaɪ/ n alibi m inv

alien /'eɪlɪən/ [1] adj straniero; fig estraneo
[2] n straniero, -a mf; (from space) alieno, -a mf

alienate /'eɪlɪəneɪt/ vt alienare

alienation /eɪlɪə'neɪʃn/ n alienazione f

alight¹ /ə'laɪt/ vi scendere; ‹bird› posarsi

a

alight² *adj* be ∼ essere in fiamme; **set** ∼ dar fuoco a

align /ə'laɪn/ *vt* allineare

alignment /ə'laɪnmənt/ *n* allineamento *m*; **out of** ∼ non allineato

alike /ə'laɪk/ ① *adj* simile; **be** ∼ rassomigliarsi
② *adv* in modo simile; **look** ∼ rassomigliarsi; **summer and winter** ∼ sia d'estate che d'inverno

alimentary /ælɪ'mentərɪ/ *adj* ‹system› digerente; ‹process› digestivo

alimentary canal *n* tubo *m* digerente

alimony /'ælɪmənɪ/ *n* alimenti *mpl*

♂ **alive** /ə'laɪv/ *adj* vivo; ∼ **with** brulicante di; ∼ **to** sensibile a; ∼ **and kicking** vivo e vegeto

alkali /'ælkəlaɪ/ *n* alcali *m*

alkaline /'ælkəlaɪn/ *adj* alcalino

♂ **all** /ɔːl/ ① *adj* tutto; ∼ **the children,** ∼ **children** tutti i bambini; ∼ **day** tutto il giorno; **he refused** ∼ **help** ha rifiutato qualsiasi aiuto; **for** ∼ **that** (nevertheless) perciò; **in** ∼ **sincerity** in tutta sincerità; **be** ∼ **for** essere favorevole a
② *pron* tutto; ∼ **of you/them** tutti voi/loro; ∼ **of it** tutto; ∼**of the town** tutta la città; ∼ **but one** tutti tranne uno; **in** ∼ in tutto; ∼ **in** ∼ tutto sommato; **most of** ∼ più di ogni altra cosa; **once and for** ∼ una volta per tutte; ∼ **being well** salvo complicazioni
③ *adv* completamente; ∼ **but** quasi; ∼ **at once** (at the same time) tutto in una volta; ∼ **at once,** ∼ **of a sudden** all'improvviso; ∼ **too soon** troppo presto; ∼ **the same** (nevertheless) ciononostante; ∼ **the better** meglio ancora; **she's not** ∼ **that good an actress** non è poi così brava come attrice; ∼ **in** in tutto; fam esausto; **thirty/three** ∼ (in sport) trenta/tré pari; ∼ **over** (finished) tutto finito; (everywhere) dappertutto; **it's** ∼ **right** (I don't mind) non fa niente; **I'm** ∼ **right** (not hurt) non ho niente; ∼ **right!** va bene!; **be** ∼ **that** fam esp Am essere in gamba

all-American *adj* ‹record, champion› americano; ‹girl, boy, hero› tipicamente americano

all-around *adj* Am ‹improvement› generale

allay /ə'leɪ/ *vt* placare ‹suspicions, anger›

all-clear *n* Mil cessato *m* allarme/pericolo; (from doctor) autorizzazione *f*; **give somebody the** ∼ fig dare il via libera a qualcuno

all-consuming *adj* ‹passion› sfrenato; ‹ambition› smisurato

all-day *adj* ‹event› che dura tutto il giorno

allegation /ælɪ'geɪʃn/ *n* accusa *f*

♂ **allege** /ə'ledʒ/ *vt* dichiarare

alleged /ə'ledʒd/ *adj* presunto

allegedly /ə'ledʒɪdlɪ/ *adv* a quanto si dice

allegiance /ə'liːdʒəns/ *n* fedeltà *f*

allegorical /ælɪ'gɒrɪkl/ *adj* allegorico

allegory /'ælɪgərɪ/ *n* allegoria *f*

all-embracing /-əm'breɪsɪŋ/ *adj* globale

allergic /ə'lɜːdʒɪk/ *adj* allergico

allergist /'ælədʒɪst/ *n* allergologo, -a *mf*

allergy /'ælədʒɪ/ *n* allergia *f*

allergy clinic *n* clinica *f* di allergologia

alleviate /ə'liːvɪeɪt/ *vt* alleviare

alleviation /əliːvɪ'eɪʃn/ *n* alleviamento *m*, alleggerimento *m*

alley /'ælɪ/ *n* vicolo *m*; (for bowling) corsia *f*

alleyway /'ælɪweɪ/ *n* vicolo *m*

all-found *adj* £200 ∼ 200 sterline inclusi vitto e alloggio

alliance /ə'laɪəns/ *n* alleanza *f*

allied /'ælaɪd/ *adj* alleato; fig (related) connesso (**to** a)

alligator /'ælɪgeɪtə(r)/ *n* alligatore *m*

all-important *adj* essenziale

all in *adj* Br fam (exhausted) distrutto; ‹fee, price› tutto compreso

all-inclusive *adj* (fee, price) tutto compreso

all-in-one *adj* ‹garment› in un pezzo solo

all-in wresting *n* Sport catch *m*

all-night *adj* ‹party, meeting› che dura tutta la notte; ‹radio station› che trasmette tutta la notte; ‹service› notturno

allocate /'æləkeɪt/ *vt* assegnare; distribuire ‹resources›

allocation /ælə'keɪʃn/ *n* assegnazione *f*; (of resources) distribuzione *f*

all-or-nothing *adj* ‹approach, policy› senza vie di mezzo

allot /ə'lɒt/ *vt* (*pt/pp* **allotted**) distribuire

allotment /ə'lɒtmənt/ *n* distribuzione *f*; (share) parte *f*; (land) piccolo lotto *m* di terreno

all-out ① *adj* ‹effort› estremo; ‹attack› senza esclusione di colpi
② *adv* **go all out to do something/for something** mettercela tutta per fare qualcosa/per qualcosa

all-over *adj* ‹tan› integrale

all over ① *prep* ∼ **China** in/per tutta la Cina; **the news is** ∼ **the village** lo sanno tutti in paese; **be** ∼ **somebody** (fawning over) stare appiccicato a qualcuno
② *adv* **be trembling** ∼ tremare tutto; **that's Mary** ∼**!** è proprio da Mary!
③ *adj* **when it's** ∼ (finished) quando è tutto finito

♂ **allow** /ə'laʊ/ *vt* permettere; (grant) accordare; (reckon on) contare; (agree) ammettere; ∼ **somebody to do something** permettere a qualcuno di fare qualcosa; **you are not** ∼**ed to...** è vietato...; **how much are you** ∼**ed?** qual è il limite?
■ **allow for** *vt* tener conto di

allowable /ə'laʊəbl/ *adj* permissibile; Jur lecito; ‹tax› deducibile

allowance /əˈlaʊəns/ n sussidio m; Am (pocket money) paghetta f; (for petrol etc) indennità f inv; (of luggage, duty free) limite m; (for tax purposes) deduzione f; **make ~s for** essere indulgente verso ‹somebody›; tener conto di ‹something›

alloy /ˈælɔɪ/ n lega f

alloy steel n lega f d'acciaio

alloy wheel n cerchione m in lega d'acciaio

all points bulletin n Am allarme m generale

all-powerful adj onnipotente

all-purpose adj ‹building› polivalente; ‹utensil› multiuso

all right [1] adj is it ~ if...? va bene se...?; **is that ~ with you?** ti va bene?; **sounds ~ to me** per me va bene; **that's [quite] ~** (it doesn't matter) non c'è problema; **is my hair ~?** sono a posto i miei capelli?; **it's ~ for you!** è facile per te!; **she's ~** (competent) è abbastanza brava; (attractive) non è niente male; (pleasant) è piuttosto simpatica; **will you be ~?** (able to manage) te la caverai?; **feel ~** (well) sentirsi bene

[2] adv ‹function, see› bene; (not brilliantly) così così; **can I? - ~** posso? - d'accordo; **she's doing ~** (in life) le cose le vanno bene; (in health) sta bene; (in activity) se la cava bene; **she knows ~!** (without doubt) lei lo sa di sicuro!; **~, ~!** va bene! va bene!

all-risk adj ‹policy, cover› multirischi

all-round Br, **all-around** Am adj ‹improvement› generale; (athlete) completo

all-rounder /-ˈraʊndə(r)/ n **be a good ~** essere versatile

allspice /ˈɔːlspaɪs/ n pepe m della Giamaica

all square adj **be ~** ‹people› essere pari; ‹accounts› quadrare

all-time adj ‹record› assoluto, senza precedenti; **the ~ greats** (people) i grandi; **~ high** massimo m storico; **be at an ~ low** ‹person, morale› essere a terra; ‹figures, shares› toccare il minimo storico

all told adv tutto sommato

allude /əˈluːd/ vi alludere

allure /æˈljʊə(r)/ n attrattiva f

alluring /əˈljʊrɪŋ/ adj allettante, affascinante

allusion /əˈluːʒn/ n allusione f

ally¹ /ˈælaɪ/ n alleato, -a mf

ally² /əˈlaɪ/ vt (pt/pp -ied) alleare; **~ oneself with** allearsi con

almighty /ɔːlˈmaɪtɪ/ [1] adj fam (big) mega inv

[2] n **the A~** l'Onnipotente m

almond /ˈɑːmənd/ n mandorla f; (tree) mandorlo m

almost /ˈɔːlməʊst/ adv quasi

alms /ɑːmz/ npl liter elemosina f sg

aloft /əˈlɒft/ adv in alto; Naut sull'alberatura; **from ~** dall'alto

alone /əˈləʊn/ [1] adj solo; **leave me ~!** lasciami in pace!; **let ~** (not to mention) figurarsi

[2] adv da solo

along /əˈlɒŋ/ [1] prep lungo

[2] adv **~ with** assieme a; **all ~** tutto il tempo; **come ~!** (hurry up) vieni qui!; **I'll bring it ~** lo porto lì; **I'll be ~ in a minute** arrivo tra un attimo; **move ~** spostarsi; **move ~!** circolare!

alongside /əlɒŋˈsaɪd/ [1] adv lungo bordo

[2] prep lungo; **work ~ somebody** lavorare fianco a fianco con qualcuno

aloof /əˈluːf/ adj distante

aloud /əˈlaʊd/ adv ad alta voce

alpaca /ælˈpækə/ n alpaca m inv

alpha /ˈælfə/ n (letter) alfa f inv; Br Univ ≈ trenta m inv e lode

alphabet /ˈælfəbet/ n alfabeto m

alphabetical /ælfəˈbetɪkl/ adj alfabetico

alphabetically /ælfəˈbetɪklɪ/ adv in ordine alfabetico

alpha male n maschio m dominante

alpine /ˈælpaɪn/ adj alpino

Alps /ælps/ npl Alpi f pl

already /ɔːlˈredɪ/ adv già

alright /ɔːlˈraɪt/ = ALL RIGHT

Alsace /ælˈzæs/ n Alsazia f

Alsatian /ælˈseɪʃn/ n (dog) pastore m tedesco

also /ˈɔːlsəʊ/ adv anche; **~, I need...** inoltre, ho bisogno di...

altar /ˈɔːltə(r)/ n altare m

altar boy n chierichetto m

altar cloth n tovaglia f da altare

altar piece n pala f d'altare

alter /ˈɔːltə(r)/ [1] vt cambiare; aggiustare ‹clothes›

[2] vi cambiare

alteration /ɔːltəˈreɪʃn/ n modifica f

altercation /ɔːltəˈkeɪʃn/ n alterco m

alternate¹ /ˈɔːltəneɪt/ [1] vi alternarsi

[2] vt alternare

alternate² /ɔːlˈtɜːnət/ adj alterno; **on ~ days** a giorni alterni

alternately /ɔːlˈtɜːnətlɪ/ adv in modo alterno; Am (alternatively) alternativamente

alternating current /ˈɔːltəneɪtɪŋ/ n corrente f alternata

alternation /ɔːltəˈneɪʃn/ n alternanza f

alternative /ɔːlˈtɜːnətɪv/ [1] adj alternativo

[2] n alternativa f

alternative energy n energia f alternativa

alternatively /ɔːlˈtɜːnətɪvlɪ/ adv alternativamente

a

a

alternative medicine *n* medicina *f* alternativa

alternative technology *n* tecnologia *f* alternativa

alternator /'ɔːltəneɪtə(r)/ *n* Electr alternatore *m*

⚹ **although** /ɔːl'ðəʊ/ *conj* benché, sebbene

altimeter /'æltɪmiːtə(r)/ *n* altimetro *m*

altitude /'æltɪtjuːd/ *n* altitudine *f*

Alt key *n* Comput tasto *m* Alt

alto /'æltəʊ/ *n* contralto *m*

altogether /ɔːltə'geðə(r)/ *adv* (in all) in tutto; (completely) completamente; **I'm not ~ sure** non sono del tutto sicuro

altruism /'æltrʊɪzm/ *n* altruismo *m*

altruistic /æltrʊ'ɪstɪk/ *adj* altruistico

aluminium /æljʊ'mɪnɪəm/, Am **aluminum** /ə'luːmɪnəm/ *n* alluminio *m*

aluminium foil *n* carta *f* stagnola

alumna /ə'lʌmnə/ *n* Am Sch, Univ ex allieva *f*

alumnus /ə'lʌmnəs/ *n* Am Sch, Univ ex allievo *m*

⚹ **always** /'ɔːlweɪz/ *adv* sempre

Alzheimer's disease /'æltshaɪməz/ *n* morbo *m* di Alzheimer

am /æm/ ▶ BE

a.m. *abbr* (**ante meridiem**) del mattino

amalgam /ə'mælgəm/ *n* amalgama *m*

amalgamate /ə'mælgəmeɪt/ **1** *vt* fondere
2 *vi* fondersi

amalgamation /əmælgə'meɪʃn/ *n* fusione *f*; (of styles) amalgama *m*

amass /ə'mæs/ *vt* accumulare

amateur /'æmətə(r)/ **1** *n* non professionista *mf*; pej dilettante *mf*
2 *attrib* dilettante; **~ dramatics** filodrammatica *f*

amateurish /'æmətərɪʃ/ *adj* dilettantesco

amaze /ə'meɪz/ *vt* stupire

amazed /ə'meɪzd/ *adj* stupito

amazement /ə'meɪzmənt/ *n* stupore *m*; **to her ~** con suo grande stupore; **in ~** stupito

⚹ **amazing** /ə'meɪzɪŋ/ *adj* incredibile

amazingly /ə'meɪzɪŋlɪ/ *adv* incredibilmente

Amazon /'æməzən/ **1** *n* (in myths) Amazzone *f*, fig (strong woman) amazzone *f*; (river) Rio *m* delle Amazzoni
2 *attrib* ‹basin, forest, tribe› amazzonico

ambassador /æm'bæsədə(r)/ *n* ambasciatore, -trice *mf*

ambassador-at-large *n* Am ambasciatore, -trice *mf* a disposizione

amber /'æmbə(r)/ **1** *n* ambra *f*
2 *adj* (colour) ambra *inv*

ambidextrous /æmbɪ'dekstrəs/ *adj* ambidestro

⚹ indicates a very frequent word

ambience /'æmbɪəns/ *n* atmosfera *f*

ambient /'æmbɪənt/ *adj* ‹temperature› ambiente *inv*; (noise) circostante

ambiguity /æmbɪ'gjuːətɪ/ *n* ambiguità *f inv*

ambiguous /æm'bɪgjʊəs/ *adj* ambiguo

ambiguously /æm'bɪgjʊəslɪ/ *adv* in modo ambiguo

ambition /æm'bɪʃn/ *n* ambizione *f*; (aim) aspirazione *f*

ambitious /æm'bɪʃəs/ *adj* ambizioso

ambivalence /æm'bɪvələns/ *n* ambivalenza *f*

ambivalent /æm'bɪvələnt/ *adj* ambivalente

amble /'æmb(ə)l/ *vi* camminare senza fretta

ambulance /'æmbjʊləns/ *n* ambulanza *f*

ambulance man *n* guidatore *m* di ambulanze

ambush /'æmbʊʃ/ **1** *n* imboscata *f*
2 *vt* tendere un'imboscata a

ameba /ə'miːbə/ *n* Am ameba *f*

amen /ɑː'men/ *int* amen

amenability /əmiːnə'bɪlɪtɪ/ *n* arrendevolezza *f*

amenable /ə'miːnəbl/ *adj* conciliante; **~ to** sensibile a

amend /ə'mend/ **1** *vt* modificare
2 *npl* **make ~s** fare ammenda (**for** di, per)

amendment /ə'mendmənt/ *n* modifica *f*

amenities /ə'miːnətɪz/ *npl* comodità *fpl*

America /ə'merɪkə/ *n* America *f*

⚹ **American** /ə'merɪkən/ *adj & n* americano, -a *f*

American Civil War *n* guerra *f* di secessione [americana]

American English *n* inglese *m* americano

American Indian *n* indiano, -a *mf* d'America

Americanism /ə'merɪkənɪzm/ *n* americanismo *m*

amethyst /'æməθɪst/ *n* (gem) ametista *f*

Amex /'æmeks/ *n abbr* 1 (**American Stock Exchange**) Borsa *f* valori americana
2 (**American Express**)

amiable /'eɪmɪəbl/ *adj* amabile

amicable /'æmɪkəbl/ *adj* amichevole

amicably /'æmɪkəblɪ/ *adv* amichevolmente

amid[st] /ə'mɪd[st]/ *prep* in mezzo a

amino acid /ə'miːnəʊ/ *n* amminoacido *m*

amiss /ə'mɪs/ **1** *adj* **there's something ~** c'è qualcosa che non va
2 *adv* **take something ~** prendersela [a male]; **it won't come ~** non sarebbe sgradito

ammo /'æməʊ/ *n abbr* (**ammunition**) munizioni *fpl*

ammonia /ə'məʊnɪə/ *n* ammoniaca *f*

ammunition /æmjʊ'nɪʃn/ *n* munizioni *fpl*

amnesia /æm'niːzɪə/ *n* amnesia *f*

amnesty /'æmnəstɪ/ *n* amnistia *f*

amoeba /ə'miːbə/ *n* ameba *f*

amoebic /ə'miːbɪk/ *adj* ‹*dysentry*› amebico

amok /ə'mɒk/ *adv* run ∼ essere in preda a furore; ‹*imagination*› scatenarsi

ꜰ **among[st]** /ə'mʌŋ[st]/ *prep* tra, fra; **talk** ∼ **yourselves** parlate tra [di] voi

amoral /eɪ'mɒrəl/ *adj* amorale

amorality /eɪmə'rælətɪ/ *n* amoralità *f*

amorous /'æmərəs/ *adj* amoroso

amorphous /ə'mɔːfəs/ *adj* Chem amorfo; ‹*ideas, plans*› confuso; ‹*shape, collection*› informe

ꜰ **amount** /ə'maʊnt/ **1** *n* quantità *f inv*; (sum of money) montante *m* **2** *v*

■ **amount to** *vt* ammontare a; fig equivalere a

amp /æmp/ *n* ampere *m inv*

ampere /'æmpeə(r)/ *n* ampere *m inv*

ampersand /'æmpəsænd/ *n* e *f inv* commerciale

amphetamine /æm'fetəmiːn/ *n* anfetamina *f*

amphibian /æm'fɪbɪən/ *n* anfibio *m*

amphibious /æm'fɪbɪəs/ *adj* anfibio

amphitheatre /'æmfɪθiːətə(r)/ *n* anfiteatro *m*

ample /'æmpl/ *adj* (large) grande; ‹*proportions*› ampio; (enough) largamente sufficiente

amplifier /'æmplɪfaɪə(r)/ *n* amplificatore *m*

amplify /'æmplɪfaɪ/ *vt* (*pt/pp* **-ied**) amplificare ‹*sound*›

amply /'æmplɪ/ *adv* largamente

amputate /'æmpjʊteɪt/ *vt* amputare

amputation /æmpjʊ'teɪʃn/ *n* amputazione *f*

amputee /æmpjʊ'tiː/ *n* mutilato, -a *mf* (*in seguito ad amputazione*)

amuse /ə'mjuːz/ *vt* divertire

amused /ə'mjuːzd/ *adj* divertito

amusement /ə'mjuːzmənt/ *n* divertimento *m*

amusement arcade *n* sala *f* giochi

amusement park *n* luna park *m inv*

amusing /ə'mjuːzɪŋ/ *adj* divertente

an /ən/ *stressed* /æn/ ▶ A¹

anabolic steroid /ænə'bɒlɪk/ *n* anabolizzante *m*

anachronism /ə'nækrənɪzm/ *n* be an ∼ ‹*object, custom etc*› essere anacronistico

anaemia /ə'niːmɪə/ *n* anemia *f*

anaemic /ə'niːmɪk/ *adj* anemico

anaerobic /æneə'rəʊbɪk/ *adj* anerobico

anaesthesia /ænəs'θiːzɪə/ *n* anestesia *f*

anaesthetic /ænəs'θetɪk/ *n* anestesia *f*; **give somebody an** ∼ somministrare a qualcuno l'anestesia

anaesthetist /ə'niːsθətɪst/ *n* anestesista *mf*

anaesthetize /ə'niːsθətaɪz/ *vt* anestetizzare

anagram /'ænəgræm/ *n* anagramma *m*

analgesic /ænəl'dʒiːzɪk/ *adj & n* analgesico *m*

analogous /ə'næləgəs/ *adj* analogo

analog[ue] /'ænəlɒg/ *adj* analogico

analogy /ə'nælədʒɪ/ *n* analogia *f*

ꜰ **analyse** /'ænəlaɪz/ *vt* analizzare

ꜰ **analysis** /ə'næləsɪs/ *n* analisi *f inv*

analyst /'ænəlɪst/ *n* analista *mf*

analytical /ænə'lɪtɪkl/ *adj* analitico

anaphylaxis, anaphylactic shock /ænəfɪ'læksɪs/ *n* anafilassi *f*, shock *m* anafilattico

anarchic[al] /ə'nɑːkɪk[l]/ *adj* anarchico

anarchist /'ænəkɪst/ *n* anarchico, -a *mf*

anarchy /'ænəkɪ/ *n* anarchia *f*

anathema /ə'næθəmə/ *n* eresia *f*

anatomical /ænə'tɒmɪkl/ *adj* anatomico

anatomically /ænə'tɒmɪklɪ/ *adv* anatomicamente

anatomy /ə'nætəmɪ/ *n* anatomia *f*

ANC *n abbr* (**African National Congress**) Congresso *m* Nazionale Africano

ancestor /'ænsestə(r)/ *n* antenato, -a *mf*

ancestral /æn'sestrəl/ *adj* ancestrale; ‹*home*› avito

ancestry /'ænsestrɪ/ *n* antenati *mpl*

anchor /'æŋkə(r)/ **1** *n* ancora *f* **2** *vi* gettare l'ancora **3** *vt* ancorare

anchorage /'æŋkərɪdʒ/ *n* ancoraggio *m*

anchorman /'æŋkəmæn/ *n* Radio, TV anchor man *m inv*; Sport staffettista *m* dell'ultima frazione

anchorwoman /'æŋkəwʊmən/ *n* Radio, TV anchor woman *f inv*

anchovy /'æntʃəvɪ/ *n* acciuga *f*

ꜰ **ancient** /'eɪnʃənt/ *adj* antico; fam vecchio; ∼ **Rome** l'antica Roma *f*

ancillary /æn'sɪlərɪ/ *adj* ausiliario

ꜰ **and** /ənd/, *accentato* /ænd/ *conj* e; ∼ **so on** e così via; **two** ∼ **two** due più due; **six hundred** ∼ **two** seicentodue; **more** ∼ **more** sempre più; **nice** ∼ **warm** bello caldo; **try** ∼ **come** cerca di venire; **go** ∼ **get** vai a prendere

Andean /'ændɪən/ *adj* andino

Andes /'ændiːz/ *npl* the ∼ le Ande

Andorra /æn'dɔːrə/ *n* Andorra *f*

a

anecdote /ˈænɪkdəʊt/ n aneddoto m

anemone /əˈnemənɪ/ n Bot anemone m

anew /əˈnjuː/ adv di nuovo

angel /ˈeɪndʒl/ n angelo m

angel cake n dolce m di pan di Spagna

angelfish /ˈeɪndʒlfɪʃ/ n angelo m di mare

angelic /ænˈdʒelɪk/ adj angelico

◆ **anger** /ˈæŋgə(r)/ ① n rabbia f
② vt far arrabbiare

angina [pectoris]
/ænˈdʒaɪnə(ˈpektərɪs)/ n angina f pectoris

angle¹ /ˈæŋgl/ n angolo m; fig angolazione f;
at an ∼ storto

angle² vi pescare con la lenza; ∼ **for** fig
cercare di ottenere

angle bracket n Techn parentesi f inv
uncinata

Anglepoise [lamp] /ˈæŋglpɔɪz/ n
lampada f a braccio estensibile

angler /ˈæŋglə(r)/ n pescatore, -trice mf

Anglican /ˈæŋglɪkən/ adj & n anglicano,
-a mf

anglicism /ˈæŋglɪsɪzm/ n anglicismo m

anglicize /ˈæŋglɪsaɪz/ vt anglicizzare

angling /ˈæŋglɪŋ/ n pesca f con la lenza

Anglo+ /ˈæŋgləʊ/ pref anglo+

Anglo-American adj & n
angloamericano, -a mf

Anglophone /ˈæŋgləfəʊn/ adj & n
anglofono, -a mf

Anglo-Saxon /æŋgləʊˈsæksn/ adj & n
anglosassone mf

Angola /æŋˈgəʊlə/ n Angola f

angora /ænˈgɔːrə/ n lana f d'angora

angrily /ˈæŋgrɪlɪ/ adv rabbiosamente

◆ **angry** /ˈæŋgrɪ/ adj (**-ier**, **-iest**) arrabbiato;
get ∼ arrabbiarsi; ∼ **with** or **at somebody**
arrabbiato con qualcuno; ∼ **at** or **about**
something arrabbiato per qualcosa

anguish /ˈæŋgwɪʃ/ n angoscia f; **in** ∼ in
preda all'angoscia

anguished /ˈæŋgwɪʃt/ adj (suffering)
straziante; ‹person› angosciato

angular /ˈæŋgjʊlə(r)/ adj angolare

◆ **animal** /ˈænɪm(ə)l/ adj & n animale m

animal experiment n esperimento m
sugli animali

animal husbandry /ˈhʌzbəndrɪ/ n
allevamento m

animal kingdom n regno m animale

animal lover n amante mf degli animali

animal product n prodotto m di origine
animale

animal rights npl diritti mpl degli
animali

animal rights activist n animalista mf

animal sanctuary n rifugio m per
animali

animal testing n sperimentazione f
sugli animali

animate¹ /ˈænɪmət/ adj animato

animate² /ˈænɪmeɪt/ vt animare

animated /ˈænɪmeɪtɪd/ adj animato;
‹person› vivace

animation /ænɪˈmeɪʃn/ n animazione f

animator /ˈænɪmeɪtə(r)/ n (film cartoonist)
animatore, -trice mf; (director) regista mf di
film d'animazione

animatronics /ænɪməˈtrɒnɪks/ n
animazione f elettronica

animosity /ænɪˈmɒsətɪ/ n animosità f inv

aniseed /ˈænɪsiːd/ n anice f

ankle /ˈæŋk(ə)l/ n caviglia f

anklebone n astragalo m

ankle-deep adj be ∼ **in mud** adj essere
nel fango fino alle caviglie

ankle-length adj (dress) alla caviglia

ankle sock n calzino m

annals /ˈænəlz/ npl go down in the ∼ [of
history] passare agli annali

annex /əˈneks/ vt annettere

annexation /ænekˈseɪʃn/ n (action)
annessione f; (land annexed) territorio m
annesso

annex[e] /ˈæneks/ n annesso m

annihilate /əˈnaɪəleɪt/ vt annientare

annihilation /ənaɪəˈleɪʃn/ n
annientamento m

anniversary /ænɪˈvɜːsərɪ/ n anniversario
m

Anno Domini /ænəʊˈdɒmɪnaɪ/ adv dopo
Cristo

annotate /ˈænəteɪt/ vt annotare

◆ **announce** /əˈnaʊns/ vt annunciare

announcement /əˈnaʊnsmənt/ n
annuncio m

announcer /əˈnaʊnsə(r)/ n annunciatore,
-trice mf

annoy /əˈnɔɪ/ vt dare fastidio a

annoyance /əˈnɔɪəns/ n seccatura f;
(anger) irritazione f

annoyed /əˈnɔɪd/ adj irritato; get ∼
irritarsi; ∼ **with somebody** irritato con
qualcuno; ∼ **at/about something** irritato per
qualcosa; ∼ **that** irritato che

annoying /əˈnɔɪɪŋ/ adj fastidioso

◆ **annual** /ˈænjʊəl/ ① adj annuale; ‹income›
annuo
② n Bot pianta f annua; (children's book)
almanacco m

Annual General Meeting n
assemblea f generale annuale

annually /ˈænjʊəlɪ/ adv annualmente; **she
earns £50,000**∼ guadagna 50.000 sterline
all'anno

annual report n resoconto m annuale

annuity /əˈnjuːətɪ/ n annualità f inv

◆ indicates a very frequent word

annul /əˈnʌl/ vt (pt/pp **annulled**)
annullare

Annunciation /ənʌnsɪˈeɪʃn/ n
Annunciazione f

anode /ˈænəʊd/ n anodo m

anodyne /ˈænədaɪn/ adj liter (bland)
anodino; (inoffensive) innocuo

anoint /əˈnɔɪnt/ vt ungere

anomalous /əˈnɒmələs/ adj anomalo

anomaly /əˈnɒməlɪ/ n anomalia f

anon /əˈnɒn/ abbr (**anonymous**)
anonimo

anonymity /ænəˈnɪmətɪ/ n anonimità f

anonymous /əˈnɒnɪməs/ adj anonimo;
remain ~ mantenere l'anonimato

anonymously /əˈnɒnɪməslɪ/ adv
anonimamente

anorak /ˈænəræk/ n giacca f a vento

anorexia /ˈænəˈreksɪə/ n anoressia f

anorexic /ænəˈreksɪk/ adj & n anoressico,
-a mf

✔ **another** /əˈnʌðə(r)/ adj & pron ~ [one] un
altro, un'altra; ~ day un altro giorno; in ~
way diversamente; ~ time un'altra volta;
one ~ l'un l'altro

✔ **answer** /ˈɑːnsə(r)/ [1] n risposta f; (solution)
soluzione f
[2] vt rispondere a ‹person, question,
letter›; esaudire ‹prayer›; ~ the door aprire
la porta; ~ the telephone rispondere al
telefono
[3] vi rispondere
■ **answer back** vi ribattere
■ **answer for** vt rispondere di

answerable /ˈɑːnsərəbl/ adj responsabile;
be ~ to somebody rispondere a qualcuno

answering machine n Teleph segreteria
f telefonica

answering service n servizio m di
segreteria telefonica

answerphone /ˈɑːnsəfəʊn/ n segreteria
f telefonica

ant /ænt/ n formica f

antacid /æntˈæsɪd/ adj & n antiacido m

antagonism /ænˈtæɡənɪzm/ n
antagonismo m

antagonistic /æntæɡəˈnɪstɪk/ adj
antagonistico

antagonize /ænˈtæɡənaɪz/ vt provocare
l'ostilità di

Antarctic /ænˈtɑːktɪk/ [1] n Antartico m
[2] adj antartico

Antarctica /ænˈtɑːktɪkə/ n Antartide f

Antarctic Circle n Circolo m polare
antartico

Antarctic Ocean n mare m antartico

anteater /ˈæntiːtə(r)/ n formichiere m

antecedent /æntɪˈsiːdənt/ n (precedent)
antecedente m; (ancestor) antenato, -a mf

antedate /æntɪˈdeɪt/ vt (put earlier date on)
retrodatare; (predate) precedere

antediluvian /æntɪdɪˈluːvɪən/ adj
antidiluviano

antelope /ˈæntɪləʊp/ n antilope m

antenatal /æntɪˈneɪtl/ adj prenatale

antenatal class n corso m di
preparazione al parto

antenatal clinic n Br assistenza f medica
prenatale

antenna /ænˈtenə/ n antenna f

anterior /ænˈtɪərɪə/ adj anteriore

anteroom /ˈæntɪ-/ n anticamera f

antheap /ˈænthiːp/ = ANTHILL

anthem /ˈænθəm/ n inno m

anthill /ˈænthɪl/ n formicaio m

anthology /ænˈθɒlədʒɪ/ n antologia f

anthracite /ˈænθrəsaɪt/ n antracite f

anthrax /ˈænθræks/ n (disease) carbonchio
m; (pustule) pustola f di carbonchio

anthropological /ænθrəpəˈlɒdʒɪkl/ adj
antropologico

anthropologist /ænθrəˈpɒlədʒɪst/ n
antropologo, -a mf

anthropology /ænθrəˈpɒlədʒɪ/ n
antropologia f

anti /ˈæntɪ/ [1] pref anti
[2] prep be ~ essere contro

anti-abortion adj antiabortista

anti-abortionist n antiabortista mf

anti-aircraft adj antiaereo

anti-apartheid adj antiapartheid inv

antibacterial /æntɪbækˈtɪərɪəl/ adj
antibatterico

antiballistic missile
/æntɪbəlɪstɪkˈmɪsaɪl/ n missile m antimissile

antibiotic /æntɪbaɪˈɒtɪk/ n antibiotico m

antibody /ˈæntɪbɒdɪ/ n anticorpo m

anticipate /ænˈtɪsɪpeɪt/ vt prevedere;
(forestall) anticipare

anticipation /æntɪsɪˈpeɪʃn/ n anticipo m;
(excitement) attesa f; in ~ of in previsione di

anticlimax /æntɪˈklaɪmæks/ n delusione f

anticlockwise /æntɪˈklɒkwaɪz/ adj &
adv in senso antiorario

antics /ˈæntɪks/ npl gesti mpl buffi

anticyclone /æntɪˈsaɪkləʊn/ n anticiclone
m

antidepressant /æntɪdɪˈpres(ə)nt/ adj &
n antidepressivo m

antidote /ˈæntɪdəʊt/ n antidoto m

anti-establishment adj contestatario

antifreeze /ˈæntɪfriːz/ n antigelo m

antiglare /æntɪˈɡleə(r)/ adj ‹screen›
antiriflesso inv

antihistamine /æntɪˈhɪstəmiːn/ n
antistaminico m

anti-inflammatory /-ɪnˈflæmətrɪ/ adj &
n antinfiammatorio m

a

anti-inflation *adj* anti-inflazione *inv*

anti-inflationary /-ɪn'fleɪʃnəri/ *adj* antinflazionistico

anti-lock *adj* antibloccaggio *inv*

antipathy /æn'tɪpəθɪ/ *n* antipatia *f*

antiperspirant /æntɪ'pɜːspɪrənt/ *n* deodorante *m* antitraspirante

antipodean /æntɪpə'diːən/ *adj & n* australiano, -a, e/o neozelandese *mf*

Antipodes /æn'tɪpədiːz/ *npl* Br the ~ gli antipodi

antiquarian /æntɪ'kweərɪən/ *adj* antiquario; ~ **bookshop** negozio *m* di libri antichi

antiquated /'æntɪkweɪtɪd/ *adj* antiquato

antique /æn'tiːk/ **1** *adj* antico **2** *n* antichità *f inv*

antique dealer *n* antiquario, -a *mf*

antiques fair *n* fiera *f* dell'antiquariato

antique shop *n* negozio *m* d'antiquariato

antiques trade *n* antiquariato *m*

antiquity /æn'tɪkwətɪ/ *n* antichità *f*

anti-racism *n* antirazzismo *m*

anti-racist *adj* antirazzista

antiretroviral /æntiretrʊ‚vaɪrəl/ *adj* antiretrovirale

anti-riot *adj* ‹police› antisommossa *inv*

anti-rust *adj* antiruggine *inv*

anti-Semitic /æntɪsɪ'mɪtɪk/ *adj* antisemita

anti-Semitism /æntɪ'semɪtɪzm/ *n* antisemitismo *m*

antiseptic /æntɪ'septɪk/ *adj & n* antisettico *m*

anti-skid *adj* antiscivolo *inv*

anti-smoking *adj* contro il fumo, antifumo

antisocial /æntɪ'səʊʃəl/ *adj* ‹behaviour› antisociale; ‹person› asociale

anti-terrorist *adj* antiterrorista

anti-theft *adj* ‹lock, device› antifurto *inv*; ‹camera› di sorveglianza; ~ **steering lock** bloccasterzo *m*

antithesis /æn'tɪθəsɪs/ *n* antitesi *f*

antitrust /æntɪ'trʌst/ *adj* antitrust *inv*

antivirus program /æntɪ'vaɪrəs/ *n* Comput programma *m* antivirus

antivirus software *n* Comput programma *m* antivirus

antivivisectionist /æntɪvɪvɪ'sekʃənɪst/ **1** *n* antivivisezionista *mf* **2** *adj* antivivisezionistico

anti-war *adj* antimilitarista

antlers /'æntləz/ *npl* corna *fpl*

antonym /'æntənɪm/ *n* antonimo *m*

Antwerp /'æntwɜːp/ *n* Anversa *f*

anus /'eɪnəs/ *n* ano *m*

anvil /'ænvɪl/ *n* incudine *f*

anxiety /æŋ'zaɪətɪ/ *n* ansia *f*

anxious /'æŋkʃəs/ *adj* ansioso

anxiously /'æŋkʃəslɪ/ *adv* con ansia

✎ **any** /'enɪ/ **1** *adj* (no matter which) qualsiasi, qualunque; **have we ~ wine/biscuits?** abbiamo del vino/dei biscotti?; **have we ~ jam/apples?** abbiamo della marmellata/ delle mele?; ~ **colour/number you like** qualsiasi colore/numero ti piaccia; **we don't have ~ wine/biscuits** non abbiamo vino/ biscotti; **I don't have ~ reason to lie** non ho nessun motivo per mentire; **for ~ reason** per qualsiasi ragione **2** *pron* (some) né; (no matter which) uno qualsiasi; **I don't want ~ [of it]** non ne voglio [nessuno]; **there aren't ~** non ce ne sono; **have we ~?** ne abbiamo?; **have you read ~ of her books?** hai letto qualcuno dei suoi libri? **3** *adv* **I can't go ~ quicker** non posso andare più in fretta; **is it ~ better?** va un po' meglio?; **would you like ~ more?** ne vuoi ancora?; **I can't eat ~ more** non posso mangiare più niente

anybody /'enɪbʌdɪ/ *pron* chiunque; (after negative) nessuno; ~ **can do that** chiunque può farlo; **I haven't seen ~** non ho visto nessuno

anyhow /'enɪhaʊ/ *adv* ad ogni modo, comunque; (badly) non importa come

✎ **anyone** /'enɪwʌn/ *pron* = ANYBODY

anyplace /'enɪpleɪs/ *adv* Am = ANYWHERE

✎ **anything** /'enɪθɪŋ/ *pron* qualche cosa, qualcosa; (no matter what) qualsiasi cosa; (after negative) niente; **take/buy ~ you like** prendi/ compra quello che vuoi; **I don't remember ~** non mi ricordo niente; **he's ~ but stupid** è tutto fuorché stupido; **I'll do ~ but that** farò qualsiasi cosa, tranne quello

anytime /'enɪtaɪm/ *adv* **if at ~ you feel lonely...** se mai ti dovessi sentire solo...; **he could arrive ~ now** potrebbe arrivare da un momento all'altro; ~ **after 2 pm** a qualsiasi ora dopo le due; **at ~ of the day or night** a qualsiasi ora del giorno o della notte; ~ **you like** quando vuoi

✎ **anyway** /'enɪweɪ/ *adv* ad ogni modo, comunque

✎ **anywhere** /'enɪweə(r)/ *adv* dovunque; (after negative) da nessuna parte; **put it ~** mettilo dove vuoi; **I can't find it ~** non lo trovo da nessuna parte; ~ **else** da qualche altra parte; **I don't want to go ~ else** non voglio andare da nessun'altra parte

aorta /eɪ'ɔːtə/ *n* aorta *f*

Aosta /æ'ɒstə/ *n* Aosta *f*

apace /ə'peɪs/ *adv* liter rapidamente

✎ **apart** /ə'pɑːt/ *adv* lontano; **live ~** vivere separati; **100 miles ~** lontani 100 miglia; **born 20 minutes ~** nati a distanza di

---

✎ indicates a very frequent word

20 minuti; ~ from a parte; **you can't tell them** ~ non si possono distinguere; **joking** ~ scherzi a parte

apartheid /ə'pɑːthaɪt/ n apartheid f

ƒ **apartment** /ə'pɑːtmənt/ n Am (flat) appartamento m; **in my** ~ a casa mia

apartment block n stabile m

apartment house n stabile m

apathetic /æpə'θetɪk/ adj (by nature) apatico; ~ **about something/towards somebody** (from illness, depression) indifferente a qualcosa/nei confronti di qualcuno

apathy /'æpəθɪ/ n apatia f

ape /eɪp/ ① n scimmia f
② vt scimmiottare

Apennines /'æpənaɪnz/ npl **the** ~ gli Appennini

aperitif /ə'perəti:f/ n aperitivo m

aperture /'æpətʃə(r)/ n apertura f

apex /'eɪpeks/ n vertice m

aphid /'eɪfɪd/ n afide m

aphrodisiac /æfrə'dɪzɪæk/ adj & n afrodisiaco m

apiary /'eɪpɪərɪ/ n apiario m

apiece /ə'piːs/ adv ciascuno

aplenty /ə'plentɪ/ adv **there were goals** ~ c'è stata una valanga di gol

apocalypse /ə'pɒkəlɪps/ n Apocalisse f; (disaster, destruction) apocalisse f

apocalyptic /əpɒkə'lɪptɪk/ adj apocalittico

apocryphal /ə'pɒkrɪfəl/ adj apocrifo

apogee /'æpədʒiː/ n apogeo m

apolitical /eɪpə'lɪtɪkl/ adj apolitico

Apollo /ə'pɒləʊ/ n also fig Apollo m

apologetic /əpɒlə'dʒetɪk/ adj ‹air, remark› di scusa; **be** ~ essere spiacente

apologetically /əpɒlə'dʒetɪklɪ/ adv per scusarsi

apologist /ə'pɒlədʒɪst/ n apologeta mf (for di)

apologize /ə'pɒlədʒaɪz/ vi scusarsi (for per)

apology /ə'pɒlədʒɪ/ n scusa f; fig **an** ~ **for a dinner** una sottospecie di cena

apoplectic /æpə'plektɪk/ adj (furious) furibondo; ‹fit, attack› apoplettico

apoplexy /'æpəpleksɪ/ n Med apoplessia f; (rage) rabbia f

apostle /ə'pɒsl/ n apostolo m

apostrophe /ə'pɒstrəfɪ/ n apostrofo m

apotheosis /əpɒθɪ'əʊsɪs/ n apoteosi f inv

app n abbr (**application**) Comput fam applicazione f

appal /ə'pɔːl/ vt (pt/pp **appalled**) sconvolgere

Appalachians /æpə'leɪtʃnz/ npl **the** ~ gli Appalachi

appalling /ə'pɔːlɪŋ/ adj sconvolgente; **he's an** ~ **teacher** fig è un disastro come

professore

appallingly /ə'pɔːlɪŋlɪ/ adv ‹behave, treat› orribilmente; **unemployment figures are** ~ **high** il tasso di disoccupazione è spaventosamente alto; **furnished in** ~ **bad taste** arredato con pessimo gusto

apparatus /æpə'reɪtəs/ n apparato m

apparel /ə'pærəl/ n abbigliamento m

ƒ **apparent** /ə'pærənt/ adj evidente; (seeming) apparente

ƒ **apparently** /ə'pærəntlɪ/ adv apparentemente

apparition /æpə'rɪʃn/ n apparizione f

ƒ **appeal** /ə'piːl/ ① n appello m; (attraction) attrattiva f
② vi fare appello; ~ **to** (be attractive to) attrarre

appeal fund n raccolta f di fondi

appealing /ə'piːlɪŋ/ adj attraente

appealingly /ə'piːlɪŋlɪ/ adv (beseechingly) in modo supplichevole; (attractively) in modo attraente

appeal[s] court n corte f d'appello

ƒ **appear** /ə'pɪə(r)/ vi apparire; (seem) sembrare; ‹publication› uscire; Theat esibirsi; **he finally** ~**ed at…** fam si è fatto finalmente vedere alle…; ~ **in court** comparire in giudizio

ƒ **appearance** /ə'pɪərəns/ n apparizione f; (look) aspetto m; **to all** ~**s** a giudicare dalle apparenze; **keep up** ~**s** salvare le apparenze

appease /ə'piːz/ vt placare

appeasement /ə'piːzmənt/ n **a policy of** ~ una politica troppo conciliante

append /ə'pend/ vt apporre ‹signature› (to a)

appendage /ə'pendɪdʒ/ n appendice f

appendicitis /əpendɪ'saɪtɪs/ n appendicite f

appendix /ə'pendɪks/ n (of book) (pl **-ices**) /-əsiːz/ appendice f (pl **-es**) Anat appendice f

appertain /æpə'teɪn/ vi ~ **to** essere pertinente a

appetite /'æpɪtaɪt/ n appetito m

appetite suppressant n pillola f antifame

appetizer /'æpɪtaɪzə(r)/ n (drink) aperitivo m; (starter) antipasto m; (biscuit, olive etc) stuzzichino m

appetizing /'æpɪtaɪzɪŋ/ adj appetitoso

applaud /ə'plɔːd/ vt/i applaudire

applause /ə'plɔːz/ n applauso m

apple /'æpl/ n mela f; **she's the** ~ **of his eye** è la luce dei suoi occhi

apple core n torsolo m di mela

apple orchard n meleto m

applet /'æplɪt/ n Comput applet f

apple tree n melo m

appliance /ə'plaɪəns/ n attrezzo m; [electrical] ~ elettrodomestico m

applicable /'æplɪkəbl/ adj be ~ to essere valido per; **not** ~ (on form) non applicabile

applicant /'æplɪkənt/ n candidato, -a mf

◆ **application** /æplɪ'keɪʃn/ n Comput (general) applicazione f; (request) domanda f; (for job) candidatura f; **on** ~ su richiesta

application form n modulo m di domanda

applicator /'æplɪkeɪtə(r)/ n applicatore m

applied /ə'plaɪd/ adj applicato

appliqué /ə'pliːkeɪ/ ⚊ n applicazione f ⚋ attrib ‹motif, decoration› applicato

◆ **apply** /ə'plaɪ/ ⚊ vt (pt/pp **-ied**) applicare; ~ **oneself** applicarsi; ~ **the brakes** frenare ⚋ vi applicarsi; ‹law› essere applicabile; ~ **to** (ask) rivolgersi a; ~ **for** fare domanda per ‹job etc›

◆ **appoint** /ə'pɔɪnt/ vt nominare; fissare ‹time›; **well ~ed** ben equipaggiato

appointee /əpɔɪn'tiː/ n incaricato, -a mf

appointment /ə'pɔɪntmənt/ n appuntamento m; (to job) nomina f; (job) posto m

apportion /ə'pɔːʃn/ vt ripartire, attribuire

apposite /'æpəzɪt/ adj appropriato

apposition /æpə'zɪʃn/ n apposizione f

appraisal /ə'preɪzəl/ n valutazione f; **make an** ~ **of something** valutare qualcosa

appraise /ə'preɪz/ vt valutare

appreciable /ə'priːʃəbl/ adj sensibile

appreciably /ə'priːʃəblɪ/ adv sensibilmente

◆ **appreciate** /ə'priːʃɪeɪt/ ⚊ vt apprezzare; (understand) comprendere ⚋ vi (increase in value) aumentare di valore

appreciation /əpriːsɪ'eɪʃn/ n (gratitude) riconoscenza f; (enjoyment) apprezzamento m; (understanding) comprensione f; (in value) aumento m; **in** ~ come segno di riconoscenza (of per)

appreciative /ə'priːʃətɪv/ adj riconoscente

apprehend /æprɪ'hend/ vt arrestare

apprehension /æprɪ'henʃn/ n arresto m; (fear) apprensione f

apprehensive /æprɪ'hensɪv/ adj apprensivo

apprehensively /æprɪ'hensɪvlɪ/ adv con apprensione

apprentice /ə'prentɪs/ n apprendista mf

apprenticeship /ə'prentɪsʃɪp/ n apprendistato m

apprise /ə'praɪz/ vt fml informare (of di)

◆ **approach** /ə'prəʊtʃ/ ⚊ n avvicinamento m; (to problem) approccio m; (access) accesso m; **make** ~**es to** fare degli approcci con

───────────────────────

◆ indicates a very frequent word

⚋ vi avvicinarsi

⚌ vt avvicinarsi a; (with request) rivolgersi a; affrontare ‹problem›

approachable /ə'prəʊtʃəbl/ adj accessibile

approach lights npl Aeron sentiero m luminoso di avvicinamento

approach path n Aeron rotta f di avvicinamento

approach road n strada f d'accesso

approbation /æprə'beɪʃn/ n approvazione f

◆ **appropriate¹** /ə'prəʊprɪət/ adj appropriato

appropriate² /ə'prəʊprɪeɪt/ vt appropriarsi di

appropriately /ə'prəʊprɪətlɪ/ adv (suitably) in modo appropriato; ‹sited› convenientemente; ‹designed, chosen, behave› adeguatamente

appropriation /əprəʊprɪ'eɪʃn/ n Am Comm stanziamento m; Jur (removal) appropriazione f

approval /ə'pruːvl/ n approvazione f; **on** ~ in prova

◆ **approve** /ə'pruːv/ ⚊ vt approvare ⚋ vi ~ **of** approvare ‹something›; avere una buona opinione di ‹somebody›

approving /ə'pruːvɪŋ/ adj ‹smile, nod› d'approvazione

approvingly /ə'pruːvɪŋlɪ/ adv con approvazione

approximate¹ /ə'prɒksɪmeɪt/ vi ~ **to** avvicinarsi a

approximate² /ə'prɒksɪmət/ adj approssimativo

◆ **approximately** /ə'prɒksɪmətlɪ/ adv approssimativamente

approximation /əprɒksɪ'meɪʃn/ n approssimazione f

APR n (**annual percentage rate**) tasso m percentuale annuo

apricot /'eɪprɪkɒt/ n albicocca f; ~ **tree** albicocco m

◆ **April** /'eɪprəl/ n aprile m; **make an** ~ **Fool of somebody** fare un pesce d'aprile a qualcuno

April Fools' Day n il primo d'aprile m

apron /'eɪprən/ n grembiule m

apropos /'æprəpəʊ/ adv ~ [**of**] a proposito [di]

apse /æps/ n abside f

apt /æpt/ adj appropriato; ‹pupil› dotato; **be** ~ **to do something** avere tendenza a fare qualcosa

aptitude /'æptɪtjuːd/ n disposizione f

aptitude test n test m inv attitudinale

aptly /'æptlɪ/ adv appropriatamente

Apulia /ə'pjuːlɪə/ n Puglia f

aqualung /'ækwəlʌŋ/ n autorespiratore m

aquamarine /ˌækwəmə'riːn/ *adj & n* acquamarina *f*

aquaplane /'ækwəpleɪn/ *vi* Sport praticare l'acquaplano; Br Auto andare in aquaplaning

aquarium /ə'kweərɪəm/ *n* acquario *m*

Aquarius /ə'kweərɪəs/ *n* Astr Acquario *m*; **be** ∼ essere dell' Acquario

aquarobics /ˌækwə'rɒbɪks/ *n* acquagym *f inv*

aquatic /ə'kwætɪk/ *adj* acquatico

aqueduct /'ækwədʌkt/ *n* acquedotto *m*

aquiline /'ækwɪlaɪn/ *adj* ‹nose, features› aquilino

Arab /'ærəb/ *adj & n* arabo, -a *mf*

Arabia /ə'reɪbɪə/ *n* Arabia *f*

Arabian /ə'reɪbɪən/ *adj* arabo

Arabic /'ærəbɪk/ ⚊ *adj* arabo; ∼ **numerals** numeri *mpl* arabi
⚋ *n* arabo *m*

Arab-Israeli *adj* arabo-israeliano

arable /'ærəbl/ *adj* coltivabile

arbiter /'ɑːbɪtə(r)/ *n* arbitro *m*

arbitrarily /ɑːbɪ'trerɪlɪ/ *adv* arbitrariamente

arbitrary /'ɑːbɪtrərɪ/ *adj* arbitrario

arbitrate /'ɑːbɪtreɪt/ *vi* arbitrare

arbitration /ɑːbɪ'treɪʃn/ *n* arbitraggio *m*

arbitrator /'ɑːbɪtreɪtə(r)/ *n* arbitro *m*

arbour /'ɑːbə(r)/ *n* pergolato *m*

arc /ɑːk/ *n* arco *m*

arcade /ɑː'keɪd/ *n* portico *m*; (shops) galleria *f*

arcane /ɑː'keɪn/ *adj* arcano

arch /ɑːtʃ/ ⚊ *n* arco *m*; (of foot) dorso *m* del piede
⚋ *vt* **the cat** ∼**ed its back** il gatto ha arcuato la schiena

archaeological /ɑːkɪə'lɒdʒɪkl/ *adj* archeologico

archaeologist /ɑːkɪ'ɒlədʒɪst/ *n* archeologo, -a *mf*

archaeology /ɑːkɪ'ɒlədʒɪ/ *n* archeologia *f*

archaic /ɑː'keɪɪk/ *adj* arcaico

archbishop /ɑːtʃ'bɪʃəp/ *n* arcivescovo *m*

arched /ɑːtʃt/ *adj* (eyebrows) arcuato

arch-enemy *n* acerrimo nemico *m*

archer /'ɑːtʃə(r)/ *n* arciere *m*

archery /'ɑːtʃərɪ/ *n* tiro *m* con l'arco

archetypal /ɑːkɪ'taɪpl/ *adj* **the** ∼ **hero** il prototipo dell'eroe

archetype /'ɑːkɪtaɪp/ *n* archetipo *m*

archipelago /ɑːkɪ'peləgəʊ/ *n* arcipelago *m*

architect /'ɑːkɪtekt/ *n* architetto *m*

architectural /ɑːkɪ'tektʃərəl/ *adj* architettonico

architecturally /ɑːkɪ'tektʃərəlɪ/ *adv* architettonicamente

architecture /'ɑːkɪtektʃə(r)/ *n* architettura *f*

archive /'ɑːkaɪv/ *vt* also Comput archiviare

archives /'ɑːkaɪvz/ *npl* archivi *mpl*

archiving /'ɑːkaɪvɪŋ/ *n* Comput archiviazione *f*

archway /'ɑːtʃweɪ/ *n* arco *m*

Arctic /'ɑːktɪk/ ⚊ *adj* artico
⚋ *n* **the** ∼ l'Artico

Arctic Circle *n* Circolo *m* polare artico

Arctic Ocean *n* mare *m* artico

ardent /'ɑːdənt/ *adj* ardente

ardently /'ɑːdəntlɪ/ *adv* ardentemente

ardour /'ɑːdə(r)/ *n* ardore *m*

arduous /'ɑːdjʊəs/ *adj* arduo

arduously /'ɑːdjʊəslɪ/ *adv* con fatica, con difficoltà

are /ɑː(r)/ ▶ BE

✒ **area** /'eərɪə/ *n* area *f*; (region) zona *f*; fig (field) campo *m*

area code *n* prefisso *m* [telefonico]

area manager *n* direttore, -trice *mf* di zona

arena /ə'riːnə/ *n* arena *f*

aren't /ɑːnt/ *are not* ▶ BE

Argentina /ɑːdʒən'tiːnə/ *n* Argentina *f*

Argentine /'ɑːdʒəntaɪn/ *adj* argentino

Argentinian /ɑːdʒən'tɪnɪən/ *adj & n* argentino, -a *mf*

arguable /'ɑːgjʊəbl/ *adj* **it's** ∼ **that…** si può sostenere che…

arguably /'ɑːgjʊəblɪ/ *adv* **he is** ∼**…** è probabilmente…

✒ **argue** /'ɑːgjuː/ ⚊ *vi* litigare (about su); (debate) dibattere; **don't** ∼**!** non discutere!
⚋ *vt* (debate) dibattere; (reason) ∼ **that** sostenere che

✒ **argument** /'ɑːgjʊmənt/ *n* argomento *m*; (reasoning) ragionamento *m*; **have an** ∼ litigare

argumentative /ɑːgjʊ'mentətɪv/ *adj* polemico

aria /'ɑːrɪə/ *n* aria *f*

arid /'ærɪd/ *adj* arido

aridity /ə'rɪdətɪ/ *n* also fig aridità *f*

Aries /'eəriːz/ *n* Astr Ariete *m*; **be** ∼ essere dell'Ariete

✒ **arise** /ə'raɪz/ *vi* (*pt* **arose**, *pp* **arisen**) ‹opportunity, need, problem› presentarsi; (result) derivare

aristocracy /ærɪ'stɒkrəsɪ/ *n* aristocrazia *f*

aristocrat /'ærɪstəkræt/ *n* aristocratico, -a *mf*

aristocratic /ærɪstə'krætɪk/ *adj* aristocratico

arithmetic /ə'rɪθmətɪk/ *n* aritmetica *f*

arithmetical /ærɪθ'metɪkl/ *adj* aritmetico

ark /ɑːk/ *n* **Noah's Ark** l'Arca *f* di Noè

a

✧ **arm** /ɑːm/ **1** *n* braccio *m*; (of chair) bracciolo *m*; ~s *pl* (weapons) armi *fpl*; ~ **in** ~ a braccetto; **up in** ~**s** fam furioso (**about** per); *fig* **with open** ~**s** a braccia aperte **2** *vt* armare

armadillo /ɑːməˈdɪləʊ/ *n* armadillo *m*

armaments /ˈɑːməmənts/ *npl* armamenti *mpl*

armband /ˈɑːmbænd/ *n* (for swimmer) bracciolo *m* (*per nuotare*) (for mourner) fascia *f* al braccio

armchair /ˈɑːmtʃeə(r)/ *n* poltrona *f*

armchair traveller *n persona* (*f*) *che si interessa di viaggi senza viaggiare*

armed /ɑːmd/ *adj* armato

armed forces /ˈfɔːsɪz/ *npl* forze *fpl* armate

armed robbery *n* rapina *f* a mano armata

Armenia /ɑːˈmiːnɪə/ *n* Armenia *f*

Armenian /ɑːˈmiːnɪən/ *adj & n* (person) armeno, -a *mf*; (language) armeno *m*

armful /ˈɑːmfʊl/ *n* bracciata *f*

armhole /ˈɑːmhəʊl/ *n* giro *m* manica *inv*

armistice /ˈɑːmɪstɪs/ *n* armistizio *m*

Armistice Day *n* l'Anniversario *m* dell'Armistizio (*11 nov. 1918*)

armour /ˈɑːmə(r)/ *n* armatura *f*

armour-clad /-ˈklæd/ *adj* ‹vehicle› blindato; ‹ship› corazzato

armoured /ˈɑːməd/ *adj* ‹vehicle› blindato

armoured car *n* autoblinda[ta] *f*

armour plate, **armour plating** /ˈpleɪtɪŋ/ *n* corazzatura *f*

armour-plated /-ˈpleɪtɪd/ *adj* corazzato

armoury /ˈɑːmərɪ/ *n* (factory) fabbrica *f* d'armi; (store) arsenale *m*, armeria *f*

armpit /ˈɑːmpɪt/ *n* ascella *f*

armrest /ˈɑːmrest/ *n* bracciolo *m* (*di sedia*)

arms control *n* controllo *m* degli armamenti

arms dealer *n* trafficante *mf* d'armi

arms dump *n* deposito *m* d'armi

arms embargo *n* embargo *m* sulle armi

arms limitation *n* controllo *m* degli armamenti

arms manufacturer *n* fabbricante *mf* d'armi

arms race *n* corsa *f* agli armamenti

arms treaty *n* trattato *m* sul controllo degli armamenti

arm-twisting /ˈɑːmtwɪstɪŋ/ *n* pressioni *fpl*

arm-wrestling *n* braccio *m* di ferro

✧ **army** /ˈɑːmɪ/ *n* esercito *m*; **join the** ~ arruolarsi

A road *n* Br [strada *f*] statale *f*

─────────────

✧ indicates a very frequent word

aroma /əˈrəʊmə/ *n* aroma *f*

aromatherapist /əˌrəʊməˈθerəpɪst/ *n* aromaterapeuta *mf*

aromatherapy /ərəʊməˈθerəpɪ/ *n* aromaterapia *f*

aromatic /ærəˈmætɪk/ *adj* aromatico

arose /əˈrəʊz/ ▶ ARISE

✧ **around** /əˈraʊnd/ **1** *adv* intorno; **all** ~ tutt'intorno; **I'm not from** ~ **here** non sono di qui; **he's not** ~ non c'è **2** *prep* intorno a; in giro per ‹room, shops, world›

arousal /əˈraʊzl/ *n* eccitazione *f*

arouse /əˈraʊz/ *vt* svegliare; (sexually) eccitare

arpeggio /ɑːˈpedʒɪəʊ/ *n* arpeggio *m*

arrange /əˈreɪndʒ/ *vt* sistemare ‹furniture, books›; organizzare ‹meeting›; fissare ‹date, time›; ~ **to do something** combinare di fare qualcosa

✧ **arrangement** /əˈreɪndʒmənt/ *n* (of furniture) sistemazione *f*; Mus arrangiamento *m*; (agreement) accordo; (of flowers) composizione *f*; **make** ~**s** prendere disposizioni; **I've made other** ~**s** ho preso altri impegni

array /əˈreɪ/ **1** *n* (clothes) abbigliamento *m*; (of troops, people) schieramento *m*; (of numbers) tabella *f*; (of weaponry) apparato *m*; (of goods, products) assortimento *m*; Comput matrice *f* **2** *vt* ~**ed in ceremonial robes** abbigliato da gran cerimonia

arrears /əˈrɪəz/ *npl* arretrati *mpl*; **be in** ~ essere in arretrato; **paid in** ~ pagato a lavoro eseguito

✧ **arrest** /əˈrest/ **1** *n* arresto *m*; **under** ~ in stato d'arresto **2** *vt* arrestare

arresting /əˈrestɪŋ/ *adj* (striking) che colpisce

arrival /əˈraɪvl/ *n* arrivo *m*; **new** ~**s** *pl* nuovi arrivati *mpl*

arrivals board *n* tabellone *m* degli arrivi

arrival(s) lounge *n* sala *f* arrivi

arrival time *n* ora *f* d'arrivo

✧ **arrive** /əˈraɪv/ *vi* arrivare; ~ **at** *fig* raggiungere

arrogance /ˈærəg(ə)ns/ *n* arroganza *f*

arrogant /ˈærəg(ə)nt/ *adj* arrogante

arrogantly /ˈærəg(ə)ntlɪ/ *adv* con arroganza

arrow /ˈærəʊ/ *n* freccia *f*

arrowhead /ˈærəʊhed/ *n* punta *f* di freccia

arse /ɑːs/ *n* Br vulg culo *m* ■ **arse about**, **arse around** *vi* vulg coglioneggiare

arsenal /ˈɑːsən(ə)l/ *n* arsenale *m*

arsenic /ˈɑːsənɪk/ *n* arsenico *m*

arson /'ɑːsən/ *n* incendio *m* doloso

arsonist /'ɑːsənɪst/ *n* incendiario, -a *mf*

ꝰ **art** /ɑːt/ *n* arte *f*; **work of** ~ opera *f* d'arte; ~**s and crafts** *pl* artigianato *m*; **the A**~**s** *pl* l'arte *f*; **A**~**s degree** Univ laurea *f* in Lettere

art collection *n* collezione *f* d'arte

art collector *n* collezionista *mf* d'arte

art college *n* ≈ accademia *f* di belle arti

art dealer *n* commerciante *mf* di oggetti d'arte

art deco *n* art déco *f*

artefact /'ɑːtɪfækt/ *n* manufatto *m*

arterial /ɑːˈtɪərɪəl/ *adj* Anat arterioso

arterial road *n* arteria *f* [stradale]

artery /'ɑːtərɪ/ *n* arteria *f*

art exhibition *n* mostra *f* d'arte

art form *n* forma *f* d'arte

artful /'ɑːtfl/ *adj* scaltro

artfully /'ɑːtfʊlɪ/ *adv* astutamente

art gallery *n* galleria *f* d'arte

arthritic /ɑːˈθrɪtɪk/ *adj* & *n* artritico, -a *mf*

arthritis /ɑːˈθraɪtɪs/ *n* artrite *f*

artichoke /'ɑːtɪtʃəʊk/ *n* carciofo *m*

ꝰ **article** /'ɑːtɪkl/ *n* articolo *m*; ~ **of clothing** capo *m* d'abbigliamento

articulate¹ /ɑːˈtɪkjʊlət/ *adj* ‹speech› chiaro; **be** ~ esprimersi bene

articulate² /ɑːˈtɪkjʊleɪt/ *vt* scandire ‹words›

articulated lorry /ɑːˈtɪkjʊleɪtɪd/ *n* autotreno *m*

articulately /ɑːˈtɪkjʊlətlɪ/ *adv* chiaramente

articulation /ɑːˌtɪkjʊˈleɪʃn/ *n* (pronunciation, Anat) articolazione *f*; (expression) espressione *f*

artifice /'ɑːtɪfɪs/ *n* artificio *m*

artificial /ɑːtɪˈfɪʃl/ *adj* artificiale

artificial insemination *n* inseminazione *f* artificiale

artificial intelligence *n* intelligenza *f* artificiale

artificiality /ɑːtɪfɪʃɪˈælətɪ/ *n* artificiosità *f*

artificial limb *n* arto *m* artificiale

artificially /ɑːtɪˈfɪʃəlɪ/ *adv* artificialmente; ‹smile› artificiosamente

artificial respiration *n* respirazione *f* artificiale

artillery /ɑːˈtɪlərɪ/ *n* artiglieria *f*

artisan /ɑːtɪˈzæn/ *n* artigiano, -a *mf*

ꝰ **artist** /'ɑːtɪst/ *n* artista *mf*

artiste /ɑːˈtiːst/ *n* Theat artista *mf*

artistic /ɑːˈtɪstɪk/ *adj* artistico

artistically /ɑːˈtɪstɪklɪ/ *adv* artisticamente

artistry /'ɑːtɪstrɪ/ *n* arte *f*, talento *m*

artless /'ɑːtlɪs/ *adj* spontaneo

artlessly /'ɑːtlɪslɪ/ *adv* ‹smile› ingenuamente

art nouveau /ɑːnuːˈvəʊ/ *adj* & *n* liberty *m*

art school *n* ≈ accademia *f* di belle arti

arts degree *n* laurea *f* in Lettere

arts funding *n* sovvenzioni *fpl* alle arti

arts student *n* studente, -essa *mf* di Lettere

art student *n* studente, -essa *mf* di belle arti

artwork /'ɑːtwɜːk/ *n* illustrazioni *fpl*

arty /'ɑːtɪ/ *adj* fam ‹person› intellettualoide; ‹district› degli intellettuali

AS *n* esame (*m*) sostenuto al termine del primo anno del biennio di preparazione agli A-Level

ꝰ **as** /æz/ ☐1 *conj* come; (since) siccome; (while) mentre; **as he grew older** diventando vecchio; **as you get to know her** conoscendola meglio; **young as she is** per quanto sia giovane

☐2 *prep* come; **as a friend** come amico; **as a child** da bambino; **as a foreigner** in quanto straniero; **disguised as** travestito da

☐3 *adv* **as well** also anche; **as soon as I get home** [non] appena arrivo a casa; **as quick as you** veloce quanto te; **as quick as you can** più veloce che puoi; **as far as** (distance) fino a; **as far as I'm concerned** per quanto mi riguarda; **as long as** finché; (provided that) purché

asap /'eɪsæp/ *adv abbr* (**as quickly as possible**) prima possibile

asbestos /æzˈbɛstɒs/ *n* amianto *m*

ASBO /'æzbəʊ/ *n abbr* Br (**Antisocial Behaviour Order**) ordinanza (*f*) giudiziaria emessa contro chi ha comportamenti contrari all'ordine pubblico

ascend /əˈsend/ ☐1 *vi* salire

☐2 *vi* salire a ‹throne›

ascendancy /əˈsend(ə)nsɪ/ *n* **gain the** ~ **over somebody** acquisire una posizione dominante su qualcuno

ascendant /əˈsend(ə)nt/ *n* **be in the** ~ Astr essere in ascendente; fig ‹person› essere in auge

Ascension /əˈsenʃn/ *n* Relig Ascensione *f*

ascent /əˈsent/ *n* ascesa *f*

ascertain /æsəˈteɪn/ *vt* accertare

ascetic /əˈsetɪk/ *adj* & *n* ascetico, -a *mf*

asceticism /əˈsetɪsɪzm/ *n* ascesi *f*

ascribable /əˈskraɪbəbl/ *adj* attribuibile

ascribe /əˈskraɪb/ *vt* attribuire

aseptic /eɪˈseptɪk/ *adj* asettico

asexual /eɪˈseksjʊəl/ *adj* asessuale, asessuato

ash¹ /æʃ/ *n* (tree) frassino *m*

ash² *n* cenere *f*

ashamed /əˈʃeɪmd/ *adj* **be/feel** ~ vergognarsi

ash blond *adj* biondo cenere

a

ashen /'æʃ(ə)n/ adj (complexion) cinereo

ashore /ə'ʃɔː(r)/ adv a terra; **go ~** sbarcare

ashtray n portacenere m

ash tree n frassino m

Ash Wednesday n mercoledì m inv delle Ceneri

Asia /'eɪʒə/ n Asia f

Asia Minor n Asia f Minore

Asian /'eɪʒ(ə)n/ adj & n asiatico, -a mf; Br (Indian, Pakistani) indiano, -a mf

Asiatic /eɪʒɪ'ætɪk/ adj asiatico

ℰ **aside** /ə'saɪd/ ① adv take somebody ~ prendere qualcuno a parte; **put something ~** mettere qualcosa da parte; **~ from you** Am a parte te; **~ from his injuries** Am a parte le sue ferite
② n in an ~ tra parentesi

asinine /'æsɪnaɪn/ adj sciocco

ℰ **ask** /ɑːsk/ ① vt fare ‹question›; (invite) invitare; **~ somebody something** domandare or chiedere qualcosa a qualcuno; **~ somebody to do something** domandare or chiedere a qualcuno di fare qualcosa
② vi **~ about something** informarsi su qualcosa
■ **ask after** vt chiedere [notizie] di ‹somebody›
■ **ask for** vt chiedere ‹something›; chiedere di ‹somebody›; **~ for trouble** fam andare in cerca di guai
■ **ask in** vt **~ somebody in** invitare qualcuno ad entrare
■ **ask out** vt **~ somebody out** chiedere a qualcuno di uscire

askance /ə'skɑːns/ adv **look ~ at somebody/something** guardare qualcuno/qualcosa di traverso

askew /ə'skjuː/ adj & adv di traverso

asking price /'ɑːskɪŋ/ n prezzo m trattabile

asleep /ə'sliːp/ adj **be ~** dormire; **fall ~** addormentarsi

asparagus /ə'spærəgəs/ n asparagi mpl

ℰ **aspect** /'æspekt/ n aspetto m

aspen /'æspən/ n pioppo m tremulo

aspersions /ə'spɜːʃnz/ npl **cast ~ on** diffamare

asphalt /'æsfælt/ n asfalto m

asphyxia /əs'fɪksɪə/ n asfissia f

asphyxiate /əs'fɪksɪeɪt/ vt asfissiare

asphyxiation /əsfɪksɪ'eɪʃn/ n asfissia f

aspic /'æspɪk/ n aspic m inv

aspirate¹ /'æspəreɪt/ vt aspirare

aspirate² /'æspɪrət/ adj aspirato

aspirations /æspə'reɪʃnz/ npl aspirazioni fpl

aspire /ə'spaɪə(r)/ vi **~ to** aspirare a

aspirin /'æspərɪn/ n aspirina f

aspiring /ə'spaɪərɪŋ/ adj **~ authors/ journalists** aspiranti scrittori/giornalisti

ass /æs/ n (animal) asino m; Am vulg (part of body) culo m

assailant /ə'seɪlənt/ n assalitore, -trice mf

assassin /ə'sæsɪn/ n assassino, -a mf

assassinate /ə'sæsɪneɪt/ vt assassinare

assassination /əsæsɪ'neɪʃn/ n assassinio m

assault /ə'sɔːlt/ ① n Mil assalto m; Jur aggressione f
② vt aggredire

assault and battery n Jur lesioni fpl personali

assault course n Mil percorso m di guerra

assemblage /ə'semblɪdʒ/ assemblaggio m

assemble /ə'sembl/ ① vi radunarsi
② vi radunare; Techn montare

assembler /ə'semblə(r)/ n (in factory) montatore, -trice mf; Comput [programma] m, assemblatore m

assembly /ə'semblɪ/ n assemblea f; Sch assemblea f giornaliera di alunni e professori di una scuola; Techn montaggio m

assembly line n catena f di montaggio

assent /ə'sent/ ① n assenso m
② vi acconsentire

assert /ə'sɜːt/ vt asserire; far valere ‹one's rights›; **~ oneself** farsi valere

assertion /ə'sɜːʃn/ n asserzione f

assertive /ə'sɜːtɪv/ adj **be ~** farsi valere

assertiveness /ə'sɜːtɪvnɪs/ n capacità f di farsi valere; **lack of ~** scarsa sicurezza f di sé

ℰ **assess** /ə'ses/ vt valutare; (for tax purposes) stabilire l'imponibile di

ℰ **assessment** /ə'sesmənt/ n valutazione f; (of tax) accertamento m

assessor /ə'sesə(r)/ n Jur (in insurance) perito m; (tax) agente m del fisco

ℰ **asset** /'æset/ n (advantage) vantaggio m; (person) elemento m prezioso; **~s** pl beni mpl; (on balance sheet) attivo msg

asset stripping /'æsetstrɪpɪŋ/ n rilevamento (m) di un'azienda per rivenderne le single attività fisse

assiduity /æsɪ'djuːətɪ/ n assiduità f

assiduous /ə'sɪdjʊəs/ adj assiduo

assign /ə'saɪn/ vt assegnare

assignation /æsɪg'neɪʃn/ n hum appuntamento m galante

assignment /ə'saɪnmənt/ n (task) incarico m

assimilate /ə'sɪmɪleɪt/ vt assimilare; integrare ‹person›

assimilation /əsɪmɪ'leɪʃn/ n assimilazione f

ℰ indicates a very frequent word

assist /əˈsɪst/ *vt/i* assistere; ~ somebody to do something assistere qualcuno nel fare qualcosa

assistance /əˈsɪstəns/ *n* assistenza *f*

assistant /əˈsɪstənt/ *n* assistente *mf*; (in shop) commesso, -a *mf*

assistant manager *n* vicedirettore, -trice *mf*

assistant professor *n* Am Univ docente *mf* universitario, -a del grado più basso

assisted suicide /əˈsɪstɪd ˈsuːɪsaɪd/ *n* suicidio *m* assistito, eutanasia *f*

associate¹ /əˈsəʊʃɪeɪt/ **1** *vt* associare (with a); be ~d with something (involved in) essere coinvolto in qualcosa
2 *vi* ~ with frequentare

associate² /əˈsəʊʃɪət/ **1** *adj* associato
2 *n* collega *mf*; (member) socio, -a *mf*

associate company *n* consociata *f*

associate director *n* Comm amministratore *m* aggiunto

associate editor *n* co-redattore, -trice *mf*

associate member *n* membro *m* associato

association /əsəʊsɪˈeɪʃn/ *n* associazione *f*

Association Football *n* [gioco *m* del] calcio *m*

assorted /əˈsɔːtɪd/ *adj* assortito

assortment /əˈsɔːtmənt/ *n* assortimento *m*

assuage /əˈsweɪdʒ/ *vt* liter alleviare

assume /əˈsjuːm/ *vt* presumere; assumere ‹controb›; ~ office entrare in carica; assuming that you're right,... ammettendo che tu abbia ragione, ...

assumption /əˈsʌmpʃn/ *n* supposizione *f*; on the ~ that partendo dal presupposto che; the A~ Relig l'Assunzione *f*

assurance /əˈʃʊərəns/ *n* assicurazione *f*; (confidence) sicurezza *f*

assure /əˈʃʊə(r)/ *vt* assicurare; he ~d me of his innocence mi ha assicurato di essere innocente

assured /əˈʃʊəd/ *adj* sicuro

Assyria /əˈsɪrɪə/ *n* Assiria *f*

asterisk /ˈæstərɪsk/ *n* asterisco *m*

astern /əˈstɜːn/ *adv* a poppa

asteroid /ˈæstərɔɪd/ *n* asteroide *m*

asthma /ˈæsmə/ *n* asma *f*

asthmatic /æsˈmætɪk/ *adj* asmatico

astigmatism /əˈstɪgmətɪzm/ *n* astigmatismo *m*

astonish /əˈstɒnɪʃ/ *vt* stupire

astonished /əˈstɒnɪʃt/ *adj* sorpreso

astonishing /əˈstɒnɪʃɪŋ/ *adj* stupefacente

astonishingly /əˈstɒnɪʃɪŋlɪ/ *adv* sorprendentemente

astonishment /əˈstɒnɪʃmənt/ *n* stupore *m*

astound /əˈstaʊnd/ *vt* stupire

astounding /əˈstaʊndɪŋ/ *adj* incredible

astrakhan /æstrəˈkæn/ *n* astrakan *m*

astray /əˈstreɪ/ *adv* go ~ smarrirsi; (morally) uscire dalla retta via; lead ~ traviare

astride /əˈstraɪd/ **1** *adv* [a] cavalcioni
2 *prep* a cavalcioni di

astringent /əˈstrɪndʒənt/ **1** *adj* astringente; fig austero
2 *n* astringente *m*

astrologer /əˈstrɒlədʒə(r)/ *n* astrologo, -a *mf*

astrological /æstrəˈlɒdʒɪkl/ *adj* astrologico

astrology /əˈstrɒlədʒɪ/ *n* astrologia *f*

astronaut /ˈæstrənɔːt/ *n* astronauta *mf*

astronomer /əˈstrɒnəmə(r)/ *n* astronomo, -a *mf*

astronomic /æstrəˈnɒmɪk/ *adj* fig astronomico

astronomical /æstrəˈnɒmɪkl/ *adj* also fig astronomico

astronomically /æstrəˈnɒmɪklɪ/ *adv* ~ expensive dal prezzo astronomico; prices are ~ high i prezzi sono astronomici

astronomy /əˈstrɒnəmɪ/ *n* astronomia *f*

astrophysicist /æstrəʊˈfɪzɪsɪst/ *n* astrofisico, -a *mf*

astrophysics /æstrəʊˈfɪzɪks/ *n* astrofisica *f*

astute /əˈstjuːt/ *adj* astuto

astutely /əˈstjuːtlɪ/ *adv* con astuzia

astuteness /əˈstjuːtnɪs/ *n* astuzia *f*

asylum /əˈsaɪləm/ *n* [political] ~ asilo *m* politico; [lunatic] ~ manicomio *m*

asylum-seeker /əˈsaɪləmsiːkə(r)/ *n* persona *f* che chiede asilo politico

asymmetric[al] /æsɪˈmetrɪk[l]/ *adj* asimmetrico

at /ət/, *accentato* /æt/ *prep* at the station/ the market alla stazione/al mercato; at the office/the bank in ufficio/banca; at the beginning all'inizio; at John's da John; at the hairdresser's dal parrucchiere; at home a casa; at work al lavoro; at school a scuola; at a party/wedding a una festa/un matrimonio; at one o'clock all'una; at 50 km an hour a 50 all'ora; at Christmas/Easter a Natale/Pasqua; at times talvolta; two at a time due alla volta; good at languages bravo nelle lingue; at sb's request su richiesta di qualcuno; are you at all worried? sei preoccupato?

atavistic /ætəˈvɪstɪk/ *adj* atavico

ate /et/ ▶ EAT

atheism /ˈeɪθɪɪzm/ *n* ateismo *m*

atheist /ˈeɪθɪɪst/ *n* ateo, -a *mf*

atheistic /eɪθɪˈɪstɪk/ adj ‹principle› ateistico; ‹person› ateo

Athenian /əˈθiːnɪən/ adj & n ateniese mf

Athens /ˈæθənz/ n Atene f

athlete /ˈæθliːt/ n atleta mf

athlete's foot n micosi f

athletic /æθˈletɪk/ adj atletico

athletics /æθˈletɪks/ n atletica fsg

Atlantic /ətˈlæntɪk/ adj & n the ~ [Ocean] l'[Oceano m] Atlantico m

atlas /ˈætləs/ n atlante m

Atlas Mountains npl Monti mpl dell'Atlante

ATM n abbr (**automatic teller machine**) cassa f continua di prelevamento

atmosphere /ˈætməsfɪə(r)/ n atmosfera f

atmospheric /ætməsˈferɪk/ adj atmosferico

atom /ˈætəm/ n atomo m

atom bomb n bomba f atomica

atomic /əˈtɒmɪk/ adj atomico

atomic physics n fisica f atomica

atomic power station n centrale f atomica

atomic reactor n reattore m nucleare

atomic scientist n fisico, -a mf nucleare

atomize /ˈætəmaɪz/ vt atomizzare

atomizer /ˈætəmaɪzə(r)/ n atomizzatore m

atone /əˈtəʊn/ vi ~ for pagare per

atonement /əˈtəʊnmənt/ n espiazione f

at-risk adj a rischio; the ~ **register** l'elenco dei soggetti a rischio

atrocious /əˈtrəʊʃəs/ adj atroce; fam ‹meal, weather› abominevole

atrociously /əˈtrəʊʃəslɪ/ adv atrocemente; ‹rude etc› terribilmente

atrocity /əˈtrɒsətɪ/ n atrocità f inv

atrophy /ˈætrəfɪ/ [1] n Med atrofia f [2] vi Med fig atrofizzarsi

at sign n Comput chiocciola f

⚘ **attach** /əˈtætʃ/ vt attaccare; attribuire ‹importance›; **be** ~**ed to** fig essere attaccato a

attaché /əˈtæʃeɪ/ n addetto m

attaché case n ventiquattrore f inv

attached /əˈtætʃt/ adj ‹document› allegato; (fond) ~ **to** affezionato a

attachment /əˈtætʃmənt/ n (affection) attaccamento m; (accessory) accessorio m; Comput allegato m

⚘ **attack** /əˈtæk/ [1] n attacco m; (physical) aggressione f [2] vt attaccare; (physically) aggredire

attacker /əˈtækə(r)/ n assalitore, -trice mf; (critic) detrattore, -trice mf

attain /əˈteɪn/ vt realizzare ‹ambition›; raggiungere ‹success, age, goal›

attainable /əˈteɪnəbl/ adj ‹ambition› realizzabile; ‹success› raggiungibile

attainment /əˈteɪnmənt/ n (of knowledge) acquisizione f; (of goal) realizzazione f, raggiungimento m; (success) risultato m

⚘ **attempt** /əˈtempt/ [1] n tentativo m [2] vt tentare

⚘ **attend** /əˈtend/ [1] vt essere presente a; (go regularly to) frequentare; (accompany) accompagnare; ‹doctor› avere in cura [2] vi essere presente; (pay attention) prestare attenzione

■ **attend to** vt occuparsi di; (in shop) servire

attendance /əˈtendəns/ n presenza f

attendance record n (of MP, committee member, schoolchild) tasso m di presenza

attendance register n Sch registro m

attendant /əˈtendənt/ n guardiano, -a mf

attendee /æten'diː/ n partecipante mf

⚘ **attention** /əˈtenʃn/ n attenzione f; Mil ~! attenti!; **pay** ~ prestare attenzione; **need** ~ aver bisogno di attenzioni; ‹skin, hair, plant› dover essere curato; ‹car, tyres› dover essere riparato; **for the** ~ **of** all'attenzione di

attention deficit disorder n Med disturbo m da deficit dell'attenzione

attention-seeking /əˈtenʃnsiːkɪŋ/ [1] n bisogno m di attirare l'attenzione [2] adj ‹person› che cerca di attirare l'attenzione

attention span n he has a very short ~ non è capace di mantenere a lungo la concentrazione

attentive /əˈtentɪv/ adj ‹pupil, audience› attento; ‹son› premuroso

attentively /əˈtentɪvlɪ/ adv attentamente

attentiveness /əˈtentɪvnɪs/ n (concentration) attenzione f; (solicitude) sollecitudine f

attenuate /əˈtenjʊeɪt/ vt attenuare

attest /əˈtest/ vt/i attestare

attic /ˈætɪk/ n soffitta f

attic room n mansarda f

attic window n lucernario m

attire /əˈtaɪə(r)/ [1] n abiti mpl [2] vt vestire (**in** con)

⚘ **attitude** /ˈætɪtjuːd/ n atteggiamento m

attn. abbr (**attention**) c.a.

attorney /əˈtɜːnɪ/ n Am (lawyer) avvocato m; **power of** ~ delega f

Attorney General n Br ≈ Procuratore m Generale; Am ≈ Ministro m di Grazia e Giustizia

⚘ **attract** /əˈtrækt/ vt attirare

attraction /əˈtrækʃn/ n attrazione f; (feature) attrattiva f

attractive /əˈtræktɪv/ adj ‹person› attraente; ‹proposal, price› allettante

attractiveness /əˈtræktɪvnɪs/ n (of person, place) fascino m; (of proposal) carattere

---

⚘ indicates a very frequent word

m allettante; (of investment) covenienza *f*

attributable /ə'trɪbjʊtəbl/ *adj* (error, fall, loss etc) attribuibile; **be ∼ to** ‹change, profit, success etc› essere dovuto a

attribute¹ /'ætrɪbjuːt/ *n* attributo *m*

attribute² /ə'trɪbjuːt/ *vt* attribuire

attribution /ætrɪ'bjuːʃn/ *n* attribuzione *f*

attributive /ə'tribjʊtɪv/ *adj* attributivo

attrition /ə'trɪʃn/ *n* **war of ∼** guerra *f* di logoramento

attune /ə'tjuːn/ *vt* **be ∼d to** (in harmony with) essere sintonizzato con; (accustomed to) essere abituato a

aubergine /'əʊbəʒiːn/ *n* melanzana *f*

auburn /'ɔːbən/ *adj* castano ramato

auction /'ɔːkʃn/ ① *n* asta *f* ② *vt* vendere all'asta

auctioneer /ɔːkʃə'nɪə(r)/ *n* banditore *m*

auction house *n* casa *f* d'aste

auction rooms *npl* sala *f* d'aste

auction sale *n* vendita *f* all'asta

audacious /ɔː'deɪʃəs/ *adj* sfacciato; (daring) audace

audaciously /ɔː'deɪʃəslɪ/ *adv* sfacciatamente; (daringly) con audacia

audacity /ɔː'dæsətɪ/ *n* sfacciataggine *f*; (daring) audacia *f*

audible /'ɔːdəbl/ *adj* udibile

⚘ **audience** /'ɔːdɪəns/ *n* Theat pubblico *m*; TV telespettatori *mpl*; Radio ascoltatori *mpl*; (meeting) udienza *f*

audience participation *n* partecipazione *f* del pubblico

audience ratings *npl* indici *mpl* di ascolto

audience research *n* sondaggio *m* tra il pubblico

audio /'ɔːdɪəʊ/ *pref* audio

audiobook *n* audiolibro *m*

audio cassette *n* audiocassetta *f*

audio system *n* impianto *m* stereo

audiotape *n* audiocassetta *f*

audiotyping *n* trascrizione *f* da audiocassetta

audio typist *n* dattilografo, -a *mf* (che trascrive registrazioni)

audiovisual *adj* audiovisivo

audit /'ɔːdɪt/ ① *n* verifica *f* del bilancio ② *vt* verificare

auditing /'ɔːdɪtɪŋ/ *n* auditing *m inv*

audition /ɔː'dɪʃn/ ① *n* audizione *f* ② *vi* fare un'audizione

auditor /'ɔːdɪtə(r)/ *n* revisore *m* di conti

auditorium /ɔːdɪ'tɔːrɪəm/ *n* sala *f*

auditory /'ɔːdɪt(ə)rɪ/ *adj* acustico, uditivo

augment /ɔːg'ment/ *vt* aumentare

augur /'ɔːgə(r)/ *vi* **∼ well/ill** essere di buon/cattivo augurio

⚘ **August** /'ɔːgəst/ *n* agosto *m*

august /ɔː'gʌst/ *adj* augusto

Augustinian /ɔːgə'stɪnɪən/ *adj* agostiniano

aunt /ɑːnt/ *n* zia *f*

auntie, **aunty** /'ɑːntɪ/ *n* fam zietta *f*

au pair /əʊ'peə(r)/ *n* **∼ [girl]** ragazza *f* alla pari

aura /'ɔːrə/ *n* aura *f*

aural /'ɔːrəl/ ① *adj* uditivo; Sch ‹comprehension, test› orale; Med ‹test› audiometrico ② *n* Sch esercizio *m* di comprensione ed espressione orale; Mus ≈ dettato *m* musicale

aurora australis/borealis /ɔː'rɔːrəʊ'strɑːlɪs / bɔːrɪ'ɑːlɪs/ *n* aurora *f* australe/boreale

auspices /'ɔːspɪsɪz/ *npl* **under the ∼ of** sotto l'egida di

auspicious /ɔː'spɪʃəs/ *adj* di buon augurio

Aussie /'ɒzɪ/ *adj* & *n* fam australiano, -a *mf*

austere /ɒ'stɪə(r)/ *adj* austero

austerity /ɒ'sterətɪ/ *n* austerità *f*

Australasia /ɒstrə'leɪʒə/ *n* Australasia *f*

Australia /ɒ'streɪlɪə/ *n* Australia *f*

⚘ **Australian** /ɒ'streɪlɪən/ *adj* & *n* australiano, -a *mf*

Austria /'ɒstrɪə/ *n* Austria *f*

Austrian /'ɒstrɪən/ *adj* & *n* austriaco, -a *mf*

Austro-Hungarian /ɒstrəʊhʌŋ'geərɪən/ *adj* austroungarico

autarchy /'ɔːtɑːkɪ/ *n* autarchia *f*

authentic /ɔː'θentɪk/ *adj* autentico

authenticate /ɔː'θentɪkeɪt/ *vt* autenticare

authenticity /ɔːθen'tɪsətɪ/ *n* autenticità *f*

⚘ **author** /'ɔːθə(r)/ *n* autore *m*

authoritarian /ɔːθɒrɪ'teərɪən/ *adj* autoritario

authoritative /ɔː'θɒrɪtətɪv/ *adj* autorevole; ‹manner› autoritario

⚘ **authority** /ɔː'θɒrətɪ/ *n* autorità *f*; (permission) autorizzazione *f*; **who's in ∼ here?** chi è il responsabile qui?; **be in ∼ over** avere autorità su; **be an ∼ on** essere un'autorità in materia di

authorization /ɔːθəraɪ'zeɪʃn/ *n* autorizzazione *f*

authorize /'ɔːθəraɪz/ *vt* autorizzare

authorized dealer /'ɔːθəraɪzd/ rivenditore *m* autorizzato

autism /'ɔːtɪzm/ *n* autismo *m*

autistic /ɔː'tɪstɪk/ *adj* autistico

autistic spectrum disorder *n* disordine *m* dello spettro autistico

auto /'ɔːtəʊ/ ① *n* Am fam auto *f* ② *attrib* ‹industry› automobilistico; ‹workers› dell'industria automobilistica

autobiographical /ɔːtəbaɪə'ɡræfɪkl/ *adj* autobiografico

a

autobiography /ɔ:təbaɪˈɒɡrəfɪ/ n
autobiografia f
autocrat /ˈɔ:təkræt/ n autocrate m
autocratic /ɔ:təˈkrætɪk/ adj autocratico
autocue /ˈɔ:təʊkju:/ n TV gobbo m
auto-destruct vi ‹spacecraft, missile›
autodistruggersi
autograph /ˈɔ:təɡrɑ:f/ [1] n autografo m
[2] vt autografare
autoimmune /ɔ:təʊɪˈmju:n/ adj ‹disease,
system› autoimmune
automate /ˈɔ:təmeɪt/ vt automatizzare
automatic /ɔ:təˈmætɪk/ [1] adj
automatico
[2] n (car) macchina f col cambio
automatico; (washing machine) lavatrice f
automatica
automatically /ɔ:təˈmætɪklɪ/ adv
automaticamente
automatic pilot n (device) pilota m
automatico; **be on** ~ also fig viaggiare con il
pilota automatico inserito
automatic teller machine /ˈtelə/ n
cassa f continua di prelevamento
automation /ɔ:təˈmeɪʃn/ n automazione f
automaton /ɔ:ˈtɒmətən/ n automa m
automobile /ˈɔ:təməbi:l/ n Am automobile
f
automotive /ɔ:təˈməʊtɪv/ adj (self-
propelling) autopropulso; ‹design, industry›
automobilistico
autonomous /ɔ:ˈtɒnəməs/ adj autonomo
autonomously /ɔ:ˈtɒnəməslɪ/ adv
autonomamente
autonomy /ɔ:ˈtɒnəmɪ/ n autonomia f
autopilot /ˈɔ:təʊpaɪlət/ n Aeron fig pilota m
automatico
autopsy /ˈɔ:tɒpsɪ/ n autopsia f
auto-suggestion /ɔ:təʊsəˈdʒestʃən/ n
autosuggestione f
◆ **autumn** /ˈɔ:təm/ n autunno m
autumnal /ɔ:ˈtʌmnl/ adj autunnale
auxiliary /ɔ:ɡˈzɪlɪərɪ/ [1] adj ausiliario
[2] n ausiliare m
auxiliary nurse n infermiere, -a mf
ausiliario
auxiliary verb n ausiliare m
avail /əˈveɪl/ [1] n to no ~ invano
[2] vi ~ oneself of approfittare di
availability /əveɪləˈbɪlətɪ/ n (option,
service) disponibilità f; (of drugs) reperibilità
f, disponibilità f; **subject to** ~ fino ad
esaurimento
◆ **available** /əˈveɪləbl/ adj disponibile; ‹book,
record etc› in vendita
avalanche /ˈævəlɑ:nʃ/ n valanga f
avant-garde /ævɒ̃ˈɡɑ:d/ [1] n
avanguardia f

[2] adj d'avanguardia
avarice /ˈævərɪs/ n avidità f
avaricious /ævəˈrɪʃəs/ adj avido
Ave abbr (**Avenue**) V.le
avenge /əˈvendʒ/ vt vendicare
avenger /əˈvendʒə(r)/ n vendicatore, -trice
mf
avenging /əˈvendʒɪŋ/ adj vendicatore
avenue /ˈævənju:/ n viale m; fig strada f
◆ **average** /ˈævərɪdʒ/ [1] adj medio;
(mediocre) mediocre
[2] n media f; **on** ~ in media; **above** ~
superiore al normale
[3] vt ‹sales, attendance etc› raggiungere una
media di
■ **average out at** vt risultare in media
averse /əˈvɜ:s/ adj not be ~ to something
non essere contro qualcosa
aversion /əˈvɜ:ʃn/ n avversione f (to per)
avert /əˈvɜ:t/ vt evitare ‹crisis›; distogliere
‹eyes›
aviary /ˈeɪvɪərɪ/ n uccelliera f
aviation /eɪvɪˈeɪʃn/ n aviazione f
aviation fuel n benzina f avio
aviation industry n industria f
aeronautica
aviator /ˈeɪvɪeɪtə(r)/ n aviatore, -trice mf
avid /ˈævɪd/ adj avido (for di); ‹reader›
appassionato
avidity /əˈvɪdətɪ/ n avidità
avidly /ˈævɪdlɪ/ adv ‹read, collect›
avidamente; ‹support› con entusiasmo
avocado /ævəˈkɑ:dəʊ/ n avocado m
◆ **avoid** /əˈvɔɪd/ vt evitare
avoidable /əˈvɔɪdəbl/ adj evitabile
avoidance /əˈvɔɪdəns/ n ~ **of one's duty**
astensione f dal proprio dovere
avowed /əˈvaʊd/ adj dichiarato
avuncular /əˈvʌŋkʊlə(r)/ adj benevolo
await /əˈweɪt/ vt attendere
awake /əˈweɪk/ [1] adj sveglio; **wide** ~
completamente sveglio
[2] vi (pt **awoke**, pp **awoken**) svegliarsi
awaken /əˈweɪkn/ [1] vt svegliare
[2] vi svegliarsi
awakening /əˈweɪknɪŋ/ n risveglio m
◆ **award** /əˈwɔ:d/ [1] n premio m; (medal)
riconoscimento m; (of prize) assegnazione f
[2] vt assegnare; ‹hand over› consegnare
award ceremony n cerimonia f di
premiazione
award winner n vincitore, -trice mf di
un premio
award-winning adj ‹book, film, design›
premiato
◆ **aware** /əˈweə(r)/ adj be ~ of (sense)
percepire; (know) essere conscio di; **become**
~ of accorgersi di; (learn) venire a sapere di;
be ~ **that** rendersi conto che

◆ indicates a very frequent word

awareness /ə'weənɪs/ n percezione f; (knowledge) consapevolezza f

awash /ə'wɒʃ/ adj inondato (**with** di)

🞦 **away** /ə'weɪ/ adv via; **go/stay** ~ andare/ stare via; **he's** ~ **from his desk/the office** non è alla sua scrivania/in ufficio; **far** ~ lontano; **four kilometres** ~ a quattro chilometri; **play** ~ Sport giocare fuori casa

away game n partita f fuori casa

awe /ɔː/ n soggezione f; **stand in** ~ **of somebody** avere soggezione di qualcuno

awe-inspiring adj maestoso

awesome /'ɔːsəm/ adj imponente

awful /'ɔːf(ə)l/ ① adj terribile; **that's an** ~ **pity** è un gran peccato
② adv fam estremamente

awfully /'ɔːf(ʊ)lɪ/ adv terribilmente; ⟨pretty⟩ estremamente; **that's** ~ **nice of you** è veramente gentile da parte tua; **thanks** ~ grazie mille

awhile /ə'waɪl/ adv per un po'

awkward /'ɔːkwəd/ adj ⟨movement⟩ goffo; ⟨moment, situation⟩ imbarazzante; ⟨time⟩ scomodo

awkwardly /'ɔːkwədlɪ/ adv ⟨move⟩ goffamente; ⟨say⟩ con imbarazzo; **the meeting is** ~ **timed** la riunione è ad un orario scomodo

awkwardness /'ɔːkwədnɪs/ n ⟨clumsiness⟩ goffaggine f; (inconvenience) scomodità f; (embarrassment) imbarazzo m; (delicacy of situation) delicatezza f

awl /ɔːl/ n (for wood etc) punteruolo m

awning /'ɔːnɪŋ/ n tendone m

awoke(n) /ə'wəʊk(ən)/ ▶ AWAKE

AWOL /'eɪwɒl/ adj & adv abbr (**absent without leave**) be/go ~ Mil assentarsi senza permesso; hum volatilizzarsi

awry /ə'raɪ/ adv storto

axe /æks/ ① n scure f; **have an** ~ **to grind** fig avere il proprio tornaconto
② vt (pres p **axing**) fare dei tagli a ⟨budget⟩; sopprimere ⟨jobs⟩; annullare ⟨project⟩

axiom /'æksɪəm/ n assioma m

axiomatic /æksɪə'mætɪk/ adj **it is** ~ **that...** è indiscutibile che...

axis /'æksɪs/ n (pl **axes** /-siːz/) asse m

axle /'æksl/ n Techn asse m

ay[e] /aɪ/ ① adv sì
② n sì m inv

Azerbaijan /æzəbaɪ'dʒɑːn/ n Azerbaigiano m

Azerbaijani /æzəbaɪ'dʒɑːnɪ/ adj & n (person) azerbaigiano, -a m f; (language) azerbaigiano m

Azores /ə'zɔːz/ npl **the** ~ le Azzorre

Aztec /'æztek/ adj & n (person) azteco, -a m f; (language) azteco m

azure /'eɪʒə(r)/ adj & n azzurro m

B b

b¹, **B** /biː/ n (letter) b, B f inv; Mus si m inv

b² abbr (**born**) nato (n.)

b. & b. abbr (**bed and breakfast**)

BA abbr (**Bachelor of Arts**) (diploma (m) di) dottore in discipline umanistiche

BAA n abbr (**British Airports Authority**) ente (m) che gestisce gli aeroporti britannici

baa /bɑː/ ① vi belare
② int bee

babble /'bæbl/ vi farfugliare; ⟨stream⟩ gorgogliare

babe /beɪb/ n liter bimbo, -a m f; fam (woman) ragazza f; fam (form of address) bella f; **a** ~ **in arms** un bimbo in fasce; fig uno sprovveduto

baboon /bə'buːn/ n babbuino m

🞦 **baby** /'beɪbɪ/ n bambino, -a m f; fam (darling) tesoro m

baby bird n uccellino m

baby boom n baby boom m inv

baby boomer n persona (f) nata durante il baby boom

baby buggy n Br carrozzina f

baby carriage n Am carrozzina f

baby carrier n zaino m portabimbo inv

baby-faced adj ⟨person⟩ con la faccia da bambino

babyish /'beɪbɪɪʃ/ adj bambinesco

baby shower n Am festa (f) in cui si portano regali a una mamma in attesa

baby-sit vi fare da baby-sitter

baby-sitter n baby-sitter m f

baby-sitting n do ~ fare il/la baby-sitter

baby talk n linguaggio m infantile

baby tooth n dente m di latte

baby walker n girello m

babywear n abbigliamento m per bambini

bachelor /'bætʃələ(r)/ n scapolo m; **B**~ **of Arts/Science** laureato, -a m f in lettere/ in scienze

bachelor apartment, bachelor flat
Br *n* appartamento *m* da scapolo
bachelorhood /'bætʃələhʊd/ *n* celibato
m
bacillus /bə'sɪləs/ *n* (*pl* -**lli**) bacillo *m*
⚔ **back** /bæk/ **1** *n* schiena *f*; (of horse, hand)
dorso *m*; (of chair) schienale *m*; (of house,
cheque, page) retro *m*; (in football) difesa *f*; **at
the** ~ in fondo; **in the** ~ Auto dietro; **stand** ~
to ~ stare in piedi schiena contro schiena;
~ **to front** ‹*sweater*› il davanti di dietro;
you've got it all ~ **to front** fig hai capito tutto
all'incontrario; **at the** ~ **of beyond** in un
posto sperduto
2 *adj* posteriore; ‹*taxes, payments*›
arretrato
3 *adv* indietro; (returned) di ritorno; **turn/
move** ~ tornare/spostarsi indietro; **put it**
~ **here/there** rimettilo qui/là; ~ **at home**
di ritorno a casa; **I'll be** ~ **in five minutes**
torno fra cinque minuti; **I'm just** ~ sono
appena tornato; **when do you want the book**
~**?** quando rivuoi il libro?; **pay** ~ ripagare
‹*somebody*›; restituire ‹*money*›; ~ **in power** di
nuovo al potere
4 *vt* (support) sostenere; (with money)
finanziare; puntare su ‹*horse*›; (cover the back
of) rivestire il retro di
5 *vi* Auto fare retromarcia
▪ **back away** *vi* tirarsi indietro
▪ **back down** *vi* battere in ritirata
▪ **back in** *vi* Auto entrare in retromarcia;
‹*person*› entrare camminando all'indietro
▪ **back out** *vi* Auto uscire in retromarcia;
‹*person*› uscire camminando all'indietro; fig
tirarsi indietro (**of** da)
▪ **back up** **1** *vt* sostenere; confermare
‹*person's alibi*›; Comput fare una copia di
salvataggio di; **be** ~**ed up** ‹*traffic*› essere
congestionato
2 *vi* Auto fare retromarcia
backache *n* mal *m* di schiena
backbench *n* Br Pol *scanni (mpl) del
Parlamento dove siedono i parlamentari
ordinari*
backbencher *n* Br Pol parlamentare *mf*
ordinario, -a
backbiting *n* maldicenza *f*
backboard *n* (in basketball) tabellone *m*
back boiler *n* caldaia *f* (*posta dietro un
caminetto*)
backbone *n* spina *f* dorsale
back-breaking *adj* massacrante
back burner *n* put something on the ~
rimandare qualcosa
backchat *n* risposta *f* impertinente
backcloth *n* Theat fondale *m*; fig sfondo *m*
back comb *vt* cotonare
back copy *n* numero *m* arretrato
back cover *n* retro *m* di copertina

⚔ indicates a very frequent word

backdate *vt* retrodatare ‹*cheque*›; ~**d to**
valido a partire da
back door *n* porta *f* di servizio
backdrop *n* Theat fondale *m*; fig sfondo *m*
back-end *n* (rear) fondo *m*
backer /'bækə(r)/ *n* sostenitore, -trice *mf*;
(with money) finanziatore, -trice *mf*
backfire *vi* Auto avere un ritorno di
fiamma; fig ‹*plan*› fallire; **the joke** ~**d on him**
lo scherzo si è ritorto contro di lui
backgammon *n* backgammon *m*
⚔ **background** *n* sfondo *m*; (environment)
ambiente *m*
background noise *n* rumore *m* di
sottofondo
background reading *n* letture *fpl*
generali
backhand *n* Tennis rovescio *m*
backhanded *adj* ‹*compliment*› implicito
backhander *n* fam (bribe) bustarella *f*
backing /'bækɪŋ/ *n* (support)
supporto *m*; (material used) fondo *m*;
Mus accompagnamento *m*; ~ **singer/
vocals/group** cantante/voci/gruppo
d'accompagnamento
back issue *n* numero *m* arretrato
backlash /'bæklæʃ/ *n* fig reazione *f*
opposta
backless /'bæklɪs/ *adj* ‹*dress*› scollato
dietro
backlist *n* opere *fpl* pubblicate
backlog *n* ~ **of work** lavoro *m* arretrato
back marker *n* Sport ultimo, -a *mf*
back number *n* numero *m* arretrato
backpack *n* zaino *m*
backpacker *n* saccopelista *mf*
backpacking *n* **go** ~ viaggiare con zaino
e sacco a pelo
back passage *n* Anat retto *m*
back pay *n* arretrato *m* di stipendio
back-pedal *vi* pedalare all'indietro; fig
fare marcia indietro
back pocket *n* tasca *f* di dietro
backrest *n* schienale *m*
back room *n* stanza *f* sul retro
back room boys *npl* esperti (*mpl) che
lavorano dietro le quinte*
back-scratcher *n* manina *f*
grattaschiena *inv*
back seat *n* sedile *m* posteriore
back-seat driver *n* persona (*f*) che dà
consigli non richiesti
backside *n* fam fondoschiena *m inv*
backslash *n* Typ backslash *nm inv*
back-space *n* Comput backspace *m*
back-stage *adj* & *adv* dietro le quinte
backstairs *npl* scale *f* di servizio

backstitch [1] *n* impuntura *f*
[2] *vi* impunturare
backstop *n* Sport ricevitore *m*
backstory *n* vicende *fpl* passate
back straight *n* Sport rettilineo *m*
backstreet [1] *n* vicolo *m*
[2] *attrib* ‹abortionist› clandestino
backstroke *n* dorso *m*
backtalk *n* Am backchat
backtrack *vi* tornare indietro; fig fare
marcia indietro
back translation *n* traduzione *f* di una
traduzione
backup *n* rinforzi *mpl*; Comput riserva *f*,
backup *m inv*; **do a** ~ realizzare un backup
backup copy *n* copia *f* di riserva
backup light *n* Am luce *f* di retromarcia
backward /'bækwəd/ *adj* ‹step› indietro;
‹child› lento nell'apprendimento; ‹country›
arretrato
backward-looking /'bækwədlʊkɪŋ/ *adj*
retrogrado
backwards Br, **backward** Am
/'bækwəd[z]/ *adv* indietro; ‹fall, walk›
all'indietro; ~ **and forwards** avanti e
indietro
backwater /'bækwɔːtə(r)/ *n* fig luogo *m*
arretrato
backyard /bæk'jɑːd/ *n* cortile *m*; **not in my**
~ **yard** fam non a casa mia
bacon /'beɪk(ə)n/ *n* ≈ pancetta *f*
bacon-slicer /'beɪkənslaɪsə(r)/ *n*
affettatrice *f*
bacteria /bæk'tɪərɪə/ *npl* batteri *mpl*
bacterial /bæk'tɪərɪəl/ *adj* batterico
bacteriology /bæktɪərɪ'ɒlədʒɪ/ *n*
batteriologia *f*
◦ **bad** /bæd/ *adj* (**worse, worst**) cattivo;
‹weather, habit, news, accident› brutto;
‹apple etc› marcio; **the light is** ~ non c'è
una buona luce; **my eyesight is** ~ non ho
una buona vista; **use** ~ **language** dire delle
parolacce; **she's going through a** ~ **patch**
sta attraversando un brutto periodo; **feel** ~
sentirsi male; (feel guilty) sentirsi in colpa;
have a ~ **back** avere dei problemi alla
schiena; **smoking is** ~ **for you** fumare fa
male; **go** ~ andare a male; **that's just too** ~!
pazienza!; **not** ~ niente male; **things have
gone from** ~ **to worse** le cose sono andate di
male in peggio
bad blood *n* there is ~ between them tra
loro non corre buon sangue
bad boy *n* ragazzaccio *m*
bad breath *n* alito *m* cattivo
bad cheque *n* assegno *m* a vuoto
bad debt *n* credito *m* inesigibile
baddie, baddy /'bædɪ/ *n* fam cattivo, -a *mf*
bade /bæd/ ▶ BID¹
bad faith *n* malafede *f*

badge /bædʒ/ *n* distintivo *m*
badger /'bædʒə(r)/ [1] *n* tasso *m*
[2] *vt* tormentare
badly /'bædlɪ/ *adv* male; ‹hurt› gravemente;
~ **off** povero; ~ **behaved** maleducato; **need**
~ aver estremamente bisogno di
bad-mannered /-'mænəd/ *adj*
maleducato
badminton /'bædmɪntən/ *n* badminton *m*
bad-tempered /-'tempəd/ *adj* irascibile
baffle /'bæfl/ *vt* confondere
baffled /'bæfld/ *adj* sconcertato
baffling /'bæflɪŋ/ *adj* sconcertante
BAFTA, Bafta /'bæftə/ *n abbr* (**British
Academy of Film and Television
Arts**) società (*m*) britannica delle arti
cinematografiche e televisive
◦ **bag** /bæg/ [1] *n* borsa *f*; (of paper) sacchetto
m; **old** ~ sl megera *f*; ~**s under the eyes**
occhiaie *fpl*; ~**s of** fam un sacco di; **it's in the**
~ fig è fatta
[2] *vt* (*pt/pp* **bagged**) fam (take)
accaparrarsi; ~ **somebody a seat** tenere un
posto a qualcuno
bagel /'beɪgəl/ *n* panino (*m*) a forma di
ciambella
baggage /'bægɪdʒ/ *n* bagagli *mpl*
baggage allowance *n* franchigia *f*
bagaglio
baggage car *n* Rail bagagliaio *m*
baggage carousel *n* nastro *m*
trasportatore per ritiro bagagli
baggage check *n* controllo *m* bagagli
baggage handler *n* addetto, -a *mf* ai
bagagli
baggage locker *n* armadietto *m* per
deposito bagagli
baggage reclaim *n* ritiro *m* bagagli
baggy /'bægɪ/ *adj* ‹clothes› ampio
Baghdad /bæg'dæd/ *n* Baghdad *f*
bag lady *n* fam barbona *f*
bag person *n* fam barbone, -a *mf*
bagpipes *npl* cornamusa *fsg*
bag snatcher *n* scippatore, -trice *mf*
baguette /bæg'et/ *n* baguette *f inv*
Bahamas /bə'hɑːməz/ *npl* the ~ le
Bahamas
Bahrain, Bahrein /bɑː'reɪn/ *n* Bahrein *m*
bail /beɪl/ *n* cauzione *f*; **on** ~ su cauzione
■ **bail out** [1] *vt* Naut aggottare; ~ **somebody
out** Jur pagare la cauzione per qualcuno; fig
trarre qualcuno d'impaccio
[2] *vi* Aeron paracadutarsi
bail bond *n* Am Jur cauzione *f*
bailiff /'beɪlɪf/ *n* ufficiale *m* giudiziario; (of
estate) fattore *m*
bait /beɪt/ [1] *n* esca *f*; **rise to the** ~
abboccare [all'amo]
[2] *vt* innescare; fig (torment) tormentare

b

baize /beɪz/ n panno m (di tavolo da gioco e da biliardo)

bake /beɪk/ **1** vt cuocere al forno; (make) fare
2 vi cuocersi al forno

baked beans /beɪkt'biːnz/ n Culin fagioli mpl al pomodoro

baked potato n patata (f) cotta al forno (con la buccia)

baker /'beɪkə(r)/ n fornaio, -a mf, panettiere, -a mf

baker's [shop] Br /'beɪkəz/, **bakeshop** Am n panetteria

bakery /'beɪkəri/ n panificio m, forno m

baking /'beɪkɪŋ/ n cottura f al forno

baking powder n lievito m in polvere

baking soda n Culin bicarbonato m di sodio

baking tin n teglia f

balaclava /bælə'klɑːvə/ n passamontagna m inv

✓ **balance** /'bæləns/ **1** n (equilibrium) equilibrio m; Comm bilancio m; (outstanding sum) saldo m; **[bank]** ~ saldo m; **be** or **hang in the** ~ fig essere in sospeso; **on** ~ tutto sommato
2 vt bilanciare; equilibrare ‹budget›; Comm fare il bilancio di ‹books›
3 vi bilanciarsi; Comm essere in pareggio

balanced /'bælənst/ adj equilibrato

balance of payments n bilancia f dei pagamenti

balance of power n Pol equilibrio m delle forze

balance of trade n bilancia f commerciale

balance sheet n bilancio m patrimoniale

balancing act /'bælənsɪŋ/ n fig **do a** ~ fare equilibrismo

balcony /'bælkəni/ n balcone m

bald /bɔːld/ adj ‹person› calvo; ‹tyre› liscio; ‹statement› nudo e crudo; **go** ~ perdere i capelli

balderdash /'bɔːldədæʃ/ n sciocchezze fpl

balding /'bɔːldɪŋ/ adj **be** ~ stare perdendo i capelli

baldly /'bɔːldli/ adv ‹state› in modo nudo e crudo

baldness /'bɔːldnɪs/ n calvizie f

bale /beɪl/ n balla f

Balearic Islands /bæleɪ'ærɪk/ npl isole fpl Baleari

baleful /'beɪlfl/ adj malvagio; (sad) triste

balefully /'beɪlfʊli/ adv con malvagità

Bali /'bɑːli/ pr n Bali f

balk /bɔːlk/ **1** vt ostacolare
2 vi ~ **at** ‹horse› impennarsi davanti a; fig

✓ indicates a very frequent word

---

tirarsi indietro davanti a

Balkan /'bɔːlkən/ adj dei Balcani

Balkans /'bɔːlknz/ npl Balcani mpl

✓ **ball¹** /bɔːl/ n palla f; (football) pallone m; (of yarn) gomitolo m; **on the** ~ fam sveglio

ball² n (dance) ballo m

ballad /'bæləd/ n ballata f

ball and chain n palla f al piede

ball-and-socket joint n giunto m sferico

ballast /'bæləst/ n zavorra f

ball-bearing n cuscinetto m a sfera

ballboy n Tennis raccattapalle m inv

ballcock n Techn galleggiante m (in serbatoio)

ball control n controllo m della palla

ball dress n abito m da sera

ballerina /bælə'riːnə/ n ballerina f [classica]

ballet /'bæleɪ/ n balletto m; (art form) danza f

ballet dancer n ballerino, -a mf [classico, -a]

ballet dress n tutù m inv

ballet shoes npl scarpe fpl da danza

ballgame n gioco m con la palla; Am partita f di baseball; **that's a whole different** ~ fig è tutto un altro paio di maniche

ballgirl n Tennis raccattapalle f inv

ball gown n abito m da sera

ballistic /bə'lɪstɪk/ adj balistico

ballistics n balistica fsg

balloon /bə'luːn/ n pallone m; Aeron mongolfiera f

balloonist /bə'luːnɪst/ n aeronauta mf

ballot /'bælət/ n votazione f

ballot box n urna f

ballot paper n scheda f di votazione

ballpark n Am stadio m di baseball

ballpark figure n fam cifra f approssimativa

ball-point [pen] n penna f a sfera

ballroom n sala f da ballo

ballroom dancing n ballo m liscio

balls up vulg **1** vi incasinarsi
2 vt incasinare

ballyhoo /bælɪ'huː/ n (publicity) battage m inv pubblicitario; (uproar) baccano m

balm /bɑːm/ n balsamo m

balmy /'bɑːmi/ adj (-ier, -iest) mite; fam (crazy) strampalato

balsam /'bɒlsəm/ n (oily) balsamo m

Baltic /'bɔːltɪk/ adj & n **the** ~ **[Sea]** il [mar] Baltico

balustrade /bælə'streɪd/ n balaustra f

bamboo /bæm'buː/ n bambù m

bamboozle /bæm'buːzl/ vt fam (mystify) confondere

ban /bæn/ **1** n proibizione f

2 *vt* (*pt/pp* **banned**) proibire; ~ **from**
espellere da ‹*club*›; **she was ~ned from
driving** le hanno ritirato la patente

banal /bə'nɑːl/ *adj* banale

banality /bə'nælɪtɪ/ *n* banalità *f inv*

banana /bə'nɑːnə/ *n* banana *f*

banana republic *n* pej repubblica *f* delle
banane

banana skin *n* buccia *f* di banana

◦ᶠ **band** /bænd/ *n* banda *f*; (stripe) nastro *m*; Mus
(pop group) complesso *m*; Mus (brass ~) banda
f; Mil fanfara *f*

■ **band together** *vi* riunirsi

bandage /'bændɪdʒ/ **1** *n* benda *f*
2 *vt* fasciare

■ **bandage up** *vt* fasciare

Band-Aid *n* Med cerotto *m*

bandanna, bandana /bæn'dænə/ *n*
bandana *f*

bandit /'bændɪt/ *n* bandito *m*

band leader *n* leader *mf* di un complesso

bandmaster *n* capobanda *m* (*di banda
musicale*)

band saw *n* segatrice *f* a nastro

bandsman *n* bandista *m*

bandstand *n* palco *m* coperto
[dell'orchestra].

bandwagon *n* **jump on the ~** fig seguire
la corrente

bandy¹ /'bændɪ/ *vt* (*pt/pp* **-ied**) scambiarsi
‹*words*›

■ **bandy about** *vt* far circolare

bandy² *adj* (**-ier, -iest**) **be ~** avere le
gambe storte

bandy-legged /-'legd/ *adj* con le gambe
storte

bane /beɪn/ *n* **she/it is the ~ of my life!** è la
mia rovina!

bang /bæŋ/ **1** *n* (noise) fragore *m*; (of gun,
firework) scoppio *m*; (blow) colpo *m*; **go with a
~** fam essere una cannonata
2 *adv* **~ in the middle of** fam proprio nel
mezzo di; **go ~** ‹*gun*› sparare; ‹*balloon*›
esplodere
3 *int* bum!
4 *vt* battere ‹*fist*›; battere su ‹*table*›;
sbattere ‹*door, head*›
5 *vi* scoppiare; ‹*door*› sbattere

■ **bang about, bang around** *vi* far
rumore

■ **bang into** *vt* sbattere contro

banger /'bæŋə(r)/ *n* (firework) petardo
m; fam (sausage) salsiccia *f*; **old ~** fam (car)
macinino *m*

Bangladesh /bæŋglə'deʃ/ *n* Bangladesh
m

Bangladeshi /ˌbæŋglə'deʃɪ/ **1** *adj* del
Bangladesh
2 *n* persona *f* del Bangladesh

bangle /'bæŋgl/ *n* braccialetto *m*

banish /'bænɪʃ/ *vt* bandire

banishment /'bænɪʃmənt/ *n* bando *m*

banister /'bænɪstə/ *n* ringhiera *f*

banjo /'bændʒəʊ/ *n* banjo *m inv*

bank¹ /bæŋk/ **1** *n* (of river) sponda *f*; (slope)
scarpata *f*
2 *vi* Aeron inclinarsi in virata

◦ᶠ **bank²** **1** *n* banca *f*
2 *vt* depositare in banca
3 *vi* ~ **with** avere un conto [bancario]
presso

■ **bank on** *vt* contare su

bank account *n* conto *m* in banca

bank balance *n* saldo *m*

bank-book *n* libretto *m* di risparmio

bank borrowings *npl* prestiti *mpl*
bancari

bank card *n* carta *f* assegni

bank charges *npl* spese *fpl* bancarie,
commissioni *fpl*

bank clerk *n* bancario, -a *mf*

bank details *npl* coordinate *fpl* bancarie

banker /'bæŋkə(r)/ *n* banchiere *m*

banker's draft *n* tratta *f* bancaria

banker's order *n* ordine *m* di pagamento

Bank Giro Credit *n* Br accreditamento
m tramite bancogiro

bank holiday *n* giorno *m* festivo

banking /'bæŋkɪŋ/ *n* bancario *m*

banking hours *npl* orario *m* di sportello
(*in banca*)

bank manager *n* direttore, -trice *mf* di
banca

banknote *n* banconota *f*

bank raid *n* rapina *f* in banca

bank robber *n* rapinatore, -trice *mf* di
banca

bank robbery *n* rapina *f* in banca

bankroll **1** *n* finanziamento *m*
2 *vt* finanziare ‹*person, party*›

bankrupt /'bæŋkrʌpt/ **1** *adj* fallito; **go
~** fallire
2 *n* persona *f* che ha fatto fallimento
3 *vt* far fallire

bankruptcy /'bæŋkrʌptsɪ/ *n* bancarotta *f*

bankruptcy court *n* tribunale *m*
fallimentare

bankruptcy proceedings *npl*
procedura *f* fallimentare

bank statement *n* estratto *m* conto

bank transfer *n* bonifico *m* bancario

banner /'bænə(r)/ *n* stendardo *m*; (of
demonstrators) striscione *m*

banner headline *n* titolo *m* a tutta
pagina

banns /bænz/ *npl* Relig pubblicazioni *fpl* [di
matrimonio]

banquet /'bæŋkwɪt/ *n* banchetto *m*

bantam /'bæntəm/ *n* gallo *m* bantam

banter /'bæntə(r)/ *n* battute *fpl* di spirito
baptism /'bæptɪzm/ *n* battesimo *m*; ~ of fire fig battesimo *m* del fuoco
Baptist /'bæptɪst/ *adj* & *n* battista *mf*
baptize /bæp'taɪz/ *vt* battezzare
◆ **bar** /bɑ:(r)/ [1] *n* sbarra *f*; Jur ordine *m* degli avvocati; (of chocolate) tavoletta *f*; (café) bar *m inv*; (counter) banco *m*; Mus battuta *f*; fig (obstacle) ostacolo *m*; ~ of soap/gold saponetta *f* /lingotto *m*; be called to the ~ Jur entrare a far parte dell'ordine degli avvocati; behind ~s fam dietro le sbarre
[2] *vt* (*pt/pp* **barred**) sbarrare ‹way›; sprangare ‹door›; escludere ‹person›
[3] *prep* tranne; ~ **none** in assoluto
barb /bɑ:b/ *n* barbiglio *m*; fig (remark) frecciata *f*
Barbados /bɑ:'beɪdɒs/ *n* Barbados *fsg*
barbarian /bɑ:'beərɪən/ *n* barbaro, -a *mf*
barbaric /bɑ:'bærɪk/ *adj* barbarico
barbarism /'bɑ:bərɪzm/ *n* (brutality, primitiveness) barbarie *f inv*; (error of style) barbarismo *m*
barbarity /bɑ:'bærətɪ/ *n* barbarie *f inv*
barbarous /'bɑ:bərəs/ *adj* barbaro
barbecue /'bɑ:bɪkju:/ [1] *n* barbecue *m inv*; (party) grigliata *f*, barbecue *m inv*
[2] *vt* arrostire sul barbecue
barbed /bɑ:bd/ *adj* ~ **wire** filo *m* spinato
barber /'bɑ:bə(r)/ *n* barbiere *m*
barber's shop *n* barbiere *m*
barbiturate /bɑ:'bɪtjʊrət/ *n* barbiturico *m*
bar chart *n* istogramma *m*
bar code *n* codice *m* a barre
bar-coded *adj* con codice a barre
bar code reader *n* lettore *m* di codice a barre
bard /bɑ:d/ *n* liter bardo *m*
bare /beə(r)/ [1] *adj* nudo; ‹tree, room› spoglio; ‹floor› senza moquette; the ~ **bones** l'essenziale *m*
[2] *vt* scoprire; mostrare ‹teeth›
bareback *adv* senza sella
barefaced *adj* sfacciato
barefoot *adv* scalzo
bare-headed *adj* a capo scoperto
◆ **barely** /'beəlɪ/ *adv* appena
bareness /'beənɪs/ *n* nudità *f*
bargain /'bɑ:gɪn/ [1] *n* (agreement) patto *m*; (good buy) affare *m*; into the ~ per di più
[2] *vi* contrattare; (haggle) trattare
■ **bargain for** *vt* (expect) aspettarsi
bargain basement *n* reparto *m* occasioni
bargaining /'bɑ:gɪnɪŋ/ [1] *n* (over pay) contrattazione *f*
[2] *attrib* ‹power, rights› contrattuale; ‹position› di negoziato

barge /bɑ:dʒ/ *n* barcone *m*
■ **barge in** *vi* fam (to room) piombare dentro; (into conversation) interrompere bruscamente; ~ **into** piombare dentro a ‹room›; venire addosso a ‹person›; venire addosso a ‹person›
bargepole /'bɑ:dʒpəʊl/ *n* I wouldn't touch him/it with a ~ non lo toccherei nemmeno con un dito
barista /bə'rɪstə/ *n* esp Am barista *mf*
baritone /'bærɪtəʊn/ *n* baritono *m*
bark¹ /bɑ:k/ *n* (of tree) corteccia *f*
bark² [1] *n* abbaio *m*
[2] *vi* abbaiare
barking /'bɑ:kɪŋ/ [1] *n* abbaio *m*
[2] *adj* ‹dog› che abbaia; ‹cough, laugh› convulso
[3] *adv* be ~ **mad** Br fam essere matto da legare
barley /'bɑ:lɪ/ *n* orzo *m*
barleycorn *n* orzo *m*; (grain) chicco *m* d'orzo
barley sugar *n* caramella *f* d'orzo
barley water *n* Br orzata *f*
barley wine *n* Br birra *f* molto forte
barmaid /'bɑ:meɪd/ *n* barista *f*
barman /'bɑ:mən/ *n* barista *m*
barmy /'bɑ:mɪ/ *adj* fam strampalato
barn /bɑ:n/ *n* granaio *m*
barnacle /'bɑ:nəkl/ *n* cirripede *m*
barn dance *n* ballo (*m*) tradizionale statunitense; (social gathering) festa (*f*) negli USA in cui si fanno balli tradizionali
barn owl *n* barbagianni *m inv*
barnstorming *adj* sensazionale
barnyard *n* aia *f*
barometer /bə'rɒmɪtə(r)/ *n* barometro *m*
baron /'bærən/ *n* barone *m*
baroness /'bærənɪs/ *n* baronessa *f*
baronial /bə'rəʊnɪəl/ *adj* baronale
baroque /bə'rɒk/ *adj* & *n* barocco *m*
barracking /'bærəkɪŋ/ *n* fischi *mpl* e insulti *mpl*
barrack room [1] *n* camerata *f*
[2] *attrib* pej ‹language› da caserma
barracks /'bærəks/ *npl* caserma *fsg*
barrage /'bærɑ:ʒ/ *n* (in river) [opera *f* di] sbarramento *m*; Mil sbarramento *m*; fig (of criticism, abuse) sfilza *f*
barrage balloon *n* pallone *m* di sbarramento
barrel /'bærəl/ *n* barile *m*, botte *f*; (of gun) canna *f*
barrel organ *n* organetto *m* [a cilindro]
barren /'bærən/ *adj* sterile; ‹landscape› brullo
barrette /bæ'ret/ *n* Am (for hair) molletta *f*
barricade /bærɪ'keɪd/ [1] *n* barricata *f*
[2] *vt* barricare

◆ indicates a very frequent word

barrier /'bærɪə(r)/ n barriera f; Rail cancello m; fig ostacolo m

barrier cream n crema f protettiva

barrier method n Med metodo m anti-concezionale meccanico

barrier reef n barriera f corallina

barring /'bɑːrɪŋ/ prep ∼ **accidents** salvo imprevisti

barrister /'bærɪstə(r)/ n avvocato m

barrow /'bærəʊ/ n carretto m; (wheel ∼) carriola f

bar stool n sgabello m da bar

bartender /'bɑːtendə(r)/ n barista mf

barter /'bɑːtə(r)/ vi barattare (**for** con)

⚬ᶠ **base** /beɪs/ ① n base f
② adj vile
③ vt basare; **be** ∼**d on** basarsi su

baseball /'beɪsbɔːl/ n baseball m

baseball cap n berretto m da baseball

base camp n campo m base inv

base form n (of verb) forma f non coniugata di un verbo

base lending rate n tasso m base inv di interesse

baseless /'beɪslɪs/ adj infondato

baseline /'beɪslaɪn/ n Tennis linea f di fondo; fig riferimento m

basement /'beɪsmənt/ n seminterrato m

basement flat n appartamento m nel seminterrato

base metal n metallo m vile inv

base rate n tasso m base inv

bash /bæʃ/ ① n colpo m violento; **have a** ∼**!** fam provaci!
② vt colpire [violentemente]; (dent) ammaccare; ∼**ed in** ammaccato

∎ **bash down** vt sfondare ‹door›

∎ **bash into** vt imbattersi in ‹person›; sbattere contro ‹wall, tree›

bashful /'bæʃfl/ adj timido

bashfully /'bæʃfʊlɪ/ adv timidamente

bashing /'bæʃɪŋ/ n fam (beating) pestaggio m; (criticism) critica f feroce; (defeat) batosta f; **take a** ∼ prendere una batosta

⚬ᶠ **basic** /'beɪsɪk/ adj di base; ‹condition, requirement› basilare; ‹living conditions› povero; **my Italian is pretty** ∼ il mio italiano è abbastanza rudimentale; **the** ∼**s** (of language, science) i rudimenti; (essentials) l'essenziale m

⚬ᶠ **basically** /'beɪsɪklɪ/ adv fondamentalmente

basic rate n tariffa f minima; (in tax) aliquota f minima

basil /'bæzɪl/ n basilico m

basilica /bə'zɪlɪkə/ n basilica f

basin /'beɪsn/ n bacinella f; (wash-hand ∼) lavabo m; (for food) recipiente m; Geog bacino m

basinful /'beɪsɪnfʊl/ n bacinella f (contenuto)

⚬ᶠ **basis** /'beɪsɪs/ n (pl **-ses** /'beɪsiːz/) base f

bask /bɑːsk/ vi crogiolarsi

basket /'bɑːskɪt/ n cestino m

basketball n pallacanestro f

basket chair n sedia m di vimini

basketwork n (objects) oggetti mpl in vimini; (craft) lavoro m artigianale di oggetti in vimini

Basle /bɑːl/ n Basilea f

Basque /bæsk/ adj & n (person) basco, -a mf; (language) basco m

bass /beɪs/ ① adj basso; ∼ **voice** voce f di basso
② n basso m

bass-baritone n baritono m basso

bass clef n chiave f di basso

bass drum n grancassa f

basset hound /'bæsɪt/ n basset hound m inv

bass guitar n (chitarra f) basso m

bassist /'beɪsɪst/ n bassista mf

bassoon /bə'suːn/ n fagotto m

bastard /'bɑːstəd/ n (illegitimate child) bastardo, -a mf; sl figlio m di puttana

baste¹ /beɪst/ vt (sew) imbastire

baste² vt Culin ungere con grasso

bastion /'bæstɪən/ n bastione m

bat¹ /bæt/ ① n mazza f; (for table tennis) racchetta f; **off one's own** ∼ fam tutto da solo
② vt (pt/pp **batted**) battere; **she didn't** ∼ **an eyelid** fig non ha battuto ciglio

bat² n Zool pipistrello m

batch /bætʃ/ n gruppo m; (of goods) partita f; (of bread) infornata f

batch file n Comput batch file m inv

batch processing /'prəʊsesɪŋ/ n Comput elaborazione f a gruppi

bated /'beɪtɪd/ adj **with** ∼ **breath** col fiato sospeso

bath /bɑːθ/ ① n (pl ∼**s** /bɑːðz/) bagno m; (tub) vasca f da bagno; ∼**s** pl piscina f; **have a** ∼ fare un bagno
② vt fare il bagno a
③ vi fare il bagno

bathe /beɪð/ ① n bagno m
② vi fare il bagno
③ vt lavare ‹wound›

bather /'beɪðə(r)/ n bagnante mf

bathing /'beɪðɪŋ/ n bagni mpl

bathing cap n cuffia f

bathing costume n costume m da bagno

bathing hut n cabina f (al mare)

bathing suit n costume m da bagno

bathing trunks n calzoncini mpl da bagno

bath mat n tappetino m da bagno

b

bathrobe /'bæθrəʊb/ n accappatoio m

bathroom /'bæθruːm/ n also (toilet) bagno m

bathroom cabinet n armadietto m del bagno

bathroom fittings npl accessori mpl per il bagno

bathroom scales npl bilancia f pesapersone

bath salts npl sali mpl da bagno

bath-towel n asciugamano m da bagno

bathtub n vasca f da bagno

baton /'bæt(ə)n/ n Mus bacchetta f

baton charge n Br carica f con lo sfollagente

baton round n Br proiettile m di gomma

batsman /'bætsmən/ n Sport battitore m

battalion /bə'tæljən/ n battaglione m

batten /'bætn/ n assicella f

batter /'bætə(r)/ n Culin pastella f

battered /'bætəd/ adj ‹car› malandato; ‹wife, baby› maltrattato

battering /'bæt(ə)rɪŋ/ n **take a ~** (from bombs, storm, waves) essere colpito; (from other team) prendersi una batosta; (from other boxer) prenderle

battering ram n ariete m

battery /'bætərɪ/ n batteria f; (of torch, radio) pila f

battery charger n caricabatterie m inv

battery chicken n pollo m di allevamento in batteria

battery controlled adj a pile

battery farming n allevamento m in batteria

battery hen n gallina f d'allevamento in batteria

battery life n autonomia f

battery operated, battery powered adj a pile

battery pack n battery pack m inv

✊ **battle** /'bæt(ə)l/ **1** n battaglia f; fig lotta f **2** vi fig lottare

battleaxe n fam virago f inv

battle cry n also fig grido m di battaglia

battle dress n uniforme f da combattimento

battlefield, battleground n campo m di battaglia; fig terreno m di scontro

battle lines npl Mil schieramenti mpl

battlements /'bætlmənts/ npl bordo m merlato; (crenellations) merlatura f

battle order n also fig ordine m di battaglia

battle-scarred adj aguerrito; fig segnato dalla vita

battleship n corazzata f

batty /'bætɪ/ adj fam strampalato

bauble /'bɔːb(ə)l/ n (ornament) gingillo m; (jewellery) ninnolo m

bawdiness /'bɔːdɪnɪs/ n oscenità f

bawdy /'bɔːdɪ/ adj (**-ier, -iest**) piccante

bawl /bɔːl/ vt/i urlare

■ **bawl out** vt fam urlare ‹name, order›; fare una sfuriata a ‹somebody›

bay[1] /beɪ/ n Geog baia f

bay[2] n **keep at ~** tenere a bada

bay[3] n Bot alloro m

bay[4] n (horse) baio m

bay leaf n foglia f d'alloro

bayonet /'beɪənet/ n baionetta f

bay window n bay window f inv (grande finestra sporgente)

bazaar /bə'zɑː(r)/ n bazar m inv

bazooka /bə'zuːkə/ n bazooka m inv

BBC n abbr (**British Broadcasting Corporation**) BBC f

BBQ abbr (**barbecue**) barbecue m inv

BC abbr (**before Christ**) a.C.

Bcc n abbr (**blind carbon copy**) ccn f

BE abbr (**bill of exchange**) cambiale f

✊ **be** /biː/ **1** vi (pres **am, are, is, are**, pt **was, were**, pp **been**) essere; **he is a teacher** è insegnante, fa l'insegnante; **what do you want to be?** cosa vuoi fare?; **be quiet!** sta'zitto!; **I am cold/hot** ho freddo/caldo; **it's cold/hot, isn't it?** fa freddo/caldo, vero?; **how are you?** come stai?; **I am well** sto bene; **there is** c'è; **there are** ci sono; **I have been to Venice** sono stato a Venezia; **has the postman been?** è passato il postino?; **you're coming too, aren't you?** vieni anche tu, no?; **it's yours, is it?** è tuo, vero?; **was John there? – yes, he was** c'era John? – sì; **John wasn't there – yes he was!** John non c'era – sì che c'era!; **three and three are six** tre più tre fanno sei; **he is five** ha cinque anni; **that will be £10, please** fanno 10 sterline, per favore; **how much is it?** quanto costa?; **that's £5 you owe me** mi devi 5 sterline **2** v aux **I am coming/reading** sto venendo/leggendo; **I'm staying** (not leaving) resto; **I am being lazy** sono pigro; **I was thinking of you** stavo pensando a te; **you are not to tell him** non devi dirglielo; **you are to do that immediately** devi farlo subito **3** passive essere; **I have been robbed** sono stato derubato

beach /biːtʃ/ n spiaggia f

beach ball n pallone m da spiaggia

beach buggy n dune buggy f inv

beach-comber /-kəʊmə(r)/ n persona (f) che vive rivendendo gli oggetti trovati sulla spiaggia

beachhead n testa f di sbarco

beach hut n cabina f [da spiaggia]

beachrobe n accappatoio m

✊ indicates a very frequent word

beachwear n abbigliamento m da spiaggia

beacon /'biːk(ə)n/ n faro m; Naut, Aeron fanale m

bead /biːd/ n perlina f

beady-eyed /biːdɪˈaɪd/ adj (sharp-eyed) a cui non sfugge niente

beagle /'biːg(ə)l/ n beagle m inv, bracchetto m

beak /biːk/ n becco m

beaker /'biːkə(r)/ n coppa f; (in laboratory) becher m inv

beam /biːm/ n ❶ n trave f; (of light) raggio m ❷ vi irradiare; ⟨person⟩ essere raggiante; ∼at somebody fare un gran sorriso a qualcuno

beaming /'biːmɪŋ/ adj raggiante

bean /biːn/ n fagiolo m; (of coffee) chicco m; **spill the** ∼s fam spiattellare tutto

bean bag n (seat) poltrona (f) imbottita di pallini di polistirolo

beanfeast n fam festa f

beanie /'biːnɪ/ n zucchetto m

beanpole n fig fam (tall thin person) spilungone, -a mf

beansprout n germoglio m di soia

bear¹ /beə(r)/ n orso m

bear² v (pt **bore**, pp **borne**) ❶ vt (endure) sopportare; mettere al mondo ⟨child⟩; (carry) portare; ∼ **in mind** tenere presente; ∼ **fruit** ⟨tree⟩ produrre; fig dare frutto ❷ vi ∼**left/right** andare a sinistra/a destra
- **bear out** vt confermare ⟨story, statement⟩
- **bear with** vt aver pazienza con
- **bear up** vi tirare avanti

bearable /'beərəbl/ adj sopportabile

bear cub n cucciolo m di orso

beard /bɪəd/ n barba f; **have a** ∼ avere la barba

bearded /'bɪədɪd/ adj barbuto

bearer /'beərə(r)/ n portatore, -trice mf; (of passport) titolare mf

bearing /'beərɪŋ/ n portamento m; Techn cuscinetto m [a sfera]; **have a** ∼ **on** avere attinenza con; **get one's** ∼s orientarsi; **lose one's** ∼s perdere l'orientamento

bear market n Fin mercato m al ribasso

bearskin n (pelt) pelle f d'orso; (hat) colbacco m militare

beast /biːst/ n bestia f; fam (person) animale m

beastly /'biːstlɪ/ adj (-ier, -iest) fam orribile

beat /biːt/ ❶ n battito m; (rhythm) battuta f; (of policeman) giro m d'ispezione ❷ vt (pt **beat**, pp **beaten**) battere; picchiare ⟨person⟩; ∼ **a retreat** Mil battere in ritirata; ∼ **it!** fam darsela a gambe!; **it** ∼**s me why...** fam non capisco proprio perché...
- **beat back** vt respingere ⟨flames, crowd⟩

- **beat down** ❶ vt buttare giù ⟨door⟩ ❷ vi ⟨sun⟩ battere a picco
- **beat off** vt respingere ⟨attacker⟩
- **beat out** vt domare ⟨flames⟩
- **beat up** vt picchiare

beaten /'biːtn/ adj off the ∼ **track** fuori mano

beatify /bɪˈætɪfaɪ/ vt beatificare

beating /'biːtɪŋ/ n bastonata f; **get a** ∼ (with fists) essere preso a pugni; ⟨team, player⟩ prendere una batosta

beating-up n fam pestaggio m

beat-up adj fam ⟨car⟩ sfasciato

beau /bəʊ/ n liter, hum spasimante m

Beaufort scale /'bəʊfət/ n scala f Beaufort

beautician /bjuːˈtɪʃn/ n estetista mf

beautiful /'bjuːtɪfl/ adj bello; **the** ∼ **people** il bel mondo

beautifully /'bjuːtɪfʊlɪ/ adv splendidamente

beautify /'bjuːtɪfaɪ/ vt (pt/pp **-ied**) abbellire

beauty /'bjuːtɪ/ n bellezza f

beauty contest n concorso m di bellezza

beauty editor n redattore, -trice mf di articoli di bellezza

beauty parlour n istituto m di bellezza

beauty queen n reginetta f di bellezza

beauty salon n istituto m di bellezza

beauty sleep n hum need one's ∼ aver bisogno delle proprie ore di sonno

beauty spot n neo m; (place) luogo m pittoresco

beaver /'biːvə(r)/ n castoro m
- **beaver away** vi fam (work hard) sgobbare

becalmed /bɪˈkɑːmd/ adj in bonaccia

became /bɪˈkeɪm/ ▶ BECOME

because /bɪˈkɒz/ ❶ conj perché; (at start of sentence) poiché ❷ adv ∼ **of** a causa di

beck /bek/ n be at sb's ∼ **and call** dover essere a completa disposizione di qualcuno

beckon /'bekn/ vt/i ∼ **[to]** chiamare con un cenno

become /bɪˈkʌm/ v (pt **became**, pp **become**) ❶ vt diventare ❷ vi diventare; **what has** ∼ **of her?** che ne è di lei?

becoming /bɪˈkʌmɪŋ/ adj ⟨clothes⟩ bello

bed /bed/ n letto m; (of sea, lake) fondo m; (layer) strato m; (of flowers) aiuola f; **in** ∼ a letto; **go to** ∼ andare a letto

BEd n abbr (**Bachelor of Education**) ≈ laurea f in magistero

bed and board n vitto e alloggio m

bed and breakfast n bed and breakfast m

bed base n fondo m del letto

bed bath *n* give somebody a ~ lavare qualcuno a letto

bedbug *n* cimice *f*

bedchamber *n* camera *f* da letto

bedclothes *npl* lenzuola e coperte *fpl*

bedding /'bedɪŋ/ *n biancheria (f) per il letto, materasso e guanciali*

bed down *vi* coricarsi

bedeck /bɪ'dek/ *vt* ornare

bedevil /bɪ'devəl/ *vt* tormentare ‹person›; intralciare ‹plans›

bedfellow *n* make strange ~s fig fare una strana coppia

bedhead *n* testata *f* del letto

bed jacket *n* liseuse *f inv*

bedlam /'bedləm/ *n* baraonda *f*

bed linen *n* biancheria *f* per il letto

bedpan /'bedpæn/ *n* padella *f*

bedraggled /bɪ'drægld/ *adj* inzaccherato

bedridden /'bedrɪdən/ *adj* allettato

bedrock /'bedrɒk/ *n* basamento *m*; fig fondamento *m*

bedroom /'bedru:m/ *n* camera *f* da letto

bedroom farce *n* Theat pochade *f inv*

bedroom slipper *n* pantofola *f*

bedroom suburb *n* Am città *f inv* dormitorio

bed-settee *n* divano *m* letto

bedside /'bedsaɪd/ *n* at his ~ al suo capezzale

bedside lamp *n* abat-jour *m inv*

bedside manner *n* modo *m* di trattare i pazienti; have a good ~ saperci fare con i pazienti

bedside rug *n* scendiletto *m*

bedside table *n* comodino *m*

bed sit, **bed-sitter**, **bedsitting-room** *n* camera *f* ammobiliata [fornita di cucina]

bedsock *n* calzino *m* da notte

bedsore *n* piaga *f* da decubito

bedspread *n* copriletto *m*

bedstead *n* fusto *m* del letto

bedtime *n* l'ora *f* di andare a letto

bedwetting *n* il bagnare il letto

bee /bi:/ *n* ape *f*

beech /bi:tʃ/ *n* faggio *m*

beef /bi:f/ *n* manzo *m*

beefburger *n* hamburger *m inv*

beefeater *n* guardia (*f*) della Torre di Londra

beefsteak *n* bistecca *f*

beefsteak tomato *n* grosso pomodoro *m*

beef stew *n* stufato *m* di manzo

beef tea *n* brodo *m* di manzo

♂ indicates a very frequent word

beefy /'bi:fɪ/ *adj ‹flavour›* di manzo; fam ‹man› grande e grosso

beehive /'bi:haɪv/ *n* alveare *m*

bee-keeper *n* apicoltore, -trice *mf*

bee-keeping *n* apicoltura *f*

bee-line *n* make a ~ for fam precipitarsi verso

been /bi:n/ ▶ BE

beep /bi:p/ ① *n* (of car) suono *m* di clacson; (of telephone) segnale *m* acustico; (of electronic device, radio) bip *m inv*
② *vi* ‹car, driver› clacsonare; ‹device› fare bip
③ *vt* (with beeper) chiamare con il cercapersone; ~ the horn clacsonare

beeper /'bi:pə(r)/ *n* cercapersone *m inv*

beer /bɪə(r)/ *n* birra *f*

beer belly *n* pancia *f* da beone

beer bottle *n* bottiglia *f* da birra

beer garden *n* giardino *m* di un pub

beer mat *n* sottobicchiere *m*

beer money *n* fam quattro soldi *mpl*

beerswilling *adj* pej ubriacone

beer tent *n* spazio (*m*) per incontri con mescita di birra

bee sting *n* puntura *f* d'ape

beeswax /'bi:zwæks/ *n* cera *f* d'api

beet /bi:t/ *n* Am (beetroot) barbabietola *f*; sugar] ~ barbabietola *f* da zucchero

beetle /'bi:tl/ *n* scarafaggio *m*

■ **beetle off** *vi* fam (hurry away) scappare

beetroot /'bi:tru:t/ *n* barbabietola *f*

befall /bɪ'fɔ:l/ *vt* liter accadere a

befit /bɪ'fɪt/ *vt* liter addirsi a

befitting /bɪ'fɪtɪŋ/ *adj ‹modesty, honesty›* opportuno

♂ **before** /bɪ'fɔ:(r)/ ① *prep* prima di; the day ~ yesterday ieri l'altro; ~ long fra poco
② *adv* prima; never ~ have I seen... non ho mai visto prima...; ~ that prima; ~ going prima di andare
③ *conj* (time) prima che; ~ you go prima che tu vada

beforehand /bɪ'fɔ:hænd/ *adv* in anticipo

before tax *adj ‹profit, income›* lordo, al lordo di imposte

befriend /bɪ'frend/ *vt* trattare da amico

befuddle /bɪ'fʌdl/ *vt* confondere ‹mind›

beg /beg/ *v* (*pt/pp* **begged**) ① *vi* mendicare
② *vt* pregare; chiedere ‹favour, forgiveness›

began /bɪ'gæn/ ▶ BEGIN

beggar /'begə(r)/ *n* mendicante *mf*; you lucky ~! che fortuna sfacciata!; poor ~! povero cristo!; you little ~! monellaccio!

beggarly /'begəlɪ/ *adj ‹existence, meal›* miserabile; ‹wage› da fame

begging bowl /'begɪŋ/ n ciotola f del mendicante

begging letter n lettera (f) che sollecita offerte in denaro

◆ **begin** /bɪ'gɪn/ vt/i (pt **began**, pp **begun**, pres p **beginning**) cominciare; **well, to ~ with** dunque, per cominciare

beginner /bɪ'gɪnə(r)/ n principiante mf

◆ **beginning** /bɪ'gɪnɪŋ/ n principio m

begonia /bɪ'gəʊnɪə/ n begonia f

begrudge /bɪ'grʌdʒ/ vt (envy) essere invidioso di; dare malvolentieri ‹money›

beguile /bɪ'gaɪl/ vt (charm) affascinare; (cheat) ingannare

beguiling /bɪ'gaɪlɪŋ/ adj accattivante

begun /bɪ'gʌn/ ▸ BEGIN

behalf /bɪ'hɑːf/ n on ~ of a nome di; on my ~ a nome mio; **say hello on my ~** salutalo da parte mia

behave /bɪ'heɪv/ vi comportarsi; ~ **[oneself]** comportarsi bene

◆ **behaviour** /bɪ'heɪvjə(r)/ n comportamento m; (of prisoner, soldier) condotta f

behavioural /bɪ'heɪvjərəl/ adj comportamentale

behaviourist /bɪ'heɪvjərɪst/ adj & n comportamentista mf

behaviour pattern n modello m comportamentale

behead /bɪ'hed/ vt decapitare

beheld /bɪ'held/ ▸ BEHOLD

◆ **behind** /bɪ'haɪnd/ **1** prep dietro; (with pronoun) dietro di; **be ~ something** fig stare dietro qualcosa
2 adv dietro, indietro; (late) in ritardo; **a long way ~** molto indietro; **in the car ~** nella macchina dietro
3 n fam didietro m

behindhand /bɪ'haɪndhænd/ adv indietro

behold /bɪ'həʊld/ vt (pt/pp **beheld**) liter vedere

beholden /bɪ'həʊldn/ adj obbligato (to verso)

beholder /bɪ'həʊldə(r)/ n **beauty is in the eye of the ~** è bello ciò che piace

beige /beɪʒ/ adj & n beige m inv

Beijing /beɪ'dʒɪŋ/ n Pechino f

◆ **being** /'biːɪŋ/ n essere m; **come into ~** nascere

Beirut /beɪ'ruːt/ n Beirut f

bejewelled /bɪ'dʒuːəld/ adj ingioiellato

Belarus /ˌbjeləʊ'rus/ n Bielorussia f

belated /bɪ'leɪtɪd/ adj tardivo

belatedly /bɪ'leɪtɪdlɪ/ adv tardi

belch /beltʃ/ **1** vi ruttare
2 vt ~**[out]** eruttare ‹smoke›

beleaguered /bɪ'liːgəd/ adj ‹city› assediato; ‹troops› accerchiato; fig ‹person› tormentato; fig ‹company› in difficoltà

Belfast /bel'fɑːst/ n Belfast f

belfry /'belfrɪ/ n campanile m

Belgian /'beldʒən/ adj & n belga mf

Belgium /'beldʒəm/ n Belgio m

Belgrade /bel'greɪd/ n Belgrado f

belie /bɪ'laɪ/ vt (give false impression of) dissimulare; (disprove) smentire

◆ **belief** /bɪ'liːf/ n fede f; (opinion) convinzione f

believable /bɪ'liːvəbl/ adj credibile

◆ **believe** /bɪ'liːv/ vt/i credere
■ **believe in** vt avere fiducia in ‹person›; credere a ‹ghosts›

believer /bɪ'liːvə(r)/ n Relig credente mf; **be a great ~ in** credere fermamente in

belittle /bɪ'lɪtl/ vt sminuire ‹person, achievements›

belittling /bɪ'lɪtlɪŋ/ adj ‹comment› che sminuisce

Belize /be'liːz/ n Belize m

bell /bel/ n campana f; (on door) campanello m; **that rings a ~** fig mi dice qualcosa

bell-bottoms npl pantaloni mpl a zampa d'elefante

bellboy /'belbɔɪ/ n Am fattorino m d'albergo

belle /bel/ n bella f

bellhop /'belhɒp/ n Am fattorino m d'albergo

belligerence /bɪ'lɪdʒərəns/ n bellicosità f; (pol) belligeranza f

belligerent /bɪ'lɪdʒərənt/ adj belligerante; (aggressive) bellicoso

bell-jar n campana f di vetro

bellow /'beləʊ/ vi gridare a squarciagola; ‹animal› muggire
■ **bellow out** vt urlare ‹name, order›

bellows /'beləʊz/ npl (for fire) soffietto m

bell-pull n (rope) cordone m di campanello

bell-push n pulsante m di campanello

bell-ringer n campanaro m

bell-shaped adj a campana

bell-tower n campanile m

belly /'belɪ/ n pancia f

bellyache **1** n fam mal m di pancia
2 vi fam lamentarsi

belly button n fam ombelico m

belly dancer n danzatrice f del ventre

belly flop n (in swimming) spanciata f

bellyful /'belɪfʊl/ n fam **have had a ~ of something** avere le tasche piene di qualcosa

◆ **belong** /bɪ'lɒŋ/ vi appartenere (**to** a); (be member) essere socio (**to** di)

belongings /bɪ'lɒŋɪŋz/ npl cose fpl

beloved /bɪ'lʌvɪd/ adj & n amato, -a mf

◆ **below** /bɪ'ləʊ/ **1** prep sotto; (with numbers) al di sotto di
2 adv sotto, di sotto; Naut sotto coperta; **see ~** vedi qui di seguito

belt /belt/ **1** n cintura f; (area) zona f; Techn cinghia f ⋯▸

2 *vi* fam (rush) ~ **along** filare velocemente
3 *vt* fam (hit) picchiare
■ **belt out** *vt* cantare a squarciagola ‹song›
■ **belt up** *vi* (in car) mettersi la cintura [di sicurezza]; ~ **up!** sl (be quiet) stai zitto!

bemoan /bɪˈməʊn/ *vt* lamentare

bemused /bɪˈmjuːzd/ *adj* confuso

bench /bentʃ/ *n* panchina *f*; (work ~) piano *m* da lavoro; **the B** ~ Jur la magistratura

benchmark /ˈbentʃmɑːk/ *n* punto *m* di riferimento; Comput paragone *m* con un campione; Fin (price) prezzo *m* di riferimento

bench-test *vt* Comput testare

bend /bend/ **1** *n* curva *f*; (of river) ansa *f*; **round the** ~ fam fuori di testa
2 *vt* (*pt/pp* **bent**) piegare
3 *vi* piegarsi; ‹road› curvare; ~ **[down]** chinarsi
■ **bend over** *vi* inchinarsi

beneath /bɪˈniːθ/ **1** *prep* sotto, al di sotto di; **he thinks it's** ~ **him** fig pensa che sia sotto al suo livello; ~ **contempt** indegno
2 *adv* giù

Benedictine /benɪˈdɪktiːn/ *adj & n* Relig benedettino *m*

benediction /benɪˈdɪkʃn/ *n* Relig benedizione *f*

benefactor /ˈbenɪfæktə(r)/ *n* benefattore, -trice *mf*

beneficial /benɪˈfɪʃl/ *adj* benefico

beneficiary /benɪˈfɪʃərɪ/ *n* beneficiario, -a *mf*

⚜ **benefit** /ˈbenɪfɪt/ **1** *n* vantaggio *m*; (allowance) indennità *f inv*
2 *vt* (*pt/pp* -**fited**, *pres p* -**fiting**) giovare a
3 *vi* trarre vantaggio (**from** da)

Benelux /ˈbenɪlʌks/ **1** *n* Benelux *m*
2 *attrib* ‹countries, organization› del Benelux

benevolence /bɪˈnevələns/ *n* benevolenza *f*

benevolent /bɪˈnevələnt/ *adj* benevolo

benevolently /bɪˈnevələntlɪ/ *adv* con benevolenza

Bengal /beŋˈgɔːl/ *n* Bengala *m*

benign /bɪˈnaɪn/ *adj* benevolo; Med benigno

benignly /bɪˈnaɪnlɪ/ *adv* con benevolenza

Benin /beˈniːn/ *n* Benin *m*

bent /bent/ **1** ▶ BEND
2 *adj* ‹person› ricurvo; (distorted) curvato; fam (dishonest) corrotto; **be** ~ **on doing something** essere ben deciso a fare qualcosa
3 *n* predisposizione *f*

benzene /ˈbenziːn/ *n* benzene *m*

benzine /ˈbenziːn/ *n* benzina *f*

bequeath /bɪˈkwiːð/ *vt* lasciare in eredità

bequest /bɪˈkwest/ *n* lascito *m*

berate /bɪˈreɪt/ *vt* fml redarguire

bereaved /bɪˈriːvd/ *n* **the** ~ *pl* i familiari del defunto

bereavement /bɪˈriːvmənt/ *n* lutto *m*

bereft /bɪˈreft/ *adj* ~ **of** privo di

beret /ˈbereɪ/ *n* berretto *m*

Berlin /bɜːˈlɪn/ *n* Berlino *f*

Berliner /bɜːˈlɪnə(r)/ *n* berlinese *mf*

Bermuda /bəˈmjuːdə/ *n* le Bermuda

Bermuda shorts *npl* bermuda *m inv*

Berne /bɜːn/ *n* Berna *f*

berry /ˈberɪ/ *n* bacca *f*

berserk /bəˈsɜːk/ *adj* **go** ~ diventare una belva

berth /bɜːθ/ **1** *n* (bed) cuccetta *f*; (anchorage) ormeggio *m*; **give a wide** ~ **to** fam stare alla larga da
2 *vi* ormeggiare

beseech /bɪˈsiːtʃ/ *vt* (*pt/pp* **beseeched** *or* **besought**) supplicare

beseeching /bɪˈsiːtʃɪŋ/ *adj* implorante

beset /bɪˈset/ *adj* **a country** ~ **by strikes** un paese vessato dagli scioperi

⚜ **beside** /bɪˈsaɪd/ *prep* accanto a; ~ **oneself** fuori di sé

besides /bɪˈsaɪdz/ **1** *prep* oltre a
2 *adv* inoltre

besiege /bɪˈsiːdʒ/ *vt* assediare

besotted /bɪˈsɒtɪd/ *adj* infatuato (**with** di)

besought /bɪˈsɔːt/ ▶ BESEECH

bespatter /bɪˈspætə(r)/ *vt* schizzare

bespectacled /bɪˈspektək(ə)ld/ *adj* con gli occhiali

bespoke /bɪˈspəʊk/ *adj* ‹suit› su misura; ‹tailor› che lavora su ordinazione

best /best/ **1** *adj* migliore; **the** ~ **part of a year** la maggior parte dell'anno; ~ **before** Comm preferibilmente prima di; ~ **wishes** migliori auguri
2 *n* **the** ~ il meglio; (person) il/la migliore; **at** ~ tutt'al più; **all the** ~**!** tanti auguri!; **do one's** ~ fare del proprio meglio; **to the** ~ **of my knowledge** per quel che ne so; **make the** ~ **of it** cogliere il lato buono della cosa
3 *adv* meglio, nel modo migliore; **as** ~ **I could** come meglio ho potuto; **like** ~ preferire

best before date *n* data *f* di scadenza

best friend *n* migliore amico, -a *mf*

bestial /ˈbestɪəl/ *adj* also fig bestiale

bestiality /bestɪˈælətɪ/ *n* bestialità *f*

best man *n* testimone *m*

bestow /bɪˈstəʊ/ *vt* conferire (**on** a)

best-seller /-ˈselə(r)/ *n* bestseller *m inv*

best-selling /-ˈselɪŋ/ *adj* ‹novelist› più venduto

bet /bet/ **1** *n* scommessa *f*
2 *vt/i* (*pt/pp* **bet** *or* **betted**) scommettere

⚜ indicates a very frequent word

beta blocker /ˈbiːtəblʊkə(r)/ n
betabloccante m

beta-test /ˈbiːtətest/ vt Comput testare la
versione beta di

Bethlehem /ˈbeθlɪhem/ n Betlemme f

betray /bɪˈtreɪ/ vt tradire

betrayal /bɪˈtreɪəl/ n tradimento m

betrothal /bɪˈtrəʊðl/ n fidanzamento m

betrothed /bɪˈtrəʊðd/ n liter hum promesso
sposo m; promessa sposa f; **be ~** essere
fidanzato

better /ˈbetə(r)/ **1** adj migliore, meglio;
get ~ migliorare; (after illness) rimettersi;
I waited the ~ part of a week ho aspettato
buona parte della settimana
2 adv meglio; **~ off** meglio; (wealthier) più
ricco; **all the ~** tanto meglio; **the sooner the
~** prima è meglio è; **I've thought ~ of it** ci
ho ripensato; **you'd ~ stay** faresti meglio a
restare; **I'd ~ not** è meglio che non lo faccia
3 vt migliorare; **~ oneself** migliorare le
proprie condizioni

betting /ˈbetɪŋ/ n (activity) scommesse fpl;
what's the ~ that…? quanto scommettiamo
che…?

betting shop n ricevitoria f
(dell'allibratore)

⚐ **between** /bɪˈtwiːn/ **1** prep fra, tra; **~ you
and me** detto fra di noi; **~ us** (together) tra
me e te
2 adv [in] **~** in mezzo; (time) frattempo

betwixt /bɪˈtwɪkst/ adv **be ~ and between**
essere una via di mezzo

bevel /ˈbevl/ **1** n (edge) spigolo m
smussato; (tool) squadra f falsa
2 vt smussare ‹mirror, edge›

beverage /ˈbevərɪdʒ/ n bevanda f

bevy /ˈbevɪ/ n frotta f

beware /bɪˈweə(r)/ vi guardarsi (of da);
~ of the dog! attenti al cane!

bewilder /bɪˈwɪldə(r)/ vt disorientare

bewildered /bɪˈwɪldəd/ adj ‹look, person›
perplesso, sconcertato

bewildering /bɪˈwɪldərɪŋ/ adj
sconcertante

bewilderment /bɪˈwɪldəmənt/ n
perplessità f

bewitch /bɪˈwɪtʃ/ vt stregare; fig
affascinare completamente

⚐ **beyond** /bɪˈjɒnd/ **1** prep oltre; **~ reach**
irraggiungibile; **~ doubt** senza alcun
dubbio; **~ belief** da non credere; **it's ~ me**
fam non riesco proprio a capire
2 adv più in là

B film n film m inv di serie B

Bhutan /buːˈtɑːn/ n Bhutan m

bias /ˈbaɪəs/ **1** n (preference) preferenza f;
pej pregiudizio m
2 vt (pt/pp **biased**) (influence) influenzare

bias binding, **bias tape** /ˈbaɪndɪŋ/ n (in
sewing) fettuccia f in sbieco

biased /ˈbaɪəst/ adj parziale

bib /bɪb/ n bavaglino m

Bible /ˈbaɪbl/ n Bibbia f

Bible Belt n zona (f) del sud degli
USA, dove predomina il fondamentalismo
protestante

biblical /ˈbɪblɪkl/ adj biblico

bibliographic[al] /bɪblɪəˈgræfɪk[l]/ adj
bibliografico

bibliography /bɪblɪˈɒgrəfɪ/ n bibliografia
f

bicarbonate /baɪˈkɑːbənət/ n **~ of soda**
bicarbonato m di sodio

bicentenary /baɪsenˈtiːnərɪ/ **1** n
bicentenario m
2 attrib ‹celebration, year› bicentenario

biceps /ˈbaɪseps/ n bicipite m

bicker /ˈbɪkə(r)/ vi litigare

bickering /ˈbɪkərɪŋ/ n bisticci mpl

bicycle /ˈbaɪsɪkl/ **1** n bicicletta f
2 vi andare in bicicletta

bicycle clip n molletta f (per pantaloni)

bicycle lane n pista f ciclabile

bicycle rack n (in yard) rastrelliera f per
biciclette; (on car) portabiciclette m inv

⚐ **bid**[1] /bɪd/ **1** n offerta f; (attempt) tentativo m
2 vt/i (pt/pp **bid**, pres p **bidding**) offrire;
(in cards) dichiarare

bid[2] vt (pt **bade** or **bid**, pp **bidden** or **bid**,
pres p **bidding**) liter (command) comandare;
~ somebody welcome dare il benvenuto a
qualcuno

bidder /ˈbɪdə(r)/ n offerente mf

bidding /ˈbɪdɪŋ/ n offerte fpl (durante
un'asta)

bide /baɪd/ vt **~ one's time** aspettare il
momento buono

bidet /ˈbiːdeɪ/ n bidè m inv

biennial /baɪˈenɪəl/ adj biennale

bier /bɪə(r)/ n catafalco m

bifocals /baɪˈfəʊklz/ npl occhiali mpl
bifocali

⚐ **big** /bɪg/ **1** adj (**bigger**, **biggest**)
grande; ‹brother, sister› più grande; fam
(generous) generoso; **make ~ money** fare i
soldi
2 adv **talk ~** fam sparlare grosse

bigamist /ˈbɪgəmɪst/ n bigamo, -a mf

bigamous /ˈbɪgəməs/ adj bigamo

bigamy /ˈbɪgəmɪ/ n bigamia f

big bang n (in astronomy) big bang m

big business n le grandi imprese; **be ~**
essere un grosso affare

big cat n grosso felino m

big deal n fam **~!** bella forza!

big dipper n Br (at fair) montagne fpl russe

big game hunting n caccia f grossa

bighead n fam montato, -a mf, gasato, -a mf

big-headed adj fam montato, gasato

big-hearted *adj* generoso

bigmouth *n* fam pej chiacchierone, -a *mf*; he's such a ∼! (indiscreet) ha una lingua lunga!

big name *n* (in film, art) grosso nome *m*

big noise *n* fam pezzo *m* grosso

bigot /'bɪgət/ *n* fanatico, -a *mf*

bigoted /'bɪgətɪd/ *adj* di mentalità ristretta

bigotry /'bɪgətrɪ/ *n* mentalità *f* ristretta

big screen *n* grande schermo *m*

big shot *n* fam pezzo *m* grosso

Big Smoke *n* Br hum Londra *f*

big time ① *n* make *or* hit the ∼ fam raggiungere il successo
② *attrib* big-time ‹crook› di alto livello

big toe *n* alluce *m*

big top *n* ‹tent› tendone *m* del circo; fig (circus) circo *m*

bigwig *n* fam pezzo *m* grosso

bike /baɪk/ ① *n* fam bici *f inv*
② *vi* andare in bici
③ *vt* mandare per corriere

biker /'baɪkə(r)/ *n* motociclista *mf*

biker['s] jacket /'baɪkə(z)dʒækɪt/ *n* fam giubbotto *m* di pelle

bikini /bɪ'kiːnɪ/ *n* bikini *m inv*

bilateral /baɪ'lætrəl/ *adj* bilaterale

bilberry /'bɪlbərɪ/ *n* mirtillo *m*

bile /baɪl/ *n* bile *f*

bilge /bɪldʒ/ *n* Naut (place) carena *f*; (substance) sentina *f*; fam (nonsense) idiozie *fpl*

bilingual /baɪ'lɪŋgwəl/ *adj* bilingue

bilingual secretary *n* segretario, -a *mf* bilingue

bilious /'bɪljəs/ *adj* Med ∼ **attack** attacco *m* di bile

✔ **bill¹** /bɪl/ ① *n* fattura *f*; (in restaurant etc) conto *m*; (poster) manifesto *m*; Pol progetto *m* di legge; Am (note) biglietto *m* di banca; Theat be top of the ∼ essere in testa al cartellone
② *vt* fatturare

bill² *n* (beak) becco *m*

billboard /'bɪlbɔːd/ *n* cartellone *m* pubblicitario

billet /'bɪlɪt/ ① *n* Mil alloggio *m*
② *vt* (*pt/pp* **billeted**) alloggiare (on presso)

billfold *n* Am portafoglio *m*

billiard ball *n* palla *f* da biliardo

billiards /'bɪljədz/ *n* biliardo *m*

billiard table /'bɪljəd/ tavolo *m* da biliardo

billing /'bɪlɪŋ/ *n* Comm fatturazione *f*; get top ∼ Theat comparire in testa al cartellone

✔ **billion** /'bɪljən/ *n* (thousand million) miliardo *m*; old-fashioned Br (million million) mille miliardi *mpl*

billionaire /bɪljə'neə(r)/ *n* miliardario, -a *mf*

bill of exchange *n* cambiale *f*

bill of fare *n* menù *m inv*

bill of rights *n* dichiarazione *f* dei diritti

bill of sale *n* atto *m* di vendita

billow /'bɪləʊ/ ① *n* (of smoke) nube *f*
② *vi* alzarsi in volute
∎ **billow out** *vi* (skirt, sail) gonfiarsi; (smoke, cloud) levarsi in volute

billposter /'bɪlpəʊstə(r)/ *n* attacchino *m*

billy /'bɪlɪ/ *n* Am (truncheon) sfollagente *m inv*

billycan /'bɪlɪkæn/ *n* gamella *f*

billy goat *n* caprone *m*

bimbo /'bɪmbəʊ/ *n* pej fam bambolona *f*; his latest ∼ la sua ultima amichetta

bin /bɪn/ *n* bidone *m*

binary /'baɪnərɪ/ *adj* binario

bin bag *n* sacco *m* per l'immondizia

bind /baɪnd/ *vt* (*pt/pp* **bound**) legare (to a); (bandage) fasciare; Jur obbligare

binder /'baɪndə(r)/ *n* (for papers) raccoglitore *m*; (for cement, paint) agglomerante *m*

binding /'baɪndɪŋ/ ① *adj* ‹promise, contract› vincolante
② *n* (of book) rilegatura *f*; (on ski) attacco *m*

binge /bɪndʒ/ ① *n* fam have a ∼ fare baldoria; (eat a lot) abbuffarsi
② *vi* abbuffarsi (on di)

binge-drinking /,bɪndʒ'drɪŋkɪŋ/ *n* il bere smodatamente in particolari occasioni, specialmente nelle sere del week-end

bingo /'bɪŋgəʊ/ *n* ≈ tombola *f*

bin liner *n* Br sacchetto *m* per la spazzatura

binoculars /bɪ'nɒkjʊləz/ *npl* [pair of] ∼ binocolo *msg*

biochemist /baɪəʊ'kemɪst/ *n* biochimico, -a *mf*

biochemistry /baɪəʊ'kemɪstrɪ/ *n* biochimica *f*

biocompatible /,baɪəʊkəm'pætəbl/ *adj* biocompatibile

biodegradable /baɪəʊdɪ'greɪdəbl/ *adj* biodegradabile

biodiesel /'baɪəʊdiːzl/ *n* biodiesel *m*

biodiversity /baɪəʊdaɪ'vɜːsətɪ/ *n* biodiversità *f*

bioengineering /baɪəʊendʒɪ'nɪərɪŋ/ *n* bioingegneria *f*

biographer /baɪ'ɒgrəfə(r)/ *n* biografo, -a *mf*

biographical /baɪə'græfɪkl/ *adj* biografico

biography /baɪ'ɒgrəfɪ/ *n* biografia *f*

biological /baɪə'lɒdʒɪkl/ *adj* biologico

biological clock *n* orologio *m* biologico

biologically /baɪə'lɒdʒɪklɪ/ *adv* biologicamente

✔ indicates a very frequent word

biological powder n detersivo m biologico

biological warfare n guerra f biologica

biologist /baɪˈɒlədʒɪst/ n biologo, -a mf

biology /baɪˈɒlədʒi/ n biologia f

bionic /baɪˈɒnɪk/ adj bionico

biopic /ˈbaɪəʊpɪk/ n Cin film (m) basato su una biografia

biopsy /ˈbaɪɒpsi/ n biopsia f

biorhythm /ˈbaɪəʊrɪðəm/ n bioritmo m

biosphere /ˈbaɪəʊsfɪə(r)/ n biosfera f

biotechnology /baɪəʊtekˈnɒlədʒi/ n biotecnologia f

bioterrorism /baɪəʊˌterərizəm/ n bioterrorismo m

bipartisan /baɪpɑːˈtɪˈzæn/ adj Pol bipartitico

bipartite /baɪˈpɑːtaɪt/ adj bipartito

bipolar disorder /baɪˈpəʊlədɪsˌɔːdə(r)/ n disturbo m bipolare

birch /bɜːtʃ/ n (tree) betulla f

♂ **bird** /bɜːd/ n uccello m, fam (girl) ragazza f; **kill two ~s with one stone** prendere due piccioni con una fava

birdbrain /ˈbɜːdbreɪn/ n fam **he's such a ~** ha un cervello da gallina

bird call n cinguettio m

bird flu n influenza f aviaria, influenza f dei polli

birdie /ˈbɜːdi/ n (in golf) birdie m

birdlike /ˈbɜːdlaɪk/ adj come un uccello

bird of paradise n uccello m del paradiso

bird of prey n [uccello m] rapace m

bird sanctuary n riserva f per uccelli

birdseed n becchime m

bird's eye view n veduta f panoramica dall'alto

bird's nest n nido m di uccello

bird's nest soup n zuppa f di nido di rondine

birdsong n canto m degli uccelli

birdwatcher n persona (f) che pratica il bird-watching

bird-watching n **go ~** fare del bird-watching

Biro® /ˈbaɪrəʊ/ n biro® f inv

♂ **birth** /bɜːθ/ n nascita f; **give ~** partorire; **give ~ to** partorire

birth certificate n certificato m di nascita

birth-control n controllo m delle nascite

♂ **birthday** n compleanno m

birthday party n festa f di compleanno

birthing pool n piccola piscina f per il parto

birthmark n voglia f

birth mother n madre f biologica

birthplace n luogo m di nascita

birth-rate n natalità f

birthright n diritto m di nascita

births column n annunci mpl delle nascite (sul giornale)

birth sign n segno m zodiacale

births, marriages, and deaths npl annunci mpl di nascite, di matrimonio, mortuari (sul giornale)

biscuit /ˈbɪskɪt/ n biscotto m

biscuit barrel, **biscuit tin** n biscottiera f

bisect /baɪˈsekt/ vt dividere in due [parti]

bisexual /baɪˈseksjʊəl/ adj & n bisessuale mf

bishop /ˈbɪʃəp/ n vescovo m; Chess alfiere m

bistro /ˈbiːstrəʊ/ n bistrò m inv

♂ **bit¹** /bɪt/ n pezzo m; (smaller) pezzetto m; (for horse) morso m; Comput bit m inv; **a ~ of** un pezzo di ‹cheese, paper›; un po' di ‹time, rain, silence›; **~ by ~** poco a poco; **do one's ~** fare la propria parte

bit² ▸ BITE

bitch /bɪtʃ/ n cagna f; sl arpia f

bitchy /ˈbɪtʃi/ adj velenoso

bite /baɪt/ [1] n morso m; (insect ~) puntura f; (mouthful) boccone m
[2] vt (pt **bit**, pp **bitten**) mordere; ‹insect› pungere; **~ one's nails** mangiarsi le unghie
[3] vi mordere; ‹insect› pungere
■ **bite off** vt staccare (con un morso)

biting /ˈbaɪtɪŋ/ adj ‹wind, criticism› pungente; ‹remark› mordace

bit part n Theat particina f

bitter /ˈbɪtə(r)/ [1] adj amaro
[2] n Br birra f amara

bitter almond n mandorla f amara

bitter lemon n limonata f amara

bitterly /ˈbɪtəli/ adv amaramente; **it's ~ cold** c'è un freddo pungente

bitterness /ˈbɪtənɪs/ n amarezza f

bittersweet /bɪtəˈswiːt/ adj liter agrodolce

bitty /ˈbɪti/ adj Br fam frammentario

bitumen /ˈbɪtjʊmɪn/ n bitume m

bivouac /ˈbɪvʊæk/ [1] n bivacco m
[2] vi bivaccare

bizarre /bɪˈzɑː(r)/ adj bizzarro

blab /blæb/ vi (pt/pp **blabbed**) cianciare

♂ **black** /blæk/ [1] adj nero; **be ~ and blue** essere coperto di lividi
[2] n nero m
[3] vt boicottare ‹goods›
■ **black out** [1] vt cancellare
[2] vi (lose consciousness) perdere coscienza

Black Africa n Africa f nera

Black American n negro, -a, americano, -a mf

black and white n bianco e nero

blackball vt dare voto contrario a

black belt n cintura f nera

blackberry n mora f
blackberry bush n rovo m
blackbird n merlo m
blackboard n Sch lavagna f
black box n Aeron scatola f nera
black bread n pane m nero
blackcurrant n ribes m inv nero
blacken /'blækən/ vt annerire
black eye n occhio m nero
Black Forest gateau n dolce (m) a base di cioccolato, panna e ciliegie
black gold n fam oro m nero
blackguard /'blægəd/ n hum brigante m
blackhead n Med punto m nero
black-headed gull n gabbiano m comune
black humour umorismo m nero
black ice n ghiaccio m (sulla strada)
blacking /'blækɪŋ/ Br (boycotting) boicottaggio m; (polish) lucido m nero (per scarpe)
blackish /'blækɪʃ/ adj nerastro
blackjack n blackjack m
blackleg n Br crumiro m
blacklist vt mettere sulla lista nera
blackmail 1 n ricatto m
2 vt ricattare
blackmailer n ricattatore, -trice mf
black mark n fig neo m
black market n borsa f nera
black marketeer n borsanerista mf
black mass n messa f nera
blackness /'blæknɪs/ n nero m; (evilness) cattiveria f; (of moods) scontrosità f
black-out n blackout m inv; **have a ~** Med perdere coscienza
black pepper n pepe m nero
black pudding n ≈ sanguinaccio m
Black Sea n Mar m Nero
black sheep n fig pecora f nera
Blackshirt n camicia f nera
blacksmith n fabbro m
black spot n fig luogo (m) conosciuto per gli incidenti stradali
black swan n cigno m nero
black tie (on invitation) abito scuro
black widow [spider] n vedova f nera
bladder /'blædə(r)/ n Anat vescica f
blade /bleɪd/ n lama f; (of grass) filo m
◢ **blame** /bleɪm/ 1 n colpa f
2 vt dare la colpa a; **~ somebody for doing something** dare la colpa a qualcuno per aver fatto qualcosa; **no one is to ~** non è colpa di nessuno
blameless /'bleɪmlɪs/ adj innocente

blameworthy /'bleɪmwɜːðɪ/ adj biasimevole
blanch /blɑːntʃ/ 1 vi sbiancare
2 vt Culin sbollentare
blancmange /blə'mɒnʒ/ n biancomangiare m
bland /blænd/ adj ‹food› insipido; ‹person› insulso
blandly /'blændlɪ/ adv ‹say› in modo piatto
blank /blæŋk/ 1 adj bianco; ‹look› vuoto
2 n spazio m vuoto; (cartridge) cartuccia f a salve
3 vt ignorare; **she completely ~ed me** mi ha completamente ignorato
■ **blank out** vt (memory) cancellare dalla memoria
blank cheque n assegno m in bianco
blanket /'blæŋkɪt/ n coperta f; **wet ~** fam guastafeste mf inv
blanket box, blanket chest n Br cassapanca f
blanket cover n (in insurance) assicurazione f che copre tutti i rischi
blanket stitch n punto m di rinforzo
blankly /'blæŋklɪ/ adv (uncomprehendingly) con espressione attonita; (without expression) senza espressione
blank verse n versi mpl sciolti
blare /bleə(r)/ vi suonare a tutto volume
■ **blare out** vt strombazzare rumorosamente
blarney /'blɑːnɪ/ n fam lusinga f
blasé /'blɑːzeɪ/ adj blasé inv
blaspheme /blæs'fiːm/ vi bestemmiare
blasphemous /'blæsfəməs/ adj blasfemo
blasphemy /'blæsfəmɪ/ n bestemmia f
blast /blɑːst/ 1 n (gust) raffica f; (sound) scoppio m
2 vt (with explosive) far saltare
3 int sl maledizione!
■ **blast off** vi (rocket) decollare
blasted /'blɑːstɪd/ adj sl maledetto
blast furnace n altoforno m
blasting /'blɑːstɪŋ/ n brillamento m
blast-off n (of missile) lancio m
blatant /'bleɪtənt/ adj sfacciato
blatantly /'bleɪtəntlɪ/ adv ‹copy, disregard› sfacciatamente; **it's ~ obvious** è lampante
blather /'blæðə(r)/ vi fam blaterare
blaze /bleɪz/ 1 n incendio m; **a ~ of colour** un'esplosione f di colori
2 vi ardere
■ **blaze down** vi ‹sun› essere cocente
blazer /'bleɪzə(r)/ n blazer m inv
blazing /'bleɪzɪŋ/ adj ‹row› acceso; ‹fire› violento; ‹building› in fiamme
bleach /bliːtʃ/ 1 n decolorante m; (for cleaning) candeggina f, varecchina f
2 vt sbiancare; ossigenare ‹hair›
bleak /bliːk/ adj desolato; fig ‹prospects, future› tetro

_____
◢ indicates a very frequent word

bleakly /'bli:klɪ/ *adv* ‹stare, say› in modo tetro

bleakness /'bli:knɪs/ *n* (of weather) tetraggine *f*; (of surroundings, future) desolazione *f*

bleary-eyed /blɪərɪ'aɪd/ *adj* be ~ avere gli occhi gonfi

bleat /bli:t/ ① *vi* belare
② *n* belato *m*

bleed /bli:d/ *v* (*pt/pp* **bled**) ① *vi* sanguinare
② *vt* spurgare ‹brakes, radiator›

bleeding /'bli:dɪŋ/ ① *n* perdita di sangue *f*; (heavy) emorragia *f*; (deliberate) salasso *m*
② *adj* ‹wound, hand› sanguinante; sl = BLOODY

bleeding heart *n* fig pej cuore *m* troppo tenero

bleep /bli:p/ ① *n* bip *m*
② *vi* suonare
③ *vt* chiamare col cercapersone

bleeper /'bli:pə(r)/ *n* cercapersone *m inv*

blemish /'blemɪʃ/ *n* macchia *f*

blend /blend/ ① *n* (of tea, coffee, whisky) miscela *f*; (of colours) insieme *m*
② *vt* mescolare
③ *vi* ‹colours, sounds› fondersi (**with** con)
▪ **blend in** ① *vi* ‹person› passare inosservato; ~ **in with** mescolarsi con
② *vt* ~ **something** in mescolare qualcosa

blender /'blendə(r)/ *n* Culin frullatore *m*

blending /'blendɪŋ/ *n* (of coffees, whiskies) miscela *f*

bless /bles/ *vt* benedire

blessed /'blesɪd/ *adj also* sl benedetto

blessing /'blesɪŋ/ *n* benedizione *f*

blew /blu:/ ▸ BLOW²

blight /blaɪt/ ① *n* Bot ruggine *f*
② *vt* far avvizzire ‹plants›

blighter /'blaɪtə(r)/ Br fam (annoying person) idiota *mf*; **you lucky** ~ hai una fortuna sfacciata!; **poor** ~ povero diavolo *m*

blimey /'blaɪmɪ/ *int* Br fam accidenti!

blind /blaɪnd/ ① *adj* cieco; ~ **man/woman** cieco/cieca
② *npl* **the** ~ i ciechi
③ *vt* accecare
④ *n* [**roller**] ~ avvolgibile *m*; [**Venetian**] ~ veneziana *f*

blind alley *n* vicolo *m* cieco

blind date *n* appuntamento (*m*) galante con una persona sconosciuta

blind drunk *adj* ubriaco fradicio

blindfold ① *adv* con gli occhi bendati
② *adj* be ~ avere gli occhi bendati
③ *n* benda *f*
④ *vt* bendare gli occhi a

blinding /'blaɪndɪŋ/ *adj* ‹light› accecante; ‹headache› da impazzire, tremendo

blindingly /'blaɪndɪŋlɪ/ *adv* ‹shine› in modo accecante; **be** ~ **obvious** essere così lampante

blindly /'blaɪndlɪ/ *adv* ciecamente

blind-man's buff *n* moscacieca *f*

blindness /'blaɪndnɪs/ *n* cecità *f*

blind spot *n* (in car, on hill) punto *m* privo di visibilità; (in eye) punto *m* cieco; fig (point of ignorance) punto *m* debole

blind trust *n* blind trust *m*

bling bling /blɪŋ 'blɪŋ/ *n* sl gioielli e abiti molto appariscenti, specialmente con riferimento a quelli indossati dai rapper americani

blink /blɪŋk/ *vi* sbattere le palpebre; ‹light› tremolare

blinkered /'blɪŋkəd/ *adj* ‹attitude, approach› ottuso; **be** ~ avere i paraocchi

blinkers /'blɪŋkəz/ *npl* paraocchi *mpl*

blinking /'blɪŋkɪŋ/ *n* (of light) intermittenza *f*; (of eye) battere *m*

blip /blɪp/ *n* (on screen) segnale *m* luminoso a intermittenza; (on graph, line) piccola irregolarità *f*, (sound) ticchettio *m*; (hitch) intoppo *m*

bliss /blɪs/ *n* Rel beatitudine *f*; (happiness) felicità *f*

blissful /'blɪsfʊl/ *adj* beato; (happy) meraviglioso

blissfully /'blɪsfəlɪ/ *adv* beatamente; ~ **ignorant** beatamente ignaro

blister /'blɪstə(r)/ ① *n* Med vescica *f*; (in paint) bolla *f*
② *vi* ‹paint› formare una bolla/delle bolle

blistering /'blɪst(ə)rɪŋ/ ① *n* (of skin) vescica *f*; (of paint) bolle *fpl*
② *adj* ‹sun› scottante; ‹heat› soffocante; ‹attack, criticism› feroce

blister pack *n* blister *m inv*

blithe /blaɪð/ *adj* (cheerful) gioioso; (nonchalant) spensierato

blithely /'blaɪðlɪ/ *adv* (nonchalantly) spensieratamente

blitz /blɪts/ *n* bombardamento *m* aereo; **have a** ~ **on something** fig darci sotto con qualcosa

blitzkrieg /'blɪtskri:g/ *n* guerra *f* lampo

blizzard /'blɪzəd/ *n* tormenta *f*

bloated /'bləʊtɪd/ *adj* gonfio

blob /blɒb/ *n* goccia *f*

bloc /blɒk/ *n* Pol blocco *m*

✍ **block** /blɒk/ ① *n* blocco *m*; (building) isolato *m*; (building ~) cubo *m* (*per giochi di costruzione*); ~ **of flats** palazzo *m*
② *vt* bloccare
▪ **block out** *vt* coprire ‹light, sun›
▪ **block up** *vt* bloccare

blockade /blɒ'keɪd/ ① *n* blocco *m*
② *vt* bloccare

blockage /'blɒkɪdʒ/ *n* ostruzione *f*

block and tackle n paranco m
block book vt prenotare in blocco
block booking n prenotazione f in blocco
block-buster n fam (book, film) successone m; Mil bomba f potente
block capital n in ∼s in stampatello
blockhead n fam testone, -a mf
blockhouse n Mil fortino m
block letters npl stampatello m
block vote n voto m per delega
block voting n votazione f per delega
blog /blɒg/ Comput ① n blog m
② vi bloggare
blogger /'blɒgə(r)/ n Comput blogger m
blogosphere /'blɒgəʊsfɪə(r)/ n blogosfera f
bloke /bləʊk/ n fam tizio m
blonde /blɒnd/ ① adj biondo
② n bionda f
⚡ **blood** /blʌd/ n sangue m
blood-and-thunder adj ‹novel, film› pieno di sangue
blood bank n banca f del sangue
blood bath n bagno m di sangue
blood blister n vescica f di sangue
blood brother n fratello m di sangue
blood cell, **blood corpuscle** n globulo m
blood count n esame m emocromocitometrico
blood-curdling adj raccapricciante
blood donor n donatore, -trice mf di sangue
blood group n gruppo m sanguigno
bloodhound n segugio m
bloodless /'blʌdlɪs/ adj (pale) esangue; (revolution, coup) senza spargimento di sangue
blood-letting n Med salasso m; (killing) spargimento m di sangue
blood lust n sete f di sangue
blood money n compenso versato ad un killer o delatore
blood orange n arancia f sanguigna
blood poisoning n setticemia f
blood pressure n pressione f del sangue
blood-red adj rosso sangue inv
blood relative n parente mf consanguineo, -a
bloodshed n spargimento m di sangue
bloodshot adj iniettato di sangue
blood sports npl sport mpl cruenti
bloodstained adj macchiato di sangue
bloodstream n sangue m
bloodsucker n also fig sanguisuga f
blood test n analisi f inv del sangue

⚡ indicates a very frequent word

bloodthirsty adj assetato di sangue
blood transfusion n trasfusione f del sangue
blood type n gruppo m sanguigno
blood vessel n vaso m sanguigno
bloody /'blʌdɪ/ ① adj (-ier, -iest) insanguinato; sl maledetto
② adv sl ∼ easy/difficult facile/difficile da matti; ∼ tired/funny stanco/divertente da morire; you ∼ well will! e, accidenti, lo farai!
bloody-minded /blʌdɪ'maɪndɪd/ adj scorbutico
bloom /bluːm/ ① n fiore m; in ∼ (of flower) sbocciato; (of tree) in fiore
② vi fiorire; fig essere in forma smagliante
bloomer /'bluːmə(r)/ n fam papera f
bloomers /'bluːməz/ npl mutandoni mpl da donna
blooming /'bluːmɪŋ/ adj fam maledetto
blossom /'blɒsəm/ ① n fiori mpl (d'albero); (single one) fiore m
② vi sbocciare
■ **blossom out** vi fig trasformarsi
blot /blɒt/ n also fig macchia f
■ **blot out**: vt blotted fig cancellare
blotch /blɒtʃ/ n macchia f
blotchy /'blɒtʃɪ/ adj chiazzato
blotter /'blɒtə(r)/ n tampone m di carta assorbente; Am (police) registro m di polizia
blotting paper /'blɒtɪŋ/ n carta f assorbente
blotto /'blɒtəʊ/ adj fam ubriaco fradicio
blouse /blaʊz/ n camicetta f
blow¹ /bləʊ/ n colpo m
⚡ **blow²** v (pt **blew**, pp **blown**) ① vi ‹wind› soffiare; ‹fuse› saltare
② vt fam (squander) sperperare; ∼ one's nose soffiarsi il naso; ∼ one's top fam andare in bestia
■ **blow away** ① vt far volar via ‹papers›
② vi ‹papers› volare via
■ **blow down** ① vt abbattere
② vi abbattersi al suolo
■ **blow off** ① vt ‹wind› portar via
② vi ‹hat, roof› volare via
■ **blow out** ① vt (extinguish) soffiare
② vi ‹candle› spegnersi
■ **blow over** ① vt ‹wind› buttare giù
② vi ‹storm› passare; fig ‹fuss, trouble› dissiparsi
■ **blow up** ① vt (inflate) gonfiare; (enlarge) ingrandire ‹photograph›; (shatter by explosion) far esplodere
② vi esplodere
blow-by-blow adj ‹account› particolareggiato
blow-dry vt asciugare con l'asciugacapelli
blowfly n moscone m (della carne)
blowhole n (of whale) sfiatatoio m
blowlamp n fiamma f ossidrica

blown /bləʊn/ ▶ BLOW²

blowout n Elec corto circuito m; (in oil or gas well) fuga f; (of tyre) scoppio m; fam (meal) abbuffata f

blowpipe n cerbottana f

blowtorch n cannello m ossidrico

blow-up [1] n Phot ingrandimento m
[2] adj ‹doll, toy, dinghy› gonfiabile

blowy /ˈbləʊɪ/ adj ventoso

blowzy /ˈblaʊzɪ/ adj pej ‹woman› volgarmente appariscente

BLT n abbr (**bacon, lettuce, and tomato**) sandwich m con bacon, lattuga e pomodoro

blubber /ˈblʌbə(r)/ [1] n (of whale) grasso m di balena; fam (of person) ciccia f
[2] vi Am (to cry) fam piagnucolare

bludgeon /ˈblʌdʒən/ vt manganellare

blue /bluː/ [1] adj (pale) celeste; (navy) blu inv; (royal) azzurro; **feel** ~ essere giù di corda; ~ **with cold** livido per il freddo; **once in a** ~ **moon** una volta ogni morte di papa
[2] n blu m inv; **the** ~**s** Music il blues; **have the** ~**s** essere giù di corda; **out of the** ~ inaspettatamente; **a bolt from the** ~ un fulmine a ciel sereno

bluebell n giacinto m di bosco

Blue Berets npl Mil Caschi blu mpl

blueberry n mirtillo m

blue blood n sangue m blu

blue-blooded adj di sangue blu

bluebottle n moscone m

blue cheese n formaggio m erborinato

blue chip adj ‹company› di altissimo livello; ‹investment› sicuro

blue-collar job n lavoro m manuale

blue-collar worker n operaio m

blue-eyed adj con gli occhi azzurri

blue-eyed boy n Br fig fam prediletto m

blue film n film m a luci rosse

blue jeans npl blue jeans mpl inv

blue light n (on emergency vehicles) luce (f) delle auto della polizia

blueness /ˈbluːnɪs/ n azzurro m

blue pencil n go through something with the ~ (censor) censurare qualcosa; (edit) fare una revisione di qualcosa

blueprint n fig progetto m

blue rinse n she's had a ~ si è tinta i capelli color grigio argentato

blue-stocking n pej [donna] intellettualoide f

blue tit n cinciarella f

Bluetooth® n Bluetooth® m

blue whale n balenottera f azzurra

bluff /blʌf/ [1] n bluff m inv
[2] vi bluffare

bluish /ˈbluːɪʃ/ adj bluastro, azzurrognolo

blunder /ˈblʌndə(r)/ [1] n gaffe f inv
[2] vi fare una/delle gaffe

blundering /ˈblʌnd(ə)rɪŋ/ adj ~ idiot rimbecillito m

blunt /blʌnt/ adj spuntato; ‹person› reciso

bluntly /ˈblʌntlɪ/ adv schiettamente

bluntness /ˈblʌntnɪs/ n (of manner) rudezza f; (of person) brutale schiettezza f

blur /blɜː(r)/ [1] n It's all a ~ fig è tutto confuso
[2] vt (pt/pp **blurred**) rendere confuso

blurb /blɜːb/ n soffietto m editoriale

blurred /blɜːd/ adj ‹vision, photo› sfocato

blurt /blɜːt/ v
■ **blurt out** vt spifferare

blush /blʌʃ/ [1] n rossore m
[2] vi arrossire

blusher /ˈblʌʃə(r)/ n fard m inv

bluster /ˈblʌstə(r)/ n (showing off) sbruffonata f

blustering /ˈblʌst(ə)rɪŋ/ [1] n (rage) sfuriata f; (boasting) spacconata f
[2] adj (angry) infuriato; (boastful) sbruffone

blustery /ˈblʌst(ə)rɪ/ adj ‹wind› furioso; ‹day, weather› molto ventoso

blu-tak® /ˈbluːtæk/ n blu-tak® m

BMI n abbr (**body mass index**) IMC m

B movie n film m inv di serie B

BO n fam puzza f di sudore

boa /ˈbəʊə/ n boa m inv

boa constrictor /kənˈstrɪktə(r)/ boa m inv

boar /bɔː(r)/ n cinghiale m

board /bɔːd/ [1] n tavola f; (for notices) tabellone m; (committee) assemblea f; (of directors) consiglio m; ~ **of directors** consiglio m di amministrazione; **full** ~ Br pensione f completa; **half** ~ Br mezza pensione f; ~ **and lodging** vitto e alloggio m; **go by the** ~ fam andare a monte
[2] vt Naut, Aeron salire a bordo di
[3] vi ‹passengers› salire a bordo; ~ **with** stare a pensione da
■ **board up** vt sbarrare con delle assi

boarder /ˈbɔːdə(r)/ n pensionante mf; Sch convittore, -trice mf

board game n gioco m da tavolo

boarding /ˈbɔːdɪŋ/ n Aeron, Naut imbarco m; (by customs officer) ispezione f; Mil abbordaggio m

boarding card n carta f di imbarco

boarding house n pensione f

boarding party n squadra f d'ispezione

boarding school n collegio m

board meeting n riunione f del consiglio di amministrazione

boardroom n sala f consiglio, sala f riunioni del consiglio di amministrazione

boardwalk n Am (by sea) lungomare m

boast /bəʊst/ [1] vi vantarsi (**about** di)
[2] vt vantare

boaster /'bəʊstə(r)/ n sbruffone, -a mf

boastful /'bəʊstfʊl/ adj vanaglorioso

ᕹ **boat** /bəʊt/ n barca f; (ship) nave f

boater /'bəʊtə(r)/ n (hat) paglietta f

boat-hook n gaffa f

boathouse /'bəʊthaʊs/ n rimessa f [per imbarcazioni]

boating /'bəʊtɪŋ/ ① n canottaggio m
② adj ‹accident› di navigazione

boating trip n traversata f per mare

boatload n carico m; ~s of tourists navi fpl cariche di turisti

boatswain /'bəʊs(ə)n/ n nostromo m

boatyard n cantiere m per imbarcazioni

bob /bɒb/ ① n (hairstyle) caschetto m
② vi (pt/pp **bobbed**) (also ~ **up and down**) andare su e giù

bobbin /'bɒbɪn/ n bobina f

bobble hat /'bɒblhæt/ n berretto m a pompon

bobby /'bɒbɪ/ n Br fam poliziotto m

bobcat /'bɒbkæt/ n lince f

bobsleigh /'bɒbsleɪ/, **bobsled** /'bɒbsleɪ/
① n bob m inv
② vi andare sul bob

bode /bəʊd/ vi ~ well/ill essere di buono/cattivo augurio

bodge /bɒdʒ/ Br = BOTCH

bodice /'bɒdɪs/ n corpetto m

bodily /'bɒdɪlɪ/ ① adj fisico
② adv (forcibly) fisicamente

ᕹ **body** /'bɒdɪ/ n corpo m; (organization) ente m; (amount: of poems etc) quantità f; **over my dead** ~! fam devi passare prima sul mio corpo!

body blow n deal a ~ **to** fig assestare un duro colpo a

bodyboarding n bodyboarding m inv

bodybuilder n culturista mf

body-building n culturismo m

bodyguard n guardia f del corpo

body heat n calore m del corpo

body language n linguaggio m del corpo

body mass index n indice m di massa corporea

body odour n fam puzza f di sudore

body piercing n piercing m inv

body politic n corpo m sociale

body shop n autocarrozzeria f

body snatching n furto m dei cadaveri

body stocking, **body suit** n body m inv

body warmer n gilet m inv imbottito

bodywork n Auto carrozzeria f

boffin /'bɒfɪn/ n Br fam scienziato m

bog /bɒg/ n palude f
■ **bog down**: vt (pt/pp **bogged**) get ~ged down impantanarsi

bogey /'bəʊgɪ/ n (evil spirit) spirito m malvagio; (to frighten people) spauracchio m

boggle /'bɒg(ə)l/ vi the mind ~s non posso neanche immaginarlo

boggy /'bɒgɪ/ adj (swampy) paludoso; (muddy) fangoso

bog-standard /bɒg,stændəd/ adj fam ordinario

bogus /'bəʊgəs/ adj falso

bohemian /bəʊ'hiːmɪən/ adj ‹lifestyle, person› bohémien

boil¹ /bɔɪl/ n Med foruncolo m

boil² ① n **bring/come to the** ~ portare/arrivare ad ebollizione
② vt [far] bollire
③ vi bollire; fig (with anger) ribollire; **the water** or **kettle's** ~**ing** l'acqua bolle
■ **boil away** vi ‹water› evaporare
■ **boil down to** vi fig ridursi a
■ **boil over** vi straboccare (bollendo)
■ **boil up** vt far bollire

boiler /'bɔɪlə(r)/ n caldaia f

boiler house n caldaia f

boiler room n locale m per la caldaia

boiler suit n tuta f

boiling /'bɔɪlɪŋ/ adj ‹water› bollente; **it's** ~ **in here!** qui si bolle!

boiling hot adj fam ‹liquid› bollente; ‹day› torrido

boiling point n punto m di ebollizione

boisterous /'bɔɪstərəs/ adj chiassoso

bold /bəʊld/ ① adj audace
② n Typ neretto m

boldly /'bəʊldlɪ/ adv audacemente

boldness /'bəʊldnɪs/ n audacia f

Bolivia /bə'lɪvɪə/ n Bolivia f

bollard /'bɒlɑːd/ n colonnina m di sbarramento al traffico

Bolognese /bɒlə'neɪz/ n ragù m

boloney /bə'ləʊnɪ/ n fam idiozie fpl

bolshy /'bɒlʃɪ/ adj Br fam (on one occasion) brontolone; **he's/she's** ~ (by temperament) è un/una piantagrane; **get** ~ fare [delle] storie

bolster /'bəʊlstə(r)/ ① n cuscino m (cilindrico)
② vt ~ **[up]** sostenere

bolt /bəʊlt/ ① n (for door) catenaccio m; (for fixing) bullone m
② vt fissare [con bulloni] (**to** a); chiudere col chiavistello ‹door›; ingurgitare ‹food›
③ vi svignarsela; ‹horse› scappar via
④ adv ~ **upright** diritto come un fuso

bolt-hole n Br rifugio m

ᕹ **bomb** /bɒm/ ① n bomba f
② vt bombardare
■ **bomb along** vi fam (move quickly) sfrecciare

bombard /bɒm'bɑːd/ vt also fig bombardare

bombardment /bɒmˈbɑːdmənt/ n bombardamento m

bombastic /bɒmˈbæstɪk/ adj ampolloso

bomb attack n bombardamento m

bomb blast n esplosione f

bomb disposal n disinnesco m

bomb disposal expert n artificiere m

bomb disposal squad n squadra f artificieri

bomber /ˈbɒmə(r)/ n Aviat bombardiere m; (person) dinamitardo m

bomber jacket n bomber m inv

bombing /ˈbɒmɪŋ/ n Mil bombardamento m; (by terrorists) attentato m dinamitardo

bombproof adj a prova di bomba

bombscare n stato (m) di allarme per la presunta presenza di una bomba

bombshell n fig (news) bomba f; **blonde ∼** bionda f esplosiva

bomb shelter n rifugio m antiaereo

bombsite n zona f bombardata; fig (mess) campo f di battaglia

Bomb Squad n squadra f artificieri

bona fide /bəʊnəˈfaɪdɪ/ adj ‹member, refugee› autentico; ‹attempt› genuino; ‹offer› serio

bonanza /bəˈnænzə/ n (windfall) momento m di prosperità; (in mining) filone m d'oro/ d'argento

bond /bɒnd/ [1] n fig legame m; Comm obbligazione f
[2] vt ‹glue› attaccare

bondage /ˈbɒndɪdʒ/ n schiavitù f

bonded warehouse /ˈbɒndɪd/ n magazzino m doganale

bonding /ˈbɒndɪŋ/ n (between mother and baby) legame m madre-figlio; **male ∼** solidarietà f maschile

✓ **bone** /bəʊn/ [1] n osso m; (of fish) spina f
[2] vt disossare ‹meat›; togliere le spine da ‹fish›

bone china n porcellana f fine

boned /bəʊnd/ adj ‹joint, leg, chicken› disossato; ‹fish› senza lische; ‹corset, bodice› con le stecche

bone-dry adj secco

bonehead n fam cretino, -a mf

bone idle adj fam fannullone

boneless /ˈbəʊnlɪs/ adj ‹chicken› disossato; ‹chicken breast› senz'osso; ‹fish› senza lische

bone marrow n midollo m osseo

bone-marrow transplant n trapianto m di midollo osseo

bonemeal n farina f d'ossa

bonfire /ˈbɒnfaɪə(r)/ n falò m inv

Bonfire Night n Br sera (f) del 5 novembre festeggiata con falò e fuochi d'artificio

bonk /bɒŋk/ vt sl scopare

bonkers /ˈbɒŋkəz/ adj fam suonato

bonnet /ˈbɒnɪt/ n cuffia f; (of car) cofano m

bonus /ˈbəʊnəs/ n (individual) gratifica f; (production)premio m; (life insurance) dividendo m; **a ∼** fig qualcosa in più

bonus point n five **∼s** un bonus di cinque punti

bony /ˈbəʊnɪ/ adj (**-ier, -iest**) ossuto; ‹fish› pieno di spine

boo /buː/ [1] interj (to surprise or frighten) bu!
[2] vt/i fischiare

boob /buːb/ [1] n fam (mistake) gaffe f inv; (breast) tetta f
[2] vi fam fare una gaffe

booboo /ˈbuːbuː/ n fam gaffe f inv

booby prize /ˈbuːbɪ/ n premio (m) di consolazione per il peggior contendente

booby trap [1] n Mil ordigno (m) che esplode al contatto, (joke) trabocchetto m
[2] vt Mil mettere un ordigno esplosivo in

boogie /ˈbuːgɪ/ n fam boogie m

booing /ˈbuːɪŋ/ n fischi mpl

✓ **book** /bʊk/ [1] n libro m; (of tickets) blocchetto m; **keep the ∼s** Comm tenere la contabilità; **be in sb's bad/good ∼s** essere nel libro nero/nelle grazie di qualcuno; **do something by the ∼** seguire strettamente le regole
[2] vt (reserve) prenotare; (for offence) multare
[3] vi (reserve) prenotare

bookable /ˈbʊkəbl/ adj ‹event, ticket› che si può prenotare; ‹offence› che può essere multato

bookbinder n rilegatore, -trice mf

bookbinding n rilegatura f

bookcase n libreria f

book club n club m inv del libro

book-ends npl reggilibri mpl

book fair n fiera f del libro

bookie /ˈbʊkɪ/ n fam bookmaker m inv, allibratore m

booking /ˈbʊkɪŋ/ n Br (reservation) prenotazione f; **make a ∼** fare una prenotazione; **get a ∼** Br (from referee) ricevere un'ammonizione

booking clerk n Br impiegato, -a mf in un ufficio prenotazioni

booking form n Br modulo m di prenotazione

booking office n biglietteria f

bookish /ˈbʊkɪʃ/ adj ‹person› secchione

book jacket n sopraccoperta f

bookkeeper n contabile mf

bookkeeping n contabilità f

booklet /ˈbʊklɪt/ n opuscolo m

book lover n amante mf della lettura

bookmaker n allibratore m

bookmark n segnalibro m

bookplate n ex libris m inv

bookrest n leggio m

bookseller n libraio, -a mf
bookshelf n (single) scaffale f; (bookcase) libreria f
bookshop n libreria f
bookstall n edicola f
bookstore n Am libreria f
book token n Br buono m acquisto per libri
bookworm n topo m di biblioteca
boom /bu:m/ ① n Comm boom m inv; (upturn) impennata f; (of thunder, gun) rimbombo m
　② vi ‹thunder, gun› rimbombare; fig prosperare
boomerang /'bu:məræŋ/ ① n boomerang m inv
　② vi ~ on somebody ‹plan› ritorcersi contro qualcuno
boomerang effect n effetto m boomerang
booming /'bu:mɪŋ/ adj ‹sound› sonoro; ‹voice› tonante; ‹economy› fiorente; ‹demand, exports, sales› in crescita
boom microphone n microfono m a stelo
boon /bu:n/ n benedizione f
boor /bʊə(r)/ n zoticone m
boorish /'bʊərɪʃ/ adj maleducato
boost /bu:st/ ① n spinta f
　② vt stimolare ‹sales›; sollevare ‹morale›; far crescere ‹hopes›
booster /'bu:stə(r)/ n Med dose f supplementare
boot /bu:t/ ① n stivale m; (up to ankle) stivaletto m; (football) scarpetta f; (climbing) scarpone m; Auto portabagagli m inv
　② vt Comput mettere in funzione
■ **boot out** vt fam cacciare
■ **boot up** Comput ① vi caricarsi
　② vt caricare
boot black n lustrascarpe mf inv
boot drive n Comput unità f inv di inizializzazione
bootee /bu:'ti:/ n (knitted) babbuccia f di lana; (leather) stivaletto m
booth /bu:ð/ n (for phoning, voting) cabina f; (at market) bancarella f
bootlace n laccio m, stringa f
bootlegger n Am contrabbandiere m di alcolici
bootlicker n leccapiedi mf inv
bootmaker n calzolaio m
boot polish n lucido m da scarpe
boot scraper n puliscipiedi m inv
bootstrap n (on boot) linguetta f calzastivali; Comput lancio m; pull oneself up by one's ~s riuscire con le proprie forze
boot-up n Comput boot m inv

✓ indicates a very frequent word

booty /'bu:tɪ/ n bottino m
booze /bu:z/ n fam alcolici mpl
boozer /'bu:zə(r)/ n fam (person) beone, -a mf; Br (pub) bar m inv
booze-up n bella bevuta f
boozy /'bu:zɪ/ adj fam ‹laughter› da ubriaco; ‹meal› in cui si beve molto
bop /bɒp/ fam ① n (blow) colpo m
　② vt dare un colpo a
　③ vi Br (dance) ballare
✓ **border** /'bɔ:də(r)/ ① n bordo m; (frontier) frontiera f; (in garden) bordura f
　② vt confinare con; fig essere ai confini di
■ **border on** vt ‹country, land› confinare con; ‹madness, hysteria› essere al limite di
border dispute n (fight) conflitto m al confine; (disagreement) contesa f sul confine
border guard n guardia f di frontiera
borderline n linea f di demarcazione; ~ case caso m dubbio
border raid n incursione f
bore¹ /bɔ:(r)/ ▶ BEAR²
bore² vt Techn forare
bore³ ① n (of gun) calibro m; (person) seccatore, -trice mf; (thing) seccatura f
　② vt annoiare
bored /bɔ:d/ adj annoiato, stufo; be ~ to tears or to death annoiarsi (da morire)
boredom /'bɔ:dəm/ n noia f
boring /'bɔ:rɪŋ/ adj noioso
✓ **born** /bɔ:n/ ① pp be ~ nascere; I was ~ in 1963 sono nato nel 1963
　② adj nato; a ~ liar/actor un bugiardo/un attore nato
born-again adj convertito alla chiesa evangelica
borne /bɔ:n/ ▶ BEAR²
Borneo /'bɔ:nɪəʊ/ n Borneo m
borough /'bʌrə/ n municipalità f inv
borough council n Br ≈ comune m
borrow /'bɒrəʊ/ vt prendere in prestito (from da); can I ~ your pen? mi presti la tua penna?
borrower /'bɒrəʊə(r)/ n debitore, -trice mf
borrowing /'bɒrəʊɪŋ/ n prestito m; increase in ~ Fin aumento m dell'indebitamento
borrowing costs n Fin costo m del denaro
borstal /'bɔ:stəl/ n Br riformatorio m
Bosnia /'bɒznɪə/ n Bosnia f
Bosnia-Herzegovina /-hɜ:tsəgəʊ'vi:nə/ n Bosnia-Erzegovina f
Bosnian /'bɒznɪən/ adj & n bosniaco, -a mf
bosom /'bʊzm/ n seno m
bosom buddy, bosom friend n fam amico, -a mf del cuore
✓ **boss** /bɒs/ ① n direttore, -trice mf
　② vt (also ~ about) comandare a bacchetta

bossy /'bɒsɪ/ *adj* autoritario
bosun /'bəʊsən/ *n* nostromo *m*
botanical /bə'tænɪkl/ *adj* botanico
botanist /'bɒtənɪst/ *n* botanico, -a *mf*
botany /'bɒtənɪ/ *n* botanica *f*
botch /bɒtʃ/ *vt* fare un pasticcio con
⚡ **both** /bəʊθ/ **1** *adj & pron* tutti e due, entrambi
2 *adv* ~ men and women sia uomini che donne; ~ [of] the children tutti e due i bambini; they are ~ dead sono morti entrambi; ~ of them tutti e due
⚡ **bother** /'bɒðə(r)/ **1** *n* preoccupazione *f*; (minor trouble) fastidio *m*; it's no ~ non c'è problema
2 *int* fam che seccatura!
3 *vt* (annoy) dare fastidio a; (disturb) disturbare
4 *vi* preoccuparsi (about di); don't ~ lascia perdere
Botswana /bɒt'swɑːnə/ *n* Botswana *m*
⚡ **bottle** /'bɒt(ə)l/ **1** *n* bottiglia *f*; (baby's) biberon *m inv*
2 *vt* imbottigliare
■ **bottle up** *vt* fig reprimere
bottle bank *n* contenitore *m* per la raccolta del vetro
bottle-feed *vt* allattare col biberon
bottle-feeding *n* allattamento *m* col biberon
bottle green *adj & n* verde *m* bottiglia *inv*
bottleneck *n* fig ingorgo *m*
bottle-opener *n* apribottiglie *m inv*
bottle top *n* tappo *m* di bottiglia
bottle-washer *n* hum chief cook and ~ tuttofare *mf inv*
⚡ **bottom** /'bɒtm/ **1** *adj* ultimo; the ~ shelf l'ultimo scaffale in basso
2 *n* (of container) fondo *m*; (of river) fondale *m*; (of hill) piedi *mpl*, (buttocks) sedere *m*; at the ~ in fondo; at the ~ of the page in fondo alla pagina; get to the ~ of fig vedere cosa c'è sotto
■ **bottom out** *vi* ⟨inflation, unemployment etc⟩ assestarsi
bottom drawer *n* fig corredo *m*
bottom gear *n* Br Auto prima *f*
bottomless /'bɒtəmlɪs/ *adj* senza fondo
bottom line *n* Fin utile *m*; that's the ~ (decisive factor) la questione è tutta qui
botulism /'bɒtjʊlɪzm/ *n* botulismo *m*
bouffant /'buːfɒ̃/ *adj* ⟨hair, hairstyle⟩ cotonato; ⟨sleeve⟩ a sbuffo
bough /baʊ/ *n* ramoscello *m*
bought /bɔːt/ ▶ BUY
boulder /'bəʊldə(r)/ *n* masso *m*
bounce /baʊns/ **1** *vi* rimbalzare; fam ⟨cheque⟩ essere respinto
2 *vt* far rimbalzare ⟨ball⟩

■ **bounce back** *vi* fig riprendersi; ⟨email⟩ tornare indietro
bouncer /'baʊnsə(r)/ *n* fam buttafuori *m inv*
bouncy /'baʊnsɪ/ *adj* ⟨ball⟩ che rimbalza bene; ⟨mattress, walk⟩ molleggiato; fig ⟨person⟩ esuberante
bound¹ /baʊnd/ **1** *n* balzo *m*
2 *vi* balzare
bound² **1** ▶ BIND
2 *adj* ~ for ⟨ship⟩ diretto a; be ~ to do (likely) dovere fare per forza; (obliged) essere costretto a fare
boundary /'baʊndərɪ/ *n* limite *m*
boundless /'baʊndlɪs/ *adj* illimitato
bounds /baʊndz/ *npl* fig limiti *mpl*; out of ~ fuori dai limiti
bounty /'baʊntɪ/ *n* (gift) dono *m*; (generosity) munificenza *f*
bounty hunter *n* cacciatore *m* di taglie
bouquet /bʊ'keɪ/ *n* mazzo *m* di fiori; (of wine) bouquet *m*
bourbon /'bʊəbən/ *n* bourbon *m inv*
bourgeois /'bʊəʒwɑː/ *adj* pej borghese
bourgeoisie /bʊəʒwɑː'ziː/ *n* borghesia *f*
bout /baʊt/ *n* Med attacco *m*; Sport incontro *m*
boutique /buː'tiːk/ *n* negozio *m*; fashion ~ negozio *m* di abbigliamento
bovine /'bəʊvaɪn/ *adj* bovino
bow¹ /bəʊ/ *n* (weapon) arco *m*; Mus archetto *m*; (knot) nodo *m*
bow² /baʊ/ **1** *n* inchino *m*
2 *vi* inchinarsi
3 *vt* piegare ⟨head⟩
bow³ /baʊ/ *n* Naut prua *f*
■ **bow out** *vi* (withdraw) ritirarsi (of da)
bowel /'baʊəl/ *n* intestino *m*; have a ~ movement andare di corpo; ~s *pl* intestini *mpl*
bower /'baʊə(r)/ *n* (in garden) pergolato *m*; liter (chamber) salottino *m*
bowl¹ /bəʊl/ *n* (for soup, cereal) scodella *f*; (of pipe) fornello *m*
bowl² **1** *n* (ball) boccia *f*
2 *vt* lanciare
3 *vi* Cricket servire; (in bowls) lanciare
■ **bowl along** *vi* (in car etc) andare spedito
■ **bowl over** *vt* buttar giù; fig (leave speechless) lasciare senza parole
bow-legged /bəʊ'legd/ *adj* dalle gambe storte
bowler¹ /'bəʊlə(r)/ *n* Cricket lanciatore *m*; Bowls giocatore *m* di bocce
bowler² *n* ~ [hat] bombetta *f*
bowling /'bəʊlɪŋ/ *n* gioco *m* delle bocce
bowling alley /'bəʊlɪŋælɪ/ *n* pista *f* da bowling
bowling green *n* prato *m* da bocce
bowls /bəʊlz/ *n* gioco *m* delle bocce

b

bowstring n corda f d'arco
bow tie n cravatta f a farfalla
bow window n bow window f inv
✍ **box¹** /bɒks/ n scatola f; Theat palco m
box² ① vi Sport fare il pugile
② vt ∼ **sb's ears** dare uno scapaccione a qualcuno
boxer /'bɒksə(r)/ n pugile m
boxer shorts npl boxer mpl
boxing /'bɒksɪŋ/ n pugilato m
Boxing Day n Br [giorno m di] Santo Stefano m
box number n casella f
box office n Theat botteghino m
boxroom n Br sgabuzzino m
boxwood n bosso m
✍ **boy** /bɔɪ/ n ragazzo m; (younger) bambino m
boy band n boy band f inv
boycott /'bɔɪkɒt/ ① n boicottaggio m
② vt boicottare
boyfriend /'bɔɪfrend/ n ragazzo m
boyhood /'bɔɪhʊd/ n (childhood) infanzia f; (adolescence) adolescenza f
boyish /'bɔɪɪʃ/ adj da ragazzino
boy scout n boy scout m inv
bpm abbr (**beats per minute**) bpm mpl
bps abbr (**bits per second**) Comput bps mpl
BR abbr (**British Rail**) ente (m) ferroviario britannico ≈ FS
bra /brɑː/ n reggiseno m
brace /breɪs/ ① n sostegno m; (dental) apparecchio m
② vt ∼ **oneself** fig farsi forza (**for** per affrontare)
bracelet /'breɪslɪt/ n braccialetto m
braces /'breɪsɪz/ npl bretelle fpl
bracing /'breɪsɪŋ/ adj tonificante
bracken /'brækn/ n felce f
bracket /'brækɪt/ ① n mensola f; (group) categoria f; Typ parentesi f inv
② vt mettere fra parentesi
brackish /'brækɪʃ/ adj salmastro
bradawl /'brædɔːl/ n punteruolo m
brag /bræg/ vi (pt/pp **bragged**) vantarsi (**about** di)
bragging /'brægɪŋ/ n vanterie fpl
Brahmin /'brɑːmɪn/ n Relig bramino m
braid /breɪd/ n (edging) passamano m
braille /breɪl/ n braille m
✍ **brain** /breɪn/ n cervello m; ∼**s** pl fig testa fsg
brainbox n fam capoccione m
brainchild n invenzione f personale
brain damage n lesione f cerebrale
brain-dead adj Med cerebralmente morto; fig senza cervello

brain death n morte f cerebrale
brain drain n fuga f di cervelli
brainless /'breɪnlɪs/ adj senza cervello
brain scan n scansione m inv del cervello
brain scanner n scanner m inv (per il cervello)
brainstorm n Med fig eccesso m di pazzia; Am (brainwave) lampo m di genio
brainstorming session n brainstorming m inv
brains trust n brain trust m inv, gruppo m di esperti
brain surgeon n neurochirurgo m
brain surgery n neurochirurgia f
brain teaser n fam rompicapo m
brainwash vt fare il lavaggio del cervello a
brainwashing n lavaggio m del cervello
brainwave n lampo m di genio
brainy /'breɪnɪ/ adj (-ier, -iest) intelligente
braise /breɪz/ vt brasare
brake /breɪk/ ① n freno m
② vi frenare
brake block n pastiglia f
brake disc n disco m dei freni
brake drum n tamburo m del freno
brake fluid n liquido m dei freni
brake-light n stop m inv
brake lining n guarnizione f del freno
brake pad n ganascia f del freno
brake pedal n pedale m del freno
bramble /'bræmb(ə)l/ n rovo m; (fruit) mora f
bran /bræn/ n crusca f
✍ **branch** /brɑːntʃ/ ① n also fig ramo m; Comm succursale f; filiale f; (of bank) agenzia f; **our Oxford St** ∼ (of store) il negozio di Oxford St
② vi ⟨road⟩ biforcarsi
▪ **branch off** vi biforcarsi
▪ **branch out** vi ∼ **out into** allargare le proprie attività nel ramo di
branch line n linea f secondaria
branch manager n (of bank) direttore, -trice mf di agenzia; (of company) direttore, -trice mf di filiale; (of shop) direttore, -trice mf di succursale
branch office n filiale f; (of bank) agenzia f
✍ **brand** /brænd/ ① n marca f; (on animal) marchio m
② vt marcare ⟨animal⟩; fig tacciare (**as** di)
branded /'brændɪd/ adj ⟨goods⟩ di marca
brand image n brand image f
brandish /'brændɪʃ/ vt brandire
brand leader n marca f leader inv
brand name n marca f
brand-new adj nuovo fiammante
brandy /'brændɪ/ n brandy m inv

brash /bræʃ/ *adj* sfrontato

brass /brɑːs/ *n* ottone *m*; **the ∼** Mus gli ottoni *mpl*; **top ∼** fam pezzi *mpl* grossi

brass band *n* banda *f (di soli ottoni)*

brassiere /'bræzɪə(r)/ Am *n* fml reggiseno *m*

brass instrument *n* Mus ottone *m*

brass neck *n* Br fam faccia *f* tosta

brass rubbing *n* ricalco (*m*) di iscrizione tombale o commemorativa

brassy /'brɑːsɪ/ *adj* (**-ier, -iest**) fam volgare

brat /bræt/ *n* pej marmocchio, -a *mf*

bravado /brə'vɑːdəʊ/ *n* bravata *f*

brave /breɪv/ **1** *adj* coraggioso **2** *vt* affrontare

bravely /'breɪvlɪ/ *adv* con coraggio

bravery /'breɪvərɪ/ *n* coraggio *m*

bravo /bruː'vəʊ/ *int* bravo!

bravura /brə'vjʊərə/ *n* virtuosismo *m*

brawl /brɔːl/ **1** *n* rissa *f* **2** *vi* azzuffarsi

brawn /brɔːn/ *n* Culin ≈ soppressata *f*

brawny /'brɔːnɪ/ *adj* muscoloso

bray /breɪ/ *vi ‹donkey›* ragliare

brazen /'breɪzn/ *adj* sfrontato
■ **brazen out** *vt* affrontare con piglio sicuro

brazier /'breɪzɪə(r)/ *n* braciere *m*

Brazil /brə'zɪl/ *n* Brasile *m*

Brazilian /brə'zɪlɪən/ *adj & n* brasiliano, -a *mf*

Brazil [nut] *n* noce *f* del Brasile

breach /briːtʃ/ **1** *n* (of law) violazione *f*; (gap) breccia *f*; fig (in party) frattura *f* **2** *vt* recedere *‹contract›*

breach of contract *n* Jur inadempienza *f* contrattuale

breach of promise *n* Jur inadempienza *f* a una promessa di matrimonio

breach of the peace *n* Jur violazione *f* dell'ordine pubblico

breach of trust *n* Jur abuso *m* di fiducia

bread /bred/ *n* pane *m*; **a slice of ∼ and butter** una fetta di pane imburrato

bread and butter *n* fig fonte *f* di guadagno principale

breadbasket *n* cestino *m* per il pane; fig granaio *m*

breadbin *n* Br cassetta *f* portapane *inv*

breadboard *n* tagliere *m* per il pane

breadcrumbs *npl* briciole *fpl*; Culin pangrattato *m*

breadfruit *n* frutto *m* dell'albero del pane

breadknife *n* coltello *m* per il pane

breadline *n* **be on the ∼** essere povero in canna

bread roll *n* panino *m*

breadstick *n* filoncino *m*

breadth /bredθ/ *n* larghezza *f*

breadwinner /'bredwɪnə(r)/ *n* quello, -a *mf* che porta i soldi a casa

✧ **break** /breɪk/ **1** *n* rottura *f*; (interval) intervallo *m*; (interruption) interruzione *f*; fam (chance) opportunità *f inv* **2** *vt* (*pt* **broke**, *pp* **broken**) rompere; (interrupt) interrompere; **∼ one's arm** rompersi un braccio **3** *vi* rompersi; *‹day›* spuntare; *‹storm›* scoppiare; *‹news›* diffondersi; *‹boy's voice›* cambiare
■ **break away** *vi* scappare; fig chiudere (**from** con)
■ **break down** **1** *vi ‹machine, car›* guastarsi; *‹negotiations›* interrompersi; (in tears) scoppiare in lacrime **2** *vt* sfondare *‹door›*; ripartire *‹figures›*
■ **break in** *vi ‹burglar›* introdursi
■ **break into** *vt* introdursi con la forza in; forzare *‹car›*
■ **break off** **1** *vt* rompere *‹engagement›* **2** *vi ‹part of whole›* rompersi; (when speaking) interrompersi
■ **break out** *vi ‹argument, war›* scoppiare
■ **break through** *vi ‹sun›* spuntare
■ **break up** **1** *vt* far cessare *‹fight›*; disperdere *‹crowd›* **2** *vi ‹crowd›* disperdersi; *‹marriage›* naufragare; *‹couple›* separarsi; Sch iniziare le vacanze

breakable /'breɪkəbl/ *adj* fragile

breakage /'breɪkɪdʒ/ *n* rottura *f*

breakaway /'breɪkəweɪ/ **1** *n* (from person) separazione *f*, allontanamento *m*; (from organization) scissione *f*; Sport contropiede *m* **2** *attrib ‹faction, group, state›* separatista

breakdown /'breɪkdaʊn/ *n* (of car, machine) guasto *m*; Med esaurimento *m* nervoso; (of figures) analisi *f inv*

breaker /'breɪkə(r)/ *n* (wave) frangente *m*

breaker's yard *n* Auto cimitero *m* delle macchine

break even *vi* andare in pareggio

break-even point *n* punto *m* di pareggio, punto *m* di equilibrio

breakfast /'brekfəst/ *n* [prima] colazione *f*

breakfast bar *n* tavolo *m* a penisola

breakfast bowl *n* scodella *f* per i cereali

breakfast cereals *npl* cereali *mpl* per la colazione

breakfast television, breakfast TV *n* programmi *mpl* televisivi del mattino

break free *vi* fuggire

break-in *n* irruzione *f*

breaking /'breɪkɪŋ/ *n* (of glass, seal, contract) rottura *f*; (of bone) frattura *f*; (of law, treaty) violazione *f*; (of voice) cambiamento *m*; (of promise) venuta *f* meno; (of horse) domatura *f*; (of link, sequence, tie) interruzione *f*

b

breaking and entering /ˈbreɪkɪŋənd
ˈentərɪŋ/ n Jur effrazione f con scasso
breaking point n Techn punto m di
rottura; fig limite m di sopportazione
breakneck adj ‹pace, speed› a rotta di
collo
break-out n (from prison) evasione f
breakpoint n Tennis breakpoint m inv
breakthrough n (discovery) scoperta f; (in
negotiations) passo m avanti
break-up n (of family, company)
disgregazione f; (of alliance, relationship) rottura
f; (of marriage) dissoluzione f
breakwater n frangiflutti m inv
breast /brest/ n seno m
breastbone n sterno m
breastfeed vt allattare al seno
breast pocket n taschino m
breast-stroke n nuoto m a rana
ꝰ **breath** /breθ/ n respiro m, fiato m; out of ∼
senza fiato; **under one's** ∼ sottovoce; a ∼ of
air un filo d'aria
breathalyse /ˈbreθəlaɪz/ vt sottoporre
alla prova del palloncino
breathalyser® Br, **breathalyzer**®
/ˈbreθəlaɪzə(r)/ n alcoltest m inv
breathe /briːð/ vt/i respirare; ∼ a sigh of
relief tirare un sospiro di sollievo
■ **breath in** [1] vi inspirare
[2] vt respirare ‹scent, air›
■ **breathe out** vt/i espirare
breather /ˈbriːðə(r)/ n pausa f
breathing /ˈbriːðɪŋ/ n respirazione f
breathing apparatus n respiratore m
breathing space n (respite) tregua f; give
oneself a ∼ riprendere fiato
breathless /ˈbreθlɪs/ adj senza fiato
breathlessly /ˈbreθlɪslɪ/ adv senza fiato
breathtaking /ˈbreθteɪkɪŋ/ adj
mozzafiato
breathtakingly /ˈbreθteɪkɪŋlɪ/ adv
∼ **audacious** di un'audacia stupefacente;
∼ **beautiful** di una bellezza mozzafiato
breath test n prova f del palloncino
bred /bred/ ▶ BREED
breech /briːtʃ/ n Med natiche fpl; (of gun)
culatta f
breed /briːd/ [1] n razza f
[2] vt (pt/pp **bred**) allevare; (give rise to)
generare
[3] vi riprodursi
breeder /ˈbriːdə(r)/ n allevatore, -trice mf
breeding /ˈbriːdɪŋ/ n allevamento m; fig
educazione f
breeding ground n zona f di
riproduzione; fig terreno m fertile
breeding period, **breeding season**
n stagione f di riproduzione

ꝰ indicates a very frequent word

breeze /briːz/ n brezza f
breeze block n Br mattone (m) fatto con
scorie di coke
breezily /ˈbriːzɪlɪ/ adv (confidently) con
sicurezza; (casually) con disinvoltura;
(cheerfully) allegramente
breezy /ˈbriːzɪ/ adj ventoso
brevity /ˈbrevətɪ/ n brevità f
brew /bruː/ [1] n infuso m
[2] vt mettere in infusione ‹tea›; produrre
‹beer›
[3] vi fig ‹trouble› essere nell'aria
brewer /ˈbruːə(r)/ n birraio m
brewery /ˈbruːərɪ/ n fabbrica f di birra
brew-up n Br fam tè m inv
briar /ˈbraɪə(r)/ n rosa f selvatica; (heather)
erica f; (thorns) rovo m; (pipe) pipa f in radica
bribe /braɪb/ [1] n (money) bustarella f;
(large sum of money) tangente f
[2] vt corrompere
bribery /ˈbraɪbərɪ/ n corruzione f
brick /brɪk/ n mattone m
■ **brick up** vt murare
brickbat n fig critica f spietata
brick-built adj di mattoni
bricklayer n muratore m
bricklaying n muratura f
brick red adj rosso mattone inv
bricks-and-mortar adj ‹company,
business› di tipo tradizionale
brickwork n muratura f di mattoni
brickworks n fabbrica f di mattoni
bridal /ˈbraɪdl/ adj nuziale
bridal party n corteo m nuziale
bridal suite n camera f nuziale
bridal wear n confezioni fpl da sposa
bride /braɪd/ n sposa f
bridegroom /ˈbraɪdgruːm/ n sposo m
bridesmaid /ˈbraɪdzmeɪd/ n damigella f
d'onore
bridge¹ /brɪdʒ/ [1] n ponte m; (of nose) setto
m nasale; (of spectacles) ponticello m
[2] vt fig colmare ‹gap›
bridge² n Cards bridge m
bridge-building n costruzione f di ponti
provvisori; fig mediazione f
bridging loan /ˈbrɪdʒɪŋ/ n Br Fin pre-
finanziamento m, credito m provvisorio
bridle /ˈbraɪd(ə)l/ n briglia f
bridle path, **bridleway** /ˈbraɪd(ə)lweɪ/
n sentiero m per cavalli
ꝰ **brief¹** /briːf/ adj breve; in ∼ in breve
brief² [1] n istruzioni fpl; Jur (case) causa f
[2] vt dare istruzioni a; Jur affidare la causa a
briefcase /ˈbriːfkeɪs/ n cartella f
briefing /ˈbriːfɪŋ/ n briefing m inv
briefly /ˈbriːflɪ/ adv brevemente; **briefly,...**
in breve,...
briefness /ˈbriːfnɪs/ n brevità f

briefs /briːfs/ npl slip m inv

brigade /brɪˈɡeɪd/ n brigata f

brigadier /brɪɡəˈdɪə(r)/ n generale m di brigata

⚡ **bright** /braɪt/ adj ‹metal, idea› brillante; ‹day, room, future› luminoso; (clever) intelligente; ~ **red** rosso m acceso

brighten /ˈbraɪt(ə)n/ v ~ **[up]** **1** vt ravvivare; rallegrare ‹person› **2** vi ‹weather› schiarirsi; ‹face› illuminarsi; ‹person› rallegrarsi

brightly /ˈbraɪtlɪ/ adv ‹shine› intensamente; ‹smile› allegramente

brightness /ˈbraɪtnɪs/ n luminosità f; (intelligence) intelligenza f

bright spark n Br fam genio m

bright young things npl Br i giovani di belle speranze

brill /brɪl/ **1** n Zool rombo m liscio **2** adj Br fam fantastico

brilliance /ˈbrɪljəns/ n luminosità f; (of person) genialità f

brilliant /ˈbrɪljənt/ adj (very good) eccezionale; (very intelligent) brillante; ‹sunshine› splendente

brilliantly /ˈbrɪljəntlɪ/ adv ‹shine› intensamente; ‹perform› in modo eccezionale

Brillo pad® /ˈbrɪləʊ/ n paglietta f d'acciaio

brim /brɪm/ n bordo m; (of hat) tesa f
■ **brim over** vi (pt/pp **brimmed**) traboccare

brine /braɪn/ n salamoia f

⚡ **bring** /brɪŋ/ vt (pt/pp **brought**) portare ‹person, object›
■ **bring about** vt causare
■ **bring along** vt portare [con sé]
■ **bring back** vt restituire ‹something borrowed›; reintrodurre ‹hanging›; fare ritornare in mente ‹memories›
■ **bring down** vt portare giù; fare cadere ‹government›; fare abbassare ‹price›
■ **bring forward** vt anticipare ‹meeting, date›; **the meeting has been brought forward to this afternoon** la riunione è stata anticipata al pomeriggio
■ **bring in** vt introdurre ‹legislation›; **his job ~s in £30,000 a year** guadagna 30.000 sterline all'anno
■ **bring off**: vt ~ **something off** riuscire a fare qualcosa
■ **bring on** vt (cause) provocare
■ **bring out** vt (emphasize) mettere in evidenza; pubblicare ‹book›
■ **bring round** vt portare; (persuade) convincere; far rinvenire ‹unconscious person›
■ **bring up** vt (vomit) rimettere; allevare ‹children›; tirare fuori ‹question, subject›

bring and buy sale n Br vendita f di beneficenza

brink /brɪŋk/ n orlo m; **on the ~ of disaster** sull'orlo del disastro

brinkmanship /ˈbrɪŋkmənʃɪp/ n strategia f del rischio calcolato

brisk /brɪsk/ adj svelto; ‹person› sbrigativo; ‹trade, business› redditizio; ‹walk› a passo spedito

brisket /ˈbrɪskɪt/ n Culin punta f di petto

briskly /ˈbrɪsklɪ/ adv velocemente; ‹say› frettolosamente; ‹walk› di buon passo

bristle /ˈbrɪsl/ **1** n setola f **2** vi **bristling with** pieno di

bristly /ˈbrɪslɪ/ adj ‹chin› ispido

Britain /ˈbrɪtn/ n Gran Bretagna f

⚡ **British** /ˈbrɪtɪʃ/ **1** adj britannico; ‹ambassador› della Gran Bretagna **2** npl **the ~** il popolo britannico

British Airports Authority n ente (m) che gestisce gli aeroporti britannici

British Broadcasting Corporation n ente (m) radio-televisivo nazionale britannico

British Columbia n Columbia f Britannica

Britisher /ˈbrɪtɪʃə(r)/ n Am britannico, -a mf

British Gas n Br società (f) del gas britannica

British Isles npl Isole fpl Britanniche

British Rail n ente (m) ferroviario britannico

British Telecom n Br società (f) britannica di telecomunicazioni

Briton /ˈbrɪtən/ n cittadino, -a, britannico, -a mf

Brittany /ˈbrɪtənɪ/ n Bretagna f

brittle /ˈbrɪtl/ adj fragile

brittle-bone disease n decalcificazione f ossea, osteoporosi f

broach /brəʊtʃ/ vt toccare ‹subject›

B road n Br ≈ strada f provinciale

⚡ **broad** /brɔːd/ adj ampio; ‹hint› chiaro; ‹accent› marcato; **two metres ~** largo due metri; **in ~ daylight** in pieno giorno

broadband /ˈbrɔːdbænd/ n Comput banda f larga; **on ~** a banda larga; ~ **connection** connessione f a banda larga

broad-based /ˈbeɪst/ adj ‹coalition, education› diversificato; ‹approach, campaign› su larga scala; ‹consensus› generale

broad bean n fava f

broadcast /ˈbrɔːdkæst/ **1** n trasmissione f **2** vt/i (pt/pp **-cast**) trasmettere

broadcaster /ˈbrɔːdkæstə(r)/ n giornalista mf radiotelevisivo, -a

broadcasting /ˈbrɔːdkæstɪŋ/ n diffusione f radiotelevisiva; **be in ~** lavorare per la televisione/radio

b

broad-chested adj con il torace robusto
broaden /'brɔ:dn/ **1** vt allargare; ~ one's horizons allargare i propri orizzonti
2 vi allargarsi
broadly /'brɔ:dlɪ/ adv largamente; ~ [speaking] generalmente
broad-minded /-'maɪndɪd/ adj di larghe vedute
broadness /'brɔ:dnɪs/ n larghezza f
broadsheet n quotidiano m di grande formato
broad-shouldered adj con le spalle larghe
broadside **1** n Naut (of ship) fiancata f; (enemy fire) bordata f; n (criticism) attacco m; deliver a ~ lanciare un attacco
2 adv di fianco
brocade /brə'keɪd/ n broccato m
broccoli /'brɒkəlɪ/ n inv broccoli mpl
brochure /'brəʊʃə(r)/ n opuscolo m; (travel) dépliant m inv
brogue /'brəʊg/ n (shoe) scarpa m da passeggio; (accent) cadenza f dialettale
broil /brɔɪl/ Am **1** vt Culin cuocere alla griglia ‹meat›
2 vi cuocere alla griglia; fig arrostire
broiler /'brɔɪlə(r)/ n (chicken) pollastro m; Am (grill) griglia f
broke /brəʊk/ **1** ▶ BREAK
2 adj fam al verde
broken /'brəʊk(ə)n/ **1** ▶ BREAK
2 adj rotto; ~ English inglese m stentato
broken-down adj ‹machine› guasto; ‹wall› pericolante
broken heart n cuore m infranto; die of a ~ essere distrutto da una delusione amorosa
broken-hearted /-'hɑ:tɪd/ adj affranto
broken home n he comes from a ~ i suoi sono divisi
broken marriage n matrimonio m fallito
broker /'brəʊkə(r)/ n broker m inv
brokerage /'brəʊkərɪdʒ/ n (fee, business) intermediazione f
broking /'brəʊkɪŋ/ n attività f di intermediazione
brolly /'brɒlɪ/ n fam ombrello m
bromide /'brəʊmaɪd/ n (in pharmacy printing) bromuro m; fig (comment) banalità f inv
bronchial /'brɒŋkɪəl/ adj ‹infection› bronchiale; ‹wheeze, cough› di petto
bronchitis /brɒŋ'kaɪtɪs/ n bronchite f
bronze /brɒnz/ **1** n bronzo m
2 attrib di bronzo
Bronze Age n età f del Bronzo
brooch /brəʊtʃ/ n spilla f

brood /bru:d/ **1** n covata f; hum (children) prole f
2 vi covare; fig rimuginare
brooding /'bru:dɪŋ/ adj ‹person, face› pensieroso; ‹landscape› sinistro
broody /'bru:dɪ/ adj (depressed) pensieroso; feel ~ Br fam ‹woman› desiderare un figlio
broody hen n chioccia f
brook[1] /brʊk/ n ruscello m
brook[2] vt sopportare
broom /bru:m/ n scopa f; Bot ginestra f
broom cupboard n ripostiglio m
broom handle n Br manico m di scopa
broomstick n manico m di scopa
Bros. abbr (**brothers**) F.lli
broth /brɒθ/ n brodo m
brothel /'brɒθ(ə)l/ n bordello m
ꝺ **brother** /'brʌðə(r)/ n fratello m
brotherhood /'brʌðəhʊd/ n (bond) fratellanza f; (of monks) confraternita f
brother-in-law n (pl **brothers-in-law**) cognato m
brotherly /'brʌðəlɪ/ adj fraterno
brought /brɔ:t/ ▶ BRING
brow /braʊ/ n fronte f; (eyebrow) sopracciglio m; (of hill) cima f
browbeat /'braʊbi:t/ vt (pt **-beat**, pp **-beaten**) intimidire
ꝺ **brown** /braʊn/ **1** adj marrone; ‹hair› castano
2 n marrone m
3 vt rosolare ‹meat›
4 vi ‹meat› rosolarsi
brown ale n Br birra f scura
brown bear n orso m bruno
brown bread n pane m integrale
browned-off /braʊnd'ɒf/ adj Br fam stufo (with di)
brown envelope n busta f di carta da pacchi
Brownie /'braʊnɪ/ n coccinella f (negli scout)
brownie point n fam punto m di merito
brownish /'braʊnɪʃ/ adj sul marrone
brownout n Am oscuramento m parziale
brown owl n allocco m
brown paper n carta f da pacchi
brown rice n riso m integrale
brown-skinned /-'skɪnd/ adj scuro di pelle
brownstone n Am (house) palazzo m in arenaria
brown sugar n Culin zucchero m greggio
browse /braʊz/ **1** vi (read) leggicchiare; (in shop) curiosare; (on Internet) navigare
2 vt visitare ‹Internet, web site›
browser /'braʊzə(r)/ n Comput (program) browser m inv; (in shop) persona f che curiosa

---

ꝺ indicates a very frequent word

bruise /bruːz/ **1** *n* livido *m*; (on fruit) ammaccatura *f*

2 *vt* ammaccare ‹fruit›; ∼ **one's arm** farsi un livido sul braccio

bruised /bruːzd/ *adj* (physically) contuso; ‹eye› pesto; ‹fruit› ammaccato; ‹ego, spirit› ferito

bruiser /'bruːzə(r)/ *n* fam omaccione *m*

bruising /'bruːzɪŋ/ **1** *n* livido *m*, contusione *f*

2 *adj* ‹game› violento; (emotionally) ‹remark› pesante; ‹campaign, encounter› traumatizzante; ‹defeat› cocente

brunch /brʌntʃ/ *n* brunch *m inv*

Brunei /bruːˈnaɪ/ *n* Brunei *m*

brunette /bruːˈnet/ *n* bruna *f*

brunt /brʌnt/ *n* **bear the** ∼ **of something** subire maggiormente qualcosa

brush /brʌʃ/ **1** *n* spazzola *f*; (with long handle) spazzolone *m*; (for paint) pennello *m*; (bushes) boscaglia *f*, fig (conflict) breve scontro *m*

2 *vt* spazzolare ‹hair›; lavarsi ‹teeth›; scopare ‹stairs, floor›

■ **brush against** *vt* sfiorare

■ **brush aside** *vt* fig ignorare

■ **brush off** *vt* spazzolare; (with hands) togliere; ignorare ‹criticism›

■ **brush up**: *vt/i* fig ∼ **up [on]** rinfrescare

brush-off *n* fam **give somebody the** ∼ mandare qualcuno a quel paese

brushstroke *n* pennellata *f*

brushup *n* Br **have a [wash and] brushup** darsi una ripulita

brushwood /'brʌʃwʊd/ *n* sterpaglie *fpl*

brushwork *n* tocco *m*

brusque /brʊsk/ *adj* brusco

brusquely /'brʊsklɪ/ *adv* bruscamente

Brussels /'brʌsəlz/ *n* Bruxelles *f*

Brussels sprouts *npl* cavolini *mpl* di Bruxelles

brutal /'bruːt(ə)l/ *adj* brutale

brutality /bruːˈtælətɪ/ *n* brutalità *f inv*

brutalize /'bruːtəlaɪz/ *vt* brutalizzare

brutally /'bruːtəlɪ/ *adv* brutalmente

brute /bruːt/ *n* bruto *m*; ∼ **force** forza *f* bruta

brutish /'bruːtɪʃ/ *adj* da bruto

BSc, Am **BS** *abbr* (**Bachelor of Science**) (diploma (*m*) di) dottore in discipline scientifiche

BSE *n abbr* (**bovine spongiform encephalitis**) encefalite *f* bovina spongiforme

B side *n* (of record) lato *m* B

BST *abbr* (**British Summer Time**) ora *f* legale in Gran Bretagna

B2B /biːtəˈbiː/ *abbr* (**business to business**) ‹trade, directory› B2B

btw *n abbr* (**by the way**) a proposito

bubble /'bʌbl/ *n* bolla *f*; (in drink) bollicina *f*

bubble bath *n* bagnoschiuma *m inv*

bubble car *n* Br fam auto (*f*) monoposto a tre ruote

bubblegum *n* gomma *f* da masticare

bubble pack *n* Br (for pills) blister *m inv*; (for small item) involucro *m* di plastica

bubble wrap *n* plastica *f* a bolle

bubbling /'bʌblɪŋ/ **1** *n* (sound) gorgoglio *m*

2 *adj* che ribolle

bubbly /'bʌblɪ/ **1** *n* fam champagne *m inv*, spumante *m*

2 *adj* ‹liquid› effervescente; ‹personality› spumeggiante

bubonic plague /bjuːbɒnɪkˈpleɪg/ *n* peste *f* bubbonica

buccaneer /bʌkəˈnɪə(r)/ *n* bucaniere *m*

Bucharest /bjuːkəˈrest/ *n* Bucarest *f*

buck¹ /bʌk/ **1** *n* maschio *m* del cervo; (rabbit) maschio *m* del coniglio

2 *vi* ‹horse› saltare a quattro zampe

buck² *n* Am fam dollaro *m*

buck³ *n* **pass the** ∼ scaricare la responsabilità

■ **buck up 1** *vi* fam tirarsi su; (hurry) sbrigarsi

2 *vt* **you'll have to** ∼ **your ideas up** fam dovresti darti una regolata

bucket /'bʌkɪt/ **1** *n* secchio *m*; **kick the** ∼ fam (die) crepare

2 *vi* **it's** ∼**ing down** fam piove a catinelle

bucketful /'bʌkɪtfʊl/ *n* secchio *m*

bucket seat *n* Auto, Aeron sedile *m* anatomico

bucket shop *n* Br fam agenzia (*f*) di viaggi che vende biglietti a prezzi scontati

bucking bronco /bʌkɪŋˈbrɒŋkəʊ/ *n* cavallo *m* da rodeo

buckle /'bʌkl/ **1** *n* fibbia *f*

2 *vt* allacciare

3 *vi* ‹shelf› piegarsi; ‹wheel› storcersi

■ **buckle down** *vi* (to work) mettersi sotto

■ **buckle in** *vt* legare

buckram *n* tela *f* rigida

buckshot *n* pallettoni *mpl*

buckskin *n* pelle *f* di daino

buck teeth *npl* denti *mpl* da coniglio

buckwheat *n* grano *m* saraceno

bucolic /bjuːˈkɒlɪk/ *adj & n* bucolico *m*

bud /bʌd/ *n* bocciolo *m*

Buddha /'bʊdə/ *n* Budda *m inv*

Buddhism /'bʊdɪzm/ *n* buddismo *m*

Buddhist /'bʊdɪst/ *adj & n* buddista *mf*

budding /'bʌdɪŋ/ *adj* Bot (into leaf) in germoglio; (into flower) in boccio; ‹athlete, champion, artist› in erba; ‹talent, romance› nascente; ‹career› promettente

buddy /'bʌdɪ/ *n* fam amico, -a *mf*

budge /bʌdʒ/ **1** *vt* spostare

2 *vi* spostarsi

■ **budge over**, **budge up** *vi* fam farsi più in là

budgerigar /'bʌdʒərɪgɑ:(r)/ n cocorita f

✧ **budget** /'bʌdʒɪt/ ① n bilancio m; (allotted to specific activity) budget m inv; **I'm on a ~** cerco di limitare le spese
② vi (pt/pp **budgeted**) prevedere le spese; **~ for something** includere qualcosa nelle spese previste

budgetary /'bʌdʒɪt(ə)rɪ/ adj budgetario; **~ year** esercizio m finanziario

budget day n Br Pol giorno (m) della presentazione del bilancio dello Stato

budgie /'bʌdʒɪ/ n fam = BUDGERIGAR

buff /bʌf/ ① adj (colour) [color] camoscio
② n color m, camoscio m; fam fanatico, -a mf
③ vt lucidare

buffalo /'bʌfələʊ/ n (inv or pl **-es**) bufalo m

buffer /'bʌfə(r)/ n Rail respingente m; Comput buffer m inv; **old ~** fam vecchio bacucco m

buffer state n stato m cuscinetto inv

buffer zone n zona f cuscinetto inv

buffet¹ /'bʊfeɪ/ n (meal, in station) buffet m inv

buffet² /'bʌfɪt/ vt (pt/pp **buffeted**) sferzare

buffet car n Br Rail carrozza f ristorante

buffoon /bə'fu:n/ n buffone, -a mf

bug /bʌg/ ① n (insect) insetto m; Comput bug m inv; fam (device) cimice f
② vt (pt/pp **bugged**) fam installare delle microspie in ‹room›; mettere sotto controllo ‹telephone›; fam (annoy) scocciare

bugbear /'bʌgbeə(r)/ n (problem, annoyance) spauracchio m

bugger /'bʌgə(r)/ fam ① n bastardo m
② int merda!
■ **bugger about, bugger around** fam
① vi (behave stupidly) fare il cretino
② vt **~ somebody about** creare problemi a qualcuno
■ **bugger off** vi fam (go away) andarsene; **~ off!** vai a farti friggere!

bugging device /'bʌgɪŋ/ n microfono m spia

buggy /'bʌgɪ/ n [baby] **~** passeggino m

bugle /'bju:g(ə)l/ n tromba f

bugler /'bju:glə(r)/ n trombettiere m

✧ **build** /bɪld/ ① n (of person) corporatura f
② vt/i (pt/pp **built**) costruire
■ **build on** vt aggiungere ‹extra storey›; sviluppare ‹previous work›
■ **build up**: ① vt **~ up one's strength** rimettersi in forza
② vi ‹pressure, traffic› aumentare; ‹excitement, tension› crescere

builder /'bɪldə(r)/ n (company) costruttore m; (worker) muratore m

builder's labourer n muratore m

builder's merchant n fornitore m di materiale da costruzione

✧ **building** /'bɪldɪŋ/ n edificio m

building block n (child's toy) pezzo m delle costruzioni; (basic element) componente m

building contractor n imprenditore m edile

building land n terreno m edificabile

building materials npl materiali mpl da costruzione

building permit n licenza f edilizia

building plot n terreno m edificabile

building site n cantiere m [di costruzione]

building society n istituto m di credito immobiliare

building trade n edilizia f

building worker n Br muratore m

build-up n (increase) aumento m; (in tension, of gas, in weapons) accumulo m; (publicity) battage m inv pubblicitario; **give something a good ~** (publicity) fare buona pubblicità a qualcosa

built /bɪlt/ ▶ BUILD

built-in adj ‹unit› a muro; fig ‹feature› incorporato

built-up adj (region) urbanizzato; **~ area** centro m abitato

bulb /bʌlb/ n bulbo m; Electr lampadina f

bulbous /'bʌlbəs/ adj grassoccio

Bulgaria /bʌl'geərɪə/ n Bulgaria f

Bulgarian /bʌl'geərɪən/ adj & n bulgaro, -a mf

bulge /bʌldʒ/ ① n rigonfiamento m; **it shows all my ~s** mette in evidenza tutti i miei cuscinetti [di grasso]
② vi esser gonfio (with di); ‹stomach, wall› sporgere; ‹eyes, with surprise› uscire dalle orbite

bulging /'bʌldʒɪŋ/ adj gonfio; ‹eyes› sporgente

bulimia [nervosa] /bʊ'lɪmɪə(nɜ:'vəʊsə)/ n bulimia f

bulimic /bʊ'lɪmɪk/ adj & n bulimico, -a mf

bulk /bʌlk/ n volume m; (greater part) grosso m; **in ~** in grande quantità; (loose) sfuso

bulk-buy vt/i comprare in grandi quantità

bulk-buying n acquisto m in grande quantità

bulk carrier n mezzo m per il trasporto di rinfuse

bulkhead n Naut, Aeron paratia f

bulky /'bʌlkɪ/ adj voluminoso

bull /bʊl/ n toro m; **take the ~ by the horns** fig prendere il toro per le corna

bull bars npl Auto paraurti mpl tubolari rigidi

bulldog n bulldog m inv

bulldog clip n fermafogli m inv

✧ indicates a very frequent word

bulldoze *vt* (knock down) demolire [con bulldozer]; (clear) spianare [con bulldozer]; fig (force) costringere

bulldozer /ˈbʊldəʊzə(r)/ *n* bulldozer *m inv*

bullet /ˈbʊlɪt/ *n* pallottola *f*

bulletin /ˈbʊlɪtɪn/ *n* bollettino *m*

bulletin board *n* Comput bacheca *f* elettronica

bulletproof /ˈbʊlɪtpruːf/ *adj* antiproiettile *inv*; ‹vehicle› blindato

bulletproof vest giubbotto *m* antiproiettile

bullfight /ˈbʊlfaɪt/ *n* corrida *f*

bullfighter /ˈbʊlfaɪtə(r)/ *n* torero *m*

bullfighting /ˈbʊlfaɪtɪŋ/ *n* corride *fpl*

bullion /ˈbʊlɪən/ *n* **gold** ∼ oro *m* in lingotti

bullish /ˈbʊlɪʃ/ *adj* (optimistic) ottimistico; ‹market, shares, stocks› al rialzo

bull market *n* Fin mercato *m* al rialzo

bullock /ˈbʊlək/ *n* manzo *m*

bullring /ˈbʊlrɪŋ/ *n* arena *f*

bull's-eye /ˈbʊlzaɪ/ *n* centro *m* del bersaglio; **score a** ∼ fare centro

bully /ˈbʊlɪ/ **1** *n* prepotente *mf*
2 *vt* fare il/la prepotente con

bullying /ˈbʊlɪŋ/ *n* prepotenze *fpl*

bulrush /ˈbʊlrʌʃ/ *n* giunco *m* di palude

bulwark /ˈbʊlwək/ *n* Mil fig baluardo *m*; Naut parapetto *m*; (breakwater) frangiflutti *m inv*

bum¹ /bʌm/ *n* sl sedere *m*

bum² *n* Am fam vagabondo, -a *mf*
■ **bum around** *vi* fam vagabondare

bumbag /ˈbʌmbæg/ *n* Br fam marsupio *m*

bumble-bee /ˈbʌmblbiː/ *n* calabrone *m*

bumbling /ˈbʌmblɪŋ/ *adj* ‹attempt› maldestro; ‹person› inconcludente

bumf /bʌmf/ *n* Br (toilet paper) carta *f* igienica; fam (documents) scartoffie *f pl*

bump /bʌmp/ **1** *n* botta *f*; (swelling) bozzo *m*, gonfiore *m*; (in road) protuberanza *f*
2 *vt* sbattere
■ **bump into** *vt* sbattere contro; (meet) imbattersi in
■ **bump off** *vt* fam far fuori
■ **bump up** *vt* fam [far] aumentare ‹prices, salaries›

bumper /ˈbʌmpə(r)/ **1** *n* Auto paraurti *m inv*
2 *adj* abbondante

bumper car *n* autoscontro *m*

bumph /bʌmf/ *n* = BUMF

bumpkin /ˈbʌmpkɪn/ *n* **country** ∼ zoticone, -a *mf*

bumptious /ˈbʌmpʃəs/ *adj* presuntuoso

bumpy /ˈbʌmpɪ/ *adj* ‹road› accidentato; ‹flight› turbolento

bun /bʌn/ *n* focaccina *f* (dolce); (hair) chignon *m inv*

bunch /bʌntʃ/ *n* (of flowers, keys) mazzo *m*; (of bananas) casco *m*; (of people) gruppo *m*; ∼ **of grapes** grappolo *m* d'uva

bundle /ˈbʌndl/ **1** *n* fascio *m*; (of money) mazzetta *f*; **a** ∼ **of nerves** fam un fascio di nervi
2 *vt* ∼ **[up]** affastellare

bundled software /ˈbʌndld-/ *n* Comput software *m inv* in bundle

bung /bʌŋ/ *vt* fam (throw) buttare
■ **bung up** *vt* (block) otturare

bungalow /ˈbʌŋɡələʊ/ *n* bungalow *m inv*

bungee jump /ˈbʌndʒɪdʒʌmp/ *n* salto *m* con l'elastico

bungee jumping /ˈbʌndʒɪdʒʌmpɪŋ/ *n* salto (*m*) da ponti, grattacieli, ecc. con un cavo elastico attaccato alla caviglia

bungle /ˈbʌŋɡl/ *vt* fare un pasticcio di

bunion /ˈbʌnjən/ *n* Med callo *m* all'alluce

bunk /bʌŋk/ **1** *n* cuccetta *f*; **do a** ∼ fam svignarsela
2 *vi* ∼ **off**/∼ **off school** fam marinare la scuola

bunk beds *npl* letti *mpl* a castello

bunker /ˈbʌŋkə(r)/ *n* (for coal) carbonaia *f*; (golf) ostacolo *m*; Mil bunker *m inv*

bunkum /ˈbʌŋkəm/ *n* fandonie *fpl*

bunny /ˈbʌnɪ/ *n* fam coniglietto *m*

Bunsen [burner] /ˈbʌnsən[bɜːnə(r)]/ *n* becco *m* Bunsen

bunting /ˈbʌntɪŋ/ *n* (flags on ship) gran pavese *m*; Zool zigolo *m*

buoy /bɔɪ/ *n* boa *f*
■ **buoy up** *vt* fig sostenere ‹prices›; tirare su ‹person›

buoyancy /ˈbɔɪənsɪ/ *n* galleggiabilità *f*

buoyancy aid *n* salvagente *m*

buoyant /ˈbɔɪənt/ *adj* ‹boat› galleggiante; ‹water› che aiuta a galleggiare; fig ‹person› allegro; ‹prices› in aumento

burble /ˈbɜːb(ə)l/ **1** *n* (of stream) gorgoglio *m*; (of voices) borbottio *m*
2 *vi* ‹stream› gorgogliare; ∼ **on about something** ‹person› blaterare di qualcosa

burbling /ˈbɜːblɪŋ/ **1** *n* (of stream) gorgoglio *m*; (rambling talk) borbottio *m*
2 *adj* ‹stream› gorgogliante; ‹voice› che borbotta

burden /ˈbɜːdn/ **1** *n* carico *m*
2 *vt* caricare

burdensome /ˈbɜːdnsəm/ *adj* gravoso

bureau /ˈbjʊərəʊ/ *n* (*pl* **-x** /ˈbjʊərəʊz/ or ∼**s**) (desk) scrivania *f*; (office) ufficio *m*

bureaucracy /bjʊəˈrɒkrəsɪ/ *n* burocrazia *f*

bureaucrat /ˈbjʊərəkræt/ *n* burocrate *mf*

bureaucratic /bjʊərəˈkrætɪk/ *adj* burocratico

burgeon /ˈbɜːdʒən/ *vi* ‹plant› germogliare; fig (flourish) fiorire; fig (multiply) moltiplicarsi rapidamente, crescere rapidamente

burgeoning /'bɜːdʒənɪŋ/ *adj* fiorente
burger /'bɜːgə(r)/ *n* hamburger *m inv*
burger bar *n* fast-food *m inv*
burglar /'bɜːglə(r)/ *n* svaligiatore, -trice *mf*
burglar alarm *n* antifurto *m inv*
burglarize /'bɜːgləraɪz/ *vt* Am svaligiare
burglar-proof *adj* a prova di ladro
burglary /'bɜːglərɪ/ *n* furto *m* con scasso
burgle /'bɜːgl/ *vt* svaligiare; **they have been ~d** sono stati svaligiati
Burgundy /'bɜːgəndɪ/ **1** *n* Borgogna *f*; **burgundy (wine)** borgogna *m inv*
    2 *adj* (colour) rosso scuro
burial /'berɪəl/ *n* sepoltura *f*
burial ground *n* cimitero *m*
burka /'bɜːkə/ *n* burka *m*
Burkina [Faso] /'bɜːkinə ('fæsəʊ)/ *n* Burkina Faso *m*
burlesque /bɜː'lesk/ *n* parodia *f*
burly /'bɜːlɪ/ *adj* (**-ier, -iest**) corpulento
Burma /'bɜːmə/ *n* Birmania *f*
Burmese /bɜː'miːz/ *adj* & *n* birmano, -a *mf*
⚜ **burn** /bɜːn/ **1** *n* bruciatura *f*
    2 *vt* (*pt/pp* **burnt** *or* **burned**) bruciare; **~ one's boats** *or* **bridges** fig tagliarsi i ponti alle spalle; Comput masterizzare ‹*CD, DVD*›
    3 *vi* bruciare
■ **burn down** *vt/i* bruciare
■ **burn out** *vi* fig esaurirsi
■ **burn up** *vt* fig bruciare ‹*calories, energy*›
burned-out *adj* = BURNT-OUT
burner /'bɜːnə(r)/ *n* (on stove) bruciatore *m*
burning /'bɜːnɪŋ/ **1** *n* (setting on fire) incendio *m*; **I can smell ~!** sento odore di bruciato!
    2 *adj* ‹*ember, coal*› acceso; (on fire) in fiamme; fig ‹*fever, desire*› bruciante; **a ~ sensation** una sensazione di bruciore; **a ~ question** una questione scottante
burnish /'bɜːnɪʃ/ *vt* lucidare
burns unit *n* Med reparto *m* grandi ustionati
burnt /bɜːnt/ ▶ BURN
burnt-out *adj* ‹*building, car*› distrutto dalle fiamme; fig ‹*person*› sfinito
burp /bɜːp/ **1** *n* fam rutto *m*
    2 *vi* fam ruttare
burr /bɜː(r)/ *n* Bot lappa *f*; (in language) erre *f* moscia
burrow /'bʌrəʊ/ **1** *n* tana *f*
    2 *vt* scavare ‹*hole*›
bursar /'bɜːsə(r)/ *n* economo, -a *mf*
bursary /'bɜːsərɪ/ *n* borsa *f* di studio
burst /bɜːst/ **1** *n* (of gunfire, energy, laughter) scoppio *m*; (of speed) scatto *m*
    2 *vt* (*pt/pp* **burst**) far scoppiare; **~ its banks** ‹*river*› rompere gli argini
    3 *vi* scoppiare; **~ into tears** scoppiare in lacrime; **~ into flames** andare in fiamme;

she **~ into the room** ha fatto irruzione nella stanza; **be ~ing at the seams** ‹*room*› scoppiare
■ **burst in** *vi* (enter suddenly) fare irruzione
■ **burst out**: *vi* **~ out laughing/crying** scoppiare a ridere/piangere
Burundi /bʊ'rʊndɪ/ *n* Burundi *m*
bury /'berɪ/ *vt* (*pt/pp* **-ied**) seppellire; (hide) nascondere
⚜ **bus** /bʌs/ **1** *n* autobus *m inv*, pullman *m inv*; (long distance) pullman *m inv*, corriera *f*
    2 *vt* (*pt/pp* **bussed**) trasportare in autobus
busby /'bʌzbɪ/ *n* colbacco *m* militare
bus conductor *n* ≈ bigliettaio *m*
bus conductress *n* ≈ bigliettaia *f*
bus driver *n* conducente *mf* di autobus
bush /bʊʃ/ *n* cespuglio *m*; (land) boscaglia *f*
bushed /bʊʃt/ *adj* fam (tired) distrutto
bushel /'bʊʃ(ə)l/ *n* **hide one's light under a ~** essere troppo modesto; Am fam **~s of** un sacco di
bushfighting *n* Mil guerriglia *f*
bushfire *n* incendio *m* in aperta campagna
bush telegraph *n* fig hum tamtam *m inv*
bushy /'bʊʃɪ/ *adj* (**-ier, -iest**) folto
busily /'bɪzɪlɪ/ *adv* con grande impegno
⚜ **business** /'bɪznɪs/ *n* affare *m*; Comm affari *mpl*; (establishment) attività *f* di commercio; **on ~** per affari; **he has no ~ to** non ha alcun diritto di; **mind one's own ~** farsi gli affari propri; **that's none of your ~** non sono affari tuoi
business activity *n* attività *f inv* economica; (of single company) attività *f inv* aziendale
business analyst *n* analista *mf* finanziario, -a
business associate *n* socio, -a *mf*
business call *n* (phone call) telefonata *f* di lavoro; (visit) appuntamento *m* di lavoro
business card *n* biglietto *m* da visita
business centre *n* centro *m* affari
business class *n* Aeron business class *f inv*
business college *n* scuola *f* di amministrazione aziendale
business contact *n* contatto *m* di lavoro
business cycle *n* ciclo *m* economico
business deal *n* operazione *f* commerciale
business expenses *npl* spese *fpl* di lavoro
business failures *npl* chiusura *f* di aziende
business hours *npl* (in office) orario *m* d'ufficio; (of shop) orario *m* d'apertura
business-like *adj* efficiente

⚜ indicates a very frequent word

business lunch ···▶ buy ····

business lunch *n* pranzo *m* di lavoro *or* d'affari

businessman /'bɪznɪsmən/ *n* uomo *m* d'affari

business management *n* amministrazione *f* aziendale

business park *n* centro *m* affari

business plan *n* piano *m* economico; (of single company) programma *m* aziendale

business premises *npl* sede *f* di un'azienda

business proposition *n* proposta *f* d'affari

business reply envelope *n* busta *f* affrancata

business school *n* scuola *f* di amministrazione aziendale

business software *n* software *m* per l'ufficio

business studies *npl* economia *f* e commercio

business suit *n* (for man) abito *m* scuro

business trip *n* viaggio *m* di lavoro

businesswoman /'bɪznɪswʊmən/ *n* donna *f* d'affari

busk /bʌsk/ *vi* Br ‹singer› cantare per strada; ‹musician› suonare per strada

busker /'bʌskə(r)/ *n* suonatore, -trice *mf* ambulante

bus lane *n* corsia *f* autobus

busload /'bʌsləʊd/ *n* **a** ~ **of tourists** una comitiva di turisti; **by the** ~ **in** massa

busman's holiday /bʌsmənz'hɒlɪdeɪ/ *n* Br *vacanze (fpl) passate a fare quello che si fa normalmente*

bus pass *n* abbonamento *m* all'autobus

bus route *n* percorso *m* dell'autobus

bus shelter *n* pensilina *f* alla fermata dell'autobus

bus station *n* stazione *f* degli autobus

bus stop *n* fermata *f* d'autobus

bust¹ /bʌst/ *n* busto *m*; (chest) petto *m*

bust² 1 *adj* fam rotto; **go** ~ fallire
2 *vt* (*pt/pp* **busted** *or* **bust**) fam far scoppiare
3 *vi* scoppiare

bustle /'bʌsl/ *n* (activity) trambusto *m*
■ **bustle about** *vi* affannarsi

bustling /'bʌslɪŋ/ *adj* animato

bust size *n* circonferenza *f* del torace

bust-up *n* fam lite *f*

♂ **busy** /'bɪzɪ/ 1 *adj* (**-ier, -iest**) occupato; ‹day, time› intenso; ‹street› affollato; (with traffic) pieno di traffico; **be** ~ **doing** essere occupato a fare
2 *vt* ~ **oneself** darsi da fare

busybody /'bɪzɪbɒdɪ/ *n* ficcanaso *m f* inv

♂ **but** /bʌt/ *atono* /bət/ 1 *conj* ma
2 *prep* eccetto, tranne; **nobody** ~ **you** nessuno tranne te; ~ **for** (without) se non

fosse stato per; **the last** ~ **one** il penultimo; **the next** ~ **one** il secondo
3 *adv* soltanto; **there were** ~ **two** ce n'erano soltanto due

butane /'bjuːteɪn/ *n* butano *m*

butch /bʊtʃ/ *adj* fam ‹man› macho inv; ‹woman› mascolino

butcher /'bʊtʃə(r)/ 1 *n* macellaio *m*
2 *vt* macellare; fig massacrare

butcher's [shop] /'bʊtʃəz[ʃɒp]/ *n* macelleria *f*

butchery /'bʊtʃərɪ/ *n* (trade) macelleria *f*; (slaughter) massacro *m*

butler /'bʌtlə(r)/ *n* maggiordomo *m*

butt /bʌt/ 1 *n* (of gun) calcio *m*; (of cigarette) mozzicone *m*; (for water) barile *m*; fig (target) bersaglio *m*
2 *vt* dare una testata a; ‹goat› dare un'incornata a
■ **butt in** *vi* interrompere

butter /'bʌtə(r)/ 1 *n* burro *m*
2 *vt* imburrare
■ **butter up** *vt* fam arruffianarsi

butter-bean *n* fagiolo *m* bianco

buttercup *n* ranuncolo *m*

butter dish *n* portaburro *m* inv

butter-fingered *adj* con le mani di pasta frolla

butter-fingers *n* fam mani *fpl* di pasta frolla

butterfly /'bʌtəflaɪ/ *n* farfalla *f*

butterfly net *n* retino *m* per farfalle

butterfly nut *n* dado *m* ad alette

butterfly stroke *n* nuoto *m* a farfalla

buttermilk /'bʌtəmɪlk/ *n* latticello *m*

butterscotch /'bʌtəskɒtʃ/ *n caramella (f) dura a base di burro e zucchero*

buttocks /'bʌtəks/ *npl* natiche *fpl*

button /'bʌtn/ 1 *n* bottone *m*; (on mouse, of status bar) pulsante *m*
2 *vt* ~ **[up]** abbottonare
3 *vi* ~ **[up]** abbottonarsi

button battery *n* batteria *f* a bottone

button-down *adj* ‹collar› button down, coi bottoni; ‹shirt› con il colletto coi bottoni, button down

buttonhole *n* occhiello *m*, asola *f*

buttonhook *n* asola *f*, occhiello *m*

button mushroom *n* piccolo champignon *m* inv

buttress /'bʌtrɪs/ 1 *n* contrafforte *m*
2 *vt* fig sostenere

buxom /'bʌksəm/ *adj* formosa

♂ **buy** /baɪ/ 1 *n* **good/bad** ~ buon/cattivo acquisto *m*
2 *vt* (*pt/pp* **bought**) comprare; ~ **somebody a drink** pagare da bere a qualcuno; **I'll** ~ **this one** (drink) questo lo offro io
■ **buy into** *vt* (accept) accettare ···▶

■ **buy off** *vt* (bribe) comprare
■ **buy out** *vt* rilevare la quota di ‹one's partner›
■ **buy up** *vt* (buy all of) accaparrarsi
buyer /'baɪə(r)/ *n* compratore, -trice *mf*
buyout /'baɪaʊt/ *n* Comm rilevamento *m*
buzz /bʌz/ ❙1❙ *n* ronzio *m*; **give somebody a ~** fam (on phone) dare un colpo di telefono a qualcuno; (excite) mettere in fermento qualcuno
❙2❙ *vi* ronzare
❙3❙ *vt* **~ somebody** chiamare qualcuno col cicalino
■ **buzz off** *vi* fam levarsi di torno
buzzard /'bʌzəd/ *n* poiana *f*
buzzer /'bʌzə(r)/ *n* cicalino *m*
buzzing /'bʌzɪŋ/ ❙1❙ *n* (of buzzer) trillo *m*; (of insects) ronzio *m*
❙2❙ *adj* ‹party, atmosphere, town› molto animato
buzzword /'bʌzwɜːd/ *n* fam parola *f* di moda
♂ **by** /baɪ/ ❙1❙ *prep* (near, next to) vicino a; (at the latest) per; **by Mozart** di Mozart; **he was run over by a bus** è stato investito da un autobus; **by oneself** da solo; **by the sea** al mare; **by sea** via mare; **by car/bus** in macchina/autobus; **by day/night** di giorno/notte; **by the hour/metre** a ore/metri; **six metres by four** sei metri per quattro; **he won by six metres** ha vinto di sei metri; **I missed the train by a minute** ho perso il treno per un minuto; **I'll be home by six** sarò a casa per le sei; **by this time next week** a quest'ora tra una settimana; **he rushed by me** mi è passato accanto di corsa

❙2❙ *adv* **she'll be here by and by** sarà qui fra poco; **by and by the police arrived** poco dopo è arrivata la polizia; **by and large** nel complesso; **put by** mettere da parte; **go/pass by** passare
bye /baɪ/ *int* fam ciao!
bye-bye /baɪ'baɪ/ *int* fam ciao, arrivederci; **go ~s** Br (baby talk) andare a fare la nanna
by-election *n* elezione (*f*) straordinaria indetta per coprire una carica rimasta vacante in Parlamento
Byelorussia /bjeləʊ'rʌʃə/ *n* Bielorussia *f*
Byelorussian /bjeləʊ'rʌʃn/ *adj & n* bielorusso
bygone *adj* passato
by-law *n* legge *f* locale
by-line *n* (in newspaper) nome *m* dell'autore; Sport linea *f* laterale
BYO, BYOB *adj abbr* (**bring your own bottle**) di ristorante o festa, in cui ciascuno si porta le proprie bevande, specialmente alcoliche
bypass ❙1❙ *n* circonvallazione *f*; Med by-pass *m inv*
❙2❙ *vt* evitare
by-product *n* sottoprodotto *m*
by-road *n* strada *f* secondaria
bystander *n* spettatore, -trice *mf*
byte /baɪt/ *n* Comput byte *m inv*
byway *n* strada *f* secondaria
byword *n* **be a ~ for** essere sinonimo di
by-your-leave *n* **without so much as a ~** senza neanche chiedere il permesso
Byzantine /bɪ'zæntaɪn/ *adj* bizantino

Cc

---

c¹, C /siː/ *n* (letter) c, C *f inv*; Br Sch (grade) voto (*m*) scolastico corrispondente alla sufficienza; Mus do *m inv*
c², C *abbr* 1 (**Celsius, centigrade**) C
2 (**cent(s)**) c
3 (**circa**) ca
C4 *abbr* Br (**channel four**) rete (*f*) televisiva britannica
CA *abbr* 1 Br (**Chartered Accountant**) [dottore *m*] commercialista *m*
2 Am (**California**) Cal
3 (**Central America**) America *f* centrale
CAA *n abbr* Br (**Civil Aviation Authority**) organismo (*m*) di controllo dell'aviazione civile

CAB *n abbr* Br (**Citizens' Advice Bureau**) ufficio (*m*) di consulenza legale gratuita per i cittadini
cab /kæb/ *n* taxi *m inv*; (of lorry, train) cabina *f*
cabana /kə'bɑːnə/ *n* Am (hut) cabina *f* da spiaggia
cabaret /'kæbəreɪ/ *n* cabaret *m inv*
cabbage /'kæbɪdʒ/ *n* cavolo *m*
cabby /'kæbɪ/ *n* fam tassista *mf*
cab driver *n* tassista *mf*
cabin /'kæbɪn/ *n* (of plane, ship) cabina *f*; (hut) capanna *f*
cabin boy *n* mozzo *m*
cabin crew *n* Aeron equipaggio *m*
cabin cruiser *n* cabinato *m*

---

cabinet /'kæbɪnɪt/ n armadietto m; [display] ∼ vetrina f; **C**∼ Pol consiglio m dei ministri

cabinet-maker n ebanista mf

cabinet meeting n Br riunione f del governo

cabinet minister n Br ministro m

cabinet reshuffle n Br rimpasto m ministeriale

cable /'keɪb(ə)l/ n cavo m; TV TV f via cavo; **this channel is only available on** ∼ questo canale è disponibile solo sulla TV via cavo

cable car n cabina f (della funivia)

cable company n rete f televisiva via cavo

cablegram n cablogramma m

cable-knit adj ‹sweater› a trecce

cable railway n funicolare f

cable-ready adj predisposto per la TV via cavo

cable television n televisione f via cavo

cable TV n TV f inv via cavo

cableway n (for people) funivia f

caboodle /kə'bu:dl/ n fam **the whole** ∼ baracca e burattini

cab rank, cab stand n posteggio m dei taxi

cache /kæʃ/ n nascondiglio m; ∼ **of arms** deposito m segreto di armi

cache memory n Comput memoria f (cache)

cachet /'kæʃeɪ/ n prestigio m

cackle /'kækl/ vi ridacchiare

cacophony /kə'kɒfənɪ/ n cacofonia f

cactus /'kæktəs/ n (pl **-ti** /'kæktaɪ/ or **-tuses**) cactus m inv

CAD /kæd/ n abbr (**computer-aided design**) CAD m inv

cadaver /kə'dɑ:və(r)/ n cadavere m

cadaverous /kə'dævərəs/ adj cadaverico

CADCAM /'kædkæm/ n abbr (**computer-aided design and computer-aided manufacture**) CADCAM m inv

caddie /'kædɪ/ n portabastoni m inv

caddy /'kædɪ/ n [tea-] ∼ barattolo m del tè

cadence /'keɪdəns/ n cadenza f

cadet /kə'det/ n cadetto m

cadet corps n Mil corpo m dei cadetti

cadet school n scuola f allievi ufficiali

cadge /kædʒ/ vt/i fam scroccare

cadre /'kɑ:dr(ə)/ n Admin, Pol quadri mpl

CAE n abbr (**computer-aided engineering**) CAE m inv

Caesarean, Caesarian /sɪ'zeərɪən/ n parto m cesareo

café /'kæfeɪ/ n caffè m inv

cafeteria /kæfə'tɪərɪə/ n tavola f calda

cafetière /kæfə,tjeə(r)/ n caffettiera f a stantuffo

caffeine /'kæfi:n/ n caffeina f

cage /keɪdʒ/ n gabbia f

cage bird n uccello m da gabbia

cagey /'keɪdʒɪ/ adj fam riservato (**about** su)

cagoule /kə'gu:l/ n Br K-way® m inv

cahoots /kə'hu:ts/ npl fam **be in** ∼ essere in combutta

cairn /keən/ n (of stones) tumulo m di pietre

Cairo /'kaɪrəʊ/ n il Cairo

cajole /kə'dʒəʊl/ vt persuadere con le lusinghe

cake /keɪk/ n torta f; (small) pasticcino m; ∼ **of soap** saponetta f; **it was a piece of** ∼ fam è stato un gioco da ragazzi; **you can't have your** ∼ **and eat it** fig non si può avere la botte piena e la moglie ubriaca; **sell like hot** ∼**s** andare a ruba

caked /keɪkt/ adj incrostato (**with** di)

cake mix n miscela f per torte

cake shop n pasticceria f

cake tin n (for baking) tortiera f, (for storing) scatola f di latta (per torte)

CAL abbr (**computer-assisted learning**) CAL m

Calabria /kə'læbrɪə/ n Calabria f

Calabrian /kə'læbrɪən/ adj & n calabrese

calamine lotion /'kæləmaɪn/ n lozione f alla calamina

calamitous /kə'læmɪtəs/ adj disastroso

calamity /kə'læmətɪ/ n calamità f inv

calcify /'kælsɪfaɪ/ vt calcificarsi

calcium /'kælsɪəm/ n calcio m

✓ **calculate** /'kælkjʊleɪt/ vt calcolare

calculated /'kælkjʊleɪtɪd/ adj ‹risk, insult, decision› calcolato; ‹crime› premeditato

calculating /'kælkjʊleɪtɪŋ/ adj fig calcolatore

calculating machine n calcolatrice f

calculation /kælkjʊ'leɪʃn/ n calcolo m

calculator /'kælkjʊleɪtə(r)/ n calcolatrice f

calculus /'kælkjʊləs/ n Math, Med calcolo m

calendar /'kælɪndə(r)/ n calendario m

calendar month n mese m civile

calendar year n anno m civile

calf[1] /kɑ:f/ n (pl **calves**) vitello m

calf[2] n (pl **calves**) Anat polpaccio m

calfskin /'kɑ:fskɪn/ n [pelle f di] vitello m

calibrate /'kælɪbreɪt/ vt calibrare ‹instrument›; tarare ‹scales›

calibre /'kælɪbə(r)/ n calibro m

calico /'kælɪkəʊ/ n cotone m grezzo

California /kælɪ'fɔ:nɪə/ n California f

Californian /kælɪ'fɔ:nɪən/ adj & n californiano, -a mf

C

CALL n abbr (**computer-assisted language learning**) CALL m inv

ꟸ **call** /kɔːl/ ① n grido m; Teleph telefonata f; (visit) visita f; **be on ∼** ⟨doctor⟩ essere di guardia; **good/bad ∼** fam buona/pessima idea

② vt chiamare; indire ⟨strike⟩; **be ∼ed** chiamarsi

③ vi chiamare; **∼ [in or round]** passare

■ **call back** vt/i richiamare

■ **call by** vi (make brief visit) passare

■ **call for** vt (ask for) chiedere; (require) richiedere; (fetch) passare a prendere

■ **call in** ① vi (make brief visit) passare
② vt chiamare ⟨patient, client⟩; interpellare ⟨expert⟩

■ **call off** vt richiamare ⟨dog⟩; disdire ⟨meeting⟩; revocare ⟨strike⟩

■ **call on** vt chiamare; (appeal to) fare un appello a; (visit) visitare

■ **call out** vt/i chiamare ad alta voce

■ **call together** vt riunire

■ **call up** vt Mil chiamare alle armi; Teleph chiamare

callback facility /'kɔːlbæk/ n Teleph servizio (m) telefonico che permette di individuare il numero che ha chiamato

call barring n blocco m chiamate

call box n cabina f telefonica

call centre Br, **call center** Am n call center m inv

caller /'kɔːlə(r)/ n visitatore, -trice mf; Teleph persona (f) che telefona

caller identification n identificativo m del chiamante

call-girl n call-girl f inv [ragazza f] squillo f inv

calligrapher /kə'lɪgrəfə(r)/ n calligrafo, -a mf

calligraphy /kə'lɪgrəfɪ/ n calligrafia f

calling /'kɔːlɪŋ/ n vocazione f

calliper /'kælɪpə(r)/ (for measuring) calibro m; (leg support) tutore m

callisthenics /kælɪs'θenɪks/ n ginnastica f

callous /'kæləs/ adj insensibile

callousness /'kæləsnɪs/ n insensibilità f

call-out n (doctor) visita f a domicilio; (plumber, electrician) chiamata f

call-out charge n costo m della chiamata

callow /'kæləʊ/ adj immaturo

call screening n filtro m chiamate

call sign n Radio segnale m di chiamata

call-up n Mil chiamata f alle armi

call-up papers npl cartolina f precetto

call waiting n avviso m di chiamata in linea

calm /kɑːm/ ① adj calmo

ꟸ indicates a very frequent word

② n calma f

■ **calm down** ① vt calmare
② vi calmarsi

calmly /'kɑːmlɪ/ adv con calma

calmness /'kɑːmnɪs/ n calma f

Calor gas® /'kælə/ n Br liquigas® m inv

calorie /'kælərɪ/ n caloria f

calorific /kælə'rɪfɪk/ adj calorico

calve /kɑːv/ vi figliare

calves /kɑːvz/ npl ▶ CALF[1] & CALF[2]

cam /kæm/ n Techn camma f

camaraderie /kæmə'rædərɪ/ n cameratismo m

camber /'kæmbə(r)/ n curvatura f

Cambodia /kæm'bəʊdɪə/ n Cambogia f

Cambodian /kæm'bəʊdɪən/ adj & n cambogiano, -a mf

camcorder /'kæmkɔːdə(r)/ n videocamera f

came /keɪm/ ▶ COME

camel /'kæml/ n cammello m

camel hair n cammello m

camellia /kə'miːlɪə/ n camelia f

cameo /'kæmɪəʊ/ n cammeo m

cameo role n Theat, Cinema breve apparizione f

ꟸ **camera** /'kæmərə/ n macchina f fotografica; TV telecamera f

camera crew n troupe f inv televisiva

cameraman /'kæmərəmæn/ n operatore m [televisivo], cameraman m inv

camera phone n telefono m con fotocamera, telefono m con videocamera

Cameroon /'kæməruːn/ n il Camerun

camisole /'kæmɪsəʊl/ n canotta f

camomile /'kæməmaɪl/ n camomilla f

camouflage /'kæməflɑːʒ/ ① n mimetizzazione f
② vt mimetizzare

ꟸ **camp¹** /kæmp/ ① n campeggio f; Mil campo m
② vi campeggiare; Mil accamparsi

camp² adj (affected) affettato

ꟸ **campaign** /kæm'peɪn/ ① n campagna f
② vi fare una campagna

campaigner /kæm'peɪnə(r)/ n partecipante mf a una campagna

campaign trail n **be on the ∼** fare la campagna elettorale

campaign worker n Br Pol membro m dello staff di una campagna elettorale

camp bed n letto m da campo

camper /'kæmpə(r)/ n campeggiatore, -trice mf; Auto camper m inv

campfire /'kæmpfaɪə(r)/ n fuoco m di bivacco

camphor /'kæmfə(r)/ n canfora f

camping /'kæmpɪŋ/ n campeggio m

camping equipment n attrezzatura f da campeggio

camping gas n gas m inv da campeggio

camping holiday n vacanza f in tenda

camping site n campeggio m

camping stool n Br sgabello m pieghevole

camping stove n fornello m da campeggio

campsite /'kæmpsaɪt/ n campeggio m

campus /'kæmpəs/ n (pl **-puses**) Univ città f universitaria, campus m inv

camshaft /'kæmʃɑːft/ n albero m a camme

can¹ /kæn/ [1] n (for petrol) latta f; (tin) scatola f; ~ **of beer** lattina f di birra [2] vt mettere in scatola

ˢ **can²** /kæn/, atono /kən/ v aux (pres **can**, pt **could**) (be able to) potere; (know how to) sapere; **I cannot** or **can't go** non posso andare; **he could not** or **couldn't go** non poteva andare; **she can't swim** non sa nuotare; **I ~ smell something burning** sento odor di bruciato

Canada /'kænədə/ n Canada m

Canadian /kə'neɪdɪən/ adj & n canadese mf

canal /kə'næl/ n canale m

canal boat, **canal barge** n chiatta f

canapé /'kænəpeɪ/ n canapè m inv

Canaries /kə'neərɪz/ npl Canarie fpl

canary /kə'neərɪ/ n canarino m

cancel /'kænsl/ v (pt/pp **cancelled**) [1] vt disdire ‹meeting, newspaper›; revocare ‹contract, order›; annullare ‹reservation, appointment, stamp› [2] vi ‹guest, host› annullare

cancellation /kænsə'leɪʃn/ n (of meeting, contract) revoca f; (in hotel, restaurant, for flight) cancellazione f

ˢ **cancer** /'kænsə(r)/ n cancro m; **C~** Astr Cancro m

cancerous /'kænsərəs/ adj canceroso

cancer patient n malato, -a mf di cancro

cancer research n ricerca f sul cancro

candelabra /kændə'lɑːbrə/ n candelabro m

candid /'kændɪd/ adj franco

candidacy /'kændɪdəsɪ/ n Pol candidatura f

ˢ **candidate** /'kændɪdət/ n candidato, -a mf

candidly /'kændɪdlɪ/ adv francamente

candied /'kændɪd/ adj candito

candle /'kænd(ə)l/ n candela f

candlelight /'kænd(ə)llaɪt/ n **by ~** a lume di candela

candlelit dinner /'kænd(ə)llɪt/ n cena f a lume di candela

candlestick /'kænd(ə)lstɪk/ n portacandele m inv

candlewick bedspread /'kænd(ə)lwɪk/ n copriletto m inv di ciniglia

candour /'kændə(r)/ n franchezza f

candy /'kændɪ/ n Am caramella f; **a [piece of]** ~ una caramella

candyfloss /'kændɪflɒs/ n zucchero m filato

candy-striped /straɪpt/ adj (blue) a righe bianche e celesti; (pink) a righe bianche e rosa

cane /keɪn/ [1] n (stick) bastone m; Sch bacchetta f [2] vt prendere a bacchettate ‹pupil›

cane sugar n zucchero m di canna

canine /'keɪnaɪn/ adj canino

canine tooth n canino m

canister /'kænɪstə(r)/ n barattolo m

cannabis /'kænəbɪs/ n cannabis f

canned /kænd/ adj in scatola; ~ **music** fam musica f registrata

cannibal /'kænɪbl/ n cannibale mf

cannibalism /'kænɪbəlɪzm/ n cannibalismo m

cannibalize /'kænɪbəlaɪz/ vt riciclare parti di

cannon /'kænən/ n inv cannone m

cannon ball n palla f di cannone

cannon fodder n carne f da cannone, carne f da macello

ˢ **cannot** /'kænɒt/ ▶ CAN²

canny /'kænɪ/ adj astuto

canoe /kə'nuː/ [1] n canoa f [2] vi andare in canoa

canoeing /kə'nuːɪŋ/ n canoismo m

canon /'kænən/ n (rule) canone m; (person) canonico m

canonization /kænənaɪ'zeɪʃn/ n canonizzazione f

canonize /'kænənaɪz/ vt canonizzare

canoodle /kə'nuːdl/ vi fam sbaciucchiarsi

can-opener n apriscatole m inv

canopy /'kænəpɪ/ n baldacchino f; (of parachute) calotta f

cant /kænt/ n (hypocrisy) ipocrisia f; (jargon) gergo m

can't /kɑːnt/ = CANNOT, ▶ CAN²

cantankerous /kæn'tæŋkərəs/ adj stizzoso

cantata /kæn'tɑːtə/ n Mus cantata f

canteen /kæn'tiːn/ n mensa f; ~ **of cutlery** servizio m di posate

canter /'kæntə(r)/ [1] n piccolo galoppo m [2] vi andare a piccolo galoppo

cantilever /'kæntɪliːvə(r)/ n cantilever m inv, trave f a sbalzo

cantonal /'kæntənəl/ adj cantonale

canvas /'kænvəs/ n tela f; (painting) dipinto m su tela

canvass /'kænvəs/ *vi* Pol fare propaganda elettorale

canvasser /'kænvəsə(r)/ *n* propagandista *mf* elettorale (porta a porta)

canvassing /'kænvəsɪŋ/ *n* (door to door for votes) propaganda *f* porta a porta; (door to door for sales) vendita *f* porta a porta

canyon /'kænjən/ *n* canyon *m inv*

canyoning /'kænjənɪŋ/ *n* canyoning *m inv*

cap /kæp/ ① *n* berretto *m*; (nurse's) cuffia *f*; (top, lid) tappo *m*
② *vt* (*pt/pp* **capped**) fig (do better than) superare

capability /keɪpə'bɪlətɪ/ *n* capacità *f*

✧ **capable** /'keɪpəbl/ *adj* capace; (skilful) abile; **be** ∼ **of doing something** essere capace di fare qualcosa

capably /'keɪpəblɪ/ *adv* con abilità

capacious /kə'peɪʃəs/ *adj* ‹pocket, car boot› capace

✧ **capacity** /kə'pæsətɪ/ *n* capacità *f*; (function) qualità *f*; **in my** ∼ **as** in qualità di

cape[1] /keɪp/ *n* (cloak) cappa *f*

cape[2] *n* Geog capo *m*

Cape of Good Hope *n* Capo *m* di Buona Speranza

caper[1] /'keɪpə(r)/ ① *vi* saltellare
② *n* fam birichinata *f*

caper[2] *n* Culin cappero *m*

Cape Town *n* Città *f* del Capo

Cape Verde /vɜːd/ *n* Capo Verde *m*

capful /'kæpfʊl/ *n* tappo *m*

cap gun *n* pistola *f* a capsule

capillary /kə'pɪlərɪ/ *adj* & *n* capillare *m*

✧ **capital** /'kæpɪtl/ *n* (town) capitale *f*; (money) capitale *m*; (letter) lettera *f* maiuscola

capital allowances *npl* detrazioni *mpl* per ammortamento

capital city *n* capitale *f*

capital expenditure *n* spese *fpl* in conto capitale; (personal) spese *fpl* di capitale

capital gains tax *n* imposta *f* sui redditi di capitale

capital goods *npl* beni *mpl* strumentali

capital-intensive *adj* ad uso intensivo di capitale

capital investment *n* investimento *m* di capitale

capitalism /'kæpɪtəlɪzm/ *n* capitalismo *m*

capitalist /'kæpɪtəlɪst/ *adj* & *n* capitalista *mf*

capitalize /'kæpɪtəlaɪz/ *vi* ∼ **on** fig trarre vantaggio da

capital letter *n* lettera *f* maiuscola

capital punishment *n* pena *f* capitale

capital spending *n* spese *fpl* in conto capitale

✧ indicates a very frequent word

capital transfer tax *n* imposta *f* sui trasferimenti di capitale

capitulate /kə'pɪtjʊleɪt/ *vi* capitolare

capitulation /kəpɪtjʊ'leɪʃn/ *n* capitolazione *f*

capon /'keɪpɒn/ *n* cappone *m*

caprice /kə'priːs/ *n* (whim) capriccio *m*

capricious /kə'prɪʃəs/ *adj* capriccioso

Capricorn /'kæprɪkɔːn/ *n* Astr Capricorno *m*

caps /kæps/ *npl abbr* (**capital letters**) maius. *fpl*

capsicum /'kæpsɪkəm/ *n* peperone *m*

capsize /kæp'saɪz/ ① *vi* capovolgersi
② *vt* capovolgere

caps lock *n* Comput bloccamaiuscole *m inv*

capstan /'kæpstən/ *n* argano *m*

capsule /'kæpsjuːl/ *n* capsula *f*

captain /'kæptɪn/ ① *n* capitano *m*
② *vt* comandare ‹team›

caption /'kæpʃn/ *n* intestazione *f*; (of illustration) didascalia *f*

captious /'kæpʃəs/ *adj* ‹remark› ipercritico

captivate /'kæptɪveɪt/ *vt* incantare

captive /'kæptɪv/ ① *adj* prigioniero; **hold/ take** ∼ tenere/fare prigioniero
② *n* prigioniero, -a *mf*

captivity /kæp'tɪvətɪ/ *n* prigionia *f*; (animals) cattività *f*

captor /'kæptə(r)/ *n* (of person) persona (*f*) che tiene prigioniero qualcuno; (of person for ransom) rapitore, -trice *mf*

✧ **capture** /'kæptʃə(r)/ ① *n* cattura *f*
② *vt* catturare; attirare ‹attention›

✧ **car** /kɑː(r)/ *n* macchina *f*; **by** ∼ in macchina

carafe /kə'ræf/ *n* caraffa *f*

car alarm *n* antifurto *m* della macchina

caramel /'kærəməl/ *n* (sweet) caramella *f* al mou; Culin caramello *m*

carat /'kærət/ *n* carato *m*

caravan /'kærəvæn/ *n* roulotte *f inv*; (horsedrawn) carovana *f*

caravan site *n* area *f* per roulotte

caraway /'kærəweɪ/ *n* (plant) cumino *m* dei prati

carbohydrate /kɑːbə'haɪdreɪt/ *n* carboidrato *m*

carbolic /kɑː'bɒlɪk/ *adj* (soap) al fenolo

car bomb *n* autobomba *f*

carbon /'kɑːbən/ *n* carbonio *m*; (paper) carta *f* carbone; (copy) copia *f* in carta carbone

carbon copy *n* copia *f* in carta carbone; fig (person) ritratto *m*

carbon-date *vt* datare con il carbonio 14

carbon dating *n* datazione *f* con il carbonio 14

carbon dioxide *n* anidride *f* carbonica

carbon filter *n* filtro *m* al carbone

carbon footprint *n* impronta *f* ecologica

carbon monoxide *n* monossido *m* di carbonio

carbon neutral *adj* a emissioni zero, a zero emissioni

carbon paper *n* carta *f* carbone

car boot sale *n* Br *mercatino* (*m*) *di oggetti usati, esposti nei bagagliai delle macchine*

carbuncle /'kɑ:bʌŋk(ə)l/ *n* Med foruncolo *m*

carburettor /kɑ:bjʊ'retə(r)/ *n* carburatore *m*

carcass /'kɑ:kəs/ *n* carcassa *f*

carcinogen /kɑ:'sɪnədʒən/ *n* cancerogeno *m*

carcinogenic /kɑ:sɪnə'dʒenɪk/ *adj* cancerogeno

car crash *n* scontro *m* automobilistico

ᵒ⁄ **card** /kɑ:d/ *n* (for birthday, Christmas etc) biglietto *m* di auguri; (playing ∼) carta *f* [da gioco]; (membership ∼) tessera *f*; (business ∼) biglietto *m* da visita; (credit ∼) carta *f* di credito; Comput scheda *f*

cardboard /'kɑ:dbɔ:d/ *n* cartone *m*

cardboard box *n* scatola *f* di cartone; (large) scatolone *m*

cardboard city *n* fam *zona* (*f*) *in cui vivono i senzatetto*

car deck *n* (on ferry) ponte *m* auto

card game *n* gioco *m* di carte

cardiac /'kɑ:dɪæk/ *adj* cardiaco

cardiac arrest *n* arresto *m* cardiaco

cardigan /'kɑ:dɪgən/ *n* cardigan *m inv*

cardinal /'kɑ:dɪnl/ [1] *adj* cardinale; ∼ **number** numero *m* cardinale
[2] *n* Relig cardinale *m*

card index *n* schedario *m*

cardiologist /kɑ:dɪ'ɒlədʒɪst/ *n* cardiologo, -a *mf*

cardiology /kɑ:dɪ'ɒlədʒɪ/ *n* cardiologia *f*

cardiovascular /kɑ:dɪə'væskjʊlə(r)/ *adj* cardiovascolare

card key *n* scheda *f* magnetica

cardphone *n* telefono *m* a scheda

card table *n* tappeto *m* verde

card trick *n* trucco *m* con le carte

ᵒ⁄ **care** /keə(r)/ [1] *n* cura *f*; (caution) attenzione *f*; (worry) preoccupazione *f*; ∼ **of** (on letter abbr **c/o**) presso; **take** ∼ (be cautious) fare attenzione; **bye, take** ∼ ciao, stammi bene; **take** ∼ **of** occuparsi di; **be taken into** ∼ essere preso in custodia da un ente assistenziale; **'[handle] with** ∼' 'fragile'
[2] *vi* ∼ **about** interessarsi di; ∼ **for** (feel affection for) volere bene a; (look after) aver cura di; **I don't** ∼ **for chocolate** non mi piace il cioccolato; **I don't** ∼ non me ne importa; **I couldn't** ∼ **less** Br *or* **I could care less** Am; non potrebbe importarmene; **who** ∼**s?** chi

se ne frega?; **for all I** ∼ per quello che me ne importa

care assistant *n* Br Med assistente *mf* a domicilio

ᵒ⁄ **career** /kə'rɪə(r)/ [1] *n* carriera *f*; (profession) professione *f*; ∼ **woman** *n* donna in carriera
[2] *vi* andare a tutta velocità

career break *n* pausa *f* nella carriera

career move *n* passo *m* utile per un avanzamento di carriera

careers adviser *n* consulente *mf* di orientamento professionale

careers office *n* centro *m* di orientamento professionale

careers service *n* servizio *m* di orientamento professionale

carefree /'keəfri:/ *adj* spensierato

careful /'keəfʊl/ *adj* attento; ⟨driver⟩ prudente

ᵒ⁄ **carefully** /'keəfʊlɪ/ *adv* con attenzione

caregiver *n* Am familiare *m* che assiste un anziano o un handicappato

care home *n* casa *f* famiglia

careless /'keəlɪs/ *adj* irresponsabile; (in work) trascurato; ⟨work⟩ fatto con poca cura; ⟨driver⟩ distratto

carelessly /'keəlɪslɪ/ *adv* negligentemente

carelessness /'keəlɪsnɪs/ *n* trascuratezza *f*

carer /'keərə(r)/ *n* Br (relative) *familiare* (*m*) *che assiste un anziano o un handicappato*; (professional) badante *mf*, assistente *mf* a domicilio

caress /kə'res/ [1] *n* carezza *f*
[2] *vt* accarezzare

caretaker /'keəteɪkə(r)/ *n* custode *mf*; (in school) bidello *m*

care worker *n* assistente *mf* sociosanitario

careworn /'keəwɔ:n/ *adj* ⟨face⟩ segnato dalle preoccupazioni

car ferry *n* traghetto *m* (*per il trasporto di auto*)

car-free *adj* ⟨environment⟩ senza macchine

cargo /'kɑ:gəʊ/ *n* (*pl* **-es**) carico *m*

cargo plane *n* aereo *m* da carico

cargo ship *n* nave *f* da carico

car hire *n* autonoleggio *m*

Caribbean /kærɪ'bi:ən/ [1] *n* the ∼ (sea) il Mar *m* dei Caraibi
[2] *adj* caraibico

caricature /'kærɪkətjʊə(r)/ [1] *n* caricatura *f*
[2] *vt* fare una caricatura di

caricaturist /'kærɪkətjʊərɪst/ *n* caricaturista *mf*

caring /'keərɪŋ/ *adj* ⟨parent⟩ premuroso; ⟨attitude⟩ altruista; **the** ∼ **professions** le attività assistenziali

carjack /'kɑːdʒæk/ *vt furto* (m) *d'auto con minaccia o violenza al conducente*

carjacker /'kɑːdʒækə(r)/ *n chi effettua un furto d'auto con minaccia o violenza al conducente*

carjacking /'kɑːdʒækɪŋ/ *n furto* (m) *d'auto con aggressione al conducente*

carload /'kɑːləʊd/ *n* a ~ **of people** un'automobile *f* piena di persone

carnage /'kɑːnɪdʒ/ *n* carneficina *f*

carnal /'kɑːn(ə)l/ *adj* carnale

carnation /kɑːˈneɪʃn/ *n* garofano *m*

carnival /'kɑːnɪvl/ *n* carnevale *m*

carnivore /'kɑːnɪvɔː(r)/ *n* carnivoro *m*

carnivorous /kɑːˈnɪvərəs/ *adj* carnivoro

carob /'kærəb/ *n* (pod) carruba *f*; (tree) carrubo *m*

carol /'kærəl/ *n* [Christmas] ~ canto *m* natalizio; ~ **concert** concerto *m* natalizio; **go** ~ **singing** andare a cantare le canzoni natalizie per le strade

carousel /kærʊˈsel/ *n* (merry-go-round) giostra *f*; (for luggage) nastro *m* trasportatore; (for slides) caricatore *m* circolare

carp[1] /kɑːp/ *n inv* carpa *f*

carp[2] *vi* lamentarsi; ~ **at** trovare da ridire su

car park *n* parcheggio *m*

carpenter /'kɑːpəntə(r)/ *n* falegname *m*

carpentry /'kɑːpəntrɪ/ *n* falegnameria *f*

carpet /'kɑːpɪt/ 1 *n* tappeto *m*; (wall-to-wall) moquette *f inv*; **be on the** ~ fig essere ammonito
2 *vt* mettere la moquette in ⟨room⟩

carpet-bomb *vt* bombardare a tappeto

carpet fitter *n* artigiano *m* che mette in opera la moquette

carpet slipper *n* pantofola *f*

carpet sweeper *n* battitappeto *m inv*

carpet tile *n* riquadro *m* di moquette

car phone *n* telefono *m* in macchina

car radio *n* autoradio *f inv*

carriage /'kærɪdʒ/ *n* carrozza *f*; (of typewriter) carrello *m*; (of goods) trasporto *m*; (cost) spese *fpl* di trasporto; (bearing) portamento *m*; ~ **paid** Comm franco di porto

carriage clock *n* orologio *m* da tavolo

carriageway /'kærɪdʒweɪ/ *n* strada *f* carrozzabile; **north-bound** ~ carreggiata *f* nord

carrier /'kærɪə(r)/ *n* (company) impresa *f* di trasporti; Aeron compagnia *f* di trasporto aereo; (of disease) portatore *m*

carrier [bag] *n* borsa *f* [per la spesa]

carrier pigeon *n* piccione *m* viaggiatore

carrot /'kærət/ *n* carota *f*

♂' **carry** /'kærɪ/ *v* (*pt/pp* -**ied**) 1 *vt* portare; (transport) trasportare; Math riportare; **get**

carried away fam lasciarsi prender la mano
2 *vi* ⟨sound⟩ trasmettersi

■ **carry forward** *vt* riportare ⟨balance, figure⟩

■ **carry off** *vt* portare via; vincere ⟨prize⟩

■ **carry on** 1 *vi* continuare; fam (make scene) fare delle storie; ~ **on with something** continuare qualcosa; ~ **on with somebody** fam intendersela con qualcuno
2 *vt* mantenere ⟨business⟩; ~ **on doing something** continuare a fare qualcosa

■ **carry out** *vt* portare fuori; eseguire ⟨instructions, task⟩; mettere in atto ⟨threat⟩; effettuare ⟨experiment, survey⟩

carryall *n* Am borsone *m*

carrycot /'kærɪkʊt/ *n* porte-enfant *m inv*

carry-on *n* fam (complicated procedure) impresa *f*; (bad behaviour) storie *fpl*

carryout /'kærɪaʊt/ *n* Am piatti *mpl* da asporto

car seat *n* (for baby or child) seggiolino *m* per auto

carsick /'kɑːsɪk/ *adj* **be** ~ avere il mal d'auto

cart /kɑːt/ 1 *n* carretto *m*; **put the** ~ **before the horse** fig mettere il carro davanti ai buoi
2 *vt* fam (carry) portare

cartel /kɑːˈtel/ *n* cartello *m*

car theft *n* furto *m* d'auto

carthorse /'kɑːθɔːs/ *n* cavallo *m* da tiro

cartilage /'kɑːtɪlɪdʒ/ *n* Anat cartilagine *f*

cartographer /kɑːˈtɒɡrəfə(r)/ *n* cartografo, -a *mf*

cartography /kɑːˈtɒɡrəfɪ/ *n* cartografia *f*

carton /'kɑːt(ə)n/ *n* scatola *f* di cartone; (for drink) cartone *m*; (of cream, yoghurt) vasetto *m*; (of cigarettes) stecca *f*

cartoon /kɑːˈtuːn/ *n* vignetta *f*; (strip) vignette *fpl*; (film) cartone *m* animato; (in art) bozzetto *m*

cartoonist /kɑːˈtuːnɪst/ *n* vignettista *mf*; (for films) disegnatore, -trice *mf* di cartoni animati

cartridge /'kɑːtrɪdʒ/ *n* cartuccia *f*; (for film) bobina *f*; (of record player) testina *f*

cartwheel /'kɑːtwiːl/ *n* (of cart) ruota *f* di carro; (in gymnastics) ruota *f*; **do a** ~ (in gymnastics) fare la ruota

carve /kɑːv/ *vt* scolpire; tagliare ⟨meat⟩

■ **carve out** *vt* crearsi ⟨name, reputation, market⟩

■ **carve up** *vt* spartire ⟨estate, territory, proceeds⟩

carving /'kɑːvɪŋ/ *n* scultura *f*

carving knife *n* trinciante *m*

car wash *n* autolavaggio *m inv*

car worker *n* operaio, -a *mf* dell'industria automobilistica

Casanova /'kæsənəʊvə/ *n* Casanova *m inv*

♂' indicates a very frequent word

cascade /kæs'keɪd/ **1** *vi* scendere a cascata
2 *n* cascata *f*

⚡ **case¹** /keɪs/ *n* caso *m*; **in any** ~ in ogni caso; **in that** ~ in questo caso; **just in** ~ per sicurezza; **in** ~ **he comes** nel caso in cui venisse; **in** ~ **of emergency** in caso d'emergenza

case² *n* (container) scatola *f*; (crate) cassa *f*; (for spectacles) astuccio *m*; (suitcase) valigia *f*; (for display) vetrina *f*

case history *n* Med cartella *f* clinica

casement window /'keɪsmənt/ *n* finestra *f* a battenti

casenotes *npl* pratica *f*

case study *n* analisi *f inv*

casework *n* **do** ~ occuparsi di assistenza sociale

⚡ **cash** /kæʃ/ **1** *n* denaro *m* contante; fam (money) contanti *mpl*; **pay [in]** ~ pagare in contanti; ~ **on delivery** pagamento alla consegna
2 *vt* incassare (cheque)

■ **cash in** *vt* riscuotere ‹bond, policy›; Am incassare ‹check›

■ **cash in on** *vt* fam approfittarsi di

cash-and-carry *n* cash and carry *m inv*

cashback *n* contanti (mpl) che si possono richiedere alla cassa di un negozio quando si effettua un pagamento con carta di debito

cash box *n* cassetta *f* portavalori

cash card *n* bancomat® *m inv*

cash desk *n* cassa *f*

cash dispenser *n* sportello *m* automatico, cassa *f* automatica

cashew [nut] /kə'ʃuː/ *n* anacardio *m*

cash flow *n* flusso *m* di cassa; ~ **difficulties** difficoltà *fpl* di flusso di cassa; ~ **management** gestione *f* del flusso di cassa

cashier /kæ'ʃɪə(r)/ *n* cassiere, -a *mf*

cashless /'kæʃlɪs/ *adj* ‹society, transaction› basato sull'uso di carte di credito, assegni ecc. anziché sul contante

cash machine *n* (sportello) bancomat® *m inv*

cashmere /'kæʃmɪə(r)/ *n* cachemire *m inv*

cash on delivery *n* pagamento *m* alla consegna

cashpoint *n* (sportello) bancomat® *m inv*

cash register *n* registratore *m* di cassa

casing /'keɪsɪŋ/ *n* (of machinery) rivestimento *m*; (of gearbox) scatola *f*; (of tyre) copertone *m*

casino /kə'siːnəʊ/ *n* casinò *m inv*

cask /kɑːsk/ *n* barile *m*

casket /'kɑːskɪt/ *n* scrigno *m*; Am (coffin) bara *f*

casserole /'kæsərəʊl/ *n* casseruola *f*; (stew) stufato *m*

cassette /kə'set/ *n* cassetta *f*

cassette deck *n* piastra *f* di registrazione

cassette player *n* mangiacassette *m inv*

cassette recorder *n* registratore *m* (a cassette)

cassette tape *n* cassetta *f*

cassock /'kæsək/ *n* tonaca *f*

cast /kɑːst/ **1** *n* (throw) lancio *m*; (mould) forma *f*; Theat cast *m inv*; **[plaster]** ~ Med ingessatura *f*
2 *vt* (*pt/pp* **cast**) dare ‹vote›; Theat assegnare le parti di ‹play›; fondere ‹metal›; (throw) gettare; (shed) sbarazzarsi di; ~ **an actor as** dare ad un attore il ruolo di; ~ **a glance at** lanciare uno sguardo a

■ **cast off** **1** *vi* Naut sganciare gli ormeggi
2 *vt* (in knitting) diminuire

■ **cast on** *vt* (in knitting) avviare

castanets /kæstə'nets/ *npl* nacchere *fpl*

castaway /'kɑːstəweɪ/ *n* naufrago, -a *mf*

caste /kɑːst/ *n* casta *f*

caster /'kɑːstə(r)/ *n* (wheel) rotella *f*

caster sugar *n* zucchero *m* raffinato

casting /'kɑːstɪŋ, US 'kæst-/ *n* casting *m inv*

casting director /'kɑːstɪŋ/ *n* direttore *m* del casting

casting vote *n* voto *m* decisivo

cast iron **1** *n* ghisa *f*
2 *adj* cast-iron di ghisa; fig solido

castle /'kɑːsl/ *n* castello *m*; (in chess) torre *f*

cast-offs *npl* abiti *mpl* smessi

castor /'kɑːstə(r)/ *n* (wheel) rotella *f*

castor oil *n* olio *m* di ricino

castor sugar *n* zucchero *m* raffinato

castrate /kæ'streɪt/ *vt* castrare

castration /kæ'streɪʃn/ *n* castrazione *f*

castrato /kæs'trɑːtəʊ/ *n* castrato *m*

casual /'kæʒʊəl/ *adj* (chance) casuale; (remark) senza importanza; ‹glance› di sfuggita; ‹attitude, approach› disinvolto; ‹chat› informale; ‹clothes› casual *inv*; ‹work› saltuario; ~ **wear** abbigliamento *m* casual

casualize /'kæʒʊəlaɪz/ *vt* impiegare con contratto a termine ‹labour›

casually /'kæʒʊəlɪ/ *adv* ‹dress› casual; ‹meet› casualmente

casualty /'kæʒʊəltɪ/ *n* (injured person) ferito *m*; (killed) vittima *f*

casualty [department] *n* pronto soccorso *m*

⚡ **cat** /kæt/ *n* gatto *m*; pej arpia *f*

catacombs /'kætəkuːmz/ *npl* catacombe *fpl*

catalogue /'kætəlɒg/ **1** *n* catalogo *m*
2 *vt* catalogare

catalyst /'kætəlɪst/ *n* Chem fig catalizzatore *m*

catalytic converter /kætə'lɪtɪk/ n Auto marmitta f catalitica

catamaran /kætəmə'ræn/ n catamarano m

catapult /'kætəpʌlt/ **1** n catapulta f; (child's) fionda f
2 vt fig catapultare

cataract /'kætərækt/ n Med cataratta f

catarrh /kə'tɑː(r)/ n catarro m

catastrophe /kə'tæstrəfɪ/ n catastrofe f

catastrophic /kætə'strɒfɪk/ adj catastrofico

cat burglar n Br scassinatore, -trice mf acrobata

♂ **catch** /kætʃ/ **1** n (of fish) pesca f; (fastener) fermaglio m; (on door) fermo m; (on window) gancio m; fam (snag) tranello m
2 vt (pt/pp **caught**) acchiappare ‹ball›; (grab) afferrare; prendere ‹illness, fugitive, train›; ~ **a cold** prendersi un raffreddore; ~ **sight of** scorgere; **I caught him stealing** l'ho sorpreso mentre rubava; ~ **one's finger in the door** chiudersi il dito nella porta; ~ **sb's eye** or **attention** attirare l'attenzione di qualcuno
3 vi ‹fire› prendere; (get stuck) impigliarsi
■ **catch on** vi fam (understand) afferrare; (become popular) diventare popolare
■ **catch out** vt (show to be wrong) prendere in castagna
■ **catch up** **1** vt raggiungere
2 vi recuperare; ‹runner› riguadagnare terreno; ~ **up with** raggiungere ‹somebody›; mettersi in pari con ‹work›

catch-22 situation /kætʃtwentɪ'tuː/ n situazione f senza uscita

catch-all adj ‹term› polivalente; ‹clause› che comprende tutte le possibilità

catching /'kætʃɪŋ/ adj contagioso

catchment area /'kætʃmənt/ n bacino m d'utenza

catchphrase /'kætʃfreɪz/ n tormentone m

catchword /'kætʃwɜːd/ n slogan m inv

catchy /'kætʃɪ/ adj (**-ier**, **-iest**) orecchiabile

catechism /'kætɪkɪzm/ n catechismo m

categorical /kætɪ'gɒrɪkl/ adj categorico

categorically /kætə'gɒrɪklɪ/ adv categoricamente

categorize /'kætəgəraɪz/ vt categorizzare

♂ **category** /'kætɪgərɪ/ n categoria f

cater /'keɪtə(r)/ **1** vi ~ **for** provvedere a ‹needs›; fig venire incontro alle esigenze di
2 vt occuparsi del rinfresco di ‹party›

caterer /'keɪtərə(r)/ n persona f che si occupa di ristorazione

catering /'keɪtərɪŋ/ n (trade) ristorazione f; (food) rinfresco m

♂ indicates a very frequent word

caterpillar /'kætəpɪlə(r)/ n bruco m

caterwaul /'kætəwɔːl/ vi miagolare

catfish n pesce m gatto

catflap n gattaiola f

catgut n catgut m inv

cathedral /kə'θiːdrl/ n cattedrale f

Catherine wheel /'kæθ(ə)rɪn/ n girandola f

catheter /'kæθɪtə(r)/ n catetere m

cathode-ray tube /kæθəʊd'reɪ/ n tubo m a raggi catodici

Catholic /'kæθəlɪk/ adj & n cattolico, -a mf

Catholicism /kə'θɒlɪsɪzm/ n cattolicesimo m

catkin /'kætkɪn/ n Bot amento m

cat litter n lettiera f del gatto

catnap vi fare un pisolino, pisolino m

cat-o'-nine-tails n gatto m a nove code

CAT scan n TAC f

cat's-eye n Br catarifrangente m (inserito nell'asfalto)

catsuit n tuta f

cattery /'kætərɪ/ n pensione f per gatti

cattle /'kæt(ə)l/ npl bestiame msg

cattle grid n recinto (m) metallico che impedisce al bestiame di accedere a una strada

cattle market n mercato m del bestiame; fig fam ‹for sexual encounters› locale (m) dove la gente va per rimorchiare

cattle shed n stalla f

catty /'kætɪ/ adj (**-ier**, **-iest**) dispettoso

catwalk /'kætwɔːk/ n passerella f

Caucasian /kɔː'keɪʒ(ə)n/ **1** n Geog (inhabitant) caucasico, -a mf; (white person) bianco, -a mf
2 Geog caucasico; ‹race, man› bianco

caught /kɔːt/ ▶ CATCH

cauldron /'kɔːldrən/ n calderone m

cauliflower /'kɒlɪflaʊə(r)/ n cavolfiore m

cauliflower cheese n cavolfiori mpl gratinati

causal /'kɔːzəl/ adj causale

♂ **cause** /kɔːz/ **1** n causa f; (reason) motivo m; **good** ~ buona causa
2 vt causare; ~ **somebody to do something** far fare qualcosa a qualcuno

causeway /'kɔːzweɪ/ n strada f sopraelevata

caustic /'kɔːstɪk/ adj caustico

cauterize /'kɔːtəraɪz/ vt cauterizzare

caution /'kɔːʃn/ **1** n cautela f; (warning) ammonizione f
2 vt mettere in guardia; Jur ammonire

cautionary /'kɔːʃənərɪ, US -nerɪ/ adj ‹tale› di ammonimento

cautious /'kɔːʃəs/ adj cauto

cautiously /'kɔːʃəslɪ/ adv cautamente

cavalcade /kævəl'keɪd/ n sfilata f

cavalier /kævə'lɪə(r)/ **1** *adj* noncurante **2** *n* **C**∼ sostenitore, -trice *mf* di Carlo I durante la guerra civile inglese

cavalry /'kævəlrɪ/ *n* cavalleria *f*

cave /keɪv/ *n* caverna *f*
■ **cave in** *vi* ‹roof› crollare; fig (give in) capitolare

caveat /'kævɪæt/ *n* avvertimento *m*

cave dweller *n* cavernicolo, -a *mf*

caveman *n* cavernicolo *m*

cave painting *n* pittura *f* rupestre

caver /'keɪvə(r)/ *n* speleologo, -a *mf*

cavern /'kævən/ *n* caverna *f*

caviare /'kævɪɑː(r)/ *n* caviale *m*

caving /'keɪvɪŋ/ *n* speleologia *f*

cavity /'kævətɪ/ *n* cavità *f inv*; (in tooth) carie *f inv*

cavity wall insulation *n* isolamento *m* per muri a intercapedine

cavort /kə'vɔːt/ *vi* saltellare

caw /kɔː/ **1** *n* (noise) gracchio *m* **2** *vi* gracchiare

cayenne pepper /'kaɪen/ *n* pepe *m* di Caienna

cayman /'keɪmən/ *n* caimano *m*

CB **1** *n abbr* (**Citizens' Band**) CB *f inv* **2** *attrib* ‹equipment, radio, wavelength› CB

CBI *n abbr* Br (**Confederation of British Industry**) ≈ Confindustria *f*

cc *abbr* 1 (**cubic centimetre**) cc *m* 2 (**carbon copy**) cc

CCJ *n abbr* Br (**County Court Judgement**) sentenza *f* del tribunale di contea

CCTV *abbr* (**closed-circuit television**) televisione *f* a circuito chiuso

CD *n abbr* 1 (**Civil Defence**) difesa *f* civile 2 (**compact disc**) CD *m inv* 3 Am (**Congressional District**) circoscrizione *f* del Congresso 4 (**corps diplomatique**) CD *m inv*

CD burner, CD writer *n* masterizzatore *m* di CD

CD-I *abbr* (**compact disc interactive**) CD-I *m*

CD player *n* lettore *m* [di] compact, lettore *m* di CD

CD-R *abbr* (**compact disc recordable**) CD-R *m*

CD-Rom /si:di:'rɒm/ *n* CD-Rom *m inv*

CD-Rom drive *n* lettore *m* CD-Rom

CD-RW *abbr* (**compact disc rewritable**) CD-RW *m*

cease /si:s/ **1** *n* without ∼ incessantemente **2** *vt/i* cessare

ceasefire /'si:sfaɪə(r)/ *n* cessate il fuoco *m inv*

ceaseless /'si:slɪs/ *adj* incessante

ceaselessly /'si:slɪslɪ/ *adv* incessantemente

cedar /'si:də(r)/ *n* cedro *m*

cede /si:d/ *vt* cedere

cedilla /sɪ'dɪlə/ *n* cedilla *f*

ceiling /'si:lɪŋ/ *n* soffitto *m*; fig tetto *m* [massimo]

ꞔ **celebrate** /'selɪbreɪt/ **1** *vt* festeggiare ‹birthday, victory› **2** *vi* far festa

celebrated /'selɪbreɪtɪd/ *adj* celebre (**for** per)

celebration /selɪ'breɪʃn/ *n* celebrazione *f*

celebrity /sɪ'lebrətɪ/ *n* celebrità *f inv*

celeriac /sɪ'lerɪæk/ *n* sedano *m* rapa

celery /'selərɪ/ *n* sedano *m*

celestial /sɪ'lestɪəl/ *adj* celestiale

celibacy /'selɪbəsɪ/ *n* celibato *m*

celibate /'selɪbət/ *adj* ‹man› celibe; ‹woman› nubile

ꞔ **cell** /sel/ *n* cella *f*; Biol cellula *f*

cellar /'selə(r)/ *n* scantinato *m*; (for wine) cantina *f*

cellist /'tʃelɪst/ *n* violoncellista *mf*

cello /'tʃeləʊ/ *n* violoncello *m*

Cellophane® /'seləfeɪn/ *n* cellophane® *m inv*

cellphone /'selfəʊn/ *n* [telefono *m*] cellulare *m*

cellular phone /seljʊlə'fəʊn/ *n* [telefono *m*] cellulare *m*

cellulite /'seljʊlaɪt/ *n* cellulite *f*

celluloid /'seljʊlɔɪd/ *n* celluloide *f*

Celsius /'selsɪəs/ *adj* Celsius

Celt /kelt/ *n* celta *mf*

Celtic /'keltɪk/ *adj* celtico

cement /sɪ'ment/ **1** *n* cemento *m*; (adhesive) mastice *m* **2** *vt* cementare; (stick) attaccare col mastice; fig consolidare

cement mixer *n* betoniera *f*

cemetery /'semətrɪ/ *n* cimitero *m*

cenotaph /'senətæf/ *n* cenotafio *m*

censor /'sensə(r)/ **1** *n* censore *m* **2** *vt* censurare

censorship /'sensəʃɪp/ *n* censura *f*

censure /'senʃə(r)/ **1** *n* biasimo *m* **2** *vt* biasimare

census /'sensəs/ *n* censimento *m*

cent /sent/ *n* (coin) centesimo *m*

centenary /sen'ti:nərɪ/ Am **centennial** /sen'tenɪəl/ *n* centenario *m*

center /'sentə(r)/ *n* Am = CENTRE

centigrade /'sentɪgreɪd/ *adj* centigrado

centilitre /'sentɪli:tə(r)/ *n* centilitro *m*

centimetre /'sentɪmi:tə(r)/ *n* centimetro *m*

centipede /'sentɪpi:d/ *n* centopiedi *m inv*

✔ **central** /'sentrəl/ *adj* centrale

Central African Republic *n*
Repubblica *f* Centrafricana

Central America *n* America *f* centrale

central heating *n* riscaldamento *m*
autonomo

centralize /'sentrəlaɪz/ *vt* centralizzare

central locking *n* Auto chiusura *f*
centralizzata

centrally /'sentrəlɪ/ *adv* al centro;
~ **heated** con riscaldamento autonomo

central nervous system *n* sistema *m*
nervoso centrale

central processing unit *n* Comput
unità *f inv* centrale di elaborazione

central reservation *n* Auto banchina *f*
spartitraffico *inv*

✔ **centre** Br, **center** Am /'sentə(r)/ [1] *n*
centro *m*
[2] *vt* (*pt/pp* **centred**) centrare
■ **centre on, centre around** *vt*
‹activities, life› imperniasi su; ‹industry,
people› incentrarsi su; ‹thoughts› concentrarsi
su

centrefold *n* (pin-up picture) paginone *m*;
(model) pin-up *f inv*

centre forward *n* centravanti *m inv*

centre ground Br, **center ground**
Am *n* fig centro *m*

centre half *n* Sport centromediano *m*

centre of gravity *n* centro *m* di gravità

centrepiece *n* (of table) centrotavola *m*; fig
(of exhibition) pezzo *m* forte

centre spread *n* paginone *m*

centre stage *n* Theat centro *m* della
scena; **stand** ~ tenersi al centro della scena;
take/occupy ~ fig essere/mettersi in primo
piano

centrifugal /sentrɪ'fjʊɡl/ *adj* ~ **force**
forza *f* centrifuga

✔ **century** /'sentʃərɪ/ *n* secolo *m*

CEO *n abbr* (**Chief Executive Officer**)
direttore, -trice *mf* generale

ceramic /sɪ'ræmɪk/ *adj* ceramico

ceramics /sɪ'ræmɪks/ *n* (art) ceramica *fsg*;
(objects) ceramiche *fpl*

cereal /'sɪərɪəl/ *n* cereale *m*

cerebral /'serɪbrl/ *adj* cerebrale

cerebral palsy /'pɔ:lzɪ/ *n* paralisi *f*
cerebrale

ceremonial /serɪ'məʊnɪəl/ [1] *adj* da
cerimonia
[2] *n* cerimoniale *m*

ceremonially /serɪ'məʊnɪəlɪ/ *adv*
secondo il rituale

ceremonious /serɪ'məʊnɪəs/ *adj*
cerimonioso

ceremoniously /serɪ'məʊnɪəslɪ/ *adv* in
modo cerimonioso

✔ indicates a very frequent word

ceremony /'serɪmənɪ/ *n* cerimonia *f*;
without ~ senza cerimonie

cert /sɜ:t/ *n* Br fam **it's a [dead]** ~! ci puoi
scommettere!

✔ **certain** /'sɜ:tn/ *adj* certo; **for** ~ di sicuro;
make ~ accertarsi; **he is** ~ **to win** è certo di
vincere; **it's not** ~ **whether he'll come** non è
sicuro che venga

✔ **certainly** /'sɜ:tnlɪ/ *adv* certamente; ~ **not!**
no di certo!

certainty /'sɜ:tntɪ/ *n* certezza *f*; **it's a** ~ è
una cosa certa

certifiable /'sɜ:tɪfaɪəbl/ *adj* ‹verifiable
statement, evidence› dimostrabile; (mad)
pazzo

certificate /sə'tɪfɪkət/ *n* certificato *m*

certified /'sɜ:tɪfaɪd/ *adj* autenticato

certified mail *n* Am (lettera)
raccomandata *f*

certified public accountant *n* Am
≈ commercialista *mf*

certify /'sɜ:tɪfaɪ/ *vt* (*pt/pp* **-ied**) certificare;
(declare insane) dichiarare malato di mente

certitude /'sɜ:tɪtju:d/ *n* certezza *f*

cervical /'sɜ:vɪkl/ *adj* cervicale

cervical cancer *n* tumore *m* del collo
dell'utero

cervical smear *n* Pap test *m inv*,
striscio *m*

cervix /'sɜ:vɪks/ *n* cervice *f* uterina, collo
m dell'utero

cessation /se'seɪʃn/ *n* cessazione *f*

cesspool /'sespu:l/ *n* pozzo *m* nero

cf. *abbr* (**compare**) cf, cfr

CFC *n abbr* (**chlorofluorocarbon**) CFC
m inv

CFC-free *adj* ‹product, spray› senza CFC

CFE *abbr* (**College of Further
Education**) istituto (*m*) di istruzione
superiore

CGI *abbr* Comput (**common graphical
interface**) CGI *f*

Chad /tʃæd/ *n* Chad *m*

chafe /tʃeɪf/ *vt* irritare

chaff /tʃɑ:f/ *n* pula *f*

chaffinch /'tʃæfɪntʃ/ *n* fringuello *m*

chagrin /'ʃæɡrɪn/ *n* **much to his** ~ con suo
grande dispiacere

✔ **chain** /tʃeɪn/ [1] *n* catena *f*
[2] *vt* incatenare ‹prisoner›; attaccare con la
catena ‹dog› **(to a)**
■ **chain up** *vt* legare alla catena ‹dog›

chain gang *n* gruppo *m* di prigionieri
incatenati

chain letter *n* lettera *f* della catena di
Sant'Antonio

chain mail *n* cotta *f* di maglia

chain reaction *n* reazione *f* a catena

chain saw *n* motosega *f*

chain-smoke *vi* fumare una sigaretta dopo l'altra

chain-smoker *n* fumatore, -trice *mf* accanito, -a

chain store *n* negozio *m* appartenente ad una catena

✓ **chair** /tʃeə(r)/ **1** *n* sedia *f*; Univ cattedra *f*
2 *vt* presiedere

chairlift /'tʃeəlɪft/ *n* seggiovia *f*

✓ **chairman** /'tʃeəmən/ *n* presidente *m*; **∼ and managing director** presidente *m* direttore generale

chairperson /'tʃeəpɜːs(ə)n/ *n* presidente *m*, -essa *f*

chairwoman /'tʃeəwʊmən/ *n* presidentessa *f*

chalet /'ʃæleɪ/ *n* chalet *m inv*; (in holiday camp) bungalow *m inv*

chalice /'tʃælɪs/ *n* Relig calice *m*

chalk /tʃɔːk/ *n* gesso *m*

chalky /'tʃɔːkɪ/ *adj* gessoso

✓ **challenge** /'tʃælɪndʒ/ **1** *n* sfida *f*; Mil intimazione *f*
2 *vt* sfidare; Mil intimare il chi va là a; fig mettere in dubbio ‹statement›

challenger /'tʃælɪndʒə(r)/ *n* sfidante *mf*

challenging /'tʃælɪndʒɪŋ/ *adj* ‹job› impegnativo

chamber /'tʃeɪmbə(r)/ *n* camera *f*

chambermaid *n* cameriera *f* ai piani

chamber music *n* musica *f* da camera

Chamber of Commerce *n* Camera *f* di Commercio

chamber orchestra *n* orchestra *f* da camera

chamber pot *n* vaso *m* da notte

chambers /'tʃeɪmbəz/ *n pl* Jur studio *m* [legale]

chameleon /kə'miːlɪən/ *n* also fig camaleonte *m*

chamois¹ /'ʃæmwɑː/ *n inv* (animal) camoscio *m*

chamois² /'ʃæmɪ/ ∼[-leather] [pelle *f* di] camoscio *m*

champagne /ʃæm'peɪn/ *n* champagne *m inv*

✓ **champion** /'tʃæmpɪən/ **1** *n* Sport campione *m*; (of cause) difensore *m*, difenditrice *f*
2 *vt* (defend) difendere; (fight for) lottare per

championship /'tʃæmpɪənʃɪp/ *n* Sport campionato *m*

✓ **chance** /tʃɑːns/ **1** *n* caso *m*; (possibility) possibilità *f inv*; (opportunity) occasione *f*; **by ∼** per caso; **take a ∼** provarci; **give somebody a second ∼** dare un'altra possibilità a qualcuno
2 *attrib* fortuito
3 *vt* **if you ∼ to see him** se ti capita di

vederlo; **I'll ∼ it** fam corro il rischio

chancel /'tʃɑːnsəl/ *n* Archit coro *m*

chancellor /'tʃɑːnsələ(r)/ *n* cancelliere *m*; Univ rettore *m*; **C∼ of the Exchequer** ≈ ministro *m* del tesoro

chancy /'tʃɑːnsɪ/ *adj* rischioso

chandelier /ʃændə'lɪə(r)/ *n* lampadario *m*

chandler /'tʃɑːndlə(r)/ *n* fornitore *m* navale

✓ **change** /tʃeɪndʒ/ **1** *n* cambiamento *m*; (money) resto *m*; (small coins) spiccioli *mpl*; **for a ∼** tanto per cambiare; **have a ∼ of heart** cambiare idea; **a ∼ of clothes** un cambio di vestiti; **∼ of address** cambiamento *m* d'indirizzo; **a ∼ of scene** also fig un cambiamento di scena; **the ∼ [of life]** la menopausa
2 *vt* cambiare; (substitute) scambiare, for con; **∼ one's clothes** cambiarsi [i vestiti]; **∼ trains** cambiare treno
3 *vi* cambiare; (∼ clothes) cambiarsi; **all ∼!** stazione terminale!

■ **change down** *vi* Auto passare alla marcia inferiore

■ **change up** *vi* Auto passare alla marcia superiore

changeability /tʃeɪndʒə'bɪlɪtɪ/ *n* (of weather) instabilità *f*

changeable /'tʃeɪndʒəbl/ *adj* mutevole; ‹weather› variable

changeless /'tʃeɪndʒlɪs/ *adj* ‹appearance› inalterabile; ‹character› costante; ‹law, routine› immutabile

change machine *n* distributore *m* di monete

changeover /'tʃeɪndʒəʊvə(r)/ *n* (time period) periodo *m* di transizione; (transition) passaggio *m*; (of leaders) subentro *m*; (of employees, guards) cambio *m*; Sport (in relay) passaggio *m* del testimone; Sport (of ends) cambiamento *m*

changing /'tʃeɪndʒɪŋ/ *adj* in mutamento

changing-room *n* camerino *m*; (for sports) spogliatoio *m*

✓ **channel** /'tʃænl/ **1** *n* canale *m*; **the [English] C∼** la Manica
2 *vt* (*pt/pp* **channelled**) **∼ one's energies into something** convogliare le proprie energie in qualcosa

channel ferry *n* traghetto *m* attraverso la Manica

channel-hop *vi* Br fare lo zapping

channel-hopping *n* Br zapping *m inv*

Channel Islands *npl* Isole *fpl* del Canale

channel-surf *vi* Am fare lo zapping

channel-surfing *n* Am zapping *m inv*

Channel Tunnel *n* tunnel *m inv* sotto la Manica

chant /tʃɑːnt/ **1** *n* cantilena *f*; (of demonstrators) slogan *m inv* di protesta
2 *vt* cantare; ‹demonstrators› gridare ⋯✲

c

③ vi ‹demonstrators› gridare slogan di protesta

chaos /'keɪɒs/ n caos m

chaotic /keɪ'ɒtɪk/ adj caotico

chap /tʃæp/ n fam tipo m

chapel /'tʃæpl/ n cappella f

chaperone, chaperon /'ʃæpərəʊn/
① n chaperon m inv
② vt fare da chaperon a ‹qualcuno›

chaplain /'tʃæplɪn/ n cappellano m

chapped /tʃæpt/ adj ‹skin, lips› screpolato

ⅆ **chapter** /'tʃæptə(r)/ n capitolo m

char¹ /tʃɑː(r)/ n fam donna f delle pulizie

char² vt (pt/pp **charred**) (burn) carbonizzare

ⅆ **character** /'kærɪktə(r)/ n carattere m;
(in novel, play) personaggio m; **that's out of**
~ non è da te/lui; **quite a** ~ fam un tipo particolare

character actor n caratterista mf

character assassination n denigrazione f

characteristic /kærəktə'rɪstɪk/ ① adj caratteristico
② n caratteristica f

characteristically /kærəktə'rɪstɪklɪ/ adv tipicamente

characterization /kærɪktəraɪ'zeɪʃn/ n caratterizzazione f

characterize /'kærɪktəraɪz/ vt caratterizzare

character reference n referenze fpl (relative al carattere)

charade /ʃə'rɑːd/ n farsa f; ~s sciarada fsg

charcoal /'tʃɑːkəʊl/ n carbonella f

ⅆ **charge** /tʃɑːdʒ/ ① n (cost) prezzo m; Electr,
Mil carica f; Jur accusa f; **free of** ~ gratuito;
be in ~ essere responsabile (of di); **take**
~ assumersi la responsabilità; **take** ~ **of**
occuparsi di
② vt far pagare ‹fee›; far pagare a ‹person›;
Electr, Mil caricare; Jur accusare (**with** di);
~ **somebody for something** far pagare
qualcosa a qualcuno; **what do you** ~?
quanto prende?; ~ **it to my account** lo
addebiti sul mio conto
③ vi (attack) caricare

charge account n (in store) apertura m
di credito presso un negozio

charge card n (credit card) carta f di
addebito; (store card) carta f di credito [di un
negozio]

charged /tʃɑːdʒd/ adj Phys carico;
emotionally ~ ‹atmosphere› carico di
emozione

chargé d'affaires /ʃɑːʒeɪdæ'feə(r)/ n
incaricato m d'affari

charge hand n caposquadra mf

charge nurse n caposala mf

char-grilled /-'grɪld/ adj alla brace

chariot /'tʃærɪət/ n cocchio m

charisma /kə'rɪzmə/ n carisma m

charismatic /kærɪz'mætɪk/ adj
carismatico

charitable /'tʃærɪtəbl/ adj caritatevole;
(kind) indulgente

charity /'tʃærəti/ n carità f; (organization)
associazione f di beneficenza; **concert given**
for ~ concerto m di beneficenza; **live on** ~
vivere di elemosina

charity box n (in church) cassetta f delle
offerte

charity shop n negozio (m) dell'usato a
scopo di beneficenza

charity work n lavoro m volontario (per
beneficenza)

charlady /'tʃɑːleɪdɪ/ n Br donna f delle
pulizie

charlatan /'ʃɑːlətən/ n ciarlatano, -a mf

charm /tʃɑːm/ ① n fascino m; (object)
ciondolo m
② vt affascinare

charmer /'tʃɑːmə(r)/ n **he's a real** ~ è un
vero seduttore

charming /'tʃɑːmɪŋ/ adj affascinante

charmingly /'tʃɑːmɪŋlɪ/ adv in modo
affascinante

charred /tʃɑːd/ adj carbonizzato

chart /tʃɑːt/ n carta f nautica; (table) tabella
f

charter /'tʃɑːtə(r)/ ① n ~ **[flight]** [volo m]
charter m inv
② vt noleggiare

chartered accountant n
commercialista mf

chartered flight n Br volo m charter inv

chartered surveyor n Br perito m edile

charter plane n Br charter m inv

charwoman /'tʃɑːwʊmən/ n donna f delle
pulizie

chase /tʃeɪs/ ① n inseguimento m; **give** ~
mettersi all'inseguimento
② vt inseguire

■ **chase away, chase off** vt cacciare via

■ **chase up** vt fam cercare

chaser /'tʃeɪsə(r)/ n fam (drink) liquore (m)
bevuto dopo la birra

chasm /'kæz(ə)m/ n abisso m

chassis /'ʃæsɪ/ n (pl **chassis** /'ʃæsɪz/)
telaio m

chaste /tʃeɪst/ adj casto

chasten /'tʃeɪs(ə)n/ vt castigare; **they**
looked suitably ~**ed** avevano l'aria
mortificata

chastise /tʃæ'staɪz/ vt castigare

chastity /'tʃæstəti/ n castità f

ⅆ indicates a very frequent word

chat /tʃæt/ [1] *n* chiacchierata *f*; **have a ~ with** fare quattro chiacchiere con; Comput chat *f inv*
[2] *vi* (*pt/pp* **chatted**) chiacchierare; Comput chattare
■ **chat up** *vt* abbordare

chatline *n* Teleph chat line *f inv*

chatroom *n* Comput chat room *f inv*

chat show *n* talk show *m inv*

chatshow host *n* presentatore, -trice *mf* di talk show

chattel /'tʃæt(ə)l/ *n* Jur **goods and ~s** beni *mpl* mobili

chatter /'tʃætə(r)/ [1] *n* chiacchiere *fpl*
[2] *vi* chiacchierare; ‹teeth› battere

chatterbox /'tʃætəbɒks/ *n* fam chiacchierone, -a *mf*

chatty /'tʃætɪ/ *adj* (**-ier**, **-iest**) chiacchierone; ‹style› familiare

chauffeur /'ʃəʊfə(r)/ *n* autista *mf*

chauvinism /'ʃəʊvɪnɪzm/ *n* sciovinismo *m*

chauvinist /'ʃəʊvɪnɪst/ *n* sciovinista *mf*; **male ~** fam maschilista *m*

⚡ **cheap** /tʃiːp/ [1] *adj* a buon mercato; ‹rate› economico; (vulgar) grossolano; (of poor quality) scadente
[2] *adv* a buon mercato

cheapen /'tʃiːp(ə)n/ *vt* **~ oneself** screditarsi

cheaply /'tʃiːplɪ/ *adv* a buon mercato

cheap rate *adj & adv* Teleph a tariffa ridotta

cheat /tʃiːt/ [1] *n* imbroglione, -a *mf*; (at cards) baro *m*
[2] *vt* imbrogliare; **~ somebody out of something** sottrarre qualcosa a qualcuno con l'inganno
[3] *vi* imbrogliare; (at cards) barare
■ **cheat on** *vt* fam tradire ‹wife›

Chechnya /ˌtʃetʃˈniːə/ *n* Cecenia *f*

check¹ /tʃek/ [1] *adj* ‹pattern› a quadri
[2] *n* disegno *m* a quadri

⚡ **check²** [1] *n* verifica *f*; (of tickets) controllo *m*; (in chess) scacco *m*; Am (bill) conto *m*; Am (cheque) assegno *m*; Am (tick) segnetto *m*; **keep a ~ on** controllare; **keep in ~** tenere sotto controllo
[2] *vt* verificare; controllare ‹tickets›; (restrain) contenere; (stop) bloccare
[3] *vi* controllare; **~ on something** controllare qualcosa
■ **check in** [1] *vi* registrarsi all'arrivo (*in albergo*); Aeron fare il check-in
[2] *vt* registrarsi all'arrivo (*in albergo*)
■ **check off** *vt* spuntare ‹item on list›
■ **check out** [1] *vi* (of hotel) saldare il conto
[2] *vt* fam (investigate) controllare
■ **check up** *vi* accertarsi
■ **check up on** *vt* prendere informazioni su

checkbook *n* Am libretto *m* d'assegni

checked /tʃekt/ *adj* a quadri

checkered /'tʃekəd/ *adj* Am ‹cloth, pattern› a quadretti; ‹career› con alti e bassi

checkers /'tʃekəz/ *n* Am dama *f*

check-in *n* accettazione *f*, check-in *m inv*

check-in desk *n* banco *m* dell'accettazione, banco *m* del check-in

checking account /'tʃekɪŋ/ *n* Am conto *m* corrente

check-in time *n* check-in *m inv*

checklist *n* lista *f* di controllo

check mark *n* Am segnetto *m*

checkmate *int* scacco matto

checkout *n* (in supermarket) cassa *f*

checkout assistant, checkout operator *n* Br cassiere, -a *mf*

checkpoint *n* posto *m* di blocco

checkroom *n* Am deposito *m* bagagli

check-up *n* Med visita *f* di controllo, check-up *m inv*

cheddar /'tʃedə(r)/ *n* formaggio (*m*) semi-stagionato

cheek /tʃiːk/ *n* guancia *f*, (impudence) sfacciataggine *f*

cheekbone /'tʃiːkbəʊn/ *n* zigomo *m*

cheekily /'tʃiːkɪlɪ/ *adv* sfacciatamente

cheeky /'tʃiːkɪ/ *adj* sfacciato

cheep /tʃiːp/ *vi* pigolare

cheer /tʃɪə(r)/ [1] *n* evviva *m inv*; **three ~s** tre urrà; **~s!** salute!; (goodbye) arrivederci; (thanks) grazie
[2] *vt/i* acclamare
■ **cheer up** [1] *vt* tirare su [di morale]
[2] *vi* tirarsi su [di morale]; **~ up!** su con la vita!

cheerful /'tʃɪəfʊl/ *adj* allegro

cheerfully /'tʃɪəfʊlɪ/ *adv* allegramente; **I could ~ strangle him!** lo strangolerei volentieri!

cheerfulness /'tʃɪəfʊlnɪs/ *n* allegria *f*

cheerily /'tʃɪərɪlɪ/ *adv* allegramente

cheering /'tʃɪərɪŋ/ *n* acclamazione *f*

cheerio /tʃɪərɪˈəʊ/ *int* fam arrivederci

cheerleader /'tʃɪəliːdə(r)/ *n* leader *mf* dei tifosi

cheerless /'tʃɪəlɪs/ *adj* triste, tetro

cheery /'tʃɪərɪ/ *adj* allegro

cheese /tʃiːz/ *n* formaggio *m*
■ **cheese off**: *vt* fam be **~d off with one's job** essere stufo del proprio lavoro; **I'm really ~d off about it** ne ho le scatole piene

cheeseboard *n* (object) vassoio *m* dei formaggi; (selection) piatto *m* di formaggi

cheeseburger *n* cheeseburger *m inv*

cheesecake *n* dolce *m* al formaggio

cheesecloth *n* mussola *f*, tela *f* indiana

cheese counter *n* banco *m* dei formaggi

cheesy /'tʃiːzɪ/ *adj* ‹smell› di formaggio; ‹grin› smagliante

cheetah /'tʃiːtə/ n ghepardo m
chef /ʃef/ **1** n cuoco, -a mf, chef m inv
2 vi (pt/pp **cheffed**) fam fare lo chef
chemical /'kemɪkl/ **1** adj chimico
2 n prodotto m chimico
chemically /'kemɪklɪ/ adv chimicamente
chemise /ʃə'miːz/ n (undergarment)
sottoveste f inv; (dress) chemisier m inv
chemist /'kemɪst/ n (pharmacist) farmacista
mf; (scientist) chimico, -a mf
chemistry /'kemɪstrɪ/ n chimica f
chemist's [shop] n farmacia f
chemotherapy /kiːməʊ'θerəpɪ/ n
chemioterapia f
cheque /tʃek/ n assegno m
chequebook /'tʃekbʊk/ n libretto m degli
assegni
cheque card n carta f assegni
chequer /'tʃekə(r)/ n (square) scacco m;
(pattern) motivo m a scacchi; (in game) pedina
f
chequered /'tʃekəd/ adj (patterned) a
scacchi; fig ‹career, history› movimentato
chequers /'tʃekəz/ n dama f
cherish /'tʃerɪʃ/ vt curare teneramente;
(love) avere caro; nutrire ‹hope›
cherry /'tʃerɪ/ n ciliegia f; (tree) ciliegio m
cherry brandy n cherry-brandy m inv
cherry-pick vt scegliere accuratamente
cherry tree n ciliegio m
cherub /'tʃerəb/ n cherubino m
chervil /'tʃɜːvɪl/ n cerfoglio m
chess /tʃes/ n scacchi mpl
chessboard n scacchiera f
chessman n pezzo m degli scacchi
chessplayer n scacchista mf
chess set n scacchi mpl
❖ **chest** /tʃest/ n petto m; (box) cassapanca f;
get something off one's ~ fig levarsi un peso
[dallo stomaco]
chest freezer n freezer m inv
orizzontale, congelatore m orizzontale
chestnut /'tʃesnʌt/ n castagna f; (tree)
castagno m
chest of drawers n cassettone m, comò
m inv
chesty /'tʃestɪ/ adj ‹person› che soffre di
bronchite; ‹cough› bronchitico
chew /tʃuː/ vt masticare
■ **chew over** vt fam (think about carefully)
rimuginare su
chewing gum /'tʃuːɪŋ/ n gomma f da
masticare
chewy /'tʃuːɪ/ adj ‹meat› legnoso; ‹toffee›
gommoso
chic /ʃiːk/ adj chic inv
chick /tʃɪk/ n pulcino m; fam (girl) ragazza f

ꝰ indicates a very frequent word

chicken /'tʃɪkn/ **1** n pollo m
2 attrib ‹soup, casserole› di pollo
3 adj fam fifone
■ **chicken out**: vi fam he ~ed out gli è
venuta fifa
chicken breast n petto m di pollo
chicken curry n pollo m al curry
chicken feed n mangime m per i polli;
fam (paltry sum) miseria f
chicken livers npl fegatini mpl di pollo
chicken noodle soup n vermicelli mpl
in brodo di pollo
chickenpox n varicella f
chicken wire n rete f metallica (a maglia
esagonale)
chick flick n fam film (m inv) mirato ad un
pubblico femminile
chick lit n fam romanzi (mpl) mirati ad un
pubblico femminile
chickpea /'tʃɪkpiː/ n cece m
chicory /'tʃɪkərɪ/ n cicoria f
❖ **chief** /tʃiːf/ **1** adj principale
2 n capo m
chief executive n direttore, -trice mf
generale
chief executive officer n direttore,
-trice mf generale
chief inspector n Br (of police) ispettore
m capo
chiefly /'tʃiːflɪ/ adv principalmente
chief of police n capo m della polizia
Chief of Staff n Mil capo m di stato
maggiore; (of the White House) segretario m
generale
chief superintendent n Br (of police)
commissario m capo
chiffon /'ʃɪfɒn/ **1** n chiffon m
2 adj ‹dress, scarf› di chiffon
chilblain /'tʃɪlbleɪn/ n gelone m
❖ **child** /tʃaɪld/ n (pl ~ren) bambino, -a mf;
(son/daughter) figlio, -a mf
child abuse n violenza f sui minori;
(sexual) violenza f sessuale sui minori
childbearing n gravidanza f; of ~ age in
età feconda
child benefit n Br assegni mpl familiari
childbirth n parto m
childcare n (bringing up children) educazione
f dei bambini; (nurseries etc) strutture fpl di
assistenza ai bambini
childhood /'tʃaɪldhʊd/ n infanzia f
childish /'tʃaɪldɪʃ/ adj infantile
childishness /'tʃaɪldɪʃnɪs/ n puerilità f
childless /'tʃaɪldlɪs/ adj senza figli
childlike /'tʃaɪldlaɪk/ adj ingenuo
child-minder n baby-sitter mf inv
child molester n molestatore, -trice mf
di bambini
child pornography n pedopornografia f
child prodigy n bambino prodigio

child-proof *adj* ‹container› a prova
di bambino; ~ **lock** sicura *f* a prova di
bambino

children /ˈtʃɪldrən/ *npl* ▶ CHILD

children's home *n* istituto *m* per
l'infanzia

child seat *n* seggiolino *m* per bambini

Chile /ˈtʃɪli/ *n* Cile *m*

Chilean /ˈtʃɪliən/ *adj & n* cileno, -a *mf*

chill /tʃɪl/ ⟦1⟧ *n* freddo *m*; (illness)
infreddatura *f*
⟦2⟧ *vt* raffreddare
■ **chill out** *vi* (relax) rilassarsi

chilli /ˈtʃɪli/ *n* (*pl* **-es**) ~ **[pepper]**
peperoncino *m*

chilly /ˈtʃɪli/ *adj* freddo

chime /tʃaɪm/ *vi* suonare

chimera /kɪˈmɪərə/ *n* (beast, idea) chimera *f*

chimney /ˈtʃɪmnɪ/ *n* camino *m*

chimneybreast *n* bocca *f* del camino

chimney-pot *n* comignolo *m*

chimney-sweep *n* spazzacamino *m*

chimp /tʃɪmp/ *n* fam scimpanzé *m*

chimpanzee /ˈtʃɪmpænˈziː/ *n* scimpanzé
m inv

chin /tʃɪn/ *n* mento *m*

China /ˈtʃaɪnə/ *n* Cina *f*

china *n* porcellana *f*

China Sea *n* Mar *m* Cinese

China tea *n* tè *m inv* cinese

Chinatown *n* quartiere *m* cinese

ᵒᶠ **Chinese** /tʃaɪˈniːz/ *adj & n* cinese *mf*;
(language) cinese *m*; **the** ~ *pl* i cinesi

Chinese lantern *n* lanterna *f* cinese

chink¹ /tʃɪŋk/ *n* (slit) fessura *f*

chink² ⟦1⟧ *n* (noise) tintinnio *m*
⟦2⟧ *vi* tintinnare

chinos /ˈtʃiːnəʊz/ *npl* pantaloni *mpl* cachi
di cotone

chintz /tʃɪnts/ *n* chintz *m inv*

chip /tʃɪp/ ⟦1⟧ *n* (fragment) scheggia *f*; (in
china, paintwork) scheggiatura *f*; Comput chip
m inv; (in gambling) fiche *f inv*; ~**s** *pl* Br Culin
patatine *fpl* fritte; Am Culin patatine *fpl*; **have
a** ~ **on one's shoulder** avere un complesso
di inferiorità
⟦2⟧ *vt* (*pt/pp* **chipped**) (damage) scheggiare
■ **chip in** fam *vi* intromettersi; (with money)
contribuire

chip and PIN *n sistema di pagamento
con carta di credito in cui il possessore della
carta deve digitare il proprio PIN invece che
apporre una firma*

chipboard /ˈtʃɪpbɔːd/ *n* truciolato *m*

chipmunk /ˈtʃɪpmʌŋk/ *n* tamia *m inv*

chip pan *n* friggitrice *f*

chipped /tʃɪpt/ *adj* (damaged) scheggiato

chippings /ˈtʃɪpɪŋz/ *npl* (on road) breccia *f*;
'loose ~' 'attenzione: breccia'

chippy /ˈtʃɪpɪ/ *n* Br fam (chip shop) negozio *m*
di fish and chips

chip shop *n* Br negozio *m* di fish and chips

chiropodist /kɪˈrɒpədɪst/ *n* podiatra *mf
inv*

chiropody /kɪˈrɒpədɪ/ *n* podiatria *f*

chiropractor /ˈkaɪərəʊpræktə(r)/ *n*
chiropratico, -a *mf*

chirp /tʃɜːp/ *vi* cinguettare; ‹cricket› fare
cri cri

chirpy /ˈtʃɜːpɪ/ *adj* fam pimpante

chisel /ˈtʃɪzl/ ⟦1⟧ *n* scalpello *m*
⟦2⟧ *vt* (*pt/pp* **chiselled**) scalpellare

chit /tʃɪt/ *n* bigliettino *m*

chitchat /ˈtʃɪ(t)tʃæt/ *n* fam chiacchiere
fpl; **spend one's time in idle** ~ fam perdere
tempo in chiacchiere

chivalrous /ˈʃɪvlrəs/ *adj* cavalleresco

chivalrously /ˈʃɪvlrəslɪ/ *adv* con cavalleria

chivalry /ˈʃɪvlrɪ/ *n* cavalleria *f*

chives /tʃaɪvz/ *npl* erba *f* cipollina

chlorine /ˈklɔːriːn/ *n* cloro *m*

chlorofluorocarbon
/klɔːrəʊflʊərəʊˈkɑːb(ə)n/ *n*
clorofluorocarburo *m*

chloroform /ˈklɒrəfɔːm/ *n* cloroformio *m*

chlorophyll /ˈklɒrəfɪl/ *n* clorofilla *f*

choc ice *n* Br gelato *m* ricoperto di
cioccolato

chock /tʃɒk/ *n* zeppa *f*

chock-a-block /tʃɒkəˈblɒk/, **chock-
full** /tʃɒkˈfʊl/ *adj* pieno zeppo

chocolate /ˈtʃɒkələt/ *n* cioccolato *m*;
(drink) cioccolata *f*; **a** ~ un cioccolatino

ᶜ **choice** /tʃɔɪs/ ⟦1⟧ *n* scelta *f*
⟦2⟧ *adj* scelto

choir /ˈkwaɪə(r)/ *n* coro *m*

choirboy /ˈkwaɪəbɔɪ/ *n* corista *m*

choirgirl /ˈkwaɪəgɜːl/ *n* corista *f*

choke /tʃəʊk/ ⟦1⟧ *n* Auto aria *f*
⟦2⟧ *vt/i* soffocare; **I** ~**d on a fishbone** mi è
rimasta in gola una lisca
■ **choke back** *vt* soffocare ‹tears, sob›

choker /ˈtʃəʊkə(r)/ *n* girocollo *m*

cholera /ˈkɒlərə/ *n* colera *m*

cholesterol /kəˈlestərɒl/ *n* colesterolo *m*

chomp /tʃɒmp/
■ **chomp on** *vt* fam masticare rumorosamente

ᶜ **choose** /tʃuːz/ *vt/i* (*pt* **chose**, *pp*
chosen) scegliere; ~ **to do something**
scegliere di fare qualcosa; **as you** ~ come
vuoi

choos[e]y /ˈtʃuːzɪ/ *adj* fam difficile

chop /tʃɒp/ ⟦1⟧ *n* (blow) colpo *m* (*d'ascia*);
Culin costata *f*; **get the** ~ fam ‹employee›
essere licenziato; ‹project› essere bocciato
⟦2⟧ *vt* (*pt/pp* **chopped**) tagliare
■ **chop down** *vt* abbattere ‹tree›
■ **chop off** *vt* spaccare

C

chopper /'tʃɒpə(r)/ n accetta f; fam elicottero m

chopping block n ceppo m; **put one's head on the ~** fig esporsi a rischi

chopping board n tagliere m

chopping knife n coltello m

choppy /'tʃɒpɪ/ adj increspato

chopsticks /'tʃɒpstɪks/ npl bastoncini mpl cinesi

choral /'kɔːrəl/ adj corale; **~ society** coro m

chord /kɔːd/ n Mus corda f

chore /tʃɔː(r)/ n corvè f inv; **[household]** **~s** faccende fpl domestiche

choreograph /'kɒrɪəɡrɑːf, US -ɡræf/ vt coreografare

choreographer /kɒrɪ'ɒɡrəfə(r)/ n coreografo, -a mf

choreography /kɒrɪ'ɒɡrəfɪ/ n coreografia f

chorister /'kɒrɪstə(r)/ n corista mf

chortle /'tʃɔːtl/ vi ridacchiare

chorus /'kɔːrəs/ n coro m; (of song) ritornello m

chorus girl n ballerina f di varietà

chose, chosen /tʃəʊz, 'tʃəʊzn/ ▶ CHOOSE

chowder /'tʃaʊdə(r)/ n zuppa m di pesce

chow mein /tʃaʊ'meɪn/ n piatto (m) cinese di spaghettini fritti con gamberetti, ecc. e verdure

Christ /kraɪst/ n Cristo m; **~ Almighty!** fam porca miseria!

christen /'krɪs(ə)n/ vt battezzare

christening /'krɪsnɪŋ/ n battesimo m

✓ **Christian** /'krɪstʃən/ adj & n cristiano, -a mf

Christianity /krɪstɪ'ænətɪ/ n cristianesimo m

Christian name n nome m di battesimo

✓ **Christmas** /'krɪsməs/ 1 n Natale m 2 attrib di Natale

Christmas box n Br mancia f natalizia

Christmas card n biglietto m d'auguri di Natale

Christmas carol n canto m natalizio, canto m di Natale

Christmas cracker n tubo (m) di cartone colorato contente una sorpresa

Christmas Day n il giorno di Natale

Christmas Eve n la vigilia di Natale

Christmas present n regalo m di Natale

Christmas stocking n calza f (per i doni di Babbo Natale)

Christmas tree n albero m di Natale

chrome /krəʊm/ **chromium** /'krəʊmɪəm/ n cromo m

chromium-plated /-'pleɪtɪd/ adj cromato

chromosome /'krəʊməsəʊm/ n cromosoma m

chronic /'krɒnɪk/ adj cronico

chronicle /'krɒnɪkl/ n cronaca f

chronological /krɒnə'lɒdʒɪkl/ adj cronologico

chronologically /krɒnə'lɒdʒɪklɪ/ adv ‹ordered› in ordine cronologico

chrysalis /'krɪsəlɪs/ n crisalide f

chrysanthemum /krɪ'sænθəməm/ n crisantemo m

chubby /'tʃʌbɪ/ adj (**-ier, -iest**) paffuto

chuck /tʃʌk/ vt fam buttare

■ **chuck in** vt fam mollare ‹job, boyfriend›

■ **chuck out** vt fam buttare via ‹object›; buttare fuori ‹person›

■ **chuck up** vt fam vomitare

chuckle /'tʃʌk(ə)l/ vi ridacchiare

chuffed /tʃʌft/ adj fam felice come una Pasqua

chug /tʃʌɡ/ vi **the train ~ged into/out of the station** il treno è entrato nella/uscito dalla stazione sbuffando

chum /tʃʌm/ n fam amico, -a mf

chummy /'tʃʌmɪ/ adj fam **be ~ with** essere amico di

chump /tʃʌmp/ n fam zuccone, -a mf; Culin braciola f

chunk /tʃʌŋk/ n grosso pezzo m

chunky /'tʃʌŋkɪ/ adj ‹sweater› di lana grossa; ‹jewellery› massiccio; fam ‹person› tarchiato

Chunnel /'tʃʌnl/ n Br fam tunnel m inv sotto la Manica

✓ **church** /tʃɜːtʃ/ n chiesa f

churchgoer n praticante mf

church hall n sala f parrocchiale

churchyard /'tʃɜːtʃjɑːd/ n cimitero m

churlish /'tʃɜːlɪʃ/ adj sgarbato

churn /tʃɜːn/ 1 n zangola f; (for milk) bidone m 2 vt fare ‹butter›; far rivoltare ‹stomach›

■ **churn out** vt sfornare ‹novels, products›

■ **churn up** vt agitare ‹water›

chute /ʃuːt/ n scivolo m; (for rubbish) canale m di scarico

chutney /'tʃʌtnɪ/ n salsa (f) piccante a base di frutti e spezie

CIA n abbr Am (**Central Intelligence Agency**) CIA f

cicada /sɪ'kɑːdə, US -'keɪdə/ n cicala f

CID abbr (**Criminal Investigation Department**) dipartimento (m) di investigazione criminale

cider /'saɪdə(r)/ n sidro m

cigar /sɪ'ɡɑː(r)/ n sigaro m

cigarette /sɪɡə'ret/ n sigaretta f

cigarette butt, cigarette end n cicca f, mozzicone m di sigaretta

cigarette lighter n accendino m

✓ indicates a very frequent word

cinch /sɪntʃ/ n fam it's a ~ è un gioco da ragazzi

cinder /'sɪndə(r)/ n (glowing) brace f; **burn something to a** ~ carbonizzare qualcosa

Cinderella /sɪndə'relə/ n Cenerentola f

cinder track n pista f di cenere

cine-camera /'sɪnɪ-/ n cinepresa f

cine-film n filmino m a passo ridotto

cinema /'sɪnɪmə/ n cinema m inv

cinema complex n cinema m inv multisale

cinemagoer /'sɪnɪməgəʊə(r)/ n (spectator) spettatore, -trice mf; (regular) cinefilo, -a mf

cinematography /sɪnəmə'tɒgrəfɪ/ n cinematografia f

cinnamon /'sɪnəmən/ n cannella f

cipher /'saɪfə(r)/ n (code) cifre fpl; fig nullità f inv

circa /'sɜ:kə/ prep circa

⚬ **circle** /'sɜ:kl/ **1** n cerchio m; Theat galleria f; **in a** ~ in cerchio
2 vt girare intorno a; cerchiare ‹mistake›
3 vi descrivere dei cerchi

circuit /'sɜ:kɪt/ n circuito m; (lap) giro m

circuit board n circuito m stampato

circuit breaker n salvavita m

circuitous /sə'kju:ɪtəs/ adj ~ **route** percorso m lungo e indiretto

circular /'sɜ:kjʊlə(r)/ adj & n circolare f; ~ **letter** n circolare f

circular saw n sega f circolare

circulate /'sɜ:kjʊleɪt/ **1** vt far circolare
2 vi circolare

circulation /sɜ:kjʊ'leɪʃn/ n circolazione f; (of newspaper) tiratura f

circulatory /sɜ:kjʊ'leɪtərɪ/ adj Med circolatorio

circumcise /'sɜ:kəmsaɪz/ vt circoncidere

circumcision /sɜ:kəm'sɪʒn/ n circoncisione f

circumference /ʃə'kʌmfərəns/ n circonferenza f

circumflex /'sɜ:kəmfleks/ n accento m circonflesso

circumnavigate /sɜ:kəm'nævɪgeɪt/ vt doppiare ‹cape›; circumnavigare ‹world›

circumnavigation /sɜ:kəmnævɪ'geɪʃn/ n circumnavigazione f

circumspect /'sɜ:kəmspekt/ adj circospetto

circumspectly /'sɜ:kəmspektlɪ/ adv in modo circospetto

⚬ **circumstance** /'sɜ:kəmstəns/ n circostanza f; ~**s** pl (financial) condizioni fpl finanziarie

circumstantial /sɜ:kəm'stænʃl/ adj Jur ‹evidence› indiziario; (detailed) circostanziato

circus /'sɜ:kəs/ n circo m

cirrhosis /sɪ'rəʊsɪs/ n cirrosi f inv

CIS abbr (**Commonwealth of Independent States**) CSI f

cistern /'sɪstən/ n (tank) cisterna f; (of WC) serbatoio m

citadel /'sɪtədel/ n cittadella f

cite /saɪt/ vt citare

⚬ **citizen** /'sɪtɪzn/ n cittadino, -a mf; (of town) abitante mf

Citizens' Advice Bureau n ufficio (m) di consulenza legale gratuita per i cittadini

citizen's arrest n arresto m effettuato da un privato cittadino

citizens' band n Radio banda f cittadina

citizenship /'sɪtɪznʃɪp/ n cittadinanza f

citric acid /sɪtrɪk'æsɪd/ acido m citrico

citrus /'sɪtrəs/ n ~ [**fruit**] agrume m

⚬ **city** /'sɪtɪ/ n città f inv; **the C**~ la City [di Londra]

city centre n Br centro m [della città]

city slicker n fam cittadino m sofisticato

civic /'sɪvɪk/ **1** adj civico
2 npl ~**s** npl educazione f sg civica

civic centre n centro m municipale

⚬ **civil** /'ʃɪvl/ adj civile

civil engineer n ingegnere m civile

civil engineering n ingegneria f civile

civilian /sɪ'vɪljən/ **1** adj civile; **in** ~ **clothes** in borghese
2 n civile mf

civility /sɪ'vɪlətɪ/ n cortesia f

civilization /sɪvɪlaɪ'zeɪʃn/ n civiltà f inv

civilize /'sɪvɪlaɪz/ vt civilizzare

civilized /'sɪvɪlaɪzd/ adj ‹country› civilizzato; ‹person, behaviour› civile; **become** ~ civilizzarsi

civil law n diritto m civile

civil liability n Jur responsabilità f inv civile

civil liberty n libertà f inv civile

civilly /'sɪvɪlɪ/ adv civilmente

civil rights **1** npl diritti mpl civili
2 attrib ‹march, activist› per i diritti civili

civil servant n impiegato, -a mf statale

Civil Service n pubblica amministrazione f

civil war n guerra f civile

civil wedding n matrimonio m civile

civvies /'sɪvɪz/ npl fam **in** ~ in borghese

CJD n abbr (**Creutzfeldt-Jakob disease**) morbo m di Creutzfeldt Jakob

cl abbr (**centilitre(s)**) cl

clad /klæd/ adj vestito (**in** di)

cladding /'klædɪŋ/ n rivestimento m

⚬ **claim** /kleɪm/ **1** n richiesta f; (right) diritto m; (assertion) dichiarazione f; **lay** ~ **to something** rivendicare qualcosa
2 vt richiedere; reclamare ‹lost property›; rivendicare ‹ownership›; ~ **that** sostenere che
■ **claim back** vt reclamare ‹money›

claimant /'kleɪmənt/ n richiedente mf; (to throne) pretendente mf

claim form n modulo m di richiesta

clairvoyant /kleə'vɔɪənt/ n chiaroveggente mf

clam /klæm/ n Culin vongola f
■ **clam up** vi zittirsi

clamber /'klæmbə(r)/ vi arrampicarsi

clammy /'klæmɪ/ adj (-ier, -iest) appiccicaticcio

clamour /'klæmə(r)/ 1 n (noise) clamore m; (protest) rimostranza f
2 vi ~ **for** chiedere a gran voce

clamp /klæmp/ 1 n morsa f
2 vt ammorsare; Auto mettere i ceppi bloccaruote a
■ **clamp down** vi fam essere duro
■ **clamp down on** vt reprimere

clampdown n fig giro m di vite

clan /klæn/ n clan m inv

clandestine /klæn'destɪn/ adj clandestino

clang /klæŋ/ n suono m metallico

clanger /'klæŋə(r)/ n fam gaffe f inv

clank /klæŋk/ 1 n rumore m metallico
2 vi fare un rumore metallico

clannish /'klænɪʃ/ adj pej ‹family, profession› chiuso

clap /klæp/ 1 n give somebody a ~ applaudire qualcuno; ~ **of thunder** tuono m
2 vt/i (pt/pp **clapped**) applaudire; ~ **one's hands** applaudire

clapboard /'klæpbɔːd/ 1 n Am rivestimento m di legno
2 attrib Am rivestito di legno

clapped out /klæpt/ adj fam (past it) sfinito; (exhausted) stanco morto; ‹car, machine› scassato

clapping /'klæpɪŋ/ n applausi mpl

claptrap /'klæptræp/ n fam sciocchezze fpl

claret /'klærət/ n claret m inv

clarification /klærɪfɪ'keɪʃn/ n chiarimento m

clarify /'klærɪfaɪ/ vt/i (pt/pp **-ied**) chiarire

clarinet /klærɪ'net/ n clarinetto m

clarinettist /klærɪ'netɪst/ n clarinettista mf

clarity /'klærətɪ/ n chiarezza f

clash /klæʃ/ 1 n scontro m; (noise) fragore m
2 vi scontrarsi; ‹colours› stonare; ‹events› coincidere

clasp /klɑːsp/ 1 n chiusura f
2 vt agganciare; (hold) stringere

ơ **class** /klɑːs/ 1 n classe f; (lesson) corso m
2 vt classificare

class-conscious adj classista

class-consciousness n classismo m

classic /'klæsɪk/ 1 adj classico
2 n classico m; ~**s** pl Univ lettere fpl classiche

classical /'klæsɪk(ə)l/ adj classico

classification /klæsɪfɪ'keɪʃn/ n classificazione f

classified /'klæsɪfaɪd/ adj (secret) riservato

classified ad /klæsɪfaɪd'æd/ n annuncio m

classified section n pagina f degli annunci

classify /'klæsɪfaɪ/ vt (pt/pp **-led**) classificare

classmate n compagno, -a mf di classe

classroom n aula f

class system n sistema m classista

classy /'klɑːsɪ/ adj (-ier, -iest) fam d'alta classe

clatter /'klætə(r)/ 1 n fracasso m
2 vi far fracasso

clause /klɔːz/ n clausola f; Gram preposizione f

claustrophobia /klɒstrə'fəʊbɪə/ n claustrofobia f

claustrophobic /klɒstrə'fəʊbɪk/ adj claustrofobico

clavichord /klævɪkɔːd/ n clavicordo m

clavicle /'klævɪkl/ n clavicola f

claw /klɔː/ 1 n artiglio m; (of crab, lobster & Techn) tenaglia f
2 vt ‹cat› graffiare

clay /kleɪ/ n argilla f

clayey /'kleɪɪ/ adj ‹soil› argilloso

clay pigeon shooting n tiro m al piattello

ơ **clean** /kliːn/ 1 adj pulito, lindo
2 adv completamente
3 vt pulire ‹shoes, windows›; ~ **one's teeth** lavarsi i denti; **have a coat** ~**ed** portare un cappotto in lavanderia
■ **clean out** vt ripulire ‹room›; **be** ~**ed out** fig (have no money) essere senza un soldo
■ **clean up** 1 vt pulire
2 vi (far) pulizia

clean-cut adj ‹image, person› rispettabile

cleaner /'kliːnə(r)/ n uomo m donna f delle pulizie; (substance) detersivo m; **[dry]** ~**'s** lavanderia f, tintoria f

cleaning /'kliːnɪŋ/ n pulizia f; **do the** ~ fare le pulizie

cleaning lady n donna f delle pulizie

cleaning product n detergente m

cleanliness /'klenlɪnɪs/ n pulizia f

clean-living /-'lɪvɪŋ/ 1 n vita f integra
2 adj ‹person› integro

cleanse /klenz/ vt pulire

cleanser /'klenzə(r)/ n detergente m

clean-shaven /-'ʃeɪvən/ adj sbarbato

ơ indicates a very frequent word

clean sheet *n* start with a ∼ fig voltare pagina

cleansing cream /'klenzɪŋ/ *n* latte *m* detergente

✧ **clear** /klɪə(r)/ **1** *adj* chiaro; ‹conscience› pulito; ‹road› libero; ‹profit, advantage, majority› netto; ‹sky› sereno; ‹water› limpido; ‹glass› trasparente; **make something** ∼ mettere qualcosa in chiaro; **have I made myself** ∼**?** mi sono fatto capire?; **I'm not** ∼ **about what I have to do** non mi è ben chiaro quello che devo fare; **five** ∼ **days** cinque giorni buoni; **be in the** ∼ essere a posto **2** *adv* **stand** ∼ **of** allontanarsi da; **keep** ∼ **of** tenersi alla larga da **3** *vt* sgombrare ‹room, street›; sparecchiare ‹table›; (acquit) scagionare; (authorize) autorizzare; scavalcare senza toccare ‹fence, wall›; guadagnare ‹sum of money›; passare ‹Customs›; ∼ **one's throat** schiarirsi la gola **4** *vi* ‹face, sky› rasserenarsi; ‹fog› dissiparsi

■ **clear away** *vt* metter via

■ **clear off** *vi* fam filar via

■ **clear out** **1** *vt* sgombrare **2** *vi* fam filar via

■ **clear up** **1** *vt* (tidy) mettere a posto; chiarire ‹mystery› **2** *vi* ‹weather› schiarirsi

clearance /'klɪərəns/ *n* (space) spazio *m* libero; (authorization) autorizzazione *f*; Customs sdoganamento *m*

clearance sale *n* liquidazione *f*

clear-cut *adj* ‹plan, division› ben definito; ‹problem, rule› chiaro; ‹difference, outline› netto; **the matter is not so** ∼ la faccenda non è così semplice

clear-headed /-'hedɪd/ *adj* lucido

clearing /'klɪərɪŋ/ *n* radura *f*

✧ **clearly** /'klɪəlɪ/ *adv* chiaramente

clear-out /'klɪəraʊt/ *n* ripulita *f*

clear-sighted /-'saɪtɪd/ *adj* perspicace

clearway /'klɪəweɪ/ *n* Auto strada *f* con divieto di sosta

cleavage /'kli:vɪdʒ/ *n* (woman's) décolleté *m inv*

cleave /kli:v/ *vt* spaccare

cleaver /'kli:və(r)/ *n* mannaia *f*

clef /klef/ *n* Mus chiave *f*

cleft /kleft/ *n* fenditura *f*

clemency /'klemənsɪ/ *n* clemenza *f*

clement /'klemənt/ *adj* clemente

clench /klentʃ/ *vt* serrare

clergy /'klɜːdʒɪ/ *npl* clero *m*

clergyman /'klɜːdʒɪmən/ *n* ecclesiastico *m*

cleric /'klerɪk/ *n* ecclesiastico *m*

clerical /'klerɪkl/ *adj* impiegatizio; Relig clericale

clerical assistant *n* impiegato, -a *mf*

clerk /klɑːk/ Am /klɜːk/ *n* impiegato, -a *mf*; Am (shop assistant) commesso, -a *mf*

clever /'klevə(r)/ *adj* intelligente; (skilful) abile

cleverly /'klevəlɪ/ *adv* intelligentemente; (skilfully) abilmente

cliché /'kli:ʃeɪ/ *n* cliché *m inv*

clichéd /'kli:ʃeɪd/ *adj* ‹idea, technique› convenzionale; ‹art, music› stereotipato; ∼ **expression** frase *f* fatta

click /klɪk/ **1** *vi* scattare; Comput (with mouse) cliccare **2** *n* Comput (with mouse) clic *m inv*

■ **click on** *vt* Comput cliccare su

✧ **client** /'klaɪənt/ *n* cliente *mf*

clientele /kli:ɒn'tel/ *n* clientela *f*

cliff /klɪf/ *n* scogliera *f*

cliffhanger /'klɪfhæŋə(r)/ *n* **it was a real** ∼ ci ha lasciato in sospeso

climate /'klaɪmət/ *n* clima *f*

climate change *n* cambiamento *m* climatico

climatic /klaɪ'mætɪk/ *adj* climatico

climax /'klaɪmæks/ *n* punto *m* culminante

✧ **climb** /klaɪm/ **1** *n* salita *f* **2** *vt* scalare ‹mountain›; arrampicarsi su ‹ladder, tree› **3** *vi* arrampicarsi; (rise) salire; ‹road› salire

■ **climb down** *vi* scendere; (from ladder, tree) scendere; fig tornare sui propri passi

■ **climb over** *vt* scavalcare ‹fence, wall›

■ **climb up** *vt* salire su ‹hill›

climber /'klaɪmə(r)/ *n* alpinista *mf*; (plant) rampicante *m*

climbing /'klaɪmɪŋ/ *adj* rampicante

climbing boot *n* scarpone *m* da alpinismo

climbing expedition *n* scalata *f*

climbing frame *n* struttura (*f*) su cui possono arrampicarsi i bambini

clinch /klɪntʃ/ **1** *vt* fam concludere ‹deal› **2** *n* (in boxing) clinch *m inv*

clincher /'klɪntʃə(r)/ *n* fam (act, remark) fattore *m* decisivo; (argument) argomento *m* decisivo

cling /klɪŋ/ *vi* (*pt/pp* **clung**) aggrapparsi; (stick) aderire

cling film *n* pellicola *f* trasparente

clingy /'klɪŋɪ/ *adj* ‹dress› attillato; ‹person› appiccicoso

clinic /'klɪnɪk/ *n* ambulatorio *m*

✧ **clinical** /'klɪnɪkl/ *adj* clinico

clinically /'klɪnɪklɪ/ *adv* clinicamente

clink /klɪŋk/ **1** *n* tintinnio *m*; fam (prison) galera *f* **2** *vi* tintinnare

clip¹ /klɪp/ **1** *n* fermaglio *m*; (jewellery) spilla *f* **2** *vt* (*pt/pp* **clipped**) attaccare

clip² **1** *n* (extract) taglio *m* **2** *vt* obliterare ‹ticket›

clipart *n* clip art *f inv*

clipboard *n* fermablocco *m*

clip-clop *n* rumore (*m*) fatto dagli zoccoli dei cavalli

clip frame *n* cornice *f* a giorno

clip-on *adj* ‹bow tie› con la clip

clip-on microphone *n* microfono *m* con la clip

clip-ons *npl* (earrings) orecchini *mpl* con le clip

clippers /'klɪpəz/ *npl* (for hair) rasoio *m*; (for hedge) tosasiepi *m inv*; (for nails) tronchesina *f*

clipping /'klɪpɪŋ/ *n* (from newspaper) ritaglio *m*

clique /kliːk/ *n* cricca *f*

cliquey, cliquish /'kliːkɪ, 'kliːkɪʃ/ *adj* ‹atmosphere› esclusivo; ‹profession, group› chiuso

cloak /kləʊk/ *n* mantello *m*

cloak-and-dagger *adj* ‹film› d'avventura; (surreptitious) clandestino

cloakroom *n* guardaroba *m inv*; (toilet) bagno *m*

cloakroom attendant *n* Br (at toilets) addetto, -a *mf* ai bagni; (in hotel) guardarobiere, -a *mf*

cloakroom ticket *n* scontrino *m* del guardaroba

clobber /'klɒbə(r)/ **1** *n* fam armamentario *m*

2 *vt* fam (hit) colpire; (defeat) stracciare

cloche /klɒʃ/ *n* (in garden) campana *f* di vetro

cloche hat *n* cloche *f inv*

clock /klɒk/ *n* orologio *m*; fam (speedometer) tachimetro *m*

■ **clock in, clock on** *vi* attaccare

■ **clock out, clock off** *vi* staccare

clock face *n* quadrante *m*

clockmaker *n* orologiaio, -a *mf*

clock radio *n* radiosveglia *f*

clock speed *n* Comput velocità *f* di clock

clock tower *n* torre *f* dell'orologio

clock-watch *vi* guardare continuamente l'orologio

clockwise *adj & adv* in senso orario

clockwork **1** *n* meccanismo *m*; **like ∼** fam alla perfezione

2 *attrib* a molla

clod /klɒd/ *n* zolla *f*

clog /klɒg/ **1** *n* zoccolo *m*

2 *vt* (*pt/pp* **clogged**) ∼ [up] intasare ‹drain›; inceppare ‹mechanism›

3 *vi* ‹drain› intasarsi

cloister /'klɔɪstə(r)/ *n* chiostro *m*

clone /kləʊn/ **1** *n* Biol, Comput, fig clone *m*

2 *vt* clonare

cloning /'kləʊnɪŋ/ *n* clonazione *f*

⚹ indicates a very frequent word

⚹ **close¹** /kləʊs/ **1** *adj* vicino; ‹friend› intimo; ‹weather› afoso; **have a ∼ shave** fam scamparla bella; **be ∼ to somebody** essere unito a qualcuno

2 *adv* vicino; **∼ by** vicino; **it's ∼ on five o'clock** sono quasi le cinque

⚹ **close²** /kləʊz/ **1** *n* fine *f*; **draw to a ∼** concludere

2 *vt* chiudere

3 *vi* chiudersi; ‹shop› chiudere

■ **close down** **1** *vt* chiudere

2 *vi* ‹TV station› interrompere la trasmissione; ‹factory› chiudere

■ **close in** *vi* ‹mist› calare; ‹enemy› avvicinarsi da ogni lato

■ **close up** **1** *vi* (come closer together) stringersi; ‹shop› chiudere

2 *vt* (bring closer together) avvicinare; chiudere ‹shop›

close combat *n* corpo a corpo *m inv*

close-cropped /-'krɒpt/ *adj* ‹hair› rasato

closed-circuit television /kləʊzdsɜːkɪt-telɪ'vɪʒən/ *n* televisione *f* a circuito chiuso

closed shop /kləʊzd'ʃɒp/ *n* azienda (*f*) che assume solo personale aderente ad un dato sindacato

close-fitting /kləʊs'fɪtɪŋ/ *adj* ‹garment› attillato

close-knit /kləʊs'nɪt/ *adj* fig ‹family, group› affiatato

⚹ **closely** /'kləʊslɪ/ *adv* da vicino; ‹watch, listen› attentamente

close-run *adj* ‹race, competition› combattutissimo

close season /kləʊs/ *n* stagione (*f*) di chiusura della caccia e della pesca

closet /'klɒzɪt/ *n* Am armadio *m*

close-up /'kləʊs-/ *n* primo piano *m*

closing /'kləʊzɪŋ/ *adj* ‹stages, minutes, words, scene› ultimo

closing date *n* data *f* di scadenza

closing-down sale *n* liquidazione *f* totale [per cessata attività]

closing time *n* orario *m* di chiusura

closure /'kləʊʒə(r)/ *n* chiusura *f*

clot /klɒt/ **1** *n* grumo *m*; fam (idiot) tonto, -a *mf*

2 *vi* (*pt/pp* **clotted**) ‹blood› coagularsi

cloth /klɒθ/ *n* (fabric) tessuto *m*; (duster etc) straccio *m*

clothe /kləʊð/ *vt* vestire

⚹ **clothes** /kləʊðz/ *npl* vestiti *mpl*, abiti *mpl*

clothes-brush *n* spazzola *f* per abiti

clotheshanger *n* gruccia *f* appendiabiti

clothes horse *n* stendibiancheria *m inv*

clothes-line *n* corda *f* stendibiancheria

clothes peg *n* molletta *f* per bucato

clothes shop *n* negozio *m* di abbigliamento

clothing /'kləʊðɪŋ/ n abbigliamento m

clotted cream n Br panna f rappresa (*ottenuta scaldando il latte*)

cloud /klaʊd/ n nuvola f
■ **cloud over** vi rannuvolarsi

cloudburst /'klaʊdbɜːst/ n acquazzone m

cloudy /'klaʊdɪ/ adj (**-ier**, **-iest**) nuvoloso; ‹*liquid*› torbido

clout /klaʊt/ 1 n fam colpo m; (influence) impatto m (**with** su)
2 vt fam colpire

clove /kləʊv/ n chiodo m di garofano; ~ **of garlic** spicchio m d'aglio

cloven foot, **cloven hoof** /'kləʊvən/ n (of animal) zoccolo m fesso; (of devil) piede m biforcuto

clover /'kləʊvə(r)/ n trifoglio m

clover leaf n raccordo m di due autostrade

clown /klaʊn/ 1 n pagliaccio m
2 vi ~ [about/around] fare il pagliaccio

🗝 **club** /klʌb/ 1 n club m inv; (weapon) clava f; Sport mazza f; ~s pl Cards fiori mpl
2 vt (pt/pp **clubbed**) bastonare
■ **club together** vi unirsi

club car n Am carrozza (f) ferroviaria con sala bar

club class n business class f inv

club foot n piede m deformato

clubhouse n (for socializing) circolo m; Am (for changing) spogliatoio m

club sandwich n club-sandwich m inv

cluck /klʌk/ vi chiocciare

clue /kluː/ n indizio m; (in crossword) definizione f; **I haven't a** ~ fam non ne ho idea

clued-up /kluːd'ʌp/ adj Br fam ben informato

clueless /'kluːlɪs/ adj Br fam incapace

clump /klʌmp/ n gruppo m

clump about, **clump around** vi (walk noisily) camminare con passo pesante

clumsily /'klʌmzɪlɪ/ adv in modo maldestro; ‹remark› senza tatto

clumsiness /'klʌmzɪnɪs/ n goffaggine f

clumsy /'klʌmzɪ/ adj (**-ier**, **-iest**) maldestro; ‹tool› scomodo; ‹remark› senza tatto

clung /klʌŋ/ ▶ CLING

cluster /'klʌstə(r)/ 1 n gruppo m
2 vi raggrupparsi (**round** intorno a)

clutch /klʌtʃ/ 1 n stretta f; Auto frizione f; **be in sb's** ~**es** essere in balia di qualcuno
2 vt stringere; (grab) afferrare
3 vi ~ **at** afferrare

clutch bag n pochette f inv

clutch cable n cavo m della frizione

clutter /'klʌtə(r)/ 1 n caos m
2 vt ~ [up] ingombrare

cm abbr (**centimetre(s)**) cm

CND n abbr (**Campaign for Nuclear Disarmament**) campagna f per il disarmo nucleare

Co. abbr 1 (**company**) C., C.ia; **and** ~ hum e compagnia
2 (**county**) contea f

c/o abbr (**care of**) c/o, presso

🗝 **coach** /kəʊtʃ/ 1 n pullman m inv; Rail vagone m; (horse-drawn) carrozza f; Sport allenatore, -trice mf
2 vt far esercitare; Sport allenare

coach party n Br gruppo m di gitanti (in pullman)

coach station n Br stazione f dei pullman

coach trip n viaggio m in pullman

coachwork n Br carrozzeria f

coagulate /kəʊ'æɡjʊleɪt/ vi coagularsi

coagulation /kəʊæɡjʊ'leɪʃn/ n coagulazione f

coal /kəʊl/ n carbone m

coalfield n bacino m carbonifero

coal fire n caminetto m alimentato a carbone

coalition /kəʊə'lɪʃn/ n coalizione f

coal-mine n miniera f di carbone

coalminer n minatore m

coal scuttle n secchio m del carbone

coal seam n giacimento m di carbone

coarse /kɔːs/ adj grossolano; ‹joke› spinto

coarse-grained /-'ɡreɪnd/ adj ‹texture› a grana grossa

coarsely /'kɔːslɪ/ adv ‹ground› grossolanamente; ‹joke› in modo spinto

coast /kəʊst/ 1 n costa f
2 vi (freewheel) scendere a ruota libera; Auto scendere in folle

coastal /'kəʊstəl/ adj costiero

coaster /'kəʊstə(r)/ n (mat) sottobicchiere m inv

coastguard /'kəʊs(t)ɡɑːd/ n guardia f costiera

coastline /'kəʊstlaɪn/ n litorale m

coat /kəʊt/ 1 n cappotto m; (of animal) manto m; (of paint) mano f; ~ **of arms** stemma f
2 vt coprire; (with paint) ricoprire

coat-hanger n gruccia f

coat-hook n gancio m [appendiabiti]

coating /'kəʊtɪŋ/ n rivestimento m; (of paint) stato m

coat rack n attaccapanni m a muro

coat-tails npl falde fpl; **be always hanging on sb's** ~ attaccarsi sempre alle falde di qualcuno

coax /kəʊks/ vt convincere con le moine

cob /kɒb/ n (of corn) pannocchia f

cobble /'kɒbl/ vt ~ **together** raffazzonare

cobbler /'kɒblə(r)/ n ciabattino m

cobblestones /'kɒbəlstəʊnz/ *npl* acciottolato *msg*

cobra /'kəʊbrə/ *n* cobra *m inv*

cobweb /'kɒbweb/ *n* ragnatela *f*

cocaine /kə'keɪn/ *n* cocaina *f*

coccyx /'kɒksɪks/ *n* coccige *m*

cock /kɒk/ **1** *n* gallo *m*; (any male bird) maschio *m*; vulg cazzo *m*
2 *vt* sollevare il grilletto di ‹gun›; ~ **its ears** ‹animal› drizzare le orecchie
■ **cock up** fam **1** *vt* incasinare
2 *vi* incasinarsi

cock-a-doodle-doo /kɒkədu:d(ə)l'du:/ *int* chicchirichì

cock-a-hoop *adj* fam al settimo cielo

cock-and-bull story *n* fam panzana *f*

cockatoo /kɒkə'tu:/ *n* cacatoa *m inv*

cockcrow /'kɒkkrəʊ/ *n* **at** ~ al primo canto del gallo

cocked hat /kɒkt'hæt/ *n* fam **knock somebody/something into a** ~ schiacciare qualcuno/qualcosa

cockerel /'kɒkərəl/ *n* galletto *m*

cocker spaniel /'kɒkə(r)/ *n* cocker *m inv* [spaniel]

cock-eyed /-'aɪd/ *adj* fam storto; (absurd) assurdo

cockfighting /'kɒkfaɪtɪŋ/ *n* combattimenti *mpl* di galli

cockle /'kɒkl/ *n* cardio *m*

cockney /'kɒknɪ/ *n* (dialect) dialetto *m* londinese; (person) abitante *mf* dell'est di Londra

cockpit /'kɒkpɪt/ *n* Aeron cabina *f*

cockroach /'kɒkrəʊtʃ/ *n* scarafaggio *m*

cocksure /kɒk'ʃʊə(r)/ *adj* ‹person, manner, attitude› presuntuoso

cocktail /'kɒkteɪl/ *n* cocktail *m inv*

cocktail bar *n* [cocktail] bar *m inv*

cocktail dress *n* abito *m* da cocktail *m inv*

cocktail party *n* cocktail-party *m inv*

cocktail shaker *n* shaker *m inv*

cocktail stick *n* stecchino *m*

cock-up *n* sl **make a** ~ fare un casino (**of** con)

cocky /'kɒkɪ/ *adj* (**-ier, -iest**) fam presuntuoso

cocoa /'kəʊkəʊ/ *n* cacao *m*

coconut /'kəʊkənʌt/ *n* noce *f* di cocco

coconut palm *n* palma *f* di cocco

coconut shy *n* Br tiro (*m*) *al bersaglio in cui si devono abbattere noci di cocco*

cocoon /kə'ku:n/ *n* bozzolo *m*

COD *abbr* (**cash on delivery**) pagamento *m* alla consegna

cod /kɒd/ *n inv* merluzzo *m*

coddle /'kɒd(ə)l/ *vt* coccolare

✓ **code** /kəʊd/ *n* codice *m*

coded /'kəʊdɪd/ *adj* codificato

codeine /'kəʊdi:n/ *n* codeina *f*

code name *n* nome *m* in codice

codeword *n* parola *f* d'ordine

coding /'kəʊdɪŋ/ *n* Comput codifica *f*

cod-liver oil *n* olio *m* di fegato di merluzzo

coeducational /kəʊedjʊ'keɪʃənəl/ *adj* misto

coefficient /kəʊɪ'fɪʃənt/ *n* coefficiente *m*

coeliac Br, **celiac** Am /'si:lɪæk/ *adj* celiaco

coerce /kəʊ'ɜ:s/ *vt* costringere

coercion /kəʊ'ɜ:ʃn/ *n* coercizione *f*

coexist /kəʊɪg'zɪst/ *vi* coesistere

coexistence /kəʊɪg'zɪstəns/ *n* coesistenza *f*

C of E *abbr* (**Church of England**) Chiesa *f* anglicana

✓ **coffee** /'kɒfɪ/ *n* caffè *m inv*

coffee bar *n* caffè *m inv*, bar *m inv*

coffee bean *n* chicco *m* di caffè

coffee break *n* pausa *f* per il caffè

coffee grinder *n* macinacaffè *m inv*

coffee machine *n* (in café) macchina *f* per l'espresso

coffee-maker *n* (on stove) caffettiera *f*; (electric) macchina *f* per il caffè (*con il filtro*)

coffee morning *n* Br *riunione* (*m*) *mattutina in cui viene servito il caffè*

coffee percolator *n* (on stove) caffettiera *f*; (electric) macchina *f* per il caffè (*con il filtro*)

coffee-pot *n* caffettiera *f*

coffee shop *n* torrefazione *f*; (café) caffè *m inv*, bar *m inv*

coffee table *n* tavolino *m*

coffer /'kɒfə(r)/ *n* forziere *m*

coffin /'kɒfɪn/ *n* bara *f*

cog /kɒg/ *n* Techn dente *m*

cogent /'kəʊdʒənt/ *adj* convincente

cogitate /'kɒdʒɪteɪt/ *vi* cogitare

cognac /'kɒnjæk/ *n* Cognac *m*

cognoscenti /kɒnə'ʃentɪ/ *npl* intenditori *mpl*

cogwheel /'kɒgwi:l/ *n* ruota *f* dentata

cohabit /kəʊ'hæbɪt/ *vi* Jur convivere

coherent /kəʊ'hɪərənt/ *adj* coerente; (when speaking) logico

cohesion /kəʊ'hi:ʒən/ *n* coesione *f*

cohort /'kəʊhɔ:t/ *n* fig seguito *m*

coil /kɔɪl/ **1** *n* rotolo *m*; Electr bobina *f*; ~**s** *pl* spire *fpl*
2 *vt* ~ **[up]** avvolgere

coin /kɔɪn/ **1** *n* moneta *f*
2 *vt* coniare ‹word›

---

coinage /'kɔɪnɪdʒ/ n (of coins, currency) coniatura f; (word, phrase) neologismo m

coin box n (pay phone) telefono m a monete; (on pay phone, in laundromat) gettoniera f

coincide /kəʊɪn'saɪd/ vi coincidere

coincidence /kəʊ'ɪnsɪdəns/ n coincidenza f

coincidental /kəʊɪnsɪ'dentl/ adj casuale

coincidentally /kəʊɪnsɪ'dentlɪ/ adv casualmente

coin operated adj a gettone

Coke® /kəʊk/ n Coca® f

coke n carbone m, coke m

Col. abbr (**Colonel**) Col. m

colander /'kʌləndə(r)/ n Culin colapasta m inv

ℱ **cold** /kəʊld/ ① adj freddo; **I'm ~** ho freddo; **get ~ feet** farsi prendere dalla fifa; **give somebody the ~ shoulder** trattare qualcuno freddamente
② n freddo m; Med raffreddore m

cold-blooded /-'blʌdɪd/ adj spietato

cold calling n Comm visita f senza preavviso

cold comfort n magra consolazione f

cold frame n telaio (m) coperto di vetro per proteggere le piante dal gelo

cold-hearted /-'hɑːtɪd/ adj insensibile

coldly /'kəʊldlɪ/ adv freddamente

cold meat n salumi mpl

coldness /'kəʊldnɪs/ n freddezza f

cold snap n ondata f di freddo

cold sore n herpes m inv

cold store n cella f frigorifera

cold sweat n sudore m freddo; **bring somebody out in a ~** far sudare freddo qualcuno

cold turkey n (reaction) crisi f inv di astinenza; **be ~** avere una crisi di astinenza; **quit ~** smettere di colpo di drogarsi

Cold War n guerra f fredda

coleslaw /'kəʊlslɔː/ n insalata (f) di cavolo crudo, cipolle e carote in maionese

colic /'kɒlɪk/ n colica f

collaborate /kə'læbəreɪt/ vi collaborare; **~ on something** collaborare a qualcosa

collaboration /kəlæbə'reɪʃn/ n collaborazione f; (with enemy) collaborazionismo m

collaborator /kə'læbəreɪtə(r)/ n collaboratore, -trice mf; (with enemy) collaborazionista mf

collage /kɒ'lɑːʒ/ n collage m inv; (film) montaggio m

collapse /kə'læps/ ① n crollo m
② vi ⟨person⟩ svenire; ⟨roof, building⟩ crollare

collapsible /kə'læpsəbl/ adj pieghevole

collar /'kɒlə(r)/ n colletto m; (for animal) collare m

collarbone /'kɒləbəʊn/ n clavicola f

collar size n taglia f di camicia

collate /kə'leɪt/ vt collazionare

collateral /kə'lætərəl/ n garanzia f collaterale; **put up ~** offrire una garanzia collaterale

collateral damage n danni mpl collaterali

collateral loan adj Fin prestito m con garanzia collaterale

ℱ **colleague** /'kɒliːg/ n collega mf

ℱ **collect** /kə'lekt/ ① vt andare a prendere ⟨person⟩; ritirare ⟨parcel, tickets⟩; riscuotere ⟨taxes⟩; raccogliere ⟨rubbish⟩; (as hobby) collezionare
② vi riunirsi
③ adv **call ~** Am telefonare a carico del destinatario

collected /kə'lektɪd/ adj controllato

ℱ **collection** /kə'lekʃn/ n collezione f; (in church) questua f; (of rubbish) raccolta f; (of post) levata f

collective /kə'lektɪv/ adj collettivo

collective bargaining n contrattazione f collettiva

collective farm n comune f

collective noun n nome m collettivo

collective ownership n comproprietà f

collector /kə'lektə(r)/ n (of stamps etc) collezionista mf

collector's item n pezzo m da collezionista

ℱ **college** /'kɒlɪdʒ/ n istituto m parauniversitario; **C~ of …** Scuola f di …

college of education n Br ≈ facoltà f inv di magistero

college of further education n Br istituto m parauniversitario

collide /kə'laɪd/ vi scontrarsi

collie /'kɒlɪ/ n pastore m scozzese, collie m inv

colliery /'kɒlɪərɪ/ n miniera f di carbone

collision /kə'lɪʒn/ n scontro m; **be on a ~ course** essere in rotta di collisione

colloquial /kə'ləʊkwɪəl/ adj colloquiale

colloquialism /kə'ləʊkwɪəlɪzm/ n espressione f colloquiale

colloquially /kə'ləʊkwɪəlɪ/ adv colloquialmente

colloquium /kə'ləʊkwɪəm/ n colloquio m

collude /kə'l(j)uːd/ vi complottare

collusion /kə'l(j)uːʒn/ n collusione f; **in ~ with** in accordo con

cologne /kə'ləʊn/ n colonia f

Colombia /kə'lɒmbɪə/ n Colombia f

c

Colombian /kə'lɒmbɪən/ *adj* & *n*
colombiano, -a *mf*

colon /'kəʊlən/ *n* due punti *mpl*; Anat colon
m inv

colonel /'kɜ:nl/ *n* colonnello *m*

colonial /kə'ləʊnɪəl/ *adj* coloniale

colonialist /kə'ləʊnɪəlɪst/ *adj* & *n*
colonialista *mf*

colonization /ˌkɒlənaɪ'zeɪʃn, US -nɪ'z-/ *n*
colonizzazione *f*

colonize /'kɒlənaɪz/ *vt* colonizzare

colonizer /'kɒlənaɪzə(r)/ *n* colonizzatore,
-trice *mf*

colonnade /kɒlə'neɪd/ *n* colonnato *m*

colony /'kɒlənɪ/ *n* colonia *f*

Colorado beetle /kɒlə'rɑːdəʊ/ *n*
dorifora *f*

colossal /kə'lɒsl/ *adj* colossale

⚘ **colour** /'kʌlə(r)/ [1] *n* colore *m*; (complexion)
colorito *m*; ~s *pl* (flag) bandiera *fsg*; **show
one's true ~s** fig buttare giù la maschera; **in
~** a colori; **off ~** fam giù di tono
[2] *vt* colorare; ~ **[in]** colorare
[3] *vi* (blush) arrossire

colour bar *n* discriminazione *f* razziale

colour-blind *adj* daltonico

colour code *vt* distinguere per mezzo di
colori diversi

coloured /'kʌləd/ [1] *adj* colorato; ⟨person⟩
di colore
[2] *n* (person) persona *f* di colore

colour fast *adj* dai colori resistenti

colour film *n* film *m inv* a colori

colourful /'kʌləfʊl/ *adj* pieno di colore

colouring /'kʌlərɪŋ/ *n* (of plant, animal)
colorazione *f*; (complexion) colorito *m*; (dye: for
hair) tinta *f*; (for food) colorante *m*

colouring book *n* album *m inv* da
colorare

colourless /'kʌlələs/ *adj* incolore

colour photo[graph] *n* fotografia *f* a
colori

colour scheme *n* [combinazione *f* di]
colori *mpl*

colour sense *n* senso *m* del colore

colour supplement *n* supplemento *m*
illustrato a colori

colour television *n* televisione *f* a colori

colt /kəʊlt/ *n* puledro *m*

⚘ **column** /'kɒləm/ *n* colonna *f*

columnist /'kɒləmnɪst/ *n* giornalista *mf*
che cura una rubrica

coma /'kəʊmə/ *n* coma *m inv*

comatose /'kəʊmətəʊz/ *adj* Med in stato
comatoso

comb /kəʊm/ [1] *n* pettine *m*; (for wearing)
pettinino *m*
[2] *vt* pettinare; fig (search) setacciare; ~

one's hair pettinarsi i capelli

■ **comb through** *vt* setacciare ⟨files, desk⟩

combat /'kɒmbæt/ [1] *n* combattimento *m*
[2] *vt* (*pt/pp* **combated**) combattere

combat jacket *n* giubba *f* da
combattimento

⚘ **combination** /kɒmbɪ'neɪʃn/ *n*
combinazione *f*

⚘ **combine**[1] /kəm'baɪn/ [1] *vt* unire; ~ **a job
with being a mother** conciliare il lavoro con
il ruolo di madre
[2] *vi* ⟨chemical elements⟩ combinarsi

combine[2] /'kɒmbaɪn/ *n* Comm associazione
f

combined /kəm'baɪnd/ *adj* combinato

combine [harvester] *n* mietitrebbia *f*

combustible /kəm'bʌstəbl/ *adj*
combustibile

combustion /kəm'bʌstʃn/ *n* combustione *f*

⚘ **come** /kʌm/ *vi* (*pt* **came**, *pp* **come**)
venire; **after coming all this way** dopo tutta
questa strada; **where do you ~ from?** da
dove vieni?; ~ **to** (reach) arrivare a; **that ~s
to £10** fanno 10 sterline; **I've ~ to appreciate
her** ho finito per apprezzarla; **I don't know
what the world is coming to** mi chiedo dove
andremo a finire; ~ **into money** ricevere
dei soldi; **that's what comes of being …**
ecco cosa significa essere…; ~ **true/open**
verificarsi/aprirsi; ~ **first** arrivare primo;
fig venire prima di tutto; ~ **in two sizes**
esistere in due misure; **the years to ~** gli
anni a venire; **how ~?** fam come mai?

■ **come about** *vi* succedere

■ **come across**: [1] *vi* ~ **across as being**
fam dare l'impressione di essere
[2] *vt* (find) imbattersi in

■ **come after** *vt* (follow) venire dopo; (chase,
pursue) inseguire

■ **come along** *vi* venire; ⟨job, opportunity⟩
presentarsi; (progress) andare bene

■ **come apart** *vi* smontarsi; (break) rompersi

■ **come at** *vt* (attack) avventarsi su

■ **come away** *vi* venir via; ⟨button, fastener⟩
staccarsi

■ **come back** *vi* ritornare

■ **come before** *vt* (precede) precedere; (be
more important than) venire prima di

■ **come by** [1] *vi* passare
[2] *vt* (obtain) avere

■ **come down** *vi* scendere; ~ **down to** (reach)
arrivare a; **the situation ~s down to …** la
situazione si riduce a…; **don't ~ down too
hard on her** vacci piano con lei; ~ **down with
flu** prendersi l'influenza

■ **come forward** *vi* farsi avanti

■ **come in** *vi* entrare; (in race) arrivare; ⟨tide⟩
salire; ~ **in with somebody** (in an undertaking)
associarsi a qualcuno

■ **come in for**: *vt* ~ **in for criticism** essere
criticato

■ **come into** *vt* (inherit) ereditare ⟨money,
inheritance⟩

⚘ indicates a very frequent word

■ **come off** *vi* staccarsi; (take place) esserci; (succeed) riuscire; ∼ **off it!** non farmi ridere!

■ **come on** *vi* (make progress) migliorare; ∼ **on!** (hurry) dai!; (indicating disbelief) ma va là!

■ **come out** *vi* venir fuori; ‹*book, sun*› uscire; ‹*stain*› andar via; ‹*homosexual*› rivelare la propria omosessualità; ∼ **out [on strike]** scioperare

■ **come out with** *vt* venir fuori con ‹*joke, suggestion*›

■ **come over** *vi* venire; **what's** ∼ **over you?** cosa ti prende?

■ **come round, come around** *vi* venire; (after fainting) riaversi; (change one's mind) farsi convincere

■ **come through** ① *vi* ‹*news*› arrivare ② *vt* attraversare ‹*operation*›

■ **come to** *vi* (after fainting) riaversi

■ **come under** *vi* trovarsi sotto

■ **come up** *vi* salire; ‹*sun*› sorgere; ‹*plant*› crescere; ‹*name, subject*› venir fuori; ‹*job, opportunity*› presentarsi; **something came up** (I was prevented) ho avuto un imprevisto

■ **come up against** *vt* incontrare

■ **come up to** *vt* (reach) arrivare a; essere all'altezza di ‹*expectations*›

■ **come up with** *vt* tirar fuori

come-back *n* ritorno *m*

comedian /kə'mi:dɪən/ *n* [attore] *m*, comico *m*

comedienne /kəmi:dɪ'en/ *n* attrice *f* comica

come-down *n* passo *m* indietro

comedy /'kɒmədɪ/ *n* commedia *f*

comer /'kʌmə(r)/ *n* **open to all** ∼**s** aperto a tutti; **take on all** ∼**s** battersi contro tutti gli sfidanti

comet /'kɒmɪt/ *n* cometa *f*

come-uppance /kʌm'ʌpəns/ *n* **get one's** ∼ fam avere quel che si merita

comfort /'kʌmfət/ ① *n* benessere *m*; (consolation) conforto *m*, **all the** ∼**s** tutti i comfort ② *vt* confortare

♂ **comfortable** /'kʌmfətəbl/ *adj* comodo; **be** ∼ ‹*person*› stare comodo; fig ‹*in situation*› essere a proprio agio; (financially) star bene

comfortably /'kʌmfətəblɪ/ *adv* comodamente

comforting /'kʌmfətɪŋ/ *adj* confortante

comfort station *n* Am bagno *m* pubblico

comfy /'kʌmfɪ/ *adj* fam comodo

comic /'kɒmɪk/ ① *adj* comico ② *n* comico, -a *mf*; (periodical) fumetto *m*

comical /'kɒmɪk(ə)l/ *adj* comico

comically /'kɒmɪk(ə)lɪ/ *adv* comicamente

comic book *n* giornalino *m* [a fumetti]

comic relief *n* Theat **provide some** ∼ fare una parentesi comica; fig sdrammatizzare

comic strip *n* striscia *f* di fumetti

coming /'kʌmɪŋ/ ① *adj* promettente ② *n* venuta *f*; ∼**s and goings** viavai *m*

comma /'kɒmə/ *n* virgola *f*

♂ **command** /kə'mɑ:nd/ ① *n* (also Comput) comando *m*; (order) ordine *m*; (mastery) padronanza *f*; **in** ∼ al comando ② *vt* ordinare; comandare ‹*army*›

commandant /'kɒmədænt/ *n* Mil comandante *m*

command centre Br, **command center** Am *n* centro *m* di comando

commandeer /kɒmən'dɪə(r)/ *vt* requisire

commander /kə'mɑ:ndə(r)/ *n* comandante *m*

commanding /kə'mɑ:ndɪŋ/ *adj* ‹*view*› imponente; ‹*lead*› dominante

commanding officer *n* comandante *m*

commandment /kə'mɑ:ndmənt/ *n* comandamento *m*

commando /kə'mɑ:ndəʊ/ *n* commando *m inv*

command performance *n* Br Theat serata (*f*) di gala (su richiesta del capo di stato)

commemorate /kə'meməreɪt/ *vt* commemorare

commemoration /kəmemə'reɪʃn/ *n* commemorazione *f*

commemorative /kə'memərətɪv/ *adj* commemorativo

commence /kə'mens/ *vt/i* cominciare

commencement /kə'mensmənt/ *n* inizio *m*

commend /kə'mend/ *vt* complimentarsi con (**on** per); (recommend) raccomandare (**to** a)

commendable /kə'mendəbl/ *adj* lodevole

commendation /kɒmen'deɪʃn/ *n* elogio *m*; (for bravery) riconoscimento *m*

commensurate /kə'menʃərət/ *adj* proporzionato (**with** a)

♂ **comment** /'kɒment/ ① *n* commento *m*; **no** ∼**!** no comment! ② *vi* fare commenti (**on** su)

commentary /'kɒməntrɪ/ *n* commento *m*; [running] ∼ (on radio, TV) cronaca *f* diretta

commentate /'kɒmənteɪt/ *vt* ∼ **on** TV, Radio fare la cronaca di

■ **commentate on** *vt* fare la radiocronaca/ telecronaca di ‹*sporting event*›

commentator /'kɒmənteɪtə(r)/ *n* cronista *mf*

commerce /'kɒmɜ:s/ *n* commercio *m*

♂ **commercial** /kə'mɜ:ʃl/ ① *adj* commerciale ② *n* TV pubblicità *f inv*

commercial break *n* spot *m inv* [pubblicitario], interruzione *f* pubblicitaria

commercialism /kə'mɜːʃ(ə)lɪzm/ n pej
affarismo m

commercialize /kə'mɜːʃ(ə)laɪz/ vt
commercializzare

commercial law n diritto m
commerciale

commercially /kə'mɜːʃ(ə)lɪ/ adv
commercialmente

commercial traveller commesso m
viaggiatore

commiserate /kə'mɪzəreɪt/ vi esprimere
il proprio rincrescimento (**with** a)

commissar /kɒmɪ'sɑː(r)/ n commissario
m

✧ **commission** /kə'mɪʃn/ **1** n
commissione f; **receive one's** ~ Mil essere
promosso ufficiale; **out of** ~ fuori uso
2 vt commissionare; Mil promuovere
ufficiale; ~ **a painting from somebody,** ~
somebody to do a painting commissionare
un dipinto a qualcuno

commissionaire /kəmɪʃə'neə(r)/ n
portiere m

commissioner /kə'mɪʃənə(r)/ n
commissario m; **C~ for Oaths** ≈ notaio m

✧ **commit** /kə'mɪt/ vt (pt/pp **committed**)
commettere; (to prison, hospital) affidare (**to** a);
impegnare ‹funds›; ~ **oneself** impegnarsi;
~ **something to memory** imparare qualcosa
a memoria

✧ **commitment** /kə'mɪtmənt/ n impegno m;
(involvement) compromissione f

committed /kə'mɪtɪd/ adj impegnato

✧ **committee** /kə'mɪtɪ/ n comitato m

commodity /kə'mɒdətɪ/ n prodotto m

commodore /'kɒmədɔː(r)/ n commodoro
m

✧ **common** /'kɒmən/ **1** adj comune; (vulgar)
volgare
2 n prato m pubblico; **have in** ~ avere
in comune; **House of C~s** Camera f dei
Comuni

common cold n raffreddore m

commoner /'kɒmənə(r)/ n persona (f)
non nobile

common ground n fig terreno m d'intesa

common-law n diritto m
consuetudinario

common-law husband n convivente
m (more uxorio)

common-law marriage n matrimonio
m di fatto

common-law wife n convivente f (more
uxorio)

commonly /'kɒmənlɪ/ adv comunemente

Common Market n Mercato m Comune

common-or-garden adj ordinario

commonplace adj banale

✧ indicates a very frequent word

common-room n sala f dei professori/
degli studenti

commonsense n buon senso m

Commonwealth **1** n Br
Commonwealth m inv
2 attrib ‹country, Games› del
Commonwealth

**Commonwealth of Independent
States** n Comunità f degli stati
indipendenti

commotion /kə'məʊʃn/ n confusione f

communal /'kɒmjʊnəl/ adj comune

commune /'kɒmjuːn/ **1** n comune f
2 /kə'mjuːn/ vi ~ **with** essere in
comunione con ‹nature›; comunicare con
(person)

communicable /kə'mjuːnɪkəbl/ adj
‹disease› trasmissibile

communicate /kə'mjuːnɪkeɪt/ vt/i
comunicare

✧ **communication** /kəmjuːnɪ'keɪʃn/ n
comunicazione f; (of disease) trasmissione
f; **be in** ~ **with somebody** essere in
contatto con qualcuno; ~**s** pl (technology)
telecomunicazioni fpl

communication cord n fermata f
d'emergenza

communications company n società
f di telecomunicazioni

communications satellite n satellite
m per telecomunicazioni

communications software n
software m di comunicazione

communication studies /'stʌdɪz/ n
studi mpl di comunicazione

communicative /kə'mjuːnɪkətɪv/ adj
comunicativo

Communion /kə'mjuːnɪən/ n [Holy] ~
comunione f

communiqué /kə'mjuːnɪkeɪ/ n
comunicato m stampa

Communism /'kɒmjʊnɪzm/ n comunismo
m

Communist /'kɒmjʊnɪst/ adj & n
comunista mf

Communist Party n partito m
comunista

✧ **community** /kə'mjuːnətɪ/ n comunità f

community care n cura (f) fuori
dell'ambito ospedaliero

community centre n centro m sociale

community policing n polizia f di
quartiere

community service n servizio m civile
(in sostituzione di pene per reati minori)

community spirit n spirito m civico

commute /kə'mjuːt/ **1** vi fare il
pendolare
2 vt Jur commutare

commuter /kə'mjuːtə(r)/ n pendolare mf

commuter belt n zona f suburbana abitata dai pendolari

commuter train n treno m dei pendolari

Comoros /'kɒmərəʊz/ npl the ∼ (Islands) le (isole) Comore fpl

compact¹ /kəm'pækt/ adj compatto

compact² /'kɒmpækt/ n portacipria m inv

compact disc n compact disc m inv

compact disc player n lettore m di compact disc

companion /kəm'pænjən/ n compagno, -a mf

companionable /kəm'pænjənəbl/ adj ‹person› socievole; ‹silence› non pesante

companionship /kəm'pænjənʃɪp/ n compagnia f

⚜ **company** /'kʌmpənɪ/ n compagnia f; (guests) ospiti mpl; I didn't know you had ∼ pensavo che fossi solo

company brochure n opuscolo m dell'azienda

company car n macchina f della ditta

company director n dirigente mf d'azienda

company letterhead n carta f intestata dell'azienda

company pension scheme n piano m di pensionamento aziendale

company policy n politica f aziendale

company secretary n direttore, -trice mf amministrativo, -a

comparable /'kɒmpərəbl/ adj paragonabile

comparative /kəm'pærətɪv/ [1] adj comparativo; (relative) relativo [2] n Gram comparativo m

comparatively /kəm'pærətɪvlɪ/ adv relativamente

⚜ **compare** /kəm'peə(r)/ [1] vt paragonare (with/to a) [2] vi it can't ∼ non ha paragoni

⚜ **comparison** /kəm'pærɪsn/ n paragone m

compartment /kəm'pɑːtmənt/ n compartimento m; Rail scompartimento m

compass /'kʌmpəs/ n bussola f

compasses /'kʌmpəsɪz/ npl pair of ∼ compasso msg

compassion /kəm'pæʃn/ n compassione f

compassionate /kəm'pæʃənət/ adj compassionevole

compatible /kəm'pætəbl/ adj compatibile; be ∼ ‹people› avere caratteri compatibili

compatriot /kəm'pætrɪət/ n compatriota mf

compel /kəm'pel/ vt (pt/pp **compelled**) costringere

compelling /kəm'pelɪŋ/ adj ‹reason, argument› convincente; ‹performance, film, speaker› avvincente

compendium /kəm'pendɪəm/ n (handbook) compendio m; Br (box of games) scatola f di giochi

compensate /'kɒmpənseɪt/ [1] vt risarcire [2] vi ∼ for fig compensare di

compensation /kɒmpən'seɪʃn/ n risarcimento m; fig (comfort) consolazione f

compère /'kɒmpeə(r)/ n presentatore, -trice mf

⚜ **compete** /kəm'piːt/ vi competere; (take part) gareggiare

competence /'kɒmpɪtəns/ n competenza f

competent /'kɒmpɪtənt/ adj competente

⚜ **competition** /kɒmpə'tɪʃn/ n concorrenza f; (contest) gara f

competitive /kəm'petɪtɪv/ adj competitivo; ∼ prices prezzi mpl concorrenziali

competitor /kəm'petɪtə(r)/ n concorrente mf

compilation /kɒmpɪ'leɪʃn/ n compilazione f; (collection) raccolta f

compile /kəm'paɪl/ vt compilare

complacency /kəm'pleɪsənsɪ/ n compiacimento m

complacent /kəm'pleɪsənt/ adj compiaciuto

complacently /kəm'pleɪsəntlɪ/ adv con compiacimento

⚜ **complain** /kəm'pleɪn/ vi lamentarsi (about di); (formally) reclamare; ∼ of Med accusare

⚜ **complaint** /kəm'pleɪnt/ n lamentela f; (formal) reclamo m, Med disturbo m

complement¹ /'kɒmplɪmənt/ n complemento m; with a full ∼ of 25 con un effettivo al completo di 25

complement² /'kɒmplɪment/ vt complementare; ∼ each other complementarsi a vicenda

complementary /kɒmplɪ'mentərɪ/ adj complementare

complementary medicine n medicina f alternativa

⚜ **complete** /kəm'pliːt/ [1] adj completo; (utter) finito [2] vt completare; compilare ‹form›

⚜ **completely** /kəm'pliːtlɪ/ adv completamente

completion /kəm'pliːʃn/ n fine f

⚜ **complex** /'kɒmpleks/ adj & n complesso m

complexion /kəm'plekʃn/ n carnagione f; that puts a different ∼ on the matter questo mette la questione in una luce nuova

complexity /kəm'pleksətɪ/ n complessità f inv

compliance /kəm'plaɪəns/ n accettazione f; (with rules) osservanza f; in ∼ with in osservanza a ‹law›; conformemente a ‹request›

compliant /kəm'plaɪənt/ *adj*
accondiscendente; Comput conforme; **~ with**
conforme a

complicate /'kɒmplɪkeɪt/ *vt* complicare

complicated /'kɒmplɪkeɪtɪd/ *adj*
complicato

complication /kɒmplɪ'keɪʃn/ *n*
complicazione *f*

complicity /kəm'plɪsəti/ *n* complicità *f*

compliment /'kɒmplɪmənt/ ① *n*
complimento *m*; **~s** *pl* omaggi *mpl*
② *vt* complimentare

complimentary /kɒmplɪ'mentəri/ *adj*
complimentoso; (given free) in omaggio

comply /kəm'plaɪ/ *vi* (*pt/pp* **-ied**) **~ with**
conformarsi a

ⴜ **component** /kəm'pəʊnənt/ *adj & n* **~**
[part] componente *m*

compose /kəm'pəʊz/ *vt* comporre;
~ oneself ricomporsi; **be ~d of** essere
composto da

composed /kəm'pəʊzd/ *adj* (calm)
composto

composer /kəm'pəʊzə(r)/ *n* compositore,
-trice *mf*

composite /'kɒmpəzɪt/ *adj* composto;
‹style› composito

composition /kɒmpə'zɪʃn/ *n*
composizione *f*, (essay) tema *m*

compos mentis /kɒmpɒs'mentɪs/ *adj*
nel pieno possesso delle proprie facoltà

compost /'kɒmpɒst/ *n* composta *f*

composting /'kɒmpɒstɪŋ/ *n*
compostaggio *m*

composure /kəm'pəʊʒə(r)/ *n* calma *f*

compound[1] /kəm'paʊnd/ *vt* (make worse)
aggravare

compound[2] /'kɒmpaʊnd/ ① *adj*
composto
② *n* Chem composto *m*; Gram parola *f*
composta; (enclosure) recinto *m*

compound fracture *n* frattura *f*
esposta

compound interest *n* interesse *m*
composto

comprehend /kɒmprɪ'hend/ *vt*
comprendere

comprehensible /kɒmprɪ'hensəbl/ *adj*
comprensibile

comprehensibly /kɒmprɪ'hensəbli/ *adv*
comprensibilmente

comprehension /kɒmprɪ'henʃn/ *n*
comprensione *f*

comprehensive /kɒmprɪ'hensɪv/ *adj*
& n comprensivo; **~ [school]** scuola (*f*)
media in cui gli allievi hanno capacità
d'apprendimento diverse

comprehensive insurance *n* Auto
polizza *f* casco

compress[1] /'kɒmpres/ *n* compressa *f*

compress[2] /kəm'pres/ *vt* (also Comput)
comprimere

compressed air /kəm'prest/ *n* aria *f*
compressa

compression /kəm'preʃn/ *n*
compressione *f*

comprise /kəm'praɪz/ *vt* comprendere;
(form) costituire

compromise /'kɒmprəmaɪz/ ① *n*
compromesso
② *vt* compromettere
③ *vi* fare un compromesso

compromising /'kɒmprəmaɪzɪŋ/ *adj*
‹situation› compromettente

compulsion /kəm'pʌlʃn/ *n* desiderio *m*
irresistibile

compulsive /kəm'pʌlsɪv/ *adj* Psych
patologico; **~ eating** voglia *f* ossessiva di
mangiare

compulsory /kəm'pʌlsəri/ *adj*
obbligatorio; **~ subject** materia *f*
obbligatoria

compulsory purchase *n* Br
espropriazione *f* (*per pubblica utilità*)

compunction /kəm'pʌŋkʃn/ *n* liter
scrupolo *m*

computation /kɒmpjʊ'teɪʃn/ *n* calcolo *m*

ⴜ **computer** /kəm'pju:tə(r)/ *n* computer *m*
inv

computer-aided *adj* assistito da
computer

computer-aided design *n*
progettazione *f* assistita da computer

computer-aided learning *n*
apprendimento *m* assistito dal computer

computer-assisted language
learning *n* apprendimento *m* della lingua
assistito da computer

computer crime *n* reati *mpl* informatici

computer dating *n* possibilità (*f*) di
incontrare l'anima gemella tramite agenzie
in rete

computer dating service *n* servizio
m di ricerca dell'anima gemella in rete

computer engineer *n* tecnico *m*
informatico

computer error *n* errore *m* informatico

computer game *n* gioco *m* su computer;
~s intelligiochi *mpl*

computer graphics *n* grafica *f*
computerizzata

computer hacker *n* pirata *m*
informatico

computerization /kəmpju:təraɪ'zeɪʃn/ *n*
computerizzazione *f*

computerize /kəm'pju:təraɪz/ *vt*
computerizzare

ⴜ indicates a very frequent word

computer-literate adj che sa usare il computer

computer operator n terminalista mf

computer program n programma m [informatico]

computer programmer n programmatore, -trice mf di computer

computer science n informatica f

computer scientist n esperto, -a mf di informatica

computer virus n virus m inv [su computer]

computing /kəm'pju:tɪŋ/ n informatica f

comrade /'kɒmreɪd/ n camerata m; Pol compagno, -a mf

comradeship /'kɒmreɪdʃɪp/ n cameratismo m

con¹ /kɒn/ ▶ PRO

con² [1] n fam fregatura f
[2] vt (pt/pp **conned**) fam fregare

concave /'kɒŋkeɪv/ adj concavo

conceal /kən'si:l/ vt nascondere

concealment /kən'si:lmənt/ n dissimulazione f

concede /kən'si:d/ vt (admit) ammettere; (give up) rinunciare a; lasciar fare ‹goal›

conceit /kən'si:t/ n presunzione f

conceited /kən'si:tɪd/ adj presuntuoso

conceivable /kən'si:vəbl/ adj concepibile

conceive /kən'si:v/ [1] vt Biol concepire
[2] vi aver figli; ~ **of** fig concepire

concentrate /'kɒnsəntreɪt/ [1] vt concentrare
[2] vi concentrarsi
[3] n concentrato m

concentration /kɒnsən'treɪʃn/ n concentrazione f

concentration camp n campo m di concentramento

concentric /kən'sentrɪk/ adj concentrico

concept /'kɒnsept/ n concetto m

conception /kən'sepʃn/ n concezione f; (idea) idea f

conceptual /kən'septjʊəl/ adj concettuale

concern /kən'sɜ:n/ [1] n preoccupazione f; Comm attività f inv
[2] vt (be about, affect) riguardare; (worry) preoccupare; ~ **oneself with** preoccuparsi di; **as far as I am** ~**ed** per quanto mi riguarda

concerned /kən'sɜ:nd/ adj (worried) preoccupato; **be** ~ **about** essere preoccupato per; (involved) interessato; **all (those)** ~ tutti gli interessati

concerning /kən'sɜ:nɪŋ/ prep riguardo a

concert /'kɒnsət/ n concerto m

concerted /kən'sɜ:tɪd/ adj collettivo

concert hall n sala f da concerti

concertina /kɒnsə'ti:nə/ n piccola fisarmonica f

concert master n Am primo violino m

concerto /kən'tʃeətəʊ/ n concerto m

concession /kən'seʃn/ n concessione f; (reduction) sconto m

concessionary /kən'seʃənrɪ/ adj (reduced) scontato

conciliate /kən'sɪlɪeɪt/ vt blandire

conciliation /kənsɪlɪ'eɪʃn/ n conciliazione f

conciliator /kən'sɪlɪeɪtə(r)/ n mediatore, -trice mf

conciliatory /kən'sɪlɪətərɪ, US -tɔ:rɪ/ adj conciliatorio

concise /kən'saɪs/ adj conciso

concisely /kən'saɪslɪ/ adv in modo conciso

conciseness /kən'saɪsnɪs/ n concisione f

conclude /kən'klu:d/ [1] vt concludere
[2] vi concludersi

concluding /kən'klu:dɪn/ adj finale, conclusivo

conclusion /kən'klu:ʒn/ n conclusione f; **in** ~ per concludere

conclusive /kən'klu:sɪv/ adj definitivo

conclusively /kən'klu:sɪvlɪ/ adv in modo definitivo

concoct /kən'kɒkt/ vt confezionare; fig inventare

concoction /kən'kɒkʃn/ n mistura f; (drink) intruglio m

concord /'kɒŋkɔ:d/ n concordia f

concordance /kən'kɔ:dəns/ n accordo m; (index) concordanze fpl; **be in** ~ **with** essere in accordo con

concourse /'kɒŋkɔ:s/ n atrio m

concrete /'kɒŋkri:t/ [1] adj concreto
[2] n calcestruzzo m
[3] vt ricoprire di calcestruzzo

concrete jungle n giungla f d'asfalto

concrete mixer n betoniera f

concur /kən'kɜ:(r)/ vi (pt/pp **concurred**) essere d'accordo

concurrently /kən'kʌrəntlɪ/ adv contemporaneamente

concuss /kən'kʌs/ vt **be** ~**ed** avere una commozione cerebrale

concussion /kən'kʌʃn/ n commozione f cerebrale

condemn /kən'dem/ vt condannare; dichiarare inagibile ‹building›

condemnation /kɒndem'neɪʃn/ n condanna f

condensation /kɒnden'seɪʃn/ n condensazione f

condense /kən'dens/ [1] vt condensare; Phys condensare
[2] vi condensarsi

condensed milk /kəndenst'mɪlk/ *n* latte *m* condensato

condescend /kɒndɪ'send/ *vi* degnarsi

condescending /kɒndɪ'sendɪŋ/ *adj* condiscendente

condescendingly /kɒndɪ'sendɪŋlɪ/ *adv* in modo condiscendente

condiment /'kɒndɪmənt/ *n* condimento *m*

⚡ **condition** /kən'dɪʃn/ [1] *n* condizione *f*; **on** ∼ **that** a condizione che [2] *vt* Psych condizionare

conditional /kən'dɪʃənəl/ [1] *adj* ‹acceptance› condizionato; Gram condizionale; **be** ∼ **on** essere condizionato da [2] *n* Gram condizionale

conditionally /kən'dɪʃənəlɪ/ *adv* condizionatamente

conditioner /kən'dɪʃənə(r)/ *n* balsamo *m*; (for fabrics) ammorbidente *m*

conditioning /kən'dɪʃənɪŋ/ [1] *n* (of hair) balsamo *m*; Psych condizionamento *m* [2] *adj* ‹shampoo, lotion etc› trattante

condole /kən'dəʊl/ *vi* fare le condoglianze (with a)

condolences /kən'dəʊlənsɪz/ *npl* condoglianze *fpl*

condom /'kɒndəm/ *n* preservativo *m*

condo[minium] /'kɒndəʊ, kɒndə'mɪnɪəm/ *n* Am condominio *m*

condone /kən'dəʊn/ *vt* passare sopra a

conducive /kən'djuːsɪv/ *adj* **be** ∼ **to** contribuire a

conduct[1] /'kɒndʌkt/ *n* condotta *f*

⚡ **conduct**[2] /kən'dʌkt/ *vt* condurre; dirigere ‹orchestra›

conduction /kən'dʌkʃn/ *n* conduzione *f*

conductor /kən'dʌktə(r)/ *n* direttore *m* d'orchestra; (of bus) bigliettaio *m*; Phys conduttore *m*

conductress /kən'dʌktrɪs/ *n* bigliettaia *f*

cone /kəʊn/ *n* cono *m*; Bot pigna *f*; Auto birillo *m*
■ **cone off**: *vt* **be** ∼**d off** Auto essere chiuso da birilli

confection /kən'fekʃn/ *n* (cake, dessert) dolce *m*; **a** ∼ **of** (combination) una combinazione di

confectioner /kən'fekʃənə(r)/ *n* pasticciere, -a *mf*

confectionery /kən'fekʃənərɪ/ *n* pasticceria *f*

confederation /kənfedə'reɪʃn/ *n* confederazione *f*

confer /kən'fɜː(r)/ *v* (*pt/pp* **conferred**) [1] *vt* conferire (on a) [2] *vi* (discuss) conferire

⚡ **conference** /'kɒnfərəns/ *n* conferenza *f*

conference room *n* sala *f* riunioni

⚡ indicates a very frequent word

confess /kən'fes/ [1] *vt* confessare [2] *vi* confessare; Relig confessarsi

confession /kən'feʃn/ *n* confessione *f*

confessional /kən'feʃənəl/ *n* confessionale *m*

confessor /kən'fesə(r)/ *n* confessore *m*

confetti /kən'fetɪ/ *n* coriandoli *mpl*

confide /kən'faɪd/ *vt* confidare
■ **confide in**: *vt* ∼ **in somebody** fidarsi di

⚡ **confidence** /'kɒnfɪdəns/ *n* (trust) fiducia *f*; (self-assurance) sicurezza *f* di sé; (secret) confidenza *f*; **in** ∼ in confidenza

confidence trick *n* truffa *f*

confidence trickster /'kɒnfɪdənstrɪkstə(r)/ *n* imbroglione, -a *mf*

confident /'kɒnfɪdənt/ *adj* fiducioso; (self-assured) sicuro di sé

confidential /kɒnfɪ'denʃl/ *adj* confidenziale

confidentiality /kɒnfɪdenʃɪ'ælətɪ/ *n* riservatezza *f*

confidentially /kɒnfɪ'denʃəlɪ/ *adv* confidenzialmente

confidently /'kɒnfɪdəntlɪ/ *adv* con aria fiduciosa; **we** ∼ **expect to win** siamo fiduciosi nella vittoria

confine /kən'faɪn/ *vt* rinchiudere; (limit) limitare; **be** ∼**d to bed** essere confinato a letto

confined /kən'faɪnd/ *adj* ‹space› limitato

confinement /kən'faɪnmənt/ *n* detenzione *f*; Med parto *m*

confines /'kɒnfaɪnz/ *npl* confini *mpl*

⚡ **confirm** /kən'fɜːm/ *vt* confermare; Relig cresimare

confirmation /kɒnfə'meɪʃn/ *n* conferma *f*; Relig cresima *f*

confirmed /kən'fɜːmd/ *adj* incallito; ∼ **bachelor** scapolo *m* impenitente

confiscate /'kɒnfɪskeɪt/ *vt* confiscare

confiscation /kɒnfɪs'keɪʃn/ *n* confisca *f*

conflagration /kɒnflə'greɪʃn/ *n* conflagrazione *f*

conflate /kən'fleɪt/ *vt* fondere

⚡ **conflict**[1] /'kɒnflɪkt/ *n* conflitto *m*

conflict[2] /kən'flɪkt/ *vi* essere in contraddizione

conflicting /kən'flɪktɪŋ/ *adj* contraddittorio

confluence /'kɒnfluəns/ *n* (of rivers) confluenza *f*; fig convergenza *f*

conform /kən'fɔːm/ *vi* ‹person› conformarsi; ‹thing› essere conforme (to a)

conformist /kən'fɔːmɪst/ *n* conformista *mf*

conformity /kən'fɔːmɪtɪ/ *n* conformità *f*; Relig ortodossia *f*; **in** ∼ **with** in conformità a

confound /kən'faʊnd/ *vt* (perplex) confondere; (show to be wrong) confutare

confounded /kən'faʊndɪd/ *adj* fam maledetto

confront /kən'frʌnt/ *vt* affrontare; **the problems ~ing us** i problemi che dobbiamo affrontare

confrontation /kɒnfrʌn'teɪʃn/ *n* confronto *m*

confrontational /ˌkɒnfrən'teɪʃənəl/ *adj* provocatorio

⚐ **confuse** /kən'fjuːz/ *vt* confondere

confused /kən'fjuːzd/ *adj* ⟨presentation, idea⟩ ingarbugliato

confusing /kən'fjuːzɪŋ/ *adj* che confonde

confusion /kən'fjuːʒn/ *n* confusione *f*

congeal /kən'dʒiːl/ *vi* ⟨blood⟩ coagularsi

congenial /kən'dʒiːnɪəl/ *adj* congeniale

congenital /kən'dʒenɪtl/ *adj* congenito

congested /kən'dʒestɪd/ *adj* congestionato

congestion /kən'dʒestʃn/ *n* congestione *f*

congestion charge *n pedaggio* (*m*) *per circolare nelle strade del centro di Londra*

conglomerate /kən'glɒmərət/ *n* conglomerato *m*

Congo /'kɒŋgəʊ/ *n* Congo *m*

Congolese /kɒŋgə'liːz/ *adj & n* congolese *mf*

congratulate /kən'grætjʊleɪt/ *vt* congratularsi con (**on** per)

congratulations /kəngrætjʊ'leɪʃnz/ *npl* congratulazioni *fpl*

congregate /'kɒŋgrɪgeɪt/ *vi* radunarsi

congregation /kɒŋgrɪ'geɪʃn/ *n* Relig assemblea *f*

⚐ **congress** /'kɒŋgres/ *n* congresso *m*

congressman /'kɒŋgresmən/ *n* Am Pol membro *m* del congresso

conical /'kɒnɪkl/ *adj* conico

conifer /'kɒnɪfə(r)/ *n* conifera *f*

conjecture /kən'dʒektʃə(r)/ 1 *n* congettura *f*
2 *vt* congetturare
3 *vi* fare congetture

conjugal /'kɒndʒʊgl/ *adj* coniugale

conjugate /'kɒndʒʊgeɪt/ *vt* coniugare

conjugation /kɒndʒʊ'geɪʃn/ *n* coniugazione *f*

conjunction /kən'dʒʌŋkʃn/ *n* congiunzione *f*; **in ~ with** insieme a

conjunctivitis /kəndʒʌŋktɪ'vaɪtɪs/ *n* congiuntivite *f*

conjure up /'kʌndʒə(r)/ *vt* evocare ⟨image⟩; tirar fuori dal nulla ⟨meal⟩

conjuring /'kʌndʒərɪŋ/ *n* giochi *mpl* di prestigio

conjuring trick /'kʌndʒərɪŋ/ *n* gioco *m* di prestigio

conjuror, **conjurer** /'kʌndʒərə(r)/ *n* prestigiatore, -trice *mf*

conk /kɒŋk/ *vi* ~ **out** fam ⟨machine⟩ guastarsi; ⟨person⟩ crollare

conker /'kɒŋkə(r)/ *n* fam castagna *f* (*d'ippocastano*)

conman /'kɒnmæn/ *n* fam truffatore *m*

⚐ **connect** /kə'nekt/ 1 *vt* collegare; **be ~ed with** avere legami con; (be related to) essere imparentato con; **be well ~ed** aver conoscenze influenti
2 *vi* essere collegato (**with** a); ⟨train⟩ fare coincidenza

connecting /kə'nektɪŋ/ *adj* ⟨room⟩ di comunicazione

connecting flight *n* coincidenza *f*

⚐ **connection** /kə'nekʃn/ *n* (between ideas) nesso *m*; (in travel) coincidenza *f*; Electr, Comput collegamento *m*; **in ~ with** con riferimento a; **~s** *p* (people) conoscenze *fpl*

connectivity /ˌkɒnek'tɪvɪti/ *n* Comput connettività *f*

connector /kə'nektə(r)/ *n* Comput connettore *m*

connivance /kə'naɪvəns/ *n* connivenza *f*

connive /kə'naɪv/ *vi* ~ **at** essere connivente in

connoisseur /kɒnə'sɜː(r)/ *n* intenditore, -trice *mf*

connotation /kɒnə'teɪʃn/ *n* connotazione *f*

connote /kə'nəʊt/ *vt* evocare; (in linguistics) connotare

conquer /'kɒŋkə(r)/ *vt* conquistare; fig superare ⟨fear⟩

conqueror /'kɒŋkərə(r)/ *n* conquistatore *m*

conquest /'kɒŋkwest/ *n* conquista *f*

conscience /'kɒnʃəns/ *n* coscienza *f*

conscientious /kɒnʃɪ'enʃəs/ *adj* coscienzioso

conscientiously /kɒnʃɪ'enʃəslɪ/ *adv* coscienziosamente

conscientious objector /əb'dʒektə(r)/ *n* obiettore *m* di coscienza

conscious /'kɒnʃəs/ *adj* conscio; ⟨decision⟩ meditato; [**fully**] ~ cosciente; **be/ become ~ of something** rendersi conto di qualcosa

consciously /'kɒnʃəslɪ/ *adv* consapevolmente

consciousness /'kɒnʃəsnɪs/ *n* consapevolezza *f*; Med conoscenza *f*

conscript¹ /'kɒnskrɪpt/ *n* coscritto *m*

conscript² /kən'skrɪpt/ *vt* Mil chiamare alle armi; ~ **somebody to do something** fig reclutare qualcuno per fare qualcosa

conscription /kən'skrɪpʃn/ *n* coscrizione *f*, leva *f*

consecrate /'kɒnsɪkreɪt/ *vt* consacrare

consecration /kɒnsɪ'kreɪʃn/ *n* consacrazione *f*

c

consecutive /kən'sekjʊtɪv/ *adj*
consecutivo

consecutively /kən'sekjʊtɪvlɪ/ *adv*
consecutivamente

consensus /kən'sensəs/ *n* consenso *m*

consent /kən'sent/ **1** *n* consenso *m*
2 *vi* acconsentire

⚡ **consequence** /'kɒnsɪkwəns/ *n*
conseguenza *f*; (importance) importanza *f*

consequent /'kɒnsɪkwənt/ *adj*
conseguente

consequently /'kɒnsɪkwəntlɪ/ *adv* di
conseguenza

conservation /kɒnsə'veɪʃn/ *n*
conservazione *f*

conservation area *n* area *f* soggetta a
vincoli ambientali

conservationist /kɒnsə'veɪʃənɪst/ *n*
fautore, -trice *mf* della tutela ambientale

conservatism /kən'sɜːvətɪzm/ *n*
conservatorismo *m*

conservative /kən'sɜːvətɪv/ **1** *adj*
conservativo; ‹estimate› ottimistico; C~ Pol
adj conservatore
2 *n* conservatore, -trice *mf*

Conservative Party *n* partito *m*
conservatore

conservatory /kən'sɜːvətrɪ/ *n* spazio (*m*)
chiuso da vetrate adiacente alla casa

conserve /kən'sɜːv/ *vt* conservare

⚡ **consider** /kən'sɪdə(r)/ *vt* considerare; ~
doing something considerare la possibilità
di fare qualcosa

considerable /kən'sɪdərəbl/ *adj*
considerevole

considerably /kən'sɪdərəblɪ/ *adv*
considerevolmente

considerate /kən'sɪdərət/ *adj* pieno di
riguardo

considerately /kən'sɪdərətlɪ/ *adv* con
riguardo

⚡ **consideration** /kənsɪdə'reɪʃn/ *n*
considerazione *f*; (thoughtfulness) attenzione *f*;
(respect) riguardo *m*; (payment) compenso *m*;
take into ~ prendere in considerazione

considering /kən'sɪdərɪŋ/ *prep*
considerando; ~ **that** considerando che

consign /kən'saɪn/ *vt* affidare

consignment /kən'saɪnmənt/ *n* consegna
f

⚡ **consist** /kən'sɪst/ *vi* ~ **of** consistere di

consistency /kən'sɪstənsɪ/ *n* coerenza *f*;
(density) consistenza *f*

⚡ **consistent** /kən'sɪstənt/ *adj* coerente;
‹loyalty› costante; **be** ~ **with** far pensare a

consistently /kən'sɪstəntlɪ/ *adv*
coerentemente; ‹late, loyal› costantemente

consolation /kɒnsə'leɪʃn/ *n* consolazione
f

consolation prize *n* premio *m* di
consolazione

console /kən'səʊl/ *vt* consolare

consolidate /kən'sɒlɪdeɪt/ *vt* consolidare

consolidation /kənsɒlɪ'deɪʃn/ *n* (of
knowledge, position) consolidamento *m*

consoling /kən'səʊlɪŋ/ *adj* consolante

consonant /'kɒnsənənt/ *n* consonante *f*

consort¹ /'kɒnsɔːt/ *n* consorte *mf*

consort² /kən'sɔːt/ *vi* ~ **with** frequentare

consortium /kən'sɔːtɪəm/ *n* consorzio *m*

conspicuous /kən'spɪkjʊəs/ *adj*
facilmente distinguibile; **be** ~ **by one's**
absence brillare per la propria assenza

conspicuously /kən'spɪkjʊəslɪ/ *adv*
‹dressed› vistosamente; ‹placed› in evidenza;
(silent, empty) in modo evidente

conspiracy /kən'spɪrəsɪ/ *n* cospirazione *f*

conspiracy theory *n* teoria *f* del
complotto

conspirator /kən'spɪrətə(r)/ *n*
cospiratore, -trice *mf*

conspire /kən'spaɪə(r)/ *vi* cospirare

constable /'kʌnstəbl/ *n* agente *m* [di
polizia]

constabulary /kən'stæbjʊlərɪ/ *n* Br
polizia *f*

constancy /'kɒnstənsɪ/ *n* costanza *f*

⚡ **constant** /'kɒnstənt/ *adj* costante

constantly /'kɒnstəntlɪ/ *adv*
costantemente

constellation /kɒnstə'leɪʃn/ *n*
costellazione *f*

consternation /kɒnstə'neɪʃn/ *n*
costernazione *f*

constipated /'kɒnstɪpeɪtɪd/ *adj* stitico

constipation /kɒnstɪ'peɪʃn/ *n* stitichezza
f

constituency /kən'stɪtjʊənsɪ/ *n collegio*
(*m*) *elettorale di un deputato nel Regno Unito*

constituent /kən'stɪtjʊənt/ *n* costituente
m; Pol elettore, -trice *mf*

constitute /'kɒnstɪtjuːt/ *vt* costituire

constitution /kɒnstɪ'tjuːʃn/ *n*
costituzione *f*

constitutional /kɒnstɪ'tjuːʃənl/ **1** *adj*
costituzionale
2 *n* passeggiata *f* salutare

constitutionally /kɒnstɪ'tjuːʃənəlɪ/
adv Pol costituzionalmente; (innately) di
costituzione

constrain /kən'streɪn/ *vt* costringere

constraint /kən'streɪnt/ *n* costrizione
f; (restriction) restrizione *f*; (strained manner)
disagio *m*

⚡ indicates a very frequent word

constrict /kən'strɪkt/ vt ‹tight jacket›
stringere

constriction /kən'strɪkʃn/ n (of chest,
throat) senso m di oppressione; (constraint)
costrizione f; (of blood vessel) restrizione f

✓ **construct** /kən'strʌkt/ vt costruire

✓ **construction** /kən'strʌkʃn/ n
costruzione f; (interpretation) interpretazione f;
under ~ in costruzione

construction engineer n ingegnere
m edile

construction paper n Am cartoncino m

construction site n cantiere m

construction worker n [operaio m]
edile m

constructive /kən'strʌktɪv/ adj
costruttivo

constructively /kən'strʌktɪvlɪ/ adv in
modo costruttivo

construe /kən'stru:/ vt interpretare

consul /'kɒnsl/ n console m

consular /'kɒnsjʊlə(r)/ adj consolare

consulate /'kɒnsjʊlət/ n consolato m

consult /kən'sʌlt/ vt consultare

consultancy /kən'sʌltənsɪ/ ① n (advice)
consulenza f; (firm) ufficio m di consulenza;
Br Med posto m di specialista; **do** ~ fare il/
la consulente

② attrib ‹fees, service, work› di consulenza

consultant /kən'sʌltənt/ n consulente mf;
Med specialista mf

consultation /kɒnsl'teɪʃn/ n
consultazione f; Med consulto m

consultative /kən'sʌltətɪv/ adj di
consulenza

consulting hours /kən'sʌltɪŋ/ npl Med
orario m di visita

consulting room n Med ambulatorio m

consumable /kən'sju:məbl/ n bene m di
consumo

consume /kən'sju:m/ vt consumare

✓ **consumer** /kən'sju:mə(r)/ n consumatore,
-trice mf

consumer advice n consigli mpl ai
consumatori

consumer confidence n fiducia f del
consumatore

consumer goods npl beni mpl di
consumo

consumerism /kən'sju:mərɪzm/ n
consumismo m

consumer organization n
organizzazione f per la tutela dei
consumatori

consumer products npl beni mpl di
consumo

consumer protection n tutela f dei
consumatori

consumer society n società f inv
consumista, società f inv dei consumi

consuming /kən'sju:mɪŋ/ adj ‹passion›
struggente; ‹urge› pressante; ‹hatred›
insaziabile

consummate /'kɒnsjʊmeɪt/ vt
consumare

consummation /kɒnsjʊ'meɪʃn/ n
consumazione f

consumption /kən'sʌmpʃn/ n consumo
m

cont. /kɒnt/ abbr (**continued**) segue

✓ **contact** /'kɒntækt/ ① n contatto m;
(person) conoscenza f
② vt mettersi in contatto con

contactable /'kɒntæktəbl/ adj ‹person›
reperibile

contact lenses npl lenti fpl a contatto

contactless /'kɒntæktləs/ adj senza
contatti

contagious /kən'teɪdʒəs/ adj contagioso

✓ **contain** /kən'teɪn/ vt contenere; ~ **oneself**
controllarsi

container /kən'teɪnə(r)/ n recipiente m;
(for transport) container m inv

container port n porto m container

container ship n [nave f] portacontainer f inv

container truck n [autocarro m]
portacontainer m inv

contaminate /kən'tæmɪneɪt/ vt
contaminare

contamination /kəntæmɪ'neɪʃn/ n
contaminazione f

contd abbr (**continued**) segue

contemplate /'kɒntəmpleɪt/ vt
contemplare; (consider) considerare; ~ **doing
something** considerare di fare qualcosa

contemplation /kɒntəm'pleɪʃn/ n
contemplazione f

contemplative /kən'templətɪv/ adj
contemplativo

contemporaneous /kəntempə'reɪnɪəs/
adj contemporaneo (with a)

contemporaneously
/kəntempə'reɪnɪəslɪ/ adv
contemporaneamente (with a)

✓ **contemporary** /kən'tempərərɪ/ adj & n
contemporaneo, -a mf

contempt /kən'tempt/ n disprezzo m;
beneath ~ più che vergognoso; ~ **of court**
oltraggio m alla Corte

contemptible /kən'tem(p)təbl/ adj
spregevole

contemptuous /kən'tem(p)tjʊəs/ adj
sprezzante

contemptuously /kən'tem(p)tjʊəslɪ/ adv
sprezzantemente

contend /kən'tend/ ① vi ~ **with**
occuparsi di
② vt (assert) sostenere

contender /kən'tendə(r)/ n concorrente mf

♂ **content¹** /'kɒntent/ n contenuto m

content² /kən'tent/ [1] adj soddisfatto [2] n to one's heart's ∼ finché se ne ha voglia [3] vt ∼ oneself accontentarsi (with di)

contented /kən'tentɪd/ adj soddisfatto

contentedly /kən'tentɪdlɪ/ adv con aria soddisfatta

contention /kən'tenʃn/ n (assertion) opinione f

contentious /kən'tenʃəs/ adj ‹subject› controverso; ‹view› discutibile; ‹person, group› polemico

contentment /kən'tentmənt/ n soddisfazione f

contents /'kɒntents/ npl contenuto m

contest¹ /'kɒntest/ n gara f

contest² /kən'test/ vt contestare ‹statement›; impugnare ‹will›; Pol ‹candidates› contendersi; ‹one candidate› aspirare a

contestant /kən'testənt/ n concorrente mf

♂ **context** /'kɒntekst/ n contesto m

continent /'kɒntɪnənt/ n continente m; the Continent l'Europa f continentale

continental /kɒntɪ'nentl/ adj continentale

continental breakfast n prima colazione (f) a base di pane, burro, marmellata, croissant ecc

continental quilt n piumone m

contingency /kən'tɪndʒənsɪ/ n eventualità f inv

contingency fund n fondo m sopravvenienze passive

contingency plan n piano m d'emergenza

contingent /kən'tɪndʒənt/ [1] adj be ∼ on dipendere da [2] n Mil contingente m

continual /kən'tɪnjʊəl/ adj continuo

continually /kən'tɪnjʊəlɪ/ adv continuamente

continuation /kəntɪnjʊ'eɪʃn/ n continuazione f

♂ **continue** /kən'tɪnju:/ [1] vt continuare; ∼ doing or to do something continuare a fare qualcosa; to be ∼d continua [2] vi continuare

continued /kən'tɪnju:d/ adj continuo

continuity /kɒntɪ'nju:ətɪ/ n continuità f

continuity announcer n annunciatore, -trice mf

continuity girl n segretaria f di produzione

continuous /kən'tɪnjʊəs/ adj continuo

continuously /kən'tɪnjʊəslɪ/ adv continuamente

continuum /kən'tɪnjʊəm/ n continuum m inv

contort /kən'tɔ:t/ vt contorcere

contortion /kən'tɔ:ʃn/ n contorsione f

contortionist /kən'tɔ:ʃənɪst/ n contorsionista mf

contour /'kɒntʊə(r)/ n contorno m; (line) curva f di livello

contraband /'kɒntrəbænd/ n contrabbando m

contraception /kɒntrə'sepʃn/ n contraccezione f; use ∼ ricorrere alla contraccezione

contraceptive /kɒntrə'septɪv/ adj & n contraccettivo m

♂ **contract¹** /'kɒntrækt/ n contratto m

contract² /kən'trækt/ [1] vi (get smaller) contrarsi [2] vt contrarre ‹illness›

contraction /kən'trækʃn/ n contrazione f

contract killer n sicario m

contractor /kən'træktə(r)/ n imprenditore, -trice mf

contractual /kən'træktjʊəl/ adj contrattuale

contract work n lavoro m su commissione

contract worker n lavoratore, -trice mf con contratto a termine

contradict /kɒntrə'dɪkt/ vt contraddire

contradiction /kɒntrə'dɪkʃn/ n contraddizione f

contradictory /kɒntrə'dɪktərɪ/ adj contraddittorio

contraflow /'kɒntrəfləʊ/ n utilizzazione (f) di una corsia nei due sensi di marcia durante lavori stradali

contraindication /kɒntrəɪndɪ'keɪʃn/ n controindicazione f

contralto /kən'træltəʊ/ n contralto m

contraption /kən'træpʃn/ n fam aggeggio m

contrariness /kən'treərɪnɪs/ n spirito m di contraddizione

contrariwise /kən'treərɪwaɪz/ adv (conversely) d'altra parte, d'altro canto; (in the opposite direction) in direzione opposta

contrary¹ /'kɒntrərɪ/ [1] adj contrario [2] adv ∼ to contrariamente a [3] n contrario m; on the ∼ al contrario

contrary² /kən'treərɪ/ adj disobbediente

♂ **contrast¹** /'kɒntrɑ:st/ n contrasto m

contrast² /kən'trɑ:st/ [1] vt confrontare [2] vi contrastare

contrasting /kən'trɑ:stɪŋ/ adj contrastante

contravene /kɒntrə'vi:n/ vt trasgredire

contravention /kɒntrə'venʃn/ n
trasgressione f

✧ **contribute** /kən'trɪbjuːt/ vt/i contribuire

✧ **contribution** /kɒntrɪ'bjuːʃn/ n
contribuzione f; (what is contributed) contributo
m

contributor /kən'trɪbjʊtə(r)/ n
contributore, -trice mf

contributory /kən'trɪbjʊtərɪ/ adj ‹factor›
concomitante; **be ~ to** contribuire a

con trick n raggiro m, truffa f

contrite /kən'traɪt/ adj contrito

contrive /kən'traɪv/ vt escogitare; **~ to do
something** riuscire a fare qualcosa

contrived /kən'traɪvd/ adj ‹style, effect›
artificioso; ‹plot, ending› forzato; ‹incident,
meeting› non fortuito

✧ **control** /kən'trəʊl/ **1** n controllo m; **~s**
pl (of car, plane) comandi mpl; **get out of ~**
sfuggire al controllo
2 vt (pt/pp **controlled**) controllare;
~ oneself controllarsi

control column n Aeron cloche f inv

control key n Comput tasto m di controllo

controlled /kən'trəʊld/ adj ‹explosion,
performance, person› controllato; **Labour-~**
dominato dai laburisti

controller /kən'trəʊlə(r)/ n controllore m;
Fin controllore m [della gestione]; Radio, TV
direttore, -trice mf

control panel n (on machine) quadro m dei
comandi; (for plane) quadro m di comando

control room n sala f di comando; Radio,
TV sala f di regia

control tower n torre f di controllo

controversial /kɒntrə'vɜːʃl/ adj
controverso

controversy /'kɒntrəvɜːsɪ/ n controversia f

conundrum /kə'nʌndrəm/ n enigma m

conurbation /kɒnɜː'beɪʃn/ n
conturbazione f

convalesce /kɒnvə'les/ vi essere in
convalescenza

convalescence /kɒnvə'lesəns/ n
convalescenza f

convalescent /kɒnvə'lesənt/ adj
convalescente

convalescent home n
convalescenziario m

convection /kən'vekʃn/ n convezione f

convector /kən'vektə(r)/ n **~ [heater]**
convettore m

convene /kən'viːn/ **1** vt convocare
2 vi riunirsi

convener /kən'viːnə(r)/ n (organizer)
organizzatore, -trice mf; (chair) presidente m

convenience /kən'viːnɪəns/ n convenienza
f; **[public] ~** gabinetti mpl pubblici; **with all
modern ~s** con tutti i comfort

convenience foods npl cibi mpl
precotti

convenience store n negozio m aperto
fino a tardi

convenient /kən'viːnɪənt/ adj comodo; **be
~ for somebody** andar bene per qualcuno; **if
it is ~ [for you]** se ti va bene

conveniently /kən'viːnɪəntlɪ/ adv
comodamente; **~ located** in una posizione
comoda

convent /'kɒnvənt/ n convento m

convention /kən'venʃn/ n convenzione f;
(assembly) convegno m

conventional /kən'venʃnəl/ adj
convenzionale

conventionally /kən'venʃnəlɪ/ adv
convenzionalmente

convention centre n palazzo m dei
congressi

convent school n scuola f retta da
religiose

converge /kən'vɜːdʒ/ vi convergere

conversant /kən'vɜːsənt/ adj **~ with**
pratico di

✧ **conversation** /kɒnvə'seɪʃn/ n
conversazione f

conversational /kɒnvə'seɪʃnəl/ adj di
conversazione

conversationalist /kɒnvə'seɪʃnəlɪst/ n
conversatore, -trice mf

converse¹ /kən'vɜːs/ vi conversare

converse² /'kɒnvɜːs/ n inverso m

conversely /'kɒnvɜːslɪ/ adv viceversa

conversion /kən'vɜːʃn/ n conversione f

conversion rate n tasso m di cambio m

conversion table n tabella f di
conversione

✧ **convert¹** /'kɒnvɜːt/ n convertito, -a mf

convert² /kən'vɜːt/ vt convertire (**into** in);
sconsacrare ‹church›

converter /kən'vɜːtə(r)/ n Electr
convertitore m

convertible /kən'vɜːtəbl/ **1** adj
convertibile
2 n Auto macchina f decappottabile

convex /'kɒnveks/ adj convesso

convey /kən'veɪ/ vt portare; trasmettere
‹idea, message›

conveyance /kən'veɪəns/ n trasporto m;
(vehicle) mezzo m di trasporto

conveyancing /kən'veɪənsɪŋ/ n Jur
passaggio m di proprietà

conveyor /kən'veɪə(r)/ n (of goods, persons)
trasportatore m

conveyor belt n nastro m trasportatore

convict¹ /'kɒnvɪkt/ n condannato, -a mf

convict² /kən'vɪkt/ vt guidicare colpevole

conviction /kən'vɪkʃn/ n condanna f;
(belief) convinzione f; **previous ~** precedente
m penale

convince /kən'vɪns/ vt convincere

convincing /kən'vɪnsɪŋ/ adj convincente

convincingly /kən'vɪnsɪŋlɪ/ adv in modo convincente

convivial /kən'vɪvɪəl/ adj conviviale

convoluted /'kɒnvəlu:tɪd/ adj contorto

convoy /'kɒnvɔɪ/ n convoglio m

convulse /kən'vʌls/ vt sconvolgere; **be ~d with laughter** contorcersi dalle risa

convulsion /kən'vʌlʃn/ n convulsione f

convulsive /kən'vʌlsɪv/ adj convulso; Med convulsivo

convulsively /kən'vʌlsɪvlɪ/ adv convulsamente

coo /ku:/ vi tubare

cooing /'ku:ɪŋ/ n (of bird, lovers) tubare m inv

cook /kʊk/ ① n cuoco, -a mf
  ② vt cucinare; **is it ~ed?** è cotto?; **~ the books** fam truccare i libri contabili
  ③ vi ‹food› cuocere; ‹person› cucinare
  ■ **cook up** vt fam inventare ‹excuse, story etc›

cookbook /'kʊkbʊk/ n libro m di cucina

cook-chill adj ‹foods, products› precotto e surgelato

cooked meats /kʊkt'mi:ts/ npl salumi mpl

cooker /'kʊkə(r)/ n cucina f; (apple) mela f da cuocere

cookery /'kʊkərɪ/ n cucina f

cookery book n libro m di cucina

cookie /'kʊkɪ/ n Am biscotto m

cooking /'kʊkɪŋ/ n cucina f; **be good at ~** saper cucinare bene; **do the ~** cucinare

cooking apple n mela f da cuocere

cooking chocolate n cioccolato m da pasticceria

cooking foil n carta f stagnola

cooking salt n sale m da cucina

cooking time n tempo m di cottura

✧ **cool** /ku:l/ ① adj fresco; (calm) calmo; (unfriendly) freddo; fam (excellent or attractive) fantastico; **a ~ T-shirt** una maglietta fantastica; **'I won!' '~!'** 'ho vinto!' 'fantastico!'
  ② n fresco m; **keep/lose one's ~** mantenere/perdere la calma
  ③ vt rinfrescare
  ④ vi rinfrescarsi
  ■ **cool down** ① vi ‹soup, tea etc› raffreddarsi; fig (become calm) calmarsi
  ② vt raffreddare ‹soup, tea etc›; fig calmare

cool bag n Br borsa f frigo

cool-box n borsa f termica

cool-headed adj equilibrato

cooling /'ku:lɪŋ/ ① n raffreddamento m
  ② adj ‹agent› refrigerante; ‹system, tower› di raffreddamento; ‹drink, swim› rinfrescante

---

✧ indicates a very frequent word

cooling-off period n (in industrial relations) periodo m di tregua [sindacale]; Comm fase f di riflessione

coolly /'ku:llɪ/ adv freddamente

coolness /'ku:lnɪs/ n freddezza f

coop /ku:p/ ① n stia f
  ② vt **~ up** rinchiudere

co-op /'kəʊɒp/ n abbr (**cooperative**) cooperativa f

cooperate /kəʊ'ɒpəreɪt/ vi cooperare

cooperation /kəʊɒpə'reɪʃn/ n cooperazione f

cooperative /kəʊ'ɒpərətɪv/ adj & n cooperativa f

co-opt /kəʊ'ɒpt/ vt eleggere

coordinate /kəʊ'ɔ:dɪneɪt/ vt coordinare

coordinated /kəʊ'ɔ:dɪneɪtɪd/ adj coordinato

coordinates /kəʊ'ɔ:dɪnəts/ npl (clothes) coordinato m sg

coordination /kəʊɔ:dɪ'neɪʃn/ n coordinazione f

coordinator /kəʊ'ɔ:dɪneɪtə(r)/ n coordinatore, -trice mf

co-owner /kəʊ'əʊnə(r)/ n comproprietario, -a mf

cop /kɒp/ n fam poliziotto m

co-parent /kəʊ'peərənt/ vt condividere la responsabilità dell'educazione dei figli

co-parenting /'kəʊ,peərəntɪŋ/ n condivisione (f) della responsabilità dell'educazione dei figli

cope /kəʊp/ vi fam farcela; **can she ~ by herself?** ce la fa da sola?; **~ with** farcela con; **I couldn't ~ with five kids** non ce la farei con cinque bambini

Copenhagen /kəʊpən'heɪgən/ n Copenaghen f

copier /'kɒpɪə(r)/ n fotocopiatrice f

co-pilot /'kəʊpaɪlət/ n copilota m

copious /'kəʊpɪəs/ adj abbondante

copiously /'kəʊpɪəslɪ/ adv abbondantemente

cop-out n fam (evasive act) bidone m; (excuse) scappatoia f

copper¹ /'kɒpə(r)/ ① n rame m; **~s** pl monete fpl da uno o due penny
  ② attrib di rame

copper² n fam poliziotto m

copper beech n faggio m rosso

copper-coloured adj [color] rame inv; ‹hair› ramato

copperplate n calligrafia f ornata

coppice /'kɒpɪs/, **copse** /kɒps/ n boschetto m

co-property /'kəʊprɒpətɪ/ n comproprietà f inv

copulate /'kɒpjʊleɪt/ vi accoppiarsi

copulation /kɒpjʊ'leɪʃn/ n copulazione f

copy /'kɒpɪ/ **1** *n* copia *f*
2 *vt* (*pt/pp* **-ied**) copiare
■ **copy down** *vt* = COPY
■ **copy out** *vt* = COPY

copybook *n* blot one's ~ rovinarsi la reputazione

copycat **1** *n* pej fam copione, -a *mf*
2 *adj* ‹crime, murder› ispirato da un altro

copy editor *n* segretario, -a *mf* di redazione

copyright *n* diritti *mpl* d'autore

copy-typist *n* dattilografo, -a *mf*

copywriter *n* copywriter *mf inv*

coquetry /'kɒkɪtrɪ/ *n* civetteria *f*

coquettish /kɒ'ketɪʃ/ *adj* civettuolo

coral /'kɒrəl/ *n* corallo *m*

coral island *n* isola *f* di corallo

coral pink *adj & n* rosa *m inv* corallo

coral reef *n* barriera *f* corallina

cord /kɔːd/ *n* corda *f*; (thinner) cordoncino *m*; (fabric) velluto *m* a coste; ~s *pl* pantaloni *mpl* di velluto a coste

cordial /'kɔːdɪəl/ **1** *adj* cordiale
2 *n* analcolico *m*

cordially /'kɔːdɪəlɪ/ *adv* con tutto il cuore

cordless /'kɔːdlɪs/ *adj* ‹phone, kettle› cordless

cordless telephone /'kɔːdlɪs/ *adj* telefono *m* cordless

cordon /'kɔːdn/ *n* cordone *m* (*di persone*)
■ **cordon off** *vt* bloccare

corduroy /'kɔːdərɔɪ/ *n* velluto *m* a coste

core /kɔː(r)/ *n* (of apple, pear) torsolo *m*; fig (of organization) cuore *m*; (of problem, theory) nocciolo *m*

core curriculum *n* materie *fpl* fondamentali (del programma scolastico)

co-respondent /kəʊrɪ'spɒndənt/ *n* Jur correo, -a *mf* in adulterio

Corfu /kɔː'fuː/ *n* Corfù *f*

coriander /kɒrɪ'ændə(r)/ *n* coriandolo *m*

cork /kɔːk/ *n* sughero *m*; (for bottle) turacciolo *m*

corkage /'kɔːkɪdʒ/ *n* somma (*f*) pagata a un ristorante per servire una bottiglia di vino portata da fuori

corker /'kɔːkə(r)/ *n* Br fam (story) storia *f* strabiliante; (stroke, shot) tiro *m* da maestro

corkscrew /'kɔːkskruː/ *n* cavatappi *m inv*

corkscrew curls *npl* boccoli *mpl*

corn¹ /kɔːn/ *n* grano *m*; Am (maize) granturco *m*

corn² *n* Med callo *m*

corncob /'kɔːnkɒb/ *n* pannocchia *f* [di mais]

cornea /'kɔːnɪə/ *n* cornea *f*

corned beef /kɔːnd'biːf/ *n* manzo *m* sotto sale

corner /'kɔːnə(r)/ **1** *n* angolo *m*; (football) calcio *m* d'angolo, corner *m inv*
2 *vt* bloccare; Comm accaparrarsi ‹market›

corner shop *n* negozio *m* di quartiere

cornerstone /'kɔːnəstəʊn/ *n* pietra *f* angolare

cornet /'kɔːnɪt/ *n* Mus cornetta *f*; (for ice-cream) cono *m*

cornfield /'kɔːnfiːld/ *n* campo *m* di grano; (sweetcorn) campo *m* di mais

cornflour /'kɔːnflaʊə(r)/ *n* farina *f* finissima di mais

cornflower /'kɔːnflaʊə(r)/ *n* fiordaliso *m*

cornice /'kɔːnɪs/ *n* (inside) cornice *f*; (outside) cornicione *m*

Cornish pasty /kɔːnɪʃ'pæstɪ/ *n* fagottino (*m*) *di pasta sfoglia ripieno di carne e verdura*

corn oil *n* olio *m* di mais

corn on the cob *n* pannocchia *f* cotta

corn plaster *n* [cerotto *m*] callifugo *m*

cornstarch *n* Am fecola *f* di mais

cornucopia /kɔːnjʊ'kəʊpɪə/ *n* cornucopia *f*; fig abbondanza *f*

Cornwall /'kɔːnwɔːl/ *n* Cornovaglia *f*

corny /'kɔːnɪ/ *adj* (**-ier**, **-iest**) fam ‹joke, film› scontato; ‹person› banale; (sentimental) sdolcinato

corollary /kə'rɒlərɪ/ *n* corollario *m*

coronary /'kɒrənərɪ/ **1** *adj* coronario
2 *n* ~ [**thrombosis**] trombosi *f* coronarica

coronation /kɒrə'neɪʃn/ *n* incoronazione *f*

coroner /'kɒrənə(r)/ *n* coroner *m inv* (*nel diritto britannico, ufficiale incaricato delle indagini su morti sospette*)

coronet /'kɒrənet/ *n* coroncina *f*

corporal¹ /'kɔːpərəl/ *n* Mil caporale *m*

corporal² *adj* corporale; ~ **punishment** punizione *f* corporale

corporate /'kɔːpərət/ *adj* ‹decision, policy, image› aziendale; ~ **life** la vita in un'azienda

corporate hospitality *n* omaggi (*mpl*) offerti dalla ditta ai clienti importanti

corporate identity *n* logo *m* dell'azienda

corporate image *n* immagine *f* aziendale

corporate lawyer *n* legale *mf* specializzato, -a in diritto aziendale

corporate planning *n* pianificazione *f* aziendale

corporate raider *n* finanziere *m* d'assalto

corporation /kɔːpə'reɪʃn/ *n* ente *m*; (of town) ≈ consiglio *m* comunale

corporation tax *n* Br imposta *f* sul reddito delle aziende

corps /kɔː(r)/ *n* (*pl* **corps** /kɔːz/) corpo *m*

corps de ballet /kɔːdə'bæleɪ/ n corpo m di ballo

corpse /kɔːps/ n cadavere m

corpulent /'kɔːpjʊlənt/ adj corpulento

corpus /'kɔːpəs/ n (of words) corpus m inv

corpuscle /'kɔːpʌsl/ n globulo m

✧ **correct** /kə'rekt/ ① adj corretto; be ~ ‹person› aver ragione; ~! esatto!
② vt correggere

correcting fluid n bianchetto m

correction /kə'rekʃn/ n correzione f

corrective /kə'rektɪv/ n correttivo m

correctly /kə'rektlɪ/ adv correttamente

correlate /'kɒrəleɪt/ ① vt correlare
② vi essere correlato

correlation /kɒrə'leɪʃn/ n correlazione f

correspond /kɒrɪ'spɒnd/ vi corrispondere (to a); ‹two things› corrispondere; (write) scriversi

correspondence /kɒrɪ'spɒndəns/ n corrispondenza f

correspondence course n corso m per corrispondenza

correspondent /kɒrɪ'spɒndənt/ n corrispondente mf

corresponding /kɒrɪ'spɒndɪŋ/ adj corrispondente

correspondingly /kɒrɪ'spɒndɪŋlɪ/ adv in modo corrispondente

corridor /'kɒrɪdɔː(r)/ n corridoio m

corroborate /kə'rɒbəreɪt/ vt corroborare

corrode /kə'rəʊd/ ① vt corrodere
② vi corrodersi

corrosion /kə'rəʊʒn/ n corrosione f

corrugated /'kɒrəgeɪtɪd/ adj ondulato

corrugated iron n lamiera f ondulata

corrupt /kə'rʌpt/ ① adj corrotto
② vt corrompere

corruption /kə'rʌpʃn/ n corruzione f

corset /'kɔːsɪt/ n & s pl busto m

Corsica /'kɔːsɪkə/ n Corsica f

Corsican /'kɔːsɪkən/ adj & n corso, -a mf

cortège /kɔː'teɪʒ/ n [funeral] ~ corteo m funebre

cosh /kɒʃ/ n randello m

co-signatory /kəʊ'sɪgnətrɪ/ n cofirmatario, -a mf

cosily /'kəʊzɪlɪ/ adv ‹sit, lie› in modo confortevole

cosiness /'kəʊzɪnɪs/ n (of room) comodità f; (intimacy) intimità f

cos lettuce /kɒs/ n lattuga f romana

cosmetic /kɒz'metɪk/ ① adj cosmetico
② n ~s pl cosmetici mpl

cosmetic surgery n chirurgia f estetica

cosmic /'kɒzmɪk/ adj cosmico

cosmonaut /'kɒzmənɔːt/ n cosmonauta mf

cosmopolitan /kɒzmə'pɒlɪtən/ adj cosmopolita

cosmos /'kɒzmɒs/ n cosmo m

Cossack /'kɒsæk/ adj & n cosacco, -a mf

cosset /'kɒsɪt/ vt coccolare

✧ **cost** /kɒst/ ① n costo m; ~s pl Jur spese fpl processuali; at all ~s a tutti i costi; I learnt to my ~ ho imparato a mie spese
② vt (pt/pp cost) costare; it ~ me £20 mi è costato 20 sterline
③ vt (pt/pp costed) ~ [out] stabilire il prezzo di

co-star /'kəʊstɑː/ ① n Cinema, Theat coprotagonista mf ② vi/t film ~ ring X and Y un film con X e Y come protagonisti

Costa Rica n Costa Rica m

cost centre n centro m di costi

cost-cutting n tagli mpl sulle spese; as a ~ exercise [come misura] per ridurre le spese

cost-effective adj conveniente

cost-effectiveness n convenienza f

costing /'kɒstɪŋ/ n (process) determinazione f dei costi; (discipline) costing m inv

costly /'kɒstlɪ/ adj -ier, -iest costoso

cost of living n costo m della vita

cost-of-living index n indice m del costo della vita

cost price n prezzo m di costo

costume /'kɒstjuːm/ n costume m

costume drama n dramma m storico

costume jewellery n bigiotteria f

cosy /'kəʊzɪ/ ① adj -ier, -iest ‹pub, chat› intimo; it's nice and ~ in here si sta bene qui
② n tea ~ copriteiera m inv

cot /kɒt/ n lettino m; Am (camp bed) branda f

cot death n Br morte (f) inspiegabile di un neonato nel sonno

Côte d'Azur /kəʊtdæ'zʊə(r)/ n Costa f Azzurra

cottage /'kɒtɪdʒ/ n casetta f

cottage cheese n fiocchi mpl di latte

cottage hospital n Br piccolo ospedale m (in zona rurale)

cottage industry n attività (f inv) artigianale basata sul lavoro a domicilio

cottage loaf n pagnotta f casereccia

cottage pie n Br pasticcio (m) di patate e carne macinata

cotton /'kɒtn/ ① n cotone m
② attrib di cotone
■ **cotton on** vi fam capire

cotton bud n cotton fioc® m inv

cotton mill n cotonificio m

cotton reel n rocchetto m, spagnoletta f

cotton wool n Br cotone m idrofilo

✧ indicates a very frequent word

couch /kaʊtʃ/ n divano m
couchette /kuːˈʃet/ n cuccetta f
couch potato n pantofolaio, -a mf
cougar /ˈkuːgə(r)/ n coguaro m
cough /kɒf/ [1] n tosse f
  [2] vi tossire
  ▪ **cough up** vt/i sputare; fam (pay) sborsare
cough mixture n sciroppo m per la tosse
ꝗ **could** /kʊd/ atono /kəd/ v aux ▶ (also CAN²)
  ∼ I have a glass of water? potrei aver un
  bicchier d'acqua?; I ∼n't do it even if I wanted
  to non potrei farlo nemmeno se lo volessi; I
  ∼n't care less non potrebbe importarmene di
  meno; he ∼n't have done it without help non
  avrebbe potuto farlo senza aiuto; you ∼ have
  phoned avresti potuto telefonare
ꝗ **council** /ˈkaʊnsl/ n consiglio m
council estate n Br complesso m di case
  popolari
council house n casa f popolare
council housing n Br case fpl popolari
councillor /ˈkaʊnsələ(r)/ n consigliere,
  -a mf
council scheme n ▶ COUNCIL ESTATE
council tax n imposta f locale sugli
  immobili
counsel /ˈkaʊnsl/ [1] n consigli mpl; Jur
  avvocato m
  [2] vt (pt/pp counselled) consigliare a
  ‹person›
counselling Am **counseling**
  /ˈkaʊnsəlɪŋ/ [1] n (psychological) terapia
  f [psichiatrica]; Sch orientamento m
  scolastico; careers ∼ orientamento m
  professionale
  [2] attrib ‹group, centre, service› di
  assistenza
counsellor /ˈkaʊnsələ(r)/ n consigliere,
  -a mf
count¹ /kaʊnt/ n (nobleman) conte m
ꝗ **count²** [1] n conto m; keep ∼ tenere il
  conto
  [2] vt/i contare
  ▪ **count against** vt ‹inexperience, police
  record› deporre a sfavore di
  ▪ **count among**: vt ∼ somebody among
  one's friends annoverare qualcuno tra i
  propri amici
  ▪ **count in** vt (include) includere; ∼ me in!
  io ci sto!
  ▪ **count on** vt contare su
  ▪ **count out** vt contare ‹money›; ∼ me out!
  fate senza di me!
  ▪ **count up** [1] vt contare
  [2] vi ∼ to ten contare fino a dieci
countable /ˈkaʊntəbl/ adj ‹noun›
  numerabile
countdown /ˈkaʊntdaʊn/ n conto m alla
  rovescia
countenance /ˈkaʊntənəns/ [1] n
  espressione f
  [2] vt approvare

counter¹ /ˈkaʊntə(r)/ n banco m; (in games)
  gettone m
counter² [1] adv ∼ to contro, in contrasto
  a; go ∼ to something andare contro
  qualcosa
  [2] vt/i opporre ‹measure, effect›; parare
  ‹blow›
counteract /kaʊntərˈækt/ vt
  neutralizzare
counter-attack n contrattacco m
counterbalance /ˈkaʊntəbæləns/ [1] n
  contrappeso m
  [2] vt controbilanciare
counter-claim n replica f
counter-clockwise /ˌkaʊntəˈklɒkwaɪz/
  Am [1] adj antiorario
  [2] adv in senso antiorario
counter-culture /ˈkaʊntəkʌltʃə(r)/ n
  controcultura f
counter-espionage n controspionaggio
  m
counterfeit /ˈkaʊntəfɪt/ [1] adj
  contraffatto
  [2] n contraffazione f
  [3] vt contraffare
counterfoil /ˈkaʊntəfɔɪl/ n matrice f
counter-inflationary /-ɪnˈfleɪʃənərɪ/
  adj antinflazionistico
counter-insurgency /-ɪnˈsɜːdʒənsɪ/
  attrib per reprimere un'insurrezione
counter-intelligence n
  controspionaggio m
countermeasure /ˈkaʊntəmeʒə(r)/ n
  contromisura f
counter-offensive n controffensiva f
counterpane /ˈkaʊntəpeɪn/ n copriletto
  m
counterpart /ˈkaʊntəpɑːt/ n equivalente
  mf
counterpoint /ˈkaʊntəpɔɪnt/ n
  contrappunto mf
counter-productive adj
  controproduttivo
countersign /ˈkaʊntəsaɪn/ vt
  controfirmare
countersignature n controfirma f
counter staff n commessi mpl
counter-terrorism n antiterrorismo m
countertop n Am piano m di lavoro
countess /ˈkaʊntɪs/ n contessa f
countless /ˈkaʊntlɪs/ adj innumerevole
countrified /ˈkʌntrɪfaɪd/ adj ‹person›
  campagnolo
ꝗ **country** /ˈkʌntrɪ/ n nazione f, paese m;
  (native land) patria f, (countryside) campagna f;
  in the ∼ in campagna; go to the ∼ andare in
  campagna; Pol indire le elezioni politiche
country and western n country m inv
country bumpkin n pej buzzurro, -a mf

country club n club (m inv) sportivo e ricreativo in campagna

country cousin n pej provinciale mf

country dancing n danza f folcloristica

country house n villa f di campagna

countryman n uomo m di campagna; (fellow ∼man) compatriota m

country music n country m inv

countryside n campagna f

countrywide adj & adv in tutto il paese

✐ **county** /'kaʊntɪ/ n contea f (unità amministrativa britannica)

county council n Br Pol consiglio m di contea

county court n Br Jur tribunale m di contea

coup /ku:/ n Pol colpo m di stato

✐ **couple** /'kʌpl/ n coppia f; **a** ∼ **of** un paio di

coupon /'ku:pɒn/ n tagliando m; (for discount) buono m sconto

courage /'kʌrɪdʒ/ n coraggio m

courageous /kə'reɪdʒəs/ adj coraggioso

courageously /kə'reɪdʒəslɪ/ adv coraggiosamente

courgette /kʊə'ʒet/ n Br zucchino m

courier /'kʊrɪə(r)/ n corriere m; (for tourists) guida f

✐ **course** /kɔ:s/ n Sch corso m; Naut rotta f; Culin portata f; (for golf) campo m; ∼ **of treatment** Med serie f inv di cure; **of** ∼ naturalmente; **in the** ∼ **of** durante; **in due** ∼ a tempo debito; ∼ **of action** linea f d'azione

course book n libro m di testo

coursework /kɔ:swɜ:k/ n Sch, Univ esercitazioni fpl scritte che contano per la media

✐ **court** /kɔ:t/ **1** n tribunale m; Sport campo m; **take somebody to** ∼ citare qualcuno in giudizio **2** vt fare la corte a ‹woman›; sfidare ‹danger›; ∼**ng couples** coppiette fpl

court case n caso m giudiziario

court circular n bollettino quotidiano f di corte

courteous /'kɜ:tɪəs/ adj cortese

courteously /'kɜ:tɪəslɪ/ adv cortesemente

courtesy /'kɜ:təsɪ/ n cortesia f

courtesy bus n servizio m bus navetta

courtesy car n vettura f di cortesia

courthouse /'kɔ:thaʊs/ n Jur palazzo m di giustizia, tribunale m

courtier /'kɔ:tɪə(r)/ n cortigiano, -a mf

court martial **1** n (pl ∼s martial) corte f marziale **2** court-martial vt (pt ∼led) portare davanti alla corte marziale

court of inquiry n commissione f d'inchiesta

court of law n Jur corte f di giustizia

court order n Jur ingiunzione f

courtroom n Jur aula f [di tribunale]

courtship /'kɔ:tʃɪp/ n corteggiamento m

courtyard /'kɔ:tjɑ:d/ n cortile m

cousin /'kʌzn/ n cugino, -a mf

cove /kəʊv/ n insenatura f

covenant /'kʌvənənt/ n (agreement) accordo m; (payment agreement) impegno m scritto a pagare

✐ **cover** /'kʌvə(r)/ **1** n copertura f; (of cushion, to protect something) fodera f; (of book, magazine) copertina f; **take** ∼ mettersi al riparo; **under separate** ∼ a parte **2** vt coprire; foderare ‹cushion›; Journ fare un servizio su

■ **cover for** vt (replace) sostituire ‹somebody›

■ **cover up** vt coprire; fig soffocare ‹scandal›

■ **cover up for** vt fare da copertura a ‹somebody›

✐ **coverage** /'kʌvərɪdʒ/ n Journ **it got a lot of** ∼ i media gli hanno dedicato molto spazio

cover charge n coperto m

covered market n mercato m coperto

covered wagon n carro m coperto

cover girl n ragazza f copertina

covering /'kʌv(ə)rɪŋ/ n copertura f; (for floor) rivestimento m; ∼ **of snow** strato m di neve

covering fire n fuoco m di copertura

covering letter n lettera f d'accompagnamento

cover note n (from insurance company) polizza f provvisoria

cover story n (in paper) articolo m di prima pagina

covert /'kəʊvɜ:t/ adj ‹threat› velato; ‹operation› segreto; ‹glance› furtivo

covertly /'kəʊvɜ:tlɪ/ adv furtivamente; ‹operate› in segreto

cover-up n messa f a tacere

cover version n Mus versione f non originale

covet /'kʌvɪt/ vt bramare

covetous /'kʌvətəs/ adj avido

covetously /'kʌvətəslɪ/ adv avidamente

cow /kaʊ/ n vacca f, mucca f

coward /'kaʊəd/ n vigliacco, -a mf

cowardice /'kaʊədɪs/ n vigliaccheria f

cowardly /'kaʊədlɪ/ adj da vigliacco

cowbell /'kaʊbel/ n campanaccio m

cowboy /'kaʊbɔɪ/ n cowboy m inv; fig fam buffone m

cower /'kaʊə(r)/ vi acquattarsi

cowherd /'kaʊhɜ:d/ n vaccaro m

cowhide /'kaʊhaɪd/ n (leather) vacchetta f

cowl /kaʊl/ n cappuccio m

cowlick /'kaʊlɪk/ n fam ciocca f ribelle

cowl neck n collo m ad anello

cowpat /'kaʊpæt/ n sterco m di vacca

✐ indicates a very frequent word

cowshed /'kaʊʃed/ n stalla f

cox /kɒks/, **coxswain** /'kɒks(ə)n/ n timoniere, -a mf

coy /kɔɪ/ adj falsamente timido; (flirtatiously) civettuolo; **be ~ about something** essere evasivo su qualcosa

coyly /'kɔɪlɪ/ adv con falsa modestia; ‹flirtatiously› con civetteria

cozy /'kəʊzɪ/ adj Am = cosy

CPU n abbr (**central processing unit**) CPU f inv

crab /kræb/ n granchio m

crab apple n mela f selvatica

crack /kræk/ **1** n (in wall) crepa f; (in china, glass, bone) incrinatura f; (noise) scoppio m; fam (joke) battuta f; **have a ~** (try) fare un tentativo
2 adj fam (best) di prim'ordine
3 vt incrinare ‹china, glass›; schiacciare ‹nut›; decifrare ‹code›; fam risolvere ‹problem›; **~ a joke** fam fare una battuta
4 vt ‹china, glass› incrinarsi; ‹whip› schioccare
■ **crack down** vi fam prendere seri provvedimenti
■ **crack down on** vt fam prendere seri provvedimenti contro
■ **crack up** vi crollare

crackdown /'krækdaʊn/ n misure fpl (**on** contro)

cracked /krækt/ adj ‹plaster› crepato; ‹skin› screpolato; ‹rib› incrinato; fam (crazy) svitato

cracker /'krækə(r)/ n (biscuit) cracker m inv; (firework) petardo m; **[Christmas] ~** cilindro (m) di cartone contenente una sorpresa che produce una piccola esplosione quando viene aperto

crackers /'krækəz/ adj fam matto

cracking /'krækɪŋ/ adj Br fam eccellente; **at a ~ pace** a ritmo incalzante

crackle /'krækl/ vi crepitare

crackling /'kræklɪŋ/ n (on radio) disturbo m; (of foil, cellophane) sfregamento m; (of fire) crepitio m; (crisp pork) cotenna f arrostita

crackpot /'krækpɒt/ fam **1** n pazzo, -a mf
2 adj da pazzi

cradle /'kreɪdl/ n culla f

cradle-snatcher n fam he's/she's a ~ se la intende con i ragazzini/le ragazzine

craft¹ /krɑːft/ n inv (boat) imbarcazione f

craft² n mestiere m; (technique) arte f

craft fair n mostra f dell'artigianato

craftily /'krɑːftɪlɪ/ adv con astuzia

craftsman /'krɑːftsmən/ n artigiano m

craftsmanship /'krɑːftsmənʃɪp/ n maestria f

crafty /'krɑːftɪ/ adj (**-ier**, **-iest**) astuto

crag /kræg/ n rupe f

craggy /'krægɪ/ adj scosceso; ‹face› dai lineamenti marcati

cram /kræm/ v (pt/pp **crammed**) **1** vt stipare (**into** in)
2 vi (for exams) sgobbare

crammer /'kræmə(r)/ n Br fam (school) ≈ istituto m di recupero

cramp /kræmp/ n crampo m

cramped /kræmpt/ adj ‹room› stretto; ‹handwriting› appiccicato; **it's a bit ~ed in here** si sta un po' stretti qui

crampon /'kræmpən/ n rampone m

cranberry /'krænbərɪ/ n Culin mirtillo m rosso

crane /kreɪn/ **1** n (at docks, bird) gru f inv
2 vt ~ **one's neck** allungare il collo

cranium /'kreɪnɪəm/ n cranio m

crank¹ /kræŋk/ n tipo, -a mf strampalato

crank² n Techn manovella f

crankshaft /'kræŋkʃɑːft/ n albero m a gomiti

cranky /'kræŋkɪ/ adj strampalato; Am (irritable) irritabile

cranny /'krænɪ/ n fessura f

crap /kræp/ n sl (faeces) merda f; (film, book etc) schifezza f; (nonsense) stronzate fpl; **have a ~** cacare

crappy /'kræpɪ/ adj sl di merda

crash /kræʃ/ **1** n (noise) fragore m; Auto, Aeron incidente m; Comm crollo m; Comput crash m inv
2 vi schiantarsi (**into** contro); ‹plane› precipitare
3 vt schiantare ‹car›
■ **crash out** vi sl (go to sleep) crollare; (on sofa etc) dormire

crash barrier n guardrail m inv

crash course n corso m intensivo

crash diet n dieta f drastica

crash-helmet n casco m

crash-land vi fare un atterraggio di fortuna

crash-landing n atterraggio m di fortuna

crass /kræs/ adj ‹ignorance› crasso

crate /kreɪt/ n (for packing) cassa f

crater /'kreɪtə(r)/ n cratere m

cravat /krə'væt/ n foulard m inv

crave /kreɪv/ vt morire dalla voglia di

craving /'kreɪvɪŋ/ n voglia f smodata

crawl /krɔːl/ **1** n (swimming) stile m libero; **do the ~** nuotare a stile libero; **at a ~** a passo di lumaca
2 vi andare carponi; ~ **with** brulicare di

crawler lane /'krɔːlə/ n Auto corsia f riservata al traffico lento

crayfish /'kreɪfɪʃ/ n gambero m d'acqua dolce

crayon /'kreɪən/ n pastello m a cera; (pencil) matita f colorata

craze /kreɪz/ n mania f

crazed /kreɪzd/ adj ‹china, glaze›
screpolato; ‹animal, person› impazzito;
power-~ ubriaco di potere

crazy /ˈkreɪzɪ/ adj (**-ier, -iest**) matto; **be ~
about** andar matto per

crazy golf n Br minigolf m inv

crazy paving n Br pavimentazione f a
mosaico irregolare

creak /kriːk/ **1** n scricchiolio m
2 vi scricchiolare

creaky /ˈkriːkɪ/ adj ‹leather› che cigola;
‹door, hinge› cigolante; ‹joint, bone,
floorboard› scricchiolante; fig fam ‹alibi,
policy› traballante

cream /kriːm/ **1** n crema f; (fresh) panna f
2 adj ‹colour› [bianco] panna inv
3 vt Culin sbattere

■ **cream off** vt accaparrarsi ‹top pupils,
scientists etc›

cream cheese n formaggio m cremoso

cream cracker n Br cracker m inv

cream puff n sfogliatina f alla panna inv

cream soda n soda f aromatizzata alla
vaniglia

cream tea n Br tè (m inv) servito con
pasticcini da mangiare con marmellata e
panna

creamy /ˈkriːmɪ/ adj (**-ier, -iest**) cremoso

crease /kriːs/ **1** n piega f
2 vt stropicciare
3 vi stropicciarsi

crease-resistant adj che non si
stropiccia

◆ **create** /kriːˈeɪt/ vt creare

◆ **creation** /kriːˈeɪʃn/ n creazione f

◆ **creative** /kriːˈeɪtɪv/ adj creativo

creative director n direttore, -trice mf
creativo

creative writing n (school subject)
composizione f

creativity /kriːerˈtɪvətɪ/ n creatività f

creator /kriːˈeɪtə(r)/ n creatore, -trice mf

creature /ˈkriːtʃə(r)/ n creatura f

creature comforts npl comodità fpl;
like one's ~ amare le proprie comodità

crèche /kreʃ/ n asilo m nido inv

credence /ˈkriːdəns/ n credito m; **give ~
to something** (believe) dare credito a qualcosa

credentials /krɪˈdenʃlz/ npl credenziali
fpl

credibility /kredəˈbɪlətɪ/ n credibilità f

credible /ˈkredəbl/ adj credibile

◆ **credit** /ˈkredɪt/ **1** n credito m; (honour)
merito m; **take the ~ for** prendersi il merito
di
2 vt accreditare; **~ somebody with
something** Comm accreditare qualcosa a

qualcuno; fig attribuire qualcosa a qualcuno

creditable /ˈkredɪtəbl/ adj lodevole

credit balance n saldo m attivo

credit card n carta f di credito

credit control n controllo m del credito

credit crunch n stretta f creditizia,
stretta f del credito

credit facilities npl facilitazioni fpl
creditizie

credit limit n limite m di credito

credit note n Comm nota f di accredito

creditor /ˈkredɪtə(r)/ n creditore, -trice mf

credits /ˈkredɪts/ npl titoli mpl di coda

credit side n **on the ~** tra i lati positivi

credit squeeze n stretta f creditizia

credit terms npl condizioni fpl di credito

credit transfer n bonifico m

creditworthiness /ˈkredɪ(t)wɜːðɪnɪs/ n
capacità f di credito

creditworthy /ˈkredɪ(t)wɜːðɪ/ adj
meritevole di credito

credulity /krɪˈdjuːlətɪ/ n credulità f; **strain
sb's ~** essere ai limiti della credibilità

credulous /ˈkredjʊləs/ adj credulo

creed /kriːd/ n credo m inv

creek /kriːk/ n insenatura f; Am (stream)
torrente m; **up the ~** fam (in trouble) nei guai

creep /kriːp/ **1** vi (pt/pp **crept**)
muoversi furtivamente
2 n fam tipo m viscido; **it gives me the ~s**
mi fa venire i brividi

creeper /ˈkriːpə(r)/ n pianta f rampicante

creepy /ˈkriːpɪ/ adj che fa venire i brividi

creepy-crawly /-ˈkrɔːlɪ/ n fam insetto m

cremate /krɪˈmeɪt/ vt cremare

cremation /krɪˈmeɪʃn/ n cremazione f

crematorium /kreməˈtɔːrɪəm/ n
crematorio m

crepe /kreɪp/ n (fabric) crespo m

crepe bandage n fascia f elastica

crepe paper n carta f crespata

crepe soles npl suole fpl di para

crept /krept/ ▶ CREEP

crescendo /krɪˈʃendəʊ/ n Mus crescendo
m; **reach a ~** fig ‹noise, protests› raggiungere
il picco; ‹campaign› raggiungere il culmine

crescent /ˈkresənt/ n mezzaluna f

crescent moon n mezzaluna f

cress /kres/ n crescione m

crest /krest/ n cresta f; (coat of arms)
cimiero m; **be on the ~ of a wave** essere
sulla cresta dell'onda

crestfallen /ˈkrestfɔːlən/ adj mogio

Crete /kriːt/ n Creta f

Creutzfeldt-Jakob disease
/ˈkrɔɪtsfelt'jækɒb/ n morbo m di Creutzfeldt
Jakob

crevasse /krɪˈvæs/ n crepaccio m

crevice /ˈkrevɪs/ n crepa f

◆ indicates a very frequent word

⚹ **crew** /kru:/ n equipaggio m; (gang) équipe f inv

crew cut n capelli mpl a spazzola

crew neck n girocollo m

crew neck sweater n maglione m a girocollo

crib¹ /krɪb/ n (for baby) culla f

crib² vt/i (pt/pp **cribbed**) fam copiare

cribbage /'krɪbɪdʒ/ n gioco (m) di carte

crick /krɪk/ n ∼ **in the neck** torcicollo m

cricket¹ /'krɪkɪt/ n (insect) grillo m

cricket² n cricket m

cricketer /'krɪkɪtə(r)/ n giocatore m di cricket

⚹ **crime** /kraɪm/ n crimine m; (criminality) criminalità f; **it's a** ∼ fig è un delitto

crime of passion n delitto m passionale

crime prevention n prevenzione f della criminalità

⚹ **criminal** /'krɪmɪnl/ **1** adj criminale; ⟨law, court⟩ penale
2 n criminale mf

criminal charges npl **face** ∼ essere imputato

criminal investigation n inchiesta f giudiziaria

Criminal Investigation Department n Br ≈ polizia f giudiziaria

criminal justice n sistema m penale

criminal law n diritto m penale

criminally insane /'krɪmɪnəlɪ/ adj pazzo criminale

criminal offence n reato m

criminal record n **have a/no** ∼ avere la fedina penale sporca/pulita

criminology /krɪmɪ'nɒlədʒɪ/ n criminologia f

crimp /krɪmp/ vt pieghettare ⟨fabric⟩; increspare ⟨pastry⟩; arricciare ⟨hair⟩

crimson /'krɪmz(ə)n/ adj cremisi inv

cringe /krɪndʒ/ vi (cower) acquattarsi; (at bad joke etc) fare una smorfia

crinkle /'krɪŋk(ə)l/ **1** vt spiegazzare
2 vi spiegazzarsi

crinkly /'krɪŋklɪ/ adj ⟨paper, material⟩ crespato; ⟨hair⟩ crespo

cripple /'krɪpl/ **1** n storpio, -a mf
2 vt storpiare; fig danneggiare

crippled /'krɪpld/ adj ⟨person⟩ storpio; ⟨ship⟩ danneggiato

crippling /'krɪplɪŋ/ adj ⟨taxes, debts⟩ esorbitante; ⟨disease⟩ devastante; ⟨strike, effect⟩ paralizzante

⚹ **crisis** /'kraɪsɪs/ n (pl -ses /'kraɪsiːz/) crisi f inv

crisp /krɪsp/ adj croccante; ⟨air⟩ frizzante; ⟨style⟩ incisivo

crispbread /'krɪs(p)bred/ n crostini mpl di pane

crisps /krɪsps/ npl patatine fpl

crispy /'krɪspɪ/ adj croccante

criss-cross /'krɪs-/ adj a linee incrociate

criterion /kraɪ'tɪərɪən/ n (pl -ria /kraɪ'tɪərɪə/) criterio m

⚹ **critic** /'krɪtɪk/ n critico, -a mf

⚹ **critical** /'krɪtɪkl/ adj critico

critically /'krɪtɪklɪ/ adv in modo critico; ∼ **ill** gravemente malato

critical path analysis n analisi f inv del percorso critico

⚹ **criticism** /'krɪtɪsɪzm/ n critica f; **he doesn't like** ∼ non ama le critiche

criticize /'krɪtɪsaɪz/ vt criticare

croak /krəʊk/ vi gracchiare; ⟨frog⟩ gracidare

Croatia /krəʊ'eɪʃə/ n Croazia f

crochet /'krəʊʃeɪ/ **1** n lavoro m all'uncinetto
2 vt fare all'uncinetto

crochet-hook n uncinetto m

crock /krɒk/ n fam **old** ∼ (person) rudere m; (car) macinino m

crockery /'krɒkərɪ/ n terrecotte fpl

crocodile /'krɒkədaɪl/ n coccodrillo m

crocodile tears npl lacrime fpl di coccodrillo

crocus /'krəʊkəs/ n (pl -es) croco m

croft /krɒft/ n piccola fattoria f

croissant /'krwæsã/ n cornetto m, croissant m inv

crone /krəʊn/ n pej vecchiaccia f

crony /'krəʊnɪ/ n compare m

crook /krʊk/ n fam (criminal) truffatore, -trice mf

crooked /'krʊkɪd/ adj storto; ⟨limb⟩ storpiato; fam (dishonest) disonesto; ∼ **deal** fregatura f

croon /kru:n/ vt/i canticchiare

crop /krɒp/ **1** n raccolto m; fig quantità f inv
2 vt (pt/pp **cropped**) coltivare
■ **crop up** vi fam presentarsi

crop rotation n rotazione f delle colture

crop spraying /'krɒpspreɪɪŋ/ n irrorazione f

croquet /'krəʊkeɪ/ n croquet m

croquette /krəʊ'ket/ n crocchetta f

⚹ **cross** /krɒs/ **1** adj (annoyed) arrabbiato; **talk at** ∼ **purposes** fraintendersi
2 n croce f; Bot, Zool incrocio m
3 vt sbarrare ⟨cheque⟩; incrociare ⟨road, animals⟩; ∼ **oneself** farsi il segno della croce; ∼ **one's arms** incrociare le braccia; ∼ **one's legs** accavallare le gambe; **keep one's fingers** ∼**ed for somebody** tenere le dita incrociate per qualcuno; **it** ∼**ed my mind** mi è venuto in mente
4 vi (go across) attraversare; ⟨lines⟩ incrociarsi

⋯⋗

■ **cross off** *vt* (from list) depennare

■ **cross out** *vt* sbarrare; (from list) depennare

crossbar *n* (of goal) traversa *f*; (on bicycle) canna *f*

cross-border *adj* oltreconfine

crossbow *n* balestra *f*

crossbred *adj* ibrido

crossbreed ① *vt* ibridare, incrociare *‹animals, plants›*
② *n* (animal) incrocio *m*, ibrido *m*

cross-Channel *adj* attraverso la Manica; *‹ferry›* che attraversa la Manica

cross-check ① *n* controprova *f*
② *vt* fare la controprova di

cross-contamination *n* contaminazione *f* incrociata

cross-country *n* Sport corsa *f* campestre

cross-country skiing *n* sci *m* di fondo

cross-court *adj* *‹shot, volley›* diagonale

cross-cultural *adj* multiculturale

crosscurrent *n* corrente *f* trasversale

cross-dressing *n* travestitismo *m*

cross-examination *n* controinterrogatorio *m*

cross-examine *vt* sottoporre a controinterrogatorio

cross-eyed /'krɒsaɪd/ *adj* strabico

crossfire *n* fuoco *m* incrociato

crossing /'krɒsɪŋ/ *n* (for pedestrians) passaggio *m* pedonale; (sea journey) traversata *f*

cross-legged /krɒs'legd/ *adj & adv* con le gambe incrociate

crossly /'krɒslɪ/ *adv* con rabbia

crossover *adj* *‹straps›* incrociato

cross-party *adj* *‹talks, committee›* interpartitico

cross-purposes *npl* **we are at ∼** non ci siamo capiti

cross-question *vt* interrogare *‹person›*

cross-reference *n* rimando *m*

crossroads *n* incrocio *m*; **reach a ∼** fig arrivare a un bivio

cross-section *n* sezione *f*; (of community) campione *m*

cross-stitch *n* punto *m* croce

crosswalk *n* Am attraversamento *m* pedonale

crosswind *n* vento *m* di traverso

crosswise *adv* in diagonale

crossword *n* ∼ **[puzzle]** parole *fpl* crociate

crotch /krɒtʃ/ *n* Anat inforcatura *f*; (in trousers) cavallo *m*

crotchet /'krɒtʃɪt/ *n* Mus semiminima *f*

crotchety /'krɒtʃətɪ/ *adj* irritabile

crouch /krautʃ/ *vi* accovacciarsi

croupier /'kru:pɪə(r)/ *n* croupier *m inv*

crouton /'kru:tɒn/ *n* crostino *m*

crow /krəʊ/ ① *n* corvo *m*; **as the ∼ flies** in linea d'aria
② *vi* cantare

crowbar /'krəʊbɑ:/ *n* piede *m* di porco

Ⓐ **crowd** /kraʊd/ ① *n* folla *f*
② *vt* affollare
③ *vi* affollarsi

crowd control *n* controllo *m* della folla

crowded /'kraʊdɪd/ *adj* affollato

crowd-puller /'kraʊdpʊlə(r)/ *n* (event) grande attrazione *f*

crowd scene *n* Cinema, Theat scena *f* di massa

crown /kraʊn/ ① *n* corona *f*
② *vt* incoronare; incapsulare *‹tooth›*

Crown court *n* Br Jur ≈ corte *f* d'Assise

crowning glory /'kraʊnɪŋ/ *n* culmine *m*; **her hair is her ∼** i capelli sono il suo punto forte

crown jewels *npl* gioielli *mpl* della corona

crown prince *n* principe *m* ereditario

crow's feet /krəʊz'fi:t/ *npl* (on face) zampe *fpl* di gallina

crow's nest /krəʊz'nest/ *n* coffa *f*

Ⓐ **crucial** /'kru:ʃl/ *adj* cruciale

crucially /'kru:ʃəlɪ/ *adv* ∼ **important** di vitale importanza

crucifix /'kru:sɪfɪks/ *n* crocifisso *m*

crucifixion /kru:sɪ'fɪkʃn/ *n* crocifissione *f*

crucify /'kru:sɪfaɪ/ *vt* (*pt/pp* **-ied**) crocifiggere

crude /kru:d/ *adj* *‹oil›* greggio; *‹language›* crudo; *‹person›* rozzo

crudely /'kru:dlɪ/ *adv* (vulgarly) in modo crudo; (simply) schematicamente; (roughly: assembled) sommariamente; *‹painted, made›* rozzamente; ∼ **speaking** in parole povere

crudity /'kru:dətɪ/ *n* (vulgarity) volgarità *f*

cruel /'kru:əl/ *adj* (**-ler, -lest**) crudele (**to** verso)

cruelly /'kru:əlɪ/ *adv* con crudeltà

cruelty /'kru:əltɪ/ *n* crudeltà *f*

cruelty-free *adj* *‹cosmetics›* non testato sugli animali

cruise /kru:z/ ① *n* crociera *f*
② *vi* fare una crociera; *‹car›* andare a velocità di crociera

cruise liner *n* nave *f* da crociera

cruise missile *n* missile *m* cruise *inv*

cruiser /'kru:zə(r)/ *n* Mil incrociatore *m*; (motor boat) motoscafo *m*

cruising speed /'kru:zɪŋ/ *n* velocità *m inv* di crociera

crumb /krʌm/ *n* briciola *f*

crumble /'krʌmbl/ ① *vt* sbriciolare
② *vi* sbriciolarsi; *‹building, society›* sgretolarsi

Ⓐ indicates a very frequent word

crumbling /'krʌmblɪŋ/ *adj* fatiscente

crumbly /'krʌmblɪ/ *adj* friabile

crummy /'krʌmɪ/ *adj* fam (substandard) scadente; Am (unwell) malato

crumpet /'krʌmpɪt/ *n* Culin focaccina (*f*) da tostare e mangiare con burro e marmellata

crumple /'krʌmpl/ **1** *vt* spiegazzare
2 *vi* spiegazzarsi

crunch /krʌntʃ/ **1** *n* fam when it comes to the ~ quando si viene al dunque
2 *vt* sgranocchiare
3 *vi* ‹snow› scricchiolare

crunchy /'krʌntʃɪ/ *adj* ‹vegetables, biscuits› croccante

crusade /kru:'seɪd/ *n* crociata *f*

crusader /kru:'seɪdə(r)/ *n* crociato *m*

crush /krʌʃ/ **1** *n* (crowd) calca *f*; have a ~ on somebody essersi preso una cotta per qualcuno
2 *vt* schiacciare; sgualcire ‹clothes›

crushed ice /krʌʃt'aɪs/ *n* ghiaccio *m* tritato

crushed velvet *n* velluto *m* stazzonato

crushing /'krʌʃɪŋ/ *adj* ‹defeat, weight, blow› schiacciante; ‹blow› tremendo

crust /krʌst/ *n* crosta *f*

crustacean /krʌ'steɪʃn/ *n* crostaceo *m*

crusty /'krʌstɪ/ *adj* ‹bread› croccante; (irritable) scontroso

crutch /krʌtʃ/ *n* gruccia *f*, Anat inforcatura *f*

crux /krʌks/ *n* fig punto *m* cruciale; ~ of the matter nodo *m* della questione

⚬ **cry** /kraɪ/ **1** *n* grido *m*; ~ for help grido d'aiuto; have a ~ farsi un pianto; a far ~ from fig tutta un'altra cosa rispetto a
2 *vi* (*pt/pp* **cried**) (weep) piangere; (call) gridare
■ **cry off** *vi* Br (cancel) disdire
■ **cry out** *vi* (shout) urlare

cryogenics /ˌkraɪə'dʒenɪks/ *n* criogenia *f*

crypt /krɪpt/ *n* cripta *f*

cryptic /'krɪptɪk/ *adj* criptico

cryptically /'krɪptɪklɪ/ *adv* ‹say, speak› in modo enigmatico; ~ worded espresso in maniera sibillina

crystal /'krɪstl/ *n* cristallo *m*; (glassware) cristalli *mpl*

crystal ball *n* sfera *f* di cristallo

crystal clear *adj* ‹water, sound› cristallino; let me make it ~ lasciatemelo spiegare chiaramente

crystal-gazing /'krɪstlgeɪzɪŋ/ *n* predizione *f* del futuro (con la sfera di cristallo)

crystallize /'krɪstəlaɪz/ *vi* (become clear) concretizzarsi

CS gas *n* Br gas *m inv* lacrimogeno

CST *abbr* Am (**Central Standard Time**) ora (*f*) solare della zona centrale dell'America settentrionale

C2C *abbr* (**consumer to consumer**) C2C

cub /kʌb/ *n* (animal) cucciolo *m*; C~ [Scout] lupetto *m*

Cuba /'kju:bə/ *n* Cuba *f*

Cuban /'kju:bən/ *adj & n* cubano, -a *mf*

cubby-hole /'kʌbɪ-/ *n* (compartment) scomparto *m*; (room) ripostiglio *m*

cube /kju:b/ *n* cubo *m*

cubic /'kju:bɪk/ *adj* cubico

cubicle /'kju:bɪkl/ *n* cabina *f*

cubism /'kju:bɪzm/ *n* cubismo *m*

cubist /'kju:bɪst/ *adj & n* cubista *mf*

cub reporter *n* cronista *mf* alle prime armi

cuckoo /'kʊku:/ *n* cuculo *m*

cuckoo clock *n* orologio *m* a cucù

cucumber /'kju:kʌmbə(r)/ *n* cetriolo *m*

cud /kʌd/ *n* also fig chew the ~ ruminare

cuddle /'kʌd(ə)l/ **1** *vt* coccolare
2 *vi* ~ up to starsene accoccolato insieme a
3 *n* have a ~ ‹child› farsi coccolare; ‹lovers› abbracciarsi

cuddly /'kʌd(ə)lɪ/ *adj* tenerone; (wanting cuddles) coccolone

cuddly toy *n* peluche *m inv*

cudgel /'kʌdʒl/ *n* randello *m*

cue¹ /kju:/ *n* segnale *m*; Theat battuta *f* d'entrata

cue² *n* (in billiards) stecca *f*

cue ball *n* pallino *m*

cuff /kʌf/ **1** *n* polsino *m*; Am (turn-up) orlo *m*; (blow) scapaccione *m*; off the ~ improvvisando
2 *vt* dare una pacca a

cuff link *n* gemello *m*

cuisine /kwɪ'zi:n/ *n* cucina *f*; haute ~ /əʊt/ haute cuisine *f*

cul-de-sac /'kʌldəsæk/ *n* vicolo *m* cieco

culinary /'kʌlɪnərɪ/ *adj* culinario

cull /kʌl/ *vt* (farming) selezionare ‹livestock›; (hunting) uccidere, massacrare ‹seal, whale›; abbattere ‹fox›

culminate /'kʌlmɪneɪt/ *vi* culminare

culmination /kʌlmɪ'neɪʃn/ *n* culmine *m*

culottes /kju:'lɒts/ *npl* gonna *fsg* pantalone

culpable /'kʌlpəbl/ *adj* colpevole

culpable homicide *n* Jur omicidio *m* colposo

culprit /'kʌlprɪt/ *n* colpevole *mf*

cult /kʌlt/ *n* culto *m*

cultivate /'kʌltɪveɪt/ *vt* coltivare; fig coltivarsi ‹person›

cultivated /'kʌltɪveɪtɪd/ *adj* ‹soil› lavorato; ‹person› colto

⚬ **cultural** /'kʌltʃərəl/ *adj* culturale

cultural attaché *n* addetto *m* culturale

⚬ **culture** /'kʌltʃə(r)/ *n* cultura *f*

cultured /'kʌltʃəd/ *adj* colto

cultured pearl *n* perla *f* coltivata

culture shock *n* shock *m inv* culturale
culture vulture *n* fam fanatico, -a *mf* di cultura
culvert /'kʌlvət/ *n* condotto *m* sotterraneo
cumbersome /'kʌmbəsəm/ *adj* ingombrante
cumin /'kjuːmɪn/ *n* cumino *m* nero
cummerbund /'kʌməbʌnd/ *n* fascia *f* (*dello smoking*)
cumulative /'kjuːmjʊlətɪv/ *adj* cumulativo
cunning /'kʌnɪŋ/ **1** *adj* astuto **2** *n* astuzia *f*
⚘ **cup** /kʌp/ *n* tazza *f*; (prize, of bra) coppa *f*
cupboard /'kʌbəd/ *n* armadio *m*
cupboard love *n* Br hum amore *m* interessato
cupboard space *n* spazio *m* negli armadi
Cup Final *n* finale *f* di coppa
cupful /'kʌpfʊl/ *n* tazza *f* (*contenuto*)
Cupid /'kjuːpɪd/ *n* Cupido *m*
cupola /'kjuːpələ/ *n* Archit cupola *f*
cup tie *n* Br partita *f* eliminatoria
cur /kɜː(r)/ *n* pej (dog) cagnaccio *m*
curable /'kjʊərəbl/ *adj* curabile
curate /'kjʊərət/ *n* curato *m*
curator /kjʊə'reɪtə(r)/ *n* direttore, -trice *mf* (*di museo*)
curb /kɜːb/ *vt* tenere a freno
curd cheese /kɜːd/ *n* cagliata *f*
curdle /'kɜːdl/ *vi* coagularsi
cure /kjʊə(r)/ **1** *n* cura *f* **2** *vt* curare; (salt) mettere sotto sale; (smoke) affumicare
cure-all *n* toccasana *m inv*, panacea *f*
curfew /'kɜːfjuː/ *n* coprifuoco *m*
curio /'kjʊərɪəʊ/ *n* curiosità *f inv*
curiosity /kjʊərɪ'ɒsətɪ/ *n* curiosità *f*
curious /'kjʊərɪəs/ *adj* curioso
curiously /'kjʊərɪəslɪ/ *adv* curiosamente
curl /kɜːl/ **1** *n* ricciolo *m* **2** *vt* arricciare **3** *vi* arricciarsi
■ **curl up** *vi* raggomitolarsi
curler /'kɜːlə(r)/ *n* bigodino *m*
curling /'kɜːlɪŋ/ *n* Sport curling *m*
curly /'kɜːlɪ/ *adj* (-ier, -iest) riccio
curly-haired, curly-headed /-'heəd, -'hedɪd/ *adj* (tight curls) dai capelli crespi; (loose curls) riccio
currant /'kʌrənt/ *n* (dried) uvetta *f*
currency /'kʌrənsɪ/ *n* valuta *f*; (of word) ricorrenza *f*; **foreign** ~ valuta *f* estera
⚘ **current** /'kʌrənt/ **1** *adj* corrente **2** *n* corrente *f*
current account *n* Br conto *m* corrente

current affairs *npl* attualità *f*
current assets *npl* Fin disponibilità *fpl* correnti
current liabilities *npl* Fin passività *fpl* correnti
⚘ **currently** /'kʌrəntlɪ/ *adv* attualmente
curriculum /kə'rɪkjʊləm/ *n* programma *m* di studi
curriculum vitae /'viːtaɪ/ *n* curriculum vitae *m inv*
curry /'kʌrɪ/ **1** *n* curry *m inv*; (meal) piatto *m* al curry **2** *vt* (*pt/pp* **-ied**) ~ **favour with somebody** cercare d'ingraziarsi qualcuno
curry powder *n* curry *m* in polvere
curse /kɜːs/ **1** *n* maledizione *f*; (oath) imprecazione *f* **2** *vt* maledire **3** *vi* imprecare
cursor /'kɜːsə(r)/ *n* cursore *m*
cursor keys *npl* tasti *mpl* cursore
cursory /'kɜːsərɪ/ *adj* sbrigativo
curt /kɜːt/ *adj* brusco
curtail /kə'teɪl/ *vt* ridurre
curtailment /kə'teɪlmənt/ *n* (of rights, freedom) limitazione *f*; (of expenditure, service) riduzione *f*; (of holiday) interruzione *f*
curtain /'kɜːtn/ *n* tenda *f*; Theat sipario *m*
■ **curtain off** *vt* separare con una tenda
curtain call *n* Theat chiamata *f* alla ribalta
curtly /'kɜːtlɪ/ *adv* bruscamente
curtsy, curtsey /'kɜːtsɪ/ **1** *n* inchino *m* **2** *vi* (*pt/pp* **-ied**) fare l'inchino
curvaceous /kɜː'veɪʃəs/ *adj* formoso
curve /kɜːv/ **1** *n* curva *f* **2** *vi* curvare; ~ **to the right/left** curvare a destra/sinistra
curved /kɜːvd/ *adj* curvo
curvy /'kɜːvɪ/ *adj* (-ier, -iest) ‹woman› formoso
cushion /'kʊʃn/ **1** *n* cuscino *m* **2** *vt* attutire; (protect) proteggere
cushy /'kʊʃɪ/ *adj* (-ier, -iest) fam facile
custard /'kʌstəd/ *n* (liquid) crema *f* pasticcera
custard cream *n* Br biscotto *m* farcito alla crema
custard pie *n* torta *f* alla crema (*nei film comici*)
custard tart *n* torta *f* alla crema
custodial sentence /kʌ'stəʊdɪəl/ *n* condanna *f* ad una pena detentiva
custodian /kʌ'stəʊdɪən/ *n* custode *mf*
custody /'kʌstədɪ/ *n* (of child) custodia *f*; (imprisonment) detenzione *f* preventiva
custom /'kʌstəm/ *n* usanza *f*; Jur consuetudine *f*; Comm clientela *f*

⚘ indicates a very frequent word

customary /'kʌstəmərɪ/ adj (habitual) abituale; **it's ~ to...** è consuetudine...

custom-built /-'bɪlt/ adj ‹house› ad hoc

custom car n vettura f personalizzata

ˢ **customer** /'kʌstəmə(r)/ n cliente mf

customer care n assistenza f alla clientela

customer feedback n feedback m inv dai clienti

customer relations npl rapporto m con i clienti

customer service n assistenza f ai clienti

customize /'kʌstəmaɪz/ vt personalizzare

custom-made /-'meɪd/ adj su misura

customs /'kʌstəmz/ npl dogana f

Customs and Excise n Br ufficio m Dazi e Dogana

customs clearance n sdoganamento m

customs declaration n dichiarazione f doganale

customs duties npl dazi mpl doganali

customs hall n dogana f

customs officer n doganiere m, guardia f di finanza

ˢ **cut** /kʌt/ **1** n (with knife etc, of clothes) taglio m; (reduction) riduzione f; (in public spending) taglio m
2 vt/i (pt/pp cut, pres p **cutting**) tagliare; (reduce) ridurre; **~ one's finger** tagliarsi il dito; **~ sb' hair** tagliare i capelli a qualcuno
3 vi (with cards) alzare
■ **cut away** vt tagliar via
■ **cut back** vt tagliare ‹hair›; potare ‹hedge›; (reduce) ridurre
■ **cut back on** vt (reduce) ridurre
■ **cut down** vt abbattere ‹tree›; (reduce) ridurre
■ **cut in 1** vi Auto tagliare la strada; (into conversation) interrompere
2 vt **~ somebody in on a deal** dare una percentuale a qualcuno
■ **cut off** vt tagliar via; (disconnect) interrompere; fig isolare; **I was ~ off** Teleph la linea è caduta
■ **cut out** vt ritagliare; (delete) eliminare; **be ~ out for** fam essere tagliato per; **~ it out!** fam dacci un taglio!
■ **cut short** vt interrompere ‹holiday, discussion›
■ **cut up** vt (slice) tagliare a pezzi

cut-and-dried adj ‹answer, solution› ovvio; **I like everything to be ~** mi piace che tutto sia ben chiaro e definito

cut and paste 1 n taglia e incolla m
2 vt tagliare e incollare

cut and thrust n **the ~ of debate** gli scambi mpl animati del dibattito

cutback /'kʌtbæk/ n riduzione f; (in government spending) taglio m

cute /kjuːt/ adj fam (in appearance) carino; (clever) acuto

cut glass n vetro m intagliato

cuticle /'kjuːtɪkl/ n cuticola f

cutlery /'kʌtlərɪ/ n posate fpl

cutlet /'kʌtlɪt/ n cotoletta f

cut-off n (upper limit) limite m [massimo]

cut-off date n data f di scadenza

cut-off point n limite m; Comm data f di scadenza

cut-offs npl (jeans) jeans mpl tagliati

cut-out n (outline) ritaglio m

cut-price adj a prezzo ridotto; ‹shop› che fa prezzi ridotti

cutter /'kʌtə(r)/ n (ship) cutter m inv; (on ship) lancia f; (for metal, glass) taglierina f

cut-throat 1 n assassino, -a mf
2 adj ‹competition› spietato

cut-throat razor n Br rasoio m da barbiere

cutting /'kʌtɪŋ/ **1** adj ‹remark› tagliente
2 n (from newspaper) ritaglio m; (of plant) talea f

cutting edge n (blade) filo m; **be at the ~** fig essere all'avanguardia

cuttingly /'kʌtɪŋlɪ/ adv ‹speak› in maniera tagliente

cutting room n Cinema **end up on the ~ floor** essere tagliato in fase di montaggio

CV n abbr (**Curriculum Vitae**) CV m

cwt abbr (**hundredweight**) Br ≈ 50 kg, Am ≈ 45 kg

cyanide /'saɪənaɪd/ n cianuro m

cyber attack /'saɪbər ə,tæk/ n cyber-attacco m

cybercafe /'saɪbəkæfeɪ/ n caffè m Internet

cyberculture /'saɪbəkʌltʃə(r)/ n cybercultura f

cybernetics /saɪbə'netɪks/ n cibernetica f

cyberspace /'saɪbəspeɪs/ n ciberspazio m

cyclamen /'sɪkləmən/ n ciclamino m

ˢ **cycle** /'saɪk(ə)l/ **1** n ciclo m; (bicycle) bicicletta f, fam bici f inv
2 vi andare in bicicletta

cycle clip n fermacalzoni m inv

cycle lane n pista f ciclabile

cycle race n corsa f ciclistica

cycle rack n portabiciclette m inv

cycle track, **cycle path** n pista f ciclabile

cyclical /'saɪklɪkl/ adj ciclico

cycling /'saɪklɪŋ/ n ciclismo m

cycling holiday n Br vacanza f in bicicletta; **go on a ~** fare una vacanza in bicicletta

cycling shorts npl pantaloncini mpl da ciclista

cyclist /'saɪklɪst/ n ciclista mf
cyclo-cross /'saɪkləʊ-/ n ciclocross m inv
cyclone /'saɪkləʊn/ n ciclone m
cygnet /'sɪgnɪt/ n cigno m giovane
cylinder /'sɪlɪndə(r)/ n cilindro m
cylindrical /sɪ'lɪndrɪkl/ adj cilindrico
cymbals /'sɪmblz/ npl Mus piatti mpl
cynic /'sɪnɪk/ n cinico, -a mf
cynical /'sɪnɪk(ə)l/ adj cinico
cynically /'sɪnɪklɪ/ adv cinicamente
cynicism /'sɪnɪsɪzm/ n cinismo m
cypress /'saɪprəs/ n cipresso m

Cypriot /'sɪprɪət/ adj & n cipriota mf
Cyprus /'saɪprəs/ n Cipro m
Cyrillic /sɪ'rɪlɪk/ adj cirillico
cyst /sɪst/ n ciste f
cystitis /sɪ'staɪtɪs/ n cistite f
Czar, czar /zɑ:(r)/ n zar m inv
Czech /tʃek/ adj & n ceco, -a mf
Czechoslovak /tʃekə'sləʊvæk/ adj cecoslovacco
Czechoslovakia /tʃekəslə'vækɪə/ n Cecoslovacchia f
Czech Republic n Repubblica f Ceca

···············

D d

···············

d¹, D /di:/ n (letter) d, D f inv; Mus re m inv
d² abbr (died) morto
dab /dæb/ ① n colpetto m; **a ~ of** un pochino di
② vt (pt/pp **dabbed**) toccare leggermente ‹eyes›
■ **dab on** vt mettere un po' di ‹paint etc›
dabble /'dæbl/ vi **~ in something** fig occuparsi di qualcosa a tempo perso
dachshund /'dækshʊnd/ n bassotto m
✧ **dad[dy]** /'dæd[ɪ]/ n fam papà m inv, babbo m
daddy-long-legs n zanzarone m [dei boschi]; Am (spider) ragno m
daffodil /'dæfədɪl/ n giunchiglia f
daft /dɑ:ft/ adj sciocco
dagger /'dægə(r)/ n stiletto m; Typ croce f; **be at ~s drawn** fam essere ai ferri corti
dahlia /'deɪlɪə/ n dalia f
✧ **daily** /'deɪlɪ/ ① adj giornaliero
② adv giornalmente
③ n (newspaper) quotidiano m; fam (cleaner) donna f delle pulizie
daintily /'deɪntɪlɪ/ adv delicatamente
dainty /'deɪntɪ/ adj (**-ier, -iest**) grazioso; ‹movement› delicato
dairy /'deərɪ/ n caseificio m; (shop) latteria f
dairy cow n mucca f da latte
dairyman /'deərɪmən/ n (on farm) operaio m addetto all'allevamento di mucche [da latte]; Am (farmer) allevatore m
dairy products npl latticini mpl
dais /'deɪɪs/ n pedana f
daisy /'deɪzɪ/ n margheritina f; (larger) margherita f
dale /deɪl/ n liter valle f

✧ indicates a very frequent word

dally /'dælɪ/ vi (pt/pp **-ied**) stare a gingillarsi
dam /dæm/ ① n diga f
② vt (pt/pp **dammed**) costruire una diga su
✧ **damage** /'dæmɪdʒ/ ① n danno m (**to** a); **~s** pl Jur risarcimento msg
② vt danneggiare; fig nuocere a
damage limitation exercise n manovra f per contenere i danni
damaging /'dæmɪdʒɪŋ/ adj dannoso
damask /'dæməsk/ n damasco m
dame /deɪm/ n liter dama f; Am sl donna f
dammit /'dæmɪt/ int Br fam accidenti!
damn /dæm/ ① adj fam maledetto
② adv ‹lucky, late› maledettamente
③ n **I don't care** or **give a ~** fam non me ne frega un accidente
④ vt dannare
damnation /dæm'neɪʃn/ ① n dannazione f
② int fam accidenti!
damnedest /'dæmdɪst/ ① n **do one's ~ (to do)** fam (hardest) fare del proprio meglio (per fare)
② adj **it was the ~ thing** (surprising) era la cosa più straordinaria
damning /'dæmɪŋ/ adj schiacciante
damp /dæmp/ ① adj umido
② n umidità f
③ vt = DAMPEN
dampen /'dæmpən/ vt inumidire; fig raffreddare ‹enthusiasm›
damper /'dæmpə(r)/ n **the news put a ~ on the evening** fam la notizia ha raggelato l'atmosfera della serata
dampness /'dæmpnɪs/ n umidità f
damson /'dæmzən/ n (fruit) susina f selvatica, prugna f selvatica

ᕫ **dance** /dɑːns/ **1** n ballo m
2 vt/i ballare
■ **dance about, dance up and down** vi
saltellare qua e là
dance hall n sala f da ballo
dance music n musica f da ballo
dancer /'dɑːnsə(r)/ n ballerino, -a mf
dancing /'dɑːnsɪŋ, US 'dænsɪŋ/ n ballo m
dandelion /'dændɪlaɪən/ n dente m di
leone
dandruff /'dændrʌf/ n forfora f
Dane /deɪn/ n danese mf; **Great ~** danese m
ᕫ **danger** /'deɪndʒə(r)/ n pericolo m; **in/out of
~** in/fuori pericolo
danger level n livello m di guardia
danger list n **on the ~** in prognosi
riservata; **off the ~** fuori pericolo
danger money n indennità f di rischio
ᕫ **dangerous** /'deɪndʒərəs/ adj pericoloso
dangerously /'deɪndʒərəslɪ/ adv
pericolosamente; **~ ill** in pericolo di vita
danger signal n also fig segnale m di
pericolo
dangle /'dæŋgl/ **1** vi penzolare; fig **leave
somebody dangling** lasciare qualcuno in
sospeso
2 vt far penzolare
Danish /'deɪnɪʃ/ **1** adj danese
2 n (language) danese m
Danish pastry n dolce (m) di pasta
sfoglia contenente pasta di mandorle, mele ecc
dank /dæŋk/ adj umido e freddo
Danube /'dænjuːb/ n Danubio m
dapper /'dæpə(r)/ adj azzimato
dappled /'dæp(ə)ld/ adj ⟨grey, horse⟩
pomellato; ⟨sky⟩ screziato; ⟨shade, surface⟩
chiazzato
dare /deə(r)/ **1** vt/i osare; (challenge)
sfidare (**to** a); **~ [to] do something** osare fare
qualcosa; **I ~ say!** molto probabilmente!
2 n sfida f
daredevil /'deədevl/ n spericolato, -a mf
daring /'deərɪŋ/ **1** adj audace
2 n audacia f
ᕫ **dark** /dɑːk/ **1** adj buio; **~ blue/brown**
blu/marrone scuro; **It's getting ~** sta
cominciando a fare buio; **~ horse** fig (in race,
contest) vincitore m imprevisto; (not much
known about) misterioso m; **keep something ~**
fig tenere qualcosa nascosto
2 n **after ~** col buio; **in the ~** al buio;
keep somebody in the ~ fig tenere qualcuno
all'oscuro
Dark Ages n alto Medioevo m
dark chocolate n cioccolato m fondente
darken /'dɑːkn/ **1** vt oscurare
2 vi oscurarsi
dark-eyed /-'aɪd/ adj ⟨person⟩ dagli occhi
scuri
dark glasses npl occhiali mpl scuri

darkly /'dɑːklɪ/ adv ⟨mutter, hint⟩
cupamente
dark matter n materia f oscura
darkness /'dɑːknɪs/ n buio m
darkroom /'dɑːkruːm/ n camera f oscura
dark-skinned adj ⟨person⟩ dalla pelle
scura
darling /'dɑːlɪŋ/ **1** adj adorabile; **my ~
Joan** carissima Joan
2 n tesoro m; **be a ~ and...** sii gentile e…
darn /dɑːn/ vt rammendare
darning needle /'dɑːnɪŋ/ n ago m da
rammendo
dart /dɑːt/ **1** n dardo m; (in sewing) pince f
inv; **~s** sg (game) freccette fpl
2 vi lanciarsi
dartboard /'dɑːtbɔːd/ n bersaglio m [per
freccette]
dash /dæʃ/ **1** n Typ trattino m; (in Morse)
linea f; **a ~ of milk** un goccio di latte; **make a
~ for** lanciarsi verso
2 vi **I must ~** devo scappare
3 vt far svanire ⟨hopes⟩; (hurl) gettare
■ **dash off** **1** vi scappar via
2 vt (write quickly) buttare giù
■ **dash out** vi uscire di corsa
dashboard /'dæʃbɔːd/ n cruscotto m
dashing /'dæʃɪŋ/ adj (bold) ardito; (in
appearance) affascinante
DAT abbr (**digital audio tape**) DAT f
inv
ᕫ **data** /'deɪtə/ npl & sg dati mpl
databank n banca f di dati
database n banca f dati, database m inv
database management system n
sistema m di gestione di data base
data capture n registrazione f di dati
data communications npl
comunicazione f dati, telematica f
data compression n compressione f
dati
data disk n dischetto m di dati
data entry n immissione f [di] dati
data file n file m inv dati
data handling n manipolazione f [di]
dati
data input n input m dati
data link n collegamento m dati
data processing n elaborazione f [di]
dati
data protection n protezione f dati
data protection act n Jur legge
(f) britannica per la salvaguardia delle
informazioni personali
data retrieval n recupero m dati
data security n sicurezza f dei dati
data storage n archiviazione f dati
data storage device n unità f archivio
dati

d

data transmission n trasmissione f dati

date¹ /deɪt/ n (fruit) dattero m

✦ **date²** **1** n data f; (meeting) appuntamento m; **to ~** fino ad oggi; **out of ~** (not fashionable) fuori moda; (expired) scaduto; ‹information› non aggiornato; **make a ~ with somebody** dare un appuntamento a qualcuno; **be up to ~** essere aggiornato
2 vt/i datare; (go out with) uscire con
■ **date back to** vi risalire a

dated /'deɪtɪd/ adj fuori moda; ‹language› antiquato

date line n linea f [del cambiamento] di data

date of issue n data f di emissione

date rape n stupro (m) perpetrato da persona nota alla vittima

date stamp n (mark) timbro m con la data

dating agency /'deɪtɪŋ/ n agenzia f matrimoniale

dative /'deɪtɪv/ n dativo m

daub /dɔ:b/ vt imbrattare ‹walls›

✦ **daughter** /'dɔ:tə(r)/ n figlia f

daughter-in-law n (pl ~s-in-law) nuora f

daunt /dɔ:nt/ vt scoraggiare; **nothing ~ed** per niente scoraggiato

daunting /'dɔ:ntɪŋ/ adj ‹task, prospect› poco allettante; ‹person› che intimidisce; **I'm faced with a ~ amount of work** mi aspetta una quantità di lavoro preoccupante; **it can be (quite) ~** può essere (piuttosto) allarmante

dauntless /'dɔ:ntlɪs/ adj intrepido

dawdle /'dɔ:dl/ vi bighellonare; (over work) cincischiarsi

dawn /dɔ:n/ **1** n alba f; **at ~** all'alba
2 vi albeggiare; **it ~ed on me** fig mi è apparso chiaro

dawn raid n (police) raid m della polizia all'alba; (stock market) dawn raid m inv

✦ **day** /deɪ/ n giorno m; (whole day) giornata f; (period) epoca f; **~ by ~** giorno per giorno; **~ after ~** giorno dopo giorno; **these ~s** oggigiorno; **In those ~s** a quei tempi; **it's had its ~** fam ha fatto il suo tempo

day-boy n Br Sch alunno m esterno

daybreak n **at ~** allo spuntar del giorno

day-care n (for young children) scuola f materna

day centre n centro m di accoglienza

day-dream **1** n sogno m ad occhi aperti
2 vi sognare ad occhi aperti

day-girl n Sch alunna f esterna

daylight n luce del giorno f

daylight robbery n fam **it's ~** è un furto!

daylight saving time n ora f legale

---

day nursery n (0–3 years) asilo m nido; (3–6 years) scuola f materna

day off n giorno m di riposo

day pass n biglietto m giornaliero

day release n giorno (m) di congedo settimanale dal lavoro da dedicare a corsi di formazione

day return n (ticket) biglietto (m) di andata e ritorno con validità giornaliera

day school n scuola (f) che non fornisce alloggio

daytime n giorno m; **in the ~** di giorno

daytime TV n programmi (mpl) televisivi trasmessi durante il giorno

day-to-day adj quotidiano; **on a ~ basis** giorno per giorno

day trader n day trader m inv

day trading n day trading m inv

day trip n gita f (di un giorno)

day tripper n gitante mf

daze /deɪz/ n **in a ~** stordito; fig sbalordito

dazed /deɪzd/ adj stordito; fig sbalordito

dazzle /'dæzl/ vt abbagliare

dazzling /'dæzlɪŋ/ adj abbagliante

DBMS n abbr (**database management system**) DBMS m

D-day n Mil D-day m inv; (important day) giorno m fatidico

deacon /'di:k(ə)n/ n diacono m

✦ **dead** /ded/ **1** adj morto; (numb) intorpidito; **~ and buried** morto e sepolto; **~ body** morto m; **~ centre** pieno centro m
2 adv **~ tired** stanco morto; **~ slow/easy** lentissimo/facilissimo; **you're ~ right** hai perfettamente ragione; **stop ~** fermarsi di colpo; **be ~ on time** essere in perfetto orario
3 n **the ~** pl i morti; **in the ~ of night** nel cuore della notte

deaden /'ded(ə)n/ vt attutire ‹sound›; calmare ‹pain›

dead end **1** n vicolo m cieco
2 attrib dead-end ‹job› senza prospettive

dead heat n **it was a ~** è finita a pari merito

deadline n scadenza f

deadlock n **reach ~** fig giungere ad un punto morto

dead loss n fam (person) buono, -a mf a nulla; (thing) oggetto m inutile

deadly /'dedlɪ/ adj (-ier, -iest) mortale; fam (dreary) barboso; **~ sins** peccati mpl capitali

dead on arrival adj Med deceduto durante il trasporto

deadpan adj impassibile; ‹humour› all'inglese

dead ringer n fam **be a ~ for somebody** essere la copia spiccicata di qualcuno

Dead Sea n Mar m Morto

dead weight n fig (burden) peso m morto

dead wood *n* Br fig zavorra *f*

deaf /def/ *adj* sordo; ~ **and dumb** sordomuto

deaf aid *n* apparecchio *m* acustico

deafen /'def(ə)n/ *vt* assordare; (permanently) render sordo

deafening /'defənɪŋ/ *adj* assordante

deaf mute *adj & n* sordomuto, -a *mf*

deafness /'defnɪs/ *n* sordità *f*

deaf without speech *adj* sordomuto, -a *mf*

⚬ **deal** /di:l/ ① *n* (agreement) patto *m*; (in business) accordo *m*; **who's ~?** Cards a chi tocca dare le carte?; **a good** *or* **great ~** molto; **get a raw ~** fam ricevere un trattamento ingiusto
  ② *vt* (*pt/pp* **dealt** /delt/) (in cards) dare; ~ **somebody a blow** dare un colpo a qualcuno
  ∎ **deal in** *vt* trattare in
  ∎ **deal out** *vt* ⟨hand out⟩ distribuire
  ∎ **deal with** *vt* (handle) occuparsi di; trattare con ⟨company⟩; (be about) trattare di; **that's been ~t with** è stato risolto

dealer /'di:lə(r)/ *n* commerciante *mf*; (in drugs) spacciatore, -trice *mf*

dealership /'di:ləʃɪp/ *n* Comm concessione *f*

dealing /'di:lɪŋ/ *n* (in drugs) traffico *m*, spaccio *m*

dealing room /'di:lɪŋ/ *n* Fin borsino *m*

dealings /'di:lɪŋz/ *npl* **have ~ with** avere a che fare con

dean /di:n/ *n* decano *m*; Univ preside *mf* di facoltà

dear /dɪə(r)/ ① *adj* caro; (in letter) Caro; (formal) Gentile
  ② *n* caro, -a *mf*
  ③ *int* **oh ~!** Dio mio!

dearly /'dɪəlɪ/ *adv* ⟨love⟩ profondamente; ⟨pay⟩ profumatamente

dearth /dɜ:θ/ *n* penuria *f*

⚬ **death** /deθ/ *n* morte *f*

deathbed *n* letto *m* di morte

death camp *n* campo *m* di sterminio

death certificate *n* certificato *m* di morte

death duty *n* tassa *f* di successione

death knell *n* campane *fpl* a morto; fig tramonto *m*

death list *n* lista *f* dei bersagli (di un assassino)

deathly /'deθlɪ/ ① *adj* ~ **silence** silenzio *m* di tomba
  ② *adv* ~ **pale** di un pallore cadaverico

death mask *n* maschera *f* mortuaria

death penalty *n* pena *f* di morte

death rate *n* tasso *m* di mortalità

death ray *n* raggio *m* mortale

death row /rəʊ/ *n* Am braccio *m* della morte

death sentence *n* also fig condanna *f* a morte

death's head *n* teschio *m*

death threat *n* minaccia *f* di morte

death throes *npl* also fig agonia *f*

death toll *n* bilancio *m* delle vittime

death trap *n* trappola *f* mortale

death warrant *n* ordine *m* di esecuzione di una condanna a morte

death wish *n* desiderio *m* di morire

debacle /deɪ'bɑ:k(ə)l/ *n* sfacelo *m*

debar /dɪ'bɑ:(r)/ *vt* (*pt/pp* **debarred**) escludere

debase /dɪ'beɪs/ *vt* degradare

debatable /dɪ'beɪtəbl/ *adj* discutibile

⚬ **debate** /dɪ'beɪt/ ① *n* dibattito *m*
  ② *vt* discutere; (in formal debate) dibattere
  ③ *vi* ~ **whether to…** considerare se

debauchery /dɪ'bɔ:tʃərɪ/ *n* dissolutezza *f*

debenture bond /dɪ'bentʃə(r)/ *n* obbligazione *f* non garantita

debilitating /dɪ'bɪlɪteɪtɪŋ/ *adj* ⟨disease⟩ debilitante

debility /dɪ'bɪlətɪ/ *n* debilitazione *f*

debit /'debɪt/ ① *n* debito *m*
  ② *vt* (*pt/pp* **debited**) Comm addebitare ⟨sum, account⟩

debit card *n* carta *f* di debito

debonair /debə'neə(r)/ *adj* ⟨person⟩ elegante e cortese

debrief /di:'bri:f/ *vt* chiamare a rapporto; **be ~ed** ⟨defector, freed hostage⟩ essere interrogato; ⟨diplomat, agent⟩ essere chiamato a rapporto

debriefing /di:'bri:fɪŋ/ *n* (of hostage, detector) interrogatorio *m*

debris /'debri:/ *n* macerie *fpl*

⚬ **debt** /det/ *n* debito *m*; **be in ~** avere dei debiti

debt collection *n* esazione *f* crediti

debt collection agency *n* agenzia *f* di recupero crediti

debt collector *n* esattore *m* dei crediti

debtor /'detə(r)/ *n* debitore, -trice *mf*

debt relief *n* cancellazione *f* del debito

debug /di:'bʌg/ *vt* (*pt/pp* **debugged**) Comput correggere gli errori di; togliere i microfoni spia da ⟨room⟩

debunk /dɪ'bʌŋk/ *vt* ridicolizzare ⟨theory, myth⟩

début /'deɪbu:/ *n* debutto *m*

⚬ **decade** /'dekeɪd/ *n* decennio *m*

decadence /'dekədəns/ *n* decadenza *f*

decadent /'dekədənt/ *adj* decadente

decaffeinated /di:'kæfɪneɪtɪd/ *adj* decaffeinato

decalitre /'dekəli:tə(r)/ *n* decalitro *m*

decametre /'dekəmi:tə(r)/ *n* decametro *m*

d

decamp /dɪ'kæmp/ vi sgattaiolare via; ~ **with something** (steal) squagliarsela con qualcosa

decant /dɪ'kænt/ vt travasare

decanter /dɪ'kæntə(r)/ n caraffa f (di cristallo)

decapitate /dɪ'kæpɪteɪt/ vt decapitare

decathlon /dɪ'kæθlɒn/ n decathlon m inv

decay /dɪ'keɪ/ ① n also fig decadenza f; (rot) decomposizione f; (of tooth) carie f inv ② vi imputridire; (rot) decomporsi; ‹tooth› cariarsi

deceased /dɪ'si:st/ ① adj defunto ② n the ~ il defunto; la defunta

deceit /dɪ'si:t/ n inganno m

deceitful /dɪ'si:tfʊl/ adj falso

deceitfully /dɪ'si:tfʊlɪ/ adv falsamente

deceive /dɪ'si:v/ vt ingannare

decelerate /di:'seləreɪt/ vi decelerare

deceleration /di:selə'reɪʃn/ n decelerazione f

🔹 **December** /dɪ'sembə(r)/ n Dicembre m

decency /'di:sənsɪ/ n decenza f

decent /'di:sənt/ adj decente; (respectable) rispettabile; **very ~ of you** molto gentile da parte tua

decently /'di:səntlɪ/ adv decentemente; (kindly) gentilmente

decentralization /di:sentrəlaɪ'zeɪʃn/ n decentramento m

decentralize /di:'sentrəlaɪz/ vt decentrare

deception /dɪ'sepʃn/ n inganno m

deceptive /dɪ'septɪv/ adj ingannevole

deceptively /dɪ'septɪvlɪ/ adv ingannevolmente; **it looks ~ easy** sembra facile ma non lo è

decibel /'desɪbel/ n decibel m inv

🔹 **decide** /dɪ'saɪd/ ① vt decidere; **that's ~d then** siamo d'accordo, allora ② vi decidere (**on** di)

■ **decide on** vt scegliere ‹date, outfit, course of action›

decided /dɪ'saɪdɪd/ adj risoluto

decidedly /dɪ'saɪdɪdlɪ/ adv risolutamente; (without doubt) senza dubbio

decider /dɪ'saɪdə(r)/ n (point) punto m decisivo; (goal) goal m inv decisivo; (game) spareggio m

deciduous /dɪ'sɪdjʊəs/ adj a foglie decidue

decigram[me] /'desɪgræm/ n decigrammo m

decilitre /'desɪli:tə(r)/ n decilitro m

decimal /'desɪml/ ① adj decimale ② n numero m decimale

decimal point n virgola f

decimal system n sistema m decimale

decimate /'desɪmeɪt/ vt decimare

decimetre /'desɪmi:tə(r)/ n decimetro m

decipher /dɪ'saɪfə(r)/ vt decifrare

🔹 **decision** /dɪ'sɪʒn/ n decisione f

decision-maker /dɪ'sɪʒnmeɪkə(r)/ n persona (f) che ama o ha il potere di prendere decisioni

decision-making /dɪ'sɪʒnmeɪkɪŋ/ n **be good/bad at ~** saper/non saper prendere decisioni; **~ process** n processo m decisionale

decisive /dɪ'saɪsɪv/ adj decisivo

decisively /dɪ'saɪsɪvlɪ/ adv con decisione

deck¹ /dek/ vt abbigliare

deck² n Naut ponte m; **on ~** in coperta; **top ~** (of bus) piano m di sopra; **~ of cards** mazzo m

deckchair /'dektʃeə(r)/ n [sedia f a] sdraio f inv

declaration /deklə'reɪʃn/ n dichiarazione f

🔹 **declare** /dɪ'kleə(r)/ vt dichiarare; **anything to ~?** niente da dichiarare?; **~ one's love** dichiararsi

declassify /di:'klæsɪfaɪ/ vt rimuovere dai vincoli di segretezza ‹document, information›

declension /dɪ'klenʃn/ n declinazione f

🔹 **decline** /dɪ'klaɪn/ ① n declino m ② vt (also Gram) declinare ③ vi (decrease) diminuire; ‹health› deperire; (say no) rifiutare

declutch /di:'klʌtʃ/ vi Br lasciare la frizione

decode /di:'kəʊd/ vt decifrare; Comput decodificare

decoding /di:'kəʊdɪŋ/ n decodifica f, decodificazione f

décolleté /deɪ'kɒlteɪ/ adj décolleté inv, scollato

decompose /di:kəm'pəʊz/ vi decomporsi

decomposition /di:kɒmpə'zɪʃn/ n scomposizione f

decompress /di:kəm'pres/ vt decomprimere

decompression /di:kəm'preʃn/ n decompressione f

decontaminate /di:kən'tæmɪneɪt/ vt decontaminare

décor /'deɪkɔ:(r)/ n decorazione f; (including furniture) arredamento m

decorate /'dekəreɪt/ vt decorare; (paint) pitturare; (wallpaper) tappezzare

decoration /dekə'reɪʃn/ n decorazione f

decorative /'dekərətɪv/ adj decorativo

decorator /'dekəreɪtə(r)/ n **painter and ~** imbianchino m

decorous /'dekərəs/ adj decoroso

decorously /'dekərəslɪ/ adv decorosamente

🔹 indicates a very frequent word

decorum /dɪ'kɔːrəm/ n decoro m

decoy¹ /'diːkɔɪ/ n esca f

decoy² /dɪ'kɔɪ/ vt adescare

decrease¹ /'diːkriːs/ n diminuzione f; be on the ∼ essere in diminuzione

◈ **decrease²** /dɪ'kriːs/ vt/i diminuire

decreasing /dɪ'kriːsɪŋ/ adj in diminuzione

decreasingly /dɪ'kriːsɪŋlɪ/ adv sempre meno

decree /dɪ'kriː/ **1** n decreto m **2** vt decretare

decrepit /dɪ'krepɪt/ adj decrepito

decriminalization /diːkrɪmɪnəlaɪ'zeɪʃn/ n depenalizzazione f

decriminalize /diː'krɪmɪnəlaɪz/ vt depenalizzare

dedicate /'dedɪkeɪt/ vt dedicare

dedicated /'dedɪkeɪtɪd/ adj ‹person› scrupoloso

dedication /dedɪ'keɪʃn/ n dedizione f; (in book) dedica f

deduce /dɪ'djuːs/ vt dedurre (**from** da)

deduct /dɪ'dʌkt/ vt dedurre

deduction /dɪ'dʌkʃn/ n deduzione f

deed /diːd/ n azione f; Jur atto m di proprietà

deed of covenant n Jur accordo (m) accessorio ad un contratto immobiliare

deed poll n change one's name by ∼ cambiare nome con un atto unilaterale

deem /diːm/ vt ritenere

◈ **deep** /diːp/ adj profondo; go off the ∼ end fam arrabbiarsi

deepen /'diːpn/ **1** vt approfondire; scavare più profondamente ‹trench› **2** vi approfondirsi; fig ‹mystery› infittirsi

deep-fat-fryer n friggitrice f

deepfelt adj profondo

deep-freeze n congelatore m

deep-fried adj fritto (in molto olio)

deep-frozen adj surgelato

deep-fry vt friggere (in molto olio)

◈ **deeply** adv profondamente

deep-rooted adj ‹habit, prejudice› radicato

deep-sea adj ‹exploration, diving› in profondità; ‹fisherman, fishing› d'alto mare

deep-sea diver n palombaro m

deep-seated adj radicato

deep-set adj ‹eyes› infossato

deep South n Am il profondo Sud

deep-vein thrombosis n trombosi f venosa profonda

deer /dɪə(r)/ n inv cervo m

de-escalate /diː'eskəleɪt/ vt ridurre ‹crisis, violence›

deface /dɪ'feɪs/ vt sfigurare ‹picture›; deturpare ‹monument›

defamation /defə'meɪʃn/ n diffamazione f

defamatory /dɪ'fæmətərɪ/ adj diffamatorio

default /dɪ'fɔːlt/ **1** n Jur (non-payment) morosità f; (failure to appear) contumacia f; Comput default m inv; win by ∼ Sport vincere per abbandono dell'avversario; in ∼ of per mancanza di **2** adj ∼ drive Comput lettore m di default **3** vi (not pay) venir meno ad un pagamento; Comput ∼ to something ritornare all'impostazione di default

defeat /dɪ'fiːt/ **1** n sconfitta f **2** vt sconfiggere; (frustrate) vanificare ‹attempts›; that ∼s the object questo fa fallire l'obiettivo

defeatist /dɪ'fiːtɪst/ adj & n disfattista mf

defecate /'defəkeɪt/ vi defecare

defect¹ /dɪ'fekt/ vi Pol fare defezione

defect² /'diːfekt/ n difetto m

defective /dɪ'fektɪv/ adj difettoso

defector /dɪ'fektə(r)/ n (from party) defezionista mf; (from country) fuor[i]uscito, -a mf

◈ **defence** /dɪ'fens/ n difesa f

defenceless /dɪ'fenslɪs/ adj indifeso

Defence Minister n ministro m della difesa

◈ **defend** /dɪ'fend/ vt difendere; (justify) giustificare

defendant /dɪ'fendənt/ n Jur imputato, -a mf

defender /dɪ'fendə(r)/ n difensore m, -ditrice f

defensive /dɪ'fensɪv/ **1** adj difensivo **2** n difensiva f; on the ∼ sulla difensiva

defer /dɪ'fɜː(r)/ **1** vt (pt/pp **deferred**) (postpone) rinviare **2** vi ∼ to somebody rimettersi a qualcuno

deference /'defərəns/ n deferenza f

deferential /defə'renʃl/ adj deferente

deferentially /defə'renʃəlɪ/ adv con deferenza

deferment, deferral /dɪ'fɜːmənt, dɪ'fɜːrəl/ n (postponement) rinvio m

defiance /dɪ'faɪəns/ n sfida f; in ∼ of sfidando

defiant /dɪ'faɪənt/ adj ‹person› ribelle; ‹gesture, attitude› di sfida

defiantly /dɪ'faɪəntlɪ/ adv con aria di sfida

deficiency /dɪ'fɪʃənsɪ/ n insufficienza f

deficient /dɪ'fɪʃənt/ adj insufficiente; be ∼ in mancare di

deficit /'defɪsɪt/ n deficit m inv

defile /dɪ'faɪl/ vt fig contaminare

◈ **define** /dɪ'faɪn/ vt definire

defined adj ‹role› definito

definite /'defɪnɪt/ adj definito; (certain) ‹answer, yes› definitivo; ‹improvement, difference› netto; he was ∼ about it è stato chiaro in proposito

d

definite article n (grammatical) articolo m determinativo

♂ **definitely** /'defɪnɪtlɪ/ adv sicuramente

♂ **definition** /defɪ'nɪʃn/ n definizione f

definitive /dɪ'fɪnətɪv/ adj definitivo

deflate /dɪ'fleɪt/ vt sgonfiare

deflation /dɪ'fleɪʃn/ n Comm deflazione f

deflationary /dɪ'fleɪʃənrɪ/ adj deflazionistico

deflect /dɪ'flekt/ vt deflettere

deformed /dɪ'fɔːmd/ adj deforme

deformity /dɪ'fɔːmətɪ/ n deformità f inv

DEFRA /'defrə/ abbr Br (**Department for Environment, Food, and Rural Affairs**) ≈ Ministero m per le Politiche Agricole e Forestali

defrag /'diːfræg/ vt fam deframmentare

defragment /'diːfræg'ment/ vt Comput deframmentare

defragmentation /diːfrægmen'teɪʃn/ n Comput deframmentazione f

defraud /dɪ'frɔːd/ vt defraudare

defray /dɪ'freɪ/ vt fml sostenere

defrost /diː'frɒst/ vt sbrinare ‹fridge›; scongelare ‹food›

deft /deft/ adj abile

deftly /'deftlɪ/ adv con destrezza

deftness /'deftnɪs/ n destrezza f

defunct /dɪ'fʌŋkt/ adj morto e sepolto; ‹law› caduto in disuso

defuse /diː'fjuːz/ vt disinnescare; calmare ‹situation›

defy /dɪ'faɪ/ vt (pt/pp -ied) (challenge) sfidare; resistere a ‹attempt›; (not obey) disobbedire a

degenerate¹ /dɪ'dʒenəreɪt/ vi degenerare; ~ into fig degenerare in

degenerate² /dɪ'dʒenərət/ adj degenerato

degeneration /dɪdʒenə'reɪʃn/ n degenerazione f

degenerative /dɪ'dʒenərətɪv/ adj degenerativo

degradation /degrə'deɪʃn/ n (debasement) degradazione f; (of culture) deterioramento m; (squalor) desolazione f

degrade /dɪ'greɪd/ vt (humiliate) degradare ‹person›; (damage) deteriorare ‹environment›

degrading /dɪ'greɪdɪŋ/ adj degradante

♂ **degree** /dɪ'griː/ n grado m; Univ laurea f; **20 ~s** 20 gradi; **not to the same ~** non allo stesso livello

degree ceremony n Br Univ cerimonia f di consegna delle lauree

degree course n Br Univ corso m di laurea

dehydrate /diːhaɪ'dreɪt/ vt disidratare

dehydrated /diːhaɪ'dreɪtɪd/ adj disidratato

dehydration /diːhaɪ'dreɪʃn/ n disidratazione f

de-ice /diː'aɪs/ vt togliere il ghiaccio da

de-icer /diː'aɪsə(r)/ n (mechanical) sbrinatore m; (chemical) liquido m scongelante

deign /deɪn/ vi ~ **to do something** degnarsi di fare qualcosa

deity /'diːətɪ/ n divinità f inv

déjà vu /deɪʒɑː'vuː/ n déjà vu m inv

dejected /dɪ'dʒektɪd/ adj demoralizzato

dejectedly /dɪ'dʒektɪdlɪ/ adv con aria demoralizzata

dejection /dɪ'dʒekʃn/ n abbacchiamento m

delay /dɪ'leɪ/ [1] n ritardo m; **without ~** senza indugio
[2] vt ritardare; **be ~ed** ‹person› essere trattenuto; ‹train, aircraft› essere in ritardo
[3] vi indugiare

delayed action /dɪ'leɪd/ adj ad azione ritardata; ‹bomb› a scoppio ritardato

delegate¹ /'delɪgət/ n delegato, -a mf

delegate² /'delɪgeɪt/ vt delegare

delegation /delɪ'geɪʃn/ n delegazione f

delete /dɪ'liːt/ vt cancellare

delete [key] n tasto m di cancellazione

deletion /dɪ'liːʃn/ n cancellatura f

deliberate¹ /dɪ'lɪbərət/ adj deliberato; (slow) posato

deliberate² /dɪ'lɪbəreɪt/ vi/i deliberare

deliberately /dɪ'lɪbərətlɪ/ adv deliberatamente; (slowly) in modo posato

deliberation /dɪlɪbə'reɪʃn/ n deliberazione f; **with ~** in modo posato

delicacy /'delɪkəsɪ/ n delicatezza f; (food) prelibatezza f

delicate /'delɪkət/ adj delicato

delicately /'delɪkətlɪ/ adv ‹handle, phrase› con delicatezza; ‹crafted, flavoured› con raffinatezza

delicatessen /delɪkə'tesn/ n negozio m di specialità gastronomiche

delicious /dɪ'lɪʃəs/ adj delizioso

delight /dɪ'laɪt/ [1] n piacere m
[2] vt deliziare
[3] vi ~ **in** dilettarsi con

delighted /dɪ'laɪtɪd/ adj lieto

delightful /dɪ'laɪtfʊl/ adj delizioso

delineate /dɪ'lɪnɪeɪt/ vt also fig delineare

delineation /dɪlɪnɪ'eɪʃn/ n delineazione f

delinquency /dɪ'lɪŋkwənsɪ/ n delinquenza f

delinquent /dɪ'lɪŋkwənt/ [1] adj delinquente
[2] n delinquente mf

delirious /dɪ'lɪrɪəs/ adj **be ~** delirare; fig (very happy) essere pazzo di gioia

---
♂ indicates a very frequent word

delirium /dɪˈlɪrɪəm/ n delirio m

◆ **deliver** /dɪˈlɪvə(r)/ vt consegnare; recapitare ‹post, newspaper›; tenere ‹speech›; dare ‹message›; tirare ‹blow›; (set free) liberare; ~ **a baby** far nascere un bambino

deliverance /dɪˈlɪv(ə)rəns/ n liberazione f

◆ **delivery** /dɪˈlɪvəri/ n consegna f; (of post) distribuzione f; Med parto m; **cash on** ~ pagamento m alla consegna

delivery address n indirizzo m del destinatario

delivery man n fattorino m

delivery room n Med sala f parto

delta /ˈdeltə/ n delta m inv

delude /dɪˈluːd/ vt ingannare; ~ **oneself** illudersi

deluge /ˈdeljuːdʒ/ [1] n diluvio m [2] vt fig (with requests etc) inondare

delusion /dɪˈluːʒn/ n illusione; ~**s of grandeur** mania f di grandezza

de luxe /dəˈlʌks/ adj di lusso

delve /delv/ vi ~ **into** (into pocket etc) frugare in; (into notes, the past) fare ricerche in

demagnetize /diːˈmægnətaɪz/ vt smagnetizzare

◆ **demand** /dɪˈmɑːnd/ [1] n richiesta f; Comm domanda f; **in** ~ richiesto; **on** ~ a richiesta [2] vt esigere (**of/from** da)

demanding /dɪˈmɑːndɪŋ/ adj esigente

demanning /diːˈmænɪŋ/ n Br taglio m di personale

demarcation /diːmɑːˈkeɪʃn/ n demarcazione f

demean /dɪˈmiːn/ vt ~ **oneself** abbassarsi (**to** a)

demeaning /dɪˈmiːnɪŋ/ adj degradante

demeanour /dɪˈmiːnə(r)/ n comportamento m

demented /dɪˈmentɪd/ adj demente

dementia /dɪˈmenʃə/ n demenza f

demerara [sugar] /deməˈreərə/ n zucchero m grezzo di canna

demilitarization /diːmɪlɪtəraɪˈzeɪʃn/ n demilitarizzazione f

demilitarize /diːˈmɪlɪtəraɪz/ vt smilitarizzare

demise /dɪˈmaɪz/ n decesso m

demister /diːˈmɪstə(r)/ n Auto sbrinatore m

demo /ˈdeməʊ/ n (pl ~**s**) fam manifestazione f

demobilize /diːˈməʊbəlaɪz/ vt Mil smobilitare

◆ **democracy** /dɪˈmɒkrəsi/ n democrazia f

democrat /ˈdeməkræt/ n democratico, -a mf

democratic /deməˈkrætɪk/ adj democratico

democratically /deməˈkrætɪkli/ adv democraticamente

demo disk n Comput demo disk m inv

demographic /deməˈgræfɪk/ adj demografico

demolish /dɪˈmɒlɪʃ/ vt demolire

demolition /deməˈlɪʃn/ n demolizione f

demon /ˈdiːmən/ n demonio m

demonic /dɪˈmɒnɪk/ adj ‹aspect, power› demoniaco

demonize /ˈdiːmənaɪz/ vt demonizzare

demonstrable /ˈdemənstrəbl/ adj dimostrabile

demonstrably /ˈdemənstrəbli/ adv ‹false, untrue› manifestamente

◆ **demonstrate** /ˈdemənstreɪt/ [1] vt dimostrare; dare una dimostrazione dell'uso di ‹appliance› [2] vi Pol manifestare

demonstration /demənˈstreɪʃn/ n dimostrazione f; Pol manifestazione f

demonstrative /dɪˈmɒnstrətɪv/ adj Gram dimostrativo; **be** ~ essere espansivo

demonstrator /ˈdemənstreɪtə(r)/ n Pol manifestante mf; (for product) dimostratore, -trice mf

demoralize /dɪˈmɒrəlaɪz/ vt demoralizzare

demoralizing /dɪˈmɒrəlaɪzɪŋ/ adj demoralizzante, avvilente

demote /dɪˈməʊt/ vt retrocedere di grado; Mil degradare

demur /dɪˈmɜː/ [1] vi (pt/pp **demurred**) (complain) protestare; (disagree) obiettare [2] n **without** ~ senza obiezioni

demure /dɪˈmjʊə(r)/ adj schivo

demurely /dɪˈmjʊəli/ adv in modo schivo

den /den/ n tana f; (room) rifugio m

denationalize /diːˈnæʃ(ə)nəlaɪz/ vt denazionalizzare

denial /dɪˈnaɪəl/ n smentita f

denier /ˈdenɪə(r)/ n denaro m

denigrate /ˈdenɪgreɪt/ vt denigrare

denigrating /ˈdenɪgreɪtɪŋ/ adj denigratore

denim /ˈdenɪm/ n [tessuto m] jeans m; ~**s** pl [blue-]jeans mpl

Denmark /ˈdenmɑːk/ n Danimarca f

denomination /dɪnɒmɪˈneɪʃn/ n Relig confessione f; (money) valore f

denote /dɪˈnəʊt/ vt denotare

denounce /dɪˈnaʊns/ vt denunciare

dense /dens/ adj denso; ‹crowd, forest› fitto; (stupid) ottuso

densely /ˈdensli/ adv ‹populated› densamente; ~ **wooded** fittamente ricoperto di alberi

density /ˈdensəti/ n densità f inv; (of forest) fittezza f

dent /dent/ [1] n ammaccatura f [2] vt ammaccare

dental /'dentl/ *adj* dei denti; ‹treatment› dentistico; ‹hygiene› dentale

dental appointment *n* appuntamento *m* dal dentista

dental clinic *n* (hospital) clinica *f* odontoiatrica; (part of hospital) reparto *m* odontoiatrico

dental floss *n* filo *m* interdentale

dental plate *n* dentiera *f*

dental surgeon *n* odontoiatra *mf*, medico *m* dentista

dental surgery *n* Br (premises) studio *m* dentistico; (treatment) visita *f* dentistica

dented /'dentɪd/ *adj* ammaccato; ~ **pride** orgoglio *m* ferito

dentist /'dentɪst/ *n* dentista *mf*

dentistry /'dentɪstrɪ/ *n* odontoiatria *f*

dentures /'dentʃəz/ *npl* dentiera *fsg*

denude /dɪ'nju:d/ *vt* denudare

denunciation /dɪnʌnsɪ'eɪʃn/ *n* denuncia *f*

Denver boot /'denvə/ *n* Am = WHEEL CLAMP

ᑐ **deny** /dɪ'naɪ/ *vt* (*pt/pp* **-ied**) negare; (officially) smentire; ~ **somebody something** negare qualcosa a qualcuno; **I can't ~it** non posso negarlo

deodorant /di:'əʊdərənt/ *n* deodorante *m*

deodorize /di:'əʊdəraɪz/ *vt* deodorare

depart /dɪ'pɑ:t/ *vi* ‹plane, train› partire; liter ‹person› andare via; (deviate) allontanarsi (from da)

departed /dɪ'pɑ:tɪd/ *adj* euph (dead) scomparso

ᑐ **department** /dɪ'pɑ:tmənt/ *n* reparto *m*; Pol ministero *m*; (of company) sezione *f*; Univ dipartimento *m*

departmental /di:pɑ:t'mentl/ *adj* Pol ‹colleague, meeting› di sezione; (in business) di reparto

department head *n* caporeparto *mf*; Univ direttore, -trice *mf* d'istituto

department manager *n* (of business) direttore, -trice *mf* di reparto; (of store) caporeparto *mf inv*

Department of Defense *n* Am ministero *m* della Difesa

Department of Energy *n* Am ≈ ministero *m* dell'Industria

Department of Health *n* ministero *m* della Sanità

Department of Homeland Security *n* Am ≈ Dipartimento *m* per la sicurezza nazionale

Department of Social Security *n* Br ≈ Istituto *m* Nazionale della Previdenza Sociale

Department of the Environment *n* Br ministero *m* dell'Ambiente

---

ᑐ indicates a very frequent word

Department of Trade and Industry *n* Br ministero *m* del Commercio e dell'Industria

department store *n* grande magazzino *m*

departure /dɪ'pɑ:tʃə(r)/ *n* partenza *f*; (from rule) allontanamento *m*; **new ~** svolta *f*

departure gate *n* (at airport) uscita *f*

departure lounge *n* (at airport) sala *f* d'attesa

departure platform *n* Rail binario *m*

departures board *n* tabellone *m* delle partenze

ᑐ **depend** /dɪ'pend/ *vi* dipendere (**on** da); (rely) contare (**on** su); **it all ~s** dipende; ~**ing on what he says** a seconda di quello che dice

dependability /dɪpendə'bɪlətɪ/ *n* affidabilità *f*

dependable /dɪ'pendəbl/ *adj* fidato

dependant /dɪ'pendənt/ *n* persona *f* a carico

dependence /dɪ'pendəns/ *n* dipendenza *f*

dependent /dɪ'pendənt/ *adj* dipendente (**on** da)

depict /dɪ'pɪkt/ *vt* (in writing) dipingere; (with picture) rappresentare

depiction /dɪ'pɪkʃn/ *n* rappresentazione *f*

depilatory /dɪ'pɪlətərɪ/ *n* (cream) crema *f* depilatoria

deplete /dɪ'pli:t/ *vt* ridurre; **totally ~d** completamente esaurito

depletion /dɪ'pli:ʃn/ *n* (of resources, funds) impoverimento *m*

deplorable /dɪ'plɔ:rəbl/ *adj* deplorevole

deplore /dɪ'plɔ:(r)/ *vt* deplorare

deploy /dɪ'plɔɪ/ **1** *vt* Mil spiegare **2** *vi* schierarsi

deployment /dɪ'plɔɪmənt/ *n* schieramento *m*

depoliticize /di:pə'lɪtɪsaɪz/ *vt* depoliticizzare

depopulate /di:'pɒpjʊleɪt/ *vt* spopolare

depopulation /di:ˌpɒpjʊ'leɪʃn/ *n* spopolamento *m*

deport /dɪ'pɔ:t/ *vt* deportare

deportation /di:pɔ:'teɪʃn/ *n* deportazione *f*

deportee /di:pɔ:'ti:/ *n* deportato, -a *mf*

deportment /dɪ'pɔ:tmənt/ *n* portamento *m*

depose /dɪ'pəʊz/ *vt* deporre

deposit /dɪ'pɒzɪt/ **1** *n* deposito *m*; (against damage) cauzione *f*; (first instalment) acconto *m* **2** *vt* depositare

deposit account *n* libretto *m* di risparmio; (without instant access) conto *m* vincolato

depositor /dɪ'pɒzɪtə(r)/ *n* Fin depositante *mf*

deposit slip *n* (in bank) distinta *f* di versamento

depot /'depəʊ/ *n* deposito *m*; Am Rail stazione *f* ferroviaria

deprave /dɪ'preɪv/ *vt* depravare

depraved /dɪ'preɪvd/ *adj* depravato

depravity /dɪ'prævətɪ/ *n* depravazione *f*

deprecate /'deprəkeɪt/ *vt* disapprovare

deprecatory /deprɪ'keɪtərɪ/ *adj* (disapproving) di disapprovazione; (apologetic) di scusa

depreciate /dɪ'priːʃɪeɪt/ *vi* deprezzarsi

depreciation /dɪpriːsɪ'eɪʃn/ *n* deprezzameto *m*

depress /dɪ'pres/ *vt* deprimere; (press down) premere

depressed /dɪ'prest/ *adj* depresso; ~ area zona *f* depressa

depressing /dɪ'presɪŋ/ *adj* deprimente

depression /dɪ'preʃn/ *n* depressione *f*

depressive /dɪ'presɪv/ ① *adj* depressivo ② *n* depresso, -a *mf*

depressurize /diː'preʃəraɪz/ *vi* depressurizzare

deprivation /deprɪ'veɪʃn/ *n* privazione *f*

deprive /dɪ'praɪv/ *vt* ~ somebody of something privare qualcuno di qualcosa

deprived /dɪ'praɪvd/ *adj* ‹area, childhood› disagiato

dept *abbr* (**department**) dipartimento *m* (dip.)

depth /depθ/ *n* profondità *f inv*; in ~ ‹study, analyse› in modo approfondito; in the ~s of winter in pieno inverno; in the ~s of despair nella più profonda disperazione; be out of one's ~ (in water) non toccare il fondo; fig sentirsi in alto mare

deputation /depjʊ'teɪʃn/ *n* deputazione *f*

deputize /'depjʊtaɪz/ *vi* ~ for fare le veci di

deputy /'depjʊtɪ/ *n* vice *mf*; (temporary) sostituto, -a *mf*

deputy chairman *n* vicepresidente *m*

deputy leader *n* Br Pol sottosegretario *m*

deputy premier, **deputy prime minister** *n* Pol vice primo ministro *m*

deputy president *n* vicepresidente *mf*

derail /dɪ'reɪl/ *vt* be ~ed ‹train› essere deragliato

derailleur gears /dɪ'reɪljə/ *npl* deragliatore *msg*

derailment /dɪ'reɪlmənt/ *n* deragliamento *m*

deranged /dɪ'reɪndʒd/ *adj* squilibrato

deregulate /diː'regjʊleɪt/ *vt* deregolamentare ‹market›

deregulation /diːregjʊ'leɪʃn/ *n* deregolamentazione *f*

derelict /'derəlɪkt/ *adj* abbandonato

deride /dɪ'raɪd/ *vt* deridere

derision /dɪ'rɪʒn/ *n* derisione *f*

derisive /dɪ'raɪsɪv/ *adj* derisorio

derisory /dɪ'raɪsərɪ/ *adj* ‹laughter› derisorio; ‹offer› irrisorio

derivation /derɪ'veɪʃn/ *n* derivazione *f*

derivative /dɪ'rɪvətɪv/ ① *adj* derivato ② *n* derivato *m*

derive /dɪ'raɪv/ ① *vt* (obtain) derivare; be ~d from ‹word› derivare da ② *vi* ~ from derivare da

dermatitis /dɜːmə'taɪtɪs/ *n* dermatite *f*

dermatologist /dɜːmə'tɒlədʒɪst/ *n* dermatologo, -a *mf*

derogatory /dɪ'rɒgətrɪ/ *adj* ‹comments› peggiorativo

derrick /'derɪk/ *n* derrick *m inv*

derv /dɜːv/ *n* Br gasolio *m*

descaler /diː'skeɪlə(r)/ *n* Br disincrostante *m*

descend /dɪ'send/ ① *vi* scendere; be ~ed from discendere da ② *vt* scendere da

■ **descend on** *vt* (attack) piombare su; (visit) capitare [all'improvviso]

descendant /dɪ'sendənt/ *n* discendente *mf*

descent /dɪ'sent/ *n* discesa *f*; (lineage) origine *f*

descrambler /diː'skræmblə(r)/ *n* Teleph, TV decodificatore *m*

✓ **describe** /dɪ'skraɪb/ *vt* descrivere

✓ **description** /dɪ'skrɪpʃn/ *n* descrizione *f*; they had no help of any ~ non hanno avuto proprio nessun aiuto

descriptive /dɪ'skrɪptɪv/ *adj* descrittivo; (vivid) vivido

desecrate /'desɪkreɪt/ *vt* profanare

desecration /desɪ'kreɪʃn/ *n* profanazione *f*

desegregate /diː'segrɪgeɪt/ *vt* abolire la segregazione razziale in ‹school›

deselect /diːsɪ'lekt/ *vt* Br be ~ed non avere riconferma della candidatura alle elezioni da parte del proprio partito

desensitize /diː'sensɪtaɪz/ *vt* desensibilizzare

desert[1] /'dezət/ ① *n* deserto *m* ② *adj* deserto; ~ island isola *f* deserta

desert[2] /dɪ'zɜːt/ ① *vt* abbandonare ② *vi* disertare

desert boot *n* scarponcino *m* Clark®

deserted /dɪ'zɜːtɪd/ *adj* deserto

deserter /dɪ'zɜːtə(r)/ *n* Mil disertore *m*

desertion /dɪ'zɜːʃn/ *n* Mil diserzione *f*; (of family) abbandono *m*

deserts /dɪ'zɜːts/ *npl* get one's just ~ ottenere ciò che ci si merita

deserve /dɪˈzɜːv/ vt meritare
deservedly /dɪˈzɜːvədlɪ/ adv meritatamente
deserving /dɪˈzɜːvɪŋ/ adj meritevole; ~ **cause** opera f meritoria
desiccated /ˈdesɪkeɪtɪd/ adj essiccato; pej (dried up) secco
design /dɪˈzaɪn/ **1** n progettazione f; (fashion ~, appearance) design m inv; (pattern) modello m; (aim) proposito m; **have ~s on** aver mire su
2 vt progettare; disegnare ‹clothes, furniture, model›; **be ~ed for** essere fatto per
designate /ˈdezɪgneɪt/ vt designare
designation /dezɪgˈneɪʃn/ n designazione f
design consultant n progettista mf
designer /dɪˈzaɪnə(r)/ n progettista mf; (of clothes) stilista mf; Theat (of set) scenografo, -a mf
design fault n difetto m di concezione
design feature n prestazione f
designing /dɪˈzaɪnɪŋ/ adj pej calcolatore
desirable /dɪˈzaɪərəbl/ adj desiderabile
desire /dɪˈzaɪə(r)/ **1** n desiderio m
2 vt desiderare
desist /dɪˈzɪst/ vi desistere (**from** da)
desk /desk/ n scrivania f; (in school) banco m; (in hotel) reception f inv; **cash ~** cassa f; **check-in ~** check-in m inv
deskbound adj ‹job› sedentario
desk diary n agenda da tavolo
desk pad n (blotter) tampone m; (notebook) block-notes m inv
desktop n piano m della scrivania; (computer) [computer m inv] desktop m inv
desktop publishing n desktop publishing m inv, editoria f da tavolo
desolate /ˈdesələt/ adj desolato
desolation /desəˈleɪʃn/ n desolazione f
despair /dɪˈspeə(r)/ **1** n disperazione f; **in ~** disperato; ‹say› per disperazione
2 vi **I ~ of that boy** quel ragazzo mi fa disperare
desperate /ˈdespərət/ adj disperato; **be ~** ‹criminal› essere un disperato; **be ~ for something** morire dalla voglia di
desperately /ˈdespərətlɪ/ adv disperatamente; **he said ~** ha detto, disperato
desperation /despəˈreɪʃn/ n disperazione f; **in ~** per disperazione
despicable /dɪˈspɪkəbl/ adj disprezzevole
despise /dɪˈspaɪz/ vt disprezzare
despite /dɪˈspaɪt/ prep malgrado
despondency /dɪˈspɒndənsɪ/ n abbattimento m
despondent /dɪˈspɒndənt/ adj abbattuto

despot /ˈdespɒt/ n despota m
despotism /ˈdespətɪzm/ n dispotismo m
des res /dezˈrez/ n abbr fam (**desirable residence**) abitazione f desiderabile
dessert /dɪˈzɜːt/ n dolce m
dessert spoon n cucchiaio m da dolce
dessert wine n vino m da dessert
destabilize /diːˈsteɪbɪlaɪz/ vt destabilizzare
destination /destɪˈneɪʃn/ n destinazione f
destine /ˈdestɪn/ vt destinare; **be ~d for something** essere destinato a qualcosa; **~d for each other** fatti l'uno per l'altra
destined /ˈdestɪnd/ adj ~ **for Paris** ‹train, package› con destinazione Parigi; **It was ~ to happen** era destino che succedesse
destiny /ˈdestɪnɪ/ n destino m
destitute /ˈdestɪtjuːt/ adj bisognoso
destitution /destɪˈtjuːʃn/ n indigenza f
destroy /dɪˈstrɔɪ/ vt distruggere
destroyer /dɪˈstrɔɪə(r)/ n Naut cacciatorpediniere m
destruct /dɪˈstrʌkt/ vi distruggersi
destruction /dɪˈstrʌkʃn/ n distruzione f
destructive /dɪˈstrʌktɪv/ adj distruttivo; fig ‹criticism› negativo
destructiveness /dɪˈstrʌktɪvnɪs/ n distruttività f
desultory /ˈdesəltrɪ/ adj ‹conversation› sconnesso; ‹friendship› incostante; ‹attempt› poco convinto
detach /dɪˈtætʃ/ vt staccare
detachable /dɪˈtætʃəbl/ adj separabile
detached /dɪˈtætʃt/ adj fig distaccato; ~ **house** villetta f
detached retina n Med retina f distaccata
detachment /dɪˈtætʃmənt/ n distacco m; Mil distaccamento m
detail /ˈdiːteɪl/ **1** n particolare m, dettaglio m; **in ~** particolareggiatamente
2 vt esporre con tutti i particolari; Mil assegnare
detail drawing n disegno m dettagliato
detailed /ˈdiːteɪld/ adj particolareggiato, dettagliato
detain /dɪˈteɪn/ vt ‹police› trattenere; (delay) far ritardare
detainee /diːteɪˈniː/ n detenuto, -a mf
detect /dɪˈtekt/ vt individuare; (perceive) percepire
detectable /dɪˈtektəbl/ adj individuabile
detection /dɪˈtekʃn/ n scoperta f
detective /dɪˈtektɪv/ n investigatore, -trice mf
detective constable n Br agente mf della polizia giudiziaria
detective inspector n Br ispettore, -trice mf della polizia giudiziaria

---

∂ indicates a very frequent word

detective story n racconto m poliziesco

detective work n indagini fpl

detector /dɪ'tektə(r)/ n (for metal) cercametalli m inv, metal detector m inv

detention /dɪ'tenʃn/ n detenzione f; Sch punizione f

detention centre n centro m di accoglienza

deter /dɪ'tɜ:(r)/ vt (pt/pp deterred) impedire; ~ somebody from doing something impedire a qualcuno di fare qualcosa

detergent /dɪ'tɜ:dʒənt/ n detersivo m

deteriorate /dɪ'tɪərɪəreɪt/ vi deteriorarsi

deterioration /dɪtɪərɪə'reɪʃn/ n deterioramento m

determination /dɪtɜ:mɪ'neɪʃn/ n determinazione f

✧ **determine** /dɪ'tɜ:mɪn/ vt (ascertain) determinare; ~ to (resolve) decidere di

determined /dɪ'tɜ:mɪnd/ adj deciso

determining /dɪ'tɜ:mɪnɪŋ/ adj determinante

deterrent /dɪ'terənt/ n deterrente m

detest /dɪ'test/ vt detestare

detestable /dɪ'testəbl/ adj detestabile

detonate /'detəneɪt/ **1** vt far detonare **2** vi detonare

detonation /detə'neɪʃn/ n detonazione f

detonator /'detəneɪtə(r)/ n detonatore m

detour /'di:tʊə(r)/ n deviazione f

detox /,di:'tɒks/ **1** n disintossicazione f **2** vi disintossicarsi

detoxify /di:'tɒksɪfaɪ/ vt disintossicare

detract /dɪ'trækt/ vi ~ from sminuire ‹merit›; rovinare ‹pleasure, beauty›

detractor /dɪ'træktə(r)/ n detrattore, -trice mf

detriment /'detrɪmənt/ n to the ~ of a danno di

detrimental /detrɪ'mentl/ adj dannoso

detritus /dɪ'traɪtəs/ n detriti mpl

deuce /dju:s/ n Tennis deuce m inv

devaluation /di:væljʊ'eɪʃn/ n svalutazione f

devalue /di:'vælju:/ vt svalutare ‹currency›

devastate /'devəsteɪt/ vt devastare

devastated /'devəsteɪtɪd/ adj fam sconvolto

devastating /'devəsteɪtɪŋ/ adj devastante; ‹news› sconvolgente

devastation /devə'steɪʃn/ n devastazione f

✧ **develop** /dɪ'veləp/ **1** vt sviluppare; contrarre ‹illness›; (add to value of) valorizzare ‹area› **2** vi svilupparsi; ~ into divenire

developer /dɪ'veləpə(r)/ n [property] ~ imprenditore, -trice mf edile

developing bath n Phot bagno m di sviluppo, bagno m rivelatore

developing country n paese m in via di sviluppo

developing tank n Phot vasca f di sviluppo

✧ **development** /dɪ'veləpmənt/ n sviluppo m; (of vaccine etc) messa f a punto

development company n (for property) impresa f edile

deviant /'di:vɪənt/ adj deviato

deviate /'di:vɪeɪt/ vi deviare

deviation /di:vɪ'eɪʃn/ n deviazione f

✧ **device** /dɪ'vaɪs/ n dispositivo m; leave somebody to his own ~s lasciare qualcuno per conto suo

devil /'devl/ n diavolo m

devilish /'dev(ə)lɪʃ/ adj diabolico

devilishly /'dev(ə)lɪʃlɪ/ adv fig fam terribilmente

devil-may-care adj menefreghista

devilment /'dev(ə)lmənt/ n Br cattiveria f

devil's advocate n avvocato m del diavolo

devil worship n culto m satanico

devious /'di:vɪəs/ adj ‹person› subdolo; ‹route› tortuoso

deviously /'di:vɪəslɪ/ adv subdolamente

devise /dɪ'vaɪz/ vt escogitare

devoid /dɪ'vɔɪd/ adj ~ of privo di

devolution /di:və'lu:ʃn/ n (of power) decentramento m

devote /dɪ'vəʊt/ vt dedicare

devoted /dɪ'vəʊtɪd/ adj ‹daughter etc› affezionato; be ~ to something consacrarsi a qualcosa

devotedly /dɪ'vəʊtɪdlɪ/ adv con dedizione

devotee /devə'ti:/ n appassionato, -a mf

devotion /dɪ'vəʊʃn/ n dedizione f; ~s pl Relig devozione f sg

devour /dɪ'vaʊə(r)/ vt divorare

devout /dɪ'vaʊt/ adj devoto

devoutly /dɪ'vaʊtlɪ/ adv Relig devotamente; (sincerely) fervidamente

dew /dju:/ n rugiada f

dewy /'dju:ɪ/ adj rugiadoso

dewy-eyed /-'aɪd/ adj (moved) con gli occhi lucidi; (naive) ingenuo

dexterity /dek'sterətɪ/ n destrezza f

dexterous /'dekstrəs/ adj ‹person, movement› agile, destro; ‹hand› abile; ‹mind› acuto

dexterously /'dekstrəslɪ/ adv ‹move› agilmente; ‹manage› abilmente

DfES abbr Br (Department for Education and Skills) ≈ Ministero m dell'Istruzione

dg abbr (decigram) dg m

diabetes /daɪə'bi:ti:z/ n diabete m

diabetic /daɪə'betɪk/ adj & n diabetico, -a mf

diabolical /daɪə'bɒlɪkl/ adj diabolico

diabolically /daɪə'bɒlɪklɪ/ adv (wickedly) diabolicamente; fam (badly) orribilmente

diacritic /daɪə'krɪtrɪk/ adj (accent, mark) diacritico

diaeresis /daɪ'erɪsɪs/ n dieresi f inv

diagnose /'daɪəgnəʊz/ vt diagnosticare

diagnosis /daɪəg'nəʊsɪs/ n (pl **-oses** /daɪəg'nəʊsiːz/) diagnosi f inv

diagnostic /daɪəg'nɒstɪk/ adj diagnostico

diagnostics /daɪəg'nɒstɪks/ n Med diagnostica f

diagonal /daɪ'æɡənl/ adj & n diagonale f

diagonally /daɪ'æɡənlɪ/ adv diagonalmente

diagram /'daɪəɡræm/ n diagramma m

dial /'daɪəl/ ① n (of clock, machine) quadrante m; Teleph disco m combinatore
② vi (pt/pp **dialled**) Teleph fare il numero; ~ **direct** chiamare in teleselezione
③ vt fare ⟨number⟩

dialect /'daɪəlekt/ n dialetto m

dialectic /daɪə'lektɪk/ ① n dialettica f
② adj dialettico

dialectics /daɪə'lektɪks/ n dialettica f

dialling code /'daɪəlɪŋ/ n prefisso m

dialling tone n segnale m di linea libera

dialogue /'daɪəlɒg/ n dialogo m

dialogue box n Comput finestra f di dialogo

dial tone n Am Teleph segnale m di linea libera

dial-up adj ⟨connection, access⟩ dial-up

dialysis /daɪ'ælɪsɪs/ n dialisi f

dialysis machine n rene m artificiale

diameter /daɪ'æmɪtə(r)/ n diametro m

diametrically /daɪə'metrɪklɪ/ adv ~ **opposed** diametralmente opposto

diamond /'daɪəmənd/ n diamante m, brillante m; (shape) losanga f; ~**s** pl (in cards) quadri mpl

diamond jubilee n sessantesimo anniversario m

diamond-shaped adj romboidale

diamond wedding [anniversary] n nozze fpl di diamante

diaper /'daɪəpə(r)/ n Am pannolino m

diaphanous /daɪ'æfənəs/ adj diafano

diaphragm /'daɪəfræm/ n diaframma m

diarist /'daɪərɪst/ n (author) diarista mf; (journalist) giornalista mf di piccola cronaca

diarrhoea /daɪə'riːə/ n diarrea f

diary /'daɪərɪ/ n (for appointments) agenda f; (for writing in) diario m

diatribe /'daɪətraɪb/ n diatriba f

✓ indicates a very frequent word

dice /daɪs/ ① n inv dadi mpl
② vt Culin tagliare a dadini

dicey /'daɪsɪ/ adj fam rischioso

dichotomy /daɪ'kɒtəmɪ/ n dicotomia f

dicky /'dɪkɪ/ ① n (shirt front) pettino m, sparato m
② adj Br fam ⟨heart⟩ malandato

dictate /dɪk'teɪt/ vt/i dettare

dictation /dɪk'teɪʃn/ n dettato m

dictator /dɪk'teɪtə(r)/ n dittatore m

dictatorial /dɪktə'tɔːrɪəl/ adj dittatoriale

dictatorship /dɪk'teɪtəʃɪp/ n dittatura f

diction /'dɪkʃn/ n dizione f

dictionary /'dɪkʃənrɪ/ n dizionario m

dictum /'dɪktəm/ n (maxim) massima f; (statement) affermazione f

did /dɪd/ ▶ DO

didactic /dɪ'dæktɪk/ adj didattico

diddle /'dɪdl/ vt fam gabbare

didn't /'dɪdnt/ =DID not

die¹ /daɪ/ n Techn (metal mould) stampo m; (for cutting) matrice f

✓ **die²** vi (pres p **dying**) morire (**of** di); **be dying to do something** fam morire dalla voglia di fare qualcosa; **be dying for a drink** fam morire dalla voglia di bere qualcosa
■ **die away** vi ⟨noise, applause⟩ smorzarsi
■ **die down** vi calmarsi; ⟨fire, flames⟩ spegnersi
■ **die off** vi morire uno dopo l'altro
■ **die out** vi estinguersi; ⟨custom⟩ morire

diehard /'daɪhɑːd/ n Pol (in party) fanatico, -a mf; (stubborn person) ultraconservatore mf

diesel /'diːzl/ n diesel m

diesel engine n motore m diesel

diesel train n treno m con locomotiva diesel

diet /'daɪət/ ① n regime m alimentare; (restricted) dieta f; **be on a** ~ essere a dieta
② vi essere a dieta

dietary /'daɪətrɪ/ adj ⟨habit⟩ alimentare

dietary fibre n fibre fpl alimentari

dietary supplement n integratore m dietetico

dietician /daɪə'tɪʃn/ n dietologo, -a mf

differ /'dɪfə(r)/ vi differire; (disagree) non essere d'accordo

✓ **difference** /'dɪfrəns/ n differenza f; (disagreement) divergenza f

✓ **different** /'dɪfrənt/ adj diverso, differente; (various) diversi; **be** ~ **from** essere diverso da

differential /dɪfə'renʃl/ ① adj differenziale
② n differenziale m

differentiate /dɪfə'renʃɪeɪt/ vt distinguere (**between** fra); (discriminate) discriminare (**between** fra); (make different) differenziare

differentiation /dɪfərenʃɪ'eɪʃn/ n differenziazione f

differently /'dɪfrəntlɪ/ *adv* in modo diverso; ~ **from** diversamente da

differently abled /'eɪbld/ *adj* diversamente abile

🔹 **difficult** /'dɪfɪkəlt/ *adj* difficile

🔹 **difficulty** /'dɪfɪkəltɪ/ *n* difficoltà *f inv*; **with** ~ con difficoltà

diffidence /'dɪfɪdəns/ *n* mancanza *f* di sicurezza

diffident /'dɪfɪdənt/ *adj* senza fiducia in se stesso

diffidently /'dɪfɪdəntlɪ/ *adv* senza fiducia in se stesso

diffuse[1] /dɪ'fju:s/ *adj* diffuso; (wordy) prolisso

diffuse[2] /dɪ'fju:z/ *vt* Phys diffondere

diffuseness /dɪ'fju:snɪs/ *n* (of organization) estensione *f*; (of argument) prolissità *f*

dig /dɪg/ 🔲 *n* (poke) spinta *f*; (remark) frecciata *f*; Archaeol scavo *m*; ~**s** *pl* fam camera *fsg* ammobiliata
🔲 *vt/i* (*pt/pp* **dug**, *pres p* **digging**) scavare ‹hole›, vangare ‹garden›, (thrust) conficcare; ~ **somebody in the ribs** dare una gomitata a qualcuno
■ **dig out** *vt* fig tirar fuori
■ **dig up** *vt* scavare ‹garden, street, object›; sradicare ‹tree, plant›; fig (find) scovare

digest[1] /'daɪdʒest/ *n* compendio *m*

digest[2] /daɪ'dʒest/ *vt* digerire

digestible /daɪ'dʒestəbl/ *adj* digeribile

digestion /daɪ'dʒestʃn/ *n* digestione *f*

digestive /daɪ'dʒestɪv/ *adj* digestivo

digestive [biscuit] *n* Br biscotto (*m*) di farina integrale

digestive system *n* apparato *m* digerente

digestive tract *n* apparato *m* digerente

digger /'dɪgə(r)/ *n* Techn scavatrice *f*

diggings /'dɪgɪŋz/ *npl* (in archaeology) scavi *mpl*

digicam /'dɪdʒɪkæm/ *n* fam fotocamera *f* digitale

digit /'dɪdʒɪt/ *n* cifra *f*; (finger) dito *m*

🔹 **digital** /'dɪdʒɪtl/ *adj* digitale

digital [television] *n* TV *f* digitale

digital audio tape *n* audiocassetta *f* digitale

digital camera *n* fotocamera *f* digitale

digital clock *n* orologio *m* digitale

digital computer *n* computer *m* digitale

digital fingerprinting *n* (identificazione *f* con) impronte digitali

digitalize /'dɪdʒɪtəlaɪz/ *vt* digitalizzare

digitization /dɪdʒɪtaɪ'zeɪʃn/ *n* digitalizzazione *f*

digitizer /'dɪdʒɪtaɪzə(r)/ *n* Comput tavoletta *f* grafica

dignified /'dɪgnɪfaɪd/ *adj* dignitoso

dignify /'dɪgnɪfaɪ/ *vt* nobilitare ‹occasion, building›

dignitary /'dɪgnɪtərɪ/ *n* dignitario *m*

dignity /'dɪgnətɪ/ *n* dignità *f*

digress /daɪ'gres/ *vi* divagare

digression /daɪ'greʃn/ *n* digressione *f*

dike /daɪk/ *n* diga *f*

dilapidated /dɪ'læpɪdeɪtɪd/ *adj* cadente

dilapidation /dɪlæpɪ'deɪʃn/ *n* rovina *f*

dilate /daɪ'leɪt/ 🔲 *vt* dilatare
🔲 *vi* dilatarsi

dilation /daɪ'leɪʃn/ *n* dilatazione *f*

dilatory /'dɪlətərɪ/ *adj* dilatorio

dilemma /dɪ'lemə/ *n* dilemma *m*

dilettante /dɪlɪ'tæntɪ/ *n* dilettante *mf*

diligence /'dɪlɪdʒəns/ *n* diligenza *f*

diligent /'dɪlɪdʒənt/ *adj* diligente

dill /dɪl/ *n* aneto *m*

dilly-dally /'dɪlɪdælɪ/ *vi* (*pt/pp* **-ied**) fam tentennare

dilute /daɪ'lju:t/ *vt* diluire

dilution /daɪ'lju:ʃn/ *n also fig* diluizione *f*

dim /dɪm/ 🔲 *adj* (**dimmer, dimmest**) ‹light› debole; (dark) scuro; ‹prospect, chance› scarso; (indistinct) impreciso; fam (stupid) tonto
🔲 *vt/i* (*pt/pp* **dimmed**) affievolire

dime /daɪm/ *n* Am moneta *f* da dieci centesimi

dimension /daɪ'menʃn/ *n* dimensione *f*

dime store *n* Am *grande magazzino (m) con prezzi molto bassi*

diminish /dɪ'mɪnɪʃ/ *vt/i* diminuire

diminished /dɪ'mɪnɪʃt/ *adj* ridotto; Mus diminuito; **on grounds of** ~ **responsibility** Jur per seminfermità mentale

diminutive /dɪ'mɪnjʊtɪv/ *adj & n* diminutivo *m*

dimly /'dɪmlɪ/ *adv* ‹see, remember› indistintamente; ‹shine› debolmente

dimmer /'dɪmə(r)/ *n* interruttore *m* a reostato

dimple /'dɪmpl/ *n* fossetta *f*

dimwit /'dɪmwɪt/ *n* fam stupido *m*

dim-witted /-'wɪtɪd/ *adj* fam stupido

din /dɪn/ *n* baccano *m*
■ **din into**: *vt* ~ **something into somebody** ficcare qualcosa in testa a qualcuno

dine /daɪn/ *vi* pranzare

diner /'daɪnə(r)/ *n* Am (restaurant) tavola *f* calda; **the last** ~ **in the restaurant** l'ultimo cliente nel ristorante

dingdong /'dɪŋdɒŋ/ *n* dindon *m*

dingdong battle *n* Br battibecco *m*

dinghy /'dɪŋgɪ/ *n* dinghy *m*; (inflatable) canotto *m* pneumatico

dingy /'dɪndʒɪ/ *adj* (**-ier, -iest**) squallido e tetro

dining car *n* carrozza *f* ristorante

dining hall *n* refettorio *m*

d

dining room n sala f da pranzo

dining table n tavolo m da pranzo

dinky /'dɪŋkɪ/ adj Br fam carino

✔ **dinner** /'dɪnə(r)/ n cena f; (at midday) pranzo m

dinner dance n cena f danzante

dinner fork n forchetta f

dinner hour n Br Sch pausa f del pranzo

dinner jacket n smoking m inv

dinner knife n coltello m

dinner money n Br Sch soldi (mpl) dati dai genitori agli scolari per il pranzo

dinner party n cena f (con invitati)

dinner plate n piatto m piano

dinner service, dinner set n servizio m da tavola

dinner time n (evening) ora f di cena; (midday) ora f di pranzo

dinnerware /'dɪnəweə(r)/ n Am servizio m da tavola

dinosaur /'daɪnəsɔː(r)/ n dinosauro m

dint /dɪnt/ n **by ~ of** a forza di

diocese /'daɪəsɪs/ n diocesi f inv

diode /'daɪəʊd/ n diodo m

dioxide /daɪ'ɒksaɪd/ n biossido m

dip /dɪp/ **1** n (in ground) inclinazione f; Culin salsina f; **go for a ~** andare a fare una nuotata
2 vt (pt/pp **dipped**) (in liquid) immergere; abbassare ‹head, headlights›
3 vi ‹land› formare un avvallamento
■ **dip into** vt scorrere ‹book›

diphtheria /dɪf'θɪərɪə/ n difterite f

diphthong /'dɪfθɒŋ/ n dittongo m

diploma /dɪ'pləʊmə/ n diploma m

diplomacy /dɪ'pləʊməsɪ/ n diplomazia f

diplomat /'dɪpləmæt/ n diplomatico, -a mf

diplomatic /dɪplə'mætɪk/ adj diplomatico

diplomatically /dɪplə'mætɪklɪ/ adv con diplomazia

diplomatic bag n valigia f diplomatica

diplomatic immunity n immunità f diplomatica

dippy /'dɪpɪ/ adj fam (crazy, weird) pazzo

dipstick /'dɪpstɪk/ n Auto astina f dell'olio

dire /'daɪə(r)/ adj ‹situation, consequences› terribile

✔ **direct** /daɪ'rekt/ **1** adj diretto
2 adv direttamente
3 vt (aim) rivolgere ‹attention, criticism›; (control) dirigere; fare la regia di ‹film, play›; **~ somebody** (show the way) indicare la strada a qualcuno; **~ somebody to do something** ordinare a qualcuno di fare qualcosa

direct access n Comput accesso m diretto

direct current n corrente m continua

direct debit n addebitamento m diretto

✔ indicates a very frequent word

direct dialling n teleselezione f

direct hit n Mil colpo m diretto

✔ **direction** /dɪ'rekʃn/ n direzione f; (of play, film) regia f; **~s** pl indicazioni fpl; **~s for use** istruzioni fpl per l'uso

directional /daɪ'rekʃənəl/ adj direzionale

directive /daɪ'rektɪv/ n direttiva f

direct line n linea f diretta

✔ **directly** /daɪ'rektlɪ/ **1** adv direttamente; (at once) immediatamente
2 conj [non] appena

direct mail n mailing m inv

directness /daɪ'rektnɪs/ n (of person, attitude) franchezza f; (of play, work, writing) chiarezza f

direct object n complemento m oggetto

✔ **director** /dɪ'rektə(r)/ n Comm direttore, -trice mf; (of play, film) regista mf

directorate /daɪ'rektərət/ n (board) consiglio m d'amministrazione

director general n presidente mf

Director of Public Prosecutions n Br ≈ Procuratore m della Repubblica

directorship /dɪ'rektəʃɪp/ n posto m di direttore

directory /dɪ'rektərɪ/ n elenco m; Teleph elenco m [telefonico]; (of streets) stradario m

directory assistance n Am servizio m informazioni abbonati

directory enquiries npl Br servizio m informazioni abbonati

direct rule n Pol sottomissione f al governo centrale

direct speech n discorso m diretto

direct transfer n trasferimento m automatico

dirt /dɜːt/ n sporco m; **~ cheap** fam ad [un] prezzo stracciato

dirtiness /'dɜːtɪnɪs/ n (of person etc) sporcizia f

dirt track n (road) strada f sterrata; Sport pista f sterrata

dirty /'dɜːtɪ/ **1** adj (**-ier, -iest**) sporco
2 vt sporcare

dirty bomb n bomba f sporca

dirty-minded /-'maɪndɪd/ adj fissato sul sesso

dirty trick n brutto scherzo m

dirty tricks npl Pol faccende fpl sporche

dirty weekend n fam weekend m inv clandestino con l'amante

dirty word n parolaccia f

disability /dɪsə'bɪlətɪ/ n infermità f inv

disable /dɪ'seɪbl/ vt (make useless) mettere fuori uso ‹machine›; (in accident) rendere invalido; Comput disabilitare; **be ~d by arthritis** essere menomato dall'artrite

disabled /dɪ'seɪbld/ adj invalido

disabled access n (to public building etc) accesso m per gli invalidi

disabled driver n guidatore, -trice mf invalido, -a

disabled person n invalido, -a mf

disabuse /dɪsə'bju:z/ vt disingannare

disadvantage /dɪsəd'vɑ:ntɪdʒ/ n svantaggio m; **at a ~** in una posizione di svantaggio

disadvantaged /dɪsəd'vɑ:ntɪdʒd/ adj svantaggiato

disadvantageous /dɪsædvən'teɪdʒəs/ adj svantaggioso

disaffected /dɪsə'fektɪd/ adj disilluso

disagree /dɪsə'gri:/ vi non essere d'accordo; **~ with** ⟨food⟩ far male a

disagreeable /dɪsə'gri:əbl/ adj sgradevole

disagreement /dɪsə'gri:mənt/ n disaccordo m; (quarrel) dissidio m

disallow /dɪsə'laʊ/ vt respingere; Sport annullare

disappear /dɪsə'pɪə(r)/ vi scomparire

disappearance /dɪsə'pɪərəns/ n scomparsa f

disappoint /dɪsə'pɔɪnt/ vt deludere

disappointed /dɪsə'pɔɪntɪd/ adj deluso; **I am ~ in you** mi hai deluso

disappointing /dɪsə'pɔɪntɪŋ/ adj deludente

disappointment /dɪsə'pɔɪntmənt/ n delusione f

disapproval /dɪsə'pru:vəl/ n disapprovazione f

disapprove /dɪsə'pru:v/ vi disapprovare; **~ of somebody/something** disapprovare qualcuno/qualcosa

disapproving /dɪsə'pru:vɪŋ/ adj ⟨look, gesture⟩ di disapprovazione

disarm /dɪs'ɑ:m/ **1** vt disarmare **2** vi Mil disarmarsi

disarmament /dɪs'ɑ:məmənt/ n disarmo m

disarming /dɪs'ɑ:mɪŋ/ adj ⟨frankness etc⟩ disarmante

disarrange /dɪsə'reɪndʒ/ vt scompigliare

disarray /dɪsə'reɪ/ n **in ~** in disordine

disaster /dɪ'zɑ:stə(r)/ n disastro m

disaster area n zona f disastrata; fig (person) disastro m

disaster fund n fondi mpl a favore dei disastrati

disaster movie n film m inv catastrofico

disaster relief n soccorso m disastri

disaster victim n disastrato, -a mf

disastrous /dɪ'zɑ:strəs/ adj disastroso

disastrously /dɪ'zɑ:strəslɪ/ adv ⟨fail⟩ disastrosamente; ⟨end, turn out⟩ in modo catastrofico; **go ~ wrong** essere un disastro

disband /dɪs'bænd/ **1** vt sciogliere; smobilitare ⟨troops⟩ **2** vi sciogliersi; ⟨regiment⟩ essere smobilitato

disbelief /dɪsbɪ'li:f/ n incredulità f; **in ~** con incredulità

disbelieve /dɪsbɪ'li:v/ vt non credere

disc /dɪsk/ n disco m; (CD) compact disc m inv

discard /dɪ'skɑ:d/ vt scartare; (throw away) eliminare; scaricare ⟨boyfriend⟩

disc brakes npl Auto freni mpl a disco

discern /dɪ'sɜ:n/ vt discernere

discernible /dɪ'sɜ:nəbl/ adj discernibile

discerning /dɪ'sɜ:nɪŋ/ adj perspicace

discharge¹ /'dɪstʃɑ:dʒ/ n Electr scarica f; (dismissal) licenziamento m; Mil congedo m; Med (of blood) emissione f; (of cargo) scarico m

discharge² /dɪs'tʃɑ:dʒ/ **1** vt scaricare ⟨battery, cargo⟩; (dismiss) licenziare; Mil congedare; Jur assolvere ⟨accused⟩; dimettere ⟨patient⟩; **~ one's duty** esaurire il proprio compito **2** vi Electr scaricarsi

disciple /dɪ'saɪpl/ n discepolo m

disciplinarian /dɪsɪplɪ'neərɪən/ n persona f autoritaria

disciplinary /'dɪsɪplɪnərɪ/ adj disciplinare

discipline /'dɪsɪplɪn/ **1** n disciplina f **2** vt disciplinare; (punish) punire

disciplined /'dɪsɪplɪnd/ adj ⟨person, approach⟩ sistematico

disc jockey n disc jockey m inv

disclaim /dɪs'kleɪm/ vt negare

disclaimer /dɪs'kleɪmə(r)/ n rifiuto m

disclose /dɪs'kləʊz/ vt svelare

disclosure /dɪs'kləʊʒə(r)/ n rivelazione f

disco /'dɪskəʊ/ n discoteca f

discoloration /dɪskʌlə'reɪʃn/ n (process) scolorimento m; (spot) macchia f scolorita

discolour /dɪs'kʌlə(r)/ **1** vt scolorire **2** vi scolorirsi

discomfort /dɪs'kʌmfət/ n scomodità f; fig disagio m

disconcert /dɪskən'sɜ:t/ vt sconcertare

disconcerting /dɪskən'sɜ:tɪŋ/ adj sconcertante

disconnect /dɪskə'nekt/ vt disconnettere

disconsolate /dɪs'kɒnsələt/ adj sconsolato

discontent /dɪskən'tent/ n scontentezza f

discontented /dɪskən'tentɪd/ adj scontento

discontinue /dɪskən'tɪnju:/ vt cessare, smettere; Comm sospendere la produzione di; **~d line** fine f serie

discontinuity /dɪskɒntɪ'nju:ɪtɪ/ n discontinuità f

d

discord /'dɪskɔːd/ n discordia f; Mus
dissonanza f

discordant /dɪ'skɔːdənt/ adj ∼ **note** nota
f discordante

discothèque /'dɪskətek/ n discoteca f

discount[1] /'dɪskaʊnt/ n sconto m

discount[2] /dɪs'kaʊnt/ vt (not believe) non
credere a; (leave out of consideration) non tener
conto di

discount card n tessera f di sconto

discount flight n volo m a prezzo ridotto

discount store n discount m inv

discourage /dɪs'kʌrɪdʒ/ vt scoraggiare;
(dissuade) dissuadere

discouragement /dɪs'kʌrɪdʒmənt/ n
(despondency) scoraggiamento m; (disincentive)
disincentivo m

discourse /'dɪskɔːs/ n discorso m

discourteous /dɪs'kɜːtɪəs/ adj scortese

discourteously /dɪs'kɜːtɪəslɪ/ adv
scortesemente

✔ **discover** /dɪ'skʌvə(r)/ vt scoprire

discovery /dɪs'kʌvərɪ/ n scoperta f

discredit /dɪs'kredɪt/ **1** n discredito m
2 vt screditare

discreet /dɪ'skriːt/ adj discreto

discreetly /dɪ'skriːtlɪ/ adv discretamente

discrepancy /dɪ'skrepənsɪ/ n
discrepanza f

discretion /dɪ'skreʃn/ n discrezione f

discriminate /dɪ'skrɪmɪneɪt/ vi
discriminare (**against** contro); ∼ **between**
distinguere tra

discriminating /dɪ'skrɪmɪneɪtɪŋ/ adj
esigente

discrimination /dɪskrɪmɪ'neɪʃn/ n
discriminazione f; (quality) discernimento m

discriminatory /dɪs'krɪmɪnətərɪ/ adj
discriminatorio, discriminativo

discus /'dɪskəs/ n disco m

✔ **discuss** /dɪ'skʌs/ vt discutere; (examine
critically) esaminare

✔ **discussion** /dɪ'skʌʃn/ n discussione f

**discussion document, discussion
paper** n documento m in abbozzo

disdain /dɪs'deɪn/ **1** n sdegno f
2 vt sdegnare

disdainful /dɪs'deɪnfʊl/ adj sdegnoso

✔ **disease** /dɪ'ziːz/ n malattia f

diseased /dɪ'ziːzd/ adj malato

disembark /dɪsem'bɑːk/ vi sbarcare

disembodied /dɪsem'bɒdɪd/ adj ⟨voice⟩
evanescente; ⟨head⟩ senza corpo; ⟨soul⟩
disincarnato

disenchant /dɪsen'tʃɑːnt/ vt disincantare

disenchanted /ˌdɪsɪn'tʃɑːntɪd, US
-'tʃænt-/ adj disincantato

disenchantment /dɪsen'tʃɑːntmənt/ n
disincanto m

disenfranchise /dɪsen'fræntʃaɪz/ vt
privare del diritto di voto

disengage /dɪsen'geɪdʒ/ vt disimpegnare;
disinnestare ⟨clutch⟩

disentangle /dɪsen'tæŋgəl/ vt districare

disfavour /dɪs'feɪvə(r)/ n sfavore m; **fall
into** ∼ perdere il favore

disfigure /dɪs'fɪɡə(r)/ vt deformare

disgorge /dɪs'ɡɔːdʒ/ vt rigettare

disgrace /dɪz'ɡreɪs/ **1** n vergogna f; **fail
into** ∼ cadere in disgrazia; **I am in** ∼ sono
caduto in disgrazia; **it's a** ∼ è una vergogna
2 vt disonorare

disgraceful /dɪz'ɡreɪsfʊl/ adj vergognoso

disgruntled /dɪs'ɡrʌntld/ adj
malcontento

disguise /dɪs'ɡaɪz/ **1** n travestimento m;
in ∼ travestito
2 vt contraffare ⟨voice⟩; dissimulare
⟨emotions⟩; ∼**d as** travestito da

disgust /dɪs'ɡʌst/ **1** n disgusto m; **in** ∼
con aria disgustata
2 vt disgustare

disgusting /dɪs'ɡʌstɪŋ/ adj disgustoso

dish /dɪʃ/ n piatto m; **do the** ∼**es** lavare i
piatti

■ **dish out** vt (serve) servire; (distribute)
distribuire

■ **dish up** vt servire

dishcloth /'dɪʃklɒθ/ n strofinaccio m

dishearten /dɪs'hɑːt(ə)n/ vt scoraggiare

disheartening /dɪs'hɑːt(ə)nɪŋ/ adj
scoraggiante

dishevelled /dɪ'ʃevld/ adj scompigliato

dishonest /dɪs'ɒnɪst/ adj disonesto

dishonestly /dɪs'ɒnɪstlɪ/ adv
disonestamente

dishonesty /dɪs'ɒnɪstɪ/ n disonestà f

dishonour /dɪs'ɒnə(r)/ **1** n disonore m
2 vt disonorare ⟨family⟩; non onorare
⟨cheque⟩

dishonourable /dɪs'ɒnərəbl/ adj
disonorevole

dishonourably /dɪs'ɒnərəblɪ/ adv in
modo disonorevole

dishtowel n strofinaccio m per i piatti

dishwasher /'dɪʃwɒʃə(r)/ n lavapiatti
f inv

dishwasher-safe adj lavabile in
lavastoviglie

dishy /'dɪʃɪ/ adj (**-ier**, **est**) Br fam ⟨man,
woman⟩ fico, figo

disillusion /dɪsɪ'luːʒn/ vt disilludere

disillusioned /dɪsɪ'luːʒnd/ adj deluso
(**with** di)

disillusionment /dɪsɪ'luːʒnmənt/ n
disillusione f

✔ indicates a very frequent word

disincentive /dɪsɪn'sentɪv/ n disincentivo m

disinclined /dɪsɪn'klaɪnd/ adj riluttante

disinfect /dɪsɪn'fekt/ vt disinfettare

disinfectant /dɪsɪn'fektənt/ n disinfettante m

disingenuous /dɪsɪn'dʒenjʊəs/ adj ‹comment› insincero; ‹smile› falso

disinherit /dɪsɪn'herɪt/ vt diseredare

disintegrate /dɪs'ɪntəgreɪt/ vi disintegrarsi

disintegration /dɪsɪntɪ'greɪʃn/ n disgregazione f

disinterested /dɪs'ɪntərestɪd/ adj disinteressato

disjointed /dɪs'dʒɔɪntɪd/ adj sconnesso

disk /dɪsk/ n Comput disco m; (diskette) dischetto m

disk drive n lettore m [di disco]

disk operating system /'dɪskɒpəreɪtɪŋ/ n sistema m operativo su disco

dislike /dɪs'laɪk/ **1** n avversione f; **your likes and ~s** i tuoi gusti **2** vt I **~ him/it** non mi piace; **I don't ~ him/ it** non mi dispiace

dislocate /'dɪsləkeɪt/ vt slogare; **~ one's shoulder** slogarsi una spalla

dislocation /dɪslə'keɪʃn/ n (of hip, knee) lussazione f

dislodge /dɪs'lɒdʒ/ vt sloggiare

disloyal /dɪs'lɔɪəl/ adj sleale

disloyally /dɪs'lɔɪəlɪ/ adv slealmente

disloyalty /dɪs'lɔɪəltɪ/ n slealtà f

dismal /'dɪzməl/ adj ‹person› abbacchiato; ‹news, weather› deprimente; ‹performance› mediocre

dismantle /dɪs'mæntl/ vt smontare ‹tent, machine›; fig smantellare

dismay /dɪs'meɪ/ n sgomento m; **much to my ~** con mio grande sgomento

dismayed /dɪs'meɪd/ adj sgomento

dismember /dɪs'membə(r)/ vt also fig smembrare

⚡ **dismiss** /dɪs'mɪs/ vt licenziare ‹employee›; (reject) scartare ‹idea, suggestion›

dismissal /dɪs'mɪsəl/ n licenziamento m

dismissive /dɪs'mɪsɪv/ adj ‹person, attitude› sprezzante; **be ~ of** essere sprezzante verso

dismount /dɪs'maʊnt/ vi smontare

disobedience /dɪsə'biːdɪəns/ n disubbidienza f

disobedient /dɪsə'biːdɪənt/ adj disubbidiente

disobey /dɪsə'beɪ/ **1** vt disubbidire a ‹rule› **2** vi disubbidire

disorder /dɪs'ɔːdə(r)/ n disordine m; Med disturbo m

disordered /dɪs'ɔːdəd/ adj ‹life› disordinato; ‹mind› disturbato

disorderly /dɪs'ɔːdəlɪ/ adj disordinato; ‹crowd› turbolento; **~ conduct** turbamento m della quiete pubblica

disorganization /dɪsɔːgənaɪ'zeɪʃn/ n disorganizzazione f

disorganized /dɪs'ɔːgənaɪzd/ adj disorganizzato

disorientate /dɪs'ɔːrɪənteɪt/ vt disorientare

disorientation /dɪsɔːrɪen'teɪʃn/ n disorientamento m

disown /dɪs'əʊn/ vt disconoscere; **I'll ~ you** fam faccio finta di non conoscerti

disparaging /dɪ'spærɪdʒɪŋ/ adj sprezzante

disparagingly /dɪ'spærɪdʒɪŋlɪ/ adv sprezzantemente

disparate /'dɪspərət/ adj (different) eterogeneo; ‹incompatible› disparato

disparity /dɪ'spærətɪ/ n disparità f inv

dispassionate /dɪ'spæʃənət/ adj spassionato

dispassionately /dɪs'pæʃənətlɪ/ adv spassionatamente

dispatch /dɪ'spætʃ/ **1** n Comm spedizione f; Mil (report) dispaccio m; **with ~** con prontezza **2** vt spedire; (kill) spedire al creatore

Dispatch Box n Br Pol postazione (f) da cui parlano i ministri nel Parlamento britannico

dispatch box n valigia f diplomatica

dispatch rider n staffetta f

dispel /dɪ'spel/ vt (pt/pp **dispelled**) dissipare

dispensable /dɪ'spensəbl/ adj dispensabile

dispensary /dɪ'spensərɪ/ n farmacia f

dispense /dɪ'spens/ vt distribuire; **~ with** fare a meno di

dispenser /dɪ'spensə(r)/ n (device) distributore m

dispensing chemist /dɪ'spensɪŋ/ n farmacista mf; (shop) farmacia f

dispensing optician n Br ottico m

dispersal /dɪ'spɜːsl/ n dispersione f

disperse /dɪ'spɜːs/ **1** vt disperdere **2** vi disperdersi

dispersion /dɪ'spɜːʃn/ n dispersione f

dispirited /dɪ'spɪrɪtɪd/ adj scoraggiato

displace /dɪs'pleɪs/ vt spostare

displaced person n profugo, -a mf

displacement /dɪs'pleɪsmənt/ n spostamento m

⚡ **display** /dɪ'spleɪ/ **1** n mostra f; Comm esposizione f; (of feelings) manifestazione f; pej ostentazione f; Comput display m inv ⸱⸱⸱⸼

2 *vt* mostrare; esporre ‹*goods*›; manifestare ‹*feelings*›; Comput visualizzare

display advertisement *n* annuncio *m* pubblicitario di grande formato

display cabinet, **display case** *n* vetrina *f*

display rack *n* espositore *m*

display window *n* vetrina *f*

displease /dɪs'pliːz/ *vt* non piacere a; **be ∼d with** essere scontento di

displeasure /dɪs'pleʒə(r)/ *n* malcontento *m*; **incur sb's ∼** scontentare qualcuno

disposable /dɪ'spəʊzəbl/ *adj* (throwaway) usa e getta; ‹*income*› disponibile

disposal /dɪ'spəʊzl/ *n* (getting rid of) eliminazione *f*; **be at sb's ∼** essere a disposizione di qualcuno

dispose /dɪ'spəʊz/ *vi* **∼ of** (get rid of) disfarsi di; **be well ∼d** essere ben disposto (**to** verso)

disposition /dɪspə'zɪʃn/ *n* disposizione *f*; (nature) indole *f*

dispossessed /dɪspə'zest/ *adj* ‹*family*› spossessato; ‹*son*› diseredato

disproportionate /dɪsprə'pɔːʃənət/ *adj* sproporzionato

disproportionately /dɪsprə'pɔːʃənətlɪ/ *adv* in modo sproporzionato

disprove /dɪs'pruːv/ *vt* confutare

dispute /dɪ'spjuːt/ **1** *n* disputa *f*; (industrial) contestazione *f*
2 *vt* contestare ‹*statement*›

disqualification /dɪskwɒlɪfɪ'keɪʃn/ *n* squalifica *f*; (from driving) ritiro *m* della patente

disqualify /dɪs'kwɒlɪfaɪ/ *vt* escludere; Sport squalificare; **∼ somebody from driving** ritirare la patente a qualcuno

disquiet /dɪs'kwaɪət/ *n* inquietudine *f*

disquieting /dɪs'kwaɪətɪŋ/ *adj* allarmante

disregard /dɪsrɪ'gɑːd/ **1** *n* mancanza *f* di considerazione
2 *vt* ignorare

disrepair /dɪsrɪ'peə(r)/ *n* **fall into ∼** deteriorarsi; **in a state of ∼** in cattivo stato

disreputable /dɪs'repjʊtəbl/ *adj* malfamato

disrepute /dɪsrɪ'pjuːt/ *n* discredito *m*; **bring somebody into ∼** rovinare la reputazione a qualcuno

disrespect /dɪsrɪ'spekt/ *n* mancanza *f* di rispetto

disrespectful /dɪsrɪ'spektfʊl/ *adj* irrispettoso

disrespectfully /dɪsrɪ'spektfʊlɪ/ *adv* irrispettosamente

disrupt /dɪs'rʌpt/ *vt* creare scompiglio in; sconvolgere ‹*plans*›

❖ indicates a very frequent word

disruption /dɪs'rʌpʃn/ *n* scompiglio *m*; (of plans) sconvolgimento *m*

disruptive /dɪs'rʌptɪv/ *adj* ‹*person, behaviour*› indisciplinato

dissatisfaction /dɪ(s)sætɪs'fækʃn/ *n* malcontento *m*

dissatisfied /dɪ(s)'sætɪsfaɪd/ *adj* scontento

dissect /dɪ'sekt/ *vt* sezionare

dissection /dɪ'sekʃn/ *n* dissezione *f*

disseminate /dɪ'semɪneɪt/ *vt* divulgare

dissemination /dɪsemɪ'neɪʃn/ *n* divulgazione *f*

dissension /dɪ'senʃn/ *n* (discord) dissenso *m*

dissent /dɪ'sent/ **1** *n* dissenso *m*
2 *vi* dissentire

dissertation /dɪsə'teɪʃn/ *n* tesi *f inv*

disservice /dɪ(s)'sɜːvɪs/ *n* **do somebody/ oneself a ∼** rendere un cattivo servizio a qualcuno/se stesso

dissidence /'dɪsɪdəns/ *n* dissidenza *f*

dissident /'dɪsɪdənt/ *n* dissidente *mf*

dissimilar /dɪ(s)'sɪmɪlə(r)/ *adj* dissimile (**to** da)

dissimilarity /dɪs(s)ɪmɪ'lærətɪ/ *n* diversità *f inv*

dissipate /'dɪsɪpeɪt/ *vt* dissipare ‹*hope, enthusiasm*›

dissipated /'dɪsɪpeɪtɪd/ *adj* dissipato

dissipation *n* dissipatezza *f*, sregolatezza *f*

dissociate /dɪ'səʊʃɪeɪt/ *vt* dissociare; **∼ oneself from** dissociarsi da

dissolute /'dɪsəluːt/ *adj* dissoluto

dissolution /dɪsə'luːʃn/ *n* scioglimento *m*

dissolve /dɪ'zɒlv/ **1** *vt* dissolvere
2 *vi* dissolversi

dissonance /'dɪsənəns/ *n* dissonanza *f*

dissonant /'dɪsənənt/ *adj* Mus dissonante

dissuade /dɪ'sweɪd/ *vt* dissuadere

❖ **distance** /'dɪstəns/ *n* distanza *f*; **it's a short ∼ from here to the station** la stazione non è lontana da qui; **in the ∼** in lontananza; **from a ∼** da lontano

distance learning *n* corsi *mpl* di studio a distanza

distant /'dɪstənt/ *adj* distante; ‹*relative*› lontano

distantly /'dɪstəntlɪ/ *adv* ‹*reply*› con distacco

distaste /dɪs'teɪst/ *n* avversione *f*

distasteful /dɪs'teɪstfʊl/ *adj* spiacevole

distemper /dɪ'stempə(r)/ *n* (paint) tempera *f*; (in horses, dogs) cimurro *m*

distend /dɪ'stend/ *vi* dilatarsi

distil /dɪ'stɪl/ *vt* (*pt/pp* **distilled**) distillare

distillation /dɪstɪ'leɪʃn/ *n* distillazione *f*

distillery /dɪ'stɪlərɪ/ *n* distilleria *f*

distinct /dɪˈstɪŋkt/ *adj* chiaro; (different) distinto

distinction /dɪˈstɪŋkʃn/ *n* distinzione *f*; Sch massimo *m* dei voti

distinctive /dɪˈstɪŋktɪv/ *adj* caratteristico

distinctly /dɪˈstɪŋktlɪ/ *adv* chiaramente

distinguish /dɪˈstɪŋgwɪʃ/ *vt/i* distinguere; ∼ oneself distinguersi

distinguishable /dɪˈstɪŋgwɪʃəbl/ *adj* distinguibile

distinguished /dɪˈstɪŋgwɪʃt/ *adj* rinomato; ‹appearance› distinto; ‹career› brillante

distinguishing /dɪˈstɪŋgwɪʃɪŋ/ *adj* ‹feature› distintivo

distort /dɪˈstɔːt/ *vt* distorcere

distortion /dɪˈstɔːʃn/ *n* distorsione *f*

distract /dɪˈstrækt/ *vt* distrarre

distracted /dɪˈstræktɪd/ *adj* assente; fam (worried) preoccupato

distracting /dɪˈstræktɪŋ/ *adj* che distrae; I found the noise too ∼ il rumore mi disturbava troppo

distraction /dɪˈstrækʃn/ *n* distrazione *f*; (despair) disperazione *f*; drive somebody to ∼ portare qualcuno alla disperazione

distraught /dɪˈstrɔːt/ *adj* sconvolto

distress /dɪˈstres/ **1** *n* angoscia *f*; (pain) sofferenza *f*; (danger) difficoltà *f* **2** *vt* sconvolgere; (sadden) affliggere

distressed /dɪˈstrest/ *adj* (upset) turbato; (stronger) afflitto

distressing /dɪˈstresɪŋ/ *adj* penoso; (shocking) sconvolgente

distress signal *n* segnale *m* di richiesta di soccorso

distribute /dɪˈstrɪbjuːt/ *vt* distribuire

⚡ **distribution** /dɪstrɪˈbjuːʃn/ *n* distribuzione *f*

distribution network *n* rete *f* di distribuzione

distributor /dɪˈstrɪbjʊtə(r)/ *n* distributore *m*

⚡ **district** /ˈdɪstrɪkt/ *n* regione *f*; Admin distretto *m*

district attorney *n* Am procuratore *m* distrettuale

district council *n* Br consiglio *m* distrettuale

district court *n* Am corte *f* distrettuale federale

district manager *n* direttore, -trice *mf* di zona

district nurse *n* infermiere, -a *mf* che fa visite a domicilio

distrust /dɪsˈtrʌst/ **1** *n* sfiducia *f* **2** *vt* non fidarsi di

distrustful /dɪsˈtrʌstfʊl/ *adj* diffidente

disturb /dɪˈstɜːb/ *vt* disturbare; (emotionally) turbare; spostare ‹papers›

disturbance /dɪˈstɜːbəns/ *n* disturbo *m*; ∼s *pl* (rioting etc) disordini *mpl*

disturbed /dɪˈstɜːbd/ *adj* turbato; [mentally] ∼ malato di mente

disturbing /dɪˈstɜːbɪŋ/ *adj* inquietante

disuse /dɪsˈjuːs/ *n* fall into ∼ cadere in disuso

disused /dɪsˈjuːzd/ *adj* non utilizzato

ditch /dɪtʃ/ **1** *n* fosso *m* **2** *vt* fam (abandon) abbandonare ‹plan, car›; piantare ‹lover›

ditchwater /ˈdɪtʃwɔːtə(r)/ *n* as dull as ∼ una barba

dither /ˈdɪðə(r)/ *vi* titubare

ditto /ˈdɪtəʊ/ *adv* idem; (in list) idem come sopra

ditto marks *npl* virgolette *fpl*

divan /dɪˈvæn/ *n* divano *m*

dive /daɪv/ **1** *n* tuffo *m*; Aeron picchiata *f*; fam (place) bettola *f* **2** *vi* tuffarsi; (when in water) immergersi; Aeron scendere in picchiata; fam (rush) precipitarsi

dive-bomb *vt* Mil bombardare in picchiata

diver /ˈdaɪvə(r)/ *n* (from board) tuffatore, -trice *mf*; (scuba) sommozzatore, -trice *mf*; (deep sea) palombaro *m*

diverge /daɪˈvɜːdʒ/ *vi* divergere

divergent /daɪˈvɜːdʒənt/ *adj* divergente

diverse /daɪˈvɜːs/ *adj* vario

diversify /daɪˈvɜːsɪfaɪ/ *vt/i* (*pt/pp* -ied) Comm diversificare

diversion /daɪˈvɜːʃn/ *n* deviazione *f*; (distraction) diversivo *m*

diversionary /daɪˈvɜːʃənərɪ/ *adj* ‹tactic, attack› diversivo

diversity /daɪˈvɜːsətɪ/ *n* varietà *f*

divert /daɪˈvɜːt/ *vt* deviare ‹traffic›; distogliere ‹attention›

divest /daɪˈvest/ *vt* privare (of di)

⚡ **divide** /dɪˈvaɪd/ **1** *vt* dividere (by per); six ∼d by two sei diviso due **2** *vi* dividersi

■ **divide out** *vt* = DIVIDE

■ **divide up** *vt* = DIVIDE

dividend /ˈdɪvɪdend/ *n* dividendo *m*; pay ∼s fig ripagare

divider /dɪˈvaɪdə(r)/ *n* (in room) divisorio *m*; (in file) cartoncino *m* separatore

dividers /dɪˈvaɪdəz/ *npl* compasso *m* a punte fisse

dividing /dɪˈvaɪdɪŋ/ *adj* ‹wall, fence› divisorio

dividing line *n* linea *f* di demarcazione

divine /dɪˈvaɪn/ *adj* divino

divinely /dɪˈvaɪnlɪ/ *adv* also fam divinamente

diving /ˈdaɪvɪŋ/ *n* (from board) tuffi *mpl*; (scuba) immersione *f*

diving board *n* trampolino *m*

diving mask *n* maschera *f* [subacquea]

diving suit *n* muta *f*; (deep sea) scafandro *m*

divinity /dɪˈvɪnətɪ/ *n* divinità *f inv*; (subject) teologia *f*; (at school) religione *f*

divisible /dɪˈvɪzəbl/ *adj* divisibile (**by** per)

✓ **division** /dɪˈvɪʒn/ *n* divisione *f*; (in sports league) serie *f*

divisional /dɪˈvɪʃənəl/ *adj* ‹commander, officer› di divisione

divisive /dɪˈvaɪsɪv/ *adj* ‹policy› che crea discordia; **be socially** ∼ creare delle divisioni sociali

divorce /dɪˈvɔːs/ ① *n* divorzio *m*
② *vt* divorziare da

divorced /dɪˈvɔːst/ *adj* divorziato; **get** ∼ divorziare

divorcee /dɪvɔːˈsiː/ *n* divorziato, -a *mf*

divulge /daɪˈvʌldʒ/ *vt* rendere pubblico

■ **divvy up** *vt* fam =DIVIDE up

DIY *abbr* (**do-it-yourself**) *fai da te, bricolage*

dizziness /ˈdɪzɪnɪs/ *n* giramenti *mpl* di testa

dizzy /ˈdɪzɪ/ *adj* (**-ier, -iest**) vertiginoso; **I feel** ∼ mi gira la testa

DJ *n abbr* 1 (**disc jockey**) DJ *m inv*
2 Br (**dinner jacket**) smoking *m inv*

Djibouti /dʒɪˈbuːtɪ/ *n* Gibuti *f*

DNA ① *n abbr* (**deoxyribonucleic acid**) DNA *m inv*
② *attrib* ‹testing› del DNA

DNR *abbr* Am 1 (**Department of Natural Resources**) ≈ Ministero *m* dell'Ambiente e della Tutela del Territorio
2 (**do not resuscitate**) non rianimare

✓ **do** /duː/ ① *n* (*pl* **dos** or **do's**) fam festa *f*
② *vt* (3 *sg pres tense* **does**, *pt* **did**, *pp* **done**) fare; fam (cheat) fregare; **do somebody out of something** (money) fregare qualcosa a qualcuno; (opportunity) defraudare qualcuno di qualcosa; **be done** Culin essere cotto; **well done** bravo; Culin ben cotto; **do the flowers** sistemare i fiori; **do the washing up** lavare i piatti; **do one's hair** farsi i capelli
③ *vi* (be suitable) andare; (be enough) bastare; **this will do** questo va bene; **that will do!** basta così!; **do well/badly** cavarsela bene/ male; **how is he doing?** come sta?
④ *v aux* **do you speak Italian?** parli italiano?; **you don't like him, do you?** non ti piace, vero?; (expressing astonishment) non dirmi che ti piace!; **yes, I do** sì; (emphatic) invece sì; **no, I don't** no; **I don't smoke** non fumo; **don't you/doesn't he?** vero?; **so do I** anch'io; **do come in, John** entra, John; **how do you do?** piacere

■ **do away with** *vt* abolire ‹rule›

■ **do for** *vt* (ruin) rovinare

■ **do in** *vt* fam (kill) uccidere; farsi male a ‹back›; **done in** fam esausto

✓ *indicates a very frequent word*

■ **do up** *vt* (fasten) abbottonare; (renovate) rimettere a nuovo; (wrap) avvolgere

■ **do with:** *vt* **I could do with a spanner** mi ci vorrebbe una chiave inglese

■ **do without** *vt* fare a meno di

d.o.b. *abbr* (**date of birth**) data *f* di nascita

docile /ˈdəʊsaɪl/ *adj* docile

dock¹ /dɒk/ *n* Jur banco *m* degli imputati

dock² ① *n* Naut bacino *m*
② *vi* entrare in porto; ‹spaceship› congiungersi

docker /ˈdɒkə(r)/ *n* portuale *m*

docket /ˈdɒkɪt/ ① *n* Comm (label) etichetta *f*; (customs certificate) ricevuta *f* doganale
② *vt* Comm etichettare ‹parcel, package›

docking /ˈdɒkɪŋ/ *n* Naut ormeggio *m*; (of spaceshuttle) aggancio *m*

docks /dɒks/ *npl* porto *m*

dockworker /ˈdɒkwɜːkə(r)/ *n* portuale *m*

dockyard /ˈdɒkjɑːd/ *n* cantiere *m* navale

✓ **doctor** /ˈdɒktə(r)/ ① *n* dottore *m*, dottoressa *f*
② *vt* alterare ‹drink›; castrare ‹cat›

doctorate /ˈdɒktərət/ *n* dottorato *m*

Doctor of Philosophy *n* titolare *mf* di un dottorato di ricerca

doctor's note /ˈdɒktəz/ *n* certificato *m* medico

doctrine /ˈdɒktrɪn/ *n* dottrina *f*

docudrama /ˈdɒkjʊdrɑːmə/ *n* film *m inv* verità

✓ **document** /ˈdɒkjʊmənt/ *n* documento *m*

documentary /dɒkjʊˈmentərɪ/ *adj & n* documentario *m*

documentation /dɒkjʊmenˈteɪʃn/ *n* documentazione *f*

document holder *n* (for keyboarder) leggio *m*

document wallet *n* (folder) cartellina *f*

doddery /ˈdɒdərɪ/ *adj* fam barcollante

doddle /ˈdɒd(ə)l/ *n* Br fam **it's a** ∼ è un gioco da ragazzi

dodge /dɒdʒ/ ① *n* fam trucco *m*
② *vt* schivare ‹blow›; evitare ‹person›
③ *vi* scansarsi; ∼ **out of the way** scansarsi

dodgems /ˈdɒdʒəmz/ *npl* autoscontro *msg*

dodgy /ˈdɒdʒɪ/ *adj* (**-ier, -iest**) fam (dubious) sospetto

DOE *n abbr* 1 Br (**Department of the Environment**) ministero *m* dell'Ambiente
2 Am (**Department of Energy**) ≈ ministero *m* dell'Industria

doe /dəʊ/ *n* femmina *f* (di daino, renna, lepre); (rabbit) coniglia *f*

does /dʌz/ ▶ DO

doesn't /ˈdʌznt/ =DOES not

✓ **dog** /dɒg/ ① *n* cane *m*
② *vt* (*pt/pp* **dogged**) ‹illness, bad luck› perseguitare

dog biscuit *n* biscotto *m* per cani
dog breeder *n* allevatore, -trice *mf* di cani
dog collar *n* collare *m* (*per cani*)
dog-eared /-ɪəd/ *adj* con le orecchie
dog-end *n* fam cicca *f*
dogfight *n* combattimento *m* di cani; Aeron combattimento *m* aereo
dogged /'dɒgɪd/ *adj* ostinato
doggedly /'dɒgɪdlɪ/ *adv* ostinatamente
doggy bag /'dɒgɪ/ *n* sacchetto (*m*) per portarsi a casa gli avanzi di un pasto al ristorante
doggy-paddle *n* fam nuoto *m* a cagnolino
dog handler *n* addestratore, -trice *mf* di cani
doghouse /'dɒghaʊs/ *n* Am canile *m*; in the ~ Br & Am fam in disgrazia
dogma /'dɒgmə/ *n* dogma *m*
dogmatic /dɒg'mætɪk/ *adj* dogmatico
do-gooder /duː'gʊdə(r)/ *n* pej pseudo benefattore, -trice *mf*
dog-paddle *n* nuoto *m* a cagnolino
dogsbody *n* fam tirapiedi *mf inv*
dog tag *n* Am Mil fam piastrina *f* di riconoscimento
doh /dəʊ/ *n* Mus do *m*
doily /'dɔɪlɪ/ *n* centrino *m*
doing /'duːɪŋ/ *n* it's none of my ~ non sono stato io; this is her ~ questa è opera sua; it takes some ~! ce ne vuole!
do-it-yourself /duːɪtjə'self/ *n* fai da te *m*, bricolage *m*
do-it-yourself shop *n* negozio *m* di bricolage
doldrums /'dɒldrəmz/ *npl* be in the ~ essere giù di corda; ‹business› essere in fase di stasi
dole /dəʊl/ *n* sussidio *m* di disoccupazione: be on the ~ essere disoccupato
■ **dole out** *vt* distribuire
doleful /'dəʊlfl/ *adj* triste
dolefully /'dəʊlfʊlɪ/ *adv* tristemente
dole queue *n* Br coda (*f*) per riscuotere il sussidio di disoccupazione; fig (number of unemployed) numero *m* dei disoccupati
doll /dɒl/ *n* bambola *f*
■ **doll up**: *vt* fam ~ oneself up mettersi in ghingheri
✧ **dollar** /'dɒlə(r)/ *n* dollaro *m*
dollar bill *n* banconota *f* da un dollaro
dollar diplomacy *n* politica (*f*) di investimenti all'estero
dollar sign *n* simbolo *m* del dollaro
dollop /'dɒləp/ *n* fam cucchiaiata *f*
dolly /'dɒlɪ/ *n* fam (doll) bambola *f*; Cinema, TV dolly *m inv*
Dolomites /'dɒləmaɪts/ *npl* Dolomiti *mpl*

dolphin /'dɒlfɪn/ *n* delfino *m*
domain /də'meɪn/ *n* dominio *m*
domain name *n* Comput nome *m* di dominio
dome /dəʊm/ *n* cupola *f*
domed /dəʊmd/ *adj* ‹skyline, city› ricco di cupole; ‹roof, ceiling› a cupola; ‹forehead, helmet› bombato
✧ **domestic** /də'mestɪk/ *adj* domestico; Pol interno; Comm nazionale
domestic animal *n* animale *m* domestico
domestic appliance *n* elettrodomestico *m*
domesticate /də'mestɪkeɪt/ *vt* addomesticare
domesticated /də'mestɪkeɪtɪd/ *adj* ‹animal› addomesticato
domestic flight *n* volo *m* nazionale
domestic help *n* collaboratore, -trice *mf* familiare
domesticity /dɒme'stɪsətɪ/ *n* ‹home life› vita *f* di famiglia; ‹household duties› faccende *fpl* domestiche
domestic servant *n* domestico, -a *mf*
domiciliary /dɒmɪ'sɪlɪərɪ/ *adj* ‹visit, care› a domicilio
dominance /'dɒmɪnəns/ *n* Biol, Zool dominanza *f*; (domination) predominio *m*; (numerical strength) preponderanza *f*
dominant /'dɒmɪnənt/ *adj* dominante
✧ **dominate** /'dɒmɪneɪt/ *vt/i* dominare
domination /dɒmɪ'neɪʃn/ *n* dominio *m*
domineering /dɒmɪ'nɪərɪŋ/ *adj* autoritario
Dominica /də'mɪnɪkə/ *n* Dominica *f*
Dominican Republic /də'mɪnɪkən/ *n* Repubblica *f* Dominicana
dominion /də'mɪnjən/ *n* Br Pol dominio *m inv*
domino /'dɒmɪnəʊ/ *n* (*pl* -es) tessera *f* del domino; ~es *sg* (game) domino *m*
don[1] /dɒn/ *vt* (*pt/pp* **donned**) liter indossare
don[2] *n* docente *mf* universitario, -a
donate /dəʊ'neɪt/ *vt* donare
donation /dəʊ'neɪʃn/ *n* donazione *f*
done /dʌn/ ▶ DO
donkey /'dɒŋkɪ/ *n* asino *m*
donkey jacket *n* giacca *f* pesante
donkey's years fam not for ~ non da secoli
donkey-work *n* sgobbata *f*
donor /'dəʊnə(r)/ *n* donatore, -trice *mf*
donor card *n* tessera *f* del donatore di organi
don't /dəʊnt/ = DO not
doodle /'duːdl/ *vi* scarabocchiare
doom /duːm/ [1] *n* fato *m*; (ruin) rovina *f* ⋯▷

2 *vt* be ∼ed **to failure** essere destinato al fallimento

doomed /'duːmd/ *adj* ‹vessel› destinato ad affondare

doomsday /'duːmzdeɪ/ *n* giorno *m* del giudizio

doomwatch /'duːmwɒtʃ/ *n* catastrofismo *m*

door /dɔː(r)/ *n* porta *f*; (of car) portiera *f*; **out of** ∼**s** all'aperto

door bell *n* campanello *m*

doorman *n* portiere *m*

doormat *n* zerbino *m*

door plate *n* (of doctor etc) targa *f*

doorstep *n* gradino *m* della porta

doorstop *n* fermaporta *m inv*

door-to-door **1** *adj* ‹canvassing, selling› porta a porta
2 *adv* ‹sell› porta a porta

doorway *n* vano *m* della porta

dope /dəʊp/ **1** *n* fam (drug) droga *f* leggera; (information) indiscrezioni *fpl*; (idiot) idiota *mf*
2 *vt* drogare; Sport dopare

dope test *n* Sport antidoping *m inv*

dopey /'dəʊpɪ/ *adj* fam addormentato

dormant /'dɔːmənt/ *adj* latente; ‹volcano› inattivo

dormer /'dɔːmə(r)/ *n* ∼ **[window]** abbaino *m*

dormitory /'dɔːmɪtərɪ/ *n* dormitorio *m*

dormitory town *n* città *f inv* dormitorio

dormouse /'dɔːmaʊs/ *n* (*pl* **dormice** /'dɔːmaɪs/) ghiro *m*

dosage /'dəʊsɪdʒ/ *n* dosaggio *m*

dose /dəʊs/ *n* dose *f*

doss /dɒs/ *vi* sl accamparsi
■ **doss down** *vi* sistemarsi [a dormire]

dosser /'dɒsə(r)/ *n* barbone, -a *mf*

doss-house *n* dormitorio *m* pubblico

dot /dɒt/ *n* punto *m*; **at 8 o'clock on the** ∼ alle 8 in punto

dotage /'dəʊtɪdʒ/ *n* be in one's ∼ essere un vecchio rimbambito

dot-com /dɒt'kɒm/ **1** *adj* ‹company› che opera in Internet; ‹millionaire› arricchito grazie a Internet
2 *n* azienda *f* che opera in Internet

dot-com bubble *n* bolla *f* delle dot-com

dote /dəʊt/ ∼ **on** stravedere per

dot matrix [printer] *n* stampante *f* a matrice di punti

dotted /'dɒtɪd/ *adj* ∼ **line** linea *f* punteggiata; **sign on the** ∼ **line** firmare nell'apposito spazio; **be** ∼ **with** essere punteggiato di

dotty /'dɒtɪ/ *adj* (**-ier, -iest**) fam tocco; ‹idea› folle

double /'dʌbl/ **1** *adj* doppio

2 *adv* **cost** ∼ costare il doppio; **see** ∼ vedere doppio; ∼ **the amount** la quantità doppia

3 *n* doppio *m*; (person) sosia *m inv*; ∼**s** *pl* Tennis doppio *m*; **at the** ∼ di corsa

4 *vt* raddoppiare; (fold) piegare in due

5 *vi* raddoppiare

■ **double back** *vi* (go back) fare dietro front

■ **double up** *vi* (bend over) piegarsi in due (**with** per); (share) dividere una stanza

double act *n* Theat, fig numero *m* eseguito da due attori

double-barrelled /-'bærəld/ *adj* ‹gun› a doppia canna

double-barrelled surname *n* cognome *m* doppio

double-bass *n* contrabbasso *m*

double bed *n* letto *m* matrimoniale

double bend *n* Auto doppia curva *f*

double bill *n* Theat rappresentazione *f* di due spettacoli

double bluff *n* atto (*m*) del dire la verità *facendola sembrare una menzogna*

double-book **1** *vi* ‹hotel, airline, company› fare prenotazioni doppie
2 *vt* ∼ **a room/seat etc** riservare la stessa camera/lo stesso posto a due persone

double-breasted *adj* a doppio petto

double-check **1** *vt/i* ricontrollare
2 *n* **double check** ulteriore controllo *m*

double chin *n* doppio mento *m*

double-click /dʌbl'klɪk/ *vi* Comput fare doppio click; ∼ **on** fare doppio click su

double cream *n* Br ≈ panna *f* densa

double-cross *vt* ingannare

double cuff *n* polsino *m* con risvolto

double-dealing **1** *n* doppio gioco *m*
2 *adj* doppio

double-decker *n* autobus *m inv* a due piani

double door[s] *n* porta *f* a due battenti

double Dutch *n* fam ostrogoto *m*

double-edged /-'edʒd/ *adj* also fig a doppio taglio

double entendre /duːblɒ'tɒdr(ə)/ *n* doppio senso *m*

double entry book-keeping *n* contabilità *f* in partita doppia

double exposure *n* Phot sovrimpressione *f*

double fault *n* Tennis doppio fallo *m*

double feature *n* Cinema proiezione (*f*) di due film con biglietto unico

double-fronted /-'frʌntɪd/ *adj* ‹house› con due finestre ai lati della porta principale

double glazing *n* doppio vetro *m*

double-jointed *adj* ‹person, limb› snodato

double knitting [wool] *n* lana *f* grossa

double lock *vt* chiudere a doppia mandata

ꞔ indicates a very frequent word

double-park *vt/i* parcheggiare in doppia fila

double-quick [1] *adv* rapidissimamente [2] *adj* **in ~ time** in un baleno

double room *n* camera *f* doppia

double saucepan *n* Br bagnomaria *m inv*

double spacing *n* Typ interlinea *f* doppia

double spread *n* Journ articolo *m*/ pubblicità *f* su due pagine

double standard *n* **have ~s** usare metri diversi

double take *n* **do a ~** reagire a scoppio ritardato

double talk *n* pej discorso *m* ambiguo

double time *n* Am Mil marcia *f* forzata; **be paid ~** ricevere doppia paga per lo straordinario

double vision *n* **have ~** vederci doppio

double whammy *n* fam (two bits of bad luck) sfortuna *f* doppia

double yellow line[s] *n*[*pl*] Br Aut *due linee* (*fpl*) *gialle continue indicanti divieto di fermata e di sosta*

doubly /'dʌblɪ/ *adv* doppiamente

⚲ **doubt** /daʊt/ [1] *n* dubbio *m* [2] *vt* dubitare di

doubtful /'daʊtfʊl/ *adj* dubbio; (having doubts) in dubbio

doubtfully /'daʊtfʊlɪ/ *adv* con aria dubbiosa

doubtless /'daʊtlɪs/ *adv* indubbiamente

douche /duːʃ/ *n* Med (vaginal) irrigazione *f*

dough /dəʊ/ *n* pasta *f*; (for bread) impasto *m*; fam (money) quattrini *mpl*

doughnut /'dəʊnʌt/ *n* bombolone *m*, krapfen *m inv*

dour /'dʊə(r)/ *adj* ‹mood, landscape› cupo; ‹person, expression› arcigno; ‹building› austero

douse /daʊs/ *vt* spegnere

dove /dʌv/ *n* colomba *f*

dovecot[e] /'dʌvkɒt/ *n* colombaia *f*

dovetail /'dʌvteɪl/ *n* Techn incastro *m* a coda di rondine

dowdy /'daʊdɪ/ *adj* (**-ier, -iest**) trasandato

down¹ /daʊn/ *n* (feathers) piumino *m*

⚲ **down²** /daʊn/ [1] *adv* giù; **go/come ~** scendere; **~ there** laggiù; **sales are ~** le vendite sono diminuite; **£50 ~** 50 sterline d'acconto; **~ 10%** ridotto del 10%; **~ with…!** abbasso…! [2] *prep* **walk ~ the road** camminare per strada; **~ the stairs** giù per le scale; **fall ~ the stairs** cadere giù dalle scale; **get that ~ you!** fam butta giù!; **be ~ the pub** fam essere al pub [3] *vt* bere tutto d'un fiato ‹drink›; **~ tools** staccare; (in protest) interrompere il lavoro per protesta

down-and-out *n* spiantato, -a *mf*

downbeat *adj* (pessimistic) pessimistico; (laidback) distaccato

downcast *adj* abbattuto

downfall *n* caduta *f*; (of person) rovina *f*

downgrade *vt* (in seniority) degradare

down-hearted /-'hɑːtɪd/ *adj* scoraggiato

downhill *adv* in discesa; **go ~** fig essere in declino

downhill skiing *n* sci *m* di fondo

down-in-the-mouth *adj* fam abbattuto

download *vt* Comput scaricare

down-market *adj* ‹newspaper, programme› rivolto al pubblico delle fasce basse; ‹products› dozzinale; ‹area› popolare; ‹hotel, restaurant› economico

down payment *n* deposito *m*

downpipe *n* Br tubo *m* di scolo

downplay *vt* minimizzare

downpour *n* acquazzone *m*

downright [1] *adj* (absolute) totale; ‹lie› bell'e buono; (idiot) perfetto [2] *adv* (completely) completamente

downs /daʊnz/ *npl* Br (hills) colline (*fpl*) di gesso nell'Inghilterra meridionale

downside /'daʊnsaɪd/ *n* svantaggio *m*

downside up *adj & adv* Am sottosopra

downsize /'daʊnsaɪz/ [1] *vt* ‹company› ridurre l'organico di [2] *vi* ridurre l'organico

Down's syndrome /'daʊnz/ *n* sindrome *f* di Down

downstairs [1] *adv* al piano di sotto [2] *adj* del piano di sotto

downstream *adv* a valle

down-to-earth *adj* (person) con i piedi per terra

downtown *adv* Am in centro

downtrodden /'daʊntrɒd(ə)n/ *adj* oppresso

downturn *n* (in economy) fase *f* discendente; (in career) svolta *f* negativa

down under *adv* fam in Australia e/o Nuova Zelanda

downward[s] /'daʊnwəd[z]/ [1] *adj* verso il basso; ‹slope› in discesa [2] *adv* verso il basso

downwind /daʊn'wɪnd/ *adv* sottovento

downy /'daʊnɪ/ *adj* (**-ier, -iest**) coperto di peluria

dowry /'daʊrɪ/ *n* dote *f*

doz *abbr* (**dozen**) dozzina *f*

doze /dəʊz/ [1] *n* sonnellino *m* [2] *vi* sonnecchiare
■ **doze off** *vi* assopirsi

dozen /'dʌzn/ *n* dozzina *f*; **~s of books** libri a dozzine

DPhil *n abbr* (**Doctor of Philosophy**) titolare *mf* di un dottorato di ricerca

DPP *n abbr* Br (**Director of Public Prosecutions**) ≈ Procuratore *m* della Repubblica

Dr *abbr* 1 (**doctor**) Dott. *m*, Dott.essa *f* 2 (**drive**) ≈ via *f*

drab /dræb/ *adj* ‹colour› spento; ‹building› tetro; ‹life› scialbo

draft¹ /drɑːft/ [1] *n* abbozzo *m*; Comm cambiale *f*; Am Mil leva *f*
[2] *vt* abbozzare; Am Mil arruolare
■ **draft in** *vt* chiamare ‹reinforcements, police›

draft² *n* Am = DRAUGHT

draft dodger *n* renitente *mf* alla leva

draftsman /ˈdrɑːftsmən/ *n* Am = DRAUGHTSMAN

drag /dræg/ [1] *n* fam scocciatura *f*; in ~ fam ‹man› travestito da donna
[2] *vt* (*pt/pp* **dragged**) trascinare; dragare ‹river›
■ **drag on** *vi* ‹time, meeting› trascinarsi
■ **drag out** *vt* tirare per le lunghe ‹discussion›; ~ **something out of somebody** tirar fuori qualcosa a qualcuno con le pinze
■ **drag up** *vt* (mention unnecessarily) tirare in ballo

drag and drop *vt* Comput trascinare e rilasciare

dragon /ˈdrægən/ *n* drago *m*

dragonfly /ˈdrægənflaɪ/ *n* libellula *f*

drag show *n* spettacolo *m* di travestiti

drain /dreɪn/ [1] *n* tubo *m* di scarico; (grid) tombino *m*; **the ~s** le fognature; **be a ~ on sb's finances** prosciugare le finanze di qualcuno
[2] *vt* drenare ‹land, wound›; scolare ‹liquid, vegetables›; svuotare ‹tank glass, person›
[3] *vi* ~ [away] andar via; **leave something to ~** lasciare qualcosa a scolare

drainage /ˈdreɪnɪdʒ/ *n* (system) drenaggio *m*; (of land) scolo *m*

draining board /ˈdreɪnɪŋ/ *n* scolapiatti *m inv*

drainpipe /ˈdreɪnpaɪp/ *n* tubo *m* di scarico

drainpipe trousers *npl* pantaloni *mpl* a tubo

drake /dreɪk/ *n* maschio *m* dell'anatra

drama /ˈdrɑːmə/ *n* arte *f* drammatica; (play) opera *f* teatrale; (event) dramma *m*

dramatic /drəˈmætɪk/ *adj* drammatico

dramatically /drəˈmætɪklɪ/ *adv* in modo drammatico

dramatics /drəˈmætɪks/ *npl* arte *f* drammatica; pej atteggiamento *m* teatrale

dramatist /ˈdræmətɪst/ *n* drammaturgo, -a *mf*

dramatization /dræmətaɪˈzeɪʃn/ *n* (for cinema) adattamento *m* cinematografico;

(for stage) adattamento *m* teatrale; (for TV) adattamento *m* televisivo; (exaggeration) drammatizzazione *f*

dramatize /ˈdræmətaɪz/ *vt* adattare per il teatro; fig drammatizzare

drank /dræŋk/ ▶ DRINK

drape /dreɪp/ [1] *n* Am tenda *f*
[2] *vt* appoggiare (**over** su)

drastic /ˈdræstɪk/ *adj* drastico

drastically /ˈdræstɪklɪ/ *adv* drasticamente

draught /drɑːft/ *n* corrente *f* [d'aria]

draught beer *n* birra *f* alla spina

draught-proof [1] *adj* a tenuta d'aria
[2] *vt* tappare le fessure di

draughts /drɑːfts/ *n sg* (game) [gioco *m* della] dama *fsg*

draughtsman /ˈdrɑːftsmən/ *n* disegnatore, -trice *mf*

draughty /ˈdrɑːftɪ/ *adj* pieno di correnti d'aria; **it's ~** c'è corrente

✧ **draw** /drɔː/ [1] *n* (attraction) attrazione *f*; Sport pareggio *m*; (in lottery) sorteggio *m*
[2] *vt* (*pt* **drew**, *pp* **drawn**) tirare; (attract) attirare; disegnare ‹picture›; tracciare ‹line›; ritirare ‹money›; attingere ‹water›; ~ **lots** tirare a sorte
[3] *vi* ‹tea› essere in infusione; Sport pareggiare; ~ **near** avvicinarsi
■ **draw away** *vi* (go ahead) distanziarsi; (move off) allontanarsi
■ **draw back** [1] *vt* tirare indietro; ritirare ‹hand›; tirare ‹curtains›
[2] *vi* (recoil) tirarsi indietro
■ **draw in** [1] *vt* ritrarre ‹claws etc›
[2] *vi* ‹train› arrivare; ‹days› accorciarsi
■ **draw on** *vt* attingere a ‹savings, sb's experience›
■ **draw out** [1] *vt* (pull out) tirar fuori; ritirare ‹money›
[2] *vi* ‹train› partire; ‹days› allungarsi
■ **draw up** [1] *vt* redigere ‹document›; accostare ‹chair›; ~ **oneself up [to one's full height]** drizzarsi
[2] *vi* (stop) fermarsi

drawback /ˈdrɔːbæk/ *n* inconveniente *m*

drawbridge /ˈdrɔːbrɪdʒ/ *n* ponte *m* levatoio

drawee *n* trattario *m*

drawer /drɔː(r)/ *n* cassetto *m*; Fin traente *mf*

drawing /ˈdrɔːɪŋ/ *n* disegno *m*

drawing board *n* tavolo *m* da disegno; fig **go back to the ~** ricominciare da capo

drawing pin *n* puntina *f*

drawing rights *npl* Fin diritti *mf* di prelievo

drawing room *n* salotto *m*

drawl /drɔːl/ *n* pronuncia *f* strascicata

drawn /drɔːn/ ▶ DRAW

✧ indicates a very frequent word

dread /dred/ **1** *n* terrore *m*
2 *vt* aver il terrore di
dreadful /'dredfʊl/ *adj* terribile
dreadfully /'dredfʊlɪ/ *adv* terribilmente
⚲ **dream** /driːm/ **1** *n* sogno *m*
2 *attrib* di sogno
3 *vt/i* (*pt/pp* **dreamt** /dremt/ *or* **dreamed**) sognare (**about/of** di)
■ **dream up** *vt* escogitare ‹*plan, idea*›
dreamer /'driːmə(r)/ *n* (idealist) sognatore, -trice *mf*; (inattentive) persona *f* con la testa fra le nuvole
dream-world *n* live in a ∼ vivere tra le nuvole
dreamy /'driːmɪ/ *adj* fam ‹*house etc*› di sogno; ‹*person*› che è un sogno; (distracted) distratto; ‹*sound, music*› dolce
dreary /'drɪərɪ/ *adj* (-**ier**, -**iest**) tetro; (boring) monotono
dredge /dredʒ/ *vt/i* dragare
■ **dredge up** *vt* riesumare ‹*the past*›
dredger /'dredʒə(r)/ *n* draga *f*
dregs /dregz/ *npl* feccia *fsg*
drench /drentʃ/ *vt* get ∼ed inzupparsi
drenched /drentʃt/ *adj* zuppo
⚲ **dress** /dres/ **1** *n* (woman's) vestito *m*; (clothing) abbigliamento *m*
2 *vt* vestire; (decorate) adornare; Culin condire; Med fasciare; ∼ oneself, get ∼ed vestirsi
3 *vi* vestirsi
■ **dress up** *vi* mettersi elegante; (in disguise) travestirsi (**as** da)
dress circle *n* Theat prima galleria *f*
dress designer *n* stilista *mf*
dresser /'dresə(r)/ *n* (furniture) credenza *f*; Am (dressing table) toilette *f inv*
dressing /'dresɪŋ/ *n* Culin condimento *m*; Med fasciatura *f*
dressing down *n* fam sgridata *f*
dressing gown *n* vestaglia *f*
dressing room *n* (in gym) spogliatoio *m*; Theat camerino *m*
dressing table *n* toilette *f inv*
dressmaker *n* sarta *f*
dressmaking *n* confezioni *fpl* (per donna)
dress rehearsal *n* prova *f* generale
dress sense *n* have ∼ saper abbinare i capi d'abbigliamento
dressy /'dresɪ/ *adj* (-**ier**, -**iest**) elegante
drew /druː/ ▶ DRAW
dribble /'drɪbl/ *vi* gocciolare; ‹*baby*› sbavare; Sport dribblare
dribs and drabs /'drɪbzən'dræbz/ *npl* in ∼ alla spicciolata
dried /draɪd/ *adj* ‹*food*› essiccato
drier /'draɪə(r)/ *n* asciugabiancheria *m inv*
drift /drɪft/ **1** *n* movimento *m* lento; ‹*of snow*› cumulo *m*; (meaning) senso *m*

2 *vi* (off course) andare alla deriva; ‹*snow*› accumularsi; fig ‹*person*› procedere senza meta
■ **drift apart** *vi* ‹*people*› allontanarsi l'uno dall'altro
drifter /'drɪftə(r)/ *n* persona *f* senza meta
driftwood /'drɪftwʊd/ *n* pezzi *mpl* di legno galleggianti
drill /drɪl/ **1** *n* trapano *m*; Mil esercitazione *f*
2 *vt* trapanare; Mil fare esercitare
3 *vi* Mil esercitarsi; ∼ for oil trivellare in cerca di petrolio
drily /'draɪlɪ/ *adv* seccamente
⚲ **drink** /drɪŋk/ **1** *n* bevanda *f*; (alcoholic) bicchierino *m*; have a ∼ bere qualcosa; a ∼ of water un po' d'acqua
2 *vt/i* (*pt* **drank**, *pp* **drunk**) bere
■ **drink to** *vt* (toast) brindare a
■ **drink up** *vt* finire
drinkable /'drɪŋkəbl/ *adj* potabile
drink-driving *n* Br guida *f* in stato di ebbrezza
drinker /'drɪŋkə(r)/ *n* bevitore, -trice *mf*
drinking chocolate /'drɪŋkɪŋ/ *n* Br cioccolata *f* in polvere
drinking water *n* acqua *f* potabile
drink problem *n* Br he has a ∼ beve
drinks cupboard *n* Br mobile *m* bar
drinks dispenser *n* Br distributore *m* di bevande
drinks machine *n* Br distributore *m* di bevande
drinks party *n* Br cocktail *m inv*
drip /drɪp/ **1** *n* gocciolamento *m*; (drop) goccia *f*; Med flebo *f inv*; fam (person) mollaccione, -a *mf*
2 *vi* (*pt/pp* **dripped**) gocciolare
drip-dry *adj* che non si stira
drip-feed *n* flebo [clisi] *f inv*
dripping /'drɪpɪŋ/ **1** *n* (from meat) grasso *m* d'arrosto
2 *adj* ∼ [wet] fradicio
⚲ **drive** /draɪv/ **1** *n* (in car) giro *m*; (entrance) viale *m*; (energy) grinta *f*; Psych pulsione *f*; (organized effort) operazione *f*; Techn motore *m*; Comput lettore *m*, unità *f inv*
2 *vt* (*pt* **drove**, *pp* **driven**) portare ‹*person by car*›; guidare ‹*car*›; Sport (hit) mandare; Techn far funzionare; ∼ somebody mad far diventare matto qualcuno
3 *vi* guidare
■ **drive at**: *vt* what are you driving at? dove vuoi arrivare?
■ **drive away** **1** *vt* portare via in macchina; (chase) cacciare
2 *vi* andare via in macchina
■ **drive back** **1** *vt* respingere ‹*people, animals*›; (in car) riportare
2 *vi* ritornare in macchina
■ **drive in** **1** *vt* piantare ‹*nail*›

⋯⟶

2 *vi* arrivare [in macchina]
■ **drive off** 1 *vt* portare via in macchina; (chase) cacciare
2 *vi* andare via in macchina
■ **drive on** *vi* proseguire; ~ **on!** avanti!
■ **drive up** *vi* arrivare (*in macchina*)
drive-by shooting *n* sparatoria *f* da auto in corsa
drive-in *adj* ~ **cinema** cinema *m inv* drive-in
drivel /'drɪvl/ *n* fam sciocchezze *fpl*
driven /'drɪvn/ ▶ DRIVE
⚘ **driver** /'draɪvə(r)/ *n* guidatore, -trice *mf*; (of train) conducente *mf*
driver's license *n* Am patente *f* di guida
drive-through *n* Am drive-in *m inv*
driveway /'draɪvweɪ/ *n* strada *f* d'accesso
driving /'draɪvɪŋ/ 1 *adj* ‹rain› violento; ‹force› motore
2 *n* guida *f*
driving force *n* spinta *f*; (person behind) forza *f* trainante
driving instructor *n* istruttore, -trice *mf* di guida
driving lesson *n* lezione *f* di guida
driving licence *n* patente *f* di guida
driving mirror *n* (rearview) specchietto *m* retrovisore
driving school *n* scuola *f* guida
driving seat *n* be in the ~ essere alla guida
driving test *n* esame *m* di guida; **take one's** ~ fare l'esame di guida
drizzle /'drɪzl/ 1 *n* pioggerella *f*
2 *vi* piovigginare
droll /drəʊl/ *adj* divertente
drone /drəʊn/ *n* (bee) fuco *m*; (sound) ronzio *m*
■ **drone on** *vi* (talk boringly) tirarla per le lunghe
drool /druːl/ *vi* sbavare; ~ **over something/ somebody** fig fam sbavare per qualcosa/ qualcuno
droop /druːp/ *vi* abbassarsi; ‹flowers› afflosciarsi
⚘ **drop** /drɒp/ 1 *n* (of liquid) goccia *f*; (fall) caduta *f*; (in price, temperature) calo *m*
2 *vt* (*pt/pp* **dropped**) far cadere; sganciare ‹bomb›; (omit) omettere; (give up) abbandonare; ~ **the subject** cambiare discorso
3 *vi* cadere; ‹price, temperature, wind› calare; ‹ground› essere in pendenza
■ **drop behind** *vi* rimanere indietro
■ **drop by** *vi* = DROP IN
■ **drop in** *vi* passare
■ **drop off** 1 *vt* depositare ‹person›
2 *vi* cadere; (fall asleep) assopirsi
■ **drop out** *vi* cadere; (from race, society) ritirarsi; ~ **out of school** lasciare la scuola

⚘ indicates a very frequent word

drop-dead /'drɒpded/ *adv* fam ~ **gorgeous** stupendo
drop-down menu *n* Comput menu *m inv* a tendina
drop handlebars *npl* manubrio *m* ricurvo
drop-out *n* persona *f* contro il sistema sociale
droppings /'drɒpɪŋz/ *npl* sterco *m*
drop shot *n* Sport drop shot *m inv*, smorzata *f*
drop zone *n* (for supplies etc) zona *f* di lancio
drought /draʊt/ *n* siccità *f*
drove /drəʊv/ ▶ DRIVE
droves /drəʊvz/ *npl* in ~ in massa
drown /draʊn/ 1 *vi* annegare
2 *vt* annegare; coprire ‹noise›; **he was** ~**ed** è annegato
drowning /'draʊnɪŋ/ *n* annegamento *m*
drowse /draʊz/ *vi* sonnecchiare; (be very sleepy) essere sonnolento
drowsiness /'draʊzɪnɪs/ *n* sonnolenza *f*
drowsy /'draʊzɪ/ *adj* sonnolento
drudgery /'drʌdʒərɪ/ *n* lavoro *m* pesante e noioso
⚘ **drug** /drʌg/ 1 *n* droga *f*; Med farmaco *m*; **take** ~**s** drogarsi
2 *vt* (*pt/pp* **drugged**) drogare
drug abuse *n* abuso *m* di stupefacenti
drug addict *n* tossicomane, -a *mf*
drug addiction *n* tossicodipendenza *f*
drug dealer *n* spacciatore, -trice *mf* [di droga]
drugged /drʌgd/ *adj* drogato
druggist /'drʌgɪst/ *n* Am farmacista *mf*
drug habit *n* tossicodipendenza *f*
drug mule *n* corriere *m* della droga
Drug Squad *n* Br [squadra *f*] narcotici *f*
drugs raid *n* operazione *f* antidroga
drugs ring *n* rete *f* di narcotrafficanti
drugstore /'drʌgstɔː(r)/ *n* Am negozio (*m*) di generi vari, inclusi medicinali, che funge anche da bar; (dispensing) farmacia *f*
drug-taking *n* consumo *m* di stupefacenti; Sport doping *m inv*
drug test *n* Sport antidoping *m inv*
drug user *n* tossicomane, -a *mf*
drum /drʌm/ 1 *n* tamburo *m*; (for oil) bidone *m*; ~**s** *pl* (in pop group) batteria *f*
2 *vi* (*pt/pp* **drummed**) suonare il tamburo; (in pop group) suonare la batteria
3 *vt* ~ **something into somebody** fam ripetere qualcosa a qualcuno cento volte; ~ **one's fingers on the table** tamburellare con le dita sul tavolo
■ **drum up** *vt* ottenere ‹business, customers, support›
drum kit *n* batteria *f*

drummer /'drʌmə(r)/ n percussionista mf; (in pop group) batterista mf

drumstick /'drʌmstɪk/ n bacchetta f; (of chicken, turkey) coscia f

drunk /drʌŋk/ ⟨1⟩ ▶ DRINK
⟨2⟩ adj ubriaco; get ~ urbiacarsi
⟨3⟩ n ubriaco, -a mf

drunkard /'drʌŋkəd/ n ubriacone, -a mf

drunken /'drʌŋkən/ adj ubriaco

drunken driving n guida f in stato di ebbrezza

ℱ **dry** /draɪ/ ⟨1⟩ adj (**drier, driest**) asciutto; ⟨climate, country⟩ secco
⟨2⟩ vt/i asciugare; ~ one's eyes asciugarsi le lacrime

■ **dry out** vi ⟨clothes⟩ asciugarsi; ⟨alcoholic⟩ disintossicarsi

■ **dry up** vi seccarsi; fig ⟨source⟩ prosciugarsi; fam (be quiet) stare zitto; (do dishes) asciugare i piatti

dry cell n cella f a secco

dry-clean vt pulire a secco

dry-cleaner's n (shop) tintoria f

dryer /'draɪə/ n = DRIER

dry ice n ghiaccio m secco

drying-up /draɪɪŋ-/ n Br do the ~ asciugare i piatti

dryness /'draɪnɪs/ n secchezza f

dry rot n carie f del legno

DSS n abbr Br (**Department of Social Security**) (local office) ≈ Ufficio m della Previdenza Sociale; (ministry) ≈ Istituto m Nazionale della Previdenza Sociale

DTI n abbr Br (**Department of Trade and Industry**) ≈ ministero m del Commercio e dell'Industria

DTP n abbr (**desktop publishing**) DTP m

dual /'dju:əl/ adj doppio

dual carriageway n strada f a due carreggiate

dual nationality n doppia nazionalità f

dual-purpose adj a doppio uso

dub /dʌb/ vt (pt/pp **dubbed**) doppiare ⟨film⟩; (name) soprannominare

dubbing /'dʌbɪŋ/ n doppiaggio m

dubious /'dju:bɪəs/ adj dubbio; be ~ about avere dei dubbi riguardo

dubiously /'dju:bɪəslɪ/ adv ⟨look at⟩ con aria dubbiosa; (say) con esitazione

Dublin /'dʌblɪn/ n Dublino f

duchess /'dʌtʃɪs/ n duchessa f

duck /dʌk/ ⟨1⟩ n anatra f
⟨2⟩ vt (in water) immergere; ~ one's head abbassare la testa
⟨3⟩ vi abbassarsi

■ **duck out of** vt sottrarsi a ⟨task⟩

duckling /'dʌklɪŋ/ n anatroccolo m

duct /dʌkt/ n condotto m; Anat dotto m

dud /dʌd/ ⟨1⟩ adj Mil fam disattivato; ⟨coin⟩ falso; ⟨cheque⟩ a vuoto
⟨2⟩ n fam (banknote) banconota f falsa; Mil (shell) granata f disattivata

ℱ **due** /dju:/ ⟨1⟩ adj dovuto; be ~ ⟨train⟩ essere previsto; the baby is ~ next week il bambino dovrebbe nascere la settimana prossima; ~ to (owing to) a causa di; be ~ to (causally) essere dovuto a; I'm ~ to... dovrei...; in ~ course a tempo debito
⟨2⟩ adv ~ north direttamente a nord

duel /'dju:əl/ n duello m

dues /dju:z/ npl quota f [di iscrizione]

duet /dju:'et/ n duetto m

duffel bag n sacca f da viaggio

duffel coat /'dʌf(ə)l/ n montgomery m inv

dug /dʌg/ ▶ DIG

duke /dju:k/ n duca m

dull /dʌl/ ⟨1⟩ adj (overcast, not bright) cupo; (not shiny) opaco; ⟨sound⟩ soffocato; (boring) monotono; (stupid) ottuso
⟨2⟩ vt intorpidire ⟨mind⟩; attenuare ⟨pain⟩

dullness /'dʌlnɪs/ n (of life) monotonia f; (of company, conversation) noia f; (no shine) opacità f

dully /'dʌllɪ/ adv ⟨say, repeat⟩ monotonamente

duly /'dju:lɪ/ adv debitamente

dumb /dʌm/ adj muto; fam (stupid) ottuso

■ **dumb down** vt abbassare il livello intellettuale di ⟨course, programme⟩

dumbfounded /dʌm'faʊndɪd/ adj sbigottito

dummy /'dʌmɪ/ n (tailor's) manichino m; (for baby) succhiotto m; (model) riproduzione f

dummy run n (trial) prova f

dump /dʌmp/ ⟨1⟩ n (for refuse) scarico m; fam (town) mortorio m; be down in the ~s fam essere depresso
⟨2⟩ vt scaricare; fam (put down) lasciare; fam (get rid of) liberarsi di

dumping /'dʌmpɪŋ/ n Fin dumping m inv, esportazione f sottocosto; no ~ divieto m di scarico

dumpling /'dʌmplɪŋ/ n gnocco m

dumpy /'dʌmpɪ/ adj (plump) tracagnotto

dunce /dʌns/ n zuccone, -a mf

dune /dju:n/ n duna f

dung /dʌŋ/ n sterco m

dungarees /dʌŋgə'ri:z/ npl tuta f sg

dungeon /'dʌndʒən/ n prigione f sotterranea

dunk /dʌŋk/ vt inzuppare

dunno /də'nəʊ/ fam (I don't know) boh

duo /'dju:əʊ/ n duo m inv; Mus duetto m

dupe /dju:p/ ⟨1⟩ n zimbello m
⟨2⟩ vt gabbare

duplicate¹ /'dju:plɪkət/ ⟨1⟩ adj doppio
⟨2⟩ n duplicato m; (document) copia f; in ~ in duplicato

d

duplicate² /'dju:plɪkeɪt/ *vt* fare un duplicato di; ‹*research*› essere una ripetizione di ‹*work*›

duplicator /'dju:plɪkeɪtə(r)/ *n* duplicatore *m*

duplicity /dju'plɪsətɪ/ *n* duplicità *f*, doppiezza *f*

durable /'djʊərəbl/ *adj* resistente; ‹*basis, institution*› durevole

duration /djʊə'reɪʃn/ *n* durata *f*

duress /djʊə'res/ *n* costrizione *f*; **under ~** sotto minaccia

ℰ **during** /'djʊərɪŋ/ *prep* durante

dusk /dʌsk/ *n* crepuscolo *m*

dusky /'dʌskɪ/ *adj* ‹*complexion*› scuro

dust /dʌst/ ① *n* polvere *f*
② *vt* spolverare; (sprinkle) cospargere ‹*cake*› (with di)
③ *vi* spolverare

dustbin *n* pattumiera *f*

dustbin man *n* Br netturbino *m*

dust-cart *n* camion *m* della nettezza urbana

dust cover *n* (on book) sopraccoperta *f*; (on furniture) telo *m* di protezione

duster /'dʌstə(r)/ *n* strofinaccio *m*

dust-jacket *n* sopraccoperta *f*

dustman *n* spazzino *m*

dustpan *n* paletta *f* per la spazzatura

dust sheet *n* (on furniture) telo *m* di protezione

dusty /'dʌstɪ/ *adj* (**-ier, -iest**) polveroso

Dutch /dʌtʃ/ ① *adj* olandese; **go ~** fam fare alla romana
② *n* (language) olandese *m*; **the ~** *pl* gli olandesi

Dutch courage *n* spavalderia *f* ispirata dall'alcool

Dutchman /'dʌtʃmən/ *n* olandese *m*

dutiable /'dju:tɪəbl/ *adj* soggetto a imposta

dutiful /'dju:tɪfl/ *adj* rispettoso

dutifully /'dju:tɪfʊlɪ/ *adv* a dovere

ℰ **duty** /'dju:tɪ/ *n* dovere *m*; (task) compito *m*; (tax) dogana *f*; **be on ~** essere di servizio

duty chemist *n* farmacia *f* di turno

duty-free ① *adj* esente da dogana

② *n* duty-free *m inv*

duty-free allowance *n* limite (*m*) d'acquisto di merci esenti da dogana

duty roster, duty rota *n* tabella *f* dei turni

duvet /'du:veɪ/ *n* piumone *m*

duvet cover *n* Br copripiumone *m*

DVD *n abbr* (**digital video disc**) DVD *m*

DVD player *n* lettore *m* DVD

DVT *abbr* (**deep-vein thrombosis**) TVP *f*

dwarf /dwɔ:f/ ① *n* (*pl* **-s** *or* **dwarves**) nano, -a *mf*
② *vt* rimpicciolire

dweeb /dwi:b/ *n* esp Am fam secchione, -a *mf*

dwell /dwel/ *vi* (*pt/pp* **dwelt**) liter dimorare
∎ **dwell on** *vt* fig soffermarsi su

dweller /'dwelə(r)/ *n* **city/town ~** cittadino, -a *mf*

dwelling /'dwelɪŋ/ *n* abitazione *f*

dwindle /'dwɪndl/ *vi* diminuire

dwindling /'dwɪndlɪŋ/ *adj* (strength, health) in calo; ‹*resources, audience, interest*› in diminuzione

DWP *abbr* Br (**Department for Work and Pensions**) ≈ Ministero *m* del Lavoro e delle Politiche Sociali

dye /daɪ/ ① *n* tintura *f*
② *vt* (*pres p* **dyeing**) tingere

dyed-in-the-wool /daɪdɪnðə'wʊl/ *adj* inveterato

dying /'daɪɪŋ/ ▶ DIE²

dyke /daɪk/ *n* (to prevent flooding) diga *f*; (beside ditch) argine *m*; Br (ditch) canale *m* di scolo

dynamic /daɪ'næmɪk/ *adj* dinamico

dynamics /daɪ'næmɪks/ *n* dinamica *f sg*

dynamism /daɪnə'mɪzm/ *n* dinamismo *m*

dynamite /'daɪnəmaɪt/ *n* dinamite *f*

dynamo /'daɪnəməʊ/ *n* dinamo *f inv*

dynasty /'dɪnəstɪ/ *n* dinastia *f*

dysentery /'dɪsəntrɪ/ *n* dissenteria *f*

dysfunctional /dɪs'fʌŋkʃənl/ *adj* disfunzionale

dyslexia /dɪs'leksɪə/ *n* dislessia *f*

dyslexic /dɪs'leksɪk/ *adj* dislessico

Ee

e¹, **E** /iː/ n (letter) e, E f inv; Mus mi m

e² abbr (**euro**) EUR m

E abbr (**east**) E

⚬ **each** /iːtʃ/ **1** adj ogni

2 pron ognuno; **£1** ∼ una sterlina ciascuno; **they love/hate** ∼ **other** si amano/odiano; **we lend** ∼ **other money** ci prestiamo i soldi; **bet on a horse** ∼ **way** puntare su un cavallo piazzato e vincente

eager /'iːɡə(r)/ adj ansioso (**to do** di fare); ⟨pupil⟩ avido di sapere

eager beaver n fam **be an** ∼ essere pieno di zelo

eagerly /'iːɡəlɪ/ adv ⟨wait⟩ ansiosamente; ⟨offer⟩ premurosamente

eagerness /'iːɡənɪs/ n premura f

eagle /'iːɡl/ n aquila f

eagle-eyed /'-aɪd/ adj (sharp-eyed) che ha un occhio di falco

⚬ **ear** /ɪə(r)/ n orecchio m; (of corn) spiga f

earache /'ɪəreɪk/ n mal m d'orecchi

eardrum /'ɪədrʌm/ n timpano m

earl /ɜːl/ n conte m

ear lobe n lobo m dell'orecchio

⚬ **early** /'ɜːlɪ/ **1** adj (**-ier, -iest**) (before expected time) in anticipo; ⟨spring⟩ prematuro; ⟨reply⟩ pronto; ⟨works, writings⟩ primo; **be here** ∼! sii puntuale!; **you're** ∼! sei in anticipo!; ∼ **morning walk** passeggiata f mattutina; **in the** ∼ **morning** la mattina presto; **in the** ∼ **spring** all'inizio della primavera

2 adv presto; (ahead of time) in anticipo; ∼ **in the morning** la mattina presto

early retirement n prepensionamento m; **take** ∼ andare in prepensionamento

early warning n **come as an** ∼ **of something** essere il segno premonitore di qualcosa

early warning system n Mil sistema m d'allarme avanzato

earmark /'ɪəmɑːk/ vt riservare (**for** a)

earmuffs /'ɪəmʌfs/ npl paraorecchie m inv

⚬ **earn** /ɜːn/ vt guadagnare; (deserve) meritare

earned income /ɜːnd/ n reddito m da lavoro

earner /'ɜːnə(r)/ n (person) persona (f) che guadagna; **the main [revenue]** ∼ la principale fonte di sostentamento; **a nice little** ∼ fam un'ottima fonte di guadagno

earnest /'ɜːnɪst/ **1** adj serio

2 n **in** ∼ sul serio

earnestly /'ɜːnɪstlɪ/ adv con aria seria

earning power /'ɜːnɪŋ/ n (of person) capacità f di guadagno; (of company) redditività f inv

earnings /'ɜːnɪŋz/ npl guadagni mpl; (salary) stipendio m

ear nose and throat department n reparto m otorinolaringoiatrico

earphones npl cuffia fsg

earplug n (for noise) tappo m per le orecchie

ear-ring n orecchino m

earshot n **within** ∼ a portata d'orecchio; **he is out of** ∼ non può sentire

ear-splitting /'ɪəsplɪtɪŋ/ adj ⟨scream, shout⟩ lacerante

⚬ **earth** /ɜːθ/ **1** n terra f; (of fox) tana f; **where/what on** ∼? dove/che diavolo?

2 vt Electr mettere a terra

earthenware /'ɜːθnweə/ n terraglia f

earthly /'ɜːθlɪ/ adj terrestre; **be no** ∼ **use** fam essere praticamente inutile

earthquake n terremoto m

earth sciences npl scienze fpl della terra

earthshaking adj fam ⟨news⟩ sconvolgente; ⟨experience⟩ travolgente

earth tremor n scossa f sismica

earthwork n (embankment) terrapieno m; (excavation work) lavori mpl di scavo

earthworm n lombrico m

earthy /'ɜːθɪ/ adj terroso; (coarse) grossolano

earwax /'ɪəwæks/ n cerume m

earwig /'ɪəwɪg/ n forbicina f

ease /iːz/ **1** n **at** ∼ a proprio agio; **at** ∼! Mil riposo!; **ill at** ∼ a disagio; **with** ∼ con facilità

2 vt calmare ⟨pain⟩; alleviare ⟨tension, shortage⟩; (slow down) rallentare; (loosen) allentare

3 vi ⟨pain, situation, wind⟩ calmarsi

■ **ease off 1** vi ⟨pain, pressure, tension⟩ attenuarsi

2 vt (remove gently) togliere con delicatezza

■ **ease up** vi = EASE OFF

easel /'iːzl/ n cavalletto m

⚬ **easily** /'iːzɪlɪ/ adv con facilità; ∼ **the best** certamente il meglio

⚬ **east** /iːst/ **1** n est m; **to the** ∼ **of** a est di

2 adj dell'est

3 adv verso est

East Africa n Africa f orientale

East Berlin n Berlino f Est

eastbound adj ‹carriageway, traffic›
diretto a est

East End n quartiere (m) nella zona est di
Londra

Easter /'i:stə(r)/ n Pasqua f

Easter egg n uovo m di Pasqua

easterly /'i:stəlɪ/ adj da levante

Easter Monday n lunedì m dell'Angelo,
Pasquetta f

eastern /'i:stən/ adj orientale

Eastern block n paesi mpl dell'est

Easter Sunday n [domenica f di] Pasqua
f

East German n Pol tedesco, -a mf dell'est

East Germany n Pol Germania f est

East Indies npl Indie fpl orientali

East Timor n Timor Est m

eastwards Br, **eastward** Am /
'i:stwəd[z]/ adv verso est

⚐ **easy** /'i:zɪ/ adj (-ier, -iest) facile; **take it** or
things ~ prendersela con calma; **take it** ~!
(don't get excited) calma!; **go** ~ **with** andarci
piano con

easy-care adj facilmente lavabile

easy chair n poltrona f

easy-going adj conciliante; **too** ~ troppo
accomodante

easy money n facili guadagni mpl

easy terms npl facilitazioni fpl di
pagamento

⚐ **eat** /i:t/ vt/i (pt **ate**, pp **eaten**) mangiare

■ **eat into** vt intaccare

■ **eat out** vi mangiar fuori

■ **eat up** vt mangiare tutto ‹food›; fig
inghiottire ‹profits›

eatable /'i:təbl/ adj mangiabile

eater /'i:tə(r)/ n (apple) mela f da tavola; **be**
a big ~ ‹person› essere una buona forchetta;
he's a fast ~ mangia sempre in fretta

eatery /'i:tərɪ/ n fam tavola f calda

eating apple n mela (f) non da cuocere

eating disorder n disoressia f

eating habits npl abitudini fpl
alimentari

eau-de-Cologne /əʊdəkə'ləʊn/ n acqua
f di colonia

eaves /i:vz/ npl cornicione msg

eavesdrop /'i:vzdrɒp/ vi (pt/pp
-dropped) origliare; ~ **on** ascoltare di
nascosto

e-banking /'i:bæŋkɪŋ/ n e-banking m

ebb /eb/ ① n (tide) riflusso m; **at a low** ~
fig a terra
② vi rifluire; fig declinare

ebony /'ebənɪ/ n ebano m

EBRD n abbr (**European Bank for**
Reconstruction and Development)
BERS f

⚐ indicates a very frequent word

ebullient /ɪ'bʌlɪənt/ adj esuberante

e-business /'i:bɪznɪs/ n e-business m inv

EC n abbr (**European Community**) CE f

e-cash /'i:kæʃ/ n denaro m virtuale

eccentric /ek'sentrɪk/ adj & n eccentrico,
-a mf

eccentricity /eksen'trɪsətɪ/ n
eccentricità f inv

ecclesiastical /ɪkli:zɪ'æstɪkl/ adj
ecclesiastico

ECG n abbr (**electrocardiogram**) ECG
m

echo /'ekəʊ/ ① n (pl **-es**) eco f or m
② vt (pt/pp **echoed**, pres p **echoing**)
echeggiare; ripetere ‹words›
③ vi risuonare (**with** di)

eclectic /ɪ'klektɪk/ n eclettico

eclipse /ɪ'klɪps/ ① n Astr eclissi f inv
② vt fig eclissare

eco+ /'i:kəʊ/ pref eco+

eco-friendly adj che rispetta l'ambiente

ecological /i:kə'lɒdʒɪkl/ adj ecologico

ecological footprint n impronta f
ecologica

ecologist /ɪ'kɒlədʒɪst/ ① n ecologo, -a mf
② adj ecologico

ecology /ɪ'kɒlədʒɪ/ n ecologia f

e-commerce /'i:kɒmɜ:s/ n e-commerce
m inv

⚐ **economic** /i:kə'nɒmɪk/ adj economico

economical /i:kə'nɒmɪkl/ adj economico

economically /i:kə'nɒmɪklɪ/ adv
economicamente; ‹thriftily› in economia;
~ **priced** a prezzo economico

economic analyst n analista mf
economico, -a

economic migrant n chi emigra
per motivi esclusivamente economici, in
contrapposizione a chi cerca asilo politico

economics /i:kə'nɒmɪks/ n economia f

economist /ɪ'kɒnəmɪst/ n economista mf

economize /ɪ'kɒnəmaɪz/ vi economizzare
(**on** su)

⚐ **economy** /ɪ'kɒnəmɪ/ n economia f

economy class n Aeron classe f turistica

economy drive n campagna f di
risparmio

economy pack, economy size n
confezione f economica inv

ecosystem /'i:kəʊsɪstəm/ n ecosistema m

ecoterrorism n ecoterrorismo m

eco-warrior /'i:kəʊwɒrɪə(r)/, US -wɔ:r-/ n
eco-guerrigliero, -a mf

ecstasy /'ekstəsɪ/ n estasi f inv; (drug)
ecstasy f

ecstatic /ɪk'stætɪk/ adj estatico

ecstatically /ɪk'stætɪklɪ/ adv
estaticamente

ectopic pregnancy /ek'tɒpɪk/ n gravidanza f extrauterina

Ecuador /'ekwədɔː(r)/ n Ecuador m

ecumenical /iːkjʊ'menɪkl/ adj ecumenico

eczema /'eksɪmə/ n eczema m

eddy /'edɪ/ n vortice m

Eden /'iːd(ə)n/ n eden m, paradiso m terrestre

⚬ **edge** /edʒ/ **1** n bordo m; (of knife) filo m; (of road) ciglio m; **on** ~ con i nervi tesi; **have the** ~ **on** fam avere un vantaggio su
2 vt bordare

■ **edge forward** vi avanzare lentamente

edgeways /'edʒweɪz/ adv di fianco;
I couldn't get a word in ~ non ho potuto infilare neanche mezza parola nel discorso

edging /'edʒɪŋ/ n bordo m

edgy /'edʒɪ/ adj (nervous) nervoso; fam (modern) all'avanguardia

edible /'edəbl/ adj commestibile; **this pizza's not** ~ questa pizza è immangiabile

edict /'iːdɪkt/ n editto m

edifice /'edɪfɪs/ n edificio m

edify /'edɪfaɪ/ vt (pt/pp -**ied**) edificare

edifying /'edɪfaɪɪŋ/ adj edificante

Edinburgh /'edɪmb(ə)rə/ n Edimburgo f

edit /'edɪt/ vt (pt/pp **edited**) far la revisione di ‹text›; curare l'edizione di ‹anthology, dictionary›; dirigere ‹newspaper›; montare ‹film›; editare ‹tape›; ~**ed by** ‹book› a cura di

■ **edit out** vt tagliare

edition /ɪ'dɪʃn/ n edizione f

⚬ **editor** /'edɪtə(r)/ n (of anthology, dictionary) curatore, -trice mf; (of newspaper) redattore, -trice mf; (of film) responsabile mf del montaggio

editorial /edɪ'tɔːrɪəl/ **1** adj redazionale
2 n Journ editoriale m

EDP n abbr (**electronic data processing**) EDP m, EED f

EDT abbr Am (**Eastern Daylight Time**) ora (f) legale degli stati orientali dell'America settentrionale

educate /'edjʊkeɪt/ vt istruire; educare ‹public, mind›; **be** ~**d at Eton** essere educato a Eton

educated /'edjʊkeɪtɪd/ adj istruito

⚬ **education** /edjʊ'keɪʃn/ n istruzione f; (culture) cultura f, educazione f

educational /edjʊ'keɪʃnəl/ adj istruttivo; ‹visit› educativo; ‹publishing› didattico

educationalist /edjʊ'keɪʃnəlɪst/ n studioso, -a mf di pedagogia

educationally /edjʊ'keɪʃnəlɪ/ adv ‹disadvantaged, privileged› dal punto di vista degli studi; ‹useless, useful› dal punto di vista didattico

educational psychology n psicopedagogia f, psicologia f

dell'educazione

educational television n televisione f scolastica

education authority n Br autorità f pl scolastiche

education committee n Br consiglio m scolastico

education department n Br ministero m della pubblica istruzione; (in local government) provveditorato m agli studi; (in university) istituto m di pedagogia

educative /'edjʊkətɪv/ adj educativo, istruttivo

educator /'edjʊkeɪtə(r)/ n educatore, -trice mf

Edwardian /ed'wɔːdɪən/ n del regno di Edoardo VII

EEA abbr (**European Economic Area**) EEA f

EEC **1** n abbr (**European Economic Community**) CEE f
2 attrib ‹policy, directive› della CEE

eel /iːl/ n anguilla f

eerie /'ɪərɪ/ adj (-**ier**, -**iest**) inquietante

efface /ɪ'feɪs/ vt cancellare

⚬ **effect** /ɪ'fekt/ **1** n effetto m; **in** ~ in effetti; **take** ~ ‹law› entrare in vigore; ‹medicine› fare effetto
2 vt effettuare

⚬ **effective** /ɪ'fektɪv/ adj efficace; (striking) che colpisce; (actual) di fatto; ~ **from** in vigore a partire da

⚬ **effectively** /ɪ'fektɪvlɪ/ adv efficacemente; (actually) di fatto

effectiveness /ɪ'fektɪvnɪs/ n efficacia f

effeminate /ɪ'temɪnət/ adj effeminato

effervescent /efə'vesnt/ adj effervescente

effete /ɪ'fiːt/ adj ‹person› senza nerbo; ‹civilization› che ha fatto il suo tempo

efficacious /efɪ'keɪʃəs/ adj efficace

efficacy /'efɪkəsɪ/ n efficacia f

efficiency /ɪ'fɪʃənsɪ/ n efficienza f; (of machine) rendimento m

efficient /ɪ'fɪʃənt/ adj efficiente

efficiently /ɪ'fɪʃəntlɪ/ adv efficientemente

effigy /'efɪdʒɪ/ n effigie f

effluent /'efluənt/ **1** n (waste) refluo m; (river) emissario m
2 attrib ‹treatment, management› dei reflui

⚬ **effort** /'efət/ n sforzo m; **make an** ~ sforzarsi

effortless /'efətlɪs/ adj facile

effortlessly /'efətlɪslɪ/ adv con facilità

effrontery /ɪ'frʌntərɪ/ n sfrontatezza f

effusion /ɪ'fjuːʒn/ n (emotional) effusione f

effusive /ɪ'fjuːsɪv/ adj espansivo; ‹speech› caloroso

e-fit /'iːfɪt/ n identikit m inv elettronico

EFL ① *n abbr* (**English as a Foreign Language**) EFL *m*
② *attrib* ‹teacher, course› di inglese come lingua straniera

EFT *n abbr* (**electronic funds transfer**) trasferimento *m* fondi elettronico

EFTA /'eftə/ *n abbr* (**European Free Trade Association**) EFTA *f*

✧ **e.g.** *abbr* (**exempli gratia**) per es.

egalitarian /ɪɡælɪ'teərɪən/ *adj* egalitario

✧ **egg** /eɡ/ *n* uovo *m*
■ **egg on** *vt* fam incitare

egg box *n* cartone *m* di uova

eggcup *n* portauovo *m inv*

egg custard *n* crema *f* pasticciera

egghead *n* (pej fam) intellettuale *mf*

eggplant *n* Am melanzana *f*

eggshaped /'eɡʃeɪpt/ *adj* ovale

eggshell *n* guscio *m* d'uovo

egg-timer *n* clessidra (*f*) *per misurare il tempo di cottura delle uova*

egg whisk *n* frusta *f*

egg white *n* albume *m*, bianco *m* d'uovo

egg yolk *n* tuorlo *m*, rosso *m*

ego /'iːɡəʊ/ *n* ego *m*

egocentric /iːɡəʊ'sentrɪk/ *adj* egocentrico

egoism /'eɡəʊɪzm/ *n* egoismo *m*

egoist /'eɡəʊɪst/ *n* egoista *mf*

egotism /'eɡəʊtɪzm/ *n* egotismo *m*

egotist /'eɡəʊtɪst/ *n* egotista *mf*

Egypt /'iːdʒɪpt/ *n* Egitto *m*

Egyptian /ɪ'dʒɪpʃn/ *adj & n* egiziano, -a *mf*

EHIC *n abbr* (**European Health Insurance Card**) TEAM *f*

Eid al-Adha /ˌiːdʊl'ɑːdə/ *n* Aid al-adha *f*

eiderdown /'aɪdədaʊn/ *n* (quilt) piumino *m*

✧ **eight** /eɪt/ *adj & n* otto *m*

eighteen /eɪ'tiːn/ *adj & n* diciotto *m*

eighteenth /eɪ'tiːnθ/ *adj & n* diciottesimo, -a *mf*

eighth /eɪtθ/ *adj & n* ottavo, -a *mf*

eighties /'eɪtɪz/ *npl* (period) **the** ~ gli anni Ottanta *mpl*; (age) ottant'anni *mpl*

eightieth /'eɪtɪɪθ/ *adj & n* ottantesimo, -a *mf*

eighty /'eɪtɪ/ *adj & n* ottanta *m*

Eire /'eərə/ *n* Repubblica *f* d'Irlanda

✧ **either** /'aɪðə(r)/ ① *adj & pron* ~ **[of them]** l'uno o l'altro; **I don't like** ~ **[of them]** non mi piace né l'uno né l'altro; **on** ~ **side** da tutte e due le parti
② *adv* **I don't** ~ nemmeno io; **I don't like John or his brother** ~ non mi piace John e nemmeno suo fratello
③ *conj* ~ **John or his brother will be there** ci saranno o John o suo fratello; **I don't**

indicates a very frequent word

like ~ **John or his brother** non mi piacciono né John né suo fratello; ~ **you go to bed or [else]...** o vai a letto o [altrimenti]...

ejaculate /ɪ'dʒækjʊleɪt/ ① *vi* eiaculare
② *vt* (exclaim) prorompere

ejaculation /ɪ'dʒækjʊleɪʃn/ *n* eiaculazione *f*; (exclamation) esclamazione *f*

eject /ɪ'dʒekt/ *vt* eiettare ‹pilot›; espellere ‹tape, drunk›

eject button *n* tasto *m* eject

ejection /ɪ'dʒekʃn/ *n* (of gases, waste, troublemaker) espulsione *f*; (of lava) emissione *f*; Aeron eiezione *f*

eke /iːk/ *vt* ~ **out** far bastare; (increase) arrotondare; ~ **out a living** arrangiarsi

elaborate¹ /ɪ'læbərət/ *adj* elaborato

elaborate² /ɪ'læbəreɪt/ *vi* entrare nei particolari (**on** di)

elaborately /ɪ'læbərətlɪ/ *adv* in modo elaborato

elaboration /ɪlæbə'reɪʃn/ *n* (of plan, theory) elaborazione *f*

elapse /ɪ'læps/ *vi* trascorrere

elastic /ɪ'læstɪk/ ① *adj* elastico
② *n* elastico *m*

elasticated /ɪ'læstɪkeɪtɪd/ *adj* ‹waistband, bandage› elastico; ‹material› elasticizzato

elastic band *n* elastico *m*

elasticity /ɪlæs'tɪsətɪ/ *n* elasticità

elated /ɪ'leɪtɪd/ *adj* esultante

elation /ɪ'leɪʃn/ *n* euforia *f*

elbow /'elbəʊ/ *n* gomito *m*

elbow grease *n* fam olio *m* di gomito

elbow room *n* (room to move) spazio *m* vitale; **there isn't much** ~ **in this kitchen** si è un po' allo stretto in questa cucina

elder¹ /'eldə(r)/ *n* (tree) sambuco *m*

elder² ① *adj* maggiore
② *n* **the** ~ il/la maggiore

elderberry /'eldəbərɪ/ *n* bacca *f* di sambuco

elderly /'eldəlɪ/ *adj* anziano

elder statesman *n* decano *m* della politica

eldest /'eldɪst/ ① *adj* maggiore
② *n* **the** ~ il/la maggiore

e-learning /'iːlɜːnɪŋ/ *n* Comput formazione *f* in rete

✧ **elect** /ɪ'lekt/ ① *adj* **the president** ~ il futuro presidente
② *vt* eleggere; ~ **to do something** decidere di fare qualcosa

✧ **election** /ɪ'lekʃn/ *n* elezione *f*

election campaign *n* campagna *f* elettorale

electioneering /ɪlekʃə'nɪərɪŋ/ *n* (campaigning) propaganda *f* elettorale; pej elettoralismo *m*

elective /ɪ'lektɪv/ *adj* ‹office, official› elettivo, eletto; (empowered to elect) elettorale;

elector ⋯⟶ elude ⋯⋯

Sch, Univ facoltativo; ~ **surgery** interventi *mpl* chirurgici facoltativi

elector /ɪˈlektə(r)/ *n* elettore, -trice *mf*

electoral /ɪˈlektərəl/ *adj* elettorale

electoral roll *n* liste *fpl* elettorali

electorate /ɪˈlektərət/ *n* elettorato *m*

electric /ɪˈlektrɪk/ *adj* elettrico

electrical /ɪˈlektrɪkl/ *adj* elettrico

electrical engineer *n* elettrotecnico *m*

electrical engineering *n* elettrotecnica *f*

electrically /ɪˈlektrɪk(ə)lɪ/ *adv* ~ **driven** [a motore] elettrico

electric blanket *n* termocoperta *f*

electric fire *n* stufa *f* elettrica

electrician /ɪlekˈtrɪʃn/ *n* elettricista *m*

electricity /ɪlekˈtrɪsətɪ/ *n* elettricità

electricity board *n* Br azienda *f* elettrica

electricity supply *n* alimentazione *f* elettrica

electric shock *n* **get an** ~ prendere la scossa

electric storm *n* temporale *m*

electrify /ɪˈlektrɪfaɪ/ *vt* (*pt/pp* **-ied**) elettrificare; fig elettrizzare

electrifying /ɪˈlektrɪfaɪɪŋ/ *adj* fig elettrizzante

electrocute /ɪˈlektrəkjuːt/ *vt* fulminare; (execute) giustiziare sulla sedia elettrica

electrocution /ɪlektrəˈkjuːʃn/ *n* elettrocuzione *f*

electrode /ɪˈlektrəʊd/ *n* elettrodo *m*

electrolysis /ɪlekˈtrɒlɪsɪs/ *n* Chem elettrolisi *f*; (hair removal) depilazione *f* diatermica

electron /ɪˈlektrɒn/ *n* elettrone *m*

electronic /ɪlekˈtrɒnɪk/ *adj* elettronico

electronic banking *n* servizi *mpl* bancari telematici

electronic engineer *n* tecnico *m* elettronico; (with diploma) perito *m* elettronico; (with degree) ingegnere *m* elettronico

electronic engineering *n* ingegneria *f* elettronica

electronic eye *n* cellula *f* fotoelettrica

electronic funds transfer *n* sistemi *mpl* telematici di trasferimento fondi

electronic mail *n* posta *f* elettronica

electronic organizer *n* Comput agenda *f* elettronica

electronic publishing *n* editoria *f* elettronica

electronics /ɪlekˈtrɒnɪks/ *n* elettronica *f*

electronic tagging *n* sorveglianza *f* tramite braccialetto elettronico

electro-shock therapy, **electroshock treatment** /ɪˈlektrəʊ-/ *n* terapia *f* elettroshock

elegance /ˈelɪɡəns/ *n* eleganza *f*

elegant /ˈelɪɡənt/ *adj* elegante

elegantly /ˈelɪɡəntlɪ/ *adv* elegantemente

elegy /ˈelədʒɪ/ *n* elegia *f*

✓ **element** /ˈelɪmənt/ *n* elemento *m*

elementary /elɪˈmentərɪ/ *adj* elementare

elephant /ˈelɪfənt/ *n* elefante *m*

elephantine /elɪˈfæntaɪn/ *adj* ‹person› mastodontico

elevate /ˈelɪveɪt/ *vt* elevare

elevated /ˈelɪveɪtɪd/ *adj* ‹language, rank› elevato; ‹walkway, railway› soprelevato

elevation /elɪˈveɪʃn/ *n* elevazione *f*; (height) altitudine *f*; (angle) alzo *m*

elevator /ˈelɪveɪtə(r)/ *n* Am ascensore *m*

eleven /ɪˈlevn/ *adj & n* undici *m*

eleven plus *n* (formerly) esame (*m*) di ammissione alla scuola secondaria inglese

elevenses /ɪˈlevənzɪz/ *n* Br fam pausa *f* per il caffè (a metà mattina)

eleventh /ɪˈlevənθ/ *adj & n* undicesimo, -a *mf*; **at the** ~ **hour** fam all'ultimo momento

elf /elf/ *n* (*pl* **elves**) elfo *m*

elicit /ɪˈlɪsɪt/ *vt* ottenere

eligible /ˈelɪdʒəbl/ *adj* eleggibile; ~ **young man** buon partito; **be** ~ **for** aver diritto a

eliminate /ɪˈlɪmɪneɪt/ *vt* eliminare

elimination /ɪlɪmɪˈneɪʃn/ *n* eliminazione *f*; **by a process of** ~ procedendo per eliminazione

élite /erˈliːt/ *n* fior fiore *m*

élitist /ɪˈliːtɪst/ *adj* elitista

ellipse /ɪˈlɪps/ *n* ellisse *f*

elliptical /ɪˈlɪptɪk(ə)l/ *adj* also fig ellittico

elm /elm/ *n* olmo *m*

elocution /eləˈkjuːʃn/ *n* elocuzione *f*

elongate /ˈiːlɒŋɡeɪt/ *vt* allungare

elongated /ˈiːlɒŋɡeɪtɪd, US ɪˈlɔːŋ-/ *adj* allungato

elope /ɪˈləʊp/ *vi* fuggire [per sposarsi]

elopement /ɪˈləʊpmənt/ *n* fuga *f* romantica

eloquence /ˈeləkwəns/ *n* eloquenza *f*

eloquent /ˈeləkwənt/ *adj* eloquente

eloquently /ˈeləkwəntlɪ/ *adv* con eloquenza

El Salvador /elˈsælvədɔː(r)/ *n* El Salvador *m*; **in** ~ nel Salvador

✓ **else** /els/ *adv* altro; **who** ~? e chi altro?; **he did of course, who** ~? l'ha fatto lui e chi, se no?; **nothing** ~ nient'altro; **or** ~ altrimenti; **someone** ~ qualcun altro; **somewhere** ~ da qualche altra parte; **anyone** ~ chiunque altro; (as question) nessun'altro?; **anything** ~ qualunque altra cosa; (as question) altro?

✓ **elsewhere** /elsˈweə(r)/ *adv* altrove

elucidate /ɪˈluːsɪdeɪt/ *vt* delucidare

elude /ɪˈluːd/ *vt* eludere; (avoid) evitare; **the name** ~**s me** il nome mi sfugge

elusive /ɪˈluːsɪv/ adj elusivo

emaciated /ɪˈmeɪsɪeɪtɪd/ adj emaciato

⚜ **e-mail** ① n e-mail f, posta f elettronica
② vt spedire per e-mail

e-mail account n account m inv di posta
elettronica

e-mail address n indirizzo m di posta
elettronica

emanate /ˈeməneɪt/ vi emanare

emancipate /ɪˈmænsɪpeɪt/ vt emancipare

emancipated /ɪˈmænsɪpeɪtɪd/ adj
emancipato

emancipation /ɪmænsɪˈpeɪʃn/ n
emancipazione f; (of slaves) liberazione f

e-marketing /ˈiːmɑːkɪtɪŋ/ n e-marketing
m inv

emasculate /ɪˈmæskjʊleɪt/ vt evirare; fig
svigorire

embalm /ɪmˈbɑːm/ vt imbalsamare

embankment /ɪmˈbæŋkmənt/ n argine
m; Rail massicciata f

embargo /emˈbɑːgəʊ/ n (pl -es) embargo
m

embark /ɪmˈbɑːk/ vi imbarcarsi; ~ on
intraprendere

embarkation /embɑːˈkeɪʃn/ n imbarco m

embarrass /emˈbærəs/ vt imbarazzare

embarrassed /emˈbærəst/ adj
imbarazzato

embarrassing /emˈbærəsɪŋ/ adj
imbarazzante

embarrassment /emˈbærəsmənt/ n
imbarazzo m

embassy /ˈembəsɪ/ n ambasciata f

embed /ɪmˈbed/ vt Comput integrare
‹command›; ~ded in ‹gem› incastonato in;
‹plant› piantato in; ‹sharp object› conficcato
in; ‹rock› incluso in; ~ded ‹traditions,
feelings› radicato; be ~ded in fig radicarsi in

embellish /ɪmˈbelɪʃ/ vt abbellire

embers /ˈembəz/ npl braci fpl

embezzle /ɪmˈbezl/ vt appropriarsi
indebitamente di

embezzlement /ɪmˈbez(ə)lmənt/ n
appropriazione f indebita

embitter /ɪmˈbɪtə(r)/ vt amareggiare

emblem /ˈembləm/ n emblema m

emblematic /embləˈmætɪk/ adj
emblematico

embodiment /ɪmˈbɒdɪmənt/ n
incarnazione f

embody /ɪmˈbɒdɪ/ vt (pt/pp -ied)
incorporare; ~ what is best in…
rappresentare quanto c'è di meglio di…

embolism /ˈembəlɪzm/ n Med embolia f

emboss /ɪmˈbɒs/ vt sbalzare ‹metal›;
stampare in rilievo ‹paper›

embossed /ɪmˈbɒst/ adj in rilievo

⚜ indicates a very frequent word

embrace /ɪmˈbreɪs/ ① n abbraccio m
② vt abbracciare
③ vi abbracciarsi

embroider /ɪmˈbrɔɪdə(r)/ vt ricamare
‹design›; fig abbellire

embroidery /ɪmˈbrɔɪdərɪ/ n ricamo m

embroil /ɪmˈbrɔɪl/ vt become ~ed in
something rimanere invischiato in qualcosa

embryo /ˈembrɪəʊ/ n embrione m

embryonic /embrɪˈɒnɪk/ adj Biol fig
embrionale

emend /ɪˈmend/ vt emendare

emerald /ˈemərəld/ n smeraldo m

⚜ **emerge** /ɪˈmɜːdʒ/ vi emergere; (come into
being: nation) nascere; ‹sun, flowers› spuntare
fuori

emergence /ɪˈmɜːdʒəns/ n emergere m;
(of new country) nascita f

⚜ **emergency** /ɪˈmɜːdʒənsɪ/ n emergenza f;
in an ~ in caso di emergenza

emergency ambulance service n
pronto soccorso m autoambulanze

emergency case n Med caso m di
emergenza

emergency centre n (for refugees etc)
centro m di accoglienza; Med centro m di
soccorso mobile

emergency exit n uscita f di sicurezza

emergency landing n Aeron atterraggio
m di fortuna

emergency laws npl Pol leggi fpl
straordinarie

emergency number n numero m di
emergenza

emergency powers npl Pol poteri mpl
straordinari

emergency rations npl viveri mpl di
sopravvivenza

emergency service n Med servizio m
di pronto soccorso

emergency services npl servizi mpl
di pronto intervento

emergency surgery n undergo ~
essere operato d'urgenza

emergency ward n [reparto m di]
pronto soccorso m

emergency worker n addetto m a
operazioni di soccorso

emergent /ɪˈmɜːdʒənt/ adj ‹industry,
nation› emergente

emery board /ˈemərɪ/ n limetta f per le
unghie (di carta)

emery paper n carta f vetrata

emigrant /ˈemɪgrənt/ n emigrante mf

emigrate /ˈemɪgreɪt/ vi emigrare

emigration /emɪˈgreɪʃn/ n emigrazione f

eminence /ˈemɪnəns/ n (fame) eminenza f,
gloria f; (honour) distinzione f; (hill) altura f

eminent /ˈemɪnənt/ adj eminente

eminently /'emɪnəntlɪ/ adv
eminentemente

emirate /'emɪərət/ n emirato m

emissary /'emɪsərɪ/ n emissario m (**to** di)

emission /ɪ'mɪʃn/ n emissione f; (of fumes)
esalazione f

emit /ɪ'mɪt/ vt (pt/pp **emitted**) emettere;
esalare ‹fumes›

Emmy /'emɪ/ n Emmy m (Oscar (m inv)
televisivo americano)

emoticon /ɪ'məʊtɪkɒn, -'mɒtɪ-/ n Comput
emoticon m inv

ꞩ **emotion** /ɪ'məʊʃn/ n emozione f

ꞩ **emotional** /ɪ'məʊʃənəl/ adj denso di
emozione; ‹person, reaction› emotivo;
become ~ avere una reazione emotiva;
don't get so ~ non lasciarti prendere dalle
emozioni

emotionally /ɪ'məʊʃənəlɪ/ adv ‹speak›
emotivamente; ~ **disturbed** con turbe
emotive

emotionless /ɪ'məʊʃənlɪs/ adj
impassibile

emotive /ɪ'məʊtɪv/ adj emotivo

empathize /'empəθaɪz/ vi ~ **with
somebody** immedesimarsi nei problemi di
qualcuno

empathy /'empəθɪ/ n comprensione f

emperor /'empərə(r)/ n imperatore m

emphasis /'emfəsɪs/ n enfasi f; **put the** ~
on something accentuare qualcosa

ꞩ **emphasize** /'emfəsaɪz/ vt accentuare
‹word, syllable›; sottolineare ‹need›

emphatic /ɪm'fætɪk/ adj categorico

emphatically /ɪm'fætɪklɪ/ adv
categoricamente

empire /'empaɪə(r)/ n impero m

empirical /em'pɪrɪkl/ adj empirico

empiricism /em'pɪrɪsɪzm/ n empirismo m

ꞩ **employ** /em'plɔɪ/ vt impiegare; fig usare
‹tact›

employable /em'plɔɪəbl/ adj ‹person› che
ha i requisiti per svolgere un lavoro

ꞩ **employee** /emplɔɪ'iː/ n impiegato, -a mf

employee buyout n rilevamento m
dipendenti

ꞩ **employer** /em'plɔɪə(r)/ n datore m di
lavoro

ꞩ **employment** /em'plɔɪmənt/ n
occupazione f; (work) lavoro m

employment agency n ufficio m di
collocamento

employment contract n contratto m
di lavoro

employment exchange n agenzia f di
collocamento

employment figures npl dati mpl
sull'occupazione

**Employment Minister,
Employment Secretary** n ministro

m del lavoro

emporium /em'pɔːrɪəm/ n hum emporio m

empower /ɪm'paʊə(r)/ vt autorizzare;
(enable) mettere in grado

empowerment /ɪm'paʊəmənt/ n
empowerment m inv

empress /'emprɪs/ n imperatrice f

empties /'emptɪz/ npl vuoti mpl

emptiness /'emptɪnɪs/ n vuoto m

ꞩ **empty** /'emptɪ/ **1** adj vuoto; ‹promise,
threat› vano
2 vt (pt/pp -**ied**) vuotare ‹container›
3 vi vuotarsi

∎ **empty out** vt/i = EMPTY

empty-handed /-'hændɪd/ adj ‹arrive,
leave› a mani vuote

empty-headed /-'hedɪd/ adj scriteriato

EMS n abbr (**European Monetary
System**) SME m

EMU abbr (**European Monetary
Union**) UME f

emulate /'emjʊleɪt/ vt emulare

emulsify /ɪ'mʌlsɪfaɪ/ v (pt/pp -**ied**) **1** vt
emulsionare
2 vi emulsionarsi

emulsion /ɪ'mʌlʃn/ n emulsione f

ꞩ **enable** /ɪ'neɪbl/ vt ~ **somebody to** mettere
qualcuno in grado di

enact /ɪ'nækt/ vt Theat rappresentare;
decretare ‹law›

enamel /ɪ'næml/ **1** n smalto m
2 vt (pt/pp **enamelled**) smaltare

enamelling /ɪ'næməlɪŋ/ n (process)
smaltatura f; (art) decorazione f a smalto

enamoured /ɪ'næməd/ adj be ~ of essere
innamorato di

enc. abbr (**enclosures**) all.

encampment /ɪn'kæmpmənt/ n
accampamento m

encapsulate /ɪn'kæpsjʊleɪt/ vt (include)
incapsulare; (summarize) sintetizzare

encase /ɪn'keɪs/ vt rivestire (**in** di)

encash /ɪn'kæʃ/ vt Br incassare

encephalogram /ɪn'kefələɡræm/ n
encefalogramma m

enchant /ɪn'tʃɑːnt/ vt incantare

enchanting /ɪn'tʃɑːntɪŋ/ adj incantevole

enchantment /ɪn'tʃɑːntmənt/ n incanto
m

encircle /ɪn'sɜːkl/ vt circondare

encl abbr (**enclosed, enclosure**) all.

enclave /'enkleɪv/ n enclave f inv; fig
territorio m

enclose /ɪn'kləʊz/ vt circondare ‹land›; (in
letter) allegare (**with** a)

enclosed /ɪn'kləʊzd/ adj ‹space› chiuso; (in
letter) allegato

enclosure /ɪn'kləʊʒə(r)/ n (at zoo) recinto
m; (in letter) allegato m

encode /ɪnˈkəʊd/ vt codificare

encoder /ɪnˈkəʊdə(r)/ n codificatore, -trice mf

encompass /ɪnˈkʌmpəs/ vt (include) comprendere

encore /ˈɒŋkɔ:(r)/ n & int bis m inv

encounter /ɪnˈkaʊntə(r)/ **1** n incontro m; (battle) scontro m
2 vt incontrare

✎ **encourage** /ɪnˈkʌrɪdʒ/ vt incoraggiare; promuovere ‹the arts, independence›

encouragement /ɪnˈkʌrɪdʒmənt/ n incoraggiamento m; (of the arts) promozione f

encouraging /ɪnˈkʌrɪdʒɪŋ/ adj incoraggiante; ‹smile› di incoraggiamento

encroach /ɪnˈkrəʊtʃ/ vt ~ on invadere ‹land, privacy›; abusare di ‹time›; interferire con ‹rights›

encrust /enˈkrʌst/ vt be ~ed with ‹ice› essere incrostato di; ‹jewels› essere tempestato di

encrypt /enˈkrɪpt/ vt criptare

encumber /ɪnˈkʌmbə(r)/ vt be ~ed with essere carico di ‹children, suitcases›; ingombro di ‹furniture›

encumbrance /ɪnˈkʌmbrəns/ n peso m

encyclop[a]edia /ɪnsaɪkləˈpi:dɪə/ n enciclopedia f

encyclop[a]edic /ɪnsaɪkləˈpi:dɪk/ adj enciclopedico

✎ **end** /end/ **1** n fine f; (of box, table, piece of string) estremità f; (of town, room) parte f; (purpose) fine m; **in the ~** alla fine; **at the ~ of May** alla fine di maggio; **at the ~ of the street/garden** in fondo alla strada/ al giardino; **on ~** (upright) in piedi; **for days on ~** per giorni e giorni; **for six days on ~** per sei giorni di fila; **put an ~ to something** mettere fine a qualcosa; **make ~s meet** fam sbarcare il lunario; **no ~ of** fam un sacco di
2 vt/i finire
∎ **end in** vt ‹word› terminare in; finire in ‹failure, argument›
∎ **end off** vt concludere ‹meal, speech›
∎ **end up** vi finire; ~ **up doing something** finire col fare qualcosa

endanger /ɪnˈdeɪndʒə(r)/ vt rischiare ‹one's life›; mettere a repentaglio ‹somebody else, success of something›

endangered species /ɪnˈdeɪndʒə(d)/ n specie f a rischio

endear /ɪnˈdɪə(r)/ vt ~ **oneself to somebody** conquistarsi la simpatia di qualcuno; ~ **somebody to** conquistare a qualcuno la simpatia di

endearing /ɪnˈdɪərɪŋ/ adj accattivante

endearingly /ɪnˈdɪərɪŋlɪ/ adv ‹smile› in modo accattivante; ~ **honest** di un'onestà disarmante

endearment /ɪnˈdɪəmənt/ n **term of ~** vezzeggiativo m

endeavour /ɪnˈdevə(r)/ **1** n tentativo m
2 vi sforzarsi (**to** di)

endemic /enˈdemɪk/ **1** adj endemico
2 n (situation) endemia f

ending /ˈendɪŋ/ n fine f; Gram desinenza f

endive /ˈendaɪv/ n indivia f

endless /ˈendlɪs/ adj interminabile; ‹patience› infinito

endlessly /ˈendlɪslɪ/ adv continuamente; ‹patient› infinitamente

endocrinology /endəʊkrɪˈnɒlədʒɪ/ n endocrinologia f

endorse /enˈdɔ:s/ vt girare ‹cheque›; ‹sports personality› fare pubblicità a ‹product›; approvare ‹plan›

endorsement /enˈdɔ:smənt/ n (of cheque) girata f; (of plan) conferma f; (on driving licence) registrazione f su patente di un'infrazione

endow /ɪnˈdaʊ/ vt dotare

endowment insurance /ɪnˈdaʊmənt/ n assicurazione (f) sulla vita che fornisce un reddito in caso di sopravvivenza

endpaper n risguardo m

end product n prodotto m finito

end result n risultato m finale

endurable /ɪnˈdjʊərəbl/ adj sopportabile

endurance /ɪnˈdjʊrəns/ n resistenza f; **it is beyond ~** è insopportabile

endurance test n prova f di resistenza

endure /ɪnˈdjʊə(r)/ **1** vt sopportare
2 vi durare

enduring /ɪnˈdjʊərɪŋ/ adj duraturo

end user n utente m finale

enema /ˈenɪmə/ n Med clistere m

✎ **enemy** /ˈenəmɪ/ **1** n nemico, -a mf
2 attrib nemico

energetic /enəˈdʒetɪk/ adj energico

energetically /enəˈdʒetɪklɪ/ adv ‹speak, promote, publicize› vigorosamente; ‹work, exercise› con energia; ‹deny› risolutamente

energize /ˈenədʒaɪz/ vt stimolare; Electr alimentare [elettricamente]

energizing /ˈenədʒaɪzɪŋ/ adj ‹influence› stimolante

✎ **energy** /ˈenədʒɪ/ n energia f

energy efficiency n razionalizzazione f del consumo energetico

energy-efficient adj a consumo ottimale di energia

energy policy n politica f energetica

energy resources npl risorse fpl energetiche

energy saving n risparmio m energetico

energy-saving adj ‹device› che fa risparmiare energia; ‹measure› per risparmiare energia

enervate /ˈenəveɪt/ vt snervare

✎ indicates a very frequent word

enfold /en'fəʊld/ vt avvolgere

enforce /ɪn'fɔːs/ vt far rispettare ‹law›

enforced /ɪn'fɔːst/ adj forzato

enforcement /ɪn'fɔːsmənt/ n applicazione f; (of discipline) imposizione f

ENG abbr (**electronic news gathering**) ENG m

⚘ **engage** /ɪn'geɪdʒ/ ① vt assumere ‹staff›; Theat ingaggiare; Auto ingranare ‹gear›; ~ **somebody in conversation** fare conversazione con qualcuno
② vi Techn ingranare; ~ **in** impegnarsi in

engaged /ɪn'geɪdʒd/ adj (in use, busy) occupato; ‹person› impegnato; (to be married) fidanzato; **get** ~ fidanzarsi (**to** con)

engaged tone n Br segnale m di occupato

engagement /ɪn'geɪdʒmənt/ n fidanzamento m; (appointment) appuntamento m; Mil combattimento m

engagement ring n anello m di fidanzamento

engagements book n agenda f

engaging /ɪn'geɪdʒɪŋ/ adj attraente

engender /ɪn'dʒendə(r)/ vt fig generare

⚘ **engine** /'endʒɪn/ n motore m; Rail locomotrice f

engine drive n macchinista m

engineer /endʒɪ'nɪə(r)/ ① n ingegnere m; (service, installation) tecnico m; Naut, Am Rail macchinista m
② vt fig architettare

engineering /endʒɪ'nɪərɪŋ/ n ingegneria f

engine failure n guasto m [al motore]; (in jet) avaria f

engine oil n olio m [del] motore

engine room n sala f macchine

engine shed n Rail deposito m

England /'ɪŋglənd/ n Inghilterra f

⚘ **English** /'ɪŋglɪʃ/ ① adj inglese; **the** ~ **Channel** la Manica
② n (language) inglese m; **the** ~ pl gli inglesi

English as a Foreign Language n inglese m come lingua straniera

English as a Second Language n inglese m come seconda lingua

Englishman n inglese m

English rose n donna (f) dalla bellezza tipicamente inglese

English speaker n anglofono, -a mf

English-speaking adj anglofono

Englishwoman n inglese f

engrave /ɪn'greɪv/ vt incidere

engraving /ɪn'greɪvɪŋ/ n incisione f

engross /ɪn'grəʊs/ vt ~**ed in** assorto in

engrossing /ɪn'grəʊsɪŋ/ adj avvincente

engulf /ɪn'gʌlf/ vt ‹fire, waves› inghiottire

⚘ **enhance** /ɪn'hɑːns/ vt accrescere ‹beauty, reputation›; migliorare ‹performance›

enigma /ɪ'nɪgmə/ n enigma m

enigmatic /enɪg'mætɪk/ adj enigmatico

⚘ **enjoy** /ɪn'dʒɔɪ/ vt godere di ‹good health›; ~ **oneself** divertirsi; **I** ~ **cooking/painting** mi piace cucinare/dipingere; **I** ~**ed the meal/film** mi è piaciuto il pranzo/il film; ~ **your meal** buon appetito

enjoyable /ɪn'dʒɔɪəbl/ adj piacevole

enjoyment /ɪn'dʒɔɪmənt/ n piacere m

enlarge /ɪn'lɑːdʒ/ ① vt ingrandire
② vi ~ **upon** dilungarsi su

enlargement /ɪn'lɑːdʒmənt/ n ingrandimento m

enlarger /ɪn'lɑːdʒə(r)/ n Phot ingranditore m

enlighten /ɪn'laɪtn/ vt illuminare

enlightened /ɪn'laɪtənd/ adj progressista

enlightening /ɪn'laɪtnɪŋ/ adj istruttivo

enlightenment /ɪn'laɪtənmənt/ n **The E**~ l'Illuminismo m

enlist /ɪn'lɪst/ ① vt Mil reclutare; ~ **sb's help** farsi aiutare da qualcuno
② vi Mil arruolarsi

enliven /ɪn'laɪvn/ vt animare

enmesh /en'meʃ/ vt **become** ~**ed in** fig impegolarsi in

enmity /'enmətɪ/ n inimicizia f

ennoble /en'nəʊbl/ vt nobilitare

enormity /ɪ'nɔːmətɪ/ n enormità f

enormous /ɪ'nɔːməs/ adj enorme

enormously /ɪ'nɔːməslɪ/ adv estremamente; ‹grateful› infinitamente

⚘ **enough** /ɪ'nʌf/ ① adj & n abbastanza; **I didn't bring** ~ **clothes** non ho portato abbastanza vestiti; **have you had** ~**?** (to eat/ drink) hai mangiato/bevuto abbastanza?; **I've had** ~**!** fam ne ho abbastanza!; **is that** ~**?** basta?; **that's** ~**!** basta così!; **£50 isn't** ~ 50 sterline non sono sufficienti
② adv abbastanza; **you're not working fast** ~ non lavori abbastanza in fretta; **funnily** ~ stranamente

enquire /ɪn'kwaɪə(r)/ vi domandare; ~ **about** chiedere informazioni su

enquiring /ɪn'kwaɪərɪŋ/ adj ‹look› indagatore; ‹mind› avido di sapere

enquiry /ɪn'kwaɪərɪ/ n domanda f; (investigation) inchiesta f

enrage /ɪn'reɪdʒ/ vt fare arrabbiare

enrich /ɪn'rɪtʃ/ vt arricchire; (improve) migliorare ‹vocabulary›

enrol /ɪn'rəʊl/ vt (pt/pp -**rolled**) (for exam, in club) iscriversi (**for, in** a)

enrolment /ɪn'rəʊlmənt/ n iscrizione f

ensconced /ɪn'skɒnst/ adj comodamente sistemato (**in** in)

ensemble /ɒn'sɒmbl/ n (clothing & Mus) complesso m

ensign /'ensaɪn/ n insegna f

enslave /ɪn'sleɪv/ vt render schiavo

ensue /ɪn'sju:/ vi seguire; ~ **from** sorgere da; **the ensuing discussion** la discussione che ne è seguita

en suite /ɒ̃'swi:t/ **1** n (bathroom) camera f con bagno annesso
2 adj ‹bathroom› annesso; ‹room› con bagno

ꝫ **ensure** /ɪn'ʃʊə(r)/ vt assicurare; ~ **that** ‹person› assicurarsi che; ‹measure› garantire che

ENT n abbr (**Ear Nose and Throat**) otorino m

entail /ɪn'teɪl/ vt comportare; **what does it ~?** in che cosa consiste?

entangle /ɪn'tæŋgl/ vt **get ~d in** rimanere impigliato in; fig rimanere coinvolto in

entanglement /ɪn'tæŋg(ə)lmənt/ n (emotional) legame m sentimentale; (complicated situation) pasticcio m

ꝫ **enter** /'entə(r)/ **1** vt entrare in; iscrivere ‹horse, runner in race›; cominciare ‹university›; partecipare a ‹competition›; Comput immettere ‹data›; (write down) scrivere
2 vi entrare; Theat entrare in scena; (register as competitor) iscriversi; (take part) partecipare (in a)
3 n Comput invio m
■ **enter into** vt (begin) intavolare ‹negotiations, an argument›

enteritis /entə'raɪtɪs/ n enterite f

enterprise /'entəpraɪz/ n impresa f; (quality) iniziativa f

enterprising /'entəpraɪzɪŋ/ adj intraprendente

entertain /entə'teɪn/ **1** vt intrattenere; (invite) ricevere; nutrire ‹ideas, hopes›; prendere in considerazione ‹possibility›
2 vi intrattenersi; (have guests) ricevere

entertainer /entə'teɪnə(r)/ n artista mf

entertaining /entə'teɪnɪŋ/ adj ‹person› di gradevole compagnia; ‹evening, film, play› divertente

entertainment /entə'teɪnmənt/ n (amusement) intrattenimento m

entertainment industry n l'industria f dello spettacolo

enthral /ɪn'θrɔːl/ vt (pt/pp **enthralled**) **be ~led** essere affascinato (**by** da)

enthralling /ɪn'θrɔːlɪŋ/ adj ‹novel, performance› affascinante

enthuse /ɪn'θjuːz/ vi ~ **over** entusiasmarsi per

enthusiasm /ɪn'θjuːzɪæzm/ n entusiasmo m

enthusiast /ɪn'θjuːzɪæst/ n entusiasta mf

enthusiastic /ɪnθjuːzɪ'æstɪk/ adj entusiastico

enthusiastically /ɪnθjuːzɪ'æstɪklɪ/ adv entusiasticamente

entice /ɪn'taɪs/ vt attirare

enticement /ɪn'taɪsmənt/ n (incentive) incentivo m

enticing /ɪn'taɪsɪŋ/ adj ‹prospect, offer› allettante; ‹person› seducente; ‹food, smell› invitante

ꝫ **entire** /ɪn'taɪə(r)/ adj intero

ꝫ **entirely** /ɪn'taɪəlɪ/ adv del tutto; **I'm not ~ satisfied** non sono completamente soddisfatto

entirety /ɪn'taɪərətɪ/ n **in its ~** nell'insieme

ꝫ **entitle** /ɪn'taɪtl/ vt dare diritto a; ~ **somebody to something** dare a qualcuno il diritto di qualcosa

entitled /ɪn'taɪtld/ adj ‹book› intitolato; **be ~ to something** aver diritto a qualcosa

entitlement /ɪn'taɪtlmənt/ n diritto m

entity /'entɪtɪ/ n entità f

entomology /entə'mɒlədʒɪ/ n entomologia f

entourage /'ɒntʊrɑːʒ/ n entourage m inv

entrails /'entreɪlz/ npl intestini mpl

entrance[1] /'entrəns/ n entrata f; Theat entrata f in scena; (right to enter) ammissione f; **'no ~'** 'ingresso vietato'

entrance[2] /ɪn'trɑːns/ vt estasiare

entrance examination n esame m di ammissione

entrance fee n **how much is the ~?** quanto costa il biglietto di ingresso?

entrance hall n (in house) ingresso m

entrance requirements npl requisiti mpl di ammissione

entrance ticket n biglietto m d'ingresso

entrancing /ɪn'trɑːnsɪŋ/ adj incantevole

entrant /'entrənt/ n concorrente mf

entreat /ɪn'triːt/ vt supplicare

entreatingly /ɪn'triːtɪŋlɪ/ adv ‹beg, ask› in tono implorante

entreaty /ɪn'triːtɪ/ n supplica f

entrée /'ɒtreɪ/ n Br (starter) primo m; Am (main course) secondo m; **her wealth gave her an ~ into high society** il denaro le ha aperto le porte dell'alta società

entrenched /ɪn'trentʃt/ adj ‹ideas, views› radicato

entrepreneur /ɒntrəprə'nɜː(r)/ n imprenditore, -trice mf

entrepreneurial /ɒntrəprə'nɜːrɪəl/ adj imprenditoriale; **have ~ skills** avere il senso degli affari

entrust /ɪn'trʌst/ vt ~ **somebody with something**, ~ **something to somebody** affidare qualcosa a qualcuno

ꝫ **entry** /'entrɪ/ n ingresso m; (way in) entrata f; (in directory etc) voce f; (in appointment diary)

ꝫ indicates a very frequent word

appuntamento m; **no** ~ ingresso vietato; Auto accesso vietato

entry fee n quota f di iscrizione

entry form n modulo m di ammissione

entry permit n visto m di entrata

entryphone n citofono m

entry requirements npl requisiti mpl di ammissione

entry visa n visto m di ingresso

entwine /ɪn'twaɪn/ vt also fig intrecciare

E-number n Br sigla f degli additivi

enumerate /ɪ'njuːməreɪt/ vt enumerare

enumeration /ɪnjuːmə'reɪʃn/ n (list) enumerazione f; (counting) conto m

enunciate /ɪ'nʌnsɪeɪt/ vt enunciare

enunciation /ɪnʌnsɪ'eɪʃn/ n (of principle, facts) enunciazione f; (of word) articolazione f

envelop /ɪn'veləp/ vt (pt/pp **enveloped**) avviluppare

envelope /'envələʊp/ n busta f

enviable /'envɪəbl/ adj invidiabile

envious /'envɪəs/ adj invidioso

enviously /'envɪəslɪ/ adv con invidia

ᶠ **environment** /ɪn'vaɪrənmənt/ n ambiente m

ᶠ **environmental** /ɪnvaɪrən'mentl/ adj ambientale

environmental health n salute f pubblica

environmentalist /ɪnvaɪrən'mentəlɪst/ n ambientalista mf

environmentally /ɪnvaɪrən'mentəlɪ/ adv ~ **friendly** che rispetta l'ambiente

environmental scientist n studioso, -a mf di ecologia applicata

Environmental Studies npl Br Sch ecogeografia f e ecobiologia f

envisage /ɪn'vɪzɪdʒ/ vt prevedere

envoy /'envɔɪ/ n inviato, -a mf

envy /'envɪ/ 1 n invidia f
2 vt (pt/pp **-ied**) ~ **somebody something** invidiare qualcuno per qualcosa

enzyme /'enzaɪm/ n enzima m

EOF abbr Comput (**end of file**) EOF m

ephemeral /ɪ'femərəl/ adj effimero

epic /'epɪk/ 1 adj epico
2 n epopea f

epicentre /'epɪsentə(r)/ n epicentro m

epidemic /epɪ'demɪk/ n epidemia f

epidermis /epɪ'dɜːmɪs/ n epidermide f

epidural /epɪ'djʊərəl/ n Med anestesia f epidurale

epigram /'epɪɡræm/ n epigramma m

epilepsy /'epɪlepsɪ/ n epilessia f

epileptic /epɪ'leptɪk/ adj & n epilettico, -a mf

epilogue /'epɪlɒɡ/ n epilogo m

Epiphany /ɪ'pɪfənɪ/ n Epifania f

ᶠ **episode** /'epɪsəʊd/ n episodio m

episodic /epɪ'sɒdɪk/ adj episodico

epistle /ɪ'pɪsl/ n liter epistola f

epitaph /'epɪtɑːf/ n epitaffio m

epithet /'epɪθet/ n epiteto m

epitome /ɪ'pɪtəmɪ/ n epitome f

epitomize /ɪ'pɪtəmaɪz/ vt essere il classico esempio di

epoch /'iːpɒk/ n epoca f

epoch-making adj che fa epoca

eponymous /ɪ'pɒnɪməs/ adj eponimo

EQ abbr (**graphic equalizer**) EQ m

equable /'ekwəbl/ adj ‹climate› temperato; ‹temperament› equilibrato

equably /'ekwəblɪ/ adv con serenità

ᶠ **equal** /'iːkwl/ 1 adj ‹parts, amounts› uguale; of ~ **height** della stessa altezza; **be ~ to the task** essere all'altezza del compito
2 n pari m inv; **treat somebody as an** ~ trattare qualcuno da pari a pari
3 vt (pt/pp **equalled**) (be same in quantity as) essere pari a; (rival) uguagliare; **5 plus 5** ~**s 10** 5 più 5 [è] uguale a 10

equality /ɪ'kwɒlətɪ/ n uguaglianza f

equalize /'iːkwəlaɪz/ vi Sport pareggiare

equalizer /'iːkwəlaɪzə(r)/ n Sport pareggio m; **get the** ~ pareggiare

ᶠ **equally** /'iːkwəlɪ/ adv ‹divide› in parti uguali; ~ **intelligent** della stessa intelligenza; ~,... allo stesso tempo ...

equal opportunities npl uguaglianza f dei diritti

Equal Opportunities Commission n Br commissione (f) per l'uguaglianza dei diritti nei rapporti di lavoro

equal opportunity attrib ‹legislation› per l'uguaglianza dei diritti nei rapporti di lavoro; ‹employer› che applica l'uguaglianza dei diritti

equal rights npl parità f dei diritti

equals sign n segno m uguale

equanimity /ekwə'nɪmətɪ/ n equanimità f

equate /ɪ'kweɪt/ vt ~ **something with something** equiparare qualcosa a qualcosa

equation /ɪ'kweɪʒn/ n Math equazione f

equator /ɪ'kweɪtə(r)/ n equatore m

equatorial /ekwə'tɔːrɪəl/ adj equatoriale

Equatorial Guinea n Guinea Equatoriale f

equestrian /ɪ'kwestrɪən/ adj equestre

equidistant /iːkwɪ'dɪstənt/ adj equidistante

equilateral /iːkwɪ'lætərəl/ adj equilatero

equilibrium /iːkwɪ'lɪbrɪəm/ n equilibrio m

equine /'ekwaɪn/ adj ‹disease, species› equino; ‹features› cavallino

equinox /'iːkwɪnɒks/ n equinozio m

e

equip /ɪ'kwɪp/ vt (pt/pp **equipped**)
equipaggiare; attrezzare ‹kitchen, office›

✦ **equipment** /ɪ'kwɪpmənt/ n attrezzatura f

equitable /'ekwɪtəbl/ adj giusto

equity /'ekwətɪ/ n (justness) equità f; Comm
azioni fpl

equity capital n Fin capitale m azionario

equity financing n Fin finanziamento m
attraverso l'emissione di azioni

equity market n Fin mercato m azionario

equivalent /ɪ'kwɪvələnt/ 1 adj
equivalente; **be** ~ **to** equivalere a
2 n equivalente m

equivocal /ɪ'kwɪvəkl/ adj equivoco

equivocate /ɪ'kwɪvəkeɪt/ vi parlare in
modo equivoco, giocare sull'equivoco

equivocation /ɪkwɪvə'keɪʃn/ n
affermazione f equivoca; **too much** ~ troppi
equivoci

✦ **era** /'ɪərə/ n età f; (geological) era f

eradicate /ɪ'rædɪkeɪt/ vt eradicare

erase /ɪ'reɪz/ vt cancellare

erase head n Comput testina f di
cancellazione

eraser /ɪ'reɪzə(r)/ n gomma f [da
cancellare]; (for blackboard) cancellino m

erasure /ɪ'reɪʒə(r)/ n (act) cancellazione f;
(on paper) cancellatura f

erect /ɪ'rekt/ 1 adj eretto
2 vt erigere

erection /ɪ'rekʃn/ n erezione f

ergonomic /ɜ:gə'nɒmɪk/ adj ergonomico;
‹seat› anatomico

ergonomics /ɜ:gə'nɒmɪks/ n ergonomia

Erie /'ɪərɪ/ n **Lake E**~ il lago Erie

Eritrea /erɪ'treɪə/ n Eritrea f

ERM n abbr (**Exchange Rate
Mechanism**) sistema (m) di cambio dello
SME

ermine /'ɜ:mɪn/ n ermellino m

erode /ɪ'rəʊd/ vt ‹water› erodere; ‹acid›
corrodere

erogenous /ɪ'rɒdʒɪnəs/ adj erogeno

erosion /ɪ'rəʊʒn/ n erosione f; (by acid)
corrosione f

erotic /ɪ'rɒtɪk/ adj erotico

erotica /ɪ'rɒtɪkə/ npl (art) arte f erotica;
(literature) letteratura f erotica; Cinema film
mpl erotici

eroticism /ɪ'rɒtɪsɪzm/ n erotismo m

err /ɜ:(r)/ vi errare; (sin) peccare

errand /'erənd/ n commissione f

errant /'erənt/ adj ‹husband, wife› infedele

erratic /ɪ'rætɪk/ adj irregolare; ‹person,
moods› imprevedibile; ‹exchange rate›
incostante

erroneous /ɪ'rəʊnɪəs/ adj erroneo

erroneously /ɪ'rəʊnɪəslɪ/ adv
erroneamente

✦ **error** /'erə(r)/ n errore m; **in** ~ per errore

error message n Comput messaggio m
di errore

ersatz /'ɜ:sæts/ n surrogato m; ~ **tobacco**
surrogato del tabacco

erudite /'erʊdaɪt/ adj erudito

erudition /erʊ'dɪʃn/ n erudizione f

erupt /ɪ'rʌpt/ vi eruttare; ‹spots› spuntare;
fig (in anger) dare in escandescenze

eruption /ɪ'rʌpʃn/ n eruzione f; fig scoppio
m

escalate /'eskəleɪt/ 1 vi intensificarsi
2 vt intensificare

escalation /eskə'leɪʃn/ n escalation f inv

escalator /'eskəleɪtə(r)/ n scala f mobile

escapade /'eskəpeɪd/ n scappatella f

✦ **escape** /ɪ'skeɪp/ 1 n fuga f; (from prison)
evasione f; **have a narrow** ~ cavarsela per
un pelo
2 vi ‹prisoner› evadere (**from** da);
sfuggire (**from somebody** alla sorveglianza
di qualcuno); ‹animal› scappare; ‹gas›
fuoriuscire
3 vt ~ **notice** passare inosservato; **the
name** ~**s me** mi sfugge il nome

escape [key] n (tasto) escape m inv

escape chute n Aeron scivolo m

escape clause n clausola f di recesso

escapee /ɪskeɪ'pi:/ n evaso m

escape hatch n Naut portello m di
sicurezza

escape route n (for fugitives) itinerario
m di fuga; (in case of fire etc) percorso m di
emergenza

escapism /ɪ'skeɪpɪzm/ n evasione f dalla
realtà

escapologist /eskə'pɒlədʒɪst/ n
illusionista (mf) capace di liberarsi dalle
catene

escarpment /es'kɑ:pmənt/ n scarpata f

eschew /ɪs'tʃu:/ vt evitare ‹discussion›;
rifuggire ‹temptation›; rifuggire da ‹violence›

escort[1] /'eskɔ:t/ n (of person)
accompagnatore, -trice mf; Mil etc scorta f

escort[2] /ɪ'skɔ:t/ vt accompagnare; Mil etc
scortare

Eskimo /'eskɪməʊ/ n esquimese mf

esophagus /ɪ'sɒfəgəs/ n Am esofago m

esoteric /esə'terɪk/ adj esoterico

ESP n abbr 1 (**extrasensory
perception**) ESP f
2 (**English for Special Purposes**)

esp abbr (**especially**) specialmente

especial /ɪ'speʃl/ adj speciale

✦ **especially** /ɪ'speʃəlɪ/ adv specialmente;
‹kind› particolarmente

espionage /'espɪənɑ:ʒ/ n spionaggio m

✦ indicates a very frequent word

espouse /ɪˈspaʊz/ *vt* abbracciare ‹cause›

espresso /eˈspresəʊ/ *n* (coffee) espresso *m*

Esq *abbr* Br (**esquire**) James McBride, ∼ Egr. Sig. James McBride

essay /ˈeseɪ/ *n* saggio *m*; Sch tema *f*

essence /ˈesns/ *n* essenza *f*; **in** ∼ in sostanza

⚹ **essential** /ɪˈsenʃl/ 1 *adj* essenziale
2 *n* **the** ∼**s** *pl* l'essenziale *m*

essentially /ɪˈsenʃəlɪ/ *adv* essenzialmente

essential oil *n* olio *m* essenziale

est *abbr* (**established**) fondato nel

EST *abbr* Am (**Eastern Standard Time**) *ora* (*f*) *solare degli stati orientali dell'America settentrionale*

⚹ **establish** /ɪˈstæblɪʃ/ *vt* stabilire ‹contact, lead›; fondare ‹firm›; (prove) accertare; ∼ **oneself as** affermarsi come

established /ɪˈstæblɪʃt/ *adj* ‹way of doing something, view› generalmente accettato; ‹company› affidabile; ‹brand› riconosciuto; **a well** ∼ **fact** un dato di fatto; **the** ∼ **church** la religione di Stato

establishment /ɪˈstæblɪʃmənt/ *n* (firm) azienda *f*; **the E**∼ l'establishment *m*

⚹ **estate** /ɪˈsteɪt/ *n* tenuta *f*; (possessions) patrimonio *m*; (housing) quartiere *m* residenziale

estate agency *n* agenzia *f* immobiliare

estate agent *n* agente *m* immobiliare

estate car *n* giardiniera *f*

estate duty *n* Br imposta *f* di successione

esteem /ɪˈstiːm/ 1 *n* stima *f*
2 *vt* stimare; (consider) giudicare

ester /ˈestə(r)/ *n* estere *m*

estimate[1] /ˈestɪmət/ *n* valutazione *f*; Comm preventivo *m*; **at a rough** ∼ a occhio e croce

⚹ **estimate**[2] /ˈestɪmeɪt/ *vt* stimare

estimated time of arrival /ˈestɪmeɪtɪd/ *n* ora *f* prevista di arrivo

estimation /estɪˈmeɪʃn/ *n* (esteem) stima *f*; **in my** ∼ (judgement) a mio giudizio

estimator /ˈestɪmeɪtə(r)/ *n* Am *geometra* (*mf*) *che calcola quantità e costo di materiali da costruzione*

Estonia /ɪˈstəʊnɪə/ *n* Estonia *f*

estrange /ɪˈstreɪndʒ/ *vt* estraniare; ∼**d from somebody** separato da qualcuno; **her** ∼**d husband** il marito da cui è separata

estrangement /ɪˈstreɪndʒmənt/ *n* disamoramento *m*

estuary /ˈestjʊərɪ/ *n* estuario *m*

ETA *n abbr* (**estimated time of arrival**) *ora* (*f*) *prevista di arrivo*

et al /etˈæl/ *abbr* (**et alii**) e altri

⚹ **etc** /etˈsetərə/ *abbr* (**et cetera**) ecc

et cetera, etcetera /etˈsetərə/ *adv* eccetera

etch /etʃ/ *vt* incidere all'acquaforte; ∼**ed on her memory** fig impresso nella sua memoria

etching /ˈetʃɪŋ/ *n* acquaforte *f*

eternal /ɪˈtɜːnl/ *adj* eterno

eternal life *n* vita *f* eterna

eternally /ɪˈtɜːnəlɪ/ *adv* eternamente

eternal triangle *n* eterno triangolo *m*

eternity /ɪˈtɜːnətɪ/ *n* eternità

ether /ˈiːθə(r)/ *n* etere *m*

ethereal /ɪˈθɪərɪəl/ *adj* etereo

ethic /ˈeθɪk/ *n* etica *f*

ethical /ˈeθɪkl/ *adj* etico

ethical bank *n* banca *f* etica

ethics /ˈeθɪks/ *n* etica *f*

Ethiopia /iːθɪˈəʊpɪə/ *n* Etiopia *f*

ethnic /ˈeθnɪk/ *adj* etnico

ethnically /ˈeθnɪklɪ/ *adv* etnicamente

ethnic cleansing *n* epurazione *f* etnica

ethnic minority *n* minoranza *f* etnica

ethnology /eθˈnɒlədʒɪ/ *n* etnologia *f*

ethos /ˈiːθɒs/ *n* **company** ∼ filosofia *f* dell'azienda

e-ticket /ˈiːtɪkɪt/ *n* Comput biglietto *m* elettronico

etiquette /ˈetɪket/ *n* etichetta *f*

etymology /etɪˈmɒlədʒɪ/ *n* etimologia *f*

EU *n abbr* (**European Union**) UE *f*

eucalyptus /juːkəˈlɪptəs/ *n* eucalipto *m*

eugenics /juːˈdʒenɪks/ *n* eugenetica *f*

eulogize /ˈjuːlədʒaɪz/ 1 *vt* fare il panegirico di
2 *vi* ∼ **over something** tessere le lodi di qualcosa

eulogy /ˈjuːlədʒɪ/ *n* elogio *m*

eunuch /ˈjuːnək/ *n* eunuco *m*

euphemism /ˈjuːfəmɪzm/ *n* eufemismo *m*

euphemistic /juːfəˈmɪstɪk/ *adj* eufemistico

euphemistically /juːfəˈmɪstɪklɪ/ *adv* eufemisticamente

euphoria /juːˈfɔːrɪə/ *n* euforia *f*

euphoric /juːˈfɒrɪk/ *adj* euforico

Eurasian /jʊəˈreɪʒ(ə)n/ *adj* ‹people, region› eurasiatico

EURATOM /jʊəˈrætəm/ *n abbr* (**European Atomic Energy Community**) EURATOM *f*

eurhythmics /jʊˈrɪðmɪks/ *n* ginnastica *f* ritmica

euro /ˈjʊərəʊ/ *n* euro *m inv*

eurobond *n* eurobbligazione *f*

Eurocheque *n* eurochèque *m inv*

Eurocrat /ˈjʊərəʊkræt/ *n* eurocrate *mf*

eurocurrency *n* eurovaluta *f*

Eurodollar *n* eurodollaro *m*

euromarket *n* euromercato *m*

Euro-MP *n* eurodeputato, -a *mf*

Europe /'jʊərəp/ n Europa f

♂ **European** /jʊərə'pɪən/ adj & n europeo, -a mf

European Bank for Reconstruction and Development n Banca f Europea per la Ricostruzione e lo Sviluppo

European Commission n Commissione f Europea

European Community n Comunità f Europea

European Court of Human Rights n Corte f europea per i diritti dell'uomo

European Court of Justice n Corte f europea di giustizia

European Economic Community n Comunità f Economica Europea

European Free Trade Association n Associazione f Europea di Libero Scambio

European Health Insurance Card n Tessera f Europea Assicurazione Malattia

European Monetary System n Sistema m Monetario Europeo

European Monetary Union n Unione f Monetaria Europea

European Parliament n Parlamento m Europeo

European Union n Unione f Europea

Euro-sceptic n Br euroscettico, -a mf

euthanasia /juθə'neɪzɪə/ n eutanasia f

evacuate /ɪ'vækjʊeɪt/ vt evacuare ‹building, area›

evacuation /ɪvækjʊ'eɪʃn/ n evacuazione f

evacuee /ɪvæjʊ'iː/ n sfollato m

evade /ɪ'veɪd/ vt evadere ‹taxes›; evitare ‹the enemy, authorities›; ~ **the issue** evitare l'argomento

evaluate /ɪ'væljʊeɪt/ vt valutare

evaluation /ɪvæljʊ'eɪʃn/ n valutazione f, stima f

evangelical /iːvæn'dʒelɪkl/ adj evangelico

evangelist /ɪ'vændʒəlɪst/ n evangelista m

evaporate /ɪ'væpəreɪt/ vi evaporare; fig svanire

evaporated milk n latte m condensato

evaporation /ɪvæpə'reɪʃn/ n evaporazione f

evasion /ɪ'veɪʒn/ n evasione f

evasive /ɪ'veɪsɪv/ adj evasivo

evasively /ɪ'veɪsɪvlɪ/ adv in modo evasivo

eve /iːv/ n liter vigilia f

♂ **even** /'iːvn/ [1] adj (level) piatto; (same, equal) uguale; (regular) regolare; ‹number› pari; **get ~ with** vendicarsi di; **now we're ~** adesso siamo pari
[2] adv anche, ancora; ~ **if** anche se; ~ **so**

con tutto ciò; **not ~** nemmeno; ~ **bigger/hotter** ancora più grande/caldo
[3] vt ~ **the score** Sport pareggiare
■ **even out** vi livellarsi
■ **even up** vt livellare

even-handed /-'hændɪd/ adj imparziale

♂ **evening** /'iːvnɪŋ/ n sera f; (whole evening) serata f; **this ~** stasera; **in the ~** la sera

evening class n corso m serale

evening dress n (man's) abito m scuro; (woman's) abito m da sera

evening performance n spettacolo m serale

evening primrose n enotera f

evening star n Venere f

evenly /'iːvnlɪ/ adv ‹distributed› uniformemente; ‹breathe› regolarmente; ‹divided› in uguali parti

♂ **event** /ɪ'vent/ n avvenimento m; (function) manifestazione f; Sport gara f; **in the ~ of** nell'eventualità di; **in the ~** alla fine

even-tempered /-'tempəd/ adj pacato

eventful /ɪ'ventfʊl/ adj movimentato

eventing /ɪ'ventɪŋ/ n Br concorso m ippico completo

eventual /ɪ'ventjʊəl/ adj **the ~ winner was...** alla fine il vincitore è stato ...

eventuality /ɪventjʊ'ælətɪ/ n eventualità

♂ **eventually** /ɪ'ventjʊəlɪ/ adv alla fine; ~! finalmente!

♂ **ever** /'evə(r)/ adv mai; **I haven't ~...** non ho mai ...; **for ~** per sempre; **hardly ~** quasi mai; ~ **since** da quando; (since that time) da allora; ~ **so** fam veramente

evergreen /'evəgriːn/ n sempreverde m

everlasting /evə'lɑːstɪŋ/ adj eterno

♂ **every** /'evrɪ/ adj ogni; ~ **one** ciascuno; ~ **other day** un giorno sì un giorno no

♂ **everybody** /'evrɪbɒdɪ/ pron tutti pl

everyday /'evrɪdeɪ/ adj quotidiano, di ogni giorno

♂ **everyone** /'evrɪwʌn/ pron tutti pl; ~ **else** tutti gli altri

everyplace /'evrɪpleɪs/ adv Am fam = EVERYWHERE

♂ **everything** /'evrɪθɪŋ/ pron tutto; ~ **else** tutto il resto

everywhere /'evrɪweə(r)/ adv dappertutto; (wherever) dovunque

evict /ɪ'vɪkt/ vt sfrattare

eviction /ɪ'vɪkʃn/ n sfratto m

♂ **evidence** /'evɪdəns/ n evidenza f; Jur testimonianza f; **give ~** testimoniare

evident /'evɪdənt/ adj evidente

evidently /'evɪdəntlɪ/ adv evidentemente

evil /'iːvl/ [1] adj cattivo
[2] n male m

evil-smelling /-'smelɪŋ/ adj puzzolente

evocative /ɪ'vɒkətɪv/ adj evocativo; **be ~ of** evocare

evoke /ɪ'vəʊk/ vt evocare

evolution /i:və'lu:ʃn/ n evoluzione f

evolutionary /i:və'lu:ʃn(ə)rɪ/ adj evolutivo

evolve /ɪ'vɒlv/ **1** vt evolvere
2 vi evolversi

ewe /ju:/ n pecora f

ex /eks/ n fam (former partner) ex mf

ex+ pref ex+

exacerbate /ɪg'sæsəbeɪt/ vt esacerbare ‹situation›

exact /ɪg'zækt/ **1** adj esatto
2 vt esigere

exacting /ɪg'zæktɪŋ/ adj esigente

exactitude /ɪg'zæktɪtju:d/ n esattezza f

exactly /ɪg'zæktlɪ/ adv esattamente; not ~ non proprio

exactness /ɪg'zæktnɪs/ n precisione f

exaggerate /ɪg'zædʒəreɪt/ vt/i esagerare

exaggerated /ɪg'zædʒəreɪtɪd/ adj esagerato; he has an ~ sense of his own importance si crede chissà chi

exaggeration /ɪgzædʒə'reɪʃn/ n esagerazione f

exalt /ɪg'zɔ:lt/ vt elevare; (praise) vantare

exam /ɪg'zæm/ n esame m

examination /ɪgzæmɪ'neɪʃn/ n esame m; (of patient) visita f; (of wreckage) ispezione f

examination paper n testo m d'esame

examine /ɪg'zæmɪn/ vt esaminare; visitare ‹patient›

examinee /ɪgzæmɪ'ni:/ n esaminando m

examiner /ɪg'zæmɪnə(r)/ n Sch esaminatore, -trice mf

example /ɪg'zɑ:mpl/ n esempio m; for ~ per esempio; make an ~ of somebody punire qualcuno per dare un esempio; be an ~ to somebody dare il buon esempio a qualcuno

exasperate /ɪg'zæspəreɪt/ vt esasperare

exasperation /ɪgzæspə'reɪʃn/ n esasperazione f

excavate /'ekskəveɪt/ vt scavare; Archaeol fare gli scavi di

excavation /ekskə'veɪʃn/ n scavo m

excavator /'ekskəveɪtə(r)/ n (machine) escavatrice f, escavatore m

exceed /ɪk'si:d/ vt eccedere

exceedingly /ɪk'si:dɪŋlɪ/ adv estremamente

excel /ɪk'sel/ v (pt/pp excelled) **1** vi eccellere
2 vt ~ oneself superare se stessi

excellence /'eksələns/ n eccellenza f

Excellency /'eksələnsɪ/ n (title) Eccellenza f

excellent /'eksələnt/ adj eccellente

excellently /'eksələntlɪ/ adv in modo eccellente

except /ɪk'sept/ **1** prep eccetto, tranne; ~ for eccetto, tranne; ~ that ... eccetto che ...
2 vt eccettuare

excepting /ɪk'septɪŋ/ prep eccetto, tranne

exception /ɪk'sepʃn/ n eccezione f; take ~ to fare obiezioni a

exceptional /ɪk'sepʃənəl/ adj eccezionale

exceptionally /ɪk'sepʃənəlɪ/ adv eccezionalmente

excerpt /'eksɜ:pt/ n estratto m

excess /ɪk'ses/ n eccesso m; in ~ of oltre

excess baggage n bagaglio m eccedente

excess fare n supplemento m

excessive /ɪk'sesɪv/ adj eccessivo

excessively /ɪk'sesɪvlɪ/ adv eccessivamente

excess postage n soprattassa f postale

excess profits npl sovraprofitto m

exchange /ɪks'tʃeɪndʒ/ **1** n scambio m; Teleph centrale f; Comm cambio m; [stock] ~ borsa f valori; in ~ in cambio (for di)
2 vt scambiare (for con), cambiare ‹money›; ~ views scambiarsi i punti di vista; ~ contracts fare il rogito
3 vi (on house purchase) fare il rogito

exchange control n controllo m dei cambi

exchange controls npl misure fpl di controllo dei cambi

exchange rate n tasso m di cambio

Exchange Rate Mechanism n meccanismo m di cambio dello Sme

exchequer /ɪks'tʃekə(r)/ n Pol tesoro m

excise[1] /'eksaɪz/ n dazio m

excise[2] /ek'saɪz/ vt recidere

excise duty n dazio m

excitable /ɪk'saɪtəbl/ adj eccitabile

excite /ɪk'saɪt/ vt eccitare

excited /ɪk'saɪtɪd/ adj eccitato; get ~ eccitarsi

excitedly /ɪk'saɪtɪdlɪ/ adv tutto eccitato

excitement /ɪk'saɪtmənt/ n eccitazione f

exciting /ɪk'saɪtɪŋ/ adj eccitante; ‹story, film› appassionante; ‹holiday› entusiasmante

excl abbr (excluding) escluso

exclaim /ɪk'skleɪm/ vt/i esclamare

exclamation /eksklə'meɪʃn/ n esclamazione f

exclamation mark, Am **exclamation point** n punto m esclamativo

exclude /ɪk'sklu:d/ vt escludere

excluding /ɪk'sklu:dɪŋ/ pron escluso

exclusion /ɪk'sklu:ʒn/ n esclusione f

exclusion zone n zona f proibita

exclusive /ɪk'sklu:sɪv/ adj ‹rights, club› esclusivo; ‹interview› in esclusiva; ~ of ... ...escluso

exclusively /ɪk'skluːsɪvlɪ/ adv
esclusivamente

excommunicate /ekskə'mjuːnɪkeɪt/ vt
scomunicare

excrement /'ekskrɪmənt/ n escremento m

excreta /ɪk'skriːtə/ npl escrementi mpl

excrete /ɪk'skriːt/ vt espellere; secernere
‹liquid›

excretion /ɪk'skriːʃn/ n (of animal, human)
escremento m

excruciating /ɪk'skruːʃɪeɪtɪŋ/ adj ‹pain›
atroce; fam (very bad) spaventoso

excursion /ɪk'skɜːʃn/ n escursione f

excusable /ɪk'skjuːzəbl/ adj perdonabile

excuse¹ /ɪk'skjuːs/ n scusa f

excuse² /ɪk'skjuːz/ vt scusare; ~ **from**
esonerare da; ~ **me!** (to get attention) scusi!;
(to get past) permesso!, scusi!; (indignant) come
ha detto?

ex-directory adj **be** ~ non figurare
sull'elenco telefonico

exec /ɪg'zek/ n abbr Am fam (**executive**)
executive mf, dirigente mf

execrable /'eksɪkrəbl/ adj esecrabile

executable file /'eksɪkjuːtəbl/ n Comput
eseguibile m

execute /'eksɪkjuːt/ vt eseguire; (put to
death) giustiziare; attuare ‹plan›

execution /eksɪ'kjuːʃn/ n esecuzione f; (of
plan) attuazione f

executioner /eksɪ'kjuːʃənə(r)/ n boia
m inv

◦' **executive** /ɪg'zekjʊtɪv/ **1** adj esecutivo
2 n dirigente mf; Pol esecutivo m

executive committee n comitato m
esecutivo

executive director n direttore, -trice
mf [esecutivo, -a]

executive jet n jet m inv privato

executive producer n Cinema direttore,
-trice mf di produzione

executive secretary n segretario, -a
mf di direzione

executor /ɪg'zekjʊtə(r)/ n Jur esecutore,
-trice mf

exemplary /ɪg'zemplərɪ/ adj esemplare

exemplify /ɪg'zemplɪfaɪ/ vt (pt/pp **-ied**)
esemplificare

exempt /ɪg'zempt/ **1** adj esente
2 vt esentare (**from** da)

exemption /ɪg'zempʃn/ n esenzione f

◦' **exercise** /'eksəsaɪz/ **1** n esercizio m; Mil
esercitazione f; **physical** ~**s** ginnastica f;
take ~ fare del moto; **you need more** ~ devi
muoverti di più
2 vt esercitare ‹muscles, horse›; portare
a spasso ‹dog›; usare ‹patience›; mettere in
pratica ‹skills›
3 vi esercitarsi; ~ **more** fare più moto

◦' indicates a very frequent word

exercise bike n cyclette® f inv

exercise book n quaderno m

exert /ɪg'zɜːt/ vt esercitare; ~ **oneself**
sforzarsi

exertion /ɪg'zɜːʃn/ n sforzo m

ex gratia /eks'greɪʃə/ adj ‹award,
payment› a titolo di favore

exhale /eks'heɪl/ vt/i esalare

exhaust /ɪg'zɔːst/ n Auto scappamento m;
(pipe) tubo m di scappamento

exhausted /ɪg'zɔːstɪd/ adj esausto

exhaust fumes **1** npl fumi mpl di
scarico m
2 vt esaurire

exhausting /ɪg'zɔːstɪŋ/ adj estenuante;
‹climate, person› sfibrante

exhaustion /ɪg'zɔːstʃn/ n esaurimento m

exhaustive /ɪg'zɔːstɪv/ adj fig esauriente

exhibit /ɪg'zɪbɪt/ **1** n oggetto m esposto;
Jur reperto m
2 vt esporre; fig dimostrare

◦' **exhibition** /eksɪ'bɪʃn/ n mostra f; (of
strength, skill) dimostrazione f

exhibition centre n palazzo m delle
esposizioni

exhibitionist /eksɪ'bɪʃənɪst/ n
esibizionista mf

exhibitor /ɪg'zɪbɪtə(r)/ n espositore, -trice
mf

exhilarated /ɪg'zɪləreɪtɪd/ adj rallegrato

exhilarating /ɪg'zɪləreɪtɪŋ/ adj
stimolante; ‹mountain air› tonificante

exhilaration /ɪgzɪlə'reɪʃn/ n allegria f

exhort /ɪg'zɔːt/ vt esortare

exhume /ɪg'zjuːm/ vt esumare

exile /'eksaɪl/ **1** n esilio m; (person) esule
mf
2 vt esiliare

◦' **exist** /ɪg'zɪst/ vi esistere

◦' **existence** /ɪg'zɪstəns/ n esistenza f; **in** ~
esistente; **be in** ~ esistere

existential /egzɪ'stenʃ(ə)l/ adj
esistenziale

existentialism /egzɪ'stenʃəlɪzm/ n
esistenzialismo m

existing /ɪg'zɪstɪŋ/ adj ‹policy,
management, leadership› attuale; ‹laws,
order› vigente

exit /'eksɪt/ **1** n uscita f; Theat uscita f di
scena
2 vi Theat uscire di scena; Comput uscire
(**from** da)

exit sign n cartello m di uscita

exodus /'eksədəs/ n esodo m

ex officio /eksə'fɪʃɪəʊ/ adj ‹member› di
diritto

exonerate /ɪg'zɒnəreɪt/ vt esonerare

exorbitant /ɪg'zɔːbɪtənt/ adj esorbitante

exorcism /'eksɔːsɪzm/ n esorcismo m

exorcist /'eksɔːsɪst/ n esorcista mf
exorcize /'eksɔːsaɪz/ vt esorcizzare
exotic /ɪg'zɒtɪk/ adj esotico
exotica /ɪg'zɒtɪkə/ npl oggetti mpl esotici
⚬ **expand** /ɪk'spænd/ [1] vt espandere; sviluppare ‹economy›
[2] vi espandersi; Comm svilupparsi; ‹metal› dilatarsi
■ **expand on** vt (explain better) approfondire
expandable /ɪk'spændəbl/ adj Comput ‹memory› espandibile
expanding /ɪk'spændɪŋ/ adj ‹file› a soffietto inv; ‹population, sector› in espansione; ‹bracelet› allungabile
expanse /ɪk'spæns/ n estensione f
expansion /ɪk'spænʃn/ n espansione f; Comm sviluppo m; (of metal) dilatazione f
expansion board, expansion card n Comput scheda f di espansione
expansionist /ɪk'spænʃənɪst/ n & adj espansionista mf
expansion slot n Comput fessura f [per la scheda] di espansione, slot m di espansione
expansive /ɪk'spænsɪv/ adj espansivo
expatriate /eks'pætrɪət/ n espatriato, -a mf
⚬ **expect** /ɪk'spekt/ vt aspettare ‹letter, baby›; (suppose) pensare; (demand) esigere; I ~ so penso di sì; we ~ to arrive on Monday contiamo di arrivare lunedì; I didn't ~ that questo non me lo aspettavo; she ~s too much from him pretende troppo da lui; be ~ing essere in stato interessante
expectancy /ɪk'spektənsɪ/ n aspettativa f
expectant /ɪk'spektənt/ adj in attesa; ~ mother donna f incinta
expectantly /ɪk'spektəntlɪ/ adv con impazienza
⚬ **expectation** /ekspek'teɪʃn/ n aspettativa f, speranza f
expediency /ɪk'spiːdɪənsɪ/ n (appropriateness) opportunità, (self-interest) opportunismo m
expedient /ɪk'spiːdɪənt/ [1] adj conveniente
[2] n espediente m
expedite /'ekspɪdaɪt/ vt fml accelerare
expedition /ekspɪ'dɪʃn/ n spedizione f
expeditionary /ekspɪ'dɪʃənərɪ/ adj Mil di spedizione
expeditionary force n corpo m di spedizione
expel /ɪk'spel/ vt (pt/pp **expelled**) espellere
expend /ɪk'spend/ vt consumare
expendable /ɪk'spendəbl/ adj sacrificabile
expenditure /ɪk'spendɪtʃə(r)/ n spesa f
⚬ **expense** /ɪk'spens/ n spesa f; business ~s pl spese fpl; at my ~ a mie spese; at the ~ of fig a spese di

expense account n conto m spese
⚬ **expensive** /ɪk'spensɪv/ adj caro, costoso
expensively /ɪk'spensɪvlɪ/ adv costosamente
⚬ **experience** /ɪk'spɪərɪəns/ [1] n esperienza f
[2] vt provare ‹sensation›; avere ‹problem›
experienced /ɪk'spɪərɪənst/ adj esperto
⚬ **experiment** /ɪk'sperɪmənt/ [1] n esperimento
[2] /ɪk'sperɪment/ vi sperimentare
experimental /ɪksperɪ'mentl/ adj sperimentale
experimentation /ɪksperɪmen'teɪʃn/ n sperimentazione f; ~ with drugs esperienza f della droga
⚬ **expert** /'ekspɜːt/ adj & n esperto, -a mf
expertise /ekspɜː'tiːz/ n competenza f
expertly /'ekspɜːtlɪ/ adv abilmente
expiate /'ekspɪeɪt/ vt espiare ‹crime, sin›; fare ammenda per ‹guilt›
expiration /ekspɪ'reɪʃn/ n (end, exhalation) espirazione f
expire /ɪk'spaɪə(r)/ vi scadere
expiry /ɪk'spaɪərɪ/ n scadenza f
expiry date n data f di scadenza
⚬ **explain** /ɪk'spleɪn/ vt spiegare
■ **explain away** vt (give reasons for) trovare delle giustificazioni per
⚬ **explanation** /eksplə'neɪʃn/ n spiegazione f
explanatory /ɪk'splænətərɪ/ adj esplicativo
expletive /ɪk'spliːtɪv/ n imprecazione f
explicit /ɪk'splɪsɪt/ adj esplicito
explicitly /ɪk'splɪsɪtlɪ/ adv esplicitamente
explode /ɪk'spləʊd/ [1] vi esplodere
[2] vt fare esplodere
exploit¹ /'eksplɔɪt/ n impresa f
exploit² /ɪk'splɔɪt/ vt sfruttare
exploitation /eksplɔɪ'teɪʃn/ n sfruttamento m
exploitative /ɪk'splɔɪtətɪv/ adj inteso a sfruttare gli individui; ‹attitude, system› a carattere di sfruttamento
exploration /eksplə'reɪʃn/ n esplorazione f
exploratory /ɪk'splɒrətərɪ/ adj esplorativo
⚬ **explore** /ɪk'splɔː(r)/ vt esplorare; fig studiare ‹implications›
explorer /ɪk'splɔːrə(r)/ n esploratore, -trice mf
explosion /ɪk'spləʊʒn/ n esplosione f
explosive /ɪk'spləʊsɪv/ adj & n esplosivo m
exponent /ɪk'spəʊnənt/ n esponente mf
exponential /ekspə'nenʃəl/ adj esponenziale

e

export¹ /'ekspɔːt/ n esportazione f

export² /ek'spɔːt/ vt esportare

export agent n esportatore, -trice mf

export control n controllo m delle esportazioni

export credit n credito m all'esportazione

export drive n campagna f di esportazione

export duty n tassa f di esportazione

export earnings npl ricavato m delle esportazioni

exporter /ek'spɔːtə(r)/ n esportatore, -trice mf

export finance n finanziamento m delle esportazioni

export-import company n azienda di import-export

export licence n licenza f di esportazione

export market n mercato m delle esportazioni

export trade n commercio m di esportazione

⚘ **expose** /ɪk'spəʊz/ vt esporre; ‹reveal› svelare; smascherare ‹traitor etc›

exposée /ɪk'spəʊzeɪ/ n (of scandal) rivelazioni fpl

exposition /ekspə'zɪʃn/ n (of facts) esposizione f

⚘ **exposure** /ɪk'spəʊʒə(r)/ n esposizione f; Med espozione f prolungata al freddo/caldo; (of crimes) smascheramento m; **24 ~s** Phot 24 pose

exposure meter n Phot esposimetro m

exposure time n Phot tempo m di esposizione

expound /ɪk'spaʊnd/ vt esporre

⚘ **express** /ɪk'spres/ **1** adj espresso
2 adv ‹send› per espresso
3 n (train) espresso m
4 vt esprimere; ~ **oneself** esprimersi

⚘ **expression** /ɪk'spreʃn/ n espressione f

expressionless /ɪk'spreʃənlɪs/ adj ‹tone, voice› distaccato; ‹playing› piatto; ‹eyes, face› inespressivo

expressive /ɪk'spresɪv/ adj espressivo

expressively /ɪk'spresɪvlɪ/ adv espressamente

express lane n corsia f a scorrimento veloce

expulsion /ɪk'spʌlʃn/ n espulsione f

expurgate /'ekspəgeɪt/ vt espurgare

exquisite /ek'skwɪzɪt/ adj squisito

exquisitely /ek'skwɪzɪtlɪ/ adv ‹dressed, written› in modo elegante e raffinato; ~ **beautiful** di una bellezza fine

⚘ indicates a very frequent word

ex-serviceman /'sɜːvɪsmən/ n ex-combattente m

ex-servicewoman /'sɜːvɪswʊmən/ n ex-combattente f

extant /ɪk'stænt/ adj ancora esistente

extempore /ɪk'stempərɪ/ adv ‹speak› senza preparazione

⚘ **extend** /ɪk'stend/ **1** vt prolungare ‹visit, road›; prorogare ‹visa, contract›; ampliare ‹building, knowledge›; (stretch out) allungare; tendere ‹hand›
2 vi ‹garden, knowledge› estendersi

extendable /ɪk'stendəbl/ adj (cable) allungabile; ‹contract› prorogabile

extension /ɪk'stenʃn/ n prolungamento m; (of visa, contract) proroga f; (of treaty) ampliamento m; (part of building) annesso m; (length of cable) prolunga f; Teleph interno m; ~ **226** interno 226; (hair) ~s le extension

extension ladder n scala f allungabile

extension lead n Electr prolunga f

extensive /ɪk'stensɪv/ adj ampio, vasto

extensively /ɪk'stensɪvlɪ/ adv ampiamente

⚘ **extent** /ɪk'stent/ n (scope) portata f; **to a certain ~** fino a un certo punto; **to such an ~ that …** fino al punto che …

extenuating /ɪk'stenjʊeɪtɪŋ/ adj ~ **circumstances** attenuanti fpl

exterior /ɪk'stɪərɪə(r)/ adj & n esterno m

exterminate /ɪk'stɜːmɪneɪt/ vt sterminare

extermination /ɪkstɜːmɪ'neɪʃn/ n sterminio m

external /ɪk'stɜːnl/ adj esterno; **for ~ use only** Med per uso esterno

externalize /ɪk'stɜːnəlaɪz/ vt esteriorizzare

externally /ɪk'stɜːnəlɪ/ adv esternamente

externals /ɪk'stɜːn(ə)lz/ npl apparenze fpl

extinct /ɪk'stɪŋkt/ adj estinto

extinction /ɪk'stɪŋkʃn/ n estinzione f

extinguish /ɪk'stɪŋgwɪʃ/ vt estinguere

extinguisher /ɪk'stɪŋgwɪʃə(r)/ n estintore m

extol /ɪk'stəʊl/ vt (pt/pp **extolled**) lodare

extort /ɪk'stɔːt/ vt estorcere

extortion /ɪk'stɔːʃn/ n estorsione f

extortionate /ɪk'stɔːʃənət/ adj esorbitante

⚘ **extra** /'ekstrə/ **1** adj in più; ‹train› straordinario; **an ~ £10** 10 sterline extra, 10 sterline in più
2 adv in più; (especially) più; **pay ~** pagare in più, pagare extra; ~ **strong/busy** fortissimo/occupatissimo
3 n Theat comparsa f; ~**s** pl extra mpl

extra charge n supplemento m; **at no ~** senza ulteriori spese

extract¹ /'ekstrækt/ n estratto m

extract ⸱⸱⸱▸ e-zine ⸱⸱⸱⸱

extract² /ɪk'strækt/ *vt* estrarre ‹*tooth, oil*›; strappare ‹*secret*›; ricavare ‹*truth*›

extraction /ɪk'strækʃn/ *n* (process) estrazione *f*; **of French** ~ di origine francese

extractor [fan] /ɪk'stræktə(r)/ *n* aspiratore *m*

extra-curricular /-kə'rɪkjʊlə(r)/ *adj* extrascolastico

extradite /'ekstrədaɪt/ *vt* Jur estradare

extradition /ekstrə'dɪʃn/ *n* estradizione *f*

extra-dry *adj* ‹*sherry, wine*› extra dry *inv*

extra-fast *adj* ultrarapido

extra-large *adj* ‹*pullover, shirt*› extra large *inv*

extramarital /ekstrə'mærɪtəl/ *adj* extraconiugale

extramural /ekstrə'mjʊərəl/ *adj* Br Univ ‹*course, lecture*› organizzato dall'università e aperto a tutti

extraneous /ɪk'streɪnɪəs/ *adj* (not essential) inessenziale; ‹*issue, detail*› superfluo

extraordinarily /ɪk'strɔːdmərɪlɪ/ *adv* straordinariamente

extraordinary /ɪk'strɔːdmərɪ/ *adj* straordinario

extrapolate /ɪk'stræpəleɪt/ *vt* arguire; Math estrapolare

extrasensory perception /ekstrə'sensərɪ/ *n* percezione *f* extrasensoriale

extra-special *adj* eccezionale

extra-strong *adj* ‹*thread*› robustissimo; ‹*coffee*› fortissimo; ‹*disinfectant, weed killer*› potentissimo; ‹*paper*› ultraresistente *inv*

extraterrestrial /ekstrətɪ'restrɪəl/ *n* & *adj* extraterrestre *mf*

extra time *n* tempo *m* supplementare; **play** ~ giocare i tempi supplementari

extravagance /ɪk'strævəgəns/ *n* (with money) prodigalità *f*; (of behaviour) stravaganza *f*

extravagant /ɪk'strævəgənt/ *adj* spendaccione; (bizarre) stravagante; ‹*claim*› esagerato

extravagantly /ɪk'strævəgəntlɪ/ *adv* dispendiosamente

extravaganza /ɪkstrævə'gænzə/ *n* rappresentazione *f* spettacolare

extra virgin olive oil *n* olio *m* extravergine d'oliva

extreme /ɪk'striːm/ ① *adj* estremo ② *n* estremo *m*; **in the** ~ al massimo

⚡ **extremely** /ɪk'striːmlɪ/ *adv* estremamente

extreme sports *npl* sport *mpl* estremi

extremism /ɪk'striːmɪzm/ *n* estremismo *m*

extremist /ɪk'striːmɪst/ *n* estremista *mf*

extremity /ɪk'stremətɪ/ *n* (end) estremità *f inv*

extricate /'ekstrɪkeɪt/ *vt* districare

extrovert /'ekstrəvɜːt/ *n* estroverso, -a *mf*

exuberance /ɪg'zjuːbərəns/ *n* esuberanza *f*

exuberant /ɪg'zjuːbərənt/ *adj* esuberante

exude /ɪg'zjuːd/ *vt* also fig trasudare

exult /ɪg'zʌlt/ *vi* esultare

exultant /ɪg'zʌltənt/ *adj* esultante; ‹*cry*› di esultanza

exultantly /ɪg'zʌltəntlɪ/ *adv* con esultanza

ex-works *adj* ‹*price, value*› franco fabbrica

⚡ **eye** /aɪ/ ① *n* occhio *m*; (of needle) cruna *f*; **keep an** ~ **on** tener d'occhio; **see** ~ **to** ~ aver le stesse idee ② *vt* (*pt/pp* **eyed**, *pres p* **ey[e]ing**) guardare

■ **eye up** *vt* adocchiare ‹*somebody*›

eyeball *n* bulbo *m* oculare

eyebath *n* bagno *m* oculare

eyebrow *n* sopracciglio *m* (*pl* sopracciglia *f*)

eyebrow pencil *n* matita *f* per le sopracciglia

eye-catching /'aɪkætʃɪŋ/ *adj* che attira l'attenzione

eye contact *n* **avoid eye contact with somebody** evitare di incrociare lo sguardo di qualcuno; **try to make eye contact with somebody** tentare di incrociare lo sguardo di qualcuno

eyedrops *n pl* collirio *m*

eyeful /'aɪfʊl/ *n* **get an** ~ (of something) avere gli occhi pieni (di qualcosa); fam (good look) lustrarsi la vista

eyeglass *n* (monocle) monocolo *m*

eyeglasses *n pl* Am occhiali *mpl* [da vista]

eyelash *n* ciglio *m* (*pl* ciglia *f*)

eyelet /'aɪlɪt/ *n* occhiello *m*

eye-level *adj* ‹*grill, shelf*› all'altezza degli occhi

eyelid *n* palpebra *f*

eye liner *n* eye liner *m inv*

eye make-up *n* trucco *m* per gli occhi

eye-opener *n* rivelazione *f*

eyepatch *n* benda *f* per gli occhi

eye-shade *n* visiera *f*

eyeshadow *n* ombretto *m*

eyesight *n* vista *f*

eyesore *n* fam pugno *m* nell'occhio

eye strain *n* affaticamento *m* degli occhi

eye test *n* esame *m* della vista

eyewash *n* bagno *m* oculare; fig (nonsense) fumo *m* negli occhi

eyewitness *n* testimone *mf* oculare

eyrie /'ɪərɪ/ *n* nido *m* d'aquila

e-zine /'iːziːn/ *n* Comput e-zine *f inv*

e

Ff

F *abbr* (**Fahrenheit**) F

f, F /ef/ *n* (letter) f, F *f inv*; Mus fa *m inv*

FA *n abbr* Br (**Football Association**) associazione *f* calcistica britannica, ≈ FIGC *f*

fable /'feɪbl/ *n* favola *f*

fabric /'fæbrɪk/ *n* also fig tessuto *m*

fabricate /'fæbrɪkeɪt/ *vt* fabbricare; inventare ⟨*story*⟩

fabrication /fæbrɪˈkeɪʃn/ *n* invenzione *f*; (manufacture) fabbricazione *f*

fabric softener /sɒfnə(r)/ *n* ammorbidente *m*

fabulous /'fæbjʊləs/ *adj* fam favoloso

façade /fəˈsaːd/ *n* (of building, person) facciata *f*

⚜ **face** /feɪs/ ① *n* faccia *f*, viso *m*; (grimace) smorfia *f*; (surface) faccia *f*; (of clock) quadrante *m*; **pull ~s** far boccacce; **in the ~ of** di fronte a; **on the ~ of it** in apparenza ② *vt* essere di fronte a; (confront) affrontare; **~ north** ⟨*house*⟩ dare a nord; **~ the fact that** arrendersi al fatto che

■ **face up to** *vt* accettare ⟨*facts*⟩; affrontare ⟨*person*⟩

face flannel *n* ≈ guanto *m* di spugna

faceless /'feɪslɪs/ *adj* anonimo

facelift /'feɪslɪft/ *n* plastica *f* facciale

face mask *n* (cosmetic) maschera *f* viso

face pack *n* maschera *f* di bellezza

face powder *n* cipria *f*

face saving *adj* ⟨*plan, solution*⟩ per salvare la faccia

facet /'fæsɪt/ *n* sfaccettatura *f*; fig aspetto *m*

facetious /fəˈsiːʃəs/ *adj* spiritoso; **~ remarks** spiritosaggini *mpl*

face to face ① *adj* ⟨*meeting*⟩ a quattr'occhi ② *adv* ⟨*be seated*⟩ faccia a faccia; **meet somebody ~ to ~** avere un incontro a quattr'occhi con qualcuno; **come ~ to ~ with** trovarsi di fronte a

face value *n* (of money) valore *m* nominale; **take someone/something at ~** fermarsi alle apparenze

facial /'feɪʃl/ ① *adj* facciale ② *n* trattamento *m* di bellezza al viso

facile /'fæsaɪl/ *adj* semplicistico

facilitate /fəˈsɪlɪteɪt/ *vt* rendere possibile; (make easier) facilitare

facilitator /fəˈsɪlɪteɪtə(r)/ *n* mediatore *m*

⚜ **facility** /fəˈsɪlətɪ/ *n* facilità *f*; **facilities** *pl* (of area, in hotel etc) attrezzature *fpl*; **credit facilities** *pl* facilitazioni *fpl* di pagamento

facing /'feɪsɪŋ/ *prep* **~ the sea** ⟨*house*⟩ che dà sul mare; **the person ~ me** la persona di fronte a me

facsimile /fækˈsɪmɪlɪ/ *n* facsimile *m*

⚜ **fact** /fækt/ *n* fatto *m*; **in ~** infatti

fact finding *adj* ⟨*mission, tour, trip*⟩ di inchiesta

faction /'fækʃn/ *n* fazione *f*

factional /'fækʃnəl/ *adj* ⟨*leader, activity*⟩ di una fazione; ⟨*fighting, arguments*⟩ tra fazioni

⚜ **factor** /'fæktə(r)/ *n* fattore *m*

factory /'fæktərɪ/ *n* fabbrica *f*

factory farming *n* allevamento *m* su scala industriale

factory floor *n* (place) reparto *m* produzione; (workers) operai *mpl*

factory inspector *n* verificatore, -trice *mf*

factory made *adj* prodotto in fabbrica

factory shop *n* negozio (*m*) di vendita diretta dalla fabbrica al consumatore

factory unit *n* unità *f inv* di produzione

factory worker *n* operaio, -a *mf*

fact sheet *n* (one issue) prospetto *m* illustrativo; (periodical) bollettino *m* d'informazione

factual /'fæktʃʊəl/ *adj* **be ~** attenersi ai fatti

factually /'fæktʃʊəlɪ/ *adv* ⟨*inaccurate*⟩ dal punto di vista dei fatti

faculty /'fækəltɪ/ *n* facoltà *f inv*

fad /fæd/ *n* capriccio *m*

faddish /'fædɪʃ/ *adj* ⟨*person*⟩ sempre in preda a una nuova mania

fade /feɪd/ *vi* sbiadire; ⟨*sound, light*⟩ affievolirsi; ⟨*flower*⟩ appassire

■ **fade away** *vi* ⟨*sound*⟩ affievolirsi; (dying person) spegnersi

■ **fade in** *vt* cominciare in dissolvenza ⟨*picture*⟩

■ **fade out** *vt* finire in dissolvenza ⟨*picture*⟩

faded /'feɪdɪd/ *adj* ⟨*clothing, carpet, colour*⟩ sbiadito; ⟨*flower, beauty*⟩ appassito; ⟨*glory*⟩ svanito

faeces /'fiːsiːz/ *npl* feci *fpl*

fag /fæg/ *n* (chore) fatica *f*; fam (cigarette) sigaretta *f*; Am sl (homosexual) frocio *m*

fag end *n* fam mozzicone *m* di sigaretta, cicca *f*; (of day, decade, conversation) fine *f*; (of material) scampolo *m*

fagged /fægd/ *adj* **~ out** fam stanco morto

⚜ indicates a very frequent word

faggot /'fægət/ n (meatball) polpetta f di carne; (firewood) fascina f

Fahrenheit /'færənhaɪt/ adj Fahrenheit

✱ **fail** /feɪl/ ① n without ~ senz'altro

② vi ‹attempt› fallire; ‹eyesight, memory› indebolirsi; ‹engine, machine› guastarsi; ‹marriage› andare a rotoli; (in exam) essere bocciato; ~ **to do something** non fare qualcosa; **I tried but I** ~ed ho provato ma non ci sono riuscito; **a** ~**ed politician** un politico fallito

③ vt non superare ‹exam›; bocciare ‹candidate›; (disappoint) deludere; **words** ~ **me** mi mancano le parole; **unless my memory** ~**s me** se la memoria non mi tradisce

failing /'feɪlɪŋ/ ① n difetto m

② prep ~ **that** altrimenti

fail-safe adj ‹device, system› di sicurezza

✱ **failure** /'feɪljə(r)/ n fallimento m; (mechanical) guasto m; (person) incapace mf

faint /feɪnt/ ① adj leggero; ‹memory› vago; **feel** ~ sentirsi mancare

② n svenimento m

③ vi svenire

faint-hearted /-'hɑːtɪd/ adj timido

fainting fit /'feɪntɪŋ/ n svenimento m

faintly /'feɪntlɪ/ adv (slightly) leggermente

faintness /'feɪntnɪs/ n (physical) debolezza f

fair¹ /feə(r)/ n fiera f

✱ **fair**² ① adj ‹hair, person› biondo; ‹skin› chiaro; ‹weather› bello; (just) giusto; (quite good) discreto; Sch abbastanza bene; **a** ~ **amount** abbastanza

② adv **play** ~ fare un gioco pulito

fair copy n bella copia f

fairground /'feəgraʊnd/ n luna park m inv

fair-haired adj dai capelli chiari

✱ **fairly** /'feəlɪ/ adv con giustizia; (rather) discretamente, abbastanza

fair-minded /feə'maɪndɪd/ adj equo

fairness /'feənɪs/ n giustizia f

fair play n fair play m inv

fair skinned /-'skɪnd/ adj di carnagione chiara

fair trade n commercio m equo e solidale, commercio m equosolidale

fairway n Naut via f d'acqua navigabile; (in golf) fairway m inv

fair weather friend n pej amico m finché tutto va bene

fairy /'feərɪ/ n fata f; **good** ~ fata [buona]; **wicked** ~ strega f

fairy godmother n fata f buona

fairy lights npl Br lampadine fpl colorate

fairy story, fairy-tale n fiaba f

✱ **faith** /feɪθ/ n fede f; (trust) fiducia f; **in good/ bad** ~ in buona/mala fede

faithful /'feɪθfl/ adj fedele

faithfully /'feɪθfʊlɪ/ adv fedelmente; **yours** ~ distinti saluti

faithfulness /'feɪθfʊlnɪs/ n fedeltà f

faith-healer /-hiːlə(r)/ n guaritore, -trice mf

faith healing n guarigione f per fede

faithless /'feɪθlɪs/ adj ‹friend, servant› sleale; ‹husband› infedele

faith school n insegnamento m religioso

fake /feɪk/ ① adj falso

② n falsificazione f; (person) impostore m

③ vt falsificare; (pretend) fingere

falcon /'fɔːlkən/ n falcone m

Falklands /'fɔːkləndz/ npl le isole Falkland, le isole Malvine

✱ **fall** /fɔːl/ ① n caduta f; (in prices) ribasso m; Am (autumn) autunno m; **have a** ~ fare una caduta

② vi (pt **fell**, pp **fallen**) cadere; ‹night› scendere; ~ **in love** innamorarsi

■ **fall about** vi (with laughter) morire dal ridere

■ **fall apart** vi ‹table, car, house› cadere a pezzi; ‹shoes› rompersi; fig ‹person› crollare

■ **fall back** vi indietreggiare; ‹army› ritirarsi

■ **fall back on** vt ritornare su

■ **fall behind** vi rimanere indietro; ~ **behind with** Br or in Am essere indietro con ‹work, project, payments›

■ **fall down** vi cadere; ‹building› crollare

■ **fall for** vt fam innamorarsi di ‹person›; cascarci ‹something, trick›

■ **fall in** vi caderci dentro; (collapse) crollare; Mil mettersi in riga; ~ **in with** concordare con ‹suggestion, plan›

■ **fall off** vi cadere; (diminish) diminuire

■ **fall open** vi ‹book› aprirsi (cadendo); ‹robe› aprirsi

■ **fall out** vi (quarrel) litigare; **his hair is** ~**ing out** perde i capelli

■ **fall over** vt cadere

■ **fall through** vt ‹plan› andare a monte

fallacious /fə'leɪʃəs/ adj fallace

fallacy /'fæləsɪ/ n errore m

fallible /'fæləbl/ adj fallibile

Fallopian tube /fə'ləʊpɪən/ n tromba f di Falloppio

fallout /'fɔːlaʊt/ n pioggia f radioattiva

fallout shelter n rifugio m antiatomico

fallow /'fæləʊ/ adj lie ~ essere a maggese

false /fɔːls/ adj falso

false alarm n falso allarme m

false bottom n doppio fondo m

falsehood /'fɔːlshʊd/ n menzogna f

falsely /'fɔːlslɪ/ adv falsamente

falseness /'fɔːlsnɪs/ n falsità f

false pretences npl under ~ sotto false spoglie; Jur con la frode

false start n Sport falsa partenza f

false teeth npl dentiera f

falsetto /fɔːl'setəʊ/ ① n (voice) falsetto m inv

② adj in falsetto

falsification /ˌfɔːlsɪfɪˈkeɪʃn/ n (of document, figures) falsificazione f; (of truth, facts) deformazione f

falsify /ˈfɔːlsɪfaɪ/ vt (pt/pp **-ied**) falsificare

falsity /ˈfɔːlsətɪ/ n falsità f

falter /ˈfɔːltə(r)/ vi vacillare; (making speech) esitare

faltering /ˈfɔːltərɪŋ/ adj ‹economy› vacillante; ‹voice› esitante

fame /feɪm/ n fama f

famed /feɪmd/ adj rinomato

◆ **familiar** /fəˈmɪljə(r)/ adj familiare; **be ～ with** (know) conoscere; **become too ～** prendersi troppe confidenze

familiarity /fəˌmɪlɪˈærətɪ/ n familiarità f

familiarize /fəˈmɪlɪəraɪz/ vt familiarizzare; **～ oneself with something** familiarizzarsi con qualcosa

◆ **family** /ˈfæməlɪ/ n famiglia f

family allowance n assegni mpl familiari

family circle n (group) cerchia f familiare; Am Theat seconda galleria f

family doctor n medico m di famiglia

family life n vita f familiare

family name n cognome m

family planning n pianificazione f familiare

family tree n albero m genealogico

family unit n nucleo m familiare

famine /ˈfæmɪn/ n carestia f

famished /ˈfæmɪʃt/ adj **be ～** fam avere una fame da lupo

◆ **famous** /ˈfeɪməs/ adj famoso

fan¹ /fæn/ [1] n ventilatore m; (handheld) ventaglio m
[2] vt (pt/pp **fanned**) far vento a; **～ oneself** sventagliarsi; fig **～ the flames** soffiare sul fuoco
■ **fan out** vi spiegarsi a ventaglio

◆ **fan²** n (admirer) ammiratore, -trice mf, fan mf; Sport tifoso m; (of Verdi etc) appassionato, -a mf

fanatic /fəˈnætɪk/ n fanatico, -a mf

fanatical /fəˈnætɪkl/ adj fanatico

fanatically /fəˈnætɪklɪ/ adv con fanatismo

fanaticism /fəˈnætɪsɪzm/ n fanatismo m

fan belt n cinghia f per ventilatore

fanciful /ˈfænsɪfl/ adj fantasioso

fancy /ˈfænsɪ/ [1] n fantasia f; **I've taken a real ～ to him** mi è molto simpatico; **as the ～ takes you** come ti pare
[2] adj fantasia inv
[3] vt (believe) credere; fam (want) aver voglia di; **he fancies you** fam gli piaci; **～ that!** ma guarda un po'!

fancy dress n costume m

fancy dress party n festa f mascherata

◆ indicates a very frequent word

fanfare /ˈfænfeə(r)/ n fanfara f

fang /fæŋ/ n zanna f; (of snake) dente m

fan heater n termoventilatore m

fanlight n lunetta f

fan mail n posta f dei fan

fantasize /ˈfæntəsaɪz/ vi fantasticare

fantastic /fænˈtæstɪk/ adj fantastico

fantasy /ˈfæntəsɪ/ n fantasia f

fanzine /ˈfænziːn/ n fanzine f inv

FAQ abbr (**frequently asked questions**) FAQ fpl

◆ **far** /fɑː(r)/ [1] adv lontano; (much) molto; **by ～ di** gran lunga; **～ away** lontano; **as ～ as the church** fino alla chiesa; **how ～ is it from here?** quanto dista da qui?; **as ～ as I know** per quanto io sappia
[2] adj ‹end, side› altro; **the F～ East** l'Estremo Oriente m; **in the ～ distance** in lontananza

faraway /ˈfɑːrəweɪ/ adj ‹land› lontano; ‹look› assente

farce /fɑːs/ n farsa f

farcical /ˈfɑːsɪkl/ adj ridicolo

fare /feə(r)/ n tariffa f; (food) vitto m

fare-dodger /-dɒdʒə(r)/ n passeggero, -a mf senza biglietto

farewell /feəˈwel/ [1] int liter addio!
[2] n addio m; **～ dinner** cena f d'addio

far-fetched /-ˈfetʃt/ adj improbabile

far flung /-ˈflʌŋ/ adj (remote) remoto; (widely distributed) sparpagliato; ‹network› esteso

◆ **farm** /fɑːm/ [1] n fattoria f, azienda f agricola
[2] vi fare l'agricoltore
[3] vt coltivare ‹land›
■ **farm out** vt dare in appalto ‹work›

◆ **farmer** /ˈfɑːmə(r)/ n agricoltore m

farmers' market n vendita (f) diretta dal produttore agricolo al consumatore

farmhand /ˈfɑːmhænd/ n bracciante m

farmhouse /ˈfɑːmhaʊs/ n casa f colonica

farming /ˈfɑːmɪŋ/ n agricoltura f

farm produce n prodotto m agricolo

farmyard /ˈfɑːmjɑːd/ n aia f

far-off adj lontano

far-reaching /-ˈriːtʃɪŋ/ adj ‹programme, plan, proposal› di larga portata; ‹effect, implication, change› notevole

far-sighted /-ˈsaɪtɪd/ adj ‹policy› lungimirante; Am (long-sighted) presbite

fart /fɑːt/ fam [1] n scoreggia f
[2] vi scoreggiare

farther /ˈfɑːðə(r)/ [1] adv più lontano
[2] adj **at the ～ end of** all'altra estremità di

farthest /ˈfɑːðɪst/ adj & adv = FURTHEST

fascia /ˈfeɪʃɪə/ n Br (dashboard) cruscotto m; (for mobile phone) guscio m

fascinate /ˈfæsɪneɪt/ vt affascinare

fascinating /ˈfæsɪneɪtɪŋ/ adj affascinante

fascination /fæsɪ'neɪʃn/ n fascino m

fascism /'fæʃɪzm/ n fascismo m

fascist /'fæʃɪst/ adj & n fascista mf

✔ **fashion** /'fæʃn/ **1** n moda f; (manner) maniera f; **in** ∼ di moda; **out of** ∼ non più di moda
2 vt modellare

fashionable /'fæʃ(ə)nəbl/ adj di moda; **be** ∼ essere alla moda

fashionably /'fæʃ(ə)nəblɪ/ adv alla moda

fashion designer n stilista mf

fashion house n casa f di moda

fashion model n indossatore, -trice mf, modello, -a mf

fashion show n sfilata f di moda

✔ **fast¹** /fɑːst/ **1** adj veloce; ⟨colour⟩ indelebile; **be** ∼ ⟨clock⟩ andare avanti
2 adv velocemente; (firmly) saldamente; ∼**er!** più in fretta!; **be** ∼ **asleep** dormire profondamente

fast² **1** n digiuno m
2 vi digiunare

fasten /'fɑːsn/ **1** vt allacciare; chiudere ⟨window⟩; (stop flapping) mettere un fermo a
2 vi allacciarsi

fastener /'fɑːsnə(r)/, **fastening** /'fɑːsnɪŋ/ n chiusura f

fast food **1** n fast food m inv
2 attrib ⟨chain⟩ di fast food; ∼ **restaurant** n fast food m inv

fast forward **1** n avanzamento m veloce
2 vt far avanzare velocemente ⟨tape⟩
3 attrib ⟨key, button⟩ di avanzamento veloce

fast growing adj in rapida espansione

fastidious /fə'stɪdɪəs/ adj esigente

fast lane n Auto corsia f di sorpasso; **life in the** ∼ fig vita f frenetica

fast-talking adj ⟨salesperson⟩ che raggira con la sua parlantina

fast track n corsia f preferenziale

fast-track /ˌfɑːst'træk, US ˌfæst-/ vt accelerare la carriera di qualcuno

fat /fæt/ **1** adj (**fatter, fattest**) ⟨person, cheque⟩ grasso; fam **that's a** ∼ **lot of use** non serve a un accidente
2 n grasso m

fatal /'feɪtl/ adj mortale; ⟨error⟩ fatale

fatalism /'feɪtəlɪzm/ n fatalismo m

fatalist /'feɪtəlɪst/ n fatalista mf

fatality /fə'tælətɪ/ n morte f

fatally /'feɪtəlɪ/ adv mortalmente

fate /feɪt/ n destino m

fated /'feɪtɪd/ adj destinato; **it was** ∼ era destino

fateful /'feɪtfʊl/ adj fatidico

fat free adj magro

fat-head n fam zuccone, -a mf

✔ **father** /'fɑːðə(r)/ **1** n padre m
2 vt generare ⟨child⟩

Father Christmas Babbo m Natale

father confessor n Relig confessore m

father figure n figura f paterna

fatherhood n paternità f

father-in-law n (pl ∼**s-in-law**) suocero m

fatherland n patria f

fatherly /'fɑːðəlɪ/ adj paterno

Father's Day /'fɑːðəz/ n la festa del papà

fathom /'fæðəm/ **1** n Naut braccio m
2 vt ∼ **[out]** comprendere

fatigue /fə'tiːg/ **1** n fatica f
2 vt affaticare

fatness /'fætnɪs/ n grassezza f

fatten /'fætn/ vt ingrassare ⟨animal⟩

fattening /'fætnɪŋ/ adj **cream is** ∼ la panna fa ingrassare

fatty /'fætɪ/ **1** adj grasso
2 n fam ciccione, -a mf

fatuous /'fætjʊəs/ adj fatuo

faucet /'fɔːsɪt/ n Am rubinetto m

✔ **fault** /fɔːlt/ **1** n difetto m; Geol faglia f; Tennis fallo m; **be at** ∼ avere torto; **find** ∼ **with** trovare da ridire su; **it's your** ∼ è colpa tua
2 vt criticare

fault-finding /'fɔːltfaɪndɪŋ/ **1** n (of person) atteggiamento m ipercritico; Techn localizzazione f del guasto
2 adj ⟨attitude⟩ da criticone; ⟨person⟩ ipercritico

faultless /'fɔːltlɪs/ adj impeccabile

faultlessly /'fɔːltlɪslɪ/ adv impeccabilmente

faulty /'fɔːltɪ/ adj difettoso

fauna /'fɔːnə/ n fauna f

faux pas /fəʊ'pɑː/ n gaffe f inv

✔ **favour** /'feɪvə(r)/ **1** n favore m; **be in** ∼ **of something** essere a favore di qualcosa; **do somebody a** ∼ fare un piacere a qualcuno
2 vt (prefer) preferire

favourable /'feɪv(ə)rəbl/ adj favorevole

favourably /'feɪv(ə)rəblɪ/ adv favorevolmente

✔ **favourite** /'feɪv(ə)rɪt/ **1** adj preferito
2 n preferito, -a mf; Sport favorito, -a mf

favouritism /'feɪv(ə)rɪtɪzm/ n favoritismo m

fawn /fɔːn/ **1** adj fulvo
2 n (animal) cerbiatto m

fax /fæks/ **1** n (document, machine) fax m inv; **by** ∼ per fax
2 vt faxare

fax machine n fax m inv

fax-modem n fax-modem m inv

fax number n numero m di fax

faze /feɪz/ vt fam scompaginare

FBI *n abbr* Am (**Federal Bureau of Investigation**) FBI *m*

FC *abbr* (**football club**) FC

✔ **fear** /fɪə(r)/ **1** *n* paura *f*; **no ~!** fam vai tranquillo!
  2 *vt* temere
  3 *vi* **~ for something** temere per qualcosa

fearful /ˈfɪəfl/ *adj* pauroso; (awful) terribile

fearless /ˈfɪəlɪs/ *adj* impavido

fearlessly /ˈfɪəlɪslɪ/ *adv* senza paura

fearsome /ˈfɪəsəm/ *adj* spaventoso

feasibility /fiːzɪˈbɪlətɪ/ *n* praticabilità *f*

feasible /ˈfiːzəbl/ *adj* fattibile; (possible) probabile

feast /fiːst/ **1** *n* festa *f*; (banquet) banchetto *m*
  2 *vi* banchettare
  ■ **feast on** *vt* gedersi

feat /fiːt/ *n* impresa *f*

feather /ˈfeðə(r)/ *n* piuma *f*; **you could have knocked me down with a ~** sono rimasto di sasso

feather-brained /-breɪnd/ *adj* che non ha un briciolo di cervello

feather duster *n* piumino *m* (*per spolverare*)

featherweight *n* peso *m* piuma *inv*

✔ **feature** /ˈfiːtʃə(r)/ **1** *n* (quality) caratteristica *f*; Journ articolo *m*; **~s** *pl* (of face) lineamenti *mpl*
  2 *vt* ⟨*film*⟩ avere come protagonista
  3 *vi* (on a list etc) comparire

feature film *n* lungometraggio *m*

feature length film *n* lungometraggio *m*

✔ **February** /ˈfebrʊərɪ/ *n* febbraio *m*

feces /ˈfiːsiːz/ *npl* feci *fpl*

feckless /ˈfeklɪs/ *adj* inetto

fecund /ˈfekənd/ *adj* fecondo

fed /fed/ **1** ▶ FEED
  2 *adj* be **~ up** fam essere stufo (**with** di)

✔ **federal** /ˈfed(ə)rəl/ *adj* federale

federalist /ˈfed(ə)rəlɪst/ *n & adj* federalista *mf*

Federal Republic of Germany *n* Repubblica *f* Federale Tedesca

federate /ˈfed(ə)rət/ *adj* federato

federation /fedəˈreɪʃn/ *n* federazione *f*

✔ **fee** /fiː/ *n* tariffa *f*; (lawyer's, doctor's) onorario *m*; (for membership, school) quota *f*

feeble /ˈfiːbl/ *adj* debole; ⟨*excuse*⟩ fiacco

feeble minded /-ˈmaɪndɪd/ *adj* deficiente

feebleness /ˈfiːblnɪs/ *n* debolezza *f*

✔ **feed** /fiːd/ **1** *n* mangiare *m*; (for baby) pappa *f*; **five ~s a day** cinque pasti al giorno
  2 *vt* (*pt/pp* **fed**) dar da mangiare a ⟨*animal*⟩; (support) nutrire; **~ something into something** inserire qualcosa in qualcosa;

~ **paper into the printer** alimentare la stampante con fogli
  3 *vi* mangiare
  ■ **feed up** *vt* ingrassare ⟨*somebody*⟩

feedback /ˈfiːdbæk/ *n* controreazione *f*; (of information) reazione *f*, feedback *m*

feeder /ˈfiːdə(r)/ *n* (for printer, photocopier) mettifoglio *m inv*; Br (bib) bavaglino *m*; (road) raccordo *m*

feeding bottle /ˈfiːdɪŋ/ *n* Br biberon *m inv*

feeding time *n* (in zoo) l'ora *f* del pasto degli animali

✔ **feel** /fiːl/ *v* (*pt/pp* **felt**) **1** *vt* sentire; (experience) provare; (think) pensare; (touch: searching) tastare; (touch: for texture) toccare
  2 *vi* **~ soft/hard** essere duro/morbido al tatto; **~ hot/hungry** aver caldo/fame; **~ ill** sentirsi male; **I don't ~ like it** non ne ho voglia; **how do you ~ about it?** (opinion) che te ne pare?; **it doesn't ~ right** non mi sembra giusto
  ■ **feel for** *vt* (feel sympathy for) dispiacersi per
  ■ **feel up to:** *vt* **~ up to doing something** sentirsi in grado di fare qualcosa; **I don't ~ up to it** non me la sento

feeler /ˈfiːlə(r)/ *n* (of animal) antenna *f*; **put out ~s** fig tastare il terreno

feel-good factor *n* sensazione *f* di benessere

✔ **feeling** /ˈfiːlɪŋ/ *n* sentimento *m*; (awareness) sensazione *f*

fee paying *adj* ⟨*school*⟩ a pagamento, privato; ⟨*parent, pupil*⟩ che paga l'iscrizione (*a una scuola privata*)

feet /fiːt/ ▶ FOOT

feign /feɪn/ *vt* simulare

feint /feɪnt/ *n* finta *f*

feisty /ˈfaɪstɪ/ *adj* Am (quarrelsome) stizzoso; fam (lively) esuberante

felicitous /fəˈlɪsɪtəs/ *adj* felice

feline /ˈfiːlaɪn/ *adj* felino

fell¹ /fel/ *vt* (knock down) abbattere

fell² ▶ FALL

✔ **fellow** /ˈfeləʊ/ *n* (of society) socio *m*; fam (man) tipo *m*

fellow citizen *n* concittadino, -a *mf*

fellow countryman *n* compatriota *m*

fellow men *npl* prossimi *mpl*

fellowship /ˈfeləʊʃɪp/ *n* cameratismo *m*; (group) associazione *f*; Univ incarico *m* di ricercatore, -trice *mf*

fellow traveller *n* compagno, -a *mf* di viaggio; Pol, fig compagno, -a *mf* di strada

felon /ˈfelən/ *n* Jur criminale *mf*

felony /ˈfelənɪ/ *n* delitto *m*

felt¹ /felt/ ▶ FEEL

felt² *n* feltro *m*

felt-tipped pen /-tɪptˈpen/ *n* pennarello *m*

✔ **female** /ˈfiːmeɪl/ **1** *adj* femminile; **the ~ antelope** l'antilope femmina
  2 *n* femmina *f*

✔ indicates a very frequent word

feminine /'femɪnɪn/ ① *adj* femminile
② *n* Gram femminile *m*

femininity /femɪ'nɪnəti/ *n* femminilità *f*

feminist /'femɪnɪst/ *adj & n* femminista *mf*

fen /fen/ *n* zona *f* paludosa

fence /fens/ ① *n* recinto *m*; fam (person)
ricettatore *m*
② *vi* Sport tirar di scherma

■ **fence in** *vt* chiudere in un recinto

fencer /'fensə(r)/ *n* schermidore *m*

fencing /'fensɪŋ/ *n* steccato *m*; Sport
scherma *f*

fend /fend/ *vi* ~ **for oneself** badare a se
stesso

■ **fend off** *vt* parare; difendersi da ‹criticisms›

fender /'fendə(r)/ *n* parafuoco *m inv*; Naut
parabordo *m*; Am (on car) parafango *m*

fennel /'fenl/ *n* finocchio *m*

ferment[1] /'fɜ:ment/ *n* fermento *m*

ferment[2] /fə'ment/ ① *vi* fermentare
② *vt* far fermentare

fermentation /fɜ:men'teɪʃn/ *n*
fermentazione *f*

fern /fɜ:n/ *n* felce *f*

ferocious /fə'rəʊʃəs/ *adj* feroce

ferocity /fə'rɒsəti/ *n* ferocia *f*

ferret /'ferɪt/ *n* furetto *m*

■ **ferret about** *vi* curiosare; ~ **about in**
curiosare in

■ **ferret out** *vt* scovare

ferrous /'ferəs/ *adj* ferroso

ferry /'feri/ ① *n* traghetto *m*
② *vt* (*pt/pp* **-ied**) traghettare

ferryman /'feriмən/ *n* traghettatore *m*

fertile /'fɜ:taɪl/ *adj* fertile

fertility /fə'tɪləti/ *n* fertilità *f*

fertility drug *n* farmaco *m* contro la
sterilità

fertility treatment *n* cura *f* della
fertilità

fertilize /'fɜ:tɪlaɪz/ *vt* fertilizzare ‹land,
ovum›

fertilizer /'fɜ:tɪlaɪzə(r)/ *n* fertilizzante *m*

fervent /'fɜ:vənt/ *adj* fervente

fervour /'fɜ:və(r)/ *n* fervore *m*

fester /'festə(r)/ *vi* suppurare

ⷮ **festival** /'festɪvl/ *n* Mus, Theat festival *m*;
Relig festa *f*

festive /'festɪv/ *adj* festivo; ~ **season**
periodo *m* delle feste natalizie

festivities /fe'stɪvətɪz/ *npl* festeggiamenti
mpl

festoon /fe'stu:n/ *vt* ~ **with** ornare di

fetch /fetʃ/ *vt* andare/venire a prendere;
(be sold for) raggiungere [il prezzo di]

fetching /'fetʃɪŋ/ *adj* attraente

fête /feɪt/ ① *n* festa *f*
② *vt* festeggiare

fetid /'fetɪd/ *adj* fetido

fetish /'fetɪʃ/ *n* feticcio *m*

fetter /'fetə(r)/ *vt* incatenare

fettle /'fetl/ *n* in fine ~ in buona forma

fetus /'fi:təs/ *n* (*pl* **-tuses**) feto *m*

feud /fju:d/ *n* faida *f*

feudal /'fju:dl/ *adj* feudale

fever /'fi:və(r)/ *n* febbre *f*

fevered /'fi:vəd/ *adj* ‹brow› febbricitante;
‹imagination› febbrile

feverish /'fi:vərɪʃ/ *adj* febbricitante; fig
febbrile

fever pitch *n* bring a crowd to ~ esaltare
la folla

ⷮ **few** /fju:/ ① *adj* pochi; every ~ **days**
ogni due o tre giorni; a ~ **people** alcuni;
~ **people know that** poche persone lo sanno;
~er reservations meno prenotazioni; the
~est number il numero più basso
② *pron* pochi; ~ **of us** pochi di noi; a ~
alcuni; quite a ~ parecchi; ~er than last
year meno dell'anno scorso

fez /fez/ *n* fez *m inv*

fiancé /fi'ɒnseɪ/ *n* fidanzato *m*

fiancée /fi'ɒnseɪ/ *n* fidanzata *f*

fiasco /fi'æskəʊ/ *n* fiasco *m*

fib /fɪb/ *n* storia *f*; tell a ~ raccontare una
storia

fibber /'fɪbə(r)/ *n* fam contaballe *mf inv*

fibre /'faɪbə(r)/ *n* fibra *f*

fibreglass ① *n* fibra *f* di vetro
② *attrib* in fibra di vetro

fibre optic *adj* ‹cable› a fibre ottiche

fibre optics *n* fibra *f* ottica

fibroid /'faɪbrɔɪd/ ① *n* fibroma *m*
② *adj* fibroso

fibula /'fɪbjʊla/ *n* Anat perone *m*

fiche /fi:ʃ/ *n* microscheda *f*

fickle /'fɪkl/ *adj* incostante

fiction /'fɪkʃn/ *n* [works of] ~ narrativa *f*;
(fabrication) finzione *f*

fictional /'fɪkʃənəl/ *adj* immaginario

fictionalize /'fɪkʃənəlaɪz/ *vt* romanzare

fictitious /fɪk'tɪʃəs/ *adj* fittizio

fiddle /'fɪdl/ ① *n* fam violino *m*; (cheating)
imbroglio *m*
② *vi* gingillarsi (with con)
③ *vt* fam truccare ‹accounts›

fiddly /'fɪdlɪ/ *adj* intricato

fidelity /fɪ'delətɪ/ *n* fedeltà *f*

fidget /'fɪdʒɪt/ *vi* agitarsi

fidgety /'fɪdʒətɪ/ *adj* agitato

ⷮ **field** /fi:ld/ *n* campo *m*

field day *n* have a ~ ‹press, critics›
godersela; (make money) fare affari d'oro

fielder /'fi:ldə(r)/ *n* Sport esterno *m*

field events *npl* atletica *fsg* leggera

field glasses *npl* binocolo *msg*

Field Marshal *n* feldmaresciallo *m*

field mouse *n* topo *m* campagnolo

field trip *n* gita *f* didattica

fieldwork *n* ricerche *fpl* sul terreno

fiend /fiːnd/ *n* demonio *m*

fiendish /ˈfiːndɪʃ/ *adj* diabolico

fierce /fɪəs/ *adj* feroce

fiercely /ˈfɪəslɪ/ *adv* ferocemente

fierceness /ˈfɪəsnɪs/ *n* ferocia *f*

fiery /ˈfaɪərɪ/ *adj* (**-ier, -iest**) focoso

fiesta /frˈestə/ *n* sagra *f*

fife /faɪf/ *n* piffero *m*

fifteen /fɪftiːn/ *adj & n* quindici *m*

fifteenth /fɪfˈtiːnθ/ *adj & n* quindicesimo, -a *mf*

fifth /fɪfθ/ *adj & n* quinto, -a *mf*

fifties /ˈfɪftɪz/ *npl* (period) the ~ gli anni Cinquanta *mpl*; (age) cinquant'anni *mpl*

fiftieth /ˈfɪftɪɪθ/ *adj & n* cinquantesimo, -a *mf*

fifty /ˈfɪftɪ/ *adj & n* cinquanta *m*

fifty-fifty ⊡ *adj* have a ~ chance avere una probabilità su due
　⊡ *adv* go ~ fare [a] metà e metà; split something ~ dividersi qualcosa a metà

fig /fɪg/ *n* fico *m*

fig. *abbr* (**figure**) fig.

✓ **fight** /faɪt/ ⊡ *n* lotta *f*; (brawl) zuffa *f*; (argument) litigio *m*; (boxing) incontro *m*
　⊡ *vt* (*pt/pp* **fought**) also fig combattere
　③ *vi* combattere; (brawl) azzuffarsi; (argue) litigare
　■ **fight back** ⊡ *vi* reagire
　⊡ *vt* frenare ‹tears›
　■ **fight for** *vt* lottare per ‹freedom, independence›
　■ **fight off** *vt* combattere ‹cold›

fighter /ˈfaɪtə(r)/ *n* combattente *mf*; Aeron caccia *m inv*; he's a ~ ha uno spirito combattivo

fighter-bomber *n* cacciabombardiere *m*

fighter pilot *n* pilota *m* di cacciabombardiere

fighting /ˈfaɪtɪŋ/ *n* combattimento *m*

fighting chance *n* have a ~ avere buone probabilità

fighting fit *adj* in piena forma

figment /ˈfɪgmənt/ *n* it's a ~ of your imagination questo è tutta una tua invenzione

fig tree *n* fico *m*

figurative /ˈfɪgərətɪv/ *adj* ‹sense› figurato; ‹art› figurativo

figuratively /ˈfɪgərətɪvlɪ/ *adv* ‹use› in senso figurato

✓ **figure** /ˈfɪgə(r)/ ⊡ *n* (digit) cifra *f*; (carving, sculpture, illustration, form) figura *f*; (body shape) linea *f*; ~ **of speech** modo *m* di dire
　⊡ *vi* (appear) figurare

③ *vt* Am (think) pensare
■ **figure out** *vt* dedurre; capire ‹person›

figurehead *n* figura *f* simbolica

figure of speech *n* modo *m* di dire; (literary device) figura *f* retorica

figure skating *n* pattinaggio *m* artistico

figurine /ˈfɪgəriːn/ *n* statuetta *f*

Fiji /fiːˈdʒiː/ *n* Figi *fpl*

filament /ˈfɪləmənt/ *n* filamento *m*

filch /fɪltʃ/ *vt* fam rubacchiare

✓ **file¹** /faɪl/ ⊡ *n* scheda *f*; (set of documents) incartamento *m*; (folder) cartellina *f*; Comput file *m inv*
　⊡ *vt* archiviare ‹documents›

file² *n* (line) fila *f*; in single ~ in fila

file³ ⊡ *n* Techn lima *f*
　⊡ *vt* limare

file cabinet *n* Am = FILING CABINET

file extension *n* Comput estensione *f* del file

file manager *n* Comput file manager *m inv*

filename *n* Comput nome *m* del file

file sharing *n* file sharing *m*

file transfer protocol *n* Comput protocollo *m* per il trasferimento di file

filial /ˈfɪlɪəl/ *adj* filiale

filibuster /ˈfɪlɪbʌstə(r)/ *n* ostruzionismo *m* parlamentare

filigree /ˈfɪlɪgriː/ *n* filigrana *f*

filing /ˈfaɪlɪŋ/ *n* archiviazione *f*

filing cabinet *n* schedario *m*, classificatore *m*

filing card *n* scheda *f*

filing clerk *n* archivista *mf*

filings /ˈfaɪlɪŋz/ *npl* limatura *fsg*

filing system *n* sistema *m* di classificazione, sistema *m* di archivio

✓ **fill** /fɪl/ ⊡ *n* eat one's ~ mangiare a sazietà
　⊡ *vt* riempire; otturare ‹tooth›
　③ *vi* riempirsi
　■ **fill in** *vt* compilare ‹form›
　■ **fill in for sb** *vt* rimpiazzare qualcuno
　■ **fill in on**: *vt* ~ somebody in on something mettere qualcuno al corrente di qualcosa
　■ **fill out** *vt* compilare ‹form›
　■ **fill up** ⊡ *vi* ‹room, tank› riempirsi; Auto far il pieno
　⊡ *vt* riempire

filler /ˈfɪlə(r)/ *n* mastice *m*

fillet /ˈfɪlɪt/ ⊡ *n* filetto *m*
　⊡ *vt* (*pt/pp* **filleted**) disossare

fillet steak *n* bistecca *f* di filetto

fill in *n* fam (replacement) rimpiazzo *m*

filling /ˈfɪlɪŋ/ *n* Culin ripieno *m*; (of tooth) piombatura *f*

filling station *n* stazione *f* di rifornimento

filly /ˈfɪlɪ/ *n* puledra *f*

✓ indicates a very frequent word

⚲ **film** /fɪlm/ **1** *n* Cinema film *m inv*; Phot pellicola *f*; **[cling]** ~ pellicola *f* per alimenti **2** *vt/i* filmare

film buff *n* cinefilo, -a *mf*

film festival *n* festival *m* cinematografico

film-goer /ˈfɪlmɡəʊə(r)/ *n* Br frequentatore, -trice *mf* di cinema

film industry *n* industria *f* cinematografica

filming /ˈfɪlmɪŋ/ *n* riprese *fpl*

filmset *n* allestimento *m* scenico

film star *n* star *f inv*, divo, -a *mf*

film studio *n* studio *m* cinematografico

filmy /ˈfɪlmɪ/ *adj* (thin) ‹fabric, screen› trasparente; (thin) sottilissimo

filter /ˈfɪltə(r)/ **1** *n* filtro *m* **2** *vt* filtrare

■ **filter through** *vi* ‹news› trapelare

filter cigarette *n* sigaretta *f* con filtro

filter coffee *n* (ground coffee) caffè *m* macinato per filtro; (cup of coffee) caffè *m inv* fatto con il filtro

filter-paper *n* carta *f* da filtro

filter tip *n* filtro *m*; (cigarette) sigaretta *f* col filtro

filth /fɪlθ/ *n* sudiciume *m*

filthy /ˈfɪlθɪ/ *adj* (-ier, -iest) sudicio; ‹language› sconcio

filthy rich *adj* fam ricco sfondato

fin /fɪn/ *n* pinna *f*

⚲ **final** /ˈfaɪnl/ **1** *adj* finale; (conclusive) decisivo **2** *n* Sport finale *f*, ~s *pl* Univ esami *mpl* finali

finale /fɪˈnɑːlɪ/ *n* finale *m*

finalist /ˈfaɪnəlɪst/ *n* finalista *mf*

finality /faɪˈnælətɪ/ *n* finalità *f*

finalize /ˈfaɪnəlaɪz/ *vt* mettere a punto ‹text›; definire ‹agreement›

⚲ **finally** /ˈfaɪnəlɪ/ *adv* (at last) finalmente; (at the end) alla fine; (to conclude) per finire

finance /ˈfaɪnæns/ **1** *n* finanza *f* **2** *vt* finanziare

finance company, **finance house** *n* società *f* finanziaria

finance director *n* direttore, -trice *mf* finanziario, -a

finances *npl* finanze *fpl*

⚲ **financial** /faɪˈnænʃl/ *adj* finanziario

financially /faɪˈnænʃəlɪ/ *adv* finanziariamente

financial year *n* Br esercizio *m* [finanziario]

finch /fɪntʃ/ *n* fringuello *m*

⚲ **find** /faɪnd/ **1** *n* scoperta *f* **2** *vt* (*pt/pp* **found**) trovare; (establish) scoprire; ~ **somebody guilty** Jur dichiarare qualcuno colpevole

■ **find out** **1** *vt* scoprire

2 *vi* (enquire) informarsi

⚲ **findings** /ˈfaɪndɪŋz/ *npl* conclusioni *fpl*

⚲ **fine¹** /faɪn/ **1** *n* (penalty) multa *f* **2** *vt* multare

⚲ **fine²** **1** *adj* bello; (slender) fine; **he's** ~ (in health) sta bene **2** *adv* bene; **that's cutting it** ~ non ci lascia molto tempo **3** *int* [va] bene

fine art *n* belle arti *fpl*

fine arts *npl* belle arti *fpl*

finely /ˈfaɪnlɪ/ *adv* ‹cut› finemente

finery /ˈfaɪnərɪ/ *n* splendore *m*

finesse /fɪˈnes/ *n* finezza *f*

fine-tooth[ed] comb /-tuːθ[t]/ *n* **go over something with a** ~ passare qualcosa al setaccio

fine-tune *vt* mettere a punto

fine tuning *n* messa *f* a punto

⚲ **finger** /ˈfɪŋɡə(r)/ **1** *n* dito *m* (*pl* dita *f*) **2** *vt* tastare

finger bowl *n* lavadita *m inv*

finger hole *n* Mus foro *m*

fingermark *n* ditata *f*

fingernail *n* unghia *f*

finger-paint *vi* dipingere con le dita

fingerprint *n* impronta *f* digitale

fingertip *n* punta *f* del dito; **have something at one's** ~s sapere qualcosa a menadito; (close at hand) avere qualcosa a portata di mano

finicky /ˈfɪnɪkɪ/ *adj* (person) pignolo; ‹task› intricato

⚲ **finish** /ˈfɪnɪʃ/ **1** *n* fine *f*; (finishing line) traguardo *m*; (of product) finitura *f*; **have a good** ~ ‹runner› avere un buon finale **2** *vt* finire; ~ **reading** finire di leggere **3** *vi* finire

■ **finish off** *vt* finire ‹something›; fam (exhaust) sfinire

■ **finish with** *vt* (no longer be using) finire (di adoperare); (end relationship with) lasciare

■ **finish up** *vt* finire ‹drink, meal›

finishing line /ˈfɪnɪʃɪŋlaɪn/ *n* traguardo *m*

finishing touches /ˈtʌtʃɪz/ *npl* ritocchi *mpl*

finite /ˈfaɪnaɪt/ *adj* limitato

Finland /ˈfɪnlənd/ *n* Finlandia *f*

Finn /fɪn/ *n* finlandese *mf*

Finnish /ˈfɪnɪʃ/ **1** *adj* finlandese **2** *n* (language) finnico *m*

fiord /fjɔːd/ *n* fiordo *m*

fir /fɜː(r)/ *n* abete *m*

fir cone *n* pigna *f* (di abete)

⚲ **fire** /ˈfaɪə(r)/ **1** *n* fuoco *m*; (forest, house) incendio *m*; **be on** ~ bruciare; **catch** ~ prendere fuoco; **set** ~ **to** dar fuoco a; **under** ~ sotto il fuoco **2** *vt* cuocere ‹pottery›; sparare ‹shot›; tirare ⋯⟶

⟨gun⟩; fam (dismiss) buttar fuori
③ *vi* sparare (**at a**)

fire alarm *n* allarme *m* antincendio *inv*

firearm *n* arma *f* da fuoco

firebomb /ˈfaɪəbɒm/ ① *n* ordigno *m* incendiario
② *vt* lanciare ordigni incendiari contro ⟨building⟩

fire brigade *n* vigili *mpl* del fuoco

fire door *n* porta *f* antincendio

fire drill *n* esercitazione *f* per l'evacuazione in caso di incendio

fire engine *n* autopompa *f*

fire escape *n* uscita *f* di sicurezza

fire exit *n* uscita *f* di sicurezza

fire extinguisher *n* estintore *m*

firefighter *n* vigile *m* del fuoco

fireguard *n* parafuoco *m* inv

fireman *n* pompiere *m*, vigile *m* del fuoco

fireplace *n* caminetto *m*

fireproof /ˈfaɪəpruːf/ *adj* ⟨door⟩ antincendio; ⟨clothing⟩ ignifugo

fire-retardant /rɪˈtɑːdənt/ *adj* ⟨material⟩ ignifugo

fire service *n* vigili *mpl* del fuoco

fireside *n* **by** *or* **at the** ~ accanto al fuoco

fire station *n* caserma *f* dei pompieri

firewall /ˈfaɪəwɔːl/ *n* Comput firewall *m inv*

firewood *n* legna *f* (**da ardere**)

firework *n* fuoco *m* d'artificio; ~**s** *pl* (display) fuochi *mpl* d'artificio

firing line *n* **be in the** ~ essere sulla linea di tiro

firing squad /ˈfaɪərɪŋ/ *n* plotone *m* d'esecuzione

✧ **firm¹** /fɜːm/ *n* ditta *f*, azienda *f*

firm² *adj* fermo; ⟨soil⟩ compatto; (stable, properly fixed) solido; (resolute) risoluto

firmly /ˈfɜːmlɪ/ *adv* ⟨hold⟩ stretto; ⟨say⟩ con fermezza

✧ **first** /fɜːst/ ① *adj & n* primo, -a *mf*; **at** ~ all'inizio; **who's** ~? chi è il primo?; **from the** ~ [fin] dall'inizio
② *adv* ⟨arrive, leave⟩ per primo; (beforehand) prima; (in listing) prima di tutto, innanzitutto

first aid *n* pronto soccorso *m*

first-aid kit *n* cassetta *f* di pronto soccorso

first-class ① *adj* di prim'ordine; Rail di prima classe
② *adv* ⟨travel⟩ in prima classe

first cousin *n* cugino, -a *mf* di primo grado

first edition *n* prima edizione *f*

first floor *n* primo piano *m*; Am (ground floor) pianterreno *m*

first grade *n* Am prima *f* elementare

firsthand /ˌfɜːstˈhænd/ *adj & adv* di prima mano

firstly /ˈfɜːstlɪ/ *adv* in primo luogo

first name *n* nome *m* di battesimo

first night *n* Theat prima *f*

first-rate *adj* ottimo

first time buyer *n* acquirente *mf* della prima casa

firth /fɜːθ/ *n* foce *f*

fiscal /ˈfɪskəl/ *adj* fiscale

fiscal year *n* Am esercizio *m* finanziario

✧ **fish** /fɪʃ/ ① *n* pesce *m*
② *vt/i* pescare
∎ **fish out** *vt* tirar fuori

fish and chips *n* pesce (*m*) fritto e patatine

fish and chip shop *n* friggitoria (*f*) dove si vende pesce fritto e patatine

fishbone /ˈfɪʃbəʊn/ *n* lisca *f*

fishbowl *n* boccia *f* dei pesci rossi

fisherman /ˈfɪʃəmən/ *n* pescatore *m*

fish farm *n* vivaio *m*

fish finger *n* Br bastoncino *m* di pesce

fishing /ˈfɪʃɪŋ/ *n* pesca *f*

fishing boat *n* peschereccio *m*

fishing rod *n* canna *f* da pesca

fish market *n* mercato *m* del pesce

fishmonger /ˈfɪʃmʌŋɡə(r)/ *n* pescivendolo *m*

fishnet /ˈfɪʃnet/ *adj* ⟨stockings⟩ a rete

fish slice *n* paletta *f* per fritti

fish stick *n* Am bastoncino *m* di pesce

fish tank *n* acquario *m*

fishy /ˈfɪʃɪ/ *adj* fam (suspicious) sospetto

fission /ˈfɪʃn/ *n* Phys fissione *f*

fist /fɪst/ *n* pugno *m*

fistful /ˈfɪstfʊl/ *n* manciata *f*, pugno *m*

fit¹ /fɪt/ *n* (attack) attacco *m*; (of rage) accesso *m*; (of generosity) slancio *m*

fit² *adj* (**fitter, fittest**) (suitable) adatto; (healthy) in buona salute; Sport in forma; **be** ~ **to do something** essere in grado di fare qualcosa; ~ **to eat** buono da mangiare; **keep** ~ tenersi in forma; **do as you see** ~ fai come ritieni meglio

✧ **fit³** ① *n* (of clothes) taglio *m*; **it's a good** ~ ⟨coat etc⟩ ti/le sta bene
② *vi* (*pt/pp* **fitted**) (be the right size) andare bene; **it won't** ~ (no room) non ci sta
③ *vt* (fix) applicare (**to** a); (install) installare; **it doesn't** ~ **me** ⟨coat etc⟩ non mi va bene; ~ **with** fornire di
∎ **fit in** ① *vi* ⟨person⟩ adattarsi; **it won't** ~ **in** (no room) non ci sta
② *vt* (in schedule, vehicle) trovare un buco per

fitful /ˈfɪtfl/ *adj* irregolare

fitfully /ˈfɪtfʊlɪ/ *adv* ⟨sleep⟩ a sprazzi

fitment /ˈfɪtmənt/ *n* ~**s** (in house) impianti *mpl* fissi

---

✧ indicates a very frequent word

fitness /'fɪtnɪs/ *n* (suitability) capacità *f*; [physical] ∼ forma *f*, fitness *m*

fitness programme *n* programma *m* di fitness

fitness video *n* video *m* di fitness

fitted /'fɪtɪd/ *adj* ‹wardrobe› a muro; ‹kitchen, bedroom› componibile; ‹jacket› attillato

fitted carpet *n* moquette *f inv*

fitted cupboard *n* armadio *m* a muro; (smaller) armadietto *m* a muro

fitted kitchen *n* cucina *f* componibile

fitted sheet *n* lenzuolo *m* con angoli

fitter /'fɪtə(r)/ *n* installatore, -trice *mf*

fitting /'fɪtɪŋ/ ⓵ *adj* appropriato
   ⓶ *n* (of clothes) prova *f*; Techn montaggio *m*; ∼s *pl* accessori *mpl*

fitting room *n* camerino *m*

✓ **five** /faɪv/ *adj & n* cinque *m*

five-a-side *n* Br (football) calcio *m* a cinque

fiver /'faɪvə(r)/ *n* fam biglietto *m* da cinque sterline

✓ **fix** /fɪks/ ⓵ *n* sl (drugs) pera *f*; **be in a** ∼ fam essere nei guai
   ⓶ *vt* fissare; (repair) aggiustare; preparare ‹meal›
  ■ **fix up** *vt* fissare ‹meeting›

fixation /fɪk'seɪʃn/ *n* fissazione *f*

fixative /'fɪksətɪv/ *n* fissativo *m*

fixed /'fɪkst/ *adj* fisso

fixed assets *npl* attività *fpl* fisse, immobilizzazioni *fpl*

fixed price *n* prezzo *m* a forfait

fixed-term contract *n* contratto *m* a tempo determinato

fixer /'fɪksə(r)/ *n* Phot fissatore *m*; fam (person) trafficone, -a *mf*

fixture /'fɪkstʃə(r)/ *n* Sport incontro *m*; ∼s **and fittings** impianti *mpl* fissi

fizz /fɪz/ *vi* frizzare

fizzle /'fɪzl/ *vi* ∼ **out** finire in nulla

fizzy /'fɪzɪ/ *adj* gassoso

fizzy drink *n* bibita *f* gassata

fjord /fjɔːd/ *n* fiordo *m*

flab /flæb/ *n* fam ciccia *f* cascante

flabbergasted /'flæbəgɑːstɪd/ *adj* **be** ∼ rimanere a bocca aperta

flabby /'flæbɪ/ *adj* floscio

flag¹ /flæg/ *n* bandiera *f*

flag² *vi* (*pt/pp* **flagged**) cedere
  ■ **flag down** *vt* (*pt/pp* **flagged**) far segno di fermarsi a ‹taxi›

flagellation /flædʒə'leɪʃn/ *n* flagellazione *f*

flagon /'flægən/ *n* bottiglione *m*

flagpole /'flægpəʊl/ *n* asta *f* della bandiera

flagrant /'fleɪgrənt/ *adj* flagrante

flagship /'flægʃɪp/ *n* Naut nave *f* ammiraglia; fig fiore *m* all'occhiello

flagstone /'flægstəʊn/ *n* pietra *f* per lastricato

flail /fleɪl/ ⓵ *n* (for threshing corn etc) correggiato *m*
   ⓶ *vt* battere ‹corn›
  ■ **flail about, flail around** *vi* ‹arms, legs› agitare

flair /fleə(r)/ *n* (skill) talento *m*; (style) stile *m*

flak /flæk/ *n* Mil artiglieria *f* antiaerea; fig fam (criticism) valanga *f* di critiche; **take a lot of** ∼ subire molte critiche

flake /fleɪk/ ⓵ *n* fiocco *m*
   ⓶ *vi* ∼ **[off]** cadere in fiocchi

flaky /'fleɪkɪ/ *adj* a scaglie

flaky pastry *n* pasta *f* sfoglia

flamboyant /flæm'bɔɪənt/ *adj* ‹personality› brillante; ‹tie› sgargiante

flame /fleɪm/ *n* fiamma *f*

flamenco /flə'meŋkəʊ/ *n* flamenco *m*

flamer /'fleɪmə(r)/ *n* Comput flamer *m* (*utente* (*mf*) *email che manda messaggi offensivi*)

flame retardant /rɪtə'dənt/ *adj* ‹substance, chemical ›ignifugo; ‹furniture, fabric› ignifugato

flame-thrower /-θrəʊə(r)/ *n* Mil lanciafiamme *m inv*

flaming /'fleɪmɪŋ/ ⓵ *adj* ‹row› acceso; ‹building› in fiamme
   ⓶ *n* Comput flaming *m inv* (*invio* (*m*) *di messaggi offensivi*)

flamingo /flə'mɪŋgəʊ/ *n* fenicottero *m*

flammable /'flæməbl/ *adj* infiammabile

flan /flæn/ *n* [fruit] ∼ crostata *f*

flange /flændʒ/ *n* (on pipe etc) flangia *f*

flank /flæŋk/ ⓵ *n* fianco *m*
   ⓶ *vt* fiancheggiare

flannel /'flæn(ə)l/ *n* flanella *f*; (for washing) ≈ guanto *m* di spugna

flannelette /flænə'let/ *n* flanella *f* di cotone

flannels /'flæn(ə)lz/ *npl* (trousers) pantaloni *mpl* di flanella

flap /flæp/ ⓵ *n* (of pocket, envelope) risvolto *m*; (of table) ribalta *f*; **in a** ∼ fam in grande agitazione
   ⓶ *vi* (*pt/pp* **flapped**) sbattere; fam agitarsi
   ⓷ *vt* ∼ **its wings** battere le ali

flapjack /'flæpdʒæk/ *n* Br dolcetto (*m*) di fiocchi d'avena; Am frittella *f*

flare /fleə(r)/ *n* fiammata *f*; (device) razzo *m*
  ■ **flare up** *vi* ‹rash› venire fuori; ‹fire› fare una fiammata; ‹person, situation› esplodere

flared /fleəd/ *adj* ‹garment› svasato

flares /fleəz/ *npl* (trousers) pantaloni *mpl* a zampa d'elefante

flash /flæʃ/ ⓵ *n* lampo *m*; **in a** ∼ fam in un attimo
   ⓶ *vi* lampeggiare; ∼ **past** passare come un bolide
                                                   ⋯⟶

3 *vt* lanciare ⟨*smile*⟩; ~ **one's headlights** lampeggiare; ~ **a torch at** puntare una torcia su

■ **flash by** *vi* ⟨*person, years, landscape*⟩ passare come un lampo

flashback *n* scena *f* retrospettiva

flashbulb *n* Phot flash *m inv*

flashcard *n* Sch scheda *f* didattica

flasher /'flæʃə(r)/ *n* Auto lampeggiatore *m*

flash flood *n* alluvione *f* improvvisa

flashgun *n* Phot flash *m inv*

flashing /'flæʃɪŋ/ *adj* ⟨*light*⟩ lampeggiante

flashlight *n* Phot flash *m inv*; Am (torch) torcia *f* [elettrica]

flashpoint *n* (trouble spot) punto *m* caldo; Chem punto *m* di infiammabilità

flashy /'flæʃɪ/ *adj* vistoso

flask /flɑːsk/ *n* fiasco *m*; (vacuum ~) termos *m inv*

flat /flæt/ **1** *adj* (**flatter**, **flattest**) piatto; ⟨*refusal*⟩ reciso; ⟨*beer*⟩ sgassato; ⟨*battery*⟩ scarico; ⟨*tyre*⟩ a terra; **A** ~ Mus la bemolle **2** *n* appartamento *m*; Mus bemolle *m*; (puncture) gomma *f* a terra

flat broke *adj* fam completamente al verde

flat feet *npl* piedi *mpl* piatti

flatfish *n* pesce *m* piatto

flat-footed /-'fʊtɪd/ *adj* be ~ avere i piedi piatti

flat hunting *n* Br **go** ~ andare in cerca di un appartamento

flatly /'flætlɪ/ *adv* ⟨*refuse*⟩ categoricamente

flatmate *n* Br persona (*f*) con cui si divide un appartamento

flat out *adv* ⟨*drive, work*⟩ a tutto gas; **it only does 120 kph** ~ arriva a 120 km all'ora andando a tutta manetta; **go** ~ **for something** mettercela tutta per fare qualcosa

flat racing *n* corse *fpl* piane

flat rate **1** *n* forfait *m inv*; (unitary rate) tariffa *f* unica **2** *attrib* ⟨*fee, tax*⟩ forfettario

flat spin *n* Aeron virata *f* piatta; **be in a** ~ fam essere in fibrillazione

flatten /'flætn/ *vt* appiattire

flatter /'flætə(r)/ *vt* adulare

flattering /'flætərɪŋ/ *adj* ⟨*comments*⟩ lusinghiero; ⟨*colour, dress*⟩ che fa sembrare più bello

flattery /'flætərɪ/ *n* adulazione *f*

flat tyre *n* gomma *f* a terra

flatulence /'flætjʊləns/ *n* flatulenza *f*

flaunt /flɔːnt/ *vt* ostentare

flautist /'flɔːtɪst/ *n* flautista *mf*

flavour /'fleɪvə(r)/ **1** *n* sapore *m* **2** *vt* condire; **chocolate** ~**ed** al sapore di cioccolato

◆ indicates a very frequent word

flavour-enhancer /-ɪnhɑːnsə(r)/ *n* esaltatore *m* dell'aroma

flavouring /'fleɪvərɪŋ/ *n* condimento *m*

flavourless /'fleɪvəlɪs/ *adj* insipido

flaw /flɔː/ *n* difetto *m*

flawed /flɔːd/ *adj* difettoso

flawless /'flɔːlɪs/ *adj* perfetto

flax /flæks/ *n* lino *m*

flaxen /'flæksən/ *adj* ⟨*hair*⟩ biondo platino

flea /fliː/ *n* pulce *f*

flea-bitten /'fliːbɪtən/ *adj* infestato dalle pulci; fig pidocchioso

flea market *n* mercato *m* delle pulci

fleapit *n* Br fam pej pidocchietto *m*

fleck /flek/ *n* macchiolina *f*

fled /fled/ ▶ FLEE

fledg[e]ling /'fledʒlɪŋ/ **1** *n* uccellino *m* (*che ha appena messo le ali*) **2** *attrib* fig ⟨*democracy, enterprise*⟩ giovane; ⟨*party, group*⟩ alle prime armi

flee /fliː/ *vt/i* (*pt/pp* **fled**) fuggire (**from** da)

fleece /fliːs/ **1** *n* pelliccia *f* **2** *vt* fam spennare

fleecy /'fliːsɪ/ *adj* ⟨*lining*⟩ felpato

fleet /fliːt/ *n* flotta *f*; (of cars) parco *m*

fleeting /'fliːtɪŋ/ *adj* **catch a** ~ **glance of something** intravedere qualcosa; **for a** ~ **moment** per un attimo

Flemish /'flemɪʃ/ *adj* fiammingo

flesh /fleʃ/ *n* carne *f*; **in the** ~ in persona; **one's own** ~ **and blood** il proprio sangue

■ **flesh out** *vt* dare più consistenza a ⟨*essay etc*⟩

flesh eating /-iːtɪŋ/ *adj* carnivoro

flesh wound *n* ferita *f* superficiale

fleshy /'fleʃɪ/ *adj* carnoso

flew /fluː/ ▶ FLY²

flex¹ /fleks/ *vt* flettere ⟨*muscle*⟩

flex² *n* Electr filo *m*

flexibility /fleksə'bɪlətɪ/ *n* flessibilità *f*

flexible /'fleksəbl/ *adj* flessibile

flexitime Br, **flextime** Am /'fleks(ɪ)taɪm/ *n* orario *m* flessibile

flick /flɪk/ *vt* dare un buffetto a; ~ **something off something** togliere qualcosa da qualcosa con un colpetto

■ **flick through** *vt* sfogliare

flicker /'flɪkə(r)/ *vi* tremolare

flick knife *n* Br coltello *m* a scatto

flier /'flaɪə(r)/ *n* = FLYER

flight¹ /flaɪt/ *n* (fleeing) fuga *f*; **take** ~ darsi alla fuga

◆ **flight²** *n* (flying) volo *m*; ~ **of stairs** rampa *f*

flight attendant *n* assistente *mf* di volo

flight bag *n* bagaglio *m* a mano

flight deck *n* Aeron cabina *f* di pilotaggio; Naut ponte *m* di volo

flight engineer *n* motorista *mf* di bordo

flight lieutenant n Mil capitano m

flight path n traiettoria f di volo

flight recorder n registratore m di volo

flighty /'flaɪtɪ/ adj (-ier, -iest) frivolo

flimsy /'flɪmzɪ/ adj (-ier, -iest) ‹material› leggero; ‹shelves› poco robusto; ‹excuse› debole

flinch /flɪntʃ/ vi (wince) sussultare; (draw back) ritirarsi; ~ **from a task** fig sottrarsi a un compito

fling /flɪŋ/ **1** n **have a** ~ fam (affair) avere un'avventura

2 vt (pt/pp **flung**) gettare

■ **fling away** vt gettar via

■ **fling open** vt spalancare ‹door, window›

flint /flɪnt/ n pietra f focaia; (for lighter) pietrina f

flip /flɪp/ v (pt/pp **flipped**) **1** vt dare un colpetto a; buttare in aria ‹coin›

2 vi fam uscire dai gangheri; (go mad) impazzire

■ **flip through** vt sfogliare

flip chart n lavagna f a fogli mobili

flip-flop n (sandal) infradito m inv; Comput (device) flip-flop m inv, multivibratore m bistabile; Am (about face) voltafaccia m inv

flippant /'flɪpənt/ adj irriverente

flipper /'flɪpə(r)/ n pinna f

flipping /'flɪpɪŋ/ Br fam **1** adj maledetto

2 adv ‹stupid, painful, cold› maledettamente

flip side n (of record) retro m; fig (other side) rovescio m

flirt /flɜːt/ **1** n civetta f

2 vi flirtare

flirtation /flɜː'teɪʃn/ n flirt m inv

flirtatious /flɜː'teɪʃəs/ adj civettuolo

flit /flɪt/ vi (pt/pp **flitted**) volteggiare

float /fləʊt/ **1** n galleggiante m; (in procession) carro m; (money) riserva f di cassa

2 vi galleggiare; Fin fluttuare

■ **float off** vi ‹boat› andare alla deriva; ‹balloon› volare via

floating /'fləʊtɪŋ/ adj ‹bridge› galleggiante; ‹population› fluttuante

floating rate interest /'fləʊtɪŋ/ n Fin interesse m a tasso variabile

floating voter n Pol elettore, -trice mf indeciso, -a

flock /flɒk/ **1** n gregge m; (of birds) stormo m

2 vi affollarsi

floe /fləʊ/ n banchisa f

flog /flɒg/ vt (pt/pp **flogged**) bastonare; fam (sell) vendere

flood /flʌd/ **1** n alluvione f; (of river) straripamento m; fig (of replies, letters, tears) diluvio m; **be in** ~ ‹river› essere straripato

2 vt allagare

3 vi ‹river› straripare

flood control n prevenzione f delle inondazioni

flood damage n danno m provocato da un'inondazione

floodgate n chiusa f; **open the** ~**s** fig spalancare le porte

floodlight **1** n riflettore m

2 vt (pt/pp **floodlit**) illuminare con riflettori

floodplain n pianura f alluvionale

flood tide n marea f montante

flood waters npl acque fpl alluvionali

⚹ **floor** /flɔː(r)/ **1** n pavimento m; (storey) piano m; (for dancing) pista f

2 vt (baffle) confondere; (knock down) stendere ‹person›

floorboard n asse f del pavimento

floorcloth n straccio m per lavare il pavimento

floor exercises npl esercizi mpl a terra

floor manager n TV direttore, -trice mf di studio; Comm gerente mf di un negozio

floor polish n cera f per il pavimento

floor show n spettacolo m di varietà

floor space n superficie f; **we don't have the** ~ non abbiamo lo spazio

flop /flɒp/ **1** n fam (failure) tonfo m; Theat fiasco m

2 vi (pt/pp **flopped**) fam (fail) far fiasco

■ **flop down** vi accasciarsi

floppy /'flɒpɪ/ adj floscio

floppy disk n floppy disk m inv

floppy [disk] drive n lettore m di floppy

flora /'flɔːrə/ n flora f

floral /'flɔːrəl/ adj floreale

Florence /'flɒrəns/ n Firenze f

Florentine /'flɒrəntaɪn/ adj fiorentino

florid /'flɒrɪd/ adj ‹complexion› florido; ‹style› troppo ricercato

florist /'flɒrɪst/ n fioraio, -a mf

floss /flɒs, US flɔːs/ **1** n filo m interdentale

2 vt ~ **one's teeth** usare il filo interdentale

3 vi usare il filo interdentale

flotsam /'flɒtsəm/ n relitti mpl alla deriva

flounce /flaʊns/ **1** n balza f

2 vi ~ **out** uscire con aria melodrammatica

flounder¹ /'flaʊndə(r)/ vi dibattersi; ‹speaker› impappinarsi

flounder² n (fish) passera f di mare

flour /'flaʊə(r)/ n farina f

flourish /'flʌrɪʃ/ **1** n gesto m drammatico; (scroll) ghirigoro m

2 vi prosperare

3 vt brandire

flourishing /'flʌrɪʃɪŋ/ adj ‹industry, business› fiorente; ‹garden› rigoglioso

floury /'flaʊərɪ/ adj farinoso

flout /flaʊt/ vt fregarsene di ‹rules›

⚡ **flow** /fləʊ/ **1** n flusso m
2 vi scorrere; (hang loosely) ricadere
flow chart n diagramma m di flusso
⚡ **flower** /'flaʊə(r)/ **1** n fiore m
2 vi fiorire
flower arrangement n composizione
f floreale
flower arranging n composizione f
floreale
flower bed n aiuola f
flowered /'flaʊəd/ adj a fiori
flower garden n giardino m fiorito
flowering /'flaʊərɪŋ/ **1** n Bot fioritura f;
fig (development) espansione f
2 adj ‹shrub, tree› in fiore; **early/late** ~ a
fioritura precoce/tardiva
flowerpot n vaso m [per i fiori]
flower shop n fiorista m
flower show n mostra f floreale
flowery /'flaʊərɪ/ adj fiorito
flown /fləʊn/ ▶ FLY²
fl oz abbr (**fluid ounce(s)**) oncia f fluida
flu /fluː/ n influenza f
fluctuate /'flʌktjʊeɪt/ vi fluttuare
fluctuation /flʌktjʊ'eɪʃn/ n fluttuazione f
flue /fluː/ n (of chimney, stove) canna f fumaria
fluency /'fluːənsɪ/ n (in speaking)
competenza f; (in writing) padronanza f
fluent /'fluːənt/ adj spedito; **speak** ~ **Italian**
parlare correntemente l'italiano
fluently /'fluːəntlɪ/ adv speditamente
fluff /flʌf/ n peluria f
fluffy /'flʌfɪ/ adj (**-ier, -iest**) vaporoso; ‹toy›
di peluche
fluid /'fluːɪd/ **1** adj fluido
2 n fluido m
fluid ounce n oncia f fluida
fluke /fluːk/ n colpo m di fortuna
flummox /'flʌməks/ vt fam sbalestrare
flung /flʌŋ/ ▶ FLING
flunk /flʌŋk/ vt Am fam essere bocciato in
fluorescent /flʊə'resnt/ adj fluorescente
fluorescent lighting n luce f
fluorescente
fluoride /'flʊəraɪd/ n fluoruro m
flurry /'flʌrɪ/ n (snow) raffica f; fig agitazione
f
flush /flʌʃ/ **1** n (blush) [vampata f di]
rossore m
2 vi arrossire
3 vt lavare con un getto d'acqua; ~ **the
toilet** tirare l'acqua
4 adj a livello (**with** di); fam (affluent) pieno
di soldi
■ **flush out** vt snidare ‹spy›
flushed /flʌʃt/ adj ‹cheeks› rosso; ~ **with**
eccitato da ‹success›; raggiante di ‹pride›

fluster /'flʌstə(r)/ vt agitare
flustered /'flʌstəd/ adj in agitazione; **get**
~ mettersi in agitazione
flute /fluːt/ n flauto m
flutter /'flʌtə(r)/ **1** n battito m
2 vi svolazzare
flux /flʌks/ n **in a state of** ~ in uno stato
di flusso
fly¹ /flaɪ/ n (pl **flies**) mosca f
⚡ **fly²** **1** vi (pt **flew**, pp **flown**) volare; (go
by plane) andare in aereo; ‹flag› sventolare;
(rush) precipitarsi; ~ **open** spalancarsi
2 vt pilotare ‹plane›; trasportare [in aereo]
‹troops, supplies›; volare con ‹Alitalia etc›
■ **fly away** vi volare via
fly³ n **flies** pl (on trousers) patta f
flyaway /'flaɪəweɪ/ adj ‹hair› che non
stanno a posto
fly-by-night adj ‹person› irresponsabile;
‹company› non affidabile
flycatcher /'flaɪkætʃə(r)/ n pigliamosche
m inv
fly-drive adj con la formula aereo più auto
flyer /'flaɪə(r)/ n aviatore m; (leaflet)
volantino m
fly-fishing n pesca f con la mosca
flying /'flaɪɪŋ/ n aviazione f
flying buttress n arco m rampante
flying colours: with ~ a pieni voti
flying saucer n disco m volante
flying start n ottima partenza f; **get off to
a flying start** partire benissimo
flying visit n visita f lampo inv
flyleaf n risguardo m
fly on the wall adj ‹documentary› con
telecamera nascosta
flyover n cavalcavia m inv
fly-past n Br Aeron parata f aerea
flysheet n (handbill) volantino m; (of tent)
soprattenda m inv
fly spray n moschicida m
FM abbr (**Frequency Modulation**) FM
foal /fəʊl/ n puledro m
foam /fəʊm/ **1** n schiuma f; (synthetic)
gommapiuma® f
2 vi spumare; ~ **at the mouth** far la bava
alla bocca
foam bath n bagnoschiuma m
foam rubber n gommapiuma® f
fob /fɒb/ vt (pt/pp **fobbed**) ~ **something
off** affibbiare qualcosa (**on somebody** a
qualcuno); ~ **somebody off** liquidare
qualcuno
focal /'fəʊkl/ adj focale
focal point n (of village, building) centro m di
attrazione; (main concern) punto m centrale;
(in optics) fuoco m; **the room lacks a** ~
nella stanza manca un punto che focalizzi
l'attenzione

⚡ indicates a very frequent word

◦ focus /'fəʊkəs/ **1** n fuoco m; **in ~** a fuoco; **out of ~** sfocato
2 vt (pt/pp **focused** or **focussed**) fig concentrare (**on** su)
3 vi **~ on something** Phot mettere a fuoco qualcosa; fig concentrarsi su qualcosa

fodder /'fɒdə(r)/ n foraggio m

foe /fəʊ/ n nemico, -a mf

foetal /'fiːtl/ adj fetale

foetid /'fetɪd/ adj fetido

foetus /'fiːtəs/ n (pl **-tuses**) feto m

fog /fɒg/ n nebbia f

fog bank n banco m di nebbia

fogey /'fəʊgɪ/ n old **~** persona f antiquata

foggy /'fɒgɪ/ adj (**foggier**, **foggiest**) nebbioso; **it's ~** c'è nebbia; **I haven't got the foggiest [idea]** fam hon ne ho la più pallida idea

foghorn /'fɒghɔːn/ n sirena f da nebbia

fog lamp, foglight /'fɒglaɪt/ n Auto [faro m] antinebbia m inv

foible /'fɔɪbl/ n punto m debole

foil¹ /fɔɪl/ n lamina f di metallo

foil² vt (thwart) frustrare

foil³ n (sword) fioretto m

foist /fɔɪst/ vt appioppare (**on somebody** a qualcuno)

fold¹ /fəʊld/ n (for sheep) ovile m

fold² **1** n piega f
2 vt piegare; **~ one's arms** incrociare le braccia
3 vi piegarsi, (fail) crollare
■ **fold back** vt ripiegare ‹sheets›; aprire ‹shutters›
■ **fold in** vt incorporare ‹flour, eggs›
■ **fold up** **1** vt ripiegare ‹chair›
2 vi essere pieghevole; fam ‹business› collassare

foldaway /'fəʊldəweɪ/ adj ‹bed› pieghevole; ‹table› estraibile

folder /'fəʊldə(r)/ n cartella f

folding /'fəʊldɪŋ/ adj pieghevole

folding seat n strapuntino m, sedile m pieghevole

folding stool n sgabello m pieghevole

fold-out n (in magazine) pieghevole m

foliage /'fəʊlɪdʒ/ n fogliame m

◦ folk /fəʊk/ npl gente f; **my ~s** (family) i miei; **hello there ~s** ciao a tutti

folk dance n danza f popolare

folklore n folclore m

folk medicine n rimedio m della nonna

folk memory n memoria f collettiva

folk music n musica f folk

folk song n canto m popolare

folk wisdom n saggezza f popolare

◦ follow /'fɒləʊ/ vt/i seguire; **it doesn't ~** non è necessariamente così; **~ suit** fig fare lo stesso; **as ~s** come segue

■ **follow through** vt portare avanti ‹project, idea›

■ **follow up** vt fare seguito a ‹letter›

follower /'fɒləʊə(r)/ n seguace mf

following /'fɒləʊɪŋ/ **1** adj seguente
2 n seguito m; (supporters) seguaci mpl
3 prep in seguito a

follow-on n seguito m

follow-up **1** n (of social work case) controllo m; (of patient, ex inmate) visita f di controllo; (film, record, single, programme) seguito m
2 attrib ‹survey, work, interview› successivo; **~ letter** lettera f che fa seguito

folly /'fɒlɪ/ n follia f

foment /fə'ment/ vt fig fomentare

fond /fɒnd/ adj affezionato; ‹hope› vivo; **be ~ of** essere appassionato di ‹music› **I'm ~ of ...** ‹food, person› mi piace moltissimo...

fondle /'fɒndl/ vt coccolare

fondly /'fɒndlɪ/ adv ‹hope› ingenuamente

fondness /'fɒndnɪs/ n affetto m; (for things) amore m

font /fɒnt/ n fonte f battesimale; Typ carattere m di stampa

◦ food /fuːd/ n cibo m; (for animals, groceries) mangiare m; **let's buy some ~** compriamo qualcosa da mangiare

food aid n aiuti mpl alimentari

foodie /'fuːdɪ/ n fam buongustaio, -a mf

food mixer n frullatore m

food poisoning n intossicazione f alimentare

food processor n tritatutto m inv elettrico

foodstuffs npl generi mpl alimentari

fool¹ /fuːl/ **1** n sciocco, -a mf; **she's no ~** non è una stupida; **make a ~ of oneself** rendersi ridicolo
2 vt prendere in giro
3 vi **~ around** giocare; ‹husband, wife› avere l'amante

fool² n Culin crema f

foolhardy /'fuːlhɑːdɪ/ adj temerario

foolish /'fuːlɪʃ/ adj stolto

foolishly /'fuːlɪʃlɪ/ adv scioccamente

foolishness /'fuːlɪʃnɪs/ n sciocchezza f

foolproof /'fuːlpruːf/ adj facilissimo

foolscap /'fuːlskæp/ n Br (paper) carta f protocollo

◦ foot /fʊt/ n (pl **feet**) piede m; (of animal) zampa f; (measure) piede (=30, 48 cm); **on ~** a piedi; **on one's feet** in piedi; **put one's ~ in it** fam fare una gaffe

footage /'fʊtɪdʒ/ n (piece of film) spezzone m; **news ~** servizio m [filmato]

foot-and-mouth disease n afta f epizootica

◦ football n calcio m; (ball) pallone m

footballer n giocatore m di calcio

football pools npl totocalcio m

footbrake n freno m a pedale

f

footbridge n passerella f

foothills npl colline fpl pedemontane

foothold n punto m d'appoggio

footing n lose one's ~ perdere l'appiglio; **on an equal ~** in condizioni di parità

footlights npl luci npl della ribalta

footloose and fancy-free adj libero come l'aria

footman n valletto m

footnote n nota f a piè di pagina

foot passenger n (on boat) passeggero, -a mf

footpath n sentiero m

footprint n orma f; (of machine) ingombro m

footrest n poggiapiedi m inv

footsore adj be ~ avere male ai piedi

footstep n passo m; **follow in somebody's ~s** fig seguire l'esempio di qualcuno

footstool n sgabellino m

footwear n calzature fpl

ꞏ**for** /fə(r), accentato fɔː(r)/ [1] prep per; ~ **this reason** per questa ragione; **I have lived here ~ ten years** vivo qui da dieci anni; ~ **supper** per cena; ~ **all that** nonostante questo; **what ~?** a che scopo?; **send ~ a doctor** chiamare un dottore; **fight ~ a cause** lottare per una causa; **go ~ a walk** andare a fare una passeggiata; **there's no need ~ you to go** non c'è bisogno che tu vada; **it's not ~ me to say** non sta a me dirlo; **now you're ~ it** ora sei nei pasticci [2] conj poiché, perché

forage /'fɒrɪdʒ/ [1] n foraggio m [2] vi ~ **for** cercare

foray /'fɒreɪ/ n Mil incursione f; **make a ~ into** ⟨politics, acting⟩ tentare la strada di

forbade /fə'bæd/ ▶ FORBID

forbearance /fɔː'beərəns/ n pazienza f

forbearing /fɔː'beərɪŋ/ adj tollerante

forbid /fə'bɪd/ vt (pt **forbade**, pp **forbidden**) proibire

forbidden /fə'bɪdn/ adj ⟨fruit, place⟩ proibito

forbidding /fə'bɪdɪŋ/ adj ⟨prospect⟩ che spaventa; (stern) severo

ꞏ**force** /fɔːs/ [1] n forza f; **in ~** in vigore; (in large numbers) in massa; **come into ~** entrare in vigore; **the [armed] ~s** pl le forze armate [2] vt forzare; ~ **something on somebody** ⟨decision⟩ imporre qualcosa a qualcuno; ⟨drink⟩ costringere qualcuno a fare qualcosa

■ **force back** vt trattenere ⟨tears⟩

■ **force down** vt buttar giù (controvoglia) ⟨food, drink⟩

forced /fɔːst/ adj forzato

forced landing n atterraggio m forzato

force-feed vt (pt/pp **-fed**) nutrire a forza

forceful /'fɔːsfʊl/ adj energico

forcefully /'fɔːsfʊlɪ/ adv ⟨say, argue⟩ con forza

forceps /'fɔːseps/ npl forcipe m

forcible /'fɔːsəbl/ adj forzato

forcibly /'fɔːsəblɪ/ adv forzatamente

ford /fɔːd/ [1] n guado m [2] vt guadare

fore /fɔː(r)/ n **to the ~** in vista; **come to the ~** salire alla ribalta

forearm /'fɔːrɑːm/ n avambraccio m

forebears /'fɔːbeəz/ npl antenati mpl

foreboding /fɔː'bəʊdɪŋ/ n presentimento m

forecast /'fɔːkɑːst/ [1] n previsione f [2] vt (pt/pp **forecast**) prevedere

forecaster /'fɔːkɑːstə(r)/ n pronosticatore, -trice mf; (economic) analista mf della congiuntura; (of weather) meteorologo, -a mf

forecourt n (of garage) spiazzo m [antistante]

forefathers npl antenati mpl

forefinger n [dito m] indice m

forefront n **be in the ~** essere all'avanguardia

foregone adj **be a ~ conclusion** essere una cosa scontata

foreground n primo piano m

forehand n Tennis diritto m

forehead /'fɔːhed, 'fɒrɪd/ n fronte f

ꞏ**foreign** /'fɒrən/ adj straniero; ⟨trade⟩ estero; (not belonging) estraneo; **he is ~** è uno straniero

foreign affairs npl affari mpl esteri

foreign body n corpo m estraneo

foreign correspondent n corrispondente mf estero

foreign currency n valuta f estera

foreigner /'fɒrənə(r)/ n straniero, -a mf

foreign exchange n (currency) valuta f estera

foreign exchange market n mercato m dei cambi

foreign language n lingua f straniera

foreign minister n ministro m degli Esteri

Foreign Office n ministero m degli [affari] Esteri

Foreign Secretary n Ministro m degli Esteri

foreleg /'fɔːleg/ n zampa f anteriore

foreman /'fɔːmən/ n caporeparto m

foremost /'fɔːməʊst/ [1] adj principale [2] adv **first and ~** in primo luogo

forename /'fɔːneɪm/ n nome m di battesimo

forensic /fə'rensɪk/ adj ~ **medicine** medicina legale

forensic evidence n prova f medico-legale

forensic science n medicina f legale

ꞏ indicates a very frequent word

forensic scientist *n* medico *m* legale

forensic tests *npl* perizia *f sg* medico-legale

forerunner /'fɔːrʌnə(r)/ *n* precursore *m*

foresee /fɔːˈsiː/ *vt* (*pt* **-saw**, *pp* **-seen**) prevedere

foreseeable /fɔːˈsiːəbl/ *adj* in the ~ future nel futuro immediato

foreshadow /fɔːˈʃædəʊ/ *vt* prevedere

foresight /'fɔːsaɪt/ *n* previdenza *f*

foreskin /'fɔːskɪn/ *n* Anat prepuzio *m*

✦ **forest** /'fɒrɪst/ *n* foresta *f*

forestall /fɔːˈstɔːl/ *vt* prevenire

forester /'fɒrɪstə(r)/ *n* guardia *f* forestale

forest fire *n* incendio *m* nei boschi

forest ranger /'reɪndʒə(r)/ *n* Am guardia *f* forestale

forestry /'fɒrɪstrɪ/ *n* silvicoltura *f*

foretaste /'fɔːteɪst/ *n* pregustazione *f*

foretell /fɔːˈtel/ *vt* (*pt/pp* **-told**) predire

forethought /'fɔːθɔːt/ *n* accortezza *f*, previdenza *f*

✦ **forever** /fəˈrevə(r)/ *adv* per sempre; he's ~ complaining si lamenta sempre

forewarn /fɔːˈwɔːn/ *vt* avvertire

foreword /'fɔːwɜːd/ *n* prefazione *f*

forfeit /'fɔːfɪt/ **1** *n* (in game) pegno *m*; Jur penalità *f* **2** *vt* perdere

forfeiture /'fɔːfɪtʃə(r)/ *n* (of right) perdita *f*; (of property) confisca *f*

forgave /fəˈgeɪv/ ▶ FORGIVE

forge¹ /fɔːdʒ/ *vi* ~ ahead ⟨runner⟩ lasciarsi indietro gli altri; fig farsi strada

forge² **1** *n* fucina *f* **2** *vt* fucinare; (counterfeit) contraffare

forger /'fɔːdʒə(r)/ *n* contraffattore *m*

forgery /'fɔːdʒərɪ/ *n* contraffazione *f*

✦ **forget** /fəˈget/ *vt/i* (*pt* **-got**, *pp* **-gotten**) dimenticare; dimenticarsi di ⟨language, skill⟩; ~ oneself perdere la padronanza di sé
■ **forget about** *vt* dimenticarsi di

forgetful /fəˈgetful/ *adj* smemorato

forgetfulness /fəˈgetfulnɪs/ *n* smemoratezza *f*

forget-me-not *n* non-ti-scordar-di-mè *m inv*

forgettable /fəˈgetəbl/ *adj* ⟨day, fact, film⟩ da dimenticare

forgive /fəˈgɪv/ *vt* (*pt* **-gave**, *pp* **-given**) ~ somebody for something perdonare qualcuno per qualcosa

forgiveness /fəˈgɪvnɪs/ *n* perdono *m*

forgiving /fəˈgɪvɪŋ/ *adj* ⟨person⟩ indulgente

forgo /fɔːˈgəʊ/ *vt* (*pt* **-went**, *pp* **-gone**) rinunciare a

forgot(ten) /fəˈgɒt(n)/ ▶ FORGET

fork /fɔːk/ **1** *n* forchetta *f*; (for digging) forca *f*; (in road) bivio *m*

2 *vi* ⟨road⟩ biforcarsi; ~ right prendere a destra
■ **fork out** **1** *vt* fam sborsare **2** *vi* sborsare soldi

forked lightning /fɔːkt/ *n* fulmine *m* ramificato

fork-lift truck *n* elevatore *m*

forlorn /fəˈlɔːn/ *adj* ⟨look⟩ perduto; ⟨place⟩ derelitto; ~ hope speranza *f* vana

✦ **form** /fɔːm/ **1** *n* forma *f*; (document) modulo *m*; Sch classe *f*
2 *vt* formare; formulare ⟨opinion⟩
3 *vi* formarsi

formal /'fɔːml/ *adj* formale

formal dress *n* abito *m* da cerimonia

formalin /'fɔːməlɪn/ *n* formalina *f*

formality /fɔːˈmælətɪ/ *n* formalità *f inv*

formally /'fɔːməlɪ/ *adv* in modo formale; (officially) ufficialmente

format /'fɔːmæt/ **1** *n* formato *m* **2** *vt* formattare ⟨disk, page⟩

✦ **formation** /fɔːˈmeɪʃn/ *n* formazione *f*

formative /'fɔːmətɪv/ *adj* ~ years anni formativi

✦ **former** /'fɔːmə(r)/ *adj* precedente; ⟨PM, colleague⟩ ex; the ~, the latter il primo, l'ultimo

formerly /'fɔːməlɪ/ *adv* precedentemente; (in olden times) in altri tempi

formidable /'fɔːmɪdəbl/ *adj* formidabile

formless /'fɔːmlɪs/ *adj* ⟨mass⟩ informe; ⟨novel⟩ che manca di struttura

form teacher *n* Br Sch ≈ coordinatore, -trice *mf* del consiglio di classe

formula /'fɔːjʊlə/ *n* (*pl* **-ae** /'fɔːmjʊliː/ or **-s**) formula *f*

formulate /'fɔːmjʊleɪt/ *vt* formulare

formulation /fɔːmjʊˈleɪʃn/ *n* formulazione *f*

fornication /fɔːnɪˈkeɪʃn/ *n* fornicazione *f*

forsake /fəˈseɪk/ *vt* (*pt* **-sook** /fəˈsʊk/; *pp* **-saken**) abbandonare

forseeable /fəˈsiːəbl/ *adj* in the ~ future in futuro per quanto si possa prevedere

forswear /fɔːˈsweə(r)/ *vt* (renounce) abiurare

fort /fɔːt/ *n* Mil forte *m*

forte /'fɔːteɪ/ *n* [pezzo *m*] forte *m*

forth /fɔːθ/ *adv* back and ~ avanti e indietro; and so ~ e così via

forthcoming /fɔːθˈkʌmɪŋ/ *adj* prossimo; (communicative) comunicativo; no response was ~ non arrivava nessuna risposta

forthright /'fɔːθraɪt/ *adj* schietto

forthwith /fɔːθˈwɪð/ *adv* immediatamente

forties /'fɔːtɪz/ *npl* the ~ gli anni Quaranta *mpl*; (age) quarant'anni *mpl*; a man in his ~ un quarantenne

fortieth /'fɔːtɪɪθ/ *adj* & *n* quarantesimo, -a *mf*

f

fortification /ˌfɔːtɪfɪˈkeɪʃn/ n fortificazione f

fortified /ˈfɔːtɪfaɪd/ adj fortificato; ~ **wine** vino liquoroso; ~ **with vitamins** arricchito con vitamine

fortify /ˈfɔːtɪfaɪ/ vt (pt/pp **-ied**) fortificare; fig rendere forte

fortitude /ˈfɔːtɪtjuːd/ n coraggio m

fortnight /ˈfɔːtnaɪt/ n Br quindicina f

fortnightly /ˈfɔːtnaɪtlɪ/ **1** adj bimensile **2** adv ogni due settimane

fortress /ˈfɔːtrɪs/ n fortezza f

fortuitous /fɔːˈtjuːɪtəs/ adj fortuito

fortunate /ˈfɔːtʃənət/ adj fortunato; **that's** ~! meno male!

fortunately /ˈfɔːtʃənətlɪ/ adv fortunatamente

fortune /ˈfɔːtʃuːn/ n fortuna f

fortune cookie n Am biscottino (m) che racchiude un foglietto con una predizione

fortune-teller n indovino, -a mf

forty /ˈfɔːtɪ/ adj & n quaranta m; **have** ~ **winks** fam fare un pisolino

forum /ˈfɔːrəm/ n foro m

⚜ **forward** /ˈfɔːwəd/ **1** adv avanti; (towards the front) in avanti; **move** ~ andare avanti **2** adj in avanti; (presumptuous) sfacciato **3** n Sport attaccante m **4** vt inoltrare ⟨letter⟩; spedire ⟨goods⟩

forward buying n Fin acquisto m a termine

forwarding address n indirizzo (m) a cui inoltrare la corrispondenza

forward-looking adj ⟨company, person⟩ lungimirante

forward planning n pianificazione f a lungo termine

forwards /ˈfɔːwədz/ adv avanti

forward slash n slash m inv

fossil /ˈfɒs(ə)l/ n fossile m

fossil fuel n combustibile m fossile

fossilized /ˈfɒsɪlaɪzd/ adj fossile; ⟨ideas⟩ fossilizzato

foster /ˈfɒstə(r)/ vt allevare ⟨child⟩

foster child n figlio, -a mf in affidamento

foster family n famiglia f affidataria

foster home n famiglia f affidataria

foster mother n madre f affidataria

fought /fɔːt/ ▶ FIGHT

foul /faʊl/ **1** adj ⟨smell, taste⟩ cattivo; ⟨air⟩ viziato; ⟨language⟩ osceno; ⟨mood, weather⟩ orrendo **2** vt inquinare ⟨water⟩; Sport commettere un fallo contro; ⟨nets, rope⟩ impigliarsi in ■ **foul up 1** vt fam (spoil) mandare in malora **2** n fam intoppo m

foul-mouthed /-ˈmaʊðd/ adj sboccato

foul play 1 n Jur delitto m

2 n Sport fallo m

foul-smelling /-ˈsmelɪŋ/ adj puzzo

foul-up n pasticcio m

found¹ /faʊnd/ ▶ FIND

found² vt fondare

foundation /faʊnˈdeɪʃn/ n (basis) fondamento m; (charitable) fondazione f; ~**s** pl (of building) fondamenta fpl; **lay the** ~**-stone** porre la prima pietra

foundation course n Br Univ corso m propedeutico

founder¹ /ˈfaʊndə(r)/ n fondatore, trice mf

founder² vi ⟨ship⟩ affondare

foundry /ˈfaʊndrɪ/ n fonderia f

fount /faʊnt/ n Typ carattere m [stampa]

fountain /ˈfaʊntɪn/ n fontana f

fountain pen n penna f stilografica

⚜ **four** /fɔː(r)/ adj & n quattro m

four-by-four /ˌfɔːbaɪˈfɔː(r)/ n (vehicle) quattro per quattro f

four four time n Mus quattro quarti

four-letter word n parolaccia f

four-poster [bed] n letto m a baldacchino

foursome /ˈfɔːsəm/ n quartetto m

four-star /ˈfɔːstɑː(r)/ **1** adj ⟨hotel, restaurant⟩ a quattro stelle **2** n (petrol) super f

four-stroke adj ⟨engine⟩ a quattro tempi

fourteen /fɔːˈtiːn/ adj & n quattordici m

fourteenth /fɔːˈtiːnθ/ adj & n quattordicesimo, -a mf

⚜ **fourth** /fɔːθ/ adj & n quarto, -a mf

fourthly /ˈfɔːθlɪ/ adv in quarto luogo

fourth rate adj ⟨job, hotel, film⟩ di terz'ordine

four-wheel drive [vehicle] n quattro per quattro m inv

fowl /faʊl/ n pollame m

fox /fɒks/ **1** n volpe f **2** vt (puzzle) ingannare

fox cub n volpacchiotto m

fox fur n pelliccia f di volpe

foxglove n digitale f

foxhound n foxhound m inv

fox-hunt n caccia f alla volpe

fox hunting n caccia f alla volpe

fox terrier n fox-terrier m inv

foxtrot n fox-trot m inv

foxy /ˈfɒksɪ/ adj (-ier, -iest) fam (sexy) sexy inv; (crafty) scaltro

foyer /ˈfɔɪeɪ/ n Theat ridotto m; (in hotel) salone m d'ingresso

fracas /ˈfrækɑː/ n baruffa f

fraction /ˈfrækʃn/ n frazione f

fractionally /ˈfrækʃənəlɪ/ adv (slightly) leggermente

fracture /ˈfræktʃə(r)/ **1** n frattura f

⚜ indicates a very frequent word

2 *vt* fratturare
3 *vi* fratturarsi

fragile /'frædʒaɪl/ *adj* fragile

fragment /'frægmənt/ *n* frammento *m*

fragmentary /'frægm(ə)ntərɪ/ *adj* frammentario

fragrance /'freɪɡrəns/ *n* fragranza *f*

fragrant /'freɪɡrənt/ *adj* fragrante

frail /freɪl/ *adj* gracile

frailty /'freɪltɪ/ *n* (imperfection) debolezza *f*; (of person: moral) fragilità *f inv*; (of person: physical) gracilità *f*; (of health, state) precarietà *f inv*

✔ **frame** /freɪm/ **1** *n* (of picture, door, window) cornice *f*; (of spectacles) montatura *f*; Anat ossatura *f*; (structure, of bike) telaio *m*; ~ **of mind** stato *m* d'animo
2 *vt* incorniciare ‹picture›; fig formulare; sl (incriminate) montare

frame of mind *n* stato *m* d'animo

framework /'freɪmwɜːk/ *n* struttura *f*; **within the** ~ **of the law** nell'ambito della legge

franc /fræŋk/ *n* franco *m*

France /frɑːns/ *n* Francia *f*

franchise /'fræntʃaɪz/ *n* Pol diritto *m* di voto; Comm franchigia *f*

Franciscan /fræn'sɪskən/ *n* francescano *m*

frank[1] /fræŋk/ *vt* affrancare ‹letter›

frank[2] *adj* franco

Frankfurt /'fræŋkfɜːt/ *n* Francoforte *f*

frankfurter /'fræŋkfɜːtə(r)/ *n* würstel *m inv*

frankincense /'fræŋkɪnsens/ *n* incenso *m*

franking machine /'fræŋkɪŋ/ *n* affrancatrice *f*

frankly /'fræŋklɪ/ *adv* francamente

frantic /'fræntɪk/ *adj* frenetico; **be** ~ **with worry** essere agitatissimo

frantically /'fræntɪklɪ/ *adv* freneticamente

fraternal /frə'tɜːnl/ *adj* fraterno

fraternity /frə'tɜːnətɪ/ *n* (club) associazione *f*; (spirit, brotherhood) fratellanza *f*

fraud /frɔːd/ *n* frode *f*; (person) impostore *m*

fraudulent /'frɔːdjʊlənt/ *adj* fraudolento

fraught /frɔːt/ *adj* ~ **with** pieno di

fray[1] /freɪ/ *n* mischia *f*

fray[2] *vi* sfilacciarsi

frayed /freɪd/ *adj* ‹cuffs› sfilacciato; ‹nerves› a pezzi

frazzle /'fræz(ə)l/ *n* **be worn to a** ~ essere ridotto uno straccio; **burn something to a** ~ carbonizzare qualcosa

freak /friːk/ **1** *n* fenomeno *m*; (person) scherzo *m* di natura; fam (weird person) tipo *m* strambo
2 *adj* anormale

■ **freak out** *vi* fam (lose control, go crazy) andar fuori di testa

freakish /'friːkɪʃ/ *adj* strambo

freckle /'frekl/ *n* lentiggine *f*

freckled /'frekld/ *adj* lentigginoso

✔ **free** /friː/ **1** *adj* (**freer, freest**) libero; ‹ticket, copy› gratuito; (lavish) generoso; ~ **of charge** gratuito; **set** ~ liberare; ~ **with**... Comm in omaggio per...
2 *vt* (*pt/pp* **freed**) liberare

free agent *n* persona *f* libera di agire come vuole

free and easy *adj* disinvolto

freebee, freebie /'friːbɪ/ *n* fam (free gift) omaggio *m*; (trip) viaggio *m* gratuito; (newspaper) giornale *m* gratuito

✔ **freedom** /'friːdəm/ *n* libertà *f*

freedom fighter *n* combattente *mf* per la libertà

free enterprise *n* liberalismo *m* economico

free fall *n* caduta *f* libera

Freefone®, **Freephone** /'friːfəʊn/ *n* numero *m* verde

free-for-all *n* (disorganized situation, fight) baraonda *f*

free gift *n* omaggio *m*

freehand *adv* a mano libera

freehold *n* proprietà *f* [fondiaria] assoluta

free house *n* Br pub (*m inv*) che non è legato a nessun produttore di birra

free-kick *n* calcio *m* di punizione

freelance *adj* & *adv* indipendente

freeloader *n* fam scroccone *m*

freely /'friːlɪ/ *adv* liberamente; (generously) generosamente; **I** ~ **admit that**... devo ammettere che...

free market *n* economia *f* di libero mercato

Freemason *n* massone *m*

Freemasonry *n* massoneria *f*

Freephone *n* = FREEFONE

freephone number *n* numero *m* verde

freepost /'friːpəʊst/ *n* Br affrancatura *f* a carico del destinatario

free-range *adj* ‹eggs› di allevamento a terra; ‹hens› allevato a terra

free-range egg *n* uovo *m* di gallina ruspante

free sample *n* campione *m* gratuito

free speech *n* libertà *f* di parola

free spirit *n* persona *f* che ama la sua indipendenza

free-standing *adj* ‹heater› non incassato; ‹statue› a tutto tondo; ‹lamp› a stelo

freestyle *n* stile *m* libero

free trade *n* libero scambio *m*

free trial period *n* periodo *m* di prova gratuito

freeware /'fri:weə(r)/ n Comput freeware m inv

freeway n Am autostrada f

freewheel vi ‹car› (in neutral) andare in folle; (with engine switched off) andare a motore spento; ‹bicycle› andare a ruota libera

free will n of one's own ∼ di spontanea volontà

freeze /fri:z/ ❶ vt (pt **froze**, pp **frozen**) gelare; bloccare ‹wages› ❷ vi ‹water› gelare; **it's freezing** si gela; **my hands are freezing** ho le mani congelate

freeze-dried adj liofilizzato

freeze-frame n (video) fermo m immagine

freezer /'fri:zə(r)/ n freezer m inv, congelatore m

freezer compartment n scomparto m freezer

freezing /'fri:zɪŋ/ ❶ adj gelido ❷ n below ∼ sotto zero

freezing cold adj gelido

freezing fog n nebbia f ghiacciata

freezing point n punto m di congelamento

freight /freɪt/ n carico m

freight charges npl costi mpl di spedizione

freighter /'freɪtə(r)/ n nave f da carico

freight forwarder n spedizioniere m

freight train n Am treno m merci

ꞎ **French** /frentʃ/ ❶ adj francese ❷ n (language) francese m; **the** ∼ pl i francesi

French beans npl fagiolini mpl [verdi]

French bread n filone m (di pane)

French Canadian ❶ n canadese mf francofono, -a ❷ adj del Canada francofono

French doors npl porta-finestra f inv

French dressing n Br vinaigrette f inv

French fries npl patate fpl fritte

French horn n corno m da caccia

French kiss n bacio m profondo

French knickers npl culottes fpl

Frenchman n francese m

French polish n vernice f a olio e gommalacca

French-speaking adj francofono

French toast n pane (m) immerso nell'uovo sbattuto e fritto

French window n porta-finestra f

Frenchwoman n francese f

frenetic /frənetɪk/ adj ‹activity› frenetico

frenzied /'frenzɪd/ adj frenetico

frenzy /'frenzɪ/ n frenesia f

ꞎ **frequency** /'fri:kwənsɪ/ n frequenza f

frequent¹ /'fri:kwənt/ adj frequente

frequent² /frɪ'kwent/ vt frequentare

frequent-flyer miles npl Am miglia fpl aeree

ꞎ **frequently** /'fri:kwəntlɪ/ adv frequentemente

fresco /'freskəʊ/ n affresco m

ꞎ **fresh** /freʃ/ adj fresco; (new) nuovo; Am (cheeky) sfacciato

fresh air n aria f fresca; **get some** ∼ prendere una boccata d'aria

freshen /'freʃn/ vi ‹wind› rinfrescare ■ **freshen up** ❶ vt dare una rinfrescata a ❷ vi rinfrescarsi

fresh-faced /-'feɪst/ adj dalla faccia giovanile

freshly /'freʃlɪ/ adv di recente

freshman /'freʃmən/ n Am matricola f; fig (in congress, in firm) nuovo arrivato m

freshness /'freʃnɪs/ n freschezza f

freshwater /'freʃwɔːtə(r)/ adj di acqua dolce

fret /fret/ vi (pt/pp **fretted**) inquietarsi

fretful /'fretfʊl/ adj irritabile

fretsaw /'fretsɔː/ n seghetto m da traforo

fretwork /'fretwɜːk/ n [lavoro m di] traforo m

Freudian slip /'frɔɪdɪən/ n lapsus m inv freudiano

friar /'fraɪə(r)/ n frate m

friction /'frɪkʃn/ n frizione f

ꞎ **Friday** /'fraɪdeɪ/ n venerdì m inv

fridge /frɪdʒ/ n frigo m

fridge-freezer /ˌfrɪdʒ'fri:zə(r)/ n frigocongelatore m

fried /fraɪd/ ❶ ▶ FRY¹ ❷ adj fritto; ∼ **egg** uovo m fritto

ꞎ **friend** /frend/ n amico, -a mf

friendly /'frendlɪ/ adj (**-ier**, **-iest**) ‹relations, meeting, match› amichevole; ‹neighbourhood, smile› piacevole; ‹software› di facile uso; **be** ∼ **with** essere amico di

friendly fire n fuoco m amico

friendship /'frendʃɪp/ n amicizia f

fries /fraɪz/ n pl Am fam patatine fpl fritte

frieze /fri:z/ n fregio m

frigate /'frɪgət/ n fregata f

fright /fraɪt/ n paura f; **take** ∼ spaventarsi

frighten /'fraɪt(ə)n/ vt spaventare ■ **frighten away** vt far scappare ‹bird, intruder›

frightened /'fraɪtənd/ adj spaventato; **be** ∼ aver paura (**of** di)

frightening /'fraɪt(ə)nɪŋ/ adj spaventoso

frightful /'fraɪtfl/ adj terribile

frightfully /'fraɪtfʊlɪ/ adv terribilmente

frigid /'frɪdʒɪd/ adj frigido

ꞎ indicates a very frequent word

frigidity /frɪˈdʒɪdətɪ/ n freddezza f; Psych frigidità f

frill /frɪl/ n volant m inv

frilly /ˈfrɪlɪ/ adj ‹dress› con tanti volant

fringe /frɪndʒ/ n frangia f; (of hair) frangetta f; fig (edge) margine m

fringe benefits npl benefici mpl supplementari

frisk /frɪsk/ vt (search) perquisire

frisky /ˈfrɪskɪ/ adj (-ier, -iest) vispo

fritter /ˈfrɪtə(r)/ n frittella f

■ **fritter away** vt sprecare

frivolity /frɪˈvɒlətɪ/ n frivolezza f

frivolous /ˈfrɪvələs/ adj frivolo

frizzy /ˈfrɪzɪ/ adj (-ier, -iest) crespo

fro /frəʊ/ ▶ TO

frock /frɒk/ n abito m

frog /frɒg/ n rana f

frogman n uomo m rana inv

frogmarch vt Br portare via a forza

frogs' legs npl cosce fpl di rana

frogspawn n uova fpl di rana

frolic /ˈfrɒlɪk/ vi (pt/pp **frolicked**) ‹lambs› sgambettare; fam ‹people› folleggiare

⚲ **from** /frɒm/ prep da; ~ Monday da lunedì; ~ that day da quel giorno; he's ~ London è di Londra; this is a letter ~ my brother questa è una lettera di mio fratello; documents ~ the 16th century documenti del XVI secolo; made ~ fatto con; she felt ill ~ fatigue si sentiva male dalla stanchezza; ~ now on d'ora in poi

⚲ **front** /frʌnt/ 1 n parte f anteriore; fig (organization etc) facciata f; (of garment) davanti m; sea ~ lungomare m; Mil, Pol, Meteorol fronte m; in ~ of davanti a; in or at the ~ davanti; to the ~ avanti
2 adj davanti; ‹page, row, wheel› anteriore

frontage /ˈfrʌntɪdʒ/ n (of house) facciata f; with ocean/river ~ (access) prospiciente l'oceano/il fiume

frontal /ˈfrʌntl/ adj frontale

front bench n Br Pol parlamentari mpl di maggiore importanza

front door n porta f d'entrata

front garden n giardino m sul davanti

frontier /ˈfrʌntɪə(r)/ n frontiera f

front line n Mil prima linea f; be in the ~ fig essere in prima linea

front of house n Br Theat foyer m inv

front page 1 n prima pagina f
2 adj ‹picture, spread› in prima pagina

front runner n Sport concorrente mf in testa; (favourite) favorito, -a mf

front-wheel drive n trazione f anteriore

frost /frɒst/ n gelo m; hoar ~ brina f

frostbite /ˈfrɒs(t)baɪt/ n congelamento m

frostbitten /ˈfrɒs(t)bɪtən/ adj congelato

frosted /ˈfrɒstɪd/ adj ~ glass vetro m smerigliato

frostily /ˈfrɒstɪlɪ/ adv gelidamente

frosting /ˈfrɒstɪŋ/ n Am Culin glassa f

frosty /ˈfrɒstɪ/ adj (-ier, -iest) also fig gelido

froth /frɒθ/ 1 n schiuma f
2 vi far schiuma

frothy /ˈfrɒθɪ/ adj (-ier, -iest) schiumoso

frown /fraʊn/ 1 n cipiglio m
2 vi aggrottare le sopracciglia

■ **frown on** vt disapprovare

froze /frəʊz/ ▶ FREEZE

frozen /ˈfrəʊzn/ 1 ▶ FREEZE
2 adj ‹corpse, hand› congelato; ‹wastes› gelido; Culin surgelato; I'm ~ sono gelato

frozen food n surgelati mpl

frugal /ˈfruːgl/ adj frugale

frugally /ˈfruːgəlɪ/ adv frugalmente

⚲ **fruit** /fruːt/ n frutto m; (collectively) frutta f; eat more ~ mangia più frutta

fruit bowl n fruttiera f

fruit cake n dolce (m) con frutta candita

fruit cocktail n macedonia f [di frutta]

fruit drop n drop m inv alla frutta

fruiterer /ˈfruːtərə(r)/ n fruttivendolo, -a mf

fruit farmer n frutticoltore m

fruit fly n moscerino m della frutta

fruitful /ˈfruːtfʊl/ adj fig fruttuoso

fruit gum n caramella f alla frutta

fruition /fruːˈɪʃn/ n come to ~ dare dei frutti

fruit juice n succo m di frutta

fruitless /ˈfruːtlɪs/ adj infruttuoso

fruitlessly /ˈfruːtlɪslɪ/ adv senza risultato

fruit machine n macchinetta f mangiasoldi

fruit salad n macedonia f [di frutta]

fruity /ˈfruːtɪ/ adj ‹wine› fruttato

frump /frʌmp/ n donna f scialba

frumpy /ˈfrʌmpɪ/ adj scialbo

frustrate /frʌˈstreɪt/ vt frustrare; rovinare ‹plans›

frustrated /frʌˈstreɪtɪd, US ˈfrʌst-/ adj frustrato

frustrating /frʌˈstreɪtɪŋ/ adj frustrante

frustration /frʌˈstreɪʃn/ n frustrazione f

fry¹ /fraɪ/ n inv small ~ fig pesce m piccolo

fry² vt/i (pt/pp **fried**) friggere

frying pan /ˈfraɪɪŋ/ n padella f

ft. abbr (**foot** or **feet**) piede, piedi

ftp abbr (**file transfer protocol**) Comput FTP m

fuchsia /ˈfjuːʃə/ n fucsia f

fuck /fʌk/ vulg 1 vt/i scopare
2 n I don't give a ~ me ne sbatto; what the ~ are you doing? che cazzo fai?
3 int cazzo!

⸪⸪

■ **fuck off**: *vi* vulg ∼ **off!** vaffanculo!

■ **fuck up** *vt* vulg (ruin) mandare a puttane

fucking /ˈfʌkɪŋ/ *adj* vulg del cazzo

fuddled /ˈfʌdɪd(ə)ld/ *adj* (confused) confuso; (slightly drunk) brillo

fuddy-duddy /ˈfʌdɪdʌdɪ/ *n* fam matusa *mf inv*

fudge /fʌdʒ/ *n* caramella (*f*) a base di zucchero, burro e latte

✦ **fuel** /ˈfjuːəl/ **1** *n* carburante *m*; fig nutrimento *m*
2 *vt* fig alimentare

fuel consumption *n* consumo *m* di carburante

fuel economy *n* risparmio *m* di carburante

fuel efficient *adj* economico

fuel injection *n* iniezione *f*

fuel injection engine *n* motore *m* a iniezione

fuel oil *n* nafta *f*

fuel pump *n* pompa *f* della benzina

fuel tank *n* serbatoio *m*

fuggy /ˈfʌgɪ/ *adj* Br (smoky) fumoso

fugitive /ˈfjuːdʒɪtɪv/ *n* fuggiasco, -a *mf*

fugue /fjuːg/ *n* Mus fuga *f*

fulcrum /ˈfʊlkrəm/ *n* fulcro *m*

fulfil /fʊlˈfɪl/ *vt* (*pt/pp* -**filled**) soddisfare ‹conditions, need›; adempiere a ‹promise›; realizzare ‹dream, desire›; ∼ **oneself** realizzarsi

fulfilling /fʊlˈfɪlɪŋ/ *adj* soddisfacente

fulfilment /fʊlˈfɪlmənt/ *n* **sense of** ∼ senso *m* di appagamento

✦ **full** /fʊl/ **1** *adj* pieno (**of** di); (detailed) esauriente; ‹bus, hotel› completo; ‹skirt› ampio; **at** ∼ **speed** a tutta velocità; **in** ∼ **swing** in pieno fervore
2 *adv* in pieno; **you known** ∼ **well that** sai benissimo che
3 *n* **in** ∼ per intero

full-back *n* difensore *m*

full beam *n* Auto [fari *mpl*] abbaglianti *mpl*

full blast *adv* fam **the TV was on** ∼ c'era la TV a manetta

full-blown /-ˈbləʊn/ *adj* ‹epidemic› vero a e proprio; ‹disease› conclamato

full board *n* pensione *f* completa

full-bodied /-ˈbɒdɪd/ *adj* ‹wine› corposo

full-cream milk *n* latte *m* intero

full-frontal *adj* ‹photograph› di nudo frontale

full house *n* Theat tutto esaurito *m inv*; (in poker) full *m inv*

full-length *adj* ‹dress› lungo; ‹curtain› lungo fino a terra; ‹portrait› intero; ∼ **film** lungometraggio *m*

full moon *n* luna *f* piena

✦ indicates a very frequent word

full name *n* nome *m* per esteso

full price *n* prezzo *m* intero

full-scale *adj* ‹model› in scala reale; ‹alert› di massima gravità

full stop *n* punto *m*

full-time *adj* & *adv* a tempo pieno

✦ **fully** /ˈfʊlɪ/ *adv* completamente; (in detail) dettagliatamente; ∼ **booked** ‹hotel, restaurant› tutto prenotato

fully fledged /-ˈfledʒd/ *adj* ‹bird› che ha messo tutte le penne; ‹lawyer› con tutte le qualifiche; ‹member› a tutti gli effetti

fulsome /ˈfʊlsəm/ *adj* esagerato

fumble /ˈfʌmbl/ *vi* ∼ **in** rovistare in; ∼ **with** armeggiare con; ∼ **for one's keys** rovistare alla ricerca delle chiavi

■ **fumble about** *vi* (in dark) andare a tentoni; ∼ **in** rovistare in ‹bag›

fume /fjuːm/ *vi* (be angry) essere furioso

fumes /fjuːmz/ *npl* fumi *mpl*; (from car) gas *mpl* di scarico

fumigate /ˈfjuːmɪgeɪt/ *vt* suffumicare

✦ **fun** /fʌn/ *n* divertimento *m*; **for** ∼ per ridere; **make** ∼ **of** prendere in giro; **have** ∼ divertirsi

✦ **function** /ˈfʌŋkʃn/ **1** *n* funzione *f*; (event) cerimonia *f*
2 *vi* funzionare; ∼ **as** (serve as) funzionare da

functional /ˈfʌŋkʃ(ə)nəl/ *adj* funzionale

function key *n* Comput tasto *m* [di] funzioni

function room *n* sala *f* di ricevimento

✦ **fund** /fʌnd/ **1** *n* fondo *m*; fig pozzo *m*; ∼**s** *pl* fondi *mpl*
2 *vt* finanziare

fundamental /fʌndəˈmentl/ *adj* fondamentale

fundamentalist /fʌndəˈmentəlɪst/ *n* fondamentalista *mf*

✦ **funding** /ˈfʌndɪŋ/ *n* (financial aid) finanziamento *m*; (of debt) consolidamento *m*

fund-raiser /-reɪzə(r)/ *n* (person) promotore, -trice *mf* di raccolte di fondi; (event) manifestazione *f* per la raccolta di fondi

fund-raising /-reɪzɪŋ/ *n* raccolta *f* di fondi

funeral /ˈfjuːnərəl/ *n* funerale *m*

funeral directors *n* impresa *f* di pompe funebri

funeral home, funeral parlour Am *n* camera *f* ardente

funeral march *n* marcia *f* funebre

funeral service *n* rito *m* funebre

funereal /fjuːˈnɪərɪəl/ *adj* lugubre

funfair /ˈfʌnfeə(r)/ *n* luna park *m inv*

fungal /ˈfʌŋgəl/ *adj* ‹infection› micotico

fungus /ˈfʌŋgəs/ *n* (*pl* -**gi** /-gaɪ/) fungo *m*

funicular /fjuːˈnɪkjʊlə(r)/ *n* funicolare *f*

fun loving /'fʌnlʌvɪŋ/ *adj* ‹person› amante del divertimento

funnel /'fʌnl/ *n* imbuto *m*; (on ship) ciminiera *f*

funnily /'fʌnɪlɪ/ *adv* comicamente; (oddly) stranamente; ∼ **enough** strano a dirsi

✧ **funny** /'fʌnɪ/ *adj* (**-ier, -iest**) buffo; (odd) strano

funny bone *n* osso *m* del gomito

funny business *n* fam affare *m* losco

fur /fɜ:(r)/ *n* pelo *m*; (for clothing) pelliccia *f*; (in kettle) deposito *m*

fur coat *n* pelliccia *f*

furious /'fjʊərɪəs/ *adj* furioso

furiously /'fjʊərɪəslɪ/ *adv* furiosamente

furl /fɜ:l/ *vt* serrare ‹sail›

furnace /'fɜ:nɪs/ *n* fornace *f*

furnish /'fɜnɪʃ/ *vt* ammobiliare ‹flat›; fornire ‹supplies›

furnished /'fɜ:nɪʃt/ *adj* ∼ **room** stanza *f* ammobiliata

furnishings /'fɜ:nɪʃɪŋz/ *npl* mobili *mpl*

furniture /'fɜ:nɪtʃə(r)/ *n* mobili *mpl*

furniture remover /rɪmu:və(r)/ *n* Br impresa *f* di traslochi

furniture van *n* furgone *m* per i traslochi

furore /fjʊ'rɔ:rɪ/ *n* (outrage, criticism) scalpore *m*; (acclaim) entusiasmo *m*

furred /fɜ:d/ *adj* ‹tongue› impastato

furrow /'fʌrəʊ/ *n* solco *m*

furry /'fɜ:rɪ/ *adj* ‹animal› peloso; ‹toy› di peluche

✧ **further** /'fɜ:ðə(r)/ **1** *adj* (additional) ulteriore; **at the** ∼ **end** all'altra estremità; **until** ∼ **notice** fino a nuovo avviso **2** *adv* più lontano; ∼,... inoltre,...; ∼ **off** più lontano **3** *vt* promuovere

further education *n* istruzione *f* parauniversitaria

furthermore /fɜ:ðə'mɔ:(r)/ *adv* per di più

furthest /'fɜ:ðɪst/ **1** *adj* più lontano **2** *adv* più lontano; **the** ∼ **advanced of the students** lo studente più avanti

furtive /'fɜ:tɪv/ *adj* furtivo

furtively /'fɜ:tɪvlɪ/ *adv* furtivamente

fury /'fjʊərɪ/ *n* furore *m*

fuse¹ /fju:z/ *n* (of bomb) detonatore *m*; (cord) miccia *f*

fuse² **1** *n* Electr fusibile *m* **2** *vt* fondere; Electr far saltare **3** *vi* fondersi; Electr saltare; **the lights have**∼**d** sono saltate le luci

fuse box *n* scatola *f* dei fusibili

fuselage /'fju:zəla:ʒ/ *n* Aeron fusoliera *f*

fuse wire *n* [filo *m* di] fusibile *m*

fusillade /fju:zɪl'ɑ:d/ *n* Mil scarica *f*; fig raffica *f*

fusion /'fju:ʒn/ *n* fusione *f*

fuss /fʌs/ **1** *n* storie *fpl*; **make a** ∼ fare storie; **make a** ∼ **of** colmare di attenzioni **2** *vi* fare storie

fussy /'fʌsɪ/ *adj* (**-ier, -iest**) ‹person› difficile da accontentare; ‹clothes etc› pieno di fronzoli

fusty /'fʌstɪ/ *adj* che odora di stantio; ‹smell› di stantio

futile /'fju:taɪl/ *adj* inutile

futility /fjʊ'tɪlətɪ/ *n* futilità *f*

✧ **future** /'fju:tʃə(r)/ *adj & n* futuro; **in** ∼ in futuro

future perfect *n* futuro *m* anteriore

futures *npl* Fin contratti *mpl* a termine

futuristic /fju:tʃə'rɪstɪk/ *adj* futuristico

fuze /fju:z/ *n & v* Am = FUSE¹, FUSE²

fuzz /fʌz/ *n* **the** ∼ sl (police) la pula

fuzzy /'fʌzɪ/ *adj* (**-ier, -iest**) ‹hair› crespo; ‹photo› sfuocato

FYI *abbr* (**for your information**) per vostra informazione

G g

g¹, G /dʒi:/ *n* (letter) g, G *f inv*; Mus sol *m inv*

g² *abbr* (**gram(s)**) g

G8 *n abbr* (**group of 8**) G8 *mpl*

gab /gæb/ *n* fam **have the gift of the** ∼ avere la parlantina

gabardine /gæbə'di:n/ *n* gabardine *f*

gabble /'gæb(ə)l/ *vi* parlare troppo in fretta

gable /'geɪb(ə)l/ *n* frontone *m*

Gabon /gə'bɒn/ *n* Gabon *m*

gad /gæd/ *vi* (*pt/pp* **gadded**) ∼ **about** andarsene in giro

gadget /'gædʒɪt/ *n* aggeggio *m*

Gaelic /'geɪlɪk/ *adj & n* gaelico *m*

gaff /gæf/ *n* Br fam **blow the** ∼ spifferare un segreto; **blow the** ∼ **on something** svelare la verità su qualcosa

gaffe /gæf/ *n* gaffe *f inv*

gaffer /'gæfə(r)/ *n* Br (foreman) caposquadra *m*; Br (boss) capo *m*; Cinema, TV tecnico *m* delle luci

gag /gæg/ [1] n bavaglio m; (joke) battuta f
[2] vt (pt/pp **gagged**) imbavagliare

gaga /'gɑːgɑː/ adj fam rimbambito

gage /geɪdʒ/ n & vt Am = GAUGE

gaiety /'geɪətɪ/ n allegria f

gaily /'geɪlɪ/ adv allegramente

✧ **gain** /geɪn/ [1] n guadagno m; (increase) aumento m
[2] vt acquisire; ~ **weight** aumentare di peso; ~ **access** accedere
[3] vi ‹clock› andare avanti
■ **gain on** vt guadagnare terreno su ‹runner, car›

gainful /'geɪnfʊl/ adj ~ **employment** lavoro m remunerativo

gainsay /geɪn'seɪ/ vt contraddire ‹person›; contestare ‹argument›

gait /geɪt/ n andatura f

gala /'gɑːlə/ [1] n gala f; swimming ~ manifestazione f di nuoto
[2] attrib di gala

galaxy /'gæləksɪ/ n galassia f

gale /geɪl/ n bufera f

gale warning n avviso m di imminente bufera

gall /gɔːl/ n (impudence) impudenza f

gallant /'gælənt/ adj coraggioso; (chivalrous) galante

gallantly /'gæləntlɪ/ adv galantemente

gallantry /'gæləntrɪ/ n coraggio m

gall bladder n cistifellea f

gallery /'gælərɪ/ n galleria f

galley /'gælɪ/ n (ship's kitchen) cambusa f

galley [proof] n bozza f in colonna

Gallic /'gælɪk/ adj francese

galling /'gɔːlɪŋ/ adj irritante

gallivant /'gælɪvænt/ vi fam andare in giro

gallon /'gælən/ n gallone m (Br = 4,5 l; Am = 3,7 l)

gallop /'gæləp/ [1] n galoppo m
[2] vi galoppare

gallows /'gæləʊz/ n forca f

gallstone /'gɔːlstəʊn/ n calcolo m biliare

galore /gə'lɔː(r)/ adv a bizzeffe

galvanize /'gælvənaɪz/ vt Techn galvanizzare; fig stimolare (**into** a)

Gambia /'gæmbɪə/ n Gambia m

gambit /'gæmbɪt/ n prima mossa f

gamble /'gæmbl/ [1] n (risk) azzardo m
[2] vi giocare; (on Stock Exchange) speculare; ~ **on** (rely) contare su

gambler /'gæmblə(r)/ n giocatore, -trice mf [d'azzardo]

gambling /'gæmblɪŋ/ n gioco m [d'azzardo]

gambol /'gæmb(ə)l/ vi saltellare

✧ indicates a very frequent word

✧ **game** /geɪm/ [1] n gioco m; (match) partita f; (animals, birds) selvaggina f; ~**s** pl Sch ≈ ginnastica f
[2] adj (brave) coraggioso; **are you** ~? ti va?; **be** ~ **for** essere pronto per

game bird n uccello m da cacciagione

gamekeeper n guardacaccia m inv

game park n game reserve

game plan n tattica f

game point n Tennis game point m inv

game reserve n (for hunting) riserva f di caccia; (for preservation) parco m naturale [faunistico]

games console n console f per videogiochi

game show n ≈ quiz m inv televisivo

gamesmanship /'geɪmzmənʃɪp/ n stratagemmi mpl

games room n sala f giochi

games software n computer game m inv

game warden n guardacaccia m inv

gaming /'geɪmɪŋ/ n **on-line** ~ giochi online

gaming laws /'geɪmɪŋ/ npl leggi fpl che regolano il gioco d'azzardo

gaming machine n slot machine f inv

gaming zone n sito (m) su cui giocare online

gammon /'gæmən/ n coscia (f) di maiale affumicata

gamut /'gæmət/ n fig gamma f

gander /'gændə(r)/ n oca f maschio; **take a** ~ **at something** fam dare un'occhiata a qualcosa

gang /gæŋ/ n banda f; (of workmen) squadra f
■ **gang up** vi far comunella (**on** contro)

gangland /'gæŋlænd/ n malavita f

gangleader /'gæŋliːdə(r)/ n capobanda mf inv

gangling /'gæŋglɪŋ/ adj spilungone

gangplank /'gæŋplæŋk/ n passerella f

gang rape n stupro m collettivo

gangrene /'gæŋgriːn/ n cancrena f

gangrenous /'gæŋgrɪnəs/ adj cancrenoso

gangster /'gæŋstə(r)/ n gangster m inv

gangway /'gæŋweɪ/ n passaggio m; Naut, Aeron passerella f

gaol /dʒeɪl/ [1] n carcere m
[2] vt incarcerare

gaoler /'dʒeɪlə(r)/ n carceriere m

✧ **gap** /gæp/ n spazio m; (in ages, between teeth) scarto m; (in memory) vuoto m; (in story) punto m oscuro

gape /geɪp/ vi stare a bocca aperta; (be wide open) spalancarsi; ~ **at** guardare a bocca aperta

gaping /'geɪpɪŋ/ adj aperto

gap year n anno (m) sabbatico tra la fine della scuola superiore e l'inizio dell'università

garage /'gærɑːʒ/ n garage m inv; (for repairs) meccanico m; (for petrol) stazione f di servizio

garage mechanic n meccanico m

garage sale n vendita (f) di articoli usati a casa propria

garb /gɑːb/ n tenuta f

garbage /'gɑːbɪdʒ/ n immondizia f; (nonsense) idiozie fpl

garbage can n Am bidone m dell'immondizia

garbage truck n Am camion m della nettezza urbana

garbled /'gɑːbld/ adj confuso

◆ garden /'gɑːdn/ **1** n giardino m; [public] ～s pl giardini mpl pubblici **2** vi fare giardinaggio

garden centre n Br vivaio m (che vende anche articoli da giardinaggio)

garden city n città f inv giardino

gardener /'gɑːdnə(r)/ n giardiniere, -a mf

garden flat n appartamento (m) al pianterreno o seminterrato che dà sul giardino

gardening /'gɑːdnɪŋ/ n giardinaggio m

garden shears npl cesoie fpl

garden spider n epeira f

garden suburb n periferia f verde

garden-variety adj Am ‹writer; book› insignificante

gargle /'gɑːgl/ **1** n gargarismo m **2** vi fare gargarismi

gargoyle /'gɑːgɔɪl/ n gargouille f inv

garish /'geərɪʃ/ adj sgargiante

garland /'gɑːlənd/ n ghirlanda f

garlic /'gɑːlɪk/ n aglio m

garlic bread n pane m condito con aglio

garlic press n spremiaglio m inv

garment /'gɑːmənt/ n indumento m

garnet /'gɑːnɪt/ n granato m

garnish /'gɑːnɪʃ/ **1** n guarnizione f **2** vt guarnire

garret /'gærɪt/ n soffitta f

garrison /'gærɪsn/ n guarnigione f

garrotte /gə'rɒt/ **1** n Br garrotta f **2** vt (strangle) strangolare

garrulous /'gærʊləs/ adj chiacchierone

garter /'gɑːtə(r)/ n giarrettiera f; Am (for man's socks) reggicalze m inv da uomo

◆ gas /gæs/ **1** n gas m inv; Am fam (petrol) benzina f **2** vt (pt/pp **gassed**) asfissiare **3** vi fam blaterare

gas burner n becco m a gas

gas chamber n camera f a gas

gas cooker n cucina f a gas

gaseous /'gæsɪəs/ adj gassoso

gas fire n stufa f a gas

gas-fired /-faɪəd/ adj ‹boiler, water heater› a gas

gash /gæʃ/ **1** n taglio m **2** vt tagliare; ～ one's arm farsi un taglio nel braccio

gasket /'gæskɪt/ n Techn guarnizione f

gas main n conduttura f del gas

gas mask n maschera f antigas

gas meter n contatore m del gas

gasoline /'gæsəliːn/ n Am benzina f

gas oven n forno m a gas

gasp /gɑːsp/ vi avere il fiato mozzato

gas pedal n Am pedale m dell'acceleratore

gas ring n Br (fixed) bruciatore m; (portable) fornelletto m [portatile]

gas station n Am distributore m di benzina

gassy /'gæsɪ/ adj ‹drink› gassato

gastric /'gæstrɪk/ adj gastrico

gastric flu n influenza f gastro-intestinale

gastric ulcer n ulcera f gastrica

gastritis /gæ'straɪtɪs/ n gastrite f

gastroenteritis /gæstrəʊentə'raɪtɪs/ n gastroenterite f

gastronomy /gæ'strɒnəmɪ/ n gastronomia f

gate /geɪt/ n cancello m; (at airport) uscita f

gâteau /'gætəʊ/ n torta f

gatecrash **1** vt entrare senza invito a **2** vi entrare senza invito

gatecrasher n intruso, -a mf

gatehouse n (to castle) corpo m di guardia; (to park) casa f del custode

gatekeeper n custode mf

gatepost n palo m del cancello

gateway n ingresso m

gateway drug n droga f di passaggio

◆ gather /'gæðə(r)/ **1** vt raccogliere; (conclude) dedurre; (in sewing) arricciare; ～ speed acquistare velocità; ～ together radunare ‹people, belongings›; (obtain gradually) acquistare **2** vi ‹people› radunarsi; **a storm is** ～**ing** si sta preparando un acquazzone

gathering /'gæðərɪŋ/ n family ～ ritrovo m di famiglia

GATT /gæt/ abbr (**General Agreement on Tariffs and Trade**) GATT m

gauche /gəʊʃ/ adj ‹person, attitude› impacciato; ‹remark› inopportuno

gaudy /'gɔːdɪ/ adj (**-ier, -iest**) pacchiano

gauge /geɪdʒ/ **1** n calibro m; Rail scartamento m; (device) indicatore m **2** vt misurare; fig stimare

gaunt /gɔːnt/ adj (thin) smunto

gauntlet /'gɔːntlɪt/ n throw down the ～ lanciare il guanto della sfida

gauze /gɔːz/ n garza f

gave /geɪv/ ▶ GIVE

gawky /'gɔːkɪ/ adj (**-ier, -iest**) sgraziato

gawp /gɔːp/ *vi* ~ **(at)** fam guardare con aria da ebete

◆ **gay** /geɪ/ *adj* gaio; (homosexual) omosessuale; ‹*bar, club*› gay

Gaza strip /ˈgɑːzə/ *n* la striscia *f* di Gaza

gaze /geɪz/ ⓵ *n* sguardo *m* fisso
⓶ *vi* guardare; ~ **at** fissare; ~ **into space** avere lo sguardo perso nel vuoto

gazelle /gəˈzel/ *n* gazzella *f*

gazette /gəˈzet/ *n* (official journal) bollettino *m* ufficiale; (newspaper title) gazzetta *f*

gazetteer /gæzɪˈtɪə(r)/ *n* (book) dizionario *m* geografico; (part of book) indice *m* dei nomi geografici

gazump /gəˈzʌmp/ *vt* Comm sl **we've been ~ed** il proprietario della casa ha optato per un'offerta migliore dopo avere accettato la nostra

gazunder /gəˈzʌndə(r)/ *vt* Br *cercare di indurre qualcuno a cedere un immobile a un prezzo inferiore a quello pattuito*

GB *abbr* (**Great Britain**) GB

GBH *n abbr* (**grievous bodily harm**) lesioni *fpl* personali gravi

GCSE *n abbr* Br (**General Certificate of Secondary Education**) *esami (mpl) conclusivi della scuola dell'obbligo*

GDP *n abbr* (**gross domestic product**) PIL *m*

gear /gɪə(r)/ ⓵ *n* equipaggiamento *m*; Techn ingranaggio *m*; Auto marcia *f*; **in** ~ con la marcia innestata; **change** ~ cambiare marcia
⓶ *vt* finalizzare (**to a**)
⓷ *vi* ~ **up for** prepararsi per ‹*election*›; ~ **up to do something** prepararsi per fare qualcosa

gearbox /ˈgɪəbɒks/ *n* Auto scatola *f* del cambio

gear lever, **gearstick** Am, **gear shift** *n* leva *f* del cambio

gear wheel *n* moltiplica *f*

geese /giːs/ ▶ GOOSE

geezer /ˈgiːzə(r)/ *n* sl tipo *m*

gel /dʒel/ *n* gel *m inv*

gelatine /ˈdʒelətɪn/ *n* gelatina *f*

gelatinous /dʒɪˈlætɪnəs/ *adj* gelatinoso

gelding /ˈgeldɪŋ/ *n* (horse) castrone *m*; (castration) castrazione *f*

gelignite /ˈdʒelɪgnaɪt/ *n* gelatina *f* esplosiva

gem /dʒem/ *n* gemma *f*

Gemini /ˈdʒemɪnaɪ/ *n* Astr Gemelli *mpl*

gen /dʒen/ *n* Br fam informazioni *fpl*; **what's the ~ on this?** cosa c'è da sapere su questo?

gender /ˈdʒendə(r)/ *n* Gram genere *m*

gene /dʒiːn/ *n* gene *m*

genealogy /dʒiːnɪˈælədʒɪ/ *n* genealogia *f*

gene library *n* genoteca *f*

gene pool *n* pool *m* genetico

◆ **general** /ˈdʒenrəl/ ⓵ *adj* generale
⓶ *n* generale *m*; **in** ~ in generale

general election *n* elezioni *fpl* politiche

generalization /dʒenrəlaɪˈzeɪʃn/ *n* generalizzazione *f*

generalize /ˈdʒenrəlaɪz/ *vi* generalizzare

general knowledge *n* cultura *f* generale

◆ **generally** /ˈdʒenrəlɪ/ *adv* generalmente

general practitioner *n* medico *m* generico

general public *n* [grande] pubblico *m*

general-purpose *adj* multiuso *inv*

general strike *n* sciopero *m* generale

◆ **generate** /ˈdʒenəreɪt/ *vt* generare

◆ **generation** /dʒenəˈreɪʃn/ *n* generazione *f*

generation gap *n* gap *m inv* generazionale

generator /ˈdʒenəreɪtə(r)/ *n* generatore *m*

generic /dʒɪˈnerɪk/ *adj* ~ **term** termine *m* generico

generosity /dʒenəˈrɒsətɪ/ *n* generosità *f*

generous /ˈdʒenərəs/ *adj* generoso

generously /ˈdʒenərəslɪ/ *adv* generosamente

genesis /ˈdʒenəsɪs/ *n* fig genesi *f inv*

gene therapy *n* terapia *f* genica

genetic /dʒɪˈnetɪk/ *adj* genetico

genetically modified /dʒɪnetɪklɪ ˈmɒdɪfaɪd/ *adj* ‹*crops*› modificato geneticamente

genetic engineering *n* ingegneria *f* genetica

genetic fingerprinting /ˈfɪŋgəprɪntɪŋ/ *n* impronte *fpl* genetiche

geneticist /dʒɪˈnetɪsɪst/ *n* genetista *mf*

genetics /dʒɪˈnetɪks/ *n* genetica *f*

genetic testing *n* test *mpl* genetici

Geneva /dʒɪˈniːvə/ *n* Ginevra *f*

genial /ˈdʒiːnɪəl/ *adj* gioviale

genially /ˈdʒiːnɪəlɪ/ *adv* con giovialità

genie /ˈdʒiːnɪ/ *n* genio *m*

genitals /ˈdʒenɪtlz/ *npl* genitali *mpl*

genitive /ˈdʒenɪtɪv/ *adj & n* ~ **[case]** genitivo *m*

genius /ˈdʒiːnɪəs/ *n* (*pl* **-uses**) genio *m*

Genoa /ˈdʒenəʊə/ *n* Genova *f*

genocide /ˈdʒenəsaɪd/ *n* genocidio *m*

genome /ˈdʒiːnəʊm/ *n* genoma *m*

genre /ˈʒɒrə/ *n* genere *m* [letterario]

gent /dʒent/ *n* fam signore *m*; **the ~s** *sg* il bagno per uomini

genteel /dʒenˈtiːl/ *adj* raffinato

gentle /ˈdʒentl/ *adj* delicato; ‹*breeze, tap, slope*› leggero

gentleman /ˈdʒentlmən/ *n* signore *m*; (well-mannered) gentiluomo *m*

◆ indicates a very frequent word

gentleness /ˈdʒentlnɪs/ n delicatezza f
gently /ˈdʒentlɪ/ adv delicatamente
gentry /ˈdʒentrɪ/ n alta borghesia f
genuine /ˈdʒenjʊɪn/ adj genuino
genuinely /ˈdʒenjʊɪnlɪ/ adv ‹sorry›
  sinceramente
genus /ˈdʒiːnəs/ n Biol genere m
geoengineering /ˌdʒiəʊˌendʒɪˈnɪərɪŋ/ n
  geoingegneria f
geographer /dʒɪˈɒɡrəfə(r)/ n geografo m
geographical /dʒɪəˈɡræfɪkl/ adj
  geografico
geographically /dʒɪəˈɡræfɪklɪ/ adv
  geograficamente
geography /dʒɪˈɒɡrəfɪ/ n geografia f
geological /dʒɪəˈlɒdʒɪkl/ adj geologico
geologist /dʒɪˈɒlədʒɪst/ n geologo, -a mf
geology /dʒɪˈɒlədʒɪ/ n geologia f
geometric[al] /dʒɪəˈmetrɪk[l]/ adj
  geometrico
geometry /dʒɪˈɒmətrɪ/ n geometria f
geophysics /dʒɪəʊˈfɪzɪks/ n geofisica f
geopolitical /dʒiːəʊpəˈlɪtɪkl/ adj
  geopolitico
Georgia /ˈdʒɔːdʒə/ n Georgia f
Georgian /ˈdʒɔːdʒən/ n & adj georgiano, -a
  mf; (language) georgiano m
geranium /dʒəˈreɪnɪəm/ n geranio m
gerbil /ˈdʒɜːbəl/ n gerbillo m
geriatric /dʒerɪˈætrɪk/ adj geriatrico
geriatrics /dʒerɪˈætrɪks/ n geriatria f
geriatric ward n reparto m geriatria
germ /dʒɜːm/ n germe m; ~**s** pl microbi
  mpl
♂ **German** /ˈdʒɜːmən/ n & adj tedesco, -a mf;
  (language) tedesco m
germane /dʒəˈmeɪn/ adj ‹point, remark›
  pertinente
Germanic /dʒəˈmænɪk/ adj germanico f
German measles n rosolia f
German shepherd n pastore m tedesco
Germany /ˈdʒɜːmənɪ/ n Germania f
germinate /ˈdʒɜːmɪneɪt/ vi germogliare
germ warfare n guerra f batteriologica
gerrymandering /ˈdʒerɪmænd(ə)rɪŋ/
  n manipolazione (f) dei confini di una
  circoscrizione elettorale
gerund /ˈdʒerənd/ n gerundio m
gestate /dʒeˈsteɪt/ vi Biol essere incinta; fig
  maturare
gestation /dʒeˈsteɪʃən/ n gestazione f
gesticulate /dʒeˈstɪkjʊleɪt/ vi gesticolare
gesture /ˈdʒestʃə(r)/ n gesto m
♂ **get** /get/ **1** vt (pt/pp **got**, pp Am also
  gotten, pres p **getting**) (receive) ricevere;
  (obtain) ottenere; (buy, catch,
  fetch) prendere; (transport, deliver to airport etc)
  portare; (reach on telephone) trovare; fam
  (understand) comprendere; preparare ‹meal›;

~ **somebody to do something** far fare
  qualcosa a qualcuno
2 vi (become) ~ **tired/bored/angry**
  stancarsi/annoiarsi/arrabbiarsi; **I'm** ~**ting
  hungry** mi sta venendo fame; ~ **real!** fatti
  furbo!; ~ **dressed/married** vestirsi/sposarsi;
  ~ **something ready** preparare qualcosa;
  ~ **nowhere** non concludere nulla; **this is**
  ~**ting us nowhere** questo non ci è di nessun
  aiuto; ~ **to** (reach) arrivare a
■ **get about** vi ‹person› muoversi; ‹rumour›
  circolare
■ **get across** vt far capire ‹message,
  meaning›; ~ **something across to somebody**
  far capire qualcosa a qualcuno
■ **get ahead** vi (progress) fare progressi
■ **get along** vi GET ON
■ **get along with** vt andare d'accordo con
  ‹somebody›
■ **get around** vi GET ABOUT
■ **get at** vi (criticize) criticare; **I see what
  you're** ~**ting at** ho capito cosa vuoi dire; **what
  are you** ~**ting at?** dove vuoi andare a parare?
■ **get away** vi (leave) andarsene; (escape)
  scappare
■ **get away with** vt restare impunito per
■ **get behind with** vt rimanere indietro con
■ **get by** vi passare; (manage) cavarsela
■ **get down 1** vi scendere; ~ **down to work**
  mettersi al lavoro
  2 vt (depress) buttare giù
■ **get in 1** vi entrare
  2 vt mettere dentro ‹washing›; far venire
  ‹plumber›
■ **get into** vt penetrare in ‹building›;
  mettersi in ‹trouble›; (squeeze into) entrare in
  ‹dress›
■ **get off 1** vi scendere; (from work)
  andarsene; Jur essere assolto; ~ **off the bus/
  one's bike** scendere dal pullman/dalla bici
  2 vt (remove) togliere
■ **get on** vi salire; (be on good terms) andare
  d'accordo; (make progress) andare avanti; (in
  life) riuscire; **on the bus/one's bike** salire sul
  pullman/sulla bici; **how are you** ~**ting on?**
  come va?
■ **get on with** vt andare d'accordo con
  ‹person›; andare avanti in ‹work›
■ **get out 1** vi uscire; (of car) scendere;
  ~ **out!** fuori!
  2 vt togliere ‹cork, stain›
■ **get out of** vt (avoid doing) evitare
■ **get over 1** vi andare al di là
  2 vt fig riprendersi da ‹illness›
■ **get round 1** vt aggirare ‹rule›; rigirare
  ‹person›
  2 vi **I never** ~ **round to it** non mi sono mai
  deciso a farlo
■ **get through** vi (on telephone) prendere la
  linea
■ **get together 1** vi (meet) incontrarsi
  2 vt mettere insieme ‹people, money,
  report›
■ **get up 1** vi alzarsi; (climb) salire

2 *vt* salire su; ~ **up a hill** salire su una collina

■ **get up to** *vt* combinare ‹*mischief*›

getaway *n* fuga *f*

get-together *n* incontro *m* fra amici

get-up *n* tenuta *f*

get-up-and-go *n* dinamismo *m*

geyser /'giːzə(r)/ *n* scaldabagno *m*; Geol geyser *m inv*

G-force *n* forza *f* di gravità

Ghana /'gɑːnə/ *n* Ghana *m*

ghastly /'gɑːstlɪ/ *adj* (**-ier, -iest**) terribile; feel ~ sentirsi da cani

gherkin /'gɜːkɪn/ *n* cetriolino *m*

ghetto /'getəʊ/ *n* ghetto *m*

ghetto blaster /blɑːstə(r)/ *n* fam radio-registratore *m* stereo portatile

ghost /gəʊst/ *n* fantasma *m*

ghostly /'gəʊstlɪ/ *adj* spettrale

ghost town *n* città *f inv* fantasma

ghost writer *n* negro *m*

ghoulish /'guːlɪʃ/ *adj* macabro

giant /'dʒaɪənt/ **1** *n* gigante *m*
  2 *adj* gigante

gibberish /'dʒɪbərɪʃ/ *n* stupidaggini *fpl*

gibe /dʒaɪb/ **1** *n* malignità *f inv*
  2 *vi* beffarsi (**at** di)

giblets /'dʒɪblɪts/ *npl* frattaglie *fpl*

giddiness /'gɪdɪnɪs/ *n* vertigini *fpl*

giddy /'gɪdɪ/ *adj* (**-ier, -iest**) vertiginoso; feel ~ avere le vertigini

giddy spell *n* giramento *m* di testa

ꞙ **gift** /gɪft/ *n* dono *m*; (made to charity) donazione *f*

gifted /'gɪftɪd/ *adj* dotato

gift shop *n* negozio *m* di souvenir

gift token *n* Br buono *m* acquisto

gift voucher *n* Br buono *m* acquisto

gift-wrap *vt* impacchettare in carta da regalo

gig /gɪg/ *n* Mus fam concerto *m*

gigantic /dʒaɪ'gæntɪk/ *adj* gigantesco

giggle /'gɪg(ə)l/ **1** *n* risatina *f*
  2 *vi* ridacchiare

giggly /'gɪglɪ/ *adj* ‹*person*› che ha la ridarella

gild /gɪld/ *vt* dorare

gilding /'gɪldɪŋ/ *n* doratura *f*

gill /dʒɪl/ *n* (measure) quarto *m* di pinta

gills /gɪlz/ *npl* branchia *fsg*

gilt /gɪlt/ **1** *adj* dorato
  2 *n* doratura *f*

gilt-edged stock /-edʒd/ *n* Fin investimento *m* sicuro

gimlet /'gɪmlɪt/ *n* succhiello *m*

gimmick /'gɪmɪk/ *n* trovata *f*

gimmicky /'gɪmɪkɪ/ *adj* ‹*production*› pieno di trovate a effetto

gin /dʒɪn/ *n* gin *m inv*

ginger /'dʒɪndʒə(r)/ **1** *adj* rosso fuoco *inv*; ‹*cat*› rosso
  2 *n* zenzero *m*

ginger ale *n* bibita *f* gassata allo zenzero

ginger beer *n* bibita *f* allo zenzero

gingerbread *n* panpepato *m*

ginger-haired /-'heəd/ *adj* con i capelli rossi

gingerly /'dʒɪndʒəlɪ/ *adv* con precauzione

ginger nut, ginger snap *n* biscotto *m* allo zenzero

gingham /'gɪŋəm/ *n* tessuto *m* vichy

gin rummy *n variante* (*f*) *del gioco del ramino*

gipsy /'dʒɪpsɪ/ *n* = GYPSY

giraffe /dʒɪ'rɑːf/ *n* giraffa *f*

girder /'gɜːdə(r)/ *n* Techn trave *f*

girdle /'gɜːdl/ *n* cintura *f*; (corset) busto *m*

ꞙ **girl** /gɜːl/ *n* ragazza *f*; (female child) femmina *f*

girl Friday *n* segretaria *f* tuttofare *inv*

girlfriend *n* amica *f*; (of boy) ragazza *f*

girl guide *n* Br giovane esploratrice *f*

girlish /'gɜːlɪʃ/ *adj* da ragazza

giro /'dʒaɪərəʊ/ *n* bancogiro *m*; (cheque) sussidio *m* di disoccupazione

girth /gɜːθ/ *n* circonferenza *f*

gist /dʒɪst/ *n* the ~ la sostanza

ꞙ **give** /gɪv/ **1** *n* elasticità *f*
  2 *vt* (*pt* **gave**, *pp* **given**) dare; (as present) regalare (**to** a); fare ‹*lecture, present, shriek*›; donare ‹*blood*›; ~ **birth** partorire
  3 *vi* (to charity) fare delle donazioni; (yield) cedere

■ **give away** *vt* dar via; (betray) tradire; (distribute) assegnare; ~ **away the bride** portare la sposa all'altare

■ **give back** *vt* restituire

■ **give in** **1** *vt* consegnare
  2 *vi* (yield) arrendersi

■ **give off** *vt* emanare

■ **give out** **1** *vi* ‹*supplies, patience*› esaurirsi; ‹*engine, heart*› fermarsi
  2 *vt* (distribute) distribuire; diffondere ‹*heat*›

■ **give over**: *vi* ~ **over!** piantala!

■ **give up** **1** *vt* rinunciare a; ~ **oneself up** arrendersi
  2 *vt* rinunciare

■ **give way** *vi* cedere; Auto dare la precedenza; (collapse) crollare

give-and-take *n* concessioni *fpl* reciproche

giveaway /'gɪvəweɪ/ *n* **to be a dead** ~ essere un indizio ovvio

given /'gɪvn/ ▶ GIVE

given name *n* nome *m* di battesimo

GLA *n abbr* Br (**Greater London Authority**) *organismo* (*m*) *di governo di Londra*

ꞙ indicates a very frequent word

glacier /'glæsɪə(r)/ n ghiacciaio m

✦ **glad** /glæd/ adj contento (**of** di)

gladden /'glædn/ vt rallegrare

glade /gleɪd/ n radura f

gladiator /'glædɪeɪtə(r)/ n gladiatore m

gladiolus /glædɪ'əʊləs/ n gladiolo m

gladly /'glædlɪ/ adv volentieri

glamorize /'glæməraɪz/ vt rendere affascinante

glamorous /'glæmərəs/ adj affascinante

glamour /'glæmə(r)/ n fascino m

✦ **glance** /glɑːns/ ① n sguardo m
  ② vi ~ **at** dare un'occhiata a
  ■ **glance off** vt ‹bullet, stone› rimbalzare contro
  ■ **glance up** vi alzare gli occhi

gland /glænd/ n ghiandola f

glandular /'glændjʊlə(r)/ adj ghiandolare

glandular fever n mononucleosi f

glare /gleə(r)/ ① n bagliore m; (look) occhiataccia f
  ② vi ~ **at** dare un'occhiataccia a

glaring /'gleərɪŋ/ adj sfolgorante; ‹mistake› madornale

✦ **glass** /glɑːs/ n vetro m; (for drinking) bicchiere m

glass ceiling n barriera (f) invisibile che impedisce alle donne di avanzare nella carriera

glasses /'glɑːsɪz/ npl (spectacles) occhiali mpl

glasshouse /'glɑːshaʊs/ n serra f

glassy /'glɑːsɪ/ adj vitreo

glassy-eyed /-'aɪd/ adj (from drink, illness) che ha gli occhi vitrei

glaucoma /glɔː'kəʊmə/ n glaucoma m

glaze /gleɪz/ ① n smalto m
  ② vt mettere i vetri a ‹door, window›; smaltare ‹pottery›; Culin spennellare

glazed /gleɪzd/ adj ‹eyes› vitreo

glazier /'gleɪzɪə(r)/ n vetraio m

gleam /gliːm/ ① n luccichio m
  ② vi luccicare

gleaming /'gliːmɪŋ/ adj (clean) splendente; ~ white teeth denti bianchi splendenti

glean /gliːn/ vt racimolare ‹information›

glee /gliː/ n gioia f

gleeful /'gliːfʊl/ adj gioioso

gleefully /'gliːfʊlɪ/ adv gioiosamente

glen /glen/ n vallone m

glib /glɪb/ adj pej insincero

glibly /'glɪblɪ/ adv pej senza sincerità

glide /glaɪd/ vi scorrere; (through the air) planare

glider /'glaɪdə(r)/ n aliante m

gliding /'glaɪdɪŋ/ n volo m a vela

glimmer /'glɪmə(r)/ ① n barlume m
  ② vi emettere un barlume

glimpse /glɪmps/ ① n occhiata f; **catch a** ~ **of** intravedere
  ② vt intravedere

glint /glɪnt/ ① n luccichio m
  ② vi luccicare

glisten /'glɪsn/ vi luccicare

glitch /glɪtʃ/ n Comput problema m tecnico

glitter /'glɪtə(r)/ vi brillare

gloat /gləʊt/ vi gongolare (**over** su)

✦ **global** /'gləʊbl/ adj mondiale

globalization /ˌgləʊbəlaɪˈzeɪʃən/ n globalizzazione f

global warming n riscaldamento m dell'atmosfera terrestre

globe /gləʊb/ n globo m; (as a map) mappamondo m

globe-trotting /-trɒtɪŋ/ ① n viaggi mpl intorno al mondo
  ② adj ‹life› da giramondo; ‹person› giramondo

globule /'glɒbjuːl/ n globulo m

gloom /gluːm/ n oscurità f; (sadness) tristezza f

gloomily /'gluːmɪlɪ/ adv (sadly) con aria cupa

gloomy /'gluːmɪ/ adj (-ier, -iest) cupo

glorify /'glɔːrɪfaɪ/ vt (pt/pp -ied) glorificare; **a glorified waitress** niente più che una cameriera

glorious /'glɔːrɪəs/ adj splendido; ‹deed, hero› glorioso

glory /'glɔːrɪ/ ① n gloria f; (splendour) splendore m; (cause for pride) vanto m
  ② vi ~ **in** vantarsi di

glory-hole n fam ripostiglio m

gloss /glɒs/ n lucentezza f
  ■ **gloss over** vt sorvolare su

glossary /'glɒsərɪ/ n glossario m

gloss paint n vernice f lucida

glossy /'glɒsɪ/ adj (-ier, -iest) lucido; ‹paper› patinato; ~ **[magazine]** rivista f femminile

glossy magazine n rivista f patinata

glottal stop /'glɒt(ə)l/ n occlusiva f glottale

glove /glʌv/ n guanto m

glove compartment n Auto cruscotto m

glove puppet n burattino m

glow /gləʊ/ ① n splendore m; (in cheeks) rossore m; (of candle) luce f soffusa
  ② vi risplendere; ‹candle› brillare; ‹person› avvampare

glower /'glaʊə(r)/ vi ~ **(at)** guardare in cagnesco

glowing /'gləʊɪŋ/ adj ardente; ‹account› entusiastico

glow-worm n lucciola f

glucose /'gluːkəʊs/ n glucosio m

glue /gluː/ ⟦1⟧ *n* colla *f*
⟦2⟧ *vt* incollare
glue sniffer *n* persona *f* che sniffa colla
glue-sniffing /-snɪfɪŋ/ *n* sniffare *m* la colla
glum /glʌm/ *adj* (**glummer, glummest**) tetro
glumly /'glʌmlɪ/ *adv* con aria tetra
glut /glʌt/ *n* eccesso *m*
glutinous /'gluːtɪnəs/ *adj* colloso
glutton /'glʌtən/ *n* ghiottone, -a *mf*
gluttonous /'glʌtənəs/ *adj* ghiotto
gluttony /'glʌtənɪ/ *n* ghiottoneria *f*
glycerine /'glɪsəriːn/ *n* glicerina *f*
GM *abbr* (**genetically modified**) MG
gm *abbr* (**gram**) g
GMO *abbr* (**genetically modified organism**) OGM *m inv*
GMT *abbr* (**Greenwich mean time**) GMT
gnarled /nɑːld/ *adj* nodoso
gnash /næʃ/ *vt* ~ **one's teeth** digrignare i denti
gnat /næt/ *n* moscerino *m*
gnaw /nɔː/ *vt* rosicchiare
gnome /nəʊm/ *n* gnomo *m*
GNP *abbr* (**gross national product**) PNL *m*
GNVQ *n abbr* Br (**General National Vocational Qualification**) *diploma* (*m*) *di istituto tecnico*

✧ **go** /gəʊ/ ⟦1⟧ *n* (*pl* **goes**) energia *f*; (attempt) tentativo *m*; **on the go** in movimento; **at one go** in una sola volta; **it's your go** tocca a te; **make a go of it** riuscire
⟦2⟧ *vi* (*pt* **went**, *pp* **gone**) andare; (leave) andar via; (vanish) sparire; (become) diventare; (be sold) vendersi; **go and see** andare a vedere; **go swimming/shopping** andare a nuotare/fare spese; **where's the time gone?** come ha fatto il tempo a volare così?; **it's all gone** è finito; **be going to do** stare per fare; **I'm not going to** non ne ho nessuna intenzione; **to go** Am ⟨*hamburgers etc*⟩ da asporto; **a coffee to go** un caffè da portar via
■ **go about** ⟦1⟧ *vi* andare in giro
⟦2⟧ *vt* affrontare ⟨*task*⟩
■ **go after** *vt* (chase, pursue) correr dietro a
■ **go ahead** *vi* (event) aver luogo; **go ahead with** mandare avanti ⟨*plans, wedding*⟩
■ **go along**: *vi* **make something up as you ~ along** inventare qualcosa mentre si va avanti
■ **go along with** *vt* concordare con ⟨*person, view, plan*⟩
■ **go around** *vi* ⟨*rumour*⟩ girare; **~ around with** (person) andare in giro con
■ **go around together** *vi* ⟨*people*⟩ andare in giro insieme

✧ indicates a very frequent word

■ **go away** *vi* andarsene
■ **go back** *vi* ritornare
■ **go back on** *vt* rimangiarsi ⟨*promise*⟩; tornare su ⟨*decision*⟩
■ **go by** *vi* passare
■ **go down** *vi* scendere; ⟨*sun*⟩ tramontare; ⟨*ship*⟩ affondare; (become) diminuire
■ **go for** *vt* andare a prendere; andare a cercare ⟨*doctor*⟩; (choose) optare per; fam (attack) aggredire; **he's not the kind I go for** non è il genere che mi attira
■ **go in** *vi* entrare
■ **go in for** *vt* partecipare a ⟨*competition*⟩; darsi a ⟨*tennis*⟩
■ **go into** *vt* entrare in ⟨*building*⟩; (discuss) discutere
■ **go off** *vi* andarsene; ⟨*alarm*⟩ scattare; ⟨*gun, bomb*⟩ esplodere; ⟨*food, milk*⟩ andare a male; **go off well** riuscire
■ **go on** *vi* andare avanti; **what's going on?** cosa succede?
■ **go on at** *vt* fam scocciare
■ **go on with** *vt* (continue) andare avanti con
■ **go out** *vi* uscire; ⟨*light, fire*⟩ spegnersi
■ **go out with** *vt* uscire con (somebody)
■ **go over** ⟦1⟧ *vi* andare
⟦2⟧ *vt* (check) controllare
■ **go round** *vi* andare in giro; (visit) andare; (turn) girare; **is there enough to go round?** ce n'è abbastanza per tutti?
■ **go through** ⟦1⟧ *vi* ⟨*bill, proposal*⟩ passare
⟦2⟧ *vt* (suffer) subire; (check) controllare; (read) leggere
■ **go through with** *vt* portare a termine ⟨*plan*⟩
■ **go under** *vi* passare sotto; ⟨*ship, swimmer*⟩ andare sott'acqua; (fail) fallire
■ **go up** *vi* salire; Theat ⟨*curtain*⟩ aprirsi
■ **go with** *vt* accompagnare
■ **go without** ⟦1⟧ *vt* fare a meno di ⟨*supper; sleep*⟩
⟦2⟧ *vi* fare senza
goad /gəʊd/ *vt* spingere (**into** a); (taunt) spronare
go-ahead ⟦1⟧ *adj* ⟨*person, company*⟩ intraprendente
⟦2⟧ *n* okay *m*
✧ **goal** /gəʊl/ *n* porta *f*; (point scored) gol *m inv*; (in life) obiettivo *m*; **score a ~** segnare
goalie /'gəʊlɪ/ fam **goalkeeper** /'gəʊlkiːpə(r)/ *n* portiere *m*
goalpost /'gəʊlpəʊst/ *n* palo *m*
goat /gəʊt/ *n* capra *f*
goatee /gəʊ'tiː/ *n* pizzetto *m*
gobble /'gɒbl/ *vi* ⟨*turkey*⟩ fare glu glu
■ **gobble up** *vt* trangugiare
gobbledygook /'gɒb(ə)ldɪguːk/ *n* ostrogoto *m*
go-between *n* intermediario, -a *mf*
goblet /'gɒblɪt/ *n* calice *m*
goblin /'gɒblɪn/ *n* folletto *m*

gobsmacked /ˈgɒbsmækt/ adj Br fam I was ~ sono rimasto a bocca aperta

⚬ **God, god** /gɒd/ n Dio m, dio m

godchild n figlioccio, -a mf

goddamn adj maledetto

god-daughter n figlioccia f

goddess /ˈgɒdes/ n dea f

godfather n padrino m

god-fearing /-fɪərɪŋ/ adj timorato di Dio

god-forsaken /-fəseɪkən/ adj dimenticato da Dio

godless /ˈgɒdlɪs/ adj empio

godlike /ˈgɒdlaɪk/ adj divino

godly /ˈgɒdlɪ/ adj (-ier, -iest) pio

godmother n madrina f

godparents npl padrino m e madrina f

godsend n manna f

godson n figlioccio m

goer /ˈgəʊə(r)/ n Br be a ~ ‹car› essere una bomba

go-getter /ˈgəʊgetə(r)/ n persona f intraprendente

go-getting /-getɪŋ/ adj intraprendente

goggle /ˈgɒgl/ vi fam ~ at fissare con gli occhi sgranati

goggles npl occhiali mpl; (of swimmer) occhialini mpl [da piscina]; (of worker) occhiali mpl protettivi

going /ˈgəʊɪŋ/ [1] adj ‹price, rate› corrente; ~ **concern** azienda f florida [2] n it's hard ~ è una faticaccia; **while the** ~ **is good** finché si può

going-over n (cleaning) pulizia f da cima a fondo; (examination) revisione f; **the doctor gave me a thorough** ~ il dottore mi ha fatto una visita completa; **give somebody a** ~ (beat up) dare una manica di botte a qualcuno

goings-on npl avvenimenti mpl

go-kart /-kɑːt/ n go-kart m inv

go-karting /-kɑːtɪŋ/ n kartismo m; **go** ~ fare del kartismo

gold /gəʊld/ [1] n oro m [2] adj d'oro

gold-digger n fig cacciatore, -trice mf di dote

gold dust n polvere f d'oro; fig cosa f rara

golden /ˈgəʊldn/ adj dorato

golden handshake n Br buonuscita f (al termine di un rapporto di lavoro)

golden rule n regola f fondamentale

golden wedding n nozze fpl d'oro

goldfish n inv pesce m rosso

gold medal n medaglia f d'oro

gold medallist n (vincitore, -trice mf della) medaglia f d'oro

gold mine n miniera f d'oro

gold-plated /ˈpleɪtɪd/ adj placcato d'oro

gold rush n corsa f all'oro

goldsmith n orefice m

golf /gɒlf/ n golf m

golf club n circolo m di golf; (implement) mazza f da golf

golf course n campo m di golf

golfer /ˈgɒlfə(r)/ n giocatore, -trice mf di golf

golliwog /ˈgɒlɪwɒg/ n bambolotto m negro

gondola /ˈgɒndələ/ n gondola f

gondolier /gɒndəˈlɪə(r)/ n gondoliere m

gone /gɒn/ ▶ GO

goner /ˈgɒnə(r)/ n fam be a ~ essere spacciato

gong /gɒŋ/ n gong m inv

gonorrh[o]ea /gɒnəˈrɪə/ n gonorrea f

⚬ **good** /gʊd/ [1] adj (**better, best**) buono; ‹child, footballer, singer› bravo; ‹holiday, film› bello; ~ **at** bravo in; **a** ~ **deal of anger** molta rabbia; **as** ~ **as** (almost) quasi; ~ **morning,** ~ **afternoon** buon giorno; ~ **evening** buona sera; ~ **night** buona notte; **have a** ~ **time** divertirsi [2] n bene m; **for** ~ per sempre; **do** ~ far del bene; **do somebody** ~ far bene a qualcuno; **it's no** ~ è inutile; **be up to no** ~ combinare qualcosa

goodbye /gʊdˈbaɪ/ int arrivederci

good-for-nothing [1] n buono, -a mf a nulla [2] adj her ~ **son** quel buono a nulla di suo figlio

Good Friday n Venerdì m Santo

good-humoured /-ˈhjuːməd/ adj amichevole; ‹remark, smile› bonario

goodies /ˈgʊdɪz/ npl fam (to eat) bontà fpl

good-looking /-ˈlʊkɪŋ/ adj bello

good-natured /-ˈneɪtʃəd/ adj be ~ avere un buon carattere

goodness /ˈgʊdnɪs/ n bontà f; **my** ~! santo cielo!; **thank** ~! grazie al cielo!

goods /gʊdz/ npl prodotti mpl

goods train n treno m merci

good-time girl n (fun-loving) ragazza f allegra; euph (prostitute) donnina f allegra

goodwill /gʊdˈwɪl/ n buona f volontà; Comm avviamento m

goody /ˈgʊdɪ/ n fam (person) buono m

goody bag n omaggi (mpl) consegnati ai visitatori di una fiera dalle aziende espositrici

goody-goody n santarellino, -a mf

gooey /ˈguːɪ/ adj fam appiccicaticcio; fig sdolcinato

goof /guːf/ vi fam cannare

goofy /ˈguːfɪ/ adj fam sciocco

google /ˈguːgl/ vi usare Google

goon /guːn/ n (clown) svitato m; (thug) picchiatore m

goose /guːs/ n (pl **geese**) oca f

gooseberry /'gʊzbərɪ/ n uva f spina
goose-flesh n, **goose-pimples** npl
pelle fsg d'oca
goose-step n passo m dell'oca
gore¹ /gɔː(r)/ n sangue m
gore² vt incornare
gorge /gɔːdʒ/ **1** n Geog gola f
2 vt ~ oneself ingozzarsi
gorgeous /'gɔːdʒəs/ adj stupendo
gorilla /gə'rɪlə/ n gorilla m inv
gormless /'gɔːmlɪs/ adj fam stupido
gorse /gɔːs/ n ginestrone m
gory /'gɔːrɪ/ adj (**-ier, -iest**) cruento
gosh /gɒʃ/ int fam caspita
gosling /'gɒzlɪŋ/ n ochetta f
go-slow n forma (f) di protesta che consiste
in un rallentamento del ritmo di lavoro
gospel /'gɒspl/ n vangelo m
gospel music n musica f gospel
gospel truth n sacrosanta verità f
gossamer /'gɒsəmə(r)/ n (fabric) mussola f;
(cobweb) fili mpl di ragnatela
gossip /'gɒsɪp/ **1** n pettegolezzi mpl;
(person) pettegolo, -a mf
2 vi pettegolare
gossip column n cronaca f mondana
gossipy /'gɒsɪpɪ/ adj pettegolo
got /gɒt/ ▶ GET; **have ~ avere; have ~ to do
something** dover fare qualcosa
Gothic /'gɒθɪk/ adj gotico
gotten /'gɒtn/ Am ▶ GET
gouge /gaʊdʒ/ vt ~ out cavare
goulash /'guːlæʃ/ n gulash m inv
gourd /gʊəd/ n (fruit) zucca f
gourmet /'gʊəmeɪ/ n buongustaio, -a mf
gout /gaʊt/ n gotta f
govern /'gʌv(ə)n/ vt/i governare; (determine)
determinare
governess /'gʌvənɪs/ n istitutrice f
governing /'gʌvənɪŋ/ adj ‹party› al potere;
‹class› dirigente; **the ~ body** (school governors)
il consiglio d'istituto
✤ **government** /'gʌvnmənt/ n governo m
governmental /gʌvn'mentl/ adj
governativo
government health warning n
avviso m a cura del ministero della salute
government stocks npl titoli mpl di
stato
governor /'gʌvənə(r)/ n governatore m; (of
school) amministratore, -trice mf; (of prison)
direttore, -trice mf; fam (boss) capo m
gown /gaʊn/ n vestito m; Univ, Jur toga f
GP abbr (**general practitioner**) medico
m generico
GPA n abbr Am (**grade point average**)
media f scolastica

✤ indicates a very frequent word

✤ **grab** /græb/ vt (pt/pp **grabbed**) ~
[hold of] afferrare
Grace n his/your ~ (duke) il signor duca;
(archbishop) Sua Eccellenza; her/your ~
(duchess) la signora duchessa
grace /greɪs/ n grazia f; (before meal)
benedicite m inv; **with good ~** volentieri;
say ~ dire il benedicite; **three days' ~** tre
giorni di proroga
graceful /'greɪsfʊl/ adj aggraziato
gracefully /'greɪsfʊlɪ/ adv con grazia
gracious /'greɪʃəs/ adj cortese; (elegant)
lussuoso
gradation /grə'deɪʃn/ n gradazione f
✤ **grade** /greɪd/ **1** n livello m; Comm qualità
f; Sch voto m; Am Sch (class) classe f; Am
= GRADIENT
2 vt Comm classificare; Sch dare il voto a
grade crossing n Am passaggio m a
livello
grade school n Am scuola f elementare
gradient /'greɪdɪənt/ n pendenza f
gradual /'grædʒʊəl/ adj graduale
gradually /'grædʒʊəlɪ/ adv gradualmente
graduate¹ /'grædʒʊət/ n laureato, -a mf
graduate² /'grædʒʊeɪt/ vi Univ laurearsi
graduated /'grædʒʊeɪtɪd/ adj ‹container›
graduato
graduate training scheme n
formazione f professionale postlaurea
graduation /grædʒʊ'eɪʃn/ n laurea f;
(calibration) graduazione f
graduation ceremony n cerimonia f
di consegna dei diplomi di laurea
graffiti /grə'fiːtɪ/ npl graffiti mpl
graffiti artist n pittore, -trice mf di
graffiti
graft /grɑːft/ **1** n Bot, Med innesto m; Med
(organ) trapianto m; fam (hard work) duro
lavoro m; fam (corruption) corruzione f
2 vt innestare; trapiantare ‹organ›
grain /greɪn/ n (of sand, salt) granello m; (of
rice) chicco m; (cereals) cereali mpl; (in wood)
venatura f; **it goes against the ~** fig è contro
la mia/sua natura
grainy /'greɪnɪ/ adj ‹photograph› sgranato;
‹paintwork› granulato
gram /græm/ n grammo m
grammar /'græmə(r)/ n grammatica f
grammarian /grə'meərɪən/ n
grammatico, -a mf
grammar school n ≈ liceo m
grammatical /grə'mætɪkl/ adj
grammaticale
grammatically /grə'mætɪklɪ/ adv
grammaticalmente
gran /græn/ n fam nonna f
granary /'grænərɪ/ n granaio m
granary bread n pane m integrale

grand /grænd/ adj grandioso; fam eccellente

grandad /'grændæd/ n fam nonno m

grandchild n nipote mf

granddaughter n nipote f

grandeur /'grændʒə(r)/ n grandiosità f

grandfather n nonno m

grandfather clock n pendolo m (che poggia a terra)

grandiose /'grændɪəʊs/ adj grandioso

grandma /'grænmɑː/ n nonna f

grandmother n nonna f

grandpa /'grændpɑː/ n nonno m

grandparents npl nonni mpl

grand piano n pianoforte m a coda

grand slam® n vittoria (f) di tutte le fasi di una gara

grandson n nipote m

grandstand n tribuna f

grand total n totale m complessivo

granite /'grænɪt/ n granito m

granny /'grænɪ/ n fam nonna f

granny flat n Br appartamentino (m) indipendente per genitori anziani annesso all'abitazione principale

⚓ **grant** /grɑːnt/ ① n (money) sussidio m; Univ borsa f di studio
   ② vt accordare; (admit) ammettere; **take something for ~ed** dare per scontato qualcosa; **take somebody for ~ed** considerare quello che qualcuno fa come dovuto

granular /'grænjʊlə(r)/ adj granulare

granulated /'grænjʊleɪtɪd/ adj ~ **sugar** zucchero m semolato

granule /'grænjuːl/ n granello m

grape /greɪp/ n acino m; ~s pl uva fsg

grapefruit /'greɪpfruːt/ n inv pompelmo m

grapeseed oil n olio m di vinaccioli

grapevine /'greɪpvaɪn/ n vite f; **hear something on the** ~ sentir dire in giro qualcosa

graph /grɑːf/ n grafico m

graphic /'græfɪk/ adj grafico; (vivid) vivido

graphically /'græfɪklɪ/ adv graficamente; (vividly) vividamente

graphic design n grafica f

graphic designer n grafico, -a mf

graphics /'græfɪks/ n grafica f

graphics card n Comput scheda f grafica

graphics interface n Comput interfaccia f grafica

graphite /'græfaɪt/ n grafite f

graphologist /græ'fɒlədʒɪst/ n grafologo, -a mf

graph paper n carta f millimetrata

grapple /'græpl/ vi ~ **with** also fig essere alle prese con

grasp /grɑːsp/ ① n stretta f; (understanding) comprensione f
   ② vt afferrare

grasping /'grɑːspɪŋ/ adj avido

grass /grɑːs/ n erba f

grass court n campo m in erba

grasshopper n cavalletta f

grassland n prateria f

grassroots npl base f; **at the** ~ alla base

grass snake n biscia f

grassy /'grɑːsɪ/ adj erboso

grate¹ /greɪt/ n grata f

grate² ① vt Culin grattugiare; ~ **one's teeth** far stridere i denti
   ② vi stridere

grateful /'greɪtfl/ adj grato

gratefully /'greɪtfʊlɪ/ adv con gratitudine

grater /'greɪtə(r)/ n Culin grattugia f

gratification /grætɪfɪ'keɪʃn/ n soddisfazione f

gratified /'grætɪfaɪd/ adj appagato

gratify /'grætɪfaɪ/ vt (pt/pp **-ied**) appagare

gratifying /'grætɪfaɪɪŋ/ adj appagante

grating /'greɪtɪŋ/ n grata f

gratis /'grɑːtɪs/ adv gratis

gratitude /'grætɪtjuːd/ n gratitudine f

gratuitous /grə'tjuːɪtəs/ adj gratuito

gratuity /grə'tjuːɪtɪ/ n gratifica f

grave¹ /greɪv/ adj grave

grave² n tomba f

gravedigger /'greɪvdɪgə(r)/ n becchino m

gravel /'grævl/ n ghiaia f

gravelly /'grævəlɪ/ adj ‹voice› rauco

gravely /'greɪvlɪ/ adv gravemente

graven image /'greɪvən/ n idolo m

gravestone /'greɪvstəʊn/ n lapide f

graveyard /'greɪvjɑːd/ n cimitero m

gravitate /'grævɪteɪt/ vi gravitare

gravity /'grævɪtɪ/ n gravità f

gravy /'greɪvɪ/ n sugo m della carne

gravy boat n salsiera f

gray /greɪ/ adj Am = GREY

graze¹ /greɪz/ vi ‹animal› pascolare

graze² ① n escoriazione f
   ② vt (touch lightly) sfiorare; (scrape) escoriare; sbucciarsi ‹knee›

grease /griːs/ ① n grasso m
   ② vt ungere

greasepaint /'griːspeɪnt/ n cerone m

greaseproof paper /griːspruːf'peɪpə(r)/ n carta f oleata

greaser /'griːsə(r)/ n (motorcyclist) componente (m) di una banda giovanile di motociclisti

greasy /'griːsɪ/ adj (**-ier**, **-iest**) untuoso; ‹hair, skin› grasso

⚓ **great** /greɪt/ adj grande; fam (marvellous) eccezionale

great-aunt n prozia f
great big adj enorme
Great Britain n Gran Bretagna f
Great Dane n danese m
great-grandchildren npl pronipoti mpl
great-grandfather n bisnonno m
great-grandmother n bisnonna f
great-great-grandchildren npl pronipoti mpl
greatly /'greɪtlɪ/ adv enormemente
greatness /'greɪtnɪs/ n grandezza f
great-uncle n prozio m
Grecian /'gri:ʃ(ə)n/ adj greco
Greece /gri:s/ n Grecia f
greed /gri:d/ n avidità f; (for food) ingordigia f
greedily /'gri:dɪlɪ/ adv avidamente; ‹eat› con ingordigia
greedy /'gri:dɪ/ adj (-ier, -iest) avido; (for food) ingordo
Greek /gri:k/ adj & n greco, -a mf; (language) greco m
♂ **green** /gri:n/ **1** adj verde; fig (inexperienced) immaturo
   2 n verde m; (grass) prato m; (in golf) green m inv; ∼s pl verdura f; **the G∼s** pl Pol i verdi
green beans n fagiolini mpl
green belt n zona (f) verde intorno a una città
green card n carta f verde; Am permesso m di soggiorno
greenery /'gri:nərɪ/ n verde m
green-eyed monster /-aɪd'mɒnstə(r)/ n gelosia f
greenfield site /'gri:nfi:ld/ n terreno (m) su cui non sono mai esistiti insediamenti urbani
greenfinch n verdone m
green fingers npl **have** ∼ avere il pollice verde
greenfly n afide m
greengage n susina f verde
greengrocer Br, **greengrocery** Am n fruttivendolo, -a mf
greenhorn n (new) novellino m; (gullible) pivello m
greenhouse n serra f
greenhouse effect n effetto m serra
Greenland n Groenlandia f
green light n fam verde m
green onion n Am cipollotto m
green salad n insalata f verde
greet /gri:t/ vt salutare; (welcome) accogliere
greeting /'gri:tɪŋ/ n saluto m; (welcome) accoglienza f
greetings card /'gri:tɪŋz/ n biglietto m d'auguri

gregarious /grɪ'geərɪəs/ adj gregario; (person) socievole
gremlin /'gremlɪn/ n hum spirito m maligno
Grenada /grə'neɪdə/ n Grenada f
grenade /grɪ'neɪd/ n granata f
grenadier /grenə'dɪə(r)/ n Mil guardia (f) reale inglese
grew /gru:/ ▶ GROW
grey Br, **gray** Am /greɪ/ **1** adj grigio; ‹hair› bianco
   2 n grigio m
   3 vi diventare bianco
■ **grey out** vt Comput visualizzare con sfondo azzurro ombreggiato
grey area n zona f oscura
grey-haired /heəd/ adj dai capelli grigi
greyhound n levriero m
grey matter n (brain) materia f grigia
grey squirrel n scoiattolo m grigio
grid /grɪd/ n griglia f; (on map) reticolato m; Electr rete f
griddle /'grɪd(ə)l/ n (for meat) piastra f
gridiron n griglia f; Am campo m di football americano
gridlock n fig (deadlock) situazione f di stallo; (in traffic) imbottigliamento m
grid reference n coordinate fpl
grief /gri:f/ n dolore m; **come to** ∼ ‹plans› naufragare
grief-stricken /-strɪkən/ adj affranto dal dolore
grievance /'gri:vəns/ n lamentela f
grieve /gri:v/ **1** vt addolorare
   2 vi essere addolorato
grievous /'gri:vəs/ adj doloroso
grievous bodily harm n lesioni fpl personali gravi
grievously /'gri:vəslɪ/ adv tristemente
grill /grɪl/ **1** n graticola f; (for grilling) griglia f; **mixed** ∼ grigliata f mista
   2 vt/i cuocere alla griglia; (interrogate) sottoporre al terzo grado
grille /grɪl/ n grata f
grim /grɪm/ adj (**grimmer**, **grimmest**) arcigno; ‹determination› accanito
grimace /'grɪməs/ **1** n smorfia f
   2 vi fare una smorfia
grime /graɪm/ n sudiciume m
grimly /'grɪmlɪ/ adv accanitamente
Grim Reaper n Morte f
grimy /'graɪmɪ/ adj (-ier, -iest) sudicio
♂ **grin** /grɪn/ **1** n sorriso m
   2 vi (pt/pp **grinned**) fare un gran sorriso
grind /graɪnd/ **1** n fam (hard work) sfacchinata f
   2 vt (pt/pp **ground**) macinare; affilare ‹knife›; Am (mince) tritare; ∼ **one's teeth** digrignare i denti

---

♂ indicates a very frequent word

grindstone /'graɪndstəʊn/ n mola
f; **keep one's nose to the ~** lavorare
indefessamente

grip /grɪp/ **1** n presa f; fig controllo m; (bag)
borsone m; **be in the ~ of** essere in preda a;
get a ~ of oneself controllarsi
2 vt (pt/pp **gripped**) afferrare; ‹tyres› far
presa su; tenere avvinto ‹attention›

gripe /graɪp/ vi fam (grumble) lagnarsi

gripping /'grɪpɪŋ/ adj avvincente

grisly /'grɪzlɪ/ adj (**-ier, -iest**)
raccapricciante

gristle /'grɪsl/ n cartilagine f

grit /grɪt/ **1** n graniglia f; (for roads) sabbia
f; (courage) coraggio m
2 vt (pt/pp **gritted**) spargere sabbia su
‹road›; **~ one's teeth** serrare i denti

gritter /'grɪtə(r)/ n Br Auto spandighiaia
m inv

gritty /'grɪtɪ/ adj (sandy) pieno di terra;
(gravelly) ghiaioso; (hard, determined) grintoso;
(novel, film) crudo

grizzle /'grɪzl/ vi piagnucolare

grizzly /'grɪzlɪ/ n (bear) grizzly m inv

groan /grəʊn/ **1** n gemito m
2 vi gemere

grocer /'grəʊsə(r)/ n droghiere, -a mf

groceries /'grəʊsərɪz/ npl generi mpl
alimentari

grocer's [shop] Br, **grocery** Am n
drogheria f

groggy /'grɒgɪ/ adj (**-ier, -iest**) stordito;
(unsteady) barcollante

groin /grɔɪn/ n Anat inguine m

groom /gruːm/ **1** n sposo m; (for horse)
stalliere m
2 vt strigliare ‹horse›; fig preparare; **well-
~ed** ben curato

groove /gruːv/ n scanalatura f

grope /grəʊp/ vi brancolare; **~ for** cercare
a tastoni

gross /grəʊs/ **1** adj obeso; (coarse)
volgare; (glaring) grossolano; ‹salary, weight›
lordo
2 n inv grossa f

gross domestic product n prodotto
m interno lordo

gross indecency n Jur oltraggio m al
pudore

grossly /'grəʊslɪ/ adv (very) enormemente

gross national product n prodotto m
nazionale lordo

grotesque /grəʊ'tesk/ adj grottesco

grotesquely /grəʊ'tesklɪ/ adv in modo
grottesco

grotto /'grɒtəʊ/ n (pl **-es**) grotta f

grotty /'grɒtɪ/ adj (**-ier, -iest**) fam ‹flat,
street› squallido

grouch /graʊtʃ/ vi brontolare (**about**
contro)

grouchy /'graʊtʃɪ/ adj brontolone

ground¹ /graʊnd/ ▸ GRIND

⚬ **ground²** **1** n terra f; Sport terreno m;
(reason) ragione f; **~s** pl (park) giardini mpl;
(of coffee) fondi mpl
2 vi ‹ship› arenarsi
3 vt bloccare a terra ‹aircraft›; Am Electr
mettere a terra

ground control n base f di controllo

ground crew n personale m di terra

ground floor n pianterreno m

grounding /'graʊndɪŋ/ n base f

groundless /'graʊndlɪs/ adj infondato

groundnut oil n olio m d'arachidi

ground rules npl principi mpl
fondamentali

groundsheet n telone m impermeabile

ground troops npl truppe fpl di terra

groundwork n lavoro m di preparazione

⚬ **group** /gruːp/ **1** n gruppo m
2 vt raggruppare
3 vi raggrupparsi

groupage /'gruːpɪdʒ/ n Comm
raggruppamento m

group booking n prenotazione f di
gruppo

group leader n capogruppo m

group therapy n terapia f di gruppo

group work n lavoro m di gruppo

grouse¹ /graʊs/ n inv gallo m cedrone

grouse² vi fam brontolare

grove /grəʊv/ n boschetto m

grovel /'grɒvl/ vi (pt/pp **grovelled**)
strisciare

grovelling /'grɒv(ə)lɪŋ/ adj leccapiedi inv

⚬ **grow** /grəʊ/ **1** vi (pt **grew**, pp **grown**)
crescere; (become) diventare; ‹unemployment,
fear› aumentare; ‹town› ingrandirsi
2 vt coltivare; **~ one's hair** farsi crescere
i capelli

■ **grow apart** vi ‹friends, couple›
disamorarsi

■ **grow on**: vt fam (become pleasing to) **it'll ~ on
you** finirà per piacerti

■ **grow out of**: vt **he's ~n out of his jumper**
il golf gli è diventato troppo piccolo

■ **grow up** vi crescere; ‹town› svilupparsi

growbag /'grəʊbæg/ n sacco (m) di
terriccio dentro cui si coltivano piante

grower /'grəʊə(r)/ n coltivatore, -trice mf

growing pains /'grəʊɪŋ/ npl (of child)
dolori mpl della crescita; fig (of firm, project)
difficoltà fpl iniziali nello sviluppo

growl /graʊl/ **1** n grugnito m
2 vi ringhiare

grown /grəʊn/ **1** ▸ GROW
2 adj adulto

grown-up adj & n adulto, -a mf

⚬ **growth** /grəʊθ/ n crescita f; (increase)
aumento m; Med tumore m

growth area n area f di sviluppo

growth industry n industria f in rapida crescita

growth rate n tasso m di crescita

groyne /grɔɪn/ n Br pennello m (*per difendere le spiagge dall'erosione*)

grub /grʌb/ n larva f, fam (food) mangiare m

grubby /'grʌbɪ/ adj (**-ier, -iest**) sporco

grudge /grʌdʒ/ **1** n rancore m; **bear somebody a ~** portare rancore a qualcuno **2** vt dare a malincuore

grudging /'grʌdʒɪŋ/ adj riluttante

grudgingly /'grʌdʒɪŋlɪ/ adv a malincuore

gruelling /'gru:əlɪŋ/ adj estenuante

gruesome /'gru:səm/ adj macabro

gruff /grʌf/ adj burbero

gruffly /'grʌflɪ/ adv in modo burbero

grumble /'grʌmbl/ vi brontolare (**at** contro)

grumpy /'grʌmpɪ/ adj (**-ier, -iest**) scorbutico

grunge /grʌndʒ/ n (dirt) lerciume m; (style) grunge m inv

grunt /grʌnt/ **1** n grugnito m **2** vi fare un grugnito

G-string n (garment) tanga m inv

guarantee /gærən'ti:/ **1** n garanzia f **2** vt garantire

guarantor /gærən'tɔ:(r)/ n garante mf

♂ **guard** /gɑ:d/ **1** n guardia f, (security) guardiano m; (on train) capotreno m; Am (in prison) guardia f carceraria; Techn schermo m protettivo; **be on ~** essere di guardia; **on one's ~** in guardia **2** vt sorvegliare; (protect) proteggere

■ **guard against** vt guardarsi da

guard-dog n cane m da guardia

guarded /'gɑ:dɪd/ adj guardingo

guardian /'gɑ:dɪən/ n (of minor) tutore, -trice mf

guardian angel n also fig angelo m custode

guard of honour n guardia f d'onore

guardroom n corpo m di guardia

guard's van n Br Rail carrozza f bagagliaio

Guatemala /ˌgwɑ:tə'mɑ:lə/ n Guatemala m

guava /'gwɑ:və/ n (fruit) guava f, (tree) albero m di guava

Guernsey /'gɜ:nzɪ/ n Guernsey f

guerrilla /gə'rɪlə/ n guerrigliero, -a mf

guerrilla warfare n guerriglia f

♂ **guess** /ges/ **1** n supposizione f **2** vt indovinare **3** vi indovinare; Am (suppose) supporre

guesstimate /'gestɪmət/ n calcolo m approssimativo

guesswork /'geswɜ:k/ n supposizione f

♂ **guest** /gest/ n ospite mf, (in hotel) cliente mf

guest house n pensione f

guest room n camera f degli ospiti

guest worker n lavoratore m immigrato; lavoratrice f immigrata

guff /gʌf/ n (nonsense) stupidaggini fpl

guffaw /gʌ'fɔ:/ **1** n sghignazzata f **2** vi sghignazzare

guidance /'gaɪdəns/ n guida f, (advice) consigli mpl

guide /gaɪd/ **1** n guida f, [Girl] G~ giovane esploratrice f **2** vt guidare

guidebook /'gaɪdbʊk/ n guida f turistica

guided missile /'gaɪdɪd/ n missile m teleguidato

guide dog n cane m per ciechi

guided tour n giro m guidato

guidelines /'gaɪdlaɪnz/ npl direttive fpl

guiding principle /gaɪdɪŋ'prɪnsɪp(ə)l/ n direttrice f

guild /gɪld/ n corporazione f

guile /gaɪl/ n astuzia f

guileless /'gaɪllɪs/ adj senza malizia

guillotine /'gɪləti:n/ n ghigliottina f, (for paper) taglierina f

guilt /gɪlt/ n colpa f

guiltily /'gɪltɪlɪ/ adv con aria colpevole

♂ **guilty** /'gɪltɪ/ adj (**-ier, -iest**) colpevole; **have a ~ conscience** avere la coscienza sporca

Guinea /'gɪnɪ/ n Guinea f

guinea /'gɪnɪ/ n ghinea f

Guinea-Bissau /-bɪ'saʊ/ n Guinea-Bissau f

guinea fowl faraona f

guinea pig n porcellino m d'India; (in experiments) cavia f

guise /gaɪz/ n **in the ~ of** sotto le spoglie di

guitar /gɪ'tɑ:(r)/ n chitarra f

guitarist /gɪ'tɑ:rɪst/ n chitarrista mf

Gulag /'gu:læg/ n gulag m inv

gulch /gʌltʃ/ n Am burrone m

gulf /gʌlf/ n Geog golfo m; fig abisso m

Gulf States npl gli stati mpl del Golfo

Gulf War n la guerra f del Golfo

gull /gʌl/ n gabbiano m

gullet /'gʌlɪt/ n esofago m; (throat) gola f

gullible /'gʌləbl/ adj credulone

gully /'gʌlɪ/ n burrone m; (drain) canale m di scolo

gulp /gʌlp/ **1** n azione f di deglutire; (of food) boccone m; (of liquid) sorso m **2** vi deglutire

■ **gulp down** vt tranguiare ‹food›; scolarsi ‹liquid›

gum¹ /gʌm/ n Anat gengiva f

gum² **1** n gomma f, (chewing-gum) gomma f da masticare, chewing-gum m inv **2** vt (pt/pp **gummed**) ingommare (**to a**)

gumboot /'gʌmbuːt/ n stivale m di gomma

gummed /gʌmd/ **1** ▶ GUM²
2 adj ‹label› adesivo

gumption /'gʌmpʃn/ n fam buon senso m

gumshoe /'gʌmʃuː/ n fam (private investigator) investigatore m privato

gum tree n fam be up a ∼ essere in difficoltà

◊ **gun** /gʌn/ n pistola f; (rifle) fucile m; (cannon) cannone m; **he had a** ∼ era armato
■ **gun down** vt (pt/pp **gunned**) freddare

gun barrel n canna f di fucile

gunboat n cannoniera f

gun dog n cane m da caccia

gunfire n spari mpl; (of cannon) colpi mpl [di cannone]

gunge /gʌndʒ/ n Br poltiglia f [disgustosa]

gung-ho /gʌn'həʊ/ adj hum (eager for war) guerrafondaio; (overzealous) esaltato

gun laws npl leggi fpl sulle armi

gun licence n porto m d'armi

gunman /'gʌnmən/ n uomo m armato

gunner /'gʌnə(r)/ n artigliere m

gunpoint n hold somebody up at ∼ assalire qualcuno a mano armata

gunpowder n polvere f da sparo

gunshot n colpo m [di pistola]

gunshot wound n ferita f d'arma da fuoco

gunslinger n pistolero m

gurgle /'gɜːgl/ vi gorgogliare; ‹baby› fare degli urletti

guru /'guruː/ n guru m inv

gush /gʌʃ/ vi sgorgare; (enthuse) parlare con troppo entusiasmo (**over** di)
■ **gush out** vi sgorgare

gushing /'gʌʃɪŋ/ adj eccessivamente entusiastico

gusset /'gʌsɪt/ n gherone m

gust /gʌst/ n (of wind) raffica f

gusto /'gʌstəʊ/ n with ∼ con trasporto

gusty /'gʌstɪ/ adj ventoso

gut /gʌt/ **1** n intestino m; ∼**s** pl pancia f; fam (courage) fegato m
2 vt (pt/pp **gutted**) Culin svuotare delle interiora; ∼**ted by fire** sventrato da un incendio

gutsy /'gʌtsɪ/ adj (brave) coraggioso; (spirited) gagliardo

gutter /'gʌtə(r)/ n canale m di scolo; (on roof) grondaia f; fig bassifondi mpl

guttering /gʌtərɪŋ/ n grondaie fpl

gutter press n stampa f scandalistica

guttersnipe /'gʌtəsnaɪp/ n ragazzo, -a mf di strada

guttural /'gʌtərəl/ adj gutturale

guv, guvnor /gʌv, 'gʌvnə(r)/ n Br fam (boss) capo m

◊ **guy** /gaɪ/ n fam tipo m, tizio m

Guyana /gaɪ'ænə/ n Guyana f

Guy Fawkes Day /fɔːks/ n Br anniversario (m) del fallimento della Congiura delle Polveri (5 novembre)

guzzle /'gʌzl/ vt ingozzarsi con ‹food›; **he's** ∼**d the lot** si è sbafato tutto

gym /dʒɪm/ n fam palestra f; (gymnastics) ginnastica f

gymkhana /dʒɪm'kɑːnə/ n manifestazione f equestre

gymnasium /dʒɪm'neɪzɪəm/ n palestra f

gymnast /'dʒɪmnæst/ n ginnasta mf

gymnastics /dʒɪm'næstɪks/ n ginnastica f

gym shoes npl scarpe fpl da ginnastica

gym-slip n Sch ≈ grembiule m (da bambina)

gynaecologist /gaɪnɪ'kɒlədʒɪst/ n ginecologo, -a mf

gynaecology /gaɪnɪ'kɒlədʒɪ/ n ginecologia f

gyp /dʒɪp/ n Br my back is giving me ∼ ho un terribile mal di schiena

gypsum /'dʒɪpsəm/ n gesso m

gypsy /'dʒɪpsɪ/ n zingaro, -a mf

gyrate /dʒaɪ'reɪt/ vi roteare

Hh

h, H /eɪtʃ/ n h, H f inv

ha! ha! /hɑː'hɑː/ int ah! ah!

haberdashery /hæbə'dæʃərɪ/ n merceria f; Am negozio m d'abbigliamento da uomo

habit /'hæbɪt/ n abitudine f; Relig (costume) tonaca f; **be in the** ∼ **of doing something** avere l'abitudine di fare qualcosa

habitable /'hæbɪtəbl/ adj abitabile

habitat /'hæbɪtæt/ n habitat m inv

habitation /hæbɪ'teɪʃn/ n unfit for human ∼ inagibile

habit-forming /-fɔːmɪŋ/ adj be ∼ creare assuefazione

habitual /həˈbɪtjʊəl/ *adj* abituale; ‹*smoker, liar*› inveterato

habitually /həˈbɪtjʊəlɪ/ *adv* regolarmente

habitual offender *n* delinquente *mf* recidivo

hack¹ /hæk/ *n* (writer) scribacchino, -a *mf*

hack² *vt* tagliare; ~ **to pieces** tagliare a pezzi

hacker /ˈhækə(r)/ *n* Comput pirata *m* informatico

hacking /ˈhækɪŋ/ *n* Comput pirateria *f* informatica

hacking cough *n* brutta tosse *f*

hackles /ˈhæk(ə)lz/ *npl* (on animal) pelo *m* del collo; (on bird) piumaggio *m* del collo; **make sb's ~ rise** fig far imbestialire qualcuno

hackney cab /ˈhæknɪ/ *n* fml taxi *m inv*

hackneyed /ˈhæknɪd/ *adj* trito [e ritrito]

hacksaw /ˈhæksɔː/ *n* seghetto *m*

had /hæd/ ▶ HAVE

haddock /ˈhædək/ *n inv* eglefino *m*

haematoma /hiːməˈtəʊmə/ *n* ematoma *m*

haemoglobin /hiːməˈgləʊbɪn/ *n* emoglobina *f*

haemophilia /hiːməˈfɪlɪə/ *n* emofilia *f*

haemophiliac /hiːməˈfɪlɪæk/ *n* emofiliaco, -a *mf*

haemorrhage /ˈhemərɪdʒ/ *n* emorragia *f*

haemorrhoids /ˈhemərɔɪdz/ *npl* emorroidi *fpl*

hag /hæg/ *n* old ~ vecchia befana *f*

haggard /ˈhægəd/ *adj* sfatto

haggis /ˈhægɪs/ *n* piatto (*m*) scozzese a base di frattaglie di pecora e avena

haggle /ˈhægl/ *vi* contrattare (**over** per)

Hague /heɪg/ *n* **the ~** l'Aia *f*

hail¹ /heɪl/ ① *vt* salutare; far segno a ‹*taxi*› ② *vi* ~ **from** provenire da

hail² ① *n* grandine *f* ② *vi* grandinare

hailstone /ˈheɪlstəʊn/ *n* chicco *m* di grandine

hailstorm /ˈheɪlstɔːm/ *n* grandinata *f*

◆ **hair** /heə(r)/ *n* capelli *mpl*; (on body, of animal) pelo *m*; **wash one's ~** lavarsi i capelli

hairband *n* (rigid) cerchietto *m*; (elastic) fascia *f* [per capelli]

hairbrush *n* spazzola *f* per capelli

hair curler *n* arricciacapelli *m inv*

haircut *n* taglio *m* di capelli; **have a ~** farsi tagliare i capelli

hairdo *n* fam pettinatura *f*

hairdresser *n* parrucchiere, -a *mf*

hairdryer, hairdrier *n* fon *m inv*; (with hood) casco *m* (asciugacapelli)

hair gel *n* gel *m inv* [per capelli]

◆ indicates a very frequent word

hairgrip *n* molletta *f*

hairless /ˈheəlɪs/ *adj* ‹*animal*› senza peli; ‹*body*› (chin) glabro

hairline *n* (on head) attaccatura *f* dei capelli

hairline crack *n* incrinatura *f* sottilissima

hairline fracture *n* Med frattura *f* capillare

hairnet *n* retina *f* per capelli

hairpiece *n* toupet *m inv*

hairpin *n* forcina *f*

hairpin bend *n* tornante *m*, curva *f* a gomito

hair-raising /ˈheəreɪzɪŋ/ *adj* terrificante

hair remover *n* crema *f* depilatoria

hairslide *n* Br fermacapelli *m inv*

hair-splitting /ˈheəsplɪtɪŋ/ *n* pedanteria *f*

hairspray *n* lacca *f* [per capelli]

hair straighteners /ˈheə(r) ˌstreɪtnəz/ *n pl* piastra *f* stirante

hairstyle *n* acconciatura *f*

hairstylist *n* parrucchiere, -a *mf*

hair transplant *n* trapianto *m* di capelli

hairy /ˈheərɪ/ *adj* (**-ier, -iest**) peloso; fam (frightening) spaventoso

Haiti /ˈheɪtɪ/ *n* Haiti *m*

Haitian /ˈheɪʃ(ə)n/ *n & adj* haitiano, -a *mf*; (language) haitiano *m*

hake /heɪk/ *n inv* nasello *m*

halal /hɑːˈlɑːl/ *adj* ‹*meat, butcher*› halal

halcyon days /ˈhælsɪən/ *npl* bei tempi *mpl* andati

hale /heɪl/ *adj* ~ **and hearty** in piena forma

◆ **half** /hɑːf/ ① *n* (*pl* **halves**) metà *f inv*; **cut in ~** tagliare a metà; **one and a ~** uno e mezzo; ~ **a dozen** mezza dozzina; ~ **an hour** mezz'ora
② *adj* mezzo; **[at] ~ price** [a] metà prezzo
③ *adv* a metà; ~ **past two** le due e mezza

half-and-half ① *adj* mezzo e mezzo
② *adv* a metà; **go ~** fare a metà

half-back *n* mediano *m*

half-baked *adj* fam che non sta in piedi

half board *n* mezza pensione *f*

half-breed *n & adj* mezzosangue *mf inv*

half-brother *n* fratellastro *m*

half-caste *n* meticcio, -a *mf*

half-century *n* mezzo secolo *m*

half cock *n* **go off at ~** partire col piede sbagliato

half-conscious *adj* semicosciente

halfcrown, half a crown *n* Br mezza corona *f*

half-cut *adj* fam (drunk) ciucco

half day *n* mezza giornata *f*

half-dead *adj* also fig mezzo morto

half-dozen *n* mezza dozzina *f*

half fare *n* metà tariffa *f*

half-hearted /-ˈhɑːtɪd/ *adj* esitante

half-heartedly /-'hɑːtɪdlɪ/ *adv* senza entusiasmo

half hour *n* mezz'ora *f*

halfhourly *adj & adv* ogni mezz'ora

half-length *adj* ‹portrait› a mezzo busto

half-light *n* penombra *f*

half mast *n* at ∼ a mezz'asta

half measures *npl* mezze misure *fpl*

half-moon ① *n* mezzaluna *f*; (of fingernail) lunula *f*
② *attrib* ‹spectacles› a mezzaluna

half pay *n* metà stipendio *m*

halfpenny /'heɪpnɪ/ *n* Br mezzo penny *m inv*

half-pint *n* mezza pinta *f* (*Br = 0,28 l, Am = 0,24 l*); (beer) piccola *f*; fig mezza calzetta *f*

half price ① *adj* a metà prezzo
② *adv* [a] metà prezzo

half-sister *n* sorellastra *f*

half size ① *n* (of shoe) mezzo numero *m*
② *adj* ‹copy› ridotto della metà

half smile *n* mezzo sorriso *m*

half-starved *adj* mezzo morto di fame

half-term *n* vacanza *f* di metà trimestre

half-time *n* Sport intervallo *m*

half-truth *n* mezza verità *f inv*

halfway ① *adj* the ∼ mark/stage il livello intermedio
② *adv* a metà strada; get ∼ fig arrivare a metà

halfway house *n* (compromise) via *f* di mezzo; (rehabilitation centre) centro *m* di riabilitazione per ex detenuti

halfway line *n* Sport linea *f* mediana

halfwit *n* idiota *mf*

half-year ① *n* Fin, Comm semestre *m*
② *attrib* ‹profit, results› semestrale

half-yearly *adj* ‹meeting, payment› semestrale

halibut /'hælɪbət/ *n inv* ippoglosso *m*

halitosis /hælɪ'təʊsɪs/ *n* alitosi *f inv*

⚡ **hall** /hɔːl/ *n* (entrance) ingresso *m*; (room) sala *f*; (mansion) residenza *f* di campagna; ∼ of residence Univ casa *f* dello studente

hallelujah /(h)ælɪ'luːjə/ *int* alleluia!

hallmark /'hɔːlmɑːk/ *n* marchio *m* di garanzia; fig marchio *m*

hallo /hə'ləʊ/ *int* ciao!; (on telephone) pronto!; say ∼ to salutare

hall of residence *n* residenza *f* universitaria

hallowed /'hæləʊd/ *adj* ‹ground› consacrato; ‹tradition› sacro

Halloween /hæləʊ'iːn/ *n* vigilia (*f*) d'Ognissanti e notte delle streghe, celebrata soprattutto dai bambini

hallucinate /hə'luːsɪneɪt/ *vi* avere le allucinazioni

hallucination /həluːsɪ'neɪʃn/ *n* allucinazione *f*

hallucinatory /hə'luːsɪnət(ə)rɪ/ *adj* ‹drug› allucinogeno

hallucinogen /hə'luːsɪnədʒən/ *n* sostanza *f* allucinante

hallucinogenic /həluːsɪnə'dʒenɪk/ *adj* allucinogeno

hallway /'hɔːlweɪ/ *n* ingresso *m*

halo /'heɪləʊ/ *n* (*pl* **-es**) aureola *f*; Astr alone *m*

halogen /'hælədʒən/ *n* alogeno *m*

halt /hɔːlt/ ① *n* alt *m inv*; come to a ∼ fermarsi; ‹traffic› bloccarsi
② *vi* fermarsi; ∼! alt!
③ *vt* fermare

halter /'hɔːltə(r)/ *n* (for horse) cavezza *f*

halter-neck *n* modello (*m*) con allacciatura dietro il collo che lascia la schiena scoperta

halting /'hɔːltɪŋ/ *adj* esitante

haltingly /'hɔːltɪŋlɪ/ *adv* con esitazione

halve /hɑːv/ *vt* dividere a metà; (reduce) dimezzare

ham /hæm/ *n* prosciutto *m*; Theat attore, -trice *mf* da strapazzo

hamburger /'hæmbɜːgə(r)/ *n* hamburger *m inv*

ham-fisted /-'fɪstɪd/ *adj* Br fam maldestro

hamlet /'hæmlɪt/ *n* paesino *m*

hammer /'hæmə(r)/ ① *n* martello *m*
② *vt* martellare
③ *vi* ∼ at/on picchiare a
■ **hammer in** *vt* piantare ‹nail›
■ **hammer out** *vt* definire con grandi sforzi ‹agreement, policy›

hammer and sickle *n* falce *f* e martello *m*

hammered /'hæməd/ *adj* fam (drunk) sbronzo

hammock /'hæmək/ *n* amaca *f*

hamper[1] /'hæmpə(r)/ *n* cesto *m*; [gift] ∼ cestino *m*

hamper[2] *vt* ostacolare

hamster /'hæmstə(r)/ *n* criceto *m*

hamstring /'hæmstrɪŋ/ ① *n* (of horse) tendine *m* del garretto; (of human) tendine *m* del ginocchio
② *vt* fig rendere impotente

⚡ **hand** /hænd/ ① *n* mano *f*; (of clock) lancetta *f*; (writing) scrittura *f*; (worker) manovale *m*; all ∼s Naut l'equipaggio al completo; at ∼, to ∼ a portata di mano; by ∼ a mano; on the one ∼ da un lato; on the other ∼ d'altra parte; out of ∼ incontrollabile; (summarily) su due piedi; in ∼ in corso; ‹situation› sotto controllo; (available) disponibile; give somebody a ∼ dare una mano a qualcuno; ∼ in ∼ ‹run, walk› mano nella mano; go ∼ in ∼ fig andare di pari passo (with con)
② *vt* porgere ⋯⋗

■ **hand back** *vt* restituire ‹*something*›
■ **hand down** *vt* tramandare
■ **hand in** *vt* consegnare
■ **hand on** *vt* passare
■ **hand out** *vt* distribuire
■ **hand over** *vt* passare; (to police) consegnare
handbag *n* borsa *f* (*da signora*)
hand baggage *n* bagaglio *m* a mano
handball *n* pallamano *f*; (fault in football) fallo *m* di mano; ~! mano!
handbasin *n* lavandino *m*
handbook *n* manuale *m*
handbrake *n* freno *m* a mano
handcart *n* carretto *m*
hand cream *n* crema *f* per le mani
handcuffs *npl* manette *fpl*
hand-dryer, hand-drier *n* asciugamani *m inv* ad aria
hand-eye coordination *n* coordinazione *f* occhio-mano
handful /'hændfʊl/ *n* manciata *f*; **be [quite] a ~** fam essere difficile da tenere a freno
hand grenade *n* bomba *f* a mano
handgun *n* pistola *f*
hand-held *adj* a mano
handicap /'hændɪkæp/ *n* handicap *m inv*
handicapped /'hændɪkæpt/ *adj* **mentally/ physically ~** mentalmente/fisicamente handicappato
handicraft /'hændɪkrɑːft/ *n* artigianato *m*
handiwork /'hændɪwɜːk/ *n* opera *f*
handkerchief /'hæŋkətʃɪf/ *n* (*pl* -**s** & -**chieves**) fazzoletto *m*
ꝯ **handle** /'hændl/ **1** *n* manico *m*; (of door) maniglia *f*; **fly off the ~** fam far perdere le staffe **2** *vt* maneggiare; occuparsi di ‹*problem, customer*›; prendere ‹*difficult person*›; trattare ‹*subject*›; **be good at handling somebody** saperci fare con qualcuno
handlebar moustache /hændlbɑːməˈstɑːʃ/ *n* baffi *mpl* a manubrio
handlebars /'hændlbɑːz/ *npl* manubrio *m*
handler /'hændlə(r)/ *n* (of dog) addestratore, -trice *mf*
handling /'hændlɪŋ/ *n* (touching, holding) manipolazione *f*; (of weapon) maneggio *m*; (dealing with) gestione *f*
handling charge *n* (for goods) spese *fpl* di movimentazione; (administrative) spese *fpl* di amministrazione
hand lotion *n* lozione *f* per le mani
hand-luggage *n* bagaglio *m* a mano
handmade *adj* fatto a mano
handout *n* (at lecture) foglio *m* informativo; fam (money) elemosina *f*
handover *n* (of prisoner, ransom) consegna *f*; (of property, territory) cessione *f*; ~ **of power** passaggio *m* delle consegne

ꝯ indicates a very frequent word

hand-pick *vt* scegliere ‹*produce*›; selezionare con cura ‹*staff*›
handrail *n* corrimano *m*
hand-reared /-'rɪəd/ *adj* ‹*animal*› allattato con il biberon
handset *n* Teleph ricevitore *m*
handshake *n* stretta *f* di mano
hand signal *n* Auto segnalazione *f* con la mano
hands-off *adj* ‹*policy*› di non intervento; ‹*manager*› che delega le responsabilità
handsome /'hænsəm/ *adj* bello; fig (generous) generoso; ‹*salary*› considerevole
hands-on *adj* ‹*experience*› pratico; ‹*approach*› pragmatico; ‹*control*› diretto; ‹*manager*› che segue direttamente le varie attività
handspring *n* salto *m* sulle mani
handstand *n* verticale *f*
hand-to-hand *adj* & *adv* ‹*fight*› corpo a corpo
hand-to-mouth *adj* ‹*existence*› precario
hand towel *n* asciugamano *m*
hand-woven /-'wəʊvən/ *adj* tessuto a mano
handwriting *n* calligrafia *f*
handwritten *adj* scritto a mano
handy /'hændɪ/ *adj* (-**ier**, -**iest**) pratico; ‹*person*› abile; **have/keep ~** avere/tenere a portata di mano
handyman /'hændɪmæn/ *n* tuttofare *m inv*
ꝯ **hang** /hæŋ/ **1** *vt* (*pt/pp* **hung**) appendere ‹*picture*›; (*pt/pp* **hanged**) impiccare ‹*criminal*›; ~ **oneself** impiccarsi; ~ **wallpaper** tappezzare **2** *vi* (*pt/pp* **hung**) pendere; ‹*hair*› scendere **3** *n* **get the ~ of it** fam afferrare
■ **hang about** *vi* gironzolare
■ **hang around** *vi* = HANG ABOUT
■ **hang back** *vi* (hesitate) esitare
■ **hang down** *vi* ‹*hem*› pendere
■ **hang on** *vi* tenersi stretto; fam (wait) aspettare; Teleph restare in linea
■ **hang on to** *vt* tenersi stretto a; (keep) tenere
■ **hang out 1** *vi* spuntare; **where does he usually ~ out?** fam dove bazzica di solito? **2** *vt* stendere ‹*washing*›
■ **hang up 1** *vt* appendere; Teleph riattaccare **2** *vi* essere appeso; Teleph riattaccare
hangar /'hæŋə(r)/ *n* hangar *m inv*
hanger /'hæŋə(r)/ *n* gruccia *f*
hanger-on *n* leccapiedi *mf inv*
hang-glider *n* deltaplano *m*
hang-gliding *n* deltaplano *m*
hanging /'hæŋɪŋ/ *n* (of person) impiccagione *f*; (curtain) tendaggio *m*; (on wall) arazzo *m*

hangman n boia m

hangover n postumi mpl della sbornia

hang-up n fam complesso m

hank /hæŋk/ n (of hair) ciocca f; (of wool etc) matassa f

hanker /'hæŋkə(r)/ vi ~ **after something** smaniare per qualcosa

hanky, hankie /'hæŋkɪ/ n fam fazzoletto m

hanky-panky /hæŋkɪ'pæŋkɪ/ n fam qualcosa m di losco

ha'penny /'heɪpnɪ/ n abbr Br (**halfpenny**) mezzo penny m inv

haphazard /hæp'hæzəd/ adj a casaccio; **in a ~ fashion** a casaccio

haphazardly /hæp'hæzədlɪ/ adv a casaccio

hapless /'hæplɪs/ adj sventurato

⋆ **happen** /'hæpn/ vi capitare, succedere; **as it ~s** per caso; **I ~ed to meet him** mi è capitato di incontrarlo; **what has ~ed to him?** cosa gli è capitato?; (become of) che fine ha fatto?

happening /'hæp(ə)nɪŋ/ n avvenimento m

happily /'hæpɪlɪ/ adv felicemente; (fortunately) fortunatamente

happiness /'hæpɪnɪs/ n felicità f

⋆ **happy** /'hæpɪ/ adj (-ier, -iest) contento, felice

happy ending n lieto fine m

happy-go-lucky adj spensierato

happy hour n ora (f) in cui nei pub le bevande vengono vendute a prezzi scontati

happy medium n giusto mezzo m

harangue /hə'ræŋ/ vt ‹morally› fare un sermone a; ‹politically› arringare

harass /'hærəs/ vt perseguitare

harassed /'hærəst/ adj stressato

harassment /'hærəsmənt/ n persecuzione f; **sexual ~** molestie fpl sessuali

harbinger /'hɑːbɪndʒə(r)/ n liter segnale m; (person) precursore m; precorritrice f

harbour /'hɑːbə(r)/ **1** n porto m **2** vt dare asilo a; nutrire ‹grudge›

⋆ **hard** /hɑːd/ **1** adj duro; ‹question, problem› difficile; **~ of hearing** duro d'orecchi; **be ~ on somebody** ‹person› essere duro con qualcuno **2** adv ‹work› duramente; ‹pull, hit, rain, snow› forte; **~ hit by unemployment** duramente colpito dalla disoccupazione; **take something ~** non accettare qualcosa; **think ~!** pensaci bene!; **try ~** mettercela tutta; **try ~er** metterci più impegno; **~ done by** fam trattato ingiustamente

hard and fast adj ‹rule, distinction› preciso

hardback n edizione f rilegata

hardboard n truciolato m

hard-boiled /-'bɔɪld/ adj ‹egg› sodo

hard cash n contante m

hard copy n copia f stampata

hard core **1** n (in construction) massicciata f; (of group, demonstrators) zoccolo m duro **2** adj ‹pornography, video› hard-core; ‹supporter, opponent› irriducibile

hard court n campo m in superficie dura

hard disk n hard disk m inv, disco m rigido

hard drive n Comput hard drive m

hard drug n droga f pesante

hard-earned /-'ɜːnd/ adj ‹cash› sudato

harden /'hɑːdn/ vi indurirsi

hardened /'hɑːdnd/ adj ‹criminal› inveterato; ‹drinker› cronico

hard-faced /-'feɪst/ adj ‹person› dai tratti duri

hard-fought adj ‹battle› accanito

hard hat n casco m

hard-headed /-'hedɪd/ adj pratico; ‹businessman› dal sangue freddo

hardhearted /-'hɑːtɪd/ adj dal cuore duro

hard-hitting /-'hɪtɪŋ/ adj ‹report, speech› incisivo

hard labour n Br lavori mpl forzati

hard lens n lente f a contatto rigida

hardline **1** adj ‹policy, regime› duro **2** n linea f dura; **~ lines!** che sfortuna!

hardliner n Pol fautore, -trice mf della linea dura

hard luck n sfortuna f

hard-luck story n **give somebody a ~** raccontare a qualcuno le proprie disgrazie

⋆ **hardly** /'hɑːdlɪ/ adv appena; **~ ever** quasi mai

hardness /'hɑːdnɪs/ n durezza f

hard-nosed /-'nəʊzd/ adj ‹attitude, businessman, government› duro

hard of hearing adj duro d'orecchio

hard-on n fam erezione f

hard porn n pornografia f hard-core

hard-pressed /-'prest/ adj in difficoltà; (for time) a corto di tempo

hard-pushed /-'pʊʃt/ adj (having problems) in difficoltà

hard rock n Mus hard rock m

hard sell n tecnica f di vendita aggressiva

hardship /'hɑːdʃɪp/ n avversità f inv

hard shoulder n Auto corsia f d'emergenza

hard up adj fam a corto di soldi; **~ up for something** a corto di qualcosa

hardware n ferramenta fpl; Comput hardware m inv

hardware shop n negozio m di ferramenta

hard-wearing /-'weərɪŋ/ adj resistente

hardwood n legno m duro

hard-working /-'wɜːkɪŋ/ *adj* be ~ essere un gran lavoratore

hardy /'hɑːdɪ/ *adj* (**-ier, -iest**) dal fisico resistente; ‹plant› che sopporta il gelo

hare /heə(r)/ *n* lepre *f*

hare-brained /'heəbreɪnd/ *adj* ‹scheme› da scervellati; ‹person› scervellato

harelip /heə'lɪp/ *n* labbro *m* leporino

harem /'hɑːriːm/ *n* serraglio *m*

haricot [bean] /'hærɪkəʊ/ *n* fagiolo *m* bianco

hark /hɑːk/ *v*

■ **hark back** *vt* fig ~ **back to** ritornare su

harm /hɑːm/ **1** *n* male *m*; (damage) danni *mpl*; out of ~'s way in un posto sicuro; it won't do any ~ non farà certo male **2** *vt* far male a; (damage) danneggiare

harmful /'hɑːmfʊl/ *adj* dannoso

harmless /'hɑːmlɪs/ *adj* innocuo

harmonica /hɑː'mɒnɪkə/ *n* armonica *f* [a bocca]

harmonious /hɑː'məʊnɪəs/ *adj* armonioso

harmoniously /hɑː'məʊnɪəslɪ/ *adv* in armonia

harmonize /'hɑːmənaɪz/ *vi* fig armonizzare

harmony /'hɑːmənɪ/ *n* armonia *f*

harness /'hɑːnɪs/ **1** *n* finimenti *mpl*; (of parachute) imbracatura *f* **2** *vt* bardare ‹horse›; sfruttare ‹resources›

harp /hɑːp/ *n* arpa *f*

■ **harp on** *vi* fam insistere (**about** su)

harpist /'hɑːpɪst/ *n* arpista *mf*

harpoon /hɑː'puːn/ *n* arpione *m*

harpsichord /'hɑːpsɪkɔːd/ *n* clavicembalo *m*

harrow /'hærəʊ/ *n* erpice *m*

harrowing /'hærəʊɪŋ/ *adj* straziante

harry /'hærɪ/ *vt* (pursue, harass) assillare

harsh /hɑːʃ/ *adj* duro; ‹light› abbagliante

harshly /'hɑːʃlɪ/ *adv* duramente

harshness /'hɑːʃnɪs/ *n* durezza *f*

harvest /'hɑːvɪst/ **1** *n* raccolta *f*; (of grapes) vendemmia *f*; (crop) raccolto *m* **2** *vt* raccogliere

harvester /'hɑːvɪstə(r)/ *n* (person) mietitore, -trice *mf*; (machine) mietitrice *f*

harvest festival *n* festa *f* del raccolto

has /hæz/ ▶ HAVE

has-been /-biːn/ *n* fam (person) persona *f* che ha fatto il suo tempo; (thing) anticaglia *f*

hash /hæʃ/ *n* make a ~ of fam fare un casino con

hash [sign] *n* cancelletto *m*

hashish /'hæʃɪʃ/ *n* hashish *m*

hassle /'hæsl/ **1** *n* fam rottura *f* **2** *vt* rompere le scatole a

hassock /'hæsək/ *n* cuscino *m* di inginocchiatoio

♂ indicates a very frequent word

haste /heɪst/ *n* fretta *f*; **make** ~ affrettarsi

hasten /'heɪsn/ **1** *vi* affrettarsi **2** *vt* affrettare

hastily /'heɪstɪlɪ/ *adv* frettolosamente

hasty /'heɪstɪ/ *adj* (**-ier, -iest**) frettoloso; ‹decision› affrettato

hat /hæt/ *n* cappello *m*

hatbox /'hætbɒks/ *n* cappelliera *f*

hatch¹ /hætʃ/ *n* (for food) sportello *m* passavivande *inv*; Naut boccaporto *m*

hatch² **1** *vi* ~ **[out]** rompere il guscio; ‹egg› schiudersi **2** *vt* covare; tramare ‹plot›

■ **hatch up** *vt* tramare ‹plot›

hatchback /'hætʃbæk/ *n* Auto tre/cinque porte *m inv*; (door) porta *f* del bagagliaio

hatchet /'hætʃɪt/ *n* ascia *f*

♂ **hate** /heɪt/ **1** *n* odio *m* **2** *vt* odiare

hateful /'heɪtfʊl/ *adj* odioso

hate mail *n* lettere *fpl* offensive o minatorie

hatpin /'hætpɪn/ *n* spillone *m*

hatred /'heɪtrɪd/ *n* odio *m*

hat-trick *n* tripletta *f*

haughtily /'hɔːtɪlɪ/ *adv* altezzosamente

haughty /'hɔːtɪ/ *adj* (**-ier, -iest**) altezzoso

haul /hɔːl/ **1** *n* (fish) pescata *f*; (loot) bottino *m*; (pull) tirata *f* **2** *vt* tirare; trasportare ‹goods› **3** *vi* ~ **on** tirare

haulage /'hɔːlɪdʒ/ *n* trasporto *m*

haulier /'hɔːlɪə(r)/ *n* autotrasportatore *m*

haunch /hɔːntʃ/ *n* anca *f*

haunt /hɔːnt/ **1** *n* ritrovo *m* **2** *vt* frequentare; (linger in the mind) perseguitare; **this house is** ~**ed** questa casa è abitata da fantasmi

haunted /'hɔːntɪd/ *adj* ‹house› infestato dai fantasmi; ‹look› tormentato

haunting /'hɔːntɪŋ/ *adj* ‹memory, melody› ossessionante

♂ **have** /hæv/ **1** *vt* (*3 sg pres tense* **has**, *pt/pp* **had**) avere; fare ‹breakfast, bath, walk etc›; ~ **a drink** bere qualcosa; ~ **lunch/dinner** pranzare/cenare; ~ **a rest** riposarsi; **I had my hair cut** mi sono tagliata i capelli; **we had the flat painted** abbiamo fatto tinteggiare la casa; **I had it made** l'ho fatto fare; ~ **to do something** dover fare qualcosa; ~ **him telephone me tomorrow** digli di telefonarmi domani; **he has** *or* **he's got two houses** ha due case; **you've got the money,** ~**n't you?** hai i soldi, no? **2** *v aux* avere; (*with verbs of motion & some others*) essere; **I** ~ **seen him** l'ho visto; **he has never been there** non ci è mai stato **3** *npl* **the** ~**s and the** ~**-nots** i ricchi e i poveri

■ **have in** *vt* avere in casa/ufficio etc ‹builders etc›

■ **have off**: *vt* fam **he's having it off with his secretary** si fa la segretaria

■ **have on** *vt* (be wearing) portare; (dupe) prendere in giro; **I've got something on tonight** ho un impegno stasera; **you're having me on!** tu mi stai prendendo in giro!

■ **have out**: *vt* ► **it out with somebody** chiarire le cose con qualcuno; ~ **a tooth out** farsi togliere un dente

haven /'heɪvn/ *n* fig rifugio *m*

haver /'heɪvə(r)/ *vi* (dither) titubare

haversack /'hævəsæk/ *n* zaino *m*

havoc /'hævək/ *n* strage *f*; **play ~ with** fig scombussolare

haw /hɔː/ ► HUM

Hawaii /həˈwaɪɪ/ *n* le Hawaii

Hawaiian /həˈwaɪən/ *n & adj* hawaiano, -a *mf*; (language) hawaiano *m*

hawk¹ /hɔːk/ *n* falco *m*

hawk² *vt* vendere in giro

hawker /'hɔːkə(r)/ *n* venditore, -trice *mf* ambulante

hawkish /'hɔːkɪʃ/ *adj* Pol intransigente

hawthorn /'hɔːθɔːn/ *n* biancospino *m*

hay /heɪ/ *n* fieno *m*

hay fever *n* raffreddore *m* da fieno

hayloft *n* fienile *m*

haymaking *n* fienagione *f*

haystack *n* pagliaio *m*

haywire *adj* fam **go ~** dare i numeri; ‹plans› andare all'aria

hazard /'hæzəd/ [1] *n* (risk) rischio *m* [2] *vt* rischiare; **~ a guess** azzardare un'ipotesi

hazardous /'hæzədəs/ *adj* rischioso

hazard [warning] lights *npl* Auto luci *fpl* d'emergenza

haze /heɪz/ *n* foschia *f*

hazel /'heɪz(ə)l/ *n* nocciolo *m*; (colour) [color] *m* nocciola *m*

hazelnut /'heɪz(ə)lnʌt/ *n* nocciola *f*

hazy /'heɪzɪ/ *adj* (-ier, -iest) nebbioso; fig ‹person› confuso; ‹memories› vago

HDTV *abbr* (**high-definition television**) HDTV *f*

♂ **he** /hiː/ *pron* lui; **he's tired** è stanco; **I'm going but he's not** io vengo, ma lui no

♂ **head** /hed/ [1] *n* testa *f*; (of firm) capo *m*; (of primary school) direttore, -trice *mf*; (of secondary school) preside *mf*; (on beer) schiuma *f*; **use your ~!** usa la testa!; **be off one's ~** essere fuori di testa; **have a good ~ for business** avere il senso degli affari; **have a good ~ for heights** non soffrire di vertigini; **10 pounds a ~** 10 sterline a testa; **20 ~ of cattle** 20 capi di bestiame; **~ first** a capofitto; **~ over heels in love** innamorato pazzo; **~s or tails?** testa o croce?

[2] *vt* essere a capo di; essere in testa a ‹list›; colpire di testa ‹ball›

[3] *vi* **~ for** dirigersi verso

headache *n* mal *m* di testa

headband *n* fascia *f* per capelli

head boy *n* Br Sch alunno (*m*) *che rappresenta la scuola nelle manifestazioni ufficiali e che ha responsabilità speciali*

head-butt *vt* dare una testata a

head case *n* fam **be a ~** essere matto da legare

head cold *n* raffreddore *m* di testa

headcount *n* **do a ~** contare i presenti

headdress *n* acconciatura *f*

header /'hedə(r)/ *n* colpo *m* di testa; (dive) tuffo *m* di testa; (on document) intestazione *f*

headfirst /ˌhedˈfɜːst/ *adv* ‹dive, fall› di testa; ‹rush into› a testa bassa

headgear *n* copricapo *m*

head girl *n* Br Sch alunna (*f*) *che rappresenta la scuola nelle manifestazioni ufficiali e che ha responsabilità speciali*

headhunt *vt* cercare per assumere

headhunter *n* (also Comm) cacciatore, -trice *mf* di teste

headhunting *n* Comm ricerca *f* ad hoc di personale

heading *n* (in list etc) titolo *m*

headlamp *n* Auto fanale *m*

headland *n* promontorio *m*

headlight *n* Auto fanale *m*

headline *n* titolo *m*

headlong *adj & adv* a capofitto

head louse *n* pidocchio *m*

headmaster *n* (of primary school) direttore *m*; (of secondary school) preside *m*

headmistress *n* (of primary school) direttrice *f*; (of secondary school) preside *f*

head of department *n* capo *mf* reparto

head office *n* sede *f* centrale

head-on [1] *adj* ‹collision› frontale [2] *adv* frontalmente

headphones *npl* cuffie *fpl*

headquarters *npl* sede *fsg*; Mil quartier *msg* generale

headrest *n* poggiatesta *m inv*

headroom *n* sottotetto *m*; (of bridge) altezza *f* libera di passaggio

headscarf *n* foulard *m inv*, fazzoletto *m*

headset *n* cuffia *f* con microfono

headstand *n* **do a ~** fare la verticale

head start *n* **have a ~** partire avvantaggiato

headstone *n* (of grave) lapide *f*

headstrong *adj* testardo

head teacher *n* (of primary school) direttore, -trice *mf*; (of secondary school) preside *mf*

head-to-head [1] *n* confronto *m* diretto [2] *adj* diretto

head waiter *n* capocameriere *m*

h

headway n progresso m
headwind n vento m di prua
heady /'hedɪ/ adj che dà alla testa
heal /hi:l/ vt/i guarire
healer /'hi:lə(r)/ n guaritore, -trice mf; time
is a great ~ il tempo guarisce tutti i mali
healing /'hi:lɪŋ/ adj ⟨power, effect⟩ curativo;
the ~ **process** il processo di guarigione
⚘ **health** /helθ/ n salute f
health care n assistenza f sanitaria
health centre n Br ambulatorio m
health check n controllo m
health club n club m ginnico
health farm n centro m di rimessa in
forma
health foods npl alimenti mpl
macrobiotici
health-food shop n negozio m di
macrobiotica
health hazard n pericolo m per la salute
healthily /'helθɪlɪ/ adv in modo sano
health insurance n assicurazione f
contro malattie
health officer n ufficiale m sanitario
health resort n (in mountains, by sea)
stazione f climatica; (spa town) stazione f
termale
Health Service n Br (for public) servizio m
sanitario; Am Univ infermeria f
health visitor n Br infermiere -a (mf) che
fa visite a domicilio
health warning n avviso m del
ministero della sanità
⚘ **healthy** /'helθɪ/ adj (-ier, -iest) sano
heap /hi:p/ **1** n mucchio m; ~s **of** fam un
sacco di
2 vt ~ **[up]** ammucchiare; ~ed **teaspoon**
un cucchiaino abbondante
heaped /hi:pt/ adj a ~ **spoonful** un
cucchiaio colmo
⚘ **hear** /hɪə(r)/ vt/i (pt/pp **heard**) sentire;
~, ~! bravo!
■ **hear about** vt (learn of) sentir parlare di
■ **hear from** vi aver notizie di
■ **hear of** vi sentir parlare di; he would not
~ **of it** non ne ha voluto sentir parlare
⚘ **hearing** /'hɪərɪŋ/ n udito m; Jur udienza f
hearing aid n apparecchio m acustico
hearing-impaired /-ɪm'peəd/ adj
audioleso
hearsay /'hɪəseɪ/ n **from** ~ per sentito dire
hearse /hɜ:s/ n carro m funebre
⚘ **heart** /hɑ:t/ n cuore m; ~s pl Cards cuori
mpl; **at** ~ di natura; **by** ~ a memoria
heartache n pena f
heart attack n infarto m
heartbeat n battito m cardiaco

heartbreak n afflizione f
heartbreaking adj straziante
heart-broken adj **be** ~ avere il cuore
spezzato
heartburn n mal m di stomaco
heart disease n malattia f cardiaca
hearten /'hɑ:t(ə)n/ vt rincuorare
heartening /'hɑ:tnɪŋ/ adj rincuorante
heart failure n arresto m cardiaco
heartfelt /'hɑ:tfelt/ adj di cuore
hearth /hɑ:θ/ n focolare m
hearthrug /'hɑ:θrʌg/ n tappeto (m)
davanti al camino
heartily /'hɑ:tɪlɪ/ adv di cuore; ⟨eat⟩ con
appetito; **be** ~ **sick of something** non
poterne più di qualcosa
heartland /'hɑ:tlænd/ n (industrial, rural)
cuore m; Pol roccaforte f
heartless /'hɑ:tlɪs/ adj spietato
heartlessly /'hɑ:tlɪslɪ/ adv in modo
spietato
heart-lung machine n polmone m
artificiale
heart rate n battito m cardiaco
heart-rending /-rendɪŋ/ adj ⟨sigh, story⟩
straziante
heart-searching n esame m di coscienza
heart surgeon n cardiochirurgo, -a mf
heartthrob n fam rubacuori m inv
heart-to-heart **1** n conversazione f a
cuore aperto
2 adj a cuore aperto
heart transplant n trapianto m di cuore
heart-warming adj toccante
hearty /'hɑ:tɪ/ adj caloroso; ⟨meal⟩ copioso;
⟨person⟩ gioviale
⚘ **heat** /hi:t/ **1** n calore m; Sport prova f
eliminatoria
2 vt scaldare
3 vi scaldarsi
■ **heat up** vt scaldare ⟨food, drink⟩; riscaldare
⟨room⟩
heated /'hi:tɪd/ adj ⟨swimming pool⟩
riscaldato; ⟨discussion⟩ animato
heater /'hi:tə(r)/ n (for room) stufa f; (for
water) boiler m inv; Auto riscaldamento m
heath /hi:θ/ n brughiera f
heat haze n foschia f (dovuta all'afa)
heathen /'hi:ð(ə)n/ adj & n pagano, -a mf
heather /'heðə(r)/ n erica f
heating /'hi:tɪŋ/ n riscaldamento m
heat loss n perdita f di calore
heat-resistant adj resistente al calore
heat sink n dissipatore m termico
heatstroke n colpo m di sole
heat treatment n Med termoterapia f
heatwave n ondata f di calore
heave /hi:v/ **1** vt tirare; (lift) tirare su; fam
(throw) gettare; emettere ⟨sigh⟩

⚘ indicates a very frequent word

2 *vi* tirare; **my stomach** ~**d** avevo la nausea

heaven /'hev(ə)n/ *n* paradiso *m*; ~ **help you if...** Dio vi scampi se...; **raise one's eyes to** ~ alzare gli occhi al cielo; **H**~**s!** santo cielo!

heavenly /'hev(ə)nlı/ *adj* celeste; *fam* delizioso

heaven-sent /-'sent/ *adj* ‹opportunity› provvidenziale

heavily /'hevılı/ *adv* pesantemente; ‹smoke, drink etc› molto

heaviness /'hevınıs/ *n* pesantezza *f*

⚘ **heavy** /'hevı/ *adj* (-ier, -iest) pesante; ‹traffic› intenso; ‹rain, cold› forte; **be a** ~ **smoker/drinker** essere un gran fumatore/bevitore

heavy-duty *adj* ‹equipment, shoes› molto resistente

heavy goods vehicle *n* veicolo *m* pesante da trasporto

heavy-handed /-'hændıd/ *adj* (severe) severo; (clumsy) maldestro

heavy industry *n* industria *f* pesante

heavy metal *n* Mus heavy metal *m*

heavyweight *n* peso *m* massimo

Hebrew /'hi:bru:/ *adj & n* ebreo

heck /hek/ *fam* **1** *int* cavolo

2 *n* **a** ~ **of a lot of** un sacco di; **what the** ~**!** chi se ne frega!; **what the** ~ **is going on?** che cavolo succede?

heckle /'hekl/ *vt* interrompere di continuo

heckler /'heklə(r)/ *n* disturbatore, -trice *mf*

hectare /'hekteə(r)/ *n* ettaro *m*

hectic /'hektık/ *adj* frenetico

hectoring /'hektərıŋ/ *adj* prepotente

hedge /hedʒ/ **1** *n* siepe *f*

2 *vi* fig essere evasivo

hedge-clippers *npl* cesoie *fpl*

hedge fund *n* hedge fund *m*

hedgehog *n* riccio *m*

hedgerow *n* siepe *f*

hedonism /'hi:dənızm/ *n* edonismo *m*

hedonistic /hi:də'nıstık/ *adj* edonistico

heebie-jeebies /hi:bı'dʒi:bız/ *npl* fam **give somebody the** ~ far venire i brividi a qualcuno

heed /hi:d/ **1** *n* **pay** ~ **to** prestare ascolto a

2 *vt* prestare ascolto a

heedless /'hi:dlıs/ *adj* noncurante

heel[1] /hi:l/ *n* tallone *m*; (of shoe) tacco *m*; **down at** ~ fig trasandato; **take to one's** ~**s** fam darsela a gambe

heel[2] *vi* ~ **over** Naut inclinarsi

heel bar *n* calzolaio *m*

hefty /'heftı/ *adj* (-ier, -iest) massiccio

heifer /'hefə(r)/ *n* giovenca *f*

height /haıt/ *n* altezza *f*; (of plane) altitudine *f*; (of season, fame) culmine *m*

heighten /'haıt(ə)n/ *vt* fig accrescere

heinous /'hi:nəs/ *adj* abominevole

heir /eə(r)/ *n* erede *mf*

heiress /eə'res/ *n* ereditiera *f*

heirloom /'eəlu:m/ *n* cimelio *m* di famiglia

heist /haıst/ *adj* Am fam furto *m*; (armed) rapina *f*

held /held/ ▶ HOLD[2]

helicopter /'helıkɒptə(r)/ *n* elicottero *m*

heliport /'helıpɔ:t/ *n* eliporto *m*

helium /'hi:lıəm/ *n* elio *m*

helix /'hi:lıks/ *n* elica *f*

hell /hel/ **1** *n* inferno *m*; **go to** ~**!** sl va' al diavolo!; **make sb's life** ~ rendere la vita infernale a qualcuno

2 *int* porca miseria!

hell-bent *adj* ~ **on doing something** deciso a tutti i costi a fare qualcosa

Hellenic /hı'lenık/ *adj* ellenico

hellfire /'helfaıə(r)/ *n* pene *fpl* dell' inferno

hell-for-leather *adv* fam **go** ~ andare a spron battuto

hello /hə'ləʊ/ *int & n* = HALLO

Hell's angel *n* Hell's angel *m* inv

helm /helm/ *n* timone *m*; **at the** ~ fig al timone

helmet /'helmıt/ *n* casco *m*

⚘ **help** /help/ **1** *n* aiuto *m*; (employee) aiuto *m* domestico; **that's no** ~ non è d'aiuto

2 *vt* aiutare; ~ **oneself to something** servirsi di qualcosa; ~ **yourself** (at table) serviti pure; **I could not** ~ **laughing** non ho potuto trattenermi dal ridere; **it cannot be** ~**ed** non c'è niente da fare; **I can't** ~ **it** non ci posso far niente

3 *vi* aiutare

■ **help out** **1** *vt* dare una mano a

2 *vi* dare una mano

help desk *n* help desk *m* inv

helper /'helpə(r)/ *n* aiutante *mf*

helpful /'helpfʊl/ *adj* ‹person› di aiuto; ‹advice› utile

helping /'helpıŋ/ *n* porzione *f*

helping hand *n* **give somebody a** ~ dare una mano a qualcuno

helpless /'helplıs/ *adj* (unable to manage) incapace; (powerless) impotente

helplessly /'helplıslı/ *adv* con impotenza; ‹laugh› incontrollatamente

helpline *n* assistenza *f* telefonica

help window *n* Comput finestrella *f* di aiuto

helter-skelter /heltə'skeltə(r)/ **1** *adv* in fretta e furia

2 *n* scivolo (*m*) *a spirale nei luna park*

hem /hem/ **1** *n* orlo *m*

2 *vt* (*pt/pp* **hemmed**) orlare

■ **hem in** *vt* intrappolare

hemisphere /'hemɪsfɪə(r)/ n emisfero m
hemline /'hemlaɪn/ n orlo m
hemlock /'hemlɒk/ n cicuta f
hemophilia n Am = HAEMOPHILIA
hemp /hemp/ n canapa f
hen /hen/ n gallina f; (any female bird) femmina f
hence /hens/ adv (for this reason) quindi; (from now on) a partire da ora; (from here) da qui
henceforth /hens'fɔ:θ/ adv fml (from that time on) da allora in poi; (from now on) d'ora in poi
henchman /'hentʃmən/ n pej tirapiedi m inv
hen-coop n stia f
hen house n pollaio m
henna /'henə/ n hennè m
hen night n fam addio m al nubilato
hen party n fam festa f di addio al nubilato
henpecked /'henpekt/ adj tiranneggiato dalla moglie
hepatitis /hepə'taɪtɪs/ n epatite f
♂ **her** /hɜ:(r)/ **1** poss adj suo m, sua f, suoi mpl, sue fpl; ~ **job/house** il suo lavoro/la sua casa; **her mother/father** sua madre/suo padre
2 pers pron (direct object) la; (indirect object) le; (after prep) lei; **I know** ~ la conosco; **give** ~ **the money** dalle i soldi; **give it to** ~ daglielo; **I came with** ~ sono venuto con lei; **it's** ~ è lei; **I've seen** ~ l'ho vista; **I've seen** ~, **but not him** ho visto lei, ma non lui
herald /'herəld/ vt annunciare
heraldic /he'rældɪk/ adj araldico
heraldry /'herəldrɪ/ n araldica f
herb /hɜ:b/ n erba f
herbaceous /hɜ:'beɪʃəs/ adj erbaceo; ~ **border** aiuola f
herbal /'hɜ:b(ə)l/ adj alle erbe
herbalist /'hɜ:bəlɪst/ n erborista mf
herbal tea n tisana f
herb garden n aromatario m
herbs /hɜ:bz/ npl (for cooking) aromi mpl [da cucina]; (medicinal) erbe fpl
herb tea n tisana f
herculean /hɜ:kju'li:ən/ adj ⟨task⟩ erculeo
herd /hɜ:d/ **1** n gregge m
2 vt (tend) sorvegliare; (drive) far muovere; fig ammassare
■ **herd together 1** vi raggrupparsi
2 vt raggruppare
♂ **here** /hɪə(r)/ adv (qui) qua; **in** ~ qui dentro; **come/bring** ~ vieni/porta qui; ~ **is...**, ~ **are...** ecco...; ~ **you are!** ecco qua!
hereabouts /hɪərə'baʊts/ Br, **hereabout** Am adv da queste parti
hereafter adv in futuro

here and now 1 adv seduta stante
2 n the ~ il presente
hereby adv con la presente
hereditary /hɪ'redɪtərɪ/ adj ereditario
heredity /hɪ'redətɪ/ n ereditarietà f
heresy /'herəsɪ/ n eresia f
heretic /'herətɪk/ n eretico, -a mf
herewith /hɪə'wɪð/ adv Comm con la presente
heritage /'herɪtɪdʒ/ n eredità f
hermetic /hɜ:'metɪk/ adj ermetico
hermetically /hɜ:'metɪklɪ/ adv ermeticamente
hermit /'hɜ:mɪt/ n eremita mf
hernia /'hɜ:nɪə/ n ernia f
♂ **hero** /'hɪərəʊ/ n (pl -es) eroe m
heroic /hɪ'rəʊɪk/ adj eroico
heroically /hɪ'rəʊɪklɪ/ adv eroicamente
heroin /'herəʊɪn/ n eroina f (droga)
heroin addict n eroinomane mf
heroine /'herəʊɪn/ n eroina f
heroism /'herəʊɪzm/ n eroismo m
heron /'herən/ n airone m
hero-worship 1 n culto m degli eroi
2 vt venerare
herpes /'hɜ:pi:z/ n herpes m
herring /'herɪŋ/ n aringa f
herringbone /'herɪŋbəʊn/ adj ⟨pattern⟩ spigato
hers /hɜ:z/ poss pron il suo m, la sua f, i suoi mpl, le sue fpl; **a friend of** ~ un suo amico; **friends of** ~ dei suoi amici; **that is** ~ quello è suo; (as opposed to mine) quello è il suo
♂ **herself** /hə'self/ pers pron (reflexive) si; (emphatic) lei stessa; (after prep) sé, se stessa; **she poured** ~ **a drink** si è versata da bere; **she told me so** ~ me lo ha detto lei stessa; **she's proud of** ~ è fiera di sé; **by** ~ da sola
hesitant /'hezɪtənt/ adj esitante
hesitantly /'hezɪtəntlɪ/ adv con esitazione
hesitate /'hezɪteɪt/ vi esitare
hesitation /hezɪ'teɪʃn/ n esitazione f
hessian /'hesɪən/ n tela f di iuta
heterogeneous /hetərə'dʒi:nɪəs/ adj eterogeneo
heterosexual /hetərəʊ'sekʃʊəl/ adj eterosessuale
het up /het/ adj fam agitato
hew /hju:/ vt (pt **hewed**, pp **hewed** or **hewn**) spaccare
hexagon /'heksəgən/ n esagono m
hexagonal /hek'sægənl/ adj esagonale
♂ **hey** /heɪ/ int ehi!
heyday /'heɪdeɪ/ n tempi mpl d'oro
hey presto /heɪ'prestəʊ/ int (magic) e voilà!
HGV abbr (**heavy goods vehicle**) TIR m

♂ indicates a very frequent word

hi /haɪ/ *int* ciao!

hiatus /haɪˈeɪtəs/ *n* (*pl* **-tuses**) iato *m*

hibernate /ˈhaɪbəneɪt/ *vi* andare in letargo

hibernation /haɪbəˈneɪʃn/ *n* letargo *m*

hiccup /ˈhɪkʌp/ ⒈ *n* singhiozzo *m*; fam (hitch) intoppo *m*; **have the ∼s** avere il singhiozzo
⒉ *vi* fare un singhiozzo

hick /hɪk/ *n* Am fam buzzurro, -a *mf*

hick town *n* Am fam città *f inv* provinciale

hid /hɪd/, **hidden** /ˈhɪdn/ ▶ HIDE²

hide¹ /haɪd/ *n* (leather) pelle *f* (*di animale*)

◆ **hide²** ⒈ *vt* (*pt* **hid**, *pp* **hidden**) nascondere
⒉ *vi* nascondersi

hide-and-seek *n* play ∼ giocare a nascondino

hideaway /ˈhaɪdəweɪ/ *n* (secluded place) rifugio *m*; (hiding place) nascondiglio *m*

hidebound /ˈhaɪdbaʊnd/ *adj* (conventional) limitato

hideous /ˈhɪdɪəs/ *adj* orribile

hideously /ˈhɪdɪəslɪ/ *adv* orribilmente

hideout /ˈhaɪdaʊt/ *n* nascondiglio *m*

hiding¹ /ˈhaɪdɪŋ/ *n* fam (beating) bastonata; (defeat) batosta *f*

hiding² *n* go into ∼ sparire dalla circolazione

hiding place *n* nascondiglio *m*

hierarchic[al] /haɪəˈrɑːkɪk[l]/ *adj* gerarchico

hierarchy /ˈhaɪərɑːkɪ/ *n* gerarchia *f*

hieroglyphics /haɪərəˈglɪfɪks/, **hieroglyphs** *npl* geroglifici *mpl*

hi-fi /ˈhaɪfaɪ/ *n abbr* (**high fidelity**) hi-fi *m inv*; (set of equipment) impianto *m* hi-fi, stereo *m inv*

higgledy-piggledy /hɪgldɪˈpɪgldɪ/ *adv* alla rinfusa

◆ **high** /haɪ/ ⒈ *adj* alto; ‹meat› che comincia ad andare a male; ‹wind› forte; (on drugs) fatto; **it's ∼ time we did something about it** è ora di fare qualcosa in proposito
⒉ *adv* in alto; ∼ **and low** in lungo e in largo
⒊ *n* massimo *m*; (temperature) massima *f*; **from on ∼** dall'alto; **be on a ∼** fam essere fatto

high and dry *adj* fig leave somebody ∼ piantare in asso qualcuno

high-beam *n* Am abbagliante *m*

high-born *adj* nobile

highbrow *adj* & *n* intellettuale *mf*

high chair *n* seggiolone *m*

high-class *adj* ‹hotel, shop, car› d'alta classe; ‹prostitute› di alto bordo

high command *n* stato *m* maggiore

High Commission *n* alto commissariato *m*

High Commissioner *n* alto commissario *m*

High Court *n* ≈ Corte *f* Suprema

high-definition *adj* ad alta definizione

high-definition television *n* televisione *f* ad alta definizione

high diving *n* tuffo *m*

high-end *adj* ‹product, model› della fascia più alta

higher education /haɪərˈedjʊˈkeɪʃn/ *n* istruzione *f* universitaria

higher mathematics *n* matematica *f* avanzata

highfaluting /haɪfəˈluːtɪŋ/ *adj* fam ‹ideas› pretenzioso; ‹language› pomposo

high fashion *n* alta moda *f*

high-fibre *adj* ‹diet› ricco di fibre

high-fidelity ⒈ *n* alta fedeltà
⒉ *adj* ad alta fedeltà

high finance *n* alta finanza *f*

high-flier *n* (person) persona *f* che mira alto

high-flown *adj* ‹phrases› ampolloso

high-flying *adj* ‹aircraft› da alta quota; ‹career› ambizioso; ‹person› che mira alto

high-frequency *adj* alta frequenza *f*

High German *n* alto tedesco *m*

high-grade *adj* ‹oil, mineral, product› di prima qualità

high ground *n* collina *f*; **take the moral ∼** assumere un atteggiamento moralistico

high-handed /-ˈhændɪd/ *adj* dispotico

high-handedly /-ˈhændɪdlɪ/ *adv* dispoticamente

highheeled /-ˈhiːld/ *adj* coi tacchi alti

high heels *npl* tacchi *mpl* alti

high jinks /dʒɪŋks/ *npl* baldoria *f*

high jump *n* salto *m* in alto

Highland games /haɪlənd/ *n* manifestazione (*f*) tradizionale scozzese con gare sportive e musicali

Highlands /ˈhaɪləndz/ *npl* Highlands *fpl* (*regione della Scozia del nord*)

high-level *adj* ‹talks› ad alto livello; ‹official› di alto livello

high life *n* bella vita *f*

highlight /ˈhaɪlaɪt/ ⒈ *vt* (emphasize, with pen) evidenziare
⒉ *n* (in art) luce *f*; (in hair) riflesso *m*, colpo *m* di sole; (of exhibition) parte *f* saliente; (of week, year) avvenimento *m* saliente; (of match, show) momento *m* clou

highlighter /ˈhaɪlaɪtə(r)/ *n* (marker) evidenziatore *m*

◆ **highly** /ˈhaɪlɪ/ *adv* molto; **speak ∼ of** lodare; **think ∼ of** avere un'alta opinione di

highly-paid /-ˈpeɪd/ *adj* ben pagato

highlystrung /-ˈstrʌŋ/ *adj* nervoso

High Mass *n* messa *f* solenne

high-minded /-'maɪndɪd/ adj ‹person› di animo nobile

high-necked /-'nekt/ adj a collo alto

Highness /'haɪnɪs/ n altezza f; **Your ~** Sua Altezza

high noon n mezzogiorno m in punto

high-performance adj ad alta prestazione

high-pitched /-'pɪtʃt/ adj ‹voice, sound› acuto

high point n momento m culminante

high-powered adj ‹car, engine› molto potente; ‹job› di alta responsabilità; ‹person› dinamico

high pressure ① n Meteorol alta pressione f
② attrib Techn ad alta pressione; ‹job› stressante

high priest n Relig gran sacerdote m; fig guru m inv

high priestess n Relig, fig gran sacerdotessa f

high-principled adj ‹person› di alti principi

high-profile adj ‹politician, group› di spicco; ‹visit› di grande risonanza

high-ranking adj di alto rango

high-rise ① adj ‹building› molto alto
② n edificio m molto alto

high road n strada f principale

high school n Am ≈ scuola f superiore; Br ≈ scuola f media e superiore

high sea n on the **~s** in alto mare

high season n alta stagione f

high society n alta società f

high-sounding /-'saʊndɪŋ/ adj ‹title› altisonante

high-speed adj ‹train, film› rapido

high-spirited adj pieno di brio

high spirits npl brio m

high spot n momento m culminante

high street n strada f principale

high-street shop n negozio m popolare

high-street spending n acquisto m di beni di consumo

high tea n pasto (m) pomeridiano servito insieme al tè

high tech /'tek/ n high tech f

high tide n alta marea f

high treason n alto tradimento m

high voltage n alta tensione f

highway /'haɪweɪ/ n Am (motorway) superstrada f; **public ~** strada f pubblica

Highway Code n Br Codice m stradale

highwayman n brigante m

highway robbery n brigantaggio m

high wire n filo m (per acrobati)

hijack /'haɪdʒæk/ ① vt dirottare
② n dirottamento m

hijacker /'haɪdʒækə(r)/ n dirottatore, -trice mf

hijacking /'haɪdʒækɪŋ/ n dirottamento m

hike /haɪk/ ① n escursione f a piedi; (in price) aumento m
② vi fare un'escursione a piedi

hiker /'haɪkə(r)/ n escursionista mf

hiking /'haɪkɪŋ/ n escursionismo m

hiking boots npl pedule fpl

hilarious /hɪ'leərɪəs/ adj da morir dal ridere

hilarity /hɪ'lærətɪ/ n ilarità f

hill /hɪl/ n collina f; (mound) collinetta f; (slope) altura f

hill-billy /-bɪlɪ/ n Am montanaro m degli Stati Uniti sudorientali

hillock /'hɪlək/ n poggio m

hillside /'hɪlsaɪd/ n pendio m

hilltop /'hɪltɒp/ n sommità f inv di una collina

hilly /'hɪlɪ/ adj collinoso

hilt /hɪlt/ n impugnatura f; **to the ~** fam ‹support› fino in fondo; ‹mortgaged› fino al collo

♂ **him** /hɪm/ pers pron (direct object) lo; (indirect object) gli; (with prep) lui; **I know ~** lo conosco; **give ~ the money** dagli i soldi; **give it to ~** daglielo; **I spoke to ~** gli ho parlato; **it's ~** è lui; **she loves ~** lo ama; **she loves ~, not you** ama lui, non te

Himalayas /hɪmə'leɪəz/ npl Himalaia msg

♂ **himself** /hɪm'self/ pers pron (reflexive) si; (emphatic) lui stesso; (after prep) sé, se stesso; **he poured ~ out a drink** si è versato da bere; **he told me so ~** me lo ha detto lui stesso; **he's proud of ~** è fiero di sé; **by ~** da solo

hind /haɪnd/ adj posteriore

hinder /'hɪndə(r)/ vt intralciare

hind legs npl zampe fpl posteriori

hindquarters /'haɪn(d)kwɔːtəz/ npl didietro m

hindrance /'hɪndrəns/ n intralcio m

hindsight /'haɪndsaɪt/ n **with ~** con il senno del poi

Hindu /'hɪnduː/ adj & n indù mf inv

Hinduism /'hɪndʊɪzm/ n induismo m

hinge /hɪndʒ/ ① n cardine m
② vi **~ on** fig dipendere da

hint /hɪnt/ ① n (clue) accenno m; (advice) suggerimento m; (indirect suggestion) allusione f; (trace) tocco m
② vt **~ that ...** far capire che...
③ vi **~ at** alludere a

hinterland /'hɪntəlænd/ n entroterra m inv, hinterland m inv

hip /hɪp/ n fianco m

hip bone n ileo m

hip flask n fiaschetta f

♂ indicates a very frequent word

hippie /'hɪpɪ/ n hippy mf inv

hippo /'hɪpəʊ/ n fam ippopotamo m

hip pocket n tasca f posteriore

Hippocratic oath /hɪpəˈkrætɪk/ adj giuramento m d'Ippocrate

hippopotamus /hɪpəˈpɒtəməs/ n (pl **-muses** or **-mi** /hɪpəˈpɒtəmaɪ/) ippopotamo m

hip replacement n protesi f inv all'anca

✎ **hire** /'haɪə(r)/ [1] vt affittare; assumere ‹person›; **~ [out]** affittare
[2] n noleggio m; **'for ~'** 'affittasi'

hire car n macchina f a noleggio

hire purchase n Br acquisto m rateale; **on ~** a rate

✎ **his** /hɪz/ [1] poss adj suo m, sua f, suoi mpl, sue fpl; **~ job/house** il suo lavoro/la sua casa; **~ mother/father** sua madre/suo padre
[2] poss pron il suo m, la sua f, i suoi mpl, le sue fpl; **a friend of ~** un suo amico; **friends of ~** dei suoi amici; **that is ~** questo è suo; (as opposed to mine) questo è il suo

Hispanic /hɪˈspænɪk/ adj ispanico

hiss /hɪs/ [1] n sibilo m; (of disapproval) fischio m
[2] vt fischiare
[3] vi sibilare; (in disapproval) fischiare

historian /hɪˈstɔːrɪən/ n storico, -a mf

historic /hɪˈstɒrɪk/ adj storico

✎ **historical** /hɪˈstɒrɪkl/ adj storico

historically /hɪˈstɒrɪklɪ/ adv storicamente

✎ **history** /'hɪstərɪ/ n storia f; **make ~** passare alla storia

histrionic /hɪstrɪˈɒnɪk/ adj istrionico

histrionics /hɪstrɪˈɒnɪks/ npl scene fpl

✎ **hit** /hɪt/ [1] n (blow) colpo m; fam (success) successo m; **score a direct ~** ‹missile› colpire in pieno
[2] vt (pt/pp **hit**, pres p **hitting**) colpire; **~ one's head on the table** battere la testa contro il tavolo; **the car ~ the wall** la macchina ha sbattuto contro il muro; **~ the target** colpire il bersaglio; **~ the nail on the head** fare centro; **~ the roof** fam perdere le staffe
∎ **hit back** vi ‹retaliate› ribattere
∎ **hit off**: vt **~ it off** andare d'accordo
∎ **hit on** vt fig trovare

hit-and-miss adj ‹affair, undertaking› imprevedibile; ‹method› a casaccio

hit-and-run adj ‹raid, attack› lampo inv; ‹accident› causato da un pirata della strada

hit-and-run driver adj pirata m della strada

hitch /hɪtʃ/ [1] n intoppo m; **technical ~** problema m tecnico
[2] vt attaccare; **~ a lift** chiedere un passaggio
∎ **hitch up** vt tirarsi su ‹trousers›

hitch-hike vi fare l'autostop

hitchhiker n autostoppista mf

hitch-hiking n autostop m

hi-tech adj HIGH TECH

hither /'hɪðə(r)/ adv **~ and thither** di qua e di là

hitherto /hɪðəˈtuː/ adv finora

hit list n lista f degli obiettivi

hit man n sicario m

hit-or-miss adj **on a very ~ basis** all'improvvisata

hit parade n hit parade f inv, classifica f

hit single n singolo m di successo

HIV n abbr (**human immunodeficiency virus**) HIV; **~ positive** sieropositivo; **~ negative** sieronegativo

hive /haɪv/ n alveare m; **~ of industry** fucina f di lavoro
∎ **hive off** vt Comm separare

HIV positive adj sieropositivo

HM abbr (**Her Majesty** or **His Majesty**) SM

HMS abbr (**His/Her Majesty's Ship**) nave (f) di Sua Maestà

hoard /hɔːd/ [1] n provvista f; (of money) gruzzolo m
[2] vt accumulare

hoarding /'hɔːdɪŋ/ n palizzata f; (with advertisements) tabellone m per manifesti pubblicitari

hoar frost /'hɔː(r)/ n brina f

hoarse /hɔːs/ adj rauco

hoarsely /'hɔːslɪ/ adv con voce rauca

hoarseness /'hɔːsnɪs/ n raucedine f

hoary /'hɔːrɪ/ adj ‹person› con i capelli bianchi; **~ old joke** barzelletta f vecchia

hoax /həʊks/ n scherzo m; (false alarm) falso allarme m

hoaxer /'həʊksə(r)/ n burlone, -a mf

hob /hɒb/ n Br piano m di cottura

hobble /'hɒbl/ vi zoppicare

hobby /'hɒbɪ/ n hobby m inv

hobby horse n fig fissazione f

hobnailed /'hɒbneɪld/ adj **~ boots** pl scarponi mpl chiodati

hobnob /'hɒbnɒb/ v
∎ **hobnob with** vt (pt/pp **hobnobbed**) frequentare

hobo /'həʊbəʊ/ n Am vagabondo, -a mf

hock /hɒk/ n vino m bianco del Reno

hockey /'hɒkɪ/ n hockey m

hocus-pocus /həʊkəsˈpəʊkəs/ n (trickery) trucco m

hod /hɒd/ n (for coal) secchio m del carbone; (for bricks) cassetta f (per trasportare mattoni)

hoe /həʊ/ [1] n zappa f
[2] vt (pres p **hoeing**) zappare

hog /hɒg/ [1] n maiale m
[2] vt (pt/pp **hogged**) fam monopolizzare

hog-tie /'hɒgtaɪ/ vt legare le quattro zampe di ‹pig, cow›; Am fig ostacolare ‹person›

hogwash /ˈhɒgwɒʃ/ n fam cretinate fpl

hoi polloi /hɔɪpɒˈlɔɪ/ npl plebaglia fsg

hoist /hɔɪst/ **1** n montacarichi m inv; fam (push) spinta f in su
2 vt sollevare; innalzare ‹flag›; levare ‹anchor›

hoity-toity /hɔɪtɪˈtɔɪtɪ/ adj fam altezzoso

hokum /ˈhəʊkəm/ n Am fam (sentimentality) polpettone m sentimentale; (nonsense) cretinate fpl

hold¹ /həʊld/ n Naut, Aeron stiva f

🗸 **hold²** **1** n presa f; fig (influence) ascendente m; **get ~ of** trovare; procurarsi ‹information›
2 vt (pt/pp held) tenere; ‹container› contenere; essere titolare di ‹licence, passport›; trattenere ‹breath, suspect›; mantenere vivo ‹interest›; ‹civil servant etc› occupare ‹position›; (retain) mantenere; **~ sb' hand** tenere qualcuno per mano; **~ one's tongue** tenere la bocca chiusa; **~ somebody responsible** considerare qualcuno responsabile; **~ that** (believe) ritenere che
3 vi tenere; ‹weather, luck› durare; ‹offer› essere valido; Teleph restare in linea; **I don't ~ with the idea that…** fam non sono d'accordo sul fatto che…
▪ **hold against**: vt ~ something against somebody avercela con qualcuno per qualcosa
▪ **hold back** **1** vt rallentare
2 vi esitare
▪ **hold down** vt tenere a bada ‹somebody›
▪ **hold on** vi (wait) attendere; Teleph restare in linea
▪ **hold on to** vt aggrapparsi a; (keep) tenersi
▪ **hold out** **1** vt porgere ‹hand›; fig offrire ‹possibility›
2 vi (resist) resistere
▪ **hold to**: vt ~ somebody to something far mantenere qualcosa a qualcuno
▪ **hold up** vt tenere su; (delay) rallentare; (rob) assalire; **~ one's head up** fig tenere la testa alta

holdall /ˈhəʊldɔːl/ n borsone m

holder /ˈhəʊldə(r)/ n titolare mf; (of record) detentore, -trice mf; (container) astuccio m

holding /ˈhəʊldɪŋ/ n (land) terreno m in affitto; Comm azioni fpl

holding company n società f inv finanziaria

hold-up n ritardo m; (attack) rapina f a mano armata

🗸 **hole** /həʊl/ n buco m

hole-in-the-wall n fam sportello m del Bancomat®

🗸 **holiday** /ˈhɒlɪdeɪ/ **1** n vacanza f; (public) giorno m festivo; (day off) giorno m di ferie; **go on ~** andare in vacanza
2 vi andare in vacanza

🗸 indicates a very frequent word

holiday home n casa f per le vacanze

holiday job n Br (in summer) lavoretto m estivo

holiday-maker n vacanziere mf

holiday resort n luogo m di villeggiatura

holier-than-thou /həʊlɪəðənˈðaʊ/ adj ‹attitude› da santerellino

holiness /ˈhəʊlɪnɪs/ n santità f; **Your H~** Sua Santità

Holland /ˈhɒlənd/ n Olanda f

holler /ˈhɒlə(r)/ vi urlare (**at** contro)

hollow /ˈhɒləʊ/ **1** adj cavo; ‹promise› a vuoto; ‹voice› assente; ‹cheeks› infossato
2 n cavità f inv; (in ground) affossamento m
▪ **hollow out** vt scavare

holly /ˈhɒlɪ/ n agrifoglio m

hollyhock /ˈhɒlɪhɒk/ n malvone m

holocaust /ˈhɒləkɔːst/ n olocausto m

hologram /ˈhɒləgræm/ n ologramma m

holograph /ˈhɒləgrɑːf/ n documento m olografo

hols /hɒlz/ n Br fam (**holidays**) vacanze fpl

holster /ˈhəʊlstə(r)/ n fondina f

holy /ˈhəʊlɪ/ adj (-ier, -est) santo; ‹water› benedetto

Holy Bible n Sacra Bibbia f

Holy Ghost, **Holy Spirit** n Spirito m Santo

Holy Land n Terra f Santa

Holy Scriptures sacre scritture fpl

Holy Week n settimana f santa

homage /ˈhɒmɪdʒ/ n omaggio m; **pay ~ to** rendere omaggio a

homburg /ˈhɒmbɜːg/ n cappello m di feltro

🗸 **home** /həʊm/ **1** n casa f; (for children) istituto m; (for old people) casa f di riposo; (native land) patria f
2 adv **at ~** a casa; (football) in casa; **feel at ~** sentirsi a casa propria; **come/go ~** venire/andare a casa; **drive a nail ~** piantare un chiodo a fondo
3 adj domestico; ‹movie, video› casalingo; ‹team› ospitante; Pol nazionale

home address n indirizzo m di casa

home brew n (beer) birra f fatta in casa

home cinema [system], **home entertainment system** n (sistema di) home cinema m

homecoming n (return home) ritorno m a casa

home computer n computer m inv da casa

home cooking n cucina f casalinga

Home Counties npl contee (fpl) intorno a Londra

home economics n Sch economia f domestica

home front n (during war) fronte m interno; (in politics) politica f interna

home game *n* partita *f* in casa

home ground *n* play on one's ~ giocare in casa

home-grown /-'grəʊn/ *adj* ‹produce› del proprio orto; fig nostrano

home help *n* aiuto *m* domestico (*per persone non autosufficienti*)

homeland *n* patria *f*

homeless /'həʊmlɪs/ *adj* senza tetto

home loan *n* mutuo *m* per la casa

homeloving /'həʊmlʌvɪŋ/ *adj* casalingo

homely /'həʊmlɪ/ *adj* (**-ier, -iest**) *adj* semplice; ‹atmosphere› familiare; Am (ugly) bruttino

home-made *adj* fatto in casa

home market *n* mercato *m* interno

Home Office *n* Br ministero *m* degli interni

homeopathic /həʊmɪə'pæθɪk/ *adj* omeopatico

homeopathy /həʊmɪ'ɒpəθɪ/ *n* omeopatia *f*

homeowner *n* proprietario, -a *mf* immobiliare

home page *n* Comput home page *f inv*

home rule *n* autogoverno *m*

Home Secretary *n* Br ≈ ministro *m* degli interni

home shopping *n* acquisti *mpl* attraverso la televisione

homesick *adj* be ~ avere nostalgia (**for** di)

homesickness *n* nostalgia *f* di casa

homestead *n* fattoria *f*

home town *n* città *f inv* natia

home truth *n* tell somebody a few ~s dirne quattro a qualcuno

home video *n* filmato *m* di videoamatore

homeward /'həʊmwəd/ **1** *adj* di ritorno **2** *adv* ~[s] verso casa; ~ **bound** sulla strada del ritorno; **travel** ~[s] tornare a casa

homework /'həʊmwɜːk/ *n* Sch compiti *mpl*

homeworker /'həʊmwɜːkə(r)/ *n* lavoratore, -trice *mf* a domicilio

homeworking /'həʊmwɜːkɪŋ/ *n* lavoro *m* a domicilio

homey /'həʊmɪ/ *adj* (home-loving) casalingo; (cosy) accogliente

homicidal /ˌhɒmɪ'saɪdl/ *adj* omicida

homicide /'hɒmɪsaɪd/ *n* (crime) omicidio *m*

homily /'hɒmɪlɪ/ *n* omelia *f*

homing /'həʊmɪŋ/ *adj* ‹missile, device› autoguidato

homing pigeon piccione *f* homing

homoeopathic /həʊmɪə'pæθɪk/ *adj* omeopatico

homoeopathy /həʊmɪ'ɒpəθɪ/ *n* omeopatia *f*

homogeneous /hɒmə'dʒiːnɪəs/ *adj* omogeneo

homogenize /hə'mɒdʒənaɪz/ *vt* omogeneizzare

homogenous /hə'mɒdʒənəs/ *adj* omogeneo

homograph /'hɒməgrɑːf/ *n* omografo *m*

homonym /'hɒmənɪm/ *n* omonimo *m*

homophobia /həʊmə'fəʊbɪə/ *n* omofobia *f*

homosexual /həʊmə'sekʃʊəl/ *adj & n* omosessuale *mf*

homosexuality /ˌhɒmə,sekʃʊ'ælətɪ/ *n* omosessualità *f*

Hon. *abbr* (**Honourable**) On.

Honduras /hɒn'djʊərəs/ *n* Honduras *m*

hone /həʊn/ *vt* (sharpen) affilare; (perfect) affinare

honest /'ɒnɪst/ *adj* onesto; (frank) sincero

honestly /'ɒnɪstlɪ/ *adv* onestamente; (frankly) sinceramente; ~! ma insomma!

honesty /'ɒnɪstɪ/ *n* onestà *f*; ‹frankness› sincerità *f*

honey /'hʌnɪ/ *n* miele *m*; fam (darling) tesoro *m*

honeycomb /'hʌnɪkəʊm/ *n* favo *m*

honeydew melon /'hʌnɪdjuː/ *n* melone *m* (*dalla buccia gialla*)

honeymoon /'hʌnɪmuːn/ *n* luna *f* di miele

honeysuckle /'hʌnɪsʌkl/ *n* caprifoglio *m*

honey trap *n* trappola (*f*) tesa a qualcuno servendosi di una collaboratrice graziosa

Hong Kong /hɒŋ'kɒŋ/ *n* Hong Kong *f*

honk /hɒŋk/ *vi* Auto clacsonare

honky-tonk /'hɒŋkɪtɒŋk/ *adj* ‹piano› honkytonky *inv*

honor /'ɒnə(r)/ *n* Am → HONOUR

honorary /'ɒnərərɪ/ *adj* onorario

honorific /ɒnə'rɪfɪk/ *adj* onorifico

✐ **honour** /'ɒnə(r)/ **1** *n* onore *m* **2** *vt* onorare

honourable /'ɒnərəbl/ *adj* onorevole

honourably /'ɒnərəblɪ/ *adv* con onore

honours degree /'ɒnəz/ *n* ≈ diploma *m* di laurea

hood /hʊd/ *n* cappuccio *m*; (of pram) tettuccio *m*; (over cooker) cappa *f*; Am Auto cofano *m*

hoodlum /'huːdləm/ *n* teppista *m*

hoodwink /'hʊdwɪŋk/ *vt* fam infinocchiare

hoody, hoodie /'hʊdɪ/ *n* fam maglia *f* con cappuccio

hoof /huːf/ *n* (*pl* ~s *or* **hooves**) zoccolo *m*

hoo-ha /'huːhɑː/ *n* fam cause a ~ fare scalpore

hook /hʊk/ **1** *n* gancio *m*; (for crochet) uncinetto *m*; (for fishing) amo *m*; **off the** ~ Teleph staccato; fig fuori pericolo; **by** ~ **or by crook** in un modo o nell' altro **2** *vt* agganciare

h

3 *vi* agganciarsi

hookah /'hʊkə/ *n* narghilè *m inv*

hook and eye *n* gancino *m*

hooked /hʊkt/ *adj* ‹nose› adunco; ~ **on** fam (drugs) dedito a; **be** ~ **on skiing** essere un fanatico dello sci

hooker /'hʊkə(r)/ *n* Am sl battona *f*

hookey /'hʊkɪ/ *n* play ~ Am fam marinare la scuola

hooligan /'huːlɪgən/ *n* teppista *f*

hooliganism /'huːlɪgənɪzm/ *n* teppismo *m*

hoop /huːp/ *n* cerchio *m*

hoopla /'huːplɑː/ *n* Br (at fair) lancio *m* degli anelli *(nei luna park)*; Am (fuss) trambusto *m*

hooray /hʊ'reɪ/ *int & n* = HURRAH

hoot /huːt/ **1** *n* colpo *m* di clacson; (of siren) ululato *m*; (of owl) grido *m*; ~**s of laughter** risate *fpl*
2 *vi* ‹owl› gridare; ‹car› clacsonare; ‹siren› ululare; (jeer) fischiare

hooter /'huːtə(r)/ *n* (siren) sirena *f*; Auto clacson *m inv*; Br fam (nose) nasone *m*

hoover® /'huːvə(r)/ **1** *n* aspirapolvere *m inv*
2 *vt* passare l'aspirapolvere su ‹carpet›; passare l'aspirapolvere in ‹room›
3 *vi* passare l'aspirapolvere

hop¹ /hɒp/ *n* luppolo *m*

hop² **1** *n* saltello *m*; **catch somebody on the** ~ fam prendere qualcuno alla sprovvista
2 *vi* (*pt/pp* **hopped**) saltellare; ~ **it!** fam tela!
■ **hop in** *vi* fam saltar su
■ **hop out** *vi* fam saltar giù; ~ **to the shops** fare un salto ai negozi

⚹ **hope** /həʊp/ **1** *n* speranza *f*; **there's no** ~ **of that happening** non c'è nessuna speranza che succeda
2 *vi* sperare (**for** in); **I** ~ **so/not** spero di sì/no
3 *vt* ~ **that** sperare che

hopeful /'həʊpfʊl/ *adj* pieno di speranza; (promising) promettente; **be** ~ **that** avere buone speranze che

hopefully /'həʊpfʊlɪ/ *adv* con speranza; (it is hoped) se tutto va bene

hopeless /'həʊplɪs/ *adj* senza speranze; (useless) impossibile; (incompetent) incapace

hopelessly /'həʊplɪslɪ/ *adv* disperatamente; ‹inefficient, lost› completamente

hopelessness /'həʊplɪsnɪs/ *n* disperazione *f*

hopscotch /'hɒpskɒtʃ/ *n* campana *f* (*gioco*)

horde /hɔːd/ *n* orda *f*

horizon /hə'raɪzn/ *n* orizzonte *m*; **on the** ~ all'orizzonte

horizontal /hɒrɪ'zɒntl/ *adj* orizzontale

horizontal bar *n* sbarra *f* orizzontale

horizontally /hɒrɪ'zɒntəlɪ/ *adv* orizzontalmente

hormonal /hɔː'məʊnəl/ *adj* ormonale; (moody) lunatico

hormone /'hɔːməʊn/ *n* ormone *m*

hormone replacement therapy *n* terapia *f* ormonale sostitutiva

horn /hɔːn/ *n* corno *m*; Auto clacson *m inv*

hornet /'hɔːnɪt/ *n* calabrone *m*

horn-rimmed /-rɪmd/ *adj* ‹spectacles› con la montatura di tartaruga

horny /'hɔːnɪ/ *adj* calloso; fam (sexually) arrapato

horoscope /'hɒrəskəʊp/ *n* oroscopo *m*

horrendous /hə'rendəs/ *adj* spaventoso

horrible /'hɒrəbl/ *adj* orribile

horribly /'hɒrəblɪ/ *adv* orribilmente

horrid /'hɒrɪd/ *adj* orrendo

horrific /hə'rɪfɪk/ *adj* raccapricciante; fam ‹accident, prices, story› terrificante

horrify /'hɒrɪfaɪ/ *vt* (*pt/pp* **-ied**) far inorridire; **I was horrified** ero inorridito

horrifying /'hɒrɪfaɪɪŋ/ *adj* terrificante

horror /'hɒrə(r)/ *n* orrore *m*

horror film *n* film *m inv* dell'orrore

horror story *n* racconto *m* dell'orrore

hors-d'œuvre /ɔː'dɜːvr/ *n* antipasto *m*

⚹ **horse** /hɔːs/ *n* cavallo *m*
■ **horse around** *vi* fare il pagliaccio

horseback *n* **on** ~ a cavallo

horseback riding *n* Am equitazione *f*

horsebox *n* furgone *m* per il trasporto dei cavalli

horse chestnut *n* ippocastano *m*

horsefly *n* tafano *m*

horsehair *n* crine *m* di cavallo

horseman *n* cavaliere *m*

horse manure *n* concime *m*

horseplay *n* gioco *m* pesante

horsepower *n* cavallo *m* [vapore]

horse race *n* corsa *f* ippica

horse racing *n* corse *fpl* di cavalli

horseradish *n* rafano *m*

horseradish sauce *n* salsa *f* di rafano

horseriding *n* equitazione *f*

horseshoe *n* ferro *m* di cavallo

horseshow *n* concorso *m* ippico

hors[e]y /'hɔːsɪ/ *adj* ‹person› che adora i cavalli; ‹face› cavallino

horticultural /hɔːtɪ'kʌltʃʊrəl/ *adj* di orticoltura

horticulture /'hɔːtɪkʌltʃə(r)/ *n* orticoltura *f*

hose /həʊz/ *n* (pipe) manichetta *f*
■ **hose down** *vt* lavare con la manichetta

hosepipe /'həʊzpaɪp/ *n* manichetta *f*

hosiery /'həʊʒərɪ/ *n* maglieria *f*

hospice /'hɒspɪs/ *n* (for the terminally ill) ospedale *m* per i malati in fase terminale

hospitable /hɒ'spɪtəbl/ *adj* ospitale

hospitably /hɒ'spɪtəblɪ/ *adv* con ospitalità

ꞏ **hospital** /'hɒspɪtl/ *n* ospedale *m*

hospitality /hɒspɪ'tælətɪ/ *n* ospitalità *f*

hospitalize /'hɒspɪtəlaɪz/ *vt* ricoverare [in ospedale]

host[1] /həʊst/ *n* **a ∼ of** una moltitudine di

ꞏ **host**[2] *n* ospite *m*

host[3] *n* Relig ostia *f*

hostage /'hɒstɪdʒ/ *n* ostaggio *m*; **hold somebody ∼** tenere qualcuno in ostaggio

host country *n* paese *m* ospitante

hostel /'hɒstl/ *n* ostello *m*

hostess /'həʊstɪs/ *n* padrona *f* di casa; Aeron hostess *f inv*

hostile /'hɒstaɪl/ *adj* ostile

hostility /hɒ'stɪlətɪ/ *n* ostilità *f*; **hostilities** *pl* ostilità *fpl*

ꞏ **hot** /hɒt/ *adj* (**hotter, hottest**) caldo; (spicy) piccante; **I am** *or* **feel ∼** ho caldo; **it is ∼** fa caldo; **in ∼ water** fig nei guai

hot-air balloon *n* mongolfiera *f*

hotbed *n* fig focolaio *m*

hot-blooded /-'blʌdɪd/ *adj* ‹person› focoso; ‹reaction› passionale

hot cake *n* **sell like ∼s** andare a ruba

hotchpotch /'hɒtʃpɒtʃ/ *n* miscuglio *m*

hot cross bun *n* panino (*m*) dolce con spezie e uvette, tipicamente pasquale

hot dog *n* hot dog *m inv*

hotdogging *n* sci *m* acrobatico

ꞏ **hotel** /həʊ'tel/ *n* hotel *m inv*, albergo *m*

hoteller /həʊ'teliə(r)/ *n* albergatore, -trice *mf*

hotfoot *adv* hum ‹go› di gran carriera

hothead *n* persona *f* impetuosa

hot-headed /-'hedɪd/ *adj* impetuoso

hothouse *n* serra *f*

hotline *n* linea *f* diretta; Mil, Pol telefono *m* rosso

hotly /'hɒtlɪ/ *adv* fig accanitamente

hotplate *n* piastra *f* riscaldante

hot seat *n* **be in the ∼** essere in una posizione difficile

hotshot *n* fam persona *f* di successo; pej carrierista *mf*

hot spot *n* (trouble zone) zona *f* calda; (sunny place) luogo *m* assolato

hot tap *n* rubinetto *m* dell'acqua calda

hot-tempered /-'tempəd/ *adj* irascibile

hot-water bottle *n* borsa *f* dell'acqua calda

hound /haʊnd/ ⓵ *n* cane da caccia *m* ⓶ *vt* fig perseguire

ꞏ **hour** /'aʊə(r)/ *n* ora *f*

hourglass /'aʊəɡlɑːs/ *n* clessidra *f*

hourly /'aʊəlɪ/ ⓵ *adj* ad ogni ora; ‹pay, rate› a ora ⓶ *adv* ogni ora

ꞏ **house**[1] /haʊs/ *n* casa *f*; Pol Camera *f*; Theat sala *f*; **at my ∼** a casa mia, da me

house[2] /haʊz/ *vt* alloggiare ‹person›; incastrare ‹machine›

houseboat *n* casa *f* galleggiante

housebound /'haʊsbaʊnd/ *adj* costretto in casa

housebreaking *n* furto *m* con scasso

house call *n* visita *f* a domicilio

ꞏ **household** *n* casa *f*, famiglia *f*

household appliance *n* elettrodomestico *m*

householder *n* capo *m* di famiglia

household name *n* noto *m*

house husband *n* casalingo *m*

housekeeper *n* governante *f* di casa

housekeeping *n* governo *m* della casa; (money) soldi *mpl* per le spese di casa

House of Commons *n* Camera *f* dei Comuni

House of Lords *n* Camera *f* dei Lord

House of Representatives *n* Camera *f* dei Rappresentanti

house plant *n* pianta *f* da appartamento

house-proud *adj* orgoglioso della propria casa

Houses of Parliament *npl* Parlamento *m*

house-to-house *adj* ‹search› casa per casa

house-trained /-treɪnd/ *adj* che non sporca in casa

house-warming [party] *n* festa *f* di inaugurazione della nuova casa

housewife *n* casalinga *f*

housework *n* lavori *mpl* domestici

ꞏ **housing** /'haʊzɪŋ/ *n* alloggio *m*; Techn alloggiamento *m*

housing estate *n* zona *f* residenziale

hovel /'hɒvl/ *n* tugurio *m*

hover /'hɒvə(r)/ *vi* librarsi; (linger) indugiare; **∼ on the brink of doing something** essere sul punto di fare qualcosa

hovercraft /'hɒvəkrɑːft/ *n* hovercraft *m inv*

ꞏ **how** /haʊ/ *adv* come; **∼ are you?** come stai?; **∼ about a coffee/going on holiday?** che ne diresti di un caffè/di andare in vacanza?; **∼ do you do?** molto lieto!; **∼ old are you?** quanti anni hai?; **∼ long** quanto tempo; **∼ many** quanti; **∼ much** quanto; **∼ often** ogni quanto; **and ∼!** eccome!; **∼ odd!** che strano!

ꞏ **however** /haʊ'evə(r)/ *adv* (nevertheless) comunque; **∼ small** per quanto piccolo

howl /haʊl/ ⓵ *n* ululato *m* ⓶ *vi* ululare; (cry with laughter) singhiozzare

howler /'haʊlə(r)/ n fam strafalcione m

HP abbr **1 (hire purchase)**
2 (horse power) C. V.

HQ n abbr Mil **(headquarters)** Q.G.

HR abbr **(human resources)** RU

HRT abbr **(hormone replacement
therapy)** TOS f

HTML abbr **(hypertext markup
language)** Comput HTML m

HTTP abbr **(hypertext transfer
protocol)** Comput HTTP m

hub /hʌb/ n mozzo m; fig centro m

hubbub /'hʌbʌb/ n baccano m

hubcap /'hʌbkæp/ n coprimozzo m

huckleberry /'hʌklbərɪ/ n Am mirtillo m
americano

huddle /'hʌdl/ vi ~ together rannicchiarsi
l'uno contro l'altro

hue¹ /hju:/ n colore m

hue² n ~ **and cry** clamore m

huff /hʌf/ n be in a/go into a ~ fare il broncio

hug /hʌg/ **1** n abbraccio m; **give
somebody a** ~ abbracciare qualcuno
2 vt (pt/pp **hugged**) abbracciare; (keep
close to) tenersi vicino a; aggrapparsi a ‹wall›

✎ **huge** /hju:dʒ/ adj enorme

hugely /'hju:dʒlɪ/ adv enormemente

huh /hʌ/ int (inquiry) eh?; (in surprise) oh!

hulk /hʌlk/ n (of ship, tank etc) carcassa f

hulking /'hʌlkɪŋ/ adj fam grosso

hull /hʌl/ n Naut scafo m

hullabaloo /hʌləbə'lu:/ n fam (noise)
trambusto m; (outcry) fracasso m

hullo /hə'ləʊ/ int = HALLO

hum /hʌm/ **1** n ronzio m
2 vt (pt/pp **hummed**) canticchiare
3 vi ‹motor› ronzare; fig fervere di attività;
~ **and haw** esitare

✎ **human** /'hju:mən/ **1** adj umano
2 n essere m umano

human being n essere m umano

humane /hju:'meɪn/ adj umano

humanely /hju:'meɪnlɪ/ adv umanamente

human interest story n storia f di vita
vissuta

humanitarian /hju:mænɪ'teərɪən/ adj &
n umanitario, -a mf

humanities /hju:'mænɪtɪz/ pl Univ dottrine
fpl umanistiche

humanity /hju:'mænətɪ/ n umanità f

human nature n natura f umana

human resources npl risorse fpl
umane

human resources manager n
responsabile mf delle risorse umane

humble /'hʌmbl/ **1** adj umile
2 vt umiliare

humbly /'hʌmblɪ/ adv umilmente

humbug /'hʌmbʌg/ n (nonsense)
sciocchezze fpl; (dishonesty) falsità f; Br (sweet)
caramella f alla menta

humdrum /'hʌmdrʌm/ adj noioso

humid /'hju:mɪd/ adj umido

humidifier /hju:'mɪdɪfaɪə(r)/ n
umidificatore m

humidity /hju:'mɪdətɪ/ n umidità f

humiliate /hju:'mɪlɪeɪt/ vt umiliare

humiliating /hju:'mɪlɪeɪtɪŋ/ adj avvilente

humiliation /hju:mɪlɪ'eɪʃn/ n umiliazione
f

humility /hju:'mɪlətɪ/ n umiltà f

hummingbird /'hʌmɪŋbɜ:d/ n colibrì
m inv

hummock /'hʌmək/ n (of earth) poggio m

hummus /'hʊməs/ n hummus m, purè m
di ceci

humorist /'hju:mərɪst/ n umorista mf

humorous /'hju:mərəs/ adj umoristico

humorously /'hju:mərəslɪ/ adv con
spirito

humour /'hju:mə(r)/ **1** n umorismo m;
(mood) umore m; **have a sense of** ~ avere il
senso dell' umorismo
2 vt compiacere

hump /hʌmp/ n protuberanza f; (of camel,
hunchback) gobba f; **he's got the** ~ sl è di
malumore

humpback[ed] bridge /'hʌm(p)bæk[t]/
n ponte m a schiena d'asino

humus /'hju:məs/ n humus m

hunch /hʌntʃ/ n (idea) intuizione f

hunchback /'hʌntʃbæk/ n gobbo, -a mf

hunched /hʌntʃt/ adj ~ up incurvato

✎ **hundred** /'hʌndrəd/ **1** adj one/a ~ cento
2 n cento m inv; ~s of centinaia di

hundredfold /'hʌndrədfəʊld/ adv
increase a ~ centuplicare

hundredth /'hʌndrədθ/ adj & n centesimo
m

hundredweight /'hʌndrədweɪt/ n
cinquanta chili m

hung /hʌŋ/ ▶ HANG

Hungarian /hʌŋ'geərɪən/ n & adj
ungherese mf; (language) ungherese m

Hungary /'hʌŋgərɪ/ n Ungheria f

hunger /'hʌŋgə(r)/ n fame f
■ **hunger for** vt aver fame di

hunger strike n sciopero m della fame

hung-over adj be ~ avere i postumi della
sbornia

hungrily /'hʌŋgrɪlɪ/ adv con appetito

hungry /'hʌŋgrɪ/ adj (-ier, -iest)
affamato; **be** ~ aver fame

hung-up adj fam (tense) complessato; **be** ~
on somebody/something (obsessed) essere
fissato con qualcosa

✎ indicates a very frequent word

h

hunk /hʌŋk/ n grosso pezzo m; fam (man) figo m

hunky-dory /hʌŋkɪ'dɔːrɪ/ adj fam perfetto

hunt /hʌnt/ ① n caccia f
② vt andare a caccia di ‹animal›; dare la caccia a ‹criminal›
③ vi andare a caccia; ~ for cercare

hunter /'hʌntə(r)/ n cacciatore m

hunting /'hʌntɪŋ/ n caccia f

hunt saboteur n Br sabotatore, -trice mf della caccia

huntsman /'hʌntsmən/ n (hunter) cacciatore m; (fox-hunter) cacciatore m di volpe

hurdle /'hɜːdl/ n Sport fig ostacolo m

hurdler /'hɜːdlə(r)/ n ostacolista mf

hurdy-gurdy /hɜːdɪ'gɜːdɪ/ n organino m

hurl /hɜːl/ vt scagliare

hurly-burly /hɜːlɪ'bɜːlɪ/ n chiasso m

hurrah /hʊ'rɑː/, **hurray** /hʊ'reɪ/ ① int urrà!
② n urrà m

hurricane /'hʌrɪkən/ n uragano m

hurried /'hʌrɪd/ adj affrettato; ‹job› fatto in fretta

hurriedly /'hʌrɪdlɪ/ adv in fretta

hurry /'hʌrɪ/ ① n fretta f; be in a ~ aver fretta
② vi (pt/pp -ied) affrettarsi
■ **hurry up** ① vi sbrigarsi
② vt mettere fretta a ‹person›; accelerare ‹things›

⚡ **hurt** /hɜːt/ ① n male m
② vt (pt/pp **hurt**) far male a; (offend) ferire
③ vi far male; **my leg ~s** mi fa male la gamba

hurtful /'hɜːtfʊl/ adj fig offensivo

hurtle /'hɜːtl/ vi ~ along andare a tutta velocità

⚡ **husband** /'hʌzbənd/ n marito m

hush /hʌʃ/ n silenzio m
■ **hush up** vt mettere a tacere

hushed /hʌʃt/ adj ‹voice› sommesso

hush-hush adj fam segretissimo

husky /'hʌskɪ/ adj (-ier, -iest) ‹voice› rauco

hussar /hʊ'zɑː(r)/ n ussaro m

hustings /'hʌstɪŋz/ n on the ~ in campagna elettorale

hustle /'hʌsl/ ① vt affrettare
② n attività f incessante; ~ and bustle trambusto m

hut /hʌt/ n capanna f

hutch /hʌtʃ/ n conigliera f

hyacinth /'haɪəsɪnθ/ n giacinto m

hybrid /'haɪbrɪd/ ① adj ibrido
② n ibrido m

hydrangea /haɪ'dreɪndʒə/ n ortensia f

hydrant /'haɪdrənt/ n [fire] ~ idrante m

hydraulic /haɪ'drɔːlɪk/ adj idraulico

hydrocarbon /haɪdrəʊ'kɑːbən/ n idrocarburo m

hydrochloric /haɪdrə'klɒrɪk/ adj ~ **acid** acido m cloridrico

hydroelectric /haɪdrəʊɪ'lektrɪk/ adj idroelettrico

hydroelectricity /ˌhaɪdrəʊɪlek'trɪsətɪ/ n energia f idroelettrica

hydroelectric power station n centrale f idroelettrica

hydrofoil /'haɪdrəfɔɪl/ n aliscafo m

hydrogen /'haɪdrədʒən/ n idrogeno m

hydrolysis /haɪ'drɒləsɪs/ n idrolisi f

hydrophobia /haɪdrə'fəʊbɪə/ n idrofobia f

hydroplane /'haɪdrəpleɪn/ n (boat) aliscafo m; Am (seaplane) idrovolante m

hydrotherapy /haɪdrəʊ'θerəpɪ/ n idroterapia f

hyena /haɪ'iːnə/ n iena f

hygiene /'haɪdʒiːn/ n igiene m

hygienic /haɪ'dʒiːnɪk/ adj igienico

hygienically /haɪ'dʒiːnɪklɪ/ adv igienicamente

hymn /hɪm/ n inno m

hymn book n libro m dei canti

hype /haɪp/ n fam grande pubblicità f; **media ~** battage m pubblicitario
■ **hype up** vt fam fare grande pubblicità a ‹film, star, book›; (exaggerate) gonfiare

hyper /'haɪpə(r)/ adj fam eccitato

hyperactive /haɪpər'æktɪv/ adj iperattivo

hyperactivity /haɪpəræk'tɪvɪtɪ/ n iperattività f

hyperbole /haɪ'pɜːbəlɪ/ n iperbole f

hypercritical /haɪpə'krɪtɪkl/ adj ipercritico

hyperlink /'haɪpəlɪŋk/ n Comput hyperlink m inv, collegamento m ipertestuale

hypermarket /'haɪpəmɑːkɪt/ n ipermercato m

hypersensitive /haɪpə'sensɪtɪv/ adj pej permaloso; (physically) ipersensibile

hypertension /haɪpə'tenʃn/ n ipertensione f

hypertext /'haɪpətekst/ n Comput ipertesto m

hypertext markup language n Comput linguaggio m per la marcatura di ipertesti

hypertext transfer protocol n Comput protocollo m per il trasferimento di ipertesti

hyperventilate /haɪpə'ventɪleɪt/ vi iperventilare

hyphen /'haɪfn/ n trattino m

hyphenate /'haɪfəneɪt/ vt unire con trattino

hypnosis /hɪp'nəʊsɪs/ n ipnosi f

hypnotherapy /hɪpnəʊ'θerəpɪ/ n
ipnoterapia f
hypnotic /hɪp'nɒtɪk/ adj ipnotico
hypnotism /'hɪpnətɪzm/ n ipnotismo m
hypnotist /'hɪpnətɪst/ n ipnotizzatore,
-trice mf
hypnotize /'hɪpnətaɪz/ vt ipnotizzare
hypoallergenic /haɪpəʊælə'dʒenɪk/ adj
anallergico
hypochondria /haɪpə'kɒndrɪə/ n
ipocondria f
hypochondriac /haɪpə'kɒndrɪæk/ adj &
n ipocondriaco, -a mf
hypocrisy /hɪ'pɒkrəsɪ/ n ipocrisia f
hypocrite /'hɪpəkrɪt/ n ipocrita mf
hypocritical /hɪpə'krɪtɪkl/ adj ipocrita
hypocritically /hɪpə'krɪtɪklɪ/ adv
ipocriticamente

hypodermic /haɪpə'dɜːmɪk/ adj & n ~
[syringe] siringa f ipodermica
hypotenuse /haɪ'pɒtənjuːz/ n ipotenusa f
hypothermia /haɪpəʊ'θɜːmɪə/ n
ipotermia f
hypothesis /haɪ'pɒθəsɪs/ n ipotesi f inv
hypothetical /haɪpə'θetɪkl/ adj ipotetico
hypothetically /haɪpə'θetɪklɪ/ adv in
teoria; ‹speak› per ipotesi
hysterectomy /hɪstə'rektəmɪ/ n
isterectomia f
hysteria /hɪ'stɪərɪə/ n isterismo m
hysterical /hɪ'sterɪkl/ adj isterico
hysterically /hɪ'sterɪklɪ/ adv
istericamente; ~ **funny** da morir dal ridere
hysterics /hɪ'sterɪks/ npl attacco m
isterico

I i

i, I /aɪ/ n (letter) i, I f inv
🖉 **I** /aɪ/ pron io; **I'm tired** sono stanco; **he's
going, but I'm not** lui va, ma io no
IAP n abbr (**internet access provider**)
Comput IAP m
IBA n abbr (**Independent
Broadcasting Authority**) organismo
(m) indipendente di vigilanza sulla
radiotelevisione
IBAN n abbr (**International Bank
Account Number**) IBAN m
ibex /'aɪbeks/ n stambecco m
ICC n abbr (**International Criminal
Court**) TPI m
🖉 **ice** /aɪs/ 1 n ghiaccio m
2 vt glassare ‹cake›
■ **ice over, ice up** vi ghiacciarsi
ice age n era f glaciale
ice axe n piccozza f per il ghiaccio
iceberg n iceberg m inv
icebox n Am frigorifero m
ice-breaker n Naut rompighiaccio m inv
ice bucket n secchiello m del ghiaccio
ice cap n calotta f glaciale
ice-cold adj ghiacciato
ice cream n gelato m
ice-cream parlour n gelateria f
ice-cream sundae n coppa f [di] gelato
guarnita
ice cube n cubetto m di ghiaccio

ice dancer n ballerino, -a mf sul ghiaccio
ice floe n banco m di ghiaccio
ice hockey hockey m su ghiaccio
Iceland /'aɪslənd/ n Islanda f
Icelander /'aɪsləndə(r)/ n islandese mf
Icelandic /aɪs'lændɪk/ adj & n islandese m
ice lolly n ghiacciolo m
ice pack n impacco m di ghiaccio
ice pick n piccone m da ghiaccio
ice rink n pista f di pattinaggio
ice-skate n pattino m da ghiaccio
ice-skater pattinatore, -trice mf sul
ghiaccio
ice-skating pattinaggio m sul ghiaccio
ice-tray n vaschetta f per il ghiaccio
icicle /'aɪsɪkl/ n ghiacciolo m
icily /'aɪsɪlɪ/ adv gelidamente
icing /'aɪsɪŋ/ n glassa f
icing sugar n zucchero m a velo
icon /'aɪkɒn/ n icona f
iconize /'aɪkənaɪz/ vt Comput iconizzare
ICT n abbr (**information and
communication technology**) ICT f
icy /'aɪsɪ/ adj (**-ier, -iest**) ghiacciato; fig gelido
id /ɪd/ n the ~ l'Es m
ID n abbr (**identification, identity**)
documento m d'identità; **ID card** n carta f
d'identità
🖉 **idea** /aɪ'dɪə/ n idea f; **I've no ~!** non ne ho
idea!
ideal /aɪ'dɪəl/ 1 adj ideale
2 n ideale m

🖉 indicates a very frequent word

idealism ⋯⟶ illuminations ⋯⋯

idealism /aɪˈdɪəlɪzm/ n idealismo m
idealist /aɪˈdɪəlɪst/ n idealista mf
idealistic /aɪdɪəˈlɪstɪk/ adj idealistico
idealize /aɪˈdɪəlaɪz/ vt idealizzare
ideally /aɪˈdɪəlɪ/ adv idealmente
identical /aɪˈdentɪkl/ adj identico
identical twin n gemello, -a mf
monozigote
identifiable /aɪdentɪˈfaɪəbl/ adj
identificabile
identification /aɪdentɪfɪˈkeɪʃn/ n
identificazione f; (proof of identity) documento
m di riconoscimento
identify /aɪˈdentɪfaɪ/ **1** vt (pt/pp -ied)
identificare
2 vi ~ with identificarsi con
identikit® /aɪˈdentɪkɪt/ n identikit m inv
identikit® **picture** n identikit m inv
♂ **identity** /aɪˈdentətɪ/ n identità f inv
identity bracelet n braccialetto m
identificativo
identity card n carta f d'identità
identity parade n confronto m
all'americana
identity theft n l'utilizzare il nome e
i dati personali di qualcuno allo scopo di
ottenere carte di credito, prelevare denaro da
conti bancari ecc.
ideological /aɪdɪəˈlɒdʒɪkl/ adj ideologico
ideology /aɪdɪˈɒlədʒɪ/ n ideologia f
idiocy /ˈɪdɪəsɪ/ n idiozia f
idiom /ˈɪdɪəm/ n idioma f
idiomatic /ɪdɪəˈmætɪk/ adj idiomatico
idiomatically /ɪdɪəˈmætɪklɪ/ adv in modo
idiomatico
idiosyncrasy /ɪdɪəˈsɪŋkrəsɪ/ n
idiosincrasia f
idiosyncratic /ˌɪdɪəsɪŋˈkrætɪk/ adj
particolare
idiot /ˈɪdɪət/ n idiota mf
idiotic /ɪdɪˈɒtɪk/ adj idiota
idle /ˈaɪd(ə)l/ **1** adj (lazy) pigro, ozioso;
(empty) vano; ‹machine› fermo
2 vi oziare; ‹engine› girare a vuoto
■ **idle away** vt passare nell'ozio ‹day, time›
idleness /ˈaɪd(ə)lnɪs/ n ozio m
idly /ˈaɪdlɪ/ adv oziosamente
idol /ˈaɪd(ə)l/ n idolo m
idolize /ˈaɪdəlaɪz/ vt idolatrare
idyll /ˈɪdɪl/ n idillio m
idyllic /ɪˈdɪlɪk/ adj idillico
♂ **i.e.** abbr (**id est**) cioè
♂ **if** /ɪf/ conj se; **as if** come se
iffy /ˈɪfɪ/ adj incerto
igloo /ˈɪgluː/ n igloo m inv
ignite /ɪgˈnaɪt/ **1** vt dar fuoco a
2 vi prender fuoco
ignition /ɪgˈnɪʃn/ n Auto accensione f
ignition key n chiave f d'accensione

ignoramus /ɪgnəˈreɪməs/ n ignorante mf
ignorance /ˈɪgnərəns/ n ignoranza f
ignorant /ˈɪgnərənt/ adj (lacking knowledge)
ignaro; (rude) ignorante
♂ **ignore** /ɪgˈnɔː(r)/ vt ignorare
ill /ɪl/ **1** adj ammalato; **feel** ~ **at ease**
sentirsi a disagio
2 adv male
3 n male m
ill-advised /-ədˈvaɪzd/ adj avventato
ill-bred /-ˈbred/ adj maleducato
ill-considered /-kənˈsɪdəd/ adj ‹measure,
remark› avventato
ill effect n effetto m negativo
♂ **illegal** /ɪˈliːgl/ adj illegale
illegality /ɪlɪˈgælətɪ/ n illegalità f
illegally /ɪˈliːgəlɪ/ adv illegalmente
illegible /ɪˈledʒəbl/ adj illeggibile
illegibly /ɪˈledʒəblɪ/ adv in modo
illeggibile
illegitimacy /ɪlɪˈdʒɪtɪməsɪ/ n illegittimità
f
illegitimate /ɪlɪˈdʒɪtɪmət/ adj illegittimo
ill-equipped /-ɪˈkwɪpt/ adj non
equipaggiato
ill-fated /-ˈfeɪtɪd/ adj sfortunato
ill feeling n rancore m
ill-fitting adj ‹garment, shoe› che non va
bene
ill-founded /-ˈfaʊndɪd/ adj ‹argument,
gossip› infondato
ill-gotten gains /ɪlgɒ(t)nˈgeɪmz/ adj
guadagni mpl illeciti
ill health n problemi mpl di salute
illicit /ɪˈlɪsɪt/ adj illecito
illicitly /ɪˈlɪsɪtlɪ/ adv illecitamente
ill-informed /-ɪnˈfɔːmd/ adj ‹person› male
informato
illiteracy /ɪˈlɪtərəsɪ/ n analfabetismo m
illiterate /ɪˈlɪtərət/ adj & n analfabeta mf
ill-mannered /-ˈmænəd/ adj maleducato
♂ **illness** /ˈɪlnɪs/ n malattia f
illogical /ɪˈlɒdʒɪkl/ adj illogico
illogically /ɪˈlɒdʒɪklɪ/ adv illogicamente
ill-prepared /-prɪˈpeəd/ adj impreparato
ill-timed /-ˈtaɪmd/ adj ‹arrival›
inopportuno; ‹campaign› fatto al momento
sbagliato
ill-treat vt maltrattare
ill-treatment n maltrattamento m
illuminate /ɪˈluːmɪneɪt/ vt illuminare
illuminated /ɪˈluːmɪneɪtɪd/ adj ‹sign›
luminoso
illuminating /ɪˈluːmɪneɪtɪŋ/ adj
chiarificatore
illumination /ɪluːmɪˈneɪʃn/ n
illuminazione f
illuminations npl Br luminarie fpl

illusion /ɪˈluːʒn/ n illusione f; **be under the ~ that** avere l'illusione che
illusory /ɪˈluːsərɪ/ adj illusorio
illustrate /ˈɪləstreɪt/ vt illustrare
illustration /ɪləˈstreɪʃn/ n illustrazione f
illustrative /ˈɪləstrətɪv/ adj illustrativo
illustrator /ˈɪləstreɪtə(r)/ n illustratore, -trice mf
illustrious /ɪˈlʌstrɪəs/ adj illustre
ill will n malanimo m
◆ **image** /ˈɪmɪdʒ/ n immagine f; (exact likeness) ritratto m
image-conscious adj attento all'immagine
image maker n persona f che cura l'immagine
image processing n trattamento m dell'immagine
imagery /ˈɪmɪdʒərɪ/ n immagini fpl
imaginable /ɪˈmædʒɪnəbl/ adj immaginabile
imaginary /ɪˈmædʒɪnərɪ/ adj immaginario
imagination /ɪmædʒɪˈneɪʃn/ n immaginazione f, fantasia f; **it's your ~** è solo una tua idea
imaginative /ɪˈmædʒɪnətɪv/ adj fantasioso
imaginatively /ɪˈmædʒɪnətɪvlɪ/ adv con fantasia or immaginazione
◆ **imagine** /ɪˈmædʒɪn/ vt immaginare; (wrongly) inventare
IMAP abbr (**Internet mail access protocol**) Comput protocollo m di gestione remota della posta elettronica
imbalance /ɪmˈbæləns/ n squilibrio m
imbecile /ˈɪmbəsiːl/ n imbecille mf
imbibe /ɪmˈbaɪb/ **1** vt ingerire; fig assorbire
2 vi hum bere
imbue /ɪmˈbjuː/ vt **~d with** impregnato di
IMF n abbr (**International Monetary Fund**) FMI m
imitate /ˈɪmɪteɪt/ vt imitare
imitation /ɪmɪˈteɪʃn/ n imitazione f
imitative /ˈɪmɪtətɪv/ adj imitativo
imitator /ˈɪmɪteɪtə(r)/ n imitatore, -trice mf
immaculate /ɪˈmækjʊlət/ adj immacolato
immaculately /ɪˈmækjʊlətlɪ/ adv immacolatamente
immaterial /ɪməˈtɪərɪəl/ adj (unimportant) irrilevante
immature /ɪməˈtʃʊə(r)/ adj immaturo
immeasurable /ɪˈmeʒərəbl/ adj incommensurabile
immediacy /ɪˈmiːdɪəsɪ/ n immediatezza f
◆ **immediate** /ɪˈmiːdɪət/ adj immediato; (relative) stretto; **in the ~ vicinity** nelle

◆ indicates a very frequent word

immediate vicinanze
◆ **immediately** /ɪˈmiːdɪətlɪ/ **1** adv immediatamente; **~ next to** subito accanto a **2** conj (non) appena
immemorial /ɪmɪˈmɔːrɪəl/ adj **from time ~** da tempo immemorabile
immense /ɪˈmens/ adj immenso
immensely /ɪˈmenslɪ/ adv immensamente
immensity /ɪˈmensətɪ/ n immensità f
immerse /ɪˈmɜːs/ vt immergere; **be ~d in** fig essere immerso in
immersion /ɪˈmɜːʃn/ n immersione f
immersion course n Br corso m full immersion
immersion heater n scaldabagno m elettrico
immigrant /ˈɪmɪgrənt/ n immigrante mf
immigrate /ˈɪmɪgreɪt/ vi immigrare
immigration /ɪmɪˈgreɪʃn/ n immigrazione f
immigration control n controllo m dell'immigrazione
imminence /ˈɪmɪnəns/ n imminenza f
imminent /ˈɪmɪnənt/ adj imminente
immobile /ɪˈməʊbaɪl/ adj immobile
immobilize /ɪˈməʊbɪlaɪz/ vt immobilizzare
immobilizer /ɪˈməʊbɪlaɪzə(r)/ n Auto immobilizzatore m elettronico
immoderate /ɪˈmɒdərət/ adj smodato
immodest /ɪˈmɒdɪst/ adj immodesto
immoral /ɪˈmɒrəl/ adj immorale
immorality /ɪməˈrælətɪ/ n immoralità f
immortal /ɪˈmɔːtl/ adj immortale
immortality /ɪmɔːˈtælətɪ/ n immortalità f
immortalize /ɪˈmɔːtəlaɪz/ vt immortalare
immovable /ɪˈmuːvəbl/ adj fig irremovibile
immune /ɪˈmjuːn/ adj immune (**to/from** da)
immune system n sistema m immunitario
immunity /ɪˈmjuːnətɪ/ n immunità f
immunization /ɪmjʊnaɪˈzeɪʃn/ n immunizzazione f
immunize /ˈɪmjʊnaɪz/ vt immunizzare
immunodeficiency /ɪmjʊnəʊdɪˈfɪʃənsɪ/ n immunodeficienza f
immunodepressant /ɪmjʊnəʊdɪˈpres(ə)nt/ **1** adj immunodepressivo **2** n immunodepressivo m
immunology /ɪmjʊˈnɒlədʒɪ/ n immunologia f
immutable /ɪˈmjuːtəbl/ adj immutabile
imp /ɪmp/ n diavoletto m
◆ **impact** /ˈɪmpækt/ n impatto m
impacted /ɪmˈpæktɪd/ adj (tooth) incluso; (fracture) incuneato
impair /ɪmˈpeə(r)/ vt danneggiare
impaired /ɪmˈpeəd/ adj **hearing ~** audioleso; **visually ~** videoleso

impale ⋯⟩ import duty ⋯⋯

impale /ɪmˈpeɪl/ *vt* impalare

impalpable /ɪmˈpælpəbl/ *adj* (intangible) impalpabile

impart /ɪmˈpɑːt/ *vt* impartire

impartial /ɪmˈpɑːʃəl/ *adj* imparziale

impartiality /ɪmpɑːʃɪˈælətɪ/ *n* imparzialità *f*

impassable /ɪmˈpɑːsəbl/ *adj* impraticabile

impasse /æmˈpɑːs/ *n* fig impasse *f inv*

impassioned /ɪmˈpæʃnd/ *adj* appassionato

impassive /ɪmˈpæsɪv/ *adj* impassibile

impassively /ɪmˈpæsɪvlɪ/ *adv* impassibilmente

impatience /ɪmˈpeɪʃns/ *n* impazienza *f*

impatient /ɪmˈpeɪʃnt/ *adj* impaziente

impatiently /ɪmˈpeɪʃntlɪ/ *adv* impazientemente

impeach /ɪmˈpiːtʃ/ *vt* accusare

impeccable /ɪmˈpekəbl/ *adj* impeccabile

impeccably /ɪmˈpekəblɪ/ *adv* in modo impeccabile

impede /ɪmˈpiːd/ *vt* impedire

impediment /ɪmˈpedɪmənt/ *n* impedimento *m*; (in speech) difetto *m*

impel /ɪmˈpel/ *vt* (*pt/pp* **impelled**) costringere; **feel ~led to** sentire l'obbligo di

impending /ɪmˈpendɪŋ/ *adj* imminente

impenetrable /ɪmˈpenɪtrəbl/ *adj* impenetrabile

imperative /ɪmˈperətɪv/ ① *adj* imperativo
② *n* Gram imperativo *m*

imperceptible /ɪmpəˈseptəbl/ *adj* impercettibile

imperfect /ɪmˈpɜːfɪkt/ ① *adj* imperfetto; (faulty) difettoso
② *n* Gram imperfetto *m*

imperfection /ɪmpəˈfekʃn/ *n* imperfezione *f*

imperial /ɪmˈpɪərɪəl/ *adj* imperiale

imperialism /ɪmˈpɪərɪəlɪzm/ *n* imperialismo *m*

imperialist /ɪmˈpɪərɪəlɪst/ *n* imperialista *mf*

imperil /ɪmˈperəl/ *vt* (*pt/pp* **imperilled**) mettere in pericolo

imperious /ɪmˈpɪərɪəs/ *adj* imperioso

imperiously /ɪmˈpɪərɪəslɪ/ *adv* in modo imperioso

impermeable /ɪmˈpɜːmɪəbl/ *adj* impermeabile

impersonal /ɪmˈpɜːsənəl/ *adj* impersonale

impersonate /ɪmˈpɜːsəneɪt/ *vt* impersonare

impersonation /ɪmpɜːsəˈneɪʃn/ *n* imitazione *f*

impersonator /ɪmˈpɜːsəneɪtə(r)/ *n* imitatore, -trice *mf*

impertinence /ɪmˈpɜːtɪnəns/ *n* impertinenza *f*

impertinent /ɪmˈpɜːtɪnənt/ *adj* impertinente

imperturbable /ɪmpəˈtɜːbəbl/ *adj* imperturbabile

impervious /ɪmˈpɜːvɪəs/ *adj* ~ **to** fig indifferente a

impetuous /ɪmˈpetjʊəs/ *adj* impetuoso

impetuously /ɪmˈpetjʊəslɪ/ *adv* impetuosamente

impetus /ˈɪmpɪtəs/ *n* impeto *m*

impiety /ɪmˈpaɪətɪ/ *n* Relig empietà *f*

impinge /ɪmˈpɪndʒ/ *v*
■ **impinge on** *vt* (affect) influire su; (restrict) condizionare

impious /ˈɪmpɪəs/ *adj* Relig empio

impish /ˈɪmpɪʃ/ *adj* birichino

implacable /ɪmˈplækəbl/ *adj* implacabile

implant¹ /ɪmˈplɑːnt/ *vt* trapiantare; fig inculcare

implant² /ˈɪmplɑːnt/ *n* trapianto *m*

implausible /ɪmˈplɔːzəbl/ *adj* poco plausibile

implement¹ /ˈɪmplɪmənt/ *n* attrezzo *m*

implement² /ˈɪmplɪment/ *vt* mettere in atto

implementation /ˌɪmplɪmenˈteɪʃn/ *n* (of law, policy, idea) attuazione *f*; Comput implementazione *f*

implicate /ˈɪmplɪkeɪt/ *vt* implicare

implication /ɪmplɪˈkeɪʃn/ *n* implicazione *f*; **by ~** implicitamente

implicit /ɪmˈplɪsɪt/ *adj* implicito; (absolute) assoluto

implicitly /ɪmˈplɪsɪtlɪ/ *adv* implicitamente; (absolutely) completamente

implied /ɪmˈplaɪd/ *adj* implicito, sottinteso

implore /ɪmˈplɔː(r)/ *vt* implorare

imploring /ɪmˈplɔːrɪŋ/ *adj* implorante

implosion /ɪmˈpləʊʒn/ *n* implosione *f*

imply /ɪmˈplaɪ/ *vt* (*pt/pp* **-ied**) implicare; **what are you ~ing?** che cosa vorresti insinuare?

impolite /ɪmpəˈlaɪt/ *adj* sgarbato

impolitely /ɪmpəˈlaɪtlɪ/ *adv* sgarbatamente

import¹ /ˈɪmpɔːt/ *n* Comm importazione *f*; (importance) importanza *f*; (meaning) rilevanza *f*

import² /ɪmˈpɔːt/ *vt* importare

importance /ɪmˈpɔːtəns/ *n* importanza *f*

important /ɪmˈpɔːtənt/ *adj* importante

importation /ɪmpɔːˈteɪʃn/ *n* Comm importazione *f*

import duty /ˈɪmpɔːt/ *n* dazio *m* d'importazione

importer /ɪmˈpɔːtə(r)/ n importatore, -trice mf

import-export /ˈɪmpɔːtˈekspɔːt/ n import-export m

importing country /ɪmˈpɔːtɪŋ/ n paese m di importazione

✧ **impose** /ɪmˈpəʊz/ ① vt imporre (on a) ② vi imporsi; ~ **on** abusare di

imposing /ɪmˈpəʊzɪŋ/ adj imponente

imposition /ɪmpəˈzɪʃn/ n imposizione f

impossibility /ɪmˈpɒsɪbɪlətɪ/ n impossibilità f

✧ **impossible** /ɪmˈpɒsəbl/ adj impossibile

impossibly /ɪmˈpɒsəblɪ/ adv impossibilmente

impostor /ɪmˈpɒstə(r)/ n impostore, -a mf

impotence /ˈɪmpətəns/ n impotenza f

impotent /ˈɪmpətənt/ adj impotente

impound /ɪmˈpaʊnd/ vt confiscare

impoverished /ɪmˈpɒvərɪʃt/ adj impoverito

impracticable /ɪmˈpræktɪkəbl/ adj impraticabile

impractical /ɪmˈpræktɪkl/ adj non pratico

imprecise /ɪmprɪˈsaɪs/ adj impreciso

impregnable /ɪmˈpregnəbl/ adj imprendibile

impregnate /ˈɪmpregneɪt/ vt impregnare (with di); Biol fecondare

impresario /ɪmprɪˈsɑːrɪəʊ/ n (pl **-os**) impresario m (di spettacoli)

impress /ɪmˈpres/ vt imprimere; fig colpire (positivamente); ~ **something [up]on somebody** fare capire qualcosa a qualcuno

impression /ɪmˈpreʃn/ n impressione f; (imitation) imitazione f

impressionable /ɪmˈpreʃənəbl/ adj ‹child, mind› influenzabile

impressionism /ɪmˈpreʃənɪzm/ n impressionismo m

impressionist /ɪmˈpreʃənɪst/ n imitatore, -trice mf; (artist) impressionista mf

impressionistic /ɪmpreʃəˈnɪstɪk/ adj impressionista; ‹account› approssimativo

✧ **impressive** /ɪmˈpresɪv/ adj imponente

imprint¹ /ˈɪmprɪnt/ n impressione f

imprint² /ɪmˈprɪnt/ vt imprimere; ~**ed on my mind** impresso nella mia memoria

imprison /ɪmˈprɪzən/ vt incarcerare

imprisonment /ɪmˈprɪzənmənt/ n reclusione f

improbable /ɪmˈprɒbəbl/ adj improbabile

impromptu /ɪmˈprɒmptjuː/ ① adj improvvisato
② adv in modo improvvisato

improper /ɪmˈprɒpə(r)/ adj ‹use› improprio; ‹behaviour› scorretto

---

improperly /ɪmˈprɒpəlɪ/ adv scorrettamente

impropriety /ɪmprəˈpraɪətɪ/ n scorrettezza f

✧ **improve** /ɪmˈpruːv/ vt/i migliorare
■ **improve [up]on** vt perfezionare

✧ **improvement** /ɪmˈpruːvmənt/ n miglioramento m

improvident /ɪmˈprɒvɪdənt/ adj (heedless of the future) imprevidente

improvisation /ɪmprəvaɪˈzeɪʃn/ n improvvisazione f

improvise /ˈɪmprəvaɪz/ vt/i improvvisare

imprudent /ɪmˈpruːdənt/ adj imprudente

impudence /ˈɪmpjʊdəns/ n sfrontatezza f

impudent /ˈɪmpjʊdənt/ adj sfrontato

impudently /ˈɪmpjʊdəntlɪ/ adv sfrontatamente

impulse /ˈɪmpʌls/ n impulso m; **on [an]** ~ impulsivamente

impulse buy n acquisto m d'impulso

impulse buying n acquisti mpl fatti d'impulso

impulsive /ɪmˈpʌlsɪv/ adj impulsivo

impulsively /ɪmˈpʌlsɪvlɪ/ adv impulsivamente

impunity /ɪmˈpjuːnətɪ/ n **with** ~ impunemente

impure /ɪmˈpjʊə(r)/ adj impuro

impurity /ɪmˈpjʊərətɪ/ n impurità f inv; **impurities** pl impurità fpl

impute /ɪmˈpjuːt/ vt imputare (to a)

✧ **in** /ɪn/ ① prep in; (with names of towns) a; **in the garden** in giardino; **in the street** in or per strada; **in bed/hospital** a letto/all'ospedale; **in the world** nel mondo; **in the rain** sotto la pioggia; **in the sun** al sole; **in this heat** con questo caldo; **in summer/winter** in estate/inverno; **in 1995** nel 1995; **in the evening** la sera; **he's arriving in two hours' time** arriva fra due ore; **deaf in one ear** sordo da un orecchio; **in the army** nell'esercito; **in English/Italian** in inglese/italiano; **in ink/pencil** a penna/matita; **in red** ‹dressed, circled› di rosso; **the man in the raincoat** l'uomo con l'impermeabile; **in a soft/loud voice** a voce bassa/alta; **one in ten people** una persona su dieci; **in doing this, he...** nel far questo, ...; **in itself** in sé; **in that** in quanto ② adv (at home) a casa; (indoors) dentro; **he's not in yet** non è ancora arrivato; **in there/here** li/qui dentro; **ten in all** dieci in tutto; **day in, day out** giorno dopo giorno; **have it in for somebody** fam avercela con qualcuno; **send him in** fallo entrare; **come in** entrare; **bring in the washing** portare dentro i panni ③ adj fam (in fashion) di moda ④ n **the ins and outs** i dettagli

in. abbr (**inch**) pollice m

inability /məˈbɪlətɪ/ n incapacità f

✧ indicates a very frequent word

inaccessible /ɪnæk'sesəbl/ *adj*
inaccessibile

inaccuracy /ɪn'ækjʊrəsɪ/ *n* inesattezza *f*

inaccurate /ɪn'ækjʊrət/ *adj* inesatto

inaccurately /ɪn'ækjʊrətlɪ/ *adv* in modo
inesatto

inaction /ɪn'ækʃn/ *n* (not being active)
inazione *f*; (failure to act) inerzia *f*

inactive /ɪn'æktɪv/ *adj* inattivo

inactivity /ɪnæk'tɪvətɪ/ *n* inattività *f*

inadequacy /ɪn'ædɪkwəsɪ/ *n*
inadeguatezza *f*

inadequate /ɪn'ædɪkwət/ *adj* inadeguato

inadequately /ɪn'ædɪkwətlɪ/ *adv*
inadeguatamente

inadmissible /ɪnæd'mɪsəbl/ *adj*
inammissibile

inadvertent /ɪnəd'vɜːtənt/ *adj*
involontario

inadvertently /ɪnəd'vɜːtəntlɪ/ *adv*
inavvertitamente

inadvisable /ɪnæd'vaɪzəbl/ *adj*
sconsigliabile

inalienable /ɪn'eɪlɪənəbl/ *adj* inalienabile

inane /ɪ'neɪn/ *adj* futile

inanely /ɪ'neɪnlɪ/ *adv* in modo vacuo

inanimate /ɪn'ænɪmət/ *adj* esanime

inanity /ɪ'nænətɪ/ *n* stupidità *f inv*

inapplicable /ɪnə'plɪkəbl/ *adj*
inapplicabile

inappropriate /ɪnə'prəʊprɪət/ *adj*
inadatto

inapt /ɪn'æpt/ *adj* (inappropriate)
inappropriato

inarticulate /ɪnɑːtɪkjʊlət/ *adj*
inarticolato

inasmuch /ɪnəz'mʌtʃ/ *conj* ~ **as** (insofar as)
in quanto; (seeing that) poiché

inattention /ɪnə'tenʃn/ *n* disattenzione *f*

inattentive /ɪnə'tentɪv/ *adj* disattento

inaudible /ɪn'ɔːdəbl/ *adj* impercettibile

inaudibly /ɪn'ɔːdəblɪ/ *adv* in modo
impercettibile

inaugural /ɪ'nɔːgjʊrəl/ *adj* inaugurale

inaugurate /ɪ'nɔːgjʊreɪt/ *vt* inaugurare

inauguration /ɪnɔːgjʊ'reɪʃn/ *n*
inaugurazione *f*

inauspicious /ɪnɔː'spɪʃəs/ *adj* infausto

in-between *adj* intermedio

inborn /'ɪnbɔːn/ *adj* innato

inbox /'ɪnbɒks/ *n* posta *f* in arrivo

inbred /ɪn'bred/ *adj* congenito

inbreeding /ɪn'briːdɪŋ/ *n* (in animals)
inbreeding *m*; (in humans) unioni *mpl* fra
consanguinei

inbuilt /ɪn'bɪlt/ *adj* ‹feeling› innato

Inc. *abbr* (**Incorporated**) Spa *f*

incalculable /ɪn'kælkjʊləbl/ *adj*
incalcolabile

incandescence /ɪnkæn'desəns/ *n* liter
incandescenza *f*

incandescent /ɪnkæn'desənt/ *adj* liter
incandescente

incapable /ɪn'keɪpəbl/ *adj* incapace

incapacitate /ɪnkə'pæsɪteɪt/ *vt* rendere
incapace

incapacity /ɪnkə'pæsɪtɪ/ *n* (also Jur)
incapacità *f*

incarcerate /ɪn'kɑːsəreɪt/ *vt* incarcerare

incarnate /ɪn'kɑːnət/ *adj* **the devil** ~ il
diavolo in carne e ossa

incarnation /ɪnkɑː'neɪʃn/ *n* incarnazione
f

incendiary /ɪn'sendɪərɪ/ ◱ **1** *adj*
incendiario
◱ **2** *n* ~ [bomb] bomba *f* incendiaria

incendiary device *n* ordigno *m*
incendiario

incense¹ /'ɪnsens/ *n* incenso *m*

incense² /ɪn'sens/ *vt* esasperare

incensed /ɪn'senst/ *adj* furibondo

incentive /ɪn'sentɪv/ *n* incentivo *m*

incentive scheme *n* piano *m* di
incentivi

inception /ɪn'sepʃn/ *n* inizio *m*

incessant /ɪn'sesənt/ *adj* incessante

incessantly /ɪn'sesəntlɪ/ *adv*
incessantemente

incest /'ɪnsest/ *n* incesto *m*

incestuous /ɪn'sestjʊəs/ *adj* incestuoso

⚲ **inch** /ɪntʃ/ ◱ **1** *n* pollice *m* (= 2.54 cm)
◱ **2** *vi* ~ **forward** avanzare gradatamente

incidence /'ɪnsɪdəns/ *n* incidenza *f*

⚲ **incident** /'ɪnsɪdənt/ *n* incidente *m*

incidental /ɪnsɪ'dentl/ *adj* incidentale;
~ **expenses** spese *fpl* accessorie

incidentally /ɪnsɪ'dent(ə)lɪ/ *adv*
incidentalmente; (by the way) a proposito

incident room *n* (for criminal investigation)
centrale *f* operativa

incinerate /ɪn'sɪnəreɪt/ *vt* incenerire

incinerator /ɪn'sɪnəreɪtə(r)/ *n*
inceneritore *m*

incipient /ɪn'sɪpɪənt/ *adj* incipiente

incision /ɪn'sɪʒn/ *n* incisione *f*

incisive /ɪn'saɪsɪv/ *adj* incisivo

incisor /ɪn'saɪzə(r)/ *n* incisivo *m*

incite /ɪn'saɪt/ *vt* incitare

incitement /ɪn'saɪtmənt/ *n* incitamento *m*

incivility /ɪnsɪ'vɪlətɪ/ *n* scortesia *f*

incl *abbr* **1** (**inclusive**) comprensivo
2 (**including**) incluso

inclement /ɪn'klemənt/ *adj* inclemente

inclination /ɪnklɪ'neɪʃn/ *n* inclinazione *f*

incline¹ /ɪn'klaɪn/ ◱ **1** *vt* inclinare; **be** ~**d**
to do something essere propenso a fare
qualcosa
◱ **2** *vi* inclinarsi

incline² /'ınklaın/ *n* pendio *m*

⚘ **include** /ın'klu:d/ *vt* includere

including /ın'klu:dıŋ/ *prep* incluso

inclusion /ın'klu:ʒn/ *n* inclusione *f*

inclusive /ın'klu:sıv/ ▢ *adj* incluso; ~ **of** comprendente; **be** ~ **of** comprendere ▢ *adv* incluso

incognito /ınkɒg'ni:təʊ/ *adv* incognito

incoherent /ınkə'hıərənt/ *adj* incoerente; (because drunk etc) incomprensibile

incoherently /ınkə'hıərəntlı/ *adv* incoerentemente; (because drunk etc) incomprensibilmente

⚘ **income** /'ınkəm/ *n* reddito *m*

income bracket *n* fascia *f* di reddito

income tax *n* imposta *f* sul reddito

income tax return *n* dichiarazione *f* dei redditi

incoming /'ınkʌmıŋ/ *adj* in arrivo; ~ **tide** marea *f* montante

incommunicado /ınkəmju:nı'ka:dəʊ/ *adj* (involuntarily) segregato; **he's** ~ (in meeting) non vuole essere disturbato

incomparable /ın'kɒmp(ə)rəbl/ *adj* incomparabile

incompatibility /ınkəmpætı'bılətı/ *n* incompatibilità *f*

incompatible /ınkəm'pætəbl/ *adj* incompatibile

incompetence /ın'kɒmpıtəns/ *n* incompetenza *f*

incompetent /ın'kɒmpıtənt/ *adj* incompetente

incomplete /ınkəm'pli:t/ *adj* incompleto

incomprehensible /ınkɒmprı'hensəbl/ *adj* incomprensibile

inconceivable /ınkən'si:vəbl/ *adj* inconcepibile

inconclusive /ınkən'klu:sıv/ *adj* inconcludente

incongruity /ınkɒŋ'gru:ətı/ *n* (of appearance) contrasto *m*; (of situation) assurdità *f inv*

incongruous /ın'kɒŋgrʊəs/ *adj* contrastante

inconsequential /ınkɒnsı'kwenʃl/ *adj* senza importanza

inconsiderate /ınkən'sıdərət/ *adj* trascurabile

inconsistency /ınkən'sıstənsı/ *n* incoerenza *f*

inconsistent /ınkən'sıstənt/ *adj* incoerente; **be** ~ **with** non essere coerente con

inconsistently /ınkən'sıstəntlı/ *adv* in modo incoerente

inconsolable /ınkən'səʊləbl/ *adj* inconsolabile

inconspicuous /ınkən'spıkjʊəs/ *adj* non appariscente

inconspicuously /ınkən'spıkjʊəslı/ *adv* modestamente

inconstancy /ın'kɒnstənsı/ *n* incostanza *f*

inconstant /ın'kɒnstənt/ *adj* ‹conditions› variabile; ‹lover› volubile

incontestable /ınkən'testəbl/ *adj* incontestabile

incontinence /ın'kɒntınəns/ *n* incontinenza *f*

incontinent /ın'kɒntınənt/ *adj* incontinente

inconvenience /ınkən'vi:nıəns/ *n* scomodità *f*; (drawback) inconveniente *m*; **put somebody to** ~ dare disturbo a qualcuno

inconvenient /ınkən'vi:nıənt/ *adj* scomodo; ‹time, place› inopportuno

inconveniently /ınkən'vi:nıəntlı/ *adv* in modo inopportuno

incorporate /ın'kɔ:pəreıt/ *vt* incorporare; (contain) comprendere

incorrect /ınkə'rekt/ *adj* incorretto

incorrectly /ınkə'rektlı/ *adv* scorrettamente

incorrigible /ın'kɒrıdʒəbl/ *adj* incorreggibile

incorruptible /ınkə'rʌptəbl/ *adj* incorruttibile

increase¹ /'ınkri:s/ *n* aumento *m*; **on the** ~ in aumento

⚘ **increase²** /ın'kri:s/ *vt/i* aumentare

increased *adj* ‹demand, risk› maggiore

increasing /ın'kri:sıŋ/ *adj* ‹impatience etc› crescente; ‹numbers› in aumento

⚘ **increasingly** /ın'kri:sıŋlı/ *adv* sempre più

incredible /ın'kredəbl/ *adj* incredibile

incredibly /ın'kredəblı/ *adv* incredibilmente

incredulity /ınkrə'dju:lətı/ *n* incredulità *f*

incredulous /ın'kredjʊləs/ *adj* incredulo

increment /'ınkrımənt/ *n* incremento *m*

incremental /ınkrı'mentəl/ *adj* Comput, Math incrementale; ‹effect, measures› progressivo

incriminate /ın'krımıneıt/ *vt* Jur incriminare

incriminating /ın'krımıneıtıŋ/ *adj* ‹evidence› incriminante

in-crowd *n* **be in with the** ~ frequentare gente alla moda

incubate /'ıŋkjʊbeıt/ *vt* incubare

incubation /ıŋkjʊ'beıʃn/ *n* incubazione *f*

incubation period *n* Med periodo *m* di incubazione

incubator /'ıŋkjʊbeıtə(r)/ *n* (for baby) incubatrice *f*

⚘ indicates a very frequent word

inculcate /'ɪnkʌlkeɪt/ vt inculcare

incumbent /ɪn'kʌmbənt/ adj be ∼ on somebody incombere a qualcuno

incur /ɪn'kɜ:(r)/ vt (pt/pp **incurred**) incorrere; contrarre ‹debts›

incurable /ɪn'kjʊərəbl/ adj incurabile

incurably /ɪn'kjʊərəblɪ/ adv incurabilmente

incursion /ɪn'kɜ:ʃn/ n incursione f

indebted /ɪn'detɪd/ adj obbligato (to verso)

indecency /ɪn'di:sənsɪ/ n oscenità f; (offence) atti mpl osceni; **gross** ∼ atti mpl osceni

indecent /ɪn'di:sənt/ adj indecente

indecent assault n atti mpl di libidine violenta

indecent exposure n esibizionismo m (dei genitali)

indecipherable /ɪndɪ'saɪfərəbl/ adj indecifrabile

indecision /ɪndɪ'sɪʒn/ n indecisione f

indecisive /ɪndɪ'saɪsɪv/ adj indeciso

indecisiveness /ɪndɪ'saɪsɪvnɪs/ n indecisione f

⚓ **indeed** /ɪn'di:d/ adv (in fact) difatti; **yes** ∼! sì, certamente!; ∼ **I am/do** veramente!; **very much** ∼ moltissimo; **thank you very much** ∼ grazie infinite; ∼? davvero?

indefatigable /ɪndɪ'fætɪgəbl/ adj instancabile

indefensible /ɪndɪ'fensəbl/ adj Mil indifendibile; (morally) ingiustificabile; (logically) insostenibile

indefinable /ɪndɪ'faɪnəbl/ adj indefinibile

indefinite /ɪn'defnɪt/ adj indefinito

indefinitely /ɪn'defnɪtlɪ/ adv indefinitamente; ‹postpone› a tempo indeterminato

indelible /ɪn'deləbl/ adj indelebile

indelibly /ɪn'deləblɪ/ adv in modo indelebile

indelicacy /ɪn'delɪkəsɪ/ n (tactlessness) mancanza f di tatto; (coarseness) rozzezza f

indelicate /ɪn'delɪkət/ adj (tactless) privo di tatto; (coarse) rozzo

indemnity /ɪn'demnətɪ/ n indennità f inv

indent¹ /'ɪndent/ n Typ rientranza f dal margine

indent² /ɪn'dent/ vt Typ fare rientrare dal margine

indentation /ɪnden'teɪʃn/ n (notch) intaccatura f

independence /ɪndɪ'pendəns/ n indipendenza f

Independence Day n Am = anniversario (m) dell'Indipendenza degli USA (4 luglio)

⚓ **independent** /ɪndɪ'pendənt/ adj indipendente

independently /ɪndɪ'pendəntlɪ/ adv indipendentemente

in-depth adj ‹analysis, study, knowledge› approfondito

indescribable /ɪndɪ'skraɪbəbl/ adj indescrivibile

indescribably /ɪndɪ'skraɪbəblɪ/ adv indescrivibilmente

indestructible /ɪndɪ'strʌktəbl/ adj indistruttibile

indeterminate /ɪndɪ'tɜ:mɪnət/ adj indeterminato

index /'ɪndeks/ n indice m

indexation /ɪndek'seɪʃn/ n indicizzazione f

index card n scheda f

index finger n dito m indice

index-linked adj ‹pension› legato al costo della vita

India /'ɪndɪə/ n India f

⚓ **Indian** /'ɪndɪən/ **1** adj indiano; (American) indiano [d'America]
2 n indiano, -a mf; (American) indiano [d'America], pellerossa mf inv

Indian elephant n elefante m indiano

Indian ink n inchiostro m di china

Indian Ocean n oceano m Indiano

Indian summer n estate f di San Martino

⚓ **indicate** /'ɪndɪkeɪt/ **1** vt indicare; (register) segnare
2 vi Auto mettere la freccia; ∼ **left** mettere la freccia a sinistra

indication /ɪndɪ'keɪʃn/ n indicazione f

indicative /ɪn'dɪkətɪv/ **1** adj be ∼ of essere indicativo di
2 n Gram indicativo m

indicator /'ɪndɪkeɪtə(r)/ n Auto freccia f

indict /ɪn'daɪt/ vt accusare

indictment /ɪn'daɪtmənt/ n Jur imputazione f

indie /'ɪndɪ/ **1** adj fam Cinema, Mus indipendente
2 n (band) gruppo (m) musicale legato a una casa discografica indipendente; (film) film (m) prodotto da una casa di produzione indipendente

indifference /ɪn'dɪf(ə)rəns/ n indifferenza f

indifferent /ɪn'dɪf(ə)rənt/ adj indifferente; (not good) mediocre

indifferently /ɪn'dɪf(ə)rəntlɪ/ adv in modo indifferente; (not well) in modo mediocre

indigenous /ɪn'dɪdʒɪnəs/ adj indigeno

indigestible /ɪndɪ'dʒestəbl/ adj indigesto

indigestion /ɪndɪ'dʒestʃn/ n indigestione f

indignant /ɪn'dɪgnənt/ adj indignato

indignantly /ɪn'dɪgnəntlɪ/ adv con indignazione

indignation /ɪndɪg'neɪʃn/ n indignazione f

indignity /ɪn'dɪɡnətɪ/ n umiliazione f
indigo /'ɪndɪɡəʊ/ n indaco m
indirect /ɪndaɪ'rekt/ adj indiretto
indirectly /ɪndaɪ'rektlɪ/ adv
indirettamente
indirect speech n discorso m indiretto
indiscernible /ɪndɪ'sɜ:nəbl/ adj
indistinguibile
indiscreet /ɪndɪ'skri:t/ adj indiscreto
indiscretion /ɪndɪ'skreʃn/ n
indiscrezione f
indiscriminate /ɪndɪ'skrɪmɪnət/ adj
indiscriminato
indiscriminately /ɪndɪ'skrɪmɪnətlɪ/ adv
senza distinzione
indispensable /ɪndɪ'spensəbl/ adj
indispensabile
indisposed /ɪndɪ'spəʊzd/ adj indisposto
indisputable /ɪndɪ'spju:təbl/ adj
indisputabile
indisputably /ɪndɪ'spju:təblɪ/ adv
indisputabilmente
indistinct /ɪndɪ'stɪŋkt/ adj indistinto
indistinctly /ɪndɪ'stɪŋktlɪ/ adv
indistintamente
indistinguishable /ɪndɪ'stɪŋɡwɪʃəbl/
adj indistinguibile
✔ **individual** /ɪndɪ'vɪdjʊəl/ ① adj
individuale
② n individuo m
individualist /ɪndɪ'vɪdjʊəlɪst/ n
individualista mf
individualistic /ɪndɪvɪdjʊə'lɪstɪk/ adj
individualistico
individuality /ɪndɪvɪdjʊ'ælətɪ/ n
individualità f
individually /ɪndɪ'vɪdjʊəlɪ/ adv
individualmente
indivisible /ɪndɪ'vɪzəbl/ adj indivisibile
Indochina /ɪndəʊ'tʃaɪnə/ n Indocina f
indoctrinate /ɪn'dɒktrɪneɪt/ vt
indottrinare
Indo-European /ɪndəʊjʊərə'pɪən/ adj
indoeuropeo
indolence /'ɪndələns/ n indolenza
indolent /'ɪndələnt/ adj indolente
indomitable /ɪn'dɒmɪtəbl/ adj indomito
Indonesia /ɪndə'ni:zjə/ n Indonesia f
Indonesian /ɪndə'ni:zjən/ adj & n (person)
indonesiano, -a mf; (language) indonesiano m
indoor /'ɪndɔ:(r)/ adj interno; ‹shoes› per
casa; ‹plant› da appartamento; ‹swimming
pool etc› coperto
indoors /ɪn'dɔ:z/ adv dentro; **go ~** andare
dentro
indubitable /ɪn'dju:bɪtəbl/ adj
indubitabile

✔ indicates a very frequent word

indubitably /ɪn'dju:bɪtəblɪ/ adv
indubitabilmente
induce /ɪn'dju:s/ vt indurre (**to** a); (produce)
causare
inducement /ɪn'dju:smənt/ n (incentive)
incentivo m
induction /ɪn'dʌkʃn/ n (inauguration)
introduzione f; (of labour) parto m indotto;
Electr induzione f
induction ceremony n cerimonia f
inaugurale
induction course n corso m
introduttivo
induction loop n sistema m di
amplificazione sonora
indulge /ɪn'dʌldʒ/ ① vt soddisfare; viziare
‹child›
② vi **~ in** concedersi
indulgence /ɪn'dʌldʒəns/ n lusso m;
(leniency) indulgenza f
indulgent /ɪn'dʌldʒənt/ adj indulgente
✔ **industrial** /ɪn'dʌstrɪəl/ adj industriale
industrial accident n infortunio m
sul lavoro
industrial action n sciopero m; **take
industrial action** scioperare
industrial dispute n vertenza f
sindacale
industrial espionage n spionaggio m
industriale
industrial estate n zona f industriale
industrialist /ɪn'dʌstrɪəlɪst/ n industriale
mf
industrialized /ɪn'dʌstrɪəlaɪzd/ adj
industrializzato
industrial relations npl relazioni fpl
industriali
industrial tribunal n tribunale (m)
competente per i conflitti di lavoro
industrial waste n rifiuti mpl
industriali
industrious /ɪn'dʌstrɪəs/ adj industrioso
industriously /ɪn'dʌstrɪəslɪ/ adv in modo
industrioso
✔ **industry** /'ɪndəstrɪ/ n industria f; (zeal)
operosità f
inebriated /ɪ'ni:brɪeɪtɪd/ adj ebbro
inedible /ɪn'edəbl/ adj immangiabile
ineffective /ɪnɪ'fektɪv/ adj inefficace
ineffectively /ɪnɪ'fektɪvlɪ/ adv
inutilmente, invano
ineffectual /ɪnɪ'fektʃʊəl/ adj inutile;
‹person› inconcludente
inefficiency /ɪnɪ'fɪʃənsɪ/ n inefficienza f
inefficient /ɪnɪ'fɪʃnt/ adj inefficiente
ineligible /ɪn'elɪdʒəbl/ adj inadatto
inept /ɪ'nept/ adj inetto
ineptitude /ɪ'neptɪtju:d/ n inettitudine f
inequality /ɪnɪ'kwɒlətɪ/ n ineguaglianza f

inert /ɪˈnɜːt/ *adj* inerte
inertia /ɪˈnɜːʃə/ *n* inerzia *f*
inescapable /ɪnɪˈskeɪpəbl/ *adj* inevitabile
inestimable /ɪnˈestɪməbl/ *adj* inestimabile
inevitable /ɪnˈevɪtəbl/ *adj* inevitabile
inevitably /ɪnˈevɪtəblɪ/ *adv* inevitabilmente
inexact /ɪnɪgˈzækt/ *adj* inesatto
inexcusable /ɪnɪkˈskjuːzəbl/ *adj* imperdonabile
inexhaustible /ɪnɪgˈzɔːstəbl/ *adj* inesauribile
inexorable /ɪnˈeksərəbl/ *adj* inesorabile
inexorably /ɪnˈegzərəblɪ/ *adv* inesorabilmente
inexpensive /ɪnɪkˈspensɪv/ *adj* poco costoso
inexpensively /ɪnɪkˈspensɪvlɪ/ *adv* a buon mercato
inexperience /ɪnɪkˈspɪərɪəns/ *n* inesperienza *f*
inexperienced /ɪnɪkˈspɪərɪənst/ *adj* inesperto
inexplicable /ɪnɪkˈsplɪkəbl/ *adj* inesplicabile
inexplicably /ɪnɪkˈsplɪkəblɪ/ *adv* inesplicabilmente, inspiegabilmente
inextricable /ɪnɪkˈstrɪkəbl/ *adj* inestricabile
inextricably /ɪnɪkˈstrɪkəblɪ/ *adv* inestricabilmente
infallibility /ɪnfælɪˈbɪlətɪ/ *n* infallibilità *f*
infallible /ɪnˈfæləbl/ *adj* infallibile
infamous /ˈɪnfəməs/ *adj* infame; ‹person› famigerato
infamy /ˈɪnfəmɪ/ *n* infamia *f*
infancy /ˈɪnfənsɪ/ *n* infanzia *f*, **in its ～** fig agli inizi
infant /ˈɪnfənt/ *n* bambino, -a *mf* piccolo
infanticide /ɪnˈfæntɪsaɪd/ *n* infanticidio *m*
infantile /ˈɪnfəntaɪl/ *adj* infantile
infantry /ˈɪnfəntrɪ/ *n* fanteria *f*
infant school *n* scuola (*f*) *elementare per bambini dai 5 ai 7 anni*
infatuated /ɪnˈfætʃʊeɪtɪd/ *adj* infatuato (with di)
infatuation /ɪnfætʃʊˈeɪʃn/ *n* infatuazione *f*
infect /ɪnˈfekt/ *vt* infettare; become ～ed ‹wound› infettarsi
ⱷ **infection** /ɪnˈfekʃn/ infezione *f*
infectious /ɪnˈfekʃəs/ *adj* infettivo
infer /ɪnˈfɜː(r)/ *vt* (*pt/pp* **inferred**) dedurre (from da); (imply) implicare
inference /ˈɪnfərəns/ *n* deduzione *f*
inferior /ɪnˈfɪərɪə(r)/ **1** *adj* inferiore; ‹goods› scadente; (in rank) subalterno

2 *n* inferiore *mf*; (in rank) subalterno, -a *mf*
inferiority /ɪnfɪərɪˈɒrətɪ/ *n* inferiorità *f*
inferiority complex *n* complesso *m* di inferiorità
infernal /ɪnˈfɜːnl/ *adj* infernale
inferno /ɪnˈfɜːnəʊ/ *n* inferno *m*
infertile /ɪnˈfɜːtaɪl/ *adj* sterile
infertility /ɪnfəˈtɪlətɪ/ *n* sterilità *f*
infest /ɪnˈfest/ *vt* be ～ed with essere infestato di
infestation /ɪnfeˈsteɪʃn/ *n* infestazione *f*
infidelity /ɪnfɪˈdelətɪ/ *n* infedeltà *f inv*
infighting /ˈɪnfaɪtɪŋ/ *n* fig lotta *f* per il potere
infiltrate /ˈɪnfɪltreɪt/ *vt* infiltrare; Pol infiltrarsi in
infiltration /ɪnfɪlˈtreɪʃn/ *n* infiltrazione *f*
infinite /ˈɪnfɪnɪt/ *adj* infinito
infinitely /ˈɪnfɪnɪtlɪ/ *adv* infinitamente
infinitesimal /ɪnfɪnɪˈtesɪml/ *adj* infinitesimo
infinitive /ɪnˈfɪnətɪv/ *n* Gram infinito *m*
infinity /ɪnˈfɪnətɪ/ *n* infinità *f*
infirm /ɪnˈfɜːm/ *adj* debole
infirmary /ɪnˈfɜːm(ə)rɪ/ *n* infermeria *f*
infirmity /ɪnˈfɜːmətɪ/ *n* debolezza *f*
in flagrante delicto /ɪnflægræntɪdɪˈlɪktəʊ/ *adv* in flagrante
inflame /ɪnˈfleɪm/ *vt* infiammare
inflamed /ɪnˈfleɪmd/ *adj* infiammato; become ～ infiammarsi
inflammable /ɪnˈflæməbl/ *adj* infiammabile
inflammation /ɪnfləˈmeɪʃn/ *n* infiammazione *f*
inflammatory /ɪnˈflæmətrɪ/ *adj* incendiario
inflatable /ɪnˈfleɪtəbl/ *adj* gonfiabile
inflate /ɪnˈfleɪt/ *vt* gonfiare
inflated /ɪnˈfleɪtɪd/ *adj* ‹price, fee, claim› eccessivo; ‹style› ampolloso; ‹tyre› gonfio; **an ～ ego** un'alta opinione di sé
inflation /ɪnˈfleɪʃn/ *n* inflazione *f*
inflationary /ɪnˈfleɪʃənərɪ/ *adj* inflazionario
inflect /ɪnˈflekt/ *vt* flettere ‹noun, adjective›; modulare ‹voice›
inflected /ɪnˈflektɪd/ *adj* ‹language› flessivo; ‹form› flesso
inflection /ɪnˈflekʃn/ *n* (of voice) modulazione *f*
inflexible /ɪnˈfleksəbl/ *adj* inflessibile
inflexion /ɪnˈflekʃn/ *n* inflessione *f*
inflict /ɪnˈflɪkt/ *vt* infliggere (on a)
in-flight *adj* a bordo
ⱷ **influence** /ˈɪnflʊəns/ **1** *n* influenza *f*; use one's ～ esercitare la propria influenza **2** *vt* influenzare
influential /ɪnflʊˈenʃl/ *adj* influente

influenza /ˌɪnfluˈenzə/ n influenza f

influx /ˈɪnflʌks/ n affluenza f

info /ˈɪnfəʊ/ n fam informazione f

✦ **inform** /ɪnˈfɔːm/ **1** vt informare; **keep somebody ~ed** tenere qualcuno al corrente **2** vi ~ **against** denunciare

informal /ɪnˈfɔːməl/ adj informale; ‹agreement› ufficioso

informality /ˌɪnfəˈmælɪtɪ/ n informalità f inv

informally /ɪnˈfɔːməlɪ/ adv in modo informale

informant /ɪnˈfɔːmənt/ n informatore, -trice mf

✦ **information** /ˌɪnfəˈmeɪʃn/ n informazioni fpl; **a piece of ~** un'informazione

information and communication technology n tecnologia f dell'informazione e della comunicazione

information desk n banco m informazioni

information highway n autostrada f telematica

information officer n addetto, -a mf stampa

information pack n pacchetto m informativo

information processing n elaborazione f dati

information superhighway n Comput autostrada f dell'informazione

information system n sistema m informativo

information technology n informatica f

informative /ɪnˈfɔːmətɪv/ adj informativo; ‹film, book› istruttivo

informer /ɪnˈfɔːmə(r)/ n informatore, -trice mf; Pol delatore, -trice mf

infra-red /ɪnfrəˈred/ adj infrarosso

infrastructure /ˈɪnfrəstrʌktʃə(r)/ n infrastruttura f

infrequent /ɪnˈfriːkwənt/ adj infrequente

infrequently /ɪnˈfriːkwəntlɪ/ adv raramente

infringe /ɪnˈfrɪndʒ/ vt ~ **on** usurpare

infringement /ɪnˈfrɪndʒmənt/ n violazione f

infuriate /ɪnˈfjʊərɪeɪt/ vt infuriare

infuriating /ɪnˈfjʊərɪeɪtɪŋ/ adj esasperante

infuse /ɪnˈfjuːz/ vi ‹tea› restare in infusione

infusion /ɪnˈfjuːʒn/ n (drink) infusione f; (of capital, new blood) afflusso m

ingenious /ɪnˈdʒiːnɪəs/ adj ingegnoso

ingenuity /ɪndʒɪˈnjuːətɪ/ n ingegnosità f

ingenuous /ɪnˈdʒenjʊəs/ adj ingenuo

ingest /ɪnˈdʒest/ vt ingerire ‹food›; assimilare ‹fact›

ingot /ˈɪŋgət/ n lingotto m

ingrained /ɪnˈgreɪnd/ adj (in person) radicato; ‹dirt› incrostato

ingratiate /ɪnˈgreɪʃɪeɪt/ vt ~ **oneself with somebody** ingraziarsi qualcuno

ingratitude /ɪnˈgrætɪtjuːd/ n ingratitudine f

ingredient /ɪnˈgriːdɪənt/ n ingrediente m

ingrowing /ˈɪngrəʊɪŋ/ adj ‹nail› incarnito

inhabit /ɪnˈhæbɪt/ vt abitare

inhabitable /ɪnˈhæbɪtəbl/ adj abitabile

inhabitant /ɪnˈhæbɪtənt/ n abitante mf

inhale /ɪnˈheɪl/ **1** vt aspirare; Med inalare **2** vi inspirare; (when smoking) aspirare

inhaler /ɪnˈheɪlə(r)/ n (device) inalatore m

inherent /ɪnˈhɪərənt/ adj inerente

inherit /ɪnˈherɪt/ vt ereditare

inheritance /ɪnˈherɪtəns/ n eredità f inv

inhibit /ɪnˈhɪbɪt/ vt inibire

inhibited /ɪnˈhɪbɪtɪd/ adj inibito

inhibition /ɪnhɪˈbɪʃn/ n inibizione f

inhospitable /ɪnhɒˈspɪtəbl/ adj inospitale

in-house adj ‹training› interno all'azienda; ‹magazine› aziendale

inhuman /ɪnˈhjuːmən/ adj disumano

inhumanity /ˌɪnhjuːˈmænətɪ/ n disumanità f

inimitable /ɪˈnɪmɪtəbl/ adj inimitabile

iniquitous /ɪˈnɪkwɪtəs/ adj iniquo

✦ **initial** /ɪˈnɪʃl/ **1** adj iniziale **2** n iniziale f **3** vt (pt/pp **initialled**) siglare

✦ **initially** /ɪˈnɪʃəlɪ/ adv all'inizio

initiate /ɪˈnɪʃɪeɪt/ vt iniziare

initiation /ɪnɪʃɪˈeɪʃn/ n iniziazione f

✦ **initiative** /ɪˈnɪʃətɪv/ n iniziativa f; **take the ~** prendere l'iniziativa

inject /ɪnˈdʒekt/ vt iniettare

injection /ɪnˈdʒekʃn/ n iniezione f

in-joke n **it's an ~** è una battuta tra di noi/ loro

injunction /ɪnˈdʒʌŋkʃn/ n ingiunzione f

✦ **injure** /ˈɪndʒə(r)/ vt ferire; (wrong) nuocere

injured /ˈɪndʒəd/ **1** adj ferito; Jur **the ~ party** la parte lesa **2** npl **the ~** i feriti

✦ **injury** /ˈɪndʒərɪ/ n ferita f; (wrong) torto m

injury time n Sport recupero m

injustice /ɪnˈdʒʌstɪs/ n ingiustizia f; **do somebody an ~** giudicare qualcuno in modo sbagliato

ink /ɪŋk/ n inchiostro m

ink-jet printer n stampante f a getto d'inchiostro

inkling /ˈɪŋklɪŋ/ n sentore m

inky /ˈɪŋkɪ/ adj macchiato d'inchiostro

inlaid /ɪnˈleɪd/ adj intarsiato

✦ indicates a very frequent word

inland /'ɪnlənd/ **1** *adj* interno
2 *adv* all'interno
Inland Revenue *n* fisco *m*
in-laws /'ɪnlɔːz/ *npl* fam parenti *mpl* acquisiti
inlay /'ɪnleɪ/ *n* intarsio *m*
inlet /'ɪnlet/ *n* insenatura *f*; Techn entrata *f*
inmate /'ɪnmeɪt/ *n* (of hospital) degente *mf*; (of prison) detenuto, -a *mf*
inn /ɪn/ *n* locanda *f*
innards /'ɪnədz/ *npl* fam frattaglie *fpl*
innate /ɪ'neɪt/ *adj* innato
inner /'ɪnə(r)/ *adj* interno
inner city **1** *n* quartieri (*mpl*) *nel centro di una città caratterizzati da problemi sociali*
2 *attrib* ‹problems› dell'area urbana con problemi sociali
inner ear *n* orecchio *m* interno
innermost /'ɪnəməʊst/ *adj* il più profondo
inner tube *n* camera *f* d'aria
innings /'ɪnɪŋz/ *nsg* (in cricket) turno *m* di battuta; **have had a good ~** Br fig (when leaving job etc) aver avuto una carriera lunga e gratificante; (when dead) aver avuto una vita lunga e piena di soddisfazioni
innkeeper /'ɪnkiːpə(r)/ *n* locandiere, -a *mf*
innocence /'ɪnəsns/ *n* innocenza *f*
innocent /'ɪnəsnt/ *adj* innocente
innocently /'ɪnəsntlɪ/ *adv* innocentemente
innocuous /ɪ'nɒkjʊəs/ *adj* innocuo
innovate /'ɪnəveɪt/ *vi* innovare
innovation /ɪnə'veɪʃn/ *n* innovazione *f*
innovative /'ɪnəvətɪv/ *adj* innovativo
innovator /'ɪnəveɪtə(r)/ *n* innovatore, -trice *mf*
innuendo /ɪnjʊ'endəʊ/ *n* (*pl* -es) insinuazione *f*
innumerable /ɪ'njuːmərəbl/ *adj* innumerevole
inoculate /ɪ'nɒkjʊleɪt/ *vt* vaccinare
inoculation /ɪnɒkjʊ'leɪʃn/ *n* vaccinazione *f*
inoffensive /ɪnə'fensɪv/ *adj* inoffensivo
inoperable /ɪn'ɒpərəbl/ *adj* inoperabile
inopportune /ɪn'ɒpətjuːn/ *adj* inopportuno
inordinate /ɪ'nɔːdmət/ *adj* smodato
inordinately /ɪ'nɔːdmətlɪ/ *adv* smodatamente
inorganic /ɪnɔː'gænɪk/ *adj* inorganico
in-patient *n* degente *mf*
input /'ɪnpʊt/ *n* input *m inv*, ingresso *m*
inquest /'ɪnkwest/ *n* inchiesta *f*
inquire /ɪn'kwaɪə(r)/ **1** *vi* informarsi (about su); **~ into** far indagini su
2 *vt* domandare
inquiring /ɪn'kwaɪərɪŋ/ *adj* ‹mind› curioso; ‹look, voice› interrogativo

⚷ **inquiry** /ɪn'kwaɪərɪ/ *n* domanda *f*; (investigation) inchiesta *f*
inquisitive /ɪn'kwɪzətɪv/ *adj* curioso
inquisitively /ɪn'kwɪzɪtɪvlɪ/ *adv* con molta curiosità
inroad /'ɪnrəʊd/ *n* **make ~s into** intaccare ‹savings›; cominciare a risolvere ‹problem›
INS *n abbr* Am (**Immigration and Naturalization Service**) *ufficio* (*m*) *immigrazione e naturalizzazione*
insalubrious /ɪnsə'luːbrɪəs/ *adj* (dirty) insalubre; (sleazy) sordido
insane /ɪn'seɪn/ *adj* pazzo; fig insensato
insanitary /ɪn'sænɪt(ə)rɪ/ *adj* malsano
insanity /ɪn'sænətɪ/ *n* pazzia *f*
insatiable /ɪn'seɪʃəbl/ *adj* insaziabile
inscribe /ɪn'skraɪb/ *vt* iscrivere
inscription /ɪn'skrɪpʃn/ *n* iscrizione *f*
inscrutable /ɪn'skruːtəbl/ *adj* impenetrabile
insect /'ɪnsekt/ *n* insetto *m*
insecticide /ɪn'sektɪsaɪd/ *n* insetticida *m*
insect repellent *n* insettifugo *m*
insecure /ɪnsɪ'kjʊə(r)/ *adj* malsicuro; fig ‹person› insicuro
insecurity /ɪnsɪ'kjʊərətɪ/ *n* mancanza *f* di sicurezza
insemination /ɪnsemɪ'neɪʃn/ *n* inseminazione *f*
insensitive /ɪn'sensɪtɪv/ *adj* insensibile
inseparable /ɪn'sep(ə)rəbl/ *adj* inseparabile
insert¹ /'ɪnsɜːt/ *n* inserto *m*
insert² /ɪn'sɜːt/ *vt* inserire
insertion /ɪn'sɜːʃn/ *n* inserzione *f*
inset /'ɪnset/ **1** *n* (map, photo) dettaglio *m*
2 *adj* **~ with** ‹necklace› incastonato di; ‹table› intarsiato di
inshore /'ɪnʃɔː(r)/ **1** *adj* ‹current› diretta a riva; ‹fishing, waters, current› costiero; ‹wind› dal mare
2 *adv* ‹fish› sotto costa
⚷ **inside** /ɪn'saɪd/ **1** *n* interno *m*; **~s** *pl* fam pancia *f*
2 *adv* dentro; **~ out** a rovescio; (thoroughly) a fondo
3 *prep* dentro; (of time) entro
inside lane *n* Auto corsia *f* interna
inside leg *n* interno *m* della gamba
insider /ɪn'saɪdə(r)/ *n* persona *f* all'interno
insider dealer, insider trader *n* Fin persona (*f*) *che pratica l'insider trading*
insider dealing, insider trading /'diːlɪŋ/, /'treɪdɪŋ/ *n* Fin insider trading *m*
insidious /ɪn'sɪdɪəs/ *adj* insidioso
insidiously /ɪn'sɪdɪəslɪ/ *adv* insidiosamente
insight /'ɪnsaɪt/ *n* intuito *m* (into per); **an ~ into** un quadro di

insignia /ɪnˈsɪɡnɪə/ *npl* insegne *fpl*

insignificant /ɪnsɪɡˈnɪfɪkənt/ *adj* insignificante

insincere /ɪnsɪnˈsɪə(r)/ *adj* poco sincero

insincerity /ɪnsɪnˈserətɪ/ *n* mancanza *f* di sincerità

insinuate /ɪnˈsɪnjʊeɪt/ *vt* insinuare

insinuation /ɪnsɪnjʊˈeɪʃn/ *n* insinuazione *f*

insipid /ɪnˈsɪpɪd/ *adj* insipido

✎ **insist** /ɪnˈsɪst/ ❶ *vi* insistere (**on** per) ❷ *vt* ∼ **that** insistere che

insistence /ɪnˈsɪstəns/ *n* insistenza *f*

insistent /ɪnˈsɪstənt/ *adj* insistente

insistently /ɪnˈsɪstəntlɪ/ *adv* insistentemente

insofar /ɪnsəˈfɑː(r)/ *conj* ∼ **as** (to the extent that) nella misura in cui; (seeing that) in quanto; ∼ **as I know** per quanto ne sappia

insole /ˈɪnsəʊl/ *n* soletta *f*

insolence /ˈɪnsələns/ *n* insolenza *f*

insolent /ˈɪnsələnt/ *adj* insolente

insolently /ˈɪnsələntlɪ/ *adv* con insolenza

insoluble /ɪnˈsɒljʊbl/ *adj* insolubile

insolvency /ɪnˈsɒlvənsɪ/ *n* insolvenza *f*

insolvent /ɪnˈsɒlvənt/ *adj* insolvente

insomnia /ɪnˈsɒmnɪə/ *n* insonnia *f*

insomniac /ɪnˈsɒmnɪæk/ *n persona* (*f*) *che soffre di insonnia*

insomuch /ɪnsəˈmʌtʃ/ *conj* ∼ **as** (to the extent that) nella misura in cui; (seeing that) in quanto

inspect /ɪnˈspekt/ *vt* ispezionare; controllare ‹ticket›

inspection /ɪnˈspekʃn/ *n* ispezione *f*; (of ticket) controllo *m*

inspector /ɪnˈspektə(r)/ *n* ispettore, -trice *mf*; (of tickets) controllore *m*

inspiration /ɪnspəˈreɪʃn/ *n* ispirazione *f*

✎ **inspire** /ɪnˈspaɪə(r)/ *vt* ispirare

inspired /ɪnˈspaɪəd/ *adj* ‹person, performance› ispirato; ‹idea› luminosa

inspiring /ɪnˈspaɪərɪŋ/ *adj* ‹person, speech› entusiasmante

instability /ɪnstəˈbɪlətɪ/ *n* instabilità *f*

✎ **install** /ɪnˈstɔːl/ *vt* installare; insediare ‹person›

installation /ɪnstəˈleɪʃn/ *n* installazione *f*

instalment /ɪnˈstɔːlmənt/ *n* Comm rata *f*; (of serial) puntata *f*; (of publication) fascicolo *m*

✎ **instance** /ˈɪnstəns/ *n* (case) caso *m*; (example) esempio *m*; **in the first** ∼ in primo luogo; **for** ∼ per esempio

instant /ˈɪnstənt/ ❶ *adj* immediato; Culin espresso ❷ *n* istante *m*

instantaneous /ɪnstənˈteɪnɪəs/ *adj* istantaneo

instant camera *n* polaroid® *f inv*

instant coffee *n* caffè *m inv* solubile

instantly /ˈɪnstəntlɪ/ *adv* immediatamente

instant messaging *n* instant messaging *m*, messaggistica *f* instantanea

instant replay *n* Sport replay *m inv*

✎ **instead** /ɪnˈsted/ *adv* invece; ∼ **of doing** anziché fare; ∼ **of me** al mio posto; ∼ **of going** invece di andare

instep /ˈɪnstep/ *n* collo *m* del piede

instigate /ˈɪnstɪɡeɪt/ *vt* istigare

instigation /ɪnstɪˈɡeɪʃn/ *n* istigazione *f*; **at his** ∼ dietro suo suggerimento

instigator /ˈɪnstɪɡeɪtə(r)/ *n* istigatore, -trice *mf*

instil /ɪnˈstɪl/ *vt* (*pt/pp* **instilled**) inculcare (**into** in)

instinct /ˈɪnstɪŋkt/ *n* istinto *m*

instinctive /ɪnˈstɪŋktɪv/ *adj* istintivo

instinctively /ɪnˈstɪŋktɪvlɪ/ *adv* istintivamente

✎ **institute** /ˈɪnstɪtjuːt/ ❶ *n* istituto *m* ❷ *vt* istituire ‹scheme›; iniziare ‹search›; intentare ‹legal action›

✎ **institution** /ɪnstɪˈtjuːʃn/ *n* istituzione *f*; (home for elderly) istituto *m* per anziani; (for mentally ill) istituto *m* per malati di mente

institutionalize /ɪnstɪˈtjuːʃənəlaɪz/ *vt* istituzionalizzare

institutionalized /ɪnstɪˈtjuːʃənəlaɪzd/ *adj* ‹racism, violence› istituzionalizzato; **become** ∼ (officially established) essere istituzionalizzato; **be** ∼**d** ‹person› non essere autonomo a causa di un lungo soggiorno in ospedale psichiatrico

instruct /ɪnˈstrʌkt/ *vt* istruire; (order) ordinare

instruction /ɪnˈstrʌkʃn/ *n* istruzione *f*; ∼**s** *pl* (orders) ordini *mpl*

instruction book *n* libretto *m* di istruzioni

instructive /ɪnˈstrʌktɪv/ *adj* istruttivo

instructor /ɪnˈstrʌktə(r)/ *n* istruttore, -trice *mf*

✎ **instrument** /ˈɪnstrʊmənt/ *n* strumento *m*

instrumental /ɪnstrʊˈment(ə)l/ *adj* strumentale; **be** ∼ **in** contribuire a

instrumentalist /ɪnstrʊˈmentəlɪst/ *n* strumentista *mf*

instrument panel *n* quadro *m* degli strumenti

insubordinate /ɪnsəˈbɔːdɪnət/ *adj* insubordinato

insubordination /ɪnsəbɔːdɪˈneɪʃn/ *n* insubordinazione *f*

insubstantial /ɪnsəbˈstænʃəl/ *adj* (unreal) irreale; ‹evidence› inconsistente; ‹flimsy, building› poco solido; ‹meal› poco sostanzioso

---

✎ indicates a very frequent word

insufferable /ɪnˈsʌf(ə)rəbl/ *adj*
insopportabile

insufficient /ɪnsəˈfɪʃənt/ *adj* insufficiente

insufficiently /ɪnsəˈfɪʃəntlɪ/ *adv*
insufficientemente

insular /ˈɪnsjʊlə(r)/ *adj* fig gretto

insulate /ˈɪnsjʊleɪt/ *vt* isolare

insulating tape /ˈɪnsjʊleɪtɪŋ/ *n* nastro
m isolante

insulation /ɪnsjʊˈleɪʃn/ *n* isolamento *m*

insulator /ˈɪnsjʊleɪtə(r)/ *n* isolante *m*

insulin /ˈɪnsjʊlɪn/ *n* insulina *f*

insult¹ /ˈɪnsʌlt/ *n* insulto *m*

insult² /ɪnˈsʌlt/ *vt* insultare

insuperable /ɪnˈsuːpərəbl/ *adj*
insuperabile

insurable value /ɪnˈʃʊərəbl/ *n* valore *m*
assicurabile

⚘ **insurance** /ɪnˈʃʊərəns/ *n* assicurazione *f*

insurance broker *n* broker *mf inv*
d'assicurazioni

Insurance claim *n* richiesta *f* di
indennizzo (*ad assicurazione*)

insurance policy *n* polizza *f*
d'assicurazione

insurance premium *n* premio *m*
assicurativo

insure /ɪnˈʃʊə(r)/ *vt* assicurare

insurgent /ɪnˈsɜːdʒənt/ *n* rivoltoso, -a *mf*

insurmountable /ɪnsəˈmaʊntəbl/ *adj*
insormontabile

insurrection /ɪnsəˈrekʃn/ *n* insurrezione
f

intact /ɪnˈtækt/ *adj* intatto

intake /ˈɪnteɪk/ *n* immissione *f*; (*of food*)
consumo *m*

intangible /ɪnˈtændʒəbl/ *adj* intangibile

integral /ˈɪntɪɡrəl/ *adj* integrale

integrate /ˈɪntɪɡreɪt/ **1** *vt* integrare
2 *vi* integrarsi

integration /ɪntɪˈɡreɪʃn/ *n* integrazione *f*

integrity /ɪnˈteɡrətɪ/ *n* integrità *f*

intellect /ˈɪntəlekt/ *n* intelletto *m*

intellectual /ɪntəˈlektjʊəl/ *adj & n*
intellettuale *mf*

⚘ **intelligence** /ɪnˈtelɪdʒəns/ *n* intelligenza
f; Mil informazioni *fpl*

intelligent /ɪnˈtelɪdʒənt/ *adj* intelligente

intelligently /ɪnˈtelɪdʒəntlɪ/ *adv*
intelligentemente

intelligentsia /ɪntelɪˈdʒentsɪə/ *n*
intellighenzia *f*

intelligible /ɪnˈtelɪdʒəbl/ *adj* intelligibile

intemperate /ɪnˈtemp(ə)rət/ *adj*
(*language, person*) intemperante; (*weather*)
rigido; (*attack*) violento

⚘ **intend** /ɪnˈtend/ *vt* destinare; (have in
mind) aver intenzione di; **be ~ed for** essere
destinato a

intended /ɪnˈtendɪd/ **1** *adj* (*visit,
purchase*) programmato; (*result*) voluto,
desiderato
2 *n* **her ~** hum il suo fidanzato; **his ~** hum
la sua fidanzata

intense /ɪnˈtens/ *adj* intenso; (*person*) dai
sentimenti intensi

intensely /ɪnˈtenslɪ/ *adv* intensamente;
(very) estremamente

intensification /ɪntensɪfɪˈkeɪʃn/ *n*
intensificazione *f*

intensify /ɪnˈtensɪfaɪ/ *v* (*pt/pp* **-ied**) **1** *vt*
intensificare
2 *vi* intensificarsi

intensity /ɪnˈtensətɪ/ *n* intensità *f*

intensive /ɪnˈtensɪv/ *adj* intensivo; **~ care**
terapia *f* intensiva

intensive care [unit] *n* [reparto *m*]
rianimazione *f*

intensively /ɪnˈtensɪvlɪ/ *adv*
intensivamente

intent /ɪnˈtent/ **1** *adj* intento; **~ on**
(absorbed in) preso da; **be ~ on doing
something** essere intento a fare qualcosa
2 *n* intenzione *f*; **to all ~s and purposes** a
tutti gli effetti

⚘ **intention** /ɪnˈtenʃn/ *n* intenzione *f*

intentional /ɪnˈtenʃənəl/ *adj* intenzionale

intentionally /ɪnˈtenʃənəlɪ/ *adv*
intenzionalmente

intently /ɪnˈtentlɪ/ *adv* attentamente

inter /ɪnˈtɜː(r)/ *vt* (*pt/pp* **interred**) fml
interrare

interact /ɪntərˈækt/ *vi* (*two factors, people*)
interagire; Comput dialogare

interaction /ɪntərˈækʃn/ *n* cooperazione *f*

interactive /ɪntərˈæktɪv/ *adj* interattivo

interactive television *n* televisione *f*
interattiva

interactive video *n* video *m* interattivo

interactive whiteboard
/ˌɪntəræktɪvˈwaɪtbɔːd/ *n* lavagna *f* interattiva

interbreed /ɪntəˈbriːd/ **1** *vt* ibridare
2 *vi* incrociarsi

interbreeding /ɪntəˈbriːdɪŋ/ *n*
ibridazione *f*

intercede /ɪntəˈsiːd/ *vi* intercedere (**on
behalf of** a favore di)

intercept /ɪntəˈsept/ *vt* intercettare

interchange /ˈɪntətʃeɪndʒ/ *n* scambio *m*;
Auto raccordo *m* [autostradale]

interchangeable /ɪntəˈtʃeɪndʒəbl/ *adj*
interscambiabile

intercity /ɪntəˈsɪtɪ/ **1** *n* Br (train) intercity
m inv
2 *adj* intercity

intercom /ˈɪntəkɒm/ *n* citofono *m*

interconnecting /ɪntəkəˈnektɪŋ/ *adj*
(*rooms*) comunicante

intercontinental /ˌɪntəkɒntɪˈnentəl/ *adj*
intercontinentale

intercourse /ˈɪntəkɔːs/ *n* (sexual) rapporti
mpl [sessuali]

interdepartmental /ˌɪntədiːpɑːtˈment(ə)l/
adj Univ, Comm interdipartimentale; Pol
interministeriale

interdependent /ˌɪntədɪˈpendənt/ *adj*
interdipendente

interdisciplinary /ˌɪntədɪsɪˈplɪnərɪ/ *adj*
interdisciplinare

✓ **interest** /ˈɪntrəst/ **1** *n* interesse *m*; **have
an ∼ in** Comm essere cointeressato in; **be of
∼** essere interessante
  2 *vt* interessare
  3 *adj* interessato

interest-bearing *adj* fruttifero

interested /ˈɪntrəstɪd/ *adj* interessato

interest-free *adj* senza interessi

interest-free loan *n* prestito *m* senza
interessi

✓ **interesting** /ˈɪnt(ə)rəstɪŋ/ *adj*
interessante

interest rate *n* tasso *m* di interesse

interface /ˈɪntəfeɪs/ **1** *n* Comput, fig
interfaccia *f*
  2 *vi* interfacciarsi
  3 *vt* interfacciare

interfere /ɪntəˈfɪə(r)/ *vi* interferire; **∼ with**
interferire con

interference /ɪntəˈfɪərəns/ *n* interferenza
f

interfering /ˌɪntəˈfɪərɪŋ/ *adj* ‹person›
impiccione

interim /ˈɪntərɪm/ **1** *adj* temporaneo;
∼ payment acconto *m*
  2 *n* **in the ∼** nel frattempo

interior /ɪnˈtɪərɪə(r)/ **1** *adj* interiore
  2 *n* interno *m*

interior decorator *n* arredatore, -trice
mf

interior designer *n* (of colours, fabrics
etc) arredatore, -trice *mf*; (of walls, space)
architetto *m* d'interni

interject /ɪntəˈdʒekt/ *vt* intervenire

interjection /ɪntəˈdʒekʃn/ *n* Gram
interiezione *f*; (remark) intervento *m*

interlink /ɪntəˈlɪŋk/ *vt* connettere; **be ∼ed
with** essere connesso con

interlock /ɪntəˈlɒk/ *vi* ‹parts› incastrarsi

interlocking /ˈɪntəlɒkɪŋ/ *adj* a incastro

interloper /ˈɪntələʊpə(r)/ *n* intruso, -a *mf*

interlude /ˈɪntəluːd/ *n* intervallo *m*

intermarry /ɪntəˈmærɪ/ *vi* sposarsi
tra parenti; ‹different groups› contrarre
matrimoni misti

intermediary /ɪntəˈmiːdɪərɪ/ *n*
intermediario, -a *mf*

✓ indicates a very frequent word

intermediate /ɪntəˈmiːdɪət/ *adj*
intermedio

interminable /ɪnˈtɜːmɪnəbl/ *adj*
interminabile

intermission /ɪntəˈmɪʃn/ *n* intervallo *m*

intermittent /ɪntəˈmɪtənt/ *adj*
intermittente

intermittently /ɪntəˈmɪtəntlɪ/ *adv* a
intermittenza

intern /ɪnˈtɜːn/ *vt* internare

✓ **internal** /ɪnˈtɜːnl/ *adj* interno

internal combustion engine *n*
motore *m* a scoppio

internally /ɪnˈtɜːnəlɪ/ *adv* internamente;
‹deal with› all'interno

✓ **international** /ɪntəˈnæʃ(ə)nəl/ **1** *adj*
internazionale
  2 *n* (game) incontro *m* internazionale;
(player) competitore, -trice *mf* in gare
internazionali

internationally /ɪntəˈnæʃ(ə)nəlɪ/ *adv*
internazionalmente; **it applies ∼** ha validità
internazionale

international money order *n* vaglia
m inv postale internazionale

International Phonetic Alphabet
n Alfabeto *m* Fonetico Internazionale

international reply coupon *n*
tagliando *m* di risposta internazionale

internee /ˌɪntɜːˈniː/ *n* internato, -a *mf*

✓ **internet** /ˈɪntənet/ *n* Internet *m*

Internet access *n* Comput accesso *m*
Internet

Internet access provider *n* Comput
fornitore *m* di accesso ai servizi Internet

Internet café *n* caffè *m* Internet

Internet kiosk *n* Internet point *m inv*

Internet protocol *n* Comput protocollo
m Internet

Internet service provider *n* Comput
fornitore *m* di servizi Internet

Internet user *n* utente *mf* di Internet

internist /ɪnˈtɜːnɪst/ *n* Am internista *mf*

internment /ɪnˈtɜːnmənt/ *n* internamento
m

interplay /ˈɪntəpleɪ/ *n* azione *f* reciproca

interpolate /ɪnˈtɜːpəleɪt/ *vt* interpolare

interpose /ɪntəˈpəʊz/ *vt* (insert) frapporre;
interrompere con ‹comment, remark›

interpret /ɪnˈtɜːprɪt/ **1** *vt* interpretare
  2 *vi* fare l'interprete

interpretation /ɪntɜːprɪˈteɪʃn/ *n*
interpretazione *f*

interpreter /ɪnˈtɜːprɪtə(r)/ *n* interprete *mf*

interpreting /ɪnˈtɜːprɪtɪŋ/ *n*
interpretariato *m*

interrelated /ɪntərɪˈleɪtɪd/ *adj* ‹facts› in
correlazione

interrogate /ɪnˈterəgeɪt/ *vt* interrogare

interrogation /ɪnterəˈɡeɪʃn/ *n*
interrogazione *f*; (by police) interrogatorio *m*

interrogative /ɪntəˈrɒɡətɪv/ *adj & n*
~ [pronoun] interrogativo *m*

interrupt /ɪntəˈrʌpt/ *vt/i* interrompere

interruption /ɪntəˈrʌpʃn/ *n* interruzione *f*

intersect /ɪntəˈsekt/ 1 *vi* intersecarsi
2 *vt* intersecare

intersection /ɪntəˈsekʃn/ *n* intersezione
f; (of street) incrocio *m*

interspersed /ɪntəˈspɜːst/ *adj* ~ with
inframmezzato di

interstate /ˈɪntəsteɪt/ Am 1 *n*
superstrada *f* fra stati
2 *adj* ‹commerce, links› fra stati

intertwine /ɪntəˈtwaɪn/ *vi* attorcigliarsi

interval /ˈɪntəvl/ *n* intervallo *m*; bright ~s
pl schiarite *fpl*

intervene /ɪntəˈviːn/ *vi* intervenire

⚜ **intervention** /ɪntəˈvenʃn/ *n* intervento *m*

⚜ **interview** /ˈɪntəvjuː/ 1 *n* Journ intervista
f; (for job) colloquio *m* [di lavoro]
2 *vt* intervistare

interviewee /ɪntəvjuːˈiː/ *n* (on TV, radio, in
survey) intervistato, -a *mf*; (for job) persona *f*
sottoposta a un colloquio di lavoro

interviewer /ˈɪntəvjuːə(r)/ *n*
intervistatore, -trice *mf*

interwar /ˌɪntəˈwɔː(r)/ *adj* the ~ years gli
anni tra le due guerre

interweave /ɪntəˈwiːv/ *vt* intrecciare
‹themes, threads›; mischiare ‹rhythms›

intestinal /ɪnteˈstaɪnəl/ *adj* intestinale

intestine /ɪnˈtestɪn/ *n* intestino *m*

intimacy /ˈɪntɪməsɪ/ *n* intimità *f*

intimate¹ /ˈɪntɪmət/ *adj* intimo; be ~ with
(sexually) avere relazioni intime con

intimate² /ˈɪntɪmeɪt/ *vt* far capire; (imply)
suggerire

intimately /ˈɪntɪmətlɪ/ *adv* intimamente

intimidate /ɪnˈtɪmɪdeɪt/ *vt* intimidire

intimidating /ɪnˈtɪmɪdeɪtɪŋ/ *adj*
‹behaviour, person› intimidatorio; ‹prospect›
impressionante

intimidation /ɪntɪmɪˈdeɪʃn/ *n*
intimidazione *f*

⚜ **into** /ˈɪntə/, *di fronte a una vocale* /ˈɪntʊ/
prep dentro, in; go ~ the house andare
dentro [casa] *or* in casa; be ~ fam (like) essere
appassionato di; I'm not ~ that questo
non mi piace; 7 ~ 21 goes 3 il 7 nel 21 ci
sta 3 volte; translate ~ French tradurre in
francese; get ~ trouble mettersi nei guai

intolerable /ɪnˈtɒlərəbl/ *adj* intollerabile

intolerance /ɪnˈtɒlərəns/ *n* intolleranza *f*

intolerant /ɪnˈtɒlərənt/ *adj* intollerante

intonation /ɪntəˈneɪʃn/ *n* intonazione *f*

intone /ɪnˈtəʊn/ *vt* recitare ‹prayer›

intoxicated /ɪnˈtɒksɪkeɪtɪd/ *adj* inebriato

intoxicating /ɪnˈtɒksɪkeɪtɪŋ/ *adj* ‹drink›
alcolico; ‹smell, sight› inebriante

intoxication /ɪntɒksɪˈkeɪʃn/ *n* ebbrezza *f*

intractable /ɪnˈtræktəbl/ *adj* intrattabile;
‹problem› insolubile

intramural /ɪntrəˈmjʊərəl/ *adj* ‹studies›
tenuto in sede

intranet /ˈɪntrənet/ *n* Comput intranet *f*

intransigence /ɪnˈtrænzɪdʒəns/ *n*
intransigenza *f*

intransigent /ɪnˈtrænzɪdʒənt/ *adj*
intransigente

intransitive /ɪnˈtrænzɪtɪv/ *adj*
intransitivo

intransitively /ɪnˈtrænzɪtɪvlɪ/ *adv*
intransitivamente

intrauterine device
/ɪntrəjuːˈtərəmdɪˈvaɪs/ *n* Med spirale *f*,
dispositivo *m* anticoncezionale intrauterino

intravenous /ɪntrəˈviːnəs/ *adj*
endovenoso

intravenous drip *n* flebo[clisi] *f inv*

intravenous drug user *n* tossicomane
mf che si inietta in vena

intravenously /ɪntrəˈviːnəslɪ/ *adv* per via
endovenosa

in-tray *n* vassoio *m* per pratiche e
corrispondenza da evadere

intrepid /ɪnˈtrepɪd/ *adj* intrepido

intricacy /ˈɪntrɪkəsɪ/ *n* complessità *f*

intricate /ˈɪntrɪkət/ *adj* complesso

intrigue /ɪnˈtriːɡ/ 1 *n* intrigo *m*
2 *vt* intrigare
3 *vi* tramare

intriguing /ɪnˈtriːɡɪŋ/ *adj* intrigante

intrinsic /ɪnˈtrɪnsɪk/ *adj* intrinseco

⚜ **introduce** /ɪntrəˈdjuːs/ *vt* presentare; (bring
in, insert) introdurre

⚜ **introduction** /ɪntrəˈdʌkʃn/ *n*
introduzione *f*; (to person) presentazione *f*; (to
book) prefazione *f*

introductory /ɪntrəˈdʌktərɪ/ *adj*
introduttivo

introspective /ɪntrəˈspektɪv/ *adj*
introspettivo

introvert /ˈɪntrəvɜːt/ *n* introverso, -a *mf*

introverted /ˈɪntrəvɜːtɪd/ *adj* introverso

intrude /ɪnˈtruːd/ *vi* intromettersi

intruder /ɪnˈtruːdə(r)/ *n* intruso, -a *mf*

intrusion /ɪnˈtruːʒn/ *n* intrusione *f*

intrusive /ɪnˈtruːsɪv/ *adj* ‹camera,
question› indiscreto

intuition /ɪntjʊˈɪʃn/ *n* intuito *m*

intuitive /ɪnˈtjuːɪtɪv/ *adj* intuitivo

intuitively /ɪnˈtjuːɪtɪvlɪ/ *adv*
intuitivamente

inundate /ˈɪnʌndeɪt/ *vt* fig inondare (with
di)

inure /ɪnˈjʊə(r)/ *vt* become ∼d to something assuefarsi a qualcosa
invade /ɪnˈveɪd/ *vt* invadere
invader /ɪnˈveɪdə(r)/ *n* invasore *m*
invalid¹ /ˈɪnvəlɪd/ *n* invalido, -a *mf*
invalid² /ɪnˈvælɪd/ *adj* non valido
invalidate /ɪnˈvælɪdeɪt/ *vt* invalidare
invaluable /ɪnˈvæljʊ(ə)bl/ *adj* prezioso; (priceless) inestimabile
invariable /ɪnˈveərɪəbl/ *adj* invariabile
invariably /ɪnˈveərɪəblɪ/ *adv* invariabilmente
invasion /ɪnˈveɪʒn/ *n* invasione *f*
invective /ɪnˈvektɪv/ *n* invettiva *f*
invent /ɪnvent/ *vt* inventare
invention /ɪnˈvenʃn/ *n* invenzione *f*
inventive /ɪnˈventɪv/ *adj* inventivo
inventor /ɪnˈventə(r)/ *n* inventore, -trice *mf*
inventory /ˈɪnvəntrɪ/ *n* inventario *m*
inverse /ɪnˈvɜːs/ 1 *adj* inverso 2 *n* inverso *m*
inversely /ɪnˈvɜːslɪ/ *adv* inversamente
invert /ɪnˈvɜːt/ *vt* invertire; in ∼ed commas tra virgolette
invertebrate /ɪnˈvɜːtɪbrət/ *adj & n* invertebrato *m*
✓ **invest** /ɪnˈvest/ 1 *vt* investire 2 *vi* fare investimenti; ∼ in fam (buy) comprarsi
✓ **investigate** /ɪnˈvestɪgeɪt/ *vt* investigare
✓ **investigation** /ɪnvestɪˈgeɪʃn/ *n* investigazione *f*
investigative journalism /ɪnˈvestɪgətɪv/ *n* dietrologia *f*
investiture /ɪnˈvestɪtʃə(r)/ *n* investitura *f*
✓ **investment** /ɪnˈvestmənt/ *n* investimento *m*
investment capital *n* capitale *m* di investimento
investment income *n* reddito *m* di investimento
investment manager *n* responsabile *mf* della gestione del portafoglio fondi di investimento
investment trust *n* fondo *m* comune di investimento
✓ **investor** /ɪnˈvestə(r)/ *n* investitore, -trice *mf*
inveterate /ɪnˈvetərət/ *adj* inveterato
invidious /ɪnˈvɪdɪəs/ *adj* ingiusto; ⟨position⟩ antipatico
invigilate /ɪnˈvɪdʒɪleɪt/ *vi* Sch sorvegliare lo svolgimento di un esame
invigilator /ɪnˈvɪdʒɪleɪtə(r)/ *n* persona (*f*) che sorveglia lo svolgimento di un esame
invigorate /ɪnˈvɪgəreɪt/ *vt* rinvigorire
invigorating /ɪnˈvɪgəreɪtɪŋ/ *adj* tonificante

✓ indicates a very frequent word

invincible /ɪnˈvɪnsəbl/ *adj* invincibile
inviolable /ɪnˈvaɪələbl/ *adj* inviolabile
invisible /ɪnˈvɪzəbl/ *adj* invisibile
invisible ink *n* inchiostro *m* simpatico
invitation /ɪnvɪˈteɪʃn/ *n* invito *m*
invitation card *n* biglietto *m* d'invito
✓ **invite** /ɪnˈvaɪt/ *vt* invitare; (attract) attirare
■ **invite in** *vt* invitare a entrare
■ **invite round** *vt* invitare a casa
inviting /ɪnˈvaɪtɪŋ/ *adj* invitante
in vitro fertilization /ɪnviːtrəʊfɜːtɪlaɪˈzeɪʃn/ *n* fecondazione *f* in vitro
invoice /ˈɪnvɔɪs/ 1 *n* fattura *f* 2 *vt* ∼ somebody emettere una fattura a qualcuno
invoke /ɪnˈvəʊk/ *vt* invocare
involuntarily /ɪnˈvɒlʌntərɪlɪ/ *adv* involontariamente
involuntary /ɪnˈvɒləntrɪ/ *adj* involontario
✓ **involve** /ɪnˈvɒlv/ *vt* comportare; (affect, include) coinvolgere; (entail) implicare; get ∼d with somebody legarsi a qualcuno; (romantically) legarsi sentimentalmente a qualcuno
involved /ɪnˈvɒlvd/ *adj* complesso
involvement /ɪnˈvɒlvmənt/ *n* coinvolgimento *m*
invulnerable /ɪnˈvʌln(ə)rəbl/ *adj* invulnerabile; ⟨position⟩ inattaccabile
inward /ˈɪnwəd/ *adj* interno; ⟨thoughts etc⟩ interiore
inward investment *n* Comm investimento *m* di capitali stranieri
inward-looking /ˈɪnwədlʊkɪŋ/ *adj* ⟨person⟩ egocentrico; ⟨society, policy⟩ chiuso
inwardly /ˈɪnwədlɪ/ *adv* interiormente
inward[s] /ˈɪnwəd[z]/ *adv* verso l'interno
in-your-face *adj* fam aggressivo
iodine /ˈaɪədiːn/ *n* iodio *m*
Ionian Sea /aɪəʊnɪən/ *n* mar *m* Ionio
iota /aɪˈəʊtə/ *n* briciolo *m*
IOU *abbr* (**I owe you**) pagherò *m inv*
IPA *n abbr* (**International Phonetic Alphabet**) AFI *m*
IQ *abbr* (**intelligence quotient**) Q.I. *m*
IRA *abbr* (**Irish Republican Army**) I.R.A. *f*
Iran /ɪˈrɑːn/ *n* Iran *m*
Iranian /ɪˈreɪnɪən/ *adj & n* iraniano, -a *mf*
Iraq /ɪˈrɑːk/ *n* Iraq *m*
Iraqi /ɪˈrɑːkɪ/ *adj & n* iracheno, -a *mf*
irascible /ɪˈræsəbl/ *adj* irascibile
irate /aɪˈreɪt/ *adj* adirato
Ireland /ˈaɪələnd/ *n* Irlanda *f*
iris /ˈaɪrɪs/ *n* Anat iride *f*; Bot iris *f inv*
✓ **Irish** /ˈaɪrɪʃ/ 1 *adj* irlandese 2 *n* the I∼ *pl* gli irlandesi
Irishman /ˈaɪrɪʃmən/ *n* irlandese *m*

Irish Republic *n* Repubblica *f* d'Irlanda

Irish sea *n* mare *m* d'Irlanda

Irishwoman /'aɪrɪʃwʊmən/ *n* irlandese *f*

irk /ɜːk/ *vt* infastidire

irksome /'ɜːksəm/ *adj* fastidioso

iron /'aɪən/ **1** *adj* di ferro

2 *n* ferro *m*; (appliance) ferro *m* [da stiro]

3 *vt/i* stirare

■ **iron out** *vt* eliminare stirando; fig appianare

Iron Curtain *n* cortina *f* di ferro

iron fist *n* fig pugno *m* di ferro

ironic[al] /aɪ'rɒnɪk[l]/ *adj* ironico

ironing /'aɪənɪŋ/ *n* stirare *m*; (articles) roba *f* da stirare; **do the ~** stirare

ironing board *n* asse *f* da stiro

iron lung *n* polmone *m* d'acciaio

ironmonger /'aɪənmʌŋgə(r)/ *n* ~**'s [shop]** negozio *m* di ferramenta

irony /'aɪərənɪ/ *n* ironia *f*

irradiate /ɪ'reɪdɪeɪt/ *vt* irradiare

irrational /ɪ'ræʃənl/ *adj* irrazionale

irreconcilable /ɪ'rekənsaɪləbl/ *adj* irreconciliabile

irrecoverable /ɪrɪ'kʌv(ə)rəbl/ *adj* ‹debt, object› irrecuperabile; ‹loss› irreparabile

irredeemable /ɪrɪ'diːməbl/ *adj* Fin ‹shares, loan› irredimibile; ‹loss› irreparabile; Relig ‹sinner› che non è redimibile

irrefutable /ɪrɪ'fjuːtəbl/ *adj* irrefutabile

irregular /ɪ'regʊlə(r)/ *adj* irregolare

irregularity /ɪregjʊ'lærətɪ/ *n* irregolarità *f inv*

irregularly /ɪ'regjʊlərlɪ/ *adv* in modo irregolare

irrelevant /ɪ'reləvənt/ *adj* non pertinente

irreligious /ˌɪrɪ'lɪdʒəs/ *adj* irreligioso

irreparable /ɪ'repərəbl/ *adj* irreparabile

irreparably /ɪ'rep(ə)rəblɪ/ *adv* irreparabilmente

irreplaceable /ɪrɪ'pleɪsəbl/ *adj* insostituibile

irrepressible /ɪrɪ'presəbl/ *adj* irrefrenabile; ‹person› incontenibile

irreproachable /ɪrɪ'prəʊtʃəbl/ *adj* irreprensibile

irresistible /ɪrɪ'zɪstəbl/ *adj* irresistibile

irresolute /ɪ'rezəluːt/ *adj* irresoluto

irrespective /ɪrɪ'spektɪv/ *adj* ~ **of** senza riguardo per

irresponsible /ɪrɪ'spɒnsəbl/ *adj* irresponsabile

irresponsibly /ɪrɪ'spɒnsəblɪ/ *adv* irresponsabilmente

irretrievable /ɪrɪ'triːvəbl/ *adj* ‹loss, harm› irreparabile

irreverence /ɪ'revərəns/ *n* irriverenza *f*

irreverent /ɪ'revərənt/ *adj* irriverente

irreverently /ɪ'revərəntlɪ/ *adv* in modo irriverente

irreversible /ɪrɪ'vɜːsəbl/ *adj* irreversibile

irreversibly /ɪrɪ'vɜːsɪblɪ/ *adv* irreversibilmente

irrevocable /ɪ'revəkəbl/ *adj* irrevocabile

irrevocably /ɪ'revəkəblɪ/ *adv* irrevocabilmente

irrigate /'ɪrɪgeɪt/ *vt* irrigare

irrigation /ɪrɪ'geɪʃn/ *n* irrigazione *f*

irritability /ɪrɪtə'bɪlətɪ/ *n* irritabilità *f*

irritable /'ɪrɪtəbl/ *adj* irritabile

irritable bowel syndrome *n* sindrome *f* da colon irritabile

irritant /'ɪrɪtənt/ *n* sostanza *f* irritante; fig (person) persona *f* irritante

irritate /'ɪrɪteɪt/ *vt* irritare

irritated /'ɪrɪteɪtɪd/ *adj* irritato, stizzito

irritating /'ɪrɪteɪtɪŋ/ *adj* irritante

irritation /ɪrɪ'teɪʃn/ *n* irritazione *f*

IRS *n abbr* Am (**Internal Revenue Service**) fisco *m*

is /ɪz/ ▶ BE

Islam /'ɪzlɑːm/ *n* Islam *m*

Islamic /ɪz'læmɪk/ *adj* islamico

Islamist /'ɪzləmɪst/ *n* (fundamentalist) estremista *mf* islamico, (-a); (scholar) islamista *mf*

⚈ **island** /'aɪlənd/ *n* isola *f*; (in road) isola *f* spartitraffico

islander /'aɪləndə(r)/ *n* isolano, -a *mf*

island hopping /'aɪləndhɒpɪŋ/ *n* **go ~** andare di isola in isola

isle /aɪl/ *n* liter isola *f*

Isle of Man *n* l'isola *f* di Man

isms /'ɪz(ə)mz/ *npl* pej ismi *mpl*

isobar /'aɪsəbɑː(r)/ *n* isobara *f*

isolate /'aɪsəleɪt/ *vt* isolare

isolated /'aɪsəleɪtɪd/ *adj* isolato

isolation /aɪsə'leɪʃn/ *n* isolamento *m*

isosceles /aɪ'sɒsəliːz/ *adj* isoscele

ISP *n abbr* (**Internet service provider**) Comput ISP *m*

Israel /'ɪzreɪl/ *n* Israele *m*

Israeli /ɪz'reɪlɪ/ *adj* & *n* israeliano, -a *mf*

⚈ **issue** /'ɪʃuː/ **1** *n* (outcome) risultato *m*; (of magazine) numero *m*; (of stamps etc) emissione *f*; (offspring) figli *mpl*; (matter, question) questione *f*; **at ~** in questione; **take ~ with somebody** prendere posizione contro qualcuno

2 *vt* distribuire ‹supplies›; rilasciare ‹passport›; emettere ‹stamps, order›; pubblicare ‹book›; **be ~d with something** ricevere qualcosa

3 *vi* ~ **from** uscire da

isthmus /'ɪsməs/ *n* (*pl* -**muses**) istmo *m*

⚈ **it** /ɪt/ *pron* (direct object) lo *m*, la *f*; (indirect object) gli *m*, le *f*; **it's broken** è rotto/rotta; **will** ⋯▷

it be enough? basterà?; **it's hot** fa caldo; **it's raining** piove; **it's me** sono io; **who is it?** chi è?; **it's two o'clock** sono le due; **I doubt it** ne dubito; **take it with you** prendilo con te; **give it a wipe** dagli una pulita

IT *n abbr* (**information technology**) informatica *f*

Italian /ɪ'tæljən/ *adj & n* italiano, -a *mf*; (language) italiano *m*

Italian-American *adj & n* italoamericano

italic /ɪ'tælɪk/ *adj* in corsivo

italics /ɪ'tælɪks/ *npl* corsivo *msg*; **in** ∼ in corsivo

Italy /'ɪtəlɪ/ *n* Italia *f*

itch /ɪtʃ/ [1] *n* prurito *m*
[2] *vi* avere prurito, prudere; **be** ∼**ing to** fam avere una voglia matta di

itching powder /'ɪtʃɪŋ/ *n* polverina *f* che dà prurito

itchy /'ɪtʃɪ/ *adj* che prude; **my foot is** ∼ ho prurito al piede; **have** ∼ **feet** fig avere la terra che scotta sotto i piedi

♂ **item** /'aɪtəm/ *n* articolo *m*; (on agenda, programme) punto *m*; (on invoice) voce *f*; ∼ **[of**

news] notizia *f*

itemize /'aɪtəmaɪz/ *vt* dettagliare ‹bill›

itinerant /aɪ'tɪnərənt/ *adj* itinerante

itinerary /aɪ'tɪnərərɪ/ *n* itinerario *m*

ITN *n abbr* Br (**independent television**) rete (*f*) televisiva britannica

♂ **its** /ɪts/ *poss pron* suo *m*, sua *f*, suoi *mpl*, sue *fpl*; ∼ **mother/cage** sua madre/la sua gabbia

it's = it is, it has

♂ **itself** /ɪt'self/ *pron* (reflexive) si; (emphatic) essa stessa; **the baby looked at** ∼ **in the mirror** il bambino si è guardato nello specchio; **by** ∼ da solo; **the machine in** ∼ **is simple** la macchina di per sé è semplice

ITV *abbr* (**Independent Television**) stazione (*f*) televisiva privata

IUD *n abbr* (**intrauterine device**) spirale *f*

IVF *n abbr* (**in vitro fertilization**) FIV *f*

ivory /'aɪvərɪ/ [1] *n* avorio *m*
[2] *attrib* d'avorio

Ivory Coast *n* Costa *f* d'Avorio

ivory tower *n* fig torre *f* d'avorio

ivy /'aɪvɪ/ *n* edera *f*

J j

j, J /dʒeɪ/ *n* (letter) j, J *f inv*

jab /dʒæb/ [1] *n* colpo *m* secco; fam (injection) puntura *f*
[2] *vt* (*pt/pp* **jabbed**) punzecchiare

jabber /'dʒæbə(r)/ *vi* borbottare

jack /dʒæk/ *n* Auto cric *m inv*; Teleph jack *m inv*; (in cards) fante *m*, jack *m inv*
■ **jack in** *vt* sl piantare ‹job›
■ **jack up** *vt* Auto sollevare [con il cric]; fam aumentare di molto ‹salary etc›

jackal /'dʒæk(ə)l/ *n* sciacallo *m*

jackboot /'dʒækbuːt/ *n* stivale *m* militare

jackdaw /'dʒækdɔː/ *n* taccola *f*

jacket /'dʒækɪt/ *n* giacca *f*; (of book) sopraccopertina *f*

jacket potato *n* patata (*f*) cotta al forno con la buccia

jack-in-the-box *n* scatola (*f*) a sorpresa contenente un pupazzo a molla

jackknife /'dʒæknaɪf/ [1] *n* coltello *m* a serramanico
[2] *vi* sbandare finendo di traverso rispetto al rimorchio

jackpot /'dʒækpɒt/ *n* premio *m* (*di una lotteria*); **win the** ∼ vincere alla lotteria; **hit**

the ∼ fig fare un colpo grosso

jackrabbit /'dʒækræbɪt/ *n* lepre *f* americana

jade /dʒeɪd/ [1] *n* giada *f*
[2] *attrib* di giada

jaded /'dʒeɪdɪd/ *adj* spossato

jagged /'dʒægɪd/ *adj* dentellato

jail /dʒeɪl/ = GAOL

jailbird *n* avanzo *m* di galera

jailbreak *n* evasione *f*

jail sentence *n* condanna *f* al carcere

jalopy /dʒə'lɒpɪ/ *n* fam vecchia carretta *f*

jam¹ /dʒæm/ *n* marmellata *f*

jam² [1] *n* Auto ingorgo *m*; fam (difficulty) guaio *m*
[2] *vt* (*pt/pp* **jammed**) (cram) pigiare; disturbare ‹broadcast›; inceppare ‹mechanism, drawer etc.›; **be** ∼**med** ‹roads› essere congestionato
[3] *vi* ‹mechanism› incepparsi; ‹window, drawer› incastrarsi
■ **jam on**: *vt* ∼ **on the brakes** inchiodare

Jamaica /dʒə'meɪkə/ *n* Giamaica *f*

Jamaican /dʒə'meɪkən/ *adj & n* giamaicano, -a *mf*

jam jar *n* barattolo *m* per la marmellata

♂ indicates a very frequent word

jam-packed *adj* fam pieno zeppo

jampot *n* vasetto *m* per la marmellata

jangle /'dʒæŋgl/ ① *vt* far squillare
② *vi* squillare

janitor /'dʒænɪtə(r)/ *n* (caretaker) custode *m*;
(in school) bidello, -a *mf*

☛ **January** /'dʒænjʊərɪ/ *n* gennaio *m*

Japan /dʒə'pæn/ *n* Giappone *m*

☛ **Japanese** /dʒæpə'niːz/ *adj* & *n* giapponese
mf; (language) giapponese *m*

jar¹ /dʒɑː(r)/ *n* (glass) barattolo *m*

jar² *vi* (*pt/pp* **jarred**) ‹sound› stridere

jargon /'dʒɑːgən/ *n* gergo *m*

jarring /'dʒɑːrɪŋ/ *adj* stridente

jasmine /'dʒæsmɪn/ *n* gelsomino *m*

jaundice /'dʒɔːndɪs/ *n* itterizia *f*

jaundiced /'dʒɔːndɪst/ *adj* fig inacidito

jaunt /dʒɔːnt/ *n* gita *f*

jaunty /'dʒɔːntɪ/ *adj* (**-ier, -iest**)
sbarazzino

javelin /'dʒævlɪn/ *n* giavellotto *m*

jaw /dʒɔː/ ① *n* mascella *f*; (bone) mandibola
f
② *vi* fam ciarlare

jawbone /'dʒɔːbəʊn/ *n* Anat osso *m*
mascellare

jawline *n* mento *m*

jay /dʒeɪ/ *n* ghiandaia *f*

jaywalker /'dʒeɪwɔːkə(r)/ *n* pedone *m*
indisciplinato

jazz /dʒæz/ *n* jazz *m*
■ **jazz up** *vt* ravvivare

jazz band *n* complesso *m* di jazz

jazzy /'dʒæzɪ/ *adj* vistoso

jealous /'dʒeləs/ *adj* geloso

jealously /'dʒeləslɪ/ *adv* gelosamente

jealousy /'dʒeləsɪ/ *n* gelosia *f*

jeans /dʒiːnz/ *npl* [blue] jeans *mpl*

jeep /dʒiːp/ *n* jeep *f inv*

jeer /dʒɪə(r)/ ① *n* scherno *m*
② *vi* schernire; ~ **at** prendersi gioco di
③ *vt* (boo) fischiare

jeering /'dʒɪərɪŋ/ *n* fischi *mpl*

jell /dʒel/ *vi* concretarsi

jellied /'dʒelɪd/ *adj* ‹eels› in gelatina

Jell-o® /'dʒeləʊ/ *n* Am dolce (*m*) di gelatina
di frutta

jelly /'dʒelɪ/ *n* gelatina *f*

jelly baby *n* caramella (*f*) gommosa a
forma di pupazzetto

jelly bean *n* caramella (*f*) di gelatina di
frutta

jellyfish *n* medusa *f*

jemmy /'dʒemɪ/ *n* piede *m* di porco

jeopardize /'dʒepədaɪz/ *vt* mettere in
pericolo

jeopardy /'dʒepədɪ/ *n* **in** ~ in pericolo

jerk /dʒɜːk/ ① *n* scatto *m*, scossa *f*

② *vt* scattare
③ *vi* sobbalzare; ‹limb, muscle› muoversi
a scatti

jerkily /'dʒɜːkɪlɪ/ *adv* a scatti

jerkin /'dʒɜːkɪn/ *n* gilè *m inv*

jerky /'dʒɜːkɪ/ *adj* traballante

jerry-built /'dʒerɪbɪlt/ *adj* pej costruito alla
bell'e meglio

jersey /'dʒɜːzɪ/ *n* maglia *f*; Sport maglietta *f*;
(fabric) jersey *m*

Jerusalem /dʒə'ruːsələm/ *n*
Gerusalemme *f*

jest /dʒest/ ① *n* scherzo *m*; **in** ~ per
scherzo
② *vi* scherzare

jester /'dʒestə(r)/ *n* buffone *m*

Jesuit /'dʒezjʊɪt/ ① *n* gesuita *m*
② *adj* gesuitico

Jesus /'dʒiːzəs/ *n* Gesù *m*

jet¹ /dʒet/ *n* (stone) giaietto *m*

jet² *n* (of water) getto *m*; (nozzle) becco *m*;
(plane) aviogetto *m*, jet *m inv*

jet-black *adj* nero ebano

jet engine *n* motore *m* a reazione

jet fighter *n* caccia *m inv* a reazione

jetfoil *n* aliscafo *m*

jet lag *n* scombussolamento *m* da fuso
orario

jet-lagged *adj* **be** ~ soffrire di jet lag

jetpropelled /-prə'peld/ *adj* a reazione

jet propulsion *n* propulsione *f* a getto

jet setter *n* **be a** ~ appartenere al jet set

jet ski *n* moto *m* d'acqua

jet-skier *n* persona *m* che fa moto d'acqua

jet-skiing *n* moto *m* d'acqua

jettison /'dʒetɪsn/ *vt* gettare a mare, fig
abbandonare

jetty /'dʒetɪ/ *n* molo *m*

Jew /dʒuː/ *n* ebreo *m*

jewel /'dʒuːəl/ *n* gioiello *m*

jewelled /'dʒuːəld/ *adj* ornato di pietre
preziose

jeweller /'dʒuːələ(r)/ *n* gioielliere *m*; ~**'s**
[shop] gioielleria *f*

jewellery /'dʒuːəlrɪ/ *n* gioielli *mpl*

Jewess /'dʒuːɪs/ *n* ebrea *f*

Jewish /'dʒuːɪʃ/ *adj* ebreo

Jew's harp *n* Mus scacciapensieri *m inv*

jib /dʒɪb/ *vi* (*pt/pp* **jibbed**) fig mostrarsi
riluttante (**at** a)

jibe /dʒaɪb/ *n* ▶ GIBE

jiffy /'dʒɪfɪ/ *n* fam **in a** ~ in un batter
d'occhio

Jiffy bag® *n* busta *f* imbottita

jig /dʒɪg/ *n* Mus giga *f* (danza popolare)

jiggle /'dʒɪg(ə)l/ *vt* scuotere

jigsaw /'dʒɪgsɔː/ *n* ~ **[puzzle]** puzzle *m inv*

jilt /dʒɪlt/ *vt* piantare

jingle /'dʒɪŋgl/ **1** n (rhyme) canzoncina f pubblicitaria
2 vi tintinnare
3 vt far tintinnare
jingoist /'dʒɪŋgəʊɪst/ n Pol sciovinista mf
jingoistic /dʒɪŋgəʊ'ɪstɪk/ adj Pol sciovinistico
jinx /dʒɪŋks/ n fam (person) iettatore, -trice mf; It's got a ∼ on it è iellato
jinxed /dʒɪŋkst/ adj be ∼ essere iellato
jitters /'dʒɪtəz/ npl fam have the ∼ aver una gran fifa
jittery /'dʒɪtərɪ/ adj fam in preda alla fifa
jive /dʒaɪv/ n Am fam (talk) storie fpl
Jnr abbr (**junior**) junior (jr)
⚜ **job** /dʒɒb/ n lavoro m; this is going to be quite a ∼ fam [questa] non sarà un'impresa facile; it's a good ∼ that ... meno male che ...
jobcentre n ufficio m statale di collocamento
job creation scheme n Br programma m di creazione di posti di lavoro
job description n mansionario m
job-hunting n ricerca f impiego
jobless /'dʒɒblɪs/ adj senza lavoro
job lot n (at auction) insieme (m) di oggetti disparati
job market n mercato m del lavoro
job satisfaction n soddisfazione f nel lavoro
job security n sicurezza f di impiego
job seeker n persona f che cerca lavoro
job seeker's allowance n Br indennità f di disoccupazione
job-share **1** n (position) posto m condiviso
2 attrib ‹scheme› di condivisione del posto di lavoro
job-sharing /-'ʃeərɪŋ/ n job sharing m inv
jockey /'dʒɒkɪ/ n fantino m
jockey shorts npl boxer mpl
jockstrap n sospensorio m
jocular /'dʒɒkjʊlə(r)/ adj scherzoso
jocularly /'dʒɒkjʊləlɪ/ adv scherzosamente
jodhpurs /'dʒɒdpəz/ npl calzoni mpl alla cavallerizza
Joe Bloggs /dʒəʊ'blɒgz/ n l'uomo qualunque
jog /dʒɒg/ **1** n colpetto m; at a ∼ in un balzo; Sport go for a ∼ andare a fare jogging
2 vt (pt/pp **jogged**) (hit) urtare; ∼ sb's memory farlo ritornare in mente a qualcuno
3 vi Sport fare jogging
▪ **jog along** vi fig tirare avanti
jogger /'dʒɒgə(r)/ n persona f che fa jogging
jogging /'dʒɒgɪŋ/ n jogging m
john /dʒɒn/ n Am fam (toilet) gabinetto m
John Bull n il tipico inglese

John Doe n Am uomo m non identificato
⚜ **join** /dʒɔɪn/ **1** n giuntura f
2 vt raggiungere, unire; raggiungere ‹person›; (become member of) iscriversi a; entrare in ‹firm›
3 vi ‹roads› congiungersi
▪ **join in** vi partecipare
▪ **join up** **1** vi Mil arruolarsi
2 vt unire
▪ **join up with** vt (meet) raggiungere ‹friends›; congiungersi a ‹road; river›
joiner /'dʒɔɪnə(r)/ n falegname m
⚜ **joint** /dʒɔɪnt/ **1** adj comune
2 n articolazione f; (in wood, brickwork) giuntura f; Culin arrosto m; fam (bar) bettola f; sl (drug) spinello m
joint account n conto m [corrente] comune
joint agreement n accordo m collettivo
jointed /'dʒɔɪntɪd/ adj Culin ‹chicken› tagliato a pezzi; ‹doll, puppet› snodabile; ‹rod, pole› smontabile
joint effort n collaborazione f
joint honours npl Br Univ laurea (f) in due discipline
jointly /'dʒɔɪntlɪ/ adv unitamente
joint owner n comproprietario, -a mf
joint venture n joint venture f inv
joist /dʒɔɪst/ n travetto m
joke /dʒəʊk/ **1** n (trick) scherzo m; (funny story) barzelletta f
2 vi scherzare
joker /'dʒəʊkə(r)/ n burlone, -a mf; (in cards) jolly m inv
joking /'dʒəʊkɪŋ/ n ∼ apart scherzi a parte
jokingly /'dʒəʊkɪŋlɪ/ adv per scherzo
jollity /'dʒɒlətɪ/ n allegria f
jolly /'dʒɒlɪ/ **1** adj (-ier, -iest) allegro
2 adv fam molto
Jolly Roger /'rɒdʒə(r)/ n bandiera f dei pirati
jolt /dʒəʊlt/ **1** n scossa f, sobbalzo m
2 vt far sobbalzare
3 vi sobbalzare
Jordan /'dʒɔːdn/ n Giordania f; (river) Giordano m
Jordanian /dʒɔː'deɪnɪən/ adj & n giordano, -a mf
joss stick /'dʒɒs/ n bastoncino m d'incenso
jostle /'dʒɒsl/ vt spingere
jot /dʒɒt/ n nulla f
▪ **jot down** vt (pt/pp **jotted**) annotare
jotter /'dʒɒtə(r)/ n taccuino m; (with a spine) quaderno m
jottings /'dʒɒtɪŋz/ npl annotazioni fpl
journal /'dʒɜːnl/ n giornale m; (diary) diario m

⚜ indicates a very frequent word

journalese /dʒɜːnəˈliːz/ n gergo m giornalistico

journalism /ˈdʒɜːnəlɪzm/ n giornalismo m

◆ **journalist** /ˈdʒɜːnəlɪst/ n giornalista mf

◆ **journey** /ˈdʒɜːnɪ/ [1] n viaggio m
[2] vi viaggiare

jovial /ˈdʒəʊvɪəl/ adj gioviale

jowl /dʒaʊl/ n (jaw) mascella f; (fleshy fold) guancia f; **cheek by ~ with somebody** fianco a fianco con qualcuno

joy /dʒɔɪ/ n gioia f

joyful /ˈdʒɔɪfʊl/ adj gioioso

joyfully /ˈdʒɔɪfʊlɪ/ adv con gioia

joyless /ˈdʒɔɪlɪs/ adj ‹occasion› triste; ‹marriage› infelice

joypad n Comput joypad m

joyride n fam giro (m) con una macchina rubata

joyrider n fam persona (f) che ruba una macchina per andare a fare un giro

joyriding /ˈdʒɔɪraɪdɪŋ/ n giri mpl su una macchina rubata

joystick n Comput joystick m inv

JP n abbr Br (**Justice of the Peace**) giudice m di pace

Jr abbr (**junior**)

jubilant /ˈdʒuːbɪlənt/ adj giubilante

jubilation /dʒuːbɪˈleɪʃn/ n giubilo m

jubilee /ˈdʒuːbɪliː/ n giubileo m

Judaism /ˈdʒuːdeɪɪzm/ n giudaismo m

judder /ˈdʒʌdə(r)/ vi vibrare violentemente

◆ **judge** /dʒʌdʒ/ [1] n giudice m
[2] vt giudicare; (estimate) valutare; (consider) ritenere
[3] vi giudicare (**by** da)

◆ **judgement, judgment** /ˈdʒʌdʒmənt/ n giudizio m; Jur sentenza f

judicial /dʒuːˈdɪʃl/ adj giudiziario

judiciary /dʒuːˈdɪʃərɪ/ n magistratura f

judicious /dʒuːˈdɪʃəs/ adj giudizioso

judo /ˈdʒuːdəʊ/ n judo m

jug /dʒʌg/ n brocca f; (small) bricco m

juggernaut /ˈdʒʌgənɔːt/ n fam grosso autotreno m

juggle /ˈdʒʌgl/ vi fare giochi di destrezza

juggler /ˈdʒʌglə(r)/ n giocoliere, -a mf

jugular /ˈdʒʌgjʊlə(r)/ n giugulare f; **go straight for the ~** fig colpire nel punto debole

juice /dʒuːs/ n succo m; **~ extractor** n spremiagrumi m inv elettrico

juicy /ˈdʒuːsɪ/ adj (**-ier, -iest**) succoso; fam ‹story› piccante

ju-jitsu /dʒuːˈdʒɪtsuː/ n jujitsu m

jukebox /ˈdʒuːkbɒks/ n juke-box m inv

◆ **July** /dʒʊˈlaɪ/ n luglio m

jumble /ˈdʒʌmbl/ [1] n accozzaglia f
[2] vt **~ [up]** mischiare

jumble sale n vendita f di beneficenza

jumbo /ˈdʒʌmbəʊ/ n **~ [jet]** jumbo jet m inv

◆ **jump** /dʒʌmp/ [1] n salto m; (in prices) balzo m; (in horse racing) ostacolo m
[2] vi saltare; (with fright) sussultare; ‹prices› salire rapidamente; **~ to conclusions** saltare alle conclusioni
[3] vt saltare; **~ the gun** fig precipitarsi; **~ the queue** non rispettare la fila

■ **jump at** vt fig accettare con entusiasmo ‹offer›

■ **jump back** vi fare un salto indietro

■ **jump down**: vt **~ down sb's throat** saltare addosso a qualcuno

■ **jump in** vi (to vehicle) saltar su

■ **jump on** vt saltare su ‹bus, train, bike, horse›; (attack) aggredire ‹somebody›

■ **jump out** vi saltare fuori; **~ out of something** saltare giù da qualcosa ‹window, train, bed›

■ **jump up** vi rizzarsi in piedi

jumped-up /dʒʌmptˈʌp/ adj montato

jumper /ˈdʒʌmpə(r)/ n (sweater) golf m inv

jump jet n aeroplano m a decollo e atterraggio verticali

jump leads npl cavi mpl per batteria

jump-start vt far partire con i cavi da batteria

jumpsuit n tuta f

jumpy /ˈdʒʌmpɪ/ adj nervoso

junction /ˈdʒʌŋkʃn/ n (of roads) incrocio m; Rail nodo m ferroviario

juncture /ˈdʒʌŋktʃə(r)/ n **at this ~** a questo punto

◆ **June** /dʒuːn/ n giugno m

Jungian /ˈjʊŋɪən/ adj junghiano

jungle /ˈdʒʌŋgl/ n giungla f

junior /ˈdʒuːnɪə(r)/ [1] adj giovane; (in rank) subalterno; Sport Junior inv
[2] n the **~s** pl Sch i più giovani

junior doctor n assistente mf ospedaliero, -a

junior high school n Am scuola f media inferiore

junior minister n sottosegretario m

junior school n scuola f elementare

juniper /ˈdʒuːnɪpə(r)/ n ginepro m

junk /dʒʌŋk/ n cianfrusaglie fpl

junk food n fam cibo m poco sano, porcherie fpl

junkie /ˈdʒʌŋkɪ/ n sl tossico, -a mf

junk mail n posta f spazzatura

junk shop n negozio m di rigattiere

junkyard n (for scrap) rottamaio m; (for old cars) cimitero m delle macchine

junta /ˈdʒʌntə/ n giunta f militare

Jupiter /ˈdʒuːpɪtə(r)/ n Giove m

jurisdiction /dʒʊərɪsˈdɪkʃn/ n giurisdizione f

jurisprudence /dʒʊərɪsˈpruːdəns/ n giurisprudenza f

jurist /ˈdʒʊərɪst/ n giurista mf

juror /'dʒʊərə(r)/ n giurato, -a mf

jury /'dʒʊərɪ/ n giuria f

jury box n banco m dei giurati

jury duty n esp Am = JURY SERVICE

jury service n do ~ far parte di una giuria popolare

◆ **just** /dʒʌst/ ❶ adj giusto
❷ adv (barely) appena; (simply) solo; (exactly) esattamente; ~ **as tall** altrettanto alto; ~ **as I was leaving** proprio quando stavo andando via; **I've** ~ **seen her** l'ho appena vista; **it's** ~ **as well** meno male; ~ **at that moment** proprio in quel momento; ~ **listen!** almeno ascolta!; **I'm** ~ **going** sto andando proprio ora

◆ **justice** /'dʒʌstɪs/ n giustizia f; **do** ~ **to** rendere giustizia a

Justice Department n Am ministero m di Grazia e Giustizia

Justice of the Peace n giudice m di pace

justifiable /dʒʌstɪ'faɪəbl/ adj giustificabile

justifiably /dʒʌstɪ'faɪəblɪ/ adv in modo giustificato

justification /dʒʌstɪfɪ'keɪʃn/ n giustificazione f

justified /'dʒʌstɪfaɪd/ adj ‹action› motivato

◆ **justify** /'dʒʌstɪfaɪ/ vt (pt/pp -**ied**) giustificare

justly /'dʒʌstlɪ/ adv giustamente

justness /'dʒʌstnɪs/ n (of decision) giustezza f; (of claim, request) legittimità f

jut /dʒʌt/ vi (pt/pp **jutted**) ~ **out** sporgere

jute /dʒuːt/ n iuta f

juvenile /'dʒuːvənaɪl/ ❶ adj giovanile; (childish) infantile; (for the young) per i giovani
❷ n giovane mf

juvenile crime n delinquenza f minorile

juvenile delinquency n delinquenza f minorile

juvenile delinquent n delinquente mf minorile

juvenile offender n Jur imputato, -a mf minorenne

juxtapose /dʒʌkstə'pəʊz/ vt giustapporre

K k

k¹, K /keɪ/ n (letter) k, K f inv

K² abbr 1 (**kilo**) k
2 (**kilobyte**) KB, Kbyte m inv
3 (**thousand pounds**) **he earns £50 K** guadagna 50 mila sterline

kale /keɪl/, **curly kale** n cavolo m riccio

kaleidoscope /kə'laɪdəskəʊp/ n caleidoscopio m

kangaroo /kæŋgə'ruː/ n canguro m

kaput /kə'pʊt/ adj fam kaputt inv

karaoke /kærɪ'əʊkɪ/ n karaoke m inv

karaoke machine n apparecchio m per il karaoke

karate /kə'rɑːtɪ/ n karatè m

kart /kɑːt/ n kart m inv

Kashmir /kæʃ'mɪə(r)/ n Kashmir m

Kashmiri /kæʃ'mɪərɪ/ ❶ adj del Kashmir
❷ n nativo, -a mf del Kashmir

kayak /'kaɪæk/ n kayak m inv

Kazakhstan /ˌkɑːzɑːk'stɑːn, ˌkæz-/ n Kazakistan m

KB n abbr (**kilobyte**) KB, Kbyte m inv

kebab /kɪ'bæb/ n Culin spiedino m di carne

kedgeree /'kedʒəriː/ n Br piatto (m) indiano a base di pesce, riso e uova

keel /kiːl/ n chiglia f

■ **keel over** vi capovolgersi

keen /kiːn/ adj (intense) acuto; ‹interest› vivo; ‹eager› entusiastico; ‹competition› feroce; ‹wind, knife› tagliente; ~ **on** entusiasta di; **she's** ~ **on him** le piace molto; **be** ~ **to do something** avere voglia di fare qualcosa

keenly /'kiːnlɪ/ adv intensamente

keenness /'kiːnnɪs/ n entusiasmo m

◆ **keep** /kiːp/ ❶ n (maintenance) mantenimento m; (of castle) maschio m; **for** ~**s** per sempre
❷ vt (pt/pp **kept**) tenere; (not throw away) conservare; (detain) trattenere; mantenere ‹family, promise›; tenere ‹shop›; allevare ‹animals›; rispettare ‹law, rules›; ~ **something hot** tenere qualcosa in caldo; ~ **somebody waiting** far aspettare qualcuno; ~ **something to oneself** tenere qualcosa per sé
❸ vi (remain) rimanere; ‹food› conservarsi; ~ **calm** rimanere calmo; ~ **left/right** tenere la sinistra/la destra; ~ **[on] doing something** continuare a fare qualcosa
■ **keep at**: vt (persevere with) ~ **at it!** non mollare!
■ **keep away** ❶ vi non avvicinarsi, stare alla larga
❷ vt tenere lontano
■ **keep away from** vt non avvicinarsi

◆ indicates a very frequent word

a ‹fire›; stare alla larga da ‹somebody›; ~ **somebody away from something** tener qualcuno lontano da qualcosa
■ **keep back** ①️ *vt* trattenere ‹person›; ~ **something back from somebody** tenere nascosto qualcosa a qualcuno ②️ *vi* tenersi indietro
■ **keep down** ①️ *vi* star giù ②️ *vt* mandar giù ‹food›; mantenere basso ‹prices, inflation etc›; ~ **one's voice down** non alzare la voce
■ **keep from**: *vt* ~ **somebody from doing something** impedire a qualcuno di fare qualcosa; ~ **somebody from impedire a** qualcuno di ‹falling›; ~ **somebody from their work** distogliere qualcuno dal lavoro; ~ **something from somebody** tenere nascosto qualcosa a qualcuno; ~ **the truth from somebody** nascondere la verità a qualcuno
■ **keep in** *vt* (in school) trattenere oltre l'orario per punizione; reprimere ‹indignation, anger etc›
■ **keep in with** *vt* mantenersi in buoni rapporti con
■ **keep off** *vt* (avoid) astenersi da ‹cigarettes, chocolate etc›; evitare ‹delicate subject›
■ **keep on** ①️ *vi* (continue one's journey) proseguire; fam assillare (**at somebody** qualcuno) ②️ *vt* non togliersi ‹coat, hat›; tenere ‹employee›
■ **keep out** ①️ *vt* tenere fuori; ~ **out!** alla larga! ②️ *vt* non far entrare ‹person, animal›
■ **keep out of** *vt* ‹person› non entrare in ‹place›; tenersi fuori da ‹argument›; ~ **somebody out of** tenere qualcuno alla larga da ‹place›; ~ **me out of this!** lasciamene fuori!
■ **keep to** *vt* non deviare da ‹path, subject›; ~ **something to oneself** tenere qualcosa per sé
■ **keep up** ①️ *vi* ‹remain level› stare al passo; ‹rain, good weather› mantenersi ②️ *vt* (continue) continuare; (prevent from going to bed) tenere alzato; mantenere alto ‹prices›; tener su ‹trousers›
■ **keep up with** *vt* (in race) stare al passo con ‹person, fashion›; ‹wages› seguire il corso di ‹inflation›
keeper /'kiːpə(r)/ *n* custode *mf*
keep-fit *n* ginnastica *f*
keeping /'kiːpɪŋ/ *n* custodia *f*; **be in** ~ **with** essere in armonia con
keepsake /'kiːpseɪk/ *n* ricordo *m*
keg /keg/ *n* barilotto *m*
kelp /kelp/ *n* laminaria *f*, fuco *m*
kennel /'kenl/ *n* canile *m*; ~**s** *pl* (boarding) canile *m*; (breeding) allevamento *m* di cani
Kenya /'kenjə/ *n* Kenya *m*
Kenyan /'kenjən/ *adj & n* keniota *mf*
kept /kept/ ▸ KEEP
kerb /kɜːb/ *n* bordo *m* del marciapiede

kernel /'kɜːnl/ *n* nocciolo *m*
kerosene /'kerəsiːn/ *n* Am cherosene *m*
kestrel /'kestrəl/ *n* gheppio *m*
ketchup /'ketʃʌp/ *n* ketchup *m*
kettle /'ket(ə)l/ *n* bollitore *m*; **put the** ~ **on** mettere l'acqua a bollire
kettledrum /'ket(ə)ldrʌm/ *n* timpano *m*
✔ **key** /kiː/ ①️ *n* (also Mus) chiave *f*; (of piano, typewriter) tasto *m* ②️ *vt* ~ **[in]** digitare ‹character›; **could you** ~ **this?** puoi battere questo?
keyboard *n* Comput, Mus tastiera *f*
keyboarder *n* tastierista *mf*
keyboard player *n* tastierista *mf*
keyboards *npl* Mus tastiere *fpl*
keyed-up /kiːd'ʌp/ *adj* (excited) teso; (anxious) estremamente agitato; (ready to act) psicologicamente preparato
keyhole *n* buco *m* della serratura
keyhole surgery *n* chirurgia *f* endoscopica
key money *n* (for apartment) somma (*f*) richiesta ad un affittuario quando si trasferisce nell'abitazione
keynote *n* Mus tonica *f*; (main theme) tema *m* principale
keynote speech *n* discorso *m* programmatico
keypad *n* Comput tastierino *m* numerico
keyring *n* portachiavi *m inv*
key signature *n* Mus armatura *f* di chiave
keystroke *n* Comput keystroke *m inv*
keyword *n* parola *f* chiave
key worker *n* chi lavora in settori, come l'insegnamento, la sanità, la sicurezza, ritenuti essenziali per la vita di una comunità
kg *abbr* (**kilogram**) kg
khaki /'kɑːkɪ/ ①️ *adj* cachi *inv* ②️ *n* cachi *m*
kibbutz /kɪ'bʊts/ *n* (*pl* -**es** *or* -**im**) kibbutz *m inv*
kibosh /'kaɪbʊʃ/ *n* fam **put the** ~ **on something** mandare all'aria qualcosa
✔ **kick** /kɪk/ ①️ *n* calcio *m*; fam (thrill) piacere *m*; **for** ~**s** fam per spasso; **get a** ~ **out of something** trovare un piacere incredibile in qualcosa ②️ *vt* dar calci a; ~ **the bucket** fam crepare ③️ *vi* ‹animal› scalciare; ‹person› dare calci
■ **kick around** ①️ *vi* fam essere in giro ②️ *vt* buttar giù ‹idea›
■ **kick in** *vt* sfondare a calci ‹door›
■ **kick off** *vi* Sport dare il calcio d'inizio; fam iniziare
■ **kick out** *vt* fam (of school, club etc) sbatter fuori
■ **kick up**: *vt* ~ **up a row** fare una scenata
kickback /'kɪkbæk/ *n* fam tangente *f*

k

kick-off n Sport calcio m d'inizio; **for a ~** fam tanto per cominciare

kick-start /'kɪksta:t/ vt mettere in moto ‹motorbike›; rilanciare ‹economy›

◆ **kid** /kɪd/ **1** n capretto m; fam (child) ragazzino, -a mf
2 vt (pt/pp **kidded**) fam prendere in giro
3 vi fam scherzare

kid gloves npl guanti mpl di capretto; **handle somebody with ~** trattare qualcuno con i guanti

kidnap /'kɪdnæp/ vt (pt/pp **napped**) rapire, sequestrare

kidnapper /'kɪdnæpə(r)/ n sequestratore, -trice mf, rapitore, -trice mf

kidnapping /'kɪdnæpɪŋ/ n rapimento m, sequestro m [di persona]

kidney /'kɪdnɪ/ n rene m; Culin rognone m

kidney bean n fagiolo m comune

kidney dialysis n dialisi

kidney failure n collasso m renale

kidney machine n rene m artificiale

kidney-shaped /'kɪdnɪʃeɪpt/ adj a forma di fagiolo

kidney stone n calcolo m renale

◆ **kill** /kɪl/ vt uccidere; fig metter fine a; ammazzare ‹time›
■ **kill off** vt eliminare ‹people›; distruggere ‹plants, insects›

killer /'kɪlə(r)/ n assassino, -a mf; **it was a real ~** fig è stato micidiale

killer instinct n istinto m di uccidere; fig spietatezza f

killer whale n orca f

killing /'kɪlɪŋ/ n uccisione f; (murder) omicidio m

killjoy /'kɪldʒɔɪ/ n guastafeste mf inv

kiln /kɪln/ n fornace f

kilo /'ki:ləʊ/ n chilo m

kilobyte n kilobyte m inv

kilogram n chilogrammo m

kilohertz n chilohertz m inv

kilometre n chilometro m

kilowatt n chilowatt m inv

kilt /kɪlt/ n kilt m inv (gonnellino degli scozzesi)

kimono /kɪ'məʊnəʊ/ n kimono m inv, kimono m inv

kin /kɪn/ n congiunti mpl; **next of ~** parente m stretto

◆ **kind¹** /kaɪnd/ n genere m, specie f; (brand, type) tipo m; **what ~ of car?** che tipo di macchina?; **~ of** fam alquanto; **two of a ~** due della stessa specie

kind² adj gentile, buono; **~ to animals** amante degli animali; **~ regards** cordiali saluti

kindergarten /'kɪndəga:tn/ n asilo m infantile

kind-hearted /-'ha:tɪd/ adj ‹person› di [buon] cuore

kindle /'kɪndl/ vt accendere

kindly /'kaɪndlɪ/ **1** adj (**-ier, -iest**) benevolo
2 adv gentilmente; (if you please) per favore

kindness /'kaɪndnɪs/ n gentilezza f

kindred /'kɪndrɪd/ adj **she's a ~ spirit** è la mia/sua/tua anima gemella

kinetic /kɪ'netɪk/ adj cinetico

kinetics /kɪ'netɪks/ n cinetica f

◆ **king** /kɪŋ/ n re m inv

kingdom /'kɪŋdəm/ n regno m

kingfisher /'kɪŋfɪʃə(r)/ n martin m inv pescatore

kingly /'kɪŋlɪ/ adj also fig regale

king-sized /'kɪŋsaɪzd/ adj ‹cigarette› king-size inv, lungo; ‹bed› matrimoniale grande

kink /kɪŋk/ n attorcigliamento m

kinky /'kɪŋkɪ/ adj fam bizzarro

kinship /'kɪnʃɪp/ n (blood relationship) parentela f; (empathy) affinità f

kiosk /'ki:ɒsk/ n chiosco m; (Teleph) cabina f telefonica

kip /kɪp/ **1** n fam pisolino m; **have a ~** schiacciare un pisolino
2 vi (pt/pp **kipped**) fam dormire

kipper /'kɪpə(r)/ n aringa f affumicata

kirk /kɜ:k/ n Scottish chiesa f

◆ **kiss** /kɪs/ **1** n bacio m
2 vt baciare
3 vi baciarsi

kiss of death n colpo m di grazia

kiss of life n respirazione f bocca a bocca; **give somebody the ~** fare la respirazione bocca a bocca a qualcuno

kissogram /'kɪsəgræm/ n servizio (m) commerciale in cui un messaggio di auguri viene scherzosamente recapitato con un bacio da una ragazza in abiti succinti

kit /kɪt/ **1** n equipaggiamento m, kit m inv; (tools) attrezzi mpl; (construction kit) pezzi mpl da montare, kit m inv
2 vt (pt/pp **kitted**) **~ out** equipaggiare

kitbag /'kɪtbæg/ n sacco m a spalla

◆ **kitchen** /'kɪtʃɪn/ **1** n cucina f
2 attrib di cucina

kitchenette /kɪtʃɪ'net/ n cucinino m

kitchen foil n carta f di alluminio

kitchen garden n orto m

kitchen paper n carta f da cucina

kitchen roll n Scottex® m inv

kitchen scales npl bilancia f da cucina

kitchen sink n lavello m; **everything bar the ~** fig proprio tutto quanto

kitchen-sink drama n teatro m neorealista

kitchen towel n Scottex® m inv

◆ indicates a very frequent word

kitchen unit *n* elemento *m* componibile da cucina

kitchenware *n* (crockery) stoviglie *fpl*; (implements) utensili *mpl* da cucina

kite /kaɪt/ *n* aquilone *m*

kitemark /'kaɪtmɑːk/ *n* Br marchio *m* di conformità alle norme britanniche

kith /kɪθ/ *n* ~ **and kin** amici e parenti *mpl*

kitsch /kɪtʃ/ *n* kitsch *m inv*

kitten /'kɪtn/ *n* gattino *m*

kitty /'kɪtɪ/ *n* (money) cassa *f* comune

kiwi /'kiːwiː/ *n* Zool kiwi *m inv*

kiwi fruit *n* kiwi *m inv*

kleptomania /kleptə'meɪnɪə/ *n* cleptomania *f*

kleptomaniac /kleptə'meɪnɪæk/ *n* cleptomane *mf*

km *abbr* (**kilometre**) km

kmh *abbr* (**kilometres per hour**) km/h

knack /næk/ *n* tecnica *f*; **have the ~ for doing something** avere la capacità di fare qualcosa

knapsack /'næpsæk/ *n* sacco *m* da montagna

knave /neɪv/ *n* (in cards) fante *m*; (rogue) furfante *m*

knead /niːd/ *vt* impastare

⚔ **knee** /niː/ *n* ginocchio *m*; **go down on one's ~s to somebody** inginocchiarsi davanti a qualcuno

kneecap /'niːkæp/ *n* rotula *f*

knee-deep /ˌniː'diːp/ *adj* **the water was ~** l'acqua arrivava alle ginocchia

kneel /niːl/ *vi* (*pt/pp* **knelt**) ~ **[down]** inginocchiarsi; **be ~ing** essere inginocchiato

knee-length *adj* ‹boots› alto; ‹skirt› al ginocchio; ‹socks› lungo

knee-pad *n* ginocchiera *f*

knees-up /'niːzʌp/ *n* Br fam festa *f*

knell /nel/ *n* campana *f* a morto; **sound the death ~ for something** segnare la fine di qualcosa

knelt /nelt/ ▶ KNEEL

knew /njuː/ ▶ KNOW

knickerbocker glory /nɪkəbɒkə'ɡlɔːrɪ/ *n* coppa *f* [gelato] gigante

knickers /'nɪkəz/ *npl* mutandine *fpl*

knick-knacks /'nɪknæks/ *npl* ninnoli *mpl*

knife /naɪf/ ⃞1 *n* (*pl* **knives**) coltello *m* ⃞2 *vt* fam accoltellare

knife-edge *n* **be on a ~** ‹person› trovarsi sul filo del rasoio; ‹negotiations› essere appeso a un filo

knifepoint *n* **at ~** sotto la minaccia di un coltello

knife sharpener *n* affilacoltelli *m inv*

knight /naɪt/ ⃞1 *n* cavaliere *m*; (in chess) cavallo *m* ⃞2 *vt* nominare cavaliere

knighthood /'naɪthʊd/ *n* **receive a ~** ricevere il titolo di cavaliere

knit /nɪt/ *vt/i* (*pt/pp* **knitted**) lavorare a maglia; **~ one, purl one** un diritto, un rovescio; **~ one's brow** aggrottare le sopracciglia

knitted /'nɪtɪd/ *adj* lavorato a maglia

knitting /'nɪtɪŋ/ *n* lavorare *m* a maglia; (product) lavoro *m* a maglia

knitting needle *n* ferro *m* da calza

knitwear /'nɪtweə(r)/ *n* maglieria *f*

knives /naɪvz/ *npl* ▶ KNIFE

knob /nɒb/ *n* pomello *m*; (of stick) pomo *m*; (of butter) noce *f*

knobbly /'nɒblɪ/ *adj* nodoso; (bony) spigoloso

⚔ **knock** /nɒk/ ⃞1 *n* colpo *m*; **there was a ~ at the door** hanno bussato alla porta ⃞2 *vt* bussare a ‹door›; fam (criticize) denigrare; **~ a hole in something** fare un buco in qualcosa; **~ one's head** battere la testa (**on** contro) ⃞3 *vi* (at door) bussare

■ **knock about** ⃞1 *vt* malmenare ⃞2 *vi* fam girovagare

■ **knock back** *vt* fam (drink quickly) buttar giù tutto d'un fiato

■ **knock down** *vt* far cadere; (with fist) stendere con un pugno; (in car) investire; (demolish) abbattere; fam (reduce) ribassare ‹price›

■ **knock off** ⃞1 *vt* fam (steal) fregare, fam (complete quickly) fare alla bell'e meglio ⃞2 *vi* fam (cease work) staccare

■ **knock out** *vt* eliminare, (make unconscious) mettere K.O.; fam (anaesthetize) addormentare

■ **knock over** *vt* rovesciare; (in car) investire

■ **knock up** *vt* fam (prepare quickly) buttare giù; sl (make pregnant) mettere incinta

knockabout *n* Sport **have a ~** palleggiare

knock-down furniture *n* mobili *mpl* scomponibili

knock-down price *n* prezzo *m* stracciato

knocker /'nɒkə(r)/ *n* battente *m*; (critic) denigratore, -trice *mf*

knocking /'nɒkɪŋ/ *n* (on door) colpi *mpl*; Auto battito *m* in testa

knocking-off time /nɒkɪŋ'ɒf/ *n* **~ is five o'clock** si stacca alle cinque

knock-kneed /-'niːd/ *adj* con gambe storte

knock-on effect *n* implicazioni *fpl*

knock-out *n* knock-out *m inv*; **be a ~** fig essere uno schianto

knoll /nəʊl/ *n* collinetta *f*

knot /nɒt/ ⃞1 *n* nodo *m*; **to tie the ~** fam convolare a giuste nozze ···⊱

2 *vt* (*pt/pp* **knotted**) annodare; Br fam **get**
~**ted!** vai a farti friggere!
knotty /'nɒtɪ/ *adj* (**-ier, -iest**) fam spinoso
ⓢ **know** /nəʊ/ 1 *vt* (*pt* **knew**, *pp* **known**)
sapere; conoscere ‹person, place›; (recognize)
riconoscere; **get to** ~ **somebody** conoscere
qualcuno; ~ **how to swim** sapere nuotare;
~ **right from wrong** saper distinguere il
bene dal male
2 *vi* sapere; **did you** ~ **about this?** lo
sapevi?
3 *n* **in the** ~ fam al corrente
■ **know of** *vt* conoscere; **not that I** ~ **of** non
che io sappia
know-all *n* fam sapientone, -a *mf*
know-how *n* know-how *m inv*
knowing /'nəʊɪŋ/ *adj* d'intesa
knowingly /'nəʊɪŋlɪ/ *adv* (intentionally)
consapevolmente; ‹smile etc› con un aria
d'intesa
ⓢ **knowledge** /'nɒlɪdʒ/ *n* conoscenza *f*
knowledgeable, knowledgable
/'nɒlɪdʒəbl/ *adj* ben informato
known /nəʊn/ 1 ▶ KNOW
2 *adj* noto
knuckle /'nʌkl/ *n* nocca *f*
■ **knuckle down** *vi* darci sotto (**to** con)

■ **knuckle under** *vi* sottomettersi
knuckle-duster *n* tirapugni *m inv*
koala [bear] /kəʊˈɑːlə/ *n* koala *m inv*
Koran /kəˈrɑːn/ *n* Corano *m*
Korea /kəˈrɪə/ *n* Corea *f*
Korean /kəˈrɪən/ *adj* & *n* coreano, -a *mf*;
(language) coreano *m*
kosher /'kəʊʃə(r)/ *adj* kasher *inv*
Kosovan /'kɒsəvən/ 1 *adj* kosovaro
2 *n* kosovaro, -a *mf*
Kosovo /'kɒsəvəʊ/ *n* Kosovo *m*
kowtow /kaʊˈtaʊ/ *vi* piegarsi
kph *abbr* (**kilometres per hour**) km/h
kudos /'kjuːdɒs/ *n* fam gloria *f*
Kurd /'kɜːd/ 1 *n* curdo, -a *mf*
2 *adj* curdo
Kurdish /'kɜːdɪʃ/ *adj* & *n* (language) curdo *m*
Kurdistan /kɜːdɪˈstɑːn/ *n* Kurdistan *m*
Kuwait /kʊˈweɪt/ *n* Kuwait *m*
Kuwaiti /kʊˈweɪtɪ/ *adj* & *n* kuwaitiano,
-a *mf*
kW *abbr* (**kilowatt**) kW
kWh *abbr* (**kilowatt-hour**) kWh
Kyrgyzstan /ˌkɪəgɪˈstɑːn, kɜːgɪ-, -ˈstæn/ *n*
Kirghizistan *m*

L l

l, L /el/ *n* (letter) l, L *f inv*
L *abbr* 1 (**lake**) L
2 (**large**) L
3 (**learner**) P
4 (**left**) sinistra *f*
5 (**line**) v
6 (**litre(s)**) l
lab /læb/ *n* fam laboratorio *m*
lab assistant *n* assistente *mf* di
laboratorio
lab coat *n* camice *m*
label /'leɪbl/ 1 *n* etichetta *f*
2 *vt* (*pt/pp* **labelled**) mettere
un'etichetta a; fig etichettare ‹person›
labelling /'leɪbəlɪŋ/ *n* (act) etichettatura *f*
labor /'leɪbə(r)/ *n* & *v* Am = LABOUR
laboratory /ləˈbɒrətrɪ/ *n* laboratorio *m*
laborer /'leɪbərə(r)/ *n* Am = LABOURER
laborious /ləˈbɔːrɪəs/ *adj* laborioso
laboriously /ləˈbɔːrɪəslɪ/ *adv* in modo
laborioso
labor union /'leɪbə/ *n* Am sindacato *m*

ⓢ **labour** /'leɪbə(r)/ 1 *n* lavoro *m*; (workers)
manodopera *f*; Med doglie *fpl*; **be in** ~ avere
le doglie; **L**~ Pol partito *m* laburista
2 *attrib* Pol laburista
3 *vi* lavorare
4 *vt* ~ **the point** fig ribadire il concetto
labour camp *n* campo *m* di lavoro
laboured /'leɪbəd/ *adj* ‹breathing›
affannato
labourer /'leɪbərə(r)/ *n* manovale *m*
labour exchange *n* (old) ufficio *m* di
collocamento
labour force *n* manodopera *f*
labouring /'leɪbərɪŋ/ *n* lavoro *m* manuale
labour-intensive *adj* ad uso intensivo di
lavoro; **be** ~ richiedere molta manodopera
labour market *n* mercato *m* del lavoro
Labour Party *n* Partito *m* laburista
labour relations *npl* relazioni *fpl*
industriali
labour-saving /'leɪbəseɪvɪŋ/ *adj* che fa
risparmiare lavoro e fatica
labour ward *n* reparto *m* maternità
labrador /'læbrədɔː(r)/ *n* (dog) labrador
m inv

ⓢ indicates a very frequent word

lab technician *n* tecnico, -a *mf* di laboratorio

laburnum /lə'bɜːnəm/ *n* maggiociondolo *m*

labyrinth /'læbərɪnθ/ *n* labirinto *m*

lace /leɪs/ **1** *n* pizzo *m*; (of shoe) laccio *m*
2 *attrib* di pizzo
3 *vt* allacciare ‹shoes›; correggere ‹drink›

lacerate /'læsəreɪt/ *vt* lacerare

laceration /læsə'reɪʃn/ *n* lacerazione *f*

lace-up [shoe] *n* scarpa *f* stringata

◆ **lack** /læk/ **1** *n* mancanza *f*; ∼ **of interest** disinteressamento *m*; ∼ **of evidence** insufficienza *f* di prove
2 *vt* **the programme** ∼**s originality** il programma manca di originalità; **I** ∼ **the time** mi manca il tempo
3 *vi* **be** ∼**ing** mancare; **be** ∼**ing in something** mancare di qualcosa

lackadaisical /lækə'deɪzɪkl/ *adj* senza entusiasmo

lackey /'lækɪ/ *n* lacchè *m inv*

lackluster /'læklʌstə(r)/ *adj* Am = LACKLUSTRE

lacklustre /'læklʌstə(r)/ *adj* scialbo

laconic /lə'kɒnɪk/ *adj* laconico

laconically /lə'kɒnɪklɪ/ *adv* laconicamente

lacquer /'lækə(r)/ *n* lacca *f*

lactate /læk'teɪt/ *vi* produrre latte

lactation /læk'teɪʃn/ *n* lattazione *f*

lacy /'leɪsɪ/ *adj* di pizzo

lad /læd/ *n* ragazzo *m*

ladder /'lædə(r)/ **1** *n* scala *f*; (in tights) smagliatura *f*
2 *vi* smagliarsi

ladderproof /'lædəpruːf/ *adj* ‹stockings› indemagliabile

laddish /'lædɪʃ/ *adj* fam da ragazzacci

laden /'leɪdn/ *adj* carico (with di)

la-di-da /lɑːdɪ'dɑː/ *adj* affettato

ladle /'leɪdl/ **1** *n* mestolo *m*
2 *vt* ∼ **[out]** versare (col mestolo)

◆ **lady** /'leɪdɪ/ *n* signora *f*; (title) Lady *f*; **ladies [room]** *n* bagno *m* per donne

ladybird, Am **ladybug** *n* coccinella *f*

lady-in-waiting /-weɪtɪŋ/ *n* dama *f* di corte

ladykiller *n* fam dongiovanni *m inv*

ladylike /'leɪdɪlaɪk/ *adj* signorile

lady mayoress *n* moglie *f* del Lord Mayor

Ladyship *n* **her/your L**∼ (to aristocrat) ≈ Signora Contessa

lady's maid *n* cameriera *f* personale

lag¹ /læg/ *vi* (*pt/pp* **lagged**) ∼ **behind** restare indietro

lag² *vt* (*pt/pp* **lagged**) isolare ‹pipes›

lager /'lɑːgə(r)/ *n* birra *f* chiara

lager lout *n* Br pej giovinastro *m* ubriaco

lagging /'lægɪn/ *n* (for pipes) materiale *m* isolante

lagoon /lə'guːn/ *n* laguna *f*

laid /leɪd/ **1** ▶ LAY³
2 sl **get** ∼ farsi scopare

laid-back *adj* fam rilassato

laid up *adj* **be** ∼ essere allettato

lain /leɪn/ ▶ LIE²

lair /leə(r)/ *n* tana *f*

laird /leəd/ *n* (in Scotland) proprietario *m* terriero

laity /'leɪətɪ/ *n* laicato *m*

lake /leɪk/ *n* lago *m*; **L**∼ **Garda** lago di Garda

lakeside /'leɪksaɪd/ **1** *n* riva *f* del lago
2 *attrib* ‹café, scenery› della/sulla riva del lago

lama /'lɑːmə/ *n* lama *m inv*

lamb /læm/ *n* agnello *m*

lambast[e] /læm'beɪst/ *vt* biasimare ‹person, organization›

lamb chop *n* cotoletta *f* d'agnello

lambskin *n* pelle *f* d'agnello

lambswool *n* lana *f* d'agnello, lambswool *m inv*

lame /leɪm/ *adj* zoppo; fig ‹argument› zoppicante; ‹excuse› traballante

lamé /'lɑːmeɪ/ *n* lamé *m*

lame duck *n* (person) inetto, -a *mf*; (firm) azienda *f* in cattive acque

lament /lə'ment/ **1** *n* lamento *m*
2 *vt* lamentare
3 *vi* lamentarsi

lamentable /'læməntəbl/ *adj* deplorevole

laminated /'læmineɪtɪd/ *adj* laminato

lamp /læmp/ *n* lampada *f*; (in street) lampione *m*

lampoon /læm'puːn/ **1** *n* satira *f*
2 *vt* fare oggetto di satira

lamp-post *n* lampione *m*

lampshade /'læmpʃeɪd/ *n* paralume *m*

lance /lɑːns/ **1** *n* lancia *f*
2 *vt* Med incidere

lance corporal *n* appuntato *m*

lancet /'lɑːnsɪt/ *n* Med bisturi *m inv*

◆ **land** /lænd/ **1** *n* terreno *m*; (country) paese *m*; (as opposed to sea) terra *f*; **plot of** ∼ pezzo *m* di terreno
2 *vt* Naut sbarcare; fam ‹obtain› assicurarsi; **be** ∼**ed with something** fam ritrovarsi fra capo e collo qualcosa
3 *vi* Aeron atterrare; (fall) cadere; ∼ **on one's feet** fig cadere in piedi
■ **land up** *vi* fam finire

land agent *n* (on estate) fattore *m*

land army *n* gruppo (*m*) di lavoratrici agricole durante la seconda guerra mondiale

landfall *n* Naut approdo *m*; **make** ∼ (reach) approdare; (sight) avvistare terra

landfill site *n* discarica (*f*) in cui i rifiuti vengono interrati

landing /ˈlændɪŋ/ *n* Naut sbarco *m*; Aeron atterraggio *m*; (top of stairs) pianerottolo *m*

landing card *n* Aeron, Naut carta *f* di sbarco

landing craft *n* mezzo *m* da sbarco

landing gear *n* Aeron carrello *m* d'atterraggio

landing lights *npl* luci *fpl* d'atterraggio

landing party *n* Mil reparto *m* da sbarco

landing-stage *n* pontile *m* da sbarco

landing strip *n* pista *f* d'atterraggio

landlady *n* proprietaria *f*; (of flat) padrona *f* di casa

landlocked *adj* privo di sbocco sul mare

landlord *n* proprietario *m*; (of flat) padrone *m* di casa

landlubber *n* marinaio *m* d'acqua dolce

landmark *n* punto *m* di riferimento; fig pietra *f* miliare

land mass *n* continente *m*

landmine *n* Mil mina *f* terrestre

landowner *n* proprietario, -a *mf* terriero, -a

landscape *n* paesaggio *m*

landscape architect *n* paesaggista *mf*

landscape gardener *n* paesaggista *mf*

landslide *n* frana *f*; Pol valanga *f* di voti

landslip *n* smottamento *m*

lane /leɪn/ *n* sentiero *m*; Auto, Sport corsia *f*

lane closure *n* (on motorway) chiusura *f* di corsia

lane markings *n* (on road) [strisce *fpl* di] mezzeria *f*

langoustine /ˈlɒŋɡustiːn/ *n* scampo *m*

ꞔ **language** /ˈlæŋɡwɪdʒ/ *n* lingua *f*; (speech, style, Comput) linguaggio *m*

language barrier *n* barriera *f* linguistica

language laboratory *n* laboratorio *m* linguistico

languid /ˈlæŋɡwɪd/ *adj* languido

languidly /ˈlæŋɡwɪdlɪ/ *adv* languidamente

languish /ˈlæŋɡwɪʃ/ *vi* languire

languor /ˈlæŋɡə(r)/ *n* languore *m*

lank /læŋk/ *adj* ‹hair› liscio

lanky /ˈlæŋkɪ/ *adj* (**-ier**, **-iest**) allampanato

lanolin /ˈlænəlɪn/ *n* lanolina *f*

lantern /ˈlæntən/ *n* lanterna *f*

lanyard /ˈlænjəd/ *n* Naut (rope) cima *f*

Laos /ˈlɑːɒs, laʊs/ *n* Laos *m*

lap¹ /læp/ *n* grembo *m*

lap² ⬜1 *n* Sport (of journey) tappa *f*; ~ **of honour** giro *m* d'onore
⬜2 *vi* (*pt/pp* **lapped**) ‹water› ~ **against** lambire
⬜3 *vt* Sport doppiare

lap³ *vt* (*pt/pp* **lapped**) ~ **up** bere avidamente; bersi completamente ‹lies›; credere ciecamente a ‹praise›

lap and shoulder belt *n* Auto, Aeron cintura *f* di sicurezza

laparoscope /ˈlæpərəskəʊp/ *n* laparoscopio *m*

laparoscopy /læpəˈrɒskəpɪ/ *n* laparoscopia *f*

lap belt *n* Auto, Aeron cintura *f* di sicurezza addominale

lapdog /ˈlæpdɒɡ/ *n* cane *m* da salotto; **he's her** ~ è il suo cagnolino

lapel /ləˈpel/ *n* bavero *m*

Lapland /ˈlæplænd/ *n* Lapponia *f*

lapse /læps/ ⬜1 *n* sbaglio *m*; (moral) sbandamento *m* [morale]; (of time) intervallo *m*
⬜2 *vi* (expire) scadere; (morally) scivolare; ~ **into** cadere in

laptop /ˈlæptɒp/ *n* ~ **[computer]** computer *m inv* portatile, laptop *m inv*

larceny /ˈlɑːsənɪ/ *n* furto *m*

larch /lɑːtʃ/ *n* larice *m*

lard /lɑːd/ *n* strutto *m*

larder /ˈlɑːdə(r)/ *n* dispensa *f*

ꞔ **large** /lɑːdʒ/ *adj & adv* grande; ‹number, amount› grande, grosso; **by and** ~ in complesso; **at** ~ in libertà; (in general) ampiamente

large intestine *n* intestino *m* crasso

largely /ˈlɑːdʒlɪ/ *adv* ~ **because of** in gran parte a causa di

largeness /ˈlɑːdʒnɪs/ *n* grandezza *f*

large-scale *adj* ‹map› a grande scala; ‹operation› su larga scala

largesse /lɑːˈʒes/ *n* generosità *f*

lark¹ /lɑːk/ *n* (bird) allodola *f*

lark² *n* (joke) burla *f*

■ **lark about** *vi* giocherellare

larva /ˈlɑːvə/ *n* (*pl* **-vae** /ˈlɑːviː/) larva *f*

laryngitis /lærɪnˈdʒaɪtɪs/ *n* laringite *f*

larynx /ˈlærɪŋks/ *n* laringe *f*

lasagne /ləˈzænjə/ *n* lasagne *fpi*

lascivious /ləˈsɪvɪəs/ *adj* lascivo

laser /ˈleɪzə(r)/ *n* laser *m inv*

laser disc *n* disco *m* laser

laser printer *n* stampante *f* laser

laser treatment *n* laserterapia *f*

lash /læʃ/ ⬜1 *n* frustata *f*; (eyelash) ciglio *m*
⬜2 *vt* (whip) frustare; (tie) legare fermamente

■ **lash out** *vi* attaccare; (spend) sperperare (on in)

lashings /ˈlæʃɪŋz/ *npl* ~ **of** fam una marea di

lass /læs/ *n* ragazzina *f*

lasso /ləˈsuː/ *n* lazo *m*

ꞔ **last** /lɑːst/ ⬜1 *adj* (final) ultimo; (recent) scorso; ~ **year** l'anno scorso; ~ **night** ieri

sera; **at ∼** alla fine; **at ∼!** finalmente!; **that's the ∼ straw** fam questa è l'ultima goccia
2 *n* ultimo, -a *mf*; **the ∼ but one** il penultimo
3 *adv* per ultimo; (last time) l'ultima volta; **∼ but not least** per ultimo ma non il meno importante
4 *vi* durare

last-ditch *adj* ‹attempt› disperato

lasting /'lɑ:stɪŋ/ *adj* durevole

lastly /'lɑ:stlɪ/ *adv* infine

last-minute *adj* all'ultimo minuto

last name *n* (surname) cognome *m*

last rites *npl* Relig estrema unzione *f*

Last Supper *n* Ultima Cena *f*

latch /lætʃ/ *n* chiavistello *m*; (on gate) saliscendi *m inv*; **leave the door on the ∼** chiudere la porta senza far scattare la serratura
■ **latch on to** *vt* fissarsi con ‹person, idea›

latchkey /lætʃki:/ *n* chiave *f* di casa

latchkey child *n* bambino (*m*) che ha le chiavi di casa in quanto i genitori lavorano

✦ **late** /leɪt/ 1 *adj* (delayed) in ritardo; (at a late hour) tardo; (deceased) defunto; **it's ∼** (at night) è tardi; **in ∼** November alla fine di novembre; **of ∼** recentemente; **be a ∼ developer** ‹child› essere lento nell'apprendimento
2 *adv* tardi; **stay up ∼** stare alzati fino a tardi

latecomer /'leɪtkʌmə(r)/ *n* ritardatario, -a *mf*, (to political party etc) nuovo, -a arrivato, -a *mf*

late developer *n* (child) **be a ∼** essere tardivo

lately /'leɪtlɪ/ *adv* recentemente

lateness /'leɪtnɪs/ *n* ora *f* tarda; (delay) ritardo *m*

late-night *adj* ‹film› ultimo; **it's ∼ shopping on Thursdays** i negozi rimangono aperti fino a tardi il giovedì

latent /'leɪtnt/ *adj* latente

✦ **later** /'leɪtə(r)/ 1 *adj* ‹train› che parte più tardi; ‹edition› più recente
2 *adv* più tardi; **∼ on** più tardi, dopo

lateral /'lætərəl/ *adj* laterale

late riser /'raɪzə(r)/ *n* dormiglione, -a *mf*

latest /'leɪtɪst/ 1 *adj* ultimo; (most recent) più recente; **the ∼ [news]** le ultime notizie
2 *n* **six o'clock at the ∼** alle sei al più tardi

latex /'leɪteks/ *n* la[t]tice *m*

lath /læθ/ *n* assicella *f*

lathe /leɪð/ *n* tornio *m*

lather /'lɑ:ðə(r)/ 1 *n* schiuma *f*
2 *vt* insaponare
3 *vi* far schiuma

Latin /'lætɪn/ 1 *adj* latino
2 *n* latino *m*

Latin America *n* America *f* Latina

Latin American *n & adj* latino-americano *mf*

Latino /lə'ti:nəʊ/ *n* Am latino-americano, -a *mf*

latitude /'lætɪtjuːd/ *n* Geog latitudine *f*; fig libertà *f* d'azione

latrine /lə'triːn/ *n* latrina *f*

✦ **latter** /'lætə(r)/ 1 *adj* ultimo
2 *n* **the ∼** quest'ultimo

latter-day *adj* moderno

latterly /'lætəlɪ/ *adv* ultimamente

lattice /'lætɪs/ *n* traliccio *m*

lattice window *n* finestra *f* con vetri a losanghe

lattice-work *n* intelaiatura *f* a traliccio

Latvia /'lætvɪə/ *n* Lettonia *f*

Latvian /'lætvɪən/ *adj & n* lettone *mf*; (language) lettone *m*

laudable /'lɔːdəbl/ *adj* lodevole

laudatory /'lɔːdətrɪ/ *adj* elogiativo

✦ **laugh** /lɑːf/ 1 *n* risata *f*
2 *vi* ridere (**at/about** di); **∼ at somebody** (mock) prendere in giro qualcuno
■ **laugh off** *vt* ridere di ‹criticism›

laughable /'lɑːfəbl/ *adj* ridicolo

laughing gas /'lɑːfɪŋ/ *n* gas *m inv* esilarante

laughing stock *n* zimbello *m*

laughter /'lɑːftə(r)/ *n* risata *f*

launch¹ /lɔːntʃ/ *n* (boat) lancia *f*

✦ **launch²** 1 *n* lancio *m*; (of ship) varo *m*
2 *vt* lanciare ‹rocket, product›, varare ‹ship›; sferrare ‹attack›
■ **launch into** *vt* intraprendere ‹career›; imbarcarsi in ‹speech›

launch[ing] pad /'lɔːntʃ[ɪŋ]/ *n* piattaforma *f* di lancio; fig trampolino *m* di lancio

launcher /'lɔːntʃə(r)/ *n* lanciamissili *m inv*

launch pad *n* piattaforma *f* di lancio

launder /'lɔːndə(r)/ *vt* lavare e stirare; **∼ money** fig riciclare denaro sporco

launderette /lɔːndə'ret/ *n* lavanderia *f* automatica

laundry /'lɔːndrɪ/ *n* lavanderia *f*; (clothes) bucato *m*

laureate /'lɒrɪət/ *adj* **poet ∼** poeta *m* di corte; **Nobel ∼** vincitore, -trice *mf* del Nobel

laurel /'lɒrəl/ *n* alloro *m*; **rest on one's ∼s** fig dormire sugli allori

lav /læv/ *n* Br fam gabinetto *m*

lava /'lɑːvə/ *n* lava *f*

lavatorial /lævə'tɔːrɪəl/ *adj* ‹humour› scatologico

lavatory /'lævətrɪ/ *n* gabinetto *m*

lavender /'lævəndə(r)/ *n* lavanda *f*

lavender blue *adj* color lavanda

lavish /'lævɪʃ/ 1 *adj* copioso; (wasteful) prodigo; **on a ∼ scale** su vasta scala ····❯

2 *vt* ~ **something on somebody** ricoprire qualcuno di qualcosa

lavishly /ˈlævɪʃlɪ/ *adv* copiosamente

✓ **law** /lɔː/ *n* legge *f*; **study** ~ studiare giurisprudenza, studiare legge; ~ **and order** ordine *m* pubblico; **take the** ~ **into one's own hands** farsi giustizia da sé; ~ **of the jungle** legge della giungla

law-abiding /ˈlɔːəbaɪdɪŋ/ *adj* che rispetta la legge

law and order *n* ordine *m* pubblico

lawbreaker /ˈlɔːbreɪkə(r)/ *n* persona *f* che infrange la legge

law court *n* tribunale *m*

lawful /ˈlɔːfʊl/ *adj* legittimo

lawfully /ˈlɔːfʊlɪ/ *adv* legittimamente

lawfulness /ˈlɔːfʊlnɪs/ *n* legalità *f*

lawless /ˈlɔːlɪs/ *adj* senza legge

lawmaker /ˈlɔːmeɪkə(r)/ *n* legislatore *m*

lawn /lɔːn/ *n* prato *m* [all'inglese]

lawnmower /ˈlɔːnməʊə(r)/ *n* tosaerba *m inv*

law school *n* facoltà *f* di giurisprudenza

lawsuit /ˈlɔːsuːt/ *n* causa *f*

✓ **lawyer** /ˈlɔːjə(r)/ *n* avvocato *m*

lax /læks/ *adj* negligente; ‹morals etc› lassista

laxative /ˈlæksətɪv/ *n* lassativo *m*

laxity /ˈlæksətɪ/ *n* lassismo *m*

lay¹ /leɪ/ *adj* laico, profano fig

lay² ▶ LIE²

✓ **lay³** **1** *vt* (*pt/pp* **laid**) porre, mettere; apparecchiare ‹table›
2 *vi* ‹hen› fare le uova
■ **lay aside** *vt* mettere da parte
■ **lay down** *vt* posare; stabilire ‹rules, conditions›
■ **lay in** *vt* farsi una scorta di ‹coal, supplies etc›
■ **lay into** *vt* sl picchiare
■ **lay off** **1** *vt* licenziare ‹workers›
2 *vi* fam (stop) ~ **off!** smettila!
■ **lay on** *vt* (organize) organizzare
■ **lay out** *vt* (display, set forth) esporre; (plan) pianificare ‹garden›; (spend) sborsare; Typ impaginare
■ **lay up**: *vt* **I was laid up in bed for a week** sono stato costretto a letto per una settimana

layabout /ˈleɪəbaʊt/ *n* fannullone, -a *mf*

lay-by *n* piazzola *f* di sosta

✓ **layer** /ˈleɪə(r)/ *n* strato *m*

layette /leɪˈet/ *n* corredino *m*

layman /ˈleɪmən/ *n* profano *m*

lay-off /ˈleɪɒf/ *n* (permanent) licenziamento *m*; (temporary) sospensione *f*

layout /ˈleɪaʊt/ *n* disposizione *f*; Typ impaginazione *f*, layout *m inv*

lay preacher *n* predicatore *m* laico

───────────────

✓ indicates a very frequent word

laze /leɪz/ *vi* ~ **[about]** oziare

lazily /ˈleɪzɪlɪ/ *adv* ‹move, wander etc› pigramente

laziness /ˈleɪzɪnɪs/ *n* pigrizia *f*

lazy /ˈleɪzɪ/ *adj* (**-ier, -iest**) pigro

lazybones /ˈleɪzɪbəʊnz/ *n* poltrone, -a *mf*

lazy eye *n* ambliopia *f*

lb *abbr* (**pound**) libbra

LCD *n abbr* (**liquid crystal display**) LCD *m*

lead¹ /led/ *n* piombo *m*; (of pencil) mina *f*

✓ **lead²** /liːd/ **1** *n* guida *f*; (leash) guinzaglio *m*; (flex) filo *m*; (clue) indizio *m*; Theat parte *f* principale; (distance ahead) distanza *f* (**over** su); **in the** ~ in testa; **follow sb's** ~ seguire l'esempio di qualcuno
2 *vt* (*pt/pp* **led**) condurre; dirigere ‹expedition, party etc›; (induce) indurre; ~ **the way** mettersi, in testa; ~ **into temptation** indurre in tentazione
3 *vi* (be in front) condurre; (in race, competition) essere in testa
■ **lead astray** *vt* sviare
■ **lead away** *vt* portar via
■ **lead on** *vt* ingannare
■ **lead off** **1** *vi* (begin) cominciare
2 *vt* (take away) portare via
■ **lead to** *vt* portare a
■ **lead up to** *vt* preludere a; **the period** ~**ing up to the election** il periodo precedente le elezioni; **what's this** ~**ing up to?** dove porta questo?

leaded /ˈledɪd/ *adj* con piombo

leaded petrol Br, **leaded gasoline** Am *n* benzina *f* con piombo

leaden /ˈledən/ *adj* di piombo

✓ **leader** /ˈliːdə(r)/ *n* capo *m*; (of orchestra) primo violino *m*; (in newspaper) articolo *m* di fondo

✓ **leadership** /ˈliːdəʃɪp/ *n* direzione *f*, leadership *f inv*; **show** ~ mostrare capacità di comando

leadership contest *n* elezione *f* alla direzione del partito

lead-free /ˈledfriː/ *adj* senza piombo

lead-in /ˈliːdɪn/ *n* presentazione *f*

leading¹ /ˈliːdɪŋ/ *adj* principale

leading² /ˈledɪŋ/ *n* Typ interlinea *f*

leading article *n* articolo *m* di fondo

leading edge *n* Aeron bordo *m* d'attacco; **at the** ~ **of** (technology) all'avanguardia in

leading lady attrice *f* principale

leading light *n* personaggio *m* di spicco

leading man attore *m* principale

leading question *n* domanda *f* che influenza la risposta

lead poisoning *n* saturnismo *m*

lead story *n* articolo *f* principale

✓ **leaf** /liːf/ *n* (*pl* **leaves**) foglia *f*; (of table) asse *f*; fig **take a** ~ **out of sb's book** imparare

la lezione di qualcuno; **turn over a new ~** voltare pagina
■ **leaf through** *vt* sfogliare

leaflet /'li:flɪt/ *n* dépliant *m inv*; (advertising) dépliant *m inv* pubblicitario; (political) manifestino *m*

leafy /'li:fɪ/ *adj* ‹tree› ricco di foglie; ‹wood› molto verde; ‹suburb, area› ricco di verde

⚐ **league** /li:g/ *n* lega *f*; Sport campionato *m*; **be in ~ with** essere in combutta con

league table *n* classifica *f* del campionato

leak /li:k/ **1** *n* (hole) fessura *f*; Naut falla *f*; (of gas & fig) fuga *f*
2 *vi* colare; ‹ship› fare acqua; ‹liquid, gas› fuoriuscire
3 *vt* **~ something to somebody** fig far trapelare qualcosa a qualcuno

leakage /'li:kɪdʒ/ *n* perdita *f*; (of gas & fig) fuga *f*

leaky /'li:kɪ/ *adj* che perde; Naut che fa acqua

lean¹ /li:n/ *adj* magro

⚐ **lean²** **1** *vt* (*pt/pp* **leaned** or **leant** /lent/) appoggiare (**against/on** contro/su); **~ one's elbows on the table** appoggiare i gomiti sul tavolo
2 *vi* appoggiarsi (**against/on** contro/su); (not be straight) pendere; **be ~ing against** essere appoggiato contro; **~ on somebody** (depend on) appoggiarsi a qualcuno; fam (exert pressure on) stare alle calcagna di qualcuno
■ **lean back** *vi* sporgersi indietro
■ **lean forward** *vi* piegarsi in avanti
■ **lean out** *vi* sporgersi
■ **lean over** *vi* piegarsi
■ **lean towards** *vt* (favour) propendere per

leaning /'li:nɪŋ/ **1** *adj* pendente; **the L~ Tower of Pisa** la torre di Pisa, la torre pendente
2 *n* tendenza *f*

leanness /'li:nnɪs/ *n* magrezza *f*

lean-to *n* garage (*m inv*) *adiacente alla casa*

leap /li:p/ **1** *n* salto *m*
2 *vi* (*pt/pp* **leapt** /lept/ or **leaped**) saltare; **he leapt at it** fam l'ha preso al volo

leapfrog /'li:pfrɒg/ *n* cavallina *f*

leap year *n* anno *m* bisestile

⚐ **learn** /lɜ:n/ **1** *vt* (*pt/pp* **learnt** Br or **learned**) imparare; **~ to swim** imparare a nuotare; **I have ~ed that…** (heard) sono venuto a sapere che…; fig **he's ~t his lesson** ha imparato la lezione
2 *vi* imparare; **as I've ~t to my cost** come ho imparato a mie spese

learned /'lɜ:nɪd/ *adj* colto

learner /'lɜ:nə(r)/ *n* also Auto principiante *mf*

⚐ **learning** /'lɜ:nɪŋ/ *n* cultura *f*

learning curve *n* curva *f* di apprendimento

learning difficulties *npl* (of schoolchildren) difficoltà *fpl* d'apprendimento

learning disability *n* difficoltà *fpl* d'apprendimento

lease /li:s/ **1** *n* contratto *m* d'affitto; (rental) affitto *m*; **the job has given him a new ~ of life** grazie al lavoro ha ripreso gusto alla vita
2 *vt* affittare

leasehold /'li:shəʊld/ *n* proprietà *f* in affitto

leaseholder /'li:shəʊldə(r)/ *n titolare* (*mf*) *di un contratto d'affitto*

leash /li:ʃ/ *n* guinzaglio *m*

leasing /'li:sɪŋ/ *n* (by company) leasing *m*; **~ scheme** piano di leasing

⚐ **least** /li:st/ **1** *adj* più piccolo; (smallest amount) meno; **you've got ~ luggage** hai meno bagagli di tutti
2 *n* **the ~** il meno; **that's the ~ of my worries** questa è la cosa che mi preoccupa di meno; **at ~** almeno; **not in the ~** niente affatto
3 *adv* meno; **the ~ expensive wine** il vino meno caro

leather /'leðə(r)/ **1** *n* pelle *f*; (of soles) cuoio *m*
2 *attrib* di pelle/cuoio; **~ jacket** giubbotto *m* di pelle

leathery /'leðərɪ/ *adj* (meat, skin) duro

⚐ **leave** /li:v/ **1** *n* (holiday) congedo *m*; Mil licenza *f*; **on ~** in congedo/licenza; **take one's ~** accomiatarsi; **~ of absence** aspettativa *f*
2 *vt* (*pt/pp* **left**) lasciare; uscire da ‹house, office›; (forget) dimenticare; **there is nothing left** non è rimasto niente; **~ somebody in peace** lasciare in pace qualcuno
3 *vi* andare via; ‹train, bus› partire
■ **leave aside** *vt* (disregard) lasciare da parte
■ **leave behind** *vt* lasciare; (forget) dimenticare
■ **leave out** *vt* omettere; (not put away) lasciare fuori

leaves /li:vz/ ▶ LEAF

leaving /'li:vɪŋ/ *adj* ‹party, present› d'addio

Lebanese /lebə'ni:z/ *adj* & *n* libanese *mf*

Lebanon /'lebənən/ *n* Libano *m*

lecher /'letʃə(r)/ *n* libertino *m*

lecherous /'letʃərəs/ *adj* lascivo

lechery /'letʃərɪ/ *n* lascivia *f*

lectern /'lektɜ:n/ *n* leggio *m*, scannello *m*

lecture /'lektʃə(r)/ **1** *n* conferenza *f*; Univ lezione *f*; (reproof) ramanzina *f*
2 *vi* fare una conferenza (**on** su); Univ insegnare (**on something** qualcosa)
3 *vt* **~ somebody** rimproverare qualcuno

lecturer /'lektʃərə(r)/ *n* conferenziere, -a *mf*; Univ docente *mf* universitario, -a

lecture room *n* Br Univ aula *f* magna

lectureship /'lektʃəʃɪp/ n Br Univ docenza f universitaria

lecture theatre n Br Univ aula f magna

led /led/ ▶ LEAD²

LED abbr (**light-emitting diode**) LED m inv

ledge /ledʒ/ n cornice f; (of window) davanzale m

ledger /'ledʒə(r)/ n libro m mastro

leech /li:tʃ/ n sanguisuga f

leek /li:k/ n porro m

leer /lɪə(r)/ **1** n sguardo m libidinoso
2 vi ~ (**at**) guardare in modo libidinoso

lees /li:z/ npl (wine sediment) fondi mpl

leeway /'li:weɪ/ n fig libertà f di azione

left¹ /left/ ▶ LEAVE

✦**left²** **1** adj sinistro
2 adv a sinistra
3 n (also Pol) sinistra f; **on the ~** a sinistra

left-hand /ˌleft'hænd/ adj di sinistra; **on the ~ side** sulla sinistra

left-hand drive adj ‹car› con la guida a sinistra

left-handed /-'hændɪd/ adj mancino; ‹scissors etc› per mancini

leftie /'leftɪ/ n sinistrorso, -a mf

leftist /'leftɪst/ adj & n sinistrorso, -a mf

left luggage [office] n deposito m bagagli

left-luggage lockers npl deposito m bagagli automatico

leftovers npl rimasugli mpl

left wing n Pol sinistra f; Sport ala f sinistra

left-wing adj Pol di sinistra

left-winger n Pol persona f di sinistra; Sport ala f sinistra

✦**leg** /leg/ **1** n gamba f; ((of animal)) zampa f; (of journey) tappa f; Culin (of chicken) coscia f; (of lamb) cosciotto m; **be on one's last ~s** ‹machine› funzionare per miracolo; **not have a ~ to stand on** non avere una ragione che regga
2 vi ~ **it** fam darsela a gambe

legacy /'legəsɪ/ n lascito m

✦**legal** /'li:gl/ adj legale; **take ~ action** intentare un'azione legale

legal adviser n consulente mf legale

legal aid n gratuito patrocinio m

legal eagle n hum principe m del foro

legal holiday n Am festa f nazionale

legality /lɪ'gælətɪ/ n legalità f

legalization /li:gəlaɪ'zeɪʃn/ n legalizzazione f

legalize /'li:gəlaɪz/ vt legalizzare

legally /'li:gəlɪ/ adv legalmente

legal proceedings npl procedimento m sg giudiziario

legal tender n valuta f a corso legale

legend /'ledʒənd/ n leggenda f

legendary /'ledʒəndərɪ/ adj leggendario

leggings /'legɪŋz/ npl (for baby) ghette fpl; (for woman) pantacollant mpl; (for man) gambali mpl

leggy /'legɪ/ adj ‹person› con le gambe lunghe

Leghorn /'legho:n/ n Livorno f

legibility /ledʒə'bɪlətɪ/ n leggibilità f

legible /'ledʒəbl/ adj leggibile

legibly /'ledʒəblɪ/ adv in modo leggibile

legion /'li:dʒn/ n legione f

legionnaire /li:dʒə'neə(r)/ n Mil legionario m

legionnaire's disease n legionellosi f

✦**legislate** /'ledʒɪsleɪt/ vi legiferare

✦**legislation** /ledʒɪs'leɪʃn/ n legislazione f

legislative /'ledʒɪslətɪv/ adj legislativo

legislator /'ledʒɪsleɪtə(r)/ n legislatore m

legislature /'ledʒɪsleɪtʃə(r)/ n legislatura f

legitimacy /lɪ'dʒɪtɪməsɪ/ n (lawfulness) legittimità f; (of argument) validità f

legitimate /lɪ'dʒɪtɪmət/ adj legittimo; ‹excuse› valido

legitimately /lɪ'dʒɪtɪmətlɪ/ adv legittimamente

legitimize /lɪdʒɪtɪ'maɪz/ vt rendere legittimo

legless /'leglɪs/ adj senza gambe; Br (drunk) ubriaco fradicio

leg-pulling n presa f in giro

legroom n spazio m per le gambe

leg warmer n scaldamuscoli m inv

legwork n fatica f; **do the ~** fare da galoppino

leisure /'leʒə(r)/ n tempo m libero; **at your ~** con comodo

leisure centre n centro m sportivo e ricreativo

leisurely /'leʒəlɪ/ adj senza fretta

leisure time n tempo m libero

leisurewear /'leʒəweə(r)/ n abbigliamento m per il tempo libero

lemming /'lemɪŋ/ n lemming m inv

lemon /'lemən/ n limone m

lemonade /lemə'neɪd/ n limonata f

lemon curd n crema f al limone

lemon juice n (drink) succo m di limone

lemon sole n sogliola f limanda

lemon squash n sciroppo m di limone

lemon tea n tè m inv al limone

lemon tree n limone m

lemon yellow **1** n giallo m limone
2 adj giallo limone

lend /lend/ vt (pt/pp **lent**) prestare; **~ a hand** fig dare una mano; **~ an ear** prestare ascolto; **~ itself to** prestarsi a

---

✦ indicates a very frequent word

lender /'lendə(r)/ n prestatore, -trice mf

lending library /'lendɪn/ n biblioteca f per il prestito

⚡ **length** /leŋθ/ n lunghezza f; (piece) pezzo m; (of wallpaper) parte f; (of visit) durata f; **at ~ a** lungo; (at last) alla fine

lengthen /'leŋθən/ ① vt allungare ② vi allungarsi

lengthways /'leŋθweɪz/ adv per lungo

lengthwise /'leŋθwaɪz/ adv longitudinale

lengthy /'leŋθɪ/ adj (**-ier, -iest**) lungo

lenience /'li:nɪəns/ n indulgenza f

lenient /'li:nɪənt/ adj indulgente

leniently /'li:nɪəntlɪ/ adv con indulgenza

lens /lenz/ n lente f; Phot obiettivo m; (of eye) cristallino m

lens cap n copriobiettivo m

lent ▶ LEND

Lent /lent/ n Quaresima f

lentil /'lentl/ n Bot lenticchia f

Leo /'li:əʊ/ n Astr Leone m

leopard /'lepəd/ n leopardo m

leopardskin /'lepədskɪn/ ① n pelle f di leopardo ② attrib di [pelle di] leopardo

leotard /'li:ətɑːd/ n body m inv

leper /'lepə(r)/ n lebbroso, -a mf; fig appestato, -a mf

leprosy /'leprəsɪ/ n lebbra f

lesbian /'lezbɪən/ ① adj lesbico ② n lesbica f

lesbianism /'lezbɪənɪzm/ n lesbismo m

lesion /'li:ʒn/ n lesione f

Lesotho /lɪ'su:tʊ, lə'səʊtʊ/ n Lesotho m

⚡ **less** /les/ ① adj meno di; **~ and ~** sempre meno ② adv & prep meno ③ n meno m

lessee /le'si:/ n Jur affittuario, -a mf

lessen /'lesn/ vt/i diminuire

lesser /'lesə(r)/ adj minore; **the ~ of two evils** il minore fra i due mali

⚡ **lesson** /'lesn/ n lezione f; **teach somebody a ~** fig dare una lezione a qualcuno

lessor /le'sɔ:/ n Jur locatore, -trice mf

lest /lest/ conj liter per timore che

⚡ **let** /let/ ① vt (pt/pp **let**, pres p **letting**) lasciare, permettere; (rent) affittare; **~ alone** (not to mention) tanto meno; 'to ~' 'affittasi'; **~ us go** andiamo; **~ somebody do something** lasciare fare qualcosa a qualcuno, permettere a qualcuno di fare qualcosa; **~ me know** fammi sapere; **just ~ him try!** che ci provi solamente!; **~ onself in for something** fam impelagarsi in qualcosa ② n Tennis colpo m nullo; Br (lease) contratto m d'affitto ③ vi **~ fly at somebody** aggredire qualcuno

■ **let down** vt sciogliersi ‹hair›; abbassare ‹blinds›; (lengthen) allungare; (disappoint) deludere; **don't ~ me down** conto su di te

■ **let go** ① vi mollare; **~ go of** lasciare andare ② vt mollare ‹rope, person›; **~ somebody go** rilasciare ‹prisoner›; licenziare ‹employee›; **~ oneself go** lasciarsi andare

■ **let in** vt far entrare

■ **let off** vt far partire; (not punish) perdonare; **~ somebody off doing something** abbonare qualcosa a qualcuno; **~ off steam** fig scaricarsi

■ **let on**: vi sl **don't ~ on** non spifferare niente

■ **let out** vt far uscire; (make larger) allargare; emettere ‹scream, groan›

■ **let through** vt far passare

■ **let up** vi fam diminuire

let-down n delusione f

lethal /'li:θl/ adj letale; **~ dose** n dose f letale

lethargic /lɪ'θɑ:dʒɪk/ adj apatico

lethargy /'leθədʒɪ/ n apatia f

let-out n fam via f d'uscita

⚡ **letter** /'letə(r)/ n lettera f

letter bomb n lettera f esplosiva

letter box n buca f per le lettere

letterhead n (heading) intestazione f; (paper) carta f intestata

lettering /'letərɪŋ/ n caratteri mpl

letter of apology n lettera f di scuse

letter of credit n Comm lettera f di credito

letter of introduction n lettera f di presentazione

lettuce /'letɪs/ n lattuga f

let-up n fam pausa f

leukaemia /lu:'ki:mɪə/ n leucemia f

⚡ **level** /'levl/ ① adj piano; (in height, competition) allo stesso livello; ‹spoonful› raso; **draw ~ with somebody** affiancare qualcuno; **do one's ~ best** fare del proprio meglio ② n livello m; **on the ~** fam giusto ③ vt (pt/pp **levelled**) livellare; (aim) puntare (**at** su)

■ **level off** vi ‹inflation, unemployment› stabilizzarsi

■ **level out** vi ‹surface› diventare pianeggiante; ‹aircraft› mettersi in orizzontale

■ **level with** vt fam (be honest with) essere franco con

level crossing n passaggio m a livello

level-headed /-'hedɪd/ adj posato

level pegging n **it's ~ so far** finora sono alla pari

lever /'li:və(r)/ n leva f

■ **lever off**, **lever up** vt sollevare (con una leva)

leverage /'li:vərɪdʒ/ n azione f di una leva; fig influenza f

leveret /'levərət/ n leprotto m

levitate /'levɪteɪt/ vi levitare

levity /'levətɪ/ n leggerezza f

levy /'levɪ/ vt (pt/pp **levied**) imporre ⟨tax⟩

lewd /lju:d/ adj osceno

lexical /'leksɪkəl/ adj lessicale

lexicographer /leksɪ'kɒgrəfə(r)/ n lessicografo, -a mf

lexicographic /leksɪkə'græfɪk/ adj lessicografico

lexicography /leksɪ'kɒgrəfɪ/ n lessicografia f

lexicon /'leksɪkən/ n lessico m

liability /laɪə'bɪlətɪ/ n responsabilità f; fam (burden) peso m; **liabilities** pl passività fpl

liable /'laɪəbl/ adj responsabile (**for** di); **be ~ to** ⟨rain, break etc⟩ rischiare di; (tend to) tendere a

liaise /lɪ'eɪz/ vi fam essere in contatto

liaison /lɪ'eɪzɒn/ n contatti mpl; Mil collegamento m; (affair) relazione f

liar /'laɪə(r)/ n bugiardo, -a mf

Lib Dem /lɪb'dem/ abbr Br Pol (**Liberal Democrat**) liberal democratico

libel /'laɪbl/ ① n diffamazione f
② vt (pt/pp **libelled**) diffamare

libellous Br, **libelous** Am adj diffamatorio

liberal /'lɪb(ə)rəl/ ① adj (tolerant) di larghe vedute; (generous) generoso; **L~** adj Pol liberale
② n liberale mf

Liberal Democrat n Br Pol liberal-democratico, -a mf

liberalism /'lɪbərəlɪzəm/ n liberalismo m

liberalization /lɪbərəlar'zeɪʃn/ n (of trade) liberalizzazione f

liberalize /'lɪbərəlaɪz/ vt liberalizzare

liberally /'lɪbrəlɪ/ adv liberalmente

liberate /'lɪbəret/ vt liberare

liberated /'lɪbəretɪd/ adj ⟨woman⟩ emancipata

liberating /'lɪbəretɪŋ/ adj liberatorio

liberation /lɪbə'reɪʃn/ n liberazione f; (of women) emancipazione f

liberator /'lɪbəreɪtə(r)/ n liberatore, -trice mf

Liberia /laɪ'bɪərɪə/ n Liberia f

libertarian /lɪbə'teərɪən/ adj & n liberale mf

libertarianism /lɪbə'teərɪənɪzm/ n liberalismo m

liberty /'lɪbətɪ/ n libertà f; **take the ~ of doing something** prendersi la libertà di fare qualcosa; **take liberties** prendersi delle libertà; **be at ~ to do something** essere libero di fare qualcosa

libido /lɪ'bi:dəʊ/ n libido f inv

Libra /'li:brə/ n Astr Bilancia f

librarian /laɪ'breərɪən/ n bibliotecario, -a mf

♂ **library** /'laɪbrərɪ/ n biblioteca f

libretto /lɪ'bretəʊ/ n (pl **-tti** or **-ttos**) libretto m di opera

Libya /'lɪbɪə/ n Libia f

Libyan /'lɪbɪən/ adj & n libico, -a mf

lice /laɪs/ ▶ LOUSE

♂ **licence** /'laɪsns/ n licenza f; (for TV) canone m televisivo; (for driving) patente f; (freedom) sregolatezza f

licence number n numero m di targa

licence plate n targa f

license /'laɪsns/ vt autorizzare; **be ~d** ⟨car⟩ avere il bollo; ⟨restaurant⟩ essere autorizzato alla vendita di alcolici

licensee /laɪsən'si:/ n titolare mf di licenza (per la vendita di alcolici)

licensing hours /'laɪsənsɪŋ/ npl Br orario (m) in cui è permessa la vendita di alcolici

licensing laws npl Br normativa f sg sulla vendita di alcolici

licentious /laɪ'senʃəs/ adj licenzioso

licentiousness /laɪ'senʃəsnɪs/ n licenziosità f

lichen /'laɪkən/ n Bot lichene m

lick /lɪk/ ① n leccata f; **a ~ of paint** una passata leggera di pittura
② vt leccare; fam (defeat) battere; leccarsi ⟨lips⟩; fam **~ somebody into shape** rendere qualcuno efficiente

licorice /'lɪkərɪs/ n Am = LIQUORICE

lid /lɪd/ n coperchio m; (of eye) palpebra f; **keep the ~ on something** fam non lasciare trapelare qualcosa

lido /'li:dəʊ/ n (beach) lido m; Br ⟨pool⟩ piscina f scoperta

lie¹ /laɪ/ ① n bugia f; **tell a ~** mentire
② vi (pt/pp **lied**, pres p **lying**) mentire

♂ **lie**² vi (pt **lay**, pp **lain**, pres p **lying**) ⟨person⟩ sdraiarsi; ⟨object⟩ stare; (remain) rimanere; **leave something lying about** or **around** lasciare qualcosa in giro; **here ~s...** qui giace...; **~ low** tenersi nascosto
■ **lie around** ① vi ⟨person⟩ girellare
② vt girellare in ⟨house⟩
■ **lie back** vi (relax) rilassarsi
■ **lie down** vi sdraiarsi
■ **lie in** vi (stay in bed) rimanere a letto

Liechtenstein /'lɪktənstaɪn/ n Liechtenstein m

lie detector n macchina f della verità

lie-down n **have a ~** fare un riposino

lie-in n fam **have a ~** restare a letto fino a tardi

lieu /lju:/ n **in ~ of** in luogo di

lieutenant /leftenənt/ n tenente m

♂ **life** /laɪf/ n (pl **lives**) vita f; **give one's ~ for somebody/one's country** dare la vita per qualcuno/la patria; **give one's** ∼ **to** (devote oneself to) dedicare la propria vita a; **lose one's** ∼ perdere la vita; **for dear** ∼ per salvare la pelle; **not on your** ∼! fam neanche morto!

life-and-death adj ‹struggle› disperato

lifebelt n salvagente m

lifeblood n fig linfa f vitale

lifeboat n lancia f di salvataggio; (on ship) scialuppa f di salvataggio

lifebuoy n salvagente m

life coach n life coach mf inv

life drawing n disegno m dal vero

life expectancy n vita f media

life form n forma f di vita

lifeguard n (on beach etc) bagnino, -a mf

life-imprisonment n ergastolo m

life insurance n assicurazione f sulla vita

life jacket n giubbotto m di salvataggio

lifeless /'laɪflɪs/ adj inanimato

lifelike adj realistico

lifeline n sagola f di salvataggio

lifelong adj di tutta la vita

lifer /'laɪfə(r)/ n fam ergastolano, -a mf

lifesaving /'laɪfseɪvɪŋ/ n salvataggio m

life sentence n condanna f all'ergastolo

life-size[d] /'laɪfsaɪz[d]/ adj a grandezza naturale

lifespan n durata f della vita

life story n biografia f

lifestyle n stile m di vita

lifestyle drug n medicinale (m) che migliora la qualità della vita

life support n Med respirazione f assistita; **on** ∼ attaccato al respiratore artificiale; ∼ **machine** respiratore artificiale

lifetime n vita f; **the chance of a** ∼ un'occasione unica; ∼ **guarantee** garanzia f a vita

⚡ **lift** /lɪft/ **1** n ascensore m; Auto passaggio m; **give somebody a** ∼ dare un passaggio a qualcuno; **I got a** ∼ mi hanno dato un passaggio
2 vt sollevare; revocare ‹restrictions›; fam (steal) rubare
3 vi ‹fog› alzarsi
■ **lift off** vi ‹rocket› partire
■ **lift up** vt sollevare

liftboy n Br lift m inv

lift-off n decollo m (di razzo)

ligament /'lɪgəmənt/ n Anat legamento m

⚡ **light¹** /laɪt/ **1** adj (not dark) luminoso; ∼ **green** verde chiaro
2 n luce f; (lamp) lampada f; **in the** ∼ **of** fig alla luce di; **have you got a** ∼? ha da accendere?; **come to** ∼ essere rivelato
3 vt (pt/pp **lit** or **lighted**) accendere; (illuminate) illuminare
■ **light up** **1** vt accendere ‹pipe, cigarette›;

illuminare ‹face›; rischiarare ‹sky›
2 vi ‹face› illuminarsi

light² **1** adj (not heavy) leggero; **make** ∼ **of** non dare peso a
2 adv **travel** ∼ viaggiare con poco bagaglio

light bulb n lampadina f

lighten¹ /'laɪtn/ vt illuminare

lighten² vt alleggerire ‹load›

light entertainment n varietà m inv

lighter /'laɪtə(r)/ n accendino m

lighter fuel n (liquid) gas m inv da accendino

light-fingered /-'fɪŋgəd/ adj svelto di mano

light-headed /-'hedɪd/ adj sventato

light-hearted /-'hɑtɪd/ adj spensierato

lighthouse n faro m

light industry n industria f leggera

lighting /'laɪtɪŋ/ n illuminazione f

lightly /'laɪtlɪ/ adv leggermente; ‹accuse› con leggerezza; ‹take something› alla leggera; (without concern) senza dare importanza alla cosa; **get off** ∼ cavarsela a buon mercato

lightness /'laɪtnɪs/ n leggerezza f

lightning /'laɪtnɪŋ/ n lampo m, fulmine m

lightning conductor n parafulmine m

lightning strike n sciopero m a sorpresa

light-pen n (for computer screen) penna f ottica

light pollution n inquinamento m luminoso

lightweight **1** adj leggero
2 n (in boxing) peso m leggero

light year n anno m luce; **it was** ∼**s ago** è stato secoli fa

like¹ /laɪk/ **1** adj simile
2 prep come; ∼ **this/that** così; **what's he** ∼? com'è?
3 conj fam (as) come; Am (as if) come se

⚡ **like²** **1** vt piacere, gradire; **I should** or **would** ∼ vorrei, gradirei; **I** ∼ **him** mi piace, **I** ∼ **this car** mi piace questa macchina; **I** ∼ **dancing** mi piace ballare; **I** ∼ **that!** fam questa mi è piaciuta!; ∼ **it or lump it!** abbozzala!
2 n ∼**s and dislikes** pl gusti mpl

likeable /'laɪkəbl/ adj simpatico

likelihood /'laɪklɪhʊd/ n probabilità f

⚡ **likely** /'laɪklɪ/ **1** adj (-ier, -iest) probabile
2 adv probabilmente; **not** ∼! fam neanche per sogno!

like-minded /laɪk'maɪndɪd/ adj con gusti affini

liken /'laɪkən/ vt paragonare (**to** a)

likeness /'laɪknɪs/ n somiglianza f

likewise /'laɪkwaɪz/ adv lo stesso

liking /'laɪkɪŋ/ n gusto m; **is it to your** ∼? è di suo gusto?; **take a** ∼ **to somebody** prendere qualcuno in simpatia

lilac /'laɪlək/ 1 n lillà m
2 adj lilla
Lilo® /'laɪləʊ/ n materassino m gonfiabile
lilting /'lɪltɪŋ/ adj cadenzato
lily /'lɪlɪ/ n giglio m
lily of the valley n mughetto m
lily pond n stagno m con ninfee
limb /lɪm/ n arto m
limber /'lɪmbə(r)/ vi ~ up sciogliersi i
muscoli
limbo /'lɪmbəʊ/ n Relig fig (dance) limbo m;
be in ~ ‹person› essere nel limbo del dubbio;
‹future of something› essere in sospeso
lime¹ /laɪm/ n (fruit) limetta f; (tree) tiglio m
lime² n calce f
lime-green adj & n verde m limone
limelight /'laɪmlaɪt/ n be in the ~ essere
molto in vista
limestone /'laɪmstəʊn/ n calcare m
⚜ **limit** /'lɪmɪt/ 1 n limite m; be the ~ essere
il colmo; that's the ~! fam questo è troppo!
2 vt limitare (to a)
limitation /lɪmɪ'teɪʃn/ n limite m
⚜ **limited** /'lɪmɪtɪd/ adj ristretto
limited company n società f inv a
responsabilità limitata
limited edition n (book, lithograph)
edizione f limitata
limited liability n responsabilità f
limitata
limitless /'lɪmɪtlɪs/ adj infinito
limousine /'lɪməziːn/ n limousine f inv
limp¹ /lɪmp/ 1 n andatura f zoppicante;
have a ~ zoppicare
2 vi zoppicare
limp² adj floscio
limpet /'lɪmpɪt/ n be like a ~ fig essere
attaccaticcio
limpid /'lɪmpɪd/ adj limpido
limp-wristed /-'rɪstɪd/ adj pej effeminato
linchpin /'lɪntʃpɪn/ n fig (essential element)
perno m
⚜ **line¹** /laɪn/ 1 n linea f; (length of rope, cord)
filo m; (of writing) riga f; (of poem) verso m;
(row) fila f; (wrinkle) ruga f; (of business) settore
m; Am (queue) coda f; in ~ with in conformità
con; bring into ~ mettere al passo ‹structure,
law›; in the ~ of duty (of policeman)
nell'esercizio delle proprie funzioni; ~ of
fire linea f di tiro; stand in ~ Am (queue) fare
la coda; in ~ for ‹promotion etc› in lista per;
on the ~ ‹job, career› in serio pericolo; read
between the ~s fig leggere tra le righe
2 vt segnare; fiancheggiare ‹street›;
foderare ‹garment›
■ **line up** 1 vi allinearsi
2 vt allineare
lineage /'lɪnɪɪdʒ/ n lignaggio m

⚜ indicates a very frequent word

linear /'lɪnɪə(r)/ adj lineare
lined¹ /laɪnd/ adj ‹face› rugoso; ‹paper› a
righe
lined² adj ‹garment› foderato
line manager n line manager m inv
linen /'lɪnɪn/ 1 n lino m; (articles)
biancheria f
2 attrib di lino
linen basket n cesto m della biancheria
liner /'laɪnə(r)/ n nave f di linea
linesman /'laɪnzmən/ n Sport guardalinee
m inv
line-up n (personnel, Sport) formazione f;
(identification) confronto m all'americana
linger /'lɪŋgə(r)/ vi indugiare
lingerie /'lɒ̃ʒərɪ/ n biancheria f intima (da
donna)
lingering /'lɪŋgərɪŋ/ adj ‹illness› lento;
‹look› prolungato; ‹doubt› persistente
linguist /'lɪŋgwɪst/ n linguista mf
linguistic /lɪŋ'gwɪstɪk/ adj linguistico
linguistically /lɪŋ'gwɪstɪklɪ/ adv
linguisticamente
linguistics /lɪŋ'gwɪstɪks/ n linguistica fsg
lining /'laɪnɪŋ/ n (of garment) fodera f; (of
brakes) guarnizione f
⚜ **link** /lɪŋk/ 1 n (of chain) anello m; fig legame
m
2 vt collegare; ~ arms prendersi
sottobraccio; Comput ‹web pages› linkare
■ **link up** TV vi unirsi (with a); TV collegarsi
linkage /'lɪŋkɪdʒ/ n (connection) connessione
f; (in genetics) associazione f
link road n bretella f
links /lɪŋks/ n or npl campo msg da golf
link-up n collegamento m
lino /'laɪnəʊ/, **linoleum** /lɪ'nəʊlɪəm/ n
linoleum m
linseed oil /'lɪnsiːdɔɪl/ n olio m [di semi]
di lino
lint /lɪnt/ n garza f
lintel /'lɪntəl/ n architrave m
lion /'laɪən/ n leone m; get the ~'s share fig
prendersi la fetta più grossa
lion cub n leoncino m
lioness /'laɪənɪs/ n leonessa f
⚜ **lip** /lɪp/ n labbro m (pl labbra f) (edge) bordo
m
lip gloss n lucidalabbra m inv
liposuction /'laɪpəʊsʌkʃn/ n liposuzione f
lip-read vi leggere le labbra
lip-reading n lettura f delle labbra
lipsalve n burro m [di] cacao
lip-service n pay ~ to approvare soltanto
a parole
lipstick n rossetto m
liquefy /'lɪkwɪfaɪ/ v (pt/pp -ied) 1 vt
liquefare
2 vi liquefarsi

liqueur /lɪˈkjʊə(r)/ *n* liquore *m*
liquid /ˈlɪkwɪd/ **1** *n* liquido *m*
　2 *adj* liquido
liquidate /ˈlɪkwɪdeɪt/ *vt* liquidare
liquidation /lɪkwɪˈdeɪʃn/ *n* liquidazione *f*;
　go into ∼ Comm andare in liquidazione
liquidator /lɪkwɪdeɪtə(r)/ *n* liquidatore,
　-trice *mf*
liquid crystal display *n* visualizzatore
　m a cristalli liquidi
liquidize /ˈlɪkwɪdaɪz/ *vt* rendere liquido
liquidizer /ˈlɪkwɪdaɪzə(r)/ *n* Culin frullatore
　m
liquor /ˈlɪkə(r)/ *n* bevanda *f* alcolica
liquorice /ˈlɪkərɪs/ *n* liquirizia *f*
liquor store *n* Am negozio *m* di alcolici
lira /ˈlɪərə/ *n* (old) lira *f*; **50,000 lire** 50.000 lire
lisp /lɪsp/ **1** *n* pronuncia *f* con la lisca;
　have a ∼ parlare con la lisca
　2 *vi* parlare con la lisca
⚔ **list¹** /lɪst/ **1** *n* lista *f*
　2 *vt* elencare
list² *vi* ⟨ship⟩ inclinarsi
⚔ **listen** /ˈlɪsn/ *vi* ascoltare; ∼ **to** ascoltare
　■ **listen in** *vi* (secretly) origliare; ∼ **in on**
　ascoltare di nascosto ⟨conversation⟩
listener /ˈlɪs(ə)nə(r)/ *n* ascoltatore, -trice
　mf
listeria /lɪˈstɪərɪə/ *n* (illness) listeriosi *f*;
　(bacteria) listeria *f*
listings /ˈlɪstɪŋz/ *npl* rubrica *f* degli
　spettacoli
listless /ˈlɪstlɪs/ *adj* svogliato
listlessly /ˈlɪstlɪslɪ/ *adv* in modo svogliato
list price *n* prezzo *m* di listino
lit /lɪt/ ▶ LIGHT¹
litany /ˈlɪtənɪ/ *n* litania *f*
literacy /ˈlɪtərəsɪ/ *n* alfabetizzazione *f*
literal /ˈlɪtərəl/ *adj* letterale
literally /ˈlɪt(ə)rəlɪ/ *adv* letteralmente
literary /ˈlɪtərərɪ/ *adj* letterario
literary critic *n* critico, -a *mf* letterario
literary criticism *n* critica *f* letteraria
literate /ˈlɪtərət/ *adj* **be** ∼ saper leggere e
　scrivere
literati /lɪtəˈrɑːtiː/ *npl* letterati *mpl*
⚔ **literature** /ˈlɪtrətʃə(r)/ *n* letteratura *f*
lithe /laɪð/ *adj* flessuoso
lithographer /lɪˈθɒɡrəfə(r)/ *n* litografo,
　-a *mf*
lithography /lɪˈθɒɡrəfɪ/ *n* litografia *f*
Lithuania /lɪθjʊˈeɪnɪə/ *n* Lituania *f*
Lithuanian /lɪθjʊˈeɪnɪən/ *adj & n* lituano,
　-a *mf*; (language) lituano *m*
litigation /lɪtɪˈgeɪʃn/ *n* causa *f*
　[giudiziaria]
litmus paper /ˈlɪtməs/ *n* cartina *f* di
　tornasole

litmus test *n* Chem test *m inv* con cartina
　di tornasole; fig prova *f* del nove
litre /ˈliːtə(r)/ *n* litro *m*
litter /ˈlɪtə(r)/ **1** *n* immondizie *fpl*; Zool
　figliata *f*
　2 *vt* **be** ∼**ed with something** essere
　ingombrato di qualcosa
litter-bin *n* bidone *m* della spazzatura
litterbug /ˈlɪtəbʌɡ/ *n persona (f) che butta
　per terra cartacce e rifiuti*
⚔ **little** /ˈlɪtl/ **1** *adj* piccolo; (not much) poco
　2 *adv & n* poco *m*; **a** ∼ un po'; **a** ∼ **water**
　un po' d'acqua; **a** ∼ **better** un po' meglio;
　∼ **by** ∼ a poco a poco
little finger *n* mignolo *m* (della mano)
little-known *adj* poco noto
liturgical /lɪˈtɜːdʒɪkl/ *adj* liturgico
liturgy /ˈlɪtədʒɪ/ *n* liturgia *f*
live¹ /laɪv/ **1** *adj* vivo; ⟨ammunition⟩
　carico; ∼ **broadcast** trasmissione *f* in
　diretta; **be** ∼ Electr essere sotto tensione;
　∼ **wire** *n* fig persona *f* dinamica
　2 *adv* ⟨broadcast⟩ in diretta
⚔ **live²** /lɪv/ *vi* vivere; (reside) abitare; ∼ **with**
　convivere con
　■ **live down** *vt* far dimenticare
　■ **live for** *vt* vivere solo per ⟨one's work,
　family⟩
　■ **live in** *vi* ⟨nanny, au-pair⟩ abitare sul posto
　di lavoro
　■ **live off** *vt* vivere alle spalle di
　■ **live on 1** *vt* vivere di
　　2 *vi* sopravvivere
　■ **live through** *vt* vivere
　■ **live together** *vi* ⟨friends⟩ vivere insieme;
　⟨lovers⟩ convivere
　■ **live up:** *vt* ∼ **it up** far la bella vita
　■ **live up to** *vt* essere all'altezza di
　■ **live with** *vt* convivere con ⟨lover, situation⟩;
　vivere con ⟨mother etc⟩
lived-in /ˈlɪvdɪn/ *adj* **have that** ∼ **look**
　⟨room, flat⟩ avere un'aria vissuta
live-in *adj* ⟨maid, nanny⟩ che vive in casa
livelihood /ˈlaɪvlɪhʊd/ *n* mezzi *mpl* di
　sostentamento
liveliness /ˈlaɪvlɪnɪs/ *n* vivacità *f*
lively /ˈlaɪvlɪ/ *adj* (-ier, -iest) vivace
　■ **liven up 1** *vt* vivacizzare
　　2 *vi* vivacizzarsi
liver /ˈlɪvə(r)/ *n* fegato *m*
liver pâté *n* pâté *m inv* di fegato
Liverpudlian /lɪvəˈpʌdlɪən/ *n* ⟨born there⟩
　originario, -a *mf* di Liverpool; ⟨living there⟩
　abitante *mf* di Liverpool
livery /ˈlɪvərɪ/ *n* (uniform) livrea *f*
lives /laɪvz/ ▶ LIFE
livestock /ˈlaɪvstɒk/ *n* bestiame *m*
live wire *n* fig **be a** ∼ essere
　superdinamico
livid /ˈlɪvɪd/ *adj* fam livido
⚔ **living** /ˈlɪvɪŋ/ **1** *adj* vivo ⋯⟶

2 *n* earn one's ∼ guadagnarsi da vivere; the ∼ *pl* i vivi

living room *n* soggiorno *m*

living will *n* testamento *m* biologico

lizard /'lɪzəd/ *n* lucertola *f*

llama /'lɑːmə/ *n* lama *m*

LLB *abbr* (**Bachelor of Laws**) laureato, -a *mf* in legge

load /ləʊd/ **1** *n* carico *m*; ∼**s of** fam un sacco di; **that's a** ∼ **off my mind** mi sono tolto un peso [dallo stomaco]
  2 *vt* ∼ [**up**] caricare

loaded /'ləʊdɪd/ *adj* carico; fam (rich) ricchissimo; ∼ **question** domanda *f* esplosiva

loading bay /'ləʊdɪŋ/ *n* piazzola *f* di carico e scarico

loaf¹ /ləʊf/ *n* (*pl* **loaves**) pane *m*; (round) pagnotta *f*; **use one's** ∼ fam pensare con il proprio cervello

loaf², ∼ **about** *or* **around** *vi* oziare

loafer /'ləʊfə(r)/ *n* (idler) scansafatiche *mf inv*; (shoe) mocassino *m*

❖ **loan** /ləʊn/ **1** *n* prestito *m*; **on** ∼ in prestito
  2 *vt* prestare

loan shark *n* fam strozzino, -a *mf*

loath /ləʊθ/ *adj* **be** ∼ **to do something** essere restio a fare qualcosa

loathe /ləʊð/ *vt* detestare

loathing /'ləʊðɪŋ/ *n* disgusto *m*

loathsome /'ləʊðsəm/ *adj* disgustoso

loaves /ləʊvz/ ▸ LOAF¹

lob /lɒb/ **1** *vt* (*pres p etc* **-bb-**) lanciare in alto; Sport respingere a pallonetto
  2 *n* Sport pallonetto *m*

lobby /'lɒbɪ/ *n* atrio *m*; Pol gruppo *m* di pressione, lobby *f inv*

lobbying /'lɒbɪɪŋ/ *n* lobbismo *m*; ∼ **for something** fare pressioni per qualcosa

lobbyist /'lɒbɪɪst/ *n* lobbista *mf*

lobe /ləʊb/ *n* (of ear) lobo *m*

lobelia /lə'biːlɪə/ *n* lobelia *f*

lobster /'lɒbstə(r)/ *n* aragosta *f*

lobster pot *n* nassa *f* per aragoste

❖ **local** /'ləʊkl/ **1** *adj* locale; **under** ∼ **anaesthetic** sotto anestesia locale; **I'm not** ∼ non sono del posto
  2 *n* abitante *mf* del luogo; fam (public house) pub *m inv* locale

local authority *n* autorità *f* locale

local bus *n* bus *m* locale

local call *n* Teleph telefonata *f* urbana

local election *n* elezioni *fpl* amministrative

local government *n* autorità *f inv* locale

locality /ləʊ'kælətɪ/ *n* zona *f*

localized /'ləʊkəlaɪzd/ *adj* localizzato

locally /'ləʊkəlɪ/ *adv* localmente; ‹live, work› nei paraggi

local network *n* Comput rete *f* locale

❖ **locate** /ləʊ'keɪt/ *vt* situare; trovare ‹person›; **be** ∼**d** essere situato

❖ **location** /ləʊ'keɪʃn/ *n* posizione *f*; **filmed on** ∼ girato in esterni

loch /lɒx/ *n* lago *m*

lock¹ /lɒk/ *n* (of hair) ciocca *f*

❖ **lock²** **1** *n* (on door) serratura *f*; (on canal) chiusa *f*
  2 *vt* chiudere a chiave; bloccare ‹wheels›
  3 *vi* chiudersi
  ▪ **lock in** *vt* chiudere dentro
  ▪ **lock out** *vt* chiudere fuori
  ▪ **lock together** *vi* ‹pieces› incastrarsi
  ▪ **lock up** **1** *vt* (in prison) mettere dentro
    2 *vi* chiudere

locker /'lɒkə(r)/ *n* armadietto *m*

locker room *n* spogliatoio *m*

locket /'lɒkɪt/ *n* medaglione *m*

lockout *n* serrata *f*

locksmith *n* fabbro *m*

lock-up *n* (prison) guardina *f*

loco /'ləʊkəʊ/ *adj* Br (crazy) toccato

locomotion /ləʊkə'məʊʃn/ *n* locomozione *f*

locomotive /ləʊkə'məʊtɪv/ *n* locomotiva *f*

locum /'ləʊkəm/ *n* sostituto, -a *mf*

locust /'ləʊkəst/ *n* locusta *f*

lodge /lɒdʒ/ **1** *n* (porter's) portineria *f*; (masonic) loggia *f*
  2 *vt* presentare ‹claim, complaint›; (with bank, solicitor) depositare; **be** ∼**d** essersi conficcato
  3 *vi* essere a pensione (**with** da); (become fixed) conficcarsi

lodger /'lɒdʒə(r)/ *n* inquilino, -a *mf*

lodgings /'lɒdʒɪŋz/ *npl* camere *fpl* in affitto

loft /lɒft/ *n* soffitta *f*

loft conversion *n* soppalco *f* abitabile

lofty /'lɒftɪ/ *adj* (**-ier**, **-iest**) alto; (haughty) altezzoso

log /lɒg/ **1** *n* ceppo *m*; Auto libretto *m* di circolazione; Naut giornale *m* di bordo; **sleep like a** ∼ fam dormire come un ghiro
  2 *vt* (*pt/pp* **logged**) registrare
  ▪ **log in** *vi* aprire una sessione
  ▪ **log off** *vi* disconnettersi
  ▪ **log on** *vi* connettersi (**to** a)
  ▪ **log out** *vi* chiudere una sessione

logarithm /'lɒgərɪθm/ *n* logaritmo *m*

logbook /'lɒgbʊk/ *n* Naut giornale *m* di bordo; Auto libretto *m* di circolazione

log cabin *n* capanna *f* di tronchi

logger /'lɒgə(r)/ *n* bosacaiolo *m*

loggerheads /'lɒgəhedz/ *npl* **be at** ∼ fam essere in totale disaccordo

logic /'lɒdʒɪk/ *n* logica *f*

❖ indicates a very frequent word

logical /'lɒdʒɪkl/ *adj* logico
logically /'lɒdʒɪklɪ/ *adv* logicamente
logistics /lə'dʒɪstɪks/ *npl* logistica *f*
logo /'ləʊɡəʊ/ *n* logo *m inv*
loin /lɔɪn/ *n* Culin lombata *f*
loin chop *n* lombatina *f*
loincloth /'lɔɪnklɒθ/ *n* perizoma *m*
loiter /'lɔɪtə(r)/ *vi* gironzolare
loll /lɒl/ *vi* ~ **about** (posture) stravaccarsi; (do nothing) starsene in panciolle
lollipop /'lɒlɪpɒp/ *n* lecca-lecca *m inv*
lollop /'lɒləp/ *vi* ‹rabbit, person› avanzare a balzi
lolly /'lɒlɪ/ *n* lecca-lecca *m inv*; fam (money) quattrini *mpl*
Lombardy /'lɒmbədɪ/ *n* Lombardia *f*
London /'lʌndən/ [1] *n* Londra *f*
[2] *attrib* londinese, di Londra
Londoner /'lʌndənə(r)/ *n* londinese *mf*
lone /ləʊn/ *adj* solitario
loneliness /'ləʊnlɪnɪs/ *n* solitudine *f*
lonely /'ləʊnlɪ/ *adj* (**-ier, -iest**) solitario; ‹person› solo
lonely hearts' column *n* rubrica *f* dei cuori solitari
loner /'ləʊnə(r)/ *n* persona *f* solitaria
lonesome /'ləʊnsəm/ *adj* solo
⚲ **long¹** /lɒŋ/ [1] *adj* (**-er** /'lɒŋɡə(r)/ **-est** /'lɒŋɡɪst/) lungo; **a** ~ **time** molto tempo; **a** ~ **way** distante; **in the** ~ **run** a lungo andare; (in the end) alla fin fine
[2] *adv* a lungo, lungamente; **how** ~ **is it** quanto è lungo?; ‹in time› quanto dura?; **all day** ~ tutto il giorno; **not** ~ **ago** non molto tempo fa; **before** ~ fra breve; **he's no** ~**er here** non è più qui; **as** *or* **so** ~ **as** finché; (provided that) purché; **so** ~ fam ciao!; **will you be** ~**?** ti ci vuole molto?
long² *vi* ~ **for** desiderare ardentemente
long-awaited *adj* tanto atteso
long-distance *adj* a grande distanza; Sport di fondo; ‹call› interurbano
long division *n* divisione *f*
longevity /lɒn'dʒevətɪ/ *n* longevità *f*
long face *n* muso *m* lungo
longhand /'lɒŋhænd/ *n* **in** ~ in scrittura ordinaria
long-haul *attrib* su lunga distanza; ‹plane› per lunghi tragitti
longing /'lɒŋɪŋ/ [1] *adj* desideroso
[2] *n* brama *f*
longingly /'lɒŋɪŋlɪ/ *adv* con desiderio
longitude /'lɒŋɡɪtjuːd/ *n* Geog longitudine *f*
long jump *n* salto *m* in lungo
long-life milk *n* latte *m* a lunga conservazione
long-lived /-'lɪvd/ *adj* longevo
long-playing record *n* 33 giri *m inv*

long-range *adj* Mil, Aeron a lunga portata; ‹forecast› a lungo termine
long-sighted /-'saɪtɪd/ *adj* presbite
long-sleeved /-'sliːvd/ *adj* a maniche lunghe
long-standing *adj* di vecchia data
long-suffering *adj* infinitamente paziente
long-term *adj* a lunga scadenza
long-time *adj* ‹partner› di lunga data
long wave *n* onde *fpl* lunghe
long-winded /-'wɪndɪd/ *adj* prolisso
loo /luː/ *n* fam gabinetto *m*
⚲ **look** /lʊk/ [1] *n* occhiata *f*; (appearance) aspetto *m*; [good] ~**s** *pl* bellezza *f*; **have a** ~ **at** dare un'occhiata a
[2] *vi* guardare; ~ **here!** mi ascolti bene!; ~ **at** guardare; ~ **for** cercare; ~ **somebody in the eye** guardare negli occhi qualcuno; ~ **somebody up and down** guardare qualcuno dall'alto in basso; ~ **a fool** fare la figura del cretino; ~ **young/old for one's age** portarsi bene/male gli anni; ~ **like** (resemble) assomigliare a; **it** ~ **s as if it's going to rain** sembra che stia per piovere; ~ **sharp** fam (hurry up) darsi una mossa
■ **look after** *vt* badare a
■ **look ahead** *vi* (think of the future) guardare al futuro
■ **look back** *vi* girarsi; (think of the past) guardare indietro
■ **look down** *vi* guardare in basso; ~ **down on somebody** fig guardare dall'alto in basso qualcuno
■ **look forward to** *vt* essere impaziente di
■ **look in on** *vt* passare da
■ **look into** *vt* (examine) esaminare
■ **look on** [1] *vi* (watch) guardare
[2] *vt* ~ **somebody/something as** (consider to be) considerare qualcuno/qualcosa come
■ **look on to** *vt* ‹room› dare su
■ **look out** [1] *vi* guardare fuori; (take care) fare attenzione; ~ **out!** attento!
[2] *vt* cercare ‹something for somebody›
■ **look out for** *vt* cercare
■ **look over** *vt* riguardare ‹notes›; ispezionare ‹house›
■ **look round** *vi* girarsi; (in shop, town etc) dare un'occhiata
■ **look through** *vt* dare un'occhiata a ‹script, notes›
■ **look to** *vt* (rely on) contare su
■ **look up** [1] *vi* guardare in alto
[2] *vt* cercare [nel dizionario] ‹word›; (visit) andare a trovare
■ **look up to** *vt* fig rispettare
look-alike *n* sosia *mf inv*
looker-on /lʊkər'ɒn/ *n* (*pl* **lookers-on**) spettatore, -trice *mf*
look-in *n* Br fam **give somebody a** ~ dare una chance a qualcuno; **get a** ~ avere una chance

lookout /'lʊkaʊt/ n guardia f; (prospect) prospettiva f; **be on the** ∼ **for** tenere gli occhi aperti per

loom¹ /luːm/ n telaio m

loom² vi apparire; fig profilarsi

loony /'luːnɪ/ adj & n fam matto, -a mf; ∼ **bin** manicomio m

loop /luːp/ n cappio m; (on garment) passante m; **be in/out of the** ∼ essere/non essere tra quelli che contano o nella stanza dei bottoni

loophole /'luːphəʊl/ n (in the law) scappatoia f

loopy /'luːpɪ/ adj fam matto

loose /luːs/ adj libero; ⟨knot⟩ allentato; ⟨page⟩ staccato; ⟨clothes⟩ largo; ⟨morals⟩ dissoluto; (inexact) vago; **be at a** ∼ **end** non sapere cosa fare; **come** ∼ ⟨knot⟩ sciogliersi; **set** ∼ liberare

loose change n spiccioli mpl

loose chippings npl ghiaino m

loose-leaf notebook n raccoglitore m di fogli

loosely /'luːslɪ/ adv scorrevolmente; ⟨defined⟩ vagamente

loosely knit adj ⟨group⟩ poco unito

loosen /'luːsn/ vt sciogliere

■ **loosen up** ① vt sciogliere ⟨muscles⟩ ② vi fam (relax) rilassarsi

loot /luːt/ ① n bottino m ② vt/i depredare

looter /luːtə(r)/ n saccheggiatore, -trice mf

looting /'luːtɪŋ/ n saccheggio m

lop vt (pt/pp **lopped**) ∼ **off** potare

lope vi ∼ **off** andarsene a passi lunghi

lop-eared /lɒpɪəd/ adj con le orecchie [a] penzoloni

lopsided /lɒp'saɪdɪd/ adj sbilenco

loquacious /lə'kweɪʃəs/ adj loquace

◇ **lord** /lɔːd/ n signore m; (title) Lord m; **House of L**∼**s** Camera f dei Lord; **the L**∼**'s Prayer** il Padrenostro; **good L**∼**!** Dio Mio!

Lord Mayor n sindaco (m) della City di Londra

Lordship /'lɔːdʃɪp/ n **your/his L**∼ (of noble) Sua Signoria; **your L**∼ (to judge) Signor Giudice

lore /lɔː(r)/ n tradizioni fpl

lorry /'lɒrɪ/ n camion m inv

lorry driver n camionista mf

◇ **lose** /luːz/ ① vt (pt/pp **lost**) perdere; ∼ **heart** perdersi d'animo; ∼ **one's inhibitions** disinibirsi; ∼ **one's nerve** farsi prendere dalla paura; ∼ **sight of** perdere di vista, perdere d' occhio; ∼ **touch with** perdere di vista; ∼ **track of time** perdere la nozione del tempo; ∼ **weight** calare di peso ② vi perdere; ⟨clock⟩ essere indietro

■ **lose out** vi rimetterci

***

◇ indicates a very frequent word

loser /'luːzə(r)/ n perdente mf

losing battle /'luːzɪŋ/ n battaglia f persa

◇ **loss** /lɒs/ n perdita f; ∼**es** pl Comm perdite fpl; **be at a** ∼ essere perplesso; **be at a** ∼ **for words** non trovare le parole; **make a** ∼ Comm subire una perdita

loss adjuster /'lɒsədʒʌstə(r)/ n Comm perito m di assicurazione

loss-leader n articolo m civetta

loss-making /'lɒsmeɪkɪŋ/ adj ⟨company⟩ in passivo; ⟨product⟩ che non vende

lost /lɒst/ ① ▶ LOSE
② adj perduto; **get** ∼ perdersi; **get** ∼**!** fam va' a quel paese!

lost and found n Am oggetti mpl smarriti

lost property n Br oggetti mpl smarriti

lost property office n ufficio m oggetti smarriti

lot¹ /lɒt/ n (at auction) lotto m; (piece of land) lotto m; **draw** ∼**s** tirare a sorte

◇ **lot²** n **the** ∼ il tutto; **a** ∼ **of**, ∼**s of** molti; **the** ∼ **of you** tutti voi; **it has changed a** ∼ è cambiato molto

lotion /'ləʊʃn/ n lozione f

lottery /'lɒtərɪ/ n lotteria f

lottery ticket n biglietto m della lotteria

◇ **loud** /laʊd/ ① adj sonoro, alto; ⟨colours⟩ sgargiante
② adv forte; **out** ∼ ad alta voce

loud hailer /'heɪlə(r)/ n megafono m

loudly /'laʊdlɪ/ adv forte

loudspeaker /laʊd'spiːkə(r)/ n altoparlante m

lounge /laʊndʒ/ ① n salotto m; (in hotel) salone m
② vi poltrire

■ **lounge about** vi stare in panciolle

lounge suit n vestito m da uomo (formale)

louse /laʊs/ n (pl **lice**) pidocchio m

■ **louse up** vt fam (ruin) guastare

lousy /'laʊzɪ/ adj (-ier, -iest) fam schifoso

lout /laʊt/ n zoticone m

loutish /laʊtɪʃ/ adj rozzo

louvred /'luːvəd/ adj ⟨door, blinds⟩ con le gelosie

lovable /'lʌvəbl/ adj adorabile

◇ **love** /lʌv/ ① n amore m; Tennis zero m; **in** ∼ innamorato (**with** di)
② vt amare ⟨person, country⟩

love affair n relazione f [sentimentale]

lovebite n succhiotto m

love letter n lettera f d'amore

love life n vita f sentimentale

lovely /'lʌvlɪ/ adj (-ier, -iest) bello; (in looks) bello, attraente; (in character) piacevole; ⟨meal⟩ delizioso; **have a** ∼ **time** divertirsi molto

lovemaking n il fare l'amore

lover /'lʌvə(r)/ n amante mf

love song *n* canzone *f* d'amore

love story *n* storia *f* d'amore

lovey-dovey /lʌvɪ'dʌvɪ/ *adj* Br fam **get all** ~ fare i piccioncini

loving /'lʌvɪŋ/ *adj* affettuoso

lovingly /'lʌvɪŋlɪ/ *adv* affettuosamente

↗ **low** /ləʊ/ ▫1 *adj* basso; (depressed) giù *inv*
▫2 *adv* basso; **feel** ~ sentirsi giù
▫3 *n* minimo *m*; Meteorol depressione *f*; **at an all-time** ~ ‹prices etc› al livello minimo

low-alcohol *adj* ‹beer› a bassa gradazione alcolica

lowbrow /'ləʊbraʊ/ *adj* di scarsa cultura

low-budget *adj* ‹flight, airline› low-cost *inv*

low-calorie *adj* ipocalorico

low-cost *adj* low-cost *inv*

low-cut *adj* ‹dress› scollato

low-down /'ləʊdaʊn/ ▫1 *adj* fam ‹trick› mancino
▫2 *n* (details) informazioni *fpl*

lower /'ləʊə(r)/ ▫1 *adj & adv* ▸ LOW
▫2 *vt* abbassare; ~ **oneself** abbassarsi

lower class ▫1 *adj* del ceto basso
▫2 *n* ceto *m* basso

lowest common denominator
/'ləʊɪst, dɪ'nɒmɪneɪtə(r)/ *n* minimo denominatore *m* comune

low-fat *adj* ‹diet› a basso contenuto di grassi; ‹cheese, milk› magro

low gear *n* Auto marcia *f* bassa

low-grade *adj* di qualità inferiore

low-income *adj* ‹families› a basso reddito

low-key *adj* fig moderato

lowlands *npl* pianure *fpl*

low-level *adj* ‹talks› informale; ‹radiation› debole; ‹bombing› a bassa quota

lowly /'ləʊlɪ/ *adj* (-ier, -iest) umile

low-lying *adj* ‹land› a bassa quota

low maintenance *adj* a ~ garden un giardino che richiede poca manutenzione

low-paid *adj* ‹job, worker› mal pagato

low-priced *adj* a basso prezzo

low profile *n* **keep a** ~ mantenere un profilo basso

low-profile *adj* ‹campaign› di basso profilo

low-quality *adj* scadente

low-risk *adj* a basso rischio

low season *n* bassa stagione *f*

low-tech *adj* a bassa tecnologia

low tide *n* bassa marea *f*

loyal /'lɔɪəl/ *adj* leale

loyally /'lɔɪəlɪ/ *adv* lealmente

loyalty /'lɔɪəltɪ/ *n* lealtà *f*

loyalty card *n* carta *f* fedeltà

lozenge /'lɒzɪndʒ/ *n* losanga *f*; (tablet) pastiglia

LP *n abbr* (**long-playing record**) LP *m inv*

L-plate *n* Br Auto cartello (*m*) che indica che il conducente non ha ancora preso la patente

LSD *n* LSD *m*

LST *abbr* (**local standard time**) ora *f* locale

Ltd *abbr* (**Limited**) s.r.l.

lubricant /'luːbrɪkənt/ *n* lubrificante *m*

lubricate /'luːbrɪkeɪt/ *vt* lubrificare

lubrication /luːbrɪ'keɪʃn/ *n* lubrificazione *f*

lucid /'luːsɪd/ *adj* ‹explanation› chiaro; (sane) lucido

lucidity /luː'sɪdətɪ/ *n* lucidità *f*; (of explanation) chiarezza *f*

luck /lʌk/ *n* fortuna *f*; **bad** ~ sfortuna *f*; **good** ~ buona fortuna!

luckily /'lʌkɪlɪ/ *adv* fortunatamente

↗ **lucky** /'lʌkɪ/ *adj* (-ier, -iest) fortunato; **be** ~ essere fortunato; ‹thing› portare fortuna

lucky charm *n* portafortuna *m inv*

lucky dip *n* pesca *f* di beneficenza

lucrative /'luːkrətɪv/ *adj* lucrativo

lucre /'luːkə(r)/ *n* fam (money) soldi *mpl*

ludicrous /'luːdɪkrəs/ *adj* ridicolo

ludicrously /'luːdɪkrəslɪ/ *adv* ‹expensive, complex› eccessivamente

ludo /'luːdəʊ/ *n* Br gioco (*m*) da tavolo

lug /lʌg/ *vt* (*pt/pp* **lugged**) fam trascinare

luggage /'lʌgɪdʒ/ *n* bagaglio

luggage-rack *n* portabagagli *m inv*

luggage trolley *n* carrello *m* portabagagli

luggage van *n* bagagliaio *m*

lughole /'lʌghəʊl/ *n* Br fam (ear) orecchio *m*

lugubrious /lʊ'guːbrɪəs/ *adj* lugubre

lukewarm /'luːkwɔːm/ *adj* tiepido; fig poco entusiasta

lull /lʌl/ ▫1 *n* pausa *f*
▫2 *vt* ~ **to sleep** cullare

lullaby /'lʌləbaɪ/ *n* ninnananna *f*

lumbago /lʌm'beɪgəʊ/ *n* lombaggine *f*

lumbar /'lʌmbə(r)/ *adj* lombare

lumber /'lʌmbə(r)/ ▫1 *n* cianfrusaglie *fpl*; Am (timber) legname *m*
▫2 *vt* fam ~ **somebody with something** affibbiare qualcosa a qualcuno

lumberjack /'lʌmbədʒæk/ *n* tagliaboschi *m inv*

luminary /'luːmɪnərɪ/ *n* fig (person) luminare *mf*

luminous /'luːmɪnəs/ *adj* luminoso

lump¹ /lʌmp/ ▫1 *n* (of sugar) zolletta *f*; (swelling) gonfiore *m*; (in breast) nodulo *m*; (in sauce) grumo *m*; **a** ~ **in one's throat** un groppo alla gola
▫2 *vt* ~ **together** ammucchiare

lump² *vt* ~ **it** fam **you'll just have to** ~ **it** che ti piaccia o no è così

lump sugar *n* zucchero *m* in zollette

lump sum *n* somma *f* globale

lumpy /'lʌmpɪ/ *adj* (**-ier, -iest**) grumoso

lunacy /'lu:nəsɪ/ *n* follia *f*

lunar /'lu:nə(r)/ *adj* lunare

lunatic /'lu:nətɪk/ *n* pazzo, -a *mf*

✒ **lunch** /lʌntʃ/ ① *n* pranzo *m*; **she's gone to** ~ è andata a pranzo; **let's have** ~ **together sometime** pranziamo qualche volta insieme ② *vi* pranzare

lunch box *n* cestino *m* del pranzo

lunchbreak *n* pausa *f* pranzo

luncheon /'lʌntʃn/ *n* (formal) pranzo *m*

luncheon meat *n* carne (*f*) in scatola

luncheon voucher *n* buono *m* pasto

lunch hour *n* pausa *f* pranzo

lunchtime /'lʌntʃtaɪm/ *n* ora *f* di pranzo

lung /lʌŋ/ *n* polmone *m*

lung cancer *n* cancro *m* al polmone

lunge /lʌndʒ/ *vi* lanciarsi (**at** su)

lurch¹ /lɜ:tʃ/ *n* **leave in the** ~ fam lasciare nei guai

lurch² *vi* barcollare

lure /lʊə(r)/ ① *n* esca *f*; fig lusinga *f* ② *vt* adescare

lurid /'lʊərɪd/ *adj* (gaudy) sgargiante; (sensational) sensazionalistico

lurk /lɜ:k/ *vi* appostarsi

luscious /'lʌʃəs/ *adj* saporito; fig sexy *inv*

lush /lʌʃ/ *adj* lussureggiante

lust /lʌst/ ① *n* lussuria *f* ② *vi* ~ **after** desiderare [fortemente]

lustful /'lʌstfʊl/ *adj* lussurioso

lustre /'lʌstə(r)/ *n* lustro *m*

lusty /'lʌstɪ/ *adj* (**-ier, -iest**) vigoroso

lute /lu:t/ *n* liuto *m*

luvvy, luvvie /'lʌvɪ/ *n* fam attore, -trice *mf* pretenzioso

Luxembourg /'lʌksəmbɜ:g/ *n* (city) Lussemburgo *f*; (state) Lussemburgo *m*

luxuriant /lʌg'ʒʊərɪənt/ *adj* lussureggiante, rigoglioso

luxuriantly /lʌg'ʒʊərɪəntlɪ/ *adv* rigogliosamente

luxurious /lʌg'ʒʊərɪəs/ *adj* lussuoso

luxuriously /lʌg'ʒʊərɪəslɪ/ *adv* lussuosamente

luxury /'lʌkʃərɪ/ ① *n* lusso *m*; **live in** ~ vivere nel lusso ② *attrib* di lusso

LV *abbr* (**luncheon voucher**) buono *m* mensa, ticket

LW *abbr* (**long wave**) OL

lychee /'laɪtʃi:/ *n* litchi *m inv*

lych-gate /'lɪtʃ-/ *n* entrata (*f*) coperta di un cimitero

lycra® /'laɪkrə/ *n* lycra *f*

lying /'laɪɪŋ/ ① ▶ LIE¹, ▶ LIE² ② *n* mentire *m*

lymph gland /'lɪmf/ *n* linfoghiandola *f*

lymph node *n* linfonodo *m*

lynch /lɪntʃ/ *vt* linciare

lynch mob *n* linciatori *mpl*

lynchpin /'lɪntʃpɪn/ *n* fig pilastro *m*

lynx /lɪŋks/ *n* lince *f*

lyric /'lɪrɪk/ *adj* lirico

lyrical /'lɪrɪkl/ *adj* lirico; fam (enthusiastic) entusiasta; ~ **poetry** *n* poesia *f* lirica

lyricism /'lɪrɪsɪzm/ *n* lirismo *m*

lyricist /'lɪrɪsɪst/ *n* paroliere, -a *mf*

lyrics /'lɪrɪks/ *npl* parole *fpl*

M m

m¹, M /em/ *n* (letter) m, M *f inv*

m² *abbr* **1** (**metre(s)**) m

 2 (**million**) milione *m*

 3 (**mile(s)**) miglio

MA *n abbr* **1** (**Master of Arts**) (diploma) laurea *f* in lettere; (person) laureato, -a *mf* in lettere

 2 Am (**Massachusetts**)

ma'am /mɑ:m/ *int* signora; (to queen) Sua Altezza

mac /mæk/ *n* fam impermeabile *m*

macabre /mə'kɑ:br/ *adj* macabro

macaroni /mækə'rəʊnɪ/ *n* maccheroni *mpl*

macaroni cheese *n* maccheroni *mpl* gratinati al formaggio

macaroon /mækə'ru:n/ *n* ≈ amaretto *m*

mace¹ /meɪs/ *n* (staff) mazza *f*

mace² *n* (spice) macis *mf*

Macedonia /mæsə'dəʊnɪə/ *n* Macedonia *f*

machete /mə'ʃetɪ/ *n* machete *m inv*

Machiavellian /mækɪə'velɪən/ *adj* machiavellico

machinations /mækɪ'neɪʃnz/ *n* macchinazioni *fpl*

✒ **machine** /mə'ʃi:n/ ① *n* macchina *f*

✒ indicates a very frequent word

2 vt (sew) cucire a macchina; Techn lavorare a macchina

machine-gun n mitragliatrice f

machine operator n addetto, -a mf alle macchine

machine-readable adj ‹data, text› leggibile dalla macchina

machinery /məˈʃiːnərɪ/ n macchinario m; fig meccanismo m

machine-stitch vt cucire a macchina

machine tool n macchina f utensile

machine translation n traduzione f elettronica

machinist /məˈʃiːnɪst/ n macchinista mf; (on sewing machine) lavorante mf addetto, -a alla macchina da cucire

machismo /mæˈkɪzməʊ/ n machismo m

macho /ˈmætʃəʊ/ adj macho inv

mackerel /ˈmækr(ə)l/ n inv sgombro m

mackintosh /ˈmækɪntɒʃ/ n impermeabile m

macro /ˈmækrəʊ/ n Comput macro f inv

macrocosm /ˈmækrəʊkɒzm/ n macrocosmo m

mad /mæd/ adj (**madder**, **maddest**) pazzo, matto; fam (angry) furioso (**at** con); **like ~** fam come un pazzo; **be ~ about somebody/something** fam (keen on) andare matto per qualcuno/qualcosa

Madagascar /mædəˈgæskə(r)/ n Madagascar m

madam /ˈmædəm/ n signora f

mad cow disease n fam – BSE

madden /ˈmædən/ vt (make angry) far diventare matto

maddening /ˈmæd(ə)nɪŋ/ adj ‹delay, person› esasperante

made /meɪd/ ▶ MAKE

Madeira cake /məˈdɪərə/ n pan m di Spagna

made to measure adj [fatto] su misura

made-up adj (wearing make-up) truccato; ‹road› asfaltata; ‹story› inventato

madhouse /ˈmædhaʊs/ n fam manicomio m; **it's like a ~ in here!** sembra di essere in un manicomio

madly /ˈmædlɪ/ adv fam follemente; **~ in love** innamorato follemente

madman /ˈmædmən/ n pazzo m

madness /ˈmædnɪs/ n pazzia f

madonna /məˈdɒnə/ n madonna f

madwoman /ˈmædwʊmən/ n pazza f

mafia /ˈmæfɪə/ n also fig mafia f

mag /mæg/ n abbr (**magazine**) rivista f

ɔ **magazine** /mægəˈziːn/ n rivista f; Mil, Phot magazzino m

maggot /ˈmægət/ n verme m

maggoty /ˈmægətɪ/ adj coi vermi

Magi /ˈmeɪdʒaɪ/ npl **the M~** i Re Magi

magic /ˈmædʒɪk/ **1** n magia f; (tricks) giochi mpl di prestigio
2 adj magico; ‹trick› di prestigio

magical /ˈmædʒɪkl/ adj magico

magic carpet n tappeto m volante

magician /məˈdʒɪʃn/ n mago, -a mf; (entertainer) prestigiatore, -trice mf

magistrate /ˈmædʒɪstreɪt/ n magistrato m

magistrate's court n ≈ pretura f

magnanimity /mægnəˈnɪmətɪ/ n magnanimità f

magnanimous /mægˈnænɪməs/ adj magnanimo

magnate /ˈmægneɪt/ n magnate m

magnesia /mægˈniːʃə/ n magnesia f

magnesium /mægˈniːzɪəm/ n magnesio m

magnet /ˈmægnɪt/ n magnete m, calamita f

magnetic /mægˈnetɪk/ adj magnetico

magnetic resonance imaging n Med risonanza f magnetica

magnetic tape n nastro m magnetico

magnetism /ˈmægnətɪzm/ n magnetismo m

magnetize /ˈmægnətaɪz/ vt magnetizzare

magnification /mægnɪfɪˈkeɪʃn/ n ingrandimento m

magnificence /mægˈnɪfɪsəns/ n magnificenza f

magnificent /mægˈnɪfɪsənt/ adj magnifico

magnificently /mægˈnɪfɪsəntlɪ/ adv magnificamente

magnify /ˈmægnɪfaɪ/ vt (pt/pp -**ied**) ingrandire; (exaggerate) ingigantire

magnifying glass /ˈmægnɪfaɪɪŋ/ n lente f d'ingrandimento

magnitude /ˈmægnɪtjuːd/ n grandezza f; (importance) importanza f; **a project of this ~** un progetto di tale portata

magnolia /mægˈnəʊlɪə/ n (tree) magnolia f; (colour) crema m

magnum opus /mægnəmˈɒpəs/ n opera f principale

magpie /ˈmægpaɪ/ n gazza f

mahogany /məˈhɒgənɪ/ **1** n mogano m
2 attrib di mogano

maid /meɪd/ n cameriera f; **old ~** pej zitella f

maiden /ˈmeɪdn/ **1** n liter fanciulla f
2 adj ‹speech, voyage› inaugurale

maiden aunt n zia f zitella

maiden name n nome m da ragazza

mail /meɪl/ **1** n posta f
2 vt impostare

mailbag n sacco m postale

mail bomb n pacco m esplosivo (arrivato per posta)

mailbox n Am cassetta f delle lettere; (e-mail) casella f postale

mail coach n Rail vagone m postale

mail delivery n consegna f della posta

mailing /'meɪlɪŋ/ n (action) mailing m inv; (document) pubblicità f

mailing address /'meɪlɪŋ/ n recapito m postale

mailing list n elenco (m) d'indirizzi per un mailing

mailman /'meɪlmən/ n Am postino m

mail order ① n vendita f per corrispondenza
② attrib ‹business› di vendita per corrispondenza; ‹goods› comprati per corrispondenza

mail-order catalogue catalogo m di vendita per corrispondenza

mail-order firm n ditta f di vendita per corrispondenza

mail room n reparto m spedizioni

mail server n Comput server m inv di posta

mailshot n mailing m inv

mail train n treno m postale

mail van n (delivery vehicle) furgone m postale; (in train) vagone m postale

maim /meɪm/ vt menomare

main¹ /meɪn/ n (water; gas, electricity) conduttura f principale

✧ **main²** ① adj principale; the ～ thing is to … la cosa essenziale è di…
② n in the ～ in complesso

main course n secondo m

main deck n ponte m di coperta

mainframe n Comput mainframe m inv

mainland n continente m

main line ① n Rail linea f principale
② attrib ‹station, terminus, train› della linea principale

✧ **mainly** /'meɪnlɪ/ adv principalmente

main memory n Comput memoria f principale

main office n (of company) sede f centrale

main road n strada f principale

mainsail n randa f, vela f di taglio

mainstay n fig pilastro m

mainstream /'meɪnstriːm/ ① adj (conventional) tradizionale
② n corrente f principale

main street n via f principale

✧ **maintain** /meɪn'teɪn/ vt mantenere; (keep in repair) curare la manutenzione di; ‹claim› sostenere

maintenance /'meɪntənəns/ n mantenimento m; (care) manutenzione f; (allowance) alimenti mpl

maintenance grant n (for student) presalario m

maintenance order n Br obbligo m degli alimenti

maisonette /meɪzə'net/ n appartamento m a due piani

maize /meɪz/ n granoturco m

Maj abbr (**Major**) Mag

majestic /mə'dʒestɪk/ adj maestoso

majestically /mə'dʒæestɪklɪ/ adv maestosamente

majesty /'mædʒəstɪ/ n maestà f inv; **His/ Her M～** Sua Maestà

✧ **major** /'meɪdʒə(r)/ ① adj maggiore; ～ **road** strada f con diritto di precedenza
② n Mil, Mus maggiore m
③ vi Am ～ **in** specializzarsi in

Majorca /mə'jɔːkə/ n Maiorca f

major general n generale m di divisione

✧ **majority** /mə'dʒɒrətɪ/ n maggioranza f; **be in the ～** avere la maggioranza

✧ **make** /meɪk/ ① n (brand) marca f
② vt (pt/pp **made**) fare; (earn) guadagnare; rendere ‹happy, clear›; prendere ‹decision›; ～ **somebody laugh** far ridere qualcuno; ～ **somebody do something** far fare qualcosa a qualcuno; ～ **it** (to party, top of hill etc) farcela; **what time do you ～ it?** che ore fai?
③ vi ～ **as if to** fare per
■ **make after** vt (chase) inseguire
■ **make do** vi arrangiarsi
■ **make for** vt dirigersi verso
■ **make good** ① vi riuscire
② vt compensare ‹loss›; risarcire ‹damage›
■ make off vi fuggire
■ **make off with** vt (steal) sgraffignare
■ **make out** vt (distinguish) distinguere; (write out) rilasciare ‹cheque›; compilare ‹list›; (claim) far credere
■ **make over** vt cedere
■ **make up** ① vt (constitute) comporre; (complete) completare; (invent) inventare; (apply cosmetics to) truccare; fare ‹parcel›; ～ **up one's mind** decidersi; ～ **it up** (after quarrel) riconciliarsi
② vi (after quarrel) fare la pace
■ make up for vt compensare; ～ **up for lost time** recuperare il tempo perso
■ **make up to** vt arruffianarsi

make-believe ① adj finto
② n finzione f

make-do-and-mend vi arrangiarsi col poco che si ha

make-over n trasformazione f

maker /'meɪkə(r)/ n fabbricante mf; **M～** Relig Creatore m; **send somebody to meet his/her ～** spedire qualcuno all'altro mondo

makeshift ① adj di fortuna
② n espediente m

make-up n trucco m; (character) natura f

make-up artist n truccatore, -trice mf

make-up bag n astuccio m per il trucco

make-up remover n struccante m

making /'meɪkɪŋ/ n (manufacture) fabbricazione f; **be the ～ of** essere la causa

---

✧ indicates a very frequent word

del successo di; **have the ~s of** aver la stoffa di; **in the ~** in formazione

maladjusted /mælə'dʒʌstɪd/ *adj* disadattato

maladjustment /mælə'dʒʌstmənt/ *n* disadattamento *m*

Malagasy /mælə'gæzɪ/ *n* (native of Madagascar) malgascio, -a *mf*; (language) malgascio *m*

malaise /mə'leɪz/ *n* fig malessere *m*

malaria /mə'leərɪə/ *n* malaria *f*

Malawi /mə'lɑːwɪ/ *n* Malawi *m*

Malaysia /mə'leɪʒə/ *n* Malesia *f*

Malaysian /mə'leɪʒən/ *n* & *adj* malese *mf*

Maldives /'mɔːldɪvz/ *npl* **the ~** le Maldive

ℰ **male** /meɪl/ ① *adj* maschile
② *n* maschio *m*

male chauvinism *n* maschilismo *m*

male chauvinist [pig] *n* [sporco *m*] maschilista *m*

male menopause *n* andropausa *f*

male model *n* indossatore *m*

male nurse *n* infermiere *m*

male voice choir *n* coro *m* maschile

malevolence /mə'levələns/ *n* malevolenza *f*

malevolent /mə'levələnt/ *adj* malevolo

malformation /mælfɔː'meɪʃn/ *n* malformazione *f*

malformed /mæl'fɔːmd/ *adj* malformato

malfunction /mæl'fʌŋkʃn/ ① *n* funzionamento *m* imperfetto
② *vi* funzionare male

Mali /'mɑːlɪ/ *n* Mali *m*

malice /'mælɪs/ *n* malignità; **bear somebody ~** voler del male a qualcuno

malicious /mə'lɪʃəs/ *adj* maligno

maliciously /mə'lɪʃəslɪ/ *adv* con malignità

malign /mə'laɪn/ *vt* malignare su

malignancy /mə'lɪɡnənsɪ/ *n* malignità *f*

malignant /mə'lɪɡnənt/ *adj* maligno

malinger /mə'lɪŋɡə(r)/ *vi* fingersi malato

malingerer /mə'lɪŋɡərə(r)/ *n* scansafatiche *mf inv*

mall /mæl/ *n* (shopping arcade, in suburb) centro *m* commerciale; Am (street) strada *f* pedonale

mallard /'mælɑːd/ *n* germano *m* reale

malleable /'mælɪəbl/ *adj* malleabile

mallet /'mælɪt/ *n* martello *m* di legno

malnourished /mæl'nʌrɪʃt/ *adj* malnutrito

malnutrition /mælnjʊ'trɪʃn/ *n* malnutrizione *f*

malpractice /mæl'præktɪs/ *n* negligenza *f*

malt /mɔːlt/ *n* malto *m*

Malta /'mɔːltə/ *n* Malta *f*

Maltese /mɔːl'tiːz/ *adj* & *n* maltese *mf*

maltreat /mæl'triːt/ *vt* maltrattare

maltreatment /mæl'triːtmənt/ *n* maltrattamento *m*

malt whisky *n* whisky *m inv* di malto

mammal /'mæml/ *n* mammifero *m*

mammary /'mæmərɪ/ *adj* mammario

mammograph /'mæməɡrɑːf/ *n* mammografia *f*

mammoth /'mæməθ/ ① *adj* mastodontico
② *n* mammut *m inv*

ℰ **man** /mæn/ ① *n* (*pl* **men**) uomo *m*; (chess, draughts) pedina *f*; **the ~ in the street** l'uomo della strada; **~ to ~** da uomo a uomo
② *vt* (*pt/pp* **manned**) equipaggiare; far funzionare ⟨*pump*⟩; essere di servizio a ⟨*counter, telephones*⟩

manacle /'mænəkl/ *vt* ammanettare

ℰ **manage** /'mænɪdʒ/ ① *vt* dirigere; gestire ⟨*shop, affairs*⟩; (cope with) farcela; **~ to do something** riuscire a fare qualcosa
② *vi* riuscire; (cope) farcela (**on** con)

manageable /'mænɪdʒəbl/ *adj* ⟨*hair*⟩ docile; ⟨*size*⟩ maneggevole

ℰ **management** /'mænɪdʒmənt/ *n* gestione *f*; **the ~** la direzione

management accounting *n* contabilità *f* di gestione

management buyout *n* buyout *m inv* da parte dei manager, rilevamento *m* dirigenti

management consultancy *n* (firm) consulente *m* aziendale; (activity) consulenza *f* aziendale

management consultant *n* consulente *mf* aziendale

ℰ **manager** /'mænɪdʒə(r)/ *n* direttore *m*; (of shop, bar) gestore *m*; Sport manager *m inv*

manageress /mænɪdʒə'res/ *n* direttrice *f*

managerial /mænɪ'dʒɪərɪəl/ *adj* **~ staff** personale *m* direttivo

managing director *n* direttore, -trice *mf* generale

mandarin /'mændərɪn/ *n* **~ [orange]** mandarino *m*

mandate /'mændeɪt/ *n* mandato *m*

mandatory /'mændətrɪ/ *adj* obbligatorio

mandolin /'mændəlɪn/ *n* mandolino *m*

mandrake /'mændreɪk/ *n* mandragola *f*

mane /meɪn/ *n* criniera *f*

manful /'mænfl/ *adj* coraggioso

manfully /'mænfʊlɪ/ *adv* coraggiosamente

manger /'meɪndʒə(r)/ *n* mangiatoia *f*

mangle /'mæŋgl/ *vt* (damage) maciullare

mango /'mæŋɡəʊ/ *n* (*pl* **-es**) mango *m*

mangrove /'mæŋɡrəʊv/ *n* mangrovia *f*

mangy /'meɪndʒɪ/ *adj* ⟨*dog*⟩ rognoso

manhandle /'mænhændl/ *vt* malmenare

manhole /'mænhəʊl/ *n* botola *f*

m

manhole cover n tombino m
manhood /'mænhʊd/ n età f adulta; (quality) virilità f
man-hour n ora f lavorativa
manhunt /'mænhʌnt/ n caccia f all'uomo
mania /'meɪnɪə/ n mania f
maniac /'meɪnɪæk/ n maniaco, -a mf
manic /'mænɪk/ adj (obsessive) maniacale; (frenetic) frenetico
manic depression n psicosi f inv maniaco-depressiva
manic-depressive adj maniaco-depressivo
manicure /'mænɪkjʊə(r)/ ① n manicure f inv
② vt fare la manicure a
manicurist /'mænɪkjʊərɪst/ n manicure f inv
manifest /'mænɪfest/ ① adj manifesto
② n Comm manifesto m
③ vt manifestare; ~ itself manifestarsi
manifestation /mænɪfe'steɪʃn/ n manifestazione f
manifestly /'mænɪfestlɪ/ adv palesemente
manifesto /mænɪ'festəʊ/ n manifesto m
manifold /'mænɪfəʊld/ adj molteplice
manipulate /mə'nɪpjʊleɪt/ vt manipolare
manipulation /mənɪpjʊ'leɪʃn/ n manipolazione f
manipulative /mə'nɪpjʊlətɪv/ adj manipolatore
mankind /mæn'kaɪnd/ n genere m umano
manly /'mænlɪ/ adj virile
man-made adj artificiale; ~ fibre n fibra f sintetica
manna /'mænə/ n manna f; ~ from heaven fig manna f dal cielo
mannequin /'mænɪkɪn/ n manichino m
⚜ **manner** /'mænə(r)/ n maniera f; in this ~ in questo modo; have no ~s avere dei pessimi modi; good/bad ~s buone/cattive maniere
mannered /'mænəd/ adj pej manierato
mannerism /'mænərɪzm/ n affettazione f
mannish /'mænɪʃ/ adj mascolino
manoeuvrable /mə'nuːvrəbl/ adj manovrabile
manoeuvre /mə'nuːvə(r)/ ① n manovra f
② vt fare manovra con ⟨vehicle⟩; manovrare ⟨person⟩
manor /'mænə(r)/ n maniero m
manpower /'mænpaʊə(r)/ n manodopera f
manse /mæns/ n canonica f
mansion /'mænʃn/ n palazzo m
manslaughter /'mænslɔːtə(r)/ n omicidio m colposo

mantelpiece /'mæntlpiːs/ n mensola f di caminetto
mantis /'mæntɪs/ n mantide f
Mantua /'mæntjʊə/ n Mantova f
manual /'mænjʊəl/ ① adj manuale
② n manuale m
manufacture /mænjʊ'fæktʃə(r)/ ① vt fabbricare
② n manifattura f
⚜ **manufacturer** /mænjʊ'fæktʃərə(r)/ n fabbricante m
manure /mə'njʊə(r)/ n concime m
manuscript /'mænjʊskrɪpt/ n manoscritto m
Manx /mæŋks/ n (language) lingua f parlata nell'isola di Man; the M~ pl (people) gli abitanti dell'isola di Man
⚜ **many** /'menɪ/ adj & pron molti; there are as ~ boys as girls ci sono tanti ragazzi quante ragazze; as ~ as 500 ben 500; as ~ as that così tanti; as ~ altrettanti; very ~, a good/great ~ moltissimi; ~ a time molte volte
many-sided /-'saɪdɪd/ adj ⟨personality, phenomenon⟩ sfaccettato
⚜ **map** /mæp/ n carta f geografica; (of town) mappa f
▪ **map out** vt (pt/pp **mapped**) fig programmare
maple /'meɪpl/ n acero m
mar /mɑː(r)/ vt (pt/pp **marred**) rovinare
marathon /'mærəθən/ n maratona f
marauder /mə'rɔːdə(r)/ n predone m
marble /'mɑːbl/ ① n marmo m; (for game) pallina f
② attrib di marmo
march ① n marcia f; (protest) dimostrazione f
② vi marciare
③ vt far marciare; ~ somebody off scortare qualcuno fuori
⚜ **March** /mɑːtʃ/ n marzo m
marcher /'mɑːtʃə(r)/ n (in procession, band) persona (f) che marcia in una processione, in un corteo ecc; (in demonstration) dimostrante mf
marchioness /mɑːʃə'nes/ n marchesa f
march past n sfilata f
mare /'meə(r)/ n giumenta f
margarine /mɑdʒə'riːn/ n margarina f
marge /mɑdʒ/ n Br fam (margarine) margarina f
margin /'mɑdʒɪn/ n margine m
marginal /'mɑdʒɪnəl/ adj marginale
marginalize /'mɑːdʒɪnəlaɪz/ vt marginalizzare
marginally /'mɑdʒɪnəlɪ/ adv marginalmente
marigold /'mærɪgəʊld/ n calendula f
marijuana /mærʊ'wɑːnə/ n marijuana f
marina /mə'riːnə/ n porticciolo m

⚜ indicates a very frequent word

marinade /mærɪˈneɪd/ ① *n* marinata *f*
② *vt* marinare

marine /məˈriːn/ ① *adj* marino
② *n* (sailor) soldato *m* di fanteria marina

Marine Corps *n* i Marine

marine engineer *n* ingegnere *m* navale;
(works in engine room) macchinista *m*

marionette /mærɪəˈnet/ *n* marionetta *f*

marital /ˈmærɪtl/ *adj* coniugale; ~ **status**
stato *m* civile

maritime /ˈmærɪtaɪm/ *adj* marittimo

marjoram /ˈmɑːdʒərəm/ *n* maggiorana *f*

mark¹ /mɑːk/ *n* (currency) marco *m*

◆ **mark²** ① *n* (stain) macchia *f*; (sign, indication)
segno *m*; Sch voto *m*; **be the ~ of** designare
② *vt* segnare; (stain) macchiare; Sch
correggere; Sport marcare; ~ **time** Mil
segnare il passo; fig non far progressi; ~ **my**
words ricordati quello che dico
■ **mark down** *vt* (reduce the price of) ribassare
■ **mark out** *vt* delimitare; fig designare
■ **mark up** *vt* (increase the price of) aumentare

marked /mɑːkt/ *adj* marcato

markedly /ˈmɑːkɪdlɪ/ *adv* notevolmente

marker /ˈmɑːkə(r)/ *n* (for highlighting)
evidenziatore *m*; Sport marcatore *m*; (of exam)
esaminatore, -trice *mf*

marker pen *n* evidenziatore *m*

◆ **market** /ˈmɑːkɪt/ ① *n* mercato *m*
② *vt* vendere al mercato; (launch)
commercializzare; **on the ~** sul mercato

market analyst *n* analista *mf* di mercato

market day *n* giorno *m* di mercato

market economy *n* economia *f* di
mercato

market forces *npl* forze *fpl* di mercato

market garden *n* orto *m*

market gardener *n* ortofrutticoltore,
-trice *mf*

market gardening *n* ortofrutticoltura *f*

◆ **marketing** /ˈmɑːkɪtɪŋ/ *n* marketing *m*

marketing campaign *n* campagna *f*
promozionale *or* pubblicitaria

marketing department *n* ufficio *m*
marketing

marketing man *n* addetto, -a *mf* al
marketing

marketing mix *n* mix *m* *inv* del
marketing

marketing strategy *n* strategia *f* di
marketing

market leader *n* (company, product) leader
m *inv* del mercato

market place *n* (square, Fin) mercato *m*.

market price *n* prezzo *m* di mercato

market research *n* ricerca *f* di mercato

market square *n* piazza *f* del mercato

market stall *n* banco *m* del mercato

market survey *n* indagine *f* di mercato

market town *n* cittadina (*f*) *dove si tiene*
il mercato

market trader *n* venditore, -trice *mf* al
mercato

market value *n* valore *m* di mercato

markings /ˈmɑːkɪŋz/ *npl* (on animal) colori
mpl

marksman /ˈmɑːksmən/ *n* tiratore *m*
scelto

marksmanship /ˈmɑːksmənʃɪp/ *n* abilità
f nel tiro

mark-up *n* (margin) margine *m* di vendita;
(price increase) aumento *m*

marmalade /ˈmɑːməleɪd/ *n* marmellata
f d'arance

maroon /məˈruːn/ *adj* marrone rossastro

marooned /məˈruːnd/ *adj* abbandonato

marquee /mɑːˈkiː/ *n* tendone *m*; Am
(awning) pensilina *f* con pubblicità

marquess /ˈmɑːkwɪs/ *n* marchese *m*

marquetry /ˈmɑːkɪtrɪ/ *n* intarsio *m*

marquis /ˈmɑːkwɪs/ *n* marchese *m*

◆ **marriage** /ˈmærɪdʒ/ *n* matrimonio *m*

marriage ceremony *n* cerimonia *f*
nuziale

marriage certificate *n* certificato *m* di
matrimonio

marriage guidance counsellor *n*
consulente *mf* matrimoniale

marriage of convenience *n*
matrimonio *m* di convenienza

married /ˈmærɪd/ *adj* sposato; ‹life›
coniugale

marrow /ˈmærəʊ/ *n* Anat midollo *m*;
(vegetable) zucca *f*

marrowbone /ˈmærəʊbəʊn/ *n* midollo
m osseo

◆ **marry** /ˈmærɪ/ (*pt/pp* **-ied**) ① *vt* (*pt/pp*
-ied) sposare; **get married** sposarsi
② *vi* sposarsi

Mars /mɑːz/ *n* Marte *m*

marsh /mɑːʃ/ *n* palude *f*

marshal /ˈmɑːʃl/ ① *n* (steward)
cerimoniere *m*
② *vt* (*pt/pp* **marshalled**) fig organizzare
‹arguments›

Marshall Islands *npl* the ~ le isole
Marshall

marshmallow /mɑːʃˈmæləʊ/ *n* caramella
f gommosa e pastosa

marshy /ˈmɑːʃɪ/ *adj* paludoso

marsupial /mɑːˈsuːpɪəl/ *n* marsupiale *m*

marten /ˈmɑːtɪn/ *n* martora *f*

martial /ˈmɑːʃl/ *adj* marziale

Martian /ˈmɑːʃn/ *adj* & *n* marziano, -a *mf*

martinet /mɑːtɪˈnet/ *n* fanatico, -a *mf* della
disciplina

martyr /ˈmɑːtə(r)/ ① *n* martire *mf*
② *vt* martirizzare

martyrdom /'mɑ:tədəm/ n martirio m

martyred /'mɑ:təd/ adj fam da martire

marvel /'mɑ:vl/ [1] n meraviglia f
[2] vi (pt/pp **marvelled**) meravigliarsi (at di)

marvellous /'mɑ:vələs/ adj meraviglioso

marvellously /'mɑ:vələslɪ/ adv meravigliosamente

Marxism /'mɑ:ksɪzm/ n marxismo m

Marxist /'mɑ:ksɪst/ adj & n marxista mf

marzipan /'mɑ:zɪpæn/ n marzapane m

mascara /mæ'skɑrə/ n mascara m inv

mascot /'mæskət/ n mascotte f inv

masculine /'mæskjʊlɪn/ [1] adj maschile
[2] n Gram maschile m

masculinity /mæskjʊ'lɪnətɪ/ n mascolinità f

mash /mæʃ/ [1] n Culin fam purè m inv
[2] vt impastare

mashed potatoes /mæʃt/ npl purè m inv di patate

mask /mɑ:sk/ [1] n maschera f
[2] vt mascherare

masked ball /mɑ:skt'bɔl/ n ballo m in maschera

masking tape /'mɑ:skɪŋ/ n nastro m di carta adesiva

masochism /'mæsəkɪzm/ n masochismo m

masochist /'mæsəkɪst/ n masochista mf

mason n muratore m

Mason /'meɪsn/ n massone m

Masonic /mə'sɒnɪk/ adj massonico

masonry /'meɪsnrɪ/ n muratura f; **two tons of** ∼ due tonnellate di pietre

masquerade /mæskə'reɪd/ [1] n fig mascherata f
[2] vi ∼ **as** (pose) farsi passare per

mass¹ /mæs/ n Relig messa f

⚘ **mass²** [1] n massa f; ∼**es of** fam un sacco di
[2] vi ammassarsi

massacre /'mæsəkə(r)/ [1] n massacro m
[2] vt massacrare

massage /'mæsɑ:ʒ/ [1] n massaggio m
[2] vt massaggiare; fig manipolare ‹statistics›

masseur /mæ'sɜ:(r)/ n massaggiatore m

masseuse /mæ'sɜ:z/ n massaggiatrice f

mass grave n fossa f comune

mass hysteria n isterismo m di massa

⚘ **massive** /'mæsɪv/ adj enorme

massively /'mæsɪvlɪ/ adv estremamente

mass market [1] n mercato m di massa
[2] attrib del mercato di massa

mass-marketing /mæs'mɑ:kɪtɪŋ/ n commercializzazione f di massa

mass media npl mezzi mpl di comunicazione di massa, mass media mpl

---

⚘ indicates a very frequent word

mass murder n omicidio m di massa

mass murderer n omicida mf di massa

mass-produce vt produrre in serie

mass production n produzione f in serie

mass screening n Med controllo m su larga scala

mast /mɑ:st/ n Naut albero m; (for radio) antenna f

⚘ **master** /'mɑ:stə(r)/ [1] n maestro m, padrone m; ((teacher)) professore m; (of ship) capitano m; **M**∼ (boy) signorino m
[2] vt imparare perfettamente; avere padronanza di ‹language›

master bedroom n camera f da letto principale

master builder n capomastro m

master copy n originale m

master disk n Comput disco m master

master key n passe-partout m inv

masterly /'mæstəlɪ/ adj magistrale

mastermind [1] n cervello m
[2] vt ideare e dirigere

Master of Arts n (diploma) laurea f in lettere; (person) laureato, -a mf in lettere

master of ceremonies n (presenting entertainment) presentatore m; (of formal occasion) maestro m di cerimonie

Master of Science n (diploma) laurea f in discipline scientifiche; (person) laureato, -a mf in discipline scientifiche

masterpiece n capolavoro m

master plan n piano m generale

master race n razza f superiore

master stroke n colpo m da maestro

master tape n nastro m matrice

mastery /'mæstərɪ/ n (of subject) padronanza f

masticate /'mæstɪkeɪt/ vi masticare

masturbate /'mæstəbeɪt/ vi masturbarsi

masturbation /mæstə'beɪʃn/ n masturbazione f

mat /mæt/ n stuoia f; (on table) sottopiatto m

⚘ **match¹** /mætʃ/ [1] n Sport partita f; (equal) uguale mf; (marriage) matrimonio m; (person to marry) partito m; **be a good** ∼ ‹colours› intonarsi bene; **be no** ∼ **for** non essere dello stesso livello di
[2] vt (equal) uguagliare; (be like) andare bene con
[3] vi intonarsi

match² n fiammifero m

matchbox /'mætʃbɒks/ n scatola f di fiammiferi

matching /'mætʃɪŋ/ adj intonato

matchmaker n he's a successful ∼ (for couples) è stato l'artefice di molti matrimoni

match point n Tennis match point m inv

matchstick n fiammifero m

mate¹ /meɪt/ **1** n compagno, -a mf; (assistant) aiuto m; Naut secondo m; fam (friend) amico, -a mf
  2 vi accoppiarsi
  3 vt accoppiare

mate² n (in chess) scacco m matto

material /məˈtɪərɪəl/ **1** n materiale m; (fabric) stoffa f; **raw ~s** pl materie fpl prime
  2 adj materiale

materialism /məˈtɪərɪəlɪzm/ n materialismo m

materialistic /mətɪərɪəˈlɪstɪk/ adj materialistico

materialize /məˈtɪərɪəlaɪz/ vi materializzarsi

maternal /məˈtɜːnl/ adj materno

maternity /məˈtɜːnətɪ/ n maternità f

maternity clothes npl abiti mpl pre-maman

maternity department n (in store) reparto m pre-maman

maternity hospital n maternità f inv

maternity leave n congedo m per maternità

maternity unit n reparto m maternità

maternity ward n maternità f inv

matey /ˈmeɪtɪ/ adj fam amichevole

math /mæθ/ n Am matematica f

mathematical /mæθəˈmætɪkl/ adj matematico

mathematically /mæθəˈmætɪklɪ/ adv matematicamente

mathematician /mæθəməˈtɪʃn/ n matematico, -a mf

mathematics /mæθˈmætɪks/ n matematica fsg

maths /mæθs/ n fam matematica fsg

matinée /ˈmætɪneɪ/ n Theat matinée f inv

mating /ˈmeɪtɪŋ/ n accoppiamento m

mating call n richiamo m [per l'accoppiamento]

mating season n stagione f degli amori

matriarchal /meɪtrɪˈɑːkl/ adj matriarcale

matriarchy /ˈmeɪtrɪɑːkɪ/ n matriarchia f

matrices /ˈmeɪtrɪsiːz/ ▶ MATRIX

matriculate /məˈtrɪkjʊleɪt/ vi immatricolarsi

matriculation /mətrɪkjʊˈleɪʃn/ n immatricolazione f

matrimonial /mætrɪˈməʊnɪəl/ adj matrimoniale

matrimony /ˈmætrɪmənɪ/ n matrimonio m

matrix /ˈmeɪtrɪks/ n (pl **matrices** /ˈmeɪtrɪsiːz/) matrice f

matron /ˈmeɪtrən/ n (of hospital) capoinfermiera f; (of school) governante f

matronly /ˈmeɪtrənlɪ/ adj matronale

matron of honour n Br damigella f d'onore (sposata)

matt /mæt/ adj opaco

matted /ˈmætɪd/ adj ~ **hair** capelli mpl tutti appiccicati tra loro

matter /ˈmætə(r)/ **1** n (affair) faccenda f; (question) questione f; (pus) pus m; Phys (substance) materia f; **money ~s** questioni fpl di soldi; **as a ~ of fact** a dire la verità; **what is the ~?** che cosa c'è?
  2 vi importare; **~ to somebody** essere importante per qualcuno; **it doesn't ~** non importa

matter-of-fact adj pratico

matting /ˈmætɪŋ/ n materiale m per stuoie

mattress /ˈmætrɪs/ n materasso m

maturation /mætʃʊˈreɪʃn/ n (of tree, body) sviluppo m; (of whisky, wine) invecchiamento m; (of cheese) stagionatura f

mature /məˈtʃʊə(r)/ **1** adj maturo; Comm in scadenza
  2 vi maturare
  3 vt far maturare

mature student n Br persona (f) che riprende gli studi universitari dopo i 25 anni

maturity /məˈtʃʊərətɪ/ n maturità f; Comm maturazione f

maudlin /ˈmɔːdlɪn/ adj (song) sdolcinato; (person) piagnucoloso

maul /mɔːl/ vt malmenare

Maundy /ˈmɔːndɪ/ n **M~ Thursday** giovedì m santo

Mauritania /mɒrɪˈteɪnɪə/ n Mauritania f

Mauritius /məˈrɪʃəs/ n [isola f di] Maurizio f

mausoleum /mɔːsəˈlɪəm/ n mausoleo m

mauve /məʊv/ adj malva

maverick /ˈmævərɪk/ n, adj anticonformista mf

mawkish /ˈmɔːkɪʃ/ adj sdolcinato

max. abbr (**maximum**) max. m

maxi /ˈmæksɪ/ n (dress) vestito m alla caviglia, (skirt) gonna f alla caviglia

maxim /ˈmæksɪm/ n massima f

maximization /mæksɪmaɪˈzeɪʃn/ n massimizzazione f

maximize /ˈmæksɪmaɪz/ vt massimizzare (profits, sales); Comput ingrandire (window)

maximum /ˈmæksɪməm/ **1** adj massimo; **ten minutes ~** dieci minuti al massimo
  2 n (pl **-ima**) massimo m

maximum security prison n carcere m di massima sicurezza

may v aux (only in present) potere; **~ I come in?** posso entrare?; **if I ~ say so** se mi posso permettere; **~ you both be very happy** siate felici; **I ~ as well stay** potrei anche rimanere; **it ~ be true** potrebbe esser vero; **she ~ be old, but…** sarà anche vecchia, ma…

May /meɪ/ n maggio m

maybe /ˈmeɪbɪ/ adv forse, può darsi

May-bug n maggiolino m

Mayday n Radio mayday m inv

May Day n il primo maggio

mayhem /'meɪhem/ n create ~ creare scompiglio

mayonnaise /meɪə'neɪz/ n maionese f

mayor /'meə(r)/ n sindaco m

mayoress /meə'res/ n sindaco m; (wife of mayor) moglie f del sindaco

maypole /'meɪpəʊl/ n palo m (intorno al quale si balla durante la celebrazione del primo maggio)

May queen n reginetta f di calendimaggio

maze /meɪz/ n labirinto m

Mb abbr (**megabyte**) MB m inv

MBA n abbr (**Master of Business Administration**) laurea f inv in economia e commercio

MBE n abbr Br (**Member of the Order of the British Empire**) onorificenza (f) britannica

MBO n abbr (**management buyout**) acquisto (m) di tutte le azioni di una società da parte dei suoi dirigenti

MC n abbr 1 (**Master of Ceremonies**) (in cabaret) presentatore m; (at banquet) maestro m delle cerimonie
2 Am (**Member of Congress**) membro m del Congresso

McCoy /mə'kɔɪ/ n this whisky is the real ~ questo è un vero whisky

MD abbr 1 (**Managing Director**) direttore, -trice mf generale
2 (**Doctor of Medicine**) dottore m in medicina
3 Am (**Maryland**)

ᕲ **me** /miː/ pers pron (object) mi; (with preposition) me; he knows me mi conosce; she called me, not you ha chiamato me, non te; give me the money dammi i soldi; give it to me dammelo; he explained it to me me lo ha spiegato; it's me sono io

ME n abbr 1 (**myalgic encephalomyelitis**) encefalomielite f mialgica
2 Am (**Maine**)

mead /miːd/ n idromele m

meadow /'medəʊ/ n prato m

meagre /'miːgə(r)/ adj scarso

ᕲ **meal¹** /miːl/ n pasto m; did you enjoy your ~? ha mangiato bene?

meal² n (grain) farina f

meal ticket n fig (quality, qualification) fonte f di guadagno; he's only a ~ to her le interessano solo i suoi soldi

mealy-mouthed /miːlɪ'maʊðd/ adj ambiguo

mean¹ /miːn/ adj avaro; (unkind) meschino; (low in rank) basso; (accommodation) misero

mean² 1 adj medio
2 n (average) media f; Greenwich ~ time ora f media di Greenwich

ᕲ **mean³** vt (pt/pp **meant**) voler dire; (signify) significare; (intend) intendere; I ~ it lo dico seriamente; ~ well avere buone intenzioni; be ~t for ⟨present⟩ essere destinato a; ⟨remark⟩ essere riferito a

meander /mɪ'ændə(r)/ vi vagare

ᕲ **meaning** /'miːnɪŋ/ n significato m

meaningful /'miːnɪŋfʊl/ adj significativo

meaningless /'miːnɪŋlɪs/ adj senza senso

meanness /'miːnnɪs/ n (with money) avarizia f; (unkindness) meschinità f

means /miːnz/ 1 n mezzo m; ~ of transport mezzo m di trasporto; by ~ of per mezzo di; by all ~! certamente!; by no ~ niente affatto
2 npl (resources) mezzi mpl; ~ test n accertamento m patrimoniale

meant /ment/ ▶ MEAN³

meantime /'miːntaɪm/ 1 n in the ~ nel frattempo
2 adv intanto

ᕲ **meanwhile** /'miːnwaɪl/ adv intanto

measles /'miːzlz/ nsg morbillo m

measly /'miːzlɪ/ adj fam misero

measurable /'meʒərəbl/ adj misurabile

ᕲ **measure** /'meʒə(r)/ 1 n misura f
2 vt/i misurare
■ **measure out** vt dosare ⟨amount⟩
■ **measure up** vi fig avere i requisiti richiesti
■ **measure up to** vt fig essere all'altezza di

measured /'meʒed/ adj misurato

measurement /'meʒəmənt/ n misura f

measuring jug /'meʒərɪŋ/ n dosatore m

measuring spoon n misurino m

meat /miːt/ n carne f

meatball n Culin polpetta f di carne

meat-eater n (animal) carnivoro m; I'm not a ~ non mangio carne

meat hook n gancio m da macellaio

meat loaf n polpettone m

meat pie n tortino m di carne

meaty /'miːtɪ/ (-ier, -iest) adj (-ier, -iest) di carne; fig sostanzioso

Mecca /'mekə/ n La Mecca

mechanic /mɪ'kænɪk/ n meccanico m

mechanical /mɪ'kænɪkl/ adj meccanico

mechanical engineering n ingegneria f meccanica

mechanically /mɪ'kænɪklɪ/ adv meccanicamente

mechanics /mɪ'kænɪks/ 1 n meccanica f
2 npl meccanismo msg

ᕲ **mechanism** /'mekənɪzm/ n meccanismo m

ᕲ indicates a very frequent word

mechanization /ˌmekənərˈzeɪʃn, US -nɪˈz-/ n meccanizzazione f

mechanize /ˈmekənaɪz/ vt meccanizzare

medal /ˈmedl/ n medaglia f

medallion /mɪˈdælɪən/ n medaglione m

medallist /ˈmedəlɪst/ n vincitore, -trice mf di una medaglia

meddle /ˈmedl/ vi immischiarsi (**in** in); (tinker) armeggiare (**with** con)

⚹ **media** /ˈmiːdɪə/ [1] n ▶ MEDIUM
[2] npl the ∼ i mass media

median /ˈmiːdɪən/ adj ∼ **strip** Am banchina f spartitraffico

media studies npl scienze fpl delle comunicazioni

mediate /ˈmiːdɪeɪt/ vi fare da mediatore

mediation /miːdɪˈeɪʃn/ n mediazione f

mediator /ˈmiːdɪeɪtə(r)/ n mediatore, -trice mf

medic /ˈmedɪk/ n fam (doctor) medico m; fam (student) studente, -essa mf di medicina; Mil fam infermiere, -a mf militare

⚹ **medical** /ˈmedɪkl/ [1] adj medico
[2] n visita f medica

medical care n assistenza f medica

medical check-up n controllo m medico

medical examiner n Am = PATHOLOGIST

medical history n anamnesi f inv

medical insurance n assicurazione f sanitaria

medically /ˈmedɪklɪ/ adv ∼ **qualified** con qualifiche di medico; ∼ **fit** in buona salute

medical officer n Mil ufficiale m medico

medical profession n (occupation) professione f del medico; (doctors collectively) categoria f medica

medical student n studente, -essa mf di medicina

medicated /ˈmedɪkeɪtɪd/ adj medicato

medication /medɪˈkeɪʃn/ n (drugs) medicinali mpl; **are you on any** ∼**?** sta prendendo delle medicine?

medicinal /mɪˈdɪsɪnl/ adj medicinale

⚹ **medicine** /ˈmedsən/ n medicina f

medicine ball n palla f medica

medicine bottle n flacone m

medicine cabinet n armadietto m dei medicinali

medicine man n stregone m

medieval /medrˈiːvl/ adj medievale

mediocre /miːdrˈəʊkə(r)/ adj mediocre

mediocrity /miːdiˈɒkrətɪ/ n mediocrità f

meditate /ˈmedɪteɪt/ vi meditare (**on** su)

meditative /ˈmedɪtətɪv/ adj ‹music, person› meditativo; ‹mood, expression› meditabondo

Mediterranean /medɪtəˈreɪnɪən/ [1] n the **M**∼ [**Sea**] il [mare] Mediterraneo
[2] adj mediterraneo

medium /ˈmiːdɪəm/ [1] adj medio; Culin di media cottura
[2] n mezzo m (pl **-s**) (person) medium mf inv

medium dry adj ‹drink› semisecco

medium-length adj ‹book, film, hair› di media lunghezza

medium-range adj ‹missile› di media portata

medium-rare adj ‹meat› appena al sangue

medium-sized /ˈmiːdɪəmsaɪzd/ adj di taglia media

medium wave n onde fpl medie

medley /ˈmedlɪ/ n miscuglio m; Mus miscellanea f

meek /miːk/ adj mite, mansueto

meekly /ˈmiːklɪ/ adv docilmente

meerkat /ˈmɪəkæt/ n suricato m

⚹ **meet** /miːt/ [1] vt (pt/pp **met**) incontrare; (at station, airport) andare incontro a; (for first time) far la conoscenza di; pagare ‹bill›; soddisfare ‹requirements›
[2] vi incontrarsi; ‹committee› riunirsi; ∼ **with** incontrare ‹problem›; incontrarsi con ‹person›
[3] n raduno m (sportivo)
■ **meet up** vi ‹people› incontrarsi; ∼ **up with somebody** incontrare qualcuno

⚹ **meeting** /ˈmiːtɪŋ/ n riunione f, meeting m inv; (large) assemblea f; (by chance) incontro m; **be in a** ∼ essere in riunione

meeting-place n luogo m d'incontro

meeting-point n punto m d'incontro

mega+ /ˈmegə/ pref mega+

megabyte /ˈmegəbaɪt/ n Comput megabyte m inv

megalith /ˈmegəlɪθ/ n megalite m

megalomania /megələˈmeɪnɪə/ n megalomania f

megalomaniac /ˌmegələˈmeɪnɪæk/ adj & n megalomane mf

megaphone /ˈmegəfəʊn/ n megafono m

melancholy /ˈmelənkəlɪ/ [1] adj malinconico
[2] n malinconia f

mellow /ˈmeləʊ/ [1] adj ‹wine› generoso; ‹sound, colour› caldo; ‹person› dolce
[2] vi ‹person› addolcirsi

melodic /mɪˈlɒdɪk/ adj melodico

melodious /mɪˈləʊdɪəs/ adj melodioso

melodrama /ˈmelədrɑːmə/ n melodramma m

melodramatic /melədrəˈmætɪk/ adj melodrammatico

melodramatically /melədrəˈmætɪklɪ/ adv in modo melodrammatico

melody /ˈmelədɪ/ n melodia f

melon /ˈmelən/ n melone m

melt /melt/ [1] vt sciogliere
[2] vi sciogliersi ⋯▷

■ **melt away** *vi* ‹*snow*› sciogliersi; ‹*crowd*› disperdersi; ‹*support*› venir meno

■ **melt down** *vt* fondere

meltdown /'meltdaʊn/ *n* (in nuclear reactor) fusione *f* del nocciolo

melting point /'meltɪŋ/ *n* punto *m* di fusione

melting pot *n* fig crogiuolo *m*

♂ **member** /'membə(r)/ *n* membro *m*; be a ∼ of the family far parte della famiglia

member countries paesi *mpl* membri

Member of Congress *n* Am membro *m* del Congresso

Member of Parliament deputato, -a *mf*

Member of the European Parliament *n* eurodeputato, -a *mf*

membership /'membəʃɪp/ *n* iscrizione *f*; (members) soci *mpl*

membrane /'membreɪn/ *n* membrana *f*

memento /mɪ'mentəʊ/ *n* ricordo *m*

memo /'meməʊ/ *n* promemoria *m inv*

memoirs /'memwɑːz/ *npl* ricordi *mpl*

memo pad *n* blocchetto *m*

memorabilia /memərə'bɪlɪə/ *npl* cimeli *mpl*

memorable /'memərəbl/ *adj* memorabile

memorandum /memə'rændəm/ *n* promemoria *m inv*

memorial /mɪ'mɔːrɪəl/ *n* monumento *m*

memorial service *n* funzione *f* commemorativa

memorize /'meməraɪz/ *vt* memorizzare

♂ **memory** /'memərɪ/ *n* (also Comput) memoria *f*; (thing remembered) ricordo *m*; from ∼ a memoria; in ∼ of in ricordo di

men /men/ ▶ MAN

menace /'menəs/ **1** *n* minaccia *f*; (nuisance) piaga *f*
2 *vt* minacciare

menacing /'menəsɪŋ/ *adj* minaccioso

menacingly /'menəsɪŋlɪ/ *adv* minacciosamente

mend /mend/ **1** *vt* riparare; (darn) rammendare
2 *n* on the ∼ in via di guarigione

menfolk /'menfəʊk/ *n* uomini *mpl*

menial /'miːnɪəl/ *adj* umile

meningitis /menɪn'dʒaɪtɪs/ *n* meningite *f*

menopause /'menəpɔːz/ *n* menopausa *f*

Menorca /mɪ'nɔːkə/ *n* Minorca *f*

men's room *n* toilette *f inv* degli uomini

menstruate /'menstrʊeɪt/ *vi* mestruare

menstruation /menstrʊ'eɪʃn/ *n* mestruazione *f*

menswear /'menzweə(r)/ *n* abbigliamento *m* per uomo

♂ **mental** /'mentl/ *adj* mentale; fam (mad) pazzo

mental arithmetic *n* calcolo *m* mentale

mental block *n* blocco *m* psicologico

mental health *n* (of person) salute *f* mentale

mental health care *n* assistenza *f* psichiatrica

mental home *n* clinica *f* psichiatrica

mental illness *n* malattia *f* mentale

mentality /men'tælətɪ/ *n* mentalità *f inv*

mentally /'mentəlɪ/ *adv* mentalmente; ∼ ill malato di mente

mentholated /'menθəleɪtɪd/ *adj* al mentolo

♂ **mention** /'menʃn/ **1** *n* menzione *f*
2 *vt* menzionare; don't ∼ it non c'è di che

mentor /'mentɔː(r)/ *n* mentore *m*

menu /'menjuː/ *n* menu *m inv*

menu bar *n* Comput barra *f* dei menu

MEP *n abbr* (**Member of the European parliament**) eurodeputato, -a *mf*

mercantile /'mɜːkəntaɪl/ *adj* mercantile

mercenary /'mɜːsɪnərɪ/ **1** *adj* mercenario
2 *n* mercenario *m*

merchandise /'mɜːtʃəndaɪz/ *n* merce *f*

merchant /'mɜːtʃənt/ *n* commerciante *mf*

merchant bank *n* Br banca *f* d'affari

merchant banker *n* (owner) proprietario, -a *mf* di una banca d'affari; (executive) dirigente *mf* di banca d'affari

merchant navy *n* marina *f* mercantile

merciful /'mɜːsɪfl/ *adj* misericordioso

mercifully /'mɜːsɪfʊlɪ/ *adv* fam grazie a Dio

merciless /'mɜːsɪlɪs/ *adj* spietato

mercilessly /'mɜːsɪlɪslɪ/ *adv* senza pietà

mercurial /mɜː'kjʊərɪəl/ *adj* fig volubile

mercury /'mɜːkjʊrɪ/ *n* mercurio *m*

mercy /'mɜːsɪ/ *n* misericordia *f*; be at sb's ∼ essere alla mercé *or* in balia di qualcuno

mercy killing *n* eutanasia *f*

mere /mɪə(r)/ *adj* solo

♂ **merely** /'mɪəlɪ/ *adv* solamente

merest /'mɪərɪst/ *adj* minimo

merge /mɜːdʒ/ **1** *vi* fondersi
2 *vt* Comm fondere

merger /'mɜːdʒə(r)/ *n* fusione *f*

meridian /mə'rɪdɪən/ *n* meridiano *m*

meringue /mə'ræŋ/ *n* meringa *f*

merit /'merɪt/ **1** *n* merito *m*; (advantage) qualità *f inv*
2 *vt* meritare

mermaid /'mɜːmeɪd/ *n* sirena *f*

merrily /'merɪlɪ/ *adv* allegramente

merriment /'merɪmənt/ *n* baldoria *f*

merry /'merɪ/ (**-ier, -iest**) *adj* (**-ier, -iest**) allegro; **M~ Christmas!** Buon Natale!; **make ~ far festa**

merry-go-round *n* giostra *f*

merry-making /'merɪmeɪkɪŋ/ *n* festa *f*

mesh /meʃ/ *n* maglia *f*

mesmerize /'mezməraɪz/ *vt* ipnotizzare

mesmerized /'mezməraɪzd/ *adj* fig ipnotizzato

mess /mes/ *n* disordine *m*, casino *m* fam; (trouble) guaio *m*; (something spilt) sporco *m*; Mil mensa *f*; **make a ~ of** (botch) fare un pasticcio di
■ **mess about** ① *vi* perder tempo; **~ about with** armeggiare con
② *vt* prendere in giro ‹person›
■ **mess up** *vt* mettere in disordine, incasinare fam; (botch) mandare all'aria
■ **mess with** *vt* fam (interface with) trafficare con ‹computer, radio etc›; contrariare ‹person›

message /'mesɪdʒ/ *n* messaggio *m*

message window *n* Comput finestra *f* di messaggio

messaging /'mesɪdʒɪŋ/ *n* messaggeria *f* elettronica

mess dress *n* Mil uniforme *f* di gala

messenger /'mesɪndʒə(r)/ *n* messaggero *m*

messenger boy *n* fattorino *m*

Messiah /mɪ'saɪə/ *n* Messia *m*

Messrs /'mesəz/ *npl* (on letter) **~ Smith** Spett. ditta Smith

messy /'mesɪ/ *adj* (**-ier, -iest**) disordinato; (in dress) sciatto

met /met/ ▶ MEET

metabolism /mɪ'tæbəlɪzm/ *n* metabolismo *m*

metal /'metl/ ① *n* metallo *m*
② *adj* di metallo

metal detector *n* metal detector *m inv*

metal fatigue *n* fatica *f* del metallo

metallic /mɪ'tælɪk/ *adj* metallico

metallurgy /mɪ'tælədʒɪ/ *n* metallurgia *f*

metal polish *n* lucido *m* per metalli

metalwork /'metlwɜːk/ *n* lavorazione *f* del metallo

metamorphose /metə'mɔːfəʊz/ ① *vt* trasformare
② *vi* trasformarsi (**into** in)

metamorphosis /metə'mɔːfəsɪs/ *n* (*pl* **-phoses** /metə'mɔːfəsiːz/) metamorfosi *f inv*

metaphor /'metəfə(r)/ *n* metafora *f*

metaphorical /metə'fɒrɪkl/ *adj* metaforico

metaphorically /metə'fɒrɪklɪ/ *adv* metaforicamente

metaphysical /metə'fɪzɪkl/ *adj* metafisico; (abstract) astruso

mete /miːt/ *v*

■ **mete out** *vt* dispensare ‹punishment, justice›

meteor /'miːtɪə(r)/ *n* meteora *f*

meteoric /miːtɪ'ɒrɪk/ *adj* fig fulmineo

meteorite /'miːtɪəraɪt/ *n* meteorite *m*

meteorological /miːtɪərə'lɒdʒɪkl/ *adj* meteorologico

Meteorological Office *n* Ufficio *m* meteorologico

meteorologist /miːtɪə'rɒlədʒɪst/ *n* meteorologo, -a *mf*

meteorology /miːtɪə'rɒlədʒɪ/ *n* meteorologia *f*

meter¹ /'miːtə(r)/ *n* contatore *m*

meter² *n* Am = METRE

meter reader *n* persona (*f*) incaricata di leggere il contatore (di gas, elettricità)

methane /'miːθeɪn/ *n* metano *m*

method /'meθəd/ *n* metodo *m*

method acting *n* metodo *m* dell'Actors' Studio

method actor *n* attore (*m*) che segue il metodo dell'Actors' Studio

methodical /mɪ'θɒdɪkl/ *adj* metodico

methodically /mɪ'θɒdɪklɪ/ *adv* metodicamente

Methodist /'meθədɪst/ *n* metodista *mf*

methodology /meθə'dɒlədʒɪ/ *n* metodologia *f*

meths /meθs/ *n* fam alcol *m* denaturato

methyl /'miːθaɪl/ *n* metile *m*

methylated /'meθɪleɪtɪd/ *adj* **~ spirit(s)** alcol *m* denaturato

meticulous /mɪ'tɪkjʊləs/ *adj* meticoloso

meticulously /mɪ'tɪkjʊləslɪ/ *adv* meticolosamente

metre /'miːtə(r)/ *n* metro *m*

metric /'metrɪk/ *adj* metrico

metrication /metrɪ'keɪʃn/ *n* conversione *f* al sistema metrico

metronome /'metrənəʊm/ *n* metronomo *m*

metropolis /mɪ'trɒpəlɪs/ *n* metropoli *f inv*

metropolitan /metrə'pɒlɪtən/ *adj* metropolitano

metropolitan district *n* Br circoscrizione *f* amministrativa urbana

Metropolitan police *n* Br polizia *f* di Londra

mettle /'metl/ *n* coraggio *m*; **show one's ~** mostrare di che stoffa si è fatti

mew /mjuː/ ① *n* miao *m*
② *vi* miagolare

mews /mjuːz/ *n* Br (stables) scuderie *fpl*; (street) stradina *f*; (yard) cortile *m*

mews flat *n* Br *piccolo appartamento* (*m*) *ricavato da vecchie scuderie*

Mexican /'meksɪkən/ *adj & n* messicano, -a *mf*

m

Mexican wave *n* ola *f inv*

Mexico /'meksɪkəʊ/ *n* Messico *m*

mezzanine /'metsəniːn/ *n* mezzanino *m*

miaow /mɪ'aʊ/ ① *n* miao *m*
② *vi* miagolare

mice /maɪs/ ▶ MOUSE

Michaelmas /'mɪkəlməs/ *n* festa *f* di San
Michele (*29 settembre*)

Michaelmas daisy *n* Br margherita *f*
settembrina

Michaelmas Term *n* Br Univ primo
trimestre *m*

mickey /'mɪkɪ/ *n* take the ∼ out of
prendere in giro

Mickey Mouse *n* Topolino *m*

microbe /'maɪkrəʊb/ *n* microbo *m*

microchip /'maɪkrəʊtʃɪp/ *n* microchip
m inv

microcomputer /'maɪkrəʊkəmpjuːtə(r)/
n microcomputer *m inv*

microcosm /'maɪkrəkɒzm/ *n* microcosmo
m

microfilm *n* microfilm *m inv*

microlight /'maɪkrəʊlaɪt/ *n* ultraleggero
m

microlighting /'maɪkrəlaɪtɪŋ/ *n* volo *m*
con l'ultraleggero

micromanage /'maɪkrəʊˌmænɪdʒ/
vt gestire, controllare in modo capillare
un'impresa o un'attività

micromesh tights *npl* collant *mpl*
velati

microphone *n* microfono *m*

microphysics *n* microfisica *f*

microprocessor *n* microprocessore *m*

microscope *n* microscopio *m*

microscopic *adj* microscopico

microsite /'maɪkrəʊsaɪt/ *n* microsito *m*

microsurgery *n* microchirurgia *f*

microwave *n* microonda *f*; (oven) forno *m*
a microonde

mid /mɪd/ *adj* ∼ May metà maggio; in ∼ air
a mezz'aria

midday /mɪd'deɪ/ *n* mezzogiorno *m*

ϑ **middle** /'mɪdl/ ① *adj* di centro; the M∼
Ages il medioevo; the ∼ class(es) la classe
media; the M∼ East il Medio Oriente
② *n* mezzo *m*; in the ∼ of ‹room, floor etc› in
mezzo a; in the ∼ of the night nel pieno della
notte, a notte piena

middle-aged /-'eɪdʒd/ *adj* di mezza età

middle-age spread *n* pancetta *f* di
mezza età

Middle America *n* (social group) ceto (*m*)
medio americano a tendenza conservatrice

middlebrow *adj* ‹book› per il lettore
medio; ‹person› con interessi culturali
convenzionali

middle-class *adj* borghese

middle distance *n* Phot, Cinema secondo
piano *m*; gaze into the ∼ avere lo sguardo
perso nel vuoto

middle-eastern *adj* mediorientale

Middle English *n* medio inglese *m*

middle finger *n* dito *m* medio

middle ground *n* Pol centro *m*; occupy
the ∼ adottare una posizione intermedia

middle-income *adj* ‹person, family,
country› dal reddito medio

middleman /'mɪdlmæn/ *n* Comm
intermediario *m*

middle manager *n* quadro *m*
intermedio

middle-of-the-road *adj* (ordinary)
ordinario; ‹policy› moderato

middle-size[d] /-saɪz[d]/ *adj* di misura
media

middleweight *n* peso *m* medio

middling /'mɪdlɪŋ/ *adj* discreto

midfield /'mɪd'fiːld/ *n* centrocampo *m*

midfield player *n* centrocampista *m*

midge /mɪdʒ/ *n* moscerino *m*

midget /'mɪdʒɪt/ *n* nano, -a *mf*

Midlands /'mɪdləndz/ *npl* the M∼
l'Inghilterra *fsg* centrale

mid-life *n* mezza età *f*

mid-life crisis *n* crisi *f inv* di mezza età

midnight /'mɪdnaɪt/ *n* mezzanotte *f*

mid-range *attrib* ‹car› (in price) di prezzo
medio; (in power) di media cilindrata; ‹hotel›
intermedio; be in the ∼ ‹product, hotel›
essere nella media

midriff /'mɪdrɪf/ *n* diaframma *m*

mid-season *adj* di metà stagione

midshipman /'mɪdʃɪpmən/ *n* Br cadetto
m di marina; Am allievo *m* dell'Accademia
Navale

midst /mɪdst/ *n* in the ∼ of in mezzo a; in
our ∼ fra di noi, in mezzo a noi

midstream /mɪd'striːm/ *adv* in ∼ (in river)
nel mezzo della corrente; fig (in speech) nel
mezzo del discorso

midsummer /'mɪdsʌmə(r)/ *n* mezza
estate *f*

Midsummer's Day *n* festa *f* di San
Giovanni (*24 giugno*)

mid-term *attrib* Sch di metà trimestre; (pol)
a metà del mandato del governo

midtown /'mɪdtaʊn/ *n* Am centro *m*
(cittadino); a ∼ apartment un appartamento
in centro

midway /'mɪdweɪ/ *adv* a metà strada

midweek /mɪd'wiːk/ ① *adj* di metà
settimana
② *adv* a metà settimana

midwife /'mɪdwaɪf/ *n* ostetrica *f*

midwifery /'mɪdwɪfrɪ/ *n* ostetricia *f*

m

midwinter /mɪd'wɪntə(r)/ n pieno inverno m

miffed /mɪft/ adj fam seccato

✦ **might¹** /maɪt/ v aux I ∼ potrei; will you come?—I ∼ vieni?—può darsi; it ∼ be true potrebbe essere vero; I ∼ as well stay potrei anche restare; he asked if he ∼ go ha chiesto se poteva andare; you ∼ have drowned avresti potuto affogare; you ∼ have said so! avresti potuto dirlo!

might² n potere m

mighty /'maɪtɪ/ ① adj (-ier, -iest) potente
② adv fam molto

migraine /'miːgreɪn/ n emicrania f

migrant /'maɪgrənt/ ① adj migratore
② n (bird) migratore, -trice mf; (person: for work) emigrante mf

migrate /maɪ'greɪt/ vi migrare

migration /maɪ'greɪʃn/ n migrazione f

migratory /maɪ'greɪtərɪ/ adj ‹animal› migratore

mike /maɪk/ n fam microfono f

Milan /mɪ'læn/ n Milano f

Milanese /mɪlə'niːz/ adj milanese

mild /maɪld/ adj ‹weather› mite; ‹person› dolce; ‹flavour› delicato; ‹illness› leggero

mildew /'mɪldjuː/ n muffa f

mildly /'maɪldlɪ/ adv moderatamente; ‹say› dolcemente; to put it ∼ a dir poco, senza esagerazione

mildness /'maɪldnɪs/ n (of person, words) dolcezza f; (of weather) mitezza f

✦ **mile** /maɪl/ n miglio m (= 1,6 km); ∼s nicer fam molto più bello; ∼s too big fam eccessivamente grande

mileage /'maɪlɪdʒ/ n chilometraggio m

mileage allowance n indennità f inv di trasferta per chilometro

milestone /'maɪlstəʊn/ n pietra f miliare

milieu /mɪ'jɜː/ n ambiente m

militant /'mɪlɪtənt/ adj & n militante mf

militarism /'mɪlɪtərɪzm/ n militarismo m

militarize /'mɪlɪtəraɪz/ vt militarizzare

✦ **military** /'mɪlɪtrɪ/ adj militare

military academy n accademia f militare

military policeman n agente m di polizia militare

military service n servizio m militare

militate /'mɪlɪteɪt/ vi ∼ against opporsi a

militia /mɪ'lɪʃə/ n milizia f

milk /mɪlk/ ① n latte m
② vt mungere

milk chocolate n cioccolato m al latte

milk float n Br furgone m del lattaio

milk jug n bricco m del latte

milkman n lattaio m

milk pudding n budino (m) a base di latte

milk shake n frappé m inv

milk train n primo treno m del mattino

milky /'mɪlkɪ/ adj (-ier, -iest) latteo; ‹tea etc› con molto latte

mill /mɪl/ ① n mulino m; (factory) fabbrica f; (for coffee etc) macinino m
② vt macinare ‹grain›
■ **mill about, mill around** vi brulicare

millennium /mɪ'lenɪəm/ n millennio m

miller /'mɪlə(r)/ n mugnaio m

millet /'mɪlɪt/ n miglio m

✦ **million** /'mɪljən/ adj & n milione m; a ∼ pounds un milione di sterline

millionaire /mɪljə'neə(r)/ n miliardario, -a mf

millipede /'mɪlɪpiːd/ n millepiedi m inv

millpond n like a ∼ calmo come una tavola

millstone n a ∼ round one's neck fig un peso

mill-wheel n ruota f di mulino

milometer /maɪ'lɒmɪtə(r)/ n Br ≈ contachilometri m inv

mime /maɪm/ ① n mimo m
② vt mimare

mime artist n mimo, a mf

mimic /'mɪmɪk/ ① n imitatore, -trice mf
② vt (pt/pp mimicked) imitare

mimicry /'mɪmɪkrɪ/ n mimetismo m

mimosa /mɪ'məʊzə/ n mimosa f

min. abbr (**minute**) min.

minaret /mɪnə'ret/ n minareto m

mince /mɪns/ ① n carne f tritata
② vt Culin tritare; not ∼ words parlare senza mezzi termini

mincemeat /'mɪnsmiːt/ n miscuglio m di frutta secca; make ∼ of fig demolire

mince pie n pasticcino (m) a base di frutta secca

mincer /'mɪnsə(r)/ n tritacarne m inv

✦ **mind** /maɪnd/ ① n mente f; (sanity) ragione f; to my ∼ a mio parere; give somebody a piece of one's ∼ dire chiaro e tondo a qualcuno quello che si pensa; make up one's ∼ decidersi; have something in ∼ avere qualcosa in mente; bear something in ∼ tenere presente qualcosa; have something on one's ∼ essere preoccupato; have a good ∼ to avere una grande voglia di; I have changed my ∼ ho cambiato idea; be out of one's ∼ essere fuori di sé
② vt (look after) occuparsi di; I don't ∼ the noise il rumore non dà fastidio; I don't ∼ what we do non mi importa quello che facciamo; ∼ the step! attenzione al gradino!
③ vi I don't ∼ non mi importa; never ∼! non importa!; do you ∼ if...? ti dispiace se...?
■ **mind out**: vi ∼ out! [fai] attenzione!

mind-bending /-bendɪŋ/ *adj* ‹*problem*› complicatissimo; ∼ **drugs** psicofarmaci *mpl*

mind-blowing /-bləʊɪŋ/ *adj* fam sconvolgente

mind-boggling /-bɒglɪŋ/ *adj* fam incredibile

minded /'maɪndɪd/ *adj* **if you're so** ∼ se vuole

minder /'maɪndə(r)/ *n* Br (bodyguard) gorilla *m inv*; (for child) baby-sitter *mf inv*

mindful /'maɪndfʊl/ *adj* ∼ **of** attento a

mindless /'maɪndlɪs/ *adj* noncurante

mind-reader *n* persona *f* che legge nel pensiero; **I'm not a** ∼ non leggo nel pensiero

❡ **mine¹** /maɪn/ *poss pron* il mio *m*, la mia *f*, i miei *mpl*, le mie *fpl*; **a friend of** ∼ un mio amico; **friends of** ∼ dei miei amici; **that is** ∼ questo è mio; (as opposed to yours) questo è il mio

mine² ① *n* miniera *f*; (explosive) mina *f*
② *vt* estrarre; Mil minare

mine-detector *n* rivelatore *m* di mine

minefield /'maɪnfiːld/ *n* also fig campo *m* minato

miner /'maɪnə(r)/ *n* minatore *m*

mineral /'mɪnərəl/ ① *n* minerale *m*
② *adj* minerale

mineral oil *n* Am (paraffin) olio *m* minerale

mineral rights *npl* concessioni *fpl* minerarie

mineral water *n* acqua *f* minerale

minesweeper /'maɪnswiːpə(r)/ *n* dragamine *m inv*

mingle /'mɪŋgl/ *vi* ∼ **with** mescolarsi a

mini /'mɪnɪ/ *n* ▶ MINISKIRT

mini+ *pref* mini+

miniature /'mɪnɪtʃə(r)/ ① *adj* in miniatura
② *n* miniatura *f*

miniature golf *n* minigolf *m inv*

miniature railway *n* trenino *m*

mini-budget *n* Br Pol budget *m inv* provvisorio

minibus *n* minibus *m inv*, pulmino *m*

minicab *n* taxi *m inv*

minidisc /'mɪnɪdɪsk/ *n* minidisc *m inv*

minidisc player *n* lettore *m* di minidisc

minim /'mɪnɪm/ *n* Mus minima *f*

minimal /'mɪnɪməl/ *adj* minimo

minimalist /'mɪnɪməlɪst/ *adj* minimalista

minimally /'mɪnɪməlɪ/ *adv* (very slightly) minimamente

minimarket /'mɪnɪmɑːkɪt/ *n* minimarket *m inv*

minimize /'mɪnɪmaɪz/ *vt* minimizzare

minimum /'mɪnɪməm/ ① *n* (*pl* **-ima**) minimo *m*

② *adj* minimo; **ten minutes** ∼ minimo dieci minuti

mining /'maɪnɪŋ/ ① *n* estrazione *f*
② *attrib* estrattivo

mining engineer *n* ingegnere *m* minerario

miniskirt /'mɪnɪskɜːt/ *n* minigonna *f*

❡ **minister** /'mɪnɪstə(r)/ *n* ministro *m*; Relig pastore

ministerial /mɪnɪ'stɪərɪəl/ *adj* ministeriale

minister of state *n* Br Pol titolo (*m*) di un parlamentare con competenze specifiche in seno a un ministero

ministry /'mɪnɪstrɪ/ *n* Pol ministero *m*; **the** ∼ Relig il ministero sacerdotale

mink /mɪŋk/ *n* visone *m*

minnow /'mɪnəʊ/ *n* (fish) pesciolino *m* d'acqua dolce

❡ **minor** /'maɪnə(r)/ ① *adj* minore
② *n* minorenne *mf*

Minorca /mɪ'nɔːkə/ *n* Minorca *f*

❡ **minority** /maɪ'nɒrətɪ/ *n* minoranza *f*; (age) minore età *f*

minority leader *n* Am Pol leader *mf inv* dell'opposizione

minority rule *n* governo *m* di minoranza

minor offence *n* Br reato *m* minore

minor road *n* strada *f* secondaria

minster /'mɪnstə(r)/ *n* (cathedral) cattedrale *f*

minstrel /'mɪnstrəl/ *n* menestrello *m*

mint¹ /mɪnt/ ① *n* zecca *f*; fam patrimonio *m*
② *adj* **in** ∼ **condition** in condizione perfetta
③ *vt* coniare

mint² *n* (herb) menta *f*

mint-flavoured /-fleɪvəd/ *adj* al gusto di menta

minuet /mɪnjʊ'et/ *n* minuetto *m*

minus /'maɪnəs/ ① *prep* meno; fam (without) senza
② *n* ∼ **[sign]** meno *m*

minuscule /'mɪnəskjuːl/ *adj* minuscolo

❡ **minute¹** /'mɪnɪt/ *n* minuto *m*; **in a** ∼ (shortly) tra un minuto; ∼**s** *pl* (of meeting) verbale *msg*

minute² /maɪ'njuːt/ *adj* minuto; (precise) minuzioso

minute hand /'mɪnɪt/ *n* lancetta *f* dei minuti

minutely /maɪ'njuːtlɪ/ *adv* ‹*vary, differ*› di poco; ‹*describe, examine*› minuziosamente

minutiae /maɪ'njuːʃɪaɪ/ *npl* minuzie *fpl*

miracle /'mɪrəkl/ *n* miracolo *m*

miraculous /mɪ'rækjʊləs/ *adj* miracoloso

mirage /'mɪrɑːʒ/ *n* miraggio *m*

mire /'maɪə(r)/ *n* pantano *m*

mirror /'mɪrə(r)/ ① *n* specchio *m*
② *vt* rispecchiare

❡ indicates a very frequent word

mirror image n (exact replica) copia f esatta; (inverse) immagine f speculare

mirth /mɜːθ/ n ilarità f

misadventure /misæd'ventʃə(r)/ n disavventura f

misanthropist /mɪˈzænθrəpɪst/ n misantropo, -a mf

misapprehension /misæprɪˈhenʃn/ n malinteso m; **be under a** ∼ avere frainteso

misappropriate /misəˈprəʊprɪeɪt/ vt appropriarsi indebitamente di ‹funds›

misbehave /misbɪˈheɪv/ vi comportarsi male

misbehaviour /misbɪˈheɪvjə(r)/ n comportamento m scorretto

miscalculate /misˈkælkjʊleɪt/ vt/i calcolare male

miscalculation /miskælkjʊˈleɪʃn/ n calcolo m sbagliato

miscarriage /ˈmiskærɪdʒ/ n aborto m spontaneo; ∼ **of justice** errore m giudiziario

miscarry /misˈkæri/ vi abortire

miscellaneous /misəˈleɪnɪəs/ adj assortito

miscellany /miˈseləni/ n (of people, things) misto m; (anthology) miscellanea f

mischief /ˈmistʃif/ n malefatta f; (harm) danno m

mischievous /ˈmistʃivəs/ adj (naughty) birichino; (malicious) dannoso

mischievously /ˈmistʃivəsli/ adv in modo birichino

misconceived /miskənˈsiːvd/ adj ‹argument, project› sbagliato

misconception /miskənˈsepʃn/ n concetto m erroneo

misconduct /misˈkɒndʌkt/ n cattiva condotta f

misconstrue /miskənˈstruː/ vt fraintendere

miscount /misˈkaʊnt/ vt/i contare male

misdeed /misˈdiːd/ n misfatto m

misdemeanour /misdɪˈmiːnə(r)/ n reato m

misdirect /misdaɪˈrekt/ vt mettere l'indirizzo sbagliato su ‹letter, parcel›; dare istruzioni sbagliate a ‹jury›; **the letter was** ∼**ed to our old address** la lettera ci è stata erroneamente spedita al vecchio indirizzo

miser /ˈmaɪzə(r)/ n avaro m

miserable /ˈmizrəbl/ adj (unhappy) infelice; (wretched) miserabile; fig ‹weather› deprimente

miserably /ˈmizrəbli/ adv ‹live, fail› miseramente; ‹say› tristemente

miserly /ˈmaɪzəli/ adj avaro; ‹amount› ridicolo

misery /ˈmizəri/ n miseria f; fam (person) piagnone, -a mf

misfire /misˈfaɪə(r)/ vi ‹gun› far cilecca; ‹plan etc› non riuscire

misfit /ˈmisfit/ n disadattato, -a mf

misfortune /misˈfɔːtʃuːn/ n sfortuna f

misgivings /misˈgivɪŋz/ npl dubbi mpl

misguided /misˈgaɪdɪd/ adj fuorviato

mishandle /misˈhændl/ vt gestire male ‹operation, meeting›; non prendere per il verso giusto ‹person›; (roughly) maneggiare senza precauzioni ‹object›; maltrattare ‹person, animal›

mishap /ˈmishæp/ n disavventura f

mishear /misˈhiə(r)/ vt sentire male

mishmash /ˈmiʃmæʃ/ n fam guazzabuglio m

misinform /misinˈfɔːm/ vt informar male

misinformation /misinfəˈmeɪʃn/ n informazioni fpl sbagliate

misinterpret /misinˈtɜːprɪt/ vt fraintendere

misinterpretation /misintɜːprɪˈteɪʃn/ n interpretazione f sbagliata

misjudge /misˈdʒʌdʒ/ vt giudicar male; (estimate wrongly) valutare male

mislay /misˈleɪ/ vt (pt/pp **-laid**) smarrire

mislead /misˈliːd/ vt (pt/pp **-led**) fuorviare

misleading /misˈliːdɪŋ/ adj fuorviante

mismanage /misˈmænɪdʒ/ vt amministrare male

mismanagement /misˈmænɪdʒmənt/ n cattiva amministrazione f

mismatch /ˈmismætʃ/ n discordanza f

misname /misˈneɪm/ vt dare il nome sbagliato a

misnomer /misˈnəʊmə(r)/ n termine m improprio

misogynist /misˈɒdʒənist/ n misogino m

misplace /misˈpleɪs/ vt mettere in un posto sbagliato; ∼ **one's trust** riporre male la propria fiducia

misprint /ˈmisprint/ n errore m di stampa

mispronounce /misprəˈnaʊns/ vt pronunciare male

mispronunciation /misprənʌnsɪeɪʃn/ n (act) pronuncia f sbagliata; (instance) errore m di pronuncia

misquote /misˈkwəʊt/ vt citare erroneamente

misread /misˈriːd/ vt leggere male ‹sentence, meter›; (misinterpret) fraintendere ‹actions›

misrepresent /misreprɪˈzent/ vt rappresentare male

misrepresentation /misreprizenˈteɪʃn/ n (of facts, opinions) travisamento m

✓ **miss** ❶ n colpo m mancato
❷ vt (fail to hit or find) mancare; perdere ‹train, bus, class›; (feel the loss of) sentire la mancanza di; **I** ∼**ed that part** (failed to notice) ⋯▸

mi è sfuggita quella parte; ∼ **the point** non afferrare il punto

③ *vi* but he ∼ed (failed to hit) ma l'ha mancato

■ **miss out** *vt* saltare, omettere

Miss /mɪs/ *n* (*pl* **-es**) signorina *f*

misshapen /mɪs'ʃeɪpən/ *adj* malformato

missile /'mɪsaɪl/ *n* missile *m*

missing /'mɪsɪŋ/ *adj* mancante; ‹person› scomparso; Mil disperso; **be** ∼ essere introvabile; ∼ **in action** Mil disperso

✶ **mission** /'mɪʃn/ *n* missione *f*

missionary /'mɪʃənrɪ/ *n* missionario, -a *mf*

missive /'mɪsɪv/ *n* missiva *f*

misspell /mɪs'spel/ *vt* (*pt/pp* **-spelt**, **-spelled**) sbagliare l'ortografia di

misspent /mɪs'spent/ *adj* **a** ∼ **youth** una gioventù sprecata

mist /mɪst/ *n* (fog) foschia *f*; **because of the** ∼ **on the windows** a causa dei vetri appannati

■ **mist over** *vi* ‹eyes› velarsi

■ **mist up** *vi* appannarsi, annebbiarsi

✶ **mistake** /mɪ'steɪk/ ① *n* sbaglio *m*; **by** ∼ per sbaglio

② *vt* (*pt* **mistook**, *pp* **mistaken**) sbagliare ‹road, house›; fraintendere ‹meaning, words›; ∼ **for** prendere per

mistaken /mɪ'steɪkən/ *adj* sbagliato; **be** ∼ sbagliarsi; ∼ **identity** errore *m* di persona

mistakenly /mɪ'steɪkənlɪ/ *adv* erroneamente

mister /'mɪstə(r)/ *n* signore *m*

mistletoe /'mɪsltəʊ/ *n* vischio *m*

mistranslate /mɪstrænz'leɪt/ *vt* tradurre in modo sbagliato

mistranslation /mɪstrænz'leɪʃn/ *n* traduzione *f* sbagliata

mistreat /mɪs'triːt/ maltrattare

mistreatment /mɪs'triːtmənt/ *n* maltrattamento *m*

mistress /'mɪstrɪs/ *n* padrona *f*; (teacher) maestra *f*; (lover) amante *f*

mistrust /mɪs'trʌst/ ① *n* sfiducia *f*
② *vt* non aver fiducia in

misty /'mɪstɪ/ *adj* (**-ier**, **-iest**) nebbioso; fig indistinto

misty-eyed /-'aɪd/ *adj* ‹look› commosso; **he goes all** ∼ **about it** a parlarne si commuove

misunderstand /mɪsʌndə'stænd/ *vt* (*pt/pp* **-stood**) fraintendere

misunderstanding /mɪsʌndə'stændɪŋ/ *n* malinteso *m*

misuse¹ /mɪs'juːz/ *vt* usare male

misuse² /mɪs'juːs/ *n* cattivo uso *m*

mite /maɪt/ *n* Zool acaro *m*; (child) piccino, -a *mf*

mitigate /'mɪtɪgeɪt/ *vt* attenuare

mitigating /'mɪtɪgeɪtɪŋ/ *adj* attenuante

mitre Br, **miter** Am /'maɪtə(r)/ *n* mitra *f*

mitt /mɪt/ *n* (no separate fingers) muffola *f*; (cut-off fingers) mezzo guanto *m*; (in baseball) guantone *m*; fam (hand) mano *f*

mitten /'mɪtn/ *n* manopola *f*, muffola *f*

✶ **mix** /mɪks/ ① *n* (combination) mescolanza *f*; Culin miscuglio *m*; (ready-made) preparato *m*
② *vt* mischiare
③ *vi* mischiarsi; ‹person› inserirsi; ∼ **with** (associate with) frequentare

■ **mix in** *vt* incorporare ‹eggs, flour etc›

■ **mix up** *vt* mescolare ‹papers›; (confuse, mistake for) confondere

mixed /mɪkst/ *adj* misto; ∼ **up** (person) confuso

mixed ability *adj* ‹class, teaching› per alunni di capacità diverse

mixed bag *n* fig it was a very ∼ c'era un po' di tutto

mixed blessing *n* be a ∼ avere vantaggi e svantaggi

mixed doubles *npl* Tennis doppio *m* misto

mixed economy *n* economia *f* mista

mixed grill *n* grigliata *f* di carne mista

mixed marriage *n* matrimonio *m* misto

mixed-media *adj* multimediale

mixed metaphor *n* abbinamento (*m*) di parte di due o più metafore diverse con effetto comico

mixed race ① *adj* ‹children› con genitori di razze diverse
② *n* **she's of** ∼ i suoi genitori sono di razze diverse

mixed-up *adj* ‹person, emotions› confuso

mixed vegetables *npl* verdure *fpl* miste

mixer /'mɪksə(r)/ *n* Culin frullatore *m*, mixer *m inv*; **he's a good** ∼ è un tipo socievole

mixing /'mɪksɪŋ/ *n* (of people, objects, ingredients) mescolamento *m*; Mus mixaggio *m*

mixture /'mɪkstʃə(r)/ *n* mescolanza *f*; (medicine) sciroppo *m*; Culin miscela *f*

mix-up *n* (confusion) confusione *f*; (mistake) pasticcio *m*

mm *abbr* (**millimetre(s)**) mm

MMS *abbr* (**multimedia messaging service**) MMS *m*

MO *abbr* 1 (**medical officer**) ufficiale *m* medico
2 (**money order**) vaglia *m inv* postale
3 Am (**Missouri**)

moan /məʊn/ ① *n* lamento *m*
② *vi* lamentarsi; (complain) lagnarsi

moat /məʊt/ *n* fossato *m*

mob /mɒb/ ① *n* folla *f*; (rabble) gentaglia *f*; fam (gang) banda *f*
② *vt* (*pt/pp* **mobbed**) assalire

✶ **mobile** /'məʊbaɪl/ ① *adj* mobile

m

2 *n* composizione *f* mobile; (phone) telefono *m*, cellulare *m*

mobile home *n* casa *f* roulotte

mobile library *n* Br biblioteca *f* itinerante

mobile phone *n* (telefono *m*), cellulare *m*, telefonino *m*

mobile shop *n* furgone *m* attrezzato per la vendita

mobility /məˈbɪlətɪ/ *n* mobilità *f*

mobility allowance *n* Br indennità *f* *inv* di accompagnamento

mobilization /məʊbɪlaɪˈzeɪʃn/ *n* mobilitazione *f*

mobilize /ˈməʊbɪlaɪz/ *vt* mobilitare

mocha /ˈmɒkə/ *n* moca *m inv*

mock /mɒk/ **1** *adj* finto
2 *vt* canzonare

mockery /ˈmɒkərɪ/ *n* derisione *f*; **a ~ of** una parodia di

mock-up *n* modello *m* in scala

MoD *n abbr* (**Ministry of Defence**) Br Ministero *m* della Difesa

modal /ˈməʊdl/ *adj* **~ auxiliary** verbo *m* modale

mod con /mɒdˈkɒn/ *abbr* Br (**modern convenience**) all **~s** tutti i comfort

mode /məʊd/ *n* modo *m*; Comput modalità *f*

ⓛ **model** /ˈmɒdl/ **1** *n* modello *m*; [fashion] **~** indossatore, -trice *mf*, modello, -a *mf*
2 *adj* ‹yacht, plane› in miniatura; ‹pupil, husband› esemplare, modello
3 *vt* (*pt/pp* **modelled**) indossare ‹clothes›
4 *vi* fare l'indossatore, -trice *mf*; (for artist) posare

modelling /ˈmɒd(ə)lɪŋ/ *n* (with clay etc) modellare *m* con la creta; (of clothes) professione *f* di indossatore; **do some ~** (for artist) fare il modello

modelling clay *n* creta *f* per modellare

modem /ˈməʊdem/ **1** *n* modem *m inv*
2 *vt* mandare per modem

moderate¹ /ˈmɒdəreɪt/ **1** *vt* moderare
2 *vi* moderarsi

moderate² /ˈmɒdərət/ **1** *adj* moderato
2 *n* Pol moderato, -a *mf*

moderately /ˈmɒdərətlɪ/ *adv* ‹drink, speak etc› moderatamente; ‹good, bad etc› relativamente

moderation /mɒdəˈreɪʃn/ *n* moderazione *f*; **in ~** con moderazione

ⓛ **modern** /ˈmɒdn/ *adj* moderno

modern-day *adj* attuale

modernism /ˈmɒdənɪzm/ *n* modernismo *m*

modernity /məˈdɜːnətɪ/ *n* modernità *f*

modernization /mɒdənaɪˈzeɪʃn/ *n* modernizzazione *f*

modernize /ˈmɒdənaɪz/ *vt* modernizzare

modern languages *npl* lingue *fpl* moderne

modest /ˈmɒdɪst/ *adj* modesto

modesty /ˈmɒdɪstɪ/ *n* modestia *f*

modicum /ˈmɒdɪkəm/ *n* **a ~ of** un po' di

modification /mɒdɪfɪˈkeɪʃn/ *n* modificazione *f*

modifier /ˈmɒdɪfaɪə(r)/ *n* (in linguistics) modificatore *m*

modify /ˈmɒdɪfaɪ/ *vt* (*pt/pp* **-fied**) modificare

modular /ˈmɒdjʊlə(r)/ *adj* ‹course› a moduli; ‹construction, furniture› modulare

modulate /ˈmɒdjʊleɪt/ *vt/i* modulare

module /ˈmɒdjuːl/ *n* modulo *m*

modus operandi /məʊdəsɒpəˈrændiː/ *n* modus operandi *m inv*

mogul /ˈməʊgl/ *n* magnate *m*

Mohammed /məʊˈhæmed/ *n* Maometto *m*

mohican /məʊˈhiːkən/ *n* (hairstyle) taglio *m* [di capelli] alla moicana

moist /mɔɪst/ *adj* umido

moisten /ˈmɔɪsn/ *vt* inumidire

moisture /ˈmɔɪstʃə(r)/ *n* umidità *f*

moisturizer /ˈmɔɪstʃəraɪzə(r)/ *n* [crema *f*] idratante *m*

molar /ˈməʊlə(r)/ *n* molare *m*

molasses /məˈlæsɪz/ *n* Am melassa *f*

mold /məʊld/ Am = MOULD

Moldavia /mɒlˈdeɪvɪə/ *n* Moldavia *f*

mole¹ /məʊl/ *n* (on face etc) neo *m*

mole² *n* Zool talpa *f*

mole³ *n* (breakwater) molo *m*

molecular /məˈlekjʊlə(r)/ *adj* molecolare

molecule /ˈmɒlɪkjuːl/ *n* molecola *f*

molehill /ˈməʊlhɪl/ *n* monticello *m*

moleskin /ˈməʊlskɪn/ *n* (fur) pelliccia *f* di talpa

molest /məˈlest/ *vt* molestare

mollify /ˈmɒlɪfaɪ/ *vt* (*pt/pp* **-ied**) placare

mollusc /ˈmɒləsk/ *n* mollusco *m*

mollycoddle /ˈmɒlɪkɒdl/ *vt* tenere nella bambagia

molt /məʊlt/ Am = MOULT

molten /ˈməʊltən/ *adj* fuso

ⓛ **mom** /mɒm/ *n* Am fam mamma *f*

ⓛ **moment** /ˈməʊmənt/ *n* momento *m*; **at the ~** in questo momento

momentarily /məʊmənˈterɪlɪ/ *adv* (for an instant) per un momento; Am (at any moment) da un momento all'altro; Am (very soon) tra un momento

momentary /ˈməʊməntrɪ/ *adj* momentaneo

momentous /məˈmentəs/ *adj* molto importante

momentum /məˈmentəm/ *n* impeto *m*

Monaco /ˈmɒnəkəʊ/ *n* Principato *m* di Monaco

monarch /ˈmɒnək/ *n* monarca *m*

m

monarchist /'mɒnəkɪst/ n monarchico, -a mf

monarchy /'mɒnəkɪ/ n monarchia f

monastery /'mɒnəstrɪ/ n monastero m

monastic /mə'næstɪk/ adj monastico

ᵈ **Monday** /'mʌndeɪ/ n lunedì m inv

monetary /'mʌnətrɪ/ adj monetario

ᵈ **money** /'mʌnɪ/ n denaro m

money box n salvadanaio m

moneylender n usuraio m

moneymaker n (business) attività f redditizia; (product) prodotto m che rende bene

money order n vaglia m inv postale

Mongolia /mɒŋ'gəʊlɪə/ n Mongolia f

mongrel /'mʌŋgrəl/ n bastardino m

monitor /'mɒnɪtə(r)/ ⟨1⟩ n Techn monitor m inv
⟨2⟩ vt controllare

monk /mʌŋk/ n monaco m

monkey /'mʌŋkɪ/ n scimmia f
■ **monkey about with** vt fam (interfere with) armeggiare con

monkey business n fam (fooling) scherzi mpl; (cheating) imbrogli mpl

monkey-nut n nocciolina f americana

monkey wrench n chiave f inglese a rullino

monkfish /'mʌŋkfɪʃ/ n bottatrice f

mono /'mɒnəʊ/ n mono m

monochrome /'mɒnəkrəʊm/ adj monocromatico; Cinema, TV in bianco e nero

monocle /'mɒnəkl/ n monocolo m

monogamous /mə'nɒgəməs/ adj monogamo

monogamy /mə'nɒgəmɪ/ n monogamia f

monogram /'mɒnəgræm/ n monogramma m

monograph /'mɒnəgrɑːf/ n monografia f

monolith /'mɒnəlɪθ/ n monolito m

monologue /'mɒnəlɒg/ n monologo m

monomania /mɒnə'meɪnɪə/ n monomania f

monoplane /'mɒnəpleɪn/ n monoplano m

monopolize /mə'nɒpəlaɪz/ vt monopolizzare

monopoly /mə'nɒpəlɪ/ n monopolio m

monoski /'mɒnəʊskiː/ ⟨1⟩ n monoscì m inv
⟨2⟩ vi praticare il monoscì

monosodium glutamate /mɒnəsəʊdɪəm'gluːtəmeɪt/ n glutammato m di sodio

monosyllabic /mɒnəsɪ'læbɪk/ adj monosillabico

monosyllable /'mɒnəsɪləbl/ n monosillabo m

monotone /'mɒnətəʊn/ n speak in a ~ parlare con tono monotono

monotonous /mə'nɒtənəs/ adj monotono

monotonously /mə'nɒtənəslɪ/ adv in modo monotono

monotony /mə'nɒtənɪ/ n monotonia f

monsoon /mɒn'suːn/ n monsone m

monster /'mɒnstə(r)/ n mostro m

monstrosity /mɒn'strɒsətɪ/ n mostruosità f

monstrous /'mɒnstrəs/ adj mostruoso

montage /mɒn'tɑːʒ/ n montaggio m

Mont Blanc /mɒn'blɒ̃/ n Monte m Bianco

Montenegro /mɒntɪ'niːgrəʊ/ n Montenegro m

ᵈ **month** /mʌnθ/ n mese m

monthly /'mʌnθlɪ/ ⟨1⟩ adj mensile
⟨2⟩ adv mensilmente
⟨3⟩ n (periodical) mensile m

monument /'mɒnjʊmənt/ n monumento m

monumental /mɒnjʊ'mentl/ adj fig monumentale

monumentally /mɒnjʊ'mentəlɪ/ adv ‹boring, ignorant› enormemente

moo /muː/ ⟨1⟩ n muggito m
⟨2⟩ vi (pt/pp mooed) muggire

mooch /muːtʃ/ vi ~ about fam gironzolare; ~ about the house gironzolare per casa

ᵈ **mood** /muːd/ n umore m; be in a good/bad ~ essere di buon/cattivo umore; be in the ~ for essere in vena di

moody /'muːdɪ/ adj (-ier, -iest) (variable) lunatico; (bad-tempered) di malumore

moon /muːn/ n luna f; over the ~ fam al settimo cielo
■ **moon about**, **moon around** vi fam (wander aimlessly) gironzolare
■ **moon over** vt fam sospirare d'amore per ‹somebody›

moonbeam n raggio m di luna

moon buggy n veicolo m lunare

moonlight ⟨1⟩ n chiaro m di luna
⟨2⟩ vi fam lavorare in nero

moonlighting n fam lavoro m nero

moonlit adj illuminato dalla luna

moonshine n (nonsense) fantasie fpl; Am (liquor) liquore m di contrabbando

moor¹ /mʊə(r)/ n brughiera f

moor² vt Naut ormeggiare

moorhen /'mʊəhen/ n gallinella f d'acqua

mooring /'mʊərɪŋ/ n (place) ormeggio m; ~s pl (chains) ormeggi mpl

Moorish /'mʊərɪʃ/ adj moresco

moorland /'mʊələnd/ n brughiera f

moose /muːs/ n (pl moose) alce m

moot /muːt/ adj it's a ~ point è un punto controverso

(m)

mop /mɒp/ **1** *n* mocio® *m inv*; ~ **of hair** zazzera *f*
2 *vt* (*pt/pp* **mopped**) lavare con il mocio®
■ **mop up** *vt* (dry) asciugare con il mocio®; (clean) pulire con il mocio®

mope /məʊp/ *vi* essere depresso
■ **mope about**, **mope around** *vi* trascinarsi

moped /'məʊped/ *n* ciclomotore *m*

◊ **moral** /'mɒrəl/ **1** *adj* morale
2 *n* morale *f*

morale /mə'rɑːl/ *n* morale *m*; **be a** ~ **booster** tirare su di morale

moral fibre *n* forza *f* morale

moralistic /mɒrə'lɪstɪk/ *adj* moralistico

morality /mə'ræləti/ *n* moralità *f*

moralize /'mɒrəlaɪz/ *vi* moraleggiare

morally /'mɒrəli/ *adv* moralmente

morals /'mɒrəlz/ *npl* moralità *f*

moratorium /mɒrə'tɔːrɪəm/ *n* moratoria *f*

morbid /'mɔːbɪd/ *adj* morboso

◊ **more** /mɔː(r)/ **1** *adj* più; **a few** ~ **books** un po' più di libri; **some** ~ **tea?** ancora un po' di tè?; **there's no** ~ **bread** non c'è più pane; **there are no** ~ **apples** non ci sono più mele; **one** ~ **word and...** ancora una parola e...
2 *pron* di più; **would you like some** ~? ne vuoi ancora?; **no** ~, **thank you** non ne voglio più, grazie
3 *adv* più; ~ **interesting** più interessante; ~ **(and** ~**) quickly** (sempre) più veloce; ~ **than** più di; **I don't love him any** ~ non lo amo più; **once** ~ ancora una volta; ~ **or less** più o meno; **the** ~ **I see him, the** ~ **I like him** più lo vedo, più mi piace

moreish /'mɔːrɪʃ/ *adj* fam **be** ~ tirare per la gola

moreover /mɔːr'əʊvə(r)/ *adv* inoltre

morgue /mɔːg/ *n* obitorio *m*

MORI /'mɔːrɪ/ *n abbr* (**Market Opinion Research Institute**) *istituto* (*m*) *di sondaggio e ricerche di mercato*

moribund /'mɒrɪbʌnd/ *adj* moribondo

◊ **morning** /'mɔːnɪŋ/ *n* mattino *m*, mattina *f*; **spend the** ~ **doing something** passare la mattinata facendo qualcosa; **in the** ~ del mattino; (tomorrow) domani mattina

morning-after pill *n* pillola *f* del giorno dopo

morning coffee *n* caffè *m inv* del mattino

morning dress *n* tight *m inv*

morning sickness *n* nausea *f* mattutina

Moroccan /mə'rɒk(ə)n/ *adj & n* marocchino, -a *mf*

Morocco /mə'rɒkəʊ/ *n* Marocco *m*

morocco leather *n* marocchino *m*

moron /'mɔːrɒn/ *n* fam deficiente *mf*

morose /mə'rəʊs/ *adj* scontroso

morosely /mə'rəʊsli/ *adv* in modo scontroso

morphine /'mɔːfiːn/ *n* morfina *f*

morris dance /'mɒrɪs/ *n danza* (*f*) *tradizionale inglese*

Morse /mɔːs/ *n* ~ **[code]** [codice *m*] Morse *m*

morsel /'mɔːsl/ *n* (food) boccone *m*

mortal /'mɔːtl/ *adj & n* mortale *mf*

mortal combat *n* duello *m* mortale

mortality /mɔː'tæləti/ *n* mortalità *f*

mortally /'mɔːtəli/ *adv* ‹wounded, offended› a morte; ‹afraid› da morire

mortar /'mɔːtə(r)/ *n* mortaio *m*

mortgage /'mɔːgɪdʒ/ **1** *n* mutuo *m*; (*money raised on collateral of property*) ipoteca *f*
2 *vt* ipotecare

mortgage rate *n* tasso *m* d'interesse sui mutui

mortgage relief *n* sgravio *m* fiscale sul mutuo

mortgage repayment *n* rata *f* del mutuo

mortician /mɔː'tɪʃn/ *n* Am impresario, -a *mf* di pompe funebri

mortification /mɔːtɪfɪ'keɪʃn/ *n* (of the flesh, embarrassment) mortificazione *f*

mortify /'mɔːtɪfaɪ/ *vt* (*pt/pp* -**ied**) mortificare

mortuary /'mɔːtjʊəri/ *n* camera *f* mortuaria

mosaic /məʊ'zeɪɪk/ *n* mosaico *m*

Moscow /'mɒskəʊ/ *n* Mosca *f*

Moselle /məʊ'zel/ *n* (wine) vino *m* della Mosella

Moses /'məʊzɪz/ *n* Mosè

Moslem /'mɒzlɪm/ *adj & n* musulmano, -a *mf*

mosque /mɒsk/ *n* moschea *f*

mosquito /mɒs'kiːtəʊ/ *n* (*pl* -**es**) zanzara *f*

mosquito bite *n* puntura *m* di zanzara

mosquito net *n* zanzariera *f*

mosquito repellent *n* antizanzare *m inv*

moss /mɒs/ *n* muschio *m*

mossy /'mɒsi/ *adj* muschioso

◊ **most** /məʊst/ **1** *adj* (majority) la maggior parte di; **for the** ~ **part** per lo più
2 *adv* più, maggiormente; (very) estremamente, molto; **the** ~ **interesting day** la giornata più interessante; **a** ~ **interesting day** una giornata estremamente interessante; **the** ~ **beautiful woman in the world** la donna più bella del mondo; ~ **unlikely** veramente improbabile
3 *pron* ~ **of them** la maggior parte di loro; **at [the]** ~ al massimo; **make the** ~ **of** sfruttare al massimo; ~ **of the time** la maggior parte del tempo

m

ꝺ **mostly** /'məʊs(t)lɪ/ *adv* per lo più

MOT *n* Br revisione *f* obbligatoria di autoveicoli

motel /məʊ'tel/ *n* motel *m inv*

moth /mɒθ/ *n* falena *f*; [clothes-] ∼ tarma *f*

mothball /'mɒθbɔːl/ *n* pallina *f* di naftalina

moth-eaten /-iːtən/ *adj* tarmato

ꝺ **mother** /'mʌðə(r)/ **1** *n* madre *f*; **Mother's Day** la festa della mamma
  2 *vt* fare da madre a

motherboard /'mʌðəbɔːd/ *n* scheda *f* madre

motherhood /'mʌðəhʊd/ *n* maternità *f*

Mothering Sunday /mʌðərɪŋ'sʌndeɪ/ *n* la festa della mamma

mother-in-law *n* (*pl* **mothers-in-law**) suocera *f*

motherland /'mʌðəlænd/ *n* patria *f*

motherless /'mʌðəlɪs/ *adj* orfano, -a *mf* di madre

motherly /'mʌðəlɪ/ *adj* materno

mother-of-pearl *n* madreperla *f*

mother's boy *n* mammone *m*

Mother's Day *n* la festa della mamma

mother's help *n* Br aiuto *m* domestico

mother-to-be *n* futura mamma *f*

mother tongue *n* madrelingua *f*

mothproof /'mɒθpruːf/ *adj* antitarmico

motif /məʊ'tiːf/ *n* motivo *m*

ꝺ **motion** /'məʊʃn/ **1** *n* moto *m*; (proposal) mozione *f*; (gesture) gesto *m*
  2 *vt/i* ∼ **[to] somebody to come in** fare segno a qualcuno di entrare

motionless /'məʊʃ(ə)nlɪs/ *adj* immobile

motionlessly /'məʊʃənlɪslɪ/ *adv* senza alcun movimento

motion picture **1** *n* film *m inv* [per il cinema]
  2 *attrib* ⟨industry⟩ cinematografico

motivate /'məʊtɪveɪt/ *vt* motivare

motivated /'məʊtɪveɪtɪd/ *adj* ⟨person, student⟩ motivato; **politically/racially** ∼ ⟨act⟩ a sfondo politico/razziale

motivation /məʊtɪ'veɪʃn/ *n* motivazione *f*

motive /'məʊtɪv/ *n* motivo *m*

motley /'mɒtlɪ/ *adj* disparato

motor /'məʊtə(r)/ **1** *n* motore *m*; (car) macchina *f*
  2 *adj* a motore; Anat motore
  3 *vi* andare in macchina

Motorail /'məʊtəreɪl/ *n* treno *m* per trasporto auto

motorbike /'məʊtəbaɪk/ *n* fam moto *f inv*

motor boat *n* motoscafo *m*

motorcade /'məʊtəkeɪd/ *n* Am corteo *m* di auto

motor car *n* automobile *f*

motorcycle *n* motocicletta *f*

motorcycle escort *n* scorta *f* di motociclette

motorcycle messenger *n* corriere *m* in moto

motorcyclist *n* motociclista *mf*

motorhome *n* camper *m inv*; (towed) roulotte *f inv*

motoring /'məʊtərɪŋ/ *n* automobilismo *m*

motorist /'məʊtərɪst/ *n* automobilista *mf*

motor launch *n* motolancia *f*

motor mechanic *n* meccanico *m*

motormouth *n* fam chiacchierone, -a *mf*

motor oil *n* olio *m* lubrificante

motor racing *n* corse *fpl* automobilistiche

motor scooter *n* motorino *m*

motor vehicle *n* autoveicolo *m*

motorway *n* autostrada *f*

mottled /'mɒtld/ *adj* chiazzato

motto /'mɒtəʊ/ *n* (*pl* **-es**) motto *m*

mould¹ /'məʊld/ *n* (fungus) muffa *f*

mould² **1** *n* stampo *m*
  2 *vt* foggiare; fig formare

moulder /'məʊldə(r)/ *vi* ⟨corpse, refuse⟩ andare in decomposizione

moulding /'məʊldɪŋ/ *n* Archit cornice *f*

mouldy /'məʊldɪ/ *adj* ammuffito; fam (worthless) ridicolo

moult /məʊlt/ *vi* ⟨bird⟩ fare la muta; ⟨animal⟩ perdere il pelo

mound /maʊnd/ *n* mucchio *m*; (hill) collinetta *f*

mount /maʊnt/ **1** *n* (horse) cavalcatura *f*; (of jewel, photo, picture) montatura *f*
  2 *vt* montare a ⟨horse⟩; salire su ⟨bicycle⟩; incastonare ⟨jewel⟩; incorniciare ⟨photo, picture⟩
  3 *vi* aumentare
  ■ **mount up** *vi* aumentare

ꝺ **mountain** /'maʊntɪn/ *n* montagna *f*; **make a** ∼ **out of a molehill** fare di una mosca un elefante

mountain bike *n* mountain bike *f inv*

mountain climbing *n* alpinismo *m*

mountaineer /maʊntɪ'nɪə(r)/ *n* alpinista *mf*

mountaineering /maʊntɪ'nɪərɪŋ/ *n* alpinismo *m*

mountainous /'maʊntɪnəs/ *adj* montagnoso

mountain range *n* catena *f* montuosa

mountain top *n* cima *f* di montagna

mounted police /maʊntɪdpə'liːs/ *n* polizia *f* a cavallo

mourn /mɔːn/ **1** *vt* lamentare
  2 *vi* ∼ **for** piangere la morte di

mourner /'mɔːnə(r)/ *n* persona *f* che partecipa a un funerale

---

ꝺ indicates a very frequent word

mournful /'mɔːnfʊl/ adj triste

mournfully /'mɔːnfʊlɪ/ adv tristemente

mourning /'mɔːnɪŋ/ n in ~ in lutto

mouse /maʊs/ n (pl **mice**) topo m; Comput mouse m inv

■ **mouse over** vt puntare con il mouse su

mousehole n tana f di topi/di un topo

mouse mat n Comput tappetino m

mousetrap n trappola f [per topi]

mousse /muːs/ n Culin mousse f inv

moustache /məˈstɑːʃ/ n baffi mpl

mousy /'maʊsɪ/ adj ‹colour› grigio topo

mouth¹ /maʊð/ vt ~ **something** dire qualcosa silenziosamente muovendo solamente le labbra

☞ **mouth²** /maʊθ/ n bocca f; (of river) foce f

mouthful /'maʊθfʊl/ n boccone m

mouth organ n armonica f [a bocca]

mouthpiece n imboccatura f; fig (person) portavoce m inv

mouth-to-mouth resuscitation n respirazione f bocca a bocca

mouthwash n collutorio m

mouthwatering /-wɔːtərɪŋ/ adj che fa venire l'acquolina in bocca

movable /'muːvəbl/ adj movibile

☞ **move** /muːv/ ① n mossa f; (moving house) trasloco m; on the ~ in movimento; get a ~ on fam darsi una mossa
② vt muovere; (emotionally) commuovere; spostare ‹car, furniture›; (transfer) trasferire; (propose) proporre; ~ **house** traslocare
③ vi muoversi; (move house) traslocare; don't ~! non muoverti!

■ **move about**, **move around** vi (in house) muoversi; (in country) spostarsi

■ **move along** ① vi andare avanti
② vt muovere in avanti

■ **move away** ① vi allontanarsi; (move house) trasferirsi
② vt allontanare

■ **move forward** ① vi avanzare
② vt spostare avanti

■ **move in** vi (to a house) trasferirsi

■ **move off** vi ‹vehicle› muoversi

■ **move on** ① vi (move to another place) muoversi
② vt ‹police› far circolare

■ **move on to** vt passare a ‹new topic, next question›

■ **move out** vi (of house) andare via

■ **move over** ① vi spostarsi
② vt spostare

■ **move up** vi muoversi; (advance, increase) avanzare

☞ **movement** /'muːvmənt/ n movimento m; (of clock) meccanismo m

☞ **movie** /'muːvɪ/ n Am film m inv; go to the ~s andare al cinema

movie camera n Am cinepresa f

movie director n Am regista mf cinematografico, -a

movie-goer /'muːvɪɡəʊə(r)/ n Am frequentatore, -trice mf di cinema

movie star n Am stella f del cinema, star f inv del cinema

movie theater n Am cinema m

moving /'muːvɪŋ/ adj mobile; (touching) commovente

mow /məʊ/ vt (pt **mowed**, pp **mown** or **mowed**) tagliare ‹lawn›

■ **mow down** vt (destroy) sterminare

mower /'məʊə(r)/ n tosaerba m inv

Mozambique /ˌməʊzæmˈbiːk/ n Mozambico m

MP abbr (**Member of Parliament**) deputato, -a mf

MP3 player n lettore m di MP3

mpg abbr (**miles per gallon**) miglia al gallone

mph abbr (**miles per hour**) miglia all'ora

MPV n abbr (**multi-purpose vehicle**) MPV m

☞ **Mr** /'mɪstə(r)/ n (pl **Messrs**) Signor m

MRI n abbr (**magnetic resonance imaging**) RM f

☞ **Mrs** /'mɪsɪz/ n Signora f

MRSA n abbr (**methicillin-resistant Staphylococcus aureus**) MRSA m

Ms /mɪz/ n Signora f (modo (m) formale di rivolgersi ad una donna quando non si vuole indicarla come sposata o nubile)

MS n abbr 1 (**multiple sclerosis**) sclerosi f a placche or multipla
2 (**manuscript**) ms
3 Am (**Mississippi**)

MSc n abbr (**Master of Science**) (diploma) laurea f in discipline scientifiche; (person) laureato, -a mf in discipline scientifiche

MST abbr Am (**Mountain Standard Time**) tempo (f) medio della zona delle Montagne Rocciose

Mt. abbr (**mount**) (in place names) M.

☞ **much** /mʌtʃ/ adj, adv & pron molto; ~ **as** per quanto; I love you just as ~ as before/ him ti amo quanto prima/lui; as ~ as £5 million ben cinque milioni di sterline; as ~ as that così tanto; very ~ tantissimo, moltissimo; ~ the same quasi uguale

muck /mʌk/ n (dirt) sporcizia f; (farming) letame m; fam (filth) porcheria f

■ **muck about** vi fam perder tempo; ~ about with trafficare con

■ **muck in** vi fam dare una mano

■ **muck up** vt fam rovinare; (make dirty) sporcare

muckraking /'mʌkreɪkɪŋ/ n scandalismo m

mucky /'mʌkɪ/ adj (-ier, -iest) sudicio

m

mucus /'mju:kəs/ n muco m

mud /mʌd/ n fango m

muddle /'mʌdl/ [1] n disordine m; (mix-up) confusione f
[2] vt ~ [up] confondere ‹dates›
■ **muddle through** vi farcela alla bell'e meglio

muddle-headed /-'hedɪd/ adj ‹plan› confuso; ‹person› confusionario

muddy /'mʌdɪ/ adj (-ier, -iest) ‹path› fangoso; ‹shoes› infangato

mudflat n distesa f di fango

mudguard n parafango m

mud hut n capanna f di fango

mudpack n (for beauty treatment) maschera f di fango

mud pie n formina f di fango

mudslide n colata f di fango

mud-slinging /-slɪŋɪŋ/ n diffamazione f

muesli /'mju:zlɪ/ n muesli m inv

muffle /'mʌfl/ vt smorzare ‹sound›
■ **muffle up** vi (for warmth) imbacuccarsi

muffler /'mʌflə(r)/ n sciarpa f; Am Auto marmitta f

mug¹ /mʌg/ n tazza f; (for beer) boccale m; fam (face) muso m; fam (simpleton) pollo m

mug² vt (pt/pp **mugged**) aggredire e derubare
■ **mug up** vt fam (learn) imparare alla bell'e meglio

mugger /'mʌgə(r)/ n assalitore, -trice mf

mugging /'mʌgɪŋ/ n aggressione f per furto

muggy /'mʌgɪ/ adj (-ier, -iest) afoso

Muhammad /mə'hæmɪd/ n Maometto m

mulatto /mju:'lætəʊ/ adj & n Am mulatto, -a mf

mulberry /'mʌlb(ə)rɪ/ n Am (fruit) mora f di gelso; (tree) gelso m

mule¹ /mju:l/ n mulo m

mule² n (slipper) ciabatta f

mulish /'mju:lɪʃ/ adj testardo

mull /mʌl/ vt ~ over rimuginare su

mulled /mʌld/ adj ~ wine vin brûlé m inv

multi+ /'mʌltɪ/ pref multi+

multi-access n Comput accesso m multiplo

multichannel /mʌltɪ'tʃænəl/ adj ‹television› con molti canali

multicoloured /'mʌltɪkʌləd/ adj variopinto

multicultural /mʌltɪ'kʌltʃərəl/ adj multiculturale

multidisciplinary /mʌltɪdɪsɪ'plɪnərɪ/ adj Sch, Univ pluridisciplinare

multi-ethnic /ˌmʌltɪ'eθnɪk/ adj multietnico

---

multifaceted /mʌltɪ'fæsɪtɪd/ adj ‹gemstone› sfaccettato; ‹career› variegato; ‹personality› sfaccettato

multifunction /mʌltɪ'fʌŋkʃn/ adj multifunzionale

multigym /'mʌltɪdʒɪm/ n attrezzo m multiuso

multilateral /mʌltɪ'læt(ə)rəl/ adj Pol multilaterale

multilevel /'mʌltɪlevəl/ adj ‹parking, access› a più piani; ‹analysis› a più livelli

multilingual /mʌltɪ'lɪŋgwəl/ adj multilingue inv

multimedia /mʌltɪ'mi:dɪə/ [1] n multimedia mpl
[2] adj multimediale

multinational /mʌltɪ'næʃnəl/ [1] adj multinazionale
[2] n multinazionale f

multipack n confezione f multipla

multi-party /'mʌltɪpɑ:tɪ/ adj ‹government, system› pluripartitico

multiplayer adj Comput ‹game› in multiplayer

♂ **multiple** /'mʌltɪpl/ adj & n multiplo m

multiple choice adj scelta f multipla

multiple choice question n Sch test m inv a scelta multipla

multiple ownership n comproprietà f

multiple pileup n tamponamento m a catena

multiple sclerosis n sclerosi f a placche or multipla

multiple store n Br negozio m appartenente a una catena

multiplex. /'mʌltɪpleks/ [1] n Teleph multiplex m inv; Cinema cinema m inv multisale
[2] adj Teleph in multiplex

multiplication /mʌltɪplɪ'keɪʃn/ n moltiplicazione f

multiply /'mʌltɪplaɪ/ [1] vt (pt/pp -ied) moltiplicare (by per)
[2] vi moltiplicarsi

multi-purpose adj ‹tool, gadget› multiuso inv; ‹organization› con più scopi

multi-purpose vehicle n monovolume f

multi-racial adj multirazziale

multi-storey adj ~ car park parcheggio m a più piani

multitask vi ‹person› eseguire varie mansioni; ‹computer› eseguire il multitasking

multi-track adj ‹sound system› a più piste

multitude /'mʌltɪtju:d/ n moltitudine f; hide a ~ of sins ‹rug etc› nascondere un sacco di magagne

multi-user adj ‹system, installation› multiutente

---

mum¹ /mʌm/ *adj* **keep ~** fam non aprire bocca

mum² *n* fam mamma *f*

mumble /'mʌmbl/ *vt/i* borbottare

mumbo-jumbo /mʌmbəʊ'dʒʌmbəʊ/ *n* fam (speech, writing) paroloni *mpl*

mummy¹ /'mʌmɪ/ *n* fam mamma *f*

mummy² *n* Archaeol mummia *f*

mummy's boy *n* Br pej mammone *m*

mumps /mʌmps/ *n* orecchioni *mpl*

munch /mʌntʃ/ *vt/i* sgranocchiare

mundane /mʌn'deɪn/ *adj* (everyday) banale

municipal /mjʊ'nɪsɪpl/ *adj* municipale

munitions /mjʊ'nɪʃnz/ *npl* munizioni *fpl*

mural /'mjʊərəl/ *n* dipinto *m* murale

⚔ **murder** /'mɜːdə(r)/ **1** *n* assassinio *m*
  2 *vt* assassinare; fam (ruin) massacrare

murder case *n* caso *m* di omicidio

murder charge *n* imputazione *f* di omicidio

murderer /'mɜːdərə(r)/ *n* assassino, -a *mf*

murderess /'mɜːdərɪs/ *n* assassina *f*

murderous /'mɜːdərəs/ *adj* omicida

murky /'mɜːkɪ/ *adj* (-ier, -iest) oscuro

murmur /'mɜːmə(r)/ **1** *n* mormorio *m*
  2 *vt/i* mormorare

murmuring /'mɜːmərɪŋ/ *n* mormorio *m*; **~s** *pl* (of discontent) segnali *mpl* di malcontento

⚔ **muscle** /'mʌsl/ *n* muscolo *m*
  ■ **muscle in** *vi* si intromettersi (**to** in)

muscle strain *n* strappo *m* muscolare

muscular /'mʌskjʊlə(r)/ *adj* muscolare, (strong) muscoloso

muscular dystrophy /'dɪstrəfɪ/ *n* distrofia *f* muscolare

muse /mjuːz/ *vi* meditare (**on** su)

museum /mjuː'zɪəm/ *n* museo *m*

mushroom /'mʌʃrʊm/ **1** *n* fungo *m*
  2 *vi* fig spuntare come funghi

mushroom cloud *n* fungo *m* atomico

mushy /'mʌʃɪ/ *adj* fig sdolcinato

⚔ **music** /'mjuːzɪk/ *n* musica *f*; (written) spartito *m*; **set to ~** musicare

⚔ **musical** /'mjuːzɪkl/ **1** *adj* musicale; ⟨person⟩ dotato di senso musicale
  2 *n* commedia *f* musicale

musical box *n* carillon *m inv*

musical instrument *n* strumento *m* musicale

music box *n* carillon *m inv*

music centre *n* impianto *m* stereo

music hall *n* teatro *m* di varietà

musician /mjuː'zɪʃn/ *n* musicista *mf*

music lover *n* amante *mf* della musica

musicology /mjuːzɪ'kɒlədʒɪ/ *n* musicologia *f*

music stand *n* leggio *m*

music stool *n* sgabello *m* per pianoforte

music video *n* video clip *m inv*

musings /'mjuːzɪŋz/ *npl* riflessioni *fpl*

musk /mʌsk/ *n* muschio *m*

musket /'mʌskɪt/ *n* moschetto *m*

musketeer /mʌskə'tɪə(r)/ *n* moschettiere *m*

musky /'mʌskɪ/ *adj* muschiato

Muslim /'mʌzlɪm/ *adj & n* musulmano, -a *mf*

mussel /'mʌsl/ *n* cozza *f*

⚔ **must** /mʌst/ **1** *v aux* (only in present) dovere; **you ~ not be late** non devi essere in ritardo; **she ~ have finished by now** (probability) deve aver finito ormai
  2 *n* **a ~** fam una cosa da non perdere

mustache /mə'stɑːʃ/ *n* Am = MOUSTACHE

mustard /'mʌstəd/ *n* senape *f*

muster /'mʌstə(r)/ *vt* radunare ⟨troops⟩; fare appello a ⟨strength⟩

musty /'mʌstɪ/ *adj* (-ier, -iest) stantio

mutant /'mjuːtənt/ *n & adj* mutante *mf*

mutate /mjuː'teɪt/ **1** *vi* ⟨cell, organism⟩ subire una mutazione; **~ into** ⟨alien, monster⟩ trasformarsi in
  2 *vt* far subire una mutazione

mutation /mjuː'teɪʃn/ *n* Biol mutazione *f*

mute /mjuːt/ *adj* muto

muted /'mjuːtɪd/ *adj* smorzato

mutilate /'mjuːtɪleɪt/ *vt* mutilare

mutilation /mjuːtɪ'leɪʃn/ *n* mutilazione *f*

mutinous /'mjuːtɪnəs/ *adj* ammutinato

mutiny /'mjuːtɪnɪ/ **1** *n* ammutinamento *m*
  2 *vi* (*pt/pp* **-ied**) ammutinarsi

mutter /'mʌtə(r)/ **1** *n* borbottio *m*
  2 *vt/i* borbottare

mutton /'mʌtn/ *n* carne *f* di montone

mutual /'mjuːtjʊəl/ *adj* reciproco; fam (common) comune

mutually /'mjuːtjʊəlɪ/ *adv* reciprocamente

Muzak® /'mjuːzæk/ *n* musica *f* di sottofondo

muzzle /'mʌzl/ **1** *n* (of animal) muso *m*; (of firearm) bocca *f*; (for dog) museruola *f*
  2 *vt* fig mettere il bavaglio a

MW *abbr* (**medium wave**) OM

⚔ **my** /maɪ/ *poss adj* mio *m*, mia *f*, miei *mpl*, mie *fpl*; **my job/house** il mio lavoro/la mia casa; **my mother/father** mia madre/mio padre

myalgic encephalomyelitis /maɪældʒɪkensefələʊmaɪɪ'laɪtɪs/ *n* encefalomelite *f* mialgica

Myanmar /mjæn'mɑː(r)/ *n* Myanmar *f*

myopic /maɪ'ɒpɪk/ *adj* miope

⚔ **myself** /maɪ'self/ *pers pron* (reflexive) mi; (emphatic) me stesso; (after prep) me; **I've seen it ~** l'ho visto io stesso; **by ~** da solo; **I thought to ~** ho pensato tra me e me; **I'm proud of ~** sono fiero di me

m

mysterious /mɪˈstɪərɪəs/ *adj* misterioso
mysteriously /mɪˈstɪərɪəslɪ/ *adv*
misteriosamente
mystery /ˈmɪstərɪ/ *n* mistero *m*; ~ **[story]**
racconto *m* del mistero
mystery play *n* mistero *m* (*teatrale*)
mystery tour *n* viaggio *m* con
destinazione a sorpresa
mystic[al] /ˈmɪstɪk[l]/ *adj* mistico
mysticism /ˈmɪstɪsɪzm/ *n* misticismo *m*

mystification /ˌmɪstɪfɪˈkeɪʃn/ *n*
disorientamento *m*
mystified /ˈmɪstɪfaɪd/ *adj* disorientato
mystify /ˈmɪstɪfaɪ/ *vt* disorientare
mystique /mɪˈstiːk/ *n* mistica *f*
myth /mɪθ/ *n* mito *m*
mythical /ˈmɪθɪkl/ *adj* mitico
mythological /mɪθəˈlɒdʒɪkl/ *adj*
mitologico
mythology /mɪˈθɒlədʒɪ/ *n* mitologia *f*

N n

n, N /en/ *n* (letter) n, N *f inv*
N *abbr* (**north**) N
n/a, N/A *abbr* (**not applicable**) non
pertinente
nab /næb/ *vt* (*pt/pp* **nabbed**) fam beccare
nadir /ˈneɪdə(r)/ *n* nadir *m*; fig punto *m* più
basso, fondo *m*
naff /næf/ *adj* Br fam banale
nag¹ /næg/ *n* (horse) ronzino *m*
nag² ① *vt* (*pt/pp* **nagged**) assillare
② *vi* essere insistente
③ *n* (person) brontolone, -a *mf*
nagging /ˈnægɪŋ/ *adj* ‹pain› persistente
nail /neɪl/ *n* chiodo *m*; (of finger, toe) unghia *f*;
on the ~ fam sull'unghia
■ **nail down** *vt* inchiodare; ~ **somebody
down to a time/price** far fissare a qualcuno
un'ora/un prezzo
nail-biting /-baɪtɪŋ/ ① *n* abitudine *f* di
mangiarsi le unghie
② *adj* ‹match, finish› mozzafiato *inv*; ‹wait›
esasperante
nail brush *n* spazzolino *m* da unghie
nail clippers *npl* tronchesina *m*
nail file *n* limetta *f* da unghie
nail polish *n* smalto *m* [per unghie]
nail polish remover *n* acetone
nail scissors *npl* forbicine *fpl* da unghie
nail varnish *n* smalto *m* [per unghie]
nail varnish remover *n* solvente *m*
per smalto
naïve /naɪˈiːv/ *adj* ingenuo
naïvely /naɪˈiːvlɪ/ *adv* ingenuamente
naïvety /naɪˈiːvtɪ/ *n* ingenuità *f*
naked /ˈneɪkɪd/ *adj* nudo; with the ~ **eye** a
occhio nudo
nakedness /ˈneɪkɪdnɪs/ *n* nudità *f*

⚔ name /neɪm/ ① *n* nome *m*; **what's your
~?** come ti chiami?; **my ~ is Matthew**
mi chiamo Matthew; **I know her by ~** la
conosco di nome; **by the ~ of Bates** di nome
Bates; **make a ~ for oneself** farsi un nome;
call somebody ~s fam insultare qualcuno
② *vt* (to position) nominare; chiamare ‹baby›;
(identify) citare; **be ~d after** essere chiamato
col nome di
name day *n* Relig onomastico *m*
name-drop *vi* he's always ~ping si vanta
sempre di conoscere persone famose
nameless /ˈneɪmlɪs/ *adj* senza nome
namely /ˈneɪmlɪ/ *adv* cioè
nameplate *n* targhetta *f*
namesake *n* omonimo, -a *mf*
name tag *n* targhetta (*f*) attaccata ad un
oggetto con il nome del proprietario
name tape *n* fettuccia (*f*) attaccata ad un
oggetto con il nome del proprietario
Namibia /nəˈmɪbɪə/ *n* Namibia *f*
nanny /ˈnænɪ/ *n* bambinaia *f*
nanny goat *n* capra *f*
nanosecond /ˈnænəʊsekənd/ *n* fam
nanosecondo *m*
nanotechnology /ˌnænəʊtekˈnɒlədʒɪ/ *n*
nanotecnologia *f*
nap /næp/ ① *n* pisolino *m*; **have a ~** fare
un pisolino
② *vi* **catch somebody ~ping** cogliere
qualcuno alla sprovvista
napalm /ˈneɪpɑːm/ *n* napalm *m*
nape /neɪp/ *n* ~ **[of the neck]** nuca *f*
napkin /ˈnæpkɪn/ *n* tovagliolo *m*
Naples /ˈneɪp(ə)lz/ *n* Napoli *f*
nappy /ˈnæpɪ/ *n* pannolino *m*
nappy liner *n* filtrante *m*
nappy rash *n* Br eritema *m* da pannolini
narcotic /nɑːˈkɒtɪk/ *adj* & *n* narcotico *m*

⚔ indicates a very frequent word

narcotics agent *n* Am agente *m* della squadra antidroga

narked /nɑːkt/ *adj* fam scocciato

narrate /nəˈreɪt/ *vt* narrare

narration /nəˈreɪʃn/ *n* narrazione *f*

narrative /ˈnærətɪv/ **1** *adj* narrativo
2 *n* narrazione *f*

narrator /nəˈreɪtə(r)/ *n* narratore, -trice *mf*

narrow /ˈnærəʊ/ **1** *adj* stretto; fig ‹views› ristretto; ‹margin, majority› scarso; **have a ∼ escape** scamparla per un pelo
2 *vi* restringersi
■ **narrow down** *vt* (reduce) restringere

narrowly /ˈnærəʊlɪ/ *adv* **∼ escape death** evitare la morte per un pelo

narrow-minded /-ˈmaɪndɪd/ *adj* di idee ristrette

nasal /ˈneɪzl/ *adj* nasale

nasal spray *n* spray *m inv* nasale

nastily /ˈnɑːstɪlɪ/ *adv* (spitefully) con cattiveria

nasty /ˈnɑːstɪ/ *adj* (**-ier, -iest**) ‹smell, person, remark› cattivo; ‹injury, situation, weather› brutto; **turn ∼** ‹person› diventare cattivo; ‹situation› mettersi male; ‹weather› volgere al brutto

⚷ **nation** /ˈneɪʃn/ *n* nazione *f*

⚷ **national** /ˈnæʃən(ə)l/ **1** *adj* nazionale
2 *n* cittadino, -a *mf*

national anthem *n* inno (*m*) nazionale

National Curriculum *n* Br *programma* (*m*) *scolastico ministeriale per il Galles e l'Inghilterra*

national debt *n* debito *m* pubblico

National Front *n* Br *partito* (*m*) *britannico di estrema destra*

national grid *n* Electr rete *f* elettrica nazionale

National Health *n* Br *servizio* (*m*) *nazionale di assistenza sanitaria*

National Health Service *n* *servizio* (*m*) *sanitario britannico*

National Insurance *n* ≈ Previdenza *f* sociale

National Insurance number *n* numero *m* di Previdenza sociale

Nationalism /ˈnæʃənəlɪzm/ *n* nazionalismo *m*

nationality /næʃəˈnælətɪ/ *n* nazionalità *f inv*

nationalization /næʃənəlaɪˈzeɪʃn/ *n* nazionalizzazione *f*

nationalize /ˈnæʃənəlaɪz/ *vt* nazionalizzare

National Lottery *n* Lotteria *f* di Stato

nationally /ˈnæʃənəlɪ/ *adv* a livello nazionale

national monument *n* monumento *m* nazionale

National Savings Bank *n* Br Cassa *f* di risparmio

national service *n* Br servizio *m* militare

National Trust *n* Br *associazione* (*f*) *per la tutela del patrimonio culturale e ambientale in Gran Bretagna*

nation state *n* stato-nazione *m*

nationwide /ˈneɪʃnwaɪd/ *adj* su scala nazionale

native /ˈneɪtɪv/ **1** *adj* nativo; (innate) innato
2 *n* nativo, -a *mf*; (local inhabitant) abitante *mf* del posto; (outside Europe) indigeno, -a *mf*

Native American *adj* & *n* amerindio, -a *mf*

native land *n* paese *m* nativo

native language *n* lingua *f* madre

native speaker *n* persona *f* di madrelingua; **Italian ∼s** Italiani madrelingua

Nativity /nəˈtɪvətɪ/ *n* **the ∼** la Natività

Nativity play *n* rappresentazione sulla nascita di Gesù

Nato, NATO /ˈneɪtəʊ/ *n abbr* (**North Atlantic Treaty Organization**) NATO *f*

natter /ˈnætə(r)/ **1** *n* **have a ∼** fam fare quattro chiacchiere
2 *vi* fam chiacchierare

natty /ˈnætɪ/ *adj* fam (smart) chic *inv*; (clever) geniale

⚷ **natural** /ˈnætʃ(ə)rəl/ *adj* naturale

natural childbirth *n* parto *m* indolore

natural gas *n* metano *m*

natural history *n* storia *f* naturale

naturalist /ˈnætʃ(ə)rəlɪst/ *n* naturalista *mf*

naturalization /nætʃ(ə)rəlaɪˈzeɪʃn/ *n* naturalizzazione *f*

naturalize /ˈnætʃ(ə)rəlaɪz/ *vt* naturalizzare

naturally /ˈnætʃ(ə)rəlɪ/ *adv* (of course) naturalmente; (by nature) per natura

⚷ **nature** /ˈneɪtʃə(r)/ *n* natura *f*; **by ∼** per natura

nature conservancy *n* protezione *f* della natura

nature reserve *n* riserva *f* naturale

nature trail *n* percorso *m* ecologico

naturism /ˈneɪtʃərɪzm/ *n* nudismo *m*

naturist /ˈneɪtʃərɪst/ **1** *n* naturista *mf*
2 *adj* naturistico

naught /nɔːt/ *n* = NOUGHT

naughtily /ˈnɔːtɪlɪ/ *adv* male

naughtiness /ˈnɔːtɪnɪs/ *n* (of child, pet) birbanteria *f*; (of joke, suggestion) maliziosità *f inv*

naughty /ˈnɔːtɪ/ *adj* (**-ier, -iest**) monello; (slightly indecent) spinto

nausea /'nɔ:zɪə/ n nausea f

nauseate /'nɔ:zɪeɪt/ vt nauseare

nauseating /'nɔ:zɪeɪtɪŋ/ adj nauseante

nauseatingly /'nɔ:zɪeɪtɪŋlɪ/ adv ⟨rich, sweet⟩ disgustosamente

nauseous /'nɔ:zɪəs/ adj I feel ~ ho la nausea

nautical /'nɔ:tɪkl/ adj nautico

nautical mile n miglio m marino

naval /'neɪvl/ adj navale

naval base n base f navale

naval dockyard n cantiere m navale militare

naval officer n ufficiale m di marina

naval station n base f navale

naval stores npl (depot) magazzini mpl della marina militare

nave /neɪv/ n navata f centrale

navel /'neɪvl/ n ombelico m

navel ring n piercing m inv all'ombelico

navigable /'nævɪgəbl/ adj navigabile

navigate /'nævɪgeɪt/ [1] vi navigare; Auto fare da navigatore
[2] vt navigare su ⟨river⟩

navigation /nævɪ'geɪʃn/ n navigazione f

navigational /nævɪ'geɪʃənəl/ adj ⟨instruments⟩ di navigazione; ⟨science⟩ della navigazione

navigator /'nævɪgeɪtə(r)/ n navigatore m

navvy /'nævɪ/ n manovale m

navy /'neɪvɪ/ [1] n marina f
[2] adj ~ [blue] adj blu scuro inv
[3] n blu m inv scuro

nay /neɪ/ [1] adv anzi
[2] n (negative vote) no m

Nazi /'nɑ:tsɪ/ n & adj nazista mf

NB abbr (**nota bene = please note**) n.b. m

NBC n abbr (**National Broadcasting Company**) NBC f (rete nazionale televisiva statunitense)

NC abbr Am (**North Carolina**)

NCO n abbr (**non-commissioned officer**) sottufficiale m

ND abbr Am (**North Dakota**)

Ne abbr Am (**Nebraska**)

NE abbr (**north-east**) NE

Neapolitan /nɪə'pɒlɪtən/ adj & n napoletano, -a mf

⚐ **near** /nɪə(r)/ [1] adj vicino; ⟨future⟩ prossimo; the ~est bank la banca più vicina
[2] adv vicino; draw ~ avvicinarsi; ~ at hand a portata di mano
[3] prep vicino a; he was ~ to tears aveva le lacrime agli occhi
[4] vt avvicinarsi a

⚐ indicates a very frequent word

nearby /nɪə'baɪ/ adj & adv vicino

near-death experience n esperienza f ultraterrena

Near East n Medio Oriente m

⚐ **nearly** /'nɪəlɪ/ adv quasi; it's not ~ enough non è per niente sufficiente

near miss n have a ~ ⟨planes, cars⟩ evitare per poco uno scontro

nearness /'nɪənɪs/ n vicinanza f

nearside n Auto (in Britain) lato m sinistro; (in America, rest of Europe) lato m destro

near-sighted /-'saɪtɪd/ adj Am miope

near-sightedness n miopia f

neat /ni:t/ adj (tidy) ordinato; (clever) efficace; (undiluted) liscio

neaten /'ni:tən/ vt riordinare ⟨pile of papers⟩; dare un'aggiustatina a ⟨tie, skirt⟩

neatly /'ni:tlɪ/ adv ordinatamente; (cleverly) efficacemente

neatness /'ni:tnɪs/ n (tidiness) ordine m

⚐ **necessarily** /nesə'serɪlɪ/ adv necessariamente

⚐ **necessary** /'nesəsərɪ/ adj necessario

necessitate /nɪ'sesɪteɪt/ vt rendere necessario

necessity /nɪ'sesətɪ/ n necessità f inv

⚐ **neck** /nek/ n collo m; (of dress) colletto m; ~ and ~ testa a testa

necking /'nekɪŋ/ n fam pomiciata f

necklace /'neklɪs/ n collana f

neckline n scollatura f

necktie n cravatta f

nectar /'nektə(r)/ n nettare m

nectarine /'nektərɪn/ n nettarina f

neé /neɪ/ adj ~ Brett nata Brett

⚐ **need** /ni:d/ [1] n bisogno m; be in ~ essere bisognoso; be in ~ of avere bisogno di; if ~ be se ce ne fosse bisogno; there is a ~ for c'è bisogno di; there is no ~ for that non ce n'è bisogno; there is no ~ for you to go non c'è bisogno che tu vada
[2] vt aver bisogno di; I ~ to know devo saperlo; it ~s to be done bisogna farlo
[3] v aux you ~ not go non c'è bisogno che tu vada; ~ I come? devo venire?

needful /'ni:dfʊl/ [1] adj necessario
[2] n do the ~ fare il necessario

needle /'ni:dl/ [1] n ago m; (for knitting) uncinetto m; (of record player) puntina f
[2] vt fam (annoy) punzecchiare

needless /'ni:dlɪs/ adj inutile

needlessly /'ni:dlɪslɪ/ adv inutilmente

needlework /'ni:dlwɜ:k/ n cucito m

needs /ni:dz/ adv ~ must il dovere chiama

need-to-know adj we have a ~ policy la nostra politica consiste nel tenere informati solo i diretti interessati

needy /'ni:dɪ/ adj (-ier, -iest) bisognoso

negate /nɪ'geɪt/ vt (cancel out) annullare; mettere in forma negativa ‹sentence›; (contradict) contraddire; (deny) negare

negation /nɪ'geɪʃn/ n negazione f

✓ **negative** /'negətɪv/ [1] adj negativo
[2] n negazione f; Phot negativo m; in the ~ Gram alla forma negativa

neglect /nɪ'glekt/ [1] n trascuratezza f; state of ~ stato di abbandono
[2] vt trascurare; he ~ed to write non si è curato di scrivere

neglected /nɪ'glektɪd/ adj trascurato

neglectful /nɪ'glektfʊl/ adj negligente; be ~ of trascurare

negligée /'neglɪʒeɪ/ n négligé m inv

negligence /'neglɪdʒəns/ n negligenza f

negligent /'neglɪdʒənt/ adj negligente

negligently /'neglɪdʒəntlɪ/ adv con negligenza

negligible /'neglɪdʒbl/ adj trascurabile

negotiable /nɪ'gəʊʃəbl/ adj ‹road› transitabile; Comm negoziabile; not ~ ‹cheque› non trasferibile

negotiate /nɪ'gəʊʃɪeɪt/ [1] vt negoziare; Auto prendere ‹bend›
[2] vi negoziare

negotiating /nɪ'gəʊʃɪeɪtɪŋ/ adj ‹rights› al negoziato; ‹team, committee› che conduce le trattative; ‹ploy, position› di negoziato; the ~ table il tavolo delle trattative

negotiation /nɪgəʊʃɪ'eɪʃn/ n negoziato m

negotiator /nɪ'gəʊʃɪeɪtə(r)/ n negoziatore, -a mf

Negro /'niːgrəʊ/ adj & n (pl -es) negro, -a mf

neigh /neɪ/ vi nitrire

✓ **neighbour** /'neɪbə(r)/ n vicino, -a mf

neighbourhood /'neɪbəhʊd/ n vicinato m; in the ~ of nei dintorni di; fig circa

neighbourhood watch scheme n vigilanza f da parte della gente del quartiere

neighbouring /'neɪbərɪŋ/ adj vicino

neighbourly /'neɪbəlɪ/ adj amichevole

✓ **neither** /'naɪðə(r)/ [1] adj & pron nessuno dei due, né l'uno né l'altro
[2] adv ~... nor né... né
[3] conj nemmeno, neanche; ~ do/did I nemmeno io

neo+ /'niːəʊ/ pref neo+

neologism /nɪ'ɒlədʒɪzm/ n neologismo m

neon /'niːɒn/ n neon m

neon light n luce f al neon

Nepal /nɪ'pɔːl/ n Nepal m

nephew /'nevjuː/ n nipote m

nephritis /nɪ'fraɪtɪs/ n nefrite f

nepotism /'nepətɪzm/ n nepotismo m

Neptune /'neptjuːn/ n Nettuno m

nerve /nɜːv/ n nervo m; fam (courage) coraggio m; fam (impudence) faccia f tosta;

lose one's ~ perdersi d'animo; **you've got a ~** hai una bella faccia tosta!; **live on one's ~s** vivere con i nervi a fior di pelle; **be a bag of ~s** avere i nervi a fior di pelle

nerve-racking /'nɜːvrækɪŋ/ adj logorante

nerviness /'nɜːvɪnɪs/ n Br nervosismo m; Am grinta f

nervous /'nɜːvəs/ adj nervoso; **he makes me ~** mi mette in agitazione

nervous breakdown n esaurimento m nervoso

nervous energy n energia f in eccesso

nervously /'nɜːvəslɪ/ adv nervosamente

nervousness /'nɜːvəsnɪs/ n nervosismo m; (before important event) tensione f

nervous system n sistema m nervoso

nervous wreck n fascio m di nervi

nervy /'nɜːvɪ/ adj (-ier, -iest) nervoso; Am (impudent) sfacciato

nest /nest/ [1] n nido m
[2] vi fare il nido

nested /'nestɪd/ adj Comput nidificato

nest egg n gruzzolo m

nesting /'nestɪŋ/ [1] n Zool nidificazione f; Comput nesting m inv, nidificazione f
[2] attrib ‹habit› di nidificare; ‹place› per nidificare; ‹season› della nidificazione

nestle /'nesl/ vi accoccolarsi

■ **nestle up to** vt accoccolarsi accanto a ‹somebody›

nestling /'neslɪŋ/ n nidiace m

net¹ /net/ [1] n rete f
[2] vt (pt/pp **netted**) (catch) prendere (con la rete)

net² [1] adj netto; ~ **of VAT** al netto dell'IVA
[2] vt (pt/pp **netted**) incassare un utile netto di

netball /'netbɔːl/ n sport (m inv) femminile simile alla pallacanestro

net cord n corda f di rete; Tennis (shot) net m inv

Netherlands /'neðələndz/ npl the ~ i Paesi Bassi

netiquette /'netɪket/ n Comput netiquette f inv

netspeak /'netspiːk/ n Comput linguaggio m del net

netting /'netɪŋ/ n [wire] ~ reticolato m

nettle /'netl/ n ortica f

net ton n Am tonnellata f corta americana

✓ **network** /'netwɜːk/ n rete f

network card n Comput scheda f di rete

networked /'netwɜːkt/ adj Comput collegato in rete

networking /'netwɜːkɪŋ/ n (establishing contacts) stabilimento m di una rete di contatti; Comput collegamento m in rete

n

network television n Am network m inv televisivo

neuralgia /njʊəˈrældʒə/ n nevralgia f

neuritis /njʊəˈraɪtɪs/ n nevrite f

neurologist /njʊəˈrɒlədʒɪst/ n neurologo, -a mf

neurology /njʊəˈrɒlədʒɪ/ n neurologia f

neurosis /njʊəˈrəʊsɪs/ n (pl **-oses** /njʊəˈrəʊsiːz/) nevrosi f inv

neurosurgeon /ˈnjʊərəsɜːˈdʒən/ n neurochirurgo m

neurotic /njʊəˈrɒtɪk/ adj nevrotico

neurotically /njʊəˈrɒtɪklɪ/ adv in modo ossessivo

neuter /ˈnjuːtə(r)/ ① adj gram neutro ② n (gram) neutro m ③ vt sterilizzare

neutral /ˈnjuːtrəl/ ① adj neutro; (country, person) neutrale ② n in ~ Auto in folle

neutrality /njuːˈtrælətɪ/ n neutralità f

neutralize /ˈnjuːtrəlaɪz/ vt neutralizzare

ℱ **never** /ˈnevə(r)/ adv [non...] mai; fam (expressing disbelief) ma va'; ~ **again** mai più; **well I ~!** chi l'avrebbe detto!

never-ending adj interminabile

nevermore /nevəˈmɔː(r)/ adv mai più

never-never n fam **buy something on the** ~ comprare qualcosa a rate

never-never land n mondo m dei sogni

nevertheless /nevəðəˈles/ adv tuttavia

ℱ **new** /njuː/ adj nuovo

New Age ① n New Age f inv ② attrib ‹music, ideas, sect› New Age inv

new blood n nuove leve fpl

newborn adj neonato

new build n nuova costruzione f

New Caledonia n Nuova Caledonia f

newcomer n nuovo, -a, arrivato, -a mf

newfangled adj pej modernizzante

newfound adj nuovo

Newfoundland /ˈnjuːfən(d)lənd/ n Terranova f

New Guinea n Nuova Guinea f

newish /ˈnjuːɪʃ/ adj abbastanza nuovo

new-laid /ˈnjuːleɪd/ adj fresco

new look ① adj ‹car, team› nuovo; ‹edition, show› rinnovato; ‹product› dall'aspetto nuovo ② n **they have given the shop a completely** ~ hanno completamente rinnovato il negozio

newly /ˈnjuːlɪ/ adv (recently) di recente

newly-built adj costruito di recente

newly-weds /ˈnjuːlɪwedz/ npl sposini mpl

new moon n luna f nuova

newness /ˈnjuːnɪs/ n novità f

ℱ **news** /njuːz/ n notizie fpl; TV telegiornale m; Radio giornale m radio; **piece of** ~ notizia f

news agency n agenzia f di stampa

newsagent's n Br giornalaio m (che vende anche tabacchi, caramelle ecc)

news bulletin n notiziario m

newscast n Am notiziario m

newscaster n giornalista mf televisivo, -a/radiofonico, -a

news conference n conferenza f stampa inv

newsdealer n Am giornalaio, -a mf

news desk n (at newspaper) redazione f

news editor n caporedattore, -trice mf di servizi di cronaca

newsflash n notizia f flash

newsgroup n newsgroup m inv

news headlines npl TV titoli mpl delle principali notizie

news item n notizia f di attualità

newsletter n bollettino m d'informazione

ℱ **newspaper** /ˈnjuːzpeɪpə(r)/ n giornale m; (material) carta f di giornale

newspaperman n giornalista m

newspaper office n ufficio m della redazione

newspaperwoman n giornalista f

newspeak /ˈnjuːspiːk/ n Am giornalese m

newsprint n (paper) carta f da giornale; (ink) inchiostro m di stampa

newsreader n giornalista mf televisivo, -a/radiofonico, -a

newsreel n cinegiornale m

newsroom n redazione f

news sheet n bollettino m

newsstand n edicola f

news value n interesse m mediatico

newsworthy adj che merita di essere pubblicato

newsy /ˈnjuːzɪ/ adj ‹letter› pieno di notizie

newt /njuːt/ n tritone m

new technology n nuova tecnologia f

New Testament n Nuovo Testamento m

new wave n & adj new wave f inv

New Year n (January 1st) Capodanno m; (next year) l'anno m nuovo; **Happy** ~**!** buon anno!; **closed for** ~ chiuso per le feste di Capodanno; **see in the** ~ festeggiare il Capodanno

New Year Honours list n Br lista (f) delle persone che ricevono decorazioni il 1 gennaio

New Year's Day n Capodanno m

New Year's Eve n vigilia f di Capodanno

New Year's resolution n proposito m per l'anno nuovo

New Zealand n Nuova Zelanda f

ℱ indicates a very frequent word

New Zealander *n* neozelandese *mf*

✓ **next** /nekst/ [1] *adj* prossimo; (adjoining) vicino; **who's ∼?** a chi tocca?; **the ∼ best thing would be to** alternativamente la cosa migliore sarebbe di; **∼ door** accanto; **∼ to nothing** quasi niente; **the ∼ day** il giorno dopo; **∼ week** la settimana prossima; **the week after ∼** fra due settimane; **the ∼ thing I knew** la sola cosa che ho saputo dopo [2] *adv* dopo; **when will you see him ∼?** quando lo rivedi la prossima volta?; **∼ to** accanto a [3] *n* seguente *mf*; **∼ of kin** parente *m* prossimo

next door [1] *adj* ‹dog, bell› dei vicini; ‹office› accanto *inv*; **the girl ∼** also fig la ragazza della porta accanto [2] *adv* ‹live, move in› nella casa accanto

next-door neighbour *n* vicino *m* di casa

nexus /'neksəs/ *n* (network) rete *f*

NF *n abbr* Br Pol (**National Front**) *partito (m) nazionalista*

NH *abbr* Am (**New Hampshire**)

NHS *n abbr* (**National Health Service**) *servizio (m) sanitario nazionale*

NI *n abbr* 1 Br (**National Insurance**) previdenza *f* sociale 2 (**Northern Ireland**) Irlanda *f* del Nord

nib /nɪb/ *n* pennino *m*

nibble /'nɪbl/ *vt/i* mordicchiare

■ **nibble at, nibble on** *vt* = NIBBLE

Nicaragua /nɪkə'ræɡjʊə/ *n* Nicaragua *m*

✓ **nice** /naɪs/ *adj* ‹day, weather, holiday› bello; ‹person› gentile, simpatico; ‹food› buono; **it was ∼ meeting you** è stato un piacere conoscerla

nice-looking *adj* carino

nicely /'naɪslɪ/ *adv* gentilmente; (well) bene

niceties /'naɪsətɪz/ *npl* finezze *fpl*

niche /niːʃ/ *n* nicchia *f*

niche market *n* mercato *m* specializzato

nick /nɪk/ [1] *n* tacca *f*; (on chin etc) taglietto *m*; fam (prison) galera *f*; fam (police station) centrale *f* [di polizia]; **in the ∼ of the time** fam appena in tempo; **in good ∼** fam in buono stato [2] *vt* intaccare; fam (steal) fregare; fam (arrest) beccare; **∼ one's chin** farsi un taglietto nel mento

nickel /'nɪkl/ *n* nichel *m*; Am moneta *f* da cinque centesimi

nickel-and-dime *adj* Am fam da quattro soldi

nickelodeon /nɪkəl'əʊdɪən/ *n* Am (juke box) juke box *m inv*

nickname /'nɪkneɪm/ [1] *n* soprannome *m* [2] *vt* soprannominare

nicotine /'nɪkətiːn/ *n* nicotina *f*

nicotine patch *n* cerotto *m* (transdermico) alla nicotina

niece /niːs/ *n* nipote *f*

nifty /'nɪftɪ/ *adj* fam (skilful) geniale; (attractive) sfizioso

Niger /'naɪdʒə(r)/ *n* Niger *m*

Nigeria /naɪ'dʒɪərɪə/ *n* Nigeria *f*

Nigerian /naɪ'dʒɪərɪən/ *adj & n* nigeriano, -a *mf*

niggardly /'nɪɡədlɪ/ *adj* ‹person› tirchio; ‹salary› misero

niggle /'nɪɡl/ fam [1] *n* (complaint) cosetta *f* da ridire [2] *vi* (complain) lamentarsi in continuazione [3] *vt* (irritate) dar fastidio a

niggling /'nɪɡlɪŋ/ *adj* ‹detail› insignificante; ‹pain› fastidioso; ‹doubt› persistente

✓ **night** /naɪt/ [1] *n* notte *f*; (evening) sera *f*; **at ∼** la notte, di notte; (in the evening) la sera, di sera; **Monday ∼** lunedì notte/sera; **work ∼s** lavorare la notte [2] *adj* di notte

nightcap *n* papalina *f*; (drink) bicchierino *m* bevuto prima di andare a letto

nightclub *n* locale *m* notturno, night[-club] *m inv*

nightclubbing *n* **go ∼** andare nei night [club]

nightdress *n* camicia *f* da notte

nightfall *n* crepuscolo *m*

nightgown, fam **nightie** *n* camicia *f* da notte

nightie *n* camicia *f* da notte

nightingale /'naɪtɪŋɡeɪl, US -tŋɡ-/ *n* usignolo *m*

nightlife *n* vita *f* notturna

night light *n* lumino *m* da notte

nightly /'naɪtlɪ/ [1] *adj* di notte, di sera [2] *adv* ogni notte, ogni sera

nightmare /'naɪtmeə(r)/ *n* also fig incubo *m*

nightmarish /'naɪtmeərɪʃ/ *adj* da incubo

night owl *n* nottambulo, -a *mf*

night porter *n* portiere *m* di notte

night school *n* scuola *f* serale

nightshade *n* Bot **deadly ∼** belladonna *f*

night shelter *n* dormitorio *m* pubblico

nightshift *n* (workers) turno *m* di notte; **be on the ∼** fare il turno di notte

nightshirt *n* camicia *f* da notte (*da uomo*)

nightspot *n* night club *m inv*

nightstand *n* Am comodino *m*

nightstick *n* Am (truncheon) manganello *m*

night-time *n* **at ∼** di notte, la notte

night vision *n* visione *f* notturna

nightwatchman *n* guardiano *m* notturno

nightwear *n* indumenti *mpl* da notte

nil /nɪl/ *n* nulla *m*; Sport zero *m*

Nile /naɪl/ *n* Nilo *m*

nimble /'nɪmbl/ *adj* agile

nimbly /'nɪmblɪ/ *adv* agilmente

nincompoop /'nɪŋkəmpu:p/ *n* fam scemo *m*

ⵏ **nine** /naɪn/ *adj & n* nove *m*

ninepin /'naɪnpɪn/ *n* birillo *m*; **be falling like** ∼**s** ‹*troops, guards, candidates*› cadere come le mosche

nineteen /naɪn'ti:n/ *adj & n* diciannove *m*

nineteenth /naɪn'ti:nθ/ *adj & n* diciannovesimo, -a *mf*

nineties /'naɪntɪz/ *npl* (period) **the** ∼ gli anni Novanta *mpl*; (age) novant'anni *mpl*

ninetieth /'naɪntɪɪθ/ *adj & n* novantesimo, -a *mf*

nine-to-five [1] *adj* ‹*job*› in un ufficio; ‹*routine*› dell'ufficio
[2] *adv* ‹*work*› dalle nove alle cinque

ninety /'naɪntɪ/ *adj & n* novanta *m*

ninth /naɪnθ/ *adj & n* nono, -a *mf*

nip /nɪp/ [1] *n* pizzicotto *m*; (bite) morso *m*
[2] *vt* pizzicare; (bite) mordere; ∼ **in the bud** fig stroncare sul nascere
[3] *vi* fam (run) fare un salto

nipper /'nɪpə(r)/ *n* fam ragazzino, -a *mf*

nipple /'nɪpl/ *n* capezzolo *m*; Am (on bottle) tettarella *f*

nippy /'nɪpɪ/ *adj* (**-ier, -iest**) fam (cold) pungente; (quick) svelto

nit /nɪt/ *n* (egg) lendine *m*; (larva) larva *f* di pidocchio

nit-pick *vi* cercare il pelo nell'uovo

nitrate /'naɪtreɪt/ *n* nitrato *m*

nitric /'naɪtrɪk/ *adj* nitrico

nitrogen /'naɪtrədʒn/ *n* azoto *m*

nitty-gritty /nɪtɪ'grɪtɪ/ *n* fam **the** ∼ il nocciolo [della questione]; **get down to the** ∼ arrivare al dunque

nitwit /'nɪtwɪt/ *n* fam imbecille *mf*

NJ *abbr* Am (**New Jersey**)

NM *abbr* Am (**New Mexico**)

ⵏ **no** /nəʊ/ [1] *adv* no
[2] *n* (*pl* **noes**) no *m inv*
[3] *adj* nessuno; **I have no time** non ho tempo; **in no time** in un baleno; **'no parking'** 'sosta vietata'; **'no smoking'** 'vietato fumare'; **it's no go** è inutile

no., **No.** *abbr* (**number**) No.

Noah /'nəʊə/ *n* Noè *m*; ∼**'s Ark** l'arca *f* di Noè

nobility /nəʊ'bɪlətɪ/ *n* nobiltà *f*

noble /'nəʊbl/ *adj* nobile

nobleman /'nəʊblmən/ *n* nobile *m*

noble-minded /-'maɪndɪd/ *adj* di animo nobile

noble savage *n* buon selvaggio *m*

nobly /'nəʊblɪ/ *adv* (selflessly) generosamente; ∼ **born** di nobili natali

---

ⵏ indicates a very frequent word

ⵏ **nobody** /'nəʊbədɪ/ [1] *pron* nessuno; **he knows** ∼ non conosce nessuno; **he's** ∼ **important** non è nessuno d'importante
[2] *n* **he's a** ∼ non è nessuno

no claims bonus *n* abbuono *m* in assenza di sinistri

nocturnal /nɒk'tɜ:nl/ *adj* notturno

ⵏ **nod** /nɒd/ [1] *n* cenno *m* del capo; **give a** ∼ fare un cenno col capo
[2] *vt* (*pt/pp* **nodded**) fare un cenno col capo; (in agreement) fare di sì col capo
[3] *vi* ∼ **one's head** fare di sì col capo
■ **nod off** *vi* assopirsi

node /nəʊd/ *n* nodo *m*

nodule /'nɒdju:l/ *n* nodulo *m*

no-go *adj* fam **it's** ∼ non è possibile

no-go area *n* zona (*f*) calda a cui la polizia può accedere solo con la forza

no-hoper /nəʊ'həʊpə(r)/ *n* persona *f* senza prospettive

ⵏ **noise** /nɔɪz/ *n* rumore *m*; (loud) rumore *m*, chiasso *m*

noiseless /'nɔɪzlɪs/ *adj* silenzioso

noiselessly /'nɔɪzlɪslɪ/ *adv* silenziosamente

noise level *n* intensità *f inv* del rumore

noise pollution *n* inquinamento *m* acustico

noisily /'nɔɪzɪlɪ/ *adv* rumorosamente

noisy /'nɔɪzɪ/ *adj* (**-ier, -iest**) rumoroso

nomad /'nəʊmæd/ *n* nomade *mf*

nomadic /nəʊ'mædɪk/ *adj* nomade

nominal /'nɒmɪnl/ *adj* nominale

nominally /'nɒmɪnəlɪ/ *adv* nominalmente

nominate /'nɒmɪneɪt/ *vt* proporre come candidato; (appoint) designare

nomination /nɒmɪ'neɪʃn/ *n* nomina *f*; (person nominated) candidato, -a *mf*

nominative /'nɒmɪnətɪv/ *adj & n* gram ∼ [**case**] nominativo *m*

nominee /nɒmɪ'ni:/ *n* persona *f* nominata

non+ /nɒn/ *pref* non+, in+

non-academic *adj* ‹*course*› pratico; ‹*staff*› non insegnante

non-addictive *adj* che non dà assuefazione

non-alcoholic *adj* analcolico

non-attendance *n* mancata presenza *f*

non-believer *n* non credente *mf*

nonchalant /'nɒnʃələnt/ *adj* disinvolto

nonchalantly /'nɒnʃələntlɪ/ *adv* in modo disinvolto

non-classified *adj* ‹*information*› non confidenziale

non-combustible *adj* incombustibile

non-commercial *adj* ‹*event, activity*› senza fini di lucro

non-commissioned /-kə'mɪʃnd/ *adj* ∼ **officer** sottufficiale *m*

non-committal /-kə'mɪtəl/ *adj* che non si sbilancia

non-compliance *n* (with standards) non conformità *f* (with a); (with orders) inadempienza *f* (with a)

nonconformist /nɒnkən'fɔːmɪst/ *adj & n* anticonformista *mf*

non-cooperation *n* non cooperazione *f*

non-denominational /-dɪnɒmɪ'neɪʃənəl/ *adj* ‹church› ecumenico; ‹school› laico

nondescript /'nɒndɪskrɪpt/ *adj* qualunque

⚹ **none** /nʌn/ ① *pron* (person) nessuno; (thing) niente; ∼ **of us** nessuno di noi; ∼ **of this** niente di questo; **there's** ∼ **left** non ce n'è più
② *adv* **she's** ∼ **too pleased** non è per niente soddisfatta; **I'm** ∼ **the wiser** non ne so più di prima

non-EC *adj* ‹national› extracomunitario; ‹country› che non appartiene alla Comunità Europea

nonentity /nɒ'nentəti/ *n* nullità *f inv*

non-essentials /-ɪ'senʃlz/ *npl* (details) dettagli *mpl*; (objects) cose *fpl* accessorie

nonetheless /nʌnðə'les/ *adv* = NEVERTHELESS

non-event *n* delusione *f*

non-existent *adj* inesistente

non-family *adj* al di fuori della famiglia

non-fat *adj* magro; ‹diet› senza grassi

non-fiction *n* saggistica *f*

non-flammable *adj* non infiammabile

non-fulfilment *n* (of contract, obligation) inadempienza *f* (of a); (of desire) inappagamento *m*

non-infectious *adj* non infettivo

non-iron *adj* che non si stira

non-judgmental *adj* imparziale

non-league *adj* Sport fuori campionato

no-no *n* fam cosa *f* proibita; **that's a** ∼ è un argomento tabù

no-nonsense *adj* ‹manner, attitude› diretto; ‹tone› spiccio; ‹look, policy› pratico; ‹person› franco

non-partisan *adj* imparziale

non-party *adj* ‹issue, decision› apartitico; ‹person› indipendente

non-person *n* (insignificant person) nullità *f inv*; **officially, he is a** ∼ Pol ufficialmente non è mai esistito

nonplussed /nɒn'plʌst/ *adj* perplesso

non-professional *adj* dilettante

non-profit-making /-'prɒfɪtmeɪkɪŋ/ *adj* ‹organization› senza fini di lucro

non-redeemable *adj* Fin vincolato

non-refillable *adj* ‹lighter, pen› non ricaricabile; ‹can, bottle› non riutilizzabile

non-religious *adj* laico

non-resident ① *adj* ‹job, course› non residenziale; Comput che non risiede in permanenza nella memoria centrale
② *n* non residente *mf*

non-residential *adj* ‹guest› di passaggio; ‹student, visitor› non residente; ‹caretaker› che non alloggia sul posto; ‹area› non residenziale

non-returnable *adj* ‹bottle› a perdere

non-segregated *adj* ‹area› non segregato; ‹society› non segregazionista

nonsense /'nɒnsəns/ *n* sciocchezze *fpl*

nonsensical /nɒn'sensɪkl/ *adj* assurdo

non sequitur /nɒn'sekwɪtə(r)/ *n* affermazione (*f*) senza legame con quanto detto prima

non-skid *adj* antiscivolo *inv*

non-smoker *n* non fumatore, -trice *mf*; (compartment) scompartimento *m* non fumatori

non-smoking *adj* non fumatori *inv*

non-specialized *adj* non specializzato

non-starter *n* **be a** ∼ ‹person› non avere nessuna probabilità di riuscita; ‹plan, idea› essere destinato al fallimento

non-stick *adj* antiaderente

non-stop ① *adj* ‹talk, work, pressure, noise› continuo; ‹train› diretto; ‹journey› senza fermate; ‹flight› senza scalo
② *adv* ‹work, talk› senza sosta; ‹travel, fly› senza scalo

non-swimmer *n* persona *f* che non sa nuotare

non-taxable *adj* non imponibile

non-union *adj* ‹person› non iscritto ad un sindacato; ‹company› non sindacalizzato

non-violent *adj* non violento

non-white, non-White *n* persona *f* di colore

noodles /'nuːdlz/ *npl* taglierini *mpl*

nook /nʊk/ *n* cantuccio *m*

noon /nuːn/ *n* mezzogiorno *m*; **at** ∼ a mezzogiorno

no one *pron* nessuno

noose /nuːs/ *n* nodo *m* scorsoio

⚹ **nor** /nɔː(r)/ *adv & conj* né; ∼ **do I** neppure io

Nordic /'nɔːdɪk/ *adj* nordico

norm /nɔːm/ *n* norma *f*

⚹ **normal** /'nɔːml/ *adj* normale

normality /nɔː'mælətɪ/ *n* normalità *f*

⚹ **normally** /'nɔːməlɪ/ *adv* (usually) normalmente

Norman /'nɔːmən/ ① *adj* normanno; ‹landscape village› della Normandia
② *n* normanno *m*

Norse /nɔːs/ *adj* ‹mythology, saga› norreno

⚹ **north** /nɔːθ/ ① *n* nord *m*; **to the** ∼ **of** a nord di
② *adj* del nord, settentrionale
③ *adv* a nord

North Africa n Africa f del Nord

North African adj & n nordafricano, -a mf

North America n America f del Nord

North American adj & n nordamericano, -a mf

Northants /nɔːˈθænts/ abbr Br (**Northamptonshire**)

northbound /ˈnɔːθbaʊnd/ adj ‹traffic, carriageway› in direzione nord

Northd abbr Br (**Northumberland**)

north-east ① adj di nord-est, nordorientale
② n nord-est m
③ adv a nord-est; ‹travel› verso nord-est

north-easterly ① adj ‹point› a nord-est; ‹wind› di nord-est
② n vento m di nord-est

northeastern /nɔːˈθiːstən/ adj nordorientale

northerly /ˈnɔːðəlɪ/ adj ‹direction› nord; ‹wind› del nord

⚡ **northern** /ˈnɔːðən/ adj del nord, settentrionale

Northern Ireland n Irlanda f del Nord

Northern Lights npl aurora f boreale

North Korea n Corea f del Nord

North Pole n polo m nord

North Sea n Mare m del Nord

North Star n stella f polare

northward[s] /ˈnɔːθwəd[z]/ adv verso nord

north-west ① adj di nord-ovest, nordoccidentale
② n nord-ovest m
③ adv a nord-ovest; ‹travel› verso nord-ovest

north-westerly ① adj ‹point› a nord-ovest; ‹wind› di nord-ovest
② n vento m di nord-ovest

north-western adj nordoccidentale

Norway /ˈnɔːweɪ/ n Norvegia f

Norwegian /nɔːˈwiːdʒn/ adj & n norvegese mf

⚡ **nose** /nəʊz/ n naso m
■ **nose about** vi curiosare

nosebleed /ˈnəʊzbliːd/ n emorragia f nasale

nosedive /ˈnəʊzdaɪv/ n Aeron picchiata f; **take a** ∼ fig ‹prices› scendere vertiginosamente

nosey /ˈnəʊzɪ/ adj = NOSY

no-show n persona (f) che non si è presentata

nosily /ˈnəʊzɪlɪ/ adv in modo indiscreto

nostalgia /nɒˈstældʒɪə/ n nostalgia f

nostalgic /nɒˈstældʒɪk/ adj nostalgico

nostril /ˈnɒstrəl/ n narice f

⚡ indicates a very frequent word

nosy /ˈnəʊzɪ/ adj (**-ier, -iest**) fam ficcanaso inv

⚡ **not** /nɒt/ adv non; he is ∼ Italian non è italiano; I hope ∼ spero di no; ∼ all of us have been invited non siamo stati tutti invitati; if ∼ se no; ∼ at all niente affatto; ∼ a bit per niente; ∼ even neanche; ∼ yet non ancora; in the ∼ too distant future in un futuro non troppo lontano; ∼ only... but also... non solo... ma anche...

notable /ˈnəʊtəbl/ adj (remarkable) notevole

notably /ˈnəʊtəblɪ/ adv (in particular) in particolare

notary /ˈnəʊtərɪ/ n notaio m; ∼ public notaio m

notation /nəʊˈteɪʃn/ n notazione f

notch /nɒtʃ/ n tacca f
■ **notch up** vt (score) segnare

⚡ **note** /nəʊt/ ① n nota f; (short letter, banknote) biglietto m; (memo, written comment etc) appunto m; of ∼ ‹person› di spicco; ‹comments, event› degno di nota; **make a** ∼ **of** prendere nota di; **take** ∼ **of** (notice) prendere nota di
② vt (notice) notare; (write) annotare
■ **note down** vt annotare

notebook /ˈnəʊtbʊk/ n taccuino m; Comput notebook m inv

notebook [PC] n notebook m inv

noted /ˈnəʊtɪd/ adj noto, celebre (for per)

notepad n blocco m per appunti

notepaper n carta f da lettere

noteworthy adj degno di nota

⚡ **nothing** /ˈnʌθɪŋ/ ① pron niente, nulla
② adv niente affatto; **for** ∼ (free, in vain) per niente; (with no reason) senza motivo; ∼ **but** nient'altro che; ∼ **much** poco o nulla; ∼ **interesting** niente di interessante; **it's** ∼ **to do with you** non ti riguarda

⚡ **notice** /ˈnəʊtɪs/ ① n (on board) avviso m; (review) recensione f; (termination of employment) licenziamento m; [**advance**] ∼ preavviso m; **two months'** ∼ due mesi di preavviso; **at short** ∼ con breve preavviso; **until further** ∼ fino nuovo avviso; **give [in one's]** ∼ ‹employee› dare le dimissioni; **give an employee** ∼ dare il preavviso ad un impiegato; **take no** ∼ **of** non fare caso a; **take no** ∼! non farci caso!
② vt notare

noticeable /ˈnəʊtɪsəbl/ adj evidente

noticeably /ˈnəʊtɪsəblɪ/ adv sensibilmente

noticeboard /ˈnəʊtɪsbɔːd/ n bacheca f

notification /nəʊtɪfɪˈkeɪʃn/ n notifica f

notify /ˈnəʊtɪfaɪ/ vt (pt/pp **-ied**) notificare

⚡ **notion** /ˈnəʊʃn/ n idea f, nozione f; he hasn't the slightest ∼ of time gli manca completamente la nozione del tempo; ∼**s** pl Am (haberdashery) merceria f

notoriety /nəʊtəˈraɪətɪ/ n notorietà f

notorious /nəʊˈtɔːrɪəs/ *adj* famigerato; be ∼ for essere tristemente famoso per

notoriously /nəʊˈtɔːrɪəslɪ/ *adv* they're ∼ unreliable tutti sanno che su di loro non si può mai fare affidamento

Notts /nɒts/ *abbr* Br (**Nottinghamshire**)

notwithstanding /nɒtwɪðˈstændɪŋ/
1 *prep* malgrado
2 *adv* ciononostante

nougat /ˈnuːɡət/ *n* torrone *m*

nought /nɔːt/ *n* zero *m*

noughts and crosses *n* tris *m*

noun /naʊn/ *n* nome *m*, sostantivo *m*

nourish /ˈnʌrɪʃ/ *vt* nutrire

nourishing /ˈnʌrɪʃɪŋ/ *adj* nutriente

nourishment /ˈnʌrɪʃmənt/ *n* nutrimento *m*

✦ **novel** /ˈnɒvl/ 1 *adj* insolito
2 *n* romanzo *m*

novelette /nɒvəˈlet/ *n* (oversentimental) romanzetto *m* rosa

novelist /ˈnɒvəlɪst/ *n* romanziere, -a *mf*

novelty /ˈnɒvəltɪ/ *n* novità *f*; **novelties** *pl* (objects) oggettini *mpl*

✦ **November** /nəʊˈvembə(r)/ *n* novembre *m*

novice /ˈnɒvɪs/ *n* novizio, -a *mf*

✦ **now** /naʊ/ 1 *adv* ora, adesso; **by** ∼ ormai; **just** ∼ proprio ora; **right** ∼ subito; ∼ **and again,** ∼ **and then** ogni tanto; ∼, ∼! su!
2 *conj* ∼ [**that**] ora che, adesso che

nowadays /ˈnaʊədeɪz/ *adv* oggigiorno

nowhere /ˈnəʊweə(r)/ *adv* in nessun posto, da nessuna parte

noxious /ˈnɒkʃəs/ *adj* nocivo

nozzle /ˈnɒzl/ *n* bocchetta *f*

nr *abbr* (**near**) vicino

NSPCC *n abbr* Br (**National Society for the Prevention of Cruelty to Children**) Società *f* nazionale per la protezione dell'infanzia

NT *abbr* (**New Testament**) Nuovo Testamento (NT)

nth /enθ/ *adj* Math fig to the ∼ **power/degree** all'ennesima potenza; **for the** ∼ **time** per l'ennesima volta

nuance /ˈnjuːɒs/ *n* sfumatura *f*

nub /nʌb/ *n* the ∼ **of the matter** il nocciolo della questione

nubile /ˈnjuːbaɪl/ *adj* ‹attractive› desiderabile

✦ **nuclear** /ˈnjuːklɪə(r)/ *adj* nucleare

nuclear bomb *n* bomba *f* atomica

nuclear deterrent *n* deterrente *m* nucleare

nuclear energy *n* energia *f* nucleare

nuclear-free zone *n* Br zona *f* denuclearizzata

nuclear physics *n* fisica *f* nucleare

nuclear power *n* (energy) energia *f* nucleare; (country) potenza *f* nucleare

nuclear power station *n* centrale *f* nucleare

nuclear shelter *n* rifugio *m* antiatomico

nuclear waste *n* scorie *fpl* nucleari

nucleus /ˈnjuːklɪəs/ *n* (*pl* **-lei** /ˈnjuːklɪaɪ/) nucleo *m*

nude /njuːd/ 1 *adj* nudo
2 *n* nudo *m*; **in the** ∼ nudo

nudge /nʌdʒ/ 1 *n* colpetto *m* di gomito
2 *vt* dare un colpetto col gomito a

nudism /ˈnjuːdɪzm/ *n* nudismo *m*

nudist /ˈnjuːdɪst/ *n* nudista *mf*

nudity /ˈnjuːdətɪ/ *n* nudità *f*

nugget /ˈnʌɡɪt/ *n* pepita *f*

nuisance /ˈnjuːsəns/ *n* seccatura *f*; (person) piaga *f*; **what a** ∼! che seccatura!

nuisance call *n* Teleph telefonata *f* anonima

null /nʌl/ *adj* ∼ **and void** nullo

nullify /ˈnʌlɪfaɪ/ *vt* (*pt/pp* **-ied**) annullare

numb /nʌm/ 1 *adj* intorpidito; ∼ **with cold** intirizzito dal freddo
2 *vt* intorpidire

✦ **number** /ˈnʌmbə(r)/ 1 *n* numero *m*; **a** ∼ **of people** un certo numero di persone
2 *vt* numerare; (include) annoverare

numbering /ˈnʌmbərɪŋ/ *n* numerazione *f*

number one *n* (most important) numero uno *m*; **look after** ∼ (oneself) pensare prima di tutto a se stessi

number plate *n* targa *f*

numeracy /ˈnjuːmərəsɪ/ *n* **improve standards of** ∼ migliorare il livello nel calcolo

numeral /ˈnjuːmərəl/ *n* numero *m*, cifra *f*

numerate /ˈnjuːmərət/ *adj* be ∼ sapere far di calcolo

numerical /njuːˈmerɪkl/ *adj* numerico; **in** ∼ **order** in ordine numerico

numerically /njuːˈmerɪklɪ/ *adv* numericamente

numeric keypad /njuːˈmerɪk/ *n* Comput tastierino *m* numerico

✦ **numerous** /ˈnjuːmərəs/ *adj* numeroso

nun /nʌn/ *n* suora *f*

nuptial /ˈnʌpʃl/ 1 *adj* nuziale
2 ∼**s** *npl* nozze *fpl*

✦ **nurse** /nɜːs/ 1 *n* infermiere, -a *mf*; **children's** ∼ bambinaia *f*
2 *vt* curare

nursemaid *n* bambinaia *f*

nursery /ˈnɜːsərɪ/ *n* stanza *f* dei bambini; (for plants) vivaio *m*; [**day**] ∼ asilo *m*

nursery rhyme *n* filastrocca *f*

nursery school *n* scuola *f* materna

nursery slope *n* Br pista *f* per principianti

nurse's aid *n* Am aiuto infermiere, -a *mf*

n

nursing /'nɜːsɪŋ/ n professione f d'infermiere

nursing auxiliary n Br aiuto infermiere, -a mf

nursing home n casa f di cura per anziani

nurture /'nɜːtə(r)/ vt allevare; fig coltivare

nut /nʌt/ n noce f; Techn dado m; fam (head) zucca f

nutcrackers /'nʌtkrækəz/ npl schiaccianoci m inv

nutmeg /'nʌtmeg/ n noce f moscata

nutrient /'njuːtrɪənt/ n sostanza f nutritiva

nutrition /njuːˈtrɪʃn/ n nutrizione f

nutritional /njuːˈtrɪʃənl/, US nuː-/ adj nutritivo

nutritionist /njuːˈtrɪʃənɪst/ n nutrizionista mf

nutritious /njuːˈtrɪʃəs/ adj nutriente

nuts /nʌts/ npl frutta f secca; **be ~** fam essere svitato

nutshell /'nʌtʃel/ n guscio m di noce; **in a ~** fig in parole povere

nuzzle /'nʌzl/ vt ‹horse, dog› strofinare il muso contro

■ **nuzzle up:** vi **~ up** against or to somebody rannicchiarsi contro qualcuno

NV abbr Am (**Nevada**)

NVQ n abbr Br (**national vocational qualification**) diploma conseguito presso un istituto tecnico o professionale

NW abbr (**north-west**) NO

NY abbr Am (**New York**)

NYC abbr Am (**New York City**)

nylon /'naɪlɒn/ ① n nailon m; **~s** pl calze fpl di nailon
② attrib di nailon

nymph /nɪmf/ n ninfa f

nymphomaniac /nɪmfəˈmeɪnɪæk/ ① n ninfomane f
② adj da ninfomane

NZ abbr (**New Zealand**)

Oo

o, O /əʊ/ n (letter) o, O f inv

O /əʊ/ n Teleph zero m

oaf /əʊf/ n (pl **oafs**) zoticone, -a mf

oak /əʊk/ ① n quercia f
② attrib di quercia

OAP abbr (**old-age pensioner**) pensionato, -a mf

oar /ɔː(r)/ n remo m

oarsman /'ɔːzmən/ n vogatore m

oasis /əʊˈeɪsɪs/ n (pl **oases** /əʊˈeɪsiːz/) oasi f inv

oatcake /'əʊtkeɪk/ n galletta f di avena

oath /əʊθ/ n giuramento m; (swear-word) bestemmia f

oatmeal /'əʊtmiːl/ n farina f d'avena

oats /əʊts/ npl avena fsg; Culin [rolled] **~** fiocchi mpl d'avena

obdurate /'ɒbdjʊrət/ adj (stubborn) irremovibile; (hardhearted) insensibile

OBE n abbr Br (**Officer of the (Order of the) British Empire**) onorificenza (f) britannica

obedience /əˈbiːdɪəns/ n ubbidienza f

obedient /əˈbiːdɪənt/ adj ubbidiente

obediently /əˈbiːdɪəntlɪ/ adv ubbidientemente

obelisk /'ɒbəlɪsk/ n obelisco m

obese /əˈbiːs/ adj obeso

obesity /əˈbiːsətɪ/ n obesità f

obey /əˈbeɪ/ ① vt ubbidire a; osservare ‹instructions, rules›
② vi ubbidire

obituary /əˈbɪtjʊərɪ/ n necrologio m

♂ **object¹** /'ɒbdʒɪkt/ n oggetto m; Gram complemento m oggetto; **money is no ~** i soldi non sono un problema

object² /əbˈdʒekt/ vi (be against) opporsi (**to** a); **~ that...** obiettare che...

objection /əbˈdʒekʃn/ n obiezione f; **have no ~** non avere niente in contrario

objectionable /əbˈdʒekʃ(ə)nəbl/ adj discutibile; ‹person› sgradevole

objective /əbˈdʒektɪv/ ① adj oggettivo
② n obiettivo m

objectively /əbˈdʒektɪvlɪ/ adv obiettivamente

objectivity /ɒbdʒekˈtəvətɪ/ n oggettività f

objector /əbˈdʒektə(r)/ n oppositore, -trice mf

obligation /ɒblɪˈgeɪʃn/ n obbligo m; **be under an ~** avere un obbligo; **without ~** senza impegno

obligatory /əˈblɪgətrɪ/ adj obbligatorio

oblige /əˈblaɪdʒ/ vt (compel) obbligare; (do a small service for) fare una cortesia a; **much ~d** grazie mille

---

♂ indicates a very frequent word

obliging /ə'blaɪdʒɪŋ/ *adj* disponibile
oblique /ə'bliːk/ *adj* obliquo; fig indiretto;
~ **[stroke]** *n* barra *f*
obliterate /ə'blɪtəreɪt/ *vt* obliterare
obliteration /əblɪtə'reɪʃn/ *n* (of mark,
memory) rimozione *f*; (of city) annientamento
m
oblivion /ə'blɪvɪən/ *n* oblio *m*
oblivious /ə'blɪvɪəs/ *adj* be ~ essere
dimentico (**of, to** di)
oblong /'ɒblɒŋ/ **1** *adj* oblungo
2 *n* rettangolo *m*
obnoxious /əb'nɒkʃəs/ *adj* detestabile
oboe /'əʊbəʊ/ *n* oboe *m inv*
obscene /əb'siːn/ *adj* osceno; ⟨profits,
wealth⟩ vergognoso
obscenity /əb'senətɪ/ *n* oscenità *f inv*
obscure /əb'skjʊə(r)/ **1** *adj* oscuro
2 *vt* oscurare; (confuse) mettere in ombra
obscurity /əb'skjʊərətɪ/ *n* oscurità *f*
obsequious /əb'siːkwɪəs/ *adj* ossequioso
observable /əb'zɜːvəbl/ *adj* (discernible)
percettibile
observance /əb'zɜːvəns/ *n* (of custom)
osservanza *f*
observant /əb'zɜːvənt/ *adj* attento
✔ **observation** /ɒbzə'veɪʃn/ *n* osservazione
f
observation car *n* carrozza *f* belvedere
observation tower *n* torre *f* di
osservazione
observatory /əb'zɜːvətrɪ/ *n* osservatorio
m
✔ **observe** /əb'zɜːv/ *vt* osservare; (notice)
notare; (keep, celebrate) celebrare
observer /əb'zɜːvə(r)/ *n* osservatore,
-trice *mf*
obsess /əb'ses/ *vt* be ~ed by essere fissato
con
obsession /əb'seʃn/ *n* fissazione *f*
obsessive /əb'sesɪv/ *adj* ossessivo
obsessively /əb'sesɪvlɪ/ *adv*
ossessivamente
obsolescence /ɒbsə'lesəns/ *n*
obsolescenza *f*; **built-in** ~ obsolescenza *f*
programmata
obsolete /'ɒbsəliːt/ *adj* obsoleto; ⟨word⟩
desueto; ⟨idea⟩ sorpassato
obstacle /'ɒbstəkl/ *n* ostacolo *m*
obstacle course *n* Mil fig percorso *m* ad
ostacoli
obstacle race *n* corsa *f* ad ostacoli
obstetrician /ɒbstə'trɪʃn/ *n* ostetrico,
-a *mf*
obstetrics /ɒb'stetrɪks/ *n* ostetricia *f*
obstinacy /'ɒbstɪnɪsɪ/ *n* ostinazione *f*
obstinate /'ɒbstɪnət/ *adj* ostinato
obstinately /'ɒbstɪnɪtlɪ/ *adv*
ostinatamente

obstreperous /əb'strepərəs/ *adj*
turbolento
obstruct /əb'strʌkt/ *vt* ostruire; (hinder)
ostacolare
obstruction /əb'strʌkʃn/ *n* ostruzione *f*;
(obstacle) ostacolo *m*
obstructive /əb'strʌktɪv/ *adj* be ~
⟨person⟩ creare dei problemi
✔ **obtain** /əb'teɪn/ **1** *vt* ottenere
2 *vi* prevalere
obtainable /əb'teɪnəbl/ *adj* ottenibile
obtrusive /əb'truːsɪv/ *adj* ⟨object⟩ stonato
obtuse /əb'tjuːs/ *adj* ottuso
obverse /'ɒbvɜːs/ *adj* the ~ side/face (of
coin) l'altra faccia *f*
obviate /'ɒbvɪeɪt/ *vt* fml ovviare a
✔ **obvious** /'ɒbvɪəs/ *adj* ovvio
✔ **obviously** /'ɒbvɪəslɪ/ *adv* ovviamente
✔ **occasion** /ə'keɪʒn/ **1** *n* occasione *f*;
(event) evento *m*; **on** ~ talvolta; **on the** ~ **of**
in occasione di
2 *vt* cagionare
occasional /ə'keɪʒənl/ *adj* saltuario; **he
has the** ~ **glass of wine** ogni tanto beve un
bicchiere di vino
occasionally /ə'keɪʒənəlɪ/ *adv* ogni tanto
occult /ɒ'kʌlt/ *adj* occulto
occupancy /'ɒkjʊpənsɪ/ *n* available for
immediate ~ libero immediatamente;
change of ~ cambio *m* di inquilino
occupant /'ɒkjʊpənt/ *n* occupante *mf*; (of
vehicle) persona *f* a bordo
occupation /ɒkjʊ'peɪʃn/ *n* occupazione *f*;
(job) professione *f*
occupational /ɒkjʊ'peɪʃənəl/ *adj*
professionale
occupational hazard *n* rischio *m*
professionale
occupational health *n* medicina *f* del
lavoro
occupational pension *n* Br pensione
f di lavoro
occupational psychologist *n*
psicologo, -a *mf* del lavoro
occupational therapist *n*
ergoterapista *mf*
occupational therapy *n* ergoterapia *f*
occupier /'ɒkjʊpaɪə(r)/ *n* residente *mf*
occupy /'ɒkjʊpaɪ/ *vt* (*pt/pp* **occupied**)
occupare; (keep busy) tenere occupato
✔ **occur** /ə'kɜː(r)/ *vi* (*pt/pp* **occurred**)
accadere; (exist) trovarsi; **it** ~ **red to me that**
mi è venuto in mente che
occurrence /ə'kʌrəns/ *n* (event) fatto *m*
ocean /'əʊʃn/ *n* oceano *m*
ocean-going /'əʊʃəngəʊɪŋ/ *adj* ⟨ship⟩
d'alto mare
ochre /'əʊkə(r)/ *n & adj* (colour) ocra *f*

o

o'clock /əˈklɒk/ *adv* it's 7 ∼ sono le sette; **at 7** ∼ alle sette

octagon /ˈɒktəgən/ *n* ottagono *m*

octagonal /ɒkˈtægənl/ *adj* ottagonale

octave /ˈɒktɪv/ *n* Mus ottava *f*

octet /ɒkˈtet/ *n* Mus ottetto *m*

◆ **October** /ɒkˈtəʊbə(r)/ *n* ottobre *m*

octogenarian /ɒktədʒɪˈneərɪən/ *n & adj* ottantenne *mf*

octopus /ˈɒktəpəs/ *n* (*pl* **-puses**) polpo *m*

oculist /ˈɒkjʊlɪst/ oculista *mf*

OD *n abbr* (**overdose**) overdose *f inv*

◆ **odd** /ɒd/ *adj* ‹number› dispari; (not of set) scompagnato; (strange) strano; **forty** ∼ quaranta e rotti; ∼ **jobs** lavoretti *mpl*; **the** ∼ **one out** l'eccezione *f*; **at** ∼ **moments** a tempo perso; **have the** ∼ **glass of wine** bere un bicchiere di vino ogni tanto

oddball /ˈɒdbɔːl/ *n* fam eccentrico, -a *mf*

odd bod /ˈɒdbɒd/ *n* Br fam tipo, -a *mf* strano, -a

oddity /ˈɒdətɪ/ *n* stranezza *f*

odd-job man *n* tuttofare *m inv*

odd jobs *npl* lavoretti *mpl*

oddly /ˈɒdlɪ/ *adv* stranamente; ∼ **enough** stranamente

oddment /ˈɒdmənt/ *n* (of fabric) scampolo *m*

odds /ɒdz/ *npl* (chances) probabilità *fpl*; **at** ∼ in disaccordo; ∼ **and ends** cianfrusaglie *fpl*; **it makes no** ∼ non fa alcuna differenza

odds-on *adj* **be the** ∼ **favourite** (in betting) essere il gran favorito; **she has an** ∼ **chance of...** ha molte probabilità di...; **it is** ∼ **that** è molto probabile che

ode /əʊd/ *n* ode *f*

odious /ˈəʊdɪəs/ *adj* odioso

odium /ˈəʊdɪəm/ *n* odio *m*

odometer /əʊˈdɒmɪtə(r)/ *n* Am contachilometri *m inv*, odometro *m*

odour /ˈəʊdə(r)/ *n* odore *m*

odourless /ˈəʊdəlɪs/ *adj* inodore

odyssey /ˈɒdɪsɪ/ *n* odissea *f*

OECD *n abbr* (**Organization for Economic Cooperation and Development**) OCSE *f*

oedema /ɪˈdiːmə/ *n* edema *m*

oesophagus /ɪˈsɒfəgəs/ *n* esofago *m*

oestrogen /ˈiːstrədʒən/ *n* estrogeno *m*

◆ **of** /ɒv/ *prep* di; **a cup of tea/coffee** una tazza di tè/caffè; **the hem of my skirt** l'orlo della mia gonna; **the summer of 1989** l'estate del 1989; **the two of us** noi due; **made of** di; **that's very kind of you** è molto gentile da parte tua; **a friend of mine** un mio amico; **a child of three** un bambino di tre anni; **the fourth of January** il quattro gennaio; **within a year of their divorce** a circa un anno dal loro divorzio; **half of it** la metà; **the whole of the room** tutta la stanza

◆ **off** /ɒf/ **1** *prep* da; (distant from) lontano da; **take £10** ∼ **the price** ridurre il prezzo di 10 sterline; ∼ **the coast** presso la costa; **a street** ∼ **the main road** una traversa della via principale; (near) una strada vicina alla via principale; **get** ∼ **the ladder** scendere dalla scala; **get** ∼ **the bus** scendere dall'autobus; **leave the lid** ∼ **the saucepan** lasciare la pentola senza il coperchio **2** *adv* ‹button, handle› staccato; ‹light, machine› spento; ‹brake› disinserito; ‹tap› chiuso; **'off'** (on appliance) 'off'; **2 kilometres** ∼ a due chilometri di distanza; **a long way** ∼ molto distante; (time) lontano; ∼ **and on** di tanto in tanto; **with his hat/coat** ∼ senza il cappello/cappotto; **with the light** ∼ a luce spenta; **20%** ∼ 20% di sconto; **be** ∼ (leave) andar via; Sport essere partito; ‹food› essere andato a male; (all gone) essere finito; ‹wedding, engagement› essere cancellato; **I'm** ∼ **drugs/alcohol** ho smesso di drogarmi/ bere; **be** ∼ **one's food** non avere appetito; **she's** ∼ **today** (on holiday) è in ferie oggi; (ill) è malata oggi; **I'm** ∼ **home** vado a casa; **you'd be better** ∼ **doing...** faresti meglio a fare...; **have a day** ∼ avere un giorno di vacanza; **drive/sail** ∼ andare via

offal /ˈɒfl/ *n* Culin frattaglie *fpl*

offbeat /ˈɒfbiːt/ *adj* insolito

off-centre *adj* Br fuori centro

off chance *n* **there's an** ∼ **that** c'è una remota possibilità che; **just on the** ∼ **that** nella remota possibilità che

off colour *adj* (not well) giù di forma; ‹joke, story› sporco

◆ **offence** /əˈfens/ *n* (illegal act) reato *m*; **give** ∼ offendere; **take** ∼ offendersi (at per)

offend /əˈfend/ *vt* offendere

offender /əˈfendə(r)/ *n* Jur colpevole *mf*

offensive /əˈfensɪv/ **1** *adj* offensivo **2** *n* offensiva *f*; **go on the** ∼ passare all'offensiva

◆ **offer** /ˈɒfə(r)/ **1** *n* offerta *f*; **on special** ∼ in offerta speciale **2** *vt* offrire; opporre ‹resistance›; ∼ **somebody something** offrire qualcosa a qualcuno; ∼ **to do something** offrirsi di fare qualcosa

offering /ˈɒfərɪŋ/ *n* offerta *f*

offer price *n* Comm prezzo *m* d'offerta

offertory /ˈɒfətrɪ/ *n* Relig offertorio *m*

offhand /ɒfˈhænd/ **1** *adj* (casual) spiccio **2** *adv* su due piedi

◆ **office** /ˈɒfɪs/ *n* ufficio *m*; (post, job) carica *f*

office automation *n* burotica *f*

office block *n* Br complesso *m* di uffici

office building *n* Br complesso *m* di uffici

office hours *npl* orario *m* di ufficio

office junior *n* fattorino, -a *mf*

office politics *n* intrighi *mpl* di ufficio

◆ indicates a very frequent word

ℐ **officer** /'ɒfɪsə(r)/ *n* ufficiale *m*; (police) agente *m* [di polizia]

office worker *n* impiegato, -a *mf*

ℐ **official** /ə'fɪʃl/ 1 *adj* ufficiale

    2 *n* funzionario, -a *mf*; Sport dirigente *m*

officialdom /ə'fɪʃəldəm/ *n* burocrazia *f*

officially /ə'fɪʃəlɪ/ *adv* ufficialmente

officiate /ə'fɪʃɪeɪt/ *vi* officiare

officious /ə'fɪʃəs/ *adj* autoritario

officiously /ə'fɪʃəslɪ/ *adv* in modo autoritario

offing /'ɒfɪn/ *n* in the ∼ in vista

off-key *adj* Mus stonato

off-licence *n* negozio *m* per la vendita di alcolici

off-limits *adj* off-limits *inv*

off-line *adj* Comput fuori linea *inv*, off-line *inv*

offload /ɒf'ləʊd/ *vt* scaricare

off-message *adj* Pol be ∼ non essere in linea con la politica del governo

off-peak *adj* ‹travel› fuori dagli orari di punta; ‹electricity› a tariffa notturna ridotta; ∼ **call** Teleph telefonata *f* a tariffa ridotta

offprint /'ɒfprɪnt/ *n* estratto *m*

off-putting /-pʊtɪŋ/ *adj* fam scoraggiante

off-road *vi* viaggiare in fuoristrada

off-roader /'ɒfrəʊdə(r)/, **off-road vehicle** *n* fuoristrada

off-screen 1 *adj* ‹voice, action› fuoricampo *inv*; ‹relationship› nella vita privata

    2 *adv* nella vita privata

off-season *adj* ‹losses› di bassa stagione; ‹cruise› in bassa stagione

offset /'ɒfset/ *vt* (*pt/pp* **-set**, *pres p* **-setting**) controbilanciare

offset printing *n* offset *m inv*

offshoot /'ɒfʃuːt/ *n* ramo *m*; fig diramazione *f*

offshore /'ɒfʃɔː(r)/ *adj* ‹wind› di terra; ‹company, investment› offshore *inv*

offside /ɒf'saɪd/ *adj* Sport [in] fuori gioco; ‹wheel etc› (left) sinistro; (right) destro

offspring /'ɒfsprɪŋ/ *n* prole *f*

off-stage *adv* dietro le quinte

off-the-cuff *adj* ‹remark› spontaneo; ‹speech› improvvisato

off-the-peg *adj* ‹garment› prêt-à-porter *inv*, confezionato

off-the-record *adj* ‹comment, statement› ufficioso

off-the-shelf *adj* Comm standard *inv*

off-the-shoulder *adj* ‹dress› senza bretelle

off-the-wall *adj* fam ‹sense of humour› strano

off-white *adj* bianco sporco

ℐ **often** /'ɒfn/ *adv* spesso; **how** ∼ ogni quanto; **every so** ∼ una volta ogni tanto

ogle /'əʊgl/ *vt* mangiarsi con gli occhi

ogre /'əʊgə(r)/ *n* orco *m*

ℐ **oh** /əʊ/ *int* oh!; **oh dear** oh Dio!

OHMS *abbr* Br (**On Her/His Majesty's Service**) abbreviazione (*f*) apposta su corrispondenza ufficiale del governo britannico

OHP *n abbr* (**overhead projector**) lavagna *f* luminosa

ℐ **oil** /ɔɪl/ 1 *n* olio *m*; (petroleum) petrolio *m*; (for heating) nafta *f*

    2 *vt* oliare

oil-burning *adj* ‹stove, boiler› a nafta

oil can *n* (applicator) oliatore *m*

oil change *n* cambio *m* dell'olio

oilcloth *n* tela *f* cerata

oilfield *n* giacimento *m* di petrolio

oil filter *n* filtro *m* dell'olio

oil-fired /-faɪəd/ *adj* ‹furnace, heating› a nafta

oil gauge *n* indicatore *m* [del livello] dell'olio

oil heater *n* stufa *f* a nafta

oil lamp *n* lampada *f* a olio

oil paint *n* colore *m* a olio

oil painting *n* pittura *f* a olio

oil pipeline *n* oleodotto *m*

oil pressure *n* pressione *f* dell'olio

oil producing /-prədjuːsɪŋ/ *adj* ‹country› produttore di petrolio

oil refinery *n* raffineria *f* di petrolio

oil rig *n* piattaforma *f* petrolifera, offshore *m inv*

oilseed rape *n* colza *f*

oilskins *npl* indumenti *mpl* di tela cerata

oil slick *n* chiazza *f* di petrolio

oil spill *n* fuoriuscita *f* di petrolio

oil stove *n* stufa *f* a nafta

oil tank *n* (domestic) serbatoio *m* della nafta; (industrial) cisterna *f* della nafta

oil tanker *n* petroliera *f*

oil well *n* pozzo *m* petrolifero

oily /'ɔɪlɪ/ *adj* (**-ier, -iest**) unto; fig untuoso

ointment /'ɔɪntmənt/ *n* pomata *f*

ℐ **OK, okay** /əʊ'keɪ/ 1 *int* va bene, o.k.

    2 *adj* if that's OK with you se ti va bene; she's OK (well) sta bene; is the milk still OK? il latte è ancora buono?

    3 *adv* (well) bene

    4 *vt* (*pt/pp* **OK'd, okayed**) dare l'o.k. a

ℐ **old** /əʊld/ *adj* vecchio; ‹girlfriend› ex; how ∼ is she? quanti anni ha?; she is ten years ∼ ha dieci anni

old age *n* vecchiaia *f*

old-age pension *n* Br pensione *f* di vecchiaia

old-age pensioner *n* pensionato, -a *mf*

O

old boy n Sch ex-allievo m

old country n paese m d'origine

olden /'əʊldən/ adj the ~ **days** i tempi andati

old-established /-ɪ'stæblɪʃt/ adj di lunga data

olde-worlde /əʊldɪ'wɜːldɪ/ adj hum dall'aria falsamente antica

old-fashioned /-'fæʃ(ə)nd/ adj antiquato

old favourite n (book, play) classico m; (song, film) vecchio successo m

old flame n fam vecchia fiamma f

old girl n ex-allieva f

Old Glory n bandiera f statunitense

old hand n be an ~ **at something/at doing something** saperci fare con qualcosa/a fare qualcosa

old hat adj fam be ~ essere roba vecchia

oldie /'əʊldɪ/ n (person) vecchio, -a mf; (film, song) vecchio successo m

old lady n (elderly woman) signora f anziana; **my** ~ (mother) la mia vecchia; (wife) la mia signora

old maid n zitella f

old man n (elderly man) uomo m anziano; (old: dear chap) vecchio m mio; **my** ~ (father) il mio vecchio; (husband) mio marito m; **the** ~ (boss) il capo

old master n (work) dipinto m antico (specialmente di un pittore europeo del XIII–XVII secolo)

old people's home n casa f di riposo

old soldier n (former soldier) veterano m

Old Testament n Antico Testamento m

old-time adj di un tempo; ~ **dancing** ballo m liscio

old-timer n veterano, -a mf

old wives' tale n superstizione f

old woman n (elderly lady) donna f anziana; **my** ~ (mother) mia madre f; (wife) la mia signora; **be an** ~ pej (man) essere una donnicciola

olive /'ɒlɪv/ [1] n (fruit, colour) oliva f; (tree) olivo m

[2] adj d'oliva; (colour) olivastro

olive branch n fig ramoscello m d'olivo

olive green adj & n verde m oliva inv

olive grove n oliveto m

olive oil n olio m di oliva

olive-skinned /-'skɪnd/ adj olivastro

Olympic /ə'lɪmpɪk/ adj olimpico

Olympic Games, **Olympics** npl Olimpiadi fpl

Oman /əʊ'mɑːn/ n Oman m

ombudsman /'ɒmbʊdzmən/ n difensore m civico

omelette /'ɒmlɪt/ n omelette f inv

omen /'əʊmən/ n presagio m

ominous /'ɒmɪnəs/ adj sinistro

omission /ə'mɪʃn/ n omissione f

omit /ə'mɪt/ vt (pt/pp **omitted**) omettere; ~ **to do something** tralasciare di fare qualcosa

omnibus /'ɒmnɪbəs/ n (bus) omnibus m inv

omnibus edition n Br TV replica f delle puntate precedenti

omnipotent /ɒm'nɪpətənt/ adj onnipotente

omnipresent /ˌɒmnɪ'preznt/ adj onnipresente

✎ **on** /ɒn/ [1] prep su; (on horizontal surface) su, sopra; **on Monday** lunedì; **on Mondays** di lunedì; **on the first of May** il primo maggio; **on arriving** all'arrivo; **on one's finger** nel dito; **on foot** a piedi; **on the right/left** a destra/sinistra; **on the Rhine/Thames** sul Reno/Tamigi; **on the radio/television** alla radio/televisione; **on the bus/train** in autobus/treno; **go on the bus/train** andare in autobus/treno; **get on the bus/train** salire sull'autobus/sul treno; **on me** (with me) con me; **it's on me** fam tocca a me

[2] adv (further on) dopo; (switched on) acceso; ‹brake› inserito; (in operation) in funzione; **'on'** (on machine) 'on'; **he had his hat/coat on** portava il cappello/cappotto; **without his hat/coat on** senza cappello/cappotto; **with/ without the lid on** con/senza coperchio; **be on** ‹film, programme, event› esserci; **it's not on** fam non è giusto; **be on at** fam tormentare (to per); **on and on** senza sosta; **off and on** a intervalli; **and so on** e così via; **go on** continuare; **stick on** attaccare; **sew on** cucire

on-board /'ɒnbɔːd/ adj di bordo

✎ **once** /wʌns/ [1] adv una volta; (formerly) un tempo; ~ **upon a time there was** c'era una volta; **at** ~ subito; (at the same time) contemporaneamente; ~ **and for all** una volta per tutte

[2] conj [non] appena

once-over n fam **give somebody/ something the** ~ (look, check) dare un'occhiata veloce a qualcuno/qualcosa

oncoming /'ɒnkʌmɪŋ/ adj che si avvicina dalla direzione opposta

✎ **one** /wʌn/ [1] adj uno, una; **not** ~ **person** nemmeno una persona

[2] n uno m

[3] pron uno; (impersonal) si; ~ **another** l'un l'altro; ~ **by** ~ [a] uno a uno; ~ **never knows** non si sa mai

one-armed bandit /wʌnɑːmd'bændɪt/ n slot-machine f inv

one-dimensional /-daɪ'menʃənəl/ adj unidimensionale; **be** ~ fig ‹character› mancare di spessore

one-eyed /-'aɪd/ adj con un occhio solo

one-for-one adj = ONE-TO-ONE

✎ indicates a very frequent word

one-handed /-'hændɪd/ *adv* ‹catch, hold› con una sola mano

one-horse town *n* fam cittadina *f* di provincia

one-legged /-'legɪd/ *adj* con una sola gamba

one-liner *n* battuta *f* d'effetto

one-man *adj* ‹bobsled› monoposto *inv*; ‹for one person› per una sola persona; **she's a ∼ woman** è una donna fedele; **it's a ∼ outfit/ operation** manda avanti tutto da solo

one-man band *n* musicista (*m*) che suona più strumenti contemporaneamente; **be a ∼** fig mandare avanti tutto da solo

one-off *adj* Br ‹experiment, order, deal› unico e irripetibile; ‹event, decision, offer, payment› eccezionale; ‹example, design› unico; ‹issue magazine› speciale

one-parent family *n* famiglia *f* con un solo genitore

one-piece /'wʌnpiːs/ *adj* ∼ **swimsuit** costume intero

one-room flat, **one-room apartment** *n* monolocale *m*

one's /wʌnz/ *poss adj* one has to look after ∼ **health** ci si deve preoccupare della propria salute

oneself /wʌn'self/ *pron* (reflexive) si; (emphatic) sé, se stesso; **by ∼** da solo; **be proud of ∼** essere fieri di sé

one-shot *adj* Am = ONE-OFF

one-sided /-'saɪdɪd/ *adj* unilaterale

one-time *adj* ex *inv*

one-to-one *adj* ‹personal relationship› fra due persone; ‹private lesson› individuale; ‹correspondence› di uno a uno

one-upmanship /-'ʌpmənʃɪp/ *n* arte *f* di primeggiare

one-way *adj* ‹street› a senso unico; ‹ticket› di sola andata

one-woman *adj* **it's a ∼ outfit** manda avanti tutto da sola; **he's a ∼ man** è un uomo fedele

ongoing /'ɒngəʊɪŋ/ *adj* ‹process› continuo; ‹battle, saga› in corso

onion /'ʌnjən/ *n* cipolla *f*

⚬ **on-line** *adj* Comput in linea, on-line *inv*; **go ∼ to...** connettersi a...; ∼ **time** durata *f* del collegamento

onlooker /'ɒnlʊkə(r)/ *n* spettatore, -trice *mf*

⚬ **only** /'əʊnlɪ/ ① *adj* solo; ∼ **child** figlio, -a *mf* unico

② *adv* & *conj* solo, solamente; ∼ **just** appena

on-message /ɒn'mesɪdʒ/ *adj* Pol be ∼ essere in linea con la politica del governo

o.n.o. *abbr* Br (**or nearest offer**) trattabile

on-off *adj* ‹button, control› di accensione

onrush /'ɒnrʌʃ/ *n* (of people, water) ondata *f*

on-screen *adj* sullo schermo

onset /'ɒnset/ *n* (beginning) inizio *m*

onshore /'ɒnʃɔː(r)/ *adj* ‹wind› di mare; ‹work› a terra

onside /ɒn'saɪd/ *adj* & *adv* Sport non in fuorigioco

on-site *adj* sul posto

onslaught /'ɒnslɔːt/ *n* attacco *m*

on-stage *adj* & *adv* in scena

on-target earnings *npl* guadagni (*mpl*) previsti incluse commissioni

on-the-job *adj* ‹training› in sede

on-the-spot *adj* ‹advice, quotation› immediato

⚬ **onto**, also **on to** /'ɒntu:/ *prep* su

onus /'əʊnəs/ *n* the ∼ **is on me** spetta a me la responsabilità (**to** di)

onwards Br, **onward** Am /'ɒnwəd[z]/ *adv* in avanti; **from then ∼** da allora [in poi]

oodles /'uːdlz/ *n* fam un sacco

ooh /u:/ *int* oh!

oomph /u:mf/ *n* fam verve *f inv*

oops /u:ps/ *int* ops!

ooze /u:z/ *vi* fluire

op /ɒp/ *n* = OPERATION

opal /'əʊpl/ *n* opale *f*

opaque /əʊ'peɪk/ *adj* opaco

Opec, **OPEC** /'əʊpek/ *n abbr* (**Organization of Petroleum Exporting Countries**) OPEC *f*

⚬ **open** /'əʊpən/ ① *adj* aperto; (free to all) pubblico; ‹job› vacante; **in the ∼ air** all'aperto

② *n* **in the ∼** all'aperto; fig alla luce del sole

③ *vt* aprire

④ *vi* aprirsi; ‹shop› aprire; ‹flower› sbocciare

■ **open onto** *vt* ‹door, window,› dare su

■ **open out** ① *vi* ‹road› allargarsi; ‹flower› aprirsi

② *vt* aprire ‹map, newspaper›

■ **open up** ① *vt* aprire

② *vi* aprirsi

■ **open with** *vi* (start with) iniziare con

open-air *adj* ‹pool, market, stage› all'aperto

opencast mining *n* Br miniera *f* a cielo aperto

open competition *n* concorso *m*

open day *n* giorno *m* di apertura al pubblico

open-ended /-'endɪd/ *adj* ‹relationship, question, contract› aperto; ‹stay› a tempo indeterminato; ‹period› indeterminato; ‹strategy› flessibile

opener /'əʊpənə(r)/ *n* (for tins) apriscatole *m inv*; (for bottles) apribottiglie *m inv*

open government *n* politica *f* di trasparenza

open-handed /-'hændɪd/ *adj* generoso

O

open-heart surgery n intervento m a cuore aperto

open house n Am (open day) giornata f di apertura al pubblico; **it's always ~ at the Batemans'** i Bateman sono sempre molto ospitali

♂ **opening** /'əʊpənɪŋ/ n apertura f; (beginning) inizio m; (job) posto m libero

opening balance n Fin saldo m iniziale

opening ceremony n cerimonia f inaugurale

opening hours npl orario m d'apertura

open learning n open learning m inv

openly /'əʊpənlɪ/ adv apertamente

open market n Econ mercato m aperto

open-minded /-'maɪndɪd/ adj aperto; (broad-minded) di vedute larghe

open-mouthed /-'maʊðd/ adj bocca aperta

open-necked /-'nekt/ adj ‹shirt› col colletto sbottonato

openness /'əʊpənnɪs/ n (of government, atmosphere) trasparenza f; (candour) franchezza f; (receptiveness) apertura f mentale

open-plan adj a pianta aperta

open sandwich n tartina f

open scholarship n Univ borsa f di studio assegnata per concorso

open season n (in hunting) stagione f della caccia

open secret n segreto m di Pulcinella

open ticket n biglietto m aperto

Open University n Br Univ corsi mpl universitari per corrispondenza

open verdict n Jur verdetto (m) che dichiara non accertabili le cause della morte

opera /'ɒpərə/ n opera f

operable /'ɒpərəbl/ adj operabile

opera glasses npl binocolo msg da teatro

opera house n teatro m lirico

opera singer n cantante mf lirico, -a

♂ **operate** /'ɒpəreɪt/ **1** vt far funzionare ‹machine, lift›; azionare ‹lever, brake›; mandare avanti ‹business›
2 vi Techn funzionare; (be in action) essere in funzione; Mil fig operare
■ **operate on** vt Med operare

operatic /ɒpə'rætɪk/ adj lirico, operistico

operating costs npl spese fpl di esercizio

operating instructions npl istruzioni fpl per l'uso

operating room n Am sala f operatoria

operating system n Comput sistema m operativo

operating table n Med tavolo m operatorio

operating theatre n Br sala f operatoria

♂ **operation** /ɒpə'reɪʃn/ n operazione f; Tech funzionamento m; **in ~** Techn in funzione; **come into ~** fig entrare in funzione; ‹law› entrare in vigore; **have an ~** Med subire un'operazione

operational /ɒpə'reɪʃənəl/ adj operativo; ‹law etc› in vigore

operations room n Mil centro m operativo; (police) centrale f operativa

operative /'ɒpərətɪv/ adj operativo

operator /'ɒpəreɪtə(r)/ n (user) operatore, -trice mf; Teleph centralinista mf

operetta /ɒpə'retə/ n operetta f

ophthalmic /ɒf'θælmɪk/ adj oftalmico

♂ **opinion** /ə'pɪnjən/ n opinione f; **in my ~** secondo me

opinionated /ə'pɪnɪəneɪtɪd/ adj dogmatico

opinion poll n sondaggio m di opinione

opium /'əʊpɪəm/ n oppio m

♂ **opponent** /ə'pəʊnənt/ n avversario, -a mf

opportune /'ɒpətjuːn/ adj opportuno

opportunist /ɒpə'tjuːnɪst/ n opportunista mf

opportunistic /ɒpətjʊ'nɪstɪk/ adj opportunistico

♂ **opportunity** /ɒpə'tjuːnətɪ/ n opportunità f inv

♂ **oppose** /ə'pəʊz/ vt opporsi a; **be ~d to something** essere contrario a qualcosa; **as ~d to** al contrario di

opposing /ə'pəʊzɪŋ/ adj avversario; (opposite) opposto

opposite /'ɒpəzɪt/ **1** adj opposto; ‹house› di fronte; **~ number** fig controparte f; **the ~ sex** l'altro sesso
2 n contrario m
3 adv di fronte
4 prep di fronte a

♂ **opposition** /ɒpə'zɪʃn/ n opposizione f

oppress /ə'pres/ vt opprimere

oppression /ə'preʃn/ n oppressione f

oppressive /ə'presɪv/ adj oppressivo; ‹heat› opprimente

oppressor /ə'presə(r)/ n oppressore m

opt /ɒpt/ v
■ **opt for** vt optare per
■ **opt out** vi dissociarsi (of da)

optic /'ɒptɪk/ adj ‹nerve, disc, fibre› ottico

optical /'ɒptɪkl/ adj ottico; **~ illusion** illusione f ottica

optician /ɒp'tɪʃn/ n ottico, -a mf

optics /'ɒptɪks/ n ottica f

optimism /'ɒptɪmɪzm/ n ottimismo m

optimist /'ɒptɪmɪst/ n ottimista mf

optimistic /ɒptɪ'mɪstɪk/ adj ottimistico

optimistically /ˌɒptɪˈmɪstɪklɪ/ *adv* ottimisticamente

optimize /ˈɒptɪmaɪz/ *vt* ottimizzare

optimum /ˈɒptɪməm/ [1] *adj* ottimale [2] *n* (*pl* **-ima**) optimum *m*

⚘ **option** /ˈɒpʃn/ *n* scelta *f*; Comm opzione *f*

optional /ˈɒpʃənəl/ *adj* facoltativo; ~ **extras** optional *m inv*

opulence /ˈɒpjʊləns/ *n* opulenza *f*

opulent /ˈɒpjʊlənt/ *adj* opulento

opus /ˈəʊpəs/ *n* (*pl* **opuses** *or* **opera**) opera *f*

⚘ **or** /ɔː(r)/ *conj* o, oppure; (after negative) né; **or [else]** se no; **in a year or two** fra un anno o due

oracle /ˈɒrəkl/ *n* oracolo *m*

oral /ˈɔːrəl/ [1] *adj* orale [2] *n* fam esame *m* orale

orally /ˈɔːrəlɪ/ *adv* oralmente

orange /ˈɒrɪndʒ/ [1] *n* arancia *f*; (colour) arancione *m* [2] *adj* arancione

orangeade /ɒrɪndʒˈeɪd/ *n* aranciata *f*

orange blossom *n* fiori *mpl* d'arancio

orange juice *n* succo *m* d'arancia

orange peel *n* scorza *f* d'arancia

orange squash *n* Br succo *m* d'arancia (*diluito in acqua*)

orange tree *n* arancio *m*

oration /əˈreɪʃn/ *n* orazione *f*

orator /ˈɒrətə(r)/ *n* oratore, -trice *mf*

oratorio /ɒrəˈtɔːrɪəʊ/ *n* oratorio *m*

oratory /ˈɒrətrɪ/ *n* oratorio *m*

orbit /ˈɔːbɪt/ [1] *n* orbita *f* [2] *vt* orbitare

orbital /ˈɔːbɪtl/ *adj* ~ **road** tangenziale *f*

orchard /ˈɔːtʃəd/ *n* frutteto *m*

orchestra /ˈɔːkɪstrə/ *n* orchestra *f*

orchestral /ɔːˈkestrəl/ *adj* orchestrale

orchestra pit *n* [fossa *f* dell']orchestra *f*

orchestrate /ˈɔːkɪstreɪt/ *vt* orchestrare

orchid /ˈɔːkɪd/ *n* orchidea *f*

ordain /ɔːˈdeɪn/ *vt* decretare; Relig ordinare

ordeal /ɔːˈdiːl/ *n* fig terribile esperienza *f*

⚘ **order** /ˈɔːdə(r)/ [1] *n* ordine *m*; Comm ordinazione *f*; **out of** ~ ‹machine› fuori servizio; **in** ~ **that** affinché; **in** ~ **to** per; **take holy** ~**s** prendere i voti [2] *vt* ordinare
■ **order about, order around** *vt* (give orders to) impartire ordini a

order book *n* registro *m* degli ordini

order form *n* modulo *m* di ordinazione

orderly /ˈɔːdəlɪ/ [1] *adj* ordinato [2] *n* Mil attendente *m*; Med inserviente *m*

orderly officer *n* Mil attendente *m*

order number *n* numero *m* d'ordine

ordinal /ˈɔːdɪnəl/ *n* & *adj* ordinale *m*

ordinarily /ɔːdɪˈnerɪlɪ/ *adv* (normally) normalmente

⚘ **ordinary** /ˈɔːdɪnərɪ/ *adj* ordinario

ordination /ɔːdɪˈneɪʃn/ *n* Relig ordinazione *f*

ordnance /ˈɔːdnəns/ *n* Mil materiale *m* militare

Ordnance Survey *n* Br *istituto* (*m*) *cartografico*; **Ordnance Survey Map** carta *f* topografica dell'istituto cartografico

ore /ɔː(r)/ *n* minerale *m* grezzo

oregano /ɒrɪˈɡɑːnəʊ/ *n* origano *m*

organ /ˈɔːɡən/ *n* Anat Mus organo *m*

organ donor *n* Med donatore, -trice *mf* di organi

organic /ɔːˈɡænɪk/ *adj* organico; (without chemicals) biologico

organically /ɔːˈɡænɪklɪ/ *adv* organicamente; ~ **grown** coltivato biologicamente

organic chemistry *n* chimica *f* organica

organic farm *n* azienda *f* agricola specializzata in prodotti biologici

organic farming *n* agricoltura *f* biologica

organism /ˈɔːɡənɪzm/ *n* organismo *m*

organist /ˈɔːɡənɪst/ *n* organista *mf*

⚘ **organization** /ɔːɡənaɪˈzeɪʃn/ *n* organizzazione *f*

organizational /ɔːɡənaɪˈzeɪʃənəl/ *adj* ‹ability, role› organizzativo

⚘ **organize** /ˈɔːɡənaɪz/ *vt* organizzare

organized crime *n* /ɔːɡənaɪzd'kraɪm/ *n* criminalità *f* organizzata

organized labour *n* manodopera *f* organizzata

organizer /ˈɔːɡənaɪzə(r)/ *n* organizzatore, -trice *mf*

organ transplant *n* Med trapianto *m* di organi

orgasm /ˈɔːɡæzm/ *n* orgasmo *m*

orgy /ˈɔːdʒɪ/ *n* orgia *f*

Orient /ˈɔːrɪənt/ *n* Oriente *m*

oriental /ɔːrɪˈentl/ [1] *adj* orientale; ~ **carpet** tappeto *m* persiano [2] *n* orientale *mf*

orientate /ˈɔːrɪənteɪt/ *vt* ~ **oneself** orientarsi

orientation /ɔːrɪənˈteɪʃn/ *n* orientamento *m*

orienteering /ɔːrɪənˈtɪərɪŋ/ *n* orientamento *m*

orifice /ˈɒrɪfɪs/ *n* orifizio *m*

⚘ **origin** /ˈɒrɪdʒɪn/ *n* origine *f*

⚘ **original** /əˈrɪdʒɪnl/ [1] *adj* originario; (not copied, new) originale [2] *n* originale *m*; **in the** ~ in versione originale

O

originality /ərɪdʒɪˈnælətɪ/ *n* originalità *f*

⚡ **originally** /əˈrɪdʒnəlɪ/ *adv* originariamente

originate /əˈrɪdʒɪneɪt/ *vi* ~ **in** avere origine in

originator /əˈrɪdʒɪneɪtə(r)/ *n* ideatore, -trice *mf*

Orkney /ˈɔːknɪ/ *n* Orcadi *fpl*

ornament /ˈɔːnəmənt/ *n* ornamento *m*; (on mantelpiece etc) soprammobile *m*

ornamental /ɔːnəˈmentl/ *adj* ornamentale

ornamentation /ɔːnəmenˈteɪʃn/ *n* decorazione *f*

ornate /ɔːˈneɪt/ *adj* ornato

ornithologist /ɔːnɪˈθɒlədʒɪst/ *n* ornitologo, -a *mf*

ornithology /ɔːnɪˈθɒlədʒɪ/ *n* ornitologia *f*

orphan /ˈɔːfn/ **1** *n* orfano, -a *mf* **2** *vt* rendere orfano; **be ~ed** rimanere orfano; **be ~ed by…** essere reso orfano da…

orphanage /ˈɔːfənɪdʒ/ *n* orfanotrofio *m*

orphaned /ˈɔːfənd/ *adj* rimasto orfano

orthodox /ˈɔːθədɒks/ *adj* ortodosso

orthopaedic /ɔːθəˈpiːdɪk/ *adj* ortopedico

orthopaedics /ɔːθəˈpiːdɪks/ *n* ortopedia *f*

OS *abbr* (**outsize**) per taglie forti

oscillate /ˈɒsɪleɪt/ *vi* oscillare

osmosis /ɒzˈməʊsɪs/ *n* osmosi *f inv*; **by ~** per osmosi

ostensible /ɒˈstensəbl/ *adj* apparente

ostensibly /ɒˈstensəblɪ/ *adv* apparentemente

ostentation /ɒstenˈteɪʃn/ *n* ostentazione *f*

ostentatious /ɒstenˈteɪʃəs/ *adj* ostentato

ostentatiously /ɒstenˈteɪʃəslɪ/ *adv* ostentatamente

osteopath /ˈɒstɪəpæθ/ *n* osteopata *mf*

osteoporosis /ɒstɪəɪpəˈrəʊsɪs/ *n* osteoporosi *f*

ostracism /ˈɒstrəsɪzm/ *n* ostracismo *m*

ostracize /ˈɒstrəsaɪz/ *vt* ostracizzare

ostrich /ˈɒstrɪtʃ/ *n* struzzo *m*

OTE *abbr* (**on-target earnings**) *guadagni (mpl) previsti incluse commissioni*

⚡ **other** /ˈʌðə(r)/ **1** *adj, pron* & *n* altro, -a *mf*; **the ~ [one]** l'altro, -a *mf*; **the ~ two** gli altri due; **two ~s** altri due; ~ **people** gli altri; **any ~ questions?** altre domande?; **every ~ day** (alternate days) a giorni alterni; **the ~ day** l'altro giorno; **the ~ evening** l'altra sera; **someone/something or ~** qualcuno/qualcosa **2** *adv* ~ **than him** tranne lui; **somehow or ~** in qualche modo; **somewhere or ~** da qualche parte

⚡ **otherwise** /ˈʌðəwaɪz/ *adv* altrimenti; (differently) diversamente

⚡ *indicates a very frequent word*

other-worldly /ʌðəˈwɜːldlɪ/ *adj* disinteressato alle cose materiali

OTT *abbr* fam (**over-the-top**) esagerato

otter /ˈɒtə(r)/ *n* lontra *f*

OU *n abbr* Br (**Open University**) corsi *mpl* universitari per corrispondenza

ouch! /aʊtʃ/ *int* ahi!

ought /ɔːt/ *v aux* **I/we ~ to stay** dovrei/dovremmo rimanere; **he ~ not to have done it** non avrebbe dovuto farlo; **that ~ to be enough** questo dovrebbe bastare

ounce /aʊns/ *n* oncia *f* (= 28.35 g)

⚡ **our** /ˈaʊə(r)/ *poss adj* il nostro *m*, la nostra *f*, i nostri *mpl*, le nostre *fpl*; ~ **mother/father** nostra madre/nostro padre

ours /ˈaʊəz/ *poss pron* il nostro *m*, la nostra *f*, i nostri *mpl*, le nostre *fpl*; **a friend of ~** un nostro amico; **friends of ~** dei nostri amici; **that is ~** quello è nostro; (as opposed to yours) quello è il nostro

⚡ **ourselves** /aʊəˈselvz/ *pers pron* (reflexive) ci; (emphatic) noi, noi stessi; **we poured ~ a drink** ci siamo versati da bere; **we heard it ~** l'abbiamo sentito noi stessi; **we are proud of ~** siamo fieri di noi; **by ~** da soli

oust /aʊst/ *vt* rimuovere

⚡ **out** /aʊt/ **1** *adv* fuori; (not alight) spento; **be ~** ⟨flower⟩ essere sbocciato; ⟨workers⟩ essere in sciopero; ⟨calculation⟩ essere sbagliato; Sport essere fuori; (unconscious) aver perso i sensi; fig (not feasible) fuori questione; **the sun is ~** è uscito il sole; ~ **and about** in piedi; **get ~!** fam fuori!; **you should get ~ more** dovresti uscire più spesso; ~ **with it!** fam sputa il rospo!; **be ~ to** avere l'intenzione di **2** *prep* ~ **of** fuori da; ~ **of date** non aggiornato; ⟨passport⟩ scaduto; ~ **of order** guasto; ~ **of print/stock** esaurito; ~ **of sorts** indisposto; ~ **of tune** (singer) stonato; (instrument) scordato; **be ~ of bed/ the room** fuori dal letto/dalla stanza; ~ **of breath** senza fiato; ~ **of danger** fuori pericolo; ~ **of work** disoccupato; **nine ~ of ten** nove su dieci; **be ~ of sugar/bread** rimanere senza zucchero/pane; **go ~ of the room** uscire dalla stanza

out-and-out *adj* ⟨success, failure⟩ totale; ⟨villain, liar⟩ vero e proprio

outback /ˈaʊtbæk/ *n* entroterra *m inv* australiano

outbid /aʊtˈbɪd/ *vt* (*pt/pp* **-bid**, *pres p* **-bidding**) ~ **somebody** rilanciare l'offerta di qualcuno

outboard /ˈaʊtbɔːd/ *adj* ~ **motor** fuoribordo *m inv*

outbreak /ˈaʊtbreɪk/ *n* ((of war)) scoppio *m*; (of disease) insorgenza *f*

outbuilding /ˈaʊtbɪldɪŋ/ *n* costruzione *f* annessa

outburst /ˈaʊtbɜːst/ *n* esplosione *f*

outcast ⋯▷ outwardly ⋯⋯

outcast /'aʊtkɑːst/ *n* esule *mf*; (social) escluso *m*

outclass /aʊt'klɑːs/ *vt* surclassare

ꝰ **outcome** /'aʊtkʌm/ *n* risultato *m*

outcrop /'aʊtkrɒp/ *n* affioramento *m*

outcry /'aʊtkraɪ/ *n* protesta *f*

outdated /aʊt'deɪtɪd/ *adj* sorpassato

outdo /aʊt'duː/ *vt* (*pt* -**did**, *pp* -**done**) superare

outdoor /'aʊtdɔː(r)/ *adj* ‹life, sports› all'aperto; ~ **swimming pool** piscina *f* scoperta

outdoors /aʊt'dɔːz/ *adv* all'aria aperta; **go** ~ uscire all'aria aperta

outer /'aʊtə(r)/ *adj* esterno

outer space *n* spazio *m* cosmico

outfit /'aʊtfɪt/ *n* equipaggiamento *m*; (clothes) completo *m*; fam (organization) organizzazione *f*

outfitter /'aʊtfɪtə(r)/ *n* men's ~ 's negozio *m* di abbigliamento maschile

outflow /'aʊtfləʊ/ *n* (of money) uscite *fpl*

outgoing /'aʊtgəʊɪŋ/ |1| *adj* (president) uscente; ‹mail› in partenza; (sociable) estroverso

|2| *npl* ~**s** uscite *fpl*

outgrow /aʊt'grəʊ/ *vi* (*pt* -**grew**, *pp* -**grown**) diventare troppo grande per

outhouse /'aʊthaʊs/ *n* costruzione *f* annessa

outing /'aʊtɪŋ/ *n* gita *f*

outlandish /aʊt'lændɪʃ/ *adj* stravagante

outlast /aʊt'lɑːst/ *vt* durare più a lungo di

outlaw /'aʊtlɔː/ |1| *n* fuorilegge *mf inv*

|2| *vt* dichiarare illegale

outlay /'aʊtleɪ/ *n* spesa *f*

outlet /'aʊtlet/ *n* sbocco *m*; fig sfogo *m*; Comm punto *m* [di] vendita

outline /'aʊtlaɪn/ |1| *n* contorno *m*; (summary) sommario *m*

|2| *vt* tracciare il contorno di; (describe) descrivere

outline agreement *n* abbozzo *m* di accordo

outlive /aʊt'lɪv/ *vt* sopravvivere a

outlook /'aʊtlʊk/ *n* vista *f*; (future prospect) prospettiva *f*; (attitude) visione *f*

outlying /'aʊtlaɪɪŋ/ *adj* ~ **areas** zone *fpl* periferiche

outmanoeuvre /aʊtmə'nuːvə(r)/ *vt* ~ **somebody** passare in vantaggio su qualcuno con un'abile manovra

outmoded /aʊt'məʊdɪd/ *adj* fuori moda

outnumber /aʊt'nʌmbə(r)/ *vt* superare in numero

out-of-body experience *n* esperienza *f* extracorporea

out of bounds *adj & adv* ‹area› vietato l'accesso

out-of-date *adj* ‹theory, concept› sorpassato; ‹ticket, passport› scaduto

out-of-pocket *adj* **be out of pocket** essere in perdita; ~ **expenses** spese *fpl* extra

out-of-the-way *adj* ‹places› fuori mano

outpatient /'aʊtpeɪʃnt/ *n* paziente *mf* esterno, -a; ~**s department** ambulatorio *m*

outpost /'aʊtpəʊst/ *n* avamposto *m*

output /'aʊtpʊt/ *n* produzione *f*

outrage /'aʊtreɪdʒ/ |1| *n* oltraggio *m*

|2| *vt* oltraggiare

outrageous /aʊt'reɪdʒəs/ *adj* oltraggioso; ‹price› scandaloso

outrider /'aʊtraɪdə(r)/ *n* battistrada *m inv*

outright¹ /'aʊtraɪt/ *adj* completo; ‹refusal› netto

outright² /aʊt'raɪt/ *adv* completamente; (at once) immediatamente; (frankly) francamente

outrun /aʊt'rʌn/ *vt* superare

outsell /aʊt'sel/ *vt* vendere meglio di ‹product›

outset /'aʊtset/ *n* inizio *m*: **from the** ~ fin dall'inizio

ꝰ **outside¹** /'aʊtsaɪd/ |1| *adj* esterno

|2| *n* esterno *m*; **from the** ~ dall'esterno; **at the** ~ al massimo

outside² /aʊt'saɪd/ |1| *adv* all'esterno, fuori; (out of doors) fuori; **go** ~ andare fuori

|2| *prep* fuori da; (in front of) davanti a

outsider /aʊt'saɪdə(r)/ *n* estraneo, -a *mf*

outsize /'aʊtsaɪz/ *adj* smisurato; ‹clothes› per taglie forti

outskirts /'aʊtskɜːts/ *npl* sobborghi *mpl*

outsmart /aʊt'smɑːt/ *vt* essere più furbo di

outsource /aʊt'sɔːs/ *vt* appaltare a imprese esterne

outsourcing /'aʊtsɔːsɪŋ/ *n* appalto *m* a imprese esterne

outspoken /aʊt'spəʊkn/ *adj* schietto

outspread /'aʊtspred/ *adj* ‹wings› spiegato; ‹arms, fingers› disteso

outstanding /aʊt'stændɪŋ/ *adj* eccezionale; ‹landmark› prominente; (not settled) in sospeso

outstandingly /aʊt'stændɪŋlɪ/ *adv* eccezionalmente; ~ **good** eccezionale

outstay /aʊt'steɪ/ *vt* ~ **one's s welcome** abusare dell'ospitalità di qualcuno

outstretched /'aʊtstretʃt/ *adj* allungato

outstrip /aʊt'strɪp/ (*pt/pp* -**stripped**) *vt* (*pt/pp* -**stripped**) superare

out-tray *n* vassoio *m* per corrispondenza e pratiche evase

outvote /aʊt'vəʊt/ *vt* mettere in minoranza

outward /'aʊtwəd/ |1| *adj* esterno; (journey) di andata

|2| *adv* verso l'esterno

outwardly /'aʊtwədlɪ/ *adv* esternamente

O

outwards Br, **outward** Am /'aʊtwəd(z)/ *adv* verso l'esterno

outweigh /aʊt'weɪ/ *vt* aver maggior peso di

outwit /aʊt'wɪt/ (*pt/pp* **-witted**) *vt* (*pt/pp* **-witted**) battere in astuzia

outworker /'aʊtwɜːkə(r)/ *n* Br lavoratore, -trice *mf* a domicilio

outworn /aʊt'wɔːn/ *adj* ‹outmoded› sorpassato

oval /'əʊvl/ **1** *adj* ovale
2 *n* ovale *m*

ovary /'əʊvəri/ *n* Anat ovaia *f*

ovation /əʊ'veɪʃn/ *n* ovazione *f*

oven /'ʌvn/ *n* forno *m*

oven cleaner *n* detergente *m* per il forno

oven glove *n* guanto *m* da forno

ovenproof *adj* da forno

oven-ready *adj* pronto da mettere in forno

ꞙ **over** /'əʊvə(r)/ **1** *prep* sopra; (across) al di là di; (during) durante; (more than) più di; ~ **the phone** al telefono; ~ **the page** alla pagina seguente; **all** ~ **Italy** in tutta [l']Italia; ‹travel› per l'Italia
2 *adv* Math col resto di; (ended) finito; ~ **again** un'altra volta; ~ **and** ~ più volte; ~ **and above** oltre a; ~ **here/there** qui/là; **all** ~ (everywhere) dappertutto; **it's all** ~ è tutto finito; **I ache all** ~ ho male dappertutto; **come/bring** ~ venire/portare; **turn** ~ girare

over+ *pref* (too) troppo

overact /əʊvər'ækt/ *vi* strafare

overactive /əʊvər'æktɪv/ *adj* ‹imagination› sbrigliato

overall[1] /'əʊvərɔːl/ *n* grembiule *m*

ꞙ **overall**[2] /əʊvər'ɔːl/ **1** *adj* complessivo; (general) generale
2 *adv* complessivamente

overalls /'əʊvərɔːlz/ *npl* tuta *fsg*

overarm /'əʊvərɑːm/ *adj & adv* ‹throw› col braccio al di sopra della spalla

overawe /əʊvər'ɔː/ *vt* fig intimidire

overbalance /əʊvə'bæləns/ *vi* perdere l'equilibrio

overbearing /əʊvə'beərɪŋ/ *adj* prepotente

overblown /əʊvə'bləʊn/ *adj* ‹style› ampolloso

overboard /'əʊvəbɔːd/ *adv* Naut in mare

overbook /əʊvə'bʊk/ *vt* accettare un numero di prenotazioni superiore ai posti disponibili

overburden /əʊvə'bɜːdən/ *vt* sovraccaricare (**with** di)

overcapacity /əʊvəkə'pæsəti/ *n* eccesso *m* di capacità produttiva

---

ꞙ indicates a very frequent word

overcast /'əʊvəkɑːst/ *adj* coperto

overcharge /əʊvə'tʃɑːdʒ/ **1** *vt* ~ **somebody** far pagare più del dovuto a
2 *vi* far pagare più del dovuto

overcoat /'əʊvəkəʊt/ *n* cappotto *m*

overcome /əʊvə'kʌm/ *vt* (*pt* **-came**, *pp* **-come**) vincere; **be** ~ **by** essere sopraffatto da

overcompensate /əʊvə'kɒmpənseɪt/ *vi* compensare eccessivamente

overconfident /əʊvə'kɒnfɪdənt/ *adj* troppo sicuro di sé

overcook /əʊvə'kʊk/ *vt* cuocere troppo

overcrowded /əʊvə'kraʊdɪd/ *adj* sovraffollato

overcrowding /əʊvə'kraʊdɪŋ/ *n* (in transport) calca *f*; (in city, institution) sovraffollamento *m*

overdo /əʊvə'duː/ *vt* (*pt* **-did**, *pp* **-done**) esagerare; (cook too long) stracuocere; ~ **it** fam (do too much) strafare

overdose /'əʊvədəʊs/ *n* overdose *f inv*

overdraft /'əʊvədrɑːft/ *n* scoperto *m*; **have an** ~ avere il conto scoperto

overdraw /əʊvə'drɔː/ *vt* (*pt* **-drew**, *pp* **-drawn**) ~ **one's account** andare allo scoperto; **be** ~**n by...** ‹account› essere scoperto di...

overdressed /əʊvə'drest/ *adj* troppo elegante

overdrive /'əʊvədraɪv/ *n* Auto overdrive *m inv*

overdue /əʊvə'djuː/ *adj* in ritardo

overeat /əʊvər'iːt/ *vi* mangiare troppo

overemphasize /əʊvər'emfəsaɪz/ *vt* esagerare ‹importance›; dare troppo rilievo a ‹aspect, fact›

overenthusiastic /əʊvərɪnθjuːzɪ'æstɪk/ *adj* troppo entusiasta

overestimate /əʊvər'estɪmeɪt/ *vt* sopravvalutare

overexcited /əʊvərɪk'saɪtɪd/ *adj* sovreccitato; **get** ~ sovreccitarsi

overexert /əʊvərɪg'zɜːt/ *vt* ~ **oneself** sovraffaticarsi

overexposure /əʊvərek'spəʊʒə(r)/ *n* Phot sovresposizione *f*; (in the media) attenzione *f* eccessiva da parte dei media

overfeed /əʊvə'fiːd/ *vt* sovralimentare ‹child, pet›; concimare troppo ‹plant›

overflow[1] /'əʊvəfləʊ/ *n* (water) acqua *f* che deborda; (people) pubblico *m* in eccesso; (outlet) scarico *m*

overflow[2] /əʊvə'fləʊ/ *vi* debordare

overgenerous /əʊvə'dʒenərəs/ *adj* ‹amount› troppo generoso

overgrown /əʊvə'grəʊn/ *adj* ‹garden› coperto di erbacce

overhang[1] /'əʊvəhæŋ/ *n* sporgenza *f*

overhang² /əʊvəˈhæŋ/ ① *vi* (*pt/pp* **-hung**) sporgere
② *vt* sovrastare

overhanging /əʊvəˈhæŋɪŋ/ *adj* ‹ledge, cliff› sporgente

overhaul¹ /ˈəʊvəhɔːl/ *n* revisione *f*

overhaul² /əʊvəˈhɔːl/ *vt* Techn revisionare

overhead¹ /əʊvəˈhed/ *adv* in alto

overhead² /ˈəʊvəhed/ ① *adj* aereo; ‹railway› sopraelevato; ‹lights› da soffitto
② *n* Am, (Br ∼s *npl*) spese *fpl* generali

overhead light *n* lampada *f* da soffitto

overhead locker *n* Aeron armadietto *m* [per il bagaglio a mano]

overhead projector *n* lavagna *f* luminosa

overhear /əʊvəˈhɪə(r)/ *vt* (*pt/pp* **-heard**) sentire per caso ‹conversation›; I ∼d him saying it l'ho sentito per caso mentre lo diceva

overheat /əʊvəˈhiːt/ ① *vi* Auto surriscaldarsi
② *vt* surriscaldare

over-indulge ① *vi* eccedere
② *vt* viziare ‹child›

over-indulgence *n* (excess) eccesso *m*; (laxity towards) indulgenza *f* eccessiva

overjoyed /əʊvəˈdʒɔɪd/ *adj* felicissimo

overkill /ˈəʊvəkɪl/ *n* (exaggerated treatment) esagerazione *f*

overland /ˈəʊvəlænd/ *adj & adv* via terra; ∼ **route** via *f* terrestre

overlap /əʊvəˈlæp/ ① *vi* (*pt/pp* **-lapped**) sovrapporsi
② *vt* sovrapporre

overlay /əʊvəˈleɪ/ *vt* ricoprire

overleaf /əʊvəˈliːf/ *adv* sul retro

overload¹ /əʊvəˈləʊd/ *vt* sovraccaricare

overload² /ˈəʊvələʊd/ *n* Electr sovratensioni *fpl*

overlook /əʊvəˈlʊk/ *vt* dominare; (fail to see, ignore) lasciarsi sfuggire

overly /ˈəʊvəlɪ/ *adv* eccessivamente

overmanned /əʊvəˈmænd/ *adj* con un'eccedenza di personale

overmanning /əʊvəˈmænɪŋ/ *n* eccesso *m* di personale

overmuch /əʊvəˈmʌtʃ/ *adv* troppo

overnight¹ /ˈəʊvənaɪt/ *adj* notturno

overnight² /əʊvəˈnaɪt/ *vt* inviare tramite sistemi di spedizione notturna con consegna il mattino seguente ‹goods›

overnight bag *n* piccola borsa *f* da viaggio

overnight stay *n* sosta *f* per la notte

overpass /ˈəʊvəpɑːs/ *n* Am cavalcavia *m inv*

overpay /əʊvəˈpeɪ/ *vt* (*pt/pp* **-paid**) strapagare

overplay /əɪvəˈpleɪ/ *vt* (exaggerate) esagerare

overpopulated /əʊvəˈpɒpjʊleɪtɪd/ *adj* sovrappopolato

overpower /əʊvəˈpaʊə(r)/ *vt* sopraffare

overpowering /əʊvəˈpaʊərɪŋ/ *adj* insostenibile

overpriced /əʊvəˈpraɪst/ *adj* troppo caro

overproduce /əʊvəprəˈdjuːs/ *vt* produrre in eccesso

overqualified /əʊvəˈkwɒlɪfaɪd/ *adj* troppo qualificato

overrate /əʊvəˈreɪt/ *vt* sopravvalutare

overrated /əʊvəˈreɪtɪd/ *adj* sopravvalutato

overreach /əʊvəˈriːtʃ/ *vt* ∼ oneself puntare troppo in alto

overreact /əʊvərɪˈækt/ *vi* avere una reazione eccessiva

overreaction /əʊvərɪˈækʃn/ *n* reazione *f* eccessiva

override /əʊvəˈraɪd/ *vt* (*pt* **-rode**, *pp* **-ridden**) passare sopra a

overriding /əʊvəˈraɪdɪŋ/ *adj* prevalente

overrule /əʊvəˈruːl/ *vt* annullare ‹decision›; we were ∼d by the chairman il direttore ha prevalso su di noi

overrun /əʊvəˈrʌn/ *vt* (*pt* **-ran**, *pp* **-run**, *pres p* **-running**) invadere; oltrepassare ‹time›; be ∼ with essere invaso da

overseas¹ /əʊvəˈsiːz/ *adv* oltremare

overseas² /ˈəʊvəsiːz/ *adj* d'oltremare

oversee /əʊvəˈsiː/ *vt* (*pt* **-saw**, *pp* **-seen**) sorvegliare

oversell /əʊvəˈsel/ *vt* lodare esageratamente ‹idea, plan›

oversensitive /əʊvəˈsensɪtɪv/ *adj* ‹person› ipersensibile

oversexed /əʊvəˈsekst/ *adj* fam be ∼ essere un maniaco/una maniaca del sesso

overshadow /əʊvəˈʃædəʊ/ *vt* adombrare

overshoot /əʊvəˈʃuːt/ *vt* (*pt/pp* **-shot**) oltrepassare

oversight /ˈəʊvəsaɪt/ *n* disattenzione *f*; an ∼ una svista

oversimplification /əʊvəsɪmplɪfɪˈkeɪʃn/ *n* semplificazione *f* eccessiva

oversimplified /əʊvəˈsɪmplɪfaɪd/ *adj* semplicistico

oversimplify /əʊvəˈsɪmplɪfaɪ/ *vt* semplificare eccessivamente

oversize[d] /əʊvəˈsaɪz[d]/ *adj* più grande del normale

oversleep /əʊvəˈsliːp/ *vi* (*pt/pp* **-slept**) svegliarsi troppo tardi

overspend /əʊvəˈspend/ *vi* spendere troppo

overspending /əʊvəˈspendɪŋ/ *n* spese *fpl* eccessive; Fin spese *fpl* superiori al bilancio di previsione

o

overspill /'əʊvəspɪl/ ① n (excess amount) eccedenza f

② attrib ~ housing development città f inv satellite; ~ population popolazione f in eccesso

overstaffed /əʊvə'stɑːft/ adj be ~ avere personale in eccedenza

overstaffing /əʊvə'stɑːfɪŋ/ n eccedenza f di personale

overstate /əʊvə'steɪt/ vt esagerare; its importance cannot be ~d la sua importanza non sarà mai sottolineata a sufficienza; ~ the case esagerare le cose

overstatement /əʊvə'steɪtmənt/ n esagerazione f

overstay /əʊvə'steɪ/ vt ~ one's time trattenersi troppo a lungo; ~ one's visa trattenersi oltre la scadenza del visto

overstep /əʊvə'step/ vt (pt/pp -stepped) ~ the mark oltrepassare ogni limite

overstretched /əʊvə'stretʃt/ adj ‹person› sovraccarico [di lavoro]; ‹budget, resources› sfruttato fino al limite

oversubscribed /əʊvəsəb'skraɪbd/ adj ‹share issue› sottoscritto in eccesso; ‹offer, tickets› richiesto oltre la disponibilità

overt /əʊ'vɜːt/ adj palese

overtake /əʊvə'teɪk/ vt/i (pt -took, pp -taken) sorpassare

overtaking /əʊvə'teɪkɪŋ/ n sorpasso m; no ~ divieto di sorpasso

overtax /əʊvə'tæks/ vt fig abusare di

over-the-counter adj ‹medicines› venduto senza ricetta

over-the-top adj fam esagerato; go over the top esagerare

overthrow¹ /'əʊvəθrəʊ/ n Pol rovesciamento m

overthrow² /əʊvə'θrəʊ/ vt (pt -threw, pp -thrown) Pol rovesciare

overtime /'əʊvətaɪm/ ① n lavoro straordinario m

② adv work ~ fare lo straordinario

overtired /əʊvə'taɪəd/ adj sovraffaticato

overtly /əʊ'vɜːtlɪ/ adv apertamente

overtone /'əʊvətəʊn/ n fig sfumatura f

overture /'əʊvətjʊə(r)/ n Mus preludio m; ~s pl fig approccio msg; make ~s to mostrare un atteggiamento di apertura verso

overturn /əʊvə'tɜːn/ ① vt ribaltare

② vi ribaltarsi

overvalue /əʊvə'væljuː/ vt sopravvalutare ‹currency, property›

overview /'əʊvəvjuː/ n visione f d'insieme

overweight /əʊvə'weɪt/ adj sovrappeso

overwhelm /əʊvə'welm/ vt sommergere (with di); (with emotion) confondere

overwhelming /əʊvə'welmɪŋ/ adj travolgente; ‹victory, majority› schiacciante

overwhelmingly /əʊvə'welmɪŋlɪ/ adv ‹vote, accept, reject› con una maggioranza schiacciante; ‹generous› straordinariamente

overwork /əʊvə'wɜːk/ ① n lavoro m eccessivo

② vt far lavorare eccessivamente

③ vi lavorare eccessivamente

overworked /əʊvə'wɜːkt/ adj affaticato dal troppo lavoro

overwrite /əʊvə'raɪt/ vt Comput registrare sopra a

overwrought /əʊvə'rɔːt/ adj in stato di agitazione

ovulation /ɒvjʊ'leɪʃn/ n ovulazione f

ow /aʊ/ int ahi!

owe /əʊ/ vt also fig dovere ([to] somebody a qualcuno); ~ somebody something dovere qualcosa a qualcuno

owing /'əʊɪŋ/ ① adj be ~ ‹money› essere da pagare

② prep ~ to a causa di

owl /aʊl/ n gufo m

ⓢ **own¹** /əʊn/ ① adj proprio

② pron a car of my ~ una macchina per conto mio; on one's ~ da solo; hold one's ~ with tener testa a; get one's ~ back fam prendersi una rivincita

own² vt possedere; (confess) ammettere; I don't ~ it non mi appartiene

■ **own up** vi confessare (to something qualcosa)

ⓢ **owner** /'əʊnə(r)/ n proprietario, -a mf

owner-driver n persona (f) che guida un'auto di sua proprietà

owner-occupied /-'ɒkjʊpaɪd/ adj abitato dal proprietario

owner-occupier n persona (f) che abita in una casa di sua proprietà

ownership /'əʊnəʃɪp/ n proprietà f

ox /ɒks/ n (pl oxen) bue m pl, buoi

Oxbridge /'ɒksbrɪdʒ/ n le università di Oxford e Cambridge

oxide /'ɒksaɪd/ n ossido m

oxidize /'ɒksɪdaɪz/ ① vt ossidare

② vi ossidarsi

oxygen /'ɒksɪdʒən/ n ossigeno m

oxygen mask n maschera f ad ossigeno

oyster /'ɔɪstə(r)/ n ostrica f

oz abbr (**ounce(s)**) oncia f

ozone /'əʊzəʊn/ n ozono m

ozone depletion n distruzione f dell'ozonosfera

ozone-friendly adj che non danneggia l'ozono

ozone layer n fascia f d'ozono

ⓢ indicates a very frequent word

Pp

p, P /piː/ **1** *n* (letter) p, P *f inv*
2 *abbr* Br (**penny, pence**) penny *m*
p & p *n abbr* (**postage and packing**)
spese *fpl* di spedizione
P45 *n* Br (form) ≈ modello CUD *m*
PA *abbr* **1** (**personal assistant**)
segretario, -a *mf* personale
2 Am (**Pennsylvania**) Pennsylvania *f*
p.a. *abbr* (**per annum**) all'anno
◆ **pace** /peɪs/ **1** *n* passo *m*; (speed) ritmo *m*;
keep ~ with camminare di pari passo con
2 *vi* **~ up and down** camminare avanti e
indietro
pacemaker /'peɪsmeɪkə(r)/ *n* Med
pacemaker *m inv*; (runner) battistrada *m inv*
pace-setter *n* (athlete) battistrada *m inv*
Pacific /pə'sɪfɪk/ *adj & n* **the ~** [Ocean]
l'oceano *m* Pacifico, il Pacifico
pacifier /'pæsɪfaɪə(r)/ *n* Am ciuccio *m*,
succhiotto *m*
pacifism /'pæsɪfɪzm/ *n* pacifismo *m*
pacifist /'pæsɪfɪst/ *n* pacifista *mf*
pacify /'pæsɪfaɪ/ *vt* (*pt/pp* **-led**) placare
‹person›; pacificare ‹country›
◆ **pack** /pæk/ **1** *n* (of cards) mazzo *m*; (of
hounds) muta *f*; (of wolves, thieves) branco *m*;
(of cigarettes etc) pacchetto *m*; **a ~ of lies** un
mucchio di bugie
2 *vt* impacchettare ‹article›; fare ‹suitcase›;
mettere in valigia ‹swimsuit etc›; (press down)
comprimere; **~ed** (crowded) strapieno, pieno
zeppo
3 *vi* fare i bagagli; **send somebody ~ing**
fam mandare qualcuno a quel paese
■ **pack in** *vt* fam mollare ‹job›; **~ it in!** (stop it)
piantala!
■ **pack off** *vt* (send) spedire
■ **pack out**: *vt* be **~ed out** ‹cinema, shops›
essere strapieno, essere pieno zeppo
■ **pack up 1** *vt* impacchettare
2 *vi* fam ‹machine› guastarsi
◆ **package** /'pækɪdʒ/ **1** *n* pacco *m*
2 *vt* impacchettare
package deal *n* offerta *f* tutto compreso
package holiday *n* vacanza *f*
organizzata
package tour *n* viaggio *m* organizzato
packaging /'pækɪdʒɪŋ/ *n* (materials)
confezione *f*; (promotion: of product)
presentazione *f* pubblicitaria
packed /pækt/ *adj* pieno zeppo; **~ with**
pieno zeppo di
packed lunch /pækt/ *n* pranzo *m* al sacco

packer /'pækə(r)/ *n* (in factory) imballatore,
-trice *mf*
packet /'pækɪt/ *n* pacchetto *m*; **cost a ~**
fam costare un sacco
pack ice *n* banchisa *f*
packing /'pækɪŋ/ *n* imballaggio *m*
pact /pækt/ *n* patto *m*
pad¹ /pæd/ **1** *n* imbottitura *f*; (for writing)
bloc-notes *m inv*, taccuino *m*; fam (home)
casa *f*
2 *vt* (*pt/pp* **padded**) imbottire
pad² *vi* (*pt/pp* **padded**) camminare con
passo felpato
■ **pad out** *vt* gonfiare
padded bra *n* reggiseno *m* imbottito
padded cell *n* cella *f* con le pareti
imbottite
padded envelope *n* busta *f* imbottita
padded shoulders *npl* spalline *fpl*
imbottite
padding /'pædɪŋ/ *n* imbottitura *f*; (in written
work) fronzoli *mpl*
paddle /'pædl/ **1** *n* pagaia *f*; **go for a ~**
sguazzare
2 *vt* (row) spingere remando
3 *vi* (wade) sguazzare
paddling pool *n* (public) piscina *f* per
bambini; (inflatable) piscina *f* gonfiabile
paddock /'pædək/ *n* recinto *m*
padlock /'pædlɒk/ **1** *n* lucchetto *m*
2 *vt* chiudere con lucchetto
padre /'pɑːdreɪ/ *n* padre *m*
Padua /'pædjoə/ *n* Padova *f*
paediatric /piːdɪ'ætrɪk/ *adj* pediatrico
paediatrician /piːdɪə'trɪʃn/ *n* pediatra *mf*
paediatrics /piːdɪ'ætrɪks/ *n* pediatria *f*
paedophile /'piːdəofaɪl/ *n* pedofilo, -a *mf*
paedophilia /piːdəʊ'fɪlɪə/ *n* pedofilia *f*
pagan /'peɪgən/ *adj & n* pagano, -a *mf*
paganism /'peɪgənɪzm/ *n* paganesimo *m*
◆ **page¹** /peɪdʒ/ *n* pagina *f*
page² **1** *n* (boy) paggetto *m*; (in hotel)
fattorino *m*
2 *vt* far chiamare ‹person›
pageant /'pædʒənt/ *n* parata *f*
pageantry /'pædʒəntrɪ/ *n* cerimoniale *m*
pageboy /'peɪdʒbɔɪ/ *n* (at wedding) paggio *m*
page proof *n* bozza *f* definitiva
pager /'peɪdʒə(r)/ *n* cercapersone *m inv*
page three *n* Br terza pagina (*f*) di
*quotidiano scandalistico inglese con una
pin-up*

page three girl n Br pin-up f inv
paid /peɪd/ ① ▶ PAY
  ② adj ~ **employment** lavoro m
  remunerato; **put** ~ **to** mettere fine a
paid-up adj Br ‹member› che ha pagato la
  sua quota; ‹instalment› versato
pail /peɪl/ n secchio m
⚑ **pain** /peɪn/ ① n dolore m; **be in** ~ soffrire;
  take ~**s to do something** fare il possibile per
  fare qualcosa; ~ **in the neck** fam rottura f di
  scatole; ‹person› rompiscatole mf inv
  ② vt fig addolorare
pained /peɪnd/ adj addolorato
painful /'peɪnfʊl/ adj doloroso; (laborious)
  penoso
painfully /'peɪnfʊlɪ/ adv ~ **shy**
  incredibilmente timido
painkiller /'peɪnkɪlə(r)/ n calmante m
painkilling /'peɪnkɪlɪŋ/ adj antinevralgico
painless /'peɪnlɪs/ adj indolore
painlessly /'peɪnlɪslɪ/ adv in modo
  indolore
painstaking /'peɪnzteɪkɪŋ/ adj minuzioso
⚑ **paint** /peɪnt/ ① n pittura f; ~**s** pl colori
  mpl
  ② vt/i pitturare; ‹artist› dipingere; ~ **the**
  town red folleggiare
  ■ **paint over** vt (cover with paint) coprire di
  vernice
paintbox /'peɪntbɒks/ n scatola f di colori
paintbrush /'peɪntbrʌʃ/ n pennello m
painter /'peɪntə(r)/ n pittore, -trice mf;
  (decorator) imbianchino m
pain threshold n soglia f del dolore
⚑ **painting** /'peɪntɪŋ/ n pittura f; (picture)
  dipinto m
paintpot n latta f di pittura
paint remover n sverniciante m
paint roller n rullo m
paint spray n pistola f a spruzzo
paint stripper n (tool) macchina f
  sverniciante; (chemical) sverniciante m
paintwork n pittura f
⚑ **pair** /peə(r)/ n paio m; (of people) coppia f; **a**
  ~ **of trousers/scissors** un paio di pantaloni/
  forbici
  ■ **pair off** vi mettersi in coppia
  ■ **pair up** vi ‹dancers› fare coppia; (for game)
  formare una coppia
paisley /'peɪzlɪ/ n motivo m cachemire inv
pajamas /pə'dʒɑːməz/ npl Am pigiama msg
Pakistan /pɑːkɪ'stɑːn/ n Pakistan m
Pakistani /pɑːkɪ'stɑːnɪ/ adj & n pakistano,
  -a mf
pal /pæl/ n fam amico, -a mf
  ■ **pal up** vi fam (become friends) fare amicizia
  (with con)
palace /'pælɪs/ n palazzo m

palaentology /pælɪən'tɒlədʒɪ/ n
  paleontologia f
palaeontologist /pælɪən'tɒlədʒɪst/ n
  paleontologo, -a mf
palatable /'pælətəbl/ adj gradevole al
  gusto
palate /'pælət/ n palato m
palatial /pə'leɪʃl/ adj sontuoso
palaver /pə'lɑːvə(r)/ n fam (fuss) storie fpl
pale¹ /peɪl/ n (stake) palo m; **beyond the** ~ fig
  inaccettabile
pale² ① adj pallido
  ② vi impallidire; ~ **into insignificance**
  diventare insignificante
paleness /'peɪlnɪs/ n pallore m
Palestine /'pælɪstaɪn/ n Palestina f
Palestinian /pælə'stɪnɪən/ adj & n
  palestinese mf
palette /'pælɪt/ n tavolozza f
palette knife n spatola f
paling /'peɪlɪŋ/ n (stake) palo m; (fence)
  palizzata f
palisade /pælɪ'seɪd/ n (fence) palizzata f
pall /pɔːl/ ① n drappo m funebre; fig velo m
  di tristezza; (of smoke) cappa f
  ② vi stufare
pallet /'pælɪt/ n pallet m inv
palliative /'pælɪətɪv/ n palliativo m
pallid /'pælɪd/ adj pallido
pallor /'pælə(r)/ n pallore m
palm /pɑːm/ n palmo m; (tree) palma f
  ■ **palm off**: vt ~ **something off on somebody**
  rifilare qualcosa a qualcuno
palmist /'pɑːmɪst/ n chiromante mf
palmistry /'pɑːmɪstrɪ/ n chiromanzia f
Palm Sunday n Domenica f delle Palme
palmtop [computer] n Comput palmtop
  m inv
palpable /'pælpəbl/ adj palpabile;
  (perceptible) tangibile
palpate /pæl'peɪt/ vi palpare
palpitate /'pælpɪteɪt/ vi palpitare
palpitations /pælpɪ'teɪʃnz/ npl
  palpitazioni fpl
paltry /'pɔːltrɪ/ adj (-ler, -lest)
  insignificante
pampas /'pæmpəs/ n pampas fpl
pamper /'pæmpə(r)/ vt viziare
pamphlet /'pæmflɪt/ n opuscolo m
pan /pæn/ ① n tegame m, pentola f; (for
  frying) padella f; (of scales) piatto m
  ② vt (pt/pp **panned**) fam (criticize)
  stroncare
  ■ **pan out** vi fam (develop) mettersi
panacea /pænə'siːə/ n panacea f
panache /pə'næʃ/ n stile m
Panama /'pænəmɑː/ n Panama m; **the** ~
  Canal il canale di Panama
pancake /'pænkeɪk/ n crêpe f inv, frittella f

Pancake Day n martedì m inv grasso
pancreas /'pæŋkrıəs/ n pancreas m inv
panda /'pændə/ n panda m inv
panda car n macchina f della polizia
pandemonium /pændɪ'məʊnıəm/ n pandemonio m
pander /'pændə(r)/ vi ~ **to somebody** compiacere qualcuno
pane /peɪn/ n ~ **[of glass]** vetro m
⚘ **panel** /'pænl/ n pannello m; (group of people) giuria f; ~ **of experts** gruppo m di esperti; ~ **of judges** giuria f
panelling /'pænəlɪŋ/ n pannelli mpl
panellist /'pænəlɪst/ n Radio, TV partecipante mf
pan-fry vt friggere
pang /pæŋ/ n ~**s of hunger** morsi mpl della fame; ~**s of conscience** rimorsi mpl di coscienza
panhandler /'pænhændlə(r)/ n Am fam mendicante mf
panic /'pænɪk/ [1] n panico m
[2] vi (pt/pp **panicked**) lasciarsi prendere dal panico
panic button n fam **hit the** ~ farsi prendere dal panico
panic buying n accaparramento m
panicky /'pænɪkı/ adj che si lascia prendere dal panico facilmente
panic-stricken /'pænɪkstrɪkən/ adj in preda al panico
pannier /'pænɪə(r)/ n (on bike) borsa f; (on mule) bisaccia f
panorama /pænə'rɑːmə/ n panorama m
panoramic /pænə'ræmɪk/ adj panoramico
pan scourer n paglietta f
pansy /'pænzı/ n viola f del pensiero; fam (effeminate man) finocchio m
pant /pænt/ vi ansimare
pantechnicon /pæn'teknɪkən/ n furgone m per traslochi
panther /'pænθə(r)/ n pantera f
panties /'pæntɪz/ npl Am mutandine fpl
panting /'pæntɪŋ/ adj ansante
pantomime /'pæntəmaɪm/ n pantomima f
pantry /'pæntrı/ n dispensa f
pants /pænts/ npl (underwear) mutande fpl; (woman's) mutandine fpl; Am (trousers) pantaloni mpl
panty girdle /'pæntı/ n guaina f
pantyhose /n Am collant m inv
panty-liner n salvaslip m inv
papal /'peɪpl/ adj papale
paparazzi /pæpə'rætzı/ npl paparazzi mpl
⚘ **paper** /'peɪpə(r)/ [1] n carta f; (wallpaper) carta f da parati; (newspaper) giornale m; (exam) esame m scritto; (treatise) saggio m; ~**s** pl (documents) documenti mpl; (for identification)

documento msg [d'identità]; **on** ~ in teoria; **put down on** ~ mettere per iscritto
[2] attrib di carta; (version) su carta
[3] vt tappezzare
■ **paper over**: vt ~ **over the cracks** dissimulare le divergenze
paperback n edizione f economica
paper bank n contenitore m per la raccolta della carta
paper boy n ragazzo m che recapita i giornali a domicilio
paper chain n festone m di carta
paper chase n corsa (f) campestre in cui i partecipanti seguono una scia di pezzetti di carta
paper clip n graffetta f
paper currency n banconote fpl
paper feed tray n Comput vassoio m della carta
paperknife n tagliacarte m inv
paper mill n cartiera f
paper money n cartamoneta f
paper napkin n tovagliolo m di carta
paper round n **he does a** ~ recapita i giornali a domicilio
paper shop n edicola f
paper shredder n distruttore m di documenti
paper-thin adj sottilissimo
paper towel n (toilet) asciugamano m di carta; (kitchen) carta f asciugatutto
paper-weight n fermacarte m inv
paperwork n lavoro m d'ufficio
papery /'peɪpərı/ adj ‹texture, leaves› cartaceo
paprika /pə'priːkə/ n paprica f
Papua New Guinea n Papua Nuova Guinea f
par /pɑː(r)/ n (in golf) par m inv; **on a** ~ **with** alla pari con; **feel below** ~ essere un po' giù di tono
para¹ /'pærə/ n (paragraph) paragrafo m
para² n Br Mil para m inv
parable /'pærəbl/ n parabola f
parachute /'pærəʃuːt/ [1] n paracadute m inv
[2] vi lanciarsi col paracadute
parachute drop n (of supplies) lancio m col paracadute
parachute jump n lancio m col paracadute
parachuting /'pærəʃuːtɪŋ/ n paracadutismo m
parachutist /'pærəʃuːtɪst/ n paracadutista mf
parade /pə'reɪd/ [1] n (military) parata f militare; (display) sfoggio m
[2] vi sfilare
[3] vt (show off) far sfoggio di
parade ground n piazza f d'armi

p

paradigm /'pærədaɪm/ n paradigma m

paradise /'pærədaɪs/ n paradiso m

paradox /'pærədɒks/ n paradosso m

paradoxical /pærə'dɒksɪkl/ adj
paradossale

paradoxically /pærə'dɒksɪklɪ/ adv
paradossalmente

paraffin /'pærəfɪn/ n paraffina f; (oil)
cherosene m

paragliding /'pærəglaɪdɪŋ/ n parapendio
m

paragon /'pærəgən/ n ~ of virtue modello
m di virtù

◆ **paragraph** /'pærəgrɑːf/ n paragrafo m

Paraguay /'pærəgwaɪ/ n Paraguay m

parallel /'pærəlel/ **1** adj & adv parallelo
2 n Geog fig parallelo m; (line) parallelo f
3 vt essere paragonabile a

parallel bars npl parallele fpl

parallelogram /pærə'leləʊgræm/ n Math
parallelogramma m

parallel port n Comput porta f parallela

Paralympics /pærə'lɪmpɪks/ npl
Paraolimpiadi fpl

paralyse /'pærəlaɪz/ vt paralizzare

paralysis /pə'ræləsɪs/ n (pl **-ses**
/pə'ræləsiːz/) paralisi f inv

paralytic /pærə'lɪtɪk/ adj ‹person›
paralitico; ‹arm, leg› paralizzato; Br fam
(drunk) ubriaco fradicio

paramedic /pærə'medɪk/ n paramedico m

parameter /pə'ræmɪtə(r)/ n parametro m

paramilitary /pærə'mɪlɪtrɪ/ **1** n
appartenente mf ad un gruppo paramilitare
2 adj paramilitare

paramount /'pærəmaʊnt/ adj supremo;
be ~ essere essenziale

paranoia /pærə'nɔɪə/ n paranoia f

paranoid /'pærənɔɪd/ adj paranoico

paranormal /pærə'nɔːməl/ adj & n
paranormale m

parapet /'pærəpɪt/ n parapetto m

paraphernalia /pærəfə'neɪlɪə/ n
armamentario m

paraphrase /'pærəfreɪz/ **1** n parafrasi
f inv
2 vt parafrasare

paraplegic /pærə'pliːdʒɪk/ adj & n
paraplegico, -a mf

parascending /'pærəsendɪŋ/ n Br
paracadutismo m ascensionale

parasite /'pærəsaɪt/ n parassita mf

parasitic /pærə'sɪtɪk/ adj parassitario

parasol /'pærəsɒl/ n parasole m

paratrooper /'pærətruːpə(r)/ n
paracadutista m

parboil /'pɑːbɔɪl/ vt scottare

◆ indicates a very frequent word

parcel /'pɑːsl/ n pacco m

■ **parcel up** vt impacchettare ‹clothes etc›

parcel bomb n pacco m bomba inv

parch /pɑːtʃ/ vt disseccare; **be** ~**ed** ‹person›
morire dalla sete

parched /pɑːtʃt/ adj ‹land› riarso; (thirsty)
I'm ~ sto morendo di sete

parchment /'pɑːtʃmənt/ n pergamena f

pardon /'pɑːdn/ **1** n perdono m; Jur
grazia f; ~? prego?; **I beg your** ~? fml chiedo
scusa?; **I do beg your** ~ (sorry) chiedo scusa!
2 vt perdonare; Jur graziare

pare /peə(r)/ vt (peel) pelare

◆ **parent** /'peərənt/ n genitore m

parentage /'peərəntɪdʒ/ n natali mpl

parental /pə'rentl/ adj dei genitori

parent company n casa f madre

parenthesis /pə'renθəsɪs/ n (pl **-ses**
/pə'renθəsiːz/) parentesi f inv

parenthood /'peərənthʊd/ n (fatherhood)
paternità f; (motherhood) maternità f

parenting /'peərəntɪŋ/ n educazione f dei
figli; ~ **classes** corsi di sostegno pratico e
psicologico per nuovi genitori

parents' evening n riunione f dei
genitori degli alunni

parer /'peərə(r)/ n sbucciatore m

pariah /pə'raɪə/ n paria m

parings /'peərɪŋz/ npl (of fruit) bucce fpl; (of
nails) ritagli mpl di unghie

Paris /'pærɪs/ n Parigi f

parish /'pærɪʃ/ n parrocchia f

parishioner /pə'rɪʃənə(r)/ n
parrocchiano, -a mf

parish priest n (Catholic) parroco m;
(Protestant) pastore m

Parisian /pə'rɪzɪən/ adj & n parigino, -a mf

parity /'pærɪtɪ/ n parità f

◆ **park** /pɑːk/ **1** n parco m
2 vt Auto posteggiare, parcheggiare;
~ **oneself** fam installarsi
3 vi posteggiare, parcheggiare

parka /'pɑːkə/ n parka m inv

park-and-ride n parcheggio (m) collegato
al centro di una città da mezzi pubblici

parking /'pɑːkɪŋ/ n parcheggio m,
posteggio m; **'no** ~' 'divieto di sosta'

parking attendant n parcheggiatore,
-trice mf, posteggiatore, -trice mf

parking lot n Am posteggio m, parcheggio
m

parking meter n parchimetro m

parking space n posteggio m,
parcheggio m

parkland n parco m

park ranger, park warden n
guardaparco m inv

◆ **parliament** /'pɑːləmənt/ n parlamento m

parliamentary /pɑːləˈmentəri/ *adj* parlamentare

parlour /ˈpɑːlə(r)/ *n* salotto *m*

parochial /pəˈrəʊkɪəl/ *adj* parrocchiale; fig ristretto

parochialism /pəˈrəʊkɪəlɪzm/ *n* campanilismo *m*

parody /ˈpærədi/ ⟦1⟧ *n* parodia *f*
⟦2⟧ *vt* (*pt/pp* **-ied**) parodiare

parole /pəˈrəʊl/ ⟦1⟧ *n* **on** ∼ sulla parola; **eligible for** ∼ suscettibile di essere liberato sulla parola
⟦2⟧ *vt* mettere in libertà sulla parola

paroxysm /ˈpærəksɪzm/ *n* accesso *m*

parquet floor /ˈpɑːkeɪ/ *n* parquet *m*

parquet flooring /ˈflɔːrɪŋ/ *n* parquet *m inv*

parrot /ˈpærət/ *n* pappagallo *m*

parry /ˈpæri/ *vt* (*pt/pp* **-ied**) parare ‹*blow*›; (in fencing) eludere

parse /pɑːz/ *vt* fare l'analisi grammaticale di ‹*sentence*›; Comput analizzare la sintassi di

parsimonious /pɑːsɪˈməʊnɪəs/ *adj* parsimonioso

parsing /ˈpɑːzɪŋ/ *n* analisi *f* grammaticale; Comput analisi *f* sintattica

parsley /ˈpɑːsli/ *n* prezzemolo *m*

parsnip /ˈpɑːsnɪp/ *n* pastinaca *f*

parson /ˈpɑːsn/ *n* pastore *m*

⚬ **part** /pɑːt/ ⟦1⟧ *n* parte *f*, (of machine) pezzo *m*; **for my** ∼ per quanto mi riguarda; **on the** ∼ **of** da parte di; **take sb's** ∼ prendere le parti di qualcuno; **take** ∼ **in** prendere parte a
⟦2⟧ *adv* in parte
⟦3⟧ *vt* ∼ **one's hair** farsi la riga
⟦4⟧ *vi* ‹*people*› separarsi; ∼ **with** separarsi da

part exchange *n* **take in** ∼ prendere indietro come pagamento parziale

partial /ˈpɑːʃl/ *adj* parziale; **be** ∼ **to** aver un debole per

partiality /pɑːʃɪˈæləti/ *n* (liking) predilezione *f*

partially /ˈpɑːʃəli/ *adv* parzialmente; ∼ **sighted** parzialmente cieco

⚬ **participant** /pɑːˈtɪsɪpənt/ *n* partecipante *mf*

⚬ **participate** /pɑːˈtɪsɪpeɪt/ *vi* partecipare (**in** a)

participation /pɑːtɪsɪˈpeɪʃn/ *n* partecipazione *f*

participatory /pɑːtɪsɪˈpeɪtəri/ *adj* partecipativo

participle /ˈpɑːtɪsɪpl/ *n* participio *m*; **present/past** ∼ participio presente/passato

particle /ˈpɑːtɪkl/ *n* Phys, Gram particella *f*

⚬ **particular** /pəˈtɪkjʊlə(r)/ *adj* particolare; (precise) meticoloso; pej difficile; **in** ∼ in particolare

⚬ **particularly** /pəˈtɪkjʊləli/ *adv* particolarmente

particulars /pəˈtɪkjʊləz/ *npl* particolari *mpl*

parting /ˈpɑːtɪŋ/ ⟦1⟧ *n* separazione *f*; (in hair) scriminatura *f*
⟦2⟧ *attrib* di commiato

partisan /pɑːtɪˈzæn/ *n* partigiano, -a *mf*

partition /pɑːˈtɪʃn/ ⟦1⟧ *n* (wall) parete *f* divisoria; Pol divisione *f*
⟦2⟧ *vt* dividere
■ **partition off** *vt* separare

partly /ˈpɑːtli/ *adv* in parte

⚬ **partner** /ˈpɑːtnə(r)/ *n* Comm socio, -a *mf*; (sport, in relationship) compagno, -a *mf*

partnership /ˈpɑːtnəʃɪp/ *n* Comm società *f inv*

part of speech *n* categoria *f* grammaticale

part owner *n* comproprietario, -a *mf*

part payment *n* acconto *m*

partridge /ˈpɑːtrɪdʒ/ *n* pernice *f*

part-time *adj* & *adv* part time; **be** *or* **work** ∼ lavorare part time

part-way *adv* ∼ **through the evening** a metà serata

⚬ **party** /ˈpɑːti/ *n* ricevimento *m*, festa *f*; (group) gruppo *m*; Pol partito *m*; Jur parte *f*; **be** ∼ **to** essere parte attiva in

party animal *n* festaiolo, -a *mf*

party dress *n* abito *m* da sera

party-goer *n* festaiolo, -a *mf*

party hat *n* cappellino *m* di carta

party leader *n* dirigente *m* di partito

party line *n* Teleph duplex *m inv*; Pol linea *f* del partito

party piece *n* pezzo *m* forte; **do one's** ∼ esibirsi nel proprio pezzo forte

party political broadcast *n* comunicato (*m*) di partito (trasmesso per radio o per televisione)

party politics *n* politica *f* di partito

party wall *n* muro *m* divisorio

⚬ **pass** /pɑːs/ ⟦1⟧ *n* lasciapassare *m inv*; (in mountains) passo *m*; Sport passaggio *m*; Sch (mark) voto *m*, sufficiente *m*; **get a** ∼ Sch ottenere la sufficienza; **make a** ∼ **at** fam fare delle avances a
⟦2⟧ *vt* passare; (overtake) sorpassare; (approve) far passare; (exceed) oltrepassare; fare ‹*remark*›; esprimere ‹*judgement*›; Jur pronunciare ‹*sentence*›; ∼ **water** orinare; ∼ **the time** passare il tempo
⟦3⟧ *vi* passare; (in exam) essere promosso; **let something** ∼ fig lasciar correre qualcosa; ∼**!** (in game) passo!
■ **pass as** *vt* = PASS FOR
■ **pass away** *vi* mancare
■ **pass by** *vi* (go past) passare
■ **pass down** *vt* passare; fig trasmettere
■ **pass for** *vt* (be accepted as) passare per
■ **pass off** ⟦1⟧ *vi* (disappear) passare; (take place) svolgersi

⋯⊹

2 *vt* ~ **somebody/something off as** far passare qualcosa/qualcuno per
■ **pass on** *vt* passare ‹*message, information*›
■ **pass on to** *vt* passare a ‹*new subject, next question*›
■ **pass out** *vi* fam svenire
■ **pass over** **1** *vt* (not mention) passare sopra a; ~ **somebody over for promotion** non prendere in considerazione qualcuno per una promozione
2 *vi* (die) spirare
■ **pass round** *vt* far passare
■ **pass through** *vt* attraversare
■ **pass up** *vt* passare; fam (miss) lasciarsi scappare

passable /'pɑːsəbl/ *adj* ‹*road*› praticabile; (satisfactory) passabile
passage /'pæsɪdʒ/ *n* passaggio *m*; (corridor) corridoio *m*; (voyage) traversata *f*
pass book *n* Fin libretto *m* di risparmio
passé /'pæˈseɪ/ *adj* pej sorpassato
◌ **passenger** /'pæsɪndʒə(r)/ *n* passeggero, -a *mf*
passenger compartment *n* Br Auto abitacolo *m*
passenger ferry *n* traghetto *m*
passenger plane *n* aereo *m* passeggeri
passenger seat *n* posto *m* accanto al guidatore
passenger train *n* treno *m* passeggeri
passepartout /pæspɑːˈtuː/ *n* (key, frame) passe-partout *m inv*
passer-by /pɑːsəˈbaɪ/ *n* (*pl* **-s-by**) passante *mf*
passing /'pɑːsɪŋ, US 'pæs-/ *adj* ‹*motorist*› di passaggio; ‹*thought*› di sfuggita; ‹*reference*› en passant; ‹*resemblance*› vago
passing place /'pɑːsɪŋ/ *n* piazzola (*f*) di sosta per consentire il transito dei veicoli nei due sensi
passing shot *n* Tennis passante *m*
passion /'pæʃn/ *n* passione *f*
passionate /'pæʃənət/ *adj* appassionato
passionately /'pæʃənətlɪ/ *adv* appassionatamente
passion fruit *n* frutto *m* della passione
passive /'pæsɪv/ *adj* & *n* passivo *m*
passively /'pæsɪvlɪ/ *adv* passivamente
passiveness /'pæsɪvnɪs/ *n* passività *f*
passive resistance *n* resistenza *f* passiva
passive smoking *n* fumo *m* passivo
pass-key *n* (master-key) passe-partout *m inv*; (for access) chiave *f*
pass mark *n* Sch [voto *m*] sufficiente *m*
Passover *n* Pasqua *f* ebraica
passport *n* passaporto *m*
password *n* parola *f* d'ordine

password-protected *adj* Comput ‹*file, site*› protetto da password
◌ **past** /pɑːst/ **1** *adj* passato; (former) ex; **that's all** ~ tutto questo è passato; **in the** ~ **few days** nei giorni scorsi; **the** ~ **week** la settimana scorsa
2 *n* passato *m*
3 *prep* oltre; **at ten** ~ **two** alle due e dieci
4 *adv* oltre; **go/come** ~ passare
pasta /'pæstə/ *n* pasta [asciutta] *f*
paste /peɪst/ **1** *n* pasta *f*; (dough) impasto *m*; (adhesive) colla *f*
2 *vt* incollare
■ **paste down** *vt* incollare
■ **paste in** *vt* incollare
■ **paste up** *vt* affiggere ‹*notice, poster*›
paste jewellery *n* bigiotteria *f*
pastel /'pæstl/ **1** *n* pastello *m*
2 *attrib* pastello
pasteurization /pɑːstʃəraɪˈzeɪʃn/ *n* pastorizzazione *f*
pasteurize /'pɑːstʃəraɪz/ *vt* pastorizzare
pasteurized /'pɑːstʃəraɪzd/ *adj* pastorizzato
pastille /'pæstɪl/ *n* pastiglia *f*
pastime /'pɑːstaɪm/ *n* passatempo *m*
pasting /'peɪstɪŋ/ *n* fam (defeat, criticism) batosta *f*
past master *n* esperto, -a *mf*
pastor /'pɑːstə(r)/ *n* pastore *m*
pastoral /'pɑːstərəl/ *adj* pastorale
past participle *n* participio *m* passato
pastrami /pæˈstrɑːmɪ/ *n* carne di manzo affumicata
pastry /'peɪstrɪ/ *n* pasta *f*; **pastries** *pl* pasticcini *mpl*
past tense *n* passato *m*
pasture /'pɑːstʃə/ *n* pascolo *m*
pasty¹ /'pæstɪ/ *n* ≈ pasticcio *m*
pasty² /'peɪstɪ/ *adj* smorto
pat /pæt/ **1** *n* buffetto *m*; (of butter) pezzetto *m*
2 *adv* **have something off** ~ conoscere; (something) a menadito
3 *vt* (*pt/pp* **patted**) dare un buffetto a; ~ **somebody on the back** fig congratularsi con qualcuno
patch /pætʃ/ **1** *n* toppa *f*; (spot) chiazza; (period) periodo *m*; **not a** ~ **on** fam molto inferiore a
2 *vt* mettere una toppa su
■ **patch up** *vt* riparare alla bell'e meglio; appianare ‹*quarrel*›
patchwork /'pætʃwɜːk/ *n* patchwork *m inv*; fig mosaico *m*
patchy /'pætʃɪ/ *adj* incostante
pâté /'pæteɪ/ *n* pâté *m inv*
patent /'peɪtnt/ **1** *adj* palese
2 *n* brevetto *m*
3 *vt* brevettare

◌ indicates a very frequent word

p

patent leather *n* vernice *m*

patently /'peɪtəntlɪ/ *adv* in modo palese

paternal /pə'tɜːnl/ *adj* paterno

paternalism /pə'tɜːnəlɪzm/ *n* paternalismo *m*

paternalistic /pətɜːnə'lɪstɪk/ *adj* paternalistico

paternity /pə'tɜːnətɪ/ *n* paternità *f*

paternity leave *n* congedo *m* di paternità

paternity suit *n* causa *f* per il riconoscimento di paternità

◆ **path** /pɑːθ/ *n* (*pl* ∼s /pɑːðz/) sentiero *m*; (orbit) traiettoria *f*; fig strada *f*

pathetic /pə'θetɪk/ *adj* patetico; fam (very bad) penoso

pathological /pæθə'lɒdʒɪkl/ *adj* patologico

pathologist /pə'θɒlədʒɪst/ *n* patologo, -a *mf*

pathology /pə'θɒlədʒɪ/ *n* patologia *f*

pathos /'peɪθɒs/ *n* pathos *m*

patience /'peɪʃns/ *n* pazienza *f*; (game) solitario *m*

◆ **patient** /'peɪʃnt/ *adj & n* paziente *mf*

patiently /'peɪʃntlɪ/ *adv* pazientemente

patio /'pætɪəʊ/ *n* terrazza *f*

patio doors *npl* portafinestra *f*

patio garden *n* cortile *m*

patriarch /'peɪtrɪɑːk/ *n* patriarca *m*

patriarchal /peɪtrɪ'ɑːkəl/ *adj* patriarcale

patriarchy /'peɪtrɪɑːkɪ/ *n* patriarcato *m*

patriot /'pætrɪət/ *n* patriota *mf*

patriotic /pætrɪ'ɒtɪk/ *adj* patriottico

patriotism /'pætrɪətɪzm/ *n* patriottismo *m*

patrol /pə'trəʊl/ ⟦1⟧ *n* pattuglia *f* ⟦2⟧ *vt/i* pattugliare

patrol boat *n* motovedetta *f*

patrol car *n* autopattuglia *f*

patron /'peɪtrən/ *n* patrono *m*; (of charity) benefattore, -trice *mf*; (of the arts) mecenate *mf*; (customer) cliente *mf*

patronage /'pætrənɪdʒ/ *n* patrocinio *m*; (of shop etc) frequentazione *f*

patronize /'pætrənaɪz/ *vt* frequentare abitualmente; fig trattare con condiscendenza

patronizing /'pætrənaɪzɪŋ/ *adj* condiscendente

patronizingly /'pætrənaɪzɪŋlɪ/ *adv* con condiscendenza

patron saint *n* santo, -a *mf*, patrono, -a *mf*

patter¹ /'pætə(r)/ ⟦1⟧ *n* picchiettio *m* ⟦2⟧ *vi* picchiettare

patter² *n* (of salesman) chiacchiere *fpl*

◆ **pattern** /'pætn/ *n* motivo *m*; (for knitting, sewing, in behaviour) modello *m*

patterned /'pætənd/ *adj* ‹material› fantasia

paunch /pɔːntʃ/ *n* pancia *f*

pauper /'pɔːpə(r)/ *n* povero, -a *mf*

pause /pɔːz/ ⟦1⟧ *n* pausa *f* ⟦2⟧ *vi* fare una pausa

pave /peɪv/ *vt* pavimentare; ∼ **the way** preparare la strada (**for** a)

pavement /'peɪvmənt/ *n* marciapiede *m*

pavement café *n* caffè *m* con tavolini all'aperto

pavilion /pə'vɪljən/ *n* padiglione *m*; Cricket *costruzione* (*f*) *annessa al campo da gioco con gli spogliatoi*

paving /'peɪvɪŋ/ *n* lastricato *m*

paving slab, **paving stone** *n* lastra *f* di pietra

paw /pɔː/ ⟦1⟧ *n* zampa *f* ⟦2⟧ *vt* fam mettere le zampe addosso a

pawn¹ /pɔːn/ *n* (in chess) pedone *m*; fig pedina *f*

pawn² ⟦1⟧ *vt* impegnare ⟦2⟧ *n* in ∼ in pegno

pawnbroker /'pɔːnbrəʊkə(r)/ *n* prestatore, trice *mf* su pegno

pawnshop /'pɔːnʃɒp/ *n* monte *m* di pietà

pawpaw /'pɔːpɔː/ *n* papaia *f*

◆ **pay** /peɪ/ ⟦1⟧ *n* paga *f*; **in the** ∼ **of** al soldo di ⟦2⟧ *vt* (*pt/pp* **paid**) pagare; prestare ‹attention›; fare ‹compliment; visit›; ∼ **cash** pagare in contanti ⟦3⟧ *vi* pagare; (be profitable) rendere; **it doesn't** ∼ **to …** fig è fatica sprecata …; ∼ **in instalments** pagare a rate; ∼ **through the nose** fam pagare profumatamente

■ **pay back** *vt* ripagare

■ **pay for** *vt* pagare per

■ **pay in** *vt* versare

■ **pay off** ⟦1⟧ *vt* saldare ‹debt› ⟦2⟧ *vi* fig dare dei frutti

■ **pay out** *vt* (spend) pagare

■ **pay up** *vi* pagare

payable /'peɪəbl/ *adj* pagabile; **make** ∼ **to** intestare a

pay-as-you-go *adj* ‹tariff› a consumo

pay cheque Br, **pay check** Am *n* assegno *m* della paga

payday *n* giorno *m* di paga

PAYE Br *abbr* (**pay-as-you-earn**) *trattenute* (*fpl*) *fiscali alla fonte*

payee /peɪ'iː/ *n* beneficiario *m*

payer /'peɪə(r)/ *n* pagante *mf*

paying-in slip /peɪɪŋ'ɪn/ *n* distinta *f* di versamento

payload /'peɪləʊd/ *n* (of bomb) carica *f* esplosiva; (of aircraft, ship) carico *m* utile

◆ **payment** /'peɪmənt/ *n* pagamento *m*; ∼ **by instalments** pagamento *m* rateale

pay-packet *n* busta *f* paga *inv*

pay-per-view *n* pay per view *f*; ∼ **programme/film** un film/programma pay per view

p

payphone n telefono m pubblico

payroll n (list) libro m paga; (sum of money) paga f del personale; (employees collectively) personale m

payslip n busta f paga inv

pay television n pay tv f

pc abbr 1 (**per cent**) per cento
2 (**politically correct**) politicamente corretto
3 (**postcard**) cartolina f postale

PC abbr 1 (**personal computer**) PC m inv
2 (**police constable**) agente m di polizia

pd abbr Am (**police department**) reparto m di polizia

PDF abbr (**portable document format**) Comput PDF m; a ~ file un file PDF

PE n abbr (**physical education**) educazione f fisica

pea /piː/ n pisello m

⚡ **peace** /piːs/ n pace f; ~ **of mind** tranquillità f

peaceable /'piːsəbl/ adj pacifico

peace envoy n mediatore, -trice mf

peaceful /'piːsfʊl/ adj calmo, sereno

peacefully /'piːsfʊlɪ/ adv in pace

peacekeeping 1 n Mil, Pol mantenimento m della pace
2 attrib ‹force, troops› di mantenimento della pace

peacemaker n mediatore, -trice mf

peace process n processo m di pace

peacetime 1 n tempo m di pace
2 attrib ‹planning, government› del tempo di pace; ‹army, alliance, training› in tempo di pace

peace treaty n trattato m di pace

peach /piːtʃ/ n pesca f; (tree) pesco m

peacock /'piːkɒk/ n pavone m

pea green adj verde pisello

peak /piːk/ n picco m; fig culmine m

peaked /piːkt/ adj Am malaticcio

peaked cap /piːkt/ n berretto m a punta

peak hours npl ore fpl di punta

peak period n ora f di punta

peak rate n tariffa f ore di punta; ~ **calls** Teleph chiamate a tariffa ore di punta

peak season n alta stagione f

peak time n = PRIME TIME

peaky /'piːkɪ/ adj Br malaticcio

peal /piːl/ n (of bells) scampanio m; ~**s of laughter** fragore msg di risate

peanut /'piːnʌt/ n nocciolina f [americana]; ~**s** pl fam miseria fsg

peanut butter n burro m di arachidi

pear /peə(r)/ n pera f; (tree) pero m

pearl /pɜːl/ n perla f

pearl barley n orzo m perlato

pearl-diver n pescatore, -trice mf

pearl grey 1 n grigio m perla inv
2 adj grigio perla inv

Pearly Gates /pɜːlɪ/ npl hum porte fpl del paradiso

peasant /'peznt/ n contadino, -a mf

peat /piːt/ n torba f

pebble /'pebl/ n ciottolo m

pebble-dash n intonaco m a pinocchino

pecan /'piːkən/ n (tree) pecan m inv; (nut) noce f pecan inv

peck /pek/ 1 n beccata f; (kiss) bacetto m
2 vt beccare; (kiss) dare un bacetto a
■ **peck at** vi beccare

pecking order /'pekɪŋ/ n gerarchia f

peckish /'pekɪʃ/ adj be ~ fam avere un languorino allo stomaco

pecs /peks/ fam **pectorals** /'pektərəlz/ npl pettorali mpl

pectoral /'pektərəl/ adj & n pettorale m

peculiar /pɪ'kjuːlɪə(r)/ adj strano; (special) particolare; ~ **to** tipico di

peculiarity /pɪkjuːlɪ'ærətɪ/ n stranezza f; (feature) particolarità f inv

peculiarly /pɪ'kjuːlɪəlɪ/ adv singolarmente

pecuniary /pə'kjuːnɪərɪ/ adj pecuniario

pedagogical /pedə'gɒdʒɪkl/ adj pedagogico

pedagogy /'pedəgɒdʒɪ/ n pedagogia f

pedal /'pedl/ 1 n pedale m
2 vi pedalare

pedal bin n pattumiera f a pedale

pedant /'pedənt/ n pedante m

pedantic /pɪ'dæntɪk/ adj pedante

pedantically /pɪ'dæntɪklɪ/ adv in modo pedante

pedantry /'pedəntrɪ/ n pedanteria f

peddle /'pedl/ vt vendere porta a porta

pedestal /'pedɪstl/ n piedistallo m

pedestrian /pɪ'destrɪən/ 1 n pedone m
2 adj fig scadente

pedestrian crossing n passaggio m pedonale

pedestrian precinct n zona f pedonale

pediatrician /piːdɪə'trɪʃn/ n Am = PAEDIATRICIAN

pedicure /'pedɪkjʊə(r)/ n pedicure f inv

pedigree /'pedɪgriː/ 1 n pedigree m inv; (of person) lignaggio m
2 attrib ‹animal› di razza, con pedigree

pedlar, peddler /'pedlə(r)/ n (old) venditore, -trice mf ambulante; **drug ~** spacciatore, -trice mf di droga

pedophile /'pedəfaɪl/ n Am = PAEDOPHILE

pee /piː/ fam 1 vi (pt/pp **peed**) fare la pipì
2 n go for a ~ andare a fare la pipì

peek /piːk/ fam 1 vi sbirciare

⚡ indicates a very frequent word

2 *n* **take a** ⁓ **at something** dare una sbirciata a qualcosa

peekaboo /piːkəˈbuː/ *int* cucù

peel /piːl/ 1 *n* buccia *f*
2 *vt* sbucciare
3 *vi* ⟨nose etc⟩ spellarsi; ⟨paint⟩ staccarsi
■ **peel off** 1 *vt* togliersi ⟨item of clothing⟩
2 *vi* ⟨wallpaper⟩ staccarsi; ⟨skin⟩ squamarsi

peeler /ˈpiːlə(r)/ *n* sbucciatore *m*

peelings /ˈpiːlɪŋz/ *npl* bucce *fpl*

peep /piːp/ 1 *n* sbirciata *f*
2 *vi* sbirciare

peephole /ˈpiːphəʊl/ *n* spioncino *m*

Peeping Tom /ˈpiːpɪŋ/ *n* fam guardone *m*

peer¹ /pɪə(r)/ *vi* ⁓ **at** scrutare

peer² *n* nobile *m*; **his** ⁓**s** *pl* (in rank) i suoi pari; (in age) i suoi coetanei

peerage /ˈpɪərɪdʒ/ *n* Br Pol nobiltà *f*; (book) almanacco *m* nobiliare; **be given a** ⁓ essere elevato al rango di pari

peer group *n* (of same status) pari *mpl*; (of same age) coetanei *mpl*; ⁓ **pressure** pressione (*f*) esercitata dal gruppo cui si appartiene

peerless /ˈpɪəlɪs/ *adj* impareggiabile

peeved /piːvd/ *adj* fam irritato

peevish /ˈpiːvɪʃ/ *adj* fam irritabile

peg /peg/ 1 *n* (hook) piolo *m*; (for tent) picchetto *m*; (for clothes) molletta *f*; **off the** ⁓ fam prêt-a-porter
2 *vt* (*pt/pp* **pegged**) fissare ⟨prices⟩; stendere con le mollette ⟨washing⟩

pegboard /ˈpegbɔːd/ *n* segnapunti *m inv*

pejorative /prˈdʒɒrətɪv/ *adj* peggiorativo

pejoratively /prˈdʒɒrətɪvlɪ/ *adv* in modo peggiorativo

peke /piːk/ *n* fam (dog) pechinese *m*

pekin[g]ese /piːkɪˈniːz/ *n* pechinese *m*

Peking /piːkɪŋ/ *n* Pechino *f*

pelican /ˈpelɪkən/ *n* pellicano *m*

pelican crossing *n* passaggio *m* pedonale con semaforo

pellet /ˈpelɪt/ *n* pallottola *f*

pell-mell /pelˈmel/ *adv* alla rinfusa

pelmet /ˈpelmɪt/ *n* mantovana *f*

pelt¹ /pelt/ *n* (skin) pelliccia *f*

pelt² 1 *vt* bombardare
2 *vi* fam (run fast) catapultarsi; (rain heavily) venir giù a fiotti
■ **pelt along** *vi* (move quickly) precipitarsi lungo
■ **pelt down** *vi* ⟨rain⟩ venir giù a fiotti

pelvis /ˈpelvɪs/ *n* Anat bacino *m*

pen¹ /pen/ *n* (for animals) recinto *m*

pen² *n* penna *f*; (ball-point) penna *f* a sfera

penal /ˈpiːnl/ *adj* penale

penal code *n* codice *m* penale

penalize /ˈpiːnəlaɪz/ *vt* penalizzare

penalty /ˈpenltɪ/ *n* sanzione *f*; (fine) multa *f*; (in football) [calcio *m* di] rigore *m*

penalty area, **penalty box** *n* area *f* di rigore

penalty clause *n* Comm, Jur clausola *f* penale

penalty kick *n* [calcio *m* di] rigore *m*

penalty shoot-out *n* rigori *mpl*

penance /ˈpenəns/ *n* penitenza *f*

pence /pens/ ▶ PENNY

penchant /ˈpɒ̃ʃɒ̃/ *n* debole *m*

pencil /ˈpensl/ 1 *n* matita *f*
2 *vt* (*pt/pp* **pencilled**) scrivere a matita
■ **pencil in** *vt* annotare provvisoriamente ⟨date⟩

pencil case *n* [astuccio *m*] portamatite *m inv*

pencil sharpener *n* temperamatite *m inv*

pendant /ˈpendənt/ *n* ciondolo *m*

pending /ˈpendɪŋ/ 1 *adj* in sospeso
2 *prep* in attesa di

pendulum /ˈpendjʊləm/ *n* pendolo *m*

penetrate /ˈpenɪtreɪt/ *vt/i* penetrare

penetrating /ˈpenɪtreɪtɪŋ/ *adj* ⟨sound, stare⟩ penetrante; ⟨remark⟩ acuto

penetration /penɪˈtreɪʃn/ *n* penetrazione *f*

penfriend /ˈpenfrend/ *n* amico, -a *mf* di penna

penguin /ˈpeŋgwɪn/ *n* pinguino *m*

penicillin /penɪˈsɪlɪn/ *n* penicillina *f*

peninsula /prˈnɪnsjʊlə/ *n* penisola *f*

penis /ˈpiːnɪs/ *n* pene *m*

penitence /ˈpenɪtəns/ *n* penitenza *f*

penitent /ˈpenɪtənt/ *adj* & *n* penitente *mf*

penitentiary /penɪˈtenʃərɪ/ *n* Am penitenziario *m*

penknife /ˈpennaɪf/ *n* temperino *m*

pen-name *n* pseudonimo *m*

pennant /ˈpenənt/ *n* bandiera *f*

penniless /ˈpenɪlɪs/ *adj* senza un soldo

penny /ˈpenɪ/ *n* (*pl* **pence**; *single coins* **pennies**) penny *m*; Am centesimo *m*; **spend a** ⁓ fam andare in bagno; **the** ⁓**'s dropped!** fam ci è arrivato!

penny-farthing *n* velocipede *m*

penny-pinching /ˈpenɪpɪntʃɪŋ/ 1 *adj* taccagno
2 *n* taccagneria *f*

penny whistle *n* zufolo *m*

pen-pusher *n* fam scribacchino, -a *mf*

pension /ˈpenʃn/ *n* pensione *f*
■ **pension off** *vt* (force to retire) mandare in pensione

pensioner /ˈpenʃənə(r)/ *n* pensionato, -a *mf*

pension fund *n* fondo *m* pensioni; (of an individual) fondo *m* pensione

p

pension scheme *n* piano *m* di pensionamento

pensive /'pensəv/ *adj* pensoso

pentagon /'pentəgən/ *n* pentagono *m*; Am Pol **the P~** il Pentagono

pentagonal /pen'tægənəl/ *adj* pentagonale

pentathlete /pen'tæθli:t/ *n* pentatleta *mf*

pentathlon /pen'tæθlɒn/ *n* pentathlon *m inv*

Pentecost /'pentɪkɒst/ *n* Pentecoste *f*

penthouse /'penthaʊs/ *n* attico *m*

pent-up /'pentʌp/ *adj* represso

penultimate /pɪ'nʌltɪmət/ *adj* penultimo

penury /'penjʊrɪ/ *n* miseria *f*

peony /'pɪənɪ/ *n* peonia *f*

⚘ **people** /'pi:pl/ [1] *npl* persone *fpl*, gente *fsg*; (citizens) popolo *msg*; **a lot of ~** una marea di gente; **the ~** la gente; **English ~** gli inglesi; **~ say** si dice; **for four ~** per quattro
[2] *vt* popolare

people carrier *n* monovolume *f*

pep /pep/
■ **pep up** *vt* vivacizzare ‹party, conversation›; tirare su ‹person›

PEP /pep/ *abbr* Br (**personal equity plan**) piano *m* di investimento azionario personale

pepper /'pepə(r)/ [1] *n* pepe *m*; (vegetable) peperone *m*
[2] *vt* (season) pepare

peppercorn *n* grano *m* di pepe

peppercorn rent affitto *m* nominale

pepper mill *n* macinapepe *m inv*

peppermint *n* menta *f* piperita; (sweet) caramella *f* alla menta

pepper pot *n* pepiera *f*

pep pill /'peppɪl/ *n* fam stimolante *m*

pep talk *n* discorso *m* d'incoraggiamento

peptic /'peptɪk/ *adj* peptico

peptic ulcer *n* ulcera *f* peptica

⚘ **per** /pɜː(r)/ *prep* per

per annum /pər'ænəm/ *adv* all'anno

per capita /pə'kæpɪtə/ *adj & adv* pro capite

perceive /pə'siːv/ *vt* percepire; (interpret) interpretare

⚘ **per cent** *adv* per cento

⚘ **percentage** /pə'sentɪdʒ/ *n* percentuale *f*

perceptible /pə'septəbl/ *adj* percettibile; fig sensibile

perceptibly /pə'septɪblɪ/ *adv* percettibilmente; fig sensibilmente

perception /pə'sepʃn/ *n* percezione *f*

perceptive /pə'septɪv/ *adj* perspicace

perch¹ /pɜːtʃ/ [1] *n* pertica *f*
[2] *vi* ‹bird› appollaiarsi

perch² *n inv* (fish) pesce *m* persico

percolate /'pɜːkəleɪt/ *vi* infiltrarsi; ‹coffee› passare

percolator /'pɜːkəleɪtə(r)/ *n* caffettiera *f* a filtro

percussion /pə'kʌʃn/ *n* percussione *f*

percussion instrument *n* strumento *m* a percussione

percussionist /pə'kʌʃ(ə)nɪst/ *n* percussionista *mf*

peremptory /pə'remptərɪ/ *adj* perentorio

perennial /pə'renɪəl/ [1] *adj* perenne
[2] *n* pianta *f* perenne

⚘ **perfect¹** /'pɜːfɪkt/ [1] *adj* perfetto
[2] *n* Gram passato *m* prossimo

perfect² /pə'fekt/ *vt* perfezionare

perfection /pə'fekʃn/ *n* perfezione *f*; **to ~** alla perfezione

perfectionism /pə'fekʃənɪzm/ *n* perfezionismo *m*

perfectionist /pə'fekʃ(ə)nɪst/ *adj & n* perfezionista *mf*

⚘ **perfectly** /'pɜːfɪktlɪ/ *adv* perfettamente

perfidious /pə'fɪdɪəs/ *adj* perfido

perforate /'pɜːfəreɪt/ *vt* perforare

perforated /'pɜːfəreɪtɪd/ *adj* perforato; ‹ulcer› perforante

perforation /pɜːfə'reɪʃn/ *n* perforazione *f*

⚘ **perform** /pə'fɔːm/ [1] *vt* compiere, fare; eseguire ‹operation, sonata›; recitare ‹role›; mettere in scena ‹play›
[2] *vi* Theat recitare; Techn funzionare

⚘ **performance** /pə'fɔːməns/ *n* esecuzione *f*; (at theatre, cinema) rappresentazione *f*; Techn rendimento *m*

performance artist *n* performance artist *mf*

performance bonus *n* premio *m* di produttività

performance indicators *npl* indicatori *mpl* di performance

performance-related *adj* commensurato alla produttività

performer /pə'fɔːmə(r)/ *n* artista *mf*

performing arts /pə'fɔːmɪŋ/ *npl* arti *fpl* dello spettacolo

perfume /'pɜːfjuːm/ *n* profumo *m*

perfumed /'pɜːfjuːmd/ *adj* profumato

perfunctory /pə'fʌŋktərɪ/ *adj* superficiale

⚘ **perhaps** /pə'hæps/ *adv* forse

peril /'perɪl/ *n* pericolo *m*

perilous /'perɪləs/ *adj* pericoloso

perilously /'perɪləslɪ/ *adv* pericolosamente

perimeter /pə'rɪmɪtə(r)/ *n* perimetro *m*

⚘ **period** /'pɪərɪəd/ [1] *n* periodo *m*; (menstruation) mestruazioni *fpl*; Sch ora *f* di lezione; Am (full stop) punto *m* fermo
[2] *attrib* (costume) d'epoca; ‹furniture› in stile

⚘ indicates a very frequent word

p

periodic /pɪərɪ'ɒdɪk/ *adj* periodico
periodical /pɪərɪ'ɒdɪkl/ *n* periodico *m*, rivista *f*
periodically /pɪərɪ'ɒdɪklɪ/ *adv* periodicamente
period of notice *n* periodo *m* di preavviso
peripheral /pə'rɪfərəl/ **1** *adj* periferico **2** *n* Comput periferica *f*
periphery /pə'rɪfərɪ/ *n* periferia *f*
periscope /'perɪskəʊp/ *n* periscopio *m*
perish /'perɪʃ/ *vi* (rot) deteriorarsi; (die) perire
perishable /'perɪʃəbl/ **1** *adj* deteriorabile **2** *npl* ~s *npl* merce *f* deperibile
perished /'perɪʃt/ *adj* fam (freezing cold) be ~ essere intirizzito
perishing /'perɪʃɪŋ/ *adj* fam it's ~ fa freddo da morire
peritonitis /perɪtə'naɪtɪs/ *n* peritonite *f*
perjure /'pɜːdʒə(r)/ *vt* ~ oneself spergiurare
perjury /'pɜːdʒərɪ/ *n* spergiuro *m*
perk¹ /pɜːk/ *n* fam vantaggio *m*
perk² *vi* Am ‹coffee› passare
■ **perk up 1** *vt* tirare su **2** *vi* tirarsi su
perky /'pɜːkɪ/ *adj* allegro
perm /pɜːm/ **1** *n* permanente *f* **2** *vt* ~ **sb's hair** fare la permanente a qno
permanent /'pɜːmənənt/ **1** *adj* permanente; ‹job, address› stabile **2** *n* Am = PERM
permanently /'pɜːmənəntlɪ/ *adv* stabilmente
permeable /'pɜːmɪəbl/ *adj* permeabile
permeate /'pɜːmɪeɪt/ *vt* impregnare
permissible /pə'mɪsəbl/ *adj* ammissibile
permission /pə'mɪʃn/ *n* permesso *m*
permissive /pə'mɪsɪv/ *adj* permissivo
permit¹ /pə'mɪt/ *vt* (*pt/pp* **-mitted**) permettere; ~ **somebody to do something** permettere a qualcuno di fare qualcosa
permit² /'pɜːmɪt/ *n* autorizzazione *f*
pernicious /pə'nɪʃəs/ *adj* pernicioso
pernickety Br /pə'nɪkətɪ/, **persnickety** Am /pərs-/ fam *adj* puntiglioso, pignolo; (about food) difficile
peroxide blonde /pə'rɒksaɪd/ *n* bionda *f* ossigenata
perpendicular /pɜːpən'dɪkjʊlə(r)/ *adj* & *n* perpendicolare *f*
perpetrate /'pɜːpɪtreɪt/ *vt* perpetrare
perpetrator /'pɜːpɪtreɪtə(r)/ *n* autore, -trice *mf*
perpetual /pə'petjʊəl/ *adj* perenne
perpetually /pə'petjʊəlɪ/ *adv* perennemente

perpetuate /pə'petjʊeɪt/ *vt* perpetuare
perplex /pə'pleks/ *vt* lasciare perplesso
perplexed /pə'plekst/ *adj* perplesso
perplexity /pə'pleksɪtɪ/ *n* perplessità *f inv*
perquisite /'pɜːsɪkjuːt/ *n* fringe benefit *m inv*, beneficio *m* accessorio
per se /pɜː'seɪ/ *adv* in sé
persecute /'pɜːsɪkjuːt/ *vt* perseguitare
persecution /pɜːsɪ'kjuːʃn/ *n* persecuzione *f*
persecutor /'pɜːsɪkjuːtə(r)/ *n* persecutore, -trice *mf*
perseverance /pɜːsɪ'vɪərəns/ *n* perseveranza *f*
persevere /pɜːsɪ'vɪə(r)/ *vi* perseverare
persevering /pɜːsɪ'vɪərɪŋ/ *adj* assiduo
Persian /'pɜːʃn/ *adj* persiano
persist /pə'sɪst/ *vi* persistere; ~ **in doing something** persistere nel fare qualcosa
persistence /pə'sɪstəns/ *n* persistenza *f*
persistent /pə'sɪstənt/ *adj* persistente
persistently /pə'sɪstəntlɪ/ *adv* persistentemente
persistent offender *n* recidivo, -a *mf*
✮ **person** /'pɜːsn/ *n* persona *f*; in ~ di persona
persona /pə'səʊnə/ *n* Psych individuo *m*; Theat personaggio *m*
personable /'pɜːsənəbl/ *adj* di bella presenza
personage /'pɜːsənɪdʒ/ *n* personaggio *m*
✮ **personal** /'pɜːsənl/ *adj* personale
personal ad *n* annuncio *m* personale
personal allowance *n* (in taxation) quota *f* non imponibile
personal assistant *n* segretario, -a *mf* personale
personal belongings *npl* effetti *mpl* personali
personal column *n* rubrica *f* degli annunci personali
personal computer *n* personal computer *m inv*
personal hygiene *n* igiene *f* personale
personality /pɜːsə'nælətɪ/ *n* personalità *f inv*; (on TV) personaggio *m*
personalize /'pɜːsənəlaɪz/ *vt* personalizzare ‹stationery, clothing›; mettere sul piano personale ‹issue, dispute›
personal loan *n* prestito *m* a privato
personally /'pɜːsənəlɪ/ *adv* personalmente
personal organizer *n* Comput agenda *f* elettronica
personal stereo *n* walkman® *m inv*
personification /pəsɒnɪfɪ'keɪʃn/ *n* the ~ of la personificazione di
personify /pə'sɒnɪfaɪ/ *vt* (*pt/pp* **-ied**) personificare
personnel /pɜːsə'nel/ *n* personale *m*

p

personnel director n direttore, -trice mf del personale

personnel management n gestione f del personale

✓ **perspective** /pəˈspektɪv/ n prospettiva f

perspex® /ˈpɜːspeks/ n plexiglas® m

perspicacious /pɜːspɪˈkeɪʃəs/ adj perspicace

perspiration /pɜːspɪˈreɪʃn/ n sudore m

perspire /pəˈspaɪə(r)/ vi sudare

persuade /pəˈsweɪd/ vt persuadere

persuasion /pəˈsweɪʒn/ n persuasione f; (belief) convinzione f

persuasive /pəˈsweɪsɪv/ adj persuasivo

persuasively /pəˈsweɪsɪvlɪ/ adv in modo persuasivo

pert /pɜːt/ adj (lively) esuberante

pertinent /ˈpɜːtɪnənt/ adj pertinente (to a)

perturb /pəˈtɜːb/ vt perturbare

perturbing /pəˈtɜːbɪŋ/ adj conturbante

Peru /pəˈruː/ n Perù m

peruse /pəˈruːz/ vt leggere

Peruvian /pəˈruːvɪən/ adj & n peruviano, -a mf

pervade /pəˈveɪd/ vt pervadere

pervasive /pəˈveɪsɪv/ adj pervasivo

perverse /pəˈvɜːs/ adj perverso; (illogical) irragionevole

perversely /pəˈvɜːslɪ/ adv in modo perverso

perversion /pəˈvɜːʃn/ n perversione f

perversity /pəˈvɜːsɪtɪ/ n perversità f

pervert[1] /pəˈvɜːt/ vt deviare ‹course of justice›

pervert[2] /ˈpɜːvɜːt/ n pervertito, -a mf

perverted /pəˈvɜːtɪd/ adj perverso

pessary /ˈpesərɪ/ n candeletta f

pessimism /ˈpesɪmɪzm/ n pessimismo m

pessimist /ˈpesɪmɪst/ n pessimista mf

pessimistic /pesɪˈmɪstɪk/ adj pessimistico

pessimistically /pesɪˈmɪstɪklɪ/ adv in modo pessimistico

pest /pest/ n piaga f; fam (person) peste f

pester /ˈpestə(r)/ vt molestare

pesticide /ˈpestɪsaɪd/ n pesticida m

pestilential /pestɪˈlenʃəl/ adj hum (annoying) fastidiosissimo

pestle /ˈpesl/ n pestello m

pet /pet/ [1] n animale m domestico; (favourite) cocco, -a mf
[2] adj (favourite) prediletto
[3] vt (pt/pp **petted**) coccolare
[4] vi ‹couple› praticare il petting

petal /ˈpetl/ n petalo m

peter /ˈpiːtə(r)/ vi ~ out finire

pet food n cibo m per animali

pet hate n Br bestia f nera

petite /pəˈtiːt/ adj minuto

petition /pəˈtɪʃn/ n petizione f

pet name n vezzeggiativo m

petrified /ˈpetrɪfaɪd/ adj (frightened) pietrificato

petrify /ˈpetrɪfaɪ/ vt (pt/pp -**ied**) pietrificare

petrochemical /petrəʊˈkemɪkl/ n petrolchimico m

petrodollar /ˈpetrəʊdɒlə(r)/ n petroldollaro m

petrol /ˈpetrəl/ n Br benzina f

petrol bomb n Br bomba f, molotov f inv

petrol can n tanica f di benzina

petroleum /pɪˈtrəʊlɪəm/ n petrolio m

petroleum jelly n vaselina f

petrol-pump n Br pompa f di benzina

petrol station n Br, stazione f di servizio

petrol tank n Br serbatoio m della benzina

pet shop n negozio m di animali

petticoat /ˈpetɪkəʊt/ n sottoveste f

pettifogging /ˈpetɪfɒgɪŋ/ adj pej cavilloso

petty /ˈpetɪ/ adj (-**ier**, -**iest**) insignificante; (mean) meschino

petty cash n cassa f per piccole spese

petty crime n piccola criminalità f

petty minded /-ˈmaɪndɪd/ adj meschino

petty officer n sottufficiale m

petty theft n furto m di minore entità

petulance /ˈpetjʊləns/ n petulanza f

petulant /ˈpetjʊlənt/ adj petulante

pew /pjuː/ n banco m (di chiesa)

pewter /ˈpjuːtə(r)/ n peltro m

PGCE n abbr Br (**postgraduate certificate in education**) diploma m di specializzazione nell'insegnamento

phallic /ˈfælɪk/ adj fallico

phallic symbol n simbolo m fallico

phallus /ˈfæləs/ n fallo m

phantom /ˈfæntəm/ n fantasma m

pharaoh /ˈfeərəʊ/ n faraone m

pharmaceutical /fɑːməˈsjuːtɪkl/ adj farmaceutico

pharmacist /ˈfɑːməsɪst/ n farmacista mf

pharmacy /ˈfɑːməsɪ/ n farmacia f

✓ **phase** /feɪz/ [1] n fase f
[2] vt phase in/out introdurre/eliminare gradualmente

PhD abbr (**Doctor of Philosophy**) ≈ dottorato m di ricerca

pheasant /ˈfeznt/ n fagiano m

phenomenal /fɪˈnɒmɪnl/ adj fenomenale; (incredible) incredibile

phenomenally /fɪˈnɒmɪnəlɪ/ adv incredibilmente

phenomenon /fɪˈnɒmɪnən/ n (pl -**na**) fenomeno m

phew /fju:/ *int* (when too hot, in relief) uff!; (in surprise) oh!

philanderer /fɪˈlændərə(r)/ *n* donnaiolo *m*

philanthropic /fɪlənˈθrɒpɪk/ *adj* filantropico

philanthropist /fɪˈlænθrəpɪst/ *adj* filantropo, -a *mf*

philatelist /fɪˈlætəlɪst/ *n* filatelico, -a *mf*

philately /fɪˈlætəlɪ/ *n* filatelia *f*

philharmonic /fɪlɑːˈmɒnɪk/ **1** *n* (orchestra) orchestra *f* filarmonica **2** *adj* filarmonico

Philippines /ˈfɪlɪpiːnz/ *npl* Filippine *fpl*

philistine /ˈfɪlɪstaɪn/ *adj & n* filisteo, -a *mf*

philology /fɪˈlɒlədʒɪ/ *n* filologia *f*

philosopher /fɪˈlɒsəfə(r)/ *n* filosofo, -a *mf*

philosophical /fɪləˈsɒfɪkl/ *adj* filosofico

philosophically /fɪləˈsɒfɪklɪ/ *adv* con filosofia

philosophy /fɪˈlɒsəfɪ/ *n* filosofia *f*

phishing /ˈfɪʃɪŋ/ *n forma di frode telematica consistente nell'inviare finte e-mail di banche o altre ditte allo scopo di entrare in possesso dei dati personali del destinatario*

phlebitis /flɪˈbaɪtɪs/ *n* flebite *f*

phlegm /flem/ *n* Med flemma *f*

phlegmatic /flegˈmætɪk/ *adj* flemmatico

phobia /ˈfəʊbɪə/ *n* fobia *f*

phobic /ˈfəʊbɪk/ *adj* fobico

phoenix /ˈfiːnɪks/ *n* fenice *f*

◊ **phone** /fəʊn/ **1** *n* telefono *m*; be on the ~ avere il telefono; (be phoning) essere al telefono **2** *vt* telefonare a
■ **phone back** *vt* richiamare
■ **phone in** *vi* telefonare al lavoro; he ~d in sick ha telefonato [al lavoro] per dire che è ammalato
■ **phone up** **1** *vi* telefonare **2** *vt* dare un colpo di telefono a

phone book *n* guida *f* del telefono

phone booth *n* cabina *f* telefonica

phone box *n* cabina *f* telefonica

phone call *n* telefonata *f*

phonecard *n* scheda *f* telefonica

phone-in *n* trasmissione *f* con chiamate in diretta

phone link *n* phone link *m inv*

phoneme /ˈfəʊniːm/ *n* fonema *m*

phone number *n* numero *m* telefonico

phonetic /fəˈnetɪk/ *adj* fonetico

phonetics /fəˈnetɪks/ *n* fonetica *f*

phoney /ˈfəʊnɪ/ **1** *adj* (-ier, -iest) fasullo **2** *n* ciarlatano, -a *mf*

phonology /fəˈnɒlədʒɪ/ *n* fonologia *f*

phosphate /ˈfɒsfeɪt/ *n* fosfato *m*

phosphorus /ˈfɒsfərəs/ *n* fosforo *m*

◊ **photo** /ˈfəʊtəʊ/ *n* foto *f*

photo album *n* album *m inv* di fotografie

photo booth *n* macchina *f* fototessere *inv*

photocall *n* photo opportunity *f*

photocell *n* fotocellula *f*

photocopier *n* fotocopiatrice *f*

photocopy **1** *n* fotocopia *f* **2** *vt* fotocopiare

photoengraving *n* fotoincisione *f*

photo finish *n* fotofinish *m*

photofit® *n* Br fotofit *m inv*

photogenic /fəʊtəʊˈdʒenɪk/ *adj* fotogenico

◊ **photograph** /ˈfəʊtəɡrɑːf/ **1** *n* fotografia *f* **2** *vt* fotografare

photographer /fəˈtɒɡrəfə(r)/ *n* fotografo, -a *mf*

photographic /fəʊtəˈɡræfɪk/ *adj* fotografico

photography /fəˈtɒɡrəfɪ/ *n* fotografia *f*

photojournalism *n* fotoreportage *m*

photojournalist *n* fotogiornalista *mf*

photomontage /fəʊtəʊmɒnˈtɑːʒ/ *n* fotomontaggio *m*

photo opportunity *n* photo opportunity *f*

photosynthesis *n* fotosintesi *f*

phrase /freɪz/ **1** *n* espressione *f* **2** *vt* esprimere

phrase book *n* libro *m* di fraseologia

phut /fʌt/ *adv* fam go ~ ‹car, washing machine etc› scassarsi; ‹plan› andare in fumo

◊ **physical** /ˈfɪzɪkl/ *adj* fisico

physical education *n* educazione *f* fisica

physical fitness *n* forma *f* fisica

physically /ˈfɪzɪklɪ/ *adv* fisicamente

physically handicapped *adj* handicappato fisicamente

physician /fɪˈzɪʃn/ *n* medico *m*

physicist /ˈfɪzɪsɪst/ *n* fisico, -a *mf*

physics /ˈfɪzɪks/ *n* fisica *f*

physio /ˈfɪzɪəʊ/ *n* Br fam (physiotherapist) fisioterapista *mf*; (physiotherapy) fisioterapia *f*

physiology /fɪzɪˈɒlədʒɪ/ *n* fisiologia *f*

physiotherapist /fɪzɪəʊˈθerəpɪst/ *n* fisioterapista *mf*

physiotherapy /fɪzɪəʊˈθerəpɪ/ *n* fisioterapia *f*

physique /fɪˈziːk/ *n* fisico *m*

pianist /ˈpɪənɪst/ *n* pianista *mf*

piano /pɪˈænəʊ/ *n* piano *m*

pianola® /pɪəˈnəʊlə/ *n* pianola® *f*

piazza /pɪˈætsə/ *n* (public square) piazza *f*; Am (veranda) veranda *f*

pick[1] /pɪk/ *n* (tool) piccone *m*

◊ **pick**[2] **1** *n* scelta *f*; take your ~ prendi quello che vuoi **2** *vt* (select) scegliere; cogliere ‹flowers›; scassinare ‹lock›; borseggiare ‹pockets›; ⋯⋗

~ **one's nose** mettersi le dita nel naso; ~ **a quarrel** attaccar briga; ~ **holes in something** fam (criticize) criticare qualcosa

3 *vi* ~ **and choose** fare il difficile

■ **pick at** *vt* piluccare ‹food›; stuzzicare ‹scab›

■ **pick off** *vt* (remove) togliere

■ **pick on** *vt* fam (nag) assillare; **he always** ~**s on me** ce l'ha con me

■ **pick out** *vt* (identify) individuare

■ **pick up** 1 *vt* sollevare; raccogliere ‹fallen object, information›; prendere in braccio ‹baby›; prendere ‹passengers, habit›; ‹police› arrestare ‹criminal›; fam rimorchiare ‹girl›; prendersi ‹illness›; captare ‹signal›; (buy) comprare; (learn) imparare; (collect) andare/venire a prendere; ~ **oneself up** riprendersi

2 *vi* (improve) recuperare; ‹weather› rimettersi

pickaxe /'pɪkæks/ *n* piccone *m*

picker /'pɪkə(r)/ *n* raccoglitore, -trice *mf*

picket /'pɪkɪt/ 1 *n* picchettista *mf*

2 *vt* picchettare

picket line *n* picchetto *m*

pickings /'pɪkɪŋz/ *npl* **rich** ~ grossi guadagni

pickle /'pɪkl/ 1 *n* ~**s** *pl* sottaceti *mpl*; **in a** ~ fig nei pasticci

2 *vt* mettere sottaceto

pick-me-up *n* (alcohol) cicchetto *m*; (medicine) tonico *m*

pickpocket /'pɪkpɒkɪt/ *n* borsaiolo *m*

pick-up *n* (truck) furgone *m*; (on record-player) pickup *m inv*

picky /'pɪkɪ/ *adj* fam (choosy, fussy) difficile

picnic /'pɪknɪk/ 1 *n* picnic *m*

2 *vi* (*pt/pp* **-nicked**) fare un picnic

pictogram /'pɪktəgræm/ *n* (symbol) pittogramma *m*; (chart) tabella *f*

pictorial /pɪk'tɔːrɪəl/ *adj* illustrato

⚘ **picture** /'pɪktʃə(r)/ 1 *n* (painting) quadro *m*; (photo) fotografia *f*; (drawing) disegno *m*; (film) film *m inv*; **as pretty as a** ~ ‹girl› bella come una madonna; **put somebody in the** ~ fig mettere qualcuno al corrente; **the** ~**s** Br fam il cinema

2 *vt* (imagine) immaginare

picture [card] *n* (in pack of cards) figura *f*

picture messaging *n* Teleph picture messaging *m inv*

picturesque /pɪktʃə'resk/ *adj* pittoresco

piddle /'pɪdl/ *vi* fam fare pipì

pie /paɪ/ *n* torta *f*

⚘ **piece** /piːs/ *n* pezzo *m*; (in game) pedina *f*; **a** ~ **of bread/paper** un pezzo di pane/carta; **a** ~ **of news/advice/junk** una notizia/un consiglio/una patacca; **take to** ~**s** smontare

■ **piece together** *vt* montare; fig ricostruire

piecemeal /'piːsmiːl/ *adv* un po' alla volta

piecework /'piːswɜːk/ *n* lavoro *m* a cottimo

pie chart *n* grafico *f* a torta

Piedmont /'piːdmɒnt/ *n* Piemonte *m*

pier /pɪə(r)/ *n* molo *m*; (pillar) pilastro *m*

pierce /pɪəs/ *vt* perforare; ~ **a hole in something** fare un buco in qualcosa

piercing /'pɪəsɪŋ/ 1 *adj* penetrante

2 *n* (in body) piercing *m inv*

pig /pɪg/ *n* maiale *m*

■ **pig out** *vi* fam abbuffarsi; ~ **out on** abbuffarsi di

pigeon /'pɪdʒɪn/ *n* piccione *m*

pigeon-hole 1 *n* casella *f*

2 *vt* incasellare

pigeon-toed /-təʊd/ *adj* **be** ~ camminare con i piedi in dentro

piggery /'pɪgərɪ/ *n* (pigsty) porcile *m*; fam (overeating) ingordigia *f*

piggyback /'pɪgɪbæk/ *n* **give somebody a** ~ portare qualcuno sulle spalle

piggy bank /'pɪgɪ/ *n* salvadanaio *m*

pig-headed /-'hedɪd/ *adj* fam cocciuto

piglet /'pɪglət/ *n* maialino *m*, porcellino *m*

pigment /'pɪgmənt/ *n* pigmento *m*

pigmentation /pɪgmən'teɪʃn/ *n* pigmentazione *f*

pigpen *n* Am = PIGSTY

pigskin /'pɪgskɪn/ *n* pelle *f* di cinghiale

pigsty *n* Br porcile *m*

pigtail /'pɪgteɪl/ *n* (plait) treccina *f*

pike /paɪk/ *n inv* (fish) luccio *m*

pilchard /'pɪltʃəd/ *n* sardina *f*

pile /paɪl/ 1 *n* (heap) pila *f*

2 *vt* ~ **something on to the something** impilare qualcosa su qualcosa

■ **pile in** *vi* (enter, get on) entrare disordinatamente

■ **pile up** 1 *vt* accatastare

2 *vi* ammucchiarsi

piles /paɪlz/ *npl* emorroidi *fpl*

pile-up *n* tamponamento *m* a catena

pilfer /'pɪlfə(r)/ *vi/t* rubacchiare

pilfering /'pɪlfərɪŋ/ *n* piccoli furti *mpl*

pilgrim /'pɪlgrɪm/ *n* pellegrino, -a *mf*

pilgrimage /'pɪlgrɪmɪdʒ/ *n* pellegrinaggio *m*

pill /pɪl/ *n* pillola *f*

pillage /'pɪlɪdʒ/ *vt* saccheggiare

pillar /'pɪlə(r)/ *n* pilastro *m*

pillar box *n* buca *f* delle lettere

pillion /'pɪljən/ *n* sellino *m* posteriore; **ride** ~ viaggiare dietro

pillory /'pɪlərɪ/ *vt* (*pt/pp* **-ied**) fig mettere alla berlina

pillow /'pɪləʊ/ *n* guanciale *m*

pillowcase /'pɪləʊkeɪs/ *n* federa *f*

⚘ **pilot** /'paɪlət/ 1 *n* pilota *mf*

2 *vt* pilotare

⚘ indicates a very frequent word

pilot light *n* fiamma *f* di sicurezza
pilot scheme *n* progetto *m* pilota *inv*
pimp /pɪmp/ *n* protettore *m*
pimple /'pɪmpl/ *n* foruncolo *m*
pimply /'pɪmplɪ/ *adj* brufoloso
pin /pɪn/ **1** *n* spillo *m*; (electr) spinotto *m*; Med chiodo *m*; **I have ~s and needles in my leg** fam mi formicola una gamba **2** *vt* (*pt/pp* **pinned**) appuntare (**to/on** su); (sewing) fissare con gli spilli; (hold down) immobilizzare; **~ something on somebody** fam addossare a qualcuno la colpa di qualcosa
▪ **pin down** *vt* (physically) immobilizzare; (to date) far fissare una data a ‹*somebody*›; (identify) definire ‹*feeling, cause*›
▪ **pin up** *vt* appuntare; (on wall) affiggere
PIN /pɪn/ *n abbr* (**personal Identification number**) [numero *m* di] codice *m* segreto
pinafore /'pɪnəfɔː(r)/ *n* grembiule *m*
pinafore dress *n* scamiciato *m*
pinball /'pɪnbɔːl/ *n* flipper *m inv*
pinball machine *n* flipper *m inv*
pincers /'pɪnsəz/ *npl* tenaglie *fpl*
pinch /pɪntʃ/ **1** *n* pizzicotto *m*; (of salt) presa *f*; **at a ~** fam in caso di bisogno **2** *vt* pizzicare; fam (steal) fregare **3** *vi* ‹*shoe*› stringere
pincushion /'pɪnkʊʃən/ *n* puntaspilli *m inv*
pine[1] /paɪn/ *n* (tree) pino *m*
pine[2] *vi* she is pining for you le manchi molto
▪ **pine away** *vi* deperire
pineapple *n* ananas *m inv*
pine cone *n* pigna *f*
pine-needle *n* ago *m* di pino
pine nut *n* pinolo *m*
ping /pɪŋ/ *n* rumore *m* metallico
ping-pong *n* ping-pong *m*
pinhead /'pɪnhed/ *n* capocchia *f* di spillo; fam pej testa *f* di rapa
pink /pɪŋk/ *adj* rosa *inv*
pinking shears, pinking scissors /'pɪŋkɪŋ/ *npl* forbici *fpl* a zigzag
pinnacle /'pɪnəkl/ *n* guglia *f*
PIN number *n* codice *m* segreto
pinpoint /'pɪnpɔɪnt/ *vt* definire con precisione
pinprick /'pɪnprɪk/ *n* puntura *f* di spillo; fig (of jealousy, remorse) punta *f*
pinstripe /'pɪnstraɪp/ *adj* gessato
pint /paɪnt/ *n* pinta *f* *Br = 0,57 l, Am = 0,47 l*; **a ~** fam una birra media
pin-up *n* ragazza *f* da copertina, pin-up *f inv*
pioneer /paɪə'nɪə(r)/ **1** *n* pioniere, -a *mf* **2** *vt* essere un pioniere di

pious /'paɪəs/ *adj* pio
pip[1] /pɪp/ *n* (seed) seme *m*
pip[2] *n* **the ~s** il segnale orario; (telephone) il segnale telefonico
pip[3] *vt* (*pt/pp* **pipped**) **be ~ped at the post** essere battuto all'ultimo minuto
pipe /paɪp/ **1** *n* tubo *m*; (for smoking) pipa *f*; **the ~s** *pl* Mus la cornamusa **2** *vt* far arrivare con tubature ‹*water: gas etc*›; Culin mettere
▪ **pipe down** *vi* fam abbassare la voce; (shut up) stare zitto
▪ **pipe up**: *vi* **~ with a suggestion** venir fuori con una proposta
pipe-cleaner *n* scovolino *m*
piped music /paɪpt/ *n* musichetta *f* di sottofondo
pipe dream *n* illusione *f*
pipeline /'paɪplaɪn/ *n* conduttura *f*; **in the ~** fam in cantiere
piper /'paɪpə(r)/ *n* suonatore *m* di cornamusa
piping /'paɪpɪŋ/ *adj* **~ hot** bollente
pique /piːk/ *n* **in a fit of ~** risentito
piracy /'paɪrəsɪ/ *n* pirateria *f*
piranha /pɪ'rɑːnə/ *n* piranha *m*
pirate /'paɪrət/ **1** *n* pirata *m* **2** *vt* pirateggiare
pirate copy *n* copia *f* pirata
pirated /'paɪrətɪd/ *adj* pirateggiato
pirate radio *n* radio *f* pirata
pirouette /pɪru'et/ **1** *n* piroetta *f* **2** *vi* piroettare
Pisces /'paɪsiːz/ *n* Astr Pesci *mpl*
piss /pɪs/ **1** *sl n* piscia *f* **2** *vi* pisciare
▪ **piss about, piss around** **1** *vi* (waste time, play the fool) cazzeggiare **2** *vt* **~ somebody about** rompere le palle a qualcuno
▪ **piss down**: *vi sl* **it's ~ing down** (raining heavily) piove a dirotto
▪ **piss off** **1** *sl vt* fare incacchiare; **that type of behaviour ~es me off** questi comportamenti mi stanno sulle palle **2** *vi* (leave) filarsela; **~ off!** levati dalle palle!, va' a cagare!
pissed /pɪst/ *adj* sl sbronzo; **~ as a newt** sbronzo come una cocuzza
pissed off *adj* sl scoglionato
pistachio [nut] /pɪ'stæʃɪəʊ/ *n* pistacchio *m*
pistol /'pɪstl/ *n* pistola *f*
piston /'pɪstn/ *n* Techn pistone *m*
pit /pɪt/ **1** *n* fossa *f*; (mine) miniera *f*; (for orchestra) orchestra *f*; (of stomach) bocca *f* **2** *vt* (*pt/pp* **pitted**) fig opporre (**against** a)
pit-a-pat /'pɪtəpæt/ *n* **go ~** ‹*heart*› palpitare
pitbull [terrier] *n* pitbull *m inv*

p

pitch¹ /pɪtʃ/ **1** n (tone) tono m; (level) altezza f; (in sport) campo m; fig (degree) grado m
2 vt montare ‹tent›

pitch² n (substance) pece f
∎ **pitch in** vi fam mettersi sotto

pitch-black adj nero come la pece; ‹night› buio pesto

pitch-dark adj buio pesto

pitcher /'pɪtʃə(r)/ n brocca f

pitchfork /'pɪtʃfɔːk/ n forca f

piteous /'pɪtɪəs/ adj pietoso

pitfall /'pɪtfɔːl/ n fig trabocchetto m

pith /pɪθ/ n (of lemon, orange) interno m della buccia; fig essenza f

pithy /'pɪθɪ/ adj (**-ier, -iest**) fig conciso

pitiable /'pɪtɪəbl/ adj pietoso

pitiful /'pɪtɪfl/ adj pietoso

pitifully /'pɪtɪfʊlɪ/ adv da far pietà

pitiless /'pɪtɪlɪs/ adj spietato

pitilessly /'pɪtɪlɪslɪ/ adv senza pietà

pittance /'pɪtns/ n miseria f

pitted /'pɪtɪd/ adj ‹surface› bucherellato; ‹face, skin› butterato; ‹olive› snocciolato

pituitary /pɪ'tjuːɪt(ə)rɪ/ adj pituitario

pituitary gland n ghiandola f pituitaria, ipofisi f

pity /'pɪtɪ/ **1** n pietà f; **[what a]** ∼**!** che peccato!; **take** ∼ **on** avere compassione di
2 vt aver pietà di

pivot /'pɪvət/ **1** n perno m; fig fulcro m
2 vi imperniarsi (**on** su)

pivotal /'pɪvətl/ adj ‹role› centrale; ‹decision› cruciale

pixel /'pɪksəl/ n pixel m inv

pixie /'pɪksɪ/ n folletto m

pizza /'piːtsə/ n pizza f

placard /'plækɑːd/ n cartellone m

placate /plə'keɪt/ vt placare

✓ **place** /pleɪs/ **1** n posto m; fam (house) casa f; (in book) segno m; **feel out of** ∼ sentirsi fuori posto; **take** ∼ aver luogo; **all over the** ∼ dappertutto
2 vt collocare; (remember) identificare; ∼ **an order** fare un'ordinazione; **be** ∼**d** (in race) piazzarsi

placebo /plə'siːbəʊ/ n Med placebo m inv; fig contentino m

place mat n sottopiatto m

placement /'pleɪsmənt/ n (act: in accommodation) collocamento m; Br (job) stage m inv

place name n toponimo m

placenta /plə'sentə/ n placenta f

placid /'plæsɪd/ adj placido

plagiarism /'pleɪdʒərɪzm/ n plagio m

plagiarist /'pleɪdʒərɪst/ n plagiario, -a mf

✓ indicates a very frequent word

plagiarize /'pleɪdʒəraɪz/ vt plagiare

plague /pleɪg/ n peste f

plaice /pleɪs/ n inv platessa f

plaid /plæd/ **1** n (fabric) plaid m inv; (pattern) motivo m scozzese
2 attrib ‹scarf, shirt› scozzese

plain /pleɪn/ **1** adj chiaro; (simple) semplice; (not pretty) scialbo; (not patterned) in tinta unita; ‹chocolate› fondente; **in** ∼ **clothes** in borghese
2 adv (simply) semplicemente
3 n pianura f

plain-clothes adj ‹policeman etc› in borghese

plainly /'pleɪnlɪ/ adv francamente; (simply) semplicemente; (obviously) chiaramente

plain paper fax n fax m inv a carta comune

plain-spoken adj franco

plaintiff /'pleɪntɪf/ n Jur parte f lesa

plaintive /'pleɪntɪv/ adj lamentoso

plaintively /'pleɪntɪvlɪ/ adv con aria lamentosa

plait /plæt/ **1** n treccia f
2 vt intrecciare

✓ **plan** /plæn/ **1** n progetto m, piano m
2 vt (pt/pp **planned**) progettare; (intend) prevedere
∎ **plan ahead** vi pianificare

plane¹ /pleɪn/ n (tree) platano m

✓ **plane²** /pleɪn/ n aeroplano m; (in geometry) piano m

plane³ **1** n (tool) pialla f
2 vt piallare

plane crash n incidente m aereo

✓ **planet** /'plænɪt/ n pianeta m

plank /plæŋk/ n asse f
∎ **plank down** vt fam (put down) mollare

plankton /'plæŋktən/ n plancton m

planner /'plænə(r)/ n progettista mf; (in town planning) urbanista mf

✓ **planning** /'plænɪŋ/ n pianificazione f

planning permission n licenza f edilizia

✓ **plant** /plɑːnt/ **1** n pianta f; (machinery) impianto m; (factory) stabilimento m
2 vt piantare; ∼ **oneself in front of somebody** piantarsi davanti a qualcuno

plantation /plæn'teɪʃn/ n piantagione f

planter /'plɑːntə(r)/ n (person) piantatore, -trice mf; (machine) piantatrice f

plant life n flora f

plaque /plɑːk/ n placca f

plasma /'plæzmə/ n plasma m

plasma screen n schermo m al plasma

plaster /'plɑːstə(r)/ **1** n intonaco m; Med gesso m; (sticking ∼) cerotto m; **in** ∼ ingessato
2 vt intonacare ‹wall›; (cover) ricoprire

plaster cast n ingessatura f

plastered /'plɑːstəd/ *adj* sl (drunk) sbronzo

plasterer /'plɑːstərə(r)/ *n* intonacatore *m*

plaster of Paris *n* gesso *m*

plastic /'plæstɪk/ **1** *n* plastica *f*
2 *adj* plastico

Plasticine® /'plæstɪsiːn/ *n* Plastilina® *f*

plastic surgeon *n* chirurgo *m* plastico

plastic surgery *n* chirurgia *f* plastica

✧ **plate** /pleɪt/ **1** *n* piatto *m;* (flat sheet) placca *f;* (gold and silverware) argenteria *f;* (in book) tavola *f* fuori testo
2 *vt* (cover with metal) placcare

plateau /'plætəʊ/ **1** *n* (*pl* ∼**x** /'plætəʊz/) altopiano *m*
2 *vi* fig livellarsi

plate glass *n* lastra *f* di vetro

platform /'plætfɔːm/ *n* (stage) palco *m;* Rail marciapiede *m;* Pol piattaforma *f;* ∼ **5** binario 5

platform shoes *npl* scarpe *fpl* con la zeppa

platinum /'plætɪnəm/ **1** *n* platino *m*
2 *attr ib* di platino

platinum blonde *n* bionda *f* platinata

platitude /'plætɪtjuːd/ *n* luogo *m* comune

platonic /plə'tɒnɪk/ *adj* platonico

platoon /plə'tuːn/ *n* Mil plotone *m*

platter /'plætə(r)/ *n* piatto *m* da portata

platypus /'plætɪpəs/ *n* ornitorinco *m*

plausibility /plɔːzɪ'bɪlɪtɪ/ *n* plausibilità *f*

plausible /'plɔːzəbl/ *adj* plausibile

✧ **play** /pleɪ/ **1** *n* gioco *m;* Theat, TV dramma *m*, opera *f* teatrale; (performance) rappresentazione *f;* Radio sceneggiato *m* radiofonico; ∼**on words** gioco *m* di parole
2 *vt* giocare a; (act) recitare; suonare (instrument); giocare (card)
3 *vi* giocare; Mus suonare; ∼ **by the rules** stare alle regole; ∼ **with fire** scherzare col fuoco; ∼ **dumb** fare lo gnorri; ∼ **safe** non prendere rischi
■ **play along:** *vi* ∼ **along with somebody** fam (cooperate) fare il gioco di qualcuno
■ **play around with** *vt* (meddle with) cincischiarsi con
■ **play back** *vt* riascoltare (recording)
■ **play down** *vt* minimizzare
■ **play on 1** *vi* (continue to play) continuare a giocare
2 *vt* (exploit) giocare su
■ **play out** *vt* vivere (drama, fantasy)
■ **play up** *vi* fam fare i capricci

play-acting *n* commedia *f*

playboy /'pleɪbɔɪ/ *n* playboy *m inv*

✧ **player** /'pleɪə(r)/ *n* giocatore, -trice *mf*

playful /'pleɪfʊl/ *adj* scherzoso

playfully /'pleɪfʊlɪ/ *adv* in modo scherzoso

playground /'pleɪɡraʊnd/ *n* Sch cortile *m* (*per la ricreazione*)

playgroup /'pleɪɡruːp/ *n* asilo *m*

playhouse *n* casetta *f* per i giochi

playing card /'pleɪɪŋ/ *n* carta *f* da gioco

playing field *n* campo *m* da gioco

playlist *n* playlist *f*

playmate *n* compagno, -a *mf* di gioco

play-off /'pleɪɒf/ *n* play off *m inv*

playpen *n* box *m inv*

playroom /'pleɪruːm/ *n* ludoteca *f*

plaything *n* giocattolo *m*

playtime *n* ricreazione *f*

playwright /'pleɪraɪt/ *n* drammaturgo, -a *mf*

plaza /'plɑːzə/ *n* (public square) piazza *f;* Am (services point) area *f* di servizio; Am (toll point) casello *m;* **shopping** ∼ centro *m* commerciale

plc *abbr* (**public limited company**) s.r.l.

plea /pliː/ *n* richiesta *f;* **enter a** ∼ **of not guilty** Jur dichiararsi non colpevole; **make a** ∼ **for** fare un appello a

plead /pliːd/ **1** *vi* fare appello (**for** a); ∼ **guilty** dichiararsi colpevole; ∼ **with somebody** implorare qualcuno
2 *vt* Jur perorare (case)

pleasant /'pleznt/ *adj* piacevole

pleasantly /'plezntlɪ/ *adv* piacevolmente; (say, smile) cordialmente

pleasantry /'plezntrɪ/ *n* (joke) battuta *f;* **pleasantries** *pl* (polite remarks) convenevoli *mpl*

✧ **please** /pliːz/ **1** *adv* per favore; ∼ **do** prego
2 *vt* far contento; ∼ **oneself** fare il proprio comodo; ∼ **yourself!** come vuoi!; pej fai come ti pare!

pleased /pliːzd/ *adj* lieto; ∼ **with/about** contento di

pleasing /'pliːzɪŋ/ *adj* gradevole

pleasurable /'pleʒərəbl/ *adj* gradevole

pleasure /'pleʒə(r)/ *n* piacere *m;* **with** ∼ con piacere, volentieri

pleat /pliːt/ **1** *n* piega *f*
2 *vt* pieghettare

pleated /'pliːtɪd/ *adj* a pieghe

pleb /pleb/ *n* fam plebeo, -a *mf*

plebby /'plebɪ/ *adj* fam plebeo

plebeian /plɪ'biːən/ pej **1** *n* plebeo, -a *mf*
2 *adj* plebeo

plebiscite /'plebɪsaɪt/ *n* plebiscito *m*

pledge /pledʒ/ **1** *n* pegno *m;* (promise) promessa *f*
2 *vt* (pawn) impegnare; ∼ **to do something** impegnarsi a fare qualcosa

plenary /'pliːnərɪ/ *adj* (session) plenario; (powers) pieno; (authority) assoluto

plentiful /'plentɪfl/ *adj* abbondante

✧ **plenty** /'plentɪ/ *n* abbondanza *f;* ∼ **of money** molti soldi; ∼ **of people** molta gente; **I've got** ∼ ne ho in abbondanza

p

pleurisy /'pluərəsı/ n pleurite f

pliability /plaıə'bılıtı/ n flessibilità f

pliable /'plaıəbl/ adj flessibile

pliers /'plaıəz/ npl pinze fpl

plight /plaıt/ n triste condizione f

plimsolls /'plımsɒlz/ npl scarpe fpl da ginnastica

plinth /plınθ/ n plinto m

plod /plɒd/ vi (pt/pp **plodded**) trascinarsi; (work hard) sgobbare

■ **plod away** vi (work hard) sgobbare; ∼ **away at** sgobbare su

plodder /'plɒdə(r)/ n sgobbone, -a mf

plonk¹ /plɒŋk/ n fam vino m; (poor wine) vinaccio m

plonk² vt fam (put) sbattere

plop /plɒp/ ① n plop m inv
② vi (pt/pp **plopped**) fare plop

⚹ **plot** /plɒt/ ① n complotto m; (of novel) trama f; ∼ **of land** appezzamento m [di terreno]
② vt/i (pt/pp **plotted**) complottare

plotter /'plɒtə(r)/ n (schemer) cospiratore, -trice mf; Comput plotter m inv, tracciatore m

plough /plaʊ/ ① n aratro m
② vt/i arare

■ **plough back** vt Comm reinvestire

■ **plough into** vt (crash into) schiantarsi contro

■ **plough through** vt procedere a fatica in

ploughman /'plaʊmən/ n aratore m

ploughman's lunch n Br piatto (m) freddo a base di pane, formaggio e sottaceti

plow /plaʊ/ Am ① n aratro m
② vt/i arare

ploy /plɔı/ n fam manovra f

pluck /plʌk/ ① n fegato m
② vt strappare; depilare ⟨eyebrows⟩; spennare ⟨bird⟩; cogliere ⟨flower⟩

■ **pluck up**: vt ∼ **up courage** farsi coraggio

plucky /'plʌkı/ adj (-ier, -iest) coraggioso

plug /plʌg/ ① n tappo m; Electr spina f; Auto candela f; fam (advertisement) pubblicità f inv
② vt (pt/pp **plugged**) tappare; fam (advertise) pubblicizzare

■ **plug away** vi (work hard) lavorare sodo

■ **plug in** vt Electr inserire la spina di

plug and play n Comput plug and play m inv

plughole /'plʌghəʊl/ n Br scarico m

plug-in adj con la spina

plum /plʌm/ n susina f; (tree) susino m

plumage /'plu:mıdʒ/ n piumaggio m

plumb /plʌm/ ① adj verticale
② adv esattamente

■ **plumb in** vt collegare

plumber /'plʌmə(r)/ n idraulico m

plumbing /'plʌmıŋ/ n impianto m idraulico

plumb line n filo m a piombo

plume /plu:m/ n piuma f

plummet /'plʌmıt/ vi precipitare; ⟨prices⟩ crollare

plump /plʌmp/ adj paffuto

■ **plump down** vt (put down) lasciare cadere

■ **plump for** vt scegliere

plumpness /'plʌmpnıs/ n rotondità f

plunder /'plʌndə(r)/ ① n (booty) bottino m
② vt saccheggiare

plunge /plʌndʒ/ ① n tuffo m; **take the** ∼ fam buttarsi
② vt tuffare; fig sprofondare; ∼ **somebody into despair** piombare qualcuno nella disperazione
③ vi tuffarsi

plunger /'plʌndʒə(r)/ n (tool) sturalavandini m inv; (handle) stantuffo m

plunging /'plʌndʒıŋ/ adj ∼ **neckline** scollatura f profonda

pluperfect /plu:'pɜ:fıkt/ n trapassato m prossimo

plural /'plʊərəl/ adj & n plurale m

⚹ **plus** /plʌs/ ① prep più
② adj in più; **500** ∼ più di 500
③ n più m; (advantage) extra m inv

plush /plʌʃ/ adj ⟨hotel etc⟩ lussuoso

plus sign n (segno m) più m inv

Pluto /'plu:təʊ/ n Plutone m

plutonium /plu:'təʊnıəm/ n plutonio m

ply /plaı/ vt (pt/pp **plied**) esercitare ⟨trade⟩; ∼ **somebody with drink** continuare ad offrire da bere a qualcuno

plywood /'plaıwʊd/ n compensato m

PM abbr (**Prime Minister**) primo ministro

p.m. abbr (**post meridiem**) del pomeriggio

PMS n abbr (**premenstrual syndrome**) sindrome f premestruale

PMT n abbr (**premenstrual tension**) tensione f premestruale

pneumatic /nju:'mætık/ adj pneumatico

pneumatic drill n martello m pneumatico

pneumonia /nju:'məʊnıə/ n polmonite f

PO abbr 1 (**Post Office**) ≈ P.T.
2 (**postal order**) vaglia m inv postale

poach /pəʊtʃ/ vt Culin bollire; cacciare di frodo ⟨deer⟩; pescare di frodo ⟨salmon⟩; ∼**ed egg** uovo m in camicia

poacher /'pəʊtʃə(r)/ n bracconiere m

PO Box n abbr (**Post Office Box**) C.P. f

⚹ **pocket** /'pɒkıt/ ① n tasca f; ∼ **of resistance** sacca f di resistenza; **be out of** ∼ rimetterci
② vt intascare

pocket-book n taccuino m; (wallet) portafoglio m

⚹ indicates a very frequent word

pocket-money n denaro m per le piccole spese

pock-marked /'pɒkmɑːkt/ adj butterato

pod /pɒd/ n baccello m

podcast /'pɒdkɑːst/ n file messo a disposizione su internet per chiunque si abboni a una trasmissione periodica e scaricabile da un apposito programma

podcaster /'pɒdkɑːstə(r)/ n persona che registra e crea un podcast

podgy /'pɒdʒɪ/ adj (-ier, -iest) grassoccio

podiatrist /pə'daɪətrɪst/ n Am pedicure mf inv

podium /'pəʊdɪəm/ n podio m

⚘ **poem** /'pəʊɪm/ n poesia f

poet /'pəʊɪt/ n poeta m

poetic /pəʊ'etɪk/ adj poetico

poetic licence n licenza f poetica

Poet Laureate /'lɔːrɪət/ n poeta m laureato

poetry /'pəʊɪtrɪ/ n poesia f

po-faced /pəʊ'feɪst/ adj Br fam look/be ~ avore un'aria di disapprovazione

poignancy /'pɔɪnjənsɪ/ n pregnanza f

poignant /'pɔɪnjənt/ adj pregnante

⚘ **point** /pɔɪnt/ ① n punto m; (sharp end) punta f; (meaning, purpose) senso m; Electr presa f; **what is the ~?** a che scopo?; **the ~ is** il fatto è; **I don't see the ~** non vedo il senso; **up to a ~** fino ad un certo punto; **be on the ~ of doing something** essere sul punto di fare qualcosa; **~s** pl Rail scambio m; **good/bad ~s** aspetti mpl positivi/negativi ② vt puntare (**at** verso) ③ vi (with finger) puntare il dito; **~ at/to** ‹person› mostrare col dito; ‹indicator› indicare; **~ and click** Comput punta e clicca ▪ **point out** vt far notare ‹fact›; **~ something out to somebody** far notare qualcosa a qualcuno

point-blank adj a bruciapelo

pointed /'pɔɪntɪd/ adj appuntito; ‹question› diretto

pointer /'pɔɪntə(r)/ n (piece of advice) consiglio m

pointillism /'pwæntɪlɪzm/ n divisionismo m

pointillist /'pwæntɪlɪst/ n divisionista mf

pointing /'pɔɪntɪŋ/ n Constr rifinitura f con la malta

pointing device n Comput dispositivo m di puntamento

pointless /'pɔɪntlɪs/ adj inutile

point of order n mozione f d'ordine

point of sale n (place) punto m di vendita; (promotional material) materiale m pubblicitario

point-of-sale promotion n promozione f punto vendita

point of view n punto m di vista

poise /pɔɪz/ n padronanza f

poised /pɔɪzd/ adj in equilibrio; (composed) padrone di sé; ~ **to** sul punto di

poison /'pɔɪzn/ ① n veleno m ② vt avvelenare

poisoned /'pɔɪz(ə)nd/ adj avvelenato

poisoner /'pɔɪzənə(r)/ n avvelenatore, -trice mf

poisonous /'pɔɪzənəs/ adj velenoso

poison-pen letter n lettera f anonima diffamatoria

poke /pəʊk/ ① n spintarella f ② vt spingere; ‹fire› attizzare; (put) ficcare; ~ **fun at** prendere in giro ▪ **poke about, poke around** vi frugare ▪ **poke out** vi (protrude) spuntare

poker[1] /'pəʊkə(r)/ n attizzatoio m

poker[2] n Cards poker m

poker-faced /-'feɪst/ adj ‹person› impassibile

poky /'pəʊkɪ/ adj (-ier, -iest) angusto

Poland /'pəʊlənd/ n Polonia f

polar /'pəʊlə(r)/ adj polare

polar bear n orso m bianco

polarity /pə'lærətɪ/ n Electr, Phys fig polarità f inv

polarize /'pəʊləraɪz/ vt polarizzare

polarized adj polarizzato

pole[1] n palo m

pole[2] n Geog, Electr polo m

Pole /pəʊl/ n polacco, -a mf

pole dancing /'pəʊl ˌdɑːnsɪŋ/ n pole dance f

polemic /pə'lemɪk/ n polemica f

polemical /pə'lemɪkl/ adj polemico

pole star n stella f polare

pole vault n salto m con l'asta

⚘ **police** /pə'liːs/ ① npl polizia f ② vt pattugliare ‹area›; sorvegliare ‹behaviour›

police car n gazzella f

police constable n agente mf di polizia

Police Department n Am dipartimento m di polizia

police force n polizia f

policeman n poliziotto m

police officer n agente mf di polizia

police state n stato m militarista

police station n commissariato m

policewoman n donna f poliziotto

policing /pə'liːsɪŋ/ n (maintaining law and order) mantenimento m dell'ordine pubblico; (of demonstration, match) organizzazione f del servizio d'ordine

⚘ **policy**[1] /'pɒlɪsɪ/ n politica f

policy[2] n (insurance) polizza f

policyholder n titolare mf della polizza

policy unit n Pol comitato m responsabile della linea politica

p

polio /'pəʊlɪəʊ/ n polio f

polish /'pɒlɪʃ/ **1** n (shine) lucentezza f; (substance) lucido m; (for nails) smalto m; fig raffinatezza f

2 vt lucidare; fig smussare

■ **polish off** vt fam finire; far fuori ‹food›
■ **polish up** vt rispolverare ‹Italian›

Polish /'pəʊlɪʃ/ adj & n polacco m

polished /'pɒlɪʃt/ adj ‹manner› raffinato; ‹performance› senza sbavature

polisher /'pɒləʃə(r)/ n (machine) lucidatrice f

polite /pə'laɪt/ adj cortese

politely /pə'laɪtlɪ/ adv cortesemente

politeness /pə'laɪtnɪs/ n cortesia f

politic /'pɒlɪtɪk/ adj prudente

✧ **political** /pə'lɪtɪkl/ adj politico

politically /pə'lɪtɪklɪ/ adv dal punto di vista politico; **∼ correct** politicamente corretto

political prisoner n prigioniero, -a mf politico

✧ **politician** /pɒlɪ'tɪʃn/ n politico m

politicize /pə'lɪtɪsaɪz/ vt politicizzare

✧ **politics** /'pɒlɪtɪks/ n politica f

polka /'pɒlkə/ n polka f

polka dot **1** n pois m inv, pallino m
2 attrib a pois

✧ **poll** /pəʊl/ **1** n votazione f; (election) elezioni fpl; [opinion] ∼ sondaggio m d'opinione; **go to the ∼s** andare alle urne
2 vt ottenere ‹votes›

pollen /'pɒlən/ n polline m

polling booth /'pəʊlɪŋ/ n cabina f elettorale

polling day n giorno m delle elezioni

polling station n seggio m elettorale

pollster /'pəʊlstə(r)/ n (person) persona f che esegue un sondaggio d'opinione

poll tax n imposta (f) locale sulle persone fisiche

pollutant /pə'lu:tənt/ n sostanza f inquinante

pollute /pə'lu:t/ vt inquinare

polluted /pə'lu:tɪd/ adj inquinato

polluter /pə'lu:tə(r)/ n inquinatore, -trice mf

pollution /pə'lu:ʃn/ n inquinamento m

polo /'pəʊləʊ/ n polo m

polo neck n collo m alto

polo shirt n dolcevita f

poltergeist /'pɒltəgaɪst/ n poltergeist m inv

poly /'pɒlɪ/ n Br fam (polytechnic) politecnico m

poly bag n sacchetto m di plastica

polyester /pɒlɪ'estə(r)/ n poliestere m

polygamous /pə'lɪgəməs/ adj poligamico

polygamy /pə'lɪgəmɪ/ n poligamia f

polymath /'pɒlɪmæθ/ n erudito, -a mf

polymer /'pɒlɪmə(r)/ n polimero m

polystyrene® /pɒlɪ'staɪri:n/ n polistirolo m

polytechnic /pɒlɪ'teknɪk/ n politecnico m

polythene /'pɒlɪθi:n/ n politene m

polythene bag n sacchetto m di plastica

polyunsaturates /pɒlɪʌn'sætjʊreɪts/ npl grassi mpl polinsaturi

pomade /pə'meɪd/ n pomata f

pomegranate /'pɒmɪgrænɪt/ n melagrana f

pomp /pɒmp/ n pompa f

pompom /'pɒmpɒm/, **pompon** n pompon m

pomposity /pɒm'pɒsətɪ/ n pomposità f

pompous /'pɒmpəs/ adj pomposo

pompously /'pɒmpəslɪ/ adv pomposamente

poncy /'pɒnsɪ/ adj fam da finocchio; ‹person› finocchio

pond /pɒnd/ n stagno m

ponder /'pɒndə(r)/ vt/i ponderare

ponderous /'pɒndərəs/ adj ponderoso; fig pesante

pong /pɒŋ/ **1** n fam puzza f
2 vi puzzare

pontiff /'pɒntɪf/ n pontefice m

pontificate /pɒn'tɪfɪkeɪt/ vi pontificare

pontoon /pɒn'tu:n/ n (float) galleggiante m; (pier) pontile m; Br (game) ventuno m

pony /'pəʊnɪ/ n pony m inv

ponytail /'pəʊnɪteɪl/ n coda f di cavallo

pony-trekking /'pəʊnɪtrekɪŋ/ n escursioni fpl col pony

pooch /pu:tʃ/ n fam (dog) cagnetto m

poodle /'pu:dl/ n barboncino m

poof /pʊf/, **poofter** /'pʊftə(r)/ n Br fam (homosexual) finocchio m

pooh /pu:/ **1** int (scorn, disgust) puah!
2 n Br (baby talk) popò f inv

pooh-pooh /pu:'pu:/ vt fam ridere di ‹suggestion›

✧ **pool¹** /pu:l/ n (of water, blood) pozza f; [swimming] ∼ piscina f

pool² **1** n (common fund) cassa f comune; (in cards) piatto m; (game) biliardo m a buca; **∼s** pl ≈ totocalcio msg
2 vt mettere insieme

pool table n tavolo m da biliardo

pooped /pu:pt/ adj fam **be ∼ [out]** essere stanco morto

✧ **poor** /pʊə(r)/ **1** adj povero; (not good) scadente; **in ∼ health** in cattiva salute
2 npl **the ∼** i poveri

poorly /'pʊəlɪ/ **1** adj **be ∼** non stare bene
2 adv male

✧ indicates a very frequent word

p

pop¹ /pɒp/ **1** *n* botto *m*; (drink) bibita *f* gasata; (turn) **the tickets were £5 a ∼ i** biglietti costavano £5 l'uno
2 *vt* (*pt/pp* **popped**) fam (put) mettere; (burst) far scoppiare
3 *vi* (burst) scoppiare
■ **pop in** *vi* fam fare un salto
■ **pop out** *vi* fam uscire; ∼ **out to the shop** fare un salto al negozio
■ **pop round** *vi* fam passare; ∼ **round to Ann's** passare da Ann
■ **pop up** *vi* fam (appear unexpectedly) saltare fuori

pop² **1** *n* fam musica *f* pop
2 *attrib* pop *inv*

popcorn /'pɒpkɔːn/ *n* popcorn *m inv*
pope /pəʊp/ *n* papa *m*
poplar /'pɒplə(r)/ *n* pioppo *m*
poppy /'pɒpɪ/ *n* papavero *m*
pop sock *n* gambaletto *m*
populace /'pɒpjʊləs/ *n* popolo *m*
popular /'pɒpjʊlə(r)/ *adj* popolare; ‹belief› diffuso
popularity /pɒpjʊ'lærətɪ/ *n* popolarità *f*
popularize /'pɒpjʊləraɪz/ *vt* divulgare
populate /'pɒpjʊleɪt/ *vt* popolare
population /pɒpjʊ'leɪʃn/ *n* popolazione *f*
populist /'pɒpjʊlɪst/ *adj & n* populista *mf*
populous /'pɒpjʊləs/ *adj* popoloso
pop-up book *n* libro *m* con immagini tridimensionali
pop-up menu *n* Comput menu *m* a tendina
pop-up toaster *n* tostapane *m inv* a espulsione automatica
porcelain /'pɔːsəlɪn/ *n* porcellana *f*
porch /pɔːtʃ/ *n* portico *m*; Am veranda *f*
porcupine /'pɔːkjʊpaɪn/ *n* porcospino *m*
pore¹ /pɔː(r)/ *n* poro *m*
pore² *vi* ∼ **over** immergersi in
pork /pɔːk/ *n* carne *f* di maiale
porn /pɔːn/ *n* fam porno *m*
porno /'pɔːnəʊ/ *adj* fam porno *inv*
pornographic /pɔːnə'græfɪk/ *adj* pornografico
pornography /pɔː'nɒgrəfɪ/ *n* pornografia *f*
porous /'pɔːrəs/ *adj* poroso
porpoise /'pɔːpəs/ *n* focena *f*
porridge /'pɒrɪdʒ/ *n* farinata *f* di fiocchi d'avena
port¹ /pɔːt/ *n* porto *m*
port² *n* Naut (side) babordo *m*
port³ *n* (wine) porto *m*
portable /'pɔːtəbl/ *adj & n* portatile *m*
Portakabin® /'pɔːtəkæbɪn/ *n* casotto *m* prefabbricato
portcullis /pɔːt'kʌlɪs/ *n* saracinesca *f*
portentous /pɔː'tentəs/ *adj* (significant) solenne; (ominous) infausto

porter /'pɔːtə(r)/ *n* portiere *m*; (for luggage) facchino *m*
portfolio /pɔːt'fəʊlɪəʊ/ *n* cartella *f*; Comm portafoglio *m*
porthole /'pɔːthəʊl/ *n* oblò *m inv*
portion /'pɔːʃn/ *n* parte *f*; (of food) porzione *f*
portly /'pɔːtlɪ/ *adj* (**-ier**, **-iest**) corpulento
portrait /'pɔːtrɪt/ *n* ritratto *m*
portrait painter *n* ritrattista *mf*
portray /pɔː'treɪ/ *vt* ritrarre; (represent) descrivere; ‹actor› impersonare
portrayal /pɔː'treɪəl/ *n* ritratto *m*; (by actor) caratterizzazione *f*
Portugal /'pɔːtjʊgl/ *n* Portogallo *m*
Portuguese /pɔːtjʊ'giːz/ *adj & n* portoghese *mf*; (language) portoghese *m*
pose /pəʊz/ **1** *n* posa *f*
2 *vt* porre ‹problem, question›
3 *vi* (for painter) posare; ∼ **as** atteggiarsi a
poser /'pəʊzə(r)/ *n* fam (puzzle) rompicapo *m inv*; (person) montato, -a *mf*
posh /pɒʃ/ *adj* fam lussuoso; ‹people› danaroso
position /pə'zɪʃn/ **1** *n* posizione *f*; (job) posto *m*; (status) ceto *m* [sociale]
2 *vt* posizionare
positive /'pɒzɪtɪv/ **1** *adj* positivo; (certain) sicuro; (progress) concreto
2 *n* positivo *m*
positive discrimination *n* misure *fpl* antidiscriminatorie
positively /'pɒzɪtɪvlɪ/ *adv* positivamente; (decidedly) decisamente
posse /'pɒsɪ/ *n* gruppo *m* di volontari armati
possess /pə'zes/ *vt* possedere
possession /pə'zeʃn/ *n* possesso *m*; ∼**s** *pl* beni *mpl*
possessive /pə'zesɪv/ *adj* possessivo
possessiveness /pə'zesɪvnɪs/ *n* carattere *m* possessivo
possessor /pə'zesə(r)/ *n* possessore, -ditrice *mf*
possibility /pɒsə'bɪlətɪ/ *n* possibilità *f inv*
possible /'pɒsəbl/ *adj* possibile
possibly /'pɒsəblɪ/ *adv* possibilmente; **I couldn't ∼ accept** non mi è possibile accettare; **he can't ∼ be right** non è possibile che abbia ragione; **could you ∼…?** potrebbe per favore…?
possum /'pɒsəm/ *n* fam opossum *m inv*; **play ∼** far finta di dormire; (pretend to be dead) fare il morto
post¹ /pəʊst/ **1** *n* (pole) palo *m*
2 *vt* affiggere ‹notice›
post² **1** *n* (place of duty) posto *m*
2 *vt* appostare; (transfer) assegnare
post³ **1** *n* (mail) posta *f*; **by ∼** per posta
2 *vt* spedire; (put in letter box) imbucare;

⋯⟫

(as opposed to fax) mandare per posta; **keep somebody ~ed** tenere qualcuno al corrente

post+ *pref* post+

postage /'pəʊstɪdʒ/ *n* affrancatura *f*; **~ and packaging** spese *fpl* di posta

postage stamp *n* francobollo *m*

postal /'pəʊstl/ *adj* postale

postal order *n* vaglia *m inv* postale

postbox *n* cassetta *f* delle lettere

postcard *n* cartolina *f*

postcode *n* codice *m* postale

post-date *vt* postdatare

poster /'pəʊstə(r)/ *n* poster *m inv*; (advertising, election) cartellone *m*

posterior /pɒ'stɪərɪə(r)/ *n fam* posteriore *m*

posterity /pɒ'sterətɪ/ *n* posterità *f*

poster paint *n* pittura *f* a guazzo

postgraduate /pəʊs(t)'grædjʊət/ **1** *n* laureato, -a *mf* che continua gli studi **2** *adj* successivo alla laurea

posthumous /'pɒstjʊməs/ *adj* postumo

posthumously /'pɒstjʊməslɪ/ *adv* dopo la morte

posting /'pəʊstɪŋ/ *n* (job) incarico *m*; Br (in mail) spedizione *f*; Comput posting *m inv*

postman /'pəʊstmən/ *n* postino *m*

postmark /'pəʊstmɑːk/ *n* timbro *m* postale

postmodern /ˌpəʊst'mɒdn/ *adj* postmoderno

post-mortem /-'mɔːtəm/ *n* autopsia *f*

post-natal /-'neɪtl/ *adj* postnatale

post office *n* ufficio *m* postale

post office box *n* casella *f* postale

postpone /pəʊs(t)'pəʊn/ *vt* rimandare

postponement /pəʊs(t)'pəʊnmənt/ *n* rinvio *m*

postscript /'pəʊs(t)skrɪpt/ *n* post scriptum *m inv*

posture /'pɒstʃə(r)/ *n* posizione *f*

post-war *adj* del dopoguerra

pot /pɒt/ *n* vaso *m*; (for tea) teiera *f*; (for coffee) caffettiera *f*; (for cooking) pentola *f*; sl (marijuana) erba *f*; **~s of money** *fam* un sacco di soldi; **go to ~** *fam* andare in malora

potash /'pɒtæʃ/ *n* potassa *f*

potassium /pə'tæsɪəm/ *n* potassio *m*

potato /pə'teɪtəʊ/ *n* (*pl* **-es**) patata *f*

potato chips Am, **potato crisps** Br *npl* patatine *fpl*

potato-peeler /-'piːlə(r)/ *n* pelapatate *m inv*

pot-bellied /'pɒtbelɪd/ *adj* panciuto

pot-belly /'pɒtbelɪ/ *n fam* pancione *m*

potent /'pəʊtənt/ *adj* potente

potentate /'pəʊtənteɪt/ *n* potentato *m*

✓ **potential** /pə'tenʃl/ **1** *adj* potenziale **2** *n* potenziale *m*

potentially /pə'tenʃəlɪ/ *adv* potenzialmente

pothole *n* cavità *f inv*; (in road) buca *f*

potholer *n* speleologo, -a *mf*

potholing /'pɒthəʊlɪŋ/ *n* speleologia *f*

pot-luck *n* **take ~** affidarsi alla sorte

pot plant *n* pianta *f* da appartamento

pot-shot *n* **take a ~ at** sparare a casaccio a

potted /'pɒtɪd/ *adj* conservato; (shortened) condensato

potted plant *n* pianta *f* da appartamento

potter[1] /'pɒtə(r)/ *vi* **[about]** gingillarsi

potter[2] *n* vasaio, -a *mf*

pottery /'pɒtərɪ/ *n* lavorazione *f* della ceramica; (articles) ceramiche *fpl*; (workshop) laboratorio *m* di ceramiche

potting compost /'pɒtɪŋ/ *n* terriccio *m*

potty /'pɒtɪ/ **1** *adj* (**-ier**, **-iest**) *fam* matto **2** *n* vasino *m*

pouch /paʊtʃ/ *n* marsupio *m*

pouffe /puːf/ *n* pouf *m inv*

poultry /'pəʊltrɪ/ *n* pollame *m*

pounce /paʊns/ *vi* balzare; **~ on** saltare su

✓ **pound**[1] /paʊnd/ *n* libbra *f* (= 0,454 kg); (money) sterlina *f*

pound[2] **1** *vt* battere **2** *vi* ‹heart› battere forte; (run heavily) correre pesantemente

pound[3] *n* (for cars) deposito *m* auto

pounding /'paʊndɪŋ/ **1** *n* martellio *m* **2** *adj* martellante

pour /pɔː(r)/ **1** *vt* versare **2** *vi* riversarsi; (with rain) piovere a dirotto

■ **pour away** *vi* svuotare

■ **pour in** *vi* ‹people› arrivare in massa; ‹letters, money› arrivare a valanghe; ‹water› entrare a fiotti

■ **pour out 1** *vi* riversarsi fuori **2** *vt* versare ‹drink›; sfogare ‹troubles›

pout /paʊt/ **1** *vi* fare il broncio **2** *n* broncio

poverty /'pɒvətɪ/ *n* povertà *f*

poverty line *n* soglia *f* di povertà

poverty-stricken *adj* indigente

POW *n abbr* (**prisoner of war**) prigioniero, -a *mf* di guerra

powder /'paʊdə(r)/ **1** *n* polvere *f*; (cosmetic) cipria *f* **2** *vt* polverizzare; (face) incipriare

powdered /'paʊdəd/ *adj* ‹milk› in polvere

powder room *n euph* toilette *f inv* per signore

powdery /'paʊdərɪ/ *adj* polveroso

✓ **power** /'paʊə(r)/ *n* potere *m*; Electr corrente *f* [elettrica]; Math potenza *f*

powerboat *n* fuoribordo *m*

power cut *n* interruzione *f* di corrente

powered /'paʊəd/ *adj* **~ by electricity** alimentato da corrente elettrica

---

✓ indicates a very frequent word

ⱷ **powerful** /'paʊəfʊl/ *adj* potente

powerhouse /'paʊəhaʊs/ *n* fig (person) persona *f* dinamica ed energica; **a ~ of ideas** un vulcano di idee

powerless /'paʊəlɪs/ *adj* impotente

power line *n* linea *f* elettrica

power of attorney *n* procura *f*

power-on light *n* spia *f* di accensione

power plant *n* centrale *f* elettrica

power sharing *n* condivisione *f* del potere

power station *n* centrale *f* elettrica

power steering *n* Auto servosterzo *m*

power switch *n* pulsante *m* di alimentazione

power unit *n* (of computer etc) alimentatore *m*

power-walk [1] *n* camminata *f* a passo sostenuto
   [2] *vi* camminare a passo sostenuto

power-walker *n* persona *f* che fa camminate a passo sostenuto

power-walking *n* camminate *fpl* a passo sostenuto (come esercizio fisico)

pow-wow /'paʊwaʊ/ *n* (of American Indians) raduno *m* tribale; fam (discussion) discussione *f*

pp *abbr* 1 (**pages**) pp.
   2 (**per procurationem**) pp.

PPP *abbr* (**public-private partnership**) *partnership* (*f*) *tra un ente pubblico e un'impresa privata*

PR *n abbr* 1 (**proportional representation**) proporzionale *f*
   2 (**public relations**) pubbliche relazioni *fpl*

practicable /'præktɪkəbl/ *adj* praticabile

practical /'præktɪkl/ *adj* pratico

practicality /præktɪ'kælɪtɪ/ *n* praticità *f*

practical joke *n* scherzo *m* pratico

practically /'præktɪklɪ/ *adv* praticamente

ⱷ **practice** /'præktɪs/ *n* pratica *f*; (custom) usanza *f*; (habit) abitudine *f*; (exercise) esercizio *m*; Sport allenamento *m*; **in ~** (in reality) in pratica; **out of ~** fuori esercizio; **put into ~** mettere in pratica

practicing /'præktɪsɪŋ/ *adj* Am = PRACTISING

practise /'præktɪs/ [1] *vt* fare pratica in; (carry out) mettere in pratica; esercitare ‹profession›
   [2] *vi* esercitarsi; ‹doctor› praticare

practised /'præktɪst/ *adj* esperto

practising /'præktɪsɪŋ/ *adj* Br praticante; **a ~ lawyer** un avvocato che esercita

pragmatic /præg'mætɪk/ *adj* pragmatico

pragmatism /'prægmətɪzm/ *n* pragmatismo *m*

pragmatist /'prægmətɪst/ *n* pragmatico, -a *mf*

prairie /'preərɪ/ *n* prateria *f*

praise /preɪz/ [1] *n* lode *f*
   [2] *vt* lodare

praiseworthy /'preɪzwɜːðɪ/ *adj* lodevole

pram /præm/ *n* carrozzella *f*

prance /prɑːns/ *vi* saltellare

prank /præŋk/ *n* tiro *m*

prattle /'prætl/ *vi* parlottare

prawn /prɔːn/ *n* gambero *m*

prawn cocktail *n* cocktail *m inv* di gamberetti

pray /preɪ/ *vi* pregare

prayer /preə(r)/ *n* preghiera *f*

preach /priːtʃ/ *vt/i* predicare

preacher /'priːtʃə(r)/ *n* predicatore, -trice *mf*

preamble /priː'æmbl/ *n* preambolo *m*

pre-arrange /priː-/ *vt* predisporre

precarious /prɪ'keərɪəs/ *adj* precario

precariously /prɪ'keərɪəslɪ/ *adv* in modo precario

precast /'priːkɑːst/ *adj* ‹concrete› prefabbricato

precaution /prɪ'kɔːʃn/ *n* precauzione *f*; **as a ~** per precauzione

precautionary /prɪ'kɔːʃnərɪ/ *adj* preventivo

precede /prɪ'siːd/ *vt* precedere

precedence /'presɪdəns/ *n* precedenza *f*

precedent /'presɪdənt/ *n* precedente *m*

preceding /prɪ'siːdɪŋ/ *adj* precedente

preceptor /prɪ'septə(r)/ *n* Am Univ precettore *m*

precinct /'priːsɪŋkt/ *n* (traffic-free) zona *f* pedonale; Am (district) circoscrizione *f*

precious /'preʃəs/ [1] *adj* prezioso; ‹style› ricercato
   [2] *adv* fam **~ little** ben poco

precipice /'presɪpɪs/ *n* precipizio *m*

precipitate¹ /prɪ'sɪpɪtət/ *adj* precipitoso

precipitate² /prɪ'sɪpɪteɪt/ *vt* precipitare

precipitation /prɪsɪpɪ'teɪʃn/ *n* precipitazione *f*

précis /'preɪsɪ/ *n* (*pl* **précis** /'preɪsɪːz/) sunto *m*

precise /prɪ'saɪs/ *adj* preciso

precisely /prɪ'saɪslɪ/ *adv* precisamente

precision /prɪ'sɪʒn/ *n* precisione *f*

preclude /prɪ'kluːd/ *vt* precludere

precocious /prɪ'kəʊʃəs/ *adj* precoce

precociousness /prɪ'kəʊʃsnɪs/ *n* precocità *f*

preconceived /priːkən'siːvd/ *adj* preconcetto

preconception /priːkən'sepʃn/ *n* preconcetto *m*

precondition /priːkən'dɪʃn/ [1] *n* presupposto *m*
   [2] *vt* Psych condizionare

p

precook /priːˈkʊk/ vt cuocere in anticipo

precursor /priːˈkɜːsə(r)/ n precursore m

predate /ˌpriːˈdeɪt/ vt retrodatare ‹cheque›; ‹building, painting› essere antecedente a

predator /ˈpredətə(r)/ n predatore, -trice mf

predatory /ˈpredət(ə)rɪ/ adj rapace

predecessor /ˈpriːdɪsesə(r)/ n predecessore, -a mf

predetermine /priːdɪˈtɜːmɪn/ vt predeterminare

predicament /prɪˈdɪkəmənt/ n situazione f difficile

predicate /ˈpredɪkət/ n Gram predicato m

predicative /prɪˈdɪkətɪv/ adj predicativo

◆ **predict** /prɪˈdɪkt/ vt predire

predictable /prɪˈdɪktəbl/ adj prevedibile

prediction /prɪˈdɪkʃn/ n previsione f

predigested /priːdaɪˈdʒestɪd/ adj predigerito

predispose /ˌpriːdɪˈspəʊz/ vt predisporre

predisposition /priːdɪspəˈzɪʃn/ n predisposizione f

predominant /prɪˈdɒmɪnənt/ adj predominante

predominantly /prɪˈdɒmɪnəntlɪ/ adv prevalentemente

predominate /prɪˈdɒmɪneɪt/ vi predominare

pre-eminent /priːˈemɪnənt/ adj preminente

pre-empt /priːˈempt/ vt (prevent) prevenire

pre-emptive /priːˈemptiv/ adj preventivo

preen /priːn/ vt lisciarsi; ~ oneself fig farsi bello

prefab /ˈpriːfæb/ n fam casa f prefabbricata

prefabricated /priːˈfæbrɪkeɪtɪd/ adj prefabbricato

preface /ˈprefɪs/ n prefazione f

prefatory /ˈprefət(ə)rɪ/ adj ‹comments› preliminare; ‹pages, notes› introduttivo

prefect /ˈpriːfekt/ n Schol studente, -tessa (mf) della scuola superiore con responsabilità disciplinare ecc

◆ **prefer** /prɪˈfɜː(r)/ vt (pt/pp preferred) preferire; I ~ to walk preferisco camminare

preferable /ˈprefərəbl/ adj preferibile (to a)

preferably /ˈprefərəblɪ/ adv preferibilmente

preference /ˈprefərəns/ n preferenza f

preferential /prefəˈrenʃl/ adj preferenziale

prefigure /ˌpriːˈfɪgə(r), US -gjər/ vt preannunciare

prefix /ˈpriːfɪks/ n prefisso m

pregnancy /ˈpregnənsɪ/ n gravidanza f

pregnant /ˈpregnənt/ adj incinta

preheat /priːˈhiːt/ vt preriscaldare ‹oven›

prehensile /priːˈhensaɪl/ adj prensile

prehistoric /priːhɪsˈtɒrɪk/ adj preistorico

pre-ignition /priːɪgˈnɪʃn/ n preaccensione f

pre-installed /priːɪnˈstɔːld/ adj preinstallato

prejudge /priːˈdʒʌdʒ/ vt giudicare prematuramente ‹issue›

prejudice /ˈpredʒʊdɪs/ ⬚**1** n pregiudizio m ⬚**2** vt influenzare (**against** contro); (harm) danneggiare

prejudiced /ˈpredʒʊdɪst/ adj prevenuto

preliminary /prɪˈlɪmɪnərɪ/ adj preliminare

preloaded /priːˈləʊdɪd/ adj precaricato

prelude /ˈpreljuːd/ n preludio m

premarital /priːˈmærɪtl/ adj prematrimoniale

premarital sex n rapporti mpl prematrimoniali

premature /ˈpremətjʊə(r)/ adj prematuro

premature birth n parto m prematuro

prematurely /ˈpremətjʊəlɪ/ adv prematuramente

premeditated /priːˈmedɪteɪtɪd/ adj premeditato

premeditation /ˌpriːmedɪˈteɪʃn/ n premeditazione f

premenstrual syndrome /priːˈmenstrʊəl/ n sindrome f premestruale

premenstrual tension n tensione f premestruale

premier /ˈpremɪə(r)/ ⬚**1** adj primario ⬚**2** n Pol primo ministro m, premier m inv

première /ˈpremɪeə(r)/ n prima f

premiership /ˈpremɪəʃɪp/ n Pol carica f di primo ministro nel Regno Unito; ≈ presidenza f del consiglio

premises /ˈpremɪsɪz/ npl locali mpl; on the ~ sul posto

premium /ˈpriːmɪəm/ n premio m; be at a ~ essere una cosa rara

premium bond n obbligazione f a premio

premonition /preməˈnɪʃn/ n presentimento m

prenatal /priːˈneɪtl/ adj esp Am prenatale

prenuptial agreement /priːnʌpʃl əˈgriːmənt/ n accordo m prematrimoniale

preoccupation /ˌpriːɒkjʊˈpeɪʃn/ n preoccupazione f

preoccupied /priːˈɒkjʊpaɪd/ adj preoccupato

preoperative /priːˈɒp(ə)rətɪv/ adj preoperatorio

preordained /priːɔːˈdeɪnd/ adj prestabilito; ‹outcome› predestinato

---

◆ indicates a very frequent word

pre-owned ⋯⟶ presume

pre-owned /priːˈəʊnd/ adj ‹video, game› di seconda mano

prep /prep/ n Sch compiti mpl

pre-packed /priːˈpækt/ adj preconfezionato

prepaid /priːˈpeɪd/ adj pagato in anticipo; ‹envelope› già affrancato

preparation /prepəˈreɪʃn/ n preparazione f; ~s pl preparativi mpl

preparatory /prɪˈpærətrɪ/ adj preparatorio; ~ to come preparazione per

preparatory school n Br = PREP SCHOOL

◆ **prepare** /prɪˈpeə(r)/ ① vt preparare ② vi prepararsi (**for** per); ~d **to** disposto a

prepay /priːˈpeɪ/ vt (pt/pp **-paid**) pagare in anticipo

preponderance /prɪˈpɒndərəns/ n preponderanza f

preponderantly /prɪˈpɒndərəntlɪ/ adv in modo preponderante

preponderate /prɪˈpɒndəreɪt/ vi predominare

preposition /prepəˈzɪʃn/ n preposizione f

prepossessing /priːpəˈzesɪŋ/ adj attraente

preposterous /prɪˈpɒstərəs/ adj assurdo

pre-programmed /priːˈprəʊɡræmd/ adj programmato; Comput preprogrammato

prep school n scuola f elementare privata

pre-recorded /-rɪˈkɔːdɪd/ adj in differita

prerequisite /priːˈrekwɪzɪt/ n condizione f sine qua non

prerogative /prɪˈrɒɡətɪv/ n prerogativa f

Pres. abbr (**President**) Pres.

Presbyterian /prezbɪˈtɪərɪən/ adj & n presbiteriano, -a mf

pre-school /ˈpriːskuːl/ ① n Am scuola f materna, asilo m ② adj ‹child› in età prescolastica; ‹years› prescolastico

prescribe /prɪˈskraɪb/ vt prescrivere

prescription /prɪˈskrɪpʃn/ n Med ricetta f

prescription charges npl Br ≈ ticket m inv sui medicinali

prescriptive /prɪˈskrɪptɪv/ adj normativo

◆ **presence** /ˈprezns/ n presenza f; ~ **of mind** presenza f di spirito

presence of mind n presenza f di spirito

◆ **present¹** /ˈpreznt/ ① adj presente ② n presente m; **at** ~ attualmente

◆ **present²** n (gift) regalo m; **give somebody something as a** ~ regalare qualcosa a qualcuno

◆ **present³** /prɪˈzent/ vt presentare; ~ **somebody with an award** consegnare un premio a qualcuno

presentable /prɪˈzentəbl/ adj **be** ~ essere presentabile

◆ **presentation** /preznˈteɪʃn/ n presentazione f

present-day adj attuale

presenter /prɪˈzentə(r)/ n TV, Radio presentatore, -trice mf

presently /ˈprezntlɪ/ adv fra poco; Am (now) attualmente

present perfect n passato m prossimo

preservation /prezəˈveɪʃn/ n conservazione f

preservative /prɪˈzɜːvətɪv/ n conservante m

preserve /prɪˈzɜːv/ ① vt preservare; (maintain & Culin) conservare ② n (in hunting & fig) riserva f; (jam) marmellata f

pre-set /priːˈset/ vt programmare

pre-shrunk /priːˈʃrʌŋk/ adj ‹fabric› irrestringibile

preside /prɪˈzaɪd/ vt presiedere (**over** a)

presidency /ˈprezɪdənsɪ/ n presidenza f

◆ **president** /ˈprezɪdənt/ n presidente m

presidential /prezɪˈdenʃl/ adj presidenziale

pre-soak /priːˈsəʊk/ vt mettere in ammollo

◆ **press** /pres/ ① n (machine) pressa f; (newspapers) stampa f ② vt premere; pressare ‹flower›; (iron) stirare; (squeeze) stringere ③ vi (urge) incalzare

■ **press ahead** vi (continue) proseguire

■ **press for** vt fare pressione per; **be** ~**ed for** (short of) essere a corto di

■ **press on** vi andare avanti

press agency n agenzia f di stampa

press conference n conferenza f stampa

press cutting n ritaglio m di giornale

press-gang vt forzare

pressing /ˈpresɪŋ/ adj urgente

press release n comunicato m stampa

press stud n [bottone m] automatico m

press-up n flessione f

◆ **pressure** /ˈpreʃə/ ① n pressione f ② vt = PRESSURIZE

pressure-cooker n pentola f a pressione

pressure group n gruppo m di pressione

pressurize /ˈpreʃəraɪz/ vt far pressione su

pressurized /ˈpreʃəraɪzd/ adj ‹cabin› pressurizzato

prestige /preˈstiːʒ/ n prestigio m

prestigious /preˈstɪdʒəs/ adj prestigioso

presumably /prɪˈzjuːməblɪ/ adv presumibilmente

presume /prɪˈzjuːm/ ① vt presumere; ~ **to do something** permettersi di fare qualcosa ② vi ~ **on** approfittare di

p

presumption /prɪˈzʌmpʃn/ n presunzione f; (boldness) impertinenza f

presumptuous /prɪˈzʌmptjʊəs/ adj impertinente

presuppose /priːsəˈpəʊz/ vt presupporre

presupposition /priːsʌpəˈzɪʃn/ n presupposizione f

pre-tax /ˈpriːtæks/ adj al lordo d'imposta

pretence /prɪˈtens/ n finzione f; (pretext) pretesto m; **it's all ~** tutta una scena

pretend /prɪˈtend/ ⚀ vt fingere; (claim) pretendere
⚁ vi fare finta

pretender /prɪˈtendə(r)/ n pretendente mf

pretension /prɪˈtenʃn/ n pretesa f

pretentious /prɪˈtenʃəs/ adj pretenzioso

preterite /ˈpretərɪt/ n preterito m

pretext /ˈpriːtekst/ n pretesto m

ꜰ **pretty** /ˈprɪtɪ/ ⚀ adj (**-ier, -iest**) carino
⚁ adv fam (fairly) abbastanza

prevail /prɪˈveɪl/ vi prevalere; **~ upon somebody to do something** convincere qualcuno a fare qualcosa

prevailing /prɪˈveɪlɪŋ/ adj prevalente

prevalence /ˈprevələns/ n diffusione f

prevalent /ˈprevələnt/ adj diffuso

prevaricate /prɪˈværɪkeɪt/ vi tergiversare

ꜰ **prevent** /prɪˈvent/ vt impedire; **~ somebody [from] doing something** impedire a qualcuno di fare qualcosa

preventable /prɪˈvenʃn/ adj evitabile

prevention /prɪˈvenʃn/ n prevenzione f

preventive /prɪˈventɪv/ adj preventivo

preview /ˈpriːvjuː/ n anteprima f

ꜰ **previous** /ˈpriːvɪəs/ adj precedente

ꜰ **previously** /ˈpriːvɪəslɪ/ adv precedentemente

pre-war /priːˈwɔː(r)/ adj anteguerra

pre-wash /ˈpriːwɒʃ/ n prelavaggio m

prey /preɪ/ ⚀ n preda f; **bird of ~** uccello m rapace
⚁ vi **~ on** far preda di; **~ on sb's mind** attanagliare qualcuno

ꜰ **price** /praɪs/ ⚀ n prezzo m
⚁ vt Comm fissare il prezzo di

price-conscious adj consapevole dell'andamento dei prezzi

price cut n riduzione f di prezzo

price cutting n taglio m dei prezzi

price freeze n congelamento m dei prezzi

price increase n aumento m di prezzo

priceless /ˈpraɪslɪs/ adj inestimabile; fam (amusing) spassosissimo

price list n listino m prezzi

price/performance ratio n rapporto m prezzo/prestazioni

price range n gamma f di prezzi

ꜰ indicates a very frequent word

price rise n rialzo m dei prezzi

price tag n talloncino m del prezzo

price war n guerra f dei prezzi

pricey /ˈpraɪsɪ/ adj fam caro

pricing policy /ˈpraɪsɪŋ/ n politica f di determinazione dei prezzi

prick /prɪk/ ⚀ n puntura f; vulg (penis) cazzo m; (person) stronzo m
⚁ vt pungere
■ **prick up**: vt **~ up one's ears** rizzare le orecchie

prickle /ˈprɪkl/ n spina f; (sensation) formicolio m

prickly /ˈprɪklɪ/ adj pungente; ‹person› irritabile

pride /praɪd/ ⚀ n orgoglio m; (of lions) branco m; **~ of place** posizione f d'onore
⚁ vt **~ oneself on** vantarsi di

priest /priːst/ n prete m

priesthood /ˈpriːsthʊd/ n (clergy) clero m; (calling) sacerdozio m; **enter the ~** farsi prete

prig /prɪg/ n presuntuoso m

priggish /ˈprɪgɪʃ/ adj presuntuoso

prim /prɪm/ adj (**primmer, primmest**) perbenino

primacy /ˈpraɪməsɪ/ n primato m; (of party, power) supremazia f; Relig carica f di primate

prima facie /praɪməˈfeɪʃi/ ⚀ adv (at first) a prima vista
⚁ adj a prima vista legittimo

primal /ˈpraɪməl/ adj ‹quality, myth, feeling› primitivo

primarily /ˈpraɪmərɪlɪ/ adv in primo luogo

ꜰ **primary** /ˈpraɪmərɪ/ adj primario; (chief) principale

primary colour n colore m primario

primary school n scuola f elementare

primate /ˈpraɪmeɪt/ n Zool, Relig primate m

prime[1] /praɪm/ ⚀ adj principale, primo; (first-rate) eccellente
⚁ n **be in one's ~** essere nel fiore degli anni

prime[2] vt preparare ‹surface, person›

ꜰ **Prime Minister** n Primo Ministro m

prime mover n promotore, -trice mf

primer /ˈpraɪmə(r)/ n (paint) base f; (for detonating) innesco m

prime time ⚀ n prime time m inv, fascia f di massimo ascolto
⚁ attrib ‹advertising, programme› nella fascia di massimo ascolto

primeval /praɪˈmiːvl/ adj primitivo

primitive /ˈprɪmɪtɪv/ adj primitivo

primordial /praɪˈmɔːdɪəl/ adj primordiale

primrose /ˈprɪmrəʊz/ n primula f

prince /prɪns/ n principe m

princely /ˈprɪnslɪ/ adj ‹life, role› da principe; ‹amount, style› principesco

princess /prɪnˈses/ n principessa f

principal /'prɪnsɪpl/ **1** *adj* principale
2 *n* Sch preside *m*
principality /prɪnsɪ'pælətɪ/ *n* principato
m
principally /'prɪnsəplɪ/ *adv*
principalmente
◆ **principle** /'prɪnsəpl/ *n* principio *m*; in
∼ in teoria; on ∼ per principio; ∼s *pl*
(fundamentals) fondamenti *mpl*
print /prɪnt/ **1** *n* (mark, trace) impronta *f*;
Phot copia *f*; (letters) stampatello *m*; (picture)
stampa *f*; in ∼ (printed out) stampato; ‹book› in
commercio; out of ∼ esaurito
2 *vt/i* stampare; (write in capitals) scrivere in
stampatello
■ **print off** *vt* stampare ‹copies›
■ **print out** *vt/i* Comput stampare
printed matter /'prɪntɪd/ *n* stampe *fpl*
printer /'prɪntə(r)/ *n* stampante *f*; (person)
tipografo, -a *mf*
printer port *n* porta *f* per la stampante
printing /'prɪntɪŋ/ *n* tipografia *f*
printout /'prɪntaʊt/ *n* Comput stampa *f*
print-preview /prɪnt'priːvjuː/ *vt* Comput
fare l'anteprima di stampa di
print speed *n* velocità *f* di stampa
◆ **prior** /'praɪə(r)/ **1** *adj* precedente
2 *prep* ∼ to prima di
◆ **priority** /praɪ'ɒrətɪ/ *n* precedenza *f*; (matter)
priorità *f inv*
priory /'praɪərɪ/ *n* monastero *m*
prise /praɪz/ *vt* ∼ open/up forzare
■ **prise off** *vt* togliere facendo leva ‹lid›
prism /'prɪzm/ *n* prisma *m*
◆ **prison** /'prɪzn/ *n* prigione *f*
prison camp *n* campo *m* di prigionia
prisoner /'prɪz(ə)nə(r)/ *n* prigioniero, -a *mf*
prison officer *n* guardia *f* carceraria
prison sentence *n* pena *f* detentiva
prissy /'prɪsɪ/ *adj* ‹person› perbenista
pristine /'prɪstiːn/ *adj* originario; (unspoilt)
intatto
privacy /'prɪvəsɪ/ *n* privacy *f*
◆ **private** /'praɪvət/ **1** *adj* privato; ‹car,
secretary, letter› personale
2 *n* Mil soldato *m* semplice; in ∼ in privato
private enterprise *n* iniziativa *f*
privata
private eye *n* fam investigatore, -trice *mf*
privato
privately /'praɪvətlɪ/ *adv* ‹funded,
educated etc› privatamente; (in secret) in
segreto; (confidentially) in privato; (inwardly)
interiormente
private property *n* proprietà *f* privata
privation /praɪ'veɪʃn/ *n* privazione *f*; ∼s
pl stenti *mpl*
privatization /praɪvətaɪ'zeɪʃn/ *n*
privatizzazione *f*
privatize /'praɪvətaɪz/ *vt* privatizzare

privilege /'prɪvəlɪdʒ/ *n* privilegio *m*
privileged /'prɪvəlɪdʒd/ *adj* privilegiato
privy /'prɪvɪ/ *adj* be ∼ to essere al corrente
di
◆ **prize** /praɪz/ **1** *n* premio *m*
2 *adj* (idiot etc) perfetto
3 *vt* apprezzare
prize draw *n* estrazione *f* a premi
prize-giving /'praɪzgɪvɪŋ/ *n* premiazione *f*
prize money *n* montepremi *m*
prizewinner *n* vincitore, -trice *mf*
prize-winning *adj* vincente
pro /prəʊ/ *n* fam (professional) professionista
mf; the ∼s and cons il pro e il contro
proactive /prəʊ'æktɪv/ *adj* ‹approach›
proattivo
probability /prɒbə'bɪlətɪ/ *n* probabilità
f inv
probable /'prɒbəbl/ *adj* probabile
◆ **probably** /'prɒbəblɪ/ *adv* probabilmente
probate /'prəʊbeɪt/ *n* Jur omologazione *f*
probation /prə'beɪʃn/ *n* prova *f*; Jur libertà
f vigilata
probationary /prə'beɪʃnərɪ/ *adj* in prova;
∼ **period** periodo *m* di prova
probationer /prə'beɪʃnə(r)/ *n* (employee
on trial) impiegato, -a *mf* in prova; (trainee)
apprendista *mf*
probation officer *n* agente (*m*) addetto
alla sorveglianza di chi si trova in regime di
libertà vigilata
probe /prəʊb/ **1** *n* sonda *f*; fig (investigation)
indagine *f*
2 *vt* sondare; (investigate) esaminare a fondo
probing /'prəʊbɪŋ/ *adj* ‹question›
penetrante
◆ **problem** /'prɒbləm/ **1** *n* problema *m*
2 *attrib* difficile
problematic /prɒblə'mætɪk/ *adj*
problematico
problem page *n* posta *f* del cuore
procedural /prə'siːdʒərəl/ *adj* ‹detail,
error› procedurale
◆ **procedure** /prə'siːdʒe(r)/ *n* procedimento
m
◆ **proceed** /prə'siːd/ **1** *vi* procedere
2 *vt* ∼ to do something proseguire
facendo qualcosa
proceedings /prə'siːdɪŋz/ *npl* (report) atti
mpl; Jur azione *fsg* legale
proceeds /'prəʊsiːdz/ *npl* ricavato *msg*
◆ **process** /'prəʊses/ **1** *n* processo *m*;
(procedure) procedimento *m*; in the ∼ nel
far ciò
2 *vt* trattare; Admin occuparsi di; Phot
sviluppare
processing /'prəʊsesɪŋ, US 'prɒ-/
n trattamento *m*; food ∼ l'industria
alimentare
procession /prə'seʃn/ *n* processione *f*

processor /'prəʊsesə(r)/ n Comput
processore m; (for food) tritatutto m inv

pro-choice /prəʊ'tʃɔɪs/ adj abortista

proclaim /prə'kleɪm/ vt proclamare

proclamation /prɒklə'meɪʃn/ n
proclamazione f

proclivity /prə'klɪvəti/ n tendenza f

procrastinate /prə'kræstɪneɪt/ vi
procrastinare

procrastination /prəkræstɪ'neɪʃn/ n
procrastinazione f

procreate /'prəʊkrɪeɪt/ vi procreare

procreation /prəʊkrɪ'eɪʃn/ n
procreazione f

procure /prə'kjʊə(r)/ vt ottenere

prod /prɒd/ ⓵ n colpetto m
⓶ vt (pt/pp **prodded**) punzecchiare; fig
incitare

prodigal /'prɒdɪgl/ adj prodigo

prodigal son n figliol m prodigo

prodigious /prə'dɪdʒəs/ adj prodigioso

prodigy /'prɒdɪdʒɪ/ n [infant] ∼ bambino
m prodigio

produce¹ /'prɒdjuːs/ n prodotti mpl; ∼ of
Italy prodotto in Italia

ᴰ **produce²** /prə'djuːs/ vt produrre; (bring
out) tirar fuori; (cause) causare; fam (give birth
to) fare

ᴰ **producer** /prə'djuːsə(r)/ n produttore m

ᴰ **product** /'prɒdʌkt/ n prodotto m

ᴰ **production** /prə'dʌkʃn/ n produzione f;
Theat spettacolo m

production control n controllo m della
produzione

production director n direttore, -trice
mf della produzione

production line n catena f di montaggio

production management n gestione
f della produzione

production manager n direttore, -trice
mf della produzione

productive /prə'dʌktɪv/ adj produttivo

productivity /prɒdʌk'tɪvəti/ n
produttività f

product range n gamma f di prodotti

Prof. abbr (**Professor**) Prof.

profane /prə'feɪm/ adj profano;
(blasphemous) blasfemo

profanity /prə'fænəti/ n (oath) bestemmia f

profess /prə'fes/ vt (claim) dichiarare

professed /prə'fest/ adj (claiming to be)
sedicente

profession /prə'feʃn/ n professione f

ᴰ **professional** /prə'feʃnəl/ ⓵ adj
professionale; (not amateur) professionista;
(piece of work) da professionista; ‹man› di
professione
⓶ n professionista mf

professionalism /prə'feʃnəlɪzm/ n (of
person, organization, work) professionalità f;
Sport professionismo m

professionally /prə'feʃnəlɪ/ adv
professionalmente

ᴰ **professor** /prə'fesə(r)/ n professore m
[universitario]

professorial /prɒfə'sɔːrɪəl/ adj ‹duties,
post, salary› professorale

proffer /'prɒfə(r)/ vt (hold out) porgere; fig
(offer) offrire

proficiency /prə'fɪʃnsɪ/ n competenza f

proficient /prə'fɪʃnt/ adj competente (in
in)

profile /'prəʊfaɪl/ n profilo m

profiling /'prəʊfaɪlɪŋ/ n profilo m;
genetic ∼ profilo genetico

ᴰ **profit** /'prɒfɪt/ ⓵ n profitto m
⓶ vi ∼ from trarre profitto da

profitable /'prɒfɪtəbl/ adj proficuo

profitably /'prɒfɪtəblɪ/ adv in modo
proficuo

profit and loss account n conto m
profitti e perdite

profiteer /prɒfɪ'tɪə(r)/ n profittatore,
-trice mf

profiterole /prə'fɪtərəʊl/ n profiterole
m inv

profit margin n margine m di profitto

profit-sharing n partecipazione f agli
utili

profligate /'prɒflɪgət/ adj (extravagant)
spendaccione; (dissolute) dissoluto; (spending)
eccessivo

pro forma invoice /'fɔːmə/ n fattura f
proforma

profound /prə'faʊnd/ adj profondo

profoundly /prə'faʊndlɪ/ adv
profondamente

profuse /prə'fjuːs/ adj ∼ apologies una
profusione di scuse

profusely /prə'fjuːslɪ/ adv profusamente

profusion /prə'fjuːʒn/ n profusione f; in ∼
in abbondanza

progeny /'prɒdʒənɪ/ n progenie f inv

prognosis /prɒg'nəʊsɪs/ n (pl -**oses**)
(prediction) previsione f; Med prognosi f inv

prognosticate /prɒg'nɒstɪkeɪt/ vt
pronosticare

ᴰ **program** /'prəʊgræm/ ⓵ n Comput
programma m
⓶ vt (pt/pp **programmed**) programmare

ᴰ **programme** /'prəʊgræm/ n Br programma
m

programmer /'prəʊgræmə(r)/ n Comput
programmatore, -trice mf

programming /'prəʊgræmɪŋ/ n
programmazione f

ᴰ **progress¹** /'prəʊgres/ n progresso m; in ∼
in corso; **make** ∼ fig fare progressi

ᴰ indicates a very frequent word

progress ⋯⟶ propagator

progress² /prə'gres/ *vi* progredire; fig fare progressi

progression /prə'greʃn/ *n* (development) progresso *m*; (improvement) evoluzione *f*; (series) serie *f*

progressive /prə'gresɪv/ *adj* progressivo; (reforming) progressista

progressively /prə'gresɪvlɪ/ *adv* progressivamente

progress report *n* (on project) resoconto sull'andamento del progetto; (on patient) cartella *f* clinica

prohibit /prə'hɪbɪt/ *vt* proibire

prohibition /prəʊhɪ'bɪʃn/ *n* proibizione; P~ Am proibizionismo *m*

prohibitive /prə'hɪbɪtɪv/ *adj* proibitivo

prohibitively /prə'hɪbɪtɪvlɪ/ *adv* ‹expensive› in modo proibitivo

✏ **project¹** /'prɒdʒekt/ *n* progetto *m*; Sch ricerca *f*

project² /prə'dʒekt/ **1** *vt* proiettare ‹film, image›
 2 *vi* (jut out) sporgere

projectile /prə'dʒektaɪl/ *n* proiettile *m*

projection /prə'dʒekʃn/ *n* (of figures) proiezione *f*

project manager *n* project manager *mf inv*

projector /prə'dʒektə(r)/ *n* proiettore *m*

proletarian /prəʊlə'teərɪən/ *adj & n* proletario, -a *mf*

proletariat /prəʊlɪ'teərɪət/ *n* proletariato *m*

pro-life /prəʊ'laɪf/ *adj* antiabortista

proliferate /prə'lɪfəreɪt/ *vi* proliferare

proliferation /prəlɪfə'reɪʃn/ *n* proliferazione *f*

prolific /prə'lɪfɪk/ *adj* prolifico

prologue /'prəʊlɒg/ *n* prologo *m*

prolong /prə'lɒŋ/ *vt* prolungare

prom /prɒm/ *n* Br fam (at seaside) lungomare *m inv*; Am fam (at high school) ballo *m* studentesco

promenade /prɒmə'nɑːd/ *n* lungomare *m inv*

prominence /'prɒmɪnəns/ *n* (of person, issue) importanza *f*; (of object) sporgenza *f*; (hill) rilievo *m*

prominent /'prɒmɪnənt/ *adj* prominente; (conspicuous) di rilievo

promiscuity /prɒmɪ'skjuːətɪ/ *n* promiscuità *f*

promiscuous /prə'mɪskjʊəs/ *adj* promiscuo

✏ **promise** /'prɒmɪs/ **1** *n* promessa *f*
 2 *vt* promettere; ~ **somebody that** promettere a qualcuno che; **I ~d to** l'ho promesso

Promised Land /prɒmɪst'lænd/ *n* Terra *f* Promessa

promising /'prɒmɪsɪŋ/ *adj* promettente

promo /'prəʊməʊ/ *n* fam (of product) campagna *f* promozionale; (video) video *m inv* promozionale

promontory /'prɒmənt(ə)rɪ/ *n* promontorio *m*

✏ **promote** /prə'məʊt/ *vt* promuovere; **be ~d** essere promosso

promoter /prə'məʊtə(r)/ *n* promotore, -trice *mf*

promotion /prə'məʊʃn/ *n* promozione *f*

promotional /prə'məʊʃnəl/ *adj* Comm promozionale

promotional video *n* video *m* promozionale

prompt /prɒmpt/ **1** *adj* immediato; (punctual) puntuale
 2 *adv* in punto
 3 *vt* incitare (**to** a); Theat suggerire a
 4 *vi* suggerire
 5 *n* Comput prompt *m inv*

prompter /'prɒmptə(r)/ *n* suggeritore, -trice *mf*

promptly /'prɒmptlɪ/ *adv* puntualmente

Proms /prɒmz/ *npl rassegna (f) di concerti estivi di musica classica presso l'Albert Hall a Londra*

prone /prəʊn/ *adj* prono; **be ~ to do something** essere incline a fare qualcosa

prong /prɒŋ/ *n* dente *m*

pronoun /'prəʊnaʊn/ *n* pronome *m*

pronounce /prə'naʊns/ *vt* pronunciare; (declare) dichiarare
 ■ **pronounce on** *vt* pronunciarsi su ‹case, subject›

pronounced /prə'naʊnst/ *adj* (noticeable) pronunciato

pronouncement /prə'naʊnsmənt/ *n* dichiarazione *f*

pronunciation /prənʌnsɪ'eɪʃn/ *n* pronuncia *f*

proof /pruːf/ **1** *n* prova *f*; Typ bozza *f*, prova *f*; **12% ~** 12°
 2 *adj* ~ **against** a prova di

proof of purchase *n* ricevuta *f* d'acquisto

proof-read *vt* correggere le bozze di

proof-reader *n* correttore, -trice *mf* di bozze

proof-reading *n* revisione *f* di bozze

prop¹ /prɒp/ **1** *n* puntello *m*
 2 *vt* (*pt/pp* **propped**) ~ **open** tenere aperto; ~ **against** (lean) appoggiare a
 ■ **prop up** *vt* sostenere

prop² *n* Theat fam accessorio *m* di scena

propaganda /prɒpə'gændə/ *n* propaganda *f*

propagate /'prɒpəgeɪt/ *vt* propagare

propagator /'prɒpəgeɪtə(r)/ *n* propagatore *m*

propane /'prəupeɪn/ n propano m

propel /prə'pel/ vt (pt/pp **propelled**) spingere

propellant /prə'pelənt/ n (in aerosol) gas m inv propellente; (in rocket) propellente m

propeller /prə'pelə(r)/ n elica f

propelling pencil /prə'pelɪŋ/ n portamina m inv

propensity /prə'pensətɪ/ n tendenza f

✧ **proper** /'prɒpə(r)/ adj corretto; (suitable) adatto; fam (real) vero [e proprio]

✧ **properly** /'prɒpəlɪ/ adv correttamente

proper name, **proper noun** n nome m proprio

✧ **property** /'prɒpətɪ/ n proprietà f inv

property developer n impresa f edile; (person) impresario m edile

property market n mercato m immobiliare

prophecy /'prɒfəsɪ/ n profezia f

prophesy /'prɒfɪsaɪ/ vt (pt/pp -ied) profetizzare

prophet /'prɒfɪt/ n profeta m

prophetic /prə'fetɪk/ adj profetico

prophylactic /prɒfɪ'læktɪk/ 1 n (condom) profilattico m, preservativo m; Med (treatment) misura f profilattica 2 adj profilattico

proponent /prə'pəunənt/ n fautore, -trice mf

✧ **proportion** /prə'pɔːʃn/ n proporzione f; (share) parte f; be in ∼ essere proporzionato (to a); be out of ∼ essere sproporzionato; ∼s pl (dimensions) proporzioni f pl

proportional /prə'pɔːʃnəl/ adj proporzionale

proportionally /prə'pɔːʃnəlɪ/ adv in proporzione

proportional representation n rappresentanza f proporzionale

✧ **proposal** /prə'pəuzl/ n proposta f; (of marriage) proposta f di matrimonio

✧ **propose** /prə'pəuz/ 1 vt proporre; (intend) proporsi 2 vi fare una proposta di matrimonio

proposition /prɒpə'zɪʃn/ n proposta f; fam (task) impresa f

proprietor /prə'praɪətə(r)/ n proprietario, -a mf

propriety /prə'praɪətɪ/ n correttezza f; the proprieties pl l'etichetta f

propulsion /prə'pʌlʃn/ n propulsione f

pro rata /'rɑːtə/ adj on a ∼ basis in proporzione

prosaic /prə'zeɪɪk/ adj prosaico

proscribe vt (exile) esiliare; (ban) bandire

prose /prəuz/ n prosa f

✧ indicates a very frequent word

prosecute /'prɒsɪkjuːt/ vt intentare azione contro

prosecution /prɒsɪ'kjuːʃn/ n azione f giudiziaria; the ∼ l'accusa f

prosecutor /'prɒsɪkjuːtə(r)/ n [Public] P∼ Pubblico Ministero m

✧ **prospect¹** /'prɒspekt/ n (expectation) prospettiva f; (view) vista f

prospect² /prə'spekt/ vi ∼ for cercare

prospective /prə'spektɪv/ adj (future) futuro; (possible) potenziale

prospector /prə'spektə(r)/ n cercatore m

prospectus /prə'spektəs/ n prospetto m

prosper /'prɒspə(r)/ vi prosperare; (person) stare bene finanziariamente

prosperity /prɒ'sperətɪ/ n prosperità f

prosperous /'prɒspərəs/ adj prospero

prostate /'prɒsteɪt/ n prostata f

prosthesis /prɒs'θiːsɪs/ n protesi f

prostitute /'prɒstɪtjuːt/ 1 n prostituta f 2 vt fig prostituire

prostitution /prɒstɪ'tjuːʃn/ n prostituzione f

prostrate /'prɒstreɪt/ adj prostrato; ∼ with grief fig prostrato dal dolore

protagonist /prə'tægənɪst/ n protagonista mf

✧ **protect** /prə'tekt/ vt proteggere (from da)

✧ **protection** /prə'tekʃn/ n protezione f

protection factor n (of suntan lotion) fattore m di protezione

protection racket n racket m inv di protezione

protective /prə'tektɪv/ adj protettivo

protector /prə'tektə(r)/ n protettore, -trice mf

protégé /'prɒtɪʒeɪ/ n protetto m

protein /'prəutiːn/ n proteina f

✧ **protest¹** /'prəutest/ n protesta f

protest² /prə'test/ vt/i protestare

Protestant /'prɒtɪstənt/ adj & n protestante mf

Protestantism /'prɒtɪstəntɪzm/ n protestantesimo m

protestation /prɒtɪ'steɪʃn/ n protesta f

protester /prə'testə(r)/ n contestatore, -trice mf; (at demonstration) dimostrante mf

protocol /'prəutəkɒl/ n protocollo m

prototype /'prəutətaɪp/ n prototipo m

protract /prə'trækt/ vt protrarre

protracted /prə'træktɪd/ adj prolungato

protractor /prə'træktə(r)/ n goniometro m

protrude /prə'truːd/ vi sporgere

protruding /prə'truːdɪŋ, US prəu-/ adj (teeth, chin, ledge) sporgente

protuberance /prə'tuːbərəns/ n protuberanza f

✧ **proud** /praud/ adj fiero (of di)

proudly /'praʊdlɪ/ *adv* fieramente

✦ **prove** /pruːv/ ① *vt* provare
② *vi* ~ **to be a lie** rivelarsi una bugia

proven /'pruːvən/ *adj* dimostrato

proverb /'prɒvɜːb/ *n* proverbio *m*

proverbial /prə'vɜːbɪəl/ *adj* proverbiale

✦ **provide** /prə'vaɪd/ ① *vt* fornire;
~ **somebody with something** fornire
qualcosa a qualcuno
② *vi* ~ **for** (allow for) tenere conto di; ‹law›
prevedere

provided /prə'vaɪdɪd/ *conj* ~ **[that]** purché

providence /'prɒvɪdəns/ *n* provvidenza *f*

provident /'prɒvɪdənt/ *adj* previdenziale

providential /prɒvɪ'denʃl/ *adj*
provvidenziale

provider /prə'vaɪdə(r)/ *n* (in family) persona
f che mantiene la famiglia

providing /prə'vaɪdɪŋ/ *conj* = PROVIDED

province /'prɒvɪns/ *n* provincia *f*; fig
campo *m*

provincial /prə'vɪnʃl/ *adj* provinciale

provincialism /prə'vɪnʃəlɪzm/ *n*
provincialismo *m*

✦ **provision** /prə'vɪʒn/ *n* (of food, water)
approvvigionamento *m* (of di); (of law)
disposizione *f*; **make** ~ **for** ‹law› prevedere;
~**s** *pl* provviste *fpl*

provisional /prə'vɪʒ(ə)nəl/ *adj*
provvisorio

provisionally /prə'vɪʒ(ə)nəlɪ/ *adv*
provvisoriamente

proviso /prə'vaɪzəʊ/ *n* condizione *f*

provocation /prɒvə'keɪʃn/ *n*
provocazione *f*

provocative /prə'vɒkətɪv/ *adj*
provocatorio; (sexually) provocante

provocatively /prə'vɒkətɪvlɪ/ *adv* in
modo provocatorio; ‹smile, be dressed› in
modo provocante

provoke /prə'vəʊk/ *vt* provocare

provost /'prɒvəst/ *n* Am Univ decano *m*; Br
Univ, Sch rettore *m*; (in Scotland) sindaco *m*

prow /praʊ/ *n* prua *f*

prowess /'praʊɪs/ *n* abilità *f inv*

prowl /praʊl/ ① *vi* aggirarsi
② *n* **on the** ~ in cerca di preda

prowler /'praʊlə(r)/ *n* tipo *m* sospetto

proximity /prɒk'sɪmətɪ/ *n* prossimità *f*

proxy /'prɒksɪ/ *n* procura *f*; (person) persona
f che agisce per procura

prude /pruːd/ *n* **be a** ~ essere
eccessivamente pudico

prudence /'pruːdəns/ *n* prudenza *f*

prudent /'pruːdənt/ *adj* prudente; (wise)
oculato

prudently /'pruːdəntlɪ/ *adv* con prudenza

prudish /'pruːdɪʃ/ *adj* eccessivamente
pudico

prudishness /'pruːdɪʃnɪs/ *n* eccessivo
pudore *m*

prune¹ /pruːn/ *n* prugna *f* secca

prune² *vt* potare

pry /praɪ/ *vi* (*pt/pp* **pried**) ficcare il naso

prying /'praɪɪŋ/ *adj* curioso

PS *n abbr* (**postscriptum**) PS *m inv*

psalm /sɑːm/ *n* salmo *m*

pseud /sjuːd/ *n* fam intellettualoide *mf*

pseudonym /'sjuːdənɪm/ *n* pseudonimo *m*

PSHE *n abbr* Br (**personal social and
health education**) (school subject) *studio
(m) degli aspetti personali, sociali e sanitari
dell'individuo in relazione alla collettività*

PST *abbr* Am (**Pacific Standard Time**)
tempo (m) medio della zona del Pacifico

psych /saɪk/
▪ **psych out** *vt* fam (unnerve) snervare
▪ **psych up** *vt* fam (prepare mentally) preparare
psicologicamente

psychedelic /saɪkə'delɪk/ *adj*
psichedelico

psychiatric /saɪkɪ'ætrɪk/ *adj* psichiatrico

psychiatrist /saɪ'kaɪətrɪst/ *n* psichiatra
mf

psychiatry /saɪ'kaɪətrɪ, US sɪ-/ *n*
psichiatria *f*

psychic /'saɪkɪk/ ① *n* sensitivo, -a *mf*
② *adj* psichico; **I'm not** ~ non sono un
indovino

psychoanalyse /saɪkəʊ'ænəlaɪz/ *vt*
psicanalizzare

psychoanalysis /saɪkəʊə'nælɪsɪs/ *n*
psicanalisi *f*

psychoanalyst /saɪkəʊ'ænəlɪst/ *n*
psicanalista *mf*

psychological /saɪkə'lɒdʒɪkl/ *adj*
psicologico

psychologically /saɪkə'lɒdʒɪklɪ/ *adv*
psicologicamente

psychologist /saɪ'kɒlədʒɪst/ *n* psicologo,
-a *mf*

psychology /saɪ'kɒlədʒɪ/ *n* psicologia *f*

psychopath /'saɪkəpæθ/ *n* psicopatico,
-a *mf*

psychopathic /saɪkə'pæθɪk/ *adj*
psicopatico

psychosis /saɪ'kəʊsɪs/ *n* psicosi *f inv*

psychosomatic /saɪkəʊsə'mætɪk/ *adj*
psicosomatico

psychotherapist *n* psicoterapista *mf*,
psicoterapeuta *mf*

psychotic /saɪ'kɒtɪk/ *adj & n* psicotico,
-a *mf*

PT *n abbr* (**physical training**)
educazione *f* fisica

PTA *n abbr* (**Parent-Teacher
Association**) ≈ consiglio *m* d'istituto

PTO *abbr* (**please turn over**) vedi retro

pub /pʌb/ n fam pub m inv
puberty /'pjuːbəti/ n pubertà f
pubic hair /'pjuːbik/ n peli mpl del pube
ⁱ **public** /'pʌblɪk/ ① adj pubblico; **make** ∼ rendere pubblico
② n the ∼ il pubblico; **in** ∼ in pubblico
public address system n impianto m di amplificazione
publican /'pʌblɪkən/ n gestore, -trice mf, proprietario, -a mf di un pub
public assistance n Am assistenza f pubblica
ⁱ **publication** /pʌblɪ'keɪʃn/ n pubblicazione f
public company n società f per azioni
public convenience n gabinetti mpl pubblici
public holiday n festa f nazionale
public house n pub m inv
publicist /'pʌblɪsɪst/ n (press agent) press agent mf inv, addetto, -a mf stampa
publicity /pʌb'lɪsəti/ n pubblicità f
publicity campaign n campagna f pubblicitaria
publicity department n settore m pubblicità
publicity director n direttore, -trice mf della pubblicità
publicity stunt n trovata f pubblicitaria
publicize /'pʌblɪsaɪz/ vt pubblicizzare
public library n biblioteca f pubblica
public limited company /'lɪmɪtɪd/ n società f inv per azioni
publicly /'pʌblɪklɪ/ adv pubblicamente
public opinion n opinione f pubblica
public prosecutor n Pubblico Ministero m
public relations npl pubbliche relazioni fpl
public relations department n ufficio m pubbliche relazioni
public relations officer n addetto, -a mf alle pubbliche relazioni
public school n scuola f privata; Am scuola f pubblica
public sector n settore m pubblico
public-spirited adj be ∼ essere dotato di senso civico
public transport n mezzi mpl pubblici
ⁱ **publish** /'pʌblɪʃ/ vt pubblicare
publisher /'pʌblɪʃə(r)/ n editore m; (firm) editore m, casa f editrice
publishing /'pʌblɪʃɪŋ/ n editoria f
puce /pjuːs/ adj color bruno rossastro
puck /pʌk/ n (in ice-hockey) disco m; (sprite) folletto m
pucker /'pʌkə(r)/ vi ‹material› arricciarsi

pudding /'pʊdɪŋ/ n dolce m cotto al vapore; (course) dolce m
puddle /'pʌdl/ n pozzanghera f
pudgy /'pʌdʒɪ/ adj (-ier, -iest) grassoccio
puerile /'pjʊəraɪl/ adj puerile
puff /pʌf/ ① n (of wind) soffio m; (of smoke) tirata f; (for powder) piumino m
② vt sbuffare
■ **puff at** vt tirare boccate da ‹pipe›
■ **puff out** vt lasciare senza fiato ‹person›; spegnere ‹candle›
■ **puff up** ① vi ‹feathers› arruffarsi; ‹eye, rice› gonfiarsi
② vt arruffare ‹feathers, fur›; **puffed up with pride** gonfio d'orgoglio
puffed /pʌft/ adj (out of breath) senza fiato
puff pastry n pasta f sfoglia
puff sleeve n manica f a palloncino
puffy /'pʌfɪ/ adj gonfio
pug /pʌg/ n (dog) carlino m
pugnacious /pʌg'neɪʃəs/ adj aggressivo
ⁱ **pull** /pʊl/ ① n trazione f; fig (attraction) attrazione f; fam (influence) influenza f
② vt tirare; estrarre ‹tooth›; stirarsi ‹muscle›; ∼ **a fast one** fam giocare un brutto tiro; ∼ **faces** far boccacce; ∼ **oneself together** ricomporsi; ∼ **one's weight** mettercela tutta; ∼ **sb's leg** fam prendere in giro qualcuno
■ **pull ahead** vi (move in front) passare davanti
■ **pull apart** vt (dismantle) smontare; (destroy) fare a pezzi
■ **pull away** vi (increase one's lead) distanziarsi
■ **pull back** ① vi ‹soldiers› ritirarsi; (not act) tirarsi indietro
② vt far ritirare ‹soldiers›
■ **pull down** vt (demolish) demolire
■ **pull in** vi Auto accostare
■ **pull off** vt togliere; fam azzeccare
■ **pull out** ① vt tirar fuori
② vi Auto spostarsi; (of competition) ritirarsi
■ **pull over** vi Aut accostare
■ **pull through** vi (recover) farcela
■ **pull together** vi (co-operate) sommare le forze
■ **pull up** ① vt sradicare ‹plant›; (reprimand) rimproverare
② vi Auto fermarsi
pull-down menu n Comput menu m inv a discesa
pulley /'pʊlɪ/ n Techn puleggia f
pull-in n Br (lay-by) piazzuola f di sosta; (cafe) bar m inv sul bordo della strada
pullover /'pʊləʊvə(r)/ n pullover m inv
pulmonary /'pʌlmənərɪ/ adj polmonare
pulp /pʌlp/ n poltiglia f; (of fruit) polpa f; (for paper) pasta f
pulp fiction n letteratura f pulp
pulpit /pʌlpɪt/ n pulpito m
pulsar /'pʌlsɑː(r)/ n pulsar m inv

ⁱ indicates a very frequent word

pulsate ···⊱ pursuer····

pulsate /pʌl'seɪt/ *vi* pulsare

pulse /pʌls/ *n* polso *m*

pulse rate *n* polso *m*

pulses /'pʌlsɪz/ *npl* legumi *mpl* secchi

pulverize /'pʌlvəraɪz/ *vt* polverizzare

puma /'pju:mə/ *n* puma *m inv*

pumice /'pʌmɪs/ *n* pomice *f*

pummel /'pʌml/ *vt* (*pt/pp* **pummelled**) prendere a pugni

pump /pʌmp/ **1** *n* pompa *f*
2 *vt* pompare; fam cercare di estorcere informazioni da
■ **pump up** *vt* (inflate) gonfiare

pumpkin /'pʌmpkɪn/ *n* zucca *f*

pun /pʌn/ *n* gioco *m* di parole

punch¹ /pʌntʃ/ **1** *n* pugno *m*; (device) pinza *f* per forare
2 *vt* dare un pugno a; forare ‹ticket›; perforare ‹hole›

punch² *n* (drink) punch *m inv*

Punch-and-Judy show *n* spettacolo *m* di burattini

punchbag *n* punching bag *f inv*

punch-drunk *adj* (in boxing) groggy *inv*; fig stordito

punchline *n* battuta *f* finale

punch-up *n* rissa *f*

punctual /'pʌŋktjʊəl/ *adj* puntuale

punctuality /pʌŋktjʊ'ælətɪ/ *n* puntualità *f*

punctually /'pʌŋktjʊəlɪ/ *adv* puntualmente

punctuate /'pʌŋktjʊeɪt/ *vt* punteggiare

punctuation /pʌŋktjʊ'eɪʃn/ *n* punteggiatura *f*

punctuation mark *n* segno *m* di interpunzione

puncture /'pʌŋktʃə(r)/ **1** *n* foro *m*; (tyre) foratura *f*
2 *vt* forare

pundit /'pʌndɪt/ *n* esperto *m*

pungency /'pʌndʒənsɪ/ *n* asprezza *f*

pungent /'pʌndʒənt/ *adj* acre

punish /'pʌnɪʃ/ *vt* punire

punishable /'pʌnɪʃəbl/ *adj* punibile

punishment /'pʌnɪʃmənt/ *n* punizione *f*

punitive /'pju:nɪtɪv/ *adj* punitivo

punk /pʌŋk/ *n* punk *m inv*

punk rock *n* punk rock *m inv*

punk rocker /'rɒkə(r)/ *n* punk *mf inv*

punnet /'pʌnɪt/ *n* cestello *m*

punt /pʌnt/ *n* (boat) barchino *m*

punter /'pʌntə(r)/ *n* (gambler) scommettitore, -trice *mf*; fam (client) consumatore, -trice *mf*

puny /'pju:nɪ/ *adj* (**-ier**, **-iest**) striminzito

pup /pʌp/ *n* = PUPPY

⚬ᶠ **pupil** /'pju:pl/ *n* alunno, -a *mf*; (of eye) pupilla *f*

puppet /'pʌpɪt/ *n* marionetta *f*; (glove, fig) burattino *m*

puppy /'pʌpɪ/ *n* cucciolo *m*

⚬ᶠ **purchase** /'pɜːtʃəs/ **1** *n* acquisto *m*; (leverage) presa *f*
2 *vt* acquistare

purchase invoice *n* fattura *f* di acquisto

purchase ledger *n* libro *m* mastro degli acquisti

purchase order *n* ordine *m* di acquisto

purchase price *n* prezzo *m* di acquisto

purchaser /'pɜːtʃəsə(r)/ *n* acquirente *mf*

purchasing [department] /'pɜːtʃəsɪŋ/ *n* ufficio *m* acquisti

purchasing power *n* potere *m* d'acquisto

purdah /'pɜːdə/ *n* reclusione (*f*) delle donne in alcune società musulmane e indù

pure /pjʊə(r)/ *adj* puro

pure-bred /-'bred/ **1** *n* (horse) purosangue *m inv*
2 *adj* purosangue *inv*

purée /'pjʊəreɪ/ **1** *n* purè *m inv*
2 *vt* passare

purely /'pjʊəlɪ/ *adv* puramente

purgatory /'pɜːgətrɪ/ *n* purgatorio *m*

purge /pɜːdʒ/ Pol **1** *n* epurazione *f*
2 *vt* epurare

purification /pjʊərɪfɪ'keɪʃn/ *n* purificazione *f*

purify /'pjʊərɪfaɪ/ *vt* (*pt/pp* **-ied**) purificare

purist /'pjʊərɪst/ *adj & n* purista *mf*

puritan /'pjʊərɪtən/ **1** *n* puritano, -a *mf*
2 *adj* fig puritano

puritanical /pjʊərɪ'tænɪkl/ *adj* puritano

purity /'pjʊərɪtɪ/ *n* purità *f*

purl /pɜːl/ **1** *n* Knitting maglia *f* rovescia
2 *vt/i* lavorare a rovescio

purple /'pɜːpl/ *adj* viola *inv*

purport /pə'pɔːt/ *vt* ~ to be farsi passare per

⚬ᶠ **purpose** /'pɜːpəs/ *n* scopo *m*; (determination) fermezza *f*; on ~ apposta

purpose-built /-'bɪlt/ *adj* costruito ad hoc

purposeful /'pɜːpəsfʊl/ *adj* deciso

purposefully /'pɜːpəsfʊlɪ/ *adv* con decisione

purposely /'pɜːpəslɪ/ *adv* apposta

purpose-made *adj* Br fatto appositamente

purr /pɜː(r)/ *vi* ‹cat› fare le fusa

purse /pɜːs/ **1** *n* borsellino *m*; Am (handbag) borsa *f*
2 *vt* increspare ‹lips›

purser /'pɜːsə(r)/ *n* commissario *m* di bordo

⚬ᶠ **pursue** /pə'sju:/ *vt* inseguire; fig proseguire

pursuer /pə'sju:ə(r)/ *n* inseguitore, -trice *mf*

p

pursuit /pə'sjuːt/ *n* inseguimento *m*; fig (of happiness) ricerca *f*; (pastime) attività *f inv*; **in** ~ all'inseguimento

pus /pʌs/ *n* pus *m*

ꝺ **push** /pʊʃ/ ① *n* spinta *f*; fig (effort) sforzo *m*; (drive) iniziativa *f*; **at a** ~ in caso di bisogno; **get the** ~ fam essere licenziato
② *vt* spingere; premere ‹button›; (pressurize) far pressione su; **be ~ed for time** fam non avere tempo
③ *vi* spingere

▪ **push around** *vt* (bully) fare il prepotente con

▪ **push aside** *vt* scostare

▪ **push back** *vt* respingere

▪ **push for** *vt* fare pressione per ottenere ‹reform›

▪ **push in** ① *vi* (in queue) farsi largo spingendo
② *vt* spingere ‹button›

▪ **push off** ① *vt* togliere
② *vi* fam (leave) levarsi dai piedi

▪ **push on** *vi* (continue) continuare

▪ **push over** *vt* (cause to fall) far cadere

▪ **push through** *vt* (have accepted quickly) fare accettare

▪ **push up** *vt* alzare ‹price›

push-button *n* pulsante *m*

pushchair /'pʊʃtʃeə(r)/ *n* passeggino *m*

pusher /'pʊʃə(r)/ *n* fam (of drugs) spacciatore, -trice *mf* [di droga]

pushover *n* fam bazzecola *f*

push start ① *vt* spingere (*per far partire*) ‹vehicle›
② *n* **give something a** ~ dare una spinta a qualcosa

push-up *n* flessione *f*

pushy /'pʊʃɪ/ *adj* fam troppo intraprendente

puss /pʊs/, **pussy** /'pʊsɪ/ *n* micio *m*

pussyfoot around /'pʊsɪfʊt/ *vi* fam tergiversare

pussyfooting /'pʊsɪfʊtɪŋ/ ① *n* fam tentennamento *m*
② *adj* fam ‹attitude, behaviour› tergiversante

ꝺ **put** /pʊt/ ① *vt* (*pt/pp* put, *pres p* **putting**) mettere; ~ **the cost of something at £50** valutare il costo di qualcosa 50 sterline; ~ **an end to** porre fine *o* termine a; ~ **in writing** mettere per iscritto; ~ **into effect** mettere in opera
② *vi* ~ **to sea** salpare
③ *adj* **stay ~!** rimani lì!

▪ **put about** *vt* mettere in giro ‹rumour›

▪ **put across** *vt* raccontare ‹joke›; esprimere ‹message›

▪ **put aside** *vt* mettere da parte

▪ **put away** *vt* mettere via

▪ **put back** *vt* rimettere; mettere indietro ‹clock›

▪ **put by** *vt* mettere da parte

▪ **put down** *vt* mettere giù; (suppress) reprimere; (kill) sopprimere; (write) annotare; (criticize unfairly) sminuire; ~ **one's foot down** fam essere fermo; Auto dare un'accelerata; ~ **down to** (attribute) attribuire

▪ **put forward** *vt* avanzare; mettere avanti ‹clock›

▪ **put in** ① *vt* (insert) introdurre; (submit) presentare
② *vi* ~ **in for** far domanda di

▪ **put off** *vt* spegnere ‹light›; (postpone) rimandare; ~ **somebody off** tenere a bada qualcuno; (deter) smontare qualcuno; (disconcert) distrarre qualcuno; (deter) smontare qualcuno; (disconcert) distrarre qualcuno; ~ **somebody off something** (disgust) disgustare qualcuno di qualcosa

▪ **put on** *vt* mettersi ‹clothes›; mettere ‹brake›; Culin mettere su; accendere ‹light›; mettere in scena ‹play›; prendere ‹accent›; ~ **weight** mettere su qualche chilo; **he's just ~ting it on** è solo una messa in scena

▪ **put on to** *vt* (help find) indicare ‹doctor, restaurant etc›

▪ **put out** *vt* spegnere ‹fire, light›; tendere ‹hand›; (inconvenience) creare degli inconvenienti a

▪ **put through** *vt* far passare; Teleph **I'll ~ you through to him** glielo passo

▪ **put to**: *vt* ~ **somebody to trouble** scomodare qualcuno; **I ~ it to you that ...** ritengo che ...

▪ **put together** *vt* montare ‹machine›; fare ‹model, jigsaw›

▪ **put up** ① *vt* alzare; erigere ‹building›; montare ‹tent›; aprire ‹umbrella›; affiggere ‹notice›; aumentare ‹price›; ospitare ‹guest›; ~ **somebody up to something** mettere qualcosa in testa a qualcuno
② *vi* (at hotel) stare; ~ **up with** sopportare

put-down /'pʊtdaʊn/ *n* commento *m* umiliante

putrefaction /pjuːtrɪ'fækʃn/ *n* putrefazione *f*

putrefy /'pjuːtrɪfaɪ/ *vi* (*pt/pp* -**ied**) putrefarsi

putrid /'pjuːtrɪd/ *adj* putrido

putt /pʌt/ ① *n* putt *m inv*
② *vi* colpire leggermente

putty /'pʌtɪ/ *n* mastice *m*

put-up job *n* fam truffa *f*

puzzle /'pʌzl/ ① *n* enigma *m*; (jigsaw) puzzle *m inv*
② *vt* lasciare perplesso
③ *vi* ~ **over** scervellarsi su

▪ **puzzle out** *vt* trovare ‹solution›

puzzled /'pʌzld/ *adj* perplesso

puzzling /'pʌzlɪŋ/ *adj* inspiegabile

PVC ① *n* PVC *m*
② *attrib* di PVC

ꝺ indicates a very frequent word

pygmy ···> quartz ····

pygmy /'pɪgmɪ/ n pigmeo, -a mf
pyjamas /pə'dʒɑːməz/ npl pigiama msg
pylon /'paɪlən/ n pilone m
pyramid /'pɪrəmɪd/ n piramide f
pyre /paɪə(r)/ n pira f

Pyrex® /'paɪreks/ n Pyrex m
pyromaniac /paɪrə'meɪnɪæk/ n piromane mf
pyrotechnics /paɪrə'teknɪks/ n (display) fuochi mpl pirotecnici
python /'paɪθn/ n pitone m

Q q

q, Q /kjuː/ n (letter) q, Q f inv
Qatar /kæ'tɑː/ n Qatar m
QC n Br Jur avvocato m di rango superiore
QED abbr (**quod erat demonstrandum**) qed
quack¹ /kwæk/ ⒈ n qua qua m inv
  ⒉ vi fare qua qua
quack² n (doctor) ciarlatano m
quad /kwɒd/ n fam (court) = QUADRANGLE; ~s pl fam = QUADRUPLETS
quadrangle /'kwɒdræŋgl/ n quadrangolo m; (court) cortile m quadrangolare
quadratic equation /kwɒ'drætɪk/ n equazione f di secondo grado
quadriplegic /kwɒdrɪ'pliːdʒɪk/ adj quadriplegico
quadruped /'kwɒdrʊped/ n quadrupede m
quadruple /'kwɒdrʊpl/ ⒈ adj quadruplo
  ⒉ vt quadruplicare
  ⒊ vi quadruplicarsi
quadruplets /kwɒd'ruːplɪts/ npl quattro gemelli mpl
quadruplicate /kwɒd'ruːplɪkət/ n in ~ in quattro copie
quagmire /'kwɒgmaɪə(r)/ n pantano m
quail /kweɪl/ vi farsi prendere dalla paura
quaint /kweɪnt/ adj pittoresco; (odd) bizzarro
quake /kweɪk/ ⒈ n fam terremoto m
  ⒉ vi tremare
Quaker /'kweɪkə(r)/ n quacchero, -a mf
qualification /kwɒlɪfɪ'keɪʃn/ n qualifica f; (reservation) riserva f
qualified /'kwɒlɪfaɪd/ adj qualificato; (limited) con riserva
qualifier /'kwɒlɪfaɪə(r)/ n Sport concorrente mf qualificato, -a
qualify /'kwɒlɪfaɪ/ ⒈ vt (pt/pp -ied) ‹course› dare la qualifica a (as di); ‹entitle› dare diritto a; ‹limit› precisare
  ⒉ vi ottenere la qualifica; Sport qualificarsi
qualitative /'kwɒlɪtətɪv/ adj qualitativo
quality /'kwɒlətɪ/ n qualità f inv
quality assurance n verifica f qualità

quality control n controllo m [di] qualità
quality controller n addetto, -a mf al controllo di qualità
qualm /kwɑːm/ n scrupolo m
quandary /'kwɒndərɪ/ n dilemma m
quango /'kwæŋgəʊ/ n Br organismo (m) autonomo ma finanziato dal governo
quantifiable /'kwɒntɪfaɪəbl/ adj quantificabile
quantify /'kwɒntɪfaɪ/ vt quantificare
quantitative /'kwɒntɪtətɪv/ adj quantitativo
quantity /'kwɒntətɪ/ n quantità f inv; in ~ in grande quantità
quantity surveyor n geometra (mf) che calcola quantità e costo di materiali da costruzione
quantum leap /kwɒntəm'liːp/ n fig balzo m in avanti
quantum mechanics n meccanica f quantistica
quarantine /'kwɒrəntiːn/ n quarantena f
quarrel /'kwɒrəl/ ⒈ n lite f
  ⒉ vi (pt/pp **quarrelled**) litigare
quarrelsome /'kwɒrəlsəm/ adj litigioso
quarry¹ /'kwɒrɪ/ n (prey) preda f
quarry² n cava f
quarry tile n mattonella f grezza
quart /kwɔːt/ n = 1,14 litre
quarter /'kwɔːtə(r)/ ⒈ n quarto m; (of year) trimestre m; Am 25 centesimi mpl; ~s pl Mil quartiere msg; at [a] ~ to six alle sei meno un quarto; from all ~s da tutti i lati
  ⒉ vt dividere in quattro
quarterdeck /'kwɔːtədek/ n Naut cassero m
quarter-final n quarto m di finale
quarterly /'kwɔːtəlɪ/ ⒈ adj trimestrale
  ⒉ adv trimestralmente
quartermaster /'kwɔːtəmɑːstə(r)/ n ‹in navy› timoniere m; ‹in army› furiere m
quartet /kwɔː'tet/ n quartetto m
quartz /kwɔːts/ n quarzo m; ~ **watch** orologio m al quarzo

quash /kwɒʃ/ vt annullare; soffocare ⟨rebellion⟩

quasi+ /'kweɪzaɪ/ pref semi+

quaver /'kweɪvə(r)/ **1** n Mus croma f **2** vi tremolare

quay /kiː/ n banchina f

quayside /'kiːsaɪd/ n banchina f

queasiness /'kwiːzɪnɪs/ n nausea f

queasy /'kwiːzɪ/ adj I feel ~ ho la nausea

Quebec /kwɪ'bek/ n (province) Quebec m; (town) Quebec f

ᶠ **queen** /kwiːn/ n regina f

queen bee n ape f regina; **she thinks she's the ~** fig si crede chissà chi

queenly /'kwiːnlɪ/ adj da regina

queen mother n regina f madre

Queen's Counsel n Br Jur avvocato (m) di rango superiore

Queen's English n Br speak the ~ parlare un inglese corretto e senza accento

Queen's evidence n Br Jur turn ~ deporre contro i propri complici

Queen's Regulations npl Br Mil codice m militare

queer /kwɪə(r)/ **1** adj strano; (dubious) sospetto; fam (homosexual) finocchio **2** n fam finocchio m

quell /kwel/ vt reprimere

quench /kwentʃ/ vt ~ one's thirst dissetarsi

querulous /'kwerʊləs/ adj lamentoso

query /'kwɪərɪ/ **1** n domanda f; (question mark) punto m interrogativo **2** vt (pt/pp **-ied**) interrogare; (doubt) mettere in dubbio

quest /kwest/ n ricerca f (**for** di)

ᶠ **question** /'kwestʃən/ **1** n domanda f; (for discussion) questione f; **out of the ~** fuori discussione; **without ~** senza dubbio; **in ~** in questione **2** vt interrogare; (doubt) mettere in dubbio

questionable /'kwestʃ(ə)nəbl/ adj discutibile

questioner /'kwestʃ(ə)nə(r)/ n interrogante mf

questioning /'kwestʃ(ə)nɪŋ/ **1** n (of person) interrogatorio m; (of criteria) messa f in discussione **2** adj ⟨look, tone⟩ inquisitorio

question mark n punto m interrogativo

question master n presentatore, -trice mf di quiz

questionnaire /kwestʃə'neə(r)/ n questionario m

question tag n domanda f di conferma

queue /kjuː/ **1** n coda f, fila f **2** vi ~ [**up**] mettersi in coda (**for** per)

ᶠ indicates a very frequent word

queue-jump vi Br passare davanti alle altre persone in coda

quibble /'kwɪbl/ vi cavillare

ᶠ **quick** /kwɪk/ **1** adj veloce; **be ~** sbrigati!; **have a ~ meal** fare uno spuntino **2** adv in fretta **3** n **be cut to the ~** fig essere punto sul vivo

quick-assembly adj facile da montare

quicken /'kwɪkən/ **1** vt accelerare ⟨pace⟩ **2** vi ⟨pace⟩ accelerarsi; ⟨interest⟩ intensificarsi

quick-fire adj ⟨questions⟩ a mitraglia

quick-freeze vt surgelare

quickie /'kwɪkɪ/ n fam (question) domanda f rapida; (drink) bicchierino m rapido; (film) cortometraggio m

quicklime /'kwɪklaɪm/ n calce f viva

ᶠ **quickly** /'kwɪklɪ/ adv in fretta

quick march n Mil passo m di marcia veloce

quicksand n sabbie fpl mobili

quick-setting /-'setɪŋ/ adj a presa rapida

quicksilver n Chem argento m vivo, mercurio m

quick-tempered /-'tempəd/ adj collerico

quick time n Am marcia f veloce

quick-witted /-'wɪtɪd/ adj ⟨reaction⟩ pronto; ⟨person⟩ sveglio

quid /kwɪd/ n inv fam sterlina f

quid pro quo /kwɪdprəʊ'kwəʊ/ n contraccambio m

ᶠ **quiet** /'kwaɪət/ **1** adj (calm) tranquillo; (silent) silenzioso; (voice, music) basso; **keep ~ about** fam non raccontare a nessuno **2** n quiete f; **on the ~** di nascosto ∎ **quiet down** Am vt/i ▶ QUIETEN DOWN

quieten /'kwaɪətn/ vt calmare ∎ **quieten down** Br **1** vt calmare **2** vi calmarsi

ᶠ **quietly** /'kwaɪətlɪ/ adv (peacefully) tranquillamente; ⟨say⟩ a bassa voce

quietness /'kwaɪətnɪs/ n quiete f

quiff /kwɪf/ n Br (hair) ciuffo m

quill /kwɪl/ n penna f d'uccello; (spine) spina f

quilt /kwɪlt/ n piumino m

quilted /'kwɪltɪd/ adj trapuntato

quilting /'kwɪltɪŋ/ n (fabric) matelassé m inv

quince /kwɪns/ n cotogna f; (tree) melo m cotogno

quinine /kwɪ'niːn/ n chinino m

quins /kwɪnz/ npl fam = QUINTUPLETS

quintessential /kwɪntɪ'senʃl/ adj ⟨quality⟩ fondamentale

quintet /kwɪn'tet/ n quintetto m

quintuple /'kwɪntjʊpl/ **1** vt quintuplicare **2** adj quintuplo

quintuplets /'kwɪntjʊplɪts/ *npl* cinque gemelli *mpl*

quip /kwɪp/ **1** *n* battuta *f*
   2 *vt* (*pt/pp* **quipped**) dire scherzando

quirk /kwɜːk/ *n* stranezza *f*

quisling /'kwɪzlɪŋ/ *n* pej collaborazionista *mf*

quit /kwɪt/ **1** *vt* (*pt/pp* **-tted** *or* **quit**) lasciare; (give up) smettere (**doing** di fare); Comput uscire da
   2 *vi* fam (resign) andarsene; Comput uscire; **give somebody notice to** ~ dare a qualcuno preavviso di sfratto

⚡ **quite** /kwaɪt/ *adv* (fairly) abbastanza; (completely) completamente; (really) veramente; ~ **[so]!** proprio così!; ~ **a few** parecchi

quits /kwɪts/ *adj* pari

quiver /'kwɪvə(r)/ *vi* tremare

quiz /kwɪz/ **1** *n* (game) quiz *m inv*
   2 *vt* (*pt/pp* **quizzed**) interrogare

quiz game, quiz show *n* quiz *m inv*

quizzical /'kwɪzɪkl/ *adj* sardonico

quoit /kwɔɪt/ *n* anello *m* (*del gioco*)

quoits *n* (game) gioco *m* degli anelli

quorum /'kwɔːrəm/ *n* quorum *m inv*; **have a** ~ avere il quorum

quota /'kwəʊtə/ *n* quota *f*

quotation /kwəʊ'teɪʃn/ *n* citazione *f*; (price) preventivo *m*; (of shares) quota *f*

quotation marks *npl* virgolette *fpl*

⚡ **quote** /kwəʊt/ **1** *n* fam = QUOTATION; **in** ~**s** tra virgolette
   2 *vt* citare; quotare ‹price›; ~**d on the Stock Exchange** quotato in Borsa

Rr

r, R¹ /ɑː(r)/ *n* (letter) r, R *f inv*; **the three Rs** leggere, scrivere e contare

R *abbr* Br (**regina**) regina *f*

R & B *n* rhythm and blues *m*

R & D *n* ricerca *f* e sviluppo *m*

rabbi /'ræbaɪ/ *n* rabbino *m*; (title) rabbi

rabbit /'ræbɪt/ *n* coniglio *m*
   ■ **rabbit on**: *vi* fam **what's he** ~**ting on about now?** cosa sta blaterando?

rabbit hutch *n* conigliera *f*

rabble /'ræbl/ *n* **the** ~ la plebaglia

rabble rouser /'raʊzə(r)/ *n* agitatore, -trice *nmf*

rabble rousing *n* incitazione *f* alla violenza

rabid /'ræbɪd/ *adj* fig rabbioso

rabies /'reɪbiːz/ *n* rabbia *f*

RAC *n abbr* Br (**Royal Automobile Club**) ≈ ACI *f*

raccoon /rə'kuːn/ *n* procione *m*, orsetto *m* lavatore

race¹ /reɪs/ *n* (people) razza *f*

⚡ **race²** **1** *n* corsa *f*
   2 *vi* correre
   3 *vt* gareggiare con; fare correre ‹horse›

racecourse /'reɪskɔːs/ *n* ippodromo *m*

racehorse /'reɪshɔːs/ *n* cavallo *m* da corsa

racer /'reɪsə(r)/ *n* (bike) bicicletta *f* da corsa; (motorbike) motocicletta *f* da corsa; (car) automobile *f* da corsa; (runner, cyclist etc) corridore, -trice *mf*

race relations *npl* rapporti *mpl* tra le razze

race riots *npl* scontri *mpl* razziali

racetrack /'reɪstræk/ *n* pista *f*

racial /'reɪʃl/ *adj* razziale

racialism /'reɪʃəlɪzm/ *n* razzismo *m*

racially /'reɪʃ(ə)lɪ/ *adv* razzialmente

racing /'reɪsɪŋ/ *n* corse *fpl*; (horse-~) corse *fpl* dei cavalli

racing car *n* macchina *f* da corsa

racing driver *n* corridore *m* automobilistico

racism /'reɪsɪzm/ *n* razzismo *m*

racist /'reɪsɪst/ *adj & n* razzista *mf*

rack¹ /ræk/ **1** *n* (for bikes) rastrelliera *f*; (for luggage) portabagagli *m inv*; (for plates) scolapiatti *m inv*
   2 *vt* ~ **one's brains** scervellarsi

rack² *n* **go to** ~ **and ruin** andare in rovina

racket¹ /'rækɪt/ *n* Sport racchetta *f*

racket² *n* (din) chiasso *m*; (swindle) truffa *f*; (crime) racket *m inv*, giro *m*

racketeer /rækɪ'tɪə(r)/ *n* trafficante *m*

racketeering /rækɪ'tɪərɪŋ/ *n* traffici *mpl* illeciti

racking /'rækɪŋ/ *adj* ‹pain› atroce

raconteur /rækɒntɜː(r)/ *n* bravo narratore *m*, brava narratrice *f*

racquetball /'rækɪtbɔːl/ *n* Am = SQUASH

racy /'reɪsɪ/ *adj* (**-ier, -iest**) vivace; (risqué) osé *inv*, spinto

radar /'reɪdɑː(r)/ *n* radar *m*

radar trap *n* Auto *tratto* (*m*) *di strada sul quale la polizia controlla la velocità dei veicoli*

radial /'reɪdɪəl/ ① n (tyre) pneumatico m, radiale m
② adj ‹lines, roads› radiale
radiance /'reɪdɪəns/ n radiosità f
radiant /'reɪdɪənt/ adj raggiante
radiate /'reɪdɪeɪt/ ① vt irradiare
② vi irradiarsi
radiation /reɪdɪ'eɪʃn/ n radiazione f
radiation exposure n esposizione f a radiazioni
radiation sickness n patologia f da radiazioni
radiator /'reɪdɪeɪtə(r)/ n radiatore m
radical /'rædɪkl/ adj & n radicale mf
radicalism /'rædɪkəlɪzm/ n radicalismo m
radically /'rædɪklɪ/ adv radicalmente
✦ **radio** /'reɪdɪəʊ/ ① n radio f inv
② vt mandare via radio ‹message›
radioactive /reɪdɪəʊ'æktɪv/ adj radioattivo
radioactive waste n scorie fpl radioattive
radioactivity /reɪdɪəʊæk'tɪvətɪ/ n radioattività f
radio alarm n radiosveglia f
radio cassette player n radioregistratore m
radio-controlled adj radiocomandato
radiographer /reɪdɪ'ɒɡrəfə(r)/ n radiologo, -a mf
radiography /reɪdɪ'ɒɡrəfɪ/ n radiografia f
radio ham n radioamatore, -trice mf
radiologist /reɪdɪ'ɒlədʒɪst/ n radiologo, -a mf
radiology /ˌreɪdɪ'ɒlədʒɪ/ n radiologia f
radio station n stazione f radiofonica
radiotherapy /reɪdɪəʊ'θerəpɪ/ n radioterapia f
radish /'rædɪʃ/ n ravanello m
radius /'reɪdɪəs/ n (pl **-dii** /'reɪdɪaɪ/) raggio m
RAF n abbr Br (**Royal Air Force**) aviazione (f) militare inglese
raffle /'ræfl/ ① n lotteria f
② vt mettere in palio
raft /rɑːft/ n zattera f
rafter /'rɑːftə(r)/ n trave f
rag¹ /ræɡ/ n straccio m; pej (newspaper) giornalaccio m; in ∼s stracciato
rag² ① vt (pt/pp **ragged**) fam fare scherzi a
② n Univ festa (f) di beneficenza organizzata da studenti universitari
ragamuffin /'ræɡəmʌfɪn/ n monellaccio m
rag-and-bone man n Br rigattiere m, straccivendolo m

ragbag /'ræɡbæɡ/ n fig accozzaglia f
rage /reɪdʒ/ ① n rabbia f; **all the** ∼ fam all'ultima moda
② vi infuriarsi; ‹storm› infuriare; ‹epidemic› imperversare
ragged /'ræɡɪd/ adj logoro; ‹edge› frastagliato
raging /'reɪdʒɪŋ/ adj ‹blizzard, sea› furioso; ‹thirst, pain› atroce; ‹passion, argument› acceso
raglan /'ræɡlən/ ① adj raglan inv
② n manica f raglan
rag trade n fam settore m dell'abbigliamento
rag week n Br Univ settimana (f) di manifestazioni a scopo benefico organizzata dagli studenti
raid /reɪd/ ① n (by thieves) rapina f; Mil incursione f, raid m inv; (by police) irruzione f
② vt Mil fare un'incursione in; ‹police, thieves› fare irruzione in
raider /'reɪdə(r)/ n (of bank) rapinatore, -trice mf
rail¹ /reɪl/ n ringhiera f; Rail rotaia f; Naut parapetto m; **by** ∼ per ferrovia
rail² vi ∼ **against** or **at** inveire contro
railcard /'reɪlkɑːd/ n tessera f di riduzione ferroviaria
railings /'reɪlɪŋz/ npl ringhiera f
railroad /'reɪlrəʊd/ ① n Am = RAILWAY
② vt ∼ **somebody into doing something** spingere qualcuno a fare qualcosa
railroad car n Am vagone m ferroviario
railroad schedule n Am orario m ferroviario
rail traffic n traffico m ferroviario
railway /'reɪlweɪ/ n ferrovia f
railway carriage n Br vagone m ferroviario
railwayman /'reɪlweɪmən/ n ferroviere m
railway station n stazione f ferroviaria
✦ **rain** /reɪn/ ① n pioggia f
② vi piovere; ∼ **down on somebody** fig piovere addosso a qualcuno
③ vt ∼ **blows on somebody** tempestare qualcuno di colpi
■ **rain off:** vt be ∼ed off essere annullato a causa della pioggia
rainbow n arcobaleno m
raincheck n Am **can I take a** ∼**?** facciamo un'altra volta
raincoat n impermeabile m
raindrop n goccia f di pioggia
rainfall n precipitazione f [atmosferica]
rainforest n foresta f pluviale, foresta f equatoriale
rainstorm n temporale m
rain water n acqua f piovana
rainy /'reɪnɪ/ adj (**-ier**, **-iest**) piovoso

✦ indicates a very frequent word

rainy day *n* save something for a ∼ fig mettere qualcosa in serbo per i tempi di magra

rainy season *n* stagione *f* delle piogge

♂ **raise** /reɪz/ ① *n* Am aumento *m*
② *vt* alzare; levarsi ‹hat›; allevare ‹children, animals›; sollevare ‹question›; ottenere ‹money›; ∼ hell indiavolarsi; ∼ a laugh ‹joke, remark› far ridere; ∼ the stakes rilanciare; ∼ one's voice alzare la voce

raised /reɪzd/ *adj* ‹flowerbed, platform› soprelevato; ∼ voices urla

raisin /ˈreɪzn/ *n* uvetta *f*; ∼s *pl* uvetta *f*, uva *f* passa

Raj /rɑː3/ *n* governo *m* britannico in India

rake /reɪk/ ① *n* rastrello *m*
② *vt* rastrellare

■ **rake in** *vt* fam farsi ‹profits, money›; he's raking it in sta facendo un sacco di soldi

■ **rake together** *vt* fig racimolare ‹money›

■ **rake up** *vt* raccogliere col rastrello; fam rivangare

rake-off *n* fam parte *f*

rakish /ˈreɪkɪʃ/ *adj* (dissolute) dissoluto; (jaunty) disinvolto

rally /ˈrælɪ/ ① *n* raduno *m*; Auto rally *m* *inv*; Tennis scambio *m*; (recovery) ripresa *f*
② *vt* (*pt/pp* -ied) radunare
③ *vi* radunarsi; (recover strength) riprendersi

rallying cry, rallying call *n* slogan *m inv*

ram /ræm/ ① *n* montone *m*; Astr Ariete *m*
② *vt* (*pt/pp* **rammed**) cozzare contro

RAM /ræm/ *n* memoria *f* RAM

ramble /ˈræmbl/ ① *n* escursione *f*
② *vi* gironzolare; (in speech) divagare

■ **ramble on** *vi* fam parlare/scrivere a ruota libera

rambler /ˈræmblə(r)/ *n* escursionista *mf*; (rose) rosa *f* rampicante

rambling /ˈræmblɪŋ/ *adj* (in speech) sconnesso; ‹club› escursionistico

ramification /ræmɪfɪˈkeɪʃən/ *n* ramificazione *f*

ramify /ˈræmɪfaɪ/ *vi* (*pt/pp* -ied) ramificarsi

ramp /ræmp/ *n* rampa *f*; Auto dosso *m*

rampage /ˈræmpeɪdʒ/ ① *n* be/go on the ∼ scatenarsi
② *vi* ∼ through the streets scatenarsi per le strade

rampant /ˈræmpənt/ *adj* dilagante; (in heraldry) rampante

rampart /ˈræmpɑːt/ *n* bastione *f*

ram raid *n* rapina (*f*) in un negozio con scasso della vetrina effettuato con un'auto

ram raider *n* rapinatore (*m*) che scassa la vetrina di un negozio con un'auto

ramshackle /ˈræmʃækl/ *adj* sgangherato

ran /ræn/ ▶ RUN

ranch /rɑːntʃ/ *n* ranch *m inv*

rancher /ˈrɑːntʃə(r)/ *n* (worker) cow-boy *m inv*; (owner) proprietario *m* di ranch

rancid /ˈrænsɪd/ *adj* rancido

rancour /ˈræŋkə(r)/ *n* rancore *m*

random /ˈrændəm/ ① *adj* casuale; ∼ sample campione *m* a caso
② *n* at ∼ a casaccio

random-access *adj* ad accesso casuale

random-access memory *n* memoria *f* viva

randy /ˈrændɪ/ *adj* (-ier, -iest) fam eccitato

rang /ræŋ/ ▶ RING²

♂ **range** /reɪndʒ/ ① *n* serie *f*; Comm, Mus gamma *f*; (of mountains) catena *f*; (distance) raggio *m*; (for shooting) portata *f*; (stove) cucina *f* economica; at a ∼ of ad una distanza di
② *vi* estendersi; ∼ from...to... andare da...a...

ranger /ˈreɪndʒə(r)/ *n* guardia *f* forestale

rank¹ /ræŋk/ ① *n* (row) riga *f*; Mil grado *m*; (social position) rango *m*; the ∼ and file la base; the ∼s *pl* Mil i soldati *mpl* semplici
② *vt* (place) annoverare (among tra)
③ *vi* (be placed) collocarsi

rank² *adj* ‹smell› puzzolente; ‹plants› rigoglioso; fig vero e proprio

ranking /ˈræŋkɪŋ/ *n* classificazione *f*

rankle /ˈræŋkl/ *vi* fig bruciare; it still ∼s with him gli brucia ancora

ransack /ˈrænsæk/ *vt* rovistare; (pillage) saccheggiare

ransom /ˈrænsəm/ *n* riscatto *m*; hold somebody to ∼ tenere qualcuno in ostaggio per il riscatto

rant /rænt/ *vi* ∼ [and rave] inveire; what's he ∼ing on about? cosa sta blaterando?

rap /ræp/ ① *n* colpo *m* secco; Mus rap *m*
② *vt* (*pt/pp* **rapped**) dare colpetti a; ∼ somebody over the knuckles fig dare una tirata d'orecchie a qualcuno
③ *vi* ∼ at bussare a

rape¹ /reɪp/ *n* Bot colza *f*

rape² ① *n* (sexual) stupro *m*
② *vt* violentare, stuprare

rape[seed] oil /ˈreɪp[siːd]/ *n* olio *m* [di semi] di colza

rapid /ˈræpɪd/ *adj* rapido

rapidity /rəˈpɪdətɪ/ *n* rapidità *f*

rapidly /ˈræpɪdlɪ/ *adv* rapidamente

rapids /ˈræpɪdz/ *npl* rapida *fsg*

rapist /ˈreɪpɪst/ *n* violentatore *m*

rapper /ˈræpə(r)/ *n* Br (door-knocker) battiporta *m inv*; Mus rapper *m inv*

rapport /ræˈpɔː(r)/ *n* rapporto *m* di intesa

rapt /ræpt/ *adj* ‹look› rapito; ∼ in assorto in

rapture /ˈræptʃə(r)/ *n* estasi *f*

rapturous /ˈræptʃərəs/ *adj* entusiastico

rapturously /ˈræptʃərəslɪ/ *adv* entusiasticamente

r

⚡ **rare¹** /reə(r)/ *adj* raro
rare² *adj* Culin al sangue
rarefied /'reərɪfaɪd/ *adj* rarefatto
rarely /'reəlɪ/ *adv* raramente
raring /'reərɪŋ/ *adj* fam **be ~ to** non vedere
l'ora di
rarity /'reərətɪ/ *n* rarità *f inv*
rascal /'rɑːskl/ *n* mascalzone *m*
rash¹ /ræʃ/ *n* Med eruzione *f*
rash² *adj* avventato
rasher /'ræʃə(r)/ *n* fetta *f* di pancetta
rashly /'ræʃlɪ/ *adv* avventatamente
rashness /'ræʃnɪs/ *n* avventatezza *f*
rasp /rɑːsp/ *n* (noise) stridio *m*
raspberry /'rɑːzbərɪ/ *n* lampone *m*
rasping /'rɑːspɪŋ/ *adj* stridente
rat /ræt/ **①** *n* topo *m*; fam (person) carogna *f*;
smell a ~ fam sentire puzzo di bruciato
② *vi* (*pt/pp* **ratted**) fam **~ on** far la spia a
rat-a-tat-tat /rætətæ(t) 'tæt/ *n* toc toc
m inv
rat-catcher *n* addetto, -a *mf* alla
derattizzazione
ratchet /'rætʃɪt/ *n* (toothed rack) cremagliera
f
⚡ **rate** /reɪt/ **①** *n* (speed) velocità *f inv*; (of
payment) tariffa *f*; (of exchange) tasso *m*; **~s**
pl (taxes) imposte *fpl* comunali sui beni
immobili; **at any ~** in ogni caso; **at this ~** di
questo passo
② *vt* stimare; **~ among** annoverare tra
③ *vt* **~ as** essere considerato
ratepayer /'reɪtpeɪə(r)/ *n* contribuente *mf*
⚡ **rather** /'rɑːðə(r)/ *adv* piuttosto; **~!** eccome!;
~ too… un po' troppo…
ratification /rætɪfɪ'keɪʃn/ *n* ratifica *f*
ratify /'rætɪfaɪ/ *vt* (*pt/pp* **-ied**) ratificare
rating /'reɪtɪŋ/ *n* valutazione *f*; (class) livello
m; (sailor) marinaio *m* semplice; **~s** *pl* Radio,
TV indice *m* d'ascolto, audience *f inv*
⚡ **ratio** /'reɪʃɪəʊ/ *n* rapporto *m*; **In a ~ of two
to one** in [un] rapporto di due a uno
ration /'ræʃn/ **①** *n* razione *f*
② *vt* razionare
rational /'ræʃənl/ *adj* razionale
rationale /ræʃə'nɑːl/ *n* (logic) base *f* logica;
(reasons) ragioni *fpl*
rationalize /'ræʃ(ə)nəlaɪz/ *vt/i*
razionalizzare
rationally /'ræʃ(ə)nəlɪ/ *adv* razionalmente
rationing /'ræʃ(ə)nɪŋ/ *n* razionamento *m*
rat race *n* fam corsa *f* al successo
rat run *n* scorciatoia (*f*) usata dagli
automobilisti in zone residenziali
rattan /rə'tæn/ *n* (tree, material) malacca *f*
rattle /'rætl/ **①** *n* tintinnio *m*; (toy)
sonaglio *m*

② *vi* tintinnare
③ *vt* (shake) scuotere; fam innervosire
■ **rattle off** *vt* fam sciorinare
■ **rattle on** *vi* (talk at length) parlare
ininterrottamente
■ **rattle through** *vt* (say quickly) dire
velocemente; (do quickly) fare velocemente
rattlesnake /'rætlsneɪk/ *n* serpente *m* a
sonagli
ratty /'rætɪ/ *adj* Br fam (grumpy) irascibile; Am
(hair) sudicio
raucous /'rɔːkəs/ *adj* rauco
raunchy /'rɔːntʃɪ/ *adj* fam (performer, voice,
song) sexy *inv*; (bawdy) spinto
ravage /'rævɪdʒ/ *vt* devastare
ravages /'rævɪdʒɪz/ *npl* danni *mpl*
rave /reɪv/ *vi* vaneggiare; **~ about** andare
in estasi per
raven /'reɪvn/ *n* corvo *m* imperiale
ravenous /'rævənəs/ *adj* (person) affamato
rave-up *n* Br fam festa *f* animata
ravine /rə'viːn/ *n* gola *f*
raving /'reɪvɪŋ/ *adj* **~ mad** fam matto da
legare
ravings /'reɪvɪŋz/ *npl* vaneggiamenti *mpl*
ravioli /rævɪ'əʊlɪ/ *n* ravioli *mpl*
ravishing /'rævɪʃɪŋ/ *adj* incantevole
raw /rɔː/ *adj* crudo; (not processed) grezzo;
(weather) gelido; (inexperienced) inesperto
raw deal *n* **get a ~** fam farsi fregare
rawhide *n* (leather) cuoio *m* grezzo
Rawlplug® /'rɔːlplʌg/ *n* tassello *m*
raw materials *npl* materie *fpl* prime
ray /reɪ/ *n* raggio *m*; **~ of hope** barlume *m*
di speranza
rayon® /'reɪɒn/ *n* raion® *m*
raze /reɪz/ *vt* **~ to the ground** radere al
suolo
razor /'reɪzə(r)/ *n* rasoio *m*
razor blade *n* lametta *f* da barba
razor-sharp *adj* affilatissimo
razzle /'ræzl/ *n* Br fam **go on the ~** andare a
fare baldoria
razzle-dazzle *n* fam baldoria *f*
razzmatazz /ræzmə'tæz/ *n* fam clamore *m*
RC **①** *n abbr* (**Roman Catholic**)
cattolico, -a *mf*
② *adj* cattolico
Rd. *abbr* (**Road**) Via
re /riː/ *prep* con riferimento a
⚡ **reach** /riːtʃ/ **①** *n* portata *f*; (of river) tratto
m; **within ~** a portata di mano; **out of ~
of** fuori dalla portata di; **within easy ~**
facilmente raggiungibile
② *vt* arrivare a (place, decision); (contact)
contattare; (pass) passare; **I can't ~ it** non
ci arrivo
③ *vi* arrivare (**to** a); **I can't ~** non ci arrivo;
~ for allungare la mano per prendere

⚡ indicates a very frequent word

reaches /'riːtʃɪz/ *npl* (of river) **the upper/lower** ∼ la parte superiore/inferiore

react /rɪ'ækt/ *vi* reagire

◆ **reaction** /rɪ'ækʃn/ *n* reazione *f*

reactionary /rɪ'ækʃ(ə)nərɪ/ *adj & n* reazionario, -a *mf*

reactor /rɪ'æktə(r)/ *n* reattore *m*

◆ **read** /riːd/ ⓵ *vt* (*pt/pp* **read** /red/) leggere; Univ studiare
　⓶ *vi* leggere; ‹*instrument*› indicare
　■ **read back** *vt* (say aloud) rileggere
　■ **read on** *vi* (continue reading) continuare a leggere
　■ **read out** *vt* leggere ad alta voce
　■ **read up on** *vt* studiare a fondo

readable /'riːdəbl/ *adj* piacevole a leggersi; (legible) leggibile

◆ **reader** /'riːdə(r)/ *n* lettore, -trice *mf*; (book) antologia *f*

readership /'riːdəʃɪp/ *n* numero *m* di lettori

read head *n* Comput testina *f* di lettura

readily /'redɪlɪ/ *adv* volentieri; (easily) facilmente

readiness /'redɪnɪs/ *n* disponibilità *f*; **in** ∼ pronto

◆ **reading** /'riːdɪŋ/ *n* lettura *f*

readjust /riːə'dʒʌst/ ⓵ *vt* regolare di nuovo
　⓶ *vi* riabituarsi (**to** a)

readjustment /riːə'dʒʌstmənt/ *n* riadattamento *m*

read-only memory *n* Comput memoria *f* di sola lettura

readvertise /riː'ædvətaɪz/ *vt* far ripubblicare un'inserzione per ‹*position, item*›

◆ **ready** /'redɪ/ *adj* (**-ier**, **-iest**) pronto; (quick) veloce; **get** ∼ prepararsi

ready-made *adj* confezionato

ready-mixed *adj* già miscelato

ready money *n* contanti *mpl*

ready-to-wear *adj* prêt-à-porter

reaffirm /riːə'fɜːm/ *vt* riaffermare

reafforestation /riːəfɒrɪ'steɪʃn/ *n* rimboschimento *m*

◆ **real** /riːl/ ⓵ *adj* vero; ‹*increase*› reale
　⓶ *adv* Am fam veramente

real estate *n* beni *mpl* immobili

realign /riːə'laɪn/ ⓵ *vt* riallineare
　⓶ *vi* fig formare nuove alleanze

realignment /riːə'laɪnmənt/ *n* Pol formazione *f* di nuove alleanze; Fin riallineamento *m*

realism /'rɪəlɪzm/ *n* realismo *m*

realist /'rɪəlɪst/ *n* realista *mf*

realistic /rɪə'lɪstɪk/ *adj* realistico

realistically /rɪə'lɪstɪklɪ/ *adv* realisticamente

◆ **reality** /rɪ'ælətɪ/ *n* realtà *f inv*

reality TV *n* reality TV *f*, reality *m*, reality show *mpl*

realization /rɪəlaɪ'zeɪʃn/ *n* realizzazione *f*

◆ **realize** /'rɪəlaɪz/ *vt* realizzare

real life *n* realtà *f*; **in** ∼ **life** nella realtà

real-life *attrib* autentico

reallocate /riː'æləkeɪt/ *vt* riassegnare

reallocation /riːælə'keɪʃn/ *n* riassegnazione *f*

◆ **really** /'rɪəlɪ/ *adv* davvero

realm /relm/ *n* regno *m*

real time ⓵ *n* tempo *m* reale; **in** ∼ in tempo reale
　⓶ *adj* in tempo reale

realtor /'rɪəltə(r)/ *n* Am agente *mf* immobiliare

realty /'rɪəltɪ/ *n* Am beni *mpl* immobili

reanimate /riː'ænɪmeɪt/ *vt* rianimare

reap /riːp/ *vt* mietere

reappear /riːə'pɪə(r)/ *vi* riapparire

reappearance /riːə'pɪərəns/ *n* ricomparsa *f*

reapply /riːə'plaɪ/ *vi* (*pt/pp* **-ied**) ripresentare domanda

reappoint /riːə'pɔɪnt/ *vt* riconfermare

reappraisal /riːə'preɪzl/ *n* riconsiderazione *f*

reappraise /riːə'preɪz/ *vt* riesaminare ‹*question, policy*›; rivalutare ‹*writer, work*›

rear[1] /rɪə(r)/ *adj* posteriore; Auto di dietro

rear[2] ⓵ *vt* allevare
　⓶ *vi* ∼ **[up]** ‹*horse*› impennarsi
　⓷ *n* **the** ∼ (of building) il retro; (of bus, plane) la parte posteriore; **from the** ∼ da dietro

rear end *n* fam di dietro *m*

rearguard /'rɪəgɑːd/ *n* Mil fig retroguardia *f*

rear light *n* luce *f* posteriore

rearm /riː'ɑːm/ ⓵ *vt* riarmare
　⓶ *vi* riarmarsi

rearmament /riː'ɑːməmənt/ *n* riarmo *m*

rearmost /'rɪəməʊst/ *adj* ultimo; ‹*carriage*› di coda

rearrange /riːə'reɪndʒ/ *vt* cambiare la disposizione di

rear-view mirror *n* Auto specchietto *m* retrovisore

◆ **reason** /'riːzn/ ⓵ *n* ragione *f*; **within** ∼ nei limiti del ragionevole; **listen to** ∼ ascoltare la ragione
　⓶ *vi* ragionare; ∼ **with** cercare di far ragionare

◆ **reasonable** /'riːznəbl/ *adj* ragionevole

reasonably /'riːznəblɪ/ *adv* (in reasonable way, fairly) ragionevolmente

reasoning /'riːznɪŋ/ *n* ragionamento *m*

reassemble /riːə'semb(ə)l/ *vt* riassemblare

reassembly /riːə'semblɪ/ *n* riassemblaggio *m*

r

reassert /ˌriːəˈsɜːt/ vt riaffermare ‹authority›

reassess /riːəˈses/ vt riesaminare ‹problem, situation›; riaccertare ‹tax liability›

reassessment /riːəˈsesmənt/ n (of situation) riesame m; (of tax) nuovo accertamento m

reassurance /riːəˈʃʊərəns/ n rassicurazione f

reassure /riːəˈʃʊə(r)/ vt rassicurare; ~ somebody of something rassicurare qualcuno su qualcosa

reassuring /riːəˈʃʊərɪŋ/ adj rassicurante

reawaken /riːəˈweɪkn/ vt fig risvegliare ‹interest›

rebate /ˈriːbeɪt/ n rimborso m; (discount) deduzione f

rebel[1] /ˈrebl/ n ribelle mf

rebel[2] /rɪˈbel/ vi (pt/pp **rebelled**) ribellarsi

rebellion /rɪˈbeljən/ n ribellione f

rebellious /rɪˈbeljəs/ adj ribelle

rebelliousness /rɪˈbeljəsnɪs/ n spirito m di ribellione

rebirth /riːbɜːθ/ n rinascita f

reboot /riːˈbuːt/ vt Comput reinizializzare

reborn /riːˈbɔːn/ adj Relig be ~ rinascere; be ~ as something rinascere come qualcosa

rebound[1] /rɪˈbaʊnd/ vi rimbalzare; fig ricadere

rebound[2] /ˈriːbaʊnd/ n rimbalzo m

rebuff /rɪˈbʌf/ ① n rifiuto m ② vt respingere

rebuild /riːˈbɪld/ vt (pt/pp **-built**) ricostruire

rebuke /rɪˈbjuːk/ ① n rimprovero m ② vt rimproverare

rebut /rɪˈbʌt/ vt confutare

rebuttal /rɪˈbʌtl/ n rifiuto m

recalcitrant /rɪˈkælsɪtrənt/ adj fml ricalcitrante

recalculate /riːˈkælkjʊleɪt/ vt ricalcolare

ⓕ **recall** /rɪˈkɔːl/ ① n richiamo m; beyond ~ irrevocabile ② vt richiamare; riconvocare ‹diplomat, parliament›; (remember) rievocare

recant /rɪˈkænt/ vi abiurare

recap /ˈriːkæp/ ① vt/i fam = RECAPITULATE ② n ricapitolazione f

recapitulate /riːkəˈpɪtjʊleɪt/ vt/i ricapitolare

recapture /riːˈkæptʃə(r)/ vt riconquistare; ricatturare ‹person, animal›

recast /riːˈkɑːst/ vt rimaneggiare ‹text, plan›; riformulare ‹sentence›

recede /rɪˈsiːd/ vt allontanarsi

receding /rɪˈsiːdɪŋ/ adj ‹forehead, chin› sfuggente; have ~ hair essere stempiato

receipt /rɪˈsiːt/ n ricevuta f; (receiving) ricezione f; ~s pl Comm entrate fpl

ⓕ **receive** /rɪˈsiːv/ vt ricevere

receiver /rɪˈsiːvə(r)/ n Teleph ricevitore m; Radio, TV apparecchio m ricevente; (of stolen goods) ricettatore, -trice mf

receivership /rɪˈsiːvəʃɪp/ n Br go into ~ essere sottomesso all'amministrazione controllata

receiving /rɪˈsiːvɪŋ/ n (stolen goods) ricettazione f

receiving end /rɪˈsiːvɪŋ/ n be on the ~ essere dall'altro lato della barricata

ⓕ **recent** /ˈriːsnt/ adj recente

ⓕ **recently** /ˈriːsntlɪ/ adv recentemente

receptacle /rɪˈseptəkl/ n recipiente m

reception /rɪˈsepʃn/ n ricevimento m; (welcome) accoglienza f; Radio ricezione f; ~ [desk] (in hotel) reception f inv

receptionist /rɪˈsepʃənɪst/ n persona f alla reception

receptive /rɪˈseptɪv/ adj ricettivo

recess /rɪˈses/ n rientranza f; (holiday) vacanza f; Am Sch intervallo m

recession /rɪˈseʃn/ n recessione f

recharge /riːˈtʃɑːdʒ/ vt ricaricare

rechargeable /ˌriːˈtʃɑːdʒəbl/ adj ‹battery› ricaricabile; ‹cost› addebitabile

recidivism /rɪˈsɪdɪvɪzm/ n recidività f

recidivist /rɪˈsɪdɪvɪst/ n recidivo, -a mf

recipe /ˈresəpɪ/ n ricetta f

recipe book n libro m di ricette

recipient /rɪˈsɪpɪənt/ n (of letter, parcel) destinatario, -a mf; (of money) beneficiario, -a mf

reciprocal /rɪˈsɪprəkl/ adj reciproco

reciprocate /rɪˈsɪprəkeɪt/ vt ricambiare

recital /rɪˈsaɪtl/ n recital m inv

recitation /resɪˈteɪʃn/ n recitazione f

recite /rɪˈsaɪt/ vt recitare; (list) elencare

reckless /ˈreklɪs/ adj ‹action, decision› sconsiderato; be a ~ driver guidare in modo spericolato

recklessly /ˈreklɪslɪ/ adv in modo sconsiderato

recklessness /ˈreklɪsnɪs/ n sconsideratezza f

reckon /ˈrekən/ vt calcolare; (consider) pensare; be ~ed essere considerato

■ **reckon on, reckon with** vt fare i conti con

■ **reckon without** vt fare i conti senza

reckoning /ˈrekənɪŋ/ n stima f, calcoli mpl; by my/your etc ~ secondo i miei/tuoi ecc. calcoli

reclaim /rɪˈkleɪm/ vt reclamare; bonificare ‹land›

ⓕ indicates a very frequent word

reclaimable /rɪˈkleɪməbl/ adj ‹expenses› rimborsabile

recline /rɪˈklaɪn/ vi sdraiarsi

reclining /rɪˈklaɪnɪŋ/ adj ‹seat› reclinabile

recluse /rɪˈkluːs/ n recluso, -a mf

reclusive /rɪˈkluːsɪv/ adj solitario

recognition /rekəgˈnɪʃn/ n riconoscimento m; **In** ∼ come riconoscimento (of per); **beyond** ∼ irriconoscibile

recognizable /ˌrekəgˈnaɪzəbl, ˈrekəgnaɪzəbl/ adj riconoscibile

♦ **recognize** /ˈrekəgnaɪz/ vt riconoscere

recoil¹ /ˈriːkɔɪl/ n (of gun) rinculo m

recoil² /rɪˈkɔɪl/ vi (in fear) indietreggiare

recollect /rekəˈlekt/ vt ricordare

recollection /rekəˈlekʃn/ n ricordo m

recommence /riːkəˈmens/ vt/i ricominciare

♦ **recommend** /rekəˈmend/ vt raccomandare

recommendatlon /rekəmenˈdeɪʃn/ n raccomandazione f

recommended retail price /rekəˈmendɪd/ n Comm prezzo m di vendita raccomandato

recompense /ˈrekəmpens/ ⟦1⟧ n ricompensa f
⟦2⟧ vt ricompensare

reconcile /ˈrekənsaɪl/ vt riconciliare; conciliare ‹facts›; far quadrare ‹bank statement›; ∼ **oneself** to rassegnarsi a

reconciliation /rekənsɪlɪˈeɪʃn/ n riconciliazione f

recondition /riːkənˈdɪʃn/ vt ripristinare; ∼**ed engine** motore m che ha subito riparazioni

reconnaissance /rɪˈkɒnɪsns/ n Mil ricognizione f; **on** ∼ in ricognizione

reconnoitre /rekəˈnɔɪtə(r)/ ⟦1⟧ vi (pres p -**tring**) fare una ricognizione
⟦2⟧ vt fare una ricognizione di

reconsider /riːkənˈsɪdə(r)/ vt riconsiderare

reconstruct /riːkənˈstrʌkt/ vt ricostruire

reconstruction /riːkənˈstrʌkʃn/ n ricostruzione f

reconvene /riːkənˈviːn/ vi riunirsi nuovamente

record¹ /rɪˈkɔːd/ vt registrare; (make a note of) annotare

♦ **record²** /ˈrekɔd/ n (file) documentazione f; Mus disco m; Sport record m inv; ∼**s** pl (files) schedario msg; **keep a** ∼ **of** tener nota di; **off the** ∼ in via ufficiosa; **have a [criminal]** ∼ avere la fedina penale sporca

record book n libro m dei record

record-breaker /ˈrekɔːdbreɪkə(r)/ n **be a** ∼ battere un record

recorded /rɪˈkɔːdɪd/ adj (on tape) ‹message› registrato; (in document) ‹sighting, case› documentato

recorded delivery /rɪˈkɔːdɪd/ n raccomandata f

recorder /rɪˈkɔːdə(r)/ n Mus flauto m dolce

record-holder /ˈrekɔːdhəʊldə(r), US ˈrekərd-/ n primatista mf

recording /rɪˈkɔːdɪŋ/ n registrazione f

recording studio n sala f di registrazione

record player n giradischi m inv

recount /rɪˈkaʊnt/ vt raccontare

re-count¹ /riːˈkaʊnt/ vt ricontare

re-count² /ˈriːkaʊnt/ n Pol nuovo conteggio m

recoup /rɪˈkuːp/ vt rifarsi di ‹losses›

recourse /rɪˈkɔːs/ n **have** ∼ **to** ricorrere a

♦ **recover** /rɪˈkʌvə(r)/ vt/i recuperare

re-cover /riːˈkʌvə(r)/ vt rifoderare

recovery /rɪˈkʌvəri/ n recupero m; (of health) guarigione f

recovery vehicle n autogrù f

recreate /ˈrekrɪeɪt, ˌriːkrɪˈeɪt/ vt ricreare

recreation /rekrɪˈeɪʃn/ n ricreazione f

recreational /rekrɪˈeɪʃənəl/ adj ricreativo

recreational drug n sostanza (f) stupefacente che si assume occasionalmente

recrimination /rɪkrɪmɪˈneɪʃn/ n recriminazione f

recruit /rɪˈkruːt/ ⟦1⟧ n Mil recluta f; **new** ∼ (member) nuovo, -a, adepto, -a mf; (worker) neoassunto, -a mf
⟦2⟧ vt assumere ‹staff›

recruitment /rɪˈkruːtmənt/ n assunzione f

rectangle /ˈrektæŋgl/ n rettangolo m

rectangular /rekˈtæŋgjʊlə(r)/ adj rettangolare

rectify /ˈrektɪfaɪ/ vt (pt/pp -**ied**) rettificare

rector /ˈrektə(r)/ n Univ rettore m

rectory /ˈrektərɪ/ n presbiterio m

rectum /ˈrektəm/ n retto m

recuperate /rɪˈkjuːpəreɪt/ vi ristabilirsi

recur /rɪˈkɜː(r)/ vi (pt/pp **recurred**) ricorrere; ‹illness› ripresentarsi

recurrence /rɪˈkʌrəns/ n ricorrenza f; (of illness) ricomparsa f

recurrent /rɪˈkʌrənt/ adj ricorrente

recyclable /riːˈsaɪkləbl/ adj riciclabile

recycle /riːˈsaɪkl/ vt riciclare; ∼**d paper** carta f riciclata

recycling /riːˈsaɪklɪŋ/ n riciclaggio m

♦ **red** /red/ ⟦1⟧ adj (**redder, reddest**) rosso
⟦2⟧ n rosso m; **be in the** ∼ ‹account› essere scoperto; ‹person› avere il conto scoperto

red alert n allarme m rosso; **be on** ∼ essere in stato di massima allerta

r

redbrick *adj* Univ di recente fondazione

Red Cross *n* Croce *f* Rossa

redcurrant *n* ribes *m* rosso

redden /'redn/ ① *vt* arrossare
② *vi* arrossire

reddish /'redɪʃ/ *adj* rossastro

redecorate /riːˈdekəreɪt/ *vt* ‹paint› ridipingere; (wallpaper) ritappezzare

redeem /rɪˈdiːm/ *vt* (Relig, from pawnshop) riscattare; **∼ing quality** unico aspetto *m* positivo

redefine /riːdɪˈfaɪn/ *vt* ridefinire

redemption /rɪˈdempʃn/ *n* riscatto *m*

redeploy /riːdɪˈplɔɪ/ *vt* ridistribuire

redevelop /ˌriːdɪˈveləp/ *vt* risanare ‹area, site›

red-faced *adj* also fig paonazzo

red-haired /-ˈheəd/ *adj* con i capelli rossi

red-handed /-ˈhændɪd/ *adj* **catch somebody ∼** cogliere qualcuno con le mani nel sacco

redhead *n* rosso, -a *mf* (di capelli)

red herring *n* diversione *f*

red-hot *adj* rovente

redial /riːˈdaɪəl/ Teleph ① *vt* ricomporre
② *vi* ricomporre il numero

redial facility *n* Teleph funzione *f* di ricomposizione automatica dell'ultimo numero

redirect /riːdaɪˈrekt/ *vt* mandare al nuovo indirizzo ‹letter›

rediscover /riːdɪˈskʌvə(r)/ *vt* riscoprire

redistribute /riːdɪsˈtrɪbjuːt/ *vt* ridistribuire

redistribution /riːdɪstrɪˈbjuːʃn/ *n* ridistribuzione *f*

red-letter day *n* giorno *m* memorabile

red light *n* Auto semaforo *m* rosso; **go through a ∼** passare col rosso

red light area *n* quartiere *m* a luci rosse

red light district *n* quartiere *m* a luci rosse

red meat *n* carne *f* rossa

redness /'rednɪs/ *n* rossore *m*

redo /riːˈduː/ *vt* (*pt* **-did**, *pp* **-done**) rifare

redolent /'redələnt/ *adj* profumato (**of** di)

redouble /riːˈdʌbl/ *vt* raddoppiare

red pepper *n* peperone *m* rosso

redraft /riːˈdrɑːft/ *vt* stendere nuovamente

redress /rɪˈdres/ ① *n* riparazione *f*
② *vt* ristabilire ‹balance›

red tape *n* fam burocrazia *f*

✧ **reduce** /rɪˈdjuːs/ *vt* ridurre; Culin far consumare

reductio ad absurdum /rɪˈdʌktɪəʊædæbˈsɜːdəm/ *n* ragionamento *m* per assurdo

─────────────
✧ indicates a very frequent word

✧ **reduction** /rɪˈdʌkʃn/ *n* riduzione *f*

redundancy /rɪˈdʌndənsɪ/ *n* licenziamento *m*; (payment) cassa *f* integrazione

redundant /rɪˈdʌndənt/ *adj* superfluo; **make ∼** licenziare; **be made ∼** essere licenziato

reed /riːd/ *n* Bot canna *f*

reedy /'riːdɪ/ *adj* ‹voice, tone› acuto

reef /riːf/ *n* scogliera *f*

reefer /'riːfə(r)/ *n* (jacket) giubbotto *m* a doppio petto; fam (dope) spinello *m*

reef knot *n* nodo *m* piano

reek /riːk/ *vi* puzzare (**of** di)

reel /riːl/ ① *n* bobina *f*
② *vi* (stagger) vacillare

re-elect *vt* rieleggere

re-election *n* rielezione *f*

reel off *vt* fig snocciolare

re-emerge *vi* riemergere

re-emergence *n* ricomparsa *f*

re-enact /riːɪˈnækt/ *vt* ricostruire ‹crime›; Jur rimettere in vigore; recitare nuovamente ‹role›

re-enter /riːˈentə(r)/ *vt* rientrare in

re-entry *n* (of spacecraft) rientro *m*

re-establish *vt* ristabilire, ripristinare

re-establishment *n* ripristino *m*

re-examination *n* riesame *m*

re-examine *vt* riesaminare

ref /ref/ *n abbr* Br fam (**referee**) arbitro *m*

refectory /rɪˈfektərɪ/ *n* refettorio *m*; Univ mensa *f* universitaria

✧ **refer** /rɪˈfɜː(r)/ ① *vt* (*pt/pp* **referred**) rinviare ‹matter›; indirizzare ‹person›
② *vi* **∼ to** fare allusione a; (consult) rivolgersi a ‹book›; **are you ∼ring to me?** alludi a me?

referee /refəˈriː/ ① *n* arbitro *m*; (for job) garante *mf*
② *vt/i* (*pt/pp* **refereed**) arbitrare

✧ **reference** /'ref(ə)rəns/ *n* riferimento *m*; (in book) nota *f* bibliografica; (for job) referenza *f*; Comm **'your ∼'** 'riferimento'; **with ∼ to** con riferimento a; **make [a] ∼ to** fare riferimento a

reference book *n* libro *m* di consultazione

reference library *n* biblioteca *f* per la consultazione

reference number *n* numero *m* di riferimento

referendum /refəˈrendəm/ *n* referendum *m inv*

referral /rɪˈfɜːrəl/ *n* (of matter, problem) deferimento *m*; Med (act) *invio* (*m*) *di un paziente a un altro medico*; (person) *paziente* (*mf*) *mandato da un medico a un altro*

refill¹ /riːˈfɪl/ *vt* riempire di nuovo; ricaricare ‹pen, lighter›

refill ···⟶ register ····

refill² /'ri:fɪl/ n (for pen) ricambio m

refine /rɪ'faɪn/ vt raffinare

refined /rɪ'faɪnd/ adj raffinato

refinement /rɪ'faɪnmənt/ n raffinatezza f

refinery /rɪ'faɪnərɪ/ n raffineria f

refining /rɪ'faɪnɪŋ/ n Techn raffinazione f

refit¹ /'ri:fɪt/ n Naut raddobbo m; (of shop, factory etc) rinnovo m

refit² /ri:'fɪt/ vt raddobbare ‹ship›; rinnovare ‹shop, factory etc›

reflate /ri:'fleɪt/ vt reflazionare ‹economy›

♦ **reflect** /rɪ'flekt/ **1** vt riflettere; **be ~ed in** essere riflesso in
2 vt (think) riflettere (**on** su); **~ badly on somebody** fig mettere in cattiva luce qualcuno

reflection /rɪ'flekʃn/ n riflessione f; ‹image› riflesso m; **on ~** dopo riflessione

reflective /rɪ'flektɪv/ adj riflessivo

reflectively /rɪ'flektɪvlɪ/ adv in modo riflessivo

reflector /rɪ'flektə(r)/ n riflettore m

reflex /'ri:fleks/ **1** n riflesso m
2 attrib di riflesso

reflexive /rɪ'fleksɪv/ adj riflessivo

reflexive verb n verbo m riflessivo

refloat /ri:'fləʊt/ vt Naut, Comm rimettere a galla

reforestation /ri:forɪ'steɪʃn/ n rimboschimento m

♦ **reform** /rɪ'fɔ:m/ **1** n riforma f
2 vt riformare
3 vi correggersi

reformat /ri:'fɔ:mæt/ vt riformattare

Reformation /refə'meɪʃn/ n Relig Riforma f

reformer /rɪ'fɔ:mə(r)/ n riformatore, -trice mf

refrain¹ /rɪ'freɪn/ n ritornello m

refrain² vi astenersi (**from** da)

refresh /rɪ'freʃ/ vt rinfrescare; Comput aggiornare

refresher course /rɪ'freʃə(r)/ n corso m d'aggiornamento

refreshing /rɪ'freʃɪŋ/ adj rinfrescante

refreshments /rɪ'freʃmənts/ npl rinfreschi mpl

refrigerate /rɪ'frɪdʒəreɪt/ vt conservare in frigo; Ind refrigerare

refrigerated lorry /rɪ'frɪdʒəreɪtɪd/ n camion m inv frigorifero

refrigeration /rɪfrɪdʒə'reɪʃn/ n Ind refrigerazione f

refrigerator /rɪ'frɪdʒəreɪtə(r)/ n frigorifero m

refuel /ri:'fjʊəl/ **1** vt (pt/pp **-fuelled**) rifornire di carburante
2 vi fare rifornimento

refuge /'refju:dʒ/ n rifugio m; **take ~** rifugiarsi

refugee /refjʊ'dʒi:/ n rifugiato, -a mf

refugee camp n campo m profughi

refund¹ /'ri:fʌnd/ n rimborso m

refund² /rɪ'fʌnd/ vt rimborsare

refurbish /ri:'fɜ:bɪʃ/ vt rimettere a nuovo

refurbishment /ri:'fɜ:bɪʃmənt/ n rinnovo m

refusal /rɪ'fju:zl/ n rifiuto m

♦ **refuse¹** /rɪ'fju:z/ vt/i rifiutare; **~ to do something** rifiutare di fare qualcosa

refuse² /'refju:s/ n rifiuti mpl

refuse collection n raccolta f dei rifiuti

refuse collector n Br spazzino, -a mf

refute /rɪ'fju:t/ vt confutare

regain /rɪ'geɪn/ vt riconquistare

regal /'ri:gl/ adj regale

regale /rɪ'geɪl/ vt **~ somebody with something** deliziare qualcuno con qualcosa

regalia /rɪ'geɪlɪə/ npl insegne fpl reali

♦ **regard** /rɪ'gɑ:d/ **1** n (heed) riguardo m; (respect) considerazione f; **~s** pl saluti mpl; **send/give my ~s to your brother** salutami tuo fratello; **with ~ to** riguardo a
2 vt (consider) considerare (**as** come); **as ~s** riguardo a

regarding /rɪ'gɑ:dɪŋ/ prep riguardo a

regardless /rɪ'gɑ:dlɪs/ adv lo stesso; **~ of** senza badare a

regatta /rɪ'gætə/ n regata f

regency /'ri:dʒənsɪ/ n reggenza f

regenerate /rɪ'dʒenəreɪt/ **1** vt rigenerare
2 vi rigenerarsi

regent /'ri:dʒənt/ n reggente mf

reggae /'regeɪ/ n reggae m

♦ **regime** /reɪ'ʒi:m/ n regime m

regiment¹ /'redʒɪmənt/ n reggimento m

regiment² /'redʒɪment/ vt irreggimentare

regimental /redʒɪ'mentl/ adj reggimentale

regimentation /redʒɪmən'teɪʃn/ n irreggimentazione f

regimented /'redʒɪmentɪd/ adj irreggimentato

♦ **region** /'ri:dʒən/ n regione f; **in the ~ of** fig approssimativamente

♦ **regional** /'ri:dʒənl/ adj regionale

♦ **register** /'redʒɪstə(r)/ **1** n registro m
2 vt registrare; mandare tramite assicurata ‹letter, package›; assicurare ‹luggage›; immatricolare ‹motor vehicle›; mostrare ‹feeling›
3 vi ‹instrument› funzionare; ‹student› iscriversi (**for** a); **it didn't ~ with me** fig non ci ho fatto attenzione; **~ with** iscriversi nella lista di ‹doctor›

r

registered /'redʒɪstəd/ adj ‹voter, student› iscritto; ‹vehicle› immatricolato

registered letter /'redʒɪstəd/ n lettera f assicurata

registered trademark n marchio m depositato

registrar /redʒɪ'strɑ:(r)/ n ufficiale m di stato civile

registration /redʒɪ'streɪʃn/ n (of vehicle) immatricolazione f; (of letter, luggage) assicurazione f; (for course) iscrizione f

registration fee n tassa f d'iscrizione

registration number n Auto [numero m di] targa f

registry office /'redʒɪstrɪ/ n anagrafe f

regress /rɪ'gres/ vi Biol, Psych fig regredire

regression /rɪ'greʃən/ n regressione f

regressive /rɪ'gresɪv/ adj Biol, Psych regressivo

regret /rɪ'gret/ [1] n rammarico m
[2] vt (pt/pp **regretted**) rimpiangere; I ~ that mi rincresce che

regretfully /rɪ'gretfʊlɪ/ adv con rammarico

regrettable /rɪ'gretəbl/ adj spiacevole

regrettably /rɪ'gretəblɪ/ adv spiacevolmente; (before adjective) deplorevolmente

regroup /ri:'gru:p/ vi riorganizzarsi

◦' **regular** /'regjʊlə(r)/ [1] adj regolare; (usual) abituale
[2] n cliente mf abituale

regularity /regjʊ'lærətɪ/ n regolarità f

regularly /'regjʊləlɪ/ adv regolarmente

regulate /'regʊleɪt/ vt regolare

◦' **regulation** /regjʊ'leɪʃn/ n (rule) regolamento m

regulator /'regjʊleɪtə(r)/ n (person) regolatore, -trice mf; (device) regolatore m

regurgitate /rɪ'gɜ:dʒɪteɪt/ vt rigurgitare; fig pej ripetere meccanicamente

rehabilitate /ri:hə'bɪlɪteɪt/ vt riabilitare

rehabilitation /ri:həbɪlɪ'teɪʃn/ n riabilitazione f

rehabilitation centre Br, **rehabilitation center** Am n (after drug addiction, illness, prison) comunità f terapeutica

rehash¹ /ri:'hæʃ/ vt rimaneggiare

rehash² /'ri:hæʃ/ n rimaneggiamento m

rehearsal /rɪ'hɜ:sl/ n Theat prova f

rehearse /rɪ'hɜ:s/ vt/i provare

reheat /ri:'hi:t/ vt scaldare di nuovo

rehouse /ri:'haʊz/ vt rialloggiare

reign /reɪn/ [1] n regno m
[2] vi regnare

reimburse /ri:ɪm'bɜ:s/ vt ~ somebody for something rimborsare qualcosa a qualcuno

reimbursement /ri:ɪm'bɜ:smənt/ n rimborso m

rein /reɪn/ n redine f

reincarnate /ri:ɪn'kɑ:neɪt/ vt be ~d reincarnarsi

reincarnation /ri:ɪnkɑ:'neɪʃn/ n reincarnazione f

reindeer /'reɪndɪə(r)/ n inv renna f

reinforce /ri:ɪn'fɔ:s/ vt rinforzare

reinforced concrete n cemento m armato

reinforcement /ri:ɪn'fɔ:smənt/ n rinforzo m; ~s pl Mil rinforzi mpl

reinstall /'ri:ɪnstɔ:l/ vt Comput reinstallare ‹software, program›

reinstate /ri:ɪn'steɪt/ vt reintegrare

reinstatement /ri:ɪn'steɪtmənt/ n reintegrazione f

reinterpret /ri:ɪnt't3:prɪt/ vt reinterpretare

reinterpretation /ri:ɪnt3:prɪ'teɪʃn/ n reinterpretazione f

reintroduce /ri:ɪntrə'dju:s/ vt reintrodurre

reintroduction /ri:ɪntrə'dʌkʃn/ n reintroduzione f

reiterate /ri:'ɪtəreɪt/ vt reiterare

reiteration /ri:ɪtə'reɪʃn/ n reiterazione f

◦' **reject** /rɪ'dʒekt/ vt rifiutare

rejection /rɪ'dʒekʃn/ n rifiuto m; Med rigetto m

rejects /'ri:dʒekts/ npl Comm scarti mpl

rejig /ri:'dʒɪg/ vt (pt/pp **rejigged**) Br riorganizzare

rejoice /rɪ'dʒɔɪs/ vi liter rallegrarsi

rejoicing /rɪ'dʒɔɪsɪŋ/ n gioia f

rejoin /rɪ'dʒɔɪn/ vt riassociarsi a ‹club, party›; Mil reintegrarsi in ‹regiment›; (answer) replicare

rejuvenate /rɪ'dʒu:vəneɪt/ vt rinnovare; ringiovanire ‹person›

rejuvenation /rɪ'dʒu:vəneɪʃn/ n rinnovamento m; (of person) ringiovanimento m

rekindle /ri:'kɪndl/ vt riattizzare

relapse /rɪ'læps/ [1] n ricaduta f
[2] vi ricadere

◦' **relate** /rɪ'leɪt/ vt (tell) riportare; (connect) collegare
■ **relate to** vt riferirsi a; identificarsi con ‹person›

◦' **related** /rɪ'leɪtɪd/ adj imparentato (to a); ‹ideas etc› affine

◦' **relation** /rɪ'leɪʃn/ n rapporto m; (person) parente mf

◦' **relationship** /rɪ'leɪʃnʃɪp/ n rapporto m; (blood tie) parentela f; (affair) relazione f

◦' **relative** /'relətɪv/ [1] n parente mf
[2] adj relativo

◦' indicates a very frequent word

◆ **relatively** /'relətɪvlɪ/ *adv* relativamente

relativity /relə'tɪvətɪ/ *n* relatività *f*

relativity theory *n* Phys teoria *f* della relatività

relaunch¹ /'riːlɔːntʃ/ *n* rilancio *m*

relaunch² /riː'lɔːntʃ/ *vt* rilanciare

◆ **relax** /rɪ'læks/ ① *vt* rilassare; allentare ‹pace grip›
② *vi* rilassarsi

relaxation /riːlæk'seɪʃn/ *n* rilassamento *m*, relax *m*; (recreation) svago *m*

relaxed /rɪ'lækst/ *adj* rilassato

relaxing /rɪ'læksɪŋ/ *adj* rilassante

relay¹ /'riːleɪ/ *vt* (*pt/pp* **-layed**) trasmettere

relay² /'riːleɪ/ *n* Electr relais *m inv*; **work in** ∼**s** fare i turni

relay [race] /'riːleɪ/ *n* [corsa *f* a] staffetta *f*

◆ **release** /rɪ'liːs/ ① *n* rilascio *m*; (of film) distribuzione *f*
② *vt* liberare; lasciare ‹hand›; togliere ‹brake›; distribuire ‹film›; rilasciare ‹information etc›

relegate /'relɪgeɪt/ *vt* relegare; **be** ∼**d** Br Sport essere retrocesso

relegation /relɪ'geɪʃn/ *n* relegazione *f*; Br Sport retrocessione *f*

relent /rɪ'lent/ *vi* cedere

relentless /rɪ'lentlɪs/ *adj* inflessibile; (unceasing) incessante

relentlessly /rɪ'lentlɪslɪ/ *adv* incessantemente

◆ **relevance** /'reləvəns/ *n* pertinenza *f*

◆ **relevant** /'reləvənt/ *adj* pertinente (**to** a)

reliability /rɪlaɪə'bɪlətɪ/ *n* affidabilità *f*

reliable /rɪ'laɪəbl/ *adj* affidabile

reliably /rɪ'laɪəblɪ/ *adv* in modo affidabile; **be** ∼ **informed** sapere da fonte certa

reliance /rɪ'laɪəns/ *n* fiducia *f* (**on** in)

reliant /rɪ'laɪənt/ *adj* fiducioso (**on** in)

relic /'relɪk/ *n* Relig reliquia *f*; ∼**s** *pl* resti *mpl*

◆ **relief** /rɪ'liːf/ *n* sollievo *m*; (assistance) soccorso *m*; (distraction) diversivo *m*; (replacement) cambio *m*; (in art) rilievo *m*; **in** ∼ in rilievo

relief agency *n* organizzazione *f* umanitaria

relief map *n* carta *f* in rilievo

relief supplies *npl* soccorsi *mpl*, aiuti *mpl* umanitari

relief train *n* treno *m* supplementare

relief work *n* lavoro *m* presso un'organizzazione umanitaria

relief worker *n* persona *f* che lavora per un'organizzazione umanitaria

relieve /rɪ'liːv/ *vt* alleviare; (take over from) dare il cambio a; ∼ **of** liberare da ‹burden›

◆ **religion** /rɪ'lɪdʒən/ *n* religione *f*

◆ **religious** /rɪ'lɪdʒəs/ *adj* religioso

religiously /rɪ'lɪdʒəslɪ/ *adv* (conscientiously) scrupolosamente

relinquish /rɪ'lɪŋkwɪʃ/ *vt* abbandonare; ∼ **something to somebody** rinunciare a qualcosa in favore di qualcuno

relish /'relɪʃ/ ① *n* gusto *m*; Culin salsa *f*
② *vt* fig apprezzare

relive /riː'lɪv/ *vt* rivivere

reload /riː'ləʊd/ *vt* ricaricare

relocate /riːlə'keɪt/ ① *vt* trasferire
② *vi* trasferirsi

relocation /riːlə'keɪʃn/ *n* (of employee, company) trasferimento *m*

relocation allowance *n* indennità *f inv* di trasferimento

reluctance /rɪ'lʌktəns/ *n* riluttanza *f*

reluctant /rɪ'lʌktənt/ *adj* riluttante

reluctantly /rɪ'lʌktəntlɪ/ *adv* con riluttanza, a malincuore

◆ **rely** /rɪ'laɪ/ *vi* (*pt/pp* **-ied**) ∼ **on** dipendere da; (trust) contare su

◆ **remain** /rɪ'meɪn/ *vi* restare

remainder /rɪ'meɪndə(r)/ ① *n* resto *m*; Comm rimanenza *f*
② *vt* Comm svendere

remaining /rɪ'meɪnɪŋ/ *adj* restante

remains /rɪ'meɪnz/ *npl* resti *mpl*; (dead body) spoglie *fpl*

remake /'riːmeɪk/ *n* (of film, recording) remake *m inv*

remand /rɪ'mɑːnd/ ① *n* **on** ∼ in custodia cautelare
② *vt* ∼ **in custody** rinviare con detenzione provvisoria

remand centre *n* Br istituto *m* di carcerazione preventiva

remark /rɪ'mɑːk/ ① *n* osservazione *f*
② *vt* osservare

remarkable /rɪ'mɑːkəbl/ *adj* notevole

remarkably /rɪ'mɑːkəblɪ/ *adv* notevolmente

remarry /riː'mærɪ/ *vi* (*pt/pp* **-ied**) risposarsi

remaster /riː'mɑːstə(r)/ *vt* incidere di nuovo ‹recording›

rematch /'riːmætʃ/ *n* Sport partita *f* di ritorno; (in boxing) secondo incontro *m*

remedial /rɪ'miːdɪəl/ *adj* correttivo; Med curativo

remedy /'remədɪ/ ① *n* rimedio *m* (**for** contro)
② *vt* (*pt/pp* **-ied**) rimediare a

◆ **remember** /rɪ'membə(r)/ ① *vt* ricordare, ricordarsi; ∼ **to do something** ricordarsi di fare qualcosa; ∼ **me to him** salutamelo
② *vi* ricordarsi

Remembrance Day /rɪ'membrəns/ *n* commemorazione *f* dei caduti (*11 novembre*)

r

remind /rɪˈmaɪnd/ *vt* ~ somebody of something ricordare qualcosa a qualcuno

reminder /rɪˈmaɪndə(r)/ *n* ricordo *m*; (memo) promemoria *m inv*; (letter) lettera *f* di sollecito; (to pay) sollecitazione *f* di pagamento

reminisce /remɪˈnɪs/ *vi* rievocare il passato

reminiscences /remɪˈnɪsənsɪz/ *npl* reminiscenze *fpl*

reminiscent /remɪˈnɪsənt/ *adj* be ~ of richiamare alla memoria

remiss /rɪˈmɪs/ *adj* negligente

remission /rɪˈmɪʃn/ *n* remissione *f*; (of sentence) condono *m*

remit /rɪˈmɪt/ *vt* (*pt/pp* remitted) rimettere ‹money›

remittance /rɪˈmɪtəns/ *n* rimessa *f*

remix¹ /riːˈmɪks/ *vt* Mus rimixare

remix² /ˈriːmɪks/ *n* Mus rimixaggio *m*

remnant /ˈremnənt/ *n* resto *m*; (of material) scampolo *m*; (trace) traccia *f*

remonstrate /ˈremənstreɪt/ *vi* fare rimostranze (with somebody a qualcuno)

remorse /rɪˈmɔːs/ *n* rimorso *m*

remorseful /rɪˈmɔːsfʊl/ *adj* pieno di rimorso

remorsefully /rɪˈmɔːsfʊlɪ/ *adv* con rimorso

remorseless /rɪˈmɔːslɪs/ *adj* spietato

remorselessly /rɪˈmɔːslɪslɪ/ *adv* senza pietà

remote /rɪˈməʊt/ *adj* remoto; (slight) minimo

remote access *n* Comput accesso *m* remoto

remote control *n* telecomando *m*

remote-controlled *adj* telecomandato

remotely /rɪˈməʊtlɪ/ *adv* lontanamente; be not ~... non essere lontanamente...

remoteness /rɪˈməʊtnɪs/ *n* lontananza *f*

remould /ˈriːməʊld/ *n* pneumatico *m* ricostruito

remount /riːˈmaʊnt/ *vt* rimontare in sella a ‹bike, horse›

removable /rɪˈmuːvəbl/ *adj* rimovibile

removal /rɪˈmuːvl/ *n* rimozione *f*; (from house) trasloco *m*

removal man *n* addetto *m* ai traslochi

removal van *n* camion *m inv* da trasloco

✶ **remove** /rɪˈmuːv/ *vt* togliere; togliersi ‹clothes›; eliminare ‹stain, doubts›

removers /rɪˈmuːvəz/ *npl* fam traslocatori *mpl*

remuneration /rɪmjuːnəˈreɪʃn/ *n* rimunerazione *f*

remunerative /rɪˈmjuːnərətɪv/ *adj* rimunerativo

renaissance /rɪˈneɪsɒns/ *n* rinascita *f*; R~ Rinascimento *m*

renal /ˈriːnəl/ *adj* renale

render /ˈrendə(r)/ *vt* rendere ‹service›

rendering /ˈrend(ə)rɪŋ/ *n* Mus interpretazione *f*

rendezvous /ˈrɒndeɪvuː/ *vi esp* Mil incontrarsi

rendition /renˈdɪʃn/ *n* interpretazione *f*

renegade /ˈrenɪɡeɪd/ *n* rinnegato, -a *mf*

renege /rɪˈneɪɡ/ *vi* venire meno (on a)

renegotiate /riːnɪˈɡəʊʃɪeɪt/ *vt* rinegoziare

renegotiation /riːnɪɡəʊʃɪˈeɪʃn/ *n* rinegoziato *m*

renew /rɪˈnjuː/ *vt* rinnovare ‹contract›

renewable /rɪˈnjuːəbl/ *adj* rinnovabile

renewal /rɪˈnjuːəl/ *n* rinnovo *m*

renewed *adj* ‹strength, interest› rinnovato; ‹attack› nuovo

renounce /rɪˈnaʊns/ *vt* rinunciare a

renovate /ˈrenəveɪt/ *vt* rinnovare

renovation /renəˈveɪʃn/ *n* rinnovo *m*

renown /rɪˈnaʊn/ *n* fama *f*

renowned /rɪˈnaʊnd/ *adj* rinomato

rent /rent/ **1** *n* affitto *m*
2 *vt* affittare; ~ [out] dare in affitto

rental /ˈrentl/ *n* affitto *m*

rent boy *n* ragazzo *m* di vita

rent-free **1** *adj* ‹accommodation› gratuito
2 *adv* ‹live, use› senza pagare l'affitto

renunciation /rɪnʌnsɪˈeɪʃn/ *n* rinuncia *f*

reoffend /riːəˈfend/ *vi* recidivare

reopen /riːˈəʊpən/ *vt/i* riaprire

reorganization /riːɔːɡənaɪˈzeɪʃn/ *n* riorganizzazione *f*

reorganize /riːˈɔːɡənaɪz/ *vt* riorganizzare

rep /rep/ *n* Comm fam rappresentante *mf*; Theat ≈ teatro *m* stabile

repackage /riːˈpækɪdʒ/ *vt* Comm cambiare la confezione di; fig (change public image of) cambiare l'immagine pubblica di; cambiare i termini di ‹proposal›

repaint /riːˈpeɪnt/ *vt* ridipingere

repair /rɪˈpeə(r)/ **1** *n* riparazione *f*; In good/ bad ~ in buone/cattive condizioni
2 *vt* riparare

repairman *n* tecnico *m* (delle riparazioni)

reparation /repəˈreɪʃn/ *n* make ~s for something risarcire qualcosa

repartee /repɑːˈtiː/ *n* botta e risposta *m inv*; piece of ~ risposta *f* pronta

repatriate /riːˈpætrieɪt/ *vt* rimpatriare

repatriation /riːpætrɪˈeɪʃn/ *n* rimpatrio *m*

repay /riːˈpeɪ/ *vt* (*pt/pp* **-paid**) ripagare

repayment /riːˈpeɪmənt/ *n* rimborso *m*

repeal /rɪˈpiːl/ **1** *n* abrogazione *f*
2 *vt* abrogare

✶ **repeat** /rɪˈpiːt/ **1** *n* TV replica *f*
2 *vt/i* ripetere; ~ oneself ripetersi

✶ indicates a very frequent word

repeated /rɪ'piːtɪd/ *adj* ripetuto

repeatedly /rɪ'piːtɪdlɪ/ *adv* ripetutamente

repel /rɪ'pel/ *vt* (*pt/pp* **repelled**) respingere; fig ripugnare

repellent /rɪ'pelənt/ *adj* ripulsivo

repent /rɪ'pent/ *vi* pentirsi

repentance /rɪ'pentəns/ *n* pentimento *m*

repentant /rɪ'pentənt/ *adj* pentito

repercussions /riːpə'kʌʃnz/ *npl* ripercussioni *fbl*

repertoire /'repətwɑː(r)/ *n* repertorio *m*

repertory /'repətrɪ/ *n* ≈ teatro *m* stabile

repertory company *n* compagnia *f* di un teatro stabile

repetition /repɪ'tɪʃn/ *n* ripetizione *f*

repetitious /repɪ'tɪʃəs/, **repetitive** /rɪ'petɪtɪv/ *adj* ripetitivo

repetitive strain injury *n* patologia *f* da sforzo ripetuto

ᘓ **replace** /rɪ'pleɪs/ *vt* (put back) rimettere a posto; (take the place of) sostituire; ∼ **something with something** sostituire qualcosa con qualcosa

replacement /rɪ'pleɪsmənt/ *n* sostituzione *f*; (person) sostituto, -a *mf*

replacement part *n* pezzo *m* di ricambio

replant /riː'plɑːnt/ *vt* ripiantare

replay /'riːpleɪ/ *n* Sport partita *f* ripetuta; [action] ∼ replay *m inv*

replenish /rɪ'plenɪʃ/ *vt* rifornire ‹stocks›; (refill) riempire di nuovo

replete /rɪ'pliːt/ *adj* ∼ with riempito di

replica /'replɪkə/ *n* copia *f*

replicate /'replɪkeɪt/ *vt* ripetere ‹experiment›

ᘓ **reply** /rɪ'plaɪ/ **1** *n* risposta *f* (to a) **2** *vt* (*pt/pp* **replied**) rispondere

reply-paid envelope *n* busta *f* affrancata per rispondere

ᘓ **report** /rɪ'pɔːt/ **1** *n* rapporto *m*; TV, Radio servizio *m*; Journ cronaca *f*; Sch pagella *f*; (rumour) diceria *f* **2** *vt* riportare; ∼ **somebody to the police** denunciare qualcuno alla polizia **3** *vi* riportare; (present oneself) presentarsi (to a)

report card *n* Am scheda *f* di valutazione scolastica

reportedly /rɪ'pɔːtɪdlɪ/ *adv* secondo quanto si dice

ᘓ **reporter** /rɪ'pɔːtə(r)/ *n* cronista *mf*, reporter *mf inv*

repose /rɪ'pəʊz/ *n* riposo *m*

repository /rɪ'pɒzɪt(ə)rɪ/ *n* (place) deposito; (of secret, authority) depositario, -a *mf*

repossess /riːpə'zes/ *vt* riprendere possesso di

repossession /riːpə'zeʃn/ *n* esproprio *m*

repot /riː'pɒt/ *vt* rinvasare ‹plant›

reprehensible /reprɪ'hensəbl/ *adj* riprovevole

ᘓ **represent** /reprɪ'zent/ *vt* rappresentare

representation /reprɪzen'teɪʃn/ *n* rappresentazione *f*; **make** ∼**s to** fare delle rimostranze a

ᘓ **representative** /reprɪ'zentətɪv/ **1** *adj* rappresentativo **2** *n* rappresentante *mf*

repress /rɪ'pres/ *vt* reprimere

repression /rɪ'preʃn/ *n* repressione *f*

repressive /rɪ'presɪv/ *adj* repressivo

reprieve /rɪ'priːv/ **1** *n* commutazione *f* della pena capitale; (postponement) sospensione *f* della pena capitale; fig tregua *f* **2** *vt* sospendere la sentenza a; fig risparmiare

reprimand /'reprɪmɑːnd/ **1** *n* rimprovero *m* **2** *vt* rimproverare

reprint¹ /'riːprɪnt/ *n* ristampa *f*

reprint² /riː'prɪnt/ *vt* ristampare

reprisal /rɪ'praɪzl/ *n* rappresaglia *f*; in ∼ for per rappresaglia contro

reproach /rɪ'prəʊtʃ/ **1** *n* rimprovero *m* **2** *vt* rimproverare a (for doing something di fare qualcosa)

reproachful /rɪ'prəʊtʃfʊl/ *adj* riprovevole

reproachfully /rɪ'prəʊtʃfʊlɪ/ *adv* con aria di rimprovero

reprocess /riː'prəʊses/ *vt* trattare di nuovo

reprocessing plant *n* impianto *m* di rilavorazione (di scorie nucleari)

reproduce /riːprə'djuːs/ **1** *vt* riprodurre **2** *vi* riprodursi

reproduction /riːprə'dʌkʃn/ *n* riproduzione *f*

reproduction furniture *n* riproduzioni *fpl* di mobili antichi

reproductive /riːprə'dʌktɪv/ *adj* riproduttivo

reproof /rɪ'pruːf/ *n* rimprovero *m*

reprove /rɪ'pruːv/ *vt* rimproverare

reptile /'reptaɪl/ *n* rettile *m*

republic /rɪ'pʌblɪk/ *n* repubblica *f*

republican /rɪ'pʌblɪkn/ *adj* & *n* repubblicano, -a *mf*

republish /riː'pʌblɪʃ/ *vt* ripubblicare

repudiate /rɪ'pjuːdɪeɪt/ *vt* ripudiare; respingere ‹view, suggestion›

repugnance /rɪ'pʌgnəns/ *n* ripugnanza *f*

repugnant /rɪ'pʌgnənt/ *adj* ripugnante

repulse /rɪ'pʌls/ *vt fml* respingere ‹attack›; rifiutare ‹assistance›

repulsion /rɪ'pʌlʃn/ *n* repulsione *f*

repulsive /rɪ'pʌlsɪv/ *adj* ripugnante

reputable /'repjʊtəbl/ *adj* affidabile

r

ℴ **reputation** /repjʊ'teɪʃn/ n reputazione f

repute /rɪ'pju:t/ n reputazione f

reputed /rɪ'pju:tɪd/ adj presunto; **he is ~
to be** si presume che sia

reputedly /rɪ'pju:tɪdlɪ/ adv
presumibilmente

ℴ **request** /rɪ'kwest/ ① n richiesta f
② vt richiedere

request stop n, f fermata f a richiesta

requiem /'rekwɪəm/ n requiem m inv

ℴ **require** /rɪ'kwaɪə(r)/ vt (need) necessitare
di; (demand) esigere

required /rɪ'kwaɪəd/ adj richiesto

ℴ **requirement** /rɪ'kwaɪəmənt/ n esigenza f;
(condition) requisito m

requisite /'rekwɪzɪt/ ① adj necessario
② n **toilet/travel ~s** pl articoli mpl da
toilette/viaggio

requisition /rekwɪ'zɪʃn/ ① n ~ **[order]**
[domanda f di] requisizione f
② vt requisire

reread /ri:'ri:d/ vt rileggere

re-release /ri:rɪ'li:s/ ① n (of film) nuova
distribuzione f
② vt ridistribuire ‹film›

reroof /ri:'ru:f/ vt rifare il tetto di ‹building›

reroute /ri:'ru:t/ vt dirottare ‹flight, traffic›

rerun /'ri:rʌn/ n (of film, play) replica f; fig
(repeat) ripetizione f

resale /ri:'seɪl/ n rivendita f

reschedule /ri:'ʃedju:l/ vt (change date of)
cambiare la data di; (change time of) cambiare
l'orario di; rinegoziare ‹debt›

rescind /rɪ'sɪnd/ vt rescindere

rescue /'reskju:/ ① n salvataggio m
② vt salvare

rescuer /'reskjʊə(r)/ n salvatore, -trice mf

rescue worker n soccorritore, -trice mf

ℴ **research** /rɪ's3:tʃ/ ① n ricerca f
② vt fare ricerche su; Journ fare
un'inchiesta su
③ vi ~ **into** fare ricerche su

research and development n
ricerca f e sviluppo m

ℴ **researcher** /rɪ's3:tʃə(r)/ n ricercatore,
-trice mf

research fellow n Br Univ ricercatore,
-trice mf

resell /ri:'sel/ vt (pt/pp **resold**) rivendere

resemblance /rɪ'zembləns/ n
rassomiglianza f

resemble /rɪ'zembl/ vt rassomigliare a

resent /rɪ'zent/ vt risentirsi per

resentful /rɪ'zentfʊl/ adj pieno di
risentimento

resentfully /rɪ'zentfʊlɪ/ adv con
risentimento

resentment /rɪ'zentmənt/ n risentimento
m

reservation /rezə'veɪʃn/ n (booking)
prenotazione f; (doubt, enclosure) riserva f

reserve /rɪ'z3:v/ ① n riserva f; (shyness)
riserbo m
② vt riservare; riservarsi ‹right›

reserved /rɪ'z3:vd/ adj riservato

reservoir /'rezəvwɑ:(r)/ n bacino m idrico

reset /ri:'set/ vt riprogrammare ‹clock›;
(zero) azzerare

reshape /ri:'ʃeɪp/ vt ristrutturare

reshuffle /ri:'ʃʌfl/ ① pol n rimpasto m
② vt rimpastare

reside /rɪ'zaɪd/ vi risiedere

residence /'rezɪdəns/ n residenza f; (stay)
soggiorno m

residence permit n permesso m di
soggiorno

ℴ **resident** /'rezɪdənt/ adj & n residente mf

residential /rezɪ'denʃl/ adj residenziale

residential area n quartiere m
residenziale

residual /rɪ'zɪdjʊəl/ adj residuo

residue /'rezɪdju:/ n residuo m

resign /rɪ'zaɪn/ ① vt dimettersi da;
~ **oneself** to rassegnarsi a
② vt dare le dimissioni

resignation /rezɪg'neɪʃn/ n rassegnazione
f; (from job) dimissioni fpl

resigned /rɪ'zaɪnd/ adj rassegnato

resignedly /rɪ'zaɪnɪdlɪ/ adv con
rassegnazione

resilient /rɪ'zɪlɪənt/ adj elastico; fig con
buone capacità di ripresa

resin /'rezɪn/ n resina f

resist /rɪ'zɪst/ ① vt resistere a
② vi resistere

ℴ **resistance** /rɪ'zɪstəns/ n resistenza f

resistance fighter n combattente mf
delle forze di resistenza

resistant /rɪ'zɪstənt/ adj resistente

resit /ri:'sɪt/ Br ① vt (pt/pp **resat**) ridare
‹exam›
② n esame m di recupero

resize /ri:'saɪz/ vt ridimensionare

reskill /ri:'skɪl/ vt riqualificare ‹workers›

resolute /'rezəlu:t/ adj risoluto

resolutely /'rezəlu:tlɪ/ adv con risolutezza

ℴ **resolution** /rezə'lu:ʃn/ n risolutezza f

ℴ **resolve** /rɪ'zɒlv/ ① n risolutezza f;
(decision) risoluzione f
② vt (solve) risolvere; ~ **to do** decidere di
fare

resolved /rɪ'zɒlvd/ adj risoluto

resonance /'rezənəns/ n risonanza f

resonant /'rezənənt/ adj risonante

resonate /'rezəneɪt/ vi risuonare

ℴ indicates a very frequent word

resort /rɪ'zɔːt/ [1] *n* (place) luogo *m* di
villeggiatura; **as a last ~** come ultima
risorsa
[2] *vi* **~ to** ricorrere a

resound /rɪ'zaʊnd/ *vi* risonare (**with** di)

resounding /rɪ'zaʊndɪŋ/ *adj* ‹success›
risonante

resoundingly /rɪ'zaʊndɪŋlɪ/ *adv* in modo
risonante

✧ **resource** /rɪ'sɔːs/ *n* **~s** *pl* risorse *fpl*

resourceful /rɪ'sɔːsfʊl/ *adj* pieno di
risorse; ‹solution› ingegnoso

resourcefulness /rɪ'sɔːsfʊlnɪs/ *n*
ingegnosità *f*

✧ **respect** /rɪ'spekt/ [1] *n* rispetto *m*; (aspect)
aspetto *m*; **with ~ to** per quanto riguarda
[2] *vt* rispettare

respectability /rɪspektə'bɪlətɪ/ *n*
rispettabilità *f*

respectable /rɪ'spektəbl/ rispettabile

respectably /rɪ'spektəblɪ/ *adv*
rispettabilmente

respectful /rɪ'spektfʊl/ *adj* rispettoso

respectfully /rɪ'spektfʊlɪ/ *adv*
rispettosamente

respective /rɪ'spektɪv/ *adj* rispettivo

respectively /rɪ'spektɪvlɪ/ *adv*
rispettivamente

respiration /respɪ'reɪʃn/ *n* respirazione *f*

respirator /'respɪreɪtə(r)/ *n* (apparatus)
respiratore *m*

respiratory /rɪ'spɪrətrɪ, US -tɔːrɪ/ *adj*
respiratorio

respite /'respaɪt/ *n* respiro *m*

resplendent /rɪ'splendənt/ *adj*
risplendente

✧ **respond** /rɪ'spɒnd/ *vi* rispondere; (react)
reagire (**to** a); ‹patient› rispondere (**to** a)

respondent /rɪ'spɒndənt/ *n* Jur
convenuto, -a *mf*; (to questionnaire)
interrogato, -a *mf*

✧ **response** /rɪ'spɒns/ *n* risposta *f*; (reaction)
reazione *f*

✧ **responsibility** /rɪspɒnsɪ'bɪlətɪ/ *n*
responsabilità *f inv*

✧ **responsible** /rɪ'spɒnsəbl/ *adj*
responsabile; (trustworthy) responsabile; (job)
impegnativo

responsibly /rɪ'spɒnsəblɪ/ *adv* in modo
responsabile

responsive /rɪ'spɒnsɪv/ *adj* **be ~**
‹audience etc› reagire; ‹brakes› essere
sensibile; **she wasn't very ~** non era molto
cooperativa

respray¹ /riː'spreɪ/ *vt* riverniciare ‹vehicle›

respray² /'riːspreɪ/ *n* riverniciatura *f*; **it's
had a ~** è stato riverniciato

✧ **rest¹** /rest/ [1] *n* riposo *m*; Mus pausa *f*; **have
a ~** riposarsi
[2] *vt* riposare; (lean, place) appoggiare (**on** su)

[3] *vi* riposarsi; ‹elbows› appoggiarsi; ‹hopes›
riposare; **it ~s with you** sta a te
■ **rest up** *vi* riposarsi

✧ **rest²** *n* **the ~** il resto; (people) gli altri

restart /riː'stɑːt/ *vt* rimettere in moto
‹engine›; riprendere ‹talks›; Comput riavviare

restate /riː'steɪt/ *vt* (say differently)
riformulare; (say again) ribadire

✧ **restaurant** /'restərɒnt/ *n* ristorante *m*

restaurant car *n* vagone *m* ristorante

restful /'restfl/ *adj* riposante

rest home *n* casa *f* di riposo

restitution /restɪ'tjuːʃn/ *n* restituzione *f*

restive /'restɪv/ *adj* irrequieto

restless /'restlɪs/ *adj* nervoso

restlessly /'restlɪslɪ/ *adv* nervosamente

restlessness /'restlɪsnɪs/ *n* agitazione *f*

restock /riː'stɒk/ [1] *vt* rifornire ‹shelf,
shop›
[2] *vi* rifornirsi

restoration /restə'reɪʃn/ *n* ristabilimento
m; (of building) restauro *m*; (of stolen property
etc) restituzione *f*

restore /rɪ'stɔː(r)/ *vt* ristabilire; restaurare
‹building›; (give back) restituire

restorer /rɪ'stɔːrə(r)/ *n* (person)
restauratore, -trice *mf*

restrain /rɪ'streɪn/ *vt* trattenere; **~ oneself**
controllarsi

restrained /rɪ'streɪnd/ *adj* controllato

restraint /rɪ'streɪnt/ *n* restrizione *f*;
(moderation) ritegno *m*

restrict /rɪ'strɪkt/ *vt* limitare (**to** a)

restricted /rɪ'strɪktɪd/ *adj* ‹access,
parking› riservato; ‹growth, movement›
limitato; ‹document, information›
confidenziale

restriction /rɪ'strɪkʃn/ *n* limite *m*;
(restraint) restrizione *f*

restrictive /rɪ'strɪktɪv/ *adj* limitativo

restring /riː'strɪŋ/ *vt* rinfilare ‹necklace,
beads›; sostituire le corde di ‹instrument,
racket›

restroom /'restruːm/ *n* Am toilette *f inv*

restructure /riː'strʌktʃə(r)/ *vt*
ristrutturare

restructuring /riː'strʌktʃərɪŋ/ *n*
ristrutturazione *f*

restyle /riː'staɪl/ *vt* cambiare il taglio
di ‹hair›; cambiare la linea di ‹car›;
rimodernare ‹shop›

resubmit /riːsʌb'mɪt/ *vt* ripresentare

✧ **result** /rɪ'zʌlt/ [1] *n* risultato *m*; **as a ~** di
conseguenza; **as a ~ of** a causa di
[2] *vi* **~ from** risultare da; **~ in** portare a

resume /rɪ'zjuːm/ *vt/i* riprendere

résumé /'rezjʊmeɪ/ *n* riassunto *m*; Am
curriculum *m inv* vitae

resumption /rɪ'zʌmpʃn/ *n* ripresa *f*

r

resurface /riːˈsɜːfɪs/ [1] vi ‹sub, person, rumour› riemergere
[2] vt rifare la copertura di ‹road›

resurgence /rɪˈsɜːdʒəns/ n rinascita f

resurrect /rezəˈrekt/ vt fig risuscitare

resurrection /rezəˈrekʃn/ n **the R~** Relig la Risurrezione

resuscitate /rɪˈsʌsɪteɪt/ vt rianimare

resuscitation /rɪsʌsɪˈteɪʃn/ n rianimazione f

retail /ˈriːteɪl/ [1] n vendita f al minuto o al dettaglio
[2] adj & adv al minuto
[3] vt vendere al minuto
[4] vi ~ **at** essere venduto al pubblico al prezzo di

retailer /ˈriːteɪlə(r)/ n dettagliante mf

retail price n prezzo m al minuto

retail sales npl vendite fpl al dettaglio

retail trade n commercio m al dettaglio

ｄ **retain** /rɪˈteɪn/ vt conservare; (hold back) trattenere

retainer /rɪˈteɪnə(r)/ n (fee) anticipo m; (old: servant) servitore, -trice mf

retake¹ /riːˈteɪk/ vt Cinema girare di nuovo; Sch, Univ ridare; Mil riconquistare

retake² /ˈriːteɪk/ n Cinema ulteriore ripresa f

retaliate /rɪˈtælieɪt/ vi vendicarsi

retaliation /rɪtælɪˈeɪʃn/ n rappresaglia f; **in ~ for** per rappresaglia contro

retarded /rɪˈtɑːdɪd/ adj ritardato

retch /retʃ/ vi avere conati di vomito

retention /rɪˈtenʃn/ n conservazione f; (of information) memorizzazione f; (of fluid) ritenzione f

retentive /rɪˈtentɪv/ adj ‹memory› buono

retentiveness /rɪˈtentɪvnɪs/ n capacità f di memorizzazione

rethink /riːˈθɪŋk/ [1] vt (pt/pp **rethought**) riconsiderare
[2] n **have a ~** riconsiderare la cosa

reticence /ˈretɪsəns/ n reticenza f

reticent /ˈretɪsənt/ adj reticente

retina /ˈretɪnə/ n retina f

retinue /ˈretɪnjuː/ n seguito m

retire /rɪˈtaɪə(r)/ [1] vi andare in pensione; (withdraw) ritirarsi
[2] vt mandare in pensione ‹employee›

retired /rɪˈtaɪəd/ adj in pensione

retirement /rɪˈtaɪəmənt/ n pensione f; **since my ~** da quando sono andato in pensione

retirement age n età f della pensione

retirement home n casa f di riposo

retiring /rɪˈtaɪərɪŋ/ adj riservato

retort /rɪˈtɔːt/ [1] n replica f; Chem storta f
[2] vt ribattere

ｄ indicates a very frequent word

retouch /riːˈtʌtʃ/ vt Phot ritoccare

retouching /riːˈtʌtʃɪŋ/ n Phot ritocco m

retrace /rɪˈtreɪs/ vt ripercorrere; **~ one's steps** ritornare sui propri passi

retract /rɪˈtrækt/ [1] vt ritirare; ritrattare ‹statement, accusation›
[2] vi ritrarsi

retractable /rɪˈtræktəbl/ adj ‹landing gear› retrattile; ‹pen› con la punta retrattile

retraction /rɪˈtrækʃn/ n ritiro m; (of statement, accusation) ritrattazione f

retrain /riːˈtreɪn/ [1] vt riqualificare
[2] vi riqualificarsi

retraining /ˌriːˈtreɪnɪŋ/ n riqualificazione f

retread /ˈriːtred/ n pneumatico m ricostruito

retreat /rɪˈtriːt/ [1] n ritirata f; (place) ritiro m
[2] vi ritirarsi; Mil battere in ritirata

retrench /rɪˈtrentʃ/ vi ridurre le spese

retrenchment /rɪˈtrentʃmənt/ n riduzione f delle spese

retrial /riːˈtraɪəl/ n nuovo processo m

retribution /retrɪˈbjuːʃn/ n castigo m

retrievable /rɪˈtriːvəbl/ adj recuperabile

retrieval /rɪˈtriːvəl/ n recupero m

retrieve /rɪˈtriːv/ vt recuperare

retroactive /retrəʊˈæktɪv/ adj retroattivo

retroactively /retrəʊˈæktɪvlɪ/ adv retroattivamente

retrograde /ˈretrəgreɪd/ adj retrogrado

retrospect /ˈretrəspekt/ n **in ~** guardando indietro

retrospective /retrəˈspektɪv/ [1] adj ‹exhibit› retrospettivo; ‹legislation› retroattivo
[2] n retrospettiva f

retrospectively /retrəˈspektɪvlɪ/ adv retrospettivamente

retrovirus /ˈretrəʊvaɪərəs/ n retrovirus m inv

retry /riːˈtraɪ/ vt Jur riprocessare; Comput riprovare

ｄ **return** /rɪˈtɜːn/ [1] n ritorno m; (giving back) restituzione f; Comm profitto m; (ticket) biglietto m di andata e ritorno; **by ~ [of post]** a stretto giro di posta; **in ~** in cambio **(for** di); **many happy ~s!** cento di questi giorni!; **~ on investment** utile m sul capitale investito
[2] vi ritornare
[3] vt (give back) restituire; ricambiare ‹affection, invitation›; (put back) rimettere; (send back) mandare indietro; (elect) eleggere

returnable /rɪˈtɜːnəbl/ adj restituibile

return flight n volo m di andata e ritorno

return match n rivincita f

return ticket n biglietto m di andata e ritorno

reunification /riːjuːnɪfɪˈkeɪʃn/ *n*
riunificazione *f*

reunify /riːˈjuːnɪfaɪ/ *vt* riunificare

reunion /riːˈjuːnjən/ *n* riunione *f*

reunite /riːjʊˈnaɪt/ *vt* riunire

reusable /riːˈjuːzəbl/ *adj* riutilizzabile

reuse /riːˈjuːz/ *vt* riutilizzare

rev /rev/ [1] *n* Auto giro; ∼s per minute
regime *m* di giri
[2] *vt* ∼ **[up]** far andare su di giri
[3] *vi* andare su di giri

Rev[d] *abbr* (**Reverend**) Reverendo

revaluation /riːˈvæljʊ'eɪʃn/ *n*
rivalutazione *f*

revalue /riːˈvæljuː/ *vt* Comm rivalutare

revamp /riːˈvæmp/ *vt* riorganizzare
‹company›; rimodernare ‹building, clothing›

rev counter *n* contagiri *m*

✧ **reveal** /rɪˈviːl/ *vt* rivelare; ‹dress› scoprire

revealing /rɪˈviːlɪŋ/ *adj* rivelatore; ‹dress›
osé *inv*

revel /ˈrevl/ *vi* (*pt/pp* **revelled**) ∼ **in**
something godere di qualcosa

revelation /revəˈleɪʃn/ *n* rivelazione *f*

reveller /ˈrev(ə)lə(r)/ *n* festaiolo, -a *mf*

revelry /ˈrev(ə)lrɪ/ *n* baldoria *f*

revenge /rɪˈvendʒ/ [1] *n* vendetta *f*; Sport
rivincita *f*; **take** ∼ vendicarsi (**on somebody
for something** di qualcuno per qualcosa)
[2] *vt* vendicare

✧ **revenue** /ˈrevənjuː/ *n* reddito *m*

reverberate /rɪˈvɜːbərɪt/ *vi* riverberare

reverberations /rɪvɜːbəˈreɪʃnz/ *npl* fig
ripercussione *f*

revere /rɪˈvɪə(r)/ *vt* riverire

reverence /ˈrevərəns/ *n* riverenza *f*

Reverend /ˈrevərənd/ *adj* Reverendo

reverent /ˈrevərənt/ *adj* riverente

reverential /revəˈrenʃ(ə)l/ *adj* riverente

reverently /ˈrevərəntlɪ/ *adv*
rispettosamente

reverie /ˈrevərɪ/ *n* sogno *m* ad occhi aperti

reversal /rɪˈvɜːsl/ *n* inversione *f*

reverse /rɪˈvɜːs/ [1] *adj* opposto; **in** ∼
order in ordine inverso
[2] *n* contrario *m*; (back) rovescio *m*; Auto
marcia *m* indietro
[3] *vt* invertire; ∼ **the car into the garage**
entrare in garage a marcia indietro; ∼ **the
charges** Teleph fare una telefonata a carico
del destinatario
[4] *vi* Auto fare marcia indietro

reverse charge [phone-]call *n*
telefonata *f* a carico del destinatario

reversible /rɪˈvɜːsəbl/ *adj* ‹jacket› double-
face; ‹procedure› reversibile

reversing lights /rɪˈvɜːsɪŋ/ *npl* luci *fpl*
di retromarcia

revert /rɪˈvɜːt/ *vi* ∼ **to** tornare a

✧ **review** /rɪˈvjuː/ [1] *n* (survey) rassegna *f*;
(reexamination) riconsiderazione *f*; Mil rivista *f*;
(of book, play) recensione *f*
[2] *vt* riesaminare ‹situation›; Mil passare in
rivista; recensire ‹book, play›

reviewer /rɪˈvjuːə(r)/ *n* critico, -a *mf*

revile /rɪˈvaɪl/ *vt* ingiuriare

revise /rɪˈvaɪz/ *vt* rivedere; (for exam)
ripassare

revision /rɪˈvɪʒn/ *n* revisione *f*; (for exam)
ripasso *m*

revisionism /rɪˈvɪʒənɪzm/ *n* revisionismo
m

revisionist /rɪˈvɪʒənɪst/ *adj & n*
revisionista *mf*

revisit /riːˈvɪzɪt/ *vt* rivisitare ‹person,
museum etc›

revitalization /riːvaɪtəlaɪˈzeɪʃn/ *n*
rivitalizzazione *f*

revitalize /riːˈvaɪtəlaɪz/ *vt* rivitalizzare

revival /rɪˈvaɪvl/ *n* ritorno *m*; (of patient)
recupero *m*; (from coma) risveglio *m*

revivalist /rɪˈvaɪvəlɪst/ *adj* Relig
revivalista

revive /rɪˈvaɪv/ [1] *vt* resuscitare;
rianimare ‹person›
[2] *vi* riprendersi; ‹person› rianimarsi

revocation /revəˈkeɪʃn/ *n* (of decision,
order) revoca *f*; (of law) abrogazione *f*; (of will)
annullamento *m*

revoke /rɪˈvəʊk/ *vt* revocare ‹decision,
order›; abrogare ‹law›; annullare ‹will›

revolt /rɪˈvəʊlt/ [1] *n* rivolta *f*
[2] *vi* ribellarsi
[3] *vi* rivoltare

revolting /rɪˈvəʊltɪŋ/ *adj* rivoltante

revolution /revəˈluːʃn/ *n* rivoluzione *f*; ∼s
per minute Auto giri *mpl* al minuto

revolutionary /revəˈluːʃənərɪ/ *adj & n*
rivoluzionario, -a *mf*

revolutionize /revəˈluːʃənaɪz/ *vt*
rivoluzionare

revolve /rɪˈvɒlv/ *vi* ruotare; ∼ **around**
girare intorno a

revolver /rɪˈvɒlvə(r)/ *n* rivoltella *f*,
revolver *m inv*

revolving /rɪˈvɒlvɪŋ/ *adj* ruotante

revolving doors *npl* porta *f* girevole

revue /rɪˈvjuː/ *n* rivista *f*

revulsion /rɪˈvʌlʃn/ *n* ripulsione *f*

reward /rɪˈwɔːd/ [1] *n* ricompensa *f*
[2] *vt* ricompensare

reward card *n* = LOYALTY CARD

rewarding /rɪˈwɔːdɪŋ/ *adj* gratificante

rewind /riːˈwaɪnd/ *vt* riavvolgere ‹tape,
film›

rewind button /riːwaɪnd/ *n* tasto *m* di
riavvolgimento

rewire /riːˈwaɪə(r)/ *vt* rifare l'impianto
elettrico di

reword /ri:'wɜd/ vt esprimere con parole diverse

rework /ri:'wɜ:k/ vt modificare

rewritable /ˌri:'raɪtəbl/ adj Comput ‹CD-Rom› riscrivibile

rewrite /ri:'raɪt/ vt (pt **rewrote**, pp **rewritten**) riscrivere

rhapsody /'ræpsədɪ/ n rapsodia f

rhesus /'ri:səs/ n reso m

rhesus-negative adj Rh-negativo

rhesus-positive adj Rh-positivo

rhetoric /'retərɪk/ n retorica f

rhetorical /rɪ'tɒrɪkl/ adj retorico

rhetorically /rɪ'tɒrɪklɪ/ adv retoricamente

rhetorical question n domanda f retorica

rheumatic /rʊ'mætɪk/ adj reumatico

rheumatism /'ru:mətɪzm/ n reumatismo m

rheumatoid arthritis /'ru:mətɔɪd/ n periartrite f

Rhine /raɪn/ n Reno m

rhino /'raɪnəʊ/ n fam rinoceronte m

rhinoceros /raɪ'nɒsərəs/ n rinoceronte m

rhombus /'rɒmbəs/ n rombo m

rhubarb /'ru:bɑ:b/ n rabarbaro m

rhyme /raɪm/ ① n rima f; (poem) filastrocca f
② vi rimare; ~ **with something** far rima con qualcosa

rhythm /'rɪðm/ n ritmo m

rhythmic[al] /'rɪðmɪk[l]/ adj ritmico

rhythmically /'rɪðmɪklɪ/ adv con ritmo

rhythm method n (of contraception) metodo m Ogino-Knauss

rib /rɪb/ ① n costola f; ~**s** pl Culin costata f
② vt (pt/pp **ribbed**) fam punzecchiare

ribald /'rɪbld/ adj spinto

ribbon /'rɪbən/ n nastro m; **in** ~**s** a brandelli

ribcage /'rɪbkeɪdʒ/ n gabbia f toracica, cassa f toracica

rice /raɪs/ n riso m

ricefield /'raɪsfi:ld/ n risaia f

rice-paper n Culin carta f di riso

◀ **rich** /rɪtʃ/ ① adj ricco; ‹food› pesante
② n **the** ~ pl i ricchi; ~**es** pl ricchezze fpl

richly /'rɪtʃlɪ/ adv riccamente; ‹deserve› largamente

richness /'rɪtʃnɪs/ n (of food) pesantezza f; (of furnishings) sfarzosità f; (of person, company) ricchezza f

Richter scale /'rɪktə(r)/ n scala f Richter

rick /rɪk/ vt Br ~ **one's ankle** prendere una storta alla caviglia

rickets /'rɪkɪts/ n rachitismo m

rickety /'rɪkətɪ/ adj malfermo

rickshaw /'rɪkʃɔ:/ n risciò m inv

ricochet /'rɪkəʃeɪ/ ① vi rimbalzare
② n rimbalzo m

rid /rɪd/ vt (pt/pp **rid**, pres p **ridding**) sbarazzare (**of** di); **get** ~ **of** sbarazzarsi di

riddance /'rɪdns/ n **good** ~! che liberazione!

ridden /'rɪdn/ ▶ RIDE

riddle /'rɪdl/ n enigma m

riddled /'rɪdld/ adj ~ **with** crivellato di

◀ **ride** /raɪd/ ① n (on horse) cavalcata f; (in vehicle) giro m; (journey) viaggio m; **take somebody for a** ~ fam prendere qualcuno in giro
② vt (pt **rode**, pp **ridden**) montare ‹horse›; andare su ‹bicycle›
③ vi andare a cavallo; ‹jockey, showjumper› cavalcare; ‹cyclist› andare in bicicletta; (in vehicle) viaggiare
■ **ride out** vt superare ‹storm, crisis›
■ **ride up** vi ‹rider› arrivare; ‹skirt› salire

rider /'raɪdə(r)/ n cavallerizzo, -a mf; (in race) fantino m; (on bicycle) ciclista mf; (in document) postilla f

ridge /rɪdʒ/ n spigolo m; (on roof) punta f; (of mountain) cresta f; (of high pressure) zona f ad alta pressione [atmosferica]

ridicule /'rɪdɪkju:l/ ① n ridicolo m
② vt mettere in ridicolo

ridiculous /rɪ'dɪkjʊləs/ adj ridicolo

ridiculously /rɪ'dɪkjʊləslɪ/ adv in modo ridicolo; ~ **expensive/easy** carissimo/facilissimo

riding /'raɪdɪŋ/ ① n equitazione f
② attrib d'equitazione

rife /raɪf/ adj **be** ~ essere diffuso; ~ **with** pieno di

riff-raff /'rɪfræf/ n marmaglia f

rifle /'raɪfl/ ① n fucile m
② vt ~ **[through]** mettere a soqquadro

rifle-range n tiro m al bersaglio

rift /rɪft/ n fessura f; fig frattura f

rig¹ /rɪg/ n equipaggiamento m; (at sea) piattaforma f per trivellazioni subacquee

rig² vt (pt/pp **rigged**) manovrare ‹election›
■ **rig out** vt equipaggiare; (with clothes) parare
■ **rig up** vt allestire

rigging /'rɪgɪŋ/ n Naut sartiame m; (of election, competition) broglio m

◀ **right** /raɪt/ ① adj giusto; (not left) destro; **be** ~ ‹person› aver ragione; ‹clock› essere giusto; **put** ~ mettere all'ora ‹clock›; correggere ‹person›; rimediare a ‹situation›; **that's** ~! proprio così!; **do you have the** ~ **time?** ha l'ora esatta?
② adv (correctly) bene; (not left) a destra; (directly) proprio; (completely) completamente; ~ **away** immediatamente; **too** ~! altroché!
③ n giusto m; (not left) destra f; (what is due) diritto m; **the R**~ Pol la destra; **on/to the** ~

a destra; **be in the ~** essere nel giusto; **by ~s** secondo giustizia; **be within one's ~s** avere tutti i diritti (**in doing something** di fare qualcosa)

4 *vt* raddrizzare; **~ a wrong** fig riparare ad un torto

right angle *n* angolo *m* retto

right away *adv* subito

righteous /'raɪtʃəs/ *adj* virtuoso; ‹cause› giusto

rightful /'raɪtfl/ *adj* legittimo

rightfully /'raɪtfʊlɪ/ *adv* legittimamente

right-hand /'raɪthænd/ *adj* di destra; **on the ~ side** sulla destra

right-hand drive *n* ‹vehicle› guida *f* a destra

right-handed /-'hændɪd/ *adj* che usa la mano destra

right-hand man *n* fig braccio *m* destro

rightly /'raɪtlɪ/ *adv* giustamente

right-minded /-'maɪndɪd/ *adj* sensato

right-of-centre *adj* Pol di centrodestra

right of way *n* diritto *m* di transito; ‹path› passaggio *m*; Auto precedenza *f*

right-on **1** *int* fam bene!
2 *adj* fam **they're very ~** sono molto impegnati

rights issue *n* emissione *f* riservata agli azionisti

right-thinking *adj* sensato

right turn *n* svolta *f* a destra

right wing *n* Pol destra; Sport ala *f* destra

right-wing *adj* Pol di destra

right-winger *n* Pol persona *f* di destra; Sport ala *f* destra

rigid /'rɪdʒɪd/ *adj* rigido

rigidity /rɪ'dʒɪdətɪ/ *n* rigidità *f*

rigidly /'rɪdʒɪdlɪ/ *adv* ‹apply› rigorosamente; ‹oppose› fermamente

rigmarole /'rɪgmərəʊl/ *n* trafila *f*; ‹story› tiritera *f*

rigor mortis /rɪgə'mɔːtɪs/ *n* rigidità *f* cadaverica

rigorous /'rɪgərəs/ *adj* rigoroso

rigorously /'rɪgərəslɪ/ *adv* rigorosamente

rigour /'rɪgə(r)/ *n* rigore *m*

rig-out *n* fam ‹clothes› tenuta *f*

rile /raɪl/ *vt* fam irritare

rim /rɪm/ *n* bordo *m*; ‹of wheel› cerchione *m*

rind /raɪnd/ *n* ‹on cheese› crosta *f*; ‹on bacon› cotenna *f*

ⵙ **ring¹** /rɪŋ/ **1** *n* ‹circle› cerchio *m*; ‹on finger› anello *m*; ‹boxing› ring *m inv*; ‹for circus› pista *f*, **stand in a ~** essere in cerchio
2 *vt* accerchiare; **~ in red** fare un cerchio rosso intorno a

ⵙ **ring²** **1** *n* suono *m*; **give somebody a ~** Teleph dare un colpo di telefono a qualcuno
2 *vt* (*pt* **rang**, *pp* **rung**) suonare; Teleph

telefonare a; **it ~s a bell** fig mi dice qualcosa; **~ the changes** fig cambiare
3 *vi* suonare; Teleph telefonare; **~ true** aver l'aria di essere vero

■ **ring back** *vt/i* Teleph richiamare

■ **ring off** *vi* Teleph riattaccare

■ **ring out** *vi* ‹voice, shot etc› risuonare chiaramente

■ **ring round** *vi* Teleph fare un giro di telefonate

■ **ring up** Teleph **1** *vt* telefonare a
2 *vi* telefonare

ring-binder /'rɪŋbaɪndə(r)/ *n* raccoglitore *m* ad anelli

ring finger *n* anulare *m*

ringing /'rɪŋɪŋ/ *n* ‹noise of bell, alarm› suono *m*; ‹in ears› fischio *m*

ringleader /'rɪŋliːdə(r)/ *n* capobanda *m*

ringlet /'rɪŋlɪt/ *n* boccolo *m*

ringmaster *n* direttore *m* di circo

ring-pull *n* linguetta *f*

ring road *n* circonvallazione *f*

ringside *n* **at the ~** in prima fila; **have a ~ seat** fig essere in prima fila

ringtone *n* suoneria *f*

rink /rɪŋk/ *n* pista *f* di pattinaggio

rinse /rɪns/ **1** *n* risciacquo *m*; ‹hair colour› cachet *m inv*
2 *vt* sciacquare

■ **rinse off** *vt* sciacquare via

■ **rinse out** *vt* sciacquare ‹cup, glass›; sciacquare via ‹shampoo, soap›

riot /'raɪət/ **1** *n* rissa *f*; ‹of colour› accozzaglia *f*; **~s** *pl* disordini *mpl*; **run ~** impazzare
2 *vi* creare disordini

riot act *n* **read the ~ to somebody** fig dare una lavata di capo a qualcuno

rioter /'raɪətə(r)/ *n* dimostrante *mf*

riot gear *n* tenuta *f* antisommossa

riotous /'raɪətəs/ *adj* sfrenato

riotously /'raɪətəslɪ/ *adv* **~ funny** divertente da morire

riot police *n* DIGOS *f*, Divisione *f* Investigazioni Generali e Operazioni Speciali

rip /rɪp/ **1** *n* strappo *m*
2 *vt* (*pt/pp* **ripped**) strappare; **~ open** aprire con uno strappo
3 *vi* strapparsi; **let ~** scatenarsi

■ **rip off** *vt* ‹remove› togliere; fam ‹cheat› fregare

■ **rip through** *vt* ‹blast› squaciare ‹building›

■ **rip up** *vt* stracciare ‹letter›

RIP *abbr* (**rest in peace**) R.I.P.

ripcord /'rɪpkɔːd/ *n* cavo *m* di spiegamento

ripe /raɪp/ *adj* maturo; ‹cheese› stagionato

ripen /'raɪpn/ **1** *vi* maturare; ‹cheese› stagionarsi
2 *vt* far maturare; stagionare ‹cheese›

ripeness /'raɪpnɪs/ *n* maturazione *f*

r

rip-off *n* fam frode *f*; **these prices are a** ∼! questi prezzi sono un furto!

riposte /rɪ'pɒst/ *n* replica *f*

ripple /'rɪpl/ ① *n* increspatura *f*; ⟨sound⟩ mormorio *m*
　② *vt* increspare
　③ *vi* incresparsi

rip-roaring /'rɪprɔːrɪŋ/ *adj* fam ⟨success⟩ travolgente

✈ **rise** /raɪz/ ① *n* (of sun) levata *f*; fig (to fame, power) ascesa *f*; (increase) aumento *m*; **give** ∼ **to** dare adito a
　② *vi* (*pt* **rose**, *pp* **risen**) alzarsi; ⟨sun⟩ sorgere; ⟨dough⟩ lievitare; ⟨prices, water level⟩ aumentare; (to power, position) arrivare (**to** a); (rebel) sollevarsi; ⟨Parliament, court⟩ aggiornare la seduta; (for holidays) sospendere i lavori
　■ **rise above** *vt* superare ⟨difficulty⟩

riser /'raɪzə(r)/ *n* early ∼ persona *f* mattiniera

rising /'raɪzɪŋ/ ① *adj* ⟨sun⟩ levante; ∼ **generation** nuova generazione *f*
　② *n* (revolt) sollevazione *f*

✈ **risk** /rɪsk/ ① *n* rischio *m*; **run the** ∼ **of** correre il rischio di; **at** ∼ in pericolo; **at one's own** ∼ a proprio rischio e pericolo; **at the** ∼ **of doing something** a costo di fare qualcosa
　② *vt* rischiare

risky /'rɪskɪ/ *adj* (**-ier**, **-iest**) rischioso

risotto /rɪ'zɒtəʊ/ *n* risotto *m*

risqué /'rɪskeɪ/ *adj* spinto

rissole /'rɪsəʊl/ *n* crocchetta *f*

rite /raɪt/ *n* rito *m*; **last** ∼**s** *pl* estrema unzione *fsg*

ritual /'rɪtjʊəl/ *adj & n* rituale *m*

ritzy /'rɪtsɪ/ *adj* fam (hotel, style, decoration) lussuoso

rival /'raɪvl/ ① *adj* rivale
　② *n* rivale *mf*; ∼**s** *pl* Comm concorrenti *mpl*
　③ *vt* (*pt/pp* **rivalled**) rivaleggiare con

rivalry /'raɪv(ə)lrɪ/ *n* rivalità *f inv*; Comm concorrenza *f*

✈ **river** /'rɪvə(r)/ *n* fiume *m*

riverbank *n* riva *f* di fiume

river-bed *n* letto *m* del fiume

riverside ① *n* lungofiume *m*
　② *attrib* sul fiume

rivet /'rɪvɪt/ ① *n* rivetto *m*
　② *vt* rivettare; **be** ∼**ed by** fig essere avvinto da

riveting /'rɪvɪtɪŋ/ *adj* fig avvincente

Riviera /rɪvɪ'eərə/ *n* **the French** ∼ la Costa Azzurra; **the Italian** ∼ la riviera ligure

roach /rəʊtʃ/ *n* (fish) lasca *f*; Am fam (insect) scarafaggio *m*

✈ **road** /rəʊd/ *n* strada *f*, via *f*; **be on the** ∼ viaggiare

roadblock *n* blocco *m* stradale

road haulage *n* trasporto *m* su strada

road hog *n* fam pirata *m* della strada

road hump *n* dosso *m* di rallentamento

roadie /'rəʊdɪ/ *n* roadie *m inv*

road map *n* fig **a** ∼ **to peace** la roadmap per la pace

road safety *n* sicurezza *f* sulle strade

road sense *n* prudenza *f* (*per strada*)

roadshow *n* (play, show) spettacolo *m* di tournée; (publicity tour) giro *m* promozionale

roadside *n* bordo *m* della strada

road sign *n* cartello *m* stradale

road surface *n* fondo *m* stradale

road sweeper *n* (person) spazzino, -a *nmf*; (machine) autospazzatrice *f*

road tax *n* tassa *f* di circolazione

roadway *n* carreggiata *f*, corsia *f*

roadworks *npl* lavori *mpl* stradali

roadworthy *adj* sicuro

roam /rəʊm/ *vt/i* girovagare
　■ **roam around** *vi* girovagare

roar /rɔː(r)/ ① *n* ruggito *m*; ∼**s of laughter** scroscio *msg* di risa
　② *vi* ruggire; ⟨lorry, thunder⟩ rombare; ∼ **with laughter** ridere fragorosamente
　■ **roar out** *vt* gridare
　■ **roar past** *vi* ⟨move noisily⟩ passare rombando

roaring /'rɔːrɪŋ/ ① *adj* **do a** ∼ **trade** fam fare affari d'oro
　② *adv* ∼ **drunk** fam ubriaco fradicio

roast /rəʊst/ ① *adj* arrosto; ∼ **pork** arrosto *m* di maiale
　② *n* arrosto *m*
　③ *vt* arrostire ⟨meat⟩
　④ *vi* arrostirsi

roasting [hot] /'rəʊstɪŋ/ *adj* fam caldissimo

roasting pan *n* teglia *f* per arrosti

rob /rɒb/ *vt* (*pt/pp* **robbed**) derubare (**of** di); svaligiare ⟨bank⟩

robber /'rɒbə(r)/ *n* rapinatore, -trice *mf*

robbery /'rɒbərɪ/ *n* rapina *f*

robe /rəʊb/ *n* tunica *f*; Am (bathrobe) accappatoio *m*

robin /'rɒbɪn/ *n* pettirosso *m*

robot /'rəʊbɒt/ *n* robot *m inv*

robotic /rəʊ'bɒtɪk/ *adj* ⟨movement, voice⟩ robotico; ⟨tool, device, machine⟩ robotizzato

robotics *n* robotica *f*

robust /rəʊ'bʌst/ *adj* robusto

rock¹ /rɒk/ *n* roccia *f*; (in sea) scoglio *m*; (sweet) zucchero *m* candito; **on the** ∼**s** ⟨ship⟩ incagliato; ⟨marriage⟩ finito; ⟨drink⟩ con ghiaccio

rock² ① *vt* cullare ⟨baby⟩; (shake) far traballare; (shock) scuotere
　② *vi* dondolarsi

✈ indicates a very frequent word

◆ **rock³** *n* Mus rock *m*

rock and roll *n* rock and roll *m*

rock-bottom **1** *adj* bassissimo
2 *n* livello *m* più basso; **hit ~** toccare il fondo

rock-climber *n* scalatore, -trice *mf*

rock-climbing *n* roccia *f*

rockery /'rɒkərɪ/ *n* giardino *m* roccioso

rocket /'rɒkɪt/ **1** *n* razzo *m*; **give somebody a ~** fam fare un cicchetto a qualcuno
2 *vi* salire alle stelle

rocket launcher /'lɔːntʃə(r)/ *n* lanciarazzi *m inv*

rocket science *n* fam **it's not ~** non ci vuole la laurea!

rock face *n* parete *f* rocciosa

rockfall /'rɒkfɔːl/ *n* caduta *f* di massi

rocking chair /'rɒkɪŋ/ *n* sedia *f* a dondolo

rocking horse *n* cavallo *m* a dondolo

rock star *n* rock star *mf inv*

rocky /'rɒkɪ/ *adj* (**-ier**, **-iest**) roccioso; fig traballante

Rocky Mountains *npl* le Montagne *fpl* Rocciose

rod /rɒd/ *n* bacchetta *f*; (for fishing) canna *f*

rode /rəʊd/ ▶ RIDE

rodent /'rəʊdnt/ *n* roditore *m*

roe¹ /rəʊ/ *n* uova *fpl* di pesce; (soft) latte *m* di pesce

roe² *n* (*pl* **roe** or **roes**) ~ [deer] capriolo *m*

roebuck /'rəʊbʌk/ *n* capriolo *m* maschio

roger /'rɒdʒə(r)/ *int* Teleph ricevuto

rogue /rəʊg/ *n* farabutto *m*

rogue state *n* stato *m* canaglia

◆ **role** /rəʊl/ *n* ruolo *m*

role model *n* Psych modello *m* comportamentale

role-play, **role-playing** /'rəʊlpleɪɪŋ/ *n* Psych role playing *m inv*

◆ **roll** /rəʊl/ **1** *n* rotolo *m*; ‹bread› panino *m*; (list) lista *f*; ‹of ship, drum› rullio *m*
2 *vi* rotolare; **be ~ing in money** fam nuotare nell'oro
3 *vt* spianare ‹lawn, pastry›; **~ed into one** allo stesso tempo

■ **roll around**, **roll about** *vi* ‹person, puppy› rotolarsi; ‹ball, marbles› rotolare

■ **roll back** *vt* ridurre ‹prices›

■ **roll by** *vi* ‹time› passare

■ **roll down** *vt* srotolare ‹blind, sleeves›

■ **roll in** *vi* fam (arrive in large quantities) arrivare a valanghe; (arrive) arrivare

■ **roll on**: *vi* **~ on Friday!** non vedo l'ora che sia venerdì!

■ **roll over** *vi* rigirarsi; fam (capitulate) arrendersi

■ **roll up** **1** *vt* arrotolare; rimboccarsi ‹sleeves›
2 *vi* fam arrivare

roll-call *n* appello *m*

roller /'rəʊlə(r)/ *n* rullo *m*; (for hair) bigodino *m*

rollerblade **1** *n* pattino *m* a rotelle in linea
2 *vi* pattinare (con pattini in linea)

roller blind *n* tapparella *f*

roller coaster *n* montagne *fpl* russe

roller skate *n* pattino *m* a rotelle

roller-skating /'rəʊləskeɪtɪŋ/ *n* pattinaggio *m* a rotelle

rollicking /'rɒlɪkɪŋ/ *adj* **have a ~ time** divertirsi da pazzi

rolling pin *n* mattarello *m*

rolling stock *n* materiale *m* rotabile

rolling stone *n* fig vagabondo, -a *mf*

rollneck *n* collo *m* alto; (whole sweater) dolcevita *f*

roll-on *n* (deodorant) deodorante *m* a sfera

roll-on roll-off ferry *n* traghetto *m* roll-on roll-off

ROM /rɒm/ *n* Comput Rom *f inv*

Roma /'rəʊmə/ *npl* i rom *mpl*

Roman /'rəʊmən/ **1** *adj* (also print) romano
2 *n* romano, -a *mf*

Roman Catholic *adj & n* cattolico, -a *mf*

romance /rəʊ'mæns/ *n* (love affair) storia *f* d'amore; (book) romanzo *m* rosa

Romania /rəʊ'meɪnɪə/ *n* Romania *f*

Romanian /rəʊ'meɪnɪən/ *adj & n* rumeno, -a *mf*; (language) rumeno *m*

roman numeral *n* numero *m* romano

romantic /rəʊ'mæntɪk/ *adj* romantico

romantically /rəʊ'mæntɪklɪ/ *adv* romanticamente

romanticism /rəʊ'mæntɪsɪzm/ *n* romanticismo *m*

romanticize /rəʊ'mæntɪsaɪz/ *vt* romanticizzare

romanticized /rəʊ'mæntɪsaɪzd/ *adj* romanzato

Romany /'rɒmənɪ/ *n* rom *mf inv*

Rome /rəʊm/ *n* Roma *f*

Romeo /'rəʊmɪəʊ/ *n* fam (ladykiller) dongiovanni *m inv*

romp /rɒmp/ **1** *n* gioco *m* rumoroso
2 *vi* giocare rumorosamente

■ **romp home** *vi* (win easily) vincere senza difficoltà

rompers /'rɒmpəz/ *npl* pagliaccetto *msg*

romp through **1** *vt* passare senza difficoltà ‹exam›
2 *vi* riuscire senza difficoltà

roof /ruːf/ **1** *n* tetto *m*; (of mouth) palato *m*; **live under one ~** vivere sotto lo stesso tetto; **go through the ~** fam (increase) andare alle stelle; (be very angry) andare su tutte le furie
2 *vt* mettere un tetto su

roof-rack *n* portabagagli *m inv*

r

rooftop /'ru:ftɒp/ n tetto m; **shout it from the ~s** fig gridarlo ai quattro venti

rook /rʊk/ **1** n corvo m; (in chess) torre f **2** vt fam (swindle) fregare

rookie /'rʊkɪ/ n Am fam novellino, -a mf

◆ **room** /'ru:m/ n stanza f; (bedroom) camera f; (for functions) sala f; (space) spazio m

room-mate n Am (flatmate) compagno, -a mf di appartamento; (in same room) compagno, -a mf di stanza

room service n servizio m in camera

room temperature n temperatura f ambiente

roomy /'ru:mɪ/ adj spazioso; ‹clothes› ampio

roost /ru:st/ **1** n posatoio m **2** vi appollaiarsi

rooster /'ru:stə(r)/ n gallo m

◆ **root¹** /ru:t/ **1** n radice f; **take ~** metter radici; **put down ~s** fig metter radici **2** vi metter radici

root² vi **~ for somebody** fam fare il tifo per qualcuno

■ **root about**, **root around** vi grufolare; **~ about for something** rovistare alla ricerca di qualcosa

■ **root out** vt fig scovare

rope /rəʊp/ n corda f; **know the ~s** fam conoscere i trucchi del mestiere

■ **rope in** vt fam coinvolgere

rope ladder n scala f di corda

ropey /'rəʊpɪ/ adj Br fam scadente; **feel ~** sentirsi poco bene

rosary /'rəʊzərɪ/ n rosario m

rose¹ /rəʊz/ n rosa f; (of watering-can) bocchetta f

rose² ▶ RISE

rosé /'rəʊzeɪ/ n [vino m] rosé m inv

rosebud /'rəʊzbʌd/ n bocciolo m di rosa

rosehip /'rəʊzhɪp/ n frutto m della rosa canina

rosemary /'rəʊzmərɪ/ n rosmarino m

rose-tinted spectacles /'rəʊztɪntɪd/ npl **wear ~** vedere tutto rosa

rosette /rəʊ'zet/ n coccarda f

roster /'rɒstə(r)/ n tabella f dei turni

rostrum /'rɒstrəm/ n podio m

rosy /'rəʊzɪ/ adj (-ier, -iest) roseo

rot /rɒt/ **1** n marciume m; fam (nonsense) sciocchezze fpl **2** vi (pt/pp **rotted**) marcire

rota /'rəʊtə/ n tabella f dei turni

rotary /'rəʊtərɪ/ adj rotante

rotate /rəʊ'teɪt/ **1** vt far ruotare; avvicendare ‹crops› **2** vi ruotare

rotation /rəʊ'teɪʃn/ n rotazione f; **in ~** a turno

rote /rəʊt/ n **by ~** meccanicamente

◆ indicates a very frequent word

rotten /'rɒtn/ adj marcio; fam schifoso; ‹person› penoso

rotund /rəʊ'tʌnd/ adj paffuto

rotunda /rəʊ'tʌndə/ n rotonda f

rouble /'ru:bl/ n rublo m

rough /rʌf/ **1** adj (not smooth) ruvido; ‹ground› accidentato; ‹behaviour› rozzo; ‹sport› violento; ‹area› malfamato; ‹crossing, time› brutto; ‹estimate› approssimativo **2** adv ‹play› grossolanamente; **sleep ~** dormire sotto i ponti **3** n **do something in ~** far qualcosa alla bell'e meglio **4** vi **~ it** vivere senza confort

■ **rough out** vt abbozzare

■ **rough up** vt fam malmenare ‹person›

roughage /'rʌfɪdʒ/ n fibre fpl

rough-and-ready adj ‹person, manner› sbrigativo; ‹conditions, method› rudimentale

rough-and-tumble n (rough play) zuffa f

rough copy n brutta copia f

rough draft n abbozzo m

roughen /'rʌfən/ vt rendere ruvido ‹surface›

roughly /'rʌflɪ/ adv rozzamente; (more or less) pressappoco

roughness /'rʌfnɪs/ n ruvidità f; (of behaviour) rozzezza f

rough paper n carta f da brutta

roughshod /'rʌfʃɒd/ adv **ride ~ over** infischiarsi di ‹person, objection›; calpestare ‹feelings›

roulette /ru:'let/ n roulette f

◆ **round** /raʊnd/ **1** adj rotondo **2** n tondo m; (slice) fetta f; (of visits, drinks) giro m; (of competition) partita f; (boxing) ripresa f; round m inv; **do one's ~s** ‹doctor› fare il giro delle visite **3** prep intorno a; **open ~ the clock** aperto ventiquattr'ore **4** adv **all ~** tutt'intorno; **ask somebody ~** invitare qualcuno; **go/come ~ to** (a friend etc) andare da; **turn/look ~** girarsi; **~ about** (approximately) intorno a **5** vt arrotondare; girare ‹corner›

■ **round down** vt arrotondare (per difetto)

■ **round off** vt (end) terminare

■ **round on** vt aggredire

■ **round up** vt radunare; arrotondare ‹prices›

roundabout /'raʊndəbaʊt/ **1** adj indiretto **2** n giostra f; (for traffic) rotonda f

round bracket n parentesi f tonda

rounders /'raʊndəz/ n Br Sport gioco (m) simile al baseball

round figure n cifra f tonda

round robin n petizione f

round-shouldered /-'ʃəʊldəd/ adj con le spalle curve

round table n tavola f rotonda

round the clock adv 24 ore su 24

round-the-clock *adj* Br ‹*care,
surveillance*› ventiquattr'ore su
ventiquattro

round-the-world *adj* ‹*trip*› intorno al
mondo

round trip *n* viaggio *m* di andata e ritorno

round-up *n* (of suspects) retata *f*; (of cattle)
raduno *m*; (summary) riepilogo *m*

rouse /raʊz/ *vt* svegliare; risvegliare
‹*suspicion, interest*›

rousing /'raʊzɪŋ/ *adj* ‹*speech*› che solleva il
morale; ‹*music*› trionfale

rout /raʊt/ ① *vt* Mil fig sbaragliare
② *n* disfatta *f*

⚔ **route** /ru:t/ *n* itinerario *m*; Naut, Aeron rotta
f; (of bus) percorso *m*

routine /ru:'ti:n/ ① *adj* di routine
② *n* routine *f inv*; Theat numero *m*

routinely /ru:'ti:nlɪ/ *adv* d'ufficio

routing number /'raʊtɪŋnʌmbər/ *n* Am
numero *m* di instradamento, numero *m* di
identificazione (bancaria)

rove /rəʊv/ *vi* girovagare

roving /'rəʊvɪŋ/ *adj* ‹*reporter, ambassador*›
itinerante

roving eye *n* have a ∼ essere sempre in
cerca di avventure amorose

⚔ **row¹** /rəʊ/ *n* (line) fila *f*; **three years in a** ∼
tre anni di fila

row² ① *vi* (in boat) remare
② *vt* ∼ **a boat** remare

row³ /raʊ/ ① *n* (quarrel) litigata *f*; (noise)
baccano *m*; **we've had a** ∼ abbiamo litigato
② *vi* fam litigare

rowboat /'rəʊbəʊt/ *n* Am barca *f* a remi

rowdy /'raʊdɪ/ ① *adj* (-ier, -iest)
chiassoso
② *n* attaccabrighe *m inv*

rower /'rəʊə(r)/ *n* rematore, -trice *mf*

rowing /'rəʊɪŋ/ *n* (sport) canottaggio *m*

rowing boat /'rəʊɪŋ/ *n* barca *f* a remi

rowing machine *n* vogatore *m*

rowlock /'rɒlək/ *n* Br scalmo *m*

⚔ **royal** /'rɔɪəl/ ① *adj* reale
② *n* membro *m* della famiglia reale

royal blue *n* & *adj* blu *m* scuro

Royal Highness *n* His/Her ∼ Sua
Altezza reale; **Your** ∼ Vostra Altezza

royally /'rɔɪəlɪ/ *adv* regalmente

royalties /'rɔɪəltɪz/ *npl* (payments) diritti
mpl d'autore

royalty /'rɔɪəltɪ/ *n* appartenenza *f* alla
famiglia reale; (persons) i membri della
famiglia reale

rpm *abbr* (**revolutions per minute**)
giri *mpl* al minuto

RSI *abbr* (**repetitive strain injury**)
patologia *f* da sforzo ripetuto

RSVP *abbr* (**répondez s'il vous plaît
= please reply**) SPR, si prega rispondere

rub /rʌb/ ① *n* sfregata *f*
② *vt* (*pt/pp* **rubbed**) sfregare; ∼ **one's
hands** fregarsi le mani

■ **rub along** *vi* sopportarsi [a vicenda]

■ **rub down** *vt* frizionare ‹*person, body*›;
levigare ‹*wood*›

■ **rub in** *vt* far assorbire (*massaggiando*)
‹*cream*›; **don't** ∼**it in** fam non rigirare il
coltello nella piaga

■ **rub off** ① *vt* mandar via sfregando ‹*stain*›;
(from blackboard) cancellare
② *vi* andar via; ∼ **off on** essere trasmesso a

■ **rub out** *vt* cancellare

■ **rub up**: *vt* ∼ **somebody up the wrong way**
prendere qualcuno per il verso sbagliato

rubber /'rʌbə(r)/ *n* gomma *f*; (eraser) gomma
f [da cancellare]

rubber band *n* elastico *m*

rubber bullet *n* proiettile *m* di gomma

rubberneck *n* fam (onlooker) curioso, -a *mf*;
(tourist) turista *mf*

rubber plant *n* ficus *m inv*

rubberstamp *vt* fig approvare senza
discutere

rubber tree *n* albero *m* della gomma

rubbery /'rʌbərɪ/ *adj* gommoso

rubbish /'rʌbɪʃ/ ① *n* immondizie *fpl*; fam
(nonsense) idiozie *fpl*; fam (junk) robaccia *f*
② *vt* fam fare a pezzi

rubbish bin *n* pattumiera *f*

rubbish dump *n* discarica *f*; (official)
discarica *f* comunale

rubbishy /'rʌbɪʃɪ/ *adj* fam schifoso

rubble /'rʌbl/ *n* macerie *fpl*

rub-down *n* strofinata *f*

rubella /rʊ'belə/ *n* rosolia *f*

rubric /'ru:brɪk/ *n* rubrica *f*

ruby /'ru:bɪ/ ① *n* rubino *m*
② *attrib* di rubini; ‹*lips*› scarlatto

rucksack /'rʌksæk/ *n* zaino *m*

ructions /'rʌkʃ(ə)nz/ *npl* fam finimondo
msg; **there'll be** ∼ **if he finds out** se lo scopre
succede il finimondo

rudder /'rʌdə(r)/ *n* timone *m*

ruddy /'rʌdɪ/ *adj* (-ier, -iest) rubicondo;
fam maledetto

rude /ru:d/ *adj* scortese; (improper) spinto

rudely /'ru:dlɪ/ *adv* scortesemente

rudeness /'ru:dnɪs/ *n* scortesia *f*

rudimentary /ru:dɪ'mentərɪ/ *adj*
rudimentale

rudiments /'ru:dɪmənts/ *npl* rudimenti
mpl

rue¹ /ru:/ *vt* pentirsi di ‹*decision*›; ∼ **the day**
maledire il giorno

rue² *n* Bot ruta *f*

rueful /'ru:fl/ *adj* rassegnato

ruefully /'ru:fʊlɪ/ *adv* con rassegnazione

ruff /rʌf/ *n* (of lace) colletto *m*; (of fur, feathers)
collare *m*

r

ruffian /ˈrʌfɪən/ *n* farabutto *m*

ruffle /ˈrʌfl/ ① *n* gala *f*
② *vt* scompigliare ‹hair›

rug /rʌg/ *n* tappeto *m*; (blanket) coperta *f*

rugby /ˈrʌgbɪ/ *n* ~ **[football]** rugby *m*

rugby league *n* rugby *m* a tredici

rugby union *n* rugby *m* a quindici

rugged /ˈrʌgɪd/ *adj* ‹coastline› roccioso;
‹face, personality› duro

ruin /ˈruːɪn/ ① *n* rovina *f*; **in** ~**s** in rovina
② *vt* rovinare

ruined /ˈruːɪnd/ *adj* ‹building, clothes›
rovinato

ruinous /ˈruːɪnəs/ *adj* estremamente
costoso

⚜ **rule** /ruːl/ ① *n* regola *f*; (control)
ordinamento *m*; (for measuring) metro *m*; ~**s**
pl regolamento *msg*; **as a** ~ generalmente;
make it a ~ **to do something** fare qualcosa
sistematicamente
② *vt* governare; dominare ‹colony,
behaviour›; ~ **that** stabilire che
③ *vi* governare

■ **rule out** *vt* escludere

ruled /ruːld/ *adj* ‹paper› a righe

rule of thumb *n* principio *m* empirico

ruler /ˈruːlə(r)/ *n* capo *m* di Stato; (sovereign)
sovrano, -a *mf*; (measure) righello *m*, regolo *m*

ruling /ˈruːlɪŋ/ ① *adj* ‹class› dirigente;
‹party› di governo
② *n* decisione *f*

rum¹ /rʌm/ *n* rum *m inv*

rum² *adj* fam (peculiar) curioso

rumble /ˈrʌmbl/ ① *n* rombo *m*; (of stomach)
brontolio *m*
② *vi* rombare; ‹stomach› brontolare

rumble strip *n* banda *f* rumorosa

rumbustious /rʌmˈbʌstʃəs/ *adj* (noisy, very
lively) chiassoso

ruminant /ˈruːmɪnənt/ *n* ruminante *m*

ruminate /ˈruːmɪneɪt/ *vi* ‹animals›
ruminare; (think) rimuginare

rummage /ˈrʌmɪdʒ/ *vi* rovistare (**in**/
through in)

rummy /ˈrʌmɪ/ *n* ramino *m*

rumour /ˈruːmə(r)/ ① *n* diceria *f*
② *vt* **it is** ~**ed that** si dice che

rumour-monger /ˈruːməmʌŋgə(r)/ *n*
persona *f* che sparge pettegolezzi

rump /rʌmp/ *n* natiche *fpl*

rumple /ˈrʌmpl/ *vt* sgualcire ‹clothes,
sheets, papers›; scompigliare ‹hair›

rump steak *n* bistecca *f* di girello

rumpus /ˈrʌmpəs/ *n* fam baccano *m*

⚜ **run** /rʌn/ ① *n* (on foot) corsa *f*; (distance to
be covered) tragitto *m*; (outing) giro *m*; Theat
rappresentazioni *fpl*; (in skiing) pista *f*; Am
(ladder) smagliatura *f* (*in calze*); **at a** ~ di

corsa; ~ **of bad luck** periodo *m* sfortunato;
on the ~ in fuga; **have the** ~ of avere a
disposizione; **in the long** ~ a lungo termine
② *vi* (*pt* **ran**, *pp* **run**, *pres p* **running**)
correre; ‹river› scorrere; ‹nose, makeup›
colare; ‹bus› fare servizio; ‹play› essere in
cartellone; ‹colours› sbiadire; (in election)
presentarsi [come candidato]; ‹software›
girare; (function) funzionare; ~ **in the family**
essere di famiglia; ~ **for President**
candidarsi alla presidenza
③ *vt* (manage) dirigere; tenere ‹house›; (drive)
dare un passaggio a; correre ‹risk›; Comput
lanciare; Journ pubblicare ‹article›; (pass) far
scorrere ‹eyes, hand›; ~ **a temperature** avere
la febbre; ~ **a bath** far scorrere l'acqua per
il bagno

■ **run about** *vi* ‹children› correre di qua e di
là; (be busy) correre

■ **run across** *vt* imbattersi in

■ **run after** *vt* (chase) rincorrere; (romantically)
andare dietro a

■ **run along** *vi* (go away) andare via

■ **run away** *vi* scappare [via], andare via di
corsa; (from home) scappare di casa

■ **run away with** *vt* scappare con ‹lover,
money›; **she let her enthusiasm** ~ **away with
her** si è lasciata trasportare dall'entusiasmo

■ **run back** ① *vi* correre indietro
② *vt* (transport by car) riaccompagnare

■ **run back over** *vt* (review) rivedere

■ **run down** ① *vi* ‹clock› scaricarsi; ‹stocks›
esaurirsi
② *vt* Auto investire; (reduce) esaurire; fam
(criticize) denigrare

■ **run in** *vi* entrare di corsa

■ **run into** *vi* (meet) imbattersi in; (knock
against) urtare

■ **run off** ① *vi* scappare [via], andare via di
corsa; (from home) scappare di casa
② *vt* stampare ‹copies›

■ **run off with** *vt* = RUN AWAY WITH

■ **run on** *vi* ‹meeting› protrarsi; ‹person›
chiacchierare senza sosta

■ **run out** *vi* uscire di corsa; ‹supplies, money›
esaurirsi; ~ **out of** rimanere senza

■ **run over** ① *vi* correre; (overflow) traboccare
② *vt* (review) dare una scorsa a; Auto
investire

■ **run through** *vt* (use up) fare fuori; (be
present in) pervadere; (review) dare una scorsa a

■ **run to** *vt* (be enough for) essere sufficiente
per; (have enough money for) potersi permettere

■ **run up** ① *vi* salire di corsa; (towards)
arrivare di corsa
② *vt* accumulare ‹debts, bill›; (sew) cucire

■ **run up against** *vt* incontrare ‹difficulties›

runabout *n* (vehicle) utilitaria *f*

run-around *n* **he's giving me/her the** ~
mi/la sta menando per il naso

runaway ① *n* fuggitivo, -a *mf*, fuggiasco,
-a *mf*; (child) ragazzo, -a *mf* scappato, -a di casa
② *adj* ‹person› in fuga; ‹child› scappato
di casa; ‹inflation› galoppante; ‹success›
eclatante

⚜ indicates a very frequent word

r

run-down [1] *adj* ‹area› in abbandono; ‹person› esaurito
[2] *n* analisi *f inv*

rung¹ /rʌŋ/ *n* (of ladder) piolo *m*

rung² ▶ RING²

run-in *n* fam (argument) lite *f*

runner /'rʌnə(r)/ *n* podista *mf*; (in race) corridore, -trice *mf*; (on sledge) pattino *f*; (carpet) guida *f*

runner bean *n* fagiolino *m*

runner-up *n* secondo, -a, classificato, -a *mf*

running /'rʌnɪŋ/ [1] *adj* in corsa; ‹water› corrente; **four times** ∼ quattro volte di seguito
[2] *n* corsa *f*; (management) direzione *f*; **be in the** ∼ essere in lizza

running battle *n* lotta *f* continua

running commentary *n* cronaca *f*

running total *n* totale *m* aggiornato

runny /'rʌnɪ/ *adj* semiliquido; ∼ **nose** naso *m* che cola

run-of-the-mill *adj* ordinario

runs /rʌnz/ *npl* **the** ∼ fam (diarrhoea) la sciolta

runt /rʌnt/ *n* (of litter) cucciolo (*m*) più piccolo e debole di una figliata; pej (weakling) mezza cartuccia *f*

run-through *n* prova *f* generale

run-up *n* Sport rincorsa *f*; **the** ∼ **to** il periodo precedente

runway /'rʌnweɪ/ *n* pista *f*

rupee /ru:'pi:/ *n* rupia *f*

rupture /'rʌptʃə(r)/ [1] *n* rottura *f*; Med ernia *f*
[2] *vt* rompere; ∼ **oneself** farsi venire l'ernia
[3] *vi* rompersi

✧ **rural** /'rʊərəl/ *adj* rurale

ruse /ru:z/ *n* astuzia *f*

rush¹ /rʌʃ/ *n* Bot giunco *m*

✧ **rush²** [1] *n* fretta *f*; **in a** ∼ di fretta
[2] *vi* precipitarsi
[3] *vt* far premura a; ∼ **somebody to hospital** trasportare qualcuno di corsa

all'ospedale

■ **rush away**, **rush off** *vi* andar via in fretta

■ **rush into**: *vt* ∼ **into marriage** sposarsi senza riflettere; ∼ **into doing something** lanciarsi a fare qualcosa senza riflettere; ∼ **somebody into doing something** spingere qualcuno a fare qualcosa

■ **rush out** *vi* uscire di corsa

■ **rush through** *vt* svolgere in fretta ‹task›; ∼ **something through** fare approvare qualcosa in fretta ‹legislation, order›

rush hour [1] *n* ora *f* di punta
[2] *attrib* delle ore di punta

rusk /rʌsk/ *n* biscotto *m*

russet /'rʌsɪt/ *adj* rossastro

Russia /'rʌʃə/ *n* Russia *f*

Russian /'rʌʃən/ *adj* & *n* russo, -a *mf*; (language) russo *m*

Russian roulette *n* roulette *f* russa

rust /rʌst/ [1] *n* ruggine *f*
[2] *vi* arrugginirsi
[3] *vt* arrugginire

rustic /'rʌstɪk/ *adj* rustico

rustle /'rʌsl/ [1] *vi* frusciare
[2] *vt* far frusciare; Am rubare ‹cattle›

■ **rustle up** *vt* fam fare ‹meal, cup of coffee›

rustler /'rʌslə(r)/ *n* ladro *m* di bestiame

rustproof /'rʌstpru:f/ *adj* a prova di ruggine

rusty /'rʌstɪ/ *adj* (**-ier**, **-iest**) arrugginito

rut /rʌt/ *n* solco *m*; **in a** ∼ fam nella routine

rutabaga /ˌru:tə'beɪgə/ *n* Am rutabaga *f*; navone *m*

ruthless /'ru:θlɪs/ *adj* spietato

ruthlessly /'ru:θlɪslɪ/ *adv* spietatamente

ruthlessness /'ru:θlɪsnɪs/ *n* spietatezza *f*

rutting /'rʌtɪŋ/ *n* accoppiamento *m*

rutting season *n* stagione *f* degli amori

RV *n abbr* Am (**recreational vehicle**) camper *m*

Rwanda /rʊ'ændə/ *n* Rwanda *m*

rye /raɪ/ *n* segale *f*

rye bread *n* pane *m* di segale

Ss

s, S¹ /es/ *n* (letter) s, S *f inv*

S² *abbr* 1 (**small**)
2 (**south**) S

sabbath /'sæbəθ/ *n* domenica *f*; Jewish sabato *m*

sabbatical /sə'bætɪkl/ *n* Univ anno *m* sabbatico

sable /'seɪbl/ *n* (animal, fur) zibellino *m*

sabotage /'sæbətɑ:ʒ/ [1] *n* sabotaggio *m*
[2] *vt* sabotare

saboteur /sæbə'tɜ:(r)/ *n* sabotatore, -trice *mf*

sabre /'seɪbə(r)/ *n* sciabola *f*

sac /sæk/ n Anat, Zool sacco m; Bot sacca f; honey ~ cestella f

saccharin /'sækərɪn/ n saccarina f

sachet /'sæʃeɪ/ n bustina f; (scented) sacchetto m profumato

sack¹ /sæk/ vt (plunder) saccheggiare

sack² ① n sacco m; **get the** ~ fam essere licenziato; **give somebody the** ~ licenziare qualcuno
② vt fam licenziare

sackcloth /'sækklɒθ/ n tela f di sacco; **wear** ~ **and ashes** cospargersi il capo di cenere

sackful /'sækfʊl/ n sacco m (contenuto)

sacking /'sækɪŋ/ n tela f per sacchi; fam (dismissal) licenziamento m

sackload /'sækləʊd/ n sacco m (contenuto)

sacrament /'sækrəmənt/ n sacramento m

sacred /'seɪkrɪd/ adj sacro

sacred cow /kaʊ/ n (institution) istituzione f intoccabile; (principle) principio m inderogabile; (person) mostro m sacro

sacrifice /'sækrɪfaɪs/ ① n sacrificio m
② vt sacrificare; ~ **oneself** immolarsi

sacrificial /sækrɪ'fɪʃəl/ adj ‹victim› sacrificale

sacrilege /'sækrɪlɪdʒ/ n sacrilegio m

sacrilegious /sækrɪ'lɪdʒəs/ adj sacrilego

sacristy /'sækrɪstɪ/ n sagrestia f

sacrosanct /'sækrəʊsæŋkt/ adj sacrosanto

sacrum /'sækrʌm/ n Anat osso m sacro

✔ **sad** /sæd/ adj (**sadder, saddest**) triste

SAD /sæd/ n abbr (**seasonal affective disorder**) Med disturbi mpl affettivi stagionali

sadden /'sædn/ vt rattristare

saddle /'sædl/ ① n sella f; **be in the** ~ fig tenere le redini
② vt sellare; **I've been** ~**d with...** fig mi hanno affibbiato...

sadism /'seɪdɪzm/ n sadismo m

sadist /'seɪdɪst/ n sadico, -a mf

sadistic /sə'dɪstɪk/ adj sadico

sadistically /sə'dɪstɪklɪ/ adv sadicamente

sadly /'sædlɪ/ adv tristemente; (unfortunately) sfortunatamente

sadness /'sædnɪs/ n tristezza f

sadomasochism /seɪdəʊ'mæsəkɪzm/ n sadomasochismo m

sadomasochist /seɪdəʊ'mæsəkɪst/ n sadomasochista m

sadomasochistic /seɪdəʊ'mæsəkɪstɪk/ adj sadomasochistico

sae abbr (**stamped addressed envelope**) busta (f) preaffrancata e preindirizzata

safari /sə'fɑːrɪ/ n safari m inv

safari park n zoosafari m inv

✔ indicates a very frequent word

✔ **safe** /seɪf/ ① adj sicuro; (out of danger) salvo; ‹object› al sicuro; ~ **and sound** sano e salvo
② n cassaforte f

safe bet n it's a ~ that he will come è certo che verrà

safe-breaker n scassinatore, -trice mf

safe-conduct /seɪf'kɒndʌkt/ n salvacondotto m

safe-deposit box, safety-deposit box n cassetta f di sicurezza

safeguard ① n protezione f
② vt proteggere

safe house n rifugio m

safe keeping n custodia f; **for** ~ in custodia

safely /'seɪflɪ/ adv in modo sicuro; ‹arrive› senza incidenti; ‹assume› con certezza

safe sex n sesso m sicuro

✔ **safety** /'seɪftɪ/ n sicurezza f

safety belt n cintura f di sicurezza

safety catch n sicura f

safety curtain n tagliafuoco m

safety-deposit box n = SAFE-DEPOSIT BOX

safety glass n vetro m di sicurezza

safety net n (for acrobat) rete f di protezione; fig protezione

safety pin n spilla f di sicurezza o da balia

safety razor n rasoio m di sicurezza

safety valve n valvola f di sicurezza; fig valvola f di sfogo

saffron /'sæfrən/ n zafferano m

sag /sæg/ vi (pt/pp **sagged**) abbassarsi

saga /'sɑːgə/ n saga f

sagacity /sə'gæsətɪ/ n sagacia f

sage¹ /seɪdʒ/ n (herb) salvia f

sage² adj & n saggio, -a mf

sagely /'seɪdʒlɪ/ adv ‹reply, nod› saggiamente

Sagittarius /sædʒɪ'teərɪəs/ n Sagittario m

sago /'seɪgəʊ/ n sagù m

Sahara /sə'hɑːrə/ n Sahara m

said /sed/ ▶ SAY

sail /seɪl/ ① n vela f; (trip) giro m in barca a vela
② vi navigare; Sport praticare la vela; (leave) salpare
③ vt pilotare
■ **sail through** vt superare senza problemi ‹exam›

sailboard /'seɪlbɔːd/ n tavola f da windsurf

sailboarder /'seɪlbɔːdə(r)/ n windsurfista mf

sailboarding /'seɪlbɔːdɪŋ/ n windsurf m inv

sailboat /'seɪlbəʊt/ n Am barca f a vela

sailing /'seɪlɪŋ/ n vela f

sailing boat n barca f a vela

sailing ship n veliero m

sailor /'seɪlə(r)/ n marinaio m

saint /seɪnt/ n santo, -a mf

sainthood /'seɪnthʊd/ n santità f

saintly /'seɪntlɪ/ adj da santo

sake /seɪk/ n for the ~ of ‹person› per il bene di; ‹peace› per amor di; for the ~ of it per il gusto di farlo

salacious /sə'leɪʃəs/ adj ‹joke› salace; ‹book› licenzioso; ‹look› lascivo

salad /'sæləd/ n insalata f

salad bar n tavola f fredda

salad bowl n insalatiera f

salad cream n salsa (f) per condire l'insalata

salad days npl anni mpl verdi

salad dressing n condimento m per insalata

salami /sə'lɑːmɪ/ n salame m

salaried /'sælərɪd/ adj stipendiato

salary /'sælərɪ/ n stipendio m

salary review n revisione f dello stipendio

salary scale n tabella f retributiva

♦ **sale** /seɪl/ n vendita f; (at reduced prices) svendita f; for/on ~ in vendita; 'for ~' 'vendesi'

sale price n prezzo m scontato

sales and marketing n vendite fpl e marketing

sales and marketing department n ufficio m vendite e marketing

sales assistant n commesso, -a mf

sales director n capo mf dell'ufficio vendite

sales engineer n tecnico m commerciale

sales executive n direttore, -trice mf commerciale

sales figures npl volumi mpl d'affari

sales force n rappresentanti mpl

sales invoice n fattura f di vendita

sales ledger n partitario m vendite

salesman n venditore m; (traveller) rappresentante m

sales pitch n discorso m imbonitore

sales rep, **sales representative** n rappresentante mf di commercio

salesroom n (for auctions) sala f d'aste

sales team n team m inv vendite

saleswoman n venditrice f

salient /'seɪlɪənt/ adj saliente

saline /'seɪlaɪn/ adj salino

saliva /sə'laɪvə/ n saliva f

salivary glands /sə'laɪvərɪ/ npl ghiandole fpl salivari

salivate /'sælɪveɪt/ vi salivare; the smell of chicken roasting makes me ~ l'odore di pollo arrosto mi fa venire l'acquolina in bocca

sallow /'sæləʊ/ adj giallastro

sally /'sælɪ/ ① n (witty remark) battuta f; Mil sortita f
② vi saltar fuori

salmon /'sæmən/ n salmone m

salmonella /sælmə'nelə/ n salmonella f

salmon-pink adj rosa inv, salmone inv

salmon trout n trota f salmonata

salon /'sælɒn/ n salone m

saloon /sə'luːn/ n Auto berlina f; Am (bar) bar m

salsa /'sælsə/ n salsa f

salt /sɔːlt/ ① n sale m
② adj salato; ‹fish, meat› sotto sale
③ vt salare; ‹cure› mettere sotto sale

salt cellar n saliera f

saltiness /'sɔːltɪnɪs/ n salinità f

salt water n acqua f di mare

salt-water fish n pesce m d'acqua salata

salty /'sɔːltɪ/ adj salato

salubrious /sə'luːbrɪəs/ adj ‹neighbourhood› raccomandabile; it's not a very ~ area è una zona poco raccomandabile

salutary /'sæljʊtərɪ/ adj salutare

salute /sə'luːt/ Mil ① n saluto m
② vt salutare
③ vi fare il saluto

salvage /'sælvɪdʒ/ ① n Naut recupero m
② vt recuperare

salvation /sæl'veɪʃn/ n salvezza f

Salvation Army n Esercito m della Salvezza

salve /sælv/ vt ~ one's conscience mettersi la coscienza a posto

salver /'sælvə(r)/ n vassoio m (di metallo)

salvo /'sælvəʊ/ n salva f

Samaritan /sə'mærɪtən/ n a good ~ un buon samaritano; the ~s ≈ telefono m amico

samba /'sæmbə/ n samba f

♦ **same** /seɪm/ ① adj stesso (as di)
② pron the ~ lo stesso; be all the ~ essere tutti uguali
③ adv the ~ nello stesso modo; all the ~ (however) lo stesso; the ~ to you altrettanto

same-day adj ‹service› in giornata

same-day delivery n consegna f in giornata

same-sex /seɪmseks/ adj ‹couple, marriage› omosessuale

♦ **sample** /'sɑːmpl/ ① n campione m
② vt testare

sanatorium /sænə'tɔːrɪəm/ n casa f di cura

sanctify /'sæŋktɪfaɪ/ vt (pt/pp -fied) santificare

sanctimonious /sæŋktɪ'məʊnɪəs/ adj moraleggiante

S

sanction /'sæŋkʃn/ [1] *n* (approval)
autorizzazione *f*; (penalty) sanzione *f*
[2] *vt* autorizzare

sanctity /'sæŋktətɪ/ *n* santità *f*

sanctuary /'sæŋktjʊərɪ/ *n* Relig santuario
m; (refuge) asilo *m*; (for wildlife) riserva *f*

sanctum /'sæŋktəm/ *n* (holy place)
santuario *m*; (private place) rifugio *m*; **the
inner** ∼ Relig il Sancta Sanctorum

sand /sænd/ [1] *n* sabbia *f*
[2] *vt* ∼ **[down]** carteggiare

sandal /'sændl/ *n* sandalo *m*

sandbag *n* sacchetto *m* di sabbia

sandbank *n* banco *m* di sabbia

sandblast *vt* sabbiare

sandblasting *n* sabbiatura *f*

sandcastle *n* castello *m* di sabbia

sand dune *n* duna *f*

sander /'sændə(r)/ *n* (machine) levigatrice *f*

Sandinista /sændɪ'niːstə/ *adj & n*
sandinista

sandpaper [1] *n* carta *f* vetrata
[2] *vt* cartavetrare

sandpit *n* recinto *m* contenente sabbia
dove giocano i bambini

sandstone *n* arenaria *f*

sandstorm *n* tempesta *f* di sabbia

sandwich /'sænwɪdʒ/ [1] *n* tramezzino *m*
[2] *vt* ∼**ed between** schiacciato tra

sandwich bar *n* locale (*m*) in cui si
comprano sandwich e panini pronti o su
ordinazione

sandwich course *n* corso (*m*) che
comprende dei periodi di tirocinio

sandwich-man *n* uomo *m* sandwich

sandy /'sændɪ/ *adj* (**-ier, -iest**) ⟨beach, soil⟩
sabbioso; ⟨hair⟩ biondiccio

sane /seɪn/ *adj* (not mad) sano di mente;
(sensible) sensato

sang /sæŋ/ ▶ SING

sangria /sæŋ'griːə/ *n* sangria *f*

sanguine /'sæŋgwɪn/ *adj* ottimistico

sanitary /'sænɪtərɪ/ *adj* igienico; ⟨system⟩
sanitario

sanitary napkin, sanitary towel *n*
Am assorbente *m* igienico

sanitation /sænɪ'teɪʃn/ *n* impianti *mpl*
igienici

sanity /'sænətɪ/ *n* sanità *f* di mente;
(sensibleness) buon senso *m*

sank /sæŋk/ ▶ SINK

Santa [Claus] /'sæntə[klɔːz]/ *n* Babbo
m Natale

sap /sæp/ [1] *n* Bot linfa *f*
[2] *vt* (*pt/pp* **sapped**) indebolire

sapling /'sæplɪŋ/ *n* alberello *m*

sapper /'sæpə(r)/ *n* Br Mil geniere *m*

sapphire /'sæfaɪə(r)/ [1] *n* zaffiro *m*
[2] *attrib* blu zaffiro *inv*

sarcasm /'sɑːkæzm/ *n* sarcasmo *m*

sarcastic /sɑː'kæstɪk/ *adj* sarcastico

sarcastically /sɑː'kæstɪklɪ/ *adv*
sarcasticamente

sarcophagus /sɑː'kɒfəgəs/ *n* sarcofago *m*

sardine /sɑː'diːn/ *n* sardina *f*

Sardinia /sɑː'dɪnɪə/ *n* Sardegna *f*

Sardinian /sɑː'dɪnɪən/ *adj & n* sardo, -a *mf*

sardonic /sɑː'dɒnɪk/ *adj* sardonico

sardonically /sɑː'dɒnɪklɪ/ *adv*
sardonicamente

sari /'sɑːrɪ/ *n* sari *m inv*

sarong /sə'rɒŋ/ *n* pareo *m*

SARS /sɑːz/ *n abbr* (**severe acute
respiratory syndrome**) SARS *f*

SAS *n abbr* Br (**Special Air Service**)
commando (*mpl*) britannico per operazioni
speciali

sash /sæʃ/ *n* fascia *f*; (for dress) fusciacca *f*

sashay /'sæʃeɪ/ *vi* fam (casually) camminare
in modo disinvolto; (seductively) camminare
in modo provocante

sassy /'sæsɪ/ *adj* Am fam (cheeky) sfacciato;
(smart) chic *inv*

sat /sæt/ ▶ SIT

Satan /'seɪtən/ *n* Satana *m*

satanic /sə'tænɪk/ *adj* satanico

satchel /'sætʃl/ *n* cartella *f*

sated /'seɪtɪd/ *adj* ⟨person⟩ sazio; ⟨desire⟩
appagato; ⟨appetite⟩ soddisfatto

satellite /'sætəlaɪt/ *n* satellite *m*

satellite channel *n* rete *f* televisiva
satellitare

satellite dish *n* antenna *f* parabolica

satellite television *n* televisione *f*
satellitare

satiate /'seɪʃɪeɪt/ *vt* saziare ⟨person⟩;
appagare ⟨desire⟩; soddisfare ⟨appetite⟩

satin /'sætɪn/ [1] *n* raso *m*
[2] *attrib* di raso

satire /'sætaɪə(r)/ *n* satira *f*

satirical /sə'tɪrɪkl/ *adj* satirico

satirically /sə'tɪrɪklɪ/ *adv* satiricamente

satirist /'sætərɪst/ *n* scrittore, -trice *mf*
satirico; (comedian) comico, -a *mf* satirico

satirize /'sætɪraɪz/ *vt* satireggiare

satisfaction /sætɪs'fækʃn/ *n*
soddisfazione *f*; **be to sb's** ∼ soddisfare
qualcuno

satisfactorily /sætɪs'fækt(ə)rɪlɪ/ *adv* in
modo soddisfacente

satisfactory /sætɪs'fæktərɪ/ *adj*
soddisfacente

satisfied /'sætɪsfaɪd/ *adj* (pleased)
soddisfatto; ∼ **with** soddisfatto di; (convinced)
convinto; ∼ **that** convinto che

satisfy ⋯▷ scale model ⋯⋯

satisfy /'sætɪsfaɪ/ *vt* (*pt/pp* **-ied**) soddisfare; (convince) convincere; **be satisfied** essere soddisfatto

satisfying /'sætɪsfaɪɪŋ/ *adj* soddisfacente

satnav /'sætnæv/ *n* satnav *m*

SATs *npl abbr* Br (**standard assessment tasks**) *esami* (*mpl*) *sostenuti per tranche d'età allo scopo di testare la preparazione degli alunni*

saturate /'sætʃəreɪt/ *vt* inzuppare (**with** di); Chem fig saturare (**with** di)

saturated /'sætʃəreɪtɪd/ *adj* saturo

saturation /sætʃə'reɪʃn/ *n* reach ∼ **point** raggiungere il punto di saturazione

Saturday /'sætədeɪ/ *n* sabato *m*

Saturn /'sætən/ *n* Saturno *m*

sauce /sɔːs/ *n* salsa *f*; (cheek) impertinenza *f*

saucepan /'sɔːspən/ *n* pentola *f*

saucer /'sɔːsə(r)/ *n* piattino *m*

saucy /'sɔːsɪ/ *adj* (**-ier, -iest**) impertinente

Saudi /'saʊdɪ/ [1] *adj* saudita
[2] *n* (person) saudita *mf*; (country) Arabia *f* Saudita

Saudi Arabia /ə'reɪbɪə/ *n* Arabia *f* Saudita

Saudi Arabian *adj & n* saudita *mf*

sauerkraut /'saʊəkraʊt/ *n* crauti *mpl*

sauna /'sɔːnə/ *n* sauna *f*

saunter /'sɔːntə(r)/ *vi* andare a spasso

sausage /'sɒsɪdʒ/ *n* salsiccia *f*; (dried) salame *m*

sausage dog /'sɒsɪdʒdɒg/ *n* fam bassotto *m*

sausage roll *n involtino* (*m*) *di pasta sfoglia con salsiccia*

sauté /'saʊteɪ/ [1] *vt* rosolare
[2] *adj* rosolato

savage /'sævɪdʒ/ [1] *adj* feroce; ‹tribe, custom› selvaggio
[2] *n* selvaggio, -a *mf*
[3] *vt* fare a pezzi

savagely /'sævɪdʒlɪ/ *adv* ‹attack› selvaggiamente; ‹criticize› ferocemente

savagery /'sævɪdʒrɪ/ *n* ferocia *f*

save /seɪv/ [1] *n* Sport parata *f*
[2] *vt* salvare (**from** da); (keep, collect) tenere; risparmiare ‹time, money›; (avoid) evitare; Sport parare ‹goal›; Comput salvare, memorizzare; ∼ **face** salvar la faccia
[3] *vi* ∼ **[up]** risparmiare
[4] (prep) salvo

saver /'seɪvə(r)/ *n* risparmiatore, -trice *mf*

saving grace /seɪvɪŋ'greɪs/ *n* that's his one saving grace si salva grazie a questo

savings /'seɪvɪŋz/ *npl* (money) risparmi *mpl*

savings account *n* libretto *m* di risparmio

savings and loan association *n* Am associazione *f* mutua di risparmi e prestiti

savings bank *n* cassa *f* di risparmio

saviour /'seɪvjə(r)/ *n* salvatore *m*

savoir faire /sævwɑː'feə(r)/ *n* (social) savoir-faire *m*

savory /'seɪvərɪ/ *n* Bot santoreggia *f*

savour /'seɪvə(r)/ [1] *n* sapore *m*
[2] *vt* assaporare

savoury /'seɪvərɪ/ *adj* salato; fig rispettabile

saw¹ /sɔː/ ▶ SEE¹

saw² [1] *n* sega *f*
[2] *vt* (*pt* **sawed**, *pp* **sawn** or **sawed**) segare

sawdust /'sɔːdʌst/ *n* segatura *f*

sawmill /'sɔːmɪl/ *n* segheria *f*

sawn-off shotgun *n* fucile *m* a canne mozze

Saxon /'sæksən/ *adj & n* sassone *mf*; (language) sassone *m*

saxophone /'sæksəfəʊn/ *n* sassofono *m*

saxophonist /sæk'sɒfənɪst/ *n* sassofonista *mf*

say /seɪ/ [1] *n* have one's ∼ dire la propria; **have a** ∼ avere voce in capitolo
[2] *vt/i* (*pt/pp* **said**) dire; **that is to** ∼ cioè; **that goes without** ∼**ing** questo è ovvio; **when all is said and done** alla fine dei conti; ∼ **yes/no** dire di sì/no; **just** ∼ **the word and I'll come** tu chiama e io vengo; **what more can I** ∼? che altro dire?; **some time next week** ∼? la prossima settimana, diciamo?; **the clock** ∼**s ten to six** la sveglia fa le sei meno dieci; **you can** ∼ **that again!** puoi dirlo forte!; **the tree is said to be very old** a quanto pare l'albero è vecchissimo; **he said you were to bring the car** ha detto che dovevi portare la macchina; **it** ∼**s a lot for him that** … il fatto che… la dice lunga sul suo conto; **what have you got to** ∼ **for yourself?** che scusa hai?; **to** ∼ **nothing of** … per non parlare di…; **what would you** ∼ **to a new car?** cosa ne diresti di una macchina nuova?

saying /'seɪɪŋ/ *n* proverbio *m*

scab /skæb/ *n* crosta *f*; pej crumiro *m*

scabby /'skæbɪ/ *adj* ‹plant› coperto di galle; ‹skin› coperto di croste; ‹animal› rognoso; fam (nasty) schifoso

scaffold /'skæfəld/ *n* patibolo *m*

scaffolding /'skæfəldɪŋ/ *n* impalcatura *f*

scalar /'skeɪlə(r)/ *adj* scalare

scald /skɔːld/ [1] *vt* scottare; (milk) scaldare
[2] *n* scottatura *f*

scalding /'skɔːldɪŋ/ *adj* bollente

scale¹ /skeɪl/ *n* (of fish) scaglia *f*

scale² /skeɪl/ [1] *n* scala *f*; **on a grand** ∼ su vasta scala; **to** ∼ in scala; ∼ **of values** scala *f* di valori
[2] *vt* (climb) scalare

■ **scale down** *vt* diminuire

scale drawing *n* disegno *m* in scala

scale model *n* modello *m* in scala

scales /skeɪlz/ *npl* (for weighing) bilancia *fsg*
scallop /'skɒləp/ **1** *n* (in sewing) smerlo *m*, festone *m*; Zool pettine *m*; Culin cappasanta *f* **2** *vt* (in sewing) smerlare; ~**ed potatoes** patate *fpl* gratinate
scalp /skælp/ **1** *n* cuoio *m* capelluto **2** *vt* scalpare
scalpel /'skælpl/ *n* bisturi *m inv*
scalper /'skælpə(r)/ *n* Am bagarino *m*
scaly /'skeɪlɪ/ *adj* ‹wing, fish› squamoso; ‹plaster, wall› scrostato
scam /skæm/ *n* fam fregatura *f*
scamper /'skæmpə(r)/ *vi* ~ **away** sgattaiolare via
scampi /'skæmpɪ/ *npl* scampi *mpl*
scan /skæn/ **1** *n* Med scanning *m inv*, scansioscintigrafia *f* **2** *vt* (*pt/pp* **scanned**) scrutare; (quickly) dare una scorsa a; Med fare uno scanning di; Comput scannerizzare **3** *vi* ‹poetry› scandire
scandal /'skændl/ *n* scandalo *m*; (gossip) pettegolezzi *mpl*
scandalize /'skændəlaɪz/ *vt* scandalizzare
scandalmonger /'skænd(ə)lmʌŋgə(r)/ *n* malalingua *f*
scandalous /'skændələs/ *adj* scandaloso
Scandinavia /skændɪ'neɪvɪə/ *n* Scandinavia *f*
Scandinavian /skændɪ'neɪvɪən/ *adj & n* scandinavo, -a *mf*
scanner /'skænə(r)/ *n* Med, Comput scanner *m inv*; (radar) antenna *f* radar; (for bar codes) lettore *m* di codice a barre
scanning /'skænɪŋ/ *n* Comput scannerizzazione *f*
scant /skænt/ *adj* scarso
scantily /'skæntɪlɪ/ *adv* scarsamente; ‹clothed› succintamente
scanty /'skæntɪ/ *adj* (**-ier, -iest**) scarso; ‹clothing› succinto
scapegoat /'skeɪpgəʊt/ *n* capro *m* espiatorio
scar /skɑː(r)/ **1** *n* cicatrice *f* **2** *vt* (*pt/pp* **scarred**) lasciare una cicatrice a
scarce /skeəs/ *adj* scarso; fig raro; **make oneself** ~ fam svignarsela
scarcely /'skeəslɪ/ *adv* appena; ~ **anything** quasi niente
scarcity /'skeəsətɪ/ *n* scarsezza *f*
scare /skeə(r)/ **1** *n* spavento *m*; (panic) panico *m* **2** *vt* spaventare; **be** ~**d** aver paura (**of** di)
■ **scare away** *vt* far scappare
scarecrow /'skeəkrəʊ/ *n* spaventapasseri *m inv*

scaremonger /'skeəmʌŋgə(r)/ *n* allarmista *mf*
scaremongering /'skeəmʌŋgərɪŋ/ *n* allarmismo *m*
scarf /skɑːf/ *n* (*pl* **scarves**) sciarpa *f*; (square) foulard *m inv*
scarlet /'skɑːlət/ *adj* scarlatto
scarlet fever *n* scarlattina *f*
scarper /'skɑːpə(r)/ *vi* Br fam squagliarsela
scart connector *n* presa *f* scart *inv*
scar tissue *n* tessuto *m* di cicatrizzazione
scary /'skeərɪ/ *adj* **be** ~ far paura
scathing /'skeɪðɪŋ/ *adj* mordace
scatter /'skætə(r)/ **1** *vt* spargere; (disperse) disperdere **2** *vi* disperdersi
scatterbrained /'skætəbreɪnd/ *adj* fam scervellato
scattered /'skætəd/ *adj* sparso
scatty /'skætɪ/ *adj* (**-ier, -iest**) fam svitato
scavenge /'skævɪndʒ/ *vi* frugare nella spazzatura
scavenger /'skævɪndʒə(r)/ *n* persona (*f*) che fruga nella spazzatura
scenario /sɪ'nɑːrɪəʊ/ *n* scenario *m*
⚡ **scene** /siːn/ *n* scena *f*; (quarrel) scenata *f*; **behind the** ~**s** dietro le quinte
scene-of-crime *adj* ‹officer, team, investigation› della polizia scientifica
scenery /'siːnərɪ/ *n* scenario *m*
scenic /'siːnɪk/ *adj* panoramico
scent /sent/ *n* odore *m*; (trail) scia *f*; (perfume) profumo *m*
scented /'sentɪd/ *adj* profumato (**with** di)
sceptic /'skeptɪk/ *n* scettico, -a *mf*
sceptical /'skeptɪkl/ *adj* scettico
sceptically /'skeptɪklɪ/ *adv* in modo scettico
scepticism /'skeptɪsɪzm/ *n* scetticismo *m*
schedule /'ʃedjuːl/ **1** *n* piano *m*, programma *m*; (of work) programma *m*; Am (timetable) orario *m*; **behind** ~ indietro; **on** ~ nei tempi previsti; **according to** ~ secondo i tempi previsti **2** *vt* prevedere
scheduled flight /ʃedjuːld'flaɪt/ *n* volo *m* di linea
schematic /skɪ'mætɪk/ *adj* schematico
⚡ **scheme** /skiːm/ **1** *n* (plan) piano *m*; (plot) macchinazione *f* **2** *vi* pej macchinare
scheming /'skiːmɪŋ/ **1** *n* pej macchinazioni *fpl*, intrighi *mpl* **2** *adj* ‹person› intrigante
schism /'skɪzm/ *n* scisma *m*
schizophrenia /skɪtsə'friːnɪə/ *n* schizofrenia *f*
schizophrenic /ˌskɪtsəʊ'frenɪk/ *adj* schizofrenico

⚡ indicates a very frequent word

schmaltzy ⋯> scramble · · · ·

schmaltzy /'ʃmʊltsɪ/ *adj* sdolcinato
scholar /'skɒlə(r)/ *n* studioso, -a *mf*
scholarly /'skɒləlɪ/ *adj* erudito
scholarship /'skɒləʃɪp/ *n* erudizione *f*;
(grant) borsa *f* di studio
scholastic /skə'læstɪk/ *adj* scolastico
♂ **school** /skuːl/ **1** *n* scuola *f*; (in university)
facoltà *f*; (of fish) banco *m*
2 *vt* addestrare ‹*animal*›
school age *n* of ~ in età scolare
schoolbag *n* cartella *f* di scuola
schoolboy *n* scolaro *m*
schoolchild *n* scolaro, -a *mf*
schooldays *npl* tempi *mpl* della scuola
school fees *npl* tasse *fpl* scolastiche
schoolfriend *n* compagno, -a *mf* di scuola
schoolgirl *n* scolara *f*
schooling /'skuːlɪŋ/ *n* istruzione *f*
school leaver *n* ≈ neo diplomato, -a *mf*
school-leaving age *n* età *f* della scuola
dell'obbligo
school lunch *n* pranzo *m* della mensa
scolastica
schoolmaster *n* maestro *m*; (secondary)
insegnante *m*
schoolmistress *n* maestra *f*; (secondary)
insegnante *f*
school report *n* scheda *f* di valutazione
scolastica
schoolteacher *n* insegnante *mf*
schoolwork /'skuːlwɜːk/ *n* lavoro *m*
scolastico
schooner /'skuːnə(r)/ *n* Am (glass) boccale
m da birra; Br (glass) grande bicchiere *m* da
sherry; (boat) goletta *f*
sciatica /saɪ'ætɪkə/ *n* sciatica *f*
♂ **science** /'saɪəns/ *n* scienza *f*
science fiction *n* fantascienza *f*
♂ **scientific** /saɪən'tɪfɪk/ *adj* scientifico
scientifically /saɪən'tɪfɪklɪ/ *adv*
scientificamente
♂ **scientist** /'saɪəntɪst/ *n* scienziato, -a *mf*
sci-fi /'saɪfaɪ/ *n* fam fantascienza *f*
scintillate /'sɪntɪleɪt/ *vi* fig brillare
scintillating /'sɪntɪleɪtɪŋ/ *adj* brillante
scissors /'sɪzəz/ *npl* forbici *fpl*
scoff[1] /skɒf/ *vi* ~ at schernire
scoff[2] *vt* fam divorare
scold /skəʊld/ *vt* sgridare
scolding /'skəʊldɪŋ/ *n* sgridata *f*
scollop /'skɒləp/ = SCALLOP
scone /skɒn/ *n* pasticcino (*m*) da tè
scoop /skuːp/ *n* paletta *f*; Journ scoop *m inv*
■ **scoop out** *vt* svuotare
■ **scoop up** *vt* tirar su
scoot /skuːt/ *vi* fam filare
scooter /'skuːtə(r)/ *n* motoretta *f*

scope /skəʊp/ *n* portata *f*; (opportunity)
opportunità *f inv*
scorch /skɔːtʃ/ *vt* bruciare
scorcher /'skɔːtʃə(r)/ *n* fam giornata *f*
torrida
scorching /'skɔːtʃɪŋ/ *adj* caldissimo
♂ **score** /skɔː(r)/ **1** *n* punteggio *m*; Mus
partitura *f*; (for film, play) musica *f*; **a** ~ **[of]**
(twenty) una ventina [di]; **keep [the]** ~ tenere
il punteggio; **on that** ~ a questo proposito
2 *vt* segnare ‹*goal*›; (cut) incidere
3 *vi* far punti; (in football etc) segnare; (keep
score) tenere il punteggio
■ **score out** *vt* cancellare
scoreboard /'skɔːbɔːd/ *n* tabellone *m*
segnapunti
scorer /'skɔːrə(r)/ *n* segnapunti *m inv*; (of
goals) giocatore, -trice *mf* che segna; **top** ~
cannoniere *m*
scorn /skɔːn/ **1** *n* disprezzo *m*
2 *vt* disprezzare
scornful /'skɔːnfʊl/ *adj* sprezzante
scornfully /'skɔːnfʊlɪ/ *adv* sdegnosamente
Scorpio /'skɔːpɪəʊ/ *n* Astr Scorpione *m*
scorpion /'skɔːpɪən/ *n* scorpione *m*
Scot /skɒt/ *n* scozzese *mf*
scotch /skɒtʃ/ *vt* far cessare
Scotch **1** *adj* scozzese
2 *n* (whisky) whisky *m* [scozzese]
Scotch egg *n* Br polpetta (*f*) di salsiccia
che racchiude un uovo sodo
Scotch tape *n* Am scotch® *m inv*
scot-free *adj* get off ~ cavarsela
impunemente
Scotland /'skɒtlənd/ *n* Scozia *f*
Scots, Scottish /skɒts, 'skɒtɪʃ/ *adj*
scozzese
scoundrel /'skaʊndrəl/ *n* mascalzone *m*
scour[1] /'skaʊə(r)/ *vt* (search) perlustrare
scour[2] *vt* (clean) strofinare
scourer /'skaʊərə(r)/ *n* (pad) paglietta *f*
scourge /skɜːdʒ/ *n* flagello *m*
scouring pad /'skaʊərɪŋ/ *n* paglietta *f* in
lana d'acciaio
scout /skaʊt/ **1** *n* Mil esploratore *m*
2 *vi or* **scout around** ~ **for** andare in
cerca di
Scout *n* [Boy] ~ [boy]scout *m inv*
scowl /skaʊl/ **1** *n* sguardo *m* torvo
2 *vi* guardare storto
Scrabble® /'skræbl/ *n* Scarabeo® *m*
■ **scrabble around** *vi* (search) cercare a
tastoni
scraggy /'skrægɪ/ *adj* (-ier, -iest) pej
scarno
scram /skræm/ *vi* fam levarsi dai piedi
scramble /'skræmbl/ **1** *n* (climb)
arrampicata *f*
2 *vi* (clamber) arrampicarsi; ~ **for**
azzuffarsi per ⋯>

S

3 *vt* Teleph creare delle interferenze in; (eggs) strapazzare

scrambled eggs /'skræmbəld/ *npl* uova *fpl* strapazzate

scrambler /'skræmblə(r)/ *n* Br (motorcyclist) [moto]crossista *mf*

scrambling /'skræmblɪŋ/ *n* (sport) motocross *m*

scrap¹ /skræp/ *n* fam (fight) litigio *m*

scrap² **1** *n* pezzetto *m*; (metal) ferraglia *f*; **~s** *pl* (of food) avanzi *mpl*
2 *vt* (*pt/pp* **scrapped**) buttare via

scrapbook /'skræpbʊk/ *n* album *m inv*

scrape /skreɪp/ *vt* raschiare; (damage) graffiare
■ **scrape by** *vi* (financially) sbarcare il lunario
■ **scrape in** *vi* (to university, school) entrare per il rotto della cuffia
■ **scrape out** *vt* (empty) svuotare ‹bowl›; (clean) scrostare ‹pan›
■ **scrape through** *vi* passare per un pelo
■ **scrape together** *vt* racimolare

scraper /'skreɪpə(r)/ *n* raschietto *m*

scrap heap *n* be on the **~** fig essere inutile

scrap iron *n* ferraglia *f*

scrap merchant *n* ferrovecchio *m*

scrap paper *n* carta *f* qualsiasi

scrappy /'skræpɪ/ *adj* frammentario

scrapyard /'skræpjɑːd/ *n* deposito *m* di ferraglia; (for cars) cimitero *m* delle macchine

scratch /skrætʃ/ **1** *n* graffio *m*; (to relieve itch) grattata *f*; **start from ~** partire da zero; **up to ~** ‹work› all'altezza
2 *vt* graffiare; (to relieve itch) grattare
3 *vi* grattarsi

scratch card *n* gratta e vinci *m inv*

scratchy /'skrætʃɪ/ *adj* ‹recording› pieno di fruscii

scrawl /skrɔːl/ **1** *n* scarabocchio *m*
2 *vt/i* scarabocchiare

scrawny /'skrɔːnɪ/ *adj* (**-ier, -iest**) pej magro

◆ **scream** /skriːm/ **1** *n* strillo *m*; **be a ~** fam ‹situation, film, person› essere uno spasso
2 *vt/i* strillare

scree /skriː/ *n* ghiaione *m*

screech /skriːtʃ/ **1** *n* stridore *m*; **~ of tyres** sgommata *f*
2 *vi* stridere
3 *vt* strillare

◆ **screen** /skriːn/ **1** *n* paravento *m*; Cinema, TV, Comput schermo *m*
2 *vt* proteggere; (conceal) riparare; proiettare ‹film›; (candidates) passare al setaccio; Med sottoporre a visita medica

screening /'skriːnɪŋ/ *n* Med visita *f* medica; (of film) proiezione *f*

screenplay *n* sceneggiatura *f*

screen saver *n* Comput salvaschermo *m*

screen test *n* Cinema provino *m*

screen-writer *n* Cinema sceneggiatore, -trice *mf*

screw /skruː/ **1** *n* vite *f*
2 *vt* avvitare; vulg trombare; **~ something to something** avvitare qualcosa a qualcosa
■ **screw up** *vt* (crumple) accartocciare; strizzare ‹eyes›; storcere ‹face›; sl (bungle) mandare all'aria; **~ up one's courage** prendere il coraggio a due mani

screwdriver /'skruːdraɪvə(r)/ *n* cacciavite *m inv*

screwed up /skruːd/ *adj* fam incasinato

screw top *n* tappo *m* a vite

screwy /'skruːɪ/ *adj* (**-ier, -iest**) fam svitato

scribble /'skrɪbl/ **1** *n* scarabocchio *m*
2 *vt/i* scarabocchiare

scrimmage /'skrɪmɪdʒ/ *n* (struggle) zuffa *f*; Am (in football) mischia *f*

scrimp /skrɪmp/ *vi* risparmiare; **~ and save** risparmiare fino all'osso; **~ on something** risparmiare su qualcosa

script /skrɪpt/ *n* scrittura *f*; (of film etc) sceneggiatura *f*

Scriptures /'skrɪptʃəz/ *npl* Sacre Scritture *fpl*

scriptwriter /'skrɪptraɪtə(r)/ *n* sceneggiatore, -trice *mf*

scroll /skrəʊl/ **1** *n* rotolo *m* (di pergamena); (decoration) voluta *f*
2 *vi* Comput far scorrere
■ **scroll down** Comput *vi* scorrere in giù
■ **scroll up** Comput *vi* scorrere in su

scroll bar *n* Comput barra *f* di scorrimento

Scrooge /skruːdʒ/ *n* fam tirchio, -a *mf*

scrotum /'skrəʊtəm/ *n* scroto *m*

scrounge /skraʊndʒ/ *vt/i* scroccare

scrounger /'skraʊndʒə(r)/ *n* scroccone, -a *mf*

scrub¹ /skrʌb/ *n* (land) boscaglia *f*

scrub² *vt/i* (*pt/pp* **scrubbed**) strofinare; fam (cancel) cancellare ‹plan›
■ **scrub up** *vi* ‹doctor› lavarsi; fam **~ up well** fare un figurone

scrubbing brush /'skrʌbɪŋ/ *n* spazzolone *m*

scruff /skrʌf/ *n* by the **~ of the neck** per la collottola

scruffy /'skrʌfɪ/ *adj* (**-ier, -iest**) trasandato

scrum /skrʌm/ *n* (in rugby) mischia *f*

scrum half *n* mediano *m* di mischia

scrunch /skrʌntʃ/ **1** *vi* ‹footsteps in snow, tyres› scricchiolare
2 *n* scricchiolio *m*
■ **scrunch up** *vt* accartocciare

◆ indicates a very frequent word

S

scrunchie /'skrʌntʃɪ/ n fermacoda m inv di stoffa

scruple /'skru:pl/ n scrupolo m; **have no ∼s** essere senza scrupoli

scrupulous /'skru:pjʊləs/ adj scrupoloso

scrupulously /'skru:pjʊləslɪ/ adv scrupolosamente

scrutinize /'skru:tɪnaɪz/ vt scrutinare

scrutiny /'skru:tɪnɪ/ n (look) esame m minuzioso

scuba diver /'sku:bə/ n sommozzatore, -trice mf

scuba diving n immersione f subacquea

scud /skʌd/ vi (pt/pp **scudded**) ‹clouds› muoversi velocemente

scuff /skʌf/ vt strascicare ‹one's feet›

scuffle /'skʌfl/ n tafferuglio m

scull /skʌl/ [1] vi (with two oars) vogare di coppia; (with one oar) vogare a bratto [2] n (boat) imbarcazione f da regata con un vogatore

scullery /'skʌlərɪ/ n retrocucina m inv

sculpt /skʌlpt/ vt/i scolpire

sculptor /'skʌlptə(r)/ n scultore m

sculpture /'skʌlptʃə(r)/ n scultura f

scum /skʌm/ n schiuma f; (people) feccia f

scurrilous /'skʌrɪləs/ adj scurrile

scurry /'skʌrɪ/ vi (pt/pp **-ied**) affrettare il passo

scuttle¹ /'skʌtl/ n secchio m per il carbone

scuttle² vt affondare ‹ship›

scuttle³ vi (hurry) ∼ **away** correre via

scythe /saɪð/ n falce f

SE abbr (**south-east**) SE

⚓ **sea** /si:/ n mare m; **at ∼** in mare; fig confuso; **by ∼** via mare; **by the ∼** sul mare

seabed n fondale m marino

seabird n uccello m marino

seaboard n costiera f

seafaring adj ‹nation› marinaro

seafood n frutti mpl di mare

seafront /'si:frʌnt/ n lungomare m

seagull n gabbiano m

sea horse n cavalluccio m marino

seal¹ /si:l/ n Zool foca f

seal² [1] n sigillo m; Techn chiusura f ermetica [2] vt sigillare; Techn chiudere ermeticamente

■ **seal off** vt bloccare ‹area›

SEAL n abbr Am (**sea, air, land**) reparti mpl speciali delle forze armate

sea level n livello m del mare; **above ∼** sopra il livello del mare

sealing wax /'si:lɪŋ/ n ceralacca f

sea lion n leone m marino

seam /si:m/ n cucitura f; (of coal) strato m

seaman /'si:mən/ n marinaio m

seamless /'si:mlɪs/ adj senza cucitura

seamy /'si:mɪ/ adj ‹scandal› sordido; ‹area› malfamato

seance /'seɪɑ:ns/ n seduta f spiritica

seaplane /'si:pleɪn/ n idrovolante m

seaport /'si:pɔ:t/ n porto m di mare

sear /sɪə(r)/ vt cauterizzare ‹wound›; rosolare [a fuoco vivo] ‹meat›; (scorch) bruciacchiare

⚓ **search** /sɜ:tʃ/ [1] n ricerca f; (official) perquisizione f; **in ∼ of** alla ricerca di [2] vt frugare (**for** alla ricerca di); perlustrare ‹area›; (officially) perquisire [3] vi ∼ **for** cercare

search and replace n Comput ricerca f e sostituzione

search engine n Comput motore m di ricerca

searching /'sɜ:tʃɪŋ/ adj penetrante

searchlight n riflettore m

search party n squadra f di ricerca

search warrant n mandato m di perquisizione

searing /'sɪərɪŋ/ adj bruciante; ‹pace› travolgente; ‹pain› lancinante

sea salt n sale m marino

seascape n paesaggio m marino

seashell n conchiglia f

seashore /'si:ʃɔ:(r)/ n spiaggia f

seasick adj be/get ∼ avere il mal di mare

seaside n at/to the ∼ al mare

seaside resort n stazione f balneare

seaside town n città f di mare

⚓ **season** /'si:zn/ [1] n stagione f [2] vt (flavour) condire; **in ∼** ‹fruit› di stagione; ‹animal› in calore

seasonal /'si:zənəl/ adj stagionale

seasoned /'si:znd/ adj Culin ‹dish› condito; ‹timber› stagionato; ‹actor, politician› consumato; ‹leader› di provata capacità, ∼ **traveller** persona f che ha viaggiato molto; ∼ **soldier** veterano m

seasoning /'si:z(ə)nɪŋ/ n condimento m

season ticket n abbonamento m

⚓ **seat** /si:t/ [1] n (chair) sedia f; (in car) sedile m; (place to sit) posto m [a sedere]; (bottom) didietro m; (of government) sede f; **take a ∼** sedersi [2] vt mettere a sedere; (have seats for) aver posti [a sedere] per; **remain ∼ed** mantenere il proprio posto

seat belt n cintura f di sicurezza; **fasten one's ∼** allacciare la cintura di sicurezza

seating /'si:tɪŋ/ n (places) posti mpl a sedere; (arrangement) disposizione f dei posti a sedere

seating capacity n numero m dei posti a sedere

sea urchin n riccio m di mare

sea view n vista f sul mare

S

seaweed n alga f marina
seaworthy adj in stato di navigare
sec /sek/ [1] n fam (short instant) attimo m, secondo m
[2] abbr (**second**) s
secateurs /sekə'tɜːz/ npl cesoie fpl
secede /sɪ'siːd/ vi staccarsi
secession /sɪ'seʃn/ n secessione f
secluded /sɪ'kluːdɪd/ adj appartato
seclusion /sɪ'kluːʒn/ n isolamento m
second¹ /sɪ'kɒnd/ vt (transfer) distaccare
✧ **second²** /'sekənd/ [1] adj secondo; in
∼ **gear** Auto in seconda; on ∼ **thoughts** ripensandoci meglio; **be having** ∼ **thoughts** ripensarci
[2] n secondo m; ∼**s** pl (goods) merce fsg di seconda scelta; **have** ∼**s** (at meal) fare il bis; **John the S**∼ Giovanni Secondo
[3] adv (in race) al secondo posto
[4] vt assistere; appoggiare ‹proposal›
secondary /'sekəndrɪ/ adj secondario
secondary school n ≈ scuola f media (inferiore e superiore)
second-best adj secondo dopo il migliore; **be** ∼ pej essere un ripiego
second class adv ‹travel, send› in seconda classe
second-class adj di seconda classe
seconder /'sekəndə(r)/ n (of motion) persona f che appoggia una mozione
second-guess vt anticipare
second hand n (on watch, clock) lancetta f dei secondi
second-hand [1] adj ‹car, goods, news, information› di seconda mano; ‹clothes› usato; ‹market› dell'usato; ‹opinion› preso a prestito
[2] adv ‹sell› di seconda mano
second in command n vice mf inv; Mil vicecomandante m
secondly /'sekəndlɪ/ adv in secondo luogo
secondment /sɪ'kɒndmənt/ n on ∼ in trasferta
second name n (surname) cognome m; (middle name) secondo nome m
second-rate adj di second'ordine
secrecy /'siːkrəsɪ/ n segretezza f; in ∼ in segreto
secret /'siːkrɪt/ [1] adj segreto
[2] n segreto m; **make no** ∼ **of something** non fare mistero di qualcosa
secret agent n agente m segreto
secretarial /sekrə'teərɪəl/ adj ‹work, staff› di segreteria
secretariat /sekrə'teərɪət/ n segretariato m
✧ **secretary** /'sekrətərɪ/ n segretario, -a mf

✧ indicates a very frequent word

Secretary of State n Segretario m di Stato; Am Pol ministro m degli Esteri
secret ballot n scrutinio m segreto, votazione f a scrutinio segreto
secrete /sɪ'kriːt/ vt secernere ‹poison›
secretion /sɪ'kriːʃn/ n secrezione f
secretive /'siːkrətɪv/ adj riservato
secretly /'siːkrɪtlɪ/ adv segretamente
secretness /'siːkrɪtnɪs/ n riserbo m
secret police n polizia f segreta
secret service n servizi mpl segreti
secret society n società f segreta
secret weapon n arma f segreta
sect /sekt/ n setta f
sectarian /sek'teərɪən/ n & adj settario, -a mf
✧ **section** /'sekʃn/ n sezione f
✧ **sector** /'sektə(r)/ n settore m
secular /'sekjʊlə(r)/ adj secolare; ‹education› laico
✧ **secure** /sɪ'kjʊə(r)/ [1] adj sicuro
[2] vt proteggere; chiudere bene ‹door›; rendere stabile ‹ladder›; (obtain) assicurarsi
securely /sɪ'kjʊəlɪ/ adv saldamente
secure unit n (in psychiatric hospital, prison) reparto m di massima sicurezza
✧ **security** /sɪ'kjʊərətɪ/ n sicurezza f; (for loan) garanzia f; **securities** pl titoli mpl
security code /sɪ'kjʊərɪtɪ kəʊd/ n codice m di sicurezza
Security Council n (of the UN) Consiglio m di Sicurezza
security guard n guardia f giurata
security leak n fuga f di notizie
security risk n be a ∼ costituire un pericolo per la sicurezza
sedan /sɪ'dæn/ n Am berlina f
sedate¹ /sɪ'deɪt/ adj posato
sedate² vt somministrare sedativi a
sedately /sɪ'deɪtlɪ/ adv in modo posato
sedation /sɪ'deɪʃn/ n somministrazione f di sedativi; **be under** ∼ essere sotto l'effetto di sedativi
sedative /'sedətɪv/ [1] adj sedativo
[2] n sedativo m
sedentary /'sedəntərɪ/ adj sedentario
sediment /'sedɪmənt/ n sedimento m
seduce /sɪ'djuːs/ vt sedurre
seduction /sɪ'dʌkʃn/ n seduzione f
seductive /sɪ'dʌktɪv/ adj seducente
seductively /sɪ'dʌktɪvlɪ/ adv con aria seducente
✧ **see¹** /siː/ [1] vt (pt **saw**, pp **seen**) vedere; (understand) capire; (escort) accompagnare; **go and** ∼ andare a vedere; (visit) andare a trovare; ∼ **you!** ci vediamo!; ∼ **you later!** a più tardi!; ∼**ing that** visto che; ∼ **somebody to the door** accompagnare qualcuno alla porta; **I can't** ∼ **myself doing this forever**

non mi ci vedo a farlo per sempre; **I can't think what she ∼s** non capisco cosa trovi in lui; **∼ reason** ragionare; **you're ∼ing things** hai le traveggole
[2] *vi* vedere; (understand) capire; **∼ that** (make sure) assicurarsi che; **let me ∼** (think) fammi pensare; **I ∼** (understand) ho capito
■ **see about** *vt* occuparsi di
■ **see off** *vt* salutare alla partenza; (chase away) mandar via
■ **see out**: *vt* **∼ somebody out** accompagnare qualcuno alla porta
■ **see through** [1] *vi* vedere attraverso; fig non farsi ingannare da
[2] *vt* portare a buon fine
■ **see to** *vi* occuparsi di
see² *n* Relig diocesi *f inv*

ᴥ **seed** /siːd/ *n* seme *m*; Tennis testa *f* di serie; **go to ∼** fare seme; fig lasciarsi andare
seeded player /'siːdɪd/ *n* Tennis testa *f* di serie
seedless /'siːdlɪs/ *adj* senza semi
seedling /'siːdlɪŋ/ *n* pianticella *f*
seedy /'siːdɪ/ *adj* (**-ier, -iest**) squallido; **feel ∼** fam sentirsi poco bene

ᴥ **seek** /siːk/ *vt* (*pt/pp* **sought**) cercare
■ **seek out** *vt* scovare
seeker /'siːkə(r)/ *n* **∼ after** *or* **for something** persona *f* che è alla ricerca di qualcosa; **gold ∼** cercatore, -trice *mf* d'oro

ᴥ **seem** /siːm/ *vi* sembrare
seeming /'siːmɪŋ/ *adj* apparente
seemingly /'siːmɪŋlɪ/ *adv* apparentemente
seemly /'siːmlɪ/ *adj* decoroso
seen /siːn/ ▶ SEE¹
seep /siːp/ *vi* filtrare
seepage /'siːpɪdʒ/ *n* (leak: from container) perdita *f*; Geol trasudamento *m* superficiale; (trickle) lenta fuoriuscita *f*; (into structure, soil) infiltrazione *f*
see-saw /'siːsɔː/ *n* altalena *f*
seethe /siːð/ *vi* **∼ with anger** ribollire di rabbia
see-through *adj* trasparente
segment /'segmənt/ *n* segmento *m*; (of orange) spicchio *m*
segregate /'segrɪgeɪt/ *vt* segregare
segregated /'segrəgeɪtɪd/ *adj* segregazionistico
segregation /segrɪ'geɪʃn/ *n* segregazione *f*
seismic /'saɪzmɪk/ *adj* sismico
seismograph /'saɪzməɡrɑːf/ *n* sismografo *m*
seismology /saɪz'mɒlədʒɪ/ *n* sismologia *f*
seize /siːz/ *vt* afferrare; Jur confiscare; **∼ the opportunity** prendere la palla al balzo
■ **seize up** *vi* Techn bloccarsi
seizure /'siːʒə(r)/ *n* Jur confisca *f*; Med colpo *m* [apoplettico]

seldom /'seldəm/ *adv* raramente
ᴥ **select** /sɪ'lekt/ [1] *adj* scelto; (exclusive) esclusivo
[2] *vt* scegliere; selezionare ‹team›
ᴥ **selection** /sɪ'lekʃn/ *n* selezione *f*
selective /sɪ'lektɪv/ *adj* selettivo
selectively /sɪ'lektɪvlɪ/ *adv* con criterio
selector /sɪ'lektə(r)/ *n* Sport selezionatore, -trice *mf*
ᴥ **self** /self/ *n* io *m*
self-addressed *adj* con il proprio indirizzo
self-addressed envelope *n* busta *f* affrancata con il proprio indirizzo
self-adhesive *adj* autoadesivo
self-analysis *n* autoanalisi *f*
self-assembly *adj* da montare
self-assurance *n* sicurezza *f* di sé
self-assured *adj* sicuro di sé
self-catering *adj* in appartamento attrezzato di cucina
self-centred *adj* egocentrico
self-cleaning *adj* ‹oven› autopulente
self-confessed *adj* dichiarato
self-confidence *n* fiducia *f* in se stesso
self-confident *adj* sicuro di sé
self-conscious *adj* impacciato
self-contained *adj* ‹flat› con ingresso indipendente
self-control *n* autocontrollo *m*
self-defence *n* autodifesa *f*; Jur legittima difesa *f*
self-denial *n* abnegazione *f*
self-destruct *vi* ‹missile, spacecraft› autodistruggersi
self-destruction *n* autodistruzione *f*; fig autolesionismo *m*
self-destructive *adj* autodistruttivo
self-determination *n* autodeterminazione *f*
self-discipline *n* autodisciplina *f*
self-disciplined *adj* disciplinato
self-effacing /-ɪ'feɪsɪŋ/ *adj* modesto, schivo
self-employed *adj* che lavora in proprio; **the ∼** i lavoratori autonomi
self-esteem *n* stima *f* di sé
self-evident *adj* ovvio
self-explanatory *adj* **be ∼** parlare da sé
self-expression /ˌselfɪk'spreʃn/ *n* espressione *f* della propria personalità
self-financing /-faɪ'nænsɪŋ/ *n* autofinanziamento *m*
self-governing /-'ɡʌvənɪŋ/ *adj* autonomo
self-government *n* autogoverno *m*
self-harm *n* autolesionismo *m*
self-help *n* iniziativa *f* personale
self-image *n* immagine *f* di sé

S

self-important *adj* borioso

self-imposed /-ɪm'pəʊzd/ *adj* autoimposto

self-improvement *n* crescita *f* personale

self-induced /-ɪn'djuːst/ *adj* autoindotto

self-indulgent *adj* indulgente con se stesso

self-inflicted *adj* Anna's problems are ~ sono problemi che Anna si è creata da sé; ~ wound autolesione *f*

self-interest *n* interesse *m* personale

self-interested *adj* interessato

selfish /'selfɪʃ/ *adj* egoista

selfishly /'selfɪʃlɪ/ *adv* egoisticamente

selfishness /'selfɪʃnɪs/ *n* egoismo *m*

selfless /'selflɪs/ *adj* disinteressato

selflessly /'selflɪslɪ/ *adv* disinteressatamente

selflessness /'selflɪsnɪs/ *n* disinteresse *m*

self-locking /-'lɒkɪŋ/ *adj* ‹door› a chiusura automatica

self-made *adj* che si è fatto da sé

self-pity *n* autocommiserazione *f*

self-portrait *n* autoritratto *m*

self-possessed /-pə'zest/ *adj* padrone di sé

self-preservation *n* istinto *m* di conservazione

self-raising flour Br, **self-rising flour** Am /'reɪzɪŋ, 'raɪzɪŋ/ *n* farina *f* contenente lievito

self-reliant *adj* autosufficiente

self-respect *n* amor *m* proprio

self-respecting *adj* di rispetto

self-righteous *adj* presuntuoso

self-rising flour Am /-'reɪzɪŋ, -'raɪzɪŋ/ *n* farina (*f*) contenente lievito

self-rule *n* autogoverno *m*

self-sacrifice *n* abnegazione *f*

selfsame *adj* stesso

self-satisfied *adj* compiaciuto di sé

self-service ① *n* self-service *m inv* ② *attrib* self-service

self-styled *adj* sedicente

self-sufficiency *n* autosufficienza *f*

self-sufficient *adj* autosufficiente

self-supporting *adj* ‹person› indipendente (*economicamente*)

self-tan *n* autoabbronzante *m*

self-tanning /-'tænɪŋ/ *adj* autoabbronzante

self-taught /-'tɔːt/ *adj* ‹person› autodidatta

self-willed /-'wɪld/ *adj* ostinato

⚹ sell /sel/ ① *vt* (*pt/pp* **sold**) vendere; be sold out essere esaurito; ~ somebody on

the idea of … fam convincere qualcuno di… ② *vi* vendersi
- **sell off** *vt* liquidare
- **sell out** *vi* (of tickets, goods) andare esaurito; 'sold out' 'tutto esaurito'; ~ out of something esaurire qualcosa; (on one's principles) vendersi
- **sell up** *vi* liquidare i propri beni

sell-by date *n* data *f* di scadenza per la vendita

seller /'selə(r)/ *n* venditore, -trice *mf*

sellers' market /'seləzmɑːkɪt/ *n* mercato *m* al rialzo

selling /'selɪŋ/ ① *adj* ‹price› di vendita ② *n* vendita *f*

selling price /'selɪŋ/ *n* prezzo *m* di vendita

Sellotape® /'seləʊteɪp/ *n* nastro *m* adesivo, scotch® *m*

sell-out *n* fam (betrayal) tradimento *m*; be a ~ ‹concert› fare il tutto esaurito

selvage, selvedge /'selvɪdʒ/ *n* cimosa *f*

selves /selvz/ *pl of* SELF

semantic /sɪ'mæntɪk/ *adj* semantico

semantics /sɪ'mæntɪks/ *n* (subject) semantica *f*; that's just ~ sono solo sfumature di significato

semblance /'sembləns/ *n* parvenza *f*

semen /'siːmən/ *n* Anat liquido *m* seminale

semester /sɪ'mestə(r)/ *n* Am semestre *m*

semi /'semɪ/ *n* Br (house) villetta *f* bifamiliare; Am Auto autoarticolato *m*

semi+ *pref* semi+

semi-automatic *adj* semiautomatico

semibreve *n* Mus semibreve *f*

semicircle *n* semicerchio *m*

semicircular *adj* semicircolare

semicolon *n* punto e virgola *m*

semiconscious *adj* semiincosciente

semi-darkness *n* semioscurità *f*

semi-detached ① *adj* gemella ② *n* casa *f* gemella

semi-final *n* semifinale *f*

semifinalist *n* semifinalista *mf*

seminal /'semɪnəl/ *adj* (major) determinante

seminar /'semɪnɑː(r)/ *n* seminario *m*

seminary /'semɪnərɪ/ *n* seminario *m*

semi-precious *adj* semiprezioso; ~ stone pietra *f* dura

semi-skilled /-'skɪld/ *adj* qualificato

semi-skimmed /-'skɪmd/ *adj* parzialmente scremato

semitone *n* Mus semitono *m*

semolina /semə'liːnə/ *n* semolino *m*

senate /'senət/ *n* senato *m*

senator /'senətə(r)/ *n* senatore *m*

⚹ send /send/ *vt/i* (*pt/pp* **sent**) mandare; (by mail) spedire

---

■ **send away for** *vt* farsi spedire ‹*information etc*›

■ **send down** *vt* (send to prison) mandare in galera

■ **send for** *vt* mandare a chiamare ‹*person*›; far venire ‹*thing*›

■ **send in** *vt* presentare ‹*application*›; far entrare ‹*person*›

■ **send off** *vt* spedire ‹*letter, parcel*›; espellere ‹*footballer*›

■ **send on** *vt* spedire ‹*luggage, letter, parcel*›

■ **send out** *vt* emettere ‹*light, heat*›; mandare fuori della porta ‹*pupil*›

■ **send up** *vt* fam parodiare

sender /'sendə(r)/ *n* mittente *mf*; **return to** ∼ (on letter) rispedire al mittente

send-off *n* commiato *m*

send-up *n* Br fam parodia *f*

Senegal /ˌsenɪ'gɔːl/ *n* Senegal *m*

senile /'siːnaɪl/ *adj* arteriosclerotico

senile dementia /dɪ'menʃə/ *n* demenza *f* senile

senility /sɪ'nɪlətɪ/ *n* senilismo *m*

ꟺ **senior** /'siːnɪə(r)/ **1** *adj* più vecchio; (in rank) superiore

2 *n* (in rank) superiore *mf*; (in sport) senior *mf*; **she's two years my** ∼ è più vecchia di me di due anni

senior citizen *n* anziano, -a *mf*

senior high school *n* Am *scuola superiore*

seniority /siːnɪ'ɒrətɪ/ *n* anzianità *f* di servizio

senior management *n* alta dirigenza *f*

sensation /sen'seɪʃn/ *n* sensazione *f*; **cause a** ∼ fare scalpore

sensational /sen'seɪʃənəl/ *adj* sensazionale

sensationalist /sen'seɪʃənəlɪst/ *adj* ‹*headline, report*› sensazionalistico

sensationalize /sen'seɪʃənəlaɪz/ *vt* pej dare un tono scandalistico a

sensationally /sen'seɪʃənəlɪ/ *adv* in modo sensazionale

ꟺ **sense** /sens/ **1** *n* senso *m*; (common) ∼ buon senso *m*; buon senso *m*; **in a** ∼ in un certo senso; **make** ∼ aver senso

2 *vt* sentire

senseless /'senslɪs/ *adj* insensato; (unconscious) privo di sensi

senselessly /'senslɪslɪ/ *adv* insensatamente

sensible /'sensəbl/ *adj* sensato; (suitable) appropriato

sensibly /'sensəblɪ/ *adv* in modo appropriato

sensitive /'sensətɪv/ *adj* sensibile; (touchy) suscettibile

sensitively /'sensətɪvlɪ/ *adv* con sensibilità

sensitivity /sensə'tɪvətɪ/ *n* sensibilità *f inv*

sensitize /'sensɪtaɪz/ *vt* **become** ∼**d to** (allergic to) diventare ipersensibile a

sensor /'sensə(r)/ *n* sensore *m*

sensory /'sensərɪ/ *adj* sensoriale

sensual /'sensjʊəl/ *adj* sensuale

sensuality /sensjʊ'ælətɪ/ *n* sensualità *f inv*

sensuous /'sensjʊəs/ *adj* voluttuoso

sent /sent/ ▶ SEND

ꟺ **sentence** /'sentəns/ **1** *n* frase *f*; Jur sentenza *f*; (punishment) condanna *f*

2 *vt* ∼ **to** condannare a

sentiment /'sentɪmənt/ *n* sentimento *m*; (opinion) opinione *f*; (sentimentality) sentimentalismo *m*

sentimental /sentɪ'mentl/ *adj* sentimentale; pej sentimentalista

sentimentality /sentɪmen'tælətɪ/ *n* sentimentalità *f inv*

sentinel /'sentɪnəl/ *n* sentinella *f*

sentry /'sentrɪ/ *n* sentinella *f*

separable /'sepərəbl/ *adj* separabile

ꟺ **separate¹** /'sepərət/ *adj* separato

separate² /'sepəreɪt/ **1** *vt* separare

2 *vi* separarsi

separately /'sepərətlɪ/ *adv* separatamente

separates /'sepərəts/ *npl* [indumenti *npl*] coordinati *npl*

separation /sepə'reɪʃn/ *n* separazione *f*

separatist /'sepərətɪst/ *n* & *adj* separatista *mf*

sepia /'siːpɪə/ *n* (colour) seppia *m*

ꟺ **September** /sep'tembə(r)/ *n* settembre *m*

septic /'septɪk/ *adj* settico; **go** ∼ infettarsi

septicaemia /septɪ'siːmɪə/ *n* setticemia *f*

septic tank *n* fossa *f* biologica

sequel /'siːkwəl/ *n* seguito *m*

sequence /'siːkwəns/ *n* sequenza *f*; **in** ∼ nell'ordine giusto

sequential /sɪ'kwenʃəl/ *adj* sequenziale

sequin /'siːkwɪn/ *n* lustrino *m*, paillette *f inv*

Serb /sɜːb/ *adj* & *n* serbo, -a *mf*

Serbia /'sɜːbɪə/ *n* Serbia *f*

Serbian /'sɜːbɪən/ **1** *n* serbo, -a *mf*; (language) serbo *m*

2 *adj* serbo

Serbo-Croat[ian]
/sɜːbəʊ'krəʊæt, sɜːbəʊkrəʊ'eɪʃən/ **1** *n* (language) serbo-croato *m*

2 *adj* serbo-croato

serenade /serə'neɪd/ **1** *n* serenata *f*

2 *vt* fare una serenata a

serene /sɪ'riːn/ *adj* sereno

serenely /sɪ'riːnlɪ/ *adv* serenamente

serenity /sɪ'renətɪ/ *n* serenità *inv*

sergeant /'sɑːdʒənt/ *n* sergente *m*

sergeant major *n* sergente *m* maggiore

serial /'sɪərɪəl/ **1** *n* racconto *m* a puntate; TV sceneggiato *m* a puntate; Radio commedia *f* radiofonica a puntate
2 *adj* Comput seriale

serialize /'sɪərɪəlaɪz/ *vt* pubblicare a puntate; Radio, TV trasmettere a puntate

serial killer *n* serial killer *mf inv*

serial number *n* numero *m* di serie

serial port *n* Comput porta *f* seriale

✧ **series** /'sɪərɪːz/ *n* serie *f inv*

✧ **serious** /'sɪərɪəs/ *adj* serio; ‹illness, error› grave

✧ **seriously** /'sɪərɪəslɪ/ *adv* seriamente; ‹ill› gravemente; **take ~** prendere sul serio

seriousness /'sɪərɪəsnɪs/ *n* serietà *f*; (of situation) gravità *f*

sermon /'sɜːmən/ *n* predica *f*

seropositive /sɪərəʊ'pɒzɪtɪv/ *adj* sieropositivo

serotonin /serə'təʊnɪn/ *n* serotonina *f*

serpent /'sɜːpənt/ *n* serpente *m*

serrated /se'reɪtɪd/ *adj* dentellato

serum /'sɪərəm/ *n* siero *m*

servant /'sɜːvənt/ *n* domestico, -a *mf*

✧ **serve** /sɜːv/ **1** *n* Tennis servizio *m*
2 *vt* servire; Jur notificare ‹writ› (**on somebody** a qualcuno); scontare ‹sentence›; **~ its purpose** servire al proprio scopo; **it ~s you right!** ben ti sta!; **~s two** per due persone
3 *vi* prestare servizio; Tennis servire; **~ as** servire da

server /'sɜːvə(r)/ *n* (piece of cutlery) posata *f* da portata; (plate) piatto *m* da portata; (tray) vassoio *m* da portata; Sport giocatore, -trice *mf* che effettua il servizio; Comput server *m inv*

✧ **service** /'sɜːvɪs/ **1** *n* servizio *m*; Relig funzione *f*, (maintenance) revisione *f*; **~s** *pl* forze *fpl* armate; (on motorway) area *f* di servizio; **in the ~s** sotto le armi; **of ~ to** utile a; **out of ~** ‹machine› guasto
2 *vt* Techn revisionare

serviceable /'sɜːvɪsəbl/ *adj* utilizzabile; (hard-wearing) resistente; (practical) pratico

service area *n* area *f* di servizio

service centre Br, **service center** Am *n* (garage) officina *f*; (in shop) centro *m* di assistenza tecnica

service charge *n* servizio *m*

service company *n* compagnia *f* del settore terziario

service industry *n* industria *f* terziaria

serviceman *n* militare *m*

service provider *n* fornitore *m* di servizi Internet

service road *n* strada *f* d'accesso

service station *n* stazione *f* di servizio

servicewoman *n* soldatessa *f*

serviette /sɜːvɪ'et/ *n* tovagliolo *m*

servile /'sɜːvaɪl/ *adj* servile

servility /sə'vɪlɪtɪ/ *n* servilismo *m*

serving /'sɜːvɪŋ/ **1** *adj* ‹officer› di carriera
2 *n* (helping) porzione *f*

serving dish *n* piatto *m* da portata

serving spoon *n* cucchiaio *m* da servizio

✧ **session** /'seʃn/ *n* seduta *f*; Jur sessione *f*; Univ anno *m* accademico

✧ **set** /set/ **1** *n* serie *f inv*, set *m inv*; (of crockery, cutlery) servizio *m*; TV, Radio apparecchio *m*; Math insieme *m*; Theat scenario *m*; Cinema, Tennis set *m inv*; (of people) circolo *m*; (of hair) messa *f* in piega
2 *adj* (ready) pronto; (rigid) fisso; ‹book› in programma; **be ~ on doing something** essere risoluto a fare qualcosa; **be ~ in one's ways** essere abitudinario
3 *vt* (*pt/pp* **set**, *pres p* **setting**) mettere, porre; mettere ‹alarm clock›; assegnare ‹task, homework›; fissare ‹date, limit›; chiedere ‹questions›; montare ‹gem›; assestare ‹bone›; apparecchiare ‹table›; Typ comporre; **~ fire to** dare fuoco a; **~ free** liberare; **~ a good example** dare il buon esempio; **~ sail for** far vela per; **~ in motion** dare inizio a; **~ to music** musicare; **the film is ~ in Rome/the 18th century** il film è ambientato a Roma/nel XVIII secolo; **~ to music** musicare; **~ about doing something** mettersi a fare qualcosa
4 *vi* ‹sun› tramontare; ‹jelly, concrete› solidificarsi; **~ to work (on something)** mettersi al lavoro (su qualcosa)
■ **set apart** *vt* (distinguish) distinguere; **~ somebody** *or* **something apart from** distinguere qualcuno o qualcosa da
■ **set aside** *vt* mettere da parte ‹money, time›; riservare ‹room, area›
■ **set back** *vt* mettere indietro; (hold up) ritardare; fam (cost) costare a
■ **set down** *vt* (establish) stabilire ‹rules, conditions›; (write down) scrivere ‹facts›
■ **set in** *vi* ‹rain, infection, recession› prendere piede
■ **set off** **1** *vi* partire
2 *vt* avviare; mettere ‹alarm›; fare esplodere ‹bomb›
■ **set on**: *vt* **~ on somebody** (attack) aggredire qualcuno; **~ the dogs on somebody** aizzare i cani contro qualcuno
■ **set out** **1** *vi* partire; **~ out to do something** proporsi di fare qualcosa
2 *vt* disporre; (state) esporre
■ **set to** *vi* mettersi all'opera
■ **set up** *vt* fondare ‹company›; istituire ‹committee›

setback /'setbæk/ *n* (hitch) contrattempo *m*; Mil sconfitta *f*, scacco *m*; Fin tracollo *m*; (in health) ricaduta *f*

✧ indicates a very frequent word

set design n scenografia f
set designer n scenografo, -a mf
set meal n menù m inv fisso
settee /se'ti:/ n divano m
setter /'setə(r)/ n (dog) setter m inv
✧ **setting** /'setɪŋ/ n scenario m; (position) posizione f; (of sun) tramonto m; (of jewel) montatura f
setting-up /ˌsetɪŋ'ʌp/ n (of project, business) creazione f
✧ **settle** /'setl/ 1 vt (decide) definire; risolvere ‹argument›; fissare ‹date›; calmare ‹nerves›; saldare ‹bill›; **that's ∼d then** allora è deciso
2 vi (live) stabilirsi; ‹snow, dust, bird› posarsi; (subside) assestarsi; ‹sediment› depositarsi
■ **settle down** vi sistemarsi; (stop making noise) calmarsi
■ **settle for** vt accontentarsi di
■ **settle in** vi (in new house, job) ambientarsi
■ **settle up** vi regolare i conti
settlement /'setlmənt/ n (agreement) accordo m; (of bill) saldo m; Comm liquidazione f; (colony) insediamento m
settler /'setlə(r)/ n colonizzatore, -trice mf
set-to n fam zuffa f; (verbal) battibecco m
set-top box n decoder m inv
set-up n situazione f
✧ **seven** /'sevn/ adj & n sette m
seventeen /sevn'ti:n/ adj & n diciassette m
seventeenth /sevn'ti:n/ adj & n diciassettesimo, -a mf
seventh /'sevnθ/ adj & n settimo, -a mf
seventies /'sevntɪz/ npl (period) **the ∼** gli anni Settanta mpl, (age) settant'anni mpl
seventieth /'sevntɪθ/ adj & n settantesimo, -a mf
seventy /'sevntɪ/ adj & n settanta m
seven-year itch n fam crisi f inv del settimo anno
sever /'sevə(r)/ vt troncare ‹relations›
✧ **several** /'sevrəl/ adj & pron parecchi
severance /'sev(ə)rəns/ n ∼ **pay** trattamento m di fine rapporto
✧ **severe** /sɪ'vɪə(r)/ adj severo; ‹pain› violento; ‹illness› grave; ‹winter› rigido
severe acute respiratory syndrome n Med sindrome f respiratoria acuta severa
severely /sɪ'vɪəlɪ/ adv severamente; ‹ill› gravemente
severity /sɪ'verətɪ/ n severità f; (of pain) violenza f; (of illness) gravità f; (of winter) rigore m
sew /səʊ/ vt/i (pt **sewed**, pp **sewn** or **sewed**) cucire
■ **sew up** vt ricucire
sewage /'su:ɪdʒ/ n acque fpl di scolo

sewer /'su:ə(r)/ n fogna f
sewing /'səʊɪŋ/ n cucito m; (work) lavoro m di cucito
sewing machine n macchina f da cucire
sewn /səʊn/ ▶ SEW
✧ **sex** /seks/ n sesso m; **have ∼** avere rapporti sessuali, fare l'amore
sex appeal n sex appeal m
sex change n **have a ∼** cambiare sesso
sex change operation n intervento m per il cambiamento di sesso
sex discrimination n discriminazione f sessuale
sex education n educazione f sessuale
sexism /'seksɪzm/ n sessismo m
sexist /'seksɪst/ adj sessista mf
sex life n vita f sessuale
sex maniac n maniaco m sessuale
sex object n oggetto m sessuale
sex offender n colpevole mf di delitti a sfondo sessuale
sextet /seks'tet/ n sestetto m
sex tourism n turismo m a scopo sessuale
✧ **sexual** /'seksjʊəl/ adj sessuale
sexual abuse n abusi mpl sessuali
sexual assault n atti mpl di libidine violenta
sexual equality n parità f dei sessi
sexual harassment n molestie fpl sessuali
sexual intercourse n rapporti mpl sessuali
sexuality /seksjʊ'ælətɪ/ n sessualità f
sexually /'seksjʊəlɪ/ adv sessualmente; **be ∼ assaulted** subire atti di libidine violenta
sexually transmitted disease /trænz'mɪtɪd/ n malattia f trasmissibile per via sessuale
sexy /'seksɪ/ adj (**-ier, -iest**) sexy inv
Seychelles /seɪ'ʃelz/ npl **the ∼** le Seychelles
sh /ʃ/ int silenzio!, sst!
shabbily /'ʃæbɪlɪ/ adv in modo scialbo; ‹treat› in modo meschino
shabbiness /'ʃæbɪnɪs/ n trasandatezza f; (of treatment) meschinità f
shabby /'ʃæbɪ/ adj (**-ier, -iest**) scialbo; ‹treatment› meschino
shack /ʃæk/ n catapecchia f
shackles /'ʃæklz/ npl catene fpl
shade /ʃeɪd/ 1 n ombra f; (of colour) sfumatura f; (for lamp) paralume m; Am (for window) tapparella f; **a ∼ better** un tantino meglio
2 vt riparare dalla luce; (draw lines on) ombreggiare
shades /ʃeɪdz/ npl fam occhiali mpl da sole

S

shading /'ʃeɪdɪŋ/ n (slight variation in colour) tonalità f inv; (to give effect of darkness) ombreggiature fpl

shadow /'ʃædəʊ/ **1** n ombra f **2** vt (follow) pedinare

shadow boxing n allenamento m di boxe con l'ombra

Shadow Cabinet n governo m ombra

shadowy /'ʃædəʊɪ/ adj (indistinct) confuso

shady /'ʃeɪdɪ/ adj (-ier, -iest) ombroso; fam (disreputable) losco

shaft /ʃɑːft/ n Techn albero m; (of light) raggio m; (of lift, mine) pozzo m; ~s pl (of cart) stanghe fpl

shaggy /'ʃægɪ/ adj (-ier, -iest) irsuto; ‹animal› dal pelo arruffato

shaggy dog story n fam barzelletta (f) interminabile dal finale deludente

✔ **shake** /ʃeɪk/ **1** n scrollata f **2** vt (pt **shook**, pp **shaken**) scuotere; agitare ‹bottle›; far tremare ‹building›; ~ **hands with** stringere la mano a; ~ **one's head** scuotere la testa **3** vi tremare

■ **shake off** vt scrollarsi di dosso

■ **shake up** vt agitare ‹bottle›; ‹news, experience› scuotere ‹person›

shaken [up] /'ʃeɪkən/ adj (after accident etc) scosso

shaker /'ʃeɪkə(r)/ n (for salad) centrifuga f [asciugaverdure]; (for dice) bicchiere m; (for cocktails) shaker m inv; (for pepper) pepaiola f; (for salt) saliera f

shake-up n Pol rimpasto m; Comm ristrutturazione f

shakily /'ʃeɪkɪlɪ/ adv ‹say something› con voce tremante; ‹walk› con passo esitante

shaky /'ʃeɪkɪ/ adj (-ier, -iest) tremante; ‹table etc› traballante; (unreliable) vacillante

✔ **shall** /ʃæl/ v aux I ~ **go** andrò; **we** ~ **see** vedremo; **what** ~ **I do?** cosa faccio?; **I'll come too,** ~ **I?** vengo anch'io, no?; **thou shalt not kill** liter non uccidere; **passengers** ~ **remain seated** i passeggeri devono rimanere seduti

shallot /ʃə'lɒt/ n scalogno m

shallow /'ʃæləʊ/ adj basso, poco profondo; ‹dish› poco profondo; fig superficiale

shallows /'ʃæləʊz/ npl secche fpl

sham /ʃæm/ **1** adj falso **2** n finzione f; (person) spaccone, -a mf **3** vt (pt/pp **shammed**) simulare

shambles /'ʃæmblz/ n caos msg

shame /ʃeɪm/ n vergogna f; **It's a** ~ **that** è un peccato che; **what a** ~! che peccato!; ~ **on you!** vergognati!; **put somebody/ something to** ~ far sfigurare qualcuno/ qualcosa

shamefaced /ʃeɪm'feɪst/ adj vergognoso

shameful /'ʃeɪmfl/ adj vergognoso

shamefully /'ʃeɪmfʊlɪ/ adv vergognosamente

shameless /'ʃeɪmlɪs/ adj spudorato

shamelessly /'ʃeɪmlɪslɪ/ adv spudoratamente

shampoo /ʃæm'puː/ **1** n shampoo m inv; ~ **and set** shampoo m inv e messa in piega **2** vt fare uno shampoo a ‹carpet, person's hair etc›

shamrock /'ʃæmrɒk/ n trifoglio m (simbolo dell'Irlanda)

shandy /'ʃændɪ/ n bevanda (f) a base di birra e gassosa

shank /ʃæŋk/ n garretto m; (of knife) manico m; (of golf club) impugnatura f; (of screw) gambo m; (of anchor) fuso m; (of person) gamba f (dal ginocchio in giù)

shan't /ʃɑːnt/ = **shall not**

shanty /'ʃæntɪ/ n (hut) baracca f; (song) marinaro

shanty town /'ʃæntɪtaʊn/ n bidonville f inv, baraccopoli f inv

✔ **shape** /ʃeɪp/ **1** n forma f; (figure) ombra f; **take** ~ prendere forma; **get back in** ~ ritornare in forma; **be out of** ~ non essere in forma **2** vt dare forma a (**into** di) **3** vi ~ **[up]** mettere la testa a posto; ~ **up nicely** mettersi bene

shapeless /'ʃeɪplɪs/ adj informe

shapely /'ʃeɪplɪ/ adj (-ier, -iest) ben fatto

shard /ʃɑːd/ n frammento m; (of clay) coccio m

✔ **share** /ʃeə(r)/ **1** n porzione f; Comm azione f **2** vt dividere; condividere ‹views› **3** vi dividere; ~ **in** partecipare a

■ **share out** vt spartire; (including oneself) spartirsi

share capital n capitale m azionario

shared /ʃeəd/ adj ‹house› condiviso; ‹bathroom› in comune

share dealing n contrattazione f di azioni

shareholder n azionista mf

shareholding n titoli mpl azionari

share index n indice m azionario

share option scheme n partecipazione (f) agli utili dell'azienda tramite acquisto di azioni

shareware /'ʃeəweə(r)/ n Comput shareware m inv

shark /ʃɑːk/ n squalo m, pescecane m; fig truffatore, -trice mf

✔ **sharp** /ʃɑːp/ **1** adj ‹knife etc› tagliente; ‹pencil› appuntito; ‹drop› a picco; ‹reprimand› severo; ‹outline› marcato; (alert) acuto; (unscrupulous) senza scrupoli; ~ **pain** fitta f **2** adv **at three o'clock** ~ alle tre in punto; **look** ~! sbrigati! **3** n Mus diesis m inv

---

✔ indicates a very frequent word

s

sharpen /'ʃɑːpn/ vt affilare ‹knife›; appuntire ‹pencil›

sharpener /'ʃɑːpnə(r)/ n (for pencils) temperamatite m inv; (for knife) affilacoltelli m inv

sharply /'ʃɑːplɪ/ adv ‹turn, rise, fall› bruscamente; ‹speak› in tono brusco

shatter /'ʃætə(r)/ vt frantumare; fig mandare in frantumi

shattered /'ʃætəd/ **1** adj fam (exhausted) a pezzi

　2 vi frantumarsi

shave /ʃeɪv/ **1** n rasatura f; **have a ~** farsi la barba

　2 vt radere

　3 vi radersi

shaver /'ʃeɪvə(r)/ n rasoio m elettrico

shaving brush n pennello m da barba

shaving foam n schiuma f da barba

shavings /'ʃeɪvɪŋz/ npl (of wood, metal) trucioli mpl

shaving soap n sapone m da barba

shawl /ʃɔːl/ n scialle m

✓ **she** /ʃiː/ pers pron lei; **~ is tired** è stanca; **I'm going, but ~** io vado, ma lei no

sheaf /ʃiːf/ n (pl **sheaves**) fascio m

shear /ʃɪə(r)/ vt (pt **sheared**, pp **shorn** or **sheared**) tosare

shears /ʃɪəz/ npl (for hedge) cesoie fpl

sheath /ʃiːθ/ n (pl **~s** /ʃiːðz/) guaina f

sheathe /ʃiːð/ vt rifoderare; rivestire ‹cable›

sheaves /ʃiːvz/ ▶ SHEAF

shed¹ /ʃed/ n baracca f; (for cattle) stalla f

shed² vt (pt/pp **shed**, pres p **shedding**) perdere; versare ‹blood, tears›; **~ light on** far luce su

shedload n Br fam **~s of money** un sacco di soldi

sheen /ʃiːn/ n lucentezza f

sheep /ʃiːp/ n inv pecora f

sheepdog /'ʃiːpdɒg/ n cane m da pastore

sheepish /'ʃiːpɪʃ/ adj imbarazzato

sheepishly /'ʃiːpɪʃlɪ/ adv con aria imbarazzata

sheepskin /'ʃiːpskɪn/ n [pelle f di] montone m

sheer /ʃɪə(r)/ **1** adj puro; (steep) a picco; (transparent) trasparente

　2 adv a picco

sheet /ʃiːt/ n lenzuolo m; (of paper) foglio m; (of glass, metal) lastra f

sheet lightning n bagliore m diffuso dei lampi; (without a storm) lampi mpl di calore

sheet metal n lamiera f

sheet music n spartiti mpl

sheikh /ʃeɪk/, **sheik** n sceicco m

shelf /ʃelf/ n (pl **shelves**) ripiano m; (set of shelves) scaffale m

shelf-life n (of product) durata f di conservazione; fig (of technology, pop music) durata f di vita; fig (of politician, star) periodo m di gloria

shell /ʃel/ **1** n conchiglia f; (of egg, snail, tortoise) guscio m; (of crab) corazza f; (of unfinished building) ossatura f; Mil granata f

　2 vt sgusciare ‹peas›; Mil bombardare

■ **shell out** vi fam sborsare

shellfish n inv mollusco m; Culin frutti mpl di mare

shell-shocked /'ʃelʃɒkt/ adj ‹soldier› traumatizzato da un bombardamento; fig in stato di shock

shell suit n tuta f di acetato

shelter /'ʃeltə(r)/ **1** n rifugio m; (air raid) **~** rifugio m antiaereo; rifugio m antiaereo; **take ~** rifugiarsi

　2 vt riparare (**from** da); fig mettere al riparo; (give lodging to) dare asilo a

　3 vi rifugiarsi

sheltered /'ʃeltəd/ adj ‹spot› riparato; ‹life› ritirato

sheltered accommodation n residenza f protetta

shelve /ʃelv/ **1** vt accantonare ‹project›

　2 vi ‹slope› scendere

shelves /ʃelvz/ ▶ SHELF

shelving /'ʃelvɪŋ/ n (shelves) ripiani mpl

shepherd /'ʃepəd/ **1** n pastore m

　2 vt guidare

shepherdess /'ʃepədes/ n pastora f

shepherd's pie /ʃepədz'paɪ/ n pasticcio (m) di carne tritata e patate

sherbet /'sɜːbət/ n Br (powder) polverina f effervescente al gusto di frutta; Am (sorbet) sorbetto m

sheriff /'ʃerɪf/ n sceriffo m

Sherpa /'ʃɜːpə/ n scerpa m

sherry /'ʃerɪ/ n sherry m inv

shield /ʃiːld/ **1** n scudo m; (for eyes) maschera f; Techn schermo m

　2 vt proteggere (**from** da)

✓ **shift** /ʃɪft/ **1** n cambiamento m; (in position) spostamento m; (at work) turno m

　2 vt spostare; (take away) togliere; riversare ‹blame›

　3 vi spostarsi; ‹wind› cambiare; fam (move quickly) darsi una mossa

shift key n tasto m delle maiuscole

shiftless /'ʃɪftlɪs/ adj privo di risorse

shift work n turni mpl

shift worker n turnista mf

shifty /'ʃɪftɪ/ adj (-ier, -iest) pej losco; ‹eyes› sfuggente

Shiite /'ʃiːaɪt/ adj & n sciita mf

shilling /'ʃɪlɪŋ/ n scellino m

shilly-shally /'ʃɪlɪʃælɪ/ vi titubare

shimmer /'ʃɪmə(r)/ **1** n luccichio m

　2 vi luccicare

S

shin /ʃɪn/ ① n stinco m
② n ~ **up/down something** (climb) arrampicarsi su/scendere giù da qualcosa

shindig /'ʃɪndɪg/ n fam (party) baldoria f; (disturbance) pandemonio m

shindy /'ʃɪndɪ/ n fam (disturbance) pandemonio m; (party) baldoria f

shine /ʃaɪn/ ① n lucentezza f; **give something a ~** dare una lucidata a qualcosa
② vi (pt/pp **shone**) splendere; (reflect light) brillare; ‹hair, shoes› essere lucido
③ vt ~ **a light on** puntare una luce su
■ **shine through** vi ‹talent, ability› trasparire

shingle /'ʃɪŋgl/ n (pebbles) ghiaia f

shingles /'ʃɪŋglz/ n Med fuoco m di Sant'Antonio

shin-guard n parastinchi m inv

shining /'ʃaɪnɪŋ/ adj ‹eyes, jewel› splendente; ‹hair› lucente; **a ~ example** un fulgido esempio

shiny /'ʃaɪnɪ/ adj (**-ier, -iest**) lucido

⚜ **ship** /ʃɪp/ ① n nave f
② vt (pt, pp **-pped**) spedire; (by sea) spedire via mare

shipbuilder /'ʃɪpbɪldə(r)/ n costruttore m navale

shipbuilding /'ʃɪpbɪldɪŋ/ n costruzione f di navi

shipment /'ʃɪpmənt/ n spedizione f; (consignment) carico m

shipowner /'ʃɪpəʊnə(r)/ n armatore m

shipper /'ʃɪpə(r)/ n spedizioniere m

shipping /'ʃɪpɪŋ/ n trasporto m; (traffic) imbarcazioni fpl

shipping agent n spedizioniere m

shipping company n compagnia f di spedizione

shipshape adj & adv in perfetto ordine

shipwreck n naufragio m

shipwrecked naufragato

shipyard n cantiere m navale

shire /ʃaɪə(r)/ n Br contea f

shire-horse n cavallo m da tiro

shirk /ʃɜːk/ vt scansare

shirker /'ʃɜːkə(r)/ n scansafatiche mf inv

⚜ **shirt** /ʃɜːt/ n camicia f; **in ~-sleeves** in maniche di camicia

shirty /'ʃɜːtɪ/ adj Br fam incavolato; **get ~ with somebody** incavolarsi con qualcuno

shish kebab /ʃɪʃkɪ'bæb/ n spiedino (m) di carne e verdure

shit /ʃɪt/ ① vulg n & int merda f
② vi (pt/pp **shit**) cacare

shit-scared adj vulg be ~ farsela sotto

shiver /'ʃɪvə(r)/ ① n brivido m
② vi rabbrividire

shoal /ʃəʊl/ n (of fish) banco m

⚜ indicates a very frequent word

⚜ **shock** /ʃɒk/ ① n (impact) urto m; Electr scossa f [elettrica]; fig colpo m, shock m inv; Med shock m inv; **get a ~** Electr prendere la scossa; **in ~** Med in stato di shock
② vt scioccare

shock absorber n Auto ammortizzatore m

shocking /'ʃɒkɪŋ/ adj scioccante; fam ‹weather, handwriting etc› tremendo

shockingly /'ʃɒkɪŋlɪ/ adv ‹behave› in modo pessimo; ‹expensive› eccessivamente

shocking pink n rosa m shocking

shockproof adj antiurto

shock treatment n terapia f d'urto

shock wave n onda f d'urto

shod /ʃɒd/ ▶ SHOE

shoddily /'ʃɒdɪlɪ/ adv in modo scadente

shoddy /'ʃɒdɪ/ adj (**-ier, -iest**) scadente

⚜ **shoe** /ʃuː/ ① n scarpa f; (of horse) ferro m
② vt (pt/pp **shod**, pres p **shoeing**) ferrare ‹horse›

shoehorn n calzante m

shoelace n laccio m da scarpa

shoemaker n calzolaio m

shoe rack n scarpiera f

shoe-shop n calzoleria f

shoestring n on a ~ fam con una miseria

shoe-tree n forma f da scarpa

shone /ʃɒn/ ▶ SHINE

shoo /ʃuː/ ① vt ~ **away** cacciar via
② int sciò!

shook /ʃʊk/ ▶ SHAKE

⚜ **shoot** /ʃuːt/ ① n Bot germoglio m; (hunt) battuta f di caccia
② vt (pt/pp **shot**) sparare, girare ‹film›; ~ **oneself in the foot** fig darsi la zappa sui piedi
③ vi (hunt) andare a caccia
■ **shoot down** vt abbattere
■ **shoot out** vi (rush) precipitarsi fuori
■ **shoot up** vi (grow) crescere in fretta; ‹prices› salire di colpo

shooting /'ʃuːtɪŋ/ ① n (pastime) caccia f; (killing) uccisione f
② adj ‹pain› lancinante

shooting range n poligono m di tiro

shooting star n stella f cadente

shoot-out n fam sparatoria f

⚜ **shop** /ʃɒp/ ① n negozio m; (workshop) officina f; **talk ~** fam parlare di lavoro
② vi (pt/pp **shopped**, pres p **shopping**) far compere; **go ~ping** andare a fare compere
■ **shop around** vi confrontare i prezzi

shopaholic /ʃɒpə'hɒlɪk/ n fanatico, -a mf dello shopping

shop assistant n commesso, -a mf

shop floor n problems on the ~ problemi tra gli operai

shopkeeper n negoziante mf

shoplifter *n* taccheggiatore, -trice *mf*

shoplifting *n* taccheggio *m*

shopper /'ʃɒpə(r)/ *n* compratore, -trice *mf*

shopping /'ʃɒpɪŋ/ *n* compere *fpl*; (articles) acquisti *mpl*; **do the ~** fare la spesa

shopping bag *n* borsa *f* per la spesa

shopping basket *n* Comput (on web site) carrello *m* della spesa

shopping cart *n* carrello *m* della spesa

shopping centre *n* centro *m* commerciale

shopping list *n* lista *f* della spesa

shopping mall *n* centro *m* commerciale

shopping trolley *n* carrello *m*

shop-soiled *adj* Br ⟨garment⟩ sporco (per lunga permanenza in negozio)

shop steward *n* rappresentante *mf* sindacale

shop window *n* vetrina *f*

shopworn *adj* Am ⟨garment⟩ sporco (per lunga permanenza in negozio)

shore /ʃɔː(r)/ *n* riva *f*

■ **shore up** *vt* puntellare ⟨building, wall⟩

shorn /ʃɔːn/ ▶ SHEAR

short /ʃɔːt/ ① *adj* corto; (not lasting) breve; ⟨person⟩ basso; (curt) brusco; **a ~ time ago** poco tempo fa; **be ~ of** essere a corto di; **be in ~ supply** essere scarso; fig essere raro; **Mick is ~ for Michael** Mick è il diminutivo di Michael; **cut ~** interrompere ⟨holiday⟩; **to cut a long story ~…** per farla breve…; **In the ~ term** nell'immediato futuro, a breve termine
② *adv* bruscamente; **in ~** in breve; **~ of doing** a meno di fare; **go ~** essere privato (of di); **stop ~ of doing something** non arrivare fino a fare qualcosa; **you're 10p ~** mancano 10 pence
③ *n* Cinema cortometraggio *m*

shortage /'ʃɔːtɪdʒ/ *n* scarsità *f inv*

shortbread *n* biscotto *m* di pasta frolla

short-change *vt* dare meno resto del dovuto a; (deliberately) imbrogliare sul resto; fig imbrogliare

short circuit ① *n* corto *m* circuito
② *vt* mandare in cortocircuito
③ *vi* causare un cortocircuito

shortcoming *n* difetto *m*

shortcrust pastry *n* pasta *f* frolla

short cut *n* scorciatoia *f*

shorten /'ʃɔːtn/ *vt* abbreviare; accorciare ⟨garment⟩

shortfall *n* (in budget, accounts) deficit *m inv*

shorthand *n* stenografia *f*

short-handed /-'hændɪd/ *adj* a corto di personale

shorthand typist *n* stenodattilografo, -a *mf*

short list *n* lista (*f*) dei candidati selezionati per un lavoro

short-lived /-'lɪvd/ *adj* di breve durata

shortly /'ʃɔːtlɪ/ *adv* presto; **~ before/after** poco prima/dopo

shortness /'ʃɔːtnɪs/ *n* brevità *f inv*; (of person) bassa statura *f*

short notice *n* **at ~** con poco preavviso

short-range *adj* di breve portata

shorts /ʃɔːts/ *npl* calzoncini *mpl* corti

short-sighted /-'saɪtɪd/ *adj* miope

short-sleeved /-'sliːvd/ *adj* a maniche corte

short-staffed /-'stɑːft/ *adj* a corto di personale

short story *n* racconto *m*, novella *f*

short-tempered /-'tempəd/ *adj* irascibile

short-term *adj* a breve termine

short time *n* **be on ~** ⟨worker⟩ fare orario ridotto

short wave *n* onde *fpl* corte

short wave radio *n* radio *f inv* a onde corte

shot /ʃɒt/ ① ▶ SHOOT
② *n* colpo *m*; (pellets) piombini *mpl*; (person) tiratore *m*; Phot foto *f inv*; (injection) puntura *f*; fam (attempt) prova *f*; **like a ~** fam come un razzo

shotgun *n* fucile *m* da caccia

shot put *n* (event) lancio *m* del peso

shot-putter *n* pesista *mf*

shot-putting *n* Sport lancio *m* del peso

should /ʃʊd/ *v aux* **I ~ go** dovrei andare; **I ~ have seen him** avrei dovuto vederlo; **you ~ have seen him!** avresti dovuto vederlo!; **you ~n't have said that** non avresti dovuto dire questo; **what ~ I say?** cosa devo dire?; **this ~ be enough** questo dovrebbe bastare; **I ~ like** mi piacerebbe; **if he ~ come** se dovesse venire, se venisse

shoulder /'ʃəʊldə(r)/ ① *n* spalla *f*, **to ~** gomito a gomito
② *vt* mettersi in spalla; fig accollarsi

shoulder bag *n* borsa *f* a tracolla

shoulder blade *n* scapola *f*

shoulder-length *adj* ⟨hair⟩ lungo fino alle spalle

shoulder pad *n* spallina *f*

shoulder strap *n* spallina *f*; (of bag) tracolla *f*

shout /ʃaʊt/ ① *n* grido *m*
② *vt/i* gridare

■ **shout at** *vi* alzar la voce con

■ **shout down** *vt* azzittire gridando

shouting /'ʃaʊtɪŋ/ *n* grida *fpl*

shove /ʃʌv/ ① *n* spintone *m*
② *vt* spingere; fam (put) ficcare
③ *vi* spingere

■ **shove off** *vi* fam togliersi di torno

■ **shove up** *vi* fam (make room) farsi più in là

shovel /'ʃʌvl/ ① n pala f
② vt (pt/pp **shovelled**) spalare

⚲ **show** /ʃəʊ/ ① n (display) manifestazione f; (exhibition) mostra f; (ostentation) ostentazione f; Theat, TV spettacolo m; (programme) programma m; **on ~** esposto
② vt (pt **showed**, pp **shown**) mostrare; (put on display) esporre; proiettare ‹film›; **~ somebody to the door** accompagnare qualcuno alla porta; **~ somebody the door** mettere alla porta qualcuno
③ vi ‹film› essere proiettato; **your slip is ~ing** ti si vede la sottoveste
■ **show in** vt fare accomodare
■ **show off** ① vi fam mettersi in mostra
② vt mettere in mostra
■ **show out**: vt **~ somebody out** fare uscire qualcuno
■ **show round**: vt **~ somebody round** far visitare a qualcuno ‹house, town›
■ **show up** ① vi risaltare; fam (arrive) farsi vedere
② vt fam (embarrass) far fare una brutta figura a
showbiz /'ʃəʊbɪz/ n fam mondo m dello spettacolo
show business n mondo m dello spettacolo
showcase ① n also fig vetrina f
② attrib ‹village, prison› modello
show-down n regolamento m dei conti
shower /'ʃaʊə(r)/ ① n doccia f; (of rain) acquazzone m; **have a ~** fare la doccia
② vt **~ with** coprire di
③ vi fare la doccia
shower-cap n cuffia f da doccia
shower-curtain n tenda f della doccia
shower-head n bocchetta f
showerproof adj impermeabile
showery /'ʃaʊərɪ/ adj **it was ~** ci sono stati diversi acquazzoni
show house n casa (f) di nuova costruzione arredata per essere mostrata ad eventuali acquirenti
showjumper /'ʃəʊdʒʌmpə(r)/ n cavaliere m f
showjumping /'ʃəʊdʒʌmpɪŋ/ n concorso m ippico
shown /ʃəʊn/ ▶ SHOW
show-off n esibizionista m f
show of hands n voto m per alzata di mano
showpiece n pezzo m forte
showplace n attrazione f
showroom n salone m [per] esposizioni
showy /'ʃəʊɪ/ adj appariscente
shrank /ʃræŋk/ ▶ SHRINK
shrapnel /'ʃræpnl/ n schegge fpl di granata, shrapnel m

shred /ʃred/ ① n brandello m; fig briciolo m
② vt (pt/pp **shredded**) fare a brandelli; Culin tagliuzzare
shredder /'ʃredə(r)/ n distruttore m di documenti
shrew /ʃru:/ n Zool toporagno m; pej (woman) bisbetica f
shrewd /ʃru:d/ adj accorto
shrewdly /'ʃru:dlɪ/ adv con accortezza
shrewdness /'ʃru:dnɪs/ n accortezza f
shriek /ʃri:k/ ① n strillo m
② vt/i strillare
shrift /ʃrɪft/ n **give somebody short ~** liquidare qualcuno rapidamente
shrill /ʃrɪl/ adj penetrante
shrillness /'ʃrɪlnɪs/ n acutezza f
shrilly /'ʃrɪlɪ/ adv in modo penetrante
shrimp /ʃrɪmp/ n Am gamberetto m
shrine /ʃraɪn/ n (place) santuario m
shrink /ʃrɪŋk/ ① vi (pt **shrank**, pp **shrunk**) restringersi; (draw back) ritrarsi (from da)
② n fam strizzacervelli m f inv
shrinkage /'ʃrɪŋkɪdʒ/ n (of fabric) restringimento m; (of area, company) rimpicciolimento m; (in a shop) perdite fpl; (of resources) diminuzione f
shrinking violet /ʃrɪŋkɪŋ'vaɪələt/ n hum mammoletta f
shrink-proof adj irrestringibile
shrink-resistant adj irrestringibile
shrink-wrap ① vt avvolgere nella pellicola trasparente
② n pellicola f trasparente
shrivel /'ʃrɪvl/ vi (pt/pp **shrivelled**) raggrinzare
shroud /ʃraʊd/ n sudario m; fig manto m; **~ed in** fig avvolto in
Shrove /ʃrəʊv/ n **~ Tuesday** martedì m grasso
shrub /ʃrʌb/ n arbusto m
shrubbery /'ʃrʌbərɪ/ n (in garden) zona f piantata ad arbusti
⚲ **shrug** /ʃrʌg/ ① n scrollata f di spalle
② vt/i (pt/pp **shrugged**) **~ [one's shoulders]** scrollare le spalle
■ **shrug off** vt ignorare
shrunk /ʃrʌŋk/ ▶ SHRINK.
shudder /'ʃʌdə(r)/ ① n fremito m
② vi fremere
shuffle /'ʃʌfl/ ① vi strascicare i piedi
② vt mescolare ‹cards›
③ n strascicamento m; (at cards) mescolata f
shufty /'ʃʊftɪ/ n Br fam **have a ~ at something** dare un'occhiata a qualcosa
shun /ʃʌn/ vt (pt/pp **shunned**) rifuggire
shunt /ʃʌnt/ vt smistare
shush /ʃʊʃ/ int zitto!

S

shut /ʃʌt/ **1** vt (pt/pp **shut**, pres p **shutting**) chiudere
  2 vi chiudersi; ‹shop› chiudere
■ **shut down** vt/i chiudere
■ **shut in** vt rinchiudere ‹person, animal›
■ **shut off** vt chiudere ‹water, gas›
■ **shut out** vt bloccare ‹light›; impedire ‹view›; scacciare ‹memory›
■ **shut up** **1** vt chiudere; fam far tacere
  2 vi fam stare zitto; ~ **up!** stai zitto!
shutdown /'ʃʌtdaʊn/ n chiusura f
shut-eye n fam (short sleep) **get some** ~ fare un pisolino
shutter /'ʃʌtə(r)/ n serranda f; Phot otturatore m
shuttle /'ʃʌtl/ **1** n navetta f
  2 vi far la spola
shuttlecock /'ʃʌtlkɒk/ n volano m
shuttle service n servizio m pendolare
shy /ʃaɪ/ **1** adj (timid) timido
  2 vi (pt/pp **shied**) ‹horse› fare uno scarto
■ **shy away from** vt rifuggire da
shyly /'ʃaɪlɪ/ adv timidamente
shyness /'ʃaɪnɪs/ n timidezza f
Siamese /saɪə'miːz/ adj siamese
Siamese twins npl fratelli mpl/ sorelle fpl siamesi
Siberia /saɪ'bɪərɪə/ n Siberia f
sibling /'sɪblɪŋ/ n (brother) fratello m; (sister) sorella f; ~s pl fratelli mpl
sibling rivalry n rivalità f tra fratelli
sibylline /'sɪbɪlaɪn/ adj sibillino
Sicilian /sɪ'sɪlɪən/ adj & n siciliano, -a mf
Sicily /'sɪsɪlɪ/ n Sicilia f
sick /sɪk/ adj ammalato; ‹humour› macabro; **be** ~ (vomit) vomitare; **be** ~ **of something** fam essere stufo di qualcosa; **feel** ~ aver la nausea
sick bay n (in school) infermeria f
sick building syndrome n sindrome f da edifici malsani
sicken /'sɪkn/ **1** vt disgustare
  2 vi **be** ~**ing for something** covare qualche malanno
sickening /'sɪkənɪŋ/ adj disgustoso
sickie /'sɪkɪ/ n Br fam **throw a** ~ darsi malato
sick leave n congedo m per malattia
sickly /'sɪklɪ/ adj (-ier, -iest) malaticcio
sickness /'sɪknɪs/ n malattia f; (vomiting) nausea f
sickness benefit n sussidio m di malattia
sick note n (from doctor) certificato m medico
sickpay n indennità f di malattia
sickroom /'sɪkruːm/ n camera f dell'ammalato
side /saɪd/ **1** n lato m; (of person, mountain) fianco m; (of road) bordo m; **on the** ~ (as sideline) come attività secondaria; ~ **by** ~

fianco a fianco; **take** ~**s** immischiarsi; **take sb's** ~ prendere le parti di qualcuno; **be on the safe** ~ andare sul sicuro
  2 attrib laterale
  3 vi ~ **with** parteggiare per
sideboard n credenza f
sideboards /'saɪdbɔːdz/ npl
Br = SIDEBURNS
sideburns npl basette fpl
side effect n effetto m collaterale
side impact bars npl Auto barre fpl laterali antintrusione
sidekick n fam (companion) compare mf; (assistant) braccio m destro
sidelights npl luci fpl di posizione
sideline n attività f inv complementare
sidelong adj ~ **glance** sguincio m
side plate n piattino m
side road n strada f secondaria
side-saddle adv all'amazzone
sideshow n attrazione f
sidestep vt schivare
side street n strada f laterale
sidetrack vt sviare
sidewalk n Am marciapiede m
sideways adv obliquamente
siding /'saɪdɪŋ/ n binario m di raccordo
sidle /'saɪdl/ vi camminare furtivamente (**up to** verso)
siege /siːdʒ/ n assedio m
Sierra Leone /sɪeərələˈəʊn/ n Sierra Leone f
siesta /sɪ'estə/ n siesta f; **take a** ~ fare una siesta
sieve /sɪv/ **1** n setaccio m
  2 vt setacciare
sift /sɪft/ vt setacciare; ~ **[through]** fig passare al setaccio
sigh /saɪ/ **1** n sospiro m; **give a** ~ sospirare
  2 vi sospirare
sight /saɪt/ **1** n vista f; (on gun) mirino m; **the** ~**s** pl le cose da vedere; **at first** ~ a prima vista; **be within/out of** ~ essere in/non essere in vista; **within** ~ **of** vicino a; **lose** ~ **of** perdere di vista; **know by** ~ conoscere di vista; **have bad** ~ vederci male
  2 vt avvistare
sightseeing /'saɪtsiːɪŋ/ n **go** ~ andare a visitare posti
sightseer /'saɪtsiːə(r)/ n turista mf
sign /saɪn/ **1** n segno m; (notice) insegna f
  2 vt/i firmare
■ **sign for** vt firmare la ricevuta di ‹letter, parcel›; firmare un contratto con ‹football club›
■ **sign in** vi ‹hotel guest› firmare il registro
■ **sign on** vi (as unemployed) presentarsi all'ufficio di collocamento; Mil arruolarsi
■ **sign up** vi Mil arruolarsi; ~ **up for a course** iscriversi a un corso

S

✧ **signal** /'sɪgnl/ **1** n segnale m
2 vt (pt/pp **signalled**) segnalare
3 vi fare segnali; ~ **to somebody** far segno a qualcuno (**to** di)

signal box n cabina f di segnalazione

signalman /'sɪgnəlmən/ n casellante m

signatory /'sɪgnət(ə)rɪ/ n firmatario, -a mf

signature /'sɪgnətʃə(r)/ n firma f

signature tune n sigla f [musicale]

signet ring /'sɪgnɪt/ n anello m con sigillo

significance /sɪg'nɪfɪkəns/ n significato m

✧ **significant** /sɪg'nɪfɪkənt/ adj significativo

significantly /sɪg'nɪfɪkəntlɪ/ adv in modo significativo

signify /'sɪgnɪfaɪ/ vt (pt/pp **-ied**) indicare

signing /'saɪnɪŋ/ n (of treaty) firma f; (of footballer) ingaggio m; (footballer) nuovo acquisto m; (sign language) linguaggio m dei segni

sign language n linguaggio m dei segni

signpost /'saɪnpəʊst/ n segnalazione f stradale

Sikh /siːk/ **1** n sikh mf inv
2 adj sikh inv

silage /'saɪlɪdʒ/ n foraggio m conservato in silo

✧ **silence** /'saɪləns/ **1** n silenzio m; **in ~** in silenzio
2 vt far tacere

silencer /'saɪlənsə(r)/ n (on gun) silenziatore m; Auto marmitta f

silent /'saɪlənt/ adj silenzioso; ‹film› muto; **remain ~** rimanere in silenzio; **the ~ majority** la maggioranza silenziosa

silently /'saɪləntlɪ/ adv silenziosamente

silhouette /sɪlʊ'et/ **1** n sagoma f, silhouette f inv
2 vt **be ~d** profilarsi

silica gel /'sɪlɪkə/ n gel m inv di silice

silicon /'sɪlɪkən/ n silicio m

silicon chip n Comput chip m inv di silicio, piastrina f di silicio

silicone /'sɪlɪkəʊn/ n Chem silicone m

silicone varnish n vernice f siliconica

silk /sɪlk/ **1** n seta f
2 attrib di seta

silkworm /'sɪlkwɜːm/ n baco m da seta

silky /'sɪlkɪ/ adj (**-ier, -iest**) come la seta

sill /sɪl/ n davanzale m

silly /'sɪlɪ/ adj (**-ier, -iest**) sciocco

silo /'saɪləʊ/ n silo m

silt /sɪlt/ n melma f

silver /'sɪlvə(r)/ **1** adj d'argento; ‹paper› argentato
2 n argento m; (silverware) argenteria f

silver birch n betulla f bianca

silver foil n carta f stagnola, foglio m d'alluminio

silver-plated adj placcato d'argento

silver service n servizio (m) a tavola in cui il cameriere fa il giro dei commensali

silversmith n argentiere m

silverware n argenteria f

silver wedding n nozze fpl d'argento

silvery /'sɪlvərɪ/ adj argentino

SIM card /sɪm/ n carta f SIM

✧ **similar** /'sɪmɪlə(r)/ adj simile

similarity /sɪmɪ'lærətɪ/ n somiglianza f

similarly /'sɪmɪləlɪ/ adv in modo simile

simile /'sɪmɪlɪ/ n similitudine f

simmer /'sɪmə(r)/ **1** vi bollire lentamente
2 vt far bollire lentamente
■ **simmer down** vi calmarsi

simper /'sɪmpə(r)/ vi ostentare un sorriso

simpering /'sɪmp(ə)rɪŋ/ adj ‹smile› affettato; ‹person› smanceroso

✧ **simple** /'sɪmpl/ adj semplice; ‹person› sempliciotto

simple-minded /-'maɪndɪd/ adj sempliciotto

simpleton /'sɪmpltən/ n sempliciotto, -a mf

simplicity /sɪm'plɪsətɪ/ n semplicità f

simplification /sɪmplɪfɪ'keɪʃn/ n semplificazione f

simplify /'sɪmplɪfaɪ/ vt (pt/pp **-ied**) semplificare

simplistic /sɪm'plɪstɪk/ adj semplicistico

✧ **simply** /'sɪmplɪ/ adv semplicemente

simulate /'sɪmjʊleɪt/ vt simulare

simulation /sɪmjʊ'leɪʃn/ n simulazione f

simulator /'sɪmjʊleɪtə(r)/ n simulatore m

simulcast /'sɪməlkɑːst/ vt teleradiotrasmettere

simultaneous /sɪml'teɪnɪəs/ adj simultaneo

simultaneously /sɪməl'teɪnɪəslɪ/ adv simultaneamente

sin /sɪn/ **1** n peccato m
2 vi (pt/pp **sinned**) peccare

✧ **since** /sɪns/ (prep) **1** da; ~ **when?** da quando in qua?
2 adv da allora
3 conj da quando; (because) siccome

sincere /sɪn'sɪə(r)/ adj sincero

sincerely /sɪn'sɪəlɪ/ adv sinceramente; **Yours ~** Distinti saluti

sincerity /sɪn'serətɪ/ n sincerità f

sine /saɪn/ n Math seno m

sinew /'sɪnjuː/ n tendine m

sinful /'sɪnfl/ adj peccaminoso

✧ **sing** /sɪŋ/ vt/i (pt **sang**, pp **sung**) cantare

singalong /'sɪŋəlɒŋ/ n **have a ~** cantare [tutti] insieme

Singapore /ˌsɪŋə'pɔː(r)/ n Singapore f

singe /sɪndʒ/ vt (pres p **-geing**) bruciacchiare

singer /'sɪŋə(r)/ n cantante mf

singer-songwriter /-'sɒŋraɪtə(r)/ n cantautore, -trice mf

singing /'sɪŋɪŋ/ n canto m

✦ **single** /'sɪŋgl/ **1** adj solo; (not double) semplice; (unmarried) celibe; ‹woman› nubile; ‹room› singolo; ‹bed› a una piazza; **I haven't spoken to a ∼ person** non ho parlato con nessuno
2 n (ticket) biglietto m di sola andata; (record) singolo m

■ **single out** vt scegliere; (distinguish) distinguere

single-breasted /-'brestɪd/ adj ad un petto

single cream n panna f da cucina liquida

single currency n (in Europe) moneta f unica

single-decker /-'dekə(r)/ n autobus m inv (a un piano solo)

single file adv in fila indiana

single-handed /-'hændɪd/ adj & adv da solo

single-handedly /-'hændɪdlɪ/ adv da solo

single market n mercato m unico

single-minded /-'maɪndɪd/ adj risoluto

single mother n madre f single inv

single-parent adj ‹family› monoparentale

singles /'sɪŋglz/ npl Tennis singolo m; (people) single mpl; **the women's ∼** il singolo femminile

singles bar n bar ritrovo m inv per single

singles charts npl classifica f inv dei singoli

single-sex adj (for boys) maschile; (for girls) femminile

single-storey adj ‹house› ad un piano

singlet /'sɪŋglɪt/ n Br canottiera f

singly /'sɪŋglɪ/ adv singolarmente

sing-song Br **1** adj ‹voice, dialect› che ha una sua particolare cadenza
2 n **have a ∼** cantare [tutti] insieme

singular /'sɪŋgjʊlə(r)/ **1** adj Gram singolare; (uncommon) eccezionale
2 n singolare m

singularly /'sɪŋgjʊləlɪ/ adv singolarmente

sinister /'sɪnɪstə(r)/ adj sinistro

sink /sɪŋk/ **1** n lavandino m
2 vi (pt **sank**, pp **sunk**) affondare
3 vt affondare ‹ship›; scavare ‹shaft›; investire ‹money›

■ **sink in** vi penetrare; **it took a while to ∼ in** fam (be understood) c'è voluto un po' a capirlo

sinker /'sɪŋkə(r)/ n (in fishing) piombo m; Am Culin ≈ bombolone m

sinking /'sɪŋkɪŋ/ n affondamento m

sink unit n mobile (m) di cucina comprendente il lavandino

sinner /'sɪnə(r)/ n peccatore, -trice mf

sinuous /'sɪnjʊəs/ adj sinuoso

sinus /'saɪnəs/ n seno m paranasale

sinusitis /saɪnə'saɪtɪs/ n sinusite f

sip /sɪp/ **1** n sorso m
2 vt (pt/pp **sipped**) sorseggiare

siphon /'saɪfn/ n (bottle) sifone m

■ **siphon off** vt travasare (con sifone)

✦ **sir** /sɜː(r)/ n signore m; S∼ (title) Sir m; **Dear S∼** Egregio Signore; **Dear S∼s** Spettabile Ditta

sire /saɪə(r)/ vt generare

siren /'saɪrən/ n sirena f

sirloin /'sɜːlɔɪn/ n (of beef) controfiletto m

sirloin steak n bistecca f di controfiletto

sissy /'sɪsɪ/ n femminuccia f

✦ **sister** /'sɪstə(r)/ n sorella f; (nurse) [infermiera] f, caposala f

sisterhood /'sɪstəhʊd/ n Relig congregazione f religiosa femminile; (in feminism) solidarietà f inv femminile

sister-in-law n (pl ∼s-in-law) cognata f

sisterly /'sɪstəlɪ/ adj da sorella

Sistine Chapel /'sɪstiːn/ n Cappella f Sistina

✦ **sit** /sɪt/ **1** vi (pt/pp **sat**, pres p **sitting**) essere seduto; (sit down) sedersi; ‹committee› riunirsi
2 vt sostenere ‹exam›

■ **sit about, sit around** vi stare senza far niente

■ **sit back** vi fig starsene con le mani in mano

■ **sit by** vi starsene a guardare

■ **sit down** vi mettersi a sedere; **please ∼ down** si accomodi; **∼ down!** siediti!

■ **sit for** vi posare per ‹portrait›

■ **sit in** vi (observe) assistere; **∼ in on a class** assistere (da osservatore) a una lezione

■ **sit on** vt far parte di ‹committee›

■ **sit up** vi mettersi seduto; (not slouch) star seduto diritto; (stay up) stare alzato

sitcom /'sɪtkɒm/ n fam situation comedy f inv

sit-down n Br **have a ∼** sedersi un momento

✦ **site** /saɪt/ **1** n posto m; Archaeol sito m; (building) ∼ cantiere m
2 vt collocare

sit-in /'sɪtɪn/ n occupazione f (di fabbrica ecc) sit-in m inv

sitter /'sɪtə(r)/ n (babysitter) baby-sitter mf inv; (for artist) modello m

sitting /'sɪtɪŋ/ n seduta f; (for meals) turno m

sitting duck n fam facile bersaglio m

sitting room n salotto m

sitting target n facile bersaglio m

S

sitting tenant n locatario m residente

situate /'sɪtjʊeɪt/ vt situare

situated /'sɪtjʊeɪtɪd/ adj situato

✧ **situation** /sɪtjʊ'eɪʃn/ n situazione f; (location) posizione f; (job) posto m; '~s vacant' 'offerte di lavoro'

situation report n quadro m della situazione

sit-ups npl addominali mpl

✧ **six** /sɪks/ adj & n sei m

six-pack n confezione f da sei (di bottiglie o lattine)

sixteen /sɪks'ti:n/ adj & n sedici m

sixteenth /sɪks'ti:nθ/ adj & n sedicesimo, -a mf

sixteenth-century adj cinquecentesco

sixth /sɪksθ/ adj & n sesto, -a mf

sixth form n Sch ultimo biennio (m) facoltativo della scuola superiore

sixth form college n Br istituto (m) che prepara studenti dai 16 ai 18 anni agli esami di maturità

sixth sense n sesto senso m

sixties /'sɪkstɪz/ npl (period) the ~ gli anni Sessanta mpl; (age) sessant'anni mpl

sixtieth /'sɪkstɪɪθ/ adj & n sessantesimo, -a mf

sixty /'sɪkstɪ/ adj & n sessanta m

✧ **size** /saɪz/ n dimensioni fpl; (of clothes) taglia f, misura f; (of shoes) numero m; what ~ is the room? che dimensioni ha la stanza?

■ **size up** vt fam valutare

sizeable /'saɪzəbl/ adj piuttosto grande

sizzle /'sɪzl/ vi sfrigolare

skate¹ /skeɪt/ n inv (fish) razza f

skate² ① n pattino m
② vi pattinare

■ **skate over** vt fig glissare su

skateboard /'skeɪtbɔːd/ n skate-board m inv

skateboarder /'skeɪtbɔːdə(r)/ n persona f che va in skate-board

skateboarding /'skeɪtbɔːdɪŋ/ n skateboard m

skater /skeɪt/ n pattinatore, -trice mf

skating /'skeɪtɪŋ/ n pattinaggio m

skating rink n pista f di pattinaggio

skeletal /'skelɪtl/ adj also fig scheletrico; (disease) dello scheletro

skeleton /'skelɪtn/ n scheletro m

skeleton key n passe-partout m inv

skeleton staff n personale m ridotto

skeptic /'skeptɪk/ n Am = SCEPTIC

skeptical /'skeptɪkl/ adj Am = SCEPTICAL

skepticism /'skeptɪsɪzm/ n Am = SCEPTICISM

✧ indicates a very frequent word

sketch /sketʃ/ ① n schizzo m; Theat sketch m inv
② vt fare uno schizzo di

■ **sketch out** vt delineare

sketchbook /'sketʃbʊk/ n (for sketching) album m inv per schizzi; (book of sketches) album m inv di schizzi

sketchily /'sketʃɪlɪ/ adv in modo abbozzato

sketchpad /'sketʃpæd/ n blocco m per schizzi

sketchy /'sketʃɪ/ adj (-ier, -iest) abbozzato

skew /skju:/ vt alterare (figures)

skewer /'skjʊə(r)/ n spiedo m

ski /ski:/ ① n sci m inv
② vi (pt/pp skied, pres p skiing) sciare; go ~ing andare a sciare

ski boot n scarpone m da sci

skid /skɪd/ ① n slittata f; go into a ~ slittare
② vi (pt/pp skidded) slittare

skid mark n segno m di frenata

skier /'ski:ə(r)/ n sciatore, -trice mf

skiing /'ski:ɪŋ/ n sci m inv

ski instructor n maestro, -a mf di sci

ski jump n (competition) salto m con gli sci; (slope) trampolino m

ski jumping n salto m dal trampolino

skilful /'skɪlfl/ adj abile

skilfully /'skɪlfʊlɪ/ adv abilmente

ski lift n impianto m di risalita

✧ **skill** /skɪl/ n abilità f inv

skilled /skɪld/ adj dotato; (worker) specializzato

skillet /'skɪlət/ n Am padella f

skim /skɪm/ vt (pt/pp skimmed) schiumare; scremare (milk)

■ **skim off** vt togliere

■ **skim over** vt sfiorare (surface, subject)

■ **skim through** vt scorrere

skimmed milk /skɪmd/ n latte m scremato

skimp /skɪmp/ vi ~ on lesinare su

skimpy /'skɪmpɪ/ adj (-ier, -iest) succinto

✧ **skin** /skɪn/ ① n pelle f; (on fruit) buccia f; soaked to the ~ fradicio fino all'osso
② vt (pt/pp skinned) spellare

skin cancer n cancro m alla pelle

skincare n cura f della pelle

skin cream n crema f per la pelle

skin-deep adj superficiale

skin diver n sub mf inv

skin diving n nuoto m subacqueo

skinflint /'skɪnflɪnt/ n miserabile mf

skin graft n innesto m epidermico

skinhead /'skɪnhed/ n skinhead m inv

skinny /'skɪnɪ/ adj (-ier, -iest) molto magro

s

skint /skɪnt/ *adj* fam al verde
skintight /skɪnˈtaɪt/ *adj* aderente
skip¹ /skɪp/ *n* (container) benna *f*
skip² **1** *n* salto *m*
   2 *vi* (*pt/pp* **skipped**) saltellare; (with rope) saltare la corda
   3 *vt* omettere
ski pants *npl* pantaloni *mpl* da sci
ski pass *n* ski-pass *m inv*
ski pole *n* bastone *m* da sci
skipper /ˈskɪpə(r)/ *n* skipper *m inv*
skipping /ˈskɪpɪŋ/ *n* salto *m* della corda
skipping rope *n* corda *f* per saltare
ski rack *n* portasci *m inv*
ski resort *n* stazione *f* sciistica
skirmish /ˈskɜːmɪʃ/ *n* scaramuccia *f*
skirt /skɜːt/ **1** *n* gonna *f*
   2 *vt* costeggiare
skirting board /ˈskɜːtɪŋ/ *n* battiscopa *m inv*, zoccolo *m*
ski run *n* pista *f* da sci
ski slope *n* pista *f* da sci
ski stick *n* bastone *m* da sci
ski suit *n* tuta *f* da sci
skit /skɪt/ *n* bozzetto *m* comico
skittish /ˈskɪtɪʃ/ *adj* (difficult to handle) ombroso; (playful) giocherellone
skittle /ˈskɪtl/ *n* birillo *m*
skive /skaɪv/ *vi* fam fare lo scansafatiche
skivvy /ˈskɪvɪ/ *n* Br fam sguattera *f*
ski wax *n* sciolina *f*
skulduggery /skʌlˈdʌgərɪ/ *n* fam imbrogli *mpl*
skulk /skʌlk/ *vi* aggirarsi furtivamente
skull /skʌl/ *n* cranio *m*
skunk /skʌŋk/ *n* moffetta *f*; (person) farabutto *m*
⚥ **sky** /skaɪ/ *n* cielo *m*
skydiving *n* paracadutismo *m* in caduta libera
sky-high **1** *adj* ‹prices› alle stelle; ‹rates› esorbitante
   2 *adv* rise ~ salire alle stelle
skyjacker /ˈskaɪdʒækə(r)/ *n* dirottatore, -trice *mf* aereo
skylight *n* lucernario *m*
skyline *n* (of city) profilo *m*
skyrocket *vi* ‹prices› andare alle stelle
skyscraper *n* grattacielo *m*
slab /slæb/ *n* lastra *f*; (slice) fetta *f*; (of chocolate) tavoletta *f*
slack /slæk/ **1** *adj* lento; ‹person› fiacco
   2 *vi* fare lo scansafatiche
■ **slack off** *vi* rilassarsi
slacken /ˈslækn/ **1** *vi* allentare; ~ [off] ‹trade› rallentare; ‹speed, rain› diminuire
   2 *vt* allentare; diminuire ‹speed›
slacker /ˈslækə(r)/ *n* lazzarone *m*

slacks /slæks/ *npl* pantaloni *mpl* sportivi
slag /slæg/ *n* scorie *fpl*
■ **slag off** *vt* (*pt/pp* **slagged**) Br fam sparlare di
slain /sleɪn/ ▶ SLAY
slalom /ˈslɑːləm/ *n* slalom *m inv*
slam /slæm/ **1** *vt* (*pt/pp* **slammed**) sbattere; fam (criticize) stroncare
   2 *vi* sbattere
slammer /ˈslæmə(r)/ *n* fam (prison) galera *f*
slander /ˈslɑːndə(r)/ **1** *n* diffamazione *f*
   2 *vt* diffamare
slanderer /ˈslɑːndərə(r)/ *n* diffamatore, -trice *mf*
slanderous /ˈslɑːnd(ə)rəs/ *adj* diffamatorio
slang /slæŋ/ *n* gergo *m*
slangy /ˈslæŋɪ/ *adj* gergale
slant /slɑːnt/ **1** *n* pendenza *f*; (point of view) angolazione *f*; **on the ~** in pendenza
   2 *vt* pendere; fig distorcere ‹report›
   3 *vi* pendere
slanted /ˈslɑːntɪd/ *adj* fig ‹report› tendenzioso
slap /slæp/ **1** *n* schiaffo *m*
   2 *vt* (*pt/pp* **slapped**) schiaffeggiare; (put) schiaffare
   3 *adv* in pieno
slap bang *adv* fam he went ~ into the wall è andato a sbattere in pieno contro il muro
slapdash *adj* fam frettoloso
slapstick *n* farsa *f* da torte in faccia
slap-up *adj* fam di prim'ordine
slash /slæʃ/ **1** *n* taglio *m*; Typ barra *f*; Comput slash, *m inv*
   2 *vt* tagliare; ridurre drasticamente ‹prices›; ~ one's wrists svenarsi
slat /slæt/ *n* stecca *f*
slate /sleɪt/ **1** *n* ardesia *f*
   2 *vt* fam fare a pezzi
slater /ˈsleɪtə(r)/ *n* (roofer) addetto *m* alla ricopertura dei tetti con tegole di ardesia; Zool onisco *m*
slatted /ˈslætɪd/ *adj* ‹shutter› a stecche
slaughter /ˈslɔːtə(r)/ **1** *n* macello *m*; (of people) massacro *m*
   2 *vt* macellare; massacrare ‹people›
slaughterhouse /ˈslɔːtəhaʊs/ *n* macello *m*
Slav /slɑːv/ **1** *adj* slavo
   2 *n* slavo, -a *mf*
slave /sleɪv/ **1** *n* schiavo, -a *mf*
   2 *vi* ~ **[away]** lavorare come un negro
slave-driver *n* schiavista *mf*
slavery /ˈsleɪvərɪ/ *n* schiavitù *f*
Slavic /ˈslɑːvɪk/ *adj* slavo
slavish /ˈsleɪvɪʃ/ *adj* servile
slavishly /ˈsleɪvɪʃlɪ/ *adv* in modo servile
Slavonic /sləˈvɒnɪk/ *adj* slavo

S

slaw /slɔ:/ *n* Am = COLESLAW

slay /sleɪ/ *vt* (*pt* **slew**, *pp* **slain**) ammazzare

sleaze /sli:z/ *n* fam (pornography) pornografia *f*; (corruption) corruzione *f*

sleazy /'sli:zɪ/ *adj* (**-ier**, **-iest**) sordido

sled /sled/ **1** *n* slitta *f*
2 *vi* andare in slitta

sledge /sledʒ/ *n* slitta *f*

sledgehammer /'sledʒhæmə(r)/ *n* martello *m*

sleek /sli:k/ *adj* liscio, lucente; (well-fed) pasciuto

ⵕ **sleep** /sli:p/ **1** *n* sonno *m*; **go to ∼** addormentarsi; **put to ∼** far addormentare; **in my ∼** nel sonno; **a good night's ∼** una bella dormita
2 *vi* (*pt/pp* **slept**) dormire; **∼ like a log** dormire come un ghiro; **∼ on it** dormirci sopra; **∼ with somebody** andare a letto con qualcuno
3 *vt* **∼s six** ha sei posti letto
∎ **sleep around** *vi* andare a letto con tutti
∎ **sleep in** *vi* dormire più a lungo

sleeper /'sli:pə(r)/ *n* Rail treno *m* con vagoni letto; (compartment) vagone *m* letto; (on track) traversina *f*; **be a light/heavy ∼** avere il sonno leggero/pesante

sleepily /'sli:pɪlɪ/ *adv* con aria assonnata

sleeping bag *n* sacco *m* a pelo

sleeping car *n* vagone *m* letto

sleeping partner *n* Br Comm socio *m* accomodante

sleeping pill *n* sonnifero *m*

sleeping policeman *n* dosso *m* di rallentamento

sleepless /'sli:plɪs/ *adj* insonne; **have a ∼ night** passare una notte insonne

sleeplessness /'sli:plɪsnɪs/ *n* insonnia *f*

sleepover /'sli:pəʊvə(r)/ *n* **the kids are having a ∼** i bambini hanno invitato degli amichetti a dormire a casa

sleepsuit *n* tutina *f*

sleepwalk *vi* essere sonnambulo

sleepwalker *n* sonnambulo, -a *mf*

sleepwalking *n* sonnambulismo *m*

sleepy /'sli:pɪ/ *adj* (**-ier**, **-iest**) assonnato; **be ∼** aver sonno

sleet /sli:t/ **1** *n* nevischio *m*
2 *vi* **it is ∼ing** nevischia

sleeve /sli:v/ *n* manica *f*; (for record) copertina *f*

sleeveless /'sli:vlɪs/ *adj* senza maniche

sleigh /sleɪ/ *n* slitta *f*

sleight /slaɪt/ *n* **∼ of hand** gioco *m* di prestigio

slender /'slendə(r)/ *adj* snello; ⟨fingers, stem⟩ affusolato; fig scarso; ⟨chance⟩ magro

ⵕ indicates a very frequent word

slept /slept/ ▸ SLEEP

sleuth /slu:θ/ *n* investigatore *m*, detective *m inv*

slew¹ /slu:/ *vi* girare

slew² ▸ SLAY

slice /slaɪs/ **1** *n* fetta *f*
2 *vt* affettare; **∼d bread** pane *m* a cassetta

slick /slɪk/ **1** *adj* liscio; (cunning) astuto
2 *n* (of oil) chiazza *f* di petrolio

slide /slaɪd/ **1** *n* scivolata *f*; (in playground) scivolo *m*; (for hair) fermaglio *m* [per capelli]; Phot diapositiva *f*
2 *vi* (*pt/pp* **slid**) scivolare
3 *vt* far scivolare

slide projector *n* proiettore *m* per diapositive

slide rule *n* regolo *m* calcolatore

slide show *n* proiezione *f* di diapositive

sliding /'slaɪdɪŋ/ *adj* ⟨door, seat⟩ scorrevole

sliding scale *n* scala *f* mobile

slight /slaɪt/ **1** *adj* leggero; ⟨importance⟩ poco; (slender) esile; **∼est** minimo; **not in the ∼est** niente affatto
2 *vt* offendere
3 *n* offesa *f*

ⵕ **slightly** /'slaɪtlɪ/ *adv* leggermente

slim /slɪm/ **1** *adj* (**slimmer**, **slimmest**) snello; fig scarso; ⟨chance⟩ magro
2 *vi* dimagrire

slime /slaɪm/ *n* melma *f*

slimy /'slaɪmɪ/ *adj* melmoso; fig viscido

sling /slɪŋ/ **1** *n* Med benda *f* al collo
2 *vt* (*pt/pp* **slung**) fam lanciare

sling-back *n* sandalo *m* (chiuso davanti)

slingshot /'slɪŋʃɒt/ *n* fionda *f*

slink /slɪŋk/ *vi* (*pt/pp* **slunk**) entrare furtivamente

slinky /'slɪŋkɪ/ *adj* fam ⟨dress⟩ sexy *inv*, attillato

ⵕ **slip** /slɪp/ **1** *n* scivolata *f*; (mistake) lieve errore *m*; (petticoat) sottoveste *f*; (for pillow) federa *f*; (paper) scontrino *m*; **give somebody the ∼** fam sbarazzarsi di qualcuno; **∼ of the tongue** lapsus *m inv*
2 *vi* (*pt/pp* **slipped**) scivolare; (go quickly) sgattaiolare; (decline) retrocedere; **let something ∼** (reveal) lasciarsi sfuggire qualcosa
3 *vt* he **∼ped it into his pocket** se l'è infilato in tasca; **∼ sb's mind** sfuggire di mente a qualcuno
∎ **slip away** *vi* sgusciar via; ⟨time⟩ sfuggire
∎ **slip into** *vi* infilarsi ⟨clothes⟩
∎ **slip on** *vt* infilarsi ⟨jacket etc⟩
∎ **slip up** *vi* fam sbagliare

slip-knot *n* nodo *m* scorsoio

slip-on [shoe] *n* mocassino *m*

slipped disc /slɪpt'dɪsk/ *n* Med ernia *f* del disco

slipper /'slɪpə(r)/ *n* pantofola *f*

S

slippery /'slɪpərɪ/ *adj* scivoloso
slip road *n* bretella *f*
slipshod /'slɪpʃɒd/ *adj* trascurato
slip-up *n* fam sbaglio *m*
slit /slɪt/ ① *n* spacco *m*; (tear) strappo *m*; (hole) fessura *f*
  ② *vt* (*pt/pp* **slit**) tagliare
slither /'slɪðə(r)/ *vi* scivolare
sliver /'slɪvə(r)/ *n* scheggia *f*
slob /slɒb/ *n* fam (messy) maiale *m*; (lazy) pelandrone *m*
slobber /'slɒbə(r)/ *vi* sbavare
sloe /sləʊ/ *n* (fruit) prugnola *f*; (bush) prugnolo *m*
slog /slɒg/ ① *n* [hard] ~ sgobbata *f*
  ② *vi* (*pt/pp* **slogged**) (work) sgobbare
slogan /'sləʊgən/ *n* slogan *m inv*
slop /slɒp/ *vt* (*pt/pp* **slopped**) versare
■ **slop over** *vi* versarsi
slope /sləʊp/ ① *n* pendenza *f*; (ski) ~ pista *f*; pista *f*
  ② *vi* essere inclinato, inclinarsi
■ **slope off** *vi* scantonare
sloping /'sləʊpɪŋ/ *adj* in pendenza
sloppiness /'slɒpɪnɪs/ *n* (of work) trascuratezza *f*
sloppy /'slɒpɪ/ *adj* (**-ier, -iest**) ‹work› trascurato; ‹worker› negligente; (in dress) sciatto; (sentimental) sdolcinato
slosh /slɒʃ/ ① *vi* fam ‹person, feet› sguazzare; ‹water› scrosciare
  ② *vt* fam (hit) colpire
sloshed /slɒʃt/ *adj* fam sbronzo
slot /slɒt/ ① *n* fessura *f*; (time-~) spazio *m*
  ② *vt* (*pt/pp* **slotted**) infilare
■ **slot in** *vi* incastrarsi
■ **slot together** *vi* ‹pieces› incastrarsi
sloth /sləʊθ/ *n* accidia *f*
slot machine *n* distributore *m* automatico; (for gambling) slot-machine *f inv*
slouch /slaʊtʃ/ *vi* (in chair) stare scomposto
Slovak /'sləʊvæk/ *adj & n* slovacco, -a *mf*
Slovakia /sləʊ'vækɪə/ *n* Slovacchia *f*
Slovene /'sləʊviːn/ *adj & n* sloveno, -a *mf*
Slovenia /sləʊ'viːnɪə/ *n* Slovenia *f*
slovenliness /'slʌvənlɪnɪs/ *n* sciatteria *f*
slovenly /'slʌvnlɪ/ *adj* sciatto
slow /sləʊ/ ① *adj* lento; be ~ ‹clock› essere indietro; in ~ motion al rallentatore
  ② *adv* lentamente
■ **slow down** *vt/i* rallentare
■ **slow up** *vt/i* rallentare
slowcoach /'sləʊkəʊtʃ/ *n* fam tartaruga *f*
slowly /'sləʊlɪ/ *adv* lentamente
slow-moving *adj* ‹film, river› lento
slowness /'sləʊnɪs/ *n* lentezza *f*
slow puncture *n* foratura *f*
sludge /slʌdʒ/ *n* fanghiglia *f*
slug /slʌg/ *n* lumacone *m*; (bullet) pallottola *f*

sluggish /'slʌgɪʃ/ *adj* lento
sluggishly /'slʌgɪʃnɪs/ *adv* lentamente
sluice /sluːs/ *n* chiusa *f*
sluice gate *n* saracinesca *f* (di chiusa)
slum /slʌm/ *n* (house) tugurio *m*; ~s *pl* bassifondi *mpl*
slumber /'slʌmbə(r)/ ① *n* sonno *m*
  ② *vi* dormire
slump /slʌmp/ ① *n* crollo *m*; (economic) depressione *f*
  ② *vi* crollare
slung /slʌŋ/ ▶ SLING
slunk /slʌŋk/ ▶ SLINK
slur /slɜː(r)/ ① *n* (discredit) calunnia *f*
  ② *vt* (*pt/pp* **slurred**) biascicare
slurp /slɜːp/ *vt/i* bere rumorosamente
slurry /'slʌrɪ/ *n* (waste from animals) liquame *m*; (waste from factory) fanghiglia *f* semiliquida; (of cement) impasto *m* semiliquido
slush /slʌʃ/ *n* pantano *m* nevoso; fig sdolcinatezza *f*
slush fund *n* fondi *mpl* neri
slushy /'slʌʃɪ/ *adj* fangoso; (sentimental) sdolcinato
slut /slʌt/ *n* sgualdrina *f*
sly /slaɪ/ ① *adj* (**-ier, -iest**) scaltro
  ② *n* on the ~ di nascosto
slyly /'slaɪlɪ/ *adv* scaltramente
SM *n abbr* (**sadomasochism**) sadomasochismo
smack¹ /smæk/ ① *n* (on face) schiaffo *m*; (on bottom) sculaccione *m*
  ② *vt* (on face) schiaffeggiare; (on bottom) sculacciare; ~ one's lips far schioccare le labbra
  ③ *adv* fam in pieno
smack² *vi* ~ of fig sapere di
smacker /'smækə(r)/ *n* fam (kiss) bacio *m*; 500 ~s (£500) 500 sterline
♂ **small** /smɔːl/ ① *adj* piccolo; be out/work until the ~ hours fare le ore piccole
  ② *adv* chop up ~ fare a pezzettini
  ③ *n* the ~ of the back le reni
small ads *npl* annunci *mpl* [commerciali]
small business *n* piccola impresa *f*
small change *n* spiccioli *mpl*
small-holding *n* piccola tenuta *f*
small hours *npl* ore *fpl* piccole
small letter *n* lettera *f* minuscola
small-minded /-'maɪndɪd/ *adj* meschino
smallpox *n* vaiolo *m*
small print *n* caratteri *mpl* piccoli; read the ~ fig leggere tutto fin nei minimi particolari
small talk *n* chiacchiere *fpl*; make ~ fare conversazione
smarmy /'smɑːmɪ/ *adj* (**-ier, -iest**) fam untuoso

S

✔ **smart** /smɑːt/ 1 *adj* elegante; (clever) intelligente; (brisk) svelto; **be** ~ fam (cheeky) fare il furbo
2 *vi* (hurt) bruciare

smart alec[k] /'smɑːtælɪk/ *n* fam sapientone *m*

smart bomb *n* bomba *f* intelligente

smart card *n* carta *f* intelligente

smarten /'smɑːt(ə)n/ *vt* ~ oneself up farsi bello

smartly /'smɑːtlɪ/ *adv* elegantemente; (cleverly) intelligentemente; (briskly) velocemente; (cheekily) sfacciatamente

smart money *n* fam the ~ was on Desert Orchid gli esperti hanno puntato su Desert Orchid

smartphone *n* smartphone *m inv*

smash /smæʃ/ 1 *n* fragore *m*; (collision) scontro *m*; Tennis schiacciata *f*
2 *vt* spaccare; Tennis schiacciare
3 *vi* spaccarsi; (crash) schiantarsi (**into** contro)
■ **smash up** *vt* distruggere ‹car, bar›

smash [hit] *n* successo *m*

smash-and-grab *n* Br rapina *f* ad un negozio (*con sfascio di vetrina*)

smashed /smæʃt/ *adj* ‹window› in frantumi; ‹vehicle› sfasciato; ‹limb› fracassato; fam (on drugs) fatto; fam (on alcohol) ubriaco fradicio

smashing /'smæʃɪŋ/ *adj* fam fantastico

smattering /'smætərɪŋ/ *n* infarinatura *f*

smear /smɪə(r)/ 1 *n* macchia *f*; Med striscio *m*
2 *vt* imbrattare; (coat) spalmare (**with** di); fig calunniare
3 *vi* sbavare

smear campaign *n* campagna *f* diffamatoria

smear test *n* Med striscio *m*, Pap test *m inv*

smell /smel/ 1 *n* odore *m*; (sense) odorato *m*
2 *vt* (*pt/pp* **smelt** or **smelled**) odorare (of di); **that** ~**s good** ha un buon odore

smelling salts /'smelɪŋ/ *npl* Med sali *mpl*

smelly /'smelɪ/ *adj* (**-ier, -iest**) puzzolente

smelt[1] /smelt/ ▶ SMELL

smelt[2] *vt* fondere

smidgeon /'smɪdʒɪn/ *n* (of something to eat) pizzico *m*; (of something to drink) goccio *m*

✔ **smile** /smaɪl/ 1 *n* sorriso *m*
2 *vi* sorridere; ~ **at** sorridere a ‹somebody›; sorridere di ‹something›
■ **smile on** *vt* ‹weather, fortune› sorridere a ‹person›

smiley /'smaɪlɪ/ *n* fam smiley *m inv*, faccina *f* sorridente

smirk /smɜːk/ 1 *n* sorriso *m* compiaciuto
2 *vi* sorridere con aria compiaciuta

smithereens /smɪðə'riːnz/ *npl* **to/in** ~ in mille pezzi

smithy /'smɪðɪ/ *n* fucina *f*

smitten /'smɪtn/ *adj* ~ **with** tutto preso da

smock /smɒk/ *n* grembiule *m*

smog /smɒg/ *n* smog *m inv*

smoke /sməʊk/ 1 *n* fumo *m*
2 *vt/i* fumare

smoke alarm *n* allarme *m* antifumo *inv*

smoked /sməʊkt/ *adj* affumicato

smoke-free zone *n* zona *f* non-fumatori; '~' 'vietato fumare'

smokeless /'sməʊklɪs/ *adj* senza fumo; ‹fuel› che non fa fumo

smoker /'sməʊkə(r)/ *n* fumatore, -trice *mf*; Rail vagone *m* fumatori

smokescreen /'sməʊkskriːn/ *n* also fig cortina *f* di fumo

smoking /'sməʊkɪŋ/ *n* fumo *m*; '**no** ~' 'vietato fumare'; '~ **or non-**~?' 'fumatori o non fumatori?'

smoking-related *adj* ‹illness› legato al fumo

smoky /'sməʊkɪ/ *adj* (**-ier, -iest**) fumoso; ‹taste› di fumo

smooch /smuːtʃ/ *vi* fam pomiciare

smooth /smuːð/ 1 *adj* liscio; ‹movement› scorrevole; ‹sea› calmo; ‹manners› mellifluo
2 *vt* lisciare; ~ **things over** sistemare le cose
■ **smooth out** *vt* lisciare

smoothly /'smuːðlɪ/ *adv* in modo scorrevole; **go** ~ andare liscio

smooth-running *adj* ‹event, service› ben organizzato

smooth-tongued /-'tʌŋd/ *adj* pej mellifluo

smother /'smʌðə(r)/ *vt* soffocare

smoulder /'sməʊldə(r)/ *vi* fumare; (with rage) consumarsi

SMS *n abbr* (**short message service**) SMS *m*

SMS message *n* sms *m inv*

smudge /smʌdʒ/ 1 *n* macchia *f*
2 *vt/i* imbrattare

smug /smʌg/ *adj* (**smugger, smuggest**) compiaciuto

smuggle /'smʌgl/ *vt* contrabbandare

smuggler /'smʌglə(r)/ *n* contrabbandiere, -a *mf*

smuggling /'smʌglɪŋ/ *n* contrabbando *m*

smugly /'smʌglɪ/ *adv* con aria compiaciuta

smugness /'smʌgnɪs/ *n* compiacimento *m*

smut /smʌt/ *n* macchia *f* di fuliggine; fig sconcezza *f*

smutty /'smʌtɪ/ *adj* (**-ier, -iest**) fuligginoso; fig sconcio

snack /snæk/ *n* spuntino *m*

snack-bar *n* snack bar *m inv*

✔ indicates a very frequent word

snag[1] /snæg/ *n* (problem) intoppo *m*

snag[2] *vt* smagliarsi ‹*tights*› (**on** con)

snail /sneɪl/ *n* lumaca *f*; **at a ~'s pace** a passo di lumaca

snail mail *n* fam posta (*f*) tradizionale, così chiamata dagli utenti di email

snake /sneɪk/ *n* serpente *m*

snakebite *n* morso *m* di serpente

snake charmer *n* incantatore, -trice *mf* di serpenti

snakes and ladders *n* Br gioco *m* dell'oca

snap /snæp/ **1** *n* colpo *m* secco; (photo) istantanea *f*
2 *attrib* ‹*decision*› istantaneo
3 *vi* (*pt/pp* **snapped**) (break) spezzarsi
4 *vt* (break) spezzare; (say) dire seccamente; Phot fare un'istantanea di; schioccare ‹*fingers*›
∎ **snap at** ‹*dog*› cercare di azzannare; ‹*person*› parlare seccamente a
∎ **snap off**: *vt* ~ sb's head off fam aggredire qualcuno
∎ **snap out**: *vi* ~ out of it venirne fuori
∎ **snap up** *vt* afferrare

snappy /'snæpɪ/ *adj* (**-ier, -iest**) scorbutico; (smart) elegante; **make it ~!** sbrigati!

snapshot /'snæpʃɒt/ *n* istantanea *f*

snare /sneə(r)/ *n* trappola *f*

snarl /snɑːl/ **1** *n* ringhio *m*
2 *vi* ringhiare

snarled-up /snɑːld'ʌp/ *adj* ‹*traffic*› bloccato

snarl-up *n* (in traffic, network) ingorgo *m*

snatch /snætʃ/ **1** *n* strappo *m*; (fragment) brano *m*; (theft) scippo *m*; **make a ~ at something** cercare di afferrare qualcosa
2 *vt* strappare [di mano] (**from** a); (steal) scippare; rapire ‹*child*›

snazzy /'snæzɪ/ *adj* fam sciccoso

sneak /sniːk/ **1** *n* fam (devious person) tipo, -a *mf* subdolo; Br fam (telltale) spia *f*
2 *vt* fam (steal) fregare; rubare ‹*kiss*›; **~ a glance at** dare una sbirciatina a
3 *vi* Br fam (tell tales) fare la spia
4 *attrib* ‹*visit*› furtivo; **have a ~ preview of something** vedere qualcosa in anteprima
∎ **sneak away** *vi* sgattaiolare via
∎ **sneak in** *vi* sgattaiolare dentro
∎ **sneak out** *vi* sgattaiolare fuori

sneakers /'sniːkəz/ *npl* Am scarpe *fpl* da ginnastica

sneaking /'sniːkɪŋ/ *adj* furtivo; ‹*suspicion*› vago

sneaky /'sniːkɪ/ *adj* sornione

sneer /snɪə(r)/ **1** *n* ghigno *m*
2 *vi* sogghignare; **~ at** (mock) ridere di

sneeze /sniːz/ **1** *n* starnuto *m*
2 *vi* starnutire; **it's not to be ~d at** non ci sputerei sopra

snide /snaɪd/ *adj* fam insinuante

sniff /snɪf/ **1** *n* (of dog) annusata *f*; **give a ~** ‹*person*› tirare su col naso
2 *vi* tirare su col naso
3 *vt* odorare ‹*flower*›; sniffare ‹*glue*›; ‹*dog*› annusare

sniffer dog /'snɪfə/ *n* cane *m* poliziotto (antidroga, antiterrorismo)

sniffle /'snɪfl/ **1** *n* **have a ~ or the ~s** (slight cold) avere un po' di raffreddore; **give a ~** tirar su col naso
2 *vi* tirar su col naso

sniffy /'snɪfɪ/ *adj* fam (haughty) con la puzza sotto il naso

snigger /'snɪgə(r)/ **1** *n* risatina *f* soffocata
2 *vi* ridacchiare

snip /snɪp/ **1** *n* taglio *m*; fam (bargain) affare *m*
2 *vt/t* ~ **[at]** tagliare
∎ **snip off** *vt* tagliare via ‹*corner, end*›

snipe /snaɪp/ *vi* ~ **at** tirare su; fig sparare a zero su

sniper /'snaɪpə(r)/ *n* cecchino *m*

snippet /'snɪpɪt/ *n* **a ~ of information/ news** una breve notizia/informazione

snivel /'snɪvl/ *vi* (*pt/pp* **snivelled**) piagnucolare

snivelling /'snɪv(ə)lɪŋ/ *adj* piagnucoloso

snob /snɒb/ *n* snob *mf inv*

snobbery /'snɒbərɪ/ *n* snobismo *m*

snobbish /'snɒbɪʃ/ *adj* da snob; **be ~** ‹*person*› essere uno/una snob; ‹*club etc*› essere molto snob

snobbishness /'snɒbɪʃnɪs/ *n* snobismo *m*

snog /snɒg/ *vi* Br sl pomiciare

snooker /'snuːkə(r)/ **1** *n* (game) snooker *m*; (shot) impallatura *f*
2 *vt* Sport impallare; fig mettere in difficoltà

snoop /snuːp/ **1** *n* spia *f*
2 *vi* fam curiosare

snooper /'snuːpə(r)/ *n* ficcanaso *mf*

snooty /'snuːtɪ/ *adj* fam sdegnoso

snooze /snuːz/ **1** *n* sonnellino *m*
2 *vi* fare un sonnellino

snore /snɔː(r)/ *vi* russare

snoring /'snɔːrɪŋ/ *n* il russare

snorkel /'snɔːkl/ *n* respiratore *m*

snorkelling Br, **snorkeling** Am /'snɔːklɪŋ/ *n* snorkelling *m inv*

snort /snɔːt/ **1** *n* sbuffo *m*
2 *vi* sbuffare
3 *vt* fiutare ‹*cocaine*›

snot /snɒt/ *n* fam (mucus) moccolo *m*

snotty /'snɒtɪ/ *adj* fam ‹*nose*› moccioso; (disagreeable) sgradevole

snotty-nosed kid /-nəʊzd/ *n* moccioso, -a *mf*

snout /snaʊt/ *n* grugno *m*

snow /snəʊ/ **1** *n* neve *f*   ····▶

S

2 *vi* nevicare; ~ed under with fig sommerso di

snowball **1** *n* palla *f* di neve
2 *vi* fig fare a palle di neve

snowboard /'snəʊbɔːd/ **1** *n* snowboard *m inv*
2 *vi* fare snowboard

snowboarding /'snəʊbɔːdɪŋ/ *n* snowboard *m inv*

snowdrift *n* cumulo *m* di neve

snowdrop *n* bucaneve *m inv*

snowfall *n* nevicata *f*

snowflake *n* fiocco *m* di neve

snowman *n* pupazzo *m* di neve

snowmobile /'snəʊməbiːl/ *n* gatto *m* delle nevi

snowplough *n* spazzaneve *m inv*

snowshoe *n* racchetta *f* da neve

snowstorm *n* tormenta *f*

snow tyres *npl* pneumatici *mpl* chiodati

snowy /'snəʊɪ/ *adj* nevoso

Snr *abbr* (**Senior**) senior

snub /snʌb/ **1** *n* sgarbo *m*
2 *vt* (*pt/pp* **snubbed**) snobbare

snub-nosed /'snʌbnəʊzd/ *adj* dal naso all'insù

snuff¹ /snʌf/ *n* tabacco *m* da fiuto

snuff² *vt* ~ [out] spegnere ‹candle›; ~ it fam tirare le cuoia

snug /snʌg/ *adj* (**snugger**, **snuggest**) comodo; (tight) aderente

snuggle /'snʌgl/ *vi* rannicchiarsi (**up to** accanto a)

♂ **so** /səʊ/ **1** *adv* così; **so far** finora; **so am I** anch'io; **I see** così pare; **you've left the door open–so I have!** hai lasciato la porta aperta–è vero!; **that is so** è così; **so much** così tanto; **so much the better** tanto meglio; **so it is** proprio così; **if so** se è così; **so as to** in modo da; **so long!** fam a presto!
2 *pron* **I hope/think/am afraid so** spero/penso/temo di sì; **I told you so** te l'ho detto; **because I say so** perché lo dico io; **I did so!** l'ho fatto!; **so saying/doing,…** così dicendo/facendo,…; **or so** circa; **very much so** sì, molto; **and so forth** *or* **on** e così via
3 *conj* (therefore) perciò; (in order that) così; **so that** affinché; **so there!** ecco!; **so what?** e allora?; **so where have you been?** allora, dove sei stato?

soak /səʊk/ **1** *vt* mettere a bagno
2 *vi* stare a bagno
■ **soak in** *vi* penetrare
■ **soak into** *vt* ‹liquid› penetrare
■ **soak up** *vt* assorbire

soaked /səʊkt/ *adj* fradicio; ~ **in** something impregnato di qualcosa

soaking /'səʊkɪŋ/ **1** *n* ammollo *m*
2 *adj & adv* ~ **[wet]** fam inzuppato

♂ indicates a very frequent word

so-and-so *n* tal dei tali *mf*; (euphemism) specie *f* di imbecille

soap /səʊp/ *n* sapone *m*

soap opera *n* telenovella *f*, soap opera *f inv*

soap powder *n* detersivo *m* in polvere

soapy /'səʊpɪ/ *adj* (**-ier, -iest**) insaponato

soar /sɔː(r)/ *vi* elevarsi; ‹prices› salire alle stelle

soaring /'sɔːrɪŋ/ *adj* ‹costs, temperatures, inflation› in forte aumento

sob /sɒb/ **1** *n* singhiozzo *m*
2 *vi* (*pt/pp* **sobbed**) singhiozzare

S.O.B. *n abbr* pej Am (**son of a bitch**) figlio *m* di puttana

sobbing /'sɒbɪŋ/ *n* singhiozzi *mpl*

sober /'səʊbə(r)/ *adj* sobrio; (serious) serio
■ **sober up** *vi* ritornare sobrio

soberly /'səʊbəlɪ/ *adv* sobriamente; (seriously) con aria seria

sobriety /sə'braɪətɪ/ *n* (not drinking) sobrietà *f*; (seriousness) serietà *f*

sob story *n* storia *f* lacrimevole

so-called /'səʊkɔːld/ *adj* cosiddetto

soccer /'sɒkə(r)/ *n* calcio *m*

soccer pitch *n* campo *m* di calcio

soccer player *n* giocatore *m* di calcio

sociable /'səʊʃəbl/ *adj* socievole

♂ **social** /'səʊʃl/ *adj* sociale; (sociable) socievole

social climber *n* arrampicatore, -trice *mf* sociale

social climbing *n* arrivismo *m* sociale

social club *n* circolo *m* sociale

socialism /'səʊʃəlɪzm/ *n* socialismo *m*

socialist /'səʊʃəlɪst/ **1** *adj* socialista
2 *n* socialista *mf*

socialite /'səʊʃəlaɪt/ *n* persona *f* che fa vita mondana

socialize /'səʊʃəlaɪz/ *vi* socializzare

socially /'səʊʃəlɪ/ *adv* socialmente; **know somebody** ~ frequentare qualcuno

social mobility *n* mobilità *f* sociale

social networking site *n* sito *m* di rete sociale

social science *n* scienze *fpl* sociali

social security *n* previdenza *f* sociale

social services *npl* servizi *mpl* sociali

social work *n* assistenza *f* sociale

social worker *n* assistente *mf* sociale

♂ **society** /sə'saɪətɪ/ *n* società *f inv*

socio-economic /səʊsɪəʊiːkə'nɒmɪk/ *adj* socioeconomico

sociological /səʊsɪə'lɒdʒɪkl/ *adj* sociologico

sociologist /səʊsɪ'ɒlədʒɪst/ *n* sociologo, -a *mf*

sociology /səʊsɪ'ɒlədʒɪ/ *n* sociologia *f*

sock¹ /sɒk/ *n* calzino *m*; (kneelength) calzettone *m*

s

sock² fam ① *n* pugno *m*
  ② *vt* dare un pugno a

socket /'sɒkɪt/ *n* (of eye) orbita *f*; (wall plug) presa *f* [di corrente]; (for bulb) portalampada *m inv*

sod /sɒd/ *n* fam stronzo *m*; **you lucky** ∼! che fortuna sfacciata!
  ■ **sod off** *vi* fam togliersi dai piedi

soda /'səʊdə/ *n* soda *f*; Am gazzosa *f*

soda water *n* seltz *m inv*

sodden /'sɒdn/ *adj* inzuppato

sodium /'səʊdɪəm/ *n* sodio *m*

sodium bicarbonate *n* bicarbonato *m* di sodio

Sod's Law /sɒdz/ *n* (fam hum) *regola (f) per cui, se qualcosa può andare storto, va storto*

sofa /'səʊfə/ *n* divano *m*

sofa bed *n* divano *m* letto

♂ **soft** /sɒft/ *adj* morbido, soffice; ‹voice› sommesso; ‹light, colour› tenue; (not strict) indulgente; fam (silly) stupido

soft-boiled /-'bɔɪld/ *adj* ‹egg› bazzotto

soft contact lenses *npl* lenti *fpl* a contatto morbide

soft drink *n* bibita *f* analcolica

soft drug *n* droga *f* leggera

soften /'sɒfn/ ① *vt* ammorbidire; fig attenuare
  ② *vi* ammorbidirsi
  ■ **soften up** ① *vi* ammorbidirsi
  ② *vt* ∼ **somebody up** ammorbidire qualcuno ‹opponent, enemy, customer›

softener /'sɒf(ə)nə(r)/ *n* (for water) dolcificatore *m*; (substance) anti-calcare *m inv*; (for fabrics) ammorbidente *m*

soft furnishings *npl* tappeti *mpl* e tessuti *mpl* da arredamento

soft-hearted *adj* dal cuore tenero

soft ice-cream *n* mantecato *m*

softie /'sɒftɪ/ *n* fam = SOFTY

softly /'sɒftlɪ/ *adv* (say) sottovoce; ‹treat› con indulgenza; ‹play music› in sottofondo

soft option *n* take the ∼ scegliere la soluzione più semplice

soft-pedal *vt* fig minimizzare

soft porn *n* fam pornografia *f* soft[-core]

soft sell *n metodo (m) di vendita basato sulla persuasione*

soft skills *n pl le capacità relazionali quali la capacità di comunicare, di persuadere, di identificarsi con gli altri, ecc.*

soft soap *n* fig lusinghe *fpl*

soft-soap *vt* fig lusingare

soft-spoken *adj* dalla voce dolce

soft spot *n* have a ∼ for somebody fam avere un debole per qualcuno

soft-top *n* Auto decappottabile *f*

soft touch *n* be a ∼ lasciarsi spremere

soft toy *n* pupazzo *m* di peluche

♂ **software** /'sɒftweə(r)/ *n* software *m*

software engineer *n* softwarista *mf*

software house *n* software house *f*

software package *n* pacchetto *m* software

software piracy *n* pirateria *f* informatica

software writer *n* scrittore, -trice *mf* di programmi

softy /'sɒftɪ/ *n* fam (weak person) pappamolle *mf inv*; (indulgent person) bonaccione, -a *mf*

soggy /'sɒgɪ/ *adj* (-ier, -iest) zuppo

♂ **soil¹** /sɔɪl/ *n* suolo *m*

soil² *vt* sporcare

soiled /sɔɪld/ *adj* sporco

solace /'sɒləs/ *n* sollievo *m*

solar /'səʊlə(r)/ *adj* solare

solar eclipse *n* eclissi *f inv* di sole

solar energy *n* energia *f* solare

solar panel *n* pannello *m* solare

solar power *n* energia *f* solare

solar system *n* sistema *m* solare

sold /səʊld/ ▶ SELL

solder /'səʊldə(r)/ ① *n* lega *f* da saldatura
  ② *vt* saldare

♂ **soldier** /'səʊldʒə(r)/ *n* soldato *m*
  ■ **soldier on** *vi* perseverare

sole¹ /səʊl/ *n* (of foot) pianta *f*; (of shoe) suola *f*

sole² *n* (fish) sogliola *f*

sole³ *adj* unico, solo

sole agency *n* rappresentanza *f* esclusiva

solecism /'sɒlɪsɪzm/ *n* (social) scorrettezza *f*; (linguistic) solecismo *m*

solely /'səʊllɪ/ *adv* unicamente

solemn /'sɒləm/ *adj* solenne

solemnity /sə'lemnətɪ/ *n* solennità *f inv*

solemnly /'sɒləmlɪ/ *adv* solennemente

sol-fa /'sɒlfɑː/ *n* solfeggio *m*

solicit /sə'lɪsɪt/ ① *vt* sollecitare
  ② *vi* ‹prostitute› adescare

soliciting /sə'lɪsɪtɪŋ/ *n* Jur adescamento *m*

solicitor /sə'lɪsɪtə(r)/ *n* avvocato *m*

solicitous /sə'lɪsɪtəs/ *adj* premuroso

solicitously /sə'lɪsɪtəslɪ/ *adv* premurosamente

♂ **solid** /'sɒlɪd/ ① *adj* solido; ‹oak, gold› massiccio; **it took a** ∼ **hour** ci è voluta ben un'ora
  ② *n* (figure) solido *m*; ∼**s** *pl* (food) cibi *mpl* solidi

solidarity /sɒlɪ'dærətɪ/ *n* solidarietà *f inv*

solidify /sə'lɪdɪfaɪ/ *vi* (*pt/pp* -**ied**) solidificarsi

soliloquy /sə'lɪləkwɪ/ *n* soliloquio *m*

solitaire /sɒlɪ'teə(r)/ *n* solitario *m*

S

solitary /'sɒlɪtərɪ/ *adj* solitario; (sole) solo

solitary confinement *n* cella *f* di isolamento

solitude /'sɒlɪtjuːd/ *n* solitudine *f*

solo /'səʊləʊ/ **1** *n* Mus assolo *m*
2 *adj* ‹flight› in solitario
3 *adv* in solitario

soloist /'səʊləʊɪst/ *n* solista *mf*

solstice /'sɒlstɪs/ *n* solstizio *m*

soluble /'sɒljʊbl/ *adj* solubile

💰 **solution** /sə'luːʃn/ *n* soluzione *f*

solvable /'sɒlvəbl/ *adj* risolvibile

💰 **solve** /sɒlv/ *vt* risolvere

solvency /'sɒlvənsɪ/ *n* Fin solvibilità *f*

solvent /'sɒlvənt/ *adj & n* solvente *m*

solvent abuse *n* uso (*m*) *di solventi come stupefacenti*

Somali /səʊ'mɑːlɪ/ *adj & n* somalo, -a *mf*

Somalia /səʊ'mɑːlɪə/ *n* Somalia *f*

sombre /'sɒmbə(r)/ *adj* tetro; ‹clothes› scuro

💰 **some** /sʌm/ **1** *adj* (a certain amount of) del; (a certain number of) alcuni, dei; ~ **bread/water** del pane/dell'acqua; ~ **books/oranges** dei libri/delle arance; **I need** ~ **money/books** ho bisogno di soldi/libri; **do** ~ **shopping** fare qualche acquisto; ~ **day** un giorno o l'altro
2 *pron* (a certain amount) un po'; (a certain number) alcuni; **I want** ~ ne voglio; **would you like** ~**?** ne vuoi?; ~ **of the butter** una parte del burro; ~ **of the apples/women** alcune delle mele/donne

💰 **somebody** /'sʌmbədɪ/ **1** *pron* qualcuno *m*; ~ **else will bring it** la porterà un altro
2 *n* he thinks he's ~ si crede chissà chi

💰 **somehow** /'sʌmhaʊ/ *adv* in qualche modo; ~ **or other** in un modo o nell'altro

💰 **someone** /'sʌmwʌn/ *pron & n* = SOMEBODY

💰 **somersault** /'sʌməsɔːlt/ **1** *n* capriola *f*; **turn a** ~ fare una capriola
2 *vi* fare una capriola

💰 **something** /'sʌmθɪŋ/ *pron* qualche cosa, qualcosa; ~ **different** qualcosa di diverso; ~ **like** un po' come; (approximately) qualcosa come; **see** ~ **of somebody** vedere qualcuno ogni tanto; **she is** ~ **of an expert** è un'esperta

sometime /'sʌmtaɪm/ **1** *adv* un giorno o l'altro; ~ **last summer** durante l'estate scorsa
2 *adj* ex

💰 **sometimes** /'sʌmtaɪmz/ *adv* qualche volta

💰 **somewhat** /'sʌmwɒt/ *adv* piuttosto

💰 **somewhere** /'sʌmweə(r)/ **1** *adv* da qualche parte
2 *pron* ~ **to eat** un posto in cui mangiare

💰 **son** /sʌn/ *n* figlio *m*

💰 indicates a very frequent word

sonar /'səʊnɑː(r)/ *n* sonar *m*

sonata /sə'nɑːtə/ *n* sonata *f*

💰 **song** /sɒŋ/ *n* canzone *f*

song and dance *n* make a ~ about something (fuss) far tante storie per qualcosa

songbird *n* uccello *m* canoro

songwriter *n* compositore, -trice *mf* di canzoni

sonic /'sɒnɪk/ *adj* sonico

sonic boom *n* bang *m inv* sonico

son-in-law *n* (*pl* ~**s-in-law**) genero *m*

sonnet /'sɒnɪt/ *n* sonetto *m*

son of a bitch *n* fam figlio *m* di un cane

sonorous /'sɒnərəs/ *adj* sonoro; ‹name› altisonante

💰 **soon** /suːn/ *adv* presto; (in a short time) tra poco; **as** ~ **as** [non] appena; **as** ~ **as possible** il più presto possibile; ~**er or later** prima o poi; **the** ~**er the better** prima è meglio è; **no** ~**er had I arrived than…** ero appena arrivato quando…; **I would** ~**er go** preferirei andare; ~ **after** subito dopo

soot /sʊt/ *n* fuliggine *f*

soothe /suːð/ *vt* calmare

soothing /'suːðɪŋ/ *adj* calmante

sooty /'sʊtɪ/ *adj* fuligginoso

sop /sɒp/ *n* throw a ~ to dare un contentino a

sophisticated /sə'fɪstɪkeɪtɪd/ *adj* sofisticato; (complex) complesso

sophistication /səfɪstɪ'keɪʃn/ *n* (elegance) sofisticatezza *f*, raffinatezza *f*; (complexity) complessità *f*

soporific /sɒpə'rɪfɪk/ *adj* soporifero

soppiness /'sɒpɪnɪs/ *n* fam svenevolezza *f*

sopping /'sɒpɪŋ/ *adj & adv* be ~ [wet] essere bagnato fradicio

soppy /'sɒpɪ/ *adj* (**-ier**, **-iest**) fam svenevole

soprano /sə'prɑːnəʊ/ *n* soprano *m*

sorcerer /'sɔːsərə(r)/ *n* stregone *m*

sorceress /'sɔːsərɪs/ *n* strega *f*, maga *f*

sorcery /'sɔːsərɪ/ *n* (witchcraft) stregoneria *f*

sordid /'sɔːdɪd/ *adj* sordido

sordidness /'sɔːdɪdnɪs/ *n* sordidezza *f*

sore /sɔː(r)/ **1** *adj* dolorante; Am (vexed) arrabbiato; **it's** ~ fa male; **have a** ~ **throat** avere mal di gola; **it's a** ~ **point with her** è un punto delicato per lei
2 *n* piaga *f*

sorely /'sɔːlɪ/ *adv* ‹tempted› seriamente

soreness /'sɔːnɪs/ *n* dolore *m*

sorrel /'sɒrəl/ *n* Bot acetosa *f*

sorrow /'sɒrəʊ/ *n* tristezza *f*

sorrowful /'sɒrəfʊl/ *adj* triste

sorrowfully /'sɒrəfʊlɪ/ *adv* tristemente

💰 **sorry** /'sɒrɪ/ *adj* (**-ier**, **-iest**) (sad) spiacente; (wretched) pietoso; **you'll be** ~**!** te ne pentirai!; **I am ~** mi dispiace; **be** *or* **feel ~ for** provare compassione per; **~!** scusa!; (more polite) scusi!

sort /'sɔːt/ ① *n* tipo *m*; **it's a ~ of fish** è un tipo di pesce; **be out of ~s** fam (unwell) stare poco bene
② *vt* classificare; fam sistemare ‹problem, person›
■ **sort out** *vt* selezionare ‹papers›; fig risolvere ‹problem›; occuparsi di ‹person›

sort code *n* Fin coordinate *fpl* bancarie

sorter /'sɔːtə(r)/ *n* (on photocopier) fascicolatrice *f*, fascicolatore *m*

SOS *n* SOS *m*; fig segnale *m* di soccorso

so-so *adj & adv* così così

sotto voce /sɒtəʊ'vəʊtʃeɪ/ *adv* ‹say, add› sottovoce

soufflé /'suːfleɪ/ *n* soufflé *m*

sought /sɔːt/ ▶ SEEK

sought-after *adj* ‹job, brand, person› richiesto

soul /'səʊl/ *n* anima *f*; **poor ~** poveretto; **there was not a ~ in sight** non c'era anima viva

soul-destroying /-dɪstrɔɪɪŋ/ *adj* ‹job› che abbruttisce

soulful /'səʊlfʊl/ *adj* sentimentale

soulmate *n* anima *f* gemella

soulsearching /-sɜːtʃɪŋ/ *n* esame *m* di coscienza

soul-stirring /-stɜːrɪŋ/ *adj* molto commovente

sound¹ /saʊnd/ ① *adj* sano; (sensible) saggio; (secure) solido; ‹thrashing› clamoroso
② *adv* **~ asleep** profondamente addormentato

sound² ① *n* suono *m*; (noise) rumore *m*; **I don't like the ~ of it** fam non mi suona bene
② *vi* suonare; (seem) aver l'aria; **it ~s to me as if…** mi sa che…
③ *vt* (pronounce) pronunciare; Med auscultare ‹chest›
■ **sound off** *vi* fare grandi discorsi
■ **sound out** *vt* fig sondare

sound barrier *n* muro *m* del suono

sound bite *n* breve frase (*f*) dal forte impatto mediatico

sound card *n* Comput scheda *f* audio

sound effect *n* effetto *m* sonoro

sound engineer *n* tecnico *m* del suono

soundless /'saʊndlɪs/ *adj* silenzioso

soundlessly /'saʊndlɪslɪ/ *adv* silenziosamente

soundly /'saʊndlɪ/ *adv* ‹sleep› profondamente; ‹defeat› clamorosamente

soundproof ① *adj* impenetrabile al suono
② *vt* insonorizzare

sound system *n* (hifi) stereo *m*; (for disco etc) impianto *m* audio

soundtrack *n* colonna *f* sonora

soup /suːp/ *n* minestra *f*; **in the ~** fam nei pasticci

souped-up /suːpt'ʌp/ *adj* fam ‹engine› truccato

soup kitchen *n* mensa *f* dei poveri

soup plate *n* piatto *m* fondo

soup spoon *n* cucchiaio *m* da minestra

sour /'saʊə(r)/ *adj* agro; (not fresh & fig) acido

source /sɔːs/ *n* fonte *f*; **at ~** ‹deducted› alla fonte

source language *n* lingua *f* di partenza

sour cream *n* panna *f* acida

sourdough *n* lievito *m*

sour-faced /saʊə'feɪst/ *adj* ‹person› dall'espressione dura

sour grapes *npl* fam **it's just ~ [on his part]** fa come la volpe con l'uva

south /saʊθ/ ① *n* sud *m*; **to the ~ of a** sud di
② *adj* del sud, meridionale
③ *adv* a sud

South Africa *n* Sudafrica *f*

South African *adj & n* sudafricano, -a *mf*

South America *n* America *f* del Sud

South American *adj & n* sudamericano, -a *mf*

southbound *adj* ‹traffic› diretto a sud; ‹carriageway› sud

south-east /saʊθ'iːst/ *n* sud-est *m*

southerly /'sʌðəlɪ/ *adj* del sud

southern /'sʌðən/ *adj* del sud, meridionale; **~ Italy** il Mezzogiorno

southerner /'sʌðənə(r)/ *n* meridionale *mf*

South Korea *n* Corea *f* del Sud

southpaw /'saʊθpɔː/ *n* (in boxing) pugile *m* mancino

South Pole *n* polo *m* sud

southward[s] /'saʊθwəd[z]/ *adv* verso sud

south-west /saʊθ'west/ *n* sud-ovest *m*

south-western /saʊθ'westən/ *adj* sudoccidentale

souvenir /suːvə'nɪə(r)/ *n* ricordo *m*, souvenir *m* inv

sovereign /'sɒvrɪn/ *adj & n* sovrano, -a *mf*

sovereignty /'sɒvrɪntɪ/ *n* sovranità *f* inv

sovereign wealth funds *n pl* fondi *mpl* sovrani

Soviet /'səʊvɪət/ *adj* sovietico

Soviet Union *n* Unione *f* Sovietica

sow¹ /saʊ/ *n* scrofa *f*

sow² /səʊ/ *vt* (*pt* **sowed**, *pp* **sown** *or* **sowed**) seminare

soya Br /'sɔɪə/, **soy** Am /sɔɪ/ *n* soya *f*

soya bean Br /'sɔɪəbiːn/, **soybean** Am /'sɔɪbiːn/ *n* soia *f*

soy sauce /sɔɪ/, **soya sauce** *n* salsa *f* di soia

S

sozzled /'sɒzld/ adj fam sbronzo
spa /spɑː/ n stazione f termale
♂ **space** /speɪs/ **1** n spazio m
2 adj ‹research etc› spaziale
3 vt ~ **[out]** distanziare
space age **1** n era f spaziale
2 attrib dell'era spaziale
space bar n barra f spaziatrice
space cadet n fig fam allucinato, -a mf
space capsule n capsula f spaziale
spacecraft n navetta f spaziale
spaced out /speɪst'aʊt/ adj fam **he's completely ~** è completamente fuori di testa
space-saving adj poco ingombrante
spaceship n astronave f
space shuttle n shuttle m inv
space station n stazione f spaziale
spacesuit n tuta f spaziale
space travel n viaggi mpl nello spazio
space walk n passeggiata f nello spazio
spacing /'speɪsɪŋ/ n distanziamento m; **single/double ~** interlinea m semplice/doppia
spacious /'speɪʃəs/ adj spazioso
spade /speɪd/ n vanga f; (for child) paletta f; **~s** pl Cards picche fpl; **call a ~ a ~** dire pane al pane e vino al vino
spadework /'speɪdwɜːk/ n fig lavoro m preparatorio
spaghetti /spə'ɡetɪ/ n spaghetti mpl
spaghetti bolognese /bɒlə'neɪz/ n spaghetti mpl al ragù
spaghetti junction n fam intricato raccordo m autostradale
Spain /speɪn/ n Spagna f
spam /spæm/ n Comput spam m inv
spamming /'spæmɪŋ/ n Comput invio m di spam
span[1] /spæn/ **1** n spanna f; (of arch) luce f; (of time) arco m; (of wings) apertura f
2 vt (pt/pp **spanned**) estendersi su
span[2] ▶ SPICK
Spaniard /'spænjəd/ n spagnolo, -a mf
spaniel /'spænjəl/ n spaniel m inv
Spanish /'spænɪʃ/ **1** adj spagnolo
2 n (language) spagnolo m; **the ~** pl gli spagnoli
spank /spæŋk/ vt sculacciare
spanking /'spæŋkɪŋ/ **1** n sculacciata f
2 adj fam **at a ~ pace** con passo spedito
3 adv fam **a ~ new car** una macchina nuova di zecca
spanner /'spænə(r)/ n chiave f inglese
spar /spɑː(r)/ vi (pt/pp **sparred**) (boxing) allenarsi; (argue) litigare
spare /speə(r)/ **1** adj (surplus) in più; (additional) di riserva; **go ~** fam (be very angry)

andare su tutte le furie
2 n (part) ricambio m
3 vt risparmiare; (do without) fare a meno di; **can you ~ five minutes?** avresti cinque minuti?; **no expense was ~d** non si è badato a spese; **to ~** (surplus) in eccedenza
spare part n pezzo m di ricambio
spare ribs npl costine fpl
spare room n stanza f degli ospiti
spare time n tempo m libero
spare tyre Br, **spare tire** Am n Auto gomma f di scorta; fam (fat) trippa f
spare wheel n ruota f di scorta
sparing /'speərɪŋ/ adj parco (with di)
sparingly /'speərɪŋlɪ/ adv con parsimonia
spark /spɑːk/ n scintilla f
■ **spark off** vt Br far scoppiare
sparkle /'spɑːkl/ **1** n scintillio m
2 vi scintillare
sparkler /'spɑːklə(r)/ n candela f magica
sparkling /'spɑːklɪŋ/ adj frizzante; ‹wine› spumante
spark-plug n Auto candela f
sparrow /'spærəʊ/ n passero m
sparse /spɑːs/ adj rado
sparsely /'spɑːslɪ/ adv scarsamente; **~ populated** ‹area› a bassa densità di popolazione
sparseness /'spɑːsnɪs/ n (of vegetation) radezza f
spartan /'spɑːtn/ adj spartano
spasm /'spæzm/ n spasmo m
spasmodic /spæz'mɒdɪk/ adj spasmodico
spasmodically /spæz'mɒdɪklɪ/ adv spasmodicamente
spastic /'spæstɪk/ **1** adj spastico
2 n spastico, -a mf
spat /spæt/ ▶ SPIT[1]
spate /speɪt/ n (series) successione f; **be in full ~** essere in piena
spatial /'speɪʃl/ adj spaziale
spatio-temporal /speɪʃɪə'tempərəl/ adj spazio-temporale
spatter /'spætə(r)/ vt/i schizzare
spatula /'spætjʊlə/ n spatola f
spawn /spɔːn/ **1** n uova fpl (di pesci, rane ecc)
2 vi deporre le uova
3 vt fig generare
spay /speɪ/ vt sterilizzare
♂ **speak** /spiːk/ **1** vi (pt **spoke**, pp **spoken**) parlare (to a); **~ing!** Teleph sono io!
2 vt dire; **~ one's mind** dire quello che si pensa
■ **speak for** vt parlare a nome di; **~ for yourself!** parla per te!
■ **speak of:** vt **~ well/ill of somebody** parlare bene/male di qualcuno; **nothing to ~ of** niente di speciale; (quantity) non un

s

granché; ~**ing of holidays**... a proposito di vacanze...

■ **speak out** *vi* (protest) parlare

■ **speak up** *vi* parlare più forte; ~ **up for oneself** farsi valere

speaker /'spi:kə(r)/ *n* parlante *mf*; (in public) oratore, -trice *mf*; (of stereo) cassa *f*

speaking terms /'spi:kɪŋ/ *npl* **we are not on** ~ non ci parliamo

spear /'spɪə(r)/ **1** *n* lancia *f* **2** *vt* trafiggere

spearhead /'spɪəhed/ *vt* fig essere l'iniziatore di

spearmint /'spɪəmɪnt/ *n* menta *f* verde

spec /spek/ *n* **on** ~ fam ‹take, use› in prova; ‹go somewhere› per ispezione

❀ **special** /'speʃl/ *adj* speciale

special correspondent *n* inviato, -a *mf* speciale

special delivery *n* espresso *m*

special effect **1** *n* Cinema, TV effetto *m* speciale **2** *attrib* ~**s** ‹specialist, team› degli effetti speciali

special envoy *n* inviato, -a *mf* speciale

specialist /'speʃəlɪst/ *n* specialista *mf*

speciality /speʃɪ'ræləti/ *n* specialità *f inv*

specialize /'speʃəlaɪz/ *vi* specializzarsi

specially /'speʃəli/ *adv* specialmente; (particularly) particolarmente

special measures *n* Br *insieme di provvedimenti migliorativi di natura didattica, organizzativa, finanziaria o strutturale che una scuola deve adottare qualora non raggiunga gli standard educativi stabiliti dall'Ofsted*

special needs *npl* difficoltà *f* d'apprendimento, **children with** ~ bambini con difficoltà d'apprendimento

special offer *n* vendita *f* promozionale

special school *n* scuola *f* per bambini con difficoltà d'apprendimento

special treatment *n* trattamento *m* di riguardo

❀ **species** /'spi:ʃi:z/ *n* specie *f inv*

❀ **specific** /spə'sɪfɪk/ *adj* specifico

❀ **specifically** /spə'sɪfɪkli/ *adv* in modo specifico

specifications /spesɪfɪ'keɪʃnz/ *npl* descrizione *f*

specify /'spesɪfaɪ/ *vt* (*pt/pp* **-ied**) specificare

specimen /'spesɪmən/ *n* campione *m*

specious /'spi:ʃəs/ *adj* ‹argument, reasoning› specioso

speck /spek/ *n* macchiolina *f*; (particle) granello *m*

speckled /'spekld/ *adj* picchiettato

specs /speks/ *npl* fam occhiali *mpl*

spectacle /'spektəkl/ *n* (show) spettacolo *m*

spectacles /'spektəklz/ *npl* occhiali *mpl*

spectacular /spek'tækjʊlə(r)/ *adj* spettacolare

spectacularly /spek'tækjʊləli/ *adv* in modo spettacolare

spectator /spek'teɪtə(r)/ *n* spettatore, -trice *mf*

spectator sport *n* sport *m inv* di intrattenimento

spectre /'spektə(r)/ *n* spettro *m*

spectrum /'spektrəm/ *n* (*pl* **-tra**) spettro *m*; fig gamma *f*

speculate /'spekjʊleɪt/ *vi* speculare

speculation /spekjʊ'leɪʃn/ *n* speculazione *f*

speculative /'spekjʊlətɪv/ *adj* speculativo

speculator /'spekjʊleɪtə(r)/ *n* speculatore, -trice *mf*

sped /sped/ ▶ SPEED

❀ **speech** /spi:tʃ/ *n* linguaggio *m*; (address) discorso *m*; **make a** ~ **give a** ~ fare un discorso

speech day *n* Sch giorno *m* della premiazione

speech impediment *n* difetto *m* di pronuncia

speechless /'spi:tʃlɪs/ *adj* senza parole

speech therapist *n* logoterapista *mf*

speech therapy *n* logoterapia *f*

speech-writer *n* *persona (f) che scrive i discorsi di personaggi pubblici*

❀ **speed** /spi:d/ **1** *n* velocità *f inv*; (gear) marcia *f*; **at** ~ a tutta velocità **2** *vi* (*pt/pp* **sped**) andare veloce **3** *vi* (*pt/pp* **speeded**) (go too fast) andare a velocità eccessiva

■ **speed up** *vt/i* (*pt/pp* **speeded up**) accelerare

speedboat *n* motoscafo *m*

speed bump *n* rallentatore *m*

speed camera *n* autovelox® *m inv*

speed dial *n* composizione *f* veloce

speed hump *n* dosso *m* di rallentamento

speedily /'spi:dɪli/ *adv* rapidamente

speeding /'spi:dɪŋ/ *n* eccesso *m* di velocità

speeding fine *n* multa *f* per eccesso di velocità

speed limit *n* limite *m* di velocità

speed merchant *n* fam fanatico, -a *mf* della velocità

speedometer /spi:'dɒmɪtə(r)/ *n* tachimetro *m*

speed skating *n* pattinaggio *m* di velocità

speed trap *n* Auto *tratto (m) di strada sul quale la polizia controlla la velocità dei veicoli*

S

speedy /'spiːdɪ/ adj (-ier, -iest) rapido

speleologist /spiːlɪ'ɒlədʒɪst/ n speleologo, -a mf

speleology /spiːlɪ'ɒlədʒɪ/ n speleologia f

spell¹ /spel/ n (turn) turno m; (of weather) periodo m

spell² ① vt (pt/pp **spelled** or **spelt**) how do you ~…? come si scrive…?; could you ~ that for me? me lo può compitare?; ~ **disaster** fig essere disastroso
② vi he can't ~ fa molti errori d'ortografia

spell³ n (magic) incantesimo m
■ **spell out** vt compitare; fig spiegare

spellbound /'spelbaʊnd/ adj affascinato

spellcheck vt Comput fare il controllo ortografico di ‹document›

spellchecker /'speltʃekə(r)/ n Comput correttore m ortografico

spelling /'spelɪŋ/ n ortografia f

spelt /spelt/ ▶ SPELL²

ℐ **spend** /spend/ vt/i (pt/pp **spent**) spendere; passare ‹time›

spending cut n taglio m alla spesa

spending money /'spendɪŋ/ n soldi mpl per le piccole spese

spending power n potere m d'acquisto

spending spree n spese fpl folli

spendthrift /'spendθrɪft/ ① adj spendaccione; ‹habit, policy› dispendioso
② n spendaccione, -a mf

spent /spent/ ▶ SPEND

sperm /spɜːm/ n spermatozoo m; (semen) sperma m

sperm bank n banca f dello sperma

sperm count n conteggio m di spermatozoi

sperm donor n donatore m del seme

spermicidal /spɜːmɪ'saɪdl/ adj spermicida inv

spermicide /'spɜːmɪsaɪd/ n spermicida m

spew /spjuː/ vt/i vomitare

sphere /sfɪə(r)/ n sfera f

sphere of influence n sfera f di influenza

spherical /'sferɪkl/ adj sferico

spice /spaɪs/ n spezia f; fig pepe m

spick /spɪk/ adj ~ **and span** lindo

spicy /'spaɪsɪ/ adj piccante

spider /'spaɪdə(r)/ n ragno m

spiderweb n Am = WEB

spiel /ʃpiːl/ n fam (sales pitch) imbonimento m; (long repetitive speech) tiritera f; he gave me some ~ about… mi ha raccontato un sacco di storie su…

spike /spaɪk/ n punta f; Bot, Zool spina f; (on shoe) chiodo m

spikes npl (shoes) scarpe fpl chiodate

spiky /'spaɪkɪ/ adj ‹plant› spinoso

spill /spɪl/ ① vt (pt/pp **spilt** or **spilled**) versare ‹blood›; ~ **the beans** fam vuotare il sacco
② vi rovesciarsi
■ **spill over** vi ‹water› traboccare; ~ **over into** degenerare in ‹violence, rioting›

spillage /'spɪlɪdʒ/ n (of oil, chemical) perdita f

spin /spɪn/ ① vt (pt/pp **spun**, pres p **spinning**) far girare; filare ‹wool›; centrifugare ‹washing›
② vi girare; ‹washing machine› centrifugare
③ n rotazione f; (short drive) giretto m
■ **spin out** vt far durare
■ **spin round** ① vi (turn quickly) girare vorticosamente; ‹dancer, skater› volteggiare; ‹car› fare un testa coda
② vt ~ **somebody** or **something round** far girare qualcuno o qualcosa

spinach /'spɪnɪdʒ/ n spinaci mpl

spinal /'spaɪnl/ adj spinale

spinal column n colonna f vertebrale

spinal cord n midollo m spinale

spindle /'spɪndl/ n fuso m

spindly /'spɪndlɪ/ adj affusolato

spin doctor n persona (f) incaricata di presentare le scelte di un partito politico sotto una luce favorevole

spin-drier n centrifuga f

spine /spaɪn/ n spina f dorsale; (of book) dorso m; Bot, Zool spina f

spineless /'spaɪnlɪs/ adj fig smidollato

spinning /'spɪnɪŋ/ n filatura f

spinning wheel n filatoio m

spin-off n ricaduta f

spinster /'spɪnstə(r)/ n donna f nubile; (old maid, fam) zitella f

spiny /'spaɪnɪ/ adj ‹plant, animal› spinoso

spiral /'spaɪrəl/ ① adj a spirale
② n spirale f
③ vi (pt/pp **spiralled**) formare una spirale

spiral staircase n scala f a chiocciola

spire /'spaɪə(r)/ n guglia f

ℐ **spirit** /'spɪrɪt/ n spirito m; (courage) ardore m; ~**s** pl (alcohol) liquori mpl; in good ~**s** di buon umore; in low ~**s** abbattuto
■ **spirit away** vt far sparire

spirited /'spɪrɪtɪd/ adj vivace; (courageous) pieno d'ardore

spirit level n livella f a bolla d'aria

spirit stove n fornellino m [da campeggio]

spiritual /'spɪrɪtjʊəl/ ① adj spirituale
② n spiritual m

spiritualism /'spɪrɪtjʊəlɪzm/ n spiritismo m

spiritualist /'spɪrɪtjʊəlɪst/ n spiritista mf

spit¹ /spɪt/ n (for roasting) spiedo m

ℐ indicates a very frequent word

spit² [1] *n* sputo *m*
[2] *vt/i* (*pt/pp* **spat**, *pres p* **spitting**)
sputare; ‹*cat*› soffiare; ‹*fat*› sfrigolare; **it's**
∼ting [with rain] pioviggina; **the ∼ting**
image of il ritratto spiccicato di

spite /spaɪt/ [1] *n* dispetto *m*; **in ∼ of**
malgrado
[2] *vt* far dispetto a

spiteful /'spaɪtfʊl/ *adj* indispettito

spitefully /'spaɪtfʊlɪ/ *adv* con aria
indispettita

spit out *vt* sputare ‹*food*›; **∼ it out!** fam
sputa l'osso!

spittle /'spɪtl/ *n* saliva *f*

splash /splæʃ/ [1] *n* schizzo *m*; (of colour)
macchia *f*; fam (drop) goccio *m*
[2] *vt* schizzare; **∼ somebody with**
something schizzare qualcuno di qualcosa
[3] *vi* schizzare
▪ **splash about** *vi* schizzarsi
▪ **splash down** *vi* ‹*spacecraft*› ammarare
▪ **splash out** *vi* (spend freely) darsi alle spese
folli

splashdown /'splæʃdaʊn/ *n* ammaraggio
m

splatter /'splætə(r)/ [1] *vt* schizzare;
∼ somebody/something with something
schizzare qualcuno/qualcosa di qualcosa
[2] *vi* **∼ onto/over something** ‹*ink, paint*›
schizzare su qualcosa

splay /spleɪ/ *vt* divaricare ‹*legs, feet,*
fingers›; svasare ‹*end of pipe etc*›; strombare
‹*side of window, door*›; **∼ed** ‹*feet, fingers,*
legs› scartato

spleen /spliːn/ *n* Anat milza *f*

splendid /'splendɪd/ *adj* splendido

splendidly /'splendɪdlɪ/ *adv*
splendidamente

splendour /'splendə(r)/ *n* splendore *m*

splice /splaɪs/ *vt* aggiuntare ‹*tape, film*›

splint /splɪnt/ *n* Med stecca *f*

splinter /'splɪntə(r)/ [1] *n* scheggia *f*
[2] *vi* scheggiarsi

splinter group *n* gruppo *m* scissionista

split /splɪt/ [1] *n* fessura *f*; (quarrel) rottura *f*;
(division) scissione *f*; (tear) strappo *m*
[2] *vt* (*pt/pp* **split**, *pres p* **splitting**)
spaccare; (share, divide) dividere; (tear)
strappare; **∼ hairs** spaccare il capello in
quattro; **∼ one's sides** sbellicarsi dalle risa
[3] *vi* spaccarsi; (tear) strapparsi; (divide)
dividersi; **∼ on somebody** fam denunciare
qualcuno
[4] *adj* **a ∼ second** una frazione di secondo
▪ **split up** [1] *vt* dividersi
[2] *vi* ‹*couple*› separarsi

split ends *npl* (in hair) doppie punte *fpl*

split personality *n* sdoppiamento *m*
della personalità

split screen *n* schermo *m* diviso

splitting /'splɪtɪŋ/ *adj* **have a ∼ headache**
avere un tremendo mal di testa

splutter /'splʌtə(r)/ *vi* farfugliare

spoil /spɔɪl/ [1] *n* **∼s** *pl* bottino *msg*
[2] *vt* (*pt/pp* **spoilt** Br *or* **spoiled**)
rovinare; viziare ‹*person*›
[3] *vi* andare a male

spoiler /'spɔɪlə(r)/ *n* Auto, Aeron spoiler *m inv*

spoilsport /'spɔɪlspɔːt/ *n* guastafeste *mf*
inv

spoilt /spɔɪlt/ *adj* Br ‹*child*› viziato; **be ∼**
for choice non avere che l'imbarazzo della
scelta

spoke¹ /spəʊk/ *n* raggio *m*

spoke² ▶ SPEAK

spoken /'spəʊkən/ [1] ▶ SPEAK
[2] *adj* ‹*language*› parlato; **be ∼ for** essere
messo da parte per qualcuno

spokesman /'spəʊksmən/ *n* portavoce
m inv

spokesperson /'spəʊkspɜːsn/ *n*
portavoce *mf*

spokeswoman /'spəʊkswʊmən/ *n*
portavoce *f*

sponge /spʌndʒ/ [1] *n* spugna *f*
[2] *vt* pulire con la spugna
[3] *vi* **∼ on** fam scroccare da

sponge bag *n* nécessaire *m inv*

sponge cake *n* pan *m* di Spagna

sponger /'spʌndʒə(r)/ *n* scroccone, -a *mf*

spongy /'spʌndʒɪ/ *adj* spugnoso

sponsor /'spɒnsə(r)/ [1] *n* garante *mf*;
Radio, TV sponsor *m inv*; (god-parent) padrino
m, madrina *f*; (for membership) socio, -a *mf*
garante
[2] *vt* sponsorizzare

sponsorship /'spɒnsəʃɪp/ *n*
sponsorizzazione *f*

sponsorship deal *n* accordo *m* con uno
sponsor

spontaneity /spɒntə'neɪətɪ/ *n*
spontaneità *f*

spontaneous /spɒn'teɪnɪəs/ *adj*
spontaneo

spontaneously /spɒn'teɪnɪəslɪ/ *adv*
spontaneamente

spoof /spuːf/ *n* fam parodia *f*

spook /spuːk/ fam [1] *vt* (haunt)
perseguitare; (frighten) spaventare
[2] *n* (ghost) fantasma *m*; Am (spy) spia *f*

spooky /'spuːkɪ/ *adj* (-ier, -iest) fam
sinistro

spool /spuːl/ *n* bobina *f*

spooling /'spuːlɪŋ/ *n* Comput spooling *m*

spoon /spuːn/ [1] *n* cucchiaio *m*
[2] *vt* mettere col cucchiaio

spoonerism /'spuːnərɪzm/ *n* scambio
(*m*) delle iniziali di due parole con effetto
umoristico

spoon-feed *vt* (*pt/pp* **-fed**) fig imboccare

spoonful /'spu:nfʊl/ n cucchiaiata f
sporadic /spə'rædɪk/ adj sporadico
sporadically /spə'rædɪklɪ/ adv
sporadicamente
spore /spɔ:(r)/ n spora f
sporran /'spɒrə/ n borsa (f) di cuoio o pelo
portata alla cintura dagli scozzesi insieme
al kilt
◆ **sport** /spɔ:t/ ① n sport m inv; **be a [good]**
~! sii sportivo!
② vt sfoggiare
sporting /'spɔ:tɪŋ/ adj sportivo
sporting calendar n calendario m
sportivo
sporting chance n possibilità f inv
sports car n automobile f sportiva
sports centre Br, **sports center** Am
n centro m polisportivo
sports club n club m sportivo
sports coat n, **sports jacket** n
giacca f sportiva
sports ground n (large) stadio m; (in
school) campo m sportivo
sports jacket n giacca f sportiva
sportsman n sportivo m
sports star n star f inv dello sport
sportswear n abbigliamento m sportivo
sportswoman n sportiva f
sports writer n giornalista mf sportivo,
-a
sporty /'spɔ:tɪ/ adj (-ier, -iest) sportivo
◆ **spot** /spɒt/ ① n macchia f; (pimple) brufolo
m; (place) posto m; (in pattern) pois m inv;
(of rain) goccia f; (of water) goccio m; ~s pl
(rash) sfogo msg; **a ~ of** fam un po' di; **a ~
of bother** qualche problema; **on the ~** sul
luogo; (immediately) immediatamente; **in a
[tight] ~** fam in difficoltà
② vt (pt/pp **spotted**) macchiare; fam
(notice) individuare
spot check n (without warning) controllo m
a sorpresa; **do a ~ on something** dare una
controllata a qualcosa
spotless /'spɒtlɪs/ adj immacolato
spotlight n riflettore m; fig riflettori mpl
spot-on adj Br esatto
spot rate n Fin tasso m di cambio a vista
spotted /'spɒtɪd/ adj ‹material› a pois
spotty /'spɒtɪ/ adj (-ier, -iest) (pimply)
brufoloso
spot-weld vt saldare a punti
spouse /spaʊz/ n consorte mf
spout /spaʊt/ ① n becco m; **up the ~** fam
(ruined) all'aria
② vi zampillare (from da)
sprain /spreɪn/ ① n slogatura f
② vt slogare; ~ **one's ankle** slogarsi la
caviglia

◆ indicates a very frequent word

sprang /spræŋ/ ▶ SPRING²
sprat /spræt/ n spratto m
sprawl /sprɔ:l/ vi (in chair) stravaccarsi; ‹city
etc› estendersi; **go ~ing** (fall) cadere disteso
sprawling /'sprɔ:lɪŋ/ adj ‹suburb, city› che
si propaga disordinatamente; ‹handwriting›
che occupa tutta la pagina
spray¹ /spreɪ/ n (of flowers) rametto m;
(bouquet) mazzolino m
spray² ① n spruzzo m; (from sea) spruzzo
m; (preparation) spray m inv; (container)
spruzzatore m
② vt spruzzare
spray can n bomboletta f spray inv
spray-gun n pistola f a spruzzo
spray-on adj ‹conditioner, glitter› spray inv
◆ **spread** /spred/ ① n estensione f; (of
disease) diffusione f; (paste) crema f; fam (feast)
banchetto m
② vt (pt/pp **spread**) spargere; spalmare
‹butter, jam›; stendere ‹cloth, arms›;
diffondere ‹news, disease›; dilazionare
‹payments›; ~ **something with** spalmare
qualcosa di
③ vi spargersi; ‹butter› spalmarsi; ‹disease›
diffondersi
■ **spread out** ① vt sparpagliare
② vi sparpagliarsi
spread-eagled /-'i:gld/ adj a gambe e
braccia aperte
spreadsheet /'spredʃi:t/ n Comput foglio
m elettronico
spree /spri:/ n fam **go on a ~** far baldoria;
go on a shopping ~ fare spese folli
sprig /sprɪg/ n rametto m
sprightly /'spraɪtlɪ/ adj (-ier, -iest) vivace
◆ **spring¹** /sprɪŋ/ ① n primavera f; **in ~, in
the ~** in primavera
② attrib primaverile
spring² ① n (jump) balzo m; (water) sorgente
f; (device) molla f; (elasticity) elasticità f
② vi (pt **sprang**, pp **sprung**) balzare;
(arise) provenire (from da); ~ **to mind** saltare
in mente
③ vt **he just sprang it on me** me l'ha detto
a cose fatte
■ **spring up** vi balzare; fig spuntare
springboard n trampolino m
spring chicken n Culin pollastrello m,
pollastrella f; **she's no ~** fam non è una
giovincella
spring-clean vt pulire a fondo
spring-cleaning n pulizie fpl di Pasqua
spring onion n cipollotto m
springtime n primavera f
springy /'sprɪŋɪ/ adj ‹mattress, sofa›
molleggiato
sprinkle /'sprɪŋkl/ vt (scatter) spruzzare
‹liquid›; spargere ‹flour, cocoa›; ~ **something
with** spruzzare qualcosa di ‹liquid›;
cospargere qualcosa di ‹flour, cocoa›

sprinkler /'sprɪŋklə(r)/ n sprinkler m inv;
(for garden) irrigatore m

sprinkling /'sprɪŋklɪŋ/ n (of liquid)
spruzzatina f; (of pepper, salt) pizzico m;
(of flour, sugar) spolveratina f; (of knowledge)
infarinatura f; (of people) pugno m

sprint /sprɪnt/ **1** n sprint m inv
2 vi fare uno sprint; Sport sprintare

sprinter /'sprɪntə(r)/ n sprinter mf inv

sprite /spraɪt/ n folletto m

spritzer /'sprɪtsə(r)/ n spritz m inv,
spritzer m inv

sprout /spraʊt/ **1** n germoglio m;
[Brussels] ~s pl cavolini mpl di Bruxelles
2 vi germogliare

spruce /spruːs/ **1** adj elegante
2 n abete m
■ **spruce up** vt dare una ripulita a

sprung /sprʌŋ/ **1** ▶ SPRING²
2 adj molleggiato

spry /spraɪ/ adj (**-er**, **-est**) arzillo

spud /spʌd/ n fam patata f

spun /spʌn/ ▶ SPIN

spur /spɜː(r)/ **1** n sperone m; (stimulus)
stimolo m; (road) svincolo m; **on the ~ of the
moment** su due piedi
2 vt (pt/pp **spurred**) ~ [on] fig spronare

spurious /'spjʊərɪəs/ adj falso

spuriously /'spjʊərɪəslɪ/ adv falsamente

spurn /spɜːn/ vt sdegnare

spurt /spɜːt/ **1** n getto m; Sport scatto m;
put on a ~ fare uno scatto
2 vi sprizzare; (increase speed) scattare

sputter /'spʌtə(r)/ **1** vi (engine)
scoppiettare
2 n colpi mpl irregolari del motore

spy /spaɪ/ **1** n spia f
2 vi spiare
3 vt fam (see) spiare
■ **spy on** vt spiare
■ **spy out** vt esplorare

spying /'spaɪɪŋ/ n spionaggio m

squabble /'skwɒbl/ **1** n bisticcio m
2 vi bisticciare

squabbling /'skwɒblɪŋ/ n bisticci mpl

squad /skwɒd/ n squadra f

squad car n macchina f della volante

squaddie /'skwɒdɪ/ n Br fam soldato m
semplice

squadron /'skwɒdrən/ n Mil squadrone m;
Aeron, Naut squadriglia f

squalid /'skwɒlɪd/ adj squallido

squalidly /'skwɒlɪdlɪ/ adv squallidamente

squall /skwɔːl/ **1** n (howl) strillo m; (storm)
bufera f
2 vi strillare

squally /'skwɔːlɪ/ adj burrascoso

squalor /'skwɒlə(r)/ n squallore m

squander /'skwɒndə(r)/ vt sprecare

square /skweə(r)/ **1** adj quadrato;
(meal) sostanzioso; fam (old-fashioned) vecchio
stampo; **all ~** fam pari
2 n quadrato m; (in city) piazza f; (on
chessboard) riquadro m; **be back to ~ one**
riessere al punto di partenza
3 vt (settle) far quadrare; Math elevare al
quadrato
4 vi (agree) armonizzare
■ **square up** vi (settle accounts) saldare
■ **square up to** vt affrontare

square bracket n parentesi f inv
quadra; **in ~s** tra parentesi quadre

square dance n quadriglia f

squarely /'skweəlɪ/ adv direttamente

square root n radice f quadrata

squash /skwɒʃ/ **1** n calca f; (drink)
spremuta f; (sport) squash m; (vegetable)
zucca f
2 vt schiacciare; soffocare (rebellion)
■ **squash up** vi (move closer together)
stringersi

squashy /'skwɒʃɪ/ adj floscio

squat /skwɒt/ **1** adj tarchiato
2 n fam edificio m occupato abusivamente
3 vi (pt/pp **squatted**) accovacciarsi;
~ **in** occupare abusivamente

squatter /'skwɒtə(r)/ n occupante mf
abusivo, -a

squaw /skwɔː/ n squaw f inv

squawk /skwɔːk/ **1** n gracchio m
2 vi gracchiare

squeak /skwiːk/ **1** n squittio m; (of hinge,
brakes) cigolio m
2 vi squittire; (hinge, brakes) cigolare

squeaking /'skwiːkɪŋ/ n (of door, hinge)
cigolio m

squeaky /'skwiːkɪ/ adj (door, hinge)
cigolante

squeaky-clean adj fam (glass, hair)
lucente; (floor) tirato a specchio; fig (person)
senza vizi; (company) al di sopra di ogni
sospetto

squeal /skwiːl/ **1** n strillo m; (of brakes)
cigolio m
2 vi strillare; sl spifferare

squeamish /'skwiːmɪʃ/ adj dallo stomaco
delicato; (scrupulous) troppo scrupoloso

squeegee /'skwiːdʒiː/ n Phot rullo m
asciugatore; (for glasses) lavavetri m inv

squeeze /skwiːz/ **1** n stretta f; (crush)
pigia pigia m inv; **give sb's hand a ~** dare a
qualcuno una stretta di mano
2 vt premere; (to get juice) spremere;
stringere (hand); (force) stringere a forza; fam
(extort) estorcere (**out of** da)
■ **squeeze in/out** vi sgusciare dentro/fuori
■ **squeeze past** vi (person, car) passare
■ **squeeze up** vi stringersi

squelch /skweltʃ/ vi sguazzare

squib /skwɪb/ n petardo m

squid /skwɪd/ n calamaro m

squidgy /'skwɪdʒɪ/ adj Br fam (squashy) molliccio

squiggle /'skwɪgl/ n scarabocchio m

squint /skwɪnt/ **1** n strabismo m
2 vi essere strabico

squire /'skwaɪə(r)/ n signorotto m di campagna

squirm /skwɜːm/ vi contorcersi; (feel embarrassed) sentirsi imbarazzato

squirrel /'skwɪrəl/ n scoiattolo m

squirt /skwɜːt/ **1** n spruzzo m; fam (person) presuntuoso m
2 vt/i spruzzare

Sri Lanka n Sri Lanka m

St abbr 1 (**Saint**) S
2 (**Street**)

stab /stæb/ **1** n pugnalata f, coltellata f; (sensation) fitta f; fam (attempt) tentativo m
2 vt (pt/pp **stabbed**) pugnalare, accoltellare

stability /stə'bɪlətɪ/ n stabilità f inv

stabilization /steɪbɪlaɪ'zeɪʃn/ n stabilizzazione f

stabilize /'steɪbɪlaɪz/ **1** vt stabilizzare
2 vi stabilizzarsi

stabilizer /'steɪbɪlaɪzə(r)/ n stabilizzatore m; (on bike) rotella f; (in food) stabilizzante m

stable¹ /'steɪbl/ adj stabile

stable² n stalla f; (establishment) scuderia f

staccato /stə'kɑːtəʊ/ **1** adj Mus staccato; ⟨gasps, shots⟩ intermittente
2 adv ⟨play⟩ staccatamente

stack /stæk/ **1** n catasta f; (of chimney) comignolo m; (chimney) ciminiera f; fam (large quantity) montagna f; ~s of ⟨money, time, work⟩ un sacco di
2 vt accatastare

stadium /'steɪdɪəm/ n stadio m

♂ **staff** /stɑːf/ **1** n (stick) bastone m; (employees) personale m; (teachers) corpo m insegnante; Mil Stato m Maggiore
2 vt fornire di personale

staff meeting n riunione f del corpo insegnante

staffroom /'stɑːfruːm/ n Sch sala f insegnanti

stag /stæg/ n cervo m

♂ **stage** /steɪdʒ/ **1** n palcoscenico m; (profession) teatro m; (in journey) tappa f; (in process) stadio m; **go on the** ~ darsi al teatro; **by** or **in** ~**s** a tappe
2 vt mettere in scena; (arrange) organizzare

stagecoach n diligenza f

stage door n ingresso m degli artisti

stage fright n panico m da palcoscenico

stage-manage vt fig orchestrare

♂ indicates a very frequent word

stage manager n direttore, -trice mf di scena

stage-struck /-strʌk/ adj appassionatissimo di teatro

stagger /'stægə(r)/ **1** vi barcollare
2 vt sbalordire; scaglionare ⟨holidays, payments etc⟩; **I was** ~**ed** sono rimasto sbalordito
3 n vacillamento m

staggering /'stægərɪŋ/ adj sbalorditivo

stagnant /'stægnənt/ adj stagnante

stagnate /stæg'neɪt/ vi fig [ri]stagnare

stagnation /stæg'neɪʃn/ n fig inattività f

stag night, **stag party** n addio m al celibato

staid /steɪd/ adj posato

stain /steɪn/ **1** n macchia f; (for wood) mordente m
2 vt macchiare; ⟨wood⟩ dare il mordente a

stained glass /steɪnd'glɑːs/ n vetro m colorato

stained-glass window n vetrata f colorata

stainless /'steɪnlɪs/ adj senza macchia

stainless steel n acciaio m inossidabile

stain remover n smacchiatore m

stair /steə(r)/ n gradino m; ~**s** pl scale fpl

staircase /'steəkeɪs/ n scale fpl

stairlift n montascale m inv

stake /steɪk/ **1** n palo m; (wager) posta f; Comm partecipazione f; **at** ~ in gioco
2 vt puntellare; (wager) scommettere; ~ **a claim to something** rivendicare qualcosa
■ **stake out** vt mettere sotto sorveglianza ⟨building⟩

stake-out n fam sorveglianza f

stalactite /'stæləktaɪt/ n stalattite f

stalagmite /'stæləgmaɪt/ n stalagmite f

stale /steɪl/ adj stantio; ⟨air⟩ viziato; (uninteresting) trito [e ritrito]

stalemate /'steɪlmeɪt/ n (in chess) stallo m; (deadlock) situazione f di stallo

stalk¹ /stɔːk/ n gambo m

stalk² **1** vt inseguire
2 vi camminare impettito

stalker /'stɔːkə(r)/ n (of person) persona (f) che perseguita qualcuno per cui ha una fissazione maniacale

stalking /'stɔːkɪŋ/ n (of person) persecuzione (f) di una persona per cui si ha una fissazione maniacale

stall /stɔːl/ **1** n box m inv; (in market) bancarella f; ~**s** pl Theat platea f
2 vi ⟨engine⟩ spegnersi; fig temporeggiare
3 vt far spegnere ⟨engine⟩; tenere a bada ⟨person⟩

stallholder /'stɔːlhəʊldə(r)/ n bancarellista mf

stallion /'stæljən/ n stallone m

stalwart /'stɔ:lwət/ **1** *adj* fedele
2 *n* sostenitore *m* fedele

stamina /'stæmɪnə/ *n* [capacità *f* di]
resistenza *f*

stammer /'stæmə(r)/ **1** *n* balbettio *m*
2 *vt/i* balbettare

stamp /stæmp/ **1** *n* (postage) ~
francobollo *m*; (instrument) timbro *m*; fig
impronta *f*
2 *vt* affrancare ‹letter›; timbrare ‹bill›;
battere ‹feet›
■ **stamp out** *vt* spegnere; fig soffocare

stamp collecting *n* filatelia *f*

stamp collector *n* collezionista *mf* di
francobolli

stamped addressed envelope
busta *f* affrancata per la risposta

stampede /stæm'pi:d/ **1** *n* fuga *f*
precipitosa; fam fuggifuggi *m inv*
2 *vi* fuggire precipitosamente

stance /stɑ:ns/ *n* posizione *f*

⚹ **stand** /stænd/ **1** *n* (for bikes) rastrelliera
f; (at exhibition) stand *m inv*; (in market)
bancarella *f*; (in stadium) gradinata *f*; fig
posizione *f*
2 *vi* (*pt/pp* **stood**) stare in piedi; (rise)
alzarsi [in piedi]; (be) trovarsi; (be candidate)
essere candidato (**for** a); (stay valid) rimanere
valido; **I don't know where I** ~ non so qual
è la mia posizione; ~ **still** non muoversi;
~ **firm** fig tener duro; ~ **on ceremony**
formalizzarsi; ~ **together** essere solidali;
~ **to lose/gain** rischiare di perdere/vincere;
~ **to reason** essere logico
3 *vt* (withstand) resistere a; (endure)
sopportare; (place) mettere; ~ **a chance**
avere una possibilità; ~ **one's ground** tener
duro; ~ **the test of time** superare la prova
del tempo; ~ **somebody a beer** offrire una
birra a qualcuno
■ **stand back** *vi* (withdraw) farsi da parte
■ **stand by 1** *vi* stare a guardare; (be ready)
essere pronto
2 *vt* (support) appoggiare
■ **stand down** *vi* (retire) ritirarsi
■ **stand for** *vt* (mean) significare; (tolerate)
tollerare
■ **stand in for** *vt* sostituire
■ **stand out** *vi* spiccare
■ **stand up** *vi* alzarsi [in piedi]
■ **stand up for** *vt* prendere le difese di; ~ **up
for oneself** farsi valere
■ **stand up to** *vt* affrontare

stand-alone *adj* Comput stand-alone

⚹ **standard** /'stændəd/ **1** *adj* standard; **be**
~ **practice** essere pratica corrente
2 *n* standard *m inv*; Techn norma *f*;
(level) livello *m*; (quality) qualità *f inv*; (flag)
stendardo *m*; ~**s** *pl* (morals) valori *mpl*

Standard Assessment Tasks *n* Br
esami (mpl) sostenuti per tranche d'età allo
scopo di testare la preparazione degli alunni

standardization /stændədaɪ'zeɪʃn/ *n*
standardizzazione *f*

standardize /'stændədaɪz/ *vt*
standardizzare

standard lamp *n* lampada *f* a stelo

standard of living *n* tenore *m* di vita

standby /'stændbaɪ/ **1** *n* (person) riserva *f*
2 *attrib* ‹circuit, battery› di emergenza;
‹passenger› in lista di attesa; ‹ticket› stand-by
inv
3 *adv* ‹fly› con biglietto stand-by

stand-in *n* controfigura *f*

standing /'stændɪŋ/ **1** *adj* (erect) in piedi;
(permanent) permanente
2 *n* posizione *f*; (duration) durata *f*

standing charge *n* canone *m*

standing order *n* ordine *m* permanente

standing ovation *n* give somebody a ~
alzarsi per applaudire qualcuno

standing room *n* posti *mpl* in piedi

stand-off /'stændɒf/ *n* punto *m* morto

stand-offish /stænd'ɒfɪʃ/ *adj* scostante

standpoint *n* punto *m* di vista

standstill *n* come to a ~ fermarsi; at a ~
in un periodo di stasi

stand-up 1 *adj* ‹buffet› in piedi;
‹argument› accanito
2 *n* (comedy) recital *m inv* di un comico

stand-up comedian *comico (m) che*
intrattiene il pubblico con barzellette

stank /stæŋk/ ▶ STINK

Stanley knife® *n* cutter *m inv*

stanza /'stænzə/ *n* strofa *f*

staple[1] /'steɪpl/ *n* (product) prodotto *m*
principale

staple[2] **1** *n* graffa *f*, pinzatrice *f*
2 *vt* pinzare

staple diet *n* a ~ of una dieta basata
principalmente su

staple gun *n* pistola *f* sparachiodi

stapler /'steɪplə(r)/ *n* pinzatrice *f*, cucitrice
f

staple remover *n* levapunti *m inv*

⚹ **star** /stɑ:(r)/ **1** *n* stella *f*; (asterisk) asterisco
m; Theat, Cinema, Sport divo, -a *mf*, stella *f*
2 *vi* (*pt/pp* **starred**) essere l'interprete
principale (**in** di)

starboard /'stɑ:bəd/ *n* tribordo *m*

starch /stɑ:tʃ/ **1** *n* amido *m*
2 *vt* inamidare

starchy /'stɑ:tʃɪ/ *adj* ricco di amido; fig
compito

stardom /'stɑ:dəm/ *n* celebrità *f*

⚹ **stare** /steə(r)/ **1** *n* sguardo *m* fisso
2 *vi* it's rude to ~ è da maleducati fissare
la gente; ~ **at** fissare; ~ **into space** guardare
nel vuoto

starfish /'stɑ:fɪʃ/ *n* stella *f* di mare

stark /stɑːk/ **1** adj austero; ‹contrast› forte
2 adv completamente; ~ **naked** completamente nudo

starlet /'stɑːlɪt/ n stellina f

starling /'stɑːlɪŋ/ n storno m

starlit /'stɑːlɪt/ adj stellato

starry /'stɑːrɪ/ adj stellato

starry-eyed /-'aɪd/ adj fam ingenuo

star sign n segno m zodiacale

star-struck /-strʌk/ adj ossessionato dalle celebrità

star-studded /-stʌdɪd/ adj ‹cast, line-up› con molti interpreti famosi; ‹sky› stellato

✧ **start** /stɑːt/ **1** n inizio m; (departure) partenza f; (jump) sobbalzo m; **from the** ~ [fin] dall'inizio; **for a** ~ tanto per cominciare; **give somebody a** ~ Sport dare un vantaggio a qualcuno
2 vi [in]cominciare; (set out) avviarsi; ‹engine, car› partire; (jump) trasalire; **to** ~ **with,…** tanto per cominciare
3 vt [in]cominciare; (cause) dare inizio a; (found) mettere su; mettere in moto ‹car›; mettere in giro ‹rumour›
■ **start off** vi (begin) cominciare
■ **start on** vt fam (attack) criticare; (nag) punzecchiare
■ **start out** vi (on journey) partire
■ **start over** Am vi (with task) ricominciare
■ **start up** vt mettere in funzione ‹engine›; avviare ‹business›

starter /'stɑːtə(r)/ n Culin primo m [piatto m]; (in race: giving signal) starter m inv; (participant) concorrente mf; Auto motorino m d'avviamento

starting point /'stɑːtɪŋ/ n punto m di partenza

starting salary n stipendio m iniziale

startle /'stɑːtl/ vt far trasalire; ‹news› sconvolgere

startling /'stɑːtlɪŋ/ adj sconvolgente

start-up capital n capitale m di avviamento

starvation /stɑː'veɪʃn/ n fame f

starve /stɑːv/ **1** vi morire di fame
2 vt far morire di fame

starving /'stɑːvɪŋ/ adj **be** ~ (dying of hunger) soffrire la fame; fam (very hungry) morire di fame

stash /stæʃ/ vt fam ~ **[away]** nascondere

✧ **state** /steɪt/ **1** n stato m; Pol Stato m; (grand style) pompa f; **be in a** ~ ‹person› essere agitato; **lie in** ~ essere esposto
2 attrib di Stato; Sch pubblico; (with ceremony) di gala
3 vt dichiarare; (specify) precisare

state-aided /-'eɪdɪd/ adj sovvenzionato dallo Stato

State Department n Am Pol ministero m degli [affari] esteri

state-funded adj sovvenzionato dallo Stato

stateless /'steɪtlɪs/ adj apolide

stately /'steɪtlɪ/ adj (-ier, -iest) maestoso

stately home n dimora f signorile

✧ **statement** /'steɪtmənt/ n dichiarazione f; Jur deposizione f; (from bank) estratto m conto; (account) rapporto m

state of emergency n stato m di emergenza

state of play punteggio m

state of the art adj ‹technology› il più avanzato

stateside /'steɪtsaɪd/ **1** adj degli Stati Uniti
2 adv negli Stati Uniti

statesman /'steɪtsmən/ n statista m

static /'stætɪk/ adj statico

static electricity n elettricità f statica

✧ **station** /'steɪʃn/ **1** n stazione f; (police) commissariato m
2 vt appostare ‹guard›; **be** ~**ed in Germany** essere di stanza in Germania

stationary /'steɪʃənərɪ/ adj immobile

stationer /'steɪəʃnə(r)/ n ~**'s [shop]** cartoleria f

stationery /'steɪʃənərɪ/ n cartoleria f

station wagon n Am station-wagon f inv

statistical /stə'tɪstɪkl/ adj statistico

statistically /stə'tɪstɪklɪ/ adv statisticamente

statistician /stætɪs'tɪʃn/ n esperto m di statistica

statistics /stə'tɪstɪks/ n (subject) statistica f; pl (figures) statistiche fpl

statue /'stætjuː/ n statua f

statuesque /stætjʊ'esk/ adj statuario

stature /'stætʃə(r)/ n statura f

✧ **status** /'steɪtəs/ n condizione f; (high rank) alto rango m

status bar n Comput barra f di stato

status quo n statu quo m inv

status symbol n status symbol m inv

statute /'stætjuːt/ n statuto m

statutory /'stætjʊtərɪ/ adj statutario

staunch /stɔːntʃ/ adj fedele

staunchly /'stɔːntʃlɪ/ adv fedelmente

stave /steɪv/ vt ~ **off** tenere lontano

✧ **stay** /steɪ/ **1** n soggiorno m
2 vi restare, rimanere; (reside) alloggiare; ~ **the night** passare la notte; ~ **put** non muoversi
3 vt ~ **the course** resistere fino alla fine
■ **stay away** vi stare lontano
■ **stay behind** vi non andare con gli altri
■ **stay in** vi (at home) stare in casa; Sch restare a scuola dopo le lezioni

S

✧ indicates a very frequent word

■ **stay on** *vi* (remain) rimanere; ~ **on at school** continuare gli studi

■ **stay up** *vi* stare su; ⟨person⟩ stare alzato

staying power /'steɪɪŋ/ *n* capacità *f* di resistenza

STD *abbr* (**sexually transmitted disease**) malattia *f* sessualmente trasmissibile, MST

STD [area] code *n* Br prefisso *m* [di teleselezione]

stead /sted/ *n* in his ~ in sua vece; **stand somebody in good** ~ tornare utile a qualcuno

steadfast /'stedfɑːst/ *adj* fedele; ⟨refusal⟩ fermo

steadily /'stedɪlɪ/ *adv* (continually) continuamente

steady /'stedɪ/ **1** *adj* (**-ier, -iest**) saldo, fermo; ⟨breathing⟩ regolare; ⟨job, boyfriend⟩ fisso; (dependable) serio
2 *adv* **be going** ~ ⟨couple⟩ fare coppia fissa

steak /steɪk/ *n* (for stew) spezzatino *m*; (for grilling, frying) bistecca *f*

♂ **steal** /stiːl/ *vt* (*pt* **stole**, *pp* **stolen**) rubare (**from** da); ~ **the show** essere al centro dell'attenzione

■ **steal in/out** *vi* entrare/uscire furtivamente

stealth /stelθ/ *n* **by** ~ di nascosto

stealthily /'stelθɪlɪ/ *adv* furtivamente

stealthy /'stelθɪ/ *adj* furtivo

steam /stiːm/ **1** *n* vapore *m*; **under one's own** ~ fam da solo; **let off** ~ fig sfogarsi
2 *vt* Culin cucinare a vapore
3 *vi* fumare

■ **steam up** *vi* ⟨window⟩ appannarsi

steamed up /stiːmd'ʌp/ *adj* **get** ~ **up** (angry) andare su tutte le furie

steam engine *n* locomotiva *f*

steamer /'stiːmə(r)/ *n* piroscafo *m*; (saucepan) pentola *f* a vapore

steam iron *n* ferro *m* [da stiro] a vapore

steamroller /'stiːmrəʊlə(r)/ *n* rullo *m* compressore

steamy /'stiːmɪ/ *adj* appannato; fig ⟨scene⟩ spinto

steel /stiːl/ **1** *n* acciaio *m*
2 *vt* ~ **oneself** temprarsi

steel wool *n* lana *f* d'acciaio

steelworks *n* acciaieria *f*

steely /'stiːlɪ/ *adj* d'acciaio

steep¹ /stiːp/ *vt* (soak) lasciare a bagno; ~**ed in** fig immerso in

steep² *adj* ripido; fam ⟨price⟩ esorbitante

steeple /'stiːpl/ *n* campanile *m*

steeplechase /'stiːpltʃeɪs/ *n* corsa *f* ippica a ostacoli

steeplejack /'stiːpldʒæk/ *n persona* (*f*) *che ripara campanili e ciminiere*

steeply /'stiːplɪ/ *adv* ripidamente

steer /stɪə(r)/ *vt/i* guidare; ~ **clear of** stare alla larga da

steering /'stɪərɪŋ/ *n* Auto sterzo *m*

steering column *n* Auto piantone *m* dello sterzo

steering committee *n* comitato *m* direttivo

steering lock *n* Auto bloccasterzo *m*; (turning circle) angolo *m* di massima sterzata

steering wheel *n* volante *m*

stem¹ /stem/ **1** *n* stelo *m*; (of glass) gambo *m*; (of word) radice *f*
2 *vi* (*pt/pp* **stemmed**) ~ **from** derivare da

stem² *vt* (*pt/pp* **stemmed**) contenere

stem cell *n* cellula *f* staminale

stem ginger *n* zenzero *m* sciroppato

stench /stentʃ/ *n* fetore *m*

stencil /'stensl/ **1** *n* stampino *m*; (decoration) stampo *m*
2 *vt* (*pt/pp* **stencilled**) stampinare

stenographer /stɪ'nɒɡrəfə(r)/ *n* stenografo, -a *mf*

stenography /stɪ'nɒɡrəfɪ/ *n* stenografia *f*

♂ **step** /step/ **1** *n* passo *m*; (stair) gradino *m*; ~**s** *pl* (ladder) scaleo *m*; **in** ~ al passo; **be out of** ~ non stare al passo; ~ **by** ~ un passo alla volta
2 *vi* (*pt/pp* **stepped**) ~ **into** entrare in; ~ **into sb's shoes** succedere a qualcuno; ~ **out of** uscire da; ~ **out of line** sgarrare

■ **step back** *vi* fare un passo indietro; ~ **back from something** fig prendere le distanze da qualcosa

■ **step down** *vi* fig dimettersi

■ **step forward** *vi* farsi avanti

■ **step in** *vi* fig intervenire

■ **step up** *vt* (increase) aumentare

step aerobics *n* step *m inv*

stepbrother *n* fratellastro *m*

stepchild *n* figliastro, -a *mf*

stepdaughter *n* figliastra *f*

stepfather *n* patrigno *m*

stepladder *n* scaleo *m*

stepmother *n* matrigna *f*

stepping stone /'stepɪŋ/ *n* pietra *f* per guadare; fig trampolino *m*

stepsister /'stepsɪstə(r)/ *n* sorellastra *f*

stepson /'stepsʌn/ *n* figliastro *m*

stereo /'sterɪəʊ/ *n* stereo *m*; **in** ~ in stereofonia

stereophonic /sterɪəʊ'fɒnɪk/ *adj* stereofonico

stereoscopic /sterɪəʊ'skɒpɪk/ *adj* stereoscopico

stereotype /'sterɪətaɪp/ *n* stereotipo *m*

stereotyped /'sterɪətaɪpt/ *adj* stereotipato

sterile /'steraɪl/ *adj* sterile

sterility /stə'rɪlətɪ/ *n* sterilità *f*

S

sterilization /sterəlaɪˈzeɪʃn/ n sterilizzazione f

sterilize /ˈsterɪlaɪz/ vt sterilizzare

sterling /ˈstɜːlɪŋ/ [1] adj fig apprezzabile [2] n sterlina f

sterling silver n argento m pregiato

stern¹ /stɜːn/ adj severo

stern² n (of boat) poppa f

sternly /ˈstɜːnlɪ/ adv severamente

steroid /ˈsterɔɪd/ n steroide m

stet /stet/ (in proofreading) vive

stethoscope /ˈsteθəskəʊp/ n stetoscopio m

stetson /ˈstetsən/ n cappello m da cowboy

stew /stjuː/ [1] n stufato m; **in a ~** fam agitato
[2] vt/i cuocere in umido; **~ed fruit** frutta f cotta

steward /ˈstjuːəd/ n (at meeting) organizzatore, -trice mf; (on ship, aircraft) steward m inv

stewardess /stjuːəˈdes/ n hostess f inv

stick¹ /stɪk/ n bastone m; (of celery, rhubarb) gambo m; Sport mazza f

✔ **stick²** [1] vt (pt/pp stuck) (stab) conficcare; (glue) attaccare; fam (put) mettere; fam (endure) sopportare; **be stuck** ‹vehicle, person› essere bloccato; ‹drawer› essere incastrato; **stuck in a traffic jam** bloccato nel traffico; **be stuck for an answer** non saper cosa rispondere; **stuck on** fam attratto da; **be stuck with something** fam farsi incastrare con qualcosa
[2] vi (adhere) attaccarsi (**to** a); (jam) bloccarsi

■ **stick around** vi fam (stay) rimanere

■ **stick at**: vt **~ at it** fam tener duro; **~ at nothing** fam non fermarsi di fronte a niente

■ **stick by** vt (be faithful to) rimanere al fianco di ‹somebody›

■ **stick down** vt incollare ‹flap›; fam (write down, put down) mettere

■ **stick out** [1] vi (project) sporgere; fam (catch the eye) risaltare
[2] vt fam fare ‹tongue›; **~ it out** (endure) tener duro; **~ one's neck out** sbilanciarsi

■ **stick to** vt (keep to) attenersi a ‹rules, facts›; mantenere ‹story›; perseverare in ‹task›; **I'll ~ to beer** continuo con la birra

■ **stick together** vi ‹pages› incollarsi; (be loyal) aiutarsi a vicenda; (not split up) rimanere uniti

■ **stick up** vi (project) sporgere

■ **stick up for** vt fam difendere

■ **stick with** vt (remain with) rimanere con ‹somebody›

sticker /ˈstɪkə(r)/ n autoadesivo m

sticking plaster /ˈstɪkɪʃ/ n cerotto m

stick insect n insetto stecco m

stick-in-the-mud n retrogrado m

stickler /ˈstɪklə(r)/ n **be a ~ for** tenere molto a

stick-up n fam rapina f a mano armata

sticky /ˈstɪkɪ/ [1] adj (-ier, -iest) appiccicoso; (adhesive) adesivo; fig (difficult) difficile
[2] n fam post-it® m inv

sticky tape n fam nastro m adesivo

stiff /stɪf/ adj rigido; ‹brush, task› duro; ‹person› controllato; ‹drink› forte; ‹penalty› severo; ‹price› alto; **bored ~** fam annoiato a morte; **~ neck** torcicollo m

stiffen /ˈstɪfn/ [1] vt irrigidire
[2] vi irrigidirsi

stiffly /ˈstɪflɪ/ adv rigidamente; ‹smile, answer› in modo controllato

stiffness /ˈstɪfnɪs/ n rigidità f

stifle /ˈstaɪfl/ vt soffocare

stifling /ˈstaɪflɪŋ/ adj soffocante

stigma /ˈstɪgmə/ n marchio m

stigmatize /ˈstɪgmətaɪz/ vt bollare

stile /staɪl/ n scaletta f

stiletto /stɪˈletəʊ/ n stiletto m; **~ heels** tacchi mpl a spillo; **~s** pl (shoes) scarpe fpl coi tacchi a spillo

still¹ /stɪl/ n distilleria f

✔ **still²** [1] adj fermo; ‹drink› non gasato; **keep/stand ~** stare fermo
[2] n quiete f; (photo) posa f
[3] adv ancora; (nevertheless) nondimeno, comunque; **I'm ~ not sure** non sono ancora sicuro

stillborn /ˈstɪlbɔːn/ adj nato morto

still life n natura f morta

stilted /ˈstɪltɪd/ adj artificioso

stilts /stɪlts/ npl trampoli mpl

stimulant /ˈstɪmjʊlənt/ n eccitante m

stimulate /ˈstɪmjʊleɪt/ vt stimolare

stimulating /ˈstɪmjʊleɪtɪŋ/ adj stimolante

stimulation /stɪmjʊˈleɪʃn/ n stimolo m

stimulus /ˈstɪmjʊləs/ n (pl **-li** /ˈstɪmjʊlaɪ/) stimolo m

sting /stɪŋ/ [1] n puntura f; (organ) pungiglione m
[2] vt (pt/pp stung) pungere; ‹jellyfish› pizzicare
[3] vi ‹insect› pungere

stinging nettle /ˈstɪŋɪŋ/ n ortica f

stingy /ˈstɪndʒɪ/ adj (-ier, -iest) tirchio

stink /stɪŋk/ [1] n puzza f
[2] vi (pt stank, pp stunk) puzzare

stink bomb n fialetta f puzzolente

stinker /ˈstɪŋkə(r)/ n fam (difficult problem etc) rompicapo m

stinking /ˈstɪŋkɪŋ/ adv **be ~ rich** fam essere ricco sfondato

stint /stɪnt/ [1] n lavoro m; **do one's ~** fare la propria parte
[2] vt **~ on** lesinare su

✔ indicates a very frequent word

stipend ···❖ **stoppage** ····

stipend /'staɪpend/ *n* congrua *f*

stipulate /'stɪpjʊleɪt/ *vt* porre come condizione

stipulation /stɪpjʊ'leɪʃn/ *n* condizione *f*

stir /stɜː(r)/ [1] *n* mescolata *f*; (commotion) trambusto *m*
[2] *vt* (*pt/pp* **stirred**) muovere; (mix) mescolare
[3] *vi* muoversi
■ **stir up** *vt* fomentare ‹hatred›

stir-fry [1] *vt* saltare in padella
[2] *n* pietanza *f* saltata in padella

stirring /'stɜːrɪŋ/ *adj* ‹speech, music› commovente

stirrup /'stɪrəp/ *n* staffa *f*

stitch /stɪtʃ/ [1] *n* punto *m*; (knitting) maglia *f*; (pain) fitta *f*; **have somebody in ∼es** fam far ridere qualcuno a crepapelle
[2] *vt* cucire
■ **stitch up** *vt* ricucire ‹wound›; **the deal's ∼ed up** l'affare è concluso

stoat /stəʊt/ *n* ermellino *m*

stock /stɒk/ [1] *n* (for use or selling) scorta *f*, stock *m inv*; (livestock) bestiame *m*; (lineage) stirpe *f*; Fin titoli *mpl*; Culin brodo *m*; **in ∼** disponibile; **out of ∼** esaurito; **take ∼** fig fare il punto
[2] *adj* solito
[3] *vt* ‹shop› vendere; approvvigionare ‹shelves›
■ **stock up** *vi* far scorta (**with** di)

stockbroker *n* agente *m* di cambio

stock car *n* (for racing) stock-car *m inv*

stock-car racing *n* corsa *f* di stock car

stock cube *n* dado *m* [da brodo]

Stock Exchange *n* Borsa *f* Valori

Stockholm /'ʃtɒkhəʊm/ *n* Stoccolma *f*

stocking /'stɒkɪŋ/ *n* calza *f*

stockist /'stɒkɪst/ *n* rivenditore *m*

stockmarket *n* mercato *m* azionario

stockpile [1] *vt* fare scorta di
[2] *n* riserva *f*

stockroom *n* magazzino *m*

stock-still *adj* immobile

stocktaking *n* Comm inventario *m*

stocky /'stɒkɪ/ *adj* (**-ier, -iest**) tarchiato

stodge /stɒdʒ/ *n* Br fam (food) ammazzafame *m inv*

stodgy /'stɒdʒɪ/ *adj* indigesto

stoic /'stəʊɪk/ *n* stoico, -a *mf*

stoical /'stəʊɪkl/ *adj* stoico

stoically /'stəʊɪklɪ/ *adv* stoicamente

stoicism /'stəʊɪsɪzm/ *n* stoicismo *m*

stoke /stəʊk/ *vt* alimentare

stole¹ /stəʊl/ *n* stola *f*

stole², **stolen** /'stəʊlən/ ▶ STEAL

stolid /'stɒlɪd/ *adj* apatico

stolidly /'stɒlɪdlɪ/ *adv* apaticamente

stomach /'stʌmək/ [1] *n* pancia *f*; Anat stomaco *m*
[2] *vt* fam reggere

stomach-ache *n* mal *m* di pancia

stomp /stɒmp/ *vi* (walk heavily) camminare con passo pesante

stone /stəʊn/ [1] *n* pietra *f*; (in fruit) nocciolo *m*; Med calcolo *m*; (weight) 6,348 kg; **within a ∼'s throw of** a un tiro di schioppo da
[2] *adj* di pietra
[3] *vt* snocciolare ‹fruit›

Stone Age *n* età *f* della pietra

stone circle *n* cromlech *m inv*

stone-cold *adj* gelido

stone-cold sober *adj* perfettamente sobrio

stoned /stəʊnd/ *adj* fam (on drugs, drink) fatto

stone-deaf *adj* fam sordo come una campana

stonemason *n* scalpellino *m*

stonewall /ˌstəʊn'wɔːl/ *vi* fare muro di gomma

stone-washed *adj* ‹jeans, denim› scolorito, stone-washed

stonework *n* lavoro *m* in muratura

stony /'stəʊnɪ/ *adj* pietroso; ‹glare› glaciale

stony-broke *adj* Br fam al verde

stood /stʊd/ ▶ STAND

stooge /stuːdʒ/ *n* Theat spalla *f*; (underling) tirapiedi *mf inv*

stool /stuːl/ *n* sgabello *m*

stool-pigeon *n* fam informatore, trice *mf*

stoop /stuːp/ [1] *n* curvatura *f*; **walk with a ∼** camminare con la schiena curva
[2] *vi* stare curvo; (bend down) chinarsi; fig abbassarsi

stop /stɒp/ [1] *n* (break) sosta *f*; (for bus, train) fermata *f*; Gram punto *m*; **come to a ∼** fermarsi; **put a ∼ to something** mettere fine a qualcosa
[2] *vt* (*pt/pp* **stopped**) fermare; arrestare ‹machine›; (prevent) impedire; **∼ somebody doing something** impedire a qualcuno di fare qualcosa; **∼ doing something** smettere di fare qualcosa; **∼ that!** smettila!; **∼ a cheque** bloccare un assegno
[3] *vi* fermarsi; ‹rain› smettere
[4] *int* fermo!
■ **stop by** *vi* (make a brief visit) passare
■ **stop off** *vi* fare una sosta
■ **stop up** *vt* otturare ‹sink›; tappare ‹hole›
■ **stop with** *vi* fam (stay with) fermarsi da

stopcock *n* rubinetto *m* di arresto

stopgap *n* palliativo *m*; (person) tappabuchi *m inv*

stop lights *npl* luci *fpl* di arresto

stop-off *n* sosta *f*

stopover *n* sosta *f*; Aeron scalo *m*

stoppage /'stɒpɪdʒ/ *n* ostruzione *f*; (strike) interruzione *f*; (deduction) trattenute *fpl*

S

stopper /'stɒpə(r)/ n tappo m

stop press n ultimissime fpl

stop sign n (segnale m di) stop m inv

stopwatch /'stɒpwɒtʃ/ n cronometro m

storage /'stɔ:rɪdʒ/ n deposito m; (in warehouse) immagazzinaggio m; Comput memoria f

storage heater n caldaia f ad accumulo

♂ **store** /stɔ:(r)/ **1** n (stock) riserva f; (shop) grande magazzino m; (depot) deposito m; **in ~** in deposito; **there's trouble in ~ for him** ci sono guai in vista per lui; **what the future has in ~ for me** cosa mi riserva il futuro; **set great ~ by** tenere in gran conto **2** vt tenere; (in warehouse, Comput) immagazzinare
■ **store up** vt (accumulate) far scorte di

store card n carta (f) di credito di grandi magazzini

storekeeper n Am = SHOPKEEPER

storeroom /'stɔ:ru:m/ n magazzino m

storey /'stɔ:rɪ/ n piano m

stork /stɔ:k/ n cicogna f

storm /stɔ:m/ **1** n temporale m; (with thunder) tempesta f **2** vt prendere d'assalto

stormy /'stɔ:mɪ/ adj tempestoso

♂ **story** /'stɔ:rɪ/ n storia f; (in newspaper) articolo m

storybook /'stɔ:rɪbʊk/ n libro m di racconti

storyteller /'stɔ:rɪtelə(r)/ n (writer) narratore, -trice mf; (liar) contaballe mf inv

stout /staʊt/ **1** adj ‹shoes› resistente; (fat) robusto; ‹defence› strenuo **2** n birra f scura

stoutly /'staʊtlɪ/ adv strenuamente

stove /stəʊv/ n cucina f [economica]; (for heating) stufa f

stovetop n Am piano m di cottura

stow /stəʊ/ vt metter via
■ **stow away** vi Naut imbarcarsi clandestinamente

stowaway /'stəʊəweɪ/ n passeggero, -a mf clandestino

straddle /'strædl/ vt stare a cavalcioni su; (standing) essere a cavallo su

strafe /streɪf/ vt mitragliare a bassa quota

straggle /'strægl/ vi crescere disordinatamente; (dawdle) rimanere indietro

straggler /'stræglə(r)/ n persona f che rimane indietro

straggly /'stræglɪ/ adj **have ~ hair** avere pochi capelli sottili

♂ **straight** /streɪt/ **1** adj diritto, dritto; ‹answer, question, person› diretto; (tidy) in ordine; ‹drink, hair› liscio; **three ~ wins** tre vittorie di seguito **2** adv diritto, dritto; (directly) direttamente; **~ away** immediatamente; **~ on or ahead** diritto; **~ out** fig apertamente; **go ~** fam rigare diritto; **put something ~** mettere qualcosa in ordine; **sit/stand up ~** stare diritto; **let's get something ~** mettiamo una cosa in chiaro

straighten /'streɪtn/ **1** vt raddrizzare **2** vi raddrizzarsi; **~ [up]** ‹person› mettersi diritto
■ **straighten out** vt fig chiarire ‹situation›

straight face n **keep a ~** restare serio

straight-faced /-'feɪst/ adj con l'aria seria

straightforward adj franco; (simple) semplice

straight man n Theat spalla f

strain¹ /streɪn/ n (streak) vena f; Bot varietà f inv; (of virus) forma f

♂ **strain²** **1** n tensione f; (injury) stiramento m; **~s** pl (of music) note fpl; **put a ~ on** fig introdurre delle tensioni in; **under a lot of ~** estremamente sotto pressione **2** vt tirare; sforzare ‹eyes, voice›; stirarsi ‹muscle›; Culin scolare **3** vi sforzarsi

strained /streɪnd/ adj ‹relations› teso

strainer /'streɪnə(r)/ n colino m

strait /streɪt/ n stretto m; **in dire ~s** in serie difficoltà

straitjacket /'streɪtdʒækɪt/ n camicia f di forza

strait-laced /-'leɪst/ adj puritano

strand¹ /strænd/ n (of thread) gugliata f; (of beads) filo m; (of hair) capello m

strand² vt **be ~ed** rimanere bloccato

♂ **strange** /streɪndʒ/ adj strano; (not known) sconosciuto; (unaccustomed) estraneo

strangely /'streɪndʒlɪ/ adv stranamente; **~ enough** curiosamente

strangeness /'streɪndʒnəs/ n stranezza f

stranger /'streɪndʒə(r)/ n estraneo, -a mf

strangle /'stræŋgl/ vt strangolare; fig reprimere

stranglehold /'stræŋglhəʊld/ n (physical grip) presa f alla gola; fig (powerful control) stretta f mortale; **have a ~ on something** fig avere in pugno qualcosa

strangulation /stræŋgjʊ'leɪʃn/ n strangolamento m

strap /stræp/ **1** n cinghia f; (to grasp in vehicle) maniglia f; (of watch) cinturino m; (shoulder) ~ bretella f, spallina f **2** vt (pt/pp **strapped**) legare; **~ in/down** assicurare

strapless /'stræplɪs/ adj ‹bra, dress› senza spalline

strapped /stræpt/ adj fam **be ~ for** essere a corto di

S

strapping /'stræpɪŋ/ *adj* robusto
strata /'strɑːtə/ ▶ STRATUM
stratagem /'strætədʒəm/ *n* stratagemma *m*
strategic /strə'tiːdʒɪk/ *adj* strategico
strategically /strə'tiːdʒɪklɪ/ *adv* strategicamente
strategist /'strætədʒɪst/ *n* stratega *mf*
ⱷ **strategy** /'strætədʒɪ/ *n* strategia *f*
stratosphere /'strætəsfɪə(r)/ *n* stratosfera *f*
stratum /'strɑːtəm/ *n* (*pl* **strata**) strato *m*
straw /strɔː/ *n* paglia *f*; (single piece) fuscello *m*; (for drinking) cannuccia *f*; **the last ∼** l'ultima goccia
strawberry /'strɔːbərɪ/ *n* fragola *f*
straw poll *n* Pol sondaggio *m* d'opinione non ufficiale
stray /streɪ/ ① *adj* (animal) randagio
② *n* randagio *m*
③ *vi* andarsene per conto proprio; (deviate) deviare (**from** da)
streak /striːk/ ① *n* striatura *f*; fig (trait) vena *f*; ∼**s** *pl* (in hair) mèche *fpl*
② *vi* (move fast) sfrecciare
streaky /'striːkɪ/ *adj* striato; (bacon) grasso
stream /striːm/ ① *n* ruscello *m*; (current) corrente *f*; (of blood, people) flusso *m*; Sch classe *f*; **come on ∼** (start operating) entrare in attività; (oil) cominciare a scorrere
② *vi* scorrere
■ **stream in** *vi* entrare a fiotti
■ **stream out** *vi* uscire a fiotti
streamer /'striːmə(r)/ *n* (paper) stella *f* filante; (flag) pennone *m*
streaming /'striːmɪŋ/ ① *adj* **a ∼ cold** raffreddore con naso che cola; Comput (media, video) in streaming
② *n* (in school) divisione (*f*) degli studenti in base alle loro capacità
streamline /'striːmlaɪn/ *vt* rendere aerodinamico; (simplify) snellire
streamlined /'striːmlaɪnd/ *adj* aerodinamico; (simplified) snellito
ⱷ **street** /striːt/ *n* strada *f*
streetcar *n* Am tram *m inv*
street cred *n* fam immagine *f* pubblica
street lamp *n* lampione *m*
street market *n* mercato *m* all'aperto
street plan *n* stradario *m*
street value *n* (of drugs) valore *m* di mercato
streetwalker *n* passeggiatrice *f*
streetwise *adj* fam (person) che conosce tutti i trucchi per sopravvivere in una metropoli
ⱷ **strength** /streŋθ/ *n* forza *f*; (of wall, bridge etc) solidità *f*; ∼**s** *pl* punti *mpl* forti; **on the ∼ of** grazie a
strengthen /'streŋθən/ *vt* rinforzare

strenuous /'strenjʊəs/ *adj* faticoso; (attempt, denial) energico
strenuously /'strenjʊəslɪ/ *adv* energicamente
ⱷ **stress** /stres/ ① *n* (emphasis) insistenza *f*; Gram accento *m* tonico; (mental) stress *m inv*; Mech spinta *f*
② *vt* (emphasize) insistere su; Gram mettere l'accento (tonico) su
■ **stress out**: *vt* ∼ somebody out stressare qualcuno
stressed /strest/ *adj* (mentally) ∼ **[out]** stressato
stressful /'stresfʊl/ *adj* stressante
ⱷ **stretch** /stretʃ/ ① *n* stiramento *m*; (period) periodo *m* di tempo; (of road) tratto *m*; (elasticity) elasticità *f*; **at a ∼** di fila; **have a ∼** stirarsi
② *vt* tirare; allargare (shoes, sweater, etc); ∼ **one's legs** stendere le gambe; ∼ **a point** fare uno strappo alla regola
③ *vi* (become wider) allargarsi; (extend) estendersi; (person) stirarsi
■ **stretch out** ① *vt* allungare (one's hand, legs); allargare (arms)
② *vi* (person) sdraiarsi; (land) estendersi
stretcher /'stretʃə(r)/ *n* barella *f*
stretchy /'stretʃɪ/ *adj* elastico
strew /struː/ *vt* (*pt/pp* **strewn** or **strewed**) sparpagliare; ∼**n with** coperto di
stricken /'strɪkn/ *adj* prostrato; ∼ **with** affetto da (illness)
strict /strɪkt/ *adj* severo; (precise) preciso
strictly /'strɪktlɪ/ *adv* severamente; ∼ **speaking** in senso stretto
strictness /'strɪktnɪs/ *n* severità *f*
stricture /'strɪktʃə(r)/ *n* critica *f*; (constriction) restringimento *m*
stride /straɪd/ ① *n* [lungo] passo *m*; **make great ∼s** fig fare passi da gigante; **take something in one's ∼** accettare qualcosa con facilità
② *vi* (*pt* **strode**, *pp* **stridden**) andare a gran passi
strident /'straɪdənt/ *adj* stridente; (colour) vistoso
stridently /'straɪdəntlɪ/ *adv* con voce stridente
strife /straɪf/ *n* conflitto *m*
ⱷ **strike** /straɪk/ ① *n* sciopero *m*; Mil attacco *m*; **on ∼** in sciopero
② *vt* (*pt/pp* **struck**) colpire; accendere (match); trovare (oil, gold); (delete) depennare; (occur to) venire in mente a; Mil attaccare; ∼ **somebody a blow** colpire qualcuno
③ *vi* (lightning) cadere; (clock) suonare; Mil attaccare; (workers) scioperare; ∼ **lucky** azzeccarla
■ **strike back** *vi* fare rappresaglia; (at critics) reagire

■ **strike off** vt eliminare; **be struck off [the register]** ⟨doctor⟩ essere radiato [dall'albo]
■ **strike out** vt eliminare
■ **strike up** vt fare ⟨friendship⟩; attaccare ⟨conversation⟩
strike-breaker n persona (f) che non aderisce a uno sciopero
strike-breaking n crumiraggio m
strike force n forze fpl d'intervento
striker /'straɪkə(r)/ n scioperante mf
striking /'straɪkɪŋ/ adj impressionante; (attractive) affascinante
string /strɪŋ/ ① n spago m; (of musical instrument, racket) corda f; (of pearls) filo m; (of lies) serie f; the ∼s pl Mus gli archi; **pull** ∼s fam usare le proprie conoscenze
② vt (pt/pp **strung**) (thread) infilare ⟨beads⟩
■ **string along** ① vt fam (deceive) prendere in giro
② vi **I'll** ∼ **along** (come too) vengo anch'io; ∼ **along with somebody** andare/venire con qualcuno
■ **string out** ① vi (spread out) allinearsi
② vt disporre in fila; **be strung out** sl (on drugs) essere fatto
■ **string together** vt mettere insieme ⟨words, remarks⟩
string bean n fagiolino m
stringed /strɪŋd/ adj ⟨instrument⟩ a corda
stringent /'strɪndʒnt/ adj rigido
stringy /'strɪŋɪ/ adj ⟨person, build⟩ asciutto; ⟨hair⟩ come spaghetti; Culin filaccioso
strip /strɪp/ ① n striscia f
② vt (pt/pp **stripped**) spogliare; togliere le lenzuola da ⟨bed⟩; scrostare ⟨wood, furniture⟩; smontare ⟨machine⟩; (deprive) privare (**of** di)
③ vi (undress) spogliarsi
■ **strip down** vt smontare ⟨engine⟩
strip cartoon n striscia f
strip club n locale m di strip-tease
stripe /straɪp/ n striscia f; Mil gallone m
striped /straɪpt/ adj a strisce
stripey /'straɪpɪ/ adj a strisce, a righe
strip light n tubo m al neon
strip lighting n illuminazione f al neon
stripper /'strɪpə(r)/ n spogliarellista mf; (solvent) sverniciatore m
strip-search ① n perquisizione f (facendo spogliare qualcuno)
② vt perquisire (facendo spogliare)
striptease /'strɪptiːz/ n spogliarello m, strip-tease m inv
strive /straɪv/ vi (pt **strove**, pp **striven**) sforzarsi (**to** di); ∼ **for** sforzarsi di ottenere
strobe /strəʊb/ n luce f stroboscopica
strode /strəʊd/ ▶ STRIDE
stroke¹ /strəʊk/ n colpo m; (of pen) tratto m; (in swimming) bracciata f; Med ictus m inv;

∼ **of luck** colpo m di fortuna; **put somebody off his** ∼ far perdere il filo a qualcuno
stroke² ① vt accarezzare
② n carezza f
stroll /strəʊl/ ① n passeggiata f; **go for a** ∼ andare a far due passi
② vi passeggiare
stroller /'strəʊlə(r)/ n Am (push-chair) passeggino m
✧ **strong** /strɒŋ/ adj (**-er** /'strɒŋɡə(r)/ **-est** /'strɒŋɡɪst/) forte; ⟨argument⟩ valido
strongbox /'strɒŋbɒks/ n cassaforte f
stronghold /'strɒŋhəʊld/ n roccaforte f
strong language n (forceful terms) linguaggio m incisivo; (swearing) linguaggio m offensivo
✧ **strongly** /'strɒŋlɪ/ adv fortemente; **feel** ∼ **about something** avere molto a cuore qualcosa
strong-minded /-'maɪndɪd/ adj risoluto
strong point n punto m di forza
strongroom n camera f blindata
strong stomach n stomaco m di ferro
strong-willed /-wɪld/ adj tenace
stroppiness /'strɒpɪnɪs/ n scontrosità f
stroppy /'strɒpɪ/ adj fam scorbutico, scontroso
strove /strəʊv/ ▶ STRIVE
struck /strʌk/ ① adj ▶ STRIKE
② adj **struck on** fam entusiasta di
structural /'strʌktʃərəl/ adj strutturale
structural damage n danni mpl alla struttura portante
structurally /'strʌktʃərəlɪ/ adv strutturalmente
✧ **structure** /'strʌktʃə(r)/ ① n struttura f
② vt strutturare
✧ **struggle** /'strʌɡl/ ① n lotta f; **with a** ∼ con difficoltà
② vi lottare; ∼ **for breath** respirare con fatica; ∼ **to do something** fare fatica a fare qualcosa; ∼ **to one's feet** alzarsi con fatica
struggling /'strʌɡlɪŋ/ adj **a** ∼ **artist/ writer** un artista/uno scrittore che fatica ad affermarsi
strum /strʌm/ vt/i (pt/pp **strummed**) strimpellare
strung /strʌŋ/ ▶ STRING
strung out adj **be** ∼ (from drugs) essere fatto; **be** ∼ **on** essere dipendente da ⟨drugs⟩
strut¹ /strʌt/ n (component) puntello m
strut² vi (pt/pp **strutted**) camminare impettito
stub /stʌb/ ① n mozzicone m; (counterfoil) matrice f
② vt (pt/pp **stubbed**) ∼ **one's toe** sbattere il dito del piede (**on** contro)
■ **stub out** vt spegnere ⟨cigarette⟩
stubble /'stʌbl/ n (on face) barba f ispida
stubbly /'stʌblɪ/ adj ispido

S

stubborn /'stʌbən/ adj testardo; ‹refusal› ostinato

stubbornly /'stʌbənlɪ/ adv testardamente; ‹refuse› ostinatamente

stubbornness /'stʌbənnɪs/ n (of person) testardaggine f

stubby /'stʌbɪ/ adj (**-ier, -iest**) tozzo

stucco /'stʌkəʊ/ n stucco m

stuck /stʌk/ ▶ STICK²

stuck-up adj fam snob inv

stud¹ /stʌd/ n (on boot) tacchetto m; (on jacket) borchia f; (for ear) orecchino m [a bottone]

stud² n (of horses) scuderia f

studded with /'stʌdɪd/ adj fig tempestato di

✧ **student** /'stjuːdənt/ n (at university) studente m, studentessa f; Am (at (high) school) scolaro, -a mf

student grant n borsa f di studio

student nurse n studente, -tessa mf infermiere, -a

student teacher n insegnante mf tirocinante

student union n (organization) organizzazione f studentesca; (building) casa f dello studente

stud-horse n stallone m [da monta]

studied /'stʌdɪd/ adj intenzionale; ‹politeness› studiato

studio /'stjuːdɪəʊ/ n studio m

studio apartment n Am monolocale m

studio flat n monolocale m

studious /'stjuːdɪəs/ adj studioso; ‹attention› studiato

studiously /'stjuːdɪəslɪ/ adv studiosamente; (carefully) attentamente

stud mare n giumenta f fattrice

✧ **study** /'stʌdɪ/ [1] n studio m
[2] vt/i (pt/pp **-ied**) studiare; ~ **for an exam** preparare un esame

study aid n sussidio m didattico

✧ **stuff** /stʌf/ [1] n materiale m; fam (things) roba f
[2] vt riempire; (with padding) imbottire; Culin farcire; ~ **something into a drawer/one's pocket** ficcare qualcosa alla rinfusa in un cassetto/in tasca; ~ **oneself** ingozzarsi (**with** di); **get ~ed!** fam va' a quel paese!

stuffing /'stʌfɪŋ/ n (padding) imbottitura f; Culin ripieno m

stuffy /'stʌfɪ/ adj (**-ier, -iest**) che sa di chiuso; (old-fashioned) antiquato

stultifying /'stʌltɪfaɪŋ/ adj che abbruttisce

stumble /'stʌmbl/ vi inciampare; ~ **across** or **on** imbattersi in

stumbling block /'stʌmblɪŋ/ n ostacolo m

stump /stʌmp/ n ceppo m; (of limb) moncone m

■ **stump up** vt/i fam sganciare

stumped /stʌmpt/ adj fam perplesso

stumpy /'stʌmpɪ/ adj (**-ier, -iest**) ‹person, legs› tozzo

stun /stʌn/ vt (pt/pp **stunned**) stordire; (astonish) sbalordire

stung /stʌŋ/ ▶ STING

stunk /stʌŋk/ ▶ STINK

stunned /stʌnd/ adj ‹expression› sbalordito

stunning /'stʌnɪŋ/ adj fam favoloso; ‹blow, victory› sbalorditivo

stunt¹ /stʌnt/ n fam trovata f pubblicitaria

stunt² vt arrestare lo sviluppo di

stunted /'stʌntɪd/ adj stentato

stuntman /'stʌntmən/ n stuntman m inv, cascatore m

stuntwoman /'stʌntwʊmən/ n stuntwoman f inv

stupefaction /stjuːpɪ'fækʃn/ n stupore m

stupefy /'stjuːpɪfaɪ/ vt (pt/pp **-ied**) (astonish) stupire

stupefying /'stjuːpɪfaɪŋ/ adj stupefacente

stupendous /stjuː'pendəs/ adj stupendo

stupendously /stjuː'pendəslɪ/ adv stupendamente

✧ **stupid** /'stjuːpɪd/ adj stupido

stupidity /stjuː'pɪdətɪ/ n stupidità f

stupidly /'stjuːpɪdlɪ/ adv stupidamente

stupor /'stjuːpə(r)/ n torpore m

sturdy /'stɜːdɪ/ adj (**-ier, -iest**) robusto; ‹furniture› solido

stutter /'stʌtə(r)/ [1] n balbuzie f; **have a ~** balbettare
[2] vt/i balbettare

St Valentine's Day n san Valentino m

sty¹ /staɪ/ n (pl **sties**) porcile m

sty², **stye** n (pl **styes**) Med orzaiolo m

✧ **style** /staɪl/ n stile m; (fashion) moda f; (sort) tipo m; (hair) ~ pettinatura f; **in ~** in grande stile

styling /'staɪlɪŋ/ [1] adj ‹gel, mousse› modellante
[2] n (design) styling m; (in hairdressing) acconciatura f

stylish /'staɪlɪʃ/ adj elegante

stylishly /'staɪlɪʃlɪ/ adv con eleganza

stylist /'staɪlɪst/ n stilista mf; **hair ~** parrucchiere, -a mf

stylistic /staɪ'lɪstɪk/ adj stilistico

stylistically /staɪ'lɪstɪklɪ/ adv stilisticamente

stylized /'staɪlaɪzd/ adj stilizzato

stylus /'staɪləs/ n (on record player) puntina f

styptic pencil /'stɪptɪk/ n matita f emostatica

suave /swɑːv/ adj dai modi garbati

sub-aqua /sʌb'ækwə/ adj ‹club› di sport subacquei

S

subcommittee /'sʌbkəmɪtɪ/ *n*
sottocommissione *f*

subconscious /sʌb'kɒnʃəs/ ① *adj*
subcosciente
② *n* subcosciente *m*

subconsciously /sʌb'kɒnʃəslɪ/ *adv* in
modo inconscio

subcontinent /sʌb'kɒntɪnənt/ *n*
subcontinente *m*

subcontract /sʌbkən'trækt/ *vt*
subappaltare (**to** a)

subcontractor /'sʌbkəntræktə(r)/ *n*
subappaltatore, -trice *mf*

subdirectory /'sʌbdaɪrektərɪ/ *n* Comput
sottodirectory *f inv*

subdivide /sʌbdɪ'vaɪd/ *vt* suddividere

subdivision /'sʌbdɪvɪʒn/ *n* suddivisione *f*

subdue /səb'dju:/ *vt* sottomettere; (make
quieter) attenuare

subdued /səb'dju:d/ *adj* ‹light› attenuato;
‹person, voice› pacato

subheading /'sʌbhedɪŋ/ *n* sottotitolo *m*

subhuman /sʌb'hju:mən/ *adj* (cruel, not fit
for humans) disumano; fam ‹appearance› da
paleolitico

🞄 **subject¹** /'sʌbdʒekt/ ① *adj* ~ **to** soggetto
a; (depending on) subordinato a; ~ **to
availability** nei limiti della disponibilità
② *n* soggetto *m*; (of ruler) suddito, -a *mf*;
Sch materia *f*; **change the** ~ parlare di
qualcos'altro

subject² /səb'dʒekt/ *vt* (to attack, abuse)
sottoporre; assoggettare ‹country›

subjective /səb'dʒektɪv/ *adj* soggettivo

subjectively /səb'dʒektɪvlɪ/ *adv*
soggettivamente

subjectiveness /səb'dʒektɪvnɪs/ *n*
soggetività *f*

subjugate /'sʌbdʒʊgeɪt/ *vt* soggiogare,
sottomettere

subjugation /sʌbdʒə'geɪʃn/ *n*
sottomissione *f*

subjunctive /səb'dʒʌŋktɪv/ *adj & n*
congiuntivo *m*

sub-let /sʌb'let/ *vt* (*pt/pp* -**let**, *pres p*
-**letting**) subaffittare

sublime /sə'blaɪm/ *adj* sublime

sublimely /sə'blaɪmlɪ/ *adv* sublimamente

subliminal /sə'blɪmɪnl/ *adj* subliminale

sub-machine gun *n* mitraglietta *f*

submarine /'sʌbməri:n/ *n* sommergibile
m

submerge /səb'mɜːdʒ/ ① *vt* immergere;
be ~**d** essere sommerso
② *vi* immergersi

🞄 **submission** /səb'mɪʃn/ *n* sottomissione *f*

submissive /səb'mɪsɪv/ *adj* sottomesso

submissively /səb'mɪsɪvlɪ/ *adv*
remissivamente

submissiveness /səb'mɪsɪvnɪs/ *n*
remissività *f*

🞄 **submit** /səb'mɪt/ ① *vt* (*pt/pp* -**mitted**,
pres p -**mitting**) sottoporre
② *vi* sottomettersi

subnormal /sʌb'nɔːml/ *adj* ‹temperature›
al di sotto della norma; ‹person› subnormale

subordinate¹ /sə'bɔːdɪnɪt/ *adj & n*
subordinato, -a *mf*

subordinate² /sə'bɔːdɪneɪt/ *vt*
subordinare (**to** a)

subpoena /səb'pi:nə/ ① *n* mandato *m* di
comparizione
② *vt* citare

subprime /'sʌbpraɪm/ *n* subprime *m*

subroutine /'sʌbru:ti:n/ *n* Comput
subroutine *f*

subscribe /səb'skraɪb/ *vi* contribuire;
~ **to** abbonarsi a ‹newspaper›; sottoscrivere
‹fund›; fig aderire a ‹theory›

subscriber /səb'skraɪbə(r)/ *n* abbonato,
-a *mf*

subscription /səb'skrɪpʃn/ *n* (to club)
sottoscrizione *f*; (to newspaper) abbonamento
m

subsequent /'sʌbsɪkwənt/ *adj*
susseguente

subsequently /'sʌbsɪkwəntlɪ/ *adv* in
seguito

subservience /səb'sɜːvɪəns/ *n*
asservimento *m*

subservient /səb'sɜːvɪənt/ *adj*
subordinato; (servile) servile

subserviently /səb'sɜːvɪəntlɪ/ *adv*
servilmente

subset /'sʌbset/ *n* Math sottoinsieme *m*

subside /səb'saɪd/ *vi* sprofondare; ‹ground›
avvallarsi; ‹storm› placarsi

subsidence /'sʌbsɪdəns/ *n* (of land)
cedimento *m*

subsidiary /səb'sɪdɪərɪ/ ① *adj*
secondario
② *n* ~ **[company]** filiale *f*

subsidize /'sʌbsɪdaɪz/ *vt* sovvenzionare

subsidy /'sʌbsɪdɪ/ *n* sovvenzione *f*

subsist /səb'sɪst/ *vi* vivere (**on** di)

subsistence /səb'sɪstəns/ *n* sussistenza *f*

subsistence level *n* livello *m* di
sussistenza

substance /'sʌbstəns/ *n* sostanza *f*

sub-standard /sʌb'stændəd/ *adj* di
qualità inferiore

🞄 **substantial** /səb'stænʃl/ *adj* sostanziale;
‹meal› sostanzioso; (strong) solido

🞄 **substantially** /səb'stænʃəlɪ/ *adv*
sostanzialmente; ‹built› solidamente

substantiate /səb'stænʃɪeɪt/ *vt*
comprovare

S

substitute /'sʌbstɪtjuːt/ **1** n sostituto m
2 vt ~ A for B sostituire B con A
3 vi ~ for somebody sostituire qualcuno
substitution /sʌbstɪ'tjuːʃn/ n sostituzione f
subterfuge /'sʌbtəfjuːdʒ/ n sotterfugio m
subterranean /sʌbtə'reɪnɪən/ adj sotterraneo
subtext /'sʌbtekst/ n storia f secondaria; fig messaggio m implicito
subtitle /'sʌbtaɪtl/ **1** n sottotitolo m
2 vt sottotitolare
subtitled /'sʌbtaɪtld/ adj sottotitolato
subtle /'sʌtl/ adj sottile; ‹taste, perfume› delicato
subtlety /'sʌtltɪ/ n sottigliezza f
subtly /'sʌtlɪ/ adv sottilmente
subtotal /'sʌbtəʊtl/ n totale m parziale
subtract /səb'trækt/ vt sottrarre
subtraction /səb'trækʃn/ n sottrazione f
suburb /'sʌbɜːb/ n sobborgo m; **in the ~s** in periferia
suburban /sə'bɜːbən/ adj suburbano
suburbia /sə'bɜːbɪə/ n sobborghi mpl
subversive /səb'vɜːsɪv/ adj sovversivo
subway /'sʌbweɪ/ n sottopassaggio m; Am (railway) metropolitana f, metrò m inv
sub-zero /sʌb'zɪərəʊ/ adj sottozero inv
✧ **succeed** /sək'siːd/ **1** vi riuscire (**in doing something** a fare qualcosa); (follow) succedere (**to** a)
2 vt succedere a ‹king›
succeeding /sək'siːdɪŋ/ adj successivo
✧ **success** /sək'ses/ n successo m; **be a ~** (in life) aver successo
✧ **successful** /sək'sesfʊl/ adj riuscito; ‹businessman, artist etc› di successo
successfully /sək'sesfʊlɪ/ adv con successo
succession /sək'seʃn/ n successione f; **in ~** di seguito
successive /sək'sesɪv/ adj successivo
successively /sə'sesɪvlɪ/ adv successivamente
successor /sək'sesə(r)/ n successore m
success rate n percentuale f di promozioni
success story n successo m
succinct /sək'sɪŋkt/ adj succinto
succinctly /sək'sɪŋktlɪ/ adv succintamente
succour /'sʌkə(r)/ **1** vt soccorrere
2 n soccorso m
succulence /'sʌkjʊləns/ n succulenza f
succulent /'sʌkjʊlənt/ adj succulento
succumb /sə'kʌm/ vi soccombere (**to** a)
✧ **such** /sʌtʃ/ **1** adj tale; ~ **a book** un libro così; ~ **a thing** una cosa del genere; ~ **a long time ago** talmente tanto tempo fa; **there is**

no ~ **thing/person** non c'è una cosa/persona così
2 pron **as** ~ in quanto tale; ~ **as** come; **and** ~ e simili; ~ **as it is** per quel che vale; **if** ~ **is the case** se questo è il caso
such and such adj tale; **for** ~ **an amount** per un tot; **go on** ~ **a day at** ~ **a time** vai il tal giorno alla tal ora
suchlike /'sʌtʃlaɪk/ pron fam di tal genere
suck /sʌk/ vt succhiare
■ **suck up** vt assorbire
■ **suck up to** vt fam fare il lecchino con
sucker /'sʌkə(r)/ (n Bot) pollone m; fam (person) credulone, -a mf
suckle /'sʌkl/ vt allattare
suction /'sʌkʃn/ n aspirazione f
suction pad n ventosa f
Sudan /sʊ'dæn/ n Sudan m
Sudanese /sʊdən'iːz/ adj & n sudanese mf
sudden /'sʌdn/ **1** adj improvviso
2 n **all of a** ~ all'improvviso
sudden death n (football) sudden death f
✧ **suddenly** /'sʌdnlɪ/ adv improvvisamente
sudoku /suː'dəʊkuː/ n sudoku m inv
suds /sʌdz/ npl (foam) schiuma f; (soapy water) acqua f saponata
sue /suː/ **1** vt (pres p **suing**) fare causa a (**for** per)
2 vi fare causa
suede /sweɪd/ n pelle f scamosciata
suet /'suːɪt/ n grasso m di rognone
✧ **suffer** /'sʌfə(r)/ **1** vi soffrire (**from** per)
2 vt soffrire di ‹pain›; subire ‹loss etc›
sufferance /'sʌf(ə)rəns/ n **you're here on** ~ qui tu sei appena tollerato
sufferer /'sʌfərə(r)/ n malato, -a mf; **Aids** ~**s** malati di Aids
suffering /'sʌf(ə)rɪŋ/ n sofferenza f
suffice /sə'faɪs/ vi bastare
sufficient /sə'fɪʃənt/ adj sufficiente
sufficiently /sə'fɪʃəntlɪ/ adv sufficientemente
suffix /'sʌfɪks/ n suffisso m
suffocate /'sʌfəkeɪt/ vt/i soffocare
suffocating /'sʌfəkeɪtɪŋ/ adj ‹heat› soffocante
suffocation /sʌfə'keɪʃn/ n soffocamento m
suffrage /'sʌfrɪdʒ/ n (right) diritto m di voto; (system) suffragio m
suffragette /sʌfrə'dʒet/ n suffragetta f
sugar /'ʃʊgə(r)/ **1** n zucchero m
2 vt zuccherare; ~ **the pill** fig addolcire la pillola
sugar basin, sugar bowl n zuccheriera f
sugar beet n barbabietola f da zucchero
sugar cane n canna f da zucchero

S

sugar-coated /-'kəʊtɪd/ *adj* ricoperto di zucchero

sugar cube *n* zolletta *f*

sugar daddy *n* fam vecchio amante *m* danaroso

sugar-free *adj* senza zucchero

sugar lump *n* zolletta *f*

sugary /'ʃʊgərɪ/ *adj* zuccheroso; fig sdolcinato

♂ **suggest** /sə'dʒest/ *vt* suggerire; (indicate, insinuate) fare pensare a

suggestible /sə'dʒestəbl/ *adj* suggestionabile

♂ **suggestion** /sə'dʒestʃən/ *n* suggerimento *m*; (trace) traccia *f*

suggestive /sə'dʒestɪv/ *adj* allusivo; be ~ of fare pensare a

suggestively /sə'dʒestɪvlɪ/ *adv* in modo allusivo

suicidal /suːɪ'saɪdl/ *adj* suicida

♂ **suicide** /'suːɪsaɪd/ *n* suicidio *m*; (person) suicida *mf*; commit ~ suicidarsi

suicide attack *n* attacco *m* suicida

suicide attempt *n* tentato suicidio *m*

suicide pact *n* patto *m* suicida

♂ **suit** /suːt/ **1** *n* vestito *m*; (woman's) tailleur *m inv*; (Cards) seme *m*; Jur causa *f*; follow ~ fig fare lo stesso

2 *vt* andar bene a; (adapt) adattare (**to** a); (be convenient for) andare bene per; be ~ed to *or* for essere adatto a; ~ yourself! fa' come vuoi!

suitability /suːtə'bɪlɪtɪ/ *n* adeguatezza *f*

suitable /'suːtəbl/ *adj* adatto

suitably /'suːtəblɪ/ *adv* convenientemente

suitcase /'suːtkeɪs/ *n* valigia *f*

suite /swiːt/ *n* suite *f inv*; (of furniture) divano *m* e poltrone *fpl* assortiti

sulk /sʌlk/ *vi* fare il broncio

sulkily /'sʌlkɪlɪ/ *adv* con aria imbronciata

sulky /'sʌlkɪ/ *adj* imbronciato

sullen /'sʌlən/ *adj* svogliato

sullenly /'sʌlənlɪ/ *adv* svogliatamente

sulphur /'sʌlfə(r)/ *n* zolfo *m*

sulphur dioxide /daɪ'ɒksaɪd/ *n* anidride *f* solforosa

sulphuric acid /sʌl'fjʊərɪk/ *n* acido *m* solforico

sultana /sʌl'tɑːnə/ *n* uva *f* sultanina

sultry /'sʌltrɪ/ *adj* (**-ier, -iest**) ‹weather› afoso; fig sensuale

sum /sʌm/ *n* somma *f*; Sch addizione *f*

■ **sum up** **1** *vi* (*pt/pp* **summed**) riassumere

2 *vt* valutare

summarily /sʌ'merɪlɪ/ *adv* sommariamente; ‹dismissed› sbrigativamente

summarize /'sʌməraɪz/ *vt* riassumere

summary /'sʌmərɪ/ **1** *n* sommario *m*

2 *adj* sommario; ‹dismissal› sbrigativo

♂ **summer** /'sʌmə(r)/ *n* estate *f*; in ~, in the ~ in estate

summer camp *n* ≈ colonia *f*

summer holiday *n* vacanze *fpl* estive

summer house *n* padiglione *m*

summer school *n* corso *m* estivo

summertime *n* (season) estate *f*

summer time *n* (clock change) ora *f* legale

summery /'sʌmərɪ/ *adj* estivo

summing-up /sʌmɪŋ'ʌp/ *n* riepilogo *m*; Jur ricapitolazione *f* del processo

summit /'sʌmɪt/ *n* cima *f*

summit conference *n* vertice *m*

summon /'sʌmən/ *vt* convocare; Jur citare

■ **summon up** *vt* raccogliere ‹strength›; rievocare ‹memory›

summons /'sʌmənz/ **1** *n* Jur citazione *f*

2 *vt* citare in giudizio

sump /sʌmp/ *n* Auto coppa *f* dell'olio

sumptuous /'sʌmptjʊəs/ *adj* sontuoso

sumptuously /'sʌmptjʊəslɪ/ *adv* sontuosamente

sum total *n* totale *m*

♂ **sun** /sʌn/ **1** *n* sole *m*

2 *vt* (*pt/pp* **sunned**) ~ oneself prendere il sole

sunbathe *vi* prendere il sole

sunbed *n* lettino *m* solare

sunblock *n* prodotto *m* solare a protezione totale

sunburn *n* scottatura *f* (solare)

sunburnt *adj* scottato (dal sole)

sun cream *n* crema *f* solare

sundae /'sʌndeɪ/ *n* gelato *m* guarnito

♂ **Sunday** /'sʌndeɪ/ *n* domenica *f*

Sunday best *n* in one's ~ con l'abito della festa

Sunday trading *n* apertura *f* domenicale (dei negozi)

sundial /'sʌndaɪəl/ *n* meridiana *f*

sundress *n* prendisole *m*

sun-dried tomatoes /'sʌndraɪd/ *npl* pomodori *mpl* secchi

sundries /'sʌndrɪz/ *npl* articoli *mpl* vari

sundry /'sʌndrɪ/ *adj* svariati; all and ~ tutti quanti

sunflower /'sʌnflaʊə(r)/ *n* girasole *m*

sung /sʌŋ/ ▶ SING

sunglasses /'sʌnglɑːsɪz/ *npl* occhiali *mpl* da sole

sun hat *n* cappello *m* da sole

sunk /sʌŋk/ ▶ SINK

sunken /'sʌŋkn/ *adj* incavato

sunlamp /'sʌnlæmp/ *n* lampada *f* abbronzante

S

sunlight /'sʌnlaɪt/ *n* [luce *f* del] sole *m*

sunny /'sʌnɪ/ *adj* (**-ier, -iest**) assolato

sunrise *n* alba *f*

sunroof *n* Auto tettuccio *m* apribile

sunscreen *n* (to prevent sunburn) crema *f* solare protettiva

sunset *n* tramonto *m*

sunshade *n* parasole *m*

sunshine *n* [luce *f* del] sole *m*

sunshine roof *n* tettuccio *m* apribile

sunstroke *n* insolazione *f*

suntan *n* abbronzatura *f*

suntan lotion *n* lozione *f* solare

sun-tanned *adj* abbronzato

suntan oil *n* olio *m* solare

super /'su:pə(r)/ *adj* fam fantastico

superannuated /su:pər'ænjʊeɪtɪd/ *adj* fig che ha fatto il suo tempo

superannuation /su:pərænjʊ'eɪʃn/ *n* (contributions) contributi *mpl* pensionistici; (pension) pensione *f*

superannuation fund *n* fondo *m* pensione

superb /sʊ'pɜːb/ *adj* splendido

superbly /sʊ'pɜːblɪ/ *adv* splendidamente

supercilious /su:pə'sɪlɪəs/ *adj* altezzoso

superciliously /su:pə'sɪlɪəslɪ/ *adv* in modo altezzoso

superficial /su:pə'fɪʃl/ *adj* superficiale

superficiality /su:pəfɪʃɪ'ælɪtɪ/ *n* superficialità *f*

superficially /su:pə'fɪʃəlɪ/ *adv* superficialmente

superfluous /sʊ'pɜːflʊəs/ *adj* superfluo

superhighway /'su:pəhaɪweɪ/ *n* [information] ~ Comput autostrada *f* telematica

superhuman /su:pə'hju:mən/ *adj* sovrumano

superimpose /su:pərɪm'pəʊz/ *vt* sovrapporre ‹picture, soundtrack› (on a); ~d title titolo *m* in sovrimpressione

superintendent /su:pərɪn'tendənt/ *n* (of police) commissario *m* di polizia

superior /su:'pɪərɪə(r)/ *adj & n* superiore *mf*

superiority /su:pɪərɪ'ɒrətɪ/ *n* superiorità *f*

superlative /su:'pɜːlətɪv/ [1] *adj* eccellente
[2] *n* superlativo *m*

superlatively /su:'pɜːlətɪvlɪ/ *adv* ‹perform› in modo eccezionale; ‹good› estremamente

superman /'su:pəmæn/ *n* superuomo *m*

supermarket /'su:pəmɑːkɪt/ *n* supermercato *m*

supermodel /'su:pəmɒdl/ *n* top model *f inv*

supernatural /su:pə'nætʃrəl/ *adj* soprannaturale

superpower /'su:pəpaʊə(r)/ *n* superpotenza *f*

superscript /'su:pəskrɪpt/ *adj* ‹number, letter› all'esponente

supersede /su:pə'si:d/ *vt* rimpiazzare

supersonic /su:pə'sɒnɪk/ *adj* supersonico

superstar /'su:pəstɑː(r), 'sju:-/ *n* superstar *mf*

superstition /su:pə'stɪʃn/ *n* superstizione *f*

superstitious /su:pə'stɪʃəs/ *adj* superstizioso

superstitiously /su:pə'stɪʃəslɪ/ *adv* in modo superstizioso

superstore /'su:pəstɔː(r)/ *n* ipermercato *m*

superstructure /'su:pəstrʌktʃə(r)/ *n* sovrastruttura *f*

supertax /'su:pətæks/ *n* Fin soprattassa *f*

supervise /'su:pəvaɪz/ *vt* supervisionare

supervision /su:pə'vɪʒn/ *n* supervisione *f*

supervisor /'su:pəvaɪzə(r)/ *n* supervisore *m*

supervisory /su:pə'vaɪzərɪ/ *adj* di supervisione

superwoman /'su:pəwʊmən/ *n* superdonna *f*

supper /'sʌpə(r)/ *n* cena *f*; **have** ~ cenare

supple /'sʌpl/ *adj* slogato

supplement /'sʌplɪmənt/ [1] *n* supplemento *m*
[2] *vt* integrare

supplementary /sʌplɪ'mentərɪ/ *adj* supplementare

supplier /sə'plaɪə(r)/ *n* fornitore, -trice *mf*

✱ **supply** /sə'plaɪ/ [1] *n* fornitura *f*; Econ offerta *f*; **be in short** ~ scarseggiare; ~ **and demand** domanda *f* e offerta *f*; **supplies** *pl* Mil approvvigionamenti *mpl*
[2] *vt* (*pt/pp* **-ied**) fornire; ~ **somebody with something** fornire qualcosa a qualcuno

supply teacher *n* supplente *mf*

✱ **support** /sə'pɔːt/ [1] *n* sostegno *m*; (base) supporto *m*; (keep) sostentamento *m*
[2] *vt* sostenere; mantenere ‹family›; (give money to) mantenere finanziariamente; Sport fare il tifo per; Comput supportare

✱ **supporter** /sə'pɔːtə(r)/ *n* sostenitore, -trice *mf*; Sport tifoso, -a *mf*

support group *n* gruppo *m* di sostegno

supporting /sə'pɔːtɪŋ/ *adj* ‹actor› non protagonista

supporting actor /sə'pɔːtɪŋ/ *n* attore *m* non protagonista

supporting actress *n* attrice *f* non protagonista

supportive /sə'pɔːtɪv/ *adj* incoraggiante; **be** ~ **of somebody** dare tutto il proprio appoggio a qualcuno

S

support stockings *npl* calze *fpl* elastiche

◆ **suppose** /sə'pəʊz/ *vt* (presume) supporre; (imagine) pensare; **be** ∼**d to do** dover fare; **not be** ∼**d to** non avere il permesso di; **I** ∼ **so** suppongo di si

supposedly /sə'pəʊzɪdlɪ/ *adv* presumibilmente

supposing /sə'pəʊzɪŋ/ *conj* ∼ **(that) he agrees** supponiamo che accetti

supposition /sʌpə'zɪʃn/ *n* supposizione *f*

suppository /sʌ'pɒzɪtrɪ/ *n* supposta *f*

suppress /sə'pres/ *vt* sopprimere

suppressant /sə'presənt/ *n* Med inibitore *m*

suppression /sə'preʃn/ *n* soppressione *f*

suppurate /'sʌpjʊreɪt/ *vi* suppurare

supremacy /su:'preməsɪ/ *n* supremazia *f*

supreme /su:'pri:m/ *adj* supremo

supremo /su:'pri:məʊ/ *n* massima autorità *f inv*

Supt. *abbr* (**Superintendent**) commissario *m* di polizia

surcharge /'sɜ:tʃɑːdʒ/ *n* supplemento *m*

◆ **sure** /ʃʊə(r)/ ☐**1** *adj* sicuro, certo; **make** ∼ accertarsi; **be** ∼ **to do it** accertati di farlo ☐**2** *adv* Am fam certamente; ∼ **enough** infatti

sure-fire *adj* fam garantito

sure-footed /-'fʊtɪd/ *adj* agile

◆ **surely** /'ʃʊəlɪ/ *adv* certamente; Am (gladly) volentieri

surety /'ʃʊərətɪ/ *n* garanzia *f*; **stand** ∼ **for somebody/something** fare da garante a qualcuno/per qualcosa

surf /sɜ:f/ ☐**1** *n* schiuma *f* ☐**2** *vt* ∼ **the Net** navigare in Internet

◆ **surface** /'sɜ:fɪs/ ☐**1** *n* superficie *f*; **on the** ∼ fig in apparenza ☐**2** *vi* (emerge) emergere

surface mail *n* **by** ∼ per posta ordinaria

surface-to-air missile *n* missile *m* terra-aria

surfboard /'sɜ:fbɔːd/ *n* tavola *f* da surf

surfeit /'sɜ:fɪt/ *n* eccesso *m*

surfer /'sɜ:fə(r)/ *n* surfista *mf*

surfing /'sɜ:fɪŋ/ *n* surf *m*

surge /sɜ:dʒ/ ☐**1** *n* (of sea) ondata *f*; (of interest) aumento *m*; (in demand) impennata *f*; (of anger, pity) impeto *m* ☐**2** *vi* riversarsi; ∼ **forward** buttarsi in avanti

surgeon /'sɜ:dʒən/ *n* chirurgo *m*

◆ **surgery** /'sɜ:dʒərɪ/ *n* chirurgia *f*; (place, consulting room) ambulatorio *m*; (hours) ore *fpl* di visita; **have** ∼ subire un intervento [chirurgico]

surgical /'sɜ:dʒɪkl/ *adj* chirurgico

surgically /'sɜ:dʒɪklɪ/ *adv* chirurgicamente

surgical spirit *n* alcol *m* denaturato

Surinam /sʊərɪ'næm/ *n* Suriname *m*

surliness /'sɜ:lɪnɪs/ *n* scontrosità *f*

surly /'sɜ:lɪ/ *adj* (**-ier, -iest**) scontroso

surmise /sə'maɪz/ *vt* supporre

surmount /sə'maʊnt/ *vt* sormontare

surname /'sɜ:neɪm/ *n* cognome *m*

surpass /sə'pɑ:s/ *vt* superare

surplus /'sɜ:pləs/ ☐**1** *adj* d'avanzo; **be** ∼ **to requirements** essere in eccedenza rispetto alle necessità ☐**2** *n* sovrappiù *m*

◆ **surprise** /sə'praɪz/ ☐**1** *n* sorpresa *f* ☐**2** *vt* sorprendere; **be** ∼**d** essere sorpreso (**at** da)

surprising /sə'praɪzɪŋ/ *adj* sorprendente

surprisingly /sə'praɪzɪŋlɪ/ *adv* sorprendentemente; ∼ **enough** stranamente

surreal /sə'rɪəl/ *adj* surreale

surrealism /sə'rɪəlɪzm/ *n* surrealismo *m*

surrealist /sə'rɪəlɪst/ ☐**1** *n* surrealista *mf* ☐**2** *adj* surrealistico

surrender /sə'rendə(r)/ ☐**1** *n* resa *f* ☐**2** *vi* arrendersi ☐**3** *vt* cedere

surreptitious /sʌrəp'tɪʃəs/ *adj* furtivo

surreptitiously /sʌrəp'tɪʃəslɪ/ *adv* furtivamente

surrogate /'sʌrəgət/ *n* surrogato *m*

surrogate mother *n* madre *f* surrogata

◆ **surround** /sə'raʊnd/ *vt* circondare; ∼**ed by** circondato da

surrounding /sə'raʊndɪŋ/ *adj* circostante

surroundings /sə'raʊndɪŋz/ *npl* dintorni *mpl*

surtax /'sɜ:tæks/ *n* soprattassa *f*; (on income) imposta *f* supplementare

surveillance /sə'veɪləns/ *n* sorveglianza *f*; **under** ∼ sotto sorveglianza

◆ **survey¹** /'sɜ:veɪ/ *n* sguardo *m*; (poll) sondaggio *m*; (investigation) indagine *f*; (of land) rilevamento *m*; (of house) perizia *f*

survey² /sə'veɪ/ *vt* esaminare; fare un rilevamento di ‹land›; fare una perizia di ‹building›

surveyor /sə'veɪə(r)/ *n* perito *m*; (of land) topografo, -a *mf*

survival /sə'vaɪvl/ *n* sopravvivenza *f*; (relic) resto *m*

◆ **survive** /sə'vaɪv/ ☐**1** *vt* sopravvivere a ☐**2** *vi* sopravvivere

surviving /sə'vaɪvɪŋ/ *adj* ‹relative› sopravvissuto

survivor /sə'vaɪvə(r)/ *n* superstite *mf*; **be a** ∼ fam riuscire sempre a cavarsela

susceptible /sə'septəbl/ *adj* influenzabile; ∼ **to** sensibile a

─────────────
◆ indicates a very frequent word

S

✛ **suspect¹** /sə'spekt/ vt sospettare; (assume) supporre

suspect² /'sʌspekt/ adj & n sospetto, -a mf

suspend /sə'spend/ vt appendere; (stop, from duty) sospendere

suspended sentence n (sospensione f) condizionale f (della pena)

suspender belt /sə'spendə/ n reggicalze m inv

suspenders /sə'spendəz/ npl giarrettiere fpl; Am (braces) bretelle fpl

suspense /sə'spens/ n tensione f; (in book etc) suspense f

suspension /sə'spenʃn/ n Auto sospensione f

suspension bridge n ponte m sospeso

suspicion /sə'spɪʃn/ n sospetto m; (trace) pizzico m; **under ~** sospettato

suspicious /sə'spɪʃəs/ adj sospettoso; (arousing suspicion) sospetto

suspiciously /sə'spɪʃəslɪ/ adv sospettosamente; (arousing suspicion) in modo sospetto

suss vt **~ out** Br fam intuire ‹person›; capire ‹software, technique›; **I've got you ~ed [out]** ho scoperto il tuo piano

sustain /sə'steɪn/ vt sostenere; mantenere ‹life›; subire ‹injury›

sustainable /səs'teɪnəbl/ adj ‹development, growth› sostenibile; ‹resource, forest› rinnovabile

sustained /sə'steɪnd/ adj ‹effort› prolungato

sustenance /'sʌstɪnəns/ n nutrimento m

suture /'suːtʃə(r)/ n sutura f

SUV n abbr Am (**sports utility vehicle**) SUV f inv

SW abbr (**south-west**) SO

swab /swɒb/ n Med tampone m

swagger /'swægə(r)/ vi pavoneggiarsi

swallow¹ /'swɒləʊ/ vt/i inghiottire

■ **swallow up** vt divorare; ‹earth, crowd› inghiottire

swallow² n (bird) rondine f

swam /swæm/ ▶ SWIM

swamp /swɒmp/ ① n palude f ② vt fig sommergere

swampy /'swɒmpɪ/ adj paludoso

swan /swɒn/ n cigno m

swank /swæŋk/ vi fam darsi delle arie

swanky /'swæŋkɪ/ adj fam (posh) snob inv

swap /swɒp/ ① n fam scambio m ② vt (pt/pp **swapped**) fam scambiare (**for** con) ③ vi fare cambio

swarm /swɔːm/ ① n sciame m ② vi sciamare; **be ~ing with** fig brulicare di

swarthy /'swɔːðɪ/ adj (**-ier, -iest**) di carnagione scura

swashbuckling /'swɒʃbʌklɪŋ/ adj ‹hero, appearance› spericolato; ‹adventure, tale› di cappa e spada

swastika /'swɒstɪkə/ n svastica f

swat /swɒt/ vt (pt/pp **swatted**) schiacciare

swathe Br, **swath** Am /sweɪð/ ① n (of grass, corn) falciata f; (land) larga striscia f ② vt (in bandages, silk) avvolgere

sway /sweɪ/ ① n fig influenza f ② vi oscillare; ‹person› ondeggiare ③ vt (influence) influenzare

Swaziland /'swɑːzɪlænd/ n Swaziland m

swear /sweə(r)/ ① vt (pt **swore**, pp **sworn**) giurare; **I could have sworn that …** avrei giurato che … ② vi giurare; (curse) dire parolacce; **I'd ~ to it!** ci potrei giurare!; **~ at somebody** imprecare contro qualcuno; **~ by** (believe in) credere ciecamente in

■ **swear in** vt prestare giuramento ‹president›

■ **swear off** vt fam (give up) smettere di

swear word n parolaccia f

sweat /swet/ ① n sudore m ② vi sudare ③ vt **~ blood** sudare sangue

■ **sweat out**: vt **~ it out** (endure to the end) tener duro fino alla fine

sweatband /'swetbænd/ n fascia f per il sudore; (for wrist) polsino m

sweater /'swetə(r)/ n golf m inv

sweat pants npl Am pantaloni mpl della tuta

sweatshirt /'swetʃɜːt/ n felpa f

sweatshop n Br manifattura (f) in cui il personale viene sfruttato

sweaty /'swetɪ/ adj sudato

swede n rapa f svedese

Swede /swiːd/ n svedese mf

Sweden /'swiːdn/ n Svezia f

Swedish /'swiːdɪʃ/ adj & n svedese m

sweep /swiːp/ ① n scopata f, spazzata f; (curve) curva f; (movement) movimento m ampio; **make a clean ~** fig fare piazza pulita ② vt (pt/pp **swept**) scopare, spazzare; ‹wind› spazzare; **~ the board** fare piazza pulita ③ vi (go swiftly) andare rapidamente; ‹wind› soffiare

■ **sweep aside** vt ignorare ‹objection›

■ **sweep away** vt fig spazzare via

■ **sweep up** vt spazzare

sweeper /'swiːpə(r)/ n (machine) spazzatrice f; (person) spazzino m; (in football) libero m

sweeping /'swiːpɪʃ/ adj ‹gesture› ampio; ‹statement› generico; ‹changes› radicale

✛ **sweet** /swiːt/ ① adj dolce; **have a ~ tooth** essere goloso ② n caramella f; (dessert) dolce m

S

sweet and sour *adj* agrodolce

sweetbread *n* (veal) animella *f* di vitello; (lamb) animella di agnello

sweetcorn *n* mais *m*, granturco *m*

sweeten /'swi:tn/ *vt* addolcire

■ **sweeten up** *vt* raddolcire ‹person›

sweetener /'swi:tnə(r)/ *n* dolcificante *m*; fam (incentive) incentivo *m*; fam (bribe) bustarella *f*

sweetheart /'swi:thɑ:t/ *n* innamorato, -a *mf*; hi, ∼ ciao, tesoro

sweetly /'swi:tlɪ/ *adv* dolcemente

sweetness /'swi:tnɪs/ *n* dolcezza *f*

sweet pea *n* pisello *m* odoroso

sweet potato *n* patata *f* americana

sweetshop *n* negozio *m* di dolciumi

sweet-talk *vt* ∼ somebody into doing something convincere qualcuno a fare qualcosa con tante belle parole

swell /swel/ **1** *n* (of sea) mare *m* lungo **2** *vi* (*pt* **swelled**, *pp* **swollen** *or* **swelled**) gonfiarsi; (increase) aumentare **3** *vt* gonfiare; (increase) far salire **4** *adj* fam eccellente

swelling /'swelɪŋ/ *n* gonfiore *m*

swelter /'sweltə(r)/ *vi* soffocare [dal caldo]

sweltering /'sweltərɪŋ/ *adj* torrido

sweltering [hot] /'sweltərɪŋ/ *adj* ‹day› afoso

swept /swept/ ▶ SWEEP

swerve /swɜ:v/ *vi* deviare bruscamente

swift /swɪft/ *adj* rapido

swiftly /'swɪftlɪ/ *adv* rapidamente

swiftness /'swɪftnɪs/ *n* rapidità *f*

swig /swɪg/ fam **1** *n* sorso *m* **2** *vt* (*pt/pp* **swigged**) scolarsi

swill /swɪl/ **1** *n* (for pigs) brodaglia *f* **2** *vt* ∼ **[out]** risciacquare

swim /swɪm/ **1** *n* have a ∼ fare una nuotata **2** *vi* (*pt* **swam**, *pp* **swum**) nuotare; ‹room› girare; go ∼ming andare a nuotare; my head is ∼ming mi gira la testa **3** *vt* percorrere a nuoto ‹distance›

swimmer /'swɪmə(r)/ *n* nuotatore, -trice *mf*

swimming /'swɪmɪŋ/ *n* nuoto *m*

swimming baths *npl* piscina *fsg*

swimming costume *n* costume *m* da bagno

swimmingly /'swɪmɪŋlɪ/ *adv* go ∼ andar liscio

swimming pool *n* piscina *f*

swimming trunks *npl* calzoncini *mpl* da bagno

swimsuit /'swɪmsu:t/ *n* costume *m* da bagno

swindle /'swɪndl/ **1** *n* truffa *f* **2** *vt* truffare

swindler /'swɪndlə(r)/ *n* truffatore, -trice *mf*

swine /swaɪn/ *n* fam porco *m*

swine flu /'swaɪn flu:/ *n* influenza *f* A

swing /swɪŋ/ **1** *n* oscillazione *f*; (shift) cambiamento *m*; (seat) altalena *f*; Mus swing *m*; in full ∼ in piena attività **2** *vi* (*pt/pp* **swung**) oscillare; (on swing, sway) dondolare; (dangle) penzolare; (turn) girare **3** *vt* oscillare; far deviare ‹vote›

swing-door *n* porta *f* a vento

swingeing /'swɪndʒɪŋ/ *adj* ‹increase› drastico

swingometer /swɪŋ'ɒmɪtə(r)/ *n* strumento (*m*) che permette di seguire l'andamento delle votazioni

swipe /swaɪp/ **1** *n* fam botta *f* **2** *vt* fam colpire; fam (steal) rubare; far passare la macchinetta ‹credit card›

swipe card *n* tessera *f* magnetica

swirl /swɜ:l/ **1** *n* (of smoke, dust) turbine *m* **2** *vt* far girare **3** *vi* ‹water› fare mulinello

swish[1] /swɪʃ/ *adj* fam chic

swish[2] *vi* schioccare

Swiss /swɪs/ *adj* & *n* svizzero, -a *mf*; the ∼ *pl* gli svizzeri

Swiss roll *n* rotolo (*m*) di pan di Spagna ripieno di marmellata

switch /swɪtʃ/ **1** *n* interruttore *m*; (change) mutamento *m* **2** *vt* cambiare; (exchange) scambiare **3** *vi* cambiare; ∼ to passare a

■ **switch off** *vt* spegnere

■ **switch on** *vt* accendere

■ **switch over** *vi* TV cambiare [canale]; ∼ over to passare a

■ **switch round** *vt* (change one for the other) scambiare

switchback *n* montagne *fpl* russe

switchblade *n* Am coltello *m* a scatto

switchboard *n* centralino *m*

switchboard operator *n* centralinista *mf*

switched line /swɪtʃt/ *n* Teleph linea *f* commutata

swither /'swɪðə(r)/ *vi* fam (hesitate) tentennare

Switzerland /'swɪtsələnd/ *n* Svizzera *f*

swivel /'swɪvl/ **1** *vt* (*pt/pp* **swivelled**) girare **2** *vi* girarsi

swivel chair *n* sedia *f* girevole

swizz /swɪz/ *n* fam (swindle) fregatura *f*

swollen /'swəʊlən/ **1** ▶ SWELL **2** *adj* gonfio

swollen-headed /-'hedɪd/ *adj* presuntuoso

swoon /swu:n/ *vi* svenire

swoop /swuːp/ **1** *n* (by police) incursione *f*
2 *vi* ~ **[down]** ‹*bird*› piombare; fig fare
un'incursione

⚔ **sword** /sɔːd/ *n* spada *f*

swordfish /ˈsɔːdfɪʃ/ *n* pesce *m* spada *inv*

swore /swɔː(r)/ ▶ SWEAR

sworn /swɔːn/ ▶ SWEAR

sworn enemy *n* nemico *m* giurato

swot /swɒt/ **1** *n* fam sgobbone, -a *mf*
2 *vt* (*pt/pp* **swotted**) fam sgobbare (**for an
exam** per un esame)

swum /swʌm/ ▶ SWIM

swung /swʌŋ/ ▶ SWING

sycamore /ˈsɪkəmɔː(r)/ *n* sicomoro *m*

sycophant /ˈsɪkəfænt/ *n* adulatore, -trice
mf

sycophantic /sɪkəˈfæntɪk/ *adj* adulatorio

syllable /ˈsɪləbl/ *n* sillaba *f*

syllabus /ˈsɪləbəs/ *n* programma *m* [dei
corsi]

syllogism /ˈsɪlədʒɪzm/ *n* sillogismo *m*

sylph /sɪlf/ *n* silfide *f*

symbiosis /sɪmbaɪˈəʊsɪs/ *n* simbiosi *f inv*

symbiotic /sɪmbaɪˈɒtɪk/ *adj* simbiotico

symbol /ˈsɪmbl/ *n* simbolo *m* (**of** di)

symbolic /sɪmˈbɒlɪk/ *adj* simbolico

symbolically /sɪmˈbɒlɪklɪ/ *adv*
simbolicamente

symbolism /ˈsɪmbəlɪzm/ *n* simbolismo *m*

symbolist /ˈsɪmbəlɪst/ *n* simbolista *mf*

symbolize /ˈsɪmbəlaɪz/ *vt* simboleggiare

symmetrical /sɪˈmetrɪkl/ *adj* simmetrico

symmetrically /sɪˈmetrɪklɪ/ *adv*
simmetricamente

symmetry /ˈsɪmətrɪ/ *n* simmetria *f*

sympathetic /sɪmpəˈθetɪk/ *adj*
(understanding) comprensivo; (showing pity)
compassionevole

sympathetically /sɪmpəˈθetɪklɪ/ *adv* con
comprensione/compassione

sympathize /ˈsɪmpəθaɪz/ *vi* capire; (in
grief) solidarizzare; ~ **with somebody** capire
qualcuno/solidarizzare con qualcuno

sympathizer /ˈsɪmpəθaɪzə(r)/ *n* Pol
simpatizzante *mf*

sympathy /ˈsɪmpəθɪ/ *n* comprensione
f; (pity) compassione *f*; (condolences)
condoglianze *fpl*; **in** ~ **with** ‹*strike*› per
solidarietà con

symphonic /sɪmˈfɒnɪk/ *adj* sinfonico

symphony /ˈsɪmfənɪ/ *n* sinfonia *f*

symphony orchestra *n* orchestra *f*
sinfonica

⚔ **symptom** /ˈsɪmptəm/ *n* sintomo *m*

symptomatic /sɪmptəˈmætɪk/ *adj*
sintomatico (**of** di)

synagogue /ˈsɪnəgɒg/ *n* sinagoga *f*

sync[h] /sɪŋk/ *n* sincronia *f*; **be out
of** ~ essere sfasato; **be in** ~ essere in
sincronia; **be in** ~ **with/out of** ~ with essere
sincronizzato/sfasato rispetto a

synchronize /ˈsɪŋkrənaɪz/ *vt*
sincronizzare

synchronous /ˈsɪŋkrənəs/ *adj* sincrono

syndicate /ˈsɪndɪkət/ *n* gruppo *m*

syndrome /ˈsɪndrəʊm/ *n* sindrome *f*

synonym /ˈsɪnənɪm/ *n* sinonimo *m*

synonymous /sɪˈnɒnɪməs/ *adj* sinonimo

synopsis /sɪˈnɒpsɪs/ *n* (*pl* **-opses**
/sɪˈnɒpsiːz/) (of opera, ballet) trama *f*; (of book)
riassunto *m*

syntactic[al] /sɪnˈtæktɪk[l]/ *adj*
sintattico

syntax /ˈsɪntæks/ *n* sintassi *f inv*

synthesis /ˈsɪnθəsɪs/ *n* (*pl* **-theses**
/ˈsɪnθəsiːz/) sintesi *f inv*

synthesize /ˈsɪnθəsaɪz/ *vt* sintetizzare

synthesizer /ˈsɪnθəsaɪzə(r)/ *n* Mus
sintetizzatore *m*

synthetic /sɪnˈθetɪk/ **1** *adj* sintetico
2 *n* fibra *f* sintetica

syphilis /ˈsɪfɪlɪs/ *n* sifilide *f*

Syria /ˈsɪrɪə/ *n* Siria *f*

Syrian /ˈsɪrɪən/ *adj* & *n* siriano, -a *mf*

syringe /sɪˈrɪndʒ/ **1** *n* siringa *f*
2 *vt* siringare

syrup /ˈsɪrəp/ *n* sciroppo *m*; Br tipo *m* di
melassa

syrupy /ˈsɪrəpɪ/ *adj* sciropposo

⚔ **system** /ˈsɪstəm/ *n* sistema *m*

systematic /sɪstəˈmætɪk/ *adj* sistematico

systematically /sɪstəˈmætɪklɪ/ *adv*
sistematicamente

systems analysis *n* analisi *f* dei
sistemi

systems analyst *n* analista *mf*
programmatore, -trice *mf*

systems design *n* progettazione *f* di
sistemi

systems engineer *n* sistemista *mf*

Szechuan /seˈtʃwɑːn, ˈseʒ-/ *adj* del
Sichuan

S

Tt

t, T /tiː/ n (letter) t, T f inv

tab /tæb/ n linguetta f; (with name) etichetta f; **keep ∼s on** fam sorvegliare; **pick up the ∼** fam pagare il conto

tabby /'tæbɪ/ n gatto m tigrato

tab key n tasto m tabulatore

⚡ **table** /'teɪbl/ **1** n tavolo m; (list) tavola f; **at [the] ∼** a tavola
2 vt proporre

table-cloth n tovaglia f

table lamp n lampada f da tavolo

table mat n sottopiatto m

table of contents tavola f delle materie

table salt n sale m fine

tablespoon n cucchiaio m da tavola

tablespoonful n cucchiaiata f

tablet /'tæblɪt/ n pastiglia f; (slab) lastra f; **∼ of soap** saponetta f

table tennis n tennis m da tavolo; (everyday level) ping pong m

tabloid /'tæblɔɪd/ n tabloid m inv; pej giornale m scandalistico

taboo /tə'buː/ **1** adj tabù inv
2 n tabù m inv

tabulate /'tæbjʊleɪt/ vt tabulare

tabulation /tæbjʊ'leɪʃn/ n (of data, results) tabulazione f

tabulator /'tæbjʊleɪtə(r)/ n tabulatore m

tachograph /'tækəɡrɑːf/ n tachigrafo m

tachometer /tæ'kɒmɪtə(r)/ n tachimetro m

tacit /'tæsɪt/ adj tacito

tacitly /'tæsɪtlɪ/ adv tacitamente

taciturn /'tæsɪtɜːn/ adj taciturno

tack /tæk/ **1** n (nail) chiodino m; (stitch) imbastitura f; Naut virata f; fig linea f di condotta
2 vt inchiodare; (sew) imbastire
3 vi Naut virare

▪ **tack on** vt (add later) aggiungere ⟨ending, paragraph⟩

tackle /'tækl/ **1** n (equipment) attrezzatura f; (football etc) contrasto m, tackle m inv
2 vt affrontare

tacky /'tækɪ/ adj ⟨paint⟩ non ancora asciutto; ⟨glue⟩ appiccicoso; fig pacchiano

tact /tækt/ n tatto m

tactful /'tæktfʊl/ adj pieno di tatto; ⟨remark⟩ delicato

tactfully /'tæktfʊlɪ/ adv con tatto

tactical /'tæktɪkl/ adj tattico

tactically /'tæktɪklɪ/ adv tatticamente

tactician /tæk'tɪʃn/ n stratega mf

tactics /'tæktɪks/ npl tattica fsg

tactile /'tæktaɪl/ adj tattile

tactless /'tæktlɪs/ adj privo di tatto

tactlessly /'tæktlɪslɪ/ adv senza tatto

tactlessness /'tæktlɪsnɪs/ n mancanza f di tatto; (of remark) indelicatezza f

tadpole /'tædpəʊl/ n girino m

tae kwon do n tae-kwon-do m

taffeta /'tæfɪtə/ n taffetà m

tag¹ /tæɡ/ **1** n (label) etichetta f
2 vt (pt/pp **tagged**) attaccare l'etichetta a

tag² n (game) acchiapparello m

▪ **tag along** vi seguire passo passo

▪ **tag on** vt (attach) aggiungere

tail /teɪl/ **1** n coda f; **∼s** pl (tailcoat) frac m inv
2 vt fam (follow) pedinare

▪ **tail off** vi diminuire

tailback n coda f

tail-end n parte f finale; (of train) coda f

tailgate /'teɪlɡeɪt/ n sponda f posteriore ribaltabile

tail light n fanalino m di coda

tail-off n diminuzione f

tailor /'teɪlə(r)/ **1** n sarto m
2 vt ∼ **something to someone's needs** adattare qualcosa alle esigenze di qualcuno

tailor-made adj fatto su misura

tailspin /'teɪlspɪn/ n Aeron vite f di coda

tailwind /'teɪlwɪnd/ n vento m di coda

taint /teɪnt/ vt contaminare

Taiwan /taɪ'wɑːn/ n Taiwan f

Tajikistan /tɑːˌdʒɪkɪ'stɑːn/ n Tajikistan m

⚡ **take** /teɪk/ **1** n Cinema ripresa f; Am (takings) incassi mpl
2 vt (pt **took**, pp **taken**) prendere; (to a place) portare ⟨person, object⟩; (contain) contenere ⟨passengers etc⟩; (endure) sopportare; (require) occorrere; (teach) insegnare; (study) studiare ⟨subject⟩; fare ⟨exam, holiday, photograph, walk, bath⟩; sentire ⟨pulse⟩; misurare ⟨sb's temperature⟩; **∼ something to the cleaner's** portare qualcosa in lavanderia; **∼ somebody home** (by car) portare qualcuno a casa; **∼ somebody prisoner** fare prigioniero qualcuno; **be ∼n ill** ammalarsi; **∼ something calmly** prendere con calma qualcosa; **∼ the dog for a walk** portare a spasso il cane; **∼ one's time doing**

something fare qualcosa con calma; **this will only ~ a minute** ci vuole solo un minuto; **I ~ it that...** (assume) presumo che...; **~ it from me!** (believe me) dai retta a me!; **~ hold** ‹*idea, disease*› prendere piede; **~ part** prendere parte; **~ part in** prendere parte a; **~ place** svolgersi

3 *vi* ‹*plant*› attecchire

■ **take aback** *vt* (surprise) cogliere di sorpresa

■ **take after** *vt* assomigliare a

■ **take against** *vt* (turn against) prendere in antipatia

■ **take apart** *vt* (dismantle) smontare

■ **take away** *vt* (with one) portare via; (remove) togliere; (subtract) sottrarre; '**to ~ away**' 'da asporto'

■ **take back** *vt* riprendere; ritirare ‹*statement*›; (return) riportare [indietro]; **she took him back** (as husband, boyfriend) lo ha perdonato

■ **take down** *vt* portare giù; (remove) tirare giù; (write down) prendere nota di

■ **take in** *vt* (bring indoors) portare dentro; (to one's home) ospitare; (understand) capire; (deceive) ingannare; riprendere ‹*garment*›; (include) includere; vedere ‹*film etc*›

■ **take off** **1** *vt* togliersi ‹*clothes*›; (deduct) togliere; (mimic) imitare; **~ time off** prendere delle vacanze; **~ oneself off** andarsene

2 *vi* Aeron decollare; *fam* (leave) andarsene; (become successful) decollare

■ **take on** *vt* farsi carico di; assumere ‹*employee*›; (as opponent) prendersela con; **~ it on oneself to do something** arrogarsi il diritto di fare qualcosa

■ **take out** *vt* portare fuori; togliere ‹*word, stain*›; (withdraw) ritirare ‹*money, books*›; **~ out a subscription to something** abbonarsi a qualcosa; **she took a pen out of her pocket** ha preso una penna dalla tasca; **I'm taking my wife out tonight** esco con mia moglie stasera; **~ somebody out to dinner** portare a cena fuori qualcuno; **it'll ~ you out of yourself** (take your mind off things) servirà a distrarti; **~ it out on somebody** *fam* prendersela con qualcuno

■ **take over** **1** *vt* assumere il controllo di ‹*firm*›

2 *vi* **~ over from somebody** sostituire qualcuno; (permanently) succedere a qualcuno

■ **take to** *vt* (as a habit) darsi a; **I took to her** (liked) mi è piaciuta

■ **take up** **1** *vt* portare su; accettare ‹*offer*›; intraprendere ‹*profession*›; dedicarsi a ‹*hobby*›; prendere ‹*time*›; occupare ‹*space*›; tirare su ‹*floor-boards*›; accorciare ‹*dress*›; **~ something up with somebody** discutere qualcosa con qualcuno; **~ somebody up on something** (question further) chiedere ulteriori chiarimenti a qualcuno su qualcosa; **I'll ~ you up on your offer** (accept) accetto la tua offerta

2 *vi* **~ up with somebody** legarsi a qualcuno

takeaway /ˈteɪkəweɪ/ *n* (meal) piatto *m* da asporto; (restaurant) *ristorante (m) che prepara piatti da asporto*

take-home pay *n* stipendio *m* netto

taken /ˈteɪkən/ *adj* ‹*room etc*› occupato; **be very ~ with somebody/something** essere conquistato da qualcuno/qualcosa

take-off *n* Aeron decollo *m*

take-out /ˈteɪkaʊt/ *n* Am = TAKEAWAY

takeover *n* rilevamento *m*

takeover bid *n* offerta *f* pubblica di acquisto

takings /ˈteɪkɪnz/ *npl* incassi *mpl*

talc /tælk/ *n* (boro)talco *m*

talcum /ˈtælkəm/ *n* **~ [powder]** talco *m*

tale /teɪl/ *n* storia *f*; *pej* fandonia *f*; **tell ~s** fare la spia

🔑 **talent** /ˈtælənt/ *n* talento *m*

talent contest *n* concorso *m* per giovani talenti

talented /ˈtæləntɪd/ *adj* [ricco] di talento

talent scout *n* talent scout *mf inv*

Taliban /ˈtælɪbæn/ *n* talebani *mpl*

talisman /ˈtælɪzmən/ *n* talismano *m*

🔑 **talk** /tɔːk/ **1** *n* conversazione *f*; (lecture) conferenza *f*; (gossip) chiacchiere *fpl*; **make small ~** parlare del più e del meno

2 *vi* parlare

3 *vt* parlare di ‹*politics etc*›; **~ somebody into something** convincere qualcuno di qualcosa

■ **talk about** *vt* parlare di; **~ about bad luck!** e quando si dice la sfortuna!

■ **talk back** *vi* (reply defiantly) rispondere

■ **talk down to** *vt* (patronize) parlare con condiscendenza a

■ **talk of** *vt* parlare di; **~ing of food...** a proposito di mangiare...

■ **talk over** *vt* discutere

■ **talk to** *vt* parlare con; (reprimand) fare un discorsetto a; **~ to oneself** parlare da solo

talkative /ˈtɔːkətɪv/ *adj* loquace

talking /ˈtɔːkɪŋ/ *adj* ‹*doll, parrot*› parlante

talking book *n* audiolibro *m*

talking head /ˈtɔːkɪŋ/ *n* mezzobusto *m*

talking-to *n* sgridata *f*

talk show *n* talk show

🔑 **tall** /tɔːl/ *adj* alto; **how ~ are you?** quanto sei alto?

tallboy *n* cassettone *m*

tall order *n* impresa *f* difficile

tall story *n* frottola *f*

tally /ˈtælɪ/ **1** *n* conteggio *m*; **keep a ~ of** tenere il conto di

2 *vi* coincidere

talon /ˈtælən/ *n* artiglio *m*

tambourine /tæmbəˈriːn/ *n* tamburello *m*

tame /teɪm/ **1** *adj* ‹*animal*› domestico; (dull) insulso

2 *vt* domare

t

tamely /'teɪmlɪ/ adv docilmente

tamer /'teɪmə(r)/ n domatore, -trice mf

tamper /'tæmpə(r)/ vi ~ **with** manomettere

tampon /'tæmpɒn/ n tampone m

tan /tæn/ ☐1 adj marrone rossiccio inv
☐2 n marrone m rossiccio; (from sun) abbronzatura f
☐3 vt (pt/pp **tanned**) conciare ‹hide›
☐4 vi abbronzarsi

tandem /'tændəm/ n tandem m inv; **in** ~ in tandem

tang /tæŋ/ n sapore m forte; (smell) odore m penetrante

tanga /'tæŋgə/ n tanga m inv

tangent /'tændʒənt/ n tangente f; **go off at a** ~ fam partire per la tangente

tangerine /tændʒə'riːn/ ☐1 n (fruit) tipo m di mandarino; (colour) arancione m
☐2 adj arancione

tangible /'tændʒɪbl/ adj tangibile

tangibly /'tændʒɪblɪ/ adv tangibilmente

tangle /'tæŋgl/ ☐1 n groviglio m; (in hair) nodo m
☐2 vt ~ **[up]** aggrovigliare
☐3 vi aggrovigliarsi

tango /'tæŋgəʊ/ n tango m

tangy /'tæŋɪ/ adj forte; ‹smell› penetrante

tank /tæŋk/ n contenitore m; (for petrol) serbatoio m; (fish ~) acquario m; Mil carro m armato

tankard /'tæŋkəd/ n boccale m

tanker /'tæŋkə(r)/ n nave f cisterna; (lorry) autobotte f

tank top n canottiera f

tanned /tænd/ adj abbronzato

tannin /'tænɪn/ n tannino m

Tannoy® /'tænɔɪ/ n Br sistema m di altoparlanti

tantalize /'tæntəlaɪz/ vt tormentare

tantalizing /'tæntəlaɪzɪŋ/ adj allettante; ‹smell› stuzzicante

tantamount /'tæntəmaʊnt/ adj ~ **to** equivalente a

tantrum /'tæntrəm/ n scoppio m d'ira; **throw a** ~ fare i capricci

Tanzania /ˌtænzə'nɪə/ n Tanzania f

tap /tæp/ ☐1 n rubinetto m; (knock) colpo m; **on** ~ a disposizione
☐2 vt (pt/pp **tapped**) dare un colpetto a; sfruttare ‹resources›; mettere sotto controllo ‹telephone›
☐3 vi picchiettare

tap-dance ☐1 n tip tap
☐2 vi ballare il tip tap

tap-dancer n ballerino, -a mf di tip tap

tape /teɪp/ ☐1 n nastro m; (recording) cassetta f
☐2 vt legare con nastro; (record) registrare

◂ indicates a very frequent word

tape backup drive n Comput unità f di backup a nastro

tape deck n piastra f

tape-measure n metro m [a nastro]

taper /'teɪpə(r)/ ☐1 n candela f sottile
☐2 vi assottigliarsi
■ **taper off** vi assottigliarsi

tape-record vt registrare su nastro

tape recorder n registratore m

tape recording n registrazione f

tapered /'teɪpəd/ adj ‹trousers› affusolato

tape streamer n Comput unità f a nastro magnetico

tapestry /'tæpɪstrɪ/ n arazzo m

tapeworm /'teɪpwɜːm/ n verme m solitario, tenia f

tapping /'tæpɪŋ/ n (noise) picchiettio m

tap water n acqua f del rubinetto

tar /tɑː(r)/ ☐1 n catrame m
☐2 vt (pt/pp **tarred**) incatramare

tardy /'tɑːdɪ/ adj (**-ier**, **-iest**) tardivo

◂ **target** /'tɑːgɪt/ ☐1 n bersaglio m; fig obiettivo m
☐2 vt stabilire come obiettivo ‹market›

target language n lingua f d'arrivo

target market n mercato m obiettivo

target practice n tiro m al bersaglio

tariff /'tærɪf/ ☐1 n (price) tariffa f; (duty) dazio m
☐2 adj tariffario

tarmac ☐1 n asfalto m; Br (of airfield) pista f
☐2 attrib ‹road, footpath› asfaltato
☐3 vt asfaltare

Tarmac® /'tɑːmæk/ n macadam m al catrame

tarnish /'tɑːnɪʃ/ ☐1 vi ossidarsi
☐2 vt ossidare; fig macchiare

tarpaulin /tɑː'pɔːlɪn/ n telone m impermeabile

tarragon /'tærəgən/ n dragoncello m

tart¹ /tɑːt/ adj aspro; fig acido

tart² n crostata f; (individual) crostatina f; sl (prostitute) donnaccia f
■ **tart up**: vt fam ~ **oneself up** agghindarsi

tartan /'tɑːtn/ ☐1 n tessuto m scozzese, tartan m inv
☐2 attrib di tessuto scozzese

tartar /'tɑːtə(r)/ n (on teeth) tartaro m

tartar sauce n salsa f tartara

◂ **task** /tɑːsk/ n compito m; **take somebody to** ~ riprendere qualcuno

task bar n Comput barra f delle applicazioni

task force n Pol commissione f; Mil taskforce f inv

taskmaster /'tɑːskmɑːstə(r), US 'tæsk-/ n tiranno m; **be a hard** ~ essere molto esigente

tassel /'tæsl/ n nappa f

taste /teɪst/ ① *n* gusto *m*; (sample) assaggio *m*; **get a ~ of something** fig assaporare il gusto di qualcosa; **in good/bad ~** di buongusto/di cattivo gusto
② *vt* sentire il sapore di; (sample) assaggiare
③ *vi* sapere (**of** di); **it ~s lovely** è ottimo; **~ like something** sapere di qualcosa

taste buds *npl* papille *fpl* gustative

tasteful /'teɪs(t)fʊl/ *adj* di [buon] gusto

tastefully /'teɪs(t)fʊlɪ/ *adv* con gusto

tasteless /'teɪs(t)lɪs/ *adj* senza gusto

tastelessly /'teɪs(t)lɪslɪ/ *adv* con cattivo gusto

taster /'teɪstə(r)/ *n* (foretaste) assaggio *m*; (person) assaggiatore, -trice *mf*

tasty /'teɪstɪ/ *adj* (**-ier**, **-iest**) saporito

tat /tæt/ ▶ TIT²

tattered /'tætəd/ *adj* cencioso; ‹pages› stracciato

tatters /'tætəz/ *npl* in **~** a brandelli

tattle /'tætl/ ① *vi* spettegolare
② *n* pettegolezzo *m*

tattoo¹ /tæ'tuː/ ① *n* tatuaggio *m*
② *vt* tatuare

tattoo² *n* Mil parata *f* militare

tatty /'tætɪ/ *adj* (**-ier**, **-iest**) ‹clothes, person› trasandato; ‹book› malandato

taught /tɔːt/ ▶ TEACH

taunt /tɔːnt/ ① *n* scherno *m*
② *vt* schernire

Taurus /'tɔːrəs/ *n* Astr Toro *m*

taut /tɔːt/ *adj* teso

tauten /'tɔːtən/ ① *vt* tendere
② *vi* tendersi

tautology /tɔː'tɒlədʒɪ/ *n* tautologia *f*

tavern /'tævən/ *n* liter taverna *f*

tawdry /'tɔːdrɪ/ *adj* (**-ier**, **-iest**) pacchiano

tawny /'tɔːnɪ/ *adj* fulvo

tax /tæks/ ① *n* tassa *f*; (on income) imposte *fpl*; **before ~** ‹price› tasse escluse; ‹salary› lordo
② *vt* tassare; fig mettere alla prova; **~ with** accusare di

taxable /'tæksəbl/ *adj* tassabile; **~ income** reddito *m* imponibile

tax allowance *n* detrazione *f* di imposta

taxation /tæk'seɪʃn/ *n* tasse *fpl*; **~ at source** ritenuta *f* alla fonte

tax avoidance *n* elusione *f* fiscale

tax bracket *n* scaglione *m* d'imposta

tax break *n* agevolazione *f* fiscale

tax burden *n* aggravio *m* fiscale

tax code *n* codice *m* fiscale

tax consultant *n* fiscalista *m*

tax-deductible *adj* detraibile

tax disc *n* Auto bollo *m*

tax evader *n* evasore *m* fiscale

tax evasion *n* evasione *f* fiscale

tax exile *n* (person) espatriato, -a *mf* per motivi fiscali

tax-free *adj* esentasse

tax haven *n* paradiso *m* fiscale

taxi /'tæksɪ/ ① *n* taxi *m inv*
② *vi* (*pt/pp* **taxied**, *pres p* **taxiing**) ‹aircraft› rullare

taxi driver *n* tassista *mf*

tax incentive *n* incentivo *m* fiscale

taxing /'tæksɪŋ/ *adj* (exhausting) sfiancante

tax inspector *n* ispettore *m* delle tasse

taxi rank *n* posteggio *m* per taxi

taxman /'tæksmæn/ *n* the **~** il fisco

tax office *n* ufficio *m* delle imposte

taxpayer *n* contribuente *mf*

tax rebate *n* rimborso *m* d'imposta

tax return *n* dichiarazione *f* dei redditi

tax shelter *n* paradiso *m* fiscale

tax system *n* regime *m* fiscale

TB *n abbr* (**tuberculosis**) TBC *f*

tbsp *abbr* (**tablespoon**) cucchiaio *m*

tea /tiː/ *n* tè

tea-bag *n* bustina *f* di tè

tea-break *n* intervallo *m* per il tè

teach /tiːtʃ/ *vt/i* (*pt/pp* **taught**) insegnare; **~ somebody something** insegnare qualcosa a qualcuno; **~ somebody a lesson** fig dare una lezione a qualcuno

teacher /'tiːtʃə(r)/ *n* insegnante *mf*; (primary) maestro, -a *mf*

teacher training *n* formazione *f* professionale per insegnanti

teaching /'tiːtʃɪŋ/ *n* insegnamento *m*

teaching hospital *n* ≈ ospedale *m* universitario

teacloth *n* (for drying) asciugapiatti *m inv*

tea cosy *n* copriteiera *f*

teacup *n* tazza *f* da tè

teak /tiːk/ *n* tek *m*

tea leaves *npl* tè *m inv* sfuso; (when infused) fondi *mpl* di tè

team /tiːm/ *n* squadra *f*; fig équipe *f inv*
■ **team up** *vi* unirsi

team captain *n* caposquadra *mf*

team manager *n* direttore *m* sportivo

team-mate *n* compagno *m* di squadra

team player *n* persona (*f*) che dimostra *spirito di squadra*

team spirit *n* spirito *m* di squadra

teamwork *n* lavoro *m* di squadra; fig lavoro *m* d'équipe

teapot /'tiːpɒt/ *n* teiera *f*

tear¹ /teə(r)/ ① *n* strappo *m*
② *vt* (*pt* **tore**, *pp* **torn**) strappare; **~ to pieces** *or* **shreds** fare a pezzi; stroncare ‹book, film›

····⟩

3 *vi* strappare; *‹material›* strapparsi; (run) precipitarsi

■ **tear apart** *vt* fig (criticize) fare a pezzi; (separate) dividere

■ **tear away**: *vt* ~ oneself away from staccarsi da *‹television›*; abbandonare a malincuore *‹party›*

■ **tear into** *vt* fam (reprimand) attaccare duramente; (make a vigorous start on) dare dentro a

■ **tear off** *vt* (carefully) staccare; (violently) strappare

■ **tear open** *vt* aprire strappando

■ **tear out** *vt* staccare; ~ one's hair out mettersi le mani nei capelli

■ **tear up** *vt* strappare; rompere *‹agreement›*

ᵍ **tear²** /tɪə(r)/ *n* lacrima *f*

tearaway /'teərəweɪ/ *n* giovane teppista *mf*

tearful /'tɪəfʊl/ *adj* *‹person›* in lacrime; *‹farewell›* lacrimevole

tearfully /'t'əfʊlɪ/ *adv* in lacrime

tear gas /'tɪə/ *n* gas *m* lacrimogeno

tearing /'teərɪŋ/ *adj* be in a ~ hurry avere una gran fretta

tear-jerker /'tɪədʒɜːkə(r)/ *n* fam this film is a real ~ è davvero un film strappalacrime

tease /tiːz/ *vt* prendere in giro *‹person›*; tormentare *‹animal›*

teasel /'tiːzl/ *n* Bot cardo *m*

teaset /'tiːset/ *n* servizio *m* da tè

tea shop *n* sala *f* da tè

teasing /'tiːzɪŋ/ *adj* canzonatorio

teaspoon *n* cucchiaino *m* [da tè]

teaspoon[ful] *n* cucchiaino *m*

tea-strainer *n* colino *m* per il tè

teat /tiːt/ *n* capezzolo *m*; (on bottle) tettarella *f*

teatime *n* ora *f* del tè

tea towel *n* strofinaccio *m* [per i piatti]

ᵍ **technical** /'teknɪkl/ *adj* tecnico

technical college *n* istituto *m* tecnico professionale

technical drawing *n* (skill or process, plan) disegno *m* tecnico

technical hitch *n* contrattempo *m* tecnico

technicality /teknɪ'kælətɪ/ *n* tecnicismo *m*; Jur cavillo *m* giuridico

technically /'teknɪklɪ/ *adv* tecnicamente; (strictly) strettamente

technician /tek'nɪʃn/ *n* tecnico, -a *mf*

ᵍ **technique** /tek'niːk/ *n* tecnica *f*

techno /'teknəʊ/ *n* techno *f*

technocrat /'teknəkræt/ *n* tecnocrate *m*

technological /teknə'lɒdʒɪkl/ *adj* tecnologico

technologically /teknə'lɒdʒɪklɪ/ *adv* tecnologicamente

ᵍ **technology** /tek'nɒlədʒɪ/ *n* tecnologia *f*

technophobe /'teknəʊfəʊb/ *n* tecnofobo, -a *mf*

teddy /'tedɪ/ *n* ~ **[bear]** orsacchiotto *m*

tedious /'tiːdɪəs/ *adj* noioso

tedium /'tiːdɪəm/ *n* tedio *m*

tee /tiː/ *n* Golf tee *m inv*

teem /tiːm/ *vi* (rain) piovere a dirotto; be ~ing with (full of) pullulare di

teen /tiːn/ *adj* *‹fashion, idol›* degli adolescenti

teenage /'tiːneɪdʒ/ *adj* per ragazzi; ~ **boy**/ **girl** adolescente *mf*

teenager /'tiːneɪdʒə(r)/ *n* adolescente *mf*

teens /tiːnz/ *npl* the ~ l'adolescenza *fsg*; be in one's ~ essere adolescente

teeny /'tiːnɪ/ *adj* fam (**-ier, -iest**) piccolissimo

teeny-weeny /tiːnɪ'wiːnɪ/ *adj* fam minuscolo

tee-shirt *n* T-shirt, maglietta *f* [a maniche corte]

teeter /'tiːtə(r)/ *vi* barcollare

teeth /tiːθ/ ► TOOTH

teethe /tiːð/ *vi* mettere i primi denti

teething troubles /'tiːðɪŋ/ *npl* fig difficoltà *fpl* iniziali

teetotal /tiː'təʊtl/ *adj* astemio

teetotaller /tiː'təʊt(ə)lə(r)/ *n* astemio, -a *mf*

TEFL /'tefl/ *n* insegnamento (*m*) dell'inglese come lingua straniera

tel. *abbr* (**telephone**) tel.

telebanking /'telɪbæŋkɪŋ/ *n* servizi *mpl* bancari telematici

telecast /'telɪkɑːst/ **1** *n* trasmissione *f* televisiva

2 *vt* far vedere in televisione

telecomms /'telɪkɒmz/ *npl* telecomunicazioni *fpl*

telecommunications /telɪkəmjuːnɪ'keɪʃnz/ *npl* telecomunicazioni *fpl*

telecommuter /telɪkə'mjuːtə(r)/ *n* persona (*f*) che lavora da casa su computer

telecommuting /telɪkə'mjuːtɪŋ/ *n* lavoro (*m*) su computer da casa

teleconference /'telɪkɒnf(ə)r(ə)ns/ *n* videoconferenza *f*

telegenic /telɪ'dʒenɪk/ *adj* telegenico

telegram /'telɪgræm/ *n* telegramma *m*

telegraph /'telɪgrɑːf/ *n* telegrafo *m*

telegraphic /telɪ'græfɪk/ *adj* telegrafico

telegraph pole *n* palo *m* del telegrafo

telemarketing /'telɪmɑːkɪtɪŋ/ *n* telemarketing *m*

telematics /telɪ'mætɪks/ *n* telematica *f*

telemessage /'telɪmesɪdʒ/ n Br telegramma m

telepathic /telɪ'pæθɪk/ adj telepatico

telepathy /tɪ'lepəθɪ/ n telepatia f; **by ~** per telepatia

telephone /'telɪfəʊn/ 1 n telefono m; **be on the ~** avere il telefono; (be telephoning) essere al telefono
2 vt telefonare a
3 vi telefonare

telephone answering service n segreteria f telefonica

telephone banking n servizi mpl bancari via telefono

telephone book n elenco m telefonico

telephone booking n prenotazione f telefonica

telephone booth n telephone box n cabina f telefonica

telephone call n telefonata f

telephone conversation n conversazione f telefonica

telephone directory n elenco m telefonico

telephone helpline n servizio m telefonico

telephone message n messaggio m telefonico

telephone number n numero m di telefono

telephone operator n centralinista mf

telephone tapping n intercettazione f telefonica

telephonist /tɪ'lefənɪst/ n telefonista mf

telephoto /telɪ'fəʊtəʊ/ adj **~ lens** teleobiettivo m

teleprinter /'telɪprɪntə(r)/ n telescrivente f

telerecording /'telɪkrɪkɔːdɪŋ/ n programma m [televisivo] registrato

telesales /'telɪseɪlz/ n vendita f per telefono

telescope /'telɪskəʊp/ n telescopio m

telescopic /telɪ'skɒpɪk/ adj telescopico

teleshopping /'telɪʃɒpɪŋ/ n acquisti mpl per telefono

teletext /'telɪtekst/ n televideo m

telethon /'telɪθɒn/ n telethon m inv

televise /'telɪvaɪz/ vt trasmettere per televisione

♂ **television** /'telɪvɪʒn/ n televisione f; **watch ~** guardare la televisione; **on ~** alla televisione

television channel n rete f televisiva

television licence n abbonamento m alla televisione

television licence fee n costo m dell'abbonamento alla televisione

television programme n programma m televisivo

television screen n teleschermo m

television serial n sceneggiato m

television set n televisore m

televisual /telɪ'vɪʒʊəl/ adj televisivo

teleworking /'telɪwɜːkɪŋ/ n telelavoro m

telex /'teleks/ 1 n telex m inv
2 vt mandare via telex ‹message›; mandare un telex a ‹person›

♂ **tell** /tel/ 1 vt (pt/pp **told**) dire; raccontare ‹story›; (distinguish) distinguere (**from** da); **~ somebody something** dire qualcosa a qualcuno; **~ somebody to do something** dire a qualcuno di fare qualcosa; **~ the time** dire l'ora; **I couldn't ~ why...** non sapevo perché...; **you're ~ing me!** a chi lo dici!
2 vi (produce an effect) avere effetto; **time will ~** il tempo ce lo dirà; **his age is beginning to ~** l'età comincia a farsi sentire [per lui]; **don't ~ me** non dirmelo; **you mustn't ~** non devi dire niente
■ **tell apart** vt distinguere
■ **tell off** vt sgridare
■ **tell on** vt Sch (inform against) fare la spia a

teller /'telə(r)/ n (in bank) casslere, -a mf

telling /'telɪŋ/ adj significativo; (argument) efficace

telling-off n cicchetto m

tell-tale 1 n spione, -a mf
2 adj rivelatore

telly /'telɪ/ n fam tv f inv, tele f inv

temerity /tɪ'merətɪ/ n audacia f

temp /temp/ fam 1 n impiegato, -a mf temporaneo, -a
2 vi lavorare come impiegato, -a temporaneo, -a

temper /'tempə(r)/ 1 n (disposition) carattere m; (mood) umore m; (anger) collera f; **lose one's ~** arrabbiarsi; **be in a ~** essere arrabbiato; **keep one's ~** mantenere la calma
2 vt fig temperare

temperament /'temprəmənt/ n temperamento m

temperamental /temprə'mentl/ adj (moody) capriccioso

temperamentally /temprə'mentəlɪ/ adv **they are ~ unsuited** tra loro c'è incompatibilità di carattere

temperance /'tempərəns/ n (abstinence) astinenza f dal bere

temperate /'tempərət/ adj ‹climate› temperato

♂ **temperature** /'temprətʃə(r)/ n temperatura f; **have or run a ~** avere la febbre

tempest /'tempɪst/ n tempesta f

tempestuous /tem'pestjʊəs/ adj tempestoso

template /'templɪt/ n sagoma f

temple¹ /'templ/ n tempio m

temple² n Anat tempia f

tempo /'tempəʊ/ n ritmo m; Mus tempo m

temporal /'tempər(ə)l/ adj temporale

temporarily /'tempə'rerɪlɪ/ adv temporaneamente; ‹introduced, erected› provvisoriamente

temporary /'tempərərɪ/ adj temporaneo; ‹measure, building› provvisorio

tempt /tempt/ vt tentare; sfidare ‹fate›; ~ **somebody to** indurre qualcuno a; **be** ~**ed** essere tentato (**to** di); **I am** ~**ed by the offer** l'offerta mi tenta

temptation /temp'teɪʃn/ n tentazione f

tempting /'temptɪŋ/ adj allettante; ‹food, drink› invitante

temptress /'temptrɪs/ n seduttrice f

♂ **ten** /ten/ adj & n dieci m; **the T**~ **Commandments** i Dieci Comandamenti

tenable /'tenəbl/ adj fig sostenibile

tenacious /tɪ'neɪʃəs/ adj tenace

tenacity /tɪ'næsətɪ/ n tenacia f

tenancy /'tenənsɪ/ n locazione f

tenant /'tenənt/ n inquilino, -a mf; Comm locatario, -a mf

tend¹ /tend/ vt (look after) prendersi cura di

♂ **tend²** vi ~ **to do something** tendere a far qualcosa

tendency /'tendənsɪ/ n tendenza f

tendentious /ten'denʃəs/ adj tendenzioso

tender¹ /'tendə(r)/ **1** n Comm offerta f; **put out to** ~ dare in appalto; **be legal** ~ avere corso legale
2 vt offrire; presentare ‹resignation›

tender² adj tenero; (painful) dolorante

tender-hearted /-'hɑːtɪd/ adj dal cuore tenero

tenderize /'tendəraɪz/ vt rendere tenero ‹meat›

tenderly /'tendəlɪ/ adv teneramente

tenderness /'tendənɪs/ n tenerezza f; (painfulness) dolore m

tendon /'tendən/ n tendine m

tendril /'tendrɪl/ n (of plant) viticcio m

tenement /'tenəmənt/ n casamento m

tenet /'tenɪt/ n principio m

tenner /'tenə(r)/ n fam biglietto m da dieci sterline

tennis /'tenɪs/ n tennis m

tennis ball n palla f da tennis

tennis-court n campo m da tennis

tennis match n partita f di tennis

tennis player n tennista mf

tennis racket n racchetta f da tennis

tennis shoes npl scarpe fpl da tennis

tenor /'tenə(r)/ n tenore m

tenpin bowling Br, **tenpins** Am n bowling m

tense¹ /tens/ n Gram tempo m

tense² **1** adj teso
2 vt tendere ‹muscle›
■ **tense up** vi tendersi

tension /'tenʃn/ n tensione f

tent /tent/ n tenda f

tentacle /'tentəkl/ n tentacolo m

tentative /'tentətɪv/ adj provvisorio; ‹smile, gesture› esitante

tentatively /'tentətɪvlɪ/ adv timidamente; ‹accept› provvisoriamente

tent city n tendopoli f inv

tenterhooks /'tentəhʊks/ npl **be on** ~ essere sulle spine

tenth /tenθ/ adj & n decimo, -a mf

tenuous /'tenjʊəs/ adj fig debole

tenure /'tenjə(r)/ n (period of office) permanenza f in carica; Univ (job security) ruolo m; (of land, property) possesso m; **security of** ~ (of land, property) diritto m di possesso

tepid /'tepɪd/ adj tiepido

tercentenary /tɜː'senti:nərɪ/ n terzo centenario m

♂ **term** /tɜːm/ n periodo m; Sch, Univ trimestre m; (in Italy, Sch) quadrimestre m; Univ semestre m; (expression) termine m; ~**s** pl (conditions) condizioni fpl; ~ **of office** carica f; **in the short/long** ~ a breve/lungo termine; **be on good/bad** ~**s** essere in buoni/ cattivi rapporti; **come to** ~**s with** accettare ‹past, fact›; **easy** ~**s** facilità fpl di pagamento; ~**s of reference** pl (of committee) competenze fpl

terminal /'tɜːmɪnl/ **1** adj finale; Med terminale
2 n Aeron terminal m inv; Rail stazione f di testa; (of bus) capolinea m; (on battery) morsetto m; Comput terminale m

terminally /'tɜːmɪnəlɪ/ adv **be** ~ **ill** essere in fase terminale

terminate /'tɜːmɪneɪt/ **1** vt terminare; rescindere ‹contract›; interrompere ‹pregnancy›
2 vi terminare; ~ **in** finire in

termination /tɜːmɪ'neɪʃn/ n termine m; Med interruzione f di gravidanza

terminologist /tɜːmɪ'nɒlədʒɪst/ n linguista mf specializzato, -a in terminologia

terminology /tɜːmɪ'nɒlədʒɪ/ n terminologia f

terminus /'tɜːmɪnəs/ n (pl -**ni**) /'tɜːmɪnaɪ/ (for bus) capolinea m; (for train) stazione f di testa

term-time n **during** ~ durante il trimestre

terrace /'terəs/ n terrazza f; (houses) fila f di case a schiera; **the** ~**s** gr Sport le gradinate

terraced house /'terəsd/ n casa f a schiera

terracotta /terə'kɒtə/ n (earthenware) terracotta f; (colour) color m terracotta

terrain /teˈreɪn/ n terreno m

terrestrial /tɪˈrestrɪəl/ [1] n terrestre mf [2] adj terrestre; ~ **television** televisione f terrestre

terrible /ˈterəbl/ adj terribile

terribly /ˈterəblɪ/ adv terribilmente; I'm ~ sorry sono infinitamente spiacente

terrier /ˈterɪə(r)/ n terrier m inv

terrific /təˈrɪfɪk/ adj fam (excellent) fantastico; (huge) enorme

terrifically /təˈrɪfɪklɪ/ adv fam terribilmente

terrify /ˈterɪfaɪ/ vt (pt/pp -ied) atterrire; be terrified essere terrorizzato

terrifying /ˈterɪfaɪɪŋ/ adj terrificante

territorial /terɪˈtɔːrɪəl/ adj territoriale

territorial waters /wɔːtəz/ npl acque fpl territoriali

ℱ **territory** /ˈterɪtərɪ/ n territorio m

terror /ˈterə(r)/ n terrore m

ℱ **terrorism** /ˈterərɪzm/ n terrorismo m

ℱ **terrorist** /ˈterərɪst/ n terrorista mf

terrorize /ˈterəraɪz/ vt terrorizzare

terror-stricken adj terrorizzato

terry towelling /terɪˈtaʊəlɪŋ/ Br, **terry cloth** Am n tessuto m di spugna

terse /tɜːs/ adj conciso

tersely /ˈtɜːslɪ/ adv concisamente

tertiary /ˈtɜːʃ(ə)rɪ/ adj ‹era, industry, sector› terziario; ‹education, college› superiore

Terylene® /ˈterɪliːn/ n terilene® m

ℱ **test** /test/ [1] n esame m; (in laboratory) esperimento m; (of friendship, machine) prova f; (of intelligence, aptitude) test m inv; put to the ~ mettere alla prova; pass one's ~ Auto passare l'esame di guida
[2] vt esaminare; provare ‹machine›

testament /ˈtestəmənt/ n testamento m; Old/New T~ Antico/Nuovo Testamento m

test ban n divieto m di test nucleari

test case n caso (m) giudiziario che fa giurisprudenza

test-drive [1] vt ‹manufacturer› collaudare; ‹buyer› provare
[2] n collaudo m; prova f

tester /ˈtestə(r)/ n (person) collaudatore, -trice mf; (device) tester m inv; (sample: of make-up, perfume) campione m

testicle /ˈtestɪkl/ n testicolo m

testify /ˈtestɪfaɪ/ vt/i (pt/pp -ied) testimoniare

testily /ˈtestɪlɪ/ adv ‹say, reply› in modo scontroso

testimonial /testɪˈməʊnɪəl/ n lettera f di referenze

testimony /ˈtestɪmənɪ/ n testimonianza f

ℱ **testing** /ˈtestɪŋ/ n (of drug) test mpl; (of blood, water) analisi fpl; (of children) esami mpl

test market n mercato m di prova

test match n partita f internazionale

testosterone /tesˈtɒstərəʊn/ n testosterone m

test pilot n pilota mf collaudatore, -trice

test tube n provetta f

test tube baby n fam bambino, -a mf in provetta

testy /ˈtestɪ/ adj irascibile

tetanus /ˈtetənəs/ n tetano m

tetanus injection n antitetanica f

tetchy /ˈtetʃɪ/ adj facilmente irritabile

tether /ˈteðə(r)/ [1] n be at the end of one's ~ non poterne più
[2] vt legare

Teutonic /tjuːˈtɒnɪk/ adj teutonico

ℱ **text** /tekst/ [1] n testo m; (on mobile phone) sms m inv
[2] vi (on mobile phone) mandare sms
[3] vt mandare sms a ‹somebody›

textbook /ˈtekstbʊk/ n manuale m

textile /ˈtekstaɪl/ [1] adj tessile
[2] n stoffa f

texting /ˈtekstɪŋ/ n fam scambio m di sms

text message n sms m inv, messaggio m di testo

text messaging n scambio m di sms

textual /ˈtekstjʊəl/ adj testuale

texture /ˈtekstʊə(r)/ n (of skin) grana f; (of food) consistenza f; of a smooth ~ (to the touch) soffice al tatto

Thai /taɪ/ adj & n tailandese mf; (language) tailandese m

Thailand /ˈtaɪlænd/ n Tailandia f

Thames /temz/ n Tamigi m

ℱ **than** /ðən/ accentato /ðæn/ conj che; (with numbers, names) di; older ~ me più vecchio di me

ℱ **thank** /θæŋk/ vt ringraziare; ~ you [very much] grazie [mille]

thankful /ˈθæŋkful/ adj grato

thankfully /ˈθæŋkfulɪ/ adv con gratitudine; (happily) fortunatamente

thankless /ˈθæŋklɪs/ adj ingrato

ℱ **thanks** /θæŋks/ npl ringraziamenti mpl; ~! fam grazie!; ~ to grazie a; no ~ to you! non certo grazie a te!

thank-you letter n lettera f di ringraziamento

ℱ **that** /ðæt/ [1] adj & pron (pl those) quel, quei pl; (before s + consonant, gn, ps, z) quello, quegli pl; (before vowel) quell' mf; quegli mpl, quelle fpl; ~ shop quel negozio; those shops quei negozi; ~ mirror quello specchio; ~ man/woman quell'uomo'/quella donna; those men/women quegli uomini/quelle donne; ~ one quello; I don't like those quelli non mi piacciono; ~ is cioè; is ~ you? sei tu?; who is ~? chi è?; what did you do after ~? cosa hai fatto dopo?; like ~ in questo ⋯⟶

modo, così; **a man like** ∼ un uomo così; ∼ **is why** ecco perché; ∼ **is the reason she gave me** questa è la ragione che mi ha dato; ∼ **is the easiest thing to do** è la cosa più facile da fare; ∼'**s it!** (you've understood) ecco!; (I've finished) ecco fatto!; (I've had enough) basta così!; (there's nothing more) tutto qui!; ∼'**s** ∼! (with job) ecco fatto!; (with relationship) è tutto finito!; **and** ∼'**s** ∼! punto e basta!

2 *adv* così; **it wasn't** ∼ **good** non era poi cosè buono

3 *rel pron* che; **the man** ∼ **I spoke to** l'uomo con cui ho parlato; **the day** ∼ **I saw him** il giorno in cui l'ho visto; **all** ∼ **I know** tutto quello che so

4 *conj* che; **I think** ∼... penso che...

thatch /θætʃ/ *n* tetto *m* di paglia

thatched /θætʃt/ *adj* coperto di paglia

thaw /θɔː/ **1** *n* disgelo *m*

2 *vt* fare scongelare ⟨food⟩

3 *vi* ⟨food⟩ scongelarsi; **it's** ∼**ing** sta sgelando

ꝏ **the** /ðə/ **1** (before a vowel) /ðɪ/ (def art) il *m*, la *f*; i *mpl*, le *fpl*; (before s + consonant, gn, ps, z) lo *m*, gli *mpl*; (before vowel) l' *mf*, gli *mpl*, le *fpl*; **at** ∼ **cinema/station** al cinema/alla stazione; **from** ∼ **cinema/station** dal cinema/ dalla stazione

2 *adv* ∼ **more** ∼ **better** più ce n'è meglio è; (with reference to pl) più ce ne sono meglio è; **all** ∼ **better** tanto meglio

ꝏ **theatre** /'θɪətə(r)/ *n* teatro *m*; Med sala *f* operatoria

theatregoer /'θiːətəgəʊə(r)/ *n* persona *f* che va a teatro

theatregoing /'θiːətəgəʊɪŋ/ *n* l'andare *m* a teatro

theatrical /θɪ'ætrɪkl/ *adj* teatrale; (showy) melodrammatico

theft /θeft/ *n* furto *m*

theft-proof *adj* antiscippo

ꝏ **their** /ðeə(r)/ *poss adj* il loro *m*, la loro *f*, i loro *mpl*, le loro *fpl*; ∼ **mother/father** la loro madre/il loro padre

theirs /ðeəz/ *poss pron* il loro *m*, la loro *f*, i loro *mpl*, le loro *fpl*; **a friend of** ∼ un loro amico; **friends of** ∼ dei loro amici; **those are** ∼ quelli sono loro; (as opposed to ours) quelli sono i loro

ꝏ **them** /ðem/ *pers pron* (direct object) li *m*, le *f*; (indirect object) gli, loro fml; (after prep: with people) loro; (after preposition: with things) essi; **we haven't seen** ∼ non li/le abbiamo visti/ viste; **give** ∼ **the money** dai loro *or* dagli i soldi; **give it to** ∼ daglielo; **I've spoken to** ∼ ho parlato con loro; **it's** ∼ sono loro

ꝏ **theme** /θiːm/ *n* tema *m*

theme park *n* parco *m* a tema

theme song *n* motivo *m* conduttore

ꝏ indicates a very frequent word

ꝏ **themselves** /ðem'selvz/ *pron* (reflexive) si; (emphatic) se stessi; **they poured** ∼ **a drink** si sono versati da bere; **they said so** ∼ lo hanno detto loro stessi; **they kept it to** ∼ se lo sono tenuti per sé; **by** ∼ da soli

ꝏ **then** /ðen/ **1** *adv* allora; (next) poi; **by** ∼ (in the past) ormai; (in the future) per allora; **since** ∼ sin da allora; **before** ∼ prima di allora; **from** ∼ **on** da allora in poi; **now and** ∼ ogni tanto; **there and** ∼ all'istante

2 *adj* di allora

thence /ðens/ *adv* (from there) di là; (therefore) perciò

theologian /θɪə'ləʊdʒɪən/ *n* teologo, -a *mf*

theological /θɪə'lɒdʒɪkl/ *adj* teologico

theology /θɪ'ɒlədʒɪ/ *n* teologia *f*

theorem /'θɪərəm/ *n* teorema *m*

theoretical /θɪə'retɪkl/ *adj* teorico

theoretically /θɪə'retɪklɪ/ *adv* teoricamente

theorist /'θɪərɪst/ *n* teorico *m*

theorize /'θɪəraɪz/ *vi* teorizzare

ꝏ **theory** /'θɪərɪ/ *n* teoria *f*; **in** ∼ in teoria

therapeutic /θerə'pjuːtɪk/ *adj* terapeutico

therapist /'θerəpɪst/ *n* terapista *mf*

ꝏ **therapy** /'θerəpɪ/ *n* terapia *f*

ꝏ **there** /ðeə(r)/ **1** *adv* là, lì; **down/up** ∼ laggiù/lassù; ∼ **is/are** c'è/ci sono; ∼ **he/she is** eccolo/eccola

2 *int* ∼, ∼! dai, su!

thereabouts /ðeərə'baʊts/ *adv* (roughly) all'incirca

thereafter *adv* dopo di che

thereby *adv* in tal modo

ꝏ **therefore** /'ðeəfɔː(r)/ *adv* perciò

therein *adv* ∼ **lies**... in ciò risiede...; **contained** ∼ Jur (in contract) contenuto nello stesso

thermal /'θɜːml/ *adj* termico; ⟨treatment⟩ termale

thermal imaging *n* termografia *f*

thermal paper *n* carta *f* termica

thermal printer *n* stampante *f* termica

thermal underwear *n* biancheria (*f*) *che mantiene la temperatura corporea*

thermometer /θə'mɒmɪtə(r)/ *n* termometro *m*

Thermos® /'θɜːməs/ *n* ∼ **[flask]** termos *m inv*

thermostat /'θɜːməstæt/ *n* termostato *m*

thesaurus /θɪ'sɔːrəs/ *n* (of particular field) dizionario *m* specialistico; (of synonyms) dizionario *m* dei sinonimi

these /ðiːz/ ▶ THIS

thesis /'θiːsɪs/ *n* (*pl* **-ses** /-siːz/) tesi *f inv*

ꝏ **they** ðeɪ/ *pers pron* loro; ∼ **are tired** sono stanchi; **we're going, but** ∼ **are not** noi andiamo, ma loro no; ∼ **say** (generalizing) si dice; ∼ **are building a new road** stanno costruendo una nuova strada

thick /θɪk/ **1** adj spesso; ‹forest› fitto; ‹liquid› denso; ‹hair› folto; fam (stupid) ottuso; fam (close) molto unito; **be 5 mm ~** essere 5 mm di spessore; **give somebody a ~ ear** fam dare uno schiaffone a qualcuno **2** adv densamente **3** n **in the ~ of** nel mezzo di

thicken /'θɪkn/ **1** vt ispessire ‹sauce› **2** vi ispessirsi; ‹fog› infittirsi

thicket /'θɪkɪt/ n boscaglia f

thickhead /'θɪkhed/ n fam zuccone mf

thickie /'θɪkɪ/ n fam zucca f vuota

thickly /'θɪklɪ/ adv densamente; ‹cut› a fette spesse

thickness /'θɪknɪs/ n spessore m

thicko /'θɪkəʊ/ n fam zucca f vuota

thickset /'θɪkset/ adj tozzo

thick-skinned /-'skɪnd/ adj fam insensibile

thief /θi:f/ n (pl **thieves**) ladro, -a mf

thieving /'θi:vɪŋ/ **1** adj ladro **2** n furti mpl

thigh /θaɪ/ n coscia f

thimble /'θɪmbl/ n ditale m

thimbleful /'θɪmbəlfʊl/ n (of wine etc) goccino m

⚹ thin /θɪn/ **1** adj (**thinner, thinnest**) sottile; ‹shoes, sweater› leggero; ‹liquid› liquido; ‹person› magro; fig ‹excuse, plot› inconsistente; **be [going] ~ on top** (be going bald) perdere i capelli; **vanish into ~ air** volatilizzarsi **2** adv ≈ THINLY **3** vt (pt/pp **thinned**) diluire ‹liquid› **4** vi diradarsi ▪ **thin down 1** vt diluire ‹paint etc› **2** vi (become slimmer) dimagrire ▪ **thin out** vi diradarsi

⚹ thing /θɪŋ/ n cosa f; **~s** pl (belongings) roba fsg; **for one ~** in primo luogo; **the right ~** la cosa giusta; **just the ~!** proprio quel che ci vuole!; **how are ~s?** come vanno le cose?; **the latest ~** fam l'ultima cosa; **the best ~ would be** la cosa migliore sarebbe; **poor ~!** poveretto!; **have a ~ about** (be frightened of) aver la fobia di; (be attracted to) avere un debole per

thingumabob /'θɪŋəməbɒb/ n fam coso m

thingumajig /'θɪŋəmədʒɪg/ n fam coso m

⚹ think /θɪŋk/ vt/i (pt/pp **thought**) pensare; (believe) credere; **I ~ so** credo di sì; **what do you ~?** (what is your opinion?) cosa ne pensi?; **~ of/about** pensare a; **what do you ~ of it?** cosa ne pensi di questo?; **~ of doing something** pensare di fare qualcosa; **~ better of it** ripensarci; **~ for oneself** pensare con la propria testa ▪ **think again** vi pensarci su; **you can ~ again!** sei matto! ▪ **think ahead** vi pensare al futuro; **~ ahead to something** pensare in anticipo a qualcosa

▪ **think back**: vi **~ back to something** ripensare a qualcosa ▪ **think out** vt mettere a punto ‹strategy› ▪ **think over** vt riflettere su ▪ **think through** vt riflettere bene su ‹problem› ▪ **think up** vt escogitare; trovare ‹name›

thinker /'θɪŋkə(r)/ n pensatore, -trice mf

thinking /'θɪŋkɪŋ/ n (opinion) opinione f

think-tank n gruppo m d'esperti

thinly /'θɪnlɪ/ adv scarsamente; ‹disguised› leggermente; ‹cut› a fette sottili

thinner /'θɪnə(r)/ n diluente m

thinness /'θɪnnɪs/ n (of person) magrezza f; (of material) finezza f

thin-skinned /-'skɪnd/ adj (sensitive) permaloso

⚹ third /θɜ:d/ adj & n terzo, -a mf

third age n terza età f

third degree n **give somebody the ~** fare il terzo grado a qualcuno

third-degree burns npl ustioni fpl di terzo grado

thirdly /'θɜ:dlɪ/ adv terzo

third party n (in insurance, law) terzi mpl

third-party insurance n assicurazione f contro terzi

third person n terzo m

third-rate adj scadente

third sector n terzo settore m

Third World n Terzo Mondo m

thirst /θɜ:st/ n sete f

thirstily /'θɜ:stɪlɪ/ adv con sete

thirsty /'θɜ:stɪ/ adj assetato; **be ~** aver sete

thirteen /θɜ:'ti:n/ adj & n tredici m

thirteenth /θɜ:'ti:nθ/ adj & n tredicesimo, -a mf

thirties /'θɜ:tɪz/ npl (period) **the ~** gli anni Trenta mpl; (age) trent'anni mpl; ▸ also FORTIES

thirtieth /'θɜ:tɪθ/ adj & n trentesimo, -a mf

thirty /'θɜ:tɪ/ adj & n trenta m

thirty-something n trentenne mf

⚹ this /ðɪs/ **1** adj (pl **these**) questo; **~ man/woman** quest'uomo/questa donna; **these men/women** questi uomini/queste donne; **~ one** questo; **~ evening/morning** stamattina/stasera **2** pron (pl **these**) questo; **we talked about ~ and that** abbiamo parlato del più e del meno; **like ~** così; **~ is Peter** questo è Peter; Teleph sono Peter; **who is ~?** chi è?; Teleph chi parla?; **~ is the happiest day of my life** è il giorno più felice della mia vita **3** adv così; **~ big** così grande

thistle /'θɪsl/ n cardo m

thong /θɒŋ/ n (on whip) cinghia f; (on shoe, garment) laccetto m; (underwear) cache-sexe m inv; **~s** pl (sandals) infradito mpl or fpl

thorn /θɔ:n/ n spina f

thorny /'θɔ:nɪ/ *adj* spinoso

thorough /'θʌrə/ *adj* completo; ‹knowledge›
profondo; ‹clean, search, training› a fondo;
‹person› scrupoloso

thoroughbred *n* purosangue *m inv*

thoroughfare *n* via *f* principale; 'no ∼'
'strada non transitabile'

thoroughly /'θʌrəlɪ/ *adv* ‹clean, search,
know something› a fondo; (extremely)
estremamente

thoroughness /'θʌrənɪs/ *n* completezza *f*

those /ðəʊz/ ▶ THAT

ᵈ **though** /ðəʊ/ ① *conj* sebbene; **as** ∼ come
se
② *adv fam* tuttavia

ᵈ **thought** /θɔ:t/ ① ▶ THINK
② *n* pensiero *m*; (idea) idea *f*; **I've given this
some** ∼ ci ho pensato su

thoughtful /'θɔ:tfʊl/ *adj* pensieroso;
(considerate) premuroso

thoughtfully /'θɔ:tfʊlɪ/ *adv*
pensierosamente; (considerately)
premurosamente

thoughtfulness /'θɔ:tfʊlnɪs/ *n* (kindness)
considerazione *f*

thoughtless /'θə:tlɪs/ *adj* (inconsiderate)
sconsiderato

thoughtlessly /'θə:tlɪslɪ/ *adv* con
noncuranza

thoughtlessness /'θə:tlɪsnɪs/ *n*
sconsideratezza *f*

thought-out /,θɔ:t'aʊt/ *adj* **well/badly** ∼
ben/male progettato

thought-provoking *adj* ‹book, film etc›
che fa riflettere

ᵈ **thousand** /'θaʊznd/ ① *adj* **one/a** ∼ mille
m inv
② *n* mille *m inv*; ∼**s of** migliaia *fpl* di

thousandth /'θaʊzndθ/ *adj & n* millesimo

thrash /θræʃ/ *vt* picchiare; (defeat)
sconfiggere

■ **thrash about** *vi* dibattersi

■ **thrash out** *vt* mettere a punto

thrashing /'θræʃɪŋ/ *n* (defeat) sconfitta
f; **give somebody a** ∼ (beating) picchiare
qualcuno

thread /θred/ ① *n* filo *m*; (of screw) filetto
m
② *vt* infilare ‹beads›; ∼ **one's way through**
farsi strada fra

threadbare /'θredbeə(r)/ *adj* logoro

ᵈ **threat** /θret/ *n* minaccia *f*

ᵈ **threaten** /'θretn/ ① *vt* minacciare (**to do**
di fare)
② *vi fig* incalzare

threatening /'θretnɪŋ/ *adj* minaccioso;
‹sky, atmosphere› sinistro

threateningly /'θretnɪŋlɪ/ *adv*
minacciosamente

ᵈ indicates a very frequent word

ᵈ **three** /θri:/ *adj & n* tre *m*

three-dimensional /-daɪ'menʃ(ə)nəl/
adj tridimensionale

threefold /'θri:fəʊld/ *adj & adv* triplo

3G *adj abbr* (**third generation**)
‹technology, phone› di terza generazione

three-legged /-'legɪd/ *adj* con tre gambe

three-piece suit *n* vestito *m* da uomo
con panciotto

three-piece suite *n* insieme (*m*) di
divano e due poltrone coordinati

three-quarter length *adj* ‹portrait› di
tre quarti; ‹sleeve› a tre quarti

three-quarters *adv* ‹empty, full, done›
per tre quarti

threesome /'θri:səm/ *n* trio *m*

three-wheeler /-'wi:lə(r)/ *n* (car) auto *f
inv* a tre ruote

thresh /θreʃ/ *vt* trebbiare

threshold /'θreʃəʊld/ *n* soglia *f*

threw /θru:/ ▶ THROW

thrift /θrɪft/ *n* economia *f*

thrifty /'θrɪftɪ/ *adj* parsimonioso

thrill /θrɪl/ ① *n* emozione *f*; (of fear) brivido
m
② *vt* entusiasmare; **be** ∼**ed with** essere
entusiasta di

thriller /'θrɪlə(r)/ *n* (book) romanzo *m*, giallo
m; (film) film *m inv*, giallo *m*

thrilling /'θrɪlɪŋ/ *adj* eccitante

thrive /θraɪv/ *vi* (*pt* **thrived, or throve**,
pp **thrived**) ‹business› prosperare; ‹child,
plant› crescere bene; **I** ∼ **on pressure** mi
piace essere sotto tensione

thriving /'θraɪvɪŋ/ *adj* fiorente

throat /θrəʊt/ *n* gola *f*; **sore** ∼ mal *m* di
gola

throaty /'θrəʊtɪ/ *adj* (husky) roco; *fam* (with
sore throat) rauco

throb /θrɒb/ ① *n* pulsazione *f*; (of heart)
battito *m*
② *vi* (*pt/pp* **throbbed**) (vibrate) pulsare;
‹heart› battere

throbbing /'θrɒbɪŋ/ *adj* ‹pain› lancinante;
‹music› martellante

throes /θrəʊz/ *npl* **in the** ∼ **of** *fig* alle prese
con

thrombosis /θrɒm'bəʊsɪs/ *n* trombosi *f*

throne /θrəʊn/ *n* trono *m*

throng /θrɒŋ/ *n* calca *f*

throttle /'θrɒtl/ ① *n* (on motorbike)
manopola *f* di accelerazione
② *vt* strozzare

ᵈ **through** /θru:/ ① *prep* attraverso; (during)
durante; (by means of) tramite; (thanks to)
grazie a; **Saturday** ∼ **Tuesday** *Am* da sabato a
martedì incluso
② *adv* attraverso; ∼ **and** ∼ fino in fondo;
wet ∼ completamente bagnato; **read
something** ∼ dare una lettura a qualcosa;

let ~ lasciar passare ‹somebody›
3 adj ‹train› diretto; **be** ~ (finished) aver
finito; Teleph avere la comunicazione

⚆ **throughout** /θruː'aʊt/ **1** prep per tutto
2 adv completamente; (time) per tutto il
tempo

throughway n Am superstrada f

throve /θrəʊv/ ▶ THRIVE

⚆ **throw** /θrəʊ/ **1** n tiro m
2 vt (pt **threw**, pp **thrown**) lanciare;
(throw away) gettare; azionare ‹switch›;
disarcionare ‹rider›; fam (disconcert)
disorientare; fam dare ‹party›
■ **throw about** vt spargere; ~ one's money
about sbandierare i propri soldi
■ **throw away** vt gettare via
■ **throw back** vt ributtare in acqua ‹fish›;
rilanciare ‹ball›
■ **throw in** vt (include at no extra cost)
aggiungere [gratuitamente]; (in football)
rimettere in gioco; ~ the towel or the sponge
fig abbandonare il campo
■ **throw off** vt seminare ‹pursuers›; liberarsi
di ‹cold, infection etc›
■ **throw together** vt (assemble hastily)
mettere insieme; improvvisare ‹meal›; (bring
into contact) fare incontrare
■ **throw out** vt gettare via; rigettare ‹plan›;
buttare fuori ‹person›
■ **throw up** **1** vt alzare
2 vi (vomit) vomitare

throwaway adj ‹remark› buttato lì; ‹paper
cup› usa e getta inv

throwback n Biol atavismo m; fig
regressione f

throw-in n Sport rimessa f laterale

thrush /θrʌʃ/ n tordo m; Med mughetto m;
(in woman) candida f

thrust /θrʌst/ **1** n spinta f
2 vt (pt/pp **thrust**) (push) spingere; (insert)
conficcare; ~ [up] on imporre a

thud /θʌd/ n tonfo m

thug /θʌg/ n delinquente m

thuggish /'θʌgɪʃ/ adj violento

thumb /θʌm/ **1** n pollice m; **as a rule of** ~
come regola generale; **under sb's** ~ succube
di qualcuno
2 vt ~ **a lift** fare l'autostop
■ **thumb through** vt sfogliare

thumb-index n indice m a rubrica

thumbnail sketch n breve descrizione f

thumbs down n fam **get the** ~ non
ottenere l'ok; **give somebody/something the**
~ non dare l'ok a qualcuno/qualcosa

thumbs up n fam **get the** ~ ricevere l'ok;
give somebody/something the ~ dare l'ok a
qualcuno/qualcosa

thumbtack n Am cimice f, puntina f [da
disegno]

thump /θʌmp/ **1** n colpo m; (noise) tonfo m
2 vt battere su ‹table, door›; battere ‹fist›;

colpire ‹person›
3 vi battere (**on** su); ‹heart› battere forte
■ **thump about** vi camminare
pesantemente

thumping /'θʌmpɪŋ/ adj fam (very large)
enorme; **a** ~ **headache** un mal di testa
martellante

thunder /'θʌndə(r)/ **1** n tuono m; (loud
noise) rimbombo m
2 vi tuonare; (make loud noise) rimbombare

thunderbolt /'θʌndəbəʊlt/ n folgore f

thunderclap /'θʌndəklæp/ n rombo m
di tuono

thundering /'θʌndərɪŋ/ adj fam (very big or
great) tremendo

thunderous /'θʌndərəs/ adj ‹applause›
scrosciante

thunderstorm /'θʌndəstɔːm/ n temporale
m

thunderstruck /'θʌndəstrʌk/ adj
sbigottito

thundery /'θʌndərɪ/ adj temporalesco

⚆ **Thursday** /'θɜːzdeɪ/ n giovedì m inv

⚆ **thus** /ðʌs/ adv così

thwack /θwæk/ **1** vt colpire
2 n colpo m

thwart /θwɔːt/ vt ostacolare

thyme /taɪm/ n timo m

thyroid /'θaɪrɔɪd/ n tiroide f

tiara /tɪ'ɑːrə/ n diadema m

Tiber /'taɪbə(r)/ n Tevere m

Tibet /tɪ'bet/ n Tibet m

tick¹ /tɪk/ n **on** ~ fam a credito

tick² **1** n (sound) ticchettio m; (mark) segno
m; fam (instant) attimo m
2 vi ticchettare
■ **tick off** vt spuntare; fam sgridare
■ **tick over** vi ‹engine› andare al minimo

⚆ **ticket** /'tɪkɪt/ n biglietto m; (for item deposited,
library) tagliando m; (label) cartellino m; (fine)
multa f

ticket barrier n cancelletto m di entrata
e uscita

ticket-collector n controllore m

ticket-holder n persona f munita di
biglietto

ticket-office n biglietteria f

ticket tout n Br bagarino m

ticket window n sportello m della
biglietteria

tickle /'tɪkl/ **1** n solletico m
2 vt fare il solletico a; (amuse) divertire
3 vi fare prurito

ticklish /'tɪklɪʃ/ adj che soffre il solletico;
‹problem› delicato

tic-tac-toe /tɪktæktəʊ/ n Am tris m

tidal /'taɪdl/ adj ‹river, harbour› di marea

tidal wave n onda f di marea

tiddly /'tɪdlɪ/ adj Br fam (drunk) brillo

tiddlywinks /'tɪdlɪwɪŋks/ n gioco m delle pulci

tide /taɪd/ n marea f; (of events) corso m; **the ~ is in/out** c'è alta/bassa marea
■ **tide over**: vt ~ **somebody over** aiutare qualcuno ad andare avanti

tidemark /'taɪdmɑːk/ n linea f di marea; Br fig (line of dirt) tracce fpl di sporco (*nella vasca da bagno*)

tidily /'taɪdɪlɪ/ adv in modo ordinato

tidiness /'taɪdɪnɪs/ n ordine m

tidy /'taɪdɪ/ **1** adj (**-ier, -iest**) ordinato; fam ‹amount› bello
2 vt ordinare
■ **tidy away** vt mettere a posto ‹toys, books›
■ **tidy out** vt mettere in ordine ‹drawer, cupboard›
■ **tidy up** vt ordinare; ~ **oneself up** mettersi in ordine

✧ **tie** /taɪ/ **1** n cravatta f; (cord) legaccio m; fig (bond) legame m; (restriction) impedimento m; Sport pareggio m
2 vt (pres p **tying**) legare; fare ‹knot›; **be ~d** (in competition) essere in parità
3 vi pareggiare
■ **tie back** vt legare [dietro la nuca] ‹hair›
■ **tie down** vt also fig legare
■ **tie in with** vi corrispondere a
■ **tie on** vt attaccare
■ **tie up** vt legare; vincolare ‹capital›; **be ~d up** (busy) essere occupato

tie-break[er] n Tennis tie-break m inv; (in quiz) pareggio m

tie-dye vt tingere annodando

tie-on adj ‹label› volante

tiepin n fermacravatta m

tier /tɪə(r)/ n fila f; (of cake) piano m; (in stadium) gradinata f

tiff /tɪf/ n battibecco m

tiger /'taɪgə(r)/ n tigre f

tiger's-eye /'taɪgəz/ n occhio m di tigre

✧ **tight** /taɪt/ **1** adj stretto; (taut) teso; fam (drunk) sbronzo; fam (mean) spilorcio; ~ **corner** fam brutta situazione f
2 adv strettamente; ‹hold› forte; ‹closed› bene

tighten /'taɪtn/ **1** vt stringere; avvitare ‹screw›; intensificare ‹control›; ~ **one's belt** fig tirare la cinghia
2 vi stringersi
■ **tighten up** **1** vt stringere ‹screw›; rendere più severo ‹security›
2 vi (become stricter) diventare più severo

tight-fisted /-'fɪstɪd/ adj tirchio

tight-fitting /-'fɪtɪŋ/ adj attillato

tight-knit adj fig ‹community, group› unito

tight-lipped /-'lɪpt/ adj **they are remaining ~ about events** mantengono il riserbo sull'accaduto

tightly /'taɪtlɪ/ adv strettamente; ‹hold› forte; ‹closed› bene

tightrope /'taɪtrəʊp/ n fune f (*da funamboli*)

tightrope walker n equilibrista mf

tights /taɪts/ npl collant m inv

tigress /'taɪgrɪs/ n tigre f femmina

tile /taɪl/ **1** n mattonella f; (on roof) tegola f
2 vt rivestire di mattonelle ‹wall›; coprire con tegole ‹roof›; Comput affiancare

till¹ /tɪl/ prep & conj ▶ UNTIL

till² n cassa f

tiller /'tɪlə(r)/ n barra f del timone

tilt /tɪlt/ **1** n inclinazione f; **at full ~** a tutta velocità
2 vt inclinare
3 vi inclinarsi

timber /'tɪmbə(r)/ n legname m

✧ **time** /taɪm/ **1** n tempo m; (occasion) volta f; (by clock) ora f; **two ~s four** due volte quattro; **at any ~** in qualsiasi momento; **this ~** questa volta; **at ~s, from ~ to ~** ogni tanto; ~ **and again** cento volte; **two at a ~** due alla volta; **on ~** in orario; **in ~** in tempo; (eventually) col tempo; **in no ~** **at all** velocemente; **in a year's ~** fra un anno; **behind ~** in ritardo; **behind the ~s** antiquato; **for the ~ being** per il momento; **what is the ~?** che ora è?; **by the ~ we arrive** quando arriviamo; **do you have the ~?** (what ~ is it?) hai l'ora?; **did you have a nice ~?** ti sei divertito?; **have a good ~!** divertiti!
2 vt scegliere il momento per; cronometrare ‹race›; **be well ~d** essere ben calcolato

time bomb n bomba f a orologeria

time-consuming adj che porta via molto tempo

time difference n differenza f di fuso orario

time-frame n arco m temporale

time-honoured /-ɒnəd/ adj venerando

timekeeper n Sport cronometrista mf; **be a good ~** (be punctual) essere sempre puntuale

time lag n intervallo m [di tempo]

timeless /'taɪmlɪs/ adj eterno

time limit n limite m di tempo

timely /'taɪmlɪ/ adj opportuno

time management n gestione f del proprio tempo

time off n (leave) permesso m; **take some ~** prendere delle ferie

time-out n (break) pausa f; Sport time out m inv

timer /'taɪmə(r)/ n timer m inv

timescale n periodo m

timeshare n (apartment) appartamento m in multiproprietà; (house) casa f in multiproprietà

✧ indicates a very frequent word

time sheet n foglio m di presenza

time signal n segnale m orario

time span n arco m di tempo

time switch n interruttore m a tempo

timetable n orario m

time zone n fuso m orario

timid /'tɪmɪd/ adj (shy) timido; (fearful) timoroso

timidly /'tɪmɪdlɪ/ adv timidamente

timidness /'tɪmɪdnɪs/ n (shyness) timidezza f; (fear) paura f

timing /'taɪmɪŋ/ n Sport, Techn cronometraggio m; **the ~ of the election** il momento scelto per le elezioni; **have no sense of ~** non saper scegliere il momento opportuno

timorous /'tɪm(ə)rəs/ adj timoroso

timpani /'tɪmpənɪ/ npl timpani mpl

tin /tɪn/ [1] n stagno m; (container) barattolo m

[2] vt (pt/pp **tinned**) inscatolare

tin can n lattina f, scatoletta f

tin foil n carta f, stagnola f

tinge /tɪndʒ/ [1] n sfumatura f

[2] vt ~**d with** fig misto a

tingle /'tɪŋgl/ vi pizzicare

tinker /'tɪŋkə(r)/ vi armeggiare

tinkle /'tɪŋkl/ [1] n tintinnio m; fam (phone call) colpo m di telefono

[2] vi tintinnare

tinned /tɪnd/ adj in scatola

tinnitus /'tɪnɪtəs/ n Med ronzio m auricolare

tinny /'tɪnɪ/ adj ‹sound, music› metallico; (badly made) che sembra fatta di latta

tin-opener /-əʊpnə(r)/ n apriscatole m inv

tinpot /'tɪnpɒt/ adj pej ‹firm› da due soldi

tinsel /'tɪnsl/ n filo m d'argento

tint /tɪnt/ [1] n tinta f

[2] vt tingersi ‹hair›; ~**ed glasses** occhiali mpl colorati

⚥ **tiny** /'taɪnɪ/ adj (**-ier, -iest**) minuscolo

tip¹ /tɪp/ n (point, top) punta f

tip² [1] n (money) mancia f; (advice) consiglio m; (for rubbish) discarica f

[2] vt (pt/pp **tipped**) (tilt) inclinare; (overturn) capovolgere; (pour) versare; (reward) dare una mancia a

[3] vi inclinarsi; (overturn) capovolgersi

■ **tip off**: vt ~ **somebody off** (inform) fare una soffiata a qualcuno

■ **tip out** vt rovesciare

■ **tip over** [1] vt capovolgere

[2] vi capovolgersi

■ **tip up** vt sollevare ‹seat›; (overturn) rovesciare

tip-off n soffiata f

tipped /tɪpt/ adj ‹cigarette› col filtro

tipple /'tɪpl/ [1] vi bere [alcool]

[2] n **have a ~** prendere un bicchierino; **my favourite ~** il mio liquore preferito

tipster /'tɪpstə(r)/ n esperto (m) che dà suggerimenti su cavalli da corsa, azioni ecc

tipsy /'tɪpsɪ/ adj fam brillo

tiptoe /'tɪptəʊ/ n **on ~** in punta di piedi

tip-top adj fam in condizioni perfette

tirade /taɪ'reɪd/ n filippica f

tire /'taɪə(r)/ [1] vt stancare

[2] vi stancarsi

■ **tire out** vt (exhaust) sfinire

⚥ **tired** /'taɪəd/ adj stanco; ~ **of** stanco di; ~ **out** stanco morto

tiredness /'taɪədnɪs/ n stanchezza f

tireless /'taɪəlɪs/ adj instancabile

tirelessly /'taɪəlɪslɪ/ adv instancabilmente

tiresome /'taɪəsəm/ adj fastidioso

tiring /'taɪərɪŋ/ adj stancante

⚥ **tissue** /'tɪʃu:/ n tessuto m; (handkerchief) fazzolettino m di carta

tissue-paper n carta f velina

tit¹ /tɪt/ n (bird) cincia f

tit² n ~ **for tat** pan per focaccia

tit³ n fam (breast) tetta f; (fool) stupido m

titbit /'tɪtbɪt/ n ghiottoneria f; fig (of news) notizia f appetitosa

titillate /'tɪtɪleɪt/ vt titillare

titivate /'tɪtɪveɪt/ vt agghindare; ~ **oneself** agghindarsi

title /'taɪtl/ n titolo m

title bar n Comput barra f di titolo

title deed n atto m di proprietà

title-holder n detentore, -trice mf del titolo

title-page n frontespizio m

title role n ruolo m principale

titter /'tɪtə(r)/ [1] vi ridere nervosamente

[2] n risatina f nervosa

tittle-tattle /'tɪtltætl/ n pettegolezzi mpl

titular /'tɪtjʊlə(r)/ adj nominale

tizzy /'tɪzɪ/ n fam **in a ~** in grande agitazione

TLC n abbr fam (**tender loving care**) cura e gentilezza f

TM abbr (**trademark**) marchio m di fabbrica

⚥ **to** /tu:/, atono /tə/ [1] prep a; (to countries) in; (towards) verso; (up to, until) fino a; **I'm going to John's/the butcher's** vado da John/dal macellaio; **come/go to somebody** venire/andare da qualcuno; **to Italy/Switzerland** in Italia/Svizzera; **I've never been to Rome** non sono mai stato a Roma; **go to the market** andare al mercato; **to the toilet/my room** in bagno/camera mia; **to an exhibition** ad una mostra; **to university** all'università; **twenty/quarter to eight** le otto meno venti/un quarto; **5 to 6 kilos** da 5 a 6 chili; **to the end** alla fine; **to this day** fino a oggi; **to the best of my recollection** per quanto mi possa ricordare; **give/say something to somebody** dare/dire qualcosa a qualcuno; **give it to me** ⋯⟶

t

dammelo; **there's nothing to it** è una cosa da niente

2 (verbal constructions) **to go** andare; **learn to swim** imparare a nuotare; **I want to/ have to go** voglio/devo andare; **it's easy to forget** è facile da dimenticare; **too ill/tired to go** troppo malato/stanco per andare; **you have to** devi; **I don't want to** non voglio; **he wants to be a teacher** vuole diventare un insegnante; **live to be 90** vivere fino a 90 anni; **he was the last to arrive** è stato l'ultimo ad arrivare; **to be honest,...** per essere sincero, ...

3 *adv* **pull to** chiudere; **to and fro** avanti e indietro

toad /təʊd/ *n* rospo *m*

toadstool /'təʊdstuːl/ *n* fungo *m* velenoso

toady /'təʊdɪ/ *v*

■ **toady to** *vi* fare da leccapiedi a

toast /təʊst/ **1** *n* pane *m* tostato; (drink) brindisi *m inv*; **be** ∼ fam essere fritto; **if he finds out, we're** ∼ se lo scopre siamo fritti
2 *vt* tostare ‹*bread*›; (drink a ∼ to) brindare a

toaster /'təʊstə(r)/ *n* tostapane *m inv*

toast rack /'təʊstræk/ *n* portatoast *m inv*

tobacco /tə'bækəʊ/ *n* tabacco *m*

tobacconist's [shop] /tə'bækənɪsts [ʃɒp]/ *n* tabaccheria *f*

toboggan /tə'bɒgən/ **1** *n* toboga *m inv*
2 *vi* andare in toboga

⚘ **today** /tə'deɪ/ *adj & adv* oggi *m*; **a week** ∼ una settimana ad oggi; ∼**'s paper** il giornale di oggi

toddle /'tɒdl/ *vi* ‹*child*› cominciare a camminare; ∼ **into town** fam fare una passeggiata in centro; **I must be toddling** fam devo scappare

toddler /'tɒdlə(r)/ *n* bambino, -a *mf* piccolo

toddy /'tɒdɪ/ *n* grog *m inv*

to-do /tə'duː/ *n* fam baccano *m*

toe /təʊ/ **1** *n* dito *m* del piede; (of footwear) punta *f*; **on one's** ∼**s** fig pronto ad agire; **big** ∼ alluce *m*; **little** ∼ mignolo *m* [del piede]
2 *vt* ∼ **the line** rigar diritto

toe-curling *adj* imbarazzante

toe-hold *n* punto *m* d'appoggio

toenail *n* unghia *f* del piede

toff /tɒf/ *n* fam elegantone, -a *mf*

toffee /'tɒfɪ/ *n* caramella *f* al mou

toffee apple *n* mela *f* caramellata

toffee-nosed *adj* Br fam con la puzza sotto il naso

⚘ **together** /tə'geðə(r)/ *adv* insieme; (at the same time) allo stesso tempo; ∼ **with** insieme a

togetherness /tə'geðənɪs/ *n* intimità *f*

toggle /'tɒgl/ *n* (fastening) olivetta *f*

Togo /'təʊgəʊ/ *n* Togo *m*

toil /tɔɪl/ **1** *n* duro lavoro *m*

⚘ indicates a very frequent word

2 *vi* lavorare duramente

toilet /'tɔɪlɪt/ *n* (lavatory) gabinetto *m*

toilet bag *n* nécessaire *m inv*

toilet paper *n* carta *f* igienica

toiletries /'tɔɪlɪtrɪz/ *npl* articoli *mpl* da toilette

toilet roll *n* rotolo *m* di carta igienica

toilet soap *n* sapone *m*

toilet tissue *n* carta *f* igienica

toilet-train *vt* ∼ **a child** insegnare ad un bambino ad usare il vasino

toilet water *n* acqua *f* di colonia

token /'təʊkən/ **1** *n* segno *m*; (counter) gettone *m*; (voucher) buono *m*
2 *attrib* simbolico

told /təʊld/ **1** ▶ TELL
2 *adj* **all** ∼ in tutto

tolerable /'tɒl(ə)rəbl/ *adj* tollerabile; (not bad) discreto

tolerably /'tɒl(ə)rəblɪ/ *adv* discretamente

tolerance /'tɒl(ə)r(ə)ns/ *n* tolleranza *f*

tolerant /'tɒl(ə)r(ə)nt/ *adj* tollerante

tolerantly /'tɒl(ə)r(ə)ntlɪ/ *adv* con tolleranza

tolerate /'tɒləreɪt/ *vt* tollerare

toll¹ /təʊl/ *n* pedaggio *m*; **death** ∼ numero *m* di morti; **take a heavy** ∼ costare gravi perdite

toll² *vi* suonare a morto

toll-booth *n* casello *m*

toll call *n* Am chiamata *f* in teleselezione

toll-free number *n* Am Teleph numero *m* verde

toll motorway *n* autostrada *f* con pedaggio

tom /tɒm/ *n* (cat) gatto *m* maschio

tomato /tə'mɑːtəʊ/ *n* (*pl* **-es**) pomodoro *m*

tomato ketchup *n* ketchup *m*

tomato purée *n* concentrato *m* di pomodoro

tomato sauce *n* salsa *f* di pomodoro

tomb /tuːm/ *n* tomba *f*

tomboy /'tɒmbɔɪ/ *n* maschiaccio *m*

tombstone /'tuːmstəʊn/ *n* pietra *f* tombale

tom-cat *n* gatto *m* maschio

tome /təʊm/ *n* tomo *m*

tomfoolery /tɒm'fuːlərɪ/ *n* stupidaggini *fpl*

⚘ **tomorrow** /tə'mɒrəʊ/ *adj & adv* domani; ∼ **morning** domani mattina; **the day after** ∼ dopodomani; **see you** ∼! a domani!

tom-tom *n* tamtam *m inv*

ton /tʌn/ *n* tonnellata *f* (1, 016 kg); ∼**s of** fam un sacco di

tonal /'təʊnl/ *adj* tonale

tonality /təʊ'nælətɪ/ *n* tonalità *f inv*

⚘ **tone** /təʊn/ *n* tono *m*; (colour) tonalità *f inv*
■ **tone down** *vt* attenuare

■ **tone in** *vi* intonarsi

■ **tone up** *vt* tonificare ‹*muscles*›

tone-deaf *adj* be ~ non avere orecchio

toneless /'təʊnlɪs/ *adj* (unmusical) piatto

toner /'təʊnə(r)/ *n* toner *m*

Tonga /'tɒŋgə/ *n* Tonga *f*

tongs /tɒŋz/ *npl* pinze *fpl*

tongue /tʌŋ/ *n* lingua *f*; ~ **in cheek** fam ‹*say*› ironicamente

tongue-lashing *n* (severe reprimand) strigliata *f*

tongue stud *n* piercing *m inv* nella lingua

tongue-tied *adj* senza parole

tongue-twister *n* scioglilingua *m inv*

tonic /'tɒnɪk/ *n* tonico *m*; (for hair) lozione *f* per i capelli; fig toccasana *m inv*; ~ **[water]** acqua *f* tonica

⸱ᶠ **tonight** /tə'naɪt/ ❶ *adv* stanotte; (evening) stasera

    ❷ *n* questa notte *f*; (evening) questa sera *f*

tonnage /'tʌnɪdʒ/ *n* stazza *f*

tonne /tʌn/ *n* tonnellata *f* metrica

tonsil /'tɒnsl/ *n* Anat tonsilla *f*; **have one's** ~**s out** operarsi di tonsille

tonsillitis /tɒnsə'laɪtɪs/ *n* tonsillite *f*; **have** ~ avere la tonsillite

⸱ᶠ **too** /tu:/ *adv* troppo; *also* anche; ~ **many** troppi; ~ **much** troppo; ~ **little** troppo poco

took /tʊk/ ▶ TAKE

⸱ᶠ **tool** /tu:l/ *n* attrezzo *m*

tool-bag *n* borsa *f* degli attrezzi

toolbar *n* Comput barra *f* degli strumenti

toolbox *n* cassetta *f* degli attrezzi

tool kit *n* astuccio *m* di attrezzi

toot /tu:t/ ❶ *n* suono *m* di clacson

    ❷ *vt* Auto clacsonare

⸱ᶠ **tooth** /tu:θ/ *n* (*pl* **teeth**) dente *m*

tooth ache /'tu:θeɪk/ *n* mal *m* di denti; **have** ~ avere mal di denti

toothbrush /'tu:θbrʌʃ/ *n* spazzolino *m* da denti

toothless /'tu:θlɪs/ *adj* sdentato

toothpaste /'tu:θpeɪst/ *n* dentifricio *m*

toothpick /'tu:θpɪk/ *n* stuzzicadenti *m inv*

toothy /'tu:θɪ/ *adj* give a ~ **grin** fare un sorriso a trentadue denti

top¹ /tɒp/ *n* (toy) trottola *f*

⸱ᶠ **top²** ❶ *n* cima *f*; Sch primo, -a *mf*; (upper part or half) parte *f* superiore; (of page, list, street) inizio *m*; (upper surface) superficie *f*; (lid) coperchio *m*; (of bottle) tappo *m*; (garment) maglia *f*; (blouse) camicia *f*; Auto marcia *f* più alta; **at the** ~ fig al vertice; **at the** ~ **of one's voice** a squarciagola; **on** ~/**on** ~ **of** sopra; **on** ~ **of that** (besides) per di più; **from** ~ **to bottom** da cima a fondo; **blow one's** ~ fam perdere le staffe; **over the** ~ fam (exaggerated, too much) eccessivo

    ❷ *adj* in alto; ‹*official, floor of building*›

superiore; ‹*pupil, musician etc*› migliore; ‹*speed*› massimo

    ❸ *vt* (*pt/pp* **topped**) essere in testa a ‹*list*›; (exceed) sorpassare; ~**ped with ice-cream** ricoperto di gelato; ~ **oneself** sl suicidarsi

■ **top up** *vt* riempire

topaz /'təʊpæz/ *n* topazio *m*

top brass *n* fam pezzi *mpl* grossi

topcoat *n* (of paint) strato *m* finale

top-end *adj* ‹*computer, model*› della fascia più alta

top floor *n* ultimo piano *m*

top gear *n* Auto marcia *f* più alta

top hat *n* cilindro *m*

top-heavy *adj* con la parte superiore sovraccarica

⸱ᶠ **topic** /'tɒpɪk/ *n* soggetto *m*; (of conversation) argomento *m*

topical /'tɒpɪkl/ *adj* d'attualità; **very** ~ di grande attualità

topless /'tɒplɪs/ *adj & adv* topless

top-level *adj* ad alto livello

top management *n* dirigenza *f*

topmost /'tɒpməʊst/ *adj* più alto

top-notch *adj* fam eccellente

top-of-the-range *adj* ‹*model*› della fascia più alta

topping /'tɒpɪŋ/ *n* **with a chocolate** ~ ricoperto di cioccolato; **pizza with a ham and mushroom** ~ pizza al prosciutto e funghi

topple /'tɒpl/ ❶ *vt* rovesciare

    ❷ *vi* rovesciarsi

■ **topple off** *vi* cadere

top-ranking *adj* ‹*official*› di massimo grado

top secret *adj* segretissimo, top secret *inv*

top security *adj* di massima sicurezza

top-shelf *adj* ‹*magazine*› pornografico

topsoil *n* strato *m* superficiale del terreno

topspin *n* topspin *m inv*

topsy-turvy /tɒpsɪ'tɜ:vɪ/ *adj & adv* sottosopra

top ten *npl* primi dieci *mpl* in classifica

top-up ❶ *n* would you like a ~? ti riempio il bicchiere/la tazza?

    ❷ *vt* ‹*phone*› ricaricare

top-up card *n* ricarica *f*

torch /tɔ:tʃ/ *n* torcia *f* [elettrica]; (flaming) fiaccola *f*

torchlight procession /'tɔ:tʃlaɪt/ *n* fiaccolata *f*

tore /tɔ:(r)/ ▶ TEAR¹

torment¹ /'tɔ:ment/ *n* tormento *m*

torment² /tɔ:'ment/ *vt* tormentare

tormentor /tɔ:'mentə(r)/ *n* tormentatore, -trice *mf*

torn /tɔ:n/ ❶ ▶ TEAR¹

    ❷ *adj* bucato

t

tornado /tɔː'neɪdəʊ/ n (pl **-es**) tornado m inv

torpedo /tɔː'piːdəʊ/ ① n (pl **-es**) siluro m ② vt silurare

torpid /'tɔːpɪd/ adj intorpidito

torrent /'tɒrənt/ n torrente m

torrential /tə'renʃl/ adj ‹rain› torrenziale

torrid /'tɒrɪd/ adj torrido

torso /'tɔːsəʊ/ n torso m; (in art) busto m

tortoise /'tɔːtəs/ n tartaruga f

tortoiseshell /'tɔːtəsʃel/ n tartaruga f

tortuous /'tɔːtʃʊəs/ adj tortuoso

tortuously /'tɔːtʃʊəslɪ/ adv tortuosamente

torture /'tɔːtʃə(r)/ ① n tortura f ② vt torturare

Tory /'tɔːrɪ/ Br ① n conservatore, -trice mf (appartenente al partito britannico conservatore) ② adj del partito conservatore

toss /tɒs/ ① vt gettare; (into the air) lanciare in aria; (shake) scrollare; ‹horse› disarcionare; mescolare ‹salad›; rivoltare facendo saltare in aria ‹pancake›; ~ **a coin** fare testa o croce ② vi ~ **and turn** (in bed) rigirarsi; **let's ~ for it** facciamo testa o croce ■ **toss out** vt buttare via ‹newspaper, rubbish›; **toss somebody out** buttare fuori qualcuno

toss-up n fam **let's have a ~ to decide** facciamo testa o croce

tot¹ /tɒt/ n bimbetto, -a mf; fam (of liquor) goccio m

tot² vt (pt/pp **totted**) ~ **up** fam fare la somma di

⚡ **total** /'təʊtl/ ① adj totale ② n totale m ③ vt (pt/pp **totalled**) ammontare a; (add up) sommare

totalitarian /təʊtælɪ'teərɪən/ adj totalitario

⚡ **totally** /'təʊtəlɪ/ adv totalmente

tote bag /təʊt/ n sporta f

totem /'təʊtəm/ n totem m inv

totem pole /'təʊtəm/ n totem m inv

totter /'tɒtə(r)/ vi barcollare; ‹government› vacillare

⚡ **touch** /tʌtʃ/ ① n tocco m; (sense) tatto m; (contact) contatto m; (trace) traccia f; (of irony, humour) tocco m; **get/be in ~** mettersi/essere in contatto ② vt toccare; (lightly) sfiorare; (equal) eguagliare; fig (move) commuovere ③ vi toccarsi ■ **touch down** vi Aeron atterrare ■ **touch off** vi fig scatenare ■ **touch on** vt fig accennare a ■ **touch up** vt ritoccare ‹painting›; ~ **somebody up** (sexually) allungare le mani

su qualcuno

touch[-sensitive] screen n Comput schermo m a sfioramento

touch-and-go adj incerto

touchdown /'tʌtʃdaʊn/ n Aeron atterraggio m; Sport meta f

touché /tuː'ʃeɪ/ int fig touché!

touched /tʌtʃt/ adj (crazy) toccato

touching /'tʌtʃɪŋ/ adj commovente

touchingly /'tʌtʃɪŋlɪ/ adv in modo commovente

touchline n (in football) linea f laterale; (in rugby) touche nf inv

touchpad n Comput touchpad m inv

touch screen n Comput touch screen m inv, schermo m a sfioramento

touch-tone adj ‹telephone› a tastiera

touch-type vi dattilografare a tastiera cieca

touch-typing n dattilografia f a tastiera cieca

touch-up n (of paintwork) ritocco m

touchy /'tʌtʃɪ/ adj permaloso; ‹subject› delicato

⚡ **tough** /tʌf/ adj duro; (severe, harsh) severo; (durable) resistente; (resilient) forte; ~**!** fam (too bad) peggio per te/lui!

toughen /'tʌfn/ vt rinforzare ■ **toughen up** vt rendere più forte ‹person›

toupee /'tuːpeɪ/ n toupet m inv

⚡ **tour** /tʊə(r)/ ① n giro m; (of building, town) visita f; Theat, Sport tournée f inv; (of duty) servizio m ② vt visitare ③ vi fare un giro turistico; Theat essere in tournée

tour guide n guida f turistica

tourism /'tʊərɪzm/ n turismo m

⚡ **tourist** /'tʊərɪst/ ① n turista mf ② attrib turistico

tourist class n classe f turistica

tourist office n ufficio m turistico

tourist resort n località f turistica

tourist route n itinerario m turistico

tourist trap n locale o località per turisti dove i prezzi sono molto alti

touristy /'tʊərɪstɪ/ adj fam pej da turisti; **it's too ~ here** è troppo turistico qui

tournament /'tʊənəmənt/ n torneo m

tourniquet /'tʊənɪkeɪ/ n laccio m emostatico

tour operator n tour operator mf inv, operatore, -trice mf turistico, -a

tousle /'taʊzl/ vt spettinare

tousled /'taʊzld/ adj ‹hair› arruffato; (appearance) scarmigliato

tout /taʊt/ ① n (ticket ~) bagarino m; (horseracing) informatore m ② vi ~ **for** sollecitare

---

⚡ indicates a very frequent word

tow /təʊ/ **1** n rimorchio m; 'on ∼' 'a rimorchio'; in ∼ fam al seguito
2 vt rimorchiare
■ **tow away** vt portare via col carro attrezzi

✧ **towards** Br, **toward** Am /təˈwɔːd(z)/ prep verso; (with respect to) nei riguardi di

tow bar n barra f di rimorchio

towel /ˈtaʊəl/ n asciugamano m
■ **towel down** vt asciugare

towelling /ˈtaʊəlɪŋ/ n spugna f

towelling robe n accappatoio m

towel rail n portasciugamano m

tower /ˈtaʊə(r)/ **1** n torre f; be a ∼ of strength to somebody essere di grande conforto per qualcuno
2 vi ∼ above dominare

tower block n palazzone m

towering /ˈtaʊərɪŋ/ adj torreggiante; ⟨rage⟩ violento

tow line n cavo m da rimorchio

✧ **town** /taʊn/ n città f inv; in ∼ nel centro

town-and-country planning n pianificazione f territoriale

town centre n centro m della città

town council n municipalità f inv

town hall n municipio m

town house n casa (f) a schiera a tre o più piani

town planner n urbanista mf

town planning n urbanistica f

township /ˈtaʊnʃɪp/ n comune m; (in South Africa) township f inv

towpath /ˈtaʊpɑːθ/ n strada f alzaia

tow rope n cavo m da rimorchio

tow truck n carro m attrezzi inv

toxic /ˈtɒksɪk/ adj tossico

toxic assets /ˌtɒksɪk ˈæsets/ n pl titoli mpl tossici

toxicity /tɒkˈsɪsɪtɪ/ n tossicità f

toxicologist /tɒksɪˈkɒlədʒɪst/ n tossicologo, -a mf

toxicology /tɒksɪˈkɒlədʒɪ/ n tossicologia f

toxic waste n rifiuti mpl tossici

toxin /ˈtɒksɪn/ n tossina f

toy /tɔɪ/ n giocattolo m
■ **toy with** vt giocherellare con

toyboy /ˈtɔɪbɔɪ/ n Br fam uomo-oggetto m

toyshop /ˈtɔɪʃɒp/ n negozio m di giocattoli

trace /treɪs/ **1** n traccia f
2 vt seguire le tracce di; (find) rintracciare; (draw) tracciare; (with tracing-paper) ricalcare
■ **trace back** vt trovare tracce di ⟨family⟩
■ **trace out** vt tracciare

tracer /ˈtreɪsə(r)/ n Mil proiettile m tracciante

tracing /ˈtreɪsɪŋ/ n ricalco m

tracing-paper n carta f da ricalco

✧ **track** /træk/ **1** n traccia f; (path, Sport) pista f; Rail binario m; keep ∼ of tenere d'occhio
2 vt seguire le tracce di

■ **track down** vt scovare

trackball, tracker ball n Comput trackball f inv

tracker /ˈtrækə(r)/ n (dog) segugio m

track record n fig background m inv

tracksuit /ˈtræksuːt/ n tuta f da ginnastica

tract /trækt/ n (pamphlet) opuscolo m

tractable /ˈtræktəbl/ adj trattabile; (docile) maneggevole

traction /ˈtrækʃn/ n (of wheel) trazione f

traction engine n trattore m

tractor /ˈtræktə(r)/ n trattore m

✧ **trade** /treɪd/ **1** n commercio m; (line of business) settore m; (craft) mestiere m; by ∼ di mestiere
2 vt commerciare; ∼ something for something scambiare qualcosa per qualcosa
3 vi commerciare

■ **trade in** vt (give in part exchange) dare in pagamento parziale

■ **trade off** vt scambiare

■ **trade on** vt approfittarsi di

trade deficit n bilancio m commerciale in deficit

trade discount n sconto m commerciale

trade fair n fiera f commerciale

trade-in n permuta f come pagamento parziale

trade mark n marchio m di fabbrica

trade-name n nome m depositato

trade-off n compromesso m

trade price n prezzo m all'ingrosso

trader /ˈtreɪdə(r)/ n commerciante mf

trade secret n segreto m commerciale

tradesman /ˈtreɪdzmən/ n (joiner etc) operaio m

tradesman's entrance n entrata f di servizio

Trades Union Congress n confederazione (f) dei sindacati britannici

trade union n sindacato m

trade unionist n sindacalista mf

trade union representative n rappresentante mf sindacale

trading /ˈtreɪdɪŋ/ n commercio m

trading estate n zona f industriale

trading floor n Fin sala f delle contrattazioni

trading stamp n bollino m premio

✧ **tradition** /trəˈdɪʃn/ n tradizione f

✧ **traditional** /trəˈdɪʃnl/ adj tradizionale

traditionalist /trəˈdɪʃn(ə)lɪst/ n tradizionalista mf

traditionally /trəˈdɪʃn(ə)lɪ/ adv tradizionalmente

✧ **traffic** /ˈtræfɪk/ **1** n traffico m
2 vi trafficare

t

traffic calming n misure fpl per rallentare la circolazione

traffic calming measures npl misure fpl per rallentare il traffico in città

traffic circle n Am isola f rotatoria

traffic cone n birillo m

traffic island n isola f spartitraffico

traffic jam n ingorgo m

trafficker /'træfɪkə(r)/ n trafficante mf

traffic lights npl semaforo msg

traffic offence n infrazione f al codice della strada

traffic warden n vigile m [urbano]; (woman) vigilessa f

tragedy /'trædʒədɪ/ n tragedia f

tragic /'trædʒɪk/ adj tragico

tragically /'trædʒɪklɪ/ adv tragicamente

trail /treɪl/ ① n traccia f; (path) sentiero m ② vi strisciare; ⟨plant⟩ arrampicarsi; ∼ [behind] rimanere indietro; (in competition) essere in svantaggio ③ vt trascinare

trail bike n moto f fuoristrada

trailblazer /'treɪlbleɪzə(r)/ n pioniere, -a mf

trailblazing /'treɪlbleɪzɪŋ/ adj innovatore

trailer /'treɪlə(r)/ n Auto rimorchio m; Am (caravan) roulotte f inv; (film) presentazione f (di un film)

trailer park n Am area f di sosta per roulotte

ꝥ **train** /treɪn/ ① n treno m; (of dress) strascico m; **by** ∼ in treno; ∼ **of thought** filo m dei pensieri ② vt formare professionalmente; Sport allenare; (aim) puntare; educare ⟨child⟩; addestrare ⟨animal, soldier⟩; far crescere ⟨plant⟩ ③ vi fare il tirocinio; Sport allenarsi

trained /treɪnd/ adj ⟨animal⟩ addestrato (**to do** a fare)

trainee /treɪ'niː/ n apprendista mf

trainer /'treɪnə(r)/ n Sport allenatore, -trice mf; (in circus) domatore, -trice mf; (of dog, race-horse) addestratore, -trice mf; ∼s pl (shoes) scarpe fpl da ginnastica

ꝥ **training** /'treɪnɪŋ/ n tirocinio m; Sport allenamento m; (of animal, soldier) addestramento m

training college n istituto m professionale

training course n corso m di formazione

train set n trenino m

train spotter n appassionato, -a mf di treni

traipse /treɪps/ vi ∼ **around** fam andare in giro

trait /treɪt/ n caratteristica f

traitor /'treɪtə(r)/ n traditore, -trice mf

trajectory /trə'dʒekt(ə)rɪ/ n traiettoria f

tram /træm/ n tram m inv

tram-lines npl rotaie fpl del tram

tramp /træmp/ ① n (hike) camminata f; (vagrant) barbone, -a mf; (of feet) calpestio m ② vi camminare con passo pesante; (hike) percorrere a piedi

trample /'træmpl/ v

■ **trample on** vt calpestare

trampoline /'træmpəliːn/ n trampolino m

trance /trɑːns/ n trance f inv

tranquil /'træŋkwɪl/ adj tranquillo

tranquillity /træŋ'kwɪlətɪ/ n tranquillità f

tranquillizer /'træŋkwɪlaɪzə(r)/ n tranquillante m

transact /træn'zækt/ vt trattare

transaction /træn'zækʃn/ n transazione f

transatlantic /trænzət'læntɪk/ adj ⟨crossing, flight⟩ transatlantico; ⟨attitude, accent⟩ americano

transceiver /træn'siːvə(r)/ n ricetrasmittente f

transcend /træn'send/ vt trascendere

transcontinental /trænzkɒntɪ'nent(ə)l/ adj transcontinentale

transcribe /træn'skraɪb/ vt trascrivere

transcript /'trænskrɪpt/ n trascrizione f

transcription /træn'skrɪpʃn/ n trascrizione f

transept /'trænsept/ n transetto m

ꝥ **transfer¹** /'trænsfɜː(r)/ n trasferimento m; Sport cessione f; (design) decalcomania f

transfer² /træns'fɜː(r)/ ① vt (pt/pp **transferred**) trasferire; Sport cedere; Comput trasferire ② vi trasferirsi; (when travelling) cambiare

transferable /træns'fɜːrəbl/ adj trasferibile

transfer fee n (for footballer) prezzo m d'acquisto

transfer list n (in football) lista f di giocatori da cedere

transferred charge call n chiamata f a carico del destinatario

transfigure /træns'fɪgə(r)/ vt trasfigurare

transfix /træns'fɪks/ vt trafiggere; fig immobilizzare

transfixed /træns'fɪkst/ adj (with fascination) folgorato; (with horror) paralizzato

ꝥ **transform** /træns'fɔːm/ vt trasformare

transformation /trænsfə'meɪʃn/ n trasformazione f

transformer /træns'fɔːmə(r)/ n trasformatore m

transfusion /træns'fjuːʒn/ n trasfusione f

transgender /trænz'dʒendə(r)/ adj trans, dei trans

ꝥ indicates a very frequent word

transgression /træns'greʃn/ n Jur trasgressione f; Relig peccato m

transient /'trænzɪənt/ adj passeggero

transistor /træn'zɪstə(r)/ n transistor m inv; (radio) radiolina f a transistor

transit /'trænzɪt/ n transito m; **in ∼** (goods) in transito

transition /træn'zɪʃn/ n transizione f

transitional /træn'zɪʃənl/ adj di, transizione

transitive /'trænzɪtɪv/ adj transitivo

transitively /'trænzɪtɪvlɪ/ adv transitivamente

transit lounge n sala f d'attesa transiti

transitory /'trænzɪtərɪ/ adj transitorio

transit passenger n passeggero m in transito

translate /trænz'leɪt/ vt tradurre

translation /trænz'leɪʃn/ n traduzione f

translation agency n agenzia f di traduzioni

translator /trænz'leɪtə(r)/ n traduttore, -trice mf

translucent /trænz'luːsnt/ adj liter traslucido

transmissible /trænz'mɪsəbl/ adj trasmissibile

transmission /trænz'mɪʃn/ n trasmissione f

transmit /trænz'mɪt/ vt (pt/pp **transmitted**) trasmettere

transmitter /trænz'mɪtə(r)/ n trasmettitore m

transparency /træn'spærənsɪ/ n Phot diapositiva f

transparent /træn'spærənt/ adj trasparente

transpire /træn'spaɪə(r)/ vi emergere; fam (happen) accadere

transplant¹ /'trænsplɑːnt/ n trapianto m

transplant² /'trænsplɑːnt/ vt trapiantare

⚓ **transport**¹ /'trænspɔːt/ n trasporto m; do you have ∼? hai un mezzo di trasporto?

transport² /træn'spɔːt/ vt trasportare

transportation /trænspɔː'teɪʃn/ n trasporto m

transpose /træns'pəʊz/ vt trasporre

transsexual /trænz'seksʃʊəl/ ① n transessuale mf
② adj transessuale

trans-shipment /trænz'ʃɪpmənt/ n trasbordo m

transverse /trænz'vɜːs/ adj trasversale

transvestite /trænz'vestaɪt/ n travestito, -a mf

trap /træp/ ① n trappola f; fam (mouth) boccaccia f; (carriage) calesse m
② vt (pt/pp **trapped**) intrappolare; schiacciare ⟨finger in door⟩; **be ∼ped** essere

intrappolato

trapdoor /'træpdɔː(r)/ n botola f

trapeze /trə'piːz/ n trapezio m

trappings /'træpɪŋz/ npl (dress) ornamenti mpl; **the ∼ of wealth/success** i segni esteriori della ricchezza/del successo

traschcan /'træʃkæn/ n Am pattumiera f, secchio m della spazzatura

trash /træʃ/ n robaccia f; (rubbish) spazzatura f; (nonsense) schiocchezze fpl

trashy /'træʃɪ/ adj scadente

trauma /'trɔːmə/ n trauma m

traumatic /trɔː'mætɪk/ adj traumatico

traumatize /'trɔːmətaɪz/ vt traumatizzare

⚓ **travel** /'trævl/ ① n viaggi mpl
② vi (pt/pp **travelled**) viaggiare; ⟨to work⟩ andare
③ vt percorrere ⟨distance⟩

travel agency n agenzia f di viaggi

travel agent n agente mf di viaggio

travel card n tessera f dei trasporti pubblici

travel expenses npl spese fpl di viaggio

traveller /'trævələ(r)/ n viaggiatore, -trice mf; Comm commesso m viaggiatore; **∼s** pl (gypsies) zingari mpl

traveller's cheque n traveller's cheque m inv

travelling Br, **traveling** Am /'trævlɪŋ/ adj ⟨circus, theatre company⟩ itinerante; ⟨companion, conditions, expenses, allowance⟩ di viaggio

travelling salesman /'trævəlɪŋ/ n commesso m viaggiatore

travel news n informazioni fpl sulla viabilità

travelogue /'trævəlɒg/ n (film) documentario m di viaggio; (talk) conferenza f su un viaggio

travel-sick adj be/get ∼ (on plane) soffrire il mal d'aria; (in car) soffrire il mal d'auto; (on boat) soffrire il mal di mare

travel-sickness ① n (on plane) mal m d'aria; (in car) mal m d'auto; (on boat) mal m di mare
② attrib ⟨pills⟩ per il mal d'aria/d'auto/ di mare

traverse /trə'vɜːs/ vt traversare

travesty /'trævɪstɪ/ n fig (farce) farsa f; **a ∼ of justice** una presa in giro della giustizia

trawler /'trɔːlə(r)/ n peschereccio m

tray /treɪ/ n vassoio m; (for baking) teglia f; (for documents) vaschetta f; (of printer, photocopier) vassoio m, cassetto m

treacherous /'tretʃərəs/ adj traditore; ⟨weather, currents⟩ pericoloso

treachery /'tretʃ(ə)rɪ/ n tradimento m

treacle /'triːkl/ n melassa f

tread /tred/ ① n andatura f; (step) gradino m; (of tyre) battistrada m inv

····⟩

② *vi* (*pt* **trod**, *pp* **trodden**) (walk)
camminare

■ **tread on** *vt* calpestare ‹grass›; pestare ‹foot›

treadmill /'tredmɪl/ *n* fig solito tran tran *m*

treason /'tri:zn/ *n* tradimento *m*

treasonable /'tri:z(ə)nəbl/ *adj* proditorio

treasure /'treʒə(r)/ ① *n* tesoro *m*
② *vt* tenere in gran conto

treasurer /'treʒərə(r)/ *n* tesoriere, -a *mf*

treasury /'treʒərɪ/ *n* the T~ il Ministero
del Tesoro

ᕳ **treat** /tri:t/ ① *n* piacere *m*; (present) regalo
m; **give somebody a** ~ fare una sorpresa a
qualcuno
② *vt* trattare; Med curare; ~ **somebody
to something** offrire qualcosa a qualcuno;
~ **somebody for something** Med sottoporre
qualcuno ad una cura per qualcosa

treatise /'tri:tɪz/ *n* trattato *m*

ᕳ **treatment** /'tri:tmənt/ *n* trattamento *m*;
Med cura *f*

treaty /'tri:tɪ/ *n* trattato *m*

treble /'trebl/ ① *adj* triplo; ~ **the amount**
il triplo
② *n* Mus (voice) voce *f* bianca
③ *vt* triplicare
④ *vi* triplicarsi

treble clef *n* chiave *f* di violino

ᕳ **tree** /tri:/ *n* albero *m*

tree house *n* capanna *f* su un albero

tree stump *n* ceppo *m*

treetop *n* cima *f* di un albero

tree trunk *n* tronco *m* d'albero

trek /trek/ ① *n* scarpinata *f*; (as holiday)
trekking *m inv*
② *vi* (*pt/pp* **trekked**) farsi una
scarpinata; (on holiday) fare trekking

trekking /'trekɪŋ/ *n* trekking *m*

trellis /'trelɪs/ *n* graticolato *m*

tremble /'trembl/ *vi* tremare (**with** di)

trembling /'tremblɪŋ/ *adj* tremante

tremendous /trɪ'mendəs/ *adj* (huge)
enorme; fam (excellent) formidabile

tremendously /trɪ'mendəslɪ/ *adv* (very)
straordinariamente; (a lot) enormemente

tremor /'tremə(r)/ *n* tremito *m*; [earth] ~
scossa *f* [sismica]

tremulous /'tremjʊləs/ *adj* tremulo

trench /trentʃ/ *n* fosso *m*; Mil trincea *f*

trenchant /'trentʃənt/ *adj* ‹comment,
criticism› mordace

trench coat *n* trench *m inv*

ᕳ **trend** /trend/ *n* tendenza *f*; (fashion) moda *f*

trend-setter *n* persona *f* che detta la
moda

trend-setting *adj* che detta la moda

trendy /'trendɪ/ *adj* (**-ier, -iest**) fam di *or*
alla moda

ᕳ indicates a very frequent word

trepidation /trepɪ'deɪʃn/ *n* trepidazione *f*

trespass /'trespəs/ *vi* ~ **on** introdursi
abusivamente in; fig abusare di

trespasser /'trespəsə(r)/ *n* intruso, -a *mf*

trestle /'tresl/ *n* cavalletto *m*

trestle table *n* tavolo *m* a cavalletto

ᕳ **trial** /'traɪəl/ *n* Jur processo *m*; (test, ordeal)
prova *f*; **on** ~ in prova; Jur in giudizio; **by** ~
and error per tentativi

trial period *n* periodo *m* di prova

trial run *n* (preliminary test) prova *f*

triangle /'traɪæŋgl/ *n* triangolo *m*

triangular /traɪ'æŋgjʊlə(r)/ *adj*
triangolare

tribal /'traɪbl/ *adj* tribale

tribe /traɪb/ *n* tribù *f inv*

tribulation /trɪbjʊ'leɪʃn/ *n* tribolazione *f*

tribunal /traɪ'bju:nl/ *n* tribunale *m*

tributary /'trɪbjʊtərɪ/ *n* affluente *m*

tribute /'trɪbju:t/ *n* tributo *m*; **pay** ~
rendere omaggio

trice /traɪs/ *n* **in a** ~ in un attimo

tricentenary /traɪsen'ti:nərɪ/ ① *n* terzo
centenario *m*
② *adj* del terzo centenario

trick /trɪk/ ① *n* trucco *m*; (joke) scherzo *m*;
Cards presa *f*; **do the** ~ fam funzionare; **play a**
~ **on** fare uno scherzo a
② *vt* imbrogliare; ~ **of the trade** trucco *m*
del mestiere

■ **trick into**: *vt* ~ **somebody into doing
something** convincere qualcuno a fare
qualcosa con l'inganno

■ **trick out**: *vt* ~ **somebody out of
something** fregare qualcuno a qualcosa

trick cyclist *n* sl (psychiatrist) psichiatra *mf*

trickle /'trɪkl/ *vi* colare

■ **trickle away** *vi* ‹water› uscire lentamente;
‹people› allontanarsi lentamente

■ **trickle in** *vi* fig entrare poco per volta

■ **trickle out** *vi* fig uscire poco per volta

trick question *n* domanda *f* trabocchetto
inv

trickster /'trɪkstə(r)/ *n* imbroglione, -a *mf*

tricky /'trɪkɪ/ *adj* (**-ier, -iest**) *adj*
‹operation› complesso; ‹situation› delicato

tricolour /'trɪkələ(r)/ *n* tricolore *m*

tricycle /'traɪsɪkl/ *n* triciclo *m*

tried /traɪd/ ▶ TRY

tried and tested *adj* ‹method›
sperimentato

trifle /'traɪfl/ *n* inezia *f*; Culin zuppa *f* inglese

trifling /'traɪflɪŋ/ *adj* insignificante

trig /trɪg/ *n* fam (trigonometry) trigonometria *f*

trigger /'trɪgə(r)/ ① *n* grilletto *m*; fig
causa *f*
② *vt* ~ [**off**] scatenare

trigger-happy *adj* fam dalla pistola facile;
fig impulsivo

trigonometry ⋯⟶ trucker⋯⋯

trigonometry /trɪgə'nɒmɪtrɪ/ *n* trigonometria *f*

trilateral /traɪ'lætərəl/ *adj* trilaterale

trilby /'trɪlbɪ/ *n* cappello *m* di feltro

trill /trɪl/ *n* Mus trillo *m*

trilogy /'trɪlədʒɪ/ *n* trilogia *f*

trim /trɪm/ ① *adj* (**trimmer, trimmest**) curato; ⟨*figure*⟩ snello ② *n* (of hair, hedge) spuntata *f*; (decoration) rifinitura *f*; **in good** ~ in buono stato; ⟨*person*⟩ in forma ③ *vt* (*pt/pp* **trimmed**) spuntare ⟨*hair etc*⟩; (decorate) ornare; Naut orientare ■ **trim off** *vt* tagliare via

trimming /'trɪmɪŋ/ *n* bordo *m*; ~**s** *pl* (of pastry) ritagli *mpl*; (decorations) guarnizioni *fpl*; **with all the** ~**s** Culin guarnito

Trinidad and Tobago *n* Trinidad e Tobago *m*

Trinity /'trɪnɪtɪ/ *n* **the [Holy]** ~ la [Santissima] Trinità

trinket /'trɪŋkɪt/ *n* ninnolo *m*

trio /'triːəʊ/ *n* trio *m*

⚡ **trip** /trɪp/ ① *n* (excursion) gita *f*; (journey) viaggio *m*; (stumble) passo *m* falso ② *vt* (*pt/pp* **tripped**) far inciampare ③ *vi* inciampare (**on/over** in) ■ **trip up** *vt* far inciampare

tripartite /traɪ'pɑːtaɪt/ *adj* tripartito

tripe /traɪp/ *n* trippa *f*; sl (nonsense) fesserie *fpl*

triple /'trɪpl/ ① *adj* triplo ② *vt* triplicare ③ *vi* triplicarsi

triplets /'trɪplɪts/ *npl* tre gemelli *mpl*

triplicate /'trɪplɪkət/ *n* **in** ~ in triplice copia

tripod /'traɪpɒd/ *n* treppiede *m inv*

tripper /'trɪpə(r)/ *n* gitante *mf*

trite /traɪt/ *adj* banale

triteness /'traɪtnɪs/ *n* banalità *f*

triumph /'traɪʌmf/ ① *n* trionfo *m* ② *vi* trionfare (**over** su)

triumphant /traɪ'ʌmf(ə)nt/ *adj* trionfante

triumphantly /traɪ'ʌmf(ə)ntlɪ/ *adv* ⟨*exclaim*⟩ con tono trionfante

triumvirate /traɪ'ʌmvɪrət/ *n* triumvirato *m*

trivia /'trɪvɪə/ *npl* cose *fpl* secondarie

trivial /'trɪvɪəl/ *adj* insignificante

triviality /trɪvɪ'ælətɪ/ *n* banalità *f inv*

trivialize /'trɪvɪəlaɪz/ *vt* sminuire

trod, trodden /trɒd, 'trɒdn/ ▶ TREAD

trolley /'trɒlɪ/ *n* carrello *m*; Am (tram) tram *m inv*

trolley bus *n* filobus *m inv*

trombone /trɒm'bəʊn/ *n* trombone *m*

trombonist /trɒm'bəʊnɪst/ *n* trombonista *mf*

⚡ **troop** /truːp/ ① *n* gruppo *m*; ~**s** *pl* truppe *fpl* ② *vi* ~ **in/out** entrare/uscire in gruppo

trooper /'truːpə(r)/ *n* Mil soldato *m* di cavalleria; Am (policeman) poliziotto *m*

trophy /'trəʊfɪ/ *n* trofeo *m*

tropic /'trɒpɪk/ *n* tropico *m*; ~**s** *pl* tropici *mpl*

tropical /'trɒpɪkl/ *adj* tropicale

tropical fruit *n* frutta *f inv* esotica

trot /trɒt/ ① *n* trotto *m* ② *vi* (*pt/pp* **trotted**) trottare ■ **trot out** *vt* fam (produce) tirar fuori

trotter /'trɒtə(r)/ *n* Culin piedino *m* di maiale

⚡ **trouble** /'trʌbl/ ① *n* guaio *m*; (difficulties) problemi *mpl*; (inconvenience, Med) disturbo *m*; (conflict) conflitto *m*; **be in** ~ essere nei guai; ⟨*swimmer, climber*⟩ essere in difficoltà; **get into** ~ finire nei guai; **get somebody into** ~ mettere qualcuno nei guai; **take the** ~ **to do something** darsi la pena di far qualcosa; **it's no** ~ nessun disturbo; **the** ~ **with you is…** il tuo problema è… ② *vt* (worry) preoccupare; (inconvenience) disturbare; ⟨*conscience, old wound*⟩ tormentare ③ *vi* **don't** ~! non ti disturbare!

troubled /'trʌbld/ *adj* ⟨*mind*⟩ inquieto; ⟨*person, expression*⟩ preoccupato; ⟨*times, area*⟩ difficile; ⟨*waters, sleep*⟩ agitato

troublefree /ˌtrʌbl'friː/ *adj* senza problemi

troublemaker /'trʌblmeɪkə(r)/ *n* **be a** ~ seminare zizzania

troubleshooter /'trʌblʃuːtə(r)/ *n* rilevatore e risolutore *m* di problemi

troublesome /'trʌblsəm/ *adj* fastidioso

trouble spot *n* zona *f* calda

trough /trɒf/ *n* trogolo *m*; (atmospheric) depressione *f*

trounce /traʊns/ *vt* (in competition) schiacciare

troupe /truːp/ *n* troupe *f inv*

trouser press *n* stiracalzoni *m inv*

trousers /'traʊzəz/ *npl* pantaloni *mpl*

trouser suit *n* tailleur *m inv* pantalone

trousseau /'truːsəʊ/ *n* corredo *m*

trout /traʊt/ *n inv* trota *f*

trowel /'traʊəl/ *n* (for gardening) paletta *f*; (for builder) cazzuola *f*

truancy /'truːənsɪ/ *n* assenze *fpl* ingiustificate

truant /'truːənt/ *n* **play** ~ marinare la scuola

truce /truːs/ *n* tregua *f*

truck /trʌk/ *n* (lorry) camion *m inv*

truck driver *n* camionista *mf*

trucker /'trʌkə(r)/ *n* fam (lorry driver) camionista *mf*

truck farmer n Am ortofrutticoltore m, ortolano m

truculent /'trʌkjʊlənt/ adj aggressivo

truculently /'trʌkjʊləntlɪ/ adv aggressivamente

trudge /trʌdʒ/ **1** n camminata f faticosa **2** vi arrancare

◆ **true** /tru:/ adj vero; **come ~** avverarsi

true-life adj ‹adventure, story› vero

truffle /'trʌfl/ n tartufo m

truism /'tru:ɪzm/ n truismo m

◆ **truly** /'tru:lɪ/ adv veramente; **Yours ~** Distinti saluti

trump /trʌmp/ **1** n Cards atout m inv **2** vt prendere con l'atout
■ **trump up** vt fam inventare

trump card n fig asso m nella manica

trumped-up /,trʌmpt'ʌp/ adj ‹charges› inventato

trumpet /'trʌmpɪt/ n tromba f

trumpeter /'trʌmpɪtə(r)/ n trombettista mf

truncate /'trʌŋkeɪt/ vt tagliare ‹text›; interrompere ‹process, journey, event›

truncheon /'trʌntʃn/ n manganello m

trundle /'trʌndl/ **1** vt far rotolare **2** vi rotolare

trunk /trʌŋk/ n (of tree, body) tronco m; (of elephant) proboscide f; (for travelling, storage) baule m; Am (of car) bagagliaio m, portabagagli m inv

trunk road n statale f

trunks /trʌŋks/ npl calzoncini mpl da bagno

truss /trʌs/ n Med cinto m erniario
■ **truss up** vt legare

◆ **trust** /trʌst/ **1** n fiducia f; (group of companies) trust m inv; (organization) associazione f; **on ~** sulla parola **2** vt fidarsi di; (hope) augurarsi **3** vi ~ **in** credere in; ~ **to** affidarsi a

trust company n società f fiduciaria

trusted /'trʌstɪd/ adj fidato

trustee /trʌs'ti:/ n amministratore, -trice mf fiduciario

trustful /'trʌstfʊl/ adj fiducioso

trustfully /'trʌstfʊlɪ/ adv fiduciosamente

trust fund n fondo m fiduciario

trusting /'trʌstɪŋ/ adj fiducioso

trustworthiness /'trʌstwɜ:ðɪnɪs/ n (of person) affidabilità f; (of source) attendibilità f

trustworthy /'trʌstwɜ:ðɪ/ adj fidato

trusty /'trʌstɪ/ adj fam fidato

◆ **truth** /tru:θ/ n (pl **-s** /tru:ðz/) verità f inv

truthful /'tru:θfʊl/ adj ‹person› sincero; ‹statement› veritiero

truthfully /'tru:θfʊlɪ/ adv sinceramente

truthfulness /'tru:θfʊlnɪs/ n (of person) sincerità f; (of account) veridicità f

◆ **try** /traɪ/ **1** n tentativo m, prova f; (in rugby) meta f; **I'll give it a ~** faccio un tentativo **2** vt (pt/pp **tried**) provare; (be a strain on) mettere a dura prova; Jur processare ‹person›; discutere ‹case›; ~ **to do something** provare a fare qualcosa **3** vi provare
■ **try for** vi cercare di ottenere
■ **try on** vt provarsi ‹garment›
■ **try out** vt provare

trying /'traɪɪŋ/ adj duro; ‹person› irritante

try-out n **give somebody a ~** mettere alla prova qualcuno

tsar /zɑ:(r)/ n zar m inv

tsarina /tsɑ:'ri:nə/ n zarina f

tsarist /'tsɑ:rɪst/ adj zarista

T-shirt n maglietta f

tsp abbr (**teaspoonful**) cucchiaino m

tsunami /tsu:'nɑ:mɪ/ n tsunami m

tub /tʌb/ n tinozza f; (carton) vaschetta f; (bath) vasca f da bagno

tuba /'tju:bə/ n Mus tuba f

tubby /'tʌbɪ/ adj (-ier, -iest) tozzo

tube /tju:b/ n tubo m; (of toothpaste) tubetto m; Br Rail metro f

tuber /'tju:bə(r)/ n tubero m

tuberculosis /tju:bɜ:kjʊ'ləʊsɪs/ n tubercolosi f

tubing /'tju:bɪŋ/ n tubi mpl

tubular /'tju:bjʊlə(r)/ adj tubolare

TUC n abbr Br (**Trades Union Congress**) confederazione (f) dei sindacati britannici

tuck /tʌk/ **1** n piega f **2** vt (put) infilare
■ **tuck away** vt (put in a safe place) mettere al sicuro; (eat) spolverare
■ **tuck in 1** vt rimboccare; ~ **somebody in** rimboccare le coperte a qualcuno **2** vi fam (eat) mangiare con appetito
■ **tuck into** vt mangiare di gusto ‹meal›; ~ **something into one's pocket** infilarsi in tasca qualcosa; ~ **somebody into bed** rimboccare le coperte a qualcuno
■ **tuck up** vt rimboccarsi ‹sleeves›; (in bed) rimboccare le coperte a

◆ **Tuesday** /'tju:zdeɪ/ n martedì m inv

tuft /tʌft/ n ciuffo m

tug /tʌg/ **1** n strattone m; Naut rimorchiatore m **2** vt (pt/pp **tugged**) tirare **3** vi dare uno strattone

tug-of-love /,tʌgəv'lʌv/ n disputa (f) tra i genitori per l'affidamento dei figli

tug of war n tiro m alla fune

tuition /tju:'ɪʃn/ n lezioni fpl

tuition fees npl tasse fpl universitarie

tulip /'tju:lɪp/ n tulipano m

◆ indicates a very frequent word

tumble /'tʌmbl/ [1] *n* ruzzolone *m*
[2] *vi* ruzzolare; ~ **to something** fam (realize) afferrare qualcosa
■ **tumble down** *vi* ‹wall, building› crollare

tumbledown /'tʌmbəldaʊn/ *adj* cadente

tumble-dry /ˌtʌmbl'draɪ/ *vt* asciugare nell'asciugabiancheria

tumble-dryer, **tumble-drier** *n* asciugabiancheria *m*

tumbler /'tʌmblə(r)/ *n* bicchiere *m* (*senza stelo*)

tummy /'tʌmɪ/ *n* fam pancia *f*

tummy button *n* fam ombelico *m*

tumour /'tjuːmə(r)/ *n* tumore *m*

tumult /'tjuːmʌlt/ *n* tumulto *m*

tumultuous /tjuːˈmʌltjʊəs/ *adj* tumultuoso

tuna /'tjuːnə/ *n* tonno *m*

tune /tjuːn/ [1] *n* motivo *m*; **out of/in** ~ ‹instrument› scordato/accordato; ‹person› stonato/intonato; **to the** ~ **of** fam per la modesta somma di
[2] *vt* accordare ‹instrument›; sintonizzare ‹radio, TV›; mettere a punto ‹engine›
■ **tune in** [1] *vt* sintonizzare
[2] *vi* sintonizzarsi (**to** su)
■ **tune up** *vi* ‹orchestra› accordare gli strumenti

tuneful /'tjuːnfl/ *adj* melodioso

tuner /'tjuːnə(r)/ *n* accordatore, -trice *mf*; Radio, TV sintonizzatore *m*

tune-up *n* (of engine) messa *f* a punto

tungsten /'tʌŋstən/ *n* tungsteno *m*

tunic /'tjuːnɪk/ *n* tunica *f*; Mil giacca *f*; Sch ≈ grembiule *m*

tuning-fork /'tjuːnɪŋ/ *n* diapason *m inv*

Tunisia /tjuːˈnɪzɪə/ *n* Tunisia *f*

Tunisian /tjuːˈnɪzɪən/ *adj & n* tunisino, -a *mf*

tunnel /'tʌnl/ [1] *n* tunnel *m inv*
[2] *vi* (*pt/pp* **tunnelled**) scavare un tunnel

tunnel vision *n* Med restringimento *m* del campo visivo; fig paraocchi *m inv*

tuppence /'tʌpəns/ *n* due penny

turban /'tɜːbən/ *n* turbante *m*

turbine /'tɜːbaɪn/ *n* turbina *f*

turbo /'tɜːbəʊ/ *n* turbo *m inv*

turbocharged /'tɜːbəʊtʃɑːdʒd/ *adj* con motore turbo

turbocharger /'tɜːbəʊtʃɑːdʒə(r)/ *n* turbocompressore *m*

turbot /'tɜːbət/ *n* rombo *m* gigante

turbulence /'tɜːbjʊləns/ *n* turbolenza *f*

turbulent /'tɜːbjʊlənt/ *adj* turbolento

turd /tɜːd/ *n sl* (excrement) stronzo *m*; pej (person) stronzo, -a *mf*

tureen /tjʊˈriːn/ *n* zuppiera *f*

turf /tɜːf/ *n* erba *f*; (segment) zolla *f* erbosa
■ **turf out** *vt* fam buttar fuori

turf accountant *n* allibratore *m*

turgid /'tɜːdʒɪd/ *adj* ‹style, water› turgido

Turin /tjʊˈrɪn/ *n* Torino *m*

Turk /tɜːk/ *n* turco, -a *mf*

turkey *n* tacchino *m*

Turkey /'tɜːkɪ/ *n* Turchia *f*

Turkish /'tɜːkɪʃ/ *adj* turco

Turkish bath *n* bagno *m* turco

Turkish delight *n* cubetti *mpl* di gelatina ricoperti di zucchero a velo

Turkmenistan /ˌtɜːkmenɪˈstɑːn/ *n* Turkmenistan *m*

turmeric /'tɜːmərɪk/ *n* (spice) curcumina *f*; (plant) curcuma *f*

turmoil /'tɜːmɔɪl/ *n* tumulto *m*

ⵦ **turn** /tɜːn/ [1] *n* (rotation, short walk) giro *m*; (in road) svolta *f*, curva *f*; (development) svolta *f*; Theat numero *m*; fam (attack) crisi *f inv*; **a** ~ **for the better/worse** un miglioramento/peggioramento *m*; **do somebody a good** ~ rendere un servizio a qualcuno; **take** ~**s** fare a turno; **in** ~ a turno; **out of** ~ ‹speak› a sproposito; **It's your** ~ tocca a te
[2] *vt* girare, voltare ‹back, eyes›; dirigere ‹gun, attention›
[3] *vi* girare; ‹person› girarsi; ‹leaves› ingiallire; (become) diventare; ~ **right/left** girare a destra/sinistra; ~ **sour** inacidirsi; ~ **to somebody** girarsi verso qualcuno; fig rivolgersi a qualcuno
■ **turn against** [1] *vi* diventare ostile a
[2] *vt* mettere contro
■ **turn around** [1] *vi* ‹person› girarsi; ‹car› girare
[2] *vt* girare ‹object›; risollevare ‹company›
■ **turn away** [1] *vt* mandare via ‹people›; girare dall'altra parte ‹head›
[2] *vi* girarsi dall'altra parte
■ **turn back** [1] *vi* tornare indietro
[2] *vt* mandare indietro ‹people›; ripiegare ‹covers, sheet etc›
■ **turn down** *vt* piegare ‹collar›; abbassare ‹heat, gas, sound›; respingere ‹person, proposal›
■ **turn in** [1] *vt* ripiegare in dentro ‹edges›; consegnare ‹lost object›
[2] *vi* fam (go to bed) andare a letto; ~ **in to** **the drive** entrare nel viale
■ **turn into** *vt* (become) diventare
■ **turn off** [1] *vt* spegnere; chiudere ‹tap, water›; ~ **somebody off** fam (disgust) fare schifo a qualcuno
[2] *vi* ‹car› girare
■ **turn on** [1] *vt* accendere; aprire ‹tap, water›; fam (attract) eccitare
[2] *vi* (attack) attaccare
■ **turn out** [1] *vt* (expel) mandar via; spegnere ‹light, gas›; (produce) produrre; (empty) svuotare ‹room, cupboard›
[2] *vi* (transpire) risultare; (to see, do something) venire; ~ **out well/badly** ‹cake, dress› riuscire bene/male; ‹situation› andare bene/male ····╏

■ **turn over** ① *vt* girare; ~ **somebody over to the police** consegnare qualcuno alla polizia; **he ~ed the business over to her** le ha ceduto l'azienda
② *vi* girarsi; **please ~ over** vedi retro
■ **turn round** *vi* girarsi; ‹*car*› girare
■ **turn up** ① *vt* tirare su ‹*collar*›; alzare ‹*heat, gas, sound, radio*›
② *vi* farsi vedere

turn-about *n* fig (change of direction) cambiamento *m*

turnaround *n* (in attitude) dietrofront *m inv*; (of fortune) capovolgimento *m*; (for the better) ripresa *f*

turncoat *n* voltagabbana *mf inv*

turning /'tɜ:nɪŋ/ *n* svolta *f*

turning-point *n* svolta *f* decisiva

turnip /'tɜ:nɪp/ *n* rapa *f*

turn-off *n* strada *f* laterale; **it's a real ~** fam ti fa davvero passar la voglia

turn of mind *n* indole *f*

turn of phrase *n* espressione *f*

turn-on *n* fam **be a real ~** essere veramente eccitante

turnout *n* (of people) affluenza *f*

turnover *n* Comm giro *m* d'affari, fatturato *m*; (of staff) ricambio *m*

turnpike *n* Am autostrada *f*

turnround *n* (in policy etc) cambiamento *m*

turnstile *n* cancelletto *m* girevole

turntable *n* piattaforma *f* girevole; (on record-player) piatto *m*

turn-up *n* (of trousers) risvolto *m*

turpentine /'tɜ:pəntaɪn/ *n* trementina *f*

turquoise /'tɜ:kwɔɪz/ ① *adj* (colour) turchese
② *n* turchese *m*

turret /'tʌrɪt/ *n* torretta *f*

turtle /'tɜ:tl/ *n* tartaruga *f* acquatica

turtle-dove *n* tortora *f*

turtleneck /'tɜ:tlnek/ *n* collo *m* a lupetto; (sweater) maglia *f* a lupetto

Tuscan /'tʌskən/ *adj* toscano

Tuscany /'tʌskənɪ/ *n* Toscana *f*

tusk /tʌsk/ *n* zanna *f*

tussle /'tʌsl/ ① *n* zuffa *f*
② *vi* azzuffarsi

tussock /'tʌsək/ *n* ciuffo *m* d'erba

tut /tʌt/ ① *vi* fare un'esclamazione di disapprovazione
② *int* ts!

tutor /'tju:tə(r)/ *n* insegnante *mf* privato, -a; Univ *insegnante (mf) universitario, -a che segue individualmente un ristretto numero di studenti*

tutorial /tju:'tɔ:rɪəl/ *n* discussione *f* col (tutor)

tutorial package *n* Comput software *m* di autoapprendimento

tuxedo /tʌk'si:dəʊ/ *n* Am smoking *m inv*

❡ **TV** *abbr* (**television**) tv *f inv*, tivù *f inv*

TV dinner *n* pasto *m* pronto

twaddle /'twɒdl/ *n* scemenze *fpl*

twain /tweɪn/ *npl* **the ~** i due; **and never the ~ shall meet** e mai i due si incontreranno

twang /twæŋ/ ① *n* (in voice) suono *m* nasale
② *vt* far vibrare

tweak /twi:k/ ① *vt* tirare ‹*ear, nose*›; (adjust) apportare delle modifiche a
② *n* (adjustment) modifica *f*; **give sb's ears a ~** dare una tirata d'orecchie a qualcuno

twee /twi:/ *adj* Br fam ‹*manner*› affettato

tweed /twi:d/ *n* tweed *m inv*

tweezers /'twi:zəz/ *npl* pinzette *f*

twelfth /twelfθ/ *adj* & *n* dodicesimo, -a *mf*

twelve /twelv/ *adj* & *n* dodici *m*

twenties /'twentɪz/ *npl* (period) **the ~** gli anni Venti *mpl*; (age) vent'anni *mpl*; ▶ *also* FORTIES

twentieth /'twentɪθ/ *adj* & *n* ventesimo, -a *mf*

twenty /'twentɪ/ *adj* & *n* venti *m*

twerp /twɜ:p/ *n* fam stupido, -a *mf*

❡ **twice** /twaɪs/ *adv* due volte; **she's done ~ as much as you** ha fatto il doppio di quanto hai fatto tu

twiddle /'twɪdl/ *vt* giocherellare con; **~ one's thumbs** fig girarsi i pollici

twig[1] /twɪg/ *n* ramoscello *m*

twig[2] *vt/i* (*pt/pp* **twigged**) fam intuire

twilight /'twaɪlaɪt/ *n* crepuscolo *m*

twilight zone *n* (mysterious place or situation) zona *f* d'ombra

twill /twɪl/ *n* spigato *m*

twin /twɪn/ ① *n* gemello, -a *mf*
② *attrib* gemello

twin beds *npl* letti *mpl* gemelli

twine /twaɪn/ ① *n* spago *m*
② *vi* intrecciarsi; ‹*plant*› attorcigliarsi
③ *vt* intrecciare

twinge /twɪndʒ/ *n* fitta *f*; **~ of conscience** rimorso *m* di coscienza

twinkle /'twɪŋkl/ ① *n* scintillio *m*
② *vi* scintillare

twinning /'twɪnɪŋ/ *n* (of companies) gemellaggio *m*

twin town *n* città *f inv* gemellata

twirl /twɜ:l/ ① *vt* far roteare
② *vi* volteggiare
③ *n* piroetta *f*

twist /twɪst/ ① *n* torsione *f*; (curve) curva *f*; (in rope) attorcigliata *f*; (in book, plot) colpo *m* di scena; **round the ~** fam (crazy) ammattito
② *vt* attorcigliare ‹*rope*›; torcere ‹*metal*›; girare ‹*knob, cap*›; (distort) distorcere; **~ one's ankle** storcersi la caviglia

t

3 *vi* attorcigliarsi; ‹*road*› essere pieno di curve

twisted /'twɪstɪd/ *adj* ‹*wire, rope*› ritorto; ‹*ankle, wrist*› slogato; ‹*sense of humour, mind*› perverso

twister /'twɪstə(r)/ *n* fam imbroglione, -a *mf*; (tornado) tornado *m inv*

twit /twɪt/ *n* fam cretino, -a *mf*

twitch /twɪtʃ/ **1** *n* tic *m inv*; (jerk) strattone *m*
2 *vi* contrarsi

twitchy /'twɪtʃɪ/ *adj* fam (nervous) nervosetto

twitter /'twɪtə(r)/ **1** *n* cinguettio *m*; in a ~ fam agitato
2 *vi* cinguettare; ‹*person*› cianciare
■ **twitter on about** *vt* parlare incessantemente di

⚡ **two** /tuː/ *adj & n* due *m*; put ~ and ~ together fare due più due

two-faced /-'feɪst/ *adj* falso

twofold /'tuːfəʊld/ **1** *adj* a ~ increase un raddoppio
2 *adv* to increase ~ raddoppiare

two-piece *adj* (swimsuit) due pezzi *m inv*; (suit) completo *m*

two-seater /-'siːtə(r)/ *n* biposto *m inv*

twosome /'tuːsəm/ *n* coppia *f*

two-tier *adj* ‹*system, health service*› a due velocità

two-time *vt* fam fare le corna a

two-tone *adj* (in colour) bicolore; (in sound) bitonale

two-way *adj* ‹*traffic*› a doppio senso di marcia

two-way mirror *n* specchio *m* unidirezionale

two-way radio *n* (radio *f*) ricetrasmittente *f*

tycoon /taɪ'kuːn/ *n* magnate *m*

tying /'taɪɪŋ/ ▶ TIE

⚡ **type** /taɪp/ **1** *n* tipo *m*; (printing) carattere *m* [tipografico]
2 *vt/i* scrivere a macchina

typecast **1** *vt* Theat fig far fare sempre la stessa parte a ‹*person*›
2 *adj* a ruolo fisso

typeface *n* carattere *m* tipografico

typeset *vt* comporre

typesetter *n* compositore *m*

typewriter *n* macchina *f* da scrivere

typewritten *adj* dattiloscritto

typhoid /'taɪfɔɪd/ *n* febbre *f* tifoidea

typhoon /taɪ'fuːn/ *n* tifone *m*

⚡ **typical** /'tɪpɪkl/ *adj* tipico

typically /'tɪpɪklɪ/ *adv* tipicamente; (as usual) come al solito

typify /'tɪpɪfaɪ/ *vt* (*pt/pp* -**ied**) essere tipico di

typing /'taɪpɪŋ/ *n* dattilografia *f*

typist /'taɪpɪst/ *n* dattilografo, -a *mf*

typo /'taɪpəʊ/ *n* errore *m* di stampa; (keying error) errore *m* di battitura

typography /taɪ'pɒɡrəfɪ/ *n* tipografia *f*

tyrannical /tɪ'rænɪkl/ *adj* tirannico

tyrannize /'tɪrənaɪz/ *vt* tiranneggiare

tyranny /'tɪrənɪ/ *n* tirannia *f*

tyrant /'taɪrənt/ *n* tiranno, -a *mf*

tyre /'taɪə(r)/ *n* gomma *f*, pneumatico *m*

tyre pressure *n* pressione *f* delle gomme

Tyrrhenian Sea /tɪ'riːnɪən/ *n* mar *m* Tirreno

tzar /zaː(r)/ *n* zar *m*

tzarina /tsɑː'riːnə/ *n* zarina *f*

U u

u¹, U /juː/ *n* (letter) u, U *f inv*

u² *abbr* (**universal**) Cinema per tutti

U-bend *n* (in pipe) gomito *m*; (in road) curva *f* a gomito

ubiquitous /juː'bɪkwɪtəs/ *adj* onnipresente

UCAS /juːkæs/ *abbr* Br (**Universities and Colleges Admissions Service**) *organismo (m) di valutazione delle ammissioni all'università*

udder /'ʌdə(r)/ *n* mammella *f* (*di vacca, capra ecc*)

UEFA /juː'iːfə/ *n abbr* (**Union of European Football Associations**) UEFA *f*

UFO *abbr* (**unidentified flying object**) ufo *m inv*

Uganda /juː'gændə/ Uganda *f*

Ugandan /juː'gændən/ *adj & n* ugandese *mf*

ugliness /'ʌglɪnɪs/ *n* bruttezza *f*

ugly /'ʌglɪ/ *adj* (-**ier**, -**iest**) brutto

UHF *abbr* (**ultra-high frequency**) UHF

UHT *abbr* (**ultra-heat-treated**) ‹*milk*› UHT

UK *abbr* (**United Kingdom**) Regno Unito

Ukraine /juːˈkreɪn/ *n* Ucraina *f*

Ukrainian /juːˈkreɪnɪən/ *adj & n* ucraino, -a *mf*; (language) ucraino *m*

ulcer /ˈʌlsə(r)/ *n* ulcera *f*

ulterior /ʌlˈtɪərɪə(r)/ *adj* ∼ **motive** secondo fine *m*

ultimate /ˈʌltɪmət/ *adj* definitivo; (final) finale; (fundamental) fondamentale

ᵍ **ultimately** /ˈʌltɪmətlɪ/ *adv* alla fine

ultimatum /ʌltɪˈmeɪtəm/ *n* ultimatum *m inv*

ultramarine /ʌltrəməˈriːn/ **①** *adj* oltremarino
② *n* azzurro *m* oltremarino

ultrasound /ˈʌltrəsaʊnd/ *n* Med ecografia *f*

ultrasound scan *n* ecografia *m*

ultrasound scanner *n* scanner *m inv* per ecografia

ultraviolet /ʌltrəˈvaɪələt/ *adj* ultravioletto

umbilical /ʌmˈbɪlɪkl/ *adj* ∼ **cord** cordone *m* ombelicale

umbrage /ˈʌmbrɪdʒ/ *n* take ∼ offendersi

umbrella /ʌmˈbrelə/ *n* ombrello *m*

umbrella stand *n* portaombrelli *m inv*

umpire /ˈʌmpaɪə(r)/ **①** *n* arbitro *m*
② *vt/i* arbitrare

umpteen /ʌmpˈtiːn/ *adj* fam innumerevole

umpteenth /ʌmpˈtiːnθ/ *adj* fam ennesimo; **for the** ∼ **time** per l'ennesima volta

UN *abbr* (**United Nations**) ONU *f*

unabashed /ʌnəˈbæʃt/ *adj* spudorato

unabated /ʌnəˈbeɪtɪd/ *adj* ⟨enthusiasm⟩ inalterato; **continue** ∼ ⟨gales⟩ continuare con la stessa intensità

ᵍ **unable** /ʌnˈeɪbl/ *adj* be ∼ **to do something** non potere fare qualcosa; (not know how) non sapere fare qualcosa

unabridged /ʌnəˈbrɪdʒd/ *adj* integrale

unacceptable /ʌnəkˈseptəbl/ *adj* ⟨proposal, suggestion⟩ inaccettabile

unaccompanied /ʌnəˈkʌmpnɪd/ *adj* non accompagnato; ⟨luggage⟩ incustodito

unaccountable /ʌnəˈkaʊntəbl/ *adj* inspiegabile

unaccountably /ʌnəˈkaʊntəblɪ/ *adv* inspiegabilmente

unaccounted /ʌnəˈkaʊntɪd/ *adj* be ∼ **for** (not explained) non avere spiegazione; (not found) mancare

unaccustomed /ʌnəˈkʌstəmd/ *adj* insolito; **be** ∼ **to** non essere abituato a

unadorned /ʌnəˈdɔːnd/ *adj* ⟨walls⟩ disadorno

unadulterated /ʌnəˈdʌltəreɪtɪd/ *adj* ⟨water⟩ puro; ⟨wine⟩ non sofisticato; fig assoluto

unadventurous /ʌnədˈventʃ(ə)rəs/ *adj* ⟨person, production⟩ poco avventuroso; ⟨meal⟩ poco fantasioso

unaffected /ʌnəˈfektɪd/ *adj* (natural) semplice; **be** ∼ **by** non essere interessato da

unafraid /ʌnəˈfreɪd/ *adj* senza paura

unaided /ʌnˈeɪdɪd/ *adj* senza aiuto

unalloyed /ʌnəˈlɔɪd/ *adj* fig puro

unambiguous /ʌnæmˈbɪgjʊəs/ *adj* inequivocabile

unanimity /juːnəˈnɪmətɪ/ *n* unanimità *f*

unanimous /juːˈnænɪməs/ *adj* unanime

unanimously /juːˈnænɪməslɪ/ *adv* all'unanimità

unannounced /ʌnəˈnaʊnst/ *adj* inaspettato

unanswerable /ʌnˈɑːns(ə)rəbl/ *adj* ⟨remark, case⟩ irrefutabile; ⟨question⟩ senza risposta

unanswered /ʌnˈɑːnsəd, US ʌnˈæn-/ *adj* ⟨question, letter⟩ senza risposta

unappealing /ʌnəˈpiːlɪŋ/ *adj* poco attraente

unappetizing /ʌnˈæpetaɪzɪŋ/ *adj* poco appetitoso

unappreciated /ʌnəˈpriːʃeɪtɪd/ *adj* ⟨work of art⟩ incompreso

unappreciative /ʌnəˈpriːʃ(ɪ)ətɪv/ *adj* ⟨audience⟩ indifferente; ⟨person⟩ ingrato

unapproachable /ʌnəˈprəʊtʃəbl/ *adj* ⟨person⟩ inavvicinabile

unarmed /ʌnˈɑːmd/ *adj* disarmato

unarmed combat *n* lotta *f* senza armi

unashamedly /ʌnəˈʃeɪmd/ *adv* sfacciatamente

unasked /ʌnˈɑːskt/ *adv* **he came** ∼ è venuto senza che nessuno glielo chiedesse

unassuming /ʌnəˈsjuːmɪŋ/ *adj* senza pretese

unattached /ʌnəˈtætʃd/ *adj* staccato; ⟨person⟩ senza legami

unattainable /ʌnəˈteɪnəbl/ *adj* irraggiungibile

unattended /ʌnəˈtendɪd/ *adj* incustodito

unattractive /ʌnəˈtræktɪv/ *adj* ⟨person⟩ poco attraente; ⟨proposition⟩ poco allettante; ⟨characteristic⟩ sgradevole; ⟨building, furniture⟩ brutto

unauthorized /ʌnˈɔːθəraɪzd/ *adj* non autorizzato

unavailable /ʌnəˈveɪləbl/ *adj* non disponibile

unavoidable /ʌnəˈvɔɪdəbl/ *adj* inevitabile

unavoidably /ʌnəˈvɔɪdəblɪ/ *adv* inevitabilmente; **I was** ∼ **detained** sono stato trattenuto da cause di forza maggiore

unaware /ʌnəˈweə(r)/ *adj* be ∼ of something non rendersi conto di qualcosa

---

ᵍ indicates a very frequent word

unawares /ˌʌnə'weəz/ *adv* catch
somebody ~ prendere qualcuno alla
sprovvista

unbalanced /ʌn'bælənst/ *adj* non
equilibrato; (mentally) squilibrato

unbearable /ʌn'beərəbl/ *adj*
insopportabile

unbearably /ʌn'beərəblɪ/ *adv*
insopportabilmente

unbeatable /ʌn'biːtəbl/ *adj* imbattibile

unbeaten /ʌn'biːtən/ *adj* imbattuto

unbecoming /ʌnbɪ'kʌmɪŋ/ *adj* ‹garment›
che non dona

unbeknown /ʌnbɪ'nəʊn/ *adj* fam ~ to me
a mia insaputa

unbelievable /ʌnbɪ'liːvəbl/ *adj*
incredibile

unbend /ʌn'bend/ *vi* (*pt/pp* **-bent**) (relax)
distendersi

unbending /ʌn'bendɪŋ/ *adj* (insistent)
inflessibile

unbiased /ʌn'baɪəst/ *adj* obiettivo

unblock /ʌn'blɒk/ *vt* sbloccare

unbolt /ʌn'bəʊlt/ *vt* togliere il chiavistello
di

unborn /ʌn'bɔːn/ *adj* non ancora nato

unbreakable /ʌn'breɪkəbl/ *adj*
infrangibile

unbridled /ʌn'braɪdld/ *adj* sfrenato

unbroken /ʌn'brəʊkən/ *adj* ‹sequence,
sleep, silence› ininterrotto

unbuckle /ʌn'bʌkl/ *vt* slacciare ‹belt›

unburden /ʌn'bɜːdən/ *vt* ~ **oneself** fig
sfogarsi (**to** con)

unbutton /ʌn'bʌtən/ *vt* sbottonare

uncalled-for /ʌn'kɔːldfɔː(r)/ *adj* fuori
luogo

uncannily /ʌn'kænɪlɪ/ *adv*
incredibilmente

uncanny /ʌn'kænɪ/ *adj* sorprendente;
‹silence, feeling› inquietante

uncared-for /ʌn'keədfɔː(r)/ *adj* ‹house,
pet› trascurato

uncaring /ʌn'keərɪŋ/ *adj* ‹world›
indifferente

unceasing /ʌn'siːsɪŋ/ *adj* incessante

uncensored /ʌn'sensəd/ *adj* ‹film, book›
non censurato

unceremonious /ʌnserɪ'məʊnɪəs/ *adj*
(abrupt) brusco

unceremoniously /ʌnserɪ'məʊnɪəslɪ/
adv senza tante cerimonie

uncertain /ʌn'sɜːtən/ *adj* incerto;
‹weather› instabile; **in no ~ terms** senza
mezzi termini

uncertainty /ʌn'sɜːtəntɪ/ *n* incertezza *f*

unchallenged /ʌn'tʃæləndʒd/ *adj*
‹statement, decision› incontestato; **I can't let
that go ~** non posso non contestarlo

unchanged /ʌn'tʃeʌndʒd/ *adj* invariato

uncharacteristic /ʌnkærəktə'rɪstɪk/
adj ‹generosity› insolito

uncharitable /ʌn'tʃærɪtəbl/ *adj* duro

unchecked /ʌn'tʃekt/ *adv* incontrollato;
go ~ dilagare

uncivilized /ʌn'sɪvɪlaɪzd/ *adj* ‹people,
nation› non civilizzato; ‹treatment,
conditions› incivile

unclassified /ʌn'klæsɪfaɪd/ *adj*
‹document, information› non riservato;
‹road› non classificato

uncle /'ʌŋkl/ *n* zio *m*

unclear /ʌn'klɪːr/ *adj* ‹instructions, reason,
voice, writing› non chiaro; ‹future› incerto;
be ~ about something ‹person› non aver ben
chiaro qualcosa

unclog /ʌn'klɒg/ *vt* sturare ‹pipe›

uncoil /ʌn'kɔɪl/ *vt* srotolare

uncomfortable /ʌn'kʌmftəbl/ *adj*
scomodo; ‹silence, situation› imbarazzante;
feel ~ fig sentirsi a disagio

uncomfortably /ʌn'kʌmftəblɪ/ *adv*
‹sit› scomodamente; (causing alarm etc)
spaventosamente

uncommon /ʌn'kɒmʌn/ *adj* insolito

uncommunicative /ʌnkə'mjuːnɪkətɪv/
adj poco comunicativo

uncomplimentary /ˌʌnkɒmplɪ'mentrɪ,
US -terɪ/ *adj* poco complimentoso

uncompromising /ʌn'kɒmprəmaɪzɪŋ/
adj intransigente

unconcerned /ˌʌnkən'sɜːnd/ *adj*
indifferente

unconditional /ʌnkən'dɪʃ(ə)nl/ *adj*
incondizionato

unconditionally /ʌnkʌn'dɪʃnəlɪ/ *adv*
incondizionatamente

unconfirmed /ˌʌnkən'fɜːmd/ *adj* ‹report,
sighting› non confermato

unconnected /ˌʌnkə'nektɪd/ *adj*
‹incidents, facts› senza alcun legame tra loro

unconscious /ʌn'kɒnʃəs/ *adj* privo di
sensi; (unaware) inconsapevole; **be ~ of
something** non rendersi conto di qualcosa

unconsciously /ʌn'kɒnʃəslɪ/ *adv*
inconsapevolmente

unconstitutional /ˌʌnkɒnstɪ'tjuːʃənl/
adj incostituzionale

uncontested /ˌʌnkʌn'testɪd/ *adj* Pol ‹seat›
non disputato

uncontrollable /ˌʌnkən'trəʊləbl/ *adj*
incontrollabile; ‹sobbing› irrefrenabile

uncontrollably /ˌʌnkən'trəʊləblɪ/ *adv*
‹increase› incontrollatamente; ‹laugh, sob›
senza potersi controllare

unconventional /ˌʌnkən'venʃnəl/ *adj*
poco convenzionale

unconvincing /ˌʌnkən'vɪnsɪŋ/ *adj* poco
convincente

u

uncooked /ʌnˈkʊkt/ *adj* crudo

uncooperative /ˌʌnkəʊˈɒpr(ə)tɪv/ *adj*
poco cooperativo

uncoordinated /ˌʌnkəʊˈɔːdɪneɪtɪd/ *adj*
‹action, efforts› non coordinato; **be ~** (person)
essere scoordinato

uncork /ʌnˈkɔːk/ *vt* sturare

uncorroborated /ʌnkəˈrɒbəreɪtɪd/ *adj*
non convalidato

uncouth /ʌnˈkuːθ/ *adj* zotico

uncover /ʌnˈkʌvə(r)/ *vt* scoprire; portare
alla luce ‹buried object›

uncritical /ʌnˈkrɪtɪkl/ *adj* poco critico

uncross /ʌnˈkrɒs/ *vt* disincrociare ‹legs,
arms›

unctuous /ˈʌŋktjʊəs/ *adj* untuoso

uncultivated /ʌnˈkʌltɪveɪtɪd/ *adj* incolto

uncut /ʌnˈkʌt/ *adj* ‹film› in versione
integrale; ‹diamond› non tagliato

undamaged /ʌnˈdæmɪdʒd/ *adj* intatto

undaunted /ʌnˈdɔːntɪd/ *adj* imperterrito;
~ by something per nulla intimidito da
qualcosa

undecided /ʌndɪˈsaɪdɪd/ *adj* indeciso; (not
settled) incerto

undefined /ʌndɪˈfaɪnd/ *adj* ‹objective,
nature› indeterminato

undelivered /ʌndɪˈlɪvəd/ *adj* ‹mail› non
recapitato

undemanding /ˌʌndɪˈmɑːndɪŋ, US
-ˈmænd-/ *adj* ‹job, course› poco impegnativo

undemocratic /ˌʌndeməˈkrætɪk/ *adj*
antidemocratico

undemonstrative /ˌʌndɪˈmɒnstrətɪv/
adj poco espansivo

undeniable /ʌndɪˈnaɪəbl/ *adj* innegabile

undeniably /ʌndɪˈnaɪəblɪ/ *adv*
innegabilmente

⚡ **under** /ˈʌndə(r)/ **1** *prep* sotto; (less than)
al di sotto di; **~ there** lì sotto; **~ repair/
construction** in riparazione/costruzione;
~ way fig in corso
2 *adv* **~** (water) sott'acqua; (unconscious)
sotto anestesia

underachieve /ʌndərəˈtʃiːv/ *vi* Sch
restare al di sotto delle proprie possibilità

underachiever /ˌʌndərəˈtʃiːvə(r)/ *n* **be
an ~** non dare il meglio

underage /ˌʌndərˈeɪdʒ/ *adj* **~ drinking**
consumo di alcolici da parte dei minorenni;
be ~ essere minorenne

underarm /ˈʌndərɑːm/ *adj* ‹deodorant›
per le ascelle; ‹hair› sotto le ascelle; ‹service,
throw› dal basso verso l'alto

undercarriage /ˈʌndəkærɪdʒ/ *n* Aeron
carrello *m*

undercharge /ʌndəˈtʃɑːdʒ/ *vt* far pagare
meno del dovuto a

⚡ indicates a very frequent word

underclass /ˈʌndəklɑːs/ *n*
sottoproletariato *m*

underclothes /ˈʌndəkləʊðz/ *npl*
biancheria *fsg* intima

undercoat /ˈʌndəkəʊt/ *n* prima mano *f*

undercook /ʌndəˈkʊk/ *vt* non cuocere
abbastanza

undercover /ʌndəˈkʌvə(r)/ *adj*
clandestino

undercurrent /ˈʌndəkʌrənt/ *n* corrente *f*
sottomarina; fig sottofondo *m*

undercut /ʌndəˈkʌt/ *vt* (*pt/pp* **-cut**) Comm
vendere a minor prezzo di

underdeveloped /ʌndədɪˈveləpt/
adj ‹country› sottosviluppato; Phot non
completamente sviluppato

underdog /ˈʌndədɒg/ *n* perdente *m*

underdone /ʌndəˈdʌn/ *adj* ‹meat› al
sangue

underemployed /ʌndərɪmˈplɔɪd/ *adj*
‹person› sottoccupato; ‹resources, equipment
etc› non sfruttato completamente

underequipped /ʌndərɪˈkwɪpt/
adj ‹army, person› insufficientemente
equipaggiato; ‹schools, gym›
insufficientemente attrezzato

underestimate /ʌndərˈestɪmeɪt/ *vt*
sottovalutare

underexpose /ʌndərɪksˈpəʊz/ *vt* Phot
sottoesporre

underfed /ʌndəˈfed/ *adj* denutrito

underfloor /ˈʌndəflɔː(r)/ *adj* ‹pipes, wiring›
sotto il pavimento

underfoot /ʌndəˈfʊt/ *adv* sotto i piedi;
trample ~ calpestare

underfunded /ʌndəˈfʌndɪd/ *adj*
insufficientemente finanziato

underfunding /ʌndəˈfʌndɪŋ/ *n*
finanziamento *m* insufficiente

undergo /ʌndəˈgəʊ/ *vt* (*pt* **-went**, *pp*
-gone) subire ‹operation, treatment›;
~ repair essere in riparazione

undergraduate /ʌndəˈgrædʒʊət/ *n*
studente, -tessa *mf* universitario, -a

underground¹ /ʌndəˈgraʊnd/ *adv*
sottoterra

underground² /ˈʌndəgraʊnd/ **1** *adj*
sotterraneo; (secret) clandestino
2 *n* (railway) metropolitana *f*

underground car park *n* parcheggio
m sotterraneo

undergrowth /ˈʌndəgrəʊθ/ *n* sottobosco
m

underhand /ˈʌndəhænd/ *adj* subdolo

underlay /ˈʌndəleɪ/ *n* strato (*m*) di gomma
o feltro posto sotto la moquette

underlie /ʌndəˈlaɪ/ *vt* (*pt* **-lay**, *pp* **-lain**,
pres p **-lying**) fig essere alla base di

underline /ʌndəˈlaɪn/ *vt* sottolineare

underling /ˈʌndəlɪŋ/ *n* pej subalterno, -a *mf*

u

underlying /ʌndə'laɪɪŋ/ *adj* fig
fondamentale

undermanned /ʌndə'mænd/ *adj ‹factory›*
a corto di mano d'opera

undermentioned /ʌndə'menʃnd/ *adj*
sottoindicato

undermine /ʌndə'maɪn/ *vt* fig minare

underneath /ʌndə'niːθ/ ⓵ *prep* sotto;
~ it sotto
⓶ *adv* sotto

undernourished /ʌndə'nʌrɪʃt/ *adj*
denutrito

underpaid /ʌndə'peɪd/ *adj* mal pagato

underpants /'ʌndəpænts/ *npl* mutande
fpl

underpass /'ʌndəpɑːs/ *n* sottopassaggio *m*

underpay /ʌndə'peɪ/ *vt* sottopagare
‹employee›

underpin /ʌndə'pɪn/ *vt* puntellare *‹wall›*;
rafforzare *‹currency, power, theory›*; essere
alla base di *‹religion, society›*

underpopulated /ʌndə'pɒpjʊleɪtɪd/ *adj*
sottopopolato

underprivileged /ʌndə'prɪvɪlɪdʒd/ *adj*
non abbiente

underrate /ʌndə'reɪt/ *vt* sottovalutare

underscore /ˌʌndə'skɔː(r)/ ⓵ *n* segno *m*
di sottolineatura
⓶ *vt* sottolineare

underseal /'ʌndəsiːl/ *n* Auto antiruggine
m inv

under-secretary /ʌndə'sekrət(ə)rɪ/ *n* Br
Pol sottosegretario *m*

undersell /ʌndə'sel/ *vt* vendere a
prezzo inferiore rispetto a *‹competitor›*;
pubblicizzare poco *‹product›*

undersexed /ʌndə'sekst/ *adj* con scarsa
libido

undershirt /'ʌndəʃɜːt/ *n* Am maglia *f* della
salute

undersigned /ʌndə'saɪnd/ *adj*
sottoscritto

undersized /ʌndə'saɪzd/ *adj ‹portion›*
scarso; *‹animal›* troppo piccolo; *‹person›* di
statura inferiore alla media

understaffed /ʌndə'stɑːft/ *adj* a corto di
personale

⚐ **understand** /ʌndə'stænd/ ⓵ *vt* (*pt/pp*
-stood) capire; I ~ that... (have heard) mi
risulta che...
⓶ *vi* capire

understandable /ʌndə'stændəbl/ *adj*
comprensibile

understandably /ʌndə'stændəblɪ/ *adv*
comprensibilmente

⚐ **understanding** /ʌndə'stændɪŋ/ ⓵ *adj*
comprensivo
⓶ *n* comprensione *f*; (agreement) accordo
m; **reach an** ~ trovare un accordo; **on the** ~
that a condizione che

understatement /'ʌndəsteɪtmʌnt/ *n*
that's an ~ non è dire abbastanza

understudy /'ʌndəstʌdɪ/ *n* Theat sostituto,
a *mf*

undertake /ʌndə'teɪk/ *vt* (*pt* **-took**, *pp*
-taken) intraprendere; ~ **to do something**
impegnarsi a fare qualcosa

undertaker /'ʌndəteɪkə(r)/ *n* impresario
m di pompe funebri; **[firm of]** ~**s** *n* impresa
f di pompe funebri

undertaking /ʌndə'teɪkɪŋ/ *n* impresa *f*;
(promise) promessa *f*

under-the-counter *adj ‹goods, supply,
trade›* comprato/venduto sottobanco

undertone /'ʌndətəʊn/ *n* fig sottofondo *m*;
in an ~ sottovoce

undervalue /ʌndə'væljuː/ *vt*
sottovalutare; **the shares are** ~**d** le azioni si
sono svalutate

underwater¹ /'ʌndəwɔːtə(r)/ *adj*
subacqueo

underwater² /ʌndə'wɔːtə(r)/ *adv*
sott'acqua

under way *adj* be ~ *‹vehicle›* essere in
corsa; *‹filming, talks›* essere in corso; **get** ~
‹vehicle› mettersi in viaggio; *‹preparations,
season›* avere inizio

underwear /'ʌndəweə(r)/ *n* biancheria
f intima

underweight /ʌndə'weɪt/ *adj* sotto peso

underworld /'ʌndəwɜːld/ *n* (criminals)
malavita *f*

underwriter /'ʌndəraɪtə(r)/ *n*
assicuratore *m*

undeserved /ʌndɪ'zɜːvd/ *adj ‹praise,
reward, win›* immeritato; *‹blame, punish›*
ingiusto

undeservedly /ʌndɪ'zɜːvɪdlɪ/ *adv ‹praise,
reward, win›* immeritatamente; *‹blame,
punish›* ingiustamente

undesirable /ʌndɪ'zaɪərəbl/ *adj*
indesiderato; *‹person›* poco raccomandabile

undetected /ʌndɪ'tektɪd/ ⓵ *adj ‹crime,
cancer›* non scoperto; *‹flaw, movement,
intruder›* non visto; **go** ~ *‹cancer, crime›* non
essere scoperto; *‹person›* passare inosservato
⓶ *adv ‹break in, listen›* senza essere
scoperto

undeterred /ˌʌndɪ'tɜːd/ *adj* imperterrito

undeveloped /ʌndɪ'veləpt/ *adj* non
sviluppato; *‹land›* non sfruttato

undies /'ʌndɪz/ *npl* fam biancheria *f* intima
(*da donna*)

undignified /ʌn'dɪgnɪfaɪd/ *adj* poco
dignitoso

undisciplined /ʌn'dɪsɪplɪnd/ *adj*
indisciplinato

undiscovered /ʌndɪs'kʌvəd/ *adj ‹secret›*
non svelato; *‹crime, document›* non scoperto;
‹land› inesplorato; *‹species›* sconosciuto;
‹talent› non ancora scoperto

u

undiscriminating /ˌʌndɪsˈkrɪmɪneɪtɪŋ/ *adj* che non sa fare distinzioni

undisguised /ˌʌndɪsˈɡaɪzd/ *adj* evidente

undisputed /ˌʌndɪˈspjuːtɪd/ *adj* indiscusso

undisturbed /ˌʌndɪˈstɜːbd/ *adj* ‹sleep, night› indisturbato

undivided /ˌʌndɪˈvaɪdɪd/ *adj* ‹loyalty, attention› assoluto

undo /ʌnˈduː/ *vt* (*pt* **-did**, *pp* **-done**) disfare; slacciare ‹dress, shoes›; sbottonare ‹shirt›; fig Comput annullare

undone /ʌnˈdʌn/ *adj* ‹shirt, button› sbottonato; ‹shoes, dress› slacciato; (not accomplished) non fatto; **leave** ∼ ‹job› tralasciare

undoubted /ʌnˈdaʊtɪd/ *adj* indubbio

undoubtedly /ʌnˈdaʊtɪdlɪ/ *adv* senza dubbio

undress /ʌnˈdres/ **1** *vt* spogliare; **get** ∼**ed** spogliarsi
2 *vi* spogliarsi

undrinkable /ʌnˈdrɪŋkəbl/ *adj* (unpleasant) imbevibile; (dangerous) non potabile

undue /ʌnˈdjuː/ *adj* eccessivo

undulating /ˈʌndjʊleɪtɪŋ/ *adj* ondulato; ‹country› collinoso

unduly /ʌnˈdjuːlɪ/ *adv* eccessivamente

undying /ʌnˈdaɪɪŋ/ *adj* eterno

unearned /ʌnˈɜːnd/ *adj* immeritato; ∼ **income** rendita *f*

unearth /ʌnˈɜːθ/ *vt* dissotterrare; fig scovare; scoprire ‹secret›

unearthly /ʌnˈɜːθlɪ/ *adj* soprannaturale; **at an** ∼ **hour** fam ad un'ora impossibile

unease /ʌnˈiːz/ *n* disagio *m*

uneasily /ʌnˈiːzɪlɪ/ *adv* a disagio

uneasiness /ʌnˈiːzɪnɪs/ *n* disagio *m*

uneasy /ʌnˈiːzɪ/ *adj* a disagio; ‹person› inquieto; ‹feeling› inquietante; (truce) precario

uneatable /ʌnˈiːtəbl/ *adj* immangiabile

uneconomic /ˌʌniːkəˈnɒmɪk/ *adj* poco remunerativo

uneconomical /ˌʌniːkəˈnɒmɪkl/ *adj* poco economico

uneducated /ʌnˈedjʊkeɪtɪd/ *adj* ‹person› non istruito; ‹tastes› non raffinato; ‹accent, speech› da persona non istruita

unemotional /ˌʌnɪˈməʊʃənl/ *adj* distaccato

unemployed /ʌnemˈplɔɪd/ **1** *adj* disoccupato
2 *npl* **the** ∼ i disoccupati

unemployment /ʌnemˈplɔɪmʌnt/ *n* disoccupazione *f*

unemployment benefit *n* sussidio *m* di disoccupazione

unemployment rate *n* tasso *m* di disoccupazione

unending /ʌnˈendɪŋ/ *adj* senza fine

unenthusiastic /ʌnɪmθjuːzɪˈæstɪk/ *adj* poco entusiasta

unenviable /ʌnˈenvɪəbl/ *adj* ‹position› poco invidiabile

unequal /ʌnˈiːkwəl/ *adj* disuguale; ‹struggle› impari; **be** ∼ **to a task** non essere all'altezza di un compito

unequalled /ʌnˈiːkwəld/ *adj* ‹achievement, quality, record› ineguagliato

unequally /ʌnˈiːkwəlɪ/ *adv* in modo disuguale

unequivocal /ˌʌnəˈkwɪvəkl/ *adj* inequivocabile; ‹person› esplicito

unequivocally /ˌʌnəˈkwɪvəklɪ/ *adv* inequivocabilmente

unerring /ʌnˈɜːrɪŋ/ *adj* infallibile

unethical /ʌnˈeθɪkl/ *adj* immorale

uneven /ʌnˈiːvən/ *adj* irregolare; ‹distribution› ineguale; ‹number› dispari

unevenly /ʌnˈiːvənlɪ/ *adv* irregolarmente; ‹distributed› inegualmente

uneventful /ʌnɪˈventfʊl/ *adj* senza avvenimenti di rilievo

unexciting /ʌnɪkˈsaɪtɪŋ/ *adj* poco entusiasmante

unexpected /ʌnɪkˈspektɪd/ *adj* inaspettato

unexpectedly /ʌnɪkˈspektɪdlɪ/ *adv* inaspettatamente

unexplored /ʌnɪkˈsplɔːd/ *adj* inesplorato

unfailing /ʌnˈfeɪlɪŋ/ *adj* infallibile

unfair /ʌnˈfeə(r)/ *adj* ingiusto

unfair dismissal *n* licenziamento *m* ingiustificato

unfairly /ʌnˈfeəlɪ/ *adv* ingiustamente

unfairness /ʌnˈfeənəs/ *n* ingiustizia *f*

unfaithful /ʌnˈfeɪθfʊl/ *adj* infedele

unfamiliar /ʌnfəˈmɪljə(r)/ *adj* sconosciuto; **be** ∼ **with** non conoscere

unfashionable /ʌnˈfæʃnəbl/ *adj* fuori moda

unfasten /ʌnˈfɑːsn/ *vt* slacciare; (detach) staccare

unfathomable /ʌnˈfæð(ə)məbl/ *adj* imperscrutabile

unfavourable /ʌnˈfeɪv(ə)rəbl/ *adj* sfavorevole; ‹impression› negativo

unfeeling /ʌnˈfiːlɪŋ/ *adj* insensibile

unfinished /ʌnˈfɪnɪʃt/ *adj* da finire; ‹business› in sospeso

unfit /ʌnˈfɪt/ *adj* inadatto; (morally) indegno; Sport fuori forma; ∼ **for work** non in grado di lavorare; ∼ **for human consumption** non commestibile

unflappable /ʌnˈflæpəbl/ *adj* fam calmo

◆ indicates a very frequent word

u

unflattering /ʌnˈflæt(ə)rɪŋ/ *adj*
‹clothes, hairstyle› che non dona; ‹portrait, description› poco lusinghiero

unflinching /ʌnˈflɪntʃɪŋ/ *adj* risoluto

unfold /ʌnˈfəʊld/ **1** *vt* spiegare; (spread out) aprire; fig rivelare
2 *vi* ‹view› spiegarsi

unforeseeable /ʌnfɔːˈsiːəbl/ *adj* imprevedibile

unforeseen /ʌnfɔːˈsiːn/ *adj* imprevisto

unforgettable /ʌnfəˈgetəbl/ *adj* indimenticabile

unforgivable /ʌnfəˈgɪvəbl/ *adj* imperdonabile

unforgiving /ʌnfəˈgɪvɪŋ/ *adj* che non perdona

unfortunate /ʌnˈfɔːtʃənət/ *adj* sfortunato; (regrettable) spiacevole; ‹remark, choice› infelice

⚡ **unfortunately** /ʌnˈfɔːtʃənətlɪ/ *adv* purtroppo

unfounded /ʌnˈfaʊndɪd/ *adj* infondato

unfriendly /ʌnˈfrendlɪ/ *adj* ‹person, remark› scortese, poco amichevole; ‹place, climate, reception› ostile; ‹software› difficile da usare

unfulfilled /ʌnfʊlˈfɪld/ *adj* ‹prophecy› non avverato; ‹promise› non mantenuto; ‹ambition› non realizzato; ‹desire, need› non soddisfatto; ‹condition› non rispettato; **feel ~** essere insoddisfatto

unfurl /ʌnˈfɜːl/ **1** *vt* spiegare
2 *vi* spiegarsi

unfurnished /ʌnˈfɜːnɪʃt/ *adj* non ammobiliato

ungainly /ʌnˈgeɪnlɪ/ *adj* sgraziato

ungentlemanly /ʌnˈdʒentlmənlɪ/ *adj* non da gentiluomo

ungodly /ʌnˈgɒdlɪ/ *adj* empio; **~ hour** fam ora *f* impossibile

ungracious /ʌnˈgreɪʃəs/ *adj* sgarbato

ungrammatical /ˌʌngrəˈmætɪkl/ *adj* sgrammaticato

ungrateful /ʌnˈgreɪtfʊl/ *adj* ingrato

ungratefully /ʌnˈgreɪtfʊlɪ/ *adv* senza riconoscenza

unhappily /ʌnˈhæpɪlɪ/ *adv* infelicemente; (unfortunately) purtroppo

unhappiness /ʌnˈhæpɪnəs/ *n* infelicità *f*

unhappy /ʌnˈhæpɪ/ *adj* infelice; (not content) insoddisfatto (with di)

unharmed /ʌnˈhɑːmd/ *adj* incolume

unhealthy /ʌnˈhelθɪ/ *adj* poco sano; (insanitary) malsano

unheard-of /ʌnˈhɜːdəv/ *adj* ‹actor, brand› mai sentito; ‹levels, price› incredibile

unheated /ʌnˈhiːtɪd/ *adj* senza riscaldamento

unheeded /ʌnˈhiːdɪd/ *adj* ignorato; **go ~** ‹warning, plea› venir ignorato

unhelpful /ʌnˈhelpfʊl/ *adj* ‹person, attitude› poco disponibile; ‹witness› che non collabora; ‹remark› di poco aiuto

unhindered /ʌnˈhɪndəd/ *adj* senza intralci; **~ by** senza essere ostacolato da ‹rules, obstacles›

unholy /ʌnˈhəʊlɪ/ *adj* ‹alliance, pact› paradossale; fam ‹mess, hour› indecente

unhook /ʌnˈhʊk/ *vt* sganciare; staccare ‹picture›

unhurried /ʌnˈhʌrɪd/ *adj* tranquillo

unhurt /ʌnˈhɜːt/ *adj* illeso

unhygienic /ʌnhaɪˈdʒiːnɪk/ *adj* non igienico

unicorn /ˈjuːnɪkɔːn/ *n* unicorno *m*

unidentified /ʌnaɪˈdentɪfaɪd/ *adj* non identificato

unification /juːnɪfɪˈkeɪʃn/ *n* unificazione *f*

uniform /ˈjuːnɪfɔːm/ **1** *adj* uniforme
2 *n* uniforme *f*

uniformly /ˈjuːnɪfɔːmlɪ/ *adv* uniformemente

unify /ˈjuːnɪfaɪ/ *vt* (*pt/pp* **-ied**) unificare

unilateral /juːnɪˈlæt(ə)rəl/ *adj* unilaterale

unilaterally /juːnɪˈlæt(ə)rəlɪ/ *adv* unilateralmente

unimaginable /ʌnɪˈmædʒɪnəbl/ *adj* inimmaginabile

unimaginative /ʌnɪˈmædʒɪnətɪv/ *adj* privo di fantasia

unimpeded /ˌʌnɪmˈpiːdɪd/ *adj* ‹access› libero

unimportant /ʌnɪmˈpɔːtənt/ *adj* irrilevante

unimpressed /ˌʌnɪmˈprest/ *adj* non impressionato

uninformed /ʌnɪnˈfɔːmd/ *adj* ‹person› disinformato

uninhabitable /ˌʌnɪnˈhæbɪtəbl/ *adj* inabitabile

uninhabited /ʌnɪnˈhæbɪtɪd/ *adj* disabitato

uninhibited /ʌnɪnˈhɪbɪtɪd/ *adj* ‹person, attitude› disinibito; ‹performance, remarks› disinvolto; **be ~ about doing something** non avere problemi a fare qualcosa

uninitiated /ʌnɪˈnɪʃɪeɪtɪd/ **1** *adj* ‹person› non iniziato
2 *npl* **the ~** i profani

uninjured /ʌnˈɪndʒəd/ *adj* illeso

uninspired /ʌnɪnˈspaɪəd/ *adj* privo di immaginazione; ‹performance› piatto; ‹times› banale

unintelligible /ˌʌnɪnˈtelɪdʒəbl/ *adj* incomprensibile

unintended /ˌʌnɪnˈtendɪd/ *adj* ‹irony, consequence› non voluto

unintentional /ʌnɪnˈtenʃənl/ *adj* involontario

u

unintentionally /ˌʌnɪnˈtenʃənəlɪ/ adv involontariamente

uninterested /ʌnˈɪntrəstɪd/ adj disinteressato

uninteresting /ʌnˈɪntrəstɪŋ/ adj poco interessante

uninvited /ˌʌnɪnˈvaɪtɪd/ adj ‹attentions› non richiesto; ~ **guest** ospite mf senza invito

uninviting /ˌʌnɪnˈvaɪtɪŋ/ adj ‹room, food› poco invitante

✦ **union** /ˈjuːnɪən/ n unione f; (trade) ~ sindacato m

Unionist /ˈjuːnɪənɪst/ n unionista mf

Union Jack n bandiera f del Regno Unito

✦ **unique** /juːˈniːk/ adj unico

uniquely /juːˈniːklɪ/ adv unicamente

unisex /ˈjuːnɪseks/ adj unisex inv

unison /ˈjuːnɪsn/ n in ~ all'unisono

✦ **unit** /ˈjuːnɪt/ n unità f inv; (department) reparto m; (of furniture) elemento m

unit cost n costo m unitario

unite /juːˈnaɪt/ ① vt unire ② vi unirsi

✦ **united** /juːˈnaɪtɪd/ adj unito

United Arab Emirates npl the ~ gli Emirati Arabi Uniti

United Kingdom n Regno m Unito

United Nations n [Organizzazione f delle] Nazioni Unite fpl

United States [of America] n Stati mpl Uniti [d'America]

unit trust n Fin fondo m comune di investimento aperto

unity /ˈjuːnɪtɪ/ n unità f; (agreement) accordo m

universal /juːnɪˈvɜːsl/ adj universale

universally /juːnɪˈvɜːsəlɪ/ adv universalmente

universe /ˈjuːnɪvɜːs/ n universo m

✦ **university** /juːnɪˈvɜːsətɪ/ ① n università f inv ② attrib universitario

unjust /ʌnˈdʒʌst/ adj ingiusto

unjustifiable /ʌnˈdʒʌstɪfaɪəbl/ adj ingiustificato

unjustifiably /ʌnˈdʒʌstɪfaɪəblɪ/ adv ‹act› senza giustificazione

unjustified /ʌnˈdʒʌstɪfaɪd/ adj ‹suspicion› ingiustificato

unjustly /ʌnˈdʒʌstlɪ/ adv ingiustamente

unkempt /ʌnˈkempt/ adj trasandato; ‹hair› arruffato

unkind /ʌnˈkaɪnd/ adj scortese

unkindly /ʌnˈkaɪndlɪ/ adv in modo scortese

unkindness /ʌnˈkaɪndnɪs/ n mancanza f di gentilezza

✦ indicates a very frequent word

unknown /ʌnˈnəʊn/ adj sconosciuto

unlace /ʌnˈleɪs/ vt slacciare ‹shoes›

unlawful /ʌnˈlɔːfʊl/ adj illecito, illegale

unlawfully /ʌnˈlɔːfʊlɪ/ adv illegalmente

unleaded /ʌnˈledɪd/ adj senza piombo

unleaded petrol n benzina f senza piombo o verde

unleash /ʌnˈliːʃ/ vt fig scatenare

unleavened /ʌnˈlevnd/ adj ‹bread› non lievitato

✦ **unless** /ʌnˈles/ conj a meno che; ~ **I am mistaken** se non mi sbaglio

unlicensed /ʌnˈlaɪsnst/ adj ‹transmitter, activity› abusivo; ‹vehicle› senza bollo; ‹restaurant› non autorizzato a vendere alcolici

✦ **unlike** /ʌnˈlaɪk/ ① adj (not the same) diversi ② prep diverso da; **that's** ~ **him** non è da lui; ~ **me, he...** diversamente da me, lui...

✦ **unlikely** /ʌnˈlaɪklɪ/ adj improbabile

unlimited /ʌnˈlɪmɪtɪd/ adj illimitato

unlined /ʌnˈlaɪnd/ adj ‹face› senza rughe; ‹paper› senza righe; ‹garment, curtain› senza fodera

unlit /ʌnˈlɪt/ adj ‹cigarette, fire› spento; ‹room, street› non illuminato

unload /ʌnˈləʊd/ vt scaricare

unlock /ʌnˈlɒk/ vt aprire (con chiave); sbloccare ‹mobile phone›

unloved /ʌnˈlʌvd/ adj feel ~ ‹person› non sentirsi amato

unluckily /ʌnˈlʌkɪlɪ/ adv sfortunatamente

unlucky /ʌnˈlʌkɪ/ adj sfortunato; **it's** ~ **to...** porta sfortuna...

unmade /ʌnˈmeɪd/ adj ‹bed› sfatto

unmade-up adj ‹road› non asfaltato

unmanageable /ʌnˈmænɪdʒəbl/ adj ‹number, company› difficile da gestire; ‹hair, child, animal› ribelle; ‹size› ingombrante

unmanly /ʌnˈmænlɪ/ adj poco virile

unmanned /ʌnˈmænd/ adj senza equipaggio

unmarked /ʌnˈmɑːkt/ adj Sport smarcato; ‹skin› senza segni; ‹container› non contrassegnato; ~ **police car** auto f inv, civetta f

unmarried /ʌnˈmærɪd/ adj non sposato

unmarried mother n ragazza f madre

unmask /ʌnˈmɑːsk/ vt fig smascherare

unmentionable /ʌnˈmenʃnəbl/ adj innominabile

unmistakable /ʌnmɪˈsteɪkəbl/ adj inconfondibile

unmistakably /ʌnmɪˈsteɪkəblɪ/ adv chiaramente

unmitigated /ʌnˈmɪtɪɡeɪtɪd/ adj assoluto

unmotivated /ʌnˈməʊtɪveɪtɪd/ adj immotivato

unmoved /ʌnˈmuːvd/ adj fig impassibile

unnamed /ʌnˈneɪmd/ *adj* (not having a name) senza nome; (name not divulged) di cui non si conosce il nome; **the as yet ~ winner...** il vincitore di cui ancora non si conosce il nome...

unnatural /ʌnˈnætʃər(ə)l/ *adj* innaturale; pej anormale

unnaturally /ʌnˈnætʃər(ə)lɪ/ *adv* in modo innaturale; pej in modo anormale

unnecessarily /ʌnˈnesəs(ə)rɪlɪ/ *adv* inutilmente

unnecessary /ʌnˈnesəs(ə)rɪ/ *adj* inutile

unnerve /ʌnˈnɜːv/ *vt* scuotere

unnerving /ʌnˈnɜːvɪŋ/ *adj* inquietante

unnoticed /ʌnˈnəʊtɪst/ *adj* inosservato

unobservant /ʌnəbˈzɜːvənt/ *adj* senza spirito d'osservazione

unobserved /ʌnəbˈzɜːvd/ *adj* inosservato; **go ~** passare inosservato

unobstructed /ˌʌnəbˈstrʌktɪd/ *adj* ‹view, path› libero

unobtainable /ʌnəbˈteɪməbl/ *adj* ‹product› introvabile; ‹phone number› non ottenibile

unobtrusive /ʌnəbˈtruːsɪf/ *adj* discreto

unobtrusively /ʌnəbˈtruːsɪvlɪ/ *adv* in modo discreto

unoccupied /ʌnˈɒkjuːpaɪd/ *adj* ‹house, block, shop› vuoto; ‹table, seat› libero

unofficial /ʌnəˈfɪʃl/ *adj* non ufficiale

unofficially /ʌnəˈfɪʃ(ə)lɪ/ *adv* ufficiosamente

unopened /ʌnˈəʊpənd/ *adj* ‹bottle, packet› chiuso; ‹package› ancora incartato

unorthodox /ʌnˈɔːθədɒks/ *adj* poco ortodosso

unpack /ʌnˈpæk/ **1** *vi* disfare le valigie **2** *vt* svuotare ‹parcel›; spacchettare ‹books›; **~ one's case** disfare la valigia

unpaid /ʌnˈpeɪd/ *adj* da pagare; (work) non retribuito

unpalatable /ʌnˈpælətəbl/ *adj* sgradevole

unparalleled /ʌnˈpærəleld/ *adj* senza pari

unpasteurized /ʌnˈpɑːstʃəraɪzd/ *adj* non pastorizzato

unperturbed /ʌnpəˈtɜːbd/ *adj* imperturbato

unpick /ʌnˈpɪk/ *vt* disfare

unplanned /ʌnˈplænd/ *adj* ‹stoppage, increase› imprevisto

unpleasant /ʌnˈplezənt/ *adj* sgradevole; ‹person› maleducato

unpleasantly /ʌnˈplezəntlɪ/ *adv* sgradevolmente; ‹behave› maleducatamente

unpleasantness /ʌnˈplezəntnɪs/ *n* (bad feeling) tensioni *fpl*

unplug /ʌnˈplʌg/ *vt* (*pt/pp* **-plugged**) staccare

unpolluted /ʌnpəˈluːtɪd/ *adj* ‹water› non inquinato; ‹mind› incontaminato

unpopular /ʌnˈpɒpjʊlə(r)/ *adj* impopolare

unprecedented /ʌnˈpresɪdentɪd/ *adj* senza precedenti

unpredictable /ʌnprɪˈdɪktəbl/ *adj* imprevedibile

unprejudiced /ʌnˈpredʒʊdɪst/ *adj* ‹person› senza pregiudizi; ‹opinion, judgement› imparziale

unpremeditated /ʌnpriːˈmedɪteɪtɪd/ *adj* involontario

unprepared /ʌnprɪˈpeəd/ *adj* impreparato

unprepossessing /ʌnpriːpəˈzesɪŋ/ *adj* poco attraente

unpretentious /ʌnprɪˈtenʃəs/ *adj* senza pretese

unprincipled /ʌnˈprɪnsɪpəld/ *adj* senza principi; ‹behaviour› scorretto

unproductive /ˌʌnprəˈdʌktɪv/ *adj* ‹discussion, meeting› poco produttivo

unprofessional /ʌnprəˈfeʃnl/ *adj* non professionale; **it's ~** è una mancanza di professionalità

unprofitable /ʌnˈprɒfɪtəbl/ *adj* non redditizio

unprompted /ʌnˈprɒm(p)tɪd/ *adj* ‹offer› spontaneo; ‹answer› non suggerito

unpronounceable /ʌnprəˈnaʊnsəbl/ *adj* impronunciabile

unprotected /ˌʌnprəˈtektɪd/ *adj* ‹sex› non protetto; ‹person› indifeso

unprovoked /ʌnprəˈvəʊkt/ *adj* ‹attack, aggression› non provocato; **the attack was ~** l'attacco è avvenuto senza provocazione

unqualified /ʌnˈkwɒlɪfaɪd/ *adj* non qualificato; fig (absolute) assoluto

unquestionable /ʌnˈkwestʃənəbl/ *adj* incontestabile

unquote /ʌnˈkwəʊt/ *vi* chiudere le virgolette

unravel /ʌnˈrævl/ *vt* (*pt/pp* **-lled**) districare; (in knitting) disfare

unreal /ʌnˈrɪəl/ *adj* irreale; fam inverosimile

unrealistic /ʌnrɪəˈlɪstɪk/ *adj* ‹character, presentation› poco realistico; ‹expectation, aim› irrealistico; ‹person› poco realista

unreasonable /ʌnˈriːz(ə)nəbl/ *adj* irragionevole

unrecognizable /ʌnˈrekəgnaɪzəbl/ *adj* irriconoscibile

unrecorded /ʌnrɪˈkɔːdɪd/ *adj* non documentato; **go ~** non essere documentato

unrefined /ʌnrɪˈfaɪnd/ *adj* ‹person, manners, style› rozzo; ‹oil› greggio; ‹flour, sugar› non raffinato

unrehearsed /ʌnrɪˈhɜːst/ *adj* ‹response, action› imprevisto; ‹speech› improvvisato

u

unrelated /ʌnrɪˈleɪtɪd/ *adj* ‹facts› senza rapporto (**to** con); ‹person› non imparentato (**to** con)

unrelenting /ʌnrɪˈlentɪŋ/ *adj* ‹person› ostinato; ‹stare› insistente; ‹pursuit› continuo; ‹heat, zeal› costante

unreliable /ʌnrɪˈlaɪəbl/ *adj* inattendibile; ‹person› inaffidabile, che non dà affidamento

unremitting /ʌnrɪˈmɪtɪŋ/ *adj* costante; ‹struggle› continuo

unrepeatable /ʌnrɪˈpiːtəbl/ *adj* ‹offer, bargain› unico; his comment was ~ il commento che ha fatto è irripetibile

unrepentant /ʌnrɪˈpentənt/ *adj* irriducibile; ‹sinner› impenitente

unrequited /ʌnrɪˈkwaɪtɪd/ *adj* non corrisposto

unreservedly /ʌnrɪˈzɜːvɪdlɪ/ *adv* senza riserve; (frankly) francamente

unresolved /ʌnrɪˈzɒlvd/ *adj* irrisolto

unrest /ʌnˈrest/ *n* fermenti *mpl*

unrestricted /ʌnrɪˈstrɪktɪd/ *adj* ‹access, view› libero

unrewarding /ʌnrɪˈwɔːdɪŋ/ *adj* ‹job› poco gratificante

unripe /ʌnˈraɪp/ *adj* ‹fruit› acerbo; ‹wheat› non maturo

unrivalled /ʌnˈraɪvəld/ *adj* ineguagliato

unroll /ʌnˈrəʊl/ **1** *vt* srotolare **2** *vi* srotolarsi

unruffled /ʌnˈrʌfld/ *adj* ‹person› imperturbato; ‹hair› a posto; ‹water› non mosso; **be ~** ‹person› rimanere imperturbato; ‹person, hair› essere a posto

unruly /ʌnˈruːlɪ/ *adj* indisciplinato

unsafe /ʌnˈseɪf/ *adj* pericoloso

unsaid /ʌnˈsed/ *adj* inespresso

unsalaried /ʌnˈsælərɪd/ *adj* ‹post› non stipendiato

unsalted /ʌnˈsɔːltɪd/ *adj* non salato

unsatisfactory /ʌnsætɪsˈfækt(ə)rɪ/ *adj* poco soddisfacente

unsatisfied /ʌnˈsætɪsfaɪd/ *adj* ‹person, need› insoddisfatto

unsatisfying /ʌnˈsætɪsfaɪɪŋ/ *adj* poco soddisfacente

unsavoury /ʌnˈseɪvərɪ/ *adj* equivoco

unscathed /ʌnˈskeɪðd/ *adj* illeso

unscheduled /ʌnˈʃedjuːld/ *adj* ‹flight› supplementare; ‹appearance, speech› fuori programma; ‹stop› non programmato

unscramble /ʌnˈskræmbl/ *vt* decifrare ‹code, words›; sbrogliare ‹ideas, thoughts›

unscrew /ʌnˈskruː/ *vt* svitare

unscrupulous /ʌnˈskruːpjʊləs/ *adj* senza scrupoli

unseasoned /ʌnˈsiːznd/ *adj* ‹wood› non stagionato; ‹food› scondito

unseat /ʌnˈsiːt/ *vt* disarcionare ‹rider›

unseemly /ʌnˈsiːmlɪ/ *adj* indecoroso

unseen /ʌnˈsiːn/ *adv* ‹escape, slip away› senza essere visto

unselfconscious /ˌʌnselfˈkɒnʃəs/ *adj* naturale

unselfish /ʌnˈselfɪʃ/ *adj* disinteressato

unsentimental /ˌʌnsentɪˈmentl/ *adj* poco sentimentale

unsettled /ʌnˈsetld/ *adj* in agitazione; ‹weather› variabile; ‹bill› non saldato

unsettling /ʌnˈsetlɪŋ/ *adj* ‹experience, novel› inquietante

unshakeable /ʌnˈʃeɪkəbl/ *adj* categorico

unshaken /ʌnˈʃeɪkən/ *adj* ‹belief› saldo

unshaven /ʌnˈʃeɪvn/ *adj* non rasato

unsightly /ʌnˈsaɪtlɪ/ *adj* brutto

unsinkable /ʌnˈsɪŋkəbl/ *adj* ‹ship, object› inaffondabile; hum ‹personality› che non si deprime

unskilled /ʌnˈskɪld/ *adj* non specializzato

unskilled worker *n* manovale *m*

unsmiling /ʌnˈsmaɪlɪŋ/ *adj* ‹person› serio

unsociable /ʌnˈsəʊʃəbl/ *adj* scontroso

unsocial hours *npl* **to work ~** lavorare al di fuori degli orari standard

unsolicited /ʌnsəˈlɪsɪtɪd/ *adj* ‹help, advice› non richiesto; ‹job application› spontaneo

unsophisticated /ʌnsəˈfɪstɪkeɪtɪd/ *adj* semplice

unsound /ʌnˈsaʊnd/ *adj* ‹building, reasoning› poco solido; ‹advice› poco sensato; **of ~ mind** malato di mente

unspeakable /ʌnˈspiːkəbl/ *adj* indicibile

unspoiled /ʌnˈspɔɪld/ *adj* ‹town› non deturpato; ‹landscape› intatto; **she was ~ by fame** la fama non l'ha cambiata

unspoken /ʌnˈspəʊkən/ *adj* (implicit) tacito

unstable /ʌnˈsteɪbl/ *adj* instabile; (mentally) squilibrato

unsteadily /ʌnˈstedɪlɪ/ *adv* ‹walk, speak› in modo malsicuro

unsteady /ʌnˈstedɪ/ *adj* malsicuro

unstoppable /ʌnˈstɒpəbl/ *adj* ‹force, momentum› inarrestabile

unstressed /ʌnˈstrest/ *adj* ‹vowel, word› atono

unstuck /ʌnˈstʌk/ *adj* **come ~** staccarsi; fam (project) andare a monte

unsubscribe /ˌʌnsəbˈskraɪb/ *vi* cancellare l'iscrizione (**from** a)

unsubstantiated /ˌʌnsəbˈstænʃɪeɪtɪd/ *adj* ‹report› non corroborato

unsuccessful /ʌnsəkˈsesfʊl/ *adj* fallimentare; **be ~** (in attempt) non aver successo

unsuccessfully /ʌnsəkˈsesfʊlɪ/ *adv* senza successo

♂ indicates a very frequent word

unsuitable /ʌn'su:təbl/ *adj* (inappropriate) inadatto; (inconvenient) inopportuno

unsupervised /ʌn'su:pəvaɪzd/ *adj* ‹activity› non controllato

unsure /ʌn'ʃɔ:(r), US -'ʃʊər/ *adj* incerto; **be ∼ about** non essere sicuro di; **∼ of oneself** essere insicuro

unsuspecting /ʌnsə'spektɪŋ/ *adj* fiducioso

unsweetened /ʌn'swi:tənd/ *adj* senza zucchero

unsympathetic /ʌnsɪmpə'θetɪk/ *adj* ‹person, attitude, manner, tone› poco comprensivo; ‹person, character› antipatico; **she is ∼ to the cause** non appoggia la causa

untamed /ʌn'teɪmd/ *adj* ‹lion› non addomesticato; ‹passion, person› indomito

untangle /ʌn'tæŋgl/ *vt* sbrogliare ‹threads›; risolvere ‹difficulties, mystery›

untaxed /ʌn'tækst/ *adj* ‹goods› non imponibile; ‹income› esente da imposte

untenable /ʌn'tenəbl/ *adj* ‹position, argument› insostenibile

unthinkable /ʌn'θɪŋkəbl/ *adj* impensabile

unthought-of /ʌn'θɔ:təv/ *adj* impensato; **hitherto ∼** finora impensato

untidily /ʌn'taɪdɪlɪ/ *adv* disordinatamente

untidiness /ʌn'taɪdɪnɪs/ *n* disordine *m*

untidy /ʌn'taɪdɪ/ *adj* disordinato

untie /ʌn'taɪ/ *vt* slegare

ə⁰ **until** /ʌn'tɪl/ ▣1 *prep* fino a; **not ∼** non prima di; **∼ the evening** fino alla sera; **∼ his arrival** fino al suo arrivo
▣2 *conj* finché, fino a quando; **not ∼ you've seen it** non prima che tu l'abbia visto

untimely /ʌn'taɪmlɪ/ *adj* inopportuno; (premature) prematuro

untiring /ʌn'taɪərɪŋ/ *adj* instancabile

untold /ʌn'təʊld/ *adj* ‹wealth› incalcolabile; ‹suffering› indescrivibile; ‹story› inedito

untouched /ʌn'tʌtʃt/ *adj* (unchanged, undisturbed) intatto; (unscathed) incolume, (unaffected) non toccato; **leave one's dinner/a meal ∼** non toccare cibo

untoward /ʌntə'wɔ:d/ *adj* **if nothing ∼ happens** se non capita un imprevisto

untrained /ʌn'treɪnd/ *adj* ‹voice› non impostato; ‹eye, artist, actor› inesperto; **be ∼** ‹worker› non avere una formazione professionale

untranslatable /ʌntrænz'leɪtəbl/ *adj* intraducibile

untreated /ʌn'tri:tɪd/ *adj* ‹sewage, water› non depurato; ‹illness› non curato

untroubled /ʌn'trʌbld/ *adj* ‹sleep› tranquillo

untrue /ʌn'tru:/ *adj* falso; **that's ∼** non è vero

untrustworthy /ʌn'trʌstwɜ:ðɪ/ *adj* ‹person› inaffidabile

unused¹ /ʌn'ju:zd/ *adj* non usato

unused² /ʌn'ju:st/ *adj* **be ∼ to** non essere abituato a

unusual /ʌn'ju:ʒʊəl/ *adj* insolito

unusually /ʌn'ju:ʒʊəlɪ/ *adv* insolitamente

unveil /ʌn'veɪl/ *vt* scoprire

unversed /ʌn'vɜ:st/ *adj* inesperto (**in** di)

unwanted /ʌn'wɒntɪd/ *adj* ‹child, pet, visitor› indesiderato; ‹goods, produce› che non serve; **feel ∼** sentirsi respinto

unwarranted /ʌn'wɒrəntɪd/ *adj* ingiustificato

unwelcome /ʌn'welkəm/ *adj* sgradito

unwell /ʌn'wel/ *adj* indisposto

unwieldy /ʌn'wi:ldɪ/ *adj* ingombrante

unwilling /ʌn'wɪlɪŋ/ *adj* riluttante

unwillingly /ʌn'wɪlɪŋlɪ/ *adv* malvolentieri

unwillingness /ʌn'wɪlɪŋnɪs/ *n* riluttanza

unwind /ʌn'waɪnd/ ▣1 *vt* (*pt/pp* **unwound**) svolgere, srotolare
▣2 *vi* svolgersi, srotolarsi; fam (relax) rilassarsi

unwise /ʌn'waɪz/ *adj* imprudente

unwisely /ʌn'waɪzlɪ/ *adv* imprudentemente

unwitting /ʌn'wɪtɪŋ/ *adj* involontario; ‹victim› inconsapevole

unwittingly /ʌn'wɪtɪŋlɪ/ *adv* involontariamente

unworldly /ʌn'wɜ:ldlɪ/ *adj* (not materialistic) poco materialista; (naive) ingenuo; (spiritual) non materialista

unworthy /ʌn'wɜ:ðɪ/ *adj* non degno

unwrap /ʌn'ræp/ *vt* (*pt/pp* **-;wrapped**) scartare ‹present, parcel›

unwritten /ʌn'rɪtn/ *adj* tacito

unyielding /ʌn'ji:ldɪŋ/ *adj* rigido

unzip /ʌn'zɪp/ *vt* aprire [la cerniera di] ‹garment, bag›

ə⁰ **up** /ʌp/ ▣1 *adv* su; (not in bed) alzato; ‹road› smantellato; ‹theatre curtain, blinds› alzato; ‹shelves, tent› montato; ‹notice› affisso; ‹building› costruito; **prices are up** i prezzi sono aumentati; **be up for sale** essere in vendita; **up here/there** quassù/lassù; **time's up** tempo scaduto; **what's up?** fam cosa è successo?; **up to** (as far as) fino a; **be up to** essere all'altezza di ‹task›; **what's he up to?** fam cosa sta facendo?; (plotting) cosa sta combinando?; **I'm up to page 100** sono arrivato a pagina 100; **feel up to it** sentirsela; **be one up on somebody** fam essere in vantaggio su qualcuno; **go up** salire; **lift up** alzare; **up against** fig ale prese con
▣2 *prep* su; **the cat ran/is up the tree** il gatto è salito di corsa/è sull'albero; **further up this road** più avanti su questa strada; **row up the river** risalire il fiume; **go up the stairs** salire su per le scale; **be up the pub** fam essere al pub; **be up on** *or* **in something** essere bene informato su qualcosa
▣3 *npl* **ups and downs** alti *mpl* e bassi

u

up-and-coming *adj* promettente

upbeat /'ʌpbiːt/ *adj* ottimistico

upbringing /'ʌpbrɪŋɪŋ/ *n* educazione *f*

update /ʌp'deɪt/ *vt* aggiornare

upfront /ʌp'frʌnt/ ⓵ *adj* fam (frank) aperto; ‹money› anticipato
⓶ *adv* ‹pay› in anticipo

upgrade /ʌp'greɪd/ ⓵ *vt* promuovere ‹person›; modernizzare ‹equipment›
⓶ *n* aggiornamento *m*

upheaval /ʌp'hiːvl/ *n* scompiglio *m*

uphill /ʌp'hɪl/ ⓵ *adj* in salita; fig arduo
⓶ *adv* in salita

uphold /ʌp'həʊld/ *vt* (*pt/pp* **upheld**) sostenere ‹principle›; confermare ‹verdict›

upholster /ʌp'həʊlstə(r)/ *vt* tappezzare

upholsterer /ʌp'həʊlstərə(r)/ *n* tappezziere, -a *mf*

upholstery /ʌp'həʊlstərɪ/ *n* tappezzeria *f*

upkeep /'ʌpkiːp/ *n* mantenimento *m*

uplifting /ʌp'lɪftɪŋ/ *adj* (morally) edificante

upload /'ʌpləʊd/ *vt* Comput fare l'upload di

up-market *adj* di qualità

✧ **upon** /ə'pɒn/ *prep* su; ~ arriving home una volta arrivato a casa

upper /'ʌpə(r)/ ⓵ *adj* superiore
⓶ *n* (of shoe) tomaia *f*

upper-case *adj* maiuscolo

upper circle *n* seconda galleria *f*

upper class *n* alta borghesia *f*

upper crust *adj* hum aristocratico

upper hand *n* have the ~ avere il sopravvento

upper middle class *n* ceto *m* medio-alto

uppermost /'ʌpəməʊst/ *adj* più alto; that's ~ in my mind è la mia preoccupazione principale

upright /'ʌpraɪt/ ⓵ *adj* dritto; ‹piano› verticale; (honest) retto
⓶ *n* montante *m*

upright freezer *n* freezer *m inv* verticale

uprising /'ʌpraɪzɪŋ/ *n* rivolta *f*

upriver /ʌp'rɪvə(r)/ *adv* ‹lie› a monte; ‹sail› controcorrente

uproar /'ʌprɔː(r)/ *n* tumulto *m*; be in an ~ essere in trambusto

uproot /ʌp'ruːt/ *vt* sradicare

upset¹ /ʌp'set/ *vt* (*pt/pp* **upset**, *pres p* **upsetting**) rovesciare; sconvolgere ‹plan›; (distress) turbare; **get ~ about something** prendersela per qualcosa; **be very ~** essere sconvolto; **have an ~ stomach** avere l'intestino disturbato

upset² /'ʌpset/ *n* scombussolamento *m*

upsetting /ˌʌp'setɪŋ/ *adj* (distressing) sconvolgente; (annoying) fastidioso

upshot /'ʌpʃɒt/ *n* risultato *m*

upside down *adv* sottosopra; **turn ~** capovolgere

upstage /ʌp'steɪdʒ/ ⓵ *vt* Theat fig distogliere l'attenzione del pubblico da
⓶ *adv* Theat ‹stand› al fondo del palcoscenico; ‹move› verso il fondo del palcoscenico

upstairs¹ /ʌp'steəz/ *adv* [al piano] di sopra

upstairs² /'ʌpsteəz/ *adj* del piano superiore

upstart /'ʌpstɑːt/ *n* arrivato, -a *mf*

upstream /ʌp'striːm/ *adv* controcorrente

upsurge /'ʌpsɜːdʒ/ *n* (in sales) aumento *m* improvviso; (of enthusiasm, crime) ondata *f*

uptake /'ʌpteɪk/ *n* **be slow on the ~** essere lento nel capire; **be quick on the ~** capire le cose al volo

uptight /ʌp'taɪt/ *adj* teso

up-to-date *adj* moderno; ‹news› ultimo; ‹person, information, records› aggiornato

up-to-the-minute *adj* ‹information› dell'ultimo minuto

uptown /'ʌptaʊn/ *adj* Am (smart) dei quartieri alti

upturn /'ʌptɜːn/ *n* ripresa *f*

upward /'ʌpwəd/ ⓵ *adj* verso l'alto, in su; ~ **slope** salita *f*
⓶ *adv* ~**[s]** verso l'alto; ~**s of** oltre

upwardly mobile /ʌpwədlɪ'məʊbaɪl/ *adj* che sale nella scala sociale

uranium /jʊ'reɪnɪəm/ *n* uranio *m*

Uranus /'jʊərənəs, jʊ'reɪnəs/ *n* Urano *m*

✧ **urban** /'ɜːbən/ *adj* urbano

urban blight, **urban decay** *n* degrado *m* urbano

urbane /ɜː'beɪn/ *adj* cortese

urban myth leggenda *f* metropolitana

urban planning *n* urbanistica *f*

urchin /'ɜːtʃɪn/ *n* riccio *m* di mare

Urdu /'ʊədu:/ *n* urdu *m*

✧ **urge** /ɜːdʒ/ ⓵ *n* forte desiderio *m*
⓶ *vt* esortare (**to** a)
■ **urge on** *vt* spronare

urgency /'ɜːdʒənsɪ/ *n* urgenza *f*

urgent /'ɜːdʒənt/ *adj* urgente

urgently /'ɜːdʒəntlɪ/ *adv* urgentemente

urinal /jʊ'raɪnl/ *n* (fixture) orinale *m*; (place) vespasiano *m*

urinate /'jʊərɪneɪt/ *vi* urinare

urine /'jʊərɪn/ *n* urina *f*

URL *abbr* (**Unified Resource Locator**) URL *m*

urn /ɜːn/ *n* urna *f*; (for tea) *contenitore (m) munito di rubinetto che si trova nei self-service, mense ecc*

Uruguay /'jʊərəgwaɪ/ *n* Uruguay *m*

✧ **us** /ʌs/ *pers pron* ci; (after prep) noi; **they know us** ci conoscono; **give us the money** dateci i soldi; **give it to us** datecelo; **they showed**

✧ indicates a very frequent word

it to us ce l'hanno fatto vedere; **they meant us, not you** intendevano noi, non voi; **it's us** siamo noi; **she hates us** ci odia

US *n abbr* (**United States**) U.S.A. *mpl*

USA *n abbr* (**United States of America**) U.S.A. *mpl*

usable /ˈjuːzəbl/ *adj* usabile

usage /ˈjuːsɪdʒ/ *n* uso *m*

USB key /ˌjuːesˈbiːkiː/ *n* chiavetta *f* USB

🔊 **use¹** /juːs/ *n* uso *m*; **be of ∼** essere utile; **be of no ∼** essere inutile; **make ∼ of** usare; (exploit) sfruttare; **it is no ∼** è inutile; **what's the ∼?** a che scopo?

🔊 **use²** /juːz/ *vt* usare

■ **use up** *vt* consumare

used¹ /juːzd/ *adj* usato

used² /juːst/ *pt* **be ∼ to something** essere abituato a qualcosa; **get ∼ to** abituarsi a; **he ∼ to say** diceva; **he ∼ to live here** viveva qui

🔊 **useful** /ˈjuːsfl/ *adj* utile

usefulness /ˈjuːsflnɪs/ *n* utilità *f*

useless /ˈjuːslɪs/ *adj* inutile; fam ‹person› incapace; **you're ∼!** sei un idiota!

🔊 **user** /ˈjuːzə(r)/ *n* utente *mf*

user-friendliness *n* facilità *f* d'uso

user-friendly *adj* facile da usare

user group *n* Comput gruppo *m* di utenti

user manual *n* manuale *m* d'uso

username *n* nome *m* utente

usher /ˈʌʃə(r)/ *n* Theat maschera *f*; Jur usciere *m*; (at wedding) persona (*f*) che accompagna gli invitati ad un matrimonio ai loro posti in chiesa

■ **usher in** *vt* fare entrare ‹person›; inaugurare ‹new age›

usherette /ʌʃəˈret/ *n* maschera *f*

USS *abbr* Am (**United States Ship**) nave *f* da guerra americana

USSR *n* URSS *f*

🔊 **usual** /ˈjuːʒəl/ *adj* usuale; **as ∼** come al solito

🔊 **usually** /ˈjuːʒəlɪ/ *adv* di solito

usurp /juˈzɜːp/ *vt* usurpare

usurper /juˈzɜːpə(r)/ *n* usurpatore, -trice *mf*

utensil /juˈtensl/ *n* utensile *m*

uterus /ˈjuːtərəs/ *n* utero *m*

utilitarian /juːtɪlɪˈteərɪən/ *adj* funzionale

utility /juˈtɪlətɪ/ *n* utilità *f*; (public) servizio *m*

utility bill *n* bolletta *f*

utility company *n* servizio *m* pubblico

utility program *n* Comput [programma *m* di] utilità *f*

utility room *n* stanza (*f*) in casa privata per il lavaggio, la stiratura dei panni ecc

utilize /ˈjuːtɪlaɪz/ *vt* utilizzare

utmost /ˈʌtməʊst/ 🔢 **1** *adj* estremo 🔢 **2** *n* **one's ∼** tutto il possibile

Utopia /juːˈtəʊpɪə/ *n* utopia *f*

Utopian /juːˈtəʊpɪən/ 🔢 **1** *n* utopista *mf* 🔢 **2** *adj* utopistico

utter¹ /ˈʌtə(r)/ *adj* totale

utter² *vt* emettere ‹sigh, sound›; proferire ‹word›

utterance /ˈʌtərəns/ *n* dichiarazione *f*

utterly /ˈʌtəlɪ/ *adv* completamente

U-turn *n* Auto inversione *f* a U; fig marcia *f* indietro

UV *abbr* (**ultraviolet**) UVA *mpl*

Uzbekistan /ʌzbekɪˈstɑːn/ *n* Uzbekistan *m*

Vv

v¹, V /viː/ *n* (letter) v, V *f inv*

v² *abbr* **1** (**versus**) contro **2** (**volt**) V *m*

vac /væk/ *n abbr* Br (**vacation**) vacanze *fpl*

vacancy /ˈveɪk(ə)nsɪ/ *n* (job) posto *m* vacante; (room) stanza *f* disponibile

vacant /ˈveɪknt/ *adj* libero; ‹position› vacante; ‹look› assente

vacant possession *n* Br Jur bene *m* immobile libero

vacate /vəˈkeɪt/ *vt* lasciare libero

vacation /vəˈkeɪʃn/ *n* Univ & Am vacanza *f*

vacationer /vəˈkeɪʃənə(r)/, US veɪ-/ *n* Am vacanziere, -a *mf*

vaccinate /ˈvæksmeɪt/ *vt* vaccinare

vaccination /væksɪˈneɪʃn/ *n* vaccinazione *f*

vaccine /ˈvæksiːn/ *n* vaccino *m*

vacillate /ˈvæsɪleɪt/ *vi* tentennare

vacuous /ˈvækjʊəs/ *adj* ‹person, look, expression› vacuo; ‹person› superficiale

vacuum /ˈvækjʊəm/ 🔢 **1** *n* vuoto *m* 🔢 **2** *vt* passare l'aspirapolvere in/su

vacuum cleaner *n* aspirapolvere *m inv*

vacuum flask *n* thermos *m inv*

vacuum-pack *vt* confezionare sotto vuoto ‹food›

vacuum-packed *adj* confezionato sottovuoto

vagabond /'væɡəbɒnd/ n vagabondo, -a mf
vagaries /'veɪɡərɪz/ npl capricci mpl
vagina /və'dʒaɪnə/ n Anat vagina f
vagrancy /'veɪɡrənsɪ/ n Jur vagabondaggio m
vagrant /'veɪɡrənt/ n vagabondo, -a mf
vague /veɪɡ/ adj vago; ‹outline› impreciso; (absent-minded) distratto; **I'm still ~ about it** non ho ancora le idee chiare in proposito
vaguely /'veɪɡlɪ/ adv vagamente
vagueness /'veɪɡnɪs/ n (imprecision) vaghezza f; (of wording, proposals) indeterminatezza f; (of image) nebulosità f; (of thinking) imprecisione f
vain /veɪn/ adj vanitoso; ‹hope, attempt› vano; **in ~** invano
vainly /'veɪnlɪ/ adv vanamente
valance /'væləns/ n (above curtains) mantovana f; (on bed base) balza f
vale /veɪl/ n liter valle f
valentine /'væləntaɪn/ n (card) biglietto m di San Valentino
Valentine's Day n giorno m di San Valentino
valet /'væleɪ/ n servitore m personale
valet parking n servizio (m) di parcheggio per clienti di alberghi e ristoranti
valiant /'vælɪənt/ adj valoroso
valiantly /'vælɪəntlɪ/ adv coraggiosamente
valid /'vælɪd/ adj valido
validate /'vælɪdeɪt/ vt (confirm) convalidare
validity /və'lɪdətɪ/ n validità f
valley /'vælɪ/ n valle f
valour /'vælə(r)/ n valore m
valuable /'væljʊəbl/ adj di valore; fig prezioso
valuables /'væljʊəblz/ npl oggetti mpl di valore
valuation /væljʊ'eɪʃn/ n valutazione f
⚜ **value** /'vælju:/ ① n valore m; (usefulness) utilità f
② vt valutare; (cherish) apprezzare
value added tax /'ædɪd/ n imposta f sul valore aggiunto
valued /'vælju:d/ adj (appreciated) apprezzato
valuer /'væljʊə(r)/ n stimatore, -trice mf
valve /vælv/ n valvola f
vamp /væmp/ n vamp f inv
vampire /'væmpaɪə(r)/ n vampiro m
van /væn/ n furgone m
vandal /'vændl/ n vandalo, -a mf
vandalism /'vænd(ə)lɪzm/ n vandalismo m
vandalize /'vænd(ə)laɪz/ vt vandalizzare
vane /veɪn/ n banderola f

vanguard /'vænɡɑ:d/ n avanguardia f; **in the ~** all'avanguardia
vanilla /və'nɪlə/ n vaniglia f
vanish /'vænɪʃ/ vi svanire
vanishing cream n crema f base per il trucco
vanishing point n punto m di fuga
vanishing trick n trucco (m) da illusionista per far sparire un oggetto; **he's done his ~ again** fam è sparito come al solito
vanity /'vænɪtɪ/ n vanità f inv
vanity bag, **vanity case** n beauty-case m inv
vanity mirror n Auto specchietto m di cortesia
vanquish /'væŋkwɪʃ/ vt sconfiggere ‹enemy›
vantage point /'vɑ:ntɪdʒ/ n punto m d'osservazione; fig punto m di vista
vaporize /'veɪpəraɪz/ vt vaporizzare ‹liquid›
vaporizer /'veɪpəraɪzə(r)/ n apparecchio m per aerosol
vapour /'veɪpə(r)/ n vapore m
vapour trail n scia f
variable /'veərɪəbl/ adj variabile; (adjustable) regolabile
variance /'veərɪəns/ n **be at ~** essere in disaccordo
variant /'veərɪənt/ n variante f
⚜ **variation** /veərɪ'eɪʃn/ n variazione f
varicose /'værɪkəʊs/ adj **~ veins** vene fpl varicose
varied /'veərɪd/ adj vario; ‹diet› diversificato; ‹life› movimentato
variegated /'veərɪəɡeɪtɪd/ adj variegato
⚜ **variety** /və'raɪətɪ/ n varietà f inv
variety show n spettacolo m di varietà
varifocal /veərɪ'fəʊkl/ adj ‹lens› multifocale
varifocals /veərɪ'fəʊklz/ npl (glasses) occhiali mpl multifocali
⚜ **various** /'veərɪəs/ adj vario
variously /'veərɪəslɪ/ adv variamente
varnish /'vɑ:nɪʃ/ ① n vernice f; (for nails) smalto m
② vt verniciare; **~ one's nails** mettersi lo smalto
⚜ **vary** /'veərɪ/ vt/i (pt/pp **-ied**) variare
varying /'veərɪɪŋ/ adj variabile; (different) diverso
vascular /'væskjʊlə(r)/ adj Anat, Bot vascolare
vase /vɑ:z/ n vaso m
vasectomy /və'sektəmɪ/ n vasectomia f
⚜ **vast** /vɑ:st/ adj vasto; ‹difference, amusement› enorme
vastly /'vɑ:stlɪ/ adv ‹superior› di gran lunga; ‹different, amused› enormemente

---

⚜ indicates a very frequent word

vat /væt/ n tino m

VAT /ˌviːerˈtiː, væt/ abbr (**value added tax**) I.V.A. f

Vatican /ˈvætɪkən/ n the ~ il Vaticano; ~ **City** la città del Vaticano

vaudeville /ˈvɔːdəvɪl/ n Theat varietà m

vault¹ /vɔːlt/ n (roof) volta f; (in bank) caveau m inv; (tomb) cripta f

vault² ① n salto m
② vt/i ~ [over] saltare

VCR abbr (**video cassette recorder**) VCR m

VD abbr (**venereal disease**) malattia f venerea

VDU abbr (**visual display unit**) VDU m

veal /viːl/ ① n carne f di vitello
② attrib di vitello

vector /ˈvektə(r)/ n Biol, Math vettore m; Aeron rotta f

veer /vɪə(r)/ vi cambiare direzione; Naut, Auto virare

vegan /ˈviːgn/ ① n vegetaliano, -a mf
② adj vegetaliano

veganism /ˈviːgənɪzəm/ n vegetalismo m

vegeburger /ˈvedʒɪbɜːgə(r)/ n = VEGGIE BURGER

vegetable /ˈvedʒtəbl/ ① n (food) verdura f; (when growing) ortaggio m
② attrib ‹oil, fat› vegetale

vegetarian /vedʒɪˈteərɪən/ adj & n vegetariano, -a mf

vegetarianism /ˌvedʒɪˈteərɪənɪzəm/ n vegetarianismo m

vegetate /ˈvedʒɪteɪt/ vi vegetare

vegetation /vedʒɪˈteɪʃn/ n vegetazione f

veggie burger n hamburger m inv vegetariano

vehemence /ˈviːəməns/ n veemenza f

vehement /ˈviːəmənt/ adj veemente

vehemently /ˈviːəməntlɪ/ adv con veemenza

✓ **vehicle** /ˈviːɪkl/ n veicolo m; fig (medium) mezzo m

vehicular /vɪˈhɪkjʊlə(r)/ adj no ~ access, no ~ traffic circolazione vietata

veil /veɪl/ ① n velo m
② vt velare

veiled /veɪld/ adj ‹woman› velato, col velo; ‹threat› velato

vein /veɪn/ n vena f; (mood) umore m; (manner) tenore m

veined /veɪnd/ adj venato

Velcro® /ˈvelkrəʊ/ n ~ **fastening** chiusura f con velcro

vellum /ˈveləm/ n pergamena f

velocity /vɪˈlɒsətɪ/ n velocità f inv

velvet /ˈvelvɪt/ n velluto m

velvety /ˈvelvətɪ/ adj vellutato

venal /ˈviːnl/ adj venale

vendetta /venˈdetə/ n vendetta f

vending machine /ˈvendɪŋ/ n distributore m automatico

vendor /ˈvendə(r)/ n venditore, -trice mf

veneer /vəˈnɪə(r)/ n impiallacciatura f; fig vernice f

veneered /vəˈnɪərd/ adj impiallacciato

venerable /ˈvenərəbl/ adj venerabile

veneration /venəˈreɪʃn/ n venerazione f

venereal /vɪˈnɪərɪəl/ adj ~ **disease** malattia f venerea

Venetian /vəˈniːʃn/ adj & n veneziano, -a mf

Venetian blind n persiana f alla veneziana

Venezuela /venɪzˈweɪlə/ n Venezuela m

Venezuelan /venɪzˈweɪlən/ (a & n) venezuelano, -a mf

vengeance /ˈvendʒəns/ n vendetta f; **with a** ~ fam a più non posso

Venice /ˈvenɪs/ n Venezia f

venison /ˈvenɪsn/ n Culin carne f di cervo

venom /ˈvenəm/ n veleno m

venomous /ˈvenəməs/ adj velenoso

vent¹ /vent/ ① n presa f d'aria; **give** ~ **to** fig dar libero sfogo a
② vt fig sfogare ‹anger›

vent² n (in jacket) spacco m

ventilate /ˈventɪleɪt/ vt ventilare

ventilation /ventɪˈleɪʃn/ n ventilazione f; (installation) sistema m di ventilazione

ventilator /ˈventɪleɪtə(r)/ n ventilatore m

ventriloquist /venˈtrɪləkwɪst/ n ventriloquo, -a mf

venture /ˈventʃə(r)/ ① n impresa f
② vt azzardare
③ vi avventurarsi

venture capital n capitale m a rischio

venue /ˈvenjuː/ n luogo m (di convegno, concerto ecc)

Venus /ˈviːnəs/ n Venere f

veracity /vəˈræsətɪ/ n veridicità f

veranda /vəˈrændə/ n veranda f

verb /vɜːb/ n verbo m

verbal /ˈvɜːbl/ adj verbale

verbally /ˈvɜːb(ə)lɪ/ adv verbalmente

verbatim /vɜːˈbeɪtɪm/ ① adj letterale
② adv parola per parola

verbose /vɜːˈbəʊs/ adj prolisso

verdict /ˈvɜːdɪkt/ n verdetto m; (opinion) parere m

verdigris /ˈvɜːdɪɡriː/ n verderame m

verge /vɜːdʒ/ n orlo m; **be on the** ~ **of doing something** essere sul punto di fare qualcosa

verge on vt fig rasentare

verger /ˈvɜːdʒə(r)/ n sagrestano m

verification /verɪfɪˈkeɪʃn/ n verifica f

verify /'verɪfaɪ/ vt (pt/pp **-led**) verificare; (confirm) confermare

veritable /'verɪtəbl/ adj vero

vermicelli /vɜːmɪ'tʃelɪ/ n (pasta) capelli mpl d'angelo; (chocolate) pezzettini mpl di cioccolato per decorazione

vermilion /vəˈmɪljən/ 1 n rosso m vermiglio
2 adj vermiglio

vermin /'vɜːmɪn/ n animali mpl nocivi

vermouth /'vɜːməθ/ n vermut m inv

vernacular /vɜːˈnækjʊlə(r)/ n vernacolo m

verruca /vəˈruːkə/ n verruca f

versatile /'vɜːsətaɪl/ adj versatile

versatility /vɜːsəˈtɪlətɪ/ n versatilità f

verse /vɜːs/ n verso m; (of Bible) versetto m; (poetry) versi mpl

versed /vɜːst/ adj ∼ in versato in

versifier /'vɜːsɪfaɪə(r)/ n pej versificatore, -trice mf

♂ **version** /'vɜːʃn/ n versione f; (translation) traduzione f

versus /'vɜːsəs/ prep contro

vertebra /'vɜːtɪbrə/ n (pl **-brae** /-briː/) Anat vertebra f

vertebrate /'vɜːtɪbrət/ 1 n vertebrato m
2 adj vertebrato

vertex /'vɜːteks/ n Anat sommità f inv del capo; Math vertice m

vertical /'vɜːtɪkl/ adj & n verticale m

vertically /'vɜːtɪklɪ/ adv verticalmente

vertigo /'vɜːtɪɡəʊ/ n Med vertigine f

verve /vɜːv/ n verve f

♂ **very** /'verɪ/ 1 adv molto; ∼ much molto; ∼ little pochissimo; ∼ many moltissimi; ∼ few pochissimi; ∼ probably molto probabilmente; ∼ well benissimo; at the ∼ most tutt'al più; at the ∼ latest al più tardi
2 adj the ∼ first il primissimo; the ∼ thing proprio ciò che ci vuole; at the ∼ end/beginning proprio alla fine/all'inizio; that ∼ day proprio quel giorno; the ∼ thought la sola idea; only a ∼ little solo un pochino

vespers /'vespəz/ npl vespri mpl

vessel /'vesl/ n nave f; (receptacle) recipiente m; Anat vaso m

vest /vest/ 1 n maglia f; Am (waistcoat) gilè m inv
2 vt ∼ something in somebody investire qualcuno di qualcosa

vested interest /vestɪd'ɪntrəst/ n interesse m personale

vestige /'vestɪdʒ/ n (of past) vestigio m

vestment /'vestmənt/ n Relig paramento m

vestry /'vestrɪ/ n sagrestia f

vet /vet/ 1 n veterinario, -a mf
2 vt (pt/pp **vetted**) controllare minuziosamente

veteran /'vetərən/ n veterano, -a mf

veteran car n auto f inv d'epoca (costruita prima del 1916)

veterinarian /ˌvetərɪˈneərɪən/ n Am = VET

veterinary /'vetərɪnərɪ/ adj veterinario

veterinary surgeon n medico m veterinario

veto /'viːtəʊ/ 1 n (pl **-es**) veto m
2 vt proibire

vetting /'vetɪŋ/ n verifica f del passato di un individuo

vex /veks/ vt irritare

vexation /vek'seɪʃn/ n irritazione f

vexatious /vek'seɪʃəs/ adj ‹person› fastidioso; ‹situation› spiacevole

vexed /vekst/ adj irritato; ∼ question questione f controversa

vexing /'veksɪŋ/ adj irritante

VHF abbr (**very high frequency**) VHF

♂ **via** /'vaɪə/ prep via; (by means of) attraverso

viability /vaɪə'bɪlətɪ/ n probabilità f di sopravvivenza; (of proposition) attuabilità f

viable /'vaɪəbl/ adj ‹life form, relationship, company› in grado di sopravvivere; ‹proposition› attuabile

viaduct /'vaɪədʌkt/ n viadotto m

vibes /vaɪbz/ npl fam I'm getting good/bad ∼ provo una sensazione gradevole/sgradevole

vibrant /'vaɪbrənt/ adj fig che sprizza vitalità

vibrate /vaɪ'breɪt/ vi vibrare

vibration /vaɪ'breɪʃn/ n vibrazione f

vicar /'vɪkə(r)/ n parroco m (protestante)

vicarage /'vɪkərɪdʒ/ n casa f parrocchiale

vicarious /vɪ'keərɪəs/ adj indiretto

vice¹ /vaɪs/ n vizio m

vice² n Techn morsa f

vice-captain n Sport vicecapitano m

vice-chairman n vicepresidente mf

vice-chancellor n Br Univ vicerettore m; Am Jur vicecancelliere m

vice-president n vicepresidente mf

vice-principal n (of senior school) vicepreside mf; (of junior school, college) vicedirettore, -trice mf

vice squad n buoncostume f

vice versa /vaɪsə'vɜːsə/ adv viceversa

vicinity /vɪ'sɪnətɪ/ n vicinanza f; in the ∼ of nelle vicinanze di

vicious /'vɪʃəs/ adj cattivo; ‹attack› brutale; ‹animal› pericoloso

vicious circle n circolo m vizioso

viciously /'vɪʃəslɪ/ adv ‹attack› brutalmente

♂ **victim** /'vɪktɪm/ n vittima f

victimization /vɪktɪmaɪ'zeʃn/ n vittimizzazione f

victimize /'vɪktɪmaɪz/ vt vittimizzare

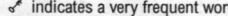
♂ indicates a very frequent word

victor /'vɪktə(r)/ n vincitore m

Victorian /vɪk'tɔːrɪən/ **1** n persona f vissuta in epoca vittoriana
2 adj ‹writer, poverty, age› vittoriano

victorious /vɪk'tɔːrɪəs/ adj vittorioso

☝ **victory** /'vɪktərɪ/ n vittoria f

☝ **video** /'vɪdɪəʊ/ **1** n video m inv; (cassette) videocassetta f; (recorder) videoregistratore m
2 attrib video
3 vt registrare

video camera n videocamera f, telecamera f

video card n scheda f video

video cassette n videocassetta f

video clip n videoclip m inv

videoconference n videoconferenza f

videoconferencing /-'kɒnfərənsɪŋ/ n videoconferenza f

videodisc n videodisco m

video game n videogioco m

video library n videoteca f

video nasty n film (m inv) con scene violente o pornografiche

videophone n videocitofono m

video recorder n videoregistratore m

video shop n negozio (m) che affitta o vende videocassette

video surveillance n videosorveglianza f

videotape n videocassetta f

vie /vaɪ/ vi (pres p **vying**) rivaleggiare

Vienna /vɪ'enə/ n Vienna f

Viennese /vɪə'niːz/ adj viennese

Vietnam /vɪet'næm/ n Vietnam m

Vietnamese /vɪetnə'miːz/ adj & n vietnamita mf; (language) vietnamita m

☝ **view** /vjuː/ **1** n vista f; (photographed, painted) veduta f; (opinion) visione f; **look at the ∼** guardare il panorama; **in my ∼** secondo me; **in ∼ of** in considerazione di; **on ∼** esposto; **with a ∼ to** con l'intenzione di
2 vt visitare ‹house›; (consider) considerare
3 vi TV guardare

viewer /'vjuːə(r)/ n TV telespettatore, -trice mf; Phot visore m

viewfinder /'vjuːfaɪndə(r)/ n Phot mirino m

viewing /'vjuːɪŋ/ **1** n TV programmi mpl della televisione; (of film) proiezione f; (of new range) presentazione f; (of exhibition, house) visita f; **it makes good ∼** TV vale la pena di vederlo; **what's tonight's ∼?** cosa danno alla tv stasera?
2 attrib ‹habits, preferences› dei telespettatori; **the ∼ public** i telespettatori

view phone n videotelefono m

viewpoint /'vjuːpɔɪnt/ n punto m di vista

vigil /'vɪdʒɪl/ n veglia f

vigilance /'vɪdʒɪləns/ n vigilanza f

vigilant /'vɪdʒɪlənt/ adj vigile

vigilante /vdʒɪ'læntɪ/ n membro (m) di un'organizzazione privata per la prevenzione della criminalità

vigorous /'vɪg(ə)rəs/ adj vigoroso

vigorously /'vɪg(ə)rəslɪ/ adv vigorosamente

vigour /'vɪgə(r)/ n vigore m

vile /vaɪl/ adj disgustoso; ‹weather› orribile; ‹temper, mood› pessimo

vilification /vɪlɪfɪ'keɪʃn/ n denigrazione f

villa /'vɪlɪ/ n (for holidays) casa f di villeggiatura

☝ **village** /'vɪlɪdʒ/ n paese m

village green n giardino (m) pubblico nel centro di un paese

village hall n sala (f) utilizzata per feste e altre attività

villager /'vɪlɪdʒə(r)/ n paesano, -a mf

villain /'vɪlɪn/ n furfante m; (in story) cattivo m

villainous /'vɪlənəs/ adj infame

vim /vɪm/ n fam energia f

vindicate /'vɪndɪkeɪt/ vt (from guilt) discolpare; **you are ∼d** ti sei dimostrato nel giusto

vindictive /vɪn'dɪktɪv/ adj vendicativo

vine /vaɪn/ n vite f

vinegar /'vɪnɪgə(r)/ n aceto m

vinegary /'vɪnɪg(ə)rɪ/ adj agro

vineyard /'vɪnjɑːd/ n vigneto m

vintage /'vɪntɪdʒ/ **1** adj ‹wine› d'annata; ‹clothes› vintage
2 n (year) annata f

vintage car n auto f inv d'epoca (costruita tra il 1917 e il 1930)

vintage year n also fig anno m memorabile

vinyl /'vaɪnɪl/ **1** n vinile m
2 attrib ‹paint› vinilico

viola /vɪ'əʊlə/ n Mus viola f

violate /'vaɪəleɪt/ vt violare

violation /vaɪə'leɪʃn/ n violazione f

☝ **violence** /'vaɪələns/ n violenza f

violent /'vaɪələnt/ adj violento

violently /'vaɪələntlɪ/ adv violentemente

violet /'vaɪələt/ **1** adj violetto
2 n (flower) violetta f; (colour) violetto m

violin /vaɪə'lɪn/ n violino m

violinist /vaɪə'lɪnɪst/ n violinista mf

VIP n abbr (**very important person**) vip mf

viper /'vaɪpə(r)/ n vipera f

virgin /'vɜːdʒɪn/ **1** adj vergine
2 n vergine f

virginal /'vɜːdʒɪn(ə)l/ adj verginale

virginals /'vɜːdʒɪn(ə)lz/ npl Mus spinetta f

Virginia creeper /vədʒɪnɪə'kriːpə(r)/ n vite f del Canada

v

virginity /vəˈdʒɪnətɪ/ n verginità f

Virgo /ˈvɜːgəʊ/ n Astr Vergine f

virile /ˈvɪraɪl/ adj virile

virility /vɪˈrɪlətɪ/ n virilità f

virologist /vaɪˈrɒlədʒɪst/ n virologo m

virtual /ˈvɜːtjʊəl/ adj effettivo

virtually /ˈvɜːtjʊəlɪ/ adv praticamente

virtual reality n realtà f virtuale

virtue /ˈvɜːtjuː/ n virtù f inv; (advantage) vantaggio m; **by** or **in ~ of** a causa di

virtuoso /vɜːtʊˈəʊzəʊ/ n (pl **-si** /-ziː/) virtuoso m

virtuous /ˈvɜːtjʊəs/ adj virtuoso

virulent /ˈvɪrʊlənt/ adj virulento

virus /ˈvaɪərəs/ n virus m inv

virus checker n Comput (programma m) antivirus m inv

virus protection n Comput protezione f antivirus

visa /ˈviːzə/ n visto m

vis-à-vis /viːzɑːˈviː/ prep rispetto a

visceral /ˈvɪs(ə)rəl/ adj ‹power, performance› viscerale

viscount /ˈvaɪkaʊnt/ n visconte m

viscous /ˈvɪskəs/ adj vischioso

visibility /vɪzəˈbɪlətɪ/ n visibilità f

visible /ˈvɪzəbl/ adj visibile

visibly /ˈvɪzəblɪ/ adv visibilmente

ơ **vision** /ˈvɪʒn/ n visione f; (sight) vista f

visionary /ˈvɪʒn(ə)rɪ/ adj & n visionario, -a mf

vision mixer n (person) tecnico m del mixaggio video; (equipment) mixaggio m video

ơ **visit** /ˈvɪzɪt/ **1** n visita f
2 vt andare a trovare ‹person›; andare da ‹doctor etc›; visitare ‹town, building›

visiting card n biglietto m da visita

visiting hours npl orario m delle visite

visiting lecturer n conferenziere, -a mf

visiting team n squadra f ospite

visiting time n orario m delle visite

ơ **visitor** /ˈvɪzɪtə(r)/ n ospite mf; (of town, museum) visitatore, -trice mf; (in hotel) cliente mf

visitor centre n centro (m) di accoglienza e di informazione per i visitatori

visitors' book n (in exhibition) albo m dei visitatori; (in hotel) registro m dei clienti

visor /ˈvaɪzə(r)/ n visiera f; Auto parasole m

vista /ˈvɪstə/ n (view) panorama m

visual /ˈvɪzjʊəl/ adj visivo

visual aids npl supporto m visivo

visual arts npl arti fpl visive

visual display unit n visualizzatore m

visualize /ˈvɪzjʊəlaɪz/ vt visualizzare

ơ indicates a very frequent word

visually /ˈvɪzjʊəlɪ/ adv visualmente; **~ handicapped** non vedente

ơ **vital** /ˈvaɪtl/ adj vitale

vitality /vaɪˈtælətɪ/ n vitalità f

vitally /ˈvaɪtəlɪ/ adv estremamente

vital statistics npl fam misure fpl

vitamin /ˈvɪtəmɪn/ n vitamina f

vitreous /ˈvɪtrɪəs/ adj vetroso; ‹enamel› vetrificato

vitriolic /vɪtrɪˈɒlɪk/ adj Chem di vetriolo; fig al vetriolo

vituperative /vɪˈtjuːp(ə)rətɪv/ adj ingiurioso

viva /ˈvaɪvə/ n Br Univ [esame m] orale m

vivacious /vɪˈveɪʃəs/ adj vivace

vivaciously /vɪˈveɪʃəslɪ/ adv vivacemente

vivacity /vɪˈvæsətɪ/ n vivacità f

vivid /ˈvɪvɪd/ adj vivido

vividly /ˈvɪvɪdlɪ/ adv in modo vivido

vivisect /vɪvɪsekt/ vt vivisezionare

vivisection /vɪvɪˈsekʃn/ n vivisezione f

vixen /ˈvɪksn/ n volpe f femmina

viz /vɪz/ adv cioè

V-neck n (neckline) scollo m a V; (sweater) maglione m con scollo a V

vocabulary /vəˈkæbjʊlərɪ/ n vocabolario m; (list) glossario m

vocal /ˈvəʊkl/ adj vocale; (vociferous) eloquente

vocal cords npl corde fpl vocali

vocalist /ˈvəʊkəlɪst/ n vocalista mf

vocalize /ˈvəʊkəlaɪz/ vt fig (express) esprimere a parole; articolare ‹sound›

vocals /ˈvəʊklz/ npl **do the ~** cantare

vocation /vəˈkeɪʃn/ n vocazione f

vocational /vəˈkeɪʃ(ə)nl/ adj di orientamento professionale

vocational course n corso m di formazione professionale

vociferous /vəˈsɪfərəs/ adj vociante

vodka /ˈvɒdkə/ n vodka f inv

vogue /vəʊg/ n moda f; **in ~** in voga

ơ **voice** /vɔɪs/ **1** n voce f
2 vt esprimere

voice box n Anat laringe f

voiceless /ˈvɔɪslɪs/ adj ‹minority› silenzioso; ‹group› privo del diritto di parola

voicemail /ˈvɔɪsmeɪl/ n posta f elettronica vocale

voice-over n voce f fuori campo

voice recognition n Comput riconoscimento m vocale

void /vɔɪd/ **1** adj (not valid) nullo; **~ of** privo di
2 n vuoto m

vol /vɒl/ abbr (**volume**) vol

volatile /ˈvɒlətaɪl/ adj volatile; ‹person› volubile

volcanic /vɒl'kænɪk/ adj vulcanico
volcano /vɒl'keɪnəʊ/ n vulcano m
volition /və'lɪʃn/ n of his own ∼ di sua spontanea volontà
volley /'vɒlɪ/ n (of gunfire) raffica f; Tennis volée f inv
volleyball /'vɒlɪbɔːl/ n pallavolo f
volt /vəʊlt/ n volt m inv
voltage /'vəʊltɪdʒ/ n Electr voltaggio m
voluble /'vɒljʊbl/ adj loquace
✔ **volume** /'vɒljuːm/ n volume m; (of work, traffic) quantità f inv
volume control n volume m
voluntarily /'vɒləntərɪlɪ/ adv volontariamente
voluntary /'vɒləntərɪ/ adj volontario
voluntary redundancy n Br dimissioni fpl volontarie
voluntary work n volontariato m
volunteer /vɒlən'tɪə(r)/ ① n volontario, -a mf
② vt offrire volontariamente ‹information›
③ vi offrirsi volontario; Mil arruolarsi come volontario
voluptuous /və'lʌptjʊəs/ adj voluttuoso
vomit /'vɒmɪt/ ① n vomito m
② vt/i vomitare
voodoo /'vuːduː/ n vudu m inv
voracious /və'reɪʃəs/ adj vorace
vortex /'vɔːteks/ n vortice m; fig turbine m
✔ **vote** /vəʊt/ ① n voto m; (ballot) votazione f; (right) diritto m di voto; **take a ∼ on** votare su
② vi votare
③ vt ∼ **somebody president** eleggere

qualcuno presidente
vote down vt (reject by vote) bocciare ai voti
vote in vt (elect) eleggere
vote of confidence n Pol fig voto m di fiducia
vote of thanks n discorso m di ringraziamento
✔ **voter** /'vəʊtə(r)/ n elettore, -trice mf
voting /'vəʊtɪŋ/ n votazione f
voting age n età f inv per votare
voting booth n cabina f elettorale
vouch /vaʊtʃ/ vi ∼ **for** garantire per
voucher /'vaʊtʃə(r)/ n buono m
vow /vaʊ/ ① n voto m
② vt giurare
vowel /'vaʊəl/ n vocale f
vox pop /vɒks'pɒp/ n TV, Radio opinione f pubblica
voyage /'vɔɪdʒ/ n viaggio m [marittimo]; (in space) viaggio m [nello spazio]
vs abbr (**versus**) contro
V-sign n (offensive gesture) gestaccio m, (victory sign) segno m di vittoria
VSO abbr (**Voluntary Service Overseas**) servizio (m) civile volontario nei paesi in via di sviluppo
vulgar /'vʌlgə(r)/ adj volgare
vulgar fraction n Math frazione f ordinaria
vulgarity /vʌl'gærətɪ/ n volgarità f inv
vulnerable /'vʌlnərəbl/ adj vulnerabile
vulture /'vʌltʃə(r)/ n avvoltoio m
vying /'vaɪɪŋ/ ▶ VIE

Ww

w, W¹ /'dʌblju:/ n (letter) w, W f inv
W² abbr 1 (**West**) O
2 Electr (**watt**) w
wad /wɒd/ n batuffolo m; (bundle) rotolo m
wadding /'wɒdɪŋ/ n ovatta f
waddle /'wɒdl/ vi camminare ondeggiando
wade /weɪd/ vi guadare
■ **wade in** vi fam (start working) mettersi al lavoro; (take part) prendere parte
■ **wade into** vt (attack) scagliarsi contro
■ **wade through** vt fam procedere faticosamente in ‹book›
wader /'weɪdə(r)/ n Zool trampoliere m; ∼s pl (boots) stivaloni mpl di gomma
wafer /'weɪfə(r)/ n cialda f, wafer m inv; Relig ostia f
wafer-thin adj sottilissimo

waffle¹ /'wɒfl/ vi fam blaterare
waffle² n Culin cialda f
waft /wɒft/ ① vt trasportare
② vi diffondersi
wag /wæg/ ① vt (pt/pp **wagged**) agitare
② vi agitarsi
wage¹ /weɪdʒ/ vt dichiarare ‹war›; lanciare ‹campaign›
✔ **wage²** n ∼s pl salario msg
wage earner n salariato, -a mf
wage packet n busta f paga
wager /'weɪdʒə(r)/ n scommessa f
wage slip n cedolino m dello stipendio
waggle /'wægl/ ① vt dimenare
② vi dimenarsi

wagon /'wægən/ *n* carro *m*; Rail vagone *m* merci; **be on the ~** fam astenersi dall'alcol

waif /weɪf/ *n* trovatello, -a *mf*

wail /weɪl/ ① *n* piagnucolio *m*; (of wind) lamento *m*; (of baby) vagito *m*
② *vi* piagnucolare; ⟨*wind*⟩ lamentarsi; ⟨*baby*⟩ vagire

Wailing Wall /'weɪlɪŋ/ *n* Muro *m* del pianto

waist /weɪst/ *n* vita *f*

waistband *n* cintura *f*

waistcoat *n* gilè *m* inv; (of man's suit) panciotto *m*

waistline *n* vita *f*

waist measurement *n* giro *m* vita

♂ **wait** /weɪt/ ① *n* attesa *f*; **lie in ~ for** appostarsi per sorprendere
② *vi* aspettare; **~ at table** servire ai tavoli; **~ for** aspettare
③ *vt* **~ one's turn** aspettare il proprio turno
■ **wait about**, **wait around** *vi* aspettare
■ **wait behind** *vi* trattenersi
■ **wait in** *vi* rimanere a casa ad aspettare
■ **wait on** *vt* servire
■ **wait up** *vi* rimanere alzato ad aspettare; **don't ~ up for me** non mi aspettare alzato

waiter /'weɪtə(r)/ *n* cameriere *m*

waiter service *n* servizio *m* al tavolo

waiting game *n* **play a ~** *n* temporeggiare

waiting list *n* lista *f* d'attesa

waiting room *n* sala *f* d'aspetto

waitress /'weɪtrɪs/ *n* cameriera *f*

waive /weɪv/ *vt* rinunciare a ⟨*claim*⟩; non tener conto di ⟨*rule*⟩

waiver /'weɪvə(r)/ *n* Jur rinuncia *f*

♂ **wake¹** /weɪk/ ① *n* veglia *f* funebre
② *vt* (*pt* **woke**, *pp* **woken**) **~ [up]** svegliare
③ *vi* svegliarsi
■ **wake up to**: *vt* **~ up to the fact that…** (realize) aprire gli occhi di fronte al fatto che…

wake² *n* Naut scia *f*; **in the ~ of** fig nella scia di

wakeful /'weɪkfʊl/ *adj* ⟨*night*⟩ insonne

waken /'weɪkn/ ① *vt* svegliare
② *vi* svegliarsi

wake-up call *n* lit sveglia *f* telefonica; fig campanello *m* d'allarme

Wales /weɪlz/ *n* Galles *m*

♂ **walk** /wɔːk/ ① *n* passeggiata *f*; (gait) andatura *f*; (path) sentiero *m*; **go for a ~** andare a fare una passeggiata; **~ of life** livello *m* sociale
② *vi* camminare; (as opposed to drive etc) andare a piedi; (ramble) passeggiare; '**~**' Am (at crossing) 'avanti'

③ *vt* portare a spasso ⟨*dog*⟩; percorrere ⟨*streets*⟩
■ **walk away** *vi* (leave) allontanarsi; **~ away from** abbandonare ⟨*place, person*⟩; disinteressarsi di ⟨*problem*⟩; (survive unscathed) uscire illeso da ⟨*accident*⟩
■ **walk away with** *vt* (win easily) vincere senza difficoltà ⟨*game, election, prize*⟩
■ **walk back** *vi* ritornare a piedi
■ **walk in** *vi* entrare all'improvviso
■ **walk into** *vt* entrare in ⟨*room*⟩; andare a sbattere contro ⟨*door, lamp post*⟩; cadere in ⟨*trap*⟩; trovare facilmente ⟨*job*⟩
■ **walk off** *vi* (leave) andarsene
■ **walk off with** *vt* (win easily) riportare senza difficoltà; (take, steal) portarsi via
■ **walk out** *vi* ⟨*husband, employee*⟩ andarsene; ⟨*workers*⟩ scioperare
■ **walk out of** *vt* uscire da ⟨*room*⟩; abbandonare ⟨*meeting*⟩
■ **walk out on** *vt* lasciare
■ **walk over**: *vt* **~ all over somebody** (defeat) stracciare qualcuno; (treat badly) trattare qualcuno come una pezza da piedi
■ **walk through** *vt* superare senza difficoltà ⟨*exam, interview*⟩
■ **walk up** *vi* (as opposed to taking the lift) salire a piedi; (approach) avvicinarsi

walkabout /'wɔːkəbaʊt/ *n* escursione (*f*) periodica degli aborigeni australiani nell'entroterra; (by royalty) incontro *m* con la folla; **go ~** ⟨*queen, politician*⟩ camminare tra la folla

walker /'wɔːkə(r)/ *n* **1** (generally) camminatore, -trice *mf*; (rambler) escursionista *mf*
2 Am (frame) deambulatore *m*

walkie-talkie /wɔːkɪ'tɔːkɪ/ *n* walkie-talkie *m* inv

walk-in *adj* **~ closet** stanzino *m*

walking /'wɔːkɪŋ/ *n* camminare *m*; (rambling) fare *m* delle escursioni

walking boots *npl* scarponi *mpl* [da trekking]

walking distance *n* **it's within ~** ci si arriva a piedi

walking frame *n* Med deambulatore *m*

walking pace *n* passo *m*

walking shoes *npl* scarpe *fpl* da passeggio

walking-stick *n* bastone *m* da passeggio

walking wounded *npl* feriti *mpl* in grado di camminare

Walkman® *n* Walkman® *m* inv

walk-on ① *n* Theat comparsa *f*
② *adj* ⟨*role*⟩ piccolo

walkout *n* sciopero *m*

walkover *n* fig vittoria *f* facile

walkway *n* passaggio *m* pedonale

♂ indicates a very frequent word

ꝺ **wall** /wɔːl/ n muro m; **go to the ~** fam andare a rotoli; **drive somebody up the ~** fam far diventare matto qualcuno
■ **wall up** vt murare

wallchart /'wɔːltʃɑːt/ n tabellone m

walled /wɔːld/ adj ‹city› fortificato

wallet /'wɒlɪt/ n portafoglio m

wallflower /'wɔːlflaʊə(r)/ n violaciocca f

wall hanging n decorazione f murale

wallop /'wɒləp/ ⓵ n fam colpo m
⓶ vt (pt/pp **walloped**) fam colpire

walloping /'wɒləpɪŋ/ fam ⓵ adj enorme
⓶ adv ~ **great** (very big) enorme
⓷ n **give somebody a ~** suonarle a qualcuno

wallow /'wɒləʊ/ vi sguazzare; (in self-pity, grief) crogiolarsi

wallpaper /'wɔːlpeɪpə(r)/ ⓵ n tappezzeria f
⓶ vt tappezzare

wall-to-wall adj che copre tutto il pavimento

walnut /'wɔːlnʌt/ n noce f

walrus /'wɔːlrəs/ n tricheco m

waltz /wɔːlts/ ⓵ n valzer m inv
⓶ vi ballare il valzer; **he came ~ing up and said** (fam è) arrivato e ha detto con nonchalance
■ **waltz off with** vt fam (take, win) portarsi via
■ **waltz through** vt superare facilmente ‹exam›

wan /wɒn/ adj esangue

wand /wɒnd/ n (magic ~) bacchetta f [magica]

wander /'wɒndə(r)/ vi girovagare; fig (digress) divagare
■ **wander about** vi andare a spasso
■ **wander away** vi allontanarsi
■ **wander off** vi allontanarsi; **I'd better be ~ing off** fam è meglio che vada

wanderer /'wɒndərə(r)/ n vagabondo, -a mf

wanderlust /'wɒndəlʌst/ n smania f dei viaggi

wane /weɪn/ ⓵ n **be on the ~** essere in fase calante
⓶ vi calare

wangle /'wæŋgl/ vt fam rimediare ‹invitation, holiday›

waning /'weɪnɪŋ/ ⓵ n (of moon) calare m; (weakening) declino m
⓶ adj ‹moon› calante; ‹popularity› in declino

wannabee /'wɒnəbiː/ n fam persona (f) che sogna di diventare famosa

ꝺ **want** /wɒnt/ ⓵ n (hardship) bisogno m; (lack) mancanza f
⓶ vt volere; (need) aver bisogno di; ~ **[to have]** something volere qualcosa; ~ **to do** something voler fare qualcosa; **we ~ to stay** vogliamo rimanere; **I ~ you to go** voglio che

tu vada; **it ~s painting** ha bisogno d'essere dipinto; **you ~ to learn to swim** bisogna che impari a nuotare
⓷ vi ~ **for** mancare di

wanted /'wɒntɪd/ adj ricercato

wanted list n lista f dei ricercati

wanting /'wɒntɪŋ/ adj **be ~** mancare; **be ~ in** mancare di

wanton /'wɒntən/ adj ‹cruelty, neglect› gratuito; (morally) debosciato

WAP /wæp/ abbr (**wireless application protocol**) WAP m; ~ **phone** telefonino WAP

WAP-enabled /-ɪ'neɪbld/ adj ‹device, system› abilitato al WAP

ꝺ **war** /wɔː(r)/ n guerra f; fig lotta f (**on** contro); **at ~** in guerra

warble /'wɔːbl/ vt/i trillare; ‹singer› gorgheggiare

war cabinet n consiglio m di guerra

war cry n grido m di guerra

ward /wɔːd/ n (in hospital) reparto m; (child) minore m sotto tutela
■ **ward off** vt evitare; parare ‹blow›

warden /'wɔːdn/ n guardiano, -a mf

warder /'wɔːdə(r)/ n guardia f carceraria

wardrobe /'wɔːdrəʊb/ n guardaroba m

wardrobe assistant n costumista mf

ward round n Med giro m delle corsie

ward sister n Br Med caposala f inv

warehouse /'weəhaʊs/ n magazzino m

wares /weəz/ npl merci mpl

warfare /'wɔːfeə(r)/ n guerra f

war game n Mil simulazione f di scontro militare

warhead n testata f

warhorse n cavallo m da battaglia; fig (campaigner) veterano m

warily /'weərɪlɪ/ adv cautamente

warlike /'wɔːlaɪk/ adj bellicoso

ꝺ **warm** /wɔːm/ ⓵ adj caldo; ‹welcome› caloroso; **be ~** ‹person› aver caldo; **it is ~** ‹weather› fa caldo
⓶ vt scaldare
■ **warm to** vt prendere in simpatia ‹person›
■ **warm up** ⓵ vt scaldare
⓶ vi scaldarsi; fig animarsi

warm-blooded /-'blʌdɪd/ adj Zool con temperatura corporea costante

war memorial n monumento m ai caduti

warm-hearted /-'hɑːtɪd/ adj espansivo

warmly /'wɔːmlɪ/ adv ‹greet› calorosamente; ‹dress› in modo pesante

warmongering /'wɔːmʌŋgərɪŋ/ ⓵ n bellicismo m
⓶ adj ‹article› bellicistico; ‹person› guerrafondaio

warmth /wɔːmθ/ n calore m

warm-up n Sport riscaldamento m; (of musicians) prove fpl

W

$\mathscr{I}$ **warn** /wɔ:n/ vt avvertire

■ **warn off** vt dare un avvertimento a

$\mathscr{I}$ **warning** /'wɔ:nɪŋ/ n avvertimento m; (advance notice) preavviso m

warning light n spia f luminosa

warning shot n sparo m d'avvertimento

warning sign n (road sign) segnale m di pericolo; (of illness) segnale m d'allarme

warning triangle n triangolo m di segnalazione

warp /wɔ:p/ ① vt deformare; fig distorcere ② vi deformarsi

warpaint /'wɔ:peɪnt/ n Mil pitture fpl di guerra

warpath /'wɔ:pɑ:θ/ n **on the** ~ sul sentiero di guerra

warped /wɔ:pt/ adj deformato; ‹personality› contorto; ‹sexuality› deviato; ‹view› distorto

warplane /'wɔ:pleɪn/ n aereo m da guerra

warrant /'wɒrənt/ ① n (for arrest, search) mandato m ② vt (justify) giustificare; (guarantee) garantire

warranty /'wɒrəntɪ/ n garanzia f

warren /'wɒr(ə)n/ n (of rabbits) area f piena di tane di conigli; (building, maze of streets) labirinto m

warring /'wɔ:rɪŋ/ adj in guerra

warrior /'wɒrɪə(r)/ n guerriero, -a mf

Warsaw /'wɔ:sɔ:/ n Varsavia f

warship /'wɔ:ʃɪp/ n nave f da guerra

wart /wɔ:t/ n porro m

wartime /'wɔ:taɪm/ n tempo m di guerra

war-torn /'wɔ:tɔ:n/ adj logorato dalla guerra

wary /'weərɪ/ adj (**-ier, -iest**) (careful) cauto; (suspicious) diffidente

was /wɒz/ ▶ BE

wash /wɒʃ/ ① n lavata f; (clothes) bucato m; (in washing machine) lavaggio m; **have a** ~ darsi una lavata ② vt lavare; ‹sea› bagnare; ~ **one's hands** lavarsi le mani ③ vi lavarsi

■ **wash away** vt ‹rain› portare via; ‹sea, floodwaters› spazzare via

■ **wash off** ① vt lavar via ‹stain, mud› ② vi andar via

■ **wash out** vt sciacquare ‹soap›; sciacquarsi ‹mouth›

■ **wash up** ① vt lavare ② vi lavare i piatti; Am lavarsi

washable /'wɒʃəbl/ adj lavabile

wash-and-wear adj che non si stira

wash bag n Br = TOILET BAG

washbasin n lavandino m

washbowl n Am = WASHBASIN

wash cloth n Am ≈ guanto m da bagno

washed out /wɒʃt'aʊt/ adj (faded) scolorito; (tired) spossato

washed up adj fam (finished) finito; (tired) distrutto

washer /'wɒʃə(r)/ n Techn guarnizione f; (machine) lavatrice f

washer-dryer /-'draɪə(r)/ n asciugabiancheria m inv

washing /'wɒʃɪŋ/ n bucato m

washing line n corda f per il bucato

washing machine n lavatrice f

washing powder n detersivo m

washing soda n soda f da bucato

washing-up n **do the** ~ lavare i piatti

washing-up bowl n bacinella f (per i piatti)

washing-up liquid n detersivo m per i piatti

washing-up water n rigovernatura f

wash load n carico m di lavatrice

wash-out n disastro m

washroom n bagno m

wash-stand n Am = WASHBASIN

wasp /wɒsp/ n vespa f

WASP, Wasp /wɒsp/ n abbr Am (**White Anglo-Saxon Protestant**) WASP m

waspish /'wɒspɪʃ/ adj pungente

wastage /'weɪstɪdʒ/ n perdita f

waste /weɪst/ ① n spreco m; (rubbish) rifiuto m; ~**s** pl distesa fsg desolata; ~ **of time** perdita f di tempo ② adj ‹product› di scarto; ‹land› desolato; **lay** ~ devastare ③ vt sprecare

■ **waste away** vi deperire

wastebasket n cestino m della carta straccia

waste bin n (for paper) cestino m della carta straccia; (for rubbish) secchio m della spazzatura

wasted /'weɪstɪd/ adj ‹energy, effort, life› sprecato; ‹limb› atrofizzato; (body) scarnito

waste disposal n smaltimento m dei rifiuti

waste disposal unit n eliminatore m di rifiuti

wasteful /'weɪstfʊl/ adj dispendioso

wasteland n area f desolata

waste paper n carta f straccia

waste-paper basket n cestino m per la carta [straccia]

waste pipe n tubo m di scarico

$\mathscr{I}$ **watch** /wɒtʃ/ ① n guardia f; (period of duty) turno m di guardia; (timepiece) orologio m; **be on the** ~ stare all'erta ② vt guardare ‹film, match, television›; (be careful of, look after) stare attento a ③ vi guardare

 w

■ **watch out** *vi* (be careful) stare attento (**for** a)
■ **watch out for** *vt* (look for) fare attenzione all'arrivo di ‹*person*›
■ **watch over** *vt* proteggere ‹*person*›
watchband *n* Am = WATCH STRAP
watchdog /'wɒtʃdɒg/ *n* cane *m* da guardia
watchful /'wɒtʃfʊl/ *adj* attento
watchfully /'wɒtʃfʊlɪ/ *adv* attentamente
watchmaker *n* orologiaio, -a *mf*
watchman *n* guardiano *m*
watch strap *n* cinturino *m* dell'orologio
watchtower *n* torre *f* di guardia
watchword *n* motto *m*
⚘ **water** /'wɔːtə(r)/ ① *n* acqua *f*; ∼**s** *pl* acque *fpl*
  ② *vt* annaffiare ‹*garden, plant*›; (dilute) annacquare; dare da bere a ‹*horse etc*›
  ③ *vi* ‹*eyes*› lacrimare; **my mouth was** ∼**ing** avevo l'acquolina in bocca
■ **water down** ① *vt* diluire
  ② *fig* attenuare
water authority *n* ente *m* dell'acqua
water bed *n* materasso *m* ad acqua
waterbird *n* uccello *m* acquatico
water birth *n* parto *m* in acqua
water bottle *n* borraccia *f*
water cannon *n* idrante *m*
watercolour *n* acquerello *m*
water company *n* società *f inv* dell'acqua
watercress *n* crescione *m*
water divining *n* rabdomanzia *f*
waterfall *n* cascata *f*
water filter *n* brocca *f* con filtro per l'acqua
waterfront *n* (by lakeside, riverside) riva *f*; (on harbour) zona *f* portuale
water-heater *n* scaldacqua *m inv*
waterhole *n* pozza *f* d'acqua
watering can /'wɔːtərɪŋ/ *n* annaffiatoio *m*
water jump *n* riviera *f*
water lily *n* ninfea *f*
waterline *n* linea *f* di galleggiamento
waterlogged *adj* inzuppato
water main *n* conduttura *f* dell'acqua
watermark *n* filigrana *f*
watermeadow *n* marcita *f*
watermelon *n* cocomero *m*, anguria *f*
watermill *n* mulino *m* ad acqua
water polo *n* pallanuoto *f*
water-power *n* energia *f* idraulica
waterproof ① *adj* ‹*coat*› impermeabile; ‹*make-up*› waterproof *inv*
  ② *n* impermeabile *m*
waterproofs *npl* sovrapantaloni *mpl* e giacca impermeabili
water rates *mpl* Br tariffe *fpl* dell'acqua

water-resistant *adj* ‹*sun cream*› resistente all'acqua; ‹*garment, watch*› impermeabile
watershed *n* spartiacque *m inv*; fig svolta *f*
waterside ① *n* riva *f*
  ② *attrib* ‹*cafe, hotel*› sulla riva
water-ski /'wɔːtəskiː/ *vi* fare sci nautico
waterskiing *n* sci *m* nautico
water slide *n* acquascivolo *m*
water softener *n* (equipment) addolcitore *m*; (substance) anticalcare *m inv*
water-soluble *adj* idrosolubile
water sport *n* sport *m inv* acquatico
water-table *n* Geog superficie *f* freatica
watertight *adj* stagno; fig irrefutabile
water tower *n* serbatoio *m* idrico a torre
waterway *n* canale *m* navigabile
water-wheel *n* ruota *f* idraulica
water wings *npl* braccioli *mpl*
waterworks *n* impianto *m* idrico; **turn on the** ∼ fam mettersi a piangere come una fontana
watery /'wɔːtərɪ/ *adj* acquoso; ‹*eyes*› lacrimoso
watt /wɒt/ *n* watt *m inv*
wattage /'wɒtɪdʒ/ *n* wattaggio *m*
⚘ **wave** /weɪv/ ① *n* onda *f*; (gesture) cenno *m*; fig ondata *f*
  ② *vt* agitare; ∼ **one's hand** agitare la mano
  ③ *vi* far segno; ‹*flag*› sventolare
■ **wave aside** *vt* respingere ‹*criticism*›
■ **wave down** *vt* far segno di fermarsi a ‹*vehicle*›
waveband /'weɪvbænd/ *n* gamma *f* d'onda
wave farm *n* centrale *f* per energia da moto ondoso
wavelength /'weɪvleŋθ/ *n* lunghezza *f* d'onda; **be on the same** ∼ fig essere sulla stessa lunghezza d'onda
waver /'weɪvə(r)/ *vi* vacillare; (hesitate) esitare
wavy /'weɪvɪ/ *adj* ondulato
wax /wæks/ *vi* ‹*moon*› crescere; fig (become) diventare
wax² ① *n* cera *f*; (in ear) cerume *m*
  ② *vt* dare la cera a
waxed jacket *n* cerata *f*
waxwork /'wækswɜːk/ *n* statua *f* di cera
waxworks /'wækswəks/ *n* museo *m* delle cere
waxy /'wæksɪ/ *adj* ‹*skin, texture*› cereo
⚘ **way** /weɪ/ ① *n* percorso *m*; (direction) direzione *f*; (manner, method) modo *m*; ∼**s** *pl* (customs) abitudini *fpl*; **be in the** ∼ essere in mezzo; **on the** ∼ **to Rome** andando a Roma; **I'll do it on the** ∼ lo faccio mentre vado; **it's on my** ∼ è sul mio percorso; **a long** ∼ **off** lontano; **this** ∼ da questa parte; (like this) così; **by the** ∼ a proposito; **by** ∼ **of** come; (via) via; **either** ∼ (whatever we do) in un modo ⋯‣

o nell'altro; **in some ~s** sotto certi aspetti; **in a ~** in un certo senso; **in a bad ~** ‹person› molto grave; **out of the ~** fuori mano; **under ~** in corso; **lead the ~** far strada; fig aprire la strada; **make ~** far posto (**for** a); **give ~** Auto dare la precedenza; **go out of one's ~** fig scomodarsi (**to** per); **get one's [own] ~** averla vinta
2 adv **~ behind** molto indietro

way in n entrata f

waylay /weɪˈleɪ/ vt (pt/pp **-laid**) aspettare al varco ‹person›; intercettare ‹letter›

way out n uscita f; fig via f d'uscita

way-out adj fam eccentrico

wayside /ˈweɪsaɪd/ n bordo m; **fall by the ~** (morally) smarrire la retta via; (fail) fallire

wayward /ˈweɪwəd/ adj capriccioso

WC abbr WC; **the WC** il gabinetto

✧ **we** /wiː/ pers pron noi; **we're the last** siamo gli ultimi; **they're going, but we're not** loro vanno, ma noi no

✧ **weak** /wiːk/ adj debole; ‹liquid› leggero; **go ~ at the knees** fam sentirsi piegare le ginocchia

weaken /ˈwiːkn/ **1** vt indebolire
2 vi indebolirsi

weakling /ˈwiːklɪŋ/ n smidollato, -a mf

weakly /ˈwiːklɪ/ adv debolmente

weak-minded /-ˈmaɪndɪd/ adj (indecisive) debole; (simple) poco intelligente

weakness /ˈwiːknɪs/ n debolezza f; (liking) debole m

weak-willed /-ˈwɪld/ adj debole

weal /wiːl/ n piaga f

wealth /welθ/ n ricchezza f; fig gran quantità f

wealthy /ˈwelθɪ/ adj (**-ier, -iest**) ricco

wean /wiːn/ vt svezzare

✧ **weapon** /ˈwepən/ n arma f

weapon of mass destruction n arma f di distruzione di massa

weaponry /ˈwepənrɪ/ n armamento m

✧ **wear** /weə(r)/ **1** n (clothing) abbigliamento m; **for everyday ~** da portare tutti i giorni; **~ [and tear]** usura f
2 vt (pt **wore**, pp **worn**) portare; (damage) consumare; **~ a hole in something** logorare qualcosa fino a fare un buco; **what shall I ~?** cosa mi metto?
3 vi consumarsi; (last) durare
■ **wear away 1** vt consumare
2 vi consumarsi
■ **wear down** vt estenuare ‹opposition etc›
■ **wear off** vi scomparire; ‹effect› finire
■ **wear out 1** vt consumare [fino in fondo]; (exhaust) estenuare
2 vi estenuarsi
■ **wear through** vi ‹elbow, knee, shoe› bucarsi

✧ indicates a very frequent word

wearable /ˈweərəbl/ adj portabile

wearily /ˈwɪərɪlɪ/ adv stancamente

weariness /ˈwɪərɪnɪs/ n stanchezza f

wearing /ˈweərɪŋ/ adj (tiring) faticoso; (irritating) fastidioso

weary /ˈwɪərɪ/ **1** adj (**-ier, -iest**) sfinito
2 vt (pt/pp **wearied**) sfinire
3 vi **~ of** stancarsi di

weasel /ˈwiːzl/ n donnola f

✧ **weather** /ˈweðə(r)/ **1** n tempo m; **in this ~** con questo tempo; **under the ~** fam giù di corda
2 vt sopravvivere a ‹storm›

weather balloon n pallone m sonda

weather-beaten /-biːtn/ adj ‹face› segnato dalle intemperie

weathercock n gallo m segnavento

weather forecast n previsioni fpl del tempo

weatherman n TV meteorologo m

weatherproof adj ‹garment, shoe› impermeabile; ‹shelter, door› resistente alle intemperie

weather-vane n banderuola f

weave¹ /wiːv/ vi (pt/pp **weaved**) (move) zigzagare

weave² **1** n Tex tessuto m
2 vt (pt **wove**, pp **woven**) tessere; intrecciare ‹flowers etc›; intrecciare le fila di ‹story etc›

weaver /ˈwiːvə(r)/ n tessitore, -trice mf

weaving /ˈwiːvɪŋ/ n tessitura f

✧ **web** /web/ n rete f; Comput web m, rete f; (of spider) ragnatela f

web-based /-beɪst/ adj ‹learning, software› basato sul web

webbed feet /webdˈfiːt/ npl piedi mpl palmati

webbing /ˈwebɪŋ/ n (material) cinghie fpl

web cam n Comput web cam f inv

web crawler /web ˌkrɔːlə(r)/ n software che analizza i contenuti di una rete in modo metodico e automatizzato

web developer n Comput sviluppatore m web

webinar /ˈwebmɑː(r)/ n seminario m via Internet

weblog /ˈweblɒg/ n Comput = BLOG

weblogger /ˈweblɒgə(r)/ n Comput = BLOGGER

webmaster n Comput webmaster mf inv

web page n Comput pagina f web

web presence n Comput presenza f in Internet

web server n Comput server m web

web site n Comput sito m web

web space n Comput spazio m web

wed /wed/ **1** vt (pt/pp **wedded**) sposare
2 vi sposarsi

wedding /'wedɪŋ/ n matrimonio m

wedding anniversary n anniversario m di nozze

wedding bells npl fig marcia f nuziale

wedding breakfast n rinfresco m di nozze

wedding cake n torta f nuziale

wedding day n giorno m del matrimonio

wedding dress n vestito m da sposa

wedding march n marcia f nuziale

wedding night n prima notte f di nozze

wedding reception n ricevimento m di nozze

wedding ring n fede f

wedding vows npl voti mpl nuziali

wedge /wedʒ/ ① n zeppa f; (for splitting wood) cuneo m; (of cheese) fetta f
② vt (fix) fissare

wedlock /'wedlɒk/ n **born out of** ∼ nato fuori dal matrimonio

✓ **Wednesday** /'wenzdeɪ/ n mercoledì m inv

wee¹ /wiː/ adj fam piccolo

wee² ① n fam **do a** ∼ fare la pipì
② vi fam fare la pipì

weed /wiːd/ ① n erbaccia f; fam (person) mollusco m
② vt estirpare le erbacce da
③ vi estirpare le erbacce

■ **weed out** vt fig eliminare

weedkiller /'wiːdkɪlə(r)/ n erbicida m

weedy /'wiːdɪ/ adj fam mingherlino

✓ **week** /wiːk/ n settimana f

weekday /'wiːkdeɪ/ n giorno m feriale

✓ **weekend** /'wiːkend/ n fine m settimana

weekend bag n piccola borsa f da viaggio

weekly /'wiːklɪ/ ① adj settimanale
② n settimanale m
③ adv settimanalmente

weep /wiːp/ vi (pt/pp **wept**) piangere

weeping willow /wiːpɪŋ'wɪləʊ/ n salice m piangente

weepy /'wiːpɪ/ adj ⟨film⟩ strappalacrime inv

weigh /weɪ/ vt/i pesare; ∼ **anchor** levare l'ancora

■ **weigh down** vt fig piegare

■ **weigh in** vi fam (join in discussion) intromettersi

■ **weigh out** vt pesare ⟨amount of flour etc⟩

■ **weigh up** vt fig soppesare; valutare ⟨person⟩

weighing machine /'weɪɪŋ/ n bilancia f

✓ **weight** /weɪt/ n peso m; **put on/lose** ∼ ingrassare/dimagrire

weighting /'weɪtɪŋ/ n (allowance) indennità f inv

weightlessness /'weɪtlɪsnɪs/ n assenza f di gravità

weightlifter n sollevatore m di pesi

weightlifting n sollevamento m pesi

weight problem n problemi mpl di peso

weight training n **do** ∼ allenarsi con i pesi

weight-watcher n (in group) persona (f) che segue una dieta dimagrante

weighty /'weɪtɪ/ adj (**-ier, -iest**) pesante; (important) di un certo peso

weir /wɪə(r)/ n chiusa f

weird /wɪəd/ adj misterioso; (bizarre) bizzarro

✓ **welcome** /'welkəm/ ① adj benvenuto; **you're** ∼! prego!; **you're** ∼ **to have it/to come** prendilo/vieni pure
② n accoglienza f
③ vt accogliere; (appreciate) gradire

welcoming /'welkəmɪŋ/ adj ⟨ceremony⟩ di benvenuto; ⟨committee, smile⟩ di accoglienza; ⟨house⟩ accogliente

weld /weld/ vt saldare

welder /'weldə(r)/ n saldatore m

welfare /'welfeə(r)/ n benessere m; (aid) assistenza f; Am previdenza f sociale

welfare services n servizi mpl sociali

Welfare State n Stato m assistenziale

welfare work n assistenza m sociale

✓ **well¹** /wel/ n pozzo m; (oil ∼) pozzo m; (of staircase) tromba f

✓ **well²** ① adv (**better, best**) bene; as ∼ anche; as ∼ as (in addition) oltre a; ∼ **done!** bravo!; **very** ∼ benissimo
② adj he is not ∼ non sta bene; **get** ∼ **soon!** guarisci presto!
③ int beh!; ∼ **I never!** ma va'!

well-attended /-ə'tendɪd/ adj ben frequentato

well-balanced /-'bælənst/ adj ⟨person, diet, meal⟩ equilibrato

well-behaved /-bɪ'heɪvd/ adj educato

well-being /'welbiːɪŋ/ n benessere m

well-bred /wel'bred/ adj beneducato

well-defined /-dɪ'faɪnd/ adj ⟨role, boundary⟩ ben definito; ⟨outline, image⟩ netto

well-disposed /-dɪ'spəʊzd/ adj benevolo; **be** ∼ **towards** essere bendisposto verso ⟨person⟩; essere favorevole a ⟨idea⟩

well done /dʌn/ adj ⟨task⟩ ben fatto; Culin ben cotto

well-educated adj istruito; (cultured) colto

well-founded /-'faʊndɪd/ adj fondato

well-heeled /-'hiːld/ adj fam danaroso

well-informed /-ɪn'fɔːmd/ adj beninformato

wellingtons /'welɪŋtənz/ npl stivali mpl di gomma

well-judged /-'dʒʌdʒd/ adj ⟨performance⟩ molto intelligente; ⟨shot⟩ ben assestato; ⟨statement, phrase⟩ ben ponderato

W

well-kept /-'kept/ adj ⟨garden⟩ curato; ⟨secret⟩ ben custodito

well-known /-'nəʊn/ adj famoso

well-liked /-'laɪkt/ adj popolare

well-made /-'meɪd/ adj benfatto

well-mannered /-'mænəd/ adj educato

well-meaning adj con buone intenzioni

well-meant /-'ment/ adj con le migliori intenzioni

well-nigh /'welnaɪ/ adv quasi

well-off adj benestante

well-read /-'red/ adj colto

well-respected /,welrɪ'spektɪd/ adj molto rispettato

well-rounded /,wel'raʊndɪd/ adj ⟨education, individual⟩ completo

well-spoken /-'spəʊkən/ adj ⟨person⟩ che parla bene

well-thought-of adj stimato

well-timed /,wel'taɪmd/ adj tempestivo

well-to-do adj ricco

well-trodden /-'trɒdn/ adj also fig battuto

well-wisher /'welwɪʃə(r)/ n simpatizzante mf

well-worn /-'wɔːn/ adj ⟨steps, floorboards⟩ consunto; ⟨carpet, garment⟩ logoro; fig ⟨argument⟩ trito e ritrito

Welsh /welʃ/ adj & n gallese mf; (language) gallese m; **the ~** pl i gallesi

Welshman /'welʃmən/ n gallese m

Welsh rabbit n toast m inv al formaggio

welt /welt/ n (on shoe) rinforzo m; (on skin) segno m di frustata

welterweight /'weltəweɪt/ n pesi mpl welter

went /went/ ▶ GO

wept /wept/ ▶ WEEP

were /wɜː(r)/ ▶ BE

ꝺ **west** /west/ ☐1 n ovest m; **to the ~ of a** ovest di; **the W~** l'Occidente m
☐2 adj occidentale
☐3 adv verso occidente; **go ~** fam andare in malora

West Bank n Cisgiordania f

West Country n sud-ovest m dell'Inghilterra

West End n zona (f) di Londra con un'alta concentrazione di teatri e negozi di lusso

westerly /'westəlɪ/ adj verso ovest; ⟨wind⟩ occidentale

western /'westən/ ☐1 adj occidentale
☐2 n western m inv

Westerner /'westənə(r)/ n occidentale mf

westernize /'westənaɪz/ vt occidentalizzare; **become ~d** occidentalizzarsi

Western Samoa n Samoa fpl Occidentali

West Germany n Germania f occidentale

West Indian adj & n antillese mf

West Indies /'ɪndɪz/ npl Antille fpl

westwards Br, **westward** Am /'westwəd[z]/ adv verso ovest

wet /wet/ ☐1 adj (**-tter**, **-test**) bagnato; ⟨paint⟩ fresco; (rainy) piovoso; fam ⟨person⟩ smidollato; **get ~** bagnarsi
☐2 vt (pt/pp **wet**, **wetted**) bagnare

wet blanket n guastafeste mf inv

wet fish n Br pesce m fresco

wet-look adj ⟨plastic, leather⟩ lucido

wet-nurse n balia f

wetsuit n muta f

whack /wæk/ ☐1 n fam colpo m
☐2 vt fam dare un colpo a

whacked /wæk/ adj fam stanco morto

whacking /'wækɪŋ/ ☐1 adj Br fam (enormous) enorme
☐2 n fam sculacciata f

whacky /'wækɪ/ adj fam ⟨joke, person etc⟩ demenziale

whale /weɪl/ n balena f; **have a ~ of a time** fam divertirsi un sacco

whaling /'weɪlɪŋ, US 'hweɪlɪŋ/ n caccia f alla balena

wham /wæm/ int bum!

wharf /wɔːf/ n banchina f

ꝺ **what** /wɒt/ ☐1 pron che, [che] cosa; **~ for?** perché?; **~ is that for?** a che cosa serve?; **~ is it?** (what do you want) cosa c'è?; **~ is it like?** com'è?; **~ is your name?** come ti chiami?; **~ is the weather like?** com'è il tempo?; **~ is the film about?** di cosa parla il film?; **~ is he talking about?** di cosa sta parlando?; **he asked me ~ she had said** mi ha chiesto cosa ha detto; **~ about going to the cinema?** e se andassimo al cinema?; **~ about the children?** (what will they do) e i bambini?; **~ if it rains?** e se piove?
☐2 adj quale, che; **take ~ books you want** prendi tutti i libri che vuoi; **~ kind of a** che tipo di; **at ~ time?** a che ora?
☐3 adv che; **~ a lovely day!** che bella giornata!
☐4 int **~** ! [che] cosa!; **~ ?** [che] cosa?

what-d'yer-call-it /'wɒtdʒəkɔːlɪt/ n fam aggeggio m

ꝺ **whatever** /wɒt'evə(r)/ ☐1 adj qualunque
☐2 pron qualsiasi cosa; **~ is it?** cos'è?; **~ he does** qualsiasi cosa faccia; **~ happens** qualunque cosa succeda; **nothing ~** proprio niente

whatnot /'wɒtnɒt/ n coso m; (stand) scaffaletto m; **and ~** (and so on) e così via

what's-her-name /'wɒtzəneɪm/ n fam cosa f

what's-his-name /'wɒtsɪzneɪm/ *n*, fam coso *m*

whatsit /'wɒtsɪt/ *n* fam aggeggio *m*, coso *m*

what's-its-name *n* fam coso, -a *mf*

whatsoever /wɒtsəʊ'evə(r)/ *adj & pron* = WHATEVER

wheat /wi:t/ *n* grano *m*, frumento *m*

wheatgerm /'wi:tdʒɜ:m/ *n* germoglio *m* di grano

wheatmeal /'wi:tmi:l/ *n* farina *f* di frumento

wheedle /'wi:dl/ *vt* ~ something out of somebody ottenere qualcosa da qualcuno con le lusinghe

wheel /wi:l/ [1] *n* ruota *f*; (steering ~) volante *m*; at the ~ al volante
[2] *vt* (push) spingere
[3] *vi* (circle) ruotare; ~ round ruotare

wheelbarrow *n* carriola *f*

wheelchair *n* sedia *f* a rotelle

wheelchair access *n* accesso *m* disabili

wheelchair-accessible *adj* accessibile alle carrozzelle, accessibile alle sedie a rotelle

wheel clamp *n* ceppo *m* bloccaruote

wheeler-dealer /wi:lə'di:lə(r)/ *n* trafficone, -a *mf*

wheelie bin *n* cassonetto *m*

wheeze /wi:z/ *vi* ansimare

wheezy /'wi:zɪ/ *adj* ‹voice, cough› dal respiro affannato

when /wen/ *adv & conj* quando; the day ~ il giorno in cui; ~ swimming/reading nuotando/leggendo

whence /wens/ *adv* liter donde

whenever /wen'evə(r)/ *adv & conj* in qualsiasi momento; (every time that) ogni volta che; ~ did it happen? quando è successo?

where /weə(r)/ *adv & conj* dove; the street ~ I live la via in cui abito; ~ do you come from? da dove vieni?

whereabouts /weərə'baʊts/ *adv* dove

whereabouts² /'weərəbaʊts/ *n* nobody knows his ~ nessuno sa dove si trovi

whereas /weər'æz/ *conj* dal momento che; (in contrast) mentre

whereby /weə'baɪ/ *adv* attraverso il quale

whereupon /weərə'pɒn/ *adv* dopo di che

wherever /weər'evə(r)/ *adv & conj* dovunque; ~ is he? dov'è mai?; ~ possible dovunque sia possibile

wherewithal /'weəwɪðɔ:l/ *n* mezzi *mpl*

whet /wet/ *vt* (*pt/pp* **whetted**) aguzzare ‹appetite›

whether /'weðə(r)/ *conj* se; ~ you like it or not che ti piaccia o no

whew /fju:/ *int* (in relief) fiuu; (when hot) uff; (in surprise) wow

which /wɪtʃ/ [1] *adj & pron* quale; ~ one? quale?; ~ one of you? chi di voi?; ~ way? (direction) in che direzione?
[2] *rel pron* (object) che; ~ he does frequently cosa che fa spesso; after ~ dopo di che; on/in ~ su/in cui

whichever /wɪtʃ'evə(r)/ *adj & pron* qualunque; ~ it is qualunque sia; ~ one of you chiunque tra voi

whiff /wɪf/ *n* zaffata *f*; have a ~ of something odorare qualcosa

while /waɪl/ [1] *n* a long ~ un bel po'; a little ~ un po'
[2] *conj* mentre; (as long as) finché; (although) sebbene; he met her ~ in exile l'ha incontrata mentre era in esilio
■ **while away** *vt* passare ‹time›

whilst /waɪlst/ *conj* = WHILE

whim /wɪm/ *n* capriccio *m*

whimper /'wɪmpə(r)/ *vi* piagnucolare; ‹dog› mugolare

whimsical /'wɪmzɪkl/ *adj* capriccioso; ‹story› fantasioso

whine /waɪn/ [1] *n* lamento *m*; (of dog) guaito *m*
[2] *vi* lamentarsi; ‹dog› guaire

whinge /wɪndʒ/ *vi* fam lagnarsi

whining /'waɪnɪŋ, US 'hwaɪn-/ [1] *adj* ‹voice, child› lagnoso
[2] *n* (complaints) lagne *fpl*; (of dog) guaiti *mpl*

whinny /'wɪnɪ/ [1] *n* nitrito *m*
[2] *vi* ‹horse› nitrire

whip /wɪp/ [1] *n* frusta *f*; Pol (person) parlamentare (*mf*) incaricato, -a di assicurarsi della presenza dei membri del suo partito alle votazioni
[2] *vt* (*pt/pp* **whipped**) frustare; Culin sbattere; (snatch) afferrare; fam (steal) fregare
■ **whip up** *vt* (incite) stimolare; fam improvvisare ‹meal›

whiplash injury /'wɪplæʃ/ *n* Med colpo *m* di frusta

whipped cream /wɪpt'kri:m/ *n* panna *f* montata

whipping boy /'wɪpɪŋ/ *n* capro *m* espiatorio

whip-round *n* fam colletta *f*; have a ~ fare una colletta

whirl /wɜ:l/ [1] *n* (movement) rotazione *f*; my mind's in a ~ ho le idee confuse
[2] *vi* girare rapidamente
[3] *vt* far girare rapidamente

whirlpool /'wɜ:lpu:l/ *n* vortice *m*

whirlpool bath *n* vasca *f* con idromassaggio

whirlwind /'wɜ:lwɪnd/ *n* turbine *m*

whirr /wɜ:(r)/ *vi* ronzare

whisk /wɪsk/ [1] *n* Culin frullino *m*
[2] *vt* Culin frullare
■ **whisk away** *vt* portare via

W

whisker /'wɪskə(r)/ n ∼s pl (of cat) baffi mpl; (on man's cheek) basette fpl; **by a ∼** per un pelo

whisky /'wɪskɪ/ n whisky m inv

🖋 **whisper** /'wɪspə(r)/ ⓵ n sussurro m; (rumour) diceria f
⓶ vt/i sussurrare

whispering gallery /'wɪspərɪŋ/ n galleria f acustica

whistle /'wɪsl/ ⓵ n fischio m; (instrument) fischietto m
⓶ vt fischiettare
⓷ vi fischiettare; ‹referee› fischiare

whistle-stop tour n Pol giro m elettorale

🖋 **white** /waɪt/ ⓵ adj bianco; **go ∼** (pale) sbiancare
⓶ n bianco m; (of egg) albume m; (person) bianco, -a mf

whitebait n bianchetti npl

white-board n lavagna f bianca

white coffee n caffè m inv macchiato

white-collar worker n colletto m bianco

white elephant n (public project) progetto m dispendioso e di scarsa efficacia; (building) cattedrale f nel deserto; (item, knick-knack) oggetto m inutile

white goods n (linen) biancheria f per la casa; (appliances) elettrodomestici mpl

Whitehall n strada (f) di Londra sede degli uffici del governo britannico; fig amministrazione f britannica

white horses npl cavalloni mpl

white-hot adj ‹metal› arroventato

White House n **the ∼** la Casa Bianca

white knight n Fin white knight m inv

white-knuckle ride n corsa f al cardiopalmo

white lie n bugia f pietosa

whiten /'waɪtn/ ⓵ vt imbiancare
⓶ vi sbiancare

whitener /'waɪt(ə)nə(r)/ n (for shoes) bianchetto m; (for clothes) sbiancante m; (for coffee, tea) surrogato m del latte

whiteness /'waɪtnɪs/ n bianchezza f

white spirit n acquaragia f

white tie n (tie) cravattino m bianco; (formal dress) frac m inv

whitewash ⓵ n intonaco m; fig copertura f
⓶ vt dare una mano d'intonaco a; fig coprire

white water n rapide fpl

white-water rafting n discesa f sulle rapide

white wedding n matrimonio m in bianco

whither /'wɪðə(r)/ adv liter dove

🖋 indicates a very frequent word

whiting /'waɪtɪŋ/ n (fish) merlano m

Whitsun /'wɪtsn/ n Pentecoste f

Whit Sunday n Pentecoste f

whittle /'wɪtl/ v
■ **whittle away** vt intaccare ‹savings›; ridurre ‹lead in race›
■ **whittle down** vt ridurre

whiz[z] /wɪz/ vi (pt/pp **whizzed**) sibilare

whiz[z]-kid n fam giovane m prodigio

🖋 **who** /huː/ ⓵ inter pron chi
⓶ rel che; **the children, ∼ were all tired, …** i bambini che erano tutti stanchi,…

WHO n abbr (**World Health Organization**) OMS f

whodunnit /huːˈdʌnɪt/ n fam [romanzo m, giallo m

whoever /huːˈevə(r)/ pron chiunque; **∼ he is** chiunque sia; **∼ can that be?** chi può mai essere?

🖋 **whole** /həʊl/ ⓵ adj tutto; (not broken) intatto; **the ∼ truth** tutta la verità; **the ∼ world** il mondo intero; **the ∼ lot** (everything) tutto; **the ∼ lot of you** tutti voi
⓶ n tutto m; **as a ∼** nell'insieme; **on the ∼** tutto considerato; **the ∼ of Italy** tutta l'Italia

wholefood n cibo m macrobiotico

wholehearted /'həʊlhɑːtɪd/ adj di tutto cuore

wholeheartedly /həʊl'hɑːtɪdlɪ/ adv ‹agree, support› senza riserve

wholemeal adj integrale

whole milk n latte m intero

whole number n numero m intero

wholesale /'həʊlseɪl/ adj & adv all'ingrosso; fig in massa

wholesaler /'həʊlseɪlə(r)/ n grossista mf

wholesome /'həʊlsəm/ adj sano

wholewheat adj = WHOLEMEAL

wholly /'həʊlɪ/ adv completamente

wholly-owned subsidiary n consociata f interamente controllata

🖋 **whom** /huːm/ ⓵ rel pron che; **the man ∼ I saw** l'uomo che ho visto; **to/with ∼** a/con cui
⓶ inter pron chi; **to ∼ did you speak?** con chi hai parlato?

whoop /wuːp/ ⓵ n (shout) grido m
⓶ vi gridare

whoopee /'wʊpɪ/ ⓵ int evviva!
⓶ n hum **make ∼** (have fun) fare baldoria; (make love) fare l'amore

whooping cough /'huːpɪŋ/ n pertosse f

whoosh /wʊʃ/ int vuum!

whopper /'wɒpə(r)/ n fam (lie) balla f; **what a ∼!** è veramente gigantesco!

whopping /'wɒpɪŋ/ adj fam enorme

whore /hɔː(r)/ n puttana f vulg

whorl /wɔːl/ n (of cream, chocolate etc) ghirigoro m; (of fingerprint) spirale f

🖋 **whose** /huːz/ ⓵ rel pron il cui; **people ∼ name begins with D** le persone i cui nomi

w

cominciano con la D

2 *inter pron* di chi; ~ **is that?** di chi è quello?

3 *adj* ~ **car did you use?** di chi è la macchina che hai usato?

Who's Who *n* pubblicazione (*f*) annuale con l'elenco delle personalità di spicco

⚘ **why** /waɪ/ **1** *adv* (inter) perché; **the reason** ~ la ragione per cui; **that's** ~ per questo

2 *int* diamine!

WI *abbr* **1** (**Women's Institute**) associazione (*f*) femminile che organizza attività culturali e sociali

2 Am (**Wisconsin**)

wick /wɪk/ *n* stoppino *m*

wicked /'wɪkɪd/ *adj* cattivo; (mischievous) malizioso

wicker /'wɪkə(r)/ **1** *n* vimini *mpl*

2 *attrib* di vimini

wicket /'wɪkɪt/ *n* (field gate) cancelletto *m*; Sport porta *f*; Am (of ticket office etc) sportello *m*; **be on a sticky** ~ fam essere in una situazione difficile

⚘ **wide** /waɪd/ **1** *adj* largo; ‹experience, knowledge› vasto; ‹difference› profondo; (far from target) lontano; **10 cm** ~ largo 10 cm; **how** ~ **is it?** quanto è largo?

2 *adv* (off target) lontano dal bersaglio; ~ **awake** del tutto sveglio; ~ **open** spalancato; **open** ~! apri bene!; **far and** ~ in lungo e in largo

wide-angle lens *n* grandangolo *m*

wide-eyed /-'aɪd/ *adj* ‹person, innocence› ingenuo; (with fear, surprise) con gli occhi sbarrati

⚘ **widely** /'waɪdlɪ/ *adv* largamente; ‹known, accepted› generalmente; ‹different› profondamente

widely read *adj* ‹student› colto; ‹writer› molto letto

widen /'waɪdn/ **1** *vt* allargare; ~ **the gap** fig accentuare il contrasto

2 *vi* allargarsi

widening /'waɪdnɪŋ/ *adj* ‹gap, division› sempre più grande

wide open *adj* ‹door, window, eyes› spalancato

wide-ranging /ˌwaɪd'reɪndʒɪŋ/ *adj* ‹interests, reforms, discussion› di ampio respiro

wide screen *n* Cinema schermo *m* panoramico

wide-screen TV *n* televisore *m* con schermo panoramico

widespread /'waɪdspred/ *adj* diffuso

widow /'wɪdəʊ/ *n* vedova *f*

widowed /'wɪdəʊd/ *adj* vedovo

widower /'wɪdəʊə(r)/ *n* vedovo *m*

width /wɪdθ/ *n* larghezza *f*; (of material) altezza *f*

widthways Br /'wɪdθweɪz/, **widthwise** Am /'wɪdθwaɪz/ *adv* trasversalmente

wield /wi:ld/ *vt* maneggiare; esercitare ‹power›

⚘ **wife** /waɪf/ *n* (*pl* **wives**) moglie *f*

wife battering /'waɪfbæt(ə)rɪŋ/ *n* maltrattamento *m* della coniuge

Wi-Fi® /'waɪfaɪ/ *n abbr* (**wireless fidelity**) Wi-Fi *m*

wig /wɪg/ *n* parrucca *f*

wiggle /'wɪgl/ **1** *vi* dimenarsi

2 *vt* dimenare

wiki /'wɪkɪ/ *n* sito web aggiornato dai suoi utilizzatori

⚘ **wild** /waɪld/ **1** *adj* selvaggio; ‹animal, flower› selvatico; (furious) furibondo; ‹applause› fragoroso; ‹idea› folle; (with joy) pazzo; ‹guess› azzardato; **be** ~ **about** (keen on) andare pazzo per

2 *adv* **run** ~ crescere senza controllo

3 *n* **in the** ~ allo stato naturale; **the** ~**s** *pl* le zone sperdute

wild boar *n* cinghiale *m*

wild card *n* jolly *m inv*; Comput carattere *m* jolly

wildcat strike *n* sciopero *m* selvaggio

wild dog *n* cane *m* randagio

wilderness /'wɪldənɪs/ *n* deserto *m*; fig (garden) giungla *f*

wild-eyed /-'aɪd/ *adj* (distressed) dall'aria angosciata; (angry) dallo sguardo minaccioso

wildfire *n* **spread like** ~ allargarsi a macchia d'olio

wild flower *n* fiore *m* di campo

wildfowl *n* (bird) uccello *m* selvatico; (birds collectively) uccelli *mpl* selvatici; (game) selvaggina *f* di penna

wild-goose chase *n* ricerca *f* inutile

wildlife *n* animali *mpl* selvatici

wildlife park *n* parco *m* naturale

wildlife reserve *n* riserva *f* naturale

wildlife sanctuary *n* riserva *f* naturale

wildly /'waɪldlɪ/ *adv* fig ‹exaggerated› estremamente; ‹speak› senza riflettere; ‹applaud› fragorosamente; ‹hit out› all'impazzata

Wild West *n* il far west *m*

wiles /waɪlz/ *npl* astuzie *fpl*

wilful /'wɪlfʊl/ *adj* intenzionale; ‹person, refusal› ostinato

wilfully /'wɪlfʊlɪ/ *adv* intenzionalmente; ‹refuse› ostinatamente

⚘ **will**[1] /wɪl/ *v aux* he ~ **arrive tomorrow** arriverà domani; **I won't tell him** non glielo dirò; **you** ~ **be back soon, won't you?** tornerai presto, no?; **he** ~ **be there, won't he?** sarà là, no?; **she** ~ **be there by now** sarà là ormai; ~ **you go?** (do you intend to go) pensi di andare?; ~ **you go to the baker's and buy…?** puoi andare dal fornaio a comprare…?; ~ **you be quiet!** vuoi stare calmo!; ~ **you have some wine?** vuoi del ⋯⟶

vino?; **the engine won't start** la macchina non parte

✓ **will²** n volontà f inv; (document) testamento m

✓ **willing** /'wɪlɪŋ/ adj disposto; (eager) volonteroso

willingly /'wɪlɪŋlɪ/ adv volentieri

willingness /'wɪlɪŋnɪs/ n buona volontà f

willow /'wɪləʊ/ n salice m

willowy /'wɪləʊɪ/ adj ⟨person, figure⟩ slanciato

will-power n forza f di volontà

willy-nilly /wɪlɪ'nɪlɪ/ adv (at random) a casaccio; (wanting to or not) volente o nolente

wilt /wɪlt/ vi appassire

wily /'waɪlɪ/ adj (-ier, -iest) astuto

wimp /wɪmp/ n rammollito, -a mf

wimpish /'wɪmpɪʃ/ adj fam ⟨behaviour⟩ da rammollito

wimpy /'wɪmpɪ/ adj fam ⟨person⟩ rammollito

✓ **win** /wɪn/ ① n vittoria f; **have a ~** riportare una vittoria
② vt (pt/pp **won**, pres p **winning**) vincere; conquistare ⟨fame⟩
③ vi vincere
■ **win back** vt recuperare
■ **win over** vt convincere
■ **win through** vi fam (be successful) uscire vittorioso

wince /wɪns/ vi contrarre il viso

winch /wɪntʃ/ n argano m
■ **winch up** vt tirare con l'argano

✓ **wind¹** /wɪnd/ ① n vento m; (breath) fiato m; fam (flatulence) aria f; **get/have the ~ up** fam aver fifa; **get ~ of** aver sentore di; **in the ~** nell'aria
② vt **~ somebody** lasciare qualcuno senza fiato; **~ a baby** far fare il ruttino ad un neonato

wind² /waɪnd/ ① vt (pt/pp **wound**) (wrap) avvolgere; (move by turning) far girare; ⟨clock⟩ caricare
② vi ⟨road⟩ serpeggiare
■ **wind down** ① vi (relax) rilassarsi; (gradually come to an end) diminuire
② vt (gradually bring to an end) metter fine in modo graduale a
■ **wind up** ① vt caricare ⟨clock⟩; concludere ⟨proceedings⟩; fam sfottere ⟨somebody⟩
② vi (end up) **~ up doing something** finire per fare qualcosa

windbreak n frangivento m

windcheater n Br giacca f a vento

windchill factor n fattore m di raffreddamento da vento

wind chimes npl campane fpl eoliche

wind energy n forza f del vento

winder /'waɪndə(r)/ n (for car window) manovella f alzacristalli; (for watch) bottone m di carica

W

windfall n fig fortuna f inaspettata; **~s** pl (fruit) frutta f abbattuta dal vento

winding /'waɪndɪŋ/ adj tortuoso

wind instrument /'wɪnd/ n strumento m a fiato

windmill /'wɪn(d)mɪl/ n mulino m a vento

✓ **window** /'wɪndəʊ/ n finestra f; (of car) finestrino m; (of shop) vetrina f

window box n cassetta f per i fiori

window cleaner n (person) lavavetri mf inv

window display n Comm esposizione f in vetrina

window dresser n vetrinista mf

window dressing n vetrinistica f; fig fumo m negli occhi

window envelope n busta f a finestra

window frame n telaio m di finestra

window ledge n davanzale m

window pane n vetro m

window seat n (in room) panca f sotto la finestra; (in plane, train) posto m accanto al finestrino

window-shopping n **go ~** andare in giro a vedere le vetrine

window sill n davanzale m

windpipe n trachea f

windpower n energia f eolica

windscreen n parabrezza m inv

windscreen washer n getto m d'acqua

windscreen-wiper n tergicristallo m

windshield n Am parabrezza m inv

wind-sleeve n manica f a vento

wind-sock n manica f a vento

windsurf vi fare windsurf

windsurfer n (person) windsurfista mf; (board) windsurf m inv

windsurfing n windsurf m inv

windswept adj esposto al vento; ⟨person⟩ scompigliato

windy /'wɪndɪ/ adj (-ier, -iest) ventoso

✓ **wine** /waɪn/ n vino m

wine bar n ≈ enoteca f

wine box n contenitore m di vino con rubinetto

wine cellar n cantina f

wine cooler n (ice bucket) secchiello m del ghiaccio; Am (drink) bibita (f) leggermente alcolica

wineglass n bicchiere m da vino

wine grower n viticultore, -trice mf

wine growing n viticultura f

wine list n carta f dei vini

wine merchant n commerciante mf di vini

wine producer n produttore, -trice mf di vini

wine rack n portabottiglie m inv

winery /'waɪnərɪ/ n Am vigneto m

wine tasting /'waɪnteɪstɪŋ/ n degustazione f di vini

wine vinegar n aceto m di vino

wine waiter n sommelier m inv

⚬⸍ **wing** /wɪŋ/ n ala f; Auto parafango m; ∼**s** pl Theat quinte fpl; **under sb's** ∼ sotto l'ala [protettiva] di qualcuno

wing chair n poltrona f con ampio schienale

wing collar n colletto m rigido

wing commander n tenente m colonnello delle forze aeree

winger /'wɪŋə(r)/ n Sport ala f

wing-half n (in soccer) mediano m

wing mirror n Br specchietto m laterale

wing nut n dado m ad alette

wingspan n apertura f alare

wlnk /wɪŋk/ [1] n strizzata f d'occhio; **not sleep a** ∼ non chiudere occhio
  [2] vi strizzare l'occhio; ‹light› lampeggiare

⚬⸍ **winner** /'wɪnə(r)/ n vincitore, -trice mf

winning /'wɪnɪŋ/ adj vincente; ‹smile› accattivante

winning post n linea f d'arrivo

winnings /'wɪnɪŋz/ npl vincite fpl

winning streak n periodo m fortunato; **be on a** ∼ essere in un periodo fortunato

winsome /'wɪnsəm/ adj accattivante

⚬⸍ **winter** /'wɪntə(r)/ n inverno m

winter sports npl sport mpl invernali

wintertime /'wɪntətaɪm/ n inverno m

wintry /'wɪntrɪ/ adj invernale

wipe /waɪp/ [1] n passata f; (to dry) asciugata f
  [2] vt strofinare; (dry) asciugare
  ■ **wipe away** vt asciugare ‹tears, sweat›; pulire ‹dirt, mark›
  ■ **wipe off** vt asciugare; (erase) cancellare
  ■ **wipe out** vt annientare; eliminare ‹village›; estinguere ‹debt›
  ■ **wipe up** vt asciugare ‹dishes›

wipe-clean adj ‹surface, cover› facile da pulire

wiper blade /'waɪpə/ n Auto bordo m gommato del tergicristallo

wire /'waɪə(r)/ n fil m di ferro; (electrical) filo m elettrico

wire brush n spazzola f metallica

wire-cutters npl tronchese msg

wire-haired /-'heəd/ adj dal pelo ispido

wireless /'waɪəlɪs/ [1] n Br Hist radio f inv
  [2] adj Techn wireless

wire mesh n rete f metallica

wire netting n rete f metallica

wire wool n lana f d'acciaio

wiring /'waɪərɪŋ/ n impianto m elettrico

wiry /'waɪərɪ/ adj (**-ier, -iest**) ‹person› dal fisico asciutto; ‹hair› ispido

wisdom /'wɪzdəm/ n saggezza f; (of action) sensatezza f

wisdom tooth n dente m del giudizio

wise /waɪz/ adj saggio; (prudent) sensato
  ■ **wise up** fam [1] vi (become more aware) aprire gli occhi
  [2] vt aprire gli occhi a (**to** su)

wisecrack /'waɪzkræk/ fam [1] n battuta f salace
  [2] vi far battute salaci

wise guy n fam sapientone m

wisely /'waɪzlɪ/ adv saggiamente; ‹act› sensatamente

Wise Men npl Re Magi mpl

⚬⸍ **wish** /wɪʃ/ [1] n desiderio m; **make a** ∼ esprimere un desiderio; **with best** ∼**es** con i migliori auguri
  [2] vt desiderare; ∼ **somebody well** fare tanti auguri a qualcuno; **I** ∼ **you every success** ti auguro buona fortuna; **I** ∼ **you could stay** vorrei che tu potessi rimanere; ∼ **something on somebody** fam sbolognare qualcosa a qualcuno
  [3] vi ∼ **for something** desiderare qualcosa

wishbone /'wɪʃbəʊn/ n forcella f (di pollo o tacchino)

wishful /'wɪʃfʊl/ adj ∼ **thinking** illusione f

wishy-washy /'wɪʃɪwɒʃɪ/ adj ‹colour› spento; ‹personality› insignificante

wisp /wɪsp/ n (of hair) ciocca f; (of smoke) filo m; (of grass) ciuffo m

wispy /'wɪspɪ/ adj ‹hair, beard› a ciocche; ‹clouds› vaporoso

wlsteria /wɪs'tɪərɪə/ n glicine m

wistful /'wɪstfʊl/ adj malinconico

wistfully /'wɪstfʊlɪ/ adv malinconicamente

wit /wɪt/ n spirito m; (person) persona f di spirito; **be at one's** ∼**s' end** non saper che pesci pigliare; **scared out of one's** ∼**s** spaventato a morte

witch /wɪtʃ/ n strega f

witchcraft n magia f

witch doctor n stregone m

witch-hunt n caccia f alle streghe

⚬⸍ **with** /wɪð/ prep con; (fear, cold, jealousy etc) di; **I'm not** ∼ **you** fam non ti seguo; **can I leave it** ∼ **you?** (task) puoi occupartene tu?; ∼ **no regrets/money** senza rimpianti/soldi; **be** ∼ **it** fam essere al passo coi tempi; (alert) essere concentrato

withdraw /wɪð'drɔː/ [1] vt (pt **-drew**, pp **-drawn**) ritirare; prelevare ‹money›
  [2] vi ritirarsi

withdrawal /wɪð'drɔː(ə)l/ n ritiro m; (of money) prelevamento m; (from drugs) crisi f inv di astinenza; Psych chiusura f in se stessi

withdrawal symptoms npl sintomi mpl da crisi di astinenza

withdrawn /wɪð'drɔːn/ [1] ▶ WITHDRAW
  [2] adj ‹person› chiuso in se stesso

W

wither /'wɪðə(r)/ *vi* ‹flower› appassire
withering /'wɪðərɪŋ/ *adj* ‹look› fulminante
withhold /wɪð'həʊld/ *vt* (*pt/pp* **-held**)
rifiutare ‹consent› (from a); nascondere
‹information› (from a); trattenere ‹smile›
✓ **within** /wɪð'ɪn/ **1** *prep* in; (before the end of)
entro; ~ **the law** legale
2 *adv* all'interno
✓ **without** /wɪð'aʊt/ *prep* senza; ~ **stopping**
senza fermarsi; **how could it have happened**
~ **you noticing it?** come è potuto succedere
senza che tu lo notassi?
withstand /wɪð'stænd/ *vt* (*pt/pp* **-stood**)
resistere a
✓ **witness** /'wɪtnɪs/ **1** *n* testimone *mf*; **bear**
~ portare testimonianza
2 *vt* ≈ autenticare ‹signature›; essere
testimone di ‹accident›
witness box, Am **witness-stand** *n*
banco *m* dei testimoni
witticism /'wɪtɪsɪzm/ *n* spiritosaggine *f*
wittingly /'wɪtɪŋlɪ/ *adv* consapevolmente
witty /'wɪtɪ/ *adj* (**-ier**, **-iest**) spiritoso
wives /waɪvz/ ▶ WIFE
wizard /'wɪzəd/ *n* mago *m*
wizardry /'wɪzədrɪ/ *n* stregoneria *f*
wizened /'wɪznd/ *adj* raggrinzito
wk *abbr* (**week**) settimana *f*
WMD *n abbr* (**weapon of mass**
destruction) ADM *fpl*
wobble /'wɒbl/ *vi* traballare
wobbly /'wɒblɪ/ *adj* traballante
wodge /wɒdʒ/ *n* fam mucchio *m*
woe /wəʊ/ *n* afflizione *f*; ~ **is me!** me
meschino!
woeful /'wəʊfʊl/ *adj* ‹story, sight› triste;
‹lack› vergognoso
woke, woken /wəʊk, 'wəʊkn/ ▶ WAKE¹
wolf /wʊlf/ **1** *n* (*pl* **wolves** /wʊlvz/) lupo
m; fam (womanizer) donnaiolo *m*
2 *vt* ~ **[down]** divorare
wolf cub *n* cucciolo *m* di lupo
wolfhound *n* Br cane *m* lupo
wolf whistle **1** *n* fischio *m*
2 *vi* ~**-whistle at somebody** fischiare
dietro a qualcuno
✓ **woman** /'wʊmən/ *n* (*pl* **women**) donna *f*
womanizer /'wʊmənaɪzə(r)/ *n* donnaiolo
m
womanly /'wʊmənlɪ/ *adj* femminile
womb /wuːm/ *n* utero *m*
women /'wɪmɪn/ ▶ WOMAN
Women's Institute *n associazione* (*f*)
che si occupa dei problemi delle donne
Women's Libber /wɪmɪnz'lɪbə(r)/ *n*
femminista *f*
Women's Liberation *n* movimento *m*
femminista

women's movement *n* movimento *m*
per l'emancipazione della donna
women's refuge *n* casa *f* rifugio *inv*
women's studies *npl* storia (*f*)
dell'emancipazione femminile
won /wʌn/ ▶ WIN
✓ **wonder** /'wʌndə(r)/ **1** *n* meraviglia
f; (surprise) stupore *m*; **no** ~**!** non c'è da
stupirsi!; **it's a** ~ **that…** è incredibile che…
2 *vi* restare in ammirazione; (be surprised)
essere sorpreso; **I** ~ è quello che mi chiedo;
I ~ **whether she is ill** mi chiedo se è malata
✓ **wonderful** /'wʌndəfʊl/ *adj* meraviglioso
wonderfully /'wʌndəfʊlɪ/ *adv*
meravigliosamente
wonderland /'wʌndəlænd/ *n* paese *m*
delle meraviglie
wonky /'wɒŋkɪ/ *adj* Br fam (faulty) difettoso;
‹furniture› traballante; (crooked) storto
wont /wəʊnt/ **1** *n* **as was his** ~ come suo
solito
2 *adj* **he was** ~ **to fall asleep** era solito
addormentarsi
won't /wəʊnt/ *will not*
woo /wuː/ *vt* corteggiare; fig cercare di
accattivarsi ‹voters›; cercare di ottenere
‹fame, fortune›
✓ **wood** /wʊd/ *n* legno *m*; (for burning) legna
f; (forest) bosco *m*; **out of the** ~ fig fuori
pericolo; **touch** ~**!** tocca ferro!
woodcarving /'wʊdkɑːvɪŋ/ *n* scultura *f*
di legno
wooded /'wʊdɪd/ *adj* boscoso
wooden /'wʊdn/ *adj* di legno; fig legnoso
wooden horse *n* cavallo *m* di Troia
wooden spoon *n* mestolo *m* di legno; fig
premio *m* di consolazione
woodland /'wʊdlənd/ *n* terreno *m*
boschivo
woodlouse *n* onisco *m*
wood-pecker *n* picchio *m*
wood pigeon *n* colombaccio *m*
wood shavings *npl* trucioli *mpl*
woodshed *n* legnaia *f*
wood stove *n* stufa *f* a legna
woodwind *n* strumenti *mpl* a fiato
woodwork *n* (wooden parts) parti *fpl* in
legno; (craft) falegnameria *f*
woodworm *n* tarlo *m*
woody /'wʊdɪ/ *adj* legnoso; ‹hill› boscoso
wool /wʊl/ **1** *n* lana *f*; **pull the** ~ **over sb's**
eyes gettar fumo negli occhi a qualcuno
2 *attrib* di lana
woollen /'wʊlən/ *adj* di lana
woollens /'wʊlənz/ *npl* capi *mpl* di lana
woolly /'wʊlɪ/ *adj* (**-ier**, **-iest**) ‹sweater› di
lana; fig confuso
woozy /'wuːzɪ/ *adj* intontito

✓ indicates a very frequent word

word /wɜːd/ n parola f; (news) notizia f; **by ~ of mouth** a viva voce; **have a ~ with** dire due parole a; **have ~s** bisticciare; **in other ~s** in altre parole; **go back on one's ~** rimangiarsi la parola

word-for-word ① adj ‹translation› letterale
② adv parola per parola

wording /'wɜːdɪŋ/ n parole fpl

word-perfect adj che sa a memoria

word processing n Comput word processing m, elaborazione f testi

word processor n sistema m di videoscrittura, word processor m inv

wordy /'wɜːdɪ/ adj prolisso

wore /wɔː(r)/ ▶ WEAR

work /wɜːk/ ① n lavoro m; (of art) opera f; **~s** pl (factory) fabbrica fsg; **at ~** al lavoro; **out of ~** disoccupato
② vi lavorare; ‹machine, ruse› funzionare; (study) studiare
③ vt far funzionare ‹machine›; far lavorare ‹employee›; far studiare ‹student›; **~ one's way through something** (read) leggere attentamente
■ **work in** vt inserire ‹comment, fact›; Culin incorporare ‹butter›
■ **work off** vt sfogare ‹anger›; lavorare per estinguere ‹debt›; fare sport per smaltire ‹weight›
■ **work on** ① vt lavorare a ‹book, report›; occuparsi di ‹problem, case›; cercare ‹solution›
② vi (continue) continuare a lavorare
■ **work out** ① vt elaborare ‹plan›; risolvere ‹problem›; calcolare ‹bill›; **I ~ed out how he did it** ho capito come l'ha fatto
② vi evolvere
■ **work up**: vt **I've ~ed up an appetite** mi è venuto appetito; **don't get ~ed up** (anxious) non farti prendere dal panico; (angry) non arrabbiarti

workable /'wɜːkəbl/ adj (feasible) fattibile

workaday /'wɜːkədeɪ/ adj ‹clothes, life› ordinario

workaholic /wɜːkə'hɒlɪk/ n stacanovista mf

workbench n banco m da lavoro

workbook n (blank) quaderno m; (with exercises) libro m di esercizi

workday n giorno m lavorativo

worker /'wɜːkə(r)/ n lavoratore, -trice mf; (manual) operaio, -a mf

work experience n esperienza f professionale; (part of training programme) stage m inv

workforce n forza f lavoro

workhorse n fig lavoratore, -trice mf indefesso, -a

working /'wɜːkɪŋ/ adj ‹clothes etc› da lavoro; ‹day› feriale; **in ~ order** funzionante

working capital n capitale m netto di esercizio

working-class adj operaio; **be ~** appartenere alla classe operaia

workings /'wɜːkɪŋz/ npl meccanismi mpl

working week n settimana f lavorativa

workload n carico m di lavoro

workman n operaio m

workmanlike adj fatto con competenza

workmanship n lavorazione f

workmate n collega mf

work of art n opera f d'arte

workout n allenamento m

work permit n permesso m di lavoro

workplace n posto m di lavoro

work-sharing n divisione (f) di un posto di lavoro tra più persone

worksheet n foglio m degli esercizi

workshop n officina f; (discussion) dibattito m

work-shy adj pigro

workstation n stazione f di lavoro

work surface n piano m di lavoro

worktop n Br piano m di lavoro

work-to-rule n sciopero m bianco

world /wɜːld/ n mondo m; **a ~ of difference** una differenza abissale; **out of this ~** favoloso; **think the ~ of somebody** andare matto per qualcuno

world-class adj di livello internazionale

World Cup n (in football) Mondiali mpl

world-famous adj di fama mondiale

world leader n (politician, company) leader m mondiale; (athlete) campione, -essa mf mondiale

worldly /'wɜːldlɪ/ adj materiale; ‹person› materialista

worldly-wise adj vissuto

world music n world music f

world power n potenza f mondiale

worldview n visione f del mondo

world war n guerra f mondiale

worldwide /'wɜːldwaɪd/ ① adj mondiale
② adv mondialmente

World Wide Web n Comput World Wide Web m

worm /wɜːm/ ① n verme m
② vt **~ one's way into sb's confidence** conquistarsi la fiducia di qualcuno in modo subdolo
■ **worm out**: vt **~ something out of somebody** carpire qualcosa a qualcuno

worm-eaten /'wɜːmiːtən/ adj ‹wood› tarlato; ‹fruit› bacato

wormhole /'wɜːmhəʊl/ n (in wood) buco m di tarlo; (in fruit, plant) buco m del verme

worn /wɔːn/ ① ▶ WEAR
② adj sciupato

worn-out adj consumato; ‹person› sfinito

W

✦ **worried** /'wʌrɪd/ *adj* preoccupato

worrier /'wʌrɪə(r)/ *n* ansioso, -a *mf*; **he's a terrible** ~ è ansioso da morire

✦ **worry** /'wʌrɪ/ **1** *n* preoccupazione *f*

2 *vt* (*pt/pp* **worried**) preoccupare; (bother) disturbare

3 *vi* preoccuparsi

■ **worry at** *vt* ‹dog› rosicchiare ‹bone, toy›; ‹person› sviscerare ‹problem›

worry beads *npl* rosario (*m*) *per scaricare la tensione*

worrying /'wʌrɪɪŋ/ *adj* preoccupante

worse /wɜːs/ **1** *adj* peggiore

2 *adv* peggio

3 *n* peggio *m*

worsen /'wɜːsn/ *vt/i* peggiorare

worsening /'wɜːsnɪŋ/ **1** *adj* ‹situation, problem› sempre più grave

2 *n* peggioramento *m*

worse off *adj* **be** ~ **than** stare peggio di; **be £100** ~ avere 100 sterline in meno

worship /'wɜːʃɪp/ **1** *n* culto *m*; (service) funzione *f*; **Your/His W**~ (to judge) signor giudice/il giudice

2 *vt* (*pt/pp* **-shipped**) venerare

3 *vi* andare a messa

worshipper /'wɜːʃɪpə(r)/ *n* fedele *mf*

worst /wɜːst/ **1** *adj* peggiore

2 *adv* peggio

3 *n* **the** ~ il peggio; **get the** ~ **of it** avere la peggio; **if the** ~ **comes to the** ~ nella peggiore delle ipotesi

worsted /'wʊstɪd/ *n* lana *f* pettinata

✦ **worth** /wɜːθ/ **1** *n* valore *m*; **£10** ~ **of petrol** 10 sterline di benzina

2 *adj* **be** ~ valere; **be** ~ **it** fig valerne la pena; **it is** ~ **trying** vale la pena provare; **it's** ~ **my while** mi conviene; **I'll make it** ~ **your while** te ne ricompenserò

worthless /'wɜːθlɪs/ *adj* senza valore

worthwhile /wɜːθ'waɪl/ *adj* che vale la pena; ‹cause› lodevole

worthy /'wɜːðɪ/ *adj* degno; ‹cause, motive› lodevole

✦ **would** /wʊd/ *v aux* **I** ~ **do it** lo farei; ~ **you go?** andresti?; ~ **you mind if I opened the window?** ti dispiace se apro la finestra?; **he** ~ **come if he could** verrebbe se potesse; **he said he** ~**n't** ha detto di no; **he said he** ~**n't have** ha detto che non lo avrebbe fatto; ~ **you like a drink?** vuoi qualcosa da bere?; **what** ~ **you like to drink?** cosa prendi da bere?; **you** ~**n't,** ~ **you?** non lo faresti, vero?

would-be *adj* pej ‹actor, singer› sedicente; ‹investor, buyer› aspirante

wound¹ /wuːnd/ **1** *n* ferita *f*

2 *vt* ferire

wound² /waʊnd/ ▶ **WIND²**

wove, woven /wəʊv, 'wəʊvn/ ▶ **WEAVE²**

wow /waʊ/ **1** *n* fam (success) successone *m*; (in sound system) wow *m*

2 *vt* fam entusiasmare ‹person›

3 *int* caspita!

WP *abbr* (**word processing**) elaborazione *f* testi

wpm *abbr* (**words per minute**) parole *fpl* al minuto

wrangle /'ræŋgl/ **1** *n* litigio *m*

2 *vi* litigare

✦ **wrap** /ræp/ **1** *n* (shawl) scialle *m*

2 *vt* (*pt/pp* **wrapped**) ~ **[up]** avvolgere; ‹present› incartare; **be** ~**ped up in** fig essere completamente preso da

3 *vi* ~ **up warmly** coprirsi bene

wraparound /'ræpəraʊnd/ *adj* ‹skirt› a pareo; ‹window, windscreen› panoramico

wraparound sunglasses *npl* occhiali *mpl* da sole avvolgenti

wrap-over *adj* ‹skirt, dress› a portafoglio

wrapper /'ræpə(r)/ *n* (for sweet) carta *f* [di caramella]

wrapping /'ræpɪŋ/ *n* materiale *m* da imballaggio

wrapping paper *n* carta *f* da pacchi; (for gift) carta *f* da regalo

wrath /rɒθ/ *n* ira *f*

wreak /riːk/ *vt* ~ **havoc with something** scombussolare qualcosa

wreath /riːθ/ *n* (*pl* ~**s** /riːðz/) corona *f*

wreathed /riːðd/ *adj* ~ **in** avvolto in ‹mists›

wreck /rek/ **1** *n* (of ship) relitto *m*; (of car) carcassa *f*; (person) rottame *m*

2 *vt* far naufragare; demolire ‹car›

wreckage /'rekɪdʒ/ *n* rottami *mpl*; fig brandelli *mpl*

wrecked /rekt/ *adj* ‹ship, car› distrutto; ‹building› demolito; fig (exhausted) distrutto

wren /ren/ *n* scricciolo *m*

wrench /rentʃ/ **1** *n* (injury) slogatura *f*; (tool) chiave *f* inglese; (pull) strattone *m*; **it was a** ~ **leaving home** fig è stato un passo difficile andarsene da casa

2 *vt* (pull) strappare; slogarsi ‹wrist, ankle etc›

wrest /rest/ *vt* strappare (**from** a)

wrestle /'resl/ *vi* lottare corpo a corpo; fig lottare

wrestler /'reslə(r)/ *n* lottatore, -trice *mf*

wrestling /'reslɪŋ/ *n* lotta *f* libera; (all-in) catch *m*

wretch /retʃ/ *n* disgraziato, -a *mf*

wretched /'retʃɪd/ *adj* odioso; ‹weather› orribile; **feel** ~ (unhappy) essere triste; (ill) sentirsi malissimo

wriggle /'rɪgl/ **1** *n* contorsione *f*

2 *vi* contorcersi; (move forward) strisciare; ~ **out of something** fam sottrarsi a qualcosa

---

✦ indicates a very frequent word

w

wriggly /ˈrɪglɪ/ *adj* ‹person› che si dimena; ‹snake, worm› che si contorce

wring /rɪŋ/ *vt* (*pt/pp* **wrung**) torcere ‹sb's neck›; strizzare ‹clothes›; ~ **something out of somebody** *fig* estorcere qualcosa a qualcuno; ~**ing wet** inzuppato

wrinkle /ˈrɪŋkl/ **1** *n* grinza *f*; (on skin) ruga *f*
   2 *vt/i* raggrinzire

wrinkled /ˈrɪŋkld/ *adj* ‹skin, face› rugoso; ‹clothes› raggrinzito

wrist /rɪst/ *n* polso *m*

wristband /ˈrɪs(t)bænd/ *n* polsino *m*; (on watch) cinturino *m*

wristwatch /ˈrɪstwɒtʃ/ *n* orologio *m* da polso

writ /rɪt/ *n* Jur mandato *m*

ℱ **write** /raɪt/ *vt/i* (*pt* **wrote**, *pp* **written**, *pres p* **writing**) scrivere
- **write away for** *vt* richiedere per posta ‹information›
- **write back** *vi* rispondere
- **write down** *vt* annotare
- **write in** *vi* scrivere
- **write off** *vt* cancellare ‹debt›; distruggere ‹car›
- **write out** *vt* fare ‹cheque, prescription›; (copy) ricopiare
- **write up** *vt* redigere; aggiornare ‹diary›; elaborare ‹notes›

write-off *n* (car) rottame *m*

write-protect *vt* Comput proteggere da sovrascrittura

ℱ **writer** /ˈraɪtə(r)/ *n* autore, -trice *mf*; **she's a** ~ è una scrittrice

writer's block *n* blocco *m* dello scrittore

write-up *n* (review) recensione *f*

writhe /raɪð/ *vi* contorcersi; ~ **with embarrassment** vergognarsi a morte

ℱ **writing** /ˈraɪtɪŋ/ *n* (occupation) scrivere *m*; (words) scritte *fpl*; (handwriting) scrittura *f*; ~**s**
pl scritti *mpl*; **in** ~ per iscritto

writing desk *n* scrivania *f*

writing pad *n* (for notes) bloc-notes *m inv*; (for letters) blocco *m* di carta da lettere

writing paper *n* carta *f* da lettere

written /ˈrɪtn/ ▶ WRITE

ℱ **wrong** /rɒŋ/ **1** *adj* sbagliato; **be** ~ ‹person› sbagliare; **what's** ~? cosa c'è che non va?
   2 *adv* ‹spelt› in modo sbagliato; **go** ~ ‹person› sbagliare; ‹machine› funzionare male; ‹plan› andar male; **don't get me** ~ non fraintendermi
   3 *n* ingiustizia *f*; **in the** ~ dalla parte del torto; **know right from** ~ distinguere il bene dal male
   4 *vt* fare torto a

wrongdoer /ˈrɒŋduːə(r)/ *n* malfattore *m*

wrong-foot *vt* Sport *fig* prendere in contropiede

wrongful /ˈrɒŋfʊl/ *adj* ingiusto

wrongfully /ˈrɒŋfʊlɪ/ *adv* ‹accuse› ingiustamente

wrongly /ˈrɒŋlɪ/ *adv* in modo sbagliato; ‹accuse, imagine› a torto; ‹informed› male

wrote /rəʊt/ ▶ WRITE

wrought iron /rɔːˈtaɪən/ **1** *n* ferro *m* battuto
   2 *attrib* di ferro battuto

wrung /rʌŋ/ ▶ WRING

wry /raɪ/ *adj* (**-er, -est**) ‹humour, smile› beffardo

WW1 *or* **WWI** *abbr* (**World War One**) prima guerra *f* mondiale

WW2 *or* **WWII** *abbr* (**World War Two**) seconda guerra *f* mondiale

WWW *abbr* (**World Wide Web**) WWW *m*

WYSIWYG /ˈwɪzɪwɪg/ *abbr* Comput (**what you see is what you get**) ciò che vedi è ciò che ottieni

X x

x¹, X /eks/ *n* (letter) x, X *f inv*; (anonymous person, place etc) X

x² *n* Math *x f inv*

X certificate *adj* Br vietato ai minori di 18 anni

xenophobia /zenəˈfəʊbɪə/ *n* xenofobia *f*

xerox® /ˈzɪərɒks/ **1** *vt* xerocopiare
   2 *n* (machine) xerocopiatrice *f*; (document) xerocopia *f*

Xmas /ˈkrɪsməs/ *n fam* Natale *m*

XML *abbr* (**extensible markup language**) Comput XML *m*

X-rated *adj* ‹film› vietato ai minori

X-ray **1** *n* (picture) radiografia *f*; **have an** ~ farsi fare una radiografia
   2 *vt* passare ai raggi X

X-ray machine *n* apparecchio *m* radiografico

X-ray unit *n* reparto *m* di radiologia

xxx *n* (at end of letter) baci *mpl*

Y y

y, Y /waɪ/ *n* (letter) y, Y *f inv*
yacht /jɒt/ *n* yacht *m inv*; (for racing) barca
f a vela
yachting /'jɒtɪŋ/ *n* vela *f*
yachtsman /'jɒtsmən/ *n* diportista *m*
yak /jæk/ *n* Zool yak
Yale® /jeɪl/ *n* (lock) serratura *f* di sicurezza
yam /jæm/ *n* (tropical) igname *m*; Am (sweet
potato) patata *f* dolce
yank *vt* fam tirare
Yank /jæŋk/ *n* fam americano, -a *mf*
Yankee /'jæŋkɪ/ *n* pej (American) yankee *m*
inv; (soldier) nordista *m*; Am (of Northern USA)
abitante *mf* degli USA settentrionali; Am
(inhabitant of New England) abitante *mf* della
Nuova Inghilterra
yap /jæp/ *vi* (*pt/pp* **yapped**) ‹dog› guaire
yapping /'jæpɪŋ/ *n* (of dogs) guaiti *mpl*; fam
(of people) ciance *fpl*
⚡ **yard¹** /jɑːd/ *n* Br (of house) cortile *m*; Am
(garden) giardino *m*; (for storage) deposito
m; **the Y~** fam Scotland Yard *f* (*polizia
londinese*)
yard² *n* iarda *f* (= 91.94 cm)
yardstick /'jɑːdstɪk/ *n* fig pietra *f* di
paragone
yarn /jɑːn/ *n* filo *m*; fam (tale) storia *f*
yashmak /'jæʃmæk/ *n* velo *m* (*delle donne
musulmane*)
yawn /jɔːn/ 1 *n* sbadiglio *m*
2 *vi* sbadigliare
yawning /'jɔːnɪŋ/ *adj* ~ gap sbadiglio *m*
yd *abbr* (**yard**) iarda *f*
⚡ **yeah** /je/ *adv* fam sì; **oh ~?** ma davvero?
⚡ **year** /jɪə(r)/ *n* anno *m*; (of wine) annata *f*; **for
~s** fam da secoli
yearbook /'jɪəbʊk/ *n* annuario *m*
yearlong *adj* ‹stay› di un anno
yearly /'jɪəlɪ/ 1 *adj* annuale
2 *adv* annualmente
yearn /jɜːn/ *vi* struggersi
yearning /'jɜːnɪŋ/ *n* desiderio *m*
struggente
year out *n* = GAP YEAR
year-round *adj* ‹supply, source›
permanente
yeast /jiːst/ *n* lievito *m*
⚡ **yell** /jel/ 1 *n* urlo *m*
2 *vi* urlare
yelling /'jelɪŋ/ *n* urla *fpl*
⚡ **yellow** /'jeləʊ/ *adj & n* giallo *m*

yellow-belly *n* fam fifone *m*
yellow card *n* Sport cartellino *m* giallo
yellowish /'jeləʊɪʃ/ *adj* giallastro
yellow pages *npl* pagine *fpl* gialle
yellowy /'jeləʊɪ/ *adj* giallastro
yelp /jelp/ 1 *n* (of dog) guaito *m*
2 *vi* ‹dog› guaire
Yemen /'jemən/ *n* Yemen *m*
Yemeni /'jemənɪ/ *adj & n* yemenita *mf*
yen /jen/ *n* forte desiderio *m* (**for** di)
yeoman /'jəʊmən/ *n* Br piccolo
proprietario *m* terriero; **Y~ of the Guard**
guardiano *m* della Torre di Londra
yep /jep/ *adv* fam sì
⚡ **yes** /jes/ 1 *adv* sì
2 *n* sì *m inv*
yes-man *n* fam tirapiedi *m inv*
⚡ **yesterday** /'jestədeɪ/ *n & adv* ieri *m inv*;
~'s paper il giornale di ieri; **the day before
~** l'altroieri; **~ afternoon** ieri pomeriggio;
~ morning ieri mattina
yesteryear /'jestəjɪə(r)/ *n* lit passato *m*; **the
music of ~** la musica del passato
⚡ **yet** /jet/ 1 *adv* ancora; **as ~** fino ad ora;
not ~ non ancora; **the best ~** il migliore
finora
2 *conj* eppure
yew /juː/ *n* tasso *m* (*albero*)
Y-fronts *npl* Br slip *m inv* da uomo con
apertura
YHA *abbr* Br (**Youth Hostels
Association**) associazione *f* degli ostelli
della gioventù
Yiddish /'jɪdɪʃ/ *n* yiddish *m*
yield /jiːld/ 1 *n* produzione *f*; ‹profit›
reddito *m*
2 *vt* produrre; fruttare ‹profit›
3 *vi* cedere; Am Auto dare la precedenza
yielding /'jiːldɪŋ/ *adj* (submissive)
arrendevole; ‹ground› cedevole; ‹person›
flessibile
YMCA *abbr* (**Young Men's Christian
Association**) Associazione *f* Cristiana
dei Giovani
yob /jɒb/, **yobbo** /'jɒbəʊ/ *n* Br fam teppista
mf
yodel /'jəʊdl/ *vi* (*pt/pp* **yodelled**) cantare
jodel
yoga /'jəʊgə/ *n* yoga *m*
yoghurt /'jɒgət/ *n* yogurt *m inv*
yoke /jəʊk/ *n* giogo *m*; (of garment) carré
m inv
yokel /'jəʊkl/ *n* zotico, -a *mf*

⚡ indicates a very frequent word

yolk /jəʊk/ n tuorlo m

yonder /'jɒndə(r)/ adv liter laggiù

yonks /jɒŋks/ npl fam **I haven't seen him for** ~ è un secolo che non lo vedo

yore /jɔː(r)/ n in days of ~ un tempo

✎ **you** /juː/ pers pron (subject) tu, voi pl; (formal) lei, voi pl; (direct/indirect object) ti, vi pl; (formal: direct object) la; (formal: indirect object) le; (after prep) te, voi pl; (formal: after prep) lei; ~ **are very kind** sg sei molto gentile; (formal) è molto gentile; (pl & formal pl) siete molto gentili; ~ **can stay, but he has to go** sg tu puoi rimanere, ma lui deve andarsene; **all of** ~ tutti voi; **I'll give** ~ **the money** sg ti darò i soldi; **I'll give it to** ~ sg te/, ve lo darò; it **does** ~ **good** sg ti//, vi fa bene; **it was** ~! sg eri tu!; ~ **have to be careful these days** si deve fare attenzione di questi tempi; ~ **can't tell the difference** non si vede la differenza

you'd /juːd/ abbr (**you would; you had**)

you-know-what pron fam sai cosa

you-know-who pron fam sai chi

you'll /juːl/ abbr (**you will**)

✎ **young** /jʌŋ/ ① adj giovane; ~ **lady** signorina f; ~ **man** giovanotto m; **her** ~ **man** (boyfriend) il suo ragazzo
② npl (animals) piccoli mpl; **the** ~ (people) i giovani

young blood n nuove leve fpl

youngish /'jʌŋɪʃ/ adj abbastanza giovane

young-looking adj dall'aria giovanile

young offender n delinquente mf minorenne

youngster /'jʌŋstə(r)/ n ragazzo, -a mf; (child) bambino, -a mf

✎ **your** /jɔː(r)/ poss adj tuo m, tua f, tuoi mpl, tue fpl; (formal) suo m, sua f, suoi mpl, sue fpl, (pl & formal pl) vostro m, vostra f, vostri mpl, vostre fpl; ~ **task/house** il tuo compito/la tua casa; (formal) il suo compito/la sua casa; (pl & formal pl) il vostro compito/la vostra casa; ~ **mother/father** tua madre/tuo padre; (formal) sua madre/suo padre; (pl & formal pl) vostra madre/vostro padre

you're /jʊə(r)/ abbr (**you are**)

yours /jɔːz/ poss pron il tuo m, la tua f, i tuoi mpl, le tue fpl; (formal) il suo m, la sua f, i suoi mpl, le sue fpl; (pl & formal pl) il vostro m, la vostra f, i vostri mpl, le vostre fpl; **a friend**

of ~ un tuo/suo/vostro amico; **friends of** ~ dei tuoi/vostri/suoi amici; **that is** ~ quello è tuo/vostro/suo; (as opposed to mine) quello è il tuo/il vostro/il suo

✎ **yourself** /jɔː'self/ pers pron (reflexive) ti; (formal) si; (emphatic) te stesso; (formal) sé, se stesso; **do pour** ~ **a drink** versati da bere; (formal) si versi da bere; **you said so** ~ lo hai detto tu stesso; (formal) lo ha detto lei stesso; **you can be proud of** ~ puoi essere fiero di te; (formal) può essere fiero di sé; **by** ~ da solo

yourselves /jɔː'selvz/ pers pron (reflexive) vi; (emphatic) voi stessi; **do pour** ~ **a drink** versatevi da bere; **you said so** ~ lo avete detto voi stessi; **you can be proud of** ~ potete essere fieri di voi; **by** ~ da soli

✎ **youth** /juːθ/ n (pl **youths** /juːðz/) gioventù f inv; (boy) giovanetto m; **the** ~ (young people) i giovani

youth club n club m per i giovani

youthful /'juːθfʊl/ adj giovanile

youth hostel n ostello m [della gioventù]

youth hostelling n viaggiare (m) pernottando in ostelli della gioventù

youth work n lavoro m di educatore

youth worker n educatore, -trice mf

you've /juːv/ abbr (**you have**)

yowl /jaʊl/ vi ‹dog› ululare; ‹cat› miagolare; ‹baby› frignare

yo-yo® /'jəʊjəʊ/ ① n yo-yo m inv
② vi (prices, inflation) andare su e giù

yr abbr (**year**) anno m

yuck /jʌk/ int Br fam bleah

yucky /'jʌkɪ/ adj Br fam schifoso

Yugoslav /'juːgəsluːv/ adj & n jugoslavo, -a mf

Yugoslavia /juːgə'slɑːvɪə/ n Jugoslavia f

Yule log /juːl/ n tronchetto m natalizio

yummy /'jʌmɪ/ fam ① adj squisito
② int gnam gnam

yup /jʌp/ adv fam sì

yuppie /'jʌpɪ/ n yuppie mf inv

yuppie flu n sindrome f da affaticamento cronico

YWCA abbr (**Young Women's Christian Association**) Associazione f Cristiana delle Giovani

Zz

z, Z /zed/ *n* (letter) z, Z *f inv*
Zaire /zɑːˈɪə/ *n* Zaire *m*
Zambia /ˈzæmbɪə/ *n* Zambia *m*
zany /ˈzeɪnɪ/ *adj* (**-ier, -iest**) demenziale
zap /zæp/ ① *n* fam (energy) energia *f*
  ② *vt* (*pt/pp* **zapped**) fam (destroy)
  distruggere ‹*town*›; far fuori ‹*person,
  animal*›; (fire at) fulminare; Comput (delete)
  cancellare
zapper /ˈzæpə(r)/ *n* fam (for TV) telecomando
  m
zeal /ziːl/ *n* zelo *m*
zealot /ˈzelət/ *n* fig fanatico *m*
zealous /ˈzeləs/ *adj* zelante
zealously /ˈzeləslɪ/ *adv* con zelo
zebra /ˈzebrə/ *n* zebra *f*
zebra crossing *n* passaggio *m* pedonale,
  zebre *fpl*
zenith /ˈzenɪθ/ *n* zenit *m inv*; fig apogeo *m*
zero /ˈzɪərəʊ/ *n* zero *m*
  ■ **zero in on** *vt* concentrarsi su ‹*problem,
  person*›; localizzare ‹*place*›; Mil mirare ‹*target*›
zero gravity *n* assenza *f* di gravità
zero hour *n* Mil ora *f* zero
zero-rated /-ˈreɪtɪd/ *adj* Br esente [da] IVA
zest /zest/ *n* gusto *m*; (peel) scorza *f* (*di
  agrumi*)
zigzag /ˈzɪgzæg/ ① *n* zigzag *m inv*
  ② *vi* (*pt/pp* **-zagged**) zigzagare
zilch /zɪltʃ/ *n* fam un tubo; **I understood** ∼
  non ho capito un tubo
Zimbabwe /zɪmˈbæbweɪ/ *n* Zimbabwe *m*
Zimmer® /ˈzɪmə(r)/ *n* Br deambulatore *m*
zinc /zɪŋk/ *n* zinco *m*
zinc oxide *n* ossido *m* di zinco

zing /zɪŋ/ ① *n* fam (energy) brio *m*; (sound)
  sibilo *m*
  ② *vt* Am (criticize) stroncare
Zionism /ˈzaɪənɪzm/ *n* sionismo *m*
zip /zɪp/ ① *n* ∼ **[fastener]** cerniera *f*
  [lampo]
  ② *vt* (*pt/pp*, **zipped**) ∼ **[up]** chiudere con
  la cerniera [lampo]
  ■ **zip along** *vi* (move quickly) procedere
  velocemente
  ■ **zip through** *vt* (do quickly) svolgere
  velocemente ‹*work*›; (read quickly) leggere
  velocemente ‹*book*›
  ■ **zip up** ① *vt* chiudere la cerniera di ‹*jacket,
  bag*›
  ② *vi* chiudersi con la cerniera
zip code *n* Am codice *m* [di avviamento]
  postale, C.A.P. *m inv*
zipper /ˈzɪpə(r)/ *n* Am cerniera *f* [lampo]
zippy /ˈzɪpɪ/ *adj* fam (vehicle) scattante
zither /ˈzɪðə(r)/ *n* cetra *f*
zodiac /ˈzəʊdɪæk/ *n* zodiaco *m*
zombie /ˈzɒmbɪ/ *n* fam zombi *mf inv*
✧ **zone** /zəʊn/ *n* zona *f*
zoning /ˈzəʊnɪŋ/ *n* zonazione *f*
zonked /zɒŋkt/ *adj* fam (on drugs, drunk, tired)
  fatto
zoo /zuː/ *n* zoo *m inv*
zoo keeper *n* guardiano, -a *mf* dello zoo
zoological /zəʊəˈlɒdʒɪkl/ *adj* zoologico
zoologist /zəʊˈɒlədʒɪst/ *n* zoologo, -a *mf*
zoology /zəʊˈɒlədʒɪ/ *n* zoologia *f*
zoom /zuːm/ *vi* sfrecciare
zoom lens *n* zoom *m inv*
zucchini /zʊˈkiːnɪ/ *n* Am zucchino *m*,
  zucchina *f*

---

z

✧ indicates a very frequent word

Summary of Italian grammar

Nouns

Gender

All Italian nouns are either masculine or feminine. As a general rule, nouns ending in **-o** are usually masculine.

il ragazzo boy	**l'amico** friend
lo sbaglio mistake	**un albero** tree
un treno train	**uno specchio** mirror

Nouns ending in **-a** are usually feminine.

la ragazza girl	**la scuola** school
l'arancia orange	**un'amica** friend
una sorella sister	**una zia** aunt

Nouns ending in **-e** can be either masculine or feminine.

il nome name	**la stazione** station
una ragione reason	**un giornale** newspaper

Plural forms

Masculine nouns ending in **-o** change to **-i** in the plural:

i ragazzi boys	**gli amici** friends
gli sbagli mistakes	

Feminine nouns ending in **-a** change to **-e**:

le ragazze girls	**le scuole** schools
le amiche friends	

All nouns ending in **-e** change to **-i**:

i genitori parents	**le stazioni** stations

Nouns ending in accented vowels do not change in the plural.

il caffè coffee	**i caffè** coffees
la città city	**le città** cities
la virtù virtue	**le virtù** virtues

Nouns ending in a consonant (imported from other languages) do not change in the plural.

il computer	**i computer**
lo sport	**gli sport**
l'autobus	**gli autobus**

The definite article

Masculine forms before:

	singular	plural	
most consonants	il	i	il treno, i treni
a, e, i, o, u	l'	gli	l'albero, gli alberi
gn, ps, z, s+ consonant	lo	gli	lo studente, gli studenti

Feminine forms before:

	singular	plural	
any consonant	la	le	la camera, le camere
a, e, i, o, u	l'	le	l'arancia, le arance

The indefinite article

Masculine forms before:

	singular	
vowel or most consonants	un	un ombrello, un caffè
gn, ps, z, s+consonant	uno	uno zoo

Feminine forms before:

	singular	
any consonant	una	una stanza
a, e, i, o, u	un'	un'aspirina

Adjectives

Adjectives agree in number and gender with the noun to which they refer.
Italian adjectives end in either **-o** or **-e**.

	singular	plural	
masculine	pigro	pigri	lazy
	felice	felici	happy
	singular	plural	
feminine	pigra	pigre	lazy
	felice	felici	happy

When you have a mixture of masculine and feminine nouns, the adjective ending is masculine.

Max e Anna sono pigri/gentili.
Max and Anna are lazy/kind.

Position

Adjectives are usually placed after the noun they describe.

Ho letto un libro interessante.
I've read an interesting book.

There are, however, a few common adjectives, such as **bello, brutto, buono, cattivo, piccolo, grande, giovane, vecchio, nuovo**, which can be placed before the noun.

Ho visto un bel film.
I have seen a lovely film.

Possessive adjectives

In Italian, the possessive adjective agrees in gender and number with what is possessed and not with the possessor. The possessive adjective is generally preceded by the definite article: **il mio ufficio**.

	singular	
	masculine	*feminine*
my	**il mio**	**la mia**
your [*informal*]	**il tuo**	**la tua**
his/her; your [*formal*]	**il suo**	**la sua**
our	**il nostro**	**la nostra**
your [*plural*]	**il vostro**	**la vostra**
their	**il loro**	**la loro**

	plural	
	masculine	*feminine*
my	**i miei**	**le mie**
your [*informal*]	**i tuoi**	**le tue**
his/her; your [*formal*]	**i suoi**	**le sue**
our	**i nostri**	**le nostre**
your [*plural*]	**i vostri**	**le vostre**
their	**i loro**	**le loro**

Except with **loro**, the definite article is dropped when the noun refers to single immediate family members – **mia sorella, tuo fratello**, but **le mie sorelle, i tuoi fratelli; la loro sorella, i loro fratelli**.

Questo and quello

Questo and **quello** can be used both as adjectives ('this'/'that') and pronouns ('this one'/'that one'). **Questo** takes the usual adjective endings (**-o/-a/-i/-e**) whether it is used as an adjective or a pronoun. **Quello** also takes these endings when used as a pronoun;

however, when it comes before a noun, it takes the same endings as the definite article.

singular	**quel, quello,**	**quella casa**
	quell', quella	**quell'amico**
plural	**quei, quegli,**	**quegli amici**
	quelle	**quelle case**

Subject pronouns

In Italian, subject pronouns are generally omitted (unless you want to place emphasis on them): the subject is shown in the verb ending.

io	I	**noi**	we
tu	you [*informal*]	**voi**	you [*plural*]
lui	he	**loro**	they
lei	she		
lei	you [*formal*]		

The **tu** form is used when speaking to a child or someone you know well;
the **lei** form when speaking to an adult you don't know well.

Object pronouns

Direct object pronouns

mi	me	**ci**	us
ti	you	**vi**	you
lo	him/it [*m*]	**li**	them [*m*]
la	her/it [*f*]	**le**	them [*f*]
la	you [*formal*]		

Indirect object pronouns

mi	to (etc.) me	**ci**	to us
ti	to you	**vi**	to you
gli	to him/to it [*m*]	**gli**	to them [*m/f*]
le	to her/to it [*f*]		
le	to you [*formal*]		

Indirect object pronouns are used with verbs which are normally followed by a preposition, such as **telefonare a** ('to telephone') and **dare a** ('to give to').

Anna telefona a Maria. Anna **le** telefona.
Anna telefona a Mario. Anna **gli** telefona.

The position of direct and indirect object pronouns

Both direct and indirect object pronouns come before the verb (or before **avere/essere** in the perfect tense). When both appear in a sentence, the indirect comes before the direct pronoun: the indirect pronoun may also change form (see below).

Ti offro un caffè.
I'll buy you a coffee.

Le scrivo domani.
I'll write to her tomorrow.

Mi piacciono quegli stivali. **Li** compro!
I like those boots. I'll buy them!

Me lo avete comprato.
You bought it for me.

When there are two verbs, and the second is an infinitive, the pronoun comes either before the first verb or combines with the infinitive.

Ti vorrei incontrare.
I'd like to meet you.

Vorrei incontrar**ti**.
I'd like to meet you.

Before a direct object pronoun, the indirect object pronouns **mi**, **ti**, **ci**, and **vi** change respectively to **me**, **te**, **ce**, and **ve**.

Ti abbiamo già dato il libro.
We have already given the book to you.

Te lo abbiamo già dato.
We have already given it to you.

Vi mando la lettera domani.
I'll send the letter to you tomorrow.

Ve la mando domani.
I'll send it to you tomorrow.

The third person indirect pronouns – **le** and **gli** – change to **glie-** and combine with **lo**, **la**, **li**, and **le** to form one word.

Mando un biglietto d'auguri ai nonni. **Glielo** mando.
I'll send a card to our grandparents.
I'll send it to them.

These forms come before the verb or can be joined to an infinitive.

Glielo dovrei dare.
I should give it to him/her/them.

Dovrei dar**glielo**.
I should give it to him/her/them.

Disjunctive pronouns

me	me	noi	us
te	you [*informal*]	voi	you [*plural*]
lui	him	loro	them
lei	her		
lei	you [*formal*]		

Disjunctive pronouns are used for emphasis and after prepositions, such as **di**, **a**, **da**, **con**, etc.:

Conosco **lui**.
I know him.

Mario gioca con **noi**.
Mario plays with us.

Lo fa per **me**.
He does it for me.

Viene con **te**?
Is he coming with you?

Possessive pronouns

These have the same form as the possessive adjectives.

Questa è la mia bicicletta.
That's my bike.

E quella è **la mia**.
And that's mine.

The definite article is used with family members in the singular.

Mia nonna abita a Roma.
My grandmother lives in Rome.

La mia abita a Napoli.
Mine lives in Naples.

ci

ci is used to refer to location. It is used to mean 'here' or 'there', although in some instances its meaning in English is understood rather than translated.
It usually comes before the verb.

Siete mai stati a Parigi? Sì, **ci** siamo andati molte volte.
Have you ever been to Paris? Yes, we've been there many times.

Quando andate a Roma? **Ci** andiamo venerdì.
When are you going to Rome? We're going (there) on Friday.

ne

ne can mean 'of it/him/her', 'about it/him/her', etc., or 'of them', 'about them', etc. In some instances it isn't translated, but it must be included.

Vorrei delle banane.
I would like some bananas.

Quante **ne** vuole?
How many (of them) do you want?

Maria parlerà delle sue vacanze.
Maria will talk about her holidays.

Maria **ne** parlerà.
Maria will talk about them.

Summary of Italian grammar

Prepositions

In addition to the general meanings of the prepositions the following uses are particularly worth noting.

a   with cities

> Abito **a** Parma.
> I live in Parma.

> Vado **a** Parigi.
> I am going to Paris.

in   with countries and regions

> Vivono **in** Italia – **in** Toscana.
> They live in Italy – in Tuscany.

di   to express possession

> la mamma **di** Federica.
> Federica's mum

da   + name of a person means 'to or at their house, shop, etc.'

> Vai **da** Paola?
> Are you going to Paola's?

> Andate **dal** giornalaio?
> Are you going to the newsagent's?

> Sei già stato **dal** dentista?
> Have you already been to the dentist's?

da   + present tense to describe an action which began in the past and which continues in the present ('for', 'since')

> È malato **da** due giorni.
> He has been ill for two days.

> **Lavorano** qui **dal** 1975.
> They have worked here since 1975.

Prepositions and articles

When the prepositions **a** ('to'), **da** ('from'), **di** ('of'), **in** ('in'), and **su** ('on') are followed by the definite article, the words combine as follows.

	singular				plural		
	il	lo	l'	la	i	gli	le
a	al	allo	all'	alla	ai	agli	alle
da	dal	dallo	dall'	dalla	dai	dagli	dalle
di	del	dello	dell'	della	dei	degli	delle
in	nel	nello	nell'	nella	nei	negli	nelle
su	sul	sullo	sull'	sulla	sui	sugli	sulle

La sveglia è **sul** comodino.
The alarm clock is on the bedside cabinet.

I pantaloni sono **nell'**armadio.
The trousers are in the wardrobe.

Adverbs

Regular adverbs

Most adverbs are formed by adding **-mente** to the feminine form of the adjective.

lento slow   **lentamente** slowly
vero true   **veramente** truly

Adjectives ending in **–e** in the singular simply add **-mente**.

triste sad   **tristemente** sadly
semplice simple   **semplicemente** simply

However, if the adjective ends in **-re** or **-le**, the **-e** is dropped:

normale normal   **normalmente** normally
regolare regular   **regolarmente** regularly

The comparative and superlative

Comparative

più … di	Lui è **più** giovane **di** lei.
	He is younger than she is.
meno … di	Lui è **meno** vivace **di** lei.
	He is less lively than she is.
(tanto) … quanto/come	Lui è alto **quanto** lei.
	He's as tall as she is.

Superlative

To say 'the most …' in Italian is **il / la / i / le più**; 'the least …' is **il / la / i / le meno**.

Mara è **la più** giovane.
Mara is the youngest.

Franco è **il più** alto.
Franco is the tallest.

After a superlative 'in' is translated by **di**.

È **la ragazza più** intelligente **della** classe.
She is the cleverest girl in her class.

È **l'albergo più** costoso **di** Venezia.
It is the most expensive hotel in Venice.

Irregular forms

Some adjectives have two different forms of the comparative and superlative. The distinctions in meaning are slight and best learnt in context.

	singular	plural
buono (good)	più buono / **migliore**	il/la più buono/a il/la **migliore**
cattivo (bad)	più cattivo / **peggiore**	il/la più cattivo/a il/la **peggiore**

Expressing quantities

di + article

Ordino **del** vino?
Shall I order some wine?

Preferisco **dell'**acqua.
I'd prefer some water.

Compra **dei** pomodori.
Buy some tomatoes.

Hai **delle** aspirine?
Do you have any aspirins®?

qualche

qualche is always followed by a singular noun.

Ho **qualche amico** a Roma.
I have some friends in Rome.

Asking questions

There are two ways of asking questions. (a) you keep the same wording as the sentence, but use a rising intonation; (b) you use a question word – then the verb and the subject change places.

È inglese?
Are you English?

Dove lavora Roberta?
Where does Roberta work?

Negatives

To make a sentence negative, you simply put **non** in front of the verb.

Sono americano.
I'm American.

Non sono americano.
I'm not American.

Numbers

1	uno	16	sedici
2	due	17	diciassette
3	tre	18	diciotto
4	quattro	19	diciannove
5	cinque	20	venti
6	sei	21	ventuno
7	sette	22	ventidue
8	otto	23	ventitré
9	nove	30	trenta
10	dieci	40	quaranta
11	undici	50	cinquanta
12	dodici	60	sessanta
13	tredici	70	settanta
14	quattordici	71	settantuno
15	quindici	72	settantadue

73	settantatré	101	centouno
74	settantaquattro, etc.	102	centodue
80	ottanta	200	duecento
81	ottantuno	202	duecentodue
82	ottantadue, etc.	999	novecentonovantanove
90	novanta	1000	mille
91	novantuno	2000	duemila
92	novantadue, etc.	2001	duemilauno
100	cento		

Verbs

The infinitive

Dictionaries and glossaries usually list verbs in the infinitive form, which in Italian has three different endings: **-are**, **-ere**, or **-ire** (apart from a few irregular forms in **-rre**). Regular verbs within each group take the same endings.

Reflexive verbs

Reflexive verbs can easily be identified by the additional **si** which appears at the end of the infinitive (**chiamarsi**): they end in **-arsi**, **-ersi**, or **–irsi**, taking the endings for **-are**, **-ere**, and **-ire** verbs respectively. They just add the reflexive pronouns **mi**, **ti**, **si**, **ci**, **vi**, and **si** in front of the verb.

	alzarsi – to get up	**divertirsi** – to enjoy oneself
(io)	*mi* alzo	*mi* diverto
(tu)	*ti* alzi	*ti* diverti
(lui/lci)	*si* alza	*si* diverte
(noi)	*ci* alziamo	*ci* divertiamo
(voi)	*vi* alzate	*vi* divertite
(loro)	*si* alzano	*si* divertono

Non **si alzano** mai prima delle otto.
They never get up before eight.

Si divertirà senz'altro.
He will definitely enjoy himself.

The imperative

The imperative is used to give orders, instructions, and advice. Irregular imperative forms are covered in the verb tables on pages 954–962.

The *tu* form of the imperative is used to address children or people you know well. The *voi* form is used to address a group of people. Except for the *tu* form of the **-are** verbs, the other forms are the same as the *tu* form of the present tense.

	parlare	credere	sentire	finire
(tu)	parla	credi	senti	finisci
(voi)	parlate	credete	sentite	finite

The imperative also has a *noi form*, translated 'let's ...'. This is the same as the *noi form* of the present tense.

	parlare	credere	sentire	finire
(noi)	parliamo	crediamo	sentiamo	finiamo

The *lei form* of the imperative is used with adults you don't know.

	parlare	credere	sentire	finire
(lei)	parli	creda	senta	finisca

The imperative and object pronouns

Direct and indirect object pronouns come *before the lei imperative*.

La guardi meglio. È tutta sporca!
Look at it more closely. It's all dirty!

Non **lo ascolti**! Scherza.
Don't listen to him. He's joking.

However, they are added to the *end of the tu, voi, and noi imperatives*.

Telefonate**gli** al più presto.
Ring him very soon.

Alziamoci alle sette.
Let's get up at seven o'clock.

Non parliamo**ne** più.
Let's not speak about it any more.

When you add a pronoun to the *tu* imperative forms of **andare, fare, dare, dire**, and **stare**, the first letter of the pronoun is doubled. The only exception to this is **gli**.

Di**mmi** la verità!
Tell me the truth!

Da**lle** questo.
Give her this.

Digli che arrivo domani.
Tell him I'll be arriving tomorrow.

The negative imperative

tu form	non + infinitive	**Non fumare**, per favore. Please don't smoke.
other forms	non + imperative	**Non fumate**, per favore. Please don't smoke.

In the negative, object pronouns come *before the lei imperative*.

Non **lo** dica!
Don't say it!

They can either come before the *tu, voi*, and *noi* imperatives or be added on to the end of it.

In the negative **tu** form, the final **-e** of the infinitive is dropped when an object pronoun is added on.

Non **dirlo**!/Non **lo dire**!
Don't say it!

The present tense

The single present tense in Italian has a wider use than its English equivalent: **io lavoro** can be translated as either 'I work' or 'I am working', according to context. Besides expressing actions which relate to the immediate present, it can also be used to express:

– actions which are done regularly

Ogni mattina **faccio** una passeggiata.
Every morning I go for a walk.

– actions which relate to a future intention.

Fra un mese **andiamo** in Spagna.
In a month we're going to Spain.

For the forms of the present tense, see the verb tables on pages 954–962.

The progressive forms

The progressive forms are used to say what is or was happening at the moment of speaking. These forms are less common in Italian than in English, because it is perfectly normal to use the simple present tense to convey the same idea.

The progressives are formed by combining the verb **stare** with the gerund, the form of the verb which ends with **-ando** or **-endo**. The present tense and the imperfect tense of **stare** are used respectively to talk about the present and the past.

parlare	prendere	dormire
sto/ stavo parlando	**sto/** stavo prendendo	**sto/** stavo dormendo
stai/ stavi parlando	**stai/** stavi prendendo	**stai/** stavi dormendo
sta/ stava parlando	**sta/** stava prendendo	**sta/** stava dormendo
stiamo/ stavamo parlando	**stiamo/** stavamo prendendo	**stiamo/** stavamo dormendo
state/ stavate parlando	**state/** stavate prendendo	**state/** stavate dormendo

• •

parlare	prendere	dormire
stanno/	**stanno/**	**stanno/**
stavano	stavano	stavano
parlando	**prendendo**	**dormendo**

Sta piovendo.
It is raining.

Che **stavi facendo?**
What were you doing?

The perfect tense

The perfect tense is used to describe a single completed event or action which took place in the past. It can be translated in one of two ways, depending on the context: for example, **ho parlato** can mean either 'I spoke' or 'I have spoken'. It is formed with the present tense of **avere** or **essere** + the past participle of the verb required. For regular verbs this is formed as follows: **-are** verbs →
-ato, -ere verbs → **-uto,** and **-ire** verbs → **-ito.**

parl**ato** cred**uto** sent**ito**

With **avere**

Most transitive verbs form the perfect tense with **avere.**

Ho mangiato troppo.
I've eaten too much.

Non **ha avuto** molta fortuna.
She didn't have much luck.

When **avere** is used, the past participle must agree with any direct object which comes before the verb. Note that **lo** and **la** shorten to **l'; li** and **le** don't.

Ho comprato una macchina. **L'ho comprata** ieri.
I bought a car. I bought it yesterday.

Hai visto Maria e Carla? Sì, **le ho viste** ieri.
Did you see Maria and Carla? Yes, I saw them yesterday.

With **essere**

Most intransitive verbs, all reflexive verbs, and a few others (such as **essere, piacere, sembrare,** etc.) form the perfect tense with **essere.** When this happens, the past participle acts like an adjective: it agrees with the subject in gender and number.

Maria **è andata** a Roma molte volte.
Maria has been to Rome many times.

Ci siamo annoiati molto.
We got really bored.

La serata **è stata** veramente piacevole.
The evening was very pleasant.

Irregular past participles

* indicates a verb forming the perfect with **essere**

infinitive	past participle
aprire (to open)	**aperto**
bere (to drink)	**bevuto**
chiedere (to ask)	**chiesto**
chiudere (to close)	**chiuso**
crescere* (to grow)	**cresciuto**
decidere (to decide)	**deciso**
dire (to say)	**detto**
essere* (to be)	**stato**
fare (to do)	**fatto**
leggere (to read)	**letto**
mettere (to put)	**messo**
morire* (to die)	**morto**
nascere* (to be born)	**nato**
perdere (to lose)	**perso**
piacere* (to please)	**piaciuto**
prendere (to take)	**preso**
rimanere* (to stay)	**rimasto**
scegliere (to choose)	**scelto**
scrivere (to write)	**scritto**
stare* (to stay, to be situated)	**stato**
succedere* (to happen)	**successo**
trascorrere (to spend)	**trascorso**
vedere (to see)	**visto**
venire* (to come)	**venuto**
vincere (to win)	**vinto**
vivere* (to live)	**vissuto**

The imperfect tense

The imperfect tense is used:

1 to describe something which used to happen frequently or regularly in the past.

   Andavamo a scuola a piedi.
   We walked/We used to walk to school.

2 to describe what was happening or what the situation was when something else happened.

   Dormivo quando Sergio **è arrivato.**
   I was sleeping when Sergio arrived.

   Aveva sei anni quando **è nata** Carla.
   He was six when Carla was born.

3 to express an emotional or physical state in the past and to refer to time, age, or the weather.

   Ieri sera Beatrice **era** stanca.
   Beatrice was tired.

   Aveva i capelli biondi.
   She had blonde hair.

Erano le sette.
It was seven o'clock.

Quando **eravamo** piccoli, ci piaceva andare al mare.
When we were little, we used to like going to the seaside.

Era una bella giornata.
It was a lovely day.

The imperfect tense is formed by adding the following endings to the stem.

	parlare	credere	sentire
(io)	parlavo	credevo	sentivo
(tu)	parlavi	credevi	sentivi
(lui/lei; lei)	parlava	credeva	sentiva
(noi)	parlavamo	credevamo	sentivamo
(voi)	parlavate	credevate	sentivate
(loro)	parlavano	credevano	sentivano

See the verb tables for details of verbs which are irregular in the imperfect.

Use of the perfect and the imperfect

The perfect is used to describe a completed or single action in the past; the imperfect describes a continuing, repeated, or habitual action. When they are used together, the imperfect is the tense that sets the scene, while the perfect is used to move the action forward.

Ho visto Marco giovedì.
I saw Marco on Thursday.

Andavo in piscina il giovedì.
I used to go swimming on Thursdays.

Poiché **faceva** caldo, **siamo andati** tutti al mare.
Because it was hot, we all went to the seaside.

The past historic tense

The past historic is a tense that refers to something that happened in the past, generally in the relatively distant past. It is formed by adding a set of endings to the verb. Before adding the endings, the infinitive ending (**-are**, **-ere**, or **-ire**) is dropped. For some **-ere** verbs there is a choice of endings for some forms; both sets of endings are commonly used. A large number of verbs form their past historic in irregular ways.

parlare	vendere	dormire
(io)	parlai	vendei	dormii
		or **vendetti**	
(tu)	parlasti	vendesti	dormisti

(lui/lei; lei)	parlò	vendé	dormì
		or **vendette**	
(noi)	parlammo	vendemmo	dormimmo
(voi)	parlaste	vendeste	dormiste
(loro)	parlarono	venderono	dormirono
		or **vendettero**	

Pagò il conto e se ne andò.
He paid the bill and left.

La città **fu fondata** nel 500 a.C.
The city was founded in 500 BC.

The pluperfect tense

The pluperfect tense is used to talk about events that happened *before* the event that is the main focus of attention. Like the perfect tense, it uses a form of **avere** or **essere** with the past participle: the past tense of **avere** (or **essere** if the verb forms its compound tenses with **essere**) is followed by the past participle. If the verb uses **essere** as an auxiliary, the past participle agrees with the subject (see the section on the perfect tense).

Li **avevo visti** l'estate prima.
I had seen them the summer before.

Ci **eravamo** già **conosciuti**.
We had already met.

The future tense

In Italian, the future can be expressed in different ways.

1 You can use the present tense with an appropriate time expression when talking about plans (as in English):

   Non **sono** libero domani.
   I'm not/I won't be available tomorrow.

   Partiamo per le vacanze lunedì prossimo.
   We're going on holiday next Monday.

2 You can use the future tense – especially when making predictions (as in weather forecasts or horoscopes) or stating a fact about the future.

   Avrete molto successo.
   You will have great success.

   Balleranno tutta la notte.
   They'll dance all night.

   Domani **nevicherà**.
   Tomorrow it will snow.

The future tense is formed by dropping the final **-e** of the infinitive and adding the future endings. In **-are** verbs, the a in the infinitive changes to **e**.

	parlare	prendere	dormire
(io)	parlerò	prenderò	dormirò
(tu)	parlerai	prenderai	dormirai
(lui)	parlerà	prenderà	dormirà
(noi)	parleremo	prenderemo	dormiremo
(voi)	parlerete	prenderete	dormirete
(loro)	parleranno	prenderanno	dormiranno

Stasera Elio **parlerà** con il padre.
Tonight Elio will talk to his father.

Non lo **lascerà** mai.
She'll never leave him.

Verbs ending in **-care** and **-gare** add an **h** before the endings to keep the hard sound of the stem.

Gli spie**gher**emo tutto noi.
We will explain everything to him.

Cer**cherete** subito lavoro?
Will you be looking for work straight away?

For irregular future forms, see the verb tables on pages 954–962.

The conditional

In Italian the conditional is used for polite requests and suggestions, and to express a wish or a probable action. The endings are the same for all conjugations and, like the future tense, are added to the infinitive minus the final **-e** (or, if irregular, to the same stem used for the future tense).
As with the future, the **a** in **-are** verbs changes to **e**. The rules affecting the spelling of **cercare**, **spiegare**, etc. also apply; see above.

	parlare	prendere	dormire
(io)	parlerei	prenderei	dormirei
(tu)	parleresti	prenderesti	dormiresti
(lui/lei; lei)	parlerebbe	prenderebbe	dormirebbe
(noi)	parleremmo	prenderemmo	dormiremmo
(voi)	parlereste	prendereste	dormireste
(loro)	parlerebbero	prenderebbero	dormirebbero

Potremmo venire con te.
We could come with you.

Dovresti andare a letto presto.
You should go to bed early.

Vorrebbe fare una partita a tennis?
Would you like to have a game of tennis?

Non **vivrebbero** mai all'estero.
They'd never live abroad.

Saresti il primo a saperlo.
You'd be the first to know.

The subjunctive

The subjunctive is a special form of the verb that expresses doubt, unlikelihood, or desire. The subjunctive is not very common in modern English, and often forms with *let, should,* etc. do the same job. In Italian the subjunctive is very common, and is obligatory in certain circumstances. The subjunctive is commonly used to show that what is being said is not a concrete fact, for example to indicate doubt or necessity, or after verbs of ordering, requiring, or persuasion. It contrasts with the *indicative,* the normal form of the verb, which always implies a greater degree of certainty. The subjunctive is sometimes translated by an infinitive in English.

The present subjunctive is generally used when the main verb in the sentence is in the present; the past subjunctive is used when the main verb is in the past, or in order to talk about hypothetical situations.

For the forms of the subjunctive, see the verb tables on pages 954–962.

Credo che tu abbia ragione.
I think you're right.

Spero che questo problema si risolva.
I hope this problem is solved.

Bisogna che tu legga tutto.
It's necessary for you to read it all.

Voglio che tu mi aiuti.
I want you to help me.

Volevo che mi aiutassi.
I wanted you to help me.

Summary of Italian grammar

. . . .

Regular verbs -are

parlare – to speak (past participle **parlato**)

	present	future	conditional	perfect	imperfect
io	parlo	parlerò	parlerei	ho parlato	parlavo
tu	parli	parlerai	parleresti	hai parlato	parlavi
lui/lei; lei	parla	parlerà	parlerebbe	ha parlato	parlava
noi	parliamo	parleremo	parleremmo	abbiamo parlato	parlavamo
voi	parlate	parlerete	parlereste	avete parlato	parlavate
loro	parlano	parleranno	parlerebbero	hanno parlato	parlavano

	pluperfect	past historic	present subjunctive	past subjunctive	imperative
io	avevo parlato	parlai	parli	parlassi	
tu	avevi parlato	parlasti	parli	parlassi	parla
lui/lei; lei	aveva parlato	parlò	parli	parlasse	parli
noi	avevamo parlato	parlammo	parliamo	parlassimo	parliamo
voi	avevate parlato	parlaste	parliate	parlaste	parlate
loro	avevano parlato	parlarono	parlino	parlassero	

Verbs ending in **-care** and **-gare**, such as **cercare**, ('to look for') or **spiegare** ('to explain'), add an **h** before **i** or **e**.

Cherchiamo un posto tranquillo. We're looking for a quiet place.

Ti spieghiamo tutto domani. We'll explain everything tomorrow.

Regular verbs -ere

credere – to believe (past participle **creduto**)

	present	future	conditional	perfect	imperfect
io	credo	crederò	crederei	ho creduto	credevo
tu	credi	crederai	crederesti	hai creduto	credevi
lui/lei; lei	crede	crederà	crederebbe	ha creduto	credeva
noi	crediamo	crederemo	crederemmo	abbiamo creduto	credevamo
voi	credete	crederete	credereste	avete creduto	credevate
loro	credono	crederanno	crederebbero	hanno creduto	credevano

	pluperfect	past historic	present subjunctive	past subjunctive	imperative
io	avevo creduto	credei or credetti	creda	credessi	
tu	avevi creduto	credesti	creda	credessi	credi
lui/lei; lei	aveva creduto	credé or credette	creda	credesse	creda
noi	avevamo creduto	credemmo	crediamo	credessimo	crediamo
voi	avevate creduto	credeste	crediate	credeste	credete
loro	avevano creduto	crederono or credettero	credano	credessero	

Summary of Italian grammar

Regular verbs -ire (1)

sentire – to hear (past participle **sentito**)

	present	future	conditional	perfect	imperfect
io	sento	sentirò	sentirei	ho sentito	sentivo
tu	senti	sentirai	sentiresti	hai sentito	sentivi
lui/lei; lei	sente	sentirà	sentirebbe	ha sentito	sentiva
noi	sentiamo	sentiremo	sentiremmo	abbiamo sentito	sentivamo
voi	sentite	sentirete	sentireste	avete sentito	sentivate
loro	sentono	sentiranno	sentirebbero	hanno sentito	sentivano

	pluperfect	past historic	present subjunctive	past subjunctive	imperative
io	avevo sentito	sentii	senta	sentissi	
tu	avevi sentito	sentisti	senta	sentissi	senti
lui/lei; lei	aveva sentito	sentì	senta	sentisse	senta
noi	avevamo sentito	sentimmo	sentiamo	sentissimo	sentiamo
voi	avevate sentito	sentiste	sentiate	sentiste	sentite
loro	avevano sentito	sentirono	sentano	sentissero	

Regular verbs -ire (2)

Some verbs ending in **-ire** insert **-isc-** between the stem and the ending in the three singular forms and in the 3rd person plural form of the present tense.

finire – to finish (past participle **finito**)

	present	future	conditional	perfect	imperfect
io	finisco	finirò	finirei	ho finito	finivo
tu	finisci	finirai	finiresti	hai finito	finivi
lui/lei; lei	finisce	finirà	finirebbe	ha finito	finiva
noi	finiamo	finiremo	finiremmo	abbiamo finito	finivamo
voi	finite	finirete	finireste	avete finito	finivate
loro	finiscono	finiranno	finirebbero	hanno finito	finivano

	pluperfect	past historic	present subjunctive	past subjunctive	imperative
io	avevo finito	finii	finisca	finissi	
tu	avevi finito	finisti	finisca	finissi	finisci
lui/lei; lei	aveva finito	finì	finisca	finisse	finisca
noi	avevamo finito	finimmo	finiamo	finissimo	finiamo
voi	avevate finito	finiste	finiate	finiste	finite
loro	avevano finito	finirono	finiscano	finissero	

Irregular verbs

....

avere – to have (past participle **avuto**)

	present	future	conditional	perfect	imperfect
io	ho	avrò	avrei	ho avuto	avevo
tu	hai	avrai	avresti	hai avuto	avevi
lui/lei; lei	ha	avrà	avrebbe	ha avuto	aveva
noi	abbiamo	avremo	avremmo	abbiamo avuto	avevamo
voi	avete	avrete	avreste	avete avuto	avevate
loro	hanno	avranno	avrebbero	hanno avuto	avevano

	pluperfect	past historic	present subjunctive	past subjunctive	imperative
io	avevo avuto	ebbi	abbia	avessi	
tu	avevi avuto	avesti	abbia	avessi	abbi
lui/lei; lei	aveva avuto	ebbe	abbia	avesse	abbia
noi	avevamo avuto	avemmo	abbiamo	avessimo	abbiamo
voi	avevate avuto	aveste	abbiate	aveste	abbiate
loro	avevano avuto	ebbero	abbiano	avessero	

essere* – to be (past participle **stato**)

	present	future	conditional	perfect	imperfect
io	sono	sarò	sarei	sono stato/stata	ero
tu	sei	sarai	saresti	sei stato/stata	eri
lui/lei; lei	è	sarà	sarebbe	è stato/stata	era
noi	siamo	saremo	saremmo	siamo stati/state	eravamo
voi	siete	sarete	sareste	siete stati/state	eravate
loro	sono	saranno	sarebbero	sono stati/state	erano

	pluperfect	past historic	present subjunctive	past subjunctive	imperative
io	ero stato/stata	fui	sia	fossi	
tu	eri stato/stata	fosti	sia	fossi	sii
lui/lei; lei	era stato/stata	fu	sia	fosse	sia
noi	eravamo stati/state	fummo	siamo	fossimo	siamo
voi	eravate stati/state	foste	siate	foste	siate
loro	erano stati/state	furono	siano	fossero	

● ●

Irregular verbs cont.

andare* – to go (past participle **andato**)

	present	future	conditional	perfect	imperfect
io	vado	andrò	andrei	sono andato/andata	andavo
tu	vai	andrai	andresti	sei andato/andata	andavi
lui/lei; lei	va	andrà	andrebbe	è andato/andata	andava
noi	andiamo	andremo	andremmo	siamo andati/andate	andavamo
voi	andate	andrete	andreste	siete andati/andate	andavate
loro	vanno	andranno	andrebbero	sono andati/andate	andavano

	pluperfect	past historic	present subjunctive	past subjunctive	imperative
io	ero andato/andata	andai	vada	andassi	
tu	eri andato/andata	andasti	vada	andassi	va'
lui/lei; lei	era andato/andata	andò	vada	andasse	vada
noi	eravamo andati/andate	andammo	andiamo	andassimo	andiamo
voi	eravate andati/andate	andaste	andiate	andaste	andate
loro	erano andati/andate	andarono	vadano	andassero	

bere – to drink (past participle **bevuto**)

	present	future	conditional	perfect	imperfect
io	bevo	berrò	berrei	ho bevuto	bevevo
tu	bevi	berrai	berresti	hai bevuto	bevevi
lui/lei; lei	beve	berrà	berrebbe	ha bevuto	beveva
noi	beviamo	berremo	berremmo	abbiamo bevuto	bevevamo
voi	bevete	berrete	berreste	avete bevuto	bevevate
loro	bevono	berranno	berrebbero	hanno bevuto	bevevano

	pluperfect	past historic	present subjunctive	past subjunctive	imperative
io	avevo bevuto	bevvi or bevetti	beva	bevessi	
tu	avevi bevuto	bevesti	beva	bevessi	bevi
lui/lei; lei	aveva bevuto	bevve or bevette	beva	bevesse	beva
noi	avevamo bevuto	bevemmo	beviamo	bevessimo	beviamo
voi	avevate bevuto	beveste	beviate	beveste	bevete
loro	avevano bevuto	bevvero or bevettero	bevano	bevessero	

Irregular verbs cont.

dare – to give (past participle dato)

	present	future	conditional	perfect	imperfect
io	do	darò	darei	ho dato	davo
tu	dai	darai	daresti	hai dato	davi
lui/lei; lei	dà	darà	darebbe	ha dato	dava
noi	diamo	daremo	daremmo	abbiamo dato	davamo
voi	date	darete	dareste	avete dato	davate
loro	danno	daranno	darebbero	hanno dato	davano

	pluperfect	past historic	present subjunctive	past subjunctive	imperative
io	avevo dato	diedi or detti	dia	dessi	
tu	avevi dato	desti	dia	dessi	da'
lui/lei; lei	aveva dato	diede or dette	dia	desse	dia
noi	avevamo dato	demmo	diamo	dessimo	diamo
voi	avevate dato	deste	diate	deste	date
loro	avevano dato	diedero or dettero	diano	dessero	

dire – to say (past participle detto)

	present	future	conditional	perfect	imperfect
io	dico	dirò	direi	ho detto	dicevo
tu	dici	dirai	diresti	hai detto	dicevi
lui/lei; lei	dice	dirà	direbbe	ha detto	diceva
noi	diciamo	diremo	diremmo	abbiamo detto	dicevamo
voi	dite	direte	direste	avete detto	dicevate
loro	dicono	diranno	direbbero	hanno detto	dicevano

	pluperfect	past historic	present subjunctive	past subjunctive	imperative
io	avevo detto	dissi	dica	dicessi	
tu	avevi detto	dicesti	dica	dicessi	di'
lui/lei; lei	aveva detto	disse	dica	dicesse	dica
noi	avevamo detto	dicemmo	diciamo	dicessimo	diciamo
voi	avevate detto	diceste	diciate	diceste	dite
loro	avevano detto	dissero	dicano	dicessero	

Irregular verbs cont.

dovere – to have to (past participle **dovuto**)

	present	future	conditional	perfect	imperfect
io	devo	dovrò	dovrei	ho dovuto	dovevo
tu	devi	dovrai	dovresti	hai dovuto	dovevi
lui/lei; lei	deve	dovrà	dovrebbe	ha dovuto	doveva
noi	dobbiamo	dovremo	dovremmo	abbiamo dovuto	dovevamo
voi	dovete	dovrete	dovreste	avete dovuto	dovevate
loro	devono	dovranno	dovrebbero	hanno dovuto	dovevano

	pluperfect	past historic	present subjunctive	past subjunctive
io	avevo dovuto	dovetti	deva	dovessi
tu	avevi dovuto	dovesti	deva	dovessi
lui/lei; lei	aveva dovuto	dovette	deva	dovesse
noi	avevamo dovuto	dovemmo	dobbiamo	dovessimo
voi	avevate dovuto	doveste	dobbiate	doveste
loro	avevano dovuto	dovettero	devano	dovessero

fare – to do, to make (past participle **fatto**)

	present	future	conditional	perfect	imperfect
io	faccio	farò	farei	ho fatto	facevo
tu	fai	farai	faresti	hai fatto	facevi
lui/lei; lei	fa	fara	farebbe	ha fatto	faceva
noi	facciamo	faremo	faremmo	abbiamo fatto	facevamo
voi	fate	farete	fareste	avete fatto	facevate
loro	fanno	faranno	farebbero	hanno fatto	facevano

	pluperfect	past historic	present subjunctive	past subjunctive	imperative
io	avevo fatto	feci	faccia	facessi	
tu	avevi fatto	facesti	faccia	facessi	fa'
lui/lei; lei	aveva fatto	fece	faccia	facesse	faccia
noi	avevamo fatto	facemmo	facciamo	facessimo	facciamo
voi	avevate fatto	faceste	facciate	faceste	fate
loro	avevano fatto	fecero	facciano	facessero	

Irregular verbs cont.

potere – to be able to (past participle **potuto**)

	present	future	conditional	perfect	imperfect
io	posso	potrò	potrei	ho potuto	potevo
tu	puoi	potrai	potresti	hai potuto	potevi
lui/lei; lei	può	potrà	potrebbe	ha potuto	poteva
noi	possiamo	potremo	potremmo	abbiamo potuto	potevamo
voi	potete	potrete	potreste	avete potuto	potevate
loro	possono	potranno	potrebbero	hanno potuto	potevano

	pluperfect	past historic	present subjunctive	past subjunctive
io	avevo potuto	potei	possa	potessi
tu	avevi potuto	potesti	possa	potessi
lui/lei; lei	aveva potuto	poté	possa	potesse
noi	avevamo potuto	potemmo	possiamo	potessimo
voi	avevate potuto	poteste	possiate	poteste
loro	avevano potuto	poterono	possano	potessero

sapere – to know (a fact, how to do something) (past participle **saputo**)

	present	future	conditional	perfect	imperfect
io	so	saprò	saprei	ho saputo	sapevo
tu	sai	saprai	sapresti	hai saputo	sapevi
lui/lei; lei	sa	saprà	saprebbe	ha saputo	sapeva
noi	sappiamo	sapremo	sapremmo	abbiamo saputo	sapevamo
voi	sapete	saprete	sapreste	avete saputo	sapevate
loro	sanno	sapranno	saprebbero	hanno saputo	sapevano

	pluperfect	past historic	present subjunctive	past subjunctive	imperative
io	avevo saputo	seppi	sappia	sapessi	
tu	avevi saputo	sapesti	sappia	sapessi	sappi
lui/lei; lei	aveva saputo	seppe	sappia	sapesse	sappia
noi	avevamo saputo	sapemmo	sappiamo	sapessimo	sappiamo
voi	avevate saputo	sapeste	sappiate	sapeste	sappiate
loro	avevano saputo	seppero	sappiano	sapessero	

. . . .

Irregular verbs cont.

stare* – to stay (past participle **stato**)

	present	future	conditional	perfect	imperfect
io	sto	starò	starei	sono stato/stata	stavo
tu	stai	starai	staresti	sei stato/stata	stavi
lui/lei; lei	sta	starà	starebbe	è stato/stata	stava
noi	stiamo	staremo	staremmo	siamo stati/state	stavamo
voi	state	starete	stareste	siete stati/state	stavate
loro	stanno	staranno	starebbero	sono stati/state	stavano

	pluperfect	past historic	present subjunctive	past subjunctive	imperative
io	ero stato/stata	stetti	stia	stessi	
tu	eri stato/stata	stesti	stia	stessi	sta'
lui/lei; lei	era stato/stata	stette	stia	stesse	stia
noi	eravamo stati/state	stemmo	stiamo	stessimo	stiamo
voi	eravate stati/state	steste	stiate	steste	state
loro	erano stati/state	stettero	stiano	stessero	

uscire* – to go out (past participle **uscito**)

	present	future	conditional	perfect	imperfect
io	esco	uscirò	uscirei	sono uscito/uscita	uscivo
tu	esci	uscirai	usciresti	sei uscito/uscita	uscivi
lui/lei; lei	esce	uscirà	uscirebbe	è uscito/uscita	usciva
noi	usciamo	usciremo	usciremmo	siamo usciti/uscite	uscivamo
voi	uscite	uscirete	uscireste	siete usciti/uscite	uscivate
loro	escono	usciranno	uscirebbero	sono usciti/uscite	uscivano

	pluperfect	past historic	present subjunctive	past subjunctive	imperative
io	ero uscito/uscita	uscii	esca	uscissi	
tu	eri uscito/uscita	uscisti	esca	uscissi	esci
lui/lei; lei	era uscito/uscita	uscì	esca	uscisse	esca
noi	eravamo usciti/uscite	uscimmo	usciamo	uscissimo	usciamo
voi	eravate usciti/uscite	usciste	usciate	usciste	uscite
loro	erano usciti/uscite	uscirono	escano	uscissero	

. . . .

Irregular verbs cont.

venire* – to come (past participle **venuto**)

	present	future	conditional	perfect	imperfect
io	vengo	verrò	verrei	sono venuto/venuta	venivo
tu	vieni	verrai	verresti	sei venuto/venuta	venivi
lui/lei; lei	viene	verrà	verrebbe	è venuto/venuta	veniva
noi	veniamo	verremo	verremmo	siamo venuti/venute	venivamo
voi	venite	verrete	verreste	siete venuti/venute	venivate
loro	vengono	verranno	verrebbero	sono venuti/venute	venivano

	pluperfect	past historic	present subjunctive	past subjunctive	imperative
io	ero venuto/venuta	venni	venga	venissi	
tu	eri venuto/venuta	venisti	venga	venissi	vieni
lui/lei; lei	era venuto/venuta	venne	venga	venisse	venga
noi	eravamo venuti/venute	venimmo	veniamo	venissimo	veniamo
voi	eravate venuti/venute	veniste	veniate	veniste	venite
loro	erano venuti/venute	vennero	vengano	venissero	

volere – to want (past participle **voluto**)

	present	future	conditional	perfect	imperfect
io	voglio	vorrò	vorrei	ho voluto	volevo
tu	vuoi	vorrai	vorresti	hai voluto	volevi
lui/lei; lei	vuole	vorrà	vorrebbe	ha voluto	voleva
noi	vogliamo	vorremo	vorremmo	abbiamo voluto	volevamo
voi	volete	vorrete	vorreste	avete voluto	volevate
loro	vogliono	vorranno	vorrebbero	hanno voluto	volevano

	pluperfect	past historic	present subjunctive	past subjunctive
io	avevo voluto	volli	voglia	volessi
tu	avevi voluto	volesti	voglia	volessi
lui/lei; lei	aveva voluto	volle	voglia	volesse
noi	avevamo voluto	volemmo	vogliamo	volessimo
voi	avevate voluto	voleste	vogliate	voleste
loro	avevano voluto	vollero	vogliano	volessero

Note sulla grammatica inglese

Gli articoli

l'articolo indeterminativo

L'articolo indeterminativo è **a** davanti a una parola che comincia con consonante o con il suono 'i + vocal' (/j/):

a ball	**a girl**	**a union**
una palla	una ragazza	un'unione

È **an** davanti a vocale o h muta:

an apple	**an hour**
una mela	un'ora

L'uso dell'articolo indeterminativo è generalmente limitato ai nomi numerabili. Da notare i seguenti usi:

- con professione

She is a doctor.	**He is an engineer.**
È medico.	È ingegnere.

- dopo una preposizione

She works as a tour guide.
Fa la guida turistica.

Anna has gone out without an umbrella.
Anna è uscita senza ombrello.

- con senso generico

A whale is larger than a frog.
La balena è più grande della rana.

l'articolo determinativo

L'articolo determinativo è **the**, sia per i nomi singolari che per i plurali:

the cat	**the owls**
il gatto	le civette

L'articolo determinativo *non* viene generalmente usato con le parole che designano:

- istituzioni

I don't go to church.
Non vado in chiesa.

He's starting school next week.
Comincia la scuola la settimana prossima.

Quando ci si riferisce all'edificio, il nome viene invece accompagnato dall'articolo:
Turn right at the school (Alla scuola, gira a destra).

- pasti

Breakfast is at 8.30.
La colazione è alle 8.30.

Dinner is ready!
La cena è pronta!

- periodi del giorno, dopo una preposizione (eccetto **in** o **during**)

I'm never out at night.
Non esco mai di sera.

They left in the morning.
Sono partiti di mattina.

- cose astratte

Hatred is a destructive force.
L'odio è una forza distruttrice.

The book is on English grammar.
Il libro è sulla grammatica inglese.

- malattie

She's got tonsillitis.
Ha la tonsillite.

- stagioni

Spring is here!
È arrivata la primavera!

It's like winter today.
Oggi, sembra inverno.

- nazioni

France	la Francia
England	l'Inghilterra

- vie, parchi, ecc.

a concert in Central Park
un concerto a Central Park

I work on Bath Street.
Lavoro in Bath Street.

L'articolo è tuttavia utilizzato nei seguenti tipi di frasi:

The breakfast he served was awful.
La colazione che ha servito era orribile.

Le seguenti categorie di nomi prendono generalmente l'articolo determinativo:

- nomi geografici plurali

the Netherlands	i Paesi Bassi
the United States	gli Stati Uniti
the Alps	le Alpi

• nomi di fiumi e oceani

the Thames il Tamigi
the Pacific il Pacifico

• nomi di hotel, pub, teatri, musei, ecc.

the Hilton
the Fox and Hounds
the Odeon

Il plurale

Il plurale di un nome è di solito formato aggiungendo **-s** in fine di parola:

dog, dogs cane, cani
tape, tapes cassetta, cassette

-es viene aggiunto a parole che terminano in **-s, -ss, -sh, -ch, -x** o **-zz**:

dress, dresses vestito, vestiti
box, boxes scatola, scatole

Nomi che terminano in consonante + y:

baby, babies bambino, bambini

Nomi che terminano in vocale + y:

valley, valleys valle, valli

I nomi che terminano in **-o** talvolta prendono **-s**, talvolta **-es**:

potato, potatoes patata, patate
tomato, tomatoes pomodoro, pomodori
solo, solos assolo, assoli
zero, zeros zero, zeri

I plurali dei nomi terminanti in **-f(e)** sono di tre tipi:

life, lives vita, vite
dwarf, dwarfs/dwarves nano, nani
roof, roofs tetto, tetti

I plurali irregolari più frequenti includono:

child, children bambino, bambini
foot, feet piede, piedi
man, men uomo, uomini
mouse, mice topo, topi
tooth, teeth dente, denti
woman, women donna, donne

I nomi composti

I nomi composti possono avere diverse forme.

nome + nome:

summer dress abito estivo
tennis shoes scarpe da tennis
record collection collezione di dischi

nome + gerundio:

disco dancing ballo da discoteca
dressmaking cucito

gerundio + nome:

parking meter parchimetro
writing course corso di scrittura
boarding card carta di imbarco

Da notare la forma di composti quali **record collection**: a **record collection** (senza la **s** del plurale in **record**), ma a **collection of records** [una collezione di dischi]; a **photo album**, ma an **album of photos** [un album di fotografie].

Nel caso di nomi numerabili, la **s** del plurale va aggiunta al secondo elemento del composto: **summer dresses** [abiti estivi], **boarding cards** [carte di imbarco].

Il femminile

L'inglese ha un numero relativamente basso di forme femminili di parole. Pertanto, **cousin** = cugino o cugina;
friend = amico o amica; **doctor** = dottore o dottoressa.

Dovendo specificare il sesso della persona alla quale ci si riferisce, si dirà, ad esempio, **a male student** (uno studente), **a woman doctor** (una dottoressa).

Il genitivo

Le regole sull'uso del genitivo – **s** preceduto dall'apostrofo (**'s**) o **s** seguito dall'apostrofo (**s'**) – sono le seguenti:

-'s viene aggiunto a nomi singolari:

the boy's book (il libro del ragazzo)

il solo apostrofo (**'**) viene aggiunto a nomi plurali terminanti in **-s**:

the boys' room (la camera dei ragazzi)
the boys' books (i libri dei ragazzi)

Se un nome plurale non termina in **-s** il genitivo si forma aggiungendo **-'s**:

the children's toys (i giocattoli dei bambini)

Con nomi propri terminanti in **-s** si possono trovare entrambe le forme **'s** e **s'**, benché **s'** sia più frequente: **Keats's poetry** o **Keats' poetry** [le poesie di Keats]. I nomi greci e romani terminanti in **s**, tuttavia, prendono in genere solo l'apostrofo: **Socrates' death** [la morte di Socrate], **Catullus' poetry** [le poesie di Catullo].

Il genitivo viene usato soprattutto con persone, animali (in particolare domestici) e paesi: **Andrew's house** [la casa di Andrew], **the lion's den** [la tana del leone], **America's foreign policy** [la politica estera dell'America].

Da notare i seguenti usi del genitivo:

We're going to Anne's.
Andiamo a casa di Anne.

We're going to Peter and Anne's.
Andiamo a casa di Peter e Anne. (Non, per lo più, **Peter's and Anne's** se Peter e Anne sono una coppia.)

Jane Austen's and George Orwell's novels
i romanzi di Jane Austen e quelli di George Orwell (Jane Austen e George Orwell sono ben distinti l'una dall'altro.)

I got it at the baker's/the chemist's.
L'ho preso dal panettiere/in farmacia (Letteralmente, nel negozio del panettiere/ del farmacista.)

Nell'inglese colloquiale il 'doppio genitivo' è frequente:

He's a friend of my brother's.
È un amico di mio fratello.

It was an idea of Anne's.
È stata un'idea di Anne.

Gli aggettivi

Gli aggettivi in inglese hanno un'unica forma, non concordano, cioè, né nel genere, né nel numero:

an old man
un uomo vecchio

three old women
tre donne vecchie

posizione dell'aggettivo

L'aggettivo può precedere il nome: **a long story** [una storia lunga] o seguire il verbo: **this story is long** [questa storia è lunga].

Alcuni aggettivi non possono essere usati davanti al nome: **The girl is upset.** [La ragazza è sconvolta.]; non si può dire **the upset girl**.

gradi comparativi

Ci sono tre gradi comparativi: la forma assoluta, il comparativo e il superlativo.

Gli aggettivi composti da una sola sillaba

formano il comparativo e il superlativo con l'aggiunta di **-(e)r** e **-(e)st**:

dull noioso
duller più noioso
dullest il più noioso

big grande
bigger
biggest

(Da notare che una consonante semplice in fine di parola viene raddoppiata.)

nice bello
nicer
nicest

Gli aggettivi di tre sillabe, per lo più, formano il comparativo e il superlativo con **more** e **most**:

generous generoso
more generous
most generous

Lo stesso vale per alcuni aggettivi di due sillabe, ad esempio **useful** [utile].

Non esistono tuttavia regole assolute per gli aggettivi bisillabici, benché **-er/-est** siano particolarmente frequenti con aggettivi terminanti in **-y, -le, -ow, -er**. Esempi:

pretty carino (da notare che **-y** diventa **-ie**)
prettier
prettiest

narrow stretto
narrower
narrowest

curious curioso
more curious
most curious

Per i participi presenti e passati si usa la forma con **more/most**:

boring noioso
more boring
most boring

bored annoiato
more bored
most bored

Most può essere inoltre usato come sinonimo di 'estremamente' o 'molto':
That was a most interesting story (Quella era una storia molto interessante).

alcuni aggettivi irregolari frequenti

bad cattivo
worse peggiore

worst il peggiore

good buono
better migliore
best il migliore

little poco
less meno
least il meno

many/much molti/molto
more più
most il più

far lontano
further
furthest (con riferimento a spazio, tempo, quantità, numero)

far lontano
farther
farthest (solo per distanza nello spazio)

old (1) vecchio
elder
eldest (usato solo per persone)

(1) Le forme regolari (**old, older, oldest** vecchio, più vecchio, il più vecchio) sono usate sia per persone che per cose.

Le comparazioni negative possono essere espresse dall'uso di **less/least**:

far lontano
less far meno lontano
least far il meno lontano

Gli aggettivi possono svolgere la funzione di nomi, in particolare quando si riferiscono a gruppi di persone: **the young** i giovani; **the old** i vecchi; **the unemployed** i disoccupati.

Gli aggettivi possessivi

Gli aggettivi possessivi sono:

my mio, mia, miei, mie
our nostro, nostra, nostri, nostre
your tuo, tua, tuoi, tue; suo,
your vostro, vostra, vostri, sua, suoi, sue vostre
his, her, its suo, sua, suoi, sue
their loro

Concordano con il possessore e non con la cosa posseduta:

his mother sua madre (la madre del ragazzo, ad esempio)

her mother sua madre (la madre della ragazza, ad esempio)

their mother la loro madre (la madre delle ragazze, o dei ragazzi, o dei ragazzi e delle ragazze)

Mantengono la stessa forma con nomi singolari e plurali:

my cat il mio gatto
my boots i miei stivali

Gli avverbi

Gli avverbi possono qualificare aggettivi:

The job was extremely dangerous.
Il lavoro era estremamente pericoloso.

verbi:

He finished quickly.
Ha finito in fretta.

altri avverbi:

very quickly
molto in fretta

Extremely, quickly e **very** sono avverbi.

Molti avverbi sono formati con il suffisso **-ly** aggiunto all'aggettivo: **sad, sadly** triste, tristemente; **brave, bravely** coraggioso, coraggiosamente; **beautiful, beautifully** bello, molto bene.

Possono tuttavia intervenire dei cambiamenti nell'ortografia: **true, truly** vero, veramente; **due, duly** dovuto, debitamente; **whole, wholly** intero, interamente.

Altri mutamenti fonetici regolari riguardano:

y in fine di parola: **ready, readily** pronto, prontamente

consonante in fine di parola + **le**: **gentle, gently** dolce, dolcemente.

Alcuni avverbi hanno forma identica all'aggettivo corrispondente; tra questi **back** dietro, **early** presto, **far** lontano, **fast** velocemente, **left** a sinistra, **little** poco, **long** a lungo, **more** più, **much** molto, **only** solo, **right** a destra, giustamente, **still** tranquillamente, **straight** dritto, **well** bene, **wrong** in modo sbagliato. Esempi:

a wrong answer (aggettivo)
una risposta sbagliata

He did it wrong. (avverbio)
L'ha fatto in modo sbagliato.

Note sulla grammatica inglese

. . . .

an early summer
un'estate precoce

Summer arrived early.
L'estate è arrivata in anticipo.

a straight road
una strada dritta

He came straight to the point.
È andato dritto al punto.

I pronomi

pronomi personali

soggetto	complemento
I io	me me, mi
you tu; lei	you te, ti; la, le
he egli, lui	him lo, gli
she essa, lei	her la, le
it esso, essa	it lo, la, gli, le
we noi	us ci
you voi	you vi
they essi, loro	them li, loro

Il soggetto di un verbo in inglese non è espresso dalla forma del verbo stesso; pertanto, la traduzione dell'italiano **vado**, ad esempio, è **I go** e non **go**.

I pronomi complemento sono usati come complemento oggetto:

Mary loves him.
Mary lo ama.

come complemento di termine:

John gave me a lift.
John mi ha dato un passaggio.

e dopo una preposizione:

The book is from her.
Il libro è da parte sua.

altri usi dei pronomi personali

he e she

Questi pronomi sono talvolta usati per indicare degli animali, specialmente domestici:

Poor Whiskers, we had to take him to the vet's.
Povero Whiskers, abbiamo dovuto portarlo dal veterinario.

it

• è usato in costruzioni impersonali:

It's sunny.
C'è il sole.

It's hard to know what to do.
È difficile sapere cosa fare.

It looks as though they were right.
Parrebbe che avessero ragione.

• in espressioni temporali e spaziali:

It's five o'clock.
Sono le cinque.

It's January the sixth.
È il sei gennaio.

How far is it to Edinburgh?
Quanto dista Edimburgo?

Va notato che **it's** è la forma contratta di **it is**, da non confondersi con il pronome possessivo **its**.

you

Rivolgendosi ad una persona, l'inglese non distingue l'uso del pronome **tu** dal pronome **lei** che vengono entrambi tradotti con **you**.

You è spesso usato in senso generico, per indicare la gente in generale:

You never know; it might be sunny this afternoon.
Non si sa mai; potrebbe esserci il sole oggi pomeriggio.

You can't buy cars like that any more.
Non si possono più comprare macchine così.

they

• è impiegato per riferirsi a un gruppo di persone sconosciute, specialmente se dotate di un qualche potere, autorità o abilità:

They don't make cars like that any more.
Non ne fanno più di macchine così.

They will have to find the murderer first.
Dovranno prima trovare l'assassino.

You'll have to get them to repair it.
Dovrai farglielo riparare.

• al posto di **he or she** (lui o lei)

The person appointed will be answerable to the director. They will be responsible for ...
La persona prescelta dovrà rispondere al direttore. Sarà responsabile di ...

A personal secretary will assist them. (= him/her)
Una segretaria personale lo/la assisterà.

• per rimandare ai pronomi indefiniti **somebody, someone** qualcuno; **anybody, anyone** chiunque; **everybody, everyone** tutti; **nobody, no one** nessuno:

• •

If anyone has seen my pen, will they please tell me.
Se qualcuno ha visto la mia penna, per favore, me lo dica.

one

One è equivalente al pronome generico **you**, ma è più formale:

One needs to get a clearer picture of what one wants.
Bisogna avere un'idea più chiara di quello che si vuole.

L'uso ripetuto di **one** viene di solito evitato.

pronomi riflessivi

myself mi	**ourselves** ci
yourself ti; si	**yourselves** vi
himself, herself, itself, oneself si	**themselves** si

Esempi dell'uso:

He burned himself badly. (complemento oggetto)
Si è bruciato seriamente.

I always buy myself a Christmas present. (complemento di termine)
Mi compro sempre un regalo di Natale.

She talks to herself. (dopo preposizione)
Parla da sola.

Do it yourself. (enfatico)
Fallo da te.

pronomi possessivi

mine il mio, la mia, i miei, le mie
yours il tuo, la tua, i tuoi, le tue
his, hers il suo, la sua, i suoi, le sue
ours il nostro, la nostra, i nostri, le nostre
yours il vostro, la vostra, i vostri, le vostre
theirs il loro, la loro, i loro, le loro

I pronomi possessivi concordano con il possessore e non con la cosa posseduta:

Whose book is this? – It's hers.
Di chi è questo libro? – È suo.

Whose shoes are these? – They're hers.
Di chi sono queste scarpe? – Sono le sue.

Whose car is that? – It's theirs.
Di chi è questa macchina? – È la loro.

Gli aggettivi e i pronomi interrogativi

who chi
whom chi
whose di chi

which quale, quali
what quale, quali, che

Who è usato per persona con funzione di soggetto:

Who is it? Chi è?

Whom è usato per persona con funzione di complemento:

To whom did you send the letter?
A chi hai spedito la lettera?

Whom did you see?
Chi hai visto?

Whom è considerato piuttosto formale e tende ad essere sostituito da **who**:

Who did you send the letter to?
A chi hai spedito la lettera?

Who did you see?
Chi hai visto?

Whose è la forma genitiva di **who**:

Whose are these?
Di chi sono questi?

Whose socks are these?
Di chi sono queste calze?

Which può designare sia persone che cose. È usato con funzione di soggetto:

Which of you are going?
Chi di voi va?

Which is bigger?
Qual è più grande?

Which box is bigger?
Quale scatola è più grande?

e di complemento:

Which of the singers/pictures do you prefer?
Quale cantante/quadro preferisci?

Which dress should I wear?
Che vestito mi metto?

What è usato esclusivamente per cose. Può avere funzione di soggetto:

What is this?
Cos'è questo?

What type of bird is that?
Che tipo di uccello è quello?

e di complemento:

What are you going to do?
Cosa farai?

What sort of books do you like?
Che tipo di libri ti piacciono?

What implica una gamma di possibilità più estesa o meno definita rispetto a **which**.

I pronomi relativi

who, whom che	which che
that chi, che	whose il cui

I pronomi relativi rimandano normalmente ad un antecedente (cioè qualcosa che è già stato menzionato). In **She phoned the man who had contacted her** (Ha telefonato all'uomo che l'aveva contattata), il pronome relativo **who** (che) si riferisce a **the man** (l'uomo).

antecedente	soggetto	complemento
persone	who/that	whom/who/that
cose	which/that	which/that

persone: soggetto

Who è il pronome relativo generalmente usato in questo caso; anche **that** viene però usato:

> **There is a prize for the student who/that gets the highest mark.**
> C'è un premio per lo studente che ottiene il voto più alto.

persone: complemento

> **The man whom/who/that she met that night was a spy.**
> L'uomo che ha incontrato quella notte era una spia.

Whom viene considerato piuttosto formale ed è generalmente sostituito da **who** o **that**.

Il pronome relativo può anche essere omesso:

> **The man she met last night was a spy.**
> L'uomo che ha incontrato la notte scorsa era una spia.

cose: soggetto

> **The book, which is on the table, was a present.**
> Il libro che è sul tavolo è un regalo.
>
> **John gave me the book which/that is on the table.**
> John mi ha dato il libro che è sul tavolo.

cose: complemento

> **His latest film, which we went to see last week, was excellent.**
> Il suo ultimo film, che siamo andati a vedere la settimana scorsa, era ottimo.
>
> **The film which/that we went to see last week was excellent.**
> Il film che siamo andati a vedere la settimana scorsa era ottimo.

Nell'ultimo esempio, il pronome relativo può anche essere omesso:

> **The film we went to see last week was excellent.**
> Il film che siamo andati a vedere la settimana scorsa era ottimo.

Whose è la forma genitiva:

> **This is the boy whose dog has been killed.**
> Questo è il ragazzo il cui cane è stato ucciso.

La forma **of which** (il cui) è usata nel linguaggio più formale o tecnico per riferirsi a cose:

> **Water, the boiling point of which is 100°C, is a colourless liquid.**
> L'acqua, il cui punto di ebollizione è a 100°C, è un liquido incolore.

Si noti che **who's** è la forma contratta di **who is** (chi è), da non confondersi con il pronome relativo **whose** (il cui).

Gli aggettivi e i pronomi indefiniti

some/any

Come aggettivi, vengono usati con nomi plurali o non numerabili:

> **Take some biscuits.**
> Prendi dei biscotti.
>
> **Take some jam.**
> Prendi della marmellata.
>
> **Have you got any biscuits?**
> Hai dei biscotti?
>
> **Have you any jam?**
> Hai della marmellata?

Come pronomi, sostituiscono nomi plurali o non numerabili:

> **We haven't got any.**
> Non ne abbiamo.

Some (aggettivo e pronome) si usa in:

- frasi affermative

> **He bought some.**
> Ne ha comprato.
>
> **He bought some jam.**
> Ha comprato della marmellata.
>
> **He bought some biscuits.**
> Ha comprato dei biscotti.

- domande alle quali ci si aspetta una risposta affermativa

Note sulla grammatica inglese

Can you lend me some money?
Mi puoi prestare dei soldi?

• offerte e richieste

Would you like some?
Ne vuoi?

Could you buy some onions for me?
Mi puoi comprare delle cipolle?

Any (aggettivo e pronome) si usa in:

• frasi negative

I haven't got any brothers or sisters.
Non ho né fratelli, né sorelle.

• domande

Have you got any bananas?
Hai delle banane?

I composti di **some** e **any** vengono usati in modo simile. Esempi:

I saw something really strange today.
Ho visto qualcosa di veramente strano oggi.

Did you meet anyone you knew?
Hai incontrato qualcuno che conoscevi?

We didn't see anything interesting.
Non abbiamo visto niente di interessante.

I verbi

L'infinito costituisce la radice o forma di base. La forma intera dell'infinito comprende **to**: **to live** vivere, **to die** morire, ecc.

Per una lista di verbi irregolari vedi p.980.

I verbi regolari vengono coniugati come segue:

infinito
want   love(1)   **stop**(2)   **prefer**(3)

participio presente/gerundio
wanting   loving   stopping   preferring

passato semplice/participio passato
wanted   loved   stopped   preferred

(1) infinito terminante in **-e**
(2) infinito monosillabico terminante in vocale + consonante semplice
(3) infinito terminante in vocale accentata + consonante semplice

Il gerundio è usato con funzione nominale:

I don't like swimming.
Non mi piace nuotare.

Dancing is fun.
Ballare è divertente.

I tempi

presente

to be essere	**to have** avere
I am sono	**I have** ho
you are sei	**you have** hai
he/she/it is è	**he/she/it has** ha
we are siamo	**we have** abbiamo
you are siete	**you have** avete
they are sono	**they have** hanno

Per gli altri verbi, la forma è la stessa della radice, con l'eccezione della terza persona singolare, che prende la desinenza **-s**:

to want (volere): **I want, you want, he/she/it wants, we want, you want, they want**

to love (amare): **I love, you love, he/she/it loves, we love, you love, they love**

La terza persona singolare dei verbi terminanti in **-s, -ss, -sh, -ch, -x** o **-zz** è formata con la desinenza **-es**:

to watch guardare: **he/she/it watches**
to kiss baciare: **he/she/it kisses**

Il presente esprime:

• azioni abituali, verità generalmente accettate ed enunciazioni di fatti:

He takes the 8 o'clock train to work.
Prende il treno delle 8 per andare al lavoro.

I work in publishing.
Lavoro nell'editoria.

• gusti e opinioni

I hate Monday mornings.
Odio i lunedì mattina.

He doesn't believe in God.
Non crede in Dio.

• percezioni sensoriali

It tastes delicious.
È squisito.

passato semplice

La forma è la stessa per tutte le persone, sia singolari che plurali:

I/you/he/she/it/we/you/they wanted

È impiegato per descrivere azioni compiute o avvenimenti del passato:

He flew to America last week.
Ha preso l'aereo per l'America la settimana scorsa.

Note sulla grammatica inglese

passato composto

È composto dal presente di **have** (avere) e il participio passato:

> **I/you have loved, he/she/it has loved, we/you/ they have loved**

Descrive azioni passate o avvenimenti che hanno una qualche rilevanza per il presente.

Si può osservare la differenza tra il passato composto e il passato semplice confrontando le seguenti frasi:

> **Have you seen Peter this morning?**
> Hai visto Peter stamattina? (è sempre mattina)

> **Did you see Peter this morning?**
> Hai visto Peter stamattina? (è ora pomeriggio o sera)

Va notato il seguente uso del present perfect:

> **I have lived in Glasgow for three years.**
> Vivo a Glasgow da tre anni.

trapassato

È composto dal tempo passato di **have** (avere) e il participio passato:

> **I/you/he/she/it/we/you/they had wanted**

Descrive azioni o avvenimenti passati precedenti rispetto ad altre azioni o avvenimenti anch'essi passati:

> **She had already left home when I arrived.**
> Era già uscita di casa quando sono arrivato.

Le forme perifrastiche

Le forme perifrastiche sono formate dal verbo **be** (essere), nel tempo e persona richiesti, e dal participio presente.

presente progressivo

I am singing sto cantando, **you are singing**, ecc.

Descrive eventi, di solito temporanei, ancora in corso:

> **What are you doing? – I'm trying to fix the television.**
> Cosa stai facendo? – Sto cercando di riparare la televisione.

> **He always interrupts when I'm reading to the children.**

> Mi interrompe sempre mentre sto leggendo per i bambini.

passato progressivo

I was singing stavo cantando, **you were singing**, ecc.

Descrive avvenimenti passati ancora in corso nel momento in cui un altro avvenimento passato ha luogo:

> **He rushed into my office while I was talking to the director.**
> Si è precipitato nel mio ufficio mentre stavo parlando al direttore.

Anche gli altri tempi verbali hanno una forma progressiva: **I have been living; I had been living; I will be living.**

Da notare il seguente uso del passato composto nella forma progressiva:

> **I have been living in Glasgow for three years.**
> Vivo a Glasgow da tre anni.

Il futuro

In inglese ci sono diversi modi per parlare del futuro.

• will/shall

Will può essere usato con tutte le persone; **shall** è usato esclusivamente con la prima persona singolare e plurale.

> **I will/shall go** andrò
> **we will/shall go** andremo

> **you will go** andrai
> **you will go** andrete

> **he/she/it will go** andrà
> **they will go** andranno

Will e le forme negative **will not** e **shall not** possono essere contratte:

> **You'll be angry.**
> Ti arrabbierai.

> **We won't/shan't stay long.**
> Non staremo a lungo.

• going to

Questa forma viene spesso usata per esprimere un'intenzione o per predire qualcosa che accadrà:

> **I'm going to go to London tomorrow.**
> Vado a Londra domani.

> **The boss is going to be furious when he hears.**
> Il capo si infurierà quando lo verrà a sapere.

• •

Going to è spesso intercambiabile con will:

The boss will be furious when he hears.
Il capo si infurierà quando lo verrà a sapere.

I wonder whether the car is going to/will start.
Mi chiedo se la macchina partirà.

• il presente

Può essere usato per esprimere qualcosa che accadrà in un momento determinato, specialmente con riferimento ad un orario:

When does term finish?
Quando finisce il trimestre?

There is a train for London at 10 o'clock.
C'è un treno per Londra alle 10.

• il presente progressivo

Viene usato in modo simile a **going to** per esprimere un'intenzione:

I'm spending Christmas in Paris.
Passerò il Natale a Parigi.

Where are you going for your holidays?
Dove vai in vacanza?

L'imperativo

La radice del verbo è usata per impartire ordini:

Be quiet!
Fai silenzio!

Shut the door!
Chiudi la porta!

L'imperativo negativo viene formato con **don't**:

Don't forget to phone Alan!
Non dimenticarti di telefonare ad Alan!

Let's viene usato per la prima persona plurale per fare delle proposte:

Let's go.
Andiamo.

Don't let's go.
Non andiamo.

Let's not go.
Non andiamo.

La forma interrogativa

La forma interrogativa di frasi contenenti il presente e il passato semplice prevede l'uso del verbo **do**, accordato con il soggetto della frase:

Do you live here?
Vivi qui?

Did you live here?
Vivevi qui?

Se la frase contiene un verbo ausiliare (**have**, **be**) o modale, la forma interrogativa è realizzata invertendo il verbo e il soggetto:

Are they going to get married?
Si sposano?

Have they seen us?
Ci hanno visti?

Can John come at eight?
Può venire alle otto John?

Con i pronomi interrogativi, i modelli sono i seguenti:

Who came?
Chi è venuto?

Who fed the cat?
Chi ha dato da mangiare al gatto?

What have they done to you?
Che cosa ti hanno fatto?

What shall we write about?
Di cosa scriviamo?

In frasi negative **not** segue il soggetto, a meno che sia utilizzata la forma contratta:

Did they not say they would come?/
Didn't they say they would come?
Non avevano detto che sarebbero venuti?

Will the director not be there?/
Won't the director be there?
Non ci sarà il direttore?

Nell'inglese parlato, l'ordine delle parole nelle domande è spesso lo stesso che nelle affermazioni, ma l'intonazione è crescente:

He told you to leave?
Ti ha detto di andartene?

He left without saying a word?
Se ne è andato senza dire una parola?

Le domande di conferma

Si tratta di domande brevi, aggiunte alla fine di una frase, per chiedere una conferma di quanto si è detto.

Una frase affermativa è di solito seguita da una domanda negativa:

You smoke, don't you?
Fumi, no?

Da notare l'ausiliare **don't** che sostituisce nella domanda il verbo **smoke**.

Una frase negativa è invece generalmente seguita da una domanda in forma affermativa:

You don't smoke, do you?
Non fumi, vero?

Se la frase contiene un verbo ausiliare o modale, questo è ripetuto nella domanda:

You aren't going, are you?
Non ci vai, vero?

You will come, won't you?
Vieni, no?

You shouldn't say that, should you?
Non dovresti dire questo, vero?

Va notata la forma della domanda quando il verbo nell'affermazione è **am**:

I am lucky, aren't I?
Sono fortunato, no?

Il tempo verbale nella domanda è lo stesso che nella frase da cui dipende:

You wanted to go home, didn't you?
Volevi andare a casa, no?

Le risposte brevi

Nelle risposte non è necessario ripetere la forma intera del verbo; si può infatti semplicemente ripetere il verbo ausiliare (**be**, **have**, **do**) o modale contenuto nella domanda.

Is it raining? – Yes, it is./No, it isn't.
Piove? – Sì./No.

Do you like fish? – Yes, I do./No, I don't.
Ti piace il pesce? – Sì./No.

Can you drive? – Yes, I can./No, I can't.
Guidi? – Sì./No.

Le frasi negative

Le proposizioni negative sono formate con l'ausiliare **do** concordato con il soggetto + **not**. Le forme contratte sono **don't** e **doesn't** per il presente e **didn't** per il passato.

They do not/don't understand English.
Non capiscono l'inglese.

We did not/didn't go anywhere yesterday.
Non siamo andati da nessuna parte ieri.

Quando il verbo è impiegato con tono enfatico, viene utilizzata la forma non contratta:

I do not approve!
Non approvo!

I verbi modali

can, could; may, might; shall, should; will, would; must; ought

I verbi modali sono invariabili: **I can, you can, he can**, ecc.

La forma interrogativa si ottiene con l'inversione del soggetto e del verbo:
Can I go now? (Posso andare ora?)

È facile trovare i modali nella forma contratta. **Will** e **shall** si contraggono in **'ll**: **I'll be going** (Andrò).

Would si contrae in **'d**: **I'd like a cup of tea** (Vorrei una tazza di tè).

La forma negativa dei verbi modali prevede l'uso di **not** (**would not, might not**, ecc.) È particolare la forma negativa di **can**: **cannot** (cioè un'unica parola nell'inglese britannico).

Le forme negative contratte sono: **can't, couldn't, mightn't, shan't, shouldn't, won't, wouldn't, mustn't, oughtn't**. (**Mayn't** non è frequente.)

can

- autorizzazione

  Can I leave the table, please?
  Posso alzarmi da tavola, per favore?

  I can have another sweet, daddy said so.
  Posso avere un'altra caramella, lo ha detto papà.

- capacità

  He can count to a hundred.
  Sa contare fino a cento.

  Can he drive?
  Sa guidare?

- possibilità

  Accidents can happen.
  Gli incidenti possono capitare.

- richieste

  Can you open the door for me, please?
  Mi puoi aprire la porta, per favore?

Note sulla grammatica inglese

could

Could è la forma passata di **can**. I suoi significati comprendono:

- autorizzazione, capacità, possibilità, richiesta, espresse nel passato

  Daddy said I could have another sweet.
  Papà ha detto che potevo avere un'altra caramella.

  By the time he was three, he could count to a hundred.
  A tre anni sapeva contare fino a cento.

  She asked if he could open the door for her.
  Gli ha chiesto se poteva aprirle la porta.

- richiesta formale

  Could I leave a message, please?
  Potrei lasciare un messaggio, per favore?

- possibilità

  I don't know where John is; I suppose he could be at Anne's.
  Non so dov'è John; forse potrebbe essere da Anne.

- indignazione

  You could have warned me!
  Avresti potuto avvertirmi!

may

- autorizzazione e richiesta formale

  May I use your phone, please?
  Potrei usare il suo telefono, per favore?

  You may not leave the examination hall until I give the sign.
  Non potete allontanarvi dalla sala d'esame prima che io abbia dato il segnale.

- possibilità

  We may get an extra day's holiday.
  Potremmo avere un giorno di vacanza in più.

  They may have left.
  Potrebbero essere andati via.

might

- possibilità

Might si differenzia da **may** in quanto spesso suggerisce che si tratta di una possibilità poco probabile:

  We might get a pay rise.
  Magari avremo un aumento di stipendio.
  (= è improbabile)

Viene usato anche nel passato:

  He was afraid he might have missed the train.
  Aveva paura di aver perso il treno.

- autorizzazione e richiesta formale

  Do you think I might have another whisky?
  Pensa che potrei avere un altro whisky?

- indignazione

  You might have phoned!
  Avresti potuto telefonare!

shall

Per l'uso di **shall** per esprimere il futuro vedi p. 971. **Shall** può essere inoltre usato per indicare:

- richieste di ordini o consigli

  Where shall we put the shopping?
  Dove mettiamo la spesa?

  What time shall I set the alarm for?
  Per che ora devo mettere la sveglia?

- offerte o suggerimenti

  Shall I make you a cup of tea?
  Ti preparo una tazza di tè?

  Shall we meet outside the station?
  Ci vediamo fuori dalla stazione?

should

Should è la forma passata di **shall** e viene inoltre impiegato per esprimere:

- convenienza o obbligo

  You shouldn't tell lies.
  Non dovresti dire le bugie.

  What do you think we should do?
  Cosa pensi che dovremmo fare?

- probabilità

  Once this job is finished, we should have more spare time.
  Una volta finito questo lavoro, dovremmo avere più tempo libero.

  They should be here by now.
  Dovrebbero essere qui ormai.

  The keys should be in that drawer. That's where I left them.
  Le chiavi dovrebbero essere in quel cassetto. È lì che le ho lasciate.

will

Per l'uso di **will** per esprimere il futuro, vedi p. 971. Per **will** in proposizioni condizionali, vedi p. 975.

• •

Will può essere anche impiegato per esprimere:

• un comportamento tipico o una caratteristica innata

The stadium will seat 4,000 people.
Lo stadio ha 4 000 posti a sedere.

Hot air will rise.
L'aria calda sale verso l'alto.

• la volontà, un desiderio, il consenso

Will you see to the post for me?
Puoi occuparti della posta per me?

I'll do what I can to help him.
Farò quello che posso per aiutarlo.

• un'offerta

Will you have another slice of cake?
Prendi un'altra fetta di dolce?

• una forte probabilità o una deduzione

There's someone at the door. That will be Kenneth.
C'è qualcuno alla porta, sarà Kenneth.

• un ordine

You will go and wash your hands immediately.
Vai subito a lavarti le mani.

would

Per l'uso di **would** in frasi condizionali, vedi Sotto. **Would** è la forma passata di **will**. Può esprimere anche:

• il 'futuro nel passato', o un'intenzione passata

He told me he would do it immediately.
Mi ha detto che l'avrebbe fatto immediatamente.

They said they wouldn't wait for me.
Hanno detto che non mi avrebbero aspettato.

• abitudini nel passato

He would always get up at 6 a.m.
Si alzava sempre alle 6.

must

• obbligo

You must make sure you lock up.
Devi assicurarti di chiudere a chiave.

I must check whether my neighbour is all right.
Devo controllare se il mio vicino sta bene.

Da notare che **mustn't** significa che non si è autorizzati a fare qualcosa:

You mustn't park there.
Non puoi parcheggiare qui. (= è vietato)

Se si vuole dire che non è necessario fare qualcosa, si può usare **don't have to** o **needn't** o **don't need to**.

You don't have to eat that./You needn't eat that./You don't need to eat that.
Non sei obbligato a mangiarlo.

• probabilità

They must be there by now.
Devono essere là ormai.

You must have been annoyed by the decision.
La decisione deve averti seccato.

ought

• obbligo

You ought to be leaving.
Dovresti andare via.

They ought to send him away.
Lo dovrebbero mandare via.

• probabilità/attesa

They ought to be there by now.
Dovrebbero essere là ormai.

Two kilos of potatoes. That ought to be enough.
Due chili di patate. Dovrebbero bastare.

Le frasi ipotetiche con *if* (se)

I modelli di base sono:

if + presente, proposizione principale con **will**:

If we hurry, we'll catch the train./We'll catch the train if we hurry.
Se ci sbrighiamo, prenderemo il treno.

if + passato semplice, proposizione principale con **would**:

If I won the lottery, I would buy a new house./I would buy a new house if I won the lottery.
Se vincessi la lotteria, mi comprerei una casa nuova.

if + trapassato, proposizione principale con **would have**:

If Paolo hadn't lost the tickets, we would have arrived on time./We would have arrived on time if Paolo hadn't lost the tickets.
Se Paolo non avesse perso i biglietti, saremmo arrivati in orario.

Note sulla grammatica inglese

· ·

I verbi frasali

Numerosi verbi possono combinarsi con una preposizione per formare i cosiddetti verbi frasali. La preposizione può cambiare il significato del verbo:

to take (prendere):

John took a book.
John ha preso un libro.

to take off:

He took off his boots./He took his boots off.
Si è tolto gli stivali.

The plane took off.
L'aereo ha decollato.

to take after:

He takes after his mother.
Assomiglia a sua madre.

Da notare che il complemento oggetto, nel primo esempio di **take off**, può trovarsi in due posizioni diverse: dopo la preposizione o tra il verbo e la preposizione.

Quando il complemento oggetto è un pronome, però, la sola posizione possibile è tra il verbo e la preposizione:

He looked it up in the dictionary.
Lo ha cercato nel dizionario.

They have put it off.
Lo hanno rimandato.

Italian verb tables

Regular verbs:

1. in **-are** (*eg* **compr**|**are**)

Present ~o, ~i, ~a, ~iamo, ~ate, ~ano
Imperfect ~avo, ~avi, ~ava, ~avamo, ~avate, ~avano
Past historic ~ai, ~asti, ~ò, ~ammo, ~aste, ~arono
Future ~erò, ~erai, ~erà, ~eremo, ~erete, ~eranno
Present subjunctive ~i, ~i, ~i, ~iamo, ~iate, ~ino
Past subjunctive ~assi, ~assi, ~asse, ~assimo, ~aste, ~assero
Present participle ~ando
Past participle ~ato
Imperative ~a (*fml* ~i), ~iamo, ~ate
Conditional ~erei, ~eresti, ~erebbe, ~eremmo, ~ereste, ~erebbero

2. in **-ere** (*eg* **vend**|**ere**)

Pres ~o, ~i, ~e, ~iamo, ~ete, ~ono
Impf ~evo, ~evi, ~eva, ~evamo, ~evate, ~evano
Past hist ~ei *or* ~etti, ~esti, ~è *or* ~ette, ~emmo, ~este, ~erono *or* ~ettero
Fut ~erò, ~erai, ~erà, ~eremo, ~erete, ~eranno
Pres sub ~a, ~a, ~a, ~iamo, ~iate, ~ano
Past sub ~essi, ~essi, ~esse, ~essimo, ~este, ~essero
Pres part ~endo
Past part ~uto
Imp ~i (*fml* ~a), ~iamo, ~ete
Cond ~erei, ~eresti, ~erebbe, ~eremmo, ~ereste, ~erebbero

3. in **-ire** (*eg* **dorm**|**ire**)

Pres ~o, ~i, ~e, ~iamo, ~ite, ~ono
Impf ~ivo, ~ivi, ~iva, ~ivamo, ~ivate, ~ivano
Past hist ~ii, ~isti, ~ì, ~immo, ~iste, ~irono
Fut ~irò, ~irai, ~irà, ~iremo, ~irete, ~iranno
Pres sub ~a, ~a, ~a, ~iamo, ~iate, ~ano
Past sub ~issi, ~issi, ~isse, ~issimo, ~iste, ~issero
Pres part ~endo
Past part ~ito
Imp ~i (*fml* ~a), ~iamo, ~ite
Cond ~irei, ~iresti, ~irebbe, ~iremmo, ~ireste, ~irebbero

Notes

- Many verbs in the third conjugation take *isc* between the stem and the ending in the first, second, and third person singular and in the third person plural of the present, the present subjunctive, and the imperative: fin|ire **Pres** ~isco, ~isci, ~isce, ~iscono. **Pres sub** ~isca, ~iscano **Imp** ~isci.

- The three forms of the imperative are the same as the corresponding forms of the present for the second and third conjugation. In the first conjugation the forms are also the same except for the second person singular: present *compri*, imperative *compra*. The negative form of the second person singular is formed by putting *non* before the infinitive for all conjugations: *non comprare*. In polite forms the third person of the present subjunctive is used instead for all conjugations: *compri*.

Italian verb tables

• •

Irregular verbs:

Certain forms of all irregular verbs are regular (except for *essere*). These are: the second person plural of the present, the past subjunctive, and the present participle. Forms not listed below can be derived from the parts given. Only those irregular verbs considered to be the most useful are shown in the tables.

accadere *as* cadere

accendere • **Past hist** accesi, accendesti • **Past part** acceso

affliggere • **Past hist** afflissi, affliggesti • **Past part** afflitto

ammettere *as* mettere

andare • **Pres** vado, vai, va, andiamo, andate, vanno • **Fut** andrò *etc* • **Pres sub** vada, vadano • **Imp** va', vada, vadano

apparire • **Pres** appaio *or* apparisco, appari *or* apparisci, appare *or* apparisce, appaiono *or* appariscono • **Past hist** apparvi *or* apparsi, apparisti, apparve *or* apparì *or* apparse, apparvero *or* apparirono *or* apparsero • **Pres sub** appaia *or* apparisca

aprire • **Pres** apro • **Past hist** aprii, apristi • **Pres sub** apra • **Past part** aperto

avere • **Pres** ho, hai, ha, abbiamo, hanno • **Past hist** ebbi, avesti, ebbe, avemmo, aveste, ebbero • **Fut** avrò *etc* • **Pres sub** abbia *etc* • **Imp** abbi, abbia, abbiate, abbiano

bere • **Pres** bevo *etc* • **Impf** bevevo *etc* • **Past hist** bevvi *or* bevetti, bevesti • **Fut** berrò *etc* • **Pres sub** beva *etc* • **Past sub** bevessi *etc* • **Pres part** bevendo • **Cond** berrei *etc*

cadere • **Past hist** caddi, cadesti • **Fut** cadrò *etc*

chiedere • **Past hist** chiesi, chiedesti • **Pres sub** chieda *etc* • **Past part** chiesto *etc*

chiudere • **Past hist** chiusi, chiudesti • **Past part** chiuso

cogliere • **Pres** colgo, colgono • **Past hist** colsi, cogliesti • **Pres sub** colga • **Past part** colto

correre • **Past hist** corsi, corresti • **Past part** corso

crescere • **Past hist** crebbi • **Past part** cresciuto

cuocere • **Pres** cuocio, cuociamo, cuociono • **Past hist** cossi, cocesti • **Past part** cotto

dare • **Pres** do, dai, da, diamo, danno • **Past hist** diedi *or* detti, desti • **Fut** darò *etc* • **Pres sub** dia *etc* • **Past sub** dessi *etc* • **Imp** da' (*fml* dia)

dire • **Pres** dico, dici, dice, diciamo, dicono • **Impf** dicevo *etc* • **Past hist** dissi, dicesti • **Fut** dirò *etc* • **Pres sub** dica, diciamo, diciate, dicano • **Past sub** dicessi *etc* • **Pres part** dicendo • **Past part** detto • **Imp** di' (*fml* dica)

dovere • **Pres** devo *or* debbo, devi, deve, dobbiamo, devono *or* debbono • **Fut** dovrò *etc* • **Pres sub** deva *or* debba, dobbiamo, dobbiate, devano *or* debbano • **Cond** dovrei *etc*

essere • **Pres** sono, sei, è, siamo, siete, sono • **Impf** ero, eri, era, eravamo, eravate, erano • **Past hist** fui, fosti, fu, fummo, foste, furono • **Fut** sarò *etc* • **Pres sub** sia *etc* • **Past sub** fossi, fossi, fosse, fossimo, foste, fossero • **Past part** stato • **Imp** sii (*fml* sia), siate • **Cond** sarei *etc*

fare • **Pres** faccio, fai, fa, facciamo, fanno • **Impf** facevo *etc* • **Past hist** feci, facesti • **Fut** farò *etc* • **Pres sub** faccia *etc* • **Past sub** facessi *etc* • **Pres part** facendo • **Past part** fatto • **Imp** fa' (*fml* faccia) • **Cond** farei *etc*

fingere • **Past hist** finsi, fingesti, finsero • **Past part** finto

giungere • **Past hist** giunsi, giungesti, giunsero • **Past part** giunto

leggere • **Past hist** lessi, leggesti • **Past part** letto

mettere • **Past hist** misi, mettesti • **Past part** messo

morire • **Pres** muoio, muori, muore, muoiono • **Fut** morirò *or* morrò *etc* • **Pres sub** muoia • **Past part** morto

muovere • **Past hist** mossi, movesti • **Past part** mosso

nascere • **Past hist** nacqui, nascesti • **Past part** nato

offrire • **Past hist** offersi *or* offrii, offristi • **Pres sub** offra • **Past part** offerto

parere • **Pres** paio, pari, pare, pariamo, paiono • **Past hist** parvi *or* parsi, paresti • **Fut** parrò *etc* • **Pres sub** paia, paiamo *or* pariamo, pariate, paiano • **Past part** parso

piacere • **Pres** piaccio, piaci, piace, piacciamo, piacciono • **Past hist** piacqui, piacesti, piacque, piacemmo, piaceste, piacquero • **Pres sub** piaccia *etc* • **Past part** piaciuto

porre • **Pres** pongo, poni, pone, poniamo, ponete, pongono • **Impf** ponevo *etc* • **Past hist** posi, ponesti • **Fut** porrò *etc* • **Pres sub** ponga, poniamo, poniate, pongano • **Past sub** ponessi *etc*

potere • **Pres** posso, puoi, può, possiamo, possono • **Fut** potrò *etc* • **Pres sub** possa, possiamo, possiate, possano • **Cond** potrei *etc*

prendere • **Past hist** presi, prendesti • **Past part** preso

ridere • **Past hist** risi, ridesti • **Past part** riso

rimanere • **Pres** rimango, rimani, rimane, rimaniamo, rimangono • **Past hist** rimasi, rimanesti • **Fut** rimarrò *etc* • **Pres sub** rimanga • **Past part** rimasto • **Cond** rimarrei

salire • **Pres** salgo, sali, sale, saliamo, salgono • **Pres sub** salga, saliate, salgano

sapere • **Pres** so, sai, sa, sappiamo, sanno • **Past hist** seppi, sapesti • **Fut** saprò *etc* • **Pres sub** sappia *etc* • **Imp** sappi (*fml* sappia), sappiate • **Cond** saprei *etc*

scegliere • **Pres** scelgo, scegli, sceglie, scegliamo, scelgono • **Past hist** scelsi, scegliesti *etc* • **Past part** scelto

scrivere • **Past hist** scrissi, scrivesti *etc* • **Past part** scritto

sedere • **Pres** siedo *or* seggo, siedi, siede, siedono • **Pres sub** sieda *or* segga

spegnere • **Pres** spengo, spengono • **Past hist** spensi, spegnesti • **Past part** spento

stare • **Pres** sto, stai, sta, stiamo, stanno • **Past hist** stetti, stesti • **Fut** starò *etc* • **Pres sub** stia *etc* • **Past sub** stessi *etc* • **Past part** stato • **Imp** sta' (*fml* stia)

tacere • **Pres** taccio, tacciono • **Past hist** tacqui, tacque, tacquero • **Pres sub** taccia

tendere • **Past hist** tesi • **Past part** teso

tenere • **Pres** tengo, tieni, tiene, tengono • **Past hist** tenni, tenesti • **Fut** terrò *etc* • **Pres sub** tenga

togliere • **Pres** tolgo, tolgono • **Past hist** tolsi, tolse, tolsero • **Pres sub** tolga, tolgano • **Past part** tolto • **Imp fml** tolga

trarre • **Pres** traggo, trai, trae, traiamo, traete, traggono • **Past hist** trassi, traesti • **Fut** trarrò *etc* • **Pres sub** tragga • **Past sub** traessi *etc* • **Past part** tratto

uscire • **Pres** esco, esci, esce, escono • **Pres sub** esca • **Imp** esci (*fml* esca)

valere • **Pres** valgo, valgono • **Past hist** valsi, valesti • **Fut** varrò *etc* • **Pres sub** valga, valgano • **Past part** valso • **Cond** varrei *etc*

vedere • **Past hist** vidi, vedesti • **Fut** vedrò *etc* • **Past part** visto *or* veduto • **Cond** vedrei *etc*

venire • **Pres** vengo, vieni, viene, vengono • **Past hist** venni, venisti • **Fut** verrò *etc*

vivere • **Past hist** vissi, vivesti • **Fut** vivrò *etc* • **Past part** vissuto • **Cond** vivrei *etc*

volere • **Pres** voglio, vuoi, vuole, vogliamo, volete, vogliono • **Past hist** volli, volesti • **Fut** vorrò *etc* • **Pres sub** voglia *etc* • **Imp** vogliate • **Cond** vorrei *etc*

Verbi inglesi

Infinitive	Past Tense	Past Participle	Infinitive	Past Tense	Past Participle
Infinito	*Passato*	*Participio passato*	*Infinito*	*Passato*	*Participio passato*
arise	arose	arisen	**fall**	fell	fallen
awake	awoke	awoken	**feed**	fed	fed
be	was	been	**feel**	felt	felt
bear	bore	borne	**fight**	fought	fought
beat	beat	beaten	**find**	found	found
become	became	become	**flee**	fled	fled
begin	began	begun	**fling**	flung	flung
behold	beheld	beheld	**fly**	flew	flown
bend	bent	bent	**forbid**	forbade	forbidden
beseech	beseeched	beseeched	**forget**	forgot	forgotten
	besought	besought	**forgive**	forgave	forgiven
bet	bet,	bet,	**forsake**	forsook	forsaken
	betted	betted	**freeze**	froze	frozen
bid	bade,	bidden,	**get**	got	got,
	bid	bid			gotten *Am*
bind	bound	bound	**give**	gave	given
bite	bit	bitten	**go**	went	gone
bleed	bled	bled	**grind**	ground	ground
blow	blew	blown	**grow**	grew	grown
break	broke	broken	**hang**	hung,	hung,
breed	bred	bred		hanged (*vt*)	hanged
bring	brought	brought	**have**	had	had
build	built	built	**hear**	heard	heard
burn	burnt,	burnt,	**hew**	hewed	hewed,
	burned	burned			hewn
burst	burst	burst	**hide**	hid	hidden
bust	busted,	busted,	**hit**	hit	hit
	bust	bust	**hold**	held	held
buy	bought	bought	**hurt**	hurt	hurt
cast	cast	cast	**keep**	kept	kept
catch	caught	caught	**kneel**	knelt	knelt
choose	chose	chosen	**know**	knew	known
cling	clung	clung	**lay**	laid	laid
come	came	come	**lead**	led	led
cost	cost,	cost,	**lean**	leaned,	leaned,
	costed (*vt*)	costed		leant	leant
creep	crept	crept	**leap**	leapt,	leapt,
cut	cut	cut		leaped	leaped
deal	dealt	dealt	**learn**	learnt,	learnt,
dig	dug	dug		learned	learned
do	did	done	**leave**	left	left
draw	drew	drawn	**lend**	lent	lent
dream	dreamt,	dreamt,	**let**	let	let
	dreamed	dreamed	**lie**	lay	lain
drink	drank	drunk	**light**	lit,	lit,
drive	drove	driven		lighted	lighted
dwell	dwelt	dwelt	**lose**	lost	lost
eat	ate	eaten	**make**	made	made

Infinitive	Past Tense	Past Participle	Infinitive	Past Tense	Past Participle
Infinito	*Passato*	*Participio passato*	*Infinito*	*Passato*	*Participio passato*
mean	meant	meant	**spell**	spelled, spelt	spelled, spelt
meet	met	met			
mow	mowed	mown, mowed	**spend**	spent	spent
overhang	overhung	overhung	**spill**	spilt, spilled	spilt, spilled
pay	paid	paid	**spin**	spun	spun
put	put	put	**spit**	spat	spat
quit	quitted, quit	quitted, quit	**split**	split	split
			spoil	spoilt, spoiled	spoilt, spoiled
read	read /red/	read /red/			
rid	rid	rid	**spread**	spread	spread
ride	rode	ridden	**spring**	sprang	sprung
ring	rang	rung	**stand**	stood	stood
rise	rose	risen	**steal**	stole	stolen
run	ran	run	**stick**	stuck	stuck
saw	sawed	sawn, sawed	**sting**	stung	stung
			stink	stank	stunk
say	said	said	**strew**	strewed	strewn, strewed
see	saw	seen			
seek	sought	sought	**stride**	strode	stridden
sell	sold	sold	**strike**	struck	struck
send	sent	sent	**string**	strung	strung
set	set	set	**strive**	strove	striven
sew	sewed	sewn, sewed	**swear**	swore	sworn
			sweep	swept	swept
shake	shook	shaken	**swell**	swelled	swollen, swelled
shear	sheared	shorn, sheared			
			swim	swam	swum
shed	shed	shed	**swing**	swung	swung
shine	shone	shone	**take**	took	taken
shit	shit	shit	**teach**	taught	taught
shoe	shod	shod	**tear**	tore	torn
shoot	shot	shot	**tell**	told	told
show	showed	shown	**think**	thought	thought
shrink	shrank	shrunk	**thrive**	thrived, throve	thrived, thriven
shut	shut	shut			
sing	sang	sung	**throw**	threw	thrown
sink	sank	sunk	**thrust**	thrust	thrust
sit	sat	sat	**tread**	trod	trodden
slay	slew	slain	**understand**	understood	understood
sleep	slept	slept	**undo**	undid	undone
slide	slid	slid	**wake**	woke	woken
sling	slung	slung	**wear**	wore	worn
slit	slit	slit	**weave**	wove	woven
smell	smelt, smelled	smelt, smelled	**weep**	wept	wept
			wet	wet, wetted	wet, wetted
sow	sowed	sown, sowed			
			win	won	won
speak	spoke	spoken	**wind**	wound	wound
speed	sped, speeded	sped, speeded	**wring**	wrung	wrung
			write	wrote	written